Little Seed Publishing
Laguna Beach, CA

Pre-press Management by New Caledonian Press
Text Design: Angie Kimbro

Cover Design and Illustrations: Kathi Dunn, www.dunn-design.com

Acknowledgement is made for permission to quote copyrighted materials.

Printed in the United States of America.

For information, contact Little Seed Publishing's operations office at Global Partnership: P.O. Box 894, Murray, KY 42071, or phone 270-753-5225 (CST).

Distributed by Global Partnership, LLC
P.O. Box 894
Murray, KY 42071

Library of Congress Cataloguing In Publication Data
Wake Up Women: BE Happy, Healthy & Wealthy
ISBN-13: 978-1-933063-16-4

$14.95 USA $14.95 Canada

Other books by Steven E, and Lee Beard

Wake Up…Live the Life You Love:

…First Edition

…Second Edition

…Inspirational How-to Stories

…In Beauty

…Living on Purpose

…Finding Your Life's Passion

…Purpose, Passion, Abundance

…Finding Personal Freedom

…Seizing Your Success

…Giving Gratitude

…On the Enlightened Path

…In Spirit

…Finding Life's Passion

…Stories of Transformation

…A Search for Purpose

...Living In Abundance

...Living In Clarity

Wake Up…Shape Up…Live the Life You Love

Wake Up...
Live the Life You Love

WAKE UP WOMEN

BE Happy, Healthy & Wealthy

compiled by Ardice Farrow, Karen Mayfield & Heidi Reagan

Table of Contents

Awaken Your Relationship

Awaken Your Emotions

Awaken Your Health

Awaken Your Career

Awaken Your Wealth

Awaken Your Spirit

Foreword

For decades I have worked with women across the country—connecting them, introducing them and bringing them together in groups that support, encourage and assist each individual in moving forward toward her dreams.

I have experienced the power, wonder and brilliance, from the newest entrepreneur to well-known national leaders, and have found that women, at the core, come from a place of commitment, community and compassion.

As women, we know that each of us can make a difference. We know that when we come together, our ability to impact and influence is amplified a thousand times.

What has been lacking are vehicles and structures to collect the wisdom and experience of women to deliver this knowledge to large audiences so that we can share our life experiences, learn from each other, come together to support and celebrate all that we are and powerfully impact the world in which we live.

The idea for *Wake Up Women* was inspired by this global need for feminine leadership and a belief in the unique value and contribution that women will make for the future of this world. The contributing authors are professional women from across the globe: Coaches, doctors, actors, authors, executives, entrepreneurs, investors and leaders who saw the vision. Each has a great story to share.

This is the very first *Wake Up Women* book in a series which is the brainchild of three dynamic women: Ardice Farrow, Karen Mayfield and Heidi Reagan. The *Wake Up Women* series is a joint venture with

Wake Up…Live books, which has published many outstanding best sellers.

Wake Up Women is an idea whose time has come.

Look forward to the exciting adventure of these three women and the platform they will create to take women to a higher level. Visit the Wake Up Women Business Exchange at *www.wuwbe.com* that will feature these authors and more.

Robbie Motter
Author, Certified Seminar Leader and Master Coach
NAFE Western & Mid Atlantic Regional Coordinator

Wake Up...
Live the Life You Love

WAKE UP WOMEN

BE Happy, Healthy & Wealthy

compiled by Ardice Farrow, Karen Mayfield & Heidi Reagan

Awaken Your Relationship

Introduction

Heidi Reagan

Every moment of your life involves some type of relationship. Which of your relationships do you value the most? People immediately think of their romantic partners, friends, co-workers—maybe even their dog groomer. Every day you make connections with the people around you who are essential to your well-being and your state of mind. Yet the most important relationship, the one we often consider last (or not at all), is the one we have with ourselves.

I have noticed throughout the years that my closest friends have been those who appreciated and accepted me for who I am. This comes without judgment or the need to change me and I tend to feel the same about them.

It doesn't matter if the rest of the world deems them odd, eccentric, or even slightly abrasive. Perhaps the same is thought about me! We are friends and I cherish the unique individuality of each one of them as they, in turn, cherish me. As friends, we support one another on our life's journey, recognizing each other's true essence.

How often do we give ourselves the same courtesy? We embrace the quirks of someone else's personality, but neglect consideration of our own eccentricities. How often do we attempt to fix them, adjust them, or even deny their expression? There is no doubt we are our harshest critics.

It's fascinating how often we assume everyone else has managed to rid their minds of this self-criticism. Observing people we consider successful, we note their good looks, their fashion sense, their intellect and their prosperity. We jump to the conclusion that somehow they have managed to escape this internal, self-judging dialogue—the negative chitter-chatter that's doing a tap dance in our own minds every minute of every day!

Can you recall the last time you unconditionally accepted yourself just the way you are? No changes necessary: no losing a few pounds, no need to color the gray roots or even brush up on your vocabulary. Often we beat ourselves up because we think we're not good enough, but whose standards are we trying to meet? What about the times when we do a job we think isn't half-bad, that we are even proud of, only to start doubting ourselves when we didn't receive the desired accolades from the person on the receiving end?

Let's say you just gave an informative and focused speech at the local women's business network. Your true light shone through and you didn't even let them see you sweat! Did you pat yourself on the back or did you fixate on the one or two imperfections?

Self-criticism interferes with our ability to connect with our own true essence. By continually focusing on the qualities that we find less than perfect, we deny ourselves the joy of embracing all that we are right now.

In the stories that follow, these amazing women share a few of their experiences from their journeys through self-discovery to self-expression. Follow their lead by allowing these stories to inspire you to celebrate every aspect of who you are now. We are all individuals with unique possibilities. Learn to focus on what you appreciate about your uniqueness. Embrace your individuality and allow others a glimpse of who you are in your true essence.

Heidi Reagan

Connected Hearts

Tereasa Jones, M.S.

Did you know when two hearts are near each other they begin to synchronize and beat together with exactly the same rhythm? It's true! Even heart muscle cells from different hearts placed in separate petri dishes near each other in the laboratory begin to synchronize their rhythms and beat together. It is almost as if our hearts are dancing together! Could it be that our hearts are more than blood-pumping muscles? Research at the Institute of HeartMath suggests our hearts have special roles to play in human emotions and connections. We are biologically wired to be connected with others. When our hearts are not connected, we become psychologically and spiritually bankrupt. Heart connections are not necessarily romantic connections. There are many different types of connected relationships in our lives and each of them is worth nurturing.

A good deal of my life was spent feeling lonely because I am an introvert. This doesn't help with the loneliness problem. I can't, however, attribute all of my loneliness to my introversion. I was often lonely simply because I lacked connected-at-the-heart friends and family. Fortunately, the more I learn about connections and how to make and keep them strong, the less lonely I feel. Most people experience loneliness but don't recognize it as such, nor do they label it as loneliness. Instead, they experience it as vague dissatisfaction.

A friend of mine recently began recognizing this dissatisfaction as loneliness. In the past, she used her occupation as a shield to hide behind. When she talked about her work, she felt comfortable in most situations; however, if she had to relate to individuals in a personal way, she felt vulnerable and withdrew. She sometimes refused social invitations because she realized she would be expected to leave her occupational cloak behind and engage with people on a personal level. By recognizing this as one of the habits that caused her loneliness she has been able to step out, take chances and build new connections.

Not long ago, a client shared with me that he has found difficultly in making friends and has become lonely since retirement. As we talked, it was obvious that he felt embarrassed by the fact that his lack of friends even mattered to him. He labeled his need to feel connected a "feminine characteristic." I assured him it was a "people characteristic." We all need to feel connected to one another.

I am amazed at the people who confide in me that they are lonely, but outwardly appear to have many friends. The ones who are courageous enough to talk with me about their loneliness confess that while they have many acquaintances, they do not feel connected-at-the-heart with many people. I read these words on the blog of a young woman: "Loneliness is an island in the middle of a sea of people." She said while others thought she had many friends, she had always struggled to belong, even within her own family. Somehow, we have learned how to fool the world into believing we have many friends and that we are well-connected. In the hearts of many of us, we feel we are standing on that island called loneliness, in the middle of a sea of people.

I have heard of friendships that have lasted for decades. My oldest daughter spends a weekend each summer catching up with girlfriends from high school and college. They have a great deal of fun, but my daughter confessed to me that when something really good or really bad happens in her life, these are not the people she calls. It is a reunion of sorts, but these girls are not connected-at-the-heart friends. They rarely talk outside of this once-a-year weekend. The friends she calls upon regularly are the ones who co-nurture their friendships.

An experience with my youngest daughter who went to Europe for a semester was the catalyst in my quest to understand the connections of our hearts. When she boarded the plane one morning in late August, I felt as if a part of my heart was being ripped from my chest. I was afraid for her. She was flying into London on the very day a group of terrorists had planned an attack on planes flying from London to the United States. I felt an odd sense of excitement that she would be experiencing her dreams, mixed with panic that something bad might happen to her. The only way to describe how we felt over the next few weeks as she struggled to free herself from my need to hold on to her and I struggled to free myself from the neurotic feelings I was experiencing was that our hearts had lost their connections.

Over the next several weeks I was able to loosen my grip on her and our hearts rediscovered their connections. I was amazed at the growth we both experienced. I asked her why she thought we had engaged in this painful dance and she wisely replied, "Mom, you were afraid I would never come back, and I was afraid I would never go." Her wisdom exceeded her years! Her words struck my heart and resonated in a way that changed me forever. That moment gave birth to my desire to reach out and help people connect their hearts to one another.

I immediately began studying relationships of all kinds and currently hold the highest certification available in relationship coaching. My passion is to help people connect with their families, co-workers, friends and those in their communities and churches, lovers and spouses. Many reasons exist for our lack of connection. I want to help people discover the art of building real, connected-at-the-heart relationships. What I want is for us to be able to invite others to join us on our islands called loneliness and connect the sea of people.

You may discover that you have more relationships than you can adequately nurture. If this is the case, you will have to decide whether to continue to cultivate them or whether you want to focus on reducing the number to a more manageable one. It is okay to relinquish a relationship that has outlived its purpose: just be gentle in the process. Make it a requirement that in order to make room for new relationships your hearts must dance!

Connect Your Hearts:

Using your journal, answer the questions or write about the following:

- List and/or write about any special, connected-at-the-heart relationships you have had in your life.
- Do these relationships still exist? Why or why not?
- Is there something you need to do to either reconnect or nurture these relationships?
- Resolve never to let a relationship die for lack of nurturing.
- Spend the time. The single most important thing you can do to connect your hearts is to spend time with one another.

Tereasa Jones, M.S.

Five Keys to Successful Interpersonal Relationships

P.S. Perkins and N.J. Mitchell

Do you want to know how to attract and experience more meaningful relationships? If you read, learn and listen with your heart, you will begin to experience the relationships you desire in life—first with yourself, then with others.

Key #1 Be the Right Person

We live in a world of have, do and be—if I have a great job, then I can do great things and everyone will know that I am great! If I have vast possessions then I can do what others cannot and I can be what others are not! The fallacy in this equation is that BEING depends on HAVING someone or something outside of you to feel whole. Wholeness comes from within. These tangibles can bring no lasting joy, as with unfulfilling relationships; their acquisition becomes a never-ending stream of "next!"

What if we turned this flawed formula around into be, do, have—if I can be compassionate, I will do compassionate things and I will have compassion. If I can be wealthy in thought, word and deed, I will do the things that attract wealth and I will have wealth. If I can be loving, and do loving actions, I will have (attract) love.

Does this formula work? Of course it does. You cannot have and keep what you are not, and what you are germinates first in the heart and mind. First comes the thought, then the thought becomes a word, then the word becomes a thing. This is the basic building block in all creation. So in order to attract the type of fulfilling relationships you desire, first be that person you want to attract.

Key #2 Choose the Right People

Compatibility is one thing the two of us can truly say has played a major role in our relationship. Our mothers are both named Betty Jean, they each had six kids, our fathers died at a young age, we both grew up in the Southern United States, we both love traveling and we are both gifted communicators. But our relationship has not been all about our compatibility list. We would be the first to tell you that there have been times when we both felt let down, betrayed or just plain angry with each other. The universe brought us together to share life, laughter, triumphs and dismay. But we always seem to get back on track with those things that are commonly important to the both of us—God, love, laughter, adventure and service. Our common goals keep us from being swallowed up by the never-ceasing agendas of other people that pervade both our lives and take us away from our common goals.

Many women seem to be attracted to the opposite of who they are within. Yes, opposites attract, but most do not stay together. Eventually, life presents the road each must travel; if you are attached to someone whose road is very divergent from your own, eventually the two will separate. Everything in nature shows us the importance of compatibility. How about you? Are you in love with Donnie Danger? Do you want to be best buds with Frolicking Frieda? Would you just love to marry Bob Billionaire?

In the science of communication, we discuss the importance of self-disclosure and sharing the details of one's life to the extent that you feel comfortable. Generally, the deeper the self-disclosure, the more close or intimate the relationship. How much time do you give to self-disclosure with your potential partners—months, days, hours, minutes? It takes time, understanding and commitment to build a healthy and successful interpersonal relationship that is mutually fulfilling.

Everyone who comes into your life comes for *a reason, a season* or *a lifetime*. Not everyone is a lifetime partner, but everyone is a learning one. Accept what life has to offer on its own terms and you will be much happier.

Key #3 Make Room for the Other Person's Reality

Human nature often lends itself to acute levels of self-preservation. My idea, my way, my desires, my pain, all resound so loudly in the average human consciousness that it is often impossible to hear another's voice. Usually it is the voice closest to us that we drown out the most.

We must understand that *PERception* is *PERsonal*! When we fall in like or love, we often make the mistake of thinking that the other individual is always on the same page. Why can't they see it your way? Because they are not you and you must learn to maturely face the truth that no matter how compatible the two of you are, you will not see everything through the same lens. Mutual respect and humility are the keys to making room for others. You learn the true nature of compromise. You learn the true nature of sharing. You learn the true nature of unconditional love.

Key #4 Maintain Empathetic Listening

What's the difference between sympathy and empathy? Empathy requires a "feeling into:" a genuine expression of, "I feel and understand your circumstance." Many relationships lose their connectedness because they stop listening to one another. Take it from your co-writers: We will be the first to admit that this has been a most difficult area for us, mainly because we are both "talkers" who usually have very strong positions about our side of the discussion. It's not always easy to listen with your heart, even when your friend may need you most.

When we stop listening with our hearts, we begin to lose touch with our common goals, dreams and intimacy. True intimacy is "into me, see?" You cannot perform this with a closed heart, mind and ears. You can easily see how making room for the other person's reality and empathetic listening go hand in hand.

Key #5 Live the Platinum Rule

We all know the "golden rule"—do unto others as you would like them to do unto you. This is a noble and important rule in life as we connect with people in our everyday affairs. But I believe that the "platinum rule" is what is missing in our most intimate relationships. The platinum rule as coined by communications practitioner Milton Bennett states "Do unto others as they would have you to do unto them."

If we only do unto others what we want done unto ourselves, then we only give to others what we want for ourselves! We will never forget a dear friend from New York whose wish for her 30th wedding anniversary was a ride in a horse-drawn carriage through New York City's Central Park. Unfortunately, her husband did not think this worthy of their 30th anniversary and wanted to give her a jewel-encrusted platinum bracelet. Well, what's wrong with that? She shared, "I have enough jewelry. I want time and romance and this is a dream I've always desired." Well, what about both? "I suggested it, but he seems to be set on getting me what he wants me to have." He was exercising the golden rule.

Our intimate, caring relationships require we go beyond our own comfort level. There is no need to guess about the desires of your beloved's heart; all you need to do is ask, look, listen and give with your heart. This will keep your relationship fresh, exciting and fun-loving, not to mention all the wonderful payback the universe loves to bestow. As the old saying goes, "You can't beat God's giving, no matter how hard you try!" Adopting the platinum rule as your own will set the example for your true soul mate and friends are sure to follow.

So, there you have it. The five keys are sure to attract and keep the relationships you so desire, with yourself first, then others who can accept you for who you are, not what you are. In our new book, *The Art and Science of Communication*, we examine these and other communication tools waiting to empower your word into positive actions and dreams come true!

5 Keys Application:
The five keys are five pearls of wisdom that will lift your relationships

to new heights. Give them an honest try. Spend just five days applying each one of the keys with a dear friend or loved one; five days using your greatest effort and watch the changes begin. But remember, it ALL begins and ends with you! And that's our word!

1. Be the Right Person
2. Choose the Right People
3. Make Room for the Other Person's Reality
4. Maintain Empathetic Listening
5. Live the Platinum Rule

P.S. Perkins and N.J. Mitchell

How I Met My Soul Mate

Arielle Ford

I have proof miracles are real, that manifestation techniques work, and I was adept at using the Law of Attraction in my already successful career. In 1997, I decided to apply those techniques to manifesting my soul mate.

On June 22, 1997, I went to see Amma (www.amma.org), the hugging saint from India. I had heard about her years earlier from Deepak Chopra, who said to me, "Amma's the real thing. If you ever have a chance to get a hug from her, do it." I signed up to attend a weekend retreat, knowing I would receive at least two hugs during this retreat. I had spent the previous year forgiving myself and others for relationships that didn't work out. I made my list and released it to the universe. I had unhooked myself energetically from past lovers, and I truly believed in my that heart my soul mate was out there. Now, I was hoping for a little cosmic power-boost to bring us together.

On the first evening of the retreat, I patiently waited in line for my hug. I was excited and a little nervous. I had a plan, but I didn't know if it would work. I had been told Amma doesn't speak English and that when you receive a hug, she may whisper or chant into your ear, but that you shouldn't converse with her. When it was my turn, I whispered in her ear while she was hugging me, "Dear Amma, please heal my heart of anything that is stopping me from finding my soul mate." She laughed as I said this and squeezed me tighter and I knew she had understood my prayer.

That night, I had a very vivid dream. In the dream, there were seven women dressed in purple, singing to me. The lyrics of the song were, "Arielle is the woman that comes after Beth." When I woke up in the morning, I was convinced it had been a sign that my soul mate was out there, but he was currently with a women named Beth.

The next evening, I had the opportunity for a second hug from Amma. This time, I whispered in her ear to please send me my soul mate and I rattled off part of my wish list. Again, she laughed and squeezed me tight.

Three weeks later, I went on an unexpected business trip to Portland, Oregon. When I landed, my client's business partner, Brian, met me at the airport. The moment I saw him, I had the thought, "I wonder who Beth is."

Later that day, I very clearly heard a voice say to me, "He's the one. This is how it happens. This is who you are going to spend your life with."

Soon after that, Brian turned to me and said, "When I picked you up at the airport, did I look familiar to you?"

I said, "Yes, why do you ask?"

He said, "Because I've been dreaming about you."

By the end of the day, he told me he had been seeing me in his dreams and had recently ended a relationship with a woman named Elizabeth!

Brian and I were engaged three weeks later. In less than two months, he moved to La Jolla to live with me. Exactly one year to the date that I asked Amma to help me find my soul mate, she married us in a Hindu ceremony in front of thousands of people.

Miracles do come true and the Law of Attraction totally works!

Arielle Ford

Get a Life!

Kathleen E. Sims

My daughter once shouted at me, "You're a powerful person hiding behind all that weight, hoping no one will notice. I'm not supposed to surpass you, so I can't lose weight until you do!"

These words burned themselves into my soul, but I didn't understand then. Everything I took pride in—my successful "Ozzie and Harriet" life, the attention I gave my children, my status as a perfect, participatory mom, the comfort and ease of our middle class household—all these achievements went out the window as my daughter continued to shout in my face.

"You're playing 'small,' pretending you're just a suburban housewife. Debbie and I have fun things we want to do with our friends after school. We don't want to come home early because you're waiting for us. Get a life! I love you and that's why I'm telling you this and I'm not going to stop until you realize it's the truth!"

Denise was my oldest daughter, a precocious teen on a fast track to her own, powerful future. She and I had just completed an intense course on empowerment and she had emerged, seeing the world and herself very differently, speaking to me like this for the first time. As our words continued to fly at each other, she told me she felt encumbered by me, that she felt that she couldn't succeed until I did, and that her own weight issue was tied up with mine. She was angry with me and wanted me to see the light immediately.

I was stunned, feeling a desperate need to defend myself and what I stood for. "Don't you love me the way I am?" I asked. "Don't you appreciate the life we created for you kids? I like my life! Leave me alone! I know who I am!"

That's when it happened. All of a sudden, I saw the truth—I am a powerful person with a lot to give the world, but because I hate conflict and rejection, I had operated in life with a "please don't notice me" attitude. I was quietly going about my business and avoiding detection.

I realized in that moment that I was protecting myself by hiding behind an extra 40 pounds, hoping no one would expect too much from me. It hit me like a ton of bricks that I had been doing this unconsciously and I hadn't even considered that there might be another way to live.

I had been restless for a long time. As a result of marrying early and becoming a teenage mother, I took on many limiting ideas that had squelched my hopes and dreams. I yearned to make a difference in the world, to counsel and teach, helping others avoid the problems I had experienced in my own challenged childhood. I had always secretly known this and had understood that within me was a dynamo of strength, but I hadn't wanted to admit it—even to myself.

With this new awareness and sudden surge of insight, I knew I was caught and could never deny my personal power and capabilities again. I saw myself completely differently. I had been a hiding visionary leader! I knew that a miracle beyond my comprehension had yet to happen to me on an internal level and there was no going back into hiding.

I was silent for three days, adjusting inside to my new sense of self. I had no idea what to do with my new identity and self-recognition, but something inside me did. The weight began to melt from my body and I lost 40 pounds in the next two months without dieting. I realized the principles I had learned in a seminar about how to be naturally thin had effortlessly kicked in and I was finally experiencing my authentic self, willing to acknowledge my God-given gifts. My limiting beliefs about who I was and what I could and could not do were also melting away. It became crystal clear—*I had to follow my lifelong calling.* Thomas Mann said, "No one remains quite what he was when he recognizes himself."

Six months later my childhood dream had come true. I became a national training director for a transformational seminar company, teaching and counseling women to discover their personal power, and training other seminar leaders. I now had the privilege of empowering people to experience their own true, authentic selves and to express them in the world as I had finally done. My work was so effective that the company expanded exponentially and I was impacting thousands of women's lives.

My daughter lost weight as well and was busy presenting her own artistic gifts to the world. She was probably the youngest, most successful personal image consultant on the planet. Our relationship had also morphed into a powerful friendship in which she spoke from her truth and I spoke from mine.

Since that time, I have followed my truth, I have listened to my heart and guidance, and I have actualized my life vision and purpose. I designed and founded my own unique counseling and seminar company 25 years ago—a business that expresses my evolving and authentic self, reflects my soul lessons and innate gifts, and fulfills my life purpose. It passes on my legacy while contributing to people and the world.

So I ask you, what has been your inner dialogue? Does it keep you "small," or does it empower your authentic self to emerge? Does it reveal your secret calling?"

Ask yourself these questions:

- *Who am I?*

- *Why am I here?*
- *How can I be of the highest value to the most people?*
- *What is my unique place in this world?*

It seems to me that, for many of us, our life purpose is doing something in the world that will help right the wrongs that occurred in our childhood. I know that is my truth and it motivates me.

One of my heroes, Buckminster Fuller, lived his life as an experiment, always living out the question, "*What can one man do for the world in his lifetime?*" I, too, have lived my life by a question. When circumstances are uncomfortable, I ask myself, "What lesson at the level of soul (not ego) is trying to emerge, and am I willing to embrace it?" This guarantees the continuous evolution of my authentic self.

As a result of the many breakthrough "pinnacle" experiences I have had in my life and my innate gift for designing processes for deep transformation, I have created several life-altering courses: *Live Your Vision, Manifest Your Soul Mate, Empowerment—Conversations from the Heart, Healing the Precious Child Within* and *Thin Inside Out.*

For me, the power and inspiration that fulfills me is my commitment to use what life presents me to advance my own evolution and that of others. In doing so, destiny unfolds before me and the torch of my legacy continues to burn brightly.

Kathleen E. Sims

THE BONUS YEARS

Anne Berry

I travel a lot on business so I frequently ride in a rental car or long-term parking shuttle buses. Recently, I arrived in Los Angeles with way too many pieces of luggage. Against my better judgment, I decided not to spend the $3 on a Smart Cart. Consequently, I was struggling to maneuver my bags to catch the long-term parking shuttle bus. As I approached the bus stop, a young woman took pity on me and helped me load my luggage on the bus. I was feeling very grateful for the assistance until I sat down and looked up at the sign posted over the seats across from me. The sign read, "Seats reserved for the elderly." It suddenly hit me there was a distinct possibility this young woman had helped me because she perceived me as an old lady unable to manage the bags by myself. As a woman in my 60s, I immediately felt indignant! How dare she think I was too old to handle my own bags! If there hadn't been other open seats, she probably would have insisted I sit in the elderly seating. How could this be happening? I am NOT old!

This event gave me much to ponder regarding this whole notion of what constitutes a senior citizen—especially for a woman. I'm guessing most women my age have heard, at one time or another, the comments made about how gray hair on a man makes him look distinguished, whereas, a gray-haired woman looks dowdy and old. Is that a conspiracy by the hair coloring and salon industries or what? I must admit I've contributed to the profitability of both industries over the last 30 years. However, about six months ago, I decided to go cold turkey and give up the hair coloring routine. It gave me a tremendous sense of freedom, but now I wondered whether that young woman would have had a different interaction with me if I were still a "blonde."

Another question surrounds what one does with this whole senior discount thing. I chose to take advantage of this phenomenon as soon as

I joined AARP. One is eligible for membership at age 50, so I figured if they considered 50 years old to be "senior," then it was absolutely fair to request a senior ticket at the local movie theater. I wasn't sure if I was insulted or relieved when my request wasn't challenged. So, my quandary was this: How can I be indignant about being perceived as a senior citizen and yet be completely willing to take advantage of the discounts offered to this population?

Another double-edged sword is I am now eligible to collect Social Security. I worked hard and contributed to the system all those years, so, by golly, I deserve to receive those funds, right? But does this mean my life is now on the down-slope? I want to be perceived as a vital, passionate woman, living her dreams and sharing her joy and happiness with the world. But, like the young woman on the shuttle bus, does the "younger" world perceive it as impossible for a female senior citizen to be just that?

My pondering has led me to the decision that I'm not going to subscribe to the image of being a senior citizen. I believe I'm entering my "bonus" years. I believe I'm now at a place where my consciousness has evolved from the lessons I have learned. I'm ready for the transition and to separate from what was. My wisdom and experience guide and direct me each day. I always have time for my reason for being. My talents shine.

These affirmations have now manifested themselves. More recently than the shuttle bus experience, I have had the pleasure of working on a project with a well-known consulting firm. One of the members of the team is a recent USC Business School graduate. She and I have been relating in a business capacity and I have very much appreciated her support in my involvement with the project. Outside of our professional relationship, the most incredible thing happened. On two different occasions she asked me for my opinion on life experience topics. I was struck by the realization that she saw value in my life experiences. I now felt like the sage or highly-respected tribal elder. Instead of feeling old, I now felt valued and respected. It was now possible that the "younger" world perceived me as a vital, passionate woman, living her dreams and sharing her joy and happiness with the world.

If you are a woman 60 or older, do you want to be a senior citizen or do you want to be the highly-revered tribal elder? If you're undecided, you might ask yourself the following questions:

- How do I know when it's time?
- What are the symptoms?
- Am I a candidate for the shift?
- What is the mindset?

You know it's time when you feel empowered rather than overpowered; you choose thoughts that support your prosperous future and you keep your intent constant.

The symptoms are increasing your awareness that your thoughts do become things, desiring to make time for fun in your life and believing (at long last) your body is healthy, strong and youthful.

You are a candidate for the shift when you live in the moment, you remember every thought perpetuates the events of the day and you appreciate your relationships as a wonderful bonus in your life.

The mindset is to accept your life experiences as having incredible value and you believe you deserve love, joy, happiness and abundance.

At the point in time this all comes together, you are no longer a senior citizen. You are a vital, passionate and respected elder in your community. Share your talents, experiences and wisdom. Spread magic fairy dust to everyone you meet!

Anne Berry

A Pro-Rated Life

Deb Holder

My parents and I lived in a one-story ranch home on 15th Avenue during the 1960s. While teenage girls fainted for John, Paul, Ringo, and George, I sang "Daydream Believer" with the Monkees, ran circles around the house with my dog Missy until we both panted for air, and picked bouquets of Queen Anne's Lace in the field next to our family home.

I was Daddy's girl: I adored him. After nearly 40 years, I still remember the melody of my father's voice. He sang as he shaved each morning, and the tapping of his razor against the bathroom sink was a soothing cadence I grew to love.

However, my parents' life together was far from perfect, and the final thread of their marriage unraveled when I was only six years old. Late one evening, as Mom watched the news coverage of Robert Kennedy's assassination, she felt compelled to check on me—something she didn't normally do once she tucked me in for the night. She left the living room and walked toward my bedroom.

When she got to the doorway, she was horrified. A brown rat—thick-bellied and as long as my mother's arm—scampered off my blanket, disappearing into the darkness. She quickly scooped me up, running to wake my father.

She had already begged him to exterminate the rodents. They were everywhere—climbing on my swing set in the backyard, dining on bags of dog food in the garage, and scratching and gnawing through our walls each day. When she raced from my bedroom to theirs, she thought it was the final wake-up call he needed to get rid of the rats. Instead, he got up, looked around my room and said, "I don't see anything," and went back to bed.

Mom didn't sleep that night. She just held me in her arms. The next day she packed our bags and said to my father, "When the rats are gone, we'll be back." He shot back at her, "If that's the way you feel, just get a divorce." So she did.

Soon after their marriage ended, my father began dating Connie, a widow with two children. That's when my pro-rated life began. He would pick me up for weekend visits, take me to my grandfather's house and forget about me until it was time to take me back home a couple of days later.

Dad and Connie married the next year and he adopted her children, Stephen and Debbie. Even though my parents called me Debbie Sue, Connie decided their family should call me Sue to "avoid confusion." The only identity I had ever known was revised by strangers. I had been demoted to a rank below my stepsister.

Soon there were new rules to follow. We lived in the same town, but they wouldn't let me have their phone number. Dad and Connie said calling would cause problems, so we became pen pals instead. I wrote to them and Connie wrote back to me. Occasionally I visited them, but I felt insecure and cut off from the father I once knew.

Over the years our visits became less frequent. Although I loved Dad, I no longer felt comfortable with him. When I was 15, I received a rare letter from him—one that would change my life from the moment I opened it. I still remember the words that both haunted and confused me:

Dear Debbie Sue,
You've caused me nothing but pain. I'm not going to pursue you any longer.

The sting of his rejection felt like a double-fisted punch to the gut. My father wanted nothing to do with me. He blamed me for the breakdown of our relationship. I had played by their rules and lost. When Mom received the final child support payment three years later it was pro-rated, minus the two days in the month after I turned 18. I was zero-balanced and paid in full.

I wore my pain like a tarnished shield. During my twenties I dated many men. If they were nice, I left them before they could leave me. The more emotionally distant they were, the more I craved unconditional love from them. I didn't realize it at the time, but I was fueled by my father's rejection. Like a magnet, my insecurities often attracted emotionally unhealthy men. By the time I was 31, I had married and divorced twice.

Two years before my second marriage ended, I wrote to my father to make peace with him. It was a risky move, but he seemed happy to hear from me. We started writing again. When I was pregnant with my son, I flew back home with my husband and two daughters to spend time with my parents—separately—during Christmas. It was my first holiday with Dad in 17 years.

When my marriage became irrevocably broken, I wrote to tell my father. I told him how much my husband had hurt me. He wasn't moved. Instead, he wrote back that "history is repeating itself." I was divorcing my husband: Mom divorced him. "You're just like your mother," he wrote.

My father's reaction was like a cold splash of water to the face first thing in the morning—just what I needed to finally wake up. The distance between us had nothing to do with me. It was about his personal struggle to give and receive love. I couldn't change him. I had to let go. I said, "Goodbye," according to his rules and wrote him a letter.

The painful moments I had with my father were now just blurred snapshots of the past. I had to leave them where they belonged.

Although they had formed me, they would no longer define me. I had a choice: I could get bitter or get better.

I realized that my worth is not a reflection of the bits and pieces of my father's fractured affection. Instead, my mother's love was the blanket that kept me warm. What my father did to me could not compare to what I had been doing to myself. I had perpetuated my insecurities by loving men who gave me what my father had given me—rules for love that I would no longer follow.

I couldn't hold my head any lower, so I had no choice but to look up. For the first time I made eye contact with the world and saw my life in perfect focus—not in the shadows, but in the reflective light. To get better, I had to step beyond the silhouette of "Sue" and become the woman I wanted to be.

My last letter to my father asked, "If someone hands you a gift and you refuse to accept it, to whom does the gift belong?"

To me, the answer was clear. I let him keep the pain and gave myself the unconditional love he could never offer.

If you're scarred by childhood wounds, you can take positive steps toward healing:

- Don't define yourself by how others treat you.
- You are your life's author. What you think, you become.
- Release your anger. Parents who hurt us act from their own pain. They're often wounded children, too.

Deb Holder

Diving In

Edith Sieg

"We are all born with a gift."—Jaycie Phelps, Gymnast

Parenting is not easy. Unlike that stubborn VCR that refuses to be programmed, kids do not come with a manual at birth and they do not always do what we ask of them. Sometimes I think they are more successful at programming us than we are at programming them. There is one more major difference between children and VCRs: You cannot take the kids back to the store and ask for a refund. You just have to dive in.

I had not given much thought to parenting when my daughter Tania arrived. Making it through pregnancy, working a full-time job, running my own business, designing an addition to our house so she could have a room of her own, learning Lamaze, picking a name, choosing the environmentally-friendly way to diaper and a myriad of other tasks and decisions demanded our attention. Then, the soon-to-be grandfather passed away during my pregnancy. I was "overwhelmed" with a capital O. Despite my general lack of preparedness for motherhood and a near-deadly start, Tania has successfully made it to adulthood.

One evening when we picked up 1-year-old Tania from the babysitter she was tired and cranky and wanted to go to the nearby playground. At the park, she tried to run to the kiddie slide but fell down and did not get up. With growing concern, I observed that she seemed out of breath for no reason. I was reluctant to call the doctor. Previously, I had the feeling that I was bothering him and was just another overanxious mother. Bracing myself for the criticism, I called. He asked a few questions, then suggested we take her to the emergency room. Tania was finally drifting off to sleep. Because she was exhausted, I did not wake her. She slept fitfully and awoke a short while later. Resignedly, we packed for a long night in the emergency room.

When we stepped into the ER lobby, we were whisked directly into the emergency room, bypassing registration and a long wait. Our doctor had not indicated that Tania's condition was critical. While I knew that being out of breath for no reason was not normal, I had no idea that her condition could be life-threatening.

The eventual diagnosis was severe chronic asthma. Over the next few years, Tania had many asthmatic episodes. Too often our best efforts to keep her healthy failed and the emergency room became our last resort. It became increasingly difficult to find day care because of her medical needs. Concern for her well-being and survival became all-consuming for me. I became a mom with a mission.

Driven by an intense desire to do everything within my power to help her be well, I turned to research. This was before the Internet, when Google was not yet a word. I read everything I could find and talked to anyone who knew about asthma and allergies. After talking to medical doctors, alternative health practitioners, people at health food stores and at work, as well as to parents of other asthmatics, I took action.

Nothing was sacred in our house. Drapes came down, hypo-allergenic sheets came in, central air filtration systems were installed and additional HEPA filters were placed in rooms where Tania spent time. Diets were strictly observed and allergenic foods banned with the vigor that would make any drill sergeant proud—even her dad's favorite chocolate bars had to go.

Little did I know that caretakers whom I trusted were feeling sorry for my little girl with curly blond hair whose smile could melt an iceberg. They were giving her foods she was desperately allergic to such as chocolate, ice cream and wheat products such as birthday cake and cookies. Occasionally, I would discover chocolate wrappers in her clothes or that she had been given a milkshake as a reward for good behavior. The next four years were, at times, extremely draining.

When Tania was entering first grade, for reasons other than her health, I decided to put my professional career on hold to homeschool her and care for her two younger siblings who were also suffering from allergies and asthma. Of course, they inconveniently had different allergies from one another and therefore had to have different foods at meals. In addition to homeschooling and caring for three health-challenged children, I thought I would write books in my spare time. Eventually I learned there were only 24 hours in a day and sleep was not optional in the long run.

Becoming my children's primary caretaker resulted in unexpected benefits. Within one year, all three of my children were completely cured! Tania changed from a child who needed as many as six medications as often as every four hours, day and night, and having regular emergency room visits, to a child who needed no medication and had no symptoms as long as we maintained the strict discipline of avoiding allergens. The asthma and immunology specialist who cared for Tania was astounded at her complete recovery.

I learned how to research and listened to my intuition when my daughter's life hung in the balance. I was willing to do whatever was necessary. Our family's determination and persistence served us well. During the nine years we homeschooled, when I felt that a textbook was not serving us or one of the children showed an interest beyond what the school books would provide, I used those same research skills to improve their homeschooling experience. I always looked for the fastest route to mastery of any subject and then moved on to another topic. My children and I became efficient learners.

During Tania's sophomore year in high school, she joined the diving team. It was not a convenient after-school activity because she did not have transportation home after practices, but she showed commitment to the sport by arranging her own transportation.

When, during her junior year, she decided she wanted to dive in college and go to an academically selective university, I knew I would do whatever was within my power to help her make that desire a reality.

By scouring the Internet and talking to people, I discovered the best summer diving programs in the country, the programs that would give her the opportunities to achieve her goals. The summer after her junior year, Tania attended three diving camps of the highest caliber. She did what she needed to do to make her dream a reality. She dove until she hurt and then kept going, often so exhausted that the walk from the pool back to her living quarters seemed an impossible task of mind over matter, willing her rubbery legs to carry her step-by-step back to her room. Tania is a winner who summons incredible strength and willpower to pursue what she truly wants, despite formidable odds.

And the odds were formidable. Many Division I college divers began diving around age seven. Tania wanted to do in three years what took many divers 10 years. I believed in her.

Tania's efforts paid off. She was admitted to an excellent university and joined the diving team. She did it!

To me, this is the ultimate collaboration between a child and a caregiver:

- Expose children to a variety of experiences.
- Encourage curiosity.
- Allow children to explore and pursue their interests and passions (and most important, drop those which are no longer of interest after exploration).
- Encourage and support them when strong desire and passion

become evident.

- Pursue your own passions and lead by example.
- Seek out the experts you need to achieve the children's and your dreams.

What will you do today to nurture a child's passion—or your own? All great endeavors start with one small step.

Edith Sieg

WHAT IF...?

Billie Willmon Jenkin

I jumped when I heard the shotgun blast from my older son's bedroom. Both my boys knew not to play with guns inside the ranch house.

"Dammit, Son! What are you...?"

As I opened his door, no question remained as to what he had done. But why had he done it? There on the carpet, bed and far wall were the remains of my firstborn, the one I had held in my heart even before I held him in my arms 17 years before, and for whom I'd had so many dreams.

He was an honor roll student, raised in church, a leader among his classmates, teachers' pet. Now dead, he left no clues to answer my "Why?"

***

As a toddler, I found imaginative ways to entertain myself. Lying on my grandparents' living room floor, gazing at the high ceiling, I often played, "*What if?*" While adults droned on, I silently speculated, "What if the ceiling is really down and the floor is up?"

In my *What if?* game, the adults seated on furniture were stuck to what was really the ceiling. I, meanwhile, floated near the ceiling and considered surprising the adults by drifting down to the empty white floor.

Today, I use my tweaked version of *What if?* to change attitudes that no longer serve me. Using this tool, I shift my own perspectives and bring emotional healing to others. Before you investigate this game-tool with me, be forewarned of the one rule: "Thou must be childlike!"

Prior to our birth, *What if* we…

- Actually chose to participate in this adventure called life? Would that mean that instead of human beings, we are spiritual beings having a human experience?
- Had a conversation in which we volunteered for certain Planet Earth assignments?
- Knew our parents' characteristics: their habits, quirks, race(s), socioeconomic level, religion (or lack thereof); and in which country on Planet Earth they would raise us?

If these *What ifs* were so, then (although we have forgotten our agreements and origin) prior to our birth, perhaps…

- We would have known the experiences our parents needed to maximize their progress along their Earth Path. (So, we lovingly chose to supply such opportunities for them. Perhaps each generation makes this agreement!)
- What if for the sake of others, some of us volunteered to be "different," including being challenged physically, emotionally or mentally; gay or transgender; a minority religion or race or a lower socioeconomic status.

Based on these possibilities, *What if* is a tool for facilitating changes in attitudes.

When my sons were in Boy Scouts, I noticed my resentment toward people who disappointed me. Following my own day of teaching, I drove 50 miles round trip to Matador, Texas, so my sons could participate in scout meetings. More than once I made the trip, only to discover that Ronnie, the scoutmaster, apparently had forgotten! Grrrr!

In planning the annual scout meeting, Ronnie agreed to reserve the school cafeteria and send announcements to parents. To promote the scouting program, the area scout representative (who lived 100 miles away) planned to meet the boys and their parents at the appointed time and place.

The day before this event, the representative phoned me, inquiring about specifics of the meeting. Self-righteously, I reported that the forgetful Ronnie apparently had overlooked the event because no announcements had been made. Consequently, there would be no big meeting. I wasn't the only one peeved about Ronnie's alleged amnesia!

Fast-forward to 5 a.m. following the scout meeting that never happened. An in-law's phone call awakened me. "Billie, is it true that the Matador School blew away last night?" he asked. "*How the hell would I know, Dummy? I try to sleep at night,*" I thought.

Turning on the news, I learned residents of the tiny west Texas town had less than 15 minutes warning to prepare for the tornado. The twister roared straight through the school. Then it reversed, retracing its path. The cafeteria, pounded twice, was totally demolished. If Ronnie's memory had been better, approximately 75 little boys and their parents—our family among them—would have been meeting in that cafeteria at that very time!

What if our local scoutmaster's "faulty" memory was a gift for this very occasion?

Yes, *What if?*

The opening story of my son's suicide came within an instant of being 100 percent accurate. At the last moment, my firstborn, shifting from victim to choice, laid the gun aside. Years later, I recognized that the harsh judgment spewed out against those who were "different" had almost robbed me of my son. And I was one of the judges who had prodded him to feelings of hopelessness and worthlessness!

Once I was willing to be open to new perspectives, I could ask *What if* Spirit* had gifted me a gay son, both for my own healing and others' growth? What if, for others' benefit, Rusty had volunteered prebirth for his unpopular role? That thought gave me new insight into "Greater love hath no man." *What if* "problems" are Spirit's priceless gifts which we have not yet unwrapped?

Viewing all our difficulties and offenses open-heartedly is *empowering for change*. Whether the others realize what they are gifting us is irrelevant to our experience. If we can believe that they gifted us (even if we do not yet know what that gift is or how we'll use it), we find there is nothing to resent, nothing to forgive.

Serendipity—making fortunate discoveries by accident—is a faculty we can cultivate through intent. We can choose to discover gifts through the most unlikely sources. The people who irritate or anger us the most, for instance, gift us by mirroring qualities we dislike in ourselves. Recognition of our own intolerance is a fortunate discovery, which provides us opportunity to shift our perspectives and see a clear image of ourselves.

Perhaps the greatest gift to ourselves is to find ways let go of the negativity we harbor. If we imagine we are that other person, we realize if we had been raised exactly the same way, made the same agreements with Spirit and had the same belief system, we would do exactly as she did. Such a "*what if*" often eliminates our judgment.

Another way to reduce our criticism is to ask ourselves, "What if that person and I switch roles in a future voyage? Would I want her to have the same attitude toward me that I currently have toward her?" Discovering we don't want to be judged the way we have judged, allows us to shift perspectives.

Great ideas and opinions, including mine, don't change lives. Perhaps

**I find Spirit to be a neutral term. If you prefer, substitute "God," "Allah," "Yahweh," "First Cause," "Supreme Intelligence" or whatever term suggests unlimited love.*

"*What if*" is an effective tool for you to replace attitudes that no longer serve you. All the ideas and tools in the world won't make a difference if they remain in the book or the box. To "hit the nail on the head," you have to "pick up the hammer."

By opening your heart and mind and using the tool of *What if*, what possibilities will you create in your life and in the lives of others?

Billie Willmon Jenkin

Hello...Your Relationship is Calling

Jennifer Morgan, BSc., CPCC

The phone call would change the course of my life.

I had already heard from my husband's company that he had been called off-site near the end of his shift and would be late getting home. But this call, a few hours later, was from the hospital. My husband was there and they asked me to get there right away.

No one told me much. I assumed there had been an accident and my husband was hurt. The hospital was 40 miles away and I had to figure out a way to get there. I had a toddler at home and no car. My mom agreed to come, and while I anxiously waited for her, I packed a change of clothes for my husband and got my daughter ready to go out.

Like many couples, my husband and I didn't always have complete conversations and sometimes took each other for granted. I kept thinking of the previous evening when he sadly said, "Don't be angry with me," as he left for work. We'd had a small argument and I was feeling angry. Of course, now I was also feeling guilty.

My life was about to take a dramatic turn. My husband never came home. He had been found unconscious in his truck at work, probably having suffered a seizure, and never regained consciousness. He died several days later and I suddenly became a 25-year-old widow with a toddler.

Through more years and relationships than I care to recall, I remained a single mom. My dating was sporadic over a 16-year period after a short-lived second marriage. I was never in another relationship that lasted longer than a year and sometimes not in a relationship at all for years.

I found a new job within a year of my husband's death. It was not what I intended, but it was good for me at the time. It was interesting and it paid the bills, but it wasn't my heart's desire.

I learned a lot about myself and relationships in those years. I realized how important it was for me to get to know myself better, to listen to my heart and to care about myself in order to attract a more fulfilling life. I learned to live in the moment.

I learned that I needed to be a more active participant in my life and my relationships in order to be more aware of what was going on, both within and around me, and to make more intentional choices.

I realized that being in alignment with my heart's desire is magical. Everything seems to flow effortlessly from this place. When I'm doing something I would happily do for free and time seems to pass very quickly, there is a flow of energy that seemingly comes out of nowhere—what I call "universal consciousness." When I become aware of that flow of energy and make choices that feel right (even if those choices are scary), I create extraordinary results.

I became aware of how much I loved being a part of other people's growth. I often volunteered to assist at personal development courses because I loved simply being part of the experience. One day, a course leader offered to pay me to not only assist, but to also manage the logistics for a regular retreat. Imagine getting paid to do something that you love. Now, *this* was my heart's desire! I have learned that being present, conscious and intentional can transform relationships.

We are often unconscious in our relationships, which may cause us to take our partner for granted over time. We can refresh our relationships by becoming more aware of what's going on in every moment and noticing what we are saying, what we are hearing from our partner and how we are feeling. We can choose to become more aware of every moment and, in each of those moments, we can choose how we want to be, how we want to react and how we want to feel about what's going on.

Each relationship has a life of its own—its own energy. You have probably walked into a room and sensed tension; it is sometimes said you could "cut the tension with a knife." When you become aware of the energy of your relationship, you become more conscious about what's actually going on in the relationship.

The magic of transformation comes from *within* our relationships. As we open ourselves up to the natural energy of each relationship and allow it to flow through us in the same way that we allow the universal consciousness to flow through us individually, we can become attuned to what the relationship wants for us. The relationship becomes more powerful when we align ourselves with that—our heart's desire—and make our choices from that place.

One of the first exercises I do with relationship clients is to explore how they want to be together, which can set the tone for the balance of our coaching sessions. For example, many couples or partners will make an agreement to be respectful and considerate of each other, to be honest and forthright or playful. They are making conscious and intentional choices.

When we become conscious and intentional participants in our conversations with each other and in making decisions about how we're going to be or what we're going to do, we make more powerful choices about what our relationship is going to look like in the future. If we want our future to be different from what it is now, we have to make different choices. The most powerful way to make different choices is to connect to the universal consciousness that flows through us, and to the relationship energy that flows between us.

My course has not been straight and narrow, and it took me a long time to get to my happy ending. I finally met a wonderful man who loves me deeply and would do anything for me. At age 50, I became happily married again. I now have a husband, a daughter and her spouse, and three step-children. I have a large, close-knit family and more friends than anyone else I know. I've had a successful career and enjoy a new part-time career that fulfills me.

Extraordinary things happen when you heed the call of your life and your relationships. Magic happens when you allow the universal consciousness to flow through you and you are in alignment with your heart's desire. Relationships are transformed when you tap into the natural energy that exists between you and every person around you. Answer that call!

To help you become more present, conscious and intentional in your relationships, ask yourself these questions. Pick one that most resonates with you at this moment and hold it in your mind for a week; perhaps journal it or meditate on it. See what you notice.

- When do I "tune out" from my relationship?
- What do I most take for granted?
- What is the energy of my relationship at this moment?
- How can I better connect to the energy of my relationship?
- What is my relationship's heart's desire?

Jennifer Morgan, BSC., CPCC

Who's Looking at Me in the Mirror?

Erica Rueschhoff

As I looked into the mirror one morning, I felt a huge sense of panic. Who is this person looking at me? Oh, that's Rebecca's mom and Dale's wife. Wow, when did she put on all that weight? Where is the sparkle in her eyes and the passion she once had to take on each new day? I asked that person in the mirror, "Is this all there is to life?" There has to be more than making one more meal, picking up messes that will be back again within minutes, scrubbing toilets and sweeping the floor, which seems a little like shoveling while it is still snowing.

Then my panic quickly turned to guilt. How can I think like this? What kind of mother am I? I have four beautiful children, a great husband, a wonderful home and the privilege of being a stay-at-home mom. Isn't this what I always wanted? Yes, but then why do I feel so restless and unhappy?

It took me a while to realize that what was really going on with me was also happening to thousands of other mothers across the world. I had somehow lost my identity in my quest to be the perfect mother and wife. I was not fulfilling my full purpose in life nor using all of my unique talents and gifts. My expectations of motherhood were completely unrealistic and had helped lead me down this path of hopelessness I was feeling. Then, one day, I realized there are no perfect mothers, wives, children and no perfect houses. My quest was unattainable; nothing would ever be perfect. It seemed I was trying to create my identity—the perfect mother—and had allowed my boundaries to blur into everyone else's needs, consuming me and leaving myself completely uncared for.

I was so busy caring for everyone else that I didn't take time to exercise, eat right, get enough sleep, read a book I might be interested in, call a friend I had lost contact with or enjoy a hobby that would bring me some relaxation. Once again, the guilty feelings surfaced. How could I be concerned with that stuff? I must give my all to my family. One day, I took a hard look at the person who was looking back at me and made the decision that day that I would find "me" in the mirror. My life is totally different today and I am happy to share my experiences with you in hopes that my words will provide some insight and direction to help find "you" in the mirror.

You may be able to relate to these feelings. Please take a minute to make yourself comfortable and really absorb what I am going to tell you. You have the most important job here on this earth. Motherhood is the highest calling for any woman. You have the biggest influence on the character, personality, behavior and values of your children. Your children are the ones who will grow up to be the leaders and centers of influence in our society. Behind every amazing leader, I'm sure you will find a pretty amazing mother. Abe Lincoln said, "All that I am or hope to be, I owe to my mother."

So, why did I feel so unfulfilled? Was it because I had the belief that my sole existence and purpose were based completely on my role as a mother? Some would argue that this is the way it is supposed to be and it is selfish to think there should be more.

However, I believe there is a huge difference between selflessness and selfishness. To truly be able to be selfless and meet others' needs day in and day out, you must take care of yourself first. Just think about being on an airplane. The flight attendant will tell you to first put the oxygen mask on yourself and then on your children. Why? Because if we do not have the proper oxygen, we are of no use to our children. It is the same in real life. If you are completely overwhelmed, stressed out, lonely, discouraged or depressed, you first have to take care of those things in order to give the very best to your family.

We each have a unique purpose in this life, beyond motherhood. We have goals and dreams that are inspired by the purpose we were meant to fulfill. Too often, mothers submerge those dreams and goals. Whenever they start to resurface, we feel guilty and push them down further. All this does is allow the "bitter bug" to take root in your soul, and before you know it, "Martyr Mom" appears, transferring that bitterness and guilt to her children.

Motherhood gives women an opportunity to expand and increase their talents and abilities. We need to rediscover the dreams and goals we have and begin finding a way to bring them to our reality. When you are truly fulfilled, you will be a better mother and wife. Your self-esteem will increase, you will feel more joy and satisfaction in what you do, and you will be a good example to your children. Your children will learn the value of taking care of themselves in order to be able to be healthy and to give back to others. You will teach them that when you have a dream, anything is possible, and to reach for their dreams.

It doesn't matter how big or small your dream or passion is. Perhaps you want to start your own business, have the best garden, keep all of your scrapbooks up-to-date, volunteer at a retirement home or something you want to do in your community. What is important is that you rediscover that passion or dream and recapture your excitement about it. Then, you will begin to realize that you can be an amazing mother while being an amazing you!

Action Steps:

- Make a decision to rediscover your passions and dreams.
- Realize this is a gift to your family and there is no need to feel guilty. Let go of any guilt and embrace your new discovery.
- Create a plan to make yourself a priority. Remember, you have to put the oxygen mask on yourself first.
- Add action to your plan, start slowly and begin to do what you wrote down in your plan.
- Get a support network. You can get a group of friends together,

join a group like Mothers of Preschoolers, an online community or hire a coach.

Erica Rueschhoff

Transforming Relationships

Dr. Carolyn Mein

For most of us, it is the closest relationship we will ever know. It ought to be the most pleasurable and important relationship, but for many of us it is a strife-ridden, anxiety-provoking problem. For me it was the doorway to a profound understanding of human relationships.

Years ago, after treating my mother, I was standing in my office wondering how I had become so dysfunctional and off-center. There were no confrontations. She was pleasant and appropriate. I couldn't pinpoint anything that should have caused me to be upset. However, I wasn't much good for the rest of the day and it was quite apparent to my staff.

I had been attending personal growth and awareness classes and workshops since I was in chiropractic college, so taking personal responsibility for my reality was my focus. Ultimately, I was given the opportunity to get in touch with my feelings of being dominated and controlled by someone who didn't understand what I needed for my own development. Basically, I did not want to be like my mother. I wanted to be my own person.

We Don't All Think Alike

When I was in high school, I understood my mother didn't think like me. Whenever I had difficulty finding something she had put away because it was not in what I thought to be a "logical" place, I would step back and silently ask, "If I were my mother, where would I put it?" Then I was able to find it immediately. My father and I communicated very well and he also had difficulty communicating with my mother. Family dinner conversations were a classic example. My mother wanted us to talk rather than watch television, so she would suggest we turn the television off and ask my father about his day. He would reply in detail and I understood him completely. My mother rarely understood, however, which never led to stimulating dinner conversation. So rather than eating dinner in silence, day after day, the television would eventually get turned back on and the cycle would repeat.

The frustration I felt growing up, particularly in high school, was predominantly from my mother's refusal to allow me to go places or do things to develop people skills. Her childhood was very sheltered. She grew up on a farm with her social contacts limited to church and family. She met my father through her sister who had been writing to him while he was in the Army. Her experience of the world was dictated by what she was told she should do. This reality was too limiting for me and wasn't preparing me for what I knew I needed to do. My way of dealing with this restriction was to say as little as possible and do as much as I could to gain the experiences I knew I needed.

There were really no major conflicts between us: just low-grade tension that I handled the best I could. My father died of cancer the morning after my graduation exercises from chiropractic college, so I continued to live at home and take my mother with me to Unity Village on Sundays. Afterward, she would help me for a couple of hours at my Missouri office. After five years, I married and moved to California. My mother followed me two years later. I had done what I have seen so many other people do: I had married someone who was very similar to the parent I had the greatest difficulty with when growing up.

My wake-up moment occurred when I was finally able to heal my relationship with my mother. This happened when I truly appreciated her for who she was, rather than who I was expecting her to be. Since our parents are our first contact with people, how we relate to them colors how we relate to ourselves. Consequently, healing my relationship with my mother reflected the healing of issues within myself, as the problems were no longer triggered by her presence.

Professionally speaking, I knew diet and nutrition were important in a person's health and emotional state. As I began researching diet more extensively, I discovered 25 different body types, each with its own unique dietary pattern. While diet is important, the most profound, valuable information I uncovered about each type was its psychological profile. This is what enabled me to understand my mother and ex-husband, and differentiate myself from both of them.

Our Answers Are Within—Unlocking Them

The plan for our life's experience is located within the body and is directed and reflected through our dominant gland, organ or system. It's the dominant one of them which determines our physical characteristics, weight gain patterns, foods that best support us, how we think, what motivates us, our core character traits and means by which we relate to the world. The 25 body types can be divided into four quadrants based on whether your dominant sense is mental/emotional and physical/spiritual. My mother's body type is Gallbladder, which is in the emotional/physical quadrant. My ex-husband is Blood, which, like my mother, is emotional/physical. That relationship was all about bringing to the surface unresolved issues I had with my mother, though I was not consciously aware of them. My father's body type was Eye, which is in the mental/spiritual quadrant. My body type is Thyroid, which is also mental/spiritual. People who are the same body type think the same way and those in the same quadrant speak the same language, which explains why it was easy for me to understand and be understood by my father, but not my mother. While everyone has all four aspects, only two are dominant. Our challenge is to develop the other two aspects and relate effectively to people in both the same and different quadrants.

The positive side of being around someone who is the same as you is that you basically think the same way and have the same strengths and challenges. This may or may not stimulate growth. The advantage of being around someone who is opposite is your opportunity to grow and develop your less expressed traits. The more we develop our weaker aspects, the more balanced, understanding and compassionate we become. The best way to learn something is to experience it, which is why opposites attract. Life has a way of bringing to us what we most need to learn.

The Gift

When I was able to understand my mother's strengths, motivations, characteristics and challenges, I was able to accept her for the sweet, conscientious, loyal, dependable person she is. She is a healthy, vibrant 80-year-old who works in my office three days a week. Our relationship is loving, appreciative and harmonious, as is my relationship with myself and those around me.

Dr. Carolyn Mein

Awaken Your Emotions

Introduction

Karen Mayfield

Cellulite: The unsightly clumps of fat cells bunched up together just under the skin.

It's a battle we cannot seem to win. We cover it up with lotions, potions, clothes and even *Photoshop*®. We completely change our lifestyles to keep it from being seen. Billions of dollars are spent covering it. Even the most privileged have it.

Emotional pain and cellulite have many similarities: We work hard to cover them, we hide them from the world, we keep them to ourselves, we spend billions of dollars on pills in an effort to manage them, and they can happen to anyone, anywhere, anytime, young or old.

EGO—Earth Guided Orientation

Emotional scars are warehoused in our world of interpretation. This warehouse is managed by the ego where feelings are manifested. How we feel will determine what we fear and how we live. The ego holds us hostage, using tactics of perception and deception.

Once our perception has been formed, that perception will become our reality. However, if our perceptions were based on falsehood, then our reality is no more than an illusion. While we may not be living a lie, we could very well be living a life that will take us further from our health, wealth and happiness.

We become devoted to emotions that have been presented by the ego. Don't blame this one on the ego. The ego's job is that of translator. Everything that happens to us is translated by the ego and the ego acts as a filter of feelings. When something happens, the ego translates the feelings to us as good or bad. With each bad feeling our DNA strand tightens, and with every good feeling our DNA relaxes. A relaxed DNA strand is free from stress, free to expand and explore, ultimately providing our physical body with the support it will need to continue the cycle of life.

The human race has intellect and intuition, two levels of awareness above that of the animal kingdom. Animals are driven; humans are influenced. The only time animals react differently to instinct is when intellect is added to their instinct through training.

When we connect instinctively with the animals we are training and apply the methods lovingly, the animals respond positively. However, when we use methods of force, fear or abuse, the animals respond negatively with dangerous reactions, or their spirits are broken and they lose the spark in their eyes. They stay that way until someone lovingly replaces painful memories with new meaning that lights every cell in their bodies and re-ignites their lives. It's the same for humans.

The ego is no more than a buffer between how we perceive something and how it feels. Until the ego is forced into positive service there will be no peace of mind. Our instinct is susceptible to the ego's direction. Our intuition is spirit speaking through our intellect. When we choose to act upon the influence of the ego, those decisions result in repercussions. To act on directions given by our intuition and intellect requires that we exercise our willpower in order to live a life filled with rewards.

The following heartfelt, inspirational and instructional stories will add to your toolbox a set of steps for moving forward to live a life you love. With each emotional cell you light with the truth, you reveal the genuine human being in you. "Yesterday is a script that cannot be erased, today you are writing your script for tomorrow." Now is the only chance you have to write a yesterday you won't want to erase. Wake up, women; it's time to be!

Karen Mayfield

Gratitude and the Power of Choice

Shoshana Allice, M.A., CPCC

Another moving day.

I've moved so many times I'm a pro by now, but, today is different. This time, I have friends who have come, seemingly out of nowhere, to rally around and support me as I get ready to move out of the home I shared with my partner of several years and into a small apartment on my own. I packed up my things and sorted out what was mine and what was his in a matter of days, a task I don't think I could have endured by myself. But, I haven't *had* to do this alone; I am receiving the most support I've ever known, and I can't figure out exactly where it came from.

The day is grey and bleak, much like my mood as I watch my ex leave our house with his new girlfriend. I choke back the tears, square my shoulders and get back to packing the last of my things, doing my best to focus on the task at hand. This has been, perhaps, the most difficult year of my life, and while moving forward is painful, it is also hopeful.

It's not long before the first of my moving crew arrives and begins to work. Friends start shifting things around the house to create a clear path for moving things out. My friend, Corina, with her two young children in tow, begins to pack up the trunk of her car, preparing to take a load to the apartment while I head out with others to get the moving truck. She assures me she is quite happy to help for as long as her toddler and still-nursing infant will allow her.

As we head through the city to get the truck, rain begins to fall. With it, I feel my chest contract and tears well up behind my eyes. I am afraid, hurt, angry and feeling guilty. I am afraid of what's coming next in my life, I am hurt by the choices my former partner has made and I am angry with him, with myself and with the weather. I am not sure how to accept all the help I've been offered, and I feel guilty that my helpers are about to get wet.

As we drive through the torrential downpour, I sit in the passenger seat and sink deeper into my misery and shame. Next to me, my friend, Renée, is driving and notices my misery. She reassures me that everything will be okay. My worries about the weather and my self-imposed shame about the impact that my move has on all involved come tumbling out of my mouth. It is a relief to share it.

We pause for a red light and she puts a hand on my leg, looking me straight in the eye. "We are your friends, we love you and we're here to help. Don't worry about the weather; we're not." She is clear that this is not an imposition; this is an act of love. I breathe her words echoed by the friend in the back seat and I feel my shoulders lower slightly as I accept her message.

In that moment, I felt gratitude. I choose to approach the day from that place of deep appreciation for all the love and help that has come my way, and to take the rest as it comes. It is a powerful choice.

We continue without incident and return to the house to start loading. I have stopped thinking about the weather altogether, and only when I get out of the truck and go to the back to open it do I realize it has stopped raining. There's not even a drop. The grass is still wet and the sky is still grey, but my friends and helpers do not have to move me in the rain. I laugh out loud.

The move is a flurry of activity: one set of helpers arrives as another has to leave. Friends of friends, whom I barely know, are there to help as well. I watch my things being taken away in unfamiliar vehicles with the absolute trust that I will see them again on the other end. My friend,

Michele, has sent her husband, whom I also barely know, and he is willing, dedicated and helpful. He will end up being the last to leave.

The bulk of the move is done in a few hours and it is time to return the truck. Two of the guys offer to do it for me, one driving the truck and another following in his car to bring them both back. The rest of the crew have left, except for Michele's husband and Renée. We head out to Renée's car for one final run to my old home to do a sweep for any forgotten items and any small cleaning I feel compelled to do.

It is on the return trip that we notice the clouds have cleared and the sun has begun to come out. Renée smiles at me and comments that it is an auspicious sign appropriate to my new beginning. My life with my former partner had been very grey and stormy for a long time. The sun coming out as I move from the home we shared feels both validating and hopeful. I smile from the inside out, feeling tears of joy and gratitude in my chest.

Later in the evening, after everyone has left, I reflect on the day. It is raining again, but I don't mind; like tears, it is cleansing. I am grateful for the friends who love and support me, for the friends of friends who came out to help because others asked them to. I am grateful that, in the midst of hurt, anger, grief and sorrow, I chose gratitude.

As I think back over the day and the difficult months leading up to it, I realize how easy it would have been for this to be a miserable day if I had chosen such. Instead, it was full of laughter, love and honest, hard work because, in that crucial moment in the pouring rain, I chose gratitude. I chose to hear the reassurances of the friends who love me. I recognized the incredible power of that choice when it would have been just as easy to choose something different.

- What area of your life could be easier if you chose gratitude? Reflect on your life today. What are five things (big or small) that you are grateful for?

- Think of one person in your life who brings you joy, love and support. Let your heart fill with gratitude for that person. Let them know how much you appreciate them.

- Explore how finding gratitude in a difficult relationship or situation might help transform or bring meaning to that experience.

- Create a gratitude journal. Make a note as often as is right for you of five things you are grateful for. Notice how this impacts your life.

With gratitude, every day can be as beautiful as you wish.

Shoshana Allice, M.A., CPCC

Letting Go—What a Feeling!

Pam Robertson, Ph.D.

As a child, I knew that I would grow up to teach. During my first day in first grade, my teacher printed her name on the chalkboard in bold, curved letters. The chalk left behind a trail of elegant printing and I can still remember thinking, "I want to do that one day—print on a chalkboard for my very own students." I thought I would be teaching children in school, but after some experimenting I discovered that school can take many forms, and students come in all ages.

My résumé tells the story of someone who has tried many things. My experience began with babysitting as a teenager. Then I got a job as a jewelry store clerk and learned about customer service and managing inventory. Toward the end of high school, I was thinking about a music career, so I joined a military band and also learned how to march and shoot. Somewhere along the way, I spent two very long, bitterly cold winter weeks as a gas pump jockey in the days of full-service gas stations. I also worked in a doctor's office as a receptionist. I eventually decided that job-hopping did not hold a future for me, so I finally buckled down and went to college to pursue a teaching degree.

I used to get really nervous in my music auditions and formal job interviews. Blood rushed to my ears, and I would stumble over words or notes. My palms were slick with sweat and my knees trembled. Performing music and teaching were not a problem. However, when it came to showing my stuff in front of administrators and managers I was terrible. I wasn't easily discouraged, and I sent out résumés for teaching jobs before the ink on my degree was dry. It took a series of very bad interviews before I began to worry. As the days ticked by and the job offers didn't flood in, I became more and more anxious.

By late summer, I was not sure how I was going to pay my bills. I swallowed my pride and started to scour the help wanted ads for anything that might work. One large ad leaped out at me for a job that I wasn't trained for in an industry in which I had no experience. At the time, I remember thinking that although I wouldn't get the job, I could sure use the interview practice. In the back of my mind was the notion that if I could just get better at being interviewed, I could showcase who I was as a teacher and be rewarded with my very own classroom.

Practice makes perfect, so I did a lot of preparation for that interview. I treated it like a rehearsal for the interviews I really wanted. I researched information about the company and the industry. I poured over copies of their annual reports. I met someone who worked for the organization and asked him what he liked and didn't like about his job. I pictured myself at work in their offices, a smile on my face, happy to have the money for looking after my girls. On the scheduled day, I arrived on time for my interview. The room felt cool and the four people interviewing me were smiling and welcoming. Seated at the boardroom table, I felt unfamiliar feelings in me. I felt odd. I didn't stammer, my voice was unwavering and clear. It dawned on me during that meeting that I felt confident. I had answered every question to the best of my ability, and when I stood to leave and shook their hands, my own palms were dry.

Despite knowing they were intent on holding two, possibly three, interviews for each position, I really wasn't intimidated. I had prepared for an interview with no expectation of a job offer. I had been confident, yet not tied to an outcome so I was surprised when they called and offered me the job based on that initial interview.

That job was my first opportunity to coach and provide training to adults, and I got it because I had stumbled upon something quite simple, but very significant. I had learned how to "detach from the outcome." This is not the same as not caring about your results; it's about relieving yourself of the pressure that comes from high expectations. It's a method of preparation that you can practice and refine so that it works for you.

To date, I have moved 21 times in 42 years, lived in two different countries and five cities and have made it through two marriages. Did I always handle things well? Heck, no! But through my journey I have learned a lot about myself and still continue to do so. I have learned things that I like about change; the anticipation of meeting new people, the fun of setting up a new kitchen or workspace, the smell of fresh paint as I roll up my sleeves and get things underway. I have learned to accept the things which I can't control. Saying goodbye to friends and knowing I may not see them again is tough, and so is finding a good doctor in a new city.

That process, as well as my first real thoughts about careers and the job search market taught me several important things I still carry with me:

- I got the job because I was not worrying about getting the job.
- Not worrying meant that I could answer questions and show case my skills in a way that was professional and not at all desperate.
- I had stumbled upon something brilliant: detaching myself from the outcome.

Today we talk much more freely about the Law of Attraction, detaching from outcomes and not having expectations. However, when this interview took place 15 years ago, I didn't have a clue about any of that. I thought that some things came easily and others were really difficult. It was a fortunate accident that showed me that I could master my thinking and take control of my life.

Does detaching yourself from the outcome always work? In the summer of 2007, I prepared for the longest move of my adult life. I led a two-car convoy with my daughter, my sister and our three dogs on a journey of 3,000 miles across the country, and we had a most amazing time finding our way and exploring the highways.

- What can you do, today or this week, to detach yourself from the outcome of something you want?

- Try to imagine what it is you want as if it's already yours and you are already enjoying it. Now, commit yourself to the process, let go of the outcome and let your dreams come true.
- If you're finding it tough, go back and re-read this story, and then assess what you can do to prepare for the process, rather than an outcome. E-mail me your efforts, or post them on my blog at *andthebandplayedonmylawn.blogspot.com*. I'd love to hear about your adventures.

Pam Robertson, Ph.D.

MOTHER'S DAY AT LAST

Dorothy Fest

"I've been waiting for this call my whole life." One evening, my mom said she had something very special to share with my twin sister and me. She began telling us one of the most beautiful stories I'd ever heard, almost like "Cinderella" or "Snow White."

"There was once a beautiful woman who lived far away who was in love with a very handsome man, but their parents did not want them to get married. Her parents sent her away to keep them apart. This made the woman very sad and lonely. Then, she found out she was pregnant. She gave birth to two beautiful babies. Even though it broke her heart, she knew she couldn't keep them and decided to give them up for adoption. She made them promise her the twins would be adopted together. In May, a little over five years ago, we adopted those twin babies. You were given to us. Being adopted means you are very special," Mom said.

Feeling like the princess in my own fairy tale, I couldn't wait to tell all my friends the next day at school. That is exactly what I did.

"Guess what?" I would say.

"What?"

"We're adopted! Do you know what that means?"

"No."

"It means we're special!" I would walk away, beaming.

Well, the next day, two girls came up and said, "You lied! I asked my mom and she said it means your real parents didn't want you. You are not special."

Almost 35 years later, after losing both my parents and giving birth to my own children, I had my wake-up moment. While attending the Landmark Forum, we were given an assignment to write to our parents. I saw how on that kindergarten playground I had unconsciously decided no one wanted me and people couldn't be trusted. I began building a wall between me and other people, which worked very nicely for many years. No one got the best of me, and for the most part, I didn't think of who I was or who my real parents were, and I surely didn't talk about being adopted. As I wrote to all of my parents, I saw how much I had cheated them out of the gratitude and acknowledgment they deserved. I saw what sheer courage it took to give away twins and the love it took to raise twins to whom you had not even given birth. I realized finding my birth parents was no longer about fixing me or finding better parents. The wall was gone. I knew it was time to create a plan to make it happen.

Step 1: Find out everything about our birth.
I learned all I could about adoption, got online, soon found our birth parents' last names and learned to request my non-identifying information. It took six months to get that information back. However, it wasn't until two years later, when I was leading seminars for Landmark Education, that I knew it was time to realize my dream or live with regret for the rest of my life.

Step 2: Connect with a birth relative by Thanksgiving.
I didn't have a clue how that would happen in less than two months. I told myself I would do whatever it took. So, I found the perfect private investigator and gave her all the information and waited.

Two days before Thanksgiving, I got a call from the investigator telling me she thought she had found my father's sister, a nun. I dialed the number, trembling. She answered, "Hello, this is Sister Anne." I immediately felt the connection. I asked her about my mom. She said, "He had the same girlfriend, Donna, all through high school but he never told me she was pregnant." Then she told me all about him. He had five children and he had passed away about 10 years earlier. "Whether I am your aunt or not, you can call me Aunt Nancy," she said. "I will see what I can find out."

Step 3: Find Mom by Valentine's Day.
Thanksgiving and the holidays came and went. In the middle of the night, my little voice screamed, "Don't give up!" The next morning, I literally woke up and went into action. I went onto *Classmates.com*, where I had looked before. This time I found her! I sent her an e-mail immediately. When I saw the confirmation, it stated her married name. I didn't wait for the reply.

I did a people search and started calling women with her name. I introduced myself saying, "I think I may know you. Is it OK if I ask you a few questions? Did you ever live in Bellevue?" The first three said "no." On the fourth call, the answer was "yes." I asked, "Is 'this' your maiden name?" "Yes." Deep breath. "Did you give birth to twins in May 1956 in San Francisco?" "Yes." My heart sank because I knew it was her. Deep breath. "Did you give them up for adoption?" "Yes."

With tears streaming down my face, I heard myself say, "If all that is true, I think you're my mom."

"If you're one of those twins, I know I am," she said. "I've been waiting for this call my whole life."

In that moment, my whole life altered and a weight was lifted off my chest.

Awkwardly, I said, "My name is Dorothy and my sister's name is

Marguerite. Let me get her on the phone and we'll call you right back."

"How did you find me?"

"I saw your posting on *Classmates.com*. It had your married name."

"That's funny. I don't even have a computer." Later, I learned that it was posted by Aunt Nancy.

"I'm glad you called today. I just came home this afternoon from surgery. If you'd called yesterday, you wouldn't have reached me. I don't even have an answering machine. You won't believe this. Seven years after you were born, I had another set of twin daughters." We talked for hours and continued to get to know everyone via phone and e-mail.

A month later, we went to meet her. We saw someone standing outside her condo and immediately knew she was one of our sisters. Our mom was at the top of the steps waving, my other sister by her side. It was a magical, surreal moment. Not only was there an almost uncanny resemblance, it was as if we'd known each other our whole lives. It was a weekend I will never forget. The date was February 12.

That Mother's Day, I flew her out to meet my children. On the drive home from the airport, she shared, "Up until this year, I spent the whole month of May in a depression. Today, I can actually say I am happy. Finally, it really feels like Mother's Day." Mother's Day at last!

Golden Nuggets:

- Have your intention and attention on them, not you. Do the work on yourself before you search, to come from a place of gratitude, love and your heart. Create a plan to help keep the search at the highest vibration.
- Let everyone know you are looking—do not wait! Include

your family and friends in the search. Trust the next perfect step will show up and take it.

- Register with the International Soundex Reunion Registry, which is the world's largest free reunion registry, *www.plum site.com/isrr.*
- Get all the information you can from family members, neighbors, the attorney or doctor, governmental or non-profit adoption agency. Send for non-identifying information. Use the Web!
- If it works for you, interview and hire an investigator.
- When your attention and intention are clear, it will happen. Don't worry about how and do not settle or give up. You deserve to celebrate and honor yourself and everyone involved in your birth.

Dorothy Fest

Let it Be!

Sheila Pearl

"No! It must be a mistake! Not me! Not now!" I thought. But it was no mistake. I was pregnant. I was a junior in college and I had big dreams. I aspired to be an opera singer and had already been a part of San Francisco Opera's junior company, performing for schools and civic organizations on radio and television. Throughout high school and college, I had purposely remained abstinent to avoid the chance of an unwanted pregnancy.

I had met Sheldon on campus. He was a brilliant poet. I became infatuated with his charm and wit, succumbing to my passion for him. Shortly after having our only sexual experience, however, I knew our personalities were mismatched for a long-term commitment. In the meantime, my momentary pleasure with him produced a long-term, life-altering result. Incredible as it seemed, I was pregnant! In the early 1960s, abortion was illegal. I didn't want to marry Sheldon or anyone else. What would I do?

I had my whole life ahead of me. I wanted to be a famous singer. I had big dreams! Nevertheless, after discussing the options with family and friends, I listened to that still, small voice inside me that said, "Keep the baby. Let it be what it is." My big dreams suddenly took a very big turn. Being a young, unmarried, pregnant woman in the 1960s was not common. The pregnancy, giving birth and becoming a mother was an awesome experience full of wonder and miracles. My daughter, whom I named Daedra, awakened every morning singing—yes, singing. She cooed and gurgled, singing sweet melodies.

I became totally dedicated to my new status as mother, finding full-time work as a secretary to support us. My dreams for a singing career and my efforts to complete college were put aside in favor of my new career. I was Daedra's mother.

When Daedra was eight months old, she developed bronchitis. One morning, I got a call from the babysitter saying, "Sheila! Come quick! I think something is very wrong. Daedra is having trouble breathing!" I called our family physician. He said I should meet him at the hospital.

I rushed to pick up her up and drive the 15 miles to San Francisco. Daedra was on the front seat next to me, sweating profusely and gasping for air. "Mama, mama!" she cried. "It's going to be okay my darling! Uncle Pat will take care of you. Mommy is here. It'll be okay," I assured her with tears streaming down my face. I had a feeling in the pit of my stomach that she was not going to be okay.

Our doctor (Uncle Pat) met us at the emergency room. "I'll take her. You just wait and we'll take care of her. Go get a cup of coffee." About an hour later, he found me in the waiting room. "Go home and rest, Sheila," he said. "We'll take care of her." Two hours later, the doorbell rang; it was Pat. He was white and he had tears in his eyes. I knew. "We did everything we could," he said. "She's gone."

What happened? How could this be? Our little angel was gone! The post-mortem revealed a congenital defect—the heart was a fibrous tissue, not muscle. She had been destined to be on this earth a very short time. My heart broke into a million pieces. I was in such unthinkable emotional pain that it seemed impossible for me to move forward. I desired to stay in that pain, as if moving beyond might mean the loss of my child did not matter.

My profound grief prevented me from returning to college for a couple of years. I was grieving not just the loss of my child, but also the loss of my role as a mother. I was faced with letting go of my newly-formed identity as "mother," and that still, small voice kept inviting me to "let it be." I cried until there were no more tears, then I was silent. In the silence, I asked myself, "What else am I? Who else can I be?"

In that same silence, I thought of Daedra's singing. I thought of the joy she had brought to me and my family. I wondered how I could honor her precious life and also honor my own. I reminded myself of my own voice. I reached deep inside my silent self, allowing myself to surrender—to accept life as it was now being presented to me. I did not choose this tragedy. I could only choose how to respond to it. At the age of 22, I had no idea that it would be this experience that would carve out my deep capacity for compassion and empathy, preparing me to care for others who would come into my life and need my love.

I never gave birth to any other children. Daedra was my only such experience. Nonetheless, life brought me countless blessings. I married a man whose children came to live with us. I became a stepmother and now have five grandchildren. My vision for a singing career morphed beyond my wildest imagination. For 25 years, I was a "cantor," singing and teaching in the synagogue rather than singing in the opera house. I turned my maternal energies toward becoming a teacher to hundreds of students. I am currently a full-time life coach to hundreds of clients. To all of these, I offer my compassionate listening and teaching skills.

What I learned about just letting life be:
Tragedies and losses happen in our lives when we least expect them. However, we have a choice in how to respond to our pain. When I have surrendered to "what is" and just let it be, miracles have happened.

In choosing my response to adversity, I surrendered to my pain, not allowing myself to become embittered. Instead, I have kept my heart open. Choosing to move forward in my life by keeping my heart and mind open to all possibilities has continued to stretch my capacities to unconditionally love my stepchildren and my grandchildren, as well as my students and my clients.

Daily Action Steps for Letting it Be:

- Get quiet and allow silence to fill the space. Meditate for 10 to 15 minutes.
- Hug someone and have a big belly laugh. Say "Thank you."
- Create "you" time—write, paint, dance, cook and enjoy.
- Ask yourself, "What do I insist on in order to be happy?" Then, let go of your insistence on anything and embrace what life is now.
- No matter what occurs in your life, look for the blessing. It's there.

Sheila Pearl

Installing Limiting Beliefs

Arlene Rannelli

Did you ever wonder, "What's the point?" How many times in your life have you wanted to attempt something new and exciting and then either talked yourself out of it or let someone else talk you out of it? Or, how many times have you simply lost your enthusiasm? Have you ever felt genuinely excited about a goal you were committed to attaining, only to realize the passion died within the first few weeks? Have you felt you had the world by the tail, then, in the next moment, you could barely speak because you felt overwhelmed by a vaguely familiar emotion you could not even describe?

Are you aware that your clarity erodes each time you say you are going to do one thing and then do another instead? I think one of the most difficult questions for most of us to answer in life is, "What do I want?" It's no wonder we have difficulty figuring it out. There have been so many times when we have said we were going to do one thing and have done another. We all stop trusting ourselves. Even if we did figure out what we want, we lose the belief in ourselves to move toward it. We do not believe any longer that we have what it takes to create results we want. We often resort to thinking, "What's the use?"

When we are born we have such strong determination. Watch a small child learning to walk and you will clearly see what I mean. There are some beliefs we have acquired in our lives that do not serve us well at all: Beliefs such as, "I'm not good enough," or, "They'll laugh at me and I will be embarrassed." Others are acquired like, "I'll never get this," or, "I'm stupid." I will give you an example of how easily we become damaged and how easily we feel inferior, insecure or unwanted. I was leading a program in Calgary many years ago and I remember this scene as clearly as if it happened this morning: I was seated in the restaurant of the hotel. It was about 8:00 a.m. and I was there alone. There was a rather large table off to my left about three feet away. There were three adults seated at the table and three or four children ranging in age from 8 to 12. Toward the entrance to the restaurant, I noticed two bobbing blonde heads moving to the table beside me. They belonged to two very lovely little girls, both about 5 years of age. My eyes became fixed on one child and I could not seem to take them off her. She was beautiful. She had cherry-colored lips, bright blue eyes and long blonde hair tied up in two very long pigtails. She pranced when she walked. Both children arrived at the table and sat down. The only child I noticed from that moment on was the little one I just described.

Within three minutes of sitting down, she held everyone, including me, in the palm of her hand. She was entertaining, charming, charismatic, beautiful, intelligent and extremely talented. Soon her mother whispered in her ear, and the child backed away, sitting quietly with her eyes down for a few moments. Then, all of a sudden, she was back. She began talking again and charming everyone. Then her mother whispered in her ear again, and the child backed away and sat quietly, saying nothing. One more time, she attempted to come out. She was enchanting. She captured everyone's attention and people genuinely enjoyed her. Then her mother, who must have been having a bad day, turned and said something to the child that must have been much more severe because the little girl stopped talking, stopped smiling, held her head down and played with the knives and forks. She never even ate anything.

I will bet you anything that in that moment the girl got a message from her mother that she was not good enough, but this was not true. As a matter of fact, it could not be further from the truth. Nonetheless, from that moment on she might have registered a belief inside her subjective mind that she is not good enough. An idea like that will negatively influence her life forever, or at least until someone she believes in and trusts tells her how talented and wonderful she really is. There is a good possibility that she will never realize her potential because of her self-doubt. There is also a good chance that she will never know why she feels that way.

That is how it begins. We form ideas based on our life experiences and the situations in which we find ourselves. For the most part, we are not consciously aware of what is going on or of how potentially debilitating certain beliefs can be. As a matter of fact, much of the time we are not even aware of the majority of our thoughts. We just know we are not getting the results we want, and we become discouraged.

I have been leading self-awareness programs for the past two decades, and I have discovered that each of us has our own unique "Essential Energy." This is a phrase I have coined to express the unique vibration that each of us is here to express and experience in this world. Essential Energy is *beingness*, not *doingness*. The little girl in my story was living in her Essential Energy when she was entertaining everyone at the table. Our Essential Energy is our unique vibration, which is our direct route to Source Energy, to Universal Mind, or to what some call "God." When we live in our Essential Energy, we feel a strong sense of belonging and know that we are part of a greater whole.

Many people settle for a life of business rather than fulfillment. Can you imagine how fulfilling it is for me to realize that my coaching practice is intended to support people in recognizing the beliefs and feelings that are not serving them? I help them change their mind about these ideas, releasing the attachment to the feelings as well.

I believe we all deserve to experience the passion, excitement and joy of living. Living in our Essential Energy, regardless of the prices we may pay for doing so, is worth everything.

Arlene Rannelli

No Tombstone Required: A Journey to Self Love

Lisa A. Fredette

One day my daughter said to me, "Mom, you're never happy anymore." Talk about a defining moment: I realized that every day when I woke up, the first thought that came to mind was, "Is this all there is?" I was only 34 and had too much living left to do to have such a mindset. That is when I started to really take a look at my life and decided it was time to find out who I really was.

During this self-discovery, I realized that there was one common thread in my life—a deep feeling of wanting someone to love me. I remember saying to myself, "I wish someone would just love me. I just want to feel that I matter." I thought that if I could only find someone to fill that void, I would be happy and all my problems would be solved.

I had tried over and over again to find someone to love me enough. Searching for love from this place brought me heartache over and over again. I continued to attract men into my life who mirrored my feelings about myself—not loving me enough. These men were also emotionally unavailable; they didn't love themselves enough to be able to make me feel loved.

The last straw came when my marriage of 16 years ended. I finally realized that I needed to make some changes. Now that I was facing the world alone, I needed to figure out how *I* could be enough for me, because I knew that I did not want to attract another man into my life who would continue to mirror my limiting beliefs.

That's when I found the magic of life coaching. Through the workshops, one-on-one and group coaching sessions with my life coach, I was able to start putting the pieces together. I first needed to learn to love myself.

I had to give myself permission to actually feel my feelings. I had become so good at shoving my feelings aside and putting on a happy face for everyone else that I no longer knew how I really felt about things. I realized that I had lost my voice. I no longer knew what got me excited, let alone what I was passionate about. In addition, I had isolated myself so much that I no longer had a circle of friends to support me in my healing. I felt truly alone. That is when I would call on my coach and she would set me straight—she would help me get out of "huge vision" mode and get into the here and now. Together we would focus on what was really going on instead of what I was projecting might be happening.

I slowly began to feel my emotions. I began to cry more, which I found to be very therapeutic—but only after I complained to my coach that I was tired of feeling all these feelings. I told her that I had cried more in the past year than I had my entire life and I was sick of it. But, when I allowed myself to feel, I found that all the emotions came back, not just the bad or sad ones. I began to get excited, I felt energized and I was actually looking forward to the future. I was slowly becoming reacquainted with my best friend, me. The two years following my separation, I recall very clearly two statements that eventually became my mantras. The first year my mantra was, "Because I can." The second year it became, "It's all about me," and remains so today.

The "Because I can" year was the year I began to embrace my independence and celebrate my freedom to make my own decisions. I began trying new things and found how exciting it was to discover something new. I remember one thing in particular. One of my co-workers talked me in to auditioning for the community play *Chicago.* Now, this show is a musical. Well, I can't sing, but I still had to audition. Talk about scary! But, with the support of my newfound mantra, "Because I can," I did it. I have to say it was an exhilarating experience dancing and singing for three separate audiences. What a high!

The "It's all about me" year was the year I gave myself permission to be selfish. I decided that I was no longer going to strive to impress others or to make them proud. All that matters is that I impress myself and make myself proud, that I live my life authentically. I found that living this way sometimes makes others uncomfortable and if I allowed them to, they would sabotage me. However, I quickly figured out that those who feel uncomfortable about my authenticity are the ones who are uncomfortable with themselves—so, in essence, I am their mirror. When you are hesitant to show your true self to the world for fear of judgment, remember that the judgment comes from the judger's own agenda and has nothing to do with you. In fact, you may be giving them the glimpse inside themselves that they can use to turn their lives around.

This journey to self love started more than six years ago and I sometimes forget how far I have come. Luckily, I was recently reminded about this journey by one of my coaching clients when she said in an almost exasperated voice, "Why can't someone just notice what a good job I do and tell me so?" Then she stopped herself and said, "Why is it that we seek outside validation to make us feel good or noticed?" That's when I shared with her my journey to self love. I also told her that when I finally realized I had gotten to the end of the journey—when I truly knew that I loved myself enough and had filled that void—was when I was walking past a cemetery that was near my home and a voice inside me said, "No tombstone required." I thought, "I don't need others to remember me with a tombstone—I am living my life fully and authentically, my memory will be in how I touch others with my life." That is when I knew I had arrived—I was enough, and there was no tombstone required.

Remember my telling you that I would attract men into my life who mirrored my feelings of not being enough? Well, after this journey to self love, I was able to attract a man into my life who mirrors the true definition of unconditional love. This was the second clue that let me know I had arrived.

Look in the mirror—what are the people in your life reflecting back to you? Take the time to learn from it and begin to heal those parts of yourself that you don't like and begin to love yourself unconditionally.

I promise you, if you stop sweeping the obstacles aside and take the time to learn from them, you will begin to put the pieces of your soul back together—before you know it, you will be having the same profound revelation that I did—you are enough and no tombstone is required.

Lisa A. Fredette

QUEEN OF SOUL

Johanna Courtleigh

I like to think about Aretha. Taking her place in the order of things. Giving us her wild-throated brilliance. Without apology. Without diminishment.

I think of what we would have missed if she'd let fear make her decisions and stayed hidden. There, in the back of the choir, head down, shame-faced, lip-syncing the words. Perhaps worried about the one next to her, with the lesser voice, and not wanting to upset, sang quietly, sang guiltily, chose not to sing at all.

I think of her, in the shower, humming softly to herself so as not to disturb the neighbors. Instead of belting herself out. Playing fragile, playing small, playing just too timid to come out with it.

Then I think about Aretha, accepting her assignment. Blowing away the heavens. Raising her hand, volunteering for the solo. "Pick me! Pick me!" Stepping forward, full-voiced, full-cleavaged. Letting it rip. Inspiring our wild, beautiful bodies with her ecstatic, brazen sound. Alive in the full soul-hood of her being.

I am often distressed, shaking my head, at how we women can turn away from our magnificence, thinking ourselves stupid, insignificant, lesser-than. Call it humility; I call it shame. Assuming self-esteem something undeserved. That it's not quite okay for us to shine like Aretha shined. Like the pure, radiant note she came to Earth to be.

And I'm awed by how tricky and tactful the ego can be. The arrogant side of us, that veils fear behind pomposity and pride. Or its evil twin, professing inadequacy. Teetering us between greater- and lesser-than. Keeping us under its thumb, till we believe that if we even begin to dare to dare, we might actually lose—love, control, r-e-s-p-e-c-t. That they might not like us any more. Or worse, not like themselves in comparison to our vast, shimmering splendor.

We become lethargic, co-dependent, imagining if we open our lives and sing, dance, write, speak, love, thrive, someone will surely crumble. So, in the service of being non-threatening, nice, accepted, we turn down the volume, mute our voices, choose to be barely seen, hardly heard. We contract, retract, back down from fully living.

I know. I've done it. Too many times. Shut myself up. Kept myself small. Not wanting to draw attention, to make someone feel bad in relation to my majesty.

Growing up, I learned that what I had to say didn't matter, that my gifts somehow weren't significant, that I was silly for even considering I might be worth bringing out and polishing to a shine. I kept myself private and diminished my life, because that's what I'd been taught I was worth. Not much. Not enough.

But that was a lie.

I remember once, in college, sharing my poems with a friend. Daring to offer myself up, out. It was one of those sunny scenes, a beautiful spring day. We were both dressed in our near-hippie best, lovely, cool, reading aloud out to each other out on the quad. And she looked at me and in a sorrowful tone said, "Your stuff is so much better than mine." I felt it like a kick in the heart, and tumbled into shame. So I did what any loyal friend would do. I closed my mouth. I hid my writing. I gave up my power and called it love, and never read to her again.

Strange paradox. I was embarrassed because I was good at something. Something that had heart and meaning for me. And thus, I, and the world, missed out.

For a while.

Till I began again to dare to dare…

Now, I see it in my clients. The beautiful artist who won't show her work. The exquisite singer who won't perform. The gorgeous mother who cannot praise the very thing she so deeply loves about herself—how she parents. The one who gave up veterinary school, because her older brother was a little "slow," and she didn't want to upstage him.

It's an undervaluing, a shyness, a turning away from the mirror of the truth of our own beauty. A lump in the stomach that reaches up and chokes us back, telling us that what we have to give will never be enough. Or is too much.

And obediently, we shut ourselves up, off, out. Forgo our royalty, staying loyal to a self-minimization that only exhausts the soul.

We come to see life as a competition; winning as losing. Because while someone may admire us, another, like my friend, may be jealous. And the caretaker in us can't abide and holds back our light, muffling a voice that has grace inherent in it. Stunting our evolution.

When what we're talking about is purely simple statement of fact.

Self-acknowledgement and self-regard.

"This is who I am." "This is what I'm good at." "This is what I love."

Nothing grandiose. Nothing lesser-than. Just life on life's terms. You, on the terms you've been given to be. For why would you have been given gifts, talents, leanings, skills, if you weren't intended to use them?

There's a big difference between being arrogant and being honest about who we are. We get that confused. We're afraid that saying we're good at something, raising our hand for the solo, singing out is somehow egotistical, conceited, unacceptable.

When it's actually about "accepting our assignments." Saying "Thank you" for and honoring ourselves. Celebrating the preciousness of this incarnation. As an act of reverence and gratitude. As appreciation for the vast, sweet mystery of our own being. Taking our place in the order of things. Thriving.

What might you be choking back in the service of staying "safe?" How do you intimidate yourself, thinking, "Not much, not enough?"

What moves you? What compels you? What invites you to open your voice, your hands, your mind, your heart? And what would it take for you to give yourself permission to truly bring yourself, full-throated, full-bodied to your one radiant life?

Who is the Aretha in you? And what might she say if she were standing beside you, whispering you on, so that, in the end, you felt well-used? That you'd done what you'd come here to do. That you'd not only received and accepted the gift, but unwrapped it, delighted in it, fulfilled it and finally said a deep, heartfelt "Thank you."

Yes, there are plenty of singers, poets, artists, cooks. Sure, there are lots of mothers, accountants, gardeners, dancers. None of them are you. None of them have your place, your face, your name. None of them have the same exact tone, the same sweet frequency. None of them have the same twist, spin, perspective. None have been given what you've been given to be.

The ones who thrive have not allowed their fear to decide. They've braved the risk, and shown up, fully. Taken the full-lunged gasp, and stepped forward to the edge of the high dive, and in a gorgeous arabesque announced, "I exist. I am here to live...."

- Find one thing you love about being you.
- Imagine it's a gift, a contract, one of the assignments you agreed to fulfill, this lifetime, for God.
- Make a list of three or four steps you need to take to turn up the volume on it, to move more fully toward it.
- Pick one, and imagine one of your heroines, or your vision of your highest, most magnificent self, is right there with you, holding your hand, coaching you on.
- Dare to risk and dream. "Be-big" versus belittle yourself!
- Take your power back and claim your reign, delighted and wild and unashamed.

The world needs each of us.

The world is waiting for you.

To take your place in the vast mysterious order of things. To claim the royalty of being you.

To be queen.

Queen of your own soul.

Johanna Courtleigh

Skyward Passion

Kara Swensen

At a bright, young nine years of age, I witnessed the space shuttle Challenger break apart with my own eyes. I remember turning my face toward that of my teacher for reassurance that the message from my eyes to my brain was horribly incorrect. As tragic as it was, the booster rockets ignited my curiosity. I knew in my soul, to the skies I would go. A few months later, Top Gun was released. When Maverick exclaimed he felt "the need for speed," he was speaking to me.

My parents recognized my drive at an early age. Bless their hearts, they would check me out of school to attend air show practices. I babysat for a family whose father, Joe, flew the F/A-18. He became the mentor in my life, and the man to whom I give much credit for always encouraging me to believe in myself. By the age of 16, I had worn the headset in the landing signal officer cabin while feeling the rumble of simulated carrier landings 20 feet away, crashed and burned the F/A-18 dome simulator and smelled the salty ocean breeze while cruising on the USS Saratoga. Now I never made it to the big leagues as a fighter pilot like Joe or as an astronaut like Christa McAuliffe, but I share something with those heroes—passion: a passion for freedom, empowerment, grace and wings. I have a passion for flight.

The day I drove away for college, my mom gave me an index card with a quotation from Leonardo da Vinci that read, "For once you have tasted flight, you will walk the earth with your eyes turned skywards, for there you have been and there you will long to return." When I graduated with an aeronautical technology degree, my announcement read, "Passion is powerful. Nothing was ever achieved without it, and nothing can take its place. No matter what you face in life, if your passion is great enough, you will find the strength to succeed. Without passion, life has no meaning. So, put your heart, mind and soul into even your smallest act: this is the essence of passion. This is the secret to life." To this day, both pieces of paper are at my fingertips and remain at the root of my wings.

Because I am a woman, most people usually stare at me with a puzzled look when I tell them I am a pilot. I have grown used to the unique look of quandary on their faces. People show a numb disbelief as if the words coming out of my mouth were spit bubbles popping into thin air the moment they slipped through my lips. Since I was nine, people have given me this look and I quickly learned to carefully choose those to whom I blow bubbles. Even as a young girl, I could sense people's thoughts about my aspirations, and these feelings suppressed my confidence. When my confidence dwindled, my passion seemed to grow exponentially. At some point, I solidified my self-esteem behind the controls of an aircraft.

My first solo cross-country flight as an 18 year-old student pilot was a 60-mile flight due west. How I ended up southwest remains a jovial mystery to my family and me. I had strapped on a Cessna 152 aluminum can and landed at an uncontrolled airport. I taxied up to an open hangar door and, while promising myself not to cry, pulled the fuel mixture and shut her down. I hopped out in my short shorts and ponytail and marched right up to the man inside. He was a hangar bum of sorts who sat in his lawn chair watching the humidity, and told his wife he had "worked on the plane all day." He shared my passion, too, but probably thought I was certainly not meant to be behind the controls when I boldly asked him, "What airport is this, sir?" He asked if I wanted a ride to a pay phone to check in with my flight instructor. Knowing I was safer in the plane than in the car of a stranger, I replied, "No sir, I'll make it home just fine." I hopped back in the plane while cursing under my breath and calling myself names. I pulled out my aeronautical chart and fired her up. I was in close contact with air traffic control which vectored me due east toward the shore due to thunderstorm buildups. Before my own eyes, my life changed. I was all alone, talking myself through my procedures, trying to keep my big girl pants on, when a space shuttle took off. One hundred miles south of me, she climbed up past my right wing and into the magnificent darkness of space.

Fast-forward many years: I have my own business selling aircraft from home and fly my own Cirrus SR22. But I had given up flying her, as the man I loved was killed in a USN Blue Angels crash in 2007. I have never known such intense sorrow and stillness. My passion for flight was gone. All I felt was numbness. My soul was quiet.

Herb, a mutual friend of ours, had bargained with Kevin to exchange a flight in a T-28 for one in a Blue Angel F/A-18. Sadly, it never came to fruition. Herb stayed in close contact with me after Kevin's death. When he realized I had given up flying, he challenged me to fly to his next air show. If I showed up, he said, he would treat me to a flight in his T-28 in honor of Kevin. A welcome and honorable challenge it was. The show was an inspiring venue: I did loopty-loops in that T-28 and I thought of Kevin each and every foot we soared.

Ironically, on my way home from the show, I heard air traffic control (ATC), speaking to Thunderbird One. My tragic loss of Kevin inspired the USAF Thunderbirds to adopt me into their family out of respect for my wounded heart. They are the "sister squadron" of the Blue Angels and the respect between the two is remarkable. I confidently requested air traffic control to send a special "Hello," to the team flying 10,000 feet directly above me. Smiling and holding my breath, I heard Thunderbird One chime in over the radio, calling out my name. Here I was on my first solo again, heading in the right direction this time, and my friends—my role models—were flying with me, sharing the passion that keeps our souls afloat.

You see, two similar tragedies illuminated my path. I continue to be enlightened by both and feel with every cell in my body that the foundation on which I grow is based upon my soul's passion. Taking leaps of faith and being my own hero have led me to be a strong woman whose path may at times be dimmed, but whose passion will forever reignite. Whenever I gaze skyward, I see my spirit flying, suspended by angel's wings, for there I have been and there I will always long to return.

Kara Swensen

LIFE'S LEADING LADY...YOU

Elaine Hendrix

As an actress, it is my job to be an expert in emotions—simple, complex and everything in between. Basically, it is my duty to be able to identify, understand, and recreate emotions with authentic and seemingly effortless representation. Eric Morris, a beloved acting coach of mine, calls actors "professional experiencers." I certainly agree that is a most perfectly fitting description.

As a "professional experiencer," it is my responsibility to have a well-rounded grasp of the human condition that is without judgment. Otherwise, it makes it impossible to hold a mirror up to society, which is, ultimately, something entertainment is beholden to as an art form. In other words, I believe reflecting life back to life is essential, and to do so accurately one cannot comment on it or alter it in any way. It has to be pure and real and raw. Otherwise, it's just bad acting.

Therefore, as an artist, my range of characters is enhanced (or hindered) by my ability (or inability) to represent any given type of human behavior, (that is, experience any given emotion)—all under imaginary circumstances.

Great! Shines a whole new light on "Hollywood," but where am I going with this, and what does it have to do with you?

Well, I firmly believe it is also my responsibility as a human, and particularly as a woman, to live my life with the same passion for understanding the human condition. Emotions seem to wreak such havoc on our sensitive feminine beings! How many times have you been knocked down, dragged out and overwhelmed with feelings that you could not control, and certainly did not care for in the least—jealousy, anger, guilt or worry? Even the "good" ones—passion, joy or elation—can sometimes be too much.

If you are anything like me, then you know well what I am talking about. I have basically gotten the [bleep] kicked out of me at times over the intensity of my emotions. Since it is my entire job to feel (and as a woman I seem to have no choice in the matter) I'm a walking nerve of sheer emotions. Yay me.

The good news is that by turning poison into medicine (that is, integrating my creative life with my personal constitution), I have learned some really valuable lessons about how to handle the turbulent storms that thunder across the seas of the creative woman.

First, emotions, in and of themselves, are meaningless. In the simplest of terms they are chemical expressions that arise from various thoughts we have about a particular subject, usually cultivated from memories of a particular situation. Because of the endless stream of thoughts and memories we tend to have, emotions can be overwhelming because they are uncontrollable. Knowing this is helpful when it comes time to sort through them. Although you might not be able to control how you feel, you can certainly control what you think and thus, what actions you take. Working with thought is a big key.

Some version of "This will never end," is one of the most challenging thoughts I have about my emotions. Next would probably be some version of "I can't handle this." And just to put the icing on the cake, another potent block is good ol' "Why me?" All three are valid questions, but not particularly helpful when your stomach is turning, your head is about to explode and you're pacing like a caged animal because you feel some lovely combination of anger, hurt, guilt and sadness. No, there are stronger questions to ask, starting with (and continuously coming back to) what might be the least obvious: "How do I feel?"

It's like trying to solve a puzzle in the dark when you don't actually know what you are feeling. So, when the heat is on (literally), it is important to stop and identify each emotion—not change, stop or push down—identify. Make the effort to learn the difference between guilt and anger, anger and sadness, sadness and disappointment, and so forth. This is the first vital step in owning your power versus continuing to spin like a manic whirling dervish, especially when the emotions are more covert and insidious, such as depression or self-doubt. First, start with what is, then move forward.

Now, depending on the intensity of the feelings (how much history you have with a particular thought) this may or may not be enough. Feelings pop up because a part of you is longing to be heard, and the more practice you have at identifying how you feel, the better you'll be at moving through your emotions with greater grace simply because you are being witness to them.

For the feelings that tend to come up over and over or roar a little more fiercely, digging deeper will be required. Everyone's story will be both universally connective and uniquely individual. Taking time to hear other people's journeys and taking time to be alone is equally beneficial. Balancing the two will help identify your own experiences, give you solid proof that you are not alone, give you practice in trusting yourself to be your own best friend and give you terrific information for options in different thoughts and behaviors.

Until you have a handle on exactly what you are feeling and the thoughts behind it, make it a habit to refrain from taking any action—or should I say, reaction. In acting terms, this is the character's "motivation" and it's the same in real life. To keep from making a big ol' mess of more emotions, it is wise to keep your motives as clear as possible. This may require some serious discipline in sitting still through some very uncomfortable moments until the emotional waters have calmed and the mental skies have cleared. It is a sure-fire way to build trust in yourself when you can let yourself feel whatever you feel and think whatever you think, but retain the power to choose the reaction.

A few other inquiries about processing feelings (and thoughts, before taking action):

- Is where I'm placing my attention worth it?
- Can I act "as if" until I get back to center?
- When have I felt this way before?
- Is this really going to last forever?
- What evidence do I have that what I feel is true?
- What evidence do I have that what I feel is not true?
- What is my motivation?

Finally, the more permission you give yourself to go through your process without judgment, the more you will learn, understand and accept yourself, and, ultimately, others. Emotions can be scary and overwhelming. We are not machines. This is why developing a system that works for you is crucial for understanding, healing and growing. Don't let the mysterious, deep, dark world of emotions derail you from being the lead in the movie of your life. You are a star! Act like one.

Elaine Hendrix

Awaken Your Health

INTRODUCTION

Heidi Reagan

We all know women are born caregivers. It is in our genetic make-up, reinforced during our childhood by the culture around us. We take on the responsibility of caring for others even when we desperately need to take care of ourselves. This nurturing is all in the name of love. It's admirable, but wouldn't it make more sense to give from a full cup rather than from one half-drained?

We split our energy by doing too much, too fast and too often for everyone else. We tax our minds and bodies to the breaking point. This creates more stress in our lives, which can contribute to a breakdown, both emotionally and physically.

The dictionary defines stress as: "A mentally or emotionally disruptive or upsetting condition occurring in response to adverse external influences and capable of affecting physical health, usually characterized by increased heart rate, a rise in blood pressure, muscular tension, irritability and depression." The dictionary definition describes the connection between the stress in our lives and the deterioration of our physical health and emotional well-being.

Think about your own patterns. How much of your physical well-being in the past has been subject to extremes? We have no time to sit and eat a balanced meal, so we hit a drive-thru, eating in our cars on the way to our next appointment. Perhaps your extreme is sleep deprivation. Procrastination prevented that report from being completed and over-scheduling put your workload in hyper-drive. We compensate by staying up until all hours to finish the day's tasks.

We want our children to be well-balanced, well-rested, healthy and happy, so what example are we setting by not taking care of ourselves?

What will it take for us to align with the signals our bodies give us and provide the rest, nutrition and exercise necessary without the guilt often associated with doing so?

Here's another aspect to self-care: Do you prioritize your eating habits based on the amount of weight you want to lose rather than the amount of nourishment you want to take in? Do you spend weeks at the gym when a class reunion is looming only to stop going once the reunion is over? When we approach our health in this way, it becomes more about our physical appearance rather than our physical well-being.

Feeling good about the way we look goes a long way toward establishing strong self-esteem. However, appearance won't provide the quality of life with our families that we want and deserve. The priority must be how we feel and how we nurture our bodies. When we feel great in our minds and in our bodies is when we will look our best as well.

This is not the time to beat ourselves up for not taking better care of ourselves. Self-acceptance will shift your perception toward an image of balance. It is about choosing equilibrium, from this point forward. You are not alone. There are many of us in the chaotic world of extremes.

The following women's stories will help you identify where you may be out of balance and provide you with action steps to self-care.

Heidi Reagan

FEELING MY PERSONAL BEST

Alice Greene

When people meet me, they can't believe I've struggled with weight or poor health, but that was my life until seven years ago.

As a child I was overweight and started my first extreme diet in high school, eating just one meal a day and taking NoDoz. I did this again two years after I graduated, when my weight was nearing 200 pounds, and I continued to diet through my 20s and 30s to maintain my thin look. Beneath my clothes, I hid how out of shape I really was, as well as the shame I felt about my body. I would periodically rally myself to go to a gym or use my home exercise equipment, but it never lasted more than a few months, and occurred only every few years. I hated exercise, having suffered through grade school gym classes and my father's insistence that I take rigorous bike rides as a kid. I did all I could to avoid exercising as an adult for more than 20 years.

Instead, I focused on my high-tech career and worked an average of 70 hours a week for years. I never made time for a balanced or healthy lifestyle and seldom took a vacation. In 2000, at the age of 43, my lack of exercise, high stress and unhealthy lifestyle took their toll. I was bedridden with a three-month chronic fatigue episode for the fourth time. I was also dealing with considerable digestive issues, chronic nausea, constant back pain and a significant weight gain of five dress sizes in just 15 months. Even worse, I didn't care anymore about the career to which I had given my life. I was exhausted, sick and burnt out.

When I was finally well enough to get out of bed, I experienced a profound, defining moment. I stood naked in front of my full-length mirror, looking at my overweight body with cellulite nearly to my knees. I discovered my inner thighs had turned into jelly fat, and I felt unsteady and weak. I knew in my heart that my body didn't reflect the real me, how I wanted to live my life or how I wanted to feel, and I knew it was up to me to do something about it. I decided that enough was enough. I was heading into perimenopause, and I had to do something before it was too late.

This wake-up call became the catalyst that made me change the way I took care of myself. Standing in front of that mirror, I decided to start using my stair machine in the basement as soon as I had the strength, and I further resolved in that moment that I would not quit before I was able to fit into my wardrobe of beautiful size six clothing. I also resolved to start tracking my foods and to follow a healthy eating regimen. I didn't want to do another diet. I didn't want to hire a full-time personal trainer again. I didn't want to go to the gym looking the way I did. I wanted to do something on my own in a way that I could live with.

I was pretty sure I knew what to do, but that didn't turn out to be the case. I did want someone who cared about my accountability and progress to guide me in the things I didn't know and to help me with motivation and encouragement. I didn't know where to find such a person and turned to myself and a girlfriend with whom I walked a few days a week. It wasn't easy.

My first time back on the stair machine was January 1, 2001, and I could barely exercise for 10 minutes. That scared me, and I wondered if I was going to fail once again. But I kept at it, and within a month I could do 30 minutes several times a week. I bought a month-at-a-glance calendar to start tracking my weekly goals and accomplishments. I created new goals each week. In the second month, I was able to reach 45 minutes, five times a week. Then, I began to increase my intensity level. My goal became to exercise five to six days a week for a minimum of 30 minutes at a time, and if I didn't reach it, I let it go. I was learning not to beat myself up if I wasn't perfect and to just do the best I could.

I was also learning to keep myself going with visualizations of being back in my size six clothes, cutting out pictures of women with the body I realistically hoped to achieve. When my inner voice resisted, I told myself, "No option, no discussion, just go do it." I found a TV show I enjoyed, and each evening during the week, I would put on my sneakers and head downstairs to watch it while I did my exercises. This helped establish a routine I could enjoy, which changed my belief that exercise was something I hated. I was beginning to look forward to it.

My greatest struggle, however, was waiting to see results. It was five months almost to the day before I experienced any difference in my size. Then, I seemed to lose a size overnight. I was thrilled and encouraged to keep going. I didn't have a scale, so I wasn't focused on my weight, and for that I was grateful. I didn't have to experience the daily anguish of seeing that the scale wasn't budging. Instead, I kept the faith and kept on climbing. Another four or five months passed before I saw another change, and again, I lost a full size. This happened again about four months later, and in the course of two years, I was finally back into my lovely clothes.

In the meantime, I shifted my lifestyle and began to make fitness a priority. I rearranged my day so I could exercise in the morning and start work at 10:00 a.m. I began cooking healthy meals instead of eating out, and I added strength training to my routine. I discovered I wasn't fighting the exercise anymore and was actually enjoying it. It has been more than seven years since I adopted a lifestyle approach to fitness. I have changed my life, career, and level of happiness. I am now 50, and look and feel my personal best.

Ask youself:

- How can you rewrite your own rules about having to be perfect and good?
- What do you want to feel or experience that will keep you motivated?

- What is your body trying to tell you in terms of stress, pain, illness or hunger?
- What beliefs about yourself or exercise are driving your decisions, and how can you change these?
- What type of fitness routine or healthier eating choices will work best for you?
- Who or what can support you to stay on track week to week?

Answer these questions and you will be on your way to feeling your personal best.

Alice Greene

ir goals and, more importantly, in making exercise and fitness part :heir lifestyles.

ved being home and closer to my family while still making a differ- :e in people's lives. I was relieved that the peer pressure was ıoved. I didn't feel the need to exercise to try to keep up with my ·rs, so the exercise became more hit-and-miss rather than a focused ention. Yet I continued to feed my inner fire to excel in my business l continued to push myself; my sense of self-worth was still wrapped in my business.

I geared up to attend my first fitness coaching conference, I felt ıflicted. It seemed to me the harder I worked, the more I felt I was nning my wheels and getting nowhere. I wasn't happy. My life was : of balance, but I loved my work.

the conference we were given a short exercise: "Write down our core ues." Examples were given, and as I sat and thought about this exer- :, the curtain slowly lifted.

ıen I put my values on paper, I saw the incongruence of my life. I s focused on my business and making choices that only met my vest core values while neglecting what really mattered. I wasn't being e to myself. The most important thing in my life was getting the st attention. No wonder my life felt so chaotic, stressful and frus- ting! It all clicked, and in that deciding moment, I changed the ›ices in my life. I began to examine living in alignment with my hest values. I wanted to focus on my marriage, family, my relation- p with God and my health, and to give myself permission to let go the need to work so much. What good was a thriving business if I sn't fulfilled?

ıen I came back from the conference, I took a hard look at how I s spending my time. It was then that I realized I hadn't done laun-

Self Care Before Sit Ups

Amy Lundberg

"You can gaze at your navel all day long and neve find answers inside you."—Anita Renfroe

I am a fitness coach who loves waffle cones, Rocco choc good burger. I would rather read a good book than spen side, hike than run a marathon, and I would avoid streng completely if I could. As someone in the fitness industry, t ties made me unique. Early in my career, I compared myse personal trainers and women and saw myself as inadequate. fit; I didn't push myself to exercise as much as I should, no as I should. Soon, my self esteem was tied to what I perce supposed to look like as a fitness professional.

I felt guilty. I wasn't spending enough time exercising, but hours at the gym, the last thing I wanted to do was stay to d workout. My passion was to help others. I loved seeing the plishments, and through their eyes I could see and feel my ow plishments in helping them achieve their fitness goals. This g inner fire to succeed in my business. Everything else that mattered to me started to fall to the wayside: Exercising and time with my husband and daughter. I didn't even notice obsession to grow my business had altered my family and ho was completely out of balance and had lost sight of what I w ing for.

When I became pregnant with my second child, I knew so had to change. It became clear that personal training wasn't ble with raising a family, so I began to look for another way to clients. I found it in fitness coaching, which allowed me to and guide my clients by phone. This was a great solution for m surprised by the impact coaching had in helping my clients dry in a year. My husband had never said a word. He had silently taken over this job and had never complained that I was no longer taking care of the household. I was dumbfounded. I wasn't sharing in the work of raising our family or maintaining the bonds of a loving marriage. I was stunned to realize how little time I was spending with my family or in keeping up with the daily activities of running the house. It was obvious how selfish I had been. One evening, Tom and I were spending time together—something we hadn't done in a long while. The business phone rang, which meant that I probably would be occupied for at least another hour before I would be back. Tom had simply asked me to spend some time with him. It hit me again.

I made the decision to start taking better care of myself and my family, and to return to prayer. I had been tolerating inactivity, a messy house and a business that was not the success I had envisioned. Above all, I had lost my connection with God. Through my renewed connection to my faith and myself, I was able to reclaim my self-esteem and was able to attain balance in my life. I changed the way I spoke to myself and how I felt about my body. I had to start practicing what I preached: self-care before sit-ups. I took an inside-out approach to release my inner conflict. I became more mindful of my food choices, got excited about training for 5k races and discovered a passion for yoga, meditating and working 3 days a week.

After my third child was born, losing weight became quite a challenge. My exercise wasn't as consistent as I wanted it to be. One evening, I sat quietly and asked myself why I didn't exercise more regularly, and a quiet voice inside me said, "Because Tom doesn't, so why should I?" I had no idea I was carrying this limiting belief. Just because my husband didn't exercise shouldn't affect my decision, or more poignantly, make me feel guilty for taking time to do it. I immediately understood that I needed to take care of myself in order to fulfill my core values. I've been exercising regularly since then, not to measure up to what I think others expect of me, but in appreciation for all that my body has done and for all that I can do in my life. Through meditation and prayer I was able to make the connection to see myself in God's eyes, instead of society's eyes. This has allowed me to be at peace with my body and to step away from the imaginary judgments I had created. I have found myself more patient and attentive with my four children, more focused during work, full of energy and finding joy and laughter in my life.

I have found my answers from within through self-care and the power of nurturing the body, mind and spirit in alignment with core values. This is how you make the best choices for yourself, your lifestyle and your health while still enjoying the chocolate. This is the missing peace.

Here's how you can start to do this for yourself:

- Identify your top five core values.
- Determine the ways your life is out of alignment and balance.
- Look at what you are tolerating and how you can reclaim your energy; consider the ways in which you feel empty and how you can be recharged.
- Connect with your inner guidance and faith.
- Take inspired action in alignment with your values.

Amy Lundberg

Wake Up, Step Up

MaryKay Mullally

The beeping of the alarm clock pierced my blissful unconsciousness. As my eyes focused, my awareness shifted to the reality of the present. I realized it was another day that I had nothing worth living for. It felt like, aside from my husband and our teen-age son and daughter, there was nothing and no one to live for. Taking a moment to ponder, I asked myself how this could this be. How could I have three degrees, a good job, a loving family, a beautiful home and financial security and feel so empty and hopeless? On the face of it, I was a virtual super mom. Since turning 40 three years earlier, I'd held down a high-powered job, raised two children, run three marathons and whittled my middle-aged body down to a sexy size two. I had put on a strong, confident face and it seemed like I had it all together. After years of being numb, unconscious and deeply resigned, I had become an imposter in my own life.

Four years earlier, I had landed what seemed like the perfect job in the perfect place—San Diego, in gorgeous southern California. Working 10 to 12-hour days, sitting behind a desk at my high-tech job and dealing with impossible deadlines and corporate politics wasn't exactly the California dream I had imagined. It also did not do much for my figure. The deadly combination of inactivity, stress, lack of sleep and a diet left to chance left me 20 pounds overweight and feeling frumpy. I had to do something about my life style and it was time to take charge of my health.

I turned to running as my stress reliever and as a way to stop the runaway weight gain. Running at night with my husband Rob became a way to connect with him and keep my promise to myself to exercise regularly. Then I took on my diet. I started by eliminating the unbridled consumption of any and every kind of candy that seemed to be a fixture of every desk in my office building. I began to actually pay attention to what I was putting into my body, making small changes and healthier choices each day. I woke up a few minutes earlier to pack a healthy lunch. I dropped a few pounds, began to feel better and, more importantly, was empowered by my action. Armed with renewed confidence and support of a colleague who was also an avid runner, I set my sights on a new goal. How great would it be to run a marathon in my 40th year? It seemed like an impossible dream but I was going to do it!

Having never run more than three miles, 26.2 miles seemed daunting. Before I knew it, I was running five, then eight, then 10 miles. I realized achieving these milestones resulted from constantly seeing myself being successful, taking one step at a time and never giving up. I ran a half marathon in January. Then two months before turning 41, barely able to see the finish line through tears of joy and disbelief, I crossed the finish line of the San Diego Marathon as the proudest mom in the world, holding hands with my 14-year-old son and 11-year-old daughter.

Now, two years and three marathons later, here I was lying awake in bed asking myself, "Is this all there really is?" I wanted more for myself and my life than a bunch of academic, professional and personal trophies to prove myself a worthy human being. I wanted to do something that I loved. I wanted to wake up excited every single day. I knew it was going to take being someone I had never been to make this quantum leap. In that moment, I knew it was my time to wake up and step up.

That wake-up call ultimately led me to put myself into the Landmark Forum: a unique educational program designed to help people be more effective in the areas of life that are important to them such as career, relationships and self-confidence. Through this education I had some of the most profound insights and breakthroughs of my life. I learned that I am really not broken. I discovered only a life lived for others is worth living and that my life was about transforming the health of the world. How? I did not know, but after losing my mom to lung cancer, my dad to colon cancer and my brother to AIDS by the time I was 35, I knew that was a life worth living.

Turning my attention outward with a commitment to making a difference for others, I founded Step Up For Life, a beginner's half-marathon training program for women. I took women who had never run before and trained them to do a half marathon in three months with support and friendly accountability. For many, it was the most profound experience of their lives. Since then, I have helped hundreds of women who had given up on themselves in their 40s and 50s to smash their "I could never do that" beliefs. Today, my business has expanded into a wellness coaching practice and I have helped hundreds more men and women lose weight and take control of their health. Today, I am living a life I love and I am living it powerfully by helping others do the same. By stepping into my power, I am transforming the health of the world one person at a time, one step at a time, starting with me. In my 40s, I am in the best shape of my life. Having the privilege of uplifting and inspiring others through my example motivates me to step up every day. I invite you to step up to a life you love.

- Focus on what you want, not on the obstacles in the way. You become what you think about. If you focus on what you want, you will begin to create it. If you focus on the lack of it or the reasons you cannot have it, you will create that, too.
- Visualize the end result and how it will make you feel. Your emotions are your internal guidance system. Your mind can't tell the difference between a dream and reality. Feel your dream like it has already been achieved and you will begin to attract people and circumstances to make it happen.
- Listen to your inner voice. You don't have to see the whole

staircase to take the next step. You may not know exactly how to achieve the perfect end result but if you listen to your inner voice and trust yourself, you will know what the next step is for you and be able to step up.

- Take action on your dreams. Despair takes you out of action, but action takes you out of despair. All it takes is one action; one step at a time.
- Be gentle with yourself. When you encounter setbacks, acknowledge the steps you have taken. Failure is simply an indication of where strength and support are missing. It doesn't mean anything is wrong with you. Look for what's missing rather that what's wrong.

MaryKay Mullally

How I Transformed from an Ugly Duckling to a Beautiful Swan

Melina Kunifas

I was born and raised in a town where your looks and money measured your personal value. So, gaining weight in my teen years and continuing to be overweight through my 20s was not only hard and painful, but it took away all confidence I might have otherwise carried over from childhood.

Wherever I went, I felt the need to prove to others and to myself that I was worthy. Consequently, I went out often, acquired a ton of friends and dressed uniquely—all to make-believe that I was at the top of the world. However, deep inside, I felt like a loser. Why couldn't I just be like everyone else? Why didn't I have the confidence my friends had?

At the same time, I didn't understand why people were judged by their looks. Weren't there other qualities in a person that determined a person's worth? I found myself fighting these social beliefs, yet casting judgment toward overweight people myself.

I would often return home from a night out, tiptoe into the kitchen, close the door so my parents wouldn't hear me and eat until I was stuffed. I needed to numb my feelings of failure and loneliness.

I was always the "guys' best friend," but never the one they actually wanted to date. However, the ones who did like me were not worth it. After all, what kind of guy would like someone like me?

I needed to prove that being overweight was my own choice. I felt embarrassed and rarely opened up with anyone about my pain.

Seventeen and depressed, I rebelled. I didn't want to go to college and

I didn't want to go out. I didn't even want to get out of bed. My mind was a blur; I couldn't see any light at the end of the tunnel. Feeling useless and not knowing what to do with my life, I felt desperate. I hoped for the day when I would lose weight and all of my problems would disappear.

I tried every gym and diet under the sun. I would begin them all and quit after a short while. I always found a good excuse to give up: I got sick, I got hurt, it was not a priority, etc. The real reason was that I didn't appreciate myself and didn't want to do "good" to someone I didn't care for. I believed I had to so I could look like everyone else, but I just hated it.

After I finished college, I left town. I moved abroad, hoping that I would find peace in a new place with new faces and new social demands. However, I carried "myself" with me, and I was far from peace internally. The problems were still there inside of me, and I was even more lost, not knowing where to go or what to do.

If you had asked me then who I would like to be, I would have answered, "Anyone but me." This, of course, meant someone thin. But even in the mist of all that pain, I always believed there ought to be a reason for my struggles. Today, I can see that reason. I had a lot to learn about myself and about life, and maybe if my life had been easier, I wouldn't know what I do now. I wouldn't be able to help others heal their pain as well. If you asked me today who I'd like to be, my answer is always the same: Me!

I now feel peace inside. I am a calm and patient mother, wife and friend. I know everything will work out for the best.

What Happened to Make Me Change?

I always waited for the day when I would have a revelation and would cease my destructive behaviors. Sometimes I even wished I was anorexic or had some sort of disease that would stop me from eating.

The revelation didn't come all at once; rather, it came in "installments" each time I was ready to learn a new lesson.

I first realized that no matter what had happened in the past, I was the only one who could really take care of myself now. I stopped looking for others to blame for my suffering, or for a savior in every person who came into my life. I finally took charge of my life, and here's what happened.

- One day I wrote positive messages to myself, like, "You're beautiful," "You're intelligent," and so on. First I couldn't use the word *I* because I didn't really believe a word I wrote. Despite my doubt, I read it every night before going to bed until one day I realized I was using the word "I" instead of "You." That's when things began to shift inside me.
- I began to treat myself as a little child who needed extra care, instead of someone I despised. When bad feelings surfaced, instead of trying to push them away with food, I welcomed them, embracing every thought until it ceased. If that didn't work, I would ask what they were trying to tell me.
- I exaggerated praise for myself in everything I did. For example, I would tell myself, "I am awesome. I remembered to do this!" I would also call my husband and say, "You are so lucky you married such an intelligent woman, listen to what I did," and so forth, until my subconscious started to believe it.
- I started to ease into changes in my habits instead of going cold turkey as I had in the past. First, I decided that my breakfast was going to be healthy, no matter how I ate the rest of the day. Then, sometime later, I began to incorporate salad into my lunch not every meal. I didn't eat celery sticks for a snack, but I had a small salad with whatever I ate for lunch. Slowly, I realized I was actually sticking to every small change. They were things I could see myself doing in the long run because they were approached in increments.
- The same thing happened with exercise. One day a friend asked me if I could run for 30 seconds. That seemed doable. A few

months later I was running for 30 minutes and actually started to enjoy it. Running is only an example; it could have been any exercise.

- I bought new clothes even though I had a nice wardrobe in my closet—that didn't fit. I started to look at myself at the mirror and appreciate that sexy, womanly body I saw. (Pretend until you believe it.)
- I got rid of the clutter in my life—physically and emotionally. I "got rid" of anyone in my life who didn't truly care for or support me. That's when I met a wonderful, loving man who appreciated me exactly the way I was extra pounds and all.
- I read a lot of books to develop myself emotionally and spiritua-lity so I could fill the hole I had previously filled with food.

I believe that self-development? physical, emotional and spiritual? is an ongoing endeavor. That's why I am always looking to perfect myself and the world around me. I believe that not only will I be a happier person, but I am also making this world a better place for everyone around me. After all, a smile can be contagious, and I am sure you, too, have the amazing power to positively influence others and yourself!

Melina Kunifas

SMILE

Nicole Brandon

"Smile, Dolly! That's all she does."

When I was a child of seven or eight, I was in a show called "Stars of Tomorrow." Young performers sang, danced and played their hearts out to audiences across the globe. I was small for my age. The host would call me out on stage and say, "Take a bow."

My little body, dressed in frills and lace, would bounce up and down, curtsy on cue and run off. "Do it again!" he'd holler. I'd run back on stage, my little shiny patent leather shoes tapping across the stage and my long hair trailing behind with my curls perfectly placed and my ruffles and bows rippling through the air as again I graced the stage, smiled, curtsied and took in the thunderous applause.

"Come on," he'd yell to the audience, "Isn't she wonderful?" They'd cheer even louder.

"Smile, Dolly," he'd scream. "That's all she does," he'd tell the audience. The crowd would go wild.

After I flew off the stage again to roaring cheers and applause, he'd call my name to come back. "Actually," he would now tell the audience, "She's a marvelous dancer." Then he'd prompt me to go and change.

I'd run off to the dressing room and change into a beautiful dance costume my mom spent hours creating for me and I'd wait in the wings to be called once again. It's true I was—and I am—a wonderful dancer. From my earliest memory, I have been able to move in a way that is heaven on earth. However, in that moment, at that second in time, my little brain believed that for people to like me I just had to smile and dress well and to impress people, well, I had to perform.

The messages we get as a children rule the way in which we see ourselves, how we feel, and how we relate to the outside world. I have spent my life smiling and dressing well and I have exhausted myself trying to impress people by doing amazing things in order to attract people's attention and to gain their love.

As a baby, I never crawled. I leap-frogged my way forward. I propelled myself to walk at just a couple months old. Anyone could see I had a gift in my legs and I needn't wear frills or lace to find joy, balance, peace, harmony or passion in life. Movement would be my world. I was an amazing athlete because I had a brother and male cousins, and no girls with whom to play. Never did I wake up and long to play football, but athletics was part of the tapestry of my body and my life's journey.

Everyone has a physical gift inside them whether it's a voice, a song, or a perfection of movement, grace and beauty that's all their own. Finding that connection is the golden chalice of life. What is beauty? What is physical perfection to you? For years I have worked with people to help them change their bodies and therefore change their lives; to be magical and scintillatingly free. To be fulfilled you must find that string—the golden thread that connects you to yourself.

So, how do you do that? If your life is a story, your version of a fairytale, then we start where all good stories start—at the beginning. Your body, the one you nurtured and created, grew and explored, the one you brought here with your eyes, your hair, your skin, your movement, your shape, your agility, your strength, your touch, your beauty and natural life, is indeed wondrous and magic.

From the beginning, the first thing your body did on its own—your first movement—was to reach.

Remember?

Someone who loved you put you on your back, while the little mobile dangled and danced in the air. Think back. You can't roll over yet, but you can reach. You reach for the faces that look in on you. You eventually reach for your toes, rattles and other pleasurable items. You learn to stand in the crib by reaching for the rail. You learn to walk by reaching toward someone. That "art" of reaching gives you a sense of balance. To be picked up, you open your arms wide. If you stopped reaching at some point in your life, your sense of balance and physical wellness may have completely gone awry. Is that you? When you master the art of reaching, you can reach for your goals, your finances, your passions and your dreams. Reaching was the first essential movement that made your body happy. It was completely individual to you.

To change your body and to find the perfect shape, weight, size and energy is easy. You just explore your body's natural instincts, choices and design. Think back to your childhood. Were you on a team or were you an individual star player? Did you play a sport or participate in an activity because someone else put you there? Did you do something because your friends were doing it and you wanted to do it, too? Is that how you exercise now?

Did your friends ride their bikes and you rode your bike just to be with them, or did you ride to explore, for the fun, the play, or the great adventure? Or, did you ride just to get away; to think, feel safe or to fly with the wind? Was that ride your personal choice, ultimate passion and desire? Was it your drive, your compulsion, your love for whatever it was, that made you move—that excited you? That made you fly out of bed? Or did you have amazing outfits that were associated with your body's joy? Perhaps a ballerina costume you never took off? A team uniform, a dress or something else that made you feel good, beautiful and proud when wearing it? When you work out, are outfits associated with how you feel and perform today?

Did you ever win any prizes or awards for anything physical you did? Are competition, achievement and challenge important to your body's wellness and to you?

Possibly, your body's natural movement and choices allowed you to travel, to miss school or to be popular? Be honest: What did it give you? How did you feel? What do you remember that was beautiful to you? Was it people, exciting places, nature or music?

I have a client who told me how beautiful she had been when she was six. She spoke of a yellow dress she loved to wear with her hair braided with ribbons and sparkle barrettes. By the time we got to age eleven, she spoke of her beautiful aunt. When did that little girl disappear? When did she stop being beautiful and when did beauty become only on the outside—–not on the inside? We had to go back to find when she disconnected from her joy, and then re-thread her life with her desires, life and glory.

Connect to your life. Did you have a favorite pair of shoes? I still have my first ballet slippers. I was two. That alone tells me something about my world. I remember how I moved in them. I danced around the living room for my elderly grandfather and felt like I was twirling on a cloud. He made me feel like the most beautiful girl in the world. This feeling I carry with me.

Finding your personal joy that comes from your perfect body means reconnecting with the perfection, image, joy, expression, creation and glory of you. Can you recall if you loved the water, the sun, the outdoors, the gym, a dance studio, your bedroom or a made-up stage? Your happiness is directly the result of your exhilaration of spirit.

Do what makes you happy. After all, shopping is very aerobic. When you thread your life from the beginning of your movement, you can eat, drink, dance, make love and move in a body bubbling with vitality, strength, sexuality, passion and pleasure which fills you up in every way.

Your body is just longing to tell you what makes it happy.

In my case, I learned I didn't need to please anyone. I didn't need applause, ringlets or beautiful clothes. I have a gift of movement and life. We all do!

It's simple. Do you want the perfect body? Just remember my words to go back to where you started. Lie back and relax. Reach for what you want. Play. Find your balance and make a move toward the perfect, happy and healthier you.

I did and still to this day, I do what I learned on that stage to do on cue.... Only this time, it's completely natural. Yes! No need for applause, but indeed, I do, SMILE.

Nicole Brandon

Managed Cost to Mangled Care

Alice R. Comer, RN, MNSc

I am not alone in my belief that a strong link exists between the body, the mind and the spirit. One cannot have a balanced life unless all three of these dimensions of being are in balance.

When we focus on the physical self, we realize that there will likely be a need to seek health care in one's lifetime. If you have had any encounters with the U.S. health care system in the past few years, you probably noticed it has become so complicated that you can easily be lost in the shuffle. Even worse is the possibility of a missed diagnosis because of system fragmentation or lack of communication. Some of us remember the "good old days" when we could go to the doctor or hospital without being obligated to pay our bills on the spot. Doctors and hospitals made money and patients were cared for comfortably by the same doctor throughout their lives. It was a simple time.

Technological advancements have fostered an increase in lifespan. Using new technology, specialists can focus on particular ailments and support continued development of life-saving techniques. However, with advancements in medical care came increasing costs. Insurance companies—including Medicare and Medicaid—freely paid for care that was rendered. Prices continued to rise to the point that those responsible for payment (usually insurance and Medicare) began to feel the crunch. As a result, in 1984, Medicare began implementing restrictions on the amount of payment for particular types of care. Other insurance companies soon followed.

The new insurance programs were called "managed care," but a better title would have been "managed cost." The concept was that one physician, usually a family practice doctor, would manage all the care needs. If a specialist was needed, the "primary care doctor" would authorize and coordinate that care. The concept was good, but a number of things contributed to the downfall of this model. Some of the issues included a proliferation of specialists, fewer primary care physicians, consumer demand and a continued increase in costs. This vicious cycle has continued and the consumer is caught in the middle. Care has become fragmented. A person could have four, five, or six doctors, each specializing in a particular body system. The downside of multiple doctors is that multiple physicians will not communicate effectively with each other. The system for adequate information sharing is not in place. This practice can contribute to unnecessary tests, hospital stays, medications, or missed diagnoses or treatments.

Insurance companies continue to squeeze providers for better care with lower costs. As it turns out, the payers are spending less for more and higher-priced specialist care. In response, the physicians try to treat more people to compensate for lower payments. The result has been an increase in the fragmentation of care, longer waits, and the possibility of health issues being overlooked. As a health care participant, I urge you to take steps to communicate with your care team. This could save your life. Remember, you are a partner in your health care.
Here are some tricks of the trade that can help make encounters with the health care system a little easier. Some of these are merely for the sake of convenience; others could save your life. Here are three of the most critical steps that will facilitate information sharing and compliance with prescribed treatments.

Tip number one: Document in writing (preferably typed) your health status, family history and any medications that are being taken. For each medication, include the name, dose, how often is taken, and for what reason or condition it is taken. This is important in maintaining consistency when accessing any type of health care. These questions are asked at any point of access for care. If your medical team does not have all the information, medical judgments may be incorrect or even dangerous. Make copies (or ask the provider to make a copy of medical records and test results) and take this information with you to every stop you make along the medical path. Don't forget to update your history as conditions change.

Tip Number Two: Maximize your appointment time. Time has become a precious commodity in health care. We feel rushed when we are with the doctor. Many times the important questions are not asked or answered. Go to appointments armed with an organized and thorough list of questions. Write them down. The physician can then focus on answering your questions. You are much more likely to encounter a positive experience.

Tip Number Three: Manage your medications. In today's advanced health care system, more tests, more treatments and more medications are driving costs higher. Medication prices make up the greatest portion of healthcare spending. It is not uncommon for individuals to leave their prescriptions unfilled due to the cost. If these are critical medications, such as those for the heart or blood pressure, conditions may worsen quickly resulting in stroke or heart attack. Many such cases are appearing at emergency rooms and doctor offices; the physician has no idea that the patient is not taking the prescribed medications. If you cannot pay for your medications, it is imperative that you discuss this with your health care provider. There are ways to secure the medications you need, but there are few ways to maintain your health without taking your prescription.

Keep these medication management tips in mind:

- If you are given a prescription, ask the doctor or nurse what condition this medication is designed to treat. You need at least a basic understanding of your prescriptions.
- Ask about the cost. Even with health insurance, some medications can be expensive.
- If it is expensive, ask about less expensive brands, or about the availability of generic versions. National chain pharmacies often

list comparison prices on their Web sites. Many pharmacies offer very low prices on popular prescriptions.

- If the medicine is too expensive, ask the doctor for samples, and keep asking until you get a "no." Call your pharmacy or search its Web site.

Attempting to navigate the complex health care system can be confusing. Take care and take control to remain healthy. The mind and the spirit depend on your body to serve as a platform for your contribution to the world.

Your body depends on you.

Alice R. Comer, RN, MNSc

Awaken Your Career

Introduction

Ardice Farrow

A job is an opportunity. A career is a privilege. And a purpose-driven career is not just a possibility, but a probability for those who are willing to wake up to their passion and talent.

Those of us who feel pulled by a unique purpose and the passion of our desire to express, share and make a difference are experiencing life at an extraordinary level.

It is never the type, the style or the scope of our vision that matters or gives it value. It is simply the privilege of allowing ourselves to see our vision and giving ourselves permission to step past our fears, concerns and doubts and follow the call of our hearts.

A purpose-driven career can be a small shop or little café; a place to paint, write or lose ourselves in artistic expression. Perhaps we want to change the world, or create new business structures and products that facilitate the growth and dreams of others. Some may apply the gift of song or the talent of acting to entertain and uplift, while others may use their knowledge to teach and lead others.

Some answer the call of the heart to assist in preserving the environment, to nurture our relationship with nature, or to support organizations which assist the less fortunate.

For some, the vision may have little to do with a profession and more to do with family, friends, or a commitment to community, touching the lives of others in ways that might be unnoticed by business and the press.

However it appears, whatever calls you, consider that you are the instrument through which universal energy is expressing itself and that something has awakened you to the unique gifts and value you alone have to share.

The term we use for nature is Mother Nature. The most abundant, creative and ceaseless experience of life is described in terms of feminine energy. As women, we are a force of nature, representing the space and energy of a world stepping through a dance of endless creation and joyful expression.

When your passion, purpose and professional expertise come together, it is a perfect alignment of expression and creation. You become a force of nature that cannot be stopped. You will change your life, and the lives of all you touch, forever.

As women in whatever career we choose, we have the opportunity to step into the invaluable role of being a feminine leader. Women are natural leaders, as we manage from the heart. As natural leaders, women come from a place of community, collaboration and creative cooperation. We soar as a contributing member of a team. We not only strive for the satisfaction of accomplishment and to generate bottom line results, but we also thrive from our sense of joy, self expression and ability to touch and impact others.

As women, we naturally understand the greatness of our vision demands that we focus on something much larger than ourselves. When we give ourselves over to vision and purpose, we are literally propelled into the highest state of selflessness by a force mightier than our tiny egos and separate identities.

Your career can be your greatest teacher and your most challenging taskmaster. To reach the heights to which you aspire and to touch the hearts and minds you long to reach will require that you leave behind all of your fears, concerns, limitations, reasons and justifications.

Imagine the creative energy of the universe as a brilliant music composer. Music in the mind of the composer is nothing if it is not heard and experienced. In order for the composer to share her vision, the composer must translate it into the language of music, which must be played on an instrument that creates a vibration. The vibration must be caught by a membrane in the ear and then translated into experience by the mind.

Consider the universe as the ultimate composer. The composition is translated into human experience, played on and through us and received and translated by the hearts and minds of others. Can you imagine a greater privilege?

Without us, without our willingness to be the instrument, life is expressed but never experienced, generated but never manifested, given but never received. We are indeed the instrument played by the universe. As we give ourselves to the visions we create, we allow the songs that inspire, uplift and ignite all to be heard.

Be willing to step into your vision, uplift your experience of life and be the change, not just in your life, but in the lives of friends, family, the community and the world.

As you read these stories, see what other women have overcome and created in their own lives. Imagine what one woman can do in a year or a lifetime; imagine what the women of the world can do together. Are you willing to step into your power as a woman and wake up, be happy, healthy and wealthy?

Ardice Farrow

Amy's Breakthrough

Amy Applebaum

I got fired! I wish I could say it was from an important job where I saved lives or changed the world, but I got fired from an uppity Italian Trattoria smack dab in the middle of Beverly Hills. My crime? I served raw oatmeal to a demanding diva of a customer who didn't understand the phrase "made to order."

This customer was in a hurry. Being concerned about her time issue, I explained that we make our oatmeal from scratch and it would take approximately 20 minutes to cook. She said, "Okay," but she clearly didn't mean it. Nine minutes later she started snapping her fingers and shouting across the restaurant, "Where's my oatmeal?" I explained to her, again, that our oatmeal was made from scratch and takes approximately 20 minutes. Her oatmeal still had another 11 minutes to go. She shouted, "Bring me my oatmeal now!" So I grabbed the oatmeal from the cook's station and placed it in front of this rude and irrational woman. As she called over the manager to complain, I knew what was coming next.

I was 25 and had moved to Los Angeles to be an actress. I performed in a Hyundai commercial that earned me $50,000 and was convinced I was going to be a star. So, I waited tables while waiting for my big break. It never came. On top of that, I slaved at this pathetic restaurant trying to meet the ridiculous expectations of these outlandish customers. This is the point to which my life had come. I was a ticking time bomb.

When the oatmeal incident ended with my boss "letting me go," I walked through the restaurant prideful and relieved. I gathered my things, got into my car and relished the fact that I was never coming back. Then, halfway across Coldwater Canyon, I lost it. My pride and relief turned into fear and humiliation. I started crying hysterically. This wasn't the life I wanted, but I didn't know how to get what I did want. Although I wasn't sad to say "goodbye" to a place that was sucking the life out of me, it was still my life and now it was gone. I was so disappointed in myself. I had always been an "achiever" and a "go-getter." I was a problem solver. I helped other people with their problems. I would set a course of action for myself and always follow through. What had happened?

I felt so depressed when I finally arrived at home. I wanted to crawl into a hole. I suffered for many weeks. I panicked. I cried. I threw things. I moped. I called myself a loser a few times an hour. I stared at the wall and I watched Oprah. In short, I surrendered. Officially declaring myself "Loser Numero Uno," my life was over.

Then, one day, I arose from the dead. Enough! I was exhausted with myself. Here I was telling my friends and anyone else who would listen how miserable I was, but I wasn't doing anything about it. This wasn't me! Everything became so clear. I had always wanted to be an entrepreneur, so it was no wonder I was so miserable as an actress and waitress where others were calling the shots. Long before I was fired, I had been settling into a life I didn't want. I don't think I ever thought about what I really wanted. All the pain and dissatisfaction I'd been experiencing came from choices I had been making. I was causing the problem. Me! I didn't have to work at that restaurant if it wasn't making me happy, but I chose to do so. I had been obsessing about my problems for months, feeling sorry for myself, blaming others and getting nowhere. I could have spent that time deciding what to do about it, moving past my problems and creating the life I wanted. Being fired actually meant I was finally free to create the amazing life I had been postponing.

In that moment, I went from feeling sorry for myself to being excited. I took a piece of paper and began writing down what I wanted to be when I grew up. I wanted to be an entrepreneur. My dad was an entrepreneur so I called him for advice. He offered me a side business he was developing—selling novelty stickers on the counters of convenience and liquor stores. Before long, these stickers were being sold in every convenience store in Los Angeles. I had become a real entrepreneur. I was doing it!

In a bizarre twist of fate, I received an e-mail from a friend letting me know he had just launched his own coaching business. I let it sit unopened in my inbox for weeks. I cannot stand clutter in my inbox and usually delete everything as fast as I can, but for some reason I kept this particular e-mail. When I finally read it, a light came on. This was it! This was the business I was born to do. I was going to launch a coaching company and I was going to have my friend guide me through it. I was so excited that I had finally found my life's purpose! Armed with the confidence of building one business, I sold my company and began plans for another.

My friend and I set two goals during our planning time together. The first goal was to create and launch my very own one-woman show. If no one was going to hire me to act, then I was going to hire myself! My second goal was to launch a coaching company. I wanted to help people create lives they loved, so they couldn't wait to wake up every day.

So, I did it. My friend helped me set a course of action and follow through. There were challenges, but with my newfound confidence and determination, I overcame them with his help. Within three months, my one-woman show was playing to a full house every night and I was training to be a life coach. I was doing it! I was living my life on my terms and loving every minute of it.

One year later, I launched Bootcamp for Your Mind.

Bootcamp for Your Mind is celebrating its seventh year. It became a reality by shifting my thinking and focusing on solutions rather than obsessing on problems. I recently found an entry in my journal I had logged five years prior to creating Bootcamp for Your Mind. I wrote, "I decided my overall goal in life is to help others succeed because it makes me feel good." There is real power in telling the world what you want. I hadn't looked at the entry in years, but it reminded me that the universe does listen. Today, when I'm not getting out of life what I truly desire, I follow the same action plan I give to all my clients. I figure out what the problem is and then ask myself what I want instead of the problem. Once that's settled, I ask myself how my thinking and my actions cause the problem. Then, I shift my thinking and take action. It never fails, and it always reminds me that being fired was one of the greatest gifts I have ever received.

Amy Applebaum

Following a Dream

Rita Oldham

Every fall, millions of young dreamers enter American colleges. More than half of them have the chance to be the first in their families to graduate. Sadly, less than half of all freshmen will graduate. What becomes of all those dreams? What can be done to save the dreams in danger of being lost forever?

Even though no one else in my family had ever gone to college, I knew from an early age that I would. Originally, I wanted to be a nurse, but along the way I discovered that science was not one of my strong suits. That did not change my desire to attend college. I didn't want to work at a minimum wage job for the rest of my life. However, leaving home for the first time at the tender age of 17 was not conducive to a life of dedicated learning. I dropped out of college after two years with only minimal progress toward a degree. At that time in my life, I simply lacked the maturity to see past tomorrow, let alone to view a horizon that was four years down the road. Little did I know how long the road would be.

During the next three years, I wanted to go back to school but lacked the funds to do so. After getting married, I started yet another dead-end job. It was then that I decided I would do whatever I had to do to go back to school. I knew the only way to better myself and get a job that I enjoyed—and not just one that paid the bills—was to earn a degree. As it turned out, getting back into school wasn't as hard as I thought. I believe this was God's will for my life, and He opened the doors to help me accomplish my goal. I did not take this opportunity for granted: Applying myself completely to my classes, I finished the semester on the Dean's List.

After only one semester back in school, I had another academic setback, but a personal joy—I became a mother. Naturally, I put my plans for a degree on hold for a little while. Becoming a mother gave me a new reason to pursue my dream with even more determination than before. This was yet another time when I felt the hand of God guiding and shaping my life. He knew that my sense of responsibility as a parent would help keep me coming back to my dream until I realized it. During the next few years, this pattern repeated itself several times. Between the times when money was too tight and I had to work instead of going to school, I earned as many credits as possible attending part-time.

I finally earned an associate's degree, but soon realized it was not enough to accomplish my goal. In the college town where I lived, there was an abundance of prospects from which employers could choose in order to fill positions at a lower pay rate. It became apparent that if I wanted to accomplish my goal, I couldn't quit yet. I didn't let this realization dishearten me. Since I could build on the foundation I already had in place, I knew I could accomplish my mission. Whenever I started to feel overwhelmed by the whirlwind of responsibilities—taking care of my family, working, and attending classes while trying to do well in school—I would remind myself of my goal. The prospect of walking across the stage in a black robe to receive a diploma in front of my family was all that kept me motivated. The vital significance of that diploma on the wall mattered even more.

During the years of struggling to complete my education, I learned lessons that have helped me in other areas of my life. One of the most important things I came to realize is I can accomplish much more than I ever thought I could. I learned the mind is a powerful force and having the right motivations can make all the difference. Finding the specific motivation that worked for me was a turning point in my quest. For a long time, I didn't think I had the support I needed to keep me excited and committed when the going got rough. It wasn't until I realized I didn't require validation from anyone else that I gained the confidence I needed to buckle down and accomplish my goal of a college education.

Although it has always been hard for me to have pride in myself, and even though it took a total of 15 years to complete my education, I felt proud of my accomplishment. At times I didn't think I would ever be able to refer to myself as a college graduate, but the day finally came. Receiving my diploma gave me a new confidence that I never had before. It was one of the few goals I had set and actually had the motivation to complete, but it was one of the most important goals I ever had. Once I graduated, I was given the opportunity that was the ultimate reward for all my hard work—I was offered a position with a company that not only respects the priority of my family in my life, but also always appreciates the work I do. This fulfilled the dream I had in mind—a career that I enjoy and not just a job that merely pays the bills. The pieces of my life have finally fallen into place. I feel so blessed to have the job I've always wanted, to have my wonderful husband and children by my side and to be living the life I love.

Action Steps:

- Set a Goal—Be specific and realistic. Don't aim to be a brain surgeon if you don't like science or to be a deep-sea diver if you live in Missouri, and don't want to relocate. Once you set your goal, commit yourself to it.
- Keep Moving Forward—Even when life throws you curve balls and sometimes knocks you off track, keep going. As long as you are gaining ground, no matter how small, you are moving forward.
- Stay Motivated, Get Motivated Again—Keep your goal in mind and remind yourself often of the end result you are trying to attain. Find the specific, personal motivation that works for you. You can't borrow someone else's.
- Be Positive—Find something good to focus on even when the going gets tough. Don't let setbacks steer you off course.
- Apply What You Learn—Take the lessons you learn in your struggles and use them to face other obstacles that come up.
- Reward Yourself—Don't be afraid to be proud of your accomplishments. You've earned it!

Rita Oldham

WALKING AWAY FROM THE "BIG BUCKS" IN THE PURSUIT OF TRUE BALANCE

Shann Vander Leek

"Any transition serious enough to alter your definition of self will require not just small adjustments in your way of living and thinking, but a full-on metamorphosis."—Martha Beck

Not too long ago, my career was dedicated to sales, mentoring, coaching and leading an exceptional sales force.

For most of my life, I was a woman who was happily married, a loyal employee and an over-achiever who traveled to exotic places, and would earn a six-figure income, live in her dream home and would be involved in the highly-charged corporate world forever!

Here is the story of my metamorphosis.

A sacred knowledge or astuteness accompanies the first foray into motherhood. The miracle of childbirth became the catalyst for my complete lifestyle transformation. While home on maternity leave, I was watching a morning news program and became drawn to an interview with a professional life coach. The attraction was profound. I contacted the television station for more information, found a local coach and began to learn about the business of professional coaching. My first coaching playbook was *Co-active Coaching—New Skills for Coaching People Toward Success in Work and Life* by Laura Whitworth, Henry Kimsey-House and Phil Sandahl.

When I returned to my career, the coaching process became a revitalizing way to lead my sales force. Coaching in the sales environment gave me volumes of practical experience for my true calling.

After a few more years, the high stress level of corporate life in someone else's board room was losing its appeal. Even though my career path resulted in the realization of my goals and dreams, I became completely disinterested in corporate culture and was unwilling to jump through any more flaming circus hoops for money. It's amusing and disheartening when you realize your dedication, work and energy—all the things you put into your career—are spent only for the sake of performing a duty and receiving a paycheck. This newfound awareness helped cement my determination to leave the business world. It was time to let go of the illusion of control that the "big bucks" created.

This realization led me to one of the most important decisions of my life. I left corporate America and gave my entrepreneurial calling a chance. I began preparing my exit strategy. No longer a company creature, my job was surely destroying my soul. I longed to spend my days undisturbed by the "powers that be." Please understand, my prior career was great fun and a great challenge for a long time. The reason I excelled and stayed on the corporate path for 18 years had much to do with the freedom I was allowed; to do what I did best. When a regime change was implemented, the corporate culture changed drastically, leading to my slow and certain suffocation. Without the discomfort, I may have never allowed myself to consider the pursuit of my dreams.

I was extremely anxious about giving up a significant income to go out on my own. For a while, I even tried to trick myself into staying with the money. Ultimately, I realized how many people before me had taken a well-planned leap of faith. Whatever you want to achieve, you can accomplish with great discipline and imagination.

After thoughtful consideration, much manic behavior and conversations with my family and confidantes, I moved forward on the path of my dreams because it was my only option. Sharing your plans and dreams with the people who know you intimately is an excellent way to receive honest feedback. These are the same people who will hold your hand through the transition. Declaring my plan for independence helped me stay on the path to personal freedom.

For about a year, many of my evenings, weekends and lunch hours were dedicated to self-awareness and studying for my professional coaching certification. This transition time included setting a new household budget, reallocating investments, setting up a line of credit and buying a new car (for the first time in 11 years). The plan was to build my coaching business and brand one day at a time until I could give my two-week notice.

Straddling two worlds was fairly easy. The job I no longer enjoyed was palatable because I could see, feel and taste the light of my future. The most difficult part of the separation was saying goodbye to my sales force. Leaving them behind was my biggest cross to bear until I allowed myself to let go and to understand that each person was amazing in his or her own right and would ultimately be fine in my absence. During this time, finding humor in the day-to-day corporate environment was the greatest blessing. Ultimately, you do whatever you can to keep from taking yourself too seriously when working through a life-changing transition. The discovery of professional humor allowed me to function well in the environment and find some peace in the moment.

Finally, after 14 years, I left my corporate life on my own terms. My former employer decided to downsize our sales management group within 60 days of my planned exodus. The interesting part of this equation is that three managers were given the responsibility of determining who would leave. Did I really jump up and say, "Pick me. Pick me!"? I was thrilled to have the "out" and volunteered to be the unlucky laid-off executive. I never looked back. Thankfully, this scenario meant an unexpected severance package. Synchronicity is such a blessing!

I packed up my office on the same day. Apparently, my willingness to leave sped up my departure. I said, "So long," to the big bucks, turned in my company SUV, let go of a cushy expense account and found the courage to walk away from a career that no longer suited me.

Fast-forward.

The business of helping people recognize their brilliance is a blast! The focus for the rest of my days is on helping people do the things they think they cannot do on their own. I will use every ounce of my business experience to inspire solo-preneurs to set big goals, achieve extraordinary results and create balance in their lives.

I am grateful for the opportunity to live the rest of my days on *my* terms.

And, the big bucks are on their way back to me again—on my terms. The characteristics that made me successful in corporate America will always benefit me as an entrepreneur. It's all about balance and moving gracefully through a profound transition.

Today, I am a woman who is happily married, mothers a sweet and healthy daughter, has earned the six-figure income plus all the perks, has traveled to many delightful places, lives in the home of her dreams and has become a successful professional life and business coach.

This caterpillar has become a butterfly.

Shann Vander Leek

Failing Forward Successfully

Debbie Allen

Can mistakes be good for your business?

If you're lucky, you make a mistake now and again, because failure can actually be good for you and your business. If you haven't made any mistakes for a while, you may be playing it too close to your comfort zone. To aim high, you must accept some of the risks that come with learning something new.

Risk is a natural part of growth, but you will want to avoid making costly mistakes or making the same mistake again. Use good common business sense. Each business or career has its share of challenges. You will constantly be tested in business as new challenges arise and your business expands.

You will always encounter new challenges in your business that stretch you past your current abilities and expertise. It may be a big sale, the start of a new business, a new opportunity or an extremely difficult challenge. All failures will help you learn more about your business and help you build your self-esteem at the same time.

Learn from your mistakes and move on.

Actually, I don't even like the word mistake. I believe mistakes are simply challenges in disguise. Realistically, most of us don't get it right the first time around. Successful people make mistakes all the time, but most of their failures go unnoticed because they keep going without giving up.

Successful people make it look easy. We don't often notice or acknowledge their failures. Successful people evaluate their failures, come up with new solutions to the challenge and try again—wiser and more experienced than before. Successful people also don't allow the fear of failure to stop them from achieving their goals.

If you study the failures and challenges of business, you will discover the ultimate success secrets of any enterprise. These are the key lessons an organization learns as it grows, expands and competes in a changing marketplace.

If you want to create shamelessly fabulous success, study all the failures. Most highly successful people were not successful from the beginning. They had to struggle to reach their peak potential. Walt Disney was actually fired from his first job because he was told he was not creative enough. Not creative enough? Luckily, he didn't listen to his clueless boss and trusted his own innovative ideas.

We all have a tendency to focus on success and fear failure when things don't go as planned. Don't be too hard on yourself if you feel you are making too many mistakes to make it to the top. Hang in there and be patient. Once you overcome the challenge, you won't have to do it again and you will be moving forward faster.

Success takes time, just as it takes time for you to adjust and learn new skills. Mistakes will continue even after you have reached a high level of success. You will always need to learn something new in business to stay innovative and on top of your game. When you think you have it all figured out and have made all the mistakes you need in order to learn, something will challenge you again and test your confidence.

I've been an entrepreneur all of my adult life and I'm still making mistakes. I plan to keep making them. Once I have it all figured out, I get bored. Making mistakes, turning them into challenges and then overcoming those obstacles in business is extremely rewarding. There is nothing that can challenge, motivate and build your confidence faster.

Mistakes and challenges are going to occur, so the sooner you learn from them, the sooner you will become more successful in whatever you do. We tend to reach conclusions about success, but until success is compared with failures, you don't truly understand the whole story of how business works.

Why don't they teach failure in school?

Failures tend to disappear from the business education curriculum. Information about business failures is often scarce or ignored completely, yet failure is inevitable. On the other hand, information on successful companies and their success strategies is in generous supply.

Companies that pursue unsuccessful strategies either change their business strategies or go out of business. A successful company is described as having used visionary management and innovative marketing strategies, while a failing business is accused of poor business management and overall bad business skills. Why don't we teach future entrepreneurs more about failure? Wouldn't that save us a ton of money from mistakes that could have been avoided in the first place?

Can you imagine telling your banker to add an additional $20,000 for the mistakes you plan to make in your new business venture? As crazy as it sounds, that is exactly what is going to happen while you develop the business. You simply must make mistakes to see what works and does not work to attract new customers. Franchise businesses have higher success rates than independent company start-ups because they have already made many of the mistakes and systemized the business around avoiding them in the future. Perhaps we should change the old saying: To err is human; to learn and grow from error is divine.

Debbie Allen

A Legacy of Passion

Marlene M. Coleman, M.D., FAAP

It all started when I was five years old, growing up in Los Angeles. My father was a doctor and I tagged along with him to his clinic, taking in the familiar sights, sounds and scents, watching him care for his patients. His personal interactions—listening, questioning, guiding—made the biggest impression on me. Following in his footsteps at age five, I was hooked. Even then, I knew helping people would be my life's passion.

To get there meant years of education. I earned my Bachelor of Science, Master of Science, and advanced master's in medical education from the University of Southern California. I attended medical school at the University of California, Irvine as one of only seven women in a class of 95 and completed my residency at White Memorial Medical Center in Los Angeles.

Even as I narrowed my specialty to pediatric medicine, I could see the single-minded pursuit of one line of work would never be enough for me. I recognized in myself wide-ranging interests, a passion for teaching and mentoring and a continual desire to expand my knowledge and capabilities. My career and my life have fulfilled those eclectic desires and, in fact, continue to broaden so I can embrace new interests.

I was very honored to be selected as one of the top pediatricians in America for 2004-2005, and to be chosen by the Consumers' Research Council of America as one of the nation's top pediatricians for 2007.

In addition to the practice of medicine, teaching is one of the most rewarding aspects of my career. As an associate professor of family medicine at the Keck School of Medicine at USC, I have a chance to share my own passion, mentor students and, most importantly, encourage them to maintain their physical, emotional and spiritual balances to create rich, full lives for themselves. My message to my students does not apply only to medical professionals: If you have integrity, honesty and love, you can do just about anything.

As a member of the Board of Trustees of the Cooperative of American Physicians/Mutual Protection Trust (CAP/MPT), a medical malpractice cooperative that now insures over 10,000 doctors, I have an opportunity to study, discuss and shape policy regarding malpractice which is an intensely important issue among doctors and patients. This role has allowed me to examine and refine my own understanding of listening, communication and physician well-being.

Small wonder that my husband, Bill, affectionately calls me "Roadrunner." If you're doing what you love, there always seems to be time to do more, especially if you're willing to examine your needs and adjust your expectations as you go.

Flexibility is a trait I developed quickly when I became stepmother to three children (ages 5, 11 and 14) more than 31 years ago. I married William Huss, an attorney who became a Los Angeles Superior Court judge. Suddenly, I found myself living in the middle of a lab course in adolescent medicine. Because with children, you have to be present when they need you, I learned to adjust my schedule so I could be with them. Today, those children, now marvelous adults, are my friends, collaborators and an enthusiastic chorus of support for my many activities.

It's probably not surprising that my varied interests would eventually find their way into print. Writing books gives me a broader audience and a chance to reach people who will never find their way into my classroom. I am also nearing completion of a soon-to-be released compact disc, *Enjoying Your Practice as a Health Professional,* that grew out of my experiences teaching first-year medical residents. I've always felt there isn't sufficient education for physicians on the importance of keeping your life in balance. The key to keeping passion alive is tolive a balanced life that reduces stress and feeds the soul. Meaningful activities and relationships lower stress, refresh the spirit and make better individuals as well as physicians. You simply can't listen to your patients if you're stressed-out about other things in your life.

I find I am often invited on radio or television to discuss a variety of health-related topics, including adolescent female medicine, college health and travel medicine. I enormously enjoy interacting with audiences and sharing my passions in whatever we are doing—traveling with a spouse, children or friends, going off to college, starting a career or making a life change—with related medical issues that can be easily overlooked. My hope is to always inspire audiences to think before they act so they will be ready to manage both planned activities and unexpected problems.

Frankly, I have a hard time with people who are too rigid, unforgiving and don't know how to laugh. In stressful times—and we all have stress—I lean on Bill, our children and my 92-year-old mother. My twin sister, a clinical psychologist, has also been extremely important to me. I try to be a good patient and follow my own advice by playing tennis, listening to music, going to the theater, spending time hiking and relaxing in the outdoors and restoring my spirits at our chalet in Big Bear, California.

Whatever success I've achieved, I know I could not have done it alone. My father showed me the way, but my family has given me their enthusiastic support. My fellow physicians, colleagues and nurses have shared their enormous wisdom and my students have listened to my words and rewarded me by turning into admirable doctors. I am fortunate and extremely grateful. These are feelings that fuel my passion to keep doing what I am doing: Teaching, learning, writing and—always—laughing.

Tips for personal success:

- Write your goals. Make a list of your personal and professional goals, both short- and long-term. Make the list as complete and detailed as possible. The more thoroughly you understand where you want to go, the more likely you are to get there. Set a time each year (such as your birthday) to revisit and revise your list.
- Set some limits. Identify the elements of your life and your work that are most rewarding and create a plan that will allow you to reach those goals. Establish priorities and set limits on your time. Use these guidelines as you make decisions about new commitments and the direction of your life and career.
- Exercise your communication skills. Your stress increases when you are not able to make yourself understood by others. Improve your communication skills by doing one thing at a time, practicing active listening, asking questions, confirming comprehension during and after meetings and conversations. Even if you are angry or extremely frustrated, avoid blaming, put-downs, generalizations, assumptions and mixed messages.
- Nurture your important relationships. The following qualities that contribute to the stability of our long-term relationships; commitment to each other's welfare and happiness; loyalty; admiration and respect; empathy; genuineness; initiative; and sharing feelings. None of these will be enough, however, if you don't spend the time with the people who are close to you in your life.

Marlene M. Coleman, M.D., FAAP

STEP BY STEP TO YOUR PERSONAL DESTINY

Mindie Kniss

What do you really want to do? If there were no constraints of money or time or education, what career would you choose? Your career is one aspect of your personal destiny that lies at the intersection of your passions, talents and the needs of the world. The secret to a fulfilling career is the integration of these three parts. Does your career align with your goals and values, or is it draining the potential you have to live a happy and healthy existence?

I asked my friend Jake what he really wanted to do. He was in the middle of yet another corporate relocation and was not looking forward to the move. "You know what's funny?" he asked. "I can't remember anyone asking me that before. I can't even remember the last time I thought about it. To be honest, I don't even know."

Jake is one of many who work on autopilot. He is successful and talented in his position, but at some point, he stopped checking in with himself about what his soul would choose to pursue. What do *you* really want to do? That is the question—not what should you do or what someone else wants you to do. What thrills you when you wake up in the morning? What motivates you throughout the day? When we are able to use our intelligence and creativity, and when our hearts play a role in our life's work, this is when we feel most alive.

Like many of my friends, I entered corporate America soon after completing college. I found the work interesting and challenging and my colleagues and I became life-long friends. Three years later, I relocated with my company to another state and started a similar cycle: Learning new policies and procedures, meeting new people and understanding the ebb and flow of my new environment.

I could finally pay my bills and the mortgage, and I enjoyed the social interactions at work, but something was missing. What began as a slight irritation became a yearning that was impossible to ignore. At first, I had dreamed of making a difference in the world and working with people, but instead I found myself in a cubicle stacked with paperwork.

I might have remained in the corporate world, but in 2006, I participated in a six-month fellowship in Nairobi, Kenya. Taking a step back from your own life can teach you to view things from a different perspective. One thing was clear: It was not the work policies and procedures that bothered me as much as it was my soul calling out, "Hey! Why are you staying with this job when everything you've ever wanted to do is out there waiting?"

I had been ignoring that question for the past six years. It was too convenient to have a regular routine and paycheck, but the nudge to make a change became stronger. It was time to act. I worked to clarify my dreams and goals, made a list of my talents, then added corresponding career ideas. I went through the list again to determine which careers would also encompass my passions. Finally, I asked myself if there was a need in the world for any of the things on my list. In the end, I narrowed it down to two options that I could do simultaneously. I wanted to work directly with people to help them embrace their highest potential and I wanted to write.

Could I find clients to fill a coaching practice or get a manuscript published? I didn't know, but I acted as if those were the only possible outcomes. I planned how I wanted a typical week to look by drawing up a schedule that allowed time for both client meetings and writing. I also looked into writing programs that I could pursue when I returned home.

This phrase kept me going: "*Whatever it takes.*" I used to have a baseball cap that read, "Whatever It Takes. Ditka 8:89." It was Mike Ditka, head coach of the Chicago Bears, who created that motto for his team.

Nearly 20 years later, I could not get it out of my head. Thanks, Coach!

I gave myself a year from the date I returned to the U.S. to get my finances in order, start a business and learn all I could about actually making it work. That was in January 2007. It was only then, when I became extraordinarily clear in what I wanted and needed to do, that things started happening. The time had come when I needed to leave corporate America. I determined my path and the universe added another bonus.

Two days before I left Nairobi, I learned that my company planned to close our site. Apparently, we would have approximately one year to transfer our projects to other sites before the final shutdown. My plan was in place to leave anyway. Synchronicity had arranged it as smoothly as possible. I made the commitment to act, and things fell into place.

The universe always supports your steps toward the call of your soul, whether through enormous action like a company closing, or in a delicate prodding that urges you forward. We are all creative beings, regardless of our various talents or career paths, and there are endless opportunities. You can do anything you like. Take it step by step and notice when synchronicity begins to guide you. At every crossroad, take the next step toward your personal destiny.

Action Steps

• Get Serious

Honestly assess your strengths and weaknesses. Does your current career utilize your talents and offer support as you grow? Dig in deep. You are a wealth of potential energy just waiting to be activated.

• Get Clear

Take stock of your current situation. Are you happy with your career? What specific actions will move your life forward?

• Get Going

Start now. No excuses. Create a plan to take action even if it consists of just one step forward. When you take that step, go for the next one. Do not beat yourself up for waiting to begin. All it takes is doing one thing differently to start the momentum.

• Get Help

Learn to ask for assistance when you need it. The most successful people in history were fueled by inspiration from a friend, a creative mastermind group or teams of people with wisdom and experience to share.

• Get On With It

Act with determination. You have started on a journey; now strengthen your resolve to persevere. Remember: "Whatever it takes." Now go and make it happen.

Mindie Kniss

Keeping the Fire Burning: Tips for Women Entrepreneurs

Aggie Kobrin

As someone fairly new to the world of entrepreneurship, I quickly discovered what any business will teach: Failure to learn the lessons fast means lost time, lost opportunities and lost money.

I've also learned that, whether you're in the corporate world or run your own business, it's easy to lose your enthusiasm, burn out, and opt out. Don't! It's all worth it. Being your own boss allows you to run the business your way, but unless you're well prepared, your way may not be the best way. We learn from one another. I want to share some of my insights with you, as so many have shared their successes and missteps with me, for which I'm forever grateful.

The key to staying motivated and inspired is to understand you don't have to do everything in one big step. By taking a number of small steps, you'll reach your goals and enjoy the journey more. It's a relatively new journey for me, but I learned hard and fast…and I'm still learning.

Here are my small steps:

Build a network of like-minded people. My business was built on networking, and I knew early on that I could succeed. Southern California is a hotbed of formal and informal networking organizations. This is an asset money can't buy. Participate. Participate. Participate. Approach the people you meet with an attitude of "How can I help you," and the rest will simply fall into place. The women's groups eWomenNetwork, TEAM Women, NAWBO and DSWA are the best of the best. Join them, and you'll find yourself having to turn business away.

Focus your vision. Find your direction—your purpose. When you combine your energy and passion with a focused vision, you create your direction and power.

We will love what we do when we honor our passions, make a contribution to those around us and live in gratitude. When we connect with our vision, we release our passion and gain a better understanding of who we are, what we stand for and where we are going.

Education matters. I don't mean just the formal education or education related to your business. Be curious and keep learning. Attend the many programs offered by the members of your networks. You never know where the next gem, the next great contact, or the next great idea will come from, but you can be certain it will come. Always work on expanding your expertise. The world of books, DVDs, magazines, the Internet—what gold lies in them! You'll be astounded by the fresh ideas that come from the assortment of learning opportunities offered by members of your network.

You can also go to school and learn. In today's Internet-savvy world, every type of course and degree is available from reputable online colleges and universities. Don't know something? The answer is only a keyboard away.

Put your know-how into action. You've learned new skills and gained new expertise; put them to work right away. If your own business doesn't call for a specific skill you want to expand, volunteer or help a friend with her business. You'll gain exponentially when you do that. You will be giving of yourself and applying your skills, and—most importantly—you'll feel great about yourself. Recognize and capitalize on every opportunity to grow.

Give of yourself. The one common element I find in my network of entrepreneurs is the strength they gain from helping one another. The more you do for others, the more you get back. Although, I found that in the corporate world, helping your colleague may not even result in a "thanks." I look for opportunities to work with my network. It gives me a real high.

The real key to success. When you ask the right questions, you create a network of "experts." The answers to your questions become a phone call or e-mail away. I am so energized every time I get an idea! I can pull the right resources together and develop the idea into a successful plan or outcome.

Keep the flames bright. Persevering and maintaining motivation is a challenge for everyone. By taking these steps, you'll stay on purpose, motivated and energized, while learning, sharing and giving back. Whatever challenges your days may hold, people and resources are available to help you meet them. Don't hold back—always think about what's best for you. Get moving toward your future today.

Examples of support available to you. Over the years, I've participated in mastermind groups, joined networking groups, and attended many conferences and meetings; they've enhanced my life in innumerable ways. The dynamics have changed; the world of women has expanded and women's roles have intensified. Mastermind groups help steer your business by providing the support, advice and brainstorming needed for success. They are your "steering committee." They bring business acumen and, most importantly, they bring love that nurtures the soul. Networking groups, conferences and events can change your life in a moment—as my friend Robbie Motter says, "It's all about showing up." It really can change your life—it has changed mine.

Tips:

- You gain confidence by getting out there and doing it. You do it and you realize the world didn't come to a screeching halt after you finished. Your confidence grows with each step.

- Failure is just a lesson in disguise. When it happens, just say: "Okay, it didn't work that way." Pick yourself up, keep going and take another path.
- Embrace whatever it is you love and go for it. It is much better to enjoy the process than to never have tried. Regret is the worst emotion you'll ever have.
- Find role models, mentors and coaches—not one, but many. Find one for finance, one for health and one for relationships. Find a role model or mentor in the business or career you want.
- You have to be willing to step out of your comfort zone. It's going to be difficult and challenging. It's going to feel uncomfortable because that is how you're going to get to your passion—by being open to the possibilities; not by being limited in your thinking, being fearful and playing small.
- Join as many groups and organizations as you can—they will help you with your business and with your life. "It's all about showing up"—I promise you!

Aggie Kobrin

A Passion, A Mission, A Dream, A Lesson

Michelle Sanchez

Because I grew up in a family business, I had an entrepreneurial spirit. Yet, instead of following my passion, I chose what I thought was the safe, practical route through corporate America.

Although I was successful, I learned some hard lessons:

- As long as you work for someone else, your financial security will always be dependent on someone else;
- Money and success have little value if you have no time or energy to enjoy them or if you sacrifice what is most important in your life to achieve them; and
- No matter how hard you work, or how successful you become, your success can be lost in one day.

I learned my first lesson when an accident at work ended my employment, leaving me devastated, both physically and financially, for nine years. The second lesson was learned when, after devoting my life once again to a company, the owner filed for bankruptcy. Suddenly, years of hard work were literally destroyed and I was unemployed again. I collapsed with the most severe bout of chronic fatigue syndrome (CFS) and fibromyalgia (FMS), compounded by more serious health challenges. I had always believed that, sometimes, out of your greatest adversity comes your greatest blessing and I was about to discover one of the greatest blessings of my life!

As my health rapidly declined, a friend insisted I try a new natural health product. Out of desperation, I finally agreed. My health improved immediately; in 90 days I had regained my health. As a result, I shared the product with many people and quickly realized I had discovered my passion. However, this presented a dilemma because I had panic-anxiety: I was not a salesperson and I wanted nothing to do with network marketing or sales, but the thrill of helping people return to a vibrantly healthy lifestyle was irresistible.

I had to make a decision. Despite the fact that everyone thought my decision was crazy, I decided to follow my passion. Over the next 90 days, I helped thousands of people, produced a near five-figure monthly income while working part-time from home, while enjoying all-expense paid dream trips to exotic destinations such as Tahiti and Hawaii. Following my passion was clearly the right decision!

However, somewhere along the line, I became sidetracked from my original mission. I had started with no training or experience—only a passion and a mission—and success came naturally as a result. Then I started learning from the "experts," using their slick sales scripts, purchasing leads, making cold calls, marketing online and using all the other tactics of the rich and famous in network marketing. I even spent two years and more than $10,000 to become a network marketing success coach. During that time, my business and my income declined, while I accumulated a massive amount of debt. My goals and dreams had been sidetracked along with my mission.

One day, I received an intriguing e-mail explaining the power of creating a dream board. At that point, I was willing to try anything. I created my own dream board online and printed it; it was eventually buried and forgotten in my paperwork. Meanwhile, the harder I worked, the more challenges I faced, including a drastic change in my company's compensation plan. This all moved me further from reaching my goals.

At that point, I was desperately looking for an additional source of income. I could not find anything I felt passionate about until a business associate called me about a unique new weight loss product which required no dieting or exercise. I was intrigued, but over the years I had tried it all without success. I finally agreed to try it, and it worked! In fact, in 30 days I went from a size 20 to a size 16 and in just 90 days, I finally reached my weight loss goal. It was a miracle! I was so excited about my results that I shared the product with my friends who also were pleased with the results and shared it with their friends, and the chain reaction started.

Suddenly, I was thrust into an exciting new business venture and achieving success at lightning speed. Finally, I had regained my passion and enthusiasm doing what I love most: helping people. I was alive and exhilarated once again! More importantly, the lives of the people I helped were forever changed and so was mine!

Five months later, I was organizing my office when I came across my dream board. I was stunned to realize I had achieved it all! The most amazing part was that my goal of "Perfect Health and Physique," symbolized by a picture of a woman measuring her midsection, was the new company's trademark. I also had set a goal to achieve the Diamond level, which is a high position and income in the company. Rather than achieving my goal of "Diamond by December," I was "Diamond by May." I had reached this goal in 30 days which was a company record. By the end of 90 days, I was Double Diamond (almost Triple) and earned more than $10,000 working part-time. I had achieved all of my dreams without even realizing it because I was so passionately focused on my mission of helping others.

Throughout this amazing journey, I experienced the thrill of creating and living the life of my dreams as well as the agony of helplessly watching my dreams slip away. Only when I became an "expert" did my passion and enthusiasm smolder, along with my business, my income and my dreams. Thankfully, along the journey, I rediscovered my mission and passion for helping others which guided me back on the path to achieving my dreams so I can help others do the same. I believe so strongly that this is the key to true success that I developed unique coaching and training programs exclusively for women networkers and appropriately named them "Heart-2-Heart Coaching," "Heart-2-Heart Networking" and "Heart-2-Heart Leadership" (www.heart2heartcoach.com).

My goal with these programs is to earn six figures per month and to reach the top position in my company in order to prove that you can achieve your dreams by passionately helping others, which will empower and inspire millions of women to do the same. This in turn will forever change the direction and reputation of Network Marketing.

It is my most sincere wish that my story empowers and inspires you to discover and follow your passion and that all your dreams come true!

Living My Passion and Living My Dream,

Michelle Sanchez

Fire Me, please!

Lisa Nack

People have always told me I am a ball of energy, that I bring commitment to any job that I take on—paid or unpaid—and I am an initiator, a quick study and a team player. So, why did I make such a lousy employee? By the time I was 22 years old, I figured out that if I was only working for the money, one of two things were going to happen: I was either going to quit or I was going to be fired. It just took a few more years to put that realization into practice.

I'll never forget the first time I was fired—or the second or third, for that matter. I was afraid to express my ideas for improving the work environment, fearing I would be labeled a complainer or a difficult worker, only to be fired because I had become a complainer and difficult to deal with. I hung onto a job because I ignored that little voice in my head that said it was time to go because people's ideas were not listened to, so I was fired because I became angry and outspoken.

Some jobs left me uninspired, unchallenged and just plain bored, but I was unable to leave because of fear—fear I wouldn't be able to pay my bills, fear no one would hire me, fear I had nothing of value to offer, fear I'd be labeled a "quitter." The list could go on and on. I realized I was just begging to be fired, and thank goodness my employers had the strength to show me the way forward. Ultimately, I found the very thing I was afraid of—unemployment.

What I have discovered over the years is that behind every fear is a wish—a desire I secretly hold.

I began to ask myself a lot of questions and listened deeply for the answers. Where did I start? I looked inside myself. I discovered that with each answer, I moved closer to the things I wanted in my life!

I asked myself who I wanted to be. What did I want to do? What did I want to have? I wanted to be kind, insightful, courageous, patient and decisive. I chose to do work that supported the creation of environments that people enjoy because they feel valued and recognized for their contributions. I chose to support others in accomplishing their goals, dreams and wishes. I chose to create the resources—time and financial freedom—that would allow me time to spend with my family, to travel, to learn, to be of service to my community and to buy the things I wanted for myself and others without worry or regret.

Once I no longer held what I wanted as a secret, the fear about my ability to take action began to loosen, and the resources and ways to make these wishes become a reality appeared.

Why did I want to be, do and have these things? Regardless of what I called it—vision, mission or goals—the "why's" had to be big enough to create "e-motion"—energy in motion. Otherwise, it was too easy to quit in the face of setbacks. My "why's" had to be personal, and they had to fuel my emotions so I was both pushed past my fears and pulled forward toward my wish.

I worked on understanding my fears. What was I so afraid of that I kept my deepest desires secret? You may have heard the acronym for fear—False Evidence Appearing Real. I realized whatever I decided to believe was true. Would the things I accepted as "true" turn out to be merely opinions when examined from a different perspective? Whose ideas, thoughts or beliefs had I built these fears upon?

Answering this question required me to challenge my beliefs—the lens through which I view the world and the convictions I hold about others and myself. What did I believe about myself, about the world of work, about being an employee, about starting a business and about being of service?

My beliefs form my thinking. My thinking forms my decisions, which, in turn, form my actions, leading to my results. What I found was that many of my beliefs had been "gifted" to me by others who meant well—parents, society, educational systems. They weren't based upon my own personal experiences or current points of reference. Some of my beliefs were outdated, yet I was allowing them to keep me locked in fear. I began to establish new points of reference from new experiences and new information in order to build new belief systems.

I started to keep a journal. Writing down my wishes moved them one step closer to coming true, and writing down my fears diminished some of the energy they carried. Some of them looked just plain silly once I saw them on paper! I also used my journal to record my action steps. It was fun to cross things off my list, and it provided me with a sense of accomplishment. It also gave me a guide I could refer to when I needed to tackle another desire or fear. It became a point of accountability because often I would share the list with a friend, coach or mentor.

Being fired presented me with opportunities that were much bigger than I had dared to wish for when I was viewing the situation through fear. I realized I wasn't alone in my idea that the workplace was a "tough" place to be, that I was capable of running my own business and that what I have to offer is valuable. I stepped into the world of organizational development 15 years ago and have never looked back.

Perhaps you are experiencing some of these same fears in your professional or personal life and, like me, you have allowed fear to stand in the way of reaching for your dreams or even daring to wish for something different.

Dare to Wish

- Put your wish in writing and share it. Create a support system.

Share your wish with a coach, mentor, or friend.

- Identify your "whys"—reasons that create a powerful response in you. Stir up feelings and emotions of desire and commitment that will carry you past setbacks and toward your wish.
- Understand your fears—List each of your fears. These are the phantoms that can become your stumbling blocks. This alone can help take some of the energy out of them. Separate fact from fiction.
- Examine your beliefs—Identify your unconscious beliefs and thoughts that are creating your current results. Change your thinking; you'll change your results.
- Take action—Identify one step you will take in the next 24 hours to move you toward your wish. Commit to taking one step every day for the next 30 days that will move you toward your wish.
- Write them down.

May all your wishes come true!

Lisa Nack

Relationship Rainmaking: Leave the Umbrella at Home

Jet Parker

I love big Texas storms, the kind resulting from the convergence of twisting winds, bright lightning and screaming thunder. More than anything, I like the raging rain that comes with a good storm. The rain, in nature and in business, brings life.

If you've been in sales, marketing or have the e-gene (entrepreneurial disposition), you probably already know I'm referring to the ultimate rain: revenue. Rainmaking is a common euphemism for sales or revenue generation and though it is important for all companies, it is the linchpin of a new start-up business or a fast-growing enterprise. Knowing the importance of rainmaking and successfully creating it are two different things and the digital age has made it both easier and more difficult at the same time.

As any seasoned CEO will tell you, sales are more easily generated through relationships than through contacts. Relationships stem from really knowing a person; contacts are nothing more than name-dropping acquaintances from your PDA. The digital age has made it more challenging to develop relationships, as technology has given us the ability to communicate with prospects and clients without ever actually meeting them. Today, people have a tendency to text rather than talk, to e-mail rather than write a personal note, to conduct Webinars rather than face-to-face meetings and to send Internet links for company sales materials rather than make personal sales calls. We conduct more "face-to-face" time through Facebook with strangers than we do person-to-person with clients, and we do more social networking online than at Starbucks.

So, how can we leverage the world's new communication dynamics to develop relationships that bring in the rain (new business) to provide the capital and cash flow to build a business? Here are a few of my favorite methods:

Start with Netgifting™, Not Networking

Netgifters focus on teaching, not telling; serving, not selling. The net value of your relationship will determine how much business you earn from a prospect. This value is determined by what you gift (support, service, timely information) to your client, not by how well you rub elbows with them.

Earn Their Trust

A study of the characteristics of great leaders in conjunction with our research at CEO IQ revealed that if you earn the respect of people, you are likely to earn their trust. However, in order to earn their trust, you must deliver three primary attributes:

> **Consistency:** Both operational and emotional. You must develop and use proven processes that ensure every task is done well by everyone and that it is done the same way every time. You must also have the emotional buoyancy to handle stress and tolerate uncertainty so that your behavior during these trials is consistently steady and sound for others.
>
> **Clarity:** You must have a crystal-clear vision of where you want to lead your client, the ability to communicate this vision and an awareness of what impedes effective information sharing.
>
> **Concern:** John C. Maxwell once stated that people don't care how much you know until they know how much you care. Influence and trust are more easily established between a rainmaker and his or her clients and prospects when he or she first expresses genuine concern for them.

Deliver Intelligence, Not Information

We can access virtually all the information in existence via the

Internet. Instead of being a benefit, it has become overwhelming to many business leaders and downright frustrating to others who fail to see how the bombardment of incessant, benign content is actually helpful to them. Your clients don't need more information; they need field intelligence, such as data that is relevant to their needs and information that will give them a market advantage. You can use e-mail messages to achieve this task, but if you want the kind of relationship with your clients and prospects that will prompt them to open and read what you send, you must be a quality supply line of *intelligence*, not just *information*.

Focus on Helping Your Clients Grow Their Companies

It's easier to build a relationship with a client or prospect when you understand the challenges he or she is facing. It's easier to identify these challenges when you determine what stage of growth the company is in by using the 5 to 7 Formula™ concept. The 5 to 7 Formula states there are seven stages of business growth: starting, surviving, building, refining, thriving, maturing and exiting. The CEO must develop and apply specific practices and processes within the five primary business functions in order to advance from one stage of business development to the next, as shown in the chart below.

7 Stages of Business Ownership

- Starting
- Surviving
- Building
- Refining
- Thriving
- Maturing
- Exiting or Transitioning

5 Key Business Functions

- Operations
- Financials

- Intellectual Capital
- Marketing/Sales
- Technology

Stellar ShowerHeads™—our moniker for super-performing rainmakers—use their energy, resources and expertise to help their clients and prospects grow their enterprise. Too often we get caught up in motivating a client to buy what we're selling rather than address what they really need. When you have a relationship with the client, your attention turns to the true needs of your client so you can help to fulfill those needs.

Leverage the Secret Slice

Most rainmakers still don't realize how much the tools in the marketing and sales toolbox have changed. Sales collateral previously consisted of a company brochure, client testimonials, rate sheets and a PowerPoint presentation, all passéé. Now the best tools are company one-sheets, client case studies, the Internet and the secret slice: zippy digital devices.

Our Favorite Rainmaking Digital Tools

We recommend the following digital devices because they actively engage your prospects and customers in the learning experience.

> **ALEX:** An Animated Learning Experience newsletter. (Go to www.ceoiq.com/ALEX to view a sample.) Rather than a stagnant online newsletter pushed to your client, ALEX pulls your prospects and customers into the learning process.
>
> **Interactive case studies:** Simply send your clients a special 800-number service where they can record a case study endorsement of your products or services in their own words and in their own voices. (To experience, e-mail: InteractiveCS@ceoiq.com.)

EDG: The first electronic business card, EDG features a high-resolution screen to showcase your company presentations. It fits in your wallet or business card holder and is perfect for handing out at trade shows or after sales appointments. Better yet, use the EDG card as a private client club card. Send clients new field intelligence each week by loading it through the EDG USB port. (See a graphic of an EDG card or a video about EDG at: EDGdemo@jumplab.com).

The American dream isn't about owning your own business; it's about building a financially viable business. You can't accomplish this without successful rainmaking. Apply these sensational methods and both your company and your clients' enterprises will flourish.

Jet Parker

Awaken Your Wealth

Introduction

Ardice Farrow

Theoretically, the universe is an abundant place. It is a place where there is no lack, limit or shortage. However, for many of us, living in such a truly abundant universe without limitation or constraint is not our day-to-day experience of life.

Instead, we often get lost in a maze of false beliefs and fears of scarcity and limitation.

Too often, we find ourselves trapped on a seesaw trying to balance feelings of "worthy" and "unworthy." Unconsciously, we are caught up in a life-long struggle of trying to do enough or work hard enough or be "good" enough so that someday the flood gates of wealth, abundance and ease with money will open.

We read, study and understand the law of attraction and alignment. We understand it is not possible to be in a state of abundance and a state of scarcity at the same time. Universally, it is impossible to be in the flow of wealth while at the same time being in fear that we will not have enough. And yet, releasing ourselves from the dilemma remains a mystery.

Some of us have had moments of ease and flow with regard to money only to have it turn around into a sea of scarcity and we are confronted once again with our need to struggle and work hard. We feel anxious as we strive to simply "get by" and we believe that true wealth will never be ours.

Where, in the midst of all of this, is the opening for ease? Where is the chance to break this rigid pattern and truly be open to the possibility of something new?

Ask yourself: What is your energetic and emotional relationship with money and wealth?

Many of us still hold deep in our hearts old myths and clichés about money: "Money is the root of all evil;" "Rich people have made their money on the backs of the poor;" "If you want to be rich, you must sacrifice your home life and your family." The list goes on.

We allow our fear-based minds to convince us that money is both an evil necessity and at the same time "the answer." We trick ourselves into believing that money will fix whatever is wrong in our lives. We want it. We see it as the "grand" solution and at the same time we are unwilling to learn how to respect it, nurture it and take care of it. We forget how to balance out giving and receiving and how to be grateful for what money enables us to accomplish, create and contribute.

With our unique pile of twisted beliefs and behaviors, no wonder money is not flowing to us naturally and easily.

Ask yourself: If you treated your spouse, partner, boyfriend or child the way you treat money, how would your loved ones feel about you? How would they treat you in return?

Then ask yourself: Instead of viewing money as something you need or want, what if you began to think of, feel and treat money like your new best friend?

Imagine, for a moment, how your life might be different if you acted as the guardian, the caretaker, the nurturer of money instead of the needy person with her hand out.

Living a wealthy life is never about money. It is all about living in the purity of the universal principle that life is an endless, creative process with no lack, limitation or constraint. It's about having a state of ceaseless gratitude and acknowledgment of all the riches of life and valuing ourselves even as we value others.

The path to freedom, ease and abundance with wealth and money is through our hearts and our humanity—not our hard work and our wallets. Once we are willing to align with the universal law of transformation, we unveil the mystery and reveal the magic deep within the laws of attraction.

Consider wealth as a state of being or a level of consciousness—not something defined by the number of commas and zeros in our bank accounts.

We invite you to open your heart to the stories that follow. Read the wise words of women, just like you, who stepped into and owned their unique values and the truth of wealth and brought the demonstration of abundance in all forms into their own lives.

Ardice Farrow

BILKING THE BILLIONAIRE BLUES

Cydney O'Sullivan

With a few overstuffed suitcases and a heart full of dreams, I left Los Angeles in 1987 to live with my new, Australian husband in his native country. I was so young I don't think I had any concept of the distance I was putting between myself and my family. The first Christmas away from them was very different.

Australia seemed to be the "land of opportunity" to a hard-working American girl with big ideas and to her young, enthusiastic husband. We threw ourselves into entrepreneurial endeavours. Over the next 15 years we purchased various start-up businesses ranging from food service to information technology. On our parents advice, we bought properties with our earnings. Christmases were a blur as we quickly shopped at whatever store was still open on Christmas Eve. We packed in as much work as we could before our much-needed January business breaks.

We moulded our lives around children and businesses, renovations and neighbourhood upgrades, and climbed our way up the ladder of social success. Eventually, one of our businesses really hit the jackpot and we sold it for a fortune.

This was when we found ourselves facing one of the toughest periods we had ever experienced. We were wealthy beyond our wildest dreams, but we had no training for such responsibility. How much do you buy your kids when you can buy them just about anything? Should you help all your family and friends when they come to you with crazy business schemes or tales of financial woe? How do you say, "No?"

We moved to a suburb that corresponded with our status and began to move with a new crowd. Eventually, my husband and I grew apart. I moved to the country and he to the waterfront. Our kids spent the weekdays living in a country town and partied in the city with their dad on the weekends.

I learned to trade the stock market while the kids were at school, and started making more money than I had ever made. Soon my income was so plentiful I couldn't relate to anyone else because I simply didn't have the problems they had. I didn't know what to do with it all. How does one manage millions of dollars? I didn't even learn to balance a check book until I was in my twenties. My husband had managed all the money in my businesses. My family had evolved from poor to middle class.

I started learning about the tax system and how to manage my money like a business. I hired some staff and took courses with wonderful teachers such as Robert Kiyosaki, Christopher Howard and Tony Robbins. I became the client of a very expensive business mentor. I dreamed of a community that taught other women in a fun environment how to find and use their own special talent to achieve financial success.

I took my kids on first-class vacations and bought beautiful homes. I bought and renovated run-down houses to rent out and was able to donate money to worthy causes.

I travelled back to Los Angeles and met with amazing people who are making a difference in the world: Director James Cameron and his passionate, socially-conscious wife Suzy; Mark Victor Hansen; and Nobel Peace Prize winner Dr. Muhammad Yunus, founder of the Grameen Bank, which has lifted more than 100 million people out of poverty. They all encouraged me to start my women's empowerment business and inspire others to tap into their inner entrepreneur.

Then, the strangest thing happened. While I was in Los Angeles planning to use my wealth for good, the economy in Sydney deteriorated at an alarming rate. The interest rates on my mortgages leapt up to 10 percent or more, the state government changed the land tax system to triple the cost of owning investment properties, the subprime crisis hit the United States and the Australian stock market halved in value in weeks.

I had lost half my wealth by taking my eye off my business and leaving it in the care of "professional advisers." The buyers in the real estate market evaporated and I started selling whatever I could in order to decrease the debt. Luckily, I liquidated my shareholdings, just in time. Brokers started imploding and many of my peers lost their businesses.

I was stunned. I didn't know who I was anymore. I didn't know where to turn for advice. Some of the very "professionals" whom I had been paying huge sums to advise me had been the catalysts for my biggest losses. I went into deep depression, with nightmares and panic attacks. The friends who rallied to my aid were not the ones I might have predicted. My ex-husband was wonderful, and a few special friends stuck by me and kept me laughing and focused on my blessings. My true friends pushed and rallied me to launch my business.

I felt like a fraud. How could I launch a business to teach women about safe investing when I didn't have a perfect record? How could I teach about choosing the right advisers when I had been defrauded?

Then I realized something, I now have experience. I know how it feels to be faced with devastating debt and the fear of losing it all. Now, more than ever, I can speak with authority and be one who cares enough to convey the message. Quitting was not an option.

I moved into action and told my staff I was closing my expensive city offices and ruthlessly reduced overhead. Amazingly, some of them stayed to work on the project, even cutting their own salaries or working for a share of future profits. Some left, but the business suddenly worked twice as efficiently. Those who left had been the people who were holding us back!

I moved back to my country home and when I saw how beautiful it was, I realized the best place to launch my business was right there. I sent out an e-mail to all the people who had been waiting for me to launch the workshops. The response was fantastic! My other successful friends were happy to share their experience with us about how to thrive in the current environment. I'm finally starting my dream business. I am helping people. It's scary, but liberating!

I was reminded of lessons I almost forgot:

It's not about your resources; it's about taking what you have and being resourceful.

Being a champion is taking what life gives you and choosing what you will make of it.

When times are tough for you, will you choose to give up or throw a party?

Dream it, live it, love it!™

Cydney O'Sullivan

CHASING THE AMERICAN DREAM

Beth Frazier

As I lie in bed with my eye lids slightly parted, drifting in and out of consciousness, I can barely read the headline flashing in front of me. The sound of a woman sobbing uncontrollably and a baby's cry in the background demanded my immediate attention. I tried to sit up and lean over to glance at the flashing red lights on my alarm clock, which read 5:45 a.m. From a distance, I could see a woman quickly gather her belongings while blood was slowly dripping down the side of her forehead. "I can't believe this," she cried. "How did this happen to me? Call my husband, there must be some mistake." The loud sound of the nearby sirens was drowning out the purity in her voice. There was something familiar about her voice. With my eyes still closed I frantically searched with one hand for the remote control so I could increase the volume. As I pressed the northbound arrow on the remote, I could barely hear the end of her sentence as she mouthed the words "My house is gone."

I could feel the pain in her voice and see the disappointment in her eyes. She felt ashamed as the journalist began to ask her probing questions about her home. "Why didn't you pay your mortgage? Could you afford this house when you bought it?" The woman screamed at the large men exiting her house with some of her valuables. As they padlocked and chained the front door, the woman's young son had to restrain her from attacking the men out of anger. "Get off of me!" she yelled, "Get off of me!" Suddenly, I could feel my husband grabbing my arms in defense and gently shaking me, as my eyes grew larger. "Are you okay? You were dreaming," he said. "Yes," I replied. "I was dreaming about our neighbor whose house was foreclosed." Although I was dreaming, I knew I had awakened to someone else's reality.

Today, stories like these are a dime a dozen. As a realtor for *The Corcoran Group* in New York, I hear so many stories of innocent people being evicted and pulled into foreclosure scams. I meet people who really can't afford the mortgage, but were given the "no money down" speech and were successful in obtaining one. I've met several people who use their houses as ATM machines, obtaining refinance after refinance, just creating more debt. On the news, we see unscrupulous people making thousands of dollars off of the elderly. Too many people have fallen into this trap. Why? Because they were "chasing the American dream." As I daydreamed about my own decision to become a homeowner, I remembered my first purchase.

In 2000, my fiancé (now husband) and I were thinking about buying a house. Although we both agreed the timing was right, we had different ideas about our first house. Like most newly-engaged women, I wanted a single-family home in the suburbs in a great school district. Ideally, I wanted a three-bedroom, two-bath house with an island in the kitchen and a two-car garage. My husband had a very different vision. He wanted a three-family town house where we would live in one unit and rent out the other two. I thought this was the dumbest idea because we were living in an apartment already. Why would I want to leave my "rent-stabilized" apartment to move into another "somewhat apartment?" In New York, rent-stabilized apartments are a valuable commodity and people don't give them up.

Looking back, I realized I was just scared of new responsibilities such as handling tenants and toilets. I didn't want to collect rent nor did I want to have to answer to nosy neighbors or hear tenants complain about the noise, leaks, etc. I listened to my family and friends tell me their nightmare stories and how crazy I was to entertain the idea of becoming a landlord. I have to admit, I believed them and wanted nothing to do with it.

As time went on, our discussions about the house became more intense and I grew more frustrated. We couldn't agree on anything. Then one rainy day at the kitchen table, we calmly discussed our options. Although we were both working at the time, he wanted me to think about the future, the "what ifs." He asked me if this first home (single family) would be my dream home. I said, "Of course not. We can't afford our dream home now." He said, "If you lose your job or have a child and decide to stay home or one of us gets sick, then that will have to be your dream home. With one salary there won't be any extra money to save for a bigger or better house."

Well, that was my wake-up moment and it hit me like a ton of bricks. It's not what I wanted to hear, but what I needed to hear. He was right. Buying a three-family town house would allow the two tenants to pay the mortgage. If we lost one salary, it wouldn't be a big deal. Back then, the houses were cheap enough to allow us to live rent-free. In addition, we would save the rent money for the down payment on the single-family home while creating equity in the three-family townhouse at the same time. It was a win-win situation and I couldn't argue with that.

Ironically, just two years later, I was eight months pregnant and laid off from my job. I was so caught up in my version of the American dream of the white house with the picket fence that I didn't think about the future. My vision of what my life should be, especially to those in the outside world, was poisoned with blurry images of the American dream. I just wanted my piece!

Are you chasing the American dream or someone else's idea of it?

Please allow me to offer some great advice and some steps you can take in your quest for home ownership:

- Budget: Make sure you find a qualified lender who can give a good understanding as to what you can afford. Obtain pre-approval before you start your search. Be sure to stick within your budget and live modestly.

- Trust you instincts: Remember the saying, "If it sounds too good to be true, it probably is."
- Teamwork: Develop a team of experts to help guide you through the process. Your team, at a minimum, should consist of a qualified lender, a realtor and an attorney. Make sure your attorney actively conducts real-estate transactions.
- Knowledge: Knowledge is not power; it is information. It's when you apply the knowledge that you become powerful. The Internet is a powerful tool, allowing you unlimited access to free information. Go to reputable Web sites like www.hud.gov and www.money.cnn.com to gain valuable insight about the market. Also, join or start your own investment club such as The NYC Women's Investment Group on meetup.com.
- Plan B: Plan ahead for future life changes such as having a baby, marriage or changing jobs. Have a contingency plan in place along with some savings in case you need it.

Buying a house is a big step, but often a rewarding one. Home ownership allows you to build equity and to access two very important tax deductions: Property tax and mortgage interest. According to the Fannie Mae Foundation, home equity is the most significant asset held by most U.S. families, and for many, it is their only asset.

I am passionate about educating women about the joys and pitfalls of home ownership. I believe it is the single most powerful investment one can have. Done properly, it can be the doorway to your American dream.

Beth Frazier

'Feng Shui' Finance: Attracting Prosperity

Melinda Day-Harper

Is finance a scary thing for you? I've been counting money since I was 7 years old when I carted a cotton candy machine in my little wagon through the neighborhood selling a cone of cotton candy for a nickel. Even if you weren't born a "numbers" person as I was, you have to agree that having a lot of money to play with is quite fun. So, how do we attract this level of prosperity into our lives?

There are three important concepts that we need to understand regarding the creation of space in your life so that you can attract prosperity.

Feng Shui

The first concept is based upon Feng Shui, which is all about creating a harmonious environment in which the flow of energy (including physical objects such as money) is maximized. De-clutter your space!

Theory of Relativity

The second concept is Albert Einstein's Theory of Relativity. Here's a way to easily grasp this concept:

1. On a piece of paper, draw a seesaw. *(I'm artistically challenged so my seesaw looks like a "T").*
2. *On the left side of the seesaw, write the letter "E".*
3. *In the middle of the seesaw, draw an equal sign (=).*
4. *On the right side of the seesaw, write* MC^2.

$E=MC^2$ is the Theory of Relativity. First, ignore the "C^2". That stands for the speed of light, which cannot change. The only thing that can change is the "E," which represents ENERGY, and the "M," which represents MASS.

Look at your seesaw. You have "E" on one side and "M" on the other. What this means is that if you increase M, or mass, what happens to the E? It drops way down to the ground. In order to get back to harmony, you have to increase E, your energy. On the simplest level, apply this method to the clutter you have in your life. If you reduce your clutter (the mass, in this case), you end up reducing the amount of energy needed to move that mass.

Your mental thought patterns are energy as well. Mental clutter—annoyances, worry and resentments—get in your way energetically, just as physical clutter does. Refer to concept one.

Law of Vacuum

The third concept is the Law of Vacuum. When one thing departs from our reality, it creates a vacuum that wants to draw in something new. Is this going to be something you want? You can *intentionally* choose what you want in your life, or you can wait to see what shows up by accident. That's your choice every day.

So what does all this have to do with prosperity? It all starts with the flow of energy around you.

Think about being a few pounds overweight. When we drop a few pounds, we not only look better, but we also have more energy for more things because we need less energy to move our mass.

The same holds true for our finances. The better organized our finances, the more physical and mental energy we have for other *intentional* activities that move us toward our purpose.

In Dr. Henry Cloud's book, *Nine Things a Leader Must Do,* he said that when we avoid facing things directly, they tend to grab us at the times when we can't address them effectively. An example is the financial issue you've been avoiding that pops into your mind the moment you lay your head down on the pillow—when you are least equipped to do something about it.

Avoidance always prolongs pain. The only way to eliminate that pain is to stop avoiding the financial issue you really don't want to deal with.

How do you do that?

Thinking for Personal Prosperity

There are five ways of thinking that will eliminate the obstacles to your prosperity attraction.

1. **One Dollar at a Time.** In society today, we want everything and we want it right now. This all-or-nothing thinking keeps us stuck in a destructive rut—sometimes for a lifetime. Buildings are built one brick at a time, and personal prosperity is created one dollar at a time.

2. **Money is a Means, Not an End.** Money is a tool, and as all matter, it's also energy, so it is meant to flow. If you hoard it and struggle or worry over it, you are cluttering your money flow. You will find yourself stuck where you are financially or, worse, it will flow elsewhere. Remember the Theory of Relativity? It's a flow of energy you want to create, so the more it flows through you, the more space you create for prosperity.

3. **Expect Abundance.** Have you ever driven on one of those new home tours where there are hundreds of opulent homes and wondered, "What in the world do all those people do to make that much money?" They're not all world-famous defense attorneys and lottery winners. The majority of them built their dreams one dollar at a time by expecting to be successful, persistently pursuing their passion and intentionally living their

purpose. They knew they would attract everything they needed to realize their dreams.

4. **The Big Picture.** In 1978, I was working full-time with a husband and a toddler. I decided to pursue my dream and go back to college. Seven years of night school later, I received my bachelor's degree. Two years later, I became a certified public accountant.

   At the beginning of that journey, if I had concentrated on how terribly hard it was going to be every day, I never would have even made it through the first semester. Instead, I opted to visualize a financially secure family, supported by my interesting, well-paid work and the use of my God-given talents.

   Even though it's important to live in the now, it's just as important to see the big picture and not let yourself get bogged down with the minutiae that happens to us every day. Instead, visualize every day having already achieved your long-term goal and concentrate on what you are doing today to make that hap pen.

5. **Start Today.** Take action. Almost any action is going to relieve some of the paralysis you feel. We all get overwhelmed and may not know what to do next, so we are indecisive. The easiest step you can take to get out of this paralyzed state is to pick one action that you can take today that will inspire you to get moving toward your purpose.

Remember the seesaw? Keep your positive thoughts and money flowing by creating space for prosperity and abundance in your life. Get rid of resentments, negative thoughts and physical stuff that clutters up your mind and your environment. Instead, focus your thoughts, time and efforts on what you want to attract.

I've been very blessed in my life. Being raised by a dad who was an outstanding businessman and who taught me that I could be and do anything I set my mind to, gave me a great start! However, the recent years I've spent studying the Law of Attraction and how the flow of energy affects everything in our lives (and minds), has catapulted me from nickel cotton candy to million-dollar deals!

Melinda Day-Harper

Conditioning, A New Conversation

Loral Langemeir

As you begin the Wealth Cycle Process, your actions will be caught up by your belief system. The conversation goes something like this: "I'm going to be wealthy," says your conscious mind.

"You?" says your subconscious. "No, you're not, you big liar."

At least that's what my brain used to do.

Your beliefs operate on two levels: The conscious, intellectual level and the subconscious, preconditioned level. It's important to understand that any limit to your thinking exists only in the paradigms ingrained in you, not in your ability to create a grand vision. I encourage you to establish a vision unencumbered by your paradigms. You created your current financial situation based on your beliefs. As you change your current financial situation, this will reprogram your brain to a new, progressive set of beliefs. Unlike processes that suggest you should think your way into thinking, the BE->Do sequence, I believe you should reprogram your brain the way it was programmed in the first place: By letting it learn from your behavior, a DO->Be sequence. It took years to be conditioned to think as you do now. That conditioning did not come from lectures and thought exercises; it came from behavior and practices. Behavior will redirect your brain. In the Wealth Cycle Process, you will act in the way you hope to be and let your brain catch up later.

I grew up on a farm in Nebraska. My family had always worked hard for its money. As a result, I always equated working hard with making money, with no idea that my beliefs could not have been farther from the truth. As I educated myself on human behavior and financial strategies, I learned the people who make their money work hard for them, rather than the people who work hard for their money are the ones who end up with more of it. Since creating my millionaire-making program, I've learned I was not alone; many people share this same myth.

Much like our views about many things—people, relationships, food and health to name a few—our beliefs came from our parents, our teachers and other adults in our lives. It goes back even further to circumstances through which they lived, what they learned from their parents, and so on. These beliefs are ingrained, and because they are usually subconscious, the cycles are continuous until someone breaks them.

You can break the cycle.

You will change your behavior. By sharing your desire for new beliefs and asking your mentors and respected friends to help you spot the subconscious limitations you may be putting on yourself, you will teach your brain to follow your behavior. Begin now by restating your beliefs.

It's time for a new conversation.

Loral Langemeir

Money Maze, Money Craze, Money Magic

Lorraine Edey, LCSW, Ph.D., ACC

What was your first memory of money? How old were you? How did you feel?

These three questions made up the catalyst that forever transformed my relationship with money. I finally began to understand the missing pieces of the puzzle.

For me, money had always equaled pain, suffering and deprivation, but these three questions later helped me to understand why money continued to come into my life only to disappear just as quickly.

My first memory of money is from age four. A tenant in my grandparents' brownstone in Brooklyn, New York, gave me a shiny silver dollar. He later told my mother I had taken the money from his room and he wanted it back. Since I was not allowed in his room, I received a spanking. That shiny silver dollar was returned to Mr. Brown and the journey of attempting to "get back" what I felt had been taken from me began.

When I was five years old, my mother left my father who was an abusive alcoholic, which forced my brother and me to live in several different places. We finally settled in upstate New York, where we lived with foster parents for five years. Though we lived on 50 acres of land and had some amazing experiences, it was here that my feelings of chronic "not-enoughness" were instilled. I did not have the same possessions, food or freedom our foster parents' children enjoyed, and there was always a sense of abandonment and loss in my soul. My saving grace was that my foster mother, Aunt Lil, was a very religious woman and took me to church regularly. Even at this tender age, I remember feeling something greater than myself and knew I was not alone in this world.

By the age of 10, I went to live with my mother and the chronic "not-enoughness" continued. I wanted things I could not have, so my mother instilled the value of working as a means of obtaining things. By the age of 12, I began traveling an hour on my own to an affluent neighborhood to help a lady cook and care for her children.

Eventually, I found a way to buy whatever I wanted through work and things were starting to look up. Money began to fill my void.

At 19, I married a young man who, at the time, always carried around large sums of money. He was unemployed and supported by his father, yet seeing him with money was very exciting to me. Here was my "knight in shining armor." He was going to rescue me and give me all the things I ever wanted.

Two years later, at 21, I had two children, had been evicted from my apartment and was living in low-income housing. Before the age of 30, I separated from my husband, was on welfare and had claimed bankruptcy. So much for my knight in shining armor. Yet through these stormy times, the spiritual foundation from my childhood kept me afloat. Somehow, I was always guided to people, places and things that would give me hope and inspiration.

Unaware that the developmental process in life was moving me forward, age "30" represented a clean slate and "30" was a magical age for me.

Living in a cooperative apartment, working two jobs and struggling as a single mom, my self-esteem was at an all-time low. Letters were posted on my apartment door stating "final notice before eviction." Feeling ashamed and filled with anxiety, I began exploring my spirituality at a deeper level by reading positive and encouraging books, attending workshops and listening to motivational speakers. One day, it clicked. I came home from work to find yet another eviction notice on my door. I decided then and there that I'd had enough! I decided to never let this happen again.

This was a defining moment in my life. I secured financial aid and went back to school to complete my bachelor's degree and later received my master's. However, the struggle with money continued. It seemed like a game. My pattern was to work hard, spend all the money then feel anxious about making more.

In all my years as a successful therapist earning a six-figure income, although I never learned the value of money or the importance of managing it, I had the uncanny ability to attract it. It showed up when I needed it, but it also controlled, over time, my entire life. My relationship with money became more and more strained. I kept asking the questions, how can I get out of this cycle of debting and spending? How can I change this pattern?

I was a committed learner. I read books on abundance and prosperity, said affirmations and attended all types of motivational classes. While this kept me in a place of attracting good into my life, I continued to struggle with deprivation, abandonment and chronic not-enoughness.

Another defining moment in my life follows the saying, "When the student is ready, the teacher appears." My teacher appeared.

There was a sequence of events that pointed me in the direction of money coaching. I found Deborah Price, author of *Money Magic*, and she changed my life. I attended a money coaching intensive and became a certified money coach. In answering the three questions, I received the answers that unlocked the unconscious patterns that kept sabotaging my relationship with money. I found freedom, and my spirit was lifted to new heights. I now know my worth is in no way related to possessions, and my inadequacies have been transformed into an unshakable strength. I am finally the victorious woman I struggled to be for so long.

Today, I am filled with gratitude for my newfound relationship with money. I have money in the bank, two homes, a 38-foot RV and a thriving money coaching business. Many people believe a person's worth is a product of material possessions. However, the wealth, abundance and richness I have in my life goes far beyond money. It is a deep peace within my soul; a balance of the material and spiritual worlds. It is wholeness.

My mission and passion is to spread the excitement I have experienced with financial freedom and solvency. You, too, can move effortlessly toward your desired financial dreams.

Use these inspired action steps to begin your daily journey toward financial freedom and peace of mind:

- **Clarity**. What are you going to do about your finances? Organize your debt and speak with significant others about your game plan.
- **Focus**. Create a clear cash-flow plan. Hold onto your vision of prosperity. Feel what it will be like when you are no longer in bondage to creditors.
- **Plan**. Design a plan that will support your success and begin exe cuting a clear 12-month action plan for eliminating debt. Begin to create the life you truly want to live.
- **Understand**. Begin to understand your conscious and unconscious patterns as they relate to money. Realize the root of your feelings and attitudes toward money.
- **Develop**. Intentionally develop a network of positive, supportive, like-minded individuals.

- **Educate**. Obtain all the information you can about money and finances. Secure a financial planner and/or a money coach. Join the Women's Institute for Financial Education (www.Wife.org) or join a Money Club (http://MoneyClubs.com)
- **Celebrate**. Give yourself credit (no pun intended) for a job well done. Celebrate your successes and keep your plan in sight.

Lorraine Edey, LCSW, Ph.D., ACC

Money and Me

Sylvia Moss

Have you noticed those people who always seem to have enough money without really having to worry about it? I was never one of them.

For most of my adult life, money and I weren't exactly on the best of terms. Finances were always a problem for me and I constantly struggled to figure out how to earn, keep and manage my money. In fact, my tumultuous relationship with money seemed to underlie every other issue in my life.

In 1985, I signed up for a workshop that promised to help me heal this ailing relationship. During a few days of intense inner examination, I discovered that my beliefs about money stemmed from my childhood. It seemed to me that my parents always had "enough" and, according to my father, the only way to have "enough" was to get a college education and pursue a career at a large corporation. If I wanted to earn a good living, I would have to set aside my dream of becoming an artist and do something practical, just as he had shelved his dream of owning a plant nursery to become an educator.

The workshop provided me with a wealth of insight into my relationship with money, revealing my deep-seated belief that I couldn't pursue my dreams *and* be wealthy. I learned positive mantras to help me shift this belief and change my expectations about the difficulty of earning money. Following the workshop, I joined a monthly support group that would help me continue the work I'd begun in the workshop. Slowly, things got better and money began to flow more easily. I had income from my divorce settlement as well as my freelance photography work and other part-time jobs. However, I found it difficult to sustain forward momentum, and my financial situation soon took a nose dive. Although I continued to live on a financial rollercoaster, I kept going to my support group, meditating and working on my inner issues.

One day, I learned that the apartment building where I lived was becoming a co-op. I was offered a buyout, but the offer wasn't high enough to allow me to relocate. Since I was happy where I was, I refused the buyout and dismissed the issue until two years later when I received another offer. This time I was shocked to discover that my apartment was valued at $100 per share—twice as much as before. Since my apartment was worth 1,445 shares, the buyout totaled $144,500. Immediately I knew that all my inner work was paying off. Maybe it really was possible to shift my belief that earning money had to be difficult. With great gratitude, I said "yes" to the buyout.

The co-op windfall allowed me to stop relying on part-time work and to embark on a more authentic career path. I began studying to become a hands-on energy healer, and my life was filled with the positive energy of following my heart's desire. However, after I graduated from the healing program and began building my practice, my funds began to dwindle. Once again, I had to face my deepest fears about not having enough money. Although I was now engaged in work that fulfilled me, I still felt uncertain about how to attract money into my life. Something was in the way, but what?

After some deep reflection, I began to see how and why I was pushing financial abundance away from myself. I realized that I was secretly afraid of succeeding at something I loved, and I uncovered several reasons for this. First, making money at my healing work meant stepping out of my family's accepted "norm." Second, I held a hidden conviction that if I did make money on my own, I would invest it unwisely and lose it. Finally, I harbored a deep fear of facing others' envy of my success.

I wish I could say that things magically improved after realizing how

I'd been blocking my money flow, but it remained an uphill battle. One beautiful autumn evening 15 years later, I was chanting my habitual money mantra as I sauntered home from work. Suddenly, I thought with utter clarity, "I'm tired of this struggle with money. I'm tired of being poor. I simply *must* have more money. I want to be a successful businesswoman."

Although the insight was vivid, it didn't immediately alter the course of my life. I continued to go about my daily routine, chanting my money mantra regularly. Then, a few months later, my brother called to inform me that our stepmother had died. By the time I arrived at her home, my brother had gone through her will and discovered that he and I were the joint beneficiaries of her investments. Since she was a retired schoolteacher who had always lived a simple life, I figured that at most there might be a couple thousand dollars for us to split. Imagine my surprise when my brother informed me that her investments had skyrocketed well into six figures. I guess my stepmother had enjoyed a much better relationship with money than I had.

Several months later, after the shock wore off and my new financial situation was in order, I had the time to wonder at the miracle of this second, much larger windfall. My astrology counselor suggested that it happened because I had been paying my dues by working on myself and helping others through pro bono healing services. Now it was payback time from the universe.

That second windfall lifted a great burden. I still face occasional challenges in my relationship with money, but I no longer need to focus every ounce of energy on survival. I now feel lighter in spirit, which makes me more effective in my private healing and guiding practice. I now lead the same money support group that I attended for so many years where I use a guided visualization that I created to help others transform negative money beliefs and issues. Last, but not least, I've set up a retirement fund. It has been exciting and a little scary to invest my money and watch it grow. I'm enjoying the process of learning how to be a successful businesswoman.

Now that I have a certain amount of expertise in the area of money manifestation, I am fiercely dedicated to helping other people step into financial ease and abundance. Here are some suggestions on how to begin:

- Find an energy healer or guidess to help you, either one-on-one or in a group.
- Find a teacher or workshop to help you delve deeper into your relationship with money.
- Be willing to get out of your own way. That means being open to what the universe brings you and learning from every situation that arises.
- Meditate daily to help yourself remain in the flow of life, rather than trying to control everything that happens.
- Be alert for uncomfortable or seemingly negative situations. These are the growth opportunities that you prayed for.
- When you feel stuck, recognize that you may be telling yourself an old story. Replace it with a new, positive one.
- Remind yourself daily that the universe is on your side. Ask for help and have faith that you will be guided.

Sylvia Moss

My Mother, Money and Me

Dorri C. Scott

Restructuring priorities, redefining dreams with a clear vision, and understanding God's life purpose that unfolds daily with great pomp and circumstance was the beginning of my journey toward high-level success. It all started with my mother's prayerful eye as she honored and understood me without judgment through the good times, lean times and all the other times in-between. She laid a solid foundation that encompassed all of me: physically, emotionally, spiritually and financially.

Yes! My mother prayed for me, and for that I am forever grateful. Lessons were often learned the hard way. The financial lessons, especially, taught me not only to respect and embrace money, but, most importantly, to take care of my money so that my money would inevitably take care of me.

For the record, my mother gave me little advice for managing a financial portfolio, building wealth or for leaving an asset-wise portfolio. That's not the kind of sense for cents she offered in her motherly way full of wit and wisdom. She was not afforded the formal education which forged the pathway for me and a generation of others to gain those wealth-building skills I acquired after graduating from the Harvard Business School. Mother did not have that to give to me. However, what she did impart was much more valuable. It surpassed all that one can see or physically touch yet produced intangible gems that remain priceless.

Those lessons and lectures talk of "making a way out of no way" and pinching pennies and prayer in hope for better tomorrows. This is what my mother, and many others from the "Mrs. Cleaver" and *Leave it to Beaver* generation gave the world. Their commitment, like hundreds who crossed the Atlantic Ocean to America's shores with only a dream and a hope to succeed, was all they had. Education was a dream and the future was where all beliefs were laid. "No begging for handouts" and one clear message, "don't spend more than you make," were their words and ways that produced dividends much more valuable than money which could be put on a balance sheet for others to boast about.

Remember, their generation is the one that burned the mortgage when it was paid. Many are enjoying pensions and a Social Security check that will become obsolete if we are not careful. Our children dare not entertain these thoughts and probably will never experience a pension, Social Security or staying on the job for 30 years or more. Those ways of living will probably become obsolete.

On average, women today earn 79 cents for every dollar men earn in the workplace. Since many women typically spend almost eight to 10 years out of the workforce due to childbearing, their earnings are even further curtailed. As a result, women are generally left with smaller retirement portfolios, lower Social Security benefits and if they are divorced, their financial security blanket will be even more compromised.

Endless conversations filled with motherly wit and wisdom are the beginnings of real success—especially as it relates to money and wealth building. With a mother's wisdom, wit and a model of working hard every day, mothers around the world generations ago instilled in daughters and sons the tools needed for long-term wealth building. Lest we forget, our parents enjoy lifestyles with pensions and homes paid for after 30-year fixed mortgages. *Please note*: adjustable rate mortgages are a new thing, created by those who desired and acted on it. Today, we have become the champions of learning financial lessons the hard way as many fumble through a house slump and a national foreclosure crisis.

Learning to value and respect money is one's greatest asset. The more quickly a woman learns to take care of her *own* money, the more she will appreciate and value how effectively money will take care of her. Incorporating those pristine values and principles that are difficult to embrace in the fast-paced world of "now" is where we as a community, and especially where we as women, must conform if we are to survive. Gas prices have driven us all to finding interesting things to do at home. Saving for a rainy day is no longer "vogue," but a necessity, lest we lose the game of keeping up with the Jones' family.

Saving and never spending more than you make must be the rule of thumb. Accepting credit card debt with interest rates in the double digits must be passéé. Review credit card applications and never sign without asking questions. It is imperative to know what the terms are. Pay as you go with cash instead of credit. Always spend within a budget and know your limits before you make a purchase. No more emotional buying no matter how fat you feel or how bad he was. He isn't worth it now and never will be. Cash must be king. Use it wisely and understand the difference between needs and greed. Women have everything to gain. Remember that your mother was right, after all.

Unafraid and not intimidated by the lull of "must have it all right now," our parents warned us of financial pitfalls. Some listened, but many, through mishaps, found themselves rebuilding in the middle of financial storms we created. Generations of women and men who proudly passed up today's wants in hopes of tomorrow's retirement live a lifestyle from which we can all learn. Financial success has its price. It requires saying no to "shop till you drop" buying and the latest and greatest bag. Shoes and a bigger house must become things of the past in order to fulfill life's dreams that build for something bigger than today.

Beginning today:

- Pay yourself first. Have an emergency fund. Every time you are paid, put something in your savings account. If you don't have one, open one and watch your money grow.
- Save a minimum of 10 percent of your earnings and enroll in a personal or company 401K plan. If you are not currently taking advantage of the money your company gives you (usually up to six percent matching) you are leaving your money on the table. Commit to you and enroll today.
- Live on a budget. Have a spending plan and don't succumb to emotional spending or buying.
- Spend less than you make.

When it's all said and done, buy that new bag, get your hair done or purchase that pair of shoes that you would die for. A girl has got to have fun. You have worked hard for it and deserve it. Just do it in moderation, remembering if you take care of your money, it will take care of you!

Dorri C. Scott

Awaken Your Spirit

INTRODUCTION

Karen Mayfield

When we discover what is beyond what we cannot see, we realize what is behind what we can see. The essence of spirit hides behind a veiled awareness.

We cannot see the air, yet we can feel it touch our face. Without it, we die.

We see the moon and stars, yet we cannot touch them. However, we know the sun, moon and stars are not just decorations for the sky.

We can't physically see spirit or touch spirit or know spirit in the same way we know everything else. Nevertheless, all beings speak to someone within when they are alone and in a sad moment. The voice addressing and helping during this time is the voice of spirit.

Body, Mind and Spirit

The human species consists of three components: body-mind (crude matter), organic material, and spirit (anti-matter; invisible energy). When a baby is born, the first breath of air ignites the brain, which sends out signals to all other parts of the body. The baby's mind is introduced to idea after idea after idea just as software is installed in a computer, and by the time the baby is three years of age, the brain has transmitted billions of signals and made thousands of synaptic connections. Long before the age of reason and logic is reached, belief systems and conditioning have begun.

The brain plays a role much like that of a receiver and transmitter. The result of brain activity is thought. Before anything can manifest into physical form or reality, it must start as a thought. So, anything that ever was, is, or will be was first a thought. This makes thought the backbone of human potential, and the human body is like an organic animated idea machine.

Instilled deep in our being is belief. Belief is one of the most powerful forces in the universe, and it exists only in the mind. Belief and instinct lie at the core of the thought process. The instincts created over thousands of years developed the ego. The ego is the part of each human that is concerned with survival. The ego believes the world is a dog-eat-dog world, and its mission is to survive.

Spiritual consciousness (the invisible energy) and ego consciousness are the two energies interacting simultaneously in the mind. Ego consciousness is easily intoxicated by the world; there is no human who will not be seized by the colorful and powerful attraction of the world. Spiritual consciousness is engaged when you learn to give for giving, love for loving and forgive your enemy.

Ego consciousness is with us at all times, and spiritual consciousness is within us at all times. There can never be peace of mind when ego consciousness has the upper hand over spiritual consciousness. In societies, governments, religions, companies or families where ego consciousness is prevalent, you will find fear, hate, control, lack, opposition and lower levels of consciousness in which every force creates another force. Spiritual consciousness fosters faith, love, freedom, abundance, collaboration and the highest levels of awareness; every action creates empowerment and a state of enlightenment.

The state of enlightenment is attained by transcending the ego. However, the physical body is dependent upon the ego for survival and the two will remain together forever. Separation from the ego is not possible. We must transcend the ego by freeing it from limiting thoughts so it no longer holds us in the lower levels of consciousness.

The stories you are about to read are delivered to you as a means of assisting you in your transcendence of the ego. Once spiritual consciousness has the upper hand over ego consciousness, the test of the world will come to an end. After reaching such a consciousness, you consider everything as energy within the one, and reach the belief, "I love the created because of the Creator."

Wake up, women. Be happy, healthy and wealthy.

Karen Mayfield

OPENING YOUR GEODE

Suzanne Strisower

The Precious "Geode" Journey—
The Four Layers of Authenticity and Well Being

A geode is a metaphor I use with my clients to find their authentic selves. This four-step process gently explores each of their inner "layers" until they reach their divine center or core.

First is the external shell: A desire to accomplish something better in life, which brings them to a life coach. We explore the thoughts and feelings that help or hinder that manifestation. The second layer focuses on their emotions and desires—the reason that people want what they do. A sense of clarity and inner connection develops, leading people to desire the knowledge of a deeper level. The third layer is the knowing or intuition which is present when our thoughts and feelings are quiet and settled as external circumstances are resolved. Finally, at the core of your being, when the geode is opened fully, you know all of the layers and how they can work for you. At this level, you also experience your connection with the Divine in whatever way you wish. My coaching motto is this: "Align your outer world with your inner being." I accomplish this by helping clients open up and discover their beautiful and unique centers.

Through the Layers of My Life

This precious geode process is demonstrated through the unfolding of my own life. I started from the outside, working inwards to manifest from my own core.

My Shell: Wanting to be Successful

My career path began with tarot card readings, as I ultimately became a professional psychic with a weekly engagement at the prestigious

Claremont Hotel and Spa in Berkeley, California. I loved helping people through intuitive guidance. However, I desired a "real" job, so I became a medical facilities interior designer and the spirit showed me how to create environments that will heal the patients. Successful but burned out, I asked myself, "What is next? What do I love to do?" The answer was working with people.

Looking Inward: Finding My Heart's Desire

I made a complete break from design and began living and working with at-risk teenagers, speaking directly to their hearts. My desire to know more led to my next career as a certified clinical hypnotherapist. I began to help people with the things that were difficult for them to experience—whether it was an emotion or an event from the past.

Living From My Center—My Creative Self Expression

The Great Spirit and the Angels of Light have guided my life for years, and I asked them what I should do to acquire a sufficient livelihood—something that would generate an income from my own resources. I channeled a new-age rune oracle, *The Runes of the Four Realms*. My intention was to create a tool for people to directly connect with their intuition, inner wisdom and divine energies.

Emanating From My Core—Manifesting My Ideal Life

My current profession and passion—intuitive life coaching—blends the best of all my skills and worlds: Working with people, using my intuition and empowering others to lead their own, inspired lives. I love taking people through their own life flow by using their emotions and desires as starting points to their inner wisdom, right livelihood and *High Havingness* (your internal fulfillment and external success).

The Four-Step Geode Process

Step One: Working From the Outside in—Looking At Your Desires

To open up to your unique process, start by exploring your thoughts, emotions and going with their flow—both positive and negative. Our regrets can show us hidden desires and our unrealized passions. The goal is to become conscious of the process, to embrace your emotions, your thoughts and what they are showing you about your life. They will show you what is working and what isn't. When people get a glimpse of the possibility for change through the shifts and resolution of their thoughts, feelings and actions, it is a special and innocent time for them.

A chiropractor and gifted healer came to me because her life was full of stress and was "in chaos." The first thing we explored was what composed her chaos—her home life, her business, her ex-husband and her finances. She said she felt burned out and didn't know how to fix things. I helped her identify the steps needed to feel refreshed and to create some order for herself. As she delved deeper into her thoughts, feelings and actions, she realized she wanted to fix things for everyone and was totally drained. We identified the "social worker" in her. This was much different from her desire to empower and help people heal through her gifts and profession. This eased her feelings and thoughts of her own inadequacy, which led to a desire for the future.

Step Two: Looking Inward—Experiencing Your Authentic Self

The second layer involves knowing the thoughts and feelings you have that naturally expose your truest inner desires and your heart's yearning for fulfillment. This will lead to those intuitive hits about things that you would like to experience. This wisdom and guidance shows you the possibility of what your inner satisfaction would look like—those things that would make you really happy and satisfied in life. Career and relationship enhancements are done wisely when one understands and honors what they feel. My job as coach is to explore desired outcomes with the clients, starting with honoring where they are and inviting them to listen to their intuition and its desired expressions, both internally and externally.

Next, my client explored how she had created this reality for herself and then shifted her thoughts, feelings and actions into alignment with who she really wanted to be. Each area of her life opened up to the image she ideally saw for herself, and she created action steps for each area. She is an inspired client who, as soon as she got it, moved into action for a positive change. She began to truly experience a sense of well-being and satisfaction from the changes she implemented.

Step Three: Living From Your Center—Your Self Expression
Your intuition takes you into a deeper layer of inspired expression and action. The goal is for your intuition to inform you about creating a life of ease and grace that can flow from the inside out. Now is the time to begin dreaming; to imagine a future that your intuition, passion and divine guidance can help to shape and create.

This same woman looked at who her ideal clients could be. With whom did she connect? Who did she really help? We looked at ways to serve these clients and enlarge her practice. She then realized she wanted to be financially empowered and to take back the control of her finances. Each time she claimed more territory for herself, I watched her expand before my eyes. This step created its own momentum within her.

Step Four: Emanating From Your Core—Your Ideal Life
Living consciously from one's core allows people to be their authentic selves and to live an ideal life. At this stage, clients experience their own core—their intuition, divine guidance and being—and let these dictate their life's direction and expression. There is a congruence and freedom people experience when they live from the inside and have worked from the outside in consciously.

My client now has a happy home life in which people interact in more healthy and empowered ways. She is creating a healing practice that reflects the people she loves to work with, and it gives her other ways to serve them. She is full of her own energy, power and promise.

I invite each one of you to explore your own precious geode, working from the outside inward through your layers to eventually emanate from your divine core and manifest your ideal life out into the world.

Suzanne Strisower

FROM TINY MOMENTS OF BLISS TO BLISS FULL MOMENTS

Amy Kelly

I never thought it would happen to me. My parents had been together for almost 40 years. They were fantastic role models for marriage. Yet, here I was, divorced and devastated.

What happened to the fairy tale relationship I'd dreamt of since I was a little girl? My prince stayed behind as I drove my chariot away from the castle and moved into a two-bedroom apartment. All of my illusions of what marriage and family should look like were split into pieces. I fell apart too.

I really didn't know how to put myself back together. For the first several months, I'd stay in my room for days except to go out to pick up ice cream. I'd return to eat it in bed. I allowed myself to wallow in my despair. Eventually, I missed my dog so much I ventured outside. My ex-husband and I had agreed to share custody of her. She was my beloved chocolate lab, Roxy. She was still a puppy and had become a best friend and teacher to me.

We lived in the foothills of Boise, Idaho, and Roxy and I loved to hike the trails. She needed exercise, and I needed to get out of the apartment—I couldn't handle looking at my ugly, dark yellow walls anymore, and I didn't have the energy to paint. I moped while Roxy ran wildly around the hillside in circles, doing anything she could to try to pull me out of my funk. Finally, I laughed through my tears. I felt a genuine moment of amusement at her attempts to make me smile.

Roxy and I began to hike together more often and I counted on those times to provide moments of laughter in the midst of my grief. Spring arrived and the wild flowers bloomed. The sunshine warmed my face as the snow melted. There was a fox in the neighborhood and hawks flew overhead. I have always loved their primal cries, as they remind me of something ancient and true at the center of my being. I noticed and appreciated these small joys more than ever before as I stopped to take them in. As I looked around I realized they had always been there. I was the one who'd closed my eyes. I called these ever-available opportunities "tiny moments of bliss" and decided I wanted to create more of them in my life.

Our hikes soon took on a more spiritual feel. We stopped beside streams, and while Roxy tore through them at full speed, I just watched the water pass, sometimes gauging the progress of a lone leaf making its way through the rocks. I felt like that leaf, and I understood its journey.

I started to hear another voice coming from inside me, speaking through my sadness. It brought feelings of comfort, assuring me I would not always feel this way. I listened and was thankful.

I'd been on a spiritual path for several years and I recognized this voice as my intuition or some higher part of me speaking through the haze of my emotions. I'd allowed it to guide me through years of spiritual musings, and now it began to navigate my healing.

I remembered times when I had been happy. Roxy and the animals we encountered reminded me that, as a child, I'd wanted to become a veterinarian. This helped me to cherish every moment in nature even more.

I recalled that when I was a teenager, all I wanted to do was dance. I had stopped dancing in college, choosing more rational and logical ways to spend my time as a biomedical engineering student.

I studied yoga and found peace in the movement and postures, discovering that it quieted my mind. I combined my passion for yoga and dance into a daily spiritual practice that helped me to open my heart and to hear my inner voice.

All the while, I honored what was. I knew it was important to feel it all—to acknowledge the darkness as well as the light—because going through the darkness helped me emerge into a brighter place. Some days I still felt depressed, but mainly I was delighted and grateful to feel genuinely happy. I'd started to engage in activities that I loved and passion flowed back into my life.

I had always thrived on relationships and friendships. After ten years as an engineer, developing medical devices for surgery, I decided to pursue a new career. I had once dreamt of finding work that would allow me to explore spirituality as a means for making a living, so I was drawn to life coaching. A good friend and coach helped me to find a training program that felt like a match for me and I enrolled. I wasn't sure if this was "it," but I was ready to try.

Halfway through the initial training course, I woke up thinking, "I've been doing this all my life." I finally felt like I was home. I'd found my new work. The next stage of my journey had begun and my soul was singing.

I continued to follow my passions while building my new business. I realized I had created my happiness. I learned that true bliss comes from within when we listen to our intuition, align with our higher selves and allow ourselves to do what we love.

I made it through another snowy winter and was ready for a change. I have wanted to live in southern California since I was nine years old, so I moved.

It's a beautiful, sunny day near San Diego. Ironically, today would have been my wedding anniversary. The tiny moments I once experienced only fleetingly have transitioned into moments full of bliss. I walk the beach several times a week, I stop to talk to the rabbits and squirrels along the path. I dance every day. I laugh often, I connect with wonderful friends and clients in deeply fulfilling relationships, and I explore my spiritual path as my work. I am not saying I have everything I want or that I am never unhappy, but I feel more fulfilled than ever before. More than anything, I do what I love.

So, in those times when we feel the pain and sadness that are part of the journey, we can notice whatever it is that makes us smile. As we begin to observe and appreciate these moments, they appear more often. When we string them together one after another, we experience greater joy. As we begin to make choices aligned with what we love, the moments grow until we eventually see that we can create them. They come from within us and we can take them wherever we go.

Amy Kelly

The Road to Knowhere

Tara Diamond

From Nowhere to
Now Here,
Standing in What I Know

I was still for a long time not wanting to move in case it would come back. I looked around for it, but I knew it was gone from the tiny room. It was nowhere and so was I, as far as my understanding of this was concerned. I hugged my knees up to my chin, wondering what just happened to me. How did I know how to heal him like that? I'd never even heard of such a thing much less know how to do it. I was left wide-eyed with wonder at the miracle that just happened.

Minutes before, I'd been watching my boyfriend lying on the bed across the room, deathly ill with nausea, severe aches, fever and vomiting. He was prone to illness just before a major workload and the next day would be one of those stress-filled days, so I didn't feel alarmed. I marveled at how he could pull off such a great act.

Then I grew concerned as I realized how sick he really was. I put down my book, sat on the edge of his bed, and calmly laid myself over his back to comfort him. Suddenly, I felt his sickness enter my body; and for a moment or two I was overcome with his nausea, fever, aches and fear. Somehow I had taken on his illness. Even though I had no idea what was going on, I wasn't afraid. I allowed the sickness to be there, and in a moment, I felt if lift off the back of my body and disappear. It's as if I had become it and then I was myself again. My boyfriend was healed and I was fine. I slowly sat up, tucked him in, and told him he would be all right. I moved to the other bed and sat there staring into space for a while. The next day, he was as good as new. I was just as I was before, physically, but I would never be the same again.

That was 25 years and thousands of healings ago. After that initiation into healing, it wasn't as easy for me to release the illnesses that came to me because I let my fears get in the way. I didn't know enough the first time to be afraid. I let love have its way with me and the energy of the illness was healed and lifted. After my boyfriend was healed, a desire to know opened me up to everything in the universe. This, of course, made me afraid of the energies streaming into me. I knew I must find my own way. I had to empower myself through knowledge and training beyond my comprehension.

My will to do it was wrapped with passion and enthusiasm, for this adventure held risks and rewards like no other. A year later, I threw caution to the wind, and following the "still, small voice" within me, I packed my easel and camera and moved to California. I had just finished an art degree and 10-years as a professional speech and language pathologist in the mountains of North Carolina. The gradual awakening of that small voice became a thunderous roar on what would be a "Road to Knowhere" as my spiritual quest took center stage in my life at the expense of everything else.

When I arrived in San Diego, I immediately began studying the "Teaching of the Inner Christ." This brilliant teaching anchored me in consistent practices of prayer and healing work. It also aligned me with the Christ consciousness of my own being on a consistent basis. I practiced the teaching for 15 years and became a minister and, later, the pastor of the center. I taught metaphysics, prayer therapy, and inner sensitivity training at night. My days were filled with inner work while I also developed myself as a professional artist.

The teaching focused on astral healing, which I needed desperately. It uses the spiritual alchemy of love and light to lift negative thoughts and emotions within our higher feeling nature. Energies from other dimensions can attach to our auras (energy fields), influence our moods, affect our choices and behaviors and even erode our health. They can make an already unhappy person even more unhappy without being able to change it. I learned to heal those suffering from grief, loss and confusion by healing on these other dimensions. It took years for me to develop the inner authority to do this work, which, in short, was my ability to stand without fear in what I know.

I ventured into many other areas of extensive study. Human design helped me understand how I'm designed to penetrate the energy fields of others and be sensitive to their thoughts and feelings. I could be intimate with people in non-threatening, compassionate ways, and sometimes take on their problems because my own energy field was so open. This deepened my spiritual focus on acceptance of myself and others while seeing the perfection of our uniqueness. However, it did not explain how I could heal people at a distance. Long-distance healing is possible when working at the higher levels of energy. I've helped people overcome social phobias, heal the debilitating effects of Epstein-Barr Virus, and make remarkable recoveries from surgery that doctors could not explain. Quite simply, I found love carries the healer and Spirit does the work.

A few things I know from my experience are vital to my health and happiness. First, keeping myself clear gives me the freedom to be myself. To remain clear, I've learned that acceptance is the foundation of everything.

We have to accept what is, regardless of our feelings about it, if we want to heal or change it. What we have not accepted within ourselves we see in others and judge, or we see it in others and long for it. Therefore, we need to develop acceptance.

Whatever we judge comes back to us again and again until we stop judging. What we judge in another, we also hold against ourselves. Therefore, we need to forgive.

Forgiveness is the release of an energy we are holding against ourselves, not someone else. The energy is held with our judgments. Examining them isn't about excusing the apparent source of conflict. Rather, it's about freeing us from the hold another seems to have on us that robs us of our power and our peace. When we forgive, we can forget. Love empowers our willingness to forgive. So, love anyway.

Finally, in developing a spiritual focus we must become aware that we're struggling with an energy, not with something personal. If we can remember that an impersonal energy is operating within the situation, we can instantly detach from it and move to acceptance and forgiveness. In doing so, we will release our judgments and bring love to it.

I know that on the "Road to Knowhere," forgiveness is the way to go. You can't make a turn without acceptance and you will never get lost if you let love show you the way. So, whatever your path or you mission, remember this simple truth: Your love is greater than your fear, always.

Tara Diamond

How Deep Is Your Love?

Christine La

Love inspires. Love quenches our desire to unify with another soul and overcome feelings of loneliness. Love can make us feel strong and whole. However, it can be a risk because it is something we cannot control. Many of us have encountered heartbreak, unfulfilled desires, difficulty communicating with our romantic partner or finally finding love after countless relationships. For some, the experience can leave you feeling empty and fearful of being vulnerable again. For others, the growth that occurs in learning about oneself is magnified by the lens of the relationship. From my experiences with patients in the therapeutic setting, I've come to realize these experiences are universal. To attain love, to learn from love and to have the ability to embrace love without fear requires that we understand ourselves.

How can we attract others to love us? According to the laws of natural selection and biological theories on relationships, the male seeks out a female who is fertile and a female searches for a male who is healthy and can protect her. In other words, our attraction to a man or woman is enhanced by an instinctive drive to perpetuate our existence. This explains why a woman may initially be attracted to a man who is stable and can take care of her and a man is focused on a woman's appearance. However, the key behind understanding attraction lies in our chemical makeup. Have you ever experienced an electric feeling of attraction when you met someone? Perhaps the chemical of attraction, dopamine, was being released and drew you to someone. I've had clients tell me about their infatuations for someone on a physical level, often after a physical encounter, which leaves them feeling confused as to why the experience never grew into a meaningful relationship. However, in order for the initial feelings of attraction to be transformed into more powerful feelings of love, it requires us to release more oxytocin, a chemical of trust and bonding that is commonly released by a man and woman through communication. Communication and the formation of a bond beyond physical desire are important elements in establishing love.

Once we have formed a physical or emotional connection, what prevents us from experiencing love completely? Why do we become fearful, angry and inhibited toward the one feeling we desire? Our identity is in large part framed by our ego, which is a sense of ourselves, and which defines us and our beliefs about others. The ego's role is entirely selfish and needs to be reinforced. If someone lives strictly to enhance his or her ego, love may be viewed only in terms of its benefits to him or her and how it makes one feel. But this is not real love. For instance, if a man objectifies a woman in order to feel powerful, that is not true love. If one is unable to value his/her partner's wishes, that is not true love. Thus, a relationship can often reveal one's weaknesses. During the process of love, your partner may threaten your ego and your view of the world. During the relationship's period of transformation, love is not experienced as a need to validate oneself, but rather as selfless. The ability to completely love requires one to transcend beyond the ego, become vulnerable and connect with one's "true self." This type of love requires a deeper level of commitment, one in which you see your partner's point of view, you question your actions and love someone even with his/her flaws.

Like a child taking his or her first steps, we experience a step-by-step metamorphosis in our relationships. For instance, a woman in her 20s or 30s may begin the courtship process based on fertility and health, which in large part is driven by a chemical attraction. From my own early experiences with relationships, my attraction to a man was based on the idealization of what a partner should be. A strong physical attraction to my partner only solidified the belief that this was true love. However, unbeknownst to me at the time, I was making decisions that were solely reinforced by my ego. I told myself I was an independent woman who deserved a man who was financially stable, successful, driven and charismatic. Being around a man who embodied these qualities reinforced my identity and made me feel loved because I loved what he represented to me. What I failed to see was that a union without depth would gradually unravel since the foundation was never created. It was a relationship based on superficial qualities of image, success and physical attraction. It lacked generosity, kindness and unconditional love. To love someone unconditionally requires us to move beyond the ego, and it is in this learning process that we discover a deeper love.

As we age, we encounter a few heartbreaks on our journey to finding love. As we evolve, our taste in men grows to encompass those characteristics that extend beyond the ego. In our early years, the mindset of a woman who loves immaturely sees the problem of love as the difficulty of *being loved* and not *of loving*. Much energy and attention are placed on *being loved* and attracting the opposite sex by superficial means. However, with experience and age, a woman learns about the *art of loving* and embraces the process. During the process, a woman may choose a partner who shares similar goals and values, embraces her flaws and supports her in her endeavors.

The process of loving may be a difficult one because it requires us to transform the identity framed by the ego which compels a woman to face her fears about intimacy and collapse them, and to cover and work on her flaws. For instance, my friend, a successful and independent professional, would often complain that she was attracting the wrong men. Through the years, she discovered the true problem stemmed from her difficulty in completely giving herself to a man due to fear of being hurt and from her own selfishness in relationships. Thus, she attracted men who embodied the very qualities she possessed. She has worked on becoming more genuine and giving in a relationship and, consequently, found herself attracted to a partner with similar traits. Today, she is married and in a loving relationship. She has embraced parts of herself beyond her ego that were once hidden, ultimately empowering herself as she learned to appreciate her inner spirit. I believe that during the process of relationships the most important lesson for a woman to learn is to look within herself and allow for the expression of her own spirit. Only by loving ourselves are we able to give love and sustain a healthy relationship.

Love is a journey where one visits distant shores and may experience heartbreak. The true mission of the journey is to discover a deeper purpose. We are born into this world as halves; a man and woman representing elements of yin and yang. Throughout our lives, we are in search of a transformational love, which will help us to unify ourselves with our other halves. Transformational love is powerful in its ability to expose the authentic self and spirit. Inherently, we seek balance in our search for a partner. We search for someone who embodies elements missing in us. We seek those who will allow us to be whole.

Words of Wisdom:

- Live and love beyond your ego.
- Embrace the art of loving by working on your own strengths and weaknesses in a relationship.
- Connect with your inner spirit.

Christine La

The Power of Your Presence

Christina South

"Don't you ever wonder why nobody told you God's inside?"—Colette Baron-Reid

A few years ago, my ordinary world was turned upside down as I noticed two golden lights following me in my home. They were beautiful, and instantly brought a feeling of peace into my heart. The lights vanished as quickly as they came. At that moment, my life was forever changed.

I began to see sparkles of light and a cobalt blue ball of light daily. My intuition also exploded. I began to know and sense things about others and future events. This was more alarming than seeing the lights because with it came memories of my childhood when I'd had similar experiences. At first, I really did not believe that my sightings and visions were real. I sought professional help to find the answer. I still had no answers after a visit to the eye doctor. I was told my vision was perfect. This left me to find answers on my own, which turned out to be one of the most joyous journeys I have ever taken.

Although I have always had a strong faith in God, I also had many more moments of doubt that often left me questioning my faith. Now I was beginning to see the supernatural world in action and I could not believe that either. Why would God allow me to see past the veil, and what purpose did it serve? I know now that God was simply answering the outcries of my heart in a way I could not deny. The more I progressed and the more I sought out God, the clearer the visions, sightings and their purpose became. God was drawing me back to myself and my spirit through heavenly assistance. I was seeing angels and still see them today.

These sightings have taught me no one is ever completely alone. This experience also created miracles in even the most mundane parts of my life and left me with the profound joy of telling others how to get their faith back.

We as humans have complicated our relationship with God. We have created rules and guidelines to get back what we never really lost. God has never left, nor will He ever leave, because you cannot leave yourself. Think about that for a moment. If God were to completely withdraw from our lives, life would not exist because we are little pieces of God in physical form. We are the hands, the feet, the ears and the voice of God. It says in John 10:34, "Is it not written in your law, I have said, you are gods." In John 14:20 it says, "On that day you will know that I am in my Father and you in me, and I in you." This is where you are at this very moment. You are an extension of the Divine and God wants you to wake up to that.

Our spiritual and daily lives are interconnected. Since we can never really be separate from God, God can never be separate from our daily lives. You may wonder how you can bring that divinity to the workplace, family or even a trip to the store. The answer is that, as a walking piece of God, your power is in your presence. When others are in your presence, you have the power to heal and connect them to their true essence. Viewing every moment of every day as a healing moment puts life into a different perspective because it gets you out of the way and allows you to focus on what is important. The most effective way you can apply this knowledge to your daily life is by being yourself. God smiles over you when you are being yourself. You heal others with your wit, your passion, your joy, your story, your ability to solve problems and your job. This is how you begin your journey. Once you recognize the healing power you have, your life will be transformed because everything you do will have meaning, so your life will have meaning. This also means that you cannot forget to work on healing yourself as well.

You must feed your spirit, as well as your body and mind. Seek out others who heal you, read books that uplift your spirit. Join a congregation or group that will help you along your spiritual path. Spend time in nature and enjoy the beauty of God's creation. Don't neglect your body. Take walks, take a yoga class or do something physical that makes you smile. Nourish your body with healthy food so that your body can feel as good as your spirit. Lastly, be who you truly are!

We offer others our greatest healing potential when we are our authentic selves. If you have to think about being yourself, then you probably are not being yourself at all. Authenticity comes when you get out of your own way and take each moment as it comes, not forcing yourselves upon that moment. It should be effortless and feel natural because being yourself is exactly how God made you. You will also be authentically you when you focus on the now instead of tomorrow or a few minutes from now. It's a lot harder to pretend when you're in the moment because you will not miss the subtle messages that you are receiving and you will rarely hear yourself say, "Could you repeat that?" Being present is a great gift you give yourself and others, and it allows you to be "you" with ease.

You may not see angels or sense things, but God is still ever-present, waiting for you to notice his presence in everyday situations. Your spirit is waiting for you to be you, for in those moments, you will truly feel your connection to God, and in those moments you will truly be living.

Christina South

A Wing, A Prayer and the Wind

Margaret Good

The key to abundant life lies in our motives. The fundamental question in every activity and relationship for us becomes "For whom am I doing this?"

One excellent example of this is Mary Kay Ash. She professed to live her life and attributed her success to putting God first, her family second and her career third. Many of the directors in her organization profess to be successful today because they have followed her practices and philosophy in life.

I now have an intimate relationship with God; a positive nurturing relationship with my daughter; a deep, loving relationship with my spouse; and a successful career which allows me to minister to others regarding God's greatness. In my early years, I would not have envisioned my life as it is today.

I grew up in the 1970's during the women's liberation movement. My perception of the message being taught was: Men were scum and motherhood was a worthless desire and a worthless occupation. Being naive, I bought into this concept and decided to go into architecture; I became a bit of a rebel. No man was going to tell me what to do and if I got married, I was still going to do my own thing no matter what. I was going to be free and no one was going to hold me back, crush my dreams or get in my way. Money, power and possessions were the only way to go. Relationships were of little value and idle chit chat was just a waste of my time.

After college, I met my future husband Rob at the construction company where we worked. We hit it off. We were both intellectuals, loved academics and he fully supported my pursuit of higher education and my dreams. Wow! Here was someone who believed in me, didn't see me as competition and wanted to see me be successful. It couldn't get any better than that!

Four months passed and Rob asked me to marry him. Being Roman Catholic, I told him divorce was not the answer to the future challenges we would face and that I was still intent on pursuing my own dreams. Having come from a broken home, he assured me that no matter what, we would be able to work it out and he could live with my strong personality and wild, adventurous spirit. Today, we laugh about it; he really had no clue what he was getting himself into when I accepted his marriage proposal.

Most people see their lives flash in front of them when they are having a near-death experience. My life flashed in front of me at the altar. I was having fun being single and on my own. Now my life, as I knew it, was over. I was becoming "one of those married women." I said my vows as life flashed in front of me and tears streamed down my face. To this day, many people think they were tears of joy. In reality, I was grieving for my life of freedom and independence.

Two weeks after we were married, I quit my job and went back to school full time. A few years later, I purchased a business without discussing it with Rob. On another occasion just two weeks before our first house closed, I was downsized from my job as assistant controller when two software companies merged. My decisions created turmoil with our finances, but my husband Rob stuck by me, no matter what.

After 15 years of marriage, we were blessed with a beautiful daughter. Through it all I dealt with my chronic depression, but God remained faithful and taught me to follow and trust in His guidelines.

God has taught me to love the diversity of others, especially in my spouse and other family members. My husband and I are opposites in many ways. He is calm, focused and methodical. After all, he is an engineer and an accountant. I jump from A to Z in a decision while he can walk you through every letter of the alphabet to get there. I sign up for all kinds of projects, trips and activities without reading the details thoroughly because it sounds like fun, knowing he is a homebody. I am action-oriented; it takes him two years to paint the hallway after stripping off the wallpaper.

Through it all, God has shown me that true love is all about our attitude. True love is patient, kind, and sees the best in the other person. Rob has always been there for me and I for him. He supported me when my depression had me bedridden for 18 months, when I wanted to own property with an unethical partner I thought I could handle, and encouraged me to go to a workshop in Sedona where I learned to become financially independent. He did all this when it was really his nature to ask me to stay home. He has willingly been there for me, quietly cheering me on.

My daughter, Stephanie, is truly a gift from God. She has taught me that motherhood has been given a bad rap. Being Stephanie's mother has taught me patience, acceptance and the meaning of unconditional love. She has taught me to laugh, to have fun, to play and to be less serious. Stephanie has taught me not to assume everyone knows even the simple things in life. Until I had my daughter, I blamed women for failing to take responsibility for their circumstances. God planted her in my life because I was a hard woman. I had no understanding of the challenges others faced in their lives. I've been shown that, despite how much we try to control our lives, someone else is in control. On my darkest days, she and Rob made me laugh and taught me that all the possessions and power in the world mean nothing if I don't have someone with whom to share them. Through relationships, diversity and love, we can achieve greater heights than when we're alone. It's more fun and more meaningful when we can bring others along for the ride. I put God first and regularly communicate with Him through prayer, thanking him for my deepest desires, knowing He will find a way to fulfill them. Jesus said, "You have not because you ask not." Our desired outcomes aren't always as we expect them. They are, however, for a greater outcome than we could ever dream of since all things of God work out for the best. God first, family second and career third have been the wind beneath my wings, and prayer is the foundation that brings it all together.

- Who has God planted in your life?
- Whose gifts will you embrace and recognize for their contributions to making your life fuller and more productive?
- With whom can you share your gifts for a more abundant life?
- Whose life are you making easier through your patience and kindness?
- Are you lifting your loved ones higher and celebrating their achievements in life?

Remember that true love is an attitude. With that attitude come the feelings that create the aura we project that attracts or repels others, thus giving us the results we have in our everyday lives.

What kinds of fruit are you harvesting from your tree of abundant life?

Margaret Good

CHOOSING TO BE CHOSEN

Terri Amos-Britt

"Okay, ladies, today we're going on an adventure!" I exclaimed to a small group of women sitting in front of me on the patio of a local bookstore. All of them were excited, but they had no idea what was in store. This wasn't any ordinary group. These women were part of my intensive Enlightened Mom course. Over the past weeks, the moms had been stretched beyond their wildest imaginations, releasing limiting beliefs that caused them anger, judgment and pain, as well as learning to love and embrace the way they were created. On this day, it was time to play.

"Your adventure today is to walk into the bookstore and be open to God's guidance. You're going to stay open and centered and allow God to show you something that you're ready to see. This is a message that will help put your life in flow and you will be more at ease."

Their eyes widened and a grin spread across each face. At that moment I was unsure if they were grins of joy, or grins to mask fear. I know some of the women were still unconvinced that they would be able to complete the assignment. They believed these kinds of miracles might happen for others but not for them.

I understood this feeling; I had once believed I was unworthy of this kind of love as well. Until I hit my mid 30s, I believed the only way to receive love was to be perfect and have the approval of others. I believed love came from the outside world. This left me empty and made me angry. In fact, I was so angry I would take it out on my loved ones and even tried to beat up my husband! Over time, I discovered that the reason I was angry was because I didn't believe it was okay for me to receive love just for being myself. The awareness that it was okay to just be me changed my life. However, there was still something missing.

I'll never forget the day I sat down at the beach and went into deep meditation. I didn't like the way I was feeling toward a friend. I was envious of her. It seemed she constantly had miracles occurring in her life and I didn't. I didn't believe I was worthy of that kind of love. So I sat in meditation and asked, "God, why does it seem that my friend is the chosen one?"

I heard a little voice in my ear say, "She's chosen to be chosen, Terri."

"What?" I asked, a little stumped.

"She has chosen to be chosen. Each of you has a choice. All you have to do is give yourself permission to receive, and then the miracles will happen."

I knew this message was true. Receiving love has nothing to do with being perfect. It comes when you make the decision that you are worthy of being loved. It's your choice. I made a choice that day. I gave myself permission to open up to God's love and miracles. I visualized "little Terri"—the little five-year-old girl inside of me—standing in front of me. She's the heart of who I am and how I was created. I imagined handing her a blue ribbon and saying, "I'm finally making you number one and giving you permission to open up to God's love."

Ironically, in making the choice to be chosen, I stepped into my life's mission. Some would say that to receive is selfish. But to truly be of service, you must open up to receive God's love and guidance. That's what I did; I allowed myself to be embraced by the love of God and created a life of passion, purpose and unconditional love. By healing my life and letting go of the need to be perfect, I saw my family heal. Anger, judgment and blame slipped away from our lives and greater communication and peace became the norm for all of us. As I saw our lives change, I was called to share my message with families all over the world. That's when I was guided to create *The Enlightened Mom*.

"So, ladies," I continued, "As you walk into the bookstore, you may feel an urge to walk to the left or walk to the right. You may even find yourself crawling on the floor. I've shared with you many times that I like to walk into a bookstore, asking for guidance, and the way I get the message is to watch for an arrow in my head. Do this if it works for you. It doesn't matter how you receive your guidance. Just trust that it's there for you.

"Before you head in to the bookstore, let's get grounded in God's light. Take a relaxing breath and say, 'I give myself permission to receive love and guidance from God.' Now, visualize a beautiful golden ball of light above your head. Imagine opening up the crown of your head like a camera lens and allow God's light to flood throughout your body, allowing all of your fear and doubt to slip away."

Each of the women had been practicing this meditation for the last eight weeks, and, as a result, had found themselves to be much more centered and at peace when dealing with their daily lives and their families. But, today wasn't going to be an ordinary day. Now it was time to put their tools to the test.

A few of the women had already experienced miracles from the first day of class, but there were others who were a little more skeptical. Stephanie was one of them. Her life had been blanketed in negativity and judgment with constant complaining. During the Enlightened Mom course, she had begun to realize that she had to change her attitude about her life, about her husband and about money. Stephanie lived with the sense that there was something lacking, and she wasn't sure she could receive the kind of guidance and love I had been talking about. Stephanie doubted she was worthy. Ironically, she was the first mom to finish the assignment.

"I'm converted! I'm converted! I'm converted!" Stephanie cried, trembling with tears of joy flowing down her face as she came back to the patio. "I can't believe it! I walked into the store and felt a nudge to turn right. Then, I felt I had to move down the aisle and turn right again. Directly in front of me was Joel Osteen's book, *Your Best Life Now.* It was staring me right in the face. I've seen him on TV or in ads every day for at least three weeks now and felt I was supposed to learn something from him, but I ignored it. So, I opened up his book and the first message I received was, 'God supplies all of your needs.' The next message was, 'Quit complaining that nothing good ever happens.' And, finally, 'Start declaring everything and command light to come in.' I can't believe I got these messages!"

Stephanie's final thoughts said it best as she threw her hands up in the air, "I get it now! I used to ask God for guidance and would get so angry because I never got any answers. Now I realize the messages were always there. All I had to do was give myself permission to open up and receive them!"

Stephanie made a choice to be chosen that day at the bookstore and finally got the message: Love and miracles are abundant when you say, "Yes!" to yourself, knowing you are worthy of a divine connection.

Terri Amos-Britt

COMPLETE

Raquel Reyna

I envision a new world of commerce. I suppose this is a lofty dream, but I believe it is the responsibility of those of us who have this vision to attempt to reach it. My story has assisted me in catching this idea and proclaiming that, through small gestures, our financial structures can slowly be reassembled. Proverbially, it is the tiny mustard seed that becomes the largest tree. In business, I feel one small act of kindness rather than many large acts of greed can redefine our finances as we know them.

As a point of reference, I turned in an assignment in college in which I attempted to reconstruct our country's most sacred document: the Constitution. My professor, clearly exasperated, exclaimed to the class that changing the Constitution simply was not an option, and no matter the argument, one's points must fall within the parameters of the given law.

For many years I pondered this. I felt trapped and caged by the very notion. Why could one not envision a new constitutional law that would bring forth higher ideals and a new world order? Is it impossible to believe new visions may exist today?

To most people, the notion of rewriting the Constitution is absurd. Perhaps this is because most people fall within the scope of a very standard, single-minded global consciousness. I believe real change begins outside, or on the fringe, of this consciousness. Along with those who are not subservient to this singular consciousness—the Michael Beckwiths and Eckhart Tolles of the world—these individuals create their own utopia right underneath the political madness milieu by living in divine harmony as instructed by their inner realities. As I started to witness the force of these role models, I began to understand it wasn't about changing the system controlled by outside forces, but about changing within. Conscious evolution is no longer an abstract notion; it is alive right now.

New philosophical consciousness would equate to a shift in financial consciousness. Most of our time and energy is entrenched in our daily work and business decisions. It currently appears that although we are evolving in consciousness, the new path to business enlightenment has not quite been forged. In the business world, we often put aside our spiritual awareness because business is business.

A new landscape of commerce would look very different than the one we know today. Let's dream for a moment together. The new world of commerce would begin with a money exchange based on each person living from his or her joy, accomplishing his or her life's work or being his or her purpose, free from the shackles of unfulfilling work. It would include the exchange of money based on selling products and services with the intention of doing good in the world, not just making money.

We should stop seeing the dollar as a god and return to the laws of divinity and natural abundance, and the divine flow of grace and goodness. I see a world where the order of the day is based on how much we can assist, how generous we can be and how kind our hearts can be. I imagine an experience where competition is eliminated and cooperation is instilled, a place where we don't "cut each other's throats" to get ahead, but instead naturally pick up the pieces if someone is broken and provide a helping hand. In this new world of commerce, one would not go armed into a business meeting with lawyers at his or her side, because people would actually *trust* each other. We would exchange money and commerce with honesty, integrity, passion and joy.

We can make new choices in each moment of business. How powerful would it be if we began choosing passion rather than duty, integrity rather than success, kindness rather than gain, and agreed to deals that benefit all rather than just one?

Is this world possible? I believe it is.

I believe this transformation begins as each individual makes different choices in the arena of business. Here is my story.

I began my life of service at the age of 30. I felt lost, and I was in between careers looking for a life of purpose. I spent my 20s building a successful dance company that began in my living room and ended up touring the country performing before thousands of people, but I knew something was missing as I indulged in all of my desires and dreams. At the height of my success, I looked around backstage at the pain, addiction, competition, lying and backstabbing that was going on to get to the top, and I thought, "Regardless of how much I am about to lose, I must leave this life and begin a career based on higher spiritual integrity." Regardless of the appearance of success, my soul was slowly diminishing into a flickering candle so weak a simple cough would extinguish my light.

The next thing I knew, I was driving down the coast with all my belongings packed up in my two-door Miata, my performance life gone and $50 in my pocket with a single thought running through my mind: "Spirit, let me live a life of service." I took a job in a small fitness facility where I made less than $10 an hour. Friends and family looked at me in complete disbelief, but my soul felt alive, free, generous, kind and fulfilled for the first time. I had a deep knowing that this was the place I belonged. I was serving women, helping some who weighed over 300 lbs. and some who had never exercised a day in their lives. Seeing their bodies come alive was a warm and satisfying feeling. Each day, I slowly began to watch my new life take shape and unfold into a path of financial riches but, more importantly, soulful riches.

I took a risk, allowed myself time to explore the mystery, and allowed the ideas in my mind to form the ones I carry today. Life and work without passion and fulfillment are meaningless. Living in service is more gratifying than any life of selfishness. As I traveled with this small fitness facility to watch it become one of the most successful franchises this country has every seen, I not only learned a lot about business, but also that my heart is a beacon I must follow. I learned a lot about a soul's integrity and the potential for life choices to be lived in vision, kindness, integrity, love and passion.

I thought about what it would be like if we all lived in a way in which we chose to contribute to the world in areas that made us feel amazing, and that helped others rather than hurt them. What if this simple thought of being generous and kind in a business deal was more important than making more money? I believe this would change the world in a huge way.

I now assist others in changing their businesses into financially successful enterprises by changing their hearts into ones of integrity, passion, excitement and learning. This helps them give stellar service because they are guided by inspiration. I see this as the absolute evolution of business. Can you imagine living in a world of givers rather than takers? Together, I believe we can make a difference in this world, one small, individual choice at a time.

Raquel Reyna

Author Index

Debbie Allen is one of the world's leading authorities on sales and marketing. She is the author of five books, including *Confessions of Shameless Self Promoters* and *Skyrocketing Sales.* Her expertise has been featured in *Entrepreneur, Selling Power* and *Sales & Marketing Excellence.* Sign up for her free six-week e-Course, *Business Success Secrets Revealed* ($97 value), and take the online business card quiz to rate your marketing online now at www.DebbieAllen.com.

Web site: www.DebbieAllen.com

Shoshana Allice is a learning specialist with more than 10 years experience educating adults in leadership, personal and career development. She is a compelling public speaker, a compassionate coach and a dynamic facilitator and trainer. Shoshana is a certified co-active coach and holds a Masters degree in Human Systems Intervention.

Called 2 Inspire...Full Potential Living.
Telephone: 604-614-5485
Web site: www.Called2Inspire.com
E-mail: Shoshana@called2inspire.ca

Terri Amos-Britt is the author of *The Enlightened Mom* and *Message Sent.* As a spiritual coach and motivational speaker, Terri shares her experiences as a wife, mom, stepmom, former Miss USA and television host, inspiring others to release the emotional chaos in their lives, creating lives of passion, purpose and love. Terri is the co-founder of The Enlightened Family Institute with her husband, Charlie Britt. Their mission is to bring hope and healing to individuals and families all over the world.

Web site: www.EnlightenedFamilyInstitute.com

Amy Applebaum is the prominent Life Coach behind the butt-kicking Boot Camp for Your Mind® coaching program. "Life coaching is the new psychology of today," says Amy. Amy's groundbreaking process allows her clients to move past barriers, allowing them to accomplish goals they never imagined possible. Amy's credentials include a BA in Speech and Organizational Communications, certifications as a life coach, hypnotherapist, timeline therapist, and trainer of neuro-linguistic programming.

Bootcamp for Your Mind, Inc.
Telephone: 1-866-988-3532
Web site: www.bootcampforyourmind.com
E-mail: info@bootcampforyourmind.com

Berry, Anne *23*

Anne is a certified Nia teacher. Nia is a body-mind-spirit fitness and lifestyle practice. Anne especially enjoys teaching women over 60 how to empower themselves to achieve physical, mental, emotional and spiritual well-being. She has struggled with how to remain vital and passionate in later life and has found true joy through dance and spiritual personal growth. To find out more about Anne and how she can help you learn to dance through the rest of your life, visit:

Web site: www.thebonusyears.com
E-mail: the bonusyears@gmail.com

Brandon, Nicole *119*

Nicole is a master fitness instructor, renowned coach and the CEO and founder of "Artistry In Motion" A.I.M. For Excellence Inc. Nicole is one of the most sought-after motivational speakers, writers and teachers across the globe today. She guides clients in the "art" of wellness, health, vitality, physical transformation and physical regeneration. Nicole rides horses, sails boats, does acrobatics, figure skates, dances and empowers others by helping people be pain free and by teaching the power of the body. Nicole inspires the beauty and the glory of the human form, which she coins "Artistry In Motion," which of course, is the way she lives.

Coleman, Marlene M., M.D. *151*

Marlene M. Coleman, M.D., is an award-winning physician, speaker, author of *Safe and Sound: Healthy Travel with Children* and co-author of *Start Your Own Medical Practice.* She is an Associate Clinical Professor of Family Medicine at USC Keck School of Medicine and an attending physician at the California Institute of Technology.

Web site: www.MedicalPracticeMentor.com

Comer, Alice R., RN, MNSc *125*

Alice Comer is a registered nurse practitioner, teacher, facilitator and dedicated friend. She is a personal coach for the Peace of Mind Principles and the Seven Secrets to Live the Life You Love. She believes there was a calling into a healing profession and now this perspective is the basis for the company she founded. Within the concept of healing, there are components of body, mind and spirit. Personal health coaching is an absolute necessity for many. Alice's challenges in life have been to discover, nurture and live her "authentic" self, while her purpose is to help others to do the same. View her site for additional information.

Web site: www.EZHealthCareOnline.com

Courtleigh, Johanna MA, LPC *85*

Johanna is a writer, teacher, Certified Coach and Licensed Professional Counselor in private practice in Portland, OR. She is also an ordained minister through the Association for the Integration of the Whole Person. An award-winning poet, her writings have been published internationally in anthologies and periodicals. Her work seeks to help people heal from the mistruths they've been taught, and to awaken a core of deeper reverence, self-love, awareness, empowerment, ease and integrity—internally and in their relationships with others. She is available for in-person and telephone counseling, coaching and consultation, as well as for workshops and speaking engagements.

Web site: www.jcourtleigh.com
E-mail: johanna@jcourtleigh.com

Day-Harper, Melinda *191*

Melinda is a speaker, author, senior certified LFE instructor and money coach, and the founder and CEO of T-Zone Consulting, Inc. T-Zone's goal is to help individuals and businesses achieve greater prosperity by teaching them to break through boundaries that limit their success.

Address: San Antonio, Texas
Web site: www.TZoneConsulting.com
E-mail: info@TZoneConsulting.com

Diamond, Tara *229*

Tara Diamond is a spiritual healer, human design analyst and professional artist in Del Mar, CA. Her deeply intuitive healing technique comes from 25 years of transpersonal healing experience. She was a minister with The Teaching of the Inner Christ for 10 years and currently is in private practice. She provides psychospiritual coaching for her clients and clears energy fields of astral influences that affect her clients' well-being.

Telephone: 858-259-7487
Web site: www.taradiamond.com
E-mail: taradiamond@msn.com (primary), tara@taradiamond.com (secondary)

Edey, Lorraine, LCSW, Ph.D., ACC *199*

Lorraine is your online money and relationship expert, coach and trainer. Lorraine is passionate about dissolving debt and supporting financial freedom. Lorraine encourages people to learn how to manage their money and how to break-free of limiting thoughts and patterns that keep them in bondage caused by debt and under-earning.

Money and Relationship Coach
Address: P.O. Box 560483
Rockledge, FL 32956-0483
Telephone: 321-288-0692
Web site: www.coachinginspirations.com

Farrow, Ardice *131, 179*

Daring, delightful and no-nonsense, Ardice Farrow is a former executive producer and creative designer for leading entertainment and technology companies and the founder, co-creator and co-publisher of Wake Up Women. In addition, Ardice is a speaker and seminar leader. Her focus is on feminine leadership and creative and innovative management. Ardice's energy is boundless and her enthusiasm is contagious as she brings together the success secrets of major media companies with her unique and playful approach to creating off-the-charts joy, satisfaction and fun.

Telephone: 866-560-8562
Web site: www.ardicefarrow.com
E-mail: ardice@wakeupwomenbe.com

Fest, Dorothy *67*

After 25 years as an award-winning elementary educator and teacher trainer, Dorothy Fest resigned to live her dreams, implementing the distinctions she gained through more than a decade of transformational work. Dorothy knows how to ride the roller-coaster of life and how to turn obstacles into opportunities and adventure. Currently, she is using her visionary and creative talents to launch her new business called, To Live Your Dreams, which provides access for all ages to live and fulfill their dreams. She is available for private and small group coaching, speaking engagements, and as a resource for you to live your dreams.

Web site: www.toliveyourdreams.com
E-mail: ToLiveYourDreams@gmail.com

Ford, Arielle *17*

Arielle believes finding true love is possible for anyone, at any age, and she points to herself as living proof. Married for the first time at age 44, she expanded on the set of skills she used to launch her highly-successful public relations firm, The Ford Group, and applied them to her love life. She is best known for helping launch the careers of many best-selling self-help and spiritual authors, including Deepak Chopra, Jack Canfield and Mark Victor Hansen of *Chicken Soup for the Soul*, Neale Donald Walsch and many others. She is the author of seven books including the *Hot Chocolate for the Mystical Soul* series. Her next book will be *The Soulmate Secret: How to Manifest the Love of Your Life with the Law of Attraction* (January 2009, Harper One). Arielle lives in La Jolla, California, with her husband, Brian Hilliard, and their feline friends.

Frazier, Beth *187*

Beth Frazier is a licensed Realtor with The Corcoran Group, a speaker and a real estate investor. She is also the founder of NYC Women's Investment Group, which provides educational seminars to women on various investing topics. Fortunate to win a contest in 2005, Beth had the unique opportunity to be mentored by renowned investor and self-help author Robert Kiyosaki, best known for his book *Rich Dad, Poor Dad.*

Address: 115 South Oxford Street, suite 521
Brooklyn, NY 11217
Telephone: 718-690-1365
Web site: beth-frazier.com
E-mail: frazierbeth@optonline.net

Fredette, Lisa *81*

Lisa Fredette is a CTA Certified Life Coach, radio host, Certified Relationship Coach, author, speaker and owner of Passionate About Life Coaching. As a coach, Lisa supports women who are ready to reclaim their relationships with themselves. The basis of her coaching is the understanding that success depends on your relationship with you. Without that foundation, success is impossible. Lisa supports her clients with one-on-one coaching, group coaching, ecourses, ebooks, teleseminars and through her coaching club.

Passionate About Life Coaching
Telephone: 814-594-5817
Web site: www.lisafredette.com
E-mail: coach@lisafredette.com

Good, Margaret *241*

Certified General Accountant

Margaret Good has an accounting practice in Canada and has been working closely with her clients since 1982 as a business coach who helps them to reach their goals and personal potential. She is actively involved in her community and holds various board appointments in organizations that advance the status of women and girls.

Address: Brampton, Ontario, Canada
Telephone: 416-804-0520
E-mail: margaret.good@rogers.com

Greene, Alice H. *103*

Alice Greene is America's healthy lifestyle coach, helping people discover ways they can succeed in making healthier choices while creating a fit, healthy and fulfilling lifestyle they can live with and feel good about. She is the author of the *Guided Healthy Living* series, *Inspired to Feel Good, Perfectionist Trap* and *The Healthy Living Challenge: Addressing the Cause of Ambivalence.* She is also co-host of Living Your Personal Best radio.

Telephone: 888-243-1737
Web sites: www.feelyourpersonalbest.com, www.feelyourpersonalbest.com/blog
www.livingyourpersonalbest.com

Hendrix, Elaine *95*

Elaine Hendrix is a world-renowned actress best known for projects such as *What the Bleep Do We Know?!, Joan of Arcadia* and *The Parent Trap.* She also happens to be a veteran film and stage producer, established singer/songwriter, classically trained dancer, published author, public speaker and avid animal activist. She manages to "have it all" by living a life of unwavering commitment to balance and authentic self-expression.

Address: c/o Innovative Artists
1505 10th St.
Santa Monica, CA 90404
Web site: Elainehendrix.com
E-mail: eteam@elainehendrix.com

Holder, Deb *27*

Deb Holder is a single mother with three teenagers, Lindsay (18), Kayla (15) and Mychal (13). She is a professional copywriter/marketing strategist and the president and CEO of Debt-Free-Mom.com—a site devoted to helping women break free from debt. Deb is also a college English instructor, diversity trainer and former mental health counselor.

Telephone: 864-980-8857
Web site: www.DebHolder.com, www.Kick-Butt-Marketing.com
E-mail: results@debholder.com

Jenkin, Billie Willmon *37*

As a teacher, Billie Willmon Jenkin saw a need for the emotional education of both teachers and students. Before retirement, she developed and facilitated a course in attitude change for adult prison inmates. Her passion for empowering others to make positive changes in their lives is evident in her writing, mentoring and speaking. *The Knock-Kneed Cowboy: A Tale of Being "Just Right" Just as We Are*, her first children's book, which she wrote and illustrated, is a joyful, empowering tale of individuality.

Web site: www.EmpoweringForChange.com
E-mail: EmpoweringForChange@gmail.com

Jones, Tereasa, M.S. *7*

Tereasa Jones is a Master Certified Relationship Coach who helps people with the art of building connected-at-the-heart relationships that will last a life-time. She offers private coaching, workshops, and teleclasses. She writes a column for her local newspaper and is available for speaking engagements.

Web site: www.CoachedLiving.com
E-mail: Tereasa@CoachedLiving.com

Kelly, Amy *225*

Amy Kelly is a life designer, specializing in supporting women who are ready to live passionately and get more out of life. Her own passion is to help her clients learn to listen to their inner voice, align with their heart, and from there, to design the life they want.

Life Designer
Web site: www.amyslifedesign.com
E-mail: amyslifedesign@gmail.com

Kniss, Mindie *155*

Mindie Kniss is a holistic life coach, writer and international speaker. She has worked in the wilderness as an adventure guide and in corporate America for a Fortune 100 company. She participated in a six-month fellowship in Nairobi, Kenya working on HIV/AIDS prevention initiatives. Mindie holds a master's degree in metaphysics and is currently pursuing an M.F.A. in creative nonfiction and a Ph.D. in metaphysics.

Awaken Consciousness Coaching, LLC
Telephone: 877-292-5320
Web site: www.awakenconsciousness.com
E-mail: awakenconsciousness@gmail.com

Kobrin, Aggie *159*

Aggie Kobrin is director of CEC Global Events and Chief Business Developer for the Elevision Network. She has produced events, conferences and film premiers for audiences of 50 to 2,000. Her companies distribute independent, motivational and inspirational films and products. Her latest initiative, The Elevision Network, is pioneering a new level of internet and television programming that will offer hundreds of hours of programs and a truly unique viewing experience. She is also managing director of the eWomenNetwork in Orange County, CA. She's an extraordinary networker and promoter and makes regular appearances on TV and radio, promoting her events and products.

Telephone: 949-257-0235, 949-727-1271
Web site: www.CECglobalevents.com

Kunifas, Melina *115*

Melina Kunifas is a Life Coach and Speaker who has struggled for years with weight and self-esteem issues. Now in a very comfortable place with herself, she thrives on helping others achieve the same.

Telephone: 617-275-8068 or 866-774-8317
Web site: www.coachingconfidence.com
E-mail: melina@coachingconfidence.com

La, Dr. Christine, M.D. *233*

Christine La, MD was born in Saigon, Vietnam, immigrated to the United States, and was raised in Orange County, CA. She received her undergraduate and medical degrees at the University of Rochester in Rochester, NY. She has received residency training at USC Medical Center in the field of psychiatry. Dr. La has worked with a variety of patients and believes in the power of the human mind and cognitive analysis to overcome mental obstacles. She is a published author. As a co-compiler and associate publisher for the Wake Up Women book series, Dr La's interest is in evaluating how women can empower themselves in relationships.

Langemeier, Loral *197*

As Founder and CEO of Live Out Loud, Loral has guided thousands across the country along their way to financial freedom. Langemeier is author of the national best seller The Millionaire Maker and two New York Times best sellers, The Millionaire Maker's Guide to Wealth Cycle Investing and The Millionaire Maker's Guide to Creating a Cash Machine for Life. In addition to her sold-out Millionaire Maker events, she has appeared frequently on CNN, CNBC and Fox News Channel and has been featured in USA Today, The Wall Street Journal, The New York Times, and on the web at ABCNews.com, Forbes.com, and BusinessWeek.com. For more information on Loral Langemeier and Live Out Loud please visit www.liveoutloud.com.

Web site: www.liveoutloud.com

Lundberg, Amy *107*

Amy's engaging, down-to-earth style and inspiring approach to achieving a healthy lifestyle makes her a fitness lifestyle coach that women of all ages can relate to. Specializing in guiding clients to build an inner foundation and harmony into all parts of their lives allows their weight loss and fitness goals to become a healthy lifestyle. It is what makes Amy's approach unique and successful.

Aim For It-Fitness Coaching LLC
Lifestyle Fitness Coach, Speaker & Author
Web sites: www.aimforfitness.com, www.selfcarebeforesitups.com
E-mail: amy@aimforfitness.com

Mayfield, Karen *57, 215*

Outgoing, expressive and humorous, Karen is the creator of the Peace of Mind Principles and the Wake Up Live Coaching Program, and is co-creator and co-publisher of Wake Up Women. Karen brings her 20 years of experience in print advertising, ad copy, print media campaigns and her 15 years in training and mid-to upper-management experience to Wake Up Women. Her focus is assisting others in building a strong foundation utilizing the Law of Attraction through her writing and inventive coaching programs. Karen's keen insight and intuitive approach to coaching combined with her passion for spiritual principles continually provide women with the resources needed to go from living a life they live to a life they love.

Mein, Dr. Carolyn *51*

Carolyn is the author of *Different Bodies, Different Diets* and *Releasing Emotional Patterns with Essential Oils*, has her doctorate in chiropractics, is a Fellow of American Council of Applied Clinical Nutrition and graduate of the International College of Applied Kinesiology. She developed a system of energy medicine for diagnosis and treatment known as Transpersonal Physiology.

Address: P.O. Box 8112, \ 16236 San Dieguito Rd.
Rancho Santa Fe, CA 92067
Telephone: 858-756-3704
Web site: www.bodytype.com
E-mail: carolyn@bodytype.com

Mitchell, N.J. *11*

NJ Mitchell, who has her MBA, is vice-president of operations at Human Communication Institute, LLC. She is co-host of the InWORD OutWORD talk show and is a Van Mar Academy Hollywood student, with several film and TV credits, including *Pirates of the Caribbean III* and the HBO series *Entourage*. She received the National Campaign Billboard for Mother's Against Gun Violence. Have a wonderful day. It's always your choice!

Web site: www.hci-global.net

Morgan, Jennifer BSc. CPCC *43*

Jennifer is trained and certified as a professional coach with the Coaches Training Institute, and has trained as an organizational and relationship systems coach with the Center for Right Relationship. Under the umbrella of her company, Trilogy Communications, Jennifer focuses on communications in personal and business relationships and is passionate about guiding people's learning to create powerful and effective results in their lives. Jennifer also co-founded a coaching partnership, Pathways to Change, which delivers leading-edge coaching skills training and relationship systems workshops in the corporate arena.

Telephone: 905-820-9019
Web site: www.trilogycommunciations.wordpress.com
E-mail: trilogy@pathcom.com

Moss, Sylvia *205*

Sylvia Moss, OM, is a gifted sound healer and spiritual teacher with a passion for helping people grow and heal. She is a Brennan Healing Science practitioner, Transformational Energetics therapist, Life Works Guidess, ordained interfaith minister and photographer. An accomplished manifester, she leads the Life Works Money Support Group and guides private clients on relationships, life issues, and manifestation. She maintains an active international healing practice and is well known for her extraordinary use of Crystal Singing Bowls in private and group healings.

Web site: www.sylviamosshealing.com
E-mail: sylviamoss@sylviamosshealing.com

Mullally, MaryKay *111*

MaryKay Mullally, MS, MBA, is a wellness and weight management coach. She is an expert in transforming body image and limiting beliefs that get in the way, helping hundreds of men and women achieve their goals. MaryKay knows how to help others overcome the barriers that get in the way of having the health, habits, lifestyle and body they want. She will empower you to be the best you can be wherever you are.

President, Step Up For Life
Health, Wellness, Cleansing and Weight Management Coaching
Telephone: 858-449-0756 or 858-720-0480
Web site: www.Stepupforlife.com
E-mail: MaryKay@stepupforlife.com

Nack, Lisa *167*

Lisa Nack is a coach, facilitator, catalyst and investor. She has partnered with organizations and individuals since 1993 to build leaders, create team environments, improve results and manage change. Lisa has the unique ability to create experientially-based training events that are safe spaces for hosting critical conversations, ensuring that learning is relevant and immediately applicable to the work place so as to catalyze individuals and organizations to take action.

Telephone: 513-742-0012
Web site: www.lisanackinternational.com
E-mail: lisa@lisanackinternational.com

Oldham, Rita ***139***

Rita Oldham lives in Kentucky with her loving husband, Jim, and her three wonderful children. After years of struggling to complete her education, she earned her Bachelor of Arts in Business from Murray State University. God has not only blessed her with a wonderful family, but a fulfilling and rewarding career. She is an executive for a magazine and book publisher and works with clients from around the world. She is truly living the life she loves.

E-mail: oldham.rita@yahoo.com

O'Sullivan, Cydney ***183***

Cydney O'Sullivan has had successful businesses spanning 20 years, including cafes, catering, fashion and retail. She has been a multi-million dollar real estate investor and made millions on the stock market using her own system of momentum investing and trading, while raising her two wonderful children. Her vision is for all women to have access to the strategies and support to create their own independence and wealth.

CEO Ms Independence Ventures
Address: Australia
Telephone: +61 414 465 843
Web sites: www.MsIndependence.com, www.TheIndependenceClub.com
Email: info@MsIndependence.com

Parker, Jet ***171***

Parker is the founder of the nation's most comprehensive talent bureau and the author of *ABCs for CEOs: 26 Vital Skills for Business Chiefs*. Jet earned a Bachelor of Science in Organizational Communications from the University of Texas, Austin. She has also trained as a stress management/conditioning facilitator and as an aerobic and kick-boxing instructor.

Telephone: 214-760-9717 or toll free 866-987-7770
Web site: www.jumplab.com
E-mail: jet@jumplab.com

Pearl, Sheila ***73***

Sheila Pearl, M.S.W., is a motivational speaker, workshop facilitator and spiritual life coach with offices in Newburgh, NY and Franklin Lakes, NJ. A graduate of Wurzweiler School of Social Work, she received coaching certification from Gail Straub, David Gershon and Neale Donald Walsch (She's been part of his coaching staff for the Conversations with God foundation since 2005). She also authored *Being Goddess Power* and *Pearl Wisdom Gifts* and co-authored *The Winning Connection* with Laura Moritz.

Telephone: 201-303-5990
Web sites: www.SheilaPearl.com, www.PearlWisdomGifts.com, www.LifeCoachSheila.com
E-mail: LifeCoachSheila@yahoo.com

Perkins, Pamela S. *11*

Pamela S. Perkins, M.A. is Founder and CEO of the Human Communication Institute, LLC. She is a graduate of the University of North Carolina at Chapel Hill and New York University. She is a professor of communication and her curriculum development skills are highly sought for corporate training. She is a featured practitioner in the film *Pass It On* and writes for a variety of magazines and periodicals. She is author of *The Art and Science of Communication*. Her effective approach to healing the communication environment has positively affected thousands of lives.

Web site: www.hci-global.net

Rannelli, Arlene *77*

Arlene is a gifted speaker, facilitator, coach and author. For the past 20 years, Arlene has designed, marketed and led adult educational programs helping people transcend their pain and negative beliefs to ultimately connect with Source Energy/God and to experience more of what they want in life. With an open heart, an understanding of human emotions and having been there herself, she is able to connect at a deep level and set people free to create long-lasting results.

Arlene Rannelli Consulting
Web site: www.masteringyouressentialenergy.com

Reagan, Heidi *5, 101*

Heidi is the owner of Establish Balance Coaching and co-creator and co-publisher of Wake Up Women. She is also the founder and creative mind behind Embrace Joy Intention Jewelry, which combines her love for art with the Law of Attraction. As an artist, Heidi unites spirit and emotion to create pieces that resonate and inspire. As a facilitator and personal coach she stimulates others to develop and enhance their entrepreneurial spirits. Heidi brings diligence, passion and sincerity to every pursuit.

Telephone: 845-337-6617
Web sites: www.establishbalance.com, www.wakeupwomen.com, www.embracejoyintentionjewelry.com
E-mail: Heidi@wakeupwomenbe.com, establishbalance@aol.com

Reyna, Raquel *249*

Reyna has a B.A. in political science and modern dance with a Master's degree in spiritual psychology. This eclectic combination of studies has established Raquel as an entrepreneur, developing and living advanced principles of spiritual consciousness in the world of franchising. Her intention is to bring a higher consciousness approach into the world of business, marketing and the exchange of money. Raquel coaches in franchising your business into successful expansion while expanding your soul's own fruitful riches!

E-mail: reynarising@gmail.com

Robertson, Pam, Ph.D. *63*

A career advocate and author, Pam loves exploring the beaches in Nova Scotia, Canada. She is also an avid bird watcher and musician. She writes and speaks professionally about careers, training and facilitation. She has a Ph.D. in career development and experience in a range of industries, the most invigorating of which was six years in the military. Pam loves to help people do what they do to the absolute best of their ability.

Address: P.O. Box 244
Lower Sackville, NS B4C 2S9
Telephone: 902-222-9212
Web site: www.mvpi.org
E-mail: pam@pamrobertson.org

Rueschhoff, Erica *47*

For 13 years, Erica Rueschhoff has been motivating and inspiring moms to embrace their role of motherhood while continuing to pursue their purpose as individuals. She will help you find balance, recapture your dreams, and put them into action. Whether you are a stay-at-home mom or a working mom, she can help you find peace and balance in your life. E-mail ericarueschhoff@gmail.com to schedule your free consultation. Visit her Web site at RealMomsRealLife.com and sign up for her free Motivating Moms to Success newsletter.

Telephone: 704-279-4219 or 980-621-1767
Web sites: www.RealMomsRealLife.com, www.MomsRealLifeUniversity.com
E-mail: ericarueschhoff@gmail.com

Sanchez, Michelle *163*

Michelle's experience includes running a multi-million dollar company and owning her own business. Michelle's journey to health led her to natural health alternatives, which in turn led her to a new career in network marketing as a Certified Network Marketing Success Coach where she passionately inspires and empowers women networkers to achieve their dreams. She is also Certified Dream Coach.

Address: 5800 79th Avenue
Pinellas Park, FL 33781
Telephone: 727-548-9898
Web sites: www.heart2heartcoach.com, www.dreamvisionnetwork.org
E-mail: michelle@heart2heartcoach.com

Scott, Dorri C. *209*

Dorri C. Scott is the founder and president of a financial advisory business consultant boutique—High Heels and High Worth. She is also employed by a Regional bank on the East Coast as a commercial banker. She hosts a weekly XM Radio show and regularly appears on radio shows as a finance expert specializing in money smart tips for women and families. Her sass and common sense for cents style is "girl friend" friendly and entertaining. She holds a BA from the College of New Jersey, a Masters in Clinical Social Work from the University of Kansas, and in 2002, she graduated from the Harvard Business School realizing a goal she set for herself at age 17. Dorri is the proud mother of two and resides in the Washington D.C. area with her 17-year-old son.

Sieg, Edith *31*

Edith Sieg is a talented and gifted professional coach and speaker. She has an uncanny, intuitive sense that guides her clients as they embark on the journey of personal awareness and discovery, gaining clarity with subsequent growth and achievement. She enables others to realize their own inherent strengths, stimulate the growth of ideas and assist with breaking through the barriers of self-imposed limitation which can lead to life altering discoveries. To find out more about coaching services or to check availability for speaking engagements, contact Edith Sieg at:

Telephone: 847-913-3900
Web site: www.escoach.com
E-mail: WakeUpWomen@esCoach.com

Sims, Kathleen E. *19*

Kathleen Sims C.H.T., C.R.C., is the founder of the "Center for Conscious Relationship" and "Lifetime Love Connection.com," offering revolutionary programs and workshops, teleseminars, audios and books. Her work is mystical, yet practical, and promotes permanent change. She is a sought after speaker, teacher, author, mentor, spiritual healer and an authority on the Law of Attraction and beyond. Kathleen answered her calling and passionately helps others discover their authentic voice, claim their birthright of living their soul's purpose, and manifest true love that promises to last a lifetime.

Telephone: 925-674-9003
Web sites: www.lifetimeloveconnection.com
E-mail: kathleen@lifetimeloveconnection.com

South, Christina CSHP *237*

Christina is a wife, mother, professional medical coder and conscious life coach whose greatest joy is assisting others in achieving their goals and dreams. She teaches yoga, offers individual and group coaching programs, conscious soul coaching, and classes on intuitive development. Life tip: If there is a dream in your heart rest assured that God planted it there. Your job is to sow it, water it and watch it grow with spirited action.

Conscious Lifestyle Coach
Address: Bryant, AR
Telephone: 501-658-7607
Web site: www.consciouslifestylecoach.com
E-mail: Christina@consciouslifestylecoach.com

Strisower, Suzanne *219*

Suzanne is a professional certified coach and an Intuitive Life Coach whose goal is to help people live conscious and authentic lives emanating from the core of their beings. For 30 years she has empowered people as an intuitive leader, social worker and clinical hypnotherapist. She is the author of *The Runes of the Four Realms* and the screenwriter for a spiritual feature film trilogy to help people connect to their spirit and possibility.

Address: P.O. Box 559
Oroville, CA 95965
Telephone: 530-589-5552
Web sites: www.yourcatalystcoach.com, www.insightfulrunes.com (free rune reading)
E-mail: Suzanne@yourcatalystcoach.com

Swensen, Kara *91*

Believing in herself has led Kara to be one of the most successful and respected aircraft brokers in the world. Kara built her aircraft sales business, Alaris Aviation LLC, from only a credit card and pure commitment. She credits her drive and accomplishments to relational leadership. Kara is an accomplished speaker who encourages all to find their passion and achieve great things, both personally and professionally.

Address: 21001 N Tatum Blvd., Ste 1630-478
Phoenix, AZ 85050
Web site: www.skywardpassion.com
E-mail: karaswensen@gmail.com

Vander Leek, Shann *143*

Shann is the Founder of True Balance Life Coaching. Shann inspires solopreneurs and women in transition to set big goals, achieve extraordinary results and create balance in their lives. Telephone and e-mail consultations make Shann accessible to clients all over the world. Visit her Web site to register for a complimentary coaching session.

Life Coach
Telephone: 231-668-1111
Web sites: www.truebalancelifecoaching.com, www.truebalancelifecoaching.blogspot.com,
E-mail: shann@truebalancelifecoaching.com

Wake Up...

Live the Life You Love

WAKE UP WOMEN

Resources

Resources: Network Groups

Getting Connected

As women, we know the value of being surrounded with focused, energized and like-minded business women. Here are just a few of the organizations we feel do a great job in supporting and accelerating the careers of women.

ewomenNetwork, www.ewomennetwork.com, www.CECglobalevents.com

The eWomenNetwork is the #1 resource for connecting and promoting women and their businesses on both a local and global scale. An online women's network with more than 20,000 members, it boasts the largest yearly women's conference. With 200,000 hits daily, it is one of the most visited businesswomen's web sites in North America. Its vision is to provide women with unprecedented access and exposure for the purpose of building their enterprise and fast tracking their career. The goal is to help women succeed, achieve and prosper.

Women In Technology Institute, www.witi.com

WITI, the leading trade association for professional women who consider technology central to their businesses, careers and professions, is committed to using technology, resources and connections to advance women worldwide.

With a global network and a market reach exceeding 2 million, WITI has established powerful strategic alliances and programs to provide connections, resources, and opportunities to empower women to achieve unimagined possibilities and transformations through technology, leadership and economic prosperity.

NAFE, www.nafe.com

In 2007, NAFE celebrated its 35th anniversary. The National

Association for Female Executives (NAFE) was founded in 1972. The organization has a rich history of providing education, networking, and public advocacy to empower its members to achieve career success and financial security. Members are female executives, women business owners and others who are committed to NAFE's mission: the advancement of women in the workplace. NAFE has affiliate networks across the country where members come together for monthly meetings Visit the NAFE National website for a local connection network in your area.

Resources: Non-Profits

Getting Involved

As women when we are inspired and uplifted we want to take action and make a difference. Below are just a few of the non-profit organizations and cause initiatives that we contribute to and which might touch your heart and move you to action.

CARE, www.care.org

CARE is a leading humanitarian organization fighting global poverty. We place special focus on working alongside poor women because, equipped with the proper resources, women have the power to help whole families and entire communities escape poverty. Women are at the heart of CARE's community-based efforts to improve basic education, prevent the spread of HIV, increase access to clean water and sanitation, expand economic opportunity and protect natural resources.

Junior Achievement World Wide, www.ja.org

JA Worldwide is a partnership between the business community, educators and volunteers—all working together to inspire young people to dream big and reach their potential. JA's hands-on, experiential programs teach the key concepts of work readiness, entrepreneurship and financial literacy to young people all over the world. 287,491 JA volunteers teach 339,261 classes to 8,358,087 students a year.

Mark Victor Hansen Foundation, www.markvictorhansenfoundation.org

The vision for The Mark Victor Hansen Foundation is a world in which innovative entrepreneurial and social enterprise solutions are used to alleviate poverty. It intends to create a lasting and impactful difference by providing literacy to end poverty and creating opportunities for citizens throughout the world in three priority areas: entrepreneurship, education, and empowerment.

Wake Up Foundation, www.wakeuplivefoundation.org

"We are going to share success with the whole world, and this is our starting place." --Steven E.

The Wake Up...Live Foundation works in conjunction with other charitable organizations to improve the quality of life in impoverished areas such as Sierra Leone. The Foundation gives successful people a mechanism for reaching out to those most in need to offer the promise of education and opportunity.

Notes And Personal Reflections

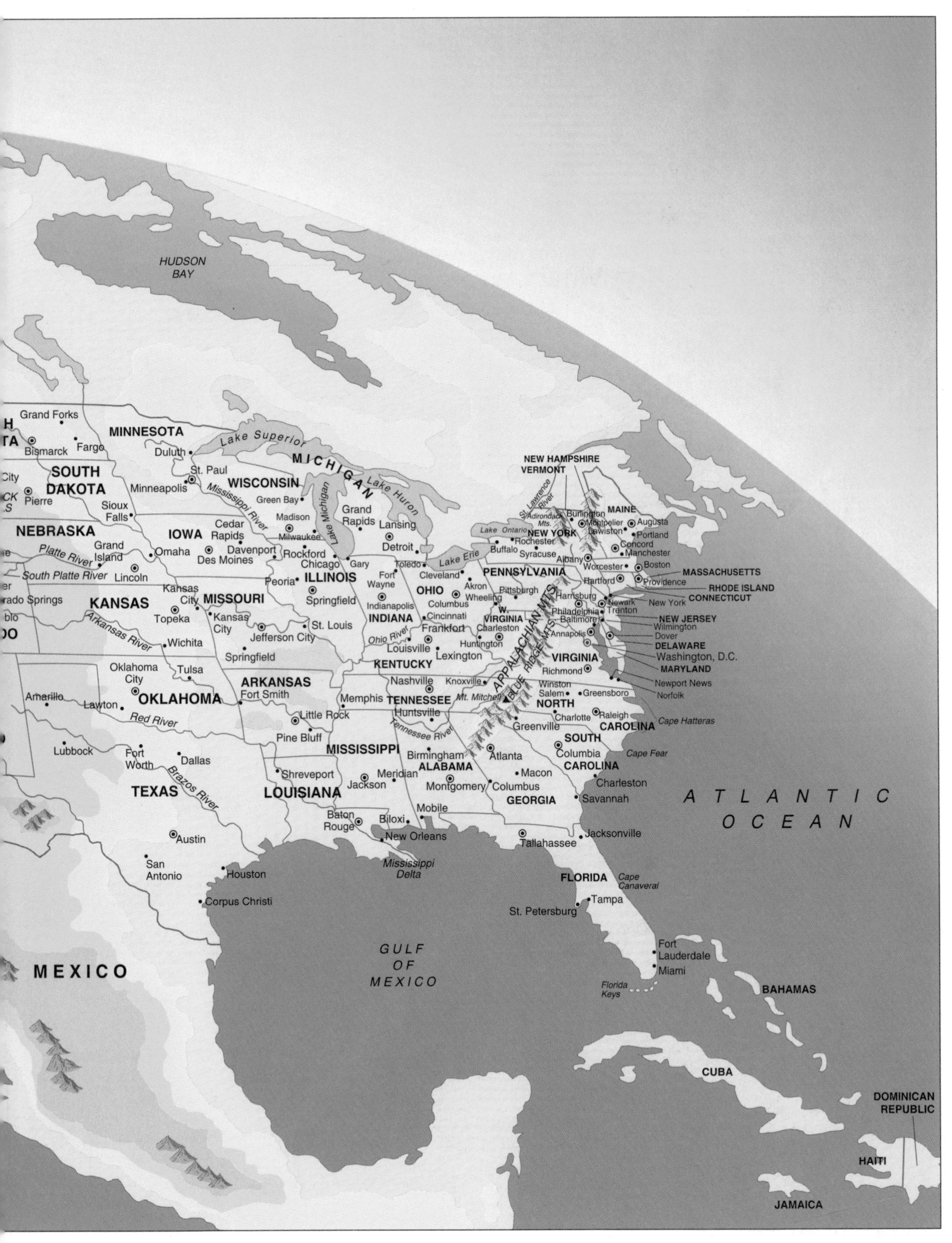

HUDSON BAY
Grand Forks
MINNESOTA
Bismarck
Fargo
Duluth
Lake Superior
MICHIGAN
SOUTH DAKOTA
St. Paul
WISCONSIN
Minneapolis
Mississippi River
Lake Huron
Pierre
Sioux Falls
Green Bay
Lake Michigan
Grand Rapids
Lansing
Madison
NEBRASKA
IOWA
Cedar Rapids
Milwaukee
Detroit
Grand Island
Omaha
Davenport
Des Moines
Rockford
Chicago
Gary
Toledo
Lake Erie
Platte River
Lincoln
South Platte River
Peoria
ILLINOIS
Fort Wayne
Cleveland
Kansas City
MISSOURI
KANSAS
Springfield
OHIO
Akron
Columbus
Indianapolis
Topeka
Kansas City
INDIANA
Cincinnati
Arkansas River
St. Louis
Jefferson City
Ohio River
Frankfort
Wichita
Louisville
Lexington
Springfield
KENTUCKY
Oklahoma City
Tulsa
ARKANSAS
Fort Smith
Amarillo
Lawton
OKLAHOMA
Memphis
TENNESSEE
Nashville
Knoxville
Red River
Little Rock
Huntsville
Tennessee River
Pine Bluff
Lubbock
Fort Worth
Dallas
MISSISSIPPI
Birmingham
ALABAMA
Shreveport
Meridian
Jackson
TEXAS
Brazos River
LOUISIANA
Montgomery
Columbus
Mobile
Baton Rouge
Biloxi
Austin
New Orleans
San Antonio
Mississippi Delta
Houston
Corpus Christi
MEXICO
GULF OF MEXICO
NEW HAMPSHIRE
VERMONT
St. Lawrence River
Adirondack Mts.
Burlington
MAINE
Montpelier
Augusta
Lewiston
Portland
Lake Ontario
NEW YORK
Rochester
Buffalo
Syracuse
Concord
Manchester
Albany
Worcester
Boston
MASSACHUSETTS
PENNSYLVANIA
Hartford
Providence
RHODE ISLAND
CONNECTICUT
Pittsburgh
Wheeling
Harrisburg
Newark
New York
Trenton
Philadelphia
Baltimore
NEW JERSEY
Wilmington
Dover
DELAWARE
W. VIRGINIA
Charleston
Huntington
Annapolis
Washington, D.C.
MARYLAND
APPALACHIAN MTS.
BLUE RIDGE MTS.
VIRGINIA
Richmond
Newport News
Norfolk
Winston Salem
Greensboro
Mt. Mitchell
NORTH CAROLINA
Charlotte
Raleigh
Cape Hatteras
Greenville
SOUTH CAROLINA
Atlanta
Columbia
Cape Fear
Macon
Charleston
GEORGIA
Savannah
ATLANTIC OCEAN
Jacksonville
Tallahassee
FLORIDA
Cape Canaveral
Tampa
St. Petersburg
Fort Lauderdale
Miami
Florida Keys
BAHAMAS
CUBA
DOMINICAN REPUBLIC
HAITI
JAMAICA

THE AMERICAN JOURNEY

A History of the United States

COMBINED VOLUME

Second Edition

DAVID GOLDFIELD

CARL ABBOTT

VIRGINIA DEJOHN ANDERSON

JO ANN E. ARGERSINGER

PETER H. ARGERSINGER

WILLIAM L. BARNEY

ROBERT M. WEIR

Upper Saddle River, New Jersey 07458

Library of Congress Cataloging-in-Publication Data

The American journey : a history of the United States / David
Goldfield . . . [et al.]. — 2nd ed.
p. cm
"Combined volume."
Includes bibliographical references and index.
ISBN 0-13-088243-7
1. United States—History. I. Goldfield, David R.,
E178.1.A4925 2001
973—dc21 00-025810

Use the Internet and eliminate mail time and postage costs
http://cip.loc.gov/cip

Editorial director: Charlyce Jones Owen
Senior acquisitions editor: Charles Cavaliere
Editor-in-chief, development: Susanna Lesan
Development editor: David Chodoff
AVP, director of production and manufacturing: Barbara Kittle
Project manager: Harriet Tellem
Prepress and manufacturing manager: Nick Sklitsis
Prepress and manufacturing buyer: Lynn Pearlman
Creative design director: Leslie Osher
Asst. creative design director: Carole Anson
Art director, interior, and cover designer: Kenny Beck
Cover art: Everett Longley Warner (1877–1963), "Along the River, New York," 1912. Oil on canvas, 32 × 10 inches. The Toledo Museum of Art, Toledo, Ohio, Museum Purchase Fund.
Photo research: Francelle Carapetyan
Manager of production services: Guy Ruggiero
Cartographers: Carto-Graphics with shaded relief from Mountain High Maps®, Digital Wisdom, Inc.
Map and art coordinator: Mirella Signoretto
Copy editor: Margaret Pinette
Interior image specialist: Beth Boyd
Mgr., rights & permissions: Kay Dellosa
Image permission coordinator: Michelina Viscusi

This book was set in 10/12 New Baskerville Roman by
TSI Graphics and was printed and bound by Von Hoffman Press, Inc.
The cover was printed by Phoenix Color Corp.

Printed in the United States of America
10 9 8 7 6 5 4 3 2

ISBN 0-13-088243-7

PEARSON EDUCATION (UK) LIMITED, *London*
PRENTICE-HALL OF AUSTRALIA PTY. LIMITED, *Sydney*
PRENTICE-HALL CANADA INC., *Toronto*
PRENTICE-HALL HISPANOAMERICANA, S.A., *Mexico*
PRENTICE-HALL OF INDIA PRIVATE LIMITED, *New Delhi*
PRENTICE-HALL OF JAPAN, INC., *Tokyo*
PEARSON EDUCATION PTE. LTD., *Singapore*
EDITORA PRENTICE-HALL DO BRASIL, LTDA., *Rio de Janeiro*

FOR OUR STUDENTS, WHO HELPED US WRITE THIS BOOK.

Brief Contents

CONTENTS

Tenochtitlán/
Mexico City

Boston
New York
Philadelphia
Jamestown

3

The Creation of New Worlds 63

4

Convergence and Conflict 1660s–1763 93

5

Imperial Breakdown 1763–1774 129

6

The War for Independence 1774–1783 155

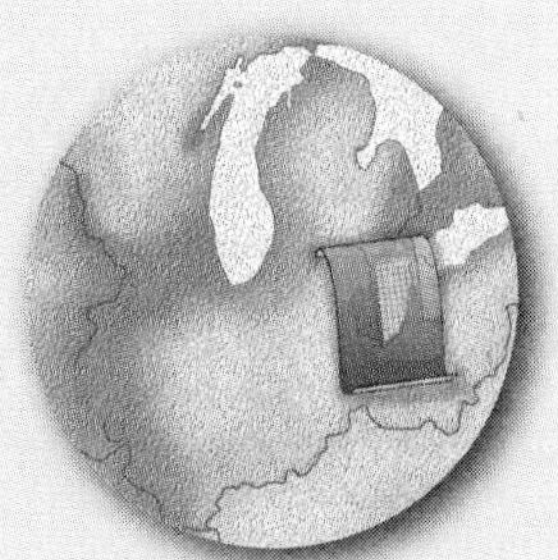

7

The First Republic 1776–1789 189

8

A New Republic and the Rise of Parties 1789–1800 219

9

The Triumph and Collapse of Jeffersonian Republicanism 1800–1824 249

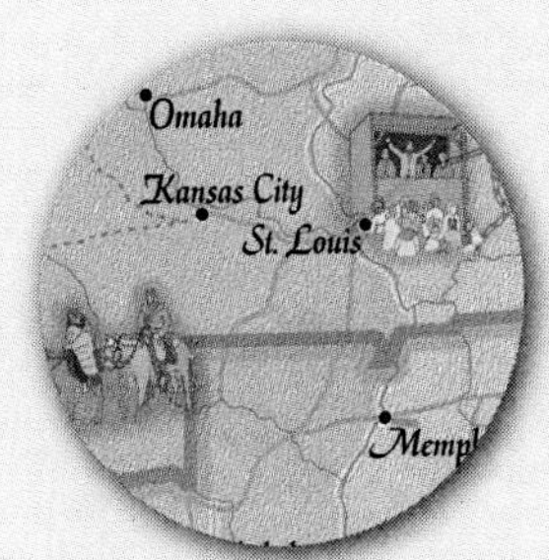

10

The Jacksonian Era 1824–1845 277

11

INDUSTRIAL CHANGE AND URBANIZATION 1820–1850 307

12

THE WAY WEST 337

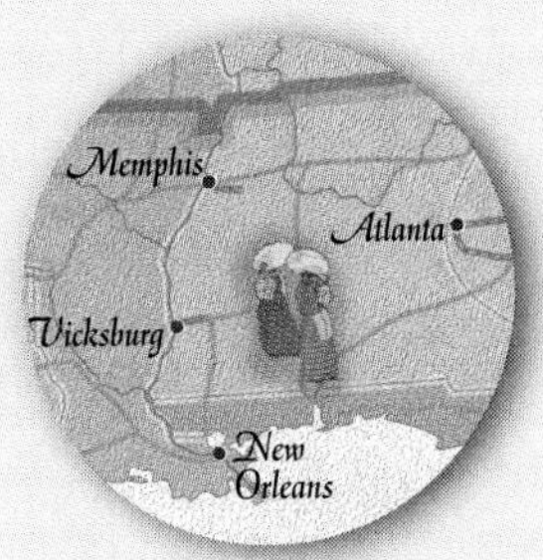

13

SLAVERY AND THE OLD SOUTH 1800–1860 367

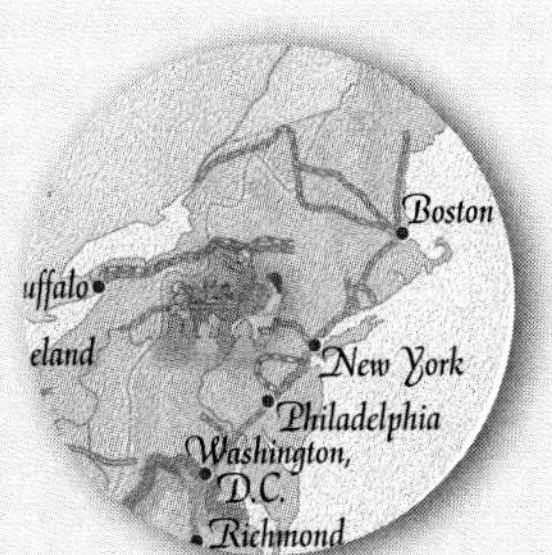

14

REFORMING ANTEBELLUM SOCIETY 1815–1850 395

15

The Politics of Sectionalism 1846–1861 423

16

Battle Cries and Freedom Songs: The Civil War, 1861–1863 459

17

The Union Preserved: The Civil War, 1863–1865 491

18

Reconstruction 1865–1877 513

19

A New South, 1877–1900 545

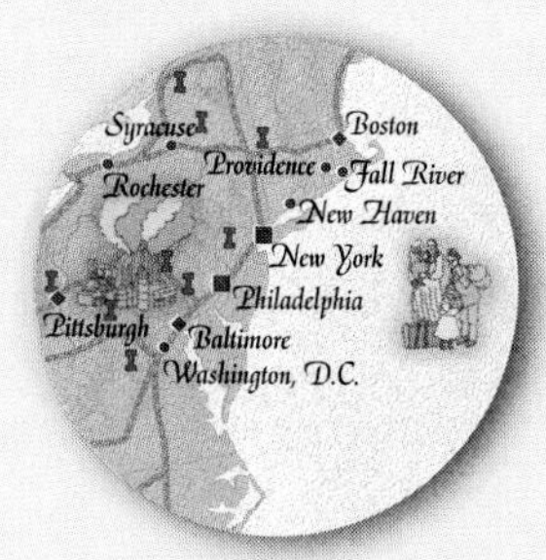

20

Industry, Immigrants, and Cities, 1870–1900 577

21

Transforming the West, 1865–1890 613

22

Politics and Government, 1877–1900 641

23

The Progressive Era, 1900–1917 669

24

Creating an Empire, 1865–1917 703

25

America and the Great War, 1914–1920 731

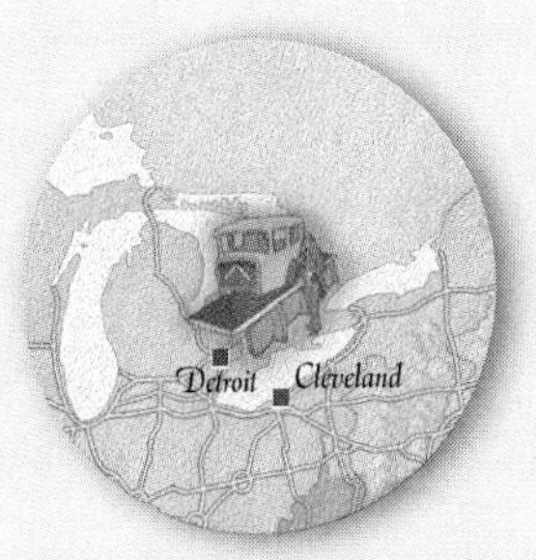

26

Toward a Modern America: The 1920s 759

27

The Great Depression and the New Deal, 1929–1939 789

28

World War II, 1939–1945 819

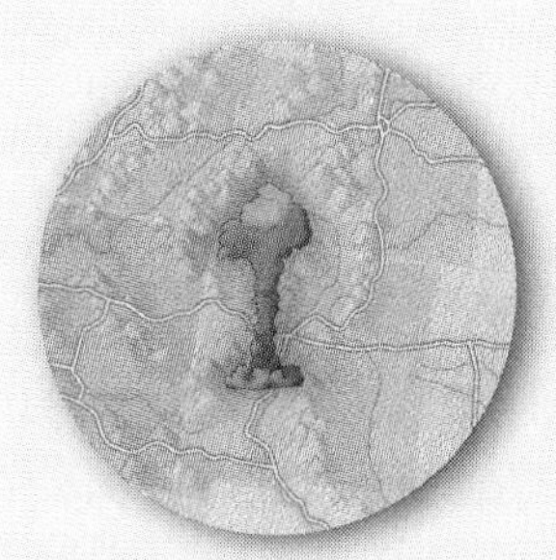

29

The Cold War at Home and Abroad, 1946–1952 851

30

The Confident Years, 1953–1964 881

31

Shaken to the Roots, 1965–1980 913

32

Shaping a New America, since 1965 943

33

SEARCHING FOR STABILITY IN A CHANGING WORLD, SINCE 1980 975

American Views

AMERICA'S JOURNEY
FROM THEN TO NOW

MAPS

FIGURES AND TABLES

FIGURES

Tables

Overview Tables

Contrasting Views of Reconstruction: President and Congress 523

Constitutional Amendments and Federal Legislation of the Reconstruction Era 528

PREFACE

The journey that led us to *The American Journey* began in the classroom with our students. We wrote this book for them and we kept their needs foremost as we set about preparing this second edition.

Over the years we have subjected our students to many American history books—including the first edition of this one—and they have let us know what they liked and disliked, what they found difficult and what they grasped easily, what they skipped and what they devoured. Most important, they have told us what connects history to their own experience and brings it alive.

Our goal is to make American history accessible to students. The key to that goal—the core of the book—is a strong clear narrative. American history is a compelling story and we seek to tell it in an engaging, forthright way. But we also provide students with an abundance of tools—including outlines, key topics lists, chronologies, overview tables, highlighted key terms, review questions, and hundreds of maps, graphs, and illustrations—to help them absorb that story and put it in context. We introduce them to the concerns of the participants in history with primary source documents. And, in a new feature called "America's Journey: From Then to Now," we connect events and issues from the past to the concerns of the present.

But if we wrote this book to appeal to our students, we also wrote it to engage their minds. We wanted to avoid academic trendiness, particularly the restricting categories that have divided the discipline of history over the last twenty years or so. We believe that the distinctions involved in the debates about multiculturalism and identity, between social and political history, between the history of the common people and the history of the elite, are unnecessarily confusing.

What we seek is integration—to combine political and social history, to fit the experience of particular groups into the broader perspective of the American past, to give voice to minor and major players alike because of their role in the story we have to tell.

Approach

In telling our story, we had some definite ideas about what we might include and emphasize that other texts do not—information we felt that the current and next generations of students will need to know about our past to function best in a new society.

CHRONOLOGICAL ORGANIZATION A strong chronological backbone supports the book. We have found that the jumping back and forth in time characteristic of some American history textbooks confuses students. They abhor dates but need to know the sequence of events in history. A chronological presentation is the best way to be sure they do.

GEOGRAPHICAL LITERACY We also want students to be geographically literate. We expect them not only to know what happened in American history, but where it happened as well. Physical locations and spatial relationships were often important in shaping historical events. The abundant maps in *The American* Journey—all numbered and called out in the text—are an integral part of our story.

COVERAGE OF THE SOUTH AND WEST The South and the West play significant roles in this text. American history is too often written from a Northeastern perspective, at least when it comes to discussing cities, economic development, and reform. But not only were the South and West developing in their own ways throughout American history, they were and remain important keys to the emerging character of the nation as a whole.

POINT OF VIEW *The American Journey* presents a balanced overview of the American past. But "balanced" does not mean bland. We do not shy away from definite positions on controversial issues, such as the nature of early contacts between Native Americans and Europeans, why the politidcal crisis of the 1850s ended in a bloody Civil War, and how Populism and its followers fit into the American political spectrum. If students and instructors disagree, that's great; discussion and dissent are important catalysts for understanding and learning.

RELIGION Nor do we shy away from some topics that play relatively minor roles in other texts, like religion. Historians are often uncomfortable writing about religion and tend to slight its influence. This text stresses the importance of religion in American society both as a source of strength and a reflection of some its more troubling aspects.

Historians mostly write for each other. That's too bad. We need to reach out and expand our audience. An American history text is a good place to start. Our students are not only our future historians, but more important, our future. Let their American journey begin.

Features of the Text

The American Journey includes an array of features and pedagogical tools designed to make American history accessible to students.

- ❖ The **Student Tool Kit** that follows this preface helps students get the most out of the text and its features. It introduces students to key conventions of historical writing and it explains how to read maps, graphs, and tables.
- ❖ A new feature, **America's Journey: From Then to Now**, relates important issues and events in each chapter to the issues and events of today, letting students see the relevance of history to their lives. Examples include "The American Revolution and the Teaching of American History" (Chapter 6), "From the Eaton Affair to Monicagate" (Chapter 10), "The Confederate Battle Flag" (Chapter 19), and "The Culture Wars" (Chapter 26).
- ❖ An **Outline** and **Key Topics** list give students a succinct overview of each chapter.
- ❖ Each chapter begins with an engaging **opening story** that highlights important themes.
- ❖ The **American Views** box in each chapter contains a relevant primary source document. Taken from letters, diaries, newspapers, government papers, and other sources, these bring the people of the past and their concerns vividly alive. An *introduction* and *prereading questions* relate the documents to the text and direct students' attention to important issues.
- ❖ **Overview Tables** in each chapter summarize complex issues.
- ❖ Chapter **chronologies** help students build a framework of key events.
- ❖ **Key Terms** are highlighted within each chapter and defined in an end-of-book **Glossary**.
- ❖ Chapter **Review Questions** help students review the material in a chapter and relate it to broader themes.
- ❖ A list of **Key Readings** and **Additional Sources** at the end of each chapter directs interested students to further information about the subject of the chapter.
- ❖ **Where To Learn More** sections describe important historical sites students can visit to gain a deeper understanding of the events discussed in the chapter.
- ❖ Abundant maps, charts, and graphs help students understand important events and trends. The *topographical detail* in many of the maps helps students understand the influence of geography on history.
- ❖ Illustrations and photographs—tied to the text with detailed captions—provide a visual dimension to history.

Supplementary Instructional Materials

The American Journey comes with an extensive package of supplementary print and multimedia materials for both instructors and students.

Print Supplements

Instructor's Resource Manual

The *Instructor's Resource Manual* contains chapter outlines, detailed chapter overviews, activities, discussion questions, readings, and information on audiovisual resources that are useful for preparing lectures and assignments.

Test Item File

The *Test Item File* includes over 1000 multiple-choice, true-false, essay, and map questions organized by chapter. A collection of blank maps can be photocopied and used for map testing or other class exercises.

Prentice Hall Custom Test

This commercial-quality computerized test management program, available for Windows and Macintosh environments, allows instructors to select items from the Test Item File and design their own exams.

Transparency Pack

This set of transparencies provides instructors with full-color acetates of all the maps, charts, and graphs in the text for use in the classroom.

Study Guide (Volumes I and II)

The *Study Guide* provides students with a brief overview of each chapter, a list of chapter objectives, study exercises, multiple-choice, short answer, and essay questions. In addition, each chapter includes two to three pages of specific map questions and exercises.

Documents in U.S. History (Volumes I and II)

This set of documents, taken from the *Retrieving the American Past* customized reader, provides five additional primary and secondary source documents—

with prereading and postreading questions—for each chapter of the textbook.

Retrieving the American Past: A Customized U.S. History Reader
This collection of documents is an on-demand history database written and developed by leading historians and educators. It offers eighty compelling modules on topics in American history, such as "Women on the Frontier," "The Salem Witchcraft Scare," "The Age of Industrial Violence," and "Native American Societies, 1870–1995." Approximately thirty-five pages in length, each module includes an introduction, several primary documents and secondary sources, follow-up questions, and recommendations for further reading. By deciding which modules to include and the order in which they will appear, instructors can compile the reader they want to use. Instructor-originated material, including other readings and exercises, can be incorporated. Contact your local Prentice Hall representative for more information about this exciting custom publishing option.

Reading Critically about History
Prepared by Rose Wassman and Lee Rinsky, DeAnza College, this brief guide provides students with helpful strategies for reading a history textbook. It is available free to students when packaged with *The American Journey*.

Understanding and Answering Essay Questions
Prepared by Mary L. Kelley, San Antonio College, this helpful guide provides analytical tools for understanding different types of essay questions and for preparing well-crafted essay answers. It is available free to students when packaged with *The American Journey*.

Themes of the Times

This special newspaper supplement is prepared jointly for students by Prentice Hall and the premier news publication, *The New York Times*. Issued twice a year, it contains recent articles pertinent to American history. These articles connect the classroom to the world. For information about a reduced-rate subscription to *The New York Times*, call toll-free: (800) 631-1222.

Multimedia Supplements

History on the Internet: A Critical Thinking Guide
This guide focuses on developing the critical thinking skills necessary to evaluate and use online sources. It provides a brief introduction to navigating the Internet with comprehensive references to History web sites. It also provides instruction on using the *Companion Website*™ available for *The American Journey*. This 96-page supplementary book is free to students with the purchase of the textbook.

Powerpoint Images CD ROM
Available in Windows and Mac formats for use with Microsoft Powerpoint™, this CD ROM provides maps, charts and graphs, summary tables, and other useful material from *The American Journey*. These resources can be used in lectures, for slide shows, printed as transparencies, or customized according to the instructor's lecture needs.

Companion Website™ and USHistory Place
Prentice Hall and Peregrine Publishers are proud to present a melding of two acclaimed interactive learning resources: Prentice Hall's ***Companion Website™*** and Peregrine's ***USHistory Place.***

Available at http://www.prenhall.com/goldfield, this new interactive history center provides materials to help students review chapter content and then test their knowledge of what they've read. *The American Journey Companion Website*™ offers students multiple choice, true-false, essay, identification, map labeling, and document questions based on material from the text. It also provides links to exciting World Wide Web destinations that expand on material in the text. Chat rooms and message boards allow students to share their ideas about American history with students from their own class or from colleges across the country. Additionally, students have access to numerous interactive maps and timelines, source documents, interactive exercises, and a comprehensive glossary from *USHistory Place* that have been keyed to the chapters in *The American Journey*. Entry to these resources is available through access codes that are provided free to students with the purchase of the text.

The *Faculty Module* contains materials for instructors, including a downloadable Microsoft Powerpoint™ presentation with maps, charts and graphs, summary tables, and other lecture material that can be presented as is or customized according to an instructor's specific lecture needs.

Instructor's Guide to USHistory Place
This guide provides helpful information for instructors on how to get the most out of *USHistory Place*. It includes a unique instructor's access code that provides entry to *USHistory Place* from *The American Journey Companion Website*™. For more information about these resources, contact your local Prentice Hall representative.

Course Management Systems

For instructors interested in distance learning, Prentice Hall offers fully customizable, online courses with enhanced content, web links, online testing, and many other course management features using the best available course management systems available, including *WebCT, Blackboard,* and *ecollege* online course architecture. Contact your local Prentice Hall representative or visit our special Demonstration Central Website at http://www.prenhall.com/demo for more information.

Acknowledgments

We would like to thank the reviewers whose thoughtful and often detailed comments helped shape this and the previous edition of *The American Journey:*

Joseph Adams, Saint Louis Community College
David Aldstadt, Houston Community College
Janet Allured, McNeese State University
Tyler Anbinder, George Washington University
Michael Batinski, Southern Illinois University
Michael Bellesiles, Emory University
Eugene Berwanger, Colorado State University
Terry Bilhartz, Sam Houston State University
Fred Blue, Youngstown State University
Eric J. Bolsteri, University of Texas at Arlington
Charles Bolton, University of Arkansas at Little Rock
James Bradford, Texas A & M University
Michael Bradley, Motlow State Community College
Henry William Brands, Texas A & M University
Neal Brooks, Essex Community College
Richard Brown, University of Connecticut
Tom Bryan, Alvin Community College
Randolph Campbell, University of North Texas
Dale Carnagey, Blinn College
E. Wayne Carp, Pacific Lutheran University
David Castle, Ohio University, Eastern Campus
Andrew Cayton, Miami University
Bill Cecil-Fronsman, Washburn University
John Chalberg, Normandale Community College
Myles Clowers, San Diego City College
David Conrad, Southern Illinois University
William Corbett, Northeastern State University
Robert Cray, Montclair State College
Richard Crepeau, University of Central Florida
Samuel Crompton, Holyoke Community College
Gilbert Cruz, Glendale Community College
Light T. Cummins, Austin College
Paul K Davis, University of Texas at San Antonio
Eugene Demody, Cerritos College
Joseph Devine, Stephen F. Austin State University
Donald Dewey, California State University
Leonard Dinnerstein, University of Arizona
Marvin Dulaney, University of Texas at Arlington
Leflett Easley, Campbell University
Iris Engstrand, University of San Diego
Robin Fabel, Auburn University
Jay Fell, University of Colorado
Nancy Gabin, Purdue University
Scott Garrett, Paducah Community College
Marilyn Geiger, Washburn University
George Gerdow, Northeastern Illinois University
Gerald Ghelfi, Rancho Santiago College
Louis Gimelli, Eastern Michigan University
James Goode, Grand Valley State University
Gregory Goodwin, Bakersfield College
Ralph Goodwin, East Texas State University
Robert Greene, Morgan State University
Mark Grimsley, Ohio State University
Ira Gruber, U.S. Military Academy
Harland Hagler, University of North Texas
Steve Haley, Shelby State Community College
Gwendolyn Hall, Rutgers University
Timothy D. Hall, Central Michigan University
David Hamilton, University of Kentucky
Joe Hapak, Moraine Valley Community College
Ronald Hatzenbuchler, Idaho State University
David G. Hogan, Heidelberg College
Alfred Hunt, SUNY Purchase
John Ingham, University of Toronto
Priscilla Jackson-Evans, Longview Community College
Donald Jacobs, Northeastern University
Frederick Jaher, University of Illinois
John Johnson, University of Northern Iowa
Wilbur Johnson, Rock Valley College
Yvonne Johnson, Central Missouri State University
Yasuhide Kawashima, University of Texas at El Paso
Joseph E. King, Texas Tech University
Gene Kirkpatrick, Tyler Junior College
Lawrence Kohl, University of Alabama at Tuscaloosa
Michael Krenn, University of Miami
Michael Krutz, Southeastern Louisiana University
Robert LaPorte, North Texas University
Armand LaPotin, SUNY Oneonta
John LaSaine, University of Georgia
Bryan LeBeau, Creighton University
Mark Leff, University of Illinois, Urbana-Champaign
Ed Lukes, Hillsborough Community College
Leo Lyman, Victor, Valley College
Ronald McArthur, Atlantic Community College
Donald McCoy, University of Kansas
David McFadden, Fairfield University
Gerald MacFarland, University of Massachusetts
Thomas McLuen, Spokane Falls Community College
Peter C. Mancell, University of Kansas
Norman Markowitz, Rutgers University
Frank Marmolejo, Irvine Valley College
James Matray, New Mexico State University
Karen Miller, Oakland University
Otis Miller, Belleville Area College
Nancy Smith Midgette, Elon College
Worth Robert Miller, Southwest Missouri State University

Timothy Morgan, Christopher Newport University
Christopher Moss, University of Texas at Arlington
Harmon Mothershead, Northwest Missouri State University
Benjamin Newcomb, Texas Technological University
Elizabeth Nybakken, Mississippi State University
Colleen O'Connor, San Diego Mesa College
Chris Padgett, Weber State University
David Parker, Kennesaw State College
Peggy Pascoe, University of Utah
Christopher Phillips, Emporia State University
Thomas L. Powers, University of South Carolina, Sumter
Kay Pulley, Trinity Valley Community College
Norman Raiford, Greenville Technical College
John Rector, Western Oregon State University
Thomas C. Reeves, University of Wisconsin, Parkside
Gary Reichard, Florida Atlantic University
Joseph Reidy, Howard University
Ronald Reitvald, California State University, Fullerton
Howard Rock, Florida International University
Hal Rothman, University of Nevada, Las Vegas
Richard Sadler, Weber State University
Henry Sage, Northern Virginia Community College, Alexandria
Bufford Satcher, University of Arkansas at Pine Bluff
Sandra Schackel, Boise State University
Michael Schaller, University of Arizona
Dale Schmitt, East Tennessee State University
Ronald Schultz, University of Wyoming
Rebecca Shoemaker, Indiana State University
Frank Siltman, U.S. Military Academy
David Sloan, University of Arkansas
J.B. Smallwood, University of North Texas
Sherry Smith, University of Texas at El Paso
Kenneth Stevens, Texas Christian University
William Stockton, Johnson County Community College
Mark Summers, University of Kentucky
William Tanner, Humbolt State University
Quintard Taylor, University of Oregon
Emily Teipe, Fullerton College
Frank Towers, Clarion University
Paula Trekel, Allegheny College
Stanley Underal, San Jose University
Andrew Wallace, Northern Arizona University
Harry Ward, University of Richmond
Ken Weatherbie, Del Mar College
Stephen Webre, Louisiana Tech University
Edward Weller, San Jacinto College, South
Michael Welsh, University of Northern Colorado
James Whittenberg, College of William and Mary
Brian Wills, Clinch Valley Community College
J. Edward Lee, Winthrop University
John Wiseman, Frostburg State University
James Woods, Georgia Southern University
Mark Wyman, Illinois State University
Neil York, Brigham Young University
William Young, Johnson County Community College
Nancy Zen, Central Oregon Community College

All of us are grateful to our families, friends, and colleagues for their support and encouragement. Jo Ann and Peter Argersinger would like in particular to thank Anna Champe, Linda Hatmaker, and John Willits; William Barney thanks Pamela Fesmire and Rosalie Radcliffe; Virginia Anderson thanks Fred Anderson, Kim Gruenwald, Ruth Helm, Eric Hinderaker, and Chidiebere Nwaubani; and David Goldfield thanks Frances Glenn and Jason Moscato. Jim Miller, Sylvia Mallory, and Sally Constable played key roles in the book's inception and initial development.

Finally, we would like to acknowledge the members of our Prentice Hall family. They are not only highly competent professionals but also pleasant people. We regard them with affection and appreciation. None of us would hesitate to work with this fine group again. We would especially like to thank David Chodoff, senior development editor, for his careful attention to detail and his insistence on clear writing; Charlyce Jones Owen, vice president and editorial director for the Humanities, who organized her team and our social functions flawlessly; Sheryl Adams, senior marketing manager, whose creative and informed marketing strategies demonstrated an appreciation for historical scholarship as well as the history textbook market; Kenny Beck and Carole Anson, art directors, and Leslie Osher, creative design director, whose creativity is evident in this book's design and layout; Harriet Tellem, senior production editor, for her efficient handling of the production process; Mirella Signoretto, line art formatter; Margret Pinette, copy editor; Francelle Carapetyan for her photo research; Susanna Lesan, editor in chief for development, for ensuring that the book had the developmental resources it needed; Nick Sklitsis, manufacturing manager, Lynn Pearlman, manufacturing buyer, and Jan Stephan, managing editor, who kept the whole team on schedule; and Phil Miller, president of Prentice Hall's Humanities and Social Sciences division, who had the good sense to let his staff run with this book.

DG
CA
VDJA
JEA
PHA
WLB
RMW

About the Authors

David Goldfield received his Ph.D. in history from the University of Maryland. Since 1982, he has been Robert Lee Baily Professor of History at the University of North Carolina in Charlotte. He is the author or editor of twelve books on various aspects of southern and urban history. Two of his works—*Cotton Fields and Skyscrapers: Southern City and Region 1607 to 1980* (1982) and *Black, White, and Southern: Race Relations and Southern Culture, 1940 to the present* (1990)—received the Mayflower award for Nonfiction. Both books were also nominated for the Pulitzer Prize in history. When he is not writing or teaching, Goldfield applies the historical craft to history museum exhibits, federal voting rights cases, and local planning and policy issues. He is currently working on a book that asks the question: Why is the South different?

Carl Abbott is a professor of Urban Studies and planning at Portland State University. He taught previously in the history departments at the University of Denver and Old Dominion University and held visiting appointments at Mesa College in Colorado and George Washington University. He holds degrees in history from Swarthmore College and the University of Chicago. He specializes in the history of cities and the American West and serves as co-editor of the *Pacific Historical Review.* His books include *The New Urban America: Growth and Politics in Sunbelt cities* (1981, 1987), *The Metropolitan Frontier: Cities in the Modern American West* (1993), *Planning a New West: The Columbia River Gorge National Scenic Area* (1997), and *Political Terrain: Washington, D.C. from Tidewater Town to Global Metropolis* (1999).

Virginia DeJohn Anderson is Associate Professor of History at the University of Colorado at Boulder. She received her B.A. from the University of Connecticut. As the recipient of a Marshall Scholarship, she earned an M.A. degree at the University of East Anglia in Norwich, England. Returning to the United States, she received her A.M. and Ph.D. degrees from Harvard University. She is the author of *New England's Generation: The Great Migration and the Formation of Society and Culture in the Seventeenth Century* (1991) and several articles on colonial history, which have appeared in such journals as the *William and Mary Quarterly* and the *New England Quarterly.*

Jo Ann E. Argersinger received her Ph.D. from George Washington University and is Professor of History at Southern Illinois University. A recipient of fellowships from the Rockefeller Foundation and the National Endowment for the Humanities, she is a historian of social, labor, and business policy. Her publications include *Toward a New Deal in Baltimore: People and Government in the Great Depression* (1988) and *Making the Amalgamated: Gender, Ethnicity, and Class in the Baltimore Clothing Industry* (1999).

Peter H. Argersinger received his Ph.D. from the University of Wisconsin and is Professor of History at Southern Illinois University. He has won several fellowships and the Binkley-Stephenson Award from the Organization of American Historians. Among his books on American political and rural history are *Populism and Politics* (1974), *Structure, Process, and Party* (1992), and *The Limits of Agrarian Radicalism* (1995). His current research focuses on the political crisis of the 1890s.

William L. Barney is Professor of History at the University of North Carolina at Chapel Hill. A native of Pennsylvania, he received his B.A. from Cornell University and his M.A. and Ph.D. from Columbia University. He has published extensively on 19th century U.S. history and has a particular interest in the Old South and the coming of the Civil War. Among his publications are *The Road to Secession* (1972), *The Secessionist Impulse* (1974), *Flawed Victory* (1975), *The Passage of the Republic* (1987), and *Battleground for the Union* (1989). He is currently finishing an edited collection of essays on nineteenth-century America and a book on the Civil War.

Robert M. Weir is Distinguished Professor of History Emeritus at the University of South Carolina. He received his B.A. from Pennsylvania State University and his Ph.D. from Case Western Reserve University. He has taught at the University of Houston and, as a visiting professor, at the University of Southampton in the United Kingdom. His articles have won prizes from the Southeastern Society for the study of the Eighteenth Century and the *William and Mary Quarterly.* Among his publications are *Colonial South Carolina: A History, "The Last of American Freemen": Studies in the Political Culture of the Colonial and Revolutionary South,* and, most recently, a chapter on the Carolinas in the new *Oxford History of the British Empire* (1998).

Student Tool Kit

When writing history, historians use maps, tables, and graphs to help their readers understand the past. What follows is an explanation of how to use the historian's tools that are contained in this book.

Text

Whether it is a biography of George Washington, an article on the Civil War, or a survey of American history such as this one, the text is the historian's basic tool for discussing the past. Historians write about the past using narration and analysis. *Narration* is the story line of history. It describes what happened in the past, who did it, and where and when it occurred. Narration is also used to describe how people in the past lived, how they passed their daily lives and even, when the historical evidence makes it possible for us to know, what they thought, felt, feared, or desired. Using *analysis,* historians explain why they think events in the past happened the way they did and offer an explanation for the story of history. In this book, narration and analysis are interwoven in each chapter.

Study Aids

A number of features in this book are designed to aid in the study of history. Each chapter begins with *Key Topics,* a short list of the most important issues that will be covered in the chapter. A *Conclusion* at the end of each chapter puts the subject of the chapter in the broader perspective of U.S. history. Both these study aids can be used to review important concepts.

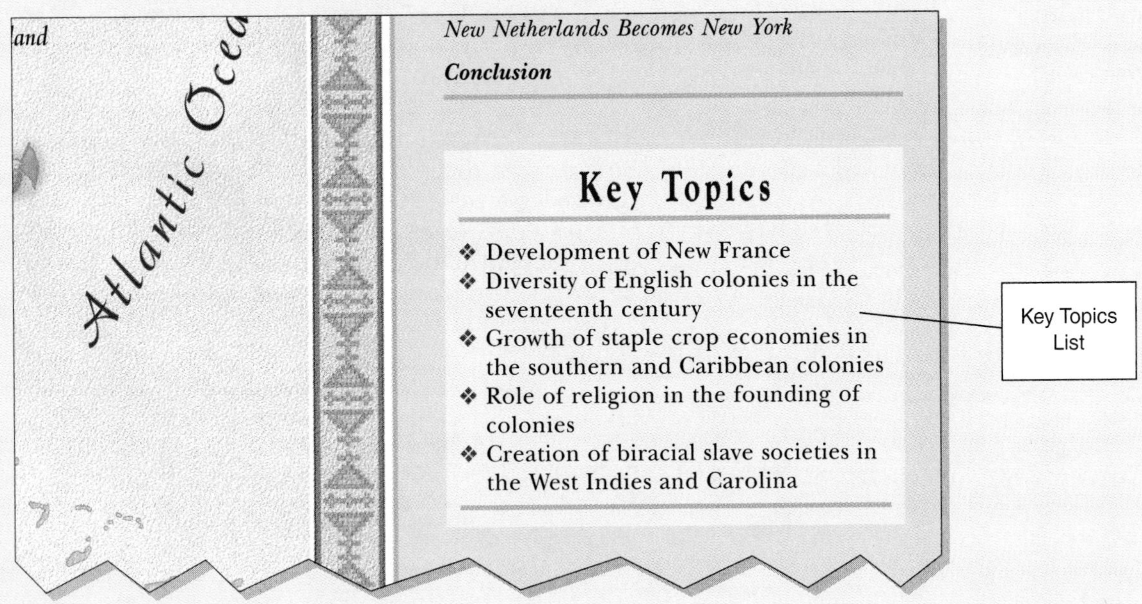

and
Atlantic Oce
New Netherlands Becomes New York
Conclusion
Key Topics
❖ Development of New France
❖ Diversity of English colonies in the seventeenth century
❖ Growth of staple crop economies in the southern and Caribbean colonies
❖ Role of religion in the founding of colonies
❖ Creation of biracial slave societies in the West Indies and Carolina
Key Topics List

Maps

Maps are important historical tools. They show how geography has affected history and concisely summarize complex relationships and events. Knowing how to read and interpret a map is important to understanding history. Map 5-1 from Chapter 5 shows the British colonies on the eastern seaboard of North America in 1763, about twelve years before the American Revolution. It has three features to help you read it: a *caption,* a *legend,* and a *scale.* The caption explains the historical significance of the map. Here the caption tells us that in 1763 the British government sought to restrict colonial settlement west of the Appalachian Mountains to prevent conflict between colonists and Indians. Colonial frustration with this policy contributed to the outbreak of the American Revolution.

The legend and the scale appear in the lower right corner of the map. The legend provides a key to what the symbols on the map mean. The solid line stretching along the Appalachian Mountains from Maine to Georgia represents the Proclamation Line of 1763—the line meant to restrict colonial settlement. Cities are marked with a dot, capitals with a star, and forts by a black square. Spanish territory west of the Mississippi River is represented in yellow-brown; territory settled by Europeans is represented in green. The scale tells us that 7/8ths of an inch on the map represents 300 miles (about 480 kilometers) on the ground. With this information, estimates of the distance between points on the map are easily made.

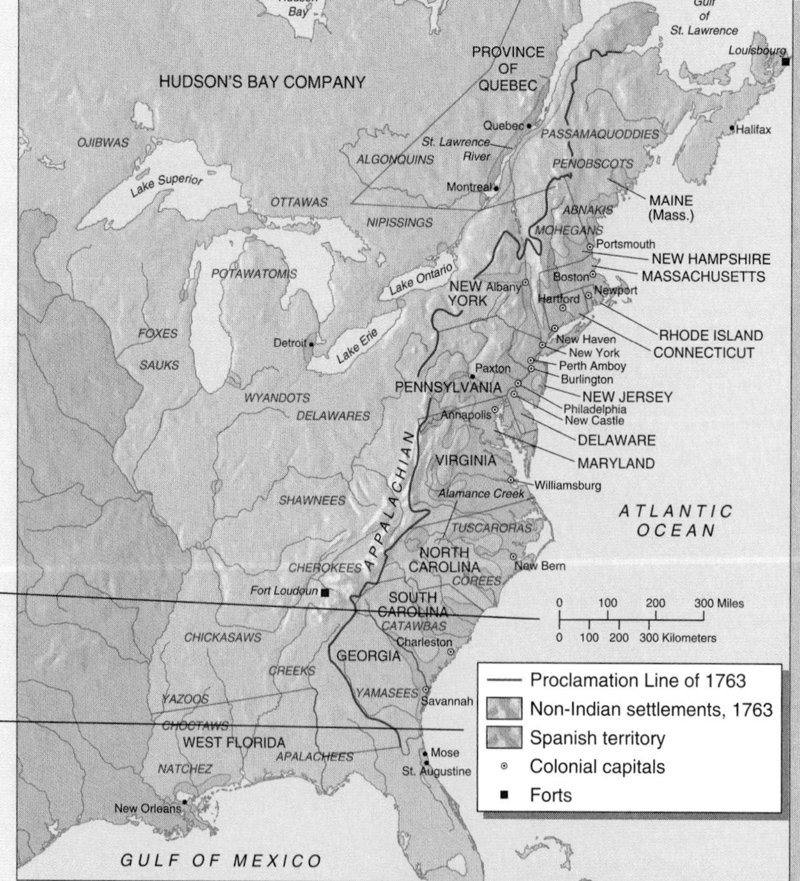

Map 5-1 Colonial Settlement and the Proclamation Line of 1763
This map depicts the regions claimed and settled by the major groups competing for territory in eastern North America. With the Proclamation Line of 1763, positioned along the crest of the Appalachian Mountains, the British government tried to stop the westward migration of settlers under its jurisdiction, and thereby limit conflict with the Indians. The result, however, was frustration and anger on the part of land-hungry settlers.

The map also shows the *topography* of the region—its mountains, rivers, and lakes. This helps us understand how geography influenced history in this case. For example, the Appalachian Mountains divide the eastern seaboard from the rest of the continent. The mountains obstructed colonial migration to the west for a long time. By running the Proclamation Line along the Appalachians, the British hoped to use this natural barrier to separate Indians and colonists. Note how small the green areas are, that is, the areas of European settlement, relative to the immense size of North America. Note also how the map shows that the Europeans tended to settle near the coasts and along rivers and across plains.

Graphs

Historians use graphs to make comparisons and summarize trends. Comparisons can be between groups of people, regions of the country, products, time periods—whatever focuses the reader's attention on an important historical development. Various types of graphs are used in this book, including *line graphs, pie charts,* and *bar graphs.* The names denote the way the graphs are drawn to make comparisons. All graphs show the numbers of some significant factor—like people, goods, or prices—at a given time or how they fluctuated over a given period. Figure 20-2 is a line graph that shows the dramatic rise in

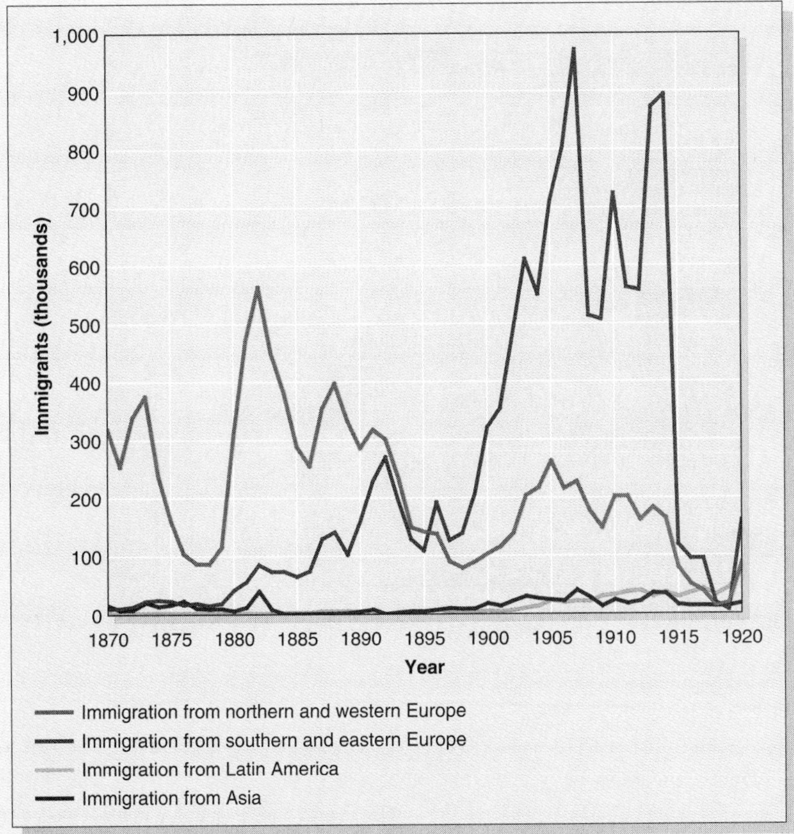

Figure 20-2 Immigration to the United States, 1870–1920
The graph illustrates the dramatic change in immigration to the United States during the late nineteenth and early twentieth centuries. As immigration from northern and western Europe slackened, the numbers of newcomers from southern and eastern Europe swelled. Latin American and Asian immigration also increased during this period as well.

immigration to the United States from eastern and southern Europe in the late nineteenth and early twentieth centuries. Figure 3-4, for example, is a pie chart—so called because it looks like a pie cut into slices. It shows the ethnic origins of the non-Indian population of the thirteen colonies at the start of the American Revolution. Figure 4-2 is a bar graph that compares the growth in population of the four major colonial regions.

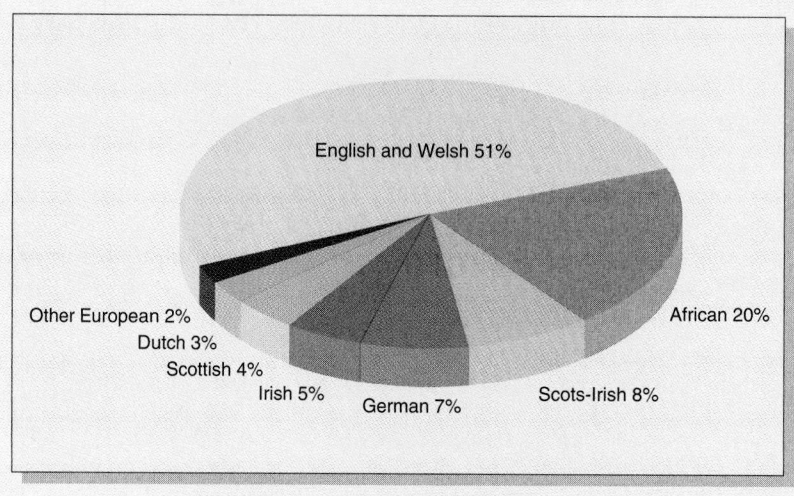

Figure 3-4 Ethnic Distribution of Non-Indian Inhabitants of British Mainland Colonies, c. 1770
By the third quarter of the eighteenth century, the colonial population was astonishingly diverse. Only two out of three settlers claimed British ancestry (from England, Wales, Scotland, or northern Ireland), while one out of five was African in origin.

Data Source: *Adapted from Thomas L. Purvis, "The European Ancestry of the* United States Population, *1790," William and Mary Quarterly, 3d series, 41 (1984), p. 98.*

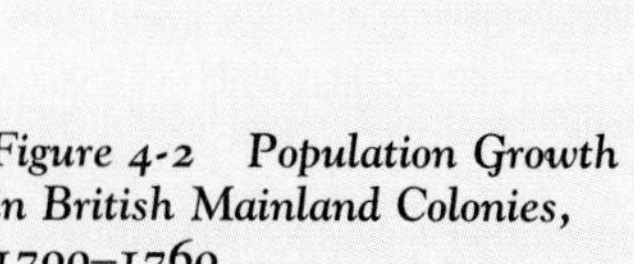

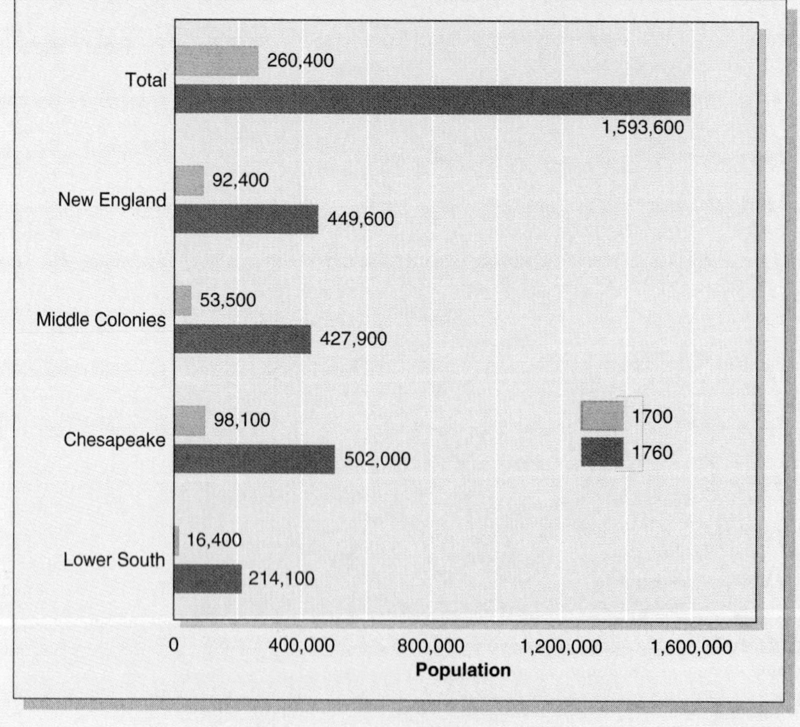

Figure 4-2 Population Growth in British Mainland Colonies, 1700–1760
Both natural increase and immigration contributed to a staggering rate of population growth in British North America. Some colonists predicted that Americans would soon outnumber Britain's inhabitants—a possibility that greatly concerned British officials.

Data Source: *John J. McCusker and Russell R. Menard,* The Economy of British America, 1607–1789, *rev. ed. (1991).*

Overview Tables

The *Overview* tables in this text are a special feature designed to highlight and summarize important topics within a chapter. The Overview table shown here, for example, summarizes the purpose and significance of the major laws and constitutional amendments passed during the Reconstruction era following the Civil War.

Overview

Constitutional Amendments and Federal Legislation of the Reconstruction Era

Amendment or Legislation	Purpose	Significance
Thirteenth Amendment (passed and ratified in 1865)	Prevented southern states from reestablishing slavery after the war	Final step toward full emancipation of slaves
Freedmen's Bureau Act (1865)	Oversight of resettlement, reflief, education, and labor for former slaves	Involved the federal government directly in assisting the transition from slavery to freedom; worked fitfully to achieve this objective during its seven-year career
Southern Homestead Act (1866)	Provided blacks preferential access to public lands in five southern states	Lack of capital and poor quality of federal land thwarted the purpose of the act

Chronologies

Each chapter includes a *Chronology,* a list of the key events discussed in the chapter arranged in chronological order. The chronology for Chapter 18 lists the dates of key events during the Reconstruction era from 1865 to 1877. Chronologies provide a review of important events and their relationship to one another.

Chronology

1863 Lincoln proposes his Ten Percent Plan.

1864 Congress proposes the Wade-Davis Bill.

1865 Sherman issues Field Order No. 15.
Freedmen's Bureau is established.
Andrew Johnson succeeds to the presidency, unveils his Reconstruction plan.
Massachusetts desegregates all public facilities.
Blacks in several southern cities organize Union Leagues.
Former Confederate states begin to pass black codes.

1866 Congress passes Southern Homestead Act, Civil Rights Act of 1866.
Ku Klux Klan is founded.
Fourteenth Amendment to the Constitution is passed (ratified in 1868).
President Johnson goes on a speaking tour.

1867 Congress passes Military Reconstruction Acts, ...ure o... Act.

Republican regimes topple in North Carolina and Georgia.

1871 Congress passes Ku Klux Klan Act.

1872 Freedmen's Bureau closes down.
Liberal Republicans emerge as a separate party.
Ulysses S. Grant is reelected.

1873 Severe depression begins.
Colfax Massacre occurs.
U.S. Supreme Court's decision in the *Slaughterhouse* cases weakens the intent of the Fourteenth Amendment.
Texas falls to the Democrats in the fall elections.

1874 White Leaguers attempt a coup against the Republican government of New Orleans.
Democrats win off-year elections across the South amid widespread fraud and violence.

1875 Congress passes Civil Rights Act of 1875.

1876 Supre... urt's decisi... *United St...* v.

Primary Source Documents

Historians find most of their information in written records, original documents that have survived from the past. These include government publications, letters, diaries, newspapers—whatever people wrote or printed, including many private documents never intended for publication. Each chapter in the book contains a feature called *American Views*—a selection from a primary source document. The example shown here compares two letters by Abraham Lincoln explaining his position on slavery. Each *American Views* feature begins with a brief introduction followed by several questions—for discussion or written response—on what the document reveals about key issues and events.

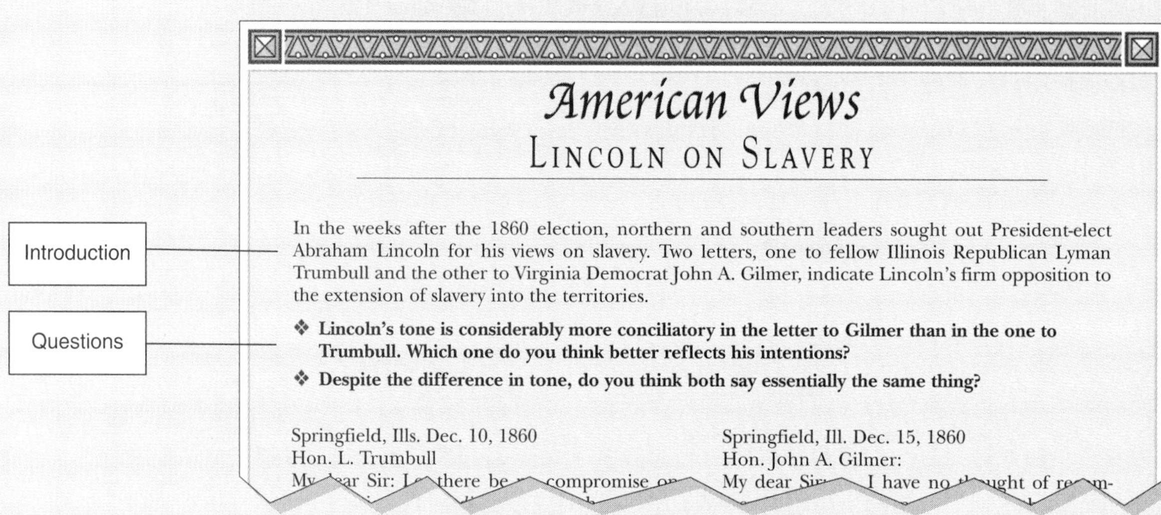

American Views

LINCOLN ON SLAVERY

In the weeks after the 1860 election, northern and southern leaders sought out President-elect Abraham Lincoln for his views on slavery. Two letters, one to fellow Illinois Republican Lyman Trumbull and the other to Virginia Democrat John A. Gilmer, indicate Lincoln's firm opposition to the extension of slavery into the territories.

❖ **Lincoln's tone is considerably more conciliatory in the letter to Gilmer than in the one to Trumbull. Which one do you think better reflects his intentions?**

❖ **Despite the difference in tone, do you think both say essentially the same thing?**

Springfield, Ills. Dec. 10, 1860
Hon. L. Trumbull
My dear Sir: Let there be no compromise on

Springfield, Ill. Dec. 15, 1860
Hon. John A. Gilmer:
My dear Sir— I have no thought of recom-

America's Journey: From Then to Now

The feature called *America's Journey: From Then to Now* connects events and trends in the past to issues that confront Americans today, illustrating the value a historical perspective can contribute to our understanding of the world we live in. The example here, from Chapter 4, traces the vitality and diversity of religion in America today to the religious diversity of the earliest colonists.

AMERICA'S JOURNEY

FROM THEN TO NOW

The Enduring Vitality and Diversity of American Religion

In a front-page story in April 1991, *The New York Times* reported on "dozens of surprises" contained in an opinion poll on religious identification in America. The poll revealed two main features of American religious life. First, organized religion was thriving. Nine out of ten people polled identified themselves with a religious denomination. Second, the American religious scene was highly di-

had become so firmly embedded in American life that people feared the establishment of a single state church far more than the consequences of having a multiplicity of faiths within a single nation. It was this fear that inspired the First Amendment to the Constitution, with its guarantee of the "free exercise" of religion, of whatever kind, and its prohibition of any religious establish-

Recommended Readings, Additional Sources, and Where to Learn More

At the end of each chapter are two lists of books—*Recommended Readings* and *Additional Sources*—that provide greater information about the topics discussed in the chapter. The section called *Where to Learn More* lists important historical sites and museums that provide first-hand exposure to historical artifacts and settings.

Where to Learn More

- ❖ **Henry Ford Museum and Greenfield Village,** Dearborn, Michigan. With 12 acres of exhibit space, the museum houses nearly 250,000 artifacts of American industry (not merely the automobile industry). The major attraction is a long-term exhibit, "Made in America: The History of the American Industrial System."
- ❖ **Edison National Historic Site,** West Orange, New Jersey. The site contains the Edison archives, including photographs, sound recordings, and industrial and scientific machinery. Its twenty historic structures dating from the 1880–1887 period include Edison's home and laboratory.
- ❖ **Japanese American National Museum,** Los Angeles, California. Housed in a converted Buddhist temple, this museum includes artifacts and photographs of early Japanese immigration

Glossary

Significant historical terms are called out in **heavy type** throughout the text. These are listed alphabetically and defined in a *glossary* at the end of the book.

Worlds Apart

Pacific Ocean
Santa Fe
Acoma Pueblo
Tenochtitlán/ Mexico City
Cahok
of Mexico
British Settlements
French Settlements
Spanish Settlements
0
400 miles
0
600 km
Tenochtitlán/ Mexico City
N
W
E
S

Chapter Outline

Different Worlds
Native American Societies before 1492
Cultural Perceptions and Misperceptions
West African Societies
Western Europe on the Eve of Discovery

Contact
The Lure of Discovery
Christopher Columbus
Spanish Conquest and Colonization
The Columbian Exchange

Competition for a Continent
Early French Efforts in North America
English Attempts in the New World

Conclusion

Key Topics

- ❖ Native American, West African, and European society on the eve of contact
- ❖ The reasons for Europe's impulse to global exploration
- ❖ The Spanish, French, and English experiences in America in the sixteenth century
- ❖ Consequences of contact between the Old and New Worlds

By October 11, 1492, the three tiny ships had been sailing westward for more than five weeks. Over three thousand miles of empty ocean separated them from their last landfall, in the Canary Islands off the coast of North Africa. Several times sailors had claimed to see land, but their sightings proved only mirages. Just the day before, frustration and fear drove officers and crew to threaten their admiral with mutiny unless they turned back for Spain. The admiral, Christopher Columbus, still confident that he could reach Asia and its riches by sailing west across the Atlantic, asked for a few more days. His men, whose yearning for home mingled with hope that their long voyage might yet prove successful, agreed. Scouring sea and sky for signs, they saw floating branches and flying birds but no land. Surely tomorrow night they would turn around.

Then, two hours after midnight on October 12, a sailor peered into the moonlight and shouted, "Land! Land!" In the pale light of dawn, a sliver of white sand beach indeed appeared. As the ships drew closer, the men thought they could smell the rich spices of the Orient. They searched the horizon for the golden-roofed temples about which they had heard so much. What they did not know was that this land was not the Orient. It was an island lying near two vast continents still invisible to them and about whose existence they had not the slightest inkling.

No one knows exactly where Columbus landed, but many historians believe it was an island in the Bahamas known to its inhabitants as Guanahani and now called Watling Island. Instead of a Chinese city, Columbus's landing party found a village of small wooden houses clustered around a central plaza. The villagers fled into the jungle when they first saw the strangers but soon emerged, bringing parrots and balls of cotton thread to trade. Remarking on their nakedness and few possessions, Columbus judged these people—part of a group called the Tainos—"a people very poor in everything," although he noticed that a few of them wore gold nose ornaments. What the Tainos thought of Columbus and his men will never be known.

Thus began one of the most momentous encounters in human history. Columbus claimed the island as a possession of the monarchs of Spain and, grateful for his safe arrival, renamed it San Salvador (Holy Savior). Still convinced that he was near Asia, he did not realize he had found what was soon to be called the New World. It was new, of course, only to Europeans ignorant of its existence, not to the people whose ancestors had lived there for thousands of years. The far-reaching consequences of Columbus's voyage, however, would ultimately bring together people who had previously lived in worlds apart—Native American, African, and European—to forge a world that was new in fact as well as name.

Different Worlds

The New World that emerged after 1492 reflected the experiences of the people who built it. Improving economic conditions in the fifteenth and early sixteenth centuries spurred Europeans to seek new opportunities for trade in overseas exploration and settlement. Spain, Portugal, France, and England, competing for political, economic, and religious domination within Europe, carried their conflict over into the Americas. Native Americans drew upon their familiarity with the land and its resources, their patterns of political and religious authority, and their systems of trade and warfare to deal with the European newcomers. Africans would not come voluntarily to the Americas but would be brought by the Europeans to work as slaves. They too would draw on their cultural heritage to cope with both a new land and a new, harsh condition of life.

Native American Societies before 1492

Convinced that he had landed in the East Indies, Columbus called the people he met *indios*. His error is preserved in the word *Indian*, used by Europeans to identify the original inhabitants of the two American continents. (The word *America* derives from the name of another Italian explorer, Amerigo Vespucci.) In their own languages, many native groups called themselves "the original people" or "the true men."

Women were the principal farmers in most Native American societies, growing corn, beans, and other crops that made up most of their food supply. This sixteenth-century French engraving shows Indian men preparing the soil for cultivation and Indian women sowing seeds in neat rows.

By 1492, the continents of North and South America were home to perhaps as many as 70 million people—nearly equal to the population of Europe at that time. The area of what is now the United States and Canada was more sparsely settled than regions further south; it is estimated that only 7 million or so people lived north of the Rio Grande. These people belonged to hundreds of groups, each with its own language or dialect, history, and way of life. They varied from nomadic hunters in the Arctic to members of the complex imperial society centered in the Aztec capital of Tenochtitlán, one of the largest cities in the world in the year Columbus sailed.

The first humans may have arrived in the Americas as long as forty thousand years ago. The earliest migrants may have come from central Siberia and made their way to southern South America. These people, and subsequent migrants from Eurasia, probably traveled across a land bridge that emerged across what is now the Bering Strait. During the last Ice Age, much of the earth's water was frozen in huge glaciers. This caused ocean levels to drop, exposing a 600-mile-wide land bridge between Asia and America. Recent research examining genetic and linguistic similarities between Asian and Native American populations suggests that there may have been later migrations as well. Asian seafarers may have crossed the Pacific to settle portions of western North and South America, while as recently as eight thousand years ago, a final migration may have brought Siberians to what is now Alaska and northern Canada.

The earliest Americans, whom archaeologists call **Paleo-Indians**, traveled in small bands, tracking and killing mammoths, bison, and other large game. Unaccustomed to the presence of humans, these animals were often easy prey. But Paleo-Indians were also highly skilled hunters. Archaeologists working near present-day Clovis, New Mexico, have found numerous carefully crafted spear points—some of which may be over thirteen thousand years old. Such efficient tools possibly contributed to overhunting, for by about 9000 B.C., mammoths, mastodons, and other large game had become extinct in the Americas. Climatic change also hastened the animals' disappearance. Around twelve thousand years ago, the world's climate began to grow warmer, turning grasslands into deserts and reducing the animals' food supply. This meant that humans too had to find other food sources.

Between roughly 8000 B.C. and 1500 B.C.—what archaeologists call the **Archaic** period—Indians adapted to regional environments, learning to use local resources efficiently. Gradually, populations grew and people began living in larger communities, some with a hundred or more residents. These villages had recognized leaders, but the rest of the inhabitants were not divided into social classes. Men and women, however, began to assume more specialized roles. Men did most of the hunting and fishing, activities that required travel. Women remained closer to home, gathering and preparing wild plant foods and caring for children. Each group made the tools it used, with men carving fishhooks and arrowheads and women making such items as bone needles and baskets.

Archaic Indians also collected local nonfood resources, including rocks, shells, and bones. They fashioned goods from these materials and traded them with other peoples, sometimes hundreds of miles away. At Indian Knoll, in western Kentucky, archaeologists have found copper from the Great Lakes area and shells from as far away as the Gulf of Mexico. Competition for control of lands where desirable materials could be found may have sparked conflict. Three bodies buried around 5000 B.C. in

CHRONOLOGY

c. 40,000–8,000 B.C.	Ancestors of Native Americans cross Bering land bridge.
c. 10,000–9000 B.C.	Paleo-Indians expand through the Americas.
c. 9000 B.C.	Extinction of large land mammals in North America.
c. 8000–1500 B.C.	Archaic Indian era.
c. 5000 B.C.	Beginnings of agriculture in Mesoamerica.
c. 1500 B.C.	Earliest mound-building culture begins.
c. 500 B.C.–A.D. 400	Adena-Hopewell mound-building culture.
c. A.D. 700–1600	Rise of West African empires.
c. 900	First mounds built at Cahokia. Anasazi expansion.
c. 1000	Spread of Islam in West Africa.
c. 1000–1500	Last mound-building culture, the Mississippian.
c. 1290s	Anasazi dispersal into smaller pueblos.
1400–1600	Renaissance in Europe.
1430s	Beginnings of Portuguese slave trade in West Africa.
1492	End of *reconquista* in Spain. Christopher Columbus's first voyage.
1494	Treaty of Tordesillas.
1497	John Cabot visits Nova Scotia and Newfoundland.
1497–1499	Vasco da Gama sails around Africa to reach India.
1517	Protestant Reformation begins in Germany.
1519–1521	Hernán Cortés conquers the Aztec empire.
1532–1533	Francisco Pizarro conquers the Inca empire.
1534–1542	Jacques Cartier explores eastern Canada for France.
1540–1542	Coronado explores southwestern North America.
1542–1543	Roberval's failed colony in Canada.
1558	Elizabeth I becomes queen of England.
1565	Spanish establish outpost at St. Augustine in Florida.
1560s–1580s	English renew attempts to conquer Ireland.
1587	Founding of "Lost Colony" of Roanoke.
1598	Spanish found colony at New Mexico.

northwestern Alabama had stone arrowheads embedded in their backbones or ribcages, clear evidence of violent death.

Ideas as well as goods circulated among Archaic Indian peoples. Across the continent, human burials became more elaborate, suggesting that ideas about death and the afterlife passed between groups. Bodies might be wrapped in woven mats or cloths and the deceased's personal possessions placed in the grave. Certain valuable trade goods, such as exotic shell beads and animal figurines, have been found in some graves, perhaps indicating that such objects had spiritual significance.

Many Indian peoples flourished by hunting and gathering, but near the end of the Archaic period, some groups made a further adaptation when they began farming. The development of agriculture appears to have occurred independently in various parts of the world. People in the Middle East began farming around 9000 B.C. A few thousand years later, farming appeared in Southeast Asia, China, India, Mexico, and Peru. Archaeologists speculate that agriculture first developed in areas where population growth threatened to outrun the supply of game and wild plants. Women, with their expertise in gathering wild plants, were probably the world's first farmers.

Agriculture in the Americas began around five thousand years ago, when the people of central Mexico started raising an ancient type of maize, or corn. At first, farming supplemented a diet still largely dependent on hunting and gathering. But agriculture gradually became more widespread. In addition to maize, the main crop in both South and North America, farmers in Mexico, Central America, and the Peruvian Andes learned to cultivate peppers, beans, pumpkins, squash, avocados, sweet and white potatoes (native to the Peruvian highlands), and tomatoes. Mexican farmers also grew cotton. Maize and bean cultivation spread from Mexico in a wide arc to the north and east. Peoples in what is now the southwestern United States began farming between 1500 and 500 B.C., and by A.D. 200, farmers tilled the soil in present-day Georgia and Florida.

Wherever agriculture took hold, important social changes followed. Populations grew, because farming produced a more secure food supply than hunting and gathering. Permanent villages appeared as farmers settled near their fields. In central Mexico, agriculture eventually sustained the populations of large cities. Trade in agricultural surpluses flowed through networks of exchange. In many Indian societies, women's status improved because of their role as the principal farmers. Specialized craft workers produced sophisticated pottery and baskets to store harvested grains. Even religious beliefs and practices reflected the centrality of farming. In describing the origins of their people, Pueblo Indians of the Southwest compared their emergence from the underworld to a maize plant sprouting from the earth.

Despite the diversity of Native American peoples, certain generalizations can be made about societies that developed within broad regions, or **culture areas** (see Map 1-1). Within each area, inhabitants shared basic patterns of subsistence and social organization, largely reflecting the natural environment to which they had adapted.

Throughout the North and West, Indians prospered without adopting agriculture. In the challenging environment of the Arctic and Subarctic, small nomadic bands moved seasonally to fish, follow game, and, in the brief summers, gather wild berries. Far to the north, Eskimos and Aleuts hunted whales, seals, and other sea mammals. Further inland, the Crees and other peoples followed migrating herds of caribou and moose. Northern peoples fashioned tools and weapons of bone and ivory, clothing and boats from animal skins, and houses of whalebones and hides or blocks of sod or snow. Many of their rituals and songs celebrated the hunt and the spiritual connection between humans and the animals on which they depended.

Along the Northwest Coast and Columbia River Plateau, abundant resources supported one of the most densely populated areas of North America. With rivers teeming with salmon and other fish and forests full of game and edible plants, people prospered without resorting to farming. Among groups like the Kwakiutls and Chinooks, extended families lived in large communal houses located in villages of up to several hundred residents. Local rulers displayed their prominence most conspicuously during potlatches, or ceremonies in which they gave away or destroyed food and other possessions. Artisans used the region's plentiful wood supply to make many items, including distinctive religious masks and memorial poles carved with images of supernatural beings.

Farther south, in present-day California, hunter-gatherers lived in smaller villages, several of which might be led by the same chief. These settlements usually adjoined oak groves, where Indians gathered acorns. Preparing the nuts was time-consuming, for they had to be ground into meal, leached with water to remove bitter acid, and then cooked. To protect their access to this important food, chiefs and villagers vigorously defended their territorial claims to the oak groves. Elsewhere, in the foothills of the Sierras, Indians periodically set fire to thick underbrush to hasten the growth of new shoots that would attract deer and other game.

Small nomadic bands in the Great Basin, where the climate was warm and dry, lived in caves and rock shelters, surviving on the region's limited resources. Shoshone hunters captured antelope in corrals and trapped small game, such as squirrels and rabbits. In what is now Utah and western Colorado, Utes hunted elk, bison, and mountain sheep and fished in mountain streams. Women gathered pinyon nuts, seeds, and wild berries. In hard times, people ate rattlesnakes, horned toads, and insects. They celebrated whenever food was plentiful and urged religious leaders to seek supernatural help when starvation loomed.

Mesoamerica, the birthplace of agriculture in North America, extends from central Mexico into Central America. A series of complex, literate, urban cultures emerged in this region beginning around 1200 B.C. Among the earliest was that of the Olmecs, who flourished on Mexico's Gulf Coast from about 1200 to 400 B.C. The Olmecs and other early Mesoamerican peoples built cities featuring large pyramids, developed religious practices that included human sacrifice, and devised calendars and writing systems. Two of the most prominent Mesoamerican civilizations to follow the Olmecs were that of the Mayans in the Yucatán and Guatemala and that of Teotihuacán in central Mexico.

Mayan civilization reached its greatest glory between about A.D. 150 and 900 in the southern Yucatán, creating Mesoamerica's most advanced writing and calendrical systems and developing a sophisticated mathematics that included the concept of zero. The Mayans of the southern Yucatán suffered a decline after 900, but there were still many

Map 1-1 North American Culture Areas, c. 1500
Over the course of centuries, Indian peoples in North America developed distinctive cultures suited to the environments in which they lived. Inhabitants of each culture area shared basic patterns of subsistence, craft work, and social organization. Most, but not all, Indian peoples combined farming with hunting and gathering.

thriving Mayan centers in the northern Yucatán in 1492. The great city of Teotihuacán dominated central Mexico from the first century to the eighth century A.D. and influenced much of the rest of Mesoamerica through trade and conquest.

Some two hundred years after the fall of Teotihuacán, the Toltecs, a warrior people, rose to prominence, dominating central Mexico from about 900 to 1100. In the wake of the Toltec collapse, the Aztecs, another warrior people, migrated from the north into the Valley of Mexico and built a great empire that soon controlled much of Mesoamerica. The magnificent Aztec capital, Tenochtitlán, was a city of great plazas, broad avenues, magnificent temples and palaces, ball courts, and busy marketplaces. Built on islands in the middle of Lake Texcoco, it was connected to the mainland by four broad causeways. In 1492, Tenochtitlán was home to some 200,000 people, making it one of the largest cities in the world at the time.

The great pyramid in Tenochtitlán's principal temple complex was the center of Aztec religious life. Here Aztec priests sacrificed human victims—by cutting open their chests and removing their still-beating hearts—to offer to the gods. Human sacrifice had been part of Mesoamerican religion since the time of the Olmecs. People believed that such ceremonies pleased the gods and prevented them from destroying the earth. The Aztecs, however, practiced sacrifice on a much larger scale than ever before. Hundreds, even thousands, of victims died in ceremonies that sometimes lasted for days.

Aztec culture expanded through continuous military conquest, driven by a quest for sacrificial victims and for wealth in the form of tribute payments of gold, food, and handcrafted goods. But as the empire grew, it became increasingly vulnerable to internal division. Neighboring peoples hated the Aztecs and submitted to them out of fear. With a powerful ally to lead them, they would readily turn on their overlords and bring the empire down.

Native societies emerging north of Mexico shared certain characteristics with those of Mesoamerica. The introduction of a drought-resistant type of maize (probably from Mexico) into the desert Southwest in 400 B.C. enabled a series of cultures to develop. Beginning about 300 B.C., the Hohokams settled in southern Arizona, eventually building permanent villages of several hundred people. Harvests of beans, corn, and squash (sometimes two a year), watered by a complex system of canals, fed Hohokam villagers. In large communities, inhabitants built ball courts similar to those found in Mexico. Artisans wove cotton cloth and made goods reflecting Mesoamerican artistic styles out of shell, turquoise, and clay. Extensive trade networks linked the Hohokams to people living as far away as California and Mexico. Their culture endured for over a thousand years but had disappeared by 1450.

Beginning about A.D. 1, the Anasazis (their name is Navajo for "ancient alien ones") settled where the borders of present-day Colorado, Utah, Arizona, and New Mexico meet. They gradually adopted agriculture, first adding maize to a diet of wild foods and later beans and squash. Scarce rainfall, routed through dams and hillside terraces, watered the crops. Networks of roads carried people and goods between villages. Artisans crafted intricate baskets and distinctive black-on-white pottery for use and trade.

The Anasazis originally lived in villages built on mesas and canyon floors. These settlements included special rooms, or **kivas**, for religious ceremonies. The largest communal dwelling, Pueblo Bonito in New Mexico's Chaco Canyon, covered 3 acres and contained 650 to 800 rooms that housed about 1,200 people. Pueblo Bonito may have been the political and ceremonial center of Anasazi society from about 900 to 1100 A.D. After about 1200, the Anasazis began carving multistoried stone houses into steep canyon walls. These spectacular dwellings were not easy places in which to live. They could be reached only by difficult climbs up steep cliffs and along narrow ledges, and water, food, and other goods had to be carried to them. Archaeologists now think that warfare and climate change worked together to force the Anasazis into these precarious homes. Around 1200, the climate of the Southwest grew colder, making it more difficult to grow enough to feed the large Anasazi population. Food scarcity, in turn, may have set village against village and encouraged attacks by outsiders. The Anasazis, then, probably resorted to cliff dwellings for defensive purposes as violence spread in the region. But Anasazi culture was doomed. By 1300, survivors abandoned the cliff dwellings and dispersed into smaller villages along the Rio Grande.

The Pueblo peoples of the Southwest, including the Hopis and Zunis, are the descendants of the Anasazis. In 1492, many lived in large communal dwellings in permanent villages (*pueblo* is the Spanish word for "village"). Pueblo men did most of the farming, tilling irrigated fields of corn, beans, squash, and sunflowers. In their religious rituals, Pueblos directed prayers to the gods for enough rain for the all-important harvest.

The Great Plains of the continent's interior were much less densely settled than the desert Southwest. Scattered villages of Mandans, Pawnees, and other groups clung to tree-lined rivers. Women raised corn, squash, beans, and sunflowers and gathered wild plants for food and medicine. Men hunted bison, whose skin and bones were used for clothing, shelter, and tools. Plains Indians moved frequently, seeking more fertile land or better hunting. Wherever they went, they traded skins, food, and obsidian (a volcanic glass used for tools and weapons) with other native peoples.

The gradual spread of agriculture transformed native societies in the Eastern Woodlands, a vast territory extending from the Mississippi Valley to the Atlantic seaboard. Although the process began

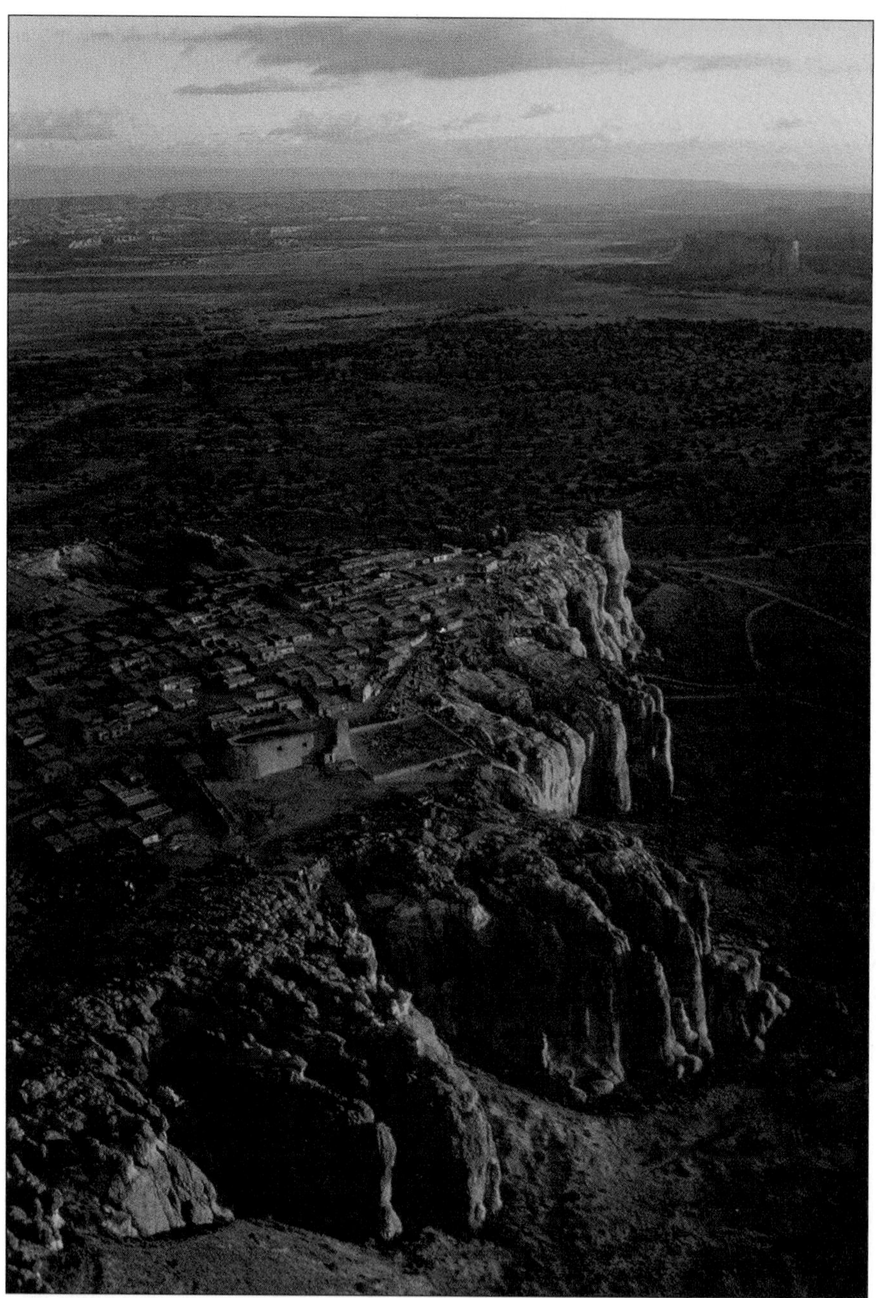

Acoma Pueblo has perched atop this 300-foot-tall mesa since the twelfth century. Now used mainly for ceremonial purposes, Acoma was once a thriving Anasazi village.

around 2500 B.C., farming was not firmly established until about A.D. 700. As agriculture spread, several "mound-building" societies—named for the large earthworks their members constructed—developed in the Ohio and Mississippi Valleys. The oldest flourished in Louisiana between 1500 and 700 B.C. The members of the Adena-Hopewell culture, which appeared in the Ohio Valley between 500 B.C. and A.D. 400, lived in small villages spread over a wide area. They built hundreds of mounds, often in the shapes of humans, birds, and serpents. Most were grave sites, where people were buried with valuable goods. Many burial objects were made from materials obtained through long-distance trade, including Wyoming obsidian, Lake Superior copper, and Florida conch shells.

The last mound-building culture, the Mississippian, emerged between 1000 and 1500 in the Mississippi Valley. Mississippian farmers raised enough maize, squash, and beans to support sizable populations and major urban centers. One of the largest of these was Cahokia, located near present-day St. Louis. By 1250, Cahokia had perhaps thirty thousand residents, making it about the same size as medieval London and the largest American city north of Mexico. Its central feature was a 100-foot-high mound, the world's largest earthwork.

Cahokia dominated the Mississippi Valley, but numerous other towns, some with hundreds or thousands of residents, dotted the Woodlands region, linked by extensive trade networks. In major towns, religious ceremonies were conducted in large temples built atop platform mounds. Powerful chiefs, thought to be related to the sun, ruled these communities. When a chief died, his wife and servants were killed in order to accompany him to the afterlife.

Mississippian culture began to decline in the thirteenth century. Food shortages and warfare drove people from the great cities into the countryside. Yet elements of the culture survived among dispersed Woodlands people, particularly methods of maize and bean agriculture. By 1492, Woodlands Indians lived part of the year in villages where women tilled lands that men had cleared. Twice a year, after crops were planted and again after the harvest, villagers separated into family groups and dispersed into the forest. Men went off to hunt, while women and children foraged for wild plants. Although the large cities of the Mississippian era had disappeared, Woodlands Indians maintained long-distance trade links throughout the region, with such precious goods as copper, shell beads, and pearls passing among groups.

Woodlands villages generally contained several extended families headed by a chief who inherited his position but ruled with the advice of a council of elders. In the North, Iroquois peoples took advantage of the demise of Cahokia to refocus trade and power in their own region, forming a confederation around 1450. The southern Woodlands region was more densely populated than the northern, largely because the warmer southern climate provided a longer growing season and more abundant wild foods. Traces of Mississippian culture lasted longer in the southern Woodlands as well. In 1492, Natchez Indians living along the lower Mississippi still erected buildings on low mounds in their towns.

This artist's rendering, based on archaeological evidence, suggests the size and magnificence of the Mississippian city of Cahokia. By the thirteenth century, it was as populous as medieval London, and served as a center of trade for the vast interior of North America.

The Caribbean islanders whom Columbus first encountered likewise descended from ancient cultures. Around 5000 B.C., mainland peoples began moving to the islands. Ancestors of the Tainos probably came from what is now Venezuela. The Guanahatabeys of western Cuba originated in Florida, and the Caribs of the easternmost islands moved from Brazil's Orinoco Valley. Surviving at first by hunting and gathering, island peoples began farming perhaps in the first century A.D. They raised manioc, sweet potatoes, maize, squash, beans, peppers, peanuts, and pineapple on clearings made in the tropical forests. Canoes carried trade goods throughout the Caribbean, as well as to Mesoamerica and coastal South America.

By 1492, as many as 4 million people may have inhabited the Caribbean islands. Powerful chiefs ruled over villages, conducted war and diplomacy, and controlled the distribution of food and other goods obtained as tribute from villagers. Island societies were divided into several ranks. An elite group aided the chief and supplied religious leaders. Below them were a large class of ordinary farmers and fishermen and a lower class of servants who worked for the elites. Elite islanders were easily recognized by their fine clothing, bright feather headdresses, and golden ear and nose ornaments—items that eventually attracted European visitors' attention.

Long before 1492, North America had witnessed centuries of dynamic change. Populations grew and spread across thousands of miles of territory. People adapted to many different environments, some of which tested their ability to survive. Farmers developed new varieties of essential food plants. Empires rose and fell. Large cities flourished and disappeared. People traded goods over vast distances. They formed alliances with trading partners and warred with groups who refused to trade. Because their histories have largely been preserved in oral traditions and archaeological evidence rather than written documents, they are less distinct, but no less real, than those of the Europeans whom they would soon meet.

Cultural Perceptions and Misperceptions

Indian and European societies had developed differently in isolation from one another. Misunderstandings inevitably arose when such dissimilar peoples encountered each other for the first time. Even simple transactions had unexpected results. When Columbus showed swords to the Tainos, for example, "they took them by the edge and through ignorance cut themselves" because they had never seen metal weapons. Similarly, French explorers choked when they tried to smoke unfamiliar Iroquois tobacco, which tasted, one of them reported, like "powdered pepper."

Many misunderstandings, however, had far graver consequences for the outcome of the encounter. Each group struggled to understand the strange behavior and customs of the other. Europeans usually decided that native practices were not just different from their own but inferior. Indians doubtless felt the same about European practices, but their opinions were rarely recorded.

Religious differences were the hardest to reconcile. Seeing no churches or recognizable religious practices among the Tainos, Columbus wrote, "I do not detect in them any religion." His comment revealed the influence of his own Christian background. Christian Europeans worshiped one God in an organized church led by trained priests. They preserved religious traditions in a written Bible. Most Indians, however, believed in a variety of gods. They considered nature itself to be sacred and understood certain beings, including plants, animals, and stars, to possess spiritual powers. Indians living north of Mexico preserved religious beliefs through oral traditions, not in writing. Their religious leaders performed ceremonies that mediated between the human and spiritual worlds. Europeans, however, thought that these men were magicians or even witches. They assumed that Indians worshiped the devil and insisted that they adopt Christianity. In the face of this demand, many native peoples doubtless shared the opinion voiced by some Iroquois: "We do not know that God, we have never seen him, we know not who he is."

Europeans also disapproved of the relative equality of men and women they observed among some Native American peoples. Reasoning from their own practices, Europeans assumed that men were naturally superior to women and should dominate them. But in North America, Europeans encountered female rulers among the Wampanoags and Powhatans and learned that among groups such as the Hurons, women helped select chiefs. They found that many Indian societies, including the Pueblos, Hurons, and Iroquois, were **matrilineal**; that is, they traced descent through the mother's family line instead of the father's, as Europeans did. In these matrilineal societies, newly married couples went to live with the wife's family. Children inherited property from their mother's brother, not their father. Rulers succeeded to their positions through their mother's family line.

In most Indian societies, men cleared the fields, but women planted and harvested the crops. Women also prepared food, cared for children, made clothing and baskets, carried burdens, and, in some regions, broke down, transported, and reassembled shelters when villages changed location. Europeans, who came from a society in which men did most agricultural work, thought that Indian women lived "a most slavish life." Misjudging the importance of Indian men's roles as hunters and warriors, Europeans scorned them as lazy husbands. Such confusion worked both ways, of course. Massachusetts Indians ridiculed English men "for spoiling good working creatures" because they did not send their wives into the fields.

Such misunderstandings fed tensions between Indians and Europeans in the centuries after 1492. But the ultimate source of conflict between them was the intention of the Europeans to dominate the lands they discovered. Encounters that often began in peace rarely ended that way. Columbus reported that at first the Tainos "became so much our friends that it was a marvel." Within three days of his arrival in America, however, he announced his intention "not to pass by any island of which I did not take possession" and soon speculated on the possibility of enslaving Indians. Native peoples everywhere challenged European claims to possession of their lands and resisted European attempts at domination.

West African Societies

Once Europeans learned of Columbus's feat, many followed his lead in exploring what they soon realized was not Asia after all. Yet in the three centuries after 1492, fully six out of seven people who crossed the Atlantic to the Americas were not Europeans but Africans, the vast majority of whom arrived as slaves. Most came from West Africa, and, like the inhabitants of North America or Europe, they belonged to many different ethnic groups, each with its own language and culture (see Map 1-2). The Wolof peoples of the Sudan differed from the Yorubas of the Guinea coast as much as the Iroquois did from the Pueblos or the English from the Spanish.

In 1492, Timbuktu, with a population of perhaps seventy thousand, was one of the greatest cities in West Africa. Located on the Niger River, the metropolis was the seat of the powerful Songhai empire. Sunni Ali ruled the empire with the support of a strong army and efficient bureaucrats. Timbuktu was a center of trade as well as government. A visitor in 1526 described its busy streets lined with "shops of artificers and merchants, and especially of such as weave linen and cotton cloth," and reported—with some exaggeration—that the inhabitants "are exceeding rich."

The Songhai empire was only the latest in a series of powerful states to develop in western Sudan, the vast plain lying south of the arid Sahara. One of the earliest, Ghana, rose to prominence in the eighth century and dominated West Africa for nearly three hundred years. Another, Mali, emerged

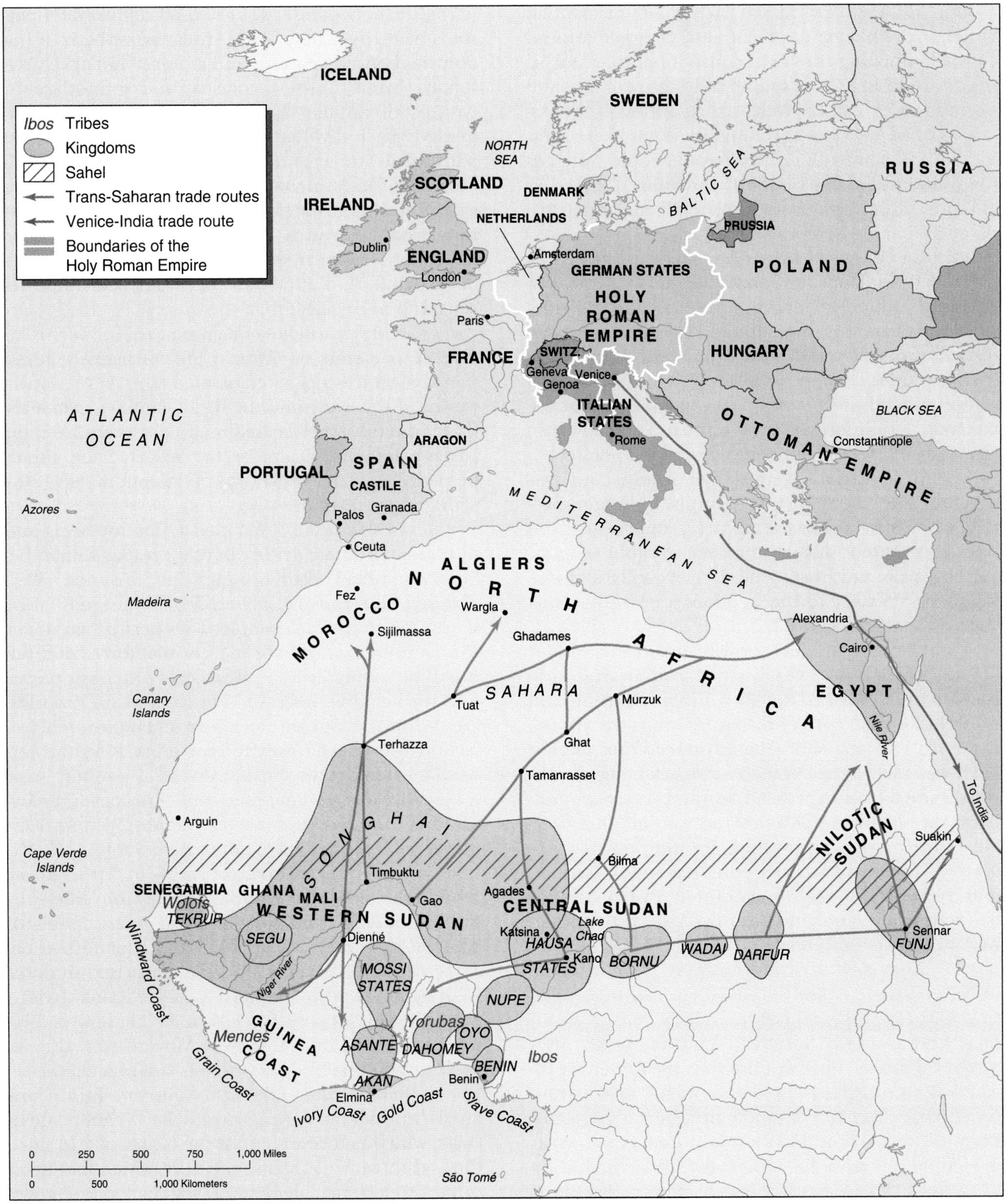

Map 1-2 West Africa and Europe in 1492
Before Columbus's voyage, Europeans knew little about the world beyond the Mediterranean basin and the coast of West Africa. Muslim merchants from North Africa largely controlled European traders' access to African gold and other materials.

around 1200 and fell in the early fifteenth century. Songhai, the largest and wealthiest, emerged around 1450, dominating the Sudan until it fell to a Moroccan invasion in 1591. Equivalently large empires did not appear in coastal West Africa, although the Asante, Dahomey, Oyo, and Bini kingdoms there grew to be quite powerful. Other coastal peoples, such as the Mendes and Ibos, were decentralized, living in autonomous villages where all adult males participated in making decisions.

Geographical as well as political differences marked the inland and coastal regions. In the vast grasslands of the Sudan, people raised cattle and cultivated millet and sorghum. In the 1500s, European visitors introduced varieties of Asian rice, which soon became another important crop. On the coast—where rain falls nearly every day—people grew yams, bananas, and various kinds of beans and peas in forest clearings. They also kept sheep, goats, and poultry.

West Africans were skilled artisans and particularly fine metalworkers. Smiths in Benin produced intricate bronze sculptures, and those from Asante designed distinctive miniature gold weights. West African smiths also used their skills to forge weapons, attesting to the frequent warfare between West African states.

Complex trade networks linked inland and coastal states, and long-distance commercial connections tied West Africa to southern Europe and the Middle East. For centuries, mines in the area of present-day Guinea and Mali produced tons of gold each year. West African merchants exchanged gold with traders from North Africa for salt, a commodity so rare in West Africa that it was sometimes literally worth its weight in gold. In addition to gold, North African merchants bought pepper, leather, and ivory. The wealth generated by this trans-Saharan trade contributed to the rise of the Songhai and earlier empires.

Most West Africans, however, were farmers, not merchants. A daily round of work, family duties, and worship defined their lives. West African men and women shared agricultural tasks. Men prepared fields for planting, while women cultivated the crops, harvested them, and dried grain for storage. Men also hunted and, in the grassland regions, herded cattle. Women in the coastal areas owned and cared for other livestock, including goats and sheep. West African women regularly traded goods, including the crops they grew, in local markets. In 1495, a Muslim African leader commented disapprovingly on the "free mixing of men and women in the markets and streets" in Timbuktu and other cities.

Family connections helped define each person's place in society. West Africans emphasized not only ties between parents and children but also those linking aunts, uncles, cousins, and grandparents. Groups of families formed clans that further extended an individual's kin ties. Most clans were **patrilineal**—tracing descent through the father's line—but some (including the Akans and Ibos) were matrilineal. Matrilineal practices did not necessarily raise women's status above that of men. But to a North African–born Muslim unfamiliar with matrilineal families, it appeared that women in them received "more respect than the men."

Religious beliefs magnified the powerful influence of family on African life. Africans believed that their ancestors acted as mediators between the worlds of the living and the dead. Families held elaborate funerals for deceased members to ensure their passage into the realm of the spirits. Such rituals helped keep the memory of ancestors alive for younger generations.

West Africans worshiped a supreme being and several subordinate deities. In other respects, their beliefs resembled Native American religions. West Africans, like Indians, believed that the gods often sent spirits to speak to people. They performed rituals to ensure the goodwill of the spiritual forces that suffused the natural world. Like Native American priests who mediated between the human and spirit worlds, West African medicine men and women provided protection against evil spirits and sorcerers. Religious ceremonies took place in sacred places—often near water—but not in buildings that Europeans recognized as churches. And like the Indians, West Africans preserved their faith through oral traditions.

Islam began to take root in West Africa around the eleventh century, probably introduced by Muslim traders from North Africa. By the fifteenth century, the cities of Timbuktu and Djenné had become centers of Islamic learning, attracting students from as far away as southern Europe. Some African rulers began keeping records in Arabic and enforcing Islamic law, but most West Africans probably retained traditional religious beliefs and practices.

Before the fifteenth century, Europeans knew little about Africa beyond its Mediterranean coast, which had been part of the Islamic world since the eighth century. Spain, much of which had been subject to Islamic rule before 1492, had stronger ties to North Africa than most of Europe. But Christian merchants from other European lands had also traded for centuries with Muslims in the North African ports. When stories of West African gold reached the ears of European traders, they tried to

Located in Djenné, Mali, this massive mosque, made of sun-hardened mud, dates from the fourteenth century. At that time, Djenné prospered as a center of trade and Islamic learning.

move deeper into the continent. But they encountered powerful Muslim merchants intent on monopolizing the gold trade.

The kingdom of Portugal, eager to expand its trade to support a spendthrift nobility, sought in the early fifteenth century to circumvent this Muslim monopoly. In 1415, Portuguese forces conquered Ceuta in Morocco and gained a foothold on the continent. Portuguese mariners gradually explored the West African coast, establishing trading posts along the way. Portuguese merchants exchanged horses, clothing, wine, lead, iron, and steel for African gold, grain, animal skins, cotton, pepper, and camels.

By the 1430s, the Portuguese had discovered perhaps the greatest source of wealth they could extract from Africa—slaves. Slavery had long been a part of West African society. African law made land available to anyone willing to cultivate it—provided that no one else was using the same plot—and the possession of a large labor force to work the land became the principal means to wealth. People became slaves in various ways. Some Africans lost their freedom as punishment for crime, but the majority of slaves were captured in war. Slave raids into neighboring territories were a regular feature of African life.

Slaves enriched their masters in a number of ways. Masters sold some slaves directly, tapping into a well-developed internal trade. Merchants from the Sahara frequently trekked to West Africa to exchange horses for slaves, and West Africans traded laborers among themselves. Most slaves worked at a variety of tasks for their owners. Many labored more or less independently as farmers, producing surplus crops for their masters. Some rulers acquired female slaves to serve as wives or concubines but also as workers. One Italian visitor to the small state of Warri reported in 1656 that its ruler had many slave wives who wove cloth for sale. Powerful Sudanese rulers employed large numbers of slaves as bureaucrats and soldiers, rewarding them for loyal service with good treatment and, occasionally, freedom.

Europeans who observed African slaves' relative freedom and variety of employment often concluded that slaves in Africa were "slaves in name only." Slavery in Africa was not necessarily a permanent status and did not automatically apply to the slaves' children. European purchasers of African slaves generally treated them much more harshly. Slavery for the unwilling African immigrants ensnared in it became even more oppressive as it developed in the Americas.

Western Europe on the Eve of Discovery

When Columbus sailed from Spain in 1492, he left a continent recovering from the devastating disease and warfare of the fourteenth century and about to embark on the devastating religious conflicts of the sixteenth. Between 1337 and 1453, England and France had exhausted each other in a series of conflicts known as the Hundred Years' War. And between 1347 and 1351, an epidemic known as the **Black Death** (probably the pneumonic form of bubonic plague) wreaked havoc on a European population already suffering from persistent malnutrition. Perhaps a third of all Europeans died, with results that were felt for more than a century.

The plague left Europe with far fewer workers than before, but the survivors learned to be more efficient. Farmers selected the most fertile land to till, and artisans adopted labor-saving techniques to increase productivity. Metalworkers, for instance, built larger furnaces with huge bellows driven by water power. Shipbuilders redesigned vessels with steering mechanisms that could be managed by smaller crews. Innovations in banking, accounting, and insurance also fostered economic recovery.

By 1500, Europe had a stronger, more productive economy than ever before, but not everyone prospered equally. In parts of England, France, Sweden, and the German states, peasants and workers rebelled against the propertied classes. These protests grew not from the workers' desperation but from a desire to protect their improving economic fortunes. They did not want to see their rising wages eaten up by higher rents and taxes.

In some parts of Europe, economic improvement encouraged an extraordinary cultural movement known as the **Renaissance**—a "rebirth" of interest in the classical civilizations of ancient Greece and Rome. The Renaissance originated in the city-states of Italy, where a prosperous and educated urban class promoted learning and artistic expression. Wealthy townspeople joined princes in becoming patrons of the arts, offering financial support to painters, sculptors, architects, writers, and musicians.

Renaissance culture gradually spread from the Italian cities to other regions. The daily lives of most Europeans, however, remained untouched by intellectual and artistic developments. Most Europeans were peasants, engaged in an annual round of agricultural labor. Within peasant families, men did most of the heavy field work, while women helped at planting and harvest time and cared for children, livestock, and the household. The economic recovery after the Black Death brought prosperity to some families, but the lives of many remained hard. Crop failures and disease often brought great suffering to villages and towns.

European states were hierarchical, with their populations divided into fairly rigid classes. Monarchs stood at the top of society. Just below were the aristocrats, who, along with the royal family, dominated government and owned most of the land, receiving rents and labor services from peasants and rural artisans. Next, in descending order, came prosperous gentry families, independent landowners, and, at the bottom, landless peasants and laborers.

European society was also **patriarchal**, with men dominating political and economic life. Europe's rulers were, with few exceptions, men, and men controlled the Catholic Church. Inheritance was patrilineal, and only men could own property. According to an ideal perhaps not always upheld, even the poorest man should be "as a king in his own house," ruling over his wife, children, and servants.

By the end of the fifteenth century, after more than a hundred years of incessant conflict, a measure of stability had returned to the countries about to embark on overseas expansion. Ferdinand and Isabella of Spain, Louis XI of France, and Henry VII of England successfully asserted royal authority over their previously fragmented realms, creating strong state bureaucracies to control political rivals. They gave special trading privileges to merchants to gain their support, creating links that would later prove important in financing overseas expeditions. At the same time, Spain and Portugal negotiated an end to a long-running dispute about the succession to the throne of Castile, one of Spain's largest kingdoms.

The consolidation of military power went hand in hand with the strengthening of political authority. Portugal developed a strong navy to defend its seaborne merchants. Louis XI of France commanded a standing army, and Ferdinand of Spain created a palace guard to use against potential opponents. Before overseas expansion began, European monarchs exerted military force to extend their authority closer to home. Louis XI and his successors used warfare and intermarriage with ruling families of nearby provinces to expand French influence. In the early sixteenth century, England's Henry VIII sent soldiers to conquer Ireland. And the Spain of 1492 was forged from the successful conclusion of the ***reconquista*** ("reconquest") of territory from Muslim control.

Muslim invaders from North Africa first entered Spain in 711 and ruled much of the Iberian peninsula (which includes Spain and Portugal) for centuries. Beginning in the mid-eleventh century, Christian armies embarked on a long effort to reclaim the region. By 1450, only the southern tip of Spain remained under Muslim control. After the marriage of Ferdinand of Aragon and Isabella of Castile in 1469 united Spain's two principal kingdoms, their combined forces completed the *reconquista*. Granada, the last Muslim stronghold, fell in 1492, shortly before Columbus set out on his first voyage.

Even as these rulers sought to unify their realms, religious conflicts began to tear Europe apart. For more than a thousand years, Catholic Christianity had united western Europeans in one faith. All Christians believed that God sent his only son, Jesus Christ, to suffer crucifixion, die, and rise from the dead in order to redeem humans from sin and give them eternal life. The Catholic Church built on this faith included an elaborate hierarchy of clergy, ranging upward from parish priests to bishops, archbishops, and cardinals, culminating in Christ's representative on earth, the pope. It also supported monastic orders whose members often lived and prayed apart from society.

By the sixteenth century, the Catholic Church had accumulated enormous wealth and power. The pope wielded influence not only as a spiritual leader but also as the political ruler of parts of Italy. The church owned considerable property throughout Europe. Many Christians, especially in northern Europe, began to criticize the worldliness of the popes and the church itself for corruption, abuse of power, and betrayal of the legacy of Christ.

In 1517, a German monk, Martin Luther, invited open debate on a set of propositions critical of church practices and doctrines. Luther believed that the church had become too insistent on the performance of good works, such as charitable donations or other actions intended to please God. He called for a return to what he understood to be the purer practices and beliefs of the early church, emphasizing that salvation came not by good deeds but only by faith in God. With the help of the newly invented printing press, his ideas spread widely, inspiring a challenge to the Catholic Church that became known as the **Reformation**.

Martin Luther (1483–1546), a German monk, sparked the Protestant Reformation with his criticisms of the worldliness of the Catholic Church. By the end of Luther's life, religious conflicts divided Europe as never before.

Lucas Cranach, Martin Luther (1483–1546). Oil on wood. The Granger Collection.

When the church refused to compromise, Luther and other critics withdrew to form their own religious organizations. Luther emphasized the direct, personal relationship of God to the individual believer. He urged people to take responsibility for their own spiritual growth by reading the Bible, which he translated for the first time into German. What started as a religious movement, however, quickly acquired an important political dimension.

Sixteenth-century Germany was a fragmented region of small kingdoms and principalities jealous of their independence. They were officially part of the **Holy Roman Empire**, but only loosely so, and many German princes resisted efforts by the Catholic empire to assert its authority. Realizing that religious protest reinforced their claims to independence, many princes supported Luther for both spiritual and secular reasons. When the Holy Roman Empire under Charles V (who was also king of Spain) tried to silence them, the reformist princes protested. From that point on, these princes—and all Europeans who supported religious reform—became known as "Protestants."

The Protestant movement took a more radical turn under the influence of the French reformer John Calvin, who emphasized the doctrine of **predestination**. Calvin maintained that an all-powerful and all-knowing God chose at the moment of creation which humans would be saved and which would be damned. Each person's fate is thus foreordained, or predestined, by God, although we cannot know our fate during our lifetimes. Good Calvinists struggled to behave as God's chosen, continually searching their souls for evidence of divine grace.

Calvin founded a religious community consistent with his principles at Geneva, a Swiss city-state near the French border. Men who claimed to be "saints," or God's chosen people, led the city's government. They drove out nonbelievers, subjected all citizens to a rigid discipline, and made Geneva the center of Protestant reform in Europe. But neither Lutherans nor Calvinists could contain the powerful Protestant impulse. In succeeding years, other groups formed, split, and split again, increasing Europe's religious fragmentation.

From Germany and Geneva the Protestant Reformation spread to France, the Netherlands, England, and Hungary. The new religious ideas particularly interested literate city-dwellers, such as merchants and skilled artisans, who were attracted to Protestant writings as well as the sermons of Protestant preachers. Peasants adopted the new ideas more slowly, although German peasants, claiming Luther as inspiration, staged an unsuccessful revolt against their masters in 1524. Luther disavowed them, however, and supported the German princes in their brutal suppression of the revolt.

The Reformation addressed spiritual needs that the Catholic Church had left unfulfilled, but it also fractured the religious unity of western Europe and spawned a century of warfare unprecedented in its bloody destructiveness. Protestants fought Catholics in France and the German states. Popes initiated a "Counter-Reformation" to strengthen the Catholic Church—in part by internal reform and in part by persecuting its opponents and reimposing religious conformity. Europe thus fragmented into warring camps just at the moment when Europeans were coming to terms with their discovery of America and seeking ways to exploit its wealth.

Contact

Religious fervor, political ambition, and the desire for wealth propelled European nations into overseas expansion as well as conflict at home. Portugal, Spain, France, and England competed to establish footholds on other continents in an intense scramble for riches and dominance. The success of these early endeavors was a reflection of Europe's prosperity and a series of technological breakthroughs that enabled its mariners to navigate beyond familiar waters.

By 1600, Spain had emerged as the apparent winner among the European competitors for New World dominance. Its astonishingly wealthy empire included vast territories in Central and South America. The conquerors of this empire attributed their success to their military superiority and God's approval of their imperial ambitions. In reality, it was the result of a complex set of interactions with native peoples as well as an unanticipated demographic catastrophe.

The Lure of Discovery

The potential rewards of overseas exploration captured the imaginations of a small but powerful segment of European society. Most people, busy making a living, cared little about distant lands. But certain princes and merchants anticipated spiritual and material benefits from voyages of discovery. The spiritual advantages included making new Christian converts and blocking Islam's expansion—a Christian goal that dated back to the eleventh-century Crusades against the Muslims in the Middle East and continued with the *reconquista*. On the material side, the voyages would contribute to Europe's prosperity by increasing trade.

Merchants especially sought access to Asian spices like pepper, cinnamon, ginger, and nutmeg that added interest to an otherwise monotonous diet and helped preserve certain foods. Wealthy Europeans paid handsomely for small quantities of spices, making it worthwhile to transport them great distances. But the overland spice trade—and the trade in other luxury goods such as silk and furs—spanned thousands of miles, involved many middlemen, and was controlled at key points by Muslim merchants. One critical center was Constantinople, the bastion of Christianity in the eastern Mediterranean. When it fell to the Ottomans—the Muslim rulers of Turkey—in 1453, Europeans feared that caravan routes to Asia would be disrupted. This encouraged merchants to turn westward and seek alternate routes.

The reorientation of European trade benefited western Italian cities such as Genoa as well as Portugal and Spain, whose ports gave access to the Mediterranean and the Atlantic Ocean. Mariners ventured farther into ocean waters, seeking direct access to the African gold trade and, eventually, a sea route around Africa to Asia. Had it not been for a set of technological developments that reduced the risks of ocean sailing, such lengthy voyages into unexplored areas would have been impossible.

Ocean voyages required sturdier ships than those that plied the Mediterranean. Because ocean-going mariners traveled beyond sight of coastal features, they also needed reliable navigational tools. In the early fifteenth century, Prince Henry of Portugal, excited by the idea of overseas discovery, sponsored the efforts of shipbuilders, mapmakers, and other workers to solve these practical problems.

By 1500, enterprising artisans had made several important advances. Iberian shipbuilders perfected the caravel, a ship whose narrow shape and steering rudder suited it for ocean travel. Ship designers combined square sails (good for speed) with triangular "lateen" sails, which increased maneuverability. Two Arab inventions—the magnetic compass and the astrolabe (which allowed mariners to determine their position in relation to a star's known location in the sky)—gained popularity among European navigators. As sailors acquired practical experience on the high seas, mapmakers recorded their observations of landfalls, wind patterns, and ocean currents.

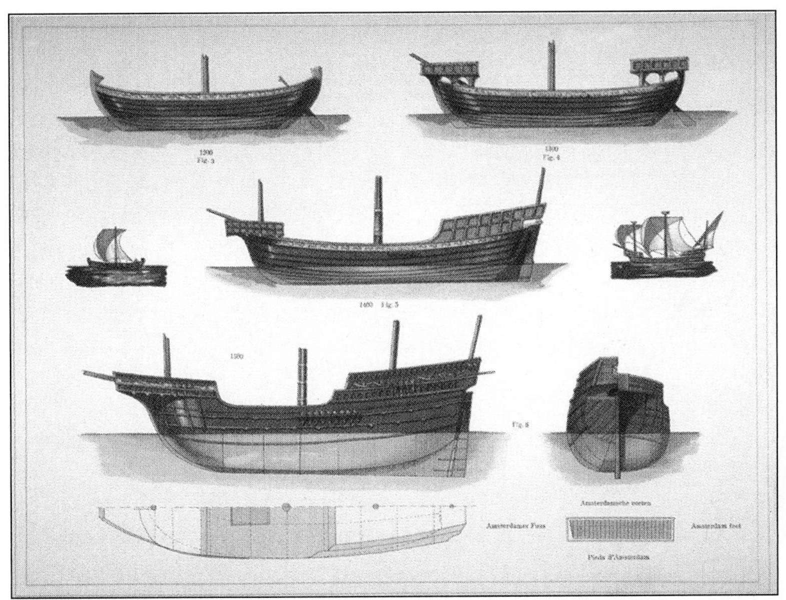

Before Europeans could safely navigate the Atlantic, they needed larger and more maneuverable ships. This drawing illustrates the evolution of sailing vessels from the late Middle Ages to the fifteenth century. Technological improvements included larger hulls, more masts, and new arrangements of sails.

After Portugal's conquest of the Moroccan city of Ceuta in 1415, its mariners slowly worked their way along Africa's western coast, establishing trading posts where they exchanged European goods for gold, ivory, and slaves (see Map 1-3). Bartolomeu Días reached the southern tip of Africa in 1488. Eleven years later, Vasco da Gama brought a Portuguese fleet around Africa to India, opening a sea route to Asia. These initiatives gave Portugal a virtual monopoly on Far Eastern trade for some time.

The new trade routes gave strategic importance to the islands that lie in the Atlantic off the west coast of Africa and Europe. Spain and Portugal vied for control of the Canary Islands, located 800 miles southwest of the Iberian peninsula. Spain eventually prevailed in 1496 by defeating the islands' inhabitants. Portugal acquired Madeira and the Cape Verde Islands, along with a set of tiny islands off Africa's Guinea Coast.

Sugar, like Asian spices, commanded high prices in Europe, so the conquerors of the Atlantic islands began to cultivate sugar cane on them, on large plantations worked by slave labor. In the Canaries, the Spanish first enslaved the native inhabitants. When disease and exhaustion reduced their numbers, the Spanish brought in African slaves, often purchased from Portuguese traders. On uninhabited islands, the Europeans imported African slaves from the start. São Tomé and the other small islands off the Guinea Coast eventually became important way stations in the transatlantic slave trade.

These island societies, in which a small European master class dominated a much larger population of native peoples or imported African slaves, were to provide a model for Spain's and Portugal's later exploitation of their American colonies. As early as 1494, Christopher Columbus wrote to Ferdinand and Isabella of Spain to suggest that Caribbean islanders could be sold as slaves in order to cover the costs of exploration. He found the inhabitants to be "a people very savage and suitable for the purpose, and well made and of very good intelligence." They "will be better than any other slaves," he went on, "and their inhumanity they will immediately lose when they are out of their own land."

Christopher Columbus

Columbus's proposal revealed him to be very much a man of his time. Born in Genoa in 1451, he later lived in Portugal and Spain and as a young man visited Africa's Guinea Coast and Madeira. He was thus thoroughly familiar with slavery and would have regarded the enslavement of Caribbean islanders as an extension of established practice.

Columbus was not the first European to believe that he could reach Asia by sailing westward. The idea developed logically during the fifteenth century as mariners gained knowledge and experience from their exploits in the Atlantic and around Africa. Columbus himself may have gained valuable experience on a voyage to Iceland. He also read widely in geographical treatises and paid close attention to the stories and rumors that circulated among mariners.

Most Europeans knew that the world was round, but most also scoffed at the idea of a westward voyage to Asia, believing that it would take so long that no ship could carry enough supplies. Columbus's confidence that he could make the voyage grew from a mathematical error. He mistakenly calculated the earth's circumference as 18,000 (rather than 24,000) miles and so concluded that Asia lay just 3,500 miles west of the Canary Islands. Columbus first sought financial support from the king of Portugal, whose advisers disputed his calculations and warned him that he would starve at sea before reaching Asia. Undaunted, he turned to Portugal's rival, Spain.

Columbus tried to convince Ferdinand and Isabella that his plan suited Spain's national goals. If he succeeded, Spain could grow rich from Asian trade, send Christian missionaries to Asia (a goal in

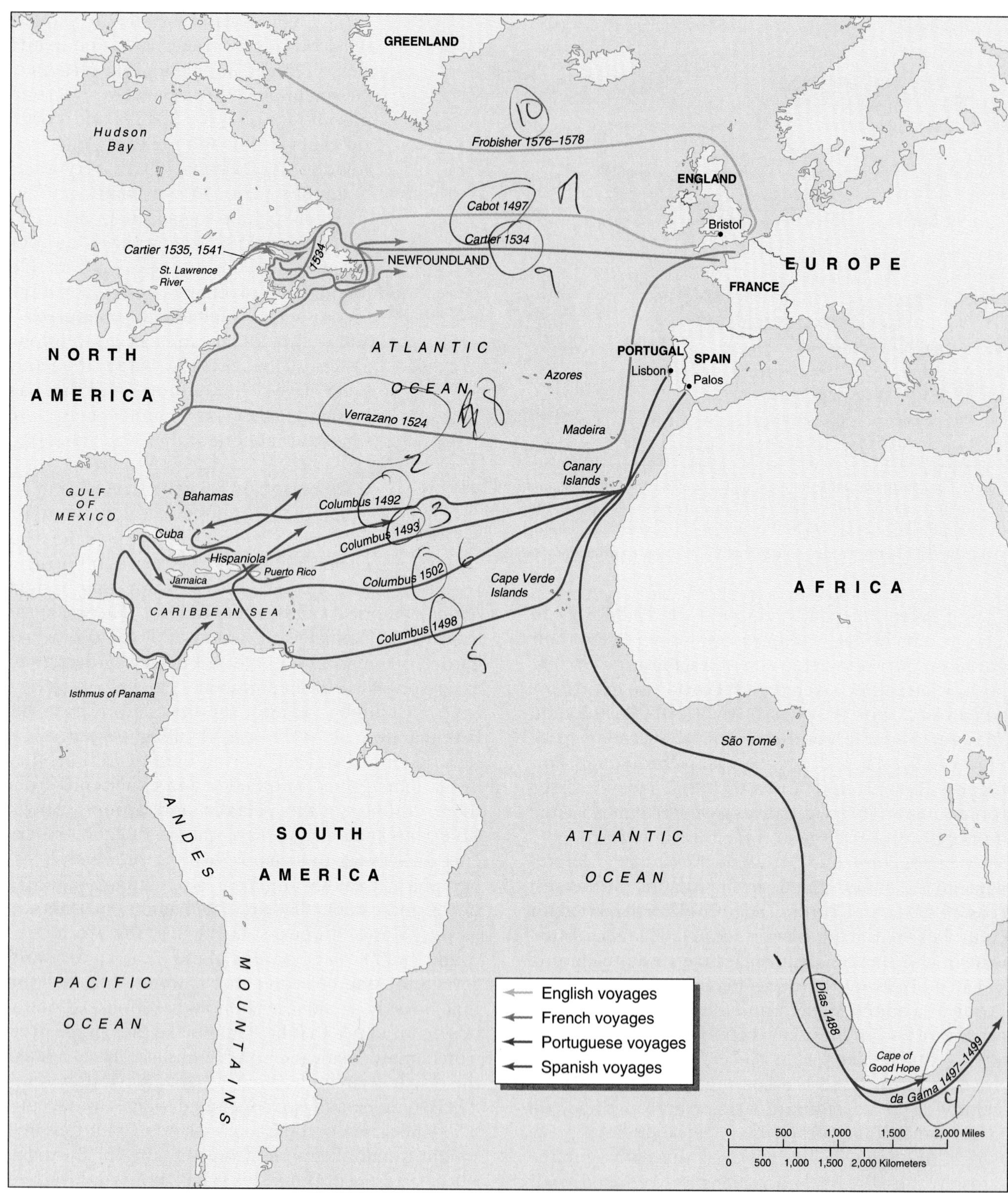

Map 1-3 European Voyages of Discovery in the Atlantic in the Fifteenth and Sixteenth Centuries

During the fifteenth and sixteenth centuries, Europeans embarked on voyages of discovery that carried them to both Asia and the Americas. Portugal dominated the ocean trade with Asia for most of this period. In the New World, reports of Spain's acquisition of vast wealth soon led France and England to attempt to establish their own territorial claims.

keeping with the religious ideals of the *reconquista*), and perhaps enlist the Great Khan of China as an ally in the long struggle with Islam. If he failed, the "enterprise of the Indies" would cost little. The Spanish monarchs nonetheless kept Columbus waiting nearly seven years—until 1492, when the last Muslim stronghold at Granada fell to Spanish forces—before they gave him their support.

After thirty-three days at sea, Columbus and his men reached the Bahamas. They spent four months exploring the Caribbean and visiting several islands, including Hispaniola (now the site of Haiti and the Dominican Republic) and Cuba. Although puzzled not to find the fabled cities of China or Japan, Columbus believed that he had reached Asia. Three more voyages, between 1493 and 1504, however, failed to yield clear evidence of an Asian landfall or samples of Asian riches. Columbus reported that the islands he encountered contained "great mines of gold and other metals" and spices in abundance, yet all he brought back to Isabella and Ferdinand were strange plants and animals, some gold ornaments, and several kidnapped Taino Indians.

Obsessed with the wealth he had promised himself and others, Columbus and his men turned violent, sacking the villages of Tainos and Caribs and demanding tribute in gold. But Caribbean gold reserves, found mainly on Hispaniola, Puerto Rico, and Cuba, were not extensive. The Spanish forced native gangs to pan rivers for the precious nuggets. Dissatisfied with the meager results, Columbus sought other sources of wealth. His plan to enslave islanders was a desperate attempt to show that the Indies could yield a profit. It earned him a sharp rebuke from Queen Isabella, who, at least initially, opposed enslaving people she considered to be new Spanish subjects. This royal fastidiousness was short-lived, however. Within thirty years of Columbus's first voyage, Spanish exploitation of native labor had brought the native populations of many Caribbean islands close to extinction.

Columbus died in Spain in 1506, still convinced he had found Asia. What he had done was to set in motion a process that would transform both sides of the Atlantic. It would eventually bring wealth to many Europeans and immense suffering to Native Americans and Africans.

Spanish Conquest and Colonization

Of all European nations, Spain was best suited to take advantage of Columbus's discovery. Its experience with the *reconquista* gave it both a religious justification for conquest (bringing Christianity to nonbelievers) and an army of seasoned soldiers—**conquistadores**—eager to seek their fortunes in America now that the last Muslims had been expelled from Spain. In addition, during the *reconquista* and the conquest of the Canary Islands, Spain's rulers had developed efficient techniques for controlling newly conquered lands that could be applied to New World colonies.

The Spanish first consolidated their control of the Caribbean, establishing outposts on Cuba, Puerto Rico, and Jamaica (see Map 1-4). The conquistadores were more interested in finding gold and slaves than in creating permanent settlements. Leaving a trail of destruction, they attacked native villages and killed or captured the inhabitants. By 1524, the Tainos had all but died out; the Caribs survived on more isolated islands until the eighteenth century. Spanish soldiers then ventured to the mainland. Juan Ponce de León led an expedition to Florida in 1513. In that same year, Vasco Núñez de Balboa arrived in Central America, crossing the isthmus of Panama to the Pacific Ocean.

In 1519, Hernán Cortés led a force of six hundred men to the coast of Mexico. "I and my companions," he declared, "suffer from a disease of the heart which can be cured only with gold." By 1521, Cortés and his men had conquered the powerful Aztec empire. The Spanish soldiers also discovered riches beyond their wildest dreams. They "picked up the gold and fingered it like monkeys," reported one Aztec witness. They were

First published in 1535, this woodcut shows Taino Indians panning for gold. Columbus and his men, desperate for riches to bring back to Spain but unaware that gold reserves on most Caribbean islands were quite small, compelled the Indians to search for the precious metal. After only a few decades of forced labor and harsh treatment, the native populations of the islands had all but disappeared.

FROM THEN TO NOW

The Columbus Quincentenary

In the early 1990s, Americans struggled over how to commemorate the upcoming quincentenary of Columbus's 1492 voyage to the New World. To celebrate the anniversary of the event that launched the "Age of Discovery," New York City arranged for an impressive display of tall ships sailing into its harbor. These plans, however, sparked a vigorous opposition. Critics urged a boycott of New York's festivities, fearing that they would encourage an "extravaganza of Nationalism, Patriotism, and self-congratulatory media messages reinforcing current-day Western mythology." They called for very different public observances, including a commemoration of five hundred years of Native American resistance to genocide and a symbolic "die-in" to coincide with the appearance of the tall ships in New York Harbor. This debate over whether the anniversary should be a cause for celebration or shame reverberated not just in New York but around the nation.

The issues at stake were at once political and moral and reflected late twentieth-century Americans' concern about the multicultural character of their society. Those who wished to celebrate Columbus's voyage as the achievement that opened the Americas to European settlement—and set in motion the long series of events that ultimately led to the establishment of the United States—placed transplanted Europeans at the center of the story. They also demonstrated faulty historical reasoning when they assumed that there was only one way that the story could have turned out. Their critics insisted on recognizing the other participants in the drama of contact between the Old World and the New, transforming it into a story of tragedy rather than triumph. While the consequences of Columbus's voyage may have been salutary for Europeans, they were disastrous for Native Americans and enslaved Africans. Any public observances, they believed, should consider the fates of all the peoples involved.

The quincentenary activities, in the end, included both celebration and serious reflection. The tall ships sailed into New York Harbor, cheered on by enormous crowds, while countless publications explored virtually every aspect—positive and negative—of the impact of Columbus's achievement. Americans agreed, for the most part, that the notion of the "discovery" of a "New World" did not adequately describe the significance of 1492. A new concept—"Columbian Encounter"—more accurately reflected the ongoing process of contact among peoples of several continents that began with Columbus's voyage. The notion of encounter provided a framework within which to understand the intertwined fates of Native Americans, African slaves, and European immigrants. It likewise provoked consideration of nonhuman transatlantic travelers—plants, animals, germs—and the dramatic ways in which they shaped history.

The debate over the Columbus Quincentenary reminded Americans that historical commemorations can be vexed affairs. Because they are public occasions, such observances invite citizens to grapple with the complexity of the past and to realize that no single perspective can illuminate experiences that affected different groups in different ways. In 1992, Americans confronted their concerns about their society's diversity and legacy of racism by debating the meaning of an event that had occurred five hundred years earlier. The result was contentious, to be sure, but reminded us that many peoples had shaped our history.

This late sixteenth-century print of Columbus's triumphant landing on Guanahani exhibits none of the ambiguity that now shapes our understanding of the meaning of his voyage. At the center are Columbus and his men, resplendent in European attire and armed with guns and metal swords. To the left, three Spaniards erect a cross to claim the land for Christianity. In the right foreground, nearly naked Indians offer gifts. Just above them we can see frightened natives running away.

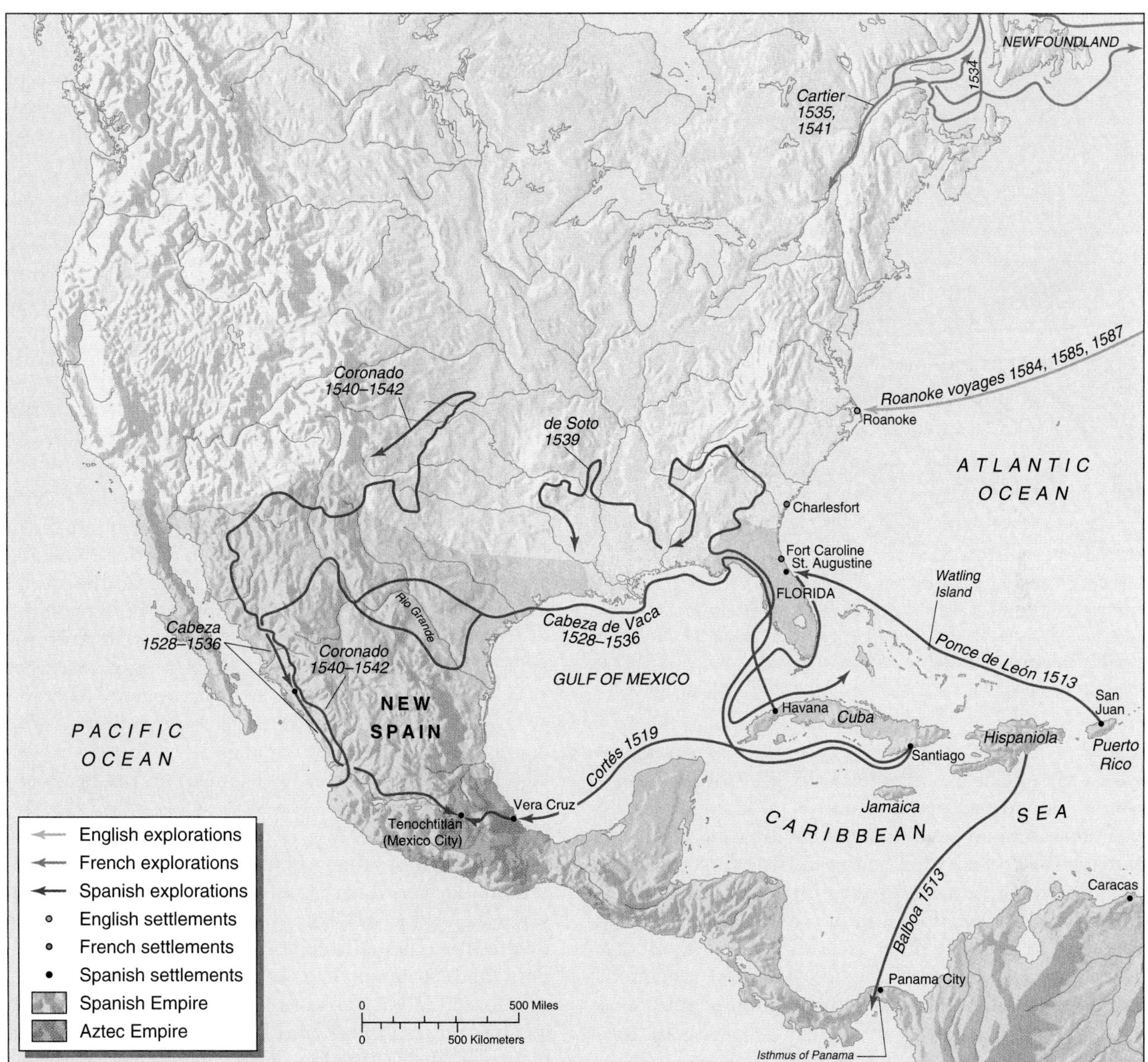

Map 1-4 Spanish, English, and French Settlements in North America in the Sixteenth Century
By the end of the sixteenth century, only Spain had established permanent settlements in North America. French outposts in Canada and at Fort Caroline, as well as the English settlement at Roanoke, failed to thrive. European rivalries for North America, however, would intensify after 1600.

"transported by joy, as if their hearts were illumined and made new."

The swift, decisive Spanish victory depended on several factors. In part, the Spanish enjoyed certain technological advantages. Their guns and horses often enabled them to overwhelm larger groups of Aztec foot soldiers armed with spears and wooden swords edged with obsidian. But technology alone cannot account for the conquest of a vastly more numerous enemy, capable of absorbing far higher losses in combat.

Cortés benefited from two other factors. First, he exploited divisions within the Aztec empire. The Spanish acquired indispensable allies among subject Indians who resented Aztec domination, tribute demands, and seizure of captives for religious sacrifice. Cortés led only six hundred Spanish soldiers but eventually gained 200,000 Indian allies eager to throw off Aztec rule.

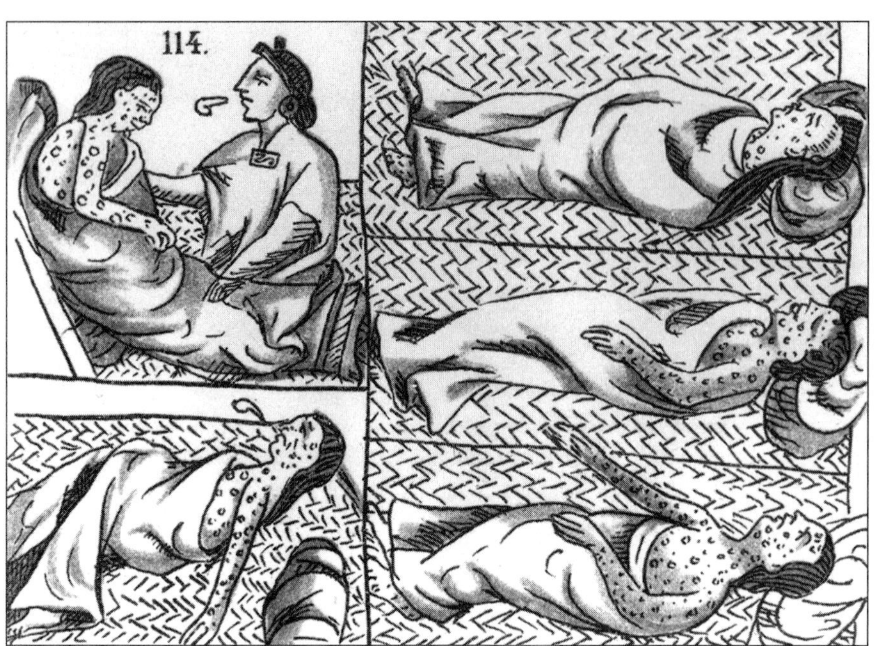

Smallpox wreaked havoc among Native Americans who lacked biological resistance to European diseases. This drawing by Aztec illustrators shows Aztec victims of a smallpox epidemic that struck Tenochtitlán in 1520. Historians estimate that up to 40 percent of the population of central Mexico died within a year. This catastrophic decline weakened the Aztecs' ability to resist the Spanish conquest of their land.

A second and more important factor was disease. One of Cortés's men was infected with smallpox, which soon devastated the native population. European diseases had been unknown in the Americas, and Indians lacked resistance to them. Historians estimate that nearly 40 percent of the inhabitants of central Mexico died of smallpox within a year. Other diseases followed, including typhus, measles, and influenza. By 1600, the population of Mexico may have declined from over 15 million to less than a million people.

Aztec society and culture collapsed in the face of appalling mortality. "The illness was so dreadful," one survivor recalled, "that no one could walk or move. The sick were so utterly helpless that they could only lie on their beds like corpses, unable to move their limbs or even their heads. . . . If they did move their bodies, they screamed with pain." The epidemic ravaged families, wiped out whole villages, and destroyed traditional political authority. Early in their bid to gain control of the Aztec empire, the Spanish seized Moctezuma, the Aztec king, and eventually put him to death. They did not have to kill his successor, however, for he died of disease less than three months after gaining the throne.

In 1532, Francisco Pizarro and 180 men, following rumors of even greater riches than those of Mexico, discovered the Inca empire high in the Peruvian Andes. The Spaniards arrived at a moment of weakness for the empire. A few years before, the Inca ruler had died, probably from smallpox, and civil war had broken out between two of his sons. The victor, Atahualpa, was on his way from the empire's northern provinces to claim his throne in Cuzco, the Inca capital, when Pizarro intercepted him. Pizarro took Atahualpa hostage and despite receiving a colossal ransom—a roomful of gold and silver—had him killed. The Spaniards then captured Cuzco, eventually extended control over the whole empire, and established a new capital at Lima.

By 1550, Spain's New World empire extended from the Caribbean through Mexico to Peru. It was administered from Spain by the Council of the Indies, which enacted laws for the empire and supervised an elaborate bureaucracy charged with their enforcement. The council aimed to project royal authority into every village in New Spain in order to maintain political control and extract as much wealth as possible from the land and its people.

For more than a century, Spanish ships crossed the Atlantic carrying seemingly limitless amounts of silver, gold, and jewels from the colonies. To extract this wealth, the colonial rulers subjected the native inhabitants of New Spain to compulsory tribute payments and forced labor. Tens of thousands of Indians toiled in silver mines in Peru and Bolivia and on sugar plantations in the Caribbean. When necessary, Spaniards imported African slaves to supplement a native labor force ravaged by disease and exhaustion.

The desire for gold eventually lured Spaniards farther into North America. In 1528, an expedition to Florida ended in disaster when the Spanish intruders provoked an attack by Apalachee Indians. Most of the Spanish survivors eventually perished, but Álvar Núñez Cabeza de Vaca and three other men (including an African slave) escaped from their captors and managed to reach Mexico after a grueling eight-year journey. In a published account of his ordeal, Cabeza de Vaca insisted that the interior of North America contained a fabulously wealthy empire (see "American Views: Cabeza de Vaca among the Indians" on page 24).

This report inspired other Spaniards to seek the treasures that had eluded its author. In 1539, Hernán de Soto—who tried unsuccessfully to get

Cabeza de Vaca to serve as a guide—led an expedition from Florida to the Mississippi River. Along the way, the Spaniards harassed native peoples, demanding provisions, burning villages, and capturing women to be servants and concubines. De Soto, who reportedly enjoyed "the sport of hunting Indians on horseback," ordered natives who resisted him to be mutilated, thrown to dogs, or burned alive. He and his men also exposed the Indians to deadly European diseases. Although weakened by native resistance, the expedition kept up its rampage for three years, turning toward Mexico only after de Soto died in 1542. In these same years, Francisco Vásquez de Coronado led three hundred troops on an equally destructive expedition through present-day Arizona, New Mexico, and Colorado on a futile search for the mythical Seven Cities of Cíbola, rumored to contain hoards of gold and precious stones.

The failure to find gold and silver halted the Spanish attempt to extend their empire to the north. By the end of the sixteenth century, they maintained just two precarious footholds north of Mexico. One was at St. Augustine, on Florida's Atlantic coast. Founded in 1565, this fortified outpost served as a naval base to defend Spanish treasure fleets from raids by English and French privateers. The other settlement was located far to the west in what is now New Mexico. Juan de Oñate, on a futile search for silver mines, claimed the region for Spain in 1598. He and his men then proceeded to antagonize the area's inhabitants. In one surprise attack, the Spaniards destroyed the ancient town at Acoma, killing or enslaving most of the residents. Having earned the enmity of the Pueblo people—astonishing even his own superiors with his brutality—Oñate barely managed to keep his tiny colony together.

Almost from the start of the conquest, the bloody tactics of men such as Oñate aroused protest back in Spain. The Indians' most eloquent advocate was Bartolomé de Las Casas, a Dominican priest shamed by his own role (as a layman) in the conquest of Hispaniola. In 1516, the Spanish king appointed him to the newly created office of Protector of the Indians, but his efforts had little effect. To publicize the horrors he saw, Las Casas wrote *In Defense of the Indians,* including graphic descriptions of native sufferings. Instead of eliciting Spanish reforms, however, his work inspired Protestant Europeans to create the "Black Legend," an exaggerated story according to which a fanatical Catholic Spain sought to spread its control at any cost.

Meanwhile, the vast riches of Central and South America glutted Spain's treasury. Between 1500 and 1650, an estimated 181 tons of gold and 16,000 tons of silver were shipped from the New World to Spain, making it the richest and most powerful state in Europe (see Figure 1-1). But this influx

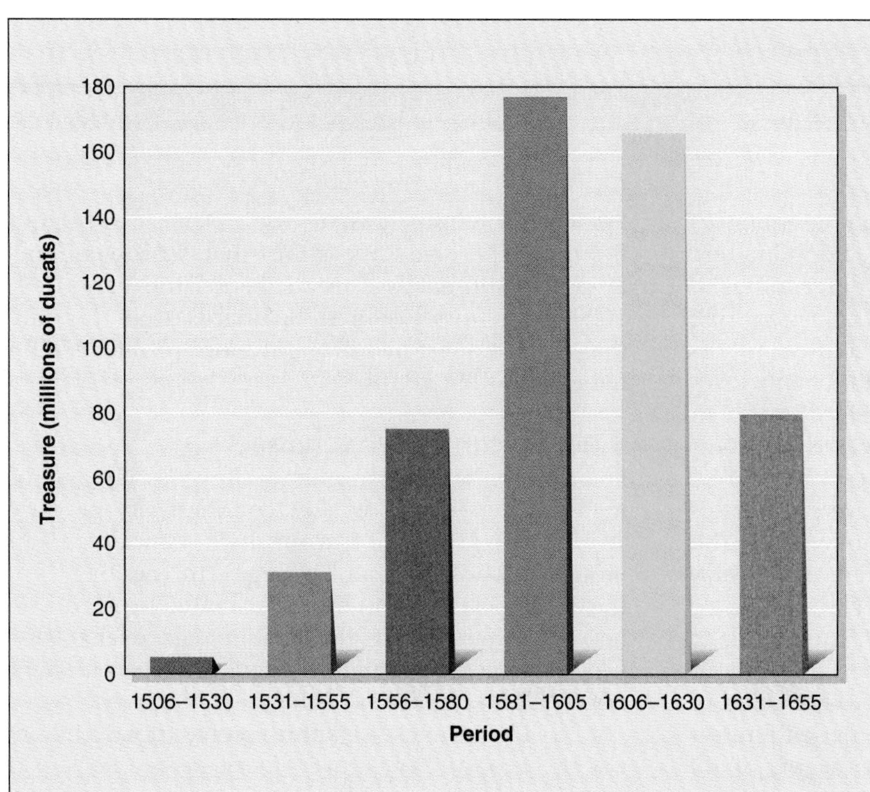

Figure 1-1 Value of New World Treasure Imported into Spain, 1506–1655

During the sixteenth and early seventeenth centuries, Spain was the only European power to reap great wealth from North America. The influx of New World treasure, however, slowed the development of Spain's economy in the long run. [Note: A ducat was a gold coin.]

Data Source: J. H. Elliott, Imperial Spain, 1469–1716 *(1964), p. 175.*

American Views

Cabeza de Vaca among the Indians (1530)

Alvar Nuñez Cabeza de Vaca came to the New World in 1527 in search of riches, not suffering. But the Spanish expedition of which he was a member met disaster shortly after it arrived in Florida on a mission to conquer the region north of the Gulf of Mexico. Of an original group of three hundred soldiers, only Cabeza de Vaca and three other men (including one African slave) survived. They did so by walking thousands of miles overland from the Gulf Coast to northern Mexico, an eight-year-long ordeal that tested the men's wits and physical endurance. Instead of entering Indian villages as proud conquistadors, Cabeza de Vaca and his companions encountered native peoples from a position of weakness. In order to survive, they had to adapt to the ways of the peoples across whose land they passed. After Cabeza de Vaca made it back to Mexico City, he described his experiences in an official report to the King of Spain. This remarkable document offers vivid descriptions of the territory extending from northern Florida to northern Mexico and the many peoples who inhabited it. It is equally interesting, as this extract suggests, for what it reveals about Cabeza de Vaca himself and the changes he made in the interest of survival.

❖ **While living among the Capoques, what sort of work did Cabeza de Vaca have to do, and why?**

❖ **Why did Cabeza de Vaca decide to become a merchant? What advantages did this way of life offer him?**

❖ **Why did the Indians welcome Cabeza de Vaca into their communities, even though he was a stranger?**

I had to stay with the Capoques more than a year. Because of the hard work they put me to, and their harsh treatment, I resolved to flee to the people of Charruco in the forests of the main. . . . My life had become unbearable. In addition to much other work, I had to grub roots

of American treasure had unforeseen consequences that would soon undermine Spanish predominance.

In 1492, the Spanish crown, determined to impose religious conformity after the *reconquista*, expelled from Spain all Jews who refused to become Christians. The refugees included many leading merchants who had contributed significantly to Spain's economy. The remaining Christian merchants, now awash in American riches, saw no reason to invest in new trade or productive enterprises that might have sustained the economy once the flow of New World treasure diminished. As a result, Spain's economy eventually stagnated.

Compounding the problem, the flood of American gold and silver inflated prices throughout Europe, hurting both workers, whose wages failed to rise as fast, and aristocrats, who were dependent on fixed rents from their estates. Most damaging of all, Spain's monarchs wasted their American wealth fighting expensive wars against their European enemies that ultimately only weakened the nation. By 1600, some disillusioned Spaniards were arguing that the conquest had brought more problems than benefits to their country.

The Columbian Exchange

Spain's long-term economic decline was just one of many consequences of the conquest of the New World. The arrival of Europeans in America set in motion a whole series of changes. In the long run, the biological consequences of contact—what one historian has called the **Columbian exchange**—proved to be the most momentous (see the summary table, "The Columbian Exchange").

The most catastrophic result of the exchange was the exposure of Native Americans to Old World in the water or from underground in the canebrakes. My fingers got so raw that if a straw touched them they would bleed. The broken canes often slashed my flesh; I had to work amidst them without benefit of clothes.

So I set to contriving how I might transfer to the forest-dwellers, who looked more propitious. My solution was to turn to trade.

[Escaping to Charruco about February 1530,] I did my best to devise ways of making my traffic profitable so I could get food and good treatment. The various Indians would beg me to go from one quarter to another for things they needed; their incessant hostilities made it impossible for them to travel cross-country or make many exchanges.

But as a neutral merchant I went into the interior as far as I pleased. . . . My principal wares were cones and other pieces of sea-snail, conchs used for cutting, sea-beads, and a fruit like a bean [from mesquite trees] which the Indians value very highly, using it for a medicine and for a ritual beverage in their dances and festivities. This is the sort of thing I carried inland. By barter I got and brought back to the coast skins, red ochre which they rub on their faces, hard canes for arrows, flint for arrowheads, with sinews and cement to attach them, and tassels of deer hair which they dye red.

This occupation suited me; I could travel where I wished, was not obliged to work, and was not a slave. Wherever I went, the Indians treated me honorably and gave me food, because they liked my commodities. They were glad to see me when I came and delighted to be brought what they wanted. I became well known; those who did not know me personally knew me by reputation and sought my acquaintance. This served my main purpose, which all the while was to determine an eventual road out.

Source: Cyclone Covey, ed., Cabeza de Vaca's Adventures in the Unknown Interior of America, *pp. 66–67.*

diseases. Europeans and Africans, long exposed to these diseases, had developed some immunity to them. Native Americans, never exposed to them, had not. The Black Death of 1347–1351, Europe's worst epidemic, killed perhaps a third of its population. Epidemics of smallpox, measles, typhus, and influenza struck Native Americans with far greater force, killing half, and sometimes as much as 90 percent, of the people in communities exposed to them. The only American disease to infect the Old World was syphilis, a serious but far less catastrophic malady, which appeared in Spain just after Columbus returned from his first voyage.

Another important aspect of the Columbian exchange was the introduction of Old World livestock to the New World, a process that began when Columbus brought horses, sheep, cattle, pigs, and goats with him on his second voyage in 1493. Native Americans had few domesticated animals (mainly dogs, and, in the Peruvian Andes, llamas and alpacas) and initially marveled at the large European beasts. The animals, however, created problems for native peoples. With few natural predators to limit their numbers, livestock populations boomed in the New World, competing with native mammals for good grazing. Moreover, the Indians' unfamiliarity with the use of horses in warfare often gave mounted European soldiers a decisive military advantage.

But for some native groups, the introduction of European livestock created opportunities. Yaquis, Pueblos, and other peoples in the American Southwest began to raise cattle and sheep. By the eighteenth century, Plains Indians had not only adopted horses but also become exceptionally skilled riders. The men found it much easier to hunt buffalo on

OVERVIEW

THE COLUMBIAN EXCHANGE

	From Old World to New World	From New World to Old World
Diseases	Smallpox, measles, plague, typhus, influenza, yellow fever, diphtheria, scarlet fever	Syphilis
Animals	Horses, cattle, pigs, sheep, goats, donkeys, mules, black rats, honeybees, cockroaches	Turkeys
Plants	Wheat, sugar, barley, coffee, rice, dandelion and other weeds	Maize, beans, peanut, potato, sweet potato, manioc, squash, papaya, guava, tomato, avocado, pineapple, chili pepper, cocoa

horseback than on foot, and the women valued horses as beasts of burden.

European ships carried unintentional passengers as well. The black rat, a carrier of disease, arrived on the first voyages. So did insects, including honeybees, previously unknown in the New World. Ships also brought weeds such as thistles and dandelions, whose seeds were often embedded in hay for animal fodder.

Europeans brought a variety of seeds and plants in order to grow familiar foods. Columbus's men planted wheat, chickpeas, melons, onions, and fruit trees on Caribbean islands. Although they optimistically reported that crops "sprouted in three days and were ready to eat by the twenty-fifth day," they—and later colonists—often found that European plants did not always fare well, at least not everywhere in the New World. As a result, Europeans learned to cultivate native foods, such as corn, tomatoes, squash, beans, and potatoes, as well as nonfood plants such as tobacco and cotton. They carried many of these plants back to Europe, enriching Old World diets with new foods. By the late seventeenth century, potatoes had become the mainstay of the Irish diet. And throughout Europe, new foods contributed to a sharp rise in population—which, in time, swelled the numbers of Europeans eager to leave their overcrowded communities for the New World.

Competition for a Continent

Spain's New World bonanza attracted the attention of other European states eager to share in the wealth. Portugal soon acquired its own profitable piece of South America. In 1494, the pope resolved the conflicting claims of Portugal and Spain with the **Treaty of Tordesillas.** The treaty drew a north–south line approximately 1,100 miles west of the Cape Verde Islands. Spain received all lands west of the line, while Portugal held sway to the east. This limited Portugal's New World empire to Brazil, where settlers followed the precedent of the Atlantic island colonies and established sugar plantations worked by slave labor. But the treaty also protected Portugal's claims in Africa and Asia, which lay east of the line.

France and England, of course, rejected the papal grant of the Western Hemisphere to Spain and Portugal. Their initial challenges to Spanish dominance in the New World, however, proved quite feeble. Domestic troubles—largely sparked by the Protestant Reformation—distracted the two countries from the pursuit of empire. By the close of the sixteenth century, both France and England insisted on their rights to New World lands, but neither had created a permanent settlement to support its claim.

Early French Efforts in North America

France was a relative latecomer to New World exploration. In 1494, French troops invaded Italy, beginning a long and ultimately unsuccessful war with the Holy Roman Empire. Preoccupied with European affairs, France's rulers paid little attention to America. But when news of Cortés's exploits in Mexico arrived in the 1520s, King Francis I wanted his own New World empire to enrich France and block further Spanish expansion.

In 1524, Francis sponsored a voyage by Giovanni da Verrazano, an Italian navigator, who mapped the North American coast from present-day South Carolina to Maine. During the 1530s and

1540s, the French mariner Jacques Cartier made three voyages in search of rich mines to rival those of Mexico and Peru. He explored the St. Lawrence River up to what is now Montreal, hoping to discover a water route through the continent to Asia (what came to be called the Northwest Passage). His second voyage, in 1535, nearly ended in disaster. Unaware of the harshness of Canadian winters, he and his crew almost froze to death and suffered from scurvy, a disease caused by a lack of vitamin C. Many men died, and the rest survived only because the Iroquois showed them how to make a vitamin-rich concoction of boiled white cedar needles and bark.

On his third voyage, in 1541, Cartier was to serve under the command of a nobleman, Jean-François de la Rocque, sieur de Roberval, who was commissioned by the king to establish a permanent settlement in Canada. Troubles in recruiting colonists delayed Roberval, who—when he finally set sail in 1542—ended up taking convicts as his settlers. Cartier sailed ahead, gathered samples of what he thought were gold and diamonds, and returned to France without Roberval's permission.

This first attempt to found a permanent French colony failed miserably. Roberval's expedition was poorly organized, and his cruel treatment of the convicts provoked several uprisings. The Iroquois, suspicious of repeated French intrusions on their lands, saw no reason to help them. A year after they arrived in Canada, Roberval and the surviving colonists were back in France. Their return coincided with news that the gold brought back by Cartier was iron pyrite ("fool's gold") and the diamonds were worthless quartz crystals.

Disappointed with their Canadian expeditions, the French made a few brief forays to the south, establishing outposts in what is now South Carolina in 1562 and Florida in 1564. They soon abandoned the Carolina colony (though not before the starving settlers resorted to cannibalism), and Spanish forces captured the Florida fort. Then, back in France, a prolonged civil war broke out between Catholics and Protestants. Renewed interest in colonization would have to await the return of peace at home.

English Attempts in the New World

The English were quicker than the French to stake a claim to the New World but no more successful at colonization. In 1497, King Henry VII sent John Cabot, an Italian mariner, to explore eastern Canada on England's behalf. But neither Henry nor his wealthier subjects would invest the funds necessary to follow up on Cabot's discoveries. For nearly half a century, English contact with America was limited to the seasonal voyages of fishermen who lived each summer in Newfoundland, fished offshore, and returned in autumn with ships full of cod.

The lapse in English activity in the New World stemmed from religious troubles at home. Between 1534 and 1558, England changed its official religion several times. King Henry VIII, who had once defended the Catholic Church against its critics, took up the Protestant cause when the pope refused to annul his marriage to Catherine of Aragon. In 1534, Henry declared himself the head of a separate Church of England and seized the Catholic Church's English property. Because many English people sympathized with the Protestant cause, there was relatively little opposition to Henry's actions. But in 1553, Mary—daughter of the spurned Catherine of Aragon—became queen and tried to bring England back to Catholicism. She had nearly three hundred Protestants burned at the stake for their beliefs (earning her the nickname "Bloody Mary"), and many others went into exile in Europe.

After Mary's brief but destructive reign, which ended with her death in 1558, her half-sister Elizabeth, a committed Protestant, became queen. Elizabeth ruled for forty-five years (1558–1603), restoring Protestantism as the state religion, bringing stability to the nation, and renewing England's interest in the New World. She and her subjects saw colonization not only as a way to gain wealth and political advantage but also as a Protestant crusade against Catholic domination.

England's first target for colonization, however, was not America but Ireland. Located less than 60 miles west of England and populated by Catholics, Ireland threatened to become a base from which Spain or another Catholic power might invade England. Henry VIII had tried, with limited success, to bring the island under English control in the 1530s and 1540s. Elizabeth renewed the attempt in the 1560s with a series of brutal expeditions that destroyed Irish villages and slaughtered the inhabitants. Several veterans of these campaigns later took part in New World colonization and drew on their Irish experience for guidance.

Two aspects of that experience were particularly important. First, the English transferred their assumptions about Irish "savages" to Native Americans. Englishmen in America frequently observed similarities between Indians and the Irish. "When they [the Indians] have their apparel on they look like Irish," noted one Englishman. "The natives of New England," he added, "are accustomed to build their houses much like the wild Irish." Because the English held the "wild Irish" in contempt, these observations encouraged them to scorn the Indians. When Indians resisted their attempts at conquest, the English recalled the Irish example, claiming that native "savagery" required brutal suppression.

Second, the Irish experience influenced English ideas about colonial settlement. English conquerors set up "plantations" surrounded by palisades on seized Irish lands. These plantations were meant to be civilized outposts in a savage land. Their aristocratic owners imported Protestant tenants from England and Scotland to farm the land. Native Irish people, considered too wild to join proper Christian communities, were excluded. English colonists in America followed this precedent when they established plantations that separated English and native peoples.

Sir Humphrey Gilbert, a notoriously cruel veteran of the Irish campaigns, became fascinated with the idea of New World colonization. He composed a treatise to convince Queen Elizabeth to support such an endeavor. The queen, who counted Gilbert among her favorite courtiers, authorized several exploratory voyages, including Martin Frobisher's three trips in 1576–1578 in search of the Northwest Passage to Asia. Frobisher failed to find the elusive passage and sent back shiploads of glittering ore that proved to be fool's gold. Elizabeth had better luck in allowing privateers, such as John Hawkins and Francis Drake, to raid Spanish ships and New World ports for gold and silver. The plunder taken during these raids enriched both the sailors and their investors—one of whom was the queen herself.

Meanwhile, Gilbert continued to promote New World settlement, arguing that it would increase England's trade and provide a place for the nation's unemployed people. Like many of his contemporaries, Gilbert believed that England's "surplus" population threatened social order. The population was indeed growing, and economic changes often made it difficult for people to support themselves. Many landlords, for instance, had been converting farmland into sheep pastures. They hoped to profit from the wool trade, but their decision threw tenant families off the land. Gilbert suggested offering free land in America to English families willing to emigrate.

In 1578, Gilbert received permission to set up a colony along the North American coast. It took him five years to organize an expedition to Newfoundland, which he claimed for England. After sailing southward seeking a more favorable site for a colony, Gilbert headed home, only to be lost at sea during an Atlantic storm. The impetus for English colonization did not die with him, however, for his half-brother, Sir Walter Raleigh (another veteran of the Irish wars), immediately took up the cause.

In 1584, Raleigh sent an expedition to find a suitable location for a colony. Learning that the Carolina coast seemed promising, Raleigh sent men in 1585 to build a settlement on Roanoke Island. Most colonists were soldiers fresh from Ireland who refused to grow their own food, insisting that the Roanoke Indians should feed them. When the local chief, Wingina, organized native resistance, they killed him. Eventually, the colonists, disappointed not to have found gold or precious stones and exhausted by a harsh winter, returned to England in 1586.

Two members of these early expeditions, however, left a more positive legacy. Thomas Hariot studied the Roanoke and Croatoan Indians and identified plants and animals in the area, hoping that some might prove to be profitable commodities. John White drew maps and painted a series of watercolors depicting the natives and the coastal landscape. When Raleigh tried once more, in 1587, to found a colony, he chose White to be its leader.

This attempt also failed. The ship captain dumped the settlers—who, for the first time, included women and children—on Roanoke Island so that he could pursue Spanish treasure ships. White waited until his granddaughter, Virginia Dare (the first English child born in America), was safely born and then sailed to England for supplies. But the outbreak of war with Spain delayed his return for three years. Spain had gathered an immense fleet to invade England, and all English ships were needed for defense. Although England defeated the Armada in 1588, White could not obtain a relief ship for Roanoke until 1590.

White found the colony deserted. Digging through the ruins of the village, he found "my books torn from the covers, the frames of some of my pictures and Maps rotten and spoiled with rain." He also saw the word CROATOAN carved on a post and assumed that the colonists had moved to nearby Croatoan Island. But bad weather prevented him from searching there. For years, English and Spanish mariners reported seeing white people along the coast of Chesapeake Bay. But no Roanoke colonists were ever found. They may have moved to the mainland and intermarried with local Indians. One historian has speculated that they survived until 1607 when Powhatan Indians, angered by the appearance of more English settlers, killed them. The actual fate of the "Lost Colony" at Roanoke will probably never be known.

At this point, Raleigh gave up on North America and turned his attention to his Irish plantations. But England's interest in colonization did not wane. In 1584, Richard Hakluyt had aroused enthusiasm for America by writing the "Discourse of Western Planting" for the queen and her advisers. He

Algonquian Indian village of Pomeiooc, North Carolina: Watercolor, c. 1585 by John White.

John White's picture of the village of Pomeiooc offers a rare glimpse of a sixteenth-century Eastern Woodlands Indian community. The village is surrounded by a palisade with two entrances; evidence suggests that White exaggerated the spacing of the poles in order to depict the houses inside. Eighteen dwellings constructed of poles and mats are clustered around the village circumference; inside some of them raised sleeping platforms can be seen. Many of the villagers are clustered around a central fire, while others are working or conversing.

argued that England would prosper from the expansion of trade and the sale of New World commodities. Once the Indians were civilized, Hakluyt added, they would eagerly purchase English goods. Equally important, England could plant "sincere religion" (that is, Protestant Christianity) in the New World and prevent the power of "the Spanish king from flowing over all the face . . . of America."

Hakluyt's arguments fired the imaginations of many people, and the defeat of the Spanish Armada only emboldened England to challenge Spain's New World dominance. The experience of Roanoke should have tempered that enthusiasm, illustrating the problems as well as benefits of colonization. The colony's fate underscored the need for adequate funding, the unsuitability of soldiers as colonists, and the need to maintain good relations with the Indians. But the English were slow to learn these lessons; when they resumed colonization efforts in 1607, they repeated Roanoke's mistakes, with disastrous results for the people involved. As it was, the sixteenth century ended with no permanent English settlement in the New World.

Conclusion

Dramatic changes occurred in North America during the century after Columbus's first voyage. Europeans, eager for wealth and power, came by the thousands to a continent that just a hundred years earlier they had not dreamed existed. Africans came in even greater numbers to the Caribbean, Mexico, and Brazil, forced to labor for white masters in unfamiliar lands. In many parts of the Americas, native peoples encountered white and black strangers whose presence disturbed—and sometimes destroyed—their accustomed ways of life.

And yet conditions in North America in 1600 bore clearer witness to the past than to the future. Only Spain had established North American colonies, and its New World dominance seemed secure. And even Spain had struggled to expand north of Mexico. Its outposts in Florida and New Mexico staked claims to territory that Spain did not really control. Virtually the entire continent north of the Rio Grande remained firmly in Indian hands. Except in Mexico and the Caribbean, Europeans had merely touched the continent's shores—often only briefly. When natives and newcomers met, the encounter was often disastrous for the Indians, who died in great numbers from European diseases and warfare. Even so, in 1600, native peoples (even in Mexico) still greatly outnumbered European and African immigrants. The next century, however, brought powerful challenges both to native control and to the Spanish monopoly of settlement.

Review Questions

1. Compare men's and women's roles in Native American, West African, and European societies. What were the similarities and differences? How did differences between European and Native American gender roles lead to misunderstandings?
2. Many of the first European colonizers in North America were military veterans. What impact did this have on their relations with Indian peoples?
3. Why did Spain so quickly become the dominant colonial power in North America? What advantages did it enjoy over France and England?
4. What role did religion play in early European efforts at overseas colonization? Did religious factors always encourage colonization, or did they occasionally interfere with European expansion?

Recommended Reading

Covey, Cyclone, ed., *Cabeza de Vaca's Adventures in the Unknown Interior of America* (1998). A remarkable account of the Spanish explorer's harrowing eight-year-long journey from Florida to Mexico.

Hassig, Ross. *Mexico and the Spanish Conquest* (1994). A brief account of Cortés's expedition, focusing on the military aspects of the Spanish conquest.

Josephy, Alvin M., Jr. *America in 1492: The World of the Indian Peoples before the Arrival of Columbus* (1991). A collection of essays describing the wide variety of Indian cultures in North America prior to contact with Europeans.

Leon-Portillo, Miguel. *The Broken Spears: The Aztec Account of the Conquest of Mexico* (1962). Reprints of translated Indian chronicles, providing a moving account of the Aztec experience of the Spanish conquest.

Phillips, William D., Jr., and Phillips, Carla Rahn. *The Worlds of Christopher Columbus* (1992). A judicious biography of Columbus that places him firmly in the context of fifteenth-century European culture.

Thornton, John. *Africa and Africans in the Making of the Atlantic World, 1400–1680* (1992). A thorough examination of the causes and consequences of the movement of Africans throughout the Atlantic world and the rise of the slave trade.

Additional Sources

Native American Cultures

Bragdon, Kathleen J. *Native People of Southern New England, 1500–1650* (1996).

Clendinnen, Inga. *Aztecs: An Interpretation* (1991).

Fagan, Brian M. *The Great Journey: The Peopling of Ancient America* (1987).

Fiedel, Stuart J. *Prehistory of the Americas,* 2d ed. (1992).

Jennings, Francis. *The Founders of America: How Indians Discovered the Land, Pioneered in It, and Created Great Classical Civilizations . . .* (1993).

Milner, George. *The Cahokia Chiefdom: The Archaeology of a Mississippian Society.* (1998).

Rouse, Irving. *The Tainos: Rise and Decline of the People Who Greeted Columbus* (1992).

West African Society

Bohannan, Paul, and Curtin, Philip. *Africa and Africans,* 3d ed. (1988).

Fage, J. D. *A History of West Africa: An Introductory Survey,* 4th ed. (1969).

Olaniyan, Richard, ed. *African History and Culture* (1982).

Europe in the Age of Discovery

Bainton, Roland H. *Here I Stand: A Life of Martin Luther* (1955).

Braudel, Fernand. *The Mediterranean and the Mediterranean World in the Age of Philip II,* 2d ed. (1966; English trans., 1972).

Burckhardt, Jacob. *The Civilization of the Renaissance in Italy* (1958).

Canny, Nicholas. *The Elizabethan Conquest of Ireland: A Pattern Established, 1565–76* (1976).

Cipolla, Carlo M. *Before the Industrial Revolution: European Society and Economy, 1100–1700* (1976).

Cipolla, Carlo M. *Guns, Sails, and Empire: Technological Innovation and the Early Phases of European Expansion, 1400–1700* (1965).

Elliott, J. H. *Imperial Spain, 1469–1716* (1964).

Lewis, Bernard. *Cultures in Conflict: Christians, Muslims, and Jews in the Age of Discovery* (1995).

Morison, Samuel Eliot. *The European Discovery of America: The Northern Voyages, A.D. 500–1600* (1971).

Morison, Samuel Eliot. *The European Discovery of America: The Southern Voyages, A.D. 1492–1616* (1974).

Scammell, G. V. *The First Imperial Age: European Overseas Expansion, c. 1400–1715* (1989).

Conquest and Colonization

Andrews, Kenneth R. *Trade, Plunder, and Settlement: Maritime Enterprise and the Genesis of the British Empire, 1480–1630* (1984).

Crosby, Alfred W., Jr. *The Columbian Exchange: Biological and Cultural Consequences of 1492* (1972).

Eccles, W. J. *France in America,* rev. ed. (1990).

Elliott, J. H. *The Old World and the New, 1492–1650* (1970).

Kupperman, Karen Ordahl. *Roanoke: The Abandoned Colony* (1984).

Meinig, D. W. *The Shaping of America, Vol. 1: Atlantic America, 1492–1800* (1986).

Seed, Patricia. *Ceremonies of Possession in Europe's Conquest of the New World 1492–1640* (1995).

Weber, David J. *The Spanish Frontier in North America* (1992).

Where to Learn More

❖ **Chillicothe, Ohio.** The Mound City Group National Monument. This site preserves a prehistoric Indian burial site. The holdings in the museum include excavated grave goods from burial mounds dating from 200 B.C. to A.D. 500. There is also a library with research materials on prehistoric Native American culture.

❖ **Washington, Connecticut.** American Indian Archaeological Institute. With both a museum and library materials, the institute preserves artifacts of Eastern Woodlands Indians and has a special collection of Algonquin baskets.

❖ **Acoma Pueblo, New Mexico.** This adobe pueblo, built on a 350-foot-high mesa, is the site of early contact between Pueblo Indians and Spanish soldiers and contains San Estevan del Rey Mission, built 1629–1642. The site is mainly used for ceremonial purposes, and travelers should obtain permission before visiting.

❖ **St. Augustine, Florida.** Founded in 1565, St. Augustine is the site of the first permanent Spanish settlement in North America. Today the restored community resembles a Spanish colonial town, with narrow, winding streets and seventeenth- and eighteenth-century buildings. The site also contains the restored Castillo de San Marcos, now a national park. The Historic St. Augustine Preservation Board owns and administers several historic house museums and offers programs in living history and craft exhibits.

TRANSPLANTATION, 1600–1685

2

Chapter Outline

The French in North America
The Development of New France
The Fur Trade

English Settlement in the Chesapeake
The Ordeal of Early Virginia
Tobacco Colony
Maryland

The Founding of New England
The Pilgrims and Plymouth Colony
Massachusetts Bay Colony and Its Offshoots
The Growth of New England

The English in the Caribbean
Sugar and Slaves
A Biracial Society

The Proprietary Colonies
Early Carolina
Pennsylvania
New Netherlands Becomes New York

Conclusion

Key Topics

- ❖ Development of New France
- ❖ Diversity of English colonies in the seventeenth century
- ❖ Growth of staple crop economies in the southern and Caribbean colonies
- ❖ Role of religion in the founding of colonies
- ❖ Creation of biracial slave societies in the West Indies and Carolina

Captain John Smith wrote his brief book, *A Description of New England,* under difficult circumstances. It was the summer of 1615, and he was being held captive aboard a French pirate ship. Smith had left England with a crew of thirty sailors, bound for the northeast coast of North America, where they planned to set up a colony. They had not gone far before being seized by the pirates, who justified their action by accusing Smith of participating in an earlier English raid on a French settlement in Maine. When Smith boarded the pirate ship to bargain for their release, his crew escaped, leaving the captain stranded. With little else to occupy him during months of captivity, Smith composed his book promoting colonization of the region he named "New England" as a challenge to rival colonies in New Spain and New France.

Smith made it back to England in 1616 and published his book. By then, England and France had joined Spain as founders of New World colonies. Smith's work (no less than his experience with the pirates) testified to the intensifying rivalry among European nations for control of North America. His book emphasized the vast wealth of Spain's empire and scolded Protestant Englishmen for allowing Spanish Catholics to spread their faith among the natives. The Spanish king, Smith declared, scarcely knew "one halfe Quarter of those Territories" he claimed, and so the English "neede not greatly feare his furie" if they created their own settlements.

John Smith's name is usually associated with the founding of Virginia, England's first permanent colony in North America, in 1607. After a brief stint as Virginia's leader, Smith was ousted in 1609 by disgruntled colonists. Back in England, he developed a plan to set up a rival colony in New England. But he never returned to America after his ill-fated voyage of 1615, and New England settlement began in 1620 without him. Even so, Smith's thwarted plans illustrated an important feature of English colonization in North America.

The seventeenth century saw not only increased rivalry among European nations for New World territory but also competition among groups of English colonists. The English king—unlike French and Spanish monarchs—exercised little direct control over his American colonies. James I and his successors preferred instead to grant land to trading companies or prominent individuals, who would then plant new settlements. This policy led to the founding of at least two dozen English colonies on the North American mainland and in the Caribbean before 1700. Some lasted only a few decades, but all attested to vigorous English expansion. Because the process lacked centralized direction, and because the experiences of colonists in different regions varied widely, the result was an English empire united more in name than in reality.

The French in North America

The English raid on the French settlement in Maine—for which the French pirates held John Smith accountable—was indeed a devastating affair. But although it virtually wiped out the tiny outpost, French influence in the area scarcely diminished. The economic base of France's New World empire, known as New France, was the fur trade, which depended more on the control of waterways and alliances with Indians than on the occupation of land. The Maine outpost disappeared, but French trade continued to flourish.

The focus of the French colony was the St. Lawrence River, which provided access to a vast interior populated by an abundance of beavers and by Indian peoples eager for trade. Because of its emphasis on the fur trade rather than extensive settlement, New France's population grew slowly in the seventeenth century. Its few, scattered villages were linked as closely to their Indian neighbors as to each other.

The Development of New France

As we saw in Chapter 1, French efforts to found American colonies in the late sixteenth century ended in failure. Preoccupied with religious conflict

Theſe are the Lines that ſhew thy Face; but thoſe
That ſhew thy Grace and Glory, brighter bee:
Thy Faire-Diſcoueries and Fowle-Overthrowes
Of Salvages, much Civillizd by thee
Beſt ſhew thy Spirit; and to it Glory Wyn;
So, thou art Braſſe without, but Golde within.

This portrait, which appeared in John Smith's Description of New England, *boldly proclaimed him to be "Admiral" of the region. A restless adventurer, Smith served as a mercenary soldier in Hungary and Turkey and then grew fascinated with the New World. He served briefly as a leader in early Virginia and later as a publicist for New England colonization.*

at home, the French government temporarily lost interest in the New World. But French fishermen, drawn to the rich fishing grounds of the Grand Banks, continued to visit the Newfoundland coast. Setting up frames onshore to dry their catch, they met Indians with furs to trade for European goods. The French quickly realized they were on to a good thing; the already strong market for furs in Europe soon expanded dramatically as broad-brimmed beaver fur hats became fashionable.

Once it was clear that a profit could be made in Canada, France's interest revived. To strengthen their claim to the region (and make some money for themselves), French kings sold exclusive trading rights to merchants willing to set up outposts in Canada. But because these outposts had to be supplied, at great expense, from France, many merchants lost money on them. To succeed, the merchants needed to bring farmers to New France to produce food and other supplies for the traders.

Quebec, organized in 1608 by Samuel de Champlain, was the first permanent French settlement in Canada (see Map 2-1). Located more than 130 miles up the St. Lawrence River, it was inhabited for its first two decades by only a few dozen settlers. Thereafter, efforts to recruit colonists to New France intensified, and French Jesuits—members of a Catholic religious order founded during the Counter-Reformation—sent missionaries to convert the Indians. In 1642, Montreal was founded as a religious and commercial center.

By 1700, New France had about fifteen thousand colonists. Many of them enjoyed a better life than peasants back in France. One observer reported that "if they are the least inclined to work," immigrants could prosper in Canada. Colonists generally lived in sturdier houses, enjoyed a better diet, and paid lower taxes than their relatives back home. They acquired land to pass on to their children with an

Map 2-1 New France, c. 1650

By 1650, New France contained a number of thinly populated settlements along the St. Lawrence River Valley and the eastern shore of Lake Huron. Most colonists lived in Quebec and Montreal; other sites served mainly as fur-trading posts and Jesuit missions to the Huron Indians.

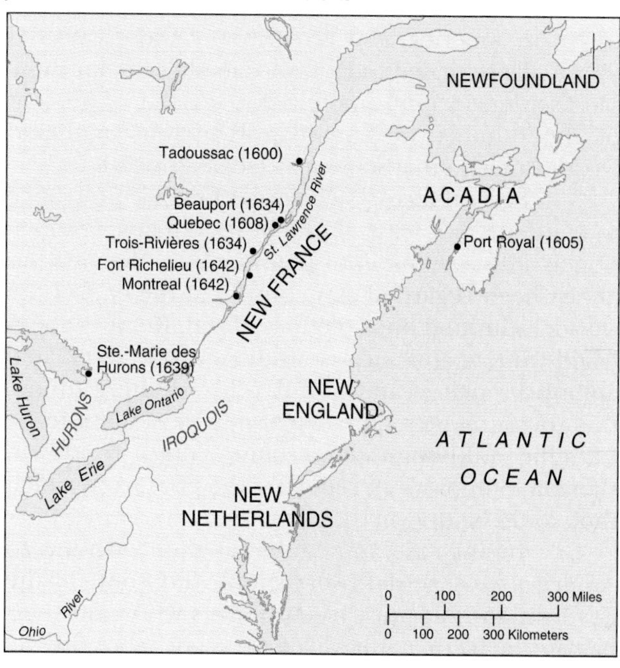

Chronology

1603–1625	James I reigns as king of England.
1607	Founding of English colonies at Jamestown and Sagadahoc.
1608	Establishment of French colony at Quebec.
1619	Virginia's House of Burgesses meets for the first time.
1620	Founding of Plymouth Colony in New England. Mayflower Compact signed.
1620s	Tobacco boom in Virginia.
1624	Dutch found colony of New Netherlands.
1625	Virginia becomes a royal colony. Fort Amsterdam founded.
1625–1649	Charles I reigns as king of England.
1627	English colony at Barbados founded.
1630	Massachusetts Bay Colony founded.
1630–1642	Great Migration to New England.
1634	Lord Baltimore (Cecilius Calvert) founds proprietary colony of Maryland.
1635–1636	Roger Williams banished from Massachusetts, founds Providence, Rhode Island.
1637	Anne Hutchinson banished from Massachusetts. Pequot War.
1638	New Haven colony founded.
1640s	Sugar cultivation and slavery established in West Indies.
1642–1660	English Civil War and Interregnum.
1649	Maryland's Act for Religious Toleration.
1660	Charles II restored to English throne; reigns until 1685.
1663	Founding of Carolina colony.
1664	New Netherlands conquered by the English, becomes New York. New Jersey established.
1673	French explorers reach the Mississippi River.
1681	Founding of Pennsylvania.

ease that French peasants could only envy. Despite these advantages, however, few French people moved to North America, and two-thirds of those who did eventually returned to France. Canada's fifteen thousand settlers in 1700 amounted to less than 7 percent of the number of English colonists in mainland North America that same year (see Figure 2-1).

Several factors accounted for this reluctance to emigrate, not least of which was Canada's reputation as a distant and inhospitable place. "Canada has always been regarded as a country at the end of the world," admitted one colonial official. Rumors about frigid winters and surprise Indian attacks circulated among French peasants and villagers. In addition, the government required prospective settlers to be Catholic (although Protestants could reside in Canada temporarily), reducing the pool from which they could be drawn.

In any case, few could pay their own way to America. Most settlers were sponsored, some by the government but most by employers who paid their passage in return for three years of labor in the colony. Those who completed their terms of service received land, but because most were young men eager to marry and raise children to help them farm, this often failed to keep them in Canada. As late as 1666, only one out of three French settlers was female, which left half of the young men without French brides. Some married Indian women (a practice the French king came to support as a way to "civilize" the natives). Others found brides from among the female orphans—called *filles du Roi,* or "king's girls"—that the French government paid to send to Canada in an attempt to remedy the sexual imbalance. (Rumors abounded that the *filles du Roi* were simply prostitutes lured from the streets of Paris and other cities, but most were poor Frenchwomen who did find Canadian husbands.) Most young men, however, chose to go home to France. Not until about 1700 did the imbalance between French men and women in Canada diminish. Nonetheless, Canada's settler population never approached that of England's North American colonies.

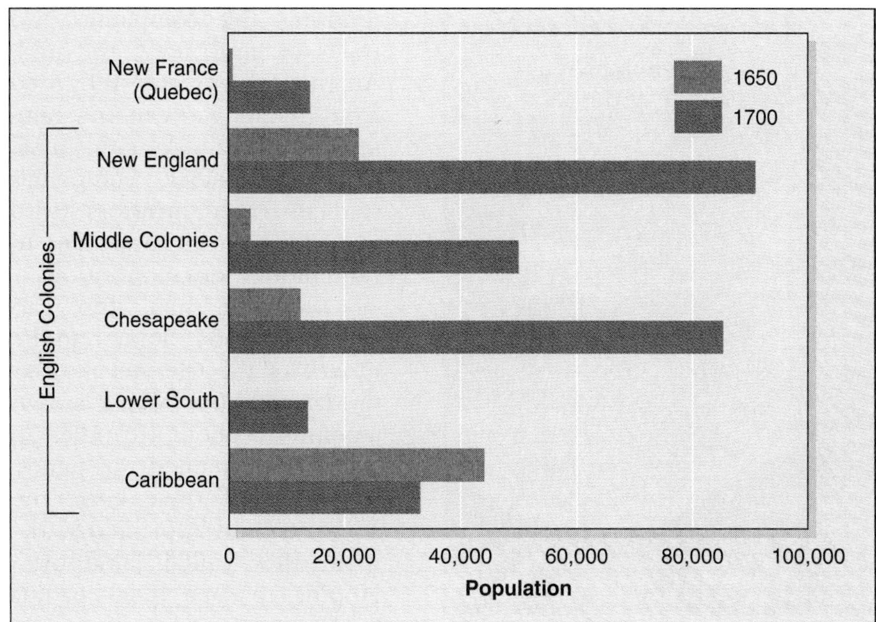

Figure 2-1 European Populations of New France (Quebec) and English Colonies in 1650 and 1700 *Although New France's population grew rapidly between 1650 and 1700, it remained only a tiny fraction of the population of England's North American colonies. By 1700, English colonists on the mainland outnumbered New France's inhabitants by a factor of about 16 to 1.*

Data Source: From John J. McCusker and Russell R. Menard, The Economy of British America, 1607–1789 *(1985). The University of North Carolina Press.*

The Fur Trade

Problems with recruiting settlers did not, in the end, limit New France's prosperity, for fur traders, not settlers, determined the colony's success. Furs were an ideal commodity—light, easy to transport, and very profitable. For the French, at least, the fur trade was also not very hard work. Indians, not Frenchmen, trapped the beavers, prepared the skins, and carried them from the interior to trading posts. French traders paid for the pelts with such goods as axes, knives, metal pots, and glass beads. The furs were then loaded on ships and sent to France. Transporting settlers to Canada was far less profitable, and merchants justified their reluctance to do so by claiming that too many settlers would displace beavers and the Indians who hunted them.

The Indians understood trade as part of a broader process of alliance that involved the exchange of gifts and mutual military assistance. As a result, the fur trade drew the French deeply into the rivalries among Indian groups. When Champlain approached the Hurons for trade, they insisted that the French agree to help them fight the Iroquois. By becoming Huron allies, the French acquired Iroquois enemies. Thereafter the security of the colony depended on the ability of its governors to handle delicate diplomatic relations with the Indians.

To manage French interests in North America, the king and his advisers created an impressive colonial bureaucracy. Beginning in 1663, the colony was ruled by a governor and ***intendant***, both of them royal appointees who in turn appointed several lesser officials. Because their affairs were controlled by appointed—not elected—officials, New France's settlers never developed institutions of self-government as English colonists did. The king also insisted on a strong military force to protect the colony from attack by Indian enemies or European rivals. He ordered the construction of forts and sent several companies of professional soldiers—a much greater investment in defense than English kings would provide for their colonies until the middle of the eighteenth century.

Yet royal control in New France was hardly absolute. Colonial officials disobeyed orders from France when it suited them. Even though instructions from Paris prohibited westward expansion—officials feared creating an empire so far-flung that it would be impossible to defend—the *intendant* in Quebec allowed explorers to move inland. By the 1670s, French traders and missionaries had reached the Mississippi River, and in 1681–1682, Robert, sieur de La Salle, followed it to the Gulf of Mexico, claiming the entire river valley (which he named Louisiana in honor of King Louis XIV) for France. Scores of independent fur traders, known as *coureurs de bois* ("woods runners"), roamed the forests, living and trading among the Indians there. This expansion of French influence alarmed the English, who had founded colonies along the Atlantic seaboard and feared a growing French presence in the west.

Because Indians expected their trading partners also to be military allies, Europeans were often drawn into native conflicts. This illustration, from Samuel de Champlain's 1613 description of the founding of New France, shows him joining his Huron allies in an attack on the Iroquois.

English Settlement in the Chesapeake

Following the Roanoke colony's disappearance after 1587, twenty years passed before the English again attempted to settle in America. When they did, in 1607, it was in the lower Chesapeake Bay region. The new settlement, Jamestown, at first seemed likely to share Roanoke's dismal fate. But it endured, eventually developing into the prosperous colony of Virginia. The reason for Virginia's success was an American plant—tobacco—that commanded good prices from European consumers. Tobacco also underlay the economy of a neighboring colony, Maryland, founded by English settlers on the northern and eastern shores of Chesapeake Bay, and had a profound influence on the development of Chesapeake society.

The Ordeal of Early Virginia

In 1606, several English merchants, convinced that they could succeed where others had failed, petitioned King James I for a charter incorporating two companies to attempt New World settlement. One, the London, or **Virginia, Company**, included merchants from the city of London; the other, the **Plymouth Company**, included merchants from England's western ports. James I issued a charter granting the companies two tracts of land along the mid-Atlantic coast but refrained from investing any money himself in such a risky enterprise. These **joint-stock companies** sold shares to investors (who expected a profit in return) to raise money for colonization.

Three small ships carried 104 settlers, all men, to the mouth of the Chesapeake Bay in May 1607 (see Map 2-2). On a peninsula about fifty miles up a river they named the James, in honor of their king, the colonists built a fortified settlement they called Jamestown. Hoping to earn quick profits for Virginia Company investors, they immediately began hunting for gold and exploring the James in search of the Northwest Passage to Asia. But Jamestown was no Mexico. All they found was disappointment and suffering. The swampy region was a perfect breeding area for malarial mosquitoes and parasites carrying other diseases. Spending all their time in search of riches, the settlers neglected to plant crops, and their food supplies dwindled. By January 1608, only thirty-eight of them were still alive.

After the disastrous first year, the colony's governing council turned to Captain John Smith for leadership. Just 28 years old, Smith was a seasoned adventurer who had fought against Spain in the Netherlands and the Ottomans in Hungary. He imposed military discipline on Jamestown, organizing settlers into work gangs and decreeing that "he that will not worke shall not eate." His high-handed methods revived the colony but antagonized certain settlers who believed that their social status exempted them from manual labor and who bristled at taking orders from a man of lower social rank. When a gunpowder explosion wounded Smith in 1609 and forced him to return to England, his enemies had him replaced as leader.

Once again, the colony nearly disintegrated. Shiploads of new settlers arrived, only to starve or die of disease. Of the five hundred people in Jamestown in the autumn of 1609, just sixty remained alive by the spring of 1610—some of whom survived only by eating their dead companions. Facing financial ruin, company officials back in England

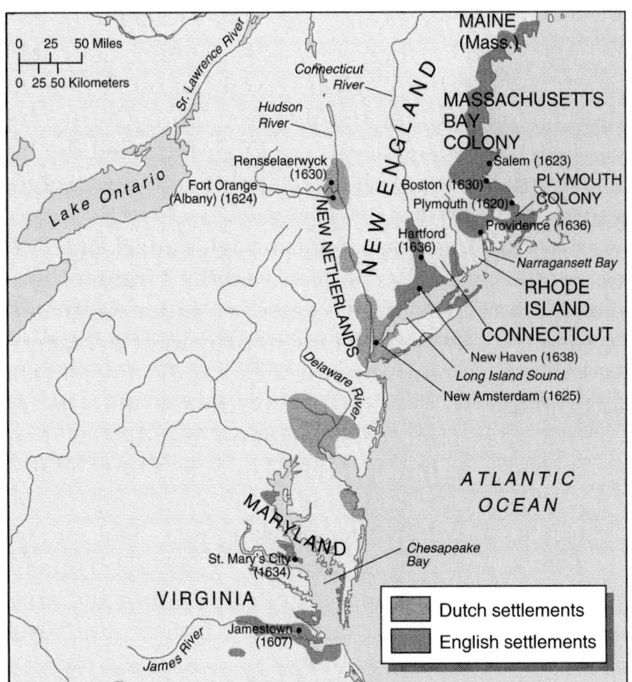

Map 2-2 *English and Dutch Mainland Colonies in North America, c. 1655*
Early English colonies clustered in two areas of the Atlantic seaboard—New England and the Chesapeake Bay. Between them lay Dutch New Netherlands, with settlements stretching up the Hudson River. The Dutch also acquired territory at the mouth of the Delaware River in 1655 when they seized a short-lived Swedish colony located there.

tried to conceal the state of the colony. They reorganized the company twice and sent more settlers, including glassmakers, winegrowers, and silkmakers, in a desperate effort to find a marketable colonial product. They experimented with harsh military discipline, instructing governors to enforce a legal code—the ***Lawes Divine, Morall and Martiall***—that prescribed the death penalty for offenses as trivial as swearing or killing a chicken. When it became clear that such severity discouraged immigration, the company tried more positive inducements.

The first settlers had been expected to work together in return for food and other necessities; only Company stockholders were to share in the colony's profits. But surviving settlers wanted land, so governors began assigning small plots to those who finished their terms of service to the company. In 1616, the company instituted the **headright** system, giving 50 acres to anyone who paid his own way to Virginia and an additional 50 for each person (or "head") he brought with him.

In 1619, three other important developments occurred. That year, the company began transporting women to become wives for planters and induce them to stay in the colony. It was also the year in which the first Africans arrived in Virginia. In addition, the company created the first legislative body in English America, the **House of Burgesses**, setting a precedent for the establishment of self-government in other English colonies. Landowners elected representatives to the House of Burgesses, which, subject to the approval of the company, made laws for Virginia. In 1621 the *Lawes Divine, Morall and Martiall* gave way to a code based on English common law.

Despite these changes, the settlers were still unable to earn the company a profit, and life in the colony barely improved. To make things worse, the headright system expanded English settlement beyond Jamestown. This strained the already tense relations between the English and the Indians onto whose lands they had intruded.

When the English arrived in 1607, they planted their settlement in the heart of territory ruled by the Indian leader Powhatan, who was then at the peak of his power. Chief of a confederacy of about thirty tribes with some fourteen thousand people, including 3,200 warriors, Powhatan had little to fear at first from the struggling English outpost. After an initial skirmish with English soldiers, he sent gifts of food, assuming that by accepting the gifts, the colonists acknowledged their dependence on him. Further action against the settlers seemed unnecessary, because they seemed fully capable of destroying themselves.

This conclusion was premature. Armed colonists began seizing corn from Indian villages whenever the natives refused to supply it voluntarily. During one raid in 1609, John Smith held a pistol to the chest of Opechancanough, Powhatan's younger brother, until the Indians ransomed him with corn. Protesting that the English came "to invade my people and possesse my Country," Powhatan besieged Jamestown and tried to starve the colony to extinction. The colony was saved by the arrival of reinforcements from England, but war with the Indians continued until 1614.

The marriage of the colonist John Rolfe to Pocahontas, Powhatan's daughter, helped seal the peace in 1614. Pocahontas had briefly been held captive by the English during the war and had been instructed in English manners and religion by Rolfe. Sent to negotiate with Powhatan in the spring of 1614, Rolfe asked the chief for his daughter's hand. Powhatan gave his consent, and Pocahontas—baptized in the Church of England and renamed Rebecca—became Rolfe's wife.

This illustration shows John Smith seizing the scalplock of Opechancanough, Chief Powhatan's brother, during an English raid on an Indian village. Smith released his prisoner only after Indians ransomed him with corn. Thirteen years later, Opechancanough led a surprise attack against the colonists.

Powhatan died in 1618, and Opechancanough succeeded him as chief. Still harboring intense resentment against the English, the new chief made plans for retaliation. Pocahontas had died on a trip to England in 1617, severing the tie between her family and the English. With new settlers arriving each year and the ranks of his warriors depleted by the ravages of European diseases, Opechancanough could not wait long to act. Early in the morning on March 22, 1622, hundreds of Indian men traveled to the scattered English settlements, as if they meant to visit or trade. Instead they attacked the unsuspecting colonists, killing 347 by the end of the day—more than one-fourth of the English population.

Opechancanough assumed that the survivors would recognize his authority and confine themselves to trading posts in Jamestown. Instead they plotted revenge. Believing that "now we have just cause to destroy them by all meanes possible," English forces struck at native villages, killing the inhabitants and burning cornfields. At peace talks held in April 1623, the English served poisoned wine to their enemies, killing two hundred more. During the ensuing nine years of war, the English treated the Indians with a ferocity that recalled their earlier subjugation of the Irish.

Although Opechancanough's attack failed to restrain the colonists, it destroyed the Virginia Company. Economic activity ceased as settlers retreated to fortified garrisons. The company went bankrupt, and a royal commission investigating the 1622 attack was shocked to discover that nearly ten times more colonists had died from starvation and disease than at the hands of Indians. King James had little choice but to dissolve the company in 1624, and Virginia became a royal colony the following year. The settlers continued to enjoy a measure of self-government through the House of Burgesses, but now the king chose the colony's governor and council, and royal advisers monitored its affairs.

Tobacco Colony

Ironically, the demise of the Virginia Company helped the colony succeed. In their search for a marketable product, settlers had begun growing tobacco after 1610. Europeans had acquired a taste for tobacco in the late sixteenth century when the Spanish brought samples from the West Indies and Florida. Initially expensive, it became popular among wealthy consumers. The high price appealed to Virginians, but they found that native Virginia leaf was of poor quality. John Rolfe began experimenting with seeds from Trinidad, which did much better. The first cargo of Virginia-grown tobacco arrived in England in 1617 and sold at a highly profitable 3 shillings per pound.

Settlers immediately planted tobacco everywhere—even in the streets of Jamestown. Company officials, unwilling to base the colony's economy on a single crop, tried to restrict annual production to 100 pounds per colonist. Colonists, busy "rooting in the ground about Tobacco like Swine" as one observer reported, ignored these restrictions. But it was only after company rule ended that tobacco planting really surged.

Between 1627 and 1669, annual tobacco exports climbed from 250,000 pounds to more than 15 million pounds. As the supply grew, the price per pound plunged from 13 pence in 1624 to a mere penny in the late 1660s, where it remained for the next half century. What had once been a luxury product thus became affordable for Europeans of average means. Now thoroughly dependent on

FROM THEN TO NOW

Tobacco and the American Economy

By the terms of a legal settlement reached in the summer of 1998, the American tobacco industry agreed to pay $206 billion to forty-six state governments as compensation for the medical costs of treating smoke-related illnesses. Health issues dominated the debates leading to the agreement, but economic questions could not help but influence the discussion. This was hardly surprising, for tobacco is the oldest commercial crop produced in what is now the United States.

The healthfulness of tobacco was a subject for debate as far back as the early seventeenth century, but its potential dangers did not deter Virginia's colonists from growing the one crop that promised them prosperity. The first small shipment of Virginia tobacco reached London markets in 1617; by the turn of the eighteenth century, colonists produced over 30 million pounds of it each year. High levels of production led to falling prices, but colonists responded by growing even more tobacco. Just before the outbreak of the American Revolution suspended trade between the colonies and England, over 55 million pounds of American-grown tobacco reached Britain.

Low prices and soil exhaustion led some eighteenth-century planters (including George Washington) to switch from tobacco to wheat, but many farmers in Virginia, Maryland, and North Carolina persisted with the crop. After the Revolution, as settlers moved westward from these former colonies across the Appalachian Mountains, they brought tobacco with them. Tobacco became a fixture of the agricultural economies of Kentucky, Tennessee, Missouri, and Ohio. By the 1890s, American farmers planted over a billion acres of land with tobacco—an acreage that was maintained or exceeded down to the early 1960s. Tobacco was so vital to the American economy into the twentieth century that the federal government subsidized its production—the only nonfood crop (besides cotton) to benefit from substantial price supports.

Thus economic decisions made by seventeenth-century Virginia colonists had unpredictable consequences that, nearly four centuries later, affect an America they could never have imagined. As the negotiations over the 1998 settlement revealed, efforts to reconfigure tobacco's place in America's economy necessarily confront the crop's historical significance. Tobacco has been around far longer than the nation itself.

The oldest commercial crop grown in what is now the United States, tobacco was key to the survival of the Chesapeake colonies and remains an important part of America's agricultural economy. During the seventeenth century, the demands of tobacco farming led to the importation of thousands of indentured servants from England.

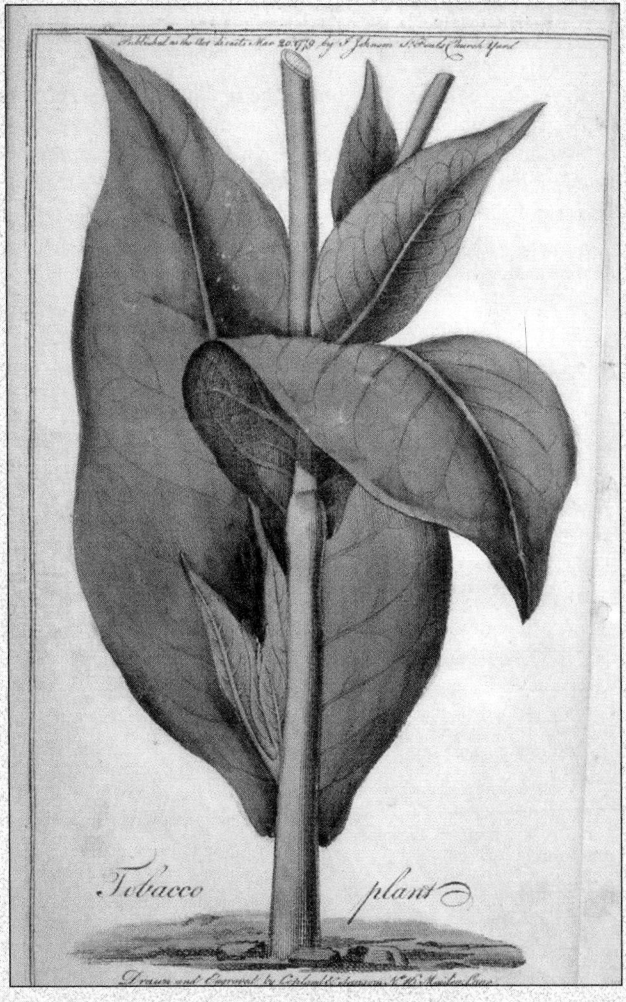

tobacco for their livelihood, the only way colonists could compensate for falling prices was to grow even more, pushing exports to England to more than 20 million pounds per year by the late 1670s (see Figure 2-2).

Tobacco shaped nearly every aspect of Virginia society, from patterns of settlement to the recruitment of colonists. Planters scrambled to claim lands near navigable rivers so that ships could easily reach their plantations and carry their crops to market. As a result, the colonists dispersed across the countryside instead of gathering in towns. People settled, one governor wrote, wherever "a choice veine of rich ground invited them, and further from neighbours the better." Colonists competed to produce the biggest and best crop and get it to market the fastest, hoping to enjoy even a small price advantage over everyone else.

The key to success was to control a large labor force. Tobacco kept workers busy nine months of the year. Planters sowed seeds in the early spring, transplanted seedlings a few weeks later, and spent the summer pinching off the tops of the plants (to produce larger leaves) and removing worms. After the harvest, the leaves were "cured"—dried in ventilated sheds—and packed in large barrels. During the winter, planters cleared and fenced more land and made barrels for next year's crop. Working on his own, one planter could tend two thousand plants, which yielded about 500 pounds of cured tobacco. Early on, when the price was high, this supplied a comfortable income. But as the price plummeted, planters could keep up only by producing more tobacco, and to do that they needed help.

The planters turned to England, importing thousands of **indentured servants**, or contract workers, who agreed to a fixed term of labor, usually four to seven years, in exchange for free passage to Virginia. The master provided food, shelter, clothing, and, at the end of the term of service, "freedom dues" paid in corn and clothing. Between 1625 and 1640, an estimated one thousand or more indentured servants arrived each year. Some were orphans; others were condemned criminals given a choice between execution and transportation to Virginia. The vast majority, however,

Figure 2-2 The Supply and Price of Chesapeake Tobacco, 1620–1700
Tobacco cultivation dominated the economy of the Chesapeake region throughout the seventeenth century. As planters brought more and more land under cultivation, the amount of tobacco exported to Britain shot up and the price plummeted. (As the dashed line indicates, no data on tobacco imports are available for the years 1650–1670.)

Data Source: From Russell R. Menard, "The Tobacco Industry in the Chesapeake Colonies, 1617–1730: An Interpretation," Research in Economic History, 5 *(1980), app. Jai Press, Inc.*

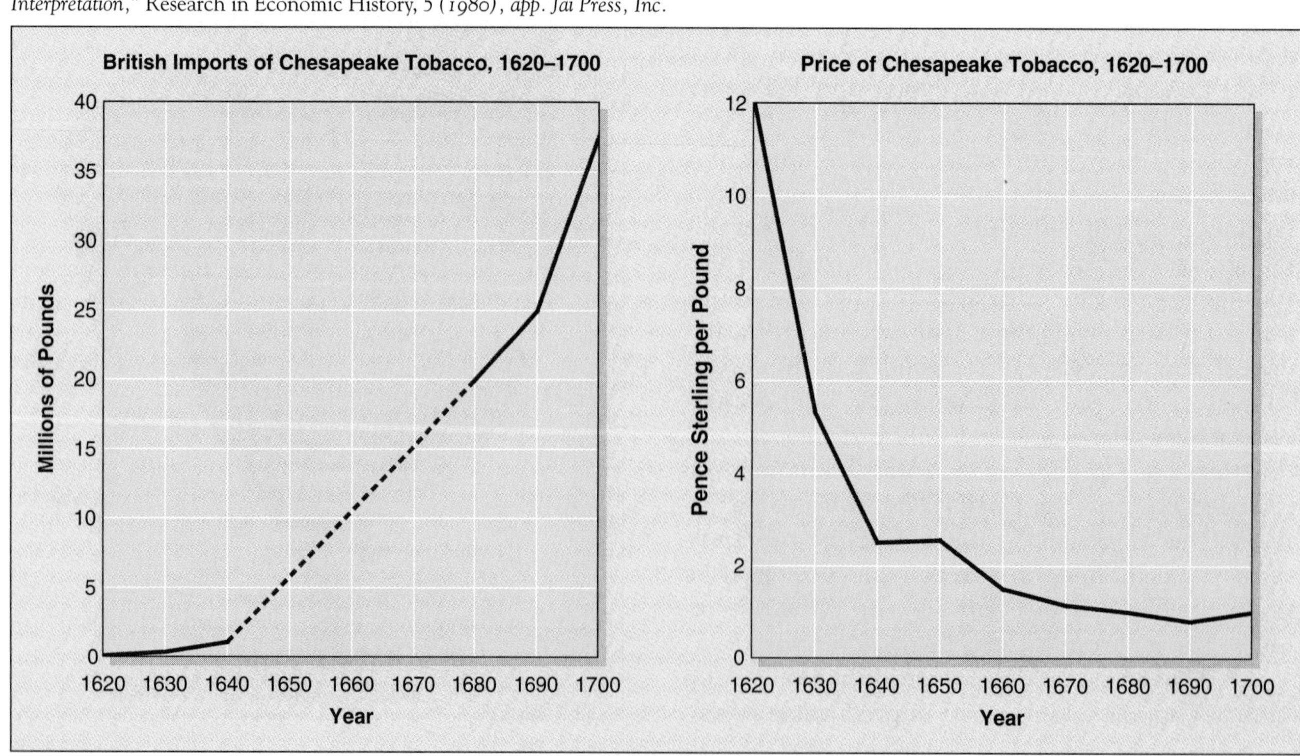

came from the ranks of England's unemployed, who emigrated in hopes of "bettering their condition in a Growing Country."

Most found such hopes quickly dashed. Servants died in alarming numbers from disease, and those who survived faced years of backbreaking labor. Masters squeezed as much work out of them as possible with long hours and harsh discipline. Some servants died from mistreatment. Richard Price beat his servant, Endymion Inleherne, for "being a common runaway and one that did use to feign himself sick," so severely that the young man died. A jury refused to charge Price with murder, reasoning that Inleherne deserved punishment and Price had not intended to kill him. Few masters matched Price's cruelty, but because the courts (administered by masters) favored masters' authority over servants' rights, those who did generally escaped prosecution.

New obstacles faced servants who managed to survive their terms of indenture. For every ex-servant who became a landholder, dozens died in poverty. To prevent freed servants from becoming economic rivals, established planters avoided selling them good land, particularly after tobacco prices hit bottom in the 1660s. Many ex-servants found land only in places less suitable for tobacco cultivation and more vulnerable to Indian attack. Forced to choose between eking a "poor living with hard labor out of the ground in a terrible Wilderness" or giving up all hope for ownership and either becoming tenants or laborers, ex-servants were a discontented group. In 1675, their discontent would flare into rebellion (discussed in Chapter 3).

By 1660, no one doubted that Virginia would survive, but few could have predicted how much it would differ from England. Because of their labor needs, masters favored young men in their teens and twenties as indentured servants, importing three or four times as many of them as women. As a result, Virginia's population in the seventeenth century was overwhelmingly young and male. Even in 1700, Virginia had three English men for every two women. Thus many free male servants found that marriage was as remote a possibility as landownership. Unlike Canadian men, very few Virginians chose Indian wives. John Rolfe's union with Pocahontas was one of only three English–Indian marriages in seventeenth-century Virginia.

Few marriages meant few children. Population growth was further slowed because servants could not marry until their indentures were completed. Many men were already in their thirties when they married, usually to women in their early twenties. Older couples had fewer children than younger couples would have had. Disease also struck with depressing regularity. Few colonists lived past 50, and many of their offspring died young. Children who survived had usually lost one or both parents by the time they reached adulthood. The experience of the Chowning family was scarcely unusual. When Robert Chowning (just 15 when he lost his own father) died in 1698, he left seven children ranging in age from 14 to 2. His eldest son, in turn, left six children under the age of 14 when he died in 1721.

Such conditions strained, but did not destroy, family ties. Surviving spouses remarried quickly, often to a widow or widower with children, creating complex households with stepparents and half-brothers and half-sisters. Widows attracted great interest because they controlled property left to them by their husbands, assuming the normally male responsibility of managing estates for their children's benefit. When she remarried, a widow chose a new spouse wisely, for he would manage the property that the children of her first marriage would inherit.

The slow rate of natural increase meant that population growth in Virginia resulted mostly from immigration. Even so, the number of settlers rose from about 2,500 in 1630 to 21,000 in 1660, thanks to the demand for indentured servants. This larger population was less vulnerable to Indian attacks. Opechancanough launched another raid in 1644 that killed nearly five hundred colonists, but this had a far less devastating effect than his attack of 1622 because the settler population now outnumbered the Indians.

The colonists' lives, however, were still far from easy. Some had acquired large estates and grew wealthy from the labor of indentured servants tilling their tobacco fields. Others, cultivating small landholdings or renting plots from more successful colonists, grew just enough food to survive and as much tobacco as they could manage. But even the most successful settlers, investing every penny of profit in labor and land, lived under quite primitive conditions.

Early colonial dwellings were often no larger than 16 by 20 feet, with one or two rooms. Only at the end of the seventeenth century did prosperous planters begin to construct grander houses with as many as ten rooms. Poor settlers slept on the floor on straw mattresses and had few other furnishings—often not even a chair or bench to sit on. Rich planters owned more goods, though often of poor quality. In 1655, for instance, William Brocas, a prominent colonial official, owned several curtains "very thin and much worn"; seven chairs, "most of them unusefull"; and seven guns, "most unfixt." Servants and poor colonists had no choice but to accept crude living conditions. Their more fortunate neighbors tolerated discomfort in order to invest in family estates where their descendants might live in greater luxury.

Maryland

Virginia's success encouraged further English colonization in the Chesapeake Bay region. In 1632, King Charles I granted 10 million acres of land north of the bay to the nobleman George Calvert, Lord Baltimore. Unlike Virginia, which was founded by a joint-stock company, Maryland was a **proprietary colony**—the sole possession of Calvert and his heirs. They owned all the land, which they could divide up as they pleased, and had the right to set up the colony's government.

Calvert, who was Catholic, intended Maryland to be a refuge for others of his faith. When Queen Elizabeth's accession made England a Protestant nation, Catholics became a disadvantaged minority. They paid double taxes and could not worship in public, hold political office, or send their children to universities. In Maryland, Calvert wanted Catholic colonists to enjoy economic and political power. He intended to divide the land into manors—large private estates like those of medieval England—and distribute them to wealthy Catholic friends. These manor lords would live on rents collected from tenant farmers, hold the most important governmental offices, and run their own law courts.

Calvert died before settlement began, and it was the sad fate of his son, Cecilius, to see his father's plans unravel. The majority of colonists, who began arriving in 1634, were Protestants who despised Catholics. Refusing to live as tenants on Catholic estates, they claimed land of their own—a process that accelerated after 1640, when Maryland adopted a headright system like Virginia's as a way to recruit settlers.

Maryland's problems intensified when civil war broke out in England in 1642. For years, political and religious disputes had divided the nation. Charles I, who became king in 1625, clashed with Protestants who called for further reform of the Church of England. He also antagonized many government leaders by dissolving Parliament in 1629 and ruling on his own for eleven years. Needing funds to suppress a rebellion in Scotland in 1640, however, Charles was forced to recall Parliament, which quickly turned against him. Both king and Parliament recruited armies and went to war in 1642. Parliamentary forces triumphed, and in 1649, they executed Charles. For the next decade, England was governed as a protectorate, not a monarchy. Oliver Cromwell, a general, ruled until his death in 1658. His son, Richard, proved an inept successor, however, and in 1660 a group of army officers invited Charles's exiled son to accept the throne.

During the 1640s and 1650s, Maryland Protestants took advantage of the upheaval in England to contest the Calverts' control of the colony. To pacify them, Cecilius Calvert established a legislature, assuming that Protestants would dominate the elective lower house while he could appoint Catholics to the upper house. In 1649, Calvert also approved the **Act for Religious Toleration**, the first law in America to call for freedom of worship for all Christians, but even this brought no peace. The Protestant majority, supported during the 1650s by Cromwell and Parliament, continued to resist Catholic political influence, at one point passing a law that prohibited Catholics from voting.

Instead of the peaceful Catholic refuge Calvert intended, Maryland soon resembled neighboring Virginia. Its settlers raised tobacco and imported as many indentured servants as possible. Because Maryland initially provided freed servants with 50 acres of land, more became landholders than in Virginia. As in Virginia, however, economic opportunity diminished after 1660 when the price of tobacco dropped. Maryland's settlers enjoyed more peaceful relations with the Indians than Virginians had, but they fought intensely among themselves. Throughout the seventeenth century, Protestants kept up their opposition to the proprietor's control of land and political power and resisted all attempts by Catholics to govern the colony that was supposed to have been theirs.

The Founding of New England

The first English attempt to settle the northeastern coast of North America, what would soon be called New England, was a miserable failure. In 1607, the same year that the Virginia Company founded Jamestown, the Plymouth Company sent two ships with 120 Englishmen (and one Indian captive from an earlier raid) to found a colony at the mouth of the Sagadahoc River in present-day Maine. The colonists alienated the Abenaki Indians who lived there, suffered through a harsh winter, and abandoned their settlement the next summer. But English explorers and fishermen continued to visit New England, among them John Smith, who published his book extolling its virtues as a site for colonization in 1616. Not long after, the English renewed their efforts to settle New England.

Six colonies appeared in the region between 1620 and 1640, settled by thousands of people troubled by religious, political, and economic upheavals in England. The society these settlers created differed markedly from the one developing in the Chesapeake—not least of all in the absence of significant Indian opposition. Between 1616 and 1618—just before any of these colonies was founded—a terrible epidemic swept through coastal New England, killing up to 90 percent of the Indians living there. The devastated survivors were unable to prevent the encroaching English from building towns where their villages had once stood.

The Pilgrims and Plymouth Colony

Plymouth Colony, the first of the New England settlements, was founded in 1620. Its origins lay in religious disputes that had plagued England since the late sixteenth century. Most of Queen Elizabeth's subjects approved of her efforts to keep England a Protestant nation, but some reformers believed that she had not rid the Church of England of all Catholic practices. The enemies of these reformers, ridiculing them for wanting to purify the Church of England (or **Anglican** Church) of all corruption, called them **Puritans**.

Following the doctrine of predestination taught by John Calvin and other Protestant reformers, English Puritans believed in an all-powerful God who, at the moment of Creation, determined which humans would be saved and which would be damned. They held that salvation came through faith alone, not good works, and urged believers to seek a direct, personal relationship with God. The centerpiece of their spiritual life was conversion: the transforming experience that occurred when individuals felt the stirrings of grace in their souls and began to hope that they were among the saved. Those who experienced conversion were considered saints and acquired new strength to live godly lives.

Puritans objected to Anglican practices that, they felt, interfered with conversion and the believer's relationship with God. They rejected the *Book of Common Prayer,* which regulated Anglican worship, insisting that ministers should pray from the heart and preach from the Bible. They objected when Anglican clergy wore rich vestments that set them apart from ordinary Christians. And they objected to any church organization above the level of individual congregations, seeing no need for bishops and archbishops. But what they hated most about the Anglican Church was that anyone could be a member. Puritans believed that everyone should attend church services, but they wanted church membership—which conferred the right to partake in the Lord's Supper, or communion—to be limited to saints who had experienced conversion.

Puritans thus insisted on further reform. Elizabeth and the rulers who followed her—who as monarchs were the "supreme heads" of the Church of England—disagreed and tried to silence them. James I viewed the Puritans' demands as a challenge to his authority and threatened to "harry them out of the land." Some Puritans, known as **separatists**, were convinced that the Church of England would never change and left it to form their own congregations. One such group, mainly artisans and middling farmers from the village of Scrooby, in Nottinghamshire, became the core of Plymouth Colony.

The Scrooby separatists, seeking a more tolerant religious environment, left England in 1607–1608, settling for more than a decade in Holland. There they worshiped in peace, but many struggled to make a living and feared that their children were being tempted by the worldly pleasures of Dutch city life. Some Scrooby separatists contemplated moving to America and contacted the Plymouth Company, which was eager to make another colonization attempt after the Sagadahoc failure. Called **Pilgrims** because they thought of themselves as spiritual wanderers, they were joined by other separatists and by nonseparatist "strangers" hired to help get the colony started. In all, 102 men, women, and children set sail on the *Mayflower* in September 1620.

After a long and miserable voyage, they landed near Massachusetts Bay. Because this was about 200 miles north of the land their charter permitted them to settle, some of the "strangers" claimed that they were no longer legally bound to obey the expedition's separatist leaders. The leaders responded by drafting the **Mayflower Compact** and urging all adult males to sign it. The Compact set out the terms for governing the new colony and became the first document to establish self-government in North America.

The Pilgrims settled at Plymouth, the site of a Wampanoag village recently depopulated by disease. William Bradford, a Pilgrim leader and Plymouth's governor for many years, described finding abandoned cornfields, a clearing "where lately a house had been," Indian graves, and baskets of corn buried underground. Although it helped feed them for a while, this corn was not enough to prevent the Pilgrims from suffering their first winter through a terrible "starving time" that left nearly half of them dead.

When two natives, Squanto and Samoset, emerged from the woods the next spring and began speaking English, the surviving Pilgrims marveled at them as "special instruments sent of God." Samoset had learned English from traders, and Squanto had learned it in England, where he lived for a time after being kidnapped by a sea captain. The two men approached the Pilgrims on behalf of Massasoit, the Wampanoag leader. Although suspicious of the newcomers, the Wampanoags were too few to threaten them and thought the Pilgrims might be useful allies against Wampanoag enemies, such as the Narragansetts, who had escaped the recent epidemics.

In 1621, the Wampanoags and the Pilgrims signed a treaty of alliance, although each side (working through translators) understood its terms differently. The Pilgrims assumed that Massasoit had submitted to the superior authority of King James, whereas Massasoit assumed that the agreement treated himself and the English king as equal partners. Despite frequent disputes caused by English assertion of authority over the Wampanoags, the two groups enjoyed relatively peaceful relations for nearly half a century.

Economic ties strengthened the alliance. The Indians taught the English how to plant corn and traded corn with them for manufactured goods. The Pilgrims also exchanged corn with other Indians to the north for furs, which they shipped back to England to help pay off their debts to English investors. In the autumn of 1621, Indians and Pilgrims gathered for a feast celebrating the settlers' first harvest—an event Americans still commemorate as the first Thanksgiving.

Plymouth remained small, poor, and weak. It never had more than seven thousand settlers and never produced more than small shipments of furs, fish, and timber to sell in England. It took the Pilgrims more than twenty years to repay their English creditors. Yet because of the idealistic visions of the founders of Plymouth Colony, who saw in the New World a chance to escape religious persecution and create peaceful communities and pure churches, it has become an important symbol in American history. It was soon overshadowed, however, by the larger and more powerful colony of Massachusetts Bay.

Massachusetts Bay Colony and Its Offshoots

The Puritans who settled Massachusetts shared many of the Pilgrims' beliefs—with one important exception. They insisted that the Anglican Church could be reformed and so were not separatists. When they went to New England, it was to create godly churches to serve as models for English reform. And England, they believed, was in more desperate need of reformation than ever.

Charles I, who became king in 1625, opposed Puritans more forcefully than his father had and supported changes in Anglican worship that recalled Catholic practices. England at the time also suffered from economic troubles—including crop failures and a depression in the wool industry—that many Puritans saw as signs of God's displeasure with their country, encouraging them to move to the New World.

In 1629, a group of Puritan merchants received a royal charter for a joint-stock enterprise, the Massachusetts Bay Company, to set up a colony north of Plymouth. They chose John Winthrop, a prosperous Puritan lawyer, as their leader. In the spring of 1630, a fleet of eleven ships carried about a thousand men, women, and children across the Atlantic.

Before Winthrop's ship landed, he preached a lay sermon, called "A Model of Christian Charity,"

John Winthrop (1588–1649) served as the Massachusetts Bay Colony's governor for most of its first two decades. Throughout his life, Winthrop—like many fellow Puritans—struggled to live a godly life in a corrupt world.

Courtesy, American Antiquarian Society.

to his fellow passengers, describing his vision of the society they were about to create. The governor reminded them of their goal "to do more service to the Lord." They should "love one another with a pure heart" and place the good of all above private ambitions. Winthrop argued that the Lord had made them his chosen people—and that as a result, "we shall be as a city upon a hill, the eyes of all people are upon us." If they failed to live up to God's expectations, he would punish them, and the spectacle of their failure would allow their enemies "to speak evil of the ways of God." With this mingled encouragement and threat ringing in their ears, the emigrants set about establishing their colony. Within a few months of their landing, they founded Boston and six adjoining towns.

Winthrop described the settlers' mission in New England as a **covenant**, or contract, with God, binding them to meet their religious obligations in return for God's favor. The settlers also created covenants to define their duties to one another. When they founded towns, colonists signed covenants agreeing to live together in peace. The settlers of Dedham, for example, agreed to "walk in a peaceable conversation," seeking "the good of each other." Worshipers in each town's church likewise wrote covenants binding themselves to live in harmony.

The desire for peace and purity could breed intolerance. Settlers scrutinized their neighbors for signs of unacceptable behavior. Standards for church membership were strict; only those who could prove they were saints by describing their conversion experiences were admitted. But the insistence on covenants and conformity also created a remarkably stable society, far more peaceable than Virginia's.

That stability was enhanced by the development of representative government. Colony leaders in effect translated the charter of the Massachusetts Bay Company into a plan of government, a process completed by 1634. The **General Court**, which initially included only the shareholders of the joint-stock company, was transformed into a two-house legislature. Freemen—adult males who held property and were church members—had the right to elect representatives to the lower house, as well as eighteen members (called "assistants") to the upper house. They also chose a governor and a deputy governor.

Between 1630 and 1642—when the outbreak of the English Civil War halted emigration—at least thirteen thousand settlers came to New England and established dozens of towns. The progress of settlement was generally untroubled in coastal Massachusetts, but when colonists moved into the Connecticut River Valley, tensions with Indians grew rapidly. These erupted in 1637 in the brief, tragic conflict called the **Pequot War**.

English settlers from Massachusetts first arrived in the Connecticut Valley in the mid-1630s. The migration accelerated in 1636 when the Reverend Thomas Hooker led part of his congregation from Cambridge, Massachusetts, to what became Hartford. The new arrivals found themselves in a dangerous situation. Dutch traders already in the region had been dealing exclusively with the Pequot Indians as partners. In 1633, however, they built an outpost near the site of Hartford and invited other Indian groups to trade. The Pequots, suffering terribly from a recent smallpox epidemic, resented losing their special trading rights and began fighting the Dutch. Initially, they saw the English settlers as potential allies against the Dutch. But when the settlers demanded Pequot submission to English authority as the price of an alliance, they turned against them too in a struggle to retain their control over the land and trade of eastern Connecticut.

The English settlers formed alliances with the Narragansetts and Mohegans, who were both rivals of the Pequots. Together they overwhelmed the Pequots in an astonishingly bloody war. In May 1637, English forces surrounded a Pequot village inhabited mainly by women and children, located on the Mystic River. They set it ablaze and shot anyone who tried to escape. Between three hundred and seven hundred Pequots died, a toll that shocked the settlers' Indian allies, who protested that English-style warfare was "too furious, and slays too many men" (see "American Views: Miantonomo's Plea for Indian Unity").

The English, for their part, marveled that God had given them "so speedy a victory over so proud and insulting an enemy." After the surviving Pequots had fled or been sold into slavery, many more settlers moved to Connecticut, which soon declared itself a separate colony. In 1639, the settlers adopted the **Fundamental Orders**, creating a government similar to that of Massachusetts, and the English government granted them a royal charter in 1662.

Massachusetts spun off other colonies as its population expanded in the 1630s and dissenters ran afoul of its intolerant government. Puritan leaders tried to suppress unorthodox religious opinions

American Views

Miantonomo's Plea for Indian Unity (1642)

Until European colonization began to force a change in outlook, the native inhabitants of North America never thought of themselves as one people, any more than Europe's residents considered themselves "Europeans." Miantonomo, a Narragansett living in Rhode Island, was one of the first native leaders to call for a unified response to English intrusion. With the gruesome lessons of the Pequot War fresh in his mind, he urged the Montauks of Long Island to put aside their differences with the Narragansetts and join them in opposing the settlers. His appeal, recorded by Lion Gardiner, an English officer during the Pequot War, was uttered in vain. Captured by the English and tried and convicted of the murder of an Indian, Miantonomo was turned over to a Mohegan rival for execution.

❖ **How did Miantonomo describe Indian life before the arrival of the English?**

❖ **What changes occurred as a result of their settlement?**

Brothers, we must be as one as the English are, or we shall all be destroyed. You know our fathers had plenty of deer and skins and our plains were full of game and turkeys, and our coves and rivers were full of fish.

But, brothers, since these Englishmen have seized our country, they have cut down the grass with scythes, and the trees with axes. Their cows and horses eat up the grass, and their hogs spoil our bed of clams; and finally we shall all starve to death; therefore, stand not in your own light, I ask you, but resolve to act like men. All the sachems both to the east and the west have joined with us, and we are resolved to fall upon them at a day appointed, and therefore I come secretly to you, [be]cause you can persuade your Indians to do what you will.

Source: Steven Mintz, ed., Native American Voices: A History and Anthology *(1995), pp. 84–85. Reprinted with permission of Brandywine Press.*

whenever they emerged, for fear that God would interpret their failure to do so as a breach of their covenant with Him. Some dissenting colonists, however, refused to be silenced.

Roger Williams, who founded Rhode Island, was one such irrepressible dissenter. Williams was a separatist minister who declared that because Massachusetts churches had not rejected the Church of England, they shared its corruption. He opposed government interference in religious affairs—such as laws requiring settlers to attend worship services—and argued for the separation of church and state. Williams even attacked the Massachusetts charter, insisting that the king had no right to grant Indian lands to English settlers.

Despite his fiery opinions, Williams was an immensely likable man—even Governor Winthrop remained on friendly terms with him and tried to persuade him to change his views. When Williams refused to be silenced, the General Court sentenced him to banishment, intending to ship him back to England. But in the winter of 1635, Williams slipped away and followed Winthrop's advice to "steer my course to Narragansett Bay." There he and a few followers found refuge among the Narragansett Indians, from whom he purchased land for the village of Providence, founded in 1636. More towns soon sprang up nearby when a new religious crisis, provoked by a woman named Anne Hutchinson, sent additional refugees to Rhode Island from Massachusetts.

Anne Hutchinson arrived in Boston from England with her husband and seven children in 1634. Welcomed by the town's women for her talents as a midwife, she also began to hold religious meetings in her house. During these meetings, she denounced several ministers, who had taught worshipers that there were certain spiritual exercises they could perform that might prepare them for sainthood. Hutchinson insisted that there was nothing humans could do to encourage God to make them saints. She implied that any minister who taught otherwise could not be a saint himself, in which case he had no authority over the true saints in his church.

Many people, including prominent Boston merchants, flocked to Hutchinson's meetings. But her critics believed her to be a dangerous antinomian (someone who claimed to be free from obedience to moral law), because she seemed to maintain that saints were accountable only to God and not to any worldly authority. Her opponents also objected to her teaching of mixed groups of men and women. Governor Winthrop complained that such behavior was neither "comely in the sight of God nor fitting for your sex." This comment suggests that Hutchinson's breach of normal gender roles, which placed women subordinate to men, upset him as much as her religious views did. Colony magistrates arrested her and tried her for sedition—that is, for advocating the overthrow of the government.

During her trial, Hutchinson mounted a lively defense. When asked to explain her views, she reminded her opponents of their objections to her teaching and asked them, "Why do you call me to teach the court?" In the end, however, the court found her guilty and banished her from the colony. With many of her followers, she moved to Rhode Island, where Roger Williams had proclaimed a policy of religious toleration. Other followers returned to England or moved north to what became in 1679 the separate colony of New Hampshire.

At the height of the Hutchinson controversy, a group of zealous Puritan emigrants led by the Reverend John Davenport arrived in Boston. Appalled by the religious turmoil, they departed for the coast of Long Island Sound, where they founded New Haven in 1638. Davenport's efforts to impose perfect Puritan conformity in his colony made Massachusetts seem easygoing in comparison. But New Haven failed to thrive, and in 1662, the poor, intolerant, and isolated colony was absorbed into Connecticut.

The Growth of New England

"This plantation and that of Virginia went not forth upon the same reasons," declared one of Massachusetts's founders. Virginians came "for profit," whereas New Englanders emigrated to bear witness to their Puritan faith. They too hoped for economic prosperity but believed that it would come only if God blessed their efforts to create a godly society. Most New England settlers arrived in the brief span between the founding of Massachusetts in 1630 and 1642, when the outbreak of the English Civil War engaged Puritans to stay at home and fight on Parliament's behalf against the king. Unlike the unmarried young men who moved in great numbers to Virginia, most New Englanders settled with their families. This had important implications for the development of New England society.

John and Anne Moulton were representative of many of New England's young couples. Both 38 years old, they brought five children (aged 3 to 14) with them from England. Like most settlers, the Moultons were neither rich nor poor. John had been a farmer in England and was wealthy enough to pay his family's passage and set himself up on a New England farm. At the time of the voyage, Anne was pregnant with her sixth child and gave birth shortly after arriving in Massachusetts. Three years later, with the

Most New Englanders came in family groups, bringing many children with them. The lace and ribbons on the clothing of the Mason children, depicted in this 1670 portrait, suggest that they came from a well-to-do family. Like many seventeenth-century portraits, this one is rich in symbolism. The cane in David Mason's hand indicates his status as the male heir, while the rose held by his sister Abigail was a symbol of childhood innocence.

Attributed to the Freake-Gibbs Painter, American, active Boston, Mass., c. 1670. The Mason Children: David, Joanna, and Abigail, 1670. Oil on canvas, 39 × 42 ½ in. The Fine Arts Museum of San Francisco, Gift of Mr. and Mrs. John D. Rockefeller 3rd, 1979.7.3.

family settled in the town of Hampton (now located in New Hampshire), she bore another daughter.

The average family in early New England, like the Moultons, had seven or eight children. Because women and men arrived in nearly equal numbers, young adults easily found spouses and produced more children. Thus the population continued to grow rapidly, even when immigration slowed after 1642. By 1660, New England's settlers numbered more than 33,000.

New Englanders—and the family ties that knitted their society together—were also largely spared from the diseases that ravaged Virginia's settlers and devastated Indian populations. It seemed a "marvelous providence of God" to Plymouth's Governor Bradford that so many settlers made it to their seventies and eighties when few of England's adults (or Virginians) lived past 60. Longevity strengthened economic security as well as emotional ties. Fathers lived long enough to build prosperous farms to pass along to their sons. They also accumulated herds of livestock and stores of household goods to give to their daughters when they married.

Unlike Chesapeake colonists, who spread out on tobacco lands near navigable rivers, New Englanders clustered in towns. The Massachusetts government strongly encouraged town formation by granting tracts of land to groups of families who promised to settle together. Once they received a grant, the families in a group divided it among themselves, allotting each family a farm of sufficient size to support all its members. Social distinctions were maintained, however, with people who had had higher standing in England receiving larger farms than those of lower standing. Land that the original families could not yet farm was held "in common" to be distributed to their children as they grew up. Settlers generally remained in their chosen towns for the rest of their lives. Grown children, inheriting parental estates and finding spouses nearby, often settled in the same community as their parents.

Towns—usually made up of fifty to a hundred families—were the focus of New England life, providing the context for religious, political, and economic activity. The importance Puritans placed on worship with fellow Christians helped promote community feeling. Every Sunday, townspeople gathered at the meetinghouse to listen to the minister preach God's word. Here church members heard their neighbors describe their experiences of conversion and decided whether to admit them.

At other times, the meetinghouse served as a town hall, where men assembled to discuss matters ranging from local taxes to making sure that everyone's fences were mended. Massachusetts law required towns with at least fifty families to support a school (so children could learn to read the Bible), and, at town meetings, men often wrangled over the choice of a schoolmaster and what salary to pay him. Townsmen tried to reach decisions by consensus in order to preserve harmony. To oversee day-to-day local affairs, men chose five to seven of their most trusted neighbors to serve as **selectmen**. Each town could also elect two men to represent it in the colony legislature. Many a town neglected to do so, however, either because its citizens could not afford to pay the men's expenses or because they lacked interest in outside political affairs.

Economic life likewise centered on the town. New England's stony soil and short growing season offered few ways to get rich, but most people achieved a modest prosperity. Farmers grew corn and other foods and raised livestock to feed their families, selling or trading what they could not use. Their goal was to achieve what they called **competency**—the possession of enough property to ensure their families' economic independence.

Maintaining competency was a family affair. Without a staple crop like tobacco to sell in an international market, New England farmers lacked resources to hire indentured servants and relied instead on their wives and children for labor. Women cared for children, cleaned, cooked, sewed and mended, milked cows, and tended poultry. Many farmwives made butter and cheese, brewed beer, preserved fruits and vegetables, salted meat, spun yarn, and wove cloth. Although they generally did not perform heavy agricultural work, women helped with planting and harvesting crops and tended gardens near their houses. If their husbands worked as merchants or craftsmen, wives might also help out in the shop.

Children undertook tasks appropriate to their age and sex, beginning work shortly after their fifth birthday. Older siblings cared for younger ones, fetched tools, and minded cattle. Around age 10, girls began learning more complicated housekeeping skills from their mothers, and boys received instruction from their fathers in such tasks as plowing, cutting hay and wood, and caring for livestock. Many children in their early teens performed tasks little different from adult duties. By the time Nathaniel Ingersoll of Salem, Massachusetts, was 11, he already knew how to handle a plow and ox team.

No family could produce all the goods that it needed, so New Englanders regularly traded with their neighbors. A skilled carpenter might erect a house—often larger and sturdier than the ramshackle dwellings of Chesapeake settlers—in return for barrels of salted beef. Men with several sons sent them to help neighbors whose children were too young to work. Midwives delivered babies in return for cheese or eggs. Women nursed sick neighbors, whom they might one day call on for similar help. These sorts of transactions allowed most New Englanders to enjoy a fairly comfortable life, one that many Virginians might have envied.

Without a staple crop like tobacco, New England prospered by exploiting a variety of resources, developing a diversified economy that was less vulnerable to depression than Virginia's. Farmers sent livestock and meat to merchants to be marketed abroad. Fishermen caught thousands of pounds of cod, haddock, and other fish to be sold in Europe. Some of the region's timber found its way abroad, but most of it ended up in shipyards. New Englanders became such skilled shipbuilders and seafaring merchants that by the 1670s, London merchants were complaining about competition from them. England itself had little use for the dried fish, livestock, salted meat, and wood products that New England vessels carried, but enterprising merchants found exactly the market they needed in the West Indies.

The English in the Caribbean

The Spanish claimed all Caribbean islands by right of Columbus's discovery, but during the early seventeenth century, French, Dutch, and English adventurers boldly defied them. By the 1640s, the English occupied Antigua, Barbados, Montserrat, Nevis, and St. Christopher; in 1655, they conquered the Spanish-held island of Jamaica (see Map 2-3). Although a few English efforts, including

Map 2-3 ***Principal European Possessions in the Caribbean in the Seventeenth Century***
Europeans scrambled for control of Caribbean islands, where they raised sugar cane with slave labor. On many islands, Africans soon formed the majority of the population. In some cases, colonists from one European country settled on lands claimed by a rival power. For instance, English settlers established bases in Belize and on the Mosquito Coast, both of which were claimed by Spain.

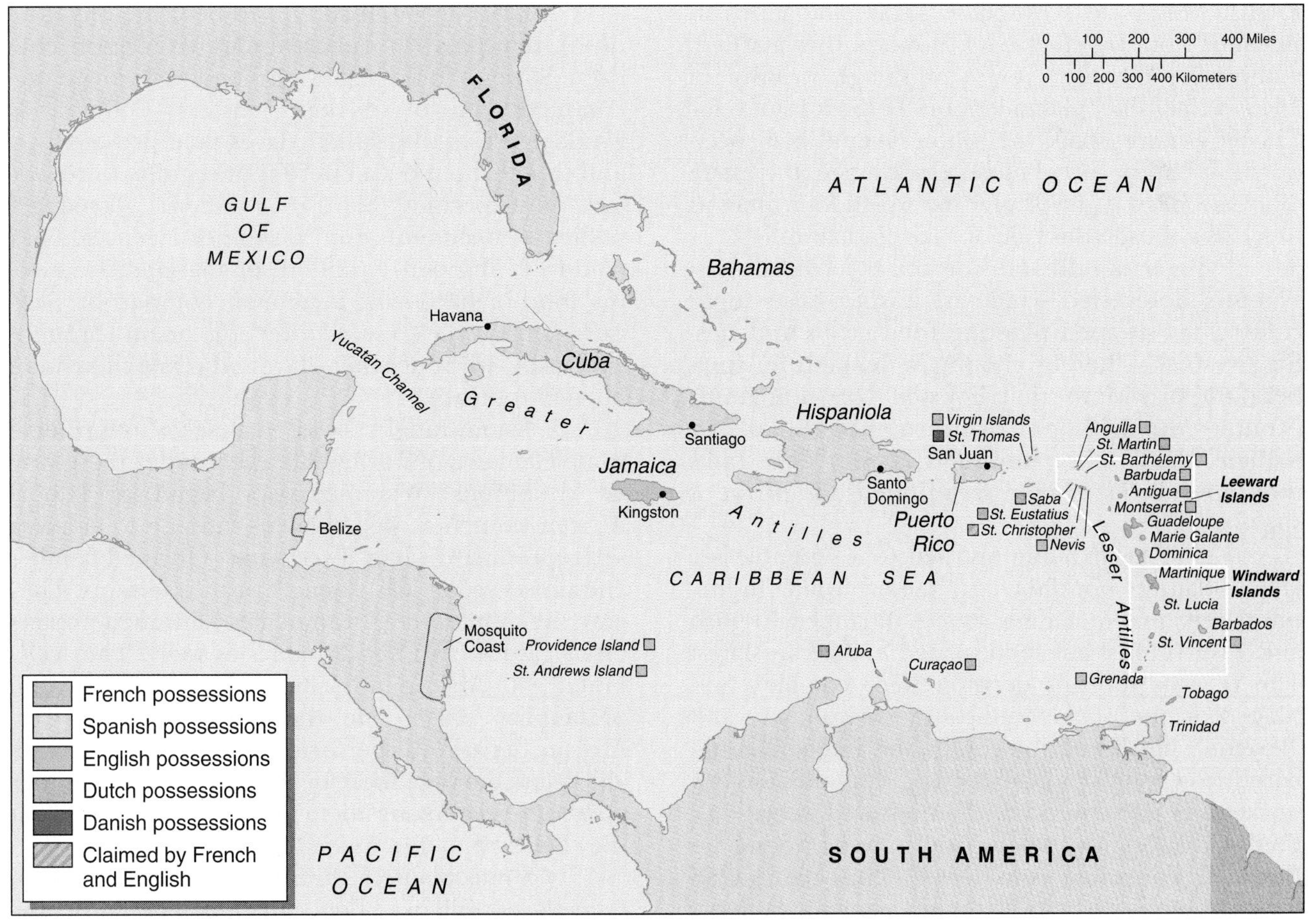

an attempt to found a Puritan colony on Providence Island off Nicaragua's coast, failed, the West Indies soon became the jewel of England's empire, producing vast wealth from the cultivation of sugar. Caribbean planters created a society totally unlike any of the mainland colonies—not least of all because their prosperity depended on the exploitation of African slaves.

Sugar and Slaves

Like the early Virginians, the first English colonists who came to the West Indies in the 1630s raised tobacco and imported indentured servants to work their fields. By that time, however, tobacco fetched low prices. Moreover, the disease environment of the West Indies proved even harsher than that of the Chesapeake, and settlers died in great numbers. That thousands came anyway during the 1620s and 1630s testified more to their hopes for prosperity than their actual chances of success.

But by the 1640s, a Barbados planter boasted of "a great change on this island of late from the worse to the better, praised be God." That change was a shift from tobacco to sugar cane. How the English learned to grow sugar is unclear. Perhaps it was from English visitors to Portuguese sugar plantations in Brazil or from Dutch traders. However they learned, many sugar planters grew astonishingly wealthy. In 1646, a 500-acre plantation on Barbados sold for £16,000—more than the whole island had been worth just a few years before. On average, the estate of a Caribbean sugar planter was worth four times as much as a prosperous Chesapeake plantation.

Sugar rapidly transformed the West Indies. Planters deforested whole islands to raise sugar cane. They stopped planting food crops and raising livestock—thereby creating a demand for lumber and provisions that boosted New England's economy. In 1647, John Winthrop noted that Barbadians "had rather buy food at very dear rates than produce it by labor, so infinite is the profit of sugar works."

The sugar boom also led to a scramble for labor. Planters continued to import white indentured servants, including some kidnapped English and Irish youths, but soon turned to African slaves. The reasons for this decision were complex and hinged on the islands' unhealthy environment and extremely harsh working conditions. England could barely meet the demand for workers, and English workers, if they survived, often proved rebellious. English visitors who saw African slaves working on Brazilian plantations considered them better suited to agricultural work in a tropical climate. And the English would not have to enslave any Africans themselves; they could simply import people who had already been enslaved by other Africans and sold to Dutch or Portuguese traders. The planters' choice has been called an "unthinking decision," but it had an enormous impact on English colonial life, first in the islands and then on the mainland, where slavery would develop later in the seventeenth century (see Chapter 3).

A Biracial Society

The West Indies had the first biracial plantation society in the English colonial world. By 1700, more than 250,000 slaves had been imported into the region, quickly becoming the most numerous segment of its population. In Barbados, black slaves increased from 50 percent to more than 70 percent of the population between 1660 and 1700. Slaves lived in wretched conditions, underfed, poorly dressed, and housed in rough huts. They labored six days a week from sunrise to sunset—except at harvest time, when they toiled seven days a week in round-the-clock shifts. Masters considered them property, often branding them like livestock and hunting them with bloodhounds when they ran away.

Laws declared slavery to be a lifelong condition that passed from slave parents to their children. Slaves had no legal rights and were under the complete control of their masters. Only rarely would masters who killed slaves face prosecution, and those who did and were found guilty were subject only to fines. Slaves, in contrast, faced appalling punishments even for minor offenses. They could be whipped, branded, or maimed for stealing food or harboring a runaway compatriot. Serious crimes such as murder or arson brought execution without trial. Slaves who rebelled were burned to death.

Astonishingly, slaves managed to preserve some elements of normal life even under these brutal conditions. When masters began to import African women as well as men—hoping to create a self-reproducing labor force—slaves formed families and preserved at least some African traditions. They gave their children African names (although masters often gave them English names as well). They celebrated with African music and worked to the rhythm of familiar songs. And they drew on their West African heritage to perform elaborate funeral rituals, often burying their dead with food and other goods to accompany them on the journey to what they believed to be a much happier afterlife.

Some planters, profiting handsomely from their slaves' toil, lived better than many English gentlemen. They indulged in large houses, fine furnishings, and expensive clothing. Even so, many hated the hot, humid West Indian climate and feared the constant threat of disease. After making their fortunes, planters often fled to England, leaving their estates under the care of hired overseers.

But sugar made relatively few white colonists wealthy. Its production required a heavy investment in land, slaves, mills, and equipment. As great planters took vast amounts of land for themselves, freed servants and small farmers struggled to survive. After 1650, many of these poor men, looking for other places to live, headed for the mainland. They were joined by planters looking for a place to expand their operations once most of the good land on the islands had been brought under cultivation.

The Proprietary Colonies

The initial burst of English colonization ended in 1640 when England tottered on the brink of civil war. With the accession of Charles II to the throne in 1660, however, interest in North America revived. Charles II needed to reward the supporters who had remained loyal to him during his long exile in France. One of the easiest ways for him to do so was with huge grants of American land. Four new colonies—Carolina, Pennsylvania, New Jersey, and New York—resulted from such grants during his reign (1660–1685) (see Map 2-4). All were proprietary colonies, essentially the private property of the people to whom they had been given. Two of them—Carolina and Pennsylvania—like the earlier proprietary colony of Maryland, provided their owners the chance to test idealistic social visions. The origins of New York and New Jersey as English colonies, in contrast, lay not in proprietary visions of social harmony but in the stern reality of military conquest (see the overview table, "English Colonies in the Seventeenth Century").

Early Carolina

In 1663, Charles II granted a group of supporters an enormous tract of land stretching from southern Virginia to northern Florida. The proprietors, who included several Barbados planters, called their colony Carolina, after the Latin form (Carolus) of the king's name. They envisioned it growing from the few English outposts already in the region, established by settlers from New England and the West Indies, into a prosperous, orderly society.

One of the proprietors, Anthony Ashley Cooper, working closely with his secretary, John Locke, devised the **Fundamental Constitutions of Carolina**, a plan to ensure the colony's stability by balancing property ownership and political rights. It called for the creation of a colonial aristocracy, who would own two-fifths of the land and wield extensive political power. Below them, a large class of freeholders would own small farms and elect representatives to an assembly. At the bottom of the social order would be slaves.

This plan never went into effect. People moved in from Virginia and the West Indies and

Courtesy of National Library of Jamaica.

Authentic portraits of West Indian slaves are extremely rare. These sketches of Jamaican slaves show them going about the mundane tasks of daily life.

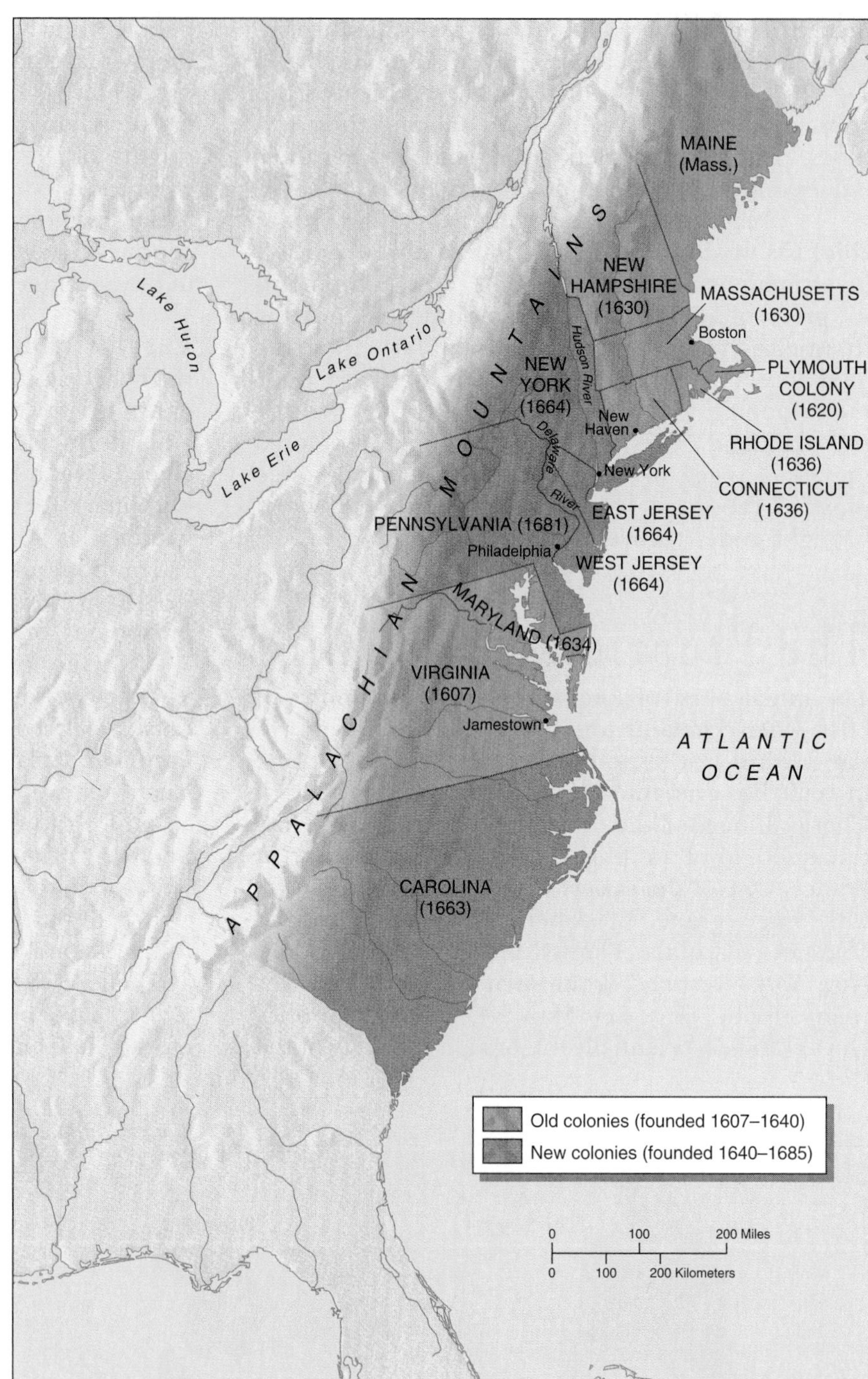

Map 2-4 English North American Colonies, c. 1685
After the restoration of Charles II in 1660, several large proprietary colonies joined earlier English settlements in New England and the Chesapeake. By 1685, a growing number of English settlers solidified England's claim to the Atlantic coast from Maine (then part of Massachusetts Bay Colony) to the southern edge of Carolina.

settled where they pleased. They even voted in the assembly to reject the Fundamental Constitutions. They antagonized the Indians in the region, who numbered perhaps fifteen thousand when settlers first arrived. When English traders first appeared, eager to buy deerskins, many Indians had welcomed them. But they grew hostile when some traders began selling guns to some tribes in exchange for captives from rival tribes whom the traders sold as slaves to the West Indies. Native resentments deepened as settlers moved onto their lands. The result was a deadly cycle of violence.

The colonists at first raised livestock to be sold to the West Indies. But the introduction of rice in Carolina in the 1690s transformed the settlers' economy, making it, as one planter noted, "as much their staple Commodity, as Sugar is to Barbadoes and Jamaica, or Tobacco to Virginia and Mary-

OVERVIEW

English Colonies in the Seventeenth Century

Colony	Date of Founding	Established Religion	Economy	Government
Virginia	1607	Anglican	Tobacco	Royal (after 1625)
Plymouth	1620	Puritan	Mixed farming	Corporate
St. Christopher	1624	Anglican	Sugar	Royal
Barbados	1627	Anglican	Sugar	Royal
Nevis	1628	Anglican	Sugar	Royal
Massachusetts (including present-day Maine)	1630	Puritan	Mixed farming, fishing, shipbuilding	Corporate
New Hampshire	1630 (first settlement, annexed to Mass. 1643–1679; royal colony after 1679)	Puritan	Mixed farming	Corporate (royal after 1679)
Antigua	1632	Anglican	Sugar	Royal
Monserrat	1632	Anglican	Sugar	Royal
Maryland	1634	None (Anglican after 1692)	Tobacco	Proprietary
Rhode Island	1636	None	Mixed farming	Corporate
Connecticut	1636	Puritan	Mixed farming	Corporate
New Haven	1638	Puritan	Mixed farming	Corporate
Jamaica	1655 (captured from Spanish)	Anglican	Sugar	Royal
Carolina	1663	Anglican	Rice	Proprietary
New York	1664 (captured from Dutch)	None	Mixed farming, furs	Proprietary (royal after 1685)
New Jersey	1664	None	Mixed farming	Proprietary
Pennsylvania	1681	None	Wheat, mixed farming	Proprietary

Thomas Coram's oil painting (c. 1770) shows the main residence and slave quarters on the Mulberry Plantation near Charleston, South Carolina. The distinctive steep-roofed design of the slave cabins on the left probably reflects African building styles. Slave quarters may not have been located quite as close to the main house as this picture suggests.

Thomas Coram, "View of Mulberry Street," (House and Street), oil on paper, 10 × 17.6 cm, Gibbs Museum of Art, Carolina Art Association.

land." The English had never grown rice, but West Africans had raised it since the 1500s. Rice cultivation in Carolina coincided with an increase in the number of African slaves there, who probably introduced it. Ironically, the profits earned from rice persuaded Carolina planters to invest even more heavily in slave labor.

Carolina society soon resembled the sugar islands from which many of its founders had come. By 1708, there were more black slaves than white settlers in the colony, and two decades after that, black people outnumbered white people by two to one. Rice farming required a substantial investment in land, labor, and equipment, including dikes and dams for flooding fields. Those who could afford such an investment set themselves up as planters in Carolina's coastal rice district, acquiring large estates and forcing poorer settlers to move elsewhere.

Some of these dislocated settlers went to the northern part of Carolina, where the land and climate were unsuited to rice. There they raised tobacco and produced pitch, tar, and timber products from the region's pine forests. So different were the two regions that the colony formally split into two provinces—North and South Carolina—in 1729.

South Carolina rice planters became some of the wealthiest colonists on the mainland. But their luxurious style of life came at a price. As Carolina began to look "more like a negro country than like a country settled by white people," planters dreaded the prospect of slave rebellion. To avert this nightmare, they enacted slave codes as harsh as those of the sugar islands.

Although John Locke went on to become one of England's most important philosophers, the visionary plan he and Cooper had devised for Carolina disintegrated on contact with American conditions. Carolina would not be a harmonious colony that balanced wealth and power; it evolved instead into a racially divided society founded on the oppression of a black majority and permeated by fear.

Pennsylvania

Even as early Carolina diverged from the plans of its founders, another Englishman dreamed of creating a colonial utopia. William Penn put his plans into action in 1681, when Charles II granted him a huge tract of land north of Maryland as payment for a royal debt owed to Penn's father. Penn intended his colony to be a model of justice and peace, as well as a refuge for members of the Society of Friends, or **Quakers**, a persecuted religious sect to which Penn himself belonged.

The Society of Friends was one of many radical religious groups that emerged in England during the civil war. Like the separatists, Quakers abandoned the Church of England as hopelessly corrupt. But they went even further in their beliefs. Rejecting predestination, they maintained that every soul had a spark of grace and that salvation was possible for all who heeded that "Inner Light." They rejected trained clergy and elaborate church rituals as unnecessary to salvation. Instead of formal religious services, Quakers held meetings at which silence reigned until someone, inspired by the Inner Light, rose to speak.

Quaker beliefs had disturbing social and political implications. Although they did not advocate complete equality of the sexes, Quakers granted women spiritual equality with men, allowing them to preach, hold separate prayer meetings, and exercise authority over "women's matters." Arguing that social distinctions were not the work of God, Quakers refused to defer to their betters. People of lower social rank were expected to remove their hats in the presence of superiors, but Quakers would not do so. And instead of the formal *you,* Quakers addressed superiors with the informal *thee* and *thou.* Because their faith required them to renounce the use of force, Quakers also refused to perform military service, which their enemies considered tantamount to treason.

When English authorities began harassing Quakers, William Penn (who was himself jailed briefly) conceived his plan for a New World refuge. He aimed to launch a "holy experiment," a harmonious society governed by brotherly love. Knowing that Quakers were unwelcome in the existing colonies—Massachusetts had hanged four of them—Penn looked elsewhere. His aristocratic background gave him advantages that other Quakers, who were mainly of humble origins, lacked. Using his father's connection with the king, he acquired the land that became Pennsylvania ("Penn's Woods") and recruited settlers from among Europe's oppressed peoples and persecuted religious sects. By 1700, eighteen thousand emigrants had left England, Wales, Scotland, Ireland, and various German provinces for the new colony.

No colonial proprietor was more idealistic than William Penn, shown here in a portrait made in about 1698 by Francis Place. Penn wanted Pennsylvania to be a place of peace, prosperity, and religious toleration—especially for his fellow Quakers. The colony eventually became an economic success but failed to achieve the social harmony that Penn had wanted.

Many came in families and settled in an area occupied by the Delaware Indians, whose numbers, though still substantial, had recently been reduced by disease and warfare. The "holy experiment" required colonists to live "as Neighbours and friends" with the Indians as well as with one another. Penn aimed to accomplish this by paying Indians for land and regulating trade. As long as Penn controlled his colony, relations between the settlers and the Indians were generally peaceful—so much so that refugee Indians from nearby colonies moved into Pennsylvania. Relations between Penn and the settlers, however, were less cordial.

In the **Frame of Government**, his constitution for Pennsylvania, Penn remained true to his Quaker principles with a provision allowing for religious freedom. But true to his aristocratic origins, he designed a legislature with limited powers and reserved considerable authority for himself. When Penn returned to England after a brief stay in the colony (1682–1684), the settlers immediately began squabbling among themselves. The governor and council—both appointed by Penn—fought with elected members of the assembly. Penn's opponents—many of whom were fellow Quakers—objected to his proprietary privileges, including his control of foreign trade and his collection of fees from landholders. Settlers on the lower Delaware River, which the crown had added to Penn's colony to give its port city, Philadelphia, access to the sea, gained autonomy for themselves with their own legislature, in effect creating an unofficial colony that later became Delaware.

A disappointed Penn lamented that the settlers had become "so brutish." He spent his fortune on his beloved colony, only to die in debt with his hopes for a harmonious society dashed. Settlers continued to fight among themselves, and with Penn's heirs, after his death. A flood of increasingly aggressive immigrants undermined peaceful relations with the Indians, forcing many natives to abandon their homelands and move west.

By 1720, Pennsylvania's ethnically and religiously diverse colonists numbered more than thirty thousand. The colony had some of the richest farmland along the Atlantic coast and was widely known as the "best poor man's country in the world." Growing wheat and other crops, the settlers lived mostly on scattered farms rather than in towns. From the busy port of Philadelphia—which William Penn had carefully designed to be a "green countrie town"—ships carried much of the harvest to markets in the West Indies and southern Europe. Penn's "holy experiment" in social harmony may have failed, but, as a thriving colony, Pennsylvania itself succeeded handsomely.

New Netherlands Becomes New York

The proprietary colonies of New York and New Jersey originated as the Dutch colony of New Netherlands. By the early seventeenth century, the Dutch Republic had become Europe's most powerful trading nation, with thousands of ships plying the world's oceans. New Netherlands was one of many outposts in its far-flung empire, which included others in the West Indies, Africa, India, and Formosa (Taiwan). Eager to supplant this rival, the English fought a series of wars with the Dutch in the 1650s and 1660s and gained control of New Netherlands in 1664.

The first Dutch colonists arrived in North America in 1624 to set up a permanent settlement at Fort Orange (Albany) in the as-yet unclaimed region between New France and English Virginia. Although Dutch traders ranged as far south as the lower Delaware and east into the Connecticut Valley, the heart of the colony was the Hudson River Valley from New Amsterdam (founded 1625) on Manhattan Island up to Fort Orange. The Dutch established a profitable trade with the Iroquois, who were eager to exchange furs for European tools and weapons.

The **Dutch West India Company**, the trading enterprise that established and governed New Netherlands, also tried to attract settlers in order to provision trading posts. In the 1630s, the company offered large landed estates (called **patroonships**), located mainly along the Hudson River, to wealthy Dutchmen willing to sponsor new emigrants. Few such estates were created, however, because most would-be patroons would not agree to company-imposed limits on their rights. In addition, few Dutchmen wanted to emigrate only to rent land from patroon landlords. At its maximum, the settler population of New Netherlands reached perhaps ten thousand.

What they lacked in numbers the colonists made up for in divisiveness. Ethnic differences prevented them from developing a sense of community. In 1643, a French Jesuit visitor reported hearing at least eighteen languages spoken on the streets of New Amsterdam. Among the colony's Dutch, German, French, English, Swedish, Portuguese, and African settlers were Calvinists, Lutherans, Quakers, Catholics, Jews, Muslims, and people of other faiths. Scattered in villages from Albany to the Atlantic, the colonists lived isolated and insecure lives.

The Dutch West India Company, more interested in making profits than keeping order, dispatched several inept but aggressive governors who made this unstable situation worse, mainly by provoking conflict with Indians. Although New Netherlands generally maintained good relations with its Iroquois trading partners at Fort Orange (Albany) on the upper Hudson River, it had far less friendly dealings with other Indian peoples along the lower Hudson, around New Amsterdam (New York City). In one particularly gruesome instance in 1645, Governor Willem Kieft ordered a massacre at an encampment of Indians who had refused to pay tribute. A horrified Dutch witness described Indian children being "thrown into the river, and when the fathers and mothers endeavoured to save them, the soldiers would not let them come on land, but made both parents and children drown." He saw victims "with their hands, some with their legs cut off, and some holding their entrails in their arms." Ten years later, Governor Peter Stuyvesant antagonized Susquehannock Indians along the Delaware River by leading Dutch forces in the seizure of a small Swedish colony where the Susquehannocks had traded.

These actions provoked retaliatory raids by the Indians, weakening a colony that increasingly looked like a poor investment to company officials back in Europe. Though profitable, the fur trade did not match the riches to be found in other parts of the Dutch empire. When an English fleet appeared off the coast in 1664 during one of the Anglo-Dutch wars, Governor Stuyvesant, in command of just 150 soldiers, surrendered without firing a shot.

Charles II made his brother James, duke of York, proprietor of this new English possession, which was renamed New York. James immediately created another colony, New Jersey, when he granted some of the land to a group of his supporters. New Jersey's proprietors struggled to control the diverse people already living there and fighting among themselves. At one point the colony split in two parts, East and West Jersey, which reunited to become a single royal colony in 1702 when the frustrated proprietors surrendered their rights to the king.

New York, which James retained for himself, was the most valuable part of the former Dutch colony. It included the port of New York City (the former New Amsterdam) and the Hudson Valley with its fur trade. James, who succeeded his brother to the English throne in 1685, encouraged Dutch colonists to remain on rather generous terms and promoted immigration from England to strengthen the colony and gain income from land sales. By 1700, the settlers numbered twenty thousand.

For nearly twenty years after its takeover by the English, New York lacked something all other English colonies had—a representative assembly. The Dutch had never created one, and James saw no reason to change that policy, despite the friction it created with his colonists. Particularly after neighboring New Jersey and Pennsylvania created their own assemblies, however, New Yorkers pressed their proprietor to follow suit. Only in 1683, when it became clear that New York might lose population to Pennsylvania, did James relent and create the assembly that brought New York into line with other English colonies.

Conclusion

During the seventeenth century, France and England joined Spain as colonial powers in North America. Far to the north, New France's small and scattered settlements clung to the St. Lawrence River Valley. The profits from the fur trade encouraged the French to maintain friendly relations with their Indian allies and ensured that French kings would monitor the colony's affairs and invest in its defense. English colonization, by contrast, was a more haphazard process. English kings granted charters—sometimes to joint-stock companies (Virginia, Plymouth, Massachusetts), sometimes to proprietors (Maryland, Carolina, New York, New Jersey, Pennsylvania)—and let the colonies develop more or less on their own. England had no equivalent in the seventeenth century of the imperial bureaucracies Spain and France created to manage their New World holdings.

The result was a highly diverse set of English colonies stretching from the Maine coast to the Caribbean. Settlers adjusted to different environments, developed different economies and labor systems, and worshiped in different churches. In many places—South Carolina, New York, Pennsylvania, the West Indies—the majority of settlers were not even of English origin. What held these colonies together—besides their establishment under English charters and their enmity toward the Spanish and French—was an overlay of common English institutions of government. By the mid-1680s, all the colonies had legislatures that provided for self-government and laws and judicial institutions based on English models.

The planting of French and English colonies not only ended Spain's monopoly of settlement in North America but also challenged the Indians' hold on the continent. Forced to deal with a rising tide of settlers and often to choose sides between European antagonists, native peoples struggled to adapt to rapidly changing circumstances. Transplanted Europeans adapted too, not only in their dealings with native peoples but also in finding and controlling the supply of laborers they needed to make their colonies prosper. For English colonists, this meant the adoption of slavery, an institution that did not exist in England itself. For millions of Africans, the result was forced migration to the New World.

Review Questions

1. The early settlers of New France and Virginia included few women. What effects did this have on the development of each colony?
2. Which English settlements were proprietary colonies? Did they share any common characteristics? What plans did the various proprietors have for their colonies, and to what extent were those plans put into effect?
3. When Virginia's settlers first arrived, they encountered a numerous and powerful confederation of Powhatan Indians. New England's colonists, in contrast, began settlement after epidemics had drastically reduced the local native population. In what ways did the presence or absence of Indians affect each region's early history?
4. In both Massachusetts and Pennsylvania, religion figured prominently as a motive for settlement. What were the religious beliefs of the settlers in each colony, and how did those beliefs help shape each colony's development?

5. Three colonial regions—the Chesapeake, the West Indies, and Carolina—developed economies dependent on staple crops. What were those crops? In what ways did staple crop agriculture shape society in each region?

Recommended Reading

Anderson, Virginia DeJohn. *New England's Generation: The Great Migration and the Formation of Society and Culture in the Seventeenth Century* (1991). Examines the experiences of nearly seven hundred emigrants to New England and explores the ways in which the composition of the settler population shaped New England society.

Dunn, Richard S. *Sugar and Slaves: The Rise of the Planter Class in the English West Indies, 1624–1713* (1972). The authoritative account of British settlement in the West Indies and the development of the slave labor system.

Eccles, W. J. *The Canadian Frontier, 1534–1760* (rev. ed., 1983). Provides a comprehensive overview of French settlement in Canada.

Morgan, Edmund S. *American Slavery, American Freedom: The Ordeal of Colonial Virginia* (1975). A vividly written account of the founding of Virginia and the development of an unfree labor system that remains the best study of an early American colony.

Wood, Peter H. *Black Majority: Negroes in Colonial South Carolina from 1670 through the Stono Rebellion* (1974). A study of the founding of South Carolina that emphasizes the contributions of the black slaves who eventually comprised a majority of the colony's settlers.

Additional Sources

New France

Choquette, Leslie. *Frenchmen into Peasants: Modernity and Tradition in the Peopling of French Canada* (1997).

Eccles, W. J. *Essays on New France* (1987).

Innis, Harold A. *The Fur Trade in Canada: An Introduction to Canadian Economic History* (1962).

Chesapeake Society

Carr, Lois Green; Menard, Russell R.; and Walsh, Lorena S. *Robert Cole's World: Agriculture and Society in Early Maryland* (1991).

Horn, James. *Adapting to a New World: English Society in the Seventeenth-Century Chesapeake* (1994).

Main, Gloria. *Tobacco Colony: Life in Early Maryland, 1650–1720* (1982).

Rutman, Darrett, and Rutman, Anita. *A Place in Time: Middlesex County, Virginia, 1650–1750* (1984).

New England

Cave, Alfred. *The Pequot War* (1996).

Demos, John. *A Little Commonwealth: Family Life in Plymouth Colony* (1970).

Hall, David D. *Worlds of Wonder, Days of Judgment: Popular Religious Belief in Early New England* (1989).

Innes, Stephen. *Creating the Commonwealth: The Economic Culture of Puritan New England* (1995).

Morgan, Edmund S. *Puritan Dilemma: The Story of John Winthrop* (1958).

Ulrich, Laurel Thatcher. *Good Wives: Image and Reality in the Lives of Women in Northern New England, 1650–1750* (1982).

The Proprietary Colonies

Dunn, Richard S., and Dunn, Mary Maples, eds. *The World of William Penn* (1986).

Goodfriend, Joyce D. *Before the Melting Pot: Society and Culture in Colonial New York City, 1664–1730* (1992).

Lemon, James T. *The Best Poor Man's Country: A Geographical Study of Early Southeastern Pennsylvania* (1972).

Levy, Barry. *Quakers and the American Family: British Settlement in the Delaware Valley* (1988).

Sirmans, M. Eugene. *Colonial South Carolina: A Political History, 1663–1763* (1966).

Where to Learn More

❖ **Jamestown Festival Park, Williamsburg, Virginia.** A museum contains indoor and outdoor exhibits on the site of the first permanent English colony in North America. The library holds material on early settlers and Virginia Indians; in addition, there are films and videotapes about early Virginia.

❖ **St. Mary's City, Maryland.** Visitors to this site of the first permanent settlement under the Calvert family may tour the area and view exhibits and living history programs that describe life in early Maryland.

❖ **Plimoth Plantation, Plymouth, Massachusetts.** A living history museum, Plimoth Plantation recreates colony life in the year 1627. There are reproductions of the English village and a Wampanoag settlement. Visitors may also see a replica of the Mayflower.

❖ **Pennsbury Manor, Morrisville, Pennsylvania.** A reconstruction of William Penn's seventeenth-century plantation, this site includes furnished buildings and restored gardens. There are also interpreters to inform visitors about agricultural life in early Pennsylvania.

The Creation of New Worlds

3

Chapter Outline

Key Topics

- Patterns of contact between Native Americans and French, Spanish, and English colonists
- The development of slavery and other unfree labor systems in early America
- The formation of African-American communities
- Causes and consequences of European immigration to America

Sometime before the spring of 1712, a Carolina slave named Harry took a terrible chance. His master, fed up with Harry's "roguery," had sold him to a new master in Virginia. But before he could be sent there, Harry ran away. This took great courage, for laws in both Virginia and Carolina prescribed mutilation and even death for recaptured runaway slaves. Harry then made the equally desperate decision to seek refuge among the Tuscarora Indians. Rather than sheltering him, the Tuscaroras might just as easily have killed him or returned him to his master for a reward.

But Harry was lucky, for he had skills that made him valuable to the Tuscaroras. He knew how to design forts and helped the Indians build a stronghold to protect themselves. From this structure, the Tuscaroras could attack the white colonists under whose oppression they too had suffered.

For years, Europeans had occupied the Tuscaroras' land, cheated them in trade, and kidnapped and enslaved them. When yet another group—this time Swiss and German settlers—marched across Tuscarora territory late in 1711, the Indians struck back, raiding frontier towns and killing or capturing their inhabitants. The Carolina government recruited a volunteer force of colonists and Indian allies and ordered it to search out and destroy Tuscarora settlements.

When these soldiers came near Harry's fort in the spring of 1712, their commander "found it strong as well by situation on the river's bank as [by] Workmanship." Under Harry's direction, the Indians had dug a deep trench around the fort and surrounded the high earthworks with "large limbs of trees [that] lay confusedly about" to make entrance difficult. They also arranged "large reeds and canes to run into people's legs" as they attacked the walls. The commander had never seen "such subtill contrivances for Defence."

Although the fort withstood a siege of nearly two months, the colonial forces ultimately prevailed. Most of the surviving Tuscaroras fled north to join the powerful Iroquois nations. Others "scattered as the wind scatters the smoke." Harry's fate is unknown.

This episode reveals three important features of the new society that was developing in England's Carolina colony. First, it had an astonishingly diverse population that included such Native American peoples as the Tuscaroras, Yamasees, Creeks, and Catawbas; Africans brought directly from Gambia, Guinea, and Angola or by way of the West Indies; and Europeans from England, Scotland, Ireland, Barbados, German provinces, and Swiss cantons. Second, the interactions among these peoples ranged from cooperation to outright violence. And third, what governed their interactions was a struggle for the control of resources, including trade goods, land, and labor. For slaves like Harry, the struggle was over nothing less than the most fundamental resource, control of one's own life—freedom.

In many ways, the history of North America in the seventeenth and eighteenth centuries is the history of early Carolina writ large. From the southwestern deserts to the Canadian forests to the Atlantic coast, diverse peoples met to trade, work, feast, worship, and fight. Their interactions, which varied from place to place and over time, created not one but many New Worlds.

Indians and Europeans

Between 1650 and 1750, a rising tide of immigrants—European and African, willing and unwilling—irrevocably altered the lives of North America's native population. By 1750, Indians had become a minority north of the Rio Grande. But despite their growing numbers, the colonists were concentrated in certain areas and did not yet dominate the entire continent. Indians living along the northern Pacific coast, for instance, met their first white men—Russian fur traders—only in the 1740s. In contrast, other native peoples—the Pueblos of the Southwest, the Hurons of Canada, and the Algonquians of the Atlantic seaboard—had by this time dealt with European colonists for a century or more.

The character of the relationship between Indians and Europeans depended on more than relative

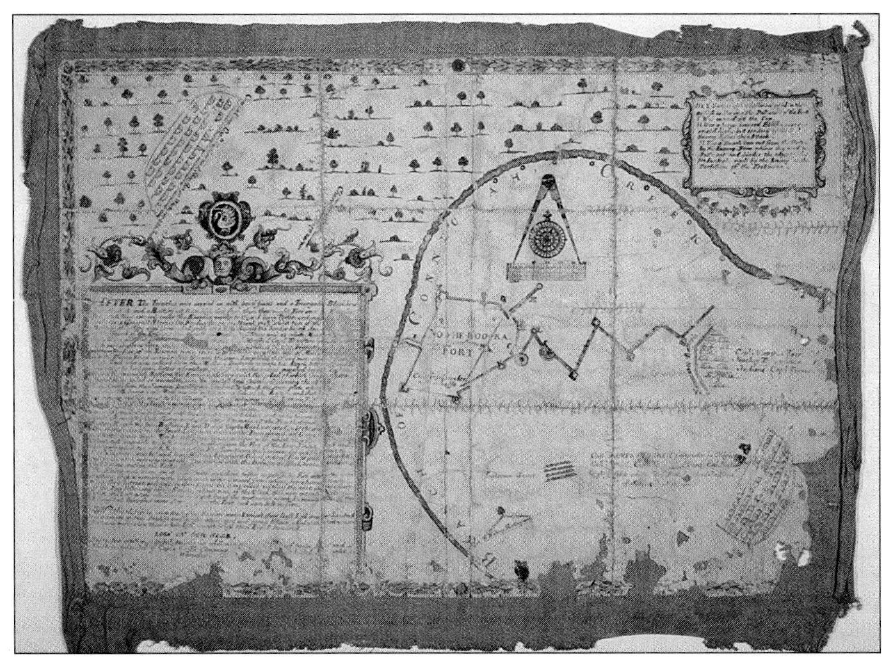

Runaway slaves occasionally found shelter among the Tuscarora Indians and, in return, helped the Indians defend their lands against white encroachment. The fort depicted here may have been constructed with help from runaway slaves during the brief Tuscarora War (1711–1713). About one-fifth of the Tuscarora population was killed or enslaved in the conflict, leading to the tribe's surrender and the migration of many of the survivors to New York.

population size and the length of time they had been in contact. It was also shaped by the intentions of the newcomers—whether they came to trade, to settle, or to gain converts—and the responses of particular Native American groups as each struggled to preserve its culture. The result was a variety of regionally distinctive New World communities. Many of the strategies Native Americans developed as they adapted to new conditions and tried to counter the intrusions of settlers would persist into the twentieth century.

The Web of Trade

Europeans eager to trade with Indians first had to enter into alliances with them. Indians refused to trade with enemies or strangers and demanded that Europeans prove their friendship by offering gifts and military aid as well as by trading goods. French traders in Canada adapted best to this practice. They brought gifts and prepared feasts for their native partners, obliging the Indians, in turn, to offer the furs that the French wanted. One seventeenth-century observer described the French governor giving the Hurons barrels of hatchets and arrowheads, in part "to waft their canoes gently homewards, [in] part to draw them to us next year." Each year the French acquired thousands of pelts, and the Indians got iron tools, kettles, cloth, beads, and—eventually—guns.

Indians could not have known that this trade would gradually destroy their way of life. One reason for this tragic outcome was that contact with traders exposed Indians to deadly European diseases (see Figure 3-1). The Huron population declined by half in just six years between 1634 and 1640. Indians trading with the Dutch in New Netherlands in the 1650s insisted that they had once been "ten times as numerous as they now are," but "their population had been melted down" by smallpox.

Trade also undermined self-sufficiency, making many Indian groups dependent on Europeans and others for essential goods. Before the French arrived, for instance, the Micmacs in easternmost Canada supported themselves mainly by fishing. But after becoming partners of the French around 1610, they trapped beaver year round, relying on others—mainly the French and New England Indians—for food. Micmac potters and basketmakers neglected to practice their crafts once their people began using French-made kettles and other goods. Only after they had trapped virtually all the beavers on their lands did the Micmacs realize the dangers of dependence. Abandoned by the French, who turned instead to the Hurons, the once-prosperous Micmacs barely survived.

Other groups would suffer a similar fate over the next century and more, growing accustomed to goods they could not produce on their own and facing hardship should their European partners withdraw from trade. "The Cloaths we wear, we cannot make ourselves," a Carolina Cherokee used to woolen garments observed in 1753. "We cannot make our Guns. . . . Every necessary Thing in Life we must have from the white People."

Another destructive aspect of European trade lay in its effect on warfare. Before European contact, most Indian bands living north of the

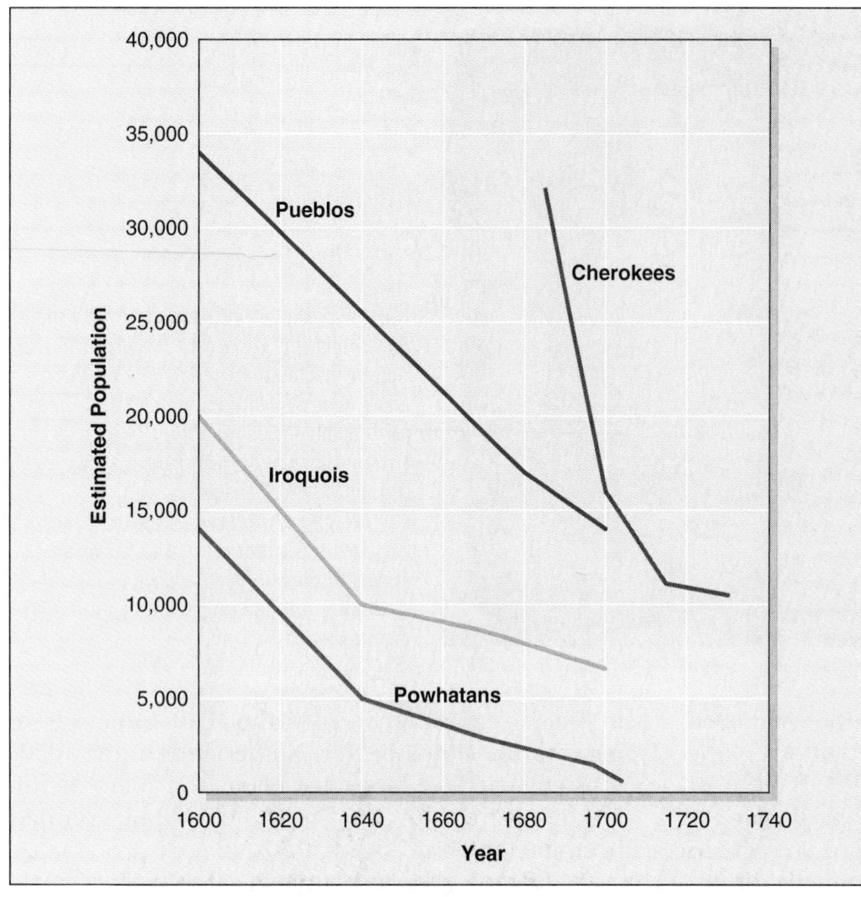

Figure 3-1 Estimated Populations of Selected Indian Peoples, 1600–1730

Indian populations shrank dramatically due to diseases brought by Europeans from the Old World. By about 1750, native peoples had become a minority of the inhabitants of America north of the Rio Grande.

Data Sources: *Daniel Richter,* The Ordeal of the Longhouse *(1992); Helen Rountree,* Pocahontas's People *(1990); David Weber,* The Spanish Frontier in North America *(1992); Peter Wood, et al., eds.,* Powhatan's Mantle *(1989).*

This eighteenth-century engraving illustrates, in idealized form, the way Indian peoples traded furs for European goods. The barrel may have contained kettles or other metalware packed in sawdust, while the bale to the left probably held cloth.

Chronology

1440s	Portuguese enter slave trade in West Africa.
c. 1450	League of the Iroquois formed.
1610–1614	First war between English settlers and Powhatan Indians.
1619	First Africans arrive in Virginia.
1622–1632	Second war between English settlers and Powhatan Indians.
1637	Pequot War in New England.
1640s	Slave labor begins to dominate in the West Indies.
	First phase of the Beaver Wars.
1651	First "praying town" established at Natick, Massachusetts.
1661	Maryland law defines slavery as lifelong, inheritable status.
1670	Virginia law defines status of slaves.
1675–1676	King Philip's War in New England.
1676	Bacon's Rebellion in Virginia.
1680	Pueblo Revolt in New Mexico.
1680s	Second phase of Beaver Wars begins.
1690s	Shift from white indentured servants to black slaves as principal labor force in the Chesapeake.
1701	Iroquois adopt policy of neutrality toward French and English.
1711–1713	Tuscarora War in Carolina.
1713	Beginnings of substantial Scottish, Scots-Irish, and German immigration to colonies.
1715–1716	Yamasee War in Carolina.
1720s	Black population begins to increase naturally in English mainland colonies.
1732	Georgia established.
1739	Stono Rebellion in South Carolina.
1741	Slave conspiracy discovered in New York City.
1750	Slavery legalized in Georgia.
1760–1775	Peak of European and African immigration to English colonies.

Rio Grande made war not to destroy their enemies or seize their lands but rather to avenge violent acts committed against their own people. Chiefs led expeditions to ambush the enemy, kill a few men, and take prisoners—some of whom might be adopted to replace victims of earlier fights. But after the Europeans arrived, Indians began to fight each other for economic advantage, and the hostilities became far more deadly. Rivalries among French, English, and Dutch traders led to conflicts among their Indian partners. The **Beaver Wars**, a long struggle between the Hurons and the Iroquois that began in the 1640s, illustrate the ferocity of such contests.

Because the French had already made the Hurons their trading partners, Dutch merchants in the Hudson River Valley seeking to break into the fur trade turned to the **Iroquois League**. Composed of five separate Indian nations—the Mohawks, Oneidas, Onondagas, Cayugas, and Senecas—the League had formed around 1450, long before the arrival of the first Europeans. For almost two hundred years it had functioned as a religious organization to preserve peace among the five nations and strengthen them in their conflicts with other Indian peoples. Envious of the Hurons' access to French trade goods, the Iroquois agreed to supply the Dutch with furs in return for similar goods.

To satisfy the European demand for furs, the Hurons and Iroquois both hunted beaver at an unsustainable rate. By the 1630s, they had killed nearly all the beavers on their own lands and began to look elsewhere for furs. The Hurons cleared new fields to increase their harvest of corn, trading the surplus for furs with Indians living north of the Great Lakes where beavers were still abundant. The Iroquois, however, began to raid Huron trading parties and then to attack Huron villages.

The Iroquois triumphed in the resulting conflict, largely because the Dutch supplied them with guns while the French were reluctant to arm the Hurons. In the end, the Hurons were destroyed. Thousands were killed or captured, and many others fled westward. A French traveler reported seeing no Hurons in "districts which, not ten years ago, I reckoned to contain eight or ten thousand men. . . . A little farther on, were but the shells of cabins abandoned to the fury of the enemy,—those who had dwelt in them having fled into the forest."

The cycle of warfare did not end with the Hurons' destruction. To maintain control over the fur supply, the victorious Iroquois went on to challenge Indian nations near the Great Lakes and in the Ohio Valley. Seeking iron kettles more durable than earthenware pots, cloth that was lighter and more colorful than animal skins, and guns that were deadlier than bows and arrows, Indians changed their lives in ways that suited their own needs as much as those of European traders.

Occupying the Land

The French and Dutch came to North America mainly to trade. The English, in contrast, came mainly to settle and had a correspondingly different impact on the native peoples on whom they intruded. Trading colonies maintained friendly relations with their Indian partners in order to keep the supply of furs flowing. The European populations of trading colonies also stayed fairly low. Even after the devastation of disease, Indians outnumbered Europeans in New France and New Netherlands. As late as 1650, there were just 657 French people in Canada (compared to perhaps ten thousand Hurons) and only three thousand Europeans in New Netherlands. By the same year, in contrast, there were more than fifty thousand Europeans and two thousand Africans in England's North American colonies.

The influx of settlers into the English colonies, as always, exposed native peoples to European diseases. To Puritan New Englanders, it looked as if the Lord was "sweeping away great multitudes of the natives . . . that he might make room for us there." So swift was the decline in native populations—and so rapid the influx of Europeans—that in coastal Massachusetts and eastern Virginia, colonists outnumbered Indians by 1650.

Largely because of the colonists' desire for land, violence between Europeans and Indians occurred with greater regularity in the English colonies than in New France or New Netherlands. The wars between Virginia's settlers and the Powhatan Indians and the Pequot War in New England, discussed in Chapter 2, were early examples of the many conflicts that marked the history of English colonization.

The first English settlers assumed that there was enough land for everyone. Colonists thrilled at the sight of what they considered vast unoccupied territory. "The Indians are not able to make use of the one fourth part of the Land," declared one New England settler. Another insisted that the natives "do but run over the grass, as do also the foxes and wild beasts" and that therefore the "spacious and void" land was free for the taking.

But the settlers misunderstood how Indians used their territory. Eastern Algonquian peoples moved frequently to take advantage of the land's diversity. They cleared areas for villages and planting fields, which native women farmed until the soil grew less fertile. Then they moved to a new location, allowing the former village site to return to forest. In ten to twenty years, they or their descendants might return to that site to clear and farm it again. Indians often built villages near the seacoast or rivers so they could fish and use reeds and grasses for weaving. In the winter, village communities broke up into small bands to hunt in the forest for deer and other animals.

Thus what the colonists considered "vacant" lands were in fact either being used for nonfarming activities or recovering from human occupation in order to be farmed in years to come. Settlers who built towns on abandoned native village sites deprived the Indians of these future planting fields. Indians tolerated such intrusions for a while, but competition from the rapidly increasing settlers threatened their survival.

Disputes between Europeans and Indians frequently arose from misunderstandings about the definition of land ownership and property rights. Indian villages claimed sovereignty over a certain territory, which their members collectively used for farming, fishing, hunting, and gathering. No Indian claimed individual ownership of a specific tract of land. Europeans, of course, did, and for them ownership conferred on an individual the exclusive right to use or sell a piece of land.

These differences created problems whenever Indians transferred land to settlers. The settlers assumed that they had obtained complete rights to the land, whereas the Indians assumed that they had given the settlers not the land itself but only the right to use it and that any Indian inhabitants would not necessarily have to leave. The Indians soon learned what the English meant by a land sale, however, because it was the English understanding that prevailed, enforced in the settlers' courts under the settlers' laws.

Many of the settlers' agricultural practices also strained relations with the Indians. Cutting down forests destroyed Indian hunting lands. When colonists dammed rivers, they disturbed Indian fishing. When they surrounded their fields with log fences and stone walls, they made trespassers of natives who crossed them. Colonial laws prohibited Indians from burning parts of the forest—something they had regularly done to destroy underbrush and make the woods suitable for hunting and travel—

because settlers feared that fires might spread to their property. Yet the colonists felt free to let their cattle and pigs loose to graze in the woods and meadows, where they could wander into unfenced Indian cornfields and damage the crops.

As their numbers grew, the colonists displaced Indian inhabitants, acquiring their lands in various ways. Some colonial leaders, such as Roger Williams in Rhode Island and William Penn of Pennsylvania, insisted on buying it. But even purchasers who tried to be fair encountered difficulties. Because Indians owned land collectively, only their leaders had the authority to negotiate sales. Settlers, however, sometimes bought land from individual Indians who had no right to sell it. Because land transfers were usually arranged through interpreters and recorded in English, Indians frequently misunderstood the terms of sale. And even Indians who willingly sold land to begin with grew resentful as colonists approached them for more. Finally, native peoples could be forced to sell land to settle debts they had run up with English creditors.

Settlers occasionally obtained land by fraud. In 1734, for instance, James Logan of Pennsylvania produced what he insisted was a copy of a deed from 1686 by which the Delaware Indians had supposedly transferred a large tract of land to William Penn. Although Logan did not have the original deed and there was no reference to it in the colony's land records, the Delawares eventually had to give up the territory. By the eighteenth century, some colonists moved farther inland, simply settled on Indian lands without any legal pretense at all, and appealed to colonial governments for help when the Indians objected. Land speculators amplified this kind of unrest on the edges of settlement as they sought to acquire land as cheaply as possible and sell it for as much as they could.

Finally, colonists often seized Indian lands in the aftermath of war, as befell, among many others, the Pequots in 1637 in Connecticut and, in Carolina, the Tuscaroras in 1713 and the Yamasees in 1715. In each case, settlers moved onto land left vacant as native peoples were killed, captured, and dispersed by colonial forces. Sometimes colonial leaders contrived for some Indian groups to help them displace others. During the Pequot War, Narragansetts aided Connecticut settlers' efforts to oust the Pequots. Carolina colonists enlisted the help of the Yamasees against the Tuscaroras and then turned to the Cherokees to help them against the Yamasees.

In the end, all these methods produced the same result. The English experience in the conquest of Ireland shaped the settlers' attitudes toward Native Americans. They viewed the Indians, like the Irish, as savages with whom it would be better not to mix. Like the English plantations in Ireland, English settlements in North America separated newcomers from natives. Colonists built communities on lands bought or taken from natives and then discouraged them from living there. In New France and New Spain, Europeans and Indians mingled more freely and even intermarried, but in the English colonies, separation prevailed.

Priests and Preachers

In addition to trade and settlement, religion played a powerful role in shaping relations between Native Americans and Europeans in colonial North America. The three major New World empires—those of Spain, France, and England—competed for Indians' souls as well as their lands and riches.

Catholic missionaries—mainly Franciscan priests—were the driving force behind Spain's efforts to control its colonies of New Mexico and Florida (see Map 3-1). Spain needed both regions more for strategic than economic reasons. Its bases in Florida helped protect Spanish ships bearing treasure from the mines of Mexico and Peru and discouraged the southward spread of English settlement. New Mexico similarly served as a buffer between the silver mines of northern Mexico and roaming Plains Indians. Neither colony attracted many settlers, however, because neither offered much opportunity for wealth. When Franciscan missionaries proposed to move in, Spanish officials—eager to back up their claims with a more visible Spanish presence—agreed and even provided financial support.

Franciscans settled near native villages in both New Mexico and Florida in order to convert their inhabitants to Christianity. The priests wore their finest vestments and displayed religious paintings and statues, trying to impress the Indians with European goods and Catholic ceremonies. They gave away bells, knives, cloth, and food. According to one Franciscan in New Mexico, these gifts functioned as bait, bringing Indians to the missions "like fish to the fish hook." The natives believed that accepting these gifts obliged them to listen to the priests' Christian message and help them build houses and churches.

After brief religious instruction, the missionaries convinced many Indians to accept baptism into the Catholic Church and with it the promise of salvation and a heavenly afterlife. Although many of these conversions were doubtless genuine, they also had practical motivations. They often followed epidemics that devastated native villages but spared the Spanish, leading many Indians to wonder if the Christian God

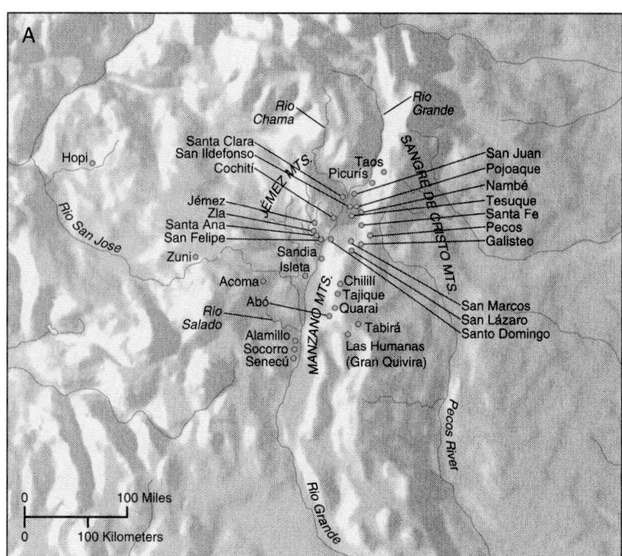

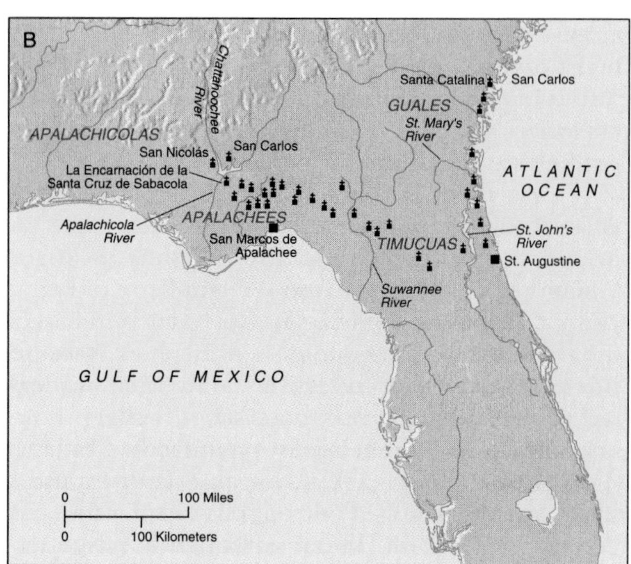

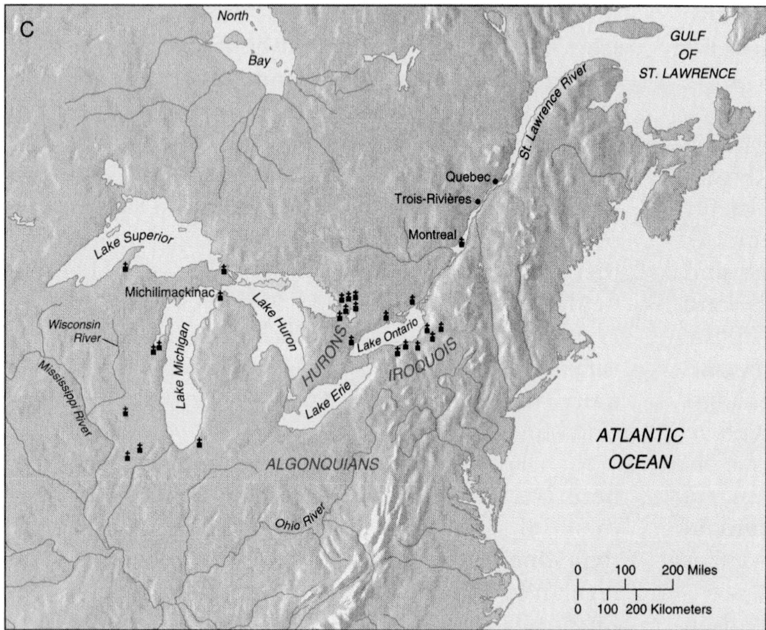

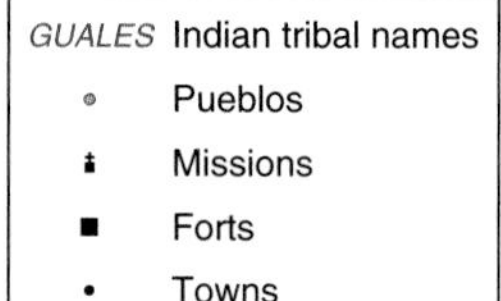

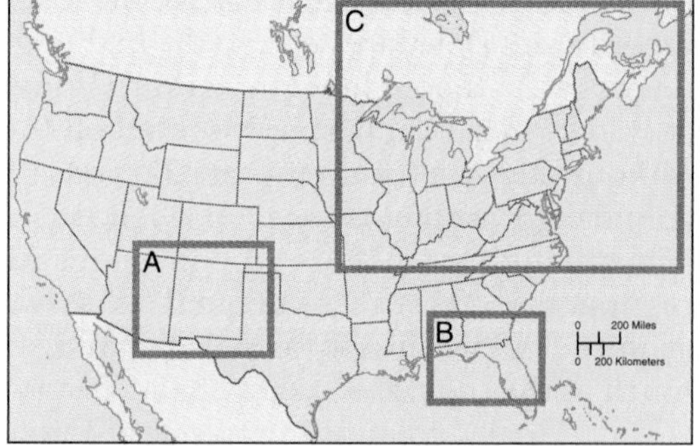

Map 3-1 Spanish and French Missions in North America
Spanish Franciscans in New Mexico (A) and Florida (B) and French Jesuits in New France (C) devoted considerable effort to converting native peoples to Catholic Christianity.

might indeed be more powerful than their own gods. In New Mexico, the Spanish offered Pueblo converts protection against Apache raids and access to Franciscan storehouses in times of famine. Ironically, the corn in the storehouses often came from the Indians' own fields, collected by the Spanish as tribute.

Many Indians did not understand that baptism committed them to a new way of life. The Franciscans insisted that converts abandon native beliefs, which they despised as devil worship. The missionaries sought to "civilize" the new converts by making them adopt Spanish food, clothing, and work routines. Priests in New Mexico, objecting to the ease with which Pueblo marriages could be dissolved, tried to enforce lifelong unions. Punishments for violating the new code were severe; in rare cases, they even led to their victims' deaths.

By the mid-seventeenth century, Spanish missionaries claimed to have baptized tens of thousands of Indians. But many converts blended Christianity with native religion, adding Jesus, Mary, and the Catholic saints to the list of Indian gods and accepting missionaries as counterparts to native priests. Many converts were ***mestizos***—people of mixed Indian and Spanish descent—who occupied a difficult position between two cultures and often practiced native rituals in secret. Some groups, such as the Zuni and Hopi peoples, rejected Christianity altogether. In the end, the spread of Christianity in the Spanish borderlands was not as complete as the Franciscans claimed.

French Catholic priests in Canada also lived among the native peoples, often at great distances from French settlements. Like the Franciscans, they tried to impress potential converts with religious rituals and material objects. Priests amazed Indians with such "magical" items as clocks and magnets and with their ability to predict eclipses and to read and write. Algonquian peoples had no written language and marveled when missionaries silently exchanged information by writing notes. "All this serves to gain their affections, and to render them more docile when we introduce the admirable and incomprehensible mysteries of our Faith," explained one priest, for the Indians would then "accept without reply what we say to them."

French missionaries resorted to economic pressure as well. They convinced merchants to sell guns only to converted Indians and to offer them other trade goods at a discount. In New France, as in New Mexico, native conversions usually followed epidemics, which undermined the survivors' faith in their own religion. And, as in the Spanish colonies, newly baptized Indians in New France often did not fully understand Christianity. But the Jesuits were generally more tolerant than the Franciscans of native ways. "One must be careful before condemning a thousand things among their customs," warned one priest, because to do so would "greatly offend minds brought up and nourished in another world."

The Protestant English were less successful at attracting Native American converts. Puritans frowned on the rituals and religious objects that drew Indian converts to Catholicism. And with its emphasis on the direct study of scripture, Protestantism required that potential converts learn to read.

Beginning in the 1650s in New England, however, Puritan ministers, such as John Eliot, established several praying towns, communities where Indians lived apart from settlers to learn Protestant Christianity and English ways. The few residents attracted to these towns were mostly survivors of groups destroyed by disease. Anglican missionaries in the southern colonies did not even begin conversion work until the eighteenth century and then often felt that the settlers needed religious instruction more urgently than the Indians. In the 1730s and 1740s, German Moravians—members of a Protestant group that stressed personal piety—managed to convert some Indians in western Pennsylvania. On the whole, however, settlers in the English colonies preferred to isolate Indians rather than convert them.

This Jesuit missionary, wearing his distinctive Catholic vestments, is baptizing an Indian in New France. French Jesuits proved to be more tolerant than most European missionaries in allowing Indian converts to retain at least some of their own customs.

After the First Hundred Years

After nearly a century of European settlement, violence between colonists and Indians erupted in all three North American empires. Each deadly encounter—**King Philip's War** in New England, **Bacon's Rebellion** in Virginia, the **Pueblo Revolt** in New Mexico, and the resumption of the Beaver Wars in New France—reflected distinctive features of English, Spanish, and French patterns of colonization.

King Philip's War, which broke out in 1675, was sparked by the growing frustration of the Wampanoags—the Indians who had befriended the Pilgrims more than half a century before—with the land-hungry settlers whose towns now surrounded them. Massasoit's younger son, Metacom—called King Philip by the English—led the Wampanoags and struggled to preserve their independence against the incursions of the colonists, who now numbered more than fifty thousand. He had little reason to trust the colonists. His older brother had died mysteriously while being questioned by colonial officials about rumors of an Indian conspiracy. Philip himself had been accused of plotting against the settlers and then forced to sign a treaty submitting to English authority.

In the spring of 1675, a colonial court found three Wampanoags guilty of murdering a Christian Indian who had warned the English of Wampanoag preparations for war. Despite Philip's protest that the evidence against the men was tainted, the court sentenced them to be hanged. This finally convinced the Wampanoags that they had to strike back against the English before it was too late. Only "a small part of the dominion of my ancestors remains," declared Philip. "I am determined not to live until I have no country."

Philip's forces attacked outlying villages in Plymouth Colony, moved into the Connecticut River Valley, and then turned eastward again to strike towns within 20 miles of Boston. As the Narragansetts and other groups joined the uprising, Philip successfully eluded the combined forces of Massachusetts, Connecticut, and Plymouth for months. By the summer of 1676, however, the Indians were exhausted, weakened by disease and food shortages. Philip moved into western New England, where his men clashed with the powerful Mohawks, long-standing enemies of the Wampanoags and allies of English fur traders in New York. Philip died in an ambush in August 1676, and the war ended soon after.

At least a thousand colonists and perhaps three thousand Indians died in King Philip's War. One out of every sixteen male colonists of military age was killed, making this the deadliest conflict in American history in terms of the proportion of casualties to total population. The Indians succeeded in forcing back the line of settlement—it would be forty years before colonists again occupied land they had first claimed before the war—but lost what remained of their independence in New England. The victorious English sold many native survivors, including Philip's wife and young son, into slavery in the West Indies. Others they employed in marginal jobs or confined in one of the few remaining praying towns. Philip's head, impaled on a stake, was left for decades just outside Plymouth as a grisly warning of the price to be paid for resisting colonial expansion.

As King Philip's War raged in New England, a bloody conflict erupted in Virginia that had a similarly devastating effect on that colony's native population. Frustrated by shrinking economic opportunities in eastern Virginia, where established planters controlled all the good land, many settlers, including wealthy new arrivals as well as recently freed indentured servants, moved to Virginia's western frontier. There they came into conflict with the region's resident Indians. In the summer of 1675, a group of frontier settlers attacked the Susquehannocks in order to seize their lands. The Indians struck back, prompting Nathaniel Bacon, a young, wealthy planter who had only recently arrived in Virginia, to lead the settlers in a violent campaign against all Indians, even those at peace with the colonial government. Governor William Berkeley ordered Bacon and his men to stop their attacks. They defied him and marched on Jamestown, turning a war between settlers and Indians into a rebellion of settlers against the colonial authorities.

The rebels believed that Berkeley and the colonial government represented the interests of established tobacco planters who wanted to keep men like themselves from emerging as potential competitors. Desperate because of the low price of tobacco, they demanded lower taxes and easier access to land—meaning, in effect, the right to take land from the Indians. Berkeley offered to build forts along the frontier to

This ball-headed war club, carved of maple wood, is thought to have been owned by King Philip, who led a confederation of Wampanoags and other New England Indians in a war against the colonists in 1675–1676. It is inlaid on both sides with pieces of white and purple wampum, which supposedly represented the number of English and Indian enemies killed.

King Philip's War Club. Published courtesy of Fruitlands Museums, Harvard, Massachusetts.

protect the settlers from the Indians, but the rebels were not interested in protection. What they wanted was help exterminating the Indians. They captured and burned the colonial capital at Jamestown, forcing Berkeley to flee. Free to direct their aggression against Indians once more, they burned Indian villages and massacred the inhabitants. Trying to appease the rebels, the House of Burgesses passed measures allowing them to seize lands belonging to Indians who had left their villages without permission—even though it was to escape the rebels that many Indians had fled. The assembly also legalized the enslavement of Indians.

By the time troops arrived from England to put down the rebellion, Bacon had died of a fever and most of his men had drifted home. Berkeley arrested and hanged twenty-three rebels, but the real victims of the rebellion were Virginia's Indians. The remnants of the once-powerful Powhatans lost their remaining lands and either moved west or lived in poverty on the edges of English settlement. In the wake of the rebellion, hatred of Indians became a permanent feature of frontier life in Virginia, and government officials appeared more eager to spend money "for extirpating all Indians" than for maintaining peaceful relations.

The Pueblo Revolt against Spanish New Mexico in 1680 had a very different outcome. Nearly twenty thousand Pueblo Indians had grown increasingly restless under the harsh rule of only 2,500 Spaniards. A prolonged drought that began in the 1660s only increased their distress. Corn harvests dwindled, and many people starved. The Apaches, who had once traded with the Pueblos for corn, now raided their storehouses instead, and Spanish soldiers could not stop them.

The spark that ignited the revolt, however, was an act of religious persecution. Spanish officials unwisely chose this troubled time to stamp out all remaining traces of Pueblo religion. In 1675, the governor arrested forty-seven native religious leaders on charges of sorcery. The court ordered most of them to be publicly whipped and released but sentenced four of them to death.

Led by Popé, one of the freed leaders, the outraged Pueblos organized for revenge. A growing network of rebels emerged as Spanish soldiers marched into Pueblo villages and destroyed kivas, the chambers that Indians used for religious ceremonies. By the summer of 1680, Popé—working from the village of Taos in northern New Mexico—had at his command an enormous force of rebels drawn from twenty Pueblo villages. On August 10, they attacked the Spanish settlements. Popé urged them to "break up and burn the images of the holy Christ, the Virgin Mary and the other saints, the crosses, and everything pertaining to Christianity" and ordered Indian converts to "plunge into the rivers and wash themselves" to remove the taint of baptism. Within a few weeks, the rebels had destroyed or damaged every Spanish building and killed more than four hundred Spaniards, including twenty-one of the colony's thirty-three missionaries. By October, all Spaniards had fled New Mexico.

They did not return for thirteen years. By then, internal rivalries had split the victorious Pueblo coalition, and Popé had been overthrown as leader. Even so, the Spanish now understood the folly of pushing the Indians too far. Fearful of inciting another rebellion, officials reduced demands for tribute, and the Franciscans eased their attacks on Pueblo religion. This spirit of accommodation opened a new century of relatively peaceful relations.

The Iroquois experience in the last phase of the Beaver Wars threatened to parallel that of the Indians of New England or Virginia rather than that of the Pueblos in New Mexico. What began as a

One of the many pueblos scattered along the Rio Grande valley, Taos served as Popé's headquarters at the start of the Pueblo Revolt in August 1680. Within a few weeks, the Indians drove the Spanish from New Mexico and destroyed most of their settlements. The Spanish did not return until 1693.

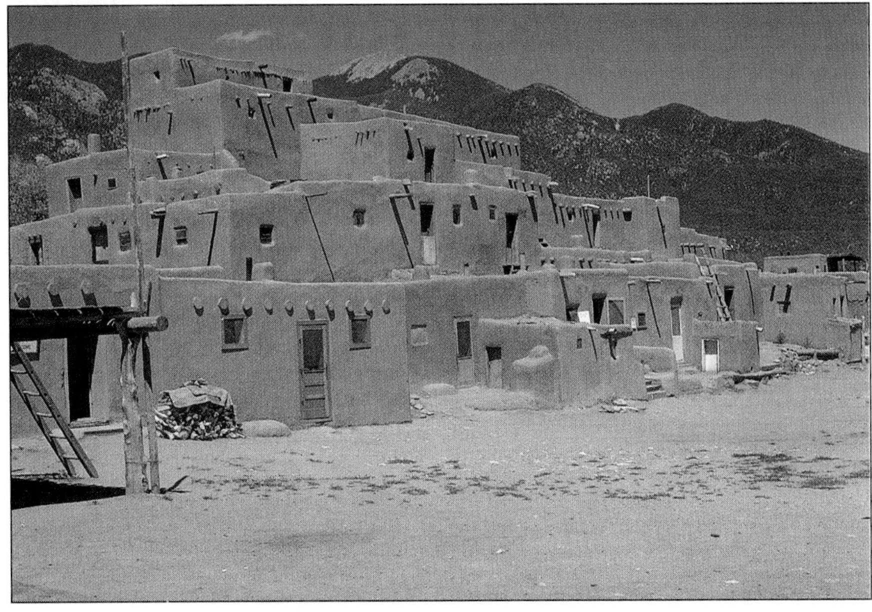

struggle between the Iroquois and western native peoples for control of the fur trade blossomed into a larger conflict as it was absorbed into the imperial rivalry between England and France. Although the Iroquois suffered devastating losses similar to those inflicted on the Indians in the English colonies, they did not similarly suffer a loss of independence. The key to Iroquois survival in the war's aftermath was the adoption of a position of neutrality between the European powers.

Looking for new trading partners to replace the Hurons, the French turned in the 1680s to the Ottawas, Wyandots, and other Indian peoples living near the Great Lakes. But the Iroquois had begun to raid these same peoples for furs and captives, much as they had attacked the Hurons in the first phase of the Beaver Wars in the 1640s. They exchanged the furs for European goods with English traders, who had replaced the Dutch as their partners after the conquest of New Netherlands. Many of the captives were adopted into Iroquois families, replacing victims of warfare and disease. When the French moved into the Great Lakes territory, the Iroquois objected to their attempt to "have all the Bevers" for themselves.

The French attacked the Iroquois to prevent them and their English allies from extending their influence in the west. In June 1687, a combined force of French and Christian Indian soldiers invaded the lands of the Senecas, the westernmost of the five nations of the Iroquois League. The Iroquois retaliated by besieging a French garrison at Niagara, where nearly two hundred soldiers starved to death, and killing hundreds of colonists in attacks on French villages along the St. Lawrence River.

The French participated much more directly and suffered greater losses in this renewal of the Beaver Wars than they had in the fighting of the 1640s. In 1689, France and England went to war in Europe, and the struggle between them and their Indian allies for control of the fur trade in North America became part of a larger imperial contest between the two countries. The European powers made peace in 1697, but calm did not immediately return to the Great Lakes region.

The conflict was even more devastating for the Iroquois. The English, still solidifying their control over their new colony of New York, provided minimal military assistance, and the Iroquois suffered heavy casualties. Perhaps a quarter of their population died from disease and warfare by 1689. The devastation encouraged Iroquois diplomats to find a way to extricate themselves from future English–French conflicts. The result, in 1701, was a pair of treaties, negotiated separately with Albany and Montreal, that recognized Iroquois neutrality and, at least for several decades, prevented either the English or the French from dominating the western lands.

Each of these late seventeenth-century conflicts between Indians and Europeans reflected the particular characteristics of each colonial power and the native peoples they were seeking to dominate. English settlers fought with Wampanoags, Powhatans, and Susquehannocks for control of land, and the losers were the outnumbered Indians. Spanish colonists clashed with Pueblos over religion, and the more numerous natives won a temporary victory and accommodation in the long run with the Spanish Catholic minority. French soldiers battled with the Iroquois over control of the fur trade until both sides agreed to an uneasy truce. In each case, nearly a century of contact culminated in a struggle that revealed how difficult, if not impossible, it was to reconcile European and native interests.

Africans and Europeans

Many more Africans than Europeans came to the New World during the colonial period. By the eighteenth century, according to an English observer, Africans had become "the strength and sinews of this western world." Virtually all of them arrived as slaves; thus the history of African experience in America is inseparable from the history of slavery and the slave trade. The evolution of slavery, its impact on both black and white lives, and the creation of a new African-American identity are essential parts of the story of the formation of New World societies.

The Evolution of Slavery in the New World

Europeans in the New World were thrilled to find that land was abundant and quite cheap by European standards. They were perplexed, however, by the unexpectedly high cost of labor. In Europe, the reverse had been true. There land was expensive but labor cheap, because competition for jobs among large numbers of workers pushed wages down.

Colonial workers commanded high wages because there were so few of them compared to the supply of land waiting to be developed. Making matters worse, few settlers wanted to work for others when they could get farms of their own. The scarcity and high cost of labor created a major problem for colonial employers, leading some to turn to enslaved Africans as a solution.

The development of slavery in the colonies was not inevitable. Europeans had owned slaves

FROM THEN TO NOW

The Legacy of Slavery

During a visit to Uganda in March 1998, President Bill Clinton made a brief statement expressing regret for America's past involvement in the enslavement of Africans. Some of his supporters had urged him to issue a formal apology for slavery, but Clinton refused to take what would have been a highly controversial step. Even so, Clinton's remarks sparked considerable public discussion.

While he was on his African tour, Clinton emphasized that the purpose of his visit was to address contemporary, and not historical, problems affecting that continent. "It is as well not to dwell too much on the past," he remarked. Yet separating modern problems from their historical antecedents is not easy. Less than a year before his trip to Africa, Clinton appointed a commission to study the persistent problem of race in America. That he selected an historian—John Hope Franklin—to head the commission suggested that Clinton recognized that America's modern problems with race are inextricably linked to the legacies of slavery.

Generations of scholars have endeavored to understand the origins of slavery and the institution's impact on race relations in America. Slavery's roots extend deep into the history of the nation, back before nationhood itself. The interconnections between race and slavery are complex, but one thing is clear. White colonists, facing a New World labor shortage in the seventeenth century, chose to fill their need for workers with enslaved Africans. Seeking to produce as much tobacco, rice, or sugar as they could for as little as possible, they left a painful legacy that has shaped America's history for centuries.

Long before the American Revolution, slavery was a fixture in every colony, and white colonists had come to associate slave status with black skin. The Revolution, with its rhetoric of freedom, challenged slavery but did not end it; it took another far bloodier war in the following century to accomplish that. But the constitutional amendments outlawing slavery and guaranteeing black people's civil rights passed after the Civil War could not eradicate the racism that had become deeply ingrained in American life. Succeeding generations have sought to reverse the legacy of slavery and make equality and justice a reality for all Americans. Yet as the controversies surrounding Clinton's speech and his decision to appoint a commission on race make clear, even at the beginning of the twenty-first century, the nation is still contending with the consequences of decisions made by some of the earliest colonists more than three hundred years ago.

Few eighteenth-century portraits depict the African slaves who were an integral part of colonial households. John Hesselius's portrait of Charles Calvert is an exception. In a graphic representation of racial and social hierarchy, it shows the young descendant of Maryland's founding proprietor in a posture of command, while his slave kneels in a subservient position at his master's side.

John Hesselius (American, 1728–1778), Charles Calvert 1761. Oil on canvas; 50¼ × 39⅞ in. The Baltimore Museum of Art. Gift of Alfred R. and Herry G. Riggs, in memory of General Lawrason Riggs BMA 1941.4.

(both white and black) long before the beginning of American colonization, but slaves formed a small—and shrinking—minority of European laborers. By the fifteenth century, slavery had all but disappeared in northern Europe, except as punishment for serious crimes. English laws in particular protected the personal freedom of the king's subjects.

Slavery persisted longer in southern Europe and the Middle East. In both regions, religion influenced who was enslaved. Because neither Christians nor Muslims would hold as slaves members of their own faiths, Arab traders turned to sub-Saharan Africa to find slaves who did not belong to either religion. Eventually the Arabic word for slave—*'abd*—became a synonym for "black man." By the fifteenth century, a durable link between slave status and black skin had been forged in European minds.

When Spanish and Portuguese adventurers needed workers to develop newly colonized Atlantic islands and New World lands, they considered slavery the best solution. Masters exercised complete control over slaves and paid them no wages. Slavery's advantages induced English colonists to adopt it in America even though it was unknown as a system of labor at home.

It was Indians, however, not Africans, whom the Europeans first forced into slavery in the Americas. Columbus's enslavement of Caribbean islanders marked only the beginning. Spaniards held Indian slaves in all their New World colonies, as did the Portuguese in Brazil. English colonists condemned Indian enemies captured in wartime to slavery as punishment for their opposition to English rule. And in early Carolina, English traders saw an opportunity to profit by enslaving Indians without any judicial niceties. They encouraged Indians "to make War amongst themselves to get Slaves" whom the traders could buy and then resell to West Indian and local planters.

Native American slaves, however, could not fill the colonists' labor needs. Everywhere disease and harsh working conditions reduced their numbers. English colonists also discovered practical reasons not to enslave Indians. When traders incited Indian wars to gain slaves, bloodshed often spread to English settlements. Enslaved Indian men refused to perform agricultural labor, which they considered women's work. Because they knew the land so well, Indians could easily escape and make their way back to their own people. As a result, although the Indian slave trade persisted in the English colonies through the eighteenth century (and there were still Indian slaves even in the nineteenth century), by 1700 it had given way to a much larger traffic in Africans.

The Spanish and Portuguese first brought Africans to the Americas, using them to replace or supplement the dwindling numbers of Indian slaves toiling in silver mines and on sugar plantations. English colonists, less familiar with slavery, adopted it more slowly. West Indian planters were the first to do so on a large scale in the 1640s, following the Portuguese example in using black slaves to grow sugar. In most other English colonies, however, a preference for white laborers or different economic conditions either postponed or prevented slavery's widespread adoption.

Black slaves first arrived in Virginia in 1619 when a Dutch trader sold "20 and odd Negroes" in Jamestown. But they did not form a significant portion of the colony's population until the end of the century (see Figure 3-2). For decades, tobacco planters saw no reason to switch from white indentured servants to slaves. Servants were cheap, available, and familiar; slaves were expensive, difficult to obtain, and exotic. Beginning in the 1680s, however, planters in the Chesapeake colonies of Virginia and Maryland began to shift from servants to slaves.

Two related developments caused this change. First, white indentured servants became harder to find. Fewer English men and women chose to emigrate as servants after 1660 because an improving economy in England provided jobs for them at home. Virginia's white population tripled between 1650 and 1700, however, rapidly increasing the number of planters now competing for a shrinking supply of laborers. Planters also faced competition from newer colonies. Pennsylvania and New Jersey, with generous land policies, attracted immigrant laborers away from the longer-settled Chesapeake colonies.

Second, even as white servants grew scarcer, African slaves became more available, largely due to changes in the slave trade. Before the 1660s, Dutch and Portuguese merchants dominated the trade and supplied mainly their own colonies and the profitable West Indian market. Beginning in 1674, however, England's Royal African Company began shipping slaves to English buyers in the Caribbean and on the mainland. The supply of slaves surged after 1698, when the Royal African Company lost its special trading rights and many English merchants—and New Englanders—entered the fiercely competitive trade.

Chesapeake planters eventually found reasons besides availability to prefer slaves to servants. Although more expensive than servants, slaves were a better long-term investment. Because slave status passed from slave mothers to their children, buying both men and women gave planters a self-reproducing labor force. Runaway black slaves were more easily recaptured than escaped servants, who blended into the white population. And unlike indentured servants, slaves were slaves for life. They would never compete as

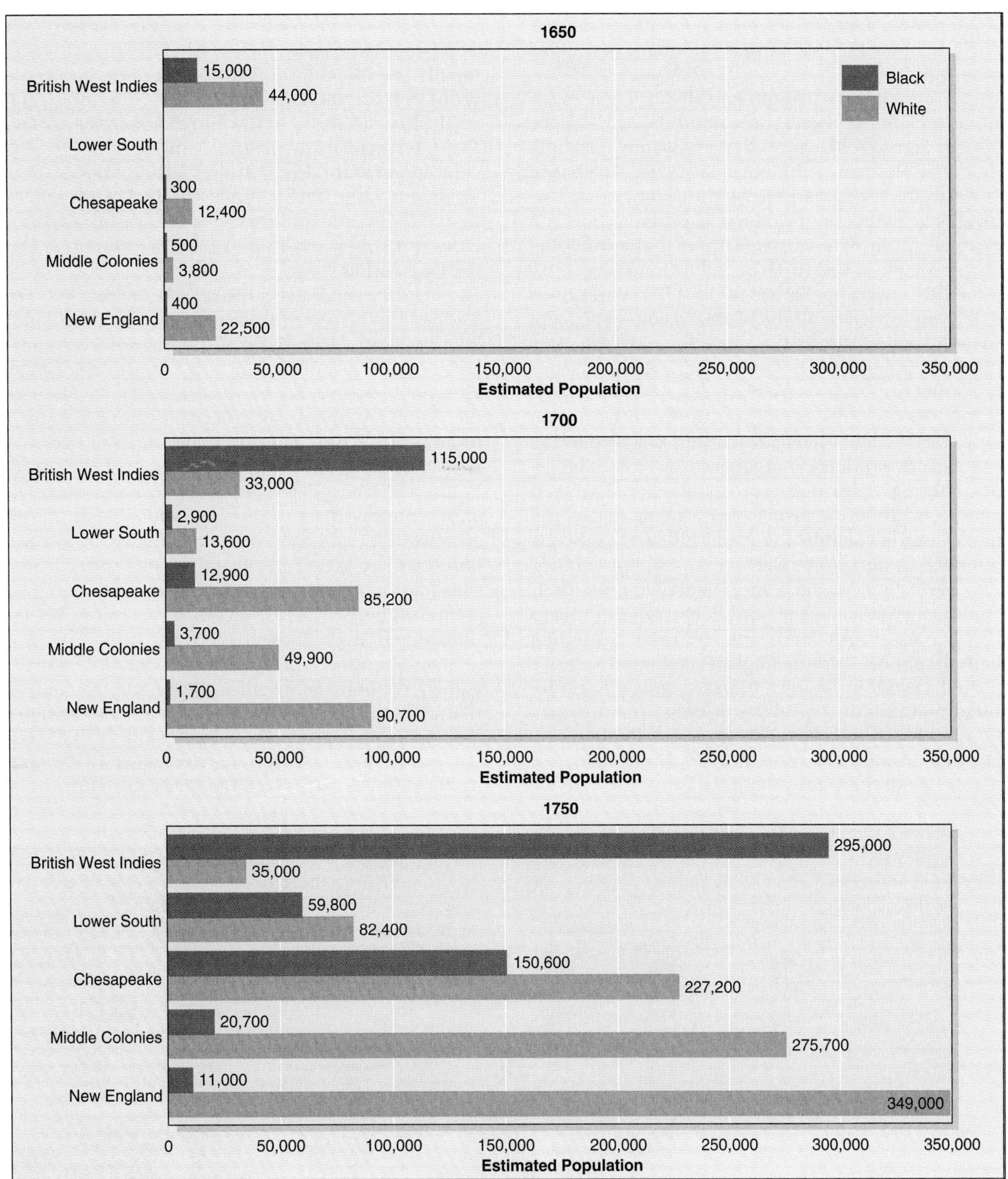

Figure 3-2 Estimated Population of Black and White Settlers in British Colonial Regions, 1650–1750

Settler populations increased rapidly in all colonial regions, but the racial composition varied. By 1750, black people overwhelmingly predominated in the West Indies and were quite numerous in the southern colonies; north of Maryland, however, their numbers remained small.

Data Source: John J. McCusker and Russell Menard, The Economy of British America, 1607–1789 *(1985).*

planters with their former masters or, like Nathaniel Bacon's followers, pose a threat to order if they failed to prosper.

Chesapeake planters had already come to see white servants as possessions, whose labor could be bought and sold like any other commodity. This attitude doubtless eased the transition in the 1680s and 1690s to the much harsher system of slavery. In Carolina, of course, the introduction of slavery was not gradual at all. Slaves arrived there right from the start, brought in the 1670s by colony founders accustomed to slavery in Barbados. By 1720, slavery was firmly embedded in all the southern colonies except sparsely settled North Carolina. In that year, one-third of Virginia's settlers—and nearly three-quarters of South Carolina's—were black.

Slavery grew rapidly in the South because it answered the labor needs of planters engaged in the commercial production of tobacco and rice. The demand for slaves became so powerful that it destroyed James Oglethorpe's plan to keep them out of the new colony of Georgia, founded in 1732. Oglethorpe intended Georgia to be a refuge for English debtors, who normally were jailed until they could repay their creditors. His idea was to send debtors to Georgia to produce exotic goods like silk and wine, benefiting both themselves and the English economy. Only rice turned a profit in Georgia, however, and colonists insisted that they needed slaves to keep up with South Carolina's planters. By 1750, Georgia's founders reluctantly legalized slavery; by 1770, slaves made up nearly half of the colony's population.

Far fewer slaves lived in the north. They were too expensive for northern farmers—who mainly produced food for their families, not staple crops for an international market—to use profitably. Instead slaves in the North generally worked as domestic servants, artisans, and day laborers. Except in areas of Long Island, where slaves grew wheat on large farms, and Rhode Island, where they raised cattle and racehorses, only in northern cities did slaves make up as much as 20 percent of the population.

Race relations in the mainland colonies were less rigid in the seventeenth century than they would later become. Before 1700, slaves did not form a majority of the population in any colony, which may have made them seem less threatening to white people. Most seventeenth-century Chesapeake planters did not own slaves. Those who did often held only a few slaves along with white servants. In these households, white and black people lived and worked in close contact. Black slaves and white servants ran away together and cooperated during Bacon's Rebellion. In some areas, free black people—often slaves who had bought their own freedom—prospered in an atmosphere of racial tolerance that would be unthinkable by the eighteenth century.

The career of an ambitious black Virginian named Anthony Johnson, for example, resembled that of many white settlers—a remarkable achievement given that he arrived in the colony in 1621 as a slave. Once free, Johnson married and raised a family. By 1651, he owned a large plantation, which en-

This late-eighteenth-century engraving, showing European slave traders on the coast of Africa, graphically illustrates the first step in the wrenching and dehumanizing process of enslavement.

abled him to provide his sons with land. He took his neighbors to court and on occasion successfully sued white settlers. He even bought a slave. The Johnsons impressed many in their community with their "hard labor and known service."

Anthony Johnson belonged to the first or what one historian has called the "charter" generation of American slaves, and his experience reveals how much slavery changed over time. These first slave immigrants mainly came from African port towns, where Europeans and Africans had mingled for generations, or by way of the West Indies or New Netherlands. Familiar with European ways, often fluent in European languages, they acquired skills and knowledge that enabled them to bargain with their masters in ways their descendants would not be able to replicate. They came in small groups, cultivated their masters as patrons, negotiated for property of their own, and often gained their freedom. They enjoyed such advantages because they came to colonies where slavery had not yet become firmly embedded, where the meaning of bondage was still being worked out.

But Johnson's descendants, and the generations of slaves who came afterwards, encountered much harsher conditions. After 1700, slavery became the dominant labor system in the Chesapeake. Tobacco planters no longer welcomed free black people, fearing that they might encourage slaves to escape. In 1699, Virginia's assembly passed a law requiring newly freed black people to leave the colony.

The condition of black people, both slave and free, swiftly deteriorated. **Slave codes**, laws governing slavery, essentially reduced an entire class of human beings to property. They defined slavery as a lifelong and inherited status—identified with black skin—that passed from slave mothers to their children. These measures deprived all black people of basic civil rights. They prohibited slaves from testifying in court against white colonists, congregating in public places, or traveling without permission, and denied them almost any possibility of freedom. Free black people, dwindling in number, were denied the right to bear arms or vote, required to pay special taxes, and punished severely for striking a white person, no matter what the cause. Interracial marriages, never common, were prohibited as "shameful Matches."

Colonists resorted to slave codes largely because of fears generated by a rising black population. In 1720, a South Carolina planter predicted that slaves would rise up against their masters because black people were "too numerous in proportion to the White Men there." The changing composition of the slave labor force also created tensions.

Unlike the charter generation, slaves who came later usually came from the African interior. Worried planters commented on the strange appearance and behavior of these people, with whom they could barely communicate. Their uneasiness, of course, scarcely compared to the Africans' harrowing experience of being torn away from the only world they knew and carried off to an unknown fate.

The Shock of Enslavement

European traders did not themselves enslave Africans. Instead, they relied on other Africans to capture slaves for them, tapping into a preexisting African slave trade and helping expand it beyond previous bounds. With the permission of local rulers, Europeans built forts and trading posts (called "factories") on the West African coast and bought slaves from African traders (see Map 3-2). African rulers occasionally enslaved and sold their own people as punishment for crimes, but most slaves were seized by one group from another. Attracted by European

Captured by Mandingo enemies and sold to a Maryland tobacco planter, Job ben Solomon accomplished the nearly impossible feat of returning to Africa as a free man. By demonstrating his talents as a Muslim scholar, including his ability to write the entire Koran from memory, he astonished his owners and eventually convinced them to let him go home.

"The Fortunate Slave, An Illustration of African Slavery in the Early Eighteenth Century," by Douglas Grant (1968). From "Some Memoirs of the Life of Job," by Thomas Bluett (1734). Photo by Robert D. Rubic/Precision Chromes, Inc., The New York Public Library, Research Libraries.

cloth, iron, liquor, guns, and other goods, West Africans fought increasingly among themselves to secure captives and began kidnapping individuals from the interior.

People of all social ranks ended up on the slave ships. Some had been slaves in Africa; others had been village leaders—and even members of royal families and the educated elite. In 1730, for example, Mandingo tribesmen captured Job ben Solomon, an accomplished Arabic scholar of the Fula tribe of Senegal, and sold him to English traders (see "American Views: Job Becomes a Slave" on page 81). In the end, slavery reduced all Africans, regardless of their social origins, to the same degraded status.

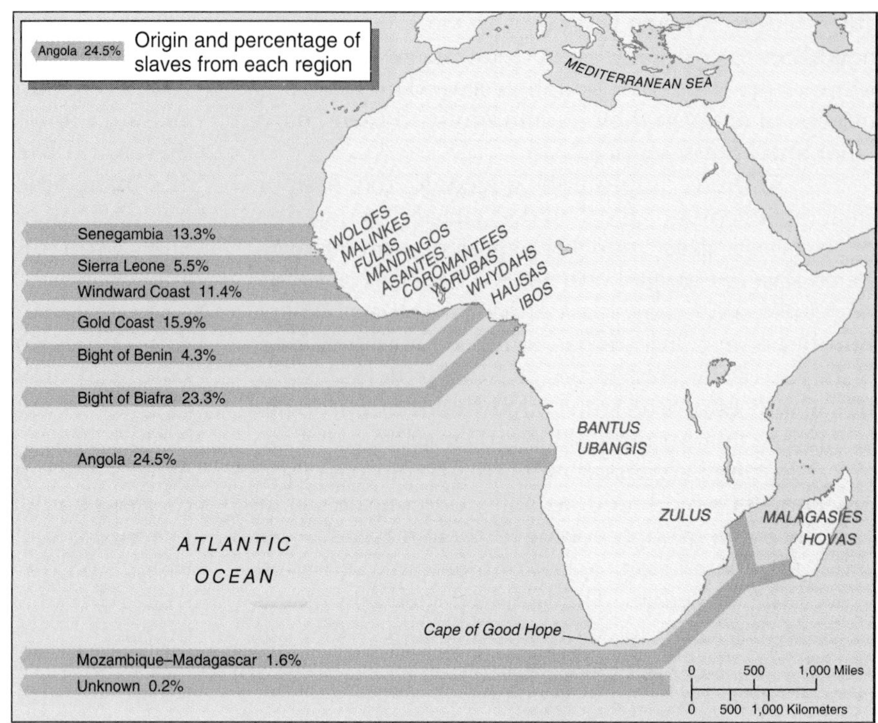

Map 3-2 ***African Origins of North American Slaves, 1690–1807***
Nearly all slaves in English North America were West Africans. Most had been captured or purchased by African slave traders, who then sold them to European merchants.

Once captured, slaves marched in chains to the coast, to be confined in cages called "barracoons" until there were enough to fill a ship. Captains examined them to ensure their fitness and branded them like cattle with a hot iron. The slaves then boarded canoes to be ferried to the ships. Desperation overwhelmed some of them, who, according to an English captain, jumped "out of the canoos . . . and kept under water till they were drowned, to avoid being taken up and saved."

Slaves brought safely to the ships suffered through a horrendous six- to eight-week-long ocean voyage known as the **Middle Passage**. Captains wedged men below decks into spaces about 6 feet long, 16 inches wide, and 30 inches high. Women and children were packed even tighter. Except for brief excursions on deck for forced exercise, slaves remained below decks, where the air grew foul from the vomit, blood, and excrement in which the terrified victims lay. No wonder that sailors sometimes heard a "howling melancholy noise" coming from below. Some slaves went insane. Others tried to commit suicide by jumping overboard or starving themselves. Captains force-fed those who refused to eat, prying their mouths open and pouring food in through a funnel. On many voyages, between 5 and 20 percent of the slaves perished from disease, but captains had usually packed the ships tightly enough to make a profit selling the rest.

Those who survived the dreadful voyage endured the fear and humiliation of sale. Sometimes buyers rushed aboard ship in a scramble to choose slaves. Planters generally preferred males and often sought slaves from particular ethnic groups. South Carolina slave owners thought that Coromantees and Whydahs from the Gold Coast and Senegambia were good workers but that Angolans had "a lazy disposition." Ship captains also sold slaves at public auctions, where purchasers poked them, looking for signs of disease. The terrified Africans often thought they were about to be eaten.

African-American Families and Communities

Only 5 percent of Africans brought to the New World ended up in the mainland English colonies; the vast majority went to New Spain, Brazil, or the West Indies (see Figure 3-3). Black communities developed slowly in early America. In the northern colonies, most slaves lived alone or in pairs with their master's family. Only in the cities, where slaves were more numerous, could they have regular contact with other black people. More slaves lived in the South, but until the eighteenth century they were

American Views

Job Becomes a Slave (1730)

Job ben Solomon was no ordinary slave. Born in Senegal to a family of Muslim clerics, he was captured by a rival African tribe, sold to an English slaver, and set to work on a Maryland plantation. He tried and failed to escape but astonished his jailers by writing a letter in Arabic describing his plight. The letter made its way to James Oglethorpe, an official of the Royal African Company as well as founder of Georgia, who bought Job and brought him to England. English observers marveled at Job's learning, which he demonstrated by writing the entire Koran from memory. Job was entertained all over London and even presented to King George, but he begged to go home. In 1734, he finally returned to Africa—an unprecedented accomplishment for an American slave. Thomas Bluett, a Maryland colonist who met Job while he was in jail, wrote and published an account of Job's experiences.

❖ **How did Job come to be captured in Africa?**

❖ **What humiliations did he suffer as a result of his enslavement?**

❖ **Does this account demonstrate any evidence of bias on the part of its English author?**

In February, 1730, Job's father hearing of an English ship at Gambia River, sent him, with two servants to attend him, to sell two Negroes, and to buy paper, and some other necessaries; but desired him not to venture over the river, because the country of the Mandingoes, who are enemies to the people of Futa, lies on the other side. Job . . . intended to go farther. Accordingly having agreed with another man, named Loumein Yoas, who understood the Mandingoe language, to go with him as his interpreter, he crossed the River Gambia, and disposed of his Negroes for some cows. As he was returning home, he stopped for some refreshment at the house of an old acquaintance; and the weather being hot, he hung up his arms in the house, while he refreshed himself. . . . It happened that a company of the Mandingoes, who live upon plunder, passing by at that time, and observing him unarmed, rushed in, to the number of seven or eight at once, at a back door, and pinioned Job, before he could get to his arms, together with his interpreter, who is a slave in Maryland still. They then shaved their heads and beards, which Job and his man resented as the highest indignity; tho' the Mandingoes meant no more by it, than to make them appear like Slaves taken in war. On the 27th of February, 1730, they carried them to Captain Pike at Gambia, who purchased them; and on the first of March they were put on board. . . .

[Job was sold to a Maryland planter] who put him to work in making tobacco; but he was soon convinced that Job had never been used to such labour. He every day showed more and more uneasiness under this exercise, and at last grew sick, being no way able to bear it; so that his master was obliged to find easier work for him, and therefore put him to tend the cattle. Job would often leave the cattle, and withdraw into the woods to pray; but a white boy frequently watched him, and whilst he was at his devotion would mock him, and throw dirt in his face. This very much disturbed Job, and added considerably to his other misfortunes; all which were increased by his ignorance of the English language, which prevented his complaining, or telling his case to any person about him.

Source: Philip D. Curtin, ed., Africa Remembered: Narratives by West Africans from the Era of the Slave Trade *(1967), pp. 39–41.*

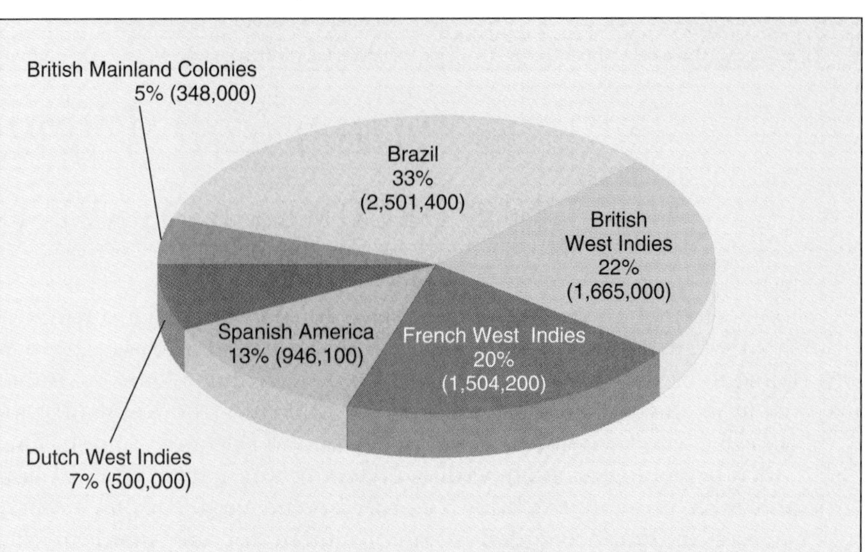

Figure 3-3 Destination of Slaves Imported from Africa to the Americas between 1451 and 1810 *Approximately 7.5 million Africans were brought as slaves to the Americas before 1810. The vast majority went to the Caribbean, Mexico, and South America, where they toiled in mines and on sugar plantations.*

Data Source: *Philip Curtin,* The Atlantic Slave Trade: A Census *(1969), p. 268.*

dispersed among a much larger white population. Slave numbers grew after 1700, but much of the increase consisted of African immigrants. These people retained their regional African ethnic identities and needed time to develop a new sense of community as African-Americans.

As bad as slavery was in North America, in one important way it was less terrible than slavery in the West Indies. On the sugar islands, many more slaves died—worked to death in a hot, disease-ridden environment—than were born, so the slave population grew only because of the constant importation of Africans. Conditions in the southern colonies, however, were less harsh, and by about 1750, more slaves there were **creoles** (American-born) than African natives. Creoles lived longer than African immigrants, and creole women usually bore twice as many children as African-born mothers. The mainland slave population therefore began to grow by natural increase and more closely resembled a normal population of men and women, children and elders.

Creole slaves grew up without personal memories of Africa, so African ethnic differences seemed less important to them. Language was no longer a barrier, for most creoles knew some English and spoke dialects they had created by mixing English and African words and speech patterns. The ability to communicate helped them develop a new identity as African-Americans that mingled aspects of their African heritage and their experience of slavery.

Kinship ties, crucial to West Africans' sense of identity, remained important to American slaves. Maintaining those ties, however, was not always under the slaves' control. Slave families were fragile units, subject to the whims of masters who did not recognize slave marriages as legal, who could break up families by sale at any time, and who could take slave women as sexual partners at will. Even so, slaves managed to form families that preserved and modified African traditions.

Households headed by mothers, common in West Africa, reappeared in America. Slave fathers often belonged to different masters than their wives and children and had to live apart from their families. Some slave husbands, like West African men, took more than one wife (a practice masters allowed because it led to more slave children). Slave parents gave their children African names, often secretly adding them to the "official" English names given by masters.

In Virginia and South Carolina, where by 1750 some plantations supported village-sized populations of slaves, communities preserved other elements of West African culture. Carolina slaves followed West African practice by building their houses of "tabby," a mixture of lime and seashells. Also following West African practice, the houses were sometimes constructed on a circular plan. Potters and basketmakers used African designs in their work. Slaves raised African food plants (millet, yams, sesame seeds) in their gardens. They also made music, performed dances, and told folk tales derived from African models.

Labor, however, consumed most of a slave's waking hours. Some slaves worked as domestic servants, but the vast majority were field hands. On tobacco plantations, slaves toiled in gangs supervised by overseers. Rice planters allowed their workers more flexibility, assigning them tasks in the morning and permitting them free time after they were finished. On large plantations, masters selected slaves to be trained as shoemakers, weavers, or tailors.

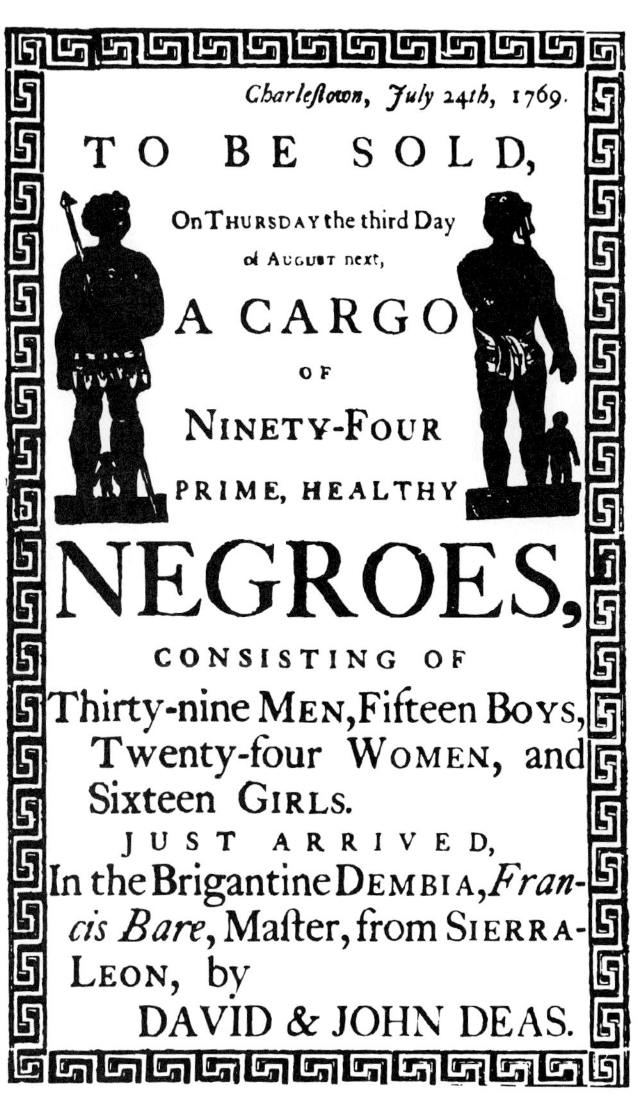

Charleſtown, July 24th, 1769.
TO BE SOLD,
On THURSDAY the third Day
of AUGUST next,
A CARGO
OF
NINETY-FOUR
PRIME, HEALTHY
NEGROES,
CONSISTING OF
Thirty-nine MEN, Fifteen BOYS,
Twenty-four WOMEN, and
Sixteen GIRLS.
JUST ARRIVED,
In the Brigantine DEMBIA, Francis Bare, Maſter, from SIERRA-LEON, by
DAVID & JOHN DEAS.

This 1769 broadside advertised the arrival of a cargo of West African slaves in Charleston, South Carolina. By that date, slaves made up over two-thirds of the colony's settlers. Note that nearly equal numbers of men and women have been imported. This practice would eventually contribute to the formation of slave families and communities.

These specialized occupations, like that of driver (or head worker), usually went to men. Only a few slave women—nurses, cooks—avoided the drudgery of field work. And after a day in the fields, slave women had to take care of their families, doing the cooking, child care, washing, and housework.

Family ties made a life in bondage more tolerable. The growth of slave communities—a slow process beginning only in the 1750s—gave a sense of belonging and dignity to people whose masters treated them as outcasts. Yet family and community ties also made it much more difficult for slaves to risk escape or contemplate rebellion. The master could use his power to break up families as a tool to ensure compliant behavior. In effect, every slave child was his hostage.

Over time, masters realized that their economic welfare and even their physical survival depended on the cooperation, or at least the submission, of their slaves, and this encouraged them to improve their treatment of their slaves. By the end of the colonial period, many masters had begun describing themselves as "fathers" to their slave "children." Few slaves, however, saw the relationship in the same benevolent light.

Resistance and Rebellion

Slaves on ships anchored off the Guinea Coast waiting to leave for America sometimes mutinied. These rebellions, fought against great odds, rarely succeeded. But the powerful desire for freedom and the spirit of resistance they represented remained strong among Africans and their descendants in America.

Running away from a master was a desperate act, but thousands of slaves did just that. Few runaways shared the mistaken impression of some new arrivals in eighteenth-century Virginia who thought they could "find the Way back to their own Country." But deciding where else to go posed a problem. Escape out of the South did not bring freedom, because slavery was legal in every colony. Some runaways went to Florida, where after 1733 Spanish officials promised them freedom. Others tried to survive on their own in the woods or join the Indians, a choice that carried the risk of capture or death. South Carolina planters paid Indians to catch escaped slaves, largely to sow seeds of distrust between the two peoples and prevent them from joining forces against white colonists. For slaves with families, running away carried the high emotional cost of separation from loved ones as well as physical danger. Many chose other ways to resist their bondage.

Landon Carter of Virginia, who complained that his slaves "seem to be quite dead hearted and either cannot or will not work," was the target of forms of resistance more subtle, but every bit as real, as running away. Slaves worked slowly, broke tools, and pretended to be ill in order to conserve strength and exert some control over their working lives. When provoked, they also took more direct action, damaging crops, stealing goods, and setting fire to their masters' barns, houses, and fields. Slaves with knowledge of poisonous plants occasionally tried to kill their white owners, although the penalty for being caught was to be burned to death.

The most serious, as well as the rarest, form of resistance was organized rebellion. South Carolinians

Abby Aldrich Rockefeller Folk Art Center, Williamsburg, VA.

This eighteenth-century painting from South Carolina records the preservation of certain African traditions in American slave communities. The dance may be Yoruba in origin, while the stringed instrument and drum were probably modeled on African instruments.

and coastal Virginians, who lived in regions where black people outnumbered white people, had a particular dread of slave revolt. Rebellions, however, required complete secrecy, careful planning, and access to weapons, which made them extremely hard to organize. No slave rebellion succeeded in the British colonies. Rumors usually leaked out before any action had been taken, prompting severe reprisals against the alleged conspirators. In Charleston, South Carolina, rumors of a planned uprising in 1740 led to the torture and execution of fifty black suspects. The following year, thirty-five alleged rebels (including four white people) were executed in New York City.

Two slave revolts did occur in the colonial period, however, and instilled lasting fear in the white colonists. In 1712 in New York City, where black people made up perhaps 20 percent of the population, about twenty slaves set a building on fire and killed nine white men who came to put it out. The revolt was quickly suppressed. The court tried forty-three rebels and sentenced twenty-four to death. Their punishments revealed the extent of white terror: thirteen were hanged, three burned at the stake, one starved to death, and one broken on the wheel. Six committed suicide before execution.

The **Stono Rebellion**, colonial America's largest slave uprising, occurred in South Carolina in 1739. It began when about twenty slaves—including several recently arrived Angolans—broke into a store and armed themselves with stolen guns. As the rebels marched southward along the Stono River, their ranks grew to perhaps a hundred. Heading for freedom in Spanish Florida, they attacked white settlements along the way. White troops (with Indian help) defeated the rebels within a week, but tensions remained high for months. The death toll, in the end, was about two dozen white people and perhaps twice as many black rebels. Planters boasted that they "did not torture one Negroe, but only put them to an easy death," although one settler claimed that white soldiers "Cutt off their heads and set them up at every Mile Post they came to."

In the wake of the Stono Rebellion, South Carolina's assembly passed a law requiring stricter supervision of slave activities. Other measures encouraged more white immigration to offset the colony's black majority. But the colony continued to rely on the labor system that generated so much fear and brutality. In South Carolina, as in the rest of the southern colonies, planters considered slavery indispensable to their economic survival and would not willingly give it up. Their slaves, in turn, obeyed when necessary, resisted when possible, and kept alive the hope that freedom would one day be theirs.

Nonslave Labor in Early America

Slavery was one of several responses to the scarcity of labor in the New World. It took hold mainly in areas where the profits from growing export crops such as sugar, rice, and tobacco offset the high purchase price of slaves and where a warm climate permitted year-round work. Elsewhere, Europeans found other means to acquire and manage laborers. Indentured servitude, forced labor, tenancy, and the extension of credit all aimed at limiting the freedom of some people in order to make them work for others.

Indian Workers in New France and the Spanish Borderlands

The French and Spanish colonies relied more heavily on native laborers than the English did. The fur trade in New France was in effect a way for the French to harness Indian labor. French officials promised military support, and merchants extended credit in order to get native hunters to trap beavers. By supplying Indians with trade goods in advance, merchants obligated them to bring in furs as payment. One year's hunting, in short, paid the previous year's debts. If Indians tried to avoid payment, merchants refused to give them any more of the trade goods on which they had come to depend. Extending credit in this way allowed the French to control native workers without having to subjugate them.

The Spanish used more direct means to control Indian labor, employing three main methods: ***encomienda***, ***repartimiento***, and ***rescate***. *Encomiendas*, granted to influential Spaniards in New Mexico, gave them the right to collect tribute—usually in the form of corn, blankets, and animal hides—from a specific group of natives. The tribute was not supposed to include forced labor but often did. Excessive demands for tribute fueled Indian anger during the Pueblo Revolt, and when the Spaniards returned to New Mexico in 1693, they did not reimpose the *encomienda* system.

In New Mexico and Florida, the *repartimiento*—a mandatory draft of native labor for public projects—set Indians to work building forts, bridges, and roads. Laws stated that native workers should be paid and limited the length of service, but the Spanish often ignored these provisions and sometimes forced Indians to work on their private estates. Spaniards also acquired laborers by ransoming captives that Indian tribes seized from one another, a practice called *rescate* ("ransom"). These "freed" Indians usually became servants in Spanish households, often for years. Some families welcomed them as foster members, but others mistreated them or even sold them into slavery.

These methods of labor control depended on two factors: the existence of sizable Indian communities and Spanish military force. Native villages provided plenty of workers as well as existing structures of government that the Spanish could use to collect tribute and organize gangs of workers. At the same time, Spanish soldiers ensured that the Indians—who outnumbered the colonists—obeyed orders. Even the Franciscans relied on military support to control native workers in the missions.

Laborers in the English Colonies

In the English colonies, slavery was just the most oppressive extreme in a spectrum of practices designed to exert control over workers and relieve the problems caused by the easy availability of land and the high cost of labor. Most colonial laborers were, in some measure, unfree (see the overview table "Principal Colonial Labor Systems, 1750").

One-half to two-thirds of all white emigrants to the English colonies arrived as indentured servants, bound by contract to serve masters for a period of years. Tens of thousands of people accepted temporary servitude in return for passage across the Atlantic and the chance for a more prosperous future in America. But indentured servants, though less costly than slaves, carried too high a price for farmers who raised crops mainly for subsistence rather than for sale. Thus servants were most common in the Chesapeake and to a lesser extent in Pennsylvania, where they produced export crops valuable enough to enable their masters to feed, clothe, and shelter them—and still make a profit.

Slaves replaced white indentured servants in Chesapeake tobacco fields during the eighteenth century. Masters continued to import servants for a while to fill skilled jobs but in time trained the more plentiful slaves to fill those positions. Thus, by the middle of the eighteenth century, white servitude, although it still existed in the Chesapeake region as well as in

OVERVIEW

PRINCIPAL COLONIAL LABOR SYSTEMS, 1750

	Colony	Labor System
New England	Massachusetts	Family farms
	Connecticut	Family farms
	New Hampshire	Family farms
	Rhode Island	Family farms
Middle Colonies	New York	Family farms, tenancy
	Pennsylvania and Delaware	Indentured servitude, tenancy, family farms
	New Jersey	Family farms, tenancy
South	Maryland	Slavery
	Virginia	Slavery
	North Carolina	Family farms, slavery
	South Carolina	Slavery

Pennsylvania and New York, was in decline as a dominant labor system.

Eighteenth-century Chesapeake planters also availed themselves of another unfree labor source: transported English convicts. Lawmakers in England saw transportation as a way of getting rid of large numbers of criminals who might otherwise be executed. Between 1718 and 1775, nearly fifty thousand convicts were sent to the colonies, 80 percent of whom ended up in the Chesapeake. Most were young, lower-class males forced by economic hardship to turn to lives of crime. Although some colonists objected to England's policy of sending its undesirables to America, labor-hungry planters eagerly bought them for seven-year terms at relatively low prices and exploited them ruthlessly. A few convicts eventually prospered in America, but most faced lives as miserable as those they had known in England.

An arrangement similar to indentured servitude—the **redemptioner** system—brought many German families to the colonies in the eighteenth century. Instead of negotiating contracts for service before leaving Europe, as indentured servants did, redemptioners promised to redeem, or pay, the costs of passage on arrival in America. They often paid part of the fare themselves before sailing. If they could not raise the rest of it soon after landing, the ship captain who brought them sold them into servitude. The length of their service depended on how much they still owed. Most Germans went to Pennsylvania, where they hoped to find friends or relatives willing to help them pay off their debt quickly.

Purchasing slaves, servants, or convicts did not make sense for everyone. Colonists who owned undeveloped land faced many tasks—cutting trees, clearing fields, building fences and barns—that brought no immediate profit. Rather than buy expensive laborers to do this, landowners rented undeveloped tracts to propertyless families. Both tenants and landlords benefited from this arrangement. Tenants enjoyed greater independence than servants and could save toward the purchase of their own farms. The landlord secured the labor necessary to transform his property into a working farm, which increased the land's value. He also received an annual rent payment, usually a portion of the tenant's crop, and eventually profited from selling the land—often to the tenant family who had rented it. Tenancy worked best in Pennsylvania, New Jersey, and the Hudson and Connecticut River Valleys, where farmers raised wheat and other grains for the market.

Merchants eager to develop New England's fisheries devised other means to fill their labor needs. Because it was fairly easy to get a farm, few New Englanders cared to take on the difficult and risky job of fishing. Moreover, few could afford the necessary equipment, which included boats, sails, provisions, and salt (used for preserving fish). Merchants learned to recruit fishermen by advancing credit to coastal villagers so they could outfit their own boats. To pay off the debt, the fishermen were legally bound to bring their catch to the merchant, who then sold it to Europe and the West Indies. Many fishermen ran up such large debts that they were obliged to continue supplying fish to their creditors, whether they wanted to or not. Toward the end of the seventeenth century, as the rising population of coastal villages lowered the cost of labor, merchants abandoned the credit system and paid fishermen wages instead.

In the northern colonies, the same conditions that made men reluctant to become fishermen deterred them from becoming farm laborers, except perhaps for high wages. Paying high wages, however, or the high purchase cost of servants or slaves was difficult, if not impossible, for New Englanders with farms that produced no export crops and could not be worked during cold winter months. So northern farmers turned to the cheapest and most dependable workers they could find—their children.

Children as young as 5 or 6 years old began with simple tasks and moved on to more complex work as they grew older. By the time they were in their late teens, girls knew how to run households, and boys knew how to farm. Instead of contracts or outright coercion, fathers used their ownership of property to prolong the time their sons worked for them.

Young men in New England could not marry and set up their own households until they could support a wife and family. New England fathers frequently postponed giving them the necessary property until the sons were in their late twenties. Often sons did not actually own any land until their fathers died and left it to them in their wills. Richard Barker's firm hold over his land in late seventeenth-century Andover, Massachusetts, kept his six sons from marrying until they were between 25 and 35 years old. Most were well into their forties before Barker died, making them at last the legal owners of land they had been tilling most of their lives.

Thus New England's labor shortage produced strong ties of dependency between generations. Fathers kept their sons working for them as long as possible; sons accepted this arrangement because they had no other way to become independent farmers. They would eventually employ their own children in the same way. As New England's population increased in the eighteenth century, and vacant land grew scarcer, the price of labor came down. Some fathers could then afford to hire occasional helpers and loosened their hold on their sons, allowing them to marry in their early twenties.

Property owners in all the English colonies found different ways to control the laborers they so desperately needed. But where property owners saw problems—high wages (often twice what workers in England received) and abundant land (which deterred colonists from working for others when they could have their own farms)—others saw opportunities. For tens of thousands of Europeans, the chance to own or rent a farm or to find steady employment made North America an irresistible magnet, promising a prosperity that was beyond their reach at home.

Transplanted Europeans

European immigrants flooded into America in the seventeenth and eighteenth centuries (see Figure 3-4). Nearly 250,000 Scots-Irish people—descendants of Protestant Scots who had settled in northern Ireland in the sixteenth and seventeenth centuries—came to the colonies after 1718 when their landlords raised rents to intolerable levels. Tens of thousands of immigrants arrived from Scotland during the same period, some seeking economic improvement and some sent as punishment for rebellions against the king in 1715 and 1745. Thousands of Irish Catholics arrived as servants, redemptioners, and convicts. By 1773, the tremendous outflow of Britons to America sparked

***Figure 3-4* Ethnic Distribution of Non-Indian Inhabitants of British Mainland Colonies, c. 1770**

By the third quarter of the eighteenth century, the colonial population was astonishingly diverse. Only two out of three settlers claimed British ancestry (from England, Wales, Scotland, or northern Ireland), while one out of five was African in origin.

Data Source: *Thomas L. Purvis, "The European Ancestry of the United States Population, 1790,"* William and Mary Quarterly, *3d series, 41 (1984), p. 98.*

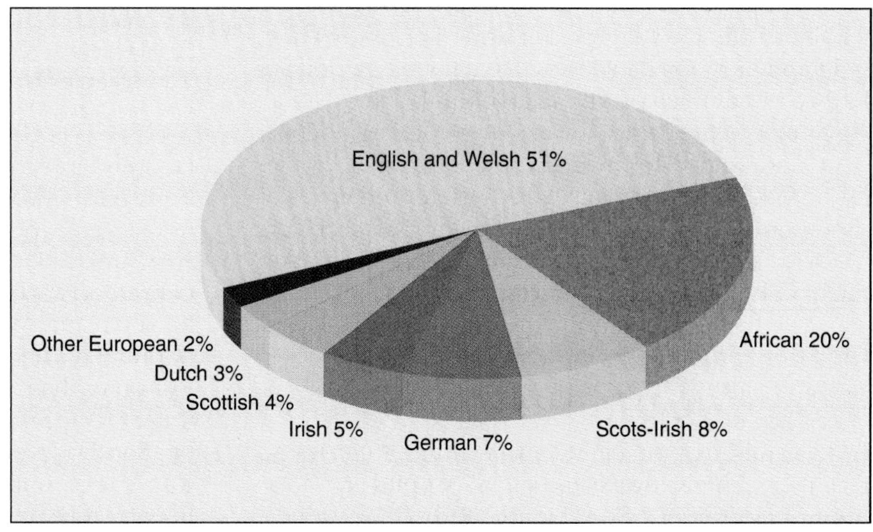

debate in England over whether emigration should be prohibited lest the British Isles themselves be left empty.

Continental Europe contributed another stream of emigrants. Perhaps 100,000 German Protestants left the Rhine Valley, where war, economic hardship, and religious persecution had brought misery. French Protestants (known as Huguenots) began emigrating after 1685, when their faith was made illegal in France, and continued to arrive for decades. Swiss Protestants likewise fled religious persecution. Even a few Poles, Greeks, Italians, and Jews reached the colonies in the eighteenth century.

Many emigrants responded to pamphlets and newspaper articles that exaggerated the bright prospects of life in America. Others studied more realistic accounts from friends and relatives who had already emigrated. One Scot who had moved to North Carolina warned his countrymen that at first "poor people will meet with many Difficulties" but they should "take courage and Come to this Country [for] it will be of Benefitt" to their families. Landowners eager for workers sent agents to port towns to recruit new arrivals to become tenants, often on generous terms. One happy immigrant wrote to his wife, who remained behind in England, that he had signed a lease for a farm in New York that exempted him from paying rent for the first five years and charged him only 7 pence an acre after that.

Streams of emigrants flowed to places where land was cheap and labor most in demand (see Map 3-3). Few went to New England, where descendants of the first settlers already occupied the best land. They also avoided areas where slavery predominated—the Chesapeake tidewater and lowland South Carolina—in favor of the foothills of the Appalachian Mountains from western Pennsylvania to the Carolinas. There, one emigrant declared, a "poor man that will incline to work may have the value of his labour."

This observation, though partly true, did not tell the whole story. Any person who came as a servant, redemptioner, or tenant learned that his master or landlord received much of "the value of his labour." Not all emigrants realized their dreams of becoming independent landowners. The scarcity of labor in the colonies led as easily to the exploitation of white workers as of slaves and Indians. Even so, for many people facing bleak prospects in Europe, the chance that emigration might bring prosperity was too tempting to ignore.

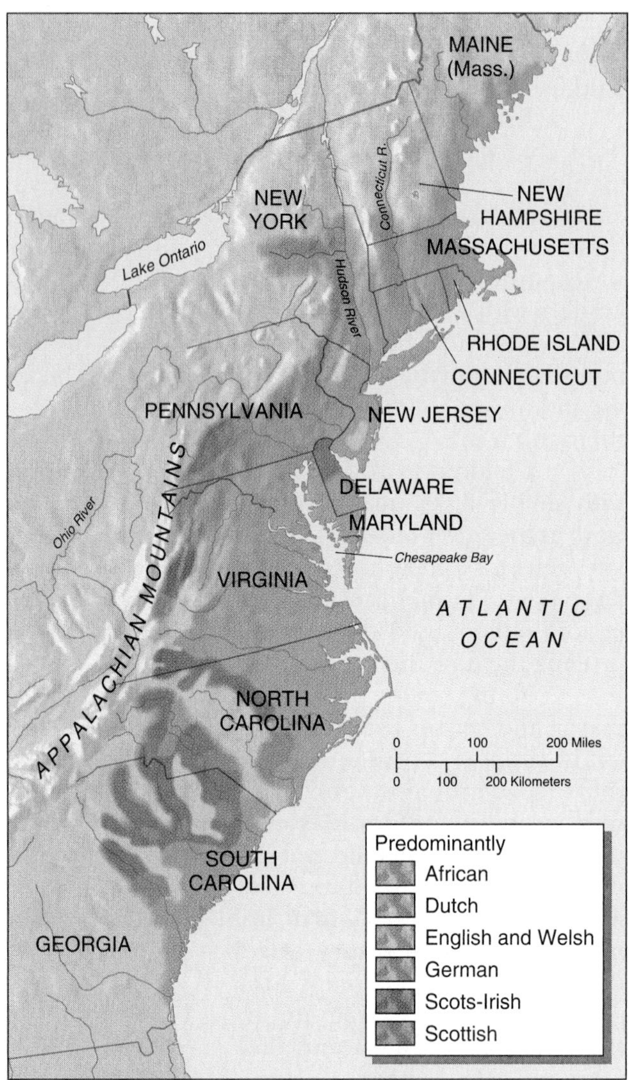

Map 3-3 Ethnic Distribution of Settler Population in British Mainland Colonies, c. 1755
Settlers of different ethnic backgrounds tended to concentrate in certain areas. Only New Englanders were predominantly English, while Africans dominated in the Chesapeake tidewater and South Carolina. German, Scottish, and Scots-Irish immigrants often settled in the backcountry.

Conclusion

By the middle of the eighteenth century, America offered a strikingly diverse mosaic of peoples and communities. Along the St. Lawrence River, for instance, lay Kahnawake, a village of Mohawks and Abenakis who had adopted Catholicism and French ways under Jesuit instruction. In Andover, Massachusetts, New Englanders tilled fields that their Puritan grandparents had cleared. German immigrants who had forsaken the world in search of spiritual perfection populated the isolated Pennsylvania settlement of Ephrata. The hundred or so slaves on Robert Carter's Virginia plantation at Nomini Hall gathered on Sunday evenings to nurture ties of community with songs and dances, while the master cultivated his very different sense of community with the neighboring planters whom he invited to the great house to sip fine wine.

In North Carolina, Swiss settlers rebuilt the coastal town of New Bern, destroyed during the Tuscarora War, while 100 miles further west, Scottish emigrants cleared land for farms near present-day Fayetteville. Catawba Indians formed new villages in the South Carolina foothills to distance themselves from white settlers. In Mose, Florida, near St. Augustine, runaway slaves farmed and gathered shellfish under the protection of Spanish soldiers. Far to the west, the Spanish, *mestizo,* and Pueblo residents of Santa Fe warily reestablished ties broken during the Pueblo Revolt.

In these and many other communities, peoples from three continents adapted to one another and to American conditions. Indians struggled with the consequences of disease, trade, religious conversion, settlement, and warfare resulting from European immigration. Africans exchanged traditional ethnic connections for a new identity as African-Americans. English settlers became landowners in unprecedented numbers, and adopted new ways to control laborers, reinventing slavery, unknown in England for centuries. No European settlement in America fully reproduced Old World patterns, and no native village fully preserved the precontact Indian way of life.

For all their divergence from European experience, the North American colonies attracted more attention from their home countries as the eighteenth century wore on. Spain, France, and England all recognized the colonies' growing economic power and strove to harness it to block the expansion of their rivals. Everywhere the effort to strengthen imperial ties created ambivalence among colonists. Because they were by far the most numerous, the English settlers' responses were most pronounced. As they saw more clearly the differences between themselves and the English, some colonists began to defend their distinctive habits, while others tried more insistently than ever to imitate English ways. The tension between new and old had, of course, characterized colonial development from the start. What made the eighteenth century distinctive were the many ways in which those tensions worked themselves out.

Review Questions

1. English colonists experienced more frequent, and more violent, conflicts with Indians than the settlers of New France did. Why was this so? What factors affected Indian–European relations in the two colonial regions?
2. Why were Catholic missionaries more successful than Protestants in converting Indians to Christianity in early America?
3. When did Chesapeake planters switch from servants to slaves? What factors contributed to their decision to make this change?
4. By about 1750, more slaves in the mainland British colonies were creoles (American-born) than African-born. What effects did this have on the formation of African-American communities in America?
5. Different labor systems predominated in various regions of British America. How did the economy of each region help determine its labor system?
6. Tens of thousands of European immigrants came to America in the eighteenth century, but they tended to settle only in certain colonial regions. What destinations did they favor and why?

Recommended Reading

Berlin, Ira. *Many Thousands Gone: The First Two Centuries of Slavery in North America* (1998). A magisterial synthesis of the evolution of slavery from its beginnings in America through the Revolution.

Cronon, William. *Changes in the Land: Indians, Colonists, and the Ecology of New England* (1983). A pathbreaking study that examines the ecological consequences of Indian settlement in New England and of the displacement of Indians by English colonists.

Delage, Denys. *Bitter Feast: Amerindians and Europeans in Northeastern North America, 1600–64* (English ed., 1993). Offers a comprehensive analysis of French, Dutch, and English colonization in northeastern North America; focuses on European strategies for trade and economic development and their impact on native peoples.

Moore, Brian. *Black Robe* (1985). A powerful novel that explores the experiences of a Jesuit missionary among the Indians in seventeenth-century New France.

Nash, Gary B. *Red, White, and Black: The Peoples of Early America* (3d ed., 1991). An important synthesis that treats the history of early America as the complex story of interactions between peoples from three major cultures—Native American, European, and African.

Vickers, Daniel. *Farmers and Fishermen: Two Centuries of Work in Essex County, Massachusetts, 1630–1830* (1994). A beautifully written and sophisticated analysis that explores the way in which settlers adapted their English experiences to deal with the shortages of labor and capital in New England.

Additional Sources

Indians and Europeans

Axtell, James. *The Indians' New South: Cultural Change in the Colonial Southeast* (1997).

Axtell, James. *The Invasion Within: The Contest of Cultures in Colonial North America* (1985).

Calloway, Colin. *New Worlds for All: Indians, Europeans, and the Remaking of Early America* (1997).

Drake, James. *King Philip's War: Civil War in New England, 1675–1676* (2000).

Gutierrez, Ramon. *When Jesus Came, the Corn Mothers Went Away: Marriage, Sexuality, and Power in New Mexico, 1500–1846* (1991).

Hinderaker, Eric. *Elusive Empires: Constructing Colonialism in the Ohio Valley, 1673–1800* (1997).

Knaut, Andrew L. *The Pueblo Revolt of 1680: Conquest and Resistance in Seventeenth-Century New Mexico* (1995).

Merrell, James H. *Into the American Woods: Negotiators on the Pennsylvania Frontier* (1999).

Merrell, James H. *The Indians' New World: Catawbas and Their Neighbors from European Contact through the Era of Removal* (1989).

Richter, Daniel. *The Ordeal of the Longhouse: The Peoples of the Iroquois League in the Era of European Colonization* (1992).

Rountree, Helen. *Pocahontas's People: The Powhatan Indians of Virginia through Four Centuries* (1990).

Salisbury, Neal. *Manitou and Providence: Indians, Europeans, and the Making of New England, 1500–1643* (1982).

Steele, Ian K. *Warpaths: Invasions of North America* (1994).

Washburn, Wilcomb E. *The Governor and the Rebel: A History of Bacon's Rebellion in Virginia* (1957).

White, Richard. *The Middle Ground: Indians, Empires, and Republics in the Great Lakes Region, 1650–1815* (1991).

Africans in America

Breen, T. H., and Innes, Stephen. *"Myne Owne Ground": Race and Freedom on Virginia's Eastern Shore, 1640–1676* (1980).

Curtin, Philip. *The Atlantic Slave Trade: A Census* (1969).

Davis, David Brion. *The Problem of Slavery in Western Culture* (1966).

Jordan, Winthrop. *White over Black: American Attitudes toward the Negro, 1550-1812* (1968).

Kulikoff, Allan. *Tobacco and Slaves: The Development of Southern Cultures in the Chesapeake, 1680–1800* (1986).

Littlefield, Daniel. *Rice and Slaves: Ethnicity and the Slave Trade in Colonial South Carolina* (1981).

Morgan, Philip. *Slave Counterpoint: Black Culture in the Eighteenth-Century Chesapeake & Lowcountry* (1998).

Mullin, Gerald W. *Flight and Rebellion: Slave Resistance in Eighteenth-Century Virginia* (1972).

Piersen, William. *Black Yankees: The Development of an Afro-American Subculture in Eighteenth-Century New England* (1988).

Wood, Betty. *The Origins of American Slavery: Freedom and Bondage in the English Colonies* (1997).

Labor Systems and European Immigration

Bailyn, Bernard. *The Peopling of British North America: An Introduction* (1986).

Bailyn, Bernard. *Voyagers to the West: A Passage in the Peopling of America on the Eve of the Revolution* (1986).

Baseler, Marilyn. *"Asylum for Mankind": America 1607-1800* (1998).

DeWolfe, Barbara, ed. *Discoveries of America: Personal Accounts of British Emigrants to America in the Revolutionary Era* (1997).

Dickson, R. J. *Ulster Emigration to Colonial America, 1718–1775* (1966).

Ekirch, A. Roger. *Bound for America: The Transportation of British Convicts to the Colonies, 1718–1775* (1987).

Innes, Stephen, ed. *Work and Labor in Early America* (1988).

Roeber, A. G. *Palatines, Liberty, and Property: German Lutherans in Colonial British America* (1993).

Salinger, Sharon V. *"To Serve Well and Faithfully": Labor and Indentured Servants in Pennsylvania, 1682–1800* (1987).

Wokeck, Marianne. *Trade in Strangers: The Beginnings of Mass Migration to North America* (1999).

Where to Learn More

❖ **Ste. Marie among the Hurons, near Midland, Ontario, Canada.** This site contains a reconstructed Jesuit mission from the seventeenth century. There is a museum with information about seventeenth-century France as well as life among the Huron Indians.

❖ **Taos Pueblo, Taos, New Mexico.** Still a residence for Pueblo Indians, portions of this multistoried pueblo date from the fifteenth century. This was the site from which Popé directed the beginnings of the Pueblo Revolt in 1680.

❖ **Ephrata Cloister, Ephrata, Pennsylvania.** Founded by German immigrants in the eighteenth century, the Ephrata community attracted religious pietists. The site now contains a museum, buildings that reflect medieval German architectural styles, and a collection of decorative art objects.

❖ **Six Nations Indian Museum, Onchiota, New York.** This museum preserves a rich collection of artifacts relating to Iroquois history and culture. It is open to the public in the summer.

❖ **Rhode Island Black Heritage Society, Providence, Rhode Island.** This organization has assembled an archive and museum collection with information about the state's black residents from the colonial period to the present.

Convergence and Conflict, 1660s–1763

4

Chapter Outline

Economic Development and Imperial Trade
The Regulation of Trade
The Colonial Export Trade
The Import Trade and Ties of Credit
Becoming More Like England

The Transformation of Culture
Goods and Houses
Shaping Minds and Manners
Colonial Religion and the Great Awakening

The Colonial Political World
The Dominion of New England and the Limits of British Control
The Legacy of the Glorious Revolution
Diverging Politics

Expanding Empires
The English in the Backcountry
The Spanish in Texas and California
The French along the Mississippi

A Century of Warfare
Imperial Conflict and the Establishment of an American Balance of Power, 1689–1738
King George's War Shifts the Balance, 1739–1754
Decision: The French and Indian War, 1754–1760
The Triumph of the British Empire, 1763

Conclusion

Key Topics

- ❖ Development of closer connections between Britain and the colonies
- ❖ Rising aspirations of the colonial elite
- ❖ Eighteenth-century religious life
- ❖ Political developments in England and the colonies
- ❖ Renewed competition among Britain, France, and Spain in North America
- ❖ Impact of imperial warfare in North America

The young man came to Williamsburg in the spring of 1763 to take his seat in Virginia's House of Burgesses. He had plenty of time, when not engaged in government business, to attend to his private affairs. His main concern was to arrange for the shipment of tobacco from his plantation to England. But he also found time to write to his tailor, Charles Lawrence of London. "Be pleased to send me," he wrote, "a genteel suit of Clothes" cut to fit a man "Six feet high & proportionably made; if any thing rather Slender than thick for a Person of that height with pretty long arms & thighs." Lawrence could choose the style and color of the suit, and when he was done he should send his bill to Robert Cary, the Virginian's financial agent in London. The colonist then wrote directly to Cary requesting that he send "4 Yards of Silk" for a dress for his wife. If the Virginian meant to impress his neighbors with his new suit, it was only fitting that his wife also display her latest London finery.

At the age of 31, this tall and "rather Slender" planter, George Washington, had joined the ranks of Virginia's leaders. In some senses he had come up the hard way. His father had died when Washington was only 11 years old, and most of the family property had gone to his older brother. Because he could not expect to inherit wealth, Washington learned surveying—a useful skill in a colony where land was constantly being divided into new farms. His maps of territory west of the Blue Ridge Mountains helped open up the region, and he became an expert at locating prime lands to buy and resell to the settlers who flooded into the area. When tensions between England and France over rival claims to those western lands flared into war, Washington took up arms to defend England's right. Military service brought him to the attention of Virginia's leaders, even as his economic fortunes improved. His older brother died and left him the family plantation at Mount Vernon, and in 1759, at age 27, Washington married a wealthy widow, Martha Custis. He thus became one of the richest men in northern Virginia.

By 1763, Washington had spent his whole adult life trying to live, look, and behave like an English country gentleman. He had served his king in battle and had assumed the local political responsibilities expected of a man of his position. He already owned vastly more land than most English gentlemen could dream of, and he prospered from the transatlantic trade that channeled tobacco and other colonial goods into British and European markets. But Washington could not be sure of what an English gentleman looked like. He had to trust his London tailor to know how he should dress.

Throughout British America, colonists who had achieved wealth and power tried, like Washington, to imitate the habits and manners of the English gentry. Their aspirations testified to important developments in the eighteenth century. Prosperity and the demand of a growing population for English manufactures tied the colonies ever more tightly into a trade network centered on the imperial metropolis, London. The flow of goods and information between England and America fueled the desires of Washington and other successful colonists for acceptance as transatlantic members of the English elite. No longer a collection of rough outposts clinging to the Atlantic seaboard, British America was growing in size and sophistication.

These developments in Britain's American colonies brought them to the attention of European statesmen, who increasingly factored North America into their political, diplomatic, and military calculations. Spain and France viewed the growth of British North America as a threat to their own colonial possessions, and they responded aggressively by expanding their territorial claims. With expansion came conflict, and with conflict, war: a series of four imperial wars, which themselves became powerful engines of change in the New World.

Economic Development and Imperial Trade in the British Colonies

The greatest assets that Great Britain could call on in its competition with other European nations were a dynamic economy and a sophisticated financial system that put commerce at the service of the state. In the century after 1690, England became the most advanced economic power in Europe. England's leaders came to see colonies as indispensable to the nation's economic welfare. Colonies supplied raw materials unavailable in the mother country, and settlers provided a healthy market for English manufactures.

As the eighteenth century progressed, colonial economies grew in tandem with England's. Parliament knitted the colonies into an empire with commercial legislation, while British merchants traded with and extended credit to growing numbers of colonial merchants and planters. Over time, these developments made colonial societies resemble England more closely than ever before and integrated the economies of the colonies with that of the metropolis in a vast transatlantic system.

The Regulation of Trade

England, Holland, and France competed vigorously in transatlantic trade. To capture a greater share of commerce, England pursued a policy of national self-sufficiency in which its American colonies played a key role. Between 1651 and 1733, Parliament passed laws that regulated trade to ensure that more wealth flowed into England's treasury than out of it (see the overview table, "British Imperial Trade Regulations, 1651–1733"). This governmental intervention in the economy for the purpose of increasing national wealth—called **mercantilism**—aimed to draw the colonies into a mutually beneficial relationship with England.

Parliament enacted four types of mercantilist regulations. The first aimed at ending Dutch dominance in England's overseas trade. Beginning with the Navigation Act of 1651, all trade in the empire had to be conducted in English or colonial ships, with crews that were at least half Englishmen or colonists. The act stimulated rapid growth in both England's merchant marine and New England's shipping industry. Shipbuilding and earnings from what was called the "carrying trade" soon became the most profitable sector of New England's economy.

Washington/Custis/Lee Collection, Washington and Lee University, Lexington, VA.

This, the earliest known portrait of George Washington, was painted by Charles Willson Peale in 1772. It depicts him in his military uniform from the French and Indian War. Military service helped to strengthen Washington's ties with the British Empire.

The second type of legislation channeled most colonial trade through England, giving it control over raw materials it would otherwise have to buy from rival nations. Certain colonial goods, called "**enumerated products**," could be shipped only to England or another English colony. They initially included tobacco, sugar, indigo, and cotton; other products, such as rice, were added later. These laws also required European goods to pass through England before they could be shipped to the colonies. When these goods entered English ports, they were taxed, which made them more expensive and encouraged colonists to buy English-made items.

The third and fourth sorts of regulation further enhanced the advantage of English manufacturers who produced for the colonial market. Parliament subsidized certain goods, including linen, gunpowder, and silks, to allow manufacturers to undersell European competitors in the colonies. Other laws protected English manufacturers from colonial competition by prohibiting colonists from manufacturing wool, felt hats, and iron on a large scale.

Chronology

1651–1733	Parliament passes series of Navigation Acts to regulate imperial trade.
1660	Charles II becomes king of England.
1662	Halfway Covenant adopted by Massachusetts clergy.
1685	James II becomes king of England.
1686–1689	Dominion of New England.
1688	Glorious Revolution in England; James II loses the throne.
1689	William and Mary become English monarchs; Leisler's Rebellion begins in New York.
1689–1697	King William's War in America.
1691–1692	Witchcraft trials in Salem, Massachusetts.
1698	First French settlements near mouth of Mississippi River.
1701	Iroquois adopt policy of neutrality toward France and Britain.
1702–1713	Queen Anne's War in America.
1718	Establishment of San Antonio, Texas; New Orleans founded.
1734–1735	Jonathan Edwards leads religious revival in Northampton, Massachusetts.
1739	Great Awakening begins in Middle Colonies with George Whitefield's arrival.
1744–1748	King George's War in America.
1754–1763	Seven Years' War in America.
1760s	Spanish begin establishing missions in California.

Although some colonists—especially tobacco and rice planters—complained about these laws, the colonies prospered. Between 1650 and 1770, the colonial economy grew twice as fast as England's did. Colonists enjoyed protected markets for their staple crops and low prices on English imports. Because colonial merchants operated on equal terms with English traders, they could take full advantage of commercial opportunities within the empire.

Occasionally, merchants evaded these laws by smuggling. Customs officials, sent over from England beginning in the 1670s, were hard-pressed to stop them. Although customs officials derived much of their income from fines collected from smugglers, they generally found it easier to accept bribes and look the other way when a suspicious ship arrived in port with, say, an illicit cargo of French West Indian sugar. Most colonial trade, however, followed the proper routes. By not pushing for perfect compliance, British officials did not put too much pressure on a system that in fact worked remarkably well.

The Colonial Export Trade and the Spirit of Enterprise

By the mid-eighteenth century, the Atlantic had become a busy thoroughfare of international commerce (see Map 4-1). Between 1700 and 1770, the number of British merchant ships nearly tripled, from 3,300 to 9,400. They, along with colonial vessels, carried goods and people from Great Britain, continental Europe, and West Africa to the British colonies and returned tons of colonial raw materials to the Old World. At the heart of Anglo-American trade lay the highly profitable commerce in staple crops, most of which were produced by slave labor.

West Indian sugar far surpassed all other colonial products in importance (see Figure 4-1). By the late 1760s, the value of sugar and sugar by-product exports reached almost £4 million per year—nearly 50 percent more than the total value of exports from all the other British American colonies combined. Prominent West Indian planters joined with the English merchants who marketed their sugar to lobby Parliament for favorable treatment. Because these planters and merchants—known as the "sugar interest"—wielded so much economic power, politicians listened. It was at their insistence that Parliament in 1733 passed the Molasses Act, which taxed sugar products from foreign sources, especially the French West Indies. Parliament also removed sugar from the list of enumerated items in 1739, allowing merchants to ship it directly from the islands to southern Europe.

Tobacco from the Chesapeake colonies was the second most valuable staple crop. Exports

OVERVIEW

British Imperial Trade Regulations, 1651–1733

Name of Act	Key Features
Navigation Act of 1651	• Aimed to eliminate Dutch competition in overseas trade • Required most goods to be carried in English or colonial ships • Required crews to be at least half English
Navigation Act of 1660	• Required all colonial trade to be carried in English ships • Required master and three-quarters of crew to be English • Created list of enumerated goods, such as tobacco and sugar, that could be shipped only to England or another English colony
Staple Act of 1663	• Required products from Europe, Asia, and Africa to be landed in England before being shipped to the colonies
Plantation Duty Act of 1673	• Attempted to reduce smuggling • Required captains of colonial ships to post bond that they would deliver enumerated goods to England or pay the "plantation duty" that would be owed in England
Navigation Act of 1696	• Plugged loopholes in earlier laws • Created vice-admiralty courts in colonies to enforce trade regulations
Woolens Act of 1699	• Forbade export of woolen cloth made in the colonies, to prevent competition with English producers
Hat Act of 1732	• Prohibited export of colonial-made hats
Molasses Act of 1733	• Placed high tax on French West Indian and other foreign molasses imported into colonies to encourage importation of British West Indian molasses

worth about £750,000 arrived each year in England during the late 1760s. Nearly 90 percent of the crop was later reexported to continental Europe. Persistent low prices, however, led many tobacco planters to sow some of their land with wheat after about 1750. This lessened their dependence on tobacco and allowed them to take advantage of the high demand for flour in southern Europe and the West Indies.

Exports of rice and indigo helped make South Carolina planters some of the richest mainland colonists. Most of the rice went to England and the West Indies, although, after 1731, Parliament permitted direct shipments to southern Europe. Parliament encouraged indigo production by granting subsidies to growers and placing stiff taxes on foreign indigo. It also subsidized colonial production of naval stores—such as tar, pitch, and turpentine—to reduce England's dependence on Swedish suppliers. The export of these items made up a small but important part of the North and South Carolina economies.

Wheat exports from the Middle Colonies boomed after 1750, when a combination of poor harvests and warfare in Europe created strong overseas demand. West Indian planters (though not their slaves) also ate bread made from Pennsylvania flour. Farmers in Great Britain grew enough wheat to supply the domestic market, so there was little demand there for colonial flour. Ships traveling from Philadelphia or New York to English ports instead carried a variety of other goods, including unrefined iron, potash (used in making soap and glass), salted meats, and wood products.

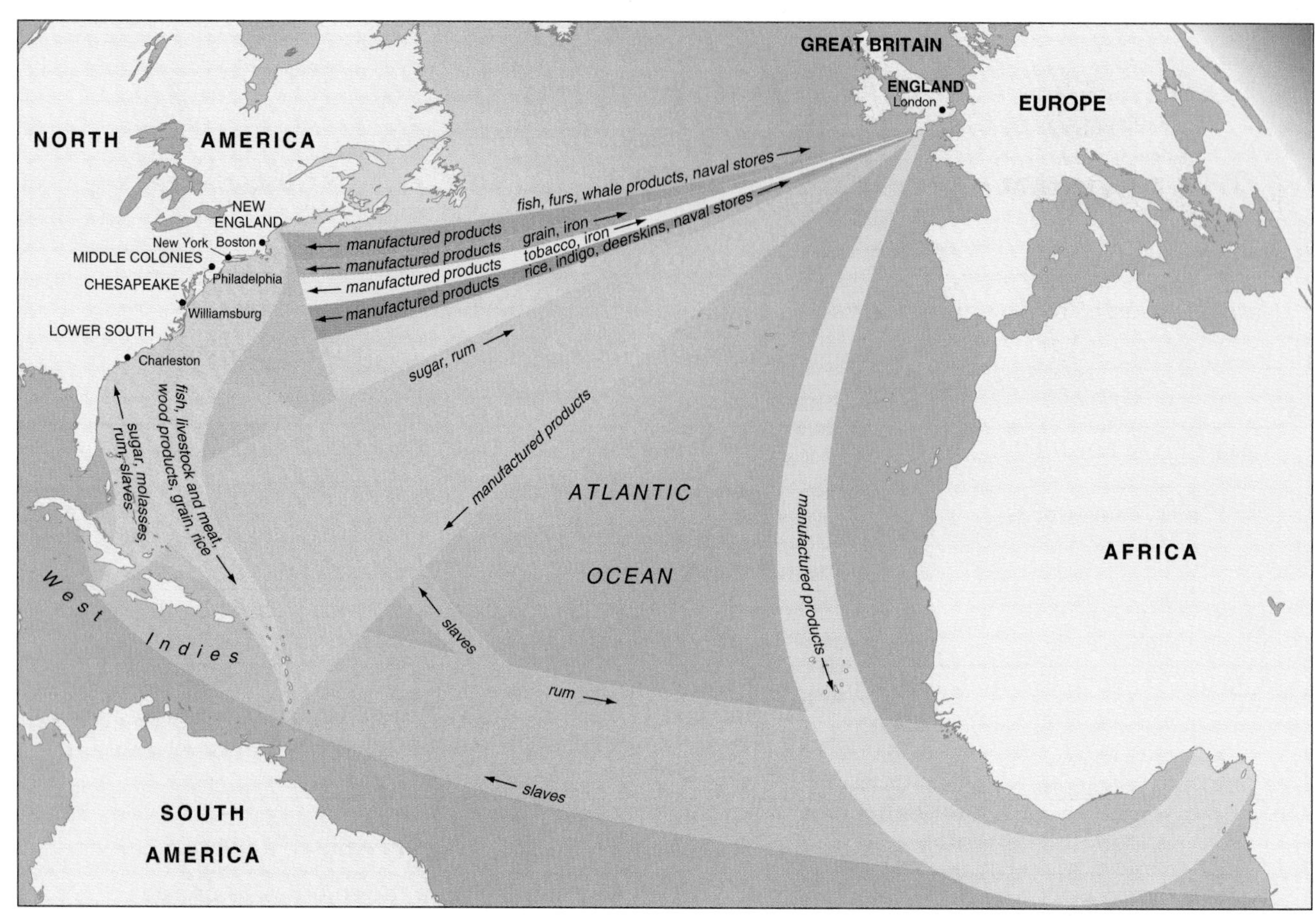

Map 4-1 ***Anglo-American Transatlantic Commerce***
By the eighteenth century, Great Britain and its colonies were enmeshed in a complex web of trade. Britain exchanged manufactured goods for colonial raw materials, while Africa provided the enslaved laborers who produced the most valuable colonial crops.

New England had no staple crop and produced little for export to Great Britain except whale products, such as oil. The region's merchants nevertheless developed a thriving transatlantic trade by grasping whatever opportunities came their way. Realizing that profits could be made from carrying other colonies' goods to market, New Englanders built thousands of vessels and eventually dominated shipping within the empire. Captains sailed from port to port, assembling mixed cargoes of goods from different regions and carrying them to England to exchange for manufactured items. By 1770, New England's earnings from shipping fees, freight charges, and insurance exceeded the total value of its own exports.

New England merchants also strengthened trade links to the West Indies that had first been forged in the 1650s. By the mid-eighteenth century, more than half of all New England exports went to the islands: salted meat for planters' dinners, salted fish for slaves, wood for sugar barrels and other equipment. Merchants accepted molasses and other sugar by-products in payment, bringing them back to New England to be distilled into cheap rum. Enterprising traders then carried rum to Africa to exchange for slaves. Although English merchants dominated the African slave trade, New Englanders also profited from it. There were few slaves in New England, but because New Englanders trafficked in human cargo and provisioned the West Indies, their commercial economy depended on the institution of slavery.

The Import Trade and Ties of Credit

By the late 1760s, the colonists imported goods worth nearly £4 million each year, almost all of which came from Great Britain. Most imports consisted of manufactured goods, which satisfied a demand for items that could not be produced—at least not cheaply—in America. Bales of English

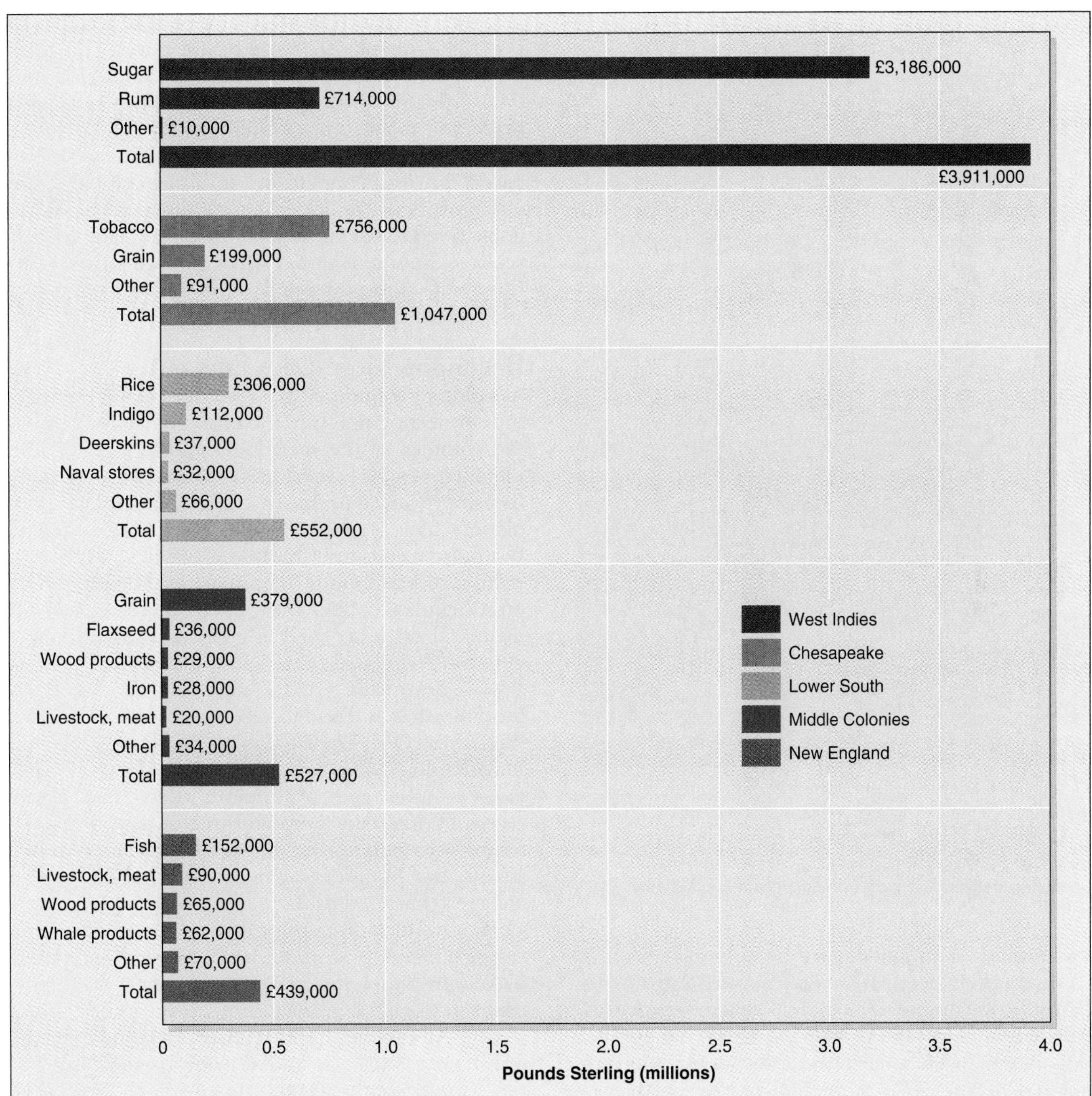

Figure 4-1 ***Average Annual Value of Colonial Exports by Region, 1768–1772***
Staple crops—especially sugar—produced by slave labor were the most valuable items exported from Britain's North American colonies.

Data Source: *John J. McCusker and Russell R. Menard,* The Economy of British America, 1607–1789, *rev. ed. (1991). University of North Carolina Press.*

cloth and leather, crates of glassware and pottery, casks of nails and lead shot piled onto the wharves of Philadelphia and New York. Dockworkers emptied ships' holds of wrought iron, brass, and copper, barrels of refined sugar, and bundles of beaverskin hats. Some of these goods—ironware, sugar, hats—were made of materials that had come from the colonies in the first place.

The colonists' consumption of manufactured goods was vital to British overseas commerce. In fact, in terms of value, colonists imported more goods than they exported. This imbalance, however,

Clothespress, 1730–40. England, London. Mahogany, glass. H: 98 in. (249 cm); W: 45¾ in. (116 cm). Gift of Albert Sack. Courtesy, Museum of Fine Arts, Boston.

During the eighteenth century, quantities of imported English manufactures began to appear in many colonial houses. This elegant mahogany clothespress, made in England in the 1740s, may have graced the Boston home of Charles Apthorp, once called "the greatest and most noble merchant" in America.

was remedied in good part by colonial earnings from shipping fees, as well as payments from the British government for colonial military expenses. The colonial economy may have run an annual deficit of £40,000 by the late 1760s, but that was only about 1 percent of a transatlantic trade worth over £4 million a year.

British merchants extended credit to colonists on generous terms, trying to make it as easy as possible for them to buy British products. Great tobacco planters, of whom Washington was typical, virtually lived on the easy credit that British merchants provided. These merchants marketed the planters' tobacco and supplied them with English goods, charging the costs of purchase and transportation against the profits they expected the next year's crop to bring.

Easy credit let planters indulge themselves, and many ordered English goods without stopping to worry about how they would pay for them. Gradually, they sank into debt. A Virginian noted that in the 1740s no planter would have dared run up a debt of £1,000, but by the 1760s "Ten times that sum is . . . spoke of with Indifference." When trade was brisk, and tobacco prices high, neither the planters nor their British creditors worried. But when tobacco prices dropped or an international crisis made overseas trading risky, creditors called in the debts owed to them. At such times, colonial debtors realized how much they (like Indians involved in European trade) depended on goods and credit supplied by distant merchants.

Becoming More Like England

As colonial commerce grew, so did colonial cities—the connecting points in the economic network tying the colonies to the metropolis. Boston, New York, Philadelphia, and Charleston were as large as many British provincial towns. By 1770, Philadelphia's population had reached 30,000, New York's 25,000, Boston's 16,000, and Charleston's 12,000. A fifth city, Baltimore, was rapidly developing at the best harbor on Chesapeake Bay. Only about 5 percent of all mainland colonists lived in cities, but the influence of urban centers far outweighed their size.

European visitors marveled at America's bustling cities and remarked on their resemblance to England's. One Englishman declared in 1759 that Philadelphia "must certainly be the object of every one's wonder and admiration." Less than eighty years old, it already boasted three thousand houses, impressive public buildings, "handsomely built" streets, two libraries, eight or ten churches, and a college (chartered as the College of Philadelphia in 1755, now the University of Pennsylvania). This same visitor judged Boston to be a "most flourishing" place with "much the air of some of our best country towns in England."

All colonial cities (like England's major ones) were seaports, and Europeans took note of the appearance and activity of their dockyards. Oceangoing ships sailed "right up to the town" of Philadelphia on the Delaware River, according to one observer. Boston had "a very fine wharf, at least half a mile long, undertaken at the expense of a number of private gentlemen" to facilitate shipping. New York, then as now, had one of the world's finest harbors, from which it conducted "a more extensive commerce than any town in the English North American provinces."

Indeed, in their bustle and cosmopolitan atmosphere, colonial cities resembled English provincial cities more than they did the farming villages of the American countryside. Cities provided all sorts of amenities, including inns, taverns, coffeehouses, theaters, and social clubs. Their populations were much more diverse in ethnic origin and religion. Dr. Alexander Hamilton, a Scottish immigrant, recalled dining at a Philadelphia tavern with "Scots, English, Dutch, Germans, and Irish" and "Roman Catholicks, Church [of England] men, Presbyterians, Quakers, Newlightmen, Methodists, Seventh day men, Moravians, Anabaptists, and one Jew." In addition, the black population in the northern colonies tended to live in cities. By 1750, slaves made up 20 percent of New York City's population, about 10 percent of Philadelphia's, and nearly 9 percent of Boston's.

Colonial cities had higher proportions of artisans than rural villages did. Perhaps two out of three adult white males living in cities worked at a craft. Many of them—shipbuilders, ropemakers, sailmakers—labored at trades directly related to overseas commerce. Others produced pottery, furniture, paper, glassware, iron tools, and various household items. Colonial products tended to be somewhat cruder and cheaper than British-made goods. Yet talented colonists such as the Boston silversmith Paul Revere and the Philadelphia furniture maker John Folwell fashioned goods that would have been prized possessions in any English gentleman's home.

John Singleton Copley's portrait of the silversmith Paul Revere, painted about 1769, depicts one of Boston's most prominent artisans. As colonists grew wealthier, some commissioned portraits for their homes to serve as emblems of their rising social aspirations. Even so, Copley despaired that America would ever provide a suitable market for his artistic talents and he eventually moved to England.

Colonial manufacturing took place not in factories but in workshops often attached to artisans' houses. Artisans managed a workforce consisting of their wives and children, along with journeymen or apprentices. Usually teenage boys, apprentices contracted to work for a master for four to seven years in order to learn the "mysteries" of his craft. Like indentured servants, they received no wages but worked for food, clothing, shelter, and a small payment at the end of their service. Once an apprentice finished his training, he became a journeyman, working for a master but now earning wages and saving until he could afford to set up his own shop. Like farmers, colonial artisans valued household independence and aimed to limit the time during which they worked for others.

Many artisans flourished in colonial cities. Adino Paddock, for example, moved from the countryside to Boston in 1736 to learn how to make the light carriages known as chaises. By 1758, he had his own shop, and, as his business prospered, Bostonians elected him to important local offices. As a gesture of public spirit, Paddock arranged for the transplanting of elm trees on Boston Common, to beautify the city where he had made his fortune, which by 1775 amounted to more than £3,000.

Paddock's rise was more spectacular than that of most craftsmen. Yet many Philadelphia artisans accumulated property worth £50 to £200, enough for a comfortable subsistence. Craft work also offered opportunities to city women that were generally unavailable to women living in the countryside. Mary Wallace and Clementia Ferguson, for instance, stitched fashionable hats and dresses for New York customers. Nonetheless, even in cities, women's options were limited. Many employed women were widows striving to maintain a family business until sons grew old enough to take over. This was true for printers such as Elizabeth Timothy, who ran the *South Carolina Gazette* after her husband's death in 1739, and Anne Catherine Green, who managed the *Maryland Gazette* for nine years.

Prosperity for urban artisans was by no means guaranteed. Workers at less skilled crafts often earned only a bare living, and ordinary laborers faced seasonal unemployment. The irregular delivery of raw materials idled even the most industrious artisans. Silversmiths, tailors, and furniture makers, relying on overseas suppliers of metal, cloth, and exotic woods, suffered when supply ships sank or wars hindered ocean traffic. Makers of luxury goods also feared downturns in the economy, for this discouraged nervous customers from purchasing their wares.

Wherever colonists engaged heavily in commerce—in cities or on plantations—the gap between rich and poor widened during the eighteenth century. In 1687, the richest 10 percent of Boston residents owned 46 percent of the taxable property in the town; by 1771, the top tenth held 63 percent of taxable wealth. Similar changes occurred in Philadelphia. In South Carolina and the Chesapeake, many planters added to the already substantial estates they had inherited. This elite group controlled vast amounts of land and slave labor. Over time, it became extremely difficult for newcomers to enter their ranks.

Some observers detected a growing problem of poverty in the colonies. Most cities built workhouses and other shelters for people who could not take care of themselves. Towns collected funds for poor relief in greater amounts than ever before. Even so, poverty had not yet become an entrenched problem. Many poor people were aged or ill, without families to help them. Able-bodied workers forced to accept public relief usually owed their misfortune to temporary downturns in the economy, more often than not the result of wartime dislocations. Such was the case in 1757, for example, when Boston's leaders complained about rising poor relief expenses. England was then at war with France, and the British commander in chief had halted Boston's overseas trade, a military expedient that hurt the city's economy.

Even in the worst of times, no more than one out of ten white colonists (mainly city-dwellers) depended on public assistance. Bad as their situation was, it scarcely matched the lot of many English people. As much as one-third of England's population regularly received relief, and the numbers swelled during hard times. Eighteenth-century colonists, on average, enjoyed a higher standard of living than most English or other Europeans. So long as land was available—even if one had to move to the edges of settlement to get it—colonists could at least eke out a bare subsistence, and many did much better.

No one would have mistaken Philadelphia for London or Virginia planters for British lords. Even so, colonial society resembled Great Britain more than ever before. The growth of cities mirrored British urban development. The widening gap between rich and poor convinced many colonists that their society had at last matured from its crude beginnings. Eighteenth-century Britons on both sides of the Atlantic believed that societies ought to be organized hierarchically, that God intended for people to be arranged in ranks from rich to poor. The more America resembled Britain, many colonists assumed, the more stable and prosperous it would be.

The Transformation of Culture

Despite the convergence of English and colonial society, many influential settlers worried that America remained culturally inferior to Great Britain. Just as Washington trusted a London tailor to make him a fashionable suit—assuming that Virginia tailors could not do the job—other colonial gentlemen tended to see American architecture, fashion, manners, and intellectual life as at best poor imitations of superior British models. During the eighteenth century, newly prosperous colonists strove to overcome this provincial sense of inferiority. They built grand houses and filled them with imported goods, cultivated what they took to be the manners of the British gentry, and followed English and European intellectual developments. Some colonial gentlemen even reshaped their religious beliefs to reflect European notions that God played only an indirect role in human affairs.

These elite aspirations, however, were not shared by most settlers. The majority of colonists, although they might purchase a few imported goods, had little interest in copying the manners of the English elite, and very few of them altered their spiritual beliefs to fit European patterns. Indeed, familiar religious practices flourished in eighteenth-century America and, when a tremendous revival swept through the colonies beginning in the 1730s, religion occupied center stage in American life.

Goods and Houses

Eighteenth-century Americans imported more manufactured products from England with every passing year. This did not simply reflect the growth of the colonial population, for the rate at which Americans bought British goods exceeded the rate of population increase. Colonists owned more goods, often of better quality, than their parents and grandparents had possessed.

In the less secure economic climate of the seventeenth century, colonists limited their purchases of goods, investing instead in land to pass on to their children. But by the eighteenth century, prosperous colonists felt secure enough to buy goods to make their lives more comfortable. Chairs replaced benches, and carpets covered wooden floors. Colonists hung mirrors and perhaps a portrait or two on their walls. At mealtimes, the table might be covered with a damask cloth and set with individual porcelain plates instead of a common wooden dish. Wealthier colonists ate with forks and knives, not just spoons.

Benjamin Franklin described such changes in his own household. Accustomed to eating his breakfast of bread and milk with a pewter spoon from an earthenware bowl, he found it one morning "in a China Bowl with a Spoon of Silver" that had cost "the enormous Sum of three and twenty Shillings." His wife, Deborah, justified the purchase by declaring "that she thought her Husband deserved a Silver Spoon & China Bowl as well as any of his Neighbors." Deborah Franklin knew that silver and china, although they served the same function as pewter and earthenware, signified her family's prosperity and good taste. Many colonists likewise acquired such goods to advertise their refined style of life.

By the 1760s, nearly every item that George Washington ordered from his London agent could have been purchased in Philadelphia. But Washington wanted the latest English styles and even worried that his agent might take advantage of him by sending goods that were no longer in fashion in England. He once complained that "instead of getting things good and fashionable . . . we often have Articles sent Us that cou[l]d only have been us[e]d by our Forefathers in the days of yore." Washington's desires were hardly unique. One visitor to Maryland, astonished at the speed with which colonists adopted English styles, declared that he was "almost inclined to believe that a new fashion is adopted earlier by the polished and affluent American than by many opulent persons" in London. Colonial shopkeepers regularly assured the "ladies and gentlemen" among their customers that their wares reflected the latest English styles.

Prosperous colonists built grand houses where they lived in greater comfort than ever before. In the seventeenth century, Virginia's governor lived in the finest house in the colony—a four-room dwelling. His eighteenth-century counterpart, however, resided in Williamsburg in the Governor's Palace, an elegant two-storied mansion designed after British architectural styles. By the 1730s, numerous southern planters had built "great houses" with expensive paneling and marble fireplaces. Others transformed older houses into more stylish residences. Washington extensively remodeled Mount Vernon, adding a second story and extra wings on each side to create a home fit for a gentleman. In the northern colonies, merchants built the most impressive houses, often following architectural pattern books imported from England.

These houses were not only larger but also different in design from the homes of less affluent colonists. Most settlers lived in one- or two-room dwellings and thus cooked, ate, and slept in the same chamber. Under such conditions, privacy was virtually unknown. But the owners of great houses could devote rooms to specialized uses. Cooking and other domestic work took place in back or in separate outbuildings. Private bedrooms were located upstairs, allowing first-floor rooms to be used for public activities. The most distinctive feature of these grand homes was the parlor, an elaborately decorated room used for receiving guests and entertaining them with music, dancing, and card games. Parlor doors often opened onto lawns and formal gardens where guests could stroll and engage in polite conversation.

Prosperous colonists did not build such homes merely to advertise their wealth. They wanted to create the proper setting for a refined way of life,

George Washington inherited Mount Vernon from his half-brother in 1754. During his lifetime, Washington rebuilt the house twice–enlarging it each time–in order for its elegance and grandeur to reflect his own position as one of Virginia's preeminent gentlemen. This late eighteenth-century picture shows Mount Vernon in its final form.

A View of Mount Vernon. Canvas 37⅝ × 43⅝; picture size 23 × 35⅛. Gift of Edgar Wm and Bernice Chysler Garbisch, 1953.

emulating the English gentry in their country estates and London townhouses. But they knew that the true measure of their gentility lay not just in where they lived and what they owned but in how they behaved.

Shaping Minds and Manners

Colonists knew that the manners of English gentlefolk set them apart from ordinary people. Many Americans thus imported "courtesy books," which contained the rules of polite behavior. In previous centuries, such books had prepared princes for life at court and their future duties as kings. Eighteenth-century versions advised would-be gentlemen on how to show regard for social rank, practice personal cleanliness, and respect other people's feelings.

The young George Washington studied such books carefully. At age 13, he copied 110 rules from *Youth's Behaviour, or Decency in Conversation among Men,* including such advice as "In the Presence of Others Sing not to yourself with a humming Noise, nor Drum with your Fingers or Feet" and "In Company of those of Higher Quality than yourself Speak not till you are ask'd a Question then Stand upright put of[f] your Hat and Answer in few words." Many colonists subscribed to English journals such as *The Tatler* and *The Spectator* that printed articles describing good manners.

Women, too, cultivated genteel manners. In Charleston, South Carolina, dozens of girls' boarding schools advertised instruction in "the different branches of Polite Education." Female pupils studied reading, writing, and arithmetic but also learned French, music, dancing, and fancy needlework. This curriculum prepared them for married lives as mistresses of great houses, mothers of future gentlemen and ladies, and hostesses of grand entertainments.

Such entertainments proliferated in the eighteenth century. Invitations to balls, musical performances, and tea parties circulated among well-bred neighbors. One gathering at Robert Carter's Virginia plantation began with an "elegant" dinner at half past four, followed at seven o'clock by dancing and card playing that lasted until nearly midnight. Such occasions excluded ordinary settlers and reinforced elite colonists' sense of themselves as a separate—and better—class of people.

Some aspiring colonial gentlemen adopted more intellectual pursuits. Literacy rates among white colonists were quite high by eighteenth-century standards. In New England, where settlers placed great emphasis on Bible study, about 70 percent of men and 45 percent of women could read and write. Farther south, literacy rates were lower, but they were still higher than in England, where only a third of all men and even fewer women could read and write. Prominent colonists, intent on developing America's intellectual life, began to participate in a transatlantic world of ideas.

These colonists, however, were more consumers of British and European ideas than producers of an American intellectual tradition. They imported thousands of books, subscribed to British journals, and established libraries in cities such as Philadelphia, Charleston, and New York where borrowing privileges could be purchased for a modest fee. Libraries and private collections contained sermons and other religious writings, classical Greek and Roman texts, political and philosophical works by prominent European thinkers, and mainly British examples of poetry, drama, essays, and novels. Colonists with literary aspirations emulated their favorite writers. Students at Harvard in Cambridge (founded in 1636) modeled their college newspaper on an English periodical, *The Spectator.* In Virginia, William Byrd—the son of an Indian trader who had risen to the rank of gentleman—composed verse in the style of contemporary English poets, and Thomas Jefferson copied out passages from the English novel *Tristram Shandy.* Benjamin Franklin honed his writing skills by rewriting essays from *The Spectator* and comparing his versions to the originals.

Educated colonists were especially interested in the new ideas that characterized what has been called the **Age of Enlightenment**. The European thinkers of the Enlightenment drew inspiration from recent advances in science—such as the English scientist Isaac Newton's explanation of the laws of gravity—that suggested that the universe operated according to natural laws that human reason could discover. They also drew on the work of the English philosopher John Locke, who maintained that God did not dictate human knowledge but rather gave us the power to acquire knowledge through experience and understanding. The hallmark of Enlightenment thought was a belief in the power of human reason to improve the human condition.

This optimistic worldview marked a profound intellectual shift. Enlightenment thinkers rejected earlier ideas about God's unknowable will and continued intervention in human and natural events. They instead assigned God a less active role as the creator of the universe, who had set the world running according to predictable laws, and then let nature—and human beings—shape events. Such ideas inspired a growing international community of scholars to try to discover the laws of nature and to work toward human progress.

Colonial intellectuals sought membership in this scholarly community. A few of them—the Reverend Cotton Mather of Massachusetts, William Byrd, Benjamin Franklin—gained election to the Royal Society of London, the most prestigious learned society in the empire. Most of their scholarly contributions were unimpressive. Byrd, for instance, sent the Royal Society a rather superficial manuscript titled "An Account of a Negro Boy That Is Dappled in Several Places of His Body with White Spots."

Benjamin Franklin, by contrast, achieved genuine intellectual prominence. Even as a youth, Franklin hungered after learning and demonstrated a particular gift for science. His experiments with a kite proved that lightning was electricity (a natural force whose properties were poorly understood at the time) and gained him an international reputation. He also found practical uses for his scientific knowledge. Franklin invented the lightning rod (which prevented fires in wooden buildings by channeling the electrical charge of a lightning bolt into the ground), bifocal spectacles, the iron "Franklin stove" (in which wood burned more efficiently than in fireplaces), and the glass harmonica, an instrument that made him famous among European musicians and composers.

If Franklin's career embodied the Enlightenment ideal of the rational exploration of nature's laws, it also revealed the limited impact of Enlightenment thought in colonial America. Only a few prosperous and educated colonists could afford such intellectual pursuits. Franklin himself came from humble origins—his father was a maker of candles and soap—but his success as a printer eventually allowed him to retire from business at age 42. Only then did he purchase the equipment for his electrical discoveries and begin his scientific work, devoting the "leisure during the rest of my life for philosophical studies and amusements." Franklin's equipment—and leisure—were as much badges of gentlemanly status as George Washington's London-made suit.

Most colonists remained ignorant of scientific advances and Enlightenment ideas. Unlike aspiring gentlemen and ladies, they had little leisure to devote to literature and polite conversation. When they found time to read, they picked up not a courtesy book or *The Spectator* but the Bible. Religion principally shaped the way in which they viewed the world and explained human and natural events.

Robert Feke (1707–1752), Portrait of Benjamin Franklin (1706–1790), c. 1746. Oil on canvas, 127 × 102 cm. Courtesy of the Harvard University Portrait Collection. Bequest of Dr. John Collins Warren, 1856.

Painted at about the time Franklin retired from his printing business, this portrait depicts the one-time craftsman as an aspiring gentleman. Wearing a wig and a shirt with ruffled cuffs, Franklin would no longer work with his hands but would pursue his scientific experiments and other studies.

Colonial Religion and the Great Awakening

Church steeples dominated the skylines of colonial cities. By the 1750s, Boston and New York each had eighteen churches, and Philadelphia boasted twenty. Churches and meetinghouses likewise dominated country towns, though more sparsely in the scattered settlements of the South than in the northern colonies. Often the largest and finest buildings in town, they bore witness to the thriving—and diverse—condition of religion in America.

In all New England colonies except Rhode Island, the Puritan (or Congregationalist) faith was the established religion. The many Congregational churches in the region, headed by ministers trained at Harvard College and Yale (founded 1701), served the majority of its colonists and received financial support from their taxes. Though proud of the Puritan tradition that had inspired New England's origins, ministers and believers nonetheless had to adapt to changing social and religious conditions.

The principal adaptation consisted of a move away from strict requirements for church membership. In order to keep their churches pure, New England's founders had required prospective members to give convincing evidence that they had experienced a spiritual conversion. Once admitted, members could receive communion and have their children baptized.

By the 1660s, however, fewer colonists sought admission under such strict standards, which left them and their unbaptized children outside the church. To address this problem, the clergy in 1662 adopted the **Halfway Covenant**, which allowed adults who had been baptized (because their parents were church members), but who had not themselves experienced conversion, to have their own children baptized. The Halfway Covenant slowly gained acceptance in the following decades. By the 1680s, some ministers made church admission even easier, requiring members only to demonstrate knowledge of the Christian faith and to live godly lives.

The Congregational Church also had to accept a measure of religious toleration in New England. In 1691, Massachusetts received a royal charter granting "liberty of Conscience" to all Protestants, bringing the colony into line with England's religious policy. Anglicans and Baptists eventually won exemptions from paying taxes to support the Congregational Church. At the same time, some Congregationalist preachers began emphasizing personal piety and good works in their sermons, ideas usually associated with Anglicanism. These changes indicated a shift away from the Puritan exclusiveness of New England's early years.

In the South, the established Church of England consolidated its authority in the early eighteenth century but never succeeded in exerting effective control over spiritual life. The bishop of London began appointing agents to oversee church matters, and the Society for the Propagation of the Gospel in Foreign Parts, founded in 1701, attempted to provide ministers for colonial parishes. Even so, these parishes often lacked trained clergy, and those who did emigrate encountered unexpected obstacles.

Many a parson in England could easily ride from one side of his parish to the other in an hour, but Anglican clergymen in the southern colonies served parishes that were vast and sparsely settled. One South Carolina parish contained 10,400 square miles—and only seven hundred white residents. Ministers also found that influential planters, who had grown used to running parishes when preachers were unavailable, resisted their efforts to take control of churches. Aware that the planters' taxes paid their salaries, many ministers found it easiest simply to preach and behave in ways that offered the least offense. Frontier regions often lacked Anglican churches and clergymen altogether. In such places, dissenting religious groups, such as Presbyterians, Quakers, and Baptists, gained followers among people neglected by the Anglican establishment.

No established church dominated in the Middle Colonies of New York, New Jersey, and Pennsylvania. The region's ethnically diverse population and William Penn's policy of religious toleration guaranteed that a multitude of groups would compete for followers. One observer, accustomed to an established church, characterized these conditions as a "soul-destroying whirlpool." Yet religion flourished in the Middle Colonies. By the mid-eighteenth century, the region had more congregations per capita than even New England.

Groups such as the Quakers and the Mennonites, who did not believe in having specially trained ministers, easily formed new congregations in response to local demand. Lutheran and German Reformed churches, however, required European-educated clergy, who were always scarce. Pious laymen held worship services in their homes even as they sent urgent letters overseas begging for ordained ministers. When more Lutheran and Reformed clergy arrived in the 1740s and 1750s, they sometimes discovered—like Anglican preachers in the South—that laymen balked at relinquishing control of the churches. Lutheran and Reformed ministers also learned that their professional training alone could not command respect. Their congregations demanded that they be powerful preachers. Because so many other religious alternatives were available, these ministers had to compete for their parishioners' allegiance.

Bewildering spiritual diversity, relentless religious competition, and a comparatively weak Anglican Church all distinguished the colonies from England. Yet in one important way, religious developments during the middle third of the eighteenth century drew the colonies closer to England. A great transatlantic religious revival, originating in Scotland and England, first touched the Middle Colonies in the 1730s. In 1740–1745, it struck the northern colonies with the force of a hurricane, and in the 1760s, the last phase of the revival spread through the South. America had never seen anything like this immense revival, which came to be called the **Great Awakening**.

By 1730, Presbyterians in Pennsylvania had split into factions over such issues as the disciplining of church members and the requirement that licensed ministers have university degrees. One group, led by an immigrant Scottish evangelist, William Tennent, Sr., and his four sons, denounced their opponents as men more interested in regulations than conversion. In the 1730s, Tennent set up the Log College in Neshaminy, Pennsylvania, to train his sons and other young men to be evangelical ministers. What began as a dispute among clergymen

FROM THEN TO NOW

The Enduring Vitality and Diversity of American Religion

In a front-page story in April 1991, *The New York Times* reported on "dozens of surprises" contained in an opinion poll on religious identification in America. The poll revealed two main features of American religious life. First, organized religion was thriving. Nine out of ten people polled identified themselves with a religious denomination. Second, the American religious scene was highly diverse. Respondents claimed affiliation with dozens of groups, from Roman Catholics (the single largest group) to Rastafarians (one of the smallest).

These results reflect an enduring religious vitality and diversity that have characterized American life since the beginning of colonization. In 1687, a governor of New York tried to describe the religious climate of the colony he had just been appointed to govern. "Here bee not many of the Church of England; few Roman Catholicks; abundance of Quakers preachers men and Women especially; Singing Quakers; Ranting Quakers; Sabbatarians; Antisabbatarians; Some Anabaptists some Independants; some Jews," he reported. The governor—himself a member of the Church of England—neglected to report that New York was also home to many Dutch Calvinists and Lutherans. For a man accustomed to living under a single established Church, this state of affairs was disconcerting. To colonists, however, religious diversity was as often as not the normal experience.

Religious enthusiasm and diversity only increased in the eighteenth century, particularly after the Great Awakening caused many churches to split into factions and go their separate ways. At the same time, the influx of immigrants from such places as northern Ireland, Scotland, and Germany added new faiths to the colonial religious mixture.

By the time of the American Revolution, religious diversity had become so firmly embedded in American life that people feared the establishment of a single state church far more than the consequences of having a multiplicity of faiths within a single nation. It was this fear that inspired the First Amendment to the Constitution, with its guarantee of the "free exercise" of religion, of whatever kind, and its prohibition of any religious establishment. The First Amendment, in turn, created the conditions under which religion could flourish in modern America.

It has also, ironically, made the federal government so wary of intervening in Americans' religious lives that the U.S. Census Bureau refuses to include any questions about religion on its decennial questionnaire. Thus it was a nongovernmental group—the City University of New York—that commissioned the report that, although surprising to New York journalists, confirmed the underlying continuities that historians have long recognized in American religious life.

Dramatically illustrating the vitality of religion in colonial New York, this woodblock of the city's skyline shows no fewer than seventeen churches and one synagogue. The variety of denominations—from Lutherans to Quakers to Jews—typified the religious experience of the Middle Colonies more than other regions, but everywhere in colonial America religious diversity increased in the eighteenth century.

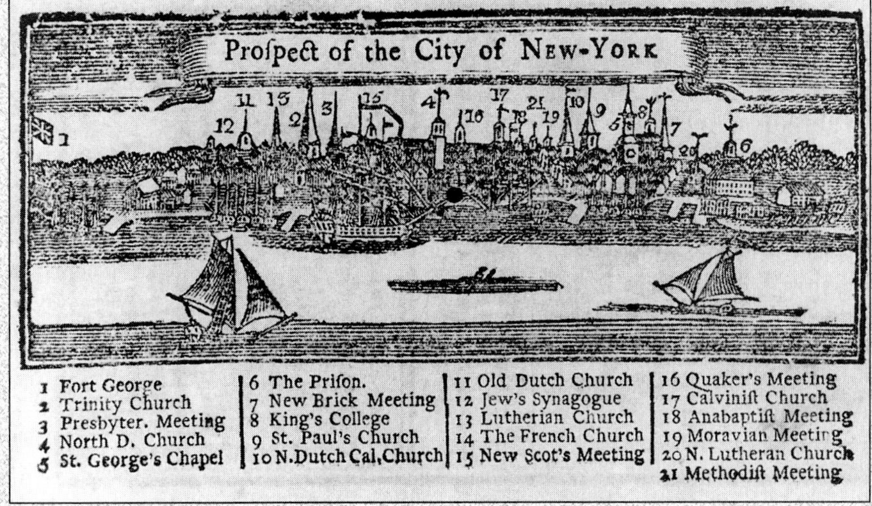

eventually blossomed into a broader challenge to religious authority. That challenge gained momentum in late 1739 when one of the most charismatic evangelists of the century, George Whitefield, arrived in the colonies from England.

Whitefield, an Anglican priest, had experienced an uncommonly intense religious conversion while he was still a university student. Already famous in Britain as a preacher of great emotional fervor, he embarked on a tour of the colonies in the winter of 1739–1740. As soon as Whitefield landed in Delaware, his admirers whipped up local enthusiasm, ensuring that he would preach to huge crowds. In Pennsylvania and New Jersey, Whitefield's powerful preaching on the experience of conversion lent support to the Presbyterian faction led by the Tennents and sparked local revivals. Whitefield then moved on to New England, where some communities had already experienced small, local awakenings. In 1734–1735, for instance, the Congregationalist minister Jonathan Edwards had led a revival in Northampton, Massachusetts, urging his parishioners to recognize their sinfulness and describing hell in such a terrifying way that many despaired of their salvation.

Whitefield's tour through the colonies knitted these scattered local revivals into the Great Awakening. Crowds gathered in city squares and open fields to listen to his sermons. Whitefield exhorted his audiences to examine their souls for evidence of the "indwelling of Christ" that would indicate that they were saved. He criticized most ministers for emphasizing good works and "head-knowledge" instead of the emotional side of religion.

Whitefield's open-air sermons scarcely resembled the colonists' accustomed form of worship. Settlers normally gathered with family and neighbors in church for formal, structured services. They sat in pews assigned on the basis of social status, with wealthier members in front and poorer folk in the back. Such worship services reinforced standards of order and community hierarchy. But Whitefield's sermons were highly dramatic performances. He preached for hours in a booming voice, accompanying his words with spirited gestures and even occasionally dissolving in tears. Thousands of strangers, jostling in crowds that often outnumbered the populations of several villages put together, wept along with him. When the sermon ended, his listeners dispersed, many never to see each other again.

In the wake of Whitefield's visits, Benjamin Franklin noted, "it seem'd as if all the World were growing Religious." Revivals and mass conversions often followed his appearances, to the happy astonishment of local clergy. But their approval evaporated when more extreme revivalists appeared. Gilbert Tennent, William's son, followed Whitefield to Boston and derided the town's ministers as unconverted "dead Drones." James Davenport—a preacher so erratic that many thought him mad—claimed that God gave him the knowledge of other ministers' spiritual state and routinely denounced by name those he "knew" to be damned. Once, in the midst of a sermon urging his audience to rid themselves of worldly finery, Davenport set an example by tearing off his velvet breeches and throwing them into a bonfire. Officials who valued civic order soon tried to silence such extremists by passing laws that prohibited them from preaching in a town without the local minister's permission.

Disputes between individuals converted in the revivals—called "**New Lights**"—and those who were not ("Old Lights") split churches. New Lights insisted, as the separatist founders of Plymouth once had, that they could not remain in churches with sinful members and unconverted ministers and so left

George Whitefield (who, contemporaries noted, was cross-eyed) enjoyed a remarkable career as a powerful preacher on both sides of the Atlantic. This portrait shows him preaching indoors to a rapt audience. During his tour of the colonies, Whitefield reportedly had a similar effect on crowds of thousands who gathered outdoors to hear his sermons.

to form new churches. "Formerly the People could bear with each other in Charity when they differ'd in Opinion," lamented one colonist, "but they now break Fellowship and Communion with one another on that Account."

The Awakening came late to the southern colonies, but it was there, in the 1760s, that it produced perhaps its greatest controversy. Many southern converts became Baptists, combining their religious criticism of the Anglicans with a condemnation of the wealthy planters' way of life. Plainly dressed Baptists criticized the rich clothes, drinking, gambling, and pride of Virginia's gentry. Planters, in turn, viewed Baptists as dangerous people who could not "meet a man upon the road, but they must ram a text of Scripture down his throat." Most of all, they hated the Baptists for their willingness to preach to slaves. More than once, irate gentlemen burst in on Baptist services and beat the preacher senseless.

Although the revivals themselves gradually waned, the Great Awakening had a lasting impact on colonial society. It forged new links between Great Britain and the colonies. Evangelical ministers on both sides of the Atlantic exchanged correspondence. Periodicals such as *The Christian History*—over which Whitefield exercised considerable control—informed British and American subscribers of advances in true religion throughout the empire.

In the colonies, the Awakening led to the founding of new colleges to serve members of different religious denominations. Middle Colony evangelicals founded the College of New Jersey (now Princeton University) in 1746. In the 1760s, New England Baptists established the College of Rhode Island (now Brown University). An evangelical wing of the Dutch Reformed Church founded Queens College (now Rutgers University) in 1766. These colleges drew students from all colonies, not just the local area.

Everywhere, the New Light challenge to established ministers and churches undermined habits of deference to authority. Revivalists urged colonists to think for themselves in choosing which church to join and which minister to follow, not just conform to what the rest of the community did. As their churches fractured, colonists—particularly New Englanders—faced more choices than ever before in their religious lives.

The exercise of religious choice also influenced political behavior. Voters took note of whether candidates for office were New or Old Lights and cast their ballots for men on their own side. Tactics first used to mobilize religious groups—organizing committees, writing petitions and letters—proved useful for political activities as well. Though hardly the intent of Whitefield or other revivalists, the Awakening thus fostered greater political awareness and participation among colonists.

The Colonial Political World

The political legacy of the Great Awakening—particularly the emphasis on individual choice and resistance to authority—corresponded to developments in the colonial political world. For most of the seventeenth century, ties within the empire developed from trade rather than governance. But as America grew in wealth and population, king and Parliament sought to manage colonial affairs more directly than before.

In the late seventeenth century, upheavals on both sides of the Atlantic seemed to confirm for both colonists and Englishmen a common interest in protecting the rights and liberties they derived from their shared heritage. The English overthrew King James II, and the people of New England successfully resisted the king's attempt to impose autocratic government in the colonies. But even as colonists and Englishmen asserted their common political culture at the dawn of the eighteenth century, differences in their political practices and ideas began to emerge.

The Dominion of New England and the Limits of British Control

Before 1650, England made little attempt to exert centralized control in North America. Each colony more or less governed itself, and most political activity occurred at the town or county level. Local officials kept the peace, resolved disputes, arranged for public works—schools, roads, bridges—and collected taxes. Busy with the routines of daily life, most colonists devoted little time—and even less interest—to politics.

When Charles II became king in 1660, he initially showed little interest in the colonies except as sources of land and government offices with which he could reward his supporters. The grandest prizes, of course, were the great proprietorships, such as Pennsylvania and Carolina, but the creation of a rudimentary imperial bureaucracy also yielded rewards for the king to distribute. With the passage of mercantilist regulations governing colonial trade, for example, Parliament required customs officers to administer the imperial trading system and thus created a certain number of jobs.

Charles's brother James, the duke of York, envisioned a more tightly controlled empire. He encouraged Charles to appoint military officers, with strong ties of loyalty to him, as royal governors in America. In 1675, James convinced Charles to create the **Lords of Trade**, a committee of the Privy Council (the group of nobles who served as royal advisers), to oversee colonial affairs.

When James became king in 1685, the whole character of the empire abruptly changed. Seeking to transform it into something much grander and more susceptible to England's control, James set out to reorganize it along the lines of Spain's empire, combining the colonies into three or four large provinces. He appointed powerful governors to carry out policies that he himself would formulate.

James began in the north, creating the **Dominion of New England** out of eight previously separate colonies stretching from Maine (then part of Massachusetts) to New Jersey. He chose Sir Edmund Andros, a former army officer, to govern the vast region with an appointive council but no elective assembly. Andros moved to Boston and initially gained some support from merchants excluded from politics by Massachusetts's insistence that only church members could vote. But he eventually antagonized them and other New Englanders by rigidly enforcing the Navigation Acts, limiting towns to just one annual meeting, remodeling the law courts, challenging property titles, and levying taxes without the colonists' consent. He even compelled Boston Puritans to share a meetinghouse with Anglicans.

Events in England ultimately sealed the fate of the Dominion. For years, English Protestants had worried about James's absolutist governing style and his conversion to Catholicism. Their fears increased in 1688 when the queen bore a son to carry on a Catholic line of succession. Parliament's leaders invited James's Protestant daughter, Mary, and her husband, William of Orange, the Stadtholder of the Netherlands, to take over the throne. In November 1688, William landed in England and gained the support of most of the English army. In December, James fled to France, ending a bloodless coup known as the **Glorious Revolution**.

Bostonians overthrew Andros the following April, even before they knew for sure that William was king, and later had him shipped back to England. Massachusetts colonists hoped that their original charter of 1629 would be reinstated, but a new one was issued in 1691. It made several important changes. Massachusetts now included within its borders what had formerly been Plymouth Colony as well as Maine. Its colonists no longer elected their governor, who would instead be appointed by the monarch. Voters no longer had to be church members, and religious toleration was extended to all Protestants.

The new charter ended exclusive Puritan control in Massachusetts but also restored political stability. During the three years between Andros's overthrow and the arrival of a royal governor in 1692, the colony lacked a legally established government. In this atmosphere of uncertainty, an outbreak of accusations of witchcraft in Salem grew to unprecedented proportions. Colonists, like most Europeans of the time, believed in the existence of witches—humans who acted as Satan's agents and used supernatural powers to hurt their enemies. Over the years, New Englanders had executed a dozen or so accused witches, usually older women. But in the winter of 1691–1692, when several young girls of Salem experienced fits and other strange behavior, hundreds of settlers were accused of witchcraft, and nineteen were hanged. Salem's crisis occurred against a backdrop of local economic change, but it gathered momentum because the courts, which would normally have intervened to settle matters, were unable to function.

The impact of the Glorious Revolution in other colonies likewise reflected local conditions. In New York, after Andros's deputy left, Jacob Leisler, a rich merchant and militia captain, gained power and ruled in a dictatorial fashion, persecuting men against whom he held personal grievances. Too slow in relinquishing command to the newly arrived royal governor in 1691, Leisler was arrested for treason and executed. In Maryland, Protestants used the occasion of William and Mary's accession to the throne to lobby for the end of the Catholic proprietorship. They were partly successful. The Calvert family lost its governing powers but retained rights to vast quantities of land. The Anglican Church became the established faith, and Catholics were barred from public office.

The colonists rejected James, not English authority in general. Their motives (especially in New England) largely reflected powerful anti-Catholic sentiment. William's firm Protestantism reassured them, and most colonists assumed that life would return to normal. But the Glorious Revolution in England and the demise of the Dominion had long-lasting effects that shaped political life in England and America for years to come.

The Legacy of the Glorious Revolution

In England, the Glorious Revolution signaled a return to political stability after years of upheaval. English people celebrated the preservation of their rights from the threat of a tyrannical king. In 1689, Parliament passed the Bill of Rights, which justified

James's ouster and bound future monarchs to abide by the rule of law. They could not suspend parliamentary laws, collect taxes or engage in foreign wars without Parliament's consent, or maintain a standing army in peacetime. Parliamentary elections and meetings would follow a regular schedule without royal interference. In sum, Parliament claimed to be the crown's equal partner in governing England.

Colonists, too, celebrated the vindication of their rights as Englishmen. They believed that their successful resistance to Andros confirmed that their membership in the empire was founded on voluntary allegiance and not forced submission to the mother country. Observing the similarity between Parliament and the colonial assemblies, they concluded that their own legislatures had a critical role in governance and in the protection of their rights and liberties. On both sides of the Atlantic, representative government had triumphed.

In fact, Parliament claimed full authority over the colonies and did not recognize their assemblies as its equal. For more than a half-century, however, it did not vigorously assert that authority. At the same time, William and his immediate successors lacked James's compulsion to control the colonies. William did make a few changes to imperial administration. In 1696, he replaced the Lords of Trade with a new committee, the **Board of Trade**. This advisory body gathered information from the colonies and recommended policy changes but itself had no executive role. William also approved the Navigation Act of 1696, which closed loopholes in earlier laws and created **vice-admiralty courts** in the colonies similar to those of England. Admiralty judges settled maritime disputes and smuggling cases without using juries.

During the early eighteenth century, Parliament and royal ministers confined their attention to matters of trade and military defense and otherwise left the colonies on their own. This mild imperial rule, later called the era of "salutary neglect," allowed the colonies to grow in wealth, population, and self-government. It also encouraged colonial self-confidence, leading colonists to assume equality with the English as members of the empire.

Diverging Politics in the Colonies and Great Britain

English people on both sides of the Atlantic believed that politics ought to reflect social organization. They often compared the state to a family. Just as fathers naturally headed families, adult men led societies. In particular, adult male property holders, who enjoyed economic independence, claimed the right to vote and hold office. Women (who generally could not own property), propertyless men, and slaves had no political role because they, like children, were subordinate to the authority of others. Their dependence on husbands, fathers, masters, or employers—who could influence their political decisions—rendered them incapable of exercising freedom of choice.

States, like families, worked best when all members fulfilled their responsibilities. Rulers ought to govern with the same fairness and benevolence that fathers presumably exercised within their families. When George II became king in 1727, he reassured Parliament of his "constant care" to "secure to All My subjects, the full Enjoyment of their religious and civil Rights." In return for protection, the people owed their rulers the same obedience that children accorded their parents. The House of Commons responded to George II's assurance of goodwill with its own promise of "Duty, Zeal and Affection to Your Majesty's Person and Government." Such phrases often disguised actual struggles between rulers and people but nevertheless expressed firmly held ideals.

Eighteenth-century people also believed that government should reflect society's hierarchical organization. In England, this idea was embodied in the institutions of monarchy and Parliament. The crown, of course, represented the interests of the royal family. Parliament represented society's two main divisions: the aristocracy in the **House of Lords** and the common people in the **House of Commons**. Americans shared the view that government should mirror social hierarchies but found it much more difficult to put the idea into practice.

American society grew closer to the British model during the eighteenth century but was never identical to it. Thus its political structure would never fully mirror that of England. One of the most obvious differences was that America lacked an aristocracy. In England, the members of this tiny privileged minority were easily recognizable by their great wealth, prestigious family lines, leisured lives, and official titles of nobility. British America had elites but no titled aristocracy. Elite colonists were often just two or three generations removed from humble beginnings. Hence the acute anxiety that inspired George Washington and other colonial gentlemen to seek refinement, to gain the automatic recognition that England's more secure elites enjoyed.

In both England and America, land ownership was the prerequisite for political participation, on the grounds that it freed people from dependence on others and gave them a stake in society. In England, this requirement sharply limited participation. By the mid-eighteenth century, only one-tenth

American Views

Boston Celebrates a New King (August 1727)

The first colonial newspaper, the *Boston News-Letter,* appeared in that city in 1704. By the 1720s, Bostonians could choose from three newspapers, and New York and Philadelphia each had one. Published weekly, these papers mainly reported on English and European affairs and often reprinted essays by prominent English political writers. Their pages carried little local news, on the assumption that colonists could learn it by word of mouth. But when truly extraordinary events occurred, such as the accession of a new British monarch, colonial newspapers reported on the local response. The following extract describes Bostonians' reaction to news that George II had become Britain's new king.

- **How did Bostonians commemorate the new king's accession?**
- **What does this reveal about their attitudes toward George II and British government in general?**
- **Who was invited to the "splendid Entertainment," and what does this reveal about the structure of Boston society?**

On Wednesday Morning by order of His Honour William Dummer, Esq., our Lieut. Governour & Commander in chief[,] three Regiments of the Militia and five Troops of horse were under arms in the great street before the State-house, making a very fine appearance. The number of Spectators exceeded the Men in Arms, covering the houses on every side. As soon as the Herauld had said his Amen to God Save the King, the loud and joyful Huzza's of so great a multitude rent the skies, the Regiments made a tripple discharge, the Castle Forts & Ships fir'd their cannon; and a splendid Entertainment follow'd for the Lieut. Governour and his Majesty's Council, Officers, Justices, and the Rev[eren]d Ministers present; with suitable provisions for the Regiments and Troops. The bells rung all the day, and in the Evening the Rejoycing was continued with Fireworks and Bonfires, and the whole Town illuminated in an extraordinary manner, the Windows of each story of the Houses in the principal streets having three or four rows of candles in them. The streets were fill'd all the Evening with the Gentry of both Sexes, who appear'd with much decency and gravity, and with gayety and chearfulness. At nine of the clock a welcome rain, after a time of much heat and drought, put an end to the Ceremony. . . . We pray God, by whom Kings reign, that the royal smiles of His Majesty King George the Second, and the happy influences of his wise and just Government, may ever be falling on all his Majesty's Dominions, and on this loyal and dutiful Province in particular. . . .

Source: New England Weekly Journal *(August 21, 1727).*

of all English heads of households owned all the country's land, and thus only a correspondingly tiny proportion of men could vote. Landholding in America, however, was much more widespread. By late in life, a large majority of white male farmers owned the land they tilled. The expansion of landholding swelled the ranks of voters. In most colonies, 50 to 75 percent of white men were eligible to vote, although not all exercised this right at election time.

Distinctive social conditions in England and America also gave rise to different notions of political representation. Electoral districts for Parliament came in a confusing mixture of shapes, reflecting their status in past centuries. Once-important towns sent representatives on the basis of their former prominence. Dunwich even retained its right to elect a parliamentary representative long after the city itself had washed into the North Sea. At the same time, rapidly growing cities, such as Manchester, lacked any representative at all. Some English radicals protested this inequity during the eighteenth century. Most of their countrymen, however, accepted the idea of **virtual representation**, which held that representatives served the interests of the nation as a whole, not just the locality from which they came. They assumed that since the colonists held interests in common with English people at home, they were virtually represented in Parliament—just like Manchester's residents.

Since the founding of their colonies, however, Americans had experienced **actual representation**—and believed that elected representatives should be directly responsive to local interests. They were accustomed to sending written instructions to their legislators, informing them how to vote on important issues. Colonial representatives, unlike members of Parliament, resided in their districts. The Americans' experience with actual representation made them extremely skeptical of Parliament's claims to virtual representation. For the first half of the eighteenth century, however, Parliament did not press this claim, and the tensions between the two ideas remained latent.

The most direct political confrontations between England and the colonies instead focused on the role of colonial governors. In every colony except Connecticut and Rhode Island, either the king or proprietors appointed the governors. Their interests thus lay with their English patrons and not the colonies. More important, governors exercised greater powers over the colonial assemblies than the king (after the Glorious Revolution) did over Parliament. Governors could veto laws enacted by the assemblies and initiate legislation in consultation with councilors whom they appointed. They could delay legislative sessions and dissolve the assemblies at will. Governors could also nominate and dismiss colonial judges as they wished.

In practice, several conditions hampered governors' efforts to exercise their legal authority. Many arrived with detailed instructions on how to govern, which limited their ability to negotiate with colonists over sensitive issues. Governors controlled few offices or other prizes with which to buy the allegiance of their opponents. They struggled to dominate assemblies that grew in size as the colonial population expanded. And in several colonies, including Massachusetts and New York, governors relied on the assemblies to appropriate the money for their salaries—a financial dependence that restrained even the most autocratic executive.

In response to the perceived, if not always realized, threat of powerful governors, colonial assemblies asserted themselves as never before. They sent agents (including such prominent figures as Benjamin Franklin) to England to lobby on behalf of colonial interests. Local factions fought for election to the increasingly important legislature, leading to some of the most contentious politics in the British Empire. Governors often stood on the sidelines, either frustrated with their inability to govern or, at times, enlisted on the side of one faction or another.

Decades of struggles with governors led colonists to exalt the assemblies' role as the guarantors of their liberties. In 1738, one Pennsylvanian went so far as to declare that the "necessity of reducing the form of this government to the British mode" by strengthening the executive was a "wicked" design. Most colonists, however, accepted the loose and sometimes contradictory political ties of empire. They assumed that their connections to Britain were voluntary, based on common identity and rights. So long as Parliament treated the Americans as partners in empire and refrained from ruling by coercion, colonists could celebrate British government as "the most perfect combination of human powers in society . . . for the preservation of liberty and the production of happiness."

By the middle of the eighteenth century, the blessings of British government extended to more colonists than ever before. The population of British America grew rapidly and spread out over vast amounts of land. The expansion of British settlement, in turn, alarmed other European powers with American colonies. Both Spain and France launched new settlements as the competition for the continent entered a new and volatile phase.

Expanding Empires

During the first half of the eighteenth century, England, Spain, and France all enlarged their North American holdings according to patterns established during the previous century. England's empire expanded in tandem with the unrelenting growth of its colonial population. Spain and France still relied on missionaries, soldiers, and traders to stake their claims to American territory. In the eighteenth century as in the seventeenth, English settlement displaced native peoples. Newly established Spanish and French colonies, however, contained small numbers of Europeans amid much larger populations of Indians. Over time, these empires came into closer contact with one another, intensifying the competition for land, trade, resources, and Indian allies (see Map 4-2).

The English in the Backcountry

Population growth in British North America during the eighteenth century was truly astonishing. Black and white settlers in the mainland colonies numbered 265,000 in 1700; by 1770, they had increased to 2.3 million (see Figure 4-2). Benjamin Franklin predicted in 1750 that if the colonial population continued to grow at this rate, within two hundred years "the greatest Number of Englishmen will be on this Side" of the Atlantic Ocean.

Much of this growth stemmed from natural increase. White families, particularly in the northern colonies, often had between five and ten children, most of whom survived to produce more offspring. The descendants of a single couple could, after three or four generations, people small towns. When 80-year-old Judith Coffin, the matriarch of an unusually large Massachusetts family, died in 1705, she had a total of 177 children and grandchildren. By the mid-eighteenth century, even the slave population, first in the Chesapeake and later in the Lower South, began to reproduce itself, although more slowly than the white population.

Immigration also boosted the population, making some regions grow faster than others. Thou-

Map 4-2 Expanding Settlement, c. 1750
Imperial rivalries drove Spain, France, and England to expand their North American empires in the mid-eighteenth century. Once again, this sparked conflict with native peoples as well as with European competitors.

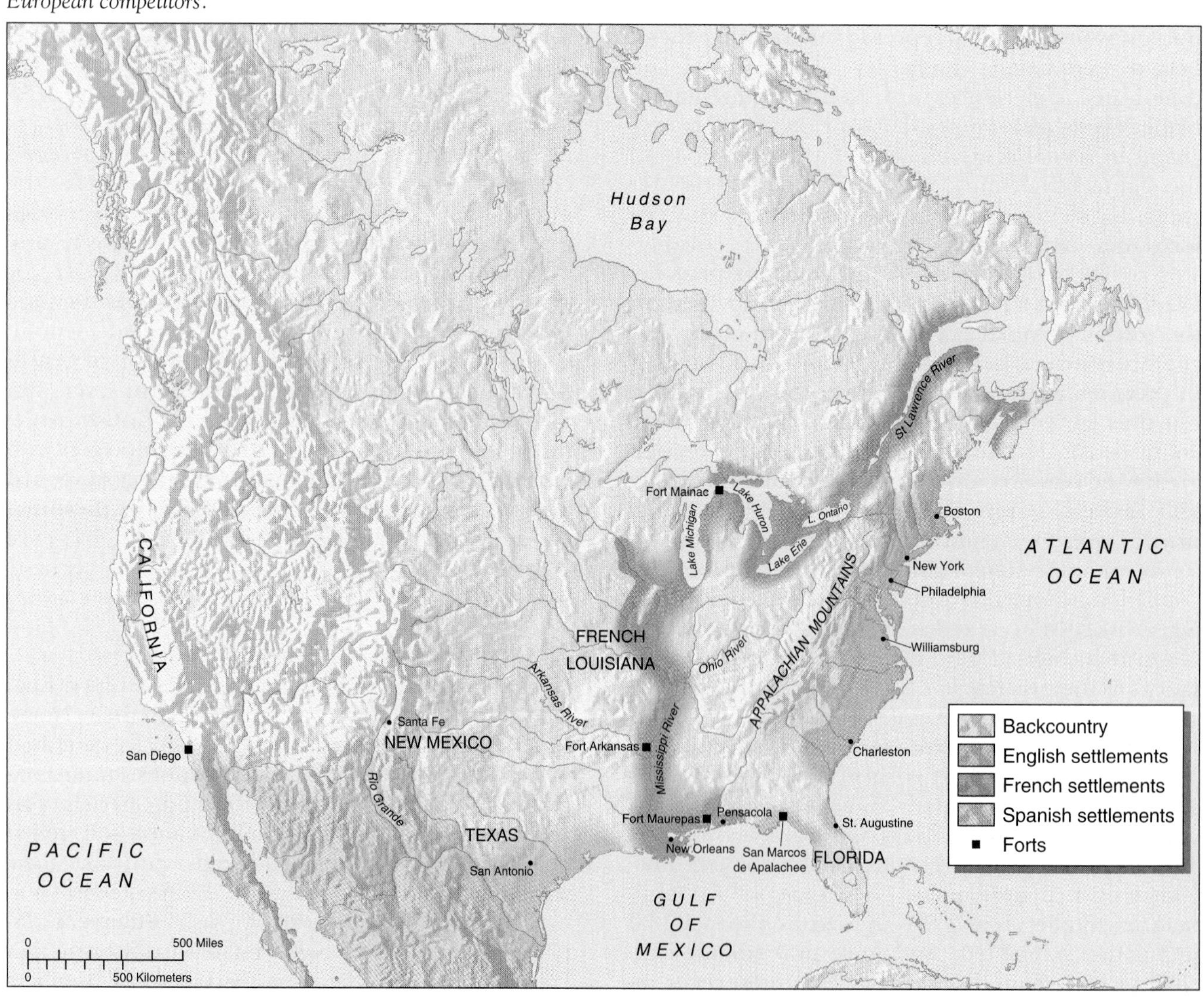

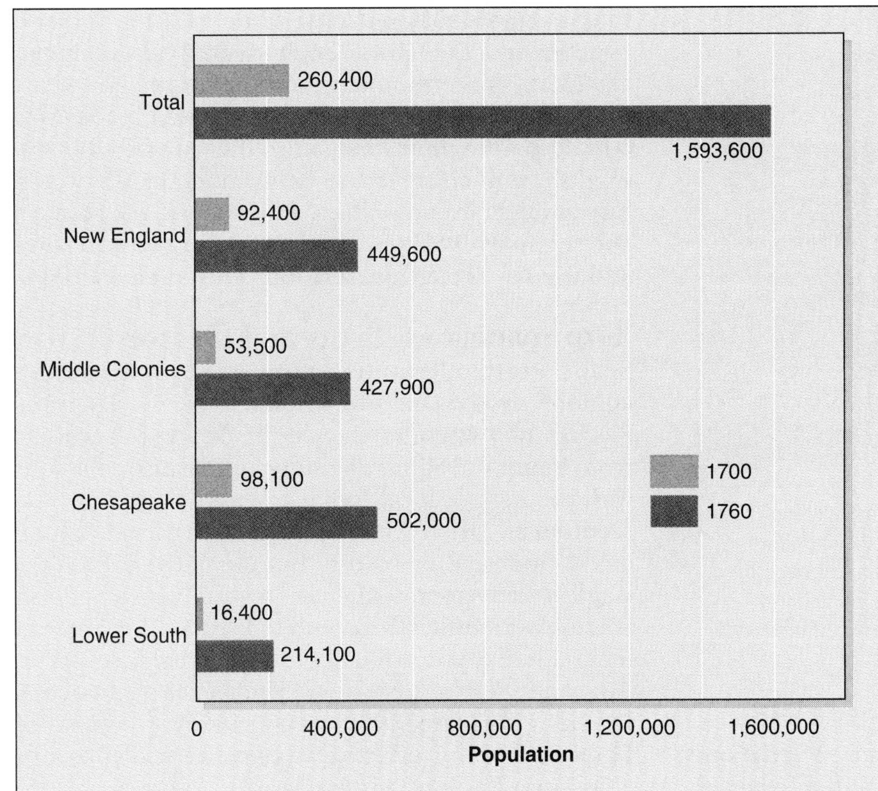

Figure 4-2 Population Growth in British Mainland Colonies, 1700–1760
Both natural increase and immigration contributed to a staggering rate of population growth in British North America. Some colonists predicted that Americans would soon outnumber Britain's inhabitants—a possibility that greatly concerned British officials.
Data Source: John J. McCusker and Russell R. Menard, The Economy of British America, 1607–1789, *rev. ed. (1991). University of North Carolina Press.*

sands of Scots-Irish and German settlers—and many involuntary African immigrants—helped the population of the Lower South increase at nearly twice the rate of New England, which attracted few immigrants (and therefore remained the most thoroughly English of all colonial regions). Pennsylvania absorbed a continuous stream of immigrants. By 1770, it had 240,000 settlers—ten times the number it had in 1710. Indeed, extensive German immigration worried Pennsylvania leaders. Like Benjamin Franklin, they feared that the newcomers would "never adopt our Language or Customs" and would soon "be so numerous as to Germanize us."

Most of the coast from Maine to Georgia was settled by 1760, forcing new immigrants to move inland. Descendants of earlier settlers often joined them, seeking farms that could no longer be had in the more crowded towns of their birth. New Englanders pushed up the Connecticut River Valley and into the hills of western Massachusetts. Settlement in New York followed the Hudson, Mohawk, and Schoharie Rivers deep into the interior. But the most dramatic expansion occurred in the foothills and valleys of the Appalachian Mountains from Pennsylvania to Georgia, a region known as the backcountry.

Between 1730 and 1770, nearly a quarter of a million German, Scots-Irish, and English colonists entered the backcountry. They mainly raised crops and livestock for subsistence on small, isolated farms. Community life developed slowly, in part because backcountry settlers often moved frequently. In addition, a surplus of men among the first settlers delayed the formation of families.

Contemporary observers derided the crudeness of frontier life. William Byrd, a wealthy planter from Virginia's Tidewater, scornfully described one backcountry house as a "castle containing of one dirty room with a dragging door to it that will neither open or shut." Charles Woodmason, an English-born Anglican missionary, was appalled by the sight of western Carolina settlers who "Live in Logg Cabbins like Hogs." Most of them, he reported, were "very loose, dissolute, Idle People—Without either Religion or Goodness." Genteel observers offered what they considered the most damaging insult by referring to such settlers as "white Indians."

These comments reflect emerging tensions between backcountry settlements and older seacoast communities. Many coastal planters—including William Byrd and George Washington—acquired vast tracts of western land with the intent to sell it to these "crude" settlers. During the 1740s and 1750s, scores of Virginia planters, northern merchants, and London investors formed companies whose purpose

This log house, built in Pennsylvania in the early eighteenth century, suggests the sort of dwellings that dotted the backcountry. Most such houses would have been smaller than this two-story example. Scandinavian colonists, who settled on the lower Delaware River in the early seventeenth century, introduced log construction to America.

was to profit from this kind of land speculation. Their interests collided with those of settlers—squatters—who occupied the land without acquiring legal title in the hope that their labor in clearing farms would establish their property rights.

Backcountry settlers often complained that rich eastern planters, who dominated the colonial legislatures, ignored western demands for adequate representation. Many argued that the crudeness of frontier life was only temporary. Perhaps the best measure of their desire to resemble eastern planters was the spread of slaveholding among prosperous backcountry farmers. In one western Virginia county in 1750, only one-fifth of the household heads owned slaves. Just nineteen years later, more than half of them did.

Tensions grew throughout the backcountry as English settlers encroached on Indian lands. Colonists who moved to Pennsylvania's fertile Susquehanna Valley displaced Delawares, Shawnees, and other native peoples who had sought refuge there from earlier white migrations. In South Carolina, the Catawbas moved to ever more remote sites to keep their distance from white settlers. Indians moving to avoid friction with whites, however, frequently encroached on lands claimed by other tribes—particularly those of the Iroquois Confederacy—leading to conflict among native peoples.

Even where English settlers had not yet appeared, English and Scottish traders could often be found, aggressively pursuing trade with the Indians. Spanish and French observers feared this commercial expansion even more than the movement of settlers. Knowing that the Indians viewed trade as a counterpart to military alliance, they worried that the English, with cheaper and better trade goods, would lure away their native allies. In response, the Spanish and French expanded their own territorial claims and tried to strengthen relations with Indian peoples.

The Spanish in Texas and California

Spain worried that its existing North American colonies would be overwhelmed by its enemies. Florida had become the target of English raiders from South Carolina, who attacked Spanish missions with the help of local Indians. Years of religious persecution and forced labor encouraged Florida's Indians to oppose the Spanish, but the natives also liked English trade goods—including guns, which Spanish traders were officially prohibited from selling. Spain maintained a precarious hold on coastal bases at St. Augustine, San Marcos de Apalachee, and Pensacola. By the mid-eighteenth century, however, control of Florida's interior effectively passed to Indian bands allied with English (and in the west, French) traders.

In 1700, New Mexico still suffered from the effects of the Pueblo Revolt. Spanish farmers and ranchers slowly moved back up the Rio Grande Valley. Franciscans returned to build fewer missions than before. Fearful of sparking another revolt, the priests eased their labor demands and avoided outright religious persecution, allowing the Pueblos to retain many of their customs and religious practices. New Mexican officials worried about news brought by Apache hunters that Frenchmen had been seen on the plains. French traders did not reach Santa Fe until 1739, but persistent rumors of their approach fueled Spanish fears that New Mexico would fall into French hands.

To create a buffer zone around their existing colonies, the Spanish moved into Texas and California. Franciscan priests led the way into east Texas, establishing several missions between 1690 and 1720. San Antonio was founded in 1718 to serve as a way station between the Rio Grande and east Texas missions; its fortified chapel, San Antonio de Valero, later became famous as the Alamo. The Spanish advance into Texas, however, met with resistance from the French (who also had outposts on the Gulf Coast) and from the Caddos and other Indians armed with French guns. Efforts to fill east Texas with settlers from Spain, Cuba, and the Canary Islands all failed when Spanish officials could not guarantee their safety. With only 1,800 settlers there as late as 1742, Spain exerted a weak hold on Texas.

Sixteenth-century Spaniards had considered building outposts in California to supply ships traveling between Mexico and the Philippines but were deterred because the coast could be reached only by a long trek across blazing deserts or a dangerous voyage around Baja California. Spanish interest revived in the 1760s when it seemed that other European powers—primarily Russia, which had built fur-trading posts in Alaska—might occupy California. Largely through the efforts of two men—José de Gálvez, a royal official, and Junípero Serra, a Franciscan priest—the Spanish constructed a string of forts and missions from San Diego north to San Francisco between 1769 and 1776.

They initially encountered little opposition from California's Indians, who lived in small, scattered villages and lacked experience with organized warfare. With no European rivals nearby to compete with them, the Spanish erected an extensive mission system designed to convert and educate Indians and set them to work. Thousands of native laborers farmed irrigated fields and tended horses, sheep, and cattle. They did so under extremely harsh conditions.

According to one observer, Indians who became Christians and settled at the missions endured a fate "worse than that of slaves." The Spanish worked them hard and maintained them in overcrowded, unsanitary dwellings. Native women suffered from sexual exploitation by Spanish soldiers. Epidemics of European diseases swept through the Indian population, reducing it from 300,000 in 1769 to about 200,000 fifty years later. Signs of native resistance met with quick and cruel punishment—including whipping, burning, and execution—so that the Indians would not (as one official later wrote) "come to know their power" over the vastly outnumbered Spanish. (As late as 1790, California had only 990 Spanish residents.) Despite the gruesome consequences, Indians staged several revolts during the eighteenth century, but Spanish soldiers usually suppressed them quickly.

Spain's empire grew, even as it weakened, during the eighteenth century. Its scattered holdings north of the Rio Grande functioned as colonies of another colony—Mexico—shielding it from foreign incursion. The scarcity of Spanish settlers, especially women, encouraged racial intermixture in the borderlands and ensured that racial distinctions would never be drawn as sharply there as in the English colonies. From the beginning, Spain's vision of empire had rested not on extensive settlement but on expansive territorial claims backed up by soldiers and missionaries who subjugated native peoples in order to control their labor for Spanish profit. After 1700, however, the limitations of this coercive approach to empire, which had served Spain well for nearly two centuries, became apparent. As their experiences in Florida and Texas vividly demonstrated, the Spanish simply could not compete with the vigorous commercial empires of France and England.

This panel of an eighteenth-century painting by an unknown Mexican artist is representative of a genre of portraits illustrating the categories Spanish colonists developed to designate the offspring of various kinds of mixed marriage. This one, labeled "Español, con India, Mestizo," *depicts a Spanish father, an Indian mother, and their* mestizo *child. The scarcity of European women made mixed marriage common in Spanish colonies. Such unions were exceedingly rare in the English colonies, where cultural preferences and the relative abundance of European women discouraged intermarriage.*

The French along the Mississippi

French expansion followed major waterways—the St. Lawrence River, the Great Lakes, the Mississippi—into the heart of North America. Explorers reached the Mississippi Valley in the 1670s. Within twenty years, French outposts appeared along the Gulf Coast. New Orleans, the capital and main port of French Louisiana, was founded in 1718. Soon forts, trading posts, and villages sprang up in the continent's interior—a chain of way stations between Canada and the Gulf of Mexico—with military garrisons strategically located on lakes and rivers. Concerned about defending scattered settlements, French officials forbade colonists to move into the interior. But colonists went anyway, building six villages along the Mississippi in a place they called the *Pays des Illinois.*

The first Illinois settlers were independent fur traders (*coureurs de bois,* or "woods runners") unwilling to return to Canada after the French government tried to prohibit their direct trade with Indians. Many found Christian Indian wives and began farming the rich lands along the river. Several hundred emigrants from Canada eventually joined them. The settlers, using the labor of their families and of black and Indian slaves, produced profitable surpluses of wheat, corn, and livestock to feed the growing population of New Orleans and the lower Mississippi Valley.

French Louisiana contained a remarkably diverse population of Indian peoples, French soldiers and settlers, German immigrants, and African slaves who, by the 1730s, outnumbered European colonists. Settlers raised some tobacco and indigo as cash crops, but Louisiana's economy depended mainly on the combined efforts of Indians, settlers, and slaves, who farmed, herded, fished, and traded deerskins. Discouraged by the lack of profits, French officials and merchants neglected Louisiana, and even Catholic missionaries failed to establish a strong presence. Significant European emigration to Louisiana essentially ceased after the 1720s.

But the French approach to empire—in Louisiana as in Canada—had always depended more on Indian alliances than on settlement. Louisiana's principal allies were the Choctaws, whom one military official called "the bulwark of the colony." The Choctaws and other native allies offered trade and military assistance in return for guns, trade goods, French help in fighting English raiders seeking Indian slaves, and occasionally French mediation of Indian disputes.

French expansion along the Mississippi Valley drove a wedge between Florida and Spain's other mainland colonies; it also blocked the westward movement of English settlers. But France's enlarged empire was only as strong as the Indian alliances on which it rested. Preserving good relations was expensive, however, requiring the constant exchange of diplomatic gifts and trade goods. When France ordered Louisiana officials to limit expenses and reduce Indian gifts in 1745, the officials objected that the Choctaws "would ask for nothing better than to have such pretexts in order to resort to the English."

The fear of losing Indian favor preoccupied officials in 1745 because at that moment France's empire in America consisted of two disconnected pieces: New France, centered in the St. Lawrence Valley and the Great Lakes basin, and Louisiana, stretching from New Orleans to the *Pays des Illinois.* Between them lay a thousand miles of wilderness through which only one thoroughfare passed—the Ohio River. For decades, communication between the two parts of France's North American empire posed no problem because Indians in the Ohio Valley allowed the French free passage through their lands. If that policy ended, however, France's New World empire would be dangerously divided.

A Century of Warfare

The expansion of empires in North America reflected the policies of European states locked in a relentless competition for power and wealth. From the time of the Glorious Revolution, English foreign policy aimed at limiting the expansion of French influence, and this, in turn, resulted in a series of four wars. As the eighteenth century wore on, the conflicts between the two countries increasingly involved their American colonies as well as Spain and its colonies. The outcome of each of the wars in America depended no less on the participation of colonists and Indians than on the policies and strategies of the European powers. The conclusion of the final conflict signaled a dramatic shift in North American history (see the overview table, "The Colonial Wars, 1689–1763").

Imperial Conflict and the Establishment of an American Balance of Power, 1689–1738

When he became king of England in 1688, the Dutch Protestant William of Orange was already fighting the **War of the League of Augsburg** against France's Catholic king, Louis XIV. Almost immediately, William brought England into the conflict. The war lasted until 1697 and ended—as most eighteenth-century European wars did—in a negotiated peace that reestablished the balance of power. Little territory changed hands, either in this

OVERVIEW

THE COLONIAL WARS, 1689–1763

Name in the Colonies	European Name and Dates	Dates in America	Results for Britain
King William's War	War of the League of Augsburg, 1688–1697	1689–1697	• Reestablished balance of power between England and France
Queen Anne's War	War of Spanish Succession, 1702–1714	1702–1713	• Britain acquired Nova Scotia
King George's War	War of Austrian Succession, 1739–1748	1744–1748	• Britain returned Louisbourg to France • British settlers began moving westward • Weakening of Iroquois neutrality
French and Indian War	Seven Years' War, 1756–1763	1754–1763	• Britain acquired Canada and all French territory east of Mississippi • Britain gained Florida from Spain

war or in the **War of the Spanish Succession** (1702–1713), which followed it.

In America, these two wars—known to British colonists as **King William's War** and **Queen Anne's War**, after the monarchs on the throne at the time—ended with equal indecisiveness. New France's Indian allies attacked New England's northern frontier with devastating success, as when they destroyed the Massachusetts town of Deerfield in 1704. New Englanders struck back at the exposed settlements of Acadia, which ultimately entered the British Empire as Nova Scotia, and tried unsuccessfully to seize Quebec. Neither war caused more than marginal changes for the colonies in North America. Both had profound effects, however, on the English state and the Iroquois League.

All European states of the eighteenth century financed their wars by borrowing. But the English were the first to realize that wartime debts did not necessarily have to be repaid during the following peace. The government instead created a funded debt. Having borrowed heavily from large joint-stock corporations, the government agreed to use tax revenues to pay interest on those loans but not to pay off the loans themselves. The corporations agreed because the interest payments amounted to a steady form of income that over the long run could amount to more than the original loans. In this way, England became the first European country to harness its national economy efficiently to military ends.

As the debt grew larger, more and more taxes were necessary to pay interest on it. Taxes also rose to pay for a powerful navy and a standing army. When the treasury created a larger and more efficient bureaucracy to collect taxes, many Englishmen grew nervous. Their anxiety emerged as a strain of thought known as **Country**, or "**Real Whig," ideology**. Country ideology stressed the threats that a standing army and a powerful state posed to personal liberty. It also emphasized the dangers of taxation to property rights and the need for property holders to retain their right to consent to taxation. Real Whig politicians publicized their fears but could not stop the growth of the state. In every successive war, the claims of national interest and patriotism—and the prospect of profit for parties rich enough to lend money to the government—overrode the objections of those who feared the expansion of state power.

In America, the first two imperial wars transformed the role of the Iroquois League. After the English took over New Netherlands in 1664, the Five Nations cultivated trading connections with them and later allied with England during King William's War. But the English offered little help when the French and their Indian allies attacked the Iroquois during that conflict. By 1700, the Iroquois League had suffered such horrendous losses—perhaps a quarter of the population had died from causes related to the war—that its leaders sought an alternative to direct alliance with the British.

With the so-called **Grand Settlement of 1701**, the Iroquois adopted a policy of neutrality with regard to the French and British Empires. Their goal was to refrain from alliances with either European power—which were likely to fight each other again—and instead maneuver between them. The Iroquois's strategic location between New France and the English colonies allowed them to serve as a geographical and diplomatic buffer between the two. Neutral Iroquois diplomats could play the English against the French, gaining favors from one side in return for promises not to ally with the other. This neutralist policy ensured that for nearly fifty years neither England nor France could gain ascendancy in North America.

This woodcut first appeared in 1758 in the midst of the French and Indian War. Symbolically representing Indian diplomatic strategy, it shows an Iroquois man considering the gifts proferred by an Englishman and a Frenchman vying for his loyalty. The ability to play the two European powers against one another ensured Iroquois supremacy in the Ohio Valley for decades, but the defeat of France in 1763 upset that delicate diplomatic balance.

Iroquois neutrality offered benefits to the Europeans as well as the Indians. The English, for instance, began to negotiate with them for land. The Iroquois claimed sovereignty over much of the country west of the Middle and Chesapeake colonies. To smooth relations with the English, the Iroquois sold them land formerly occupied by Delawares and Susquehannocks. This simultaneously helped satisfy the colonists' land hunger and enrich the Iroquois League.

Meanwhile, a neutral Iroquois League claiming control over the Ohio Valley and blocking English access across the Appalachian Mountains helped the French protect the strategic corridor of the Ohio and Mississippi Valleys that linked Canada and Louisiana. If the English ever established a permanent presence in the Ohio Valley, however, the Iroquois would cease to be of use to the French. The Iroquois remained reasonably effective at keeping the British out of the Valley until the late 1740s. The next European war, however, altered these circumstances, increasing French anxiety about their empire and compelling British strategists to incorporate their colonies into war plans more fully than ever before.

King George's War Shifts the Balance, 1739–1754

The third confrontation between Britain and France in Europe, the **War of the Austrian Succession** (**King George's War** to the British colonists) began as a small war between Britain and Spain in 1739. Its immediate cause was British attempts to poach on trade to Spain's Caribbean colonies. But in 1744, France joined in the war against Britain. An Anglo-French conflict once again erupted in North America.

New Englanders saw yet another chance to attack Canada. This time, their target was the great fortress of Louisbourg on Cape Breton Island, a naval base that dominated the Gulf of St. Lawrence. An expedition from Massachusetts and Connecticut, supported by a squadron of Royal Navy warships, captured Louisbourg in 1745. This success cut Canada off from French reinforcement and resupply. English forces should now have been able to conquer New France.

Instead, politically influential merchants in Albany, New York, chose to continue their profitable trade with the enemy over Lake Champlain, enabling Canada to hold out until the end of the war. When the peace treaty was signed in 1748, Britain, which had fared badly in the European fighting, returned Louisbourg to France. This diplomatic adjustment, routine by European standards, shocked New Englanders. At the same time, New York's illegal trade with the enemy appalled British administrators. They began thinking of ways to prevent such independent behavior in any future war.

King George's War furnished an equal share of shocks for New France, which had suffered more than in any previous conflict. Even before the war's end, aggressive English traders from Pennsylvania began moving west to buy furs from Indians who had once traded with the French. The movements of these traders, along with the appearance of Virginians in the Ohio Valley after 1748, gravely concerned the French.

In 1749, the governor general of New France set out to assert direct control over the region by building a set of forts from Lake Erie to the Forks of the Ohio (where the Monongahela and Allegheny Rivers meet to form the Ohio River). This decision signaled the end of France's commitment to Iroquois neutrality. Instead of enjoying their old position as neutral mediators, the chiefs of the Iroquois League now found themselves trapped between empires edging closer to confrontation in the Ohio Valley.

The Iroquois, in fact, had never exerted direct power in the Ohio Country. Their control instead depended on their ability to dominate the peoples who actually lived there—western Senecas, as well as the Delawares and Shawnees, both in theory Iroquois dependents. The appearance of English traders in the valley offering goods on better terms than the French or the Iroquois had ever provided undermined Iroquois dominance.

The Ohio Valley Indians increasingly ignored Iroquois claims of control and pursued their own independent course. One spur to their disaffection from the Iroquois was the 1744 **Treaty of Lancaster**, by which Iroquois chiefs had sold a group of Virginia land speculators rights to trade at the Forks of the Ohio. The Virginians assumed that these trading rights included the right to acquire land for eventual sale to settlers. The Ohio Valley Indians found this intolerable, as did the French. When, in 1754, the government of Virginia sent out a small body of soldiers under Lieutenant Colonel George Washington to protect Virginia's claims to the Forks of the Ohio, the French struck decisively to stop them.

This cartoon, the first to appear in a colonial American newspaper, was printed in the Pennsylvania Gazette in the spring of 1754. It refers to the plan for a colonial union that was put forward at the Albany Congress. The image alludes to the folk belief that a severed snake could revive if its parts were rejoined before sundown.

Decision: The French and Indian War, 1754–1760

In April 1754, French soldiers overwhelmed a group of Virginians who had been building a small fort at the Forks of the Ohio. They then erected a much larger fort of their own on the spot, Fort Duquesne. The French intended to follow up by similarly ousting Washington's weak, untrained troops, who had encamped further up the Monongahela River. However, at the end of May, Washington's men killed or captured all but one of the members of a small French reconnaissance party. The French decided to teach the Virginians a lesson. On July 3, they attacked Washington at his encampment, Fort Necessity. The next day, with a quarter of his troops killed or wounded, Washington surrendered.

Even before news of these engagements reached Britain, imperial officials worried that the Iroquois might ally with the French. Britain ordered New York's governor to convene an intercolonial meeting in Albany—known as the **Albany Congress**—to discuss matters with the Iroquois. Several prominent colonists, including Governor William Shirley of Massachusetts and Benjamin Franklin, took advantage of the occasion to put forward the **Albany Plan of Union**, which called for an intercolonial union to coordinate colonial defense, levy taxes, and regulate Indian affairs. But the colonies, too suspicious of one another to see their common interests, rejected the Albany Plan. Meanwhile, events in the west took a turn for the worse.

The French expulsion of the Virginians left the Indians of the region, Delawares and Shawnees, with no choice but to ally with the French in what came to be called the **French and Indian War** (see Map 4-3). Soon French and Indian attacks fell like hammer blows on backcountry settlements from Pennsylvania to the Carolinas. The Iroquois tried to remain neutral, but their neutrality no longer mattered. Europeans were at last contending directly for control of the Ohio Country.

The French and Indian War blazed in America for two years before it erupted as a fourth Anglo-French war in Europe in 1756. Known in Europe as the **Seven Years' War** (1756–1763), it involved fighting in the Caribbean, Africa, India, and the Philippine Islands as well as in Europe and North America. It was unlike any other eighteenth-century conflict not only in its immense scope and expense but also in its decisive outcome.

The war had two phases in North America—one from 1754 to 1758 and the other from 1758 through 1760—that corresponded to shifts in European involvement. During the first phase, the French enjoyed a string of successes as they followed what had been a proven strategy in previous conflicts—guerrilla war. Relying on Indian allies acting with Canadian soldiers, the French raided English frontier settlements, killing and capturing hundreds of civilians and forcing tens of thousands more to flee. Then they attacked fortified outposts whenever the opportunity appeared. This style of warfare allowed the Canadians' Indian allies—who came from all over the Northeast and the upper Midwest—to act independently in choosing targets and tactics.

The first full campaign of the war, in 1755, saw not only the British colonial frontiers collapsing in terror but also a notable defeat inflicted on the troops Britain had dispatched to attack Fort Duquesne. The British commander in chief, Major General Edward Braddock, with immense self-confidence and no real knowledge of the countryside or his enemy, marched to within 10 miles of Fort Duquesne, only to have his 1,450-man force surrounded and destroyed by Indians and Canadian militiamen. Braddock's defeat set the tone for virtually every military engagement of the next three years and opened a period of demoralization and internal conflict in the British colonies.

Britain responded to Braddock's defeat by sending a new commander in chief with more trained British soldiers. The new commander, Lord

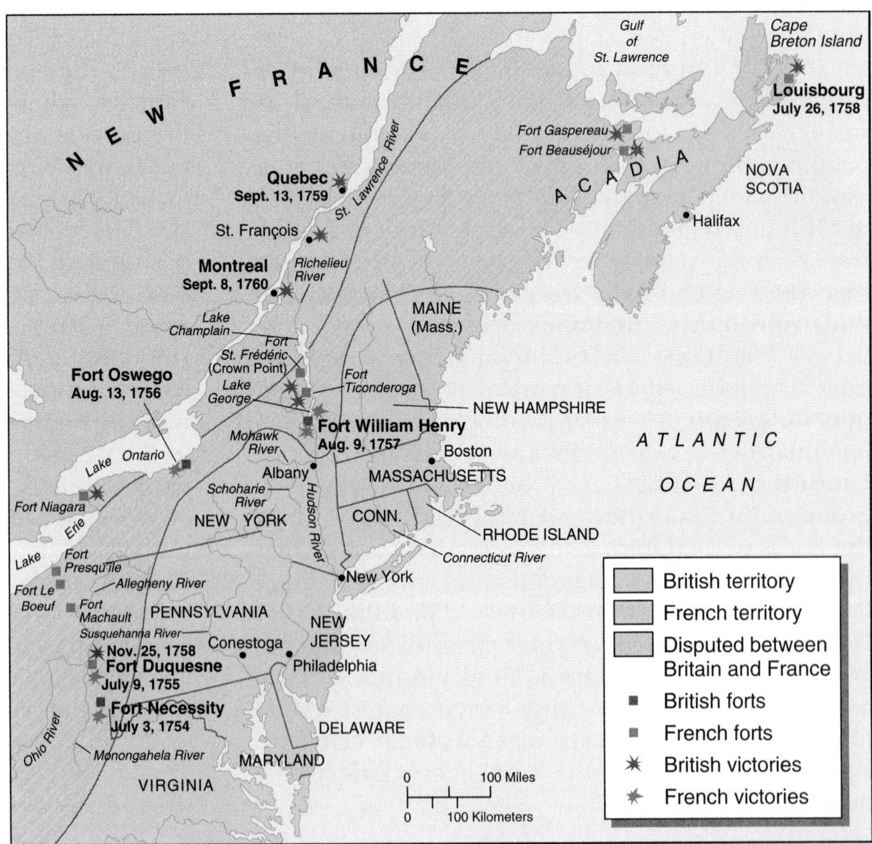

Map 4-3 ***The French and Indian War, 1754–1763***
Most of the battles of the French and Indian War occurred in the frontier regions of northern and western New York and the Ohio Valley. The influx of settlers into these areas created tensions that eventually developed into war.

Loudoun, tried to set colonial military affairs on a professional footing. He insisted on managing every aspect of the war effort, not only directing the campaigns but also dictating the amount of support, in men and money, that each colony would provide. The colonists, who had plenty of experience with war, had never experienced anything like Loudoun's high-handed style and grew increasingly stubborn in response to it. Colonial soldiers, who had volunteered to serve under their own officers, objected to Loudoun's command. By the end of 1757, a year of disastrous military campaigns, colonial assemblies were also refusing to cooperate.

Britain's aim had been to "rationalize" the war by making it conform to European professional military standards. This approach to warfare required soldiers to advance in formation in the face of massed musket fire without breaking rank. It needed iron discipline, which was enforced—as in the British army—by savage punishments, including hundreds of lashes at the whipping post. Few colonial volunteers met professional standards, and few colonists thought them necessary, especially when British soldiers suffered defeat after defeat at the hands of French and Indian guerrillas. British officers assumed that colonial soldiers were simply lazy cowards. But colonial volunteers, appalled to see men lashed "till the blood came out at the knee" of their breeches, saw British officers as brutal taskmasters. They resisted all efforts to impose such discipline on their own units, even to the point of desertion and mutiny.

Despite the astonishing success of their guerrilla tactics, the French, too, began moving toward a more European style of warfare. In the process, they destroyed their strategic and tactical advantages. In 1756, the marquis de Montcalm, a strong proponent of European professional standards of military conduct, assumed command of French forces. In his first battle, the successful siege of Fort Oswego, New York, Montcalm was horrified by the behavior of his Indian allies, which included killing wounded prisoners, taking personal captives, and collecting scalps as trophies. He came to regard the Indians—so essential to the defense of New France—as mere savages.

Following his next victory, the capture of Fort William Henry, New York, Montcalm conformed to European practice by allowing the defeated garrison to go home in return for the promise not to fight again. Montcalm's Indian allies—a thousand or more strong—were not to take prisoners, trophies, or plunder. The tragic result came to be known as the Massacre of Fort William Henry. Feeling betrayed by their French allies, the Indians took captives and trophies anyway, killing as many as 185 defenders and taking about 300 captive. This not only outraged the New England colonies (most of the victims were New Englanders) but also alienated the Indians on whom the defense of Canada depended. Ironically, Montcalm's efforts to limit the war's violence—to impose European standards of conduct—prepared the way for the British army and its colonial auxiliaries to win an unlimited victory.

For at the same time that the Europeanization of the war was weakening the French, the British moderated their policies and reached accommodation with the colonists. A remarkable politician came to power in London as England's chief war minister. William Pitt, who as secretary of state directed the British war effort from late 1757 through 1761, realized that friction between the colonists and the commander in chief arose from the colonists' sense that they were bearing all the financial burdens of the war without having any say in how the war was fought. Pitt's ingenious solutions were to promise reimbursements to the colonies in proportion to their contribution to the war effort, to deemphasize the power of the commander in chief, and to replace the arrogant Loudoun with a less objectionable officer.

Pitt's money and measures restored colonial morale. He sent thousands of British soldiers to America to fight alongside tens of thousands of colonial troops. As the Anglo-American forces grew stronger, they operated more successfully, seizing Louisbourg again in 1758. Once more, Canada experienced crippling shortages of supplies, weapons, and trade goods. But this time, unlike in 1745, the Anglo-Americans were united and able to take advantage of the situation. British emissaries persuaded the Delawares and Shawnees to abandon their French alliance, and late in 1758, an Anglo-American force again marched on Fort Duquesne. In command of its lead battalion was Colonel George Washington. The French defenders, abandoned by their native allies and confronted by overwhelming force, blew up the fort and retreated to the Great Lakes.

From this point on, the Anglo-Americans suffered no setbacks, and the French won no victories. The war became a contest in which the larger, better-supplied army would triumph. Montcalm, forced back to Quebec, decided to risk everything in a European-style, open-field battle against a British force led by General James Wolfe. At the Battle of Quebec (September 13, 1759), Montcalm lost the gamble—and his life (as did the victorious General Wolfe).

But the French had not yet lost the war. The Anglo-Americans had to hold on to their conquests. The French might still revive their Indian alliances, if only they could be resupplied from France with the weapons and trade goods the Indians demanded. What finally decided the outcome of the war in America was not the Battle of Quebec but two other developments: the Battle of Quiberon Bay in France (November 20, 1759) and the Iroquois' decision to join the Anglo-American side in 1760. The sea battle cost the French navy its ability to operate on the Atlantic, preventing it from carrying the reinforcements and supplies Canada needed to survive. Montcalm's successor could not rebuild the Indian alliances he so desperately needed. At the same time, the Iroquois decision to enter the war on the side of the Anglo-Americans tipped the balance irrevocably against the French. The last ragged, hungry defenders of Canada, surrounded at Montreal by a vastly superior Anglo-American-Iroquoian force, surrendered on September 8, 1760.

The Triumph of the British Empire, 1763

The war pitting Britain against France and Spain (which had entered the fighting as a French ally in 1762) concluded with an uninterrupted series of British victories. In the Caribbean, where every valuable sugar island the French owned came under British control, the culminating event was the surrender of Havana on August 13, 1762. Even more spectacular was Britain's capture of the Philippine capital of Manila on October 5—a victory that literally carried British power around the world.

These conquests created the unshakable conviction that British arms were invincible. An immense surge of British patriotism spread throughout the American colonies. When news of the conquest of Havana reached Massachusetts, bells rang, cannons fired salutes, and bonfires blazed. General John Winslow of Plymouth, a portly man, rejoiced by becoming "so intoxicated as to jump on the table, and break a great number of bowls."

Hostilities ended formally on February 10, 1763, with the conclusion of the **Treaty of Paris**. France regained its West Indian sugar islands—its most valuable colonial possessions—but lost the rest of its North American empire. France ceded to Britain all its claims to lands east of the Mississippi River (except the city of New Orleans) and compensated Spain for the losses it had sustained as an ally by handing over all claims to the Trans-Mississippi West and the port of New Orleans (see Map 4-4). Britain returned Cuba and the Philippines to Spain and in compensation received Florida. Now Great Britain owned everything east of the Mississippi, from the Gulf of Mexico to Hudson's Bay. With France and Spain both humbled and on the verge of financial collapse, Britain seemed preeminent in Europe and ready to dominate in the New World. Never before had Americans felt more pride in being British, members of the greatest empire on earth.

In his most famous painting, American artist Benjamin West depicted the death of the British general James Wolfe at the Battle of Quebec. He portrays Wolfe as a glorious martyr to the cause of British victory. In the left foreground, West added the figure of an Indian, a "noble savage" who contemplates the meaning of Wolfe's selfless sacrifice of his life.

Benjamin West (1738–1820), "The Death of General Wolfe," 1770, oil on canvas, 15.6 × 214.5 cm. Transfer from the Canadian War Memorials, 1921 (Gift of the 2nd Duke of Westminster, Eaton Hall, Cheshire, 1918). National Gallery of Canada, Ottawa, Canada.

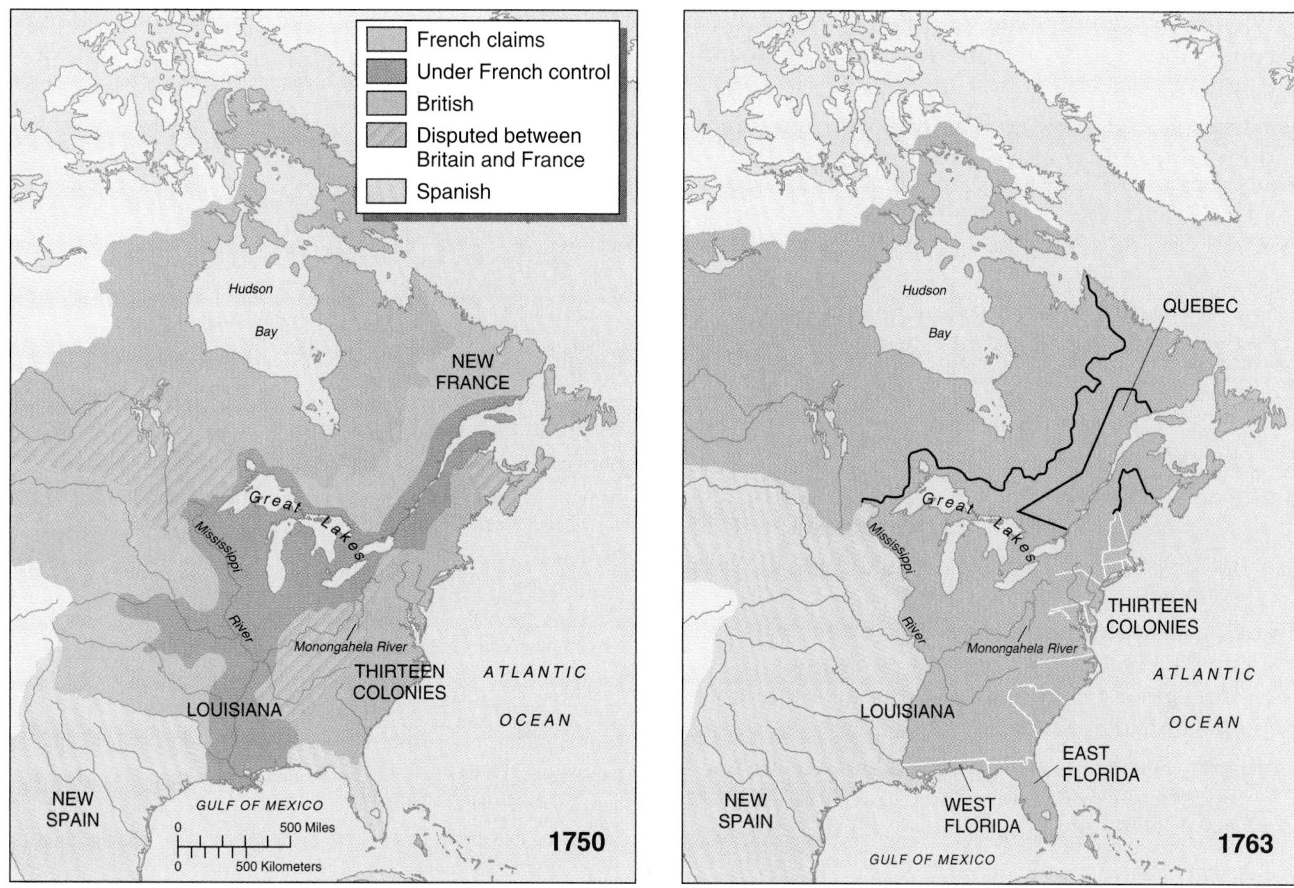

Map 4-4 European Empires in North America, 1750–1763
Great Britain's victory in the French and Indian War transformed the map of North America. France lost its mainland colonies, England claimed all lands east of the Mississippi, and Spain gained nominal control over the Trans-Mississippi West.

Conclusion

The George Washington who ordered a suit in 1763 was not a revolutionary; on the contrary, he was a man who longed to be part of the elite of the great British Empire. If he feared any threat to his position in that elite, it was not Parliament and the king but the uncomfortably large debts he owed to his London agents for the goods he and Martha wanted or perhaps the unruly Baptists who refused to acknowledge the superiority of the great planters. But those worries, though real, were merely small, nagging doubts, shared by most of his fellow planters.

What was more real to Washington was the great victory that the British Empire had just gained over France, a victory that he had helped achieve. With the French eliminated as an imperial power in North America, Washington could look forward to increasing his fortune by speculating in the western lands he knew so well. For Washington, as for virtually all other colonial leaders, 1763 was a moment of great promise and patriotic devotion to the British Empire. It was a time to rejoice in the fundamental British identity and liberty and rights that seemed to ensure that life in the colonies would be better and more prosperous than ever.

Review Questions

1. In what ways did economic ties between Britain and the colonies grow closer in the century after 1660?
2. What did elite colonists think about American society and culture in the eighteenth century? What changes did they want to introduce?
3. What was the Great Awakening, and what impact did it have on colonial society?
4. In what ways were colonial and British political ideas and practices similar? In what ways were they different?

5. Why did England, Spain, and France renew their competition for North America in the eighteenth century?
6. What role did warfare play in North America in the eighteenth century? What role did the Iroquois play?

Recommended Reading

Anderson, Fred. *Crucible of War: The Seven Years' War and the Fate of Empire in British North America, 1754–1766* (2000). A vivid narrative of the last great imperial war.

Bushman, Richard L. *The Refinement of America: Persons, Houses, Cities* (1992). A sophisticated exploration of the quest for gentility in early America.

Franklin, Benjamin. *Autobiography* (numerous editions). The classic account of Franklin's rise from poor beginnings to prominence in colonial Philadelphia.

Lambert, Frank. *Inventing the "Great Awakening"* (1999). An overview of the causes and development of the tremendous transatlantic revival.

McCusker, John J., and Menard, Russell R. *The Economy of British America, 1607–1789,* rev. ed. (1991). The most comprehensive study of the economies of each colonial region.

Additional Sources

Colonial Economic Development

Kammen, Michael. *Empire and Interest: The American Colonies and the Politics of Mercantilism* (1970).

Marshall, Peter, and Williams, Glyn, eds. *The British Atlantic Empire before the American Revolution* (1980).

Walton, Gary M., and Shepherd, James F. *The Economic Rise of Early America* (1979).

Waterhouse, Richard. *A New World Gentry: The Making of a Merchant and Planter Class in South Carolina, 1670–1770* (1989).

Religion, Society, and Culture in Early America

Bonomi, Patricia. *Under the Cope of Heaven: Religion, Society, and Politics in Colonial America* (1986).

Boyer, Paul, and Nissenbaum, Stephen. *Salem Possessed: The Social Origins of Witchcraft* (1974).

Brown, Richard D. *Knowledge Is Power: The Diffusion of Information in Early America, 1700–1865* (1991).

Bushman, Richard L. *From Puritan to Yankee: Character and the Social Order in Connecticut, 1690–1765* (1967).

Butler, Jon. *Awash in a Sea of Faith: Christianizing the American People* (1990).

Clark, Charles. *The Public Prints: The Newspaper in Anglo-American Culture, 1665–1740* (1994).

Demos, John. *Entertaining Satan: Witchcraft and the Culture of Early New England* (1982).

Karlsen, Carol. *The Devil in the Shape of a Woman: Witchcraft in Colonial New England* (1987).

May, Henry. *The Enlightenment in America* (1976).

Westercamp, Marilyn. *Triumph of the Laity: Scots-Irish Piety and the Great Awakening, 1625–1760* (1988).

Wright, Esmond. *Franklin of Philadelphia* (1986).

Colonial and Imperial Politics

Bailyn, Bernard. *The Origins of American Politics* (1968).

Brewer, John. *The Sinews of Power: War, Money, and the English State, 1688–1783* (1989).

Bushman, Richard. *King and People in Provincial Massachusetts* (1985).

Greene, Jack P. *The Quest for Power: The Lower Houses of Assembly in the Southern Royal Colonies, 1689–1776* (1963).

Johnson, Richard. *Adjustment to Empire: The New England Colonies, 1675–1715* (1981).

Jones, J. R. *Country and Court: England, 1658–1714* (1978).

Lovejoy, David S. *The Glorious Revolution in America, 1660–1692* (1972).

Morgan, Edmund S. *Inventing the People: The Rise of Popular Sovereignty in England and America* (1988).

Nash, Gary B. *The Urban Crucible: The Northern Seaports and the Origins of the American Revolution,* abr. ed. (1986).

Plumb, J. H. *The Growth of Political Stability in England, 1675–1725* (1967).

Shannon, Timothy. *Indians and Colonists at the Crossroads of Empire: The Albany Congress of 1754* (1999).

Speck, W. A. *Stability and Strife: England, 1714–1760* (1977).

The Expansion of Empires

Chipman, Donald E. *Spanish Texas, 1519–1821* (1992).

Mancall, Peter. *Valley of Opportunity: Economic Culture along the Upper Susquehanna, 1700–1800* (1991).

Usner, Daniel H., Jr. *Indians, Settlers, and Slaves in a Frontier Exchange Economy: The Lower Mississippi Valley before 1783* (1992).

Weber, David J. *The Spanish Frontier in North America* (1992).

Imperial Warfare

Dowd, Gregory. *A Spirited Resistance: The North American Indian Struggle for Unity, 1745–1815* (1992).

Jennings, Francis. *Empire of Fortune: Crowns, Colonies, and Tribes in the Seven Years' War in America* (1988).

Selesky, Harold. *War and Society in Colonial Connecticut* (1990).

Steele, Ian K. *Betrayals: Fort William Henry and the "Massacre"* (1990).

Titus, James. *The Old Dominion at War: Society, Politics, and Warfare in Late Colonial Virginia* (1991).

Where to Learn More

❖ **Mission Parkway, San Antonio, Texas.** Three Spanish missions (Mission Nuestra Señora de la Purisma Concepción, Mission San Francisco de la Espada, Mission San Juan Capestrano) founded in the early eighteenth century are located along this road. Their architecture indicates that they were intended to be fortifications as well as churches.

❖ **Ste. Genevieve Historic District, Ste. Genevieve, Missouri.** This restored site of an early-eighteenth-century French settlement in the *Pays des Illinois* contains many historic buildings open for tours.

❖ **Colonial Williamsburg, Williamsburg, Virginia.** A reconstruction of the capital of eighteenth-century Virginia, this site covers 173 acres and contains many restored and rebuilt structures, including houses, churches, the House of Burgesses, and the Governor's Palace. Many educational and cultural programs are available. Historical interpreters, dressed in period costume, provide information about eighteenth-century Chesapeake life.

❖ **Historical Society of Pennsylvania, Philadelphia, Pennsylvania.** The society preserves many documents and material objects relating to early American, and particularly Philadelphia, history. Its collections include exhibits of paintings, furniture, silver, and costumes.

IMPERIAL BREAKDOWN
1763–1774

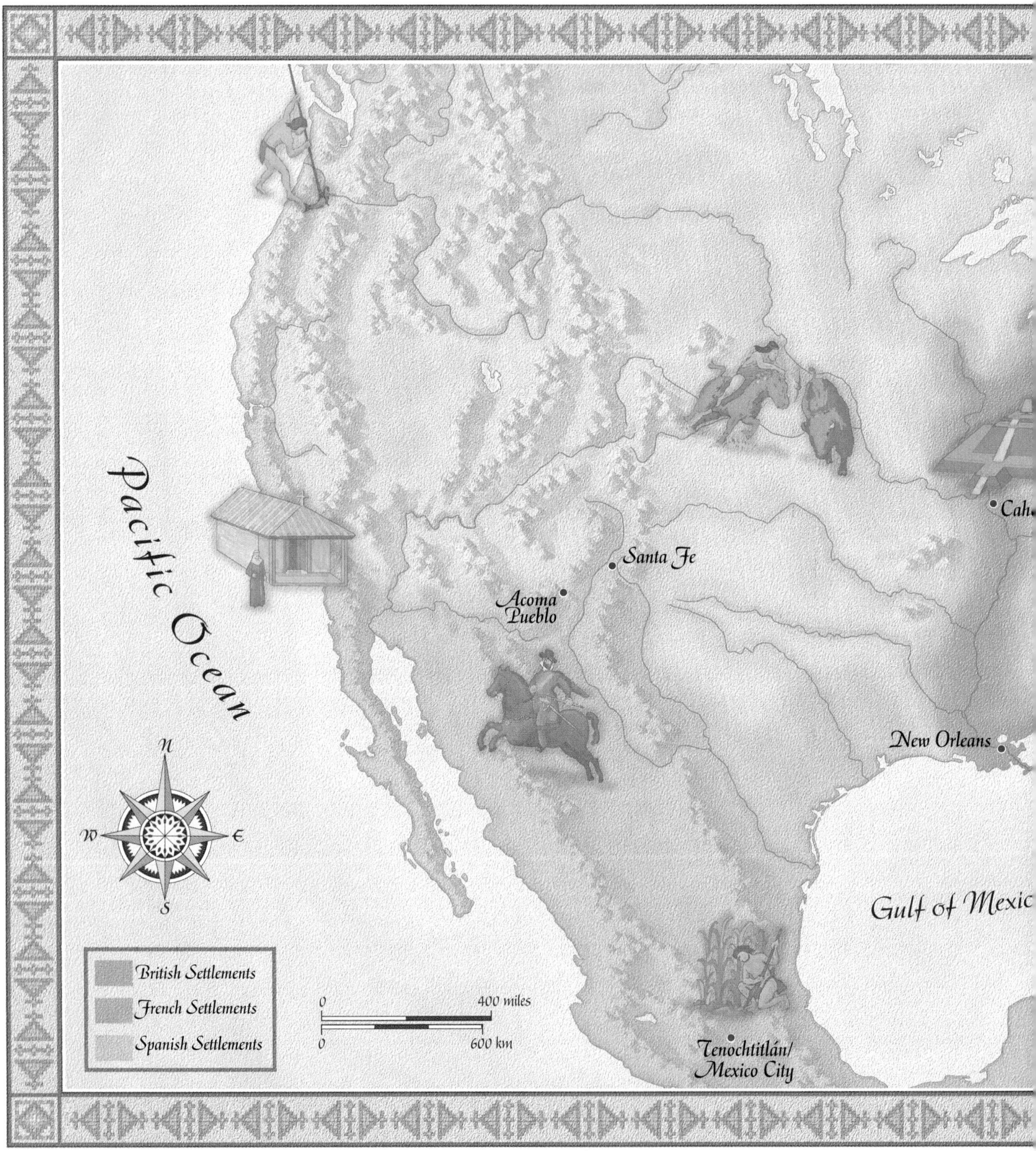

Pacific Ocean

Santa Fe

Acoma Pueblo

Cah

New Orleans

Gulf of Mexic

Tenochtitlán/
Mexico City

N
W
E
S

British Settlements
French Settlements
Spanish Settlements

0
400 miles
0
600 km

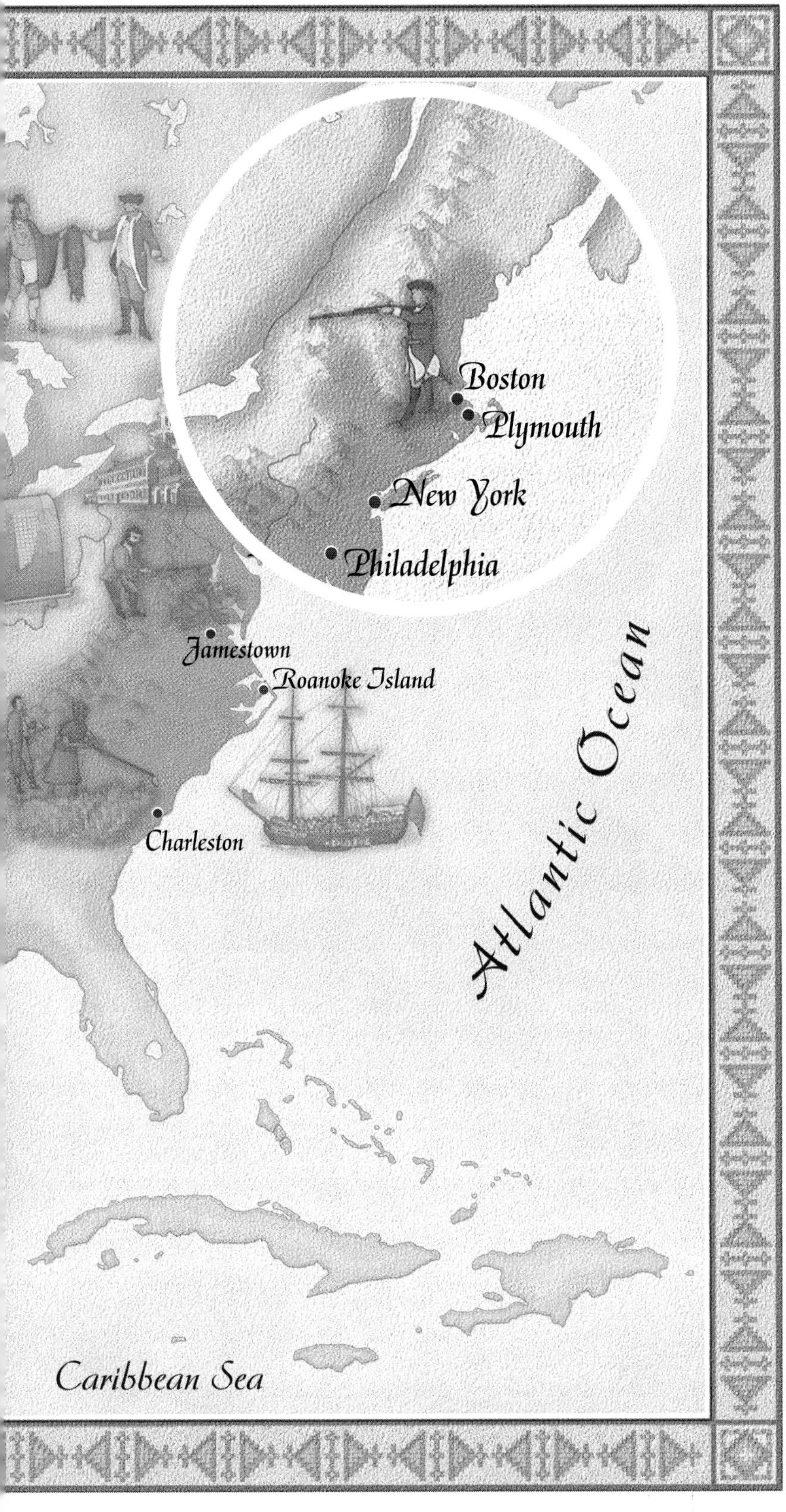

Chapter Outline

Imperial Reorganization
British Problems
Dealing with the New Territories
Indian Affairs
Curbing the Assemblies
The Sugar and Stamp Acts

American Reactions
Constitutional Issues
Taxation and the Political Culture
Protesting the Taxes

The Aftermath of Crisis
A Strained Relationship
Regulator Movements

The Townshend Crisis
Townshend's Plan/American Boycott
The Boston Massacre
The "Quiet Period"
The Boston Tea Party
The Intolerable Acts

The Road to Revolution
American Response to the Intolerable Acts
The First Continental Congress
The Continental Association
Political Divisions

Key Topics

- ❖ British problems and policies in North America after the French and Indian War
- ❖ Native Americans' conflicts with the colonists
- ❖ The American reaction to British attempts to tax the colonies
- ❖ Social tensions and the Regulator movements in the Carolinas
- ❖ Intercolonial union and resistance to British measures

In 1774, Christopher Gadsden of South Carolina reportedly announced that "were his wife and all his children in Boston, and they were there to perish by the sword, it would not alter his sentiment or proceeding for American Liberty." He wanted to make an immediate attack on the British troops who then occupied Boston. Except for his impetuosity, Gadsden was a typical member of the American political elite who led the Revolution. Like his peers, he was proud and happy to be a subject of the British monarchy until the 1770s, but, like other Americans, he would rebel against the crown. Why they felt compelled to take this drastic step is the subject of this chapter.

A zealot for American rights, Gadsden, the son of a British customs official, had been born in 1724 at Charleston, South Carolina. He had received his schooling in England and Pennsylvania, where he later served as a clerk for a Philadelphia merchant. Chance made him a supply officer aboard a royal naval vessel in the expedition that captured the French fortress of Louisbourg during King George's War (1739–1748). Gadsden then returned to South Carolina and became a merchant. Perhaps he resented the arrogance of people in England who treated colonials as backward provincials, and he doubtless believed that Great Britain subordinated American to British concerns when it returned Louisbourg to France at the end of the war. Many years later, at any rate, he became a leader of American opposition to British taxation.

Until the very eve of independence in 1776, Gadsden and others like him felt immense pride to be British subjects and part of Britain's increasingly powerful empire. They had fought the king's enemies as well as their own in a series of imperial wars and had gloried in British successes. But over the course of the eighteenth century, they had also developed a sense of their identity as Americans. Largely governing themselves through their own legislatures, they believed they enjoyed all the rights of British subjects anywhere.

In the wake of the French and Indian War, British authorities found themselves with a burdensome debt and a vastly increased territory to administer. In response, they attempted to change the way they governed the colonies and for the first time to impose direct taxes on the colonists. Most Americans saw these measures as violations of their rights and opposed them, although they divided over how far to carry their resistance.

Imperial Reorganization

At the close of the French and Indian War, British officials adopted a new and ultimately disastrous course in dealing with America. Lacking experience and led by a young and somewhat naïve monarch, they panicked at the magnitude of the problems confronting them. Trying to fix a relationship between England and the colonies that most Americans would have said was not broken, they took measures that worked mostly to the disadvantage of the colonies. As one contemporary critic observed, "A great Empire and little minds go ill together."

British Problems

Britain's empire in 1763 was indeed a great one, and the problems its rulers faced were correspondingly large. Its territories in North America stretched from Hudson's Bay in the north to the Caribbean Sea in the south and from the Atlantic Ocean west to the Mississippi River. Britain also had possessions in the Mediterranean region, Africa, and India. It still faced threats, if diminished ones, from its traditional European enemies. French territory on the North American mainland had been reduced to two tiny islands in the Gulf of St. Lawrence. But France would be eager for revenge, and French inhabitants in the recently acquired territories might prove disloyal to their new rulers in any future war between the two countries.

Spain was less powerful militarily than France but a more significant presence on the North American mainland. In the territorial settlement at the end of the French and Indian War, it surrendered East and West Florida to Britain but got back its possessions in Cuba and the Philip-

Christopher Gadsden of South Carolina was one of the most outspoken advocates of American rights during the revolutionary era. This portrait by Jeremiah Theus was probably commissioned by the colonial legislature to commemorate his attendance at the Stamp Act Congress in 1765.

pines that the British had captured. Spain acquired Louisiana from its French ally as compensation for the loss of the Floridas. Shocked by their inability to defend Cuba and the Philippines, Spanish officials stepped up the pace of reforms that they had begun making earlier in the century. Following the efficient French model of colonial government, they appointed *intendants*—generally Spaniards rather than colonials—to ensure better tax collection. Spain also expelled the Jesuit order from its dominions, because Jesuit priests were too independent of royal control to suit Spanish officials. And Spain strengthened its military forces in much of the empire, including Mexico, which then encompassed Texas, New Mexico, and California, as well as present-day Mexico.

Spain began to establish settlements in California in 1769 (see Chapter 4), but these were too weak and too far from the British colonies on the eastern seaboard to worry authorities in London. British authorities were similarly little concerned about Louisiana, though it was closer and more populated. As for Florida, under British control after 1763, the Spanish authorities evacuated it completely, taking with them not only the free black population of Mose (a settlement of former slaves who had escaped from Georgia and South Carolina) but even the bones of one of the late royal governors.

Protecting and controlling the old and new territories in North America as inexpensively as possible presented British officials with difficult questions. How should they administer the new territories? How should they deal with Indians likely to resist further encroachments on their lands? And perhaps most vexing, how could they rein in the seemingly out-of-control colonists in the old territories?

Permitting most of the new areas to have their own assemblies appeared inadvisable but unavoidable if they were to attract settlers. Believing that the increasing power of the legislatures had long since "unhinged" the government of the older colonies, British authorities hoped to avoid similar unruliness in the new territories. In fact, they had long wanted to roll back the power of the old colonial assemblies. But Britain needed the cooperation of these assemblies during the years of war with France. Now, with France vanquished, imperial officials felt they could crack down on the local governments. Some British statesmen, however, realized a danger in this new approach. With France gone from the continent, Americans would be less dependent on Britain for protection and therefore more inclined to resist unpopular restrictions.

Resentment against American conduct during the war colored British thinking. Some of the colonies failed to enlist their quota of recruits, and for this the British blamed the local assemblies. Worse yet, some Americans continued to smuggle goods to and from the enemy in the French West Indies during the war. Illicit trade was so common in New England that it cost Britain more to operate the customs service in America than it collected in duties.

England emerged from the war with what was then an immense national debt of approximately £130 million. Interest payments alone accounted for half the government's annual expenditures after the war. Alarmed by the unprecedented debt, many Britons concluded that Americans should bear more of the financial burden of running the empire. The colonists certainly appeared prosperous to British

Chronology

1759–1761	Cherokee War takes place.
1760	George III becomes king.
1761–1762	Writs of Assistance case in Massachusetts.
1763	Peace of Paris ends French and Indian War.
	Spanish accelerate imperial reforms.
	British troops remain in America.
	Proclamation Line of 1763 limits western expansion of colonial settlement.
	Pontiac's Rebellion begins.
	Paxton Boys murder peaceful Indians.
	Virginia Court decides Parson's Cause.
1764	Sugar Act passed.
	Currency Act passed.
1765	Quartering Act passed.
	Stamp Act passed.
	Stamp Act Congress meets in New York.
1766	Stamp Act repealed; Declaratory Act passed.
	New York Assembly refuses to comply with the Quartering Act.
1767	Townshend duties imposed.
	Regulator movements begin in North and South Carolina.
1770	Boston Massacre takes place.
	Tea duty retained, other Townshend duties repealed.
1771	North Carolina Regulator movement defeated.
1772	*Gaspee* burned.
	Committees of Correspondence formed.
1773	Boston Tea Party takes place.
1774	Coercive Acts passed.
	Quebec Act passed.
	First Continental Congress meets and agrees to boycott British imports.

soldiers who had served in America. But compared to the English, who paid on average perhaps a third of their income in taxes, many Americans normally rendered no more than 5 percent. An economic recession—triggered by the reduction in spending that followed the war—put further pressure on British officials to reduce taxes in England.

Dealing with the New Territories

In 1763, the British government took several important steps to deal with the new territories, protect the old colonies, and maintain peace with the Indians. One was to keep a substantial body of troops stationed in America even in peacetime. Another, announced in the **Proclamation of 1763**, was to establish civilian governments in East and West Florida (Canada remained under military rule). A third, in the same proclamation, was to temporarily forbid white settlement west of the Appalachian Mountains. The purpose of the **Proclamation Line** restricting white settlement was presumably twofold: to keep white settlers and Indians apart, preventing fighting between them, and to keep the colonists closer to the coast where they would be easier to control (see Map 5-1). Permanent arrangements for the Mississippi Valley could come later after British officials had time to ponder matters.

Neither the Proclamation Line nor the stationing of troops in America was particularly wise. The Proclamation Line provoked resentment because it threatened to deprive settlers and speculators in the rapidly developing colonies of the land they coveted. Some who had moved into the Ohio area were forcefully removed. Other Americans merely ignored the restriction. As for the troops, someone had to pay for them, forcing the British government to take additional measures that further provoked American resentment. These measures included the imposition of direct taxes and the passage of **Quartering Acts** that required colonial assemblies to provide barracks and certain supplies for the troops.

The presence of troops in peacetime alarmed Americans. Sharing the traditional English distrust of standing armies, they wondered whether the soldiers were there to coerce rather than protect them. And their presence in fact may have made imperial authorities less cautious in dealing with the colonies. Given their wariness, Americans would doubtless have objected to the troops and the taxes necessary to support them even if the troops had done an exemplary job of protecting the frontiers. But conflicts with Indians cast doubt on their ability to do even that.

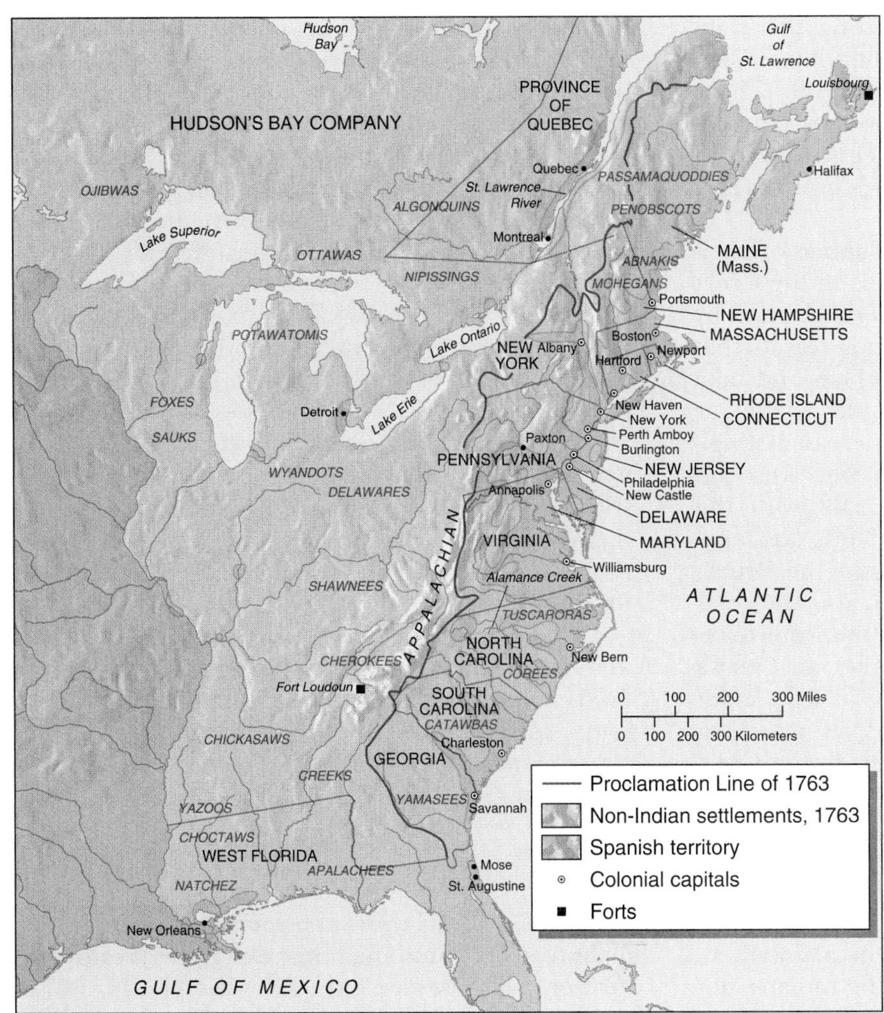

Map 5-1 Colonial Settlement and the Proclamation Line of 1763
This map depicts the regions claimed and settled by the major groups competing for territory in eastern North America. With the Proclamation Line of 1763, positioned along the crest of the Appalachian Mountains, the British government tried to stop the westward migration of settlers under its jurisdiction and thereby limit conflict with the Indians. The result, however, was frustration and anger on the part of land-hungry settlers.

Indian Affairs

If Britain confronted complex problems in North America, Native Americans would have said those problems were nothing compared to their own troubles in dealing with the British. Colonial settlers and their livestock were displacing Indians from their ancient lands. Free-flowing rum and rampant cheating among traders were making the fur and deerskin trades increasingly violent. Each of the colonies tried to regulate its Indian traders, but lack of coordination made most of these efforts ineffective.

The British victory over the French and the westward expansion of British territory undermined the Indians' traditional strategies and alignments. British officials no longer found Native American neutrality or military help as important as they once had. Increasingly superfluous as allies and unable to play the European powers off against each other, Native Americans lost much of their former ability to protect themselves by any means short of military resistance. The British took advantage of this increasing vulnerability: Traders exploited the Indians, and settlers encroached on their lands.

Two major Indian wars—one breaking out in the late 1750s during the closing years of the French and Indian War and the other erupting in its aftermath in the early 1760s—challenged British policy toward Native Americans. The first conflict, the **Cherokee War**, took place in the southern Appalachian highlands. Though increasingly alarmed at the abuses and encroachments of their white neighbors, the Cherokees had long remained allies of the British. But, in 1759, Cherokee warriors returning home from a campaign with the British against the French and their Indian allies in western Pennsylvania may have stolen horses belonging to Virginia colonists. The colonists attacked the Cherokees, killing some of them. The Cherokees retaliated with attacks on western settlements in all of the southern colonies. In 1760, they captured Fort

Loudoun in eastern Tennessee, stuffing the commander's mouth full of dirt and telling him, "Dog, since you are so hungry for land, eat your fill." Three expeditions, manned by British as well as colonial troops, eventually forced the Cherokees to agree, in a 1761 treaty, to surrender land in the Carolinas and Virginia to the colonists.

The second major conflict, **Pontiac's Rebellion**, broke out in 1763 among Indians in the Great Lakes and Ohio Valley regions formerly claimed by France. Many Native American groups feared that the British planned to exterminate them and take their lands now that the French could no longer help them. They also resented the increased stinginess of British traders and officials who were no longer forced to compete commercially with the French to secure Indian allegiance. These concerns helped inspire a united effort to resist the British and revitalize Indian cultures. Neolin, also known as the Delaware Prophet, urged Native Americans to reject European goods and ways. Pontiac, an Ottawa chief, joined other chiefs in leading at least eight major groups of Native Americans in attacking British forces and American settlers from the Great Lakes to Virginia in 1763.

Pontiac's Rebellion raged until 1766. During intermittent negotiations, Pontiac cleverly insisted that British possession of the old French forts in western Pennsylvania and Ohio did not give Great Britain title to the area. The French, he maintained, had been there merely as tenants of the Indians, not owners of the land. The British eventually forced the Indians to give up portions of their territory in return for compensation and guarantees that traditional hunting grounds in the Ohio Valley would remain theirs.

At one point during the war, a British commander used germ warfare against the Indians, sending them blankets that smallpox victims had used. Settlers in Paxton township (near modern Harrisburg, Pennsylvania) were equally unrestrained. Angered by the Pennsylvania Assembly's lack of aggressive action against the Indians, the settlers lashed out at convenient targets, massacring their peaceful neighbors, the Conestogas. Facing arrest and trial for this outrage, the so-called **Paxton Boys** marched toward Philadelphia, threatening the Pennsylvania Assembly. Benjamin Franklin convinced them to disperse. Despite the government's efforts, the Paxton Boys were never effectively prosecuted for their acts.

Pontiac's Rebellion and the Cherokee War were costly for both sides, claiming the lives of hundreds of Indians and white settlers. Hoping to prevent such outbreaks, British officials began experimenting with centralized control of Indian affairs during the 1760s. Following the recommendations of the Albany Congress in 1754 (see Chapter 4), they had already created two districts, northern and southern, for the administration of Indian affairs, each with its own superintendent. The Proclamation of 1763, and the line it established restricting further white settlement, gave these officials increased responsibility for protecting the Indians

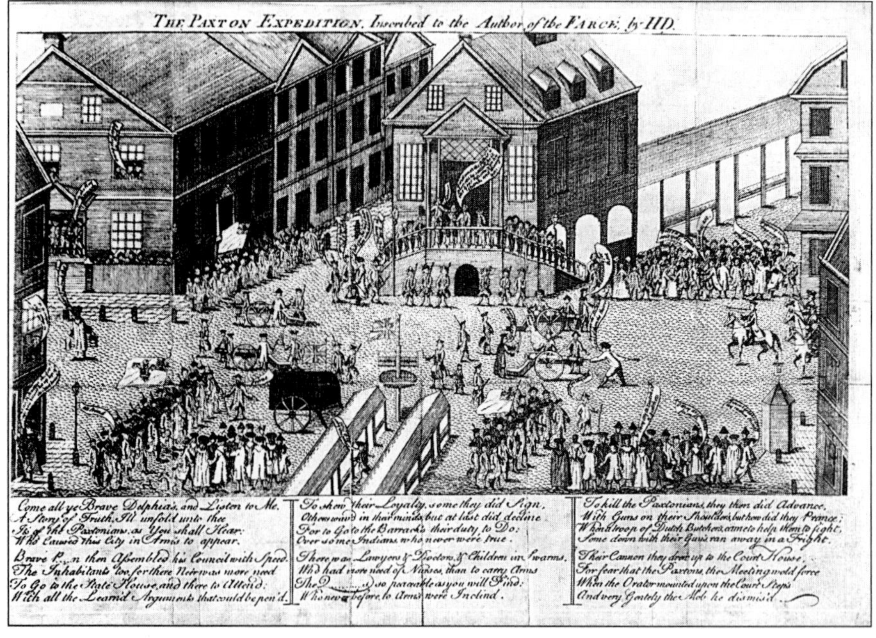

When frontiersmen from Paxton township marched on Philadelphia to demand greater protection against the Indians during Pontiac's Rebellion, Philadelphians prepared to defend themselves. This engraving by Henry Dawkins satirizes the consternation in the city and depicts the governor's representative announcing a peaceful settlement with the Paxton Boys.

AMERICA'S JOURNEY

FROM THEN TO NOW

Protecting the Land

Speaking before a backdrop of glorious fall foliage in the mountains of western Virginia in October 1999, President Bill Clinton announced that he would provide permanent protection for 40 million or more acres of forest land owned by the Federal Government. The U.S. Forest Service now manages about 192 million acres; Congress has designated about 18 percent of the total as permanently reserved wilderness areas. Clinton proposed to increase this area by administrative regulations that would bar future mining, logging, and road building (without which no commercial development could take place). Individual conservationists and environmental groups applauded the announcement; spokesmen for the timber industry and Republican legislators from the western states where logging is a big business denounced it.

Calling Clinton "King William," a senator from Idaho maintained that "these are not the King's lands, these are the people's lands, and we think he ought to come to the people's bodies [Congress] to form and shape this kind of policy." Clinton admitted that "We're going to have a big fight on this for about a year," but later added, "in the end we're going to protect all this before it's too late."

As the senator's words reflect, Clinton's proposed actions and the controversy they provoked echo a recurring theme in American history that emerged prominently in 1763, during the pre-Revolutionary period, when King George III issued a proclamation temporarily restricting colonial settlement to the eastern side of the Appalachian Mountains. His advisors had carefully considered the step and believed it to be in the public interest. Their intent was to prevent costly wars with the Indians by eliminating one of the chief causes of such conflicts—the encroachment by white settlers on Indian lands.

The prohibition, however, threatened the economic interests of many Americans. Some farmers ignored the proclamation line and squatted on prohibited land without any legal title to it. Large speculators, who needed legal titles to resell their land and make a profit, tried hard to get the policy reversed but failed until after the United States gained independence from Great Britain.

Independence, however, did not end political conflict over the allocation of the natural resources of the continent. Until the end of the nineteenth century, these conflicts usually involved lands belonging to Native Americans. Since then, attention has turned increasingly to the preservation of what remains intact of the American wilderness.

Should private interests be able to exploit the resources of public lands for economic gain, or is it in the public interest to prohibit such activity? And who defines the public interest? These have been—and will continue to be—as President Clinton suggested, hard fights.

This clearing and cabin in the Blue Ridge Mountains of the southern Appalachian chain typifies the hopes and homes of many small farmers who resented the British Proclamation Line of 1763 which barred white settlement west of the eastern continental divide.

against the encroachments of settlers. But land-hungry Americans objected to efforts to keep them off Indian lands, and white traders resented restrictions on their activities. Centralized control of the fur and deerskin trades also proved to be expensive for the British government. British authorities therefore permitted several adjustments in the Indian boundary line and in 1768 returned supervision of the Indian traders to the individual colonies. But such tacit recognition of local autonomy conflicted with imperial authorities' plans to restrict the powers of the colonial assemblies.

Curbing the Assemblies

As an episode in Virginia known as the Parson's Cause illustrates, British authorities took advantage of opportunities to curb the American legislatures as early as the 1750s. Anglican ministers in Virginia drew tax-supported salaries computed in pounds of tobacco. As a result, when a drought in the mid-1750s caused a sharp rise in tobacco prices, they expected a windfall. The Virginia House of Burgesses, however, restricted their payment to two pennies a pound, below the market value of the tobacco that backed their salaries. Lobbying by the clergy convinced the king to disallow the Two Penny Act, and some Virginia clergymen sued for the unpaid portion of their salaries.

In the most famous of these cases, the Virginia government was defended by Patrick Henry, a previously obscure young lawyer who looked like "a Presbyterian clergyman, used to haranguing the people." Henry gained instant notoriety when he declared that a king who vetoed beneficial acts became a tyrant and thereby forfeited "all right to his subjects' obedience." Given Henry's eloquence, the jury found in favor of the suing minister but awarded him only one penny in damages. This pittance reflected the hostility many Virginians of all denominations felt toward the pretensions of the Anglican clergy.

Meanwhile, still in response to the Two Penny Act, the crown further dismayed Virginians by instructing the colony's governor not to sign any new law that modified existing laws unless it contained a suspending clause making it inoperative until the king approved it. This restriction severely hampered the assembly's ability to respond to emergencies such as the drought. As one Virginian observed, it "put us under the despotic Power of a French or Turkish Government; for what is the real Difference between a French Edict and an English Instruction if they are both equally absolute?" The legislators of the colony, Virginians maintained, had the "Right to enact ANY Law they shall think necessary for their INTERNAL Government."

British authorities also sought to restrict the power of colonial legislatures to issue legal tender currency, paper notes that could be used to settle debts. These notes frequently depreciated to only a fraction of their face value in British money. Not surprisingly, British merchants who had to accept them felt cheated and complained. Parliament had responded in 1751 by forbidding further issues of legal tender paper money in New England. In the **Currency Act** of 1764, Parliament extended this restriction to the rest of the colonies, prohibiting all of them from printing their own legal tender paper money. Because the new restrictions came when most colonies were in an economic recession, Americans considered this step an especially burdensome attempt to curtail the assemblies' powers. To deprive them of their paper money was, in the words of one American, "downright Robbery." Worse, however, was yet to come.

The Sugar and Stamp Acts

In 1764, the British Parliament, under Prime Minister George Grenville, passed the American Revenue Act, commonly known as the **Sugar Act**. The main purpose of this act, as stated in its preamble, was "for improving the revenue of this kingdom." To generate funds, the Sugar Act and its accompanying legislation combined new and revised duties on colonial imports with strict provisions for collecting those duties. The act lowered the duty on molasses from the French West Indies from 6 pence a gallon to 3 pence a gallon. Smugglers had long evaded the earlier duty with bribes to customs officials. By lowering the duty and improving its collection, Grenville hoped to capture for the crown what customs officials had been siphoning off for themselves without excessively increasing the shippers' cost of business.

The Sugar Act legislation also lengthened the list of enumerated products—goods that could be sent only to England or within the empire—and required that ships carry elaborate new documents certifying the legality of their cargoes. The purpose of the new paperwork was to prevent illegal trade with other countries. A ship's captain, however, could have his entire cargo seized if any of the complicated documents were out of order.

To enforce these cumbersome regulations, the British government continued to use the Royal Navy to seize smugglers' ships, a practice begun during the French and Indian War. It also ordered colonial customs collectors to discharge their duties personally. Previously, the collectors had often lived in England, leaving the work of collection in the colonies to poorly paid deputies who were susceptible to bribes. Finally, Parliament gave responsibility for trying violations of the laws to a new vice-admiralty court in Halifax, Nova Scotia. Vice-admiralty courts had jurisdiction over maritime affairs. Unlike other courts, they normally operated without a jury and were therefore more likely to enforce trade restrictions. For this reason, and because of the remote location of the Halifax court—getting to it would be a hardship—Americans immediately opposed this provision of the Sugar Act. In response, Parliament created three more conveniently located vice-admiralty courts in Boston, Philadelphia, and Charleston, which was not exactly what the colonists had in mind.

In the spring of 1765, Parliament enacted another tax on Americans, the **Stamp Act**. This required that all valid legal documents, as well as newspapers, playing cards, and various other papers, bear a government-issued stamp for which there was a charge. The Sugar Act, though intended to raise revenue, appeared to fall within Britain's accepted authority to regulate commerce; the Stamp Act, by contrast, was the first internal tax (as opposed to an external trade duty) that Parliament had imposed on the colonies. Grenville, a lawyer, realized that it raised a constitutional issue: Did Parliament have the right to impose direct taxes on Americans when Americans had no elected representatives in Parliament? Following the principle of virtual representation—that members of Parliament served the interests of the nation as a whole, not just the locality from which they came—Grenville maintained that it did. Americans, he would find, vigorously disagreed. Nor were they without at least some support in Parliament. Colonel Isaac Barré, a member who had served in the colonies, spoke out against the Stamp Act. In one speech he referred to Americans as "Sons of Liberty," a label Americans soon would adopt for themselves.

Thursday, October 31, 1765. THE NUMB. 1195.

PENNSYLVANIA JOURNAL;
AND
WEEKLY ADVERTISER.

EXPIRING: In Hopes of a Resurrection to LIFE again.

I AM sorry to be obliged to acquaint my Readers, that as The STAMP-ACT, is fear'd to be obligatory upon us after the *First of November* ensuing, (the *fatal To-morrow*) the Publisher of this Paper unable to bear the Burthen, has thought it expedient to STOP a while, in order to deliberate, whether any Methods can be found to elude the Chains forged for us, and escape the insupportable Slavery; which it is hoped, from the just Representations now made against that Act, may be effected. Mean while, I must earnestly Request every Individual of my Subscribers, many of whom have been long behind Hand, that they would immediately Discharge their respective Arrears, that I may be able, not only to support myself during the Interval, but be better prepared to proceed again with this Paper, whenever an opening for that Purpose appears, which I hope will be soon. WILLIAM BRADFORD.

The last issue of the Pennsylvania Journal *on the day before the Stamp Act was to go into effect. Note the caricature of a stamp in the lower right corner. William Bradford, who printed this paper, was one of the organizers of the Sons of Liberty in Philadelphia.*

American Reactions

The measures Britain took to solve its financial and administrative problems first puzzled, then shocked, and eventually outraged Americans. The colonists had emerged from the French and Indian War believing that they had done their fair share and more toward making Great Britain ruler of the greatest empire the world had yet seen. They expected to be rewarded for their efforts and treated with the respect that they assumed they deserved. They were certain that as British Americans they shared in the glory and enjoyed all the rights of Englishmen in England. The new restrictions and taxes accordingly hit them like a slap in the face.

Constitutional Issues

To Americans, it was self-evident that the British measures were unfair. It was difficult to contend, however, that the British authorities had no right to impose them. The king and Parliament were considered the sovereign, or highest, authority in the empire. Then as now, the **British Constitution** was not a single written document. It consisted, rather, of the accumulated body of English law and custom, including acts of Parliament. How, then, could the colonists claim that an act of Parliament was unconstitutional?

Constitutional conflict surfaced early in Massachusetts over the issue of **writs of assistance**. These general search warrants, which gave customs officials in America the power to inspect virtually any building suspected of holding smuggled goods, had to be formally renewed at the accession of a new monarch. When George III became king in 1760, Massachusetts merchants—perhaps out of a fondness for smuggling as well as for liberty—sought to block the reissuance of the writs. Their attorney, James Otis, Jr., arguing before the Massachusetts superior court, called the writs "instruments of slavery." Parliament, he maintained, lacked the authority to empower colonial courts to issue them. Otis lost, but "then and there," a future president of the United States, John Adams, would later write, "the child independence was born."

Taxation and the Political Culture

The constitutional issue that most strained the bond between the colonies and the empire was taxation. British measures on other issues annoyed and disturbed Americans, and their cumulative effect helped alienate the colonists from England. But it was outrage over taxation—the most fundamental issue—that would be the midwife of American independence. Because Parliament had customarily refrained from taxing them, Americans assumed that it could not, and, because their own assemblies had done it, they believed that those legislatures were in fact their parliaments.

Most Americans, including many who would later side with the British, believed that to deprive them of the right to be taxed only by their own elected representatives was to deny them one of the most basic rights of Englishmen. If taxes were imposed "without our having a legal Representation where they are laid," one American asked, "are we not reduced from the Character of free Subjects to the miserable State of tributary Slaves?"

British subjects everywhere believed that Parliament's exclusive authority to impose taxes on its constituents made Britain the freest country in the world. British officials, who believed in parliamentary sovereignty, counted the colonists among those constituents. Americans, who understood that their interests might conflict with those of England, thought otherwise. Given the selfishness of human nature, they believed that to have governing officials who could do unto them without doing the same to themselves was to risk disaster.

American views on taxation and the role of government reflected the influence of country ideology. As mentioned in Chapter 4, this opposition political philosophy emerged in England in the late seventeenth and early eighteenth centuries partly in response to the development of Britain's powerful standing army and navy. It viewed these forces, and the financial measures needed to support them, as threats to personal liberty. Country ideology proceeded from two basic assumptions: that human beings are selfish and that they need governments to protect them from one another. But country ideology also held that government power, no matter how necessary or to whom entrusted, is inherently aggressive and expansive. According to the English political philosopher John Locke, rulers have the authority to enforce law "only for the public good." When government exceeds this proper function, the people have the right to change it. Only in the last resort does this right justify revolution. The preferable alternative is a system with less disruptive ways of protecting the freedom of the people.

Country ideology stressed that in the English system of government, it was the duty of Parliament, in particular the House of Commons (which represented the people as a whole), to check the executive power of the crown. The House of Commons's control of taxation enabled it to curb tyrannical rulers. When the crown did its job properly, the Commons appropriated the necessary funds; when rulers infringed on the liberty of the people, the Commons restrained them by withholding taxes.

Such important responsibilities required that the people's representatives be men of sufficient property and judgment to make independent decisions. A representative should be "virtuous" (meaning public-spirited), and he should avoid political partisanship, because divisions within the House of Commons could undermine its ability to resist or curb the executive. A representative of the appropriate social status who exhibited the proper behavior deserved the deference of his constituents. They should assume, in other words, that he was more qualified to understand and manage public affairs than they were, and they should accordingly follow his lead. But if he did not measure up, the people should be able to vote him out.

Country ideology appealed to Americans for a number of reasons. In part, colonists were drawn to it as they were to other English fashions. The works of Alexander Pope, the most widely read English poet of the eighteenth century and a proponent of a version of country ideology, appeared in many colonial libraries. So also did the works of two readable and prolific country ideology publicists, John Trenchard and Thomas Gordon, who collaborated in writing *Cato's Letters* (1720–1724) and the *Independent Whig* (1721). More important, country ideology's suspicion of those in power suited American politics on the local level, where rivalries and factionalism fostered distrust between those with and without power. And it emboldened the many Americans who feared they had no voice in the decisions of the government in London on matters of vital importance to them. Finally, with its insistence on the important political role of the propertied elite, country ideology appealed to America's local gentry. It suggested that it was their duty, as elected political officials, to safeguard the freedom of their constituents.

These ideas have had an enduring influence on American politics, surfacing even today in the suspicion of Washington and "big government." During the eighteenth century, they predisposed Americans to value local control and to expect the worst from remote governments. In so doing, they helped inspire the American Revolution. Many Americans were ready to attribute any new imperial regulations or taxes to a conspiracy of corrupt British officials to tyrannize them.

Protesting the Taxes

Given this ideological background, the initial American response to the Sugar Act was surprisingly mild. This was because the new taxes it imposed took the form of duties on trade and thus appeared consistent with the earlier Navigation Acts. The actual reaction varied from colony to colony in ways that reflected regional self-interest. The speaker of the legislature in one southern colony commented that it was "much divided" over the effects of the act and would probably not petition against it. In New England, in contrast, the Sugar Act threatened to cut into the profits of the lucrative smuggling trade with the French West Indies. As a result, people there and in other northern colonies were quicker to recognize the act's implications. The legislative body that imposed it—Parliament—and whose constituents in England stood to gain from it was not accountable to the people on whom it was imposed, the colonists. As one alarmed colonist noted, if his fellow Americans submitted to any tax imposed by Parliament, they were dumb and docile donkeys; "more Sacks, more Sacks," or burdens, were coming.

The size of the burden was less important than the principle involved. To Americans steeped in country ideology, direct taxation by London threatened to undercut the elected representatives' power of the purse and thereby remove the traditional first line of defense against a tyrannical executive. Thus all the assemblies eventually passed resolutions flatly maintaining that any parliamentary tax on America, including the Sugar Act, was unconstitutional. Colonists in New York, their assembly stated, claimed to be exempt from taxation by anyone but their own representatives not "as a Privilege" but "as their Right." By the end of 1764, New York merchants had joined the artisans and merchants of Boston in a **nonimportation** movement, an organized boycott of British manufactured goods. The goal was to cut into the profits of British employers, inducing them and the workers laid off as a result to bring pressure on the government to back down.

Unlike the Sugar Act, the Stamp Act had an equal impact throughout the colonies, and the response to it was swift and vociferous. Newspapers and pamphlets were filled with denunciations of the supposedly unconstitutional measure, and in taverns everywhere outraged patrons roundly condemned it. "The minds of the freeholders," wrote one observer, "were inflamed . . . by many a hearty damn of the Stamp Act over bottles, bowls and glasses." Parliament, Americans were convinced, did not represent them. Its members did not share their economic interests and would not pay the taxes that they imposed on Americans. Parliament therefore could not legitimately tax Americans.

The colonial legislatures were also quick to condemn the new measure. Virginia's lower house was the first to act, approving Patrick Henry's strong resolutions against the Stamp Act. These were then reprinted in newspapers throughout the colonies, and other legislatures passed similar formal objections.

Shared outrage at the Stamp Act inspired the colonies to join in unified political action. The **Sons of Liberty**, a collection of loosely organized protest groups, put pressure on stamp distributors and British authorities. In August 1765, a Boston crowd led by shoemaker Ebenezer MacIntosh demolished property belonging to a revenue agent, and another mob sacked Lieutenant Governor Thomas Hutchinson's house. The Sons of Liberty organized similar demonstrations in other cities but kept most of them more peaceful with tighter discipline.

Members of the Sons of Liberty included people from all ranks of society. The leaders, however, among them Christopher Gadsden, came mostly from the middle and upper classes. Often pushed by more radical common people, some of them doubtless joined in the hope of protecting their own positions and interests. Indeed, in Charleston, slaves paraded through the streets crying, "Liberty!" much to the dismay of their masters and the rest of the city's white population.

Movement leaders were also concerned that violence could discredit the American cause. Even the fiery Samuel Adams, one of the leading organizers of the protest in Boston, would later claim, "I am no friend to Riots." Still, he added, "when the People

Samuel Adams, the leader of the Boston radicals, as he appeared to John Singleton Copley in the early 1770s. In this famous picture, thought to be commissioned by another revolutionary leader, John Hancock, Adams points to legal documents guaranteeing American rights.

are oppressed," they will be "discontented, and they are not to be blamed."

Partly as a result of the growing unrest, leaders throughout the colonies determined to meet and agree on a unified response to Britain. As Gadsden observed at the time, "There ought to be no New England men, no New Yorker, etc. known on the Continent, but all of us Americans." Nine colonies eventually sent delegates to the **Stamp Act Congress**, which met in New York City in October 1765. A humorist in the South Carolina legislature, who had opposed sending anyone, observed that the gathering would produce a most unpalatable combination: New England would throw in fish and onions; the middle provinces, flax-seed and flour; Virginia and Maryland, tobacco; North Carolina, pitch, turpentine, and tar; South Carolina, indigo and rice—and Georgia would sprinkle the whole with sawdust. "Such an absurd jumble will you make if you attempt to form [a] union among such discordant materials as the thirteen British provinces," he concluded. A quick-witted member of the assembly shot back that he would not choose his colleague for a cook, but that the congress would prepare a dish fit for any king.

It did indeed. The congress adopted the **Declaration of Rights and Grievances**, which denied Parliament's right to tax the colonies, and petitioned both king and Parliament to repeal the Stamp and Sugar acts. Parliament, unwilling to acknowledge this challenge to its authority, refused to receive the colonial petitions.

As protests spread, the stamp distributors got the message and resigned, "for the welfare of the people." In some areas, Americans went about their business as usual without using stamped paper. In other places, they avoided activities that required taxed items. They also stepped up the boycott of British goods that had begun in response to the Sugar Act. British merchants, hurt by this economic pressure, petitioned Parliament for repeal of the Stamp Act, and a new ministry obliged them by rescinding it in March 1766. Modifications in the provisions of the Sugar Act came later in the year.

The Aftermath of Crisis

During the Stamp Act crisis, Benjamin Franklin appeared before Parliament to present American objections to the Stamp and Sugar acts. Some members apparently concluded from his remarks that the colonists would accept port duties but would oppose direct taxes. They were wrong. At this point, Americans were in no mood to accept any tax imposed by Parliament.

Americans in turn misunderstood the **Declaratory Act** that accompanied the repeal of the Stamp Act. Intended to make Parliament's retreat more acceptable to its members, this act stated that Parliament had the right to "legislate for the colonies in all cases whatsoever." Did legislate mean tax? Not necessarily, for taxes were traditionally deemed to be a voluntary gift to the king from the people acting through their own representatives. (This is why money bills, as distinct from other acts, had to originate in the House of Commons.) Americans therefore tended to consider the Declaratory Act a mere face-saving gesture. Unfortunately, it was more than that. As one colonist later observed, it created a "platform for the Invincible Reasoning from the Mouths of four and twenty pounders [cannons]."

A Strained Relationship

Most members of Parliament continued to believe that they represented everyone in the empire and that they could therefore tax people in the colonies

A satirical British engraving from 1766 showing English politicians burying the Stamp Act, "born 1765 died 1766." The warehouses in the background symbolize the revival of trade with America.

as well as in England. Americans believed just as strongly that "in taxing ourselves and making Laws for our own internal government . . . we can by no means allow our Provincial legislatures to be subordinate to any legislative power on earth."

Relations were never quite the same between England and America after the Stamp Act crisis. Each side became ever more suspicious of the other. Americans were convinced that they had forced British authorities to back down and that, if need be, they could do it again. Or so they told themselves every March 18, the anniversary of the repeal of the Stamp Act. This date became an occasion for celebration, giving Americans a national holiday before they had a nation.

An exchange between British merchants and their American correspondents in the wake of the Stamp Act's repeal illustrates how far apart Englishmen and Americans had become. The British merchants lectured the Americans, enjoining them "to express filial duty and gratitude to your parent country." To which one Virginia planter tartly replied, "We rarely see anything from your side of the water free from the authoritative style of a master to a schoolboy." This, he observed, was more than "a little ridiculous."

Events likewise testified to continuing tensions between the two sides. When British authorities required Massachusetts to compensate those who had suffered damage in the Stamp Act rioting, the legislature complied but pardoned the rioters. In 1767, an irritated Parliament then passed an act suspending the New York legislature because it had not complied with the Quartering Act of 1765. This law required colonial assemblies to provide facilities and certain supplies for royal troops. The New York legislature finally obeyed before the suspending act went into effect, and it remained in business. But such incidents boded ill for the hopes of some colonists that a British government that had repealed the Stamp Act would prove cooperative in other ways.

Regulator Movements

In 1766, a committee of the South Carolina legislature appointed to consider "the State of the Province" recommended that it establish courts in the rapidly growing backcountry and petition Parliament for repeal of the Currency Act. These suggestions were prompted by mounting unrest in the southern backcountry. Vigilante groups calling themselves **Regulators** had emerged in North Carolina in response to official corruption and in South Carolina in response to lawlessness. High taxes and high court costs in North Carolina oppressed the colony's western farmers. The Currency Act, because it reduced the amount of money in circulation, compounded their problems, leaving them "crouched beneath their sufferings" and unable to pay their debts and taxes. In South Carolina, the devastation and disruptions of the Cherokee War left a legacy of violence. Outlaws roamed the backcountry stealing livestock and raiding isolated houses. In both colonies, because representation in the assemblies failed to reflect the rapidly growing backcountry populations, legislatures were slow to respond to their needs. As a result, the Regulators did by extralegal action what they couldn't do through legal channels. In North Carolina, they closed courts and intimidated tax officials. In South Carolina, they pursued outlaws and whipped people suspected of harboring them.

These activities brought the Regulators into conflict with the local elites of both North and South Carolina. British officials, however, only made matters worse. Instead of encouraging the assemblies to increase western representation, the crown did exactly the opposite. As part of its effort to limit the power of colonial legislatures, it forbade them from increasing their size. Americans termed this instruction "perhaps [as] peculiar as any that have been given on the continent." As for the shortage of currency, Lord Hillsborough, the secretary of state for the colonies, callously informed North Carolinians that "no Consideration of a possible local inconvenience" would prompt Britain to modify the "sound Principles" of the Currency Act. And instead of approving legislation in South Carolina that would have established courts in the backcountry, British officials disallowed it because it specified that judges would hold their positions contingent on good behavior rather than at the pleasure of the crown.

Thanks to such help from London as well as to their own mistakes, a crisis confronted local authorities by 1767. In South Carolina, the assembly belatedly reapportioned itself, giving the backcountry some representation, and permitted the crown to dictate the terms of judicial appointments. These and other concessions to western residents narrowly averted bloodshed. But in North Carolina, fighting broke out in 1771. Governor William Tryon led the local militia against the Regulators who had gathered near Alamance Creek. There, he ordered the Regulators to disperse or his men would fire. "Fire and be damned," someone replied, and gunfire erupted, killing 29 men and wounding more than 150 on both sides. During the next several weeks, seven Regulators were hanged and six thousand pardoned.

The confrontation in North Carolina was the most serious of its kind, but similar social tensions were apparent in other colonies. To deal with them, colonial leaders had to understand local conditions and be able to act on their knowledge. But British attempts to reform colonial governments threatened to hamstring them.

The Townshend Crisis

British authorities had not given up the idea of taxing the colonies with the repeal of the Stamp Act in 1766. Little over a year later, Parliament passed a new collection of taxes, the Townshend duties. Another crisis ensued, lasting until an American boycott of British goods forced repeal of most of the new duties. The relatively quiet period that followed ended when Britain made a serious attempt to enforce compliance with the one duty still on the books, the duty on tea.

Townshend's Plan

Charles Townshend became the leading figure in Britain's government in 1767. A former member of the Board of Trade, he thought he understood the colonies, and he knew that many members of Parliament still wanted to tax Americans. The legislation that bears his name, the **Townshend Duty Act**, was intended to help pay the cost of government in America. It imposed new duties, or external taxes, which Townshend believed the colonists were willing to accept, but no direct, or internal, taxes like the Stamp Tax. The duties covered a number of items the colonists regularly imported—tea, paper, paint, lead, and glass. To make sure that the duties were collected, British authorities added a new board of customs commissioners for America and located its headquarters in Boston, the presumed home of many smugglers.

Coming on top of the threatened suspension of the New York legislature, the Townshend Duty Act seemed to foreshadow greater British interference in colonial affairs. And the new customs officials were in fact far more diligent than their predecessors. One of them, taking advantage of technicalities in the law, entrapped Henry Laurens, a prominent merchant in South Carolina. Other officials harassed the wealthy Boston merchant John Hancock, perhaps because he was openly contemptuous of them. Seizing his appropriately named vessel *Liberty,* they accused him of smuggling. Hancock may indeed have violated the acts of trade at times, but in this case the accusations were apparently false. The incident sparked a riot in Boston during which a crowd on the waterfront roughed up members of the customs service. British authorities responded in 1768 by sending troops to Boston. The soldiers would remain there amid mounting hostility for the next year and a half.

American Boycott

The Townshend duties, like the stamp tax, provoked resistance throughout the colonies. Rejecting the argument that duties were somehow different from taxes, John Dickinson, a wealthy lawyer who wrote under the pen name "A Farmer in Pennsylvania," asserted that a tax was a tax, whatever its form. The purpose of the taxes—to help pay the costs of government in the colonies, including the salaries of governors and judges—also seemed dangerous. Americans believed it was the role of their own assemblies to raise revenues for these costs. By bypassing the assemblies, the Townshend Act threatened to undermine their authority.

There was no equivalent to the Stamp Act Congress in response to the Townshend Act, because British officials (acting through the colonial governors) barred the assemblies from sending delegates to such a meeting. Even so, Americans gradually organized an effective nonimportation movement. When, for example, the governor of Virginia dissolved the House of Burgesses for resolutions opposing British measures, the members met on their own in the Raleigh Tavern at Williamsburg and adopted a nonimportation agreement. Once again, vigilant laborers and artisans threatened violators of the general boycott with physical violence, but few disturbances occurred. Many Americans signed subscription lists binding themselves, with the other signers, to buy only goods made in the colonies and nothing made in Great Britain. Handbills, like one urging "the Sons and Daughters of LIBERTY" to shun a particular Boston merchant, brought pressure to bear on uncooperative importers. To avoid imported English textiles, American women spun more thread and wove more cloth at home. Wearing homespun became a moral virtue, a sign of self-reliance, personal independence, and the rejection of "corrupting" English luxuries (see "American Views: Social Status and the Enforcement of the Nonimportation Movement").

The nonimportation movement forged a sense of common purpose among all who participated in it—men and women, southern planters and northern artisans alike—giving them the sense of belonging to a larger community of fellow Americans. Although it was at this point more an imagined community than a political community, it was real enough and large enough to reduce imports from Britain by 40 percent after only one year.

Because Britain had increased its exports to Europe since the Stamp Act crisis, it took longer than before for the nonimportation movement to have an effect on its economy (see Figure 5-1). Still, the troubles in America contributed to the king's decision to appoint a new prime minister, Lord North. Thinking—and even looking—remarkably alike, George III and North complemented each other. At the king's insistence, North would remain prime minister until 1782. In 1770, he was prepared to concede that the Townshend duties had been counterproductive because they interfered with British trade. But when Parliament repealed most of them, it left the duty on tea. This symbolic equivalent of the Declaratory Act served to assert Parliament's continuing right to tax the colonies.

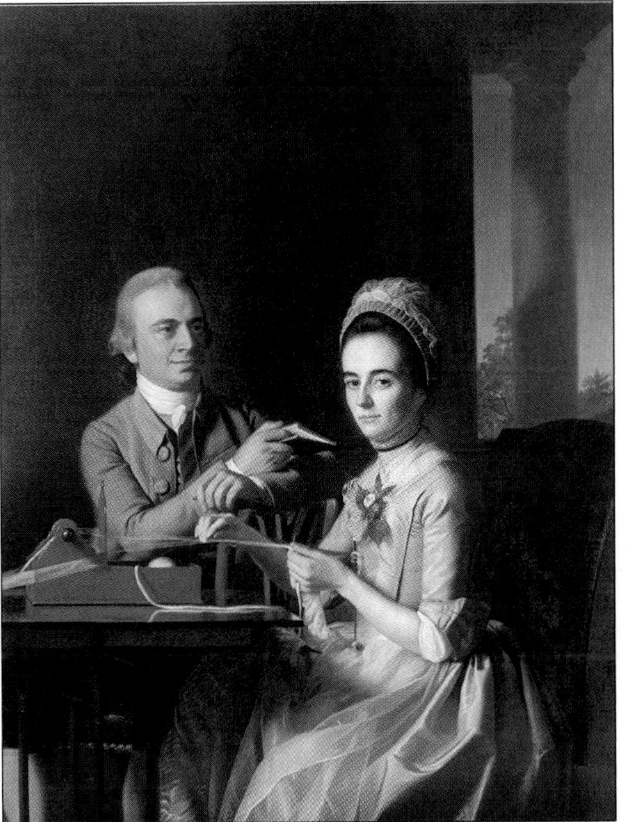

Mr. and Mrs. Mifflin by John Singleton Copley.

Mr. and Mrs. Thomas Mifflin of Philadelphia. A prominent merchant and radical opponent of British policy toward the colonies, Mifflin and his wife were visiting Boston in 1773, when John Singleton Copley painted them. Working at a small loom, Sarah Morris Mifflin weaves a decorative fringe. She no doubt did the same during the nonimportation movement against the Townshend duties, thereby helping to make importation of such goods from England unnecessary.

The Boston Massacre

Ironically, on the same day that North proposed that Parliament rescind most of the Townshend duties—March 5, 1770—British troops fired on American civilians in Boston. This incident, which came to be known as the **Boston Massacre**, resulted from months of increasing friction between townspeople and the British troops stationed in the city. The townspeople complained that the soldiers insulted them, leered at women, and competed for scarce jobs. Samuel Adams recounted these real and imagined misdeeds in a column called "A Journal of the Times" that he circulated to other American cities. The hostility was so great, complained a British officer, that "twenty" soldiers could be "knocked down in the Streets" and nothing be heard of it, but if a soldier merely kicked a resident, "the Town is immediately in an Alarm."

The Boston Massacre occurred when angry and frightened British soldiers fired on a crowd that

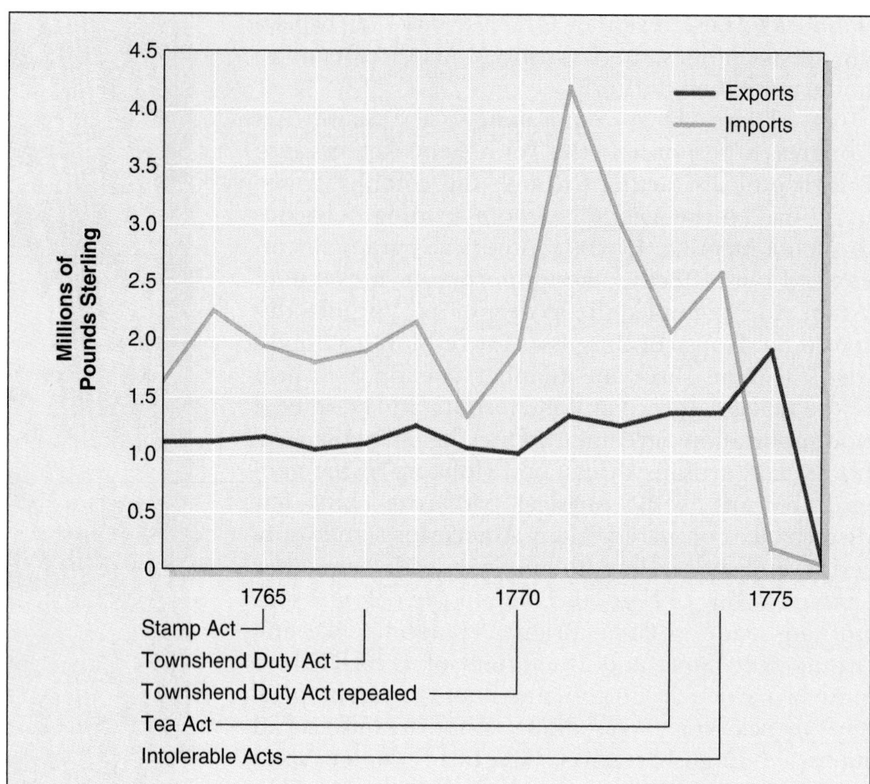

Figure 5-1 Value of American Exports to and Imports from England, 1763–1776
This figure depicts the value of American exports to and imports from England. The decrease of imports in 1765–1766 and the even sharper drop in 1769 illustrate the effect of American boycotts in response to the Stamp Act and Townshend duties.

Data Source: *U.S. Bureau of the Census,* Historical Statistics of the United States, Colonial Times to 1970, Bicentennial Edition, Part 1 (1975).

was pelting them with sticks and stones. Five men died, including Crispus Attucks—subsequently described as "that half Indian, half negro and altogether rowdy"—who has since become the most celebrated casualty of the incident. To preserve order, the troops withdrew from the city. But the damage had been done.

The "Quiet Period"

In the so-called Quiet Period that followed, no general grievance united all Americans. But in almost every colony, issues continued to simmer. In Massachusetts and South Carolina, for example, the royal governors temporarily moved the meeting places of the legislatures to small towns miles away from the capital, "for the sole Purpose," as the Declaration of Independence would later charge, "of fatiguing them into compliance" with British measures.

Local circumstances produced a more spectacular confrontation in Rhode Island. The crew of a British revenue schooner, the ***Gaspee***, had been patrolling Narragansett Bay, seizing smugglers and, it was said, stealing livestock and cutting down farmers' fruit trees for firewood. When the *Gaspee* ran aground while chasing some American ships, Rhode Islanders got even. Led by John Brown, a local merchant, they boarded the vessel, shot its captain in the buttocks, and, putting him and his crew ashore, burned the ship. The British government appointed a commission of inquiry with instructions to arrest the culprits and send them to England for trial. Despite its offer of a reward for information about the incident, the commission learned nothing. The British attempt to stamp out smuggling in the colonies was so heavy-handed that it offended the innocent more than it frightened the guilty.

Such incidents, and in particular the British threat to send Americans to England for trial, led American leaders to resolve to keep one another informed about British actions. Twelve colonies established **committees of correspondence** for this purpose. Leaders in Boston established similar committees in Massachusetts. There would soon be plenty for these organizations to do, for Boston was about to become the scene of a showdown between imperial authority and colonial resistance.

The Boston Tea Party

During the Quiet Period, Americans drank smuggled (and therefore untaxed) Dutch tea. Partly as a result, the British East India Company, which had the exclusive right to distribute tea in the British Empire, nearly went bankrupt. Lord North tried to rescue it with the **Tea Act of 1773**. The act permitted the company to ship tea from its warehouses in

The Boston Massacre, March 5, 1770, in an engraving by Paul Revere. Copied from an earlier print, Revere's widely circulated version shows—somewhat inaccurately—well-organized soldiers firing on helpless civilians; the names of the dead, including Crispus Attucks, appear below.

Britain without paying the duty normally collected there. Because its tea would therefore be cheaper, British authorities assumed that Americans would buy it and simultaneously pay the old Townshend duty. The company selected a few merchants to act as its exclusive agents in the colonies. These merchants stood to reap substantial profits from their position.

This plan angered Americans. Some may have been jealous at being excluded from the tea trade. Most, however, were outraged at the attempt to trick them into paying the tax on tea. Thousands decided not to touch the stuff. Newspapers discussed its dangers to the body as well as to the body politic and offered recipes for substitutes. "To their great honor," according to the newspapers, many women rejected the tea and put pressure on others to do likewise, while schoolboys collected and burned tea leaves.

Thomas Hutchinson, who had been lieutenant governor of Massachusetts during the Stamp Act riots, was now the colony's royal governor. Two of his sons were among those chosen to be the East India Company's agents. In most other cities, threats from the Sons of Liberty had convinced the captains of the tea ships to return to England without landing their cargo. Hutchinson, however, was determined to have the tea landed in Boston, and he barred the tea ships there from leaving. As a result, violence once again erupted in the city.

When the Sons of Liberty realized they could not force the ships to leave, they decided on dramatic action. On December 16, 1773, Samuel Adams reportedly told a large gathering at Old South Meeting House that it "could do nothing more to preserve the liberties of America." This remark was apparently a prearranged signal for what came to be known as the **Boston Tea Party**. War whoops immediately answered him from the street outside, and a well-organized band of men disguised as Indians raced aboard the tea ship *Dartmouth,* broke open 342 chests of tea, and heaved the contents in the harbor. In a similar action in 1774, residents of Annapolis, Maryland, forced some merchants to burn their own ship when it arrived with dutied tea.

"The Bostonian's Paying the Excise-Man or Tarring & Feathering." This print, published in London in 1774, satirizes American resistance to British tax measures. Five men representing a broad range of social classes pour tea down the throat of a tax collector while the Boston Tea Party takes place in the background.

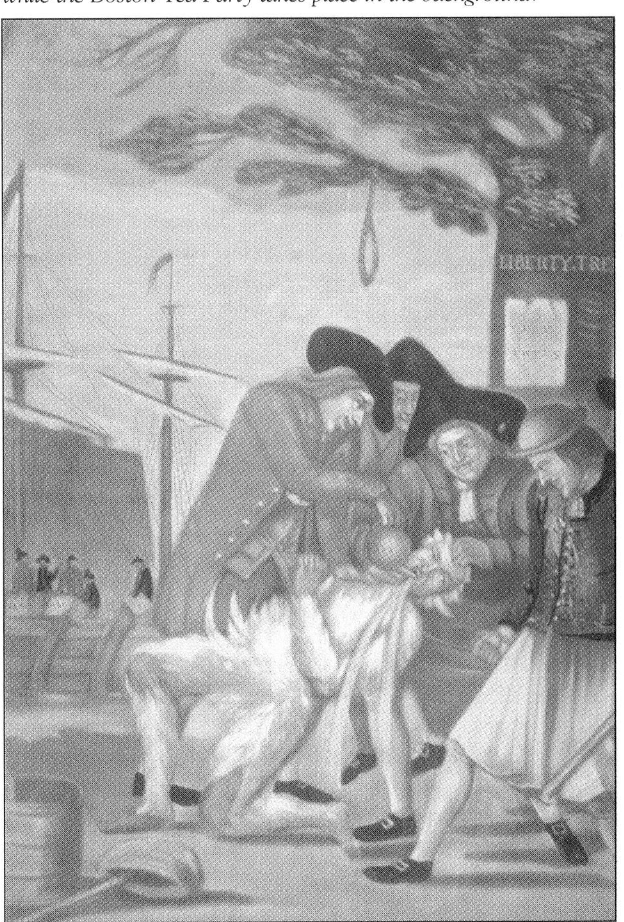

American Views

Social Status and the Enforcement of the Nonimportation Movement

Many Americans enthusiastically supported the nonimportation movement called in response to the Townshend Duty Act crisis of the late 1760s. A few, however, openly opposed it. Among these was William Henry Drayton of South Carolina, who objected to the composition of the committee that had been chosen to enforce the nonimportation agreement in his region. The committee included artisans and shopkeepers, men whom Drayton claimed should have no role in public affairs. Their education prepared them only "to cut up a beast in the market to the best advantage, to cobble an old shoe in the neatest manner, or to build a necessary house [outhouse]," not to make public policy. As the following document makes clear, they emphatically disagreed with him. Drayton was later to reverse himself and actively support the Continental Association's ban on importing British goods in 1775. "The people" wanted it, he would later explain, and "it was our duty, to satisfy our constituents; as we were only servants of the public [at large]."

- **Who makes policy in the United States today?**
- **What qualifications do you think they should have?**
- **How do your answers to these questions differ from Drayton's? From the "Mechanics"?**
- **How would you explain Drayton's later switch?**

The Mechanics of the General Committee to William Henry Drayton

The gracious Giver of all good things, has been pleased to bestow a certain principle on mankind, which properly may be called common sense: But, though every man hath a natural right to a determined portion of this ineffable ray of the Divinity, yet, to the misfortune of society, many persons fall short of this most necessary gift of God; the want of which cannot be compensated by all the learning of the schools.

The Mechanicks pretend to nothing more, than having a claim from nature, to their share in this inestimable favour, in common with Emperors and Kings, and, were it safe to carry the comparison still higher, they would say with William-Henry Drayton himself; who, in his great condescention, has been pleased to allow us a place amongst human beings: But whether it might have happened from an ill construction of his sensory, or his upper works being damaged by some rough treatment of the person who conducted his birth,

The Intolerable Acts

The destruction of property in the Boston Tea Party shocked many Americans. Surprised and angry, British officials reacted even more strongly. Parliament passed a series of repressive measures known as the **Coercive Acts**. The first of these, effective June 1, 1774, was the Boston Port Act, which closed the port of Boston to all incoming and outgoing traffic until the East India Company and the crown received payment for the destroyed tea and lost duties. The Administration of Justice Act, which followed, declared that an official who, while performing his duties, killed a colonist could be tried in England (where he would almost certainly receive sympathetic treatment) rather than in Massachusetts. The third measure, the Massachusetts Government Act, drastically modified that colony's charter of 1691. Under the old document, we know not; however so it is, that, to us, he seems highly defective in this point, whatever exalted notions he may entertain of his own abilities.

By attending to the dictates of common sense, the Mechanicks have been able to distinguish between RIGHT and WRONG; in doing which indeed no great merit is claimed, because every man's own feelings will direct him thereto, unless he obstinately, or from a pertinacious opinion of his own superior knowledge, shuts his eyes, and stoickally submits to all the illegal encroachments that may be made on his property, by an ill-designing and badly-informed ministry.

Mr. Drayton may value himself as much as he pleases, on his having had a liberal education bestowed on him, tho' the good fruits thereof have not hitherto been conspicuous either in his public or private life: He ought however to know, that this is not so absolutely necessary to these, who move in the low sphere of mechanical employments. But still, though he pretends to view them with so contemptuous and oblique an eye, these men hope, that they are in some degree useful to society, without presuming to make any comparisons between themselves and him, except with regard to love for their country; for he has amply shewn, that an attachment of this sort is not one of his ruling passions. Nor does he appear in the least to have regarded the peace and good order of that community of which he is a member; otherwise he would not wilfully, and without any cause, have knocked his head against ninety-nine out of every hundred of the people, not only in this province, but of all North-America, not one of whom bore him any malice, nor yet do, though they may entertain what opinions they please, with respect to his want of patriotism, from his having proved a Felo de se [murderer of himself] in this point.

After an avowal of principles, incompatible with the essential rights of freemen under the English constitution, surely, no parish in this province, will ever think it prudent, to trust their interests in such hands, for the time to come? Besides, who can say he ever shewed any capacity for business, when he was honoured with a seat in the House of Assembly? . . .

Mr. Drayton may be assured, that so far from being ashamed of our trades, we are in the highest degree thankful to our friends, who put us in the way of being instructed in them; and that we bless God for giving us strength and judgment to pursue them, in order to maintain our families, with a decency suitable to their stations in life. Every man is not so lucky as to have a fortune ready provided to his hand, either by his own or his wife's parents, as has been his lot; nor ought it to be so with all men; and Providence accordingly hath wisely ordained otherwise, by appointing the greatest part of mankind, to provide for their support by manual labour; and we will be bold to say, that such are the most useful people in a community. . . .

We are, Yours, &c.
MECHANICKS of the COMMITTEE.
October 3d, 1769.

Source: South Carolina Gazette, *October 5, 1769; reprinted in* The Letters of Freeman, etc.: Essays on the Nonimportation Movement in South Carolina *by William Henry Drayton, ed. Robert M. Weir (1977), University of South Carolina Press, pp. 111–114.*

the legislature had elected members to the governor's council; henceforth, the crown would appoint them. And appointed, rather than elected, sheriffs would now name juries. In addition, the Massachusetts Government Act limited the number of town meetings that could be held without the governor's prior approval. In another measure, the British government made its commander in chief in America, General Thomas Gage, the governor of Massachusetts and, in the Quartering Act of 1774, declared that the troops under his command could be lodged in virtually any uninhabited building.

On the same day that Parliament enacted these measures, it also passed the **Quebec Act**. This statute enlarged the boundaries of Quebec south to the Ohio River and stipulated that it be governed by an appointed governor and council but no elected assembly (see Map 5-2). The act also provided for the trial of civil cases without a jury and gave the Catholic Church the same privileges that it had enjoyed under the French. The colonists linked the Quebec Act with the Coercive Acts and labeled them the **Intolerable Acts**.

The Road to Revolution

Americans throughout the colonies considered the Intolerable Acts so threatening that they organized another gathering, the **First Continental Congress**, to respond to them. Congress renewed the nonimportation movement and took measures to enforce it strictly. These measures widened the gap between those who supported British authorities and those who opposed them.

Map 5-2 The Quebec Act of 1774
The Quebec Act enlarged the boundaries of the Canadian province southward to the Ohio River and westward to the Mississippi, thereby depriving several colonies of claims to the area granted to them by their original charters.

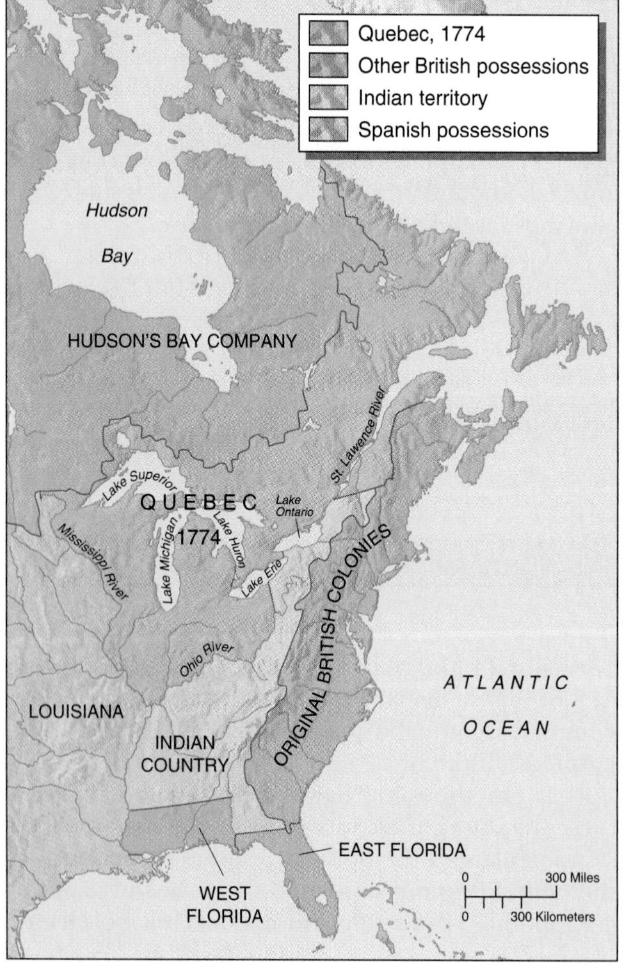

American Response to the Intolerable Acts

Americans found the territorial, administrative, and religious provisions of the Quebec Act deeply disturbing. As one royal governor observed, "The securing of lands for the rising Generation is a matter of great importance to a poor and provident Man with a large family." The Quebec Act, however, gave Canada jurisdiction over lands in the area north of the Ohio River claimed by Connecticut, Pennsylvania, and Virginia. This deprived settlers of their hoped-for homesteads and land speculators of their hoped-for profits, angering both. The administrative provisions of the act—appointed government, no assemblies, no jury for civil cases—also suggested to Americans what Britain might have in store for them.

Americans had similar fears about the religious provisions of the Quebec Act. During the 1760s, some Anglican clergymen had sought to have a bishop appointed for America. But most Americans, including Anglicans, opposed this proposal. They were convinced that the creation of such an office would strengthen the Anglican Church at the expense of other denominations, weaken local control of religious affairs, and require the payment of additional taxes. Many Americans believed that British authorities had scrapped the idea. The Quebec Act's concessions to Canadian Catholics, however, seemed to resurrect it in more ominous form. As one Virginian had observed, the hierarchical organization of the Anglican Church was "a Relick of the Papal Incroachments" on English law. The Quebec Act accordingly "gave a General Alarm to all Protestants," whose ministers throughout the continent warned their congregations that they might be "bound by Popish chains."

American reaction to the religious provisions of the Quebec Act may have been exaggerated, but some features of the Coercive Acts were cause for real concern. The Boston Port Act arbitrarily punished innocent and guilty Bostonians alike. The Administration of Justice Act—which some with vivid imaginations dubbed the "Murder Act"—seemed to declare an open season on colonists, allowing crown officials to kill them without fear of punishment. The Massachusetts Government Act raised the more realistic fear that no colonial charter was safe. A Parliament that had stripped the Massachusetts legislature of an important power might equally decide to abolish the lower houses of all the colonies.

Nightmarish scenarios filled the colonial newspapers. One clergyman observed that the terms of the Coercive Acts were such that if someone were to "make water" on the door of the royal customs house, an entire colonial city "might be laid in

Ashes." He undoubtedly knew that he exaggerated, but his words embodied real fear and anger, and many other Americans shared his feelings. Trying to make an example of Boston, British authorities had taken steps that united Americans as nothing had ever done before (see the overview table, "New Restraints and Burdens on Americans, 1759–1774").

The First Continental Congress

Massachusetts wanted to respond to the Intolerable Acts with an immediate renewal of the nonimportation movement. Leaders in other colonies wanted to organize a more coordinated response and called for another meeting like the Stamp Act Congress. The colonies accordingly agreed to send delegates to a meeting in Philadelphia that came to be called the First Continental Congress. Royal governors attempted to prevent the meeting by barring the legislatures from naming delegates, so the colonies called extralegal public meetings for the purpose. In the end, all the colonies except Georgia were represented.

The First Continental Congress met at Carpenter's Hall in Philadelphia from September 5 to October 26, 1774, with fifty-five delegates present at one time or another. All were leading figures in their home colonies, but only a few knew members from elsewhere. Each colony had one vote, irrespective of the size of its delegation. Some of the more conservative participants favored a compromise with Britain. The speaker of the Pennsylvania Assembly, Joseph Galloway, introduced a measure reminiscent of the Albany Plan of Union. It called for creation of an American "grand council" that would have veto power over parliamentary legislation dealing with America. His plan failed in the Congress by one vote. Instead, those who favored stronger measures—like Samuel Adams and his cousin John, Patrick Henry, and Christopher Gadsden—prevailed. They persuaded most of their colleagues to endorse the **Suffolk Resolves**, which had been passed at a meeting held in Suffolk County (the site of Boston). These strongly worded resolves denounced the Coercive Acts as unconstitutional, advised the people to arm, and called for general economic sanctions against Britain. Learning of them, one British official told an American, "If these Resolves of your people are to be depended on, they have declared War against us."

The Continental Association

Congress created the **Continental Association** to organize and enforce sanctions against the British. As a first step, the Association pledged Americans to cut off imports from Britain after December 1, 1774. If the dispute with Britain was not resolved by September 1775, the Association called for barring most exports to Britain and the West Indies. Voters in every district throughout the colonies were to choose committeemen to enforce the terms of the Association. All who violated them were to be considered "enemies of American liberty." Their names were to be published, and associators (people agreeing to the Association) would "break off all dealings" with them.

Congress also issued a declaration of rights and grievances summarizing its position. This declaration condemned most of the steps taken by British authorities since 1763, but "cheerfully" consented to trade regulations for the good of the whole empire. In addition, the Congress sent addresses to the people of America, to the inhabitants of Great Britain, and to the king. The address to the king asked him to use his "royal authority and interposition" to protect his loyal subjects in America. The words were significant, for protection and allegiance were considered the reciprocal duties of a sovereign and his people. After agreeing to convene again on May 10, 1775, if its grievances had not been redressed by then, the First Continental Congress adjourned.

The proceedings of the First Continental Congress revealed division as well as agreement among its delegates. All of the delegates believed that the Coercive Acts were unconstitutional, but they differed over how to resist them. Only a minority was prepared to take up arms against Britain. Most representatives tried to protect the interests of their own colonies. Those from Virginia and Maryland, for example, insisted that the embargo on exports not begin until planters had finished shipping the current tobacco crop. Even more alarming, some South Carolina delegates, in an early example of the sectional stubbornness that would culminate nearly a century later in the U.S. Civil War, threatened to walk out of the meeting unless the nonexportation agreement omitted rice, most of which went to northern Europe by way of Britain. To placate the Carolinians, northerners agreed to the exemption. Gadsden was disgusted with his self-serving South Carolina colleagues. Their actions, he felt, betrayed the spirit of united purpose Patrick Henry had spoken of so stirringly earlier in the Congress: "The distinctions between Virginians, Pennsylvanians, New Yorkers and New Englanders are no more. I am not a Virginian, but an American."

Political Divisions

In the wake of the First Continental Congress, Americans were forced to take sides for and against the Continental Association. At this point, not even such well-known radicals as Adams and Gadsden were advocating independence. Throughout the pre-Revolutionary period, most colonists hoped and

Overview

New Restraints and Burdens on Americans, 1759–1774

	Restraints on Legislative Action	Restraints on Territorial Expansion	Restraints on Colonial Trade	Imposition of New Taxes
1759	Royal instructions restrict the ability of the Virginia assembly to pass timely legislation.			
1762			Writs of assistance issued.	
1763		Proclamation Line keeps white settlement east of the Appalachians.	Peacetime use of the navy and new customs officials to enforce Navigation Acts.	
1764	Currency Act limits the colonial legislatures' ability to issue paper money.		Vice-admiralty courts strengthened for Sugar Act.	Sugar Act imposes taxes for revenue (modified 1766).
1765				Quartering Act requires assemblies to provide facilities for royal troops. Stamp Act imposes internal taxes on legal documents, newspapers, and other items (repealed 1766).
1767	Royal instructions limit the size of colonial assemblies.		Vice-admiralty courts strengthened for Townshend duties. American Customs Service established in Boston.	Townshend duties imposed on some imported goods in order to pay colonial officials. (All but tax on tea repealed, 1770.)
1773				Tea Act reduces duty and prompts Boston Tea Party.
1774 (Intolerable Acts)	Massachusetts Government Act limits town meetings, changes legislature, and violates Massachusetts charter.	Quebec Act enlarges Quebec at expense of colonies with claims in the Ohio River Valley.	Boston Port Act closes harbor until East India Company's tea is paid for.	Quartering Act of 1774 declares that troops could be lodged in virtually any uninhabited building in Boston.

expected that imperial authorities would change their policy toward America. English history, Americans believed, was full of instances in which the resolute opposition of a free people forced oppressive ministries and tyrannical kings to back down. They were confident that it could happen again.

What Americans were divided over was the extent of Parliament's authority over them and the degree to which they could legitimately challenge its power. As British officials failed, with the passing of time, to accommodate American views of their rights, Americans began in increasing numbers to challenge London's control over them. The experience of James Wilson, a Pennsylvania lawyer, illustrates this shift. In *Considerations on the Nature and Extent of the Legislative Authority of the British Parliament* (published in 1774), Wilson writes that he set out to find a reasonable dividing line between those areas in which Parliament had legitimate authority over the colonies and those in which it did not. But the more he thought, the more he became convinced "that such a line does not exist" and that there can be "no medium between acknowledging and denying that power in all cases." Wilson therefore concluded that Parliament had no authority at all over the colonies, that the colonies' only legal governing bodies were their own assemblies, and that their only link to the British Empire was through the king, to whom colonists owed allegiance. British authorities and their American supporters strongly disagreed, insisting that Parliament had complete authority over the colonies.

During 1774 and early 1775, as the British–American confrontation grew more heated, lively debates raged in newspapers and pamphlets, and the colonists became increasingly polarized. In the last months before the outbreak of the American Revolution, the advocates of colonial rights began to call themselves **Whigs** and condemned their opponents as **Tories**. These traditional English party labels dated from the late seventeenth century, when the Tories had supported the accession of the Catholic King James II; the Whigs had opposed it. By calling themselves Whigs and their opponents Tories (loyalist was a more accurate label), the advocates of colonial rights cast themselves as champions of liberty and their enemies as defenders of religious intolerance and royal absolutism.

Conclusion

All Americans, Whigs and loyalists alike, had considered themselves good British subjects. But Americans were a more diverse and more democratic people than the English. A considerably larger percentage of them could participate in government, and for all practical purposes they had been governing themselves for a long time.

British officials recognized the different character of American society and feared it might lead Americans to reject British control. But the steps they took to prevent this from happening had the opposite effect.

From Britain's perspective, the measures it took in the wake of the French and Indian War were a reasonable response to its administrative and financial problems in the colonies. Taken one by one from the colonists' perspective, however, they were a rain of blows that finally impelled them to rebel.

No wonder that Americans, whose political ideology had already made them wary of governmental power, believed that they were the victims of a conspiracy in London to deprive them of their liberty. That Parliament should be a party to this presumed conspiracy particularly shocked and offended them. Because it was the representative body in the government, Americans had long considered it their "friend," though they were certain that it was not composed of their representatives.

Yet Americans probably should not have been surprised at Parliament's role. After the Glorious Revolution, virtually the only institutional limitation on Parliament was Parliament itself. That the most powerful part of the British government should concern itself with the empire after 1763 seemed only natural in Britain; that its American counterparts should defend their own rights seemed only reasonable in America. The American assemblies, after all, had modeled themselves on Parliament. Indeed, both Parliament and the colonial assemblies were doing what similar bodies throughout Europe were also doing at roughly the same time—asserting their powers and defending their liberties against encroachments from above and below.

The attempts to protect their accustomed autonomy first brought the colonial assemblies into conflict with Parliament. Asserting their rights led the individual colonies to cooperate more among themselves. This in turn led to increasingly widespread resistance, then to rebellion, and finally to revolution. Moving imperceptibly from one stage to the next, Americans grew conscious of their common interests and their differences from the English. They became aware, as Benjamin Franklin would later write, of the need to break "through the bounds, in which a dependent people had been accustomed to think, and act" so that they might "properly comprehend the character they had assumed."

That working men and members of the elite dressed as Indians had joined in the dangerous act of defiance known as the Boston Tea Party also foreshadowed coming developments. No one now knows for certain why they adopted that particular disguise, but Indians were a traditional symbol of the new world. And those who were making a new political world were risking much—even, it would shortly turn out—life itself.

Review Questions

1. How did the British victory and French withdrawal from North America after the French and Indian War affect the relations between Native Americans and white settlers? Between British authorities and Americans?
2. What was the relationship between the French and Indian War and changes in British policy toward America? What problems were British officials trying to solve in 1763? What difficulties confronted Americans in 1763? How did the expectations of American and British authorities differ in 1763? Why were the new policies offensive to Americans?
3. How was stationing British troops in America related to British taxation of the colonists? Why did the colonists consider taxation by Parliament an especially serious threat to their freedom as well as to their pocketbooks?
4. How did Americans oppose the new measures? Who participated in the various forms of resistance? How effective were the different kinds of resistance? What were the effects of American resistance to British measures on their own sense of identity as Americans? What were the effects on their own internal politics?
5. What led to the meeting of the First Continental Congress? What steps did the Congress take? What did it expect to achieve? What were the differences between Whigs and Tories?

Recommended Reading

Bernard Bailyn, *The Ideological Origins of the American Revolution*, 2nd ed. (1992). A clear and illuminating account of how the colonists' ideas about politics prepared them to resist British measures.

Edward Countryman, *The American Revolution* (1985). A brief, readable general history of the Revolutionary period that focuses on the involvement of the common people.

Edmund S. Morgan and Helen M. Morgan, *The Stamp Act Crisis: Prologue to Revolution* (1963, 1995). The classic account of the most important pre-Revolutionary crisis, beautifully written.

Samuel Eliot Morison, ed., *Sources and Documents Illustrating the American Revolution, 1764–1788, and the Formation of the Federal Constitution* (1965). The most readily available and conveniently used collection of documents (mostly official) from the era of the American Revolution.

Additional Sources

Imperial Reorganization

John R. Alden, *John Stuart and the Southern Colonial Frontier: A Study of Indian Relations, War, Trade, and Land Problems in the Southern Wilderness, 1754–1775* (1944, 1966).

Thomas C. Barrow, *Trade and Empire: The British Customs Service in Colonial America, 1660–1775* (1967).

Colin Bonwick, *The American Revolution* (1991).

John Brooke, *King George III* (1972).

Gregory Dowd, *A Spirited Resistance: The North American Indian Struggle for Unity, 1745–1815* (1992).

Tom Hatley, *The Dividing Paths: Cherokees and South Carolinians through the Era of Revolution* (1993).

Paul Langford, *A Polite and Commercial People: England, 1727–1783* (1989).

Howard H. Peckham, *Pontiac and the Indian Uprising* (1947).

John Shy, *Toward Lexington: The Role of the British Army in the Coming of the American Revolution* (1965).

J. Russell Snapp, *John Stuart and the Struggle for Empire on the Southern Frontier* (1996).

Jack M. Sosin, *Whitehall and the Wilderness: The Middle West in British Colonial Policy, 1760–1775* (1961).

David J. Weber, *The Spanish Frontier in North America* (1992).

Richard White, *The Middle Ground: Indians, Empires, and Republics in the Great Lakes Region, 1650–1815* (1991).

American Reactions

Timothy H. Breen, "Ideology and Nationalism on the Eve of the American Revolution: Revisions Once More in Need of Revising," *Journal of American History* (1998), 13-39.

Richard D. Brown, *Revolutionary Politics in Massachusetts: The Boston Committee of Correspondence and the Towns, 1772–1774* (1970).

Richard M. Brown, *The South Carolina Regulators* (1963).

Robert M. Calhoon, *Dominion and Liberty: Ideology in the Anglo-American World, 1660–1801* (1994).

H. Trevor Colbourn, *The Lamp of Experience: Whig History and the Intellectual Origins of the American Revolution* (1965).

Edward Countryman, *A People in Revolution: The American Revolution and Political Society in New York, 1760–1790* (1981).

Marc Egnal, *A Mighty Empire: The Origins of the American Revolution* (1988).

Robert A. Ekirch, *"Poor Carolina": Politics and Society in Colonial North Carolina, 1729–1776* (1981).

Jack P. Greene, *Negotiated Authorities: Essays in Colonial Political and Constitutional History* (1994).

Jack P. Greene, *Understanding the American Revolution: Issues and Actors* (1995).

Dirk Hoerder, *Crowd Action in Revolutionary Massachusetts, 1765–1780* (1977).

Merrill Jensen, *The Founding of a Nation: A History of the American Revolution, 1763–1776* (1968).

Rachel N. Klein, *Unification of a Slave State: The Rise of the Planter Class in the South Carolina Backcountry, 1760–1808* (1990).

Bernhard Knollenberg, *Origin of the American Revolution, 1759–1766* (1960).

Stephen G. Kurtz and James H. Hutson, eds., *Essays on the American Revolution* (1973).

Benjamin W. Labaree, *The Boston Tea Party* (1964).

Pauline Maier, *From Resistance to Revolution: Colonial Radicals and the Development of American Opposition to Britain, 1765–1776* (1972).

Pauline Maier, *The Old Revolutionaries: Political Lives in the Age of Samuel Adams* (1980).

Edmund S. Morgan, *The Birth of the Republic, 1763–1789,* 3rd ed. (1992).

Gary B. Nash, *The Urban Crucible: The Northern Seaports and the Origins of the American Revolution* (1986).

John P. Reid, *Constitutional History of the American Revolution: The Power to Tax* (1987).

Richard A. Ryerson, *"The Revolution Is Now Begun": The Radical Committees of Philadelphia, 1765–1776* (1978).

Peter D. C. Thomas, *The Townshend Duties Crisis: The Second Phase of the American Revolution, 1767–1773* (1987).

Carl Ubbelohde, *The Vice-Admiralty Courts and the American Revolution* (1960).

James P. Whittenburg, "Planters, Merchants, and Lawyers: Social Change and the Origins of the North Carolina Regulation," *William and Mary Quarterly, 34* (1977), 214–238.

Hiller B. Zobel, *The Boston Massacre* (1970).

The Road to Revolution

David Ammerman, *In the Common Cause: American Response to the Coercive Acts of 1774* (1974).

Carl Bridenbaugh, *Mitre and Sceptre: Transatlantic Faiths, Ideas, Personalities, and Politics, 1689–1775* (1962).

Wallace Brown, *The Good Americans: The Loyalists in the American Revolution* (1969).

Robert M. Calhoon, *The Loyalists in Revolutionary America, 1760–1781* (1973).

J. C. D. Clark, *The Language of Liberty, 1660–1832: Political Discourse and Social Dynamics in the Anglo-American World* (1994).

William H. Nelson, *The American Tory* (1961).

Jack N. Rakove, *The Beginnings of National Politics: An Interpretive History of the Continental Congress* (1979).

Where to Learn More

❖ **Charleston, South Carolina.** Many buildings date from the eighteenth century. Local officials stored tea in one of them—the Exchange—to prevent a local version of the Boston Tea Party.

❖ **Philadelphia, Pennsylvania.** Numerous buildings and sites date from the eighteenth century. Independence National Historical Park, between Second and Sixth streets on Walnut and Chestnut streets, contains Carpenter's Hall, where the First Continental Congress met, and the Pennsylvania State House (now known as Independence Hall), where the Declaration of Independence was adopted.

❖ **Boston, Massachusetts.** Many important buildings and sites in this area date from the seventeenth and eighteenth centuries. They include Faneuil Hall (Dock Square), where many public meetings took place prior to the Revolution, and the Old State House (Washington and State streets), which overlooks the site of the Boston Massacre.

❖ **Fort Michilimackinac National Historic Landmark, Mackinaw City, Michigan.** Near the south end of the Mackinac Bridge, the present structure is a modern restoration of the fort as it was when Pontiac's Rebellion took a heavy toll of its garrison.

The War for Independence, 1774–1783

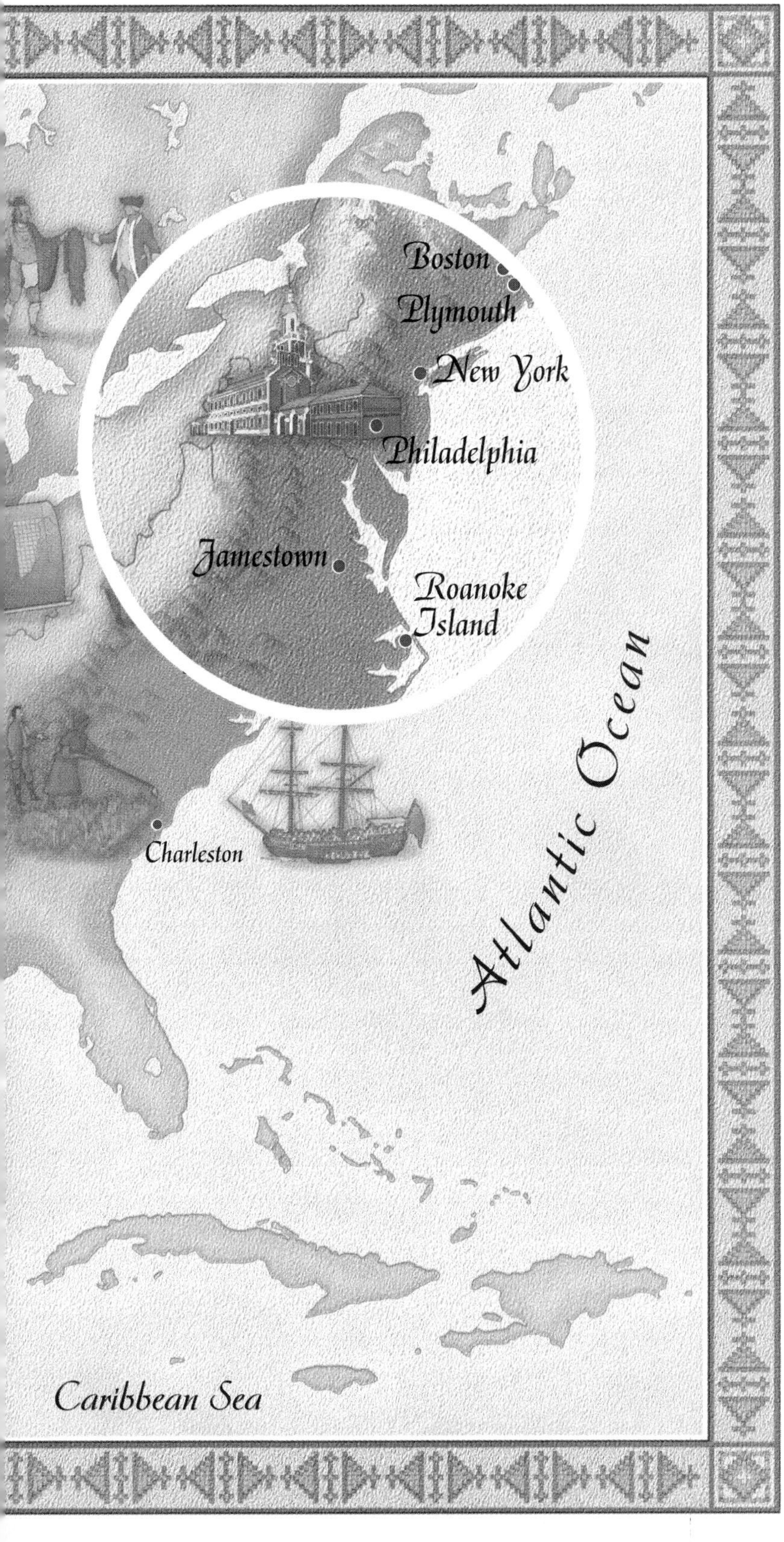

Chapter Outline

The Outbreak of War, 1774–1776
Mounting Tensions
The Loyalists' Dilemma
British Coercion and Conciliation
The Battles of Lexington and Concord
The Second Continental Congress, 1775–1776
Commander in Chief George Washington
Independence/Republicanism

The Combatants
Professional Soldiers
Women in the Contending Armies
Black and Native American Participation

The War in the North, 1776–1777
The British Army Hesitates
The Year of the Hangman

The War Widens, 1778–1781
The United States Gains an Ally
Fighting on the Frontier and at Sea
The Land War Moves South
American Counterattacks

The American Victory, 1782–1783
The Peace of Paris
The Components of Success

The War and Society, 1775–1783
The Women's War
Effect of the War on African-Americans and Native Americans
Economic Disruption/The Price of Victory

Key Topics

- ❖ Mounting tensions with Britain
- ❖ Declaring independence
- ❖ The contending forces
- ❖ The major campaigns of the Revolution
- ❖ The alliance with France
- ❖ The peace settlement
- ❖ The social effects of the war

It was May 1780, during some of the darkest days for the American Revolution. Charleston, South Carolina, was soon to fall to an advancing British army. A German officer—a professional mercenary soldier—serving with the British army saw a wounded American sergeant who had been shot and captured after venturing far in front of his unit. Asked why he had been so foolhardy, the American replied that he had been promised an officer's commission if he would successfully scout the enemy lines. His captors told him that he was mortally wounded. "He quietly lay down like a brave man," wrote the German officer, and managed to say, "Well, then, I die for my country and for its just cause." Someone handed him a glass of wine, which he "drank . . . down with relish," and he died.

American independence would be won by the dogged courage of ordinary soldiers like this nameless man. Like him, many fought in hopes of an immediate reward. And also like him, they risked death because they believed in their country's cause.

Between 1774 and 1783, the thinking of those Americans who challenged British authority changed dramatically. As late as 1774, they were still seeking self-government within the British Empire. After 1776, they were struggling for full independence from their once-revered mother country. To be sure, however, most of them, asked what was their country, would have named their home state, and asked what was their cause, would have replied, simply, "Liberty."

American political identity emerged in part from a new ideology of republicanism that combined a New Whig distrust of central authority with a belief in a government rooted in the public spirit of a virtuous citizenry. Clinging fervently to this ideology, Americans relied at the outset of the war on the efficacy of a zealous citizens' militia to defeat the British army. But as the war grew fiercer, they learned that they could prevail only by developing an equally professional fighting force of their own. With vital French assistance, the new American army overcame the enemy. But eight long years of warfare strained and in some ways profoundly altered the fabric of American society.

The Outbreak of War and the Declaration of Independence, 1774–1776

After the Boston Tea Party, both the British and the Americans knew they were approaching a crisis. A British officer in Massachusetts commented in late 1774 that "it is thought by every body here" that British forces would soon have "to take the field." "The people in general are very enraged," he explained, and some would "defend what they call their Liberties," to the death. Many Americans also expected a military confrontation but continued to hope that the king would not "reason with us only by the roar of his Cannon."

Mounting Tensions

In May 1774, General Thomas Gage, the commander in chief of the British army in America, replaced Thomas Hutchinson as governor of Massachusetts. After Gage dissolved the Massachusetts legislature, the General Court, it defied him by assembling anyway. Calling itself the Provincial Congress, the legislature in October 1774 appointed an emergency executive body, the **Committee of Safety**, headed by John Hancock, which began stockpiling weapons and organizing militia volunteers. Some localities had already provided for the formation of special companies of **Minute Men**, who were to be ready at "a minutes warning in Case of an alarm."

Enforcing the Continental Association's boycott of British goods, local committees sometimes assaulted suspected loyalists and destroyed their property. The increasingly polarized atmosphere, combined with the drift toward military confrontation, drove a growing wedge between American loyalists and the patriot anti-British American Whigs.

The Loyalists' Dilemma

Loyalists and Whigs began to part company in earnest during the fall and winter of 1774–1775 as the threat of war mounted. Much like other Americans, loyalists came from all walks of life and all social classes. Most were farmers, though officeholders and professionals were more numerous among them than in the population at large. Many recent immigrants to the colonies, as well as some locally unpopular minorities (Scots in the South, Anglicans in New England), also remained loyal because they felt the crown offered them some protection against more established Americans. Most loyalists felt, in short, that they had something to lose—including their honor—if America broke with Britain. During the War for Independence, about 19,000 American men would join British provincial units and fight to restore royal authority. (This compares with the perhaps 200,000 who served in some military capacity on the rebel side.) Including those who did not actually fight, the loyalists numbered close to half a million men and women—some 20 percent of the colonies' free population. Of these, up to 100,000 would leave with the British forces at the end of the war.

British Coercion and Conciliation

Britain held parliamentary elections in the fall of 1774, but if Americans hoped the outcome would change the government's policy toward them, they were disappointed. Few British voters paid much attention to colonial affairs or to opposition criticism of Prime Minister Lord North's handling of them. As one member of Parliament later noted, a robbery near London "would make more conversation than all the disturbances of America." North's supporters won easily. Angry and alarmed at the colonists' challenge to Parliament's sovereignty, they took a hard line. Under North's direction, Parliament resolved in February 1774 that Massachusetts was in rebellion and prohibited the New England colonies from trading outside the British Empire or sending their ships to the North Atlantic fishing grounds. Similar restrictions on most of the other colonies soon followed.

Meanwhile, in a gesture of appeasement, Parliament endorsed Lord North's **Conciliatory Proposition** pledging not to tax the colonies if they would voluntarily contribute to the defense of the empire. British authorities, however, would decide what was a sufficient contribution. Parliament, as a result, would remain sovereign and the colonial legislatures strictly subordinate to it.

Had it specified a maximum colonial contribution and had it been offered ten years earlier, the colonists might have found the Conciliatory Proposition acceptable. Now it was too late. North's government, in any case, had already sent orders to General Gage to take decisive action against the Massachusetts rebels. These orders triggered the first clash between British and American forces.

The Battles of Lexington and Concord

Gage received his orders on April 14, 1775. On the night of April 18, he assembled seven hundred men on the Boston Common and marched them toward the little towns of Lexington and Concord, some 20 miles away (see Map 6-1). Their mission was to arrest

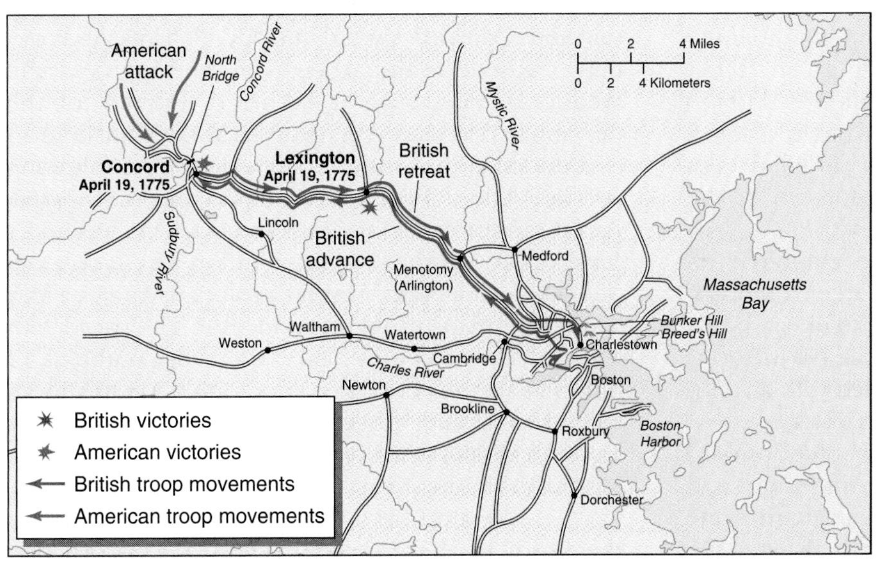

Map 6-1 The Battles of Lexington and Concord
This map shows the area around Boston, Massachusetts, where in April 1775 British and American forces fought the first military engagements of the Revolution.

Chronology

1775 April 19: Battles of Lexington and Concord.
May 10: Second Continental Congress meets.
June 17: Battle of Bunker Hill.
December 31: American attack on Quebec.

1776 January 9: Thomas Paine's *Common Sense.*
July 4: Declaration of Independence.
September 15: British take New York City.
December 26: Battle of Trenton.

1777 January 3: Battle of Princeton.
September 11: Battle of Brandywine Creek.
October 17: American victory at Saratoga.
Runaway inflation begins.
Continental Army winters at Valley Forge.

1778 February 6: France and the United States sign an alliance.
June 17: Congress refuses to negotiate with British peace commissioners.
July 4: George Rogers Clark captures British post in the Mississippi Valley.
December 29: British capture Savannah.

1779 June 21: Spain declares war on Britain.
Americans devastate the Iroquois country.
September 23: John Paul Jones captures the British ship *Serapis.*

1780 May 12: Fall of Charleston, South Carolina.
October 7: Americans win Battle of Kings Mountain.
Nathanael Greene takes command in the South.

1781 January 17: Americans defeat British at Battle of Cowpens.
March 15: Battle of Guilford Court House.
October 19: Cornwallis surrenders at Yorktown.

1783 March 15: Washington quells the Newburgh "Conspiracy."
September 3: Peace of Paris signed.
November 21: British begin evacuating New York.

rebel leaders Samuel Adams and John Hancock (then staying in Lexington) and to destroy the military supplies the Committee of Safety had assembled at Concord. Patriots in Boston got wind of the troop movements and sent out riders—one of them the silversmith Paul Revere—to warn their fellows. Adams and Hancock escaped.

When the British soldiers reached Lexington at dawn, they found about seventy armed militiamen drawn up in formation on the village green. Their precise intentions are not clear. Outnumbered ten to one, they probably did not plan to begin a fight. More likely, they were there in a show of defiance, to demonstrate that Americans would not run at the sight of a superior British force.

Months of mounting tension exploded on the Lexington green. A British major ordered the militia to disperse. They were starting to obey when a shot cracked through the dawn stillness. No one now knows who fired. The British responded with a volley that killed or wounded eighteen Americans.

The British troops pressed on to Concord and burned what few supplies the Americans had not been able to hide. When their rear guard came under patriot fire at Concord's North Bridge, the British panicked. As they retreated to Boston, patriot Minute Men and other militia harried them from both sides of the road. By the time the column reached safety, 273 British soldiers were either dead, wounded, or missing. The four thousand Americans who had shot at them along the way suffered nearly one hundred dead, wounded, and missing.

News of the fighting at the **Battles of Lexington and Concord** spread quickly. Patriots in Providence, Rhode Island, knew of it by evening of the Wednesday on which it occurred. Rumors of the fighting had already reached New York by the time an express rider confirmed them at noon the following Sunday. The Philadelphia newspaper *Pennsylvania Packet* carried the story on Monday. Williamsburg's *Virginia Gazette* printed an account on May 4, only two weeks after the event. South Carolinians knew by May 9 and Georgians probably soon after. The speed with which distant colonies heard about the outbreak of fighting suggests both the importance Americans attached to it and the extraordinary efforts patriots made to spread word of it. Everywhere, news of Lexington and Concord spurred Whigs into action.

The shots fired that April morning would, in the words of the nineteenth-century Concord phi-

"The Battle of Lexington, April 19th, 1775." OH:13¾ in.; OW:19 in. Courtesy, Winterthur Museum.

This dramatic engraving of the first battle of the American Revolution at Lexington, Massachusetts, on April 19, 1775, is not the photographic work of an eyewitness to events but a close approximation to it. Ralph Earl, a painter, and Amos Doolittle, an engraver, walked over the battlefields at Lexington and Concord a few days after the engagement, interviewed spectators and participants, and collaborated in producing four large engravings that depicted the events with considerable accuracy. This scene from the first plate shows British troops firing on the American militia at Lexington.

losopher and poet Ralph Waldo Emerson, be "heard round the world." They signaled the start of the American Revolution. And that revolution helped inspire the French Revolution in 1789 and other revolutions in Europe and Latin America.

The Second Continental Congress, 1775–1776

By the time the Second Continental Congress convened in Philadelphia on May 10, 1775, it had a war on its hands. After Gage's troops had limped back into Boston from Lexington and Concord, patriot militia surrounded the city and laid siege to it. On the day Congress met, militia forces from Vermont under Ethan Allen and from Massachusetts under Benedict Arnold overwhelmed the British garrison at **Fort Ticonderoga** at the southern end of Lake Champlain. Rebel forces elsewhere seized arms and ammunition from royal storehouses.

Assuming leadership of the rebellion, Congress in the succeeding months became, in effect, a national government. It called for the patchwork of local forces to be organized into the **Continental Army**, authorized the formation of a navy, established a post office, and authorized the printing of paper **continental dollars** to meet its expenses. Denying Parliament's claim to govern the colonies but not yet ready to declare themselves independent, the delegates sought to preserve their ties to Britain by expressing loyalty to the crown. In the **Olive Branch Petition**, addressed to George III on July 5, they asked the king to protect his American subjects from the military actions ordered by Parliament. The following day, Congress approved the **Declaration of the Causes and Necessity of Taking Up Arms**, asserting the resolve of American patriots "to die freemen, rather than to live slaves." And at the end of the month, it formally rejected North's Conciliatory Proposition.

Commander in Chief George Washington

To take command of the patriot forces around Boston—the newly named Continental Army—Congress turned to George Washington. John Adams, a Whig leader from Massachusetts, first nominated Washington. Selecting the Virginian, Adams realized, would help transform a local quarrel in New England into a continental conflict involving all of British North America. Adams and his fellow delegates also expected Washington's leadership to help attract recruits from Virginia, which was then the most populous colony. Washington claimed, despite (or perhaps because of) his experience in the French and Indian War, to feel inadequate to the task, but by attending Congress in military uniform he seemed to be volunteering for it.

He was the ideal person for the job. Some of his contemporaries had quicker minds and broader educations; Washington, however, was blessed with good judgment, a profound understanding of both the uses and the limitations of power, and a quiet air of authority. In short, he had the gift of command. He soon also realized that the fate of the patriot cause depended on the survival of the army. Early in the war, he almost suffered catastrophic military defeat at least twice, but he learned from his mistakes and thereafter did not risk lives unnecessarily. The troops in turn revered him. In a crisis, wrote a man who served under him, "his likeness was worth more . . . than the British would have given for his person"—presumably a great deal.

Early Fighting

General Gage, finding himself besieged in Boston after the fighting at Lexington and Concord, decided to seize and fortify territory south of Boston, where his cannons could command the harbor. But the Americans seized high ground first, entrenching themselves on Breeds Hill north of town. On June 17, 1775, Gage sent 2,200 well-trained soldiers to drive the 1,700 patriot men and boys from their new position.

The British succeeded, but at great cost. In three assaults, they suffered more than a thousand casualties. The Americans, who retreated when they ran short of gunpowder, lost just under four hundred dead or wounded. One glum British officer observed afterward that another such victory "would have ruined us." Misnamed for another hill nearby, this encounter has gone down in history as the **Battle of Bunker Hill** (see Map 6-2).

Washington, who arrived in Boston after the battle, took command of the American forces there in early July. Months of standoff followed, with neither side able to dislodge the other. During the winter of 1775–1776, however, the Americans dragged some sixty cannons—the largest weighed as much as a ton—300 miles through snow and over mountains from Fort Ticonderoga to Boston. In March 1776, Washington mounted the newly arrived guns overlooking Boston harbor, putting the British in an indefensible position. The British then evacuated Boston—which really had no strategic value for them—and moved their troops to Halifax, Nova Scotia. New England was for the moment secure for the patriots.

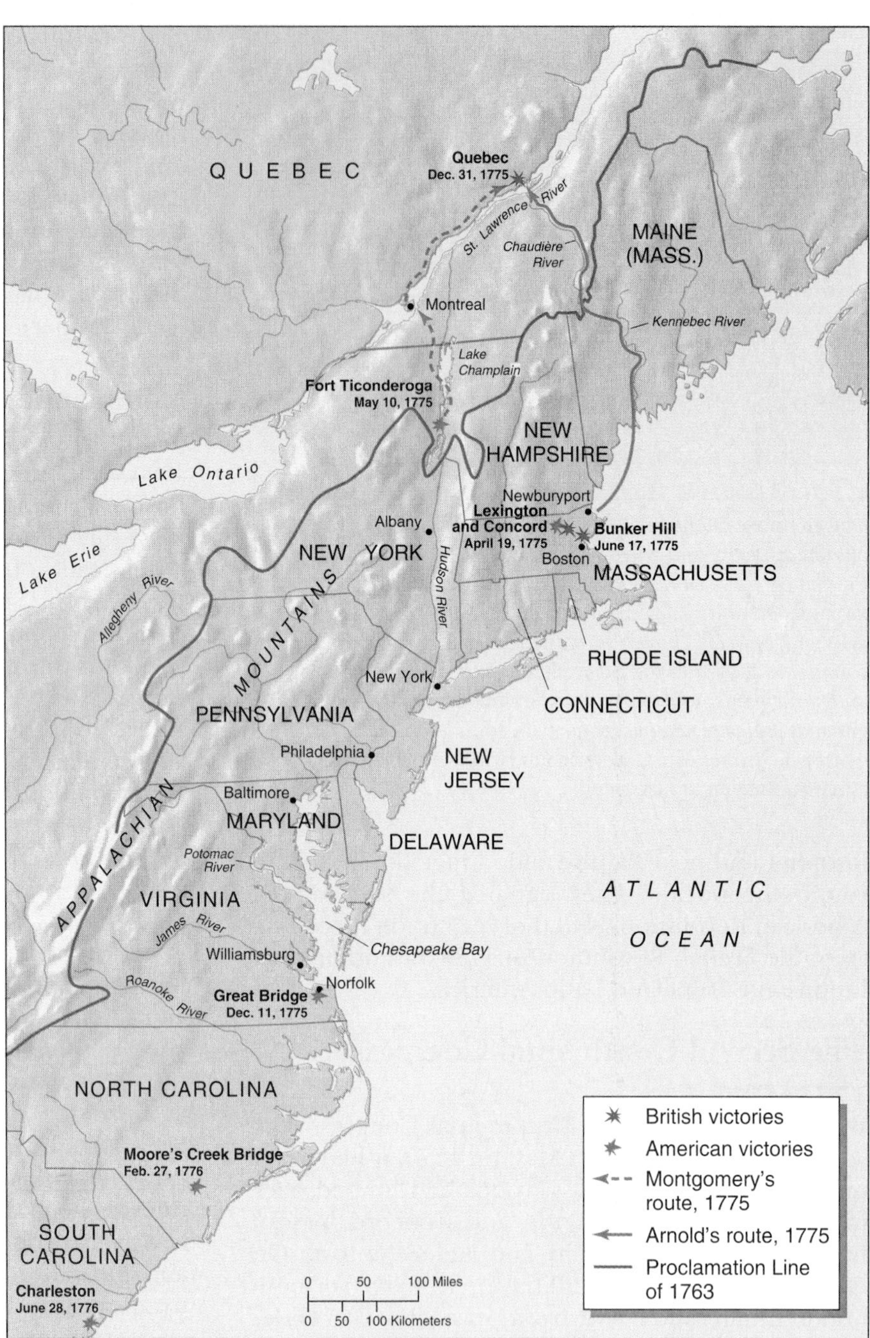

Map 6-2 Early Fighting, 1775–1776
As this map clearly reveals, even the earliest fighting occurred in widely scattered areas, thereby complicating Britain's efforts to subdue the Americans.

Initial fighting in the South also went well for the patriots. Virginia's last royal governor, Lord Dunmore, fled the capital, Williamsburg, and set up a base in nearby Norfolk. Promising freedom to slaves who joined him, he succeeded in raising a small force of black and white loyalists. On December 9, 1775, he sent these men, with some British marines, to attack a much larger force of nine hundred Virginia and North Carolina patriots at **Great Bridge**, near Norfolk. As it advanced up a long causeway, Dunmore's little band was slaughtered. It was, one British officer commented, an "extravagant Folly." On February 27, a force of loyalist Scots suffered a similar defeat at Moore's Creek Bridge in North Carolina. In June 1776, patriot forces successfully repulsed a large British expedition sent to capture Charleston, South Carolina.

In contrast, an attempt to win Canada to the patriot side met with disaster. Two American armies attacked Canada in late 1775. One quickly captured Montreal. The other, under Benedict

FROM THEN TO NOW

The American Revolution and the Teaching of American History

In October 1994, TV viewers saw politically conservative talk show host Rush Limbaugh hold up a history book and begin ripping out pages. "Here's Paul Revere. He's gone," he exclaimed, and out went a page. "Here's George Washington. . . . He's gone. . . ." More pages bit the dust. "This is what we're doing to American history with this stupid new book, folks." The volume that prompted his outburst was the *National History Standards*—"the standards from hell" according to conservative critics. In response to such outbursts, Gary Nash, a leading author of the standards and an expert in early American history, repeatedly went on television to defend them, appearing in one twenty-four hour period on ABC, NBC, and PBS.

The furor arose out of a bipartisan attempt to improve education in the nation's schools. In 1989, President George Bush and the nation's governors announced that it was time "to establish clear national performance goals, goals that will make us internationally competitive . . . in the twenty-first century." The plan called for knowledgeable professionals to establish voluntary guidelines governing what schools should expect students to know about several core subjects, including history. The development of the history standards, which involved thousands of historians and history teachers, took more than two and one-half years.

The heated reaction to the standards caught many by surprise, but it probably shouldn't have. History, Nash has pointed out, is "unceasingly controversial because it provides so much of the substance for the way a society defines itself." This is certainly true of the history of the American Revolution—the focus of much of the ire of the standard's critics—because it is from the Revolution that the founding propositions of the nation emerged.

The authors of the standards wanted students to learn the results of recent research that has given voice to African Americans, Native Americans, women, and ordinary people and documented their active role in history. But critics complained that including this material would unduly diminish coverage of prominent figures like Revere and Washington. They also worried that calling attention, say, to African-American life under slavery or to incidents like the Paxton Boys' assault on their Indian neighbors would darken the narrative of American history.

How should one tell the story of the United States? A state legislature once resolved that school textbooks should emphasize "the history of hearts and souls inspired by wonderful American principles and traditions." Those who wrote the National History Standards believed that the "governing narrative" should be "the struggle to fulfill the American ideals of liberty, equal justice, and equality" as "various groups [sought] to elbow their way under the canopy of the nation's founding promises."

Compromise eventually quieted the controversy. After the Senate rejected the history standards, blue-ribbon panels of experts reviewed them, recommended some changes, and predicted that the revised version would make an important contribution toward "developing a responsible and productive citizenry." And indeed, teachers and school administrators throughout the country now regularly consult the revised standards to help them design an appropriate history curriculum.

In this painting of The Battle of Bunker Hill, the artist John Trumbull highlighted the death of Major General Joseph Warren of the Massachusetts militia. Like Trumbull, historians have traditionally emphasized prominent historical figures. More recently, however, they have focused on the common people, such as the militiamen, black and white, who appear at the margins of this picture but who composed the majority of the American forces fighting that day.

Arnold, approached through the Maine wilderness in the face of great hardships. The two forces linked up outside heavily fortified Quebec. On December 31, their hasty attack failed, and most of the Americans who participated in it were captured. The Siege of Quebec dragged on into the spring, when a British fleet relieved the city and fresh troops forced the Americans back to Lake Champlain. Canada remained a British province.

Independence

The stunning American successes in New England and the South in late 1775 and early 1776 bolstered the patriots' confidence as attempts to promote an Anglo-American reconciliation failed.

In August 1775, King George III rejected Congress's Olive Branch Petition. Instead, he issued a proclamation declaring the colonies in rebellion and denying them his protection. In December, Parliament barred all exports from the American colonies. These aggressive actions, especially the king's, persuaded many colonists to abandon their loyalty to the crown. More and more, Whigs began to think seriously of declaring full independence from Britain.

At this critical moment, a ne'er-do-well Englishman, recently arrived on American soil, gave the cause of independence a powerful boost. Thomas Paine was by trade a corsetmaker—and twice a fired tax collector. He was also a man of radical ideas—which he expressed forcefully in the everyday English of ordinary people—and he became a powerful polemicist for the American cause. Benjamin Franklin, in London as a lobbyist for the colonies, recognized Paine's talent and gave him letters of introduction when he sailed for America in 1774. In his pamphlet ***Common Sense***, published in Philadelphia in January 1776, Paine denounced King George and made the case for independence. He ridiculed the absurdity of "supposing a continent to be perpetually governed by an island." America, he maintained, would be better off on every count if it were independent. The king, Paine said bluntly, was "the Royal Brute" whose tyranny should be thrown off. This assertion, which not long before would have shocked even Whigs, seemed self-evident now in light of the king's rejection of the Olive Branch Petition. Simple common sense, Paine concluded, dictated that " 'TIS TIME TO PART."

Common Sense, which promptly sold more than 100,000 copies throughout the colonies, helped predispose Americans toward independence. Tactical considerations also led patriot leaders toward a formal separation from Great Britain. Such a move would make it easier for America to gain desperately needed aid from foreign countries, especially from England's ancient enemy, France. Declaring independence would also give the local political elites leading the resistance to British rule a solid legal basis for their newly claimed authority. Accordingly, most of the American states (as the rebellious colonies now called themselves) either instructed or permitted their delegates in Congress to vote for independence.

On June 7, 1776, Virginian Richard Henry Lee introduced in Congress a resolution stating that the united colonies "are, and of right ought to be, free and independent States." Postponing a vote on the issue, Congress appointed a committee to draw up a declaration of independence. The committee turned to a young Virginian named Thomas Jefferson to compose the first draft. "You can write ten times better than I," John Adams supposedly told Jefferson. On June 28, after making revisions in Jefferson's proposed text, the committee presented the document to Congress. In the debate that followed, the South Carolina, Pennsylvania, and New York delegations initially opposed independence. As it became clear that the majority favored it, the Pennsylvania and South Carolina delegations switched sides, and the New York delegation decided to abstain. A few delegates—including the notable patriot leaders John Dickinson and Robert Morris of Pennsylvania—clung to the hope of maintaining loyal ties to the crown. But when Congress voted on the resolution for independence on July 2, 1776, all voting delegations approved it. After further tinkering with the wording, Congress officially adopted the **Declaration of Independence** on July 4, 1776.

Congress intended the declaration to be a justification for America's secession from the British Empire. Jefferson later maintained that he did not write any more than what everyone was thinking. The political theory that lies behind the declaration is known as the **contract theory of government**. Developed by the late-seventeenth-century English philosopher John Locke and others, the contract theory maintains that legitimate government rests on an agreement between the people and their rulers. The people are bound to obey their rulers only so long as the rulers offer them protection. Jefferson's prose, however, transformed what might have been a bland, legalistic rehash of the contract theory into one of history's great statements of human rights.

The Declaration of Independence consists of a magnificently stated opening assumption, two premises, and a powerful conclusion. The opening assumption is that all men are created equal, that they therefore have equal rights, and that they can neither give up these rights nor allow them to be taken away.

Thomas Jefferson, author of the Declaration of Independence and future president of the United States. Mather Brown, an American artist living in England, painted this picture of Jefferson for John Adams while the two men were in London on diplomatic missions in 1786. A companion portrait of Adams that Jefferson ordered for himself also survives. Brown's sensitive portrait of a thoughtful Jefferson is the earliest known likeness of him.

The first premise—that people establish governments to protect their fundamental rights to life, liberty, and property—is a restatement of contract theory. (With a wonderful flourish reflecting the Enlightenment's optimism about human potential, Jefferson changed "property" to "the pursuit of happiness.") The second premise is a long list of charges meant to prove that George III had failed to defend his American subjects' rights. This indictment, the heart of the declaration, justified the Americans' rejection of their hitherto legitimate ruler. Then followed the dramatic conclusion: that Americans could rightfully overthrow King George's rule and replace it with something more satisfactory to them.

Historians have spilled oceans of ink debating Jefferson's use of the expression "all men." Almost certainly he was thinking in the abstract and meant "humanity in general." In practice, of course, many people were excluded from full participation in eighteenth-century American society. Women had no formal political rights and limited legal rights. Propertyless white and free black men had similarly restricted rights, and slaves enjoyed no rights at all. (Although himself a slaveowner, Jefferson was deeply troubled by American slavery. He had wanted to include a denunciation of the slave trade among the charges against George III in the Declaration of Independence, but Congress took it out, believing that to blame the king for this inhumane business would appear hypocritical.) But if the words "all men are created equal" had limited practical meaning in 1776, they have ever since confronted Americans with a moral challenge to make good on them.

Republicanism

Americans reacted to news of the Declaration of Independence with mixed emotions. There was rejoicing as orators read the declaration to great crowds. Soldiers fired noisy salutes, and candles lit up the

This British engraving published in 1783 depicts one of the many public readings of the Declaration of Independence that occurred throughout the United States during the weeks following its adoption by the Second Continental Congress on July 4, 1776.

windows of public buildings at night. But even many who favored independence worried about how Americans would govern themselves. Most Whigs, animated by the political ideology known as **republicanism**, thought a republican government was best suited to American society.

John Adams once complained that republicanism was too shadowy a concept to define, and indeed it was a complex, changing body of ideas, values, and assumptions. Closely related to country (New Whig) ideology, republicanism was derived from the political ideas of classical antiquity, Renaissance Europe, and early modern England. It held that self-government—either directly by the citizens of a country or indirectly by their elected representatives—provided a more reliable foundation for the good society and individual freedom than rule by kings. Thus drawing on contract theory, as in the Declaration of Independence, republicanism called for government by consent of the governed. Drawing on country ideology, it was suspicious of excessively centralized government and insistent on the need for virtuous, public-spirited citizenry. The benefits of monarchy depended on the variable abilities of monarchs; the character of republican government depended on the virtue of the people. Republicanism therefore helped give the American Revolution a moral dimension.

But other than a state that was not ruled by a hereditary king, what was a republic? And what were the chances that one would survive? Every educated person knew, of course, that ancient Rome and Athens had been republics. Classical political theory, beginning with the ancient Greek thinkers Plato and Aristotle, had insisted that republics could endure only as long as their citizens remained virtuous and self-sacrificing. Once individual citizens, greedy for wealth and power, began fighting among themselves, a republic would certainly collapse. A failed republic would give way to the despotism of one-man rule or to oligarchy—rule by a narrow clique of rich men—or, worst of all, to the "mob rule" of ignorant and violent common people. Europe's three surviving republics in the eighteenth century—the Netherlands, Switzerland, and Venice—seemed to bear out this dismal picture. All were rather corrupt and uninspiring societies, and none of them was at all democratic.

But Americans had at hand a more recent example of a republic than ancient Athens or Rome, one more closely linked to their own history than the republics of eighteenth-century Europe. During the English Civil War of the mid-seventeenth century, English Puritans had for a time replaced the monarchy with a republican "Commonwealth," dedicated to advancing the "common weal," or common good. Most eighteenth-century Americans thought of the Puritan Commonwealth as a misguided product of fanaticism that had ended in a military dictatorship. However, some New Englanders, spiritual descendants of the Puritans, considered the Commonwealth to have been a noble experiment. To them, the American Revolution offered another chance to establish a republic of the godly.

"When the mere Politician weighs the Danger or Safety of his Country," warned one clergyman, "he computes them in Proportion to its Fortresses, Arms, Money, Provisions, Numbers of Fighting Men, and its Enemies." But, the clergyman continued, the "Christian Patriot" calculates them "by its Numbers of Sinful or praying People, and its Degrees of Holiness or Vice." Such language recalled the Great Awakening; it reached beyond the upper classes who had been directing resistance to the British and mobilized ordinary people for what their ministers repeatedly assured them was a just war against sin and despotism. Out of this fusion of republican theory (with which only the educated were familiar) and the religious heritage that all Americans understood, a common belief developed that Americans must have "resolution enough to forego Self gratification" and be willing to stake their all "upon the prospect of Securing freedom and happiness to future Generations."

The Combatants

At the outset of the American Revolution, republican fervor produced a spontaneous eruption of patriotism that to skeptical foreign observers looked like religious fanaticism. The experience of Lancaster, Pennsylvania, where more men responded to a call for volunteers than were then needed, leaving disappointed men behind, was shared elsewhere. But this enthusiastic flocking to the colors eventually waned, and in any case, its results were often unsatisfactory.

Republican theory mistrusted professional armies as the instruments of tyrants. A free people, republicans insisted, relied for defense on their own patriotism. When individual or community rights were in danger, free men should grab their muskets from over the fireplace, assemble as the local militia, take care of the problem, and go home (see "American Views: A British Woman Observes an American Militia Exercise in 1775"). But militiamen, as one American general observed, had trouble coping with "the shocking scenes of war" because they were not "steeled by habit or fortified by military pride." In real battles, they often proved unreliable. Americans

American Views

A British Woman Observes an American Militia Exercise in 1775

The following description of North Carolinians preparing for war in 1775 comes from the travel journal of Janet Schaw, a Scotswoman visiting her brother Robert in America. Robert Schaw, although he was appointed a colonel in the North Carolina militia, disapproved of the American cause and eventually refused to take the oath of allegiance to the new state government. His wife, in contrast, according to Janet Schaw, was "so rooted an American, that she detests every thing that is European." Early in June 1775 Janet Schaw saw the militia train outside of Wilmington under their commander, Robert Howe, who later became a major general in the Continental Army. She returned to Scotland in late 1775.

❖ **What does this passage suggest about Janet Schaw's own views of the American cause?**

❖ **How accurately do you think it reflects the effectiveness of milita forces?**

❖ **What does it suggest about the relationship between patriots and loyalists?**

We came down in the morning in time for the review, which the heat made as terrible to the spectators as to the soldiers, or what you please to call them. They had certainly fainted under it, had not the constant draughts of grog supported them. Their exercise was that of bush-fighting, but it appeared so confused and so perfectly different from any thing I ever saw, I cannot say whether they performed it well or not; but this I know that they were heated with rum till capable of committing the most shocking outrages. We stood in the balcony of Doctor Cobham's [a future loyalist] house and they were reviewed on a field mostly covered with what are called here scrubby oaks which are only a little better than brushwood. They at last however assembled on the plain field, and I must really laugh while I recollect their figures: 2000 men in their shirts and trousers, preceded by a very ill beat-drum and a fiddler, who was also in his shirt with a long sword and a cue at his hair, who played with all his might. They made indeed a most unmartial appearance. But the worst figure there can shoot from behind a bush and kill even a General Wolfe.

Before the review was over, I hear a cry of tar and feather. I was ready to faint at the idea of this dreadful operation. I would have gladly quitted the balcony, but was so much afraid the Victim was one of my friends, that I was not able to move; and he indeed proved to be one, tho' in a humble station. For it was Mr. Neilson's [a loyalist] poor English groom. You can hardly conceive what I felt when I saw him dragged forward, poor devil, frighted out of his wits. However at the request of some of the officers, who had been Neilson's friends, his punishment was changed into that of mounting on a table and begging pardon for having smiled at the regt. He was then drummed and fiddled out of the town, with a strict prohibition of ever being seen in it again.

Source: [Janet Schaw], Journal of a Lady of Quality; Being the Narrative of a Journey from Scotland to the West Indies, North Carolina, and Portugal, in the Years 1774 to 1776, *ed. Evangeline Walker Andrews in Collaboration with Charles McLean Andrews (1923). Yale University Press.*

therefore faced a hard choice: Develop a professional army, or lose the war. In the end, they did what they had to do. While state militias continued to offer support, it was the disciplined forces of the Continental Army that won the crucial battles. To be sure, when the war was over, Americans tried to forget about their professional troops; in American mythology, it was the "embattled farmers"—Minute Men at Lexington and Concord, swamp fighters in the South—who had won independence. But long before the struggle was over, toughened Continental soldiers knew better.

Professional Soldiers

Drawing on their colonial experience and on republican theory, the new state governments first tried to meet their military needs by relying on the militia and by creating new units based on short-term enlistments. Officers, particularly in the North, were often elected, and their positions depended on personal popularity. As a result, their orders sometimes sounded more like requests than commands, and rules were lax. Discipline became a major problem in both the militia and the new state units, and often volunteers had barely received basic training before their term of duty ended and they returned home.

Washington tightened things up in the new Continental Army. Eventually, he prevailed on Congress to adopt stricter regulations and to require enlistments for three years or the duration of the war. Although he used militia effectively, his consistent aim was to turn the Continental Army into a disciplined force that could defeat the British in the large engagements of massed troops characteristic of eighteenth-century European warfare. Guerrilla fighters shooting from behind trees like "savages" had their place in the American war effort, but they could never win a decisive, formal battle. And only such a "civilized" victory would impress the other European powers and establish the legitimacy of the United States.

Many soldiers of fortune, as well as a few idealists, offered their services to American representatives in Europe. So many came to the United States that both Washington and Congress soon regarded most of them as nuisances. But several proved especially valuable in helping Washington forge a professional army. France's 19-year-old Marquis de Lafayette was one of the youngest, wealthiest, and most idealistic. Two Poles, Tadeusz Kosciuszko, an engineer, and Kazimierz Pulaski, a cavalry commander mortally wounded at the Battle of Savannah in 1779, also rendered good service. Johann Kalb, a bogus baron from Germany, became a general and died heroically at Camden, South Carolina, in 1780. Most useful of all, probably, was Baron von Steuben. His title, too, was new, but he had experience in the Prussian army, continental Europe's best. He also knew how to get along with American soldiers by explaining the reasons for his orders. He became the Continental Army's drillmaster, and thanks partly to him, Washington's troops increasingly came to resemble their disciplined European counterparts.

The enemy British troopers—and the nearly thirty thousand German mercenaries (Americans called them "Hessians") whom the British government also employed—offered Americans the clearest model of a professional army. British regulars were not (as Americans, then and later, assumed) the "dregs of society." Most enlisted men did come from the lower classes and from economically depressed areas, but many also had skills. British officers usually came from wealthy families or had simply purchased their commissions. Only in rare cases did a man rise from the enlisted ranks to commissioned officer status.

Most British troops carried the "Brown Bess" musket. With bayonet attached, it was almost 6 feet long and weighed over 16 pounds. It fired a lead ball slightly more than 1/2 inch in diameter, which might hit its target at up to 100 yards. Skilled troops could get off more than two rounds per minute under combat conditions. In battle, soldiers usually stood close together in lines three deep. They were expected to withstand bombardment without flinching, fire on command in volleys, charge with the bayonet, and use their heavy musket stock (the wooden end) to crush the skulls of any wounded enemy they strode over.

Military life was tough. On the march, seasoned troops carrying 60-pound packs normally covered about 15 miles a day but could go 30 miles in a "forced" march. In most weather conditions, they wore heavy woolen uniforms dyed bright red for visibility on smoke-filled battlefields (hence their nickname "Redcoats"). In their barracks, British soldiers doubled up in a bed slightly over 4 feet wide; in the field, they were often wet, crawling with lice, and hungry. Under the best conditions, they ate mainly beef or salt pork and bread. They were frequently undernourished, however, and many more died of disease than of injury in battle. Medical care was, by modern standards, primitive. Treatments for illness included bleeding and purging (induced vomiting and diarrhea). Serious arm or leg wounds usually meant amputation, without antiseptics or anesthetics. But unless a man was extraordinarily lucky, a body wound or amputation usually proved fatal. If loss of blood or infection did not kill him immediately, tetanus probably would later.

Severe discipline held soldiers in line. Striking an officer or deserting could bring death; lesser offenses usually incurred a beating. Several hundred lashes, "well laid on" with the notorious cat-o'-nine-tails (a whip with multiple cords, each ending in a nasty little knot or a metal ball), were not uncommon.

Soldiers amused themselves with gambling (despite regulations against it) and drinking. As one foreign officer serving with the British lamented, America was a terrible country where one drank "to get warm, or to get cool, or . . . because you get no letters." Perhaps two-thirds of the Redcoats were illiterate, and they all suffered from loneliness and boredom. Camaraderie and a legendary loyalty to their regiments sustained them.

After the winter of 1777–1778, conditions in the Continental Army came to resemble those of the British army. Like British regulars, American recruits tended to be low on the social scale. They included young men without land, indentured servants, some criminals and vagrants—in short, men who lacked better prospects. The chances for talented enlisted men to win an officer's commission were greater in the Continental Army than the British army. As a German prisoner of war observed, American troops tended to be taller than their British counterparts. And despite their ragged uniforms, they carried themselves like soldiers. Indeed, Continental soldiers frequently had little more than "their ragged shirt flaps to cover their nakedness," and more than once their bare marching feet left bloody tracks in the snow.

Both British and American authorities had trouble supplying their troops. Both sides suffered from bureaucratic inefficiencies, but the fundamental problems of each were different. The British had plenty of hard-coin money with a stable value, which many American merchants and farmers were happy to take in payment for supplies. But the British had to rely mostly on supplies shipped to them from the British Isles. The Continental Army, in contrast, had to pay for supplies in paper money, both Continental dollars and state-issued currency, whose value sank steadily as the war progressed. After 1780, the burden of provisioning the Continental Army fell on the states, which did little better than Congress had done. Unable to obtain sufficient supplies, the army sometimes provoked resentment by threatening to seize them by force. This in turn increased the public's republican distrust of its own professional army.

Feeling themselves outcasts from an uncaring society, the professional soldiers of the Continental Army developed a community of their own. The soldiers were "as strict a band of brotherhood as Masons," one later wrote, and their spirit kept them together in the face of misery. They groused, to be sure—sometimes alarmingly. In May 1780, Connecticut troops at Washington's camp in Morristown, New Jersey, staged a brief mutiny. A more serious mutiny erupted on January 1, 1781, when armed units from Pennsylvania stationed in New Jersey marched to Philadelphia demanding their arrears in pay. The Pennsylvania Executive Council met part of the soldiers' demands, but some of the men left the service. Washington ordered subsequent mutinies by New Jersey and Pennsylvania troops suppressed by force.

Occasionally, American officers let their disgruntlement get out of hand. The most notorious such case was that of Benedict Arnold, a general who compiled a distinguished record during the first three years of the war but then came to feel himself shabbily treated by Congress and his superiors. Seeking better rewards for his abilities, he offered to surrender the strategic fort at West Point (which he commanded) to the enemy. Before he could act, however, his plot was discovered, and he fled to the British, serving with them until the end of the war. Among Americans, his name became a synonym for traitor.

What was perhaps the most serious expression of army discontent—one that threatened the future of republican institutions and civilian government in the United Sates—occurred in March 1783, after the fighting was over. At the time, Washington's troops were stationed near Newburgh, New York, waiting to disband and for Congress to decide how to settle up with them. During the war, Congress had promised officers a pension of half pay for life (the custom in Great Britain), but now many veterans demanded instead full pay for six years. When Congress failed to grant real assurances that any pay would be forthcoming, hotheaded young officers called a meeting that could have led to an armed uprising and military coup. General Washington, who had scrupulously deferred to civilian authority throughout the war, asked permission to address the gathering and, in a dramatic speech, subtly warned the men of all that they might lose by insubordination. A military coup would "open the flood Gates of Civil discord" and "deluge" the nation in blood; loyalty now, he said, would be "one more distinguished proof" of their patriotism. With the fate of the Revolution and the honor of the army hanging in the balance, the movement collapsed. Officers and politicians behind the "conspiracy" were probably only bluffing, using the threat of a discontented army to frighten the states into granting Congress the power (which it then lacked) to levy taxes so it would have the

Ye Foil'd, Ye Baffled Brittons This Behold
Nor longer urge your Pardons,Threats or Gold;
See in each virtuous face Patr'otic Zeal
To fave their Country and Promote its Weal
Difdaining Bribes to wound a righteous Caufe
While ANDRE falls a victim to the Laws.

Mezzotint, 1780–1800. Size: H. 7⅜ in., W. 9¾ in. Courtesy, Winterthur Museum.

This print Ye Foil'd, Ye Baffled Brittons, shows the capture of Major John Andre, the British agent who acted as the go-between for British authorities and the American General Benedict Arnold, who planned to turn over the American fortress at West Point to them. Probably published in Salem, Massachusetts, this print may have been the first depiction of events surrounding Arnold's shocking defection. The three militiamen who captured Andre, who was later hanged as a spy, reportedly refused a bribe for his release. The strange facial expressions of all the participants were probably the artist's crude attempt to indicate surprise.

funds to pay the army. If so, they may not have realized the potential harm they threatened. In any case, the Continental Army thereafter disbanded without further serious incidents.

Women in the Contending Armies

Women accompanied many units on both sides, as was common in eighteenth-century warfare. A few were prostitutes. Some were officers' wives or mistresses, but most were the married or common-law consorts of ordinary soldiers. These women "camp followers" cooked and washed for the troops, occasionally helped load artillery, and provided most of the nursing care. A certain number in a company were subject to military orders and were authorized to draw rations and pay.

The role of these women found its way into American folklore in the legend of Molly Pitcher (perhaps Mary Ludwig Hays, the wife of a Continental artillery sergeant), who heroically carried water to gunners to cool them and their overheated guns at the Battle of Monmouth Court House in 1778. Numberless, nameless other women accompanying the troops also found themselves under fire. A British officer fighting in New York, for example, reported discovering three American bodies, one a woman with cartridges in her hands. A few women even managed to serve in the Continental Army's ranks. One was discharged only when she was hospitalized for illness and her sex was discovered.

Black and Native American Participation in the War

Early in the war, some royal officials sought to recruit black slaves into the loyalist forces with a promise of freedom. Such was the case with Lord Dunmore, for example, whose black and white troops met disaster at Great Bridge in some of the earliest fighting of the war. Unfortunately for the British, these offers proved counterproductive, frightening and enraging potentially loyalist slaveowners and driving them to the Whig side. Thus it was not until June 30, 1779, that the British commander in chief, Sir Henry Clinton, promised to allow slaves who fled from rebel owners to join the royal troops to "follow . . . any Occupation" they wished. Hedged as this promise of freedom was, news of it spread quickly among the slave communities, and late in the war enough black people flocked to the British army in South Carolina and Georgia to make feeding and housing them a serious problem.

The British shared the racial prejudices of many Americans, however, and, despite their efforts to recruit African Americans, were reluctant to arm them. Instead, the British put most of the ex-slaves to work as agricultural or construction workers (many of the free and enslaved blacks accompanying American troops were similarly employed). A few relatively well equipped black British dragoons (mounted troops), however, saw some combat in South Carolina, much to the horror of local Whigs. Some of these troops formed the nucleus of the postwar First and Second British West India Regiments.

Approximately five thousand African Americans fought against the British and for American independence, hundreds of them in the Continental Army. Many were freemen from Massachusetts and Rhode Island. Several free black men served among the defenders at Bunker Hill, and at least one distinguished himself sufficiently for his commander to commend him as "an experienced officer as well as an excellent soldier."

Farther south, a young Carolina patriot repeatedly but vainly tried to convince the South Carolina assembly to raise and arm black troops. (On the contrary, the legislature eventually voted to give slaves confiscated from loyalists to white volunteers as a reward for their service in the state regiments.) It is therefore scarcely surprising that, as one Whig put it, many black people were "a little Toryfied," especially in the South.

Many Indians also favored the British. To Native Americans, the key issue of the American Revolution, as well as in most disputes with white settlers, was simple. As a Cherokee chief told Virginians, "Remember that *the difference is about our land.*" British Indian agents had frequently protected Native Americans against advancing settlers, and Native Americans generally feared that an American victory would sweep away any restraint on white settlers' westward movement. Many Indian peoples, including the Cherokees, therefore decided that it was in their interest to back the British. Their aid mainly took the form of attacks on white frontier settlements. Thus in one notorious incident, an Indian attack in the Hudson River Valley resulted in the mistaken scalping of Jane McCrae, the fiancée of a British officer. Whig propagandists exploited this tragedy to the fullest. Because they could not control the Indians, the British regarded their native allies as a liability as well as an asset and seldom made unrestricted use of them.

Most Native Americans, however, tried at first to remain neutral, and some important groups aided the Americans. Pulled and pushed by both sides, the Iroquois Confederation split. The Mohawks and most of the other Iroquois nations, under the leadership of Thayendanegea—known as Joseph Brant to the English and Americans—sided with the British. The Oneidas and the Tuscaroras, however, joined the Americans. Some small Indian groups, like the Catawbas of South Carolina, who lived in the midst of white settlements, also cooperated with the Americans.

This depiction of the death of Jane McCrea with Esopus (now Kingston, New York) burning in the background was part of a satirical cartoon published in London in 1778 to criticize the British conduct of the war. Jane McCrea, who was tomahawked by Indian allies of the British during General Burgoyne's invasion of the Hudson River Valley, was to be married to a British officer. A force sent northward up the Hudson River burned Esopus but failed to relieve Burgoyne, who surrendered at Saratoga.

The War in the North, 1776–1777

The Revolutionary War can be divided into three phases. In the first, from the outbreak of fighting in 1775 to 1778, most of the important battles took place in New England, New York, New Jersey, and Pennsylvania. During these years, the Americans faced the British alone. But in 1778, France entered the war on the American side, opening the second phase of the war. Fighting in the second phase would rage from 1778 to 1781 mainly in the South, at sea, and on the western frontier. The third phase of the war, from late 1781 to 1783, saw little actual fighting. With American victory assured, attention shifted to the diplomatic maneuvering leading up to the Treaty of Paris (1783), which ended the war and recognized American independence.

The British Army Hesitates

During the first phase of the war, the British concentrated on subduing New England, the hotbed of what they saw as "rebellious principles." Replacing General Gage, the government appointed Sir William Howe as commander in chief of British forces and his brother, Richard Howe, as admiral of the naval forces in North American waters. New York City had been the headquarters of the British army during the late colonial period, and the Howes decided to make it their base of operations. To counter this move, Washington had moved his forces to New York in the spring of 1776. In August 1776, the Howes landed troops on Long Island and in the **Battle of Brooklyn Heights** quickly drove the American forces deployed there from Brooklyn Heights and back to Manhattan Island (see Map 6-3).

Following instructions to negotiate peace as well as wage war, Richard Howe then met with three envoys from Congress on Staten Island on September 11, 1776. The Howes were prepared to offer fairly generous terms but could not grant independence. The Americans would accept nothing less. So despite a fine meal of cold meat and wine, the meeting produced no substantive negotiations.

In the ensuing weeks, British forces overwhelmed Washington's forces, driving them out of Manhattan and then, moving north, clearing them from the area around the city at the **Battle of White Plains**. But the Howes were hesitant to deal a crushing blow, and the Americans were able to retreat across New Jersey into Pennsylvania. The American cause seemed lost, however; Congress fled from Philadelphia to Baltimore, and the Continental Army almost melted away. The enlistments for most of his troops expired on January 1, and Washington realized that without a success, he would soon have no army left.

On Christmas night, he led his forces back across the icy Delaware from Pennsylvania and, in the **Battle of Trenton**, launched an unorthodox surprise attack on a garrison of Hessian mercenaries at Trenton, New Jersey, on the morning of December 26. Still in the midst of their Christmas celebrations, the Hessians quickly surrendered. A week later, in the **Battle of Princeton**, Washington overwhelmed a British force at Princeton, New Jersey. Thereafter, Washington withdrew to winter quarters in Morristown, New Jersey, and the Howes made no further effort to pursue him. Both sides suspended operations until the spring.

"These are the times that try men's souls." So wrote Tom Paine—briefly a volunteer in the Continental Army—of these difficult months. "The summer soldier and the sunshine patriot will, in this crisis, shrink from the service of his country; but he that stands it NOW, deserves the love and thanks of man and woman."

The victories at Trenton and Princeton boosted morale and saved the American cause. But why did the Howes not annihilate the Continental Army while they had the chance? Perhaps, as a favorite Whig ditty had it, it was because Sir William Howe was "snug" abed with his mistress in New York. More significantly, the Howe brothers themselves were not entirely in favor of the war. Seeking to restore peace as well as end the rebellion, they wanted to regain loyal subjects, not alienate them. But if they had inflicted a crushing defeat on the Americans, they would have risked making them permanent enemies of British rule. In short, the British had sound political reasons for not beating the Americans too thoroughly. By the time it later became apparent that this cautious strategy was not working and the Howes were replaced with more aggressive commanders, the British had lost their best chance to win the war.

The Year of the Hangman

Contemporaries called 1777 the Year of the Hangman because the triple sevens suggested a row of gallows. Living up to its ominous name, it was indeed a crucial year for the American cause.

The British began the year by mounting a major effort to end the rebellion. Their strategy was to send a force south from Canada down the

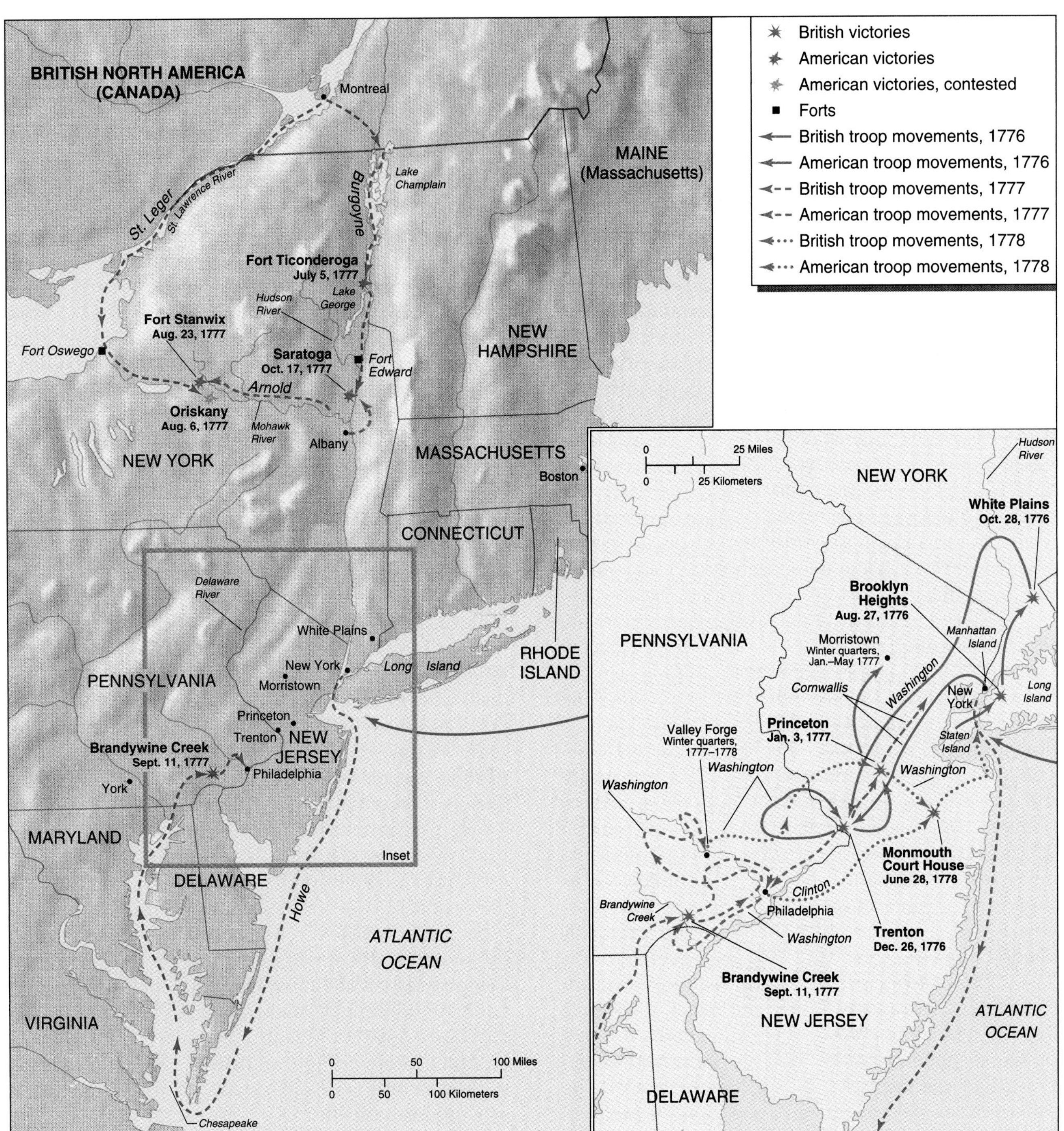

Map 6-3 The War in the North, 1776–1777
Most of the fighting between the British and Americans during the first part of the war occurred in the North, partly because British authorities assumed that the New England colonies were the most rebellious.

Hudson River to link up with the Howes in New York City, separate New England from the rest of the states, and then crush the rebellion in that most recalcitrant region. Unfortunately, there was no effort to coordinate strategy between the forces advancing from Canada and the forces under the command of the Howes in New York. Thus in the end, poorly planned, poorly executed, and unsupported from the South, the campaign ended in disaster for the British.

Some five thousand Redcoats and three thousand German mercenaries assembled in Canada during the winter of 1776–1777. Ravaged by disease, the troops were unable to bury their dead until the frozen ground thawed in the spring. (To amuse himself, the officer in charge of the morgue arranged the dead around a room in lifelike poses, which did nothing to calm the nerves of survivors.) Under the command of the jaunty, high-living, and popular "Gentleman Johnny" Burgoyne, the army finally set off in June with 1,500 horses hauling its heavy artillery and ponderous supply train. A second, smaller column, supported by an Indian force under Joseph Brant, set out to the west to capture an American fort near Oriskany, New York, and then join up with Burgoyne's main force.

Crossing Lake Champlain, Burgoyne's army made a splendid spectacle. Indians in lightly bobbing canoes led the way, followed by row after row of boats filled with uniformed regulars resplendent in the bright sunshine. On July 5, Burgoyne's army recaptured Fort Ticonderoga, but success eluded him after that.

Trouble began as the troops started moving overland through the woods at the southern end of the lake. Forced to clear away huge trees in its path felled by American axmen, the army crawled along at only 2 or 3 miles a day. Early in August, the column under Colonel Barry St. Leger that had been sent west from the Montreal area failed to capture the American fort near Oriskany and turned back to Canada. Burgoyne's Indian allies under Joseph Brant likewise went home. Promised reinforcements never arrived. Ten days later, a Whig militia force wiped out a force of eight hundred men that Burgoyne had sent into Vermont to round up badly needed horses.

By October 1777, Burgoyne's army was down to less than six thousand men and facing disaster. A force of nearly three thousand Continentals and nine thousand militia, commanded by General Horatio Gates, had now assembled to confront the British. The Americans exerted relentless pressure on the harassed and dispirited invaders. Unable to break through the American lines, Burgoyne surrendered to Gates following the **Battle of Saratoga** on October 17, 1777.

Burgoyne's defeat was a stunning reversal for the British. It also gave the American cause a significant boost in the eyes of foreign observers. It would prove an important factor in convincing the French, in particular, eager for a way to strike back at their old enemy, the British, to recognize America as an ally and join the fighting on the American side.

While Burgoyne was making his way to disaster, William Howe, rather than moving north to support him, was making plans to destroy Washington's army and capture Philadelphia. In July 1777, Howe's troops sailed from New York to Chesapeake Bay and from there marched on Philadelphia from the south. They met Washington's army on the banks of **Brandywine Creek**, near the Pennsylvania–Delaware border. An American teenager who fought for the first time that day recalled that some men stiffened their courage by drinking a concoction of liquor and gunpowder. The young man himself could not stomach it, but it may have worked for some of his companions. They put up a good fight before giving way with a loss of 1,200 killed or captured (twice as many as the British).

Howe occupied Philadelphia, and his men settled down in comfortable winter quarters. Congress fled to York, Pennsylvania, and the Continental Army established its own winter camp outside Philadelphia, at **Valley Forge**. Here Washington was joined by his wife, Martha, in a small stone farmhouse, surrounded by the log huts that his men built for themselves.

The Continental Army's miserable winter at Valley Forge has become legendary in American history. Suffering from cold, disease, and starvation, as many as 2,500 soldiers died. Meanwhile, some Congressmen and a few unhappy officers intrigued unsuccessfully to replace Washington with Gates as commander in chief. Yet despite the suffering of the troops, the Continental Army managed, over the course of the winter, to transform itself into a disciplined professional army. Under the watchful eye of General von Steuben, the soldiers drilled endlessly. Just before the encampment broke up in the spring, they put on an impressive demonstration of their new skills, including a precisely timed wave of massed musket volleys. Pleased observers felt that Washington at last had an army capable of meeting the British on equal terms. With the coming of spring, American prospects improved dramatically.

The War Widens, 1778–1781

Since late 1776, Benjamin Franklin and a team of American diplomats had been in Paris negotiating French support for the patriot cause. In the winter of 1777–1778, aware that a Franco-American alliance was close, Parliament belatedly tried to end the rebellion by giving the Americans everything they wanted except independence itself. A peace commission sailed to America with authorization to grant the former colonies full autonomy, including the exclusive right to tax themselves, in return for a resumption of allegiance to the crown. But France and the United States concluded an alliance on February 6, 1778, and news of it reached America before the British commission arrived. Seeing independence within reach, Congress refused to negotiate.

Foreign intervention would transform the American Revolution into a virtual world war, engaging British forces in heavy fighting not only in North America but also in the West Indies and India. In the end, had it not been for French assistance, the American side probably would not have won the clear-cut victory it did.

The United States Gains an Ally

If the American victory at Saratoga had persuaded the French that the United States had a viable future, Washington's defeat at Brandywine Creek suggested it was a fragile one. Hoping to get even with their old enemy, Britain, the French had already been secretly supplying some aid to the United States. They now became convinced that they needed to act quickly lest further reverses force the Americans to agree to a reconciliation with Britain. The agreements they signed with the United States included both a commercial treaty and a military alliance. Both sides promised to fight together until Britain recognized the independence of the United States, and France pledged not to seek the return of lands in North America.

French entry into the war was the first step in the consolidation of a formidable alliance of European powers eager to see Britain humbled and to gain trading rights in the former British colonies. In turn, France persuaded Spain to declare war on Britain in June 1779. Unlike France, Spain never recognized the independence of the United States and would give it only minimal financial aid. Spain did, however, contribute important logistical support. Much of the salt used to preserve American soldiers' provisions came from Spanish possessions. American agents also purchased other supplies in Spanish New Orleans, and American privateers used New Orleans as a base. More important, the Spanish fleet augmented the naval power of the countries arrayed against Great Britain.

Meanwhile, Catherine the Great of Russia suggested that European powers form a League of Armed Neutrality to protect their trade with the United States and other warring countries against British interference. Denmark and Sweden soon joined; Austria, the Netherlands, Portugal, Prussia, and Sicily eventually followed. Britain, however, quickly went to war with Holland, ostensibly over another issue (to avoid war with the League), but really to cut off Dutch trade with the United States.

Great Britain thus found itself nearly completely isolated and even, briefly, threatened with invasion. In the spring of 1779, a joint Franco-Spanish fleet tried to ferry thousands of French troops across the English Channel but abandoned the effort after weeks at sea. These threats did not frighten the British leaders into suing for peace. On the contrary, they inspired a wave of patriotism that swelled enlistments in the armed forces. But facing challenges on a worldwide scale, British officials were forced to make several important changes in policy and strategy.

Accordingly, as early in the spring of 1778, the British replaced the Howes with a tough new commander, Sir Henry Clinton, instructing him to detach some of his troops to attack the French West Indies. To replace them, Clinton sought closer cooperation with Britain's Indian and loyalist allies. Knowing he now faced a serious French threat, Clinton began consolidating his forces. He evacuated Philadelphia and pulled his troops slowly back across New Jersey to New York.

On June 28, 1778, Washington caught up with the British and engaged them at the **Battle of Monmouth Court House**. The day was hot and the battle hard-fought. For a while, it looked as if the now well-trained Americans might win, but a mix-up in orders cost Washington the victory. This inconclusive battle proved to be the last major engagement in the North for the rest of the war. Clinton withdrew to New York, and Continental troops occupied the hills along the Hudson Valley north of the city. The war shifted to other fronts.

Fighting on the Frontier and at Sea

Native Americans called Kentucky "a dark and bloody ground," a designation that took on added meaning when Indians began raiding the territory in 1777 on British instructions. The nerve center for coordinating these attacks was the British post of Detroit, and the Americans accordingly made plans to capture it. Two expeditions from Pittsburgh in 1778 failed completely. A third, under Virginian George Rogers Clark, although it never reached Detroit, was more successful (see Map 6-4). In July 1778 Clark's force of 175 frontiersmen captured three key British settlements in the Mississippi Valley: Kaskaskia, Cahokia, and Vincennes. These successes may have strengthened American claims to the West at the end of the war.

Blood also ran on the Pennsylvania and upstate New York frontiers. In the summer of 1778, a British force of one hundred loyalists and five hundred Indians struck settlers in north-central Pennsylvania's Wyoming Valley. After the Americans' Forty Fort surrendered on July 4, raiders killed the wounded and fleeing defenders. A similar mix of attackers in November 1778 burned farmsteads and slaughtered civilians at Cherry Valley, New York. Both raids became the stuff of legends and stimulated equally savage reprisals against the Indians. Congress authorized an expedition against the Iroquois, and in the late summer of 1779, more than four thousand Continental soldiers and state militia swept through the Finger Lakes region of New York, destroying forty-one Indian villages.

Anglo-American clashes at sea had begun in 1775, shortly after the Battles of Lexington and Concord, and would continue until the end of the war as Americans struggled to break the British navy's blockade. Great Britain was the preeminent sea power of the age, and the United States never came close to matching it, in either the number or the size of its ships. But Congress did its best to challenge the British at sea. In 1775, it authorized the construction of thirteen frigates—medium-sized, relatively fast ships, mounting thirty-two guns—as well as the purchase of several merchant vessels for conversion to warships. In contrast, the Royal Navy in 1779 had more than a hundred large and heavily armed "ships of the line." The Americans therefore engaged in what was essentially a guerrilla war at sea. Their naval flag, appropriately, pictured a rattlesnake and bore the motto "Don't Tread on Me."

The country's first naval hero, Scottish-born John Paul Jones, was primarily a hit-and-run

Map 6-4 The War on the Frontier, 1778–1779

Significant battles in the Mississippi Valley and the frontiers of the seaboard states added to the ferocity of the fighting and strengthened some American claims to western lands.

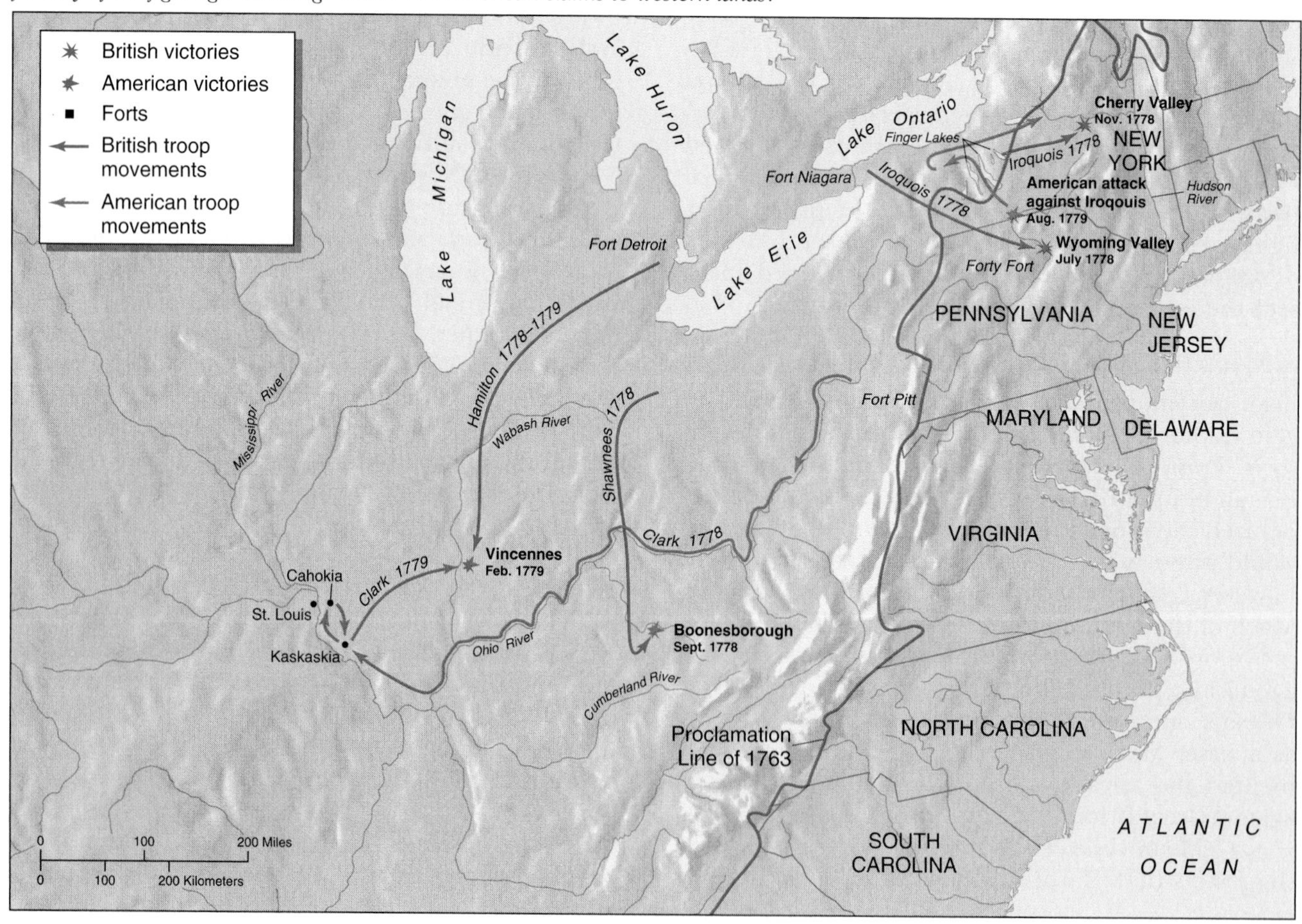

raider. Originally named only John Paul, he had gone to sea at age 12. He took the name Jones as an alias after he killed a fellow sailor during a mutiny. In the colonies by chance when the war broke out, this adventurer offered his services to Congress. As commander of the new frigate *Ranger*, it was Jones who brought news of the American victory at Saratoga to France in early 1777. After delivering the news—which helped Franklin clinch the alliance with France—Jones raided the British coast, inspiring local panic.

Franklin helped secure Jones an old French merchant ship, which he outfitted for war and renamed the *Bon Homme Richard* in honor of Franklin's famous *Poor Richard's Almanac*. After capturing seventeen enemy vessels, he encountered the formidable H.M.S. *Serapis* in the North Sea on September 23, 1779. Completely outgunned, Jones brought the *Bon Homme Richard* close enough to make his small arms fire more effective. Asked by the British if he was surrendering, Jones gave the legendary reply, "I have not yet begun to fight." Lashing the two ships together, Jones and his men battled the crew of the *Serapis* for more than four hours, much of it by moonlight. Finally, the *Serapis* surrendered. Jones's crew took possession of the British vessel and left the crippled *Bon Homme Richard* to sink.

This engraving, published in London in 1779, shows an apocryphal incident during the battle in which John Paul Jones's ship Bon Homme Richard *defeated the British* Serapis. *During the fighting, Jones supposedly shot an American sailor who attempted to lower the ship's flag as a sign of surrender; actually Jones only knocked him down with a pistol. Legend (and the artist) may have confused this incident with another earlier one—while Jones was still a Scotsman (note the bonnet)—in which Jones did kill a mutineer.*

"Paul Jones Shooting a Sailor." Color engraving from the Olds Collection #366, no negative number. Collection of The New-York Historical Society.

Congress and the individual states supplemented America's naval forces by commissioning individual sea captains to outfit their merchant vessels with guns and act as privateers. In effect legalized pirates, these privateers preyed on British shipping. They sold the goods they seized and divided the proceeds among their crews according to rank. The crews of captured vessels became prisoners of war. Successful privateering could bring wealth but required stealth and speed. One particularly fast vessel cruised off New York towing a buoy to make itself look like a lumbering merchantman under full sail. Once within range of a potential prize, the crew cut away the buoy and took the cannons out from under wraps. Such tactics paid off. Some two thousand American privateers captured more than six hundred British ships and forced the British navy to spread itself thin doing convoy duty.

The Land War Moves South

During the first three years of the war, the British had made little effort to mobilize what they believed to be considerable loyalist strength in the South. In 1778, however, facing a threat from France and with their forces in the North concentrated and inactive, they gave southern loyalists a key role in a new strategy for subduing the rebellion. After first sending Redcoats sweeping through a large area, they would leave behind a Tory militia to reestablish loyalty to the crown and suppress local Whigs. The British hoped by this strategy to recapture everything from Georgia to Virginia; they would deal with New England later.

The British southern strategy began to unfold in November 1778, when General Clinton dispatched 3,500 troops to take control of Georgia (see Map 6-5). Meeting only light resistance, they quickly seized Savannah and Augusta. Indeed, enough inhabitants seemed happy to have the British back that the old colonial government was restored under civilian control. After their initial success, however, the British suffered some serious setbacks. The Spanish entered the war and seized British outposts on the

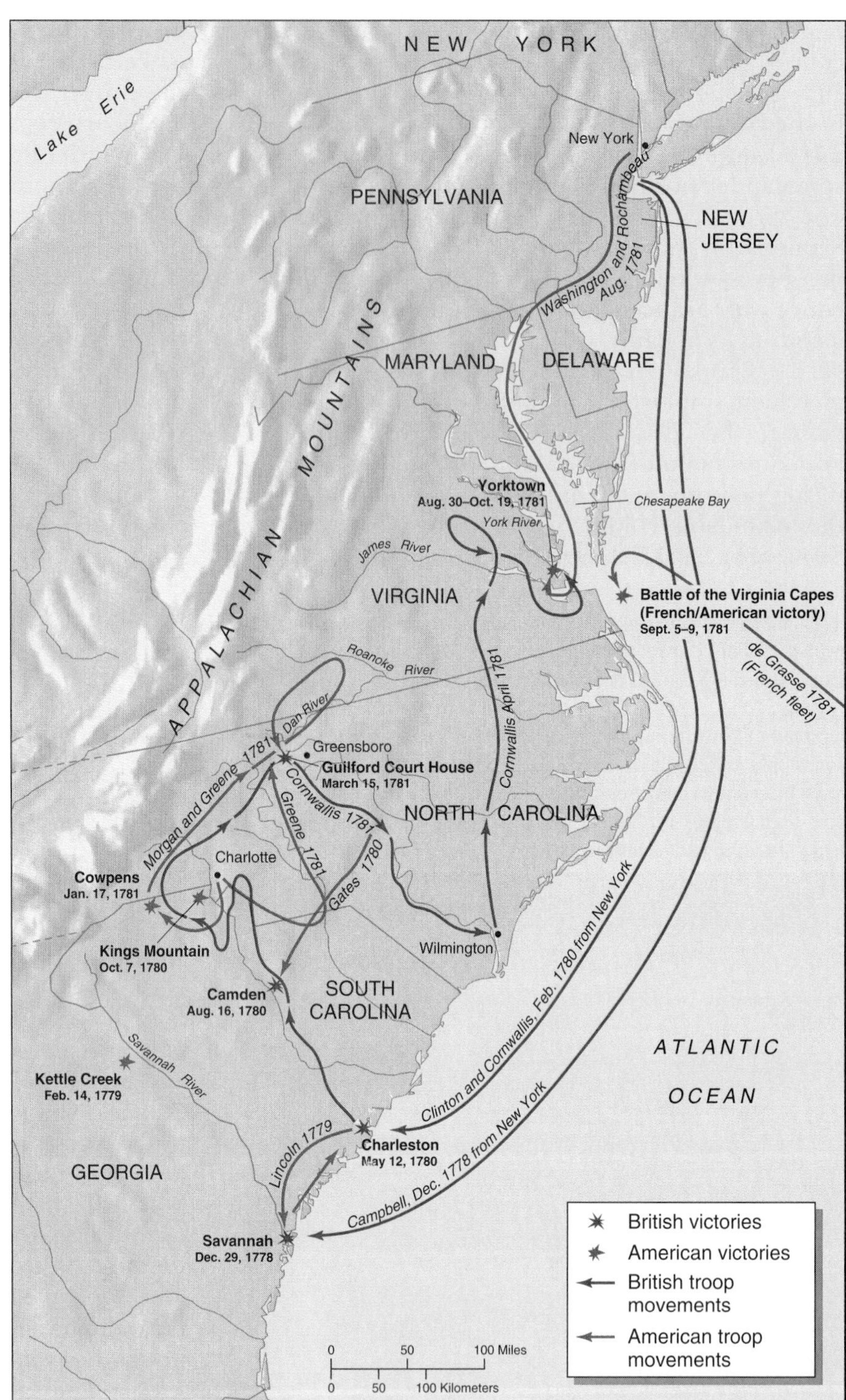

Map 6-5 The War in the South, 1778–1781
During the latter part of the war, most of the major engagements occurred in the South. British forces won most of the early ones but could not control the immense territory involved and eventually surrendered at Yorktown.

Mississippi and Mobile Rivers. And in February 1779, at the Battle of Kettle Creek, South Carolina's Whig militia decimated a loyalist militia contingent that was trying to fight its way from the North Carolina backcountry to Georgia to join up with British troops.

But the Americans could not beat the British army. In late September and early October 1779, a combined force of 5,500 American and French troops, supported by French warships, laid siege to Savannah. Moving too slowly to encircle the city, they allowed British reinforcements to get through. Then, impatient to get their ships away from the hurricane-prone coast, the French forced the Americans to launch a premature assault on the city on October 9. The assault failed, and the French sailed off.

Overview

Important Battles of the Revolutionary War

	Battle	Date	Outcome
Early Fighting	Lexington and Concord, Massachusetts	April 19, 1775	Contested
	Fort Ticonderoga, New York	May 10, 1775	American victory
	Breeds Hill ("Bunker Hill"), Boston, Massachusetts	June 17, 1775	Contested
	Great Bridge, Virginia	Dec. 9, 1775	American victory
	Quebec, Canada	Dec. 31, 1775	British repulse American assault
	Moore's Creek Bridge, North Carolina	Feb. 27, 1776	American victory
The War in the North	Brooklyn Heights, New York	Aug. 27, 1776	British victory
	White Plains, New York	Oct. 28, 1776	British victory
	Trenton, New Jersey	Dec. 26, 1776	American victory
	Princeton, New Jersey	Jan. 3, 1777	American victory
	Brandywine Creek, Pennsylvania	Sept. 11, 1777	British victory (opened way for British to take Philadelphia)
	Saratoga, New York	Sept. 19 and Oct. 17, 1777	American victory (helped persuade France to form an alliance with United States)
	Monmouth Court House, New Jersey	June 28, 1778	Contested
The War on the Frontier	Wyoming Valley, Pennsylvania	June and July 1778	British victory
	Kaskaskia and Cahokia, Illinois; Vincennes, Indiana	July 4, 1778–Feb. 23, 1779	American victories strengthen claims to Mississippi Valley
	Cherry Valley, New York	Nov. 11, 1778	British victory
The War in the South	Savannah, Georgia	Dec. 29, 1778	British victory (took control of Georgia)
	Kettle Creek, Georgia	Feb. 14, 1779	American victory
	Savannah, Georgia	Sept. 3–Oct. 28, 1779	British victory (opened way for British to take Charleston)
	Charleston, South Carolina	Feb. 11–May 12, 1780	British victory
	Camden, South Carolina	Aug. 16, 1780	British victory
	Kings Mountain, South Carolina	Oct. 7, 1780	American victory
	Cowpens, South Carolina	Jan. 17, 1781	American victory
	Guilford Court House, North Carolina	March 15, 1781	Contested
	Yorktown, Virginia	Aug. 30–Oct. 19, 1781	American victory (persuaded Britain to end the war)

The way was now open for the British to attack Charleston, the military key to the Lower South. In December 1779, Clinton sailed through storm-battered seas from New York to the Carolina coast with about nine thousand troops. In the **Battle of Charleston**, he encircled the city, trapping the patriot forces inside. On May 12, 1780, more than five thousand Continentals and militia laid down their arms—the worst American defeat of the war and the largest single loss of United States troops to a foreign army until the surrender of American forces in the Philippines to Japan in 1942.

The British were now poised to sweep all the South before them. Local Whigs, thinking the Revolution over, offered little resistance to Redcoats striking into the Carolina backcountry. At the South Carolina–North Carolina border, British troops under Colonel Banastre Tarleton overwhelmed a detachment of 350 Virginia Continentals trying to retreat homeward after coming too late to Charleston's aid. When the Continentals offered to surrender, Tarleton slaughtered most of them. So complete did the British success seem that Clinton tried to force the American troops whom he had taken prisoner to resume their duties as British subjects and join the loyalist militia. Thinking that matters were now well in hand, Clinton sailed back to New York, leaving the southern troops under the command of Lord Cornwallis.

Clinton's confidence that the South had returned securely to the loyalist camp was premature. Atrocities like Tarleton's slaughter of the Virginians inflamed anti-British feelings. And Clinton's decision to force former rebels into the loyalist militia backfired, infuriating real loyalists—who saw their enemies getting off lightly—as well as Whigs. Atrocities and reprisals mounted on both sides as Whigs continued to defy British authority. "Tarleton's Quarter" and "a Georgia parole" (a bullet in the back) became Whig euphemisms for "take no prisoners."

American Counterattacks

In the summer of 1780, Congress dispatched a substantial Continental force to the South under General Horatio Gates, the hero of Saratoga. Local patriots flocked to join him. But Gates was reckless. Pushing through North Carolina, his men tried to subsist on green corn. Weakened by diarrhea, they blundered into Cornwallis's British army near Camden, South Carolina, on August 16, and suffered a complete rout. More than one thousand Americans were killed or wounded and many captured. Gates—transformed from the hero of Saratoga to the goat of Camden—fled to Hillsborough, North Carolina.

American morale revived on October 7, 1780, when "over mountain men" (militia) from Virginia, western North and South Carolina, and what is today eastern Tennessee inflicted a defeat on the British at **Kings Mountain**, South Carolina. And in December 1780, Nathanael Greene replaced the discredited Gates, bringing competent leadership to the Continentals in the South.

The daring and resourceful Greene realized he would need an unorthodox strategy to defeat Cornwallis's larger army of seasoned professional troops. He divided his forces, keeping roughly half with him in northeastern South Carolina and sending the other half westward under General Daniel Morgan. Cornwallis ordered Tarleton to pursue Morgan's troops, who retreated northward until they reached an open area in South Carolina called Hannah's Cowpens. There Morgan rallied his men, reportedly inspiring them with the sight of his scarred back; he had been flogged by order of a British court martial during the French and Indian War. At the **Battle of Cowpens** on January 17, 1781, Morgan cleverly posted his least reliable troops, the militia, in the front line, telling them to run after firing two volleys. When Tarleton attacked, the militia fired and withdrew. Thinking that the American ranks had broken, the Redcoats charged—straight into devastating fire from Morgan's Continentals. Tarleton escaped, but his reputation for invincibility had been destroyed.

Cornwallis now badly needed a battlefield victory. Burning his army's excess baggage, he set off in hot pursuit of Greene and Morgan, who had rejoined forces. The Continentals had the advantage of knowing the country, which was laced with rain-swollen rivers. Greene's officers often arranged to have boats waiting at the deeper crossings. Finally, on February 13, 1781, Greene's tired men crossed the Dan River into Virginia, and Cornwallis gave up the chase, marching his equally exhausted Redcoats southward. To his surprise, Cornwallis now found himself pursued—though cautiously, to be sure—by Greene. On March 15, the opposing forces met at **Guilford Court House** (near present-day Greensboro, North Carolina) in one of the war's bloodiest battles. At one point, with the two sides tangled in hand-to-hand combat, the Americans drove the British back. To blunt the onslaught, Cornwallis fired grapeshot directly into the melee, mowing down friend and foe alike. Thanks to such tactics, the British still held the field at the end of the day. But, as one Englishman observed, "another such victory would destroy the British Army." Cornwallis had to retreat to the coastal town of Wilmington, North Carolina, to rest and regroup. Abandoning his most seriously wounded men, he carried the rest back in wagons, their broken bones poking through their wounds as they bounced along rutted roads.

By the late summer of 1781, British fortunes were waning in the Lower South. The Redcoats held only the larger towns and the immediately surrounding countryside. With their superior staying power, they won most major engagements, but these victories brought them no lasting gain. As General Greene observed of the Americans, "We fight, get beat, and rise and fight again." When the enemy pressed him too hard, Greene retreated out of reach, advancing again as the British withdrew.

Patriot guerrilla forces, led by such colorful figures as "Swamp Fox" Francis Marion, disrupted British communications between their Charleston headquarters and outlying garrisons. The loyalist militias that the British had hoped would pacify the countryside proved unequal to the task. Whig militiamen had often driven out any loyalists before a British sweep. And those who did welcome the British found themselves the targets of Whig retaliation once the Redcoats had left. Thus although Greene never defeated the Redcoats outright, his campaign was a strategic success. The British could not hold what they had taken; the Americans had time on their side.

Disappointed and frustrated, Cornwallis decided to conquer Virginia to cut off Greene's line of supply and to destroy Whig resolve. British forces, including units commanded by turncoat Benedict Arnold, had already been raiding the state. Cornwallis marched north to join them, reaching Yorktown, Virginia, during the summer of 1781.

The final military showdown of the war was at hand. By now, five thousand French soldiers were in America ready to fight alongside the Continentals, and a large French fleet in the West Indies had orders to support an attack on the British in North America. Faking preparations for an assault on British-occupied New York, the Continentals (commanded by Washington) and the French headed for the Chesapeake. Cornwallis and his six thousand Redcoats soon found themselves besieged behind their fortifications at **Yorktown** by 8,800 Americans and 7,800 French. A French naval victory gave the allies temporary command of the waters around Yorktown. Cornwallis had nowhere to go, and Clinton—still in New York—could not reinforce him quickly enough. On October 19, 1781, the British army surrendered. The defeated men filed between rows of American and French troops to lay down their arms while a British band mournfully played a tune reputedly called "The World Turned Upside Down." When he learned the news in London, the British prime minister, Lord North, took it like "a ball in his breast." "It is all over," he groaned.

The American Victory, 1782–1783

The British surrender at Yorktown marked the end of major fighting in North America, though skirmishes continued for another year. In April 1782,

"Surrender of Lord Cornwallis at Yorktown," by John Trumbull (American, 1756–1843). Oil on canvas, 20⅞ x 30⅝ in.

The surrender of Lord Cornwallis at Yorktown on October 19, 1781, led to the British decision to withdraw from the war. Cornwallis, who claimed to be ill, absented himself from the ceremony and is not in the picture. Washington, who is astride the horse under the American flag, designated General Benjamin Lincoln (on the white horse in the center) as the one to accept the submission of a subordinate British officer. John Trumbull, who painted The Battle of Bunker Hill *and some three hundred other scenes from the Revolutionary War, finished this painting while he was in London about fifteen years after the events depicted. A large copy of the work now hangs in the rotunda of the United States Capitol in Washington, D.C.*

the Royal Navy defeated the French fleet in the Caribbean, strengthening the British bargaining position. George III had insisted on continuing the war for so long because he feared that conceding American independence would threaten British rule in Canada and the West Indies. But the majority in Parliament now felt that enough men and money had been wasted trying to keep the Americans within the empire. In March 1782, the king accepted Lord North's resignation and appointed Lord Rockingham as prime minister, with a mandate to make peace.

The Peace of Paris

The peace negotiations, which took place in Paris, were lengthy. The Americans demanded independence, handsome territorial concessions—Franklin, the senior American negotiator, asked for all of Canada—and access to the rich, British-controlled fishing grounds in the North Atlantic. The new British prime minister, Lord Shelburne (Rockingham had died in 1782), was inclined to be conciliatory. By making concessions, he hoped to help British merchants recover their lost colonial trade. The French had achieved their objective—to weaken the British—and now wanted out of an increasingly costly worldwide war. Spain had not won its most important goal, the recovery of British-held Gibraltar, and thus gave the Americans no support at all.

The American negotiators, Franklin, John Adams, and John Jay, masterfully threaded their way among these conflicting interests. With good reason, they feared that the French and Spanish would strike a bargain with the British at the expense of the United States—one that might, for example, confine the new country to a narrow coastal strip or allow Britain to retain areas such as New York City and Charleston, which its troops still occupied. As a result, the Americans disregarded Congress's instructions to avoid making peace unilaterally. Instead, they secretly worked out their own arrangements with the British that would meet Shelburne's objective of restoring Anglo-American commercial ties. On November 30, 1782, the negotiators signed a preliminary Anglo-American treaty of peace. Its terms were embodied in the final **Peace of Paris**, signed by all the belligerents on September 3, 1783.

The Peace of Paris gave the United States nearly everything it sought except Canada (which was never really a serious issue). Great Britain acknowledged that the United States was "free, sovereign and independent." The northern boundary of the new nation extended west from the St. Croix River (which separated Maine from Nova Scotia) past the Great Lakes to what were thought to be the headwaters of the Mississippi River (see Map 6-6). The Mississippi itself—down to just north of New Orleans—formed the western border. Spain acquired the provinces of East and West Florida from Britain.

Benjamin West's painting of the American commissioners who negotiated the Peace of Paris includes, from left to right, John Jay, John Adams, Benjamin Franklin, and Franklin's grandson, who served as the commissioners' secretary. A fourth American commissioner who arrived only at the end of the negotiations, Henry Laurens, stands in the background. The British commissioners, who would have occupied the blank space on the right, did not sit for their portraits. Chagrin at the outcome of the war probably contributed to their absence, but an apocryphal story attributed it to the reluctance of Richard Oswald, who was blind in one eye, to have his portrait painted.

Benjamin West, 1783 "American Commissioners of Preliminary Negotiations." Courtesy, Winterthur Museum.

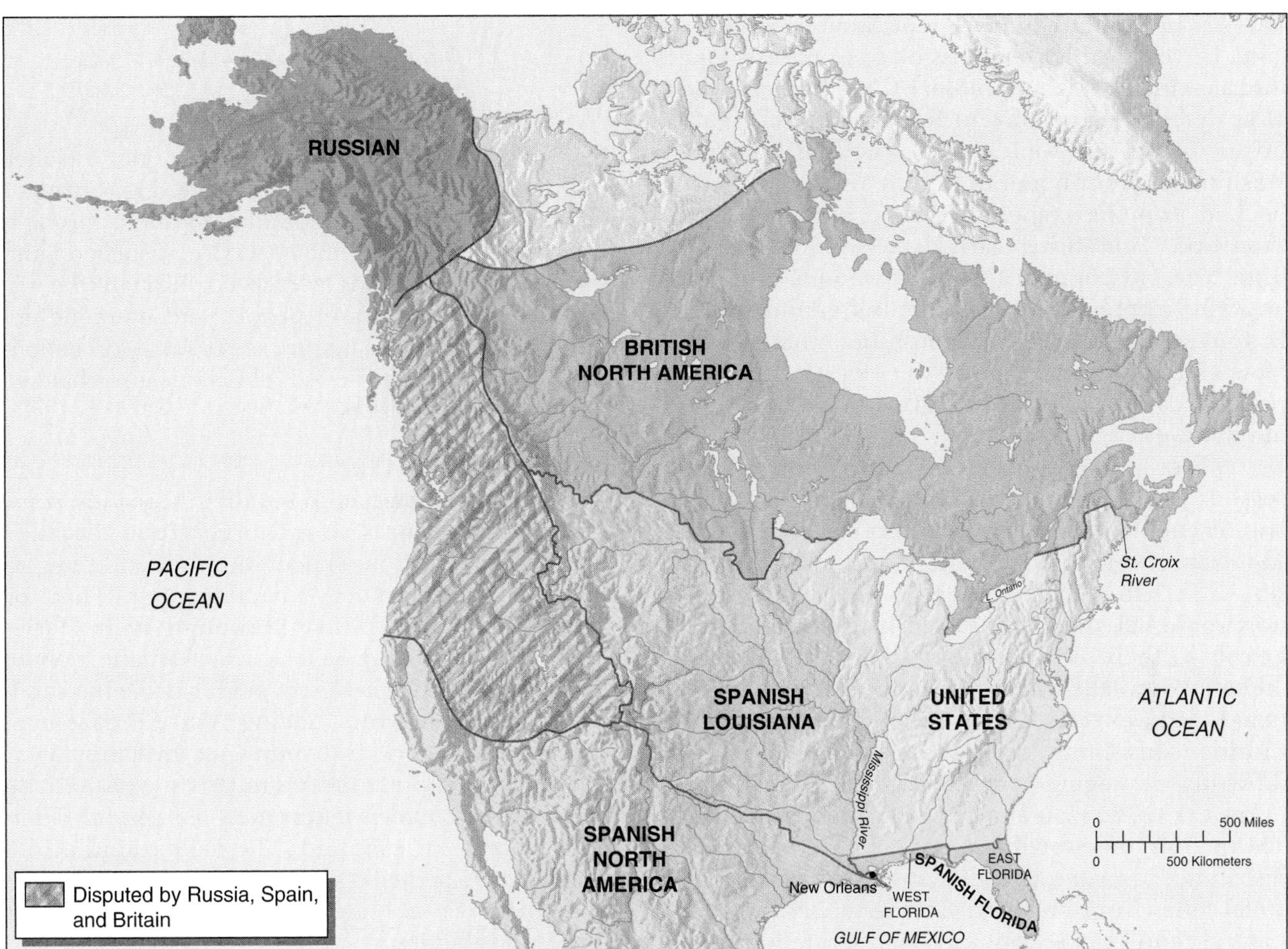

Map 6-6 North America after the Peace of Paris, 1783
The results of the American Revolution redrew the map of North America, confining Britain to Canada and giving the United States most of the area east of the Mississippi River, though Spain controlled its mouth for most of the next twenty years.

This territory included a substantial chunk of present-day Louisiana, Mississippi, Alabama, and Georgia. The treaty did not, however, provide the United States with access to the Gulf of Mexico, which would be a source of diplomatic friction for years.

Several provisions of the treaty addressed important economic issues. Adams, on behalf of his fellow New Englanders, insisted on a provision granting American fishermen access to the waters off eastern Canada. The treaty also required that British forces, on quitting American soil, were to leave behind all American-owned property, including slaves. Another provision declared existing debts between citizens of Britain and the United States still valid, giving British merchants hope of collecting on their American accounts. Congress was to "recommend" that the states restore rights and property taken from loyalists during the war. Nothing was said about the slave trade, which Jay had hoped to ban.

The Components of Success

The War for Independence was over. In December 1783, the last British transports put to sea with troops evacuated from New York. Despite the provisions of the peace treaty and the objections of southern planters, about three thousand African Americans went with them. General Guy Carleton, who had replaced Clinton as commander in chief after Yorktown, agreed to keep a list of these people, but he refused to renege on British promises of freedom for slaves who fled rebel owners. (Carleton's list survived and has recently been published.)

Washington's Continental Army had already disbanded in the summer of 1783 (but not, as we have seen, before a dispute over pay came close to provoking a military coup). On December 4, the American commander said an emotional farewell to his officers at New York City's Fraunces

Tavern, and on December 23, at Annapolis, Maryland, he resigned his commission to Congress. Like the legendary citizen-soldier Cincinnatus, who after defending the ancient Roman Republic gave up his power and went back to plowing his land, Washington went home to Mount Vernon. By now he had won the respect of friend and foe alike. "You are," one British aristocrat would write to him, "the only human being for whom I ever felt an awful reverence." Only a natural genius, other Britons said, could have accomplished what he did. How else could one explain the victory of ragtag provincials over the world's greatest military and naval power?

Washington's leadership was just one of the reasons why the Americans won the Revolutionary War. French assistance played a crucial role. Some historians contend that without the massive infusion of French men and money in 1781, the Revolution would have failed. The British also contributed heavily to their own downfall. Their fatal mistakes included bureaucratic inefficiency, hesitant command, and, worst of all, overconfidence. British authorities consistently underestimated the enormous difficulty of waging war 3,000 miles from home in an era of slow and uncertain communications. The people they sought to conquer were sparsely distributed over an area that stretched more than 1,500 miles from Maine to Georgia. There was no natural center whose capture would severely cripple the rest of the country. British forces occupied, at one time or another, most of the important seaports and state capitals—Boston, New York, Philadelphia, Charleston, and Savannah—but patriot forces driven from these centers could simply regroup in another location. Finally, Great Britain had tried to solve a political problem by military means. An occupying army is far more likely to alienate people than secure their goodwill.

Yet it took 175,000 to 200,000 soldiers—Continentals and militia troops—to prevent Great Britain from recovering the colonies. Of these, some seven thousand—like the nameless soldier recalled at the beginning of this chapter—died in battle for their "country and for its just cause." Perhaps ten thousand more succumbed to disease while on active duty, another 8,500 died while prisoners of war, and nearly 1,500 were reported missing in action. More than eight thousand were wounded and survived. Those who served in the Continental Army, probably more than half of all who fought, served the longest and saw the most action. Their casualty rate—30 to 40 percent—may have been the highest of any war in which the United States has been engaged.

War and Society, 1775–1783

Regular combatants were not the only ones to suffer during the struggle for independence. Eight years of warfare also produced profound dislocations throughout American society. Military service wrenched families apart, sporadic raids by each side brought the war home to vast numbers of people, and everyone endured economic disruptions. As a forge of nationhood, the Revolution tested all Americans, whatever their standing as citizens.

The Women's War

Everywhere women had to see their husbands, sons, brothers, and fiancés go off to fight and die. Like Mary Silliman in Connecticut, they waited, trying to stay calm until they knew "what tidings God" had for them. At first, with spirits still running high, Mary's letters to her husband, Selleck, reveal an affectionate lightheartedness. "These cold nights make me shudder for you," she wrote, adding "Oh, King George, what hardships does thy tyranny put thy late subjects to!" Selleck responded with similarly suggestive banter. Later the couple's letters grew less playful. Then her husband was captured. The daily round of domestic duties helped to keep her going, but his extended absence increased her burdens and enlarged her responsibilities.

Such circumstances elevated women's domestic status. Couples began referring to "our"—not "my" or "your"—property. Wives frequently grew more knowledgeable about a family's financial condition than long-absent husbands. "What shall I do my Dearest? I wish I had Your Advice," wrote Selleck Silliman to his wife after he had been released from captivity.

Women also assumed new public roles during the conflict. Some nursed the wounded. More wove cloth for uniforms. The Ladies' Association of Philadelphia was established in 1780 to demonstrate women's patriotism and raise money to buy shirts for the army. Though women might not be able to march "to glory by the same path as the Men," wrote the association's founder, "we should at least equal and sometimes surpass them in our love for the public good." Similar associations formed in other states.

Despite their increasing private responsibilities and new public activities, however, it did not occur to most women to encroach very far on traditional male prerogatives. When John Adams's wife, Abigail, urged him and the Second Continental Congress to "Remember the Ladies," she was not expecting equal political rights. What she wanted, rather, was some legal protections for women and recognition of their value and need for autonomy in the domestic sphere. "Remember," she cautioned, "all Men would be Tyrants if they could." Why not, then, make it impossible for "the vicious and lawless" to abuse them with impunity? "I will never consent to have our sex considered in an inferior point of light," she wrote.

Republican ideology, responding to the changing status of women, assigned them a role that was at once exalted and subordinate. It was their job to nurture wise, virtuous, and public-spirited men. It would be this view of women that would prevail in the post-Revolutionary era.

Effect of the War on African Americans and Native Americans

In the northern states, where slavery was already economically marginal and where black men were welcome as volunteers in the Continental Army, the Revolutionary War helped bring an end to slavery, although it remained legal there for some time (see Chapter 7). In the South, however, slavery was integral to the economy, and white planters viewed it as crucial to their postwar recovery. Thus although British efforts to recruit black soldiers brought freedom to thousands and temporarily undermined slavery in the South, the war ultimately strengthened the institution, especially in the Carolinas and Georgia. Of the African Americans who left with the British at the end of the war, many, both slave and free, went to the West Indies. Others settled in Canada, and some eventually went back to Africa, where Britain established the colony of Sierra Leone for them.

Survivors among the approximately thirteen thousand Native Americans who fought for the British did not have the option of leaving with them at the end of the war. How many died during the war is not known, but certainly many did. Their families and their communities also paid a high price. The Americans repeatedly invaded the Cherokees' homeland in the southern Appalachian Mountains and ravaged the Iroquois country in western New York. They also attacked the Shawnees of Ohio. In one notorious incident, militiamen even massacred peaceful Christian Indians at Gnadenhutten, Ohio. "There was no withstanding them," recalled a Cherokee chief of the many frontiersmen who assaulted his people. "They dyed their hands in the blood of many of our Women and children, burnt seventeen towns, destroyed all our provisions," and spread famine across the land.

With the peace treaty of 1783, Britain surrendered its territory east of the Mississippi, shocking and infuriating the Native Americans living there. They had not surrendered, and none of them had been at the negotiations in Paris. The Iroquois told a British commander that if the English really "had basely betrayed them by pretending to give up their Country to the Americans without their Consent, or Consulting them, it was an Act of Cruelty and injustice that Christians only were capable of doing." With the Americans now claiming their country by conquest, the Revolutionary War was a disaster for most Native Americans.

Economic Disruption

The British and American armies both needed enormous quantities of supplies. This heavy demand disrupted the normal distribution of goods and drove up real prices seven- or eightfold. The

American soldiers at Yorktown in 1781 as drawn by a young officer in the French army, Jean-Baptiste-Antoine de Verger. The African American on the left is an infantryman of the First Rhode Island Regiment; the next a musketeer; the third, with the fringed jacket, a rifleman. The man on the right is a Continental artilleryman, holding a lighted match used to fire cannons.

widespread use of depreciating paper money by the American side amplified this rise in prices and triggered severe inflation.

When the British did not simply seize what they needed, they paid for it in hard currency—gold and silver. American commanders, in contrast, had to rely on paper money because Congress and the states had almost no hard currency at their disposal. The continental dollar, however, steadily declined in value, and by March 1780, Congress was forced to admit officially that it was worthless. (The popular expression "not worth a continental" suggests that the public had long since reached this conclusion.) Thus not surprisingly, American farmers and merchants, whatever their political opinions, sometimes sold food to the British while their own forces went hungry.

Necessity, not folly, drove Congress and the states to rely on the printing press. Rather than alienate citizens by immediately raising taxes to pay for the war, the states printed paper money supposedly redeemable by future tax revenues. Because the quantity of this paper money rose faster than the supply of goods and services, prices skyrocketed, and the value of the money plunged. By April 1779, as Washington commented, "a wagon load of money will scarcely purchase a wagon load of provisions." Savvy people tried to spend money before its value could drop further, whereas those who had salable commodities like grain tended to hoard them in the hope that the price would go even higher. Prices also climbed much faster than wages, leaving many working people impoverished. As always happens in times of severe inflation, people resorted to bartering and demanded price-fixing laws. But often there was nothing to barter, and price controls never worked for long.

The rampant inflation was demoralizing and divisive. Lucky speculators and unscrupulous profiteers grew rich while ordinary and patriotic people suffered. These conditions sparked more than thirty protest demonstrations. In October 1779, frustrated Philadelphia militiamen marched on the house of a local Whig leader, demanding better enforcement of price controls. The confrontation left six people dead but otherwise achieved little. Freebooters—rovers in search of plunder—sailed Long Island Sound in boats with names like *Retrieve My Losses,* ostensibly to harry the British but all too often to trade with them. As usual, war and its deprivations brought out both the best and the worst in human nature.

Nevertheless, the successful outcome of the war and the stable peace that followed suggest that most Americans somehow managed to cope. But during the last years of the conflict, their economic and psychological reserves ran low. The total real wealth of private individuals declined by an average of 0.5 percent annually from 1774 to 1805, even with the returning prosperity of the 1790s. Such statistics suggest the true economic cost of the War for Independence. And the atrocities committed on both sides provide nearly as accurate an indicator of the conflict's psychological cost.

The Price of Victory

Most American and British commanders tried to keep hostilities "civilized"—if such a characterization can ever be applied to a war—but discipline sometimes broke down among regular troops. Controlling militias or civilians acting on their own was even more difficult, demonstrating once again that civil wars and guerrilla struggles often rank among the worst of human conflicts. Residents of contested areas near British-occupied cities such as New York and Charleston lived in almost constant danger. Their plight emerges starkly from an incident in New Jersey in 1779. A roving Tory band knocked on the door of a Whig militiaman. Entering his house, they announced that he was a dead man. Drinking his liquor and terrorizing his wife, they argued about how to execute him until one of the intruders abruptly resolved the dispute by shooting him. Whigs could be equally brutal. Late in the war, British sympathizers in the Lower South compiled a list of more than three hundred loyalists who had been massacred by Whigs—some, the survivors claimed, while they slept.

Although the British were probably the worse offenders, both sides burned, plundered, and murdered. One can see the results in a returning refugee's description of the area around Beaufort, South Carolina, in the early 1780s:

> All was desolation. . . . Robberies and murders are often committed on the public roads. The people that remain have been peeled, pillaged, and plundered. Poverty, want, and hardship appear in almost every countenance . . . , and the morals of the people are almost entirely extirpated.

Conclusion

Despite the devastation and divisiveness of the war, many people in Europe and the United States were convinced that it represented something momentous. *The Annual Register,* an influential British magazine reflecting respectable opinion, commented accurately in 1783 that the American Revolution has already overturned those favourite systems of policy and commerce, both in the old and in the new world, which the wisdom of the ages, and the power of the greatest nations, had in vain endeavored to render permanent; and it seems to have laid the seeds of still greater revolutions in the history and mutual relations of mankind.

Americans, indeed, had fired a shot heard round the world. Thanks in part to its heavy investment in the American Revolution, France suffered a grave financial crisis in the late 1780s. This in turn ushered in the political crisis that culminated in the French Revolution of 1789. The American Revolution helped inspire among French people (including soldiers returning from service in America) an intense yearning for an end to arbitrary government and undeserved social inequalities. Liberty also proved infectious to thousands of German troops who had come to America as mercenaries but elected to stay as free citizens after the war was over. Once prosperous but distant provinces of a far-flung empire, the North American states had become an independent confederation, a grand experiment in republicanism whose fate mattered to enlightened men and women throughout the Western world. In his written farewell to the rank and file of his troops at the end of October 1783, Washington maintained that "the enlarged prospects of happiness, opened by the confirmation of our independence and sovereignty, almost exceed the power of description." He urged those who had fought with him to maintain their "strong attachments to the union" and "prove themselves not less virtuous and useful as citizens, than they have been persevering and victorious as soldiers." The work of securing the promise of the American Revolution, Washington knew, would now shift from the battlefield to the political arena.

Review Questions

1. Who were the loyalists, and how many of them were there? What attempts did the British and Americans make in 1775 to avert war? Why did these steps fail?
2. What actions did the Second Continental Congress take in 1775 and 1776? Why did it choose George Washington as the commander of its army? Why was he a good choice?
3. Why did Congress declare independence in July 1776? How did Americans justify their claim to independence?
4. What was republicanism, and why was the enthusiasm that it inspired insufficient to win the war?
5. What were the chief characteristics of the British and American armies?
6. Why were most of the early battles fought in the northern states? Why did the British not crush the Americans immediately? Why did France decide to enter the war as an ally of the United States? What effect did French entry into the war have on British strategy?
7. Why did the initial British victories in the South not win the war for them? Why did the United States ultimately win? What did it obtain by winning?
8. What were the effects of the war on American society? What impact did it have on the status of women? On the lives of African Americans? Native Americans? What was the price of victory—for the victors and for the vanquished? What were the immediate results of the American victory?

Recommended Reading

Joy D. Buel and Richard Buel, Jr., *The Way of Duty: A Woman and Her Family in Revolutionary America* (1984). A readable and unusually full biography of Mary Fish of Connecticut, who lived from 1736 to 1818. Her experiences during the Revolutionary War while her husband, Selleck Silliman, was a prisoner of the British have become the subject of a good movie, *Mary Silliman's War* (1993).

Stephen Conway, *The War of American Independence, 1775–1783* (1995). A short, accessible account that emphasizes the degree to which the American Revolution was the first modern war.

John C. Dann, ed., *The Revolution Remembered: Eyewitness Accounts of the War for Independence* (1980). A collection of seventy-nine narratives by veterans seeking pensions for their Revolutionary War service; sometimes poignant and frequently illuminating.

Robert A. Gross, *The Minutemen and Their World* (1976). An example of "history from the bottom up" that provides a close look at the Minute Men of Concord from the late colonial period through the Revolution.

Pauline Maier, *American Scripture: Making the Declaration of Independence* (1997). A readable account of the adoption of the Declaration of Independence and its later reputation.

John Shy, *A People Numerous and Armed: Reflections on the Military Struggle for American Independence* (1990). A collection of essays on various aspects of the American Revolution by a perceptive military historian; full of interesting ideas.

Russell F. Weigley, *The Partisan War: The South Carolina Campaign of 1780–1782* (1970). A short, stimulating account of the American recovery of the Lower South that takes "the perspective of our recent insights into unconventional war" and the communist victory in Vietnam.

Additional Sources

The Outbreak of War and the Declaration of Independence

Willi Paul Adams and Others, "Interpreting the Declaration of Independence by Translation: A Round Table," *Journal of American History* (1999), pp. 1280–1458.

Robert M. Calhoon, *The Loyalists in Revolutionary America, 1760–1781* (1973).

Joseph Ellis, *American Sphinx: The Character of Thomas Jefferson* (1996).

David H. Fischer, *Paul Revere's Ride* (1994).

James T. Flexner, *Washington: The Indispensable Man* (1984).

Eric Foner, *Tom Paine and Revolutionary America* (1976).

Ronald Hamowy, "Jefferson and the Scottish Enlightenment: A Critique of Garry Wills's Inventing America," *William and Mary Quarterly* (1979), pp. 503–523.

Don Higginbotham, *The War of American Independence: Military Attitudes, Policies, and Practice, 1763–1789* (1971).

Robert Middlekauff, *The Glorious Cause: The American Revolution, 1763–1789* (1982).

The Combatants

George A. Billias, ed., *George Washington's Generals* (1964).

George A. Billias, ed., *George Washington's Opponents: British Generals and Admirals in the American Revolution* (1969).

Sylvia R. Frey, *The British Soldier in America: A Social History of Military Life in the Revolutionary Period* (1981).

Robert Gardiner, *Navies and the American Revolution, 1775–1783* (1996).

Holly A. Mayer, *Belonging to the Army: Camp Followers and Community during the American Revolution* (1996).

Charles P. Neimeyer, *America Goes to War: A Social History of the Continental Army* (1996).

Charles Royster, *A Revolutionary People at War: The Continental Army and American Character, 1775–1783* (1979).

Robert K. Wright, *The Continental Army* (1984).

The War in the North

Ira Ira D. Gruber, *The Howe Brothers and the American Revolution* (1972).

Lee B. Kennett, *The French Forces in America, 1780–1783* (1977).

Mark V. Kwasny, *Washington's Partisan War, 1775–1783* (1996).

James Kirby Martin, *Benedict Arnold, Revolutionary Hero: An American Warrior Reconsidered* (1997).

Steven Rosswurm, *Arms, Country, and Class: The Philadelphia Militia and "Lower Sort" during the American Revolution, 1775–1783* (1987).

William C. Stinchcombe, *The American Revolution and the French Alliance* (1969).

The War Widens

Sylvia R. Frey, *Water from the Rock: Black Resistance in a Revolutionary Age* (1991).

Barbara Graymont, *The Iroquois in the American Revolution* (1972).

Ronald Hoffman, Thad W. Tate, and Peter J. Albert, eds., *An Uncivil War: The Southern Backcountry during the American Revolution* (1985).

James H. O'Donnell, *Southern Indians in the American Revolution* (1973).

Paul H. Smith, *Loyalists and Redcoats: A Study in British Revolutionary Policy* (1964).

Theodore Thayer, *Nathanael Greene: Strategist of the American Revolution* (1960).

Franklin Wickwire and Mary Wickwire, *Cornwallis: The American Adventure* (1970).

The American Victory

Jonathan R. Dull, *A Diplomatic History of the American Revolution* (1985).

Piers Mackesy, *The War for America, 1775–1783* (1964).

James K. Martin and Mark E. Lender, *A Respectable Army: The Military Origins of the Republic, 1763–1789* (1982).

Richard B. Morris, *The Peacemakers: The Great Powers and American Independence* (1965).

Howard H. Peckham, *The Toll of Independence: Engagements and Battle Casualties of the American Revolution* (1974).

The War and Society

Wallace Brown, *The Good Americans: The Loyalists in the American Revolution* (1969).

Richard Buel Jr., *Dear Liberty: Connecticut's Mobilization for the Revolutionary War* (1980).

Colin G. Calloway, *The American Revolution in Indian Country: Crisis and Diversity in Native American Communities* (1995).

Graham Russell Hodges, ed., *The Black Loyalist Directory: African Americans in Exile after the American Revolution* (1996).

Ronald Hoffman and Peter J. Albert, eds., *The Transforming Hand of Revolution: Reconsidering the American Revolution as a Social Movement* (1995).

Ronald Hoffman and Peter J. Albert, eds., *Women in the Age of the American Revolution* (1989).

Linda Kerber, *Women of the Republic: Intellect and Ideology in Revolutionary America* (1980).

Adrian C. Leiby, *The Revolutionary War in the Hackensack Valley: The Jersey Dutch and the Neutral Ground, 1775–1783* (1962).

Mary Beth Norton, *Liberty's Daughters: The Revolutionary Experience of American Women, 1750–1800* (1980).

Alfred F. Young, ed., *The American Revolution: Explorations in the History of American Radicalism* (1976).

Where to Learn More

❖ **Gnadenhutten Monument and Schoenbrunn Village near New Philadelphia, Ohio.** Reconstructed buildings mark the Moravian Indian settlement whose inhabitants were massacred in 1782.

❖ **Independence National Historical Park, Philadelphia, Pennsylvania.** Independence Hall, where Congress adopted the Declaration of Independence, is the most historic building in Philadelphia.

❖ **Kings Mountain National Military Park and Cowpens National Battlefield, South Carolina.** Situated approximately 20 miles apart, these were the sites of two battles in October 1780 and January 1781 that turned the tide of the war in the South. Both have museums and exhibits.

❖ **Minute Man National Historical Park, Lexington and Concord, Massachusetts.** There are visitors' centers at both Lexington and Concord with explanatory displays. Visitors may also follow the self-guided Battle Road Automobile Tour.

❖ **Saratoga National Historical Park, New York.** The park preserves and commemorates the American victory that led to French entry into the war. There is a museum with artifacts from the battlefield. Both the explanatory displays and the topography of the area make this an especially illuminating site.

❖ **Valley Forge National Historical Park, Valley Forge, Pennsylvania.** Reconstructed huts convey a sense of life in the Continental Army camp at Valley Forge during the hard winter of 1777–1778.

❖ **Yorktown Battlefield, Colonial National Historical Park, Yorktown, Virginia.** The park commemorates the great American victory here. Innovative exhibits enable visitors to follow the course of the war from a multicultural perspective.

THE FIRST REPUBLIC, 1776–1789

7

Chapter Outline

Key Topics

- Republicanism and the political philosophy of the new state constitutions
- Internal problems in the United States under the Articles of Confederation
- Efforts of Britain and Spain to exploit the weaknesses of the United States after the Revolution
- The movement for a stronger national government
- The drafting and ratification of the United States Constitution

"Instead of a due reverence to authority, and submission to government . . . have you not endeavored . . . to overturn all government and order, to shake off all restraints, human and divine, to give up yourselves wholly to the power of the most restless, malevolent, destructive, tormenting passion?" With these harsh words, Chief Justice William Cushing of Massachusetts denounced the debt-ridden farmers who had taken arms against the state government—and the merchants and creditors who controlled it—during **Shays's Rebellion** of 1786–1787. Led by Daniel Shays, a former captain in the Continental Army, the rebels were protesting legislative policies that had saddled them with high taxes, left them vulnerable to the loss of their farms when they couldn't pay the taxes or repay other debts, and blocked increases in the supply of currency that would have provided them with economic relief. State forces stamped out Shays's Rebellion early in 1787, but the insurrection triggered waves of agrarian protest in other states, convincing many Americans that the republic stood on the brink of lawlessness.

More so than any other domestic disturbance in the 1780s, Shays's Rebellion dramatized the ideological, social, and economic ferment of America's first republic, its earliest years, which began in a burst of optimism following the victory over the British at Yorktown in 1781. The rebellion underscored, in particular, the clashing, if not contradictory, meanings that newly independent Americans attributed to the concept of liberty. Conservatives such as Cushing—mainly men of wealth and high social standing—equated liberty with the right of the individual to pursue wealth and amass property. They sought a society founded on the rule of law that would provide a stable foundation for an expanding economy.

Ordinary farmers, artisans, and small producers, in contrast, understood liberty more in terms of the traditional right of communities to defend their interests against the threat of moneyed and aristocratic elites. Denounced as radicals by their opponents, the Shaysites viewed themselves as the true conservatives, the preservers of republican liberties won in the Revolution against aristocratic elitists who they claimed had taken control of the Massachusetts government, shut out the popular voice, and victimized the true republicans, the common people who lived off their own labor.

During the Revolutionary War, the states had engaged in an unprecedented period of constitution writing. In 1781, they ratified the Articles of Confederation, the first attempt at a political union of the states. The years that followed were a period of trial and error marked by a running debate over the meaning of liberty and the extent of power that could safely be entrusted to a national government. A host of regional conflicts and economic problems like those that sparked Shays's Rebellion emerged, and the nation found itself caught between the need for more central power and the desire of states to protect their sovereignty. By the end of the 1780s, influential leaders favoring a strong national government had lost confidence in the Articles of Confederation and began working to replace them. They succeeded with the enactment and ratification of the Constitution of the United States in 1788.

The New Order of Republicanism

As royal authority collapsed during the Revolution, various provincial congresses and committees assumed power in each of the former colonies. The Continental Congress, seeking to build support for the war effort, was concerned that these new institutions should have a firm legal and popular foundation. In May 1776, the Congress called on the colonies to form new state governments "under the authority of the people."

This call reflected the political philosophy of republicanism that animated the Revolution (see Chapter 6). To Americans, republicanism meant first and foremost that legitimate political authority derives from the people. It is they who are sovereign, not the king or the aristocracy. The people should elect the officials who govern them, and those officials should represent the interests of the people who elected them. Another key aspect of republicanism was the revolutionary idea that the people could define and limit governmental power through written constitutions.

Thus for many Americans, the Congress's call reflected the root purpose of the Revolution—to banish aristocratic tyranny and reconstruct government in the states on republican principles. But if those principles included the idea that legitimate government flowed from the people, it was not always clear just who "the people" included.

Although Shays' Rebellion was crushed, this uprising of debt-ridden farmers shocked many Americans into accepting the need for a stronger national government.

Defining the People

When news of the peace treaty with Britain reached New Bern, North Carolina, in June 1783, the citizens held a grand celebration. As reported by Francisco de Miranda, a visiting Spanish officer, "There was a barbecue [a roast pig] and a barrel of rum, from which the leading officials and citizens of the region promiscuously drank with the meanest and lowest kind of people, holding hands and drinking from the same cup. It is impossible to imagine, without seeing it, a more purely democratic gathering."

For Miranda, this boisterous mingling of all citizens as seeming equals confirmed the central tenet of republicanism, the belief that the people were sovereign. But republicanism also taught that political rights should be limited to those who owned private property, because the independent will required for informed political judgment required economic self-sufficiency. This in effect restricted political participation to propertied white men. Virtually all others—propertyless white men, servants legally bound to others, women, slaves and most free black people, and Native Americans—were denied political rights.

Because the ownership of property was relatively widespread among white men, some 60 to 85 percent of adult white men could participate in politics—a far higher proportion than elsewhere in the world of the eighteenth century. The greatest concentration of the remaining 25 percent or so shut out of the political process were unskilled laborers and mariners living in port cities. In Philadelphia, for example, half the population of taxable adult men and women in the 1780s reported no taxable property. The city's working poor still included indentured servants, bound by contract to give personal service for a fixed time. The walking poor—vagrants and transients—might be jailed by local authorities, confined to workhouses, or hired out in public auctions for fixed terms of labor. Those who incurred debts they were unable to pay faced imprisonment.

The Revolution did little to change the traditional patriarchal assumption that politics and public life should be the exclusive domain of men. Women, according to republican beliefs, were part of the dependent class and belonged under the control of propertied men—their husbands and fathers. Under common law (the customary, largely unwritten law that Americans had inherited from Britain), women surrendered their property rights at marriage. Legally and economically, husbands had complete control over their wives. As a result, argued Theophilus Parsons of Massachusetts in 1778, women were, as a matter of course, "so situated as to have no wills of their own."

To be sure, some women saw in the political and social enthusiasm of the Revolution an

Chronology

1776 States begin writing the first constitutions.

1777 Articles of Confederation proposed.

1781 Articles ratified.

1783 Americans celebrate independence and the peace treaty with Britain.

1784 Onset of the postwar depression.
Spain closes the Mississippi.
Separatist plots in the West.
Treaty of Fort Stanwix.

1785 Land Ordinance of 1785.
States begin to issue more paper money.
Treaty of Fort McIntosh.

1786 Shays's Rebellion breaks out.
Jay–Gardoqui Treaty defeated.
Annapolis Convention.

1787 Constitutional Convention at Philadelphia.
Northwest Ordinance.

1788 Constitution ratified and goes into effect.
Publication of *The Federalist.*

opportunity to protest the most oppressive features of their subordination. "I won't have it thought that because we are the weaker sex as to bodily strength we are capable of nothing more than domestic concerns," wrote Eliza Wilkinson of South Carolina. Men, she lamented, "won't even allow us liberty of thought and that is all I want." Such protests, however, had little enduring effect. Most women were socialized to accept that their proper place was in the home with their families.

Gender-specific language—terms like "men," "Freemen," "white male inhabitants," and "free white men"—explicitly barred women from voting in almost all state constitutions of the 1770s. Only the New Jersey constitution of 1776 defined **suffrage**—the right to vote—in gender-free terms, extending it to all adults "worth fifty pounds." As a result, until 1807, when the state legislature changed the constitution, propertied women enjoyed the right to vote in New Jersey.

With the exception of New Jersey, where women meeting the property qualifications were eligible to vote, the state constitutions of the Revolutionary era prohibited women from voting.

The Revolution otherwise did bring women a few limited gains. They benefited from slightly less restrictive divorce laws and gained somewhat greater access to educational and business opportunities, changes that reflected the relative autonomy of many women during the war when their men were off fighting. The perception of women's moral status also rose. As the Philadelphia physician Benjamin Rush argued in his *Thoughts upon Female Education* (1787), educated and morally informed women were needed to instruct "their sons in the principles of liberty and government."

The Revolution had a more immediate impact on the lives of many African Americans, triggering the growth of free black communities and the development of an African-American culture. Changes begun by the Revolution were the main factor in the tremendous increase of the free black population from a few thousand at midcentury to more than 100,000 by 1800 (see Figure 7-1). One key to this increase was a shift in the religious and intellectual climate. Revolutionary principles of liberty and equality and evangelical notions of human fellowship convinced many white people for the first time to challenge slavery. In 1784, Virginia Methodists condemned slavery as "contrary to the Golden Law of God on which hang all the Laws and Prophets, and the unalienable Rights of Mankind, as well as every Principle of Revolution." As many white people grew more hostile to slavery, African Americans

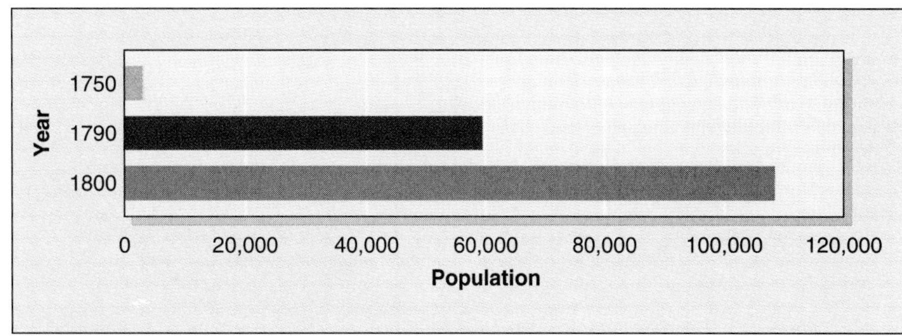

Figure 7-1 Growth of the Free Black Population between 1750 and 1800
Gradual emancipation in the North, the freeing of many slaves by their owners in the South, and the opportunities for freedom offered by the Revolution all contributed to an explosive growth in the free population of African Americans in the second half of the eighteenth century.

Data Source: A Century of Population Growth in the United States, 1790–1900 *(1909), p. 80. Data for 1750 estimated.*

began to seize opportunities for freedom that emerged from the disruptions of the war.

Upwards of fifty thousand slaves—one in ten—gained freedom as a result of the war. One route was through military service, which generally carried a promise of freedom. When the British began raising black troops, the Americans followed suit. All of the states except Georgia and South Carolina recruited black regiments. Some five thousand black men served in the Continental armies, and they, like their counterparts in British units, were mostly slaves. Most slaves who gained freedom during the war, however, were those who fled their owners and made their way to the port cities of the North.

By making slave property generally less secure, the Revolution encouraged many masters to free their slaves. Once freed, black people tried to break all the bonds of their former servitude. "Negro Soloman," his former owner griped, "now free, prefers to mould bricks rather than serve me." A Delaware mistress felt rejected when a slave she had freed spurned her offer of employment with a friend and found her own job. "I cannot help think," she sourly noted, that "it is too generally the case with all those of colour to be ungrateful." As the number of free black people increased, those still enslaved grew bolder in their efforts to gain freedom. "Henny," warned a Maryland slaveowner in 1783, "will try to pass for a free woman as several have lately been set free in this neighbourhood."

If slavery experienced some strain in the South during the Revolution, in the North, where slaves were only a small percentage of the population, it crumbled. Most northern states ended slavery between 1777 and 1784. New York followed in 1799 and New Jersey in 1804. Nonetheless, although a majority of white northerners now agreed that slavery was incompatible with the Revolution's commitment to **natural rights** (the inherent human rights to life and liberty), they refused to sanction a sudden emancipation. The laws ending slavery in most northern states called only for the children of slaves to be freed, and only when they reached adulthood.

Black northerners had to struggle to overcome white prejudice. Although black men were allowed to vote, most were too poor to meet the property qualifications. Facing discrimination in jobs and housing, barred from juries, and denied a fair share of funds for schools, they had to rely on their own resources. With the help of the small class of property holders among them, they began establishing their own churches and self-help associations.

The impact of the Revolution on Native Americans was almost entirely negative (see Chapter 6). Most Indian peoples stayed neutral during the war or fought for the British. Just as the Americans sought to shake off British control, so the Indians—especially the western tribes and most of the Iroquois Confederation—sought to free themselves from American dominance. The British defeat was thus a double blow, depriving the Indians

Phillis Wheatley was an acclaimed African-American poet. Kidnapped into slavery as a child in Africa, she was a domestic slave to the Wheatley family of Boston when her first poems were published in 1773.

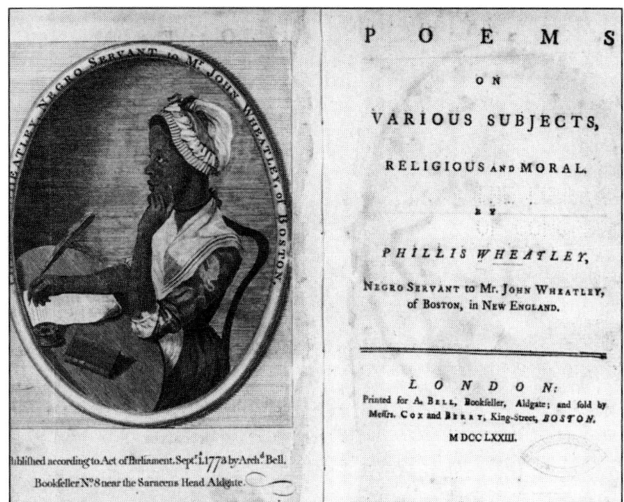

POEMS
ON
VARIOUS SUBJECTS,
RELIGIOUS AND MORAL.
BY
PHILLIS WHEATLEY,
NEGRO SERVANT to Mr. JOHN WHEATLEY, of BOSTON, in NEW ENGLAND.
LONDON:
Printed for A. BELL, Bookseller, Aldgate; and sold by Messrs. COX and BERRY, King-Street, BOSTON.
M DCC LXXIII.

The Mother Bethel Church in Philadelphia, dedicated in 1794, was home to the first independent black congregation in America and the founding establishment of the African Methodist Episcopal denomination. Churches were central to the community life of black northerners and provided leadership in the struggle for racial justice.

of a valuable ally and exposing them to the wrath of the victorious patriots. "The minds of these people appear as much agitated as those of the unhappy Loyalists," observed a British officer late in the war of the pro-British southern Indians; "they have very seriously proposed to abandon their country and accompany us [in an evacuation], having made all the world their enemies by their attachment to us."

The state governments and the Confederation Congress treated Indian lands after the Revolution as a prize of war to be distributed to white settlers. Territorial demands on the Indians escalated, even on the few tribes that had furnished troops for the American cause. White Americans did not consider Native Americans to be part of their republican society. With the exception of Massachusetts, the states denied voting and legal rights to Indians within their borders.

The State Constitutions

"Oppose everything that leans to aristocracy, of power in the hands of the rich and chief men exercised to the oppression of the poor." So the voters of Mecklenburg County, North Carolina, instructed their delegates to the state's constitutional convention in 1776. These instructions reflect a basic premise of the new state constitutions of the Revolutionary period: Power had to be checked to ensure individual liberty and safeguard against tyranny.

Ten new state constitutions were in place by the end of 1777. In Connecticut and Rhode Island, the new constitutions simply amended the existing colonial charters, which already provided for extensive self-rule, by dropping all references to royal authority. Massachusetts, the only state to hold elections for a special constitutional convention, ratified its constitution in 1780.

All of these constitutions were written documents, a striking departure from the English practice of treating a constitution as a collection of customary rights and practices that had evolved over time. In the American view, a constitution was a formal expression of the people's sovereignty, a codification of the powers of government and the rights of citizenship that functioned as a fundamental law to which all public authority was accountable.

Because Americans had come to associate tyranny with the privileges of royal governors, all the new state constitutions cut back sharply on executive power. Annual elections were now the norm for governors, who were also made subject to **impeachment**—charges of misconduct, resolved at a public trial—and limited in the number of terms they could serve. Most important, for it struck at what patriots felt was the main source of executive domination and corruption, governors lost control over **patronage**, the power to appoint executive and judicial officials.

As the new constitutions curbed the power of governors, they increased that of the legislatures, making them the focal point of government. Colonial assemblies had been in the forefront of popular opposition to British authority, and the state legislatures that succeeded them were now seen as the most trustworthy defenders of individual liberty. The new constitutions expanded the power of the legislatures to appoint officials and to oversee military and financial matters. To make the legislatures more expressive of the popular will, the new constitutions included provisions that lowered property requirements for voting and officeholding, mandated annual elections, increased the number of legislative seats, and made representation more proportional to population. Upper houses, whose members were previously appointed by the colonial governors, were made independent of the executive and opened to popular election.

Americans knew that legislatures, too, could act tyrannically, as they believed Britain's Parliament had done. So in a final check on arbitrary power, each state constitution eventually included some form of a **bill of rights** that set explicit limits on the power of government to interfere in the lives of citizens. The Virginia Declaration of Rights, written by the planter George Mason and adopted in June 1776, set the precedent for this notable republican feature. By 1784, the constitutions of all thirteen states had provisions guaranteeing religious liberty, freedom of the press, and a citizen's right to such fair legal practices as trial by jury.

The new constitutions weakened but did not always sever the traditional tie between church and state. Many Americans held, as the Massachusetts Constitution of 1780 put it, that "the happiness of a people, and the good order and preservation of civil government, essentially depend upon piety, religion, and morality." Many states, notably in New England, levied taxes for the support of religion. The states of New England also continued to maintain Congregationalism as the established, or state-supported, religion while allowing dissenting Baptists and Methodists access to funds from the compulsory religious taxes. The "common people," explained the Baptist leader Isaac Backus, insisted that they had "as good a right to judge and act for themselves in matter of religion as civil rulers or the learned clergy."

The mid-Atlantic states lacked the religious uniformity of New England. The region had several prominent denominations—Quaker, Episcopalian, Presbyterian, Dutch Reformed, and Lutheran—and this pluralism checked legislative efforts to impose religious taxes or designate any denomination as the **established church**. In the South, where many Anglican (or Episcopalian) clergymen had been Tories, the Anglican Church lost its former established status. Thomas Jefferson, in Virginia's religious freedom law of 1786, went so far as to assert that "our civil rights have no dependence on our religious opinions any more than on opinions in physics or geometry."

Although in general the executive lost power and the legislative gained power under the new state constitutions, the actual structure of each state government reflected the outcome of political struggles between those holding a radical vision of republicanism and those holding a conservative vision. The democratically inclined radicals wanted to open government to all male citizens. The conservatives, fearing "mob rule," wanted to limit government to an educated elite of substantial property holders. Although they agreed that government had to be derived from the people, most conservatives, like Jeremy Belknap of New Hampshire, thought that the people had to be "taught . . . that they are not able to govern themselves."

In South Carolina, where conservative planters gained the upper hand, the constitution mandated property qualifications that barred 90 percent of the state's white males from holding elective public office. In contrast, Pennsylvania had the most democratic and controversial constitution. Many of Pennsylvania's conservatives had discredited themselves during the Revolution by remaining neutral or loyal to the crown. The Scots-Irish farmers and Philadelphia artisans who stepped into the resulting political vacuum held an egalitarian view of republicanism. The constitution they pushed through in 1776 gave the vote to all free males who paid taxes regardless of wealth and eliminated property qualifications for officeholding. In addition, the constitution concentrated power in a unicameral (single-house) legislature, eliminating both the office of governor and the more elite upper legislative house. To prevent the formation of an entrenched class of officeholders, the constitution's framers also required legislators to stand for election annually and barred them from serving more than four years out of seven.

The constitutions of the other states, although not as bold in their democratic reforms as Pennsylvania's, typically enhanced the political influence of ordinary citizens more than the constitution of South Carolina did. Unlike the colonial assemblies, the new bicameral (two-house) legislatures included substantially more artisans and small farmers and were not controlled by men of wealth. The proportion of legislators who came from a common background—those with property valued under £200—more than tripled to 62 percent in the North and more than doubled in the South from the 1770s to the 1780s.

American Views

A French Observer Describes a New Society

In 1782, J. Hector St. John Crèvecoeur, a Frenchman who had lived and traveled in British North America, published his impressions of America. The following selection from his *Letters from an American Farmer* captures the striking optimism and sense of newness that he found. More so than any other literary work, the *Letters* stamped the new American republic, especially in the minds of Europeans, as the home of the world's freest and most equal people.

- **What is Crèvecoeur's image of America? Do you believe it was overly optimistic?**
- **Why does Crèvecoeur put such emphasis on the absence of titles and great disparities of wealth?**
- **Just what was so new about America to Crèvecoeur?**
- **Why did Crèvecoeur ignore African slaves in his definition of the American? What happened to Native Americans in his account of the making of the American?**

I wish I could be acquainted with the feelings and thoughts which must agitate the heart and present themselves to the mind of an enlightened Englishman when he first lands on this continent. . . . He is arrived on a new continent; a modern society offers itself to his contemplation, different from what he had hitherto seen. It is not composed, as in Europe, of great lords who possess everything and of a herd of people who have nothing. Here are no aristocratical families, no courts, no kings, no bishops, no ecclesiastical dominion, no invisible power giving to a few a very visible one, no great manufactures employing thousands, no great refinements of luxury. The rich and the poor are not so far removed from each other as they are in Europe. Some few towns excepted, we are all tillers of the earth, from Nova

This growing political equality was accompanied by demands that those in government be more responsive to the people. Summing up the prevailing view, William Hooper of North Carolina wrote in 1776, "Rulers must be conceived as the creatures of the people, made for their use, accountable to them, and subject to removal as soon as they act inconsistent with the purposes for which they were formed."

The Articles of Confederation

Once the Continental Congress decided on independence in 1776, it needed to create a legal basis for a permanent union of the states. John Dickinson of Pennsylvania, a reluctant supporter of independence, presented a draft plan for such a union as early as the summer of 1776. Dickinson favored a strong central government to prevent the collapse of the social order that he feared might follow the overthrow of imperial rule. Congress, however, fundamentally altered Dickinson's original plan to recognize the sovereign power of the individual states. According to the key provision of the **Articles of Confederation** that Congress finally submitted to the states in November 1777, "Each State retains its sovereignty, freedom and independence, and every power, jurisdiction and right, which is not by this confederation expressly delegated to the United States, in Congress assembled." The effect was to create a loose confederation of autonomous states.

The powers the Articles of Confederation delegated to the central government were extremely limited, in effect little more than those already exercised by the Continental Congress. There were no provisions for a national judiciary or a separate executive branch of government. The Articles made Congress the sole instrument of national au-

Scotia to West Florida. We are a people of cultivators scattered over an immense territory, communicating with each other by means of good roads and navigable rivers, united by the silken bands of mild government, all respecting the laws without dreading their power, because they are equitable. We are all animated with the spirit of an industry which is unfettered and unrestrained, because each person works for himself. . . . A pleasing uniformity of decent competence appears throughout our habitations. The meanest of our log-houses is a dry and comfortable habitation. Lawyer and merchant are the fairest titles our towns afford; that of a farmer is the only appellation of the rural inhabitants of our country. It must take some time ere he can reconcile himself to our dictionary, which is but short in words of dignity and names of honour. . . . We have no princes for whom we toil, starve, and bleed; we are the most perfect society now existing in the world. Here man is free as he ought to be, nor is this pleasing equality so transitory as many others are. Many ages will not see the shores of our great lakes replenished with inland nations, nor the unknown bounds of North America entirely peopled. . . .

The next wish of this traveller will be to know whence came all these people. They are a mixture of English, Scotch, Irish, French, Dutch, Germans, and Swedes. From this promiscuous breed, that race now called Americans have arisen. . . .

What, then, is the American, this new man? He is either an European or the descendant of an European; hence that strange mixture of blood, which you will find in no other country. . . . He is an American, who, leaving behind him all his ancient prejudices and manners, receives new ones from the new mode of life he has embraced, the new government he obeys, and the new rank he holds. He becomes an American by being received in the broad lap of our Alma Mater. Here individuals of all nations are melted into a new race of men, whose labours and posterity will one day cause great changes in the world.

Source: J. Hector St. John Crèvecoeur, Letters from an American Farmer and Sketches of Eighteenth-Century America, *ed. Albert E. Stone, Copyright © 1963, 1981 by Viking Penguin Inc. pp. 66–70. Used by permission of Penguin, a division of Penguin, Putnam, Inc.*

thority but restricted it with constitutional safeguards that kept it from threatening the interests of the states. Each state had only one vote in Congress, making each politically equal regardless of its size or population. State legislatures were to choose their congressional delegations in annual elections, and delegates could serve only three years out of six. Delegates were expected to follow the instructions of their state legislatures and could be recalled at any time. Important measures, such as those dealing with finances or war and peace, required approval from a majority of nine states. Amendments to the Articles of Confederation, including the levying of national taxes, required the unanimous consent of the states.

Congress had authority primarily in the areas of foreign policy and national defense. It could declare war, make peace, conduct foreign affairs, negotiate with Native Americans, and settle disputes between the states. It had no authority, however, to raise troops or impose taxes on its own; it could only ask the states to supply troops and money and hope that they complied.

The central principle behind the Articles was the fear of oppressive, centralized power encroaching on the freedoms for which the Revolution was fought. In the end, as Edward Rutledge, a delegate from South Carolina to the Continental Congress, put it, the new Confederation Congress was vested "with no more Power than is absolutely necessary." "It is freedom, Gentlemen, it is freedom, & not a choice of the forms of servitude for which we contend," resolved the residents of West Springfield, Massachusetts, in instructions to their congressional representatives in 1778.

Most states quickly ratified the Articles of Confederation, but Maryland stubbornly held out until March 1781. Because they needed the approval of all thirteen states, it was not until then that the Articles officially took effect. Surprisingly, given the prevailing deep suspicion of central power, what caused the delay was the demand of some states to give Congress a power not included in the Articles submitted for ratification in 1777.

The issue here concerned the unsettled lands in the West between the Appalachian Mountains and the Mississippi River (see Map 7-1). Some states claimed these lands by virtue of their colonial charter rights, and, led by Virginia and Massachusetts, they insisted on maintaining control over them. The so-called landless states—those with no claim to the West—insisted that it be set aside as a national domain, a reserve of public land controlled by Congress for the benefit of all the states. Land speculators who had purchased huge tracts of land from the Indians before the Revolution sided with the landless states. Many of them leading politicians, they expected Congress would be more likely to honor their land titles than the individual states.

The British threat to the Chesapeake area in early 1781 finally broke the impasse. Though retaining control of Kentucky, Virginia gave up its claim to a vast area extending north of the Ohio River. In turn, Maryland, the last holdout among the landless states and now desperate for military aid from Congress, agreed to ratify the Articles. After more than three years of debate and the airing of jealousies among the states, the final cementing of the original Union was decidedly anticlimactic.

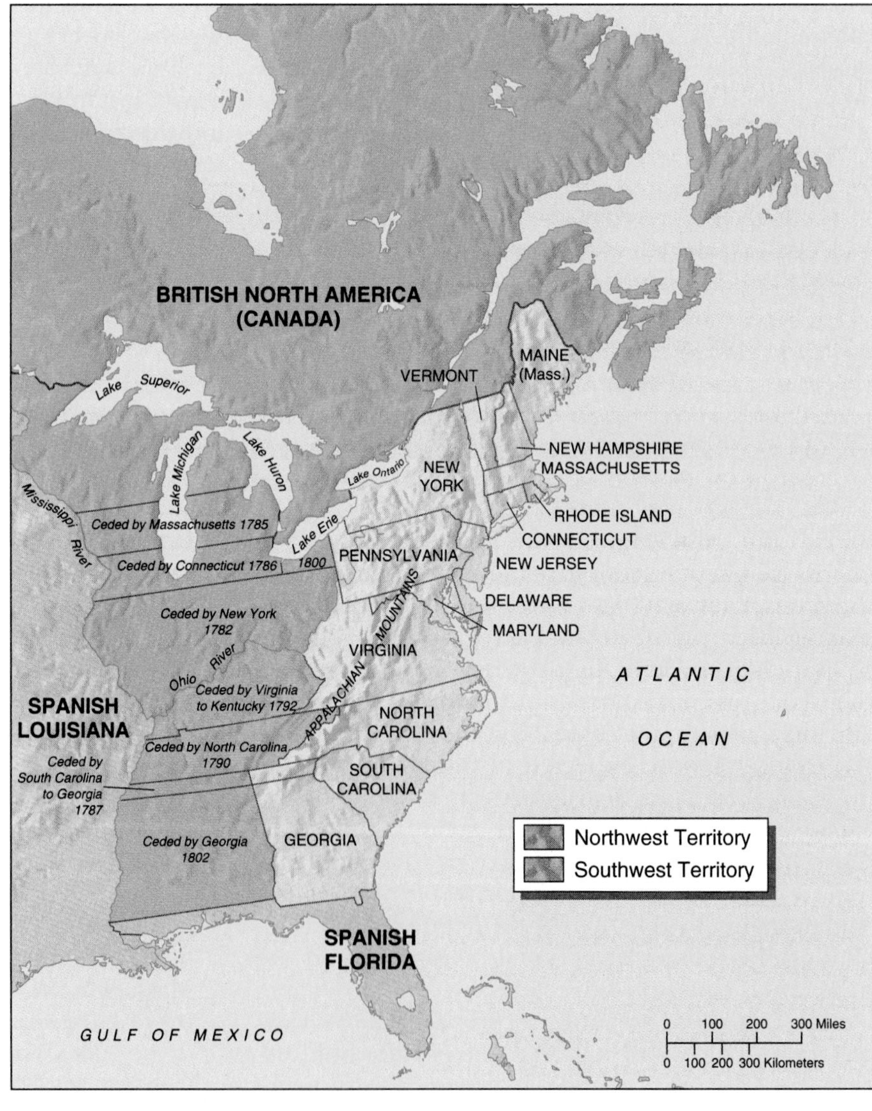

Map 7-1 Cession of Western Lands by the States
Eight states had claims to lands in the West after the Revolution, and their willingness to cede them to the national government was an essential step in the creation of a public domain administered by Congress.

Problems at Home

Neither prosperity nor political stability accompanied the return of peace in 1783. The national government struggled to avoid bankruptcy, and in 1784, an economic depression struck the country. As fiscal problems deepened, creditor and debtor groups clashed angrily in state legislatures. When legislatures passed measures that provided relief to debtors at the expense of creditors, the creditors decried what they saw as the interference of ignorant majorities with the rights of private property. Raising the cry of "legislative despotism," the abuse of power by tyrannical lawmakers, they joined their voices to those who early on had wanted the power of the states curbed by a stronger central government. The only solid accomplishment of the Confederation Congress during this troubled period was to formulate an orderly and democratic plan for the settlement of the West.

The Fiscal Crisis

The Continental Congress and the states incurred heavy debts to finance the Revolutionary War. Unable to impose and collect sufficient taxes to cover the debts and without reserves of gold or silver, they had to borrow funds and issue certificates or bonds pledging repayment. Congress had the largest responsibility for meeting the war's costs, and to do so it printed close to $250 million in paper notes backed only by its good faith. By the end of the war in 1781, these Continental dollars were nearly worthless, and the national debt—primarily certificates issued by the Continental Loan Office—stood at $11 million. As Congress issued new securities to settle claims by soldiers and civilians, this sum rose to $28 million within just a few years.

Issued in 1777, this Georgia four-dollar banknote was an example of the type of paper money used to finance the Revolutionary War.

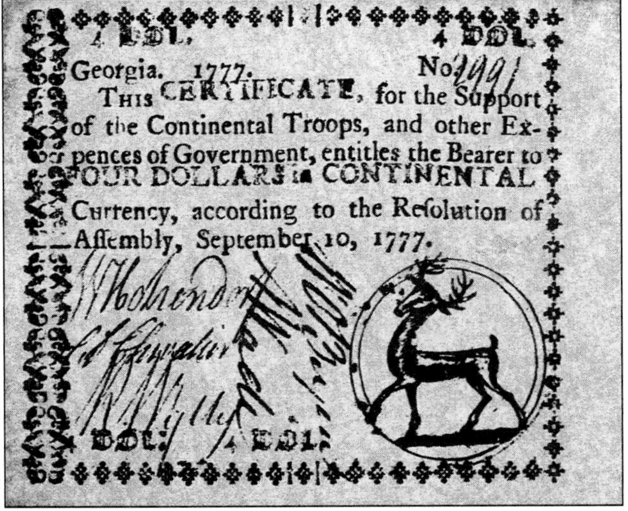

Congress never did put its tottering finances on a sound footing, and its fiscal problems ultimately discredited the Articles of Confederation in the eyes of the **nationalists**, a loose bloc of congressmen, army officers, and public creditors who wanted to strengthen the Confederation at the expense of the states. The nationalists first began to organize in the dark days of 1780 and 1781 when inflation was rampant, the army was going unpaid, Congress had ceased paying interest on the public debt, and the war effort itself seemed in danger of collapsing. Galvanized by this crisis, the nationalists rallied behind Robert Morris, a Philadelphia merchant appointed as superintendent of finance for the Confederation government.

Morris, who came to be known as the "financier of the Revolution," sought to enhance national authority through a bold program of financial and political reform. He began by securing a charter from Congress in 1781 for the Bank of North America, the nation's first commercial bank. Located in Philadelphia and partly owned by private investors, the bank had close connections to the Confederation government. Morris wanted it to serve as a national institution, and he used it to hold government funds, make loans to the government, and issue bank notes—paper money that could be used to settle debts and pay taxes owed to the United States. Morris was able to resume some specie payments, and he temporarily stabilized the nation's finances.

Morris's larger objective—central to the aims of the nationalists—was to create a "bond of union" by having Congress assume payment of the entire national debt. Settling this debt would lead the propertied classes—the people who had financed the war and held the debt—to identify their economic self-interest with the effective exercise of power by the national government.

But to achieve this political goal, Morris had to gain for Congress what it had always lacked: the power to tax. In 1781, he proposed a national impost, or tariff, of 5 percent on imported goods. Because this was a national tax, it required an amendment to the Articles of Confederation and the consent of all thirteen states. Twelve of the states quickly ratified the impost amendment, but Rhode Island—critically dependent on its own import duties to finance its war debt—rejected it. When a revised impost plan was considered two years later, New York blocked it.

These failures doomed Morris's financial reforms. He left office in 1784, and in the same year the Bank of North America severed its ties to the national government and became a private corporation in Pennsylvania. Morris remained committed to the nationalist cause and would see his ideas resurface under the financial programs of Treasury Secretary Alexander Hamilton in the 1790s (see Chapter 8).

The failure of the impost tax was one of many setbacks that put the nationalists temporarily on the defensive. With the conclusion of peace in 1783, confidence in state government returned, taking the edge off calls to invest the central government with greater authority. The states continued to balk at supplying the money requisitioned from them by Congress and denied Congress even limited authority to regulate foreign commerce. Most ominously for the nationalist cause, the states began to assume responsibility for part of the national debt. By 1786, New Jersey, Pennsylvania, Maryland, and New York had absorbed one-third of the debt by issuing state bonds to their citizens in exchange for national securities. As Morris had warned in 1781, such a policy entailed "a principle of disunion . . . which must be ruinous."

Without the power to tax, Congress was a hostage to the sovereignty of the individual states with no real authority over the nation's economic affairs. When the economy plunged into a severe depression in 1784, it could only look on helplessly.

Economic Depression

During the Revolutionary War, Britain closed its markets to American goods. After the war, the British continued this policy, hoping to keep the United States weak and dependent. In the summer of 1783, they excluded Americans from the lucrative trade with the British West Indies that before the revolution had been the colonists' primary source for the credits they needed to offset their imports from Britain.

Meanwhile, British merchants were happy to satisfy America's pent-up demand for consumer goods. A flood of cheap British imports inundated the American market, and coastal merchants made them available to inland traders and shopkeepers by extending easy credit terms. In turn, these local businessmen sold the goods to farmers and artisans in the interior. Ultimately, however, the British merchants required payment in hard currency—gold and silver coins. Without access to its former export markets, America's only source of hard currency was foreign loans obtained by Congress and what money the French army had spent during the war. This was soon exhausted as America's trade deficit with Britain—the excess of imports over exports—ballooned in the early 1780s to £5 million (see Figure 7-2).

The result was an immense bubble of credit that finally burst in 1784, triggering a depression that would linger for most of the rest of the decade. As merchants began to press debtors for immediate payment, prices collapsed (they fell more than 25 percent between 1784 and 1786), and debtors were unable to pay.

Small farmers everywhere had trouble paying their taxes. In 1786, James Swan of Massachusetts wrote of farmers in his state: "There is no family that does not want some money for some purposes, and the little which the farmer carries home from market, must be applied to other uses, besides paying off the [tax] collector's bills." Rural shop-

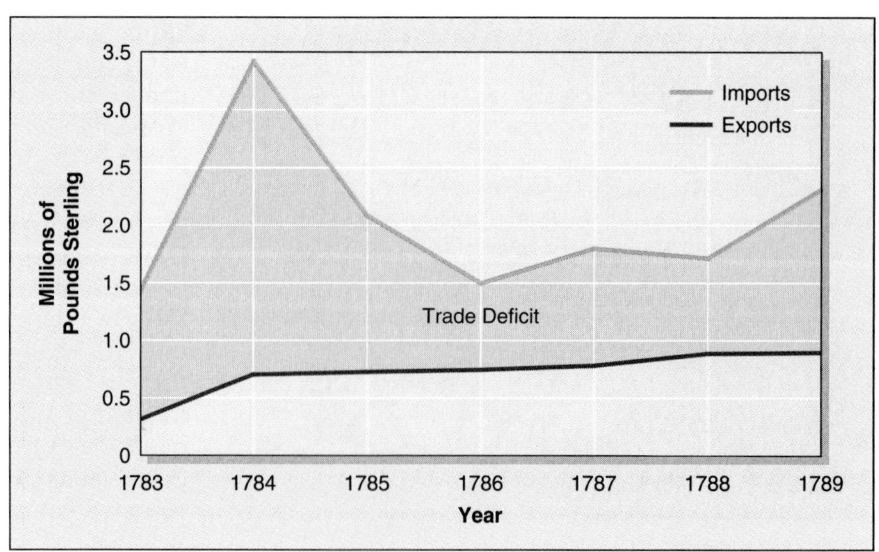

Figure 7-2 American Exports to and Imports from Britain between 1783 and 1789
During the 1780s, the United States imported far more from Britain than it exported there. The resulting huge trade deficit drained the country of gold and silver and was a major factor in the credit crisis that triggered an economic depression in the middle of the decade.

Data Source: U.S. Bureau of the Census, Historical Statistics of the United States: Colonial Times to 1970, Part 2 (1975), p. 1176.

keepers often could not move goods unless they agreed to barter them for farm produce. Abigail Dwight, who ran a small store in western Massachusetts, reported in 1785 that "most of these People sell on credit for To-Morrow at large—for very little Cash stirring this way—to be pay'd for in old Horses—cows—some Boards—cabbages—turnips—Potatoes etc."

In the cities, wages fell 25 percent between 1785 and 1789, and workers began to organize. They called for tariffs to protect them from cheap British imports and for legislative measures to promote American manufacturers. In the countryside, farmers faced a wave of lawsuits for the collection of debts and the dread possibility of losing their land. "To be tenants to landlords, we know not who," protested the farmers of Conway, Massachusetts, "and pay rent for lands, purchased with our money, and converted from howling wilderness, into fruitful fields, by the sweat of our brows, seems . . . truly shocking."

With insufficient money in circulation to raise prices and reverse the downturn, the depression fed on itself. Congress was powerless to raise cash and was unable to pay off its old debts, including what it owed to the Revolutionary soldiers. Many state governments made things worse by imposing heavy taxes payable in the paper money they had issued during the Revolution. The result was further to reduce the amount of money in circulation, forcing prices still lower.

Britain's trade policies caused particular suffering among New England merchants. No longer protected under the old Navigation Acts as British vessels, American ships were now barred from most ports in the British Empire. Incoming cargoes from the West Indies to New England fell off sharply, and the market for whale oil and fish, two of New England's major exports, dried up. The economy of the mid-Atlantic region held up somewhat better, but even there the loss of the provisioning trade to the British West Indies in grains, livestock, and dairy products cut into the income of merchants and farmers and forced layoffs among artisans who serviced the shipping trade.

In the southern states, British policies made it harder to recover from the physical damage and social disruptions of the war. Some 10 percent of the region's slaves had fled, and production levels on plantations fell. Chesapeake planters needed a full decade to restore tobacco production to its prewar levels, and a collapse in tobacco prices in 1785 left most of them in the same chronic state of indebtedness that had plagued them on the eve of the Revolution. Rice production in the Carolina lowcountry was similarly slow to recover, despite the debts planters piled up to purchase additional slaves and repair their war-damaged plantations. Burdened by new British duties on American rice, planters saw rice exports fall by 50 percent. Small farmers in the pine barrens of North Carolina likewise had to adjust to the loss of their formerly protected British market for naval stores—tar, pitch, and turpentine.

By the late 1780s, the worst of the depression was over, and an upturn was under way in the mid-Atlantic states. Food exports to continental Europe were on the rise, and American merchants were developing new trading ties with India and China. Commercial treaties with the Dutch, Swedes, and

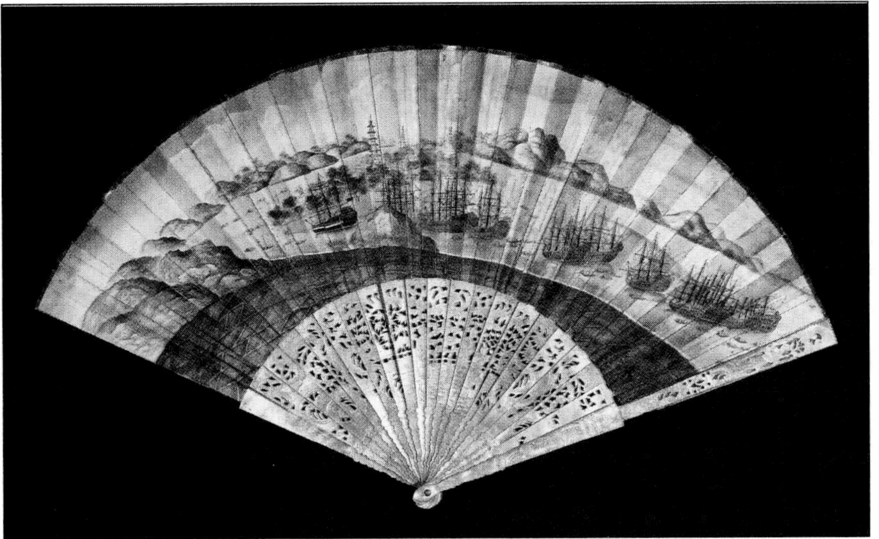

Courtesy of The Historical Society of Pennsylvania.

Depicted here in a folding fan, the Empress of China *was the first American ship to undertake an extensive trading voyage to China. Sailing out of New York in February 1784, the* Empress of China *returned on May 11, 1785, and netted a profit of $37,000 for the investors who had financed the voyage. Building trading contacts to new markets in Asia and Europe helped the United States break its economic dependence on England.*

Prussians also opened up markets that had been closed to the colonists. Nonetheless, a full recovery had to await the 1790s.

The depression of the 1780s was the culmination of a decade of painful adjustment that followed the wrenching of the American economy from its traditional moorings within the British trading empire. A stagnant economy and burdensome debt combined with a growing population (there were 50 percent more Americans in 1787 than there had been in 1775) to reduce living standards. With more losers than winners, economic conflict dominated the politics of the Confederation period.

The Economic Policies of the States

The depression had political repercussions in all the states. Britain was an obvious target of popular anger, and merchants poorly positioned to adjust to the postwar dislocations of trade led a campaign to slap retaliatory duties on British ships and special taxes on the goods they carried. Likewise artisans and workers, especially in the North, pushed for tariff barriers against cheap British goods as a way to encourage domestic manufacturing and protect their jobs and wages.

State legislatures in the North responded to the protests of artisans by passing tariffs, but the lack of a uniform, national policy doomed their efforts. Shippers evaded high tariffs by bringing their cargoes in through states with no tariffs or less restrictive ones. States without ports, like New Jersey and North Carolina, complained of economic discrimination. When they purchased foreign goods from a neighboring shipping state, they were forced to pay part of the tariff cost, but all the revenue from the tariff accrued only to the importing state. James Madison neatly summarized the plight of these states when he noted that "New Jersey, placed between Philadelphia and New York, was likened to a cask tapped at both ends; And North Carolina, between Virginia and South Carolina, to a patient bleeding at both Arms."

Tariff policies also fed sectional tensions that undermined efforts to confer on Congress the power to regulate commerce. The agrarian states of the South, which had little in the way of manufacturing to protect, had different interests than the states of the North. With the exception of Virginia, they favored free trade policies that encouraged British imports. Southern planters were also happy to take advantage of the low rates charged by British ships for transporting their crops to Europe; by doing so, they put pressure on northern shippers to reduce their rates.

The bitterest divisions exposed by the depression of the 1780s, however, were not between states but between debtors and creditors within states. As the value of debt securities the states had issued to raise money dropped during the Revolutionary War, speculators bought them up for a fraction of their face value and then put pressure on the states to raise taxes and repay the debts in full in hard currency. Wealthy landowners and merchants likewise supported higher taxes and the rapid repayment of debts in hard currency. Arrayed against these creditor groups by the mid-1780s was a broad coalition of debtors comprised of middling farmers, small shopkeepers, artisans, laborers, and people who had overextended themselves speculating in western land. The debtors wanted the states to issue paper money that they could use instead of hard money—gold and silver—to pay their debts. The paper money would have an inflationary effect, raising wages and the prices of farm commodities and reducing the value of debts contracted in hard currency. The townspeople of Atkinson, New Hampshire, expressing the feelings of many hard-pressed rural areas, put the issue this way: "For want of a suitable medium of trade the Citizens of this State are altogether unable to pay their public taxes, or private debts, or even to support the train of needless and expensive lawsuits, which alone would be an insupportable burden."

This was the economic context in which Shays's Rebellion exploded in the fall of 1786. Farm foreclosures and imprisonments for failure to pay debts had skyrocketed in western Massachusetts. Facing a collapse in farm prices and an impoverishing debt, farmers petitioned the state legislators for economic relief. They complained of heavy taxes and the shortage of money and demanded legislation that would temporarily prohibit creditors from seizing farms or pressing suits for debt collection. When the creditor and seaboard interests in the legislature refused to pass any relief measures, some two thousand farmers took up arms against the state government. Following Daniel Shays, a former Revolutionary War officer, they shut down the courts—and with them the legal machinery for collecting debts—in three counties in western Massachusetts. When they marched on the state arsenal in Springfield, alarmed state officials raised troops to crush the uprising.

Unlike the Shaysite rebels, discontented debtors elsewhere were often successful in changing the monetary policy of their states and generally stopped short of armed resistance. In 1785 and 1786, seven states enacted laws for new paper money issues. In most cases, the result was a qualified success. Controls on the supply of the new money kept it from depreciating rapidly, so its inflationary effect was mild. It was used chiefly to provide loans to farmers so they could meet their tax or mortgage payments. Combined with laws that prevented or delayed creditors from seizing property from debtors to satisfy debts, the currency issues helped keep a lid on popular discontent.

The most notorious exception to this pattern of fiscal responsibility was in Rhode Island, already nicknamed "Rogue's Island" for the sharp trading practices of its merchants. A rural party that gained control of the Rhode Island legislature in 1786 pushed through a currency law that flooded the state with paper money that could be used to pay all debts. Creditors who balked at accepting the new money at face value were subject to heavy penalties. Shocked, they went into hiding or left the state entirely, and merchants denounced the law as outright fraud.

The actions of the debtor party in Rhode Island alarmed conservatives everywhere, confirming their fears that legislative bodies dominated by common farmers and artisans rather than, as before the Revolution, by men of wealth and social distinction, were dangerous. One South Carolina conservative declared that he could see nothing but an "open and outrageous . . . violation of every principle of justice" in paper money and debt-relief laws. Conservatives, creditors, and nationalists alike now spoke of a democratic tyranny that would have to be checked if the republic were to survive and protect its property holders.

Congress and the West

The Treaty of Paris and the surrender of charter claims by the states gave Congress control of a magnificent expanse of land between the Appalachian Mountains and the Mississippi River. This was the first American West. In what would prove the most enduring accomplishment of the Confederation government, Congress set forth a series of effective provisions for its settlement, governance, and eventual absorption into the Union.

Congress took several steps to establish its jurisdiction in the West. Asserting for the national government the right to formulate Indian policy, Congress negotiated a series of treaties with the Indians, beginning in 1784, for the abandonment of their land claims in the West. By threatening to use military force, congressional commissioners in 1784 coerced the Iroquois Confederation of New York to cede half of its territory to the United States in the Treaty of Fort Stanwix. Similar tactics in 1785 resulted in the Treaty of Fort McIntosh, in which the northwestern tribes ceded much of their land in Ohio. Against the opposition of states intent on grabbing Indian lands for themselves, Congress resolved in 1787 that its treaties were binding on all the states. And anxious for revenue, Congress insisted on payment from squatters who had filtered into the West before provisions had been made for land sales.

The most pressing political challenge was to secure the loyalty of the West to the new and fragile Union. To satisfy the demands of settlers for self-government, Congress resolved as early as 1779 that new states would be carved out of the western domain with all the rights of the original states. An early plan for organizing the territories, the Ordinance of 1784, was largely the work of Thomas Jefferson. In it, he proposed to create ten districts or territories—suggesting such whimsical names for them as Assenissipia and Cherronesus—each of which could apply for admission as a state when its population equaled that of the free inhabitants in the least populous of the existing states. Jefferson also proposed that settlers be permitted to choose their own officials, and he called for the prohibition of slavery in the West after 1800. Shorn of its no-slavery features, the ordinance passed Congress but was never put into practice.

As settlers and speculators began pouring into the West in 1784, however, Congress was forced to move quickly to formulate a policy for conveying its public land into private hands. If it couldn't regulate land sales and pass on clear titles, Congress would, in effect, have surrendered its claim to govern. One way or another, settlers were going to get their land, but a pell-mell process of private acquisitions in widely scattered settlements threatened to touch off costly Indian wars, deprive the national government of vitally needed revenue, and encourage separatist movements. The members of Congress had to act on national land policy, warned a western Pennsylvanian, or else "lose the only opportunity they ever will have of extending their power and influence over this new region."

Congress responded with the **Land Ordinance of 1785**. The crucial feature of this seminal legislation was its stipulation that public lands be surveyed in a rectangular grid pattern before being offered for sale (see Figure 7-3). By requiring that land first be plotted into townships of thirty-six uniform sections of 640 acres each, the ordinance adopted the New England system of land settlement, an approach that promoted compact settlements and produced undisputed land titles. In sharp contrast was the typical southern pattern whereby settlers picked out a piece of land in a large tract ahead of a precise survey and then fought each other in the courts to secure legal title. In an effort to avoid endless litigation, Congress opted for a policy geared to order and regularity.

Congress also attempted to attract a certain type of settler to the West by offering the plots of 640 acres at the then hefty sum of no less than $640, or $1 per acre, payable in hard currency or its equivalent. The goal here was to keep out the shiftless poor and reserve the West for enterprising and presumably law-abiding farm families who could afford the entry cost. Concerned about westerners' reputation for lawlessness, Congress also set aside the income from the sale of the sixteenth section in each township for the support of public schools. Education, as a congressional report of 1783 put it, would help provide for "security against the increase of feeble, disorderly and dispersed settlements in those remote and extended territories [and] against the depravity of manners which they have a tendency to produce."

Before any land sales occurred under the Ordinance of 1785, impatient settlers continued to push north of the Ohio River and claim homesteads

Figure 7-3 Land Ordinance of 1785
The precise uniformity of the surveying system initiated in the Land Ordinance of 1785 created a rectangular grid pattern that was the model for all future land surveyed in the public domain.

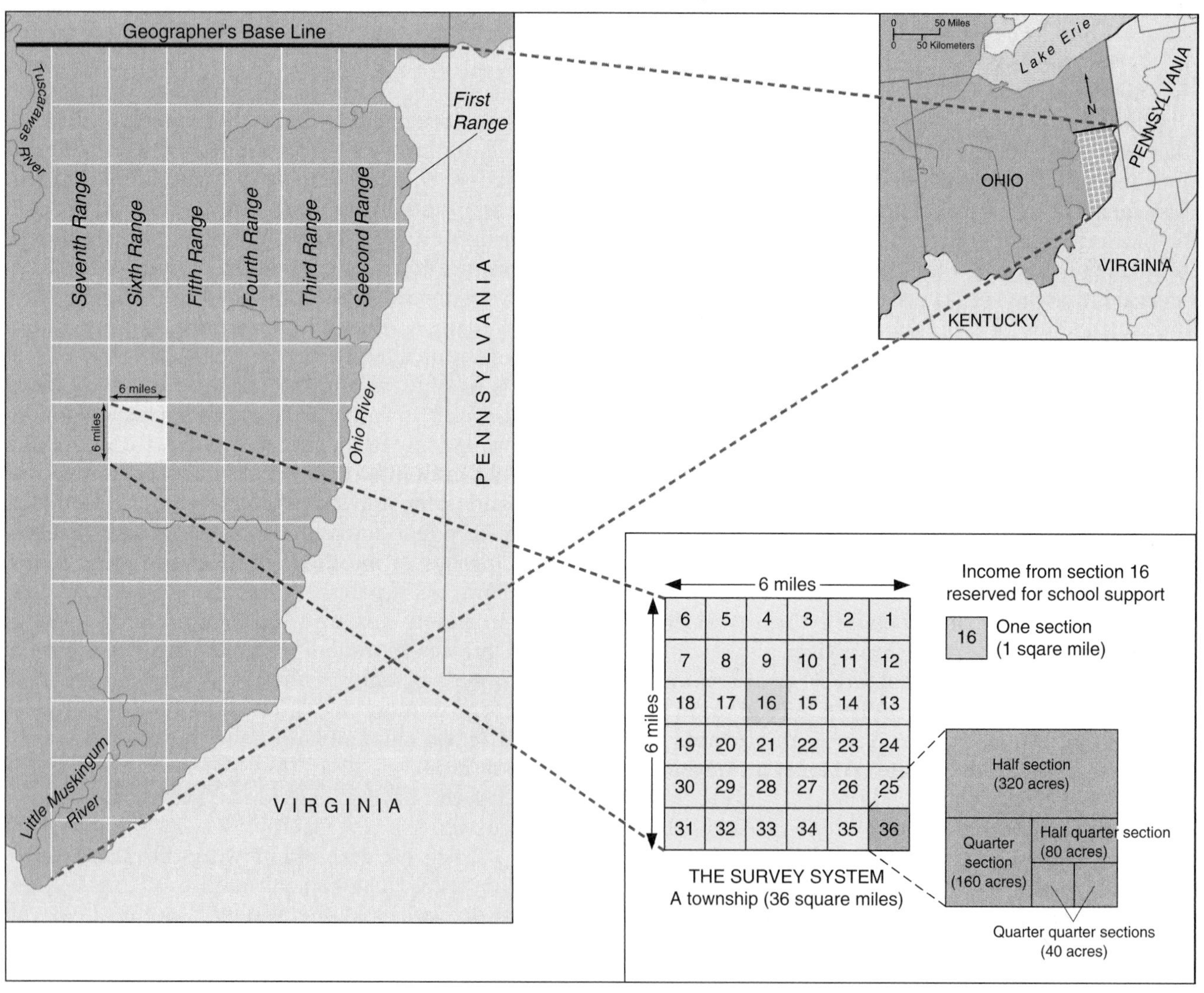

as squatters. They clashed both with local Indian tribes and the troops sent by Congress to evict them. Impatient itself with the slow process of surveying, Congress sold off a million and a half acres to a group of New England speculators organized as the Ohio Company. The speculators bought the land with greatly depreciated loan office certificates that had been issued to Revolutionary War veterans, and their cost per acre averaged less than 10 cents in hard money. They now pressed their allies in Congress to establish a governmental structure for the West that would protect their investment by bringing the unruly elements in the West under control.

Both Congress and speculators wanted political stability and economic development in the West and a degree of supervision for settlers commonly viewed in the East as "but little less savage than the Indians." What was needed, wrote James Monroe of Virginia, were temporary controls—made acceptable by the promise of eventual statehood—that "in effect" would place the western territories under "a colonial government similar to that which prevail'd in these States previous to the revolution." The **Northwest Ordinance of 1787**, the most significant legislative act of the Confederation Congress, filled this need, creating a political structure for the territories and a phased process for achieving statehood that neatly blended public and private interests.

According to the ordinance, controls on a new territory were to be strictest in the early stage of settlement, when Congress would appoint a territorial government consisting of a governor, a secretary, and three judges. When a territory reached a population of five thousand adult males, those with 50 acres of land or more could elect a legislature. The actions of the legislature, however, were subject to an absolute veto by the governor. Once a territory had a population of sixty thousand, the settlers could draft a constitution and apply for statehood "on an equal footing with the original states in all respects whatsoever."

Unlike Jefferson's Ordinance of 1784, which called for ten states, the Northwest Ordinance of 1787 stipulated that only three to five states were to be formed out of the Northwest. This was because the admission of new states would weaken the control over Congress that the original thirteen states wanted to maintain for themselves as long as possible. Although less democratic in many respects than Jefferson's plan in mandating a period of outside control by Congress, the 1787 ordinance did provide greater protection for property rights as well as a bill of rights guaranteeing individual freedoms. Most significant, it prohibited slavery.

Southern congressmen agreed to the slavery ban in part because they feared that planters in the new states would compete with them in the production of slave-produced staples such as tobacco. More important, however, they expected slavery to be permitted in the region south of the Ohio River that was still under the administrative authority of Virginia, North Carolina, and Georgia in the 1780s. Indeed, slavery was allowed in this region when the **Southwest Ordinance of 1790** brought it under national control, a decision that would have grave consequences in the future sectionalization of the United States.

Although the Northwest Ordinance applied only to the national domain north of the Ohio River, it provided the organizational blueprint by which all future territory was brought into the Union. It went into effect immediately and set the original Union on a course of dynamic expansion through the addition of new states.

Diplomatic Weaknesses

In the international arena of the 1780s, the United States was weak and often ridiculed. Under the Articles of Confederation, Congress had the authority to negotiate foreign treaties but no economic or military power to enforce them. Unable to regulate commerce or set tariffs, it had no leverage with which to pry open the restricted trading empires of France, Spain, and most important, Britain.

France and the United States, allies during the Revolutionary War, remained on friendly terms. The United States even had a favorable trade balance with France, selling more there than it bought. Britain, however, treated its former colonies with contempt, and Spain was likewise openly antagonistic to the new nation. Both Britain and Spain sought to block American expansion into the trans-Appalachian West. And a dispute with Spain over the West produced the most serious diplomatic crisis of the period, one that spilled over into domestic politics, increasing sectional tensions between northern and southern states and leading many to question the country's chances of survival.

Impasse with Britain

The Confederation Congress was unable to resolve any of the major issues that poisoned Anglo-American relations in the 1780s. Key among these were provisions in the peace treaty of 1783 that concerned prewar American debts to the British and the treatment of Loyalists by the patriots. Britain used what it claimed to be America's failure to satisfy those provisions to justify its own violations of the treaty. The result was a diplomatic deadlock that hurt American interests in the West and in foreign trade.

The peace treaty called for the payment of all prewar debts at their "full value in sterling money"—that is, in gold or silver coin. Among the most numerous of those with outstanding debts to British creditors were tobacco planters in the Chesapeake region. During the Revolution, the British army had carried off and freed many of the region's slaves without compensating the planters. Still angry, the planters were in no mood to repay their debts. Working out a scheme with their respective legislatures, they agreed only to pay the face value of their debts to their state treasuries in state or Continental paper money. Because this money was practically worthless, the planters in effect repudiated their debts.

During the Revolution, all the states had passed anti-Loyalist legislation, and many state governments had seized Loyalists' lands and goods, selling them to raise revenue for the war effort. Upwards of 100,000 Loyalists fled to Canada and England, and their property losses ran into millions of dollars. The peace treaty pledged Congress to "recommend" to the states that they stop persecuting Loyalists and restore confiscated property. But wartime animosities remained high. Despite the pleadings of John Jay, the secretary for foreign affairs in the Confederation government, the states were slow to rescind their punitive legislation or allow the recovery of property.

Combined with the matter of the unpaid debts, the continued failure of the states to make restitution to the Loyalists gave the British a convenient pretext to hold on to the forts in the West that they had promised to relinquish in the Treaty of Paris. Their refusal to abandon the forts, which extended from Lake Champlain in upstate New York westward along the Great Lakes, was part of an overall strategy to keep the United States weak, divided, and small. The continued British presence in the region effectively shut Americans out of the fur trade with the Indians. It also insulted the sovereignty of the United States and threatened the security of its northern frontier. In 1784, exasperated New Yorkers warned Congress that unless the British were forced to leave, New York would "be compelled to consider herself as left to pursue her own Councils, destitute of the Protection of the United States." Elsewhere, the British, spurred on by Canadian officials, encouraged secessionist movements in the Northwest and sought out Indian allies to fight for a possible buffer state south of the Great Lakes that would keep Americans hemmed in along the Atlantic seaboard.

Throughout the 1780s, the British also explored the possibility of entering into an economic alliance with Vermont. Created in 1777 out of land claimed by both New York and New Hampshire, Vermont proclaimed itself an independent republic, free from the control of the British Parliament and the American Congress. Ethan Allen and his brothers Ira and Levi dominated Vermont politics, and their ambitious schemes for profiting from the sale of such raw materials as lumber and naval stores depended on a favorable treaty with Britain. The Allens offered the British a treaty of friendship in exchange for recognition of Vermont's independence and trading privileges within the British Empire. The British were tempted but held back for fear of unduly antagonizing the United States. (Most Vermonters were strongly pro-American in their loyalties, and, in 1791, after settlement of the disputed land claims, Vermont joined the Union as the fourteenth state.)

Although concerned by British provocations in the West and the possibility that Vermont would become a British client state, American officials viewed Britain's retaliatory trade policies as the gravest threat to American security and prosperity. John Adams, the American minister to London, sought in vain to counter Britain's anti-American economic policies. "I may reason till I die to no purpose," Adams reported to Jay in June 1785, and he complained that he was treated as a complete "cypher."

Adams soon concluded that the British would never lift their trading and shipping restrictions until forced to do so by a uniform American system of discriminatory duties on British goods. The problem was that a uniform policy was impossible to achieve under the Articles of Confederation. Retaliatory navigation acts by individual states did little good because they left the British free to play one state off another. Adams could denounce Parliament as a "parcel of sots" for restricting American trade, but only with a strong, centralized government could Americans fashion a navigation system that would command Britain's respect.

Spain and the Mississippi River

At the close of the Revolutionary War, Spain reimposed barriers on American commerce within its empire. Anxious to maintain as large a buffer zone as possible between its Louisiana and Florida possessions and the restless Americans, Spain also refused to recognize the southern and western boundaries of the United States as specified in the treaty with Britain in 1783, holding out instead for a more northerly border (see Map 7-2). And, of greatest consequence, it denied the claim of the United

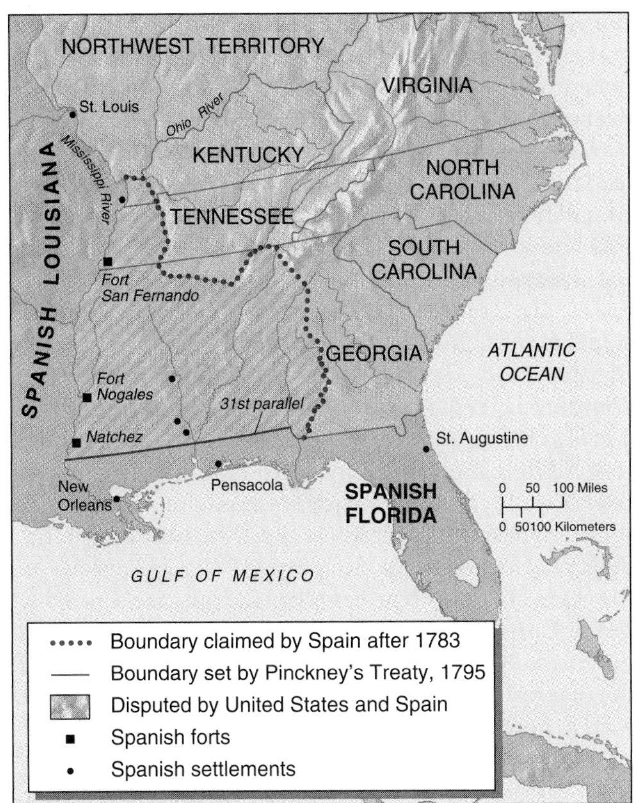

Map 7-2 Disputed Territory in the West after the Treaty of Paris
Throughout the 1780s, Spain asserted title to a large area in the West south of the Ohio River.

States to free navigation of the entire length of the Mississippi River.

The Mississippi question was explosive because on its resolution hinged American settlement and control of the entire western region south of the Ohio River. Southerners were rapidly moving into this area, and the slave South expected to gain new support for an alliance against the commercial North as new slave states were created south of the Ohio. Free navigation of the Mississippi was essential to the realization of these expectations. Only with access to the Mississippi and the commercial right of deposit at New Orleans—that is, the right to transfer cargoes to oceangoing vessels—could the region's farmers, then mostly in what would become Tennessee and Kentucky, profitably reach national and international markets.

In the wake of the Revolution, the settlers of Kentucky, which was still part of Virginia, and Tennessee, which was still part of North Carolina, flirted with the idea of secession. According to a 1785 report, settlers in Kentucky felt they did "not at present enjoy a greater portion of liberty [under Virginia] than an American colony might have done a few years ago had she been allowed a Representation in the British Parliament." Impatient to secure both political independence and the economic benefits that would come with access to the Mississippi, the separatists were not particular about whom they dealt with. They became entangled in a web of diplomatic intrigue that included the Spanish, the Indians, and American authorities east of the mountains.

Spain sought to trade on the divided loyalties of American speculators and frontier settlers to its advantage, employing some of them as spies and informers. Led by General James Wilkinson in Kentucky, these agents encouraged separatist plots and talk of a western confederation under Spanish protection. Spain likewise sought to exploit divisions among Indian groups. When the Confederation government and the state of Georgia negotiated treaties with southern Indians to open up land for white settlement, the Spanish responded by recruiting Indian groups into an alliance system of their own. The staunchest of the Spanish allies were the Creeks, a tribe of some five thousand warriors led by Alexander McGillivray, son of a trader father and a half-French, half-Creek mother.

Spain stepped up pressure on the West in the summer of 1784 when it closed the Mississippi River within Spanish territory to American trade. Hoping now to benefit from American weakness, Spain also opened negotiations for a long-term settlement with the United States. The Spanish negotiator, Don Diego de Gardoqui, offered a deal that cleverly played the interests of the North against those of the South and West. In exchange for an American agreement to surrender claims to navigate the Mississippi for thirty years, Gardoqui proposed to grant the United States significant trading concessions in the Spanish Empire that would open new markets and new sources of hard money to the financially pressed merchants of the northeastern states. John Jay, his American negotiating partner, reluctantly accepted the offer.

When Jay released the terms of the proposed treaty with Spain in 1786, Congress erupted in angry debate. Southerners, who had taken the lead in the settlement of the West, accused Jay of selling out their interests. The treaty threatened the agrarian alliance they hoped to forge with the West, increasing the odds that the West would break from the East and go its own way. Vowing that they would not surrender the West, southern congressmen united to defeat the treaty. Nine states' votes were required for ratification under the Articles, and Jay's treaty could gain only seven—all in the North.

The regional antagonisms exposed by the Jay–Gardoqui talks heightened the alarm over the

This portrait, sketched in about 1790 by John Trumbull, is the only known likeness of Alexander McGillivray, a Creek leader who effectively played off Spanish and American interests in the Southeast to gain a measure of independence for the Creeks in the 1780s.

future of the republic provoked by Shays's Rebellion earlier in 1786. The Union had never appeared more fragile nor Congress so powerless. Southerners openly calculated the value of remaining in a Union seemingly dominated by the commercial North, and Westerners warned that unless they were upheld on the Mississippi issue, they would consider themselves "relieved from all Federal Obligations and fully at Liberty to exact alliances & Connections wherever they find them." As the sense of crisis deepened in 1786, the nationalists grew in influence and numbers. Led by Alexander Hamilton of New York and James Madison of Virginia, they now argued that only a radical political change could preserve the republic.

Toward a New Union

In June 1786, a worried John Jay wrote to George Washington that he was "uneasy and apprehensive; more so than during the war. Then we had a fixed object. . . . The case is now altered; we are going and doing wrong, and therefore I look forward to evils and calamities, but without being able to guess at the instrument, nature, or measure of them." Other nationalists fully shared Jay's forebodings. Everywhere they saw unsolved problems and portents of disaster: unpaid debts, social unrest, squabbling states, sectional hostilities, the uncertain status of the West, blocked channels of trade, foreign intrigues, and a paralyzing lack of centralized authority.

In September 1786, delegates from several states met at the **Annapolis Convention**, in Annapolis, Maryland, seeking to devise a uniform system of commercial regulation for the country. While there, a group of nationalist leaders called on all the states to send delegates to a convention at Philadelphia "to devise such further provisions as shall appear to them necessary to render the constitution of the Federal Government adequate to the exigencies of the Union." The leaders who met at the **Constitutional Convention** in Philadelphia forged an entirely new framework of governance, the **Constitution of the United States**, that called for a federal republic with a powerful and effective national government. In 1788, after a close struggle in state ratifying conventions, the Constitution was adopted.

The Road to Philadelphia

The road to Philadelphia began at Mount Vernon, George Washington's estate in Virginia. Commissioners from Maryland and Virginia met there in March 1785 to resolve jurisdictional and navigational disputes over the Potomac River and Chesapeake Bay, waters shared by both states. Washington had a personal stake in hosting the conference, for he was president of the Potomac Company, a newly formed group of investors hoping to build a series of canals linking the Potomac River with the Shenandoah and Ohio Valleys. The meeting went so well that the participants invited representatives from Delaware and Pennsylvania to join them at a conference in Annapolis the following year to formulate policies for interstate commerce on the waterways that linked the Chesapeake region and the Ohio Valley. James Madison then broadened the scope of the Annapolis Conference to include representatives from all thirteen states for a general discussion of how best to promote and regulate interstate trade.

Only nine states decided to send delegates to the Annapolis Convention, and those from only five had actually arrived when the nationalists, at the prompting of Madison and Hamilton, abruptly adjourned the meeting. They then called on the states and Congress to approve a full-scale constitutional convention for Philadelphia in May 1787.

The timing of the call for the Philadelphia Convention could not have been better. During the fall and winter of 1786, the agrarian protests unleashed by Shays's Rebellion in Massachusetts spilled over into other states. For many Americans, especially those with wealth to protect, Shays's Rebellion dramatized the need for change. Coupled with talk of a dismemberment of the Union in the wake of the Jay–Gardoqui negotiations, the agrarian unrest strengthened the case of the nationalists for more centralized authority.

All the states except Rhode Island, which wanted to retain exclusive control over its own trade, sent delegates to Philadelphia. The fifty-five men who attended the convention represented an extraordinary array of talent and experience. Chiefly lawyers by training or profession, most of them had served in the Confederation Congress, and more than one-third had fought in the Revolution. Extremely well educated by the standards of the day, the delegates were members of the intellectual as well as the political and economic elite. As a group, they were far wealthier than the average American. Most had investments in land and the public securities of the United States. At least nineteen owned slaves. Their greatest asset as a working body was their common commitment to a nationalist solution to the crisis of confidence they saw gripping the republic. Strong supporters of the Articles of Confederation mostly refused to attend, perhaps because, as Patrick Henry of Virginia remarked, they "smelt a rat."

The Convention at Work

When it agreed to the Philadelphia Convention, Congress authorized only a revision of the Articles of Confederation. Almost from the start, however, the delegates set about replacing the Articles altogether. Their first action was to elect George Washington unanimously as the convention's presiding officer, gaining credibility for their deliberations from his prestige. The most ardent nationalists then immediately seized the initiative by presenting the **Virginia Plan**. Drafted by James Madison, this plan replaced the Confederation Congress with a truly national government organized like most state governments, with a bicameral legislature, an executive, and a judiciary.

Two features of the Virginia Plan stood out. First, it granted the national Congress power to legislate "in all cases in which the separate states are incompetent" and to nullify any state laws that in its judgment were contrary to the "articles of Union." Second, it made representation in both houses of Congress proportional to population. This meant that the most populous states would have more votes in Congress than the less populous states, giving them effective control of the government. In short, Madison sought to all but eliminate the independent authority of the states while also forcing the smaller states to defer to the more populous ones in national affairs.

Delegates from the small states countered with the **New Jersey Plan**, introduced on June 15 by William Paterson. This plan kept intact the basic structure of the Confederation Congress—one state, one vote—but otherwise amended the Articles by giving the national government the explicit power to tax and to regulate domestic and foreign commerce. In addition, it gave acts of Congress precedence over state legislation, making them "the supreme law of the respective states."

The New Jersey Plan was quickly voted down, and the convention remained deadlocked for another month over how to apportion state representation in the national government. The issue was finally resolved on July 16 with the so-called **Great Compromise**. Based on a proposal by Roger Sherman of Connecticut, the compromise split the differences between the small and large states. Small states were given equal footing with large states in the Senate, or upper house, where each would have two votes. In the lower house, the House of Representatives, the number of seats was made proportional to population, giving larger states the advantage. The Great Compromise also settled a sectional dispute over representation between the free (or about to be free) states and slave states. The southern states wanted slaves counted for apportioning representation in the House but excluded from direct tax assessments. The northern states wanted slaves counted for tax assessments but excluded for apportioning representation. To settle the issue, the Great Compromise settled on an expedient, if morally troubling, formula: Free residents were to be counted precisely; to that count would be added three-fifths "of all other persons," excluding Indians not taxed. Thus the slave states gained additional political representation, while the states in the North received assurances that the owners of nonvoting slaves would have to bear part of the cost of any direct taxes levied by the new government.

The Great Compromise ended the first phase of the convention, which had focused on the general framework of a stronger national government. In its next phase, the convention debated the specific powers to be delegated to the new government. It was at this point that the sectional cleavage between North and South over slavery and other issues came most prominently to the fore. As Madison had warned in late June, "the great division of interests" in the United States would arise from the effect of states "having or not having slaves."

The sectional clash first erupted over the power of Congress to regulate commerce. At issue was whether Congress could regulate trade and set tariffs by a simple majority vote. Southerners worried that a northern majority would pass navigation acts favoring northern shippers and drive up their export costs. To counter this threat, delegates from the Lower South demanded that a two-thirds majority be required to enact trade legislation. Suddenly, the central plank in the nationalists' program—the unified power to force trading concessions from Britain—was endangered. A frustrated Madison urged his fellow southerners to remember that "as we are laying the foundation of a great empire, we ought to take a permanent view of the subject."

In the end, Madison had his way; the delegates agreed that enacting trade legislation would require only a simple majority. In return, however, southerners exacted concessions on the slavery issue. When planters from South Carolina and Georgia made it clear they would agree to join a new Union only if they could continue to import slaves, the convention abandoned a proposal to ban the foreign slave trade. Instead, following the lead of Roger Sherman of Connecticut, who argued that emancipation sentiment would eventually lead to abolition of slavery anyway, antislavery New Englanders reached a compromise with the delegates from the lower South: Congress would be barred from acting against the slave trade for twenty years. In addition, bowing to the fears of planters that Congress could use its taxing power to undermine slavery, the convention denied Congress the right to tax exports from any state. And to alleviate southern concerns that slaves might escape to freedom in the North, the new Constitution included an explicit provision calling on any state to return "persons held to Service or Labour" in another.

After settling the slavery question in late August, the convention faced one last significant hurdler: the question of the national executive. For months the delegates had gone in circles debating how presidents should be elected, how long they should serve, and what their powers should be. But in early September, eager to wrap matters up, they moved quickly to resolve these issues.

In large part because of their confidence in General Washington, whom nearly everyone expected to be the first president, the delegates fashioned a chief executive office with broad discretionary powers. The prerogatives of the president included the rank of commander in chief of the armed forces, the authority to conduct foreign affairs and negotiate treaties, the right to appoint diplomatic and judicial officers, and the power to veto congressional legislation. The president's term of office was set at four years, with no limits on how often an individual could be reelected.

Determining how to elect the president proved a thorny problem. The delegates envisioned a forceful, energetic, and independent executive insulated from the whims of an uninformed public and the intrigues of the legislature. As a result, they rejected both popular election and election by Congress. The solution they hit upon was the convoluted system of an "electoral college." Each state was left free to determine how it would choose presidential electors equal to the number of its representatives and senators. These electors would then cast votes to select a president. If no candidate received a majority of the electoral votes, the election would be turned over to the House of Representatives, where each state would have one vote.

After a style committee polished the wording of the Constitution, thirty-nine of the forty-two delegates still in attendance signed it on September 17. The Preamble, which originally began with a list of the states, was reworded at the last minute to begin simply: "We the people of the United States, in order to form a more perfect Union . . ." This subtle change had significant implications. By identifying the people, and not a collection of states, as the source of authority, it emphasized the national vision of the framers and their desire to create a government quite different from a confederation of states.

Overview of the Constitution

Although not as strong as the most committed nationalists would have liked, the central government outlined in the Constitution had far more powers than those entrusted to Congress under the Articles of Confederation (see the overview table, "The Articles of Confederation and the Constitution Compared"). The Constitution's provision for a strong, single-person executive had no precedent in the Articles. Nor did the provision for a Supreme Court. The Constitution vested this Court, as well as the lower courts that Congress was empowered to establish, with the judicial power of the United States. In addition, the Constitution specifically delegated to Congress powers to tax, borrow and coin money, regulate commerce, and raise armed forces that the Confederation government had lacked.

Most of the economic powers of Congress came at the expense of the states, which were prohibited from passing tariffs, issuing money, or—in an obvious response to the debtor relief legislation in the 1780s—enacting any law that infringed on the rights of creditors to collect money from debtors.

OVERVIEW

THE ARTICLES OF CONFEDERATION AND THE CONSTITUTION COMPARED

	Articles	**Constitution**
Sovereign power of the central government	No power to tax or raise armies	Power granted on taxes and armed forces
Source of power	Individual states	Shared through federalism between states and the national government
Representation in Congress	Equal representation of states in a unicameral Congress	A bicameral legislature with equal representation of the states in the Senate and proportional representation in the House
Amendment process	Unanimous consent of the states	Consent of three-fourths of the states
Executive	None provided for	Office of the president
National judiciary	None provided for	The Supreme Court

Further curbing the sovereignty of the states was a clause stipulating that the Constitution and all national legislation and treaties were to be "the supreme law of the land." This clause has subsequently been interpreted as giving the central government the power to invalidate state laws.

A no-nonsense realism, as well as a nationalist outlook, infused the Constitution. Its underlying political philosophy was that, in Madison's wonderful phrase, "ambition must be made to counter ambition." Madison and the other members of the national elite who met at Philadelphia were convinced that self-interest, not disinterested virtue, motivated political behavior. As proof, they cited what to them was the sorry record of the state governments in protecting property rights and promoting social order. In their view, these governments were failures because they had been captured by unrestrained majorities corrupted by the selfishness of competing interest groups. Accepting interest group politics as inevitable and seeking to prevent a tyrannical majority from forming at the national level, the architects of the Constitution designed a central government in which competing blocs of power counterbalanced one another.

The Constitution placed both internal and external restraints on the powers of the central government. The division of the government into executive, legislative, and judicial branches, each with ways to limit the power of the others, created an internal system of checks and balances. For example, the Senate's authority to approve or reject presidential appointments and to ratify or reject treaties curbed the powers of the executive. The president commanded the armed forces, but only Congress could declare war. The president could veto congressional legislation, but Congress could override that veto with a two-thirds vote. To pass in the first place, legislation had to be approved by both the House of Representatives, which, with its membership proportional to population, represented the interests of the people at large, and the Senate, which represented the interests of the states. And as an ultimate check against executive power, Congress could impeach, convict, and remove a president from office for "treason, bribery, or other high crimes and misdemeanors."

Although the Constitution did not explicitly grant it, the Supreme Court soon claimed the right to invalidate acts of Congress and the president that it found to be unconstitutional. This power of **judicial review** provided another check against legislative and executive authority. To guard against an arbitrary federal judiciary, the Constitution empowered Congress to determine the size of the Supreme Court and to indict and remove federal judges appointed by the president.

The external restraints on the central government were to be found in the nature of its relationship to the state governments. This relationship was based on **federalism**, the division of power between local and central authorities. By listing specific powers for Congress, the Constitution implied that all other powers were to be retained by the states. Thus while strengthening the national government, the Constitution did not obliterate the sovereign rights of the states, leaving them free to curb the potential power of the national government in the ambiguous areas between national and state sovereignty.

This ambiguity in the federalism of the Constitution was both its greatest strength and its greatest weakness. It allowed both nationalists and advocates of states' rights to support the Constitution. But the issue of slavery, left unresolved in the gray area between state and national sovereignty, would continue to fester, sparking sectional conflict over the extent of national sovereignty that would plunge the republic into civil war three-quarters of a century later.

Overview

Federalists versus the Antifederalists

	Federalists	**Antifederalists**
Position on the Constitution	Favored the Constitution	Opposed the Constitution
Position on the Articles of Confederation	Felt the Articles had to be abandoned	Felt the Articles needed only to be amended
Position on the power of the states	Sought to curb the power of the states with a new central government	Felt the power of the states should be paramount
Position on the need for a bill of rights	Initially saw no need for a bill of rights in the Constitution	Saw the absence of a bill of rights in the proposed Constitution as a threat to individual liberties
Position on the optimum size of the republic	Believed a large republic could best safeguard personal freedoms	Believed only a small republic formed on common interests could protect individual rights
Source of support	Commercial farmers, merchants, shippers, artisans, holders of the national debt	State-centered politicians, most backcountry farmers

The Struggle over Ratification

The realism the Philadelphia delegates displayed in the drafting of the Constitution extended to the procedure they devised for implementing it. Knowing they had exceeded their instructions by proposing an entirely new government, not an amended version of the Articles, and aware that the Articles' requirement of unanimous consent by the state legislatures to any amendment would result in certain defeat, they boldly bypassed both Congress and the state legislatures.

The last article of the Constitution stipulated that it would go into effect when it had been ratified by at least nine of the states acting through specially elected popular conventions. Influenced by the nationalist sentiments of many of its members, one-third of whom had attended the Philadelphia Convention, and perhaps weary of its own impotence, Congress accepted this drastic and not clearly legal procedure, submitting the Constitution to the states in late September 1787.

The delegates in Philadelphia had excluded the public from their proceedings. The publication of the Constitution lifted this veil of secrecy and touched off a great political debate. Although those who favored the Constitution might best have been defined as nationalists, they referred to themselves as **Federalists**, a term that helped deflect charges that they favored excessive centralization. By default, the opponents of the Constitution were known as **Antifederalists**, a negative-sounding label that obscured their support of the state-centered sovereignty most Americans associated with federalism. Initially outmaneuvered in this way, the Antifederalists never did mount an effective campaign to counter the Federalists' output of pamphlets, speeches, and newspaper editorials (see the overview table, "Federalists versus Antifederalists").

The Antifederalists did attract some men of wealth and social standing. Three of them—Elbridge Gerry of Massachusetts and George Mason and Edmund Randolph of Virginia—had been delegates at Philadelphia but refused to sign the Constitution.

They feared that the new national government would swallow up the state governments.

Most Antifederalists, however, were backcountry farmers, men with mud on their boots who lived far from centers of communication and market outlets for their produce. They distrusted the social and commercial elite, and many saw in the Constitution a sinister plot by this elite "to trample the poorer part of the people under their feet that they may be rendered their servants and slaves." The Antifederalists clung to the belief that only a small republic, one composed of relatively homogeneous social interests, could secure the voluntary attachment of the people necessary for a free government. They argued that a large republic, such as the one framed by the Constitution, would inevitably become tyrannical because it was too removed from the interests of common citizen-farmers.

The Antifederalists attacked the Constitution as a danger to the individual liberties and local independence they believed the Revolution had been fought to safeguard, but they lacked the social connections, access to newspapers, and self-confidence of the more cosmopolitan and better-educated Federalists. The Federalists could also more easily mobilize their supporters, who were concentrated in the port cities and commercial farming areas along the coast.

With talent, intellect, and political savvy on their side, the Federalists skillfully built on the momentum for change that had developed out of the crisis atmosphere of 1786. They successfully portrayed the Constitution as the best opportunity to erect a governing structure capable of preserving and extending the gains of the Revolution.

Conservatives shaken by Shays's Rebellion lined up behind the Constitution. So too did groups like creditors, merchants, manufacturers, urban artisans, and commercial farmers. A stronger national government, they believed, would promote economic development by protecting the home market from British imports, enlarging foreign markets for American exports, promoting a stable and uniform currency, and raising revenues to pay off the Revolutionary War debt.

In the early stages, the Federalists scored a string of easy victories (see Map 7–3). Delaware ratified the Constitution on December 7, 1787, and within a month, so too had Pennsylvania, New Jersey, Georgia, and Connecticut. Except for Pennsylvania, these were small, sparsely populated states that stood to benefit economically or militarily from a stronger central government. The Constitution carried in the larger state of Pennsylvania because of the Federalists' strength in the commercial center of Philadelphia.

Map 7-3 The Ratification Vote on the Constitution
Aside from some frontier districts exposed to possible foreign attack, the strongest support for the Constitution came from coastal and interior areas tied into a developing commercial economy.

The Federalists faced their toughest challenge in the large states that had generally been more successful in going it alone during the 1780s. One of the most telling arguments of the Antifederalists in these and other states was the absence of a bill of rights in the Constitution. The framers had felt it unnecessary to include such an explicit protection of individual rights in a document intended to specify the powers of a national government and had barely discussed the issue. Responding to this challenge, the Federalists promised to recommend amending the Constitution with a bill of rights once it was ratified. By doing so, they split the ranks of the Antifederalists in Massachusetts. After the Federalists gained the support of two venerable heroes of the Revolution, John Hancock and Sam Adams, the Massachusetts convention approved the Constitution by a close vote in February 1788. To win over Hancock, the Federalists had played on his vanity, suggesting that they would back him for a top national post. Adams was convinced to back the Federalists by demonstrations of Boston artisans in favor of national tariff protection.

The major hurdles remaining for the Federalists were Virginia, the most populous state, and the strategically located New York. Technically, the Constitution could have gone into effect without them once Maryland, South Carolina, and New Hampshire had ratified it, bringing the total number of states to ratify to the required nine. But without Virginia, which ratified on June 25, and New York, which followed a month later, the new Union would have been weak and the Federalist victory far from assured.

As in Massachusetts, the Federalists were helped in these two crucial states by their promise of a bill of rights. And for the New York campaign, Madison, Jay, and Hamilton wrote an eloquent series of eighty-five essays known collectively as ***The Federalist*** to allay fears that the Constitution would so consolidate national power as to menace individual liberties. In the two most original and brilliant essays in *The Federalist,* essays 10 and 51, Madison turned traditional republican doctrine on its head. A large, diverse republic like the one envisaged by the Constitution, he reasoned, not a small and homogeneous one, offered the best hope for safeguarding the rights of all citizens. This was because a large republic would include a multitude of contending interest groups, making it difficult for any combination of them to coalesce into a tyrannical majority that could oppress minority rights. With this argument Madison had developed a political rationale by which Americans could have both an empire and personal freedom.

Although physically frail, James Madison, shown here in a portrait made in about 1815, was a formidable thinker whose essays in The Federalist *endure as a lasting contribution to political theory.*

North Carolina and Rhode Island did not ratify until after the new government was functioning. North Carolina joined the Union in 1789 once Congress submitted the amendments that comprised the Bill of Rights. The obstinate Rhode Islanders stayed out until 1790, when Congress forced them in with a threat of commercial reprisal.

Conclusion

In freeing themselves from British rule, Americans embarked on an unprecedented wave of constitution making that sought to put into practice abstract principles of republicanism that held that political power should derive from the people. Between 1776 and 1780, Americans developed a unique system of constitutionalism. They proclaimed the supremacy of constitutions over ordinary legislation, detailed the powers of government in a written document, provided protection for individual freedoms in bills of rights, and fashioned a process for framing governments through the election of delegates to a special constitutional convention and the popular ratification of the work of that convention. In all of these areas, Americans were pioneers in demonstrating to

FROM THEN TO NOW

Reshaping the Constitution

The U.S. Constitution remains the world's longest continuously applied written charter of government. Key to its remarkable durability has been the power of the American people to reshape it as public expectations, values, and needs have changed. The twenty-seven amendments that have been added to the Constitution since its ratification in 1788 have maintained it as a responsive, living document.

Amending the Constitution is by design a cumbersome process. The framers were keenly aware that the requirement of unanimous consent by the states to any amendment had crippled the Articles of Confederation. But they also wanted to insulate the Constitution from the whims of temporary majorities. To strike a balance they stipulated that amendments could be initiated only by a two-thirds vote of both houses of Congress or by a call of two-thirds of the states for a constitutional convention. In turn, proposed amendments would become law only when approved by three-fourths of the states. The supporters of the Constitution resorted to this process almost immediately after ratification to honor their pledge to add amendments protecting individual liberties and states' rights. The result was the ten amendments known as the Bill of Rights, which became part of the Constitution in 1791.

Only two more amendments were added before the Civil War. The Eleventh (1795), which bars a citizen of one state from bringing suit against the government of another state, was a victory for states fearful of being sued in a federal court by creditors in other states. The Twelfth (1804), which required the separate election of the president and vice president, corrected a problem in the original presidential election process that had confused the outcome of the election of 1800. Two twentieth-century amendments (the Twentieth and Twenty-fifth) have likewise addressed concerns about presidential succession and the delimiting of congressional and presidential terms.

Like the Bill of Rights, most of the fifteen amendments added since the Civil War have tended to cluster around specific themes. The three great Civil War amendments (the Thirteenth, Fourteenth, and Fifteenth) wrote Union victory into the Constitution by abolishing slavery and extending citizenship and the vote to African Americans. By nationalizing principles of freedom and equal rights, these amendments laid the basis for a new conception of American identity in the twentieth century.

The four amendments ratified between 1913 and 1920—which permitted the imposition of a national income tax, required the popular election of senators, prohibited the sale of alcoholic beverages, and extended the vote to women—reflect the reformist zeal of the Progressive era. This was a time when pressing social problems led to calls for the curbing of corporate power and the broadening of democratic governance as well as the enforcement of civic virtue. The unpopular Prohibition amendment was repealed by the Twenty-first Amendment in 1933.

Two themes have dominated amendments since the 1930s. One reflects the egalitarian reform movements of the 1960s and resulted in three amendments. The Twenty-third (1961), allowed residents of the District of Columbia to vote in presidential elections. The Twenty-fourth (1964), outlawed the poll tax, a device segregationists had used to deny the vote to poor black people. And the Twenty-sixth (1967), lowered the voting age to 18. The second theme reflects a contrary concern with the growth in the influence of the federal government and the power of the presidency that began during the Depression of the 1930s. The two amendments that stand out here are those limiting a president to two terms (the Twenty-second, 1951) and barring a congressional pay raise from taking effect until after another election for the House of Representatives has intervened (the Twenty-seventh, first submitted in 1789 with the Bill of Rights, but not ratified until 1992).

The amendment process has operated as a safety valve releasing pressures for change and realigning the framework of national governance to meet changing circumstances. It has kept the Constitution alive as a vital source of American identity.

Washington presides over the Constitutional Convention.

the rest of the world how common citizens could create their own governments.

The curbs on centralized power that characterized the state constitutions also applied to what amounted to the first national constitution, the Articles of Confederation. Indeed, the inability of the Confederation Congress to exercise effective power in the areas of taxation and foreign trade was a crippling flaw that thoroughly discredited the Articles in the eyes of the nationalist-minded leaders who had emerged during the Revolution. These leaders overthrew the Articles at the Constitutional Convention in 1787 and engineered a peaceful revolution in securing the ratification of the Constitution. Their victory in creating a new central government with real national powers was built on the foundation of constitutional concepts and mechanisms that Americans had laid down in their states The new Constitution did rest on the consent of the governed, and it endured because it could be amended to reflect shifts in popular will and to widen the circle of Americans granted the rights of political citizenship.

Accepting as a given that self-interest drove political action, the framers of the Constitution designed the new national government to turn ambition against itself. They created rival centers of power that forced selfish factions to compete in a constant struggle to form a workable majority. That struggle occurred both within the national government and between that government and the states in the American system of federalism. The Constitution thus set the stage for an entirely new kind of national politics.

Review Questions

1. How would you define republicanism? Do you believe that Americans today still believe in the basic tenets of republicanism?
2. What was so unprecedented about the new state constitutions, and what principles of government did they embody?
3. What were the problems of the economy in the 1780s, and why did clashes between debtors and creditors become so divisive? Do you think that an economic recovery could have been achieved under the Articles of Confederation?
4. What were the diplomatic weaknesses of the United States under the Articles, and what threat did they pose for national unity?
5. What sorts of men drafted the Constitution in 1787, and how representative were they of all Americans? What explains the differences between the Federalists and Antifederalists? Do you think they shared the same vision of what America should become? How widespread was the popular backing for the Constitution, and what accounts for its ratification?

Recommended Reading

Richard Beeman, Stephen Botein, and Edward C. Carter, III, eds., *Beyond Confederation: Origins of the Constitution and American National Identity* (1987). Twelve essays that offer a fine overview of the competing ideologies and issues that shaped the history of the 1880s and pushed the republic toward a new framework of government in the Constitution.

J. Hector St. John Crèvecoeur, *Letters from an American Farmer and Sketches of Eighteenth-Century America,* ed. Albert E. Stone (1986). A modern reprint of Crèvecoeur's work that provides an accessible account of Americans and their living conditions in the late eighteenth century.

Merrill Jensen, *The New Nation: A History of the United States during the Confederation, 1781–1787* (1948). A work making the strongest case for the Articles as a tentative success that was overturned in a conservative reaction that exaggerated threats to social order.

Richard B. Morris, *The Forging of the Union, 1781–1789* (1987). The best-balanced synthesis of the 1780s, documenting the creative statesmanship of the leaders of the Constitutional Convention.

Gordon Wood, *The Creation of the American Republic, 1776–1787* (1969). A masterful study indispensable for understanding the transformation in American republicanism between the winning of independence and the ratification of the Constitution.

Additional Sources

The New Order of Republicanism

Ruth H. Block, *Visionary Republic: Millennial Themes in American Thought, 1756–1800* (1985).

Sylvia R. Frey, *Water from the Rock: Black Resistance in a Revolutionary Age* (1991).

Linda Kerber, *Women of the Republic* (1980).

Marc W. Kruman, *Between Authority and Liberty: State Constitution Making in Revolutionary America* (1997).

J. R. Pole, *Political Representation in England and the Origins of the American Republic* (1966).

Gordon Wood, *The Radicalism of the American Revolution* (1992).

Problems at Home

Joseph L. Davis, *Sectionalism in American Politics, 1774–1787* (1977).

Robert A. Gross, ed., *In Debt to Shays: The Bicentennial of an Agrarian Rebellion* (1992).

Ronald L. Hoffman and Peter Albert, eds., *Sovereign States in an Age of Uncertainty* (1981).

Jackson Turner Main, *Political Parties before the Constitution* (1973).

Peter S. Onuf, *The Origins of the Federal Republic* (1983).

Diplomatic Weaknesses

Charles T. Ritcheson, *Aftermath of Revolution: British Policy toward the United States, 1783–1795* (1969).

Richard W. Van Alstyne, *The Rising American Empire* (1980).

Arthur P. Whitaker, *The Spanish-American Frontier, 1783–95* (1927, 1962 reprint).

Toward a New Nation

Charles Beard, *An Economic Interpretation of the Constitution* (1913).

Roger H. Brown, *Redeeming the Republic: Federalists, Taxation, and the Origins of the Constitution* (1993).

Christopher M. Duncan, *The Anti-Federalists and Early American Political Thought* (1995).

Michael Allen Gillespie and Michael Lienesch, eds., *Ratifying the Constitution* (1989).

Jackson Turner Main, *The Anti-Federalists: Critics of the Constitution, 1781–1788* (1961).

Forrest McDonald, *Novus Ordo Seclorum: The Intellectual Origins of the Constitution* (1985).

Richard B. Morris, *Witness at the Creation* (1985).

Where to Learn More

❖ **South Street Seaport Museum, New York City, New York.** Maritime commerce was the lifeblood of the postrevolutionary economy. The artifacts and the exhibits here offer a fine introduction to the seafaring world of the port city that became the nation's first capital in the new federal Union.

❖ **Independence National Historical Park, Philadelphia, Pennsylvania.** Walks and guided tours through this historic district enable one to grasp much of the physical setting in which the delegates to the Constitutional Convention met.

❖ **Northern Indiana Center for History, South Bend, Indiana.** The permanent exhibition on the St. Joseph River valley of northern Indiana and southern Michigan explains the material world of this region and how it changed as first Europeans and then Americans mingled and clashed with the Native American population.

A New Republic and the Rise of Parties, 1789–1800

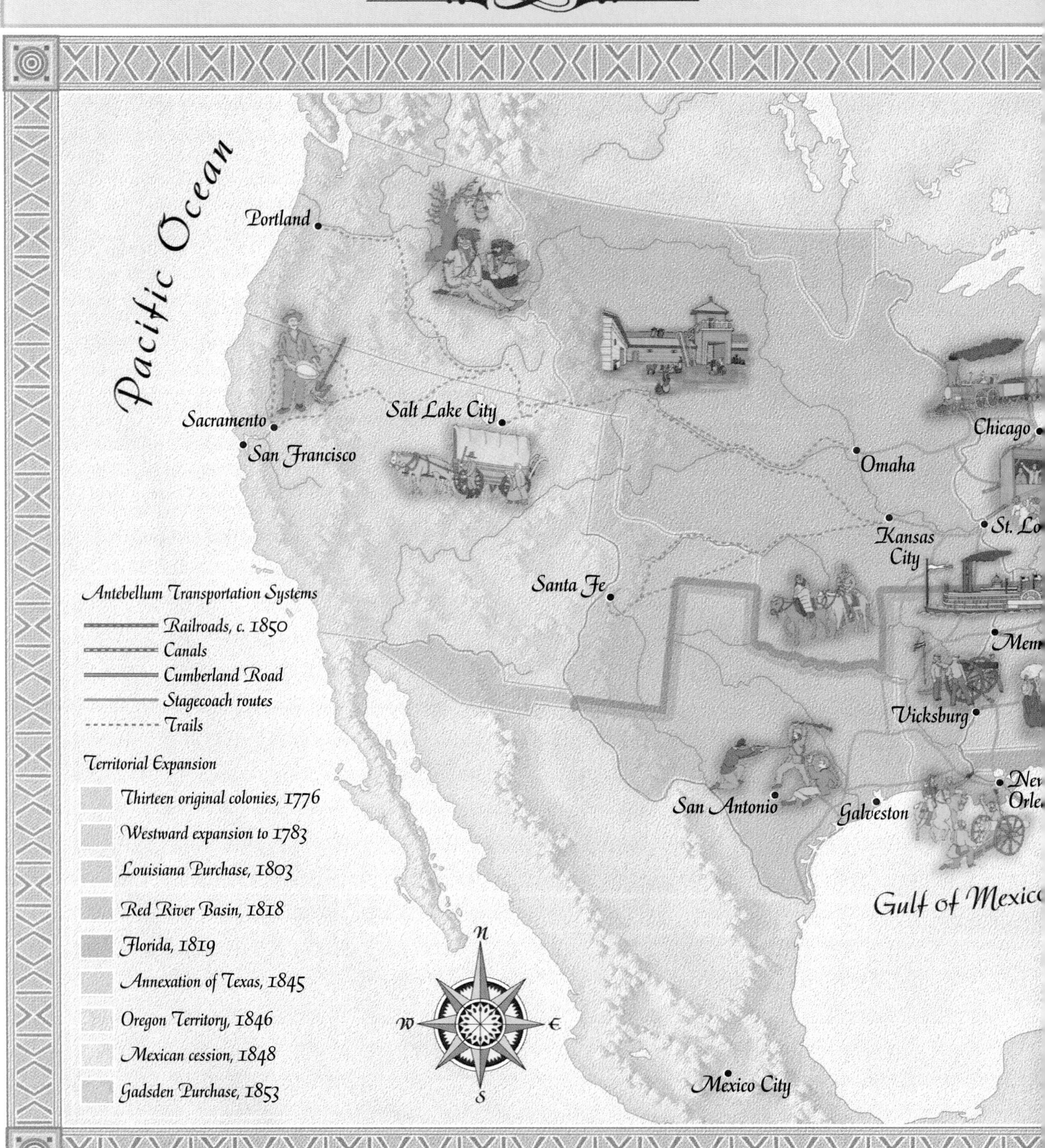

Pacific Ocean
Portland
Sacramento
San Francisco
Salt Lake City
Santa Fe
Omaha
Chicago
Kansas City
St. Lo
Mem
Vicksburg
San Antonio
Galveston
New Orle
Gulf of Mexic
Mexico City
n
w
e
s
Antebellum Transportation Systems
Railroads, c. 1850
Canals
Cumberland Road
Stagecoach routes
Trails
Territorial Expansion
Thirteen original colonies, 1776
Westward expansion to 1783
Louisiana Purchase, 1803
Red River Basin, 1818
Florida, 1819
Annexation of Texas, 1845
Oregon Territory, 1846
Mexican cession, 1848
Gadsden Purchase, 1853

Chapter Outline

Washington's America
The Uniformity of New England
The Pluralism of the Mid-Atlantic Region
The Slave South and Its Backcountry
The Growing West

Forging a New Government
"Mr. President" and the Bill of Rights
Departments and Courts
Revenue and Trade
Hamilton and the Public Credit
Reaction and Opposition

The Emergence of Parties
The French Revolution
Securing the Frontier
The Whiskey Rebellion
Treaties with Britain and Spain
The First Partisan Election

The Last Federalist Administration
The French Crisis and the XYZ Affair
Crisis at Home
The End of the Federalists

Conclusion

Key Topics

- ❖ Regional diversity of the United States in 1789
- ❖ Laying the foundations of American government during Washington's first term
- ❖ Hamilton's financial policies
- ❖ The emergence of parties during Washington's second term
- ❖ The Adams administration and the election of 1800

When George Washington took the oath of office as the first president of the United States on April 30, 1789, he struck many people as anything but presidential. He seemed to one observer "to have forgot half of what he was to say for he made a dead pause and stood for some time, to appearance, in a vacant mood." During his address to the assembled dignitaries he appeared "agitated and embarrassed more than he ever was by the leveled Cannon or pointed Musket. He trembled, and several times could scarce make out to read."

The president's shakiness reflected the shaky start of the country's new government. Two states, North Carolina and Rhode Island, had not yet ratified the Constitution and were still outside the federal Union. The newly elected members of Congress felt no urgency to assume their duties. They had been scheduled to meet in New York on March 4, 1789, to count the ballots of the electoral college and officially confirm Washington's election, but only one-quarter of them had arrived by then. A month would go by before the minimum needed to count the ballots could be mustered. Washington, his dignity ruffled by this show of congressional disinterest, dallied at Mount Vernon until formally notified of his election.

He had every reason to dread taking on the burden of the presidency. As head of the new national government, he would put at risk the legendary status he had achieved during the Revolution. Most Americans intensely feared centralized authority, which is why the framers deliberately left the word *national* out of the Constitution. Washington somehow had to establish loyalty to a new government whose main virtue in the eyes of many was the very vagueness of its defined powers.

The Constitution had created the framework for a national government, but pressing problems demanded the fleshing out of that framework. The government urgently needed revenue to begin paying off the immense debt incurred during the Revolution. It also had to address unstable conditions in the West. Remote from the seat of federal power and wooed by the British in the Old Northwest and the Spanish in the lower Mississippi Valley, western settlers wavered in their loyalties. Ultimately, the key to solving these and other problems was to establish the new republic's legitimacy. Washington and his supporters had to inspire popular backing for the government's right to exercise authority.

The realities of governing would soon shatter the nonpartisan ideal that had prevailed among the backers of the Constitution. By the end of Washington's first term, two political parties had begun to emerge. The **Federalist party**, which included Washington and his successor, John Adams, favored a strong central government. The opposition party, the **Jeffersonian Republicans**, took shape as a result of differences over financial policy and the American response to the French Revolution. Led by Thomas Jefferson, the Republicans were distrustful of excessive central power. These first American political parties are not to be confused with the Federalists and Antifederalists of the ratification debate.

The Federalists, who governed through 1800, succeeded in showing a doubting world ruled by kings and queens that the American experiment in republican government could work. But as inheritors of a political tradition that equated parties with factions—temporary coalitions of selfish private interests—the Federalists doubted the loyalty of the Republicans. When the Federalists under President Adams attempted to suppress the Republicans, the stage was set for the critical election of 1800. Jefferson's victory in that election ended both Federalist rule and the republic's first major internal crisis.

Respectful crowds greet George Washington as he arrives in New York City in this tapestry commemorating his inauguration as president.

Washington's America

Who were the Americans whom Washington was called on to lead? There is no easy answer. In 1789, as now, Americans identified and grouped themselves according to many factors, including race, sex, class, ethnicity, religion, and degree of personal freedom. Geographical factors, including climate and access to markets, further divided them into regions and sections. The resulting hodgepodge sorely tested the assumption—and it was never more than an assumption in 1789—that a single national government could govern Americans as a whole (see Figure 8-1).

The Uniformity of New England

The national census of 1790 counted nearly 4 million Americans, one in four of whom lived in New England. Although often viewed as the most typically "American" part of the young nation, New England in fact was rather atypical. It alone of the nation's formative regions had largely shut itself off from outsiders. The Puritan notions of religious liberty that prevailed in the region extended only to those who subscribed to the Calvinist orthodoxy of the dominant Congregationalist church. Geography conspired with this religious exclusiveness to limit population diversity. New England's poor soils and long, cold winters made it an impractical place to cultivate cash crops like the tobacco and rice of the South. As a result, New England farmers had little need of indentured servants or slaves. Family members, helped by neighbors and the occasional hired hand, provided labor on New England farms.

Puritan values and a harsh environment thus combined to make New England the most religiously and ethnically uniform region in the United States. Most of the people living there were descended from English immigrants who had arrived in the seventeenth century. Small pockets of Quakers, Baptists, and Catholics had gained the legal right of worship by the 1720s, but Congregationalism remained the official, state-supported religion in Connecticut and Massachusetts. Black people and Indians together barely constituted 3 percent of New England's population. The few remaining Indians lived on reservations of inferior land, which they usually left only to find work as servants or day laborers.

New Englanders found slavery incompatible with the natural rights philosophy that had emerged during the Revolution and abolished it in the 1780s. Slavery had, in any case, always been marginal in New England's economy. Owning slaves as domestic servants or artisans had been a status symbol for the urban wealthy in Boston, Portsmouth, and Newport. As a result, about 20 percent of New England's small African-American population lived in cities. In contrast 90 percent of the white population lived in the countryside.

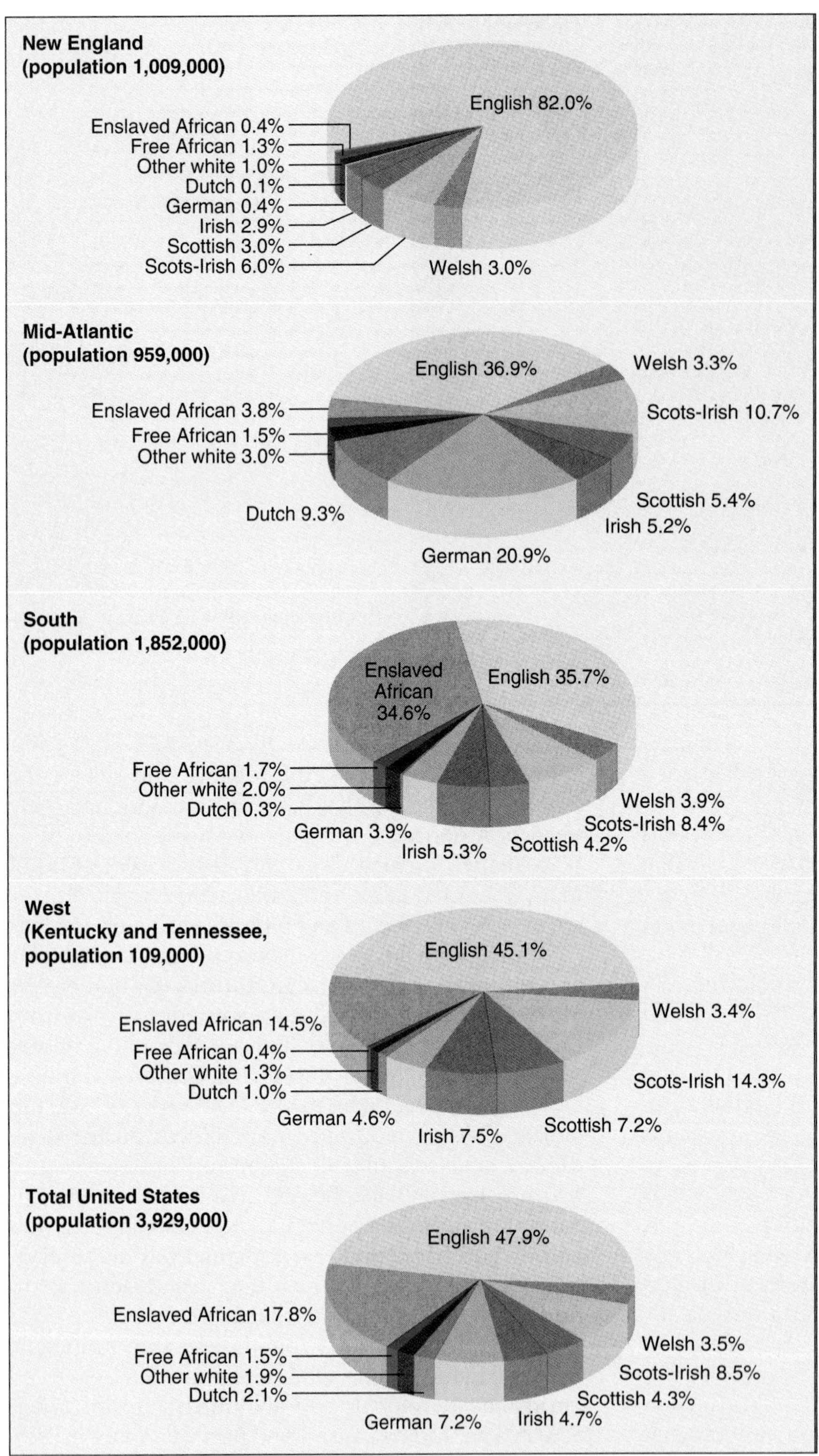

Figure 8-1 Ethnic Breakdown of the United States in 1790, by Region
Unique racial and ethnic patterns shaped each of the nation's four major regions in 1790. New England was most atypical in its lack of racial or ethnic diversity.

Data Source: The Statistics of the Population of the United States, *comp. Francis A. Walker (1872), pp. 3–7; Thomas L. Purvis, "The European Ancestry of the United States Population, 1790,"* William and Mary Quarterly, 41 *(1984), p. 98.*

Freed slaves and their descendants tended to remain in the cities, where jobs were easier to find than in rural areas.

Women outnumbered men in parts of New England in 1789. This pattern—not found in other parts of the country—was the result of the pressure of an expanding population and the practice of dividing family farms among male heirs. As farms in the older, more densely settled parts of New England were divided into ever-smaller lots, many young men migrated west in search of cheap, arable land. They first pushed into the hilly regions of northern New England and then, by the 1790s, through the Mohawk River Valley into New York. Thus, by 1789, women formed a slight majority in Connecticut, Massachusetts, and Rhode Island.

Despite their superior numbers, women in New England, as elsewhere, remained subordinate to men. Even so, the general testing of traditional authority that accompanied the Revolution led some New England women to question male power. The Massachusetts poet Judith Sargeant Murray, for example, published essays asserting that women were the intellectual equals of men. Murray was the first woman to argue publicly in favor of equal educational opportunities for young women, and she boldly asserted that women should learn how to become economically independent.

Republican ideology, emphasizing the need of women to be intellectually prepared to raise virtuous, public-spirited children, also led reformers in New England to seek equal access for women to education. In 1789, Massachusetts became the first state to allocate funds

This painting of a young woman reading (General Schumacker's Daughter, *by Jacob Maentel) reflects women's increasing access to education in the early years of the nation. Nearly four hundred female academies and seminaries were established between 1790 and 1830.*

specifically for girls' elementary education. And beginning in the 1780s, wealthy residents of eastern cities set up private academies for women that would later provide the foundation for women's higher education. Liberalized divorce laws in New England also allowed a woman to seek legal separation from an abusive or unfaithful spouse.

In other respects, politics in New England remained rooted in the Puritan past. Age, property, and reputation determined one's standing in a culture that valued a clearly defined social order. The moral code that governed town life promoted curbs on individual behavior for the benefit of the community as a whole. With their notions of collective liberty, New Englanders subscribed to a version of republicanism that favored strong government. This set them apart from most other Americans, who embraced a more individualistic idea of liberty and a republicanism suspicious of government power. New Englanders perceived government as a divine institution with a moral responsibility to intervene in people's lives. Acting through town meetings, they taxed themselves for public services at rates two to four times higher than in the rest of the country. Their courts were also far more likely than those elsewhere to punish individuals for crimes against public order (like failing to observe the Sabbath properly) and sexual misconduct.

The Pluralism of the Mid-Atlantic Region

The states of the mid-Atlantic region—New York, New Jersey, and Pennsylvania—were the most diverse in the nation. People of English descent comprised less than 40 percent of the population. Other major ethnic groups included the Dutch and Scots-Irish in New York and Germans and Scots-Irish in New Jersey and Pennsylvania. With ethnic diversity came religious diversity. Transplanted New Englanders, who brought their Congregationalism and Yankee twang with them when they settled Long Island and northern New Jersey, made up about 40 percent of New York's ethnic English population. Among others of English descent, Anglicans predominated in New York and Quakers in New Jersey and Pennsylvania. The Dutch, concentrated in the lower Hudson Valley, had their own Dutch Reformed Church, and most Germans were either Lutherans or **pietists**, such as Mennonites and Moravians, who stressed personal piety over theological doctrine. The Presbyterian Scots-Irish settled heavily in the backcountry.

This mosaic-like pattern of ethnic and religious groupings was no accident. In contrast to Puritan New England, the middle colonies had offered freedom of worship to attract settlers. In addition, economic opportunities for newcomers were much greater than in New England. The soil was better, the climate was milder, and market outlets for agricultural products were more abundant. These conditions made the mid-Atlantic region the nation's first breadbasket. It produced surpluses of wheat, flour, and corn that were shipped out of New York and Philadelphia, the two largest cities in North America by 1790. Commercial agriculture fed urban growth and created a greater demand for labor in both rural and urban areas than in New England. The influx of Germans and Scots-Irish into the region in the eighteenth century occurred in response to this demand.

The demand for labor had also been met by importing African slaves. Black people, both free and enslaved, made up 5 percent of the mid-Atlantic

Chronology

1789 Inauguration of Washington.
Congress establishes the first federal departments.
French Revolution begins.

1790 Hamilton submits the first of his financial reports to Congress.

1791 Bill of Rights ratified.
Congress charters the Bank of the United States.

1792 St. Clair's defeat along the Wabash.
Reelection of Washington.

1793 France goes to war against Britain, Spain, and Holland.
Genêt mission.
Washington issues Proclamation of Neutrality.

1794 Ohio is opened with the victory of General Anthony Wayne at the Battle of Fallen Timbers.
Suppression of the Whiskey Rebellion in western Pennsylvania.

1795 Jay's Treaty with Britain ratified.
Treaty of Greenville with Ohio Indians.

1796 Pinckney's Treaty with Spain ratified.
Washington's Farewell Address.
John Adams elected president.

1797 Beginning of the Quasi-War with France.

1798 XYZ Affair.
Alien and Sedition Acts.
Provisional army and direct tax.
Virginia and Kentucky Resolutions.

1799 Fries's Rebellion in Pennsylvania.

1800 Franco-American Accord.
Thomas Jefferson elected president.

population in 1790, and, as in New England, they were proportionally more likely than white people to live in the maritime cities. New York had more slaveholders in 1790 than any other American city except Charleston, South Carolina. About 40 percent of white families in the city's nearby rural outposts of Queens, Brooklyn, and Staten Island owned slaves, a rate as high as in Maryland and South Carolina.

Despite its considerable strength in the port cities and adjacent rural areas, slavery was never an economically vital institution in most of the mid-Atlantic region. The region's major cash crop, wheat, required seasonal labor, which did not warrant tying up capital in slaves. Commercial agriculture did not rest on a slave base, nor did it produce a politically powerful class of planters. As a result, slavery in the mid-Atlantic region gave way to the demands for emancipation inspired by the natural rights philosophy of the Revolution.

Pennsylvania in 1780, New York in 1799, and New Jersey in 1804 each passed laws of gradual emancipation. These laws did not free adult slaves but provided that children born of a slave mother were to be freed at ages ranging between 18 and 28. Soon after the laws were passed, however, adult slaves began hastening their own freedom. They ran away, set fires, and pressured their owners to accept cash payments in return for a short, fixed term of labor service. But even as they gained their freedom, African-Americans had to confront enduring white racism. The comments of one white New Yorker suggest what they were up against. "We may sincerely advocate the freedom of black men," he wrote, "and yet assert their moral and physical inferiority."

The diversity of the mid-Atlantic region created a complex political environment. Competing cultural and economic interests prevented the kind of broad consensus on the meaning of republicanism that had emerged in New England. Some mid-Atlantic groups favored a strong central government to foster economic development and maintain traditional authority. Others wanted to keep government weak so as to foster a republican equality that would promote individual freedom.

Those who supported strong government included mercantile and financial leaders in the cities and commercial farmers in the countryside. These people tended to be Anglicans, Quakers, and Congregationalists of English descent. Those opposing them and favoring a more egalitarian republicanism tended to come from the middle and lower classes. They included subsistence farmers in the backcountry and artisans and day laborers in the cities. Most were Scots-Irish Presbyterians, but they also included Dutch Calvinists and German Lutherans. Fiercely independent and proud of their liberties, they resented the claims of the wealthy to political authority. They resisted government aid to business as a form of political corruption that unfairly enriched those who were already economically powerful.

The Slave South and Its Backcountry

In the South—the region from Maryland and Delaware to Georgia—climate and soil conditions favored the production of cash staples for world markets. Cultivating these crops required backbreaking labor that white immigrants avoided. As Thomas Jefferson put it, "In a warm climate no man will work for himself, who can make another labor for him." Southern planters relied on the coerced labor of African slaves, whose numbers made the South the most populous region in the country.

Just under 40 percent of all Southerners were slaves, but their concentration varied within the region. They were a majority in the Chesapeake Tidewater region, where slave ownership was widely distributed among white tobacco planters, including small and middling growers as well as the few great plantation owners. Farther south, in the tidal swamps of the South Carolina and Georgia lowcountry, where draining and clearing the land required huge inputs of labor, black people outnumbered white people five to one. Slave ownership there was more concentrated than in the Tidewater. Large planters, the richest men in the country, worked hundreds of slaves in the production of rice, indigo, and sea-island cotton. Because yellow fever and malaria plagued the Carolina lowcountry, white people avoided the area, and the death rate among slaves was very high.

Slaves were less numerous in the Piedmont, or foothill, region of the South that lies between the coastal plain and the Appalachian highlands. Although sons of Tidewater planters had expanded tobacco production with slave labor into the Piedmont of Virginia and South Carolina, this was predominantly an area of nonslaveholding farmers who relied on family labor to raise livestock, corn, and wheat. In the southern mountains, sloping to the southwest from the Blue Ridge in Virginia, the absence of marketable crops diminished the demand for slave labor.

The free black population in the South had grown rapidly during the 1780s. Thousands of slaves fled behind British lines to win their freedom, and patriots freed others as a reward for enlisting in their forces. The Revolutionary values of liberty and equality also led many slave owners to question the morality of slavery. Legislatures in the upper South passed laws making it financially easier than before for masters to manumit (free) their slaves. In Virginia alone, ten thousand slaves were manumitted in the 1780s. Slavery, however, remained the foundation of the southern economy. As a result, no southern state undertook a general program of emancipation, and slavery survived the turbulence of the Revolutionary era.

Economic conditions in the South, where the raw poverty of the backcountry offset the great wealth of the lowcountry, stamped the region's politics and culture. Tidewater planters were predominantly Anglican and of English descent. Piedmont farmers were more likely to be Scots-Irish Presbyterians and Baptists. More evangelical in their religion and with simpler habits and tastes, the backcountry Baptists denounced the lowcountry planters for their luxury and arrogance. The planters retaliated by trying unsuccessfully to suppress the backcountry evangelicals.

The planters were indeed proud, domineering, and given to ostentatious displays of wealth. An English traveler observed that Virginia planters "are haughty and jealous of their liberties, impatient of restraint, and can scarcely bear the thought of being controlled by any superior power." Planters understood liberty to mean the power of white males, unchecked by any outside authority, to rule over others. The only acknowledged check on this power was the planter's sense of duty, his obligation to adhere to an idealized code of conduct befitting a gentleman and a man of honor.

Backcountry farmers also jealously guarded their liberties. "They are," noted a late-eighteenth-century traveler, "extremely tenacious of the rights and liberties of republicanism. They consider themselves on an equal footing with the best educated people of the country, and upon the principles of equality they intrude themselves into every company." Backcountry farmers shared with the planters a disdain for government and restraints on the individual. But they opposed the planters' belief in a social hierarchy based on wealth and birth that left both poor whites and black slaves in a subordinate position.

The Growing West

Between the Appalachian Mountains and the Mississippi River stretched the most rapidly growing region of the new nation, the West. Land-hungry settlers poured across the mountains once the British recognized the American claim to the region in the Treaty of Paris. During the 1780s, the white population of the West exploded from less than 10,000 to 200,000. The region's Native American population was, in contrast, about 150,000.

Although Indians and settlers struck many friendships and mutually advantageous ties, their relations were more generally marked by tension and sporadic violence. An example illustrates the often cruel ferocity of their conflicts. When James Boone, the eldest son of the fabled Daniel Boone, who had blazed the first trail for white settlers into Kentucky, was captured, tortured, and killed by a band of Indians, a group of settlers sought vengeance. They lured some Mingo Indians into their camp, got them drunk, and then killed and scalped them. According to one account, they strung up a pregnant Mingo woman, "sliced open her belly with a tomahawk, and impaled her unborn child on a stake."

Indians strongly resisted white claims on their lands. A confederation of tribes in the Ohio Valley, led by the Miamis and supplied with firearms by the British in exchange for furs, kept settlers out of the Old Northwest territory, the area north of the Ohio River. South of the Ohio, white settlements were largely limited to Kentucky and Tennessee. In what is today Alabama and Mississippi, the Creeks and their allies blocked American expansion.

Most white migrants in Kentucky and Tennessee were the young, rural poor from the seaboard slave states. The West offered them the opportunity to claim their own farms and gain economic independence free from the dominance of planters and the economic competition of slave labor. But planters also saw the West as a land of opportunity. The planters of Tidewater Virginia were especially likely to speculate in vast tracts of western land. And many planters' sons migrated to the West with a share of the family's slaves to become planters in their own right. This process laid the foundation for the extension of slavery into new regions. As early as 1790, slaves made up more than 10 percent of the population of Tennessee and Kentucky.

Life in the western settlements was harsh and often cruel. Mortality was high, especially among infants. Travelers from the East described settlers living in crudely built log cabins with squalid, filthy interiors infested with fleas and lice. Easterners also found an appallingly casual acceptance of violence in the West. Men commonly settled disputes in knife-slashing, eye-gouging brawls.

Isolation and uncertainty haunted frontier life. The Appalachians posed a formidable barrier to social and economic intercourse with the East. Few settlers had the labor resources, which chiefly meant slaves, to produce an agricultural surplus for shipment to market down the Ohio and Mississippi Rivers. Most farmers lived at a semisubsistence level. Many of them, mostly Scots-Irish, did not own the land they cultivated. These **squatters**, as they were called, occupied the land hoping someday to obtain clear title to it.

In Kentucky, squatters, aligned with a small class of middling landowners, spearheaded the movement for political separation from Virginia that gained statehood for the territory in 1792. (In similar fashion, white settlers in Vermont established their independence from New York and New Hampshire and gained statehood in 1791.) The settlers wanted to break the control that Tidewater

Frontier log cabins like this were squalid, rough-hewn structures that could be built in a day with the help of neighbors.

planters had gained over most of the land and lucrative government offices in Kentucky. In their minds, planters, officeholders, land speculators, and gentlemen of leisure were all part of an aristocracy tied to the distant government in Richmond and intent on robbing them of their liberty. As one proponent of statehood proudly announced, "I never was a frend to larned men for I see it is those sort of fokes who always no how to butter thare own bred and care not for others."

Despite the movement in Kentucky for statehood, the ultimate political allegiance of the West was uncertain in 1790. Westerners wanted the freedom to control their own affairs and outlets for their crops. Apparently, they were willing to strike a deal with any outside power offering to meet these needs. The British, contrary to the terms of the Treaty of Paris, had not abandoned their military posts in the Old Northwest. Using their military position and close ties with the Indians as leverage, they encouraged separatist movements north of the Ohio River.

Spain posed a more serious threat. It rejected the American claim to the 31st parallel as the southern boundary of the United States and asserted that most of the area south of the Ohio and east of the Mississippi was Spanish territory. Most important, Spain controlled New Orleans and hence the main outlet on the Mississippi River for western produce. Washington had warned in 1784 that the political loyalties of the West wavered "on a pivot," and the future of the region loomed as a major test for his administration.

Forging a New Government

The Congress that assembled in New York from 1789 to 1791 faced a challenge scarcely less daunting than that of the Constitutional Convention of 1787. It had to give form and substance to the framework of the new national government outlined in the Constitution. Executive departments had to be established, a federal judiciary organized, sources of revenue found, terms of international trade and foreign policy worked out, and a commitment to add a bill of rights to the Constitution honored.

Staunch supporters of the new government had easily carried the first national elections in 1788 and enjoyed large majorities in both houses of Congress. These people brought superb administrative talents to the task of governing. Many, however, were clumsy politicians and unsympathetic to the egalitarian sensibilities of the electorate. By 1792, they faced growing political opposition.

"Mr. President" and the Bill of Rights

The first problem for Washington and Congress was to decide just how the chief executive of the new republic should be addressed. Vice President John Adams of Massachusetts and his like-minded colleagues in the Senate wanted a title with dignity, something that imparted proper respect both for the office and for national political authority. They preferred "His Highness." In a debate that tied up Congress for a month, the more democratically inclined members of the House argued that such a title smacked of a longing for monarchical rule. Adams and the others grudgingly agreed to accept "Mr. President."

Whatever his title, Washington was intent on surrounding the presidency in a halo of respectability. Dismayed by the hordes of visitors and officeseekers who immediately invaded his rented mansion in New York, he set down strict rules for his interactions with the public. He met with visitors twice a week for an hour and bowed with republican deference to the people but refused to shake hands. He traveled outside New York in a luxurious coach pulled by six horses, and at all times he carried himself with stern reserve. After a dinner with the president, one senator remarked that "as usual the company was as grave as at a funeral."

While Washington was laying down guidelines for presidential etiquette, Congress got down to business. James Madison, now a representative from Virginia, early emerged as the most forceful leader in the House. He pushed for speedy action on the Bill of Rights, which the Federalists had promised to add to the Constitution during the ratification debate. To allay Antifederalist fears that the Constitution granted too much power to the national government, the Federalists had promised to consider amendments that protected both individual rights and liberties and the rights of states. But Madison, concerned not to have the new government immediately hobbled by concessions to states, astutely kept the focus of the amendments on personal liberties. He submitted nineteen amendments, and Congress soon settled on twelve. Ten of these amendments, known collectively as the Bill of Rights, were ratified by the states and became part of the Constitution as of December 15, 1791.

The Bill of Rights has been one of the most enduring legacies of the first Congress. The first eight amendments are concerned mostly with individual rights. They guarantee religious freedom,

freedom of expression, and the safeguarding of individuals and their property against arbitrary legal proceedings. Only three amendments speak of state interests. Citing the necessity of a "well-regulated militia" for "the security of a free State," the Second Amendment guarantees "the right of the people to keep and bear Arms." This assured the states that they could rely on their militias for protection against federal tyranny. The Ninth and Tenth Amendments stipulate that the powers not granted to the national government in the Constitution are retained by the people and the states.

The Bill of Rights broadened the government's base of popular support. Once Congress submitted the amendments to the states for ratification, North Carolina (1789) and Rhode Island (1790) overcame their lingering objections and joined the Union. The Bill of Rights also assured Americans that the central government would not try to impose on them a uniform national culture.

Departments and Courts

In the summer of 1789, Congress authorized the first executive departments: the State Department for foreign affairs, the Treasury for finances, and the War Department for the nation's defense. These departments already existed under the Articles of Confederation, and the only debate about them concerned the extent of presidential control over the officials who would head them. The Constitution gave the president the right to nominate public officials but required the consent of the Senate to confirm their appointments. The Constitution was silent, however, on whether or not the president could dismiss an official without the Senate's consent. Congress decided that the president could do so, setting an important precedent that bolstered presidential power. Department heads would now be closely bound to the president. As a group, they would evolve into the **cabinet**, the president's chief advisory body.

Greater controversy attended the creation of the federal judiciary. The Constitution called for "one Supreme Court" but left it up to Congress to authorize lower federal courts. The framers were deliberately vague about the federal judiciary because Antifederalists and proponents of states' rights did not want national courts enforcing a uniform judicial system. National courts, they argued, would be far removed from the people and would act as engines of oppression.

The **Judiciary Act of 1789** represented an artful compromise that balanced the concerns of the Antifederalists and states' rights advocates with the concerns of nationalists who strongly opposed leaving matters of national law up to state courts. It created a hierarchical national judiciary based on thirteen federal district courts, one for each state. Appeals from these courts were to be heard in one of three circuit courts, and the Supreme Court was to have the final say in contested cases. In a major concession to the Antifederalists, however, the act limited jurisdiction in federal courts to legal issues stemming from the Constitution and the laws and treaties of the national government. The distinctive legal systems and customs of the states remained intact. State courts would continue to hear and rule on the vast majority of civil and criminal cases.

Revenue and Trade

The government's most pressing need was for revenue. Aware that Congress under the Articles of Confederation had been crippled by its inability to secure a reliable source of income, Madison acted to put the finances of the new federal government on a firm footing. Nearly everyone agreed that the government's chief source of income should be a tariff on imported goods and tonnage duties (fees based on cargo capacity) on ships entering American ports. The United States imported most of its manufactured goods, as well as many raw materials, and foreign-owned ships accounted for nearly half of entering tonnage.

The **Tariff Act of 1789** was designed primarily to raise revenue, not to protect American manufacturers by keeping out foreign goods with high duties. It did, however, seek to protect a few industries thought vital to the economic health of the nation. Thus it levied a duty of 5 percent on most imported goods but imposed tariffs as high as 50 percent on items such as steel, salt, cloth, and tobacco. The debate on the Tariff Act provoked some sectional sparring. In general, manufacturers, who were concentrated in the North, wanted high tariffs for protection against foreign competition. In contrast, farmers and southern planters wanted low tariffs to keep down the cost of the manufactured goods they purchased.

Madison originally hoped to use tonnage duties not only to raise revenue but also to strike at foreign nations that had not signed a commercial treaty with the United States. He had in mind specifically Great Britain. Since the Revolution, Britain had kept its trading empire closed to American merchants while at the same time exploiting the United States as a market for its manufactured goods. In contrast, France, America's ally during the Revolution, had a commercial treaty with the United States that recognized the American position on equal trading relations and the rights of neutral shippers during war.

This painting of about 1797 captures the bustle of commercial activity in New York at the end of the eighteenth century. The large building on the left is the Tontine Coffee House, the site of insurance offices and the Stock Exchange. The spars of ships in the background reflect New York's importance as a center of trade. The new government relied on tariffs on the import trade as its main source of income.

Madison wanted to punish the British with a duty of 60 cents per ton on British ships entering American ports, twice the proposed duty on French ships. He hoped to dislodge the British from their dominant position in American markets and open up overseas trade for American and French shippers.

Madison's duties were in effect a declaration of economic warfare against Britain, but they failed to pass Congress, defeated by an unlikely coalition of sectional interests. Southerners voted against them because they feared their result would be to give New England merchants a monopoly on the carrying trade and raise the cost of shipping tobacco to Europe. But northern merchants, presumably the beneficiaries of the duties, also opposed them. They were leery of disrupting their profitable trade with Britain, especially with the economic slump of the 1780s abating. The **Tonnage Act of 1789**, as finally passed, treated all foreign ships equally. Foreign-owned and foreign-built ships were to pay a duty of 50 cents a ton; foreign-owned but American-built ships were to pay a duty of 30 cents a ton. The duty for American ships was only 6 cents a ton.

Hamilton and the Public Credit

The Treasury was the largest and most important new department. To its head, Alexander Hamilton of New York, fell the task of bringing order out of the nation's ramshackle finances. The basic problem was the huge debt left over from the Revolution. With interest going unpaid, the debt was growing, and, by 1789, it had reached $52 million. Most of this, about $40 million, was held by Americans in the form of securities and certificates issued during the Revolution. Foreigners, mostly French and Dutch, held another $12 million. In addition, state governments had debts totaling close to $25 million. Until the government set up and honored a regular schedule for paying interest, the nation's public credit would be worthless. Unable to borrow, the government would collapse.

More than any other individual, Hamilton imparted energy and purpose to the Washington administration. He was ambitious, egotistical, and overbearing. When he spoke of the people, he usually did so with a sneer. But he also had a brilliant financial mind and a sweeping vision of national greatness. He was convinced that the economic self-interests of the wealthy and well-born offered the only sound foundation for the success of the new government.

Born illegitimate in the West Indies in 1755 and orphaned at the age of 13, Hamilton craved power and social connections. Friends impressed with his potential sent him as a teenager to New York City for an education at Kings College (now Columbia University). An eager patriot, he served as Washington's personal aide during the Revolution. Washington's backing enabled him to marry into a wealthy New York family. He now had an entry into the world of the social and economic elite, and he parlayed it into a flourishing legal practice and a rising political career. With no ancestral loyalties to any individual state, he brought an unabashed nationalism to Washington's cabinet. And with a conviction born of his own rise that wealth and power were synonymous, he made no apologies for trying to link the interests of the government with those of the wealthy.

At the request of Congress, Hamilton prepared a series of reports on the nation's finances and economic condition. In the first, issued in January 1790, Hamilton proposed a bold plan to address the

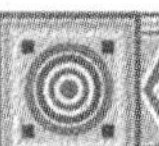

FROM THEN TO NOW

Hamilton's Legacy and the National Debt

The debate over the national debt that figured so prominently in the rise of party politics in the 1790s has continued to echo throughout American history. The tripling of the debt in the 1980s, combined with a recession that hit during the presidency of George Bush, sharpened these debates and made the debt a major issue in the election of 1992.

Well into the twentieth century, a Jeffersonian bias against a large public debt dominated the fiscal policy of the federal government. Until 1930, government revenues usually exceeded expenditures, and the surplus was used to reduce the debt. Even so, except for a brief time in the mid-1830s during Andrew Jackson's presidency, the debt was never actually extinguished. This was because economic depressions periodically reduced government income and wars periodically forced huge increases in expenditures, keeping the government perpetually in debt.

By 1860, the national debt was smaller than it had been when Alexander Hamilton took office as the first secretary of the treasury. To pay for the unprecedented expenses of the Civil War, however, the government borrowed funds, and, by 1866, the debt had skyrocketed. The government then committed itself to lowering the debt, and, by the 1890s, when a depression ended twenty-eight consecutive years of budget surplus, it had declined by two-thirds. World War I began a similar cycle—a runup of the debt followed by a gradual reduction—until the onset of the Great Depression of the 1930s began a dramatic change in government policy toward the debt.

Under President Franklin Roosevelt's New Deal, the federal government responded to the length and severity of the depression with new relief programs that drove up outlays while revenues plunged. In what was highly unusual for peacetime, budget deficits piled up, and the national debt rose. It was the cost of World War II, however, that sent the debt soaring. By 1946 it stood at $271 billion, more than the entire economic output of the country. This time, after the war, the creation of surpluses to reduce the debt did not top the government agenda. On the contrary, the onset of the Cold War began an extended period of massive defense spending. At the same time, the government built on the New Deal with new spending on domestic welfare.

Many economists argue that the government's deficit spending since World War II has kept the economy healthy and helped to avert a new depression. In any case the size of the debt relative to the economy as a whole has declined since World War II—even after the runup of the 1980s—because the economy has grown faster than the debt.

Why then were the debt and federal deficits such potent political issues in 1992? One reason was surely that the country was just then emerging from a recession. All aspects of the economy were under intense scrutiny, as voters fearful for their own jobs struggled with their own debt loads. Renewed economic growth and budgetary restraint have allayed these concerns for now. In 1998 and 1999 the budget was in surplus, and the government paid down some of the national debt. Another economic downturn, however, will likely provoke new calls for deficit spending and revive concerns about the national debt that Jeffersonians first voiced in the 1790s.

Alexander Hamilton's portrait on the ten dollar bill reflects the enduring legacy of his dynamic economic leadership, which put the young republic's finances on a sound footing.

Revolutionary War debt. The federal government, he maintained, should fund the national debt at full face value. To do this, he proposed exchanging the old debt, including accrued interest, for new government bonds bearing interest at about 4 percent. In addition, Hamilton maintained that the federal government should assume the remaining war debt of the state governments. The intent of this plan was to give the nation's creditors an economic stake in the stability of the new nation and to subordinate state financial interests to those of the central government.

In his second report, issued in December 1790, Hamilton called for an excise tax (a tax on the production, sale, or consumption of a commodity) on distilled whiskey produced within the United States. The purpose of the tax was to raise additional revenue for interest payments on the national debt. It would also establish the government's authority to levy internal taxes on its citizens.

The third report, which followed quickly after the second, recommended the chartering of a national bank, the Bank of the United States. Hamilton patterned his proposed bank after the Bank of England and intended it to meet a variety of needs. Jointly owned by the federal government and private investors, it would serve as the fiscal (financial) and depository agent of the government and make loans to businesses. Through a provision that permitted up to three-fourths of the value of bank stock to be purchased with government bonds, the bank would create a market for public securities and hence raise their value. Most important, the bank would provide the nation with a stable currency. At the time, the country had only three private banks and specie—hard currency in the form of gold and silver coins—was scarce. The government needed a reliable source of money, as did the economy as a whole. Hamilton proposed to allow the Bank of the United States to issue money in the form of paper banknotes that would be backed by a small reserve of specie and the security of government bonds. His goal was both to strengthen the economy and to consolidate the power of the national government.

Hamilton's final report, issued in December 1791, recommended government actions to promote industry. Looking, as always, to the British model of economic development, he argued that the United States would never become a great power until it diversified its largely agrarian economy. As long as the nation imported most of its manufactured goods, Hamilton warned, it would be no more than a second-rate power. Moreover, American manufacturers, saddled with both high labor costs and primitive technology, would remain at a severe competitive disadvantage unless they received government assistance. Hamilton advocated aid in the form of **protective tariffs** (high tariffs meant to make imported goods more expensive than domestic goods) for such industries as iron, steel, and shoemaking—which had already begun to establish themselves—and direct subsidies to assist with start-up costs for other industries. Hamilton believed that such "patronage," as he called it, would ultimately foster interregional economic dependence. An industrializing Northeast, for example, would depend on the South and West for foodstuffs for its workers and raw materials for its factories. In turn, farmers and planters would buy manufactured goods from the Northeast. Thus in Hamilton's vision, manufacturing, like a national currency, would be a great national unifier.

Reaction and Opposition

The breadth and boldness of Hamilton's program invited opposition. For many people, it reflected a vision of the nation that challenged their deeply held beliefs about the purpose and meaning of the American Revolution. Opposition began to emerge with the first report on the public credit, and quickly solidified along economic, ideological, and sectional lines.

About half of the members of Congress owned some of the nation's debt, and nearly all of them agreed with Hamilton that it should be paid off. Some opponents, however, were concerned that Hamilton's plan was unfair. Hard times had forced most of the original holders of the debt—by and large, ordinary citizens—to sell their certificates to speculators at a fraction of their face value. Should the government, asked Madison, reward speculators with a windfall profit when the debt was paid back in full and forget about the true patriots who had sustained the Revolution in its darkest hours?

Others objected on republican grounds that Hamilton had no intention of actually eliminating the government's debt. He envisioned instead a permanent debt, with the government making regular interest payments as they came due. The debt, in the form of government securities, would serve as a vital prop for the support of moneyed groups. One congressman saw this as a violation of "that great principle which alone was the cause of the war with Great Britain . . . that taxation and representation should go hand in hand." Future generations, he argued, would be unfairly taxed for a debt incurred by the present generation.

Opposition to Hamilton's proposal to have the federal government assume state debts reflected sectional differences. With the exception of South Carolina, the southern states had already paid back a good share of their war debts. Thus Hamilton's plan stood to benefit the northern states disproportionately. Because Hamilton had linked the funding of the national debt with the assumption of state debts, southern opposition to assumption threatened funding as well. Tensions mounted as the deadlock continued into the summer of 1790. Frustrated over southern intransigence, New Englanders muttered about seceding. Southerners responded in kind. A Virginia senator charged that disunion would be a small price to pay to escape "the rule of a fixed insolent northern majority."

Tempers cooled when a compromise was reached in July. Southerners agreed to accept funding in its original form because, as Hamilton correctly noted, it would be impractical, if not impossible, to distinguish between the original and current holders of the national debt. Assumption passed after Hamilton cut a deal with Virginians James Madison and Thomas Jefferson. In exchange for southern support of assumption, Hamilton agreed to line up northern votes for locating the nation's permanent capital on the banks of the Potomac River, where it would be surrounded by the slave states of Maryland and Virginia. The package was sweetened by extra grants of federal money to states with small debts.

Hamilton's alliance with Madison and Jefferson proved short-lived, dissolving when Madison led the congressional opposition to Hamilton's proposed bank. Madison and most other Southerners viewed the bank as evidence of a willingness to sacrifice the interests of the agrarian South in favor of the financial and industrial interests of the North. They feared that the bank, with its power to dispense economic favors, would re-create in the United States the kind of government corruption and privilege they associated with Great Britain. They argued that the Constitution did not explicitly authorize Congress to charter a bank or any other corporation.

The bank bill passed Congress on a vote that divided on sectional lines. Madison's objections, however, left Washington concerned that the bank might not be constitutional. He sought the cabinet's opinion, provoking the first great debate over how the Constitution should be interpreted. Thomas Jefferson, the secretary of state, sided with Madison and for the first time openly clashed with Hamilton. Taking a **strict constructionist** position, he argued that all powers the Constitution had not expressly delegated to the national government were reserved to the states under the Tenth Amendment. Hamilton, in a brilliant rejoinder, argued that Article 1, Section 8 of the Constitution, which declares that Congress has the right to "to make all laws which shall be necessary and proper" to exercise its powers and those of the federal government, gives Congress implicit authority beyond its explicitly enumerated powers. With this **broad constructionist** position, he won Washington to his side.

With Washington's signature on the bill, Hamilton's bank was chartered for twenty years. Congress also passed a hefty 25 percent excise tax on distilled liquor. Little, however, of Hamilton's plan to promote manufacturing survived the scrutiny of the agrarian opposition. Tariff duties were raised moderately in 1792, but no funds were forthcoming to accelerate industrial development.

The Emergence of Parties

By the end of Washington's first term, Americans were dividing into two camps. On one side stood those who still called themselves Federalists. These were the supporters of Hamilton's program—speculators, creditors, merchants, manufacturers, and commercial farmers. They were the Americans most fully integrated into the market economy and in control of it. Concentrated in the North, they included New England Congregationalists and mid-Atlantic Episcopalians (former Anglicans), members of the more socially prestigious churches. In both economic and cultural terms, the Federalists were drawn from the more privileged segments of society.

Jefferson and Madison shrewdly gave the name Republican to the party that formed in opposition to the Federalists, thus identifying it with individual liberties and the heritage of the Revolution. The Republicans accused Hamilton and the Federalists of attempting to impose a British system of economic privilege and social exploitation. The initial core of the party consisted of southern planters and backcountry Scots-Irish farmers. These were Americans outside the market economy or skeptical of its benefits. They feared that the commercial groups favored by Hamilton would corrupt politics in their pursuit of power and foster commerce and manufacturing at the expense of agriculture. The Republicans were committed to an agrarian America in which power remained in the hands of farmers and planters.

In 1792, parties were still in a formative stage. The political divisions that had appeared first in Congress and then spread to Washington's cabinet did not yet extend very deeply into the electorate. Washington remained aloof from the political infighting and was still seen as a great unifier. Unopposed, he was reelected in 1792. However, a series of crises in his second term deepened and broadened the incipient party divisions. By 1796, rival parties were contesting the presidency and vying for the support of an increasingly politically organized electorate.

Overview

Federalist Party versus Republican Party

Federalists	Republicans
Favored strong central government	Wanted to limit the role of the national government
Supported Hamilton's economic program	Opposed Hamilton's economic program
Opposed the French Revolution	Generally supported the French Revolution
Supported Jay's Treaty and closer ties to Britain	Opposed Jay's Treaty and favored closer ties to France
In response to the threat of war with France, proposed and passed the Direct Tax of 1798, the Alien and Sedition Acts, and legislation to enlarge the size of the army	Opposed the Alien and Sedition Acts and the enlarged army as threats to individual liberties
Drew strongest support from New England; lost support in the mid-Atlantic region after 1798	Drew strongest support from the South and West

The French Revolution

The French Revolution began in 1789, and, in its early phase, most Americans applauded it. France had been an ally of the United States during the Revolutionary War and now seemed to be following the example of its American friends in shaking off monarchical rule. By 1792, however, the French Revolution had turned violent and radical. Its supporters confiscated the property of aristocrats and the church, slaughtered suspected enemies, and executed the king, Louis XVI. In early 1793, republican France was at war against Britain and the European powers.

The excesses of the French Revolution and the European war that erupted in its wake touched off a bitter debate in America. Federalists drew back in horror from France's new regime. They insisted that the terror unleashed by the French was far removed from the reasoned republicanism of the American Revolution. As the Federalist *Gazette of the United States* argued: "The American Revolution, it ought to be repeated, was not accomplished as the French has been, by massacres, assassinations, or proscriptions." For the Republicans, the French remained the standard-bearers of the cause of liberty for common people everywhere. Jefferson admitted that the French Revolution was tarnished by the loss of innocent lives, "but rather than it should have failed, I would have seen half the earth desolated." He was convinced that "the liberty of the whole earth was depending on the issue in the contest."

When the new French ambassador, Edmond Genêt, arrived in the United States in April 1793—just as the debate in America over the French Revolution was heating up—French and American relations reached a turning point. The two countries were still bound to one another by the Franco-American Alliance of 1778. The alliance required the United States to assist France in the defense of its West Indian colonies and to open American ports to French privateers if France were attacked. Genêt, it soon became clear, hoped to embroil the United States in the French war against the British. He commissioned American privateers to attack British shipping and tried to enlist an army of frontiersmen to attack Spanish possessions in Louisiana and Florida.

Genêt's actions, as well as the enthusiastic receptions that greeted him as he traveled from Charleston to Philadelphia (chosen in 1790 as the temporary national capital), forced Washington to call a special cabinet meeting. The president feared that Genêt would stampede Americans into the European war, with disastrous results for the nation's finances. The bulk of America's foreign trade was with the British, and tariff duties on British imports were the main source of revenue to pay for Hamilton's assumption and funding programs. Hamilton urged Washington to declare American neutrality in the European war, maintaining that the president could commit the nation to neutrality on his own authority when Congress, as was then the case, was

American Views

The Grass-Roots Politics of a Democratic-Republican Organization

The Democratic-Republican societies that sprang up in sympathy with the French Revolution modeled themselves after the U.S. Revolutionary committees of the 1770s. Their members drew up constitutions, elected officers, issued resolutions and memorials, and drank toast after toast to the memory of the patriots who secured American independence. Above all, they insisted on the need for the constant vigilance of an informed citizenry to protect republican liberties against government encroachment. The following selection is from the constitution of the Democratic Society in Addison County, Vermont.

- ❖ **What moral principles does the society associate with republican government? What duties of citizenship does it outline? What does the society mean by a "strictly republican government"?**
- ❖ **What explains the society's suspicion of public officials? Why does it stress the need for an informed citizenry? How does the society hope to safeguard popular liberties? How practical do you feel this program would be in the United States today?**
- ❖ **Why did the Federalists oppose these ideas on popular government? How would they construe the nature of liberty and republican government differently?**

We, the undersigned, compact and associate ourselves into a Society . . . to promote the political ends expressed in the following articles, which shall be considered constitutional of our Society.

We make no apology for thus associating ourselves . . . to consider . . . and publish our sentiments, on the political interests, constitution and government of our country; this is a right, the disputation of which reflects on political freedom, and wears an appearance peculiarly absurd, proceeding from the tongue or pen of an American.

We declare the following . . . to be some of our political sentiments, and principles of government, . . . —That all men are naturally free, and possess equal rights. —That all legitimate government originates in the voluntary and social com-

not in session. Hamilton also wanted to suspend the military and commercial treaties of 1778 with France and refuse diplomatic recognition of Genêt. Jefferson, although he too wanted to avoid war, opposed Hamilton on these issues. Disputing Washington's power to act on his own, Jefferson maintained that the warmaking powers of Congress reserved for it alone the right to issue a declaration of neutrality.

Washington steered a middle course. He granted Genêt a formal (but cold) reception and took no action to suspend the Franco-American treaties. But he accepted Hamilton's argument on his authority to declare neutrality and issued a proclamation on April 22, 1793, stating that the United States would be "friendly and impartial toward the belligerent powers."

Despite this proclamation, Genêt continued meddling. He finally exceeded Washington's patience in the summer of 1793 when he grandly announced that he would take his case directly to the American people and force a cowardly administration to stand up for French rights. Washington was on the verge of forcing his recall to France in August when news arrived that a new and more radical French government had decided to bring Genêt back as a political prisoner. The president graciously permitted Genêt to remain in America as a private citizen. Had he returned to France, he would have faced almost certain execution.

Genêt quickly faded from public view, but American politics became more open and aggressive in the wake of his visit. Pro-French enthusiasm pact of the people. —That no rights of the people are surrendered to their rulers, as a price of protection and government. —That the constitution and laws of a country are the expressions of the general will of the body of the people or nation, that all officers of government are the ministers & servants of the people, and, as such, are amenable to them, for all their conduct in office. —That it is the right, and becomes the duty of a people, as a necessary means of the security and preservation of their rights, and the future peace and political happiness of the nation, to exercise watchfullness and inspection, upon the conduct of all their public officers; to approve, if they find their conduct worthy of their high and important trusts—and to reprove and censure, if it be found otherwise. That frequent elections, directly from the body of the people, of persons, to important offices of trust, have an immediate tendency to secure the public power; that compensations for public service ought to be reasonable (and even moderate, when the debts and exigencies of a nation require it) and a reward only for actual service; that a public debt (and a financial funding system to continue the same) is a burthen upon a nation, and ought . . . to be reduced and discharged; that an increase of public officers, dependent on the executive power, [is] a foolish copying of ancient corrupt and foreign governments and courts, where the equal rights of men are trampled under the feet of kings and lords; and a standing army—are all highly dangerous to liberty; and that the constitution, laws, and government of a country are always of right, liable to amendation and improvement.

We are concerned that the present political state of our country calls for the rational, wise and vigilant attention of its citizens. . . . It shall be the objects . . . of this society to study the Constitution, to avail ourselves of the journals, debates, and laws of Congress and such other publications as may be judged necessary to give information as to the proceedings of Congress and the departments of government and also of the conduct of individual officers in the discharge of their trusts. . . . And on information, we will speak; and upon deliberation, we will write and publish our sentiments. A steady zeal and firmness for the liberties of our country, and a strictly republican government, in pursuing our enquiries, & in passing our resolutions, shall be severely guided by the reason and temperance, which a sense of moral obligation, and the dread of ignorant popular convulsions, demand. . . .

Source: Philip S. Foner, ed., The Democratic-Republic Societies, 1790–1800: A Documentary Sourcebook of Constitutions, Declarations, Addresses, Resolutions, and Toasts *(Greenwood, 1976).*

lived on in a host of grassroots political organizations known as the Democratic-Republican societies. Nearly forty of these societies formed in 1793 and 1794. As their name suggests, these societies reflected a belief that democracy and republicanism were one and the same. This was a new concept in American politics. Democracy had traditionally been equated with anarchy and mob rule. The members of the new societies argued to the contrary that only democracy—meaning popular participation in politics and direct appeals by politicians to the people—could maintain the revolutionary spirit of 1776, because the people were the only true guardians of that spirit. As a letter writer to the Newark Gazette put it:

> It must be the mechanics and farmers, or the poorer class of people (as they are generally called), that must support the freedom which they and their fathers purchased with their blood—the nobility will never do it—they will be always striving to get the reins of government into their own hands, and then they can ride the people at pleasure.

The Democratic-Republican societies attacked the Washington administration for failing to assist France, and they expressed the popular feeling that Hamilton's program favored the rich over the poor. For the first time, Washington himself was personally assailed in the press.

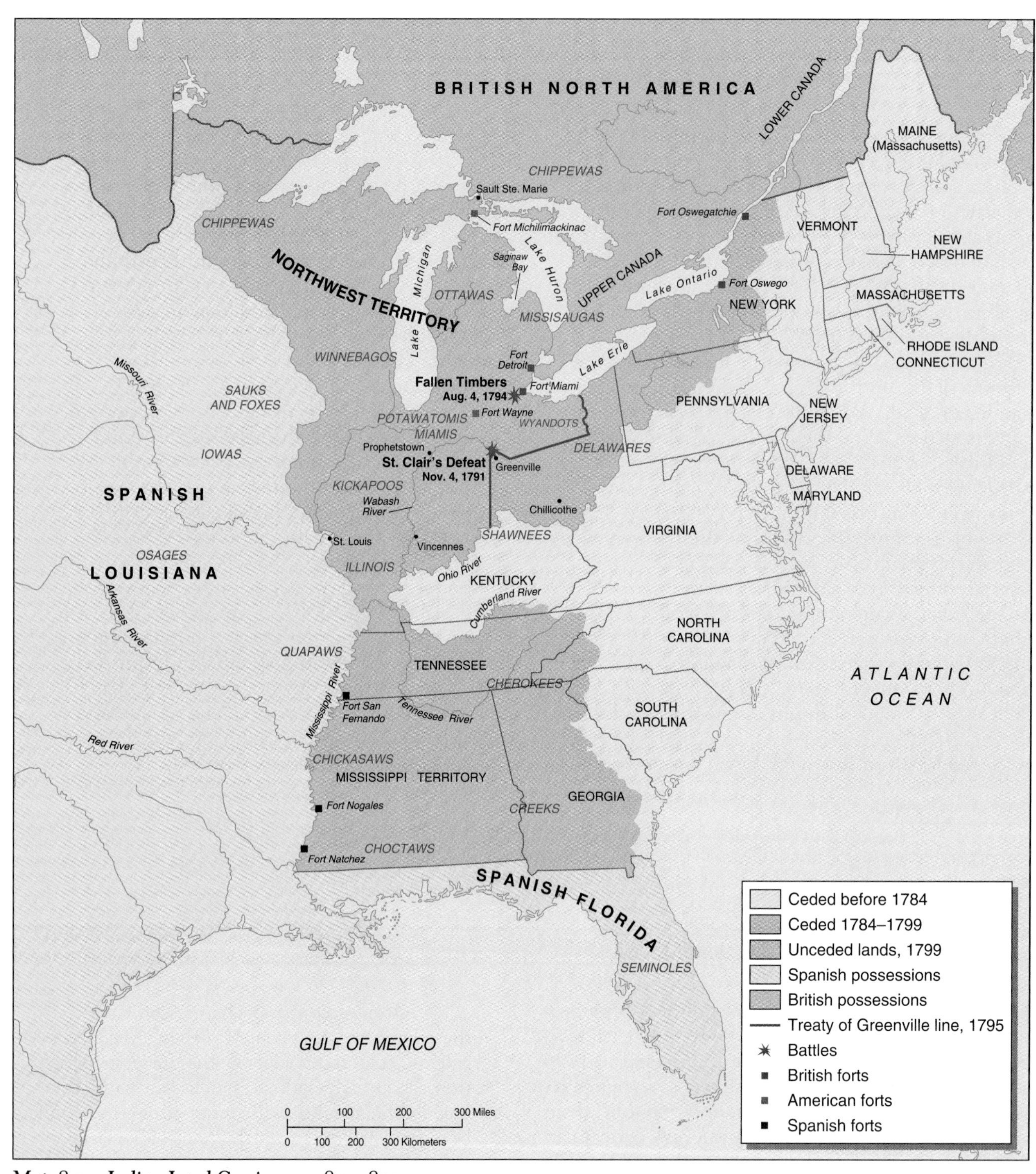

Map 8-1 Indian Land Cessions, 1784–1800
The persistent pressure of white settlers and the military forces of the new national government forced Native Americans to cede huge tracts of their western lands.

The core members of the societies were urban artisans whose egalitarian views shocked the Federalists. They expected deference, not criticism and political activism, from the people. In their view, the Democratic-Republicans were rabble-rousers trying to dictate policy to the nation's natural leaders. The Federalists harshly condemned the emergence of organized political dissent from below, but in so doing they only enhanced the popular appeal of the growing Republican opposition.

Securing the Frontier

Control of the West remained an elusive goal throughout Washington's first term. Indian resistance in the Northwest Territory prevented whites from pushing north of the Ohio River. The powerful Miami Confederacy routed two ill-trained American armies in 1790 and 1791. The 1791 encounter, which took place on the banks of the Wabash River in western Ohio, was the worst defeat an American army ever suffered in frontier fighting. More than nine hundred soldiers were killed or wounded, and the commander, General Arthur St. Clair, was lucky to survive. The southern frontier was quieter, but the Spanish continued to use the Creeks and Cherokees as a buffer against American penetration south of the Tennessee River.

By 1793, many western settlers felt abandoned by the national government. They believed that the government had broken a promise to protect them against Indians and foreigners. Much of the popularity of the Democratic-Republican societies in the West fed off these frustrations. Westerners saw the French, who were at war with Britain and Spain, as allies against the foreign threat on the frontier, and they forwarded resolutions to Congress embracing the French cause. These resolutions also demanded free and open navigation on the Mississippi River. This, in the minds of Westerners, was their natural right. Without it, they would be forever impoverished. "If the interest of Eastern America requires that we should be kept in poverty," argued the Mingo Creek society of western Pennsylvania, "it is unreasonable from such poverty to exact contributions. The first, if we cannot emerge from, we must learn to bear, but the latter, we never can be taught to submit to."

Submission to national authority, however, was precisely what the Federalists wanted from both the Indians and the western settlers. St. Clair's humiliating defeat in 1791 prompted a reorganization of the War Department. By the summer of 1794, Washington's administration felt prepared to move against the Indians. This time, it sent into the Ohio region not the usual ragtag crew of militia and unemployed city dwellers but a force built around veterans from the professional army. The commander, General Anthony Wayne, was a savvy, battle-hardened war hero.

On August 4, 1794, at the **Battle of Fallen Timbers**, near present-day Toledo, Wayne's army dealt a decisive blow to the Ohio Indians. The British, who had promised full support for an independent Indian country north of the Ohio River, backed off for fear of provoking a war with the United States. The Indians had little choice but to submit to the peace terms Wayne demanded. In the Treaty of Greenville, signed in August 1795, twelve tribes ceded most of the present state of Ohio to the U.S. government in return for an annual payment of $9,500. The Ohio country was now open to white settlement (see Map 8-1).

The Whiskey Rebellion

Within a few months of Wayne's victory at Fallen Timbers, another American army was on the move. The target this time were the so-called whiskey rebels of

Painting; P & S–1914.0001; "The Treaty of Fort Greenville, Ohio;" 1795. Artist unknown, member of Gen. Anthony Wayne's staff.

This painting by an officer on General Wayne's staff shows Little Turtle, a Miami chief, speaking through an interpreter to General Wayne (with one hand behind his back) during the negotiations that led to the Treaty of Greenville.

western Pennsylvania, who were openly resisting Hamilton's excise tax on whiskey. This tax had always been unpopular among western farmers. The high cost of transport across the mountains made it unprofitable for them to sell their grain in the east. But by distilling corn or rye into whiskey, they reduced it enough in bulk to lower transportation costs and earn a profit. Hamilton's excise tax wiped out these profits.

Hamilton was determined to enforce the tax and assert the supremacy of national laws. Although resistance to the tax was widespread, he singled out the Pennsylvania rebels. It was easier to send an army into the Pittsburgh area than the Carolina mountains. Washington, moreover, was convinced that the Democratic-Republican societies of western Pennsylvania were behind the defiance of federal authority there. He welcomed the opportunity to chastise these organizations, which he identified with the dangerous doctrines of the French Revolution.

Washington called on the governors of the mid-Atlantic states to supply militia forces to crush the **Whiskey Rebellion**. The 13,000-man army that assembled at Harrisburg and marched into western Pennsylvania in October 1794 was larger than any Washington had commanded during the Revolution. But the rebellion, as Jefferson sardonically noted, "could never be found." The army met no resistance and expended considerable effort rounding up twenty prisoners. Two men were found guilty of treason, but Washington pardoned both. Still, at Hamilton's insistence, the Federalists had made their point: When its authority was openly challenged, this national government was prepared to use military force to compel obedience.

The Whiskey Rebellion starkly revealed the conflicting visions of local liberty and national order that divided Americans of the early republic. The non-English majority on the Pennsylvania frontier—Irish, Scots-Irish, German, and Welsh—justified resistance to the whiskey tax with the same republican ideology that had fueled the American Revolution. Mostly poor farmers, artisans, and laborers, they appealed to notions of liberty, equality, and freedom from oppressive taxation that were deeply rooted in backcountry settlements from Maine to Georgia. In putting down the Pennsylvania rebels, Washington and Hamilton acted on behalf of more English and cosmopolitan groups in the East who valued central power as a check on any local resistance movement that might begin unraveling the still-fragile republic.

Treaties with Britain and Spain

Much of the unrest in the West stemmed from the menacing presence of the British and Spanish on the nation's borders. Washington's government had the resources to suppress Indians and frontier dissidents but lacked sufficient armed might to push Spain and especially Britain out of the West.

The British, embroiled in what they saw as a life-or-death struggle against revolutionary France, clamped a naval blockade on France and its colonies in the Caribbean in the fall of 1793. They also supported an uprising of slaves on the French island of Saint-Domingue (present-day Haiti), enraging southern planters fearful that slave rebellions might spread to the United States. The French countered by opening their colonial trade, which had been closed to outsiders during peacetime, to neutral shippers. American merchants stepped in and reaped profits by supplying France. The British retaliated by seizing American ships involved in the French trade. They further claimed the right to search American ships and impress, or forcibly remove, sailors they suspected of having deserted from the British navy. News of these provocations reached America in early 1794 and touched off a major war scare. Desperate to avert a war, Washington sent John Jay, the chief justice of the United States, to London to negotiate an accord.

Jay brought a weak hand to the negotiating table. Britain had enormous military resources, the United States only a small army and navy. What is more, tariffs on British trade were the main source of revenue for the United States government. But the British, too, benefited from their trade with the United States, and they wanted to keep the United States neutral.

From the American point of view, the resulting agreement, known as **Jay's Treaty**, was flawed but acceptable. Jay had to abandon the American insistence on the right of neutrals to ship goods to nations at war without interference (meaning in this case the right of the United States to continue trading with France without British harassment). He also had to grant Britain "most favored nation" status, giving up the American right to discriminate against British shipping and merchandise. And he had to reconfirm the American commitment to assure that pre-Revolutionary debts owed by Americans to the British would be repaid in full. In return for these major concessions, Britain pledged to compensate American merchants for the ships and cargoes it had seized in 1793 and 1794, to abandon the six forts it still held in the American Northwest, and to grant the United States limited trading rights in India and the British West Indies.

Signed in November 1794, Jay's Treaty caused an uproar in the United States when its terms became known in March 1795. Southerners saw in it another sellout of their interests. It required them to pay their prewar debts to British merchants but was silent about the slaves Britain had carried off during the Revolution. And the concessions Britain did make seemed to favor the North, especially New England merchants and shippers. Republicans, joined now by urban artisans, were infuriated that Jay had stripped them of their chief weapon—economic retaliation—for breaking free of British commercial dominance. The Senate ratified the treaty in June 1795, but only because Washington backed it.

Jay's Treaty, combined with a string of French victories in Europe in 1795, convinced Spain to adopt a more conciliatory attitude toward the United States. With France apparently gaining the upper hand in the war, Spain was anxious to shift its allegiance from Britain to France. But it saw the Jay treaty as the beginning of an Anglo-American alliance and decided to reach an agreement with the United States before it changed sides lest the United States and Britain combine forces to challenge its American possessions. In the **Treaty of San Lorenzo** (also known as **Pinckney's Treaty**) of 1795, Spain accepted the American position on the 31st parallel as the northern boundary of Spanish Florida and granted American farmers the right of free transit through the port of New Orleans.

The First Partisan Election

Two terms in office were more than enough for Washington. The partisan politics that emerged during his second term—and its expression in an increasingly partisan press—disgusted him. The first opposition newspaper, the *National Gazette,* appeared in 1791, and the number of newspapers more than doubled within a decade. Circulated and discussed in taverns and coffeehouses, newspapers helped draw ordinary Americans into the political process. An outgrowth of the Revolution's appeal to popular sovereignty, this democratization of political involvement in turn created a basis for two-party politics. It also produced a form of cultural warfare that left gentlemen of wealth and refinement, including the leaders of the Federalist party, on the defensive. No symbol of traditional authority, including Washington, was safe from challenge. Although he remained silent in public, Washington complained bitterly to friends that his political opponents had maligned him "in such exaggerated and indecent terms as could scarcely be applied to a . . . notorious defaulter, or even a common pickpocket."

Washington announced his decision to retire from public life in his Farewell Address of September 1796, less than two months before the presidential election. He intentionally delayed the announcement to minimize the time the Republicans would have to prepare for the campaign. Washington devoted most of his address to a denunciation of partisanship. He invoked the republican ideal of disinterested, independent statesmanship as the only sure and virtuous guide for the nation. The sectional and pro-French or pro-British bias of partisanship particularly worried him. He warned against any permanent foreign alliances and cautioned that the Union itself would be endangered if parties continued to be characterized "by geographical discriminations—*Northern* and *Southern, Atlantic* and *Western*—whence designing men may endeavor to excite a belief that there is a real difference of local interests and views."

Confirming Washington's fears, the election of 1796 was the first openly partisan election in American history. John Adams was the Federalist candidate and Thomas Jefferson the Republican candidate. Each was selected at a **party caucus**, a meeting of party leaders.

Adams won despite Alexander Hamilton's interference, which inadvertently almost threw the election to Jefferson. Now a private citizen in New York, Hamilton wanted to be the power behind the throne in any new Federalist administration. Uncomfortable with Adams, he connived to have Thomas Pinckney of South Carolina, the other Federalist running with Adams, win the election. The Constitution did not originally call for electors to cast separate ballots for president and vice president. Rather, they cast two votes; the highest vote-getter who received a majority became president, and the second highest became vice president. Nor were the electors, nearly half of whom in 1796 were chosen by state legislatures, under any obligation to cast a party ticket. In short, the Constitution was written with absolutely no thought of organized partisan competition for the presidency. Taking advantage of this weakness, Hamilton convinced some of the South Carolina electors to drop Adams from their ballots. He expected that with the solid support of the New England electors for both Adams and Pinckney, Pinkney would be elected president and Adams vice president. But the scheme backfired. When New Englanders learned of it, they refused to vote for Pinckney. As a result, Adams came in first with seventy-one votes, but Jefferson came in second with sixty-eight. Thanks to Hamilton, Adams entered office with his chief rival as vice president and a politically divided administration.

Despite the election's confused outcome, the sectional pattern in the voting was unmistakable. Only the solid support of regional elites in New England and the mid-Atlantic states enabled the Federalists to retain the presidency. Adams received all the northern electoral votes, with the exception of Pennsylvania's. Jefferson was the overwhelming favorite in the South.

The Last Federalist Administration

The Adams administration got off to a rocky start from which it never recovered. The vice president was the leader of the opposition party; key members of the cabinet, which Adams had inherited from Washington, owed their primary loyalty to Hamilton; and the French, who saw Adams as a dupe of the British, instigated a major crisis that left the threat of war hanging over the entire Adams presidency. Adams had been a lawyer before the Revolution; he was a veteran of both Continental Congresses, had been a diplomat in Europe for a decade, and had served as Washington's vice president for eight years. But despite this extraordinarily rich background in public affairs, he was politically naive. Scrupulously honest but quick to take offense, he lacked the politician's touch for inspiring personal loyalty and crafting compromises based on a realistic recognition of mutual self-interest. But putting the interests of the country before those of his party, he almost single-handedly prevented a nearly certain war with France and a possible civil war at home. The price he paid was a badly split Federalist party that refused to unite behind him when he sought reelection in 1800.

The French Crisis and the XYZ Affair

An aggressive coalition known as the Directory gained control of revolutionary France in 1795 and denounced the Jay treaty as evidence of an Anglo-American alliance against France. When Jefferson and the pro-French Republicans lost the election of 1796, the Directory turned openly hostile. In short order, the French annulled the commercial treaty of 1778 with the United States, ordered the seizure of American ships carrying goods to the British, and declared that any American sailors found on British ships, including those forcibly pressed into service, would be summarily executed. By the time Adams had been in office barely three months, the French had already confiscated more than three hundred American ships.

In the fall of 1797, Adams sent three commissioners to Paris in an effort to avoid war. The French treated the three with contempt. Having just conquered the Netherlands and detached Spain from its British alliance, France was in no mood to compromise. Through three intermediaries—identified by Adams only as X, Y, and Z when he informed Congress of the negotiations—the French foreign minister demanded a large bribe to initiate talks and an American loan of $12 million.

In April 1798, the Senate published a full account of the insulting behavior of the French in what came to be called the **XYZ Affair**. The public was indignant, and war fever swept the country. The Federalists, who had always warned against the French, enjoyed greater popularity than they ever had or ever would again. Congress acted to upgrade the navy, which had languished since the Revolutionary War. Funds were provided to build and arm forty new ships. Responsibility for naval affairs, formerly divided between the Treasury and War Departments, was consolidated in a new Department of the Navy. By the fall of 1798, American ships were waging an undeclared

With the horrors of the French Revolution forming a backdrop, this cartoon depicts France as a five-headed monster demanding a bribe from the three Americans sent by Adams. The Federalists hoped that such anti-French sentiments would lead to an open war.

This contemporary cartoon shows Republican Matthew Lyon, on the right with the fire tongs, fighting against Roger Griswold, a Connecticut Federalist. This brawl in Congress on February 15, 1798, revealed the depth of feeling that now divided the Republicans and Federalists.

war against the French in Caribbean waters, a conflict that came to be known as the **Quasi-War**.

The Federalists in Congress, dismissing Republican objections, also voted to create a vastly expanded army. They tripled the size of the regular army to ten thousand men and authorized a special provisional army of fifty thousand. Congress put the provisional army under Washington's command, but he declined to come out of retirement except for a national emergency. In the meantime, he insisted that Hamilton be appointed second in command and given charge of the provisional army's field operations. To pay for both the expanded army and the naval rearmament, the Federalists pushed through the Direct Tax of 1798, a levy on the value of land, slaves, and dwellings.

Crisis at Home

The thought of Hamilton in charge of a huge army convinced many Republicans that their worst nightmares were about to materialize. One congressman shuddered that "the monarchy-loving Hamilton is now so fixed, as to be able, with one-step, to fill the place of our present commander in chief." Adams shared such fears. He was furious that Hamilton had been forced on him as commander of the provisional army. Years later, he wrote that "the British faction was determined to have a war with France, and Alexander Hamilton at the head of the army and then Pres. of U.S. Peace with France was therefore treason against their fundamental maxims and reasons of State." As the Republicans immediately sensed and Adams came to realize, Hamilton's supporters, known as the **High Federalists**, saw the war scare with France as an opportunity to stamp out dissent, cement an alliance with the British, and strengthen and consolidate the powers of the national government.

The Federalists passed four laws in the summer of 1798, known collectively as the **Alien and Sedition Acts**, that confirmed the Republicans' fears. Three of these acts were aimed at immigrants, especially French and Irish refugees who voted for the Republicans. They convinced hundreds of immigrants to flee the country to avoid possible arrest. The Alien Enemies Act empowered the president to deport foreigners from countries at war with the United States. The more sweeping Alien Friends Act authorized the president to expel any alien resident he suspected of subversive activities. The Naturalization Act extended the residency requirement for American citizenship (and hence the right to vote) from five to fourteen years.

The most dangerous of the four acts in the minds of Republicans was the Sedition Act, a measure that made it a federal crime to engage in any combination or conspiracy against the government or to utter or print anything "false, scandalous and malicious" against the government. Federalist judges were blatantly partisan in their enforcement of the Sedition Act. Twenty-five individuals, mostly Republican editors, were indicted under the act, and ten were convicted. The most celebrated case involved Matthew Lyon, a Republican congressman from Vermont. Indicted for publishing a letter criticizing President Adams, he was reelected to Congress in December 1798 while still in jail.

Facing a Congress and a Supreme Court dominated by the Federalists, Jefferson and Madison turned to the safely Republican legislatures of Kentucky and Virginia for a forum from which to attack the constitutionality of the Alien and Sedition Acts. Taking care to keep their authorship secret, they each drafted a set of resolutions—Jefferson for the Kentucky legislature and Madison for the Virginia legislature—that challenged the entire centralizing program of the Federalists. In doing so, they produced the first significant articulation of the southern stand on **states' rights**.

The resolutions—adopted in the fall of 1798—proposed a compact theory of the Constitution. They asserted that the states had delegated specific powers to the national government for their common benefit. It followed that the states reserved the right to rule whether the national government had unconstitutionally assumed power not granted to it. If a state decided that the national government had exceeded its powers, it could "interpose" its authority to shield its citizens from a tyrannical law. In a second set of resolutions, the Kentucky legislature introduced the doctrine of **nullification**, the right of a state to render null and void a national law it deemed unconstitutional.

Jefferson and Madison hoped that these resolutions would rally voters to the Republican party as the defender of threatened American liberties. Yet not a single additional state seconded them. In the end, what aroused popular rage against the Federalists was not legislation directed against aliens and subversives but the high cost of Federalist taxes.

The Direct Tax of 1798 fell on all owners of land, dwellings, or slaves and provoked widespread resentment. Enforcing it required an army of bureaucrats—more than five hundred for the state of Pennsylvania alone. In February 1799, in the heavily German southeastern counties of Pennsylvania, a group of men led by an auctioneer named John Fries released tax evaders from prison in Bethlehem. President Adams responded to **Fries's Rebellion** with a show of force, but the fiercest resistance the soldiers he sent to Pennsylvania encountered was from irate farm wives, who doused them with hot water. Fries and two other men were arrested, convicted of treason, and sentenced to be executed (Adams later pardoned them). But the Federalists had now lost much of their support in Pennsylvania.

The End of the Federalists

The events in Pennsylvania reflected an air of menace that gripped the country as the campaign of 1800 approached. The army was chasing private citizens whose only crime in the eyes of many was that they were honoring their Revolutionary heritage by resisting hateful taxes. Federal soldiers also roughed up Republican voters at polling places. No wonder Adams later wrote that "the army was as unpopular as if it had been a ferocious wild beast let loose upon the nation to devour it." Southern Republicans talked in private of the possible need to resist Federalist tyranny by force and, failing in that, to secede from the Union. Hamilton and the High Federalists saw in the Kentucky and Virginia resolutions "a regular conspiracy to overturn the government." Reports that Virginia intended to strengthen its militia heightened their anxieties, and they proposed to meet force with force. Speaking of Virginia, Hamilton said that "the government must not merely defend itself, it must attack and arraign its enemies."

No one did more to defuse this charged atmosphere than President Adams. The Federalists depended for their popular support on the expectation of a war with France, which as late as 1798 had swept them to victory in the congressional

Short and pudgy, Adams had little of Hamilton's physical presence as a natural leader. But he had a first-rate mind and the political courage to place the nation's needs above those of his Federalist party when he peacefully ended the Quasi-War with France.

elections. Still, Adams refrained from asking for a declaration of war. The United States had been successful in the Quasi-War against France. By early 1799, French ships had been forced out of the Caribbean and American coastal waters. And in Europe, the tide of war had turned against the French. As a result, Adams believed that the French would now be more open to conciliation. Of greater importance, Adams recognized that war with France could trigger a civil war at home. Hamilton and the High Federalists, he realized, would use war as an excuse to crush the Republican opposition in Virginia. Fearful of Hamilton's intentions and unwilling to run the risk of militarizing the government and saddling it with a huge war debt, Adams broke with his party and decided to reopen negotiations with France in February 1799.

The **Franco-American Accord of 1800** that resulted from Adams's initiative released the United States from its 1778 alliance with France. It also obligated the United States to surrender all claims against the French for damages done to American shipping during the Quasi-War. The negotiations in Paris dragged on through the election of 1800, but for the Hamiltonian Federalists, the political damage had already been done. The prospect of peace with France deprived them of their trump card in the election. The Republicans could no longer be branded as the traitorous friends of an enemy state. The enlarged army, with no foe to fight, became a political embarrassment, and the Federalists dismantled it. Although rumors of possible violence continued to circulate, the Republicans grew increasingly confident that they could peacefully gain control of the government.

The Federalists nonetheless ran a very competitive race in 1800. Adams's peace policy bolstered his popularity. And because American merchants had profited from supplying both sides in the European war, the country was enjoying a period of prosperity that benefited the president and his party. The Federalists put on a show of unity when they nominated Adams and Charles C. Pinckney of South Carolina as their presidential candidates at their party caucus. But the wounds opened by Adams's decision to broker a peace with France continued to fester. Hamilton and his friends felt that Adams had betrayed them, and Hamilton wrote a scathing attack on the president in a letter that fell into the hands of Aaron Burr, a crafty politician from New York whom the Republicans had teamed up with Jefferson for the presidential election. Burr published the letter, airing the Federalists' squabblings in public.

The Federalists, hampered by party disunity, could not counter the Republicans' aggressive organizational tactics. They found it distasteful to appeal to common people. One party member lamented that the Republicans sent spokesmen "to every class of men, and even to every individual man, that can be gained. Every threshing floor, every husting, every party at work on a house-frame or raising a building, the very funerals are infected with bawlers or whisperers against government."

Wherever they organized, the Republicans attacked the Federalists as monarchists plotting to undo the gains of the Revolution. The Federalists responded with emotional appeals that depicted Jefferson as a godless revolutionary whose election would usher in a reign of terror. "The effect," intoned the Reverend William Linn, "would be to destroy religion, introduce immorality, and loosen all bonds of society."

Attacks like Linn's reflected the fears of Calvinist preachers that a tide of disbelief was about to submerge Christianity in the United States. Church attendance had declined in the 1790s, particularly among men, and perhaps no more than one in twenty Americans was a member of any church. **Deism**, an Enlightenment religious philosophy popular among the leaders of the Revolutionary era, was making inroads among common citizens as well. Deists viewed God as a kind of master clockmaker who created the laws by which the universe runs but otherwise leaves it alone. They rejected revelation for reason, maintaining that the workings of nature alone reveal God's design. In 1794, the famed pamphleteer Thomas Paine, in *The Age of Reason*, denounced churches as "human inventions set up to terrify and enslave mankind, and monopolize power and profit."

These developments convinced Calvinist ministers, nearly all of them Federalists, that the atheism of the French Revolution was infecting American republicanism. They lashed out at the Republicans, the friends of the French Revolution, as perverters of religious and social order. Jefferson, a deist known for his free thinking in religion, bore the brunt of their attack in 1800.

The Republicans won the election by mobilizing voters through strong party organizations. Voter turnout in 1800 was twice what it had been in the early 1790s, and most of the new voters were Republicans. The Direct Tax of 1798 cost the Federalists the support of commercial farmers in the mid-Atlantic states. Artisans in port cities had already switched to the Republicans in protest over Jay's

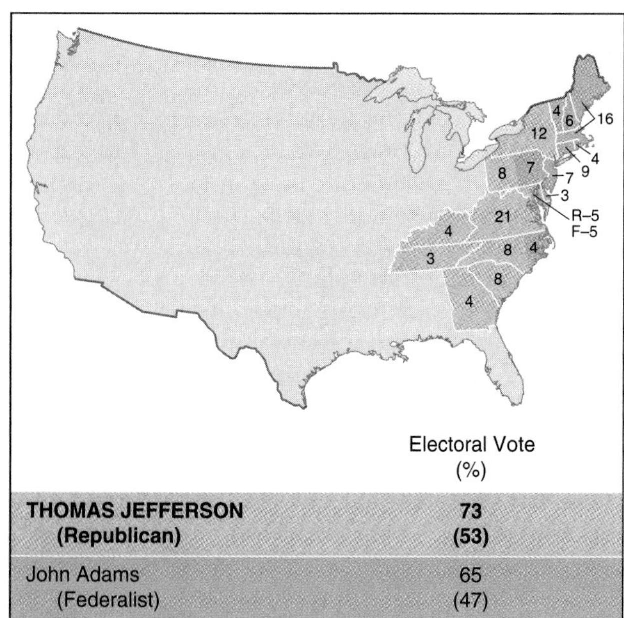

Electoral Vote
(%)
THOMAS JEFFERSON (Republican) 73 (53)
John Adams (Federalist) 65 (47)
R–5
F–5

Map 8-2 The Election of 1800
The sharp erosion of Federalist strength in New York and Pennsylvania after 1798 swung the election of 1800 to the Republicans.

Treaty, which they feared left them exposed to a flood of cheap British imports. Adams carried New England and had a smattering of support elsewhere. With New York added to their solid base in the South and the backcountry, the Jeffersonians gained an electoral majority (see Map 8-2).

Party unity among Republican electors was so strong that Jefferson and Burr each received seventy-three electoral votes. Consequently the election was thrown into the House of Representatives, which, until the newly elected Congress was seated, was still dominated by Federalists. Hoping to deny Jefferson the presidency, the Federalists in the House backed Burr. They believed that he was untainted by the Revolutionary virus that made Jefferson seem so dangerous, even though Hamilton, who faced Burr as a political rival in New York, sought to convince them otherwise. The result was a deadlock that persisted into the early months of 1801. Pennsylvania and Virginia mobilized their state militias, a clear message that the Republicans were prepared to use force against what Jefferson termed any "legislative usurpation" of the people's will as expressed in the election. On February 16, 1801, the Federalists yielded. Informed through intermediaries that Jefferson would not dismantle Hamilton's fiscal system, enough Federalists cast blank ballots to give Jefferson the majority he needed for election. The Twelfth Amendment to the Constitution, ratified in 1804, prevented a similar impasse from arising again by requiring electors to cast separate ballots for president and vice president.

Conclusion

In 1789, the American republic was little more than an experiment in self-government. The Federalists provided a firm foundation for that experiment. Hamilton's financial program, neutrality in the wars

By associating their Federalist opponents with the hated Tories of the American Revolution, the Republicans appealed to the voters as the true defenders of American liberation.

REPUBLICANS

Turn out, turn out and save your Country from ruin!

From an *Emperor*—from a *King*—from the iron grasp of a *British Tory Faction*—an unprincipled banditti of British speculators. The hireling tools and emissaries of his majesty king George the 3d have thronged our city and diffused the poison of principles among us.

DOWN WITH THE TORIES, DOWN WITH THE BRITISH FACTION,

Before they have it in their power to enslave you, and reduce your families to distress by heavy taxation. Republicans want no Tribute-liars—they want no ship Ocean-liars—they want no Rufus King's for Lords—they want no Varick to lord it over them—they want no Jones for senator, who fought with the British against the Americans in time of the war.—But they want in their places such men as

Jefferson & Clinton,

who fought their Country's Battles in the year '76

of the French Revolution, and the diplomatic settlement with Britain in Jay's Treaty bequeathed the young nation a decade of peace and prosperity.

Federalist policies, however, provoked strong opposition rooted in conflicting economic interests and contrasting regional views over the meaning of liberty and government in the new republic. Federalist leadership initially depended on a coalition of regional elites in New England, the mid-Atlantic region, and the slave districts of the South. Each of these elites favored the establishment of effective national power, though often for different reasons. Merchants in Congregationalist New England were concerned mainly with reviving their British trading connections and reversing what they saw as the social and moral decline of the 1780s. Quaker and Episcopal businessmen and commercial farmers in the middle states wanted a central government to promote economic development at home and expand markets aboard. Southern slaveholders, hoping to expand into the West, needed a national government strong enough to secure the trans-Appalachian region.

The Federalist coalition split during Washington's second term when southern planters joined urban artisans and backcountry Scots-Irish farmers in opposing Jay's Treaty and the commercially oriented program of the Federalists. When Quaker and German farmers in the mid-Atlantic states defected from the Federalists over the tax legislation of 1798, three of the four regions in Washington's America now lined up behind the Republicans. The new Republican majority was united by their belief that the actions of the New England Federalists—the expansion of the army, the imposition of new taxes, and the passage of the Alien and Sedition Acts—threatened individual liberty and regional autonomy. Non-English groups and farmers south of New England turned to the Republicans as the upholders of these threatened freedoms.

The openly partisan politics of the 1790s surprised the country's founders, who equated parties with the evils of factionalism. They had not foreseen that parties would forge a necessary link between the rulers and the ruled and create a mechanism by which group values and regional interests could be given a political voice. Party formation climaxed in the election of 1800, when the Republicans ended the Federalists' rule. The Republicans won by embracing the popular demand for a more egalitarian social and political order.

To the credit of the Federalists, they relinquished control of the national government peacefully. The importance of this precedent can scarcely be exaggerated. It marked the first time in modern political history that a party in power handed over the government to its opposition. It now remained to be seen what the Republicans would do with their newfound power.

Review Questions

1. What was distinctive about the four regions of the United States in 1790? What were the common values and goals that brought white Americans together?
2. What were the major problems confronting the Washington administration, and how effectively were they resolved?
3. Who were the Federalists and the Republicans, and how did they differ over the meaning of liberty and the power of the national government? What were the major steps in the formation of two distinct parties in the early United States?
4. Why did regional differences tend to pit the North against the South by the late 1790s?
5. How did the XYZ Affair lead to a political crisis in the United States? Why did the Federalists believe that they would benefit from a war against France?
6. Jefferson called his election in 1800 the "revolution of 1800." What do you think he meant? Would you agree with him?

Recommended Reading

Stanley Elkins and Eric McKitrick, The *Age of Federalism* (1993). A magisterial work of narrative history that includes brilliant sketches of the major political actors in the 1790s.

James T. Flexner, *George Washington and the New Nation, 1783–1793* (1969) and *George Washington: Anguish and Farewell, 1793–1799* (1972). Two volumes that stand out for their readable and informative account of Washington's political career after the Revolution.

Richard Hofstadter, *The Idea of a Party System, 1780–1840* (1969). A book that combines political and intellectual history in a graceful account of how Americans gradually came to accept political parties as a legitimate expression of the popular will.

Seymour Lipset, *The First New Nation: The United States in Historical and Comparative Perspective* (1963). Draws on insights from political sociology to show what was unique and enduring in

America's pioneering role as a new nation with a written constitution.

John C. Miller, *The Federalist Era, 1789–1801* (1960). An older work still of great value for its relatively brief and well-balanced overview of the Washington and Adams administrations.

David Waldstreicher, *In the Midst of Perpetual Fetes: The Making of American Nationalism, 1776–1820* (1997). An imaginatively conceived work that reveals how Americans in the early republic created their own sense of nationalism through popular festivals, street parades, and other forms of political celebration at the local level.

Additional Sources

Washington's America

Reginald Horseman, *The Frontier in the Formative Years, 1783–1815* (1970).

Robert McColley, *Slavery and Jeffersonian Virginia* (1964).

Gary B. Nash, *Forging Freedom: The Formation of Philadelphia's Black Community, 1720–1840* (1988).

Simon P. Newman, *Parades and the Politics of the American Street* (1997).

Billy G. Smith, The "Lower Sort": *Philadelphia's Laboring People, 1750–1800* (1990).

Laurel Thather Ulrich, *A Midwife's Tale: The Life of Martha Ballard, Based on Her Diary, 1785–1812* (1990).

Anthony F. C. Wallace, *The Death and Rebirth of the Seneca* (1970).

Betty Wood, *Women's Work, Men's Work: The Informal Slave Economies of Lowcountry Georgia* (1995).

Forging a New Government

Marcus Cunliffe, *George Washington: Man and Monument* (1958).

Ralph Ketcham, *Presidents above Party: The First American Presidency, 1789–1829* (1984).

Richard H. Kohn, *Eagle and Sword: The Federalists and the Creation of the Military Establishment in America, 1783–1802* (1975).

Glenn A. Phelps, *George Washington and American Constitutionalism* (1993).

Gerald Stourzh, *Alexander Hamilton and the Idea of Republican Government* (1970).

Leonard D. White, *The Federalists: A Study in Administrative History* (1948).

The Emergence of Parties

Joyce Appleby, *Capitalism and a New Social Order: The Republican Vision of the 1790s* (1984).

Richard Buel Jr., *Securing the Revolution: Ideology in American Politics, 1789–1815* (1972).

William N. Chambers, *Political Parties in a New Nation: The American Experience, 1776–1809* (1963).

Noble E. Cunningham Jr., *The Jeffersonian Republicans: The Formation of Party Organization, 1789–1801* (1957).

Alexander De Conde, *Entangling Alliance: Politics and Diplomacy under George Washington* (1958).

Thomas P. Slaughter, *The Whiskey Rebellion: Frontier Epilogue to the American Revolution* (1986).

Alfred F. Young, *The Democratic Republicans of New York: The Origins, 1763–1797* (1967).

The Last Federalist Administration

Manning Dauer, *The Adams Federalists* (1953).

Stephen G. Kurtz, *The Presidency of John Adams: The Collapse of Federalism, 1795–1800* (1957).

Roger Sharp, *American Politics in the Early Republic: The New Nation in Crisis* (1993).

Daniel Sisson, *The American Revolution of 1800* (1974).

James M. Smith, *Freedom's Fetters: The Alien and Sedition Laws and American Civil Liberties,* rev. ed. (1966).

William Stinchcombe, *The XYZ Affair* (1980).

Where to Learn More

❖ **Cincinnati Historical Society, Cincinnati, Ohio.** Collections include written and visual materials on the history of the Old Northwest Territory.

❖ **Federal Hall National Memorial, New York, New York.** This museum and historic site holds artifacts relating to President Washington's inauguration.

❖ **Hamilton Grange National Memorial, New York, New York.** The home of Alexander Hamilton contains materials on his life.

❖ **Adams National Historic Site, Quincy, Massachusetts.** This site preserves buildings and manuscripts associated with four generations of the Adams family.

The Triumph and Collapse of Jeffersonian Republicanism, 1800–1824

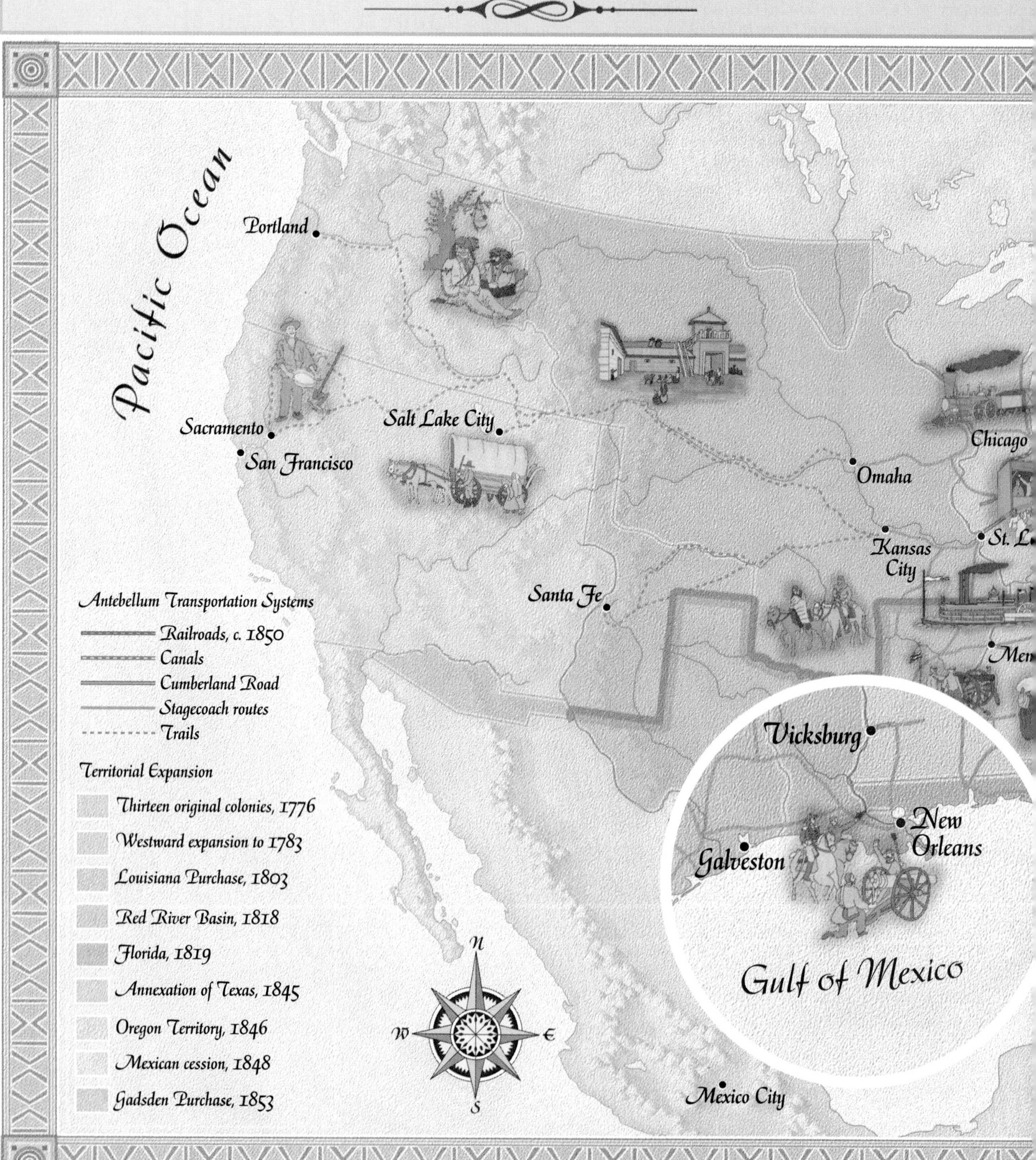

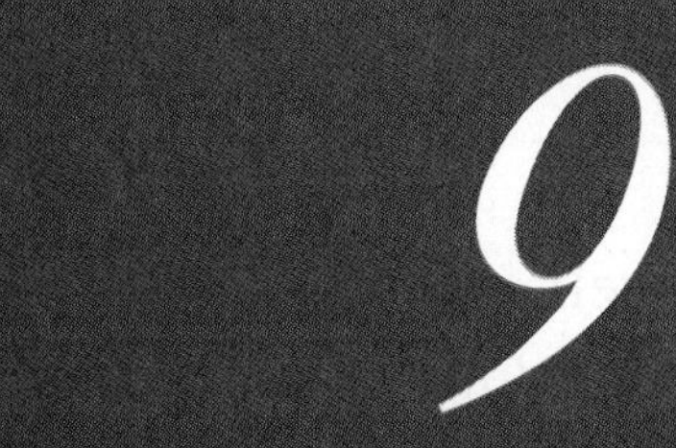

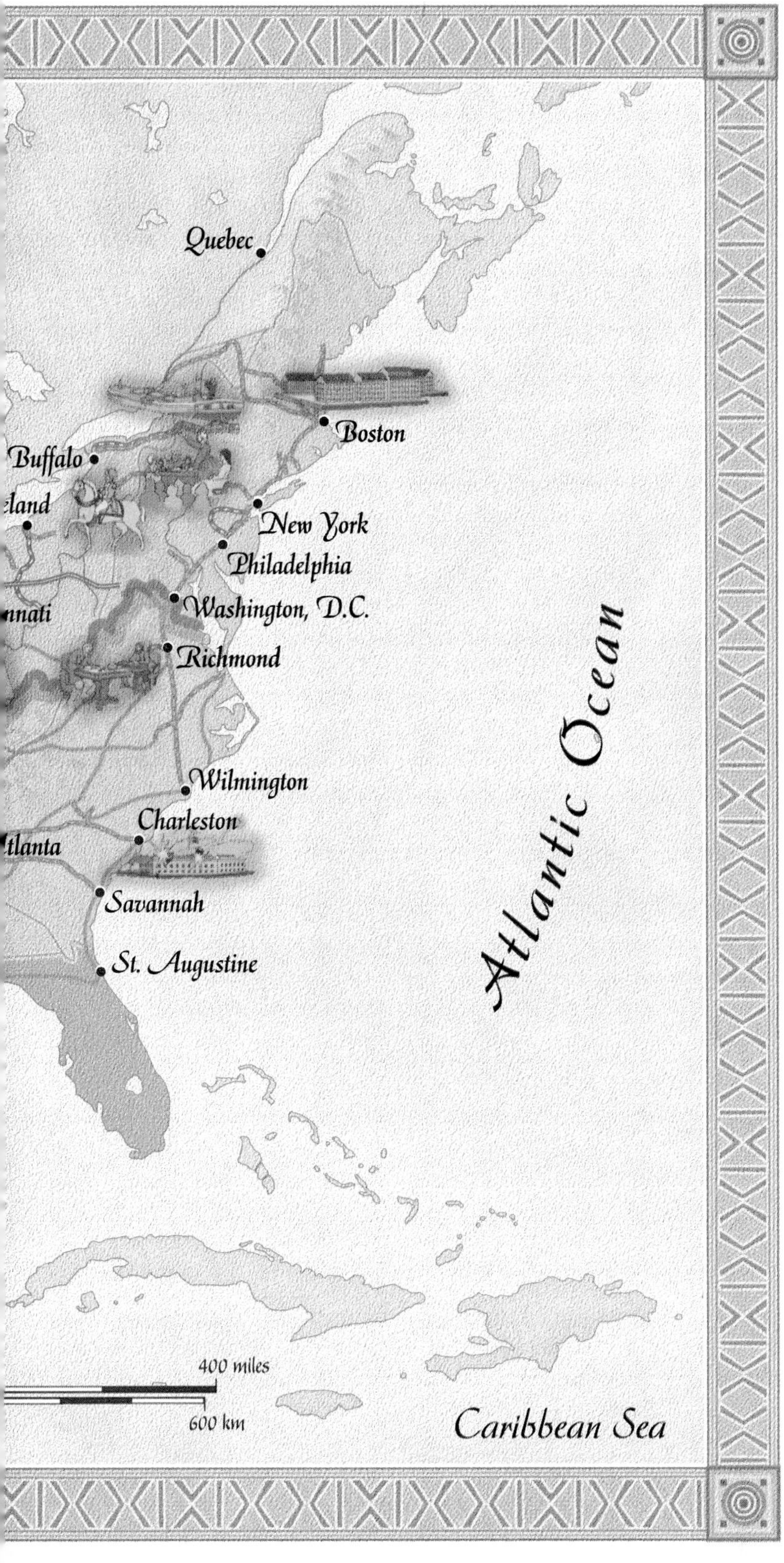

9

Chapter Outline

Jefferson's Presidency
Reform at Home
The Louisiana Purchase
Florida and Western Schemes
Embargo and a Crippled Presidency

Madison and the Coming of War
The Failure of Economic Sanctions
The Frontier and Indian Resistance
Decision for War

The War of 1812
Setbacks in Canada
Western Victories and British Offensives
The Treaty of Ghent and the Battle of New Orleans

The Era of Good Feelings
Economic Nationalism
Judicial Nationalism
Toward a Continental Empire

The Breakdown of Unity
The Panic of 1819
The Missouri Compromise
The Election of 1824

Conclusion

Key Topics

- The domination of the Republicans and the collapse of the Federalist party
- The territorial expansion of the United States to the west and the south
- The growth of nationalism and of sectional rivalry
- The first national crisis over slavery
- The collapse of the Republican party

"It is well known," related the account in the *Richmond Recorder* in September 1802, "that the man, *whom it delighteth the people to honor*, keeps, and for many years has kept, as his concubine, one of his own slaves. Her name is SALLY. . . . The name of her eldest son is TOM. His features are said to bear a striking, although sable resemblance to those of the President himself." Thus broke the sensational story of an illicit affair between Thomas Jefferson and Sally Hemings, a mulatto slave and house servant at Monticello, the president's plantation retreat. James T. Callender, a scurrilous journalist who turned against Jefferson after serving as his political employee, leveled the first accusations, and the story was gleefully picked up by Federalist newspapers across the country.

Jefferson maintained a discreet silence on the allegations, and the resounding success of his first administration defused any political damage they might have caused him. Nevertheless, the tale of a Jefferson–Hemings liaison acquired a life of its own. The oral traditions of the Hemings family insist that Jefferson was the father of Sally Hemings's five children. Another tradition, passed down by the white descendents of the Jefferson family, holds that Jefferson's nephew Peter Carr fathered the children. Recent DNA studies, which established that Jefferson *or* one of his close male kin fathered one or more of Hemings's children, have not definitively settled the issue, but combined with other evidence placing Jefferson and Hemings together at the appropriate times, they strongly support the Hemings family tradition.

The Jefferson–Hemings story highlights how the cruel and degrading institution of slavery enmeshed both the public and private lives of slaveholders in a tangle of contradictions. As John Adams observed with probably only slight exaggeration, "there was not a planter in Virginia who could not reckon among his slaves a number of his children." Indeed, Hemings was the offspring of Jefferson's father-in-law, and thus half sister to Jefferson's deceased wife. Yet no slaves, even if freed and whoever their parents, were to be treated as equals.

Whatever Jefferson's feelings toward Sally Hemings, Jeffersonian democracy was emphatically for white people only. Jefferson, whose party valued the white farmer as the ideal republican citizen, could not conceive of white and black people living peacefully in a postemancipation society. Westward expansion and free and open trade with the outside world were the keys to Jefferson's empire of liberty. His republic would escape the social hierarchy of corrupt Europe by filling North America with farm families of white yeomen. These families would feed Europe with their agricultural surpluses and accept in exchange most of the manufactured goods they needed to improve their standard of living.

To an extraordinary extent, Jefferson and his Republican successors, James Madison and James Monroe, succeeded in promoting the growth and independence of the United States in the first quarter of the nineteenth century. Expansionist policies to the south and west more than doubled the size of the republic and fueled the westward spread of slavery. A war against Britain in 1812–1814, if less than a military triumph, nonetheless freed Americans to look inward for economic development.

At the height of Republican success during the Era of Good Feelings just after the War of 1812, the Federalist party collapsed. Without an organized opposition to enforce party discipline among themselves, the Republicans soon followed the Federalists into political oblivion. The nation's expansion produced two crises—a financial panic and a battle over slavery in Missouri—that shattered the façade of Republican unity. By the mid-1820s, a new party system was emerging.

Jefferson's Presidency

Thomas Jefferson believed that a true revolution had occurred in 1800, a peaceful overthrow of the Federalist party and its hated principles of government consolidation and military force. In his eyes, the defeat of the monarchical Federalists reconfirmed the true political legacy of the Revolution by restoring the republican majority to its rightful control of the government.

Unlike the Hamiltonian Federalists, whose commercial vision of America accepted social and economic inequalities as inevitable, the Jeffersonians wanted a predominantly agrarian republic based on widespread economic equality for white yeomen families. Without such equality, Jefferson was convinced that the privileged few would threaten the people's liberties. Contemporary political thought held that all societies went through stages of economic development that ended in the consolidation of power and suppression of liberties by a wealthy minority. Jefferson hoped to break that cycle through territorial expansion that would add enough land to maintain self-reliant farmers as the guardians of republican freedoms.

Jefferson's first administration was a solid success. A unified Republican party reduced the size and scope of the federal government, allowed the Alien and Sedition Acts to lapse, and celebrated the Louisiana Purchase. An enfeebled Federalist party weakly opposed Jefferson's reelection in 1804. His second term, however, was a bitter disappointment, marked by the massive unpopularity of Jefferson's embargo on American foreign trade. The embargo, designed to compel warring Britain and France to recognize American rights as a neutral shipper, failed at home and abroad. As a result, Jefferson left his successor, James Madison, a divided party, a revived Federalism, and an unresolved crisis in foreign affairs.

Reform at Home

Jefferson set the style and tone of his administration from the beginning. He was the first president to be inaugurated in Washington, D.C., and his inauguration was as unpretentious as the raw and primitive capital city itself. Then little more than a scraggly collection of huts, a few boardinghouses, and unfinished public buildings, Washington lacked, one senator ruefully noted, "only houses, wine cellars, learned men, amiable women, and other trifles to make our city perfect." Jefferson walked from his lodgings to the Capitol building to be sworn in. His dress was neat but shorn of gentlemanly refinements such as a wig. After giving notice that an unadorned style of republican egalitarianism would now replace the aristocratic formalities of the Federalists, Jefferson emphasized in his inaugural address the overwhelming commitment of Americans to the "republican form" of government and affirmed his own support of civil liberties as an American principle.

A poor public speaker, Jefferson sent written messages to Congress to avoid having to read them in person. This change from Federalist policy both eliminated the impression of a monarch addressing his subjects and played to Jefferson's formidable skills as a writer. He replaced the stiff formalism of receptions for presidential visitors with more relaxed weekly meetings. Presidential dinners became notorious among society and the diplomatic corps for their breezy disregard of aristocratic etiquette and hierarchical seating arrangements. Jefferson welcomed dinner guests at a circular table. Still, he

When Jefferson moved into the White House in 1801, Washington was still a wilderness capital with a population that barely reached four thousand people.

Dolley Madison, the engaging young wife of James Madison, Jefferson's secretary of state, served as the unofficial social hostess in the White House during the administration of Jefferson, a widower.

served fine food and wine, and he used these dinners to cultivate party ties that enabled him to steer favored legislation through Congress.

The cornerstone of Republican domestic policy was retrenchment, a return to the frugal, simple federal establishment the Jeffersonians believed was the original intent of the Constitution. Determined to root out what they viewed as the corruption and patronage of a government bloated by the power-grasping Federalists, the Republicans began with fiscal policy. Jefferson's secretary of the treasury was Albert Gallatin, a native of Switzerland who emerged in the 1790s as the best financial mind in the Republican party. He convinced Jefferson that the Bank of the United States was essential for financial stability and blocked efforts to dismantle it. Unlike Hamilton, however, Gallatin thought that a large public debt was a curse, a drag on productive capital, and an unfair burden on future generations. He succeeded in reducing the national debt from $83 million in 1800 to $57 million by 1809.

Gallatin's conservative fiscal policies shrank both the spending and taxes of the national government. The Republicans eliminated all internal taxes, including the despised tax on whiskey. Slashes in the military budget kept government expenditures below the level of 1800. The army was cut back to three thousand men, and the navy was nearly eliminated. Jefferson's defense strategy called for gunboats and coastal fortifications. If the country were invaded, he would rely on the militia, citizen soldiers commanded by professional officers to be trained at the newly established (1802) military academy at West Point. The cuts in military spending combined with soaring revenues from customs collections left Gallatin with a surplus in the budget that he could devote to debt repayment.

Jeffersonian reform targeted the political character, as well as the size, of the national government. Of the six hundred officeholders appointed by Washington and Adams, Jefferson estimated that only six were Republicans. He moved to break the Federalist stranglehold on federal offices and appoint officials with sound Republican principles. Arch-Federalists, those Jefferson deemed guilty of misusing their offices for openly political reasons, were immediately replaced, and Republicans filled other posts opened up by attrition. By the time Jefferson left the presidency in 1809, Republicans held nearly all the appointive offices.

Jefferson moved most aggressively against the Federalists in the judiciary. Just days before they relinquished power, the Federalists passed the Judiciary Act of 1801. This act created sixteen new circuit courts; added nearly two hundred federal marshals, attorneys, and clerks; and reduced the size of the Supreme Court from six justices to five by stipulating that the next vacancy was not to be filled. The Jeffersonians were enraged. The Federalists already monopolized all federal judgeships, and this last-minute legislation both enlarged the judiciary and packed it with more Federalists appointed by Adams, the outgoing president. To add insult to injury, the Federalists had even tried to ensure that Jefferson would be unable to appoint a Republican to the Supreme Court when the first opening occurred.

The Republicans fought back. Now dominant in Congress, they quickly repealed the Judiciary Act of 1801, replacing it with a measure that eliminated the new judgeships and restored the size of the Supreme Court to six members, each with responsibility for one of the circuit courts. Frustrated Federalists now turned to John Marshall, a staunch Federalist appointed chief justice of the United States by President Adams in 1801, hoping he would rule that Congress had acted unconstitutionally in removing the recently appointed federal judges. Marshall moved carefully to avoid an open confrontation. He was aware that the Republicans contended that Congress and the president had at least a coequal right with the Supreme Court to decide constitutional questions.

Chronology

1801 Thomas Jefferson is inaugurated, the first Republican president.
John Marshall becomes chief justice.

1802 Congress repeals the Judiciary Act of 1801.

1803 *Marbury* v. *Madison* sets the precedent of judicial review by the Supreme Court.
Louisiana Purchase.

1804 Vice President Aaron Burr kills Alexander Hamilton in a duel.
Judges John Pickering and Samuel Chase impeached by Republicans.
Jefferson is reelected.

1806 Britain and France issue orders restricting neutral shipping.
Betrayal of the Burr conspiracy.

1807 Chesapeake affair.
Congress passes the Embargo Act.

1808 Congress prohibits the African slave trade.
James Madison elected president.

1809 Repeal of the Embargo Act.
Passage of the Nonintercourse Act.

1810 Macon's Bill No. 2 reopens trade with Britain and France.
United States annexes part of West Florida.
Georgia state law invalidated by the Supreme Court in *Fletcher* v. *Peck*.

1811 Battle of Tippecanoe and defeat of the Indian confederation.
Charter of the Bank of the United States expires.

1812 Congress declares war on Britain.
American loss of Detroit.
Madison reelected.

1813 Perry's victory at Battle of Put-in-Bay.
Battle of the Thames and death of Tecumseh.

1814 Jackson crushes the Creeks at the Battle of Horseshoe Bend.
British burn Washington, D.C., and attack Baltimore.
Macdonough's naval victory on Lake Champlain turns back a British invasion.
Hartford Convention meets.
Treaty of Ghent signed.

1815 Jackson routs British at the Battle of New Orleans.

1816 Congress charters the Second Bank of the United States and passes a protective tariff.
James Monroe elected president.

1817 Rush–Bagot Treaty demilitarizes the Great Lakes.

1818 Anglo-American Accords on trade and boundaries.
Jackson's border campaign in Spanish East Florida.

1819 Trans-Continental Treaty between United States and Spain.
Beginning of the Missouri controversy.
Financial panic sends economy into a depression.
Dartmouth College v. *Woodward* upholds the charter rights of corporations.
McCulloch v. *Maryland* upholds constitutionality of the Bank of the United States.

1820 Missouri Compromise on slavery in the Louisiana Purchase.
Monroe reelected.

1823 Monroe Doctrine proclaims western hemisphere closed to further European colonization.

1825 John Quincy Adams elected president by the House of Representatives.

The issue came to a head in the case of ***Marbury* v. *Madison*** (1803), which centered on Secretary of State James Madison's refusal to deliver a commission to William Marbury, one of Adams's "midnight appointments" as a justice of the peace for the District of Columbia. Marshall held that although Marbury had a legal right to his commission, the Court had no jurisdiction in the case. The Court ruled that the section of the Judiciary Act of 1789 granting it the power to order the delivery of Marbury's commission was unconstitutional because it conferred on the Court a power not specified in Article 3 of the Constitution on cases of original jurisdiction. Stating that it was "emphatically the province and duty of the judicial department to say what the law is," Marshall created the precedent of judicial review, the power of the Supreme Court to rule on the constitutionality of federal law. Although not invoked again until the Dred Scott decision of 1857, this doctrine was of pivotal importance for the future of the Court. Marshall had brilliantly turned a threatening situation into a success for the judiciary.

Marshall's assertion of the Court's power deepened Republican suspicions of judicial tyranny. Demanding popular election for all judges, radical Republicans rejected the entire notion of an appointed judiciary. Jefferson did not want to go that far, but he felt strongly that judges should be accountable to the popular will.

At the urging of the radicals, congressional Republicans brought formal charges against two notorious Federalist judges. One of them, John Pickering, a district judge from New Hampshire and a mentally unstable alcoholic, was convicted and removed from office. The other was bigger game, Justice Samuel Chase of the Supreme Court, the most obnoxious Federalist still in a position of national power. For all his blatant partisanship, however, Chase was clearly sane, and he escaped conviction in the Senate in early 1805 when the Republicans failed to show he was guilty of "high crimes and misdemeanors," the constitutionally defined grounds for removal from office. His acquittal ended the Republican offensive against the judiciary.

The Louisiana Purchase

In foreign affairs, fortune smiled on Jefferson during his first term. The European war that had almost sucked in the United States in the 1790s subsided. Britain and France agreed on a truce in 1802. Meanwhile, Jefferson, despite his distaste for a strong navy, ordered a show of force in the Mediterranean to punish the Barbary pirates who were preying on American shipping and taking American sailors hostage.

For years, the North African states of Morocco, Algeria, Tunis, and Tripoli had demanded cash tribute from foreigners trading in the Mediterranean. Jefferson stopped the payments in 1801, and when attacks on American shipping resumed, he retaliated by sending warships and marines to the Mediterranean. The tribute system continued until 1815, but thanks to the success of U.S. forces in Tripoli, Jefferson got much better terms.

The Anglo-French peace was a mixed blessing for the United States. Although it removed any immediate threat of war, the return of peace also allowed Spain and France to reclaim their colonial trade in the Western Hemisphere. American shippers were thus deprived of the windfall profits they had earned while dominating that trade during the European war. Of greater long-range concern, the new military ruler of France, Napoleon Bonaparte, was now free to develop his plans for reviving the French empire in America. In a secret treaty with Spain in 1800, Napoleon reacquired for France the Louisiana Territory, a vast, vaguely defined area stretching between the Mississippi River and the Rocky Mountains.

Sketchy, unconfirmed reports of the treaty reached Jefferson in the spring of 1801, and he was immediately alarmed. He had long believed that Spain, proud but militarily impotent, would be powerless to stem the spread of the expanding American population into its territories in western North America. Indeed, Spanish military officials in Louisiana had repeatedly called in vain for military reinforcements to block the Americans, this "new and vigorous people . . . advancing and multiplying in the silence of peace." France, in contrast, was a formidable opponent. French control of the Mississippi Valley, combined with the British presence in Canada, threatened to hem in the United States and deprive Jefferson's farmers of their empire for liberty.

Jefferson was prepared to reverse the traditional foreign policy of his party to eliminate this threat. He opened exploratory talks with the British on an Anglo-American alliance to drive the French out of Louisiana. Looking toward the possibility of war, he also strengthened American forces in the Mississippi Valley and secured congressional approval for the Lewis and Clark expedition through upper Louisiana. Although best known for its scientific discoveries, this expedition was designed initially as a military mission.

Jefferson applied diplomatic and military pressure to induce Napoleon to sell New Orleans and a small slice of coastal territory to its east to the United States. This was his main objective: to possess New Orleans and control the mouth of the Mississippi River, outlet to world markets. To his surprise, Napoleon suddenly decided in early 1803 to sell all of the immense Louisiana Territory to the Americans (see Map 9-1).

Napoleon's failure to reconquer Saint-Domingue (modern-day Haiti) was instrumental in his about-face on plans for a revived French empire in America. He had envisioned this rich sugar island as the jewel of his new empire and intended to use the Louisiana Territory as a granary to supply the island. During the upheavals of the French Revolution, the slaves on the island, led by Touissant L'Ouverture, rebelled in a bloody and successful bid for independence. Napoleon sent a large army to reassert French control, but it succumbed to the islanders' fierce resistance.

Without firm French control of St. Domingue, Louisiana was of little use to Napoleon. And when the U.S. Congress passed resolutions threatening an American attack on New Orleans, he realized he would likely have to fight to keep it. With a renewed war against Britain looming, he had better use for his troops in Europe and wanted to keep Americans neutral. For \$15 million (including about \$4 million in French debts owed to American citizens), he offered to part with the whole of Louisiana. The cost to the United States was about $3\frac{1}{2}$ cents per acre.

AMERICA'S JOURNEY

FROM THEN TO NOW

The Lewis and Clark Expedition in Their World and Ours

In its day the Lewis and Clark expedition was as daring a venture as space exploration is today. The expedition, which began in 1803, ended in 1806, and lasted 863 days, brought Americans their first knowledge of the vast territory they had secured in the Louisiana Purchase. Travelling more than seven thousand miles by foot, boat, and horseback from St. Louis to the Pacific Coast and back, the explorers compiled a detailed record of their experiences and observations. In these journals they have bequeathed to us a vivid picture of the natural environment of the trans-Mississippi West before white settlement.

The West described by Lewis and Clark was a land of change, diversity, and abundance. The Missouri River that their party of forty-five followed to the north and west up to central Montana was wild and unpredictable. Its currents were ceaselessly eroding its banks, forming and displacing sandbars, and cutting new channels as they deposited soil eroded from the Rocky Mountains onto its immense floodplain. Today, a series of dams has tamed the river, controlling floods, generating electricity, and diverting water for irrigation. But the dams have had unforeseen consequences. The fertile sediments the Missouri once deposited on its floodplain, replenishing the soil in the farm states of the midwest, now flow into the Gulf of Mexico. As Midwesterners learned in the summer of 1993, the levees and retaining walls that confine the river can sometimes result in floods far more disastrous than ever occurred under natural conditions.

Lewis and Clark passed through regions of incredible biological diversity and abundance. They catalogued 122 animals and 178 plants that were new to American science. Traveling through present-day South Dakota in September, 1804, Lewis observed "Vast herds of Buffaloe deer elk and Antilopes . . . feeding in every direction as far as the eye of the observer could reach." Upon seeing the salmon in the Columbia River in 1805, Clark wrote that their numbers were "almost inconceivable."

Before the end of the nineteenth century, the great herds of grazing animals in the West and the carnivores that stalked them had nearly been wiped out by government-sponsored extermination programs. The industrialization of the Pacific Northwest in the twentieth century reduced the natural habitat essential for the spawning and rearing of salmon, and their numbers fell sharply. Even more striking, the vast prairie landscape that Lewis and Clark crossed from the Mississippi Valley to the Rocky Mountains has mostly disappeared, replaced by uniform fields of row-to-row crops. The prairie grasslands were once the largest ecosystem in North America, a patchwork of native grasses and herbs that supported wide diversity of habitats.

Lewis and Clark were hardly romantic sentimentalists. Their West was dangerous and threatening, and their supplies included the latest in scientific equipment. They fully shared American notions of progress, and they carefully noted locations that were favorably situated for settlement. Still, the West they saw often left them with a sense of awe. For Lewis, the White Cliffs of the Missouri River in Montana were a spectacle "of visionary enchantment." He described the Great Falls of the Missouri as "the grandest sight I ever beheld."

The journals of Lewis and Clark provide a baseline from which to gauge how much the West has changed, putting Americans in a better position to preserve what is left and even restore some of what has been lost.

William Clark sketched a Columbia River salmon on this page of his journal.

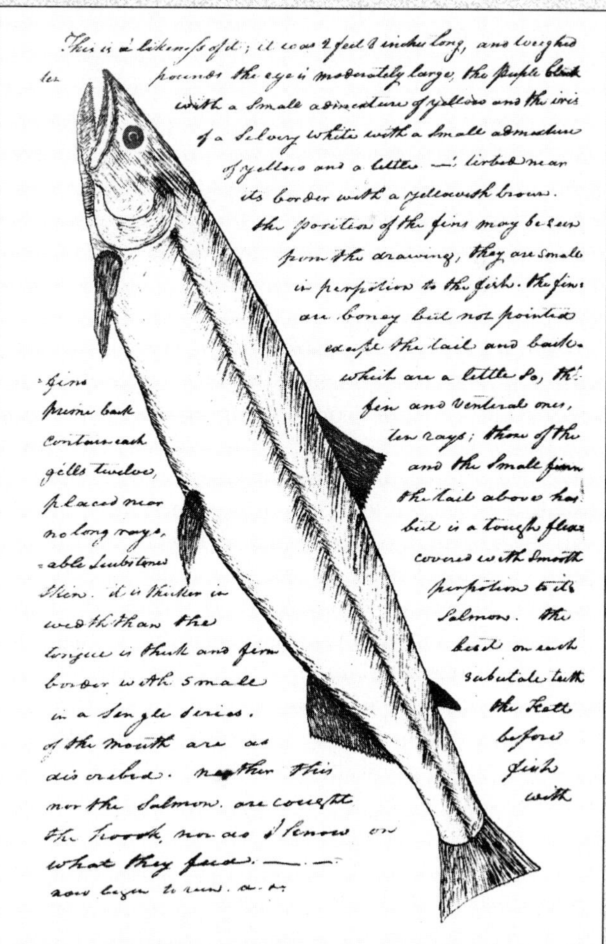

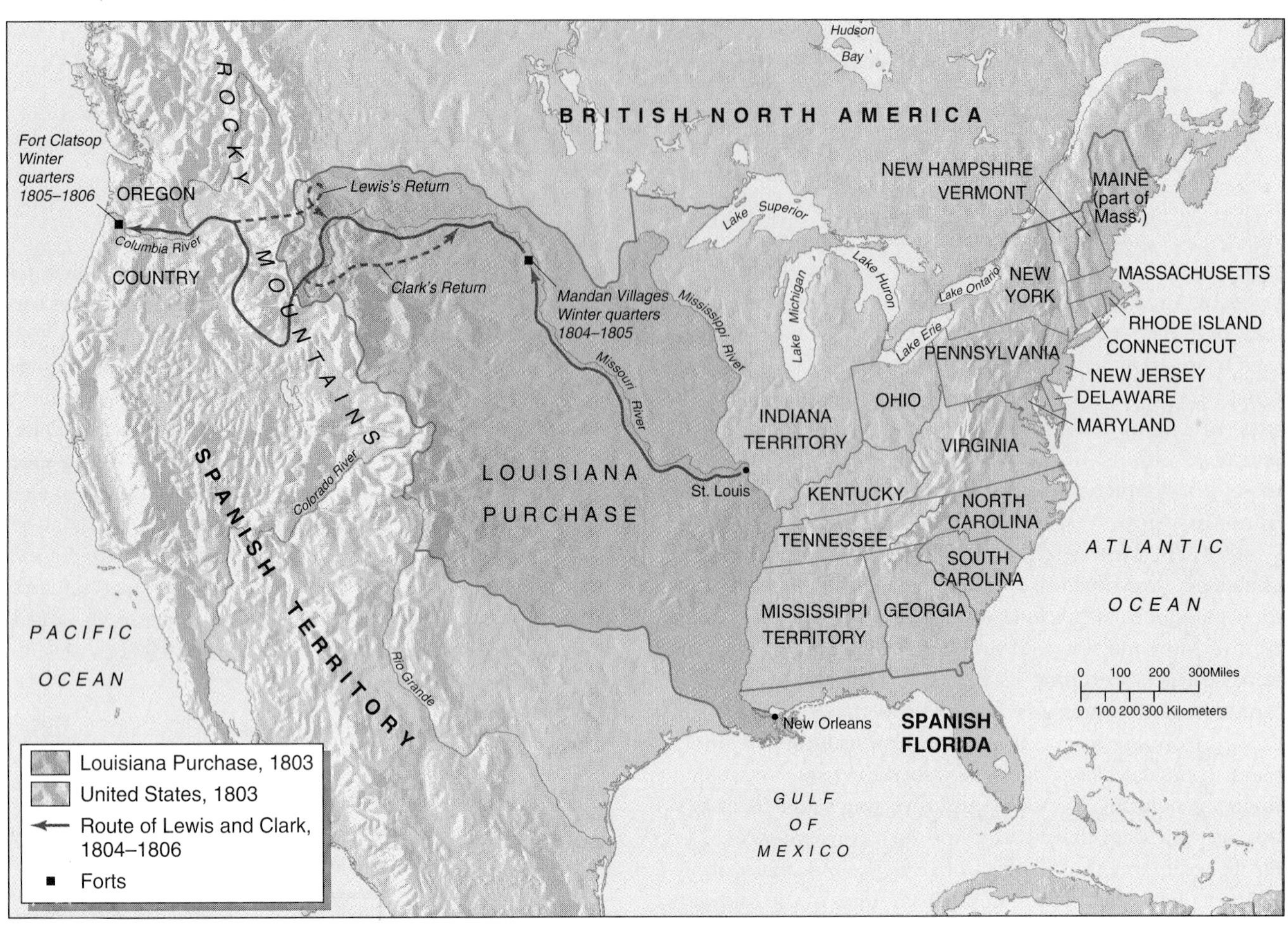

Map 9-1 The Louisiana Purchase and the Lewis and Clark Expedition
The vast expanse of the Louisiana Purchase was virtually unknown territory to Americans before the Lewis and Clark expedition gathered a mass of scientific information about it.

Jefferson, the strict constructionist, now turned pragmatist. Despite the lack of any specific authorization in the Constitution for the acquisition of foreign territory or the incorporation as American citizens of the fifty thousand French and Spanish descendants then living in Louisiana, he accepted Napoleon's deal. The **Louisiana Purchase** doubled the size of the United States and offered seemingly endless space to be settled by yeoman farmers.

Jefferson was willing, as the Federalists had been when they were in power, to stretch the Constitution to support his definition of the national good. Conversely, it was now the Federalists, fearful of a further decline in their political power, who relied on a narrow reading of the Constitution in a futile attempt to block the Louisiana acquisition.

Florida and Western Schemes

The magnificent prize of Louisiana did not satisfy Republican territorial ambitions. Still to be gained were river outlets on the Gulf Coast essential for the development of plantation agriculture in Alabama and Mississippi. As Secretary of State Madison later bluntly explained, "The free navigation of these rivers was inseparable from the very existence of the United States." The boundaries of the Louisiana Purchase were so vague that Jefferson felt justified in claiming Spanish-held Texas and the Gulf Coast eastward from New Orleans to Mobile Bay, including the Spanish province of West Florida. Against stiff Spanish opposition, he pushed ahead with his plans to acquire West Florida. This provoked the first challenge to his leadership of the party.

Once it was clear that Spain did not want to sell West Florida to the United States, Jefferson accepted Napoleon's offer to act as a middleman in the acquisition. Napoleon's price was $2 million. He soon lost interest in the project, however, and Jefferson lost prestige in 1806 when he pushed an appropriations bill through Congress to pay for Napoleon's services. Former Republican stalwarts in Congress denounced the bill as bribe money and staged a party revolt against the president's devious tactics.

Jefferson's failed bid for West Florida emboldened Westerners to demand that Americans seize the territory by force. In 1805 and 1806, Aaron Burr, Jefferson's first vice president, apparently became entangled in an attempt at just such a land grab.

Republicans had been suspicious of Burr since his dalliance with the Federalists in their bid to make him president rather than Jefferson in 1800. He further alienated the party when he involved himself with the efforts of a minority of die-hard Federalists known as the Essex Junto. The members of this group feared that incorporation of the vast Louisiana Purchase into the United States would leave New England powerless in national affairs. Picking up on states' rights themes first used by Jefferson in the Kentucky Resolutions, they concocted a plan for a northern confederacy. New York was central to their scheme. Rebuffed by Hamilton, they turned to Burr and backed him in the New York gubernatorial race of 1804. Burr lost, largely because Hamilton denounced him. The enmity between the two men reached a tragic climax in July 1804, when Burr killed Hamilton in a duel at Weehawken, New Jersey. Facing murder charges in New Jersey and New York, Burr fled to the West and lined up followers for a separatist plot.

The Burr conspiracy remains mysterious. Burr was undoubtedly eager to pry land loose from the Spanish and Indians, and he may have been thinking of carving out a separate western confederacy in the lower Mississippi Valley. Whatever he had in mind, he blundered in relying on General James Wilkinson as a coconspirator. Wilkinson, the military governor of the Louisiana Territory and also a double agent for Spain, betrayed Burr. He was tried for treason in 1807, and Jefferson made extraordinary efforts to secure his conviction. He was saved by the insistence of Chief Justice Marshall that the Constitution defined treason only as the waging of war against the United States or the rendering of aid to its enemies. The law also required the direct testimony of two witnesses to an "overt act" of treason for conviction. Lacking such witnesses, the government failed to prove its case, and Burr was acquitted.

Embargo and a Crippled Presidency

Concern about a possible war against Britain in 1807 soon quieted the uproar over Burr's trial. After Britain and France resumed their war in 1803, the United States became enmeshed in the same quarrels over neutral rights, blockades, ship seizures, and impressment of American sailors that had almost dragged the country into war in the 1790s. Britain proclaimed a blockade of the European continent, which was controlled by Napoleon, and confiscated the cargoes of ships attempting to run the blockade. Napoleon retaliated with seizures of ships that adhered to the blockade by submitting to British searches and accepting the British-imposed licensing system for trading with Europe. Caught in the middle, but eager to supply both sides, was the American merchant marine, the world's largest carrier of neutral goods.

American merchants and shippers had taken full advantage of the opportunities opened by the European war. During the flush years from 1793 to 1807, American ship tonnage tripled, and the value of exports soared fivefold. Despite French and British restrictions, American merchants traded with anyone they pleased. They dominated commerce not only between Britain and the United States but also between the European continent and the French and Spanish colonies in the West Indies. Profits were so great that merchants made money even when only one-third of their ships evaded the blockades.

In June 1807, however, a confrontation known as the ***Chesapeake* incident** nearly triggered an Anglo-American war. A British ship, the *Leopard*, ordered a U.S. frigate, the *Chesapeake*, to submit to a search in coastal waters off Norfolk. When the commander of the *Chesapeake* refused, the *Leopard* opened fire. Three Americans were killed, eighteen were wounded, and four others (one of whom was subsequently hanged) were impressed as alleged deserters from the Royal Navy. Although Federalists worried that "our rogue of a President will glory in a war with England," Jefferson resisted the popular outcry for revenge. Instead, he barred American ports to British warships and called for monetary compensation and an end to impressment.

Britain offered in response only a belated apology and a promise of reparations. Still, Jefferson desperately wanted to avoid conflict. The country was woefully unprepared for war, and he passionately believed that international law should resolve international disputes. In a resort to the Republican idealism that had animated the Revolution, Jefferson called for a trade embargo as a substitute for war. The **Embargo Act of 1807**, an expression of Jefferson's policy of "peaceable coercion," prohibited American ships from clearing port to any nation until Britain and France repealed their trading restrictions on neutral shippers.

The premise of the embargo was that Europe was so dependent on American foods and raw materials that it would do America's bidding if faced with a cutoff. This premise was not so much wrong as unrealistic. The embargo did hurt Europe, but the people who first felt the pain were British textile workers and slaves in the colonies, hardly those who wielded the levers of power. Meanwhile, politically influential landlords and manufacturers benefited from short-term shortages by jacking up prices.

The American export trade and its profits dried up with Jefferson's self-imposed blockade. Except for manufacturers, who now had the American

"And the grass literally grew upon the wharves."

The caption on this 1807 illustration of a deserted pier in Portland, Maine—"And the grass literally grew upon the wharves"—reflects the hardship Jefferson's embargo caused as it choked off the American export trade.

market to themselves, nearly all economic groups suffered under the embargo. Especially hard hit were New England shippers and merchants, and they accused the Republicans of near-criminal irresponsibility for forcing a depression on the country. Jefferson responded to these criticisms and to widespread violations of the embargo with a series of enforcement acts. These acts put real teeth into the embargo and consolidated executive powers far beyond what the Federalists themselves had been able to achieve while in power.

As the embargo tightened and the 1808 presidential election approached, the Federalist party revived. The Federalist presidential candidate, Charles C. Pinckney, running against Secretary of State Madison, Jefferson's handpicked successor, polled three times more votes than he had in 1804. Madison won only because he carried the South and the West, the Republican heartland.

Before Madison took office, the Republicans abandoned Jefferson's embargo. Britain and France had remained defiant, and at home the embargo had become an intolerable political burden. The embargo ended on March 3, 1809, and was immediately replaced by the **Nonintercourse Act**, a measure that prohibited American trade only with Britain and France. At the president's discretion, trade could be reopened with either nation after it lifted its restrictions on American shipping.

Madison and the Coming of War

Frail-looking and short, Madison struck most contemporaries as an indecisive and weaker version of Jefferson. He never did succeed in escaping from his predecessor's shadow. Nor did he succeed as president in keeping America at peace. Yet in intellectual toughness and resourcefulness he was at least Jefferson's equal. He failed because of an inherited foreign policy that was partly of his own making as Jefferson's secretary of state. The Republicans' idealistic stand on neutral rights was ultimately untenable unless backed up by military and political force. Madison concluded as much when he decided on war against Britain in the spring of 1812.

A war against America's old enemy also promised to restore unity to a Republican party increasingly divided over Madison's peaceful diplomacy. What was at stake for Madison was not just the defense of America's economic independence but the legacy of republicanism itself, now under attack by monarchists in Britain and their presumed American friends in the resurgent Federalist party. Thus did Madison and his fellow Republicans push for a war they were eager but unprepared to fight.

The Failure of Economic Sanctions

Early in his administration, Madison convinced himself that the impasse in Anglo–American relations was about to be broken. Britain benefited from the Nonintercourse Act at the expense of France. Unlike the embargo, which kept American vessels at home, nonintercourse permitted ship clearances. Once at sea, American ships were kept away from France and steered to England by the strong British navy. Perhaps in recognition of this unintended consequence of the new American policy, the British began to relax their restrictions on neutral shipping, known as the Orders in Council, in favor of U.S. commerce. At the same time, the British minister in Washington,

David Erskine, reached an agreement with Madison that called for completely rescinding the Orders in Council as they applied to the United States. In return, Madison pledged to terminate nonintercourse against Britain while maintaining it against France.

Madison set June 10, 1809, as the date for the resumption of Anglo–American trade. Unfortunately, Erskine had exceeded his instructions, and the Madison–Erskine agreement was disavowed as soon as news of it reached London. Although Madison reimposed sanctions on Britain in August, he was left looking the fool.

With Madison floundering, Congress stepped in with its own policy in 1810. Macon's Bill No. 2 threw open American trade to everyone but stipulated that if either France or England lifted its restrictions, the president would resume trading sanctions against the other. A concession to mercantile interests in New England and the mid-Atlantic states, Macon's bill also bought Madison time before he had to decide between war or submission to the British Orders in Council. Thanks to Napoleon's duplicity, however, that time was short.

Napoleon made an offer in August 1810 that Madison felt he had to accept. The French emperor promised to withdraw his decrees against American shipping on the condition that if Britain did not follow suit, Madison would force the British to respect American rights. Madison took the bait. He was under no illusion as to Napoleon's honesty, but he was desperate to apply pressure on the British to match the apparent French concessions. To Madison's chagrin, Napoleon's offer was an utter fraud. French seizures of American ships continued. By the time his duplicity became clear, Napoleon had already succeeded in worsening Anglo–American tensions. In November 1810, Madison reimposed nonintercourse against Britain, putting the two nations on a collision course.

The Frontier and Indian Resistance

Mounting frustrations in the South and West also pushed Madison toward a war against Britain. Nearly 1 million Americans lived west of the Appalachian Mountains in 1810, a tripling of the western population in just a decade. Cheap, fertile land and markets for crops down the Ohio and Mississippi River systems drew farm families from the East. Farm prices, including those for the southern staples of cotton and tobacco, plunged when Jefferson's embargo shut off exports, and they stayed low after the embargo was lifted. Blame for the persistent agricultural depression focused on the British and their stranglehold on overseas trade after 1808. As a glut of American goods piled up in English ports, prices remained depressed.

Western settlers also accused the British of inciting Indian resistance. After the *Chesapeake* incident, the British did seek alliances with Indians in the Old Northwest, reviving the strategy of using them as a buffer against any American move on Canada. However, it was the unceasing demand of Americans for ever more Indian land, not any British incitements, that triggered the **pan-Indian resistance movement** that so frightened western settlers on the eve of the War of 1812.

In the Treaty of Greenville (1795), the American government had promised that any future acquisitions of Indian land would have to be approved by all native peoples in the region. Nonetheless, government agents continued to play one group against another and divide groups from within by lavishing money and goods on the more accommodationist Christianized Indians. By such means, William Henry Harrison, the governor of the Indiana Territory, procured most of southern Indiana in the **Treaty of Vincennes** of 1804. Two extraordinary leaders, the Shawnee chief Tecumseh and his brother, the Prophet Tenskwatawa, channeled Indian outrage over this treaty into a movement to unify tribes throughout the West for a stand against the white invaders.

The Prophet Tenskwatawa was the spiritual leader of the pan-Indian movement that sought to revitalize native culture and block the spread of white settlement in the Old Northwest.

The message of pan-Indianism was unwavering: White encroachments had to be stopped and tribal and clan divisions submerged in a return to native rituals and belief systems. As preached by Tecumseh and the Prophet, Indian land could be saved and self-respect regained only through racial solidarity and a spiritual rebirth. Tenkswatawa had undergone such a rebirth when he saved himself from alcoholism, and much of the passion he brought to preaching reflected his own sense of redemption. With the assistance of Tecumseh, Tenkswatawa established the Prophet's Town in 1808. At the confluence of the Wabash and Tippecanoe Rivers in north-central Indiana, this encampment became headquarters of an intertribal confederation. As he tried to explain to the worried Governor Harrison, his goals were peaceful. He admonished his followers, "[Do] not take up the tomahawk, should it be offered by the British, or by the long knives: do not meddle with any thing that does not belong to you, but mind your own business, and cultivate the ground, that your women and your children have enough to live on."

That ground, of course, was the very reason the Indians could not live in peace and dignity. White settlers wanted it and would do anything to get it. In November 1811, Harrison marched an army to Prophet's Town and provoked the **Battle of Tippecanoe**. The Indian encampment was on land claimed by the U.S. government in the Treaty of Fort Wayne (1809). Tecumseh was absent, off on a recruiting mission among the southern tribes, and without his restraining influence, impetuous young braves attacked Harrison's army. Losses were heavy on both sides, but Harrison regrouped his forces, drove the surviving Indians away, and burned the abandoned town. Harrison's victory came at a high cost. Tecumseh now joined forces with the British, leaving the frontier more unsettled than ever.

While Harrison's aggressiveness was converting fears of a British–Indian alliance into a self-fulfilling prophecy, expansionist-minded Southerners struck at Britain through Spain, now its ally against Napoleon. With the covert support of President Madison, American adventurers staged a bloodless revolt in Spanish West Florida between Louisiana and the Pearl River. They raised the American flag and declared their independence. This "republic" was quickly recognized by the U.S. government and annexed as part of Louisiana in 1811. Spanish possession of the rest of Florida still galled southern planters anxious to remove the territory as a sanctuary for fugitive slaves.

Hatred of Native Americans, expansionist pressures, the lingering agricultural depression, and impatience with the administration's policy of economic coercion all pointed in the same direction—a war against Britain coupled with an American takeover of British Canada and Spanish Florida. This was the rallying cry of the **War Hawks**, the forty or so prowar congressmen swept into office in 1810. Generally younger men from the South and West, the War Hawks were led by Henry Clay of Kentucky. Along with other outspoken nationalists such as John C. Calhoun of South Carolina, Clay played a key role in building congressional support for Madison's growing aggressiveness on the British issue.

Decision for War

In July 1811, Madison issued a Proclamation calling Congress into an early session on November 4. By the time of the announcement, Madison had probably accepted the inevitability of war against Britain. Deceived by Napoleon and dismissed by the British as the head of a second-rate power, Madison had run out of diplomatic options and was losing control of his party.

When Congress met, Madison tried to lay the groundwork for war. Although he did not rule out a peaceful settlement, he called for military preparations and stressed his "deep sense of the crisis." In January 1812, the authorized size of the army was increased from 10,000 to 35,000 men. Still, fewer than 7,000 men were actually under arms throughout the spring, and Congress refused to enlarge the navy. The Republican-controlled Congress also balked at raising taxes to pay for a war that seemed ever more likely. In opposing Madison, many Republicans cited their party's traditional view of high taxes and a strong military as the tools of despots.

Madison secretly asked Congress on April 1 for a sixty-day embargo, a move designed to give American merchant ships time to return safely to their home ports. On June 1, he sent a war message to Congress in which he laid out the stark alternative of submission or resistance to the British control of American commerce. Madison was now convinced that British commercial restrictions were not just a defensive measure aimed at France but an aggressive attempt to reduce the United States to the permanent status of colonial dependent.

For Madison and most other Republicans, the impending conflict was a second war for independence. Free and open access to world markets was certainly at stake, but so was national pride. The arrogant British policy of impressment was a humiliating affront to American honor and headed the list of grievances in Madison's war message.

A divided Congress declared war on Britain. The vote in the House on June 4 was seventy-nine in favor and forty-nine opposed; on June 17, the Senate concurred, nineteen to thirteen. The vote split along regional, economic, and party lines. Support for the war was strongest in regions whose economies had been damaged the most by the British blockades and control of Atlantic commerce. Thus the South and the

West, trapped in an agricultural depression and anxious to eliminate foreign threats at their frontiers, favored war. Conversely, mercantile New England, a region that had, ironically, prospered as a result of British interference with ocean commerce, opposed the war.

The votes that carried the war declaration came from northern Republicans, who saw the impending struggle as a defense of America's experiment in self-government. Nine-tenths of the congressional Republicans voted for war, but not a single Federalist did so. For the Federalists, the real enemy was France, which had actually seized more American ships than the British. From their strongholds in coastal New England, the Federalists condemned the war as a French-inspired plot and predicted it would end in financial ruin.

The Federalists' anger increased when they learned that the British had been prepared to yield on one of the most prominent issues in the coming of war. On June 23, the British government revoked for one year its Orders in Council against the United States. A poor harvest and the ongoing economic pressure exerted by Madison had finally caused hard times in England and produced a policy reversal intended to placate the Americans. This concession, however, did not address impressment or monetary compensation, and news of it did not reach America until August. For Madison, it was too little too late, and he remained committed to war.

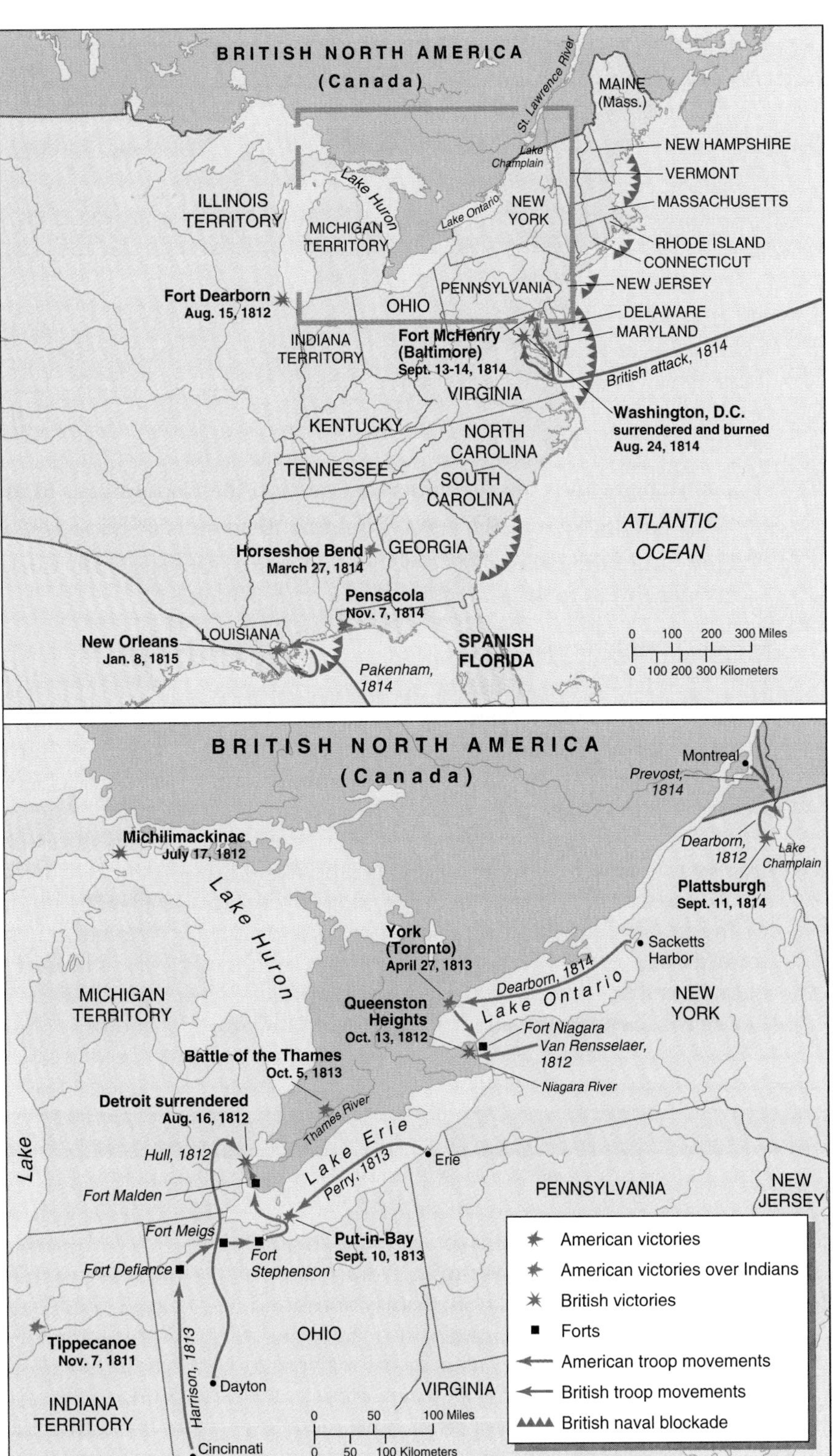

Map 9-2 The War of 1812
Most of the battles of the War of 1812 were fought along the Canadian–American border, where American armies repeatedly tried to invade Canada. Despite the effectiveness of the British naval blockade, the American navy was successful in denying the British strategic control of the Great Lakes. Andrew Jackson's smashing victory at the Battle of New Orleans convinced Americans that they had won the war.

The War of 1812

The Republicans led the nation into a war it was unprepared to fight (see Map 9-2).

American Views

Federalist Antiwar Resolutions

As the policies of the Madison administration in the spring of 1812 increasingly pointed toward war against Great Britain, New England Federalists mounted protest meetings in an effort to preserve peace. Passed at a meeting in Providence, Rhode Island, on April 7, 1812, the following resolutions make the Federalist case for the disastrous consequences of a war against Britain and reveal the depths of the party divisions over foreign policy.

❖ **On what grounds did the Federalists accuse the Republicans of an anti-British bias?**

❖ **What did the Federalists argue would be the results of a war against Britain?**

❖ **How could the Federalists now depict France, America's ally during the Revolutionary War, as a greater threat to American freedoms than Britain?**

Voted and Resolved unanimously,

That, in our opinion, the peace, prosperity and happiness of these United States, are in great jeopardy; inasmuch as, we have the strongest reasons to believe, the general government have determined to make war on Great-Britain. . . .

We are further confirmed in our apprehensions . . . by the evident partiality [the Republicans] have for a long time manifested towards one of the belligerents; and their deep-rooted enmity towards the other. The decrees of both nations equally violate our neutral rights; but France by her Berlin Decree, was the first aggressor; and still persists in capturing and burning our vessels on the high seas; and in robbing, imprisoning, and insulting our citizens; yet all these atrocities have been either palliated, or excused; while every effort has been made to excite the prejudices and animosities of our people against Great Britain. British vessels are excluded from our harbors; and our citizens are forbidden to import goods of the growth and manufacture of Britain and her dependencies; at the same time that French privateers are suffered to refit in American ports; and French goods are received, and protected, by our government. . . . All this, too, is done, when our trade to

Still, the apparent vulnerability of Canada to invasion made it possible to envision an American victory. Canada was thinly populated, poorly defended, and exposed to a potentially huge American army of militiamen. Yet bungled American invasions verged on tragicomedy, and British-Canadian forces and their Indian allies stymied American advances. For much of the war, Britain was preoccupied with Napoleon in Europe. When free to concentrate on the American sideshow in 1814, the British failed to secure naval control of the Great Lakes, their minimal strategic objective, and their counterinvasions of the United States bogged down. By the fall of 1814, both sides were eager for an end to the military stalemate.

Internal dissent endangered the Union almost as much as British troops did. The war exacerbated Federalist disenchantment with southern dominance of national affairs. Nearly all Federalists believed that pro-French fanatics and slaveholding agrarians in the Republican party had consistently sacrificed the commercial interests of New England. A minority of Federalists were convinced that New England could never regain its rightful place in shaping national policy and was prepared to lead a secession movement. Although blocked by party moderates at the **Hartford Convention** in 1814, the secessionists tarred Federalism with the brush of treason. Consequently, the Republicans, the party that brought the country to

France, is of little value; and that to England, and her dependence is, of more importance to the United States, than with all the world besides.

Resolved, That . . . believing as we most sincerely do, that a war with England, at this time, is neither necessary, nor expedient, we deem it a duty which we owe to our families, and to our country, to use our utmost efforts to avert so great a calamity; and . . . we are of opinion that this expression ought to be given in the approaching elections. If we choose Democratic [Republican] State Rulers, we choose war; if we choose Federal State Rulers, we choose peace. . . .

But should we, forgetful of our duties, elect democratic rulers, and thereby let loose this wild spirit of war, what calamities, and horrors must spread themselves over those devoted States! All the taxes proposed must fall upon us; our foreign and coasting commerce be cut off; our fisheries be destroyed; our agriculture neglected. . . . The destruction of our navigation would interrupt, and we fear, ruin our numerous, and flourishing manufactories; for, when the enemies['] ships cover our coasts, we can neither obtain the necessary materials, nor export the manufactured goods.

But these evils are only the beginning of sorrows. When war arrives, what will give protections to our harbours and maritime towns? [The enemy] will . . . make a war of frequent, and sudden descent on our long, and defenceless seacoast. Ships manned, and now moored on the other side of the Atlantic Ocean, can, in forty days, be riding on the waters of our bay and river. What could then save our sea-port towns, together with all the vessels in our harbours from conflagration, pillage, and military exaction?

Dreadful are these consequences of war: but more dreadful will await us. A war with England will bring us into alliance with France. This alliance would make the last page of our history as a nation. All the horrors of war might be endured; but who can endure to become a Slave?—If we are allied to that putrid pestilence of tyranny; our laws, freedom, independence, national name and glory, are blotted out from the memory of man—If Bonaparte sends to this country, ships, and French soldiers, and French generals, we shall soon be like Holland, and Italy, and Switzerland, and every other country where this scourge of nations has been permitted to set his foot.

Source: William S. Dudley, ed., The Naval War of 1812: A Documentary History. Vol. I: 1812 *(Naval Historical Center, Dept. of the Navy 1985), pp. 69–72.*

the brink of a military disaster, emerged from the war more powerful than ever.

Setbacks in Canada

The outbreak of the **War of 1812** unleashed deep emotions that often divided along religious lines. From their strongholds in the Congregationalist churches in New England, the Federalists preached that all true Christians opposed a war "against the nation from which we are descended, and which for many generations has been the bulwark of the religion we profess." Such antiwar sentiments, however, outraged the Baptists and Methodists, the largest and most popularly rooted denominations. They believed, as resolved by the Georgia Baptist Association in 1813, that the British government was "corrupt, arbitrary, and despotic" and that the war was "just, necessary, and indispensable."

Fiercely loyal to Madison, who had championed religious freedom in Virginia, these Methodists and Baptists harbored old grudges against the established churches of both Britain and New England for suppressing their religious rights. Especially for the Baptists, the war became something of a crusade to secure civil and religious liberties against their traditional enemies. For Spencer Houghton Cone, a lieutenant in a company of sharpshooters and a future president of the National Baptist Convention, service in the war seemed "as much the duty of the Christian as the honor of the soldier."

POLICE.

WHEREAS authentic intelligence has been received that the Government of the United States of America did, on the 18th instant, declare War against the United Kingdom of Great Britain and Ireland and its dependencies, Notice is hereby given, that all Subjects or Citizens of the said United States, and all persons claiming American Citizenship, are ordered to quit the City of Quebec, on or before TWELVE o'clock at Noon, on WEDNESDAY next, and the District of Quebec on or before 12 o'clock at noon on FRIDAY next, on pain of arrest. ROSS CUTHBERT, C. Q. S. & Inspector of Police.

The Constables of the City of Quebec are ordered to assemble in the Police Office at 10 o'clock to-morrow morning, to receive instructions.

Quebec, 29th June, 1812.

Fearful of an American invasion, Canadian authorities ordered American residents expelled at the beginning of the War of 1812.

Madison hoped to channel this Christian, anti-British patriotism into the conquest of Canada. Two out of three Canadians were native-born Americans who, it was assumed, would welcome the U.S. Army with open arms. Only five thousand British troops were initially stationed in Canada, and Canadian militia were outnumbered nine to one by their American counterparts. No wonder Madison and his advisers felt Canada was ripe for the taking, "a mere matter of marching," as Jefferson put it.

Canada was also the only area where the United States could strike directly against British forces. Although officially a war to defend America's neutrality on the high seas, the War of 1812 was largely a land war. The United States simply did not have enough ships to do more than harass the powerful British navy. Against sixteen ships in the U.S. Navy, only seven of which were top-of-the-line frigates (warships), the British could deploy more than two hundred vessels.

By seizing Canada, Madison also hoped to weaken Britain's navy and undercut its navigation system. Madison had been convinced that withholding American foodstuffs and provisions from the British West Indies would quickly force the British to yield to American economic pressure. But the British turned to Canada as an alternative source of supplies. Madison hoped to close off that source. And if, as Madison expected, Napoleon denied the British access to the naval stores of the Baltic region in Europe, an American monopoly on Canadian lumber would cripple British naval power. Facing such a threat, the British would have to end the war on American terms.

Madison's strategic vision was clear, but its execution was pathetic. Three offensives against Canada in 1812 were embarrassing failures. In the first, in July, General William Hull crossed into Canada from Detroit and invited Canadians to join the American cause. He found few takers. Meanwhile, Fort Michilimackinac fell, and Tecumseh's warriors cut Hull's communications. Hull hurried back to Detroit only to surrender his army on August 16 to the smaller British-Indian force.

The loss of Detroit, preceded a day earlier by the abandonment of Fort Dearborn (present-day Chicago) and the massacre of its inhabitants, exposed western settlements to the full fury of frontier warfare. Americans in the Indiana Territory fled outlying areas for the safety of forts in the interior. The acting territorial governor scarcely exaggerated when he proclaimed, "Our former frontiers are now wilds and our inner Settlements have become frontiers." By the end of the year, the British controlled half of the Old Northwest.

Farther east, the Americans botched two offensives in 1812. In October, an American thrust across the Niagara River was defeated when a New York state militia refused to cross the river to join the regular army troops on the Canadian side. This left the isolated forces under General Stephen Van Rensselaer an easy prey for the British at the **Battle of Queenston Heights**. Then the long-delayed third offensive, north from Lake Champlain, turned into a bloodless fiasco. It was aimed at Montreal, the center of British operations in Canada. General Henry Dearborn, the leader of the expedition, turned back in late November when he discovered, as Van Rensselaer had, that his militia would not leave their state.

Republican expectations of victory in Canada had been wishful thinking. Most Canadians fought against, not with, the Americans. Reliance on state militias proved disastrous. Poorly trained and equipped, the militias, when they did show up for battle, could not match the discipline of British soldiers or the fighting skills of their Native American allies. Nor was American generalship on a par with that of the British. Primitive land communications made the movement and coordination of troops a nightmare. New England, the obvious base for operations against the strategically critical St. Lawrence River Valley, the entry point for all British supplies and reinforcements, withheld many of its state forces from national service. Consequently, the invasions were piecemeal, ineffective forays launched from western areas where anti-British and anti-Indian sentiment ran high.

All the Republicans had to show for the first year of the war were morale-boosting but otherwise insignificant naval victories. In individual combat between ships, the small American navy acquitted itself superbly. Early in the war, American privateers harassed British merchant vessels, but the easy pickings were soon gone. British squadrons ships redeployed to protect shipping, and other warships kept up a blockade that stifled American commerce.

Military setbacks and antiwar feelings in much of the Northeast hurt the Republicans in the election of 1812. Madison won only narrowly. Federalists and other disaffected Northerners rallied behind DeWitt Clinton, an antiadministration Republican from New York. The now familiar regional pattern in voting repeated itself. Madison swept the electoral vote of the South and West. He ran poorly in the Northeast and won only because his party held on to Pennsylvania.

Western Victories and British Offensives

American forces fared better in 1813. Motivation remained high because, as Major Isaac Roach of an artillery regiment noted, many Americans believed that "it had become a jest and byword in England that this country could not be kicked into war." In September, the navy won a major engagement on Lake Erie that opened up a supply line in the western theater. Commodore Oliver Hazard Perry attacked the British fleet in the **Battle of Put-in-Bay**, on the southwestern shore of the lake, and forced the surrender of all six British ships. The victory signaled General William Henry Harrison to launch an offensive in the West.

With the loss of Lake Erie, the British were forced to abandon Detroit. Harrison caught up with the British garrison and their Indian allies on the banks of the Thames River in southern Ontario. Demonstrating bold leadership and relying on battle-tested western militias, Harrison won a decisive victory. Tecumseh, the most visionary of the Indian warriors, was killed, and the backbone of the Indian resistance broken. The Old Northwest was again safe for American settlement.

The **Battle of the Thames** ended British plans for an Indian buffer state. But by 1814, Britain had bigger goals in mind. A coalition of European powers forced Napoleon to abdicate in April 1814, thus freeing Britain to focus on the American war. It now seemed poised to break the military stalemate with a clear-cut victory.

British strategy in 1814 called for two major offensives, an invasion south from Montreal down Lake Champlain in upstate New York and an attack on Louisiana aimed at seizing New Orleans with a task force out of Jamaica. Meanwhile, diversionary raids along the mid-Atlantic coast were to pin down American forces and undermine morale. The overall objective was nothing less than a reversal of America's post-1783 expansion. If the invasions succeeded, the British would have been in a strong position to force a southward adjustment of the Canadian–American boundary and to claim the Louisiana Purchase territory.

The British attacks could hardly have come at a worse time for the Madison administration. The Treasury

Cut off from their American customers during the War of 1812, some British businessmen hoped to recoup their losses once hostilities ended by making bandanas for the American souvenir market that celebrated American naval victories in the war.

was nearly bankrupt. Against the wishes of Treasury Secretary Gallatin, Congress had refused to preserve the Bank of the United States when its charter expired in 1811. Lacking both a centralized means of directing wartime finances and any significant increase in taxes, the Treasury was forced to rely on makeshift loans. These loans were poorly subscribed, largely because the cash-rich New England banks refused to buy them. Inflation also became a problem when state banks, no longer restrained by the controls of a national bank, overissued paper money in the form of bank notes.

As the country's finances tottered toward collapse, political dissent in New England was reaching a climax. In 1814, the British extended their blockade of American commerce northward to include New England. Federalist merchants and shippers, who had earlier profited from their illegal trade with the British, now felt the economic pinch of the war. Cries for resistance against "Mr. Madison's war" culminated in a call issued by the Massachusetts legislature for a convention to consider "a radical reform of the national compact." The convention was scheduled for December in Hartford, Connecticut.

The darkest hour came in August 1814. A British amphibious force occupied and torched Washington, D.C., in retaliation for an American raid on York (now Toronto), the capital of Upper Canada. The defense of Washington was slipshod at best, and a local inhabitant can be excused for scribbling on a wall: "The capital and the Union lost by cowardice." Still, the British actions stiffened American resistance, and the failure of a follow-up attack on Baltimore deprived the British of any strategic gain. Baltimore's defenses held, stirring Francis Scott Key, a young lawyer who viewed the bombardment from a British prisoner-of-war ship, to write "The Star-Spangled Banner." Fittingly in this strange war, the future national anthem was set to the tune of a British drinking song.

The Chesapeake campaign was designed to divert American attention from the major offensive General George Prevost was leading down the shores of Lake Champlain. Prevost commanded the largest and best-equipped army the British had yet assembled. His opponent was Commodore Thomas Macdonough, one of several young, talented regional commanders Madison appointed late in the war. On September 11, at the **Battle of Plattsburgh**, Macdonough smashed a British fleet on Lake Champlain. Having counted on that fleet to protect his supply lines, Prevost retreated to Canada.

The tide had turned. When news of the setbacks at Baltimore and especially Plattsburgh reached England, the foreign office scaled back the demands it had been making on American negotiators at peace talks in the city of Ghent, in present-day Belgium. The British were ready for peace, but one of their trump cards had yet to be played—the southern offensive against New Orleans. The outcome of that campaign could still upset whatever was decided at Ghent.

The Treaty of Ghent and the Battle of New Orleans

By the fall of 1814, the British were eager to get on with redrawing the map of post-Napoleonic Europe, restoring profitable relations with America, and reducing their huge war debt. The British negotiators at Ghent agreed to a peace treaty on terms the Americans were delighted to accept. The **Treaty of Ghent**, signed on Christmas Eve, 1814, simply restored relations to their status at the start of the war. No territory changed hands, and nothing was said about impressment or the rights of neutrals.

The ink had barely dried on the Treaty of Ghent when the British government sent reinforcements to General Edward Pakenham, the commander of the Louisiana invasionary force. By this action, the British indicated that they were not irrevocably committed to the peace settlement, which, though signed, could not be formally ratified until weeks had passed while it was sent across the Atlantic. The British had always held that the Louisiana Purchase was fraudulent (they insisted that Louisiana was never Napoleon's to sell), and they were prepared to install a new government in Louisiana if Pakenham succeeded. Far from being an anticlimax to a war that was already over, the showdown between British and American forces at the **Battle of New Orleans** in January 1815 had immense strategic significance for the United States.

The hero of New Orleans, in song and legend, was Andrew Jackson. A planter-politician from Tennessee, Jackson rose to prominence during the war as a ferocious Indian fighter. The Creeks of Alabama and Georgia, much like the Shawnees farther north, had undergone a religious revival that culminated in a military effort to drive American settlers out of their tribal homelands. As a general in the Tennessee militia, Jackson crushed Indian resistance in the Old Southwest at the Battle of Horseshoe Bend in March 1814. He then forced the vanquished Creeks to cede two-thirds of their territory to the United States.

After his Indian conquests, Jackson was promoted to general in the regular army and given command of the defense of the Gulf Coast. In November 1814, he seized Pensacola in Spanish Florida to deny the British its use as a supply depot and then hurried to defend New Orleans. The overconfident British frontally attacked Jackson's lines on January 8, 1815. The result was a massacre. Artillery fire laid down by

This illustration of the Battle of New Orleans depicts the fatal wounding of British General Edward Pakenham, which prompted the massed British troops to begin fleeing the battlefield.

French-speaking cannoneers from New Orleans accounted for most of the carnage. More than two thousand British soldiers were killed or wounded. American casualties totaled twenty-one.

Strategically, Jackson's smashing victory at New Orleans ended any possibility of a British sphere of influence in Louisiana. Politically, it was a deathblow to Federalism. At the Hartford Convention in December, party moderates had forestalled talk of secession with a series of proposed constitutional amendments designed to limit southern power in national affairs. At the top of their list was a demand for eliminating the three-fifths clause by which slaves were counted for purposes of congressional representation. They also wanted to require a two-thirds majority in Congress for the admission of new states, declarations of war, and the imposition of embargoes. These demands became public as Americans were rejoicing over the Treaty of Ghent and Jackson's routing of the British. Set against the revived nationalism that marked the end of the war, the Federalists now seemed to be parochial sulkers who put regional interests above the national good. Worse yet, they struck many Americans as quasi-traitors who had been prepared to desert the country in the face of the enemy. As a significant political force, Federalism was dead.

The Era of Good Feelings

In 1817, on the occasion of a presidential visit by James Monroe, a Boston newspaper proclaimed the **Era of Good Feelings**, an expression that nicely captured the spirit of political harmony and sectional unity that washed over the republic in the immediate postwar years. National pride surged with the humbling of the British at New Orleans, the demise of the Federalists lessened political tensions, and the economy boomed. The Republicans had been vindicated, and for a short time they enjoyed *de facto* status as the only governing party.

At the end of Madison's presidency and in the first administration of his successor, James Monroe of Virginia, the Republicans embarked on a program of economic nationalism that would have pleased Alexander Hamilton. In foreign policy, they moved aggressively to stake out American leadership in the Western Hemisphere. A series of decisions handed down by the Supreme Court also reinforced the postwar nationalism. In 1819, however, an economic depression and a bitter controversy over slavery shattered the harmony. The nationalist tide set in motion by the end of the war had run its course, and the Republicans divided on sectional and economic issues.

Economic Nationalism

The War of 1812 had taught the Republicans to appreciate old Federalist doctrines on centralized national power. In his annual message of December 1815, Madison outlined a program of economic nationalism that was pushed through Congress by Henry Clay and John Calhoun, the most prominent of the new generation of young, nationalist-minded Republicans.

The first order of business was creating a new national bank. Reliance on state banks for wartime financing had proved a major mistake. The banks lacked sufficient capital reserves or, as occurred in New England, held them back. Demand for credit was met by a flood of state bank notes that fell in value because there was insufficient gold and silver to back them. Many banks suspended specie payments for their notes, and inflation was a persistent problem. After the British burned Washington, the Treasury was temporarily bankrupt, and throughout the war it could borrow only at high interest rates. Fiscal stability required the monetary coordination and restraint that only a new Bank of the United States could provide.

Introduced by Calhoun, the bank bill passed Congress in 1816. Modeled after Hamilton's original bank and also headquartered in Philadelphia, the **Second Bank of the United States** was capitalized at $35 million, making it by far the nation's largest bank. Its size and official status as the depository and dispenser of the government's funds gave the bank tremendous econonomic power. It also enjoyed the exclusive privilege of being able to establish branches in any state.

After moving to repair the fiscal damage of the war, the Republicans then acted to protect what the war had fostered. Embargoes followed by three years of war forced American businessmen to manufacture goods they previously had imported. This was especially the case with iron and textile goods long supplied by the British. In 1815 and again in 1816, the British inundated the American market with cheap imports to strangle American industry in its infancy. Responding to this challenge to the nation's economic independence, the Republicans passed the Tariff of 1816, the first protective tariff in American history. The act levied duties of 20 to 25 percent on manufactured goods that could be produced in the United States.

Responding to pressure from the War department and western states, Congress earmarked revenue from the tariff and $1.5 million from the Bank of the United States (a cash payment in return for its charter) for transportation projects. The lack of a road system in the trans-Appalachian region had severely hampered troop movements during the war. Also, as settlers after the war moved onto lands seized from the pro-British Indians, western congressmen demanded improved outlets to eastern markets.

In early 1817, an internal improvements bill passed Congress. Despite the soaring rhetoric of John Calhoun, the bill's sponsor, seeking to "bind the republic together with a perfect system of roads and canals," President Madison remained unmoved. Though in agreement with the bill's objectives, he was convinced that the Constitution did not permit federal financing of primarily local projects. He vetoed the bill just before he left office.

Congressional passage of Calhoun's internal improvements bill marked the pinnacle of the Republicans' economic nationalism. Frightened by the sectional disunity of the war years, a new generation of Republicans jettisoned many of the ideological trappings of Jefferson's original agrarian party. Their program was a call for economic, and therefore political, unity. Such unity was to be achieved through a generous program of national subsidies consisting of tariffs for manufacturers in the Northeast and transportation funds for planters and farmers in the South and West. The new national bank would provide a uniform currency and credit facilities for the internal exchange of raw materials and manufactured goods.

Support for this program was strongest in the mid-Atlantic and western states, the regions that stood to gain the most economically. Opposition centered in the Southeast, notably among die-hard proponents of states' rights in the old tobacco belt of Virginia and North Carolina, and in New England, a region not only well served already by banks and a road network but also anxious not to be politically overshadowed by the rising West. This opposition took on an increasingly hard edge in the South as the Supreme Court outlined an ever more nationalist interpretation of the Constitution.

Judicial Nationalism

Under Chief Justice John Marshall, the Supreme Court had long supported the nationalist perspective Republicans began to champion after the war. A Virginia Federalist whose nationalism was forged during his service in the Revolutionary War, Marshall dominated the Court throughout his tenure (1801–1835) by his forceful personality and the logical power of his nationalist convictions. Two principles defined Marshall's jurisprudence: the primacy of the Supreme Court in all matters of constitutional interpretation and the sanctity of contractual property rights. In *Fletcher* v. *Peck* (1810), for example, the Court ruled that a Georgia law voiding a land grant made by an earlier legislature—on the grounds that it had involved massive fraud—violated the Constitutional provision barring any state from "impairing the obligation of contracts." Marshall held that despite the fraud the original land grant constituted an unbreakable legal contract.

Out of the political limelight since the Burr trial in 1807, the Court was thrust back into it by two controversial decisions in 1819. The first involved Dartmouth College and the attempt by the New Hampshire legislature to amend its charter in the direction of greater public control over this private institution. In *Dartmouth College* v. *Woodward*, the Court ruled that Dartmouth's original royal charter of 1769 was a contract protected by the Constitution. Hence the state of New Hampshire could not alter that charter without the prior consent of the college. By so sanctifying charters or acts of incorporation as contracts, the Court prohibited states from interfering with the rights and privileges they had bestowed on private corporations.

The second important decision in 1819, *McCulloch* v. *Maryland*, rested on a positive assertion of national power over the states. The case involved the Bank of the United States. Many state bankers were jealous of the privileges of the national bank, and this resentment was shared by legislators who viewed the bank's branches as an infringement on the states' economic sovereignty. In 1818, the Maryland legislature placed a heavy tax on the branch of the Bank of the United States established in Baltimore (and on all other banks in the state established without legislative authority). James McCulloch, the cashier of the Baltimore branch, refused to pay the tax. This set up a test case that involved two fundamental legal issues: Was the bank itself constitutional, and could a state tax federal property within its borders?

A unanimous Court, in language similar to but even more sweeping than that used by Alexander Hamilton in the 1790s, upheld the constitutional authority of Congress to charter a national bank and thereby regulate the nation's currency and finances. As long as the end was legitimate "within the scope of the Constitution," Congress had full power to use any means not expressly forbidden by the Constitution to achieve that end. As for Maryland's claim of a constitutional right to tax a federal agency, Marshall stressed that "the power to tax involves the power to destroy." Surely, he reasoned, when the people of the United States ratified the Constitution, they did not intend the federal government to be controlled by the states or rendered powerless by state action. Here was the boldest statement to date of the loose or "implied powers" interpretation of the Constitution and a ringing rebuke to the compact theory of the Union outlined by Southerners in the Virginia and Kentucky Resolutions and picked up by disgruntled Federalists in New England.

This 1830 painting shows Chief Justice John Marshall in the full robes of his office. Marshall's leadership molded the Supreme Court into an effective instrument of the national government. John Marshall by Chester Harding (1792–1886). Oil on canvas, 1830. Boston Athenaeum.

John Marshall by Chester Harding (1792–1886), oil on canvas, 1830. Boston Athenaeum.

Toward a Continental Empire

Marshall's legal nationalism paralleled the diplomatic nationalism of John Quincy Adams, secretary of state from 1817 to 1825. A former Federalist and the son of the second president, Adams broke with the party over its refusal to support an expansionist policy and held several diplomatic posts under the Madison administration. Adams made few friends as a negotiator. A British statesman once described him as "doggedly and systematically repulsive." Still, he was an effective diplomat. Convinced in his Puritan soul that God and nature had ordained that America stretch from the Atlantic to the Pacific as a beacon of liberty to the world, Adams used whatever tactics were necessary to realize that vision.

Adams shrewdly exploited Britain's desire for friendly and profitable relations after the War of 1812. The British wanted access to American cotton and foodstuffs in exchange for manufactured goods and investment capital. The United States wanted more trading opportunities in the British Empire and a free hand to deal with Spain's disintegrating empire in the Americas.

The **Rush–Bagot Agreement** of 1817 signaled the new pattern of Anglo–American cooperation. The agreement strictly limited naval armaments on the Great Lakes, thus effectively demilitarizing the border with Canada. The **Anglo–American Accords** of the following year resolved several issues left hanging after the war. Of great importance to New England, the British once again recognized American fishing rights off Labrador and Newfoundland. The boundary of the Louisiana Territory abutting Canada was set at the 49th parallel, and both nations agreed to the joint occupation of Oregon, the territory in the Pacific Northwest that lay west of the Rocky Mountains.

Having secured the northern flank of the United States, Adams was now free to deal with the South and West. Adams wanted all of Florida and an undisputed American window on the Pacific. The adversary here was Spain. Much weaker than it had been in the eighteenth century and struggling to suppress independence movements in its South American possessions, Spain resorted to delaying tactics in trying to hold off the tenacious Adams. Negotiations remained deadlocked until Andrew Jackson gave Adams the leverage he needed.

In March 1818, Jackson led his troops across the border into Spanish Florida. He destroyed encampments

OVERVIEW
TERRITORIAL EXPANSION UNDER THE REPUBLICANS

Benchmark	Year	Land Area of United States and Its Territories (square miles)
Republicans gain power	1801	864,746
Louisiana Purchase	1803	1,681,828
Trans-Continental Treaty	1819	1,749,462

of the Seminole Indians, seized two Spanish forts, and executed two British subjects on the grounds that they were dealing arms to the Seminoles for raids on the Alabama–Georgia frontier. Despite later protestations to the contrary, Jackson had probably exceeded his orders. He might well have been censured by the Monroe administration had not Adams supported him, telling Spain that Jackson was defending American interests and warning that he might be unleashed again.

Spain yielded to the American threat in the **Trans-Continental Treaty of 1819** (see Map 9-3). The United States annexed East Florida, and Spain recognized the prior American seizures of West Florida in 1810 and 1813. Adams secured an American hold on the Pacific Coast by drawing a boundary between the Louisiana Purchase and the Spanish Southwest that ran stepwise up the Sabine, Red, and Arkansas Rivers to the Continental Divide and then due west along the 42nd parallel to the Pacific. Spain renounced any claim to the Pacific Northwest; the United States in turn renounced its shaky claim to Texas under the Louisiana Purchase and assumed $5 million in Spanish debts to American citizens.

Adams's success in the Spanish negotiations turned on the British refusal to threaten war or assist Spain in the wake of Jackson's highhanded actions in Florida. Spanish possessions and the lives of two British subjects were worth little when weighed against the economic advantages of retaining close trading ties with the United States. Moreover, Britain, like the United States, had a vested interest in developing trade with newly independent Latin American countries now free of Spain's former imperial monopoly. Recognizing this common interest, George Canning, the British foreign minister, proposed in August 1823 that the United States and Britain issue a joint declaration opposing any European attempt to recolonize South America or to assist Spain in regaining its colonies.

President Monroe rejected the British overture, but only at the insistence of Adams. Canning's offer had a string attached to it: a mutual pledge by the British and Americans not to annex former Spanish territory. But Adams was confident that within a generation, the United States would acquire California, Texas, and perhaps Cuba as well. He wanted to maintain the maximum freedom of action for future U.S. policy and avoid any impression that America was beholden to Britain. Thus originated the most famous diplomatic statement in early American history, the **Monroe Doctrine**.

In his annual message to Congress in December 1823, Monroe declared that the Americas "are henceforth not to be considered as subjects for future colonization by any European power." In turn, Monroe pledged that the United States would not interfere in the internal affairs of European states. With its continental empire rapidly taking shape and new Latin American republics to be courted, the United States was more than willing to proclaim a special position for itself as the guardian of New World liberties.

The Breakdown of Unity

For all the intensity with which he pursued his continental vision, John Quincy Adams worried in early 1819 that "the greatest danger of this union was in the overgrown extent of its territory, combining with the slavery question." His words were prophetic. A sectional crisis flared in 1819 over slavery and its expansion when the territory of Missouri sought admission to the Union as a slave state. Simultaneously, a financial panic ended postwar prosperity and crystallized regional discontent over banking and tariff policies. Party unity cracked under these pressures, and each region backed its own presidential candidate in the wide-open election of 1824.

The Panic of 1819

From 1815 to 1818, Americans enjoyed a wave of postwar prosperity. European markets were starved for American goods after a generation of war and trade restrictions, and farmers and planters met

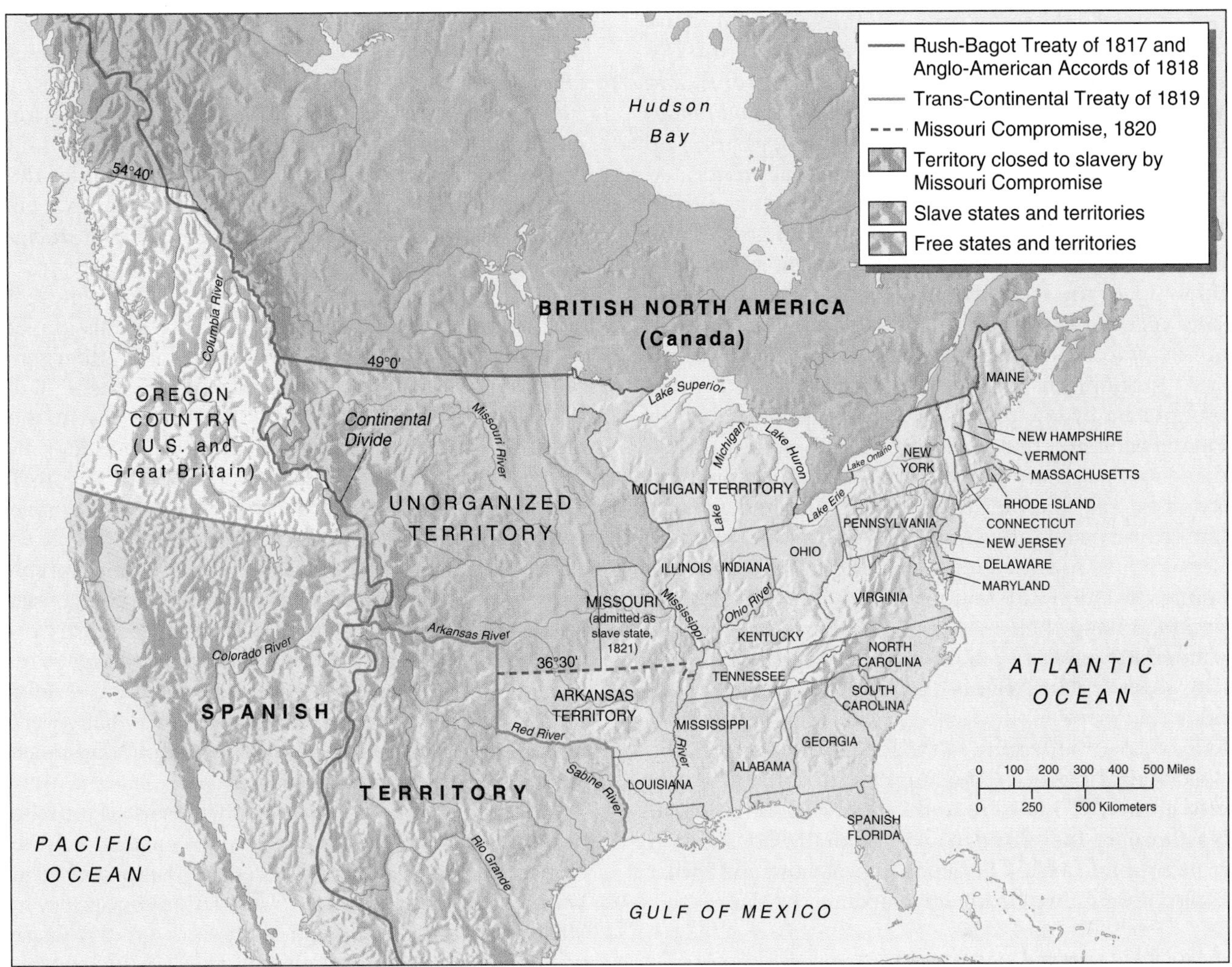

Map 9-3 The Missouri Compromise of 1820 and Territorial Treaties with Britain and Spain, 1818–1819
Treaties with Britain and Spain in 1818 and 1819 clarified and expanded the nation's boundaries. Britain accepted the 49th parallel as the boundary between Canada and the United States in the Trans-Mississippi West to the Oregon Country; Spain ceded Florida to the United States and agreed to a boundary stretching to the Pacific between the Louisiana Purchase territory and Spanish possessions in the Southwest. Sectional disputes over slavery led to the drawing of the Missouri Compromise line of 1820 that prohibited slavery in the Louisiana Territory north of 36°30'.

that demand by expanding production and bringing new land into cultivation. The availability of public land in the West on easy terms of credit sparked a speculative frenzy, and land sales soared. State banks and, worse yet, the Bank of the United States fed the speculation by making loans in the form of bank notes far in excess of their hard currency reserves. Before the bubble burst, cotton prices doubled to 30 cents a pound, real estate values became wildly inflated, and the money Westerners owed the federal government for the purchase of public lands rose to $21 million, an amount greater than the value of all western farm goods.

European markets for American cotton and food supplies returned to normal by late 1818. In January 1819, cotton prices sank in England, and the **Panic of 1819** was on. Cotton was the most valuable American export, and expected returns from the staple were the basis for an intricate credit network anchored in Britain. The fall in cotton prices triggered a credit contraction that soon engulfed the overextended American economy. Commodity prices fell across the board, and real estate values collapsed, especially in and around western cities.

A sudden shift in policy by the Bank of the United States virtually guaranteed that the economic downturn would settle into a depression. The Bank stopped all loans, called in all debts, and refused to honor drafts drawn on its branches in the South and West. Hardest hit by these policies were farmers and businessmen in the West, a region that had piled up debt in the expectation that the income generated by postwar prosperity would return a tidy profit. Bankruptcies mushroomed as creditors forced the liquidation of farms and real estate. For westerners, the Bank of the United States now became "the Monster," a ruthless institution controlled by eastern aristocrats who callously destroyed the hopes of farmers.

Southern resentment over the hard times brought on by low cotton prices focused on the tariff. Planters charged that the Tariff of 1816 unfairly raised their costs and amounted to an unconstitutional tax levied for the sole benefit of northern manufacturers. Unreconstructed Jeffersonians, now known as the Old Republicans, spearheaded a sharp reaction against the South's flirtation with nationalist policies in the postwar period. Taking their cue from John Taylor, a Virginia planter and agrarian philosopher, they demanded a return to strict states' rights doctrines. They saw an ominous pattern of unchecked and unconstitutional federal power emerging in the form of high tariffs, the judicial nationalism of the Supreme Court, and northern efforts to interfere with slavery in Missouri. If Northerners, they asked, could stretch the Constitution to incorporate a bank or impose a protective tariff, what could prevent them from emancipating the slaves?

The Missouri Compromise

Until 1819, slavery had not been a major divisive issue in American politics. The Northwest Ordinance of 1787, which banned slavery in federal territories north of the Ohio River, and the Southwest Ordinance of 1790, which permitted slavery south of the Ohio, represented a compromise that had allowed slavery in areas where climate and soil conditions favored slave-based agriculture. What was unforeseen in the 1780s, however, was the explosive demand for slave-produced cotton generated by the English textile industry in the early nineteenth century. At the republic's founding in 1787, slavery was identified with the declining tobacco economy of the South Atlantic states, and many Americans felt, perhaps wishfully, that the institution would gradually wither away.

By 1819, all hopes for the natural death of slavery were gone. Kentucky, Tennessee, Louisiana, Mississippi, and Alabama had all been added to the Union as slave states since 1787. Florida had just been annexed and surely would be another slave state. A thriving cotton market was underwriting slavery's expansion across the South, and even Missouri, a portion of the Louisiana Purchase that Northerners initially assumed would be inhospitable to slavery, had fallen under the political control of slaveholders.

The Missouri issue increased long simmering northern resentment over the spread of slavery and the southern dominance of national affairs under the Virginia presidents. In February 1819, James Tallmadge, a Republican congressman from New York, introduced an amendment in the House mandating a ban on future slave imports and a program of gradual emancipation as preconditions for the admission of Missouri as a state. Missourians, as well as Southerners in general, rejected the **Tallmadge Amendment**. The states, they argued, had absolute sovereignty in the drafting of their constitutions and any attempt by Congress to set conditions for statehood was unconstitutional. Nonetheless, a solid phalanx of northern congressmen supported the amendment.

Without a two-party system in which each of the parties had to compromise to protect its intersectional interests, voting followed sectional lines. The northern-controlled House passed the amendment, but it was repeatedly blocked in the Senate, which was evenly divided between free and slave states. The debates were heated, and Southerners spoke openly of secession if Missouri were denied admission as a slave state.

The stalemate over Missouri persisted into the next session of Congress. Finally, Speaker of the House Henry Clay engineered a compromise in March 1820. Congress put no restrictions on slavery in Missouri, and the admission of Missouri as a slave state was balanced by the admission of Maine (formerly part of Massachusetts) as a free state. In return for their concession on Missouri, northern congressmen demanded a prohibition on slavery in the remainder of the Louisiana Purchase north of the 36°30' parallel, the southern boundary of Missouri (see Map 9-3 on page 271). Except for the Arkansas Territory and what would become the Indian Territory of Oklahoma, the Louisiana Purchase was closed to slavery in the future.

The compromise almost unraveled when Missouri submitted a constitution the next November that required the state legislature to bar the entry of free black people. This mandate violated the guarantee in the U.S. Constitution that "the citizens of each State shall be entitled to all privileges and immunities of citizens in the several States." Missouri's restrictionist policy obviously denied African-American citizens this constitutional right to move from one state to any other state. Southerners were quick to point out, however, that free states as well as slave states already restricted the rights of free black people to vote or serve in the militia.

The nearly universal acceptance of white Americans of second-class citizenship for free black

Americans permitted Clay to dodge the issue. Missouri's constitution was accepted with the proviso that it "shall never be construed" to discriminate against citizens in other states. In short, with meaningless words that begged the issue of Missouri's defiance of the federal Constitution, the **Missouri Compromise** was salvaged. With this sacrifice of the claims of free black citizens for equal treatment, the Union survived its first great sectional crisis over slavery.

The Missouri crisis made white southerners aware that they were now a political minority within the Union. More rapid population growth in the North had reduced southern representation in the House to just over 40 percent. Of greater concern was the crystallization in Congress of a northern majority arraigned against the expansion of slavery. Southern threats of secession died out in the aftermath of the Missouri Compromise, but it was an open question whether the sectional settlement really solved the intertwined issues of slavery and expansion or merely sidestepped them for a day of final reckoning.

The Election of 1824

The election of 1820 made Monroe, like both his Republican predecessors, a two-term president. Monroe was the uncontested choice of his party, and the Federalists were too weak to run a candidate. Although Monroe won all but one of the electoral votes, Republican unity was more apparent than real. Voters had no choice in 1820, and without two-party competition, no outlets existed for expressing popular dissatisfaction with the Republicans. Instead, the Republicans split into factions as they began jockeying almost immediately for the election of 1824 (see Map 9-4).

The politics of personality dominated Monroe's second administration. Monroe had no obvious successor, and five candidates competed to replace him. All of them were nominal Republicans, and three were members of his cabinet. Secretary of War John Calhoun soon dropped out. He preferred to accept a nomination as vice president, confident that his turn would come in 1828. The other candidates—Secretary of the Treasury William Crawford from Georgia, Secretary of State John Quincy Adams from Massachusetts, Henry Clay from Kentucky, and Andrew Jackson from Tennessee—each had a strong regional following. As the Republican party fragmented, sectional loyalties were replacing partisan allegiances.

The early favorite was Crawford. He was the "official" party nominee in the sense that he had received the support of the congressional caucus, but most Republicans had boycotted the caucus, by now a useless relic of past party unity. Clay, Jackson, and Adams were nominated by their state legislatures. None of the candidates ran on a platform, but Crawford was identified with states' rights and Clay and Adams with centralized government. Clay in particular was associated with the national bank, protective tariffs, and federally funded internal improvements, a package of federal subsidies he called the **American System.** Jackson took no stand on any of the issues.

Jackson's noncommittal stance turned out to be a great asset. It helped him project the image of a military hero fresh from the people who was unsullied by any connection with Washington politicians, whom the public associated with hard times and sectional controversies. He was the highest vote-getter (43 percent of the popular vote), but none of the four candidates had a majority in the electoral college.

As in 1800, the election was thrown into the House of Representatives. Each state had one vote, and the choice was from among the top three in the electoral college. Clay, who had received the fewest electoral votes, was eliminated. Crawford had suffered a debilitating stroke and was no longer a viable candidate. Thus it came down to Adams or Jackson. Anxious to undercut Jackson, his chief rival in the

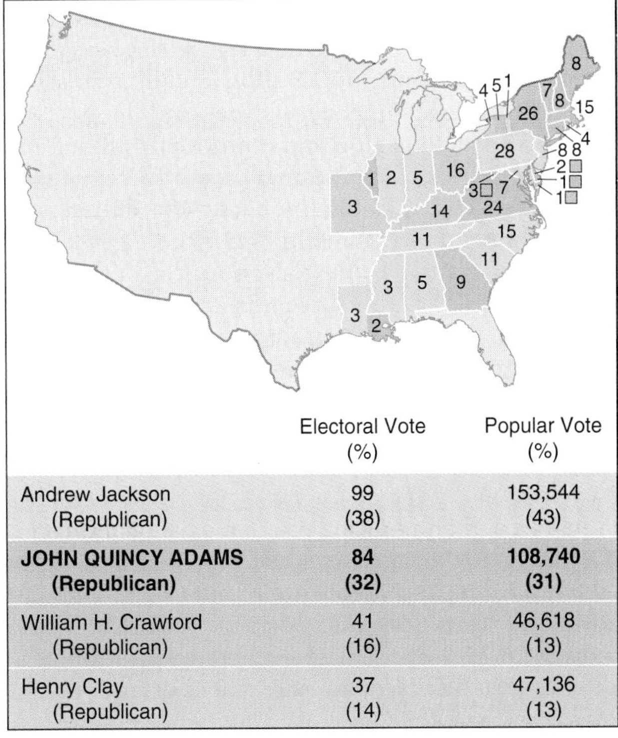

	Electoral Vote (%)	Popular Vote (%)
Andrew Jackson (Republican)	99 (38)	153,544 (43)
JOHN QUINCY ADAMS (Republican)	**84 (32)**	**108,740 (31)**
William H. Crawford (Republican)	41 (16)	46,618 (13)
Henry Clay (Republican)	37 (14)	47,136 (13)

Map 9-4* *The Election of 1824
The regional appeal of each of the four presidential candidates in the election of 1824 prevented any candidate from receiving a majority of the electoral vote. Consequently, and as set forth in the Constitution, the House of Representatives now had to choose the president from the three leading candidates. Its choice was John Quincy Adams.

West, Clay used his influence as speaker of the House to line up support for Adams, a fellow advocate of a strong centralized government.

Adams won the election, and he immediately named Clay as his secretary of state, the office traditionally viewed as a steppingstone to the presidency. Jackson and his followers were outraged. They smelled a "corrupt bargain" in which Clay had bargained away the presidency to the highest bidder. Vowing revenge, they began building a new party that would usher in a more democratic era of mass-based politics.

Conclusion

In 1800, the Republicans were an untested party whose coming to power frightened many Federalists into predicting the end of the Union and constitutional government. The Federalists were correct in sensing that their days of power had passed, but they underestimated the ideological flexibility the Republicans would reveal once in office and the imaginative ways in which Jefferson and his successors would wield executive power to expand the size of the original Union. Far from being anarchists and demagogues, the Republicans were shrewd empire builders astute enough to add to their base of political support in the South and West. They also paved the way for the nation to evolve as a democratic republic rather than the more aristocratic republic preferred by the Federalists.

Most Federalists never did learn the art of popular electioneering, and they were too elitist to have any desire to do so. Although foreign policy issues arising out of Jefferson's and Madison's attempts to assert American neutral rights during the Anglo-French war kept the Federalists alive and even briefly revived the party, the British posed the greatest test to Republican leadership. The Republicans chose war rather than surrendering their claims of American rights. Jackson's victory at the Battle of New Orleans ended the war in an American burst of glory, and the Federalists were swept aside by the postwar surge of nationalism.

By the mid-1820s, the Republicans were about to join the Federalists as political dinosaurs. The Republican era ended when the party became a victim of its own success. With no Federalist threat to enforce party discipline, the Republicans lost their organizational strength. Embracing economic nationalism after the war made the party's original focus on states' rights all but meaningless. Ideologically and organizationally adrift, the party split into regional coalitions in the wake of the Missouri controversy and the panic of 1819. But before it dissolved, the party left as its most enduring legacy the foundations of a continental empire.

Review Questions

1. What changes did the Republicans bring to the federal government? How did their policies differ from those of their Federalist predecessors?
2. Why were the Republicans so intent on expanding the boundaries of the United States, and why did the Federalists oppose an expansionist program?
3. What factors accounted for the Federalists' inability to regain national power after they lost the election of 1800?
4. What external and internal factors drew the United States into war against Britain? Could this war have been avoided?
5. What accounted for the difficulties of the United States in waging the War of 1812, and why was the war widely viewed as a great American victory? How did the war lead to an increasing pattern of diplomatic cooperation between the United States and Britain?
6. What explains the upsurge of nationalism that underlay the Era of Good Feelings? Why were the Republicans unable to maintain their party unity after 1819?

Recommended Reading

Annette Gordon-Reed, *Thomas Jefferson and Sally Hemings: An American Controversy* (1997). A model study that painstakingly weighs the evidence of Jefferson's alleged sexual involvement with his slave Sally Hemmings.

Donald R. Hickey, *The War of 1812: A Forgotten Conflict* (1989). Breaks no new ground, but presents a complete and very readable account of all aspects of the war.

Drew R. McCoy, *The Elusive Republic: Political Economy in Jeffersonian America* (1980). A gracefully written study that examines how attitudes on economic development influenced Jeffersonian notions of republicanism and were central to the Republicans' stand on free trade.

Peter S. Onuf, ed., *Jeffersonian Legacies* (1993). A collection of essays that presents the latest thinking on the extraordinary range of Jefferson's activities.

Marshall Smelser, *The Democratic Republic, 1801–1815* (1968). Gives a sound overview of the Jefferson and Madison administrations. Smelser portrays Jefferson as a political moderate adept in wielding power and offers a spirited defense of Madison's record as a war president.

Gore Vidal, *Burr* (1973). A superbly entertaining novel that satirically brings to life the leading personalities of Jefferson's America.

William Earl Weeks, *John Quincy Adams and American Global Empire* (1992). Presents Adams as a cynical, tough-minded negotiator utterly driven by his vision of an American continental empire. Though questioning his tactics, Weeks confirms Adams's reputation as America's greatest secretary of state.

Additional Sources

Jefferson's Presidency

Lance Banning, *The Jeffersonian Persuasion: Evolution of a Party Ideology* (1978).

Doron S. Ben-Atar, *The Origins of Jeffersonian Commercial Policy and Diplomacy* (1993).

Noble E. Cunningham, Jr., *The Jeffersonian Republicans in Power: Party Operations, 1801–1809* (1963).

Alexander De Conde, *This Affair of Louisiana* (1976).

Richard E. Ellis, *The Jeffersonian Crisis: Courts and Politics in the Early Republic* (1971).

David Hackett Fischer, *The Revolution of American Conservation: The Federalist Party in the Era of Jeffersonian Democracy* (1965).

Forrest McDonald, *The Presidency of Thomas Jefferson* (1976).

James Sterling Young, *The Washington Community, 1800–1828* (1966).

Madison and the Coming of War

Roger H. Brown, *The Republic in Peril* (1964).

Gregory Evans Dowd, *A Spirited Resistance: The North American Indian Struggle for Unity, 1745–1815* (1992).

R. David Edmunds, *The Shawnee Prophet* (1983) and *Tecumseh and the Quest for Indian Leadership* (1984).

Frank Lawrence Owsley, Jr., and Gene H. Smith, *Filibusters and Expansionists: Jeffersonian Manifest Destiny* (1997).

Bradford Perkins, *Prologue to War: England and the United States, 1805–1812* (1961).

Robert A. Rutland, *Madison's Alternatives: The Jeffersonian Republicans and the Coming of War, 1805–1812* (1975).

The War of 1812

James M. Banner, *To the Hartford Convention: The Federalists and the Origins of Party Politics in the Early Republic, 1789–1815* (1967).

Harry L. Coles, *The War of 1812* (1965).

William Gribbin, *The Churches Militant: The War of 1812 and American Religion* (1973).

Reginald Horsman, *The War of 1812* (1969).

J. C. A. Stagg, *Mr. Madison's War: Politics, Diplomacy, and Warfare in the Early Republic, 1783–1830* (1983).

Steven Watts, *The Republic Reborn: War and the Making of Liberal America* (1987).

The Era of Good Feelings

Samuel Flagg Bemis, *John Quincy Adams and the Foundations of American Foreign Policy* (1949).

Noble E. Cunningham, Jr., *The Presidency of James Monroe* (1996).

Shaw Livermore, *The Twilight of Federalism: The Disintegration of the Federalist Party, 1815–1830* (1962).

Ernest R. May, *The Making of the Monroe Doctrine* (1975).

G. Edward White, *The Marshall Court and Cultural Change, 1815–1835* (1991).

The Breakdown of Unity

Glover Moore, *The Missouri Compromise, 1819–1821* (1953).

Murray N. Rothbard, *The Panic of 1819: Reactions and Policies* (1962).

Where to Learn More

- ❖ **Fort McHenry National Monument, Baltimore, Maryland.** This historic site preserves the fort that was the focal point of the British attack on Baltimore and contains a museum with materials on the battle and the writing of "The Star-Spangled Banner."
- ❖ **Tippecanoe Battlefield Museum, Battle Ground, Indiana.** This museum includes artifacts from the Indian and white settlement of Indiana and visual materials on the Battle of Tippecanoe of 1811.
- ❖ **Monticello, Charlottesville, Virginia.** The architecturally unique home of Thomas Jefferson and the headquarters for his plantation serves as a museum that provides insights into Jefferson's varied interests.
- ❖ **Montpelier, Montpelier Station, Virginia.** The museum here was the home of James Madison, and it includes material on his life as a politician and planter.
- ❖ **Perry's Victory and International Peace Memorial, Put-in-Bay, Ohio.** At the site of Perry's decisive victory on Lake Erie in 1813 now stands a museum that depicts the role of the Old Northwest in the War of 1812.

THE JACKSONIAN ERA, 1824–1845

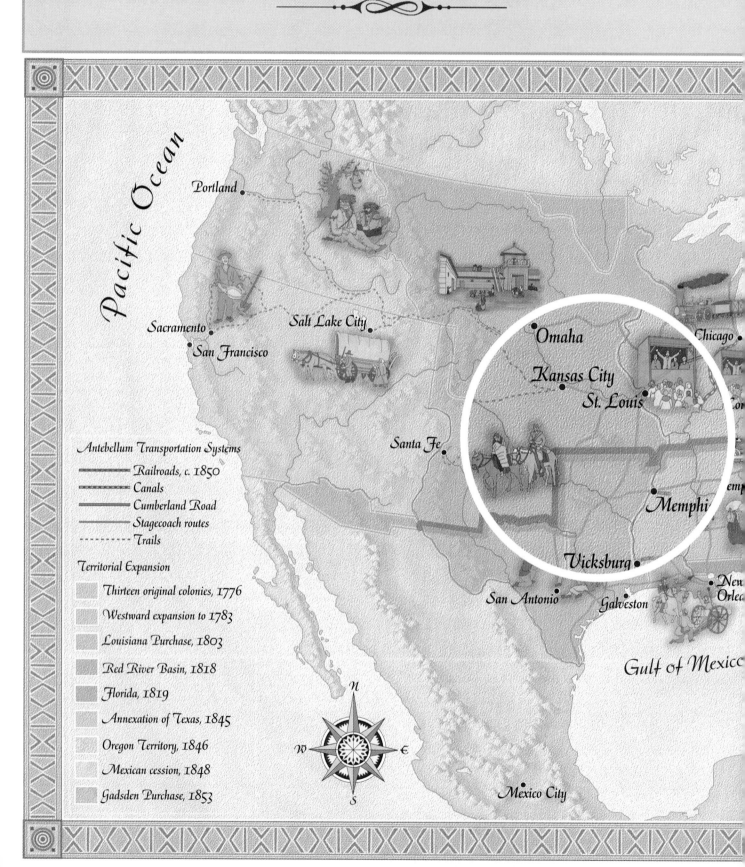

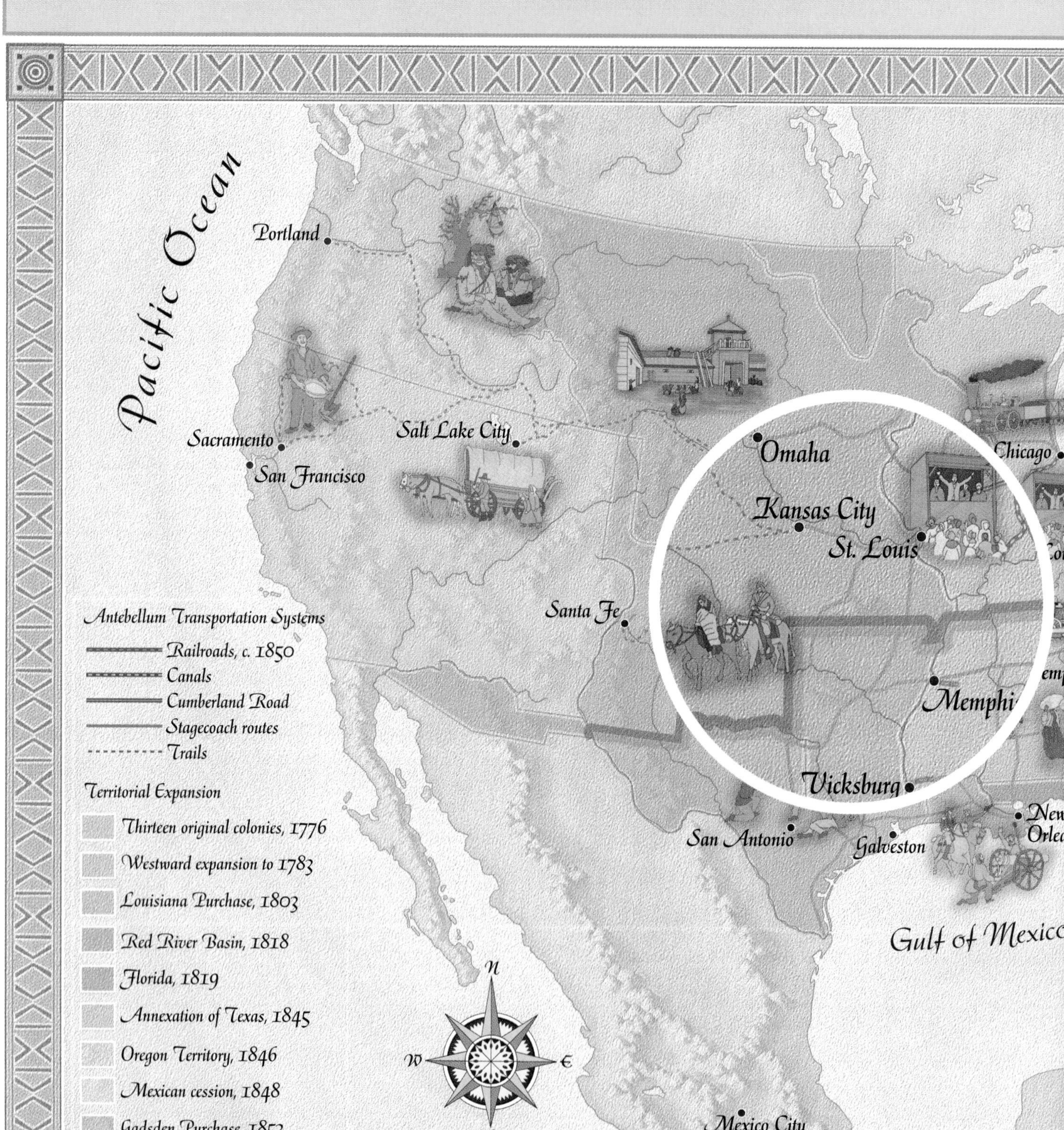

10

Chapter Outline

Key Topics

- The rise of new political parties: Jacksonian Democrats and Whigs
- The disfranchisement of free black people and women
- Birth of the Whig party
- The Second Great Awakening
- The Bank War
- The growing conflict over slavery

"Politics at the present time are the all-engrossing topic of discourse," observed a New Englander in the fall of 1828. "In the ballroom, or at the dinner table, in the Stagecoach & in the tavern; even the social chitchat of the tea table must yield to the everlasting subject." The republic had seen spirited presidential elections before, notably the Jefferson–Adams contest of 1800, but something was clearly new in 1828. Whether measured by the vulgar personal attacks launched by a partisan press, the amount of whiskey and beef consumed at political barbecues, or the huge increase in voter turnout for president, this election marked the entrance of ordinary Americans onto the political stage.

Jefferson's world, in which refined gentlemen were entrusted with office as their just due, had been left behind by the 1820s. As Jefferson lamented shortly before his death in 1826, he and the other founders of the republic were "left alone midst a new gener[ation] whom we know not, and who know not us." This "new generation" impatiently pushed for greater political and social equality. Ongoing democratization in American politics had expanded the number and potential power of the voters, and professional politicians realized that party success now depended on reaching and organizing this enlarged electorate. The "Jacksonian Democrats," named for their leader, Andrew Jackson, were the first party to learn this fundamental lesson. Trumpeting Andrew Jackson as the friend of the common man and the foe of aristocratic privilege, they won a landslide victory in 1828 and held national power through the 1830s. The Jacksonians promised to protect farmers and workers from the monied elite, whom they portrayed as the enemies of equality and the corruptors of public morality.

By the mid-1830s, the Whig party had formed in opposition to the Jacksonians. The Whigs offered an ordered vision of American progress and liberty, anchored in the use of governmental power to expand economic opportunities and promote morality. By embracing electoral techniques of popular appeal first used by the Democrats, the Whigs captured the presidency in 1840. Their triumph heralded a new party system, one based on massive voter turnouts and two-party competition in every state.

The luckless Whigs failed to capitalize on their victory in 1840. Their newly elected president, William Henry Harrison, died shortly after entering office, and Vice President John Tyler, his successor, blocked the Whigs' economic program. Spurned by the Whigs as a traitor, Tyler then reopened the explosive question of slavery and territorial expansion by pushing to annex the independent republic of Texas, where slavery was legal.

The Democrats regained power in 1844 by skillfully exploiting the Texas issue, but they set an ominous precedent. Debates over the expansion of slavery became embedded in the political system, and the greatest strength of the mass-based parties—their ability to tap and unleash popular emotions—now became their greatest weakness. The slavery issue began to take on a life of its own beyond the control of party leaders. The seeds of the Civil War were being sown.

The Egalitarian Impulse

Political democracy, defined as the majority rule of white males, was far from complete in early nineteenth-century America. Acting on the belief that only property owners with a stake in society should have a voice in governing it, the landed and commercial elites of the Revolutionary era erected legal barriers against the full expression of majority sentiments. These barriers—property requirements for voting and officeholding, the prevalence of appointed over elected offices, and the overrepresentation of older and wealthier regions in state legislatures—came under increasing attack after 1800 and were all but eliminated by the 1820s.

As politics opened to mass participation, a democratization movement in American religion also gathered momentum. Popular styles of religious

John L. Krimmel, painting, (1786–1821). Oil paint, canvas, H. 16⅜", W. 25⅝". (AN:59.131) Courtesy, Winterthur Museum, "Election Day in Philadelphia" (1815).

This early nineteenth-century painting of a polling place in Philadelphia illustrates the growing involvement of common Americans in politics. As suffrage broadened and more Americans came out to vote, elections became more heated and emotional.

leadership and worship emerged in a broad reaction to the formalism and elitism of the dominant Protestant churches. The same egalitarian impulse drove these twin democratic revolutions, and both movements represented an empowerment of the common man. Popular movements now spoke his language and appealed to his quest for republican equality. (Women would have to wait longer.) John Quincy Adams and his followers never understood the more democratic America of the 1820s. As a result, they were easily routed in the election of 1828 by those who did—the **Jacksonian Democrats**.

The Extension of White Male Democracy

In 1789, Congress set the pay of representatives and senators at $6 a day plus travel expenses. By 1816, inflation had so eroded this salary that many government clerks earned more than members of Congress. Thus Congress thought itself prudent and justified when it voted itself a hefty raise to $1,500 a year. The public thought otherwise. In a resolution typical of the popular response, the citizens of Saratoga, New York, accused Congress of "wanton extravagance" and "a daring and profligate trespass against . . . the *morals* of the *Republic*." The outcry stunned the politicians, who found themselves deluged with protests decrying their greed.

So sharp was the reaction against the Salary Act of 1816 that 70 percent of the members of Congress were turned out of office at the next election. Congress quickly repealed the salary increase, but not before John C. Calhoun spoke for many in Congress when he plaintively asked, "Are we bound in all cases to do what is popular?" The answer was apparently yes. As Richard M. Johnson of Kentucky noted, "The presumption is, that the people are always right."

The people had spoken in 1816, and the politicians got the message. The uproar over the Salary Act marked a turning point in the transition from the deferential politics of the Federalist-Republican period to the egalitarianism of the coming Jacksonian era. Since the War of 1812, demands for a greater popular voice in government had noticeably quickened the pace of democratization. The public would no longer passively accept decisions handed down by local elites or established national figures.

Individual states, not the federal government, defined who could vote. Six states—Indiana, Mississippi, Illinois, Alabama, Missouri, and Maine—entered the Union between 1816 and 1821, and none of them required voters to own property. Meanwhile, proponents for suffrage liberalization won major victories in the older eastern states. Constitutional conventions in Connecticut in 1818 and Massachusetts and New York in 1821 eliminated property requirements for voting. By the end of the 1820s, universal white male suffrage was the norm everywhere except Rhode Island, Virginia, and Louisiana.

Broadening the suffrage was part of a general democratization of political structures and procedures in the state governments. Representation in most state legislatures was made more equal by giving more seats to newer, rapidly growing regions in the backcountry. States removed or reduced property qualifications for officeholding. The selection of local officials and, in many cases, judges was taken out of the hands of governors and executive councils and given to the voters in popular elections. With the end of oral or "stand-up" voting, the act of casting a ballot became more private and freer from the intimidation of influential neighbors. Written ballots were the norm by the 1820s. Most significant for national politics, voters acquired the power to choose presidential electors. In 1800, only two states had provided for a statewide popular vote in presidential elections. By 1824, most did so, and by 1832 only South Carolina still clung to the practice of having the state legislature choose the electors (see Map 10-1).

Several currents swelled the movement for democratic reform. Limiting voting rights to those who owned landed property seemed increasingly elitist when economic changes were producing new classes—workers, clerks, and small tradesmen—whose livelihoods were not tied directly to the land. At the same time, the middling and lower ranks of society demanded the ballot and access to offices to protect themselves from the commercial and manufacturing interests, who benefited most from economic change. Propertyless laborers in Richmond argued in an 1829 petition that "virtue [and] intelligence are not among the products of the soil. Attachment to property, often a sordid sentiment, is not to be confounded with the sacred flame of patriotism."

Of greatest importance, however, was the incessant demand that all white men be treated equally. Seth Luther, an advocate for workers' rights, insisted that "we wish nothing, but those equal rights, which were designed for us all." The logical extension of the ideology of the American Revolution, with its leveling attacks against kings and aristocrats, this demand for

Map 10-1 Methods of Electing Presidential Electors, 1800 and 1824

The Constitution permits each state legislature to choose the method of electing presidential electors for its state. In 1800 the legislatures in most states appointed the electors. By 1824 most states had adopted more democratic systems in which electors pledged to specific presidential candidates were selected by popular vote in statewide elections.

Data Source: U.S. *Bureau of the Census*, Historical Statistics of the United States, Colonial Times to 1957 (1960), p. 681.

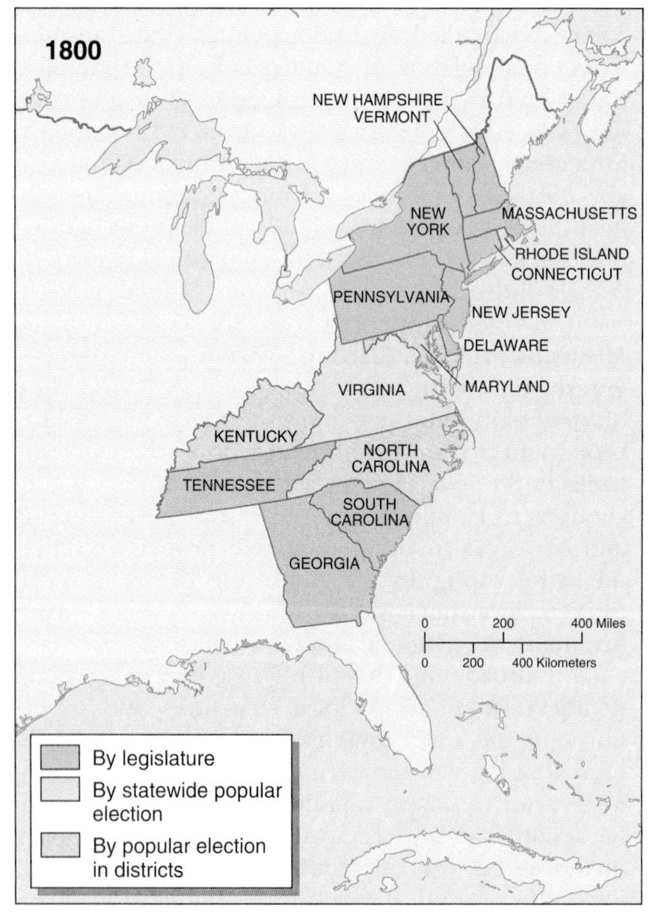

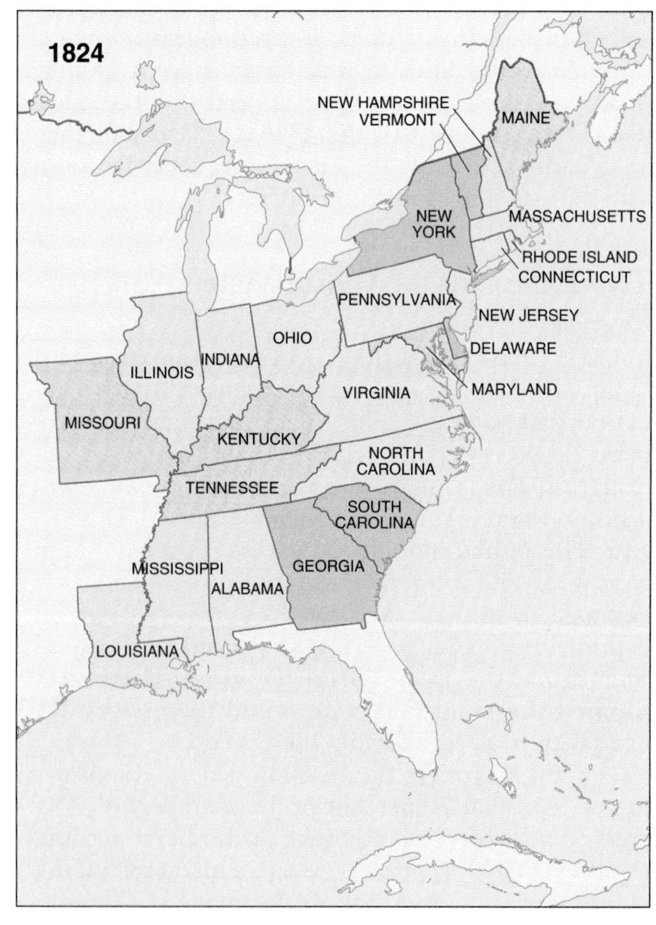

Chronology

1826 Disappearance of William Morgan.

1827 Emergence of the Anti-Masons, the first third party.

1828 Andrew Jackson elected president.

John Calhoun writes *The South Carolina Exposition and Protest.*

1830 Congress passes the Indian Removal Act.

1831 William Lloyd Garrison starts publication of *The Liberator.*

Nat Turner leads a slave uprising in Virginia.

1832 Jackson vetoes bill for rechartering the Second Bank of the United States; Bank War begins.

South Carolina nullifies the Tariffs of 1828 and 1832.

Jackson reelected.

1833 Congress passes the Force Act and the Compromise Tariff.

American Anti-Slavery Society established.

1834 Whig party begins to organize.

1836 Texas War of Independence and establishment of the Republic of Texas.

Congress passes first gag rule on abolitionist petitions.

Van Buren elected president.

1837 Panic of 1837 sets off a depression.

1840 Independent Treasury Act passes.

William Henry Harrison elected as first Whig president.

1841 John Tyler succeeds to presidency on death of Harrison.

1842 United States and Britain sign the Webster–Ashburton Treaty.

1844 Polk elected president.

Gag rule repealed.

1845 Texas admitted to the Union.

equality made republicanism by the 1820s synonymous with simple majority rule. If any white male was the equal of any other, regardless of wealth or property holdings, then only the will of the majority could be the measure of a republican government.

As political opportunities expanded for white males, they shrank for women and free black people. In the state constitutions of the Revolutionary era, free black males who met the minimum property requirements usually had the same voting rights as white males. New Jersey's constitution of 1776 was exceptional in also granting the suffrage to single women and widows who owned property. By the early 1800s, race and gender began to replace wealth and status as the basis for defining the limits of political participation. Thus when New Jersey's new constitution in 1807 broadened suffrage by requiring only a simple taxpaying qualification to vote, it specifically denied the ballot to women and free black men. In state after state, the same constitutional conventions that embraced universal suffrage for white men deprived black men of the vote or burdened them with special property qualifications. Moreover, none of the ten states that entered the Union from 1821 to 1861 allowed black suffrage. African Americans protested in vain. "Foreigners and aliens to the government and laws," complained black New Yorkers in 1837, "strangers to our institutions, are permitted to flock to this land and in a few years are endowed with all the privileges of citizens; but we native born Americans . . . are most of us shut out." By the 1850s, black males could vote only in certain New England states.

The linkage of democracy with white manhood was not accidental. Advocates of greater democratization explicitly argued that only white males had the intelligence and love of liberty to be entrusted with political rights. Women, they said, were too weak and emotional, black people too lazy and lascivious. In denouncing distinctions drawn on property as artificial and demeaning, the white egalitarians simultaneously erected new distinctions based on race and sex that were supposedly natural and hence immutable. Thus personal liberties were now to be guarded not by propertied gentlemen but by all white men, whose equality ultimately rested on assumptions of their shared political superiority over women and nonwhite people.

The Popular Religious Revolt

In religion as well as politics, ordinary Americans demanded a greater voice in the early nineteenth century. Insurgent religious movements rejected the formalism and traditional Calvinism of the Congregational and Presbyterian churches, the dominant Protestant denominations in Washington's America. In a blaze of fervor known as the **Second Great Awakening**, evangelical sects led by the Methodists and Baptists radically transformed the religious landscape between 1800 and 1840. A more popularly rooted Christianity moved outward and downward as it spread across frontier areas and converted marginalized and common folk. By 1850, one in three Americans was a regular churchgoer, a dramatic increase since 1800.

The Baptists and Methodists, both spinning off numerous splinter groups, grew spectacularly and were the largest religious denominations by the 1820s. The key to their success was their ability to give a religious expression to the same popular impulse behind democratic reform. Especially in the backcountry of the South and West, where the first revivals occurred, itinerant preachers reshaped religion to fit the needs and values of ordinary Americans.

Evangelical Christianity emphasized personal, heartfelt experience that would produce a spiritual rebirth. Preaching became a form of theater in which scenes of damnation and salvation were acted out by both preacher and audience. The emotional force unleashed at the mass revivals known as camp meetings astounded observers. "The scene that then presented itself to my mind was indescribable," recalled James Finley of the camp meeting at Cane Ridge, Kentucky, in 1801. "At one time I saw at least five hundred swept down in a moment, as if a battery of a thousand guns had been opened upon them, and then immediately followed shrieks and shouts that rent the very heavens."

The evangelical religion of the traveling preachers was democratic in its populist rejection of traditional religious canons and its encouragement of organizational forms that gave a voice to popular culture. Salvation was no longer simply bestowed by an implacable God as taught by the Calvinist doctrine of individual predestination. Ordinary people could now actively choose salvation, and this possibility was exhilarating. "Why, then, I can be saved!" exclaimed Jesse Lee upon hearing a Methodist preacher in Massachusetts. "I have been taught that only a part of the race could be saved, but if this man's singing be true, all may be saved." Evangelical churches bound the faithful into tightly knit communities that expressed and enforced local values and standards of conduct. Their hymns borrowed melodies from popular music and were accompanied by fiddles and other folk instruments.

The Second Great Awakening originated on the frontier. Preachers were adept at arousing emotional fervor, and women in particular responded to the evangelical message of spiritual equality open to all who would accept Christ into their lives.

Evangelicalism was a religion of the common people, and it appealed especially to women and African Americans. The revivals converted about twice as many women as men. Excluded from most areas of public life, women found strength and comfort in the evangelical message of Christian love and equality. Church membership offered them, as the wife of a Connecticut minister explained, a welcome release from "being treated like beasts of burden [and] drudges of domineering masters." In the first flush of evangelical excitement, female itinerant preachers spread the gospel up and down the East Coast. By thus defying social convention, these women offered a model of independent action. Other women organized their own institutions within denominations still formally controlled by men. Women activists founded and largely directed hundreds of church-affiliated charitable societies and missionary associations.

Evangelicalism also empowered black Americans. African-American Christianity experienced its first sustained growth in the generation after the Revolutionary War. As a result of their uncompromising commitment to convert slaves, the Baptists and Methodists led the way. They welcomed slaves at their revivals, encouraged black preachers, and, above all else, advocated secular and spiritual equality. Many of the early Baptist and Methodist preachers directly challenged slavery. In converting to Methodism, one slave stated that "from the sermon I heard, I felt that God had made all men free and equal, and that I ought not be a slave." Perceiving in it the promise of liberty and deliverance, the slaves received the evangelical gospel in loud, joyous, and highly emotional revivals. They made it part of their own culture, fusing Christianity with folk beliefs from their African heritage.

But for all its liberating appeal to women and African Americans, evangelicalism was eventually limited by race and gender in much the same way as the democratic reform movement. Denied positions of authority in white-dominated churches and resentful of white opposition to integrated worship, free black Northerners founded their own independent churches. As increasing numbers of planters embraced evangelicalism after the 1820s, southern evangelicals first muted their attacks on slavery and then developed a full-blown religious defense of it based on the biblical sanctioning of human bondage. They similarly cited the Old Testament patriarchs to defend the unquestioned authority of fathers over their households, the masters of slaves, women, and children. Many popular religious sects in the North also used a particular reading of the Bible to exalt the independence of white males at the expense of the dependence of everyone else.

In religion as well as politics, white men retained the power in Jacksonian America. Still, the Second Great Awakening removed a major intellectual barrier to political democracy. Traditional Protestant theology—whether Calvinist, Anglican, or Lutheran—viewed the mass of humanity as sinners predestined to damnation and hence was loath to accept the idea that those same sinners, by majority vote, should make crucial political decisions. In rejecting this theology, ordinary Americans made a fundamental intellectual breakthrough. "Salvation open to all" powerfully reinforced the legitimacy of "one man, one vote."

The Rise of the Jacksonians

The Jacksonian Democrats were the first party to mold and organize the democratizing impulse in popular culture. At the core of the Jacksonian appeal was the same rejection of established authority that was the hallmark of the secular and religious populists. Much like the revivalists and the democratic reformers, the Jacksonians also fashioned techniques of communication that tapped into the hopes and fears of ordinary Americans. In so doing, they built the first mass-based party in American history.

In Andrew Jackson the new **Democratic party** that formed between 1824 and 1828 had the perfect candidate for the increasingly democratic temperament of the 1820s. Born of Scots-Irish ancestry on the Carolina frontier in 1767, Jackson was a self-made product of the southern backcountry. Lacking any formal education, family connections, or inherited wealth to ease his way, he relied on his own wits and raw courage to carve out a career as a frontier lawyer and planter in Tennessee. He won fame as the military savior of the republic with his victory at the Battle of New Orleans. Conqueror of the British, the Spanish, and the Indians, all of whom had blocked frontier expansion, he achieved incredible popularity in his native South. His strengths and prejudices were those most valued by the restless, mobile Americans to whom he became a folk hero.

As a presidential candidate, Jackson's image was that of the antielitist champion of the people. "Take for your President a man from your own body, untainted by the corruption of a court and uninitiated in Cabinet secrets," urged a New Jersey Jackson convention in 1824. Jackson lost the election of 1824, but his defeat turned out to be a blessing in disguise. The wheeling and dealing in Congress that gave the presidency to John Quincy Adams enveloped that administration in a cloud of suspicion from the start. It also enhanced Jackson's appeal as the honest tribune of the people whose rightful claim to the presidency had been spurned by intriguing politicians in Washington. His supporters now claimed that the people, as well as Jackson, had been swindled by the "corrupt bargain" between Adams and Clay.

Moreover, the ill-fated Adams presidency virtually destroyed itself. Though the same age as Jackson, Adams seemed frozen in an eighteenth-century past in which aloof gentlemanly statesmen disdainfully refused to turn to the people for support. Uncomfortable with the give-and-take of politics or the very idea of building a coalition to support himself, Adams was out of touch with the political realities of the 1820s.

Just how out of touch was revealed when Adams delivered his first annual message to Congress in 1825. He presented a bold vision of an activist federal government promoting economic growth, social advancement, and scientific progress. Such a vision might have received a fair hearing in 1815, when postwar nationalism was in full stride. In 1825, it amounted to political suicide. Postwar nationalism had dissolved into sectional bickering and burning resentments against banks, tariffs, and the political establishment, blamed for the hard times after the Panic of 1819. The Jacksonians charged that an administration born in corruption now wanted to waste the people's money by promoting more corruption and greed. And when Adams urged Americans not "to proclaim to the world that we are palsied by the will of our constituents," the Jacksonians attacked him as an arrogant aristocrat contemptuous of the common man.

Little of Adams's program passed Congress, and his nationalist vision drove his opponents into the Jackson camp. Southern planters jumped onto the Jackson bandwagon out of fear that Adams might use federal power against slavery; more Westerners joined because Adams revived their suspicions of the East. The most important addition came from New York, where Martin Van Buren had built the **Albany Regency**, a tightly disciplined state political machine.

Van Buren was a new breed of politician, a professional who made a business out of politics. The son of a tavern keeper, he quickly grasped as a young lawyer how politics could open up career opportunities. The discipline and regularity of strict party organization gave him and others from the middling ranks a winning edge in competition against their social betters. In battling against the system of family-centered wealth and prestige on which politics had previously been based, Van Buren redefined parties as something good in and of themselves. Indeed, he and his followers argued that parties were indispensable instruments for the successful expression of the popular will against the dominance of elites.

State leaders such as Van Buren organized the first national campaign that relied extensively on new techniques of mass mobilization. In rallying support for Jackson against Adams in 1828, they put together chains of party-subsidized newspapers and coordinated a frantic schedule of meetings and rallies. Grass-roots Jackson committees reached out to the voters by knocking on their doors, pressing party literature into their hands, dispensing mass-produced medals and buttons with a likeness of Jackson, and lavishly entertaining all who would give them a hearing. Politics became a folk spectacle as torchlight parades awakened sleepy towns and political barbecues doled out whiskey and food to farmers from the surrounding countryside.

To the opponents of the Jacksonians, elections had become a degrading spectacle in which conniving Democratic politicians, such as the one shown below handing a voting ticket to the stereotypical Irishman in the light coat, were corrupting the republic's political culture.

The election of 1828 centered on personalities, not issues. This in itself was a victory for Jackson's campaign managers, who proved far more skillful in the new presidential game of image making then their Adams counterparts, now known as the National Republicans. Although both sides tried to depict the other's candidate as morally unfit, the Jackson men were more in tune with a public sentiment that identified Adams's call for a strong government with special privileges for the favored few. Thus for many voters, Adams personified a discredited elite and Jackson the voice of the people.

Jackson carried every state south and west of Pennsylvania in 1828 and polled 56 percent of the popular vote (see Map 10-2). Voter turnout shot up to 55 percent from the apathetic 25 percent of 1824. Adams ran well only in New England and in commercialized areas producing goods for outside markets. Aside from the South, where he was virtually untouchable, Jackson's appeal was strongest among ordinary Americans who valued their local independence and felt threatened by outside centers of power beyond their control. He rolled up heavy majorities from Scots-Irish farmers in the Baptist-Methodist evangelical belt of the backcountry and from unskilled workers with an Irish Catholic background. To these voters, Jackson was a double hero, for he had defeated their hated British enemy and promised to do the same to the Yankee capitalists of the Northeast and all the elitist politicians. Democracy, they were convinced, had at last come to presidential politics.

Map 10-2 The Election of 1828
Andrew Jackson won a decisive victory in 1828 by sweeping the South and West and making major inroads in the Northeast.

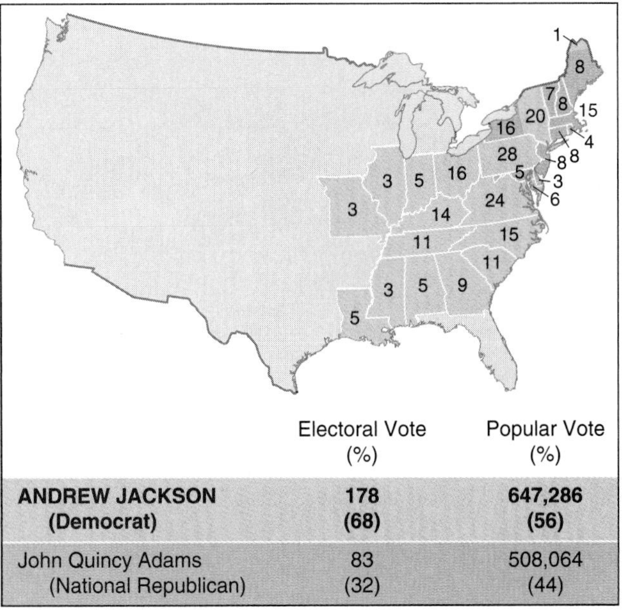

	Electoral Vote (%)	Popular Vote (%)
ANDREW JACKSON (Democrat)	**178 (68)**	**647,286 (56)**
John Quincy Adams (National Republican)	83 (32)	508,064 (44)

Jackson's Presidency

Once in office, Jackson proved to be the most forceful and energetic president since Jefferson. Like a military chieftain tolerating no interference from his subordinates, Jackson dominated his presidency with the sheer force of his personality. At one time or another, his administration angered southern planters, frightened eastern bankers and commercial interests, and outraged New England reformers. Nonetheless, Jackson remained popular because he portrayed himself as the embodiment of the people's will.

This 1845 painting captures the heroic, forceful side of Andrew Jackson that made him so appealing to many voters.

Thomas Sully, "General Andrew Jackson," 1845. Oil on canvas. In the Collection of The Corcoran Gallery of Art, Washington, D.C. Gift of William Wilson Corcoran.

The Jacksonians had no particular program in 1828, and Jackson shrewdly had avoided taking a stand on divisive issues. Apart from removing Indians to areas west of the Mississippi River, Jackson's first term was notable primarily for its political infighting. Two political struggles that came to a head in 1832–1833—the **Bank War** and the **nullification crisis**—stamped the Jacksonians with a lasting party identity. By destroying the Second Bank of the United States and rejecting the attempt of South Carolina to nullify (or annul) a national tariff, Jackson firmly established the Democrats as the enemy of special privilege, the friend of the common man, and the defender of the Union. Consequently, even when Jackson stepped down in 1836, the Democrats were so identified with the interests of the people that they were able to elect Van Buren, who had none of Jackson's personal magnetism or broad appeal.

The Jacksonian Appeal

Jackson's inauguration struck many conservatives as ushering in a vulgar new order in national affairs. A vast crowd poured into Washington to applaud their hero. They cheered loudly when Jackson took his oath of office and then rushed to the White House for a postinauguration reception. Any semblance of order broke down as they pressed in on waiters trying to serve them refreshments. Bowls of liquor-laced punch went flying, and glass and china crashed to the floor as a seeming mob surged through the White House. "But it was the People's day," reported one conservative onlooker, "and the People's President and the People would rule. God grant that one day or other, the People do not put down all rule and rulers."

Ordinary Americans identified with Jackson as with no earlier president, and he convinced them that he was using his office as the instrument of their will. Although led by wealthy planters and entrepreneurs who were hardly average Americans, the Jacksonians skillfully depicted themselves as the champions of the common man against the aristocratic interests who had enriched themselves through special privileges granted by the government. Jackson proclaimed his task as one of restoring the federal government to the ideal of Jeffersonian republicanism, in which farmers and artisans could pursue their individual liberty free of any government intervention that favored the rich and powerful.

Jackson began his assault on special privilege by proclaiming a reform of the appointment process for federal officeholders. Accusing his predecessors, especially Adams, of having created a social elite of self-serving bureaucrats, he vowed to make government service more responsive to the popular will. He insisted that federal jobs required no special expertise or training and proposed to rotate honest, hardworking citizens in and out of the civil service.

Jackson's reform of the federal bureaucracy had more style than substance. He removed only about one-fifth of the officeholders he inherited, and most of his appointees came from the same relatively high-status groups as the Adams people. But by providing a democratic rationale for government service, he opened the way for future presidents to move more aggressively against incumbents. Thus emerged the **spoils system**, in which the victorious party gave government jobs to its supporters and removed the appointees of the defeated party. This was a powerful

The inauguration of Andrew Jackson in 1829 brought out an unprecedented mob of well-wishers anxious for a glimpse of the new president.

technique for building party strength, because it tied party loyalty to the reward of a federal appointment.

When Jackson railed against economic privilege, he most often had in mind Henry Clay's American System. Clay's program called for a protective tariff, a national bank, and federal subsidies for internal improvements; his goal was to bind Americans together in an integrated national market. To the Democrats, Clay's system represented government favoritism at its worst, a set of costly benefits at the public's expense for special-interest groups who corrupted politicians in their quest for economic power. In 1830, Jackson found the perfect opportunity to strike a blow for the Democratic conception of the limited federal role in economic development. He vetoed the Maysville Road Bill, which would have provided federal money for a road to be built entirely within Kentucky. The bill was unconstitutional, he claimed, because it benefited only the citizens of Kentucky and not the American people as a whole. Moreover, since the Maysville project was within Clay's congressional district, Jackson had the added delight of embarrassing his most prominent political enemy.

On the issue of internal improvements, as well as bureaucratic reform, the Democrats placed party needs ahead of ideology. Jackson's Maysville veto did not rule out congressional appropriations for projects deemed beneficial to the general public. This pragmatic loophole gave Democrats all the room they needed to pass more internal improvement projects during Jackson's presidency than during all of the previous administrations together. Having built a mass party, the Democrats soon discovered that they had to funnel federal funds to their constituents back home.

Any support Jackson might have lost among market-minded entrepreneurs and farmers in the West by his Maysville veto was more than made up by the popularity of his Indian removal policy. Jackson's strongest base of support was in the West and South, and by driving Native Americans from these regions, he more than lived up to his billing as the friend of the common (white) man.

Indian Removal

Some 125,000 Indians lived east of the Mississippi when Jackson became president. The largest concentration was in the South, where five Indian confederations—the Cherokees, Creeks, Choctaws, Chickasaws, and Seminoles—controlled millions of acres of land in what soon would become the great cotton frontiers of southwestern Georgia and central Alabama and Mississippi. That, of course, was the problem: Native Americans held land that white farmers coveted for their own economic gain.

Pressure from the states to remove the Indians had been building since the end of the War of 1812. It was most intense in Georgia. In early 1825, Georgia authorities finalized a fraudulent treaty that ceded most of the Creek Indians' land to the state. When Adams tried to obtain fairer terms for the Creeks in a new treaty, he was brazenly denounced in Georgia, which based its case for grabbing Indian territory on the inviolability of states' rights. Georgia dared Adams to do something about it; not willing to risk an armed confrontation between federal and state authorities, Adams backed down.

In 1828, Georgia moved against the Cherokees, the best organized and most advanced (by white standards) of the Indian confederations. By now a prosperous society of small farmers with their own written alphabet and schools for their children, the Cherokees wanted to avoid the fate of their Creek neighbors. In 1827, they adopted a constitution declaring themselves an independent nation with complete sovereignty over their land. The Georgia legislature reacted by placing the Cherokees directly under state law, annulling Cherokee laws and even their right to make laws, and legally defining the Cherokees as tenants on

Sequoyah, a Cherokee scholar, developed an alphabet for the Cherokee language that enabled his people to publish a tribal newspaper in both Cherokee and English.

land belonging to the state of Georgia. By also prohibiting Indian testimony in cases against white people, the legislature stripped the Cherokees of any legal rights. They were now easy prey for white settlers, who scrambled onto Cherokee land after gold was discovered in northern Georgia in 1829. Alabama and Mississippi followed Georgia's lead in denying Indians legal rights.

Thus the stage was set for what Jackson always considered the most important measure of his early administration, the **Indian Removal Act.** Jackson had no qualms about allowing state officials to override federal protection of Native Americans. He had long considered the federal policy of negotiating with the Indians as sovereign entities a farce. But it was awkward politically for the president to declare that he had no intention of enforcing treaty obligations of the U.S. government. The way out of this dilemma was to remove Native Americans from the center of the dispute. In his first annual message, Jackson sided with state authorities in the South and advised the Indians "to emigrate beyond the Mississippi or submit to the laws of those States." This advice enabled Jackson to pose as the friend of the Indians, the wise father who would lead them out of harm's way and save them from rapacious white people.

Congress acted on Jackson's recommendation in the Indian Removal Act of 1830. The act appropriated $500,000 for the negotiation of new treaties under which the southern Indians would surrender their territory and be removed to land in the trans-Mississippi area (primarily present-day Oklahoma). Although force was not authorized and Jackson stressed that removal should be voluntary, no federal protection was provided for Indians harassed into leaving by land-hungry settlers. Ultimately, Jackson did deploy the U.S. Army, but only to round up and push out Indians who refused to comply with the new removal treaties.

And so most of the Indians left the eastern United States—the Choctaws in 1830, the Creeks and Chickasaws in 1832, and the Cherokees in 1838 (see Map 10-3). The government was ill-prepared to supervise the removal. The private groups who won the federal contracts for transporting and provisioning the Indians were those who had entered the lowest bids; they were a shady lot interested only in a quick profit. Thousands of Indians, perhaps as many as one-fourth of those who started the trek, died on the way to Oklahoma, the victims of cold, hunger, disease, and the general callousness of the white people they met along

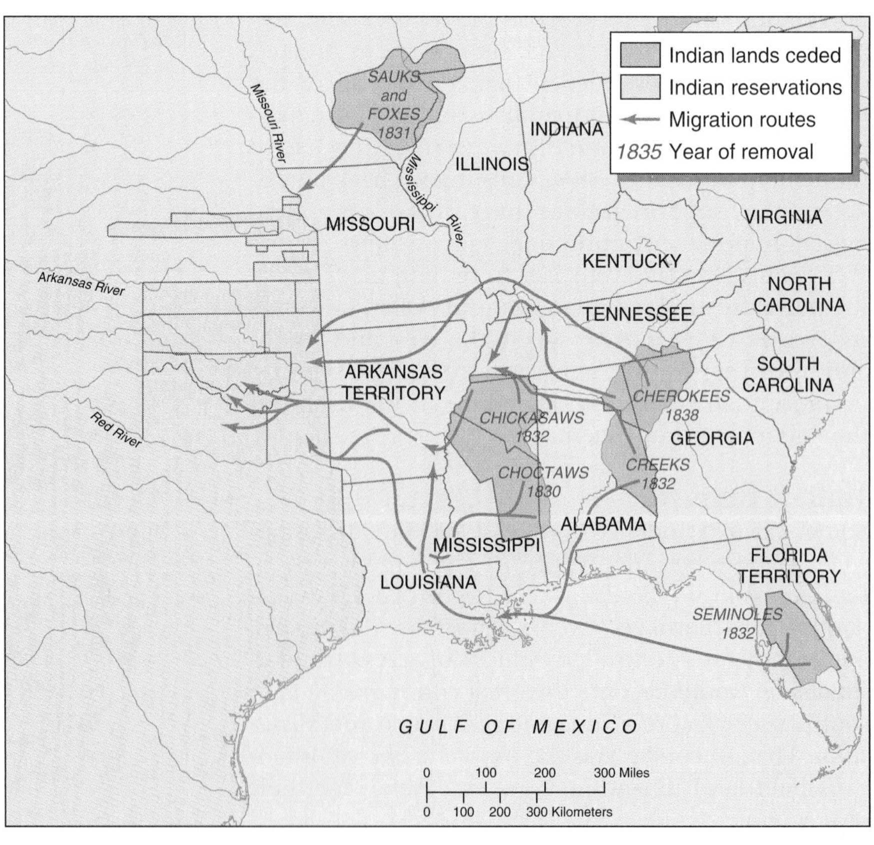

Map 10-3 Indian Removals
The fixed policy of the Jackson administration and pressure from the states forced Native Americans in the 1830s to migrate from their eastern homelands to a special Indian reserve west of the Mississippi River.

the way. "It is impossible to conceive the frightful sufferings that attend these forced migrations," noted a Frenchman who observed the Choctaw removal. It was indeed, as recalled in the collective memory of the Cherokees, a **Trail of Tears**.

Tribes that resisted removal were attacked by white armies. Federal troops joined local militias in 1832 in suppressing the Sauk and Fox Indians of Illinois and Wisconsin in what was called **Black Hawk's War**. More of a frantic attempt by the Indians to reach safety on the west bank of the Mississippi than an actual war, this affair ended in the slaughter of five hundred Indian men, women, and children by white troops and their Sioux allies. The Seminoles held out in the swamps of Florida for seven years between 1835 and 1842 in what became the longest Indian war in American history. Their resistance continued even after their leader, Osceola, was captured while negotiating under a flag of truce.

Jackson forged ahead with his removal policy despite the opposition of eastern reformers and Protestant missionaries. Aligned with conservatives concerned by Jackson's cavalier disregard of federal treaty obligations, they came within three votes of defeating the removal bill in the House of Representatives. Jackson ignored their protests (see "American Views: Memorial and Protest of the Cherokee Nation, 1836") as well as the legal rulings of the Supreme Court. In *Cherokee Nation* v. *Georgia* (1831) and *Worcester* v. *Georgia* (1832), the Court ruled that Georgia had violated the U.S. Constitution in extending its jurisdiction over the Cherokees. Chief Justice Marshall defined Indian tribes as "dependent domestic nations" subject only to the authority of the federal government. Marshall may have won the legal argument, but he was powerless to enforce his decisions without Jackson's cooperation. Aware that Southerners and Westerners were on his side, Jackson ignored the Supreme Court rulings and pushed Indian removal to its tragic conclusion.

The Nullification Crisis

Jackson's stand on Indian removal confirmed the impression of many of his followers that when state and national power conflicted, he could be trusted to side with the states. But when states' rights forces in South Carolina, known as the nullifiers, directly challenged Jackson in the early 1830s over tariff policy—the most sensitive issue involving the power of the national government—they precipitated the most serious sectional crisis since the Missouri debates of 1819–1820. And Jackson, for all his talk of states' rights when it came to Indian policy, revealed himself to be an ardent nationalist on the issue of majority rule in the Union. He won the showdown with South Carolina and established the nationalist credentials of his Democratic party. In reaction to his strong stand, however, the solid front of Democratic power in the South began to crack.

After the first protective tariff in 1816, rates increased further in 1824 and then jumped to 50 percent in 1828 in what was denounced as the "Tariff of Abominations." Southerners were especially angry over the last tariff, because it had been contrived by northern Democrats to win additional northern support for Jackson in his presidential campaign. The outcry was loudest in South Carolina, an old cotton state losing population to the West in the 1820s as cotton prices remained low after the Panic of 1819. What fueled antitariff sentiment was not just the economic argument that high tariffs worsened the agricultural depression in the state by raising the cost of manufactured goods purchased by farmers and planters and lowering the foreign demand for agricultural exports. Protective tariffs were also denounced as an unconstitutional extension of national power over the states; many southern planters feared that they were only a prelude to forced emancipation.

South Carolina was the only state where African Americans made up the majority of the population. Slaves were heavily concentrated in the marshes and tidal flats south of Charleston, the lowcountry district of huge rice plantations. Here black people outnumbered white people ten to one in the summer months. Nat Turner's Rebellion, a bloody slave uprising in Virginia in 1831, and earlier aborted rebellions in the 1820s (see Chapter 13) left fearful planters convinced that growing antislavery agitation in the North and in England was feeding slave unrest. The disturbances so far would be "nothing to what we shall see," warned the South Carolina planter James Hamilton Jr., "if we do not stand manfully at the Safety Valve of Nullification."

Led by the lowcountry planters, the antitariff forces in South Carolina controlled state politics by 1832. They called themselves the nullifiers, a name derived from the constitutional theory developed by Calhoun in an anonymous tract of 1828 titled *The South Carolina Exposition and Protest.* Pushing to its logical extreme the states' rights doctrine first outlined in the Kentucky and Virginia Resolutions of 1798, Calhoun argued that a state, acting through a popularly elected convention, had the sovereign power to declare an act of

American Views

Memorial and Protest of the Cherokee Nation, 1836

Of the major tribes in the Southeast, the Cherokees fought longest and hardest against the Jacksonian policy of Indian removal. Led by their principal chief, John Ross, the son of a Scot and a mixed-blood Cherokee woman, they submitted the following protest to Congress against the fraudulent 1835 Treaty of New Echota forced on them by the state of Georgia. Although clearly opposed by an overwhelming majority of the Cherokees, this treaty provided the legal basis for the forced removal of the Cherokee people from Georgia to the Indian Territory.

- **On what legal grounds did the Cherokees base their protest? What pledges had been made to them by the U. S. government?**
- **What did the Cherokees mean when they said they had been "taught to think and feel as the American citizen"? If the Cherokees had become "civilized" by white standards, why did most whites still insist on their removal?**
- **Why would President Jackson have allowed white intruders to remain on land reserved by treaties for the Cherokees?**
- **Do you feel that the Cherokees were justified in believing that they had been betrayed by the American government?**

The undersigned representatives of the Cherokee nation, east of the river Mississippi, impelled by duty, would respectfully submit . . . the following statement of facts: It will be seen, from the numerous treaties between the Cherokee nation and the United States, that from the earliest existence of this government, the United States, in Congress assembled, received the Cherokees and

the national government null and inoperative. Once a state nullified a law, it was to remain unenforceable within that state's borders unless three-fourths of all the states approved a constitutional amendment delegating to the national government the power that was challenged. If such an amendment passed, the nullifying state had the right to leave the Union.

Calhoun, who had been elected vice president in 1828, openly embraced nullification only after he had broken with Jackson. When Calhoun's wife and friends snubbed Peggy Eaton, the wife of Jackson's secretary of war, on the grounds that she was a "loose woman" who had driven her first husband to suicide, Jackson was convinced that Calhoun was plotting to discredit his administration. He believed that the South Carolinian wanted "to coerce me to abandon Eaton, and thereby bring on me disgrace for having appointed him, and thereby weaken me in the affections of the nation, and open the way to his preferment or my ruin." Then, in what finalized the break, friends of Van Buren, who was secretary of state, leaked the information that Calhoun, while secretary of war under President James Monroe, had favored censuring Jackson for his 1818 raid into Spanish Florida. Deceived by Calhoun as to his role in the affair, Jackson felt betrayed and vowed political revenge.

An outcast in Jackson's administration by 1830, Calhoun also faced the danger of losing con-their nation into favor and protection; and that the chiefs and warriors, for themselves and all parts of the Cherokee nation, acknowledged themselves and the said Cherokee nation to be under the protection of the United States of America, and of no other sovereign whatsoever: they also stipulated, that the said Cherokee nation will not hold any treaty with any foreign power, individual State, or with individuals of any State: that for, and in consideration of, valuable concessions made by the Cherokee nation, the United States solemnly guaranteed to said nation all their lands not ceded, and pledged the faith of the government, that "all white people who have intruded, or may hereafter intrude, on the lands reserved for the Cherokees, shall be removed by the United States, and proceeded against, according to the provisions of the act, passed 30th March, 1802," entitled "An act to regulate trade and intercourse with the Indian tribes, and to preserve peace on the frontiers." It would be useless to recapitulate the numerous provisions for the security and protection of the rights of the Cherokees, to be found in the various treaties between their nation and the United States. The Cherokees were happy and prosperous under a scrupulous observance of treaty stipulations by the government of the United States, and from the fostering hand extended over them, they made rapid advances in civilization, morals, and in the arts and sciences. Little did they anticipate, that when taught to think and feel as the American citizen, and to have with him a common interest, they were to be despoiled by their guardian, to become strangers and wanderers in the land of their fathers, forced to return to the savage life, and to seek a new home in the wilds of the far west, and that without their consent. An instrument purporting to be a treaty with the Cherokee people, has recently been made public by the President of the United States, that will have such an operation, if carried into effect. This instrument, the delegation aver before the civilized world, and in the presence of Almighty God, is fraudulent, false upon its face, made by unauthorized individuals, without the sanction, and against the wishes, of the great body of the Cherokee people. Upwards of fifteen thousand of those people have protested against it, solemnly declaring they will never acquiesce. . . .

Source: U.S. Congress, Executive Documents *(1836).*

trol of his political base in South Carolina. Unless he publicly identified himself with nullification, his leadership of the state would be threatened. With Calhoun's approval, a South Carolina convention in November 1832 nullified the tariffs of 1828 and 1832 (a compromise tariff that did not reduce rates low enough to satisfy the nullifiers). The convention decreed that customs duties were not to be collected in South Carolina after February 1, 1833.

Calhoun always insisted that nullification was not secession. He defended his doctrine as a constitutional means of protecting minority rights within a Union dominated by a tyrannical national majority. Jackson rejected such reasoning as the talk of a scheming disunionist. He considered nullification a dangerous and nonsensical perversion of the Constitution, and he vowed to crush any attempt to block the enforcement of federal laws. He told a congressman from South Carolina that "if a single drop of blood shall be shed there in opposition to the laws of the United States, I will hang the first man I can lay my hand on engaged in such treasonable conduct, upon the first tree I can reach."

In January 1833, Jackson, in the Force Bill, asked for and received from Congress full authorization to put down nullification by military force. Simultaneously, he worked to defuse nullification by supporting a new tariff that would cut duties by half within two years. Because Jackson's opponents in Congress did not want him to get political credit for

AMERICA'S JOURNEY

FROM THEN TO NOW

From the Eaton Affair to Monicagate

Sex and scandal have long been linked in Washington politics. Just as the Eaton Affair dominated the early years of Andrew Jackson's presidency, so also did the affair dubbed Monicagate rock the second administration of President Bill Clinton.

Just before Jackson's inauguration, John Eaton, a close friend soon to be appointed secretary of war, married Margaret O'Neale Timberlake, the widowed daughter of a Washington tavern keeper. In the eyes of Washington society, the flirtatious Timberlake was a fallen woman rumored to have been sexually involved with several men, including Eaton before their marriage. When the wives of Jackson's cabinet members, led by Floride Calhoun, the wife of Vice President John C. Calhoun, pointedly ostracized the Eatons and shut them out of polite society, Jackson rallied to their defense.

Jackson's wife Rachel had suffered from politically motivated scandalmongering because she had unwittingly married Jackson before securing a divorce from her first husband. Jackson saw in Margaret Eaton's detractors the same kind of slanderous political scheming he held responsible for Rachel's death in 1828. His reaction turned a social scandal into a political one. In the spring of 1831 he forced the resignations of five of his six cabinet members for their refusal to accept the Eatons. The controversy received so much attention because many Americans, dismayed by the democratization of political life, identified Margaret Eaton with the immoral forces they saw challenging proper standards of social behavior.

For the remainder of the nineteenth century, no sexual scandal matched the Eaton affair as a disruptive force in national politics. In 1884, Democratic presidential nominee Grover Cleveland defused Republican accusations that he had fathered an illegitimate child by candidly admitting he had and pulled out a narrow victory.

In the twentieth century, personality became increasingly important in presidential politics. Until recently, however, the press treated a president's private life, particularly extramarital affairs, as mostly off limits to public scrutiny. All this, of course, changed with the presidency of Bill Clinton.

The roots of this change can be traced in part to the highly publicized and praised role of the press in exposing the scandals of the Nixon administration in the 1970s. Thereafter, coverage of national affairs became more investigative and distrustful of authority. At the same time increasing competition among media organizations for ratings and profits increased the demand for sex and sensationalism in the news.

By the 1990s, presidential character was fair game for the media, and Clinton as candidate and president faced a host of questions about his sex life. These questions metastasized into a constitutional crisis in 1998 when the House of Representatives passed articles of impeachment against Clinton for alleged offenses he committed attempting to cover up his involvement with White House intern Monica Lewinsky.

Both intense partisanship and genuine outrage at the president's actions explain much of the snowballing impact of Monicagate. But more was involved. Unwittingly, Clinton, like Margaret Eaton, served as a lightning rod for pent-up anxieties over profound changes in American society. In Eaton's case, the anxieties resulted from the unsettling changes associated with the democratization of American politics. Today, the anxieties result from transformations that began in the 1960s, including the civil rights revolution, increased freedom of sexual expression, the feminist movement, and the campaign for gay liberation.

Surely an argument can be made that a national debate over the impact of these social changes is long overdue. But to be meaningful, such a debate should focus on more than the character failings of individual presidents.

Depicted in the cartoon below as a stylish dancer appearing before Jackson and his cabinet (Martin Van Buren is the leering figure at the far right), Peggy Timberlake was at the center of the first sex scandal to rock Washington politics.

brokering a compromise, they pushed through their own tariff measure. The Compromise Tariff of 1833 lowered duties to 20 percent but extended the reductions over a ten-year period. Up against this combination of the carrot and the stick, the nullifiers backed down.

Jackson reacted swiftly and decisively when challenged by the nullifiers. His stand established the principle of national supremacy grounded in the will of the majority. Despite his victory, however, states' rights doctrines remained popular both in the South and among many northern Democrats. South Carolina had been isolated in its stand on nullification, but many Southerners, and especially slaveholders, agreed that the powers of the national government had to be strictly limited. Their quarrel with the nullifiers was one of tactics, not objectives. Moreover, by dramatically affirming his right to use force against a state in defense of the Union, Jackson drove many planters out of the Democratic party. In the shock waves set off by the nullification crisis, a new anti-Jackson coalition began to form in the South.

The Bank War

What amounted to a war against the Bank of the United States became the centerpiece of Jackson's presidency and a defining event for the Democratic party. The Bank War erupted in 1832 when Jackson was presented with draft legislation for the early rechartering of the national bank. His thunderous veto kept banking and currency issues in the forefront of national politics for the remainder of the decade.

Like most Westerners, Jackson distrusted banks. Because gold and silver coins were scarce and the national government did not issue or regulate paper currency, money consisted primarily of notes issued as loans by private and state banks. These bank notes fluctuated in value in accordance with the reputation and creditworthiness of the issuing banks. In the credit-starved West, banks were particularly unreliable. Many were "wildcat" operations that made a quick profit by issuing notes without the gold or silver reserves to redeem them and then skipping town when they were on the verge of being found out. Even when issued by honest bankers, notes often could not be redeemed at face value because of market conditions. All of this struck many Americans, and especially farmers and workers, as inherently dishonest. They wanted to be paid in "real" money, gold or silver coin, and they viewed bankers as parasites who did nothing but fatten their own pockets by manipulating paper money.

The largest and most powerful bank was the Bank of the United States, and citizens who were wiped out or forced to retrench drastically by the Panic of 1819 never forgave the Bank for saving itself at the expense of its debtors. Still, under the astute leadership of a new president, Nicholas Biddle of Philadelphia, the Bank performed well in the 1820s. Prosperous times had returned, and the Bank underwrote the economic expansion with its healthy credit reserves and stable banknotes. By 1832, the Bank was as popular as it ever would be.

Beginning with his first annual message, Jackson had been making noise about not rechartering the Bank, at least in its present form. Searching for an issue to use against Jackson in the presidential campaign of 1832, Clay then forced Jackson's hand. Clay convinced Biddle to apply to Congress for a new charter, even though the current charter would not expire until 1836. Confident of congressional approval, Clay reasoned that he had Jackson trapped. If Jackson went along with the new charter, Clay could take credit for the measure. If he vetoed it, Clay could attack Jackson as the enemy of a sound banking system.

Clay's clever strategy backfired. Jackson turned on him and the Bank with a vengeance. As he told his heir apparent, "The bank, Mr. Van Buren, is trying to kill me, *but I will kill it!*" Jackson and his advisers realized that the Bank was vulnerable as a symbol of privileged monopoly, a monstrous institution that deprived common Americans of their right to compete equally for economic advantage. Moreover, many of these advisers were also state bankers and local developers who backed Jackson precisely because they wanted to be free of federal restraints on their business activities. On July 10, 1832, Jackson vetoed the rechartering bill for the Bank in a message that appealed both to state bankers and to foes of all banks. He took a ringing "stand against all new grants of monopolies and exclusive privileges, against any prostitution of our Government to the advancement of the few at the expense of the many."

The business community and eastern elites lashed out at Jackson's veto as the demagogic ravings of an economic fool. For Biddle, the veto message had "all the fury of a chained panther, biting the bars of his cage." In rejecting Jackson's claims that the Bank had fostered speculative and corrupt financial practices, the pro-Bank forces had the better of the economic argument. But Jackson won the political battle, and he went to the people in the election of 1832 as their champion against the banking aristocracy. Although his support was no stronger than

This Democratic cartoon portrays Jackson as the champion of the people attacking the Bank of the United States, a many-headed monster whose tentacles of corruption spread throughout the states.

"General Jackson caricature slaying the many-headed monster," 1836. Courtesy of Collection of The New York Historical Society.

in 1828, he easily defeated Clay, the candidate of the short-lived **National Republican party** that had also backed Adams in 1828.

Having blocked the rechartering of the Bank when Congress failed to override his veto, Jackson then set out to destroy it, claiming his reelection in 1832 as a mandate to do so. He finally found a secretary of the treasury (his first two choices refused) who agreed to sign the order removing federal deposits from the Bank in 1833. Drained of its lifeblood, the deposits, the Bank was reduced by 1836 to seeking a charter as a private corporation in the state of Pennsylvania. In the meantime, the government's monies were deposited in "pet banks," state banks controlled by loyal Democrats.

Jackson won the Bank War, but he left the impression that the Democrats had played fast and loose with the nation's credit system. The economy overheated in his second term. High commodity prices and abundant credit, both at home and abroad, propelled a buying frenzy of western lands. Prices soared, and inevitably the speculative bubble had to burst. When it did, the Democrats would be open to the charge of having squandered the people's money by shifting deposits to reckless state bankers who were part of a corrupt new alliance between the government and private economic interests. Jackson was out of office when the Panic of 1837 hit; Van Buren, his successor, paid the political price for Jackson's economic policies.

Van Buren and Hard Times

Like John Adams and James Madison, Martin Van Buren followed a forceful president who commanded a strong popular following. Fairly or not, he would come out, as they did, second best compared to his predecessor. Where Jackson forged ahead regardless of consequences, Van Buren tended to hang back, carefully calculating all the political angles. This trait served him poorly as president.

Facing a sharp economic downturn, Van Buren appeared indecisive and unwilling to advance a bold program. When the rise of a radical **abolitionist movement** in the North revived sectional tensions over slavery, he awkwardly straddled the the divisive issue. Van Buren's difficult position was made worse by his cautious political style. In the end, he undermined himself by failing to offer a compelling vision of his presidency.

The Panic of 1837

Van Buren was barely settled into the White House when the nation was rocked by a financial panic. For over a decade, the economy had benefited from a favorable business cycle. Easy credit and the availability of territories opened up by Jackson's Indian removal policy generated a stampede to buy land in the West. Government land sales ballooned from under 4 million acres in 1833 to 20 million acres by 1836. As in 1817 and 1818, Americans piled up debt on the assumption that the good times would never end. A banking crisis in 1837 painfully reintroduced economic reality.

Even as it expanded, the American economy had remained vulnerable to disruptions in the supply of foreign capital and the sale of agricultural exports that underpinned prosperity. The key foreign nation was Britain, a major source of credit and demand for exports. In late 1836, the Bank of England tightened its credit policies. Concerned with the large outflow of specie to the United States, it raised interest rates and reduced the credit lines of British merchants heavily involved in the American trade. Consequently, the British demand for cotton fell and with it the price of cotton (see Figure 10-1). Because cotton, as the leading export, was the main security for most loans issued by American banks and mercantile firms, its drop in value set off a chain reaction of contracting credit and falling prices. When panic-stricken investors rushed to the banks to redeem their notes in specie, the hard-pressed banks suspended specie payments.

The shock waves hit New Orleans in March 1837 and spread to the major New York banks by May. What began as a bank panic soon dragged down the entire economy. Bankruptcies multiplied, investment capital dried up, and business stagnated. State governments, which had borrowed lavishly in the heady optimism of the boom years to finance canals and other internal improvements, slashed their budgets and halted all construction projects. Nine states in the South and West defaulted (stopped making payments) on their bonds. Workers in the shoe, textile, mining, and

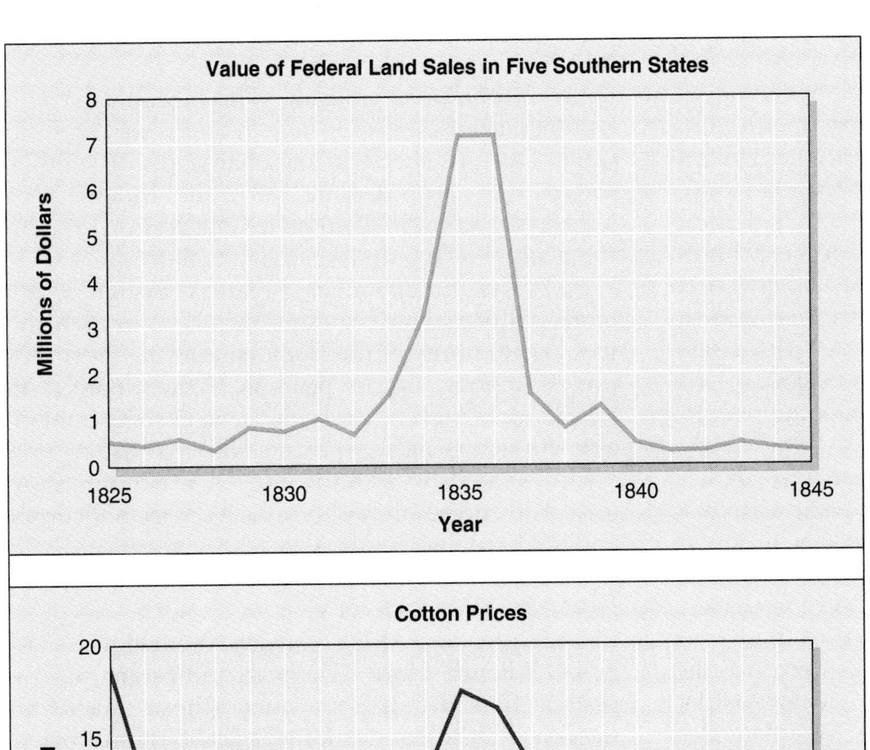

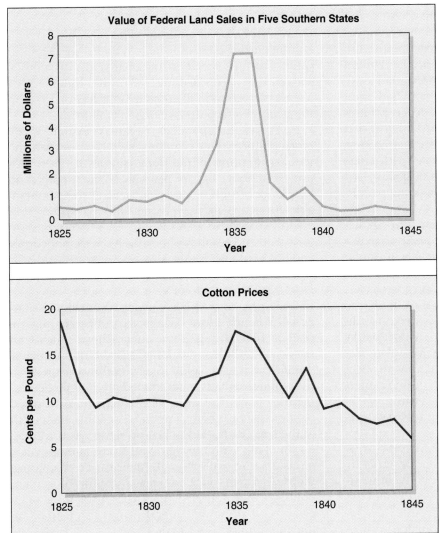

***Figure 10-1* Cotton Prices and the Value of Federal Land Sales in Five Southern States, 1825–1845**
Because the U.S. economy was heavily dependent on cotton exports as a source of credit, the collapse of cotton prices—and a corresponding plunge in the sale of federal land after a speculative runup in the newer cotton regions of the South—triggered a financial panic in the late 1830s.

Data Source: Douglas C. North, The Economic Growth of the United States, 1790–1860 *(1966), tab. A-X, p. 257.*

construction industries suddenly found themselves without jobs. As unemployment mounted and workers mobilized mass protest meetings in eastern cities, conservatives feared the worst. "Workmen thrown out of employ by the hundred daily," nervously noted a wealthy merchant in New York City in May 1837. He half expected that "we shall have a revolution here."

After a brief recovery in 1838, another round of credit contraction drove the economy into a depression that did not bottom out until 1843. In the manufacturing and commercial centers of the Northeast, unemployment reached an unheard-of 20 percent. The persistence of depressed agricultural prices meant that farmers and planters who had incurred debts in the 1830s faced the constant threat of losing their land or their slaves. Many fled west to avoid their creditors.

The Independent Treasury

Although the Democrats bore no direct responsibility for the economic downturn, they could not avoid being blamed for it. Their political opponents, now coalescing as the **Whig party**, pointed to Jackson's destruction of the Bank of the United States, which they claimed had undermined business confidence. In their view, Jackson had then compounded his error by trying to force a hard-money policy on the state banks that had received federal deposits. The "pet banks" were required to replace small-denomination bank notes with coins or hard money. This measure, it was hoped, would protect the farmers and workers from being paid in depreciated bank notes.

Jackson had taken his boldest step against paper money when he issued the **Specie Circular** of 1836, which stipulated that large tracts of public land could be bought only with specie. Aimed at breaking the speculative spiral in land purchases, the Specie Circular likely contributed to the Panic of 1837 by requiring the transfer of specie to the West for land transactions just when eastern banks were strapped for specie reserves to meet demands on their own bank notes. Bankers and speculators denounced Jackson for unwarranted government interference with the natural workings of the economy and blundering into a monetary disaster.

Conservative charges of Democratic irresponsibility were overblown, but the Democrats were caught on the horns of a dilemma. By dramatically politicizing the banking issue and removing federal monies from the national bank, the Democrats had in effect assumed the burden of protecting the people from the paper aristocrats in the banking and business community. Once they shifted treasury receipts to selected state banks, they had to try to regulate these banks. Otherwise they would be accused of creating a series of little "monsters" and feeding the paper speculation they so decried. But any regulatory policy contradicted the Democratic commitment to limiting governmental power. A restrictive policy, especially one aimed at replacing bank notes with specie, was bound to upset business interests and drive them out of the Democratic party. Worse yet, even the "pet banks" joined in the general suspension of specie payments when the Panic of 1837 hit. Thus the banks favored by the Democrats proved themselves unworthy of the people's trust.

The only way out of the dilemma was to make a clean break between the government and banking. Van Buren reestablished the Democrats' tarnished image as the party of limited government when he came out for the **Independent Treasury System**. Under this plan, the government would dispense with banks entirely. The Treasury would conduct its business only in gold and silver coin and would store its specie in regional vaults or subtreasuries. First proposed in 1837, the Independent Treasury System finally passed Congress in 1840 on the heels of a second wave of bank failures.

The Independent Treasury System made more political than economic sense. It restored the ideological purity of the Democrats as the friends of honest money, but it prolonged the depression. Specie locked up in government vaults was unavailable for loans in the private banking system that could expand the credit needed to revive the economy. The end result was to reduce the money supply and further depress prices.

Uproar over Slavery

In 1831, the year of Nat Turner's Rebellion in Virginia, William Lloyd Garrison of Boston inaugurated a radical new phase in northern attacks on slavery with the publication of his abolitionist paper *The Liberator.* The abolitionists embraced the doctrine of immediatism, an immediate moral commitment to begin the work of emancipation. Inspired by the wave of religious revivals sweeping the North in the late 1820s, they seized on slavery as the greatest sin of all. With the righteous wrath of evangelical ministers, they called on all Americans to recognize their Christian duty to end a system of human bondage that deprived the enslaved of their God-given right to be free moral beings. (For more on the abolitionists, see Chapter 14.)

Although some planters were outraged by the abolitionists from the start, most southern white people ignored them until the abolitionists launched a propaganda offensive in 1835. Taking advantage of technological improvements in the printing industry, they produced over a million pieces of antislavery literature, much of which was sent to the South through the U.S. mails. Alarmed white Southerners vilified the abolitionists as fanatics intent on enticing the slaves to revolt. Abolitionist tracts were burned, and, with the open approval of Jackson, southern postmasters violated federal law by censoring the mails to keep out antislavery materials.

Unable to receive an open hearing in the South, the abolitionists now focused on Congress. Beginning in 1836 and continuing through Van Buren's presidency, hundreds of thousands of antislavery petitions, some of them with thousands of signatures, flooded into Congress. Most of them called for the abolition of slavery in the District of Columbia. Southern congressmen responded by demanding that free speech be repressed in the name of southern white security. The enemy, they were convinced, was fanaticism, and nearly all agreed with Francis Pickens of South Carolina that they must "meet it and strangle it in its infancy." The strangling took the form of the gag rule, a procedural device whereby antislavery petitions were automatically tabled with no discussion.

The gag rule first passed in 1836 and was renewed in a series of raucous debates through 1844. Only the votes of some three-fourths of the northern Democrats enabled the southern minority to have its way. With Van Buren's reluctant support, the gag rule became a Democratic party measure, and it identified the Democrats as a prosouthern party in the minds of many Northerners. Ironically, while Van Buren was attacked in the North as a lackey of the slave interests, he was damned in the South, if only because he was a nonslaveholder from the North, as being unsafe on the slavery issue. In short, tensions over slavery and the economy seemingly doomed Van Buren to be cast as a vacillating president fully trusted by neither section.

OVERVIEW

THE SECOND PARTY SYSTEM

	Democrats	Whigs
Ideology	Favor limited role of federal government in economic affairs and in matters of individual conscience; support territorial expansion	Favor government support for economic development and controls over individual morality; opposed to expansion
Voter support	Mainly subsistence farmers, unskilled workers, and Catholic immigrants	Mainly manufacturers, commercial farmers, skilled workers, and northern evangelicals
Regional strength	South and West	New England and Upper Midwest

The Rise of the Whig Party

The early opponents of the Democrats were known as the National Republicans, a label that captured the nationalist vision of former Jeffersonian Republicans who adhered to the economic program of Henry Clay and John Quincy Adams. The Bank War and Jackson's reaction to nullification shook loose pro-Bank Democrats and many southern states' righters from the original Jacksonian coalition, and these groups joined the opposition to Jackson. By 1834, the anti-Jacksonians started to call themselves Whigs, a name associated with the eighteenth-century American and British opponents of monarchical tyranny. The name stuck because of the party's constant depiction of Jackson as King Andrew, an executive tyrant who ran roughshod over congressional prerogatives and constitutional liberties.

By 1840, the Whigs had mastered the techniques of political organization and mobilization pioneered by the Democrats in the late 1820s. They ran William Henry Harrison, their own version of a military hero, and swept to victory. The **second party system** of intense national competition between Whigs and Democrats was now in place (see the overview table, "The Second Party System"). It would dominate politics until the rise of the antislavery Republican party in the 1850s.

The Party Taking Shape

The Whig party was born in the congressional reaction to Jackson's Bank veto and his subsequent attacks on the national bank. Led by the unlikely trio of Henry Clay and Daniel Webster, nationalists from the West and New England, and John C. Calhoun, a states' righter from the South, the congressional opposition accused Jackson of demagogic appeals to the poor against the rich. What upset them, apart from the specific content of Jackson's policies, was how he enforced his will. Jackson wielded his executive power like a bludgeon. Whereas all earlier presidents together had used the veto only ten times, Jackson did so a dozen times. He openly defied the Supreme Court and Congress, be it on Indian or banking policy, and unlike any of his predecessors, he took his case directly to the people. To his opponents, Jackson was threatening to undermine the constitutional system of checks and balances and bypass the established leadership of public-spirited gentlemen who had hitherto ruled on behalf of the people.

Local and state coalitions of the Whigs sent an anti-Jackson majority to the House of Representatives in 1835. The most powerful of these coalitions was in New York, where a third party, the **Anti-Masons**, joined the Whigs. The party had originated in western New York in the late 1820s as a grassroots response to the sudden disappearance and presumed murder of William Morgan, an itinerant artisan who threatened to expose the secrets of the Order of Freemasons. An all-male order steeped in ritual and ceremony, the Masons united urban and small-town elites into a tightly knit brotherhood through personal contacts and mutual aid. When efforts to investigate Morgan's disappearance ran into a legal dead end, rumors spread that the Masons constituted a vast conspiracy that conferred special privileges and legal protection on its exclusive members. To combat this "monster," farmers and townspeople flocked to the new Anti-Masonic party. They sought, in the words of an 1831 Anti-Masonic address, "equal rights and equal privileges among the freemen of the country."

Western New York, an area of religious fervor and rapid economic change after the opening of the Erie Canal in 1825, provided fertile ground for the growth of the new party. With close ties to rural landlords and town creditors, the Masons were vulnerable to the charge of economic favoritism. In addition, evangelicals accused the Masons of desecrating the Christian faith with their secret rituals. The Anti-Masons were thus the first party to combine demands for equal opportunity with calls for the moral reform of a sinful society.

Although it spread into New England and the neighboring mid-Atlantic states, the Anti-Mason party was unable to sustain itself. Its presidential candidate in 1832, William Wirt of Maryland, won only Vermont. Recognizing that the opponents of the Anti-Masons were usually the entrenched local interests of the Democratic party, shrewd politicians, led by Thurlow Weed and William Seward of New York, took up the movement and absorbed most of it into the anti-Jackson coalition. They thus broadened the Whigs' mass base and added an egalitarian message to their appeal.

By 1836, the Whigs were strong enough to mount a serious challenge for the presidency. However, they still lacked an effective national organization that could unite their regional coalitions behind one candidate. They ran three candidates—Webster of Massachusetts, William Henry Harrison of Ohio, and Hugh Lawson White of Tennessee—and some Whigs hoped that the regional popularity of these candidates would siphon off enough votes from Van Buren to throw the election into the House of Representatives. The strategy, if such it can be called, failed. Van Buren won an electoral majority by holding on to the populous mid-Atlantic states and improving on Jackson's showing in New England. Still, the Whigs were encouraged by the results. Compared to Jackson, Van Buren did poorly in what had been the overwhelmingly Democratic South. He lost Tennessee and Georgia and barely carried the popular vote elsewhere. The South was now open to further Whig inroads.

Whig Persuasion

The Whigs, like the Democrats, based their mass appeal on the claim that they could best defend the republican liberties of the people. Whereas the Democrats attributed the threat to those liberties to privileged monopolies of government-granted power, the Whigs found it in the expansive powers of the presidency as wielded by Jackson and in the party organization that put Jackson and Van Buren into office. In 1836, the Whigs called for the election of "a president of the nation, not a president of party." Underlying this call was the persistent Whig belief that parties undermined individual liberties and the public good by fostering and rewarding the selfish interests of the party faithful. Although the Whigs dropped much of this ideology when they themselves matured as a party, they never lost their fear of the presidency as an office of unchecked, demagogic power. They always insisted that Congress should be the locus of power in the federal system.

If the Whigs were more reluctant than the Democrats to accept political change in the form of mass-based parties, they were quicker to embrace economic change in the form of banks and manufacturing corporations. Building on ideas that originated with the Clay–Adams core of the party, most Whigs viewed governmental power as a positive force to promote economic development. They favored encouraging the spread of banking and paper money, chartering corporations, passing protective tariffs to support American manufacturers, and opening up new markets for farmers through government-subsidized transportation projects. Such policies, they held, would widen economic opportunities for more and more Americans and provide positive incentives for material self-improvement.

The Whigs' economic program appealed mostly to Americans who were benefiting from economic change or expecting to do so. They drew heavily from commercial and planting interests in the South. They were also the party of bankers, manufacturers, small-town entrepreneurs, farmers prospering from the market outlets of canals and railroads, and skilled workers who valued a high tariff as protection from the competition of goods produced by cheap foreign labor. These Whig groups also tended to be native-born Protestants of New England or Yankee ancestry, particularly those caught up in the religious revivals of the 1820s and 1830s. The strongest Whig constituencies comprised an arc of Yankee settlement stretching from rural New England through central New York and around the southern shores of the Great Lakes.

Whether as economic promoters or evangelical reformers, Whigs believed in promoting social progress and harmony through an interventionist government. The Whigs favored such social reforms as prohibiting the consumption of alcohol; preserving the sanctity of the Protestant Sabbath through bans on business activities on Sundays; caring for orphans, the physically handicapped, and the mentally ill in state-run asylums and hospitals; and teaching virtuous behavior and basic knowledge through a centralized system of public education. Whig ideology blended economic, social, and spiritual reform into a unified message of uplift. An activist government would provide the economic opportunities and moral guidance for a harmonious, progressive society of freely competing individuals whose behavior would be shaped by the evangelical norms of thrift, sobriety, and self-discipline.

Much of the Whigs' reform impulse was directed against non-English and Catholic immigrants, those Americans whom the Whigs believed most needed to be taught the virtues of self-control and disciplined work habits. Not coincidentally, these groups—the Scots-Irish in the backcountry, the Reformed Dutch, and Irish and German Catholics—were the most loyal Democrats. They resented the aggressive moralism of the Whigs and the legislative attempts to interfere with their drinking habits and Sunday amusements. These Democrats were typically subsistence farmers on the periphery of market change or unskilled workers forced by industrial change to abandon their hopes of ever opening their own shops. They equated an activist government with special privileges for the economically and culturally powerful and identified with the Democrats' demand for keeping the government out of the economy and individual religious practices.

This cotton banner used by the Whigs in the campaign of 1840 celebrated their ticket as the friends of common Americans who had been raised in a log cabin.

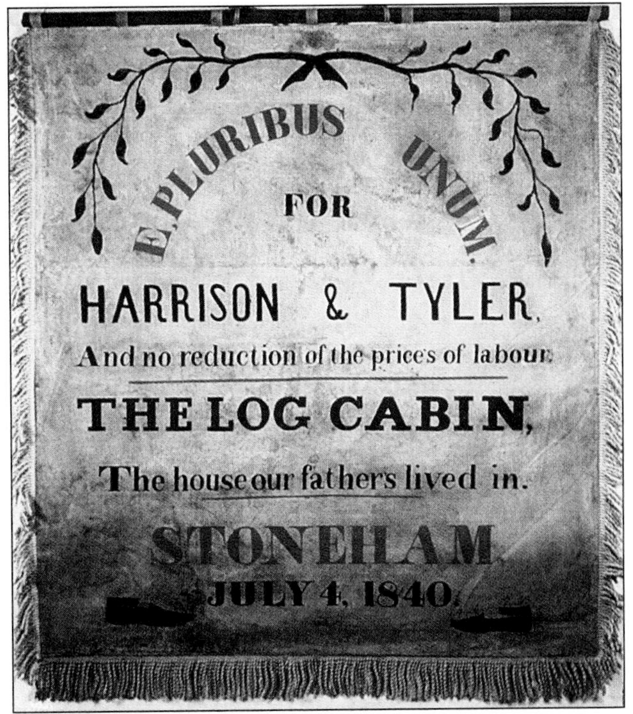

The Election of 1840

One of the signs of the Whigs' maturing as a party was their decision in 1840 to place victory above principle. Because of the lingering economic depression, Democratic rule had been discredited for many voters. Aside from the Independent Treasury Act and legislation establishing a ten-hour workday for federal employees, the Van Buren administration had no program to combat the Whig charge of helplessness in the face of economic adversity. Henry Clay, who promised that his American System would revive the economy with government aid, appeared the most likely Whig candidate for president against Van Buren in 1840. Yet the power brokers in the party dumped Clay, who represented the ideological heart of the party, for their version of a popular military hero, William Henry Harrison of Ohio.

Harrison had run surprisingly well as one of the Whigs' regional candidates in 1836 and had revealed a common touch with the voters that the Whigs generally lacked. Unlike Clay, he was untainted by any association with the Bank of the United States, the Masonic Order, or slaveholding. As the victor at the Battle of Tippecanoe and a military hero in the War of 1812, he enabled Whig image makers to cast him, like Jackson, as the honest, patriotic soldier worthy of the people's trust. In a decision that came back to haunt them, the Whigs geographically balanced their ticket by selecting John Tyler, a planter from Virginia, as Harrison's running mate. Tyler was an advocate of states' rights and a former Democrat who had broken with Jackson over the Force Bill.

The Democrats inadvertently gave the Whig campaign a tremendous boost. A Democratic editor wisecracked that "Old Granny" Harrison (he was 67) was such a simpleton that he would like nothing better than to retire to a log cabin with a government pension and a barrel of hard cider. Pouncing on this sneer, the Whigs created a Harrison who never was—a yeoman farmer of humble origins and homespun tastes whose rise to prominence was a democratic model of success for other Americans to follow. Thus Harrison, who was descended from the Virginia slaveholding aristocracy, became a symbol of the common man, and the Whigs were finally able to shed their aristocratic image. Indeed, they pinned the label of the dandified and elitist aristocrat on Van Buren. "Martin Van Ruin," as effectively portrayed by the Whigs, squandered public revenue on effete luxuries and was concerned only with the spoils of office.

The Whigs beat the Democrats at their own game of mass politics in 1840. They reversed the roles and symbolism of the Jackson–Adams election of 1828 and seized the high ground as the party of the people. In a further adaptation of earlier Democratic initiatives, the Whigs put together a frolicking campaign of slogans, parades, and pageantry. Politics became a carnival in which voters were shamelessly wooed with food, drink, and music in huge rallies complete with live animals and gigantic buckskin balls that were triumphantly rolled from one rally to another. Clay muttered with some disgust that he regretted the need "of appealing to the feelings and passions of our Countrymen, rather than to their reasons and their judgments." Nonetheless, such hoopla was now essential for electoral victory.

The Whigs gained control of both Congress and the presidency in 1840. Harrison won 53 percent of the popular vote, and for the first time the Whigs carried the South (see Map 10-4). With the arrival of politics as mass spectacle, the turnout surged to an unprecedented 78 percent of eligible voters, a whopping increase over the average of 55 percent in the three preceding presidential elections (see Figure 10-2). The Whigs claimed most of the new voters and were now fully competitive with the Democrats in all parts of the nation. As the new majority party, they finally had the opportunity, or so they thought, to implement their economic program.

Map 10-4 The Election of 1840
Building upon their strength in the commercializing North, the Whigs attracted enough rural voters in the South and West to win the election of 1840.

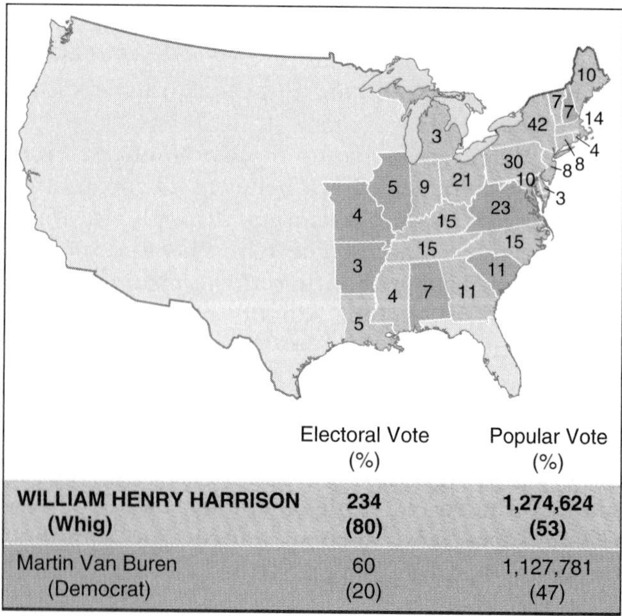

	Electoral Vote (%)	Popular Vote (%)
WILLIAM HENRY HARRISON (Whig)	**234 (80)**	**1,274,624 (53)**
Martin Van Buren (Democrat)	60 (20)	1,127,781 (47)

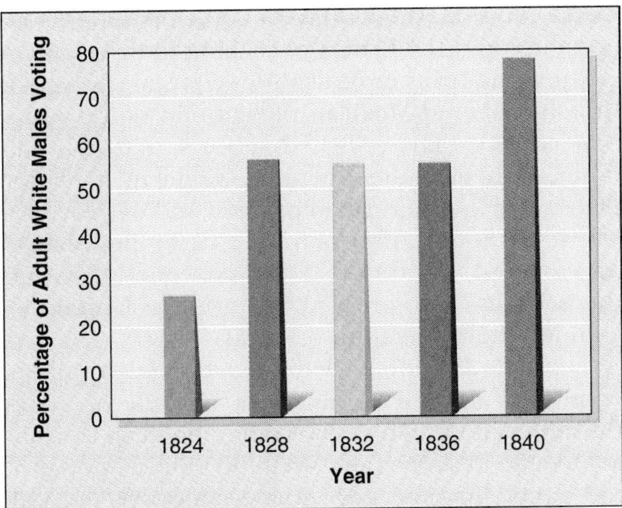

Figure 10-2 ***Voter Turnout in Presidential Elections, 1824–1840***
The creation of mass-based political parties dramatically increased voter turnout in presidential elections. Voting surged in 1828 with the emergence of the Jacksonian Democratic Party and again in 1840 when the Whig Party learned to appeal to the mass electorate.
Data Source: *Richard P. McCormick, "New Perspectives on Jacksonian Politics" in* The Nature of Jacksonian America, *ed. Douglas T. Miller (1972), p. 103.*

The Whigs in Power

Although the Whigs had been noncommittal on their plans during the campaign of 1840, it was common knowledge that Clay would move quickly on Whig economic policies by marshaling his forces in Congress and trying to dominate a pliant Harrison. But Harrison died from pneumonia in April 1841, barely a month after his inauguration, ruining Clay's plans. Tyler, Harrison's successor, was a particularly rigid states' rights ideologue who betrayed party expectations by blocking key pieces of Clay's program. The Whigs reacted by reading Tyler out of the party.

In 1843, Tyler latched on to the annexation of the slaveholding Republic of Texas as an issue that might get him back into the good graces of the Democratic party and establish his own successful record as president. At the end of his administration, Tyler did succeed in securing the annexation of Texas, but his main accomplishment was to shift the focus of national politics from economic issues to sectional ones of territorial expansion. Running on an expansionist platform, the Democrats regained the presidency in 1844.

Harrison and Tyler

Perhaps the Democrats had been right that Harrison was too old for the demands of the presidency. He fumed that "I am bothered almost to death with visitors. I have not time to attend to my person, not even to change my shirt, much less to attend to the public business." Still, for all his grumblings, he was the type of president the Whigs wanted. He had pledged to follow the dictates of party leaders in Congress and defer to the judgment of his cabinet. Bowing to Clay's demands, he agreed to call Congress into special session to act on Whig party measures. Thus his death was a real blow to Whig hopes of establishing the credibility of their party as an effective agent for positive change.

Just how serious that blow was soon became apparent when Tyler became president, the first vice president to succeed on the death of a president. Tyler was cut from quite different cloth from Harrison. This stiff, unbending planter subscribed to a states' rights agrarian philosophy that put him at odds with the urban and commercial elements of the Whig party even in his home state of Virginia. Clay's economic nationalism struck him as a program of rank corruption that surrendered the constitutional rights of the South to power-hungry politicians and manufacturers in the North. Clay refused to cultivate Tyler's prickly pride with soothing gestures, and he forged ahead with the party agenda—the repeal of the Independent Treasury System and its replacement by a new national bank, a protective tariff, and the distribution of the proceeds of the government's public land sales to the states as funds for internal improvements.

A Democratic observer predicted in mid-May 1841 that "the Whigs will be very much disappointed by the course which the President will feel himself constitutionally bound to pursue." Tyler used the negative power of presidential vetoes to stymie the Whig program. He twice vetoed bills to reestablish a national bank. The second veto led to the resignation of the cabinet he had inherited from Harrison, save for Secretary of State Daniel Webster, who was in the midst of negotiations with the British. Enraged congressional Whigs then expelled Tyler from the party.

A now desperate Clay sought to salvage what was left of his American System. He lined up southern votes for the distribution of federal funds to the states by agreeing to a ceiling of 20 percent on tariff rates. Westerners were won over by Clay's support for the Preemption Act of 1841, a measure that allowed squatters to purchase up to 160 acres of public land at the minimum government price of $1.25 per acre. This act was popular in the West because squatters no longer had to match the bids of speculators at government land sales.

Clay's legislative wizardry got him nowhere. When the Whigs passed a higher tariff in 1842 with a provision for distribution, Tyler vetoed it and forced them to settle for a protective tariff with no distribution. In the end, Clay had no national bank, no funds for internal improvements, and only a slightly higher tariff. Although Clay's leadership of the Whigs was strengthened, Tyler had deprived that leadership of meaning by denying the Whigs the legislative fruits of their victory in 1840.

The Texas Issue

Constrained by his states' rights view to a largely negative role in domestic policy, Tyler was a much more forceful president in foreign policy, an area in which the Constitution gives the chief executive considerable latitude. In 1842, Webster wrapped up his negotiations with the British. **The Webster–Ashburton Treaty** of that year settled a long-standing dispute over the boundary between British Canada and Maine and parts of the Upper Midwest. An agreement was also reached to cooperate in suppressing the African slave trade. Webster now resigned from the cabinet to join his fellow Whigs, allowing Tyler to follow a prosouthern policy of expansion that he hoped would gain him the Democratic nomination for the presidency in 1844. His goal was the annexation of Texas.

Texas had been a slaveholding republic since 1836, when rebellious Americans, joined by some *tejanos* (Texans of Mexican descent), declared their independence from Mexico. Jackson extended diplomatic recognition before leaving office, but he refused the new nation's request to be annexed to the United States out of fear of provoking a war with Mexico, which did not recognize Texan independence. But he was also aware that the addition of Texas, a potentially huge area for the expansion of plantation slavery, would inflame sectional tensions and endanger Van Buren's chances in the upcoming presidential election. In private, however, he urged Texans to seize harbors on the Pacific Coast from Mexican control and thus make annexation more attractive to the commercial interests of the Northeast.

For the sake of sectional harmony, party leaders sidestepped the Texas issue after 1836. Spurned by the Whigs and anxious to return to the Democrats, Tyler renewed the issue in 1843 to curry favor among southern and western Democrats. He replaced Webster as secretary of state with a proannexationist Virginian, Abel P. Upshur, and secretly opened negotiations with the Texans. After Upshur's death in an accidental explosion on the battleship *Princeton*, Calhoun, his successor, completed the negotiations and dramatically politicized the slavery issue. Calhoun made public his correspondence with Richard Pakenham, the British minister in Washington. In his letter, Calhoun accused the British of seeking to force emancipation on Texas in return for economic aid and a British-brokered Mexican recognition of Texan independence. These British efforts, warned Calhoun, were just the opening wedge in a master plan to block American expansion and destroy slavery in the South. After pointedly defending slavery as a benign institution, Calhoun concluded that the security and preservation of the Union demanded the annexation of Texas.

The Pakenham letter hit the Senate like a bombshell, convincing antislavery Northerners that the annexation of Texas was a slaveholders' conspiracy to extend slavery and swell the political power of the South. In June 1844, the Senate rejected Calhoun's treaty of annexation by a two-to-one margin. All but one Whig senator voted against it. Still, the issue was hardly dead. Thanks to Tyler and Calhoun, Texas dominated the election of 1844.

The Election of 1844

The Whig and Democratic National Conventions met in the spring of 1844 in the midst of the uproar over Texas. Both Clay, who had the Whig nomination locked up, and Van Buren, who was the strong favorite for the Democratic one, came out against immediate annexation. Clay's stand was consistent with Whig fears that territorial expansion would disrupt the party's plans for ordered economic development. But Van Buren's anti-Texas stand cost him his party's nomination. In a carefully devised strategy, western and southern Democrats united to deny him the necessary two-thirds vote of convention delegates. A deadlocked convention turned to James K. Polk of Tennessee, a confirmed expansionist who had the blessing of Jackson, the party's patriarch.

To counter the charge that they were a prosouthern party, the Democrats ran in 1844 on a platform that linked Oregon to Texas as territorial objectives. Oregon had first attracted public attention during the Tyler presidency. Glowing reports from Protestant missionaries of the boundless fertility of Oregon's Willamette Valley triggered a migration to the new promised land on the shores of the Pacific by midwestern farm families still reeling from the Panic of 1837. At the same time, the report of a naval expedition sent to explore the Pacific aroused the interest of New England merchants in using Oregon as a jumping-off point for expanded trade with China.

Some six thousand Americans were in Oregon by the mid-1840s, and demands mounted, especially from northern Democrats, that the United States abandon its 1818 agreement of joint occupation with the British and lay exclusive claim to Oregon as far north as the 54°40' parallel, the border with Russian-owned Alaska. These were bold, even reckless, demands, because the actual area of American settlement in Oregon was south of the Columbia River, itself well south of even the 49th parallel. Nonetheless, the Polk Democrats seemed to endorse them when they asserted an American claim "to the whole of the Territory of Oregon."

Polk's expansionist program united the Democrats and enabled them to campaign with much more enthusiasm than in 1840. Acquiring Texas and Oregon not only held out the economic hope of cheap, abundant land to debt-burdened farmers in the North and planters in the South but also played on the anti-British sentiments of many voters. In contrast, the Whig campaign was out of focus. Clay sensed that his opposition to the immediate annexation of Texas was hurting him in the South, and he started to hedge by saying that he would accept Texas if the conditions were right. This wavering, however, failed to stem the defection of proslavery southern Whigs to the Democrats and cut into his support among antislavery Whigs in the North. Clay lost to Polk by less than 2 percent of the popular vote.

Tyler claimed Polk's victory as a mandate for the immediate annexation of Texas. He knew that it would still be impossible to gain the two-thirds majority in the Senate necessary for the approval of a treaty. Thus he resorted to the constitutionally unprecedented expedient of a joint resolution in Congress inviting Texas to join the Union. By the narrow margin of twenty-seven to twenty-five, the Senate concurred with the House in favor of annexation. Tyler signed the joint resolution on March 1, 1845.

Although Tyler had failed to secure the Democratic nomination in 1844, he had gained Texas. He also had the satisfaction of getting revenge against the Whigs, the party that had disowned him. Texas, more than any other issue, defeated Clay and the Whigs in 1844.

Conclusion

The Jacksonian era ushered in a revolution in American political life. Responding to a surge of democratization that was in full swing by the 1820s, politicians learned how to appeal to a mass electorate and to build disciplined parties that channeled popular desires into distinctive party positions. In the two decades after 1824, voter participation in national elections tripled, and Democrats and Whigs competed on nearly equal terms in every region.

Although the origins of a national political culture can be traced back to the Federalists and Jeffersonian Republicans, politics did not fully enter the mainstream of American life until the rise of the second party system of Democrats and Whigs. The election of 1824 revived interest in presidential politics, and Jackson's forceful style of leadership highlighted the presidency as the focal point of American politics. Professional politicians soon mastered the art of tailoring issues and images to reach the widest popular audience. Voters in favor of government aid for economic development and a social order based on Protestant moral controls turned to the Whigs' program of economic and moral activism. Conversely, those who saw an activist government as a threat to their economic and cultural equality turned to the Democrats.

The national issues around which the Democrats and Whigs organized and battled down to 1844 were primarily economic. As long as this was the case, party competition tended to diffuse sectional tensions and strengthen a national political culture. Slavery, in the form of the Texas question, replaced the economy as the decisive issue in the election of 1844. With this shift, party appeals began to focus on the place of slavery in American society, creating an escalating politics of sectionalism. Within a decade, the slavery issue would rip apart the second party system.

Review Questions

1. Explain the democratic movements of the early nineteenth century. What role did race and gender play in these movements?
2. What distinguished Jackson's presidency from those of his predecessors? How did he redefine the role of the president?
3. How was the Bank War central to the development of the Democratic and Whig parties? Why did the political debates of the 1830s focus on financial issues?
4. In terms of ideology and voter appeal, how did the Democrats and Whigs differ? How did each party represent a distinctive response to economic and social change?
5. How would you describe the changes in American politics between 1824 and 1840? What accounted for these changes?

6. How did the annexation of Texas emerge as a political issue in the early 1840s? Why were the Democrats more in favor of territorial expansion than the Whigs?

Recommended Reading

Donald B. Cole, *The Presidency of Andrew Jackson* (1993). A revisionist look at Jackson's presidency that argues that he was an uncertain leader who failed in his efforts to resist the spread of the market revolution that was transforming America.

Daniel Feller, *The Jacksonian Promise: America, 1815–1840* (1995). An up-to-date survey that emphasizes the optimism and innovation of the Jacksonian era.

Marvin Meyers, *The Jacksonian Persuasion* (1960). A gracefully written work that explores the beliefs of the Jacksonians and concludes that their agrarian values made them fearful of economic change.

Edward Pessen, *Jacksonian America* (1985). A revisionist work that argues that Democrats and Whigs, for all their talk of democratic change, were driven primarily by the goal of acquiring office as an end in itself.

Robert V. Remini, *The Life of Andrew Jackson* (1988). A lively account of Jackson's career, written by his most noted biographer.

Arthur Schlesinger, Jr., *The Age of Jackson* (1945). Remains the enduring statement of the democratic impulse behind the Jackson movement.

Charles Sellers, *The Market Revolution: Jacksonian America, 1815–1846* (1991). A boldly conceived work that places responses to market change at the center of the era's political development.

Alexis de Tocqueville, *Democracy in America*, ed. Phillips Bradley, 2 vols. (1945). An often-quoted classic, still popular for its firsthand depiction of Jacksonian society and institutions.

Harry Watson, *Liberty and Power: The Politics of Jacksonian America* (1990). A very readable and concise synthesis of Jacksonian politics.

Additional Sources

The Egalitarian Impulse

Jon Butler, *Awash in a Sea of Faith: Christianizing the American People* (1990).

Mary W. M. Hargreaves, *The Presidency of John Quincy Adams* (1985).

Nathan O. Hatch, *The Democratization of American Christianity* (1989).

Merrill D. Peterson, ed., *Democracy, Liberty, and Property: The State Constitutional Conventions of the 1820s* (1966).

Chilton Williamson, *American Suffrage from Property to Democracy, 1760–1860* (1960).

Jackson's Presidency

Angie Debo, *And Still the Waters Run: The Betrayal of the Five Civilized Tribes* (1940; reprint, 1972).

Richard E. Ellis, *The Union at Risk: Jacksonian Democracy, States' Rights, and the Nullification Crisis* (1987).

William W. Freehling, *Prelude to Civil War: The Nullification Controversy in South Carolina, 1816–1836* (1966).

Robert V. Remini, *Andrew Jackson and the Bank War* (1967).

Michael Paul Rogin, *Fathers and Children: Andrew Jackson and the Subjugation of the American Indian* (1975).

John William Ward, *Andrew Jackson: Symbol for an Age* (1955).

Van Buren and Hard Times

John M. McFaul, *The Politics of Jacksonian Finance* (1972).

Reginald Charles McGrane, *The Panic of 1837* (1924).

Roger Sharp, *The Jacksonians versus the Banks: Politics in the States after the Panic of 1837* (1970).

Peter Temin, *The Jacksonian Economy* (1969).

Major L. Wilson, *The Presidency of Martin Van Buren* (1984).

The Rise of the Whig Party

John Ashworth, *"Agrarians" and "Aristocrats": Party Political Ideology in the United States, 1837–1846* (1983).

Daniel Walker Howe, *The Political Culture of the American Whigs* (1979).

Lawrence Frederick Kohl, *The Politics of Individualism: Parties and the American Character in the Jacksonian Era* (1989).

Richard P. McCormick, *The Second American Party System* (1966).

Merrill Peterson, *The Great Triumvirate: Webster, Clay, and Calhoun* (1987).

The Whigs in Power

William R. Brock, *Parties and Political Conscience* (1979).

Michael F. Holt, *The Rise and Fall of the American Whig Party* (1999).

Frederick Merk, *Slavery and the Annexation of Texas* (1972).

Norma Louis Peterson, *The Presidencies of William Henry Harrison and John Tyler* (1990).

Robert V. Remini, *Henry Clay: Statesman for the Union* (1991).

Where to Learn More

- ❖ **Rice Museum, Georgetown, South Carolina.** Rice planters were the leaders of the nullification movement, and the interpretive materials here on the history of rice cultivation help one understand how slave labor was employed to produce their great wealth.
- ❖ **The Hermitage, Hermitage, Tennessee.** This site, the plantation home of Andrew Jackson, includes a museum with artifacts of Jackson's life.
- ❖ **Martin Van Buren National Historic Site, Kinderhook, New York.** The site preserves Lindenwald, Van Buren's home after he left the presidency, and includes a library with materials on Van Buren and his political era.
- ❖ **The Alamo, San Antonio, Texas.** Originally a Franciscan mission, the Alamo was converted into a fort during the Texas War of Independence. The massacre of its defenders in 1836 by Santa Anna's army gave birth to the rallying cry for Texas independence, "Remember the Alamo."

INDUSTRIAL CHANGE AND URBANIZATION, 1820–1850

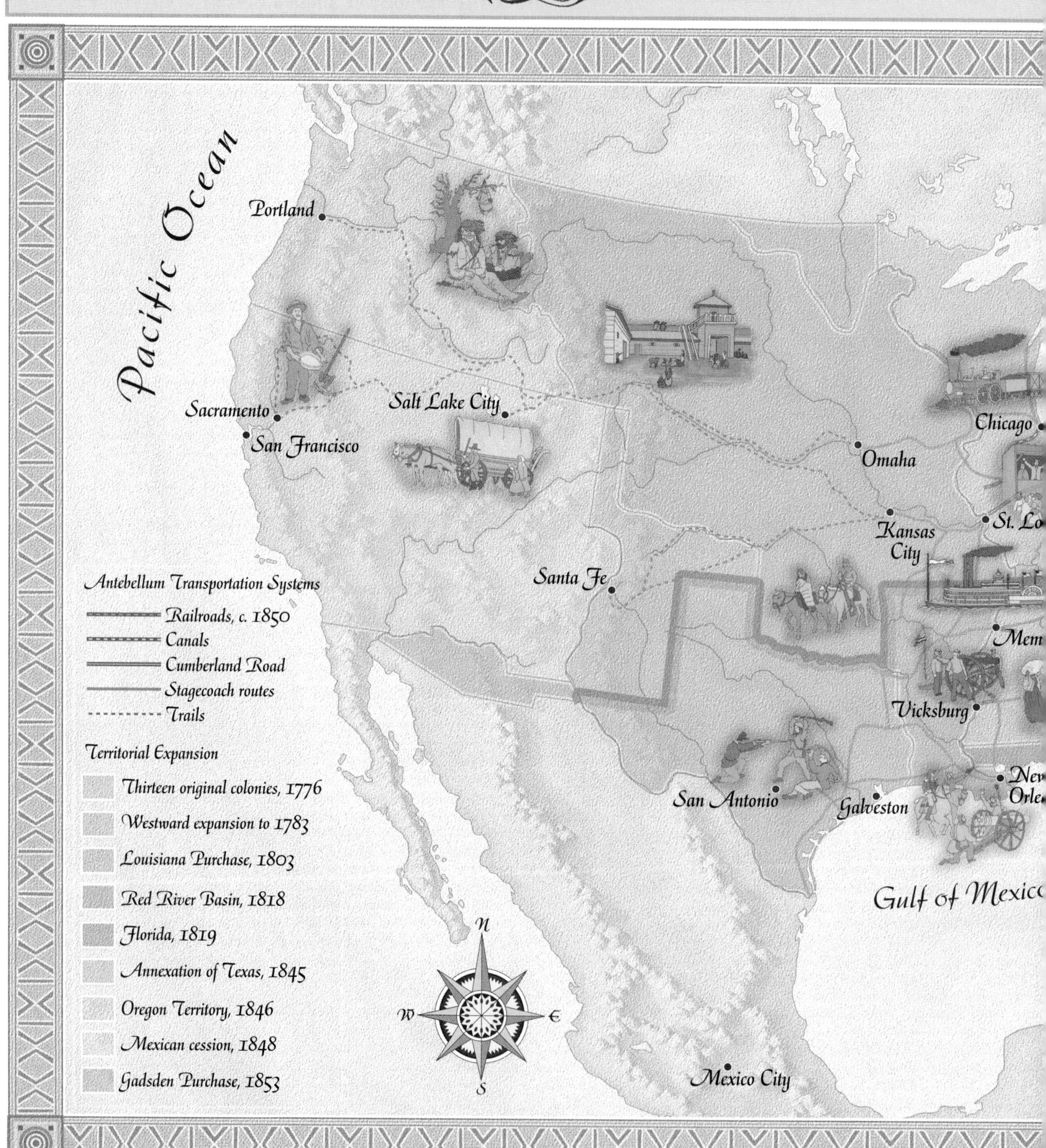

11

Chapter Outline

Key Topics

- The increasing industrialization of the U.S. economy between 1815 and 1850
- The effect of the transportation revolution on the pattern and direction of American commerce
- The growth of cities and the emergence of both a new middle-class society and a lower class of working poor
- Massive immigration starting in the 1840s, mainly from Ireland and Germany, providing a new labor force essential to industrialization
- New wealth and the increasing inequalities among the rich, the middle class, and the working classes
- The emergence of poorly paid, unskilled labor and the decline of the old artisan-mechanic class

"Oh, that I had wings!" wished Lucy Larcom as she leaned out a window in the factory at Lowell, Massachusetts, on a warm June afternoon in the 1830s. Like thousands of other young women from New England's farms, she had gone to work in the new textile mills and had become part of the nation's first large industrial work force. Larcom entered the mill when she was 11, glad to be able to relieve her widowed mother of the cost of her upkeep, and now she enjoyed the independence that came with earning her own wages. But mill work was a mixed blessing. Larcom "never cared much for machinery" and hated its noisy clatter, and she resented "being shut in to daily toil so early" in the morning. She recalled that "sometimes the confinement of the mill became very wearisome," and her "whole stifled being would cry out" for freedom. Still, she was there of her own choosing, and she conceded that the discipline of the mill had taught her self-control. "Perhaps," she mused, "I could have brought myself into the limitations of order and method in no other way."

Larcom's ambivalence typified the reaction of Americans to the wrenching social and economic changes of the Jacksonian era from 1820 to 1850. Factories were new institutions with authoritarian work rules that deprived workers of their accustomed freedoms and radically altered the self-directed rhythm of farm and artisan work. Yet the factories were just one sign of the quickening pace of economic development and social dislocation after 1820. Cities grew rapidly—indeed, at the fastest relative rate in American history. Urbanization also brought new production patterns and increasingly separated one's home from one's place of work. New middle and working classes evolved in response to such changes. These class changes were most pronounced in the Northeast, which can serve as a window through which to view the transformation of the nation's economy and social structure up to the middle of the nineteenth century.

The Transportation Revolution

In 1820, the American economy was little changed from the days of Washington's presidency. Four in five people worked in agriculture, and manufacturing played a minor role in overall economic activity. Over the next three decades, however, America joined England as a world leader in industrialization. By 1850, manufacturing accounted for one-third of total commodity output, and nonfarm employment had more than doubled to 45 percent of the labor force.

The most direct cause of this rapid and sustained surge in manufacturing was the growth of the home market, the increasing consumption within the United States of the goods the country was producing. The improvements in moving people, raw materials, and finished goods that were key to this growth are collectively known as the **transportation revolution**. Dramatically lower transportation costs and faster shipping times opened up new markets for farmers and manufacturers alike and provided an ongoing incentive for expanding production (see Table 11-1). As physical barriers to economic development fell, agricultural and manufactured goods could be exchanged more efficiently. The economy as a whole benefited, and the growing home market continually stimulated the development of American manufacturing.

Canals and Steamboats

The nation had no system of transportation in 1820. The states had chartered turnpike companies to build improved roads, graded with crushed stone, for overland transportation. Some four thousand miles of these toll roads had been built by 1820, mostly in the Northeast, but their economic impact was marginal. They made travel more comfortable for passengers on stagecoaches between coastal cities, but transporting bulky freight on them was still too slow and expensive. It cost as much to haul heavy goods by horse-drawn wagons thirty miles into the interior as to ship them three thousand miles across the Atlantic Ocean. West of the Appalachian

Table 11.1

Impact of the Transportation Revolution on Traveling Time

Route	1800	1830	1860
New York to Philadelphia	2 days	1 day	Less than 1 day
New York to Charleston	More than 1 week	5 days	2 days
New York to Chicago	6 weeks	3 weeks	2 days
New York to New Orleans	4 weeks	2 weeks	6 days

Mountains, where the need for improved transportation was the greatest, roads were mostly stump-strewn, muddy trails through forests and swamps.

Water transportation was much cheaper, but it was limited to the coast or navigable rivers. Only farmers located near a city or a river grew surplus crops for sale in an outside market. Rivers were the arteries of commerce in the West, and their southerly flow directed western farm surpluses down the Ohio and Mississippi river systems toward New Orleans. Flatboats (rafts with a deck and a steering device) could carry heavy loads with the current but were useless for upriver traffic. Although keelboats could be poled upstream, they were slow and expensive.

Steamboats provided the first transportation breakthrough. American entrepreneur-inventors had been tinkering with the design of steamboats since John Fitch launched the first one on the Delaware River in 1787, and, in 1807, Robert Fulton demonstrated their commercial practicality when he sent the *Claremont* 150 miles up the Hudson River from New York City to Albany. In 1815, the *Enterprise* carried a cargo upriver from New Orleans to Pittsburgh.

Steamboats revolutionized western river transport. By the 1820s, they had reduced the cost and the time of upriver shipments by 90 percent. Engineering changes that lightened their weight and broadened their hulls for a more shallow draft made them ideal for the western rivers and many of their tributaries. By the 1840s, more than five hundred steamboats were plying western waters. More and more farmers could now reap the economic benefits of exporting corn, pork, and other regional foodstuffs. Because freight rates for upstream cargoes dropped much more than those for downriver traffic, western produce now purchased substantially more in outside goods.

Steamboats greatly expanded trade between the South and the West. But because no natural waterways ran on an east–west axis across the mountains, western trade did not start to flow eastward until the completion in 1825 of the Erie Canal, the first and most successful of the artificial waterways designed to link eastern seaboard cities with western markets (see Map 11-1).

The Erie Canal originated in the desire of New York City merchants to reach the agricultural markets of the Old Northwest. Prodded by Governor DeWitt Clinton, the New York legislature agreed to fund the project in 1817. This was a daring and expensive undertaking. The United States had barely a hundred miles of canals, none longer than twenty-eight miles. The Erie Canal was to stretch 364 miles from Albany to Buffalo, a small port on Lake Erie. Its construction—the excavation of massive amounts of earth, the building of locks to raise and lower the water level for boats, and the clearing and grading of towpaths for the horses and mules that pulled boats along the forty-foot-wide band of water—was the greatest engineering feat of its era.

The completion of the Erie ultimately depended on the backbreaking labor of Irish immigrants, who comprised the bulk of its work gangs. They worked for less than $10 a month, part of which (at their insistence) was paid in whiskey in a daily ration of 12 to 20 ounces. The workers lived in camps built by the canal contractors. Sickness, especially fevers and cholera, was a constant danger. A thousand workers contracted a fever in the marshes around Syracuse in the summer of 1819, and many of them died.

Conditions for workers on the Erie promoted a violent culture of brawling and drinking that fed ethnic stereotypes of the Irish as drunken brutes. The reality, as an Irishman working on the Chesapeake and Ohio Canal a decade later tried to explain, was that "if the same number of the laboring class of any other country on the face of the globe, were collected on the line of the Canal, at least as many excesses would be committed by them, as by my hard working generous countrymen." Still, the stereotypes stuck, and when New York City celebrated the completion of the canal in 1825, the Irish were excluded from the festivities.

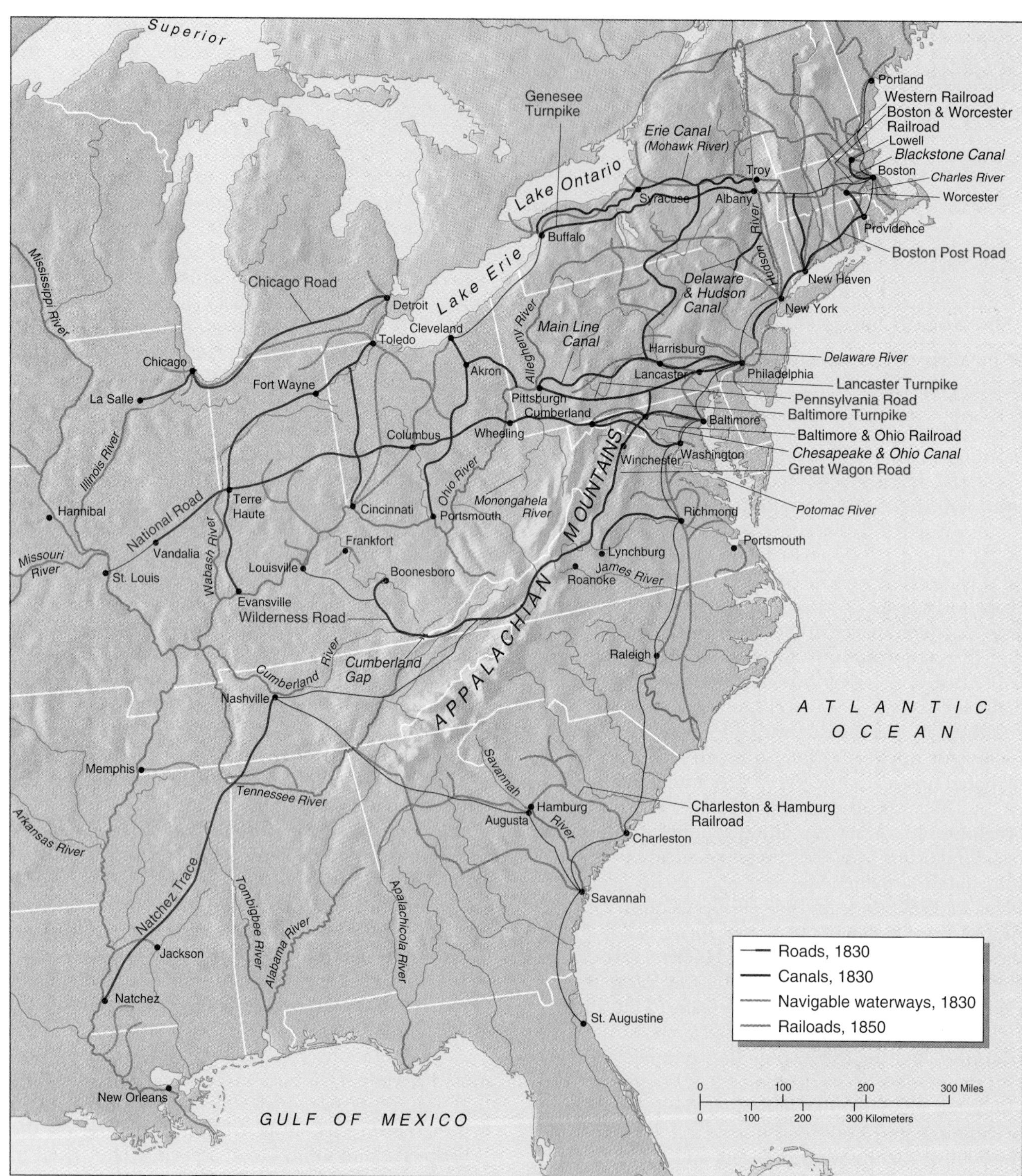

Map 11-1 The Transportation Revolution

By 1830, a network of roads, canals, and navigable rivers was spurring economic growth in the first phase of the Transportation Revolution. By 1850, railroads, the key development in the second phase of the Transportation Revolution, were opening up additional areas to commercial activity.

Chronology

1790	Samuel Slater opens the first permanent cotton mill in Rhode Island.
1793	Eli Whitney patents the first cotton gin.
1807	Robert Fulton's steamboat, the *Clermont,* makes its pioneering voyage up the Hudson River.
1811	Construction begins on the federally financed National Road at Cumberland, Maryland.
1814	The Boston Associates opens its Waltham mill, the first textile factory to mechanize all phases of production.
1817	Construction on the Erie Canal begins.
1819–1823	Economic depression.
1824	In *Gibbons* v. *Ogden,* the Supreme Court strikes down a state monopoly over steamboat navigation.
1825	Erie Canal is completed.
1828	The Baltimore and Ohio, the most important of the early railroads, is chartered.
1834	Female workers at the Lowell Mills stage their first strike. National Trades Union is formed.
1837	In *Charles River Bridge* v. *Warren Bridge,* the Supreme Court encourages economic competition by ruling that presumed rights of monopolistic privileges could not be used to block new economic enterprises.
1839–1843	Economic depression.
1842	Massachusetts Supreme Court in *Commonwealth* v. *Hunt* strengthens the legal right of workers to organize trade unions.
1845	Potato famine in Ireland sets off a mass migration of Irish to the United States.
1847	Cyrus McCormick opens his main reaper factory in Chicago.

The Erie was an immediate success. It reduced the cost of sending freight from Buffalo to New York City by more than 90 percent and redirected the southerly flow of farm surpluses in the Great Lakes region to lake ports that sent it east across the Erie. As early as 1827, New York City leapfrogged Philadelphia and Baltimore as the leading exporter of flour, and by the mid-1840s, the Erie was pulling in more western trade than was being sent south to New Orleans on the Mississippi River. Profits from the Erie were so high that the construction cost of $7 million was paid off in just twelve years.

The Erie's success touched off a boom in canal building. Pennsylvania and Maryland launched plans for competing canals to the West, and other states soon joined them. More than three thousand miles of canals were in place by 1840, but no canal matched the spectacular success of the Erie. Geography gave it a unique advantage. It ran through the only natural break in the Appalachian Mountains, the Mohawk Valley of central New York. Other major east-west canals across the Appalachians, such as Pennsylvania's Main Line Canal, were more difficult and more expensive to construct. And they could never overcome the tremendous advantage of the Erie's head start in fixing trading patterns along its route.

The Panic of 1837 abruptly ended the canal boom. Financing dried up, and states abandoned canal projects that had left them heavily in debt. Still, the canal boom had greatly accelerated economic growth. Three broad networks of canals existed by 1840. One set linked seaboard cities on the Atlantic with their agricultural hinterlands, another connected the mid-Atlantic states with the Ohio River Valley, and a third funneled western grain to ports on the Great Lakes. Canals and steamboats enlarged the profitable marketing radius of all kinds of goods and expanded the volume of interregional trade. A unified national market was starting to take shape.

Railroads

Railroads were the last and ultimately the most important link in the transportation improvements that spurred economic development in Jacksonian America. Unlike the canals, which seemed to blend into nature and complement the age-old advantages of water transport, railroads struck Americans as a radically new technology that overturned traditional notions of time and space. "What an object of wonder!" exclaimed Christopher Columbus Baldwin of Massachusetts when he saw his first railroad car in 1835. "I cannot describe the strange sensation produced on

This 1829 painting shows how the Erie Canal blended into the rural landscape of western New York. Although derided by skeptics as "Clinton's Big Ditch," the Erie was an economic success from the very beginning, and the tonnage carried on the Erie continued to grow until it reached a peak in 1880.

seeing the train of cars come up. And when I started in them . . . it seemed like a dream."

Americans remembered most the speed and noise from their first encounter with the railroads. Moving at fifteen to twenty miles per hour—four times as fast as a canal boat and twice the speed of a stagecoach—the railroads of the 1830s seemed to annihilate distance. After riding on the Western Railroad in Massachusetts, Caroline Fitch of Boston described her trip as a "lightning flash." The hissing of steam engines, squealing of iron wheels on iron rails, and gusts of air rushing into open rail cars made early rail travel an adventure; passengers felt like daring pioneers on a new technological frontier.

The railroads that were a source of such wonder emerged from humble beginnings in late eighteenth-century England. The first were horse-drawn wagons on wooden poles hauling coal from mines to British seaports. Cast-iron rails permitted much heavier loads to be hauled, and rapid technological advances gave birth to steam locomotives. In 1825, the same year the Erie Canal was completed, the world's first general-purpose steam-powered railroad, the Stockton and Darlington, opened in England. Businesspeople in the eastern cities of the United States, fearful that the canal would give New York a monopoly on the western trade, were quick to see the commercial promise of rail transport.

The construction of the first American railroads—the Baltimore and Ohio, the Boston and Worcester, and the Charleston and Hamburg—began in the late 1820s, and they all pushed outward from seaboard cities eager to connect to the western market. The Baltimore and Ohio was to cross the Appalachians and connect Baltimore with Wheeling, Virginia, on the Ohio River. Too far east to benefit from the Erie Canal, Boston merchants saw the Boston and Worcester as a link between New England and the eastern terminus of the Erie at Albany. By 1841, Boston had a rail connection to Albany. The Charleston enterprise sought to divert the lucrative cotton trade of the Carolina interior away from Savannah, Georgia. At its completion in 1833, the Charleston and Hamburg, with 136 miles of track, was the world's longest railroad.

Experimentation and innovation marked the first decade of railroad construction. American engineers received in-the-field training as they coped with problems posed by rough, mountainous terrain. They learned how to use crushed rock to cushion rails pounded by iron wheels. Stronger and sturdier iron T-rails replaced wooden rails overlaid with an iron strip. The swivel or bogie truck, loosely jointed forward wheels that turned with the curve of the track, controlled trains on sharp bends.

By 1840, U.S. rail mileage had drawn even with that of canals and was twice as extensive as the total for all of Europe. Although canals and steamboats were responsible for the greatest drop in freight rates in pre–Civil War America, competition from the railroads soon overshadowed them. Canals suffered from freezing in winter and low water in summer. The railroads were faster and more dependable and had more flexible schedules. They could serve landlocked areas beyond the reach of river and canal networks. Above all, they were more efficient. As early as 1840, a railroad could move four times as much freight as a canal for the same cost in labor and capital.

After a pause during the depression from 1839 to 1843, the railroads became the most dynamic booster of interregional trade. Whereas the canal network stopped expanding after 1840, the railroads tripled their mileage in the 1840s. Revenues from freight traffic exceeded those from passenger travel for the first time in 1849. By then, trunk lines built westward from Atlantic Coast cities had reached the Great Lakes and the Ohio Valley and were about to enter the Mississippi Valley. Short lines were being consolidated into larger systems. New York and Pennsylvania took the lead in developing trunk lines to the west.

Although the 1850s were the greatest decade of pre–Civil War rail construction, the rail network in place by midcentury was already altering the North-South sectional balance. Originating from the commercial cities of the Northeast, the major lines ran on an east–west axis that reinforced the shift in regional trade that the Erie Canal had begun. Before the coming of canals and railroads, the bulk of western trade went downriver to New Orleans. By the early 1850s, this traditional trading pattern had been reversed, and most western produce went east. Moving in the opposite direction were northern-born settlers, manufactured goods, and cultural values that increasingly unified the free states east of the Mississippi into a common economic and cultural unit. The Northeast and the Old Northwest were becoming just the North. Significantly, no direct rail connection linked the North and the South.

Government and the Economy

Both national and state government played an active part in the economy. The first major road to the West, the National Road, was a federal project. Begun in 1811, it ran from Cumberland, Maryland, to Vandalia, Illinois, by 1850. In the burst of economic nationalism after the War of 1812, Congress twice voted funds for a network of roads and canals. However, the constitutional objections and vetoes of Presidents Madison and Monroe prevented the federal government from developing a national system of transportation. Still, it was widely accepted that government should promote and regulate economic growth for the benefit of its citizens, and the constitutional scruples that held back the federal government did not apply to the individual states.

Following the lead of New York with the Erie Canal, state governments provided some 70 percent of the funding for canals. High construction costs made private investors leery of risking their scarce capital in such long-term transportation projects. Moreover, publicists for the state construction and ownership of canals argued that these transportation facilities should not be used "to pamper the cupidity and enrich the purses of our capitalists." The popular fear, as expressed by John Sergeant of Pennsylvania, was that the private owners of canals would "monopolize their benefits in perpetuity" and thereby deprive the people of part of their sovereign power. Similar arguments also induced the states to invest in the early railroads. Although the Panic of 1837 reduced their financial assistance, about half of all railroad capital before the Civil War came from the state governments.

Over time, the federal government assumed a larger role in assisting the railroads. Initially, it provided engineers for railroad surveys. Congress also lowered tariff duties on iron used in rail construction, which saved the railroads $6 million between 1830 and 1843. The most significant aid offered by Congress was grants of public land that totaled 20 million acres by 1860. Such grants had helped finance canal construction in Ohio and Indiana, and the precedent for railroads was set in 1850 when intense lobbying from southern and western congressmen secured a major grant to build the Illinois Central and the Mobile and Ohio Railroads. The Illinois Central raised the massive funds it needed for construction by mortgaging the federal lands it had received. Such federal subsidies through grants of public land were the chief means for financing the transcontinental railroads after the Civil War.

Government also encouraged economic growth through legislative and judicial actions. State courts and legislatures after the War of 1812 began to confer new rights and powers on private enterprises that had incorporated as transportation companies. Investors in these corporations received the protection of limited liability. If the corporation went bankrupt, the investors' personal assets were safe from creditors; their potential loss was limited to their direct financial stake in the company. Second, these corporations acquired the power of eminent domain, the legal right to purchase whatever land they needed for their rights-of-way. State courts upheld these enhanced legal powers. Thus farmers who did not want to sell their land for a right-of-way had no legal recourse. The courts ruled that a greater good—the development of the economy through transportation improvements—took precedence over the private property rights of an individual.

By the 1830s, the states were making it easier for businesses to incorporate. The older view of the

OVERVIEW

CHANGES PROMOTING GROWTH IN THE TRANSFORMED ECONOMY

Sector	1815	1850
Travel and transportation	By foot and horse-drawn wagon	Cheaper and faster with canals, steamboats, and railroads opening up new markets
Population	Overwhelmingly native-born, rural, and concentrated east of the Appalachian Mountains	Four times larger as a result of natural increase and surge of immigration after 1840; settlement of West and growth of cities
Wage labor	Native-born, primarily women and children in manufacturing	Expanding as rural poor and immigrants enter the manufacturing work force
Power	Water-driven mills	Steam-driven engines
Farming	Subsistence-oriented; surplus sold in localized markets	Commercialized agriculture spreading in response to improvements in transportation
Manufacturing	Small-scale production in household units and artisan shops	Large-scale production in eastern cities and factories

corporation as a privileged quasi-public institution entrusted with a communal responsibility gave way to the modern notion of the corporation as a private business that should receive no special government favors. A corporate charter had been viewed as a privilege, and each one required a special act of the legislature. As the economy expanded, incorporation was increasingly seen as a democratic right of business enterprise. Most states now enacted uniform provisions for receiving a charter that conferred no special powers as a public agency. Incorporation became an administrative process. The number of corporations grew rapidly under these new laws, and two-thirds of them were in transportation.

The proliferation of corporate charters produced legal clashes between older and newer economic interests. Artisans whose livelihoods were threatened by the spread of factories objected that incorporation "puts means into the hands of inexperienced capitalists to take from us the profits of our art which cost us so many years of labour to obtain." When railroads brought in outside goods that undersold local producers, farmers and artisans in Massachusetts accused the corporations of having delivered "the business and profits of general transportation into the hands of the capitalists." Their fears were well founded: "Scores of deserted villages in various sections of the Commonwealth bear witness to the wasting and blasting effects of this growing monopoly."

At stake also was the ability of new entrepreneurs to compete against the monopoly privileges granted to many of the early corporations. Two decisions of the Supreme Court helped open up the economy to competition. In *Gibbons v. Ogden* (1824), the Court overturned a New York law that had given Aaron Ogden a monopoly on steamboat service between New York and New Jersey. Thomas Gibbons, Ogden's competitor, had a federal license for the coastal trade. The right to compete under the national license, the Court ruled, took legal precedence over Ogden's monopoly. The decision prevented states from restricting trade within their jurisdictions and affirmed the supremacy of the national government to regulate interstate commerce.

A new Court, presided over by Chief Justice Roger B. Taney, Jackson's former secretary of the treasury (John Marshall had died in 1835), struck a bolder blow against monopoly in the landmark case of *Charles River Bridge* v. *Warren Bridge* in 1837. Taney ruled in favor of the Warren Bridge Company by deciding that the older Charles River Bridge Company had not received a monopoly from Massachusetts to collect tolls across the Charles River. Any uncertainties in the charter rights of corporations, reasoned Taney, should be resolved in favor of the broader community interests that would be served by free and open competition. His decision divested corporations of any implied charter privileges that could put a monopolistic brake on economic progress.

The Rise of Cities

When Washington became president, Philadelphia, with a population just over forty thousand, was the nation's largest city. Barely one in twenty Americans lived in an urban area (defined as a place with a population of 2,500 or more). By the 1820s, cities had begun to grow more rapidly than rural areas. At midcentury, more than one in seven Americans was a city-dweller, and the nation had ten cities whose population exceeded fifty thousand (see Map 11-2).

The transportation revolution triggered this surge in urban growth. The cities that prospered and grew were those with access to the expanding network of cheap transport on steamboats, canals, and railroads. This network opened up the rural interior for the purchase of farm commodities by city merchants and the sale of finished goods by urban importers and manufacturers. Increased commercial activity tied to interregional trade was the primary source of economic growth in the largest cities until the 1840s. Manufacturing did not begin to play a major role until the late stages of pre–Civil War urbanization. A huge influx of immigrants after the mid-1840s and simultaneous advances in steam engines provided the cheap labor and sources of power that increasingly made cities focal points of manufacturing production.

The Port Cities

America's largest cities in the early nineteenth century were its Atlantic ports: New York, Philadelphia, Baltimore, and Boston. As late as the 1820s, these four cities held more than half the total urban population. Small in size—it took only half an hour to walk entirely across any one of them in 1800—these cities packed together merchants, artisans, and laborers near the waterfronts that were their economic lifeblood. "The carters were driving in every direction," an Englishman wrote of the New York City waterfront in 1806, "and the sailors and labourers upon the wharfs, and on board the vessels, were moving their ponderous burthens from place to place. The merchants and their clerks were busily engaged in their counting-houses, or upon the piers. . . . Everything was in motion; all was life, bustle, and activity."

These Atlantic seaports all benefited from the increased trade promoted by the transportation revolution, but only New York experienced phenomenal growth. By 1810, New York had become the largest American city, and its population exceeded 800,000 by the 1850s. One-third of the nation's exports and more than three-fifths of its imports passed through New York between 1820 and 1860. No wonder poet Walt Whitman trumpeted this metropolis as "the great place of the Western Continent, the heart, the brain, the focus, the main spring, the pinnacle, the extremity, the no more beyond of the new world."

Nature had blessed New York with incomparable advantages. Its harbor, the finest on the East Coast, gave oceangoing ships direct, protected access to Manhattan Island, and from there the Hudson River provided a navigable highway flowing 150 miles north to Albany, deep in the state's agricultural interior. No other port was so ideally situated for trade. The entrepreneurial moxie of New York City merchants, the most forward-looking of all mercantile groups, enhanced these natural advantages. In 1817, the merchants established the Black Ball Line, the first line of packet ships that ran on a regular schedule for moving cargoes, passengers, and mail across the Atlantic. The city's merchants also convinced the state legislature to finance the Erie Canal, which guaranteed the ongoing commercial preeminence of the port of New York.

The Erie Canal gave New York City merchants a lucrative gateway to the West. The city benefited not only from the increased volume of western foodstuffs sent east across the canal and down the Hudson River for export to Europe but also from the swelling flow of finished goods shipped out of New York for sale in the West. Western families with access to the Erie Canal became increasingly specialized economically. New markets for the sale of agricultural surpluses encouraged them to concentrate on cash crops, and profits from the sale of these crops were spent on finished goods that no longer had to be produced within the household. One measure of this trend was that families in upstate New York had virtually stopped making their own textiles by the 1850s. The rise in the disposable income of farmers generated a demand

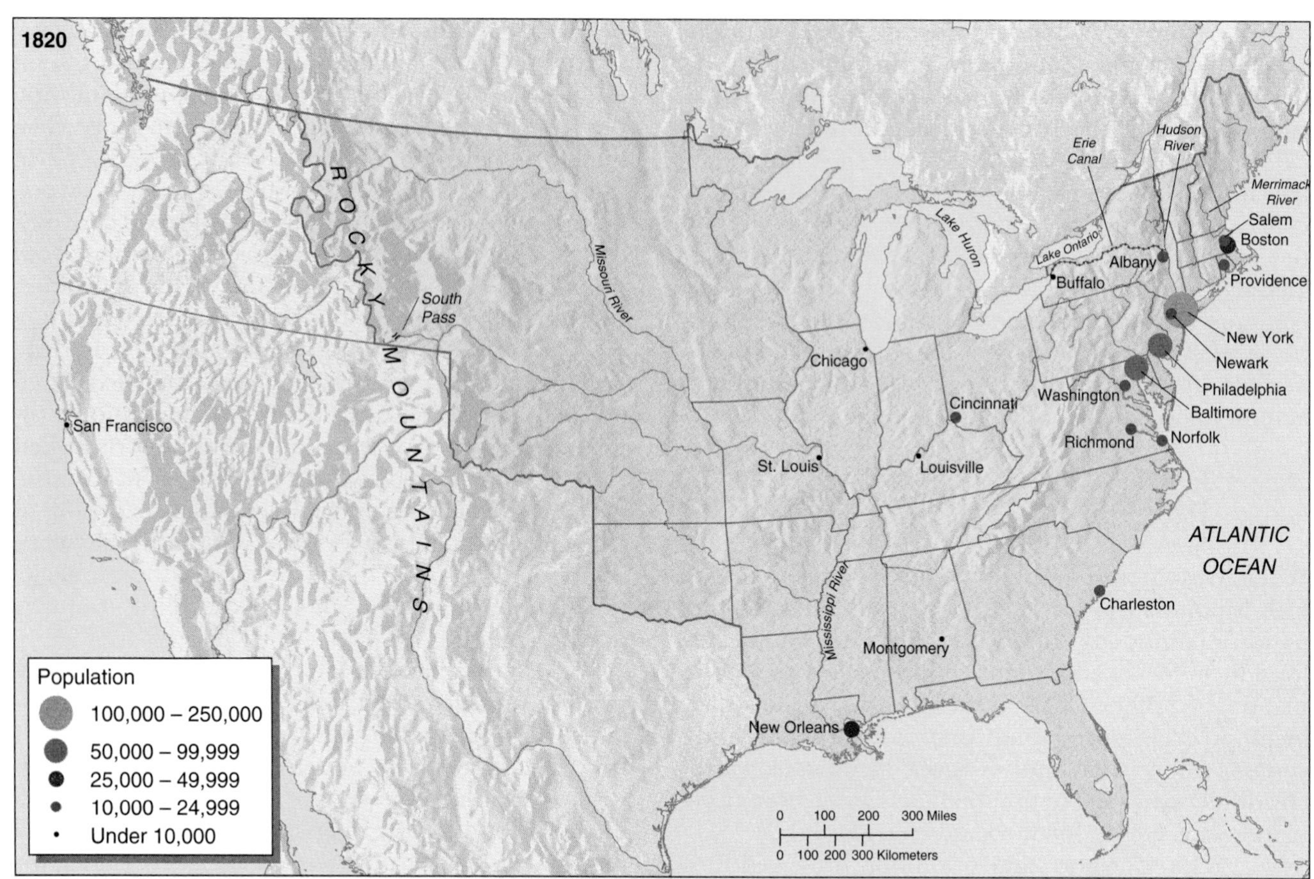

Map 11-2 The Growth of Cities, 1820–1860
In 1820 most cities were clustered along the Atlantic seaboard. By 1860, new transportation outlets—canals and railroads—had fostered the rapid growth of cities in the interior, especially at trading locations with access to navigable rivers or to the Great Lakes. Much of this growth occurred in the 1850s.

Data Source: Statistical Abstract of the United States.

for the textiles, shoes, and other consumer goods that the Erie Canal brought in. These goods came out of New York, but most were not manufactured in the city. Nonetheless, the jobs created by handling these goods and the profits derived from supplying the western market solidified the city's position as the nation's most dynamic economic center.

New Yorkers plowed the profits of this commerce into local real estate—which soared in value fiftyfold between 1823 and 1836—and into financial institutions. The New York Stock Exchange, founded in 1817, became the country's main clearinghouse for stocks, and the city's banks brought together the capital that made New York the country's chief financial center. Agents for the city's mercantile and financial interests used this capital to offer advantageous terms by which New York captured much of the southern trade and dominated commerce with South America.

Commercial rivals in other port cities could not keep pace with New York. They launched their own canal and railroad ventures to penetrate the West, but none developed a hinterland as rich or extensive as New York's. Boston and Baltimore were also handicapped by the decline in their West Indian trade after the War of 1812, and Philadelphia lagged behind New York in financing international connections. Still, these cities continued to grow and at midcentury remained the nation's largest cities behind New York.

As they grew, the Atlantic ports pioneered new forms of city transportation. Omnibuses (horse-drawn coaches carrying up to twenty passengers) and steam ferries were in common use by the 1820s. The first commuter railroad, the Boston and Worcester, began service in 1838. The greatest advance in moving people within cities came with the introduction of horse-drawn street railway lines in the 1850s. These moved at speeds of about six miles an hour,

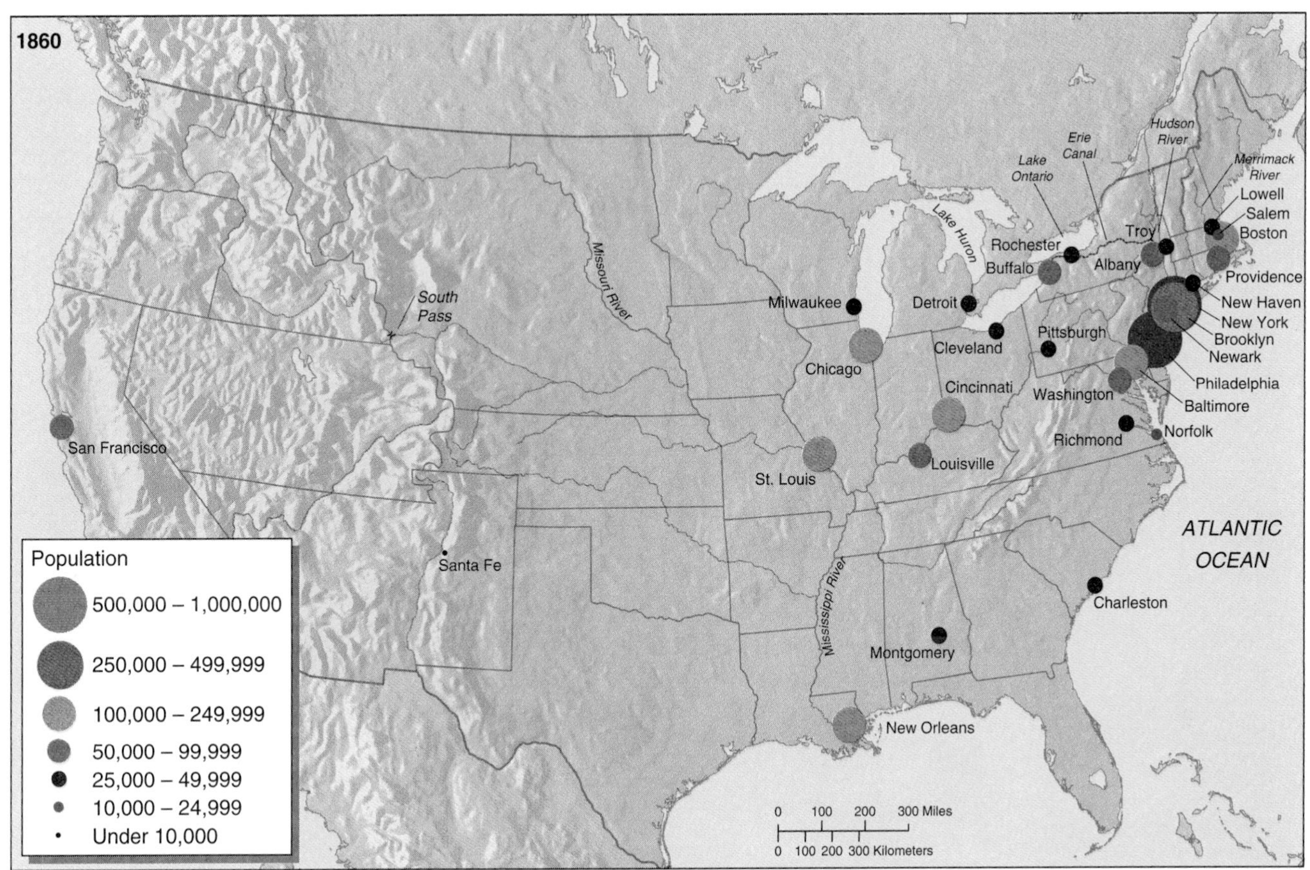

overcoming some of the limitations of the "walking cities" of the early nineteenth century. Cities began to spread outward as cheaper, faster ways of traveling to work became available.

Living conditions improved more slowly. An expanding population strained limited housing resources, and at least one in four families shared a dwelling with others. The first slums appeared, the most notorious of which was the Five Points district of New York City. In 1842, the English novelist Charles Dickens described this area of tenement houses, brothels, and saloons as "these narrow ways, diverging to the right and left, and reeking everywhere with dirt and filth."

Small, flimsy wooden structures, often crammed into a back alley, housed the working poor in cramped, fetid conditions. Indoor plumbing was not available until the 1830s and then only as a luxury for the wealthy. Backyard privies, supplemented by chamber pots, were the standard means of disposing of human wastes. These outhouses overflowed in heavy rain and often contaminated private wells, the source of drinking water. Garbage and animal wastes simply accumulated on streets, scavenged by roving packs of hogs. Rudimentary systems for disposing of sewage and for piping in water from the countryside began to emerge in the 1840s but were inadequate for urban needs.

These conditions—a densely packed population in a poorly drained, garbage-strewn setting—made cities unhealthy. Mortality rates were much higher than in rural areas, and the death rate in New York City was double that of London. Stagnant pools of water bred mosquitoes that carried yellow fever, and contaminated water supplies produced frequent epidemics of cholera and typhus. Despite these deplorable standards in public health, the cities continued to grow.

Interior Cities

The fastest-growing cities were in the interior. Their share of the urban population quadrupled from 1800 to 1840. Some of these cities were specifically designed as new manufacturing centers, and others were favorably located to tap into the expanding transportation network. Both sets of cities had a frantic sense of newness. Rochester, New York, a village that the opening of the Eric Canal rapidly transformed into a major flour-milling center, amazed one English visitor in 1827 with its spontaneous energy. "The very streets," he observed, "seemed to be starting up of

This illustration captures the boisterous disorder and cramped living conditions of the Five Points slum area in New York City.

their own accord, ready-made, and looking as fresh as new, as if they had been turned out of the workmen's hands but an hour before—or that a great boxful of new houses had been sent by steam from New York, and tumbled out on the half-cleared land."

Pittsburgh, at the head of the Ohio River, was the first western city to develop a manufacturing sector to complement its exchange function. Situated among the extensive coalfields of western Pennsylvania, Pittsburgh had access to a cheap fuel that provided the high heat needed to manufacture iron and glass. It emerged after the War of 1812 as America's best-known and most polluted manufacturing city. "It is surrounded," noted the French traveler Michel Chevalier in the 1830s, "with a dense, black smoke which, bursting forth in volumes from the foundries, forges, glass-houses, and the chimneys of all the factories and houses, falls in flakes of soot upon the dwellings and persons of the inhabitants. It is, therefore, the dirtiest town in the United States."

Cincinnati, downstream on the Ohio, soon became as famous for its hogs as Pittsburgh was for its soot. "Porkopolis," as it was called, was the West's first meatpacking center. Industries in animal by-products, such as soap, candles, shoes, and boots, gave the city a diversified manufacturing base that kept it in the forefront of western urban growth. In contrast, Louisville, at the falls of the Ohio, remained more of a distribution point and slipped from the top rank of western cities after 1840. New Orleans, the largest city in the West, kept its rank because of its unique location at the mouth of the Mississippi, the only outlet to the Atlantic for western produce before the Erie Canal began drawing trade toward the Great Lakes. Still, because its economic base remained heavily concentrated on the export of cotton, New Orleans grew more slowly in the late antebellum period.

By the 1840s, St. Louis and the Great Lakes ports of Buffalo, Cleveland, Detroit, Milwaukee, and Chicago were the dynamic centers of western urbanization. St. Louis, just below the merger of the Missouri and the Mississippi Rivers, serviced American trade with the trans-Mississippi West. This trade blossomed once the Trans-Continental Treaty of 1819 eliminated Spanish claims to the Missouri Country.

Outfitters used St. Louis as the jumping-off point for the fur trade up the middle Missouri and through the South Pass of the Rocky Mountains to rendezvous points with trappers and Native Americans in Wyoming. The city was also the eastern end of the Santa Fe Trail, a corridor of Anglo–Mexican trade that stretched across the southern plains to Santa Fe, New Mexico. St. Louis tripled in population in the 1830s, and it continued to surge after 1840 as a result of the city's importance in receiving and distributing goods for the upper Mississippi Valley. By midcentury, St. Louis was developing rail connections that linked it to the Great Lakes cities in a great transportation arc that shuttled goods and services east and west.

The success of the Erie Canal in reorienting western trade northward was the impetus behind the spectacular growth of the ports on the Great Lakes. Buffalo led the way in the 1820s, and a decade later, Cleveland and Detroit were also booming. They were soon joined by the Lake Michigan ports of Chicago and Milwaukee. The Great Lakes served as an extension of the Erie Canal, and cities on the lakes where incoming and outgoing goods had to be unloaded for transshipment benefited enormously. They attracted settlers and soon evolved into regional economic centers serving the surrounding agricultural communities. They also aggressively promoted themselves into major rail hubs and thus reaped the economic advantages of being at the juncture of both water and rail transport.

The combined populations of Cleveland, Detroit, Milwaukee, and Chicago increased twenty-five-fold between 1830 and 1850. The only other cities experiencing such phenomenal growth were the new industrial towns. The densest cluster of these was in rural New England along the fall line of rivers, where the rapidly falling water provided cheap power to drive industrial machinery. Each town supported a cluster of factories and machine shops and was tied to a transportation network that brought in raw cotton for the textile mills from the mercantile centers of Boston and Providence and shipped out the finished goods.

The most famous of these new factory cities was Lowell, Massachusetts. Indeed, it became a must stop for foreign visitors. Lowell was America's first large-scale, planned manufacturing city. Founded in 1822 by Boston businessmen, Lowell was built around

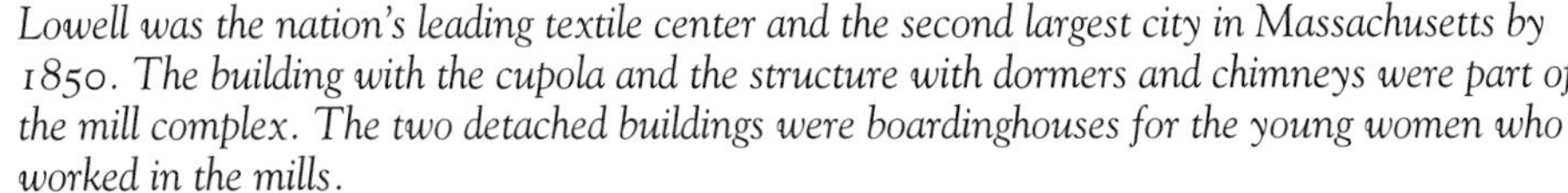

Lowell was the nation's leading textile center and the second largest city in Massachusetts by 1850. The building with the cupola and the structure with dormers and chimneys were part of the mill complex. The two detached buildings were boardinghouses for the young women who worked in the mills.

the falls of the Merrimack River. Within a decade, rural fields had been transformed into a city of eighteen thousand people. Multistoried brick factories surrounded by detached housing for the supervisory staff and large boardinghouses for the workers dominated the landscape and defined the city's industrial functions. The overall impression was one of bustling but well-ordered productive activity. "Everywhere one hears the noise of hammers, of spindles, of bells calling the hands to their work or dismissing them from their tasks, of coaches and six arriving or starting off, of the blasting of rocks to make a millrace or to level a road," noted Michel Chevalier in the mid-1830s; "It is the peaceful hum of an industrious population whose movements are regulated like clockwork." Lowell's success, like that of the Erie Canal, became a model for others to follow, and by 1840, New England led the North in both urbanization and industrialization.

Immigration

After improved transportation and a quickened economic pace provided the initial impetus for urban growth, a surge of immigrants swelled the size of the cities after the 1830s. At midcentury, most of the population in New York was foreign-born, and in all the port cities of the Northeast, immigrants dominated the manufacturing workforce.

In the half-century after the Revolution, immigration to the United States had slowed to a trickle. Before 1825, it was well under ten thousand newcomers per year. It then jumped in the 1830s to more than fifty thousand per year and soared to 140,000 in the 1840s and 280,000 in the 1850s. Most of these immigrants were Irish and Germans who settled in the Northeast (see Figure 11-1).

In the 1840s, economic and political upheavals in Europe spurred mass migration, mostly to America. No group suffered more than the Catholic peasants of Ireland. Dominated by their Protestant English landlords, these peasants eked out a subsistence as tenants on tiny plots of land. The potato was practically their only source of food, and when a blight wiped out the potato crop in 1845 and 1846, mass starvation ensued. In the next five years, about 1 million Irish died of malnutrition and disease, and another 1.5 million fled, many to America.

The Irish, like other immigrants, followed the main ocean trade routes to the New World. Most of these routes centered on New York, where two-thirds of all immigrants arrived in the 1840s and 1850s. As the poorest and most desperate of the immigrants, the Irish clustered in the ports. They had no money to buy land or move west unless they joined construction gangs for canals and rail-

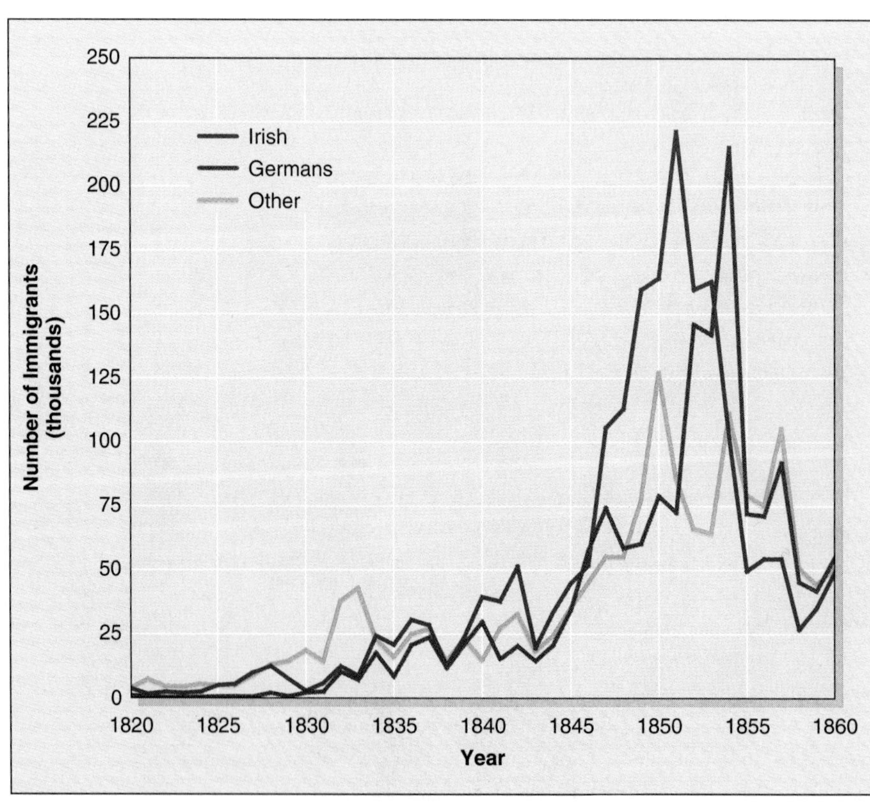

Figure 11-1 Immigration to the United States, 1820–1860
The potato famine in Ireland and economic and political unrest on the Continent led to a surge in immigration in the 1840s. The pace slackened in the mid-1850s when economic conditions in Europe improved.

Data Source: U.S. Bureau of the Census, Historical Statistics of the United States, Colonial Times to 1957 (1960), p. 57.

roads. Without marketable skills, they had to take the worst and lowest-paying jobs: ragpicker, porter, day laborer, and unskilled factory hand. Wives and daughters became laundresses and maids for the urban middle class.

The living conditions of the urban Irish were deplorable. Packed into dark cellars, unventilated attics, and rank tenements, their mortality rates were frightful. Still, cash wages and access to food made the American city enviable compared to the prospect of starvation in Ireland. The message the Irish sent home was that for all its hardships, life was better in the New World than in the Old. Urging her parents to join her, Margaret McCarthy, an Irish domestic servant, wrote in 1850 that New York was a place "where no man or woman ever Hungerd or ever will and where you will not be Seen Naked . . . where you would never want or be at a loss for a good Breakfast and Dinner."

German immigrants were second in number only to the Irish by the 1850s. Coming to America to escape poor harvests and political turmoil, they were relatively better off then their Irish counterparts. Far more of them had owned property as farmers, artisans, and shopkeepers, and so had the capital to purchase land in the West and the skills to join the ranks of small businesspeople in the cities. They were also more likely than the Irish to have entered the country through Baltimore or New Orleans, southern ports engaged in the tobacco and cotton trade with continental Europe. From there they fanned out into the Mississippi and Ohio Valleys.

Compared to the Irish, more German immigrants settled in rural areas, but they also tended to congregate in the cities. With the Irish, they made up over half of the population of St. Louis by the 1850s and were close to a majority in the other large cities of the Midwest and Northeast. With their diversified skills, the Germans found ample economic opportunities in the fast-growing cities and a setting in which to build tightly knit ethnic communities for mutual support. Centered around neighborhoods of German-speaking shops, churches, schools, and benevolent societies, these communities published their own newspapers and met most of the immigrants's cultural and economic needs.

About four in five of the 4.2 million immigrants from all nations who arrived from 1840 to 1860 settled in the New England and mid-Atlantic states. Their sheer numbers transformed the size and ethnic composition of the working class, especially in the cities of the Northeast. And their cheap labor provided the final ingredient in the expansion of industrialization that began after the War of 1812.

The Industrial Revolution

Manufacturing was the most dynamic growth sector in the American economy after 1815. Once the transportation revolution removed the physical barriers that had blocked the flow of goods, agriculture and manufacturing emerged as separate, specialized economic activities. Each fed on the other as home markets developed for the products of farms and factories. Regions, as well as individuals, had an incentive to specialize in goods that they could produce most efficiently with their labor and capital. Specialization in the scale of production, the organization of work, and the utilization of labor was also occurring. When these changes were combined with power-driven machinery in the new factories, the very meaning of the word *manufacturing* changed. Whereas before the 1820s it referred to the making of things by hand, it now came to mean the production of goods by machines in factories.

The Northeast led America's industrial revolution. In 1815, this region had the largest cities, the most developed capital markets, the readiest access to the technological skills of artisans, and the greatest supply of available labor. The first large-scale factories, the textile mills, were erected in New England in the 1820s, and for the next thirty years, the United States had the most rapidly developing industrial economy in the world.

Early Stages

The household and the small workshop were the sites of manufacturing in Jefferson's America. Household manufacturers accounted for about two-thirds of all clothing worn in the United States and a sizable percentage of such consumer items as shoes, hats, and soap. Because of the high cost of transportation in the precanal age, markets for manufactured items were localized, and the overwhelmingly rural population had to produce most of the goods it consumed. Informal trading networks in which labor and services were bartered for needed finished goods made farming communities, if not individual farm families, largely self-sufficient. Wider markets for household manufactures began to develop in the late eighteenth century with the coming of the **putting-out system**. Local merchants furnished ("put out") raw materials to rural households and paid at a piece rate for the labor that converted those raw materials into manufactured products. The supplying merchant then marketed and sold these goods.

In the cities and larger towns, most manufacturing was done by artisans, skilled craftsmen who were also known as mechanics. Working in their own shops and with their own tools, they produced small batches of finished goods. They made clothing and shoes, built houses, butchered carcasses, set type for printing, and turned out metal and wood products to order. Making up close to half of the population in the seaport cities, artisans and their families fed, clothed, and housed the urban population.

All artisans had a specific skill that set them above common laborers. For example, some knew how to gauge when a forge was just hot enough for working hand-wrought iron, and others could lay down and level the frame of a house without blueprints. These skills came from hands-on experience and craft traditions that were handed down from one generation to the next.

Artisanal skills were the "mysteries of the craft," and they were taught by master craftsmen to the **journeymen** and **apprentices** who lived with them and worked in their shops. Journeymen had learned the skills of their craft but lacked the capital to open their own shops. Before establishing their own businesses, they saved their earnings and honed their skills while working for a wage under a master. Apprentices were adolescent boys legally sent by their fathers to live with and obey a master craftsman in return for being taught a trade. By the terms of the contract, known as an **indenture**, the master also provided for the apprentice's schooling and moral upbringing. Although nothing was guaranteed in the craft hierarchy, an apprentice could reasonably expect to be promoted to journeyman in his late teens and begin advancement toward his **competency**, a secure income from an independent trade that would enable him to support a family.

As revealed in this portrait of the blacksmith Pat Lyon, the self-image of artisans was closely related to the pride and dignity they derived from their craft work.

The artisanal trades dictated a way of life bound by self-regulated rules and values. Artisans controlled entry into their trades and the process of production from start to finish. They set their own work rules and were their own bosses. The independence of their crafts and the satisfaction derived from their work were the basis of their self-identity as workers and citizens. "The Mechanics are a class [of] men," proudly wrote "Peter Single" in the *Mechanic's Free Press* of Philadelphia, "who compose that proportion of the population of our country, on whom depends its present and future welfare; from them emanates her glory, her greatness and her power."

The factory system of production that undercut both household and artisanal manufacturing was in its infancy before 1815, but it had several advantages. First, by uniting the different phases of manufacture in one setting, the factories could produce goods far more quickly and cheaply per worker than artisans or rural households. Factories subdivided the specialized skills of the artisan into a series of semiskilled tasks, a process foreshadowed by the putting-out system. Second, they pulled workers out of families and shops and put them under systematic controls. And in the final stage of industrialization, they boosted workers' productivity through the use of power-driven machinery. The earliest factories turned out cotton and woolen textiles; the most technologically advanced of the early factories was founded in 1790 by Samuel Slater in Providence, Rhode Island.

Britain pioneered the technological advances that drove early industrialization. The secrets of this technology, especially the designs for the machines that mechanized textile production, were closely guarded by the British government. Despite attempts to prohibit the emigration of artisans who knew how this machinery worked, some British mechanics got to the United States. Slater was one of them, and he took over the operation of a fledging mill started by Moses Brown, a Quaker merchant. With his knowledge of how to build water-powered spinning machinery, Slater converted the mill into the nation's first permanent cotton factory.

Slater's factory, and those modeled after it, manufactured yarn that was put out to rural housewives to be woven into cloth. The first factory to mechanize the operations of spinning and weaving and turn out finished cloth was incorporated in Waltham, Massachusetts, in 1813 by the Boston Associates, a group of wealthy merchants. The Waltham factory signaled the future direction of the textile industry. It was heavily capitalized, relied on the latest technology, and recruited its work force from rural farm families.

A rudimentary factory system was in place by 1815. The first real spurt of factory building came with the closing off of British imports during the embargo and the War of 1812. Hundreds of new cotton and woolen mills were established from 1808 to 1815. But the great test of American manufacturing came after 1815 when peace with Britain brought a flood of cheap British manufactured goods. If factories were to continue to grow, American manufacturers had to reach more consumers in their home market and overcome the British advantage of lower labor costs.

Sources of Workers in Manufacturing

The economy was at a crossroads in 1815. Its growth during the early national period had been heavily dependent on transatlantic trade, but future growth would have to come from within as capital and resources were diverted from carrying goods to producing them. As we have seen, the Erie Canal opened markets at home for American manufacturers. To expand significantly, however, the factories needed abundant cheap labor.

Industrial labor was more expensive in America than in England, where the high cost of land forced the peasantry into the cities to find work. In contrast, land was cheap and plentiful in the United States, and Americans preferred the independence of farm work to the dependence of factory labor. Consequently, the first mill workers were predominantly children. Early mill owners recruited their work force from poor, rural families, especially large ones. For example, the mills that advertised in the *Massachusetts Spy* in the 1820s called for families "of five or six children each." The owners set up the father on a plot of company-owned land, provided piecework for the mother, and put the children to work in the mills.

Although this so-called **Rhode Island system** of family employment sufficed for small mills, it was inadequate for the larger, more mechanized factories that were built in New England after the War of 1812. These mill owners needed more workers to operate their textile machinery than could be found among poor families near the mill. Following a plan pioneered at the Waltham mill, they recruited single, adolescent daughters of farmers from across New England as their laborers.

The **Waltham system** of recruitment succeeded. Throughout the 1820s and 1830s, most mill hands in New England were young farm daughters. They were the most expendable members of large rural families, whose farms could not compete with cheap western foodstuffs. As Jemima Sanborn explained when she went into the mills in Nashua, New Hampshire, they left home because of "the hard times to get a living off the farm for so large a family." Although factory wages were low (a little over a dollar per week after deductions for room and board), they were higher than what these young women could earn doing piecework in the home or hiring out as domestics. The wages also brought a liberating degree of financial independence. "When they felt the jingle of silver in their pockets," recalled Harriet Hanson Robinson of her fellow workers at Lowell in the 1830s, "there for the first time, their heads became erect and they walked as if on air." No longer directly dependent on their male-dominated families for support, these women could now spend their personal time as they pleased.

Based on what they had heard of conditions in British factories, most Americans associated mill towns with morally depraved, impoverished workers. To overcome parental fears of sending their daughters into such an unwholesome environment, New England manufacturers set up paternalistic moral controls. Single female workers had to live in boardinghouses owned or subsidized by the company. Curfews were imposed, visitors were screened, church attendance was mandatory, and special cultural activities were arranged for the mill hands (see "American Views: An Englishman's Description of Lowell").

Despite this paternalism, the mill women still worked long hours for low wages. Six days a week from dawn to dusk, the operatives tended clattering, fast-moving machinery in a work environment kept humid to minimize the snapping of threads in the machines. The market for mill cloth was very competitive, and the owners responded by slashing wages and speeding up work. In 1834 and 1836, the female hands at Lowell "turned out" to protest wage reductions in demonstrations that were the largest strikes in

Shown here working at power looms under the supervision of a male overseer, young single women comprised the bulk of the labor force in the first textile factories of New England.

American history up to that time. Drawing on the republican heritage of the Revolution, they insisted that "as our fathers resisted unto blood the lordly avarice of the British ministry, so we, their daughters, will never wear the yoke which has been prepared for us."

After the economic downturn of the late 1830s, conditions in the mills got worse. By the mid-1840s, however, laborers who would work longer for less pay than their Yankee predecessors were available. The Irish, desperate for work, sent their children into the mills at an earlier age than Yankee farm families had, and these workers stayed longer—they did not leave after two or three years when they had built up a small dowry for marriage, as many New Englanders did. The Irish soon began to replace the Yankee women in the mills. In the mid-1830s, some 95 percent of the textile operatives in New England were native-born and mostly women; by the early 1850s, more than half were Irish women.

South of New England in the mid-Atlantic region, immigrants played a larger role in the formative stages of industrialization. The farm population here was more prosperous than in New England, and fewer young women were available for factory work. Consequently, manufacturers had to rely on foreign-born labor. As early as 1820, about half of the factory workers in the mid-Atlantic states were immigrants. Many of them were the Irish, who drifted into the factories after working on the canals.

The rise in immigration after the 1820s was crucial for urban manufacturing. The port cities lacked usable water power but did have a large and cheap pool of immigrant labor. This was a decisive advantage. By drawing on this pool, manufacturers could increase the volume of production while driving down the cost. A few skilled workers supervised the most difficult part of production, and semiskilled or unskilled workers performed by hand the specialized tasks into which the rest of the manufacturing process had been subdivided.

Especially in finished consumer goods, such as the clothing and leather industries, where low-paid workers could stitch cloth or sole a shoe, urban manufacturing became labor-intensive, depending more heavily on workers than on investment in machines and other capital. Shops were enlarged, or work was contracted out at piece rates. New York and Philadelphia, followed by Boston in the 1840s, thus built up a diversified manufacturing sector in consumer goods.

Except in New England textile factories and the smaller factories and shops in the seaboard cities, native-born males were the largest group of early manufacturing workers. They dominated the production of boots and shoes, an industry that employed twice as many workers in Massachusetts as cotton textiles in the 1850s. Native-born men also supplied most of the labor in the small manufacturing centers that sprang up in the medium-sized cities of the interior. They came from the surrounding countryside and were mostly the younger sons of poor farm families who no longer had enough land to pass on to all of the heirs. Unable or unwilling to go west, they sought work at a neighboring factory, usually as unskilled laborers.

As late as 1840, women, including those working at home, made up about half of the manufacturing work force and one-quarter of the factory hands. These proportions declined by midcentury as immigrant males and displaced sons of poor American farmers became the fastest-growing source of manufacturing laborers. Regardless of their sex, few of these workers brought any specific skills to their jobs and so had little bargaining power. Economic necessity forced them to accept low wages and harsh working conditions. The sheer increase in their numbers, as opposed to any productivity gains from technological innovations, accounted by 1850 for two-thirds of the gains in manufacturing output.

The Role of Technology

Technological backwardness was the last major barrier American manufacturers overcame. Significant gains in productivity could be achieved only by applying the latest industrial technology to mechanize production. In closing the technological gap with Britain, manufacturers first relied on the trade secrets brought to America by British mechanics such as Samuel Slater. This smuggled knowledge was essential for starting up the textile industry, but elsewhere the versatile, practical skills of American mechanics provided the impetus for technological innovation.

Mechanics, especially in the countryside, had an extensive range of skills. The Dominy family of Easthampton, Long Island, for example, worked with wood and iron, built grist mills, and made clocks and watches. Mechanics understood how machines worked and were great tinkerers. They experimented with new designs, improved old ones, and patented inventions that found industrial applications outside their own crafts. Oliver Evans, a wagonmaker in the Delaware Valley, developed machinery for a highly automated flour mill in the 1780s. In the 1830s, two mechanics in Connecticut who made axes built a machine that pressed and forged hot metal into dies, devices that cut metal into special forms. A skilled worker could use their machines to expand his daily production of ax heads twenty-five times over.

The most famous early American invention was the cotton gin. Eli Whitney, a Massachusetts Yankee who had turned out knives and blades at a forge on his father's farm as a teenager, built the first prototype in 1793 while working as a tutor on a Georgia plantation. By cheaply and mechanically removing the seeds from cotton fibers, the cotton gin spurred the cultivation of cotton across the South.

Whitney also pushed the idea of basing production on interchangeable parts. After receiving a federal contract to manufacture muskets, he designed new milling machines and turret lathes that transformed the technology of machine tool production. The federal arsenal at Harpers Ferry, Virginia, developed machine tools that could manufacture standardized, interchangeable parts. The new techniques were first applied in 1815 to the manufacture of wooden clocks and by the 1840s to sewing machines, farm machinery, and watch parts. What became famous in the 1850s as the **American system of manufacturing**—low-cost, standardized mass production, built around interchangeable parts stamped out by machines—was characteristic of only about twenty industries, mostly those in metal cutting. Nonetheless, it was America's unique contribution to the industrial revolution.

As the pace of technological innovation accelerated after 1840, so did the growth of manufacturing. Indeed, the 1840s registered the highest rate of expansion in the manufacturing sector of the economy in the nineteenth century. The adoption of the stationary steam engine in urban manufacturing fueled much of this expansion.

Large cities had always offered manufacturers the advantages of concentrated pools of labor and capital, cheap transportation and trading services, and ready access to urban consumers. But these advantages were largely offset by the lack of water power to drive machinery. Thus urban manufacturing initially rested on an extensive division of labor and the hiring of more workers to expand production. This pattern began to reverse in the 1840s when high-pressure steam engines enabled power-driven industry to locate in the port cities of the Northeast.

Steam power and more mechanized manufacturing also benefited the booming cities in the Great Lakes corridor of the Old Northwest. With limited access to water power, early manufacturing in

American Views

An Englishman's Description of Lowell

Although Lowell was not a typical industrial city, it was touted as a model of the success of American manufacturing. Early visitors routinely praised Lowell's physical appearance and the character of its female operatives. As can be seen in the following account written in 1845 by the Englishman William Scoresby, many saw in Lowell confirmation of the belief that Americans could escape the social evils associated with the factory system in England.

- **How did Scorseby favorably contrast Lowell with manufacturing towns in England?**
- **Why does the account put such emphasis on the apparent "respectability" of the young women who worked at Lowell?**
- **What does Scorseby single out as the special features of industrialism in the United States?**

On entering Lowell, a stranger is naturally struck with the contrast presented by that place to an English manufacturing town. Here, in Bradford [England], every building is of stone, or brick, solid, substantial, with little of the freshness that might be looked for in so rapidly an increasing town: there, in Lowell, though the mills and boardinghouses are generally of brick, the chief part of the other buildings, houses, hotels, and even churches, are of wood, and nearly the whole as fresh looking as if built within a year. Here, with us, everything, externally, is discolored with smoke . . .: there, nothing is discolored, neither houses nor mills nor trees. . . . Hence, as to Lowell, large as it has grown, it is yet rural in its appearance, and, notwithstanding its being a city of factories, is yet fresh and cleanly. . . .

We proceeded [to] one of the factories, that we might see the factory workers as they came out to their dinners. Several hundreds of

the West was confined to the processing of farm goods—milling corn and wheat, tanning leather, packing meat, and rendering animal by-products into soap and candles. By turning to steam power and new machine tools, western manufacturers after 1840 enlarged their region's industrial base and created a new industry, the mass production of agricultural implements. The McCormick reaper factory in Chicago was one of the world's most modern industrial facilities by the 1850s. Steam-powered conveyer belts moved parts through the factory in an assembly-line system of production. The West was the center of the farm machinery industry, and the region produced 20 percent of the nation's manufacturing output by the 1850s.

By freeing industry to locate near centers of population and driving the trains that reached areas untouched by rivers or canals, steam power was beginning to transform the American landscape by the mid-nineteenth century. However, most of the change evident in the countryside by 1850 was the product of preindustrial technologies and the aftermath of impounding water for factory use.

The most obvious change involved the clearing of the land. About one-fifth of the original forest cover in the United States east of the Mississippi was gone by 1850. Most of this loss resulted from agricultural use. Clear-cutting, firing, and girdling—killing a tree by removing its bark in a continuous strip—were the cheapest ways to hack out a farm in the wilderness. The initial result was a bleak landscape of stumps and scorched trunks. Wood that was not needed for farmhouses, fences, and fuel found a ready market in the cities and factories, where it was both the primary energy source and the basic building material.

As the land was being cleared and carved into private farms, the lakes and streams continued young women, but not any children, issued from the mills, altogether very orderly in their manner, and very respectable in their appearance. They were neatly dressed and clean in their persons [with] not the slightest appearance of boldness or vulgarity; on the contrary, a very becoming propriety and respectability of manner, approaching, with some, to genteel [and] I have been led to infer that their character and moral conduct are unusually high. . . .

One great and striking difference, in the present positions of England and America, is found in the history and rise of our respective manufacturing establishments. In England, for the most part they consist of enlargements of old, and successions of new manufactories, within a previously existing manufacturing town. But in America, the manufactories consist altogether of new, or at least of very modern erections; and these are not infrequently planted, as in the case of Lowell, not as grafts upon the stock of a town venerable in age, but as the original occupants of the ground, and as the stock on which the town itself is grafted.

Hence the American manufacturing towns possess, in many cases, the advantage of a peculiar unity of construction—each part, like the mass of machinery in a factory, having an essential relation to, or connection with, the whole. There is no previously existing idle and profligate population to inoculate with its viciousness, the incoming country females; nor is there already there any unhappily pauperized population to depress with its burdensomeness the enterprise of the manufacturers. They have not, as with us it commonly happens, to contend with preexisting difficulties but . . . a clear and unembarrassed field for their manufacturing enterprises—a field wherein they can build on a plan to their liking, adopt the best models, introduce the most perfect and efficient machinery, and then order the principal contingencies, requisite for carrying on their works, on some commodious general plans.

Source: David J. Rothman and Sheila M. Rothman, eds., Sources of the American Social Tradition *(New York: Basic Books Inc., 1975), pp. 93–95.*

to be viewed as public property and became dumping grounds for agricultural and industrial wastes. The dyes and chemical sulfates used in tanneries and in clothing and textile production were released into water supplies. By 1840, the woolens industry alone was discarding some 18,000 tons of grease (which clings to raw wool and is removed in fulling mills) into rivers and streams. Water supplies were being polluted long before any sustained industrialization. What did change with the coming of large factories dependent on water power was the greater degree of private control over water resources and the extent of the ecological impact.

The Boston Associates, the merchant group that built the Waltham–Lowell system of textile mills in New England, illustrate how corporate capital was transforming water from a resource into a private commodity. To provide their mills with a steady, reliable source of water, one that would not be affected by the whims of nature, the Associates constructed a series of dams and canals that extended to the headwaters of the Merrimack River in northern New Hampshire. Inevitably, the ecology of the region under control changed. The level of lakes was altered, the flow of rivers interrupted, the upward migration of spawning fish blocked, and the foraging terrain of wild game flooded. Farmers protested when their fields and pastures were submerged, but lawyers for the Boston Associates successfully argued that water, like any other natural resource, should be treated as a commodity that could contribute to economic progress. Legal battles over water rights led to judicial decisions that cleared the way for the incorporation of nature by other business endeavors. Increasingly, the law treated nature as an economic resource to be engineered and bought and sold.

Growing Inequality and New Classes

As the economy expanded after 1815 and the industrial revolution began to take hold, per capita income doubled in the first half of the century. Living standards for most Americans improved. Houses, for those who could afford them, became larger and better furnished and heated. Food was more plentiful and varied, and factory-made consumer goods made domestic life easier and more comfortable.

There was a price to be paid, however, for the benefits of economic growth. In 1800, fully 90 percent of the free workforce was self-employed, primarily as independent farmers and artisans. By midcentury, a permanent wage-earning class and a middle class of nonmanual, salaried employees had emerged. Half of adult white males were now propertyless. Wealth had become more concentrated, and extremes of wealth and poverty eroded the Jeffersonian ideal of a republic of independent proprietors who valued liberty because they were economically free.

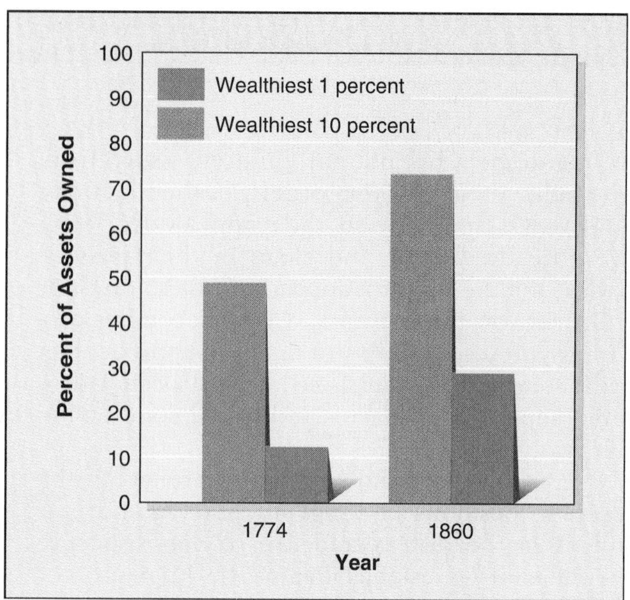

***Figure 11-2** Growth in Wealth Inequality, 1774–1860*
The two benchmark years for the gathering of data on the nationwide distribution of wealth are 1774 and 1860. Specialized studies on regions and subregions indicate that wealth inequality increased most sharply from the 1820s to 1850, the period that coincides with early industrialization.

Data Source: *Jeffrey G. Williamson and Peter H. Lindert,* American Inequality: A Macroeconomic History *(1980), p. 38.*

The Old Rich

The gap between the rich and the poor widened considerably in the early phases of industrialization (see Figure 11-2). In 1800, the richest 10 percent of Americans owned 40 to 50 percent of the national wealth. By the 1850s, that share was about 70 percent. The richest 1 percent alone saw their share more than double to 30 percent. Most of this increase occurred after 1815 when industrial development accelerated, and the most glaring discrepancies in wealth appeared in the large cities.

Owners of capital and income-producing property were most successful in generating wealth in the Atlantic seaports. By 1840, the wealthiest 1 percent of the population in New York City, Brooklyn, Philadelphia, and Boston held 40 percent of all tangible property (land, buildings, and other real estate), and their share of intangible assets (bonds, mortgages, and other paper investments) was undoubtedly much higher. The same pattern existed elsewhere. In all American cities by the 1840s, the top 10 percent of the population owned over 80 percent of urban wealth.

Most of the urban rich at midcentury had been born wealthy, the offspring of old-money families who had married and invested wisely. To be sure, there were popular stories of a rise from rags to riches, and many of them focused on John Jacob Astor. Born poor in Germany, he amassed a fortune of $25 million in the fur trade and was the richest man in New York by 1845. But for every Astor, twenty Americans benefited from inherited wealth and family connections to stay in the ranks of the very rich. Indeed, less than 10 percent of this class emerged from a background of even middling wealth.

The urban rich created their own society. As one of them noted, it was a society "characterised by a spirit of exclusiveness and persecution unknown in any other country. Its gradations not being regulated according to rank and titles, selfishness and conceit are its principal elements; and its arbitrary distinctions the more offensive, as they principally refer to fortune." The urban wealthy belonged to exclusive clubs, attended lavish balls and dinners, were waited on by a retinue of servants in their mansions, and generally recoiled from what they considered the "mob government" ushered in by the Jacksonian Democrats. This aristocracy of wealth tried to use their riches as a shield from the democratic changes in the larger society around them, and they were a constant reminder of how unequal the distribution of wealth had become in the so-called age of the common man.

This scene, entitled The Tea Room *by Henry Sargent in his 1821 painting, depicts how the wealthy elite in Boston used their social gatherings to set themselves apart as an elegantly cultured class.*

The New Middle Class

Although the rich increased their share of the economic pie during the Jacksonian era, that pie also grew larger. The economy was now growing three times faster than in the eighteenth century, and incomes were rising. New employment opportunities opened up, especially in nonmanual work. Most of these jobs were in northern cities and bustling market towns, where the need was greatest for office and store clerks, managerial personnel, sales agents, and independent retailers. The result by midcentury was a new middle class superimposed on the older one of independent farmers, artisans, shopkeepers, and professionals.

Cities provided the setting where members of the new middle class began to forge a distinctive identity, one that set them apart from the wealthy above them and the working poor beneath them. The apparent separation of work and home constituted the first step in this evolving sense of class consciousness. The preindustrial household, whether in the city or the countryside, had combined living and working arrangements in a set of personal relations controlled by the male head of the household. Master craftsmen, for example, directed the work of journeymen and apprentices who lived in their households. As the market revolution advanced, the workplace increasingly became a specialized location of production or selling. Middle-class fathers left for their jobs in the morning, while mothers governed households that were primarily residential units.

As homes lost many of their productive functions, they became places of material comfort for the rising middle class. Growing quantities of consumer goods—pianos, carpets, draperies, mirrors, oil lamps, and ornate furniture—filled their homes. Stoves replaced open fireplaces as the main source of heat, and plumbing eliminated outdoor privies. More rooms offered greater privacy, and visitors were now entertained in a parlor.

New status symbols accompanied middle-class prosperity. Having servants, the single largest field of employment in the cities, became a badge of domestic respectability. Shunned as degrading by most native-born white women, these low-paying jobs were filled by African-American and young immigrant (especially Irish) women. Work had not left the middle-class home; instead, it was disguised as the "domestic duties" of middle-class wives and scorned as the servile labor of persons said to lack the capacity for female virtue.

Etiquette books for the middle class propagated ideals of civility and explained the proper behavior needed to win social acceptance. They laid down rules for presenting oneself in public and in the home. "Don't drum with your fingers on chair, table, or window-pane. Don't hum a tune. The instinct for making noise is a survival of savagery," warned one adviser. Above all, they stressed decorum and self-restraint. Spitting and tobacco chewing, male activities that continued among the working classes, were condemned as boorish.

Besides seeking guidance from etiquette manuals on achieving respectability, the middle class also tried to shape its behavior by the tenets of evangelical religion. Revivals swept northern cities in the late 1820s. Charles G. Finney led the most dramatic and successful ones in the cities along the Erie Canal in upstate New York. Finney preached that salvation was available to those who willed it, but only by disciplining themselves to lead a Christian life could the converted hope to avoid backsliding into damnation. Moral self-determination was at the heart of northern evangelicalism, and the new middle class eagerly embraced the ethic of self-control as a moral guide for making sense of the social and economic changes that were transforming their lives.

"A self-indulgent Christian is a contradiction," insisted Finney. Both economic and moral success depended on the virtues of sobriety, self-restraint, and hard work. Aggressiveness and ambition at work were not necessarily sinful so long as businessmen reformed their own moral lives and helped others do the same. This message was immensely reassuring to employers and entrepreneurs in the urban middle class, for it confirmed and sanctified their own pursuit of economic self-interest. It also provided them with a religious inspiration for attempting to exert moral control over their communities and employees.

Merchants, manufacturers, and professionals were the first to be converted by Finney's preaching, and these business leaders, along with their wives and daughters, were in the forefront of evangelical reform. **Temperance**—the prohibition of alcoholic beverages—was the greatest of the evangelically inspired reforms, and abstinence from alcohol became the most telling evidence of middle-class respectability. (For more on reform, see Chapter 14.)

Evangelicalism also shaped middle-class conceptions of womanhood and the home. In a reversal of traditional Calvinist doctrine, the evangelical ministers of the northern middle class enshrined women as the moral superiors of men. Though considered weak and passive, women were also held to be uniquely pure and pious. Women, who easily outnumbered men at Sunday services and weeknight prayer meetings, were now responsible for converting their homes into loving, prayerful centers of domesticity. "There is a ministry that is older and deeper and more potent than ours," wrote a liberal Presbyterian clergyman; "It is the ministry that presides over the crib and impresses the first gospel influence on the infant soul."

This sanctified notion of motherhood accompanied new views of childhood. Evangelical preachers softened the Calvinist doctrine of infant damnation for children who died before baptism. Ideas about infant depravity gave way to conceptions of young children as "little immortal beings," pure and innocent, though potentially corruptible. The primary task of motherhood now became the Christian nurturing of the souls entrusted to their care. "My Children how will they get along through this World of sin and vanity?" worried Mercy Flynt Morris. "It is my duty to warn them against those vices and try to instill into their minds the importance of seeking an interest in Christ—without which they will be miserable."

These changing images of women and children reflected and reinforced shifting patterns of family life. Families became smaller as the birthrate fell by 25 percent in the first half of the nineteenth century. The decline was greatest in the urban middle class after 1820. Sexual abstinence and male withdrawal before ejaculation, not mechanical methods of contraception, explain most of this decline. Advice literature, to say nothing of wives anxious to avoid the medical risks of too-frequent pregnancies, urged men to curb their sexual desires, and middle-class fathers now had an economic incentive to do so. Children were no longer an economic asset as they had been as workers on a family farm. Middle-class couples consciously limited the size of their families, and women stopped having children at a younger age.

Beginning in the 1820s, ministers and female writers elevated the family role of middle-class women into a **cult of domesticity**. This idealized conception of womanhood insisted that the biological differences of God's natural order determined separate social roles for men and women. Characterized as strong, aggressive, and ambitious, men naturally belonged in the competitive world of business and politics. Women's providential task was to preserve religion and morality in the home and family. Held to be innately weak, nurturing, and selfless, only they possessed the moral purity necessary for rearing virtuous children and preserving the home as a refuge from the outside world.

Middle-class women thus became the moral rulers of families that were smaller and more child-centered then those of the eighteenth century. Parents were able to devote more care and financial resources to child rearing. Middle-class children lived at home longer than children had in the past and received more schooling than working-class children.

"Family Group." Davis, Joseph H., M. and M. Karolik Collection. Courtesy, Museum of Fine Arts, Boston.

This pen-and-watercolor drawing of a middle-class family in 1832 illustrates how the home, as it lost its productive functions, became idealized as a center of domestic refinement and material comfort.

Sons learned to be self-directed men who could take advantage of the educational or professional opportunities their parents had provided for them.

The middle class defined itself in terms of character, not occupational or economic status. Unlike the wealthy, whose riches were inherited, members of the middle class believed that their property was the product of hard work and self-denial. They also saw themselves as the industrious Americans whose moral fortitude and discipline enabled them to escape the clutches of poverty, the fate of those who were presumed to be lazy and undisciplined.

The Working Classes

The economic changes that produced a new middle class also fundamentally transformed the working class. In preindustrial America, the working class was predominantly native-born and of artisan origins. By midcentury, most urban workers were immigrants or the children of immigrants and had never been artisans in a skilled craft (see Figure 11-3). The size of the industrial workforce had grown tremendously, especially in the cities, and was so diverse that contemporaries spoke of it in the plural as the "working classes."

Job skills, sex, race, and ethnicity all divided workers after 1840. Master craftsmen were the most highly skilled and best-paid members of the labor force. Initially, they were in the best positions to take advantage of the growth in manufacturing. However, as industrialization proceeded, the unity of the old artisan class splintered. Ambitious master craftsmen with access to capital ignored craft traditions to rise into the ranks of small businessmen and manufacturers. They expanded output and drove down the cost of production by contracting out work at piece wages and hiring the cheapest workers they could find. The result was to transform the apprentice system into a system of exploited child labor.

By the 1830s, most journeymen were becoming a class of permanent wage earners with little prospect of opening their own shops. Threatened by declining status and income and ever more dependent on a wage for their survival, they denounced the new industrial relations as a "system of mental and physical slavery." To protect their liberties from what they considered a new aristocracy of manufacturers, they organized workingmen's political parties in the 1830s. These parties were broadly reformist

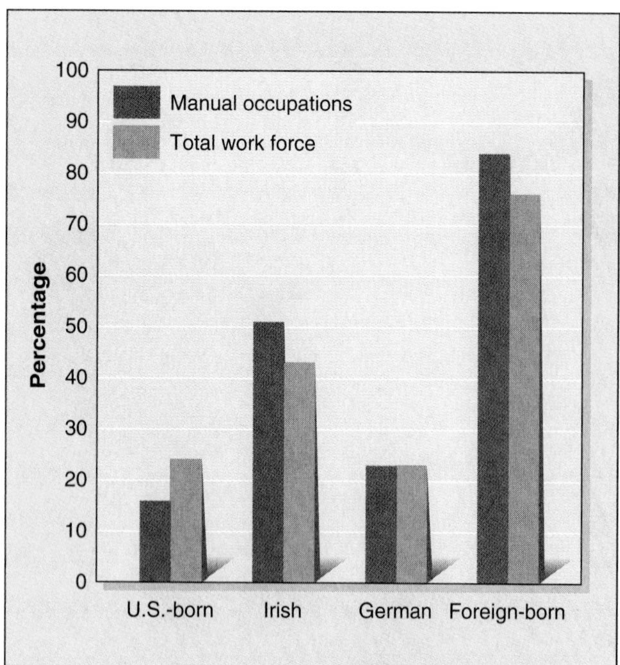

Figure 11-3 **New York City Working Class, 1855**
Especially in the large eastern cities, a new working class of wage laborers dominated by immigrants emerged by the 1850s.
Data Source: Richard B. Stott, Workers in the Metropolis: Class, Ethnicity, and Youth in Antebellum New York City (1990), p. 92.

and centered in eastern cities. At the top of their list of reforms were free public education, the abolition of imprisonment for debt, and a ten-hour workday. This independent political action was short-lived. The depression of 1839–1843 forced mechanics to concentrate on their economic survival, and the Democrats siphoned off many of their political leaders.

Journeymen also turned to trade union activity in the 1820s and 1830s to gain better wages, shorter hours, and enhanced job security. Benefiting from a strong demand for their skills, workers in the building trades organized the first unions. They were soon followed by shoemakers, printers, and weavers, workers in trades where pressure on urban journeymen was the most intense. Locals from various trades formed the National Trades Union, the first national union, in 1834. The new labor movement launched more than 150 strikes in the mid-1830s.

Although the Panic of 1837 decimated union membership, the early labor movement did achieve two notable victories. First, by the late 1830s, it had forced employers to accept the ten-hour day as the standard for most skilled workers. Second, in a landmark decision handed down in 1842, the Massachusetts Supreme Court ruled in *Commonwealth v. Hunt* that a trade union was not necessarily subject to laws against criminal conspiracies and that a strike could be used to force employers to hire only union members. Legally at least, organized labor now had more room to maneuver.

Even at the height of their strength in the mid-1830s, when they may have organized up to one-quarter of the labor force in the larger cities, the trade unions had little to offer unskilled workers and common laborers. The unions were the defenders of artisanal rights and virtues, and they ignored workers whose jobs had never had craft status. As massive immigration merged with industrialization after 1840, this basic division between workers widened. On one side was the male, Protestant, and native-born class of skilled artisans, a group under constant pressure as immigrants poured into the cities and as technological innovation and the division of labor undercut their former control over production. Artisans by midcentury accounted for only 20 percent of the manual workers in the large eastern cities, and two-thirds of these artisans were foreign-born.

On the other side was the working-class majority of factory laborers and the unskilled. These workers were predominantly immigrants and women who worked for a wage as domestic or factory hands. On average, they earned less than $500 a year, about half what skilled workers earned. Their financial survival rested on a family economy in which all members contributed whatever they could earn. The seasonal nature of manual jobs added to the uncertainties of working-class life in cramped tenements, and the tensions frequently exploded in domestic violence.

Artisans continued to think of themselves as independent craftsmen who had little in common with the growing mass of unskilled, foreign-born, and mostly Catholic workers. Indeed, increasingly fearing these workers as a threat to their job security and Protestant values, American-born artisans joined **nativist** organizations in the 1840s that sought to curb mass immigration from Europe and limit the political rights of Catholic immigrants. Ethnic workers viewed temperance as business-class meddling in their lives. In contrast, successful native-born workers tended to embrace the evangelical, middle-class ideology of temperance and self-help. The greatest unity achieved by labor was the nearly universal insistence of white workers that black workers be confined to the most menial jobs.

Gender also divided workers. Working-class men shared the dominant ideology of female dependence. They demanded women's services at home and measured their own status as husbands by their ability to keep their wives and daughters from having to work. Beginning in the 1830s, male workers argued that their wages would be higher if women were

AMERICA'S JOURNEY

FROM THEN TO NOW

Immigration and Reaction

Americans have long extended an ambivalent welcome to newcomers. In the mid-nineteenth century employment posters often read "Irish Need Not Apply," and today stepped-up border patrols seek to keep out Mexican and other Latin American immigrants. Yet America is a nation settled and built by immigrants whose founding ideals promise equality and opportunity to all. And for much of its history it has offered asylum for the world's oppressed.

In the early years of the republic, Federalists worried that immigrants from Europe might be contaminated by the radical ideas of the French revolution and sought to make it harder for them to become naturalized citizens. The nation's first naturalization law in the 1790s also barred black immigrants from citizenship. The first sustained attack against newcomers, however, emerged as a result of the surge in immigration during the 1840s and 1850s. It was directed by established immigrant groups—the descendants of settlers from Britain and northwest Europe—at unfamiliar newcomers, particularly the Irish.

Nativist arguments of that time have found an echo in all subsequent immigration debates. The Irish, it was claimed, would take jobs away from American workers and lower their wages. Taxpayers would have to foot the bill for the strains the newcomers imposed on schools, hospitals, and other civic services. The ignorant immigrants would corrupt the political process. Nativists especially feared religious contamination, claiming that the Catholicism of the Irish was alien to the Protestant values held to be indispensable to the preservation of American liberties. So many Irish arrived so quickly that many nativists were convinced of a Papal plot to undermine American freedom. "The bloody hand of the Pope," one wrote, "has stretched itself forth to our destruction."

Eventually the Irish and Germans merged into the economic and political fabric of American life. But in the late nineteenth century a massive new immigrant surge dominated by people from Southern and Eastern Europe seeking economic opportunity and fleeing religious oppression transformed American society and renewed nativist fears. This time, race replaced religion as the basis for drawing invidious comparisons between established residents and the newcomers. Pseudo-scientific theories relegated Jews, Slavs, and Mediterranean peoples, together with Africans, to an inferior status below people of Northern European and especially Anglo-Saxon descent. The newcomers, it was claimed, were unfit for democratic government and would endanger American civilization. Strict anti-immigrant legislation in the 1920s sharply curtailed immigration from outside the Western Hemisphere, banning Asians entirely and setting quotas based on national origin for others.

Recent concerns about immigration result from the unforeseen consequences of a 1965 reform in immigration law that abolished quotas. Since then, immigration has risen sharply, and the national origin of the immigrants has diverged from previous patterns. By the 1980s Europeans comprised but 10 percent of the newcomers. The bulk of the remainder came from Asia (40 percent) and Mexico, Central America, and the Caribbean. Once again, anti-immigrant voices worry that alien newcomers are threatening the cohesiveness of the nation's institutions and values. But, once again as well, a more inclusive vision of American identity and ideals seems likely to prevail as the newcomers establish themselves. As Abraham Lincoln expressed it, "There was no exclusively American race entitled to claim liberty by heredity. What held the nation together was an *idea* of equality that every newcomer could claim and defend by free choice."

This painting shows immigrants disembarking in New York City in 1855. The round building on the left is Castle Garden, the city's first immigration center.

Samuel B. Waugh, "The Bay and Harbor of New York" circa 1855. Gift of Mrs. Robert M. Littlejohn. Museum of the City of New York. 33.169.1.

barred from the workforce. A report of the National Trades Union in 1836 cited women's "ruinous competition to male labor." It insisted that a woman's "efforts to sustain herself and family are actually the same as tying a stone around the neck of her natural protector, Man, and destroying him with the weight she has brought to his assistance."

Because they equated earning wages with manliness and accepted conventional ideas that woman's proper place was in the home, male workers helped lock wage-earning women into the lowest-paying and most exploited jobs. Of the 25,000 women in 1860 working in manufacturing in New York City, two-thirds were in the clothing trades. Many were seamstresses working at home fifteen to eighteen hours a day for starvation wages of less than $100 a year. More than half of them were the sole breadwinners in their households.

"If we do not come forth in our defence, what will become of us?" asked Sarah Monroe of New York City in the midst of a strike by seamstresses in 1831. Women tried to organize as workers, but the male labor movement refused to lend much support. The men tried to channel the discontent of women workers into "proper female behavior" and generally restricted their assistance to pushing for legislation that would limit the hours worked by women and children, a stand that enhanced their male image as protectors of the family. Unable to break free from a conventional notion of domesticity, male workers continued to view women as providers at home and competitors in the workplace.

Conclusion

In 1820, the United States seemed an unlikely candidate for sustained industrialization. Manufacturing activity was a footnote in its agricultural economy. Cheap land was still abundant, and most Americans dreaded the prospect of wage labor in a factory setting. Yet with surprising speed, transportation improvements, technological innovations, and expanding markets drove the economy on a path toward industrialization. As part of this process, wealth inequality increased, old classes were reshaped, and new ones formed. These changes were sharpest in the Northeast, where capital, labor, and expanding urban markets spurred the acceleration of manufacturing.

By 1850, most of the workforce in the Northeast was no longer employed in agriculture. In New York, the nation's largest city, wage laborers made up 80 percent of the working population. Still, most Americans dreamed of a life of economic independence on a family farm. This was the great appeal of the West, the nation's fastest-growing region in the first half of the nineteenth century.

Review Questions

1. Why were improvements in transportation so essential to the growth of the economy after 1815? What were the nature and scope of these improvements?
2. What factors contributed to the rapid growth of cities in the Jacksonian era? What types of cities grew the fastest?
3. What is an industrial revolution? How can we explain the surge in manufacturing in the United States from 1815 to 1850?
4. Why did economic growth widen the gap between the rich and the poor?
5. How did the class structure change in the first half of the nineteenth century? How would you characterize the differences between the middle class and manufacturing wage laborers at midcentury?

Recommended Reading

Jeanne Boydston, *Home and Work: Housework, Wages, and the Ideology of Labor in the Early Republic* (1990). A provocative work that shows how issues of gender shaped the emergence of a market for labor and influenced the very notion of work itself.

Thomas C. Cochran, *Frontiers of Change: Early Industrialism in America* (1981). An engagingly written narrative that argues for the importance of cultural factors in the rise and scope of manufacturing in the United States before 1850.

Robert E. Gallman and John Joseph Wallis, eds., *American Economic Growth and Standards of Living before the Civil War* (1992). Interdisciplinary essays that address the economic and historical forces that propelled the American economy after 1800.

Brooke Hindle and Steven Lubar, *Engines of Change: The American Industrial Revolution, 1790–1860* (1986). A comprehensive overview that is particularly strong in explaining the role of technological innovation in the American industrial revolution.

Jack Larkin, *The Reshaping of Everyday Life, 1790–1840* (1988). A very readable depiction of how social and economic changes were reflected in the rhythms and customs of daily life in the first half of the nineteenth century.

Walter Licht, *Industrializing America: A Nineteenth Century* (1995). A smoothly written survey that interprets industrialization as both a product and a promoter of economic and social change.

George R. Taylor, *The Transportation Revolution, 1815–1860* (1951). A solid economic history and classic study that persuasively argues that improvements in transportation were the catalyst for the transformation of the nineteenth-century economy.

Additional Sources

The Transportation Revolution

Albert Fishlow, *American Railroads and the Transformation of the Ante-Bellum Economy* (1965).

Carter Goodrich, *Government Promotion of American Canals and Railroads, 1800–1890* (1960).

Louis Hartz, *Economic Policy and Democratic Thought: Pennsylvania, 1776–1860* (1948).

Erik F. Hiates, James Mak, and Gary M. Walton, *Western River Transportation: The Era of Early Internal Development, 1800–1860* (1975).

Morton J. Horowitz, *The Transformation of American Law, 1780–1860* (1977).

Ronald E. Shaw, *Canals for a Nation: The Canal Era in the United States, 1790–1860* (1990).

Peter Way, *Common Labour: Workers and the Digging of North American Canals, 1780–1860* (1993).

The Rise of Cities

Kathleen Neils Conzen, *Immigrant Milwaukee, 1836–1860* (1976).

Oscar Handlin, *Boston's Immigrants: A Study of Acculturation*, rev. ed. (1959).

Marcus L. Hansen, *The Atlantic Migration, 1607–1860 (1940).*

Edward K. Spann, *The New Metropolis: New York, 1840–1857* (1981).

Christine Stansel, *City of Women: Sex and Class in New York, 1789–1860* (1986).

Richard C. Wade, *The Urban Frontier* (1964).

The Industrial Revolution

Robert F. Dalzell, *Enterprising Elite: The Boston Associates and the World They Made* (1987).

Thomas Dublin, *Women at Work: The Transformation of Work and Community in Lowell, Massachusetts, 1826–1860* (1979).

Lucy Larcom, *A New England Girlhood* (1889; reprint, 1977).

Theodore Steinberg, *Nature Incorporated: Industrialization and the Waters of New England* (1991).

Anthony F. C. Wallace, *Rockdale: The Growth of an American Village in the Early Industrial Revolution* (1978).

Growing Inequality and New Classes

Stuart M. Blumin, *The Emergence of the Middle Class: Social Experience in the American City, 1760–1900* (1989).

Paul E. Johnson, *A Shopkeeper's Millennium: Society and Revivals in Rochester, New York, 1815–1837* (1978).

Bruce Laurie, *Artisans into Workers: Labor in Nineteenth-Century America* (1989).

Edward Pessen, *Riches, Class, and Power before the Civil War* (1973).

David Roediger, *The Wages of Whiteness: Race and the Making of the American Working Class* (1991).

Mary Ryan, *Cradle of the Middle Class: The Family in Oneida County, New York, 1790–1865* (1981).

Sean Wilentz, *Chants Democratic: New York City and the Rise of the American Working Class, 1790–1865* (1984).

Where to Learn More

❖ **Baltimore Center for Urban Archaeology, Baltimore, Maryland.** Operated by Baltimore City Life Museums, the center has a large collection of artifacts depicting urban life in the eighteenth and nineteenth centuries and a working archaeological library.

❖ **Hanford Mills Museum, East Meredith, New York.** This museum preserves and interprets water-powered machinery and explains the role played by local mills in the community life of the nineteenth century.

❖ **Arabia Museum, Kansas City, Missouri.** This private museum has a fascinating exhibit of the contents of a steamboat that sank on the Missouri River in 1856. The exhibit reveals the abundance and variety of consumer goods that were being shipped to river towns in the Midwest in the 1850s.

❖ **Slater Hill Historic Site, Pawtucket, Rhode Island.** The Sylvanus Brown House of 1758, the Slaren Mill of 1793, and the Wilkinson Mill of 1810 are on the site. An extensive library and holdings provide insight into the social and economic world of the early industrial revolution.

❖ **Erie Canal Museum, Syracuse, New York.** The museum houses extensive collections on the building and maintenance of the Erie Canal, and its photo holdings visually record much of the history of the canal.

THE WAY WEST

Pacific Ocean

Portland

Salt Lake City

Sacramento

San Francisco

Chicago

Omaha

St. Lo

Kansas City

Santa Fe

Mem

Vicksburg

San Antonio

Galveston

New Orle

Gulf of Mexic

Mexico City

N
W
E
S

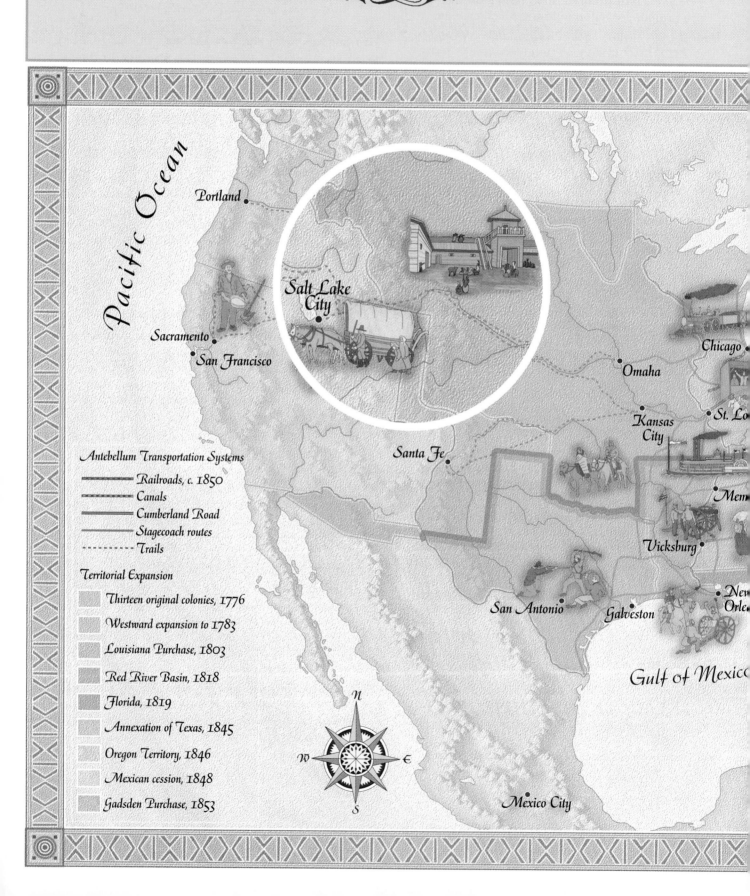

Antebellum Transportation Systems

- Railroads, c. 1850
- Canals
- Cumberland Road
- Stagecoach routes
- Trails

Territorial Expansion

- Thirteen original colonies, 1776
- Westward expansion to 1783
- Louisiana Purchase, 1803
- Red River Basin, 1818
- Florida, 1819
- Annexation of Texas, 1845
- Oregon Territory, 1846
- Mexican cession, 1848
- Gadsden Purchase, 1853

12

Chapter Outline

Key Topics

- ❖ Western migration spurred by economic and demographic pressures in the East after the War of 1812
- ❖ The development of free commercial agriculture tied to eastern markets and increased industrialization and urbanization of the Old Northwest
- ❖ The development of a plantation economy based on cotton and slavery in the Old Southwest
- ❖ Manifest Destiny and westward expansion, relegating Native Americans and Mexican-Americans to subjugated status
- ❖ U.S. annexation of Texas and the wresting of the Southwest and California from Mexico

"Out in Oregon, I can get me a square mile of land," exclaimed a Missourian to his wife in 1843. "I am done with this country. Winters it's frost and snow to freeze a body; summers the overflow from the Old Muddy drowns half my acres. Taxes take the yield of them that's left. What say, Maw . . . it's God's country." And so it proved to be for Peter Burnett. He moved his family to Oregon and then to California, where he became the first governor of the new state, acquired through war with Mexico.

Burnett's family was among the first of the some 300,000 Americans who traveled the Oregon Trail by 1860 and eventually made the United States a nation that spanned the continent. These overlanders, as they came to be known, were part of a restless surge of white settlement that eventually saw more than fifty thousand Americans a year migrate west of the Appalachians after the War of 1812. After moving into the Old Northwest and Old Southwest—the American West of the early nineteenth century—migrants headed beyond the Mississippi River in the 1840s. The edge of settlement pushed into the Louisiana Purchase territory and across a huge area of plains, desert, mountains, and ocean coast that had seen few American settlers before 1840.

The broad expanse of the trans-Mississippi region had become the new American West by mid-century. The West became a meeting ground of people from diverse cultures as Anglo-Americans came into contact and conflict with the Indians of the Plains and the Mexicans of the Southwest. Convinced of the superiority of their political and cultural values, Anglo-Americans asserted a God-given right to spread across the continent and impose their notions of liberty and democracy on peoples whose land they coveted. In the process, they defeated and subjugated those who stood in their way.

Manifest Destiny was the label for this presumed providential right, and it provided a justification for the aggressively expansionist Democratic administration of James K. Polk that came to power in 1845. The most dramatic result of these policies was the Mexican War of 1846–1848, which made California and the present-day Southwest part of the American continental empire.

The Agricultural Frontier

The U.S. population ballooned from 5.3 million in 1800 to more than 23 million by 1850. The population grew about 33 percent per decade, and four-fifths of this extraordinary gain was from natural increase—the surplus of births over deaths. As the population expanded, it shifted westward. Fewer than one in ten Americans lived west of the Appalachians in 1800; by 1850, about half did (see Map 12-1).

The tremendous amount of land available for settlement accounted for both phenomena. Through purchase and conquest, the land area of the United States more than tripled in the first half of the nineteenth century. Here was space where Americans could raise the large families of a rural society in which, on average, six to eight children survived to adolescence. Millions of fertile acres lured eastern families ever westward to the next agricultural frontier.

Declining soil fertility and rising population pressure in the rural East propelled these migrations. A common desire for greater economic opportunity, however, resulted in two distinct western societies by the 1840s. North of the Ohio River, in the Old Northwest, free labor and family farms defined the social order. South of the Ohio was the Old Southwest, a society dominated by slave labor and the plantation.

The Crowded East

Looking back at his rural youth, Omar H. Morse recalled, "My Parents were in very limited circumstances financially yet blessed with a large family of children which is a poor man's capital though capital of this kind is not considered very available in case of financial Depression." Born in 1824 in the upstate New York village of Hastings, Morse was typical of the hard-pressed eastern youth who moved west after the War of 1812. With no prospect of inheriting land from his father and tired of taking orders as a farmhand for

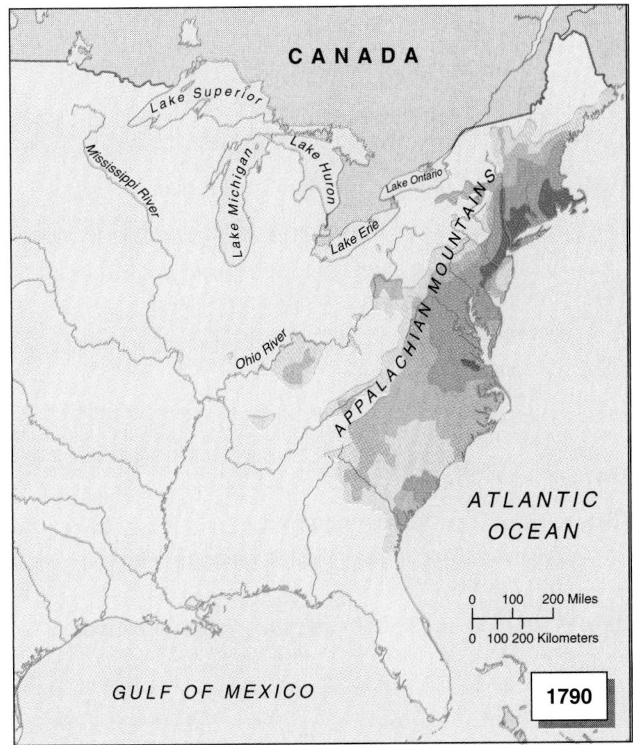

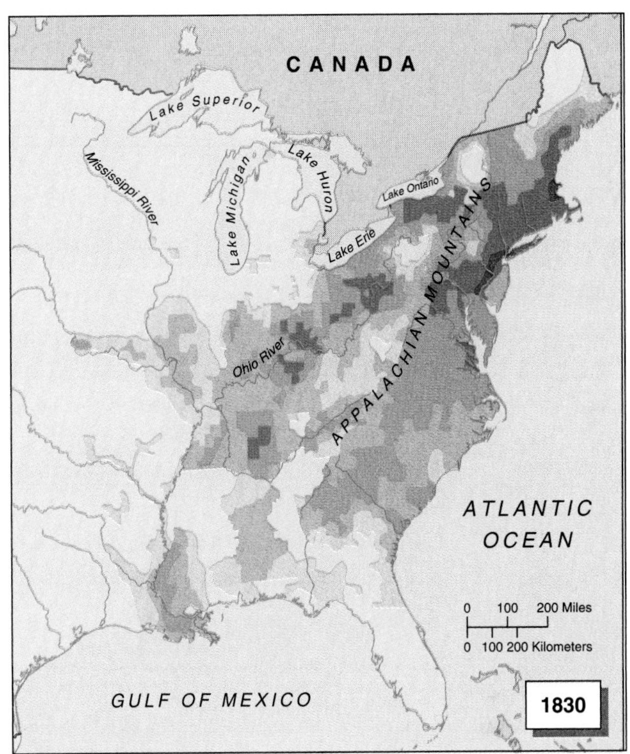

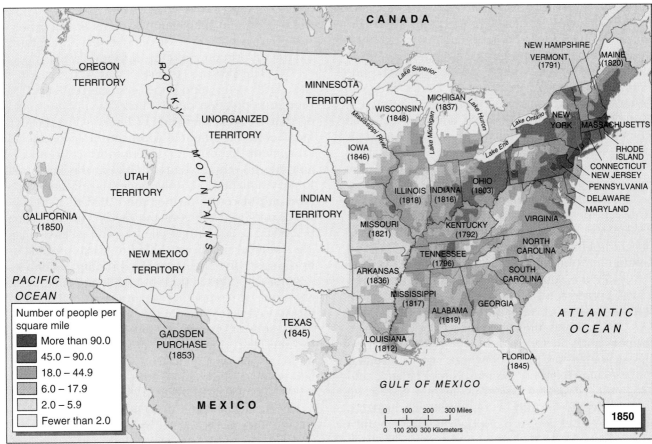

Map 12-1 The Westward Shift of the United States Population, 1790–1850
With a speed that was unimaginable in 1790, the United States quickly became a continental nation that stretched from the Atlantic to the Pacific by 1850. Particularly dramatic was the population growth in what became the Midwest.

Chronology

1803–1806	Lewis and Clark travel up the Missouri River in search of a water route to the Pacific.
1816	Settlers surge into the trans-Appalachian region.
1821	Mexico gains its independence from Spain.
	Santa Fe Trail opens.
	Stephen F. Austin establishes the first American colony in Texas.
1824	Rocky Mountain Fur Company begins the rendezvous system.
1830	Congress creates the Indian Territory.
1834	Protestant missions are established in Oregon.
	Santa Anna seizes power in Mexico.
1836	Texas wins its independence from Mexico.
1837	Smallpox epidemic hits the Plains Indians.
1842	First large parties of migrants set out on the Oregon Trail.
1845	United States annexes Texas.
	Democrats embrace Manifest Destiny.
1846	Mexican War breaks out.
	United States and Britain reach an agreement in Oregon.
1847	Mormons begin settlement of Utah.
1848	Oregon Territory is organized.
	Treaty of Guadalupe Hidalgo ends the Mexican War.
1851	Fort Laramie Treaty with the Plains Indians is signed.

temporary wages, he moved in the 1840s to Wisconsin, where he found what he thought was "the most beautiful spot of country on God's green Earth." Even after this fresh start, bad luck and too many debts prevented Morse from ever achieving landed independence. He lost three farms and eventually settled in Minnesota, where he worked at odd jobs and built houses. Heading west did not guarantee economic success, but it was the best option open to land-starved easterners who dreamed of leaving a productive farm to their children.

By the early nineteenth century, land was scarce in the East, especially in New England. After generations of population growth and subdivisions of landholdings to male heirs, most New England communities no longer had enough arable land to satisfy all the young men who wanted their own farms. Even recently opened areas such as Vermont felt the pressure of rural overpopulation.

Land was more productive and expensive farther south, in the mid-Atlantic states. Based on the major export crop of wheat, agriculture was more commercialized than in New England, and economic inequality was thus higher. Successful farmers became wealthy by specializing in wheat and hiring the rural poor to work their fields. One-third to one-half of the young men in the commercialized agricultural districts of New Jersey and Pennsylvania were landless by the end of the eighteenth century. These men and their families, many of whom were recently arrived Scots-Irish and German immigrants, led the western migration from Pennsylvania.

The pressure to move west was greatest in the slave states along the eastern seaboard. Although population density here was just two-thirds of that in New England, ordinary white farmers faced even more limited prospects of economic advancement. Landholdings were more concentrated and the soil more exhausted than in the Northeast. Repeated plantings of tobacco in Virginia and Maryland and of cotton farther south had depleted the soil throughout much of the region. In the Chesapeake states, established planters with extensive capital and labor resources shifted to wheat production or bought out their nonslaveholding neighbors. Tenants who wanted their own land and small farmers tired of competing against slave labor were forced west across the mountains. They were joined by the sons of planters. Despite marriages arranged to keep land within the wealthy families, there was no longer enough good land left to carve out plantations for all the younger sons.

By the early 1800s, the young and the poor in the rural East faced limited opportunities for social mobility and economic independence. They had every incentive to head west, where fertile land was abundant, accessible, and, at $2 to $3 per acre, far cheaper than in the East. Land was the basis of wealth and social standing, and its ownership separated the independent from the dependent, the rooted from the rootless. According to the principles of Jeffersonian democracy, the independent farmer was the backbone of the republic, the virtuous citizen who made republican government possible. "Those who labor in the earth," Jefferson wrote in 1785, "are the chosen people of God . . . whose breasts He has made his peculiar deposit for substantial and genuine virtue."

The western settler, observed a traveler on the Missouri frontier in the 1820s, wanted "to be a freeholder, to have plenty of rich land, and to be able to settle his children around him." Government policy under the Jeffersonian Republicans and Jacksonian Democrats attempted to make it easier to reach these goals. Central to the land policy of the federal government after 1800 was the conviction that political liberties rested on the broadest possible base of land ownership. Thus public policy and private aspirations merged in the belief that access to land was the key to preserving American freedom.

When Jefferson took office in 1801, the minimum price for public land was $2 per acre, and a block of 320 acres had to be purchased at one time. By the 1830s, the price was down to $1.25 per acre, and the minimum purchase was only 80 acres. Congress also protected squatters, who had settled on public land before it was surveyed, from being outbid by speculators at a land sale. The Preemption Act of 1841 guaranteed the right to purchase up to 160 acres at the minimum price of $1.25 when the public auction was held.

The Old Northwest

The number of Americans who settled in the heartland of the Old Northwest—Ohio, Indiana, and Illinois—rose tenfold from 1810 to 1840. Ohio had already entered the Union in 1803; Indiana joined in 1816, Illinois in 1818. The end of the War of 1812 and the abandonment by the British of their former Indian allies opened up the region to a flood of migrants.

Travelers passing through the Ohio Valley just after the war were astonished by the number of Americans trekking west. Wagonloads of migrants bounced along turnpikes to disembark on the Ohio River at Pittsburgh and Wheeling, where they bought flatboats to carry them down the Ohio to the interior river valleys. Moving north across the Ohio were families from the hill country of Virginia and Kentucky. These two streams of migrants, one predominantly northern and the other southern, met in the lower Midwest and viewed each other as strangers. Lucy Maynard, a New Englander living in south-central Illinois, noted that her neighbors were "principally from Indiana and Kentucky, some from Virginia, all friendly but very different from our people in their manners and language and every other way."

The Old Northwest was less a melting pot in which regional cultures merged than a mosaic of settlements in which the different values and folkways of regional cultures from throughout the East took root and expanded. Belts of migration generally ran along a line from east to west as settlers sought out soil types and ecological conditions similar to those they had left behind. Thus the same North–South cultural differences that existed along the Atlantic seaboard in 1800 were to be found half a century later in the Mississippi Valley.

A transplanted Yankee culture from New England and upstate New York spread over the upper Midwest—northern Ohio, Indiana, and Illinois, as well as Michigan and Wisconsin. These westerners were Whiggish in their politics, tended to be antislavery, and valued a communal sense of responsibility that regulated moral behavior and promoted self-improvement. The highland Southerners who settled the lower Midwest—southern Ohio, Indiana, and Illinois, as well as Kentucky—were Democrats: They fiercely distrusted any centralized authority, political or moral, and considered Yankees intolerant do-gooders. Holding the balance of cultural and political power were the migrants from Pennsylvania and New Jersey, who were accustomed to ethnic diversity and the politics of competing economic groups. They settled principally in central Ohio, Indiana, and Illinois. By emphasizing economic growth and downplaying the cultural politics that pitted Yankees against Southerners, they built a consensus around community development.

Much as they had done in the East, the early settlers practiced a diversified agriculture to feed and shelter their families. The first task was to clear the land and sow a crop of corn, a hardy grain that required little care. Wild game and livestock left to forage in the woods supplemented the corn-based diet.

It took about ten years of backbreaking labor to create an eighty-acre farm in heavily wooded sections. The Northwest Ordinance of 1787 had barred slavery north of the Ohio, so settlers had to do the work themselves or hire farmhands. The work of women was essential for the success of the farm and the production of any salable surplus. Wives and daughters helped tend the field crops, milked cows and churned butter, and produced the homespun cloth that, along with their dairy goods, found a market in the first country stores on the frontier. Charlotte

Clearing the land and erecting a log cabin were the first steps in creating a farm on the western frontier.

Webb Jacobs, from the Sugar Creek community on the Illinois prairie, proudly recalled, "I made everything that we wore; I even made my towels and table cloths, sheets and everything in the clothing line."

Because outside labor was scarce and expensive, communities pooled their efforts for such tasks as raising a cabin. Groups of settlers also acted as a cooperative unit at public land auctions. Local associations known as **claims clubs** enforced the extralegal right of squatters to enter noncompetitive bids on land they had settled and improved. Members of the clubs physically intimidated speculators who refused to step aside until local settlers had acquired the land they wanted.

The high cost of hauling goods to outside markets kept the early frontier economy barely above self-sufficiency. Any surplus was sold to newcomers moving into the area or bartered with local storekeepers for essentials such as salt, sugar, and metalwares. This initial economy, however, soon gave way to a more commercially oriented agriculture when steamboats, canals, and railroads opened up vast new markets (see Chapter 11). Western lands were at least twice as fertile as those in the East, and farmers could now profit from their bountiful yields.

The first large market was in the South, down the corridor of the Ohio and Mississippi Rivers, and its major staples were corn and hogs. By the 1830s, the Erie Canal and its feeder waterways in the upper Midwest began to reorient much of the western farm trade to the Northeast. Wheat, because of its ready marketability for milling into flour, became the major cash crop for the northern market.

Wheat production skyrocketed when settlers overcame their initial reluctance to farming in a treeless terrain and moved into the prairies of Indiana and Illinois in the 1840s. New plows—a cast-iron one patented by Jethro Wood in 1819 and a steel version developed by John Deere in 1837—helped break the thick prairie sod. The plows were followed in the 1840s by horse-drawn mechanical harvesters. Traditional harvesting methods that relied on a worker using a scythe with a cradle frame were slow and relatively expensive. An experienced worker could cut no more than two acres a day. The same worker with the new machinery could harvest twelve acres a day, and the per-acre cost of labor fell dramatically. Once railroads provided direct access to eastern markets, the Midwest became the nation's breadbasket.

Although southern cotton was the raw material that fueled New England textile factories in the first stages of industrialization, the commercialization of agriculture in the West also contributed to the growth of eastern manufacturing. The productivity of western farms supplied eastern manufacturers with inexpensive raw materials for processing into finished goods. By flooding national markets with corn and wheat, western produce not only supplied eastern workers with cheap food but also forced noncompetitive eastern farmers either to move west or to work in factories in eastern cities. In turn, the West itself became an ever-growing market for eastern factory goods. For example, nearly half of the nation's iron production in the 1830s was fashioned into farm implements.

Cyrus McCormick pioneered the development of horse-drawn mechanical reapers. Shown here demonstrating his reaper to potential customers, McCormick helped revolutionize American agriculture with labor-saving machinery that made possible far larger harvests of grain crops.

In the 1820s, the Old Northwest was just emerging from semisubsistence and depended on the southern trade. Thirty years later it had become part of a larger Midwest whose economy was increasingly integrated with that of the Northeast. Settlers continued to pour into the region, and three additional states—Michigan (1837), Iowa (1846), and Wisconsin (1848)—joined the Union.

The combination of favorable farm prices and steadily decreasing transportation costs generated a rise in disposable income that was spent on outside goods or invested in internal development. A network of canals and railroads was laid down, and manufacturing cities grew from towns favorably situated by water or rail transport. There was still room for subsistence farming, but the West north of the Ohio was now economically specialized and socially diverse.

The Old Southwest

"The *Alabama Feaver* rages here with great violence and has carried off vast numbers of our Citizens," wrote a North Carolina planter in 1817 about the westward migration from his state. "I am apprehensive, if it continues to spread as it has done, it will almost depopulate the country." The planter, James Graham, had reason to be concerned. About as many people migrated from the old slave states in the East to the Old Southwest as those states gained by natural increase in the 1820s and 1830s. By 1850, more than 600,000 white settlers from Maryland, Virginia, and the Carolinas lived in slave states to the south and west, and many of them had brought their slaves with them. Indeed, from 1790 to 1860, more than 800,000 slaves were moved from the South Atlantic region into the Old Southwest.

Soaring cotton prices after the War of 1812 and the smashing of Indian confederations during the war, which opened new lands to white settlement, propelled the first surge of migration into the Old Southwest. Before cotton prices plunged in the Panic of 1819, planters flooded into western Tennessee and the Black Belt, a crescent-shaped band of rich, black loamy soil arcing westward from Georgia through central Alabama and Mississippi. Migration surged anew in the 1830s when cotton prices were again high and the Chickasaws and Choctaws had been forced out of the incredibly fertile Delta country between the Yazoo and Mississippi Rivers (see Chapter 10). The 1840s brought Texas fever to replace the Alabama fever of the 1810s, and a steady movement to the Southwest rounded out the contours of the cotton South. In less than thirty years, six new slave states—Mississippi (1817), Alabama (1819), Missouri (1821), Arkansas (1836), Florida (1845), and Texas (1845)—joined the Union (see the overview table, "Westward Expansion and the Growth of the Union, 1815–1850").

The southwestern frontier attracted both slaveholding planters and small independent farmers. The planters, though a minority, had the capital or the credit to acquire the best lands and the slave labor to make those lands productive. In abandoning the light, sandy, and overworked soils of eastern plantations for the far richer alluvial and prairie soils of the Old Southwest, these slaveholders were responding both to the need for fresh land and to the extraordinary demand for short-staple cotton. As one North Carolina planter put it, Alabama would be a "garden of plenty" compared to the "old-fields and empty corn-houses" of his native state.

OVERVIEW

Westward Expansion and the Growth of the Union, 1815–1850

New Free States	New Slave States	Territories (1850)
Indiana, 1816	Mississippi, 1817	Minnesota
Illinois, 1818	Alabama, 1819	Oregon
Maine, 1820	Missouri, 1821	New Mexico
Michigan, 1837	Arkansas, 1836	Utah
Iowa, 1846	Florida, 1845	
Wisconsin, 1848	Texas, 1845	
California, 1850		

Short-staple cotton could be grown anywhere with a minimum of 210 consecutive frost-free days. The crop, however, was of minor commercial importance before the 1790s, when Eli Whitney's gin eliminated the problem of removing the sticky, green seeds from cotton fiber, an essential step in preparing it to be spun and woven into cloth. Meanwhile, the mechanization of the British textile industry had created a seemingly unquenchable demand for raw cotton. No place in the world was better positioned to meet that demand than the American South. Most important, a slave labor force was available to work the land. Led by the booming output of the new plantations in the Old Southwest, the South increased its share of world cotton production from 9 percent in 1800 to 68 percent in 1850.

Thanks to cotton and slavery, aggressive, hard-driving planters loomed large in the Old Southwest. But small independent yeoman farmers, most with no slaves, were far more typical on the southern frontier. Usually settling in the valleys, on the ridges, and in the hill country, they often soon sold out to neighboring planters and headed west again. Like the yeoman farmer Gideon Linecum, they relished "the pleasure of frequent change of country."

The yeomanry moved onto the frontier in two waves. The first consisted of stockmen-hunters, a restless, transient group who spread from the pine barrens in the Carolina backcountry to the coastal plain of eastern Texas. They prized unfettered independence and measured their wealth in the livestock left to roam and fatten on the sweet grasses of uncleared forests. They were quick to move on when farmers, the second wave, started to clear the land for crops.

Like the stock herders, the yeoman farmers valued self-sufficiency and the leisure to hunt and fish. In pursuit of these goals, they practiced a diversified agriculture aimed at feeding their families. Corn and pork were the mainstays of their diet, and both could readily be produced as long as there was room for the open-range herding of swine and for patches of corn and small grains. The more ambitious farmers, usually those who owned one or two slaves, grew some cotton, but most preferred to avoid the economic risks of cotton production. The yeoman's chief source of labor was his immediate family, and to expand that labor force to produce cotton meant going into debt to purchase slaves. That debt could easily cost the yeoman his farm if the price of cotton fell.

Measured by per capita income, and as a direct result of the profits from slave-produced cotton on virgin soils, the Old Southwest was a wealthier society than the Old Northwest in 1850. In the short term, the settlement of the Old Southwest was also more significant for national economic development. Cotton accounted for more than half the value of all American exports after the mid-1830s. More than any other commodity, cotton paid for American imports and underpinned national credit. But southern prosperity was not accompanied by the same economic development and social change as in the Old Northwest. Compared to the slave West in 1860, the free-labor West was twice as urbanized, and far more of its workforce was engaged in nonagricultural pursuits.

The Southwest Ordinance, enacted by Congress in 1790, opened all territories south of the Ohio River to slavery. Slaves, land, and cotton were the keys to wealth on the southern frontier, and agricultural profits were continually plowed back into more land and slaves to produce more cotton. In contrast, prosperous farmers in the Old Northwest had no slaves to work additional acres. Hence they were much more likely to invest their earnings in promotional schemes designed to attract settlers whose presence would raise land values and increase business for local merchants and entrepreneurs. As early as the 1840s, rural communities in the Old Northwest were supporting bustling towns that offered jobs in trade and manufacturing on a scale far surpassing anything in the slave West. By the 1850s, the Midwest was almost as urbanized as the Northeast had been in 1830, and nearly half its labor force no longer worked on farms.

The Old Southwest remained overwhelmingly agricultural. Once the land was settled, the children of the first generation of slaveholders and yeomen moved west to the next frontier rather than compete for the good land that was left. Relatively few newcomers took their place. By the 1850s, Kentucky, Tennessee, Alabama, and Mississippi—the core states of the Old Southwest—were all losing more migrants than they were gaining.

The Frontier of the Plains Indians

Few white Americans had ventured west of the Mississippi by 1840. What scanty knowledge there was of this huge inland expanse was the result of government-sponsored expeditions. Reports of explorations of the southern Plains by Zebulon Pike in 1806 and Stephen Long in 1819 dismissed the area as the Great American Desert, an arid, treeless landscape with little agricultural potential, fit only for the Indians being removed from the East. The vast plains and plateaus climbing westward to the foothills of the Rocky Mountains in a seemingly endless ocean of grass were unfamiliar and intimidating to farmers accustomed to the wooded, well-watered, humid East.

Moreover, Americans had no legal claim to much of the trans-Mississippi West—or merely the paper title of the Louisiana Purchase, to which none of the native inhabitants had acquiesced. Beyond Texas and the boundary line drawn by the Trans-Continental Treaty of 1819 lay the northern possessions of Mexico. Horse-mounted Indian tribes dominated by the Sioux were a formidable power on the central Plains northward to the Canadian boundary.

Before the 1840s, Americans lacked the interest, numbers, and concerted military power to control this Far West, held by other peoples. Only fur trappers and traders, who worked with and not against the powerful Sioux, had pushed across the Great Plains and into the Rockies. The 1840s brought a sudden change, a large migration westward that radically altered the ecology of the Great Plains. Farm families trapped in an agricultural depression and enticed by Oregon's bounty turned the trails blazed by the fur traders into ruts on the **Oregon Trail**, the route that led to the first large settlement of Americans on the Pacific Coast.

Tribal Lands

At least 350,000 Native Americans lived in the plains and mountains of the trans-Mississippi West in 1840. They were loosely organized into tribal groups, each with its own territory and way of life. Most of them inhabited the Great Plains region that lay north and west of the Indian Territory reserved for eastern tribes in the present state of Oklahoma. The point where the prairies of the Midwest gave way to the higher, drier plains marked a rough division between predominantly agricultural tribes to the east and nomadic, hunting tribes to the west. The Kansas, Osages, and Omahas in what is now Kansas and Iowa and the Arikaras, Mandans, and Hidatsas along the upper Missouri River grew corn, beans, and squash and lived in semipermanent villages, much as woodland Indians had in the East. On the open plains were hunting and raiding peoples, such as the western Sioux, Crows, Cheyennes, and Arapahos.

In the 1830s, the U.S. government set aside a broad stretch of country between the Platte River to the north and the Red River to the south (most of what is now Oklahoma and eastern Kansas) exclusively for Indians. This Indian Territory was reserved for tribes resettled from the East under the Indian Removal Act of 1830 and for village-living groups native to the area. Many government officials envisioned this territory as a permanent sanctuary that would separate Indians from white people and allow them to live in peace on allotments of land granted to individual tribes as compensation for the territory they had ceded to the federal government in earlier treaties. However, even as Congress was debating the idea of a permanent Indian reserve, the pressure on native peoples in the Mississippi Valley both from raiding parties of Plains Indians and the incessant demands of white farmers and speculators for land was rendering a stable Indian–white boundary untenable.

On the eve of Indian removal in the East, the Sauks, Foxes, Potawatomis, and other Indian peoples inhabited Iowa. The defeat of the Sauks and Foxes in what white Americans called Black Hawk's War of 1832 opened Iowa to white settlement and forced tribes to cede land. In 1838, Congress created the Territory of Iowa, which encompassed all the land between the Mississippi and Missouri Rivers north of the state of Missouri, which left the Indians on the verge of being pushed completely out of the region. Throughout the upper Mississippi Valley in the

1830s, other groups suffered a similar fate, and the number of displaced Indians swelled.

The first to be displaced were farming peoples whose villages straddled the woodlands to the east and the open plains to the west. These border tribes were caught in a vise between the loss of their land to advancing white people and the seizure of their horses and agricultural provisions by Indian raiders from the plains. The Pawnees were among the hardest hit.

By the 1830s, the Pawnees were primarily an agricultural people who embarked on seasonal hunts for game in the Platte River Valley. In 1833, they signed a treaty with the U.S. government in which they agreed to withdraw from south of the Platte in return for subsidies and military protection from the hostile Indians on the plains. Once they moved north of the Platte, the Pawnees were attacked by Sioux who seized control of the prime hunting grounds. Sioux raiders seeking provisions and horses also harassed Pawnee agricultural villages. When the Pawnees in desperation filtered back south of the Platte, in violation of the treaty of 1833, they encountered constant harassment from white settlers. In vain the Pawnee leaders cited the provisions of the same treaty that promised them protection from the Sioux. Forced back north of the Platte by the U.S. government, the Pawnees were eventually driven out of their Nebraska homeland by the Sioux.

The Sioux were the dominant power on the northern and central Great Plains, more than able to hold their own against white Americans in the first half of the nineteenth century. The Tetons, Yanktons, and Yanktonais comprised the main divisions of the western Sioux. In the eighteenth century, these western Sioux had separated from their woodland kin (known as the Santee Sioux), left their homeland along the headwaters of the Mississippi River, and pushed onto the Minnesota prairies. Armed with guns they had acquired from the French, the western Sioux dominated the prairies east of the Missouri River by 1800.

The Sioux learned to use the horse from the Plains Indians. Introduced to the New World by the Spanish, horses had revolutionized the lives of native peoples on the Great Plains. As they acquired more horses through trading and raids, the Plains Indians evolved a distinctly new and nomadic culture. Horses made buffalo hunting vastly more productive, they made it easier to transport bulky possessions, and they made possible an aggressive, highly mobile form of warfare. The Sioux were the most successful of all the tribes in melding two facets of white culture, the gun and the horse, into an Indian culture of warrior-hunters.

Although the Sioux frequently fought other tribes, casualties from these encounters were light. The Sioux and other Plains Indians fought not to kill the greatest number of the enemy but rather to dom-

Shown here is a Lakota shirt, c. 1850, that was specially woven for those Sioux warriors who had distinguished themselves in battle. The blue and yellow dyes symbolize sky and earth, and the strands of human hair represent the acts of bravery performed in defense of the Lakota people.

inate hunting grounds and to win individual honor by "counting coup" (touching a live foe). When an Army officer in 1819 urged the Sioux to make peace with the Chippewas, Little Crow, a Santee Sioux, explained why war was preferable: "Why, then, should we give up such an extensive country to save the life of a man or two annually?"

When the United States acquired title to the Great Plains in the Louisiana Purchase of 1803, the western Sioux economy was based on two seasonally restricted systems of hunting. In summer, they hunted buffalo on horse on the plains. In winter, they trapped beaver. In great spring trading fairs, the western Sioux exchanged their buffalo robes and beaver pelts for goods acquired by the Santee Sioux from European traders.

As the supply of beaver dwindled and the demand for buffalo hides from American and European traders increased in the early 1800s, the Sioux extended their buffalo hunts. In a loose alliance with the Cheyennes and Arapahos, Sioux war parties pushed aside or subjugated weaker tribes to the south and west of the Missouri River basin. The Sioux gained access to new sources for buffalo and raided the village tribes for horses and provisions. Reduced to a dependent status, these tribes were forced to rely on the Sioux for meat and trading goods.

Epidemic diseases brought to the plains by white traders helped Sioux expansion. Because they lived in small wandering bands, the Sioux were less susceptible to these epidemics than the more sedentary village peoples. The Sioux were also one of the first tribes to be vaccinated against smallpox by doctors sent up the Missouri River by the Bureau of Indian Affairs in the early 1830s. Smallpox reached the plains in the 1780s, and a major epidemic in 1837 probably halved the region's Indian population. Particularly hard hit were tribes attempting to resist the Sioux advance. Sioux losses were relatively light and, unlike the other tribes, their population grew.

Some 25,000 strong by 1850, the western Sioux had increased in power and numbers since they first encountered American officials during the Lewis and Clark Expedition in 1804 and 1805. Even then, Jefferson had cautioned Lewis to cultivate good relations with the Sioux "because of their immense power." "These are the vilest miscreants of the savage race," Lewis and Clark wrote of the Sioux, "and must ever remain the pirates of the Missouri, until such measures are pursued by our government as will make them feel a dependence on its will for their supply of merchandise."

Words were one thing, gaining power over the Sioux another. Americans could vilify the Sioux, but they could not force them into dependence in the first half of the nineteenth century. The Sioux continued to extend their influence, and they were shrewd enough to align themselves with the Americans whenever their interests dictated conciliation.

The Fur Traders

"Curiosity, a love of wild adventure, and perhaps also a hope of profit—for times are hard, and my best coat has a sort of sheepish hang-dog hesitation to encounter fashionable folk—combined to make me look upon the project with an eye of favour." As best he could recollect, these were the motives that induced Warren A. Ferris, a New York civil engineer, to join the American Fur Company in 1829 at the age of 19 and go west as a fur trapper and mountain man. When Ferris joined up, the American fur trade in the trans-Mississippi West—and the spirit of adventure it stirred—was at its height. During their golden age in the 1820s and 1830s, the trappers blazed the trails that far greater numbers of white settlers would follow in the 1840s.

The western fur trade originated in the rivalry between British and American companies for profitable furs, especially beaver pelts. Until the early 1820s, the Hudson's Bay Company, a well-capitalized British concern, dominated the trans-Mississippi fur trade. A breakthrough for American interests came in 1824 when two St. Louis businessmen, William Henry Ashley and Andrew Henry of the Rocky Mountain Fur Company, developed the rendezvous system, which eliminated the need for permanent and costly posts deep in Indian territory. In keeping with Indian traditions of periodic intertribal meetings, the rendezvous system brought together trappers, Indians, and traders in a grand annual fair at a designated site in the high mountain country of Wyoming. White trappers and Indians exchanged the animal skins they had gathered in the seasonal hunt for the guns, traps, tobacco, whiskey, textiles, and other trading goods that agents of the fur companies in St. Louis brought to the fair.

The mountain men signed up for two- or three-year stints with the fur companies. Except for the annual fairs, they lived isolated, hard lives in the wilderness. Their closest relations were with Indians, and about 40 percent of the trappers married Indian women, unions that often linked them economically and diplomatically to their bride's tribe.

Living conditions in the wilderness were primitive, even brutal. Mortality rates among trappers ran as high as 80 percent a year. Death often came suddenly from an accidental gunshot wound, an encounter with a grizzly, or an arrow from an Indian

The annual rendezvous in Wyoming of fur trappers and traders was a multinational affair in which Anglo-Americans, French Canadians, Mexican-Americans, and Native Americans gathered to trade, drink, and swap stories.

whose hunting grounds a trapper had transgressed. Survival required techniques that a "civilized" American would find repellent. Many a trapper avoided death from dehydration by sucking blood from the sliced vein of a horse or drinking the watery contents from the stomach of a buffalo carcass. "Peg-Leg" Smith became a legend for amputating his own leg after a bullet shattered it.

For all its dangers, the life of a trapper appealed to unattached young men like Warren Ferris. They were fleeing the confinements, as well as the comforts, of white civilization and were as free as they could be. When on a hunt with the Indians, they were part of a spectacle unknown to other white Americans, one that was already passing into history. "Fancy to yourself," Ferris asked readers of his published journals, "three thousand horses of every variety of size and colour, with trappings almost as varied as their appearance . . . ridden by a thousand souls . . . their persons fantastically ornamented. . . . Listen to the rattle of numberless lodgepoles [trailed] by packhorses. . . . Yonder see a hundred horsemen pursuing a herd of antelopes." He was describing the color, bustle, and motion at the start of a hunt with the Salish Indians of Montana in the 1830s, played out on "a beautiful level prairie, with dark blue snow-capped mountains in the distance for the locale."

Such spectacles were increasingly rare after 1840, the year of the last mountain men's rendezvous on the Green River in Wyoming. The most exploitive phase of the fur trade in the 1830s had ravaged the fur-bearing animals and accelerated the spread of smallpox among the tribes. Whiskey, the most profitable item among the white man's trading goods, had corrupted countless Indians and undermined the vitality of tribal cultures.

The mountain men were about to pass into legend, but before they did, they explored every trail and path from the front (or eastern) range of the Rockies to the Pacific. They had gone where no white people had gone before. The main trading corridor of the fur trade—up the lower Missouri to the North Platte and across the plains to the South Pass, a wide plateau crossing the Continental Divide, and into the Wyoming basin—became the main overland route to the West that migrating farm families followed in the 1840s. The mountain men had removed the mystery of western geography, and in so doing they hastened the end of the frontier conditions that had made their unique way of life possible.

The Oregon Trail

The ruts are still there. One can follow them to the horizon in the Platte River Valley of Nebraska and the dry tablelands of Wyoming, Idaho, and Nevada. They were put there by the wheels of wagons hauled by oxen on a jolting two-thousand-mile journey across plains, mountains, and deserts from Missouri to Oregon, Utah, and California (see Map 12-2). Some 150,000 Americans made this overland trek in the heyday of the Oregon Trail in the 1840s and early 1850s (see Figure 12-1). Most of them walked alongside their wagons. They covered up to fifteen miles a day on a trip that lasted close to six months.

Before the 1830s, few Americans had heard of Oregon, and practically none lived there. Under an agreement reached in 1818, the Oregon Country was still jointly administered by the United States and Great Britain. Furs—whether beaver pelts or the skins of the Pacific sea otter—had attracted a few American trappers and merchants, but the British-controlled Hudson's Bay Company dominated the region. Protestant missionaries established the first permanent white settlements in the 1830s. Under the leadership of Jason Lee, they set up their missions in the fertile Willamette Valley, south of the Columbia River. Reports of Oregon's fertility that the missionaries sent east sparked the first popular interest in the region, especially among Midwestern farmers stuck in the agricultural depression that followed the Panic of 1837.

While the missionaries were publicizing Oregon and attracting future settlers, they were failing in their efforts to convert the Indians of the region to Christianity. Unlike the trappers, the missionaries sought to change the entire structure of Indian life and beliefs. But with their numbers already thinned by the diseases brought in by the trappers, Oregon tribes such as the Cayuses refused to abandon their traditional culture based on hunting and fishing to become laborers for white farmers. During a measles epidemic in 1847, the Cayuses killed two of the most prominent missionaries, Marcus and Narcissa Whitman. In retaliation, white Americans, who now numbered more than five thousand, virtually exterminated the Cayuses.

The first large party of overlanders on the Oregon Trail left Independence, Missouri, for the Willamette Valley in 1842. Independence and St. Joseph in Missouri and, by the 1850s, Council Bluffs in Iowa

Map 12-2 Western Overland Trails
The great overland trails to the West began at the Missouri River. The Oregon Trail crossed South Pass in Wyoming and then branched off to Oregon, California, or Utah. The Santa Fe Trail carried American goods and traders to the Mexican Southwest.

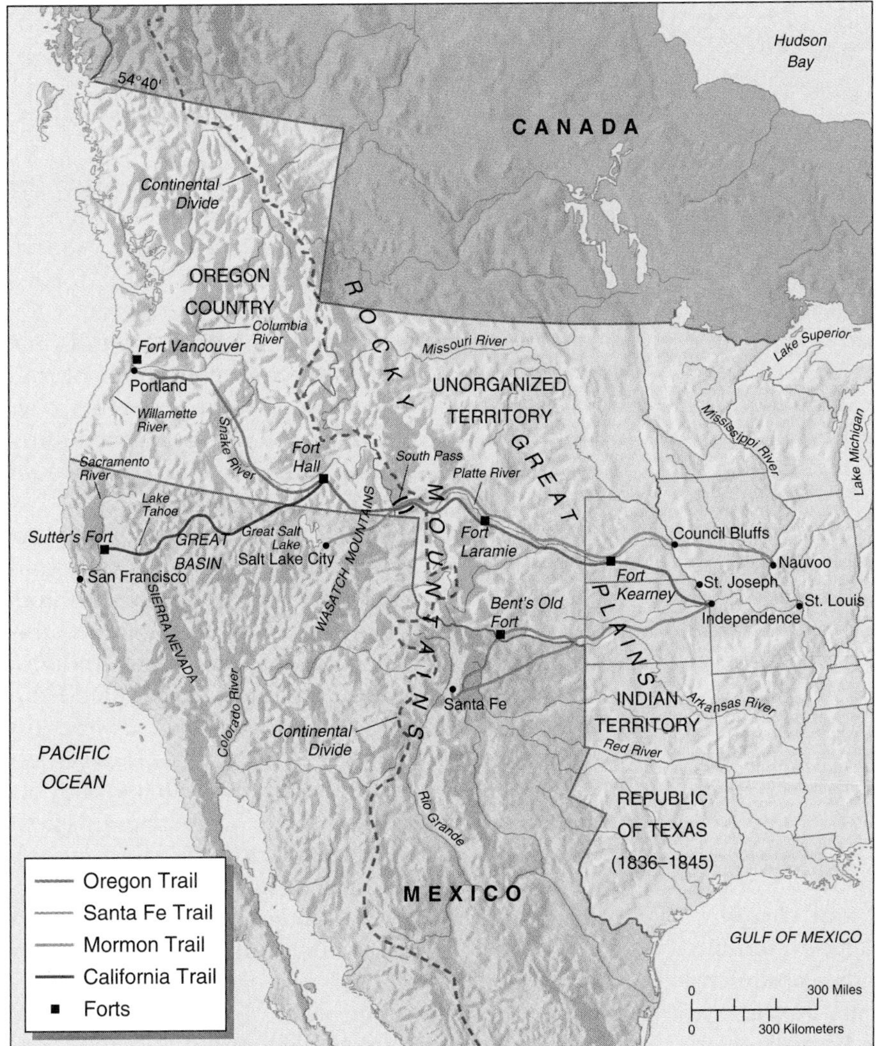

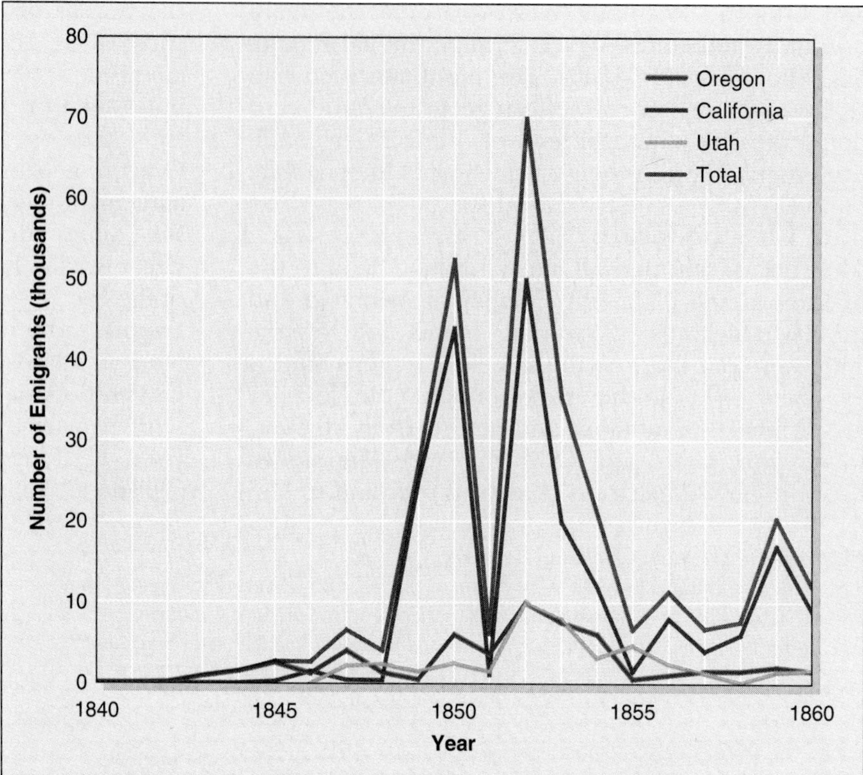

Figure 12-1 Overland Emigration to the West, 1840–1860
Emigration to the trans-Mississippi West steadily increased in the 1840s as farm families moved to Oregon or Utah. After the discovery of gold in California in 1849, California attracted the bulk of the emigrants, many of whom were single men hopeful of striking it rich.

Data Source: John D. Unruh, Jr., The Plains Across: The Overland Emigrants and the Trans-Mississippi West, 1840–60 *(1982), pp. 84–85.*

were the jumping-off points for the Oregon Trail. Each town competed to capture the lucrative trade of outfitting the migrants. There was more than enough trade to go around. Merchants profited from supplying, usually at inflated prices, wagons, mules, oxen, guns, ammunition, and staples like flour, bacon, and sugar.

Most overlanders were young farm families from the Midwest, who had moved at least once before in their restless search for the perfect farm that would keep them out of debt. Indeed, Medorum Crawford said of one family that made the journey to Oregon with him in 1842 and then quickly left for California: "They had practically lived in the wagon for more than twenty years, only remaining in one locality long enough to make a crop, which they had done in every State and Territory in the Mississippi Valley."

Usually the male head of a household made the decision to move. Women often regretted giving up ties with kin and friends, which provided security and assistance in their isolated, rural lives. They were well aware of the dangers of childbirth on a long, hard journey. Besides their usual work of minding the children and cooking and cleaning, they would now have to help drive wagons and tend livestock. Still, many women were also optimistic about the journey. "Ho—for California—at last we are on the way," exclaimed Helen Carpenter in 1857, "and with good luck may some day reach the 'promised land.'" A study of 159 women's trail diaries indicates that about one-third of the women strongly favored the move. Margaret Frink, for example, recalled that she "never had occasion to regret the prolonged hardships of the toilsome journey." By adapting to the new conditions of trail life—pitching tents, yoking oxen, cooking over open fires, and gathering buffalo chips (dried dung used for fuel)—women learned skills that would help them start a new life in the West.

The journey was long and dangerous. In the 1840s, some five thousand of the ninety thousand men, women, and children who set out on the Oregon Trail died along the way. But although the overlanders were terrified of encountering Indians, whom they assumed would be hostile, few died from Indian attacks. As long as the wagon trains were just passing through their lands, the Plains Indians left the white people alone. At first they watched with bemused curiosity, and then, as the white migrants kept coming, they traded game for clothing and ammunition. Indians killed only 115 migrants in the 1840s, and trigger-happy white migrants provoked most clashes. Disease, especially cholera, was the great killer. Second to disease were accidents, especially drownings that resulted when drivers tried to force overloaded wagons across swollen rivers.

Large wagon trains of settlers began making the overland journey to the West in the 1840s. As the parties moved across the plains, their horses and livestock depleted forage grasses by overgrazing.

Cooperation among families was the key to a successful overland crossing. The men in a party often drew up a formal, written constitution at the start of a trip spelling out the assignments and work responsibilities of each wagon. Before the trail was well marked, former mountain men hired on as captains to lead wagon trains. Timing was crucial. A wagon train had to leave late enough in the spring to get good grass in Nebraska for the oxen and mules. Too early a departure, and the wagon train risked getting bogged down in spring mud; too late a departure, and it risked being trapped in the snows of the Pacific coastal ranges.

Before "Oregon fever" had run its course, the flow of white settlers across the continent radically changed the economy and ecology of the Great Plains. Pressure mounted on plants and animals, reducing the land's ability to support all the tribes accustomed to living off it. Intertribal warfare intensified as the supply of buffalo and other game dwindled. Far from being separated from white people by a permanent line of division, the Plains Indians now stood astride the main path of white migration to the Pacific.

In response, officials in the Bureau of Indian Affairs organized a great gathering of the tribes in 1851. At this conference they pushed through the **Fort Laramie Treaty**, the first U.S. government attempt to draw boundaries within which to contain the Plains Indians. In exchange for accepting limitations on their movement and for the loss of game, the tribes were to receive annual compensation of $50,000 a year for fifty years (later reduced by the U.S. Senate to ten years).

Most of the Indians at the Fort Laramie conference were the Sioux and their allies. The Sioux viewed the treaty as confirming their dominant power on the Great Plains. When American negotiators tried to restrict Sioux hunting to north of the Platte, the Sioux demanded and received treaty rights to lands south of the Platte as well. "These lands once belonged to the Kiowas and the Crows," argued a western Sioux, "but we whipped those nations out of them, and in this we did what the white men do when they want the lands of the Indians." This was an argument white Americans could understand, and they conceded the point.

The Fort Laramie Treaty represented a standoff between the Sioux and the U.S. government, the two great powers on the Plains. If neither yielded its claims to the region, war between them would be inevitable.

The Mexican Borderlands

By the mid-1840s, parties of emigrant Americans were beginning to branch off the main Oregon Trail on their way to Utah and California. These areas were then part of the northern borderlands of Mexico. Mostly a semiarid and thinly populated land of high plateaus, dry basins, and desert bisected north to south by mountain ranges, the borderlands had been part of the Spanish empire in North America. Mexico inherited this territory when it won independence from Spain in 1821. The borderlands covered roughly 1 million square miles; today, they comprise the American Southwest from Texas to California. Mexico's hold on this region was always weak. It lost Texas in 1837, and, in the next decade,

This painting by Alfred James Miller depicts the busy interior of Fort Laramie in 1837.

the American penetration of Utah and California set the stage for the American seizure of most of the rest in the Mexican War.

The Peoples of the Southwest

Diverse peoples lived in the Southwest. Imperial Spain had divided them into four main groupings: Indians, full-blooded Native Americans who retained their own languages and customs; ***mestizos***, those of racially mixed ancestry, usually Spanish and Indian; ***criollos***, American-born whites of Spanish ancestry; and Spaniards.

By far the smallest group were the Spaniards. Compared to the English, few Spaniards emigrated to the New World, and most who did were men. Consequently, Spanish males married or lived with native women, creating a large class of *mestizos.* Despite their small numbers, the Spanish, along with the *criollos*, monopolized economic and political power. This wealthy elite controlled the labor of the *mestizos* in the predominantly ranching economy of the borderlands.

The largest single group in the borderlands were the Indians, about half the population in the 1820s. Most had not come under direct Spanish or Mexican control. Those who had were part of the **mission system**. This instrument of Spanish imperial policy forced Indians to live in a fixed area, to convert to Catholicism, and to work as agricultural laborers.

Spanish missions, most of them established by the Franciscan order, aimed both to Christianize and "civilize" the Indians, making them loyal imperial subjects. Mission Indians were forced to abandon their native economies and culture and settle in agricultural communities under the tight supervision of the friars. Spanish soldiers and royal officials, who lived in military garrisons known as *presidios*, accompanied the friars.

The largest concentration of Indians—some 300,000 when the Spanish friars arrived in the 1760s—was in California. Most of these—the Paiutes, Chumashes, Pomos, Shastas, and a host of smaller tribes—occupied their own distinct ecological zones where they gathered and processed what the rivers, forests, and grasslands provided. Fish and game were abundant, and wild plants and nuts, especially acorns, provided grain and flour. The Paiutes in the Owens Valley perfected an intricate system for irrigating wild grasses, but only the Yumans along the Colorado River in southeastern California practiced full-scale agriculture. The Spanish marveled at their lush fields of wheat, maize, beans, tobacco, and melons. The Yumans also had an elaborate religion based on an oral tradition of dream songs. (Dream songs remain a distinctive feature of Native American culture.)

The major farming Indians east of California were the Pueblo peoples of Arizona and New Mexico. Named after the adobe or stone community dwellings (*pueblo* is Spanish for "village") in which they lived atop mesas or on terraces carved into cliffs, the Pueblo Indians were a peaceful people closely bound to small, tightly knit communities. Indeed, some of their dwellings, such as those of the Hopis in Arizona or the Acomas in New Mexico, have been continuously occupied for more than five hundred years. Corn and beans were the staples of their irrigation-based agriculture. Formally a part of the Spanish mission system, they had incorporated the Catholic God and Catholic rituals into their own polytheistic religion, which stressed the harmony of all living things with the forces of nature. They continued to worship in their underground sanctuaries known as *kivas*.

Once the Pueblos made their peace with the Spaniards after their great revolt in 1680 (see Chapter 3), their major enemies were the nomadic tribes that lived by hunting and raiding. These tribes outnumbered the Pueblos four to one and controlled most of the Southwest until the 1850s. The horse, which many of the tribes acquired during Spain's temporary retreat from the region during the late seventeenth century in the wake of the Pueblo Revolt, was the basis of their way of life. As the horse frontier spread, the peoples of the southern Plains gained enormous mobility and the means of ranging far and wide for the economic resources that sustained their transformation into societies of mounted warriors.

West of the pueblos around Taos was the land of the Navajos, who herded sheep, raised some crops, and raided other tribes from their mountain fastness. Spilling over onto Navajo lands, the Southern Utes ranged up and down the canyon lands of Utah. The Gila Apaches were the dominant tribe south of Albuquerque and westward into Arizona. To the east in the Pecos River Valley roamed bands of Mescalero and Jicarillo Apaches. On the broad plains rolling northward from the Texas panhandle and southward into northern Mexico were war parties of Comanches and Kiowas.

The Comanches, a branch of the mountain Shoshonis who moved to the plains when horses became available, were the most feared of the nomadic peoples. Utterly fearless, confident, and masterful horsemen, they gained a reputation of mythic proportions for their prowess as mounted warriors. For food and clothing, they relied on the immense buffalo herds of the southern plains. For guns, horses, and other trading goods, they lived off their predatory raids. When the Santa Fe Trail opened in the early 1820s, their shrewdness as traders gave them a new source of firearms that strengthened their raiding prowess.

The three focal points of white settlement in the northern borderlands of Mexico—Texas, New Mexico, and Alta California (as distinguished from Lower, or Baja, California)—were never linked by an effective network of communications or transportation. Navigable rivers were few, and travel was limited to tortuous journeys along Indian and Spanish trails that barely indented the dry and largely barren landscape. Each of these settlements was an isolated offshoot of Hispanic culture with a semiautonomous economy based on ranching and a mostly illegal trade with French, British, and American merchants that brought in a trickle of needed goods.

Neither Spain, which tried to seal off its northern outposts from economic contact with foreigners, nor Mexico, which opened up the borderlands to outsiders, had integrated this vast region

The paintings of George Catlin are among the best visual sources for understanding the material culture of the Plains Indians. This painting, c. 1834, shows how central was the buffalo in the life of the Comanches, the most powerful tribe on the Southern Plains.

into a unified economic or political whole. Indeed, Mexico's most pressing problem in the 1820s was protecting its northern states from the Comanches. To serve as a buffer against the Comanches, the Mexican government in 1821 invited Americans into Texas, opening the way to the eventual American takeover of the territory.

The Americanization of Texas

The Mexicans faced the same problems governing Texas that the Spanish had. Mexico City was about a thousand miles from San Antonio, the center of Hispanic settlement in Texas, and communications were slow and cumbersome. The ranching elite of ***Tejanos*** (Spanish-speaking Mexicans born in Texas) had closer economic ties to American Louisiana than they did to Coahuila, the Mexican state to which Texas was formally attached. These large ranchers had long been smuggling horses and cattle into Louisiana in exchange for manufactured items and tobacco. Markets for farm crops were limited, and the ranchers and a scattered class of tenant farmers produced little surplus food. This low agricultural productivity, combined with the low birthrate among mission Indians, outbreaks of disease, and the generally hostile frontier environment, sharply restricted population growth. Only some five thousand Mexicans lived in Texas in the 1820s.

Sparsely populated and economically struggling, Mexican Texas shared a border with the United States along the Sabine River in Louisiana and the Red River in the Arkansas Territory. The threat that the nearby Americans posed to Mexico's security was obvious to Mexican officials. As one of them early noted with alarm: "If we do not take the present opportunity to people Texas, day by day the strength of the United States will grow until it will annex Texas, Coahuila, Saltillo, and Nuevo León like the Goths, Visigoths, and the other tribes that assailed the Roman Empire." However, attempts to promote immigration into Texas from other parts of Mexico failed. Reasoning that the Americans were going to come in any event and anxious to build up the population of Texas against Indian attacks, the Mexican government encouraged Americans to settle in Texas by offering huge grants of land in return for promises to accept Mexican citizenship, convert to Catholicism, and obey the authorities in Mexico City.

The first American ***empresario***—the recipient of a large grant in return for a promise to bring in settlers—was Stephen F. Austin. He had inherited a huge Spanish grant from his father, Moses Austin, a Missourian who had had business dealings with the Spanish since 1797. After having the grant confirmed by the new Mexican government in 1821, Stephen Austin founded the first American colony in Texas. The Austin grant encompassed eighteen thousand square miles. Other grants were smaller but still lavish. The *empresarios* stood to grow wealthy by leasing out land, selling parcels to settlers, and organizing the rest into large-scale farms that produced cotton with slave labor in the bottomlands of the Sabine, Colorado, and Brazos Rivers. For the Americans who followed in their wake, Texas was a dream come true—the chance to acquire good land that was so cheap it was almost free. As early as 1830, eastern and south-central Texas were becoming an extension of the plantation economy of the Gulf coastal plain. More than 25,000 white settlers, with around a thousand slaves, had poured into the region (see "American Views: A Mexican View of the Texans in 1828").

More Americans moved into Texas with slaves than the Mexicans had anticipated. Many settlers simply ignored Mexican laws, especially the Emancipation Proclamation of 1829 that forbade slavery in the Republic of Mexico. In 1830, the Mexican government attempted to assert its authority. It levied the first taxes on the Americans, prohibited the further importation of slaves, and closed the international border to additional immigration. Still, another ten thousand Americans spilled across the border in the early 1830s, and they continued to bring in slaves.

Unlike the *empresarios*, many of whom became Catholic and married into elite *Tejano* families, these newcomers lived apart from Mexicans and rejected Mexican citizenship. Cultural tensions escalated. Believing that they belonged to a superior race of liberty-loving white Anglo-Saxons, most of these new arrivals sneered at the Mexicans as a mongrelized race of black people, Indians, and Spaniards and resented having to submit to their rule. They considered Catholicism a despotic, superstitious religion and ignored legal requirements that they convert to it.

A clash became inevitable in 1835 when General Santa Anna, elected president of Mexico in 1833, overturned the liberal Mexican constitution of 1824. He established himself as a dictator in 1834, and his centralist rule ended any hope of the Americans *empresarios* and their *Tejano* allies that Texas might become an autonomous state within a federated Mexico. Skirmishing between Mexican troops and rebellious Texans began in the fall of 1835.

At first, the Anglo–*Tejano* leadership did not renounce all ties with Mexico. When these leaders drafted a constitution in November 1835, they sought to overthrow Santa Anna, restore the constitution of 1824, and win separate statehood for Texas within a liberal Mexican republic. Santa Anna, however, refused to compromise. When he raised a large army to crush the uprising, he radicalized the rebellion and pushed its leaders to declare complete independence on March 2, 1836. Four days later, a Mexican army of four thousand annihilated the 187 defenders of the **Alamo**, an abandoned mission in San Antonio. A few weeks later at Goliad, another three hundred Texans were killed after they had agreed to surrender (see Map 12-3).

"Remember the Alamo!" and "Remember Goliad!" were powerful rallying cries for the beleaguered Texans. Volunteers from the American South rushed to the aid of the main Texan army, commanded by Sam Houston. A product of the Tennessee frontier and a close friend of Andrew Jackson's, Houston did Jackson proud by catching the overconfident Santa Anna off guard in eastern Texas. Houston's victory in April 1836 at the **Battle of San Jacinto** established the independence of Texas. Captured while trying to flee, Santa Anna signed a treaty in May 1836, recognizing Texas as an independent republic with a boundary on the south and west at the Rio Grande. However, the Nueces River to the north of the Rio Grande had

Map 12-3 ***Texas and Mexico after the Texas Revolt***
The Battle of San Jacinto was the decisive American victory that gained the independence of Texas, but the border dispute between Texas and Mexico would not be resolved until the Mexican War a decade later.

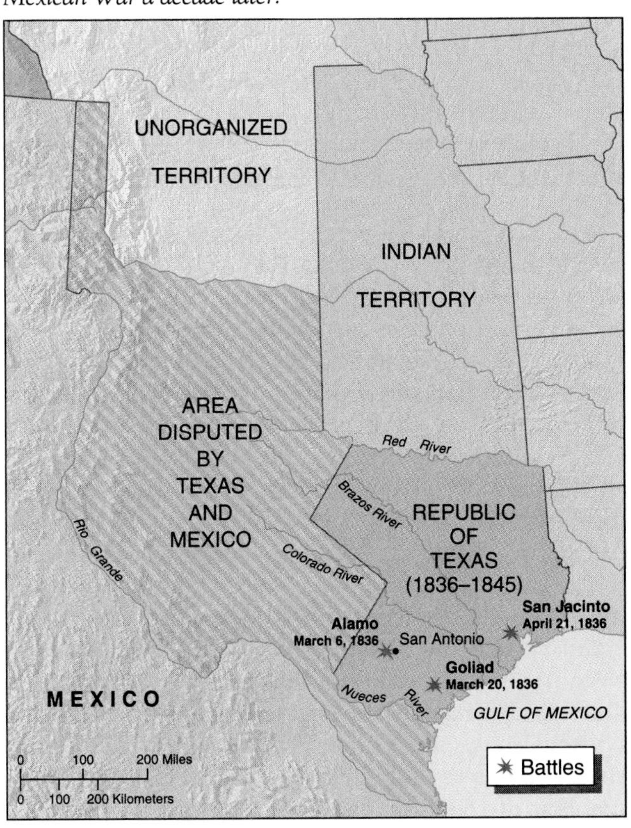

been the administrative border of Texas under Mexican rule. The Mexican Congress rejected the treaty, and the boundary remained in dispute.

Soon forgotten during the ensuing eight years of Texas independence was the support that many *Tejanos* had given to the successful revolt against Mexican rule. In part because Mexico refused to recognize the Texas Republic, Anglos feared *Tejanos* as a subversive element. Pressure mounted on them to leave, especially after Santa Anna launched a major counterattack in 1842, capturing San Antonio. Those who stayed lost much of their land and economic power as Anglos used their knowledge of American legal codes or just plain chicanery to reduce the *Tejanos* to second-class citizens.

More difficult to subordinate were the Comanches. While president of Texas, Houston tried to fix a permanent boundary between the Comanches and white settlers, but Texas pride and ongoing white encroachments on Indian land undercut his efforts. By the early 1840s, Texans and Comanches were in a state of nearly permanent war. Only the force of the federal army after the Civil War ended the Comanches' long reign as the effective rulers of the high, dry plains of northern and western Texas.

The Push into California and the Southwest

Mexican rule in California was always weak. The Sonoran desert and the resistance of the Yuman Indians in southeastern California cut off Mexico from any direct land contact with Alta California. Only irregular communications were maintained over a long sea route. For ***Californios***, Californians of Spanish descent, Mexico was literally *la otra banda*, "the other shore." In trying to strengthen its hold on this remote and thinly populated region, the Mexican government relied on a program of economic development. As in Texas, however, Mexican policy had unintended consequences.

The centerpiece of the Mexican program was the secularization of the missions. This policy opened up the landholdings of the Catholic Church to private ownership and released the mission Indians from paternalistic bondage. Small allotments of land were set aside for the Indians, but most returned to their homelands. Those who remained became a source of cheap labor for the *rancheros* who carved up the mission lands into huge cattle ranches. Thus by the 1830s, California had entered what is called the *rancho* era. The main beneficiaries of this process, however, were not Mexican authorities but the American traders who responded to the economic opportunities presented by the privatization of the California economy.

American Views

A Mexican View of the Texans in 1828

By the late 1820s, Mexico was reassessing its policy of encouraging American immigration to Texas. Concerned over the large numbers and uncertain loyalties of the American settlers, the government appointed a commission in 1827 ostensibly to survey the boundary between Louisiana and the province of Texas. The real purpose of the commission was to recommend policy changes that would strengthen Mexico's hold on Texas. The following excerpt is from a journal kept by José María Sánchez, the draftsman of the boundary commission.

❖ **Why was the Mexican government so ineffective in maintaining control over Texas?**

❖ **What was the appeal of Texas for Americans? How did most of them enter Texas and take up land?**

❖ **Why did Sánchez have such a low opinion of the Americans in the Austin colony? What did he think of Stephen Austin?**

❖ **Why did the Mexicans fear that they would lose Texas?**

The Americans from the north have taken possession of practically all the eastern part of Texas, in most cases without the permission of the authorities. They immigrate constantly, finding no one to prevent them, and take possession of the *sitio* [location] that best suits them without either asking leave or going through any formality other than that of building their homes. Thus the majority of inhabitants in the Department are North Americans, the Mexican population being reduced to only Bejar, Nacoghoches, and La Bahía del Espíritu Santo, wretched settlements that between them do not number three thousand inhabitants, and the new village of Guadalupe Victoria that has scarcely more than seventy settlers. The government of the state, with its seat at Saltillo, that

New England merchants had been trading in California since the 1780s. What first attracted them were the seal fisheries off the California coast, a source of otter pelts highly prized in the China trade. After the seals had been all but exterminated by the 1820s, Yankee merchants shipped out hides and tallow, a trade fed by the immense cattle resources of the *rancheros,* to New England for processing into shoes and candles. Ships from New England and New York sailed around Cape Horn to California ports, where they unloaded trading goods. Servicing this trade in California was a resident colony of American agents, some three hundred strong by the mid-1840s.

Whereas Yankees dominated the American colonies in coastal California, it was mostly midwestern farm families who filtered into the inner valleys of California from the Oregon Trail in the 1830s and 1840s. About one in ten of the overland parties took a cutoff on the Trail near Fort Hall on the Snake River that led them across the deserts of northern Nevada to a passage across the Sierra Nevada near Lake Tahoe. At the end of the journey, they dropped down into the fertile Sacramento River Valley. Nearly a thousand Americans had arrived by 1846.

California belonged to Mexico in name only by the early 1840s. The program of economic development had strengthened California's ties to the outside world at the expense of Mexico. American merchants and California *rancheros* ran the economy, and both groups had joined separatist movements against Mexican rule. Unlike the *Californios,* who were ambivalent about their future political allegiance, the Americans wanted to be part of the United States and assumed that California would shortly be annexed. With the outbreak of the Mexican War in 1846, their wish became reality.

should watch over the preservation of its most precious and interesting department, taking measures to prevent its being stolen by foreign hands, is the one that knows the least not only about actual conditions, but even about its territory. . . . Repeated and urgent appeals have been made to the Supreme Government of the Federation regarding the imminent danger in which this interesting Department is of becoming the prize of the ambitious North Americans, but never has it taken any measures that may be called conclusive. . . .

[Sánchez goes on to describe the village of Austin and the American colony founded by Stephen Austin.]

Its population is nearly two hundred persons, of which only ten are Mexicans, for the balance are all Americans from the North with an occasional European. Two wretched little stores supply the inhabitants of the colony: one sells only whiskey, rum, sugar, and coffee; the other, rice, flour, lard, and cheap cloth. . . . The Americans from the North, at least the great part of those I have seen, eat only salted meat, bread made by themselves out of corn meal, coffee, and home-made cheese. To these the greater part of those who live in the village add strong liquor, for they are in general, in my opinion, lazy people of vicious character. Some of them cultivate their small farms by planting corn; but this task they usually entrust to their negro slaves, whom they treat with considerable harshness. Beyond the village in an immense stretch of land formed by rolling hills are scattered the families brought by Stephen Austin, which today number more than two thousand persons. The diplomatic policy of this *empresario,* evident in all his actions, has, as one may say, lulled the authorities into a sense of security, while he works diligently for his own ends. In my judgment, the spark that will start the conflagration that will deprive us of Texas, will start from this colony. All because the government does not take vigorous measures to prevent it. Perhaps it does not realize the value of what it is about to lose.

Source: José María Sánchez, excerpted from "A Trip to Texas in 1828," trans. Carlos E. Castaneda from Southwestern Historical Quarterly, 29 *Copyright © 1926. Reprinted courtesy of Texas State Historical Association, Austin Texas. All rights reserved.*

Except for Utah, the American push into the interior of the Mexican Southwest followed the California pattern of trade preceding settlement. When Mexico liberalized the formerly restrictive trading policies of Spain, American merchants opened up the nine-hundred-mile-long **Santa Fe Trail** from Independence, Missouri, to Santa Fe, New Mexico. Starved for mercantile goods, the New Mexicans were a small but highly profitable market. They paid for their American imports with gold, silver, and furs.

Brent's Old Fort, an impregnable adobe structure built on the Arkansas River at the point where the Santa Fe Trail turned to the southwest and Taos, was the fulcrum for the growing economic influence of Americans over New Mexican affairs. Completed in 1832, the fort enabled the Brent brothers from Missouri to control a flourishing and almost monopolistic trade with Indians, trappers, caravans on the Santa Fe Trail, and the large landowners and merchants of New Mexico. This trade pulled New Mexico into the cultural and economic orbit of the United States and undermined what little sovereign power Mexico held in the region.

Although only a few hundred Americans were permanent residents of New Mexico in the 1840s, they had married into the Spanish-speaking landholding elite and were themselves beginning to receive large grants of land. Ties of blood and common economic interests linked this small group of American businessmen with an influential faction of the local elite. American merchants and New Mexican landlords were further united by their growing disdain for the instability of Mexican rule, Santa Anna's dictatorship, and sporadic attempts by Mexico to levy heavy taxes on the Santa Fe trade. Another bond was their concern over the aggressive efforts of the Texans to seize eastern New Mexico. After thwarting an 1841 Texan attempt to occupy Santa Fe, the leaders of New Mexico increasingly looked to the United States to protect their local autonomy. They quickly decided to cooperate with the American army of invasion when the Mexican War got under way. Over the opposition of the clergy and ranchers still loyal to Mexico, this group was instrumental in the American takeover of New Mexico.

At the extreme northern and inner reaches of the Mexican borderlands lay Utah. Dominated by an intermountain depression called the Great Basin, Utah was a starkly beautiful but dry region of alkaline flats, broken tablelands, cottonwood canyons, and mountain ranges. It was home to the Bannocks, Utes, Navajos, Hopis, and small bands of other Indians. Aside from trading ties with the Utes, Spain and Mexico had largely ignored this remote region. Its isolation and lack of white settlers, however, were precisely what made Utah so appealing to the leaders of the Mormons, the Church of Jesus Christ of Latter-day Saints. For the Mormons in the 1840s, Utah became the promised land in which to build a new Zion.

Founded by Joseph Smith in upstate New York in the 1820s, Mormonism grew rapidly within a communitarian framework that stressed hard work and economic cooperation under the leadership of patriarchal leaders. The economic success of close-knit Mormon communities, combined with the righteous zeal of their members, aroused the fears and hostility of non-Mormons. Harassed out of New York, Ohio, and Missouri, the Mormons thought they had found a permanent home by the late 1830s in Nauvoo, Illinois. But the murder of Joseph Smith and his brother by a mob in 1844 convinced the beleaguered Mormons that they had to leave the settled East for a refuge of their own in the West. In 1846 a group of Mormons migrated to the Great Basin in Utah. Under the leadership of Brigham Young, they established a new community in 1847 at the Great Salt Lake on the western slopes of the Wasatch Mountains. Ten thousand Mormons joined them.

The Mormons thrived in the arid desert. Their intense communitarianism was ideally suited to dispensing land and organizing an irrigation system that coordinated water rights with the amount of land under production. To their dismay, however, they learned in 1848 that they had not left the United States after all. The Union acquired Utah, along with the rest of the northern borderlands of Mexico, as a result of the Mexican War. (For more on the Mormons, see Chapter 14.)

Politics, Expansion, and War

The Democrats viewed their victory in the election of 1844 (see Chapter 10) as a popular mandate for expansion. They had campaigned on a platform that boldly demanded both Texas and the "reoccupation" of Oregon up to 54°40'.

James K. Polk, the new Democratic president, fully shared the expansionist vision of his party. The greatest prize in his eyes was California. Although silent in public on California for fear of further antagonizing the Mexicans, who had never accepted the loss of Texas, Polk made the acquisition of California the cornerstone of his foreign policy. When he was stymied in his efforts to purchase California and New Mexico, he tried to force concessions from the Mexican government by ordering American troops to the mouth of the Rio Grande, far within the territory claimed by Mexico. When the virtually inevitable clash of arms occurred in late April 1846, war broke out between the United States and Mexico.

Victory resulted in the **Mexican Cession of 1848**, which added half a million square miles to the United States. Polk's administration also finalized the acquisition of Texas and reached a compromise with the British on the Oregon Territory that recognized American sovereignty in the Pacific Northwest up to the 49th parallel. The United States was now a nation that spanned a continent.

Manifest Destiny

With a phrase that soon entered the nation's vocabulary, John L. O'Sullivan, editor and Democratic politician, proclaimed in 1845 America's "manifest destiny to overspread and to possess the whole of the continent which Providence has given us for the development of the great experiment of Liberty and federated self-government entrusted to us." Central to Manifest Destiny was the assumption that white Americans were a special people. Part of that sense of specialness was religiously inspired and dated back to the Puritans' belief that God had appointed them to establish a New Israel cleansed of the corruption of the Old World. Evangelical revivals in the early nineteenth century then added an aggressive sense of urgency to America's presumed mission to spread the benefits of Protestantism and Christian civilization. Protestant missionaries, as in Oregon, were often in the vanguard of American expansion.

What distinguished the special American mission as enunciated by Manifest Destiny was its explicitly racial component. Between 1815 and 1850, the term *Anglo-Saxon*, originally loosely applied to English-speaking peoples, acquired racial overtones, in keeping with the then current interest of European and American scientists in defining, classifying, and ranking human races (with themselves, of course, at the top). Caucasian Anglo-Saxon Americans, as the descendants of ancient Germanic tribes that purportedly brought the seeds of free institutions to England, were now said to be the foremost race in the world. Only they, it was argued, had the energy, industriousness, and innate love of liberty to establish a successful free government. This superior racial pedigree gave white Americans the natural right as a chosen people to expand westward, carrying the blessings of democracy and progress.

Advocates of Manifest Destiny insisted that American expansion would be irresistible and peaceful. They were not warmongers calling for conquest. Still, the doctrine was undeniably a self-serving justification for what other peoples would see as territorial aggrandizement. Certainly, that was true of the Mexican-Americans and Native Americans who lost land and cultural independence as they were brought under American control. Manifest Destiny and popular stereotypes lumped Indians and Mexicans together as inferior peoples. An emigrant guide of 1845 spoke of the Mexican Californians as "scarcely a visible grade in the scale of intelligence, above the barbarous tribes by whom they are surrounded." For Waddy Thompson, an American minister to Mexico in the early 1840s, the Mexicans in general were "lazy, ignorant, and, of course, vicious and dishonest." This alleged Mexican inferiority was attributed to racial intermixture with the Indians, who, it was said, were hopelessly unfit for civilization.

Manifest Destiny was closely associated with the Democratic party. For Democrats, expansionism would counterbalance the debilitating effects of industrialization and urbanization. As good Jeffersonians, they stressed the need for more land to realize the ideal of a democratic republic rooted in the virtues and rough equality of independent farmers. For their working-class Irish constituency, the Democrats touted the broad expanses of the West as the surest means to escape the misery of wage slavery. It was no coincidence that O'Sullivan was a Democrat or that he feared that the spread of factories would produce an impoverished class of workers in America as it had in England.

As a manifesto for expansion, Manifest Destiny captured the popular imagination when the country was still mired in a depression after the Panic of 1837. The way out of the depression, according to many Democrats, was to revive the export trade to soak up the agricultural surplus. Thomas Hart Benton, a Democratic senator from Missouri, was the leading spokesman for the vast potential of an American trade with India and China, a trade to be secured by American possession of the harbors on the Pacific Coast.

The Mexican War

Once in office, Polk proved far more conciliatory with the British than with the Mexicans. Despite a stridently anti-British tone in his annual message to Congress in December 1845, Polk was willing to compromise on Oregon because he dreaded the possibility of a two-front war against both the Mexicans and the British. Mexico had severed diplomatic ties with the United States over the annexation of Texas (see Chapter 11), and a war could break out at any time.

In the spring of 1846, after Polk had abrogated the agreement on the joint occupation of Oregon, the British offered a compromise that they had earlier rejected. They agreed to a boundary at the 49th parallel if they were allowed to retain Vancouver Island in Puget Sound. Polk sent the offer to the Senate, which quickly approved it in June 1846. British–American trade continued to flourish, Mexico lost a potential ally, and, most important, Polk could now concentrate on the **Mexican War** that had erupted a month earlier.

Unlike Oregon, where he backed off from extravagant territorial claims, Polk refused to budge on the American claim (inherited form the Texans, when the United States annexed Texas in 1845) that the Rio Grande was the border between Texas and Mexico. The Mexicans insisted that the Nueces River, a hundred miles to the north of the Rio Grande, was the border, as it had been when Texas was part of Mexico. An immense territory was at stake, for the headwaters of the Rio Grande were in northern New Mexico, and a boundary on the Rio Grande would more than double the size of Texas.

Citing rumors of a Mexican invasion, Polk sent 3,500 troops under General Zachary Taylor to the Nueces River in the summer of 1845. Polk also stepped up his efforts to acquire California. He instructed Thomas Larkin, the American consul in Monterey, California, to inform the *Californios* and Americans that the United States would support them if they revolted against Mexican rule. Polk also secretly ordered the U.S. Pacific naval squadron to

AMERICA'S JOURNEY

FROM THEN TO NOW

Manifest Destiny and American Foreign Policy

From the birth of the nation in 1776 to the U.S.-led NATO air strikes on Yugoslavia in 1999, a sense of mission has often imbued American foreign policy. Manifest Destiny was one expression of that sense of mission.

Thomas Paine, in *Common Sense*, declared that America had the "power to begin the world over again." The shining force of the American republic's free government, Paine believed, would redeem those suffering under despotic monarchies. According to the lofty rhetoric of Manifest Destiny, America would fulfill this divinely ordained mission by absorbing all the people of North America—at least those deemed capable of self-government—into the republic.

Manifest Destiny helped inspire the American surge to the Pacific and justify the Mexican War. But the war also provoked a contrary fear: Was the United States guilty of an imperial conquest that threatened liberty rather than promoting it? When expansionists pushed for the acquisition of all of Mexico, opponents objected. Mexicans, they claimed, were unfit to join Anglo-Saxon Americans in assuming the responsibilities of self-rule. At the same time, to subject Mexico to colonial rule would deny it the democratic liberty that Manifest Destiny promised. Consequently, the All Mexico movement soon collapsed.

After cresting in the 1840s, Manifest Destiny lost its appeal. Expansionists in the late nineteenth century invoked Manifest Destiny to justify America's acquisition of an overseas empire following the Spanish-American War, but the new empire didn't really fit that model. The advocates of Manifest Destiny had envisioned neighboring peoples in North America voluntarily joining the Republic. According to critics, the new empire, on the contrary, rested on the once-despised imperialist doctrines of Old World Europe. For former President Grover Cleveland, the annexation of the Hawaiian Islands in 1898 was "a perversion of our national mission," a signal that the nation was prepared to "abandon old landmarks and . . . follow the lights of monarchical hazards."

Cleveland and the other anti-imperialists lost the turn-of-the-century debate over whether the nation should acquire dependent possessions abroad. Still, by insisting, with Thomas Paine, that America's true mission must be to serve as the "model republic" for others to follow, they established the theme that characterized at least the public face of American diplomacy in the twentieth century. President Woodrow Wilson, for example, justified American intervention in World Was I as a moral crusade to save democracy in Europe, and he sought in vain to bring the United States into a new international body—the League of Nations—designed to curb aggressive nations and prevent future wars. Wilsonian idealism infused the foreign policy of President Franklin D. Roosevelt during World War II and inspired the formation of the United Nations. Throughout the Cold War, America identified itself as the protector of democratic freedoms from the threat of international communism. In the post–Cold War world, both Presidents George Bush and Bill Clinton have cited the need to uphold human rights as grounds for U.S. military intervention abroad.

Critics have charged that the mantle of human rights cloaks the pursuit of less noble U.S. interests in other nations. Whether or not this critique is valid, it is clear that as the twenty-first century dawns, any interventionist foreign policy must present itself in the idealistic terms of a special American mission if it is to have public support.

In this late 1872 evocation of the spirit of Manifest Destiny, Indians retreat westward as white settlers, guided by a diaphanously-clad America, spread the benefits of American civilization.

Courtesy Amon Carter Museum, Fort Worth, Texas.

This daguerreotype (an early form of photograph) is one of the few extant views of Americans volunteering for the Mexican War. Shown here are volunteers in 1846 from Exeter, New Hampshire.

seize California ports if war broke out with Mexico. Polk's final effort at peaceful expansion was the Slidell mission in November 1845. He sent John L. Slidell to Mexico City to offer $30 million to purchase California and New Mexico and to secure the Rio Grande boundary.

When Polk learned that the Mexican government had refused to receive Slidell, he set out to draw Mexico into a war that would result in the American acquisition of California. In early 1846, he ordered General Taylor to advance to the Rio Grande, deep in the disputed border region. Taylor blockaded the mouth of the Rio Grande (an aggressive act even if the river had been an international boundary) and built a fort on the northern bank across from the Mexican town of Matamoros. The Mexicans attacked and were repulsed on April 24.

Even before the news reached Washington, Polk had decided on war, on the grounds that the Mexican government had unjustifiably refused to sell territory to the United States and had fallen behind on debt payments owed to American citizens. Informed of the clash between Mexican and American troops in early May (it took ten days for the news to reach Washington), he sent a redrafted war message to Congress on May 9 asserting that Mexico "has invaded our territory, and shed American blood on American soil." Congress declared war on May 13, 1846.

The war was a stunning military success for the United States (see Map 12-4). The Mexicans fought bravely, but they lacked the leadership, modern artillery, and naval capacity to check the American advances. By the end of 1846, Polk had gained his objectives in the Mexican borderlands. An army sent west under Colonel Stephen W. Kearny occupied New Mexico. The conquest was relatively bloodless, because most of the local elite cooperated with the American authorities. Sporadic resistance was largely confined to poorer Mexicans and the Pueblo Indians, who feared that their land would be confiscated. The largest uprising, one that was ruthlessly suppressed, was the **Taos Revolt** in January 1847, led by Jesús Trujillo and Tomasito, a Pueblo chieftain. A sympathetic observer described the rebels as "those who defend to the last their country and their homes."

Kearny's army then moved to Tucson and eventually linked up in southern California with pro-American rebels and U.S. forces sent ashore by the Pacific squadron. As in New Mexico, the stiffest resistance came from ordinary Mexicans and the Spanish-speaking Indians.

Despite the loss of its northern provinces, Mexico refused to concede defeat. After Taylor had established a secure defensive line in northeastern Mexico with a victory at Monterrey in September 1846 and repulsed a Mexican counterattack at Buena Vista in February 1847, Polk directed General Winfield Scott to invade central Mexico. Following an amphibious assault on Vera Cruz in March 1847, Scott captured Mexico City in September.

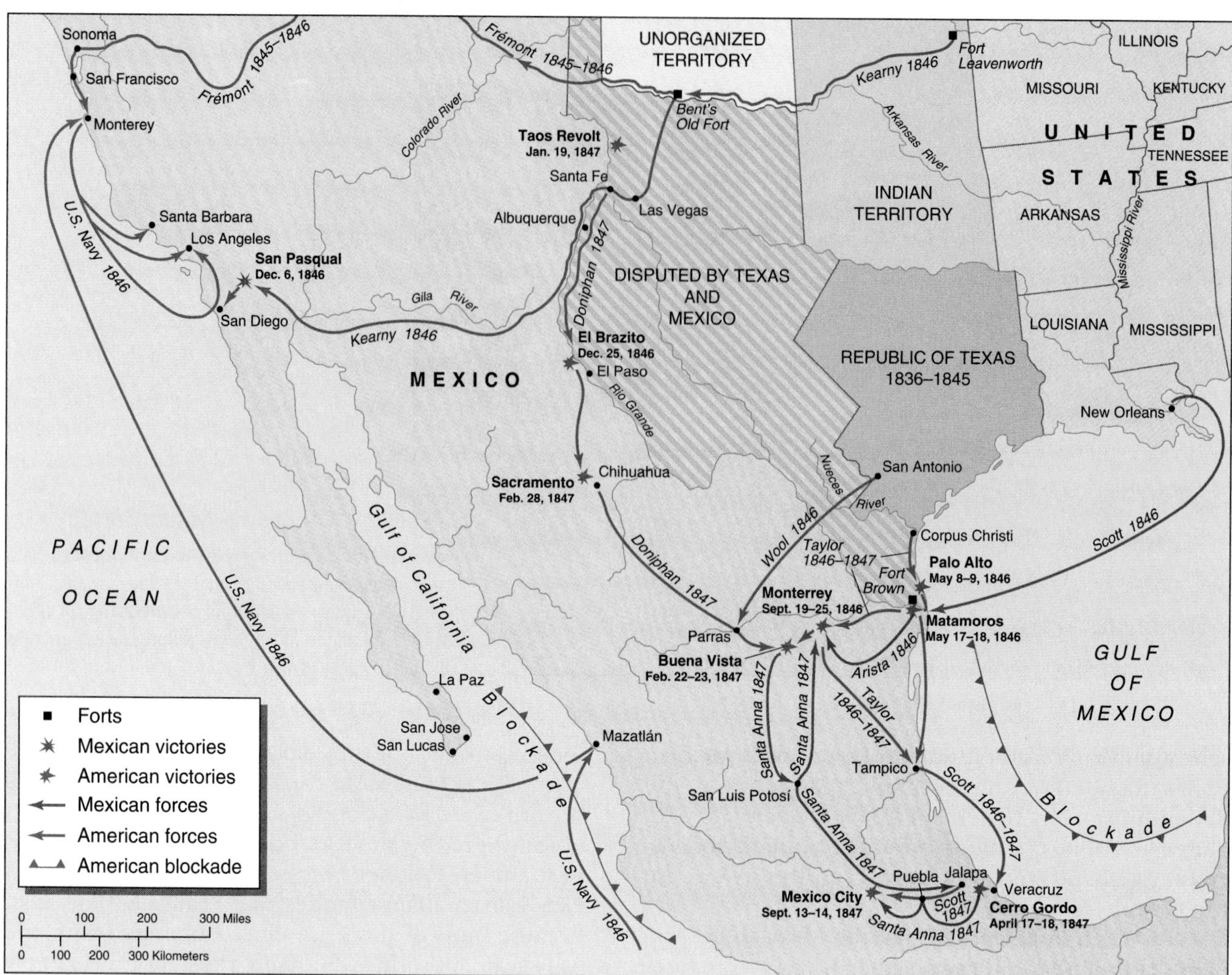

Map 12-4 The Mexican War

Victories under General Zachary Taylor in northern Mexico secured the Rio Grande as the boundary between Texas and Mexico. Colonel Stephen Kearny's expedition won control of New Mexico, and reinforcements from Kearny assured the success of American troops landed by the Pacific Squadron in gaining Alta California for the United States. The success of General Winfield Scott's amphibious invasion at Vera Cruz and his occupation of Mexico City brought the war to an end.

After a frustrating delay while Mexico reorganized its government, peace talks finally got under way and concluded in the **Treaty of Guadalupe Hidalgo**, signed on February 2, 1848. Mexico surrendered its claim to Texas north of the Rio Grande and ceded Alta California and New Mexico (including present-day Arizona, Utah, and Nevada). The United States paid $15 million, assumed over $3 million in claims of American citizens against Mexico, and agreed to grant U.S. citizenship to Mexicans resident in its new territories.

Polk had gained his strategic goals, but the cost was thirteen thousand American lives (most from diseases such as measles and dysentery), fifty thousand Mexican lives, and the poisoning of Mexican–American relations for generations. The war also, as will be seen in Chapter 15, heightened sectional tensions over slavery and weakened the political structure that was vital to preserving the Union.

Conclusion

Americans were an expansionist people. Though not necessarily proof of Manifest Destiny, their surge across the continent between 1815 and 1850 was fully in keeping with their restless desire for independence on a plot of land. Population pressure on overworked farms in the East impelled much of this westward migration, but, by the 1840s, expansion had seemingly acquired a momentum all its own, one that increasingly rejected the claims of other peoples to the land.

Far from being a process of peaceful, evolutionary, and democratic change, as was once thought, expansion involved the spread of slavery, violent confrontations, and the uprooting and displacement of native peoples. By 1850, the earlier notion of reserving the trans-Mississippi West as a permanent Indian country had been abandoned. The Sioux and Comanches were still feared by white settlers, but their final subjugation was not far off. The derogatory stereotypes of Mexican-Americans that were a staple of both popular thought and expansionist ideology showed clearly that American control after the Mexican War would relegate Spanish-speaking people to second-class status.

However misleading and false much of it was, the rhetoric of Manifest Destiny did highlight a central truth. A broad, popular base existed for expanding across the continent. As the Mexican War made clear, the United States was now unquestionably the dominant power in North America. The only serious threat to its dominance in the near future would come from inside, not outside, its continental domain.

Review Questions

1. What accounted for the westward movement of Americans? How did the presence or absence of slavery affect developmental patterns in the new settlements?
2. How was the West of the Plains Indians transformed after 1830 as peoples migrated both within the region and into it from various directions? Why were the Sioux so powerful? How did they interact with other Native Americans and the U.S. government?
3. Who lived in the Mexican borderlands of the Southwest? Why was it so difficult for Mexican authorities to maintain effective control of the region? What role did trade play in the American penetration of the Southwest?
4. What did Americans mean by Manifest Destiny? Why was territorial expansion so identified with the Democratic party?
5. Who was responsible for the outbreak of the Mexican War? Were Mexicans the victims of American aggression?

Recommended Reading

Ray Allen Billington, *The Far Western Frontier, 1830–1860* (1956). Still a useful survey and an excellent example of an older approach to the West from the perspective of white people entering the region with their values of freedom and individualism.

Richard Brandon, *The Last Americans: The Indian in American Culture* (1974). A beautifully written, panoramic account that looks at Indian cultures and their interactions with the spread of white settlement.

Patricia Nelson Limerick, *The Legacy of Conquest: The Unbroken Past of the American West* (1987). A forcefully argued work that overturns many stereotypes and places the federal government and cultural antagonisms at the center of western history.

D. W. Meinig, *The Shaping of America, Vol. 2: Continental America, 1800–1867* (1993). A comprehensive work that offers a distinctive interpretation of continental expansion from the perspective of historical geography.

Frederick Merk, *Manifest Destiny and Mission in American History* (1963). Valuable not only for its revisionist look at the appeal of Manifest Destiny in the 1840s but also for its insights into how a sense of mission influenced American foreign policy in the future.

Clyde A. Milner II, Carol A. O'Connor, and Martha A. Sandweiss, eds., *The Oxford History of the American West* (1994). A comprehensive collection of essays that summarize much of the best work in the modern rethinking of the history of the American West.

Anders Stephanson, *Manifest Destiny: American Expansionism and the Empire of Right* (1995). A tightly argued study that traces Manifest Destiny back to its roots in Puritan ideology and shows how, in revised form, it continued to influence American foreign policy well into the twentieth century.

Richard White, *"Its Your Misfortune and None of My Own": A History of the American West* (1991). An outstanding work that draws on cultural and environmental approaches to show how complex and often unequal relationships among a host of peoples shaped the history of the West.

Additional Sources

The Agricultural Frontier

Joan E. Cashin, *A Family Venture: Men and Women on the Southern Frontier* (1991).

John Mack Faragher, *Sugar Creek: Life on the Illinois Prairie* (1986).

Paul W. Gates, *The Farmer's Age: Agriculture, 1815–1860* (1962).

John Hebron Moore, *The Emergence of the Cotton Kingdom in the Old Southwest: Mississippi, 1770–1860* (1987).

John C. Hudson, *Making the Corn Belt: A Geographical History of Middle-Western Agriculture* (1994).

Malcolm J. Rohrbough, *The Trans-Appalachian Frontier: People, Societies, and Institutions, 1775–1850* (1978).

The Frontier of the Plains Indians

Malcolm Clark, Jr., *Eden Seekers: The Settlement of Oregon, 1810–1862* (1981).

Barnard De Voto, *Across the Wide Missouri* (1947).

William H. Goetzmann, *Exploration and Empire: The Explorer and Scientist in the Winning of the American West* (1966).

Julie R. Jeffrey, *Frontier Women: The Trans-Mississippi West, 1840–1880* (1979).

John H. Moore, ed., *The Political Economy of the North American Indians* (1993).

John Unruh, *The Plains Across: The Overland Emigrations and the Trans-Mississippi West, 1840–1860* (1979).

Richard White, *The Roots of Dependency: Subsistence, Environment, and Social Change among the Choctaws, Pawnees, and Navajos* (1983).

The Mexican Borderlands

Rudolfo Acuña, *Occupied America: A History of Chicanos* (1988).

Paul D. Lack, *The Texas Revolutionary Experience: A Political and Social History, 1835–1836* (1992).

Howard R. Lamar, *The Far Southwest, 1846–1912* (1966).

Janet Lecompte, *Pueblo, Hardscabble, Greenhorn: The Upper Arkansas, 1832–1856* (1978).

George Harwood Phillips, *Indians and Intruders in Central California, 1769–1849* (1993).

Andres Tijerina, *Tejanos and Texas under the Mexican Flag, 1821–1836* (1994).

David J. Weber, *The Mexican Frontier, 1821–1846: The American Southwest under Mexico* (1982).

Politics, Expansion, and War

Richard Griswold del Castillo, *The Treaty of Guadalupe Hidalgo: A Legacy of Conflict* (1990).

John S. D. Eisenhower, *So Far from God: The U.S. War with Mexico* (1989).

Thomas R. Hietala, *Manifest Design: American Aggrandizement in Late Jacksonian America* (1985).

Reginald Horsman, *Race and Manifest Destiny: The Origins of American Racial Anglo-Saxonism* (1981).

Robert W. Johannsen, *To the Halls of Montezuma: The Mexican War in the American Imagination* (1985).

Charles G. Sellers, *James K. Polk: Continentalist, 1843–1846* (1966).

Where to Learn More

❖ **Indian Pueblo Cultural Center, Albuquerque, New Mexico.** This center provides an excellent orientation to the culture, crafts, and community life of the Pueblo and Southwestern Indians. It also includes much material on archaeological findings.

❖ **Museum Association of American Frontier and Fur Trade, Chadron, Nebraska.** The library in the museum holds archives, maps, and some photographs dealing with the western fur trade.

❖ **Indian Museum of North America, Crazy Horse, South Dakota.** This is one of the best sources for learning of the culture of the Teton Sioux and other American and Canadian tribes on the Great Plains. Holdings include outstanding examples of Indian art and artifacts.

❖ **Living History Farms, Des Moines, Iowa.** This site includes several working farms, operated as they were at different points in the nineteenth century, as well as a mid-twentieth-century farm. A vintage town with a general store, church, and other buildings has also been re-created.

❖ **Scotts Bluff National Monument, Gering, Nebraska.** Scotts Bluff was a prominent landmark on the Oregon Trail, and the museum exhibits here have interpretive material on the trail and the western phase of expansion.

❖ **Conner Prairie, Noblesville, Indiana.** The museum and historic area re-create a sense of life on the Indiana frontier during the period of the Old Northwest.

❖ **Fort Union National Monument, Watrous, New Mexico.** Fort Union was a nineteenth-century military post, and the holdings and exhibits in the museum relate to frontier military life and the Santa Fe Trail.

SLAVERY AND THE OLD SOUTH, 1800–1860

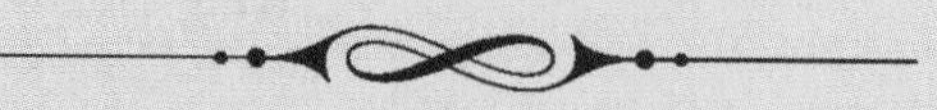

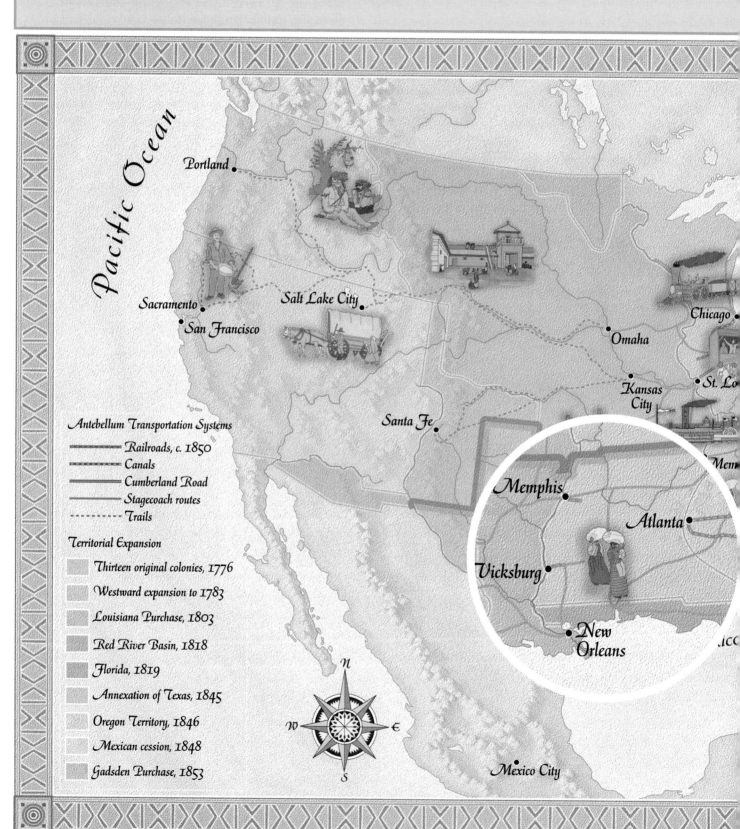

Pacific Ocean

Portland

Sacramento

San Francisco

Salt Lake City

Omaha

Chicago

Kansas City

St. Lo

Santa Fe

Mem

Memphis

Atlanta

Vicksburg

New Orleans

Mexico City

N

W

E

S

Antebellum Transportation Systems

- Railroads, c. 1850
- Canals
- Cumberland Road
- Stagecoach routes
- Trails

Territorial Expansion

- Thirteen original colonies, 1776
- Westward expansion to 1783
- Louisiana Purchase, 1803
- Red River Basin, 1818
- Florida, 1819
- Annexation of Texas, 1845
- Oregon Territory, 1846
- Mexican cession, 1848
- Gadsden Purchase, 1853

13

Chapter Outline

Key Topics

- How the increasing demand for cotton made slavery highly profitable in the Lower South
- The decline of slavery after 1800 in the increasingly diversified economy of the Upper South
- Slave culture and slave resistance
- The divisions of free white society
- The southern defense of slavery in response to increasing attacks from northern abolitionists

"This morning I had a difficulty with Matt. I tied him up and gave him a gentle admonition in the shape of a good whipping. I intended to put him in jail and keep him there until I sold him, but he seemed so penitent & promised so fairly & the other negroes promising to see that he would behave himself in future that I concluded that I would try him once more." Thus did David Golightly Harris, an upcountry South Carolina farmer who owned ten slaves, casually record in his journal for January 8, 1858, his punishment of a recalcitrant slave.

Harris was an upstanding, God-fearing member of his community, and few of his neighbors would have protested the "good whipping" he had laid on Matt's back. This was the slave South, and white Southerners routinely inflicted pain on slaves to control them and coerce them into productive labor. After all, as an overseer on a large plantation informed a northern visitor in the 1850s, "They'd never do any work at all if they were not afraid of being whipped."

Slavery, and the physical coercion on which it rested, increasingly defined the South as a distinctive region in the antebellum United States. Indeed only the widespread presence of slaves makes it possible to speak of the South as a single region despite its geographical and cultural diversity. It was black slavery that created a bond among white Southerners and cast them in a common mold.

Not only did slavery make the South distinctive, it was also the source of the region's immense agricultural wealth, the foundation on which planters built their fortunes, the basis for white upward mobility, and the means by which white people controlled a large black minority. Slavery also frightened white Southerners with a vision of what might happen to them should they not protect their own personal liberties, including, paradoxically, the liberty to enslave African Americans. Southern white men were thus quick to take offense at any challenge to their honor or independence. A code of honor for planters demanded an apology or vindication in a duel for any insult, whether real or perceived. Precisely because slavery was so deeply embedded in southern life and customs, white leadership reacted to mounting attacks on slavery after 1830 with an ever more defiant defense of the institution. That defense in turn reinforced a growing sense of sectionalism among white Southerners, the belief that their values divided them from their fellow citizens in the Union.

Economically and intellectually, the Old South developed in stages. The South of 1860 was geographically much larger and more diverse than it had been in 1800, but it was also more uniformly committed to a single cash crop, cotton. Demand for cotton had exploded as the industrial revolution made the mass production of textiles possible. New England mill owners were now as dependent on slavery as southern planters were. Cotton became king, as contemporaries put it, and it provided the economic basis for southern sectionalism. During the reign of King Cotton, however, regional differences emerged between the Lower South, where the linkage between cotton and slavery was strong, and the Upper South, where slavery was relatively less important and the economy was more diversified.

The Lower South

South and west of South Carolina in 1800 stretched some of the best cotton land in the world. A long growing season, adequate rainfall, navigable rivers, and untapped fertility gave the Lower South—consisting in 1850 of South Carolina, Georgia, Florida, Alabama, Mississippi, Louisiana, and Texas—incomparable natural advantages for growing cotton. Ambitious white Southerners exploited these advantages by extending slavery after 1800 to the newer cotton lands that opened up in the Lower South (see Map 13-1). Cotton production and slavery thus went hand in hand.

Cotton and Slaves

Before 1800, slavery was associated with the cash crops of tobacco, rice, and sea island (or long-staple) cotton. Tobacco, the mainstay of the colonial

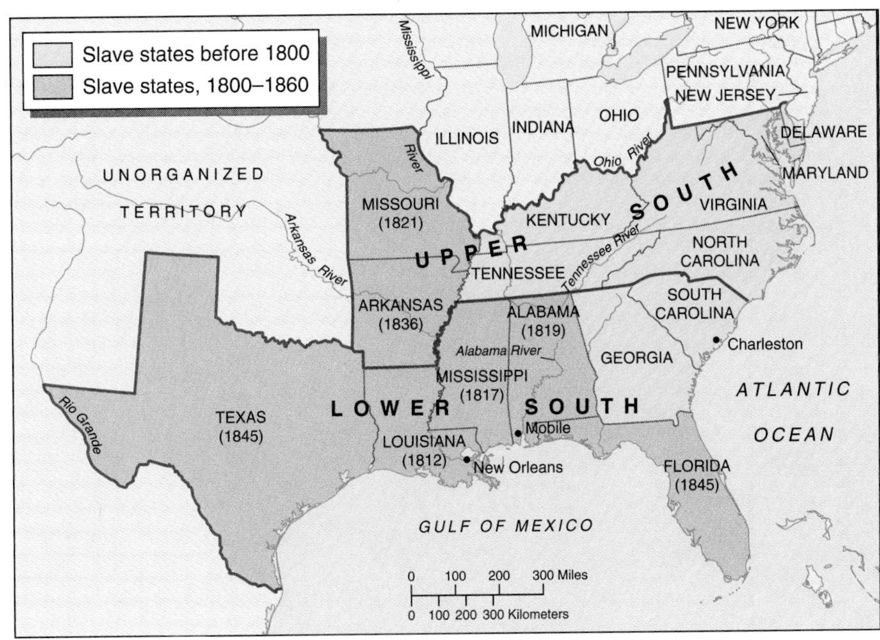

Map 13-1 The Spread of Slavery: New Slave States Entering the Union, 1800–1850
Seven slave states entered the Union after 1800 as cotton production shifted westward.

Chesapeake economy, severely depleted the soil. Its production had stagnated after the Revolutionary War when it lost its formerly protected markets in Britain. Rice and long-staple cotton, named for its long, silky fibers, were profitable but geographically limited to the humid sea islands and tidal flats off the coast of South Carolina and Georgia. Like sugar cane, introduced into Louisiana in the 1790s, they required a huge capital investment in special machinery, dikes, and labor.

Upland, or short-staple, cotton faced none of these constraints, once the cotton gin removed the technical barrier to its commercial production. It could be planted far inland, and small farmers could grow it profitably because it required no additional costs for machinery or drainage systems. As a result, after the 1790s, the production of short-staple cotton boomed. Moreover, like the South's other cash crops, upland cotton was well suited for slave labor because it required fairly continuous tending throughout most of the year. Once the harvest was in—a time when northern agricultural workers were laid off—the slaves cleared land, cut wood, and made repairs. The long work year maximized the return on capital invested in slave labor.

Despite the care required, the cultivation of cotton left plenty of time for slaves to grow food. The major grain in the southern diet was corn, which nicely complemented the labor cycle of cotton. Corn needed little attention while cotton was being harvested and could be planted earlier or later than cotton during the long growing season. Surplus corn could be fed to hogs and converted into pork. Because almost all cotton farms and plantations also raised corn and hogs, the South virtually fed itself.

The linkage of cotton and slaves was at the heart of the plantation system that spread westward after the War of 1812. From its original base in South Carolina and Georgia, the cotton kingdom moved into the Old Southwest and then into Texas and Arkansas. As wasteful agricultural practices exhausted new lands, planters moved to the next cotton frontier farther west. Cotton output exploded from 73,000 bales (each bale weighed close to five hundred pounds) in 1800 to more than 2 million bales by midcentury, thanks to the fertility of virgin land and technological changes, such as improved seed varieties and steam-powered cotton gins (see Figure 13-1). Slave labor accounted for more than 90 percent of cotton production.

Plantations, large productive units specializing in a cash crop and employing at least twenty slaves, were the leading economic institution in the Lower South. Planters were the most prestigious social group, and, though less than 5 percent of white families were in the planter class, they controlled more than 40 percent of the slaves, cotton output, and total agricultural wealth. Most had inherited or married into their wealth, but they could stay at the top of the South's class structure only by continuing to profit from slave labor.

Plantations were generally more efficient producers of cotton than small farms. Planters had the best land because only they commanded the

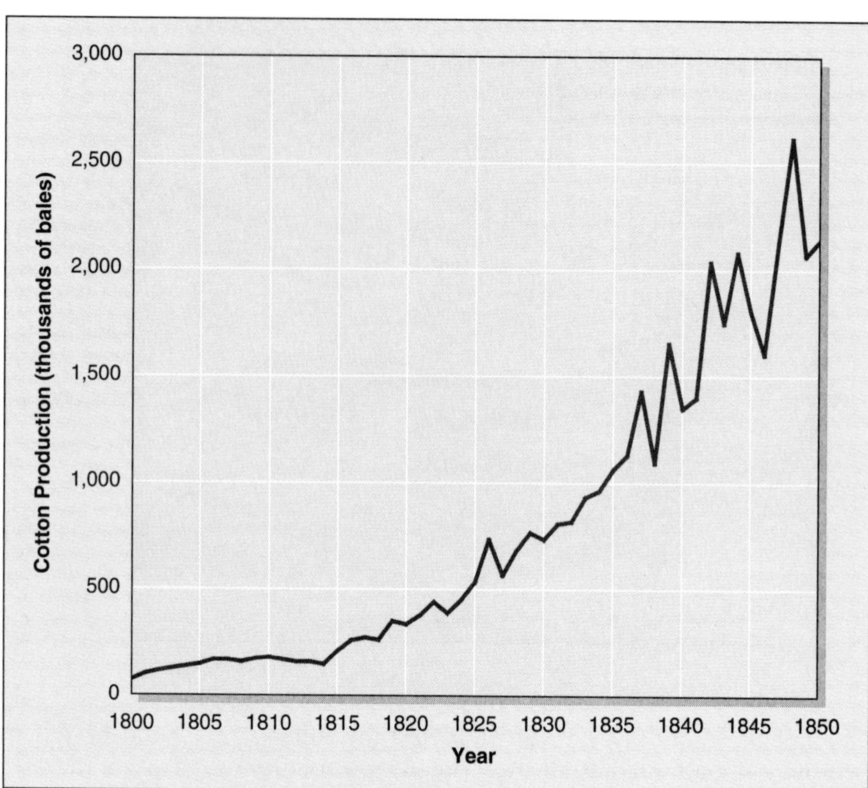

***Figure 13-1* U.S. Cotton Production, 1800–1850**
Cotton production spiraled upward after 1800, and the South became the world's leading supplier.

Data Source: U.S. Bureau of the Census, Historical Statistics of the United States (1960).

labor resources to exploit the wet bottomlands, drain the swamps, or clear the raw jungle in the Mississippi Delta. They were also more likely than farmers to belong to agricultural reform societies that made them aware of superior varieties of seed or the most progressive techniques of cultivation. Most important, the ownership of twenty or more slaves enabled planters to use gangs to do both routine and specialized agricultural work. This **gang system**, a cruder version of the division of labor that was being introduced in northern factories, permitted a regimented pace of work that would have been impossible to impose on free agricultural workers. Teams of field hands, made up of women as well as men, had to work at a steady pace or else feel the lash. They were supervised by white overseers and black drivers, slaves selected for their management skills and agricultural knowledge.

By 1850, the plantations of the Lower South were larger and more specialized than elsewhere in the South, and the wealth of their owners was more ostentatiously displayed. More clusters of slave cabins, overseers' quarters, and cotton gins dotted the countryside. The few towns were little more than a haphazard collection of plain wooden houses scattered around a tavern, country store, and blacksmith's shop. "During two days' sail on the Alabama River from Mobile to Montgomery," noted a traveler in 1860, "I did not see so many houses standing together in any one spot as could be dignified with the appellation of village."

The plantation districts of the Lower South stifled the growth of towns and the economic enterprise they fostered. Planters, as well as ordinary farmers, strove to be self-sufficient. The most significant economic exchange—exporting cotton—took place in international markets and was handled by specialized commission merchants in Charleston, Mobile, and New Orleans. The Lower South had amassed great wealth, but most outsiders saw no signs of progress there.

The Profits of Slavery

Slavery was profitable on an individual basis. Most modern studies indicate that the average rate of return on capital invested in a slave was about 10 percent a year, a rate that at least equaled what was available in alternative investments in the South or the North. Not surprisingly, the newer regions of the cotton kingdom in the Lower South, with the most productive land and the greatest commitment to plantation agriculture, consistently led the nation in per capita income.

The profitability of slavery ultimately rested on the enormous demand for cotton outside the South. This demand grew at about 5 percent a year in

Chronology

1790s	Large-scale conversions of slaves to Christianity begin.
1793	Eli Whitney patents the cotton gin.
1800	Gabriel Prosser leads a rebellion in Richmond, Virginia.
1808	Congress prohibits the African slave trade.
1811	Slaves rebel in Louisiana.
1816–1819	First cotton boom in the South.
1822	Denmark Vesey's Conspiracy fails in Charleston, South Carolina.
1831	Nat Turner leads a rebellion in Southampton County, Virginia.
1831–1832	Virginia legislature debates and rejects gradual emancipation.
1832	Thomas R. Dew publishes the first full-scale defense of slavery.
1837–1845	Slavery issue divides Presbyterians, Methodists, and Baptists into separate sectional churches.
1845	Florida and Texas, the last two slave states, are admitted to the Union.
1850s	Cotton production doubles.
1857	Hinton R. Helper publishes *The Impending Crisis of the South.*

the first half of the nineteenth century. Although cotton prices fluctuated like those of any other commodity in an unregulated market, demand was so strong that prices held steady at around 10 cents a pound in the 1850s even as southern production of cotton doubled. Textile mills in Britain were always the largest market, but demand in continental Europe and the United States grew even faster after 1840.

Southern law defined slaves as chattel, the personal property of their owners, and their market value increased along with the profitability of slavery. Prices for a male field hand rose from $250 in 1815 to $900 by 1860. Prices at any given time varied according to the age, sex, and skills of the slave, as well as overall market conditions, but the steady appreciation of prices for slaves meant that slave owners could sell their human chattel and realize a profit over and above what they had already earned from the slaves' labor. This was especially the case with slave mothers; the children they bore increased the capital assets of their owners. Slave women of childbearing age were therefore valued nearly as much as male field hands. The domestic slave trade brought buyers and sellers of slaves together. Slaves flowed from the older areas of the Upper South to the newer plantation districts in the Lower South. Indeed, when Congress ended the African slave trade in 1808 and it became difficult to smuggle in significant numbers of African slaves, planters in the Deep South had to depend on internal trade for the bulk of their labor supply. This trade was extensive: more than 800,000 slaves were moved between regions in the South from 1790 to 1860, and professional slave traders transported at least 60 percent of them. Drawing on lines of credit from banks, the traders paid cash for slaves, most of whom they bought from plantations in the Upper South. By selling these slaves in regional markets where demand had driven up the price, they turned a tidy profit.

The sheer size of the internal slave trade indicates just how profit-driven slave owners were. Few of them hesitated to break up slave families for sale when market conditions were right. About half of all slave sales separated family members. Slave children born in the Upper South after 1820 stood a one-in-three chance of being sold during their lifetime.

Most of the profits from slave labor and sales went into buying more land and slaves. As long as slaves employed in growing cash staples returned 10 percent a year, slave owners had little economic incentive to shift their capital resources into manufacturing or urban development. The predictable result was that industrialization and urbanization fell far behind the levels in the free states, creating what outsiders came to decry as southern "backwardness." The South had one-third of the nation's population in 1860 but produced by value only 10 percent of the nation's manufacturing output. Fewer than one in ten Southerners lived in a city, compared to more than one in three Northeasterners and one in seven Midwesterners.

Nowhere was the indifference of planters to economic diversification more evident than in the Lower South, which had the smallest urban population and the fewest factories. Planters here were not

The internal slave trade was the primary means by which the slaves of the Upper South were brought into the plantation markets of the Old Southwest. This illustration shows professional slave traders driving a chained group of slaves, known as a coffle, to perspective buyers in the Lower South.

opposed to economic innovations that promised greater profits, but they feared social changes that might undermine the stability of slavery. Urbanization and industrialization both entailed such risks.

Most planters suspected that the urban environment weakened slavery. An editorial in the *New Orleans Crescent* charged that slaves in the city were "demoralized to a deplorable extent, all owing to the indiscriminate license and indulgence extended them by masters, mistresses, and guardians, and to the practice of forging passes, which has now become a regular business in New Orleans." For a white person, a "demoralized" slave was one who behaved as if free. Urban slaves, though scarcely free, enjoyed a degree of personal and economic independence that blurred the line between freedom and servitude.

Urban slaves were artisans, semiskilled laborers, and domestics, and, unlike their rural counterparts, they usually lived apart from their owners. They had much more freedom than field hands to move around, interact with white people and other black people, and experiment with various social roles. Many of them, especially if they had a marketable skill such as carpentry or tailoring, could hire out their labor and retain some wages for themselves after reimbursing their owners. In short, the direct authority of the slave owner was less clear-cut in the town than in the country.

Urban slavery declined from 1820 to 1860 as slaves decreased from 22 percent to 10 percent of the urban population. This decline reflected both doubts about the stability of slavery in an urban setting and the large profits that slave labor earned for slave owners in the rural cotton economy.

The ambivalence of planters toward urban slavery also characterized their attitudes toward industrial slavery and indeed to industrialization itself. If based on free labor, industrialization risked promoting an antislavery class consciousness among manufacturing laborers that would challenge the property rights of slave owners. William Gregg, the owner of a large cotton mill in upcountry South Carolina, showed that these fears were overblown when he built a company town in the 1840s that kept his white workers under tight, paternalistic controls. Still, many planters considered free workers potential abolitionists.

But the use of slaves as factory operatives threatened slave discipline because an efficient level of production required special incentives. "Whenever a slave is made a mechanic, he is more than half freed," complained James Hammond, a South Carolina planter. Elaborating on Hammond's fears, a Virginian noted of slaves that he had hired out for industrial work, "They were worked hard, and had too much liberty, and were acquiring bad habits. They earned money by overwork, and spent it for

FROM THEN TO NOW

The Economic Legacy of Slavery

The South today enjoys one of the highest rates of economic growth in the nation and plays host to business conglomerates, bank mergers, and Olympic games. Yet as late as the 1930s the South was so impoverished that it was labeled the nation's number one economic problem. The key to this remarkable transformation was the way in which the South finally overcame the economic legacy of slavery.

Because slavery persisted in the South and was abolished in the North, the Northern and Southern economies developed separately before the Civil War. The key difference was the markedly lower level of Southern investment in manufacturing and transportation compared to the North. Slaveowners had invested two-thirds of their wealth in slaves and were reluctant to promote changes that would diversify their economy along Northern lines through the introduction of manufacturing based on low-wage labor. On the contrary, they had every incentive to keep wages high to protect the value of their investment in human labor.

The end of slavery reversed the basic dynamic shaping the Southern economy. Planters now had to derive their wealth primarily from their land, not their slaves. As a result, they encouraged low-wage policies that transformed many former slaves and poor white farmers into impoverished tenant farmers and sharecroppers. When cotton prices began a steady decline in the 1870s, Southern investors turned to manufacturing in an effort to generate economic growth, but the abundance of cheap agricultural labor kept industrial wage rates well below the national level. Consequently, the South attracted little in the way of outside labor. And with investment opportunities more attractive elsewhere, it attracted little capital for modernizing its factories. Education in the South likewise remained behind, because the white Southern elite was leery of reforms that would increase workers' skills and encourage them to leave the region in search of better wages. Thus, although Southern industry grew, it remained labor intensive and failed to keep pace with the region's rising population. By the 1930s, when the Great Depression hit, the South was mired in poverty and backwardness.

Sweeping new federal policies initiated in the wake of the Depression began fundamentally to change the Southern economy, raising wages and bringing them more in line with the national average. Farm subsidiess encouraged planters to take land out of production, forcing poor tenants and sharecroppers to leave the land and migrate out of the region. Abundant, well-paying jobs in Northern factories during World War II accelerated the outflow of the South's low-skill workers. Meanwhile, federal money poured into the South for new defense plants and war-related projects.

By the 1950s, the formerly insulated, low-wage Southern economy had turned the corner. Southern politicians dropped the region's corporate taxes to the lowest in the nation and became adept at attracting new sources of capital and large federal subsidies. After initially opposing the black-led civil rights revolution of the 1950s and 1960s, most of the white business elite backed the formal end of racial segregation in an attempt to improve the South's image. Today, well over a century after slavery had placed it on a separate path of economic development, the Southern economy has lost nearly all traces of its distinctiveness. As it did so, Southerners replaced the stigma of backwardness with the boast of being in the forefront of national economic trends.

African-American field hands return from a South Carolina cotton field in the 1860s. The economy of the prewar South was based on the production of cotton by a large enslaved labor force. The legacy of this system left the South the most impoverished region in the country for almost 100 years after the Civil War.

whisky, and got a habit of roaming about and *taking care of themselves;* because, when they were not at work in the furnace, nobody looked out for them."

The anxieties of planters over industrialization and their refusal to shift capital from plantation agriculture to finance it ensured that manufacturing played only a minor economic role in the Lower South. Planters supported industrialization only as an adjunct, not an alternative, to the plantation economy. Thus planters did invest in railroads and factories, but their holdings remained concentrated in land and slaves. They augmented their income by renting slaves to manufacturers and railroad contractors but were quick to recall these slaves to work on the plantations when needed.

No more than 5 percent of the slaves in the Lower South ever worked in manufacturing, and most of these were in rural enterprises serving local markets too small to interest northern manufacturers. Ever concerned to preserve slavery, planters would not risk slave discipline or the profits of cotton agriculture by embracing the unpredictable changes that industrialization was sure to bring.

The Upper South

Climate and geography distinguished the Upper South from the Lower South. The eight slave states of the Upper South lay north of the best growing zones for cotton. The northernmost of these states—Delaware, Maryland, Kentucky, and Missouri—bordered on free states and were known as the Border South. The four states south of them—Virginia, North Carolina, Tennessee, and Arkansas—constituted a middle zone. Slavery was entrenched in all these states, but it was less dominant than in the cotton South.

The key difference from which others followed was the suitability of the Lower South for growing cotton with gangs of slave laborers. Except for prime cotton districts in middle Tennessee, eastern Arkansas, and parts of North Carolina, the Upper South lacked the fertile soil and long growing season necessary for the commercial production of cotton, rice, or sugar (see Map 13-2). Consequently, the demand for slaves was less than in the Lower South. Two-thirds of white Southerners lived in the Upper South in 1860, but they held only 45 percent of all slaves. Percentages of slave ownership and of slaves in the overall population were roughly half those in the cotton South.

While the Lower South was undergoing a cotton boom after the War of 1812, the Upper South was mired in a long economic slump from which it did not emerge until the 1850s. The improved economy of the Upper South in the late antebellum period increasingly relied on free labor, a development that many cotton planters feared would diminish southern unity in defense of slavery.

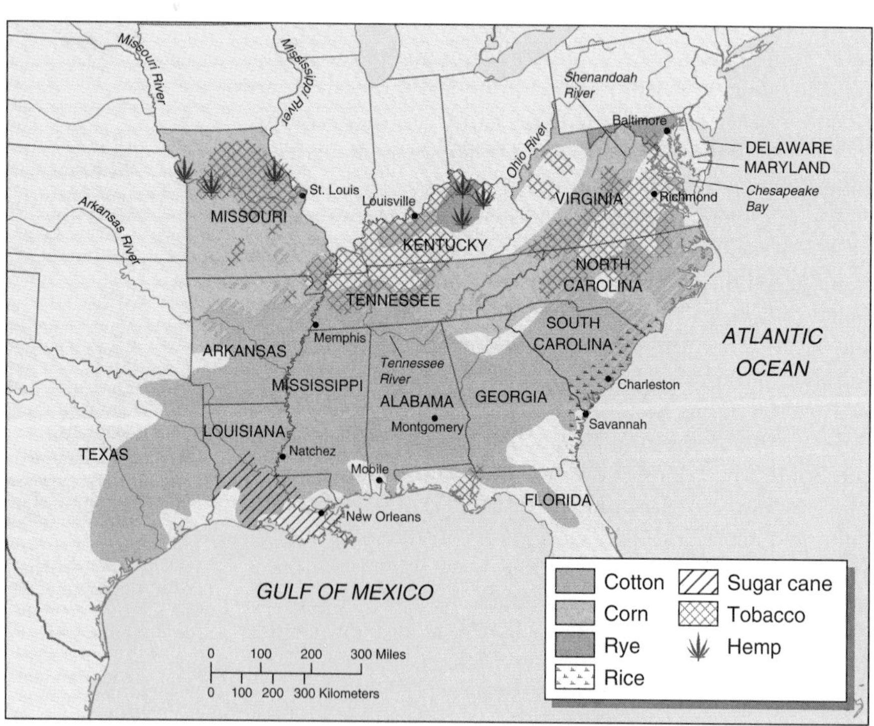

Map 13-2 Cotton and Other Crops in the South, 1860
Most of the Upper South was outside the cotton belt where the demand for slave labor was greatest.

A Period of Economic Adjustment

To inhabitants and visitors alike, vast stretches of the Upper South presented a dreary spectacle of exhausted fields and depopulation in the 1820s and 1830s. The soil was most depleted where tobacco had been cultivated extensively. Even where the land was still fertile, farmers could not compete against the agricultural commodities that the fresher lands of the Old Southwest produced. Land values fell as farmers dumped their property and headed west. "Emigration is here raging with all the strength of fanaticism," wrote a Virginian in 1837, "and nothing else can be talked of but selling estates, at a great sacrifice, and *'packing off'* for the *'far west.'*"

Agricultural reform emerged in the 1830s as one proposed solution to this economic crisis. Its leading advocate was Edmund Ruffin, a Virginia planter who tirelessly promoted the use of marl (shell deposits) to neutralize the overly acidic and worn-out soils of the Upper South. He also called for deeper plowing, systematic rotation of crops, and upgrading the breeding stock for animal husbandry.

Ruffin's efforts, and those of the agricultural societies and fairs spawned by the reform movement, met with some success, especially in the 1840s when the prices of all cash staples fell. Still, only a minority of farmers ever embraced reform. These were generally the well-educated planters who read the agricultural press and could afford to change their farming practices. The landscape of Ruffin's beloved Virginia Tidewater still provoked travelers to remark, as one did in the early 1850s, "I've heard 'em say out West that old Virginny was the mother of statesmen—reckon she must be about done, eh? This 'ere's about the barrenest look for a mother ever I see."

Although soil exhaustion and wasteful farming persisted, agriculture in the Upper South had revived by the 1850s. A rebound in the tobacco market accounted for part of this revival, but the growing profitability of general farming was responsible for most of it.

Particularly in the Border South, the trend was toward agricultural diversification. Farmers and planters lessened their dependence on slave labor or on a single cash crop and practiced a thrifty, efficient agriculture geared to producing grain and livestock for urban markets. Western Maryland and the Shenandoah Valley and northern sections of Virginia grew wheat, and in the former tobacco districts of the Virginia and North Carolina Tidewater, wheat, corn, and garden vegetables became major cash crops.

Expanding urban markets and a network of internal improvements facilitated this transition to general farming. Both of these developments were outgrowths of the movement for industrial diversification launched in the 1820s in response to the heavy outflow of population from the Upper South. Although not far advanced by northern standards, urbanization and industrialization in the Upper South were considerably greater than in the Lower South. The region had twice the percentage of urban residents of the cotton South, and it contained the leading manufacturing cities in the slave states—St. Louis, Baltimore, and Louisville. By 1860, the Upper South accounted for three-fourths of the South's manufacturing capital and output and nearly all of its heavy industry. Canals and railroads linked cities and countryside in a denser transportation grid than in the Lower South.

With an economy more balanced among agriculture, manufacturing, and trade than a generation earlier, the Upper South at midcentury was gradually becoming less tied to plantation agriculture and slave labor. The rural majority increasingly prospered by growing foodstuffs for city-dwellers and factory workers. The labor market for railroad construction and manufacturing work was strong enough to attract northern immigrants and help reduce the loss of the native-born population that had migrated to other states.

The economic adjustment in the Upper South converted the labor surplus of the 1820s into a labor scarcity by the 1850s. "It is a fact," noted Edmund Ruffin in 1859, "that labor is greatly deficient in all Virginia, and especially in the rich western counties, which, for want of labor, scarcely yet yield in the proportion of one tenth of their capacity." Ruffin's commitment to agricultural reform was exceeded only by his devotion to slavery. Like many planters in the cotton states, he feared that free labor was about to replace scarce and expensive slave labor in Virginia and much of the Upper South.

The Decline of Slavery

Slave owners tended to exaggerate all threats to slavery, and Ruffin was no exception. But slavery was clearly growing weaker in the Upper South by the 1850s (see Figure 13-2). The decline was most evident along the northern tier of the Upper South, where the proportion of slaves to the overall population fell steadily after 1830. By 1860, slaves in the Border South had dropped to 2 percent of the population in Delaware, 13 percent in Maryland, 19 percent in Kentucky, and 10 percent in Missouri. In Virginia from 1830 to 1860, slaves fell from 39 to 31 percent of the population.

Elsewhere in the Upper South, slavery was more or less holding its own by the 1850s. Tobacco

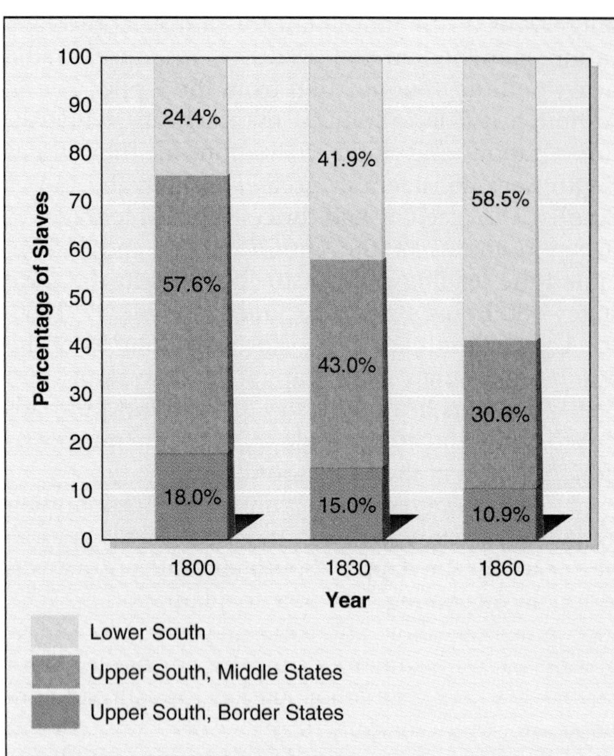

Figure 13-2 The Changing Regional Pattern of Slavery in the South, 1800–1860
As the nineteenth century progressed, slavery increasingly became identified with the cotton-growing Lower South.

and cotton planters in North Carolina and Tennessee continued to rely heavily on slave labor, but most small farmers were indifferent, if not opposed, to the institution. Only in Arkansas, whose alluvial lands along the Mississippi River offered a new frontier for plantation agriculture, was slavery growing rapidly. Slaves, however, still made up only 25 percent of the population of Arkansas in 1860 and were confined mainly to the southeastern corner of the state. Geographically dominated by the Ozark Highlands, Arkansas was best suited to general farming.

The region's role as a slave exporter to the Lower South hastened the decline of slavery in the Upper South. In every decade after 1820, the internal slave trade drained off about 10 percent of the slaves in the Upper South, virtually the entire natural increase. Slave traders initially made most of their purchases in Virginia and Maryland, but by the 1850s, they were also active in the Carolinas, Kentucky, and Missouri. New Orleans, Memphis, and Natchez, Mississippi, were the major western distribution points for the slaves, who were sent west both by sea and by land.

Selling slaves to the Lower South reinforced the Upper South's economic stake in slavery at a time when the institution was otherwise barely profitable there. The sale of surplus slaves was a windfall for planters whose slaves had become an economic burden. This same windfall gave planters the capital to embark on agricultural reform and shift out of tobacco production. Investment capital in the Upper South was not flowing into slave property but into economic diversification that expanded urban manufacturing. Both of these structural changes increasingly put slavery at a competitive disadvantage against free labor.

The wheat, small grains, and fodder crops that replaced tobacco in much of the Upper South did not require the nearly continuous attention of a work force. Unlike tobacco, wheat needed intensive labor only at planting and during the short harvest. Thus as planters abandoned tobacco, they kept fewer slaves and relied on seasonal and cheap agricultural workers to meet peak labor demand.

The cheapness and flexibility of free labor made it better suited than slave labor for general farming. Urban manufacturers likewise wanted workers who could be hired and fired at a moment's notice. Despite the successful use of slaves in tobacco manufacturing and at the large Tredegar Iron Works in Richmond, immigrant workers displaced slaves in most of the factories in the Border South. By 1860, slaves made up just 1 percent of the population in St. Louis and Baltimore, the South's major industrial cities.

Slavery was in economic retreat across the Upper South after 1830. There were still plantation districts with large concentrations of slaves, and slave owners retained enough political power to defeat all challenges to their property interests. Nevertheless, the gradual turn to free labor was unmistakable. As Alfred Iveson, a Georgia planter, noted with alarm in 1860, "Those border States can get along without slavery. Their soil and climate are appropriate to white labor; they can live and flourish without African slavery; but the cotton States cannot."

Slave Life and Culture

Nearly 4 million slaves lived in the South by 1860, a more than fivefold increase since the ratification of the Constitution. This population gain was overwhelmingly due to an excess of births over deaths, although as many as fifty thousand Africans may have been smuggled into the country until about 1860 despite the ban on the African slave trade that took effect in 1808.

Almost all southern slaves were thus native-born by the mid-nineteenth century. They were not

Africans but African-Americans, and they shared the common fate of bondage. By resisting an enslavement they could not prevent, they shaped a culture of their own that eased their pain and raised their hopes of someday being free. They managed to retain their dignity despite the humiliations to which they were subjected. In their family life and religious beliefs, slaves found the strength to sustain themselves under nearly intolerable circumstances.

Work Routines and Living Conditions

Being treated as a piece of property to be worked for a profit and bought and sold when financially advantageous to one's owners—this was the legal and economic reality that all slaves confronted. Each southern state had its own **slave codes**, laws defining the status of slaves and the rights of masters; the codes gave slave owners near-absolute power over their human property.

"The right of personal liberty in the slave is utterly inconsistent with the idea of slavery," wrote Thomas R. R. Cobb of Georgia in a legal treatise on slavery. The slave codes, accordingly, severely restricted the lives of slaves. Slaves could not own property, make contracts, possess guns or alcohol, legally marry (except in Louisiana), leave plantations without the owner's written permission, or testify against their masters or any other white person in a court of law. Many states also prohibited teaching a slave to read or write. The law assumed that the economic self-interest of masters in their slave property gave slaves adequate legal protection against injuries inflicted by others. The murder of a slave by a master was illegal, but in practice the law and community standards looked the other way if a disobedient slave was killed while being disciplined.

The slave codes penalized any challenge to a master's authority or any infraction of plantation rules. Whippings were the most common authorized punishment: twenty lashes on the bare back for leaving a plantation without a pass, one hundred lashes for writing a pass for another slave, and so on. Striking a master, committing arson, or conspiring to rebel were punishable by death.

The owner, as expressed in the Alabama Slave Code of 1852, had "the right to the time, labor and services of the slave." This of course was the whole purpose of owning a slave. Most masters recognized that it was good business sense to feed, clothe, and house their slaves well enough to ensure productive labor and to encourage a family life that would enable the slave population to reproduce itself. Thus planters' self-interest probably improved the living standards for slaves in the first half of the nineteenth century, and the slave population grew at a rate only slightly below that of white Southerners.

However, planters rarely provided more than the bare necessities. The slaves lived mainly on rations of cornmeal and salt pork supplemented with vegetables they grew on the small garden plots that many planters permitted and occasional catches of game and fish. This diet provided ample calories but often insufficient vitamins and nutrients to protect slaves (as well as the many poor whites who ate the same diet) against such diseases as beriberi and pellagra. Intestinal disorders were chronic, and dysentery and cholera were common. About 20 percent of the slaves on a typical plantation were sick at any given time. Infant mortality was twice as high among slaves as among white southerners in 1850; so was mortality among slave children up to age 14. According to one study, the life expectancy for slaves at birth was 21 to 22 years, roughly half the white life expectancy.

Planters furnished slaves with two sets of coarse clothing, one for summer and one for winter. Their housing, typically a 15-by-15-foot one-room cabin for five or six occupants, provided little more than basic shelter against the elements. "They were built of logs," a traveler noted of slave cabins in South Carolina, "with no windows—no opening at all, except the doorway, with a chimney of sticks and mud; with no trees about them, no porches, or shades, of any kind. Except for the chimney . . . I should have conjectured that it had been built for a powder-house, or perhaps an ice-house—never for an animal to sleep in."

Small and unadorned, slave cabins emphasized not only the planters' desire to minimize housing costs but also their determination to treat slaves as a regimented, collective population. Large planters placed these cabins in a row, an arrangement that projected precision and undifferentiated order. Slaves expressed their own individuality by furnishing their cabins with handmade beds and benches and by pushing for the right to put in gardens.

The diet and housing of most slaves may have been no worse than that of the poorest whites in both the North and the South, but their workload was undoubtedly heavier. Just over half of the slave population at midcentury was concentrated on plantation units with twenty or more slaves, and most of these slaves worked as field hands in gang labor. Overseers freely admitted that they relied on whippings to make slaves work in these gangs.

Most plantation slaves toiled at hard, physical labor from sunup to sundown. The work was more intense and sustained than that of white farmers or white factory hands. The fear of the whip on a bare back set the pace. At daybreak, recalled

Solomon Northrup of his enslavement on a Louisiana plantation, "the fears and labors of another day begin; and until its close there is no such thing as rest. [The slave] fears he will be caught lagging through the day; he fears to approach the gin-house with his basket-load of cotton at night; he fears, when he lies down, that he will oversleep himself in the morning."

Some 15 to 20 percent of plantation slaves were house servants or skilled artisans who had lighter and less regimented workloads than field hands. Some planters used the prospect of transfer to these relatively privileged positions as an incentive to field hands to work harder. Extra rations, time off on weekends, passes to visit a spouse on a nearby plantation, and the right to have a garden plot were among the other incentives planters used to keep labor productivity high. However, what a planter viewed as privileges benevolently bestowed, slaves quickly came to see as customary rights. Despite the power of the whip, if planters failed to respect these "rights," slave morale would decline, and the work routine would be interrupted.

Especially on large plantations, slave nursemaids cared for the young children in the white planter's family.

From the Collection of the Louisiana State Museum.

Nearly three-fourths of the slaves worked on plantations and medium-sized farms. Most of the remainder—those in units with fewer than ten slaves—worked on small farms in close contact with the master's family. Their workloads were more varied and sometimes less taxing than those of plantation hands, but these slaves were also more directly exposed to the whims of their owners and were less likely to live in complete family units. Slave couples in small holdings were more likely to live on separate farms. The owners of only a few slaves were also more vulnerable than planters to market downturns that could force them to sell slaves and further divide families.

Ten percent of slaves were not attached to the land, laboring instead at jobs that most white workers shunned. Every southern industry—but most particularly extractive industries like mining and lumbering—relied heavily on slaves. The Tredegar Iron Company in Richmond, the largest iron foundry in the South, used slaves as its main work force after 1847, partly to curb strikes by its white workers. Racial tensions often flared in southern industry, and when the races worked together, skilled white laborers typically insisted on being placed in supervisory positions.

Digging coal as miners or shoveling it as stokers for boilers on steamboats, laying down iron for the railroads or shaping hot slabs of it in a foundry, industrial slaves worked at least as hard as field hands. Compared to plantation slaves, however, they had more independence off the job and greater opportunities to earn money of their own. Because many of them had to house and feed themselves, they could also enjoy more time free from direct white scrutiny. By undertaking extra factory work, known as "overwork," industrial slaves could earn $50 or more a month, money they could use to buy goods for their families or, in rare cases, to purchase their freedom.

Families and Religion

The core institution of slave life was the family. Except in Louisiana, southern law did not recognize slave marriages, but masters permitted, even encouraged, marital unions to raise the morale of their labor force and increase its value by producing marketable children. Slaves embraced their families as a source of loving warmth and strength in a system that treated them as commodities.

Despite all the obstacles arrayed against them, many slave marriages produced enduring commitments and a supportive moral code for family members. Most slave unions remained intact until the death or, frequently, the sale of a spouse. Close to one-third of slave marriages were broken up by sales

Five generations are represented in this photograph of an African-American family on a South Carolina plantation. The photograph was taken in 1862, soon after the family gained its freedom during the Civil War.

or forced removals. A slave bitterly recalled that "the separation of slaves in this way is little thought of. A few masters regard their union as sacred, but where one does, a hundred care nothing about it."

Both parents were present in about two-thirds of slave families, the same ratio as in contemporary peasant families in western Europe. Although the father's role as protector of and provider for his wife and children had no standing under slavery, most slave fathers struggled to help feed their families by hunting and fishing, and they risked beating and death to defend their wives from sexual abuse by the overseer or master. Besides their field labor, slave mothers had all the burdens of pregnancy, child care, laundry, and cooking. After escaping from slavery, Sojourner Truth told how she placed her babies in a basket hanging from a tree while she worked in the field and had older children care for them.

No anguish under slavery was more heart-rending than that of a mother whose child was sold away from her. "Oh, my heart was too full!" recalled Charity Bowery on being told that her boy Richard was sold. "[My mistress] had sent me away on an errand, because she didn't want to be troubled with our cries. I hadn't any chance to see my poor boy. I shall never see my poor boy. I shall never see him again in this world. My heart felt as if it was under a great load."

Charity Bowery's experience was hardly unique. Slave parents had to suppress the rage they felt at their powerlessness to protect their children from the cruelties of slavery. Slave accounts are full of stories of children running in vain to their parents to save them from a whipping. Most parents could only teach their children the skills of survival in a world in which white people had a legal monopoly on violence. The most valuable of these skills was the art of hiding one's true feelings from white people and telling them what they wanted to hear. As a perceptive traveler noted: "When therefore a white man approaches [the slaves] with inquiries concerning their condition, they are at once put upon their guard, and either make indefinite and vague replies, or directly contradict their real sentiments."

Extensive kinship ties provided a support network for the vulnerable slave family. Thickest on the older and larger plantations, these networks included both blood relatives and other significant people. Children were taught to address elders as "Aunt" and "Uncle" and fellow slaves as "sister" and "brother." Parents thus helped prepare their children for the day when the family might be divided. If separated from a parent, a child could turn to relatives or the larger slave community for care and assistance.

Slaves followed West African customs by prohibiting marriage between cousins and by often naming their children after departed grandparents. They also drew on an African heritage kept alive through folklore and oral histories to create a religion that fit their needs. The ancestors of nineteenth-century slaves brought no common religion with them when they were taken to the New World. However, beliefs common to a variety of African religions survived. Once slaves began to embrace Christianity in the late eighteenth-century, they blended these beliefs into an African Christianity.

In keeping with African traditions, the religion of the slaves fused the natural and spiritual worlds, accepted the power of ghosts over the living, and relied on an expressive form of worship in which the participants shouted and swayed in rhythm with the beat of drums and other instruments. Associated with reverence for ancestors, dance was sacred in Africa. Spirituals, the religious songs of the slaves, were sung in a dance known in America as the "ring shout." Moving counterclockwise and stamping their feet to establish a beat, slaves blended dance and song in a religious ceremony that helped them endure oppression and sustain their self-confidence.

By most estimates, no more than 20 percent of slaves ever converted to Christianity. Those who did found in Christianity a message of deliverance rooted in the liberation of Moses's people from bondage in Egypt. The Jesus of the New Testament spoke to them as a compassionate God who had shared their burden of suffering so that all peoples could hope to find the Promised Land of love and justice. By blending biblical imagery into their spirituals, the slaves expressed their yearning for freedom: "Didn't my Lord deliver Daniel/Then why not every man?"

The initial exposure of slaves to Christianity usually came from evangelical revivalists, and slaves always favored the Baptists and Methodists over other denominations. The evangelical message of universal spiritual equality confirmed the slaves' sense of personal worth. Less formal in both their doctrines and organization than the Presbyterians and Episcopalians, the evangelical sects allowed the slaves more leeway to choose their own preachers and engage in their physical call-and-response pattern of worship. Perhaps because they baptized by total immersion, which evoked the purifying power of water so common in African religions, the Baptists gained the most slave converts.

Most planters were pragmatic about encouraging Christianity among their slaves. Like every other aspect of the slave's life, they favored it only if they could control it. Thus while many planters allowed black preachers at religious services on their plantations, they usually insisted that white observers be present. Worried that abolitionist propaganda might attract the slaves to Christianity as a religion of secular liberation, some planters in the late antebellum period tried to convert their slaves to their own version of Christianity. They invited white ministers to their plantations to preach a gospel of passivity and obedience centered on Paul's call for servants to "obey in all things your Masters."

Although most slaves viewed the religion of their owners as hypocritical and the sermons of white ministers as propaganda, they feigned acceptance of the religious wishes of their masters. They attended the special slave chapels some masters built and sat in segregated galleries in white churches on Sunday mornings. But in the evening, out of sight of the master or overseer, they held their own services in the woods and listened to their own preachers. As much as they could, the slaves hid their religious life from white people. Many slaves experienced religion as a spiritual rebirth that gave them the inner strength to endure their bondage. As one recalled, "I was born a slave and lived through some hard times. If it had not been for my God, I don't know what I would have done."

Resistance

Open resistance to slavery was futile. The persistently disobedient slave would be sold "down river" to a harsher master or, in extreme cases, killed. The fate of Richard, Charity Bowery's son who was sold away from her, typified that of the openly defiant slave. He resisted the efforts of his new owner in Alabama to break his will. When the owner threatened to shoot him if he did not consent to being whipped, Richard replied, "Shoot away, I won't come to be flogged." The master shot and killed him.

Although the odds of succeeding were infinitesimal, slaves as desperate as Richard did plot rebellions. Four major uprisings occurred in the nineteenth century. The first, **Gabriel Prosser's Rebellion** in 1800, involved about fifty armed slaves around Richmond, though perhaps as many as one thousand slaves knew about Prosser's plans. The failure to seize a key road to Richmond and a warning to white authorities by a slave informer doomed the rebellion before it got under way. State authorities executed Prosser and twenty-five of his followers.

A decade later, in what seems to have been a spontaneous bid for freedom, several hundred slaves in the river parishes (counties) above New Orleans marched on the city. Poorly armed, they were no match for the U.S. Army troops and militiamen who stopped them. More than sixty slaves died, and the heads of the leading rebels were posted on poles along the Mississippi River to warn others of the fate that awaited rebellious slaves.

The most carefully planned slave revolt, **Denmark Vesey's Conspiracy**, like Prosser's, failed before it got started. Vesey, a literate carpenter and lay preacher in Charleston who had purchased his freedom with the money he had won in a lottery, planned the revolt in the summer of 1822. Vesey drew on biblical passages, antislavery sentiments in Congress he had gleaned from newspaper reports on the Missouri Compromise debates, and the successful revolt of slaves in Haiti to inspire his followers. He tried to steel the courage of his coconspirators by telling them that his chief lieutenant, Gullah Jack, a conjurer, or voodoo doctor, would cast spells on their enemies. He assigned teams of rebels specific targets, such as the municipal guardhouse and arsenal. Once Charleston was secured, the rebels apparently planned to flee to Haiti. The plot collapsed when two domestic servants betrayed it. White authorities responded swiftly and savagely. They hanged thirty-five conspirators, including Vesey, and banished thirty-seven others. After destroying the African Methodist Episcopal Church where Vesey had preached and the conspirators had met, they

After eluding his white pursuers for two months, Nat Turner, the leader of the South's most famous slave revolt, was captured on October 30, 1831.

tried to seal off the city from subversive outsiders by passing the Negro Seamen's Act, which mandated the imprisonment of black sailors while their ships were berthed in Charleston.

One slave revolt, **Nat Turner's Rebellion** in Southampton County, Virginia, did erupt before it could be suppressed. Turner was a literate field hand driven by prophetic visions of black vengeance against white oppressors. Like Vesey, he was well versed in the Bible. Convinced by what he called "signs in heaven" that he should "arise and prepare myself and slay my enemies with their own weapons," he led a small band of followers on a murderous rampage in late August 1831. The first white man to be killed was Joseph Travis, Turner's owner, known for his lenient treatment of slaves. In the next two days, sixty other white people were also killed. An enraged posse, aided by slaves, captured or killed most of Turner's party. Turner hid for two months before being apprehended. He and more than thirty other slaves were executed, and panicky white people killed more than a hundred other slaves.

Slaves well understood that the odds against a successful rebellion were insurmountable. They could see who had all the guns. White people were also more numerous. In contrast to the large black majorities in the slave societies of the West Indies and Brazil—majorities made possible only by the continuous, heavy importation of Africans—slaves made up only one-third of the population of the antebellum American South. They lacked the numbers to overwhelm the white population and could not escape to mountain hideaways or large tracts of jungle. Surveillance by mounted white patrols—part of the police apparatus of slavery—limited organized rebellion by slaves to small, local affairs that were quickly suppressed.

Nor could many slaves escape to freedom. Few runaways made it to Canada or a free state. White people could stop black people and demand to see papers documenting their freedom or right to travel without a master. The **Underground Railroad**, a secret network of stations and safe houses organized by Quakers and other black and white antislavery activists, provided some assistance. However, fellow slaves or free black people, especially in the cities of the Border South, provided the only help most runaways could count on. Out of more than 3 million slaves in the 1850s, only about a thousand a year permanently escaped (see "American Views: A Letter from an Escaped Slave to His Former Master").

The few who made it to the North did so by running at night and hiding during the day. The most ingenious resorted to clever stratagems. Henry "Box" Brown arranged to have himself shipped in a box from Richmond to Philadelphia. Ellen Craft, a

After fleeing from slavery in Maryland in 1849, Harriet "Moses" Tubman, standing on the left, risked reenslavement by returning to the South on several occasions to assist other slaves in escaping. She is photographed here with some of those she helped free.

Smith College, Sophia Smith Collection, Northampton, Massachusetts.

American Views

A Letter from an Escaped Slave to His Former Master

In 1859, Jackson Whitney was one of six thousand fugitive slaves living in Canada, a sanctuary of freedom beyond the reach of the Fugitive Slave Act of 1850. Like most fugitives, he was male, and he had been forced to leave his family behind in Kentucky. His letter, as well as other direct testimony by African Americans about their experiences and feelings while enslaved, gives us information about slavery that only the slaves could provide.

- ❖ **How would you characterize the tone of Whitney's letter? How did he express his joy at being a free man?**
- ❖ **How did Whitney feel that Riley, his former owner, had betrayed him? What did Whitney mean by the phrase "a slave talking to 'massa' "? How did he indicate that he had been hiding his true feelings as a slave?**
- ❖ **How did Whitney contrast his religious beliefs and those of Riley? How did he expect Riley to be punished?**
- ❖ **What pained Whitney about his freedom in Canada, and what did he ask of Riley?**

March 18, 1859
Mr. Wm. Riley, Springfield, Ky. —Sir: I take this opportunity to dictate a few lines to you, supposing you might be curious to know my whereabouts. I am happy to inform you that I am in Canada, in good health, and have been here several days. Perhaps, by this time, you have concluded that robbing a woman of her husband, and children of their father does not pay, at least in your case; and I thought, while lying in jail by your direction, that if you had no remorse or conscience that would make you feel for a poor, broken-hearted man, and his worse-than-murdered wife and child, . . . and could not by any entreaty or permission be induced to do as you promised you would, which was to let me go with my family for $800—but contended for $1,000, when you had promised to take the same you gave for me (which

light-skinned slave who could pass as white, disguised herself as a male slaveholder accompanied by his dark-skinned servant (her husband, William). What could have been a fatal flaw in their plan as they traveled from Savannah to Philadelphia—their inability to write and hence sign their names or document their assumed identities—was overcome by having Ellen pose as a sickly, rheumatic master whose right hand had to be kept bandaged.

Running away was common, but most runaways fled no farther than to nearby swamps and woods. Most voluntarily returned or were tracked down by bloodhounds within a week. Aside from protesting a special grievance or trying to avoid punishment, these slaves usually wanted to visit a spouse or loved one. Occasionally, runaways could bargain for lenient treatment in return for faithful service in the future. Most were severely punished. Such temporary flights from the master's control siphoned off some of the anger that might otherwise have erupted in violent, self-destructive attacks on slave owners. All planters had heard about the field hand who took an ax to an overseer, the cook who poisoned her master's family, or the house servant who killed a sleeping master or mistress.

Slaves resisted complete domination by their masters in less overt ways. They mocked white people in folktales like those about Brer Rabbit, for example, was $660.) at the time you bought me, and let me go with my dear wife and children! but instead would render me miserable, and lie to me, and to your neighbors . . . and when you was at Louisville trying to sell me! then I thought it was time for me to make my feet feel for Canada, and let your conscience feel in your pocket.—Now you cannot say but that I did all that was honorable and right while I was with you, although I was a slave. I pretended all the time that I thought you, or some one else had a better right to me than I had to myself, which you know is rather hard thinking. —You know, too, that you proved a traitor to me in the time of need, and when in the most bitter distress that the human soul is capable of experiencing; and could you have carried out your purposes there would have been no relief. But I rejoice to say that an unseen, kind spirit appeared for the oppressed, and bade me take up my bed and walk—the result of which is that I am victorious and you are defeated.

I am comfortably situated in Canada, working for George Harris [another fugitive slave from Kentucky who had bought a farm in Canada]. . . .

There is only one thing to prevent me being entirely happy here, and that is the want of my dear wife and children, and you to see us enjoying ourselves together here. I wish you could realize the contrast between Freedom and Slavery; but it is not likely that we shall ever meet again on this earth. But if you want to go to the next world and meet a God of love, mercy, and justice, in peace; who says, "Inasmuch as you did it to the least of them my little ones, you did it unto me"—making the professions that you do, pretending to be a follower of Christ, and tormenting me and my little ones as you have done—[you] had better repair the breaches you have made among us in this world, by sending my wife and children to me; thus preparing to meet your God in peace; for, if God don't punish you for inflicting such distress on the poorest of His poor, then there is no use of having any God, or talking about one. . . .

I hope you will consider candidly, and see if the case does not justify every word I have said, and ten times as much. You must not consider that it is a slave talking to 'massa' now, but one as free as yourself.

I subscribe myself one of the abused of America, but one of the justified and honored of Canada.

Jackson Whitney

Source: John W. Blassingame, ed., Slave Testimony: Two Centuries of Letters, Speeches, Interviews, and Autobiographies *(Louisiana State University Press 1977).*

in which weak but wily animals cunningly outsmart their stronger enemies. Slave owners routinely complained of slaves malingering at work, abusing farm animals, losing tools, stealing food, and committing arson. These subversive acts of protest never challenged the system of slavery itself, but they did help slaves maintain a sense of dignity and self-respect.

Free Society

The abolitionists and the antislavery Republican party of the 1850s portrayed the social order of the slave South as little more than haughty planters lording it over shiftless, poor white people. The reality was considerably more complex. Planters, who set the social tone for the South as a whole, did act superior, but they were a tiny minority and had to contend with an ambitious middle class of small slaveholders and a majority of nonslaveholding farmers. Some landless white people on the margin of rural society fit the stereotype of "poor whites," but they were easily outnumbered by self-reliant farmers who worked their own land. Southern cities, though small by northern standards, provided jobs for a growing class of free workers who increasingly clashed with planters over the use of slave labor.

OVERVIEW

STRUCTURE OF FREE SOCIETY IN THE SOUTH, C. 1860

Group	Size	Characteristics
Large planters	Less than 1 percent of white families	Owned fifty or more slaves and plantations in excess of one thousand acres; the wealthiest class in America
Planters	About 3 percent of white families	Owned twenty to forty-nine slaves and plantations in excess of one hundred acres; controlled bulk of southern wealth and provided most of the political leaders
Small slaveholders	About 20 percent of white families	Owned fewer than twenty slaves and most often fewer than five; primarily farmers, though some were part of a small middle class in towns and cities
Nonslaveholding whites	About 75 percent of white families	Mostly yeomen farmers who owned their own land and stressed production for family use; one in five owned neither slaves nor land and squatted on least desirable land where they planted some corn and grazed some livestock; in cities they worked as artisans or, more typically, day laborers
Free blacks	About 3 percent of all free families	Concentrated in the Upper South; hemmed in by legal and social restrictions; mostly tenants or farm laborers; about one-third lived in cities and generally were limited to lowest-paying jobs

These same cities, notably in the Upper South, were also home to the nation's largest concentration of free black people. Their freedom, though restricted, contradicted the racial justification of slavery. They competed with white workers for jobs, and by the 1850s pressure was mounting on them to leave the South or be enslaved. The free society in the South was surely more diverse than its antislavery critics charged, but overriding racism bonded most white people together to defend the prerogatives of white supremacy.

The Slaveholding Minority

The white-columned plantation estate approached from a stately avenue of shade trees and framed by luxuriant gardens remains the most popular image of the slave South. In fact, such manorial estates were utterly unrepresentative of the lifestyle of the typical slaveholder. Only the wealthiest planters could live in such splendor, and they comprised less than 1 percent of southern white families in 1860. Yet displayed in their homes and grounds, their wealth and status were so imposing that they created an idealized image of grace and grandeur that has obscured the cruder realities of the slave regime.

Only in the rice districts of the South Carolina lowcountry and in the rich sugar parishes and cotton counties of the Mississippi Delta were large planters more than a small minority of the slaveholding class, let alone the general white population. Families of the planter class—those who held a minimum of twenty slaves—constituted only around 3 percent of all southern families in 1860. Fewer than one out of five planter families—less than 1 percent of all families—owned more than fifty slaves. Far from conspicuously exhibiting their wealth, most planters lived in drab log cabins. "The planter's home is generally a rude ungainly structure, made of logs, rough hewn from the forest; rail fences and rickety gates guard its enclosures," complained a speaker to the Alabama horticultural society in 1851. "We murder our soil with wasteful culture because there is plenty of fresh land West—and we live in tents and huts when we might live in rural palaces."

Most planters wanted to acquire wealth, not display it. They were restlessly eager to move on and

James Cameron (1817–1882), "Colonel and Mrs. James A. Whiteside, son Charles and servants." Oil on canvas; c. 1858–1859. Hunter Museum of Art, Chattanooga, Tennessee, Gift of Mr. and Mrs. Thomas Whiteside.

Colonel James A. Whiteside and his family were among the small elite of white Southerners who enjoyed the wealth and ease of life on a large plantation. Reflecting the ideal of patriarchy, this portrait, c. 1858, projects the colonel as a figure of power and authority.

abandon their homes when the allure of profits from a new cotton frontier promised to relieve them of the debts they had incurred to purchase their slaves. The sheer drive and penny-pinching materialism of these planters on the make impressed Tyrone Power, an Irish actor who visited the South in the 1830s. The slaveholders he saw carving plantations out of the wilderness were "hardy, indefatigable, and enterprising to a degree; despising and condemning luxury and refinement, courting labour, and even making a pride of the privations which they, without any necessity, continue to endure with their families."

Most planters expected their wives to help supervise the slaves and run the plantation. Besides raising her own children, the plantation mistress managed the household staff, oversaw the cooking and cleaning, gardened, dispensed medicine and clothing to the slaves, and often assisted in their religious instruction. When guests or relatives came for an extended visit, the wife had to make all the special arrangements that this entailed. When the master was called off on a business or political trip, she kept the plantation accounts. In many respects, she worked harder than her husband.

Planter wives often complained in their journals and letters of their isolation from other white women and the physical and mental toil of managing slaves. Still, they enjoyed a wealth and status unknown to most southern women and only rarely questioned the institution of slavery. Their deepest anger stemmed from their humiliation by husbands who kept slave mistresses or sexually abused slave women.

Bound by their duties as wives not to express this anger publicly and unwilling to renounce the institution that both victimized and benefited them, white women tended to vent their frustrations on black women whose alleged promiscuity they blamed for the sexual transgressions of white males. "Sometimes white mistresses will surmise that there is an intimacy between a slave woman & the master," recalled a former slave, "and perhaps she will make a great fuss & have her whipped, & perhaps there will be no peace until she is sold."

Despite the tensions and sexual jealousies that it aroused, the ownership of slaves was the surest means of social and economic advancement for most white families. Most slave owners, however, never attained planter status. Nine in ten slave owners in 1860 owned fewer than twenty slaves, and fully half of them had fewer than five. Many white people also rented a few slaves on a seasonal basis.

Generally younger than the planters, small slaveholders were a diverse lot. About 10 percent were women, and another 20 percent or so were merchants, businessmen, artisans, and urban professionals. Most were farmers trying to acquire enough land and slaves to enter the ranks of planters. To keep costs down, they often began by purchasing children, the cheapest slaves available, or a young slave family, so that they could add to their slaveholdings as the slave mother bore more children.

Other slaveholding farmers had inherited their slaves and were trying to regain their fathers' planter status. Partible inheritance—the equal division of property among children—was the norm in the nineteenth-century South. Except among the richest planter families, this division reduced the sons to modest slaveholders who had to struggle to build their own plantations.

Small slaveholders enjoyed scant economic security. A deadly outbreak of disease among their slaves or a single bad crop could destroy their credit and force them to sell their slaves to clear their debts. Owners of fewer than ten slaves stood a fifty–fifty chance within a decade of dropping out of the slaveholding class. Nor could small holders hope to compete directly with the planters. In any given area suitable for plantations, they were gradually pushed out as planters bought up land to raise livestock or more crops. In general, only slave owners who had established themselves in business or the professions had the capital reserves to rise into the planter elite.

Especially in the Lower South, owning slaves was a necessary precondition for upward mobility, but it was hardly a sufficient one. Slaveholders who failed to advance had nonetheless acquired a badge of social respectability. As a Baptist opponent of slavery put it, "Without slaves a man's children stand but poor chance to marry in reputation." Aside from conferring status, owning a few slaves could relieve a white household of much hard domestic labor. "I wish to God every head of a family in the United States had one [slave] to take the drudgery and menial service off his family," proclaimed Andrew Johnson of Tennessee in the U.S. Senate. Thanks to slavery, even average white Southerners could aspire to some relief from endless toil.

The White Majority

Three-fourths of southern white families owned no slaves in 1860. Although most numerous in the Upper South, nonslaveholders predominated wherever the soil and climate were not suitable for plantation agriculture. Most were yeoman farmers who worked their own land with family labor.

These farmers were quick to move when times were bad and their land was used up, but once settled in an area they formed intensely localized societies in which fathers and husbands held sway over their families. The community extended five to ten miles around the nearest country store or county courthouse. Networks of kin and friends provided labor services when needed, fellowship in evangelical churches, and staple goods that an individual farm could not produce. Social travel and international markets, so central to the lives of planters, had little relevance in the farmers' community-centered existence. The yeomanry aimed to be self-sufficient and limited market involvement to the sale of livestock and an occasional cotton crop that could bring in needed cash.

Yeoman farmers jealously guarded their independence, and in their tight little worlds of face-to-face relationships, they demanded that planters treat them as social equals. Ever fearful of being re-

A yeoman farmstead in New Braumfels, Texas. The yeomanry strove for self-sufficiency by growing food crops and grazing livestock.

duced to dependence, they avoided debt and sought to limit government authority. Rather than risk financial ruin by buying slaves on credit to grow cotton, they grew food crops and depended on their sons and, when needed, their wives and daughters to work the fields. Far longer than most northern farmers, and in part because poor transportation raised the cost of manufactured goods, they continued to make their own clothes, shoes, soap, and other consumer items.

Nonslaveholding farmers from the mountains and planters on the bottomlands rarely mixed, and their societies developed in isolation from each other. In areas where there were both small farms and scattered plantations, the interests of the yeomen and the planters were often complementary. Planters provided local markets for the surplus grain and livestock of nonslaveholders and, for a small fee, access to grist mills and gins for grinding corn and cleaning cotton. They lent small sums to poorer neighbors in emergencies or to pay taxes. The yeomen staffed the slave patrols and became overseers on the plantations. Both groups sought to protect property rights from outside interference and to maintain a system of racial control in which white liberties rested on black degradation.

When yeomen and planters did clash, it was usually over economic issues. Large slaveholders needing better credit and marketing facilities gravitated toward the Whig party, which called for banks and internal improvements. Nonslaveholding farmers, especially in the Lower South, tended to be Democrats who opposed banks and state-funded economic projects. They considered bankers grasping outsiders who wanted to rob them of their economic independence, and they suspected that state involvement in the economy only led to higher taxes and increased the public debt. These partisan battles, however, rarely involved a debate about the merits of slavery. As long as planters deferred to the egalitarian sensibilities of the yeomen by courting them at election time and promising to safeguard their liberties, the planters were able to maintain broad support for slavery across class lines.

Around 15 percent of rural white families owned neither land nor slaves. These were the so-called "poor whites," stigmatized by both abolitionists and planters as lazy and shiftless. The abolitionists considered them a kind of underclass who proved that slavery so degraded the dignity of labor that it led people to shun work and lapse into wretched poverty. For the planters, they were a constant nuisance and a threat to slave discipline. Planters habitually complained that poor whites demoralized their slaves by showing that a person could survive without steady labor. Planters also accused them of trading guns and alcohol with slaves for stolen plantation property.

Some landless white people did live down to their negative stereotype. Still, the "poor white trash" label with which they were stigmatized is misleading. Most were resourceful and enterprising enough to supply themselves with all the material comforts they wanted. Back in the swamps and pine barrens shunned by planters and yeomen alike, they squatted on a few acres of land, put up crude cabins for shelter, planted some corn, and grazed livestock in the surrounding woods. Aided by the mild southern climate, they had all the corn and pork they could eat. Not having to do steady work for survival, they hunted, fished, and took orders from no one. Although poor by most standards, they were also defiantly self-reliant.

Nonslaveholders were a growing majority in southern cities, especially among the working classes. These urban workers shared no agricultural interests or ties with the planters. Nor were most of them, especially in the unskilled ranks, southern-born. Northerners and immigrants dominated the urban work force.

Free workers, especially Irish and German immigrants, increasingly replaced slaves in urban labor markets. These white workers bitterly resented competition from black slaves, and their demands to exclude slaves from the urban workplace reinforced planters' belief that cities bred abolitionism. When urban laborers protested against slave competition in the 1850s, planters singled them out as the nonslaveholders most likely to attack slavery.

Free Black People

A few southern black people—6 percent of the total in 1860—were "free persons of color" and constituted 3 percent of the free population in the South (see Figure 13-3). These free black people occupied a precarious and vulnerable position between degraded enslavement and meaningful freedom. White intimidation and special legal provisions known as **black codes** (found throughout the North as well) denied them nearly all the rights of citizenship. Because of the legal presumption in the South that all black people were slaves, they had to carry freedom papers, official certificates of their freedom. They were shut out of the political process and could not testify against white people in court. Many occupations, especially those involved in the communication of ideas, such as the printing trades, were closed to them.

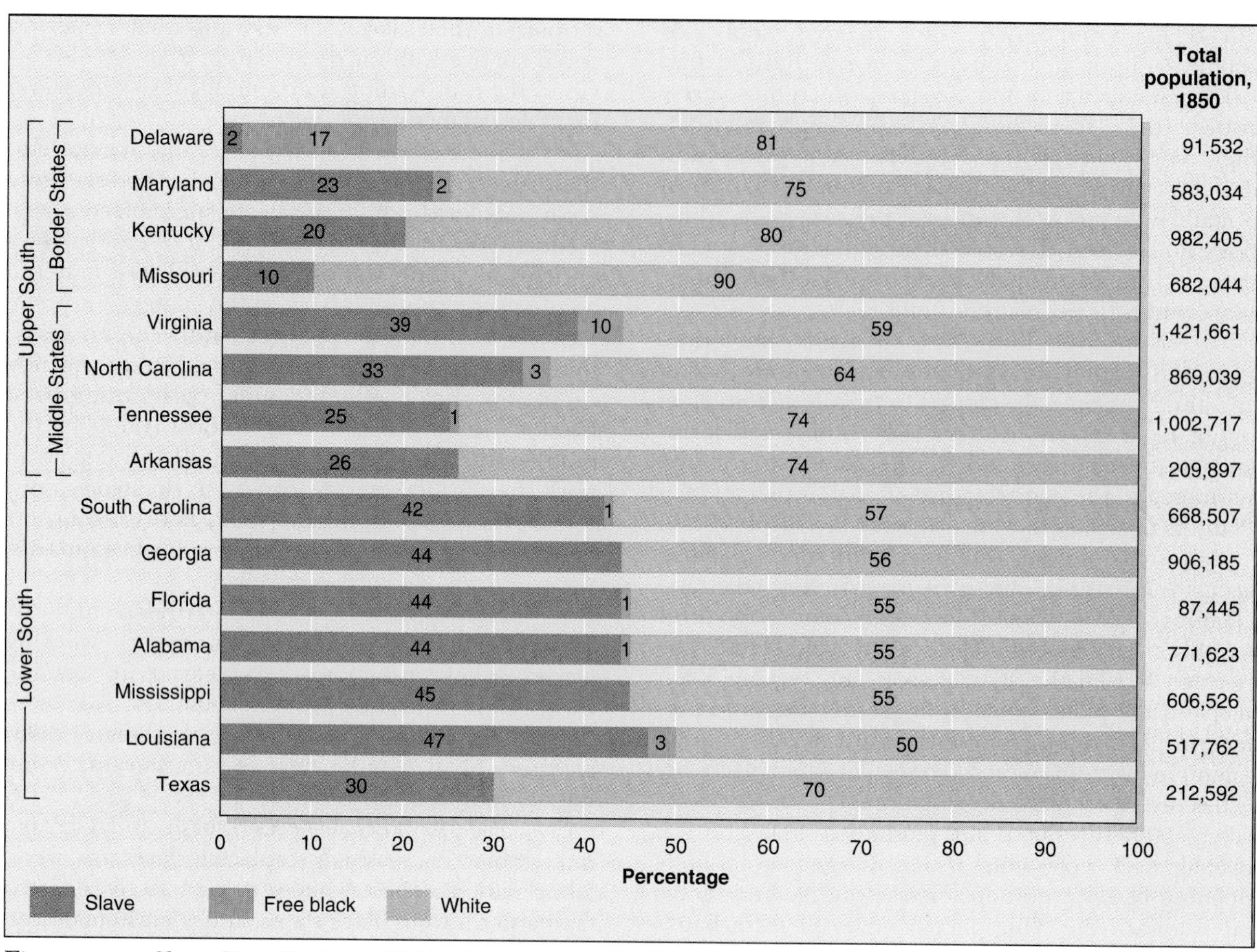

Figure 13-3 Slave, Free Black, and White Population in Southern States, 1850
Except for Texas, slaves by 1850 comprised over 40 percent of the population in every state of the Lower South. The small population of free black people was concentrated in the Upper South.

Every slave state forbade the entry of free black people, and every municipality had its own rules and regulations that forced them to live as an inferior caste. In Charleston, for example, a free black person could not smoke a cigar or carry a cane in public. Any sign of upward mobility or intimation of equal standing was ruthlessly suppressed. White people had the right of way, and a free black person who bumped into a white person on the street was likely to be flogged.

More than four-fifths of the southern free black population lived in the Upper South. Most were the offspring of slaves freed by private manumissions between 1780 and 1800 when slavery temporarily loosened in the Chesapeake region in the wake of the Revolutionary War. Manumissions dropped sharply after 1810, the result of heightened white anxieties over slave security after Prosser's Rebellion and the rising demand for slaves in the Lower South. From 1810 to 1860, only 13 percent of black people in the Upper South were free.

As in the North, legal barriers and white prejudice generally confined free black people to the poorest-paying and most menial work. In rural areas, a handful became independent farmers, but most worked as farm laborers or tenants. The best economic opportunities were in the cities, where some found factory jobs and positions in the skilled trades. Because the South had a general shortage of skilled labor, free black artisans—carpenters, barbers, shoemakers, tailors, and plasterers—could earn a respectable income. Indeed, the percentage of black people in the skilled trades was generally higher in the South than in the North. Talented artisans such as Thomas Day, widely recognized as the finest cabinetmaker in North Carolina, could command a premium in wages from white employers.

A free black wood sawyer. The skilled trades offered among the best economic opportunities for free black people in the South.

One-third of free black people in the Upper South lived in cities, a much higher proportion than among white people. Cities offered black people not only jobs but also enough social space to found their own churches and mutual-aid associations. Especially after 1840, urban African-American churches proliferated to become the center of black community life. Church Sunday schools and day schools provided black people practically their only access to education, which they persisted in pursuing despite white opposition. A "good education," declared a black schoolmaster in Baltimore, "is the *sine qua non* as regards the elevation of our people."

Less than 2 percent of the black people in the Lower South were free in 1860. Given the greater profitability of slavery there, manumissions were rare. Most of the Lower South's free black population descended from black emigrants who fled the revolutionary unrest in Haiti in the 1790s. These refugees were artisans, shopkeepers, and farmers who settled primarily in Charleston and New Orleans. Able to secure a solid economic footing, they left their descendants wealthier than any other free black people in the United States. Free black people in the Lower South were more likely than those in the Upper South to have a marketable skill, and two-thirds of them lived in cities.

A light skin also enhanced the social standing of free black people among color-conscious whites in the Lower South. Nearly 70 percent of free black people in 1860 were mulattoes, and from their ranks came nearly all of the very small number of black planters. Mulattoes could count on greater white patronage, and they monopolized the best jobs available to free black people. A mulatto elite emerged in Charleston, Mobile, and New Orleans that carefully distanced itself from most black people, slave or free. In New Orleans, where a tradition of racially mixed unions dated back to French and Spanish rule, mulattoes put on lavish "octoroon balls" attended by free women of color and white men. Even here, however, the mulatto elite remained suspended between black and white worlds, never fully accepted by either.

Despite the emergence of a three-tiered racial hierarchy in the port cities of the Lower South, white authorities insisted on making a white and black racial dichotomy the overriding social division in the South. As the racial defense of slavery intensified in the 1850s, more calls were made for laws to banish or enslave free black people. Arkansas passed such a law in 1859, and similar bills were proposed in Florida, Tennessee, Mississippi, and Missouri. Even Maryland held a referendum in 1859 on whether to reenslave its free black population, the largest in the South. Only the opposition of nonslaveholders heavily dependent on cheap free black labor defeated the referendum.

Despised and feared by white people as a subversive element in a slave society, free black Southerners were daily reminded that their freedom rested on the whims of the white majority. As white attitudes turned uglier in the late antebellum period, that freedom became ever less secure.

The Proslavery Argument

In the early nineteenth century, white Southerners made no particular effort to defend slavery because the institution was not under heavy outside attack. If pressed, most white people would have called slavery a necessary evil, an unfortunate legacy from earlier generations that was needed to maintain racial peace.

The 1830s marked a turning point. After the twin shocks of Nat Turner's Rebellion and the onset of the abolitionist crusade, white mobs emerged to stifle any open criticism of slavery in the Lower

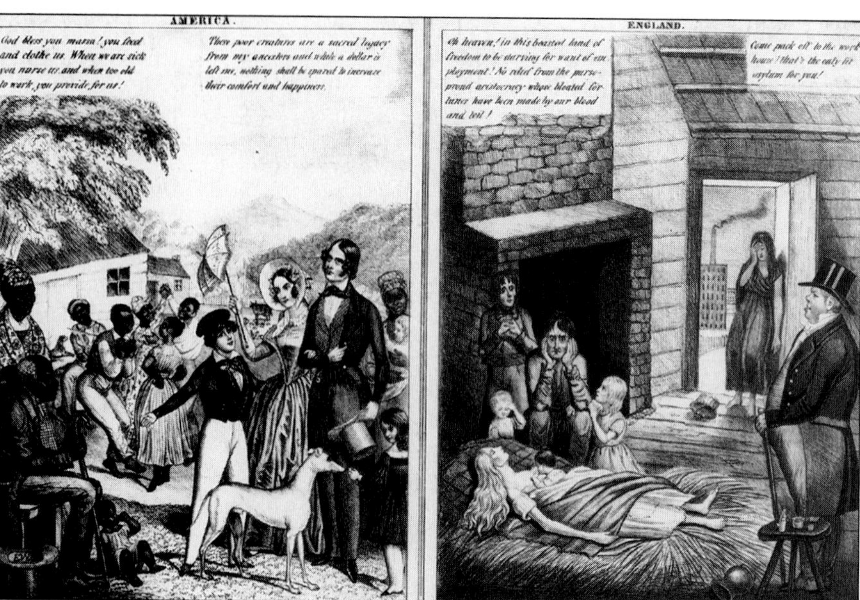

As this 1841 cartoon reflects, a staple of proslavery propaganda was to contrast the allegedly contented and healthy lot of slaves with that of starving factory workers exploited by the system of wage labor.

South. White Southerners also began to develop a defense of slavery. By the 1850s, politicians, intellectuals, and evangelical ministers were arguing that it was a positive good, an institution ordained by God as the foundation of southern prosperity, white democracy, and Christian instruction for heathen Africans. Slavery, they insisted, was a mild, paternalistic, and even caring institution.

This defense obviously portrayed slavery as the defenders imagined it, not as it was. However comforting it may have been to individual slaveholders, it failed to convince abolitionists or southern dissenters who condemned slavery on moral and economic grounds.

Evangelical Protestantism dominated southern religious expression by the 1830s, and its ministers took the lead in combating abolitionist charges that slavery was a moral and religious abomination. Except for a radical minority of antislavery evangelicals in the Upper South, a group largely silenced or driven out by the conservative reaction following Nat Turner's uprising, the southern churches had always supported slavery. This support grew more pronounced and articulate once the abolitionists stepped up their attacks on slavery in the mid-1830s.

Southern evangelicals accepted the Bible as God's literal word, and through selective reading they found abundant evidence in it to proclaim slavery fully in accord with His moral dictates. They pointed out, for example, that the patriarchs of Israel owned slaves. Slavery was practiced throughout the Roman world at the time of Christ, they noted, and the apostles urged obedience to all secular laws, including those governing slavery.

Southern evangelicals also turned to the Bible to support their argument that patriarchal authority—the unquestioned power of the father—was the basis of all Christian communities. Part of that authority extended over slaves, and slavery thus became a matter of family governance, a domestic institution in which Christian masters of slaves, unlike capitalist masters of free "wage slaves" in the North, accepted responsibility for caring for their workers in sickness and old age. Far from being a moral curse, slavery was part of God's plan to Christianize an inferior race and teach its people how to produce raw materials that benefited the world's masses.

The growing commitment of southern evangelicals to slavery as a positive good clashed with the antislavery position and the generally more liberal theology of northern evangelicals. In 1837, the Presbyterians split along sectional lines because of differences over slavery. In 1844, and as a direct result of the slavery issue, the Methodist Episcopal Church, the nation's largest, divided into northern and southern churches. The Baptists did the same a year later. These religious schisms foreshadowed the sectionalized political divisions of the 1850s; they also severed one of the main emotional bonds between white northerners and Southerners.

The religious defense of slavery was central to the slaveholding ethic of paternalism that developed after 1830. By the 1850s, planters commonly described slaves as members of an extended family who were treated better than free workers in the North. This language often reflected the psychological need of planters to feel appreciated, even loved, as caring parents by their slave dependents. Some evangelical masters tried to act as moral stewards to their slaves and to curb the worst features of their bondage. Led by Charles Colcock Jones, a minister and planter in the Georgia lowcountry, they founded religious missions to the slaves and sought reforms such as legal measures that would prevent the separation of slave families. Such slaveholders, however, were a minority, and efforts to reform slavery failed largely because masters would accept no limits on their power to control and work their slaves as they saw fit.

The crusade to sanctify slavery won few converts outside the South. Most northern churches did not endorse abolitionism but did have moral qualms about slavery. In a particularly stinging rebuke to southern church leaders in the 1850s, black abolitionists succeeded in having slaveholders barred from international religious conventions.

More common than the biblical defense of slavery was the racial argument that black people were unfit for freedom among white people. Drawing in part on the scientific wisdom of the day, the racial defense alleged that black people were naturally lazy and inherently inferior to white people. If freed, so went the argument, they would turn to crime and sexually assault white women. Only the controls of slavery enabled the races to coexist in the South.

Slavery as a necessary racial control was a central theme in Thomas R. Dew's *Review of the Debates in the Virginia Legislature of 1831 and 1832,* the first major justification of slavery by a Southerner. Dew, a Tidewater planter, was responding to a proposal for gradual emancipation that had been introduced into the Virginia legislature. Although the plan was defeated (largely because the eastern plantation counties were overrepresented in the legislature), upper-class conservatives such as Dew were alarmed by the potentially dangerous class division it had revealed between slaveholders and nonslaveholders. He tried to unite white people on the issue of race.

The racial argument resonated powerfully among white people because nearly all of them, including those otherwise opposed to slavery, dreaded emancipation. The attitude of a Tennessee farmer, as recorded by a northern traveler in the 1850s, was typical: "He said he'd always wished there hadn't been any niggers here . . . , but he wouldn't like to have them free." Unable to conceive of living in a society with many free black people, most white people could see no middle ground between slavery and the presumed social chaos of emancipation.

The existence of *black* slavery also had egalitarian implications for the nonslaveholding majority of whites. Slavery supposedly spared white Southerners from the menial, degrading labor that white northerners had to perform. Moreover, because slaves lacked political rights, champions of slavery argued that black bondage buttressed the political liberties of all white males by removing from politics the leveling demands of the poor and propertyless for a redistribution of wealth.

Despite its apparent success in forging white solidarity, the racial argument could be turned on its head and used to weaken slavery. Most white Northerners were about as racist as their southern counterparts, but they were increasingly willing to end slavery on the grounds that the stronger white race should help black people improve themselves as free persons. In short, nothing in the internal logic of racist doctrines required enslaving black people. That same logic also encouraged some white Southerners to challenge the economic prerogatives of slaveholders. Why, for example, should any white people, as members of the master race, be forced into economic competition against skilled slave artisans? Why should not all nonagricultural jobs be legally reserved for white people? Doctrines of black inferiority could not prevent white unity from cracking when the economic interests of nonslaveholders clashed with those of planters.

Conclusion

Slavery and a biracial social order defined the South as a distinctive region. The spread of plantation agriculture across the Lower South after 1830 deepened the involvement of white Southerners in cotton and slavery. At the same time, an abolitionist movement in the North attacked slavery on moral grounds and demanded that it be abolished. As southern interests became more enmeshed in an institution that outsiders condemned, religious and intellectual leaders portrayed slavery as a Christian institution and a positive good necessary for white democracy and harmonious race relations. Proslavery ideologues stridently insisted the South was separate from and superior to the rest of the nation.

The proslavery argument depicted a nearly ideal society blessed by class and racial harmony. In reality, social conditions in the slave South were contradictory and conflict-ridden. Slaves were not content in their bondage. They dreamed of freedom and sustained that dream through their own forms of Christianity and the support of family and kin. Relations between masters and their slaves were antagonistic, not affectionate, and wherever the system of control slackened, slaves resisted their owners.

Nor did all white Southerners, who confronted increasing economic inequality after 1830, accept racial slavery as in their best interests. It divided as well as united them. The publication in 1857 of Hinton Rowan Helper's *Impending Crisis of the South,* a scathing indictment by a white North Carolinian of slavery's harmful effect on economic opportunities for average white people, vividly showed that not all were convinced by the proslavery argument.

During the 1850s, the size of the slaveholding class fell from 31 percent of Southern white families to 25 percent. Slaveowners were a shrinking minority, and slavery was in decline throughout the Upper South. In the Border South, free labor was replacing slavery as the dominant means of organizing economic production. In these states, slavery was a vulnerable institution. Planters were not fooled by the public rhetoric of white unity. They knew that slavery was increasingly confined to the Lower South and that elsewhere in the South white support for it was gradually eroding.

Planters feared the double-edged challenge to their privileged positions of outside interference with slavery and internal white disloyalty. By the 1850s, many of them were concluding that the only way to resolve their dilemma was to make the South a separate nation.

Review Questions

1. What factors accounted for the tremendous expansion of cotton production in the South? How was this expansion linked to slavery and westward movement?
2. What differentiated the Upper South from the Lower South? What role did slavery play in each region after 1815?
3. How would you characterize the life of a plantation slave? Why were religion and family such key features of the world that slaves built for themselves? What evidence is there of resistance and rebellion among the slaves?
4. How did most nonslaveholding white Southerners live? What values did they prize most highly? Why did most nonslaveholders accept slavery or at least not attack it directly?
5. What was the position of free black Southerners in southern society? How were their freedoms restricted?
6. How did white Southerners attempt to defend slavery and reconcile it with Christianity?

Recommended Reading

Shearer Bowman, *Masters and Lords: Mid-19th Century U.S. Planters and Prussian Junkers* (1993). A fascinating study in comparative history that portrays southern planters as agrarian capitalists.

William W. Freehling, *The Road to Disunion: Secessionists at Bay, 1776–1854* (1990). A fine introduction to the social diversity of the Old South, especially strong in exploring the tensions over slavery between the Upper South and the Lower South.

Eugene D. Genovese, *Roll Jordan Roll: The World the Slaveholders Made* (1974). A richly textured study of slavery that is an excellent source for the interaction between masters and slaves. Genovese argues that paternalistic relations of dependent rights and obligations characterized slavery.

Christopher Morris, *Becoming Southern: The Evolution of a Way of Life, Warren County and Vicksburg, Mississippi, 1770–1860* (1995). A well-crafted study that reveals how central slavery was to the evolving self-consciousness of rural white southerners.

James Oakes, *The Ruling Race* (1982). A relatively short but provocative history of the slave-owning class that stresses the restless, acquisitive nature of the small slave owners, the most typical holders of slaves.

Kenneth M. Stampp, *The Peculiar Institution* (1956). A work that has aged well and is still the best one-volume history of southern slavery; leaves no doubt that slavery was both brutal and profitable.

Charles S. Sydnor, *The Growth of Southern Sectionalism, 1819–1848* (1948). The most thorough account of how the South moved from its nationalist stance in the early nineteenth century toward increasing sectional self-consciousness.

Bertram Wyatt-Brown, *Southern Honor: Ethics and Behavior in the Old South* (1982). Valuable for its insights into the culture of the planter class and the notions of honor that structured social relations among all white people.

Additional Sources

The Lower South

Robert W. Fogel and Stanley Engerman, *Time on the Cross: The Economics of American Negro Slavery* (1974).

Lacy K. Ford Jr., *Origins of Southern Radicalism: The South Carolina Upcountry, 1800–1860* (1988).

Stephanie McCurry, *Masters of Small Worlds* (1995).

J. Mills Thornton III, *Politics and Power in a Slave Society* (1978).

Gavin Wright, *The Political Economy of the Cotton South* (1978).

The Upper South

David F. Allmendinger, *Ruffin: Family and Reform in the Old South* (1990).

Fred Arthur Bailey, *Class and Tennessee's Confederate Generation* (1987).

David W. Crofts, *Old Southampton: Politics and Society in a Virginia County, 1834–1869* (1992).

Barbara J. Fields, *Slavery and Freedom on the Middle Ground: Maryland during the Nineteenth Century* (1985).

Robert Tracey McKenzie, *One South or Many? Plantation Belt and Upcounty in Civil War Era Tennessee* (1994).

Michael Tadman, *Speculators and Slaves: Masters, Traders, and Slaves in the Old South* (1989).

Slave Life and Culture

John W. Blassingame, *The Slave Community: Plantation Life in the Antebellum South* (1972).

Charles B. Dew, *Bond of Iron: Master and Slave at Buffalo Forge* (1994).

Herbert G. Gutman, *The Black Family in Slavery and Freedom, 1750–1925* (1974).

Peter Kolchin, *Unfree Labor: American Slavery and Russian Serfdom* (1987).

Roderick A. McDonald, *The Economy and Material Culture of Slaves* (1993).

Robert Starobin, *Industrial Slavery in the Old South* (1970).

Richard C. Wade, *Slavery in the Cities* (1964).

Free Society

Ira Berlin, *Slaves without Masters: The Free Negro in the Antebellum South* (1974).

Charles C. Bolton, *Poor Whites of the Antebellum South* (1994).

Victoria E. Bynum, *Unruly Women: The Politics of Social and Sexual Control in the Old South* (1992).

Bill Cecil-Fronsman, *Common Whites: Class and Culture in Antebellum North Carolina* (1992).

Elizabeth Fox-Genovese, *Within the Plantation Household: Black and White Women of the Old South* (1988).

J. William Harris, *Plain Folk and Gentry in a Slave Society* (1985).

Frank Owsley, *Plain Folk in the South* (1949).

The Proslavery Argument

David L. Bailey, *Shadow on the Church: Southwestern Evangelical Religion and the Issue of Slavery, 1783–1860* (1985).

George M. Fredrickson, *The Black Image in the White Mind* (1971).

Eugene D. Genovese, *The Slaveholders' Dilemma: Freedom and Progress in Southern Conservative Thought, 1820–1860* (1992).

W. S. Jenkins, *Pro-Slavery Thought in the Old South* (1935).

Donald G. Mathews, *Religion in the Old South* (1977).

Mitchell Snay, *Gospel of Disunion: Religion and Separatism in the Antebellum South* (1993).

Where to Learn More

❖ **Appalachian Museum of Berea College, Berea, Kentucky.** This museum is an excellent source for understanding the lifestyles and material culture of the nonslaveholding farmers in the Appalachian highlands.

❖ **Museum of African-American Culture, Columbia, South Carolina.** This museum provides a wealth of material on the culture of nineteenth-century black people, including the free black population in the South.

❖ **Cottonlandia Museum, Greenwood, Mississippi.** The library and museum depict the history of cotton in the Mississippi Delta. Special collections include some Native American artifacts.

❖ **Jarrell Plantation, Juliette, Georgia.** This state historic site consists of a fifteen-building farm complex that conveys a good sense of the physical dimensions of a nineteenth-century Georgia plantation.

❖ **Meadow Farm Museum, Richmond, Virginia.** The archives and museum are especially strong on southern farm life in the mid-nineteenth century.

Reforming Antebellum Society, 1815–1850

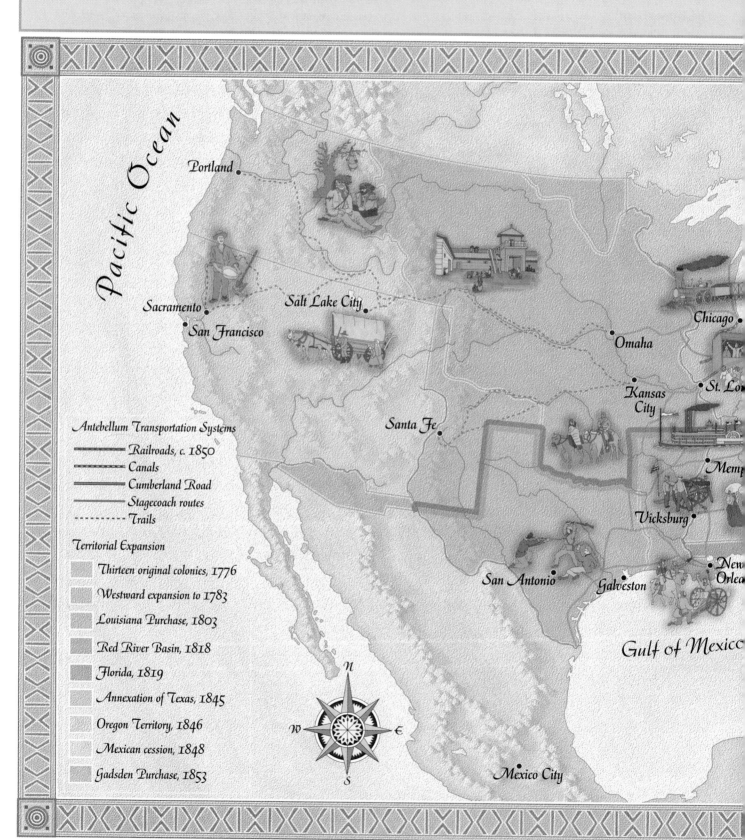

Pacific Ocean

Portland

Sacramento

San Francisco

Salt Lake City

Santa Fe

Omaha

Kansas City

Chicago

St. Lo

Memp

Vicksburg

San Antonio

Galveston

New Orlea

Gulf of Mexico

Mexico City

N S W E

Antebellum Transportation Systems

- Railroads, c. 1850
- Canals
- Cumberland Road
- Stagecoach routes
- Trails

Territorial Expansion

- Thirteen original colonies, 1776
- Westward expansion to 1783
- Louisiana Purchase, 1803
- Red River Basin, 1818
- Florida, 1819
- Annexation of Texas, 1845
- Oregon Territory, 1846
- Mexican cession, 1848
- Gadsden Purchase, 1853

14

Chapter Outline

Key Topics

- The rise of the reform movement after the War of 1812
- The spread of reform from moral to social issues in the 1820s
- The development of regimented institutions—penitentiaries, asylums, workhouses—for criminals, the poor, and the insane
- The growth of abolitionist agitation and sentiment in the North
- Women's crucial role in the reform movements and the rise of an organized women's rights movement

"Would to God this [Fourth of July] were truly—what it is not, though lying lips declare it to be—the JUBILEE OF FREEDOM! That Jubilee cannot come, so long as one slave is left to grind in his prison-house. It will come only when liberty is proclaimed throughout ALL the land, unto ALL the inhabitants thereof." The abolitionist William Lloyd Garrison issued this call for freeing the slaves in a speech on July 4, 1839. He had been instrumental in organizing an antislavery movement in the 1830s that branded slavery as a sin, an unconscionable blot on America as a Christian nation. The abolitionists demanded in the name of Christian morality and human rights that all Americans commit themselves to the immediate end of slavery.

Abolitionism was the most radical extension of the reform impulse after the War of 1812 that swept many Americans into organized movements for individual improvement and social betterment. This reform impulse was strongest in the North in areas where traditional social and economic relations were undergoing wrenching changes as a market revolution accelerated the spread of cities, factories, and commercialized farms. These were also the areas where the emotional fires of evangelical revivals burned the hottest.

The religious message of the Second Great Awakening provided a framework for responding to change. New within mainstream Protestantism was the belief that anyone who sought salvation could attain it, not just those whom God had predestined to be saved. Evangelicalism taught that in both the spiritual and secular realms, individuals were accountable for their own actions. Through Christian activism, individuals could strive toward moral perfectibility. Social evils, and the sinful consequences of change, could be cleansed if only good Christians would help others find the path of righteousness.

The first wave of reform after the War of 1812 focused on individual behavior, targeting drinking, gambling, sexual misconduct, and Sabbath-breaking. By the 1830s, a second phase of reform turned to institutional solutions for crime, poverty, and social delinquency, largely untouched by voluntary moral suasion. One group of reformers, the abolitionists, aimed to reshape the very structure of American society through their moral crusade to eliminate slavery.

Women, especially those from the evangelical middle class, were active in both these phases of reform. Gaining self-confidence and organizational experience from their activities, some began to question their subordinate place in public life. Abolitionism, more than any other reform movement, radicalized many women. Identifying with the plight of black people under slavery, female abolitionists drew parallels with their own lack of power in a male-dominated society. Coming primarily from an abolitionist background, women reformers founded a women's rights movement in the 1840s. They organized the Seneca Falls Convention of 1848, which called for extending the full rights and privileges of citizenship to women.

Women's demands that abolitionist societies treat them as equals split the abolitionist movement by 1840. Garrison supported women's rights, and abolitionists who opposed him formed an independent political party. These anti-Garrisonian abolitionists set out to win northern voters over to the antislavery stance. This was the first stage in the evolution of the politics of sectionalism that dominated national affairs in the 1850s.

Reform and Moral Order

American society was being transformed after 1815. Urbanization, industrialization, and westward migration accelerated in the generation after the War of 1812. Former restraints of family, church, and community that had once produced a sense of social order and public morality seemed to be breaking down. Religious leaders and wealthy businessmen in the East saw evidence of disorder and unchristian wickedness all around them in the more fluid, materialistic society that was emerging. In their eyes, infidelity flourished on the frontier, licentiousness was rampant in the cities, and the evils of drink were causing workers to forsake God and their families. Alarmed by what they perceived as a widespread

The second major structure from right in the illustration above is the Bible House, the headquarters of the American Bible Society on Nassau Street in New York City. The Bible House was the distribution point for hundreds of thousands of Bibles printed on the technologically most advanced steam-powered presses.

breakdown in moral authority, they sought to impose moral discipline on their fellow Americans.

These eastern elites, aided by their wives and daughters, created a network of voluntary, church-affiliated reform organizations known collectively as the **benevolent empire**. Revivals in the 1820s and 1830s then broadened the base of reform to include the newly evangelicalized middle class in northern cities and towns. From this class emerged the temperance crusade, the largest reform movement in pre–Civil War America.

The Benevolent Empire

For the Reverend Lyman Beecher, the American condition in 1814 presented "a scene of destitution and wretchedness." From his Presbyterian pulpit in Litchfield, Connecticut, and then in Boston, Beecher became the leader of a clerical drive to restore morality to America. Like other clergy with whom he created the benevolent empire, Beecher was driven by a profound fear of disorder.

The America these ministers valued was one of respectable churchgoers whose behavior conformed to Puritan and Federalist standards of freedom as defined and ordered by an educated clergy. Such a morally homogeneous America, feared Beecher, was being fragmented and corrupted by mass emigration to the unchurched West and by challenges to religious orthodoxy from populist sects. At risk was not only Beecher's vision of a Christian republic but also the stability of the Union itself. Beecher believed that only religion, as preached by "pious, intelligent, enterprising ministers through the nation," could provide the order that would preserve the Union and place it under "the moral government of God."

Evangelical businessmen in the seaboard cities backed Beecher's call to restore moral order. Worried by the increasing number of urban poor, wealthy merchants contributed vital financial support. From its origins in the Plan of Union between Congregationalists and Presbyterians in 1801, the network of reform associations grew to include the American Board of Commissioners for Foreign Missions (1810), the American Bible Society (1816), the American Sunday School Union (1824), the American Tract Society (1825), and the American Home Missionary Society (1826). Following British models, these moral agencies were cross-denominational. The constant proselytizing of the itinerant revivalists of the Second Great Awakening fed their growth and prepared the way for a national marketplace for spirituality that emerged in the 1820s.

The reform societies built on the Second Great Awakening's techniques of organization and communication. The key, as the revivalist Charles G. Finney explained, was to find the best measures to persuade the people to "vote in the Lord Jesus Christ as the governor of the Universe." Instead of relying on sporadic, individual efforts, the Christian reformers sent out speakers on regular schedules along prescribed routes. They developed organizations that maintained a constant pressure for reform. National and local boards of directors supervised the work of

Chronology

1817	American Colonization Society is founded.
1820s	Shaker colonies grow.
1825	Robert Owen begins his utopian experiment at New Harmony, Indiana.
1826	American Temperance Society launches its crusade.
1829	David Walker publishes Appeal to the Colored Citizens of the World.
1830	Joseph Smith founds the Church of Jesus Christ of Latter-day Saints.
1830–1831	Evangelical revivals are held in northern cities.
1831	William Lloyd Garrison begins publishing *The Liberator.*
1832	New England Anti-Slavery Society is founded.
1833	Slaves in the British Empire are emancipated.
	American Anti-Slavery Society is organized.
1834	New York Female Moral Reform Society is founded.
1836	Congress passes gag rule.
1837	Horace Mann begins campaign for school reform as secretary of the Massachusetts Board of Education.
	Antiabolitionist mob kills Elijah P. Lovejoy.
1838	Sarah Grimké publishes *Letters on the Equality of the Sexes and the Condition of Women.*
1840	Abolitionists split into Garrisonian and anti-Garrisonian societies.
	Political abolitionists launch the Liberty party.
1841	Brook Farm is established.
	Dorothea Dix begins her work to improve conditions for the mentally ill.
1846–1848	Mormons migrate to the West.
1847	John Humphrey Noyes establishes the Oneida Community.
1848	Seneca Falls Convention outlines a program for women's rights.

salaried managers, who inspired volunteers to combat sin among the unconverted.

Sooner even than the politicians, religious reformers grasped how technological advances in printing and papermaking enabled them to reach an increasingly literate mass audience. Steam presses and stereotype plates halved the cost of printing and dramatically increased its speed. The American Bible Society was the first to exploit this printing revolution. Between 1790 and 1830, the number of religious newspapers grew from fourteen to more than six hundred. By then, religious presses were churning out more than 1 million Bibles and 6 million tracts a year. These publications were mass-distributed by traveling agents and heavily promoted in national advertising campaigns. For the evangelicals, the printed word became the God-given means of spreading the gospel. As the *Christian Herald* editorialized in 1823, "Preaching of the gospel is a Divine institution—'printing' is no less so. . . . The PULPIT AND THE PRESS are inseparably connected."

While the largest and most nationally organized of the Protestant voluntary associations focused on missionary activity, especially on the western frontier and in the slums of eastern cities, a host of local societies concerned themselves more with stamping out individual vices. These societies of ministers and concerned laity were self-appointed moral watchdogs for their local communities. Their purpose, as summed up by a Massachusetts group, the Andover South Parish Society for the Reformation of Morals, was "to discountenance [discourage] immorality, particularly Sabbath-breaking, intemperance, and profanity, and to promote industry, order, piety, and good morals." These goals linked social and moral discipline in a way that appealed both to pious churchgoers concerned about godlessness and to profit-oriented businessmen eager to curb their workers' unruly behavior.

The reformers tried to influence the young through interdenominational Sunday schools. With volunteers drawn largely from the teenage daughters of evangelical businessmen, these schools combined elementary education with instruction in the Bible and Christian principles. The American Sunday School Union was both a coordinating agency for local efforts and a publishing house for books and periodicals. By 1832, nearly 10 percent of all American children aged five to fourteen were attending one of eight thousand Sunday schools.

The boldest expression of the drive to enhance Christian power was the **Sabbatarian movement**. Traditionally, Protestants had devoted Sunday to worship and Bible reading. But the accelerated pace of business activity by the 1820s, as well as the growth of popular forms of entertainment, such as theater, dancing, and music, intruded on the Sabbath. In 1828, evangelicals led by Lyman Beecher formed the General Union for Promoting the Observance of the Christian Sabbath.

The immediate goal of the General Union was the repeal of a law passed by Congress in 1810 directing post offices to deliver mail on Sunday, a law that to Christian reformers symbolized the moral degeneracy into which the republic had fallen. Its broader mission was to enforce local statutes that shut down business and leisure activities on Sundays. The Sabbatarians considered such statutes no less "necessary to the welfare of the state" than "laws against murder and polygamy." To their opponents, such laws were "repugnant to the rights of private property and irreconcilable with the free exercise of civil liberty."

The Sabbatarian crusade soon burned itself out, suffering a crippling setback in 1829 when the Democratic Congress rejected petitions demanding an end to Sunday mails and upheld the postal law of 1810. At the local level, the Sabbatarians outraged canal operators, hotel keepers, tavern owners, and other business owners threatened with the loss of their Sunday trade. Workingmen likewise resisted a moral crusade that threatened their one day a week of recreation. Southern evangelicals worried that the reformers' blend of moral and political activism might raise the sensitive issue of slavery. Even religious conservatives in New England felt that the Sabbath purists had gone too far. The most pressing religious needs, insisted these Calvinist ministers, were to enforce discipline within the churches and to safeguard theological doctrine.

The General Union disbanded in 1832, but it left an important legacy. It had developed techniques for converting the reform impulse into direct political action. In raising funds, training speakers, holding rallies, disseminating literature, lobbying for local Sunday regulations, and coordinating a petition to Congress, the Sabbatarians created an organizational model for other reformers to follow in mobilizing public opinion and influencing politicians. And in their failure, the Sabbatarians had revealed that heavy-handed attempts to force the "unconverted" to follow Christian standards of conduct were self-defeating. A new approach was needed that encouraged individuals to reform themselves without coercive controls. It soon emerged in the temperance movement.

The Temperance Movement

Temeperance—the drive against the consumption of alcohol—had the greatest immediate impact on the most people of any reform movement. Its success rested on what Lyman Beecher called "a new moral power." Dismayed by popular resistance to the coercive moralism of the first wave of Christian reform, evangelicals like the Reverend John Chester concluded in 1821 that "you cannot coerce a free people that are jealous to fastidiousness of their rights." Therefore, reform had to rest on persuasion, and it had to begin with the voluntary decision of individuals to free themselves from sin. The electrifying new teaching that anyone could gain salvation through self-discipline was the central message of the dramatic religious revivals that gathered up mass converts from the business and middle classes in the late 1820s and the 1830s. For evangelicals leading these revivals, the self-control to renounce alcohol became the key to creating a harmonious Christian society of self-regulating citizens.

The early temperance movement was led by former Federalists in New England who sought to substitute moral leadership for their declining political authority. Their impact was limited, and they aimed at little more than getting people to moderate their intake of alcohol. Temperance then shifted tone and organization in the mid-1820s. In 1826, evangelicals founded the **American Temperance Society** in Boston and took control of the movement. They were inspired by Beecher's *Six Sermons on Temperance*, a stirring call for voluntary associations dedicated to the belief that "the daily use of ardent spirits, in any form, or in any degree" was a sin. They now sought a radical change in American attitudes toward alcohol and its role in social life.

The temperance forces faced a daunting challenge. American consumption of alcohol increased after 1800, reaching an all-time high by 1830 of 7.1 gallons of pure alcohol per year for every American aged fourteen and over (about three times present-day levels). Alcoholic beverages were plentiful and cheaper than tea or coffee. "Liquor at that time," recalled a carpenter, "was used as commonly as the food we ate." An English observer in 1819 was shocked to discover that "you cannot go into hardly any man's house without being asked to drink wine, or spirits, even *in the morning.*"

Drinking was more than a casually accepted activity in pre-1830 America. It was a bond of male fellowship, forged wherever men gathered. Taverns easily outnumbered churches as centers of community sociability. In them men swapped stories and tested their manliness in games of chance, physical brawling, and blood sports like dogfights and cockfighting. Alcohol flowed freely when courts were in session and during election rallies and militia musters. It was used to pay both common laborers and the itinerant preachers on the early Methodist circuit. Masters and journeymen shared a drink when taking a break from work. No wedding, funeral, or meeting of friends was complete without alcohol. Indeed, not to offer a drink to guests was simply inhospitable.

For the temperance crusade to succeed, old forms of cultural and social behavior had to be abandoned and new ones learned. The reformers had to demonize alcohol and then banish it from the household and workplace. They had to finance a massive propaganda campaign and link it to an organization that could mobilize and energize thousands of people. They built such a mass movement by merging temperance into the network of churches and lay volunteers that the benevolent empire had developed and by adopting the techniques of revivals to win new converts.

Evangelical reformers denounced intemperance as the greatest sin of the land, worse even than slavery and the horrors of the African slave trade. In the words of the Reverend Herman Humphrey, it deprived "its victims of the means of grace. . . . If there is any evil which hardens the heart faster, or fills the mouth with 'cursing and bitterness' sooner, or quickens hatred [of] God and man into a more rapid and frightful maturity, I know not what it is." Alcohol represented all that was wrong in America—crime, poverty, insanity, broken families, boisterous politicking, Sabbath-breaking—and all that threatened the dawning of a Christian age of progress and prosperity.

This message, with its dark overtones of damnation but bright assurances of salvation through self-discipline, thundered from the pulpit and the public lectern. Thanks to the generous support of such wealthy benefactors as Stephen Van Rensselaer and Edward Delavan of New York, it was also broadcast in millions of tracts printed on the latest high-speed presses. This technologically advanced campaign of mass persuasion spread the

These scenes from a temperance tract depict the evils of alcohol.

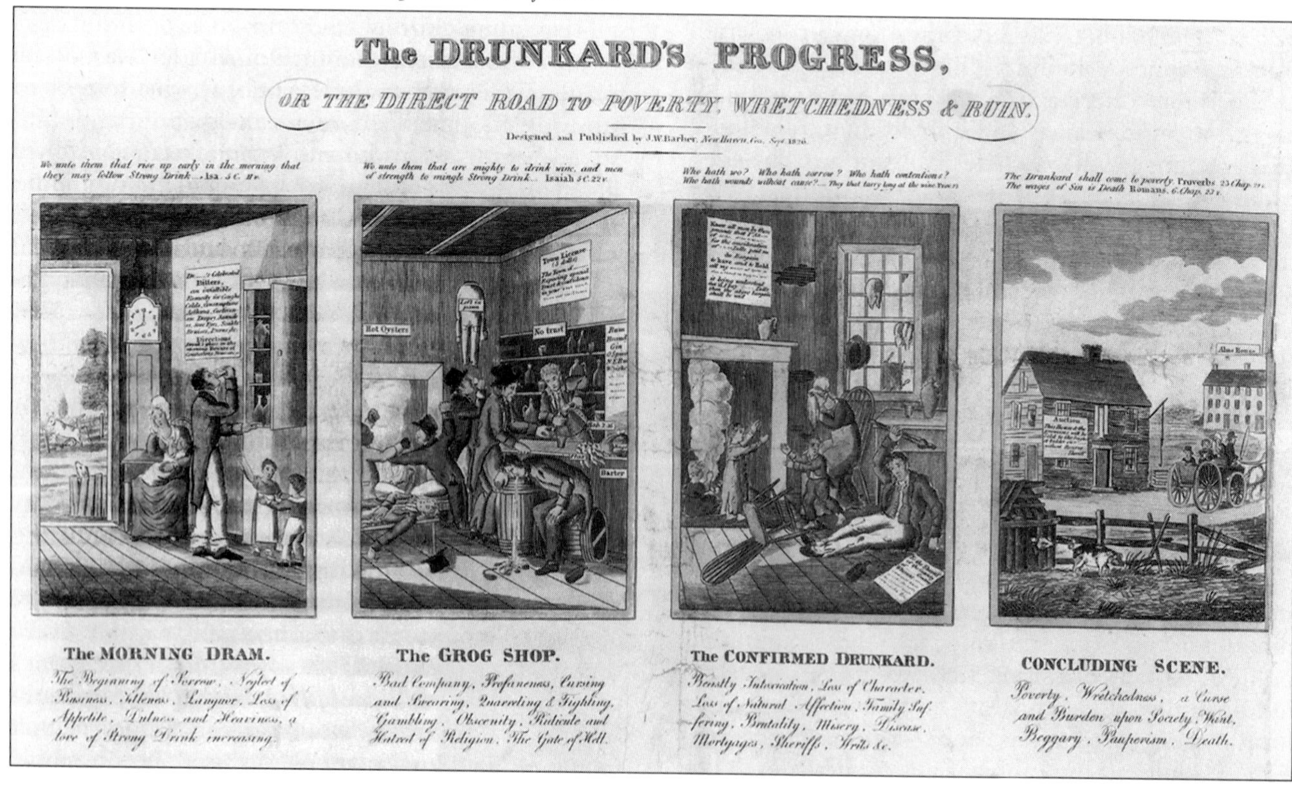

temperance message and prepared the way for the gathering in of converts. Like revivals, temperance rallies combined emotionally charged sermons with large, tearful prayer meetings to evoke guilt among sinners, who would then seek release by taking the pledge of abstinence.

The temperance crusade was stunningly successful. Within a decade, the American Temperance Society had more than five thousand local chapters and statewide affiliates. A million members had pledged abstinence by 1833. The movement, though national, was always strongest in the Northeast. New England and New York alone claimed 72 percent of all temperance societies in the mid-1830s. Most of the converts came from the upper and middle classes. Businessmen welcomed temperance as a model of self-discipline in their efforts to regiment factory work. Young, upwardly mobile professionals and petty entrepreneurs, worried about both salvation and success in the marketplace, learned in temperance how to be thrifty, self-controlled, and more respectable and creditworthy. As the *Temperance Recorder* put it, "The enterprise of this country is so great, and competition so eager in every branch of business . . ., that profit can only result from . . . *temperance.*"

Women, vulnerable to what they called "the slavery of intemperance," were indispensable to the movement. Lacking legal protection against abusive husbands who drank away the family resources, women had a compelling reason to join the crusade. They comprised 35 to 60 percent of the members in local temperance societies, but their greatest role was not in the public arena but at home. As the moral protectors of the family, they pressured their husbands to take the teetotaler's pledge and stick by it, raised sons to shun alcohol, and banished liquor from their homes. By the 1840s, temperance and middle-class domesticity had become synonymous.

Temperance made its first significant inroads among the working classes during the economic depression of 1839–1843. Joining together in what they called **Washington Temperance Societies**, small businessmen and artisans, many of them reformed drunkards, carried temperance into working-class districts. The Washingtonians gained a considerable following by insisting that workers could survive the depression only if they stopped drinking and adopted the temperance ethic of frugality and self-help. Their wives organized auxiliary societies and pledged to enforce sobriety and economic restraint at home.

In a telling measure of the temperance movement's success, per capita consumption of alcohol had fallen to less than two gallons by 1845. In 1851, Maine passed the first statewide prohibition law. Other northern states followed suit, but antitemperance coalitions soon overturned most of these laws outside New England. Nonetheless, alcohol consumption remained low. For temperance, at least, moral suasion proved able to change individual behavior.

Backlash against Benevolence

Many Americans were indifferent or hostile to the benevolent empire's do-gooding. Some of the harshest critics came out of the populist revivals of the early 1800s. Free-Will Baptists, Universalists, Disciples of Christ, and many Methodist sects spurned the entire program of the Christian reformers—its missions, Sabbath regulations, Sunday schools, tract societies, and vast network of well-financed local organizations. They considered such a program a conspiracy of orthodox Calvinists from old-line denominations to impose social and moral control on behalf of a religious and economic elite. The goal of the "orthodox party," warned the Universalist *Christian Intelligencer,* was the power of "governing the nation"; the societies they formed "are but so many strings . . ., the ultimate design of which is to draw them into power."

These fears of elite dominance sprang from more than resentment of the financial and organizational resources of the wealthier and more prestigious Presbyterians and Congregationalists, the mainstays of benevolent reform. They also reflected a profound mistrust of the emerging market society.

Evangelical reformers were drawn from the well-educated business and middle classes who were benefiting from economic change. The members of evangelical grassroots sects and the followers of itinerant preachers, in contrast, were drawn mostly from the unschooled poor who suffered from market forces beyond their control. Many were farmers forced by debt to move west or artisans and tradesmen displaced by new forms of factory production and new commercial outlets. Socially uprooted and economically stranded, they found a sense of community in their local churches and resisted control by wealthier, better-educated outsiders. Above all, they clung to beliefs that shored up the threatened authority of the father over his household.

The importance of women in evangelical reform challenged patriarchal authority. Middle-class evangelicalism in the Northeast was becoming feminized with the elevation of women to the status of moral guardians of the family and agents of benevolent reform outside the household. This new social role for women was especially threatening—indeed, galling—for men who were the causalities of the more competitive economy. Raised on farms where the father had been the unquestioned lawgiver and provider, these men attacked feminized evangelicalism for undermining their paternal authority, and they rejected the middle-class values of progress and human perfectibility that seemed to mock their own failure and lost economic independence. They found in Scripture an affirmation of patriarchal power for any man, no matter how poor or economically dependent.

The **Church of Jesus Christ of Latter-day Saints** (also known as the **Mormon Church**) represented the most enduring religious backlash of economically struggling men against the aggressive efforts of reforming middle-class evangelicals. Joseph Smith, who established the church in upstate New York in 1830, came from a New England farm family uprooted and impoverished by market speculations gone sour. He and his followers were alienated not only from the new market economy but also from what they saw as the religious and social anarchy around them. Most of the early converts to Mormonism were young men in their twenties who had not yet established themselves in northern rural society.

Based on Smith's divine revelations as set forth in *The Book of Mormon* (1830), their new faith offered them a sanctuary as a biblical people and a release from social and religious uncertainties. Like Smith, they had been confused, even angered, by the competing voices of revival ministers and the fragmenting of a father-centered rural world. They believed that the mainstream evangelical churches had corrupted Christ's original gospel and fallen under the sway of the haughty rich by identifying salvation with worldly success. "This generation abounds in ignorance, superstition, selfishness, and priestcraft," charged the Mormon John Whitmer; "for this generation is truly led by . . . hireling priests whose God is the substance of the world's goods."

Mormonism provided a defense of communal beliefs centered on male authority that was reassuring to rural families seeking refuge from individualism and economic dislocation. It assigned complete spiritual and secular authority to men. Where women often took the lead in evangelical reform, it was men who led their families into Mormonism, which taught that women could gain salvation only through subordination and obedience to their husbands.

To be a Mormon was to join a large extended family that was part of a shared enterprise. Men bonded their labor in a communal economy to benefit all the faithful. A law of tithing, instituted in 1841, required Mormons to give 10 percent of their property to the church upon conversion and 10 percent of their annual income thereafter. Driven by a strong sense of social obligation, the Mormons tried to replace selfish individualism with economic cooperation. By emphasizing the needs of the community as they strove to build their kingdom of God on earth, the Mormons forged the most successful alternative vision in antebellum America to the individualistic Christian republic of the benevolent reformers. (For the Mormons' role in the westward movement, see Chapter 12.)

Institutions and Social Improvement

Although evangelical Protestantism was its mainspring, antebellum reform also had its roots in the European Enlightenment. Enlightenment thinkers broke with Calvinist dogma by insisting that reason could lead to an understanding of the physical world and improve the human condition. Like the evangelicals inspired by religious optimism, other reformers drawing on Enlightenment doctrines of progress had unbounded faith in social improvement. They saw in America an unlimited potential to fashion a model republic of virtuous, intelligent citizens.

Studies published in the 1820s that documented increasing urban poverty, crime, and teenage delinquency created a sense of urgency for many reformers. They interpreted these studies as evidence of the failure of traditional institutions—family, community, religion—to shape American character. New public institutions that would provide the poor and the socially deviant with a morally wholesome environment free from corrupting influences were needed. Guided by the Enlightenment belief that environmental conditions shaped human character, reformers created a new system of public schooling in the North. They also prodded state legislatures to fund penitentiaries for criminals, asylums for the mentally ill, reformatories for the delinquent, and almshouses for the poor.

As reformers were implementing new institutional techniques for shaping individual character after 1820, a host of utopian communities sprang up. These communities also tapped into an impulse for human betterment, but they sought to accomplish it from outside society by the moral force of their example. They typically rejected either private property or families based on monogamous marriage. To replace these accepted social relations, they offered a communitarian life designed to help a person reach perfection. Most of these communities were

OVERVIEW

THE REFORM IMPULSE

Type	Objects of Reform	Means	Example	Origin
Moral reform	Individual failings such as drinking, sexual misconduct, Sabbath-breaking	Mass distribution of literature, speaker tours, lobbying	American Temperance Society	1810s–1820s
Institutional reform	Crime, poverty, delinquency	Penitentiaries, asylums, almshouses, state-supported schools	Massachusetts Board of Education	1830s
Utopian societies	Selfish materialism of society	New, highly structured communities	Shakers	1820s
Abolition	Slavery	Petition and mailing campaigns	American Anti-Slavery Society	1830s
Women's rights	Legal subordination of women	Lobbying, petition campaigns	Seneca Falls Convention	1840s

short-lived because the new forms of social and economic organization they promoted were far too radical for all but a handful of Americans.

School Reform

"An ignorant people always has been and always will be a degraded and oppressed people—they are always at the mercy of the corrupt and designing," cautioned Philadelphia school officials in their annual report for 1836. "If we fail by Education to awake—guide—confirm the moral energies of our people," they warned, "we are lost!" Such alarm reflected the urgency with which reformers approached public education. Secular revivalists as much as they were institutional innovators, the school reformers embarked on a crusade to save America from ignorance and vice.

Before the 1820s, schooling in America was an informal, haphazard affair that nonetheless met the needs of an overwhelmingly rural population for basic skills in reading, writing, and arithmetic. New England, largely because of the Puritans' insistence that the Bible should be accessible to all, pioneered publicly supported common schools in the seventeenth century, but even there school attendance and tax support were irregular until well into the nineteenth century. Private tutors and academies for the wealthy, a few charitable schools for the urban poor, and rural one-room schoolhouses open for a few months a year comprised formal education at the primary level. Still, except for isolated areas in the backcountry, literacy rates in America were among the highest in the Western world, and most parents supported schooling that was under local control and equipped their children for work in a rural society.

The first political demands for free tax-supported schools came from the Workingmen's movement in eastern cities in the 1820s. Decrying what the Philadelphia Working Men's Committee in 1830 described as "a monopoly of talent, which consigns the multitude to comparative ignorance, and secures the balance of knowledge on the side of the rich and the rulers," workers called for free public schooling. In pushing for what they called "equal republican education," they were also seeking to guarantee that all citizens, no matter how poor, could achieve meaningful liberty and equality. Their proposals, however, met stiff resistance from wealthier property holders who refused to be taxed to pay for the education of working-class children.

The breakthrough in school reform came in New England, where the disruptive forces of industrialization and urbanization were felt the earliest. Increasing economic inequality, growing numbers of Irish Catholic immigrants, and the emergence of a mass democracy based on nearly universal white male suffrage convinced reformers of the need for state-supported schools. Appealing to both the hopes and the fears of urban businessmen and the middle class, the reformers enlisted support for a system of "universal education" designed to restore civic virtue, train the masses in the responsibilities of political citizenship, and close the dangerous class divisions that were emerging.

In 1837, the Massachusetts legislature established the nation's first state board of education. The head of the board for the next twelve years was Horace Mann, a former Whig politician and temperance advocate who now tirelessly championed educational reform. Mann demanded that the state government assume centralized control over Massachusetts schools. He preached standardization and professionalism. All schools should have the same standards of compulsory attendance, strict discipline, common textbooks, professionally trained teachers, and graded, competitive classes of age-segregated students.

Once this system was in place, Mann promised that schools would become "the great equalizer of the conditions of men—the balance-wheel of the social machinery." Poverty would no longer threaten social disruption because the ignorant would have the knowledge to acquire property and wealth. Education, Mann stated, "does better than disarm the poor of their hostility against the rich; it prevents being poor." Trained in self-control and punctuality, youths would be able to take advantage of economic opportunities and become intelligent voters concerned with the rights of property. The children of Catholic immigrants, hapless victims of vice and superstition to most Protestants, would learn Protestant morality and thrift and become productive citizens. These children, wrote the Boston reformer Samuel Bates, must be "liberalized, Americanized."

For all its optimism, Mann's program faced stiff opposition in Massachusetts and elsewhere. Democrats in the Massachusetts legislature denounced it as "a system of centralization and of monopoly of power in a few hands, contrary in every respect, to the true spirit of our democratical institutions." The laboring poor, who depended for economic survival on the wages their children could earn, resisted compulsory attendance laws and a longer school year. Farmers fought to maintain local control over schooling and to block the higher taxes needed for a more comprehensive and professionalized system. The Catholic Church protested the thinly veiled attempts of the reformers to indoctrinate all students in the moral strictures of middle-class Protestantism. Failing to get a share of state revenues, Catholics followed the lead of Bishop John Hughes of New York City and, at great expense, began building their own parochial schools.

Mann and his allies nonetheless prevailed in most of the industrializing states. Ethnic and religious differences divided their opponents, and the educational reformers received strong support from the professional and business constituencies of the Whig party. Manufacturers hoped that the schools would turn out a more obedient and punctual labor force, and the more skilled and more prosperous workers saw in free public education a key to upward mobility for their children.

Most important for its political success, school reform appealed to the growing northern urban middle class. In the rhetoric of the reformers, state-supported education was to be the indispensable foundation for creating a harmonious society of individuals with the self-restraint necessary to improve themselves continually. Opposing both the "vicious passions" of the poor and the "idle luxury" of the rich, schools would instill the moral and economic discipline that the middle class deemed essential for a progressive and ordered society. Teaching morality and national pride was central to the educational curriculum, and from the popular McGuffey Readers used as a classroom text, students learned such lessons as "God gives a great deal of money to some persons, in order that they may assist those [who] are poor."

Out of the northern middle class also came the young female teachers who increasingly staffed elementary schools. As part of Mann's reforms for graded classes, school discipline was to rest less on corporal punishment and more on rewarding good behavior. Presumed by their nature to be more nurturing than men, women now had an entry into teaching, the first profession open to them. Besides, women could also be paid far less than men; school boards assumed they would accept low wages while waiting to be married.

Just over 50 percent of white children between five and nineteen years of age in the United States were enrolled in school in 1850—the highest percentage in the world at the time. School attendance varied by class and region. Working-class parents were quicker to pull their children out of school at an early age than higher-income middle-class parents. Planters continued to rely on private tutors or academies for their children, and southern farmers saw little need for public education. As a result, the slave states, especially in the Lower South, lagged behind the rest of the nation in public education.

Pencil/Watercolor, 13½ × 18⅞ in. M. and M. Karolik Collection of American Paintings, 1815–1865, Courtesy of Museum of Fine Arts, Boston.

The sewing table on the right in this painting, Girls' Evening School, *from about 1840, indicates how notions of women's domestic sphere limited the educational opportunities available for young women in the mid-nineteenth century. Still, women trained in female academies and seminaries increasingly displaced men as teachers in public schools.*

Prisons, Workhouses, and Asylums

The transformation of public education was part of a wider reform effort after 1820 that sought to improve society through specialized institutions of moral reformation. Up to this time, Americans had depended on voluntary efforts to cope with crime, poverty, and social deviance. Convinced that these efforts were now inadequate, reformers turned to public authorities to establish a host of new institutions—penitentiaries, workhouses, mental hospitals, orphanages, and reformatories—to deal with social problems.

All these public institutions reflected a new attitude toward conditions that had been regarded as inevitable and irreversible. Eighteenth-century Americans viewed crime, poverty, and deviance as a natural part of a divinely sanctioned order—and they expected good Christians to respond with charity and the wicked to suffer for their sinfulness. Virtually no one, for example, ever thought of rehabilitating criminals. Prisons were simple structures whose only purpose was to hold criminals before they were fined, whipped, mutilated, or executed in a public ritual that drew large crowds of festive onlookers. But the institutional reformers of the Jacksonian era believed that criminals, as well as the poor and other deviants, could be morally redeemed.

Having abandoned ideas of innate depravity, the reformers believed that people's environments shaped their character for good or evil. The Boston Children's Friend Society was devoted to the young, "whose plastic natures may be molded into images of perfect beauty, or . . . perfect repulsiveness." Samuel Gridley Howe, a prison reformer, proclaimed: "Thousands of convicts are made so in consequence of a faulty organization of society. . . . They are thrown upon society as a sacred charge; and that society is false to its trust, if it neglects any means for their reformation." The means of reformation, confidently asserted advocates for moral rehabilitation, were to be found in the properly ordered environment of new institutions. Here, discipline and moral character would be instilled in criminals and other deviants who lacked the self-control to resist the corrupting vices and temptations that pervaded society.

Reformers had particularly high expectations for the penitentiary systems pioneered in Pennsylvania and New York in the 1820s. As two French observers noted in the early 1830s, "The penitentiary system . . . to them seems the remedy for all the evils of society." Unlike earlier prisons, the penitentiaries were huge, imposing structures that isolated the prisoners from each other and the outside world. Inmates in the New York system worked in gangs during the day, but under the Pennsylvania plan, each prisoner was held in solitary confinement.

The penitentiaries were the institutional expression of the new philosophy of prisoner rehabilitation. No longer were criminals to be brutally punished or thrown together under inhumane conditions that perpetuated a cycle of moral depravity. Now, cut off from all corrupting influences, forced to learn that hard work teaches moral discipline, and uplifted by religious literature, criminals would be guided toward becoming law-abiding, productive citizens. For its proponents, the penitentiary became "a grand theatre, for the trial of all new plans in hygiene and education, in physical and moral reform."

The same philosophy of reform provided the rationale for asylums to house the poor and the insane. The number of transient poor and the size of urban slums increased as commercial capitalism uprooted farmers from the land and undercut the security of craft trades. Recognizing that families and local authorities could not cope with rising poverty, state governments in the Northeast began to intervene in the 1820s. Believing that the poor, much like criminals, had only themselves to blame, public officials and their evangelical allies prescribed a therapeutic regimen of discipline and physical labor to cure them of their moral defects. The structured setting for that regimen was the workhouse.

What the poor needed, reformers were convinced, was a wholesome environment to promote moral regeneration. The custodians of the workhouses banished drinking, gambling, and idleness. Under the workhouse rules in New York, officers could "rightly exercise . . . a measure of moral force upon the will of these persons, to induce them to do that which their own uncultivated understanding might oppose." They were to administer their duties "with strictness—severity." Their prime responsibility was to supervise the inmates in a tightly scheduled daily routine built around manual labor. Once purged of their laziness and filled with self-esteem as the result of work discipline, the poor would be released to become useful members of society.

Public insane asylums offered a similar regimen for the mentally ill. Reformers associated insanity with social disorder. A highly mobile, materialistic, competitive society, it was felt, presented people with too many choices, driving some insane. They could be cured, reformers predicted, in a highly structured and institutionally managed environment. Following the lead of New York and Massachusetts in the 1830s, twenty-eight states had established mental hospitals by 1860. These facilities set rigid rules and work assignments to teach patients how to order their lives.

Much of the public commitment to the mentally ill resulted from the crusading efforts of Dorothea Dix, a Massachusetts schoolteacher. In the early 1840s she discovered that the insane in her home state were dumped into jails and almshouses, where they suffered filthy, inhumane treatment. She found the insane "confined . . . in *cages, closets, cellars, stalls, pens! Chained, naked, beaten with rods,* and *lashed* into obedience." Horrified, Dix lobbied state legislatures across the nation for the next twenty years to improve treatment for the mentally ill.

The reformers acted out of humanitarian concerns, and they did provide social deviants with cleaner and safer living conditions. But their penitentiaries and asylums succeeded more in classifying and segregating their inmates than in reforming them. Freedom was too easily identified with tractability and submission to routine, and regimentation turned out not to be the best builder of character. What reformers praised as enlightened discipline, others denounced as a cruel new form of control. Witnessing the rigorous control of every movement of the isolated prisoners at the Eastern State Penitentiary in Philadelphia, English novelist Charles Dickens declared "this slow and daily tampering with the mysteries of the brain to be immeasurably worse than any torture of the body."

Institutionalization did not produce model citizens. After early successes, recovery rates in mental hospitals dropped. Penitentiaries, reformatories, and workhouses failed to eliminate or noticeably check poverty, crime, and vice. Refusing to question their basic premise that repressive institutions could promote individual responsibility, reformers abandoned their environmental explanations for deviance. By midcentury, they were defining deviants and dependents as permanent misfits with ingrained character defects. The asylums remained; but, stripped of their earlier optimism, they became little more than holding pens for the outcasts of society.

Utopian Alternatives

The quest for human perfectibility that underlay the reformers' early idealism found its ultimate expression in the utopian community movement in the antebellum North. Unlike the reformers, who aimed to improve the existing order by guiding individuals to greater self-discipline, the utopians sought perfection by withdrawing from society and its confining institutions. A radically new social order, not an improved old one, was their goal.

Though following different religious and secular philosophies, all the utopians wanted to fashion a more rational and personally satisfying alternative to the competitive materialism of antebellum America. Nearly all the communities sought to transform the organization and rewards of work, thus challenging the prevailing dogmas about private property. The more radical communities experimented with new roles for women by redefining family life and rejecting prevailing marriage and gender conventions.

The most successful utopian communities were religious sects whose reordering of both sexual and economic relations departed most sharply from middle-class norms. The largest of these sects were the **Shakers**. At their height in the 1830s, Shaker communities, mostly in the North, attracted some six thousand followers.

Named for the convulsive dancing that was part of their religious ceremonies, the Shakers traced their origins to the teachings of Ann Lee ("Mother Ann"). An illiterate English factory laborer anguished by the death of her four children, Lee had a revelation in 1770 that the Second Coming of Christ was to be fulfilled in her own womanly form, the embodiment of the female side of God. Fired by another vision in 1774, Lee led eight of her followers to America, where, after her death in 1784, her disciples established the first Shaker community in New Lebanon, New York.

According to Mother Ann, sexual passion and private property enslaved women as wives and mothers and enriched the wealthy at the expense of the poor. Shaker communities were thus organized around a doctrine of celibate **communism**. Members held all property in common, and the sexes worked and lived apart. Dancing during religious worship brought men and women together and provided an emotional release from enforced sexual denial. As an early Shaker leader explained, "There is evidently no labor which so fully absorbs all the faculties of soul and body, as real spiritual devotion and energetic exercise in sacred worship." Leadership rested with elders and eldresses, who exercised authority over their gender-defined spheres of community life. In worldly as well as spiritual terms, women enjoyed an equality in Shaker life that the outside world denied them. For this reason, twice as many women as men joined the Shakers.

Their rule of celibacy meant, of course, that the Shakers could propagate themselves only by recruiting new members. With fresh converts declining after 1850, they gradually dwindled. Viewed as eccentric outsiders by contemporaries, the Shakers today are best remembered for the beautiful simplicity of the furniture they made in their workshops.

John Humphrey Noyes founded another utopian community that offered women a liberating alternative to the burdens of monogamous marriage and constant childbearing. A graduate of Dartmouth who studied for the ministry at Yale, Noyes carried evangelical notions of perfectionism to their logical extreme. He preached that the millennium ushering in the Second Coming of Christ was already under way and that the converted could lead lives free from sin. Believing that marriage, the selfish "exclusive possession of one woman to one man," was the main barrier to perfection, he proposed instead "complex marriage," the mutual love of all the saved for each other. Despite the notoriety that swirled around this apparent call for free love and adultery, Noyes was not advocating the abandonment of sexual restraints. His ideal of physical love was sexual intercourse without male orgasm, and his goal was a religious society in which cooperative arrangements between men and women regulated child care and the distribution of property.

After he had been drummed out of the ministry for his radical teachings, Noyes established the **Oneida Community** in upstate New York in 1847. He

The clean, functional lines of Shaker furniture reflect the stress on order and usefulness in Shaker communities.

attracted over two hundred followers with his perfectionist vision of plural marriage, community nurseries, group discipline, and common ownership of property. The profits from the patent on an animal trap and the sale of products from its workshops gave the community a secure economic base, and it flourished for thirty years. Charged with adultery, Noyes fled to Canada in 1879. The Oneida Community, reorganized in 1881 as a joint-stock company in the United States and committed thereafter to conventional sexual mores, survived into the twentieth century.

In contrast with the Shaker and Oneida communities and a host of other experiments in religious perfectionism, secular variants of utopianism met with little success. Secular utopians aspired to perfect social relations through the rational design of planned communities. Bitter critics of the social evils of industrialization, they tried to construct models for a social order free from poverty, unemployment, and inequality. They envisioned cooperative communities that balanced agricultural and industrial pursuits in a mixed economy that recycled wealth to the laborers who produced it.

Despite their high expectations, nearly all the planned communities ran into financial difficulties and soon collapsed. The pattern was set by the first of the controversial socialist experiments, **New Harmony** in Indiana, the brainchild of the wealthy Scottish industrialist and philanthropist Robert Owen. A proponent of utopian **socialism**, Owen promised to create a new order where "the degrading and pernicious practices in which we are now trained, of buying cheap and selling dear, will be rendered unnecessary" and "union and co-operation will supersede individual interest." But within two years of its founding in 1825, New Harmony fell victim to inadequate financing and internal bickering. The economic misery of the depression of the 1840s revived interest in utopian ventures and helped popularize the ideas of Charles Fourier, a French utopian who proposed to restore dignity to labor and end poverty by dividing society into phalanxes, cooperative units of workers who lived communally. Scores of **Fourierist communities** were set up, but few survived into the 1850s.

About the only secular cooperative that gained lasting fame was **Brook Farm** in West Roxbury, Massachusetts (today part of Boston). Established in 1841, Brook Farm was a showcase for the transcendentalist philosophy of Ralph Waldo Emerson. A former Unitarian minister in Boston who turned to lecturing and writing after leaving the ministry, Emerson taught that intuition and emotion could grasp a truer ("transcendent") reality than the senses alone could. The Boston intellectuals drawn to Brook Farm in the 1840s saw it as a refuge from the pressures and coarseness of commercial society, a place where they could realize the Emersonian ideal of spontaneous creativity. Although disbanded after six years as an economic failure, Brook Farm inspired intellectuals such as Nathaniel Hawthorne, who briefly lived there. In turn, his writings and those of other writers influenced by **transcendentalism** flowed into the great renaissance of American literature in the mid-nineteenth century, an outpouring of work that grappled with Emersonian themes of individualism and the reshaping of the American character.

In an 1837 address at Harvard titled "The American Scholar," Emerson had called for a distinctly national literature devoted to the democratic possibilities of American life. "The literature of the poor, the feelings of the child, the philosophy of the street, the meaning of household life, are the topics of the time," he proclaimed. Writers soon responded to Emerson's call.

Walt Whitman, whose *Leaves of Grass* (1855) foreshadowed modern poetry in its use of free verse, shared Emerson's faith in the possibilities of individual fulfillment, and his poems celebrated the democratic variety of the American people. Henry David Thoreau, Emerson's friend and neighbor, embodied the transcendentalist fascination with nature and self-discovery by living in relative isolation for sixteen months at Walden Pond, near Concord, Massachusetts. His *Walden, or Life in the Woods* (1854), a reflection on self-reliance as a way to free oneself of the fetters and artificiality of "civilized society," became an American classic. "I went to the woods," he wrote, "because I wished to . . . confront only the essential facts of life, and see if I could not learn what it had to teach, and not, when I came to die, discover that I had not lived."

Hawthorne and Herman Melville, the greatest novelists of the American renaissance, did not share the optimism of Emerson, Whitman, and Thoreau in the democratic promise of unrestrained individualism. Both of these writers focused on evil and the human need for community. In *The Scarlet Letter* (1850) and *The House of the Seven Gables* (1851), Hawthorne probed themes of egoism and pride to reveal the dark side of the human soul. Melville's *Moby-Dick* (1851) depicted the consequences of a competitive individualism unchecked by a social conscience. In his relentless pursuit of the great white whale, Captain Ahab destroys himself and his crew.

Much of the appeal of utopian communities flowed from the same concern about the splintering and selfishness of antebellum society that animated Hawthorne and Melville. The works of these novelists have endured, but the utopian experiments, especially those without a strong, authoritarian leader or the cohesiveness of a disciplined religious vision, quickly collapsed. Promising economic security and social harmony to buttress a threatened sense of community, they failed to lure all but a few Americans from the acquisitiveness and competitive demands of the larger society.

Women's Role in Reform

Women played a central role in the major reform movements. They first entered reform through benevolent and missionary societies in the early 1800s. These women's organizations, whose members were predominately upper class, were concerned with the spiritual welfare of the poor and the widowed. Influenced by the Second Great Awakening, middle-class women turned to reform in the 1820s. Many of them staffed societies that continued the benevolent pattern of reliance on moral suasion and deference to the existing political and social order. Others, however, were more openly reformist.

A second phase of women's reform by the 1830s began to question the assumptions of a male-dominated society. Women founded or joined new organizations that took up the causes of prostitutes and slaves, previously shunned as outside the scope of respectable reform. These reformers were aggressive activists who boldly sought political support by lobbying and petitioning. They increasingly challenged the limited role American life allotted to women. Those most determined to demand fundamental change came from the abolitionist crusade.

Reform and Women's Sphere

The Cult of Domesticity that emerged in the commercializing Northeast after 1815 (see Chapter 11) promoted an idealized concept of "true womanhood" that limited women to the domestic sphere and reserved the public sphere for men. Ministers, male moralists, and many women writers redefined femininity to encompass the virtues of piety, purity, and submissiveness. These virtues made women naturally suited to a role in the home providing moral training and uplift for their families, a role all respectable women now aspired to.

The first phase of women's reform flowed from this domestic ideal. Assumptions about their unique moral qualities permitted and even encouraged women to assume the role of "social mother" by organizing on behalf of the orphaned and the widowed. Founded in 1797, the Society for the Relief of Poor Widows with Small Children in New York typified these early approaches to reform. The women in the society came from socially prominent families. Motivated by religious charity and social duty, they visited poor women and children, dispensed funds, and set up work programs. However, they limited their benevolence to the "deserving poor"—socially weak but morally strong people who had suffered personal misfortune. They screened out all who were thought to be unworthy.

The revivalist call in the 1820s for moral action inspired middle-class women to join voluntary female groups. They founded maternal associations, where they prayed and fasted for the moral strength to save the souls of their children. Other associations sponsored revivals, visited the poor, established Sunday schools, and distributed Bibles and religious tracts. These reformers widened the public role of women, but their efforts also reinforced cultural stereotypes of women as nurturing helpmates who deferred to males as the wielders of economic and political power.

A New Militancy

A second type of women's reform developed in the 1830s. Although most women still favored conservative reform—teaching Sunday school, doing missionary work among the poor, and administering charity—new, more confrontational organizations emerged. Women from the broad middle ranks of society now flocked to various moral reform and antislavery groups that aggressively pushed for an expanded female role in setting public policy.

Unlike their benevolent counterparts, the reformers in the 1830s challenged male prerogatives and moved beyond moral suasion. The crusade against prostitution exemplified the new militancy. Women seized leadership of the movement in 1834 with the founding of the New York Female Moral Reform Society. This was an exclusively female organization that replaced the New York Magdalen Society, a male-dominated group forced to disband when its first report scandalized the city fathers with its exposé of "kept women and ruined servant girls." Far from trying to spare men from embarrassment, the female reformers used their society to publicize the names of the male patrons at the city's brothels. Through the society's journal, *Advocate for Moral Reform,* they blamed prostitution on male greed—the low wages paid by male businessmen left some women no alternative—and licentiousness. They denounced lustful men for engaging in "a regular crusade against [our] sex."

In 1839, this attack on the sexual double standard became a national movement with the establishment of the **American Female Moral Reform**

Society. With 555 affiliates throughout the evangelical heartland of the North, this new national association shifted from moral pressure to legal sanctions. Female activists mounted a lobbying campaign that, unlike earlier efforts, bypassed prominent men and reached out to a mass audience for signatures. By the 1840s, such unprecedented political involvement enabled women to secure the first state laws criminalizing seduction and adultery.

Newer women's groups formed after 1830 that focused on poverty also developed a more radical critique of American society and its male leadership. The Boston Seamen's Aid Society, founded in 1833 by Sarah Josepha Hale, a widow with five children, soon rejected the benevolent tradition of distinguishing between the "respectable" and the "unworthy" poor. After opening workshops to train poor women as seamstresses and laundresses, Hale discovered that her efforts to guide them toward self-sufficiency could not counter the low wages and substandard housing that trapped them in poverty. She concluded in 1838 that "it is hardly possible for the hopeless poor to avoid being vicious." Even more shocking to the benevolent establishment and its financial backers in the business community, Hale attacked male employers for exploiting the poor. "Combinations of selfish men are formed to beat down the price of female labor," she wrote in her 1836 annual report, "and then . . . they call the diminished rate the market price."

The Appeal of Abolitionism

The rising concern of female reformers in the 1830s over the inequities of a male-controlled power structure and the injustices inflicted on women and children found its greatest expression in abolitionism. "From the beginning," noted the Boston abolitionist Lydia Maria Child in 1838, "women, by paying their money, have become members of anti-slavery societies and conventions in various free states." As Christian wives and mothers, they could identify with the plight of the black family under slavery. Abolitionist literature emphasized the anguish of families broken up by the slave trade and the sexual degradation of female slaves forced to submit to their owners' lust. The most powerful abolitionist depiction of slavery showed a chained female slave imploring, "Am I not a woman and a sister?" In a male-governed society in which husbands could abuse their wives with legal impunity and gain custody of the children after a divorce, such images of slavery spoke with special force to northern white women.

The black artist Patrick Reason made this engraving in 1835. White female abolitionists identified strongly with his image of the chained female slave.

Women established their own antislavery societies in the 1830s as auxiliaries to the national organization run and dominated by men. Initially, their gender-segregated role was limited to raising funds, circulating petitions, and visiting homes to gain converts. Their contributions as unpaid volunteers were indispensable in spreading the antislavery message. Often operating out of local churches, women were grassroots organizers of a massive petition campaign that the abolitionists launched in the mid-1830s. Women signed more than half of the antislavery memorials sent to Congress. "There would be but few abolition petitions if the ladies . . . would let us alone," complained a Mississippi congressman.

Most women accepted, or at least did not openly question, a restricted role within the antislavery movement. That role subordinated them to male power and limited their activities to those deemed proper for women. Some antislavery women, however, found in abolitionism a liberating message of individualism and equality that spoke to them as oppressed members of society. For these women, abolitionism was a bridge to feminism, a bold effort to make women the political and social equals of men.

Abolitionism and Women's Rights

Abolitionism emerged from the same religious impulse that energized reform throughout the North. Like other reformers, the abolitionists came predominantly from evangelical, middle-class families,

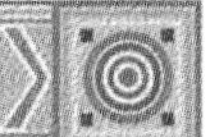

AMERICA'S JOURNEY

FROM THEN TO NOW

The Changing Nature of American Reform

The reform impulse that so animated American society before the Civil War seems largely absent today. Antebellum reformers were optimistic that they could identify and remedy social wrongs. That optimism has been replaced today with a more pessimistic approach to social problems.

This transformation has been a process of many stages. After the Civil War, issues of race, class, and sex began to divide the reform movement. With the defeat of the Confederacy and the ratification of the Thirteenth Amendment outlawing slavery, the abolitionist movement, so central to antebellum reform, appeared to have completed its mission. Some abolitionists continued to support missionary and educational efforts on behalf of freed slaves, but the movement's influence quickly waned. The ardent abolitionist Wendell Phillips became a champion of the rights of labor and an advocate of the eight-hour day, but few others followed his lead. The women's rights movement, meanwhile, divided until the 1890s in a bitter dispute over whether or not the struggle for women's equality should take a back seat to the struggle for black equality. The Women's Christian Temperance Union, organized in 1874, focused the reform efforts of most women on crusades to protect the family against the evils of alcohol and obscenity. Recoiling from the ghastly bloodshed of the Civil War, reformers in general abandoned visions of sweeping change to focus instead on themes of professionalism, organization, and discipline that they identified with the victory of the Union cause. They increasingly turned to state power to regulate private behavior and morality through laws criminalizing abortion, censoring art, suppressing information on contraceptives, and prohibiting gambling, vice, and narcotics.

A new wave of reform, known as the Progressive movement, emerged in the early twentieth century in response to decades of unregulated industrialization, urbanization, and immigration. Progressives, convinced of the need for a new ethic of social responsibility, sought to increase the role of government in the fight against social injustice with both state and federal laws to protect the rights of women, children, and industrial workers. Women reformers lobbied for a host of welfare measures designed to improve living conditions in slums and working conditions in factories. Progressives also sought, though with limited success, to regulate corporations on behalf of the public good. Concerned with social control as well as welfare, some progressives also supported prohibition, immigration restriction, and the disfranchisement of black voters. The legacy of Progressivism was thus mixed, but it did lay the foundation for the New Deal, a program of reforms created in response to the Great Depression of the 1930s. The architects of the New Deal sought to provide a safety net of social and economic benefits for all Americans.

Since the last great burst of social reform in the 1960s, Americans have grown increasingly cynical about the capacity of "big government" to improve their lives. Economic dislocations in the 1970s left many fearful and open to the conservative assertion that the private marketplace can best generate wealth, jobs, and financial security if it is unfettered by government regulation. Americans also increasingly view such social problems as poverty, violence, and inequality—which pricked the consciences of earlier reformers—as intractable and beyond remedy. Consequently, much of the New Deal's safety net has been shredded.

Today, the United States is easily the world's wealthiest and most powerful nation. But it also has the highest rate of child poverty (over 20 percent) and the highest proportion of its population in prison of any developed nation in the western world. If such disparities persist, chances are that they will eventually spark a revival of the reform tradition rooted in antebellum ideals of human justice and improvement.

The illustration on the masthead of this 1831 issue of The Liberator *condemns the relegation of slaves to the legal status of chattel, mere livestock to be bought and sold, no different from cattle or horses. Revulsion at the treatment of human beings as property was central to the abolitionist indictment of slavery.*

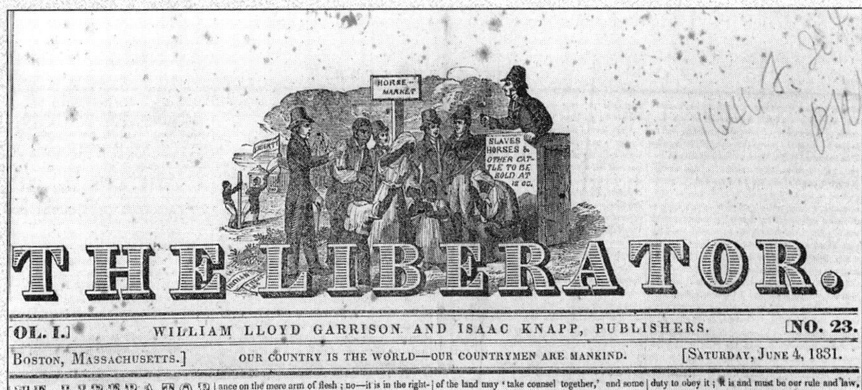

THE LIBERATOR.

OL. I.] WILLIAM LLOYD GARRISON AND ISAAC KNAPP, PUBLISHERS. [NO. 23.

BOSTON, MASSACHUSETTS.] OUR COUNTRY IS THE WORLD—OUR COUNTRYMEN ARE MANKIND. [SATURDAY, JUNE 4, 1831.

HE LIBERATOR IS PUBLISHED WEEKLY AT NO. 10, MERCHANTS' HALL.

M. LLOYD GARRISON, EDITOR.

TERMS.

Two Dollars per annum, payable in advance.

No subscription will be received for a short-

ance on the mere arm of flesh; no—it is in the righteousness of our cause, a knowledge of the attributes of Deity, combined with a consciousness of innocence under suffering, that have inspired us with a moral courage which no oppression shall shake, no fulminations overawe. Our limits will not permit us to expatiate, at this time, on the import of the terms, '*a system of measures—the sternest principles,*' &c. We would barely remark that the climax of

of the land may 'take counsel together,' and some of the professed ministers of Jesus may 'come into their secret,' but 'He that sitteth in the heavens shall laugh: the Lord shall have them in derision.' Fear not then, my colored countrymen, but press forward, with a laudable ambition, for all that heaven has intended for you and your children, remembering that the path of duty is the path of safety, and that 'righteousness' alone 'exalteth a nation.'

duty to obey it; it is and must be our rule and law, for we have no other. Thus if a heathen in offering sacrifice to his idol deities, or if St Paul in persecuting the Christians, were actuated by a principle of piety, and were obeying the dictates of their misguided consciences, how could they be criminal?

I have thus considered first what is perhaps the strongest and simplest case, that of a person who believes himself to be absolutely bound in duty to do

OVERVIEW

TYPES OF ANTISLAVERY REFORM

Type	Definition	Example
Gradualist	Accepts notions of black inferiority and attempts to end slavery gradually by purchasing the freedom of slaves and colonizing them in Africa	American Colonization Society
Immediatist	Calls for immediate steps to end slavery and denounces slavery and racial prejudice as moral sins	Abolitionists
Political Antislavery	Recognizes slavery in states where it exists but insists on keeping slavery out of the territories	Free-Soilers

particularly those of New England stock, and also like them were committed to a moral crusade that would free individual consciences and rid the nation of sin. What distinguished the abolitionists was their insistence that slavery was the great national sin, mocking American ideals of liberty and Christian morality.

Under the early leadership of William Lloyd Garrison, the abolitionist movement uncompromisingly attacked not only slaveholders but also all others whose moral apathy helped support slavery. After provoking a storm of protest in both North and South, the movement split in 1840. Crucial in this division was Garrison's support of women's rights. Most abolitionists broke with him and founded their own antislavery organization. Female abolitionists took the lead in organizing a separate women's rights movement.

The anti-Garrison abolitionists treated slavery as a political question that could be addressed through political means. Although this new approach diluted the moral intensity of the original abolitionist message, it enabled the abolitionists to begin mobilizing a constituency of voters that would soon push slavery to the center of national politics.

Rejecting Colonization

In the early nineteenth century, when slavery was expanding westward, almost all white Americans, regardless of class or region, shared a pervasive racism that inclined them against general emancipation and long shielded slavery from sustained attack. White people believed they could not live peacefully with large numbers of black people in a free republic. They feared emancipation would result in race war or the debasement of their presumed racial superiority through interbreeding. Only free black Northerners advocated slavery's immediate end. Organized antislavery activities among white people slackened once Congress prohibited the African slave trade in 1808, and most of it was confined to deeply religious farmers in the subsistence districts of the Upper South.

In 1817, antislavery reformers from North and South founded the **American Colonization Society**. Slaveholding politicians from the Upper South, notably Henry Clay, James Madison, and President James Monroe, were the leading organizers of the society, whose goal was to promote emancipation by sending freed black people to Africa. Gradual emancipation followed by the removal of black people from America was the only solution that white reformers could imagine for ridding the nation of slavery and avoiding a racial bloodbath. Their goal was to make America all free and all white.

Although the American Colonization Society clung to its program until the Civil War, it had no real chance of success. No form of emancipation, however gradual, could appeal to slave owners who could profit from the demand for their slaves in the Lower South. Moreover, the society could never afford to purchase the freedom of any significant number of slaves. Almost all the people it transported to Liberia, the West African colony it helped found, were already free. At the height of its popularity in the 1820s, the society sent only fourteen hundred colonists to Africa. During that same decade, the American slave population increased by 700,000.

Free African Americans were the harshest critics of colonization. They bitterly attacked the colonizers' central assumption that black people were unfit to live as free citizens in America. Typical of the colonizers' racist thinking was the claim by Henry Clay in 1827 that the "free coloured" were the "most vicious" of all Americans. "Contaminated themselves, they extend their vices to all around them, to the slaves and to the whites." The annual report of the American Colonization Society in 1824 approvingly quoted a New England minister who said of the free African American: "You cannot raise him from the abyss of his degradation. You may call him free . . . but you cannot bleach him into the enjoyment of freedom."

Confronted with this wall of racial prejudice, free black people condemned colonization as a scheme to prop up slavery by ridding the nation of the slaves' natural allies in the black population. Most free African Americans were native born, and they considered themselves as entitled as white Americans to the blessings of republican liberty. As a black petition in 1817 stated, banishment from America "would not only be cruel, but in direct violation of the principles, which have been the boast of this republic."

A black protest meeting in 1817 at Philadelphia's Bethel Church began black resistance to colonization. Organizing through their own churches in northern cities, free African Americans founded some fifty abolitionist societies, offered refuge to fugitive slaves, and launched the first African-American newspaper in 1827, ***Freedom's Journal.*** David Walker, a free black man who had moved from North Carolina to Massachusetts, was the Boston agent for the *Journal.* In 1829 he published his ***Appeal to the Colored Citizens of the World***, a searing indictment of white greed and hypocrisy that expressed the rage black people about their oppression. Rejecting colonization, Walker insisted that "America is more our country, than it is the whites'—we have enriched it with our *blood and tears,*" and he warned white Americans that "wo, wo, will be to you if we have to obtain our freedom by fighting."

Walker's *Appeal* shocked white America, especially after copies of it were found in the possession of slaves. As if in response to his call for revolutionary resistance, Nat Turner's Rebellion exploded in the summer of 1831 (see Chapter 13). The nation seemed on the brink of bloody slave uprisings. Both alarmed and inspired by the increased tempo of black militancy, a small group of antislavery white people abandoned all illusions about colonization and embarked on a radically new approach for eradicating slavery.

Abolitionism

The leading figure in early abolitionism was William Lloyd Garrison. A Massachusetts printer, Garrison found his life's cause in 1829 when he became coeditor of an antislavery newspaper in Baltimore. Before the year was out, Garrison was arrested and convicted of criminal libel for his editorials against a Massachusetts merchant engaged in the domestic slave trade. He spent seven weeks in jail before a wealthy New York City philanthropist paid his $100 fine. Recognizing that his lack of freedom in jail paled against that of the slave, Garrison emerged with an unquenchable hatred for slavery. Returning to Boston, he launched his own antislavery newspaper, ***The Liberator***, in 1831. A year later, he was instrumental in founding the New England Anti-Slavery Society.

Garrison instilled the antislavery movement with moral urgency. As militant as the free African Americans who comprised the bulk of the early subscribers to *The Liberator*, he thundered, "If we would not see our land deluged in blood, we must instantly burst asunder the shackles of the slaves." Repudiating the gradualism and racial prejudice of the colonizers, he committed abolitionism to the twin goals of immediatism—an immediate moral commitment to end slavery—and racial equality.

Only by striving toward these goals, he insisted, could white America ever hope to end slavery without massive violence. Slaveholders, as well as all other white people, had to realize that emancipation was a moral imperative and had to begin immediately. For black freedom to be meaningful and not the shameful mockery white prejudice had made it, white people had to accept black equality before the law as a goal that would hasten the end of slavery.

The demand of the abolitionists for the legal equality of black people was as unsettling to public opinion as their call for immediate, uncompensated emancipation. Most white people believed that only they could—or should—exercise the rights of freedom and equality. Whiteness had become a visible badge of one's fitness for republican citizenship, and discriminatory laws, aptly described by abolitionist Lydia Maria Child as "this legalized contempt of color," restricted the political and civil liberties of free African Americans in every state. Denied the vote outside New England, segregated in all public facilities, prohibited from moving into several western states, and excluded from most jobs save menial labor, free black people everywhere were walled off as an inferior caste (see "American Views: Appeal of a Female Abolitionist").

As he promised in the first issue of *The Liberator*, Garrison was harsh and uncompromising in denouncing slavery and advocating black rights. But without the organizational and financial resources of a national society, the message of the early Garrisonians rarely extended beyond free

American Views
Appeal of a Female Abolitionist

Lydia Maria Child's *Appeal*, published in Boston in 1833, was a landmark in abolitionist literature for both the thoroughness of its attack on slavery and its refutation of racist ideology and discrimination. This condemnation of racial prejudice was the most radical feature of abolitionist ideology. It directly challenged the deeply held beliefs and assumptions of nearly all white Americans, in the North as well as the South. Racism and slavery, as Child shows in this excerpt from her *Appeal*, fed off one another in the national curse of slavery.

- **How does Child argue that northern white people must bear some of the responsibility for perpetuating slavery?**
- **What arguments does Child make against racial discrimination in northern society?**
- **What did Child mean when she wrote that "the Americans are peculiarly responsible for the example they give"? Do you agree with her?**
- **How does Child deal with the charge that the abolitionists threatened the preservation of the Union?**

While we bestow our earnest disapprobation on the system of slavery, let us not flatter ourselves that we are in reality any better than our brethren of the South. Thanks to our soil and climate, and the early exhortions of the Quakers, the form of slavery does not exist among us; but the very spirit of the hateful and mischievous thing is here in all its strength. . . . Our prejudice against colored people is even more inveterate than it is at the South. The planter is often attached to his negroes, and lavishes caresses and kind words upon them, as he would on a favorite hound: but our cold-hearted, ignoble prejudice admits of no exception—no intermission.

The Southerners have long continued habit, apparent interest and dreaded danger, to palliate the wrong they do; but we stand without excuse. . . . If the free States wished to cherish the system of slavery forever, they could not take a more direct course than they now do. Those who are kind and liberal on all other subjects, unite with the selfish and the proud in their unrelenting efforts to keep the colored population in the lowest state of degradation; and the influence they unconsciously exert over children early infuses into their innocent minds the same strong feelings of contempt. . . .

black communities in the North. The success of British abolitionists in 1833 when gradual, compensated emancipation was enacted for Britain's West Indian colonies inspired white and black abolitionists to gather at Philadelphia in December 1833 and form the **American Anti-Slavery Society**. Sixty-two delegates attended the meeting, one-third of them Quakers. Most of the remainder were evangelical businessmen and ministers from other reform movements.

Arthur and Lewis Tappan, two wealthy merchants from New York City, provided financial backing, and Theodore Dwight Weld, a young evangelical minister, fused abolitionism with the moral passion of religious revivalism. Weld brought abolitionism to the West in 1834 with the revivals he preached at Lane Theological Seminary in Cincinnati. The "Lane rebels," students gathered by Weld, fanned out as itinerant agents to seek converts for abolitionism throughout the Yankee districts of the rural North. Weld's *American Slavery as It Is: Testimony of a Thousand Witnesses,* a massively documented indictment of slavery, became a best-seller in 1839. Abolitionist

The state of public feeling not only makes it difficult for the Africans to obtain information, but it prevents them from making profitable use of what knowledge they have. A colored man, however intelligent, is not allowed to pursue any business more lucrative than that of a barber, a shoe-black, or waiter. These, and all other employments, are truly respectable, whenever the duties connected with them are faithfully performed; but it is unjust that a man should, on account of his complexion, be prevented from performing more elevated uses in society. Every citizen ought to have a fair chance to try his fortune in any line of business, which he thinks he has ability to transact. Why should not colored men be employed in the manufactories of various kinds? If their ignorance is an objection, let them be enlightened, as speedily as possible. If their moral character is not sufficiently pure, remove the pressure of public scorn, and thus supply them with motives for being respectable. All this can be done. It merely requires an earnest wish to overcome a prejudice, which . . . is in fact opposed to the spirit of our religion, and contrary to the instinctive good feelings of our nature. . . . When the majority heartily desire a change, it is effected, be the difficulties what they may. The Americans are peculiarly responsible for the example they give; for in no other country does the unchecked voice of the people constitute the whole of government. . . .

The strongest and best reason that can be given for our supineness on the subject of slavery, is the fear of dissolving the Union. The Constitution of the United States demands our highest reverence. . . . But we must not forget that the Constitution provides for any change that may be required for the general good. The great machine is constructed with a safety valve, by which any rapidly increasing evil may be expelled whenever the people desire it.

If the Southern politicians are determined to make a Siamese question of this also—if they insist that the Union shall not exist without slavery—it can only be said that they join two things, which have no affinity with each other, and which cannot permanently exist together. —They chain the living and vigorous to the diseased and dying; and the former will assuredly perish in the infected neighborhood.

The universal introduction of free labor is the surest way to consolidate the Union, and enable us to live together in harmony and peace. If a history is ever written entitled "The Decay and Dissolution of the North American Republic," its author will distinctly trace our downfall to the existence of slavery among us.

Source: Lydia Maria Child, An Appeal in Favor of That Class of Americans Called Africans, *(original published 1833) ed. Carolyn L. Karcher (University of Massachusetts Press, 1996).*

women, notably Angelina Grimké, Weld's wife and the daughter of a South Carolina planter, contributed much of the research.

Revivalistic exhortations were just one of the techniques the abolitionists exploited to mobilize public opinion against slavery. They spread their message through rallies, paid lecturers, children's games and toys, and the printed word. Drawing on the experience of reformers in Bible and tract societies, the abolitionists harnessed steam printing to the cause of moral suasion. They distributed millions of antislavery tracts, and by the late 1830s, abolitionist sayings appeared on posters, emblems, song sheets, and even candy wrappers.

The abolitionists focused their energies on mass propaganda because they saw their role as social agitation. Their problem was white moral apathy regarding slavery. To break through that apathy and change public opinion, they described slavery in horrific terms of absolute moral and physical degradation to compel white people to identify as fellow human beings with the plight of the slave. This strategy convinced some to work for racial justice and the speedy end of slavery. By 1840, nearly

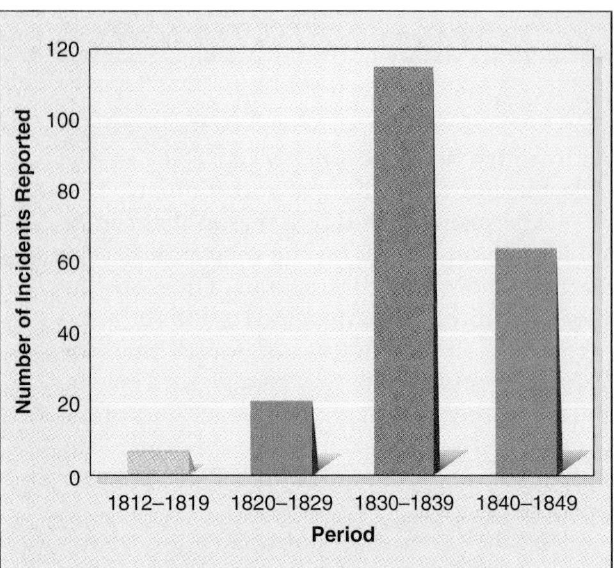

Figure 14-1 Mob Violence and the Abolitionists
Civil disturbances resulting in attacks on individuals or property increased sharply in the 1830s. The abolitionist campaign to flood the country with antislavery literature triggered much of this surge. Nearly half of the mob activity in the 1830s was directed against the abolitionists.

Data Source: *Leonard L. Richards,* "Gentlemen of Property and Standing": Anti-Abolitionist Mobs in Jacksonian America *(1970)*.

200,000 Northerners belonged to two thousand local affiliates of the American Anti-Slavery Society. Most white people, however, remained unmoved, and some violently opposed the abolitionists.

Antiabolitionist mobs in the North went on a rampage in the mid-1830s (see Figure 14-1). They disrupted antislavery meetings, beat and stoned speakers, destroyed printing presses, burned the homes of the wealthy benefactors of the movement, and vandalized free black neighborhoods in a wave of terror that drove black people from several northern cities. Although Garrison and Weld, the most frequent targets of mob violence, escaped with their lives, Elijah P. Lovejoy, an abolitionist editor in Illinois, was killed by a mob in 1837. By attacking slavery and appealing to women and children, the abolitionists had challenged the social and economic leadership of local elites, especially those with profitable ties to the slave economy of the South. These elites often incited the mobs, whose fury expressed the anxieties of semiskilled and common laborers that they might lose their jobs if freed slaves moved north.

There were few abolitionists to lynch in the South. The hostility to abolitionism there took the form of burning and censoring antislavery literature, offering rewards for the capture of leading abolitionists to stand trial for inciting slave revolts, and tightening up slave codes and the surveillance of free black people. Meanwhile, Democrats in Congress yielded to slaveholding interests in 1836 by passing a gag rule that automatically tabled antislavery petitions. Citing the fear of slave revolts in the South and the need for national harmony, Congress was now on record as infringing on the constitutional right of Americans to petition their representatives for the redress of grievances.

The hostility and violence abolitionism provoked convinced Garrison and some of his followers that American institutions and values were funda-

Elijah Lovejoy, an abolitionist editor, was shot dead in November 1837, when a mob in Alton, Illinois, burned the warehouse where he had stored his printing press.

mentally immoral. In 1838, Garrison helped found the New England Non-Resistant Society, dedicated to the belief that a complete moral regeneration, based on the renunciation of force in all human relationships, was necessary if America were ever to live up to its Christian and republican ideals. The Garrisonian nonresistants rejected all coercive authority, whether expressed in human bondage, clerical support of slavery, male dominance in the patriarchical family, the racial oppression of black people, or the police power of government. The logic of their stand as Christian **anarchists** drove them to denounce all formal political activities and even the legitimacy of the Union, based as it was on a pact with slaveholders.

Garrison's opponents within the abolitionist movement accused him of alienating the public by identifying the antislavery cause with radical attacks on traditional authority. Garrison's support for the growing demand of antislavery women to be treated as equals in the movement brought the factional bickering to a head in 1840 and split the American Anti-Slavery Society. In turn, the opposition of most male abolitionists to the public activities of their female counterparts provoked a militant faction of these women into founding their own movement to achieve equality in American society.

The Women's Rights Movement

The participation of thousands of women in antislavery and moral reform work led to the first organized movement for women's rights. Feminism grew out of abolitionism because of the parallels many women drew between the exploited lives of the slaves and their own subordinate status in northern society. Considered biologically inferior to men, women were denied the vote, deprived of property or control of any wages after marriage, and barred from most occupations and advanced education. "In striving to cut [the slave's] irons off, we found most surely that *we* were manacled *ourselves,*" argued Abby Kelley, a Quaker abolitionist.

The participation of women in abolitionism always aroused opposition, especially from conservative clergy convinced that women had no place in a movement that stirred fears of social instability and racial mixing. The issue came to a head in 1837 when Angelina and Sarah Grimké, South Carolinians born into the planter aristocracy, attracted large crowds of men and women to their antislavery lectures in New England. The Grimké sisters had moved north because of their opposition to slavery and had become Quakers. Coming from the planter class with firsthand experience of the evils of slavery, they attracted large audiences on the abolitionist lecture circuit. But by publicly lecturing to a "promiscuous" (mixed) audience of men and women, they defied restrictions on women's proper role and enraged the Congregational clergy of Massachusetts. Harshly criticized for their unwomanly behavior, the Grimkés publicly responded with an indictment of the male patriarchy and the shocking assertion that "men and women are *created equal!* They are both moral and accountable beings and whatever is right for man to do is right for woman." The clergy had unintentionally triggered the opening salvo in the campaign of women for equal citizenship.

Now more sensitive than ever to the injustice of their assigned role as men's submissive followers, antislavery women demanded an equal voice in the abolitionist movement. Despite strong opposition from many of his fellow male abolitionists, Garrison helped Abby Kelley win a seat on the business committee of the American Anti-Slavery Society at its convention in 1840. Her election ended any hope of healing the division between the Garrisonian and anti-Garrisonian abolitionists. The anti-Garrisonians walked out of the convention and formed a separate organization in 1840, the American and Foreign Anti-Slavery Society.

What was rapidly becoming known as the "woman question" also disrupted the 1840 World Anti-Slavery Convention in London. The refusal of the convention to seat the American female delegates was the final indignity that transformed the discontent of women into a self-conscious movement for women's equality. Two of the excluded delegates, Lucretia Mott and Elizabeth Cady Stanton, vowed to build an organization to "speak out for *oppressed* women."

Their work went slowly. The early feminists were overshadowed by the abolitionist crusade. Dependent on the abolitionists for most of their followers, the feminists were unable to do more than hold local meetings and sponsor occasional speaking tours. Many women sympathetic to the movement held back lest they be shunned in their communities. A minister's wife in Portsmouth, New Hampshire, spoke for many of these women when she wrote to a feminist friend, "There are but few here who think of women as anything more than slave or a plaything, and they think I am different from most women."

In 1848, Stanton and Mott were finally able to call the first national convention ever devoted to women's rights at Seneca Falls, in upstate New York. The **Seneca Falls Convention** issued the **Declaration of Sentiments**, a call for full female equality. Modeled directly on the Declaration of Independence, it identified male patriarchy as the source of women's oppression and demanded the vote for women as a

Elizabeth Cady Stanton addresses The Seneca Falls Convention with her demand for the full equality of women.

sacred and inalienable right of republican citizenship. This call for suffrage raised the prospect of women's self-determination as independent citizens.

The Seneca Falls agenda defined the goals of the women's movement for the rest of the century. The call for the vote met the stiffest opposition, and male legislators refused to budge. The feminists' few successes before the Civil War came in economic rights. By 1860, fourteen states had granted women greater control over their property and wages—most significantly under New York's Married Women's Property Act of 1860. Largely the result of the intense lobbying of Susan B. Anthony, the act established women's legal right to their own wage income and to sue fathers and husbands who tried to deprive them of their wages.

Despite these initial steps in dismantling legal and economic discrimination against women, the feminist movement did not attract broad support. Most women found in the doctrine of separate spheres a reassuring feminine identity that they could express either at home or in benevolent and reform societies. Within the reform movement as a whole, women's rights were always of minor concern. The abolitionists, those most likely to provide the feminists with a receptive audience, remained focused on emancipation.

Political Antislavery

Most abolitionists who had broken with Garrison in 1840 believed that emancipation could best be achieved by moving abolitionism into the mainstream of American politics. Political abolitionism had its roots in the petition campaign of the late 1830s. Congressional efforts to suppress the discussion of slavery backfired when John Quincy Adams, the former president who had become a Massachusetts congressman, resorted to an unending series of parliamentary ploys to get around the gag rule. A failure as president, Adams became a hero to antislavery Northerners, a champion of the constitutional right to petition Congress for redress of grievances. White Northerners who had shown no interest in abolitionism as a moral crusade for black people began to take a stand against slavery when the issue involved the civil liberties of white people and the overwhelming political power of the South. By the hundreds of thousands, they signed abolitionist petitions in 1837 and 1838 to protest the gag rule and block the admission of Texas as a slave state.

In 1840, anti-Garrison abolitionists tried to turn this new antislavery constituency into an independent political party. They formed the **Liberty party** and nominated James G. Birney, a former slaveholder converted by Weld to abolitionism, as their presidential candidate. Birney failed to draw even one percent of the total popular vote, but pockets of antislavery strength appeared in rural areas of the North dominated by evangelical New Englanders. These districts elected several antislavery congressmen, most of whom were Whigs forced by the Liberty party to take a stronger antislavery position to win the evangelical vote.

The Liberty party condemned racial discrimination in the North as well as slavery in the South and won the support of most black abolitionists. "To it," recalled Samuel Ward of New York, "I devoted my political activities; with it I lived my political life." Black abolitionists had organized state conventions in the North pressing black demands for political and civil equality. In 1843, a national African-American convention in Buffalo endorsed the Liberty party.

This political activism was part of a concerted effort by African Americans to assert leadership in an antislavery movement that rarely treated them as equals. Frederick Douglass was their most dynamic spokesman. After escaping from slavery in 1838, Douglass became a spellbinding lecturer for abolitionism and in 1845 published his classic autobiography, *Narrative of the Life of Frederick Douglass, an American Slave.* Increasingly dissatisfied with Garrison's Christian pacifism and his stand against political action, Douglass broke with Garrison in 1847 and founded a black abolitionist newspaper, ***The North Star.*** The break became irreparable in 1851 when Douglass publicly denied the Garrisonian position that the Constitution was a proslavery document. If properly interpreted, Douglass insisted, "the Constitution is a *glorious liberty document,*" and he called for a political war against slavery.

That war had started in the 1840s with the Liberty party. Although the party elected only one of its candidates to Congress (Gerrit Smith of New York), it kept slavery in the limelight of national politics. A small but vocal bloc of antislavery politicians, many of whom owed their election to the vote of Liberty men, emerged in Congress. Led by Joshua R. Giddings, an antislavery Whig from Ohio, these congressmen began to popularize the frightening concept of "the **Slave Power**"—a vast conspiracy of planters and their northern lackeys that had seized control of the federal government and was plotting to spread slavery and subvert any free institutions that opposed it. As proof, they cited the gag rule shutting off debate on slavery and the campaign of the Tyler administration to annex slaveholding Texas.

After escaping to freedom in 1838, Frederick Douglass became a commanding figure in the abolitionist movement. His speeches denouncing slavery were fiery and eloquent.

Frederick Douglass (1817?–1895). Oil on canvas, c. 1844, attr. to E. Hammond. The Granger Collection.

The notion of the Slave Power originated in abolitionist propaganda and was the basis of the Liberty party's appeal to northern white voters. Typical of that appeal were the claims of the Michigan Liberty party in 1843 that slavery was "not only a monstrous legalized system of wickedness . . . but an overwhelming political monopoly . . . which has thus tyrannically subverted the constitutional liberties of more than 12,000,000 of nominal American freemen." Moreover, the Liberty party blamed the depression of 1839–1843 on the "withering and impoverishing effect of slavery on the free States." Planters, it was charged, had reneged on their debts to northern creditors and manipulated federal policies on banking and tariffs to the advantage of the South.

The specter of the Slave Power made white liberties and not black bondage central to northern concerns about slavery. This redefined the evil of slavery to appeal to the self-interests of white Northerners who had rejected the moral appeals of the Garrisonians. People who had earlier been apathetic now began to view slavery as a threat to their rights of free speech and self-improvement through free labor untainted by the degrading competition of slave labor.

Birney again headed the Liberty party ticket in 1844, but he ran only marginally stronger than in 1840. Nonetheless, the image of the Slave Power predisposed many Northerners to see the expansionist program of the incoming Polk administration as part of a southern plot to secure more territory for slaveholders at the expense of northern farmers. Northern fears that free labor would be shut out of the new territories won in the Mexican War provided the rallying cry for the Free-Soil party of 1848, an antislavery party that foreshadowed the more powerful Republican party of the late 1850s.

Conclusion

The reform impulse driving social movements arose as a religious response to the unsettling pace of social and economic change in the decades after the War of 1812. From its beginnings in the benevolent societies of upper-class conservatives concerned with social order and the need to uphold traditional Protestant morality, the reform impulse spiraled outward into a growing critique of American institutions and values. The new evangelical Protestantism promised that human perfectibility was possible if individuals strove to free themselves from sin. Influenced by this promise, the northern middle class embraced reform causes that sought to improve human character. Temperance, the most widely accepted of these causes, changed American drinking habits and established sobriety as the cultural standard for respectable male behavior. Although benevolent efforts based on volunteerism and moral suasion continued, middle-class reform also turned to institutional solutions for what now were defined as the social problems of ignorance, crime, and poverty.

The most radical of the reform movements focused on women's equality and the elimination of slavery. Denied entry into politics and business, women found in reform work an outlet for their religious and social concerns and an affirmation of their sense of self. The women's rights movement emerged out of their involvement in reform, especially in abolitionism. By directly challenging the underlying values that kept women and African Americans in positions of social inferiority, feminism and abolitionism threatened to upset the structure of American society. Both movements triggered a backlash from the more conservative majority. This backlash prevented women from gaining legal and political equality, the major demand of the feminists, and convinced most abolitionists that they had to switch from moral agitation to political persuasion.

The most effective approach of the political abolitionists in widening the antislavery appeal was their charge that a Slave Power conspiracy threatened the freedoms of white Northerners. This image of an evil Slave Power would shape northern responses to the Mexican War and in the 1850s would mobilize Northerners against the expansion of slavery into the western territories.

Review Questions

1. What was the religious impulse behind the first wave of reform? What innovations in reaching a mass audience did the benevolent reformers pioneer?
2. How did reform movements begin to change by the 1830s? Why did temperance become the greatest and most successful reform?
3. What accounts for the initial optimism of the institutional reformers? What problems were they reacting to, and how did they expect to solve them?
4. What drew women into reform? Why did many of them feel a special affinity for abolitionism?
5. Why was abolitionism the most radical reform of all?
6. What was the Slave Power, and what role did it play in the growth of the political antislavery movement?

Recommended Reading

Robert H. Abzug, *Cosmos Crumbling: American Reform and the Religious Imagination* (1994). Provides a fresh look at antebellum reform by using the lives of individual reformers to show how Protestant Christianity inspired a rethinking of American values in a period of rapid economic change.

Whitney R. Cross, *The Burned-Over District: The Social and Intellectual History of Enthusiastic Religion in Western New York, 1800–1850* (1950). An enormously influential work that was the first to examine the linkages between the economic transformation of rural society and revivalistic waves of reform.

David Brion Davis, ed., *Antebellum American Culture* (1979). A superb collection of source materials covering all facets of the commitment to reform and institutional change.

Henry Mayer, *All on Fire: William Lloyd Garrison and the Abolition of Slavery* (1999). An excellent new biography of the individual who was arguably the predominant figure in the abolitionist movement.

Steven Mintz, *Moralists and Modernizers: America's Pre–Civil War Reformers* (1995). A recent survey that demonstrates how both the fears and possibilities of change influenced the impulse of reform.

James Brewer Stewart, *Holy Warriors: The Abolitionists and American Slavery* (1976). Provides the best overview of abolitionism and what distinguished it from the mainstream of the reform tradition.

Ronald A. Walters, *American Reformers, 1815–1860* (1978). Although superseded by later works in its discussion of the role of women, a book that remains the most insightful treatment of the entire range of antebellum reform.

Additional Sources

Reform and Moral Order

Charles I. Foster, *An Errand of Mercy: The Evangelical United Front* (1960).

Mark Y. Hanley, *Beyond a Christian Commonwealth: The Protestant Quarrel with the American Republic, 1830–1860* (1994).

Carroll Smith-Rosenberg, *Religion and the Rise of the American City* (1971).

W. J. Rorabaugh, *The Alcoholic Republic* (1979).

Kenneth H. Winn, *Exiles in a Land of Liberty: Mormons in America, 1830–1846* (1989).

Peter J. Wosh, *Spreading the Word: The Bible Business in Nineteenth-Century America* (1994).

Institutions and Social Improvement

Gerald N. Grob, *Mental Institutions in America: Social Policy to 1875* (1973).

Carl J. Guarneri, *The Utopian Alternative: Fourierism in Nineteenth-Century America* (1991).

Adam Jay Hirsch, *The Rise of the Penitentiary* (1992).

Carl F. Kaestle, *Pillars of the Republic: Common Schools and American Society, 1780–1860* (1983).

Michael B. Katz, *In the Shadow of the Poorhouse: A Social History of Welfare in America* (1986).

David Rothman, *The Discovery of the Asylum: Social Order and Disorder in the New Republic* (1971).

Stephen J. Stein, *The Shaker Experience in America* (1992).

Women's Role in Reform

Norma Basch, *In the Eyes of the Law: Women, Marriage, and Property in Nineteenth-Century New York* (1982).

Barbara I. Berg, *The Remembered Gate: Origins of American Feminism: The Woman and the City, 1800–1860* (1978).

Nancy F. Cott, *The Bonds of Womanhood: "Woman's Sphere" in New England, 1780–1835* (1977).

Ann Douglas, *The Feminization of American Culture* (1977).

Barbara Leslie Epstein, *The Politics of Domesticity: Women, Evangelicalism, and Temperance in Nineteenth-Century America* (1981).

Lori D. Ginzberg, *Women and the Work of Benevolence: Morality, Politics, and Class in the 19th-Century United States* (1990).

Nancy A. Hewitt, *Women's Activism and Social Change: Rochester, New York, 1822–1872* (1984).

Abolitionism and Women's Rights

Ellen Du Bois, *Feminism and Suffrage: The Emergence of an Independent Women's Movement, 1848–1869* (1978).

Nancy Isenberg, *Sex and Citizenship in Antebellum America* (1998).

Julie Roy Jeffrey, *The Great Silent Army of Abolitionism: Ordinary Women in the Antislavery Movement* (1998).

Leon F. Litwack, *North of Slavery: The Negro in the Free States, 1790–1860* (1961).

John R. McKivigan, *The War against Proslavery Religion: Abolitionism and the Northern Churches, 1830–1865* (1984).

Jane H. Pease and William H. Pease, *They Who Would Be Free: Blacks' Search for Freedom, 1830–1861* (1974).

C. Peter Ripley et al., eds., *Witness for Freedom: African-American Voices on Race, Slavery, and Emancipation* (1993).

Philip J. Staudenraus, *The African Colonization Movement, 1816–1865* (1961).

Where to Learn More

- **Black Freedom Trail, Boston, Massachusetts.** This walking trail includes many of the sites in antebellum Boston that figured prominently in the African-American struggle for freedom.
- **Historic New Harmony, New Harmony, Indiana.** The tours and museum holdings at this preserved site offer a glimpse into the communal living that Robert Owen tried to promote in his utopian plan.
- **Oberlin College Library, Oberlin, Ohio.** Oberlin was a hotbed of reform agitation, and the tracts, broadsides, photographs, and other memorabilia here are especially rich on the activities of white evangelicals and black abolitionists.
- **Shaker Museum at Sabbathday Lake, Poland Spring, Maine.** The exhibits, artifacts, and archives are a superb source for understanding the history and material culture of the Shakers and other radical religious sects.
- **Women's Rights Historical Park, Seneca Falls, New York.** The park provides an interpretive overview of the first women's rights convention and includes among its historical sites the restored home of Elizabeth Cady Stanton.

The Politics of Sectionalism, 1846–1861

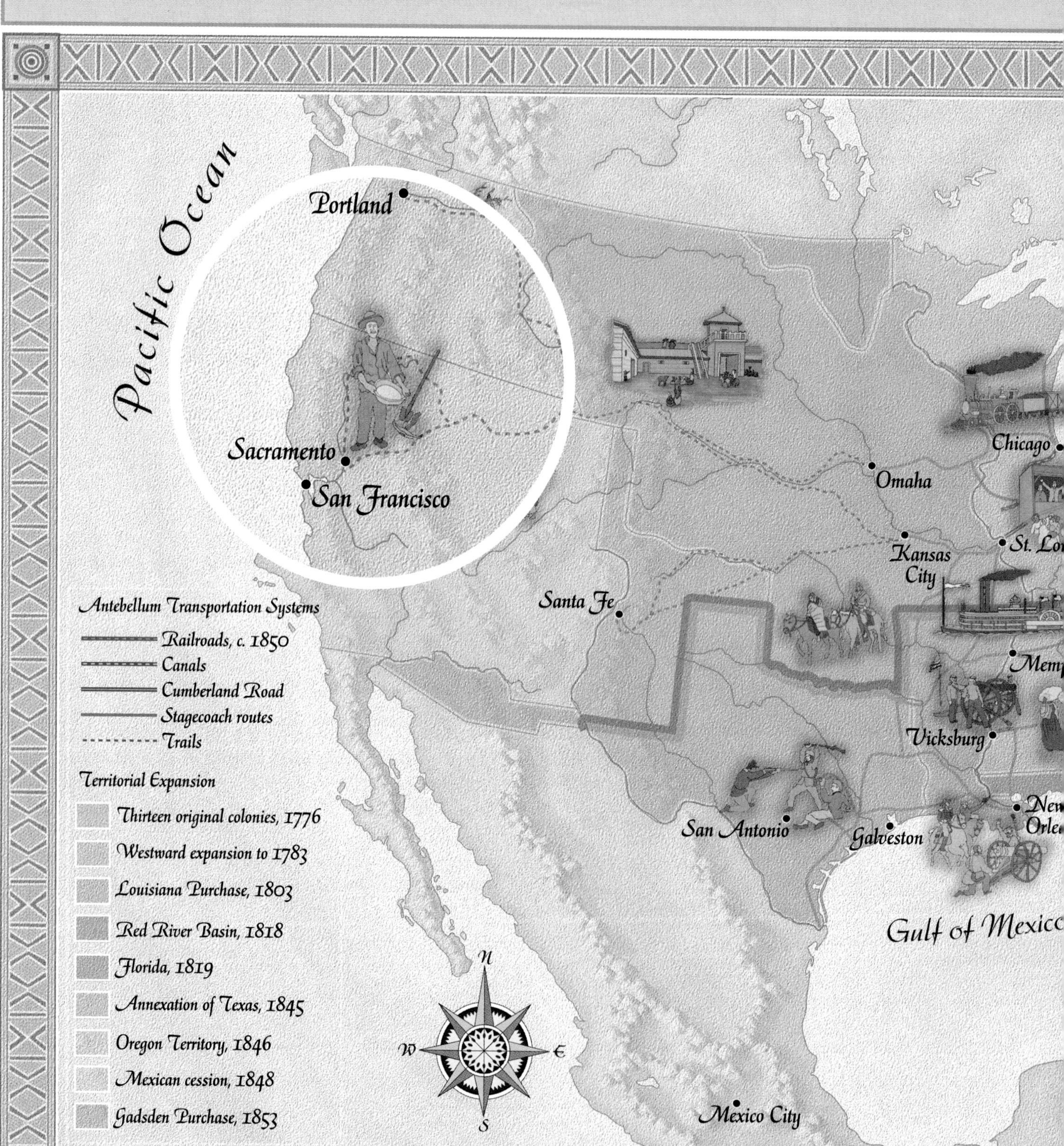

15

Chapter Outline

Key Topics

- ❖ The controversy over slavery in the territories and the attempt to resolve it
- ❖ The causes and consequences of political realignment in the 1850s
- ❖ Why Lincoln was elected in 1860
- ❖ The secession crisis and why the political system could not fix it

George N. Sanders, the American consul in London, held a dinner party on the eve of George Washington's birthday in 1854. He invited seven European revolutionaries who sat around the heavy oak table, lighted to brilliance by three ornate chandeliers and set with fine china, crystal, and silver. The party dined on Virginia ham and Carolina sweet potatoes and talked about America. The guests marveled at how the United States remained both united and committed to democracy—to rule by the consent of the governed.

Yet within six years, the United States would break apart. Northerners and Southerners accused each other of violating the country's commitment to democracy. And, unable to reconcile their differences through the political process, they went to war.

For Northerners, democracy meant majority rule and the supremacy of the central government over the states. For Southerners, it meant the protection of minority rights (although not, of course, the rights of black slaves) and the supremacy of the states over the central government. These conflicting views were as old as the Constitution itself. James Madison, the Virginian whose genius guided the Constitutional Convention of 1787, had foreseen the difficulty of balancing majority will and minority rights in a democratic society. He believed that the federal government would protect individual rights by balancing the competing claims of states and interest groups. The national government, he wrote, functioned as "a disinterested and dispassionate umpire in disputes between different passions and interests in the State." Suppose, however, that a numerical majority hostile to a geographic, religious, or ethnic minority won control of the national government. Who or what would protect the minority?

The collapse of governments was familiar to European revolutionaries. But the United States had seemed different. Americans had governed themselves for more than eighty years. They had spread across a continent and absorbed millions of newcomers from Europe without compromising their political traditions. They reveled in their diversity and bigness. Why did the nation fall apart?

In a word, slavery. The issue transformed the national government from umpire to advocate, from a force for harmonizing disparate interests to a pulpit for articulating basic differences. The nation, as Abraham Lincoln put it, could not exist half slave and half free.

But slavery had existed on the American continent since the colonial period. Colonists north and south held slaves. The Constitution acknowledged slavery's existence. And the Missouri Compromise of 1820 had apparently resolved for all time how slavery would be extended into the territories. Why did slavery become the issue that would not go away?

The answer lies in the events of the late 1840s and the 1850s. There were signs of slavery's explosive potential before then: the debate over the Missouri Compromise, the nullification controversy, and the battles in Congress over abolitionist mailings and petitions. But, by the late 1840s, the periodic clashes between northern and southern congressmen over issues relating to slavery were becoming more frequent and more difficult to resolve. In the coming years, several developments—including white Southerners' growing consciousness of themselves as a minority, the confounding of political issues and religious questions, and the rise of the Republican party—would aggravate sectional antagonism. But the flash point that first brought it to the fore was the issue of slavery in the territories acquired from Mexico.

Slavery in the Territories

Whatever its boundaries over the years, the West symbolized the hopes and dreams of white Americans. It was the region of fresh starts, of possibilities. To exclude slavery from the western territories was to exclude white Southerners from pursuing their vision of the American dream. Exclusion meant, an Alabamian declared, "that a free citizen of Massachusetts was a better man and entitled to more privileges than a free citizen of Alabama." Northern politicians disagreed. They argued that exclusion preserved

Miners in the California gold fields, 1849. Labor competition prompted white miners to favor the exclusion of black people—and slavery—from California.

equality—the equality of all white men and women to live and work without competition from slave labor or rule by despotic slaveholders. The issue of slavery in the territories became an issue of freedom for both sides.

From the late 1840s until 1861, northern and southern leaders attempted to fashion a solution to the problem of slavery in the territories. Four proposals dominated the debate:

- ❖ Outright exclusion
- ❖ Extension of the Missouri Compromise line to the Pacific
- ❖ Popular sovereignty—allowing the residents of a territory to decide the issue
- ❖ Protection of the property of slaveholders (meaning their right to own slaves) even if few lived in the territory

The first major debate on these proposals occurred during the early days of the Mexican War and culminated with the Compromise of 1850.

The Wilmot Proviso

In August 1846, David Wilmot, a Pennsylvania Democrat, offered an amendment to an appropriations bill for the Mexican War. The language of the **Wilmot Proviso** stipulated that "as an express and fundamental condition to the acquisition of any territory from the Republic of Mexico . . . neither slavery nor involuntary servitude shall ever exist in any part of said territory." This language deliberately reflected Thomas Jefferson's Northwest Ordinance of 1787, which prohibited slavery in the Old Northwest. The proviso did not apply to Texas, which had become a state before the war began.

Wilmot explained that he wanted only to preserve the territories for "the sons of toil, of my own race and own color." By thus linking the exclusion of slavery in the territories to freedom for white people, he hoped to generate support across the North regardless of party and even in some areas of the Upper South.

Linking freedom for white people to the exclusion of slaves infuriated Southerners. It implied that the mere proximity of slavery was degrading and that white Southerners were therefore a degraded people, unfit to join other Americans in the territories. Georgia's Whig senator, Robert Toombs, issued a warning that reflected the feelings of many Southerners: "I do not hesitate to avow before this House and the Country, and in the presence of the living God, that if, by your legislation, you seek to drive us from the territories of California and New Mexico, purchased by the common blood and treasure of the whole people . . . , thereby attempting to fix a national degradation upon half the states of this Confederacy, *I am for disunion.*"

Northern congressmen replied in kind. An Ohio Congressman declared, "We [the North] will establish a cordon of free states that shall surround you; and then we will light up the fires of liberty on every side until they melt your present chains and render all your people free." Now a majority in the House of Representatives (because the population of the northern states was greater than that of the southern states), Northern lawmakers passed more than fifty versions of the proviso between 1846 and 1850. In the Senate, however, where each state had equal representation, the proviso was consistently rejected and never became law.

The proviso debate sowed distrust and suspicion between Northerners and Southerners. Congress had divided along sectional lines before, but seldom had divisions become so personal. The leaders of both the Democratic and Whig parties, disturbed that the issue of slavery in the territories could so monopolize Congress and poison sectional relations, sought to defuse the issue as the presidential election of 1848 approached.

The Election of 1848

Both Democrats and Whigs wanted to avoid identification with either side of the Wilmot Proviso controversy, and they selected their presidential candidates

Chronology

1846 Wilmot Proviso is submitted to Congress but is defeated.

1848 Gold is discovered in California.

Whig party candidate Zachary Taylor defeats Democrat Lewis Cass and Free-Soiler Martin Van Buren for the presidency.

1850 California applies for statehood.

President Taylor dies; Vice President Millard Fillmore succeeds him.

Compromise of 1850 is passed.

1851 Harriet Beecher Stowe publishes *Uncle Tom's Cabin.*

1852 Democrat Franklin Pierce is elected president in a landslide over Whig candidate Winfield Scott.

Whig party disintegrates.

1853 National Black Convention called in Rochester, New York, to demand repeal of the Fugitive Slave Act.

1854 Ostend Manifesto is issued.

Kansas-Nebraska Act repeals the Missouri Compromise.

Know-Nothing and Republican parties are formed.

1855 Civil war erupts in "Bleeding Kansas."

William Walker attempts a takeover of Nicaragua.

1856 "Sack of Lawrence" occurs in Kansas; John Brown makes a retaliatory raid at Pottawatomie Creek.

Democratic congressman Preston Brooks of South Carolina canes Massachusetts senator Charles Sumner in the U.S. Senate.

Democrat James Buchanan is elected president over Republican John C. Frémont and American (Know-Nothing) candidate Millard Fillmore.

1857 Supreme Court issues *Dred Scott* decision.

Kansas territorial legislature passes the proslavery Lecompton Constitution.

Panic of 1857 begins.

1858 Senatorial candidates Abraham Lincoln and Stephen A. Douglas hold series of debates in Illinois.

1859 John Brown's Raid fails at Harpers Ferry, Virginia.

1860 Constitutional Union party forms.

Democratic party divides into northern and southern factions.

Republican candidate Abraham Lincoln is elected president over southern Democratic candidate John C. Breckinridge, northern Democratic candidate Stephen A. Douglas, and Constitutional Unionist candidate John Bell.

South Carolina secedes from the Union.

1861 The rest of the Lower South secedes from the Union.

Crittenden Plan and Tyler's Washington peace conference fail.

Jefferson Davis assumes presidency of the Confederate States of America.

Lincoln is inaugurated.

Fort Sumter is bombarded; Civil War begins.

Several Upper South states secede.

accordingly. The Democrats nominated Michigan senator Lewis Cass, a veteran party stalwart whose public career stretched back to the War of 1812. Cass understood the destructive potential of the slavery issue. In 1847, he suggested that territorial residents, not Congress, should decide slavery's fate. This solution, **popular sovereignty**, had a do-it-yourself charm: Keep the politicians out of it, and let the people decide. Cass was deliberately ambiguous, however, on when the people should decide. The timing was important. If residents could decide only when applying for statehood, slavery would be legal up to that point. The ambiguity aroused more fears than it allayed.

The Whigs were silent on the slavery issue. Reverting to their winning 1840 formula of nominating a war hero, they selected General Zachary Taylor of Mexican War fame. If the Whigs were looking for someone with no political record, they found him in the squat and craggy-faced Taylor. Taylor belonged to no party and had never voted. He was also inarticulate to the point of unintended humor. In one address, he intoned: "We are at peace with all of the world, and seek to maintain . . . amity with the rest of mankind." If one had to guess his views, his background provided some clues. He lived in Louisiana in the Lower South, he owned a one-hundred-slave plantation, and his now-deceased daughter had been married to Jefferson Davis, Mississippi's staunch proslavery senator.

Taylor's background disturbed many antislavery northern Whigs. These **Conscience Whigs** along with remnants of the old Liberty party and a scattering of northern Democrats bolted their parties and formed the **Free-Soil party**. The name reflected the party's vow to keep the territories free. Its slogan—"Free soil, free speech, free labor, free men"—was a catalog of white liberties that the South had allegedly violated over the previous decade.

The Free-Soilers' appeal centered on their opposition to slave labor in the territories. Free labor, they believed, could not compete with bonded labor. Slavery condemned the white worker to unemployment, poverty, and eventually a condition little better than slavery itself. The party nominated former president Martin Van Buren. The old New Yorker, who had remained active in state politics, had little hope of winning. But he could wield some influence if he were to prevent one of the major party candidates from winning a majority of electoral votes, thereby throwing the election into the House of Representatives.

Chalking up one out of seven northern votes, Van Buren ran strongly enough in eleven of the fifteen northern states to deny the winning candidate in those states a majority of the votes cast. But he could not overcome Taylor's strength in the South. Taylor was elected, giving the nation its first president from the Lower South.

The Compromise of 1850

Taylor had little time to savor his victory. Gold had been discovered in California in January 1848, and, in little more than a year, eighty thousand people, most of them from the North, had rushed into the territory. These **Forty-Niners**, as they were called, included free black people as well as slaves brought into the gold fields by their southern masters. Open hostility flared between white prospectors and their black competitors. When the territory's new residents began asking for statehood and drafted a state constitution, the document contained no provision for slavery. The constitution reflected antiblack rather than antislavery sentiment. Keeping California white shielded residents against social and economic interaction with black people. "Free" in the context of territorial politics became a synonym for "whites only."

If Congress accepted the residents' request for statehood, California would enter the Union as a free state. The Union at the time consisted of fifteen free states and fifteen slave states. The admission of California would tip the balance and give free states a majority in the Senate. California, with its rapidly growing population, would also add to the sixty-one-vote majority the North enjoyed in the House of Representatives. New Mexico (which then included most of present-day New Mexico, Arizona, small parts of Nevada, and Colorado) appeared poised to follow suit and enter the Union as the seventeenth free state. Southerners saw their political power slipping away. Northern leaders saw an opportunity to stop the extension of slavery and reduce southern influence in the federal government.

When Congress confronted the issue of California statehood in December 1849, partisans on both sides began marshaling forces for what promised to be a long and bitter struggle. Because nine Free-Soil candidates had won seats in the House of Representatives, neither Whigs nor Democrats held a majority there. South Carolina senator John C. Calhoun understood that only a politically unified South could protect its interests. He urged southern congressmen to ignore party ties and unite behind a plan he proposed to gain federal protection for slavery in the territories. Most southern Whigs ignored Calhoun and waited to hear from President Taylor before abandoning him and their party.

No one, at first, knew where Taylor stood. Although a political novice, the president was not stupid. Recognizing his lack of political experience, he selected Whig senator William H. Seward of New York as his adviser. Seward, a committed antislavery man, was one of the most hated politicians in the South; Taylor, a slaveholder from Louisiana, was distrusted by many northern members of his party. This odd match provided the first insight into the president's thinking on California.

He supported, it turned out, a version of popular sovereignty and favored allowing California and the other territories acquired from Mexico to decide the slavery issue for themselves. Under normal circumstances, the residents of a new territory organized a territorial government under the direction of Congress. When the territory's population approached thirty thousand or so, residents could draft a constitution and petition Congress for statehood. California already easily exceeded the population threshold. Taylor proposed bypassing the territorial stage—and congressional involvement in it—and having California and New Mexico admitted as states directly. (Before his inauguration in March 1849, he had already privately encouraged people in both territories to write state constitutions and to request admission.) The result would be to bring both into the Union as free states.

Although Seward no doubt encouraged him in it, Taylor's position was his own. The president was a nationalist and a strong believer in Manifest Destiny. He did not oppose slavery, but he abhorred the slavery issue because it threatened his vision of a continental empire. He was thus willing to forgo the extension of slavery into the territories. Southerners were certain to object strongly. But the president had a chilling message for them: "Whatever dangers may threaten [the Union] I shall stand by it and maintain it in its integrity."

Southerners resisted Taylor's plan, and Congress deadlocked on the territorial issue. Henry Clay then stepped forward with his last great compromise. To break the impasse, Clay urged that Congress should take four steps:

- ❖ Admit California as a free state, as its residents clearly preferred
- ❖ Allow the residents of the New Mexico and Utah territories to decide the slavery issue for themselves too
- ❖ End the slave trade in the District of Columbia
- ❖ Pass a new fugitive slave law to enforce the constitutional provision stating that a person "held to Service or Labor in one state . . . escaping into another . . . shall be delivered upon Claim of the party to whom such Service or Labor may be due."

Clay's proposal provoked a historic Senate debate that began in February 1850, featuring America's three most prominent statesmen—Clay, Calhoun, and Daniel Webster—together for the last time. The emaciated Calhoun, who would be dead in two months, had to be carried into the Senate chamber. Too weak to read his remarks, he passed them to Virginia senator James M. Mason. Calhoun argued that the compromise did not resolve the slavery issue to the South's satisfaction, and he proposed to give Southerners in Congress the right to veto legislation in Congress as a way to safeguard their minority rights. Webster stood up to support the compromise, at deep political peril to himself. His Massachusetts constituents detested the fugitive slave provision, which gave southern slaveholders the right to "invade" northern states to reclaim escaped slaves. Webster declared that he came to the debate "not as a Massachusetts man, nor as a Northern man, but as an American." He would swallow the fugitive slave law to save the Union.

After tumultuous deliberation that lasted into the summer of 1850, the Senate rejected the compromise. Calhoun had died at the end of March 1850, even before the debate ended. The seventy-three-year-old Clay, exhausted, left Washington to recover his health. He would die less than two years later. Webster, estranged from fellow northern Whigs, left the Senate and went to his grave a few months after Clay.

President Taylor, who had vowed to veto any compromise, died unexpectedly of a stomach ailment after overindulging in cherries and milk in the hot sun at a July 4 celebration in Washington. Vice President Millard Fillmore, a pro-Clay New Yorker, assumed the presidency after Taylor's death. Compared with Taylor, who stormed around the White House daring Southerners to attempt secession, Fillmore was a back-room man, quiet, at home with the cigar-and-brandy crowd, and effective with the deal. Fillmore let it be known that he favored Clay's package and would sign it if passed.

Although the Senate had rejected the compromise, Illinois senator Stephen A. Douglas kept it alive. A small man with a large head that gave him a mushroomlike appearance, Douglas epitomized the promise of American life for men of his generation. A native Vermonter, he migrated first to New York, then to Illinois as a teenager; read law; and developed a voracious appetite for politics. By the age of twenty-eight, he had already served as state legislator, chairman of the state Democratic party, and judge of the state supreme court. He envisioned an urban, industrial West linked to the East by a vast railroad network eventually extending to the Pacific. Above all, Douglas professed an unbending nationalism. To him, according to a biographer, "the Union was sacred, the symbol of all human progress." After his election to Congress in 1842, the "Little Giant," as his constituents affectionately called him, developed a reputation as an astute parliamentarian and a tenacious debater.

Like Webster, Douglas feared for the Union if the compromise failed. Realizing that it would never pass as a package, he proposed to break it up into its components and hold a separate vote on each. With a handful of senators voting for all parts, and with different sectional blocs supporting one provision or another, Douglas engineered a majority for the compromise, and Fillmore signed it.

The **Compromise of 1850** (see Map 15–1) was not a compromise in the sense of opposing sides consenting to certain terms desired by the other. The North gained California but would have done so in any case. Southern leaders looked to the West and saw no slave territories awaiting statehood. Their future in the Union appeared to be one of numerical and economic decline, and the survival of their institutions seemed doubtful. They gained the **Fugitive Slave Act**, which reinforced their right to seize and return to bondage slaves who had fled to free terri-

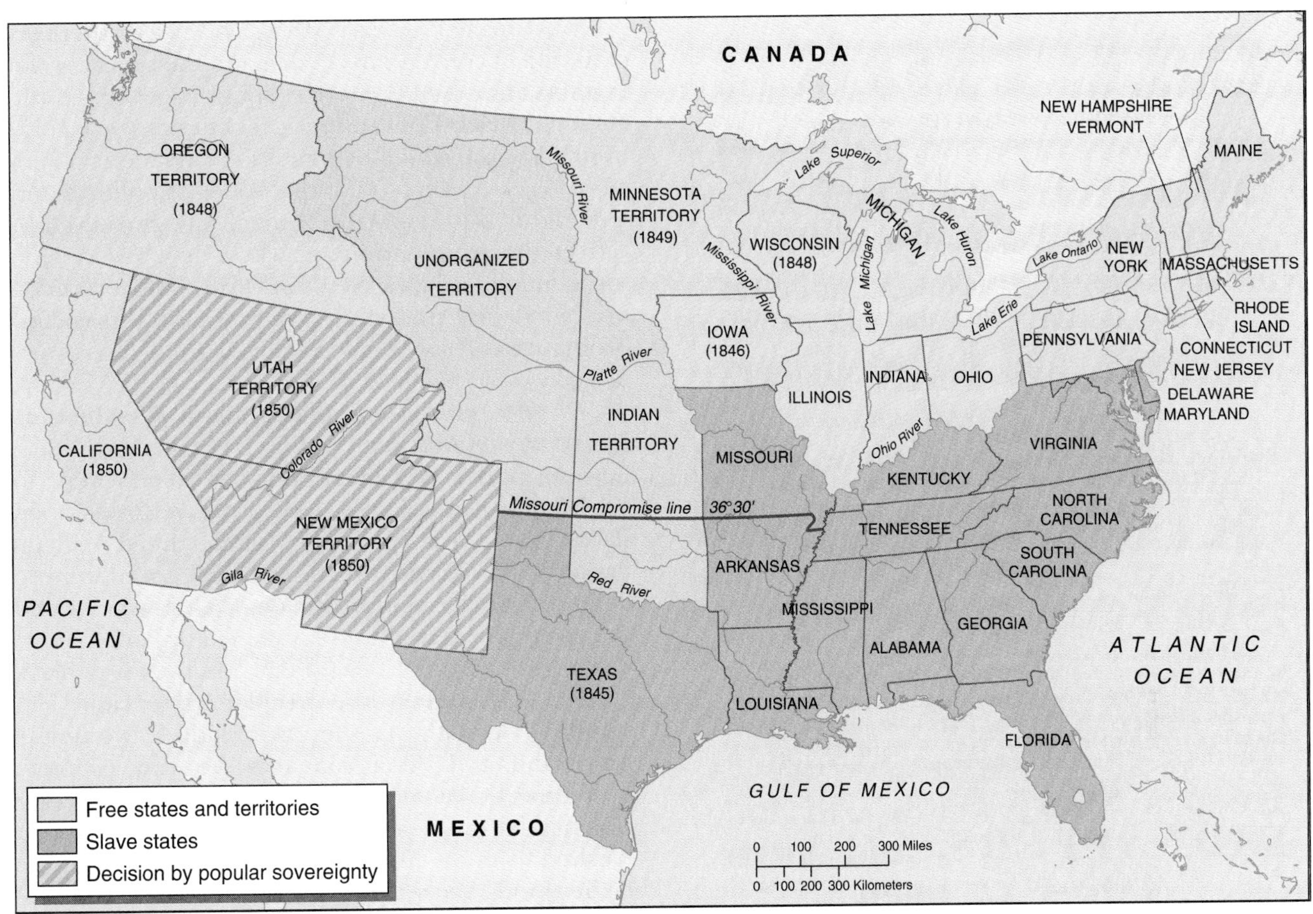

Map 15-1 The Compromise of 1850
Given the unlikely prospect that any of the western territories would opt for slavery, the compromise sealed the South's minority status in the Union.

tory, but it was slight consolation. One Lower South senator termed it "useless." Because most slaves who escaped to the North did so from neighboring slave states, the law affected mainly the states of the Upper South. Few slave owners from the Lower South would bear the expense and uncertainty of chasing an escaped slave into free territory. And the North's hostile reception to the law made Southerners doubt their commitment to the compromise.

Response to the Fugitive Slave Act

The Fugitive Slave Act was ready-made for abolitionist propaganda mills and heartrending stories. A few months after Congress passed it, a Kentucky slaveholder visited Madison, Indiana, and snatched a black man from his wife and children, claiming that the man had escaped nineteen years earlier. Black people living in northern communities feared capture, and some escaped across the Canadian border. Several northern cities and states vowed resistance, but except for a few publicized cases, northern authorities typically cooperated with southern slave owners to help them retrieve their runaway property. The effect of the act on public opinion, however, was to polarize North and South even further.

The strongest reaction to the act was in the black communities of the urban North. Previously, black abolitionists in the North had focused on freeing slaves in the South. The Fugitive Slave Act brought the danger of slavery much closer to home. No black person was safe under the new law. Mistaken identity, the support of federal courts for slaveholders' claims, and the presence of informants made reenslavement a real possibility. The lives that 400,000 black Northerners had constructed, often with great difficulty, appeared suddenly uncertain.

Black Northerners formed associations to protect each other and repel—violently, if necessary—any attempt to capture and reenslave them. Boston's black leaders created the League of Freedom. Black Chicagoans organized the Liberty Association, with teams assigned to "patrol the city, spying for possible

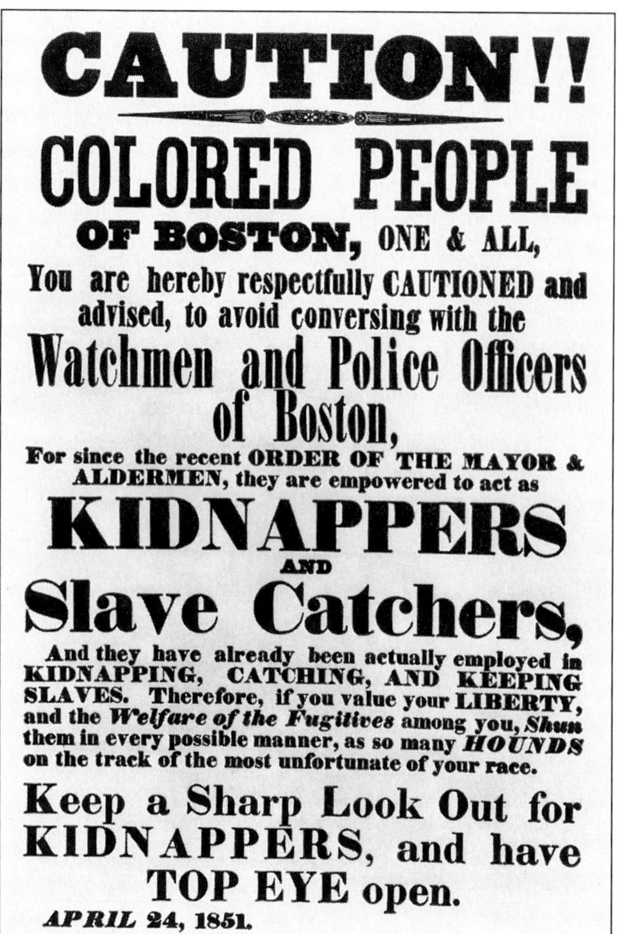
CAUTION!!
COLORED PEOPLE
OF BOSTON, ONE & ALL,
You are hereby respectfully CAUTIONED and advised, to avoid conversing with the
Watchmen and Police Officers of Boston,
For since the recent ORDER OF THE MAYOR & ALDERMEN, they are empowered to act as
KIDNAPPERS
AND
Slave Catchers,
And they have already been actually employed in KIDNAPPING, CATCHING, AND KEEPING SLAVES. Therefore, if you value your LIBERTY, and the Welfare of the Fugitives among you, Shun them in every possible manner, as so many HOUNDS on the track of the most unfortunate of your race.
Keep a Sharp Look Out for KIDNAPPERS, and have TOP EYE open.
APRIL 24, 1851.

The Fugitive Slave Act threatened the freedom of escaped slaves living in the North, and even of free black northerners. This notice, typical of warnings posted in northern cities, urged Boston's African-American population to take precautions.

slave-hunters." Similar associations appeared in Cleveland and Cincinnati. Frederick Douglass, an escaped slave himself, explained the need for such organizations: "We must be prepared . . . to see the streets . . . running with blood . . . should this law be put into operation." Some black people left the United States. In October 1850, two hundred left Pittsburgh for Ontario, Canada, vowing that "they would die before being taken back into slavery." As many as twenty thousand African Americans may have found their way across the border during the 1850s in response to fears over capture and reenslavement. Another solution was proposed by Martin Delany, a prominent black abolitionist. He argued for the establishment of a black homeland at several potential sites in Central or South America or on the west coast of Africa. "Go we must," he wrote in 1852. "To remain here in North America and be crushed to the earth in vassalage and degradation, we never will."

During the early 1850s, black Northerners gathered in conventions to demand the repeal of the Fugitive Slave Act. Frederick Douglass convened the **National Black Convention** in Rochester, New York, in July 1853, at which he established a national council of black leaders to address issues of political and civil rights. Although the council was short-lived, it reflected a growing militancy. Less than a year later, for example, a black New York City woman schoolteacher defied that city's public transit segregation ordinance and succeeded in pressing state legislators to strike down the law.

On several occasions, black Northerners fought to defend their rights. In September 1851, Edward Gorsuch, a Maryland slaveholder, went to Christiana, Pennsylvania, where two of his escaped slaves were living. A fugitive slave named William Parker had organized the town's black community to defend against such an incident. Gorsuch located the two fugitives in a house occupied by Parker and a dozen other armed black men. Another fifty black people and some white people arrived and surrounded Gorsuch, his son, two relatives, two neighbors, and a federal marshal. Gunfire erupted, wounding both Gorsuch and his son. As the elder Gorsuch lay on the ground, a group of black women "rushed from the house with corn cutters and scythe blades [and] hacked the bleeding and lifeless body."

How much of this militancy filtered down to slaves in the South is difficult to say. Slaveholders noted an increase in black resistance during the early 1850s. A white Virginian noted in 1852 that "it is useless to disguise the fact, its truth is undeniable, that a greater degree of insubordination has been manifested by the negro population within the last few months, than at any previous period in our history as a state." Southerners often concocted tales of slave plots and unrest during times of national distress. But even if the Virginia writer exaggerated, his concern reflected genuine southern anxiety.

Uncle Tom's Cabin

Sectional controversy over the Fugitive Slave Act was relatively modest compared to the firestorm abolitionist writer Harriet Beecher Stowe ignited with the publication of a novel about southern slavery. ***Uncle Tom's Cabin***, which first appeared in serial form in 1851, moved many northern white people from the sidelines of the sectional conflict to more active participation.

Stowe grew up in a remarkable family. Her father was Lyman Beecher, the prominent evangelical reformer. In Beecher's view, evangelical Christianity erased the line between public and private. Personal and societal salvation were closely con-

Southworth, Albert Sands (1811–1894), and Hawes, Josiah Johnson (1808–1901), Harriet Beecher Stowe. Daguerreotype, 4¼ × 3¼ in. The Metropolitan Museum of Art, Gift of I. N. Phelps Stokes, Edward S. Hawes, Alice Mary Hawes, and Marion Augusta Hawes, 1937.

Harriet Beecher Stowe, the daughter of a prominent Northern evangelist, catapulted to international fame with the publication of Uncle Tom's Cabin. *The novel helped raise the debate over slavery from a political to a moral level.*

nected; one could not occur without the other. In 1832, he became president of Lane Theological Seminary and moved his large family from New England to Cincinnati. He hoped, as he put it, to save the West from "Catholics and infidels." In Cincinnati, he became an active opponent of slavery.

Beecher instilled a sense of righteous indignation in his offspring. All six of his sons became ministers. Two of his three daughters, Catharine and Harriet, became accomplished nonfiction writers specializing in family and domestic advice books. Harriet married Calvin Stowe, a biblical scholar, who held views similar to Beecher's.

What first drew Harriet Beecher Stowe to the subject of slavery was her concern about its impact on family life in the South. It was not until the passage of the Fugitive Slave Act, however, that abolition became a major focus in her life. Even then, her views on black people remained ambivalent. She did not, like William Lloyd Garrison, advocate racial equality. She supported abolition, but she also believed America should be a white person's country. Like the antislavery whites who had founded the colonization movement, she thought it would be best for both races if freed slaves, after sufficient exposure to "civilization" from white evangelicals, were repatriated to Africa. As she wrote at the conclusion of *Uncle Tom's Cabin*: "Let the church of the North receive these poor sufferers until they have attained to somewhat of a moral and intellectual maturity, and then assist them in their passage to those shores where they may put in practice the lessons they have learned in America."

Slavery was an abstract concept to most white Northerners. Stowe's challenge was to personalize it in a way that would make them see it as an institution that not just oppressed black people but destroyed families and debased well-meaning Christian masters as well. Stowe herself had little experience of the South, no more than four hours spent on a Kentucky plantation. But she was familiar with the accounts of black abolitionists and counted Frederick Douglass among her friends.

At the beginning of *Uncle Tom's Cabin*, a Kentucky slave owner is reluctantly forced by financial ruin to sell some of his slaves. Among them are the son of two mulatto slaves, George and Eliza Harris, and an older slave, Tom. Eliza escapes across the ice-choked Ohio River, clutching her son to her breast as slave catchers and their bloodhounds pursue them. Tom submits to sale to a New Orleans master. When that master dies, Tom is sold to Simon Legree, who owns a plantation on the Red River in Louisiana. Legree is vicious and sadistic—the only major slaveholding character in the book whom Stowe portrays in this manner. Tom, a devout Christian, remains loyal and obedient until Legree asks him to whip another slave. When Tom refuses, Legree beats him to death. Legree, incidentally, is from Vermont.

Stowe offered not abstractions but characters who seemed real. She aimed to evoke strong emotions in the reader. The broken family, the denial of freedom, and the Christian martyr were emotional themes. The presence of mulattoes in the book testified to widespread interracial and extramarital sex, which Northerners, then in the midst of a religious revival, viewed as an abhorrent sin destructive to family life. And the depiction of southern masters struggling unsuccessfully with their consciences focused public attention on how slavery subverted Christianity.

Uncle Tom's Cabin created a sensation in the United States and abroad. The book sold ten thousand copies in its first week and 300,000 within a year. By the time of the Civil War, it had sold an unprecedented 3 million copies in the United States and tens of thousands more in Europe. Stowe's book gave slavery a face; it changed people's moral perceptions about the institution in an era of deep Protestant piety; it was a Sermon on the Mount for a generation of Northerners seeking witness for their Christianity and a crusade on behalf of their faith. It transformed abolitionism, bringing a movement whose extreme rhetoric many Northerners had previously viewed with disapproval to the edge of respectability.

For Southerners, *Uncle Tom's Cabin* was a damnable lie, a political tract disguised as literature. One Southerner denounced the book as a "criminal prostitution of the high functions of the imagination to the pernicious intrigues of sectional animosity." Some Southerners retaliated with crude plays and books of their own. In these versions of slavery, no slave families were broken up, no slaves were killed, and all masters were models of Christian behavior. Few Northerners, however, read these southern responses. The writers penned them more to convince fellow Southerners that slavery was necessary and good than to change opinions in the North.

Black Northerners embraced *Uncle Tom's Cabin.* Frederick Douglass's National Black Convention resolved that the book was "a work plainly marked by the finger of God" on behalf of black people. Some black people hoped that the popularity of *Uncle Tom's Cabin* would highlight the hypocrisy of white Northerners who were quick to perceive evil in the South but were often blind to discrimination against African Americans in the North. Despite reactions to Stowe's book, however, black Northerners continued to face voting restrictions, segregation, and official harassment.

The Election of 1852

While the nation read and reacted to *Uncle Tom's Cabin,* a presidential election campaign took place. The Compromise of 1850 had divided the Whigs deeply. Northern Whigs perceived it as a capitulation to southern slaveholding interests and refused to support the renomination of President Millard Fillmore. Many southern Whigs, angered by the suspicions and insults of their erstwhile northern colleagues, abandoned the party. Although the Whigs nominated Mexican War hero and Virginian Winfield Scott for president, few southern Whigs viewed the nonslaveholding general as a friend of their region.

The Democratic party entered the campaign more united. Despite reservations, both northern and southern wings of the party announced their support for the Compromise of 1850. Southern Democrats viewed the party's nominee, Franklin Pierce of New Hampshire, as safe on the slavery issue despite his New England heritage. Pierce satisfied Northerners as a nationalist devoted to the idea of Manifest Destiny. He belonged to **Young America**, a mostly Democratic group that advocated extending American influence into Central and South America and the Caribbean with an aggressive foreign policy. His service in the Mexican War and his good looks and charm won over doubters from both sections.

Given the disarray of the Whigs and the relative unity of the Democrats, the election results were predictable. Pierce won overwhelmingly with 254 electoral votes to Scott's 42. But Pierce's landslide victory could not obscure the deep fissures in the American party system. The Whigs, although they would continue to run local candidates through the rest of the 1850s, were finished as a national party. And the Democrats, despite their electoral success, emerged frayed from the election. In the Lower South, conflicts within the party between supporters and opponents of the Compromise of 1850 had overshadowed the contests between Democrats and Whigs. Southern Democrats had wielded great influence at the party's nominating convention and dominated party policy, clouding its prospects in the North. During the election, much of the party's support in the North had come from the first-time votes of mainly Catholic immigrants. But the growing political influence of Catholics alarmed evangelical Protestants of both parties, thus adding religious bigotry to the divisive issues undermining the structure of the national parties.

As Franklin Pierce took office in March 1853, it seemed that the only thing holding Democrats together was the thirst for political patronage. The low voter turnout in the 1852 election—Whig participation declined by 10 percent and Democratic participation by 17 percent, mostly in the Lower South—reflected public apathy and disgust at the prevailing party system. As the slavery issue confronted the nation with the most serious challenge it had faced since its inception, American voters were losing faith in their parties' ability to govern and in each other.

Political Realignment

Franklin Pierce, only forty-eight when he took office, was one of the youngest presidents in American history. He hoped to duck the slavery issue by focusing on Young America's dreams of empire. During the 1840s, the nationalist appeal of Manifest Destiny had helped elect Democrat James K. Polk to the presidency and had bolstered support for the Mexican War. Americans were still susceptible to nationalist fervor. For all their sectional, religious, ethnic, and racial differences, they shared a common language and political institutions. New technologies like the railroad and the telegraph were working to bind them together physically as well. The country was optimistic, and its possibilities for advancement seemed limitless. As Florida senator Stephen R. Mallory claimed, "It is no more possible for this country to pause in its career, than for the free and untrammeled eagle to cease to soar." But President Pierce's attempts to forge national sentiment around an aggressive foreign policy failed. And his administration's inept handling of a new territorial controversy in Kansas forced him to confront the slavery debate.

As Missouri senator Thomas Hart Benton, a Democrat, had realized during the debates over the Wilmot Proviso in 1848, no matter what policies a president pursued, Congress and the American people would interpret them in the light of their impact, real or potential, on slavery. The issue, said Benton, was like the plague of frogs that God had inflicted on the Egyptians to convince them to release the Hebrews from bondage. "You could not look upon the table but there were frogs, you could not sit down at the banquet but there were frogs, you could not go to the bridal couch and lift the sheets but there were frogs!" So it was with "this black question, forever on the table, on the nuptial couch, everywhere!"

Franklin Pierce lacked the skilled leadership the times demanded. Troubled by alcoholism, worried about his chronically ill wife, and grief-stricken over the death of three young sons, including one in a train wreck, Pierce presided weakly over the nation and increasingly deferred to proslavery interests in his policies.

Young America's Foreign Misadventures

Pierce's first missteps occurred in pursuit of Young America's foreign ambitions. The administration turned a greedy eye toward Spanish-ruled Cuba, just ninety miles off the coast of Florida. Spanish authorities were harassing American merchants exporting sugar from Cuba and the American naval vessels protecting the merchants' ships. Southerners supported an aggressive Cuba policy, seeing the island as a possible new slave state. And nationalists saw great virtue in replacing what they perceived as a despotic colonial regime with a democratic government under the guidance of the United States.

In October 1854, three American diplomats met in Ostend, Belgium, to discuss Cuba. It is not clear whether Pierce approved or even knew of their meeting, but the diplomats believed that they had the administration's blessing. One of them, the American minister to Spain, Pierre Soulé of Louisiana, was especially eager for the United States to acquire Cuba. The group composed a document on Cuba called the **Ostend Manifesto** that claimed that the island belonged "naturally to the great family of states of which the Union is the Providential Nursery." The implication was that Spain's control of Cuba was unnatural. The United States would offer to buy Cuba from Spain, but if Spain wouldn't sell, the authors warned, "by every law, human and Divine, we shall be justified in wresting it from Spain."

The Ostend Manifesto caused an uproar and embarrassed the Pierce administration when it became public. In the polite world of nineteenth-century diplomacy, it was a significant breach of etiquette. Other nations quickly denounced it as a "buccaneering document" and a "highwayman's plea." It provoked a similar reaction in the United States, raising suspicions in the North that the South was willing to provoke a war with Spain to expand the number of slaveholding states.

Meanwhile, the Pierce administration's aggressive foreign policy encouraged private citizens to pursue Young America's goals in Latin America. Such was the case of self-styled "General" William Walker and his private army, "the immortals." Newspaper reporters loved the diminutive Walker, whose exploits provided excellent copy. The popular press called him "the grey-eyed man of destiny." Walker moved from Tennessee to California, and in 1853, after gathering arms and men, he invaded Mexican-owned Baja California and proclaimed a republic. Before he could establish a permanent government and legalize slavery, the Mexican authorities tossed him out. Undaunted, Walker and his followers plunged into the civil war that had erupted in Nicaragua in May 1855. He gained control of the country by the end of the year, proclaimed himself president, and invited southern slaveholders to take up residence. The Pierce administration immediately recognized Walker's government; the people of Nicaragua did not. Backed by other Central American countries, they fought to oust the little general. Congressional pressure forced the Pierce administration to cool its support for Walker, and his financial resources dried up. His foes overthrew him in 1857, and he fled Nicaragua on an American naval vessel. After two more abortive attempts at conquest in Central America, he was executed by a Honduran firing squad in 1860.

These and other setbacks frustrated Pierce's hope that foreign adventures would mute the angry debate over slavery. Instead, the proslavery overtones of the Cuban fiasco and Walker's open courting of southern support sharpened sectional conflict. As Pierce was fumbling in foreign policy, Senator Stephen A. Douglas of Illinois was developing a national project that also promised to draw the country together—the construction of a transcontinental railroad and the settling of the land it traversed. The result was worse conflict and the first outbreak of sustained sectional violence.

Stephen Douglas's Railroad Proposal

Douglas, like many Westerners, wanted a transcontinental railroad. He himself had a personal stake in railroad building in that he owned some Chicago real estate and speculated in western lands. Railroads and the people and business they carried drove up property values. But beyond personal gain, Douglas, the supreme nationalist, understood that a transcontinental railroad would tie the nation together. Not only would it physically link East and West, it would also help spread American democracy. In short, a transcontinental railroad made good economic and political sense.

Douglas had in mind a transcontinental route extending westward from Chicago through the Nebraska Territory. Unfortunately for his plans, Indians already occupied this region, many of them on land the U.S. government had set aside as Indian Territory and barred to white settlement. "How," Douglas complained, "are we to develop, cherish, and protect our immense interests and possessions on the Pacific with a vast wilderness 1,500 miles in breadth, filled with hostile savages, and cutting off all direct communication?" Removing the "Indian barrier" and establishing white government were "first steps," in the senator's view, toward a "tide of emigration and civilization."

Once again, and not for the last time, the federal government responded by reneging on earlier promises and forcing Indians to move. In 1853, President Pierce sent agents to convince the Indians in the northern part of the Indian Territory to cede land for the railroad.

With the Indian "obstacle" removed, Douglas sought congressional approval to establish a government for the Nebraska Territory. But southern senators defeated his proposal. They objected to it not only because it called for a northern rather than southern route for the transcontinental railroad but also because the new territory lay above the Missouri Compromise line and would enter the Union as yet another free state. Bowing to southern pressure, Douglas rewrote his bill and resubmitted it in January 1854. He predicted that the new bill would "raise a hell of a storm." He was right.

The Kansas-Nebraska Act

Douglas's Kansas-Nebraska Bill split the Nebraska Territory into two territories, Kansas and Nebraska, with the implicit understanding that Kansas would become a slave state and Nebraska a free state. Consistent with Douglas's belief in popular sovereignty, it left the actual decision on slavery to the residents of the territories. But because it allowed Southerners to bring slaves into an area formerly closed to slavery, it repealed the Missouri Compromise (see Map 15-2).

Northerners of all parties were outraged. The Missouri Compromise had endured for thirty-four years as a basis for sectional accord on slavery. Now it was threatened, northern leaders charged, by the South's unquenchable desire to spread slavery and expand its political power. In defense of the bill, Douglas claimed that it was unlikely that a majority in either territory would vote for slavery. But a group of northern leaders of Douglas's own Democratic party countered vehemently that repealing the Missouri Compromise was more than a political maneuver. Using language indicative of the way religious and conspiratorial imagery had infected political debate, transforming it into a contest of good against evil, of liberty against oppression, they said it was "a gross violation of a sacred pledge," "a criminal betrayal of precious rights," and "part and parcel of an atrocious plot" to make a free territory a "dreary region of despotism, inhabited by masters and slaves." President Pierce, however, backed the bill, assuring the support of enough northern Democrats to secure it a narrow victory. The **Kansas-Nebraska Act** was law.

In August 1854, shortly after Congress adjourned, Douglas left Washington for his home in Chicago, to rest and mend political fences. He did not enjoy a pleasant journey home. "I could travel," he later recalled, ". . . by the light of my own effigy on every tree we passed." Arriving in Chicago, he addressed a large, hostile crowd outside his hotel balcony. As he departed, he lost his temper and blurted, "It is now Sunday morning. I'll go to church; you can go to hell."

"Bleeding Kansas"

Because of its fertile soil, favorable climate, and location adjacent to the slave state of Missouri, Kansas was the most likely of the new territories to support slavery. As a result, both Southerners and antislavery Northerners began an intensive drive to recruit settlers and establish a majority there. Speaking for the antislavery forces, William H. Seward said in the Senate, "We will engage in competition for the virgin soil of Kansas, and God give this victory to the side which is strong in numbers as it is in right." South Carolina editor Robert Barnwell Rhett accepted the challenge, urging fellow Southerners to "send men to Kansas, ready to cast in their lot with the proslavery

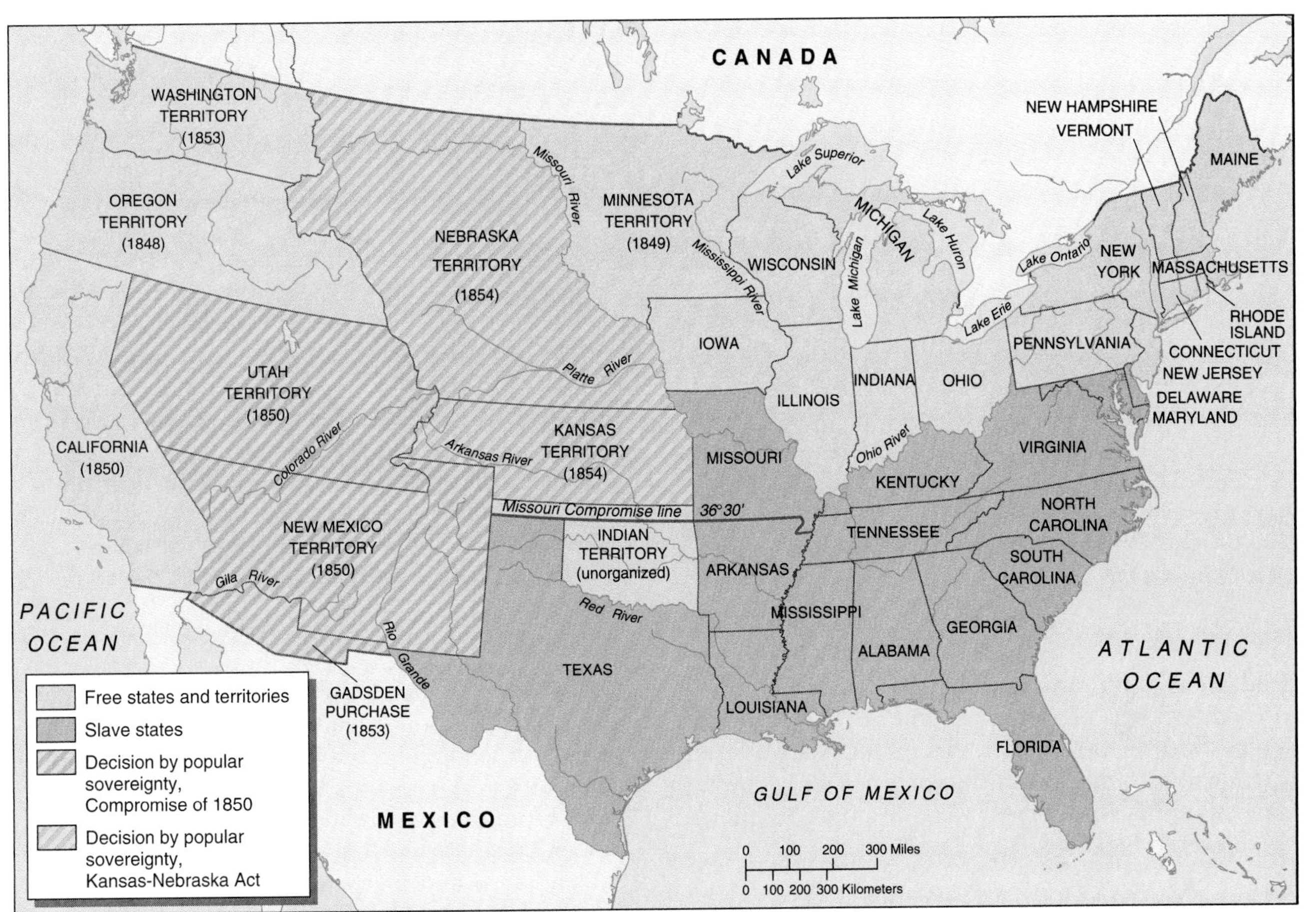

Map 15-2 The Kansas-Nebraska Act, 1854
The Kansas-Nebraska Act of 1854, which divided the Nebraska Territory in two and repealed the Missouri Compromise, reopened the incendiary issue of slavery in the territories.

part there and able to meet Abolitionism on its own issue, and with its own weapons."

As proslavery residents of Missouri poured into Kansas, antislavery organizations funded and armed their own migrants. In March 1855, proslavery forces, relying on the ineligible votes of Missouri residents, fraudulently elected a territorial legislature. This legislature promptly passed a series of harsh measures, including a law mandating the death penalty for aiding a fugitive slave and another making it a felony to question slaveholding in Kansas. For good measure, the proslavery majority expelled the few free-staters elected to the assembly. In response, free-staters established their own government in Topeka and vowed to make Kansas white.

A sporadic civil war erupted in Kansas in November 1855 and reached a climax in the spring of 1856. Journalists dubbed the conflict **"Bleeding Kansas."** On May 21, a group of proslavery officials attacked free-state stronghold Lawrence, subjecting it to a heavy artillery barrage. No one was killed, but the town suffered substantial damage. Eastern newspapers, exaggerating the incident, called it **"the sack of Lawrence."** Three days later, antislavery agitator John Brown, originally from Connecticut, went with several sympathizers to Pottawatomie Creek south of Lawrence in search of proslavery settlers. Armed with razor-sharp broadswords, they split the skulls and hacked the bodies of five men.

Kansans were not the only Americans bleeding over slavery. Five days before the "sack of Lawrence," Massachusetts senator Charles Sumner delivered a longwinded diatribe, "The Crime Against Kansas," full of personal insults against several Southerners, especially elderly South Carolina senator Andrew P. Butler. Two days after Sumner's outburst, and a day after the story of the sack of Lawrence appeared in the newspapers, Butler's cousin, South Carolina congressman Preston Brooks, entered a mostly vacant Senate chamber where Sumner sat working on a speech. Seeking to defend his cousin's honor, Brooks raised his walking cane and beat Sumner over the

Armed Missourians cross the border into Kansas to vote illegally for a proslavery government in 1855.

head. Bloody and unconscious, the senator slumped to the floor. He recovered but did not return to the Senate for over three years. His empty chair offered Northerners' mute confirmation of their growing conviction that Southerners were despotic. Southerners showered Brooks with new walking canes.

Know-Nothings and Republicans: Religion and Politics

The Sumner incident, along with the Kansas-Nebraska Bill and the civil war in Kansas, further polarized North and South, widening sectional divisions within the political parties. Some northern Democrats distanced themselves from their party and looked for political alternatives; northern Whigs seized on changing public opinion to form new coalitions; and free-soil advocates gained new adherents. From 1854 to 1856, Northerners moved into new political parties that altered the national political landscape and sharpened sectional conflict.

Although the slavery issue was mainly responsible for party realignment in the North, other factors played a role as well. Nearly 3.5 million immigrants entered the United States between 1848 and 1860, the greatest influx in American history in proportion to the total population. Some of these new-

A typical Northern view of South Carolina's Representative Preston S. Brooks attacking Massachusetts Senator Charles Sumner in 1856 for Sumner's intemperate speech against Brooks's relative, Senator Andrew P. Butler. The incident reinforced sectional antagonism.

J.L. Magee, "Southern Chivalry—Argument versus Clubs." Lithograph, 1856. Weitenkampf Collection #745, Prints Collection: Miriam and Ira D. Wallach Division of Art, Prints and Photographs, The New York Public Library, Astor, comers, especially the Germans, were escaping failed democratic revolutions in Europe. They were predominantly middle-class Protestants who, along with fewer German Catholics and Jews, settled mostly in the cities, where they established shops and other businesses. More than 1 million of the immigrants, however, were poor Irish Roman Catholics fleeing their homeland to avoid starvation.

The Irish immigrants made their homes in northern cities, at the time in the midst of Protestant revivals and reform. They also competed for jobs with native-born Protestant workers. Because the Irish would work for lower wages, the job competition bred animosity and sometimes violence. Culturally, the Irish held different views on keeping the Sabbath, and they preferred to send their children to separate sectarian schools. But it was their Roman Catholic religion that most concerned some urban Protestants. These Protestants associated Catholicism with despotism and immorality, the same evils they attributed to Southerners. For their part, the Irish made it clear that they had little use for Protestant reform, especially temperance and abolitionism. The clash of cultures would soon further disturb a political environment increasingly in flux over the slavery issue.

Democrats wooed the Irish newcomers. The champions of individual rights against intrusive government and meddling reformers, they supported the strict separation of church and state. Evangelical Protestants, especially those who were not Democrats, took a different view. They believed that the assertion of individual rights led to chaos and had to be countered by evangelically led reform. And that reform must be legislated. As a Boston minister wrote during the debate on the Wilmot Proviso, "The great problem for the Christian world now to accomplish is to effect a closer union between religion and politics. . . . We must make men to do good and be good."

Evangelicals supported government action on a wide variety of issues, from drinking to slavery to economic policy. To the reformers, every political issue had moral overtones. Those who disagreed with them were not merely political opponents but obstacles to the creation of a righteous society. These views, though, blurred the lines not only between church and state but also between the expiation of sin and the elimination of the sinner.

New parties emerged from this cauldron of religious, ethnic, and sectional strife. Anti-immigrant, anti-Catholic sentiment gave rise to the **Know-Nothing party**, which began as a secret organization in July 1854. Its name derived from the reply that members gave when asked about the party: "I know nothing." Although strongest in the North, Know-Nothing chapters blossomed in several southern cities that had experienced some immigration since 1848, among them Richmond, Louisville, New Orleans, and Savannah. The party's members in both North and South were mostly former Whigs. In addition to their biases against Catholics and foreigners, the Know-Nothings shared a fear that the slavery issue could destroy the Union. But because attempts to solve the issue seemed only to increase sectional tensions, the Know-Nothings hoped to ignore it.

Know-Nothing candidates fared surprisingly well in local and congressional elections during the fall of 1854, carrying 63 percent of the statewide vote in Massachusetts and making strong showings in New York and Pennsylvania. In office, Know-Nothings achieved some notable reforms. In Massachusetts, where they pursued an agenda similar to that of the Whigs in earlier years, they secured administrative reforms and supported public health and public education programs.

The Know-Nothings' anti-Catholicism, however, overshadowed their reform agenda. In several states and cities, they passed legislation barring Catholics from public office and unsuccessfully sought to increase the time required for an immigrant to become a citizen from one year to twenty-one years. The Know-Nothings also fostered anti-Catholic violence such as a bloody election day riot that erupted in Louisville, Kentucky, in 1855.

Ethnic and religious bigotry were weak links to hold together a national party. Southern and northern Know-Nothings soon fell to quarreling among themselves over slavery, despite their vow to avoid it, and the party split. Many northern Know-Nothings soon found a congenial home in the new **Republican party**.

The Republican party formed in the summer of 1854 from a coalition of antislavery Conscience Whigs and Democrats disgusted with the Pierce administration's Kansas policy. The Republicans supported many of the same kinds of reforms as the Know-Nothings, and, like them, the Republicans also supported strong state and national governments to promote those reforms. Most Republicans were likewise native-born white Protestants, and some shared the Know-Nothing's anti-immigrant, anti-Catholic bias. But the overriding bond among Republicans was their opposition to the extension of slavery in the territories. Unlike the Know-Nothings, the Republicans confronted the slavery issue head on.

Reflecting its opposition to slavery, the Republican party was an antisouthern sectional party. The overwhelming majority of its members were

AMERICA'S JOURNEY

FROM THEN TO NOW

Religion and Politics

When evangelical Protestantism first emerged in the late eighteenth century, its adherents advocated the separation of church and state. By the 1850s, however, the social landscape of America had changed. A wave of immigrants, many of them Roman Catholic, threatened Protestant dominance. Growing cities and rapid technological and economic change strained the traditional moral and social order. Alarmed by these changes, Evangelicals entered the political arena. Their convictions, as we saw in Chapter 14, helped drive the antebellum reform movement.

The give and take of politics, however, posed a challenge to the evangelical belief in an absolute truth grounded in the Bible. Eventually the two great evangelical crusades of the 1850s—anti-Catholicism and abolitionism—were subsumed within the Republican Party. And after the Civil War, the Republican Party gradually lost its radical fervor.

By the twentieth century, the evangelical movement had begun to turn away from politics and revert to its traditional focus on saving souls. In 1950, Jerry Falwell, an emerging evangelical leader, declared himself "a soul-winner and a separatist," meaning he wanted little involvement with society at large, much less with politics. But then came the upheavals of the 1960s and 1970s that challenged traditional morality and authority, including the Supreme Court's decision in *Roe* v. *Wade* to legalize abortion. In addition, the Internal Revenue Service began questioning the tax-exempt status of various religious groups. Once again, a changing social landscape compelled evangelicals to enter the political arena, this time to defend themselves against what they perceived to be an encroaching government. Organizations emerged to mobilize evangelical voters, including Jerry Falwell's Moral Majority in the late 1970s and Pat Robertson's Christian coalition in 1989.

In the 1850s the Northeast was the center of evangelical politics. Now evangelical political organizations speak with a mostly Southern accent. In the 1850s opposition to slavery was the focus of evangelical politics. Now it is opposition to abortion and other social issues that have risen to prominence with the end of the Cold War and the nation's growing prosperity. Evangelical activists have once again found a home in the Republican Party. The Democrats, they believe, are too permissive and too committed to abortion rights, just as nineteenth century Democrats had been committed to the defense of slavery.

And again, as in the 1850s, evangelical involvement has heated political discourse with the language of righteousness. In 1992, Randall Terry, founder of Operation Rescue, a militant antiabortion organization, wrote in his newsletter that "to vote for Bill Clinton is to sin against God." In a similar if more flowery declaration, a New England evangelical journal proclaimed the 1856 presidential contest a choice between "the bloodstained ticket of the Democratic party, responsible for the murder of your brothers and mine on the plains of Kansas," and a Republican ticket designated by "the God of peace and purity as the one that shall smile upon you."

Most Americans today, as in the 1850s, recoil from the overt intrusion of religion into politics, and groups like the Christian Coalition have had only limited success in electing their favored candidates. Despite these disappointments, they have been as wary of compromise as their nineteenth-century predecessors. As one evangelical leader explained in 1999: "I would rather go to bed with a clear conscience after losing."

But if evangelical political organizations can't gain control of Congress and the Presidency, it is unlikely that their social agenda—which, in addition to antiabortion legislation, includes school prayer, the posting of the Ten Commandments in public places, and laws restricting the rights of homosexuals—will be enacted. Today, some evangelical strategists call for a "popular front" approach, allying themselves with candidates not openly associated with the evangelical agenda. Abolitionists in the 1850s faced the same quandary between ideological purity and political pragmatism. Their support of Abraham Lincoln in 1860 reflected a bow toward pragmatism, a course that ultimately proved successful for their cause, but not without a bloody civil war.

This 1861 cartoon reproaches the self-righteousness of antislavery advocates. Preacher Henry Ward Beecher and abolitionist John Brown deny communion to George Washington, a slaveholder.

Northerners. Northern Whig merchants and entrepreneurs who joined the party were impatient with southern obstruction in Congress of federal programs for economic development, such as a transcontinental railroad, harbor and river improvements, and high tariffs to protect American industries (located mostly in the North) from foreign competition. In a bid to keep slavery out of the territories, the Republicans favored limiting homesteads in the West to 160 acres. Not incidentally, populating the territories with northern whites would ensure a western base for the new party.

Heightened sectional animosity laced with religious and ethnic prejudice fueled the emergence of new parties and the weakening of old political affiliations in the early 1850s. Accompanying the political realignment were diverging views on the proper role of government. As the nation prepared for the presidential election of 1856, the Democrats had become a party top-heavy with Southerners; the Know-Nothings splintered along sectional lines; some Whigs remained active under the old party name, mainly on the state and local levels in North and South; and the Republican party was becoming an important political force in the North and, to Southerners, the embodiment of evil.

The Election of 1856

The presidential election of 1856 proved one of the strangest in American history. The Know-Nothings and the Republicans faced a national electorate for the first time. The Democrats were deeply divided over the Kansas issue. Rejecting both Pierce and Douglas, they turned instead to a longtime insider, James Buchanan. This Pennsylvanian's major asset was that he had been absent from the country the previous three years as ambassador to Great Britain and was thus untainted by the Kansas controversy. The members of the increasingly powerful southern wing of the party supported him because he had cooperated with them during his more than thirty years in Congress. Northerners accepted him primarily because of his clean slate on Kansas and because he hailed from a state crucial to a Democratic victory.

The Republicans passed over their most likely candidate, the New York senator and former Whig William H. Seward. Instead, they followed a tried-and-true Whig precedent and nominated a military hero, John C. Frémont, a handsome, dark-haired soldier of medium height and medium intelligence. His wife, Jessie Benton, the daughter of Missouri senator Thomas Hart Benton, was his greatest asset. In effect, she ran the campaign and wisely encouraged her husband to remain silent.

The Know-Nothings split into the "South Americans" and the "North Americans." The South Americans nominated Millard Fillmore, although he was not a Know-Nothing. The North Americans eventually and reluctantly embraced Frémont, despite the widespread but mistaken belief that he was a Roman Catholic.

Openly reviling what they called the "Black Republican party," Southerners threatened disunion if Frémont won. Virginia governor Henry A. Wise declared that Frémont's election "would be an open, overt proclamation of public war." Georgia's fire-eating Senator Robert Toombs concurred, warning that "the election of Frémont would be the end of the Union, and ought to be."

Buchanan claimed to be the only national candidate on the ballot. Writing to a colleague before the election, he stated, "I consider that all incidental questions are comparatively of little importance . . . when compared with the grand and appalling issue of Union or Disunion." Voters agreed, for Buchanan bested Frémont in the North and Fillmore in the South to win the presidency.

The overall result pleased Southerners, but the details left them uncomfortable. Buchanan won by carrying every southern state and the Lower North—Pennsylvania, New Jersey, Illinois, Indiana, and California. But Frémont, a political novice running on his party's first national ticket, carried eleven free states, and the rest he lost by scant margins to Buchanan. It was a remarkable showing for a two-year-old party. In the South and border states, Fillmore managed more than 40 percent of the vote and carried Maryland, despite bearing the standard of a fragmented party.

Buchanan, who brought more than a generation of political experience to the presidency, would need every bit and more. He had scarcely settled into office when two major crises confronted him: a Supreme Court decision that challenged the right of Congress to regulate slavery in the territories and renewed conflict over Kansas.

The *Dred Scott* Case

Dred Scott was a slave owned by an army surgeon based in Missouri. In the 1830s and early 1840s, he had traveled with his master to the state of Illinois and the Wisconsin Territory before returning to Missouri. In 1846, Scott sued his master's widow for freedom on the grounds that the laws of Illinois and the Wisconsin Territory barred slavery. After a series of appeals, the case reached the Supreme Court.

Chief Justice Roger Taney of Maryland, joined by five other justices of the nine-member

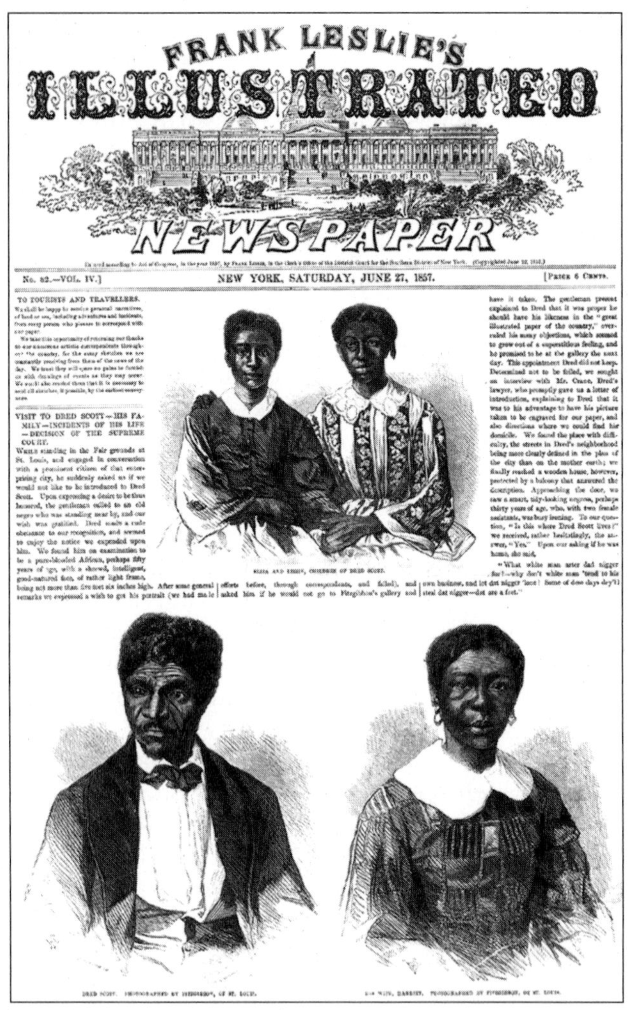

FRANK LESLIE'S ILLUSTRATED NEWSPAPER

Entered according to Act of Congress, in the year 1857, by Frank Leslie, in the Clerk's Office of the District Court for the Southern District of New York. (Copyrighted June 12, 1857.)

No. 82.—VOL. IV.] NEW YORK, SATURDAY, JUNE 27, 1857. [PRICE 6 CENTS.

TO TOURISTS AND TRAVELLERS.

We shall be happy to receive personal narratives, of land or sea, including adventures and incidents, from every person who pleases to correspond with our paper.

We take this opportunity of returning our thanks to our numerous artistic correspondents throughout the country, for the many sketches we are constantly receiving from them of the news of the day. We trust they will spare no pains to furnish us with drawings of events as they may occur. We would also remind them that it is necessary to send all sketches, if possible, by the earliest conveyance.

VISIT TO DRED SCOTT—HIS FAMILY—INCIDENTS OF HIS LIFE—DECISION OF THE SUPREME COURT.

While standing in the Fair grounds at St. Louis, and engaged in conversation with a prominent citizen of that enterprising city, he suddenly asked us if we would not like to be introduced to Dred Scott. Upon expressing a desire to be thus honored, the gentleman called to an old negro who was standing near by, and our wish was gratified. Dred made a rude obeisance to our recognition, and seemed to enjoy the notice we expended upon him. We found him on examination to be a pure-blooded African, perhaps fifty years of age, with a shrewd, intelligent, good-natured face, of rather light frame, being not more than five feet six inches high. After some general remarks we expressed a wish to get his portrait (we had made efforts before, through correspondents, and failed), and asked him if he would not go to Fitzgibbon's gallery and have it taken. The gentleman present explained to Dred that it was proper he should have his likeness in the "great illustrated paper of the country," overruled his many objections, which seemed to grow out of a superstitious feeling, and he promised to be at the gallery the next day. This appointment Dred did not keep. Determined not to be foiled, we sought an interview with Mr. Crane, Dred's lawyer, who promptly gave us a letter of introduction, explaining to Dred that it was to his advantage to have his picture taken to be engraved for our paper, and also directions where we could find his domicile. We found the place with difficulty, the streets in Dred's neighborhood being more clearly defined in the plan of the city than on the mother earth; we finally reached a wooden house, however, protected by a balcony that answered the description. Approaching the door, we saw a smart, tidy-looking negress, perhaps thirty years of age, who, with two female assistants, was busy ironing. To our question, "Is this where Dred Scott lives?" we received, rather hesitatingly, the answer, "Yes." Upon our asking if he was home, she said,

"What white man arter dat nigger for?—why don't white man 'tend to his own business, and let dat nigger 'lone? Some of dese days dey'll steal dat nigger—dat are a fact."

ELIZA AND LIZZIE, CHILDREN OF DRED SCOTT.

DRED SCOTT. PHOTOGRAPHED BY FITZGIBBON, OF ST. LOUIS.

HIS WIFE, HARRIET. PHOTOGRAPHED BY FITZGIBBON, OF ST. LOUIS.

Dred Scott and his wife Harriet are portrayed here with their children as an average middle-class family, an image that fueled Northern opposition to the Supreme Court's 1857 decision that denied both Scott's freedom and his citizenship.

Supreme Court (five of whom came from slave states), dismissed Scott's suit two days after Buchanan's inauguration in March 1857. There is evidence that Buchanan had urged the Court to issue a sweeping ruling on slavery in the territories that would set the question to rest once and for all. Although Buchanan apparently did not suggest which way he wanted the Court to rule, such contact between the executive and the judicial branches of government concerning a pending case was inappropriate. In any case, Taney's opinion, far from settling the sectional debate over slavery, deepened it.

Taney's opinion contained two bombshells. First, using dubious logic and failing to take into account the status of African Americans in several northern states, he argued that black people were not citizens of the United States. Because Scott was not a citizen, he could not sue. In reaching this conclusion, Taney noted that the framers of the Constitution had never intended citizenship for slaves. The framers, according to Taney, respected a long-standing view that slaves were "beings of an inferior order . . . so far inferior that they had no rights which the white man was bound to respect."

Second, Taney held that even if Scott had standing in court, his residence in the Wisconsin Territory did not make him a free man. This was because the Missouri Compromise, which was still in effect in the 1840s, was, in Taney's view, unconstitutional. (The Wisconsin Territory lay above the compromise line.) The compromise, the Chief Justice explained, deprived citizens of their property (slaves) without the due process of law granted by the Fifth Amendment to the U.S. Constitution. In effect, Taney ruled that Congress could not bar slavery from the territories.

Black Americans reacted bitterly to the ***Dred Scott* decision**. Throughout the struggle of black abolitionists to free their compatriots in the South, they had appealed to the basic American ideals of freedom, liberty, and self-determination. Now Taney was saying that these ideals did not apply to black people. Throughout the urban North, African Americans held meetings to denounce the decision. One gathering in Philadelphia in April 1857 resolved "that the only duty the colored man owes to a constitution under which he is declared to be an inferior and degraded being . . . is to denounce and repudiate it." A statewide black convention in Ohio objected in even stronger language: "If the Dred Scott dictum be the true . . . law of the land, then are the founders of the American Republic convicted by their descendants of base hypocrisy, and colored men absolved from all allegiance to a government which withdraws all protection." The gap between American ideals and the application of those ideals to black Americans had never been wider or more apparent.

The decision also shocked Republicans. The right of Congress to ban slavery from the territories, which Taney had apparently voided, was one of the party's central tenets. Republicans responded by ignoring the implications of the decision for the territories while promising to abide by it so far as it affected Dred Scott himself. Once in office, Republicans vowed, they would seek a reversal. This position allowed them to attack the decision without appearing to defy the law.

The *Dred Scott* decision boosted Republican fortunes in the North even as it seemed to undercut the party. Fears of a southern Slave Power conspiracy, which some had dismissed as fanciful and politically motivated, now seemed justified. If Congress could not ban slavery from the territories, Republicans asked, how secure was the right of states to ban slavery within their borders? A small group of slaveholders, they charged, was holding nonslaveholding white people hostage to the institution of slavery.

The Lecompton Constitution

Establishing a legitimate government in Kansas was the second major issue to bedevil the Buchanan administration. The president made a good start, sending his friend and fellow Pennsylvanian Robert Walker (then a resident of Mississippi) to Kansas as territorial governor to oversee the election of a constitutional convention in June 1857. Walker, though sickly, was a man of integrity.

The violence had subsided in Kansas, and prospects had grown for a peaceful settlement. But free-staters, fearing that the slavery forces planned to stuff the ballot box with fraudulent votes, announced a boycott of the June election. As a result, proslavery forces dominated the constitutional convention, which was held in Lecompton. And Walker, although a slaveholder, let it be known that he thought Kansas would never be a slave state. He thus put himself at odds with proslavery residents from the outset.

Walker convinced the free-staters to vote in October to elect a new territorial legislature. The returns gave the proslavery forces a narrow victory, but Walker discovered irregularities. In McGee, Kansas, twenty voters somehow had cast twelve hundred votes for proslavery candidates. And in Oxford, a community of a mere six houses, 1,601 names appeared on the voting rolls, all in the same handwriting and all copied from the Cincinnati city directory. Walker threw out these returns, and the free-staters took control of the territorial legislature for the first time.

Undeterred, the proslavery forces drafted a proslavery constitution at the constitutional convention in Lecompton. Buchanan, who had promised Southerners a proslavery government in Kansas, dismissed Walker before he could rule on the **Lecompton Constitution**, then ignored the recommendation of Walker's successor that he reject it. He submitted the Lecompton Constitution to the Senate for approval even though it clearly sidestepped the popular sovereignty requirement of the Kansas-Nebraska Act.

As with the Kansas-Nebraska Act, many Northerners were outraged by the Lecompton Constitution. The proslavery Kansans behind the constitution had a record of fraud, and Buchanan's own appointee had advised him against it. Northern Democrats facing reelection refused to support a president of their own party and, though the constitution passed in the Senate, Democratic opposition killed it in the House. Among Lecompton's opponents was Stephen A. Douglas, who justified his vote with an impassioned defense of popular sovereignty, which the president and proslavery Kansans had openly defied.

Douglas knew that the Dred Scott decision and Buchanan's support of the Lecompton Constitution would help the Republicans and hurt him and his fellow northern Democrats in the 1858 congressional elections. The **Panic of 1857**, a severe economic recession that lingered into 1858, also worked to the advantage of the Republicans. The Democratic administration did nothing as unemployment rose, starvation stalked the streets of northern cities, and homeless women and children begged for food and shelter. Republicans claimed that government intervention—specifically, Republican-sponsored legislation to raise certain tariffs, give western land to homesteaders, and fund transportation projects—could have prevented the panic. The Democrats' inaction, they said, reflected the southern Slave Power's insensitivity to northern workers.

Southerners disagreed. The panic had scarcely touched them. Cotton prices were high, and few southern banks failed. Cotton seemed indeed to be king. The financial crisis in the North reinforced the southern belief that northern society was corrupt and greedy. The Republicans' proposed legislative remedies, in their view, would enrich the North and beggar the South.

Such were the issues confronting Douglas as he returned home to Illinois in the summer of 1858 to begin his reelection campaign.

The Lincoln–Douglas Debates

Douglas faced a forceful opponent. The Republicans had nominated Abraham Lincoln, a forty-nine-year-old lawyer and former Whig congressman. The Kentucky-born Lincoln had risen from modest circumstances to become a prosperous lawyer in the Illinois state capital of Springfield. His marriage to wealthy and well-connected Mary Todd helped both his law practice and his pocketbook. After one term in Congress from 1847 to 1849, he returned to his law practice but maintained his interest in politics. Strongly opposed to the extension of slavery into the territories, he considered joining the Republican party after the passage of the Kansas-Nebraska Act. Lincoln had developed a reputation as an excellent stump speaker with a homespun sense of humor, a quick wit, and a self-deprecating style that fit well with the small-town residents and farmers who composed the majority of the Illinois electorate.

But substance counted more than style with Illinois voters. Most of them opposed the extension of slavery into the territories, although generally not out of concern for the slaves. Illinois residents, like most Northerners, wanted to keep the territories free for white people. Few voters would support dissolving the Union over the slavery issue. Douglas, who knew his constituents well, branded Lincoln a dangerous radical for warning, in a biblical paraphrase, that the United States, like "a house divided against itself," could not "endure permanently half slave and half free."

Lincoln could not allow the charge of radicalism to go unanswered. Little known beyond the Springfield area, he also had to find a way to gain greater exposure. So in July 1858, he challenged Douglas to a series of debates across the state. Douglas was reluctant to provide exposure for his lesser-known opponent, but he could not reject Lincoln's offer outright lest voters think he was dodging his challenger. He agreed to debates in seven of the state's nine congressional districts.

The **Lincoln–Douglas debates** were defining events in American politics. Farmers rode into market towns like Ottawa, Galesburg, Alton, and Freeport, bringing their families and picnic baskets. They settled in their wagons or on the ground under trees to hear the two great debaters confront each other on the most troubling issue of the day. What a sight it must have been, the stubby-legged, animated, barrel-chested Little Giant engaging the gangly, deliberate former rail-splitter, Abe Lincoln.

The debates put the differences between Lincoln and Douglas, Republicans and Democrats, and North and South into sharp focus. At Freeport, Lincoln asked Douglas to reconcile popular sovereignty, which Douglas had long championed, with the *Dred Scott* decision, which seemed to outlaw it by prohibiting a territorial legislature from excluding slavery before statehood. Douglas replied with what became known as the **Freeport Doctrine**. Slavery, he argued, could exist in a territory only if residents passed a law to protect it. Without such a law, no slaveholders would move in, and the territory would be free. Thus if residents did nothing, there could be no slavery in the territory.

For Douglas, slavery was not a moral issue. What mattered was what white people wanted. If they wanted slavery, fine; if they did not, fine also.

Lincoln and many Republicans had a very different view. For them, slavery was a moral issue. As such, it was independent of what the residents of a territory wanted. In the final Lincoln-Douglas debate, Lincoln turned to his rival and explained:

> The real issue in this controversy . . . is the sentiment on the part of one class that looks upon the institution of slavery *as a wrong*, and of another class that does not look upon it as a wrong. . . . The Republican party . . . look upon it as being a moral, social and political wrong . . . and one of the methods of treating it as a wrong is to *make provision that it shall grow no larger*. . . . That is the real issue. . . . It is the eternal struggle between these two principles—right and wrong—throughout the world.

Abolitionists and evangelicals had been saying much the same thing. But Lincoln was calm and nonaccusatory, his measured words more like a conversation than a sermon. And people listened.

Lincoln tempered his moralism with practical politics. He took care to distance himself from abolitionists, asserting that he abided by the Constitution and did not seek to interfere where slavery existed. Privately, however, he prayed for its demise. Nor did he agree, publicly at least, with abolitionist calls for racial equality. Several times during the debates he noted "a physical difference between the white and black races" that would "forever forbid the two races living together on terms of social and political equality." At the Springfield debate, he echoed the wishes of most white Illinoisans when he declared, "What I would most desire would be the separation of the white and black races." Indeed, he had once advocated sending freed slaves to Africa. Slavery was immoral, but inequality was not. The Republican party was antislavery, but it did not advocate racial equality.

Illinois voters retained a narrow Democratic majority in the state legislature, which reelected Douglas to the U.S. Senate. (State legislatures elected senators until 1913, when the Seventeenth Amendment provided for direct election by the people.) But Douglas alienated southern Democrats with his strong defense of popular sovereignty and lost whatever hope he had of becoming the standard-bearer of a united Democratic party in 1860. Lincoln lost the senatorial contest but won national respect and recognition.

Despite Lincoln's defeat in Illinois, the Republicans made a strong showing in the 1858 congressional elections across the North. The increased Republican presence and the sharpening sectional divisions among Democrats portended a bitter debate over slavery in the new Congress. Americans were viewing issues and each other more than ever before in sectional terms. *Northern* and *Southern* took on meanings that expressed a great deal more than geography.

The Road to Disunion

The unsatisfying Compromise of 1850, the various misadventures in the Caribbean and Central America, and the controversies over Kansas and the *Dred Scott* case convinced many Northerners that South-

OVERVIEW

SOUTH AND NORTH COMPARED IN 1860

	South	North
Population	Biracial; 35 percent African American	Overwhelmingly white; less than 2 percent African American
Economy	Growing though relatively undiversified; 84 percent of work force in agriculture	Developing through industrialization and urbanization; 40 percent of workforce in agriculture
Labor	Heavily dependent on slave labor, especially in Lower South	Free wage labor
Factories	15 percent of national total	85 percent of national total; concentrated in the Northeast
Railroads	Approximately ten thousand miles of track; primarily shorter lines, with fewer links to trunk lines	Approximately twenty thousand miles of track; more effectively linked in trunk lines connecting east and west
Literacy	17 percent illiteracy rate for free population	6 percent illiteracy rate

erners were conspiring with the federal government to restrict their political and economic liberties. Southerners interpreted the response to these same events as evidence of a northern conspiracy to gain increased power in the federal government and reduce the South's political and economic influence. There were no conspiracies, but with so little goodwill on either side, hostility predominated. Slavery, above all, accounted for the growing divide.

When abolitionist John Brown, who had avenged the "sack of Lawrence" in 1856, led a raid against a federal arsenal at Harpers Ferry, Virginia, in 1859 in the vain hope of sparking a slave revolt, he brought the frustrations of both sides of the sectional conflict to a head. The presidential election campaign of 1860 began before the uproar over the raid had subsided. In the course of that contest, one of the last nationally unifying institutions, the Democratic party, broke apart. The election of Abraham Lincoln, an avowedly sectional candidate, triggered a crisis that defied peaceful resolution.

Although the crisis spiraled into a civil war, this outcome did not signal the triumph of sectionalism over nationalism. Ironically, in defending their stands, both sides appealed to time-honored nationalist and democratic sentiments. Southern secessionists believed they were the true keepers of the ideals that had inspired the American Revolution. They were merely re-creating a more perfect Union. It was not they, but the Republicans, who had sundered the old Union by subverting the Constitution's guarantee of liberty. Lincoln similarly appealed to nationalist themes, telling Northerners that the United States was "the last best hope on earth."

Northerners and Southerners both appealed to nationalism and democracy but applied different meanings to those concepts. These differences underscored how far apart the sections had grown. When Southerners and Northerners looked at each other, they no longer saw fellow Americans; they saw enemies.

North–South Differences

Behind the ideological divide that separated North and South lay real and growing social and economic differences (see the overview table "South and North Compared in 1860"). As the North became increasingly urban and industrial, the South remained primarily rural and agricultural. The urban population of the free states increased from 10 to 26 percent between 1820 and 1860. In the South, in the same period, it increased only from 5 to 10 percent. Likewise the proportion of the northern work force in agriculture declined from 68 percent to 40 percent between 1800 and 1860, whereas in the South it increased from 82 percent to 84 percent. Northern farmers made up for the decline in farm workers by relying on machinery instead. In 1860, the free states had twice the value of farm machinery per worker as the slave states had.

The demand for farm machinery in the North reflected growing demand for manufactured products in general. The need of city-dwellers for ready-to-wear shoes and clothing, household iron products, processed foods, homes, workplaces, and public amenities boosted industrial production in the North. In contrast, in the South, the slower rate of urbanization, the lower proportion of immigrants, and the region's labor-intensive agriculture kept industrial development modest. The proportion of manufacturing capital invested in the South declined from 31 to 16 percent between 1810 and 1860. In 1810, per capita investment in industrial enterprises was 2.5 times greater in the North than in the South; in 1860, it was 3.5 times greater.

The rate of urban and industrial growth in the North was greater than anywhere else in the world in the early nineteenth century. As a result, the South inevitably suffers by comparison. Even when compared to the West, however, the South was falling behind. The South and West had about the same levels of manufacturing investment and urban population in the 1850s, but the rate of growth was even greater in the West than in the North. What is more, a vast railroad network linked the West to the Northeast rather than the South (see Map 15-3).

More subtle distinctions between North and South became evident as well by midcentury. Southerners tended to be more violent than Northerners. The slave states had a higher homicide rate than the free states, and more Southerners carried weapons. Southern values stressed courtesy, honor, and courage. Southerners were more inclined to military service than Northerners. They had proportionately more cadets enrolled in the United States Military Academy at West Point; more than 60 percent of the volunteer soldiers for the Mexican War hailed from the South; and, excluding West Point and the Naval Academy at Annapolis, seven of the nation's eight military colleges were located in the South.

The South had a high illiteracy rate, nearly three times greater than the North—eight times greater if black Southerners are included. The "ideology of literacy," as one historian called it, was not as widespread in the South as in the North. Northerners, for example, supported far more public schools and libraries than Southerners. In the South, education was barred by law to slaves and limited for most white people. Many white leaders viewed education more as a privilege for the well-to-do than a right for every citizen. A South Carolinian wrote in the 1850s that "it is better that a part should be fully and highly educated and the rest utterly ignorant."

Evangelical Protestantism attracted increasing numbers in both North and South, but its character differed in the two regions. The Methodist Church divided along sectional lines over slavery in 1844, and the Baptists split the following year. The Presbyterians splintered in 1837 over mainly doctrinal issues, but the rupture became complete in 1861. In the North, evangelical Protestants viewed social reform as a prerequisite for the Second Coming of Christ. As a result, they were in the forefront of most reform movements. Southern evangelicals generally defended slavery. Just as southern politics stressed individual rights, southern religion emphasized individual salvation over social reform. Northern churches hunted sinners outside their congregations (and often found them in Southerners) and sermonized on political issues; southern churches confined their preaching to their members and their message to the Gospel.

Slavery accounted for many of the differences between the North and the South. Investment in land and slaves limited investment in manufacturing. The availability of a large slave labor force reduced the need for farm machinery and limited the demand for manufactured products. Slaves were relatively immobile. They did not migrate to cities in massive numbers as did northern farmers. Nor could they quickly fill the labor demands of an expanding urban economy. Agriculture usually took precedence.

Slavery also divided northern from southern churches. And it accounted for the contrast between the inward, otherworldly emphasis of southern theology and the reformist theology of northern evangelicals. Southerners associated black slavery with white freedom; Northerners associated it with white degradation.

Slavery contributed to the South's martial tradition and its lukewarm attitude toward public education. Fully 95 percent of the nation's black population lived in the South in 1860, 90 percent of them slaves. As a result, the South was often a region on edge. Fearful of revolt, especially in the 1850s, when rumors of slave discontent ran rampant, white people felt compelled to maintain patrols and militias in constant readiness. The South was also determined to keep slaves as ignorant as possible. Educated

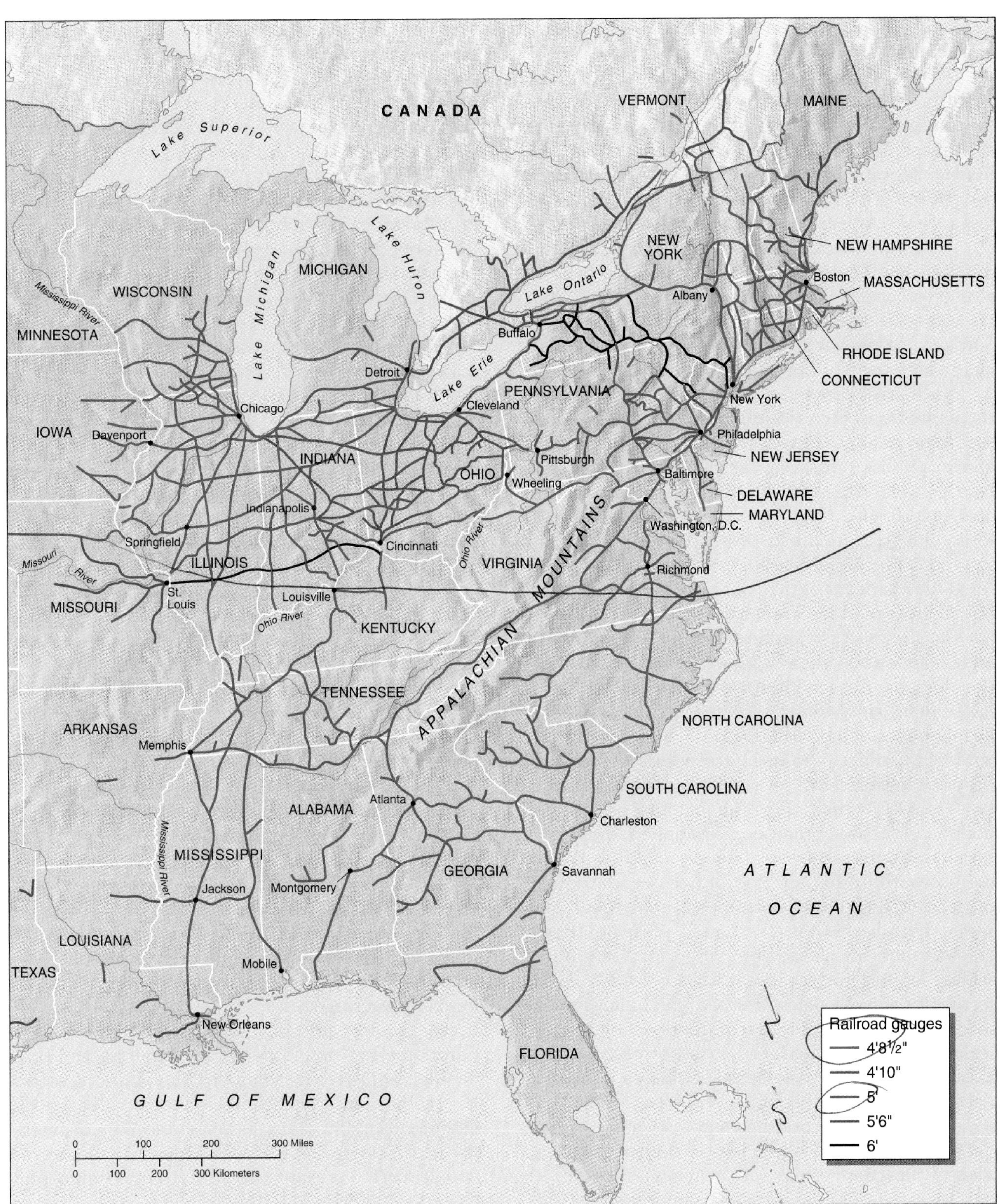

Map 15-3 Railroads in the United States, 1860
A vast network of railroads honeycombed the North and West by 1860. While the South made considerable progress in railroad construction during the 1850s, its lines had many different gauges, and it lacked suitable connections to the West.

slaves would be susceptible to abolitionist propaganda and more inclined to revolt.

The South's defense of slavery and the North's attack on it fostered an array of stereotypes that exaggerated the real differences between the sections. Like all stereotypes, these reduced individuals to dehumanized categories. They encouraged the people of each section to view those of the other less as fellow Americans than as aliens in their midst.

Southerners saw Northerners as crass and materialistic but themselves as generous and compassionate. Northerners saw Southerners as brutal and backward, themselves as progressive and temperate. Southerners perceived themselves as honorable and chaste and saw Northerners as corrupt and loose living. Northerners saw Southerners as perverse and lazy, themselves as righteous and hardworking. The South, according to Southerners, was the land of moonlight and magnolias (an image actually originated in the North), while the North was the region of muggings and mudslinging. Northerners saw Southerners as lords of the lash and themselves as angels of mercy.

Ironically, although slavery increasingly defined the character of the South in the 1850s, a growing majority of white Southerners did not own slaves. Slavery nonetheless implicated nonslaveholders in ways that assured their support for it. By satisfying the demand for labor on large plantations, it relieved many rural white Southerners from serving as farmhands and enabled them to work their own land. Slaveholders also recruited nonslaveholders to suppress slave violence or rebellion. It was nonslaveholders, for example, who often manned patrols and militia companies. Some nonslaveholders hoped to purchase slaves someday. Many dreamed of migrating westward to the next cotton frontier where they might find greater opportunity to own land and slaves. This dream not only bound white Southerners together on slavery but also prompted their strong support for southern access to the western territories. Finally, regardless of a white man's social or economic status, he shared an important feature with the largest slaveholder: As long as racial slavery existed, the color of his skin made him a member of a privileged class that could never be enslaved.

While white Southerners were more united on slavery than on other issues, their defense of slavery presented them with a major dilemma. It left them vulnerable to moral condemnation because, in the end, slavery was morally indefensible. By the 1850s, most western nations had condemned and abolished the institution. And because Northerners controlled the flow of information through the popular newspapers and the national network of communications, credit, and commerce, Southerners were likely to find themselves increasingly isolated. A minority in their own country and a lonely voice for a despised institution that was for them a significant source of wealth, Southerners were understandably jittery.

John Brown's Raid

Shortly after he completed his mayhem at Pottawatomie Creek, John Brown left Kansas and approached several New England abolitionists for funds to continue his private war in the territory. By 1857, Brown had become a rustic celebrity in New England. He had dined at Ralph Waldo Emerson's home, had tea with Henry David Thoreau, and discussed theology with the abolitionist minister Theodore Dwight Weld. Brown's frontier dress, rigid posture, reticent manner, and piercing eyes gave him the appearance of a biblical prophet. After several failed businesses, more than twenty lawsuits for nonpayment of debts, and a brush with horse rustling, he had at last found his life's calling: He had become a moderately successful fund-raiser for his own violent frontier exploits.

But when Brown returned to Kansas in late 1857, he discovered that peace had settled over that troubled territory. Residents now cared more about making money than making war. Leaving Kansas for the last time, he went east with a new plan. He proposed to attack and capture the federal arsenal at Harpers Ferry, Virginia, a small town near the Maryland border. The assault, Brown imagined, would spark a slave uprising in the area, eventually spreading to the rest of the state. With funds from his New England friends, he equipped a few dozen men and hired an English army officer to train them.

When Brown outlined his scheme to Frederick Douglass, the noted black abolitionist warned him against it. But his white New England friends were less cautious, and a group of six prominent abolitionists (the "Secret Six") gave Brown additional funds for his project.

Brown and his "army" moved to a Maryland farmhouse in the summer of 1859 to train and complete planning for the raid. On the night of October 16, 1859, he and twenty-two followers captured the federal arsenal at Harpers Ferry and waited for the slaves to rally to his banner. Meanwhile, the townspeople alerted outside authorities. The Virginia militia and a detachment of United States Marines under the command of Colonel Robert E. Lee arrived and put a quick end to **John Brown's Raid**. They wounded Brown and killed or captured most of his force.

Brown had launched the operation without provisions and at a site from which escape was impossible. Although the primary goal of the attack had been to inspire a slave insurrection, no one had bothered to inform the local slaves. And despite the secret nature of the expedition, Brown had left behind a mountain of documents at the Maryland farmhouse. He had tried to conquer the state of Virginia with twenty-two men and an ill-conceived plan. Was he crazy? As the *Boston Post* editorialized after the raid, "John Brown may be a lunatic, [but if so] then one-fourth of the people of Massachusetts are madmen."

Although the *Post* may have exaggerated, the editorial reflected an article of faith among many abolitionists that, given the signal, slaves would immediately throw off their chains, slaughter their masters, and join a rebellion. But even those slaves in the area who knew of the raid understood the odds against Brown and had the good sense not to join him. As Abraham Lincoln observed, "It was not a slave insurrection. It was an attempt by white men to get up a revolt among slaves, in which the slaves refused to participate."

The raid, though foolish and unsuccessful, played on Southerners' worst fears of slave rebellion, adding a new dimension: Here was an attack engineered not from within the South but from the North. Some southern white people may have dismissed the ability or even the desire of slaves to mount revolts on their own, but they less easily dismissed the potential impact of outside white agitators.

The state of Virginia tried Brown on the charge of treason to the state. Brown, recovering from his wounds, attended most of the trial on a stretcher. The trial was swift but fair. The jury sentenced Brown to hang. Throughout his brief imprisonment and trial, Brown maintained a quiet dignity that impressed even his jailers. The governor of Virginia spoke admiringly of him as "a man of clear head, of courage, fortitude, and simple ingenuousness." Speaking to the court after his sentencing, Brown suggested that he was God's agent in a holy war: "I believe that to have interfered as I have done . . . in behalf of [God's] despised poor, is no wrong, but right. Now, if it is deemed necessary that I should forfeit my life for the furtherance of the ends of justice, and mingle my blood further with the blood of my children and with the blood of millions in this slave country whose rights are disregarded by wicked, cruel, and unjust enactments, I say, let it be done."

Some Northerners compared Brown's execution with the death of a religious martyr. Abolitionist William Lloyd Garrison asked readers of *The Liberator* to "let the day of [Brown's] execution . . . be the occasion of such a public moral demonstration against the bloody and merciless slave system as the land has never witnessed." When the state of Virginia hanged Brown, church bells tolled across the North. Thoreau compared Brown with Jesus and called the abolitionist "an angel of light." Emerson observed that Brown would "make the gallows glorious like the cross." Writing to Margeretta Mason, wife of Virginia senator James M. Mason, abolitionist Lydia Maria Child asserted that "in this enlightened age, all despotisms ought to come to an end by the agency of moral and rational means. But if they resist such

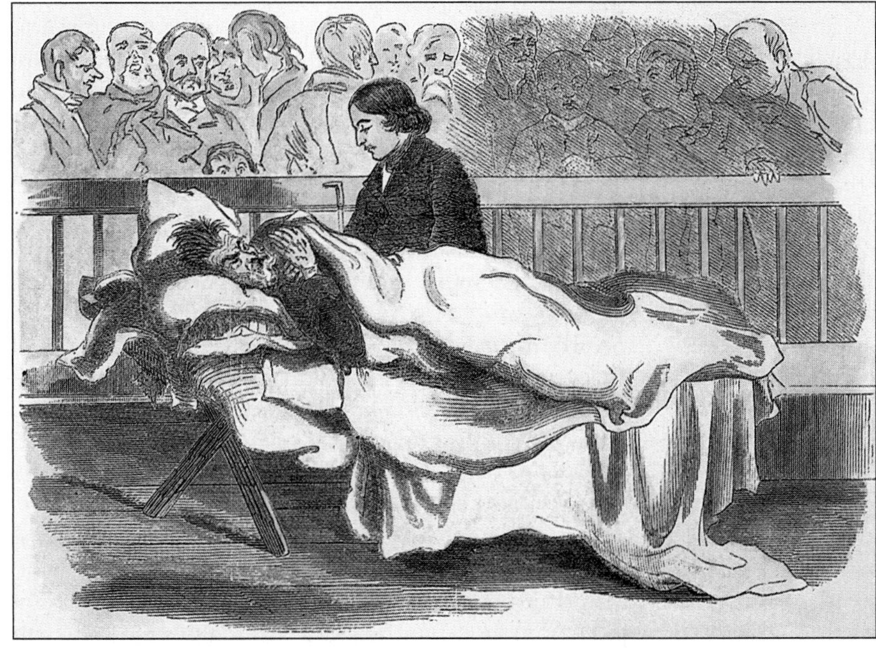

John Brown, wounded during his raid on the federal arsenal at Harpers Ferry, lies on a cot during his trial for murder and treason in Charlestown, Virginia, in 1859.

agencies, it is in the order of Providence that they must come to an end by violence." Most Northerners, however, including many Republicans, had condemned the raid. Still, the dignity of Brown's death touched many. Condemning the deed, they nevertheless embraced the cause.

The outpouring of northern grief over Brown's death convinced white Southerners that the threat to their security was not over. The discovery of Brown's correspondence at his Maryland farmhouse further fueled southern rancor, and Southerners increasingly ceased to believe northern disclaimers about the raid. Senator Mason asserted in Congress that "John Brown's invasion was condemned [in the North] only because it failed." Several members of the Secret Six had ties to the Republican party, and Southerners targeted them for special censure. Mississippi senator Jefferson Davis remarked that the Republican party "was organized on the basis of making war" against the South.

John Brown's Raid significantly changed southern public opinion. However much they defended slavery, most Southerners were for the Union. The northern reaction to John Brown's trial and death, however, troubled them. The *Richmond Whig*, a newspaper that had reflected moderate Upper South opinion for decades, observed in early 1860 that "recent events have wrought almost a complete revolution in the sentiments, the thoughts, the hopes, of the oldest and steadiest conservatives in all the southern states. . . . There are thousands upon . . . thousands of men in our midst who, a month ago, scoffed at the idea of a dissolution of the Union as a madman's dream, but who now hold the opinion that its days are numbered, its glory perished."

It was one thing to condemn slavery in the territories but another to attack it violently where it was long established. Southerners now saw in the Republican party the embodiment of John Brown's ideals and actions. So, in their view, the election of a Republican president would be a death sentence for the South.

The impact of this shifting sentiment was immediately apparent in Congress when it reconvened three days after Virginia hanged Brown. Debate quickly turned tense and ugly. South Carolina senator James H. Hammond captured the mood well, remarking of his colleagues on the Senate floor that "the only persons who do not have a revolver and a knife are those who have two revolvers." The southern and northern wings of the Democratic party were now almost totally estranged. Southern Democrats seemed concerned only to promote an extreme proslavery agenda rather than to initiate real legislation.

The Election of 1860

An atmosphere of mutual sectional distrust and animosity characterized the campaign for the presidential election of 1860. In April, the Democratic party, the sole surviving national political organization, held its convention in Charleston, South Carolina. The location was not conducive to sectional reconciliation. The city had been a hotbed of nullification sentiment during the 1830s, and talk of disunion had surfaced periodically ever since, especially in the influential *Charleston Mercury*, edited by Robert Barnwell Rhett. At the convention, Charlestonians packed the galleries and cheered for their favorite extremists.

Northern Democrats arrived in Charleston united behind Stephen A. Douglas. Although they constituted a majority of the delegates, they could not muster the two-thirds majority vote necessary to nominate their candidate. Other issues, however, were decided on a simple majority vote, permitting northern Democrats to defeat a platform proposal for a federal slave code in the territories.

Southern extremists who favored secession hoped to disrupt the convention and divide the party. They reasoned that the Republicans would then win the presidency, providing the South with the justification to secede. The platform vote gave them the opportunity they were seeking. Accompanied by spectators' cheers, delegates from five Lower South states—South Carolina, Florida, Mississippi, Louisiana, and Texas—walked out. The Arkansas and Georgia delegations joined them the following day.

Still without a nominee, the Democrats agreed to reconvene in Baltimore in June. This time, the Upper South delegations marched out when Douglas Democrats, in a commanding majority, refused to seat the Lower South delegations that had walked out in Charleston. The remaining delegates nominated Douglas for president. The bolters, who included almost all southern delegates plus a few Northerners loyal to President Buchanan, met in another hall and nominated John C. Breckinridge of Kentucky.

The disintegration of the national Democratic party alarmed those Southerners who understood that it would ensure the election of a Republican president in November. The *Memphis Appeal* warned that "the odium of the Black-Republican party has been that it is *Sectional*." Should Southerners now allow a group of "restless and reckless or misguided men to destroy the national Democratic party?" the *Appeal* asked. Its emphatic answer was, "No!"

The *Appeal* reflected the sentiment of many former Whigs, mainly from the Upper South, who would not support Breckinridge and could not support Douglas. Together with Whig allies in the North who had not defected to the Republican party, they met in Baltimore in May 1860 to form the **Constitutional Union party** and nominated John Bell of Tennessee for president.

Sensing victory, the Republicans convened in Chicago. If they could hold the states won by Frémont in 1856, add Minnesota (a new Republican-leaning state), and win Pennsylvania and one of three other Lower North states—Illinois, Indiana, or New Jersey—their candidate would win. These calculations dictated a platform and a candidate who could appeal to the four Lower North swing states where antislavery sentiment was not so strong.

The issue of slavery in the territories had dominated the Republicans' 1856 platform. Now they embraced other issues as well, presenting themselves as the party of sound economy, business, and industry. Delegates enthusiastically cheered a tariff plank calling for the protection of American industry.

In selecting an appropriate presidential nominee, the Republicans faced a dilemma. Senator William H. Seward came to Chicago as the leading Republican candidate. But his immoderate condemnation of Southerners and slavery made moderate northern voters wary of him, and these were precisely the voters the party needed for victory.

Reservations about Seward benefited Abraham Lincoln. A year after his losing 1858 Senate campaign, he had embarked on a speaking tour of the East at the invitation of influential newspaper editor Horace Greeley. Lincoln's lieutenants at the convention stressed their candidate's moderation and morality, distancing him from both the abolitionists and Seward. Moreover, Chicago was Lincoln's home turf, and he had many friends working for him at the convention. When Seward faltered, Lincoln rose and won the Republican nomination.

True to their Whig heritage, the Republicans staged a colorful campaign featuring drill teams and organized groups of young men called the **Wide Awakes** outfitted in flowing black oilcloth capes. Douglas supporters countered by enrolling teams of "Little Giants." Breckinridge and Bell followed suit, and soon large groups of young men were marching all over the country in support of one candidate or another. The theme was political, but the atmosphere was an odd mix of military parade and religious revival.

The presidential campaign of 1860 actually comprised two campaigns. In the South, the contest was between Breckinridge and Bell; in the North, it was Lincoln against Douglas. Breckinridge and Bell had scattered support in the North, as did Douglas in the South, but in the main this was a sectional election. Lincoln did not even appear on the ballot in most southern states.

Lincoln's strategy was to say practically nothing. He spent the entire campaign in Springfield, Illinois. When he did speak, it was to a reporter or friends but not in a public forum. He discounted southern threats of disunion if he were to become president. Other Republicans dismissed southern talk of secession as well. Republican leaders thought the South too fragmented to unite behind a move as drastic as disunion. "The South," Greeley wrote dismissively, "could no more unite upon a scheme of secession than a company of lunatics could conspire to break out of bedlam."

Douglas campaigned hard, trying to convince the electorate that the Union hung in the balance. Breckinridge, like Lincoln in the North, sought to assure voters that he was not the disunion candidate. And Bell ran a low-key campaign, venturing out of Tennessee infrequently. He reiterated his support of the Constitution and the Union but said little else.

States in those days held gubernatorial elections on different days, even in different months, from the national presidential election. When, in mid-October, Republicans had swept the statehouses in two crucial states, Pennsylvania and Indiana, Douglas made an extraordinary decision, but one consistent with his ardent nationalism. He abandoned his campaign and headed south at great personal peril to urge Southerners to remain in the Union now that Lincoln's election was inevitable.

Lincoln became the nation's sixteenth president with 39 percent of the popular vote (see Map 15-4). Bell won the three Upper South states of Virginia, Kentucky, and Tennessee. Douglas, though second after Lincoln in the popular balloting, won the undivided electoral vote of only one state, Missouri.

Lincoln took most northern states by significant margins and won all the region's electoral votes except three in New Jersey. This gave him a substantial majority of 180 electoral votes. Breckinridge won eleven southern states but received a majority of the popular vote cast in just four. In the South as a whole, his opponents, Bell and Douglas, together reaped 55 percent of the popular vote, confirming Republicans' skepticism about southern determination to secede.

The urban vote in the 1860 election is intriguing. Lincoln fared worst in the larger cities of the North, and urban voters drubbed Breckinridge in the South. City-dwellers tended to vote for the centrist candidates, Douglas and Bell. The close commercial ties of North and South, the tendency of immigrants in northern cities to vote Democratic, and the concern of affluent urban residents that disunion could

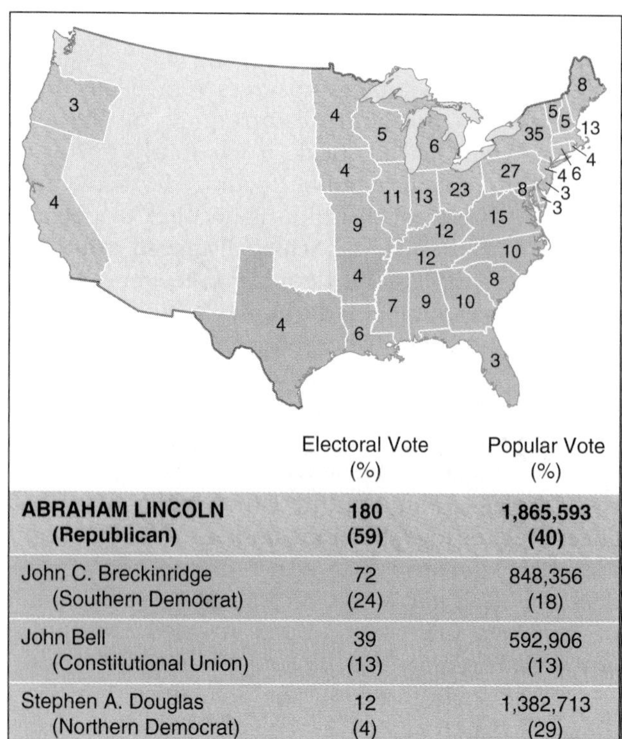

	Electoral Vote (%)	Popular Vote (%)
ABRAHAM LINCOLN (Republican)	**180 (59)**	**1,865,593 (40)**
John C. Breckinridge (Southern Democrat)	72 (24)	848,356 (18)
John Bell (Constitutional Union)	39 (13)	592,906 (13)
Stephen A. Douglas (Northern Democrat)	12 (4)	1,382,713 (29)

Map 15-4 The Election of 1860
The election returns from 1860 vividly illustrate the geography of sectionalism.

bring economic uncertainty motivated their votes. The owners of large plantations in the South similarly had a strong economic interest in preserving the Union and tended to vote for the southern centrist, Bell. But the United States was still a nation mostly of farms and small towns, and rural communities returned strong majorities for Lincoln in the North and Breckinridge in the South.

Secession Begins

The events following Lincoln's election demonstrated how wildly mistaken were those who dismissed southern threats of secession. Four days after Lincoln's victory, the South Carolina legislature called on the state's citizens to elect delegates to a convention to consider secession. Meeting on December 20, the delegates voted unanimously to leave the Union. By February 1, six other states—Mississippi, Florida, Alabama, Georgia, Louisiana, and Texas—had all held similar conventions and decided to leave the Union (see Map 15-5). Representatives from the seven seceding states met to form a separate country, the **Confederate States of America**. On February 18, Jefferson Davis was sworn in as its president.

The swiftness of secession in the Lower South obscured divisions in most states over the issue. Secessionists barely secured a majority in the Georgia and Louisiana conventions. In Mississippi, Florida, and Alabama, the secessionist majority was more comfortable, but pro-Union candidates polled a significant minority of votes. With Lincoln headed for the White House, the greatest support for secession came from large landowners in counties in which slaves comprised a majority of the population. Support for secession was weakest among small, nonslaveholding farmers.

Secessionists mounted an effective propaganda campaign, deftly using the press to convince voters to elect their delegates to the state conventions. Framing the issue as a personal challenge to every southern citizen, they argued that it would be cowardly to remain in the Union, a submission to despotism and enslavement. Southerners, they maintained, were the true heirs to the spirit of 1776. Lincoln and the Republicans were like King George III and the British—they meant to deny Southerners the right to life, liberty, and the pursuit of happiness. Republicans, the secessionists warned, would turn southern society upside down. They would use the federal government to incite slave rebellions and would drain the economy of the South with their economic legislation. In short, the secessionists presented themselves as the guardians of American democracy and the Republicans as its usurpers.

Unionists, in response, could only offer voters a wait-and-see strategy. By remaining in the Union, they argued, Southerners could extract concessions from the Republicans that would protect their institutions.

Presidential Inaction

Because Lincoln would not take office until March 4, 1861, it was the Buchanan administration that had to cope with the secession crisis during the critical months of December and January. The president's failure to work out a solution with Congress as secession fever swept the Lower South further undermined Unionist forces in the seceding states.

When Buchanan lost the support of northern Democrats over the Lecompton Constitution, he turned to the South for support and filled his cabinet with Southerners. Now, facing the secession crisis, he proposed holding a constitutional convention to amend the Constitution in ways that would satisfy the South's' demands on slavery. This outright surrender to southern demands, however, had no chance of passing in Congress.

Thereafter, Buchanan's administration quickly fell apart. As the Lower South states left the Union, their representatives and senators left Washington,

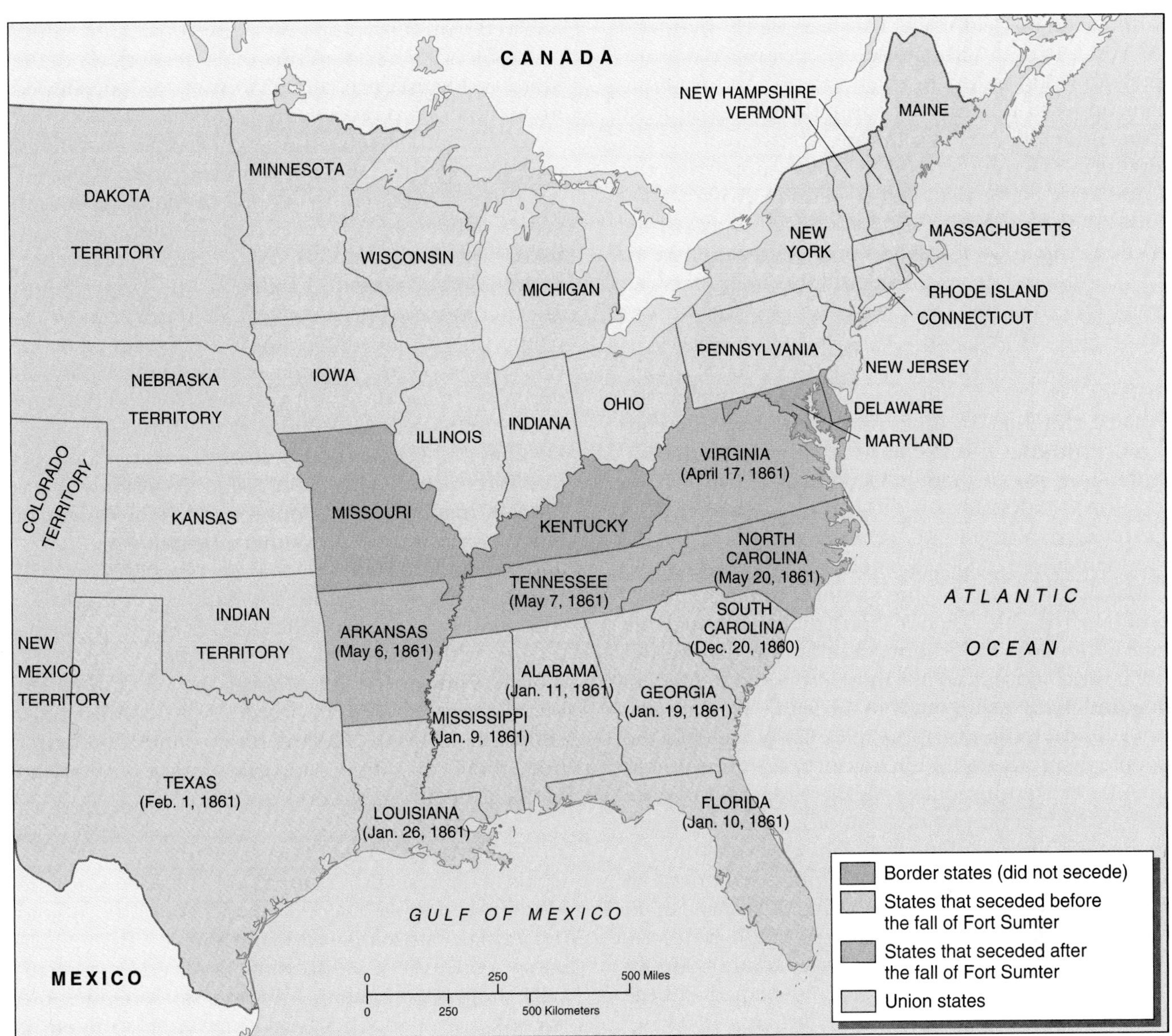

Map 15-5 The Course of Secession
Before the firing on Fort Sumter in April 1861, the Confederacy consisted primarily of states in the Lower South. After Sumter, and after President Lincoln called upon them for troops, the Upper South states of Virginia, North Carolina, Tennessee, and Arkansas seceded.

and with them went Buchanan's closest advisers and key cabinet officials. Commenting on the emotionally charged atmosphere in the Senate as prominent Southerners gave their farewells and departed, one observer wrote, "There was everywhere a feeling of suspense, as if, visibly, the pillars of the temple were being withdrawn and the great Government structure was tottering."

Buchanan, a lame duck, bereft of friends and advisers, did little more than condemn secession. He was reluctant to take action that would limit the options of the incoming administration or, worse, tip the balance in the Upper South toward secession. He hoped that waiting might bring an isolated Lower South to its senses and give efforts to mediate the sectional rift a chance to succeed.

Peace Proposals

Kentucky senator John J. Crittenden chaired a Senate committee that proposed a package of constitutional amendments in December 1860 designed to solve the sectional crisis. The central feature of the **Crittenden Plan** was the extension of the Missouri Compromise line through the territories all the way to the state of California. The plan was of marginal interest to the South, however, because it was unlikely to result in any new slave states. And Republicans opposed it because it contradicted one of their basic principles, the exclusion of slavery from the territories. Despite a flood of letters supporting the Crittenden Plan, including a petition from 38,000 citizens of New York City, Republicans successfully bottled it up in Congress and prevented action on it.

Meanwhile, ex-president John Tyler emerged from retirement to lead an effort by the border states—the Upper South and the Lower North—to forge a peace. Delegates from these states responded to Tyler's invitation and met in February 1861 at the Willard Hotel in Washington. But the plan the conference produced differed little from Crittenden's, and it, too, got nowhere in Congress.

Lincoln's Views on Secession

President-elect Lincoln monitored the secession of the Lower South states and the attempts to reach a compromise from his home in Springfield. Although he said nothing publicly, he made it known that he did not favor compromises like those proposed by Crittenden and Tyler. As he put it to a friend, "We have just carried an election on principles fairly stated to the people. Now we are told in advance, the government shall be broken up, unless we surrender to those we have beaten, before we take the offices. . . . If we surrender, it is the end of us, and of the government."

Lincoln counted on Unionist sentiment to keep the Upper South from seceding. Like Buchanan, he felt that the longer the Lower South states remained isolated, the more likely they would be to return to the fold. For a while, events seemed to bear him out. In North Carolina, the *Wilmington Herald* responded to South Carolina's secession by asking readers, "Will you suffer yourself to be spit upon in this way? Are you submissionists to the dictation of South Carolina . . . are you to be called cowards because you do not follow the crazy lead of that crazy state?"

One by one, Upper South states registered their support for the Union. North Carolinians went to the polls in February and turned down the call for a secession convention. Also in February, Virginians elected Unionists to their convention by a five-to-one margin, leading a Charleston editor to lament, "Virginia would never secede now." On the other side, a correspondent of Senator Seward rejoiced, "The Gulf Confederacy can count Virginia out of their little family arrangement—*she will never* join them." Tennesseans also refused to call a convention. In Missouri, not one secessionist won election to the state convention. In Kentucky, the legislature adjourned without taking any action on a convention or a statewide referendum on secession. And the Maryland legislature, already out of session, showed no inclination to reconvene.

A closer look, however, reveals that there were limits to the Upper South's Unionism. Most voters in the region went to the polls assuming that Congress would eventually reach a compromise based on the Crittenden proposals, Tyler's peace conference, or some other remedy. Leaders in the Upper South saw themselves as peacemakers. As one Virginian explained, "Without submission to the North or desertion of the South, Virginia has that moral position *within the Union* which will give her power to arbitrate between the sections." But what if arbitration failed? Or what if the Lower South states precipitated a crisis that forced the Upper South to choose sides? It was unlikely that the Upper South would abide the use of federal force against its southern neighbors.

Lincoln believed that the slavery issue had to come to a crisis before the nation could solve it. Although he said in public that he would never interfere with slavery in the slave states, the deep moral revulsion he felt toward the institution left him more ambivalent in private. As he confided to a colleague in 1860, "The tug has to come, and better now, than any time hereafter" (see "American Views: Lincoln on Slavery").

Fort Sumter: The Tug Comes

In his inaugural address on March 4, 1861, Abraham Lincoln denounced secession and vowed to uphold federal law but tempered his firmness with a conciliatory conclusion. Addressing Southerners specifically, he assured them, "We are not enemies but friends. . . . Though passion may have strained, it must not break our bonds of affection. The mystic chords of memory, stretching from every battlefield, and patriot grave, to every living heart and hearthstone, all over this broad land, will yet swell the chorus of the Union, when again touched, as surely they will be, by the better angels of our nature."

Southerners wanted concessions, not conciliation, however. The new president said nothing about slavery in the territories, nothing about constitutional amendments proposed by Crittenden and Tyler, and nothing about the release of federal property in the South to the Confederacy. Even some Northerners hoping for an olive branch were disappointed. As one Ohio editor wrote, Lincoln's policies would "stain the soil and color the waters of the entire continent." But Lincoln was hoping for time—time to get the Lower South states quarreling with one another, time to allow Union sentiment to build in the Upper South,

American Views
Lincoln on Slavery

In the weeks after the 1860 election, northern and southern leaders sought out President-elect Abraham Lincoln for his views on slavery. Two letters, one to fellow Illinois Republican Lyman Trumbull and the other to Virginia Democrat John A. Gilmer, indicate Lincoln's firm opposition to the extension of slavery into the territories.

❖ **Lincoln's tone is considerably more conciliatory in the letter to Gilmer than in the one to Trumbull. Which one do you think better reflects his intentions?**

❖ **Despite the difference in tone, do you think both say essentially the same thing?**

Springfield, Ills. Dec. 10, 1860
Hon. L. Trumbull
My dear Sir: Let there be no compromise on the question of extending slavery. If there be, all our labor is lost, and ere long, must be done again. The dangerous ground—that into which some of our friends have a hankering to run—is Pop[ular] Sov[ereignty]. Have none of it. Stand firm. The tug has to come, & better now, than any time hereafter. Yours as ever,
A. Lincoln

Springfield, Ill. Dec. 15, 1860
Hon. John A. Gilmer:
My dear Sir: . . . I have no thought of recommending the abolition of slavery in the District of Columbia, nor the slave trade among the slave states . . . and if I were to make such recommendation, it is quite clear Congress would not follow it. As to the use of patronage in the slave states, where there are few or no Republicans, I do not expect to inquire for the politics of the appointee, or whether he does or not own slaves. . . . In one word, I never have been, am not now, and probably never shall be, in a mood of harassing the people, either North or South. On the territorial question, I am inflexible. . . . On that, there is a difference between you and us; and it is the only substantial difference. You think slavery is right and ought to be extended; we think it is wrong and ought to be restricted. For this, neither has any just occasion to be angry with the other.
Your obt. Servt.
A. Lincoln

Source: John G. Nicolay and John Hay, eds., Works of Abraham Lincoln, *vol. 6 (New York, Century Co., 1905).*

and time to convince Northerners that the Union needed preserving. He did not get that time.

One day after Lincoln's inauguration, Major Robert Anderson (like Lincoln, a native Kentuckian), the commander of **Fort Sumter** in Charleston harbor, informed the administration that he had only four to six weeks' worth of provisions left. Sumter was one of three southern forts still under federal control. Confederate batteries had ringed the fort, and Anderson estimated that only a force of at least twenty thousand troops could run the gauntlet and provision and defend the fort. Anderson assumed that Lincoln would understand the hopeless arithmetic and order him to evacuate Fort Sumter. The commanding general of the army, Winfield Scott, advised the president accordingly, as did many members of his cabinet. Lincoln stalled.

News of Anderson's plight changed the mood in the North. The Slave Power, some said, was holding him and his men hostage. Frustration grew over Lincoln's silence and inaction. The Confederacy's bold resolve seemed to contrast sharply with the federal government's confusion and inertia. "The bird of our country," cracked New York diarist George Templeton Strong, "is a debilitated chicken, disguised in eagle feathers. . . . We are a weak, divided, disgraced people unable to maintain our institutional existence."

By the end of March, nearly a month after Anderson had informed Lincoln of the situation at Fort Sumter, the president finally moved. By this time, northern public opinion and Lincoln's cabinet (with Secretary of State Seward a notable exception) favored an effort to provision Major Anderson.

Seward made a last, desperate attempt to avert armed conflict by drawing on the reservoir of common American nationalism. He suggested that Lincoln trump up charges of Spanish and French aggression in the Caribbean and convene Congress to declare war. Seward hoped his absurd plan would draw seceding states back into the Union to make common cause against Spain and France. Lincoln politely rejected the advice and ordered an expedition to provision Fort Sumter.

The president still hoped to avoid a confrontation. He did not send the troops that Anderson had requested. Instead he ordered unarmed boats to proceed to the fort, deliver the provisions, and leave. Only if the Confederates fired on them were they to force their way into the fort with the help of armed reinforcements. Lincoln notified South Carolina authorities that he intended to do nothing more than "feed the hungry."

At Charleston, Confederate general P. G. T. Beauregard had standing orders to turn back any relief expedition. But President Davis wanted to take Sumter before the provisions arrived to avoid fighting Anderson and the reinforcements at the same time. He also realized that the outbreak of fighting could compel the Upper South to join the Confederacy. But his impatience to force the issue placed the Confederacy in the position of firing, unprovoked, on the American flag and at a man who had become a national hero.

On April 10, Davis ordered Beauregard to demand the immediate evacuation of Fort Sumter. Anderson refused but wondered what the hurry was, considering that his provisions would run out in a few days. The remark gave Beauregard pause and prompted additional negotiations. Anderson did not yield, and before dawn on April 12, 1861, the first Confederate shell whistled down on the fort. After more than a day of shelling, during which more than five thousand artillery rounds struck Fort Sumter, Anderson surrendered. Remarkably, neither side suffered any casualties, a deceptive beginning to an exceptionally bloody war.

When the verdict of Fort Sumter reached President Lincoln, he called on the southern states still in the Union to send troops to put down the rebellion. Refusing to make war on South Carolina, the Upper South states of Virginia, North Carolina, Tennessee, and Arkansas seceded, and the Confederacy expanded to eleven states.

Conclusion

When David Wilmot had submitted his amendment to ban slavery from the territories gained from Mexico, he could not have foreseen that the debate he unleashed would end in civil war just fifteen years later (see the overview table, "The Emerging Sectional Crisis"). Northerners and Southerners had lived together in one nation for nearly eighty years. During that time, they had reached accommodations on slavery at the Constitutional Convention of 1787, in the Compromises of 1820 and 1850, and on numerous lesser occasions. But they could not reach agreement during the 1850s. By that time, the slavery issue had become weighted with so much moral and political freight that it defied easy resolution. Throughout the Western world, attitudes toward slavery were changing. Northern evangelical Protestants in the 1840s and 1850s branded slavery a sin and slaveholders sinners. The overwhelming popularity of *Uncle Tom's Cabin* both tapped and fed this sentiment.

Political conflict over slavery coalesced around northern efforts to curtail southern expansion and power and southern attempts to maintain their power and influence in the federal government by planting the institution in the western territories. This conflict eventually helped undo the Compromise of 1850 and turned Stephen A. Douglas's railroad bill into a battle royal over Kansas. Unable to resolve sectional differences over slavery, the Whigs disintegrated, and the Democrats divided into northern and southern factions. The Republican party formed from the political debris. Ethnic and religious conflicts further disturbed the political landscape and contributed to party realignment.

Northerners and Southerners eventually interpreted any incident or piece of legislation as an attempt by one side to gain moral and political advantage at the other's expense. Northerners viewed the *Dred Scott* decision, the Lecompton Constitution, and the southern reaction to John Brown's Raid as evidence of a Slave Power conspiracy to deny white Northerners their constitutional rights. Southerners

OVERVIEW

THE EMERGING SECTIONAL CRISIS

Event	Year	Effect
Wilmot Proviso	1846	Congressman David Wilmot's proposal to ban slavery from territories acquired from Mexico touched off a bitter sectional dispute in Congress.
Compromise of 1850	1850	Law admitted California as a free state, granted the population of Utah and New Mexico Territories the right to decide on slavery, and established a new and stronger Fugitive Slave Act, all of which "solved" the territorial issue raised by the Wilmot Proviso but satisfied neither North nor South and planted the seeds of future conflict.
Election of 1852	1852	Results confirmed demise of the Whig party, initiating a period of political realignment.
Kansas-Nebraska Act	1854	Law created the Kansas and Nebraska Territories and repealed the Missouri Compromise of 1820 by leaving the question of slavery to the territories' residents. Its passage enraged many Northerners, prompting some to form the new Republican party.
"Bleeding Kansas"	1855–1856	Sometimes violent conflict between pro- and antislavery forces in Kansas further polarized the sectional debate.
Election of 1856	1856	Presidency was won by Democrat James Buchanan of Pennsylvania, but a surprisingly strong showing by the recently formed Republican party in the North set the stage for the 1860 election.
Dred Scott Case	1857	The Supreme Court ruling that slaves were not citizens and that Congress had no authority to ban slavery from the territories boosted Republican prospects in the North.
Lecompton Constitution	1857	Proslavery document, framed by a fraudulently elected convention in Kansas and supported by President Buchanan, further convinced Northerners that the South was subverting their rights.
John Brown's Raid	1859	Unsuccessful attempt to free the South's slaves, this attack on a federal arsenal in Harpers Ferry, Virginia, increased sectional tension.
Election of 1860	1860	Republican Abraham Lincoln won a four-way race for the presidency. The last major national party, the Democrats, disintegrated. Lower South states seceded.
Fort Sumter	1861	Confederate forces attacked the fort in April 1861, Lincoln called for troops, and several Upper South states seceded. The Civil War was underway.

interpreted northern reaction to these same events as evidence of a conspiracy to rob them of security and equality within the Union.

By 1861, the national political parties that had muted sectional animosities were gone, and so were national church organizations and fraternal associations. The ideals that had inspired the American Revolution remained in place, especially the importance of securing individual liberty against encroachment by government. But with each side interpreting them differently, these ideals served more to divide than to unite. Southerners viewed the North in general and the Republican party in particular as threats to their individual liberties. Lincoln's victory, they believed, robbed the national government of its traditional role as "a disinterested and dispassionate umpire." Northerners believed that the South was conspiring to rob them of their individual rights as well and that only a redeemed federal government stood between their freedom and the despotism of the Slave Power. Both sides claimed for themselves the role of guardian of the Revolutionary tradition. Lincoln's election left Northerners feeling vindicated and Southerners feeling vulnerable.

Ironically, as Americans in both sections talked of freedom and self-determination, the black men and women in their midst had little of either. Lincoln went to war to preserve the Union; Davis, to defend a new nation. Slavery was the spark that ignited the conflict, but white America seemed more comfortable embracing abstract ideals than real people. Northerners and Southerners would confront this irony during the bloodiest war in American history—but they would not resolve it.

Review Questions

1. How do you account for the great success of Harriet Beecher Stowe's *Uncle Tom's Cabin*?
2. If you were a Democratic representative from your state to the U.S. Congress in 1854, what would your position be on the Kansas-Nebraska Bill? What if you were a Whig?
3. Discuss the role of evangelical religion in sharpening the sectional conflict between North and South.
4. Between the time he was elected president in November and his inauguration in March, what options did Abraham Lincoln have for resolving the sectional crisis?
5. Northerners and Southerners appealed to the same American ideals in support of their respective positions. Could they both have been correct?

Recommended Reading

William W. Freehling, *The Road to Disunion, Vol. 1: Secessionists at Bay, 1776–1854* (1990). A detailed and lively treatment of events and personalities in the years leading up to passage of the Kansas-Nebraska Act.

David M. Potter, *The Impending Crisis, 1848–1861* (1976). Remains the most comprehensive analysis of the coming of the war; a balanced account that is especially strong on political events.

Harriet Beecher Stowe, *Uncle Tom's Cabin* (1852; reprint edition 1982, with notes by Kathryn Kish Sklar). Reading this book is essential for understanding why and how it generated so much controversy and intensified sectional antagonisms in the early 1850s.

Additional Sources

Slavery in the Territories

Irving H. Bartlett, *John C. Calhoun: A Biography* (1993).

Eugene H. Berwanger, *The Frontier against Slavery: Western Anti-Negro Prejudice and the Slavery Extension Controversy* (1967).

Lacy Ford Jr., "Inventing the Concurrent Majority: Madison, Calhoun, and the Problem of Majoritarianism in American Political Thought," *Journal of Southern History, 60* (February 1994): pp. 19–58.

Holman Hamilton, *Prologue to Conflict: The Crisis and Compromise of 1850* (1966).

Joan D. Hedrick, *Harriet Beecher Stowe: A Life* (1993).

Robert E. May, *The Southern Dream of a Caribbean Empire, 1854–1861* (1973).

Michael E. Morrison, *Slavery and the American West: The Eclipse of Manifest Destiny and the Coming of the Civil War* (1997).

Merrill Peterson, *The Great Triumvirate: Webster, Clay, and Calhoun* (1987).

Benjamin Quarles, *Black Abolitionists* (1969).

Malcolm J. Rohrbough, *Days of Gold: The California Gold Rush and the American Nation* (1997).

Political Realignment

Tyler Anbinder, *Nativism and Slavery: The Northern Know-Nothings and the Politics of the 1850s* (1992).

Richard J. Carwardine, *Evangelicals and Politics in Antebellum America* (1993).

William J. Cooper, Jr., *The South and the Politics of Slavery, 1828–1856* (1978).

Don E. Fehrenbacher, "The New Political History and the Coming of the Civil War," *Pacific Historical Review, 54* (May 1985): 117–142.

Don E. Fehrenbacher, *Slavery, Law, and Politics: The* Dred Scott *Case in Historical Perspective* (1981).

Eric Foner, *Free Soil, Free Labor, Free Men: The Ideology of the Republican Party before the Civil War* (1970).

William Gienapp, *Origins of the Republican Party, 1852–1856* (1987).

Michael F. Holt, *The Political Crisis of the 1850s* (1978).

Daniel Walker Howe, "The Evangelical Movement and Political Culture in the North during the Second Party System," *Journal of American History,* 77 (March 1991): 1216–1239.

Robert W. Johannsen, *The Frontier, the Union, and Stephen A. Douglas* (1989).

Robert W. Johannsen, ed., *The Lincoln–Douglas Debates of 1858* (1965).

Kathryn Teresa Long, *The Revival of 1857–58: Interpreting an American Religious Awakening* (1998).

Ganja SenGupta, *For God and Mammon: Evangelicals and Entrepreneurs, Masters and Slaves in Territorial Kansas, 1854–1860* (1996).

James A. Rawley, *Race and Politics: "Bleeding Kansas" and the Coming of the Civil War* (1969).

James Brewer Stewart, *Holy Warriors: The Abolitionists and American Slavery* (1976).

J. Mills Thornton, *Politics and Power in a Slave Society: Alabama, 1800–1860* (1978).

Gerald W. Wolff, *The Kansas-Nebraska Bill: Party, Section, and the Coming of the Civil War* (1977).

The Road to Disunion

Russell Banks, *Cloudsplitter* (1997).

William L. Barney, *The Road to Secession: A New Perspective on the Old South* (1972).

Bruce Collins, *White Society in the Antebellum South* (1985).

Avery Craven, *The Growth of Southern Nationalism, 1848–1861* (1953).

Daniel W. Crofts, *Reluctant Confederates: Upper South Unionists in the Secession Crisis* (1989).

Richard N. Current, *Lincoln and the First Shot* (1963).

David Donald, *Charles Sumner and the Coming of the Civil War* (1960).

Michael P. Johnson and James L. Roark, eds., *No Chariot Let Down: Charleston's Free People of Color on the Eve of the Civil War* (1984).

John McCardell, *The Idea of a Southern Nation: Southern Nationalists and Southern Nationalism, 1830–1860* (1979).

James M. McPherson, "Antebellum Southern Exceptionalism: A New Look at an Old Question," *Civil War History, 29* (September 1983): 230–244.

Stephen Oates, *To Purge This Land with Blood: A Biography of John Brown* (1970).

Michael Snay, *Gospel of Disunion: Religion and Separatism in the Antebellum South* (1993).

Kenneth M. Stampp, *America in 1857: A Nation on the Brink* (1990).

Kenneth M. Stampp, *And the War Came: The North and the Secession Crisis, 1860–1861* (1950).

Eric H. Walther, *The Fire-Eaters* (1992).

Where to Learn More

❖ **The Underground Railroad Freedom Center, Cincinnati, Ohio.** The Center provides information on the Northern response to the Fugitive Slave Act. It also sponsors a traveling exhibition, "Free at Last: A History of the Abolition of Slavery in America."

❖ **Adair Cabin and John Brown Museum, John Brown Memorial Park, Osawatomie, Kansas.** Maintained by the Kansas Historical Society, the cabin (which once belonged to John Brown's sister) and the museum are located on the site of the Battle of Osawatomie, one of the critical events of "Bleeding Kansas."

❖ **Constitution Hall, Lecompton, Kansas.** This site, also run by the Kansas State Historical Society, is where proslavery delegates framed the controversial Lecompton Constitution that increased sectional discord.

❖ **Harpers Ferry National Historical Park, West Virginia.** Exhibits interpret John Brown's Raid and re-create some of the atmosphere and structures of the 1850s village and the federal arsenal.

❖ **"A House Divided," mounted by the Chicago Historical Society, Chicago.** This exhibit depicts the major events of the sectional crisis during the 1850s, the election of 1860, and the coming of the Civil War. It will continue until 2001.

❖ **Fort Sumter National Monument, Charleston, South Carolina.** This historic site interprets the bombardment of the fort and the events that immediately preceded the Civil War.

Battle Cries and Freedom Songs
The Civil War, 1861–1863

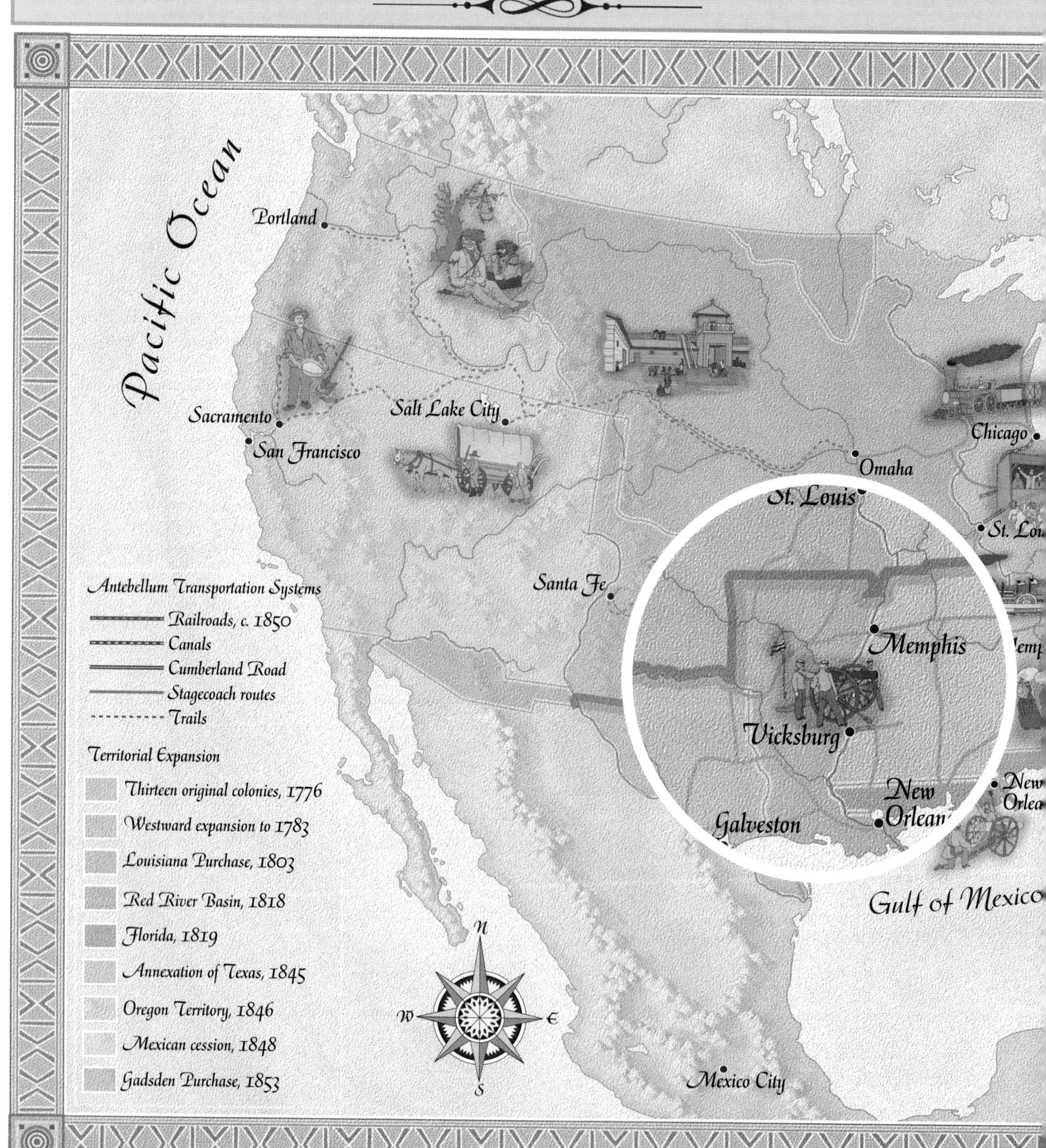

16

Chapter Outline

Key Topics

- ❖ The comparative economic and human resources of the North and South
- ❖ Confederate and Union military strategies
- ❖ Changing perceptions of the nature and length of the war
- ❖ The course of the war through 1863 and the major battles that shifted it in the North's favor
- ❖ Steps leading to the Emancipation Proclamation

In October 1862, a photographic exhibit opened in New York City. The pictures were by two photographers working for Mathew Brady. Taken a month earlier near Sharpsburg, a small town in western Maryland, they featured gently rolling hills littered with bloated corpses. Until then, most Northerners had experienced the Civil War only distantly through newspaper dispatches. Now Brady's photographers, as a *New York Times* reviewer pointed out, had "done something to bring home to us the terrible reality and earnestness of war. If he has not brought bodies and laid them in our door-yards and along streets, he has done something very like it."

For others, the face of war was more immediate. Kate Cumming, a nurse in a Confederate hospital in Chattanooga, once witnessed a stream of blood cascading from an operating table into a large tub that held a recently severed arm. The blood ran over the bucket, onto the floor, and down the stairs into the kitchen below, where the hospital staff took their meals.

On July 4, 1862, after a bloody weeklong battle, Confederate and Union soldiers laid down their arms to pick berries together. As a Confederate private described it, "Our boys and the Yanks made a bargain not to fire at each other and went out in the field . . . and gathered berries together and talked over peacefully and kindly as if they had not been engaged for the last seven days in butchering each other."

In 1862, a seventy-year-old slave woman in Georgia gathered her twenty-two children and grandchildren, seized an abandoned flatboat, and drifted forty miles down the Savannah River. When a Union vessel rescued the party, "the grandmother rose to her full height, with her youngest grandchild in her arms, and said only, 'My God! Are we free?' "

The Civil War comprised a million such stories and evoked countless emotions. The experiences of many of the people who lived through it have found their way into print. Some eighty thousand books about the war have been published since it ended in 1865, an average of more than one a day. This outpouring attests to the country's enduring need to understand, explain, and reinterpret its bloodiest conflict. The Civil War preserved the Union, abolished slavery, and killed at least 620,000 soldiers—more than in all other wars the country fought from the Revolution to the Korean conflict. To come to terms with it is to try to reconcile its great accomplishments with its awful consequences.

When the war began, only a minority of Northerners linked the preservation of the Union with the abolition of slavery. By 1863, Union and freedom had become inseparable Federal objectives. The Confederacy fought for independence and the preservation of slavery. But their own ambivalence about slavery and the contempt of outside public opinion eventually led Southerners to emphasize independence. To save their new nation, some Southerners by late 1864 favored abandoning the "peculiar institution."

The Confederate objectives dictated a defensive military strategy; the Union objectives dictated an offensive strategy. But during the war's early years, both sides faced similar problems—raising an army, financing the war effort, mobilizing the civilian population, and marshaling resources. The Confederates confronted the added burden of starting a government from scratch with relatively fewer resources than the Federals.

At the end of the war's first year, the Confederacy's strong military position east of the Appalachians belied its numerical and economic inferiority. Confederate advances resulted as much from the bungling of Union commanders as from the gallant efforts of the South's own forces. By the end of 1862, Union officers had begun to expose Southern military shortcomings, and Federal officials had expanded the North's war aims to include the abolition of slavery. Within a year, the trans-Mississippi portion of the Confederacy capitulated as dissent and despair mounted on the home front.

Mobilization, North and South

Neither side was prepared for a major war. The Confederacy lacked a national army. Each southern state had a militia, but, by the 1850s, these companies had become more social clubs than fighting units. Aside from private boats and some captured Federal vessels, the Confederacy also lacked a navy. The Union had a regular army of only sixteen thousand men, most of whom were stationed west of the Mississippi River. Their major concern had been to intervene between white settlers and Indians. The Federal navy had just three ships available for immediate service along the U.S. coast. Its sailors were trained for deep-water operations, not for coastal or inland-waterway maneuvers.

Each government augmented these meager military reserves with thousands of new recruits and developed a bureaucracy to mount a war effort. At the same time, the administrations of Presidents Lincoln and Davis secured the loyalty of their civilian populations and devised military strategies for a war of indeterminate duration. How North and South went about these tasks reflected both the different objectives of the two sides and the distinctive personalities of their leaders, Abraham Lincoln and Jefferson Davis.

War Fever

The day after Major Robert Anderson surrendered Fort Sumter, President Lincoln moved to enlarge his small, scattered army by mobilizing state militias for ninety days. Four states—Virginia, Arkansas, North Carolina, and Tennessee—refused the call and seceded from the Union. The governors of Kentucky and Missouri also declined to send troops, though these states remained in the Union. About one-third of the officer corps in the regular army, including some of the highest-ranking officers, resigned their commissions to join the

A rousing send-off for the Union's 7th Regiment in 1861 reflects the optimism and enthusiasm of citizens at the beginning of the war.

George Hayward (1834–1872), "Departure of the Seventh Regiment," N.Y.S.M., April 19, 1861. Pencil, watercolor, and gouache. M. and M. Karolik Collection, Courtesy, Museum of Fine Arts, Boston.

Chronology

1861 April:	Confederates fire on Fort Sumter; Civil War begins.
1861 July:	First Battle of Bull Run.
1862 February:	Forts Henry and Donelson fall to Union forces.
March:	Peninsula Campaign begins.
	Ironclads *Monitor* and *Virginia* (*Merrimac*) do battle.
	Battle of Pea Ridge, Arkansas.
	Battle of Glorieta Pass, New Mexico.
April:	Battle of Shiloh.
	New Orleans falls to Federal forces.
May:	Union captures Corinth, Mississippi.
July:	Seven Days' Battles end.
	Congress passes the Confiscation Act.
August:	Second Battle of Bull Run.
September:	Battle of Antietam.
December:	Battle of Fredericksburg.
1863 January:	Emancipation Proclamation takes effect.
May:	Battle of Chancellorsville; Stonewall Jackson is mortally wounded.
July:	Battle of Gettysburg.
	Vicksburg falls to Union forces.
	Black troops of the 54th Massachusetts Volunteer Infantry Regiment assault Fort Wagner outside Charleston, South Carolina.
September:	Battle of Chickamauga.
November:	Battle of Chattanooga.

Confederacy. Still, Lincoln seemed likely to meet his target of 75,000 troops.

Lincoln's modest ninety-day call-up reflected the general belief, North and South, that the war would end quickly. The *New York Times* predicted that the "local commotion" in the South would be put down "in thirty days." Union general in chief Winfield Scott was more cautious, warning that the war could last as long as ten months. Some Southerners believed that the Yankees would quit after the first battle. "Just throw three or four shells among those blue-bellied Yankees," a North Carolinian boasted, "and they'll scatter like sheep." The North's numerical superiority was inconsequential, because "the Yankee army is filled up with the scum of creation and ours with the best blood of the grand old Southland."

Not everyone thought the war would be brief. William T. Sherman, who had recently headed a Louisiana military academy and would become one of the Union's few great commanders, wrote in April 1861, "I think it is to be a long war—very long—much longer than any politician thinks."

Northerners closed ranks behind the president after the Confederacy's attack on Fort Sumter. Leading Democrat Stephen A. Douglas called on the Republican Lincoln to offer his and his party's support. "There can be no neutrals in this war," Douglas said, "*only patriots—or traitors.*" Residents of New York City, where sympathy for the South had probably been greater than anywhere else in the North, now sponsored huge public demonstrations in support of the war effort. One New Yorker exclaimed, "It seems as if we never were alive till now; never had a country till now." The city council appropriated $1 million to raise and equip Union regiments. Vigilance committees intimidated pro-Southern newspapers. And American flags flew everywhere. The New York *Daily Tribune*, an abolitionist paper, made the objective of this patriotic fervor clear: "We mean to conquer [the Southern people]—not merely to defeat, but to conquer, to SUBJUGATE them—and we shall do this the most mercifully, the more speedily we do it. But when the rebellious traitors are overwhelmed in the field, and scattered like leaves before an angry wind, it must not be to return to peaceful and contented homes. They must find poverty at their firesides, and see privation in the anxious eyes of mothers and rags of children."

Southerners were equally eager to support their new nation. A *London Times* correspondent traveling in the South witnessed large crowds with "flushed faces, wild eyes, screaming mouths." They punctuated stirring renditions of "Dixie" with the high-pitched piercing sounds that would later be known as the "rebel yell." Enlistment rallies, wild send-offs at train stations, and auctions and balls to raise money for the troops were staged throughout the Confederacy during the war's early months. As in the North, war fever fired hatred of the enemy. A Louisiana plantation overseer wrote:

> My prayer Sincerely to God is that Every Black Republican in the Hole combined whorl Either man women o chile that is opposed to negro slavery . . . shal be trubled with pestilences & calamitys of all kinds & drag out the Balance of there existence in misry & degradation with Scarsely food & rayment enughf to keep sole & body to geather and O God I pray the to Direct a bullet or a bayonet to pirce the art of every northern Soldier that invades southern Soil.

As war fever gripped North and South, volunteers on both sides rushed to join, quickly filling the quotas of both armies. The Confederates turned away 200,000 eager recruits in June and July for lack of arms and supplies. In the North, Congress responded to the clamor by authorizing the enlistment of 500,000 volunteers.

Most soldiers were motivated by patriotism, a desire to defend their homes and loved ones, and a craving for glory and adventure. A recruitment poster in one Massachusetts town promised "travel and promotion" as well as good pay. Some men succumbed to the pressure of companions and sweethearts. A young Alabamian received a package from his fiancée with a skirt, a petticoat, and a note demanding "Wear these or volunteer!"

The initial enthusiasm, however, wore off quickly. After four months of war, a young Confederate soldier admitted, "I have seen quite enough of a Soldier's life to satisfy me that it is not what it is cracked up to be." A Confederate general observed: "The first flush of patriotism led many a man to join who now regrets it."

The South in particular faced a contradiction between its ideology and the demands of full-scale war. Southerners were loyal to their localities, counties, and states. Southern leaders had been fighting for decades to defend states' rights against national authority. Now these same leaders had to forge the states of the Confederacy into a nation. By early spring 1862, the Confederate government was compelled to order the first general draft in U.S. history. It required three years' service from men between eighteen and thirty-five years of age (a range later expanded from seventeen to fifty). Several Southern politicians denounced the draft as unconstitutional and coercive. But in 1864, the Confederate Congress added a compulsory reenlistment provision. At that point, the only way a recruit could get out of the army was to die or desert.

The Confederate draft law allowed several occupational exemptions. Among them was an infamous provision that allowed one white man on any plantation with more than twenty slaves to be excused from service. The reason for the exemption was to assure the security and continued productivity of large plantations, not to protect the privileged, but it led some Southerners to conclude that the struggle had become "a rich man's war but a poor man's fight."

The initial flush of enthusiasm faded in the North as well. Responding to a Federal call for additional troops, some Northern states initiated a draft during the summer of 1862. In March 1863, Congress passed the Enrollment Act, a draft law that, like the Confederate draft, allowed for occupational exemptions. A provision that allowed a draftee to hire a substitute aroused resentment among working-class Northerners. Anger at the draft—as well as poor working conditions—sparked several riots during 1863. But the North was less dependent on conscription than the South. Only 8 percent of Union forces were drafted, compared to 20 percent for the Confederacy.

The complaints of many rank-and-file soldiers may give the impression that only people of lesser or modest means fought, but in fact the armies

Several hundred women, disguised as men, made their contribution to the war effort by enlisting. Frances Clalin served with Federal forces in Missouri. Many were found out after suffering wounds or illness.

of both sides included men from all walks of life, from common laborers to clerks to bankers. An undetermined number of women, typically disguised as men, also served in both armies. Perhaps as many as three hundred women joined the Union ranks, and about half that number enlisted in the Confederate army. They joined for the same reasons as men: adventure, patriotism, and glory.

The North's Advantage in Resources

The resources of the North—including its population, industrial and agricultural capacity, and transportation network—greatly exceeded those of the South (see Figure 16-1). The 2.1 million men who fought for the Union represented roughly half the men of military age in the North. The 900,000 men who fought for the Confederacy, in contrast, represented fully 90 percent of its eligible population. Irish and German immigrants continued to flow into the North during the war, although at a slower rate than before 1861, and thousands of them enlisted, often as substitutes for native-born Northerners. And nearly 200,000 African Americans, most of them ex-slaves from the South, took up arms for the Union. Not until the last month of the war did the Confederacy consider arming slaves.

The Confederacy compensated somewhat for its numerical disadvantage by requiring long tours of duty, which meant that its forces tended to be more experienced than those of the Union. But the Union's greater numbers left the South vulnerable to a war of attrition. As one Confederate veteran explained to a Union veteran several years after the war, "When one of your men got killed, a dozen took his place. When one of our boys died, it was just another good man gone."

At the beginning of the war, the North controlled 90 percent of the nation's industrial capacity. It had seventeen times more cotton and woolen cloth than the South, thirty times more boots and shoes, and thirty-two times more firearms. The North had dozens of facilities for producing the tools to make war material; the South had no such factories and only one munitions plant, the Tredegar Iron Works in Richmond. Northern farms, more mechanized than their Southern counterparts, produced record harvests of meat, grains, and vegetables. Southern farms were also productive, but the South lacked the North's capacity to transport and distribute food efficiently. The railroad system in the North was more than twice the size of the South's. And Northern railroads, with their main lines of a uniform track gauge, were more efficiently interlinked than Southern railroads, which were of several different gauges.

Thanks to the North's abundance of resources, no soldier in any previous army had ever been outfitted as well as the blue-uniformed Union trooper. The official color of the Confederate uniform was gray, although a dust-brown shade was more common. Most Southern soldiers, however, did not wear distinguishable uniforms, especially toward the end of the war. They also often lacked proper shoes or any footwear at all. In winter and on certain road surfaces, this shortage was a severe handicap. When Confederate general Robert E. Lee invaded Maryland in 1862, he left behind several thousand barefoot soldiers because they couldn't march on gravel roads.

Still, the South never lost a battle because of insufficient supplies or inadequate weaponry. New foundries opened, and manufacturing enterprises in Augusta, Georgia; Selma, Alabama; and elsewhere joined the Tredegar Iron Works to keep the Confederate armies equipped with the weapons and other supplies they needed to keep fighting. European imports and Northern weapons captured on the bat-

Figure 16-1 A Comparison of the Union and Confederate Control of Key Resources at the Outset of the Civil War.

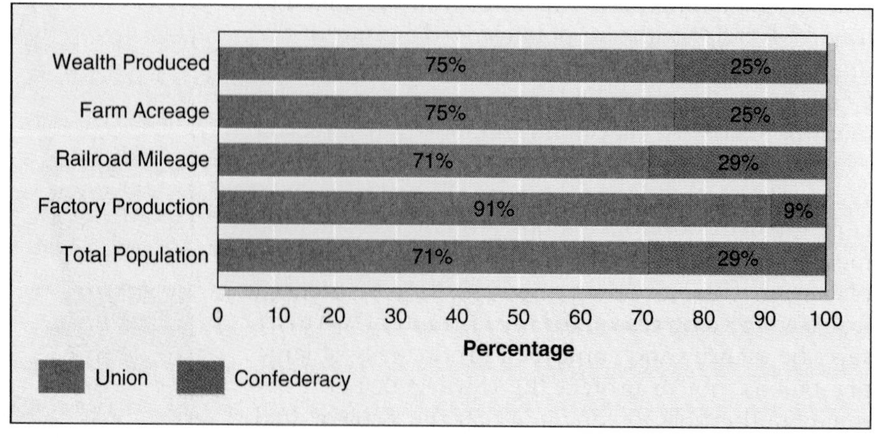

tlefield added to the South's reserve. The Confederacy's chief of ordnance—the man responsible for supplying its armies with war materiel—stated confidently in 1863, "We are now in a condition to carry on the war for an indefinite period."

Unstable finances proved more of a handicap to the Confederacy than its relatively low industrial capacity. The Confederate economy—and its treasury—depended heavily on cotton exports. But a Union naval blockade and the ability of textile manufacturers in Europe to find new sources of supply restricted this crucial source of revenue. The imposition of taxes would have improved the Confederacy's finances, but Southerners resisted taxation. They paid what taxes the government could impose—less than 1 percent of Confederate revenues—in nearly worthless state paper money. The government sold interest-bearing bonds to raise money, but as Confederate fortunes declined, so did bond sales. With few other options, the Confederacy financed more than 60 percent of the $1.5 billion it spent on the war with printing-press money. Inflation spiraled out of control, demoralizing civilians.

The Union had more abundant financial resources than the Confederacy, and the Federal government was more successful than the Confederate government at developing innovative ways to meet the great cost of the war. Its first recourse was to borrow money by selling long-term interest-bearing bonds and shorter-term interest-bearing treasury notes. Together these bonds accounted for 66 percent of the $4 billion that the Union raised to wage the war. Secretary of the Treasury Salmon P. Chase astutely hired a private entrepreneur, Jay Cooke, to market the bonds. Cooke mounted extensive newspaper and door-to-door campaigns offering the average citizen a stake in the war effort. Like the Confederacy, the Federal government issued paper money—bills derisively known as "greenbacks"—that was not backed by gold or silver. But the Federal government also offset its expenses with the country's first income tax, which citizens could pay in greenbacks, a move that bolstered the value and credibility of the paper currency. These financial measures eliminated the need for wage and price controls and rationing and warded off ruinous inflation in the North.

Leaders and Governments

Leadership ability, like resources, played an important role in the war. It was up to the leaders of the two sides to determine and administer civilian and military policy, to define the war objectives of each side, and to inspire a willingness to sacrifice in both citizens and soldiers.

Confederate president Jefferson Davis had to build a government from scratch during a war. Abraham Lincoln at least had the benefit of an established governmental structure, a standing army, healthy financial resources, and established diplomatic relations with the nations of Europe.

Davis and Lincoln were both born in Kentucky within a year and 100 miles of each other. Davis, like Lincoln, was born into modest circumstances. His forebears had moved from Philadelphia to Georgia to Kentucky and finally, a few years after Davis's birth, to Louisiana. He attended the military academy at West Point, where he was a mediocre student. He abandoned his military career after seven years of service and married the sixteen-year-old daughter of General Zachary Taylor. Davis and his bride moved to a plantation in Mississippi, where she soon died of yellow fever. Immersing himself in books and cotton farming, Davis had emerged as a gentleman planter by the 1840s and married Varina Howell in 1845. He returned to military service during the Mexican War, fought well, and used his success to become a senator from Mississippi in 1847. He served as secretary of war under President Franklin Pierce and returned to the Senate in 1857.

Although Davis's career qualified him for the prodigious task of running the Confederacy, aspects of his character compromised his effectiveness. He had a sharp intellect but related awkwardly to people and was not "one of the boys." Colleagues found him aloof. He was inclined to equate compromise with weakness and interpreted any opposition as a personal attack. His wife commented, "If anyone disagrees with Mr. Davis he resents it and ascribes the difference to the perversity of his opponent." Davis was also fatalistic. According to his wife, when he heard that the Confederate Congress had selected him as president, he spoke of it "as a man might speak of a sentence of death."

Southerners viewed themselves as the genuine heirs of the American Revolution and the true defenders of the United States Constitution. The Confederate Constitution differed in only minor particulars from the Federal document. If the South were to establish itself as a separate country, however, Southerners had to renounce their American identity and develop one of their own. But on what distinctive aspects of Southern life could the Confederacy build such an identity? Slavery was distinctively Southern, but most white Southerners, even if they believed that slavery served their interests, did not own slaves. Southerners had forcefully advanced the ideology of states' rights during the 1840s and 1850s, but, with its emphasis on the primacy of state sovereignty over central authority, states' rights too was a weak foundation on which to build a national consciousness.

Could appeals to the defense of slavery or to states' rights, or even just to Southern independence, sustain the loyalty of Southern Unionists who only reluctantly had sided with their states, of yeomen farmers who had voted against secession and who harbored political and economic resentments against slaveholding planters, of Southern women who wept through their cheers as they waved good-bye to brothers, husbands, and sons, of the countless devout Southerners who privately questioned slavery and wondered if the war might be God's final act to rid the South of the sin of human bondage? What would happen when the Confederacy began to lose men, battles, and property? Although Southerners fought for a variety of reasons, protecting their homes and families remained paramount. When these were threatened or destroyed, where would loyalty lie? Did Davis, or anyone else for that matter, possess the skill to hold together a new nation that was more like the nation it had renounced than anything that could replace it?

Structural issues that Lincoln never had to consider compounded Davis's problems. Both Davis and Lincoln made some bad appointments. But Lincoln had the advantage of an established bureaucracy staffed by experienced personnel who could at least partially compensate for incompetent cabinet officials. Davis's appointees had to build departments from nothing. The Confederate secretary of the navy lacked a navy, the postmaster general had no stamps, the secretary of the treasury had no money, and the secretary of state had no diplomatic credentials to any foreign country. Lincoln could use patronage to loyal Republicans to exert some discipline on his cabinet and the rest of his administration. The Confederacy, however, had no political parties. Davis faced shifting alliances and found it difficult to build a loyal base of support.

Northerners, like Southerners, needed a convincing reason to endure the prolonged sacrifice of the Civil War. For them, the struggle was a distant one, fought mostly on Southern soil far from their homes. Lincoln and other Northern leaders secured support by convincing their compatriots of the importance of preserving the Union. Lincoln eloquently articulated this view, framing the war as more than a military conquest. In a message to Congress on July 4, 1861, he explained that the struggle to preserve the Union was "not altogether for today; it is for a vast future." The president viewed the conflict in global terms, its results affecting the hopes for democratic government around the world. He concluded that the war "embraces more than the fate of these United States. It presents to the whole family of man, the question, whether a constitutional republic . . . can or cannot maintain its territorial integrity, against its own domestic foes."

Lincoln handled disagreement better than Davis did. He defused tense situations with folksy humor, and his simple eloquence captured the imagination of ordinary people, even if it did not persuade his political enemies. Lincoln viewed himself as a man of the people. He was not aloof, like Davis. Friends and critics alike agreed that Lincoln made himself available to them. But even if Jefferson Davis had been a more effective leader than Lincoln, it is unlikely that he could have overcome the odds against him. The key to Southern independence lay less with the Confederacy's president than with its forces on the battlefield.

Lincoln's Fight for the Border States

The secession of Virginia, Arkansas, North Carolina, and Tennessee left four border slave states—Maryland, Delaware, Kentucky, and Missouri—hanging in the balance. Were Maryland and Delaware to secede, the Federal capital at Washington, D.C., would be surrounded by Confederate territory. The loss of Kentucky and Missouri would threaten the borders of Iowa, Illinois, Indiana, and Ohio and remove the Deep South from the threat of imminent invasion. Kentucky's manpower, livestock, and waterways were as important to hold for the Union as they were to gain for the Confederacy. The state also had special symbolic significance as the birthplace of the rival presidents, Lincoln and Davis. Lincoln viewed Kentucky as the key to retaining the three other border states: "I think to lose Kentucky is nearly to lose the whole game. Kentucky gone, we cannot hold Missouri, nor, as I think, Maryland. . . . We would as well consent to separation at once, including the surrender of this capital."

Early reports from the four states were troubling. The governors of Maryland and Delaware, although they did not move to join the Confederacy, politely declined to comply with Lincoln's request for troops. The governors of Kentucky and Missouri responded less politely to the request, firing back angry denunciations of the Federal government.

Maryland's strategic location north of Washington, D.C., rendered its loyalty to the Union vital. Although a majority of its citizens opposed secession, a mob attack on Union troops passing through Baltimore in April 1861 indicated strong pro-Southern sentiment. Lincoln dispatched Federal troops to monitor the fall elections in the state, placed its legislature under military surveillance, and arrested officials who opposed the Union cause, including the mayor of Baltimore. This show of force guaranteed the pro-Union candidate for governor an overwhelming victory and saved Maryland for the Union. Delaware, although nominally a slave state, remained staunchly for the Union.

Missourians settled their indecision by combat. The fighting culminated with a Union victory in March 1862 at the Battle of Pea Ridge, Arkansas. Pro-Confederate Missourians refused to concede defeat and waged an unsuccessful guerrilla war over the next two years.

Kentucky never seceded but attempted to remain neutral at the outset of the war. The legislature was pro-Union, the governor pro-Southern. Both sides actively recruited soldiers in the state. In September 1861, when Confederate forces invaded Kentucky and Union forces moved to expel them, the state became one of the war's battlegrounds.

Although Virginia went with the Confederacy, some counties in the western part of the state opposed the state's secession and, as early as the summer of 1861, took steps to establish a pro-Union state. In June 1863, West Virginia became the nation's thirty-fifth state.

Strategies and Tactics

To a great extent, the political objectives of each side determined its military strategy. Southerners wanted independence; Northerners fought to preserve the Union. The North's goal required conquest. Federal forces had to invade the South, destroy its armies, and rout its government. Occupying a part of the Confederacy or winning a few battles might reduce the South's ability and will to fight, but as long as there were Confederate armies in the field and a functioning Confederate government, the rebellion would grind on.

The Confederacy, for its part, did not need to conquer the North. Fighting a defensive battle in its own territory, the South had only to hang on until growing Northern opposition to the war or some decisive Northern military mistake convinced the Union to stop fighting.

But the South's strategy had two weaknesses. First, it demanded more patience than the South had shown in impulsively attacking Fort Sumter. Second, the South might not have sufficient resources to draw out the war long enough to swing Northern public opinion behind peace. The question was what would break first, Northern support for the war or Southern ability to wage it?

The Early War, 1861–1862

The North's offensive strategy dictated the course of the war for the first two years. In the West, the Federal army's objectives were to hold Missouri, Kentucky, and Tennessee for the Union, to control the Mississippi River, and eventually to detach the area west of the Appalachians from the rest of the Confederacy. In the East, Union forces sought to capture Richmond, the Confederate capital. The U.S. Navy imposed a blockade along the Confederate coast and pushed into inland waterways to capture Southern ports.

The Confederates defended strategic locations throughout their territory or abandoned them when prudence required. Occasionally taking advantage of surprise or terrain, Southern forces ventured out to engage Union armies. Between engagements, each side sniped at, bushwhacked, and trapped the other.

By the end of 1862, the result remained in the balance. Although Union forces attained some success in the West, Southern armies there remained intact. In the East, where resourceful Confederate leaders several times stopped superior Union forces, Southerners clearly had the best of it.

First Bull Run

By July 1861, the border states appeared more secure for the Union than they had a few months earlier. President Lincoln shifted his attention southward and ordered Union general Irvin McDowell to move Federal forces into Virginia to take Richmond (see Map 16-1). Confronting McDowell twenty miles southwest of Washington at Manassas, an important junction in the railway that supplied the Confederate capital, was a Confederate army under General P. G. T. Beauregard.

McDowell and Beauregard's armies clashed on July 21 at the **First Battle of Bull Run** (known to the Confederacy as the First Battle of Manassas). The Union forces seemed at first on the verge of winning. But Beauregard's forces, with General Joseph E. Johnston's reinforcements, repulsed the assault, scattering not only the Union army but also hundreds of picnickers who had come out from Washington to watch the fight. At the height of the battle, General Barnard Bee of South Carolina called out to Colonel Thomas J. Jackson for assistance. Jackson, a Virginia college professor turned officer, either did not hear Bee or chose to ignore him. In exasperation, Bee shouted, "There stands Jackson—like a damned

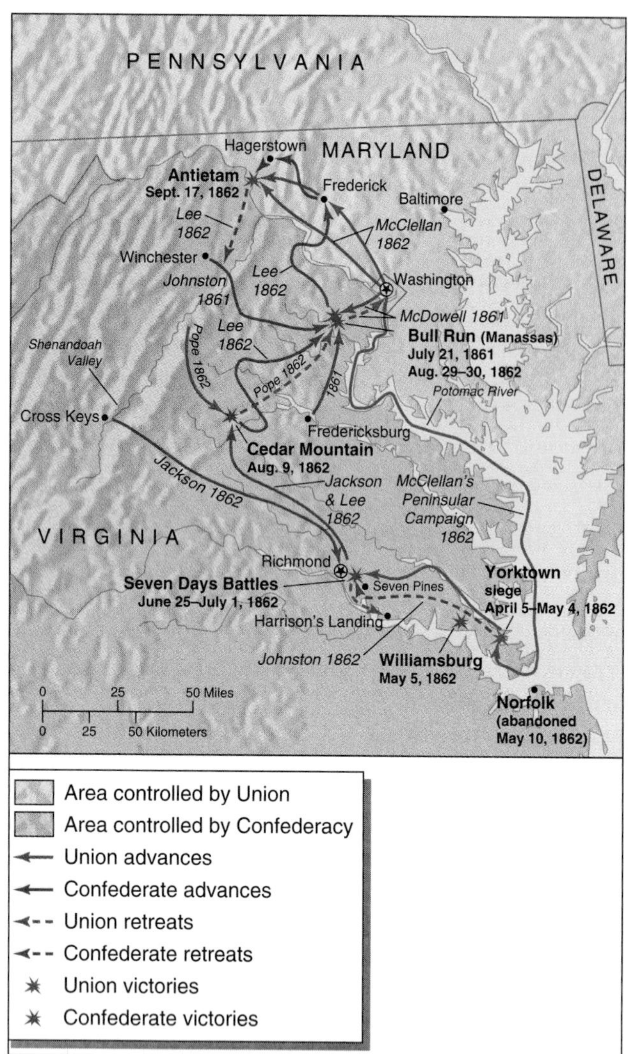

Map 16-1 From First Bull Run to Antietam: The War in the East, 1861–1862

The early stages of the war demonstrated the strategies of both Confederate and Union forces. Federal troops stormed into Virginia hoping to capture Richmond and bring a quick end to the war. Through a combination of poor generalship and Confederate tenacity, they failed. Confederate troops hoped to defend their territory, prolong the war, and eventually win their independence as Northern patience evaporated. They proved successful initially, but, with the abandonment of the defensive strategy and the invasion of Maryland in the fall of 1862, the Confederates suffered a political and morale setback at Antietam.

stone wall!" The rebuke became, in the curious alchemy of battlefield gossip, a shorthand for courage and steadfastness. Jackson's men henceforth called him "Stonewall."

Bull Run dispelled some illusions and reinforced others. It boosted Southerners' confidence and seemed to confirm their boast that one Confederate could whip ten Yankees, even though the opposing armies were of relatively equal strength when the fighting began. The Union rout planted the suspicion in Northern minds that perhaps the Confederates were invincible and destroyed the widespread belief in the North that the war would be over quickly.

The War in the West

While Federal forces retreated in Virginia, they advanced in the West. Two Confederate forts on the Tennessee–Kentucky border, **Fort Henry** on the Tennessee River and **Fort Donelson** on the Cumberland River, guarded the strategic waterways that linked Tennessee and Kentucky to the Mississippi Valley. The forts also defended Nashville, the Tennessee state capital (see Map 16-2). In February 1862, Union general Ulysses S. Grant coordinated a land and river campaign against the forts with Flag Officer Andrew H. Foote, who commanded a force of ironclad Union gunboats.

Grant, recently promoted to brigadier general, had resigned from the military in the 1850s after a mediocre career marked by bouts of excessive drinking. Before rejoining the army, he had worked in his family's struggling leather business in Illinois. A plain-looking man with dark brown hair and a beard streaked with gray, he often looked as if he had slept in his uniform. Behind the rumpled appearance lay a flexible military mind that would eventually grasp how the Civil War must be won.

Grant appreciated the strategic importance of river systems in the conquest of the western Confederacy. The Southerners, reflecting their defensive strategy, had concentrated their forces at fixed points. Grant's combined river and land campaign caught them unprepared and outflanked. By February 16, both forts had fallen. The Union victory drove a wedge into Southern territory and closed the Confederacy's quickest path to the West from Virginia and the Carolinas. The Confederacy's only safe link across the Appalachians was now through Georgia. The Confederacy never recovered the strategic advantage in the West after the loss of Forts Henry and Donelson.

Grant next moved his main army south to Pittsburg Landing on the Tennessee River to prepare for an assault on the key Mississippi River port and rail center of Vicksburg. Confederate forces interrupted his planning on April 6, 1862, with a surprise attack on a Federal outpost at **Shiloh Church** near Pittsburg Landing. The raw Federal recruits ran at the first sounds of gunfire, and the Confederates overtook their positions. But the next day, Grant sent in fresh troops and rallied his forces for a fierce counterattack that pushed the Southerners back to

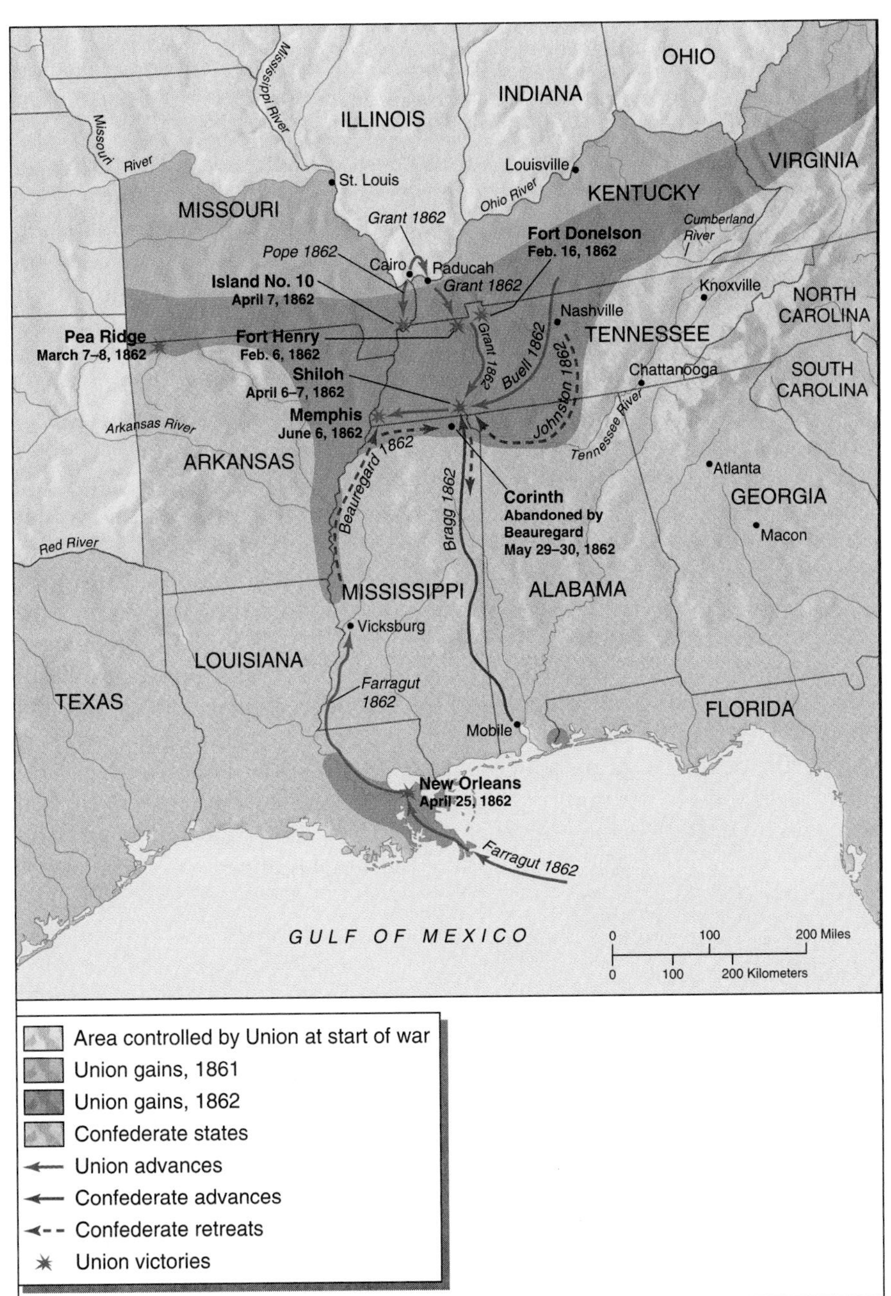

Map 16-2 The War in the West, 1861–1862

Because of the early Union emphasis on capturing Richmond, the war in the West seemed less important to Northerners. But, from a strategic standpoint, the victories at Forts Henry and Donelson, which drove a wedge into southern territory and closed the Confederacy's quickest path to the West from Virginia and the Carolinas, and the capture of New Orleans and its Mississippi River port were crucial and set the stage for greater Federal success in the West in 1863.

Corinth, Mississippi. General Henry W. Halleck, Grant's superior, assumed personal command of the Union troops and captured Corinth in May 1862, but he did not pursue the Confederate army, which slipped away to fight another day.

Federal forces complemented their victories at Shiloh and Corinth with another important success in the western Confederacy. Admiral David G. Farragut, who remained a Unionist even though born in Tennessee, blasted the Confederate river defenses protecting New Orleans and sailed a Federal fleet into the city in April 1862. The result was to open two hundred miles of the Mississippi River, the nation's most vital commercial waterway, to Union traffic. With the fall of Memphis to Union forces in June, Vicksburg remained the only major river town still in Confederate hands.

The fall of New Orleans underscored a major problem with the Confederates' defensive strategy: Their military reserves were stretched too thin to defend their vast territory. The defenses at New Orleans had been weak in part because the troops assigned to them had been shifted north to counter the Union advance in Tennessee.

The Federal offensive in the West had swept into the heart of Dixie. Vicksburg and the rich cottonfields of Mississippi were now vulnerable to Union assault. To the east lay Chattanooga, Tennessee, the last major Confederate bastion protecting Georgia and the eastern Confederacy from Union armies.

Reassessing the War

The fierce fighting at Shiloh wrought unprecedented carnage. More American soldiers were lost at Shiloh than in all of the nation's wars combined up to that time. Each side suffered more than ten thousand casualties. By the time the smoke had cleared, the soldiers' view of the war had undergone a major transformation. The initial enthusiasm and bravado was replaced by the sober realization that death or capture was a likely outcome and that heroism, courage, and piety did not guarantee survival. A hunger for peace replaced the thirst for battle. "Too shocking too horrible," a Confederate survivor of Shiloh wrote. "God grant that I may never be the partaker in such scenes again. . . . When released from this I shall ever be an advocate of peace." A Union soldier wrote of "the dead and dying lying in masses, some with arms, legs, and even their jaws shot off, bleeding to death, and no one to wait upon them to dress their wounds."

Landing in a hospital scarcely improved a wounded or ill soldier's chances of survival. Kate Cumming, a nurse at a Confederate hospital in Corinth, wrote of soldiers brought from the battle "mutilated in every imaginable way." The wounded lay packed together on the floor, and Cumming negotiated the rooms with great difficulty to avoid stepping on the dead and dying. Piercing the air were the screams of men undergoing amputations, often with little or no anesthetic. Some pleaded with physicians to kill them and end their misery. Others bore the pain stoically and entrusted last words and letters to nurses, dying with the word "Mother" on their lips.

Women on both sides played a major role in caring for the wounded and sick. As Kate Cumming explained, "In war, the men to fight, and the women to nurse." In the North, members of the U.S. Sanitary Commission attempted to upgrade hospital and medical care. This voluntary organization, formed in April 1861, was staffed mainly by women volunteers who collected and distributed medical supplies and clothing and advised on cleaning hospitals and camps. The commission made some headway during the first year of the war, but in the months after Shiloh and with the resumption of fighting in the East, the extent of casualties often overwhelmed the dedicated volunteers. And the bloodiest fighting lay ahead.

Artist Winslow Homer's depiction of the place soldiers spent most of their time: camp. A soldier's life was boredom occasionally interspersed with fierce and deadly combat.

Even if a soldier escaped death on the battlefield and survived a hospital stay, he still faced the possibility of death from disease. Roughly twice as many men died from disease as on the battlefield during the Civil War. Heaps of garbage, contaminated food and water, and swarming mosquitoes, flies, and lice created unhealthy camp conditions. Typhoid, commonly and appropriately known as "camp fever," claimed the most lives.

Many soldiers turned to religion for consolation in response to the growing carnage. The frequency of camp prayer meetings and revivals increased after Shiloh. Many a recruit carried books with titles such as *Satan's Bait* and *A Mother's Parting Words to Her Soldier Boy* in his knapsack. Soldiers often gathered with their comrades to sing hymns before retiring for the night. Stories circulated of a Bible that stopped a bullet whistling toward a soldier's heart. But veterans knew that a deck of cards did just as well, and they understood that neither Bibles nor cards offered protection against artillery.

Soldiers responded in various ways to constant danger and fear. Some talked or yelled loudly. (The Confederate rebel yell probably served to relieve some of the tension of battle as well as to frighten the enemy.) Others shook so much that they fell down, unable to control their limbs. A few soldiers could not wake up in the morning without being doused with cold water; "they wanted to stay out, they couldn't bear to remember all this mess waiting with first light."

The harsh conditions of camp life often strained relations between officers and enlisted men. Volunteers expected the army to follow the same democratic procedures they were used to in civilian life. Companies elected their officers up to the rank of lieutenant and captain, and some regiments elected officers as high as the rank of colonel. Personality rather than ability carried many elections, with incompetence and insubordination the outcome in some cases. Independent young men, unaccustomed to deferring to anyone in civilian life, did not willingly become more docile in the military.

Soldiers also suffered from boredom. Battles rarely lasted more than a day or two. While in camp between engagements, a recruit faced seemingly incessant drilling (loading and firing a rifle required nine separate steps) and heavy chores such as chopping wood and hauling water. Typically, he spent what little time remained resting, writing, reading, and eating. To relieve their anxieties, soldiers talked about home and loved ones, upcoming or recent battles, and food. Soldiers also fought the boredom and harsh physical conditions of camp life by singing, playing cards, and competing in sports like footracing and makeshift forms of football and baseball.

Women camp followers cooked, did laundry, and provided sexual services for a price. The two capitals, Washington and Richmond, had notorious vice districts. A Confederate recruit lamented that "almost half of the women in the vicinity of the army, married and unmarried, are lost to all virtue." Both armies experienced soaring rates of venereal disease.

By 1862, the war's carnage and brutality had dispelled any lingering notions of war as a chivalrous enterprise. At a battle in Virginia that year, Stonewall Jackson reprimanded a Confederate general who had ordered his men not to shoot at a Union officer riding before his own men, rallying them on. "This is no ordinary war," Jackson said, "and the brave and gallant Federal officers are the very kind that must be killed. Shoot the brave officers and the cowards will run away and take the men with them." The reluctance of some commanders to pursue retreating armies or to initiate campaigns resulted in part from their recognition of how awful the war really was.

The War in the East

With Grant and Farragut squeezing the Confederacy in the West, Lincoln ordered a new offensive against Richmond in the East that he believed would end the war. Following the defeat at Bull Run, he had shaken up the Union high command and appointed General George B. McClellan to lead what was now called the Army of the Potomac.

A West Point graduate, McClellan had served with distinction in the Mexican War. In 1857, he resigned from the military to pursue a career in business as a railroad official. He was called back into active duty at the outbreak of the Civil War. When he assumed command of the Army of the Potomac, it was no more than a collection of raw recruits and disgruntled veterans. McClellan succeeded in transforming it into a disciplined fighting force. He was well liked by his soldiers, who referred to him affectionately as "Little Mac." McClellan returned their affection, perhaps too much. A superb organizer, he would prove overly cautious on the field of battle.

In March 1862, at the outset of the **Peninsula Campaign**, McClellan moved his 112,000-man army out of Washington and maneuvered his forces by boat down the Potomac River and Chesapeake Bay to the peninsula between the York and James Rivers southeast of the Confederate capital. Union forces took Yorktown, Williamsburg, and Norfolk. The Confederates, commanded by General Joseph E. Johnston, withdrew up the Peninsula toward

Richmond, preparing for what most felt would be the decisive battle of the war.

McClellan, moving ponderously up the peninsula, clashed with Johnston's army inconclusively at Seven Pines in late May 1862. Johnston was badly wounded in the clash, and President Davis replaced him with General Robert E. Lee, who renamed the forces under his command the Army of Northern Virginia.

Lee was from a prominent Virginia family long accustomed to power and command. His father, "Light-Horse Harry" Lee, had been a Revolutionary War hero. Lee attended West Point, served with distinction in the Mexican War, and commanded the Federal force that captured John Brown at Harpers Ferry in 1859. In 1831, he married Mary Custis, the granddaughter of George Washington's adopted son. Their gracious home in Arlington, Virginia, had a commanding view of the Potomac and Washington, D.C. Before the war, it had seemed as if Lee would live out his days as a soldier-farmer much like his wife's grandfather.

In 1860, the army posted Lee to Texas, where he watched the secession drama unfold. He opposed secession but was unwilling to take up arms against his native Virginia. Refusing an offer from Winfield Scott to take command of Federal forces, he resigned from the U.S. Army and went with Virginia after it left the Union.

Lee's reserved and aristocratic bearing masked a gambler's disposition. One fellow officer noted, "His name might be Audacity. He will take more chances, and take them quicker than any other general in this country." Under his daring leadership, the Confederacy's defensive strategy underwent an important shift.

Lee seized the initiative on June 25, 1862, attacking McClellan's right flank. Although inconclusive, the attack pushed the nervous McClellan into a defensive position. For a week, the armies sparred in a series of fierce engagements known collectively as the **Seven Days' Battles**. More than thirty thousand men were killed or wounded on both sides, the deadliest week of the war so far. Although McClellan prevailed in these contests, the carnage so shocked him that he withdrew down the peninsula and away from Richmond. The retreat bitterly disappointed Lincoln, who wanted McClellan to push on to the Confederate capital. The exasperated president ordered McClellan and the Army of the Potomac back to northern Virginia and placed John Pope at the head of the newly formed Army of Virginia to carry on the fight.

Although Lee had saved Richmond, his troops had suffered frightfully. He had lost one-fourth of his eighty thousand–man army, but he remained convinced of the wisdom of his offensive-defensive strategy. Better coordination between his staff and field commanders, he believed, would have reduced his casualties and inflicted greater damage on the enemy.

A career army officer who resigned his commission to serve his state and new country, Confederate General Robert E. Lee's quiet courage and sense of duty inspired his men.

Lee and Stonewall Jackson went to work on John Pope to vindicate their tactics. A series of inconclusive skirmishes, highlighted by Jackson's lightning thrusts at Pope and young J. E. B. Stuart's daring cavalry raid on a Federal base, brought Union and Confederate armies together once more near Manassas Junction. The **Second Battle of Bull Run** was as much a disaster for the Union as the first had been. Lee's generalship completely befuddled Pope and again saved Richmond. With better coordination than they had displayed during the Peninsula Campaign, Lee's forces sustained fewer losses than Pope's army and kept the Federals from moving beyond the positions they held in Virginia at the start of the war. Lee and the Army of Northern Virginia were developing a reputation for invincibility.

Turning Points, 1862–1863

The impressive Confederate victories in the East masked the delicate condition of Southern fortunes. The longer the Confederacy held off Union offensives, the greater the likelihood of securing the South's independence. But the longer the war continued, the higher the probability that the Confederacy's shortcomings in men, finances, and materiel would erode its ability to keep fighting. Lee's offensive-defensive strategy seemed to be working, but it raised the possibility that the Confederacy could exhaust its men and resources before it sealed its independence.

The waning summer months of 1862 brought other concerns to the Davis administration in Richmond. Access to the sea was vital for the South's export economy and its financial well-being. But the Union navy was choking the South's commercial link with Europe.

Davis looked to the nations of Europe for diplomatic recognition as well as for trade. Diplomatic ties would lend legitimacy to the Confederacy's fight for independence. With them might come financial aid, offers to mediate with the North, perhaps even armed intervention against the North. For these same reasons, the Union sought to block recognition. Southern envoys and their Union counterparts sparred in the courts and parliaments of Europe.

But the most important arena of the war remained the battlefield. Diplomatic triumph, financial solvency, and civilian support depended on military success. Having stymied the Union war machine, Lee contemplated a bold move—a thrust into Northern territory to bring the conflict to the North and stoke Northerners' rising hostility to the war. It was a bold plan that might end the war and secure Southern independence—or hasten an otherwise inevitable Union victory.

President Lincoln also harbored a bold plan. Gradually during the spring and summer of 1862, the president had concluded that emancipation of the Confederacy's slaves was essential for preserving the Union. Emancipation would provide Federal forces with both moral and strategic advantages over their foes. But Lincoln was reluctant to take this step before the Union's fortunes on the battlefield improved. Without a significant victory, emancipation would appear to be an act of desperation.

As the fall of 1862 approached, both Union and Confederate governments prepared for the most significant conflicts of the war to date.

The Naval War

The Union's naval strategy was to blockade the Southern coast and capture its key seaports and river towns. The intention was to prevent arms, clothing, and food from reaching the Confederacy and keep cotton and tobacco from leaving. Destroying the South's ability to carry on trade would also prevent the Confederacy from raising money to purchase the goods it needed to wage war.

Neither side had much of a navy at the outset of the war. With more than three thousand miles of Confederate coastline to cover, the Union blockade was weak at first. As time passed and the number of ships in the Union navy grew, the blockade tightened. The skyrocketing prices of Southern staples on world markets by 1862 attested to the effectiveness of the Union strategy.

Understandably, the Confederate naval strategy was to break the blockade and defend the South's vital rivers and seaports. The Confederacy attacked the blockade with a variety of weapons. In March 1862, the South refurbished a scuttled Union vessel, the *Merrimac*, with iron plate and renamed it the *Virginia*. The *Virginia* easily destroyed two wooden Union ships blockading Hampton Roads, Virginia. But the Southern advantage was short-lived. The Union navy had outfitted an ironclad of its own, the *Monitor*, and a day after the *Virginia's* success, the two vessels dueled each other to a draw. Thereafter, the Union navy gained a superiority in ironclads, and the Confederates never seriously threatened the blockade again.

But if the Confederates could not break the blockade, they could evade it. They built several warships to serve as blockade runners and as privateers to attack Union merchant ships. The *Sumter*, under the command of Raphael Semmes, captured eighteen ships in the Caribbean and the Atlantic in 1862. Semmes did even better with his next command, the *Alabama*. In this vessel, he sailed the Atlantic for two years, preying on Union vessels. He seized sixty-four merchant ships and sank a Union warship. The Union cruiser *Kearsarge* finally sent the *Alabama* to the bottom of the Atlantic in June 1864. During the *Alabama's* rovings, merchants at English ports provided the ship with supplies, fuel, and other support, creating tensions between the Federal and British governments. Although the Confederate navy never seriously threatened Union overseas commerce, insurance rates for Northern merchants rose during the war. And more than seven hundred Union vessels flew the British flag to avoid capture. The Confederate navy also disrupted Federal coastal operations.

Historians disagree about the effectiveness of the Union naval blockade. As late as 1864, the ports

OVERVIEW

MAJOR BATTLES OF THE CIVIL WAR, 1861–1863

Battle or Campaign	Date	Outcome and Consequences
First Bull Run	July 21, 1861	Confederate victory, destroyed the widespread belief in the North that the war would end quickly, fueled Confederate sense of superiority
Forts Henry and Donelson	Feb. 6–16, 1862	Union victory, gave the North control of strategic river systems in the western Confederacy and closed an important link between the eastern and western Confederacy
Shiloh Church	Apr. 6–7, 1862	Union victory, high casualties transformed attitudes about the war on both sides
Seven Days' Battles	June 25–July 1, 1862	Standoff, halted Union General McClellan's advance on Richmond in the Peninsula Campaign
Second Bull Run	Aug. 29–30, 1862	Confederate victory, reinforced Confederate General Robert E. Lee's reputation for invincibility
Antietam	Sept. 17, 1862	Standoff, halted Lee's advance into the North, eliminated Confederacy's chance for diplomatic recognition, encouraged Lincoln to issue the Emancipation Proclamation
Fredericksburg	Dec. 13, 1862	Confederate victory, revived morale of Lee's army
Chancellorsville	May 2–6, 1863	Confederate victory, Confederate General Stonewall Jackson killed, encouraged Lee to again invade North
Gettysburg	July 1–3, 1863	Union victory, halted Confederate advance in the North, major psychological blow to Confederacy
Vicksburg	Nov. 1862–July 1863	Union victory; closed the key remaining Confederate port on the Mississippi, with Gettysburg, dealt a severe blow to Confederate cause
Chattanooga	Aug.–Nov. 1863	Union victory, solidified Union dominance in the West and cleared the way to Atlanta

of Charleston, Mobile, Wilmington (North Carolina), and Galveston remained in Confederate control and open to blockade runners. The last of these ports did not fall to the Union until January 1865. One estimate suggests that the Union navy captured only one in six blockade runners. The rest succeeded in smuggling in arms, food, and clothing to the Confederacy. With the enormous profits shipowners reaped from blockade running, they could afford to lose some of their ships. Yet high insurance rates and the threat of seizure may have caused some merchants on both sides of the Atlantic to abandon blockade running. In any case, blockade runners were small, light ships, designed for speed and evasion. Their cargo space was limited. Larger Southern vessels rarely attempted to slip through the blockade. With limited resources and capital, the Confederacy was heavily dependent on the flow of trade. Any restriction in that flow hurt the Southern cause.

The Diplomatic War

Southerners thought that the recognition of their independence by overseas governments would legitimize their cause in the eyes of the world. They also remembered the crucial role that timely French assistance had played in the American Revolution and hoped for similar support.

Great Britain had several reasons to support the Confederate cause. After two wars and a succession of diplomatic wrangles, it had no great love of the United States. If the country divided, it would pose less of a threat to British economic and territorial ambitions. Also, the aristocratic pretensions of some Southerners appealed to their British counterparts, who viewed the upstart, immigrant-clogged cities of the North with distaste. (One member of Parliament claimed that the Union army was composed of "the scum and refuse of Europe.") Finally, some British textile magnates supported the Confederacy because they feared a drastic reduction in the supply of Southern cotton.

British foreign policy, however, had been antislavery for a quarter century, and the slavery issue turned many Britons against the South. The Union cause had support in high ruling circles, especially from Queen Victoria, as well as from middle-class and working-class Britons. One working-class leader declared the Confederate cause "odious and . . . blasphemous" and hoped for a reunited America that would become "the hope of freedom, and a refuge for the oppressed of every race and of every clime."

Emperor Napoleon III of France, who had imperial designs on Mexico, favored the Confederacy. A restored Union, he thought, would pose a greater threat to his ambitions than a divided one. But Napoleon feared antagonizing the powerful British and would not intervene unilaterally in the Confederate cause.

The Russians were probably the staunchest supporters of the Union abroad. The odd friendship between the Western world's most autocratic country and its most democratic one resulted primarily from political expediency. The Russian tsar, Alexander II, saw the United States as a counterweight to British power. There was also some sympathy for the North's opposition to slavery in Russia, where the tsar had abolished serfdom (a form of slavery) in 1861.

Southerners were convinced that their cotton was so important to the world economy that they could use it as a diplomatic bargaining chip. "You dare not to make war on cotton. . . . Cotton is King." So declared South Carolina senator James H. Hammond in a warning to the North in 1858. A London Times correspondent reported that a Southerner told him, "Why, sir, we have only to shut off your supply of cotton for a few weeks and we can create a revolution in Great Britain." But King Cotton was no more successful at coercing the British—who had large cotton reserves and an alternate source of supply in Egypt—into granting recognition to the Confederacy than it was at stopping the North from going to war against the South.

The Davis administration did chalk up some minor diplomatic victories early in the war. Great Britain declared itself neutral and allowed British merchants to sell arms and supplies to both Confederate and Union forces. This policy especially benefited the Confederacy, with its limited arsenal. France followed with a similar concession. Davis almost won a more significant diplomatic victory in November 1861 when a Federal warship overtook the British mail packet *Trent* and, ignoring Britain's neutrality, seized two Confederate diplomats en route to England. The affair outraged the British and pushed Britain and the Union to the verge of war. Lincoln's secretary of state, William Seward, however, advised "one war at a time," and Lincoln agreed. The Confederates were released, and the crisis was defused.

In the end, the Confederacy's hopes for diplomatic recognition depended on its ability to show that it could secure its independence on the battlefield. After Lee's victories in Virginia in the spring of 1862 and his subsequent decision to invade the North, British intervention in the war grew more likely. The British government had more or less decided that if Lee emerged victorious from his planned invasion, it would press for mediation. The United States ambassador to Great Britain, Charles Francis Adams, worried that "unless a very few weeks show some great military result we shall have our hands full in this quarter." William Gladstone, England's future prime minister, believed that Lee would achieve his goal. He concluded that "we may anticipate with certainty the success of the Southern States so far as regards their separation from the North."

Antietam

The alarming arithmetic of the offensive-defensive strategy convinced Lee that the South could not sustain a prolonged conflict. He knew that his army must keep the pressure on Union forces and, if possible, destroy them quickly. Union success in the Mississippi Valley threatened to cut the Confederacy in two and deprive it of the resources of a vast chunk of territory. Within a year, the Confederacy might cease to exist west of the Appalachians. He desperately needed a dramatic victory.

In September 1862, Lee crossed the Potomac into Maryland as his band played "Maryland, My Maryland" for the unimpressed residents. He was on his way to cut off the Pennsylvania Railroad at Harrisburg. Lee established camp at Frederick, scattering his army at various sites, convinced that McClellan and the Army of the Potomac would not attack him.

At this point, luck intervened for the North. At an abandoned Confederate encampment, a Union corporal found three wrapped cigars on the ground, evidently tossed out by a careless Confederate officer. To the corporal's amazement, the wrapping was a copy of Lee's orders for the disposition of his army. But even with this information, "Little Mac" moved so cautiously that Lee had time to gather his and Jackson's regiments and retreat to defensive positions at Sharpsburg, Maryland, along Antietam Creek. There Lee's army of 50,000 men came to blows with McClellan's army of 75,000.

The **Battle of Antietam** saw the bloodiest single day of fighting in American history. About 2,100 Union soldiers and 2,700 Confederates died on the battlefield, and another 18,500, equally divided, were wounded. McClellan squandered his numerical superiority with uncoordinated and timid Union attacks. Although the armies had fought to a tactical draw, the battle was a strategic defeat for the Confederacy. In the battle's aftermath, Lee's troops limped back across the Potomac into Virginia. McClellan did not pursue.

Antietam marked a major turning point in the war. It kept Lee from directly threatening Northern industry and financial institutions. It prompted Britain and France to abandon plans to grant recognition to the Confederacy. And it provided Lincoln with the victory he needed to announce the abolition of slavery.

Emancipation

President Lincoln despised slavery, but he had always maintained that preserving the Union was his primary war goal. "If I could save the Union without freeing any slave I would do it," he wrote to newspaper editor Horace Greeley in August 1862, "and if I could save it by freeing all the slaves I would do it; and if I could save it by freeing some and leaving others alone, I would also do that." An astute politician, Lincoln realized that he had to stress union and equivocate on slavery to keep the Northern public united in support of the war. But from the war's outset, the possibility of emancipation as a war objective was considered in the Republican Congress, within the Union army, and among citizens throughout the Northern states. Northern soldiers, as they moved south, saw slaves building trenches, earthworks, bridges, and roads for the Confederate army as well as working Southern farms. As a result, pressure grew within the Union army to declare emancipation as a way to deprive the South and the Confederate army of its labor force.

In August 1861, fighting to keep Missouri in the Union, General John C. Frémont broadly interpreted federal legislation allowing Union commanders to confiscate Confederate property and issued a proclamation freeing the state's slaves. Frémont's decree delighted abolitionists but alarmed wavering Unionists in the border states. President Lincoln commanded Frémont to rescind it.

Lincoln said in his inaugural address that he had "no purpose, directly or indirectly, to interfere with the institution of slavery in the states where it exists." Despite the urging of some Republican colleagues, he stood by this pledge and revoked two other emancipation edicts besides Frémont's. By March 1862, however, his moral repugnance toward slavery and the military arguments for abolition led him to propose a resolution, which Congress adopted, supporting the compensated emancipation of slaves. The measure died, however, when Congress failed to appropriate funds for it and border state slaveholders expressed no interest in the plan.

Pressure from Northern civilians, Union soldiers, and Congress for some form of emancipation mounted in the spring of 1862. In response, the Republican Congress prohibited slavery in the territories and abolished slavery in the District of Columbia. The act emancipating the district's slaves called for compensating slave owners and colonizing the freed slaves in black republics such as Haiti and Liberia. Then in July 1862, Congress passed the **Confiscation Act**, which ordered the seizure of land from disloyal Southerners and the emancipation of their slaves.

Although support for emancipation had grown both in the army and among civilians, Lincoln still faced political considerations that dictated against it. Emancipation was still not favored by a majority in the North, especially not in the border states. Lincoln feared a blow to Union military morale, the loss of loyal border states, and a voter backlash in the fall 1862 congressional elections. The thousands of Irish Catholic immigrants who entered the Union army and who had competed with black workers for jobs in Northern cities during the 1850s were especially opposed to emancipation, fearing loss of economic security. They also resented the abolitionists' Protestant moralizing. Roman Catholic archbishop John Hughes of New York declared that "we Catholics, and a vast majority of our brave troops in the field, have not the slightest idea of carrying on a war that costs so much blood and treasure just to gratify a clique of Abolitionists in the North."

But other considerations favored emancipation. Freeing the slaves would appeal to the strong antislavery sentiment in Britain and gain support for the Union cause abroad. And it would weaken the Confederacy's ability to wage war by removing a crucial source of labor.

By mid-1862, the president had resolved to act on his moral convictions and proclaim emancipation. Taking the advice of Secretary of State Seward, however, he decided to wait for a battlefield victory so that the measure would not appear an act of desperation. Antietam gave the president his opening, narrow though it was, and on September 22, 1862, he announced his intention to issue the **Emancipation Proclamation**, to take effect January 1, 1863, in all states still in rebellion. The proclamation exempted slaves in the border states loyal to the Union and in areas under Federal occupation.

Southerners reacted to the Emancipation Proclamation with outrage. Some viewed it as an invitation to race war and conjured up fears of freed slaves slaying white women and children while their men were at the battlefront. Jefferson Davis, taking a positive view, thought the proclamation would invigorate the Southern war effort. Some observers abroad were skeptical. One London newspaper, noting that emancipation did not apply to all slaves, stated, "The principle is not that a human being cannot justly own another, but that he cannot own him unless he is loyal to the United States." Foreign newspapers and governments questioned the president's sincerity, but the European people supported him. English textile workers who had cause to side with the South because their jobs depended on Southern cotton, supported Lincoln's efforts to "strike off the fetters of the slave."

Northerners generally approved the Emancipation Proclamation. Although abolitionists comprised a minority of the Northern population, most civilians and soldiers accepted emancipation for its military advantages. A private in the Army of the Potomac who had previously expressed serious reservations about emancipation wrote home his support for "putting away any institution if by so doing it will help put down the rebellion." Not all sentiment in the North was so accommodating. Many Democrats opposed the move both for political and personal reasons. And some Republicans expressed regret that Lincoln's document was not more sweeping.

But the Emancipation Proclamation represented far more than its qualified words and phrases expressed. "A mighty *act*," Massachusetts governor John Andrew called it. Lincoln had freed the slaves. He and the Union war effort were now tied to the cause of freedom. What began as a war to save the Union had became a holy war of deliverance. Freedom and Union entwined in the public consciousness of the North. As Lincoln noted in his December 1862 message to Congress, "In giving freedom to the slave, we assure freedom to the free." Emancipation also unified the Republican party and strengthened the president's hand in conducting the war.

"Stealing" Freedom

As word of the Emancipation Proclamation raced through the slave grapevine, slaves rejoiced that their long-awaited day of jubilee had arrived. But the proclamation only continued a process that had begun when the first Union armies invaded the South. In the months before freedom came, many slaves had run away to Union camps, dug Union trenches, and scouted for Federal troops.

Southern masters fought to deter their slaves by severely punishing the families of black men who fled to Union lines. They used the courts and slave catchers to reclaim runaways. Some Confederate masters protected their investments by removing slaves to Texas or to areas far from Federal forces. And a few slave owners whipped, sold, and even killed their slaves to prevent them from joining Union troops.

But in the end, slaveholders could not stem the tide of slaves fleeing toward the Union lines and freedom. The 1862 Confiscation Act included slaves with other Confederate property as the "contraband" of war and subject to confiscation, a term Union general Benjamin Butler had applied to escaped slaves as early as May 1861. As they helped the

Even before the Emancipation Proclamation, slaves throughout the South "stole" their freedom. After the Proclamation, the trickle of black slaves abandoning their masters became a flood, as they sought freedom behind Union lines.

Union cause, **contrabands** also sought to help fellow slaves "steal" their freedom. When Union forces occupied part of the Georgia coast in April 1862, for example, March Haynes, a slave who had worked as a river pilot in Savannah, began smuggling slaves to Union lines. Federal general Quincy Adams Gillmore provided a swift boat for Haynes's missions. In return, Haynes supplied Gillmore with "exact and valuable information" on the strength and location of Confederate defenses.

The former slaves who arrived at Federal camps after emancipation often encountered poor conditions but relished their freedom nonetheless. A Northern missionary in occupied Louisiana wrote in 1863 that he was surrounded by "negroes in uniform, negroes in rags, negroes in frame houses, negroes living in tents, negroes living in rail pens covered with brush, and negroes living under brush piles without any rails, negroes living on the bare ground with the sky for their covering; all hopeful . . . every one pleading to be taught, willing to do anything for learning."

The Emancipation Proclamation accelerated the slaves' flight from bondage. Personally fighting to secure their freedom and liberating those still enslaved became the objective of many, for after 1863, ex-slaves served in increasing numbers in the Union army.

Black Troops in the Union Army

More than 80 percent of the roughly 180,000 black soldiers and 20,000 black sailors who fought for the Union were slaves and free black men from the South. For the typical black Southerner who joined the army, the passage from bondage to freedom came quickly. Making his escape from his master, he perhaps "stole" his family as well. He typically experienced his first days of freedom behind Union lines, where he may have learned to read and write. Finally, he put on the Federal uniform, experiencing, as one black Southern volunteer commented, "the biggest thing that ever happened in my life."

As early as August 1862, five thousand African Americans had enrolled in the Union army in the occupied Sea Islands off South Carolina despite a widely publicized Confederate directive promising to shoot black prisoners of war. This threat was later withdrawn when Union officers declared that they would do the same with Confederate prisoners. The Confederacy, however, held fast to its refusal to parole, or send back, captured black soldiers, a policy that led to the end of prisoner exchanges in early 1863 and contributed to horrible conditions in overcrowded prisoner-of-war camps on both sides.

Initially, the enlistment of black soldiers in South Carolina encountered opposition in the North. By early 1863, however, public opinion was changing. One reason was that white Northerners realized that the enlistment of African Americans relieved them in comparable numbers from military service. President Lincoln strongly advocated enlisting former slaves. In March 1863, he wrote with exaggerated enthusiasm, "The bare sight of 50,000 armed and drilled black soldiers on the banks of the Mississippi would end the rebellion at once."

On the contrary, the appearance of black Union troops infuriated the Confederates. After a battle at Milliken's Bend, Louisiana, in 1863, for example, observers found dead Confederate and black Union soldiers entangled in each other's arms and impaled on one another's bayonets.

But for black volunteers, the promise of freedom and redemption outweighed the dangers of combat. Black abolitionists campaigned tirelessly for the enlistment of free black men and fugitive slaves in the Union army. Frederick Douglass, whose son Lewis distinguished himself in the all-black 54th Massachusetts Volunteer Infantry Regiment, explained in early 1863, "Once let the black man get upon his person the brass letters, 'U.S.,' let him get an eagle on his buttons and a musket on his shoulder and bullets in his pockets, and there is no power on earth which can deny that he has earned the right to citizenship in the United States." Other black abolitionists took up the refrain. Sojourner Truth, a former slave who saw many of her thirteen children sold into slavery,

COME AND JOIN US BROTHERS.
PUBLISHED BY THE SUPERVISORY COMMITTEE FOR RECRUITING COLORED REGIMENTS
1210 CHESTNUT ST. PHILADELPHIA.

Lithograph; ICHi-22051; "Come and Join Us Brothers" Civil War; Philadelphia PA; ca. 1863. Creator P. S. Duval & Son. Chicago Historical Society.

Once orders were issued allowing the recruitment of black troops, posters like this appeared throughout the North. The illustrations stressed the dignity and manhood of military service, but also showed segregated soldiers and white officers.

canvassed northern cities to rally public opinion for the deployment of black troops.

Although black soldiers were eager to engage the enemy and fought as ably as their white comrades, they received lower pay and performed the most menial duties in camp. Abolitionists and black leaders in the North pressured President Lincoln for more equitable treatment of African-American recruits. When Frederick Douglass complained to Lincoln about the lower pay that black troops received, the president defended the practice, noting that "their enlistment was a serious offense to popular prejudice" and the fact "that they were not to receive the same pay as white soldiers seemed a necessary concession to smooth the way to their employment at all as soldiers."

Despite discrimination, black soldiers fought valiantly at Port Hudson, Louisiana; near Charleston; and, late in the war, at the siege of Petersburg, Virginia. After hearing of African-American troops fighting Confederate forces nearby, one young white Mississippian wrote in her diary, "It is said the Negro regiments fought there like mad demons." The most celebrated black encounter with Confederate troops occurred in July 1863 during a futile assault by the 54th Massachusetts Regiment on **Fort Wagner** outside Charleston (see "American Views: Lewis Douglass on the Fighting of the 54th Massachusetts Regiment"). The Northern press, previously lukewarm toward black troops, heaped praise on the effort. "Through the cannon smoke of that dark night," intoned a writer in the *Atlantic Monthly*, "the manhood of the colored race shines before many eyes that would not see."

If only President Lincoln could find such gallantry among his generals! George McClellan had failed to follow his advantage at Antietam in September 1862, allowing Lee's army to escape to Virginia and remain a formidable fighting force. And despite Union successes in the West, the Confederate forces massed there remained largely intact.

Fredericksburg and Chancellorsville

In late 1862, after Antietam, the president replaced McClellan with General Ambrose E. Burnside. The new chief of the Army of the Potomac, an imposing physical presence, sported bushy whiskers on his cheeks that came to be known as "sideburns," a transposition of the two parts of his name. Despite his commanding stature, Burnside was shy and insecure. Claiming incompetence, he had twice refused the command. His judgment proved better than Lincoln's.

Moving swiftly against Lee's dispersed army in northern Virginia, Burnside reached the Rappahannock River opposite **Fredericksburg** in November 1862 (see Map 16-3). But the pontoon bridges to ford his 120,000 soldiers across the river arrived three weeks late, giving Lee an opportunity to gather his 78,000 men. On December 13, the Union forces launched a poorly coordinated and foolish frontal assault that the Confederates repelled, inflicting heavy Federal casualties. Burnside, having

Map 16-3 From Fredericksburg to Gettysburg: The War in the East, December 1862–July 1863
By all logic, the increasingly outgunned and outfinanced Confederacy should have been showing signs of faltering by 1863. But bungling by Union generals at Fredericksburg and Chancellorsville sustained Southern fortunes and encouraged Robert E. Lee to attempt another Northern invasion.

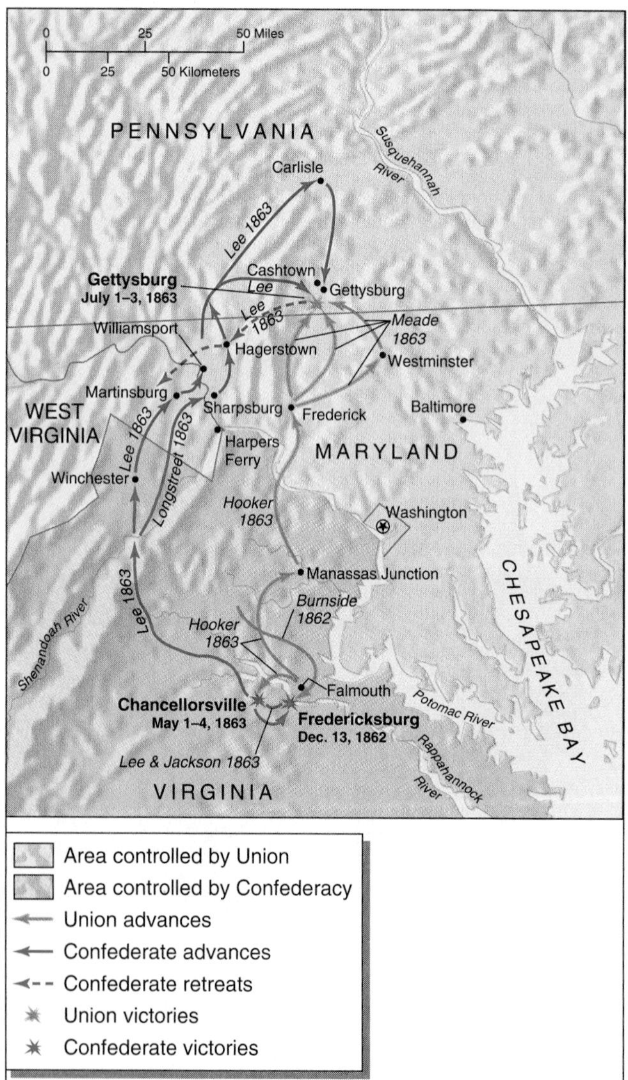

American Views

Lewis Douglass on the Fighting of the 54th Massachusetts Regiment

When the Civil War began, Union officials did not permit African Americans to enlist. But black Northerners successfully pressured the Lincoln administration to reverse that policy and began fighting in all-black units as early as 1862. The excerpt here is a letter from Lewis Douglass (son of black abolitionist Frederick Douglass) of the 54th Massachusetts Regiment to his wife after the failed Union assault on Fort Wagner in South Carolina.

❖ **What motivated black Northerners, all of whom were free, to enlist by the thousands in the Union army?**

July 20 [1863]
My Dear Amelia:
I have been in two fights, and am unhurt. I am about to go in another I believe tonight. Our men fought well on both occasions. The last one was desperate. We charged that terrible battery on . . . Fort Wagner and were repulsed. . . . I escaped unhurt from amidst that perfect hail of shot and shell. It was terrible. . . . This regiment has established its reputation as a fighting regiment. Not a man flinched, though it was a trying time. Men fell all around me. . . . Our men would close up again, but it was no use. . . . How I got out of that fight alive I cannot tell, but I am here. My dear girl, I hope again to see you. I must bid you farewell should I be killed. Remember if I die, I die in a good cause. I wish we had a hundred thousand colored troops. We would put an end to this war.

Your own loving
Lewis

Source: Carter G. Woodson, ed., The Mind of the Negro as Reflected in Letters Written during the Crisis 1800–1860 *(1926).*

performed to his own expectations, was relieved of his command, and Major General Joseph Hooker was installed in his place.

The hard-drinking Hooker lacked Burnside's humility but not his incompetence. Resuming the offensive in the spring of 1863, Hooker hoped to outflank Lee. But the Confederate commander surprised Hooker by sending Stonewall Jackson to outflank the Union right. Between May 1 and May 4, Lee's army delivered a series of crushing attacks on Hooker's forces at **Chancellorsville**. Outnumbered two to one, Lee had pulled off another stunning victory—but at a high cost. Lee lost some thirteen thousand men, fewer than Hooker's seventeen thousand, but more than the Confederacy could afford.

Lee also lost Stonewall Jackson at Chancellorsville. Nervous Confederate sentries mistakenly shot and wounded him as he returned from a reconnoitering mission, and he died a few days later. Known for his lightning strikes at the enemy and his brilliant understanding of the tactics of modern warfare, Jackson had helped Lee win some of the Confederacy's most stunning victories in 1862. Lee recognized the tragedy of Jackson's loss for himself and his country. "Any victory," the Confederate commander wrote, "would be dear at such a price. I know not how to replace him."

"Master Abraham Lincoln gets a new Toy." The "toy" in this case is Major General Joseph Hooker, who, in late 1862, became the latest in a frustrating line of musical-chair generals whom President Lincoln appointed in the hope of achieving a decisive victory over Confederate forces. Not until Grant and Sherman emerged the following year did the President find generals who were not only willing to fight but fought well.

Still, Lee appeared invincible. Chancellorsville thrust Lincoln into another bout of despair. "My God!" he exclaimed in agony, "What will the country say! What will the country say!" Meanwhile, Lee, to take advantage of the Confederacy's momentum and the Union's gloom, planned another bold move. On June 3, 1863, the 75,000-man Army of Northern Virginia broke camp and headed north once again.

Gettysburg

President Lincoln sent the Union Army of the Potomac after Lee. But General Hooker dallied, requested more troops, and allowed the Confederates to march from Maryland into Pennsylvania. An infuriated Lincoln replaced Hooker with George Gordon Meade.

Lee and Meade were personal friends—they had served together during the Mexican War—and the change in command worried the Confederate general. He had counted on the bungling Hooker as his opponent. "General Meade," he commented prophetically, "will commit no blunder in my front."

Meade set out after the Confederate army, which was encamped at Cashtown, Pennsylvania, forty-five miles from Harrisburg. That the greatest battle of the war erupted at nearby **Gettysburg** was pure chance. A Confederate brigade left Cashtown to confiscate much-needed shoes in Gettysburg. Meeting Federal cavalry resistance near the town, the brigade withdrew. On July 1, 1863, a larger Confederate force advanced toward Gettysburg to disperse the cavalry and seize the shoes. What the Confederates did not realize was that the entire Army of the Potomac was coming up behind the cavalry (see Map 16-4).

During the first day of battle, July 1, the Confederates appeared to gain the upper hand, forcing Union forces back from the town to a new position on Cemetery Hill. On the second day, the entire Union army was in place, but the Confederates seized the initiative and took several key locations along Cemetery Ridge before Federal forces pushed them back to the previous day's positions. Although the opposing sides had suffered heavy casualties, both armies were intact; and, if anything, Lee had the advantage. On July 3, the third day of the battle, Lee made a fateful error. Believing that the center of Meade's line was weak, he ordered an all-out assault against it. The night before, Meade

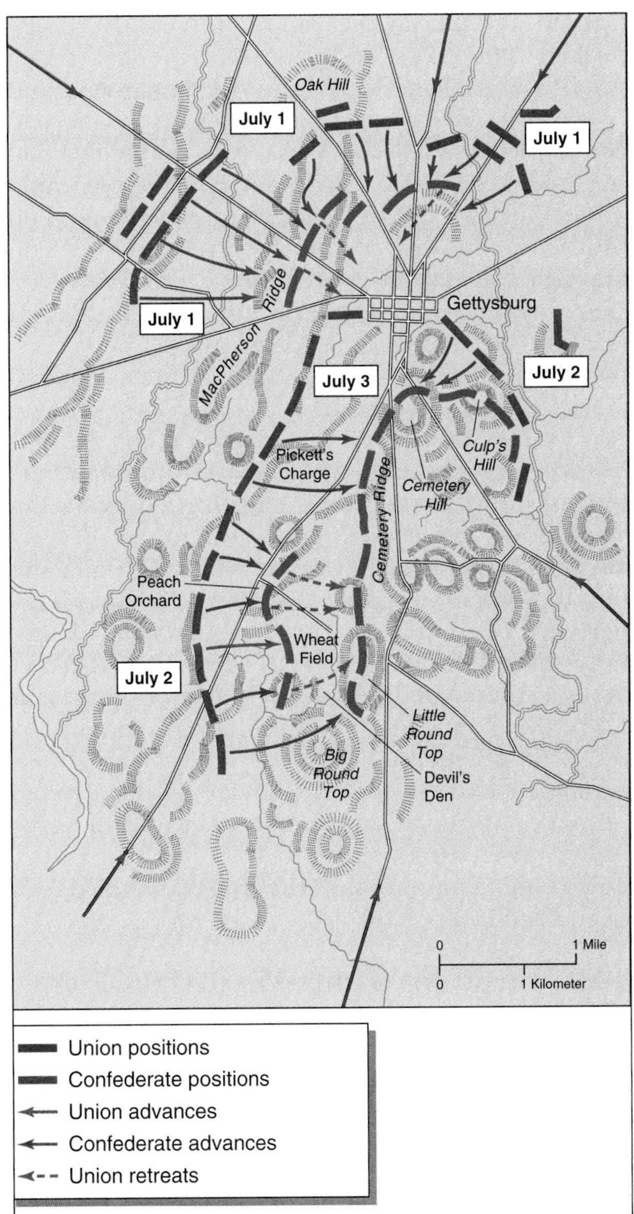

Map 16-4 The Battle of Gettysburg, July 1–3, 1863
In a war that lasted four years, it is difficult to point to the decisive battle. But clearly the outcome during those hot July days at Gettysburg set the tone for the rest of the war. The result was unclear until the final day of battle, and, even then, it might have gone either way. Winning by a whisker was enough to propel Union armies to a string of victories over the next year and throw Confederate forces back on their defenses among an increasingly despairing population. Gettysburg marked the last major Southern invasion of the North.

had remarked to his colleague, Brigadier General John Gibbon, "If Lee attacks tomorrow, it will be in your front. He has made attacks on both our flanks and failed and if he concludes to try it again, it will be on our center." Thus Meade was prepared for Lee's assault.

The next morning, a bright, hot summer day, the Confederates launched an assault on Culp's Hill, only to fall back by noon. The key battle of the day occurred at three in the afternoon at Cemetery Ridge, preceded by a fierce artillery duel. When the Union guns suddenly went silent, the Confederates, thinking they had knocked them out, began a charge led by General George Pickett. As the Confederate infantry marched out with battle colors flying, the Union artillery opened up again, supported by Federal riflemen. They tore apart the charging Southerners. Some managed to reach their objective, a low stone wall at the crest of the hill, but the Federals who held the wall outnumbered them and pushed them back. The Confederates retreated down the gentle slope strewn with their fallen comrades, the hopes of a Southern victory dashed. Half of Pickett's thirteen thousand–man division lay dead or wounded.

At Gettysburg, Lee had violated his own rule never to order a frontal assault. After the battle, he explained, "I believed my men were invincible." By the second day of the battle, he may have been suffering from combat fatigue. He managed only one message to his generals in the field that day. Meade, in contrast, remained in constant touch with his staff. After Pickett's charge, Lee rode among his troops and urged them to brace for a final Union assault. The attack never came. Meade allowed Lee to withdraw into Maryland and cross the Potomac to Virginia.

Gettysburg was the bloodiest battle of the war. The Union suffered 23,000 casualties; the Confederacy, 28,000. Yet Lincoln blasted Meade for failing to follow up on his victory. "I do not believe you appreciate the magnitude of the misfortune involved in Lee's escape," he wrote to his general. "He was within your easy grasp, and to have closed upon him would, in connection with our other late successes, have ended the war. As it is, the war will be prolonged indefinitely. . . . Your golden opportunity is gone, and I am distressed immeasurably because of it." Convinced by his aides that Meade would resign when he read the letter, Lincoln never sent it.

Vicksburg

When Lincoln mentioned "our other late successes" in his letter to Meade, he was referring to another crucial Union victory. On July 4, one day after Pickett's charge at Gettysburg, the city of **Vicksburg**, the last major Confederate stronghold on the Mississippi, surrendered to Ulysses S. Grant.

Grant is often perceived, incorrectly, as a general who ground out victories by dint of his superior numbers, with little finesse and less concern for his troops' safety. "The Butcher," as some called him later, did make mistakes, but he fretted about the lives of his troops as much as any other commander. In his campaigns in the western Confederacy, he demonstrated an ability to use his forces creatively, swiftly, and with a minimum loss of life.

Vicksburg presented Grant with several strategic obstacles (see Map 16-5). The formidable defenses on the city's western edge, which towered over the Mississippi, had thwarted a naval assault by Union admiral David G. Farragut in May 1862. And an assault by William T. Sherman later that year had failed in the labyrinth of swamps, creeks, and woods that protected the city from the north. The only feasible approaches appeared to be from the south and east.

By March 1863, Grant had devised a brilliant plan to take Vicksburg that called for rapid maneuvering and expert coordination. Grant had his twenty thousand Union troops ferried across the Mississippi from the Louisiana side at a point south of Vicksburg. Then he marched them quickly into the interior of Mississippi. Cut off from supplies, they moved northeastward, captured the Mississippi state capital at Jackson, and turned west toward Vicksburg. On May 22, 1863, Grant settled down in front of the city, less than six hundred yards from Confederate positions. Grant's tight siege and the Union navy's bombardment from the river cut the city off completely. As food stores dwindled, residents were forced to eat mules and rats to survive. Their situation hopeless, General John Pemberton and his thirty thousand–man garrison surrendered on July 4.

Chattanooga

As Grant was besieging Vicksburg in June 1863, Union general William S. Rosecrans, commanding the Army of the Cumberland, advanced on Confederate general Braxton Bragg, whose Army of Tennessee held **Chattanooga**, a "doorway" on the railroad that linked Richmond to the Lower South. The capture of the city would complete the uncoupling of the West from the eastern Confederacy.

Bragg lacked confidence in his men and consistently overestimated the force and cunning of his enemy. At Rosecrans's approach, he abandoned Chattanooga and took up positions at nearby Chickamauga Creek. When the two armies clashed at Chickamauga on September 19, Bragg pushed Rosecrans back to Chattanooga. Bragg seized the railroad leading into Chattanooga and bottled up Rosecrans there much as Grant had confined Pemberton at Vicksburg. Both sides had suffered heavily—the Federals with sixteen thousand casualties and the Confederates with eighteen thousand. But the prospect of recovering Chattanooga and capturing an entire Union army banished Confederate concerns about casualties at least for the moment. Suddenly, the Union's careful strategy for the conquest of the western Confederacy seemed in jeopardy.

The Confederate position on the heights overlooking Chattanooga appeared impregnable. But the Confederate camp was plagued by dissension. Some officers openly questioned Bragg's ability. President Davis considered replacing him but had no one else available with Bragg's experience. Instead, he ordered General James Longstreet (along with one-third of Bragg's army) on a futile expedition against Union forces at Knoxville, Tennessee. Converging on Chattanooga with reinforcements, Union generals Grant, Sherman, and Hooker took advantage of the divided Confederate army to break the siege and force Bragg's army to retreat into Georgia. The Union now dominated most of the West and faced an open road to the East.

The War in the Trans-Mississippi West

The Confederacy's reverses at Vicksburg and Chattanooga mirrored its misfortunes farther west beyond the Mississippi River. Although a relatively minor theater of war, the territory west of the Mississippi provided supplies and strategic advantages for the Confederate West. Success in the Trans-Mississippi West could occupy Federal troops and relieve pressure from other parts of the Confederacy while allowing food and munitions to reach desperate Southern armies.

The loyalties of Native Americans in the Trans-Mississippi West generally split evenly between the Union and the Confederacy. Three regiments of Cherokee Indians, led by Colonel (later Brigadier General) Stand Watie, fought for the South at the Battle of Pea Ridge in 1862. The Union won the battle and with it control of Missouri and northern Arkansas. Most battles between pro-Union and pro-Confederate Native American forces occurred in the Indian Territory (now Oklahoma).

Texas was critical to Confederate fortunes, both as a source of supply for the East and as a base

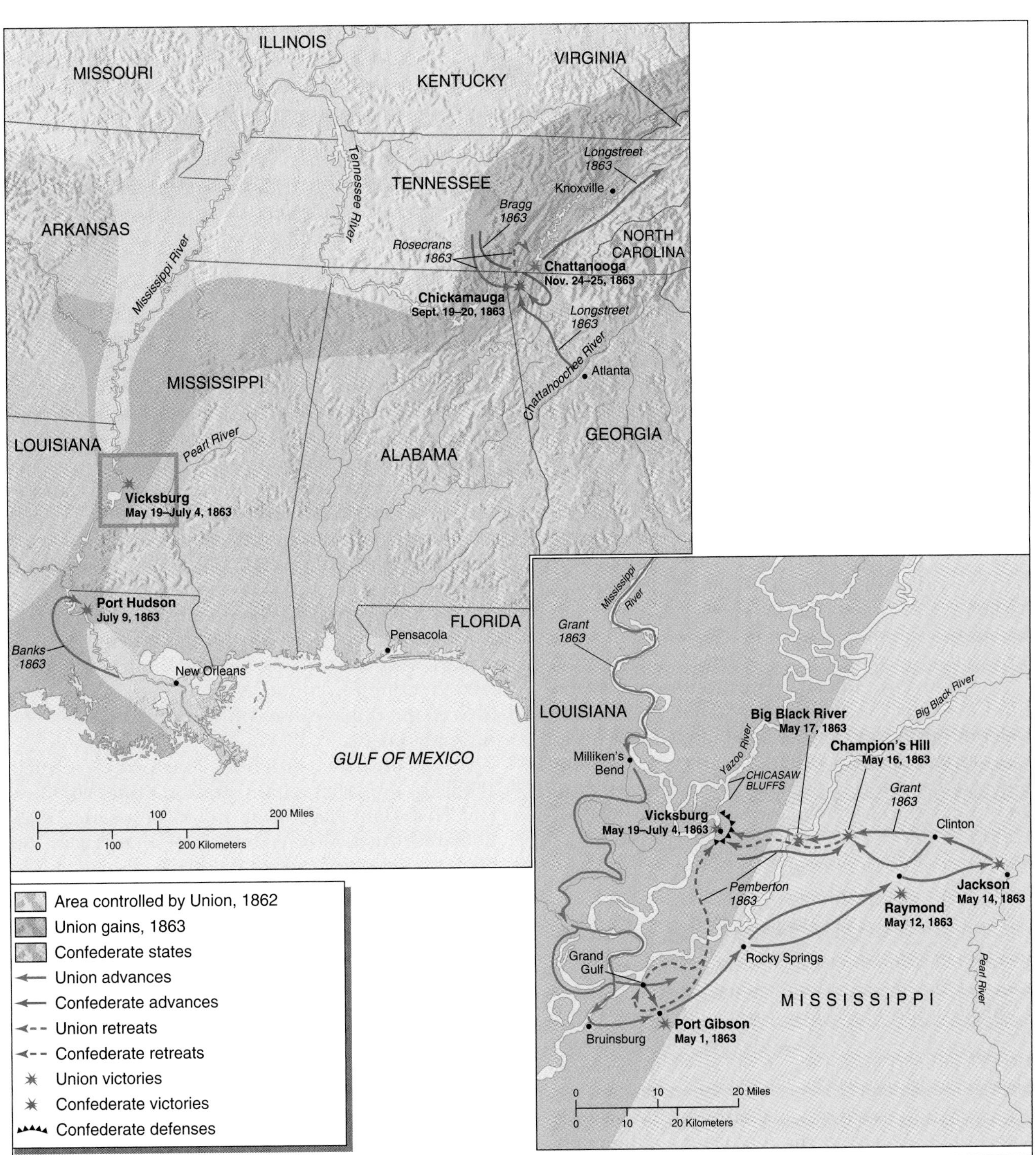

Map 16-5 Vicksburg and Chattanooga: The War in the West, 1863

Devising a brilliant strategy, Union General Ulysses S. Grant took the last major Mississippi River stronghold from Confederate hands on July 4, 1863, dealing a significant economic and morale blow to southern forces. Coupled with the defeat at Gettysburg a day earlier, the fall of Vicksburg portended a bitter finale to hopes for Southern independence. Grant completed his domination of the West by joining forces with several Union generals to capture Chattanooga and push Confederate forces into Georgia, setting the stage for the capture of that key southern state by the Federals in 1864.

for the conquest of the Far West. President Davis envisaged a continental Confederacy that included California, with its gold fields and Pacific ports. The ports would give the Confederacy access to Asian trade and, Davis reasoned, weaken the Federal naval blockade.

Texas, however, was far from secure. It suffered from internal dissent and violence on its borders. Texans, like many other Southerners, were ambivalent about secession. As early as 1862, areas of northern Texas, a Unionist stronghold before the war, rebelled against Confederate authorities and were brutally suppressed. Germans in the Fredericksburg–San Antonio area openly defied the Confederacy from 1862 until the war's end. And the Mexican population in southern Texas supported the Union. On the state's western border, Comanches raided homesteaders at will until late 1864. In the east and along the southern frontier in the lower Rio Grande Valley, Union gunboats and troops disrupted Confederate supply lines. For a time, Texas maintained commercial contact with the rest of the Confederacy through Matamoros, Mexico. But by 1864, with the Union in control of the Mississippi, Texas had lost its strategic importance.

The Confederacy's transcontinental aspirations died early in the war. In March 1862, a Confederate army seeking to conquer the Southwest was overwhelmed by Union forces at the **Battle of Glorieta Pass** in New Mexico. The Southwest from New Mexico to California would remain firmly in Union hands.

Conclusion

By late fall 1863, the Civil War was over in large portions of the former Confederacy. Northern forces controlled the Mississippi River and all the ports along its banks. Federal gunboats patrolled other rivers in the Confederate West, and Union troops garrisoned strategic forts along these waterways.

The Confederacy had also lost the war over slavery in many parts of the South. Tens of thousands of slaves abandoned plantations, farms, and towns to find freedom behind Union lines, depriving the South of their labor. And when many former slaves signed on to fight with Union armies, the South suffered doubly.

Not the least of Union advantages in the fall of 1863 was the ability of President Lincoln to articulate the meaning of the war for soldiers and civilians, for Americans and Europeans. In November, the president was asked to say a few words at the dedication of the federal cemetery at Gettysburg. There, surrounded by a somber scene of fresh graves, Lincoln bound the cause of the Union to that of the country's founders: "Fourscore and seven years ago our fathers brought forth upon this continent a new nation, conceived in liberty and dedicated to the proposition that all men are created equal. Now we are engaged in a great civil war, testing whether that nation, or any nation so conceived and so dedicated can long endure."

Many Confederate leaders had proclaimed, though less eloquently, a similar connection between their government and the Revolutionary generation. But the Emancipation Proclamation allowed Lincoln to make an even broader and bolder claim for the significance of the conflict. A Union victory would not only honor the past but also call forth a new nation, cleansed of its sins, to serve as an inspiration to oppressed peoples around the world. He called on the nation to resolve "that the nation shall, under God, have a new birth of freedom; and that government of the people, by the people, for the people, shall not perish from the earth." Not only did the two-minute Gettysburg Address capture what Union supporters were fighting for, but it also connected their sacrifices to the noble causes of freedom and democratic government.

Without battlefield victories, similar claims by the Davis administration would ring hollow. Historians have often noted how Lincoln articulated the Union cause better than Davis did the Confederate cause. Whatever shortcomings the Southern president suffered as an orator, however, the worsening situation on the battlefield left him little to say. The Confederacy's hopes now rested increasingly on Robert E. Lee and the Army of Northern Virginia. Despite two unsuccessful invasions of the North, Lee remained unbeaten on Southern soil. But time was running out for the general and his government. The incompetence of the Union commanders he had faced so far exaggerated his brilliance. Eventually, Lincoln would find a general to test the Army of Northern Virginia.

The Confederacy also faced an enemy with a seemingly endless reserve of troops and supplies. The North thrived on war and victory, while the South's economy and will faltered with defeat. The outcome of the war was not yet foreordained. The South still had armies in the field, a government in Richmond, and a heart for independence. But the Confederate cause was growing desperate.

AMERICA'S JOURNEY

FROM THEN TO NOW

Gettysburg

Each year more than 1.8 million visitors track across Pennsylvania's rolling hills to retrace the steps of the competing armies as they fought the Battle of Gettysburg in July 1863. The fascination has become big business at the Gettysburg National Military Park, where tourists spend more than $40 million annually on items ranging from Pickett's Charge T-shirts to ersatz battlefield relics. For a nation not ordinarily fixated on the past, the devotion to this battle—to which a majority of Americans have no ancestral connections—is extraordinary. What accounts for it?

The Civil War was a defining event in American history, and the Battle of Gettysburg was the defining moment of the Civil War, a guidepost on the American journey. The battle has thus become a metaphor for the national ideals the war brought into focus, symbolizing them in an enduring form for subsequent generations of Americans and serving as a reminder of the work still to be done to translate those ideals into reality for all. The battle also emerged as a symbol of national reconciliation after the fratricidal conflict of the war.

For generations of white Southerners after the Civil War, Gettysburg was the place where the young men of a doomed cause displayed incomparable courage against long odds. "For every Southern boy fourteen years old," William Faulkner wrote, "not once but whenever he wants it, there is the instant when it's still not yet two o'clock"—the hour of Pickett's charge—"on that July afternoon in 1863."

Bur today most Americans, North and South, see Gettysburg not as a missed opportunity, but, thanks to President Lincoln's famous address dedicating the battlefield cemetery, as a place that gives meaning to the sacrifices of both sides. Consecrating the battlefield to a renewal of the nation's founding ideals, Lincold asked his listeners to

> highly resolve that these dead shall not have died in vain – that this nation, under God, shall have a new birth of freedom – and that government of the people, by the people, for the people, shall not perish from the earth.

In the years after the war, veterans from both sides came to the battlefield seeking reconciliation, posing together for pictures and shaking hands. Tourists strike similar poses today.

African Americans, however, have not by and large shared the national fascination with Gettysburg and make up less than three percent of the visitors to the battlefield. "When you're black," African-American historian Allan B. Ballard explained, "the great battlefield holds mixed messages." Although the National Park Service, which oversees the site, has put up an exhibit on the role of African-American troops in the Civil War, black visitors remain ambivalent about the place. Aware of the long and continuing struggle they would face to secure true equality in American society after the Civil War, they see irony in Lincoln's call for "a new birth of freedom." Yet, if, as Ballard notes, "we are still fighting our civil wars," at Gettysburg at least, it is possible for Americans today to see and learn how their freedoms were paid for in blood and to reflect, in Lincoln's words, on the "unfinished work which they who fought here have thus far so nobly advanced."

These Union and Confederate dead at Gettysburg represent the cost of the war, the price of freedom. President Lincoln transformed the battleground from a killing field to a noble symbol of sacrifice for American ideals. Gettysburg continues to occupy a special place in our nation's history and in the memory of its citizens.

Review Question

1. How did the Union and the Confederacy compare in terms of resources, leadership, and military strategies in the period 1861–1863? What impact did these factors have on the course of the war?
2. What was the significance of the battles of Antietam and Gettysburg? In what ways were they turning points in the Civil War?
3. If you were a Confederate general, what would you have done differently at Gettysburg? At Vicksburg?
4. What effects did the Emancipation Proclamation have on both the Union and Confederate causes?

Recommended Reading

Stephen Crane, *The Red Badge of Courage* (originally published 1895; reprinted various dates). The Civil War did not inspire great American novels. But this is a notable exception that depicts not only the horrors of combat but its impact on the soldiers who fought.

Shelby Foote, *The Civil War: A Narrative*, 3 vols. (1958–1974). An excellent choice as a highly readable, if weighty, narrative of the Civil War. Although the account is thin on interpretation and obviously omits recent research on black people and women in the war, it is a balanced, comprehensive view of the conflict.

James M. McPherson, *Battle Cry of Freedom: The Civil War Era* (1982). Probably the best account of the war in print—more up-to-date than the Foote volumes and more interpretive. The author draws a number of interesting conclusions on several controversial topics from military strategy to the home front.

Additional Sources

Mobilization, North and South

Richard N. Current, *Lincoln's Loyalists: Union Soldiers from the Confederacy* (1992).

William C. Davis, *"A Government of Our Own": The Making of the Confederacy* (1994).

William C. Davis, *Jefferson Davis: The Man and His Hour* (1991).

David Donald, *Lincoln* (1995).

Paul D. Escott, *After Secession: Jefferson Davis and the Failure of Southern Nationalism* (1978).

Drew Gilpin Faust, *The Creation of Confederate Nationalism: Ideology and Identity in the Civil War* (1988).

George M. Fredrickson, *The Inner Civil War: Northern Intellectuals and the Crisis of Union* (1965).

Joseph L. Harsh, *Confederate Tide Rising: Robert E. Lee and the Making of Southern Strategy, 1861-1862* (1998).

Archer Jones, *Civil War Command and Strategy: The Process of Victory and Defeat* (1992).

George C. Rable, *The Confederate Republic: A Revolution against Politics* (1994).

Charles Royster, *The Destructive War: William Tecumseh Sherman, Stonewall Jackson, and the Americans* (1991).

The Early War, 1861–1862

Benjamin Franklin Cooling, *Forts Henry and Donelson: The Key to the Confederate Heartland* (1988).

Larry J. Daniel, *Shiloh: The Battle That Changed the Civil War* (1997).

Michael Fellman, *Inside War: The Guerrilla Conflict in Missouri during the Civil War* (1989).

Joseph Allan Frank, *With Ballot and Bayonet: The Political Socialization of American Civil War Soldiers* (1998).

Gerald F. Linderman, *Embattled Courage: The Experience of Combat in the American Civil War* (1989).

James M. McPherson, *What They Fought For, 1861–1865* (1994).

Grady McWhiney and Perry Jamieson, *Attack and Die: Civil War Military Tactics and the Southern Heritage* (1982).

Reid Mitchell, *Civil War Soldiers* (1988).

Clarence L. Mohr, *On the Threshold of Freedom: Masters and Slaves in Civil War Georgia* (1986).

Mary Panzer, *Mathew Brady and the Image of History* (1997).

James I. Robertson, *Stonewall Jackson: The Man, the Soldier, the Legend* (1997).

Stephen W. Sears, *George B. McClellan: The Young Napoleon* (1988).

Stephen W. Sears, *To the Gates of Richmond: The Peninsula Campaign* (1992).

Turning Points, 1862–1863

Ira Berlin et al., eds., *Freedom: A Documentary History of Emancipation, 1861–1867, Ser. 1, Vol. 1: The Destruction of Slavery* (1985).

Paul D. Casdorph, *Lee and Jackson: Confederate Chieftains* (1992).

Dudley T. Cornish, *The Sable Arm: Negro Troops in the Union Army, 1861–1865* (1966).

LaWanda Cox, *Lincoln and Black Freedom: A Study in Presidential Leadership* (1981).

Paul D. Escott, *Slavery Remembered: A Record of Twentieth-Century Slave Narratives* (1979).

Eric Foner, *Nothing but Freedom: Emancipation and Its Legacy* (1983).

John Hope Franklin, *The Emancipation Proclamation* (1963).

Ernest B. Furgurson, *Chancellorsville, 1863: The Souls of the Brave* (1992).

Louis S. Gerteis, *From Contraband to Freedman: Federal Policy toward Southern Blacks, 1861–1865* (1973).

Joseph T. Glatthaar, *Forged in Battle: The Civil War Alliance, Black Soldiers and White Officers* (1990).

Robert W. Johannsen, *Lincoln, the South, and Slavery: The Political Dimension* (1991).

Alvin M. Josephy Jr., *The Civil War in the American West* (1993).

William S. McFeely, *Grant: A Biography* (1981).

James M. McPherson, *The Negro's Civil War: How American Negroes Felt and Acted* (1965).

Alan T. Nolan, *Lee Considered: General Robert E. Lee and Civil War History* (1991).

Benjamin Quarles, *The Negro in the Civil War* (1953).

Carol Reardon, *Pickett's Charge in History and Memory* (1997).

Stephen W. Sears, *Landscape Turned Red: The Battle of Antietam* (1983).

David Paul Smith, *Frontier Defense in the Civil War: Texas' Rangers and Rebels* (1992).

Garry Wills, *Lincoln at Gettysburg: The Words That Remade America* (1992).

Where to Learn More

❖ **Museum of the Confederacy, Richmond, Virginia.** This museum has rotating exhibits on various aspects of the Confederate effort during the Civil War, both on the home front and on the battlefield. The Confederate White House, which is open to the public, is next door to the museum.

❖ **Gettysburg National Military Park, Gettysburg, Pennsylvania.** An excellent and balanced interpretation awaits the visitor at this national park. For a similar experience, visit Antietam National Battlefield, Sharpsburg, Maryland.

❖ **Various locations.** Many southern states, where most of the war was fought, have historic sites related to battles or significant events such as Manassas National Battlefield Park; Fredericksburg and Spotsylvania County Battlefields; Memorial National Military Park; Shiloh National Military Park; Vicksburg National Military Park; and Chickamauga and Chattanooga National Military Park. The war in the West is commemorated at Pea Ridge National Military Park, just north of Rogers, Arkansas, and at Pecos National Historical Park, the site of the Battle of Glorieta Pass, near Santa Fe, New Mexico.

THE UNION PRESERVED
THE CIVIL WAR, 1863–1865

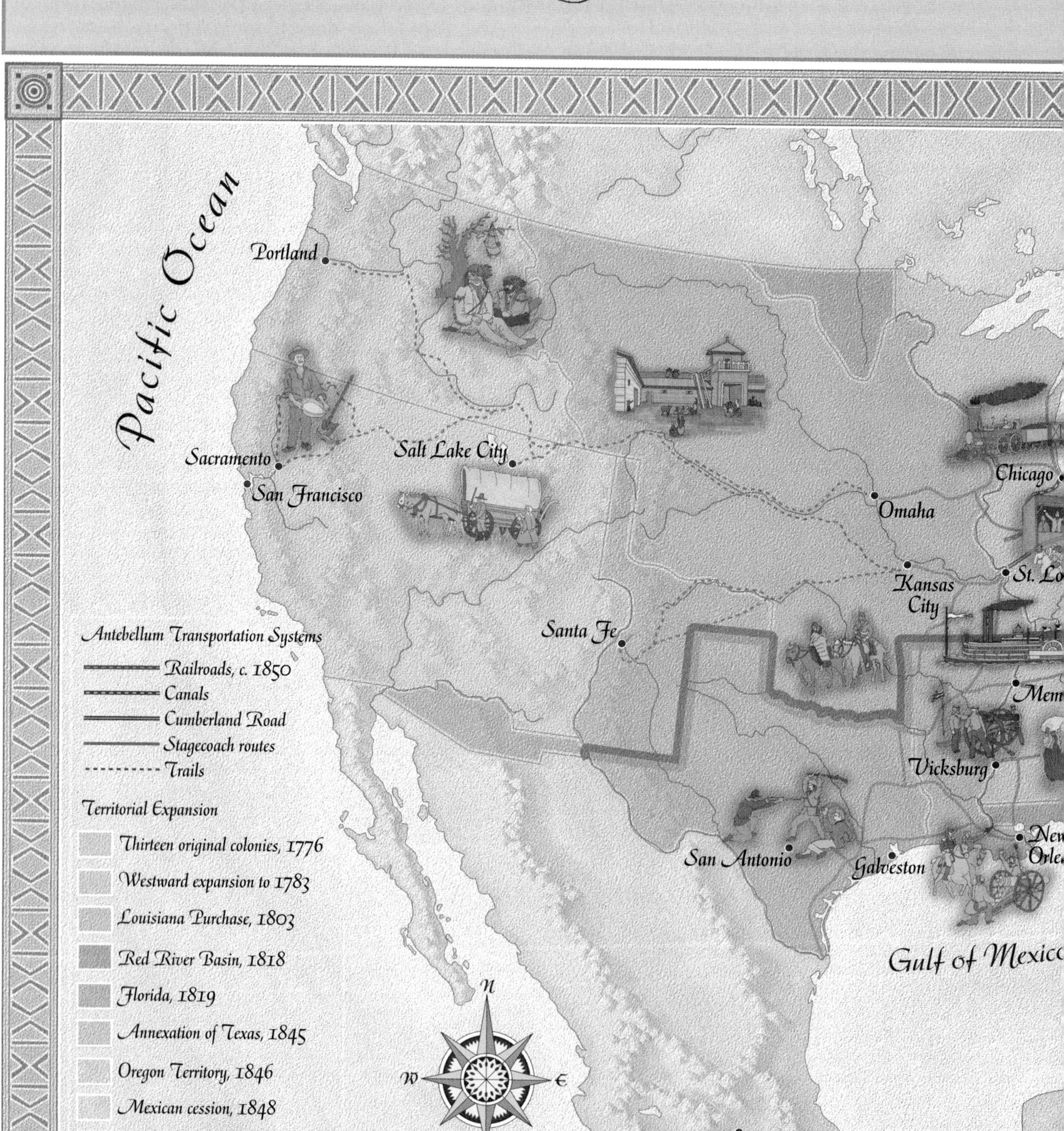

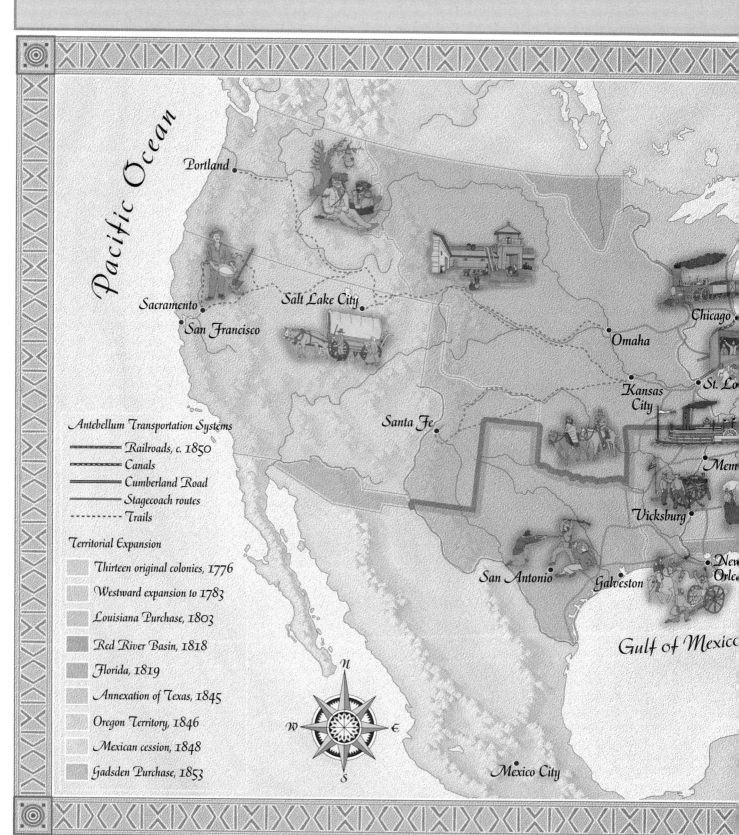

17

Chapter Outline

War Transforms the North
Wartime Legislation and Politics
Conscription and the Draft Riots
The Northern Economy
Northern Women and the War

The Confederacy Disintegrates
Southern Politics
The Southern Economy
Southern Women and the War

The Union Prevails, 1864–1865
Grant's Plan to End the War
From the Wilderness to Cold Harbor
Atlanta
The Election of 1864
Sherman's March to the Sea
Arming the Confederacy's Slaves
The Road to Appomattox
The Death of Lincoln

Conclusion

Key Topics

- ❖ The impact of the war on Northern political, economic, and social life
- ❖ How military reversals affected Confederate political and economic life and civilian morale
- ❖ The strategies and campaigns of Union generals Grant and Sherman in 1864 and 1865
- ❖ The meaning of the Civil War for the nation and its citizens

Colonel Alfred Pike of North Carolina and his men trained their rifles on the prisoner. They wanted information, but she refused to talk. Desertion from the Confederate army had increased during 1864, and Pike suspected that she knew the location of several deserters. Exasperated, Pike ordered his men to tie her thumbs together "behind her back & suspend her with a cord tied to her two thumbs thus fastened behind her to a limb so that her toes could just touch the ground." The colonel later reported with satisfaction that the woman "told some truth" after a while.

As this incident reflects, by late in the Civil War, the South was a troubled nation. Its people and government were reeling from the impact of defeat. Economic collapse, declining civilian morale, and desertion were undermining the Confederate cause as much as military setbacks were. Still, a loyal if besieged fighting force remained in the field, and enough citizens and officials still dreamed of Southern independence to prolong the conflict.

But the Union juggernaut rolled on. The North's strong economy stoked the war effort. The Lincoln administration formulated aggressive economic and military policies to win the war and secure the peace. The North, too, suffered social and political disruption, but the marvelous elixir of battlefield victory did wonders to allay these ills, if only temporarily.

For black Southerners, the war against slavery was almost over, and another war to secure the fruits of freedom had begun. Disagreement arose between North and South, black and white, Congress and president over what those fruits should be even as the Civil War raged on. The differing perceptions of freedom would haunt the nation for generations.

But for the immediate future, winning the war remained paramount for the Union. As Lincoln and his generals prepared the North's final campaigns, the South hoped General Lee could produce one last miracle.

War Transforms the North

Union successes by 1863 had a profound impact on both sides. For the North, hopes of victory and reunion increased. The Federal government expanded its bureaucracy to wage war efficiently, and a Republican-dominated Congress passed legislation that broadened Federal power and furthered the war effort. The Lincoln administration faced opposition on these measures and on its conduct of the war from within Congress, from the Democratic party, and from state leaders. But it successfully weathered dissent, thanks to the president's political skill, the desire of the Republicans to remain in power, and the Union's improving military fortunes. Boosted by Federal economic legislation and wartime demand, the Northern economy boomed. Women entered the work force in growing numbers. But labor unrest and class and racial tensions suggest that prosperity had a price.

Wartime Legislation and Politics

Before the Civil War, the Federal government rarely affected citizens' lives directly. But raising troops, protecting territory, and mobilizing the economy for war required a strong and active central government. With the departure of the South from the Union, Republicans dominated all branches of the Federal administration. This left them in a position to test the constitutional limits of federal authority.

President Lincoln began almost immediately to use executive authority to suppress opposition to the war effort in the North. Within the first few weeks of the conflict, he ordered raids on telegraph offices in the North and the seizure of telegrams to intercept seditious messages to the South. In one of his most controversial actions, he also issued a temporary suspension of the writ of habeas corpus, the constitutional requirement that authorities explain before a court their legal reasons for arresting someone. Habeas corpus protects a defendant against illegal imprisonment. Suspending it allowed authorities to

Chronology

1862 May: Congress passes Homestead Act.

1862 July: Congress passes Federal Land Grant College Act (Morrill Act).

1862 September: President Lincoln suspends the writ of habeas corpus.

1863 February: Congress passes National Banking Act.

1863 July: New York Draft Riot occurs.

1864 May: Battle of the Wilderness.

1864 June: Battle of Cold Harbor.

1864 September: Sherman captures Atlanta.

1864 November: President Lincoln is reelected.
Sherman begins his march to the sea.

1865 January: Congress passes Thirteenth Amendment to the Constitution, outlawing slavery (ratified December 1865).

1865 February: Charleston surrenders.

1865 March: Confederate Congress authorizes enlistment of black soldiers.

1865 April: Federal troops enter Richmond.
Lee surrenders to Grant at Appomattox Court House.
Lincoln is assassinated.

arrest suspected Confederate agents and hold them indefinitely. The Constitution forbids suspension of the writ except "when in cases of Rebellion or Invasion the public Safety may require it." Explaining his extraordinary actions in a July 4, 1861, message to Congress, Lincoln stated, "It became necessary for me to choose whether I should let the government fall into ruin, or whether . . . availing myself of the broader powers conferred by the Constitution in case of insurrection, I would make an effort to save it." Some citizens objected. New England abolitionist Wendell Phillips charged that "Abraham Lincoln sits today a more unlimited despot than the world knows this side of China." But most Republicans supported the president, and Congress approved his action.

Executive sanctions fell particularly hard on the Democratic party. "Disloyalty" was difficult to define in the midst of war. Though many Democrats opposed secession and supported the Union, they challenged the president on the conduct of the war, on emancipation, and on Lincoln's coolness toward peace initiatives. Those opposed to Republican policies formed secret societies in Ohio, Indiana, and Illinois. Republicans, exaggerating the danger of the societies, accused them of plotting to form a Northwest Confederacy. Most of the groups were harmless and operated under the loose guidance of the Democratic party. But a few had ties with Confederate agents. Republicans called these dissenters **"Copperheads,"** after the poisonous snake.

Federal laws were in place to punish disloyalty, but the courts enforced them poorly. Bypassing Congress and the judiciary in September 1862, Lincoln declared a suspension of habeas corpus for the duration of the war. His decree subjected antiwar protesters and, later, draft resisters and people accused of more serious activities against the administration to arbitrary arrest. Those detained faced military, not civilian, courts and were subject to military punishments. More than fourteen thousand citizens were arrested under Lincoln's decree. Few, however, lived in the North, and few were antiwar critics. Most lived in the border states and were detained for trading with the enemy, defrauding the War Department, draft evasion, blockade running, and guerrilla activities.

In April 1866, a year after the war ended, the U.S. Supreme Court in *Ex parte Milligan* held that Lincoln's declaration was unconstitutional. "Martial rule," the court decided, "can never exist where the courts are open. . . . It is . . . confined to the locality of actual war."

Despite the suspension of habeas corpus, Lincoln compiled a fairly good record for upholding basic American civil liberties. Although the authorities shut down a handful of newspapers temporarily, the administration made no attempt to control the news or subvert the electoral process. Two major elections were held during the war. In the first, the off-year election in 1862, Republicans retained control of Congress but lost several seats to Democrats. In the presidential election of 1864, Lincoln won reelection in a hard-fought contest.

While fellow Republicans sometimes chastised the president for violating civil liberties, mismanaging military command assignments, or moving too slowly on emancipation, they rarely threatened to disrupt the party or the administration over political or philosophical differences. Party discipline, though sometimes tenuous, kept most Republicans behind the administration on crucial issues. Republican governors often found common ground with the Lincoln administration. State governments supported the war to save the Union, and state leaders did not obstruct Lincoln's exercise of his role as commander in chief. Although congressional Republicans grumbled about Lincoln's expansion of executive authority, they did not attempt to override his executive decrees. In some instances, they passed complementary measures or ratified his actions, as in the Habeas Corpus Act of March 1863. The strength of the Democratic party in the North also reinforced party loyalty among Republicans.

But there was dissent in the Republican party, and it had an effect on national policy. **Radical Republicans** hounded Lincoln from early in his administration, establishing the Joint Committee on the Conduct of the War to examine and monitor military policy. Some of them accused Democratic generals, including McClellan, of deliberately subverting the war effort with their poor performance. They also pressed Lincoln for quicker action on emancipation, the enlistment of black troops, and the confiscation of rebel property. The radicals did not, however, sacrifice party unity to ideological purity. They supported the president on most crucial matters.

Lincoln likewise supported his party on an array of initiatives in Congress. Republicans used the federal government to enhance individual opportunities, especially in the West. The **Homestead Act,** passed in May 1862, granted 160 acres free to any settler in the territories who agreed to improve the land (by cultivating it and erecting a house) within five years of the grant. In addition to offering a fresh start to farmers whose land elsewhere had played out, the act was a boon for railroad companies. (Congress had passed a similar bill in 1860, but President Buchanan vetoed it.)

Other legislation to boost the nation's economy and the fortunes of individual manufacturers and farmers included the **Land Grant College Act** of 1862, a protective tariff that same year, and the **National Banking Act** of 1863. The Land Grant Act awarded the proceeds from the sale of public lands to the states for the establishment of colleges offering instruction in "agriculture and mechanical arts." (President Buchanan had also vetoed an earlier version of this act.) The tariff legislation protected Northern industry from foreign competition while raising revenue for the Union. It stimulated industrial output, contributing to the surge in manufacturing that began in the North during the Civil War and continued after it. Southern Democrats had vigorously opposed such legislation, fearing that foreign ports would retaliate by raising taxes on Southern cotton.

The National Banking Act of 1863 replaced the bank notes of individual states, which were often backed by flimsy reserves and subject to wild fluctuations in value, with a uniform national currency. It authorized existing and new banks in several cities throughout the country to issue bank notes backed by United States bonds and guaranteed by Washington. The consequences of the act would contribute to financial hardship later in the century, but when it was passed, it brought order to a chaotic monetary system and boosted the creditworthiness of the federal government.

Changes in the disposition of federal lands, the protective tariff, and the establishment of a national banking system presaged the active role the federal government would henceforth play in shaping the nation's economy. These measures helped sustain the Union war effort and enjoyed widespread support. The expansion of government into other areas, however, aroused opposition in some quarters, none more than the draft laws.

Conscription and the Draft Riots

Congress passed the first national conscription law in 1863. Almost immediately, evasion, obstruction, and weak enforcement threatened to undermine it. As military authorities began arresting draft dodgers and deserters, secret societies formed to harbor draftees and instruct them on evasion. In Wisconsin, the governor begged federal officials to send six hundred troops to enforce draft notices.

Conflicts between citizens and federal officials over the draft sometimes erupted in violence. The worst draft riot occurred in New York City in July 1863. Opposition to what many perceived as the Republican's war ran deep in New York, and support for the Democratic party was strong. The city's merchants were hurting from their lost trade in Southern cotton, and its Irish workers feared competition for jobs from freed slaves migrating to the North. Many in New York's large ethnic population found the Protestant morality and anti-immigrant nativism of some Republicans offensive.

The **New York Draft Riot** began when a mostly Irish mob protesting conscription burned the federal marshal's headquarters. Racial and class antagonisms quickly joined antidraft anger as the mob went on a rampage through the city's streets,

AMERICA'S JOURNEY

FROM THEN TO NOW

Federal–State Relations

The relationship between the states and the federal government has been contentious since the American Revolution. Our first national government under the Articles of Confederation foundered because it lacked sufficient authority over the states. The Constitution, although it created a stronger central government, left many aspects of the relationship between federal and state power unresolved. Slavery brought the issue to crisis in the Civil War.

The most fundamental issue in Federal–state relations is whether or not states have the right to secede from the Union. The war definitively resolved that they do not. But it also greatly expanded the role of the federal government. Before the war, the Post Office was the only federal agency most Americans had any direct contact with. During the war, however, the Republican-led Congress established a national banking system and a national paper currency, new taxes and the bureaucracy to collect them, and the military draft. It also ended slavery and established the nation's first federal welfare agency, the Freedmen's Bureau. Little wonder that after the war, Northerners, and soon all Americans, routinely said "the United States *is* . . ." instead of "*are* . . ." as they had before the Civil War.

Similarly, all amendments to the Constitution before the war had limited federal power. In contrast, the six amendments ratified during Reconstruction after the war all expanded federal authority.

But if the war boosted the profile of the Federal government, it was not the intent of Republican lawmakers to establish Federal supremacy. Most of them were more interested in boosting individual rights than in building the Federal bureaucracy. After Reconstruction, federal courts scaled back Federal power, and with a laissez-faire approach to government now ascendant, little attempt was made to reassert it.

War and depression, however, provoke calls for government intervention. Thus it was that the Federal government began to grow substantially again in the wake of the Great Depression of the 1930s and during World War II in the 1940s. This time, however, Federal dominance did not wane following the crises. Lyndon B. Johnson expanded the federal government substantially with his Great Society in the 1960s, and Presidents Nixon, Ford, and Carter mostly followed his lead. Although Nixon sought to share revenue with localities and states, his "New Federalism" did not significantly shift power from Washington.

Beginning with the Reagan administration, however, and continuing through the Clinton administration, in a process called devolution, Congress has been shifting responsibility for spending and administering federal funds to the states.

Today, neither of the major parties would consider expanding federal power. But Americans recognize the need for appropriate federal action. Thus the Republicans' 1994 Contract with America, which called for a revolutionary reduction in federal responsibilities, was short-lived. The recent embrace by some Republicans of "compassionate conservatism" brings them closer to the Democratic position on the role of government in social policy. According to historian Gertrude Himmelfarb, the phrase means "Good government—but preferably not the Federal Government. This is the principle of devolution: the highest authority should have a secondary function, doing only what cannot be done as well by local authorities."

In this view of federal–state relations there is no competition for power. Government remains the arbiter of social, environmental, and educational policy, among others, with authority divided between the states and Washington in a mutually agreed upon way. Perhaps this approach will finally resolve a jurisdictional problem as old as the nation itself. But don't bet on it.

The U.S. Capitol building, with its dome under construction, dominates the growing city of Washington. This Civil War illustration presents an apt metaphor for the expanding size and power of the federal government caused by the conflict.

fighting police, plundering houses of the wealthy, and crying, "Down with the rich!" The rioters hanged two black New Yorkers who wandered into their path and burned the Colored Orphan Asylum. City authorities and the police stood by unable or unwilling to stem the riot, which claimed eighty lives. It was finally quelled by army units fresh from Gettysburg, along with militia and naval units. The draft resumed a month later.

The Northern Economy

"The North," one historian has said, "was fighting the South with one hand and getting rich with the other behind its back." After an initial downturn during the uncertain months preceding the war, the Northern economy picked up quickly. High tariffs and massive federal spending soon made up for the loss of Southern markets and the closing of the Mississippi River. Profits skyrocketed for some businesses. The earnings of the Erie Railroad, for example, jumped from $5 million in 1860 to $10 million in 1863. New industries boomed, and new inventions increased manufacturing efficiency, as in the sewing machine industry, which was first commercialized in the 1850s. Technological advances there greatly increased the output of the North's garment factories. Production of petroleum, a lubricant, increased from 84,000 gallons to 128 million gallons during the war.

Despite the loss of manpower to the demands of industry and the military, the productivity of Northern agriculture grew during the war. As machines replaced men on the farm, the manufacturers of farm machinery became wealthy. Crop failures in Europe dramatically increased the demand for American grain. Exports of wheat from the United States to Great Britain jumped from less than 25,000 pounds in 1859 to 1.2 million pounds in 1862. "Old King Cotton's dead and buried; brave young Corn is king," went a popular Northern refrain of the day. Northern crops brought in $955 million in 1863 and nearly $1.5 billion a year later. The resulting profits spread throughout the economy as Northerners, according to one disapproving observer, went on a shopping spree "unexampled, even in the history of our wasteful people."

Working people should have benefited from wartime prosperity. With men off to war and immigration down, labor was in short supply. But workers reaped minimal gains. Although wages increased, prices rose more. Declining real wages led to exploitation, especially of women in garment factories.

Workers organized to combat poor working conditions and low wages. The trade union movement, which suffered a serious setback in the depression of 1857, revived. Local unions of shoemakers, carpenters, and miners emerged in 1862 across the North, and so did a few national organizations. Unions divided along racial and gender lines, and some ethnic groups formed their own workers' associations. By 1865, more than 200,000 Northern workers belonged to labor unions.

Employers struck back at union organizing by hiring strikebreakers, usually African Americans. Labor conflicts between striking white workers and black strikebreakers sparked riots in New York City and Cincinnati. The racial antagonism accounted in part for workers' opposition to Lincoln's Emancipation Proclamation and for the continued strength of the Democratic party in Northern cities. White workers supported the Democrats because they feared that freed slaves would flood Northern cities as a result of Lincoln's policies, undercutting wages and taking white workers' jobs.

The lynching of a black New Yorker during the Draft Riots in July 1863. The violence against black people during the riots reflected decades of racial tensions, especially between Irish immigrants and black residents, over jobs and housing.

The promise of enormous profits bred greed and corruption as well as exploitation. Illicit trade between North and South was inevitable when cotton could be bought at 20 cents a pound in New Orleans and sold for $1.90 a pound in Boston. Profiteers not only defied the government to trade with the enemy but also sometimes swindled the government outright. Some merchants reaped high profits supplying the army with shoddy goods at inflated prices. A writer for *Harper's Weekly* complained that "soldiers, on the first day's march or in the earliest storm, found their clothes . . . scattering to the wind in rags." Some Yankee soldiers experienced leaky tents, tainted meat, and wormy grain. With winning the war taking precedence over fiscal prudence, even parties who dealt legitimately with government agencies could expect handsome returns.

Some Northerners viewed the spending spree uneasily. They were disturbed to see older men flaunting their wealth while young men were dying on the battlefield. "The lavish profusion in which the old southern cotton aristocracy used to indulge," wrote an indignant reporter for the *New York World*, "is completely eclipsed by the dash, parade, and magnificence of the new northern shoddy aristocracy. . . . The individual who makes the most money—no matter how—and spends the most money—no matter for what—is considered the greatest man."

Exploited workers likewise resented the "shoddy aristocracy." Speaking at a labor rally in New York City, one man said bitterly of the wealthy people profiting from the war, "Union with them means no more nor less than that they want the war prolonged that they may get the whole of the capital of the country into their breeches pocket and let it out at a percentage that will rivet the chain about your neck."

Comments like these hinted at the deep social and ethical problems that were emerging in Northern society and would become more pronounced in the decades after the Civil War. For the time being, the benefits of economic development for the Union cause outweighed its negative consequences. The thriving Northern economy fed, clothed, and armed the Union's soldiers and kept most civilians employed and well fed. Prosperity and the demands of a wartime economy also provided Northern women with unprecedented opportunities.

Northern Women and the War

More than 100,000 Northern women took jobs in factories, sewing rooms, and arsenals during the Civil War. Stepping in for their absent husbands, fathers, and sons, they often performed tasks previously reserved for men but at lower pay. The expanding bureaucracy in Washington also offered opportunities for many women. The United States Treasury alone employed 447 women in the war years. And unlike private industry, the federal government paid women and men equally for the same work.

Women also had the opportunity to serve the war effort directly in another profession previously dominated by men—nursing. Physicians and officers, however, although they tolerated women nurses as nurturing morale boosters, thought little of their ability to provide medical care. Women sometimes challenged this condescending view, braving dismissal to confront the medical-military establishment head-on. Clara Barton, among the most notable nurses of the war, treated soldiers on the battlefield at great peril to her safety and to the consternation of officers. One of them remarked to her,

Nurse Ann Bell tends a fallen Union soldier. Although medical practices were primitive and many young men died from poorly treated wounds or disease, the U.S. Sanitary Commission attempted to improve care in Union hospitals during the war. The war helped open nursing as a respectable occupation for women.

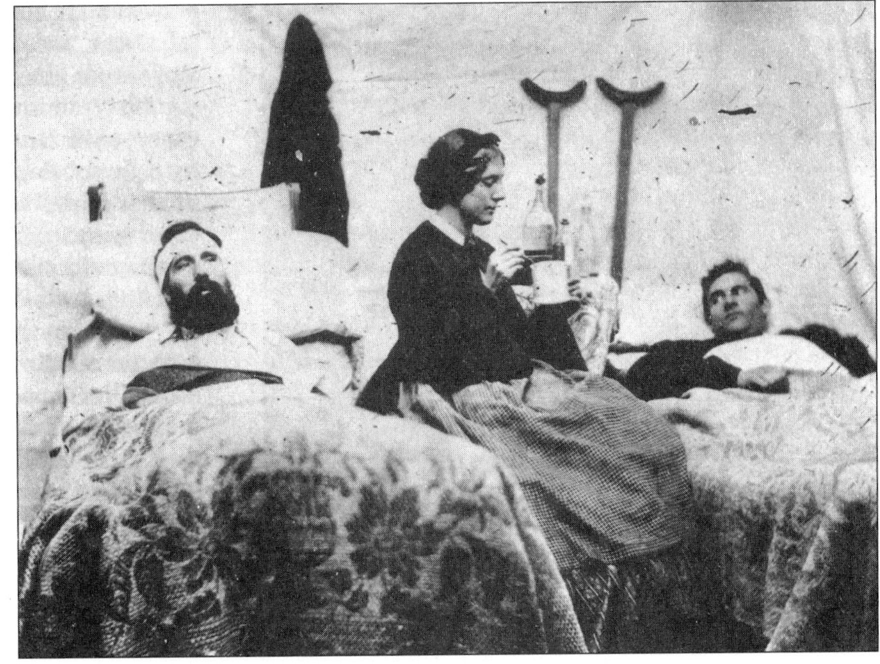

"Miss Barton, this is a rough and unseemly position for you, a woman, to occupy." She shot back, "Is it not as rough and unseemly for these pain-racked men?" The officer temporarily suspended Barton for her candor. A British journalist, impressed by Barton and the thousands of women like her, commented that no conflict in history was so much "a woman's war" as the Civil War.

If the war created opportunities for many women, it also left tens of thousands widowed and devastated. In a society that assumed that men supported women, the death of a husband could be a financial and psychological disaster. Many women were left to survive on meager pensions with few skills they could use to support themselves.

The new economic opportunities the war created for women left Northern society more open to a broader view of women's roles. One indication of this change was the admission of women to eight previously all-male state universities after the war. Like the class and racial tensions that surfaced in Northern cities, the shifting role of women during the Civil War hinted at the promises and problems of postwar life. The changing scale and nature of the American economy, the expanded role of government, and the shift in class, racial, and gender relations are all trends that signaled what historians call the "modernization" of American society. Many of these trends began before the war, but the war highlighted and accelerated them.

The Confederacy Disintegrates

Even under the best of conditions, the newly formed political and economic institutions of the Confederacy would have had difficulty maintaining control over the country's class and racial tensions. But as battlefield losses mounted, the Confederacy disintegrated.

Victory is a marvelous glue. Defeat dissolves the bonds that hold a small society like the Confederacy together and exposes the large and small divisions within it. After 1863, defeat infected Confederate politics, ruined the Southern economy, and eventually invaded the hearts and minds of the Southern people. The Davis administration tried to deal with a maddening array of dissenting or indifferent politicians. But the deteriorating military situation and the impending Confederate economic collapse doomed these efforts. The South pinned its waning hopes on its defensive military strategy. If it could prolong the conflict a little longer, perhaps a war-weary North would replace Lincoln and the Republicans in the 1864 elections with a Democratic president and Congress inclined to make peace.

Southern Politics

Dissent plagued Southern politics before the end of the war's first year and before defeat and privation sapped Confederate morale. Residents of western Virginia mounted a secession movement of their own, declaring themselves for the Union and forming the new state of West Virginia. Several counties in north Alabama, in German-speaking districts in Texas, and throughout the mountains of Tennessee and North Carolina contemplated similar action.

As the war turned against the Confederacy, southerners increasingly turned against each other. Some joined the peace societies that emerged as early as 1861 in Arkansas and soon after in most other Southern states. North Carolinians opposed to the war formed the Order of the Heroes of America, whose members not only demonstrated for peace but took control of the Piedmont and mountain sections of the state as well. Other Southerners preferred quieter dissent. They refused to join the army, pay taxes, or obey laws prohibiting trade with the enemy.

States' rights, a major principle of the seceding states, proved an obstacle to the Davis administration's efforts to exert central authority. The governors of Georgia and North Carolina gave the Richmond government particular difficulty, hoarding munitions, soldiers, supplies, food, and money. At one point, Georgia's governor contemplated a separate peace between his state and the United States. Even cooperative governors refused to allow state agents to collect taxes for the Confederacy.

Unlike Abraham Lincoln, Jefferson Davis could not appeal to party loyalty to control dissent because the Confederacy had no parties. Davis's frigid personality, his insistence on attending to minute details, and his inability to accept even constructive criticism gracefully also set him apart from Lincoln and worsened political tensions within the Confederacy.

Several parts of the South began clamoring for peace during the fateful summer of 1863. In a tour of his state that year, North Carolina political leader Jonathan Worth heard calls for the overthrow of the Davis administration and a separate peace with the North. "Every man [I] met," he concluded "was for reconstruction on the basis of the old [U.S.] constitution." By November 1864, the Confederacy suffered as much from internal disaffection as from the attacks of Union armies. Confederate authorities could not suppress civilian unrest in Virginia, North Carolina, and Tennessee, and Union spies operated openly in Mobile, Wilmington, and Richmond. Divisions among Confederate officials themselves added to the growing disarray.

Some Southern politicians and journalists, long accustomed to an opposition role in national affairs before secession, maintained it after secession. When Union general George B. McClellan crept toward Richmond in 1862, for example, the *Richmond Examiner* accused the Davis administration of dragging its feet in imposing martial law on the city. "To the dogs with Constitutional questions and moderation!" one editorial screamed. Less than two years later, however, when Davis suspended habeas corpus in several areas threatened by Union armies, the *Examiner* unleashed a tirade against the president for acting unconstitutionally, warning him that he was the people's "servant" and not their "dictator."

Davis and other Confederate leaders might have averted some of these political problems had they succeeded in building a strong sense of Confederate nationalism among soldiers and civilians. They tried several strategies to do so. For example, Davis tried to identify the Confederacy's fight for independence with the American Revolution of 1776. But egalitarian Revolutionary ideals quickly lost their appeal in the face of poverty, starvation, and defeat. Davis also tried to cast the Confederacy as a bastion of freedom standing up to Lincoln's despotic abuse of executive authority, but he, too, eventually invoked authority similar to Lincoln's. Some Southerners saw slavery as the cornerstone of the Confederacy. But Davis understood that identifying the Southern cause too closely with slavery risked alienating foreign governments and dividing white Southerners. Confederate religious leaders sought to distinguish their new nation from the North by referring to Southerners as God's "chosen people." But when Confederate military fortunes declined, religious leaders drew back from such visions of collective favor and stressed the need for individual salvation.

Secession and the early battles gave Southerners a common purpose but not a common nation. The diaries of Southern soldiers reveal devotion to God, state, locality, family, and friends but rarely to the Confederacy. Battlefield and economic reverses diminished what national feeling there was. Planters in the lower Mississippi Valley, for example, quickly succumbed to Union offers of cash for cotton. Desertion increased, and the will to resist Federal troops declined. Worn out, fed up, and homesick, some Confederate soldiers just called it quits.

In a devout society convinced it was fighting a holy war, some Southerners sought some moral failing to account for their mounting losses. Some identified slavery as the culprit. A Confederate leader in South Carolina asked in 1864, "Are we not fighting against the moral sense of the world? Can we hope to succeed in such a struggle?" In a similar vein, a Louisiana woman admitted that "always I felt that moral guilt of it [slavery], felt how impossible it must be for an owner of slaves to win his way into Heaven."

The Southern Economy

Defeat came to the South, according to one historian, "not because the government failed to mobilize the South's resources" but "because there was virtually nothing left to mobilize." By 1863, the Confederacy was having a difficult time feeding itself. Destruction of farms by both sides and growing Union control of waterways and rail lines restricted the distribution of food. Speculators held certain commodities off the market to drive up prices, making shortages worse.

Wartime food shortages, skyrocketing inflation, and rumors of hoarding and price-gouging drove women in several southern cities to protest violently. Demonstrations like the 1863 food riot shown here reflected a larger rending of southern society as Confederate losses and casualties mounted on the battlefield. Some Southern women placed survival and providing for their families ahead of boosting morale and silently supporting a war effort that had taken their men away. Their defection hurt the Confederate cause.

People ate rats and mules to supplement their meager diets. Lacking access to salt, an essential food preservative, they obtained it by evaporating sea water or by boiling the salt-saturated soil from the floors of smokehouses. Bread riots erupted in Mobile, Atlanta, and Richmond. In Mobile, a group of women marched under banners reading "Bread or Blood" and "Bread and Peace." Armed with hatchets, they looted stores for food and clothing. In a show of grim humor, people in Southern cities held "starvation parties" at which they served only water.

More than one-quarter of Alabama's population was receiving public welfare by the end of the war. "Deaths from starvation have absolutely occurred," a Confederate official in the state informed President Davis in 1864. As the price of medicines skyrocketed, Southerners tried ineffectual home remedies. One recommended treatment for diphtheria was to smear the patient with lard.

Southern soldiers had marched off to war in neat uniforms with shiny buttons, many leaving behind self-sustaining families. But in August 1863, diarist Mary Chesnut, wife of a Confederate official in Richmond, watched ten thousand men marching near Richmond and commented, "Such rags and tags as we saw now. Most garments and arms were . . . taken from the enemy." The soldiers' families were threadbare as well. The prohibitive cost of new clothing prompted a group of women in northern Georgia to raid a textile mill for calico cloth in 1863. During the winter of 1863–1864, women lined their clothes with rags and newspapers to keep warm. In the devastated areas near battle sites, civilians survived by selling fragments of dead soldiers' clothing stripped off their bodies and by collecting spent bullets and selling them for scrap.

A privileged few avoided such hardship. Mary Chesnut noted the contrast between rich ladies "in their landaus . . . with tall footmen in livery" and the shabbiness of "poor soldiers' wives . . . on the sidewalks."

The predations of both Union and Confederate soldiers further threatened civilians in the South. The women and children left alone on farms and plantations were vulnerable to stragglers and deserters from both armies. One Louisiana woman described how "for more than a year past, lawless men have been permitted to band themselves together, and roam at will . . . insulting, chastising, robbing, burning houses, murdering the families of our soldiers; and in some instances despoiling in the most brutal manner, wives, daughters and sisters of that which is dearer than life itself—their honor."

Southerners also feared that slaves on isolated plantations would rise up against their masters. Most slaves, however, were more intent on escape than revenge. There was no point in murdering the master or his family when freedom was just out the door and down the road to the Union lines. There was no point in sacking the big house when a Union regiment would make short work of the whole plantation and all others around it. Escaped slaves had children, husbands, wives, and other relatives to find and spirit away to Union camps. The business of freedom was too time-consuming to waste on white people. Leave it to God to mete out punishment for the evil of bondage.

Some slaves felt genuine affection for the families they served and stayed on with them even after the war. Some protected white Southerners from Union soldiers and hid valuables for them. But women forced to manage plantations alone could never be sure where their slaves stood. Mary Chesnut wrote in her diary about her mother's butler: "He looks over my head—he scents freedom in the air." As slaves stopped working and abandoned plantations, the women left to run them had to work the fields themselves.

As Confederate casualties mounted, more and more Southern women and children, like their Northern counterparts, faced the pain of grief. Funeral processions became commonplace in the cities and black the color of fashion. With little food, worthless money, and a husband or father gone forever, the future looked bleak.

Southern Women and the War

In the early days of the Civil War, Southern white women continued to live their lives according to antebellum conventions. Magazine articles urged them to preserve themselves as models of purity for men debased by the violence of war. The Southern woman, by her moral example, "makes the confederate soldier a gentleman of honor, courage, virtue and truth, instead of a cut-throat and vagabond," opined one magazine. She would buttress the nation's morale through the wavering fortunes of war. On her shoulders rested "the destinies of the Southern Confederacy," the *Natchez Weekly Courier* declared.

Women flooded newspapers and periodicals with patriotic verses and songs. A major theme of these works, illustrated by the following example from the *Richmond Record* in September 1863, was the need to suppress grief and fear for the good of the men at the front:

> The maid who binds her warrior's sash
> And smiling, all her pain dissembles,
> The mother who conceals her grief
> [had] shed as sacred blood as e'er
> was poured upon the plain of battle.

A Virginia woman confided to her diary, "We must learn the lesson which so many have to endure—to struggle against our feelings."

By the time of the Civil War, such emotional concealment had become second nature to Southern white women. They had long had to endure their anguish over their husbands' nocturnal visits to the slave quarters. They were used to the condescension of men who assumed them to be intellectually inferior. And they accepted in bitter, self-sacrificing silence the contradiction between the myth of the pampered leisure they were presumed to enjoy and the hard demands their lives actually entailed.

But some Southern women chafed at their supporting role and, as Confederate manpower and materiel needs became acute, took on new productive responsibilities. Initially, they did so within the domestic context: Women formed clubs to sew flags and uniforms. To raise money for the war effort, they held benefits and auctions and collected jewelry and other valuables.

Soon, however, the needs of the Confederacy drew women outside the home to fill positions vacated by men. They managed plantations. They worked in the fields alongside slaves, and, if they had worked there before, they worked harder. They worked in factories to make uniforms and munitions. They worked in government offices as clerks and secretaries. They taught school. A few, like Belle Boyd and Rose O'Neal Greenhow, spied for the Confederacy. And many, like their Northern counterparts, served as nurses. Eventually, battlefield reverses and economic collapse undermined all these roles, leaving women and men alike struggling simply to survive.

As the war dragged on and the Southern economy and the social order deteriorated, even the patriots suffered from resentment and doubt. By 1864, many women were helping their deserting husbands or relatives elude Confederate authorities. In Randolph County, North Carolina, for example, two women torched a barn belonging to a state official in charge of rounding up deserters. Incidents like these convinced authorities that women were mainly responsible for the high desertion rate in the last years of the war. A North Carolina official explained that "desertion takes place because desertion is encouraged. . . . And though the ladies may not be willing to concede the fact, they are nevertheless responsible . . . for the desertion in the army and the dissipation in the country" (see "American Views: Southern Women against the War").

By 1864, many Southern white women had tired of the war. What had begun as a sacred cause had disintegrated into a nightmare of fear and deprivation. Uprooted from their homes, some women wandered through the war-ravaged South, exposed to violence, disease, and hunger and seeking shelter where they could find it. Those women fortunate enough to remain in their homes turned to work, others to protest, and many to religion. Some devoutly religious women concluded that it was God, not the Yankees, who had brought destruction on the South for its failure to live up to its responsibilities to women and children.

The Union Prevails, 1864–1865

Despite the Union's dominant military position after Vicksburg and Gettysburg and the Confederacy's mounting home-front problems, three obstacles to Union victory remained. Federal troops under General William T. Sherman controlled Chattanooga and the gateway to Georgia, but the

White family "refugeeing." In advance of Union armies, tens of thousands of Southern families fled to safer locales, a bitter exodus that fulfilled the Federals' vow to bring the war to the South's civilian population.

American Views

Southern Women against the War

As Confederate military fortunes deteriorated during and after 1863, food shortages, marauding Yankees and deserters, and widespread poverty plagued the home front. The documents excerpted here reflect the growing desperation of the women left to cope with these conditions, the pressures on soldiers to desert and return to their families, and the inability of public officials to boost sagging Confederate morale.

- ❖ **Why did some Southern women encourage their husbands to desert?**
- ❖ **How should Confederate officials have responded to women who wanted their men to return home?**
- ❖ **What do these documents reveal about their authors' attitude toward Southern independence?**

Letter of Martha Revis to her husband
Marshall, Madison County, North Carolina, July 20, 1863

Dear Husband: I seat myself to drop you a few lines to let you know that me and Sally is well as common, and I hope these few lines will come to hand and find you well and doing well. . . . The people is all turning to Union here since the Yankees has got Vicksburg [on July 4]. I want you to come home as soon as you can after you git this letter. . . . That is all I can think of, only I want you to come home the worst that I ever did. . . . The folks is leaving here, and going North as fast as they can.

Your wife, till death.

Petition from Women of Miller County, Georgia, to President Jefferson Davis
September 8, 1863

Our crops is limited and so short . . . cannot reach the first day of march next . . . our fencing is unanamosly allmost decayed . . . But little of any sort to Rescue us and our children from a unanamus starveation. . . . An allwise god ho is slow to anger and full of grace and murcy and without Respect of persons and full of love and charity that he will send down his fury and judgement in a very grate manar [on] all those our leading men and those that are in power ef thare is no more favors shone to those the mothers and wives. . . . I tell you that with out some grate and speadly alterating in the conduckting of afares in this our little nation god will frown on it and that speadly.

Source: Paul D. Escott and David R. Goldfield, eds., Major Problems in the History of the American South *D.C. Heath, (1990).*

Confederate Army of Tennessee, commanded by Joseph E. Johnston, was still intact, blocking Sherman's path to Atlanta. Robert E. Lee's formidable Army of Northern Virginia still protected Richmond. And the Confederacy still controlled the rich Shenandoah Valley, which fed Lee's armies and supplied his cavalry with horses. In March 1864, President Lincoln brought General Ulysses S. Grant to Washington and appointed him commander of all Union armies. Grant set about devising a strategy to overcome these obstacles.

Grant's Plan to End the War

Grant brought two innovations to the final campaign. First, he coordinated the Union war effort. Before, the Union's armies in Virginia and the West

OVERVIEW

MAJOR BATTLES OF THE CIVIL WAR, 1864–1865

Battle or Campaign	Date	Outcome and Consequences
Wilderness and Cold Harbor	May and June 1864	Both Confederate victories that inflicted huge losses on Grant's army; turned public opinion against Grant but failed to force him to withdraw
Atlanta	May–September 1864	Union victory; Confederacy lost key rail depot and industrial center
Sherman's March	November 1864–March 1865	Nearly unopposed, Sherman's army cut a path of destruction through Georgia and South Carolina, breaking Southern morale
Battles of Franklin and Nashville	November and December 1864	Union victories in Tennessee; effectively destroyed Army of Tennessee
Siege of Petersburg	June 1864–April 1865	Long stalemate ended in Union victory; led to fall of Richmond and surrender of Lee's army at Appomattox Court House

had operated independently, giving Confederate leaders the opportunity to direct troops and supplies to whichever arena most needed them. Now Grant proposed to deprive them of that option. The Union's armies in Virginia and the Lower South would attack at the same time, keeping steady pressure on all fronts. Second, Grant changed the tempo of the war. Before, long periods of rest had intervened between battles. Grant, with the advantage of superior numbers, proposed nonstop warfare. As he explained, he wanted to "hammer continuously against the armed force of the enemy and his resources, until by mere attrition, if in no other way, there should be nothing left to him but an equal submission with the loyal section of our common country to the constitution and laws of the land."

Although Grant's strategy ultimately worked, several problems and miscalculations undermined its effectiveness. With Sherman advancing in Georgia, Grant's major focus was Lee's army in Virginia. But Grant underestimated Lee. The Confederate general thwarted him for almost a year and inflicted horrendous casualties on his army. Confederate forces under Jubal Early drove off Union forces from the Shenandoah Valley in June 1864, depriving Grant of troops and allowing the Confederates to maintain their supply lines. And the incompetence of General Benjamin Butler, charged with advancing up the James River to Richmond in May 1864 to relieve Lee's pressure on Grant, further eroded Grant's plan. Grant also faced administrative problems. He left General George G. Meade, the victor of Gettysburg, in command of the Army of the Potomac but accompanied the army in its campaign against Lee and directed its movements, undercutting Meade's authority. Finally, he had to contend with disaffection in his officer corps. Many officers in the Army of the Potomac felt enduring loyalty to General George McClellan, whom Lincoln had dismissed in 1862, and considered Grant a mediocrity who had triumphed in the West only because his opposition there had been third-rate.

Lee's only hope was to make Grant's campaign so costly and time-consuming that the Northern general would abandon it before the Southerners ran out of supplies and troops. But despite problems and setbacks, Grant kept relentless pressure on Lee. Tied down in Virginia, the Confederate general was unable to send troops to help slow Sherman's advance in Georgia.

From the Wilderness to Cold Harbor

Grant and Meade began their campaign against Lee in May 1864, crossing the Rapidan River near Fredericksburg, Virginia, and marching toward an area known as the Wilderness (see Map 17-1). Just a year earlier, Lee and Jackson had won a smashing victory at nearby Chancellorsville. Hoping to duplicate that earlier success, Lee attacked the Army of the Potomac, which outnumbered his 118,000 to 60,000, in the thickets of the Wilderness on May 5 and 6 before it could reach open ground. The densely wooded terrain reduced the Union army's advantage in numbers and artillery. Much of the fighting involved fierce hand-to-hand combat. Exchanges of gunfire at close range set the dry underbrush ablaze. Wounded soldiers, trapped in the fires, begged their comrades to shoot them before they burned to death. The toll was frightful—eighteen thousand casualties on the Union side, ten thousand on the Confederate side.

In the past, Union commanders would have pulled back and rested after such an encounter. But Grant startled Lee's army by pushing on. "Surprise and disappointment were the prevailing emotions," one Southerner wrote, "when we discovered after the contest in the Wilderness that General Grant was not going to retire." Lee's offensive in the **Battle of the Wilderness** was his last. From then on, his army was on the defensive against Grant's relentless pursuit.

Marching and fighting, his casualties always higher than Lee's, Grant continued South. Attacking the entrenched Confederate Army at **Spotsylvania**, his army suffered another eighteen thousand casualties to the Confederates' eleven thousand. Undeterred, Grant moved on toward **Cold Harbor**, where Lee's troops again awaited him in entrenched positions. Flinging his army against withering Confederate fire on June 3, he lost seven thousand men in eight minutes.

In less than a month of fighting, the Army of the Potomac had lost 55,000 men. The slaughter undermined Grant's support in Northern public opinion and led peace advocates to renew their quest for a cease-fire. With antiwar sentiment growing in the

Map 17-1 *Grant and Lee in Virginia, 1864–1865*
The engagements in Virginia from May 1864 to April 1865 between the two great generals for the Union and the Confederacy proved decisive in ending the Civil War. Although General Lee fared well enough in the Wilderness, Spotsylvania, and Cold Harbor campaigns, the sheer might and relentlessness of Grant and his army wore down the Confederate forces. When Petersburg fell after a prolonged siege on April 2, 1865, Richmond, Appomattox, and dreams of Southern independence soon fell as well.

Union General Ulysses Grant had the pews from a local church moved to a grove of trees where he and his officers planned the following day's assault on Confederate troops at Cold Harbor, Virginia. Grant appears at the left of the photograph, leaning over a bench and studying a map.

North as the presidential elections approached in November, Lee's defensive strategy seemed to be working.

At this point, Grant decided to change his tactics. Abandoning his march on Richmond from the north, he shifted his army south of the James River to approach the Confederate capital from the rear. Wasting no time, he crossed his army over the James and, on June 17, 1864, surprised the Confederates with an attack on **Petersburg**, a critical rail junction twenty-three miles south of Richmond. It was a brilliant maneuver, but the hesitant actions of Union corps commanders gave Lee time to reinforce the town's defenders. Both armies dug in for a lengthy siege.

In an effort to break the stalemate, Union troops dug a tunnel under the Confederate defenses and filled it with eight thousand pounds of explosive powder. They ignited it on July 30, throwing dirt, men, and guns high into the air and leaving a large crater in the ground. But Union troops were as awed by the explosion as the Confederates. They hesitated in their attack on the breach in the Confederate lines, giving Lee time to rally his forces. The attack failed, the Union lost another four thousand men, and the siege of Petersburg continued.

Atlanta

While Grant engaged Lee in Virginia, Union forces under William T. Sherman in Georgia engaged in a deadly dance with the Army of Tennessee under the command of Joseph E. Johnston as they began the

Atlanta Campaign, a scheme to take Atlanta, Georgia (see Map 17-2). Johnston had replaced the incompetent Braxton Bragg after the Confederate debacle at Chattanooga in late 1863. He shared Lee's belief that the Confederacy's best hope lay in a defensive strategy. Hoping to lure Sherman into a frontal assault, Johnston settled his forces early in May at Dalton, an important railroad junction in Georgia twenty-five miles south of Chattanooga and seventy-five miles north of Atlanta. The wily Union general declined to attack and instead made a wide swing around the Confederates, prompting Johnston to abandon Dalton, rush south, and dig in again at Resaca to prevent Sherman from cutting the railroad. Again Sherman swung around without an assault, and again Johnston rushed south to cut him off, this time at Cassville.

This waltz continued for two months until Johnston had retreated to a strong defensive position on Kennesaw Mountain, barely twenty miles north of Atlanta. At this point, early in July, Sherman decided to attack, with predictably disastrous consequences. The Union suffered three thousand casualties, the Confederates only six hundred. Sherman would not make such a mistake again. He resumed his maneuvering and by mid-July had forced Johnston into defensive positions on Peachtree Creek just north of Atlanta. President Davis feared that Johnston would let Sherman take Atlanta without a fight and waltz with the Union general until the sea stopped them both. He dismissed Johnston and installed John Bell Hood of Texas in his place. This was a grave error. Hood, in the opinion of those who fought for him, had a "lion's heart" but a "wooden head."

In late July, Hood began a series of attacks on Sherman, beginning at Peachtree Creek on July 20, and was thrown back each time with heavy losses. In less than nine days, Hood suffered thirteen thousand casualties, compared to the Union's six thousand. Davis, who three weeks earlier had eagerly sought an offensive, ordered Hood back to defensive positions in Atlanta.

Sherman launched a series of flanking maneuvers around the city in late August that left Hood in danger of being surrounded. The Confederate general had no choice but to abandon Atlanta and save his army. On the night of September 1, Hood evacuated the city, burning everything of military value.

The loss of Atlanta was a severe blow to the Confederacy. Several of the South's major railroads converged at the city, and its industries helped arm and clothe the South's armies. Atlanta's fall also left Georgia's rich farmland at the mercy of Sherman's army.

Most significant, the fall of Atlanta revived the morale of the war-weary North and helped assure Lincoln's reelection in November. The last hope of the Confederacy—that a peace candidate would replace Lincoln and end the war—had faded. As the disconsolate editor of the *Richmond Examiner* explained, the "disaster at Atlanta [came] in the very nick of time" to "save the party of Lincoln from irretrievable ruin. . . . It will obscure the prospect of peace, late so bright. It will also diffuse gloom over the South."

Map 17-2 The Atlanta Campaign and Sherman's March, 1864–1865
Sherman, a brilliant tactician who generally refused to be goaded into a frontal assault, "danced" with Confederate General Joseph E. Johnston until an impatient Jefferson Davis replaced Johnston with Hood, and soon Atlanta was in Federal hands. The fall of Atlanta opened the way to the rest of Georgia, a key supply state for the Confederacy. With orders not to harm the civilian population, Sherman's men took their wrath out on property as they made their way through Georgia and South Carolina.

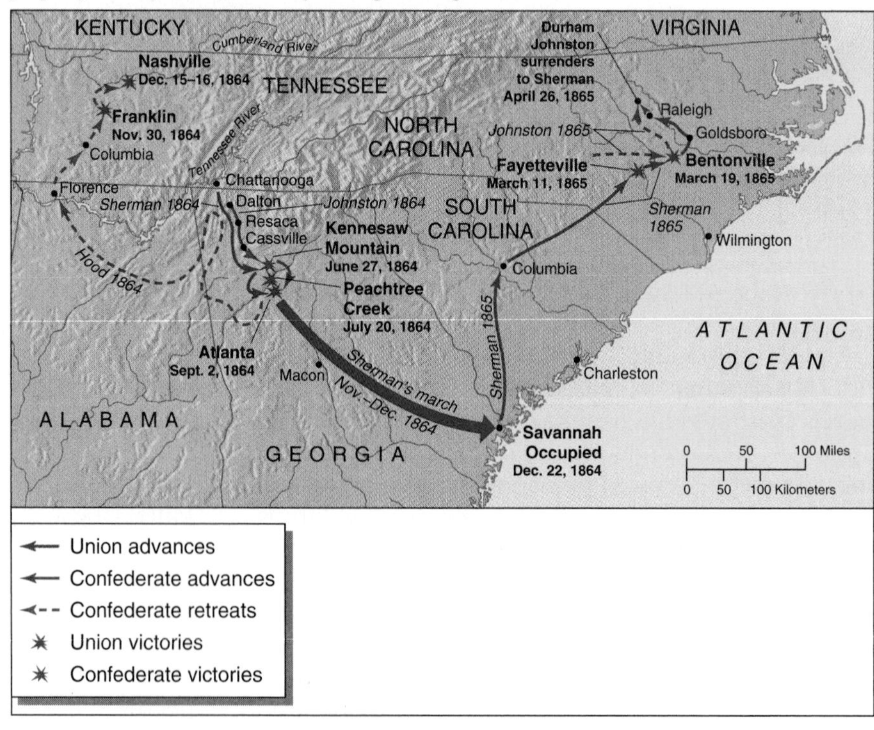

The Election of 1864

Before Sherman's victory at Atlanta, Northern dismay over Grant's enormous losses and his failure to take Richmond raised the prospect of a Democratic election victory. Nominating George B. McClellan, former commander of the Union's armies, as their presidential candidate, the Democrats appealed to the voters as the party of peace. They also appealed to the antiemancipation sentiment that was strong in some parts of the North.

The fall of Atlanta and the Union's suddenly improved military fortunes undermined Democratic prospects. Another Union victory three weeks before the elections gave Lincoln a further boost and diminished McClellan's chances. Since September, Union forces under General Philip H. Sheridan had been on the offensive in the Shenandoah Valley. In lightning cavalry raids on farms and supply depots, they destroyed valuable Confederate food reserves. And, in a decisive battle on October 19, they overwhelmed the valley's Confederate defenders. Lee had now been deprived of a vital source of supply.

In the voting on November 8, Lincoln captured 55 percent of the popular vote, losing only New Jersey, Delaware, and Kentucky. Republicans likewise swept the congressional elections, retaining control of both the Senate and the House of Representatives.

The Republican victory reinforced the Union commitment to emancipation. A proposed constitutional amendment outlawing slavery everywhere in the United States, not just those areas still in rebellion, had failed in Congress when it was introduced earlier in 1864. Reintroduced after the election, it passed Congress and was ratified as the **Thirteenth Amendment** to the U.S. Constitution in 1865. All earlier amendments related to government powers and functions; this was the first to outlaw a domestic institution previously protected by the Constitution and state law. (Ironically, an earlier Thirteenth Amendment had been proposed to the states by Congress and President Buchanan in March 1861, just before Lincoln took office and the South seceded. This amendment would have prohibited Congress from interfering with slavery wherever it existed. It lapsed when Southerners deserted Congress and the Civil War began.)

Sherman's March to the Sea

After Sherman took Atlanta, Hood withdrew his army toward Tennessee, hoping to lure Union forces away from Georgia. Grant wanted Sherman to go after Hood. But Sherman had a different idea. He proposed to break Confederate resistance once and for all by marching his army to the sea and destroying everything in its path.

Sherman's March got under way on November 15. His force of sixty thousand men encountered little resistance, prompting North Carolina's marveling governor, Zebulon Vance, to comment, "It shows what I have always believed, that the great popular heart is not now and never had been in this war!" Sherman entered Savannah on December 22, 1864, and presented the city to Lincoln as a Christmas present. Just a few weeks earlier, Union forces in Tennessee had routed Hood's army at the **Battle of Franklin** and then crushed it entirely at the **Battle of Nashville**. Hood's defeat removed any threat to Sherman's rear.

Sherman resumed his march in February 1865, heading for South Carolina, the heart of the Confederacy and the state where the Civil War had begun. "The truth is," Sherman wrote a friend, "the whole army is burning with an insatiable desire to wreak vengeance on South Carolina." South Carolinians sent taunting messages promising stiff resistance, but these served only further to provoke Sherman's troops. They pushed aside the small force that assembled to oppose them, wreaked greater destruction in South Carolina than they had in Georgia, and burned the state capitol at Columbia. Sherman sent the colonel of a black regiment to receive the surrender of Charleston and ordered black troops to be the first to take possession of the city. The soldiers marched in singing "John Brown's Body" to the cheers of the city's black population.

Sherman ended his march in Goldsboro, North Carolina, in March 1865 after repelling a surprise Confederate attack at Bentonville led by the restored Joseph E. Johnston and the remnants of the Army of Tennessee. Behind the Union army lay a barren swath 425 miles long from Savannah to Goldsboro. A wave of despair spread through what remained of the Confederacy, and desertions soared in Lee's Army of Virginia.

Arming the Confederacy's Slaves

In a move reflecting their desperation in March 1865, Confederate leaders revived a proposal that they had previously rejected to arm and free slaves. Slaves had served involuntarily in the Confederate army, and a number of free black Louisianans had volunteered for service in Southern ranks early in the war. But this proposal represented a major policy shift. President Davis hoped it would gain the Confederacy not only a military benefit but also diplomatic recognition from countries that had balked because of slavery.

The issue divided Confederate leaders. Confederate general Howell Cobb argued that "if slaves will make good soldiers, our whole theory of slavery is wrong." Others thought it was preferable to abandon

Sherman's March reached a triumphant conclusion in February 1865 when black Federal troops of the 55th Massachusetts Regiment marched into battered Charleston, South Carolina. The illustration captures both the destructiveness of the total war General Sherman waged on Georgia and South Carolina, and the hope among former slaves for a new birth of freedom.

slavery than to lose independence. A Confederate congressman from Georgia wrote to a friend in October 1864 that if the South lost the war, slavery was over anyway, and "we and our children will be slaves, while our freed negroes will lord it over us." But if the Confederacy enlisted slaves, it could "win our independence, and have liberty and homes for ourselves and our children."

Not surprisingly, slaves themselves greeted the proposal with little enthusiasm. They might have found service in the Confederate army an acceptable alternative to bondage earlier in the war, but not now, with Union victory imminent. Mary Chesnut recalled in March 1865 that early in the war, when her husband "spoke to his Negroes about it, his head men were keen to go in the army, to be free and get a bounty after the war. Now they say coolly that they don't want freedom if they have to fight for it. That means they are pretty sure of having it anyway."

On March 13, 1865, a reluctant Confederate Congress passed a bill to enlist black soldiers, but without a provision offering them freedom. President Davis and the War Office bypassed the equivocal congressional legislation ten days later, issuing a general order that promised immediate freedom to slaves who enlisted. The war ended before the order could have any effect. The irony was that in the summer of 1864, a majority of Northerners probably would have accepted reunion without emancipation had the Confederacy abandoned its fight.

The Road to Appomattox

With Sherman's triumph in Georgia and the Carolinas and Sheridan's rout of the Confederates in the Shenandoah Valley, Lee's army remained the last obstacle to Union victory. On April 1, Sheridan's cavalry seized a vital railway junction on Lee's right flank, forcing Lee to abandon Petersburg and the defense of Richmond. He tried a daring run westward toward Lynchburg, hoping to secure much-needed supplies and join Johnston's Army of Tennessee in North Carolina to continue the fight.

President Davis fled Richmond with his cabinet and headed toward North Carolina. Union troops occupied the Confederate capital on April 3, and, two days later, President Lincoln walked through its streets to the cheers of his army and an emotional reception from thousands of black people. "I know I am free," shouted one black spectator, "for I have seen Father Abraham and felt him."

Grant's army of 80,000 outran Lee's diminishing force of 35,000 and cut off his escape at **Appomattox Court House**, Virginia, on April 7. Convinced that further resistance was futile, the Confederate commander met Grant on April 9, 1865, in the McLean house at Appomattox to sign the documents of surrender. The Union general offered generous terms, allowing Lee's men to go home unmolested and to take with them horses or mules "to put in a crop." Grant reported feeling "sad and depressed" at "the downfall of a foe who had fought so long and valiantly, and had suffered so much for a cause, though that cause was, I believe, one of the worst for which a people ever fought." Lee rode through the thinned ranks of his troops, who crowded around him in silent tribute, brushing the general's boots and the withers of his horse with their hats.

The fleeing Davis met Joseph E. Johnston at Greensboro, North Carolina, hoping to convince him to continue fighting. But Johnston, like Lee, saw no point in continued bloodshed and surrendered to Sherman near Durham, North Carolina, on April 26. Davis continued south, urging the people to fight on, but the people were tired of the war and ignored him. On May 10, Union cavalry captured Davis and his companions in southern Georgia. On May 26, Texas general Kirby Smith surrendered his trans-Mississippi army, and the Civil War came to an end.

The Death of Lincoln

Washington greeted the Confederate surrender at Appomattox with predictable and raucous rejoicing—torchlight parades, cannon salutes, and crowds spontaneously bellowing "The Star-Spangled Banner." On April 11, President Lincoln addressed a large crowd from the White House balcony and spoke briefly of his plans to reconstruct the South with the help of persons loyal to the Union, including recently freed slaves. At least one listener found the speech disappointing. Sometime actor and full-time Confederate patriot John Wilkes Booth muttered to a friend in the throng, "That means nigger citizenship. Now, by God, I'll put him through. That is the last speech he will ever make."

On the evening of April 14, Good Friday, the president went to Ford's Theater in Washington to view a comedy, *Our American Cousin.* During the performance, Booth shot the president, wounding him mortally, then jumped from Lincoln's box to the stage shouting "*Sic semper tyrannis*" ("Thus ever to tyrants") and fled the theater. Union troops tracked him down to a barn in northern Virginia and killed him. Investigators arrested eight accomplices who had conspired with Booth to murder other high officials in addition to Lincoln. Four of the accomplices were hanged. Besides the president, however, the only other official attacked was Secretary of State Seward, who received serious but not fatal knife wounds.

This photograph of Abraham Lincoln was taken four days before John Wilkes Booth assassinated him in Ford's Theater.

Southerners reacted to Lincoln's assassination with surprisingly mixed emotions. Many saw in the death of the man they had regarded as their bitterest enemy for four years some slight hope of relief for the South's otherwise bleak prospects. But General Johnston and others like him understood Lincoln's influence with the radical elements in the Republican party who were pressing for harsh terms against the South. The president's death, Johnston wrote, was "the greatest possible calamity to the South."

Conclusion

Just before the war, William Sherman had warned a friend from Virginia, "You people of the South don't know what you are doing. This country will be drenched in blood. . . . War is a terrible thing." He was right. More than 365,000 Union soldiers died during the war, 110,000 in battle, and more than 256,000 Confederate soldiers, 94,000 of them in battle. Total casualties on both sides, including wounded, were more than 1 million.

Southern armies suffered disproportionately higher casualties than Northern armies. One in four Confederate soldiers died or endured debilitating wounds, compared to one in ten Federal soldiers. During the first year after the war, Mississippi allocated one-fifth of its budget for artificial limbs. Compounding the suffering of the individuals behind these gruesome statistics was the incalculable suffering—in terms of grief, fatherless children, women who never married, families never made whole—of the people close to them.

The war devastated the South. The region lost one-fourth of its white male population between the ages of 20 and 40. It also lost two-fifths of its livestock and half its farm machinery. Union armies destroyed many of the South's railroads and shattered its industry. Between 1860 and 1870, the wealth of the South declined by 60 percent, and its share of the nation's total wealth dropped from more than 30 percent to 12 percent. The wealth of the North, in contrast, increased by half in the same period.

The Union victory solved the constitutional question about the right of secession and sealed the fate of slavery. The issue that dominated the prewar sectional debate had vanished. Now when politicians intoned in Independence Day orations or campaign speeches about the ideals of democracy and freedom, the glaring reality of human bondage would no longer mock their rhetoric.

For black Southerners, emancipation was the war's most significant achievement. Journalists sponsored by the federal government who recorded the testimony of ex-slaves in the 1930s during the Great Depression, seventy years after emancipation, found their memory of the jubilee as fresh as yesterday. Lincoln entered African-American folklore as a larger-than-life figure. At age ninety-one, Fanny Burdock of Valdosta, Georgia, told a recorder a common tale of seeing Lincoln "coming all dusty and on foot" past her Georgia home.

> We run right to the fence and had the oak bucket and the dipper. When he draw up to us, he so tall, black eyes so sad. Didn't say not one word, just looked hard at all us, every one us crying. We give him nice cool water from the dipper. Then he nodded and set off and we just stood there till he get to being dust then nothing. After, didn't our owner or nobody credit it, but me and all my kin, we knowed. I still got the dipper to prove it.

The Civil War stimulated other changes that grew more significant over time. It did not make the Union an industrial nation, but it taught the effectiveness of centralized management, new financial techniques, and the coordination of production, marketing, and distribution. Entrepreneurs would apply these lessons to create the expanding corporations of the postwar American economy.

Likewise, the war did not revolutionize gender relations in American society; but, by opening new opportunities to women in fields such as nursing and teaching, it helped lay the foundation for the women's suffrage movement of the 1870s and 1880s.

For many Americans, especially black and white Southerners, the war was the most important event in their lives. It had a devastating impact on the families and friends of those who died. But it was not responsible for every postwar change in American society, and it left many features of American life intact. The experience of pulling together in a massive war effort, for example, did not soften class antagonisms. European socialist and father of communism Karl Marx hailed Lincoln as a son of the working class and predicted that "as the American War of independence initiated a new era of ascendancy for the middle class, so the American anti-slavery war will do for the working classes." But capitalism, not labor, triumphed during the war. And it was industrialists and entrepreneurs, not working people, who most benefited from the war's bonanza. Lincoln brutally suppressed strikes at defense plants and threw labor leaders into military prisons.

The war to end slavery changed some American racial attitudes, especially in the North. When Lincoln broadened the war's objectives to include the abolition of slavery, he connected the success of the Union to freedom for the slave. At the outset of the Civil War, only a small minority of Northerners considered themselves abolitionists. After the Emancipation Proclamation, every Northern soldier became a liberator. By the end of the war, perhaps a majority of Northerners supported granting freedmen the right to vote and to equal protection under the law, even if they believed (as many did) that black people were inferior to white people. The courage of black troops and the efforts of African-American leaders to link the causes of reunion and freedom were influential in bringing about this shift.

Most white Southerners did not experience a similar enlightenment. Some were relieved by the end of slavery, but most greeted it with fear, anger, and regret. For them, the freed slaves would be living reminders of the South's defeat and the end of a way of life grounded in white supremacy.

If the Civil War resolved the sectional dispute of the 1850s by ending slavery and denying the right of the Southern states to secede, it created two new equally troubling problems: how to reunite South and North and how to deal with the legacy of slavery. At his last cabinet meeting on April 14, Lincoln gave little indication of how he intended to proceed on these problems. He seemed inclined to be conciliatory, cautioning against reprisals on Confederate leaders and noting the courage of General Lee and his officers. The president said nothing about the rights of freedmen, although earlier statements indicated that he favored suffrage, but not social equality, for African Americans.

America's greatest crisis had closed. In its wake, former slaves tested their new freedom, and the nation groped for reconciliation. The struggle to preserve the Union and abolish slavery had renewed and vindicated the nation's ideals. It was time to savor the hard-fought victories before plunging into the uncertainties of Reconstruction.

Review Questions

1. Compare and contrast the roles played by women, in the North and in the South, during the Civil War, and explain how their actions and activities aided or hindered the war effort of their respective nations.

2. Some historians view the 1864 presidential election as one of the most important elections in American history. Why?
3. Looking back at the Confederacy's position after Gettysburg, defeat seemed inevitable. But even as late as the summer of 1864, many Southerners still believed that they had a fighting chance at independence. Why did they feel this way, and what happened between then and the end of the year to dash such hopes?
4. Given the enormity of the losses in lives and property, it is not surprising that some historians have attributed major changes in American society to the Civil War. But other historians claim that the Civil War's impact has been exaggerated. Analyze and assess what the Civil War did or did not accomplish.

Recommended Reading

John P. Marszalek, *Sherman: A Soldier's Passion for Order* (1993). A balanced, insightful biography that dispels many myths about the mercurial Union general whose march through Georgia became a symbol for a new type of warfare.

Emory M. Thomas, *Robert E. Lee: A Biography* (1995). Presents a balanced account of the enigmatic Confederate leader.

Additional Sources

War Transforms the North

Mark E. Neely Jr., *The Fate of Liberty: Abraham Lincoln and Civil Liberties* (1991).

Elizabeth B. Pryor, *Clara Barton: Professional Angel* (1987).

Heather Cox Richardson, *The Greatest Nation of the Earth: Republican Economic Policies during the Civil War* (1997).

Bruce Tapp, *Over Lincoln's Shoulder: The Committee on the Conduct of the War* (1998).

The Confederacy Disintegrates

Stephen V. Ash, *When the Yankees Came: Conflict and Chaos in the Occupied South, 1861–1865* (1995).

Edward D. C. Campbell, Jr., and Kym S. Rice, eds., *A Woman's War: Southern Women, Civil War, and the Confederate Legacy* (1996).

Catherine Clinton and Nina Silber, eds., *Divided Houses: Gender and the Civil War* (1992).

Robert F. Durden, *The Gray and the Black: The Confederate Debate on Emancipation* (1972).

Drew Gilpin Faust, "Altars of Sacrifice: Confederate Women and the Narratives of War," *Journal of American History,* 76 (March 1990): 1200–1228.

Gary W. Gallagher, *The Confederate War: How Popular Will, Nationalism, and Military Strategy Could Not Stave Off Defeat* (1997).

Mark Grimsely, *The Hard Hand of War: Union Policy toward Southern Civilians, 1861–1865* (1995).

LeeAnn Whites, *The Civil War as a Crisis in Gender: Augusta, Georgia, 1860-1890* (1995).

C. Vann Woodward, ed., *Mary Chesnut's Civil War* (1981).

The Union Prevails

Richard E. Beringer, Herman Hattaway, Archer Jones, and William N. Still, Jr., *Why the South Lost the Civil War* (1986).

Albert Castel, *Decision in the West: The Atlanta Campaign of 1864* (1992).

Joseph T. Glatthaar, *The March to the Sea and Beyond* (1985).

Lee Kennett, *Marching through Georgia: The Story of Soldiers and Civilians during Sherman's Campaign* (1995).

Craig L. Symonds, *Joseph E. Johnston: A Civil War Biography* (1992).

Emory Thomas, *The Confederate Nation, 1861–1865* (1979).

Where to Learn More

❖ **Cyclorama, Grant Park, Atlanta, Georgia.** This exhibit vividly depicts the 1864 Battle of Atlanta, complete with "gunfire" and oozing "blood." Interpretive literature at the site helps make sense of the panoramic depiction.

❖ **Petersburg National Battlefield, Petersburg, Virginia.** The battlefield offers a complete overview of the city's siege in 1864–65, which, when broken, led to the fall of Richmond and ultimately to the end of the war.

❖ **Ford's Theatre National Historical Site, Washington, DC.** The place where John Wilkes Booth assassinated President Abraham Lincoln not only depicts those events, including artifacts from the assassination, but also presents period plays.

❖ **Appomattox Court House, Appomattox, Virginia.** What historian Bruce Catton termed "a stillness at Appomattox" can be felt at the McLean House in this south-central Virginia town. The house is much as it was when Confederate general Robert E. Lee surrendered his forces to Union general Ulysses S. Grant on April 9, 1865. An almost reverential solitude covers the house and the well-maintained grounds today. Other sites related to the last year of the war include Kennesaw Mountain National Battlefield Park, Petersburg National Battlefield, and Richmond National Battlefield Park.

RECONSTRUCTION, 1865–1877

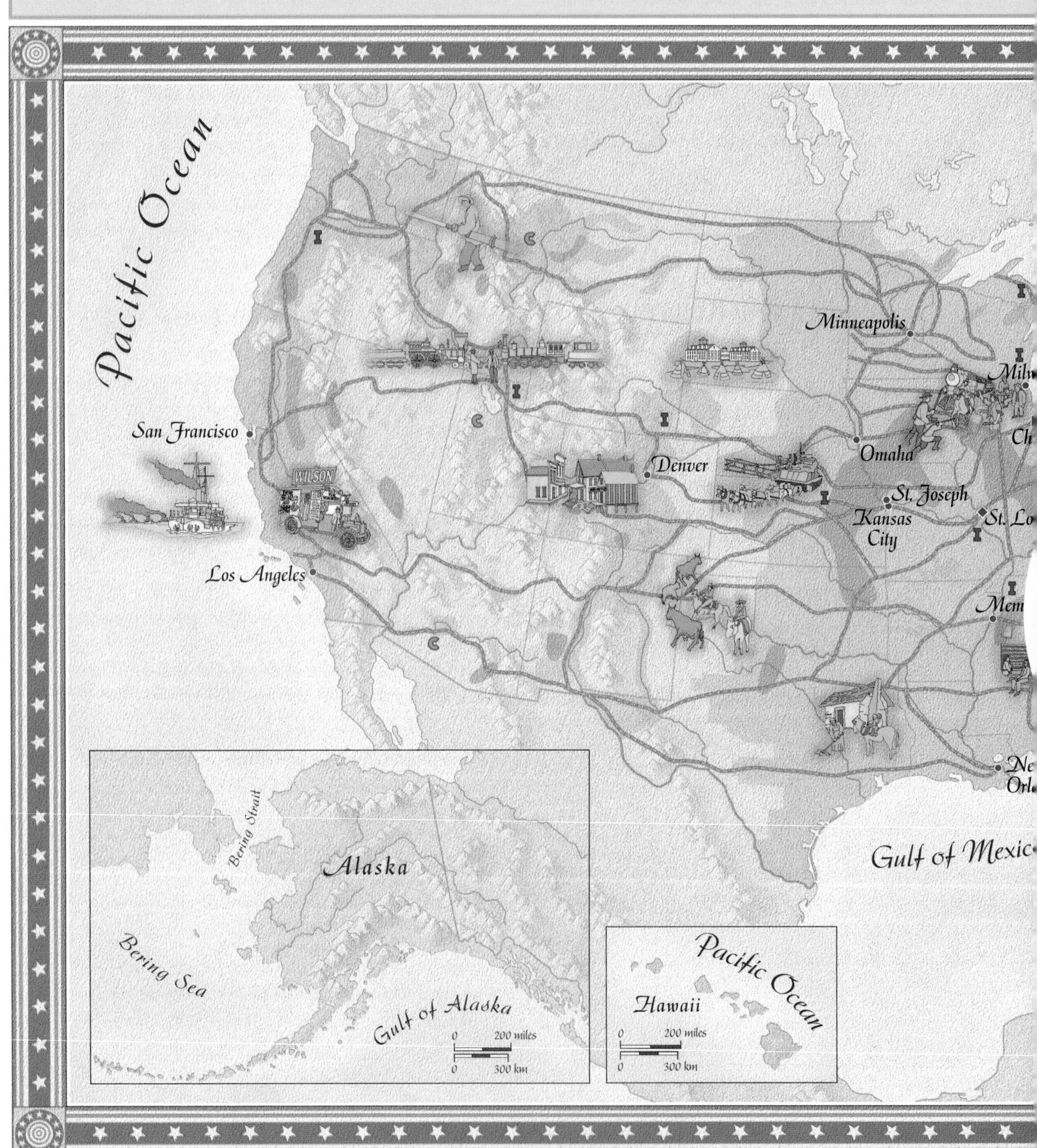

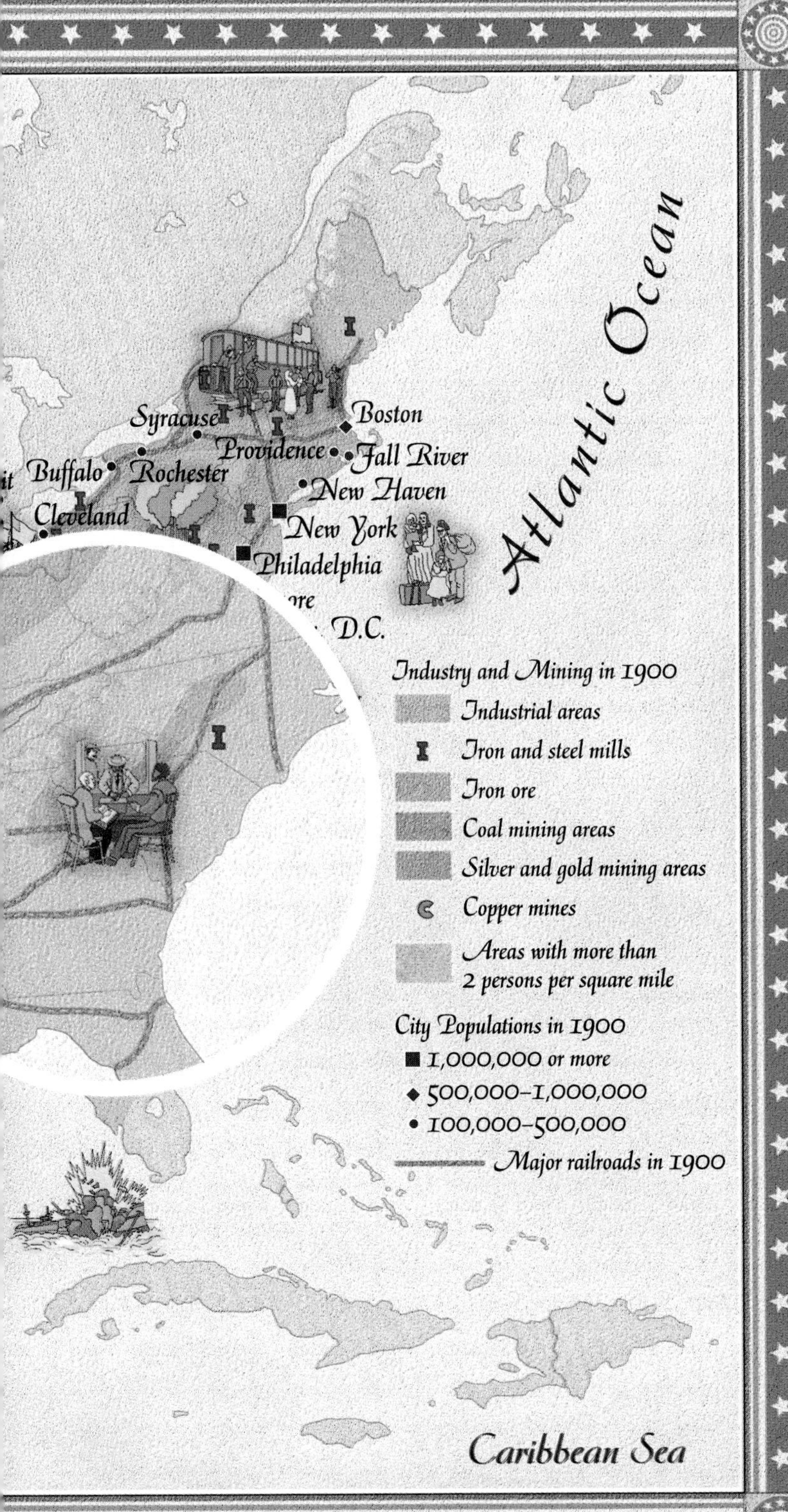

18

Chapter Outline

Key Topics

- African-American aspirations and southern white expectations
- Federal government plans to bring the South back into the Union and secure freedom for former slaves
- Southern Republican efforts to keep the allegiance of black voters and win white support
- Why and how Reconstruction ended

As Union general William T. Sherman burned his way through Georgia and South Carolina in late 1864 and early 1865, slaves left their plantations to work for and follow the conquering army. In January 1865, Sherman allowed former slaves to settle on farms abandoned by their masters along the Atlantic coast. Tom Mansart, a former slave, seized this opportunity to stake out a farm near Port Royal, South Carolina. Less than a year later, the federal government returned the land to its previous owner. Mansart found work as a stevedore in nearby Charleston and joined a labor union founded by free black people before the war. By 1871, he had married and risen to prominence in his community. He was president of his eight-hundred-member union, and his backing helped elect local Republican candidates to office.

The Mansart family's good fortune declined after 1871 as first an economic depression and then racial violence stole their dream. Tom Mansart was killed at the door of his house during the election campaign of 1876, the victim of one of the white mobs roaming through South Carolina to discourage black citizens from voting. The federal troops that had been sent to Charleston to maintain an open political process instead fraternized with the city's white leaders.

Tom Mansart's story, as told by African-American leader W. E. B. Du Bois in *The Black Flame* (1957), exemplified both the promise of the **Reconstruction** era and its eventual betrayal by white people in both the North and the South. Crossing the threshold of freedom in 1865, black Southerners saw their prospects widening. Rights formerly denied them—to move, to own property, to get an education, to keep their families together, to succeed or fail in their own endeavors—were now theirs. Freedom meant more than a change in status; it marked a rebirth. But, by 1877, African Americans again faced restrictions that, though not as severe as slavery, deprived them of the promised fruits of freedom.

The position of African Americans in American society was one of the two great issues of Reconstruction. Americans of both sections disagreed about how much freedom to grant the former slaves, almost all of whom lived in the South. The other great issue was how and under what terms to readmit the former Confederate states. The Constitution was silent on the subject. As with the issue of black equality, opinions in both sections varied widely.

The formation of a national consensus on freedom and reunification began with the demands and hopes of three broad groups. One was the Republican party, which controlled the federal government and determined its policies. Most Republicans were unwilling to accept the seceding states back in the Union without an expression of loyalty and a commitment to protecting the rights of freedmen. A second group, the more than 4 million former slaves, demanded voting rights, access to education, and the opportunity to seek economic self-sufficiency. Few black Northerners yet enjoyed all these benefits, and few white Southerners could conceive of former slaves possessing them. The third group, white Southerners, hoped to restore their shattered lives, fortunes, and dignity. In their vision of a renewed South, black people remained subservient, and the federal government stopped interfering in southern affairs.

Between 1865 and 1867, under President Andrew Johnson's Reconstruction plan, white Southerners pretty much had their way with the former slaves and with their own state governments. Congressional action between 1867 and 1870 attempted to balance black rights and home rule, with mixed results. After 1870, white Southerners gradually regained control of their states and localities, often through violence and intimidation, denying black Southerners their political gains while Republicans in Washington lost interest in policing their former enemies.

By the time the last federal troops left the South in 1877, white Southerners had prevailed. The Confederate states had returned to the Union with all of their rights and many of their leaders restored. And the freed slaves remained in mostly subservient positions with few of the rights and privileges enjoyed by other Americans.

White Southerners and the Ghosts of the Confederacy, 1865

Confederate soldiers—generals and troops alike—returned to devastated homes they could scarcely recognize. General Braxton Bragg returned to his "once prosperous" Alabama home to find "all, all was lost, except my debts." Bragg and his wife found temporary shelter in a slave cabin. Yeomen farmers, the backbone of the Confederacy, found uprooted fences, farm animals dead or gone, and buildings destroyed. With no income or savings to soften their plight, they and their families wandered about in a living nightmare, seeking shelter where they could. They lived in morbid fear of vengeful former slaves or the hated Yankee soldiers wreaking more damage. "The demoralization is complete," a Georgia girl noted.

Their cause lost and their society reviled, white Southerners lived through the summer and fall of 1865 surrounded by ghosts—the ghosts of lost loved ones, joyful times, bountiful harvests, self-assurance, and slavery. Defeat shook the basic tenets of their religious beliefs. A North Carolinian cried, "Oh, our God! What sins we must have been guilty of that we should be so humiliated by Thee now!" Some praised God for delivering the South from the sin of slavery. A Virginia woman expressed thanks that "we white people are no longer permitted to go on in such wickedness, heaping up more and more wrath of God upon our devoted heads."

But many other white Southerners refused to accept their defeat as a divine judgment. Instead, they insisted, God had spared the South for a greater purpose. They came to view the war as the **Lost Cause** and interpreted it not as a lesson in humility but as an episode in the South's journey to salvation. Robert E. Lee became the patron saint of this cause, his poignant nobility a contrast to the crassness of the Yankee warlords. White Southerners would not allow the memory of the bloody struggle to die, transforming it into a symbol of courage against great odds and piety against sin. Eventually, they believed, redemption would come.

Fifteen years after the war, Mark Twain traveled the length of the East Coast. After visiting a gentlemen's club in Boston, he recalled that the conversation had covered a variety of topics, none of which included the Civil War. Northerners had relegated that conflict to history books and moved on. This was not the case in the South. There defeat and destruction demanded rationalization and remembrance. Thus Twain reported that, unlike in the

This engraving shows Southerners decorating the graves of rebel soldiers at Hollywood Memorial Cemetery in Virginia, in 1867. Northern and Southerners alike honored their war dead. But, in the South, the practice of commemorating fallen soldiers became an important element in maintaining the myth of the Lost Cause that colored white Southerners' view of the War.

North, gentlemen's talk in Atlanta inevitably wandered to the war and to heroism and sacrifice. "In the South," Twain wrote, "the war is what A.D. is elsewhere: they date from it." Such people would not accept the changes implied by defeat. They would fight to preserve as much of their past as the victors allowed.

Most white Southerners approached the great issues of freedom and reunification with unyielding views. They saw African Americans as adversaries whose attempts at self-improvement were a direct challenge to white people's beliefs in their own racial superiority. White Southerners saw outside assistance to black Southerners as another invasion. The Yankees may have destroyed their families, their farms, and their fortunes, but they would not destroy the racial order. The war may have ended slavery, but white Southerners were determined to preserve strict racial boundaries.

More than Freedom: African-American Aspirations in 1865

If black people could have peered into the minds of white Southerners, they would have been stunned. The former slaves did not initially even dream of social equality; far less did they plot the kind of vengeful murder and mayhem white people feared. They did harbor two potentially contradictory aspirations. The first was to be left alone, free of white supervision. Responding to the key question of the time,

Chronology

1863 Lincoln proposes his Ten Percent Plan.

1864 Congress proposes the Wade-Davis Bill.

1865 Sherman issues Field Order No. 15.

Freedmen's Bureau is established.

Andrew Johnson succeeds to the presidency, unveils his Reconstruction plan.

Massachusetts desegregates all public facilities.

Black citizens in several southern cities organize Union Leagues.

Former Confederate states begin to pass black codes.

1866 Congress passes Southern Homestead Act, Civil Rights Act of 1866.

Ku Klux Klan is founded.

Fourteenth Amendment to the Constitution is passed (ratified in 1868).

President Johnson goes on a speaking tour.

1867 Congress passes Military Reconstruction Acts, Tenure of Office Act.

1868 President Johnson is impeached and tried in the Senate for defying the Tenure of Office Act.

Republican Ulysses S. Grant is elected president.

1869 Fifteenth Amendment passed (ratified 1870).

1870 Congress passes Enforcement Act.

Republican regimes topple in North Carolina and Georgia.

1871 Congress passes Ku Klux Klan Act.

1872 Freedmen's Bureau closes down.

Liberal Republicans emerge as a separate party.

Ulysses S. Grant is reelected.

1873 Severe depression begins.

Colfax Massacre occurs.

U.S. Supreme Court's decision in the *Slaughterhouse* cases weakens the intent of the Fourteenth Amendment.

Texas falls to the Democrats in the fall elections.

1874 White Leaguers attempt a coup against the Republican government of New Orleans.

Democrats win off-year elections across the South amid widespread fraud and violence.

1875 Congress passes Civil Rights Act of 1875.

1876 Supreme Court's decision in *United States* v. *Cruikshank* nullifies Enforcement Act of 1870.

Outcome of the presidential election between Republican Rutherford B. Hayes and Democrat Samuel J. Tilden is contested.

1877 Compromise of 1877 makes Hayes president and ends Reconstruction.

"What shall we do with the Negro?" former slave and abolitionist Frederick Douglass responded, "Do nothing. . . . Give him a chance to stand on his own legs! Let him alone!" But former slaves also wanted land, voting and civil rights, and education. To secure these, they needed the intervention and support of the white power structure.

In 1865, African Americans had reason to hope that their dreams of full citizenship might be realized. They enjoyed a reservoir of support for their aspirations among some Republican leaders. The views of James A. Garfield, Union veteran, U.S. congressman, and future president, were typical of these Republicans. Commenting on the ratification of the Thirteenth Amendment, Garfield asked, "What is freedom? Is it the bare privilege of not being chained? . . . If this is all, then freedom is a bitter mockery, a cruel delusion."

The first step Congress took beyond emancipation was to establish the Bureau of Refugees, Freedmen, and Abandoned Lands in March 1865. Congress envisioned the **Freedmen's Bureau**, as it came to be called, as a multipurpose agency to provide social, educational, and economic services, advice, and protection to former slaves and destitute white Southerners. The Bureau marked the federal government's first foray into social welfare legislation. Congress also authorized the bureau to rent confiscated and abandoned farmland to freedmen in forty-acre plots with an option to buy. This auspicious beginning belied the great disappointments that lay ahead.

Education

The greatest success of the Freedmen's Bureau was in education. The bureau coordinated more than fifty northern philanthropic and religious groups, which in turn established three thousand freedmen's schools in the South serving 150,000 men, women, and children.

Initially, single young women from the Northeast comprised much of the teaching force. One of them, twenty-six-year-old Martha Schofield, came to Aiken, South Carolina, from rural Pennsylvania in 1865. Like many of her colleagues, she had joined the abolitionist movement as a teenager and decided to make teaching her life's work. Her strong Quaker beliefs reflected the importance of Protestant Christianity in motivating the young missionaries. When her sponsoring agency, the Pennsylvania Freedmen's Relief Association, folded in 1871, her school closed. Undaunted, she opened another school on her own, and, despite chronic financial problems and the hostility of Aiken's white citizens, she and the school endured. (Since 1953, her school has been part of Aiken's public school system.)

By the time Schofield opened her own school in 1871, black teachers outnumbered white teachers in the "colored" schools. The financial troubles of northern missionary societies and declining interest in the freedmen's condition among white Northerners opened opportunities for black teachers. Support for them came from black churches, especially the **African Methodist Episcopal (AME) Church**.

The former slaves crowded into basements, shacks, and churches to attend school. "The children . . . hurry to school as soon as their work is over," wrote a teacher in Norfolk, Virginia, in 1867. "The plowmen hurry from the field at night to get their hour of study. Old men and women strain their dim sight with the book two and half feet distant from the eye, to catch the shape of the letter. I call this heaven-inspired interest."

At the end of the Civil War, only about 10 percent of black Southerners were literate, compared with more than 70 percent of white Southerners. Within a decade, black literacy had risen above 30 percent. Joseph Wilson, a former slave, attributed the rise to "this longing of ours for freedom of the mind as well as the body."

Some black Southerners went on to one of the thirteen colleges established by the American Missionary Association and black and white churches. Between 1860 and 1880 more than one thousand black Southerners earned college degrees at institutions still serving students today, such as Howard University in Washington, D.C., Fisk University in Nashville, Hampton Institute (now University), Tuskegee Institute, and Biddle Institute (now Johnson C. Smith University) in Charlotte.

The Freedmen's Bureau, northern churches, and missionary societies established more than three thousand schools attended by some 150,000 men, women, and children in the years after the Civil War. At first, mostly young white women from the Northeast staffed these schools.

Pursuing freedom of the mind involved challenges beyond those of learning to read and write. Many white Southerners condemned efforts at "Negro improvement." They viewed the time spent on education as wasted, forcing the former slaves to catch their lessons in bits and pieces between work, often by candlelight or on Sundays. White Southerners also harassed white female teachers, questioning their morals and threatening people who rented rooms to them. The *Atlanta Constitution,* in a vicious caricature, suggested that Harriet Beecher Stowe planned to establish a freedmen's school near Atlanta "for the benefit of mulatto children that have been born in the South since its invasion by Yankee school-marms."

After the Freedmen's Bureau folded in 1872 and

many of the northern societies that supported freedmen's education collapsed or cut back their involvement, education for black Southerners became more haphazard.

"Forty Acres and a Mule"

Although education was important to the freed slaves in their quest for civic equality, land ownership offered them the promise of economic independence. For generations, black people had worked southern farms and had received nothing for their labor. An overwhelmingly agricultural people, freedmen looked to farm ownership as a key element in their transition from slavery to freedom. "Gib us our own land and we take care of ourselves," a Charleston freedman asserted to a Northern visitor in 1865. "But without land, de ole massas can hire or starve us, as dey please."

Even before the war's end, rumors circulated through black communities in the South that the government would provide each black family with forty acres and a mule. These rumors were fueled by General William T. Sherman's **Field Order No. 15** in January 1865, which set aside a vast swath of abandoned land along the South Atlantic coast from the Charleston area to northern Florida for grants of up to forty acres. The Freedmen's Bureau likewise raised expectations when it was initially authorized to rent forty-acre plots of confiscated or abandoned land to freedmen.

By June 1865, about forty thousand former slaves had settled on "Sherman land" along the southeastern coast. In 1866, Congress passed the **Southern Homestead Act**, giving black people preferential access to public lands in five southern states. Two years later, the Republican government of South Carolina initiated a land redistribution program financed by the sale of state bonds. The state used proceeds from the bond sales to purchase farmland, which it then resold to freedmen, who paid for it with state-funded long-term low-interest loans. By the late 1870s, more than fourteen thousand African-American families had taken advantage of this program.

The highest concentration of black land ownership was in the Upper South and in areas of the Lower South with better economic conditions and less white hostility toward black people. By 1890, one out of three black farmers in the Upper South owned his land, compared to one out of five for the South as a whole. In Virginia, 43 percent of black farmers owned the land they farmed.

Land ownership did not ensure financial success. Most black-owned farms were small and on marginal land. The value of these farms in 1880 was roughly half that of white-owned farms. Black farmers also had trouble obtaining credit to purchase or expand their holdings. A lifetime of field work left some freedmen without the managerial skills to operate a farm. The hostility of white neighbors and their refusal to lend tools or animals, share work, sell land, or offer advice also played a role in thwarting black aspirations. Black farmers often had the most success when groups of families settled together, as in the farm community of Promise Land in upcountry South Carolina.

The vast majority of former slaves, however, especially those in the Lower South, never fulfilled their dreams of land ownership. Rumors to the contrary, the federal government never intended to implement a land redistribution program in the South. General Sherman viewed his field order as a temporary measure to support freedmen for the remainder of the war. President Andrew Johnson nullified the order in September 1865, returning confiscated land to its former owners. Even Republican supporters of black land ownership questioned the constitutionality of seizing privately owned real estate. Most land redistribution programs that did emerge after the war, including government-sponsored programs, required black farmers to have capital. But in the impoverished postwar economy of the South, it was difficult for them to acquire it.

Republican party rhetoric of the 1850s extolled the virtues and dignity of free labor over the degradation of slave labor. Free labor usually meant working for a wage or under some other contractual arrangement. But unlike slaves, according to the then prevailing view, free laborers could enjoy the fruits of their work and might someday become owners or entrepreneurs themselves. It was self-help, not government assistance, that guaranteed individual success. After the war, many white Northerners envisioned former slaves assuming the status of free laborers, not necessarily of independent landowners.

For most officials of the Freedmen's Bureau, who shared these views, reviving the southern economy was a higher priority than helping former slaves acquire farms. They wanted both to get the crop in the field and start the South on the road to a free labor system. They thus encouraged freedmen to work for their former masters under contract and postpone their quest for land. Bureau and military officials lectured former slaves on the virtues of staying home and working "faithfully" in the fields.

At first, agents of the Freedmen's Bureau supervised labor contracts between former slaves and masters. But after 1867, bureau surveillance declined. Agents assumed that both black laborers and white landowners had become accustomed to the mutual obligations of contracts. The bureau, however, underestimated the power of white landowners to coerce favorable terms or to ignore those they did not like. Contracts implied a mutuality that most planters could not accept in their relations with former slaves. As northern journalist Whitelaw Reid noted in 1865, planters "have no sort of conception of free labor. They do not comprehend any law for controlling laborers, save the law of force."

The former slaves had their own views of their proper place in the labor hierarchy. If they could not own land in the short term, they would strive for the best labor arrangement in the meantime. As early as 1862, slaves behind Union lines abandoned the gang system of labor, which they associated with slavery and dependence. In contracts with planters (usually their former masters) after the war, freedmen in most of the South insisted on working the land independently with their families. By contrast, freedmen in the rice districts along the South Atlantic coast retained their task system of labor, which allowed them flexibility and a degree of independence.

Throughout the South in 1865 and 1866, landlords complained of a chronic labor shortage, although few freedmen had left the region. The alleged shortage was the result of former slaves' refusal to work under conditions that resembled slavery. The withdrawal of black women from field work also contributed to the impression of a labor shortage. By staying home to care for their families, black women avoided the economic and sexual exploitation of the slavery era. They also sought to place themselves on an equal social footing with white plantation women, who likewise worked in the home and not in the fields.

Migration to Cities

While some black Southerners asserted their rights as workers on southern farms, others affirmed their freedom by moving to towns and cities. Even before the war, the city had offered slaves and free black people a measure of freedom unknown in the rural South. After the war, African Americans moved to cities to find families, seek work, escape the tedium and supervision of farm life, or simply test their right to move about.

For these same reasons, white people disapproved of black migration to the city. It reduced the labor pool for farms. It also gave black people more opportunities to associate with white people of similar social status, to compete for jobs, and to establish schools, churches, and social organizations, fueling their hopes for racial equality. White people felt confident that they could fix the freedmen's place in southern society on the farm; the city was another matter.

Between 1860 and 1870, the African-American population in every major southern city rose significantly. In Atlanta, for example, black people accounted for one in five residents in 1860 and nearly one in two by 1870.

Some freedmen came to cities initially to reunite with their families. Every city newspaper after the war carried advertisements from former slaves seeking their mates and children. In 1865, the Nashville *Colored Tennessean* carried this poignant plea: "During the year 1849, Thomas Sample carried away from this city, as his slaves, our daughter, Polly, and son. . . . We will give $100 each for them to any person who will assist them . . . to get to Nashville, or get word to us of their whereabouts."

Once in the city, freedmen had to find a home and a job. They usually settled for the cheapest accommodations in low-lying areas or on the outskirts of town where building

Milk sampling at Hampton Institute. Hampton, which opened in Virginia in 1868, was one of the first of several schools established with the help of northern philanthropic and missionary societies to allow freedmen to pursue a college education. Hampton stressed agricultural and vocational training. The military uniforms were typical for male students, black and white, at agricultural and mechanical schools.

codes did not apply. Rather than developing one large ghetto, as in many northern cities, black Southerners lived in several concentrations in and around cities.

Sometimes armed with a letter of reference from their former masters, black people went door to door to seek employment. Many found work serving white families—as guards, laundresses, maids—for very low wages. Both skilled and unskilled laborers found work rebuilding war-torn cities like Atlanta. Frederick Ayer, a Freedmen's Bureau agent in Atlanta, reported to a colleague in 1866 that "many of the whites are making most vigorous efforts to retrieve their broken fortunes and . . . rebuild their dwellings and shops. . . . This furnished employment to a large number of colored people as Masons, Carpenters, Teamsters, and Common Workmen."

Most rural black Southerners, however, arrived in cities untrained in the kinds of skills sought in an urban work force and so worked as unskilled laborers. In both Atlanta and Nashville, black people comprised more than 75 percent of the unskilled work force in 1870. Their wages were at or below subsistence level. A black laborer in Richmond admitted to a journalist in 1870 that he had difficulty making ends meet on $1.50 a day. "It's right hard," he reported. "I have to pay $15 a month rent, and only two little rooms." His family survived because his wife took in laundry while her mother watched the children. Considering the laborer's struggle, the journalist wondered, "Were not your people better off in slavery?" The man replied, "Oh, no sir! We're a heap better off now. . . . We're men now, but when our masters had us we was only change in their pockets."

Faith and Freedom

Religious faith framed and inspired the efforts of African Americans to test their freedom on the farm and in the city. White Southerners used religion to transform the Lost Cause from a shattering defeat to a premonition of a greater destiny. Black Southerners, in contrast, saw emancipation in biblical terms as the beginning of an exodus from bondage to the Promised Land.

Some black churches in the postwar South originated in the slavery era, but most split from white-dominated congregations after the war. White churchgoers deplored the expressive style of black worship, and black churchgoers were uncomfortable in congregations that treated them as inferiors. A separate church also reduced white surveillance.

The First African Baptist Church in Richmond originated in a white Baptist congregation founded before the war. An 1846 agreement allowed black worshippers to hold separate services, but only with a white minister officiating. In 1866, the white pastor resigned, noting that black worshippers "would naturally and justly prefer a minister of their own color." The white church transferred the deed to the black congregation that year, and the Reverend James Henry Holmes, a former slave, became their first black pastor. The church flourished under Holmes, paid off its debt, and by the 1870s boasted the largest black congregation in the United States.

The church became a primary focus of African-American life. It gave black people the opportunity to hone skills in self-government and administration that white-dominated society denied them. Within the supportive confines of the congregation, they could assume leadership positions, render important decisions, deal with financial matters, and engage in politics. The church also operated as an educational institution. Local governments, especially in rural areas, rarely constructed public schools for black people; churches often served that function. The desire to read the Bible inspired thousands of former slaves to attend the church school.

The church also spawned other organizations that served the black community over the next century. Burial societies, Masonic lodges, temperance groups, trade unions, and drama clubs originated in churches. By the 1870s, African Americans in Memphis had more than two hundred such organizations. They often came together to celebrate such holidays as Independence Day on July 4 and the anniversary of the Emancipation Proclamation on January 1. These commemorations antagonized white people and further divided the black and white communities.

African Americans took great pride in their churches, which became visible measures of their progress. In Charleston, the first building erected after the war was a black church. The First Colored Baptist Church in Nashville became a landmark for its imposing brick and stone façade. Black people donated a greater proportion of their earnings to their churches than white people did.

The church and the congregation were a cohesive force in black communities. They supported families under stress from discrimination and poverty. Husbands and wives joined church-affiliated societies together. Their children joined organizations such as the Young Rising Sons and Daughters of the New Testament. The church enforced family and religious values, punishing violaters guilty of such infractions as adultery. Black

The black church was the center of African-American life in the postwar urban South. Most black churches formed after the Civil War, but some, like the First African Baptist Church in Richmond, shown here in an 1874 engraving, traced their origins to before 1861.

churchwomen—both working- and middle-class—were especially prominent in the family-oriented organizations.

Most black churches looked inward to strengthen their members against the harsh realities of postwar southern society. Few ministers dared to engage in or even support protest activities. Some, especially those in the Colored Methodist Episcopal Church, counseled congregants to abide by the rules of second-class citizenship and to trust in God's will to right the wrongs of racism.

Northern-based denominations, however, notably the AME Church, were more aggressive advocates of black rights. AME ministers stressed the responsibility of individual black people to realize God's will of racial equality.

Henry McNeal Turner, probably the most influential AME minister of his day, helped expand the denomination into the South from its small primarily northern base at the end of the Civil War. The white Southern Methodist church granted the nineteen-year-old Turner a license to preach in 1853. He served as an itinerant minister for both black and white congregations during the next five years. In 1858, he joined the AME Church and moved north to lead a congregation in Baltimore. Having served as a U.S. Army chaplain, Turner moved to Georgia and evangelized former slaves who thronged to an activist church with black roots. Within five years, the AME Church had grown to 500,000 members, 80 percent of whom lived in the South. Turner entered Georgia politics in the late 1860s and held several state elective offices. His church elevated him to bishop in 1880.

Turner's career and the efforts of former slaves in the classroom, on the farm, in cities, and in the churches reflect the enthusiasm and expectations with which black Southerners greeted freedom. But the majority of white Southerners were unwilling to see those expectations fulfilled. For this reason, African Americans could not secure the fruits of their emancipation without the support and protection of the federal government. The issue of freedom was therefore inextricably linked to the other great issue of the era, the rejoining of the Confederacy to the Union, as expressed in federal Reconstruction policy.

Federal Reconstruction, 1865–1870

When the Civil War ended in 1865, no acceptable blueprint existed for reconstituting the Union. President Lincoln believed that, at heart, a majority of white Southerners were Unionists and that they could and should undertake the task of reconstruction. He favored a conciliatory policy toward the South in order, as he put it in one of his last letters, "to restore the Union, so as to make it . . . *a Union of hearts and hands as well as of States.*" He counted on the loyalists to be fair with respect to the rights of the former slaves.

The President had outlined his policy as early as 1863 when he proposed to readmit a seceding state if 10 percent of its prewar voters took an oath of loyalty to the Union and it prohibited slavery in a new state constitution. But this Ten Percent Plan did not require states to grant equal civil and political rights to former slaves, and many Republicans in Congress thought it was not stringent enough. In 1864, a group of them responded with the **Wade-Davis Bill**, which required a majority of a state's prewar voters to pledge their loyalty to the

Union and demanded guarantees of black equality before the law. The bill was passed at the end of a congressional session, but Lincoln kept it from becoming law by refusing to sign it (an action known as a "pocket veto").

The controversy over these plans reflected two obstacles to Reconstruction that would continue to plague the ruling Republicans after the war. First, neither the Constitution nor legal precedent offered any guidance on whether the president or Congress should take the lead on Reconstruction policy. Second, there was no agreement on what that policy should be. Proposals requiring various preconditions for readmitting a state—loyalty oaths, new constitutions with certain specific provisions, guarantees of freedmen's rights—all provoked vigorous debate.

President Andrew Johnson, some conservative Republicans, and most Democrats believed that because the Constitution made no mention of secession, the southern states had been in rebellion, but had never left the Union, so there was no need for a formal process to readmit them. Moderate and radical Republicans disagreed, arguing that the defeated states had forfeited their rights. Moderates and radicals parted company, however, on the conditions necessary for readmission to the Union. The radicals wanted to treat the former Confederate states as territories—or "conquered provinces"—subject to congressional legislation. Moderates wanted to grant the seceding states more autonomy and limit federal intervention in their affairs while they satisfied the conditions of readmission. No group held a majority in Congress, and legislators sometimes changed their positions (see the overview table, "Contrasting Views of Reconstruction").

Presidential Reconstruction, 1865–1867

When the Civil War ended in April 1865, Congress was not in session and would not reconvene until December. Thus the responsibility for developing a Reconstruction policy initially fell on Andrew Johnson, who succeeded to the presidency upon Lincoln's assassination. Johnson seemed well suited to the difficult task. The new president's personal and political background was promising to his Republican colleagues. Johnson was born in humble circumstances in North Carolina in 1808. He learned the tailoring trade and struck out for Tennessee as a teenager to open a tailor shop in the eastern Tennessee town of Greenville. Gaining his education informally, he prospered modestly, purchased a few slaves, and began to pursue politics. He was elected alderman, mayor, state legislator, congressmen, governor, and then, in 1856, U.S. senator.

Johnson was the only southern senator to remain in the U.S. Senate after secession. This defiant Unionism won him acclaim in the North and credibility among Republican leaders, who welcomed him into their party. During the war, as military governor of Tennessee, he solidified his Republican credentials by advocating the abolition of slavery in Tennessee and severe punishment of Confederate leaders. His views landed him on the Republican ticket as the candidate for vice president in 1864. Indiana Republican congressman George W. Julian, who advocated harsh terms for the South and broad rights for black people, viewed Johnson's accession to the presidency in 1865 as "a godsend."

Most Northerners and many Republicans approved Johnson's Reconstruction plan when he unveiled it in May 1865. Johnson extended pardons and restored property rights, except in slaves, to Southerners who swore an oath of allegiance to the Union and the Constitution. Southerners who had held prominent positions in the Confederacy, however, and those with more than $20,000 in taxable property had to petition the president directly for a pardon. The plan had nothing to say about the voting rights and civil rights of former slaves.

Northern Democrats applauded the plan's silence on these issues and its promise of a quick restoration of the southern states to the Union. They expected the southern states to favor their party and expand its political power. Republicans, although some of them would have preferred the plan to have provided for black suffrage, approved of the restoration of property rights to white Southerners. This position was consistent with their view of former slaves as laborers, not property owners. Republicans also hoped that Johnson's conciliatory terms might attract some white Southerners to the Republican party.

White Southerners, however, were not so favorably impressed with Johnson's plan, and their response turned northern public opinion against the president. On the two great issues of freedom and reunion, white Southerners quickly demonstrated their eagerness to reverse the results of the Civil War. Although most states accepted President Johnson's modest requirements, several objected to one or more of them. Mississippi and Texas refused to ratify the Thirteenth Amendment, which abolished slavery. Alabama accepted only parts of the amendment. South Carolina declined to nullify its secession ordinance. No southern state authorized black voting. When Johnson ordered special congressional elections in the South in the fall of 1865, the

OVERVIEW

CONTRASTING VIEWS OF RECONSTRUCTION: PRESIDENT AND CONGRESS

Politician or Group	Policy on Former Slaves	Policy on Readmission of Former Confederate States
President Johnson	Opposed to black suffrage Silent on protection of black civil rights Opposed to land redistribution	Maintained that rebellious states were already readmitted Granted pardons and restoration of property to all who swore allegiance to the United States
Radical Republicans	Favored black suffrage Favored protection of black civil rights Favored land redistribution	Favored treating rebellious states as territories and establishing military districts* Favored limiting franchise to black people and loyal white people
Moderate Republicans	Favored black suffrage Favored protection of civil rights Opposed land redistribution	Favored some restrictions on white suffrage* Favored requiring states to meet various requirements before being readmitted* Split on military rule

**True of most but not all members of the group.*

all-white electorate returned many prominent Confederate leaders to office.

In late 1865, the newly elected southern state legislatures revised their antebellum slave codes. The updated **black codes** allowed local officials to arrest black people who could not document employment and residence or who were "disorderly" and sentence them to forced labor on farms or road crews (see "American Views: Mississippi's 1865 Black Codes"). The codes also restricted black people to certain occupations, barred them from jury duty, and forbade them to possess firearms. Apprenticeship laws permitted judges to take black children from parents who could not, in the judges' view, adequately support them. Given the widespread poverty in the South in 1865, the law could apply to almost any freed black family. Northerners looking for contrition in the South found no sign of it. Worse, President Johnson did not seem perturbed about this turn of events.

The Republican-dominated Congress reconvened in December 1865 in a belligerent mood. A few radical Republicans pushed for swift retribution. George W. Julian thundered that he would "indict, convict and hang Jefferson Davis in the name of God; as for Robert E. Lee, unmolested in Virginia, hang him too." His colleague, Benjamin F. Wade, suggested that "if the negroes by insurrection would contrive to slay one-half of the White Southerners, the remaining half would then hold them in respect and treat them with justice." Few in Congress took these statements seriously. Nonetheless, a consensus formed among radical Republicans, who comprised nearly half of the party's strength in Congress, that to gain readmission, a state would have to extend suffrage to black citizens, protect freedmen's civil rights, and have its white citizens officially acknowledge these rights. Some radicals also supported the redistribution of land to former slaves, but few pressed for social equality. They envisioned a new South of modest farms, some owned by former slaves, and a Republican party built on an alliance between black people and white loyalists.

Thaddeus Stevens of Pennsylvania led the radical forces in the House of Representatives, while abolitionist veteran Charles Sumner of Massachusetts rallied radicals in the Senate. Stevens had established himself as a partisan for black political rights in the North as early as the 1840s. As a congressman during the Civil War, he pushed Lincoln to free and arm the slaves and later to extend them the right to vote. Stevens dreamed of a South populated by white and black yeoman farmers. With no large plantations and few landless farmers, the South would become an ideal republic, a boon to the rest of the nation instead of a burden. Few shared his vision, and when he died in 1868, a reporter noted that "no man was oftener outvoted." Yet he remained the conscience of the House, a standard of idealism in an age of growing cynicism. His epitaph read in part, "The principle which I advocated through a long life, Equality of Man before his Creator."

Sumner was among the foremost abolitionist politicians before the Civil War. His combative nature won him few friends, even within his own party. As fierce as Stevens in the promotion of black civil and political rights after the war, he also believed that the Reconstruction era offered a "golden moment" to remake the South into an egalitarian region. Sumner died in 1874 as his dream was fading. The last piece of Reconstruction legislation, the Civil Rights Act of 1875, became a posthumous tribute to his uncommon ability to overcome the racial prejudices of the day with a vision of a colorblind society.

But the radicals could not unite behind a program, and it fell to their moderate colleagues to take the first step toward a Congressional Reconstruction plan. The moderates shared the radicals' desire to protect the former slaves' civil and voting rights. But they would not support land redistribution schemes or punitive measures against prominent Confederates. The moderates' first measure, passed in early 1866, extended the life of the Freedmen's Bureau and provided it with authority to punish state officials who failed to extend to black citizens the civil rights enjoyed by white citizens. But President Johnson vetoed the legislation.

Undeterred, Congress passed the **Civil Rights Act of 1866** in direct response to the black codes. The act specified the civil rights to which all U.S. citizens were entitled. In creating a category of national citizenship with rights that superseded state laws restricting them, the act changed federal–state relations (and in the process overturned the Dred Scott decision). President Johnson vetoed the act, but it became law when Congress mustered a two-thirds majority to override his veto, the first time in American history that Congress passed major legislation over a president's veto.

Andrew Johnson's position reflected both his view of government and his racial attitudes. The Republican president remained a Democrat in spirit. Republicans had expanded federal power during the Civil War. Johnson, however, like most Democrats, favored more of a balance between federal and state power. He also shared with many of his white southern neighbors a belief in black inferiority and a view that white plantation owners had conspired to limit the economic and political power of white yeomen like himself. Johnson supported abolition assuming that, once free, black people would emigrate to Africa. Given the president's views and his inflexible temperament, a clash between him and Congress became inevitable.

"Selling a Freeman to Pay His Fine at Monticello, Florida." This 1867 engraving shows how the black codes of the early Reconstruction era in the South reduced former slaves to virtually their pre–Civil War status. Scenes such as this convinced Northerners that the white South was unrepentant and prompted Congressional Republicans to devise their own Reconstruction plan.

To keep freedmen's rights safe from presidential vetoes, state legislatures, and federal courts, the Republican-dominated Congress moved to incorporate some of the provisions of the 1866 Civil Rights Act into the Constitution. The **Fourteenth Amendment**, which Congress passed in June 1866, addressed the issues of civil and voting rights. It guaranteed every citizen equality before the law. The two key sections of the amendment prohibited states from violating the civil rights of their citizens, thus outlawing the black codes, and gave states the choice of enfranchising black people or losing representation in Congress. Some radical Republicans expressed disappointment that the amendment, in a reflection of northern ambivalence, failed to give the vote to black people outright.

The amendment also disappointed advocates of woman suffrage, for the first time using the word *male* in the Constitution to define who could vote. Wendell Phillips, a prominent abolitionist, counseled them, "One question at a time. This hour belongs to the Negro." Susan B. Anthony, who had campaigned for the abolition of slavery before the war and helped mount a petition drive that collected 400,000 signatures for the Thirteenth Amendment, formed the **American Equal Rights Association** in 1866 with her colleagues to push for woman suffrage at the state level.

The Fourteenth Amendment had little immediate impact on the South. Although enforcement of black codes diminished, white violence against black people increased. In the 1870s, several decisions by the U.S. Supreme Court would weaken the amendment's provisions. Eventually, however, it would play a major role in securing the civil rights of African Americans.

President Johnson seemed to encourage white intransigence by openly denouncing the Fourteenth Amendment. In August 1866, at the start of the congressional election campaign, he undertook an unprecedented tour of key northern states to sell his message of sectional reconciliation to the public. Although listeners appreciated Johnson's desire for peace, they questioned his claims of southern white loyalty to the Union. The president's diatribes against the Republican Congress won him followers in those northern states with a reservoir of opposition to black suffrage. But the tone and manner of his campaign offended many as undignified. In the November elections, the Democrats suffered embarrassing defeats in the North as Republicans managed better than two-thirds majorities in both the House and Senate, sufficient to override presidential vetoes. Radical Republicans, joined by moderate colleagues buoyed by the election results and revolted by the president's and the South's intransigence, seized the initiative when Congress reconvened.

Congressional Reconstruction, 1867–1870

The radicals' first salvo in their attempt to take control over Reconstruction occurred with the passage over President Johnson's veto of the **Military Reconstruction Acts**. The measures, passed in March 1867, inaugurated a period known as **Congressional Reconstruction** or Radical Reconstruction. Congress divided the ex-Confederate states (except for Tennessee, the only southern state that had ratified the Fourteenth Amendment and been readmitted to the Union) into five military districts, each headed by a general (see Map 18-1). The commanders' first order of business was to conduct voter registration campaigns to enroll black people and bar white people who had held office before the Civil War and who had supported the Confederacy. The eligible voters would then elect delegates to a state convention to write a new constitution that guaranteed **universal manhood suffrage**. Once a majority of eligible voters ratified the new constitution and the Fourteenth

Map 18-1 Congressional Reconstruction, 1865–1877
When Congress wrested control of Reconstruction policy from President Andrew Johnson, it divided the South into the five military districts depicted here. The commanding generals for each district held the authority both to hold elections and to decide who could vote.

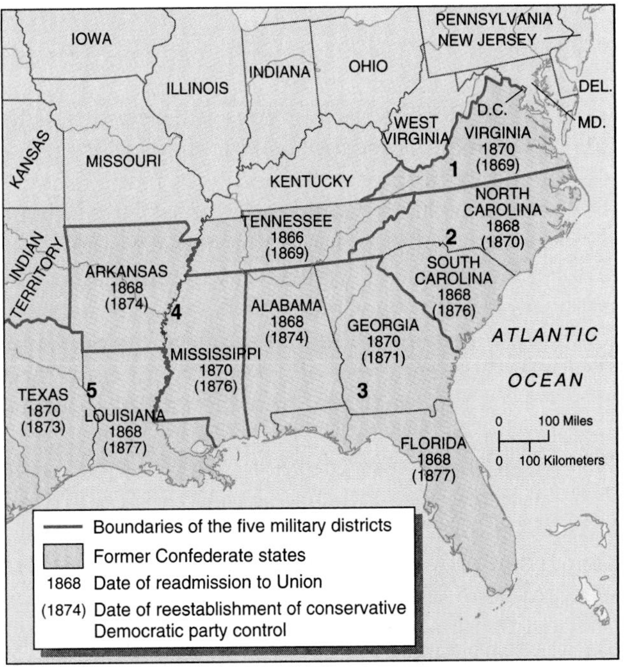

American Views

Mississippi's 1865 Black Codes

White Southerners, especially landowners and business owners, feared emancipation would produce a labor crisis; freedmen, they expected, would either refuse to work or strike hard bargains with their former masters. White Southerners also recoiled from the prospect of having to treat their former slaves as full social equals. Thus beginning in late 1865, several southern states, including Mississippi, enacted laws designed to control black labor, mobility, and social status. Northerners responded to the codes as a provocation, a bold move to deny the result of the war and its consequences.

- **How did the black codes fit into President Andrew Johnson's Reconstruction program?**
- **Some Northerners charged that the black codes were a backdoor attempt at reestablishing slavery. Do you agree?**
- **If southern states enacted black codes to stabilize labor relations, how did the provisions below effect that objective?**

From An Act to Confer Civil Rights on Freedmen, and for other Purposes

Section 1. All freedmen, free negroes and mulattoes may sue and be sued, implead and be impleaded, in all the courts of law and equity of this State, and may acquire personal property, and choose in action, by descent or purchase, and may dispose of the same in the same manner and to the same extent that white persons may: Provided, That the provisions of this section shall not be so construed as to allow any freedman, free negro or mulatto to rent or lease any lands or tenements except in incorporated cities or towns, in which places the corporate authorities shall control the same.

Amendment, their state would be eligible for readmission to the Union.

The Reconstruction Acts fulfilled the radicals' three major objectives. First, they secured the freedmen's right to vote. Second, they made it likely that southern states would be run by Republican regimes that would enforce the new constitutions, protect former slaves' rights, and maintain the Republican majority in Congress. Finally, the acts set standards for readmission that required the South to accept the consequences of defeat: the preeminence of the federal government and the end of involuntary servitude.

To limit presidential interference with their policies, Republicans passed the **Tenure of Office Act**, prohibiting the president from removing certain officeholders without the Senate's consent. Johnson, angered at what he believed was an unconstitutional attack on presidential authority, deliberately violated the act by firing Secretary of War Edwin M. Stanton, a leading radical, in February 1868. The House responded to this defiance by approving articles of impeachment against a president for the first time in American history. After a trial, the Senate voted 35 to 19 to convict the president, one vote short of the two-thirds necessary to remove him from office. The seven Republicans who voted against their party did so not out of respect for the president but because they feared a conviction would damage the office of the presidency and violate the constitutional separation of powers. The outcome weakened the radicals and eased the way for moderate Republican Ulysses S. Grant to gain the party's nomination for president in 1868.

The Republicans viewed the 1868 presidential election as a referendum on Congressional Reconstruction. They supported black suffrage in the South but equivocated on allowing African Americans to vote in the North. Black Northerners could

Section 7. Every civil officer shall, and every person may, arrest and carry back to his or her legal employer any freedman, free negro, or mulatto who shall have quit the service of his or her employer before the expiration of his or her term of service without good cause; and said officer and person shall be entitled to receive for arresting and carrying back every deserting employee aforesaid the sum of five dollars, and ten cents per mile from the place of arrest to the place of delivery; and the same shall be paid by the employer, and held as a set off for so much against the wages of said deserting employee: Provided, that said arrested party, after being so returned, may appeal to the justice of the peace or member of the board of police of the county, who, on notice to the alleged employer, shall try summarily whether said appellant is legally employed by the alleged employer, and has good cause to quit said employer. Either party shall have the right of appeal to the county court, pending which the alleged deserter shall be remanded to the alleged employer or otherwise disposed of, as shall be right and just; and the decision of the county court shall be final.

From An Act to Amend the Vagrant Laws of the State

Section 2. All freedmen, free negroes and mulattoes in this State, over the age of eighteen years, found on the second Monday in January, 1866, or thereafter, with no lawful employment or business, or found unlawful assembling themselves together, either in the day or night time, and all white persons assembling themselves with freedmen, Free negroes or mulattoes, or usually associating with freedmen, free negroes or mulattoes, on terms of equality, or living in adultery or fornication with a freed woman, freed negro or mulatto, shall be deemed vagrants, and on conviction thereof shall be fined in a sum not exceeding, in the case of a freedman, free negro or mulatto, fifty dollars, and a white man two hundred dollars, and imprisonment at the discretion of the court, the free negro not exceeding ten days, and the white man not exceeding six months.

Source: "Laws in Relation to Freedmen," 39 Congress, 2 Session, Senate Executive Document 6, Freedmen's Affairs, 182–86.

vote in only eight of the twenty-two northern states, and white Northerners had rejected equal suffrage referendums in eight of eleven states between 1865 and 1869. Republicans "waved the bloody shirt," reminding voters of Democratic disloyalty, the sacrifices of war, and the peace only Republicans could redeem. Democrats denounced Congressional Reconstruction as federal tyranny and, in openly racist appeals, warned white voters that a Republican victory would mean black rule. Grant won the election, but his margin of victory was uncomfortably narrow. Reflecting growing ambivalence in the North over issues of race and federal authority, New York's Horatio Seymour, the Democratic presidential nominee, probably carried a majority of the nation's white vote. Black voters' overwhelming support for Grant probably provided him his margin of victory.

The Republicans retained a strong majority in both houses of Congress and managed to pass another major piece of Reconstruction legislation, the **Fifteenth Amendment**, in February 1869. In response to growing concerns about voter fraud and violence against freedmen, the amendment guaranteed the right of American men to vote, regardless of race. Although the amendment provided a loophole allowing states to impose restrictions on the right to vote based on literacy or property qualifications, it was nonetheless a milestone. It made the right to vote perhaps the most distinguishing characteristic of American citizenship.

The Fifteenth Amendment allowed states to keep the franchise a male prerogative, angering many in the woman suffrage movement more than had the Fourteenth Amendment. The resulting controversy severed the ties between the movement and Republican politics. Susan B. Anthony broke with her abolitionist colleagues and opposed the amendment. Fellow abolitionist and woman suffragist Elizabeth Cady Stanton charged that the amendment created an "aristocracy of sex." In an appeal brimming with ethnic

OVERVIEW

Constitutional Amendments and Federal Legislation of the Reconstruction Era

Amendment or Legislation	Purpose	Significance
Thirteenth Amendment (passed and ratified in 1865)	Prevented southern states from reestablishing slavery after the war	Final step toward full emancipation of slaves
Freedmen's Bureau Act (1865)	Oversight of resettlement, reflief, education, and labor for former slaves	Involved the federal government directly in assisting the transition from slavery to freedom; worked fitfully to achieve this objective during its seven-year career
Southern Homestead Act (1866)	Provided black people preferential access to public lands in five southern states	Lack of capital and poor quality of federal land thwarted the purpose of the act
Civil Rights Act of 1866	Defined rights of national citizenship	Marked an important change in federal–state relations, tilting balance of power to national government
Fourteenth Amendment (passed 1866; ratified 1868)	Prohibited states from violating the rights of their citizens	Strengthened the Civil Rights Act of 1866 and guaranteed all citizens equality before the law
Military Reconstruction Acts (1867)	Set new rules for the readmission of ex-Confederate states into the Union and secured black voting rights	Initiated Congressional Reconstruction
Tenure of Office Act (1867)	Required congressional approval for the removal of any official whose appointment had required Senate confirmation confirmation	A congressional challenge to the president's right to dismiss Cabinet members that led to President Andrew Johnson's impeachment trial
Fifteenth Amendment (passed 1869; ratified 1870)	Guaranteed the right of all American male citizens to vote regardless of race	The basis for black voting rights
Civil Rights Act of 1875	Prohibited racial discrimination in jury selection, public transportation, and public accommodations	Rarely enforced; Supreme Court declared it unconstitutional in 1883

and racial animosity, Stanton warned that "if you do not wish the lower orders of Chinese, African, Germans and Irish, with their low ideas of womanhood to make laws for you and your daughters . . . awake to the danger . . . and demand that woman, too, shall be represented in the government!" Such language created a major rift in the nascent women's movement. Women who supported the amendment formed the New England Woman Suffrage Association, challenging Anthony's American Equal Rights Association.

Southern Republican Governments, 1867–1870

Away from Washington, the first order of business for the former Confederacy was to draft state constitutions. The documents embodied progressive principles new to the South. They mandated the election of numerous local and state offices. Self-perpetuating local elites could no longer appoint themselves or cronies to powerful positions. The constitutions committed southern states, many for the first time, to public education. Lawmakers enacted a variety of reforms, including social welfare, penal reform, legislative reapportionment, and universal manhood suffrage.

The Republican regimes that gained control in southern states promoted vigorous state government and the protection of civil and voting rights. Three diverse Republican constituencies supported these governments. One consisted of white natives, most of them yeomen farmers. Residing mainly in the upland regions of the South and long ignored by lowland planters and merchants in state government, some had supported the Union during the war. The conflict had left many of them devastated. They struggled to keep their land and hoped for an easing of credit and for debt-stay laws to help them escape foreclosure. They wanted public schools for their children and good roads to get their crops to market. Some urban merchants and large planters also called themselves Republicans. Many were Whigs before the war, and a few had been Unionists. They were attracted to the party's emphasis on economic development, especially railroad construction, and would become prominent in Republican leadership after 1867.

Collectively, these native white Southerners were called **scalawags**, a derogatory term for an idle or mischievous person derived from Scalloway, the name of a district on Scotland's Shetland Islands known for its scraggly livestock. The term was first applied in western New York before the Civil War to an idle person and then to a mischievous one. Although their opponents may have perceived them as a unified group, scalawags held a variety of views. Planters and merchants opposed easy debt and credit arrangements and the use of their taxes to support programs other than railroads or port improvements. Yeomen farmers desperately needed the debt and credit legislation to retain their land. And even though they supported public schools and road building—which would require increased state revenues—they opposed higher taxes.

Northern transplants, or **carpetbaggers**, as their opponents called them, constituted a second group of southern Republicans. The term also had antebellum origins, referring to a suspicious stranger. Cartoonists depicted carpetbaggers as shoddily dressed and poorly groomed, their worldly possessions in a ratty cloth satchel, slinking into a town and swindling the locals before departing with their ill-gotten gains. The reality was far different from the caricature. Thousands of Northerners came south during and after the war. Many were Union soldiers who simply enjoyed the climate and perhaps married a local woman. Most were drawn by economic opportunity. Land was cheap and the price of cotton high. Although most carpetbaggers had supported the Republican party before they moved south, few became politically active until the cotton economy nosedived in 1866. Financial concerns were not all that motivated carpetbaggers to enter politics; some hoped to aid the freedmen.

Carpetbaggers never comprised more than 2 percent of any state's population. Most white Southerners viewed them as an alien presence, instruments of a hated occupying force. They provoked resentment because they seemed to prosper while most Southerners struggled in poverty. And they further estranged themselves from their neighbors by supporting and participating in the Republican state governments that most white people despised. In Alabama, local editors organized a boycott of northern-owned shops. "STARVE THEM OUT!" they wrote. "Don't put your foot in the doors of their shops, offices, and stores. Purchase from true men and patronize those of known Southern sympathies." Because many of them tended to support extending political and civil rights to black Southerners, carpetbaggers were also often at odds with their fellow white Republicans, the scalawags.

African Americans constituted the Republican party's largest southern constituency. In three states—South Carolina, Mississippi, and Louisiana—they also constituted the majority of eligible voters. They viewed the franchise as the key to civic equality and economic opportunity and demanded an active role in party and government affairs.

Black people began to take part in southern politics even before the end of the Civil War, especially in cities occupied by Union forces. In February 1865, black people in Norfolk, Virginia, gathered to demand a say in the new government that Union supporters were forming in that portion of the state. In April, they created the Colored Monitor Union club, modeled after Republican party organizations in northern cities, called **Union Leagues**. They demanded "the right of universal suffrage" for "all loyal men, without distinction of color." Black people in other southern cities held similar meetings, seeking inclusion in the democratic process in order to protect their freedom. As a member of the Alexandria, Virginia, black Union League argued in August 1865, "The only salvation for us . . . is in the *possession of the ballot.* Give us this, and we will protect ourselves."

White Southerners viewed these developments with alarm but could not at first counter them. Despite white threats, black Southerners thronged to Union League meetings in 1867, even forging interracial alliances in states such as North Carolina and Alabama. Focusing on political education and recruitment, the leagues successfully mobilized black voters. In 1867, more than 90 percent of eligible black voters across the South turned out for elections. Black women, even though they could not vote, also played a role. During the 1868 presidential campaign, for example, black maids and cooks in the South wore buttons touting the candidacy of Republican presidential nominee Ulysses S. Grant.

Black Southerners were not content just to vote; they also demanded political office. White Republican leaders in the South often took the black vote for granted. But on several occasions after 1867, black people threatened to run independent candidates, support rival Democrats, or simply stay home unless they were represented among Republican nominees. These demands brought them some success. The number of southern black congressmen in the U.S. House of Representatives increased from two in 1869 to seven in 1873, and more than six hundred African Americans, most of them former slaves from plantation counties, were elected to southern state legislatures between 1867 and 1877.

White fears that black officeholders would enact vengeful legislation proved unfounded. African Americans generally did not promote race-specific legislation. Rather, they supported measures such as debt relief and state funding for education that benefited all poor and working-class people. Like all politicians, however, black officials in southern cities sought to enact measures beneficial to their constituents. In Atlanta, for example, black officeholders had a sidewalk laid in front of a prominent black church and diverted a road scheduled to cut through a black neighborhood. In Richmond, black people secured an ordinance forbidding the robbing of black graves to supply medical schools with corpses. And they succeeded in having a black police commissioner appointed in Jacksonville, Florida. Gains like these underscored the advantages of suffrage for the African-American community.

During the first few years of Congressional Reconstruction, Republican governments walked a tightrope, attempting to lure moderate Democrats and unaffiliated white voters into the party without slighting the black vote. They used the lure of patronage power and the attractive salaries that accompanied public office. In 1868, for example, Louisiana's Republican governor, Henry C. Warmoth, appointed white conservatives to state and local offices, which he divided equally between ex-Confederate veterans and black people, and repealed a constitutional provision disfranchising former Confederate officials.

Republicans also gained support by expanding the role of state government to a degree unprecedented in the South. Southern Republican administrations appealed to hard-pressed upland white constituents by prohibiting foreclosure and passing stay laws that allowed farm owners extra time to repay debts. They undertook building programs that benefited both black and white citizens, erecting hospitals, schools, and orphanages. Stepping further into social policy than most northern states at the time, Republican governments in the South expanded women's property rights, enacted legislation against child abuse, and required child support from fathers of mulatto children. In South Carolina, the Republican government provided medical care for the poor; in Alabama, it provided free legal aid for needy defendants.

Despite these impressive policies, southern Republicans were unable to hold their diverse constituency together. Although the party had some success among white yeoman farmers, the liberal use of patronage to attract white conservatives failed to gain it many new adherents. At the same time, it alienated the party's core supporters, who resented seeing their former enemies rewarded with lucrative offices.

The high costs of their activist policies further undermined the Republicans by forcing them to raise state taxes. Small property holders, already reeling from declining staple prices, found the taxes especially burdensome, despite liberal stay laws. Revenues nonetheless could not keep pace with expenditures. In Mississippi—where the Republican governor built a public school system for both black and white students, founded a black university, reorganized the state judiciary, built new courthouses and two state hospitals, and pushed through legislation giving black people equal access to public facilities—the state debt soared to $1.5 million between 1869 and 1873. This was in an era when state budgets rarely exceeded $1 million.

Unprecedented expenditures and the liberal use of patronage sometimes resulted in waste and corruption. Officials charged with selecting railroad routes, appointing lesser officials, and erecting public buildings were well positioned to benefit from their power. Their high salaries offended many in an otherwise impoverished region. Problems like these were not limited to the South. They were pervasive throughout the country in the 1860s and 1870s. The perception of dishonesty was nonetheless damaging to governments struggling to build legitimacy among a skeptical white electorate.

The excesses of some state governments, high taxes, contests over patronage, and conflicts over the relative roles of white and black party members opened rifts in Republican ranks. Patronage triggered intraparty warfare. Every office secured by a Democrat created a disappointed Republican. Class tensions erupted in the party as economic development policies, favored by former Whigs, sometimes superseded relief and social service legislation supported by small farmers. The failure of Alabama Republicans to deliver on promises of debt relief and land redistribution eroded the significant support the party had enjoyed among upcountry white voters. There were differences among black voters too. In the Lower South, divisions that had developed in the prewar era between urban, lighter-skinned free black people and darker, rural slaves persisted into the Reconstruction era. In many southern states, black clergy, because of their independence from white support and their important spiritual and educational role, became leaders. But most preached salvation in the next world rather than equality in this one, conceding more to white people than their rank-and-file constituents.

"The Shackle Broken by the Genius of Freedom" is the title of this 1874 lithograph of South Carolina legislator Robert B. Elliott addressing his fellow lawmakers. Born in Boston, educated in England, Elliott served with distinction in Congress and at the state level during Reconstruction.

Counter-Reconstruction, 1870–1874

Republicans might have survived battles over patronage, differences over policy, and the resentment provoked by extravagant expenditures and high taxes. But they could not overcome racism. Racism killed Republican rule in the South because it deepened divisions within the party, encouraged white violence, and eroded support in the North. Southern Democrats discovered that they could use race baiting and racial violence to create solidarity among white people that overrode their economic and class differences. Unity translated into election victories.

Northerners responded to the persistent violence in the South not with outrage but with a growing sense of tedium. They came to accept the arguments of white Southerners that it was folly to allow black people to vote and hold office. Racism became respectable. Noted intellectuals and journalists espoused "scientific" theories that claimed to demonstrate the natural superiority of white people over black people. These theories influenced the **Liberal Republicans**, followers of a new political movement that splintered the Republican party, further weakening its will to pursue Reconstruction policy.

By 1874, Americans were concerned with an array of domestic problems that overshadowed Reconstruction. A serious economic depression left them more preoccupied with survival than racial justice. Corruption convinced many that politics was part of the nation's problems, not a solution to them. With the rest of the nation thus distracted and weary, white Southerners reclaimed control of the South.

The Uses of Violence

Racial violence preceded Republican rule. As African Americans moved about, attempted to vote, haggled over labor contracts, and carried arms as part of occupying Union forces, they tested the patience of white Southerners. In a racial world turned upside down from the white perspective, any black assertion of equality seemed threatening.

Cities, where black and white people competed for jobs and where black political influence was most visible, became flashpoints for interracial violence. In May 1866, the collision of two wagons in Memphis, one driven by a white carter, the other by a black carter, touched off three days of white attacks on black people and black neighborhoods. Forty-six black people and two white people died in the fray, and five black women were raped. The white mob destroyed black churches, schools, and homes.

White paramilitary groups flourished in the South during the Reconstruction era and were responsible for much of the violence directed against African Americans. Probably the best known of these groups was the **Ku Klux Klan**. Founded in Tennessee by six Confederate veterans in 1866, the Klan was initially a social club. Prominent ex-Confederates such as General John B. Gordon and General Nathan Bedford Forrest, allegedly the first Grand Wizard of the Klan, saw the political potential of the new organization. Within a year, the Klan had spread throughout the South. In 1867, when black people entered politics in large numbers, the Klan unleashed a wave of terror against them. Klan night riders in ghostlike disguises intimidated black communities. The Klan directed much of its violence toward subverting the electoral process. One historian has estimated that roughly 10 percent of all black delegates to the 1867 state constitutional conventions in the South became victims of political violence during the next decade.

Not all Klan attacks had political objectives. Klansmen struck against anyone, black or white, whom they believed had violated racial boundaries. A Georgia Klansman murdered a freedman because he could read and write. Klansmen in Florence, South Carolina, killed a black man who rented a plantation "because such a thing ought not to be." And in 1868, Klansmen murdered three southern white Republican Georgia state legislators. Membership in the Klan crossed class lines. Race became an issue on which white people, regardless of differing economic interests, could agree.

By 1868, white paramilitary organizations permeated the South. Violence was particularly severe in election years in Louisiana, which had a large and active black electorate. Before the presidential election of 1868, for example, white Louisianans killed at least seven hundred Republicans, including black leader William R. Meadows, who was dragged from his home and shot and beheaded in front of his family. As the election neared, white mobs roamed New Orleans, attacking black people and breaking up Republican rallies. The violence cut the Republican vote in the state by 50 percent from the previous spring.

The most serious example of political violence in Louisiana, if not in the entire South, occurred in Colfax in 1873 when a white Democratic mob attempted to wrest control of local government from Republicans. For three weeks, black defenders held the town against the white onslaught. When the white mob finally broke through, they massacred the remaining black defenders, including those who had surrendered and laid down their weapons.

Racial violence and the combative reaction it provoked both among black people and Republican administrations energized white voters. Democrats regained power in North Carolina, for example, after the state's Republican governor enraged white voters by calling out the militia to counter white violence during the election of 1870. That same year, the Republican regime in Georgia fell as well.

Some Republican governments countered the violence successfully for a time. Republican governor Edmund J. Davis of Texas, for example, organized a special force of two hundred state policemen to round up Klan night riders. Between 1870 and 1872, Davis's force arrested six thousand and broke the Klan in Texas. Arkansas governor Powell Clayton launched an equally successful campaign against the Klan in 1869. But other governors hesitated to enforce laws directed at the Klan, fearing that to do so would further alienate white people.

The federal government responded with a variety of legislation. One example was the Fifteenth Amendment, ratified in 1869, which guaranteed the right to vote. Another was the Enforcement Act of 1870, which authorized the federal government to appoint supervisors in states that failed to protect voting rights. When violence and intimidation persisted, Congress followed with a second, more sweeping measure, the Ku Klux Klan Act of 1871. This law permitted federal authorities, with military assistance, if necessary, to arrest and prosecute members of groups that denied a citizen's civil rights if state authorities failed to do so. The Klan Act was not successful in curbing racial violence, as the Colfax Massacre in 1873 made vividly clear. But with it, Congress, by claiming the right to override state authority to bring individuals to justice, established a new precedent in federal–state relations.

The Failure of Northern Will

The success of political violence after 1871 reflected less the inadequacy of congressional legislation than the failure of will on the part of northern Republicans to follow through on commitments to southern

Republican administrations. The erosion of northern support for Congressional Reconstruction began as early as the presidential election of 1868. Republican candidate Ulysses S. Grant's campaign theme that year was "Let Us Have Peace," a reference to the political turmoil in the South.

The commitment to voting rights for black Southerners, widespread among Republicans in 1865 and affirmed in the Fifteenth Amendment, faded as well. American politics in the 1870s seemed increasingly corrupt and irresponsible. Scandal abounded. Democratic boss William M. Tweed and his associates transformed **Tammany Hall**, a Democratic Club, into a full-fledged political machine that robbed New York City of an astounding $100 million. Federal officials allowed private individuals to manipulate the stock market for spectacular gains. Several members of Congress and President Grant's vice president exchanged government favors for railroad stock. And the president's secretary of war was caught selling contracts to firms supplying goods to Indians.

A growing number of Americans attributed the debacle to the expansion of the right to vote. Voting was a privilege to be earned, they maintained, not a basic right of citizenship. And black people, according to some Republicans, had not earned that right.

The racist assumption behind this view found growing support among intellectuals. Racism gained an aura of scientific respectability in the late nineteenth century. Science was held in high esteem at the time, helping assure public acceptance of the putatively scientific views of the racial theorists. According to those views, some peoples are inherently inferior to others, a natural state of affairs that no government interference can change.

According to white racial theorists, it was folly to grant suffrage to African Americans because an inferior race (black) could not hold power over a superior race (white). Black people, because of their race, could not understand the basic principles of democracy. Thus Missouri's Republican senator Carl Schurz looked on with equanimity as white terror toppled Republican regimes in the South in 1872. He urged his colleagues to let affairs run their course and admit that southern black voters and officeholders "were ignorant and inexperienced; that the public business was an unknown world to them, and that in spite of the best intentions they were easily misled." Allowing an unfit people to vote resulted in a "more disastrous process than rebellion," intoned *The Nation*, a leading Republican journal, in 1872. The perpetual turmoil in the South, the extravagances of some Republican southern administrations, and their persistent inability to attract sufficient numbers of white voters all reinforced the view that these governments were unnatural.

Black people were not the only targets of racial theory. Immigrants were also said to derive from inferior races. Their growing numbers coincided with the flourishing of corrupt political machines in northern cities, fueling Republican reservations about an unrestricted franchise. Like black people, immigrants were held to be incapable of understanding the American electoral process. As one Republican leader observed, "What is bad

Two Alabama Klansmen are shown here in 1868 at the height of the Ku Klux Klan's campaign of political terror. Although Congress outlawed the Klan, political terrorist groups associated with the Democratic party continued the Klan's violent legacy in the 1870s and succeeded in reestablishing white Democratic party rule in the South.

among ignorant foreigners in New York will not be good among ignorant natives in South Carolina."

Concerns about the quality of the electorate reflected the rising stakes of public office in post–Civil War America. The urban industrial economy boomed in the five years after the war. Engineers flung railroads across the continent. Steam propelled factories to unprecedented levels of productivity and ships to new speed records. Discoveries of rich natural resources such as oil and iron presaged a new age of industrial might. Republicans promoted and benefited from the boom, and it influenced their priorities. Railroad, mining, and lumber lobbyists crowded Washington and state capitals begging for financial and land subsidies and favorable legislation. In an era before conflict-of-interest laws, leading Republicans sat on the boards of railroads, land development companies, and industrial corporations. While the federal government denied land to the freedman, it doled out millions of acres to corporations. Issues of fiscal responsibility, tariffs, and hard money replaced freedom and reunion, moving the Republican party, as *The Nation* explained in 1874, "out of the region of the Civil War."

Not all Republicans approved the party's promotion of economic development. Some questioned the prudence of government intervention in the "natural" operation of the economy. The emerging scandals of the Grant administration led to calls for reform. Republican governments, North and South, were condemned for their lavish spending and high taxes.

The reform movement attracted an assortment of groups concerned about the size, activism, and expense of government. Business leaders decried the ability of wealthy lobbyists to influence economic decisions. An influential group of intellectuals and opinion makers lamented the inability of politicians to understand "natural" laws. Some reformers expressed alarm at the federal government's increasing intervention in the affairs of the states since the Civil War. And some Republicans joined the reform movement out of fear that Democrats would capitalize on the turmoil in the South and the political scandals in the North to reap huge electoral victories in 1872.

Liberal Republicans and the Election of 1872

Liberal Republicans put forward an array of suggestions to improve government and save the Republican party. They advocated civil service reform to reduce reliance on patronage and the abuses that accompanied office seeking. To limit government and reduce artificial economic stimuli, the reformers called for tariff reduction and an end to federal land grants to railroads. For the South, they recommended a general amnesty for white people and a return to "local self-government" by men of "property and enterprise."

When the Liberals failed to convince other Republicans to adopt their program, they broke with the party. Taking advantage of this split, the Democrats forged an alliance with the Liberals. Together, they nominated journalist Horace Greeley to challenge Ulysses S. Grant for the presidency in the election of 1872. Grant won resoundingly, helped by high turnout among black voters in the South. He carried all southern states except Georgia, Tennessee, and Texas. Elsewhere, Republicans again used the tactic of waving the bloody shirt to good effect. It was the Republicans, they declared, who had saved the Union, the Democrats who had almost destroyed it. Greeley had been a staunch Republican during the Civil War and had spent most of his career attacking Democrats. Republicans used his own words against him. Many Democratic voters stayed home.

The election suggested that the excesses of the Grant administration had not yet exceeded public tolerance and that the Republican experiment in the South retained some public support. But Greeley had helped the Republicans by running an inept campaign. Within a year, an economic depression, continued violence in the South, and the persistent corruption of the Grant administration would turn public opinion against the Republicans. With this shift, support for Reconstruction and black rights would also fade.

Redemption, 1874–1877

For southern Democrats, the Republican victory in 1872 underscored the importance of turning out larger numbers of white voters and restricting the black vote. They accomplished these goals over the next four years with a surge in political violence. Southern Democrats operated in the secure knowledge that federal authorities would not intervene against them. Preoccupied with corruption and economic crisis and increasingly indifferent, if not hostile, to African-American aspirations, most Americans looked the other way. The elections of 1876—on the local, state, and national levels—affirmed the triumph of white Southerners. Reconstruction did not end; it was overthrown.

In a religious metaphor that matched their view of the Civil War as a lost crusade, southern Democrats called their victory "Redemption" and depicted themselves as **Redeemers**, holy warriors who had saved the South from the hell of black Republican rule. Generations of American boys and girls would learn this interpretation of the Reconstruction era, and it would affect race relations for nearly a century.

The Democrats' Violent Resurgence

The violence between 1874 and 1876 differed in several respects from earlier attempts to restore white government by force. Attackers operated more openly and more closely identified themselves with the Democratic party. Mounted, gray-clad ex-Confederate soldiers flanked Democratic candidates at campaign rallies and "visited" black neighborhoods afterward to discourage black people from voting. With black people intimidated and white people already prepared to vote, election days were typically quiet.

Democrats swept to victory across the South in the 1874 elections. "A perfect reign of terror" redeemed Alabama for the Democrats. The successful appeal to white supremacy inspired a massive white turnout to unseat Republicans in Virginia, Florida (legislature only), and Arkansas. Texas had fallen to the Democrats in 1873. Only South Carolina, Mississippi, and Louisiana—states with large black populations—survived the debacle. But the relentless tide of terror would soon overwhelm them as well.

In Louisiana, a group of elite Democrats in New Orleans organized a military organization known as the White League in 1874 to challenge the state's Republican government. In September 1874, more than eight thousand White Leaguers staged a coup to overthrow the Republican government of New Orleans. The city's police, commanded by former Confederate general James Longstreet, and the intervention of nearby federal troops saved the government and prevented a wholesale slaughter. But the incident only inspired White Leaguers to redouble their efforts.

Few Reconstruction politicians endured greater trials than Louisiana Republican Marshall Harvey Twitchell. Born in Vermont, he led black troops during the Civil War and settled in Louisiana after the war. He married the daughter of a prominent plantation owner and launched a successful business career. But with the advent of Congressional Reconstruction, Twitchell entered politics and built a powerful Republican organization in Red River Parish. The hospitable reception he had until then enjoyed in his adopted state quickly evaporated. During the 1874 election campaign, White Leaguers murdered his brother and two brothers-in-law. Two years later, White Leaguers shot him six times in an assassination attempt. Although he lost both arms, he survived. He left Louisiana in 1877, never to return.

The Weak Federal Response

Unrest like that in Louisiana also plagued Mississippi and South Carolina. When South Carolina governor Daniel H. Chamberlain could no longer contain the violence in his state in 1876, he asked the president for help. Grant acknowledged the gravity of Chamberlain's situation but would offer him only the lame hope that South Carolinians would exercise "better judgment and cooperation" and assist the governor in bringing offenders to justice "without aid from the federal Government."

Congress responded to the violence with the **Civil Rights Act of 1875**. Introduced by Charles Sumner, the bill went through several variations. Congress finally passed a watered-down version after Sumner's death. The act prohibited discrimination against black people in public accommodations such as theaters, parks, and trains and guaranteed freedmen's rights to serve on juries. It had no provision for voting rights, which Congress presumed the Fifteenth Amendment protected. The only way to enforce the law was for individuals to bring grievances related to it before federal courts in the South.

When black people tested the law by trying to make free use of public accommodations, they were almost always turned away. Some filed suit, with disappointing results. A Texas judge fined a Galveston theater $500 for refusing to allow black people to sit wherever they wanted, but most judges either interpreted the law narrowly or declared it unconstitutional. In 1883, the U.S. Supreme Court concurred and overturned the act, declaring that only the states, not Congress, could redress "a private wrong, or a crime of the individual."

As this Thomas Nast cartoon makes clear, the paramilitary violence against black Southerners in the early 1870s threatened not only the voting rights of freedmen, but their dreams of education, prosperity, and family life as well. In this context, the slogan, "The Union As It Was" is highly ironic.

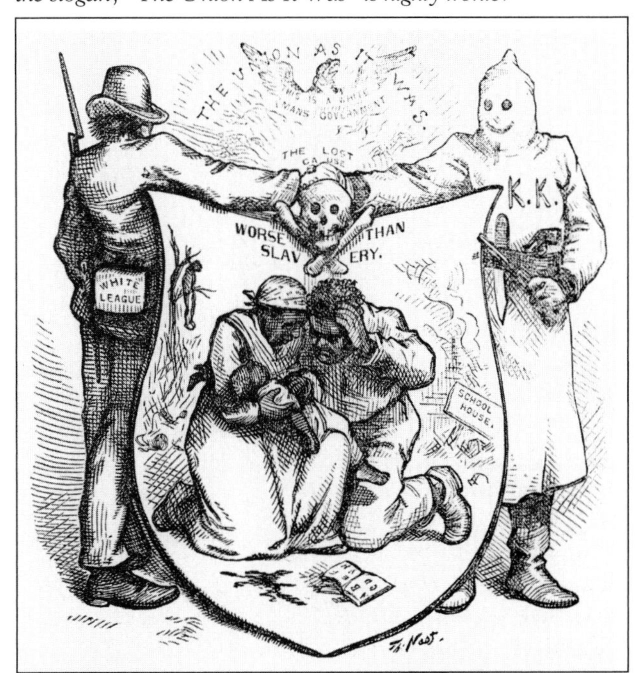

The Election of 1876 and the Compromise of 1877

Reconstruction officially ended with the presidential election of 1876 in which Democrat Samuel J. Tilden ran against Republican Rutherford B. Hayes. Republicans again waved the bloody shirt, touting their role in preserving the Union during the Civil War, but they ignored Reconstruction. The Democrats hoped that their resurgent strength in the South and a respectable showing in the North would bring them the White House. The scandals of the Grant administration, northern weariness with southern Republican governments, and the persisting economic depression worked in the Democrats' favor.

When the ballots were counted, it appeared that Tilden, a conservative New Yorker respectable enough for northern voters and Democratic enough for white southerners, had won. But despite a majority in the popular vote, disputed returns in three southern states left him with only 184 of the 185 electoral votes needed to win (see Map 18-2). The three states—Florida, South Carolina, and Louisiana—were the last in the South still to have Republican adminstrations.

Map 18-2 The Election of 1876
The Democrat Samuel J. Tilden won a majority of the popular vote but eventually fell short of an electoral vote majority when the contested electoral votes of Florida, Louisiana, and South Carolina went to his Republican opponent, Rutherford B. Hayes. The map also indicates the Republicans' failure to build a base in the South after more than a decade of Reconstruction.

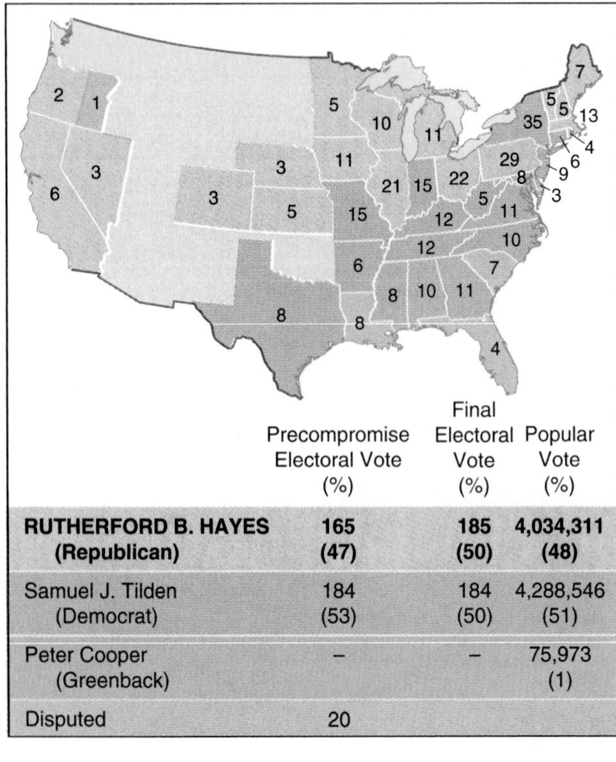

	Precompromise Electoral Vote (%)	Final Electoral Vote (%)	Popular Vote (%)
RUTHERFORD B. HAYES (Republican)	**165 (47)**	**185 (50)**	**4,034,311 (48)**
Samuel J. Tilden (Democrat)	184 (53)	184 (50)	4,288,546 (51)
Peter Cooper (Greenback)	–	–	75,973 (1)
Disputed	20		

Both camps maneuvered intensively in the months following the election to claim the disputed votes. Congress appointed a fifteen-member commission to settle the issue. Because the Republicans controlled Congress, they held a one-vote majority on the commission.

Southern Democrats wanted Tilden to win, but they wanted control of their states more. They were willing to deal. As one South Carolina newspaper editorialized in February 1877, "It matters little to us who rules in Washington, if South Carolina is allowed to have [Democratic governor Wade] Hampton and Home Rule." Hayes intended to remove federal support from the remaining southern Republican governments anyway. It thus cost him nothing to promise to do so in exchange for the contested electoral votes. Republicans also made vague promises to invest in the southern economy and support a southern transcontinental railroad, but these were secondary. What the South wanted most was to be left alone, and that is what it got. The so-called **Compromise of 1877** installed Hayes in the White House and gave Democrats control of all state governments in the South. Congress never carried through on the economic promises, and southern Democrats never pressed them to.

Southern Democrats emerged the major winners from the Compromise of 1877. President Hayes and his successors into the next century left the South alone. In practical terms, the Compromise signaled the revocation of civil rights and voting rights for black Southerners. The Fourteenth and Fifteenth Amendments would be dead letters in the South until well into the twentieth century. On the two great issues confronting the nation at the end of the Civil War, reunion and freedom, the white South had won. It reentered the Union largely on its own terms with the freedom to pursue a racial agenda consistent with its political, economic, and social interests.

The Memory of Reconstruction

Southern Democrats used the memory of Reconstruction to help maintain themselves in power. The Civil War became the glorious Lost Cause, Reconstruction the story of the Redemption against insurmountable odds from a purgatory of black rule and federal oppression. Whenever southern Democrats felt threatened over the next century, they reminded their white constituents of the sacrifices and heroism of war, the "horrors of Reconstruction," the menace of black rule, and the cruelty of Yankee occupiers. The southern view of

Reconstruction permeated textbooks, films, and standard accounts of the period. By the 1920s, if not earlier, most Americans believed that the policies of Reconstruction had been misguided and had brought great suffering to the white South. The widespread acceptance of this view allowed the South to maintain its system of racial segregation and exclusion without interference from the federal government.

Not all memories of Reconstruction conformed to this thesis. In 1913, John R. Lynch, a former black Republican congressman from Mississippi, published *The Facts of Reconstruction* to "present the other side." He hoped his book would "bring to public notice those things that were commendable and meritorious, to prevent the publication of which seems to have been the primary purpose of nearly all who have thus far written upon that important subject." But most Americans ignored his book. Two decades later, a more forceful defense, W. E. B. Du Bois's *Black Reconstruction* (1935), met a similar fate. An angry Du Bois attacked the prevailing view of Reconstruction as "one of the most stupendous efforts the world ever saw to discredit human beings, an effort involving universities, history, science, social life and religion."

The Failure of Reconstruction

Most black and white people in 1877 would have agreed on one point: Reconstruction had failed. As Republican governments and black voters succumbed to the southern white reign of terror in the early 1870s, the *Atlanta Constitution* chided black people for being so presumptuous as to want to participate in the democratic process. Politics, the *Constitution* intoned, "was not intended . . . for the blacks, but for the whites. . . . This government is still a white man's government, and will remain forever such. The superior intelligence of the white race . . . will for all time secure political ascendancy." The *Constitution* excused the freedman for his delusion, blaming the "infamous carpetbagger and the radical [Republican] party."

If the demise of Reconstruction elicited a sigh of relief from most white Americans, black Southerners greeted it with frustration. Their dreams of land ownership faded as a new labor system relegated them to a lowly position in southern agriculture. Redemption reversed their economic and political gains and deprived them of most of the civil rights they had enjoyed under Congressional Reconstruction. Although they continued to vote into the 1890s, they had by 1877 lost most of the voting strength and political offices they held. Rather than becoming part of southern society, they were increasingly set apart from it, valued only for their labor.

Still, the former slaves were better off in 1877 than in 1865. They were free, however limited their freedom. Some owned land; some held jobs in cities. They raised their families in relative peace and experienced the spiritual joys of a full religious life. They socialized freely with relatives and friends, and they moved about. But by 1877, the "golden moment"—an unprecedented opportunity for the nation to live up to its ideals by extending equal rights to all its citizens, black and white alike—had passed.

Sharecropping

When they lost political power, black Southerners also lost economic independence. As the Freedmen's Bureau retreated from supervising farm labor contracts and opportunities for black people to possess their own land dried up, the bargaining power of black farm laborers decreased, and the power of white landlords increased. The faltering southern economy contributed to the loss of labor autonomy as well. Cash wages were at first high enough and rental agreements between tenant farmers and landlords at first fair enough for black farmers to be able to buy their own tools and perhaps a few extra acres. But the dramatic decline of cotton prices soon after the war reduced cash surpluses in an already cash-poor region. Unable now to purchase their own animals or tools and lacking cash to buy food and other necessities at local stores, freedmen were forced to barter their crops for credit.

The upshot was that by the late 1870s, most former slaves in the rural South had been drawn into a subservient position in a new labor system called **sharecropping** (see Maps 18-3 and 18-4). The premise of this system was relatively simple: The landlord furnished the sharecroppers a house, a plot of land to work, seed, some farm animals, and farm implements and advanced them credit at a store the landlord typically owned. In exchange, the sharecroppers promised the landlord a share of their crop, usually one-half. The croppers kept the proceeds from the sale of the other half to pay off their debts at the store and save or spend as they and their families saw fit. In theory, a sharecropper could save enough to secure economic independence.

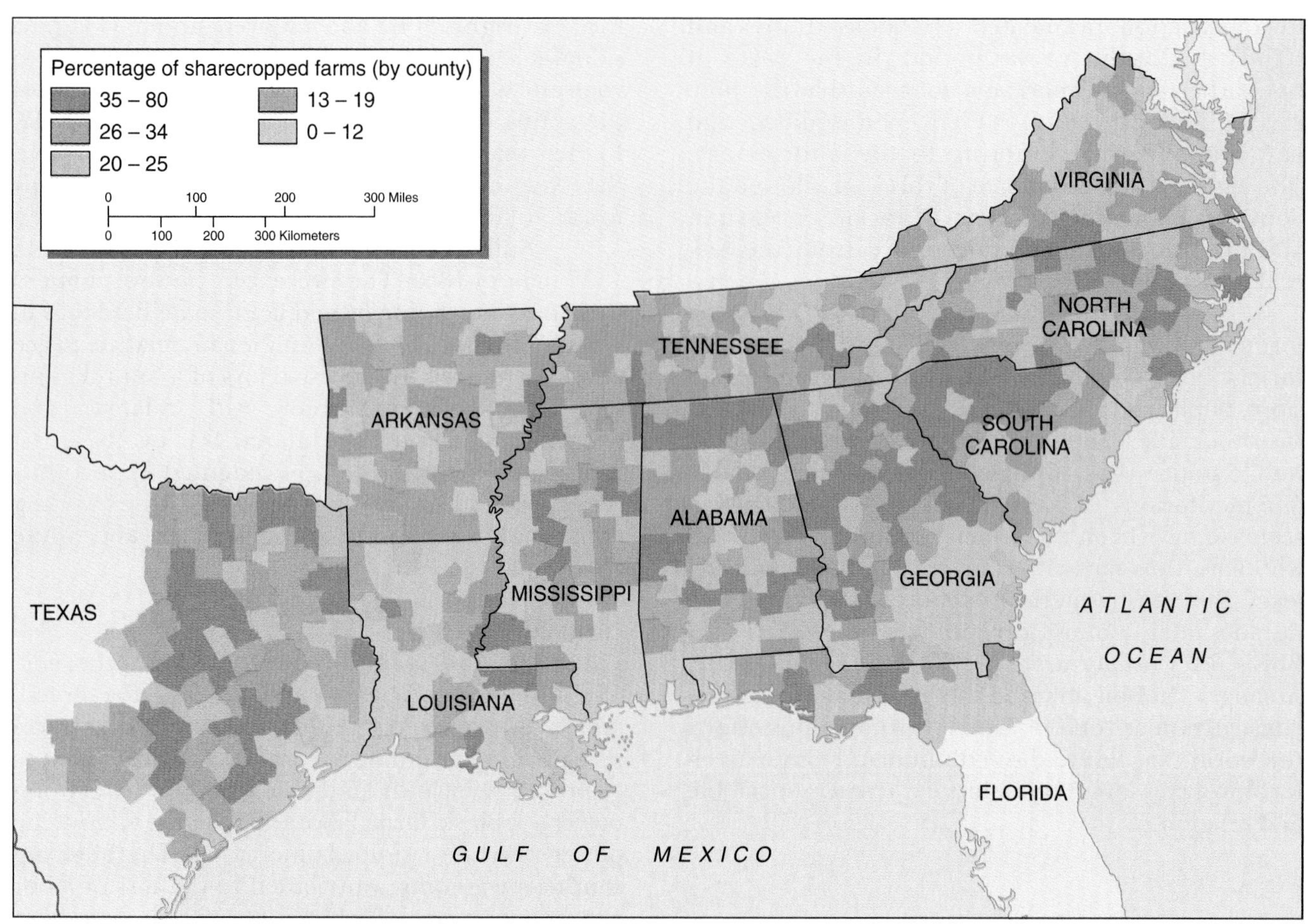

Map 18-3 The Extent of Sharecropping, 1880
Virtually unknown in 1865, sharecropping took hold in the South during the 1870s. Although both black and white farmers worked as sharecroppers, the labor system became most characteristic for black farmers.

But white landlords perceived black independence as both contradictory and subversive. With landlords holding the accounts at the store, black sharecroppers found that the proceeds from their share of the crop never left them very far ahead. In exchange for extending credit to sharecroppers, store owners felt justified in requiring collateral, but sharecroppers had no assets other than the cotton they grew. So southern states passed **crop lien laws**, which gave the store owner the right to the next year's crop in exchange for this year's credit. If the following year's harvest couldn't pay off the debt, the sharecropper sank deeper into dependence. Some found themselves in perpetual debt and worked as virtual slaves. They could not simply abandon their debts and go to another farm because the new landlord would check their references. Those found to have jumped their debts could end up on a prison chain gang. Not all white landlords cheated their tenants, but given the sharecroppers' innocence regarding accounting methods and crop pricing, the temptation to do so was great. Thus weak cotton prices conspired with white chicanery to keep black people economically dependent.

Sharecropping represented a significant step down from tenancy. Tenants owned their own draft animals, farm implements, and seed. Once they negotiated with a land owner for a fixed rent, they kept whatever profits they earned. Eventually, they could hope to purchase some land and move into the landlord class themselves. But the continued low price of cotton made such mobility less likely during the Reconstruction era. Movement in the opposite direction was more common, especially for white people who owned small farms and could not eke out an income to at least pay taxes on loans. Landowning farmers and their families slid increasingly into tenancy and sharecropping.

Historians have often depicted the sharecropping system as a compromise between white landlord and black laborer. But compromise implies a give-and-take between relatively equal negotiators. As northern and federal support for

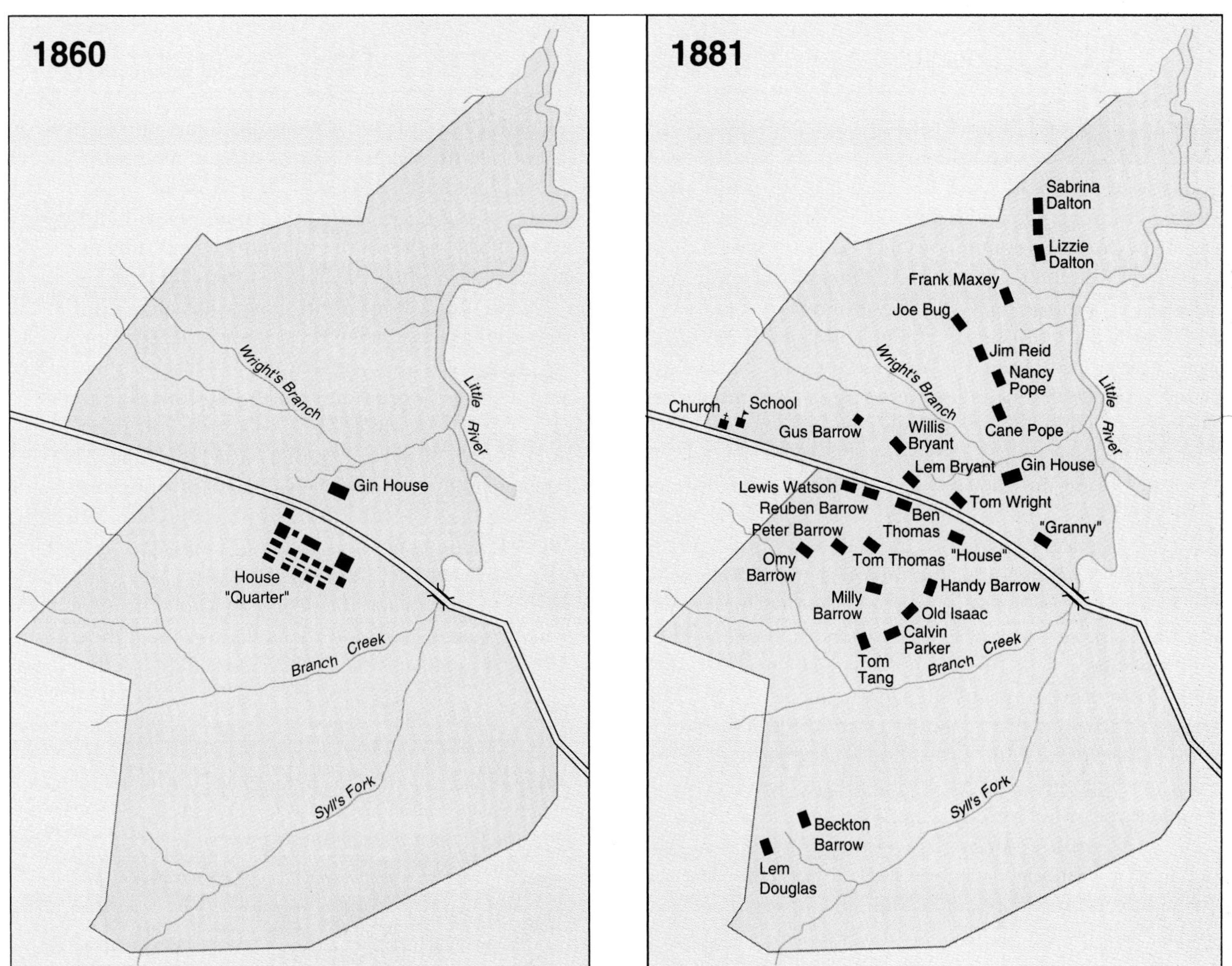

Map 18-4 The Effect of Sharecropping on the Southern Plantation: The Barrow Plantation, Oglethorpe County, Georgia
Sharecropping changed the landscape of the plantation South, cutting large estates into small holdings worked by sharecroppers and tenants.

Reconstruction waned after 1870 and southern Democrats regained political control, white power over black labor increased. Black people had no recourse to federal and state authorities or, increasingly, to the polls as a white reign of terror stripped them of their political rights. The prophecy of one Alabama planter in 1866 had come to pass: "The nigger is going to be made a serf, as sure as you live. It won't need any law for that. Planters will have an understanding among themselves: 'You won't hire my niggers, and I won't hire yours,' then what's left for them? They're attached to the soil, and we're as much their masters as ever."

Northern Republicans offered little opposition to southern labor practices after 1870. A resurgence of labor militancy and the emergence of a large industrial work force caused them to rethink the ideology of free labor they had espoused during the Civil War. They had trouble reconciling their notions of the dignity of independent labor with the aggressive, hostile, and increasingly foreign-born workers who now toiled in northern factories. The gap between worker and entrepreneur had widened between 1860 and 1870. Northern factory owners were now no more interested in encouraging upward mobility for their workers than southern landlords. Instead, they used the courts and state and local governments to keep workers in their place.

The only difference between northern and southern employers' outlook on labor was that Southerners exercised more control over their workers. What had been a triangular debate—among white Northerners, white Southerners, and

AMERICA'S JOURNEY

FROM THEN TO NOW

African-American Voting Rights in the South

Right from the end of the Civil War, white Southerners resisted African-American voting rights. Black people, with equal determination, used the franchise to assert their equal right to participate in the political process. Black voting rights proved so contentious that Congress sought to secure them with the Fourteenth and Fifteenth Amendments to the U.S. Constitution. But U.S. Supreme Court decisions in *United States* v. *Cruikshank* (1876) and in the *Civil Rights Cases* (1883) undermined federal authority to protect the rights of freedmen, including voting rights. A combination of violence, intimidation, and legislation effectively disfranchised black Southerners by the early twentieth century.

During the 1960s, a period some historians have referred to as the Second Reconstruction, Congress passed legislation designed to override state prohibitions and earlier court decisions limiting African-American voting rights. The key measure, the 1965 Voting Rights Act, not only guaranteed black Southerners (and later, other minorities) the right to register and vote but protected them from procedural subterfuges, many of which dated from the first Reconstruction era, that would dilute their votes. These protections proved necessary because of the extreme racial polarization of Southern elections: White people rarely voted for black candidates.

To ensure African-American candidates an opportunity to win elections, the federal government after 1965 insisted that states and localities establish procedures to increase the likelihood of such a result. As part of this process, the federal government also monitored state redistricting for Congressional elections, which occurs every decade in response to population shifts recorded in the national census.

By the early 1990s, states were being directed to draw districts with majority-black voting populations to ensure African-American representation in the Congress and state legislatures. The federal government cited the South's history of racial discrimination and racially polarized voting to justify these districts. But white Southerners challenged such claims, as they had more than a century earlier, and their challenges proved successful in federal court.

In 1993, the U.S. Supreme Court issued a decision in a North Carolina redistricting case, *Shaw* v. *Reno*, that struck down a majority-black Congressional district in that state. Subsequent decisions in other southern districts produced similar rulings. The general principle followed by the Court has been that if race is a key justification for drawing these districts, then they violate the Fourteenth Amendment, which, according to the Court majority, demands color-blind electoral procedures. But, as the late Supreme Court Justice William Brennan noted, "to read the Fourteenth Amendment to state an abstract principle of color-blindness is itself to be blind to history." The framers of the Reconstruction Amendments had the protection of the rights of the freedmen (including and especially voting rights) in mind when they wrote those measures. One voting rights expert has charged that the Court rulings have ushered in a "Second Redemption."

But it is also true that in 1998 black Congressional incumbents in Georgia and North Carolina, running in redrawn districts in which black voters were in the minority (and less than 40 percent at that) won reelection. These results may indicate that racially polarized voting may be diminishing in the South, although they may also reflect the power of incumbency and the weak campaigns of the challengers. In any case, the issue of African-American voting rights in the South and the degree to which the federal government may or may not intercede to protect those rights remains as much at issue as it was more than a century ago.

Casting a ballot. Black voters in Richmond vote on a state constitutional convention in 1867. A key objective of Congressional Reconstruction was to secure the voting rights of freedmen.

freedmen—had become a lopsided discourse divided along racial rather than sectional lines. In 1876, after a political campaign marked by brazen violence against Republican voters, Wade Hampton, ex-Confederate general and newly elected governor of South Carolina, provided an appropriate summary of labor perspectives in both regions. "The real North," he explained, "never liked Negroes and was not willing to attack slavery. Now that it is gone they are glad and so are we; but they no more than we want to make Negroes their equals. They want good, cheap, profitable labor and so do we."

Modest Gains and Future Victories

Black Southerners experienced some advances in the decade after the Civil War, but these owed little to Reconstruction. Black families functioned as economic and psychological buffers against unemployment and prejudice. Black churches played crucial roles in their communities. Self-help and labor organizations offered mutual friendship and financial assistance. All of these institutions existed in the slavery era, although on a smaller scale. And some of them, such as black labor groups, schools, and social welfare associations, endured because comparable white institutions excluded black people.

Black people also scored some modest economic successes during the Reconstruction era, mainly from their own pluck. In the Lower South, black per capita income increased 46 percent between 1857 and 1879, compared with a 35 percent decline in white per capita income. Sharecropping, oppressive as it was, represented an advance over forced and gang labor. Collectively, black people owned more than $68 million worth of property in 1870, a 240 percent increase over 1860, but the average worth of each was only $408. Those who had been free before the war sometimes fared worse after it, especially property-owning free black people in the Lower South. Black city dwellers, especially in the Upper South, fared somewhat better. The overwhelming majority of black people, however, were landless agricultural laborers eking out a meager income that merchants and landlords often snatched to cover debts.

The Fourteenth and Fifteenth Amendments to the Constitution are among the few bright spots in Reconstruction's otherwise dismal legacy. The Fourteenth Amendment guaranteed former slaves equality before the law; the Fifteenth Amendment protected their right to vote. Both amendments elevated the federal government over the states by protecting freedmen from state attempts to deny them their rights. But the benefits of these two landmark amendments did not accrue to African Americans until well into the twentieth century. White Southerners effectively nullified the Reconstruction amendments, and the U.S. Supreme Court virtually interpreted them, and other Reconstruction legislation, out of existence.

In the ***Slaughterhouse* cases** (1873), the Supreme Court contradicted the intent of the Fourteenth Amendment by decreeing that most citizenship rights remained under state, not federal, control. In ***United States* v. *Cruikshank*** (1876), the Court overturned the convictions of some of those responsible for the Colfax Massacre, ruling that the Enforcement Act applied only to violations of black rights by states, not individuals. Within the next two decades, the Supreme Court would uphold the legality of racial segregation and black disfranchisement, in effect declaring that the Fourteenth and Fifteenth Amendments did not apply to African Americans. The Civil War had killed secession forever, but states' rights enjoyed a remarkable revival.

As historian John Hope Franklin accurately concluded, Reconstruction "had no significant or permanent effect on the status of the black in American life. . . . [Black people] made no meaningful steps toward economic independence or even stability."

Conclusion

Formerly enslaved black Southerners had entered freedom with many hopes, among the most prominent of which was to be let alone. White Southerners, after four bloody years of unwanted attention from the federal government, also longed to be left alone. But they did not include their ex-slaves as equals in their vision of solitude. Northerners, too, began to seek escape from the issues and consequences of the war, eventually abandoning their commitment to secure civil and voting rights for black Southerners.

White Southerners robbed black Southerners of their gains and sought to reduce them again to servitude and dependence, if not to slavery. But in the processs, the majority of white Southerners lost as well. Yeoman farmers missed an opportunity to break cleanly from the Old South and establish a more equitable society. Instead, they allowed the old elites to regain power and gradually ignore their needs. They preserved the social benefit of a white skin at the cost of almost everything else. Many lost their farms and sank into tenancy, leasing land from others. Fewer had a voice in state legislatures or Congress. A new South, rid of slavery and sectional antagonism, had indeed emerged, redeemed, regenerated, and disenthralled. But the old South lingered on in the new like Spanish moss on live oaks.

As federal troops left the South to be redeployed restraining striking workers in the North and suppressing Native Americans on the Great Plains, an era of possibility for American society ended, and a new era began. "The southern question is dead," a Charleston newspaper proclaimed in 1877. "The question of labor and capital, work and wages" had moved to the forefront. The chance to redeem the sacrifice of a bloody civil war with a society that fulfilled the promise of the Declaration of Independence and the Constitution for all citizens slipped away. It would take a new generation of African Americans a long century later to revive it.

Review Questions

1. Given the devastation in the South after the Civil War and the loss of property, lives, and hope among many white Southerners, do you think they should they have supported black aspirations for civil rights, land, and suffrage? How differently would things have turned out if they had?
2. Some historians have placed a great deal of the blame for Reconstruction's failures on the backs of southern Republicans. Is this fair? Explain your response.
3. Black people did achieve some notable gains during Reconstruction, despite its overall failure. What were those gains?

Recommended Reading

W. E. B. Du Bois, *Black Reconstruction in America, 1860–1880* (1935). An early and long-ignored study by the foremost black scholar of his time that refuted the contemporary historical wisdom that Reconstruction was a horror visited on the South by an overbearing federal government and ignorant, willful black people.

Eric Foner, *Reconstruction: America's Unfinished Revolution, 1863-1877* (1988). The standard work on Reconstruction, notable for its emphasis on the experience and aspirations of black Southerners.

Gaines M. Foster, *Ghosts of the Confederacy: Defeat, the Lost Cause, and the Emergence of the New South, 1865 to 1913* (1987). A fine picture of how the memory of the Civil War affected white Southerners and their views on Reconstruction policy.

Leon Litwack, *Been in the Storm So Long: The Aftermath of Slavery* (1979). An eloquent account of the early days of freedom from the freedmen's perspective, up to 1867.

Albion W. Tourgée, *A Fool's Errand* (1879). A novel written by an Ohioan who migrated to North Carolina in 1865 to take advantage of economic opportunities in the state and eventually became involved in politics, with his frustrations with Reconstruction and his keen analysis of racism as important themes.

Additional Sources

White Southerners and the Ghosts of the Confederacy

Dan T. Carter, *When the War Was Over: The Failure of Self-Reconstruction in the South, 1865–1867* (1985).

LaWanda Cox and John Cox, *Politics, Principle, and Prejudice, 1865–1866* (1963).

Black Aspirations beyond Freedom

Ira Berlin et al., *Freedom: A Documentary History of Emancipation, 1861–1867. The Wartime Genesis of Free Labor: The Lower South* (1990).

John Blassingame, *Black New Orleans, 1860–1880* (1973).

Carol R. Bleser, *The Promised Land: The History of the South Carolina Land Commission* (1963).

Edmund L. Drago, *Black Politicians and Reconstruction in Georgia* (1982).

Michael W. Fitzgerald, *The Union League Movement in the Deep South: Politics and Agricultural Change during Reconstruction* (1989).

Herbert G. Gutman, *The Black Family in Slavery and Freedom, 1750–1925* (1976).

Gerald Jaynes, *Branches without Roots: The Genesis of the Black Working Class in the American South, 1862–1882* (1986).

Jacqueline Jones, *Labor of Love, Labor of Sorrow: Black Women, Work, and the Family from Slavery to the Present* (1985).

Peter Kolchin, *First Freedom: The Responses of Alabama's Blacks to Emancipation and Reconstruction* (1972).

Howard N. Rabinowitz, *Race Relations in the Urban South, 1865–1890* (1978).

Howard N. Rabinowitz, ed. *Southern Black Leaders of the Reconstruction Era* (1982).

Emma Lou Thornbrough, ed., *Black Reconstructionists* (1972).

Joel Williamson, *After Slavery: The Negro in South Carolina during Reconstruction, 1861–1877* (1965).

Federal Reconstruction, 1865–1870

Richard Abbott, *The Republican Party and the South, 1855–1877* (1986).

Herman Belz, *A New Birth of Freedom: The Republican Party and Freedmen's Rights, 1861–1866* (1976).

Michael Les Benedict, *A Compromise of Principle: Congressional Republicans and Reconstruction, 1863–1869* (1974).

Paul Cimbala, *Under the Guardianship of the Nation: The Freedman's Bureau and the Reconstruction of Georgia, 1865–1870* (1997).

Louis S. Gerteis, *From Contraband to Freedmen: Federal Policy toward Southern Blacks, 1861–1865* (1973).

William C. Harris, *With Charity for All: Lincoln and the Restoration of the Union* (1997).

Thomas Holt, *Black over White: Negro Political Leadership in South Carolina during Reconstruction* (1977).

William S. McFeely, *Grant: A Biography* (1981).

Carl H. Moneyhon, *Republicanism in Reconstruction Texas* (1980).

Michael Perman, *Reunion without Compromise: The South and Reconstruction, 1865–1868* (1973).

Willie Lee Rose, *Rehearsal for Reconstruction: The Port Royal Experiment* (1964).

Mark W. Summers, *Railroads, Reconstruction, and the Gospel of Prosperity: Aid under the Radical Republicans, 1865–1877* (1984).

Hans Trefousse, *The Radical Republicans: Lincoln's Vanguard for Racial Justice* (1969).

Counter-Reconstruction, 1870–1874

Richard N. Current, *Those Terrible Carpetbaggers: A Reinterpretation* (1988).

Russell Duncan, *Entrepreneur for Equality: Governor Rufus Bullock, Commerce, and Race in Post–Civil War Georgia* (1994).

Samuel C. Hyde, Jr., *Pistols and Politics: The Dilemma of Democracy in Louisiana's Florida Parishes, 1810–1899* (1996).

Michael Perman, *The Road to Redemption: Southern Politics, 1869–1879* (1984).

George C. Rable, *But There Was No Peace: The Role of Violence in the Politics of Reconstruction* (1984).

John G. Sproat, *"The Best Men": Liberal Reformers in the Gilded Age* (1968).

Allen W. Trelease, *White Terror: The Ku Klux Conspiracy and Reconstruction* (1971).

Redemption, 1874–1877

Randolph B. Campbell, *Grass-Roots Reconstruction in Texas, 1865–1880* (1997).

Laura F. Edwards, *Gendered Strife & Confusion: The Political Culture of Reconstruction* (1997).

Otto H. Olsen, ed., *Reconstruction and Redemption in the South* (1980).

Keith Ian Polakoff, *The Politics of Inertia: The Election of 1876 and the End of Reconstruction* (1973).

C. Vann Woodward, *Reunion and Reaction: The Compromise of 1877 and the End of Reconstruction* (1951).

The Failure of Reconstruction

Stephen Ward Angell, *Bishop Henry McNeal Turner and African-American Religion in the South* (1992).

John Hope Franklin, *Reconstruction after the Civil War* (1961).

James M. McPherson, *Ordeal by Fire: Reconstruction* (1982).

Roger L. Ransom and Richard Sutch, *One Kind of Freedom: The Economic Consequences of Emancipation* (1977).

James L. Roark, *Masters without Slaves: Southern Planters in the Civil War and Reconstruction* (1977).

Kenneth M. Stampp, *The Era of Reconstruction, 1865–1877* (1965).

Where to Learn More

- ❖ **Penn Center Historic District, St. Helena Island, South Carolina.** The Penn School was a sea-island experiment in the education of free black people established by northern missionaries Laura Towne and Ellen Murray in 1862 that they operated until their deaths in the early 1900s. The Penn School became Penn Community Services in 1948, serving as an educational institution, health clinic, and a social service agency.
- ❖ **Hampton University Museum, Hampton, Virginia.** Hampton University was founded by the Freedmen's Bureau in 1868 to provide "practical" training in the agricultural and mechanical fields for former slaves. In addition to a history of the institution, the museum includes one of the oldest collections of African art in the United States.
- ❖ **Beauvoir, Biloxi, Mississippi.** The exhibits at Beauvoir, the home of Jefferson Davis, evoke the importance of the Lost Cause for the white survivors of the Confederacy. Especially interesting is the Jefferson Davis Soldiers Home on the premises and the Confederate Veterans Cemetery. Davis spent his retirement in Beauvoir.
- ❖ **Levi Jordan Plantation, Brazoria County, Texas.** This site provides an excellent depiction and interpretation of the lives of sharecroppers and tenants during and immediately after the Reconstruction era. The site is especially valuable for demonstrating the transition from slavery to sharecropping.

A New South, 1877–1900

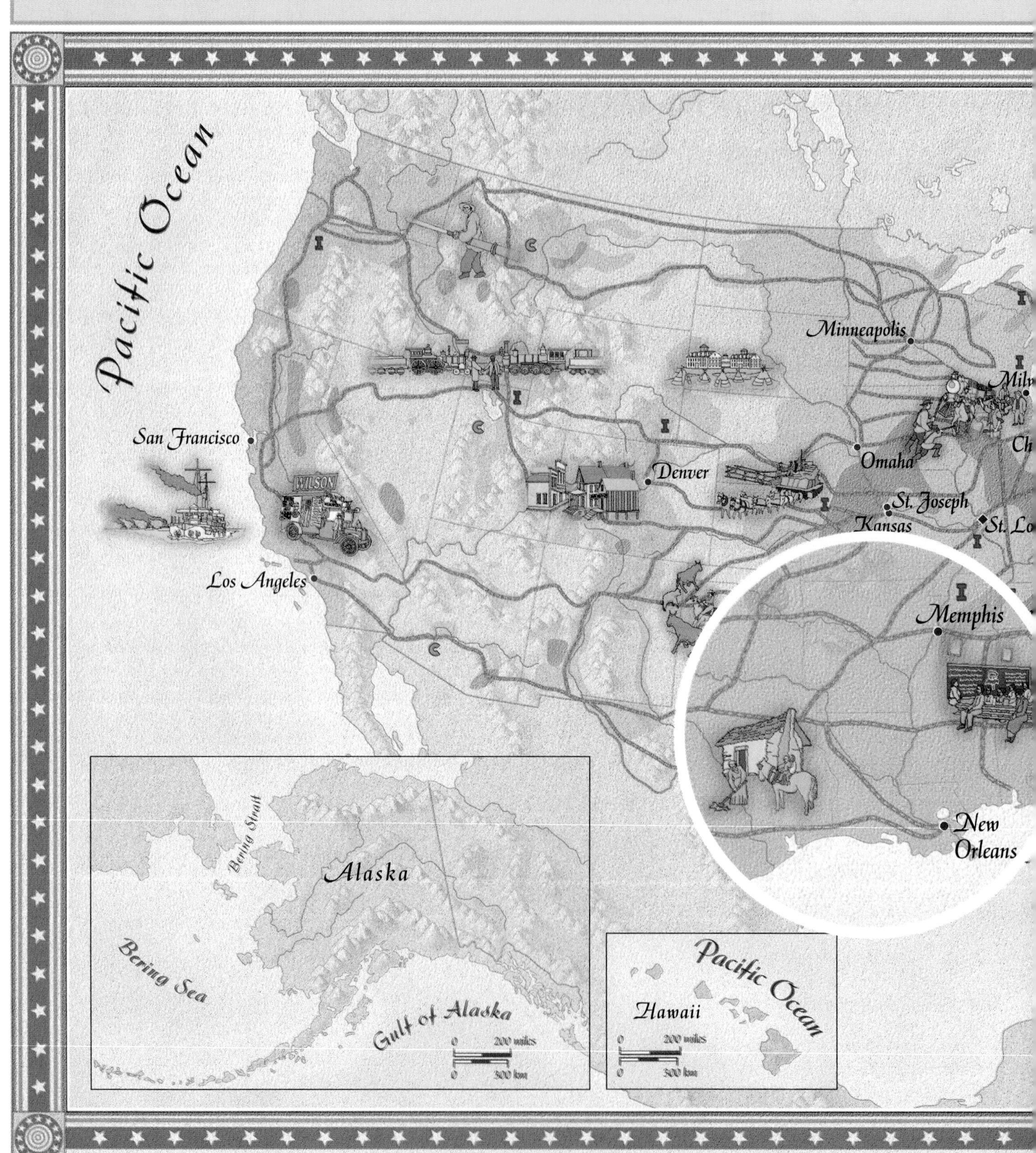
Pacific Ocean
Minneapolis
San Francisco
Denver
Omaha
St. Joseph
Kansas
St. Lo
Los Angeles
Memphis
New Orleans
WILSON
Alaska
Bering Strait
Bering Sea
Gulf of Alaska
0 200 miles
0 300 km
Pacific Ocean
Hawaii
0 200 miles
0 300 km

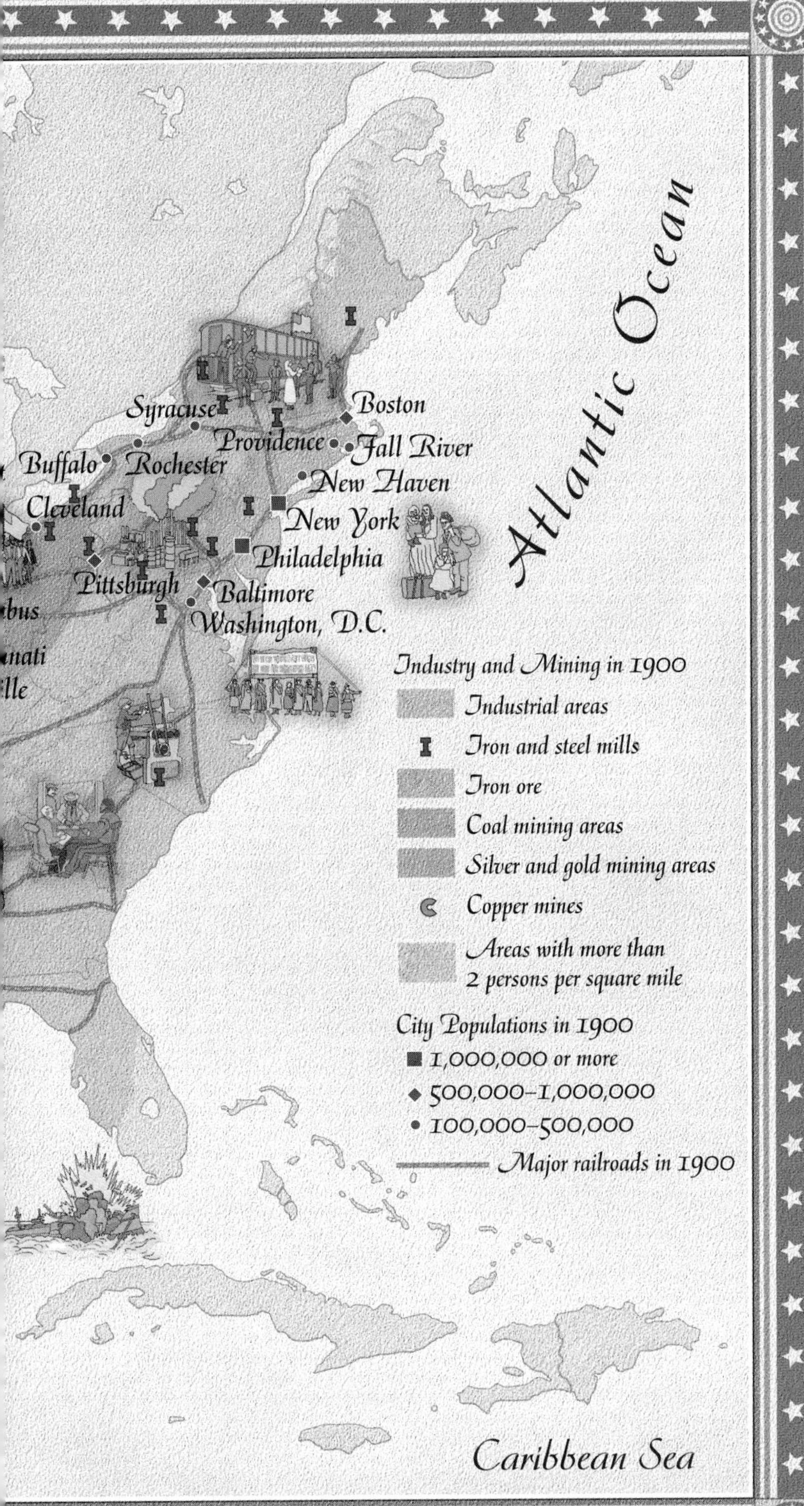

19

Chapter Outline

Key Topics

- Continuity and change between the Old South and the New South
- The origins and nature of southern Populism
- Women's roles in the New South
- How and why segregation and disfranchisement changed race relations in the South

The members of the Holtzclaw family worked hard to supplement the meager income they earned sharecropping on an Alabama farm in the late 1870s. Little more than a decade out of slavery, they hoped to rent and eventually buy a piece of land. Ten-year-old William Holtzclaw foraged for wild nuts and fruits in the swamps around the farm. William's mother cooked for a white family. His father earned extra money hauling logs from a nearby sawmill. When the timber was all gone, he found work on a railroad that kept him away from his family three months at a time.

In 1880, the Holtzclaws bought a mule, a horse, and two oxen and rented a forty-acre farm. But then bad weather and a crippling injury suffered by the elder Holtzclaw dimmed their prospects. By 1884, they had lost their crop and farm animals to debt and were once again sharecropping.

William, a member of the first generation of black Southerners born in freedom, persevered. He graduated from Tuskegee Institute, a black college in Alabama established in 1881, and worked as a teacher and administrator of black schools. He became a prominent educator and founded a vocational college for black people in Mississippi, the Utica Normal and Industrial Institute.

In 1876, while William Holtzclaw and his family were struggling in Alabama, a fourteen-year-old white youth, William Henry Belk, went to work as a store clerk in a small North Carolina town to help support his widowed mother. Over the next twelve years, he saved $750. Borrowing an additional $500, he opened his own retail store, which he called the New York Racket Store. *Racket* in those days meant "cheap," and the word fit both his prices and his merchandise. His one-price, cash-only strategy was successful in his town of 2,500 people. By 1895, he had earned enough from his modest venture to move to Charlotte and open a department store. Charlotte had excellent railroad connections to the rest of the country, so Belk could stock his store with the latest fashions from New York City and the newest household appliances and products from the industrial centers of the Northeast and Midwest. The railroad also brought people—potential Belk customers—to Charlotte. Combining brash advertising with personal attention to customers and attractive prices, Belk prospered. He expanded, opening new stores in the Carolinas. By the early 1900s, Belk owned the largest retail chain in the South.

Both these stories—Holtzclaw's and Belk's—reflect the promise and the problems of the New South that emerged after Reconstruction. Neither would have been likely in the Old South. The experience of the Holtzclaw family shows that despite rising racial hostility in the late-nineteenth-century South, African Americans could aspire to land ownership, education, and a professional career. But it also shows the tenuous plight of southern farmers, white and black alike. And it suggests how narrowing economic opportunities and growing social and political isolation made the road to recovery harder and longer for African Americans than for white Southerners. William Belk's story shows how some Southerners, especially white Southerners, could find opportunity in the South's burgeoning urban centers. Belk and others like him took advantage of the growing transportation systems centered in the cities to translate hard work, some good ideas, and a small financial stake into good fortune.

The New South was very American in the opportunities it provided its citizens through urban and industrial growth. But it was very southern in the persistence of its rural poverty and the distinctiveness of its racial institutions.

The Newness of the New South

While southern farmers, both black and white, faced limited prospects in a stagnant agricultural economy, other Southerners were building railroads, erecting factories, and moving to towns and cities. They were doing what other Americans were doing between 1877 and 1900, only on a smaller scale and with more modest results. The factories did not dramatically alter the South's rural economy, and the towns and cities did not make it an urban region. The changes nonetheless brought political and social turmoil, emboldening black people to assert their rights, encouraging women to work outside the home and pursue public careers, and frightening some white men. By 1900, southern white leaders, urban and rural, had used the banner of white supremacy to stifle dissent. They removed African Americans from political life and constricted their social and economic role. The New South was thus like a cake with fancy new layers piled high on a very old crust. The appearance was American, but the taste was southern.

The New South's "newness" was to be found primarily in its economy. After Reconstruction, new industries absorbed tens of thousands of first-time industrial workers from impoverished rural areas. Southern cities grew faster than those in any other region of the country. A burst of railroad construction linked these cities to one another and to the rest of the country, giving them increased commercial prominence. Growing in size and taking on new functions, cities extended their influence into the countryside with newspapers, consumer products, and new values. But this urban influence had important limits. It did not bring electricity, telephones, public health services, or public schools to the rural South. It did not greatly broaden the rural economy with new jobs. And it left the countryside without the daily contact with the outside world that fostered a broader perspective.

The Democratic party dominated southern politics after 1877, significantly changing the South's political system. Through various deceits, Democrats purged most black people and some white people from the electoral process and suppressed challenges to their leadership. The result was the emergence by 1900 of the **Solid South**, a period of white Democratic party rule that lasted into the 1950s.

Although most southern women remained at home or on the farm, piecing together families shattered by war, some enjoyed new options after

By the 1890s, textile mills were a common sight in towns throughout the South. The mills provided employment for impoverished rural families, especially women and children.

1877. Middle-class women in the cities, both white and black, became increasingly active in civic work and reform. They organized clubs, preserved and promoted the memories of war, lobbied for various causes, and assumed regional leadership on a number of important issues. Tens of thousands of young white women from impoverished rural areas found work in textile mills, in city factories, or as servants. These new options posed a challenge to prevailing views about the role of women but ultimately did not change them.

The status of black Southerners changed significantly between 1877 and 1900. The members of the first generation born after Emancipation sought more than just freedom as they came of age. They also expected dignity and self-respect and the right to work, to vote, to go to school, and to travel freely. White Southerners responded with the equivalent of a second Civil War—and they won. By 1900, black Southerners found themselves more isolated from white Southerners and with less political power than at any time since 1865. Despite these setbacks, they succeeded, especially in the cities, in building a rich community life and spawning a vibrant middle class.

An Industrial and Urban South

Since the 1850s, public speakers calling for economic reform in the South had been rousing audiences with the tale of the burial of a southern

Chronology

1872 Texas and Pacific Railway connects Dallas to eastern markets.

1880 First southern local of the Women's Christian Temperance Union is formed in Atlanta.

1881 Booker T. Washington establishes Tuskegee Institute.

1882 Agricultural Wheel is formed in Arkansas.

1883 Laura Haygood founds the home mission movement in Atlanta.

1884 James B. Duke automates his cigarette factory.

1886 Dr. John Pemberton creates Coca-Cola.

Southern railroads conform to national track gauge standards.

1887 Charles W. Macune expands the Southern Farmer's Alliance from its Texas base to the rest of the South.

1888 The Southern Farmers' Alliance initiates a successful boycott of jute manufacturers.

1890 Mississippi becomes the first state to restrict black suffrage with literacy tests.

1892 The Populist party forms.

1894 United Daughters of the Confederacy is founded.

Populist and Republican fusion candidates win control of North Carolina.

1895 Booker T. Washington delivers his "Atlanta Compromise" address.

1896 Populists endorse the Democratic presidential candidate and fade as a national force.

In *Plessy* v. *Ferguson*, the Supreme Court permits segregation by law.

1898 North Carolina Mutual Life Insurance is founded.

Democrats regain control of North Carolina.

1903 W. E. B. Du Bois publishes *The Souls of Black Folk.*

1905 James B. Duke forms the Southern Power Company.

Thomas Dixon publishes *The Clansman.*

1906 Bloody race riots break out in Atlanta.

1907 Pittsburgh-based U.S. Steel takes over Birmingham's largest steel producer.

compatriot. The man's headstone, his clothes, the coffin, and the gravediggers' tools all came from the North. Only the corpse and the earth of his grave were southern. The speakers urged their listeners to found industries, build railroads, and grow great cities so that the South could make its own goods and no one in the future would have to suffer the indignity of journeying to the next world accompanied by Yankee artifacts.

It is unclear whether such admonitions worked. Certainly, Southerners manufactured very little in 1877, less than 10 percent of the national total. By 1900, however, they boasted a growing iron and steel industry, textile mills that rivaled those of New England, a world-dominant tobacco industry, and a timber-processing industry that helped make the South a leading furniture-manufacturing center. A variety of regional enterprises also rose to prominence, among them the maker of what would become the world's favorite soft drink, Coca-Cola.

Birmingham, barely a scratch in the forest in 1870, exemplified one aspect of what was new about the New South. Within a decade, its iron and steel mills belched the smoke of progress across the northern Alabama hills. By 1889, Birmingham had surpassed the older southern iron center of Chattanooga, Tennessee, and was preparing to challenge Pittsburgh, the nation's preeminent steelmaking city.

The southern textile industry also experienced significant growth during the 1880s. Although the South had manufactured cotton products since the early decades of the nineteenth century, chronic shortages of labor and capital kept the industry small. In the 1870s, however, several factors drew local investors into textile enterprises. The population of the rural South was rising, but farm income was low, ensuring a steady supply of cheap labor. Cotton was plentiful and cheap. Mixing profit and southern patriotism, entrepreneurs promoted a strong textile industry as a way to make the South less dependent on northern manufactured products and capital. The entrepreneurs located their mills mostly in rural areas, not in cities. The center of the industry was in the Carolina Piedmont, a region with good railroads, plentiful labor, and cheap energy. By 1900, the South had surpassed New England to become the nation's foremost textile-manufacturing center.

The South's tobacco industry, like its textile industry, predated the Civil War. Virginia was the dominant producer, and its main product was chewing tobacco. The discovery of bright-leaf tobacco, a strain suitable for smoking in the form of cigarettes, changed Americans' tobacco habits. In 1884, James B. Duke installed the first cigarette-making machine in his Durham, North Carolina, plant. By 1900, Duke's American Tobacco Company controlled 80 percent of all tobacco manufacturing in the United States.

Although not as important as textiles or tobacco in 1900, a soft drink developed by Atlanta pharmacist Dr. John Pemberton eventually became the most renowned southern product in the world. Pemberton developed the drink—a mixture of oils, caffeine, coca leaves, and cola nuts—in his backyard in an effort to find a good-tasting cure for headaches. He called his concoction Coca-Cola. It was not an overnight success, and Pemberton, short of cash, sold the rights to it to another Atlantan, Asa Candler, in 1889. Candler tinkered with the formula to improve the taste and marketed the product heavily. By the mid-1890s, Coca-Cola enjoyed a national market. Southerners were such heavy consumers that the Georgia Baptist Association felt compelled to warn its members "the more you drink, the more you want to drink. We fear great harm will grow out of this sooner or later, to our young people in particular."

Southern railroad construction boomed in the 1880s, outpacing the rest of the nation. Overall, southern track mileage doubled between 1880 and 1890, with the greatest increases in Texas and Georgia (see Map 19-1). By 1890, nine out of ten Southerners lived in a county with a railroad running through it. In 1886, the southern railroads agreed to conform to a national standard for track width, firmly linking the region into a national transportation network and ensuring quick and direct access for southern products to the booming markets of the Northeast.

The railroads connected many formerly isolated small southern farmers to national and international agricultural markets. At the same time, it gave them access to a whole new range of products, from fertilizers to fashions. Drawn into commercial agriculture, the farmers were now subject to market fluctuations, their fortunes rising and falling with the market prices for their crops. To an extent unknown before the Civil War, the market now determined what farmers planted, how much credit they could expect, and on what terms.

The railroad also opened new areas of the South to settlement and economic development. In 1892, according to one guidebook, Florida was "in the main inaccessible to the ordinary tourist, and unopened to the average settler." But railroad construction boomed in the state in the 1890s, and by 1912, there were tourist hotels as far south as Key West. Railroads also penetrated the Appalachian Mountains, expanding markets for farmers but also opening the area to outside timber and coal-mining interests.

The railroad increased the prominence of interior cities at the expense of older cities along the southern Atlantic and Gulf Coasts. Antebellum ports such as New Orleans, Charleston, and Savannah declined as commerce rode the rails more than the water. Cities such as Dallas, Atlanta, Nashville, and Charlotte, astride great railroad trunk lines, emerged to lead southern urban growth. No fewer than five major rail lines converged on Atlanta by the 1870s. As early as 1866, it had become "the radiating point for Northern and Western trade coming Southward, and . . . the gate through which passes Southern trade and travel going northward." When the Texas and Pacific Railway linked Dallas to eastern markets in 1872, it was a small town of three thousand people. Eight years later, its population had grown to more than ten thousand, and within thirty years it had become the South's twelfth largest city. By 1920, New Orleans and Norfolk were the only coastal ports still among the ten most populous southern cities.

Railroads also spurred the growth of smaller towns that marketed and processed farm products for the surrounding countryside. A town on a rail line that invested in a cotton press and a cottonseed oil mill would become a marketing hub for the surrounding countryside within a day's wagon ride away. Local merchants would stock the latest fashions from New York, canned foods, and current issues of popular magazines such as *Atlantic* or *Harper's*. The number of towns with fewer than five thousand people doubled between 1870 and 1880 and had doubled again by 1900. During the 1880s, southern urban growth was twice the national average. By 1900, one out of six Southerners lived in an urban place.

The Limits of Industrial and Urban Growth

Rapid as it was, urban and industrial growth in the South barely kept pace with that of the booming North (see Chapter 20). Between 1860 and 1900, the South's share of the nation's manufacturing increased only marginally from 10.3 percent to 10.5 percent, and its share of the nation's capital declined slightly from 11.5 percent to 11 percent. About the same percentage of people worked in manufacturing in the southern states east of the Mississippi in 1900 as in 1850. Between 1860 and 1880, the per capita

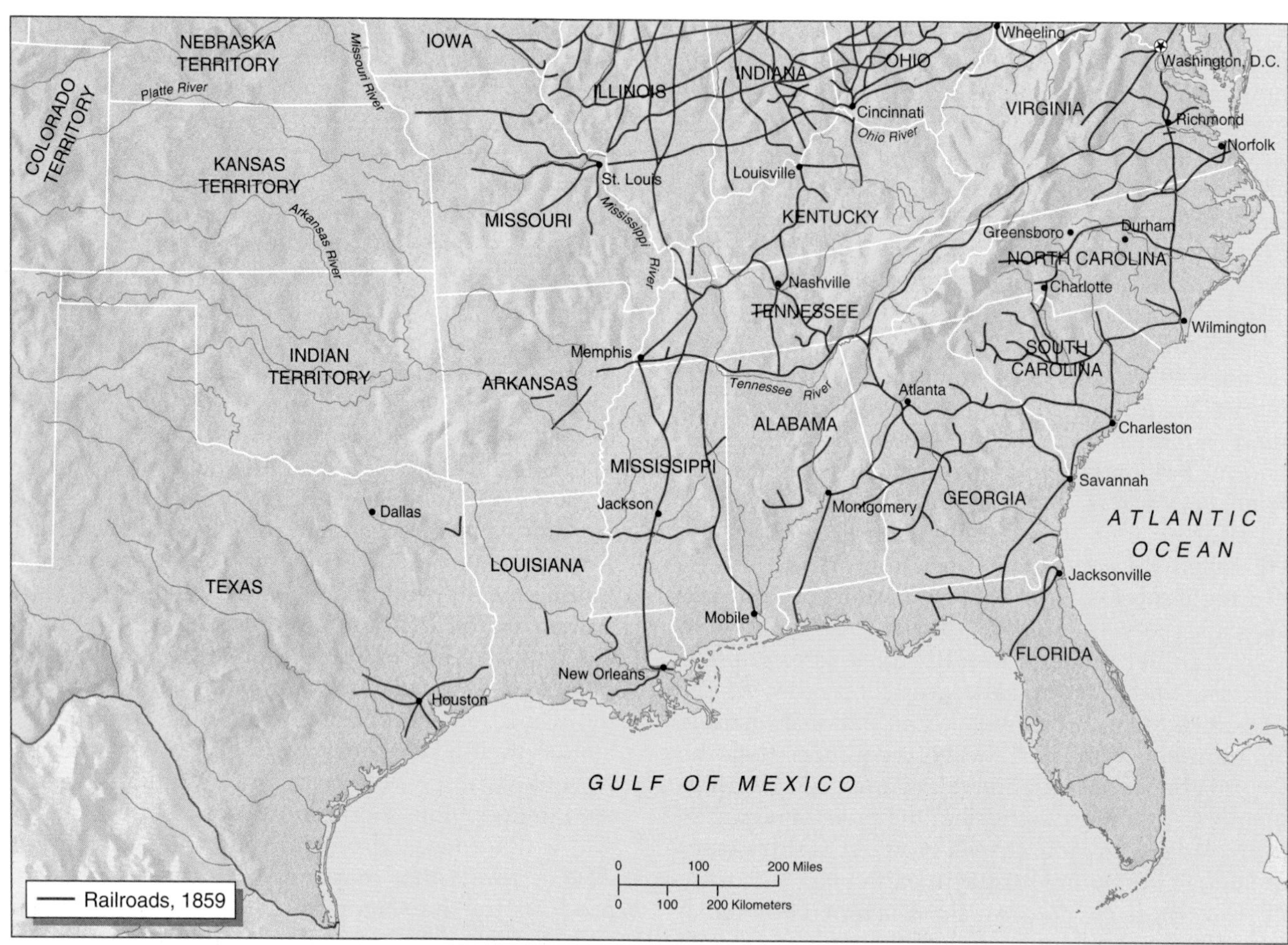

Map 19-1 Railroads in the South, 1859 and 1899
A postwar railroad construction boom promoted commercial agriculture and industry in the South. Unlike the railroads of the prewar South, uniform gauges and connections to major trunk lines in the North linked Southerners to the rest of the nation. Northern interests, however, owned the major southern railroads in 1899, and most of the products flowing northward were raw materials to be processed by northern industry or shipped elsewhere by northern merchants.

income of the South declined from 72 percent of the national average to 51 percent and by 1920 had recovered to only 62 percent (see Figure 19-1).

A weak agricultural economy and a high rural birthrate depressed wages in the South. Southern industrial workers earned roughly half the national average manufacturing wage during the late nineteenth century. Business leaders promoted the advantages of this cheap labor to northern investors. In 1904, a Memphis businessman boasted that his city "can save the northern manufacturer . . . who employs 400 hands, $50,000 a year on his labor bill."

Despite their attractiveness to industrialists, low wages undermined the southern economy in several ways. Poorly paid workers didn't buy much, keeping consumer demand low and limiting the market for southern manufactured goods. They also couldn't provide the southern states with much tax revenue, restricting the states' ability to fund services like public education. Low wages meant that mostly low-skilled, labor-intensive industries flourished in the South. Well-educated workers would have been overqualified for work in such industries. They would either go north, where factories needed skilled labor to produce high-quality goods and run complicated machinery, or agitate for higher wages and better working conditions in the South. Birmingham, Alabama, for example, probably spent more on public education than any other southern city, but the skilled workers in its steel mills tended to leave as soon as they could for higher-wage opportunities in northern cities like Pittsburgh and Cleveland. As a result, investment in education lagged in the South. Per-pupil expenditure in the region was at least 50 percent below that of the rest of the nation in 1900. North Dakota, not a wealthy state, spent ten times more per pupil than North Carolina, not the poorest state in the South.

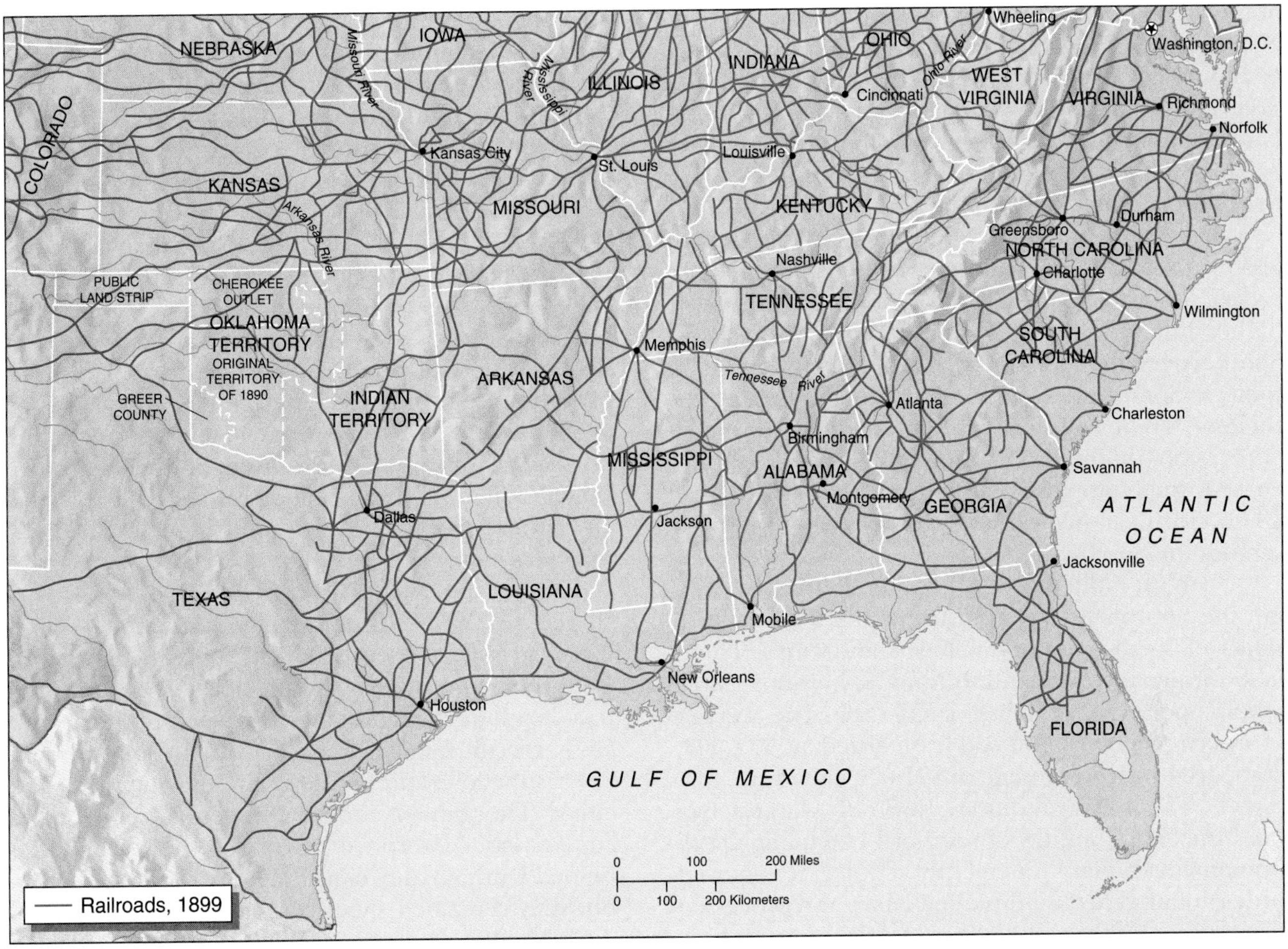

Finally, low wages kept immigrants—and the skills and energy they brought with them—out of the South. With steady work available at higher wages north of the Mason-Dixon line, only a scattering of Italian farm laborers, Chinese railroad workers, and Jewish peddlers ventured below it. Between 1860 and 1900—during one of the greatest waves of immigration the United States has yet experienced—the foreign-born population of the South actually declined from about 10 percent to less than 2 percent.

Why didn't the South do better? Why didn't it benefit more from the rapid expansion of the national economy in the last three decades of the nineteenth century? The simple answer is that despite its growing links to the national economy, the South remained a region apart.

The Civil War had wiped out the South's capital resources, leaving it in effect an economic colony of the North. Northern goods flowed into the South,

Figure 19-1 Per Capita Income in the South as a Percentage of the U.S. Average, 1860–1920

This graph illustrates the devastating effect of the Civil War on the southern economy. Southerners began a slow recovery during the 1880s that accelerated after 1900. But even as late as 1920, per capita income in the South was still lower relative to the country as a whole than it had been before the Civil War.

Data Source: Richard A. Easterlin, "Regional Economic Trends, 1840–1950," in American Economic History, *ed.* Seymour E. Harris *(1961).*

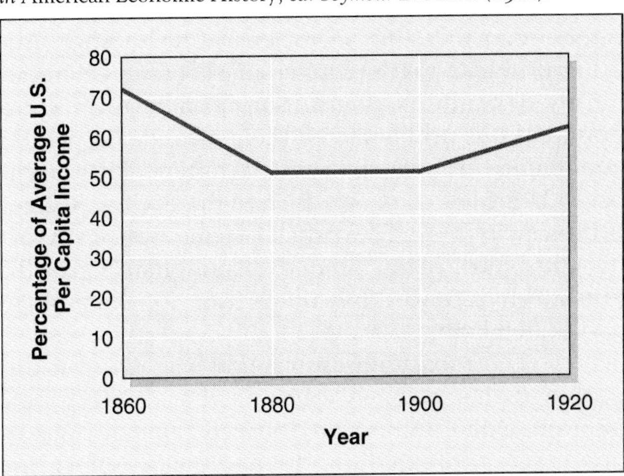

but northern capital, technology, and people did not. Northern-based national banks emerged in the wake of the Civil War to fund northern economic expansion. The South, in contrast, had few banks, and those lacked sufficient capital reserves to fuel an equivalent expansion there. In 1880, Massachusetts alone had five times as much bank capital as the entire South.

Investment in the South seemed riskier and less promising than investment in the vibrant northern economy. As a result, northern banks imposed higher interest rates and shorter terms on loans to Southerners than on loans to their northern customers. Some northern capital came south nonetheless. When southern rail lines failed during a depression in the 1870s, northern financiers purchased the companies at bargain prices. By the 1890s, northern firms owned the five major rail lines serving the South.

With limited access to other sources of capital, the South's textile industry depended on thousands of small investors in towns and cities. These investors avoided risk and shunned innovation. Most textile operations remained small-scale. The average southern firm in 1900 was capitalized at $11,000, compared with an average of $21,000 elsewhere.

The lumber industry, the South's largest, typified the shortcomings of southern economic development in the late nineteenth century. It required little capital, relied on unskilled labor, and processed its raw materials on site. After clear-cutting—felling all the trees—in one region, sawmills moved quickly to the next stand of timber, leaving behind a bare landscape, rusting machinery, and a work force no better off than before. This process—later repeated by the coal-mining industry—inflicted environmental damage on once remote areas such as Appalachia and displaced their residents.

Birmingham's iron and steel industry also suffered from financial weakness. Part of the fault lay with mill owners who relied on cheap black labor rather than investing in expensive technology. Another problem was the limited market for steel in the mostly agricultural South. Southern farmers compounded this problem with their reliance on people and mules instead of farm machinery. Pittsburgh-based U.S. Steel took over Birmingham's largest steel producer in 1907. Thereafter, pricing policies favoring Pittsburgh plants limited Birmingham's growth. Pittsburgh also won the competition for technology and skilled labor.

The tobacco industry, however, avoided the problems that plagued other southern enterprises. James B. Duke's American Tobacco Company was so immensely profitable that he became, in effect, his own bank. With more than enough capital to install the latest technology in his plants, Duke bought out his competitors. He then diversified into electric power generation, investing in an enterprise that became the Southern Power Company in 1905 (and later the Duke Power Company). He also endowed what became Duke University.

Southern industry fit into a narrow niche of late-nineteenth-century American industrialization. With an unskilled and uneducated work force, poor access to capital and technology, and a weak consumer base, the South processed raw agricultural products and produced cheap textiles, cheap lumber products, and cheap cigarettes. "Made in the South" became synonymous with bottom-of-the-line goods. When skill levels and capital resources grew after 1920, however, the quality of southern manufactured products increased.

In the North, industrialization usually occurred in an urban context and promoted rapid urban growth. This was not the case in the South. Most textile mills were typically located in the countryside, often in mill villages, where employers could easily recruit families and keep them isolated from the distractions and employment alternatives of the cities. The timber industry similarly remained a rural-based enterprise. Tobacco manufacturing helped Durham and Winston, North Carolina, grow, but they remained small compared to northern industrial cities. Duke moved his corporate headquarters to New York to be near that city's financial, advertising, and communications services.

The Impact on Southerners

If industrialization in the South was limited compared to the North, it nonetheless had an enormous impact on southern society. In the southern Piedmont, for example, textile mills erupted from the red clay and transformed a portion of the farm population into an industrial work force. Failed farmers moved to textile villages to earn a living. Entire families secured employment and often a house in exchange for their labor. Widows and single young men also moved to the mills, usually the only option outside farm work in the South. Nearly one-third of the textile mill labor force by 1900 consisted of children under the age of fourteen and women. They worked twelve hours a day, six days a week, although some firms allowed a half-day off on Saturday. They had worked long hours on the farm, too, but now they became the target of concern of middle-class urban reformers who viewed factory work as destructive of individual and family life.

Southern urban growth, which also paled in comparison with that of the North, had a similarly disproportionate impact on southern society. One observer noted the changes in a North Carolina town between 1880 and 1900. The town in 1880 presented a sorry aspect: rutted roads, a shanty for a school, a few forlorn churches, and perhaps three families of prominence. Twenty years later, another railroad, bustling commerce, and textile mills had produced a new scene: paved streets, two public schools—one for black children, one for white children—and a cosmopolitan frame of mind among its residents. "The men have a wider range of activities and the women have more clothes." Discussions changed from local gossip to "the prices of certain stocks in New York." The town now had electric lights, paved streets, and a direct train to New York. In another twenty years, the observer predicted, it will be "very like hundreds of towns in the Middle West."

In 1880, southern towns often did not differ much from the countryside in appearance, economy, religion, and outlook. Over the next twenty years, the gap between town and country widened. By 1900, a town in the New South would boast a business district and more elegant residences than before. It would have a relatively prosperous economy and more frequent contact with other parts of the country. Its influence would extend into the countryside. Mail, the telegraph, the railroad, and the newspaper brought city life to the attention of farm families. In turn, farm families visited nearby towns and cities more often. A South Carolina writer related in 1900 that "Country people who . . . went to town annually or semiannually, can now go quickly, safely, pleasantly, and cheaply several times a day." Many never returned to the farm. "Cheap coal, cheap lights, convenient water supply offer inducements; society and amusements draw the young; the chance to speculate, to make a sudden rise in fortunes, to get in the swim attracts others."

The urban South drew the region's talented and ambitious young people. White men like William Henry Belk moved to cities to open shops or take jobs as bank clerks, bookkeepers, merchants, and salesmen. White women worked as retail clerks, telephone operators, and office personnel. Black women filled the growing demand for laundresses and domestic servants. And black men also found prospects better in towns than on the farm, despite a narrow and uncertain range of occupations available to them.

The excitement that drew some Southerners to their new cities repelled others. To them, urbanization and the emphasis on wealth, new technology, and display represented a second Yankee conquest. The cities, they feared, threatened to infect the South with northern values, undermining southern grace, charm, faith, and family. Ministers warned against traffic with the urban devil, whose temptations could overcome even the most devout individual. Evangelist Sam Jones, a reformed alcoholic, chose Atlanta for his largest revivals in the 1890s, challenging its residents to keep the Sabbath holy, reject alcohol, and obey the Golden Rule.

Country people held ambivalent views of the city. Farm children looked forward to the Saturday excursion to town, when they would gaze in shop windows, watch people rushing about, wonder at the workings of electricity, and drink a "Co'Cola" at the drugstore. Their parents shared some of this excitement but experienced apprehension as well. They were disturbed by the easy blurring of class and racial distinctions in town and offended by the scorn with which town folk sometimes treated them.

White Southerners in town and country, who not long ago had lived similar lives, grew distant. Evelyn Scott recalled how rural folk looked to her when they visited her town, Clarksville, Tennessee, at the turn of the century:

> These beings [farmers and their families] I regarded as from another planet. . . . The little girls whose petticoats were never of a length with their frocks; the little boys whose misfit "store pants" were cut of material . . . uncongenial . . . to the human form; the misses in muslin dresses of [a] diluted [pink] color; . . . already-weary mothers wearing hats on which reposed entire flimsy gardens and orchards, or else pathetically alighted, stuffed birds! [They engaged] in bouts of window-shopping in which stoical hearts and vacant imaginations were replenished.

Once the backbone of the South, small landholding white farmers and their families like those Scott thought so alien had fallen on hard times. The market that lured them into commercial agriculture threatened to take away their independence. They faced the loss of their land and livelihood. Their way of life no longer served as the standard for the South. New South spokesmen promoted cities and industries and ordered farmers to get on board the train of progress before it left the station without them.

The Southern Agrarian Revolt

Even more than before the Civil War, cotton dominated southern agriculture between 1877 and 1900. And the economics of cotton brought despair to cotton farmers. Those who grew two other traditional southern cash crops—rice and tobacco—fared better. Rice and tobacco production increased, and Louisiana and Arkansas overtook South Carolina in rice production. Steady demand, however, allowed rice and tobacco growers to maintain a decent standard of living. Cotton was another matter. The size of the cotton crop continued to set annual records after 1877. Fertilizers revived supposedly exhausted soils in North and South Carolina, turning them white with cotton. The railroad opened new areas for cultivation in Mississippi and eastern Texas. But the price of cotton fell while the price of fertilizers, agricultural tools, food, and most other necessities went up (see Figure 19-2). As a result, the more cotton the farmers grew, the less money they made.

Before the Civil War, the South fed itself. After the war, with railroads providing direct access to major cotton-marketing centers, farmers cultivated more land in cotton and less in food crops. The South became an importer of food. As a common lament went in 1890, "Five-cent cotton, forty-cent meat, how in the world can a poor man eat?"

Cotton and Credit

The solution to this agrarian dilemma seemed simple: Grow less cotton. But that was not possible for several reasons. In a cash-poor economy, credit ruled. Cotton was the only commodity instantly convertible into cash and hence the only commodity accepted for credit. Food crops generated less income per acre than cotton, even in the worst years. Local merchants, themselves bound in a web of credit to merchants in larger cities, accepted cotton as collateral. As cotton prices plummeted, the merchants required their customers to grow more cotton to make up the difference. "No cotton, no credit" became a standard refrain throughout the South after 1877.

For small landowning farmers, credit proved addictive. Trapped in debt by low cotton prices and high interest rates, they lost their land in record numbers. Both black farmers, like the Holtzclaws, and white farmers were affected. But white farmers were more likely than black farmers to own their farms, and the effect on them was more dramatic. Less than one-third of white farmers in the South were tenants or sharecroppers just after the Civil War. By the 1890s, nearly half were.

Some areas did diversify. Good rail connections in Georgia, for example, made peach farming profitable for some farmers. Railroads likewise helped cattle ranching spread in Texas. But few crops or animals had the geographical range of cotton. Soil type, rainfall, animal parasites, and frost made alternatives unfeasible for many farmers. Cotton required no ma-

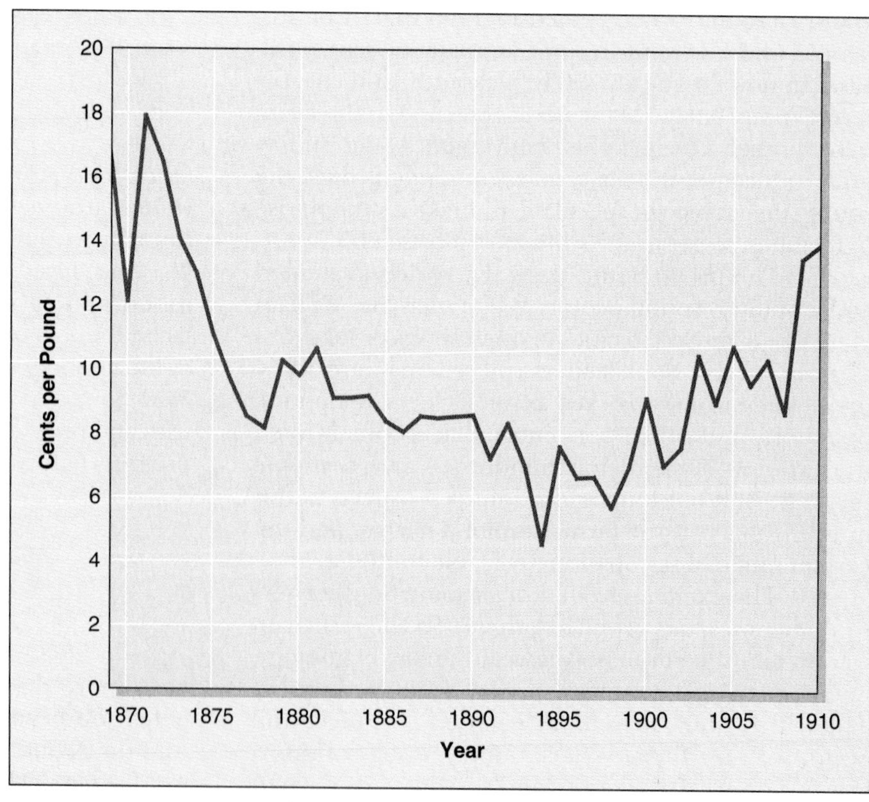

Figure 19-2 The Price of Cotton, 1869–1910

The steadily declining price of cotton after the Civil War—from 18 cents a pound to 5 cents a pound by the early 1890s—reflected extreme overproduction. Behind the numbers lay an impoverished rural South.

Data Source: *U.S. Department of Commerce,* Historical Statistics of the United States: Colonial Times to 1957.

chinery or irrigation system. James Barrett, a farmer outside Augusta, Georgia, said of his experiment with diversification in 1900: "I have diversified, and I have not made any money by diversification. . . . I grow green peas and everything I know of. I have raised horses, cows, and hogs, and I have diversified it for the last three years and have not been able to make a dollar."

Southern Farmers Organize, 1877–1892

As their circumstances deteriorated, southern farmers fought back. They engaged in barter when they could. They supplemented their income with occasional jobs off the farm and by selling eggs or vegetables. They lobbied for debt-stay laws and formed farmer organizations. They had lived a communal life of church, family, and kin. Now they would widen the circle of their community to include other farmers sharing their plight. These were not naive country folk—most owned their own land and participated in the market economy. They just wanted to make the market fairer, to lower interest rates and ease credit, to regulate railroad freight rates, and to keep the prices of necessities in check.

But these goals required legislation that neither the federal government nor southern state governments were inclined to support. No presidential administration between 1877 and 1900, Republican or Democrat, favored debt relief or extensive regulation of business. And the Redeemer Democrats who gained control of the southern state governments after Reconstruction represented large landowners and merchants, not poor farmers.

To strengthen their authority and suppress dissent, the Redeemer Democrats appealed to racial and regional solidarity among white Southerners. They portrayed themselves as having saved the South from the rule of black people and Republicans. Insurgent farmers who challenged this leadership risked being branded as disloyal.

The Democrats nonetheless faced opposition beginning soon after they had wrested control of southern state governments from the Republicans. In some states, like North Carolina, the Republicans retained support in mountain areas and among black people. In addition, disaffected white farmers mounted independent political campaigns against the Redeemers in several states in the late 1870s and early 1880s to demand currency reform and the easing of credit. But the Democrats, in firm control of the election machinery throughout the South, turned back these challenges. Although Independents at one point succeeded in gaining control of the Virginia legislature, their few other victories were confined to the local level. Hard-pressed farmers began to organize on a broader scale.

Southern farmers joined their colleagues nationwide to address common grievances related to pricing, credit, and tax policies. Though some of the southern farmers' problems resulted from conditions particular to the South, agricultural distress became widespread in the decades after 1870. By 1875, nearly 250,000 southern landowners had joined the National **Grange** of the Patrons of Husbandry or, more popularly, simply the Grange (see Chapter 22). The leaders of the Grange, however, were large landowners. Their interests were not the same as the small farmers who made up the organization's rank and file. The Grange leadership in the South, for example, while nominally concerned about issues of concern to small farmers, such as exploitative merchants and excessive railroad freight rates, favored policies—like fence laws to pen animals and protect crops and

The faces of this white sharecropper family in North Carolina reflect the harshness of farm life in the late nineteenth- and early twentieth-century South, a period when thousands of Southerners, white and black alike, slipped from land ownership to sharecropping.

controls on farm labor—that hurt small farmers. The rank-and-file members, in contrast, pushed a more radical agenda including establishing community stores, cotton gins, and warehouses to bypass the prevailing credit system.

Despite a few successes, the Grange failed to stem the reverses of small southern farmers. As a result, the farmers were drawn to new agricultural organizations that emerged in the 1880s promising to promote their interests more forcefully. In 1882, for example, a group of farmers in Arkansas formed an organization called the **Agricultural Wheel** that had attracted more than 500,000 southern farmers by 1887. Wheelers tried to purchase farm equipment directly from manufacturers, avoiding merchant middlemen. Unlike the Grange, they called for an array of federal programs to ease the credit and cash burdens of farmers, including a graduated income tax and the printing and distribution of more paper money.

The most potent agricultural reform organization, the **Southern Farmers' Alliance**, originated in Texas in the late 1870s. Alliance-sponsored farmers' **cooperatives** provided their members with discounts on supplies and credit. Members also benefited from marketing their cotton crops collectively. The Alliance was not the only organization to form cooperatives, but it was unique in the messianic zeal with which it promoted them. Although it endorsed some candidates for office, the Alliance was not a political party and did not challenge Democratic domination of the South.

The Alliance was still very much a Texas organization in 1887 when Charles W. Macune, a Wisconsin native, became its driving force. Macune sent a corps of speakers to create a network of southern cooperatives. Within two years, the Alliance had spread throughout the South and into the North and West. By 1890, it claimed more than a million members. With the exception of a few large landowners and some tenant farmers, almost all were small farmers who owned their own land. The success of the Alliance reflected both the desperate struggle of these small farmers to keep their land and the failure of other organizations to help them.

The Alliance operated like a religious denomination. Its leaders preached a message of salvation through cooperation to as many as twenty thousand people at huge revival-like rallies. Qualifications for membership included a belief in the divinity of Christ and the literal truth of the Bible. Alliance speakers, many of them rural ministers, often held meetings in churches. In their talks, they combined biblical nostrums with economic policy and stressed the importance of doing good as much as good farming. They urged members to visit "the homes where lacerated hearts are bleeding, to assuage the suffering of a brother or a sister, bury the dead, care for the widows and educate the orphans." The Alliance lobbied state legislatures to fund rural public schools. To increase the sense of community, the Alliance sponsored picnics, baseball games, and concerts.

The Alliance became for many small farmers a surrogate government and church in a region where public officials and many mainline Protestant ministers ignored their needs. It imposed strict morality on its members, prohibiting drinking, gambling, and sexual misconduct. Alliance leaders criticized many Baptist, Methodist, and Presbyterian ministers for straying from the traditional emphasis on individual salvation and for defending a status quo that benefited large planters and towns. Cyrus Thompson, North Carolina Alliance president and a prominent Methodist, declared in 1889 that "the church today stands where it has always stood, on the side of human slavery."

Some Alliance members left their churches for new religious groups. The Holiness movement, which began in the North before the Civil War, revived among Texas farmers in the mid-1880s. Holiness disciples advocated simple dress, avoided coffee and pork, and swore off all worldly amusements. The members of the Church of God, which formed in the mountains of Tennessee and North Carolina in 1886, similarly sought to cleanse themselves of secular evils. The new churches promoted a vision of an egalitarian South. They accepted women on an equal basis and occasionally black people as well. As many as a third of Holiness preachers were women.

Women also found an active role as officers and speakers in the Alliance. As a Texas woman declared, "The Alliance has come to redeem woman from her enslaved condition. She is admitted into the organization as the equal of her brother, and the ostracism which has impeded her intellectual progress in the past is not met with."

Unlike some of the new religious movements, however, the Alliance did not accept black members. Black farmers formed the first **Colored Farmers' Alliance** in Texas in 1886. The Colored Alliance had fewer landowners and more tenants and sharecroppers in its ranks than the white organization. It concerned itself with issues relevant to this constituency, such as higher wages for cotton pickers. In 1891, the Colored Alliance attempted a regionwide strike over farm wages but was unable to enforce it in the worsening southern economy.

The white Alliance had better results with a protest over price fixing. To protect cotton shipped to market, farmers wrapped it in a burlaplike material called jute. In 1888, jute manufacturers combined to raise the price from 7 cents to as much as 14 cents a yard. The Alliance initiated a jute boycott throughout the South, telling farmers to use cotton bagging as an alternative. The protest worked, forcing the chastened jute manufacturers to offer farmers their product at a mere 5 cents per yard.

This success encouraged Macune to pursue a more ambitious project. Low cotton prices and a lack of cash kept farmers poor. To address these problems, Macune proposed his **subtreasury plan**. Alliance members were to store their crops in a subtreasury (a warehouse), keeping their cotton off the market until the price rose. In the meantime, the government would loan the farmers up to 80 percent of the value of the stored crops at a low interest rate of 2 percent per year. This arrangement would free farmers from merchants' high interest rates and crop liens.

Macune urged Alliance members to endorse political candidates who supported the subtreasury scheme. Many Democratic candidates for state legislatures throughout the South did endorse it and were elected with Alliance backing in 1890. Once in office, however, they failed to deliver.

The failure of the subtreasury plan combined with a steep drop in cotton prices after 1890 undermined the Alliance. Its cooperatives collapsed as crop liens cut down small landowners as though with scythes. A Georgia Allianceman wrote in 1891 that "Hundreds of farmers will be turned adrift, and thousands of acres of our best land allowed to grow up in weeds through lack of necessary capital to work them." Alliance membership declined by two-thirds in Georgia that year. Desperate Alliance leaders merged their organization with a new national political party in 1892, the People's or **Populist party**. Populists appropriated the Alliance program and challenged Democrats in the South and Republicans in the West. The merger reflected desperation more than calculation.

Southern Populists

Northern farmers, like their southern counterparts, faced growing financial pressure in the 1880s that by the early 1890s had led them too to join the Alliance. Just as southern farmers had turned to the Democratic party to redress their grievances, northern farmers turned to the dominant party in the northern farming states—the Republican party—to redress theirs. Like the Democrats, the Republicans failed to respond. Beginning in Kansas in 1890, disillusioned farmers formed the People's party, soon called the Populist party. The Populists held their first national nominating convention in Omaha in July 1892.

The Populists supported a wide range of reforms, many adopted from the Alliance, including the direct election of United States senators by popular vote rather than by state legislatures, an income tax, woman suffrage, government ownership of railroads, and various proposals to ease credit. As we will see in Chapter 22, the Populists stirred up national politics between 1892 and 1896. In the South, they challenged the Democratic party, sometimes courting Republicans, including black voters.

Southern populists were ambivalent about African Americans. On the one hand, black people constituted a potential voting bloc the Populists could ill afford to ignore. On the other hand, appealing to black voters would expose Populists to demagogic attacks from Democrats for undermining white supremacy, frightening away potential white backers. Populists who wanted to extend the hand of fellowship to black people risked withering fire from Democrats. The *Baton Rouge Daily Advocate,* for example, informed its readers in 1892 that the Populist party was "the most dangerous and insidious foe of white supremacy." Many southern Populists, including former members of the Alliance, supported segregation and never made the gesture of racial reconciliation.

Despite the risks, in at least two southern states, Texas and Georgia, Populists openly appealed for black votes. In Texas, black Populist John B. Rayner, the "silver-tongued orator of the colored race," spoke to racially mixed audiences around the state. The Texas Populist platform called for "equal justice and protection under the law to all citizens without reference to race, color or nationality." In Georgia, Populist leader Tom Watson supported a biracial party organization and counseled white people to accept black people as partners in their common crusade. "You are kept apart," Watson told black and white Georgians, "that you may be separately fleeced of your earnings. You are made to hate each other because upon that hatred is rested the keystone of the arch of financial despotism which enslaves you both."

Despite Rayner's and Watson's efforts, most black people remained loyal to the Republican party for its role in abolishing slavery and for the few patronage crumbs the party still threw their way. Black people also suspected Populists' motives. The party appealed mainly to small, landowning farmers, not, as most black Southerners were, propertyless tenants and sharecroppers. And even the Texas Populists, while appealing for black support, opposed black officeholding and jury service.

Unwilling or unable to mobilize black voters and unsuccessful in dislodging white voters from the

Democratic party, the Populists finished a distant third in the 1892 presidential election. In the South, their only significant inroads were in the state legislatures of Texas, Alabama, and Georgia. Even in these states, widespread voter fraud among Democrats undermined Populist strength.

Despite a deepening economic depression, the Populists had only a few additional successes in the South after 1892. Their major victory was in North Carolina in 1894. Republicans had remained a political force in the state's mountain counties and among black people in its eastern part. Adopting a fusion strategy, the Populists ran candidates on a combined ticket with Republicans. The fusion candidates captured the governorship and state legislature. Once in office, they overhauled the state electoral machinery, eased voter registration procedures, and established nonpartisan electoral panels to monitor elections. Reflecting Populist influence, they also imposed limits on interest rates, increased expenditures for education, and raised taxes on railroads.

Higher cotton prices and returning prosperity in the late 1890s, however, undermined Populist support in North Carolina, as in the rest of the South. In 1896, the Populists assisted in their own nationwide demise by merging with the Democrats for the presidential election of 1896. In 1898, Democrats surged back into office in North Carolina on the strength of a virulent white supremacy campaign and promptly undid the work of the fusionists.

Women in the New South

Just as farm women found their voices in the Alliance movement of the 1880s, a growing group of middle-class white and black urban women entered the public realm and engaged in policy issues. In the late-nineteenth-century North, women became increasingly active in reform movements, including woman suffrage, labor legislation, social welfare, and city planning. Building on their antebellum activist traditions, northern women, sometimes acting in concert with men, sought to improve the status of women in society.

Antebellum reform movements, because they included abolitionism, had made little headway in the South. As a result, southern women had a meager reform tradition to build on. The war also left them ambivalent about independence. With husbands, fathers, and brothers dead or incapacitated, many women had to care for themselves and their families in the face of defeat and deprivation. Some determined never again to depend on men. Others, responding to the stress of running a farm or business, would have preferred less independence.

The response of southern white men to the war also complicated women's efforts to improve their status. Southern men had been shaken by defeat. They had lost the war and placed their families in peril. Many responded with alcoholism and violence. To regain their self-esteem, they recast the war as a noble crusade rather than a defeat. And they imagined southern white women as paragons of virtue and purity who required men to defend them. Demands for even small changes in traditional gender roles would threaten this image. Southern women understood this and never mounted an extensive reform campaign like their sisters in the North. Some middle-class women were openly hostile to reform, and others adopted conservative causes more inclined to reinforce the role of men in southern society than to challenge it.

Despite such limitations, middle-class southern women found opportunities to broaden their social role and enter the public sphere in the two decades after 1880. They found these opportunities primarily in the cities, where servants, stores, and schools freed them of many of the productive functions—like making clothing, cooking, and child care—that burdened their sisters in the country and kept them tied to the home.

Church Work and Preserving Memories

Southern women waded warily into the public arena, using channels men granted them as natural extensions of the home, such as church work. The movement to found **home mission societies**, for example, was led by single white women in the Methodist church. Home missions promoted industrial education among the poor and helped working-class women become self-sufficient. The home mission movement reflected an increased interest in missionary work among white southern evangelical churches. Laura Haygood, an Atlantan who had served as a missionary in China, founded a home mission in Atlanta when she returned in 1883. Lily Hammond, another Atlantan, extended the mission concept when she opened **settlement houses** in black and white city neighborhoods in Atlanta in the 1890s. Settlement houses, pioneered in New York in the 1880s, promoted middle-class values in poor neighborhoods and provided them with a permanent source of services. In the North, they were privately sponsored. In the South, they were supported by the Methodist church and known as Wesley Houses, after John Wesley, the founder of Methodism.

Religion also prompted southern white women to join the **Women's Christian Temperance**

Union (WCTU). The first southern local formed in Lucy Haygood's church in Atlanta in 1880. Temperance reform, unlike other church-inspired activities, involved women directly in public policy. Women framed temperance and the prohibition of alcohol as a family issue—alcohol ruined families, victimizing innocent women and children. WCTU members visited schools to educate children about the evils of alcohol, addressed prisoners, and blanketed men's meetings with literature. As a result, they became familiar with the South's abysmal school system and its archaic criminal justice system. They thus began advocating education and prison reform as well as legislation against alcohol.

By the 1890s, many WCTU members realized that they couldn't achieve their goals unless women had the vote. Rebecca Latimer Felton, an Atlanta suffragist and WCTU member, reflected the frustration of her generation of southern women in an address to working women in 1892:

> But some will say—you women might be quiet—you can't vote, you can't do anything! Exactly so—we have kept quiet for nearly a hundred years hoping to see relief come to the women of this country—and it hasn't come. How long must our children be slain? If a mad dog should come into my yard, and attempt to bite my child or myself—would you think me out of my place, if I killed him with a dull meat axe? . . . [You] would call that woman a brave woman . . . and yet are we to sit by while drink ruins our homes?

Despite the WCTU's roots in southern churches, the activism of its members alarmed some southern men. WCTU rhetoric implied a veiled attack on men. Felton, for example, often referred to men who drank as "beasts." And WCTU members had many other issues besides prohibition on their agenda. When the WCTU held its national convention in Atlanta in 1890, local Baptist and Methodist ministers launched a bitter attack against the organization, claiming that it drew women into activities contrary to the Scriptures and that its endorsement of woman suffrage subverted traditional family values.

Few women, however, had such radical objectives in mind. Rebecca Felton's own career highlighted the essentially conservative nature of the reform movement among middle-class women in the New South. Born in 1835 to a wealthy planter family, she attended college and married Dr. William H. Felton, a physician and minister twelve years her senior. During the Civil War and its aftermath, the Feltons eked out a modest living teaching school and working a small farm. Four of their five children died. Seeing southern families worse off than her own, Felton threw herself into a variety of reform activities, ranging from woman suffrage to campaigns against drinking, smoking, and Coca-Cola. She fought for child care facilities, sex education, and compulsory school attendance and pushed for the admission of women to the University of Georgia. But she strongly supported textile operators over textile workers and defended white supremacy. She had no qualms about the **lynching** of black men—executing them without trial—"a thousand times a week if necessary" to preserve the purity of white women. In 1922, she became the first woman member of the U.S. Senate. By any definition, Felton was a reformer, but like most middle-class southern women, she had no interest in challenging the class and racial inequities of the New South.

The dedication of southern women to commemorating the memory of the Confederate cause also suggested the conservative nature of middle-class women's reform in the New South. Ladies' Memorial Associations formed after the war to ensure the proper burial of Confederate soldiers and suitable markings for their graves. The associations joined with men to erect monuments to Confederate leaders and, by the 1880s, to the common soldier. These activities reinforced white solidarity and constructed a common heritage for all white Southerners regardless of class or location. By the 1890s, women planned monuments in prominent civic spaces in the urban South. Their efforts sparked interest in city planning and city beautification. A new organization, the United Daughters of the Confederacy (UDC), appeared in 1894 to preserve southern history and honor its heroes. Although men formed similar associations, women remained the most active protectors of regional memory. Work for the Lost Cause reflected traditional roles, but it also offered a way for women to hone leadership and organizational skills, preparing them for less traditional public activities in the 1890s. Gertrude Thomas, for example, one of the South's leading suffragists, played an important role in the Georgia UDC.

Women's Clubs

A broader spectrum of southern middle-class women joined women's clubs than joined church-sponsored organizations or memorial associations. Most clubs began in the 1880s as literary or self-improvement societies that had little interest in reform. By 1890, most towns and cities boasted at least several women's clubs and perhaps a federated club organization. But, also by that time, some clubs and their members had begun to discuss political issues such as child labor reform, educational improvement,

FROM THEN TO NOW

The Confederate Battle Flag

Memories of the Civil War and Reconstruction formed a crucial part of southern civic and religious culture from the late nineteenth century onward. Southerners perceived themselves and the rest of the nation through the lens of the heroic Lost Cause and the alleged abuses of Reconstruction, and the symbols associated with those events took on the status of icons. During the 1890s, the memory industry that white political and religious leaders had promoted since the end of the war became institutionalized. Organizations such as the United Daughters of the Confederacy and the Sons of the Confederate Veterans strove to educate a new generation of white Southerners on the meanings of the sacrifices of the war generation, bolstering the imposition of white supremacy through racial segregation and disfranchisement.

The Confederate battle flag emerged from this process as an icon of the Lost Cause and a symbol of white supremacy. Alabama, for example, redesigned its state flag in the 1890s to resemble more closely the battle flag. Its red St. Andrews cross on a white background symbolized the blood spilled in defense of the Southern homeland and the supremacy of the white race.

Still, the Confederate battle flag itself was displayed mostly at veterans' reunions and only rarely at other public occasions—until the late 1940s, that is, when civil rights for African Americans emerged as a national issue for the first time since the Reconstruction era. In 1948, Mississippians waved the flag at Ole Miss football games for the first time. In 1956, as the civil rights struggle in the South gained momentum, the state of Georgia incorporated the battle flag into its state flag. And, in 1962, as sit-ins and Freedom Riders spread throughout the South, officials in South Carolina—claiming to be commemorating the Civil War centennial—hoisted the battle flag above the State House in Columbia.

The centennial is long-gone, but the battle flag continues to fly in Columbia and adorn the Georgia state flag. This official display has become a focus of heated controversy. Proponents argue that the battle flag represents heritage, not hate. Opponents denounce it as a symbol of white supremacy. In the mid-1990s, South Carolina's Republican Governor David Beasley, seeking to defuse the issue, proposed removing the flag from atop the Capitol and installing it at a nearby history museum. The resulting firestorm of protest from some of the Governor's white constituents forced him to reverse himself, however, and contributed to his defeat in his bid for reelection.

The flag controversy erupted again in 1999 when South Carolina's state Democratic Party chairman urged voters to return a Democratic legislature that would, once and for all, remove the flag from the State Capitol. The angry response from both Republicans and some Democrats forced the new Democratic governor, who had been searching for a compromise on the issue since taking office in January 1999, to quickly distance himself from the proposal. Then, in July 1999 the National Association for the Advancement of Colored People (NAACP) announced a national boycott of South Carolina beginning in January 2000. Facing the loss of convention and tourist revenues, business groups pleaded with lawmakers to lower the flag.

When people in other parts of the country sometimes remark that white Southerners are still fighting the Civil War, it's controversies like that over the battle flag they have in mind. But the controversy is less about the past than it is about the way we use history to shape our understanding of the society we live in and our vision of its future. At issue is not just history, but *whose* history. In that sense the flag controversy, as much as it picks at wounds more than a century old, can to some extent at least generate positive dialogue. Even so, in the interests of reconciliation, it's surely time for Southerners to follow Robert E. Lee's final order to his men and "Furl the flag, boys."

The Confederate battle flag on this parade float reflects its emerging status as an icon of the Lost Cause in the late nineteenth century.

and prison reform. The Arkansas Federation of Women's Clubs launched a boycott of goods produced by "exploited" labor in 1903. The Lone Star (Texas) Federation scrutinized public hospitals, almshouses, and orphanages at the turn of the century. Its president asserted, "The Lone Star Federation stands for the highest and truest type of womanhood—that which lends her voice as well as her hand." Southern women's club members sought out their sisters in the North. As Georgia's federated club president, Mrs. A. O. Granger, wrote in 1906, "Women of intellectual keenness in the South could not be left out of the awakening of the women of the whole country to a realization of the responsibility which they properly had in the condition of their fellow-women and of the children."

This pursuit of solidarity with women in the North did not extend to the members of black women's clubs in the South. The activities of black women's clubs paralleled those of white women's clubs. Only rarely, however—as at some meetings of the Young Women's Christian Association (YWCA) or occasional meetings in support of prohibition—did black and white club members interact.

Some white clubwomen expressed sympathy for black women privately, but publicly they maintained white solidarity. Most were unwilling to sacrifice their own reform agenda to the cause of racial reconciliation. Women suffragists in the South, for example, did not make common cause with black people. On the contrary, some used racial solidarity as a weapon to promote white women's right to vote, arguing that the combined vote of white men and women would further white interests.

The primary interest of most southern white women's clubs was the plight of young white working-class and farm women. This interest reflected the growing number of such women in the work force. Single and adrift in the city, many worked for low wages, and some slipped into prostitution. The clubs sought to help them make the transition from rural to urban life or to improve their lives on the farm. To this end, they focused on child labor reform and on upgrading public education.

Settling the Race Issue

The assertiveness of a new generation of African Americans, especially those in urban areas, in the 1880s and 1890s provided the impetus and opportunity for white leaders to secure white solidarity. To counter black aspirations, white leaders enlisted the support of young white Southerners, convincing them that the struggle for white supremacy would place them beside the larger-than-life heroes of the Civil War generation. African Americans resisted the resulting efforts to deprive them of their remaining freedoms. Though some left the South, many more built new lives and communities within the restricted framework white Southerners allowed them.

The Fluidity of Southern Race Relations, 1877–1890

Race relations remained remarkably fluid in the South between the end of Reconstruction and the early 1890s. Despite the departure of federal troops and the end of Republican rule, many black people continued to vote and hold office. Some Democrats even courted the black electorate. Though segregation ruled in churches, schools, and in some organizations and public places after the Civil War, black people and white people continued to mingle, do business with each other, and often maintain cordial relations.

In 1885, T. McCants Stewart, a black journalist from New York, traveled to his native South Carolina expecting a rough reception once his train headed south from Washington, D.C. To his surprise, the conductor allowed him to remain in his seat while white riders sat on baggage or stood. He provoked little reaction among white passengers when he entered the dining car. Some of them struck up a conversation with him. Stewart, who admitted he had begun his journey with "a chip on my shoulder . . . [daring] any man to knock it off," now observed that "the whites of the South are really less afraid to [have] contact with colored people than the whites of the North." In Columbia, South Carolina, Stewart found that he could move about with no restrictions. "I can ride in first-class cars. . . . I can go into saloons and get refreshments even as in New York. I can stop in and drink a glass of soda and be more politely waited upon than in some parts of New England."

Other black people corroborated Stewart's experiences. John Gray Lucas, a native of Pine Bluff, Arkansas, attended law school in Boston. There, in an 1887 newspaper interview, Lucas noted that three of Pine Bluff's eight city councilmen and half the police force were black and that black people encountered no segregation or discrimination in public careers. Given the racial climate in Pine Bluff, Lucas wondered "why more colored young men from the North did not make Arkansas their home. It is an inviting field for them, and a grand opportunity to make something of themselves." Lucas followed his own advice and returned to Pine Bluff, where he embarked on a successful legal career in the 1890s.

During the 1880s, black people joined interracial labor unions and continued to be active in the Republican party. They engaged in business with white people. In the countryside, African Americans and white people hunted and fished together, worked side by side at sawmills, and traded with each other. Cities were segregated more by class than by race, and people of both races sometimes lived in the same neighborhoods. To be sure, black people faced discrimination in employment and voting and random retaliation for perceived violations of racial barriers. But those barriers were by no means fixed.

The White Backlash

The black generation that came of age in this environment demanded full participation in American society. As the young black editor of Nashville's *Fisk Herald* proclaimed in 1889, "We are not the Negro from whom the chains of slavery fell a quarter of a century ago. . . . We are now qualified, and being the equal of whites, should be treated as such." Charles Price, an educator from North Carolina, admonished colleagues in 1890, "If we do not possess the manhood and patriotism to stand up in the defense of . . . constitutional rights and protest long, loud and unitedly against their continual infringements, we are unworthy of heritage as American citizens and deserve to have fastened on us the wrongs of which many are disposed to complain."

For many in the generation of white Southerners who came of age in the same period, this assertiveness rankled. These young white people, raised on the myth of the Lost Cause, were continually reminded of the heroism and sacrifice of their fathers during the Civil War. Confronted with what was for many worse conditions than their families had enjoyed before the war, they resented the changed status of black people. For them, black people replaced the Yankees as the enemy; they saw it as their mission to preserve white purity and dominance. Echoing these sentiments, David Schenck, a Greensboro, North Carolina, businessman, wrote in 1890 that "the breach between the races widens as the young free negroes grow up and intrude themselves on white society and nothing prevents the white people of the South from annihilating the negro race but the military power of the United States Government." Using the Darwinian language popular among educated white people at the time, Schenck concluded, "I pity the Negro, but the struggle is for the survival of the fittest race."

The South's deteriorating rural economy and the volatile politics of the late 1880s and early 1890s exacerbated the growing tensions between assertive black people and threatened white people. So too did the growth of industry and cities in the South. In the cities, black and white people came in close contact, competing for jobs and jostling each other for seats on streetcars and trains. Racist rhetoric and violence against black people accelerated in the 1890s.

Lynch Law

In 1892, three prominent black men, Tom Moss, Calvin McDowell, and William Stewart, opened a grocery on the south side of Memphis, an area with a large African-American population. The People's Grocery prospered while a white-owned store across the street struggled. The proprietor of the white-owned store, W. H. Barrett, was incensed. He secured an indictment against Moss, McDowell, and Stewart for maintaining a public nuisance. Outraged black community leaders called a protest meeting at the grocery during which two people made threats against Barrett. Barrett learned of the threats, noti-

Lynching became a public spectacle, a ritual designed to reinforce white supremacy. Note the matter-of-fact satisfaction of the spectators to this gruesome murder of a black man.

fied the police, and warned the gathering at the People's Grocery that white people planned to attack and destroy the store. Nine sheriff's deputies, all white, approached the store to arrest the men who had threatened Barrett. Fearing Barrett's threatened white assault, the people in the grocery fired on the deputies, unaware who they were, and wounded three. When the deputies identified themselves, thirty black people surrendered, including Moss, McDowell, and Stewart, and were imprisoned. Four days later, deputies removed the three owners from jail, took them to a deserted area, and shot them dead.

The men at the People's Grocery had violated two of the unspoken rules that white Southerners imposed on black Southerners to maintain racial barriers: They had prospered, and they had forcefully challenged white authority. During 1892, a year of political agitation and economic depression, 235 lynchings occurred in the South. White mobs lynched nearly two thousand black Southerners between 1882 and 1903. During the 1890s, lynchings occurred at the rate of 150 a year. Most lynchers were working-class whites with rural roots who were struggling in the depressed economy of the 1890s and enraged at the fluidity of urban race relations. The men who murdered Moss, McDowell, and Stewart, for example, had recently moved to Memphis from the countryside, where they had been unable to make a living farming.

The silence or tepid disapproval of white leaders condoned this orgy of violence. The substitution of lynch law for a court of law seemed a cheap price to pay for white solidarity at a time when political and economic pressures threatened entrenched white leaders. In 1893, Atlanta's Methodist bishop, Atticus G. Haygood, typically a spokesman for racial moderation, objected to the torture some white lynchers inflicted on their victims but added, "Unless assaults by Negroes on white women and little girls come to an end, there will most probably be still further displays of vengeance that will shock the world."

Haygood's comments reflect the most common justification for lynching—the presumed threat posed by black men to the sexual virtue of white women. Sexual "crimes" could include remarks, glances, and gestures. Yet only 25 percent of the lynchings that took place in the thirty years after 1890 had some alleged sexual connection. Certainly, the men of the People's Grocery had committed no sex crime. Lynchers did not carry out their grisly crimes to end a rape epidemic; they killed to keep black men in their place and to restore their own sense of manhood and honor.

Ida B. Wells, who owned a black newspaper in Memphis, used her columns to publicize the People's Grocery lynchings. The great casualty of the lynchings, she noted, was her faith that education, wealth, and upright living guaranteed black people the equality and justice they had long sought. The reverse was true. The more black people succeeded, the greater was their threat to white people. She investigated other lynchings, countering the claim that they were the result of assaults on white women. When she suggested that, on the contrary, perhaps some white women were attracted to black men, she enraged the white citizens of Memphis, who destroyed her press and office. Exiled to Chicago, Wells devoted herself to the struggle for racial justice.

Segregation by Law

Southern white lawmakers sought to cement white solidarity and ensure black subservience in the 1890s by instituting **segregation** by law and the **disfranchisement** of black voters. Racial segregation restricting black Americans to separate and rarely equal public facilities had prevailed nationwide before the Civil

Ida B. Wells, an outspoken critic of lynching, fled to Chicago following the People's Grocery lynchings in Memphis in 1892 and became a national civil rights leader.

War. After 1870, the custom spread rapidly in southern cities. In Richmond by the early 1870s, segregation laws required black people registering to vote to enter through separate doors and registrars to count their ballots separately. The city's prison and hospitals were segregated. So too were its horse-drawn railways, its schools, and most of its restaurants, hotels, and theaters.

During the same period, many northern cities and states, often in response to protests by African Americans, were ending segregation. Massachusetts, for example, passed the nation's first public accommodations law in May 1865, desegregating all public facilities. Cities such as New York, Cleveland, and Cincinnati desegregated their streetcars. Chicago, Cleveland, Milwaukee, and the entire state of Michigan desegregated their public school systems. Roughly 95 percent of the nation's black population, however, lived in the South. Integration in the North consequently required white people to give up very little to black people. And as African-American aspirations increased in the South during the 1890s as their political power waned, they became more vulnerable to segregation by law at the state level. At the same time, migration to cities, industrial development, and technologies such as railroads and elevators increased the opportunities for racial contact and muddled the rules of racial interaction.

Much of the new legislation focused on railroads, a symbol of modernity and mobility in the New South. Local laws and customs could not control racial interaction on interstate railroads. White passengers objected to black passengers' implied assertion of economic and social equality when they sat with them in dining cars and first-class compartments. Black Southerners, in contrast, viewed equal access to railroad facilities as a sign of respectability and acceptance. When southern state legislatures required railroads to provide segregated facilities, black people protested.

The railroad segregation laws required the railroads to provide "separate but equal" accommodations for black passengers. Railroads balked at the expense involved in doing so and provided black passengers with distinctly inferior facilities. Many lines refused to sell first-class tickets to black people and treated them roughly if they sat in first-class seats or tried to eat in the dining car. In 1890, Homer Plessy, a black Louisianan, refused to leave the first-class car of a railroad traveling through the state. Arrested, he filed suit, arguing that his payment of the first-class fare entitled him to sit in the same first-class accommodations as white passengers. He claimed that under his right of citizenship guaranteed by the Fourteenth Amendment, neither the state of Louisiana nor the railroad could discriminate against him on the basis of color. The Constitution, he claimed, was colorblind.

The U.S. Supreme Court ruled on the case, ***Plessy* v. *Ferguson***, in 1896. In a seven-to-one decision, the Court held that Louisiana's railroad segregation law did not violate the Constitution as long as the railroads or the state provided equal accommodations. The decision left unclear what "equal" meant. In the Court's view, "Legislation is powerless to eradicate racial instincts," meaning that segregation of the races was natural and transcended constitutional considerations. The only justice to vote against the decision was John Marshall Harlan, a Kentuckian and former slave owner. In a stinging dissent, he predicted that the decision would result in an all-out assault on black rights. "The destinies of the two races . . . are indissolubly linked together," Harlan declared, "and the interests of both require that the common government of all shall not permit the seeds of race hate to be planted under the sanction of law."

Harlan's was a prophetic dissent. Both northern and southern states enacted new segregation laws in the wake of *Plessy* v. *Ferguson.* In practice, the separate facilities for black people these laws required, if provided at all, were rarely equal. A sense of futility, time, expense, and physical danger dissuaded black people from challenging the statutes. Protests in the press, appeals to white leaders, and occasional boycotts failed to stem the rising tide. By 1900, segregation by law extended to public conveyances, theaters, hotels, restaurants, parks, and schools.

The segregation statutes came to be known collectively as **Jim Crow laws**, after the blackface stage persona of Thomas Rice, a white northern minstrel show performer in the 1820s. Reflecting white stereotypes of African Americans, Rice caricatured Crow as a foolish, elderly, lame slave who spoke in an exaggerated dialect.

Economic segregation followed social segregation. Before the Civil War, black men had dominated crafts such as carpentry and masonry. By the 1890s, white men were replacing them in these trades and excluding them from new trades such as plumbing and electrical work. Trade unions, composed primarily of craft workers, began systematically to exclude African Americans. Although the steel and tobacco industries hired black workers, most other manufacturers turned them away. Confined increasingly to low or unskilled positions in

OVERVIEW

THE MARCH OF DISFRANCHISEMENT ACROSS THE SOUTH, 1889–1908

Year	State	Strategies
1889	Florida	Poll tax
1889	Tennessee	Poll tax
1890	Mississippi	Poll tax, literacy test, understanding clause
1891	Arkansas	Poll tax
1893, 1901	Alabama	Poll tax, literacy test, grandfather clause
1894, 1895	South Carolina	Poll tax, literacy test, understanding clause
1894, 1902	Virginia	Poll tax, literacy test, understanding clause
1897, 1898	Louisiana	Poll tax, literacy test, grandfather clause
1899, 1900	North Carolina	Poll tax, literacy test, grandfather clause
1902	Texas	Poll tax
1908	Georgia	Poll tax, literacy test, understanding clause, grandfather clause

railroad construction, the timber industry, and agriculture, black people underwent **deskilling**—a decline in workforce expertise—after 1890. With lower incomes from unskilled labor, they faced reduced opportunities for better housing and education.

Disfranchisement

With economic and social segregation came political isolation. The authority of post-Reconstruction Redeemer governments had rested on their ability to limit and control the black vote. Following the political instability of the late 1880s and the 1890s, however, white leaders determined to disfranchise black people altogether, thereby reinforcing white solidarity and eliminating the need to consider black interests. Obstacles loomed—the Fifteenth Amendment, which guaranteed freedmen the right to vote, and a Republican-dominated Congress—but with a national consensus emerging in support of white supremacy, they proved easy to circumvent.

Rural and urban white elites engineered the disfranchisement campaigns. Support for disfranchisement was especially strong among large landowners in the South's plantation districts, where heavy concentrations of black people threatened their political domination. Urban leaders, especially after the turmoil of the 1890s, looked on disfranchisement as a way to stabilize politics and make elections more predictable.

The movement to reduce or eliminate the black vote in the South began in the 1880s and continued through the early 1900s (see the overview table, "The March of Disfranchisement across the South, 1889–1908"). Democrats enacted a variety of measures to attain their objectives without violating the letter of the Fifteenth Amendment. They complicated the registration and voting processes. States enacted **poll taxes**, requiring citizens to pay to vote. They adopted the secret ballot, which confused and intimidated illiterate black voters accustomed to using ballots with colors to identify parties. States set literacy and educational qualifications for voting or required prospective registrants to "interpret" a section of the state constitution. To avoid disfranchising poor, illiterate white voters with these measures, states enacted **grandfather clauses** granting the vote automatically to anyone whose grandfather could have voted prior to 1867 (the year Congressional Reconstruction began). The grandfathers of

American Views

Robert Smalls Argues against Disfranchisement

Born in Beaufort, South Carolina, in 1839, Robert Smalls served as a slave pilot in Charleston Harbor. In 1862, he emancipated himself, with his family and friends, when he delivered a Confederate steamer, the *Planter*, to a Union fleet blockading the harbor. He entered politics in 1864 as a delegate from his state to the Republican National Convention. He helped write South Carolina's Reconstruction constitution, which, among its provisions, guaranteed the right of former slaves to vote and hold office. Smalls won election to the state house of representatives in 1869, the state senate in 1871, and the U.S. House of Representatives in 1875. With opportunities for African Americans to hold public office declining following Reconstruction, Smalls secured appointment as collector of the Port of Beaufort, a federal post he occupied until his death in 1915. In the speech excerpted here—delivered to the South Carolina Constitutional Convention of 1895—he bitterly assails the state's plan to disfranchise black voters.

- ❖ **From the white perspective, what is Smalls's most telling argument against the disfranchisement and the planned strategies to implement it?**
- ❖ **How does Smalls depict the black citizens of South Carolina?**
- ❖ **Why were white political leaders unmoved by Smalls's plea?**

Mr. President, this convention has been called for no other purpose than the disfranchisement of the negro. . . .

The negroes are paying taxes in the south on $263,000,000 worth of property. In South Carolina, according to the census, the negroes pay tax on $12,500,000 worth of property. That was in 1890. You voted down without discussion . . . a proposition for a simple property and education qualification [for voting]. What do you want? . . .

most black men in the 1890s had been slaves, ineligible to vote.

Tennessee was the first state to pass disfranchising legislation. In 1889, it required the secret ballot and a poll tax in four cities—Nashville, Memphis, Chattanooga, and Knoxville—where African Americans often held a balance of power. A year later, Mississippi amended its constitution to require voters to pass a literacy test and prove they "understood" the state constitution. The laws granted the registrar wide latitude in interpreting the accuracy of the registrant's understanding. When a journalist asked an Alabama lawmaker if Jesus Christ could pass his state's "understanding" test, the legislator replied, "That would depend entirely on which way he was going to vote."

Lawmakers sold white citizens on franchise restrictions with the promise that they would apply only to black voters and would scarcely affect white voters. This promise proved untrue. Alarmed by the Populist uprising, Democratic leaders used disfranchisement to gut dissenting parties. During the 1880s, minority parties in the South consistently polled an average of 40 percent of the statewide vote; by the mid-1890s, that figure had diminished to 30 percent, despite the Populist insurgency. Turnout dropped even more dramatically. In Mississippi, for example, voter turnout in gubernatorial races during the 1880s averaged 51 percent; during the 1890s, it was 21 percent. Black turnout in Mississippi, which averaged 39 percent in the 1880s, plummeted to near zero in the 1890s. Over-

In behalf of the 600,000 negroes in the State and the 132,000 negro voters all that I demand is that a fair and honest election law be passed. We care not what the qualifications imposed are, all that we ask is that they be fair and honest, and honorable, and with these provisos we will stand or fall by it. You have 102,000 white men over 21 years of age, 13,000 of these cannot read nor write. You dare not disfranchise them, and you know that the man who proposes it will never be elected to another office in the State of South Carolina. . . . Fifty-eight thousand negroes cannot read nor write. This leaves a majority of 14,000 white men who can read and write over the same class of negroes in this State. We are willing to accept a scheme that provides that no man who cannot read nor write can vote, if you dare pass it. How can you expect an ordinary man to "understand and explain" any section of the Constitution, to correspond to the interpretation put upon it by the manager of election, when by a very recent decision of the supreme court, composed of the most learned men in State, two of them put one construction upon a section, and the other justice put an entirely different construction upon it. To embody such a provision in the election law would be to mean that every white man would interpret it aright and every negro would interpret it wrong. . . . Some morning you may wake up to find that the bone and sinew of your country is gone. The negro is needed in the cotton fields and in the low country rice fields, and if you impose too hard conditions upon the negro in this State there will be nothing else for him to do but to leave. What then will you do about your phosphate works? No one but a negro can work them; the mines that pay the interest on your State debt. I tell you the negro is the bone and sinew of your country and you cannot do without him. I do not believe you want to get rid of the negro, else why did you impose a high tax on immigration agents who might come here to get him to leave?

Now, Mr. President we should not talk one thing and mean another. We should not deceive ourselves. Let us make a Constitution that is fair, honest and just. Let us make a Constitution for all the people, one we will be proud of and our children will receive with delight.

Source: The Columbia State, *October 27, 1895.*

all turnout, which averaged 64 percent during the 1880s, fell to only 30 percent by 1910.

Black people protested disfranchisement vigorously. When 160 South Carolina delegates gathered to amend the state constitution in 1895, the six black delegates among them mounted a passionate but futile defense of their right to vote. Black delegate W. J. Whipper noted the irony of white people clamoring for supremacy when they already held the vast majority of the state's elected offices. He also pointed out that African Americans voted responsibly where they had a majority and frequently elected white candidates. Robert Smalls, the state's leading black politician, urged delegates not to turn their backs on the state's black population (see "American Views: Robert Smalls Argues against Disfranchisement"). Such pleas fell on deaf ears.

A National Consensus on Race

How could the South get away with it? How could Southerners openly segregate, disfranchise, and lynch African Americans without a national outcry? Apparently, the majority of Americans in the 1890s subscribed to the notion that black people were inferior to white people and deserved to be treated as second-class citizens. Contemporary depictions of black people show scarcely human stereotypes: black men with bulbous lips and bulging eyes, fat black women wearing turbans and smiling vacuously, and black children contentedly eating watermelon or romping with jungle animals. These images appeared on cereal boxes, in advertisements, in children's books, in newspaper cartoons, and as lawn ornaments. Popular theater of the day featured white men in blackface cavorting in

Racial stereotypes permeated American popular culture by the turn of the twentieth century. Images like this advertisement for Pullman railroad cars, which depicts a deferential black porter attending to white passengers, reinforced racist beliefs that black people belonged in servile roles. Immersed in such images, white people assumed they depicted the natural order of things.

ridiculous fashion and singing songs such as "All Coons Look Alike to Me" and "I Wish My Color Would Fade." Among the widely read books of the era was *The Clansman,* a glorification of the rise of the Ku Klux Klan by Thomas Dixon, a North Carolinian living in New York City and an ardent white supremacist. D. W. Griffith transformed *The Clansman* into an immensely popular motion picture epic under the title *Birth of a Nation.*

Intellectual and political opinion in the North bolstered southern policy. So-called "scientific" racism purported to establish white superiority and black inferiority on biological grounds. Northern-born professional historians reinterpreted the Civil War and Reconstruction in the white South's favor. Historian William A. Dunning, the generation's leading authority on Reconstruction, wrote in 1901 that the North's "views as to the political capacity of the blacks had been irrational." Respected journals openly supported disfranchisement and segregation. The progressive journal *Outlook* hailed disfranchisement because it made it "impossible in the future for ignorant, shiftless, and corrupt negroes to misrepresent their race in political action." Harvard's Charles Francis Adams, Jr., chided colleagues who disregarded the "fundamental, scientific facts" he claimed demonstrated black inferiority. The *New York Times,* summarizing this national consensus in 1903, noted that "practically the whole country" supported the "southern solution" to the race issue, because "there was no other possible settlement."

These views permeated Congress, which made no effort to block the institutionalization of white supremacy in the South after 1890, and the courts, which upheld discriminatory legislation. As a delegate at the Alabama disfranchisement convention of 1901 noted, "The race problem is no longer confined to the States of the South, [and] we have the sympathy instead of the hostility of the North."

By the mid-1890s, Republicans were so entrenched in the North and West that they did not need southern votes to win presidential elections or to control Congress. Besides, business-oriented Republicans found common ground with conservative southern Democrats on fiscal policy and foreign affairs.

As the white consensus on race emerged, the status of African Americans slipped in the North as well as the South. Although no northern states threatened to deny black citizens the right to vote, they did increase segregation. The booming industries of the North generally did not hire black workers. Antidiscrimination laws on the books since the Civil War went unenforced. In 1904, 1906, and 1908, race riots erupted in Springfield, Ohio; Greensburg, Indiana; and Springfield, Illinois, matching similar disturbances in Wilmington, North Carolina, and Atlanta, Georgia.

Response of the Black Community

American democracy had, it seemed, hung out a "whites only" sign. How could African Americans respond to the growing political, social, and economic restrictions on their lives? Given white America's hostility, protest proved ineffective, even dangerous. African Americans organized more than a dozen boycotts of streetcar systems in the urban South between 1896 and 1908 in an effort to desegregate them, but not one succeeded. The Afro-American Council, formed in 1890 to protest the deteriorating conditions of black life, accomplished little and disbanded in 1908. W. E. B. Du Bois organized an annual Conference on Negro Problems at Atlanta University beginning in 1896, but it produced no effective plan of action.

A few black people chose to leave the South. In 1879, Benjamin "Pap" Singleton, a Nashville real estate agent, led several thousand black migrants to Kansas. Henry McNeal Turner of Georgia, an African Methodist Episcopal (AME) bishop, promoted migration to Liberia, but only a few hundred made the trip in the late 1870s, Turner not included, and most of those returned disappointed. Most black people who moved in the 1890s stayed within the South, settling in places like Mississippi, Louisiana, and Texas, where they could find work with timber companies or farming new lands that had opened to cotton and rice cultivation.

More commonly, black people withdrew to develop their own rich community life within the restricted confines white society permitted them. Particularly in the cities of the South, they could live relatively free of white surveillance and even white contact. In 1890, fully 70 percent of black city dwellers lived in the South; and between 1860 and 1900, the proportion of black people in the cities of the South rose from one in six to more than one in three. The institutions, businesses, and families that black people began painstakingly building during Reconstruction continued to grow, and in some cases flourish, after 1877.

By the 1880s, a new black middle class had emerged in the South. Urban-based, professional, business-oriented, and serving a primarily black clientele, its members fashioned an interconnected web of churches, fraternal and self-help organizations, families, and businesses. Black Baptists, AME, and AME Zion churches led reform efforts in the black community, seeking to eliminate drinking, prostitution, and other vices in black neighborhoods.

African-American fraternal and self-help groups, led by middle-class black people, functioned as surrogate welfare organizations for the poor. Some groups, such as the Colored Masons and the Colored Odd Fellows, paralleled white organizations. Black membership rates usually exceeded those in the white community. More than 50 percent of Nashville's black men, for example, belonged to various fraternal associations in the city. Fraternal orders also served as the seedbed for such business ventures as the North Carolina Mutual Life Insurance Company, founded in Durham in 1898. Within two decades, North Carolina Mutual became the largest black-owned business in the nation and helped transform Durham into the "capital of the black middle class." Durham's thriving black business district included several black-owned insurance firms, banks, and a textile mill. Most southern cities boasted active black business districts by the 1890s.

Nashville's J. C. Napier typified the activism of the African-American urban middle class in the New South era. He belonged to two of the city's prominent black churches, was active in Republican politics, played an important role in several temperance and fraternal societies, served as president of

The offices of the North Carolina Mutual Life Insurance Company, around 1900. Founded by John Merrick, C. C. Spaulding, and Dr. A. M. Moore (all of whom appear in this picture), this Durham-based insurance company became one of the most successful black enterprises in the country.

the local black YMCA chapter, and as an attorney helped his fellow African Americans with numerous legal matters. Before disfranchisement in the 1890s, Napier used his leverage to secure the appointment of black teachers for black schools and of black applicants to the police force and fire department.

The African-American middle class worked especially hard to improve black education (see Figure 19-3). Declining black political power encouraged white leaders to reduce funding for black public education. Black students in cities had only makeshift facilities; those in the countryside had almost no facilities. By the early 1900s, the student–teacher ratio in Nashville's segregated school system was thirty-three to one for white schools but seventy-one to one for black schools. To improve these conditions, black middle-class leaders solicited educational funds from northern philanthropic organizations.

Black women played an increasingly active and prominent role in African-American communities after 1877, especially in cities. The experience of Ida B. Wells illustrates this trend. When she moved to Memphis from Mississippi in 1884, she entered an environment that, despite her race and gender, offered her opportunities for intellectual growth and a professional career. In December 1886, for example, she attended a lecture at an interracial Knights of Labor meeting (see Chapter 20). Earlier that year, she witnessed a religious revival conducted by the nation's leading evangelist, Dwight Moody. The following year, Wells began her journalism career and soon purchased a one-third interest in a local black newspaper.

Black women's clubs evolved to address the new era in race relations. Most African-American women in southern cities worked as domestics or laundresses. Black women's clubs supported day care facilities for working mothers and settlement houses in poor black neighborhoods modeled after those in northern cities. Atlanta's Neighborhood Union, founded by Lugenia Burns Hope in 1908, provided playgrounds and a health center and secured a grant from a New York foundation to improve black education in the city. Black women's clubs also established homes for single black working women to protect them from sexual exploitation, and they worked for woman suffrage "to reckon with men who place no value on her [black woman's] virtue," as Nannie H. Burroughs of the **National Association of Colored Women** argued at the turn of the century.

Black clubwomen were aware of their leadership role in the first postemancipation generation.

Figure 19-3 Disfranchisement and Educational Spending in the South, 1890–1910
By barring black people from the political process, franchise restrictions limited their access to government services. Educational expenditures—which increased for white people but decreased for black people following disfranchisement—provide one measure of the result.

Data Source: Robert A. Margo, "Disfranchisement, School Finance, and the Economics of Segregated Schools in the United States South, 1890–1910," Ph.D. diss., Harvard University, 1982.

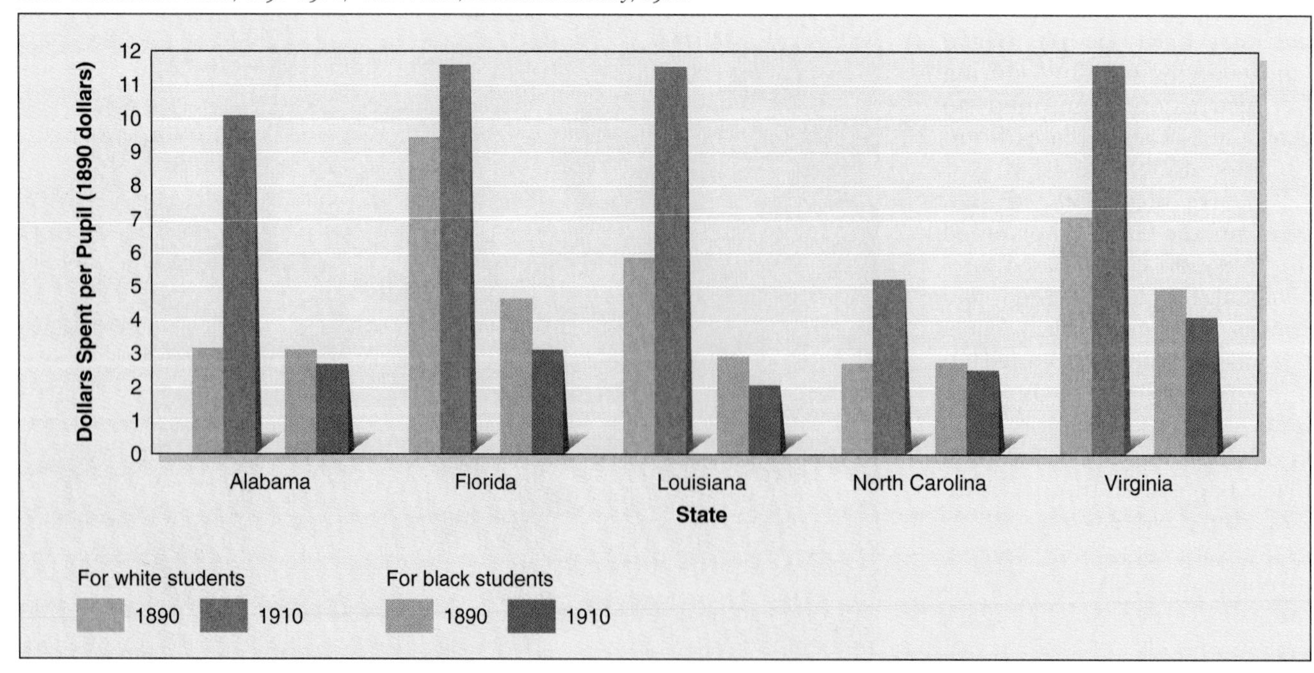

Anna J. Cooper, a Nashville clubwoman, wrote in 1892 that to be a member of this generation was "to have a heritage unique in the ages." Assertive black women did not arouse the same degree of white antagonism as assertive black men. They could operate in a broader public arena than men and speak out more forcefully. Sometimes what they spoke out about was political corruption within the black community itself. They were critical, for example, of the willingness of poor black people to accept bribes and other favors in exchange for their votes, a willingness they saw at least partially responsible for black disfranchisement.

As such views suggest, middle-class black clubwomen, like other middle-class reformers, were sometimes disdainful of the poor even as they worked to help them. Mary Church Terrell, for example, president of the National Association of Colored Women, informed her colleagues in 1900 that association-sponsored day care programs assisted their "benighted sisters in the Black Belt of Alabama . . . whose ignorance of everything that makes life sweet or worth the living, no ray of light would have penetrated but for us."

After disfranchisement, middle-class black women assumed an even more pivotal role in the black community. They often used their relations with prominent white women and organizations such as the WCTU and the Young Womens Christian Association (YWCA) to press for public commitments to improve the health and education of African Americans. Absent political pressure from black men, as well as the danger of African-American males asserting themselves in the tense racial climate after 1890, black women became critical spokespersons for their race.

The extension of black club work into rural areas of the South, where the majority of the African-American population lived, to educate families about hygiene, nutrition, and child care, anticipated similar efforts among white women after 1900. But unlike their white counterparts, these middle-class black women worked with limited resources in a context of simmering racial hostility and political and economic impotence. In response, they nurtured a self-help strategy to improve the conditions of the people they sought to help. One of the most prominent African-American leaders of the late nineteenth and early twentieth centuries, Booker T. Washington, adopted a similar approach to racial uplift.

Born a slave in Virginia in 1856, Washington and his family worked in the salt and coal mines of West Virginia after the Civil War. Ambitious and flushed with the postwar enthusiasm for advancement that gripped freedmen, he enrolled in Hampton Normal and Agricultural Institute, the premier black educational institution in the South at that time. Washington worked his way through Hampton, graduated, taught for a time, and then, in 1881, founded the **Tuskegee Institute** for black students in rural Alabama. Washington thought his students would be best served if they learned a trade and workplace discipline. By learning industrial skills, he maintained, black people could secure self-respect and economic independence. As a result, Tuskegee emphasized vocational training over the liberal arts.

Washington argued that African Americans should accommodate themselves to segregation and disfranchisement until they could prove their economic worth to American society. In exchange for this accommodation, however, white people should help provide black people with

Booker T. Washington (left) and W. E. B. Du Bois (right). The differences between these two prominent black leaders reflected in part the differences between the North and the South in the late nineteenth and early twentieth centuries. The northern-born Du Bois challenged segregation and pinned his hopes for improving the condition of African Americans on a talented elite. The southern-born Washington counseled acquiescence to segregation, maintaining that black people could ultimately gain the acceptance of white society through self-improvement and hard work.

the education and job training they would need to gain their independence. Washington articulated this position, known as the **Atlanta Compromise**, in a speech at the Atlanta Cotton States and International Exposition in 1895. Despite his conciliatory public stance, Washington secretly helped finance legal challenges to segregation and disfranchisement. The social and economic realities of the South, meanwhile, frustrated his educational mission. Increasingly, black people were shut out of the kinds of jobs for which Washington hoped to train them. Facing a depressed rural economy and growing racial violence, they had little prospect of advancement.

Another prominent African-American leader, W. E. B. Du Bois, challenged Washington's acceptance of black social inequality. Born in Massachusetts in 1868, Du Bois was the first African-American to earn a doctorate at Harvard. Du Bois promoted self-help, education, and black pride. A gifted teacher and writer, he taught at Atlanta University and wrote eighteen books on various aspects of black life in America. In *The Souls of Black Folk,* published in 1903, he described the strengths of black culture and attacked Washington's Atlanta Compromise. Du Bois was a cofounder, in 1910, of the **National Association for the Advancement of Colored People (NAACP)**, an interracial organization dedicated to restoring African-American political and social rights.

Despite their differences, which reflected their divergent backgrounds, Washington and Du Bois agreed on many issues. Both had reservations about allowing illiterate black people to vote, and both believed that black success in the South required some white assistance. As Du Bois wrote in *The Souls of Black Folk,* "Any movement for the elevation of the Southern Negro needs the cooperation, the sympathy, and the support of the best white people in order to succeed." But it became apparent to Du Bois that "the best white people" did not care to elevate black Southerners. In 1906, after a bloody race riot in Atlanta, Du Bois left the South, a decision millions of black Southerners would make over the next two decades.

A curtain had descended between black and white, North and South on the issue of race. Northerners did not care to look behind that curtain to acknowledge the injustice of southern treatment of black people. As long as it provided the raw materials for the North's new urban industrial economy and maintained the peace, the South could count on the rest of the country not to interfere in its solution to race relations. Indeed, to the extent that most white Americans concerned themselves with race, they agreed with the southern solution.

Conclusion

In many respects, the South was more like the rest of the nation in 1900 than at any other time since 1860. Southern cities hummed with activity and industries from textiles to steel dotted the southern interior. Young men and women migrated to southern cities to pursue opportunities unavailable to their parents. Advances in the production and marketing of cigarettes and soft drinks would soon make southern entrepreneurs and their products household names. Southerners ordered fashions from Sears, Roebuck catalogs and enjoyed electric lights, electric trolleys, and indoor plumbing as much as other urban Americans.

Americans idealized the South—not the urban industrial South but a mythical South of rural grace and hospitality. National magazines and publishers rushed to print stories about this land of moonlight and magnolias, offering it as a counterpoint to the crowded, immigrant-infested, factory-fouled, money-grubbing North. It was this fantasy South that white people in both the North and the South imagined as they came to a common view on race and reconciled their differences. Northern journalists offered admiring portraits of southern heroes like Robert E. Lee, of whom one declared in 1906, "the nation has a hero to place beside her greatest." The Republican-dominated Congress agreed to care for the graves of the Confederate dead and ordered the return to the South of captured Confederate flags.

White Southerners cultivated national reconciliation but remained fiercely dedicated to preserving the peculiarities of their region: a one-party political system, disfranchisement, and segregation by law. The region's urban and industrial growth, impressive from the vantage of 1865, paled before that of the North. The South remained a colonial economy characterized more by deep rural poverty than urban prosperity.

How one viewed the New South depended on one's vantage point. White Northerners accepted at face value the picture Southerners painted for them of a chastened and prosperous yet still attractive region. Middle-class white people in the urban South enjoyed the benefits of a national economy and a secure social position. Middle-class white women enjoyed increased influence in the public realm, but not to the extent of their northern sisters. And the institutionalization of white supremacy gave even poor white farmers and factory workers a place in the social hierarchy a rung or two above the bottom.

For black people, the New South proved a crueler ruse than Reconstruction. No one now stepped forward to support their cause and stem the erosion of their economic independence, political freedom, and civil rights. Yet they did not give up the American dream, nor did they give up the South for the most part. They built communities and worked as best they could to challenge restrictions on their freedom.

The New South was thus both American and southern. It shared with the rest of the country a period of rapid urban and industrial growth. But the legacy of war and slavery still lay heavily on the South, manifesting itself in rural poverty, segregation, and black disfranchisement. The burdens of this legacy would limit the attainments of both black and white Southerners for another half-century until Americans finally rejected racial inequality as an affront to their national ideals.

Review Questions

1. In what ways did the growing activism of white middle-class women, the increasing assertiveness of young urban black people, and the persistence of the agricultural depression affect the politics of the South in the late 1880s and early 1890s?
2. We associate segregation and disfranchisement with reactionary political and social views. Yet many white people who promoted both seriously believed them to be reforms. How could white people hold such a view?
3. What strategies did black Southerners employ in response to the narrowing of economic and political opportunities in the New South?
4. New South publicists promoted the South as an emerging urban and industrial region. How accurate were their assertions in 1900?

Recommended Reading

Edward L. Ayers, *The Promise of the New South: Life after Reconstruction* (1992). Illuminates how the people of the late-nineteenth-century South accommodated the conflict between the economic and cultural legacies of the slave South and the currents of modernity, such as industrialization and the creation of a national state.

Paul M. Gaston, *The New South Creed: A Study in Southern Mythmaking* (1970). Provides an important assessment of how New South booster rhetoric matched up against the economic reality; especially good at examining how New South spokesmen turned images of the Old South and other southern traditions to the ends of urban and industrial development.

Walter Hines Page, *The Rebuilding of Old Commonwealths* (1902). The classic argument for the New South from one of its most serious promoters.

Howard N. Rabinowitz, *The First New South, 1865–1920* (1992). An interpretive survey of recent research on the era that explores a continuity between the Old South and the New that may have limited the latter's potential.

Howard N. Rabinowitz, *Race Relations in the Urban South, 1865–1890* (1978). A fine survey of how African Americans built communities in the urban South despite the worsening racial situation after Reconstruction.

Joel Williamson, *The Crucible of Race: Black–White Relations in the American South since Emancipation* (1984). An innovative work that details the racial attitudes of white Southerners and reveals how elites particularly used race to further political and social objectives.

C. Vann Woodward, *Origins of the New South, 1877–1913* (1951). A classic interpretation of the New South era that stresses the discontinuities between Old South and New.

Additional Sources

The Newness of the New South

Dwight B. Billings, Jr., *Planters and the Making of a "New South"* (1979).

Orville Vernon Burton, *In My Father's House Are Many Mansions: Family and Community in Edgefield County, South Carolina* (1985).

Orville Vernon Burton and Robert C. McMath, eds., *Toward a New South?* (1982).

David L. Carlton, *Mill and Town in South Carolina, 1880–1920* (1980).

Thomas D. Clark, *Pills, Petticoats, and Plows: The Southern Country Store* (1944).

John Milton Cooper, Jr., *Walter Hines Page* (1977).

Harold E. Davis, *Henry Grady's New South: Atlanta, a Brave and Beautiful City* (1990).

Don H. Doyle, *New Men, New Cities, New South: Atlanta, Nashville, Charleston, Mobile, 1860–1910* (1990).

Robert F. Durden, *The Dukes of Durham, 1865–1929* (1975).

Ronald D. Eller, *Miners, Millhands, and Mountaineers: Industrialization of the Appalachian South, 1880–1920* (1982).

Paul D. Escott, *Many Excellent People: Power and Privilege in North Carolina, 1850–1900* (1985).

Jacqueline Dowd Hall et al., *Like a Family: The Making of a Southern Cotton Mill World* (1987).

Patrick J. Hearden, *Independence and Empire: The New South's Cotton Mill Campaign, 1865–1901* (1982).

Tony Horwitz, *Confederates in the Attic: Dispatches from the Unfinished Civil War* (1998).

Maury Klein, *The Great Richmond Terminal: A Study in Businessmen and Business Strategy* (1970).

W. David Lewis, *Sloss Furnaces and the Rise of the Birmingham District: An Industrial Epic* (1994).

Cathy McHugh, *Mill Family: The Labor System in the Southern Cotton Textile Industry, 1880–1915* (1988).

Broadus Mitchell, *The Rise of Cotton Mills in the South* (1921).

Gail W. O'Brien, *The Legal Fraternity and the Making of a New South Community, 1848–1882* (1986).

James M. Russell, *Atlanta, 1847–1890: City Building in the Old South and the New* (1988).

Laurence Shore, *Southern Capitalists: The Ideological Leadership of an Elite, 1832–1885* (1986).

John S. Spratt, *The Road to Spindletop: Economic Change in Texas, 1875–1901* (1970).

John F. Stover, *The Railroads of the South, 1865–1900* (1955).

Nannie M. Tilley, *The Bright-Tobacco Industry, 1860–1929* (1948).

Nannie M. Tilley, *The R. J. Reynolds Tobacco Company* (1985).

Gavin Wright, *Old South, New South: Revolutions in the Southern Economy since the Civil War* (1986).

Kathleen Minnix, *Laughter in the Amen Corner: The Life of Evangelist Sam Jones* (1993).

I. A. Newby, *Plain Folk in the New South: Social Change and Cultural Persistence, 1880–1915* (1989).

Ted Ownby, *Subduing Satan: Religion, Recreation, and Manhood in the Rural South, 1865–1920* (1990).

Bruce Palmer, *"Man over Money": The Southern Populist Critique of American Capitalism* (1980).

Roger Ransom and Richard Sutch, *One Kind of Freedom: The Economic Consequences of Emancipation* (1977).

Theodore Saloutos, *Farmer Movements in the South, 1865–1933* (1960).

Michael Schwartz, *Radical Politics and Social Structure: The Southern Farmers' Alliance and Cotton Tenancy, 1880–1890* (1978).

Barton C. Shaw, *The Wool-Hat Boys: A History of the Populist Party in Georgia, 1892 to 1910* (1984).

Crandall A. Shifflett, *Patronage and Poverty in the Tobacco South: Louisa County, Virginia, 1860–1900* (1982).

Peter Wallenstein, *From Slave South to New South: Public Policy in Nineteenth-Century Georgia* (1987).

Samuel L. Webb, *Two-Party Politics in the One-Party South: Alabama's Hill Country, 1874–1920* (1997).

Jonathan Wiener, *Social Origins of the New South: Alabama, 1860–1885* (1978).

Harold D. Woodman, *King Cotton and His Retainers: Financing and Marketing the Cotton Crop of the South, 1800–1925* (1968).

C. Vann Woodward, *Tom Watson: Agrarian Rebel* (1938).

The Southern Agrarian Revolt

Raymond Arsenault, *Wild Ass of the Ozarks: Jeff Davis and the Social Bases of Southern Politics, 1888–1913* (1984).

Donna Barnes, *Farmers in Rebellion: The Rise and Fall of the Southern Farmers' Alliance and People's Party in Texas* (1987).

Alwyn Barr, *Reconstruction to Reform: Texas Politics, 1876–1906* (1971).

Gregg Cantrell, *Kenneth and John B. Rayner and the Limits of Southern Dissent* (1993).

Pete Daniel, *Breaking the Land: The Transformation of Cotton, Tobacco and Rice Cultures since 1880* (1985).

Gilbert Fite, *Cotton Fields No More: Southern Agriculture, 1865–1890* (1984).

Lawrence Goodwyn, *Democratic Promise: The Populist Moment in America* (1976).

Steven Hahn, *The Roots of Southern Populism: The Transformation of the Georgia Upcountry, 1850–1890* (1983).

Michael R. Hyman, *The Anti-Redeemers: Hill-Country Political Dissenters in the Lower South from Redemption to Populism* (1990).

Albert D. Kirwan, *Revolt of the Rednecks: Mississippi Politics, 1876–1925* (1951).

Robert McMath, Jr., *The Populist Vanguard: A History of the Southern Farmers' Alliance* (1975).

Women in the New South

Virginia Bernhard et al., eds., *Southern Women: Histories and Identities* (1992).

Elizabeth York Enstam, *Women and the Creation of Urban Life: Dallas, Texas, 1843–1920* (1998).

Jean E. Friedman, *The Enclosed Garden: Women and Community in the Evangelical South, 1830–1900* (1985).

Glenda Elizabeth Gilmore, *Gender and Jim Crow: Women and Politics of White Supremacy in North Carolina, 1896–1920* (1996).

Elna C. Green, *Southern Strategies: Southern Women and the Woman Suffrage Question* (1997).

Evelyn Brooks Higginbotham, *Righteous Discontent: The Women's Movement in the Black Baptist Church, 1880–1920* (1993).

Tera W. Hunter, *To 'Joy My Freedom: Southern Black Women's Lives and Labors after the Civil War* (1997).

Katherine DuPre Lumpkin, *The Making of a Southerner* (1947).

John P. McDowell, *The Social Gospel in the South: The Woman's Home Mission Movement in the Methodist Episcopal Church, South, 1886–1939* (1982).

Anne Firor Scott, *The Southern Lady: From Pedestal to Politics, 1830–1930* (1970).

Mary Church Terrell, *A Colored Woman in a White World* (1980).

Mary Martha Thomas, *The New Woman in Alabama: Social Reforms and Suffrage, 1890–1920* (1992).

Elizabeth Hayes Turner, *Women, Culture, and Community: Religion and Reform in Galveston, 1880-1920* (1997).

Marsha Wedell, *Elite Women and the Reform Impulse in Memphis, 1875–1915* (1991).

Marjorie Spruill Wheeler, *New Women of the New South: The Leaders of the Woman Suffrage Movement in the Southern States* (1993).

Settling the Race Issue

Eric Anderson, *Race and Politics in North Carolina, 1872–1901: The Black Second* (1981).

Edward L. Ayers, *Vengeance and Justice: Crime and Punishment in the Nineteenth-Century American South* (1984).

Bess Beatty, *A Revolution Gone Backwards: The Black Response to National Politics, 1876–1896* (1987).

W. Fitzhugh Brundage, *Lynching in the New South: Georgia and Virginia, 1880–1930* (1993).

John W. Cell, *The Highest Stage of White Supremacy: The Origins of Segregation in South Africa and the American South* (1982).

Bruce Clayton, *The Savage Ideal: Intolerance and Intellectual Leadership in the South, 1890–1914* (1972).

William Cohen, *At Freedom's Edge: Black Mobility and the Southern White Quest for Racial Control, 1861–1915* (1991).

Gerald H. Gaither, *Blacks and the Populist Revolt: Ballots and Bigotry in the "New South"* (1977).

Willard B. Gatewood, Jr., *Black Americans and the White Man's Burden, 1898–1903* (1975).

Janette Thomas Greenwood, *Bittersweet Legacy: The Black and White "Better Classes" in Charlotte, 1850–1910* (1994).

Louis R. Harlan, *Booker T. Washington: The Making of a Black Leader, 1856–1901* (1972).

Stanley P. Hirshson, *Farewell to the Bloody Shirt: Northern Republicans and the Southern Negro, 1877–1893* (1962).

Gerald David Jaynes, *Branches without Roots: Genesis of the Black Working Class in the American South, 1862–1882* (1986).

Robert C. Kenzer, *Enterprising Southerners: Black Economic Success in North Carolina, 1865–1915* (1997).

J. Morgan Kousser, *The Shaping of Southern Politics: Suffrage Restriction and the Establishment of the One-Party South, 1880–1910* (1974).

Daniel Letwin, *The Challenge of Interracial Unionism: Alabama Coal Miners, 1878–1921* (1998).

Charles A. Lofgren, *The Plessy Case: A Legal-Historical Interpretation* (1987).

August Meier, *Negro Thought in America, 1880–1915: Racial Ideologies in the Age of Booker T. Washington* (1963).

H. Leon Prather, *We Have Taken a City: The Wilmington Racial Massacre and Coup of 1898* (1989).

Peter J. Rachleff, *Black Labor in the South: Richmond, Virginia, 1865–1890* (1984).

Nina Silber, *The Romance of Reunion: Northerners and the South* (1993).

George B. Tindall, *South Carolina Negroes, 1877–1900* (1952).

Stewart E. Tolnay and E. M. Beck, *A Festival of Violence: An Analysis of Southern Lynchings, 1882–1930* (1995).

Walter B. Weare, *Black Business in the New South: A Social History of the North Carolina Mutual Life Insurance Company* (1973).

C. Vann Woodward, *The Strange Career of Jim Crow* (1955).

George C. Wright, *Life behind a Veil: Blacks in Louisville, Kentucky, 1865–1930* (1985).

Where to Learn More

- ❖ **Museum of the New South, Charlotte, North Carolina.** The museum has exhibits on various New South themes. A permanent exhibit on the history of Charlotte and the Carolina Piedmont opens in the fall of 2001.
- ❖ **Atlanta History Center, Atlanta, Georgia.** The major exhibit, "Metropolitan Frontiers, 1835–2000," includes a strong segment on the New South era, including the development of separate black and white economies in Atlanta. The Herndon home, also on the grounds of the center, has an exhibit on black upper-class life in Atlanta from 1880 to 1930.
- ❖ **Sloss Furnaces National Historical Landmark, Birmingham, Alabama.** The site recalls the time when Birmingham challenged Pittsburgh as the nation's primary steel-producing center.

INDUSTRY, IMMIGRANTS, AND CITIES, 1870–1900

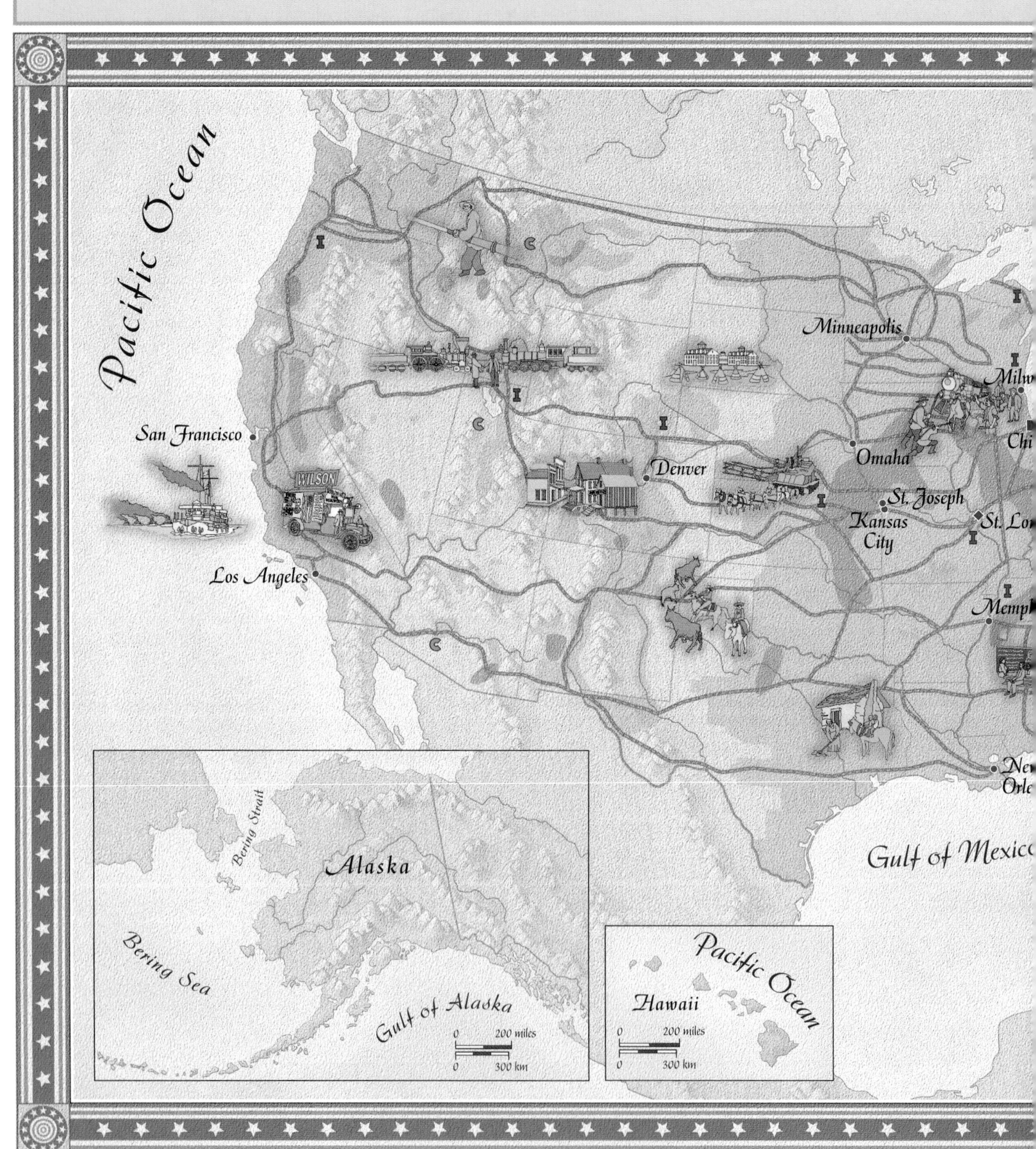

20

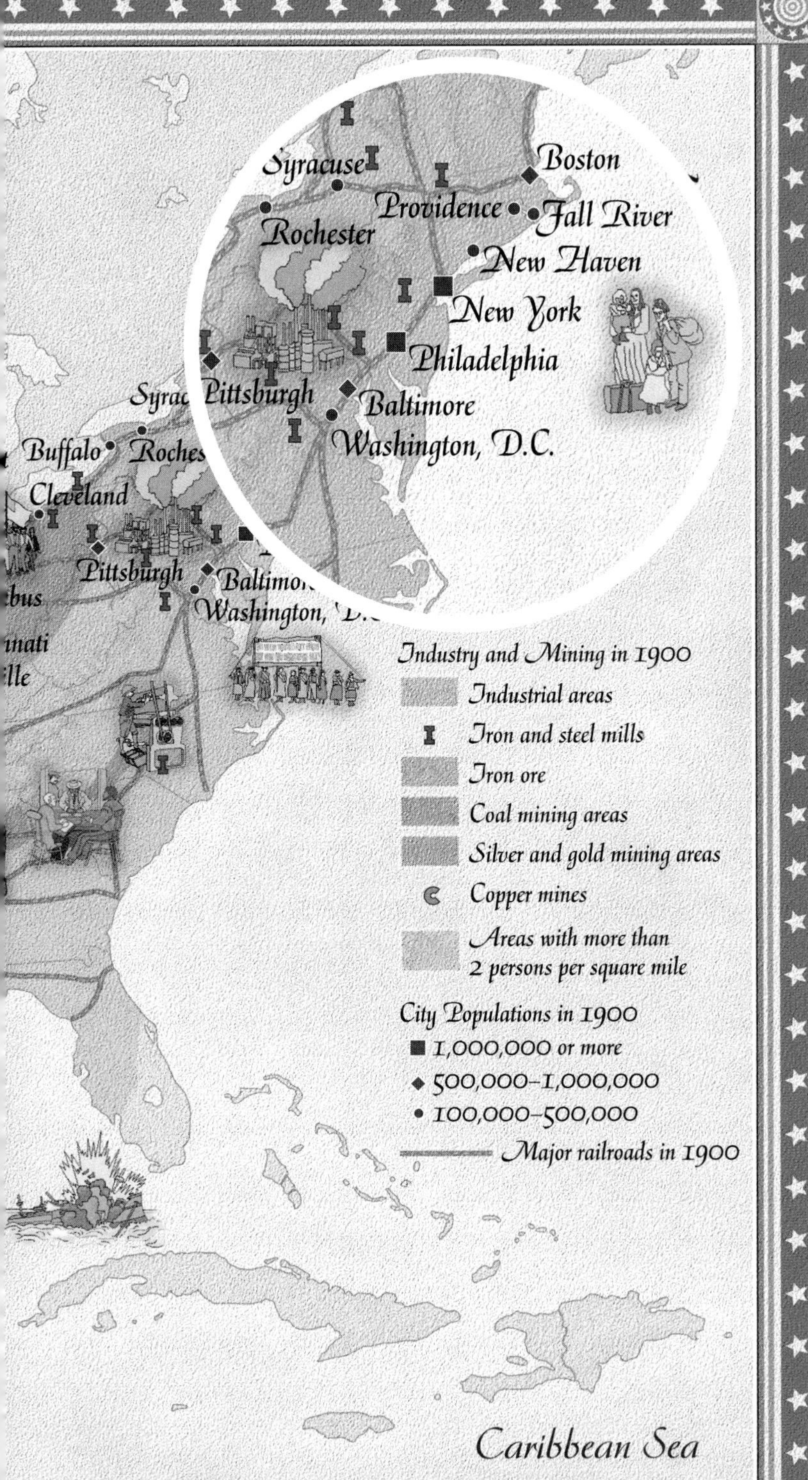

Chapter Outline

Key Topics

- The technological and organizational innovations behind the emergence of large industrial corporations
- Changes in the American workforce in the urban-industrial economy and the reaction of organized labor
- The impact of the new immigration and the start of African-American migration to the cities of the North
- The changing physical and social structure of the industrial city
- New patterns of residence and recreation in the consumer society

Philadelphia, May 10, 1876: President Ulysses S. Grant and several hundred political and military dignitaries rise to their feet as the orchestra and chorale reach the climax of Handel's "Hallelujah Chorus." A huge American flag unfurls above a nearby building, and one hundred cannons roar a deafening salute to the start of America's second century.

This ceremony opened Philadelphia's Centennial Exposition, which more than 8 million people would visit over the next six months. There they witnessed the ingenuity of the world's newest industrial power. Thomas Edison explained his new automatic telegraph, and Alexander Graham Bell demonstrated his telephone to the wonder of onlookers. A giant Corliss steam engine loomed over the entrance to Machinery Hall, dwarfing the other exhibits and providing them with power. "Yes," a visitor concluded, "it is in these things of iron and steel that the national genius most freely speaks."

For many Americans, however, the fanfare of the exposition rang hollow. The country was in the midst of a depression that had begun in 1873 and would not bottom out until 1877. Tens of thousands were out of work, and countless others had lost their savings in bank failures and sour investments. With the typical daily wage a dollar, most Philadelphians could not afford the exposition's 50-cent admission price. They celebrated instead at "Centennial City," a ragtag collection of cheap bars, seedy hotels, small restaurants, and circus sideshows hurriedly constructed of wood and tin along a muddy mile-long strip across the street from the exposition's sturdy halls and manicured lawns.

This small area of Philadelphia reflected the promise and failure of late-nineteenth century America, a period often called the **Gilded Age**. The term is taken from the title of a novel by Mark Twain that satirizes the materialistic excesses of his day. It serves as a shorthand description of the shallow worship of wealth—and the veneer of respectability and prosperity covering deep economic and social divisions—that characterized the period.

Between 1870 and 1900, the country experienced a major demographic and economic transformation. Rapid industrial development changed the nature of the work force and the workplace. Large factories staffed by semiskilled laborers displaced the skilled artisans and small shops that had dominated American industry before 1870. Industrial development also accelerated urbanization. Between the Civil War and 1900, the proportion of the nation's population living in cities—swelled by migrants from the countryside and immigrants from Europe and Asia—increased from 20 to 40 percent, a rate of growth twice that of the population as a whole. During the 1880s alone, more than 5 million immigrants came to the United States, twice as many as in any previous decade.

The changes in American life were exhilarating for some, tragic for others. New opportunities opened as old opportunities disappeared. Vast new wealth was created, but poverty increased. New technologies eased life for some but left others untouched. It would be the great dilemma of early-twentieth-century America to reconcile these contradictions and satisfy the American quest for a decent life for all within the new urban industrial order.

New Industry

Between 1870 and 1900, the United States transformed itself from an agricultural nation—a nation of farmers, merchants, and artisans—into the world's foremost industrial power, producing more than one-third of the world's manufactured goods. By the early twentieth century, factory workers made up one-fourth of the work force, and agricultural workers had dropped from a half to less than a third

In this illustration celebrating the nation's centennial and the Philadelphia Centennial Exposition, a confident Uncle Sam stands astride a continent drawn together by American technology.

(see Figure 20-1). A factory with a few dozen employees would have been judged fair-sized in 1870. By the early twentieth century, many industries employed thousands of workers in a single plant. Some industries—petroleum, steel, and meatpacking, for example—had been unknown before the Civil War.

Although the size of the industrial workforce increased dramatically, the number of firms in a given industry shrank. Mergers, changes in corporate management and the organization of the workforce, and a compliant government left a few companies in control of vast segments of the American economy. Workers, reformers, and eventually government challenged this concentration of economic power.

Inventing Technology

Technology played a major role in transforming factory work and increasing the scale of production. Steam engines like the giant Corliss engine at the Centennial Exposition and, later, electricity freed manufacturers from dependence on water power. Factories no longer had to be located by rivers. They could be built anywhere accessible to the transportation system and a concentration of labor. Technology also enabled managers to substitute machines for workers, skewing the balance of power in the workplace toward employers. And it transformed city life, making available a host of new conveniences. By the early twentieth century, electric lights, appliances, ready-made clothing, and store-bought food eased middle-class life. Electric trolleys whisked clerks, salespeople, bureaucrats, and bankers to new urban and suburban subdivisions. Electric streetlights lit up city streets at night. Amusement parks drew crowds with mechanical attractions scarcely imaginable a generation earlier. Movies entertained the masses. As historian and novelist Henry Adams put it at the turn of the century, "In the essentials of life . . . the boy of 1854 stood nearer [to] the year one than to the year 1900."

For much of the nineteenth century, the United States was dependent on the industrial nations of Europe for technological innovation. American engineers often went to England and Germany for education and training, and the textile industry, railroads, and the early steel industry benefited from German and English inventions.

In the late nineteenth century, the United States changed from a technological borrower to a technological innovator. By 1910, a million patents had been issued in the United States, 900,000 of them after 1870. Nothing represented this shift better than Thomas A. Edison's development of a practical electric lightbulb and electric generating system. Edison's invention transformed electricity into a new and versatile form of industrial energy. It also reflected a change in the relationship between science and technology. Until the late nineteenth century, advances in scientific theory usually followed technological innovation rather than the other way around. Techniques for making steel, for example, developed before scientific theories

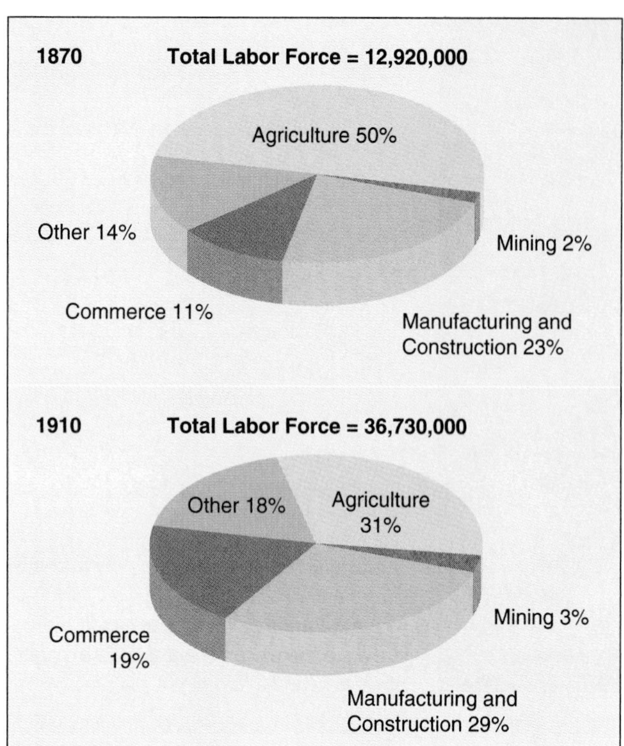

Figure 20-1 Changes in the American Labor Force, 1870–1910
The transformation of the American economy in the late nineteenth century changed the nature and type of work. By 1910 the United States was an urban, industrial nation with a matching workforce that toiled in factories and for commercial establishments (including railroads) and less frequently on farms.

emerged to explain how they worked. Textile machinery and railroad technology developed similarly. In contrast, a theoretical understanding of electricity preceded its practical use as a source of energy. Scientists had been experimenting with electricity for half a century before Edison unveiled his lightbulb in 1879. Edison's research laboratory at Menlo Park, New Jersey, also established a model for corporate-sponsored research and development that would rapidly increase the pace of technological innovation.

Edison was a problem student who had only three months of formal schooling. But he spent much of his childhood at home reading and experimenting with chemistry. In 1863, at the age of sixteen, he began working as a telegraph operator, devoting his spare time to inventing. Over the next fourteen years, he produced several practical devices, including a system for carrying multiple messages on the same telegraph wire and an improved automatic stock ticker. With the money he earned from the stock ticker, he built a factory in Newark. In 1876, he gave up the factory, established his research laboratory at Menlo Park, and turned his attention to the electric light.

Scientists had already discovered that passing an electric current through a filament in a vacuum produced light. They had not yet found a filament, however, that could last for more than a few minutes. Edison tried a variety of materials, from grass to hair from a colleague's beard, before succeeding with charred thread. In 1879, he produced a bulb that burned for an astounding forty-five hours. Then he devised a circuit that provided an even flow of current through the filament. After thrilling a crowd with the spectacle of five hundred lights ablaze on New Year's Eve in 1879, Edison went on to build a power station in New York City to serve businesses and homes by 1882. The electric age had begun.

Edison's initial success touched off a wave of research and development in Germany, Austria, Great Britain, France, and the United States. Whoever could light the world cheaply and efficiently held the key to an enormous fortune. Ultimately the prize fell not to Edison but to Elihu Thomson, a high school chemistry

A humorous view of Thomas Edison's laboratories in Menlo Park, New Jersey, around 1880. There was no joking, however, about the potential of Edison's incandescent bulb and his other practical adaptations of electricity for everyday use. Electricity would soon transform life for millions of people. Edison's methods set the precedent for corporate research and development that would accelerate the pace of new discoveries with practical applications.

Chronology

1869 The Knights of Labor is founded in Philadelphia.

1870 John D. Rockefeller forms the Standard Oil Company.

Congress passes the Naturalization Act barring Asians from citizenship.

1876 The Centennial Exposition opens in Philadelphia.

1877 The Great Uprising railroad strike, the first nationwide work stoppage in the United States, provokes violent clashes between workers and federal troops.

1879 Thomas Edison unveils the electric light bulb.

1880 Founding of the League of American Wheelmen in 1880 helps establish bicycling as one of urban America's favorite recreational activities.

1881 Assassination of Russian Tsar Alexander II begins a series of pogroms that triggers a wave of Russian Jewish immigration to the United States.

1882 Congress passes the Chinese Exclusion Act.

First country club in the United States founded in Brookline, Massachusetts.

1883 National League merges with the American Association and opens baseball to working-class fans.

1886 The Neighborhood Guild, the nation's first settlement house, opens in New York City.

Riot in Chicago's Haymarket Square breaks the Knights of Labor.

American Federation of Labor is formed.

1887 Anti-Catholic American Protective Association is formed.

1888 Wanamaker's department store introduces a "bargain room," and competitors follow suit.

1889 Jane Addams opens Hull House, the nation's most celebrated settlement house, in Chicago.

1890 Jacob A. Riis publishes *How the Other Half Lives.*

1891 African-American Chicago physician Daniel Hale Williams establishes Provident Hospital, the nation's first interracially staffed hospital.

1892 General Electric opens the first corporate research and development division in the United States.

Strike at Andrew Carnegie's Homestead steelworks fails.

1894 Pullman Sleeping Car Company strike fails.

Immigration Restriction League is formed.

1895 American-born Chinese in California form the Native Sons of the Golden State to counter nativism.

1897 George C. Tilyou opens Steeplechase Park on Coney Island in Brooklyn, New York.

1898 Congress passes the Erdman Act to provide for voluntary mediation of railroad labor disputes.

1901 Socialist Party of America is formed.

1905 Militant labor organization, the Industrial Workers of the World, is formed.

teacher in Philadelphia. Thomson, like Edison, enjoyed dabbling in electricity. Leaving teaching to devote himself to research full time, Thomson founded his own company and in 1883 moved to Connecticut, where he experimented with transformers and electric trolley equipment. Thomson purchased Edison's General Electric Company in 1892 and established the country's first corporate research and development division. His scientists produced what was then the most efficient lightbulb design, and by 1914, General Electric was producing 85 percent of the world's lightbulbs.

Following this precedent, other American companies established research and development laboratories. Standard Oil, U.S. Rubber, the chemical giant Du Pont, and the photographic company Kodak all became world leaders in their respective industries because of innovations their laboratories developed.

The process of invention that emerged in the United States gave the country a commanding technological lead. But the modernization of industry that made the United States the world's foremost industrial nation after 1900 reflected organizational as well as technological innovation. As industries sought efficient ways to apply technology and expand their markets within and beyond national borders, their workforces expanded, and their need for capital mounted. Coping with these changes required significant changes in corporate management.

The Corporation and Its Impact

The modern corporation provided the structural framework for the transformation of the American economy. A corporation is an association of individuals with legal rights and liabilities separate from those of its members. This form of business organization had existed since colonial times but became a significant factor in the American economy with the growth of railroad companies in the 1850s. A key feature of a corporation is the separation of ownership from management. A corporation can raise capital by selling stock—ownership shares—to people with no direct role in running it. The shareholders benefit from dividends drawn on profits and, if the corporation thrives, from the rising value of its stock.

The corporation had two major advantages over other forms of business organization that made it attractive to investors. First, unlike a partnership, which can dissolve when a partner dies, a corporation can outlive its founders. This durability permits long-term planning. Second, a corporation's officials and shareholders are not personally liable for its debts. If it goes bankrupt, they stand to lose only what they have invested in it.

As large corporations emerged in major American industries, they had a ripple effect on the economy. To build plants, merge with or acquire other companies, develop new technology, and hire workers, large corporations needed huge supplies of capital. They turned to the banks to help meet those needs, and the banks grew in response. The corporations stimulated technological change as they looked for ways to speed production, improve products, and lower costs. As they grew, they generated jobs.

Large industrial corporations also changed the nature of work. Into the late nineteenth century, well-paid skilled artisans, typically native-born, dominated the industrial workplace. Operating alone or in groups, they controlled the pace of their work, their output, and even the hiring and firing of coworkers. By the early twentieth century, control of the workplace was shifting to managers, and semiskilled and unskilled workers were replacing skilled artisans. These new workers, often foreign-born, performed repetitive tasks for low wages.

Because corporations usually located factories in cities, they stimulated urban growth. Large industrial districts sprawled along urban rivers and near urban rail lines. There were exceptions. Southern textile manufacturers tended to locate plants in villages and small towns and on the outskirts of larger cities. A few northern entrepreneurs also constructed industrial communities outside major cities to save on land costs and ensure control over labor. George Pullman, for example, built his railway car manufacturing plant outside of Chicago in 1880. Nonetheless, by 1900, fully 90 percent of all manufacturing occurred in cities.

Two organizational strategies—vertical integration and horizontal integration—helped successful corporations reduce competition and dominate their industries. **Vertical integration** involved the consolidation of all functions related to a particular industry, from the extraction and transport of raw materials to manufacturing and finished-product distribution and sales. Vertical integration reduced a company's dependence on outside suppliers, cutting costs and delays. Geographical dispersal went hand in hand with vertical integration. Different functions—a factory and its source of raw materials, for example—were likely to be in different places, a development made possible by advances in communication like the telephone. The multiplication of functions also prompted the growth of corporate bureaucracy.

The development of the meatpacking industry provides a good example of vertical integration. Meat is perishable and cannot be transported long distances without refrigeration. To reach eastern markets, cattlemen had to ship live animals in cattle cars from western ranges to major rail centers like Chicago. Only 40 percent of a steer is edible, so shippers were paying freight charges for a lot of commercially useless weight. In addition, some animals died in transit, and many lost weight.

Gustavus Swift, a Boston native who moved to Chicago in 1875, realized that refrigerated railway cars would make it possible to ship butchered meat, eliminating the need to transport live cattle. He invented a refrigerated car but could not sell it to the major railroads because they feared losing their substantial investment in cattle cars and pens. Swift had the cars built himself and convinced a Canadian railroad with only a small stake in cattle shipping to haul them to eastern markets. He established packing houses in Omaha and Kansas City, near the largest cattle markets; built refrigerated warehouses at key distribution points; and hired a sales force to convince eastern butchers of the quality of his product. He now controlled the production, transportation, and distribution of his product, the essence of vertical integration. By 1881, he was shipping $200,000 worth of beef a week. Competitors soon followed his example.

Horizontal integration involved the merger of competitors in the same industry. John D. Rockefeller's Standard Oil Company pioneered horizontal integration in the 1880s. Born in western New York State, the son of a traveling patent medicine salesman, Rockefeller moved to Ohio at the age of 14 in 1853. Serving as family head during his father's frequent absences, Rockefeller developed a capacity for leadership, a thirst for hard work, and a devotion to the Baptist Church. He began investing in Cleveland oil refineries by his midtwenties and formed Standard Oil in 1870. Using a variety of tactics—including threats, deceit, and price wars—Rockefeller rapidly acquired most of his competitors. Supported by investment bankers like J. P. Morgan, Standard Oil controlled 90 percent of the nation's oil refining by 1890. Acquiring oil fields and pipelines as well as refineries, it achieved both vertical and horizontal integration. Rockefeller's dominant position allowed him to impose order and predictability on the industry, ensuring a continuous flow of profits. He closed inefficient refineries, opened new ones, and kept his operations up-to-date with the latest technologies.

Other entrepreneurs achieved similar dominance in other industries and amassed similarly enormous fortunes. James B. Duke, who automated cigarette manufacturing, gained control of most of the tobacco industry. Andrew Carnegie consolidated much of the U.S. steel industry within his Carnegie Steel Company (later U.S. Steel). By 1900, Carnegie's company was producing one-quarter of the country's steel.

The concentration of American industry in the hands of a few powerful corporations alarmed many Americans. Giant corporations threatened to restrict opportunities for small entrepreneurs like the shopkeepers, farmers, and artisans who abounded at midcentury. In the words of one historian, the corporations "seemed to signal the end of an open, promising America and the beginning of a closed, unhappier society." Impersonal and governed by profit, the modern corporation challenged the ideal of the self-made man and the belief that success and advancement would reward hard work. These concerns eventually prompted the federal and state governments to respond with antitrust and other regulatory laws (see Chapters 22 and 23).

Tabloid newspapers reinforced distrust of the corporations with exposés of the sharp business practices of corporate barons like Rockefeller and Carnegie and accounts of the sumptuous lifestyles of the corporate elite. Public concern notwithstanding, however, the giant corporations helped increase the efficiency of the American economy, raise the national standard of living, and transform the United States into a major world power. Corporate expansion generated jobs that attracted rural migrants and immigrants by the millions from Europe and Asia to American cities.

The Changing Nature of Work

From the perspective of the workers, immigrant and native-born alike, the growth of giant corporations was a mixed blessing. The corporations provided abundant jobs, but they firmly controlled working conditions. A Pennsylvania coal miner spoke for many of his fellows in the 1890s when he remarked: "The working people of this country . . . find monopolies as strong as government itself. They find capital as rigid as absolute monarchy. They find their so-called independence a myth."

As late as the 1880s, shops of skilled artisans were responsible for most manufacturing in the United States. Since midcentury, however, industrialists had been introducing ways to simplify manufacturing processes so they could hire low-skilled workers. This deskilling process accelerated in the 1890s in response to new technologies, new workers, and workplace reorganization. By 1906, according to a U.S. Department of Labor report, industrial labor had been reduced to minute, low-skilled operations, making skilled artisans obsolete.

Mechanization and technological innovation did not reduce employment, although they did eliminate some jobs, most of them skilled. On the contrary, the birth of whole new industries—steel, automobiles, electrical equipment, cigarettes, food canning, and machine tools—created a huge demand for workers. Innovations in existing industries, like railroads, similarly spurred job growth. The number of people working for U.S. railroads increased from eighty thousand to more than 1 million between 1860 and 1910.

Ironically, it was a shortage of skilled workers as much as other factors that encouraged industrialists to mechanize. Unskilled workers cost less than the scarce artisans. And with massive waves of immigrants arriving from Europe and Asia between 1880 and 1920 (joined after 1910 by migrants from the American South), the supply of unskilled workers seemed limitless.

The new workers, however, shared little of the wealth generated by industrial expansion and enjoyed few of the gadgets and products generated by the new manufacturing. The eastern European immigrants who comprised three-quarters of U.S. Steel's work force during the first decade of the twentieth century received less than $12.50 a week, significantly less than the $15.00 a week a federal government survey in 1910 said an urban family needed to subsist.

Nor did large corporations put profits into improved working conditions. In 1881, on-the-job accidents maimed or killed thirty thousand railroad workers. Safety equipment existed that could have prevented many of these injuries, but the railroads refused to purchase it. At a U.S. Steel plant in Pittsburgh, injuries or death claimed one out of every four workers between 1907 and 1910. In Chicago's meat plants, injuries were commonplace. Workers grew careless from fatigue and long-term exposure to the extreme temperatures of the workplace. Meat cutters working rapidly with sharp knives often sliced fingers off their numb hands. Upton Sinclair wrote in his novel *The Jungle* (1906), a chronicle of the killing floors of meatpacking plants in Chicago, "It was to be counted as a wonder that there were not more men slaughtered than cattle."

Factory workers typically worked ten hours a day, six days a week in the 1880s. Steel workers put in twelve hours a day. Because the mills operated around the clock, once every two weeks, when the workers changed shifts, one group took a "long turn" and stayed on the job for twenty-four hours.

Long hours affected family life. By Sunday, most factory workers were too tired to do more than sit around home. During the week, they had time only to eat and sleep. As one machinist testified before a U.S. Senate investigative committee in 1883:

> They were pretty well played out when they come home, and the first thing they think of is having something to eat and sitting down, and resting, and then of striking a bed. Of course when a man is dragged out in that way he is naturally cranky, and he makes all around him cranky . . . and staring starvation in the face makes him feel sad, and the head of the house being sad, of course the whole family are the same, so the house looks like a dull prison.

Workers lived as close to the factory as possible to reduce the time and expense of getting to work. The environment around many factories, however, was almost as unwholesome as the conditions inside. A visitor to Pittsburgh in 1884 noticed "a drab twilight" hanging over the areas around the steel mills, where "gas-lights, which are left burning at mid-day, shine out of the murkiness with a dull, reddish glare." Industrial wastes fouled streams and rivers around many plants. The factories along the Cuyahoga River in Cleveland turned that waterway into an open sewer by the turn of the century.

Big factories were not characteristic of all industries after 1900. In some, like the "needle," or garment, trade, operations remained small scale. But salaries and working conditions in these industries were, if anything, worse than in the big factories. The garment industry was dominated by small manufacturers who assembled clothing for retailers from cloth provided by textile manufacturers. The manufacturers squeezed workers into small, cramped, poorly ventilated **sweatshops**. These might be in attics or lofts or even the workers' own dwellings. Workers pieced together garments on the manufacturer's sewing machines. A government investigator in Chicago in the 1890s described one sweatshop in a three-room tenement where the workers—a family of eight—both lived and worked: "The father, mother, two daughters, and a cousin work together making trousers at seventy-five cents a dozen pairs. . . . They work seven days a week. . . . Their destitution is very great."

Child Labor

Child labor was common in the garment trade and other industries. Shocked reformers in the 1890s told of the devastating effect of factory labor on children's lives, citing cases like that of a seven-year-old girl whose legs were paralyzed and deformed because she toiled "day after day with little legs crossed, pulling out bastings from garments."

Industries that employed many children were often dangerous, even for adults. In the gritty coal mines of Pennsylvania, breaker boys, youths who stood on ladders to pluck waste matter from coal tumbling down long chutes, breathed harmful coal dust all day. Girls under sixteen made up half the work force in the silk mills of Scranton and Wilkes-Barre, Pennsylvania. Girls with missing fingers from mill accidents were a common sight in those towns.

By 1900, Pennsylvania and a few other states had passed legislation regulating child labor, but enforcement of these laws was lax. Parents desperate for income often lied about their children's age, and authorities were often sympathetic toward mill or mine owners, who paid taxes and provided other civic benefits.

Working Women

Women accompanied children into the work force outside the home in increasing numbers after 1870. The comparatively low wages of unskilled male workers often required women family members to work as well. The head of the Massachusetts Bureau of Labor Statistics observed in 1882, "A family of workers can always live well, but the man with a family of small children to support, unless his wife works also, has a small chance of living properly." Between 1870 and 1920, the number of women and children in the workforce more than doubled.

Like child labor, the growing numbers of women in the workforce alarmed middle-class reformers. They worried about the impact on family life and on the women themselves. Working-class men were also concerned. The trend toward deskilling favored women. Employers, claiming that women worked only for supplemental money, paid them less than men. A U.S. Department of Labor commissioner asserted that women worked only for "dress or pleasure." In one

AMERICA'S JOURNEY

FROM THEN TO NOW

The Nature of Work

The growth of American corporate capitalism and the emergence of the United States as a major industrial power transformed the nature of work and unsettled the workforce in the late nineteenth century. As machines deskilled the workplace by taking over sophisticated tasks, laborers were left to drudge at repetitive, dead-end jobs. Wages fell as certain jobs became obsolete, and a wave of mergers reduced competition and forced layoffs. In the late twentieth century, as the country began a transition from an industrial economy to an economy based on service and information technology, many workers felt similar pressures. But capitalism, according to Nobel economist Lester Thurow, is "a process of creative destruction." Job losses and social dislocation accompanied both the industrialization of the late nineteenth century and the transition to an information economy in the late twentieth. Both also generated new wealth and created new types of work.

There are important contrasts, however, between then and now. There may be little difference in scale between the wealth of a John D. Rockefeller and the wealth of a Bill Gates, but there are significant differences in the sources of their wealth. The great moguls of industry at the turn of the twentieth century made their fortunes from natural resources such as oil and iron ore. The entrepreneurial wizards of the turn of the twenty-first century derive wealth from knowledge. Before, few Americans could command the raw materials to produce vast wealth. But now the primary resource of the economy is the mind, opening previously unimagined opportunities. One result has been to blur the line between workers, managers, and even entrepreneurs.

A second difference is the current power of the consumer. The great industries kept wages low as entrepreneurs plowed huge profits into acquiring competitors, expanding production, and building their own personal fortunes. Although a growing middle class fueled the early twentieth-century economy, its influence pales before that of today's buyers. As the wages of industrial workers improved beginning in the 1940s, the consumer base broadened, but buyers still had relatively little choice. In 1959, for example, if you wanted to purchase a car, you basically had a choice between Ford, Chrysler, and General Motors. Today, more than thirty auto makers compete for customers, dampening inflation, increasing quality, and expanding choice.

Although a global economy existed in 1900, today's version relies more on electronic mobility to shift labor and capital rapidly. Firms cast about for the best and, in some cases, the cheapest places to do business to gain a competitive edge. Why should the German car manufacturer BMW, for example, pay high wages and benefits to German workers when South Carolina workers can build their cars just as well at a lower cost?

All of these factors have made work less secure. A laborer for U.S. Steel in the early twentieth century could expect to spend his working life with that company, barring injury. And he probably could pass a job down to his son. Today, workers are likely to have several employers over time. Some work is as deadening as on the old industrial production lines, but increasingly companies are redefining work to maintain their competitive advantage in a way that offers workers new opportunities. At the Duke Energy Corporation in Charlotte, North Carolina, for example, a line technician has the authority to schedule jobs, change instructions for those jobs, and recommend and secure equipment. Some of these responsibilities were previously the province of engineers. Now, reflecting both the destructive and creative aspects of the new economy, the company needs fewer engineers. Employers today expect more flexibility and initiative from their employees, and workers have more opportunities for responsibility and advancement. But workers pay a price in diminished job security and employers in diminished worker loyalty.

Secretaries of the Metropolitan Life Insurance Company in New York City pound away on Remington typewriters. The American Industrial Revolution spawned many jobs that involved repetitive mechanical tasks, both creating and destroying employment opportunities. Before the typewriter, men dominated clerical office work.

St. Louis factory in 1896, women received $4 a week for work for which men were paid $16 a week. Women chafed under this wage system but had no recourse other than to quit. An Iowa shoe saleswoman complained in 1886, "I don't get the salary the men clerks do, although this day I am 600 sales ahead! Call this justice? But I have to grin and bear it, because I am so unfortunate as to be a woman."

Most women worked out of economic necessity. In 1900, fully 85 percent of wage-earning women were unmarried and under the age of 25. They supported siblings and contributed to their parents' income. A typical female factory worker earned $6 a week in 1900. On this wage, a married woman might help pull her family up to subsistence level. For a single woman on her own, however, it allowed little more, in writer O. Henry's words, "than marshmallows and tea." Her lodging rarely consisted of more than one room.

Working women had little opportunity for recreation or diversion. Married women could seek comfort in home and family. Cheap amusements attracted single working women. Reformer Jane Addams noted in the 1890s, "Apparently the modern city sees in these girls only two possibilities, both of them commercial: first, a chance to utilize by day their labor power in its factories and shops, and then another chance in the evening to extract from them their petty wages by pandering to their love of pleasure."

Some working-class women turned to prostitution. As with other enterprises, industrial capitalism transformed commercialized sex into big business. The consumers in this industry—mainly middle-class men—sought their pleasure in dance halls, clubs, bawdy theater reviews, and thinly veiled bordellos. The income from prostitution could exceed factory work by four or five times. "So is it any wonder," asked the Chicago Vice Commission in 1894, "that a tempted girl who receives only six dollars per week working with her hands sells her body for twenty-five dollars per week . . . ?" As much as 10 percent of New York City's female working-age population worked in the sex business in the 1890s. During depression years, the percentage was probably higher.

Despite its tacit acceptance of sexual commerce, Victorian America condemned anyone guilty of even the most trivial moral transgression to social ostracism and treated the prostitute as a social outcast. Even those who urged understanding for women who violated convention faced exclusion. Kate Chopin, a New Orleans novelist, caused a tremendous uproar in the 1890s with stories that took a compassionate view of women involved in adultery, alcoholism, and divorce. Booksellers boycotted Theodore Dreiser's 1900 novel *Sister Carrie*, whose title character lived with a succession of men, one of them married.

The mere pursuit of leisure placed working women in compromising situations. They could not afford frequent visits to amusement parks, dance halls, or theaters. Yet these were the only places where they could meet young men without supervision from their families and employers. Men often expected sexual favors in return for "treating"—paying for all the expenses on a date. Thus the pressure to conform to conventional morality conflicted with working women's desire to enjoy a break. One social reformer heard one woman commenting to a coworker: "Don't yeh know there ain't no feller going t'spend coin on yeh for nothin'? Yeh gotta be a good Indian, Kid—as we all gotta!"

Over time, more work options opened to women, but low wages and poor working conditions persisted. Women entered the needle trades after widespread introduction of the sewing machine in the 1870s. Factories gradually replaced sweatshops in the garment industry after 1900, but working conditions improved little.

The introduction of the typewriter transformed clerical office work, dominated by men until the 1870s, into a female preserve. Women were alleged to have the greater dexterity and tolerance for repetition that the new technology required. But they earned only half the salary of the men they replaced. Middle-class parents saw office work as clean and honorable compared with factory or sales work. Consequently, clerical positions drew growing numbers of native-born women into the urban work force after 1890. A top-paid office worker in the 1890s earned as much as $900 a year. Teaching, another acceptable occupation for middle-class women, typically paid only $500 a year.

By the turn of the century, women were gaining increased access to higher education. Coeducational colleges were rare, but by 1900 there were many women-only institutions. By 1910, women comprised 40 percent of all American college students, compared to 20 percent in 1870. Despite these gains, many professions—including those of physician and attorney—remained closed to women. Men still accounted for more than 95 percent of all doctors in 1900. Women also were rarely permitted to pursue doctoral degrees.

Women college graduates mostly found employment in such "nurturing" professions as nursing, teaching, and library work. Between 1900 and 1910, the number of trained women nurses increased sevenfold. In response to the growing problems of urban society, a relatively new occupation, social work, opened to women. There were one thousand women social workers in 1890 and nearly thirty thousand by

1920. Reflecting new theories on the nurturing role of women, school boards after 1900 turned exclusively to female teachers for the elementary grades.

Despite these gains, women's work remained segregated. More than 90 percent of all wage-earning women in 1900 worked at jobs where women comprised the great majority of workers. Some reforms meant to improve working conditions for women reinforced this state of affairs. **Protective legislation** restricted women to "clean" occupations and limited their ability to compete with men in other jobs. As an economist explained in 1901, "The wage bargaining power of men is weakened by the competition of women and children, hence a law restricting the hours of women and children may also be looked upon as a law to protect men in their bargaining power."

Women also confronted negative stereotypes. Most Americans in 1900 believed a woman's proper role was to care for home and family. The single working woman faced doubts about her virtue. The system of "treating" on dates reinforced stories about loose salesgirls, flirtatious secretaries, and easy factory workers. Newspapers and magazines published exposés of working girls descending into prostitution. These images encouraged sexual harassment at work, which was rarely punished.

Working women faced a difficult dilemma. To justify their desire for education and training, they had to argue that it would enhance their roles as wives and mothers. To gain improved wages and working conditions, they increasingly supported protective legislation that restricted their opportunities in the workplace.

Responses to Poverty and Wealth

Concerns about working women merged with larger anxieties about the growing numbers of impoverished workers in the nation's cities during the 1890s and the widening gap between rich and poor. While industrial magnates flaunted their fabulous wealth, working men and women led hard lives on meager salaries and in crowded dwellings. In his exposé of poverty in New York, *How the Other Half Lives* (1890), Danish-born urban reformer Jacob Riis wrote that "the half that is on top cares little for the struggles, and less for the fate of those who are underneath so long as it is able to hold them there and keep its own seat."

The urban poor included workers as well as the unemployed, aged, widowed, and disabled. The industrial economy strained working-class family life. Workplace accidents and deaths left many families with only one parent. Infant mortality among the working poor was nearly twice the citywide norm in 1900. Epidemic diseases, especially typhoid, an illness spread by impure water, devastated crowded working-class districts. Poverty compounded itself in various ways. For example, the poor paid twice as much for coal to heat their homes as better-off people because they could only afford to buy it in small quantities.

Inadequate housing was the most visible badge of poverty. Crammed into four- to six-story buildings on tiny lots, **tenement** apartments in urban **slums** were notorious for their lack of ventilation and light. According to Jacob Riis, a typical apartment in New York's Mulberry Bend neighborhood consisted of a parlor—a combined livingroom and kitchen—and "two pitch-dark coops called bedrooms." The furniture included three beds, "if the old boxes and heaps of foul straw can be called by that name," which gave off an appalling smell. In 90-degree July heat, temperatures inside soared to 115 degrees.

Authorities did nothing to enforce laws prohibiting overcrowding for fear of leaving people homeless. The population density of New York's tenement district in 1894 was 986.4 people per acre, the highest in the world at the time. (Today, the densest areas of American cities rarely exceed 400 people per acre, and only Calcutta, India, and Lagos, Nigeria, approach the crowding of turn-of-the-century New York; today Manhattan has 84 residents per acre).

One early attempt to deal with these conditions was the settlement house. The settlement house movement, which originated in England, sought to moderate the effects of poverty through neighborhood reconstruction. New York's Neighborhood Guild, established in 1886, was the first settlement house in the country; Chicago's **Hull House**, founded in 1889 by Jane Addams, a young Rockford (Illinois) College graduate, became the most famous. Addams had visited settlement houses in England and thought the idea would work well in American cities.

The settlement house typically did not dispense charity. Rather, it provided the working poor with facilities and education to help them improve their environment and, eventually, to escape it. By 1900, there were more than one hundred settlement houses throughout the country.

Hull House, a rambling old residence in a working-class immigrant neighborhood, quickly became a neighborhood institution. On Saturday evenings, Italian immigrants and their families came to settle legal disputes. Hull House also catered to native-born Americans, who formed the Young Citizens' Club to discuss municipal issues. Addams renovated an adjacent saloon and transformed it into a gym. She began a day nursery as well. When workers at a nearby knitting factory went on strike, Addams arbitrated the conflict.

The poor seldom lived near large urban parks and could not afford to join athletic clubs.

Settlement house gyms like the one Addams built for Hull House provided them with much-needed recreational space. So too did the athletic fields and playgrounds built adjacent to public schools after 1900.

Late-nineteenth-century political ideology discouraged more comprehensive efforts to remedy urban poverty until the Progressive Era (discussed in Chapter 23). According to the **Gospel of Wealth**, a theory popular among industrialists, intellectuals, and some politicians, any intervention on behalf of the poor was of doubtful benefit. Hard work and perseverance, in this view, led to wealth. Poverty, by implication, resulted from the flawed character of the poor. Steel tycoon Andrew Carnegie sought to soften this doctrine by stressing the responsibility of the affluent to set an example for the working class and to return some of their wealth to the communities in which they lived. Carnegie accordingly endowed libraries, cultural institutions, and schools throughout the country. Beneficial as they might be, however, these philanthropic efforts scarcely addressed the causes of poverty, and few industrialists followed Carnegie's example.

Social Darwinism, a flawed attempt to apply Charles Darwin's theory of biological evolution to human society, emerged as a more common justification than the Gospel of Wealth for the growing gap between rich and poor. According to social Darwinism, the human race evolves only through competition. The fit survive, the weak perish, and humanity moves forward. Wealth reflects fitness; poverty, weakness. For governments or private agencies to interfere with this natural process is futile. Thus Columbia University president Nicholas Murray Butler, claiming that "nature's cure for most social and political diseases is better than man's," warned against charity for the poor in 1900. Standard Oil's John D. Rockefeller concurred, asserting that the survival of the fittest is "the working out of a law of nature and a law of God."

Social Darwinism provided some industrialists with an excuse to do nothing to relieve the causes of poverty. Workers, caught between harsh theory and harsher reality, began to take matters into their own hands.

Workers Organize

The growing power of industrial corporations and the declining power of workers generated social tensions reminiscent of the sectional crisis that triggered the Civil War. Wild swings in the business cycle—the fluctuation between periods of growth and contraction in the economy—aggravated these tensions. Two prolonged depressions, one beginning in 1873 and the other in 1893, threw as many as 2 million laborers out of work. Skilled workers, their security undermined by deskilling, were hit particularly hard. Their hopes of becoming managers or starting their own businesses disappearing, they saw the nation "drifting," as a carpenter put it in 1870, "to that condition of society where a few were rich, and the many very poor."

Beginning after the depression of 1873 and continuing through World War I, workers fought their loss of independence to industrial capital by organizing and striking (see the overview table, "Workers Organize"). The first episode in this conflict was the railroad strike of 1877, sometimes referred to as the **Great Uprising**. The four largest railroads, in the midst of a depression and in the wake of a series of pay cuts over the previous four years, agreed to slash wages yet again. When Baltimore & Ohio Railroad workers struck in July to protest the cut, President Rutherford B. Hayes dispatched federal troops to protect the line's property. The use of federal troops infuriated railroad workers throughout the East and Midwest, and they stopped work as well. Violence

During the Great Uprising of 1877, federal troops clashed with striking workers. Here, the Maryland militia fires at strikers in Baltimore, killing twelve. As Reconstruction ended, government attention shifted from the South to quelling labor unrest.

OVERVIEW

WORKERS ORGANIZE

Organization	History	Strategies
Knights of Labor	Founded in 1869; open to all workers; declined after 1886	Disapproved of strikes; supported a broad array of labor reforms, including cooperatives; favored political involvement
American Federation of Labor	Founded in 1886; open to craft workers only and organized by craft; hostile to blacks and women; became the major U.S. labor organization after 1880s	Opposed political involvement; supported a limited number of labor reforms; approved of strikes
Industrial Workers of the World	Founded in 1905; consisted mainly of semiskilled and unskilled immigrant workers; represented a small portion of the work force; disappeared after World War I	Highly political; supported socialist programs; approved of strikes and even violence to achieve ends

erupted in Pittsburgh when the state militia opened fire on strikers and their families, killing twenty-five, including a woman and three children. As news of the violence spread, so did the strike, as far as Galveston, Texas, and San Francisco. Over the next two weeks, police and federal troops continued to clash with strikers. By the time this first nationwide work stoppage in American history ended, more than one hundred had been killed. The wage cuts remained.

Despite its ultimate failure, the Great Uprising was notable for the way workers cooperated with one another across ethnic and, in some cases, racial lines. The experience proved important in the next major upheaval, nine years later.

The **Knights of Labor**, a union of craft workers founded in Philadelphia in 1869, grew dramatically after the Great Uprising under the leadership of Terence V. Powderly. Reflecting the views of many skilled workers, the Knights saw "an inevitable . . . conflict between the wage system of labor and [the] republican system of government." Remarkably inclusive for its time, the Knights welcomed black workers and women to its ranks. Victories in several small railroad strikes in 1884 and 1885 boosted its membership to nearly one million workers by 1886.

In that year, the Knights led a movement for an eight-hour workday. Ignoring the advice of the national leadership to avoid strikes, local chapters staged more than 1,500 strikes involving more than 340,000 workers. Workers also organized boycotts against manufacturers and ran candidates for local elections. Social reformer Henry George made a strong, though losing, effort in the New York City mayoral race, and labor candidates won several local offices in Chicago.

Employers fought back. They convinced the courts to order strikers back to work and used local authorities to arrest strikers for trespassing or obstructing traffic. In early May 1886, police killed four unarmed workers during a skirmish with strikers in Chicago. Rioting broke out when a bomb exploded at a meeting in **Haymarket Square** to protest the slayings. The bomb killed seven policemen and four strikers and left one hundred people wounded. Eight strike leaders were tried for the deaths, and despite a lack of evidence linking them to the bomb, four were executed.

The Haymarket Square incident and a series of disastrous walkouts that followed it weakened the Knights of Labor. By 1890, it had shrunk to less than 100,000 members. Thereafter, the **American Federation of Labor (AFL)**, formed in 1886, became the major organizing body for skilled workers.

The AFL was much less ambitious and less inclusive than the Knights of Labor. Led by British immigrant Samuel Gompers, it emphasized **collective**

bargaining—negotiations between management and union representatives—to secure workplace concessions. The AFL also discouraged political activism. With this **business unionism**, the AFL proved more effective than the Knights of Labor at meeting the needs of skilled workers, but it left out the growing numbers of unskilled workers, black workers, and women workers to whom the Knights had given a glimmer of hope.

Rather than including all workers in one large union, the AFL organized skilled workers by craft. It then focused on a few basic workplace issues important to each craft. Workers at a given factory might be represented by five or more craft unions instead of one umbrella organization. This organizing technique assured that rank-and-file members in a union shared similar objectives. The result was greater cohesion and discipline. In 1889 and 1890, more than 60 percent of AFL-sponsored strikes were successful, a remarkable record in an era when most strikes failed. A series of work stoppages in the building trades between 1888 and 1891, for example, won an eight-hour day and a national agreement with builders.

Responding to this success, employers determined to break the power of craft unions just as they had destroyed the Knights. In 1892, Andrew Carnegie dealt the steelworkers union a major setback in the **Homestead strike**. Carnegie's manager, Henry Clay Frick, announced to workers at Carnegie's Homestead plant in Pennsylvania that he would negotiate only with workers individually and not renew the union's collective bargaining contract. Expecting a strike, Frick locked the union workers out of the plant and hired three hundred armed guards to protect the nonunion ("scab") workers he planned to hire in their place. Union workers, with the help of their families and unskilled workers, seized control of Homestead's roads and utilities. In a bloody confrontation, they drove back Frick's forces. Nine strikers and seven guards died. But Pennsylvania's governor called out the state militia to open the plant and protect the nonunion workers. After four months, the union capitulated. With this defeat skilled steelworkers lost their power on the shop floor. Eventually, mechanization cost them their jobs.

In 1894, workers suffered another setback in the **Pullman strike**, against George Pullman's Palace Sleeping Car Company. The strike began when the company cut wages for workers at its plant in the "model" suburb it built outside Chicago without a corresponding cut in the rent it charged workers for their company-owned housing. When Pullman rejected their demands, the workers appealed for support to the American Railway Union (ARU), led by Eugene V. Debs. The membership of the ARU, an independent union not affiliated with the AFL, had swelled to more than 150,000 workers after it won a strike earlier in 1894 against the Great Northern Railroad. On behalf of the Pullman strikers, Debs ordered a boycott of any trains with Pullman cars. The result was to disrupt train travel in several parts of the country. The railroads claimed to be innocent victims of a local dispute, and with growing public support, they fired workers who refused to handle trains with Pullman cars. Debs called for all ARU members to walk off the job, crippling rail travel nationwide. When Debs refused to honor a federal court injunction against the strike, President Cleveland, at the railroads' request, ordered federal troops to enforce it. Debs was arrested, and the strike and the union were broken.

These setbacks and the depression that began in 1893 left workers and their unions facing an uncertain future. But growing public opposition to the use of troops, the high-handed tactics of industrialists, and the rising concerns of Americans about the power of big business sustained the unions. Workers would call more than 22,000 strikes over the next decade, the majority of them union-sponsored. Still, no more than 7 percent of the American work force was organized by 1900.

American Workers and Socialism

Unlike American workers, European workers formed powerful labor organizations and political parties in the late nineteenth and early twentieth centuries. These parties advocated a policy of **socialism**. They called for state ownership of industry and worker control of corporations. Socialism had some influence in the American labor movement. The Greenback-Labor Party and the Socialist Labor Party attracted some workers in the 1870s. So too did the Socialist Party of America, formed in 1901. Some European immigrants brought radical ideas with them. German socialists and anarchists (who advocated the abolition of government) played prominent roles in the Haymarket affair, for example.

Although the influence of socialist ideas in the United States grew during the Progressive Era (see Chapter 23), several factors limited socialism's appeal and that of more radical leftist movements among workers. First, American socialism was terribly fragmented. One wing supported cooperation with the Democratic party and another insisted on independent action. A third group emerged during the Progressive Era that supported the **Industrial Workers of the World (IWW)**. The IWW, founded in 1905, consisted mostly of recent immigrants espousing a fiery class-conscious program of militant action.

Second, the diversity of the American workforce limited concerted political and union activity. Semiskilled and unskilled immigrant workers formed the majority of the industrial workforce after 1900. Skilled native-born workers, their ranks diminishing, were reluctant to associate with foreigners. Ethnicity divided workers as well. Some unions, such as the Jewish- and Italian-dominated textile unions in the North, successfully organized across ethnic lines. But these were the exception.

Religious differences compounded ethnic diversity. Jewish and Catholic workers demanded a different sabbath and different holidays. Workers often mixed religious and union rituals in ways that reinforced ethnic and religious unity but inhibited worker solidarity. Jewish vestmakers quoted from the Torah to justify a strike. Slavic steelworkers in Hammond, Indiana, in 1910 voted to strike at a ceremony where "the lights of the hall were extinguished. A candle stuck into a bottle was placed on a platform along with a crucifix. One by one the men came and kissed the ivory image on the cross, kneeling before it."

Some European immigrant workers saw factory work from a short-term perspective that discouraged militancy. Their goal was to save enough money to return home to a better life.

Third, Americans prized individualism and saw it threatened by collective worker action as well as by corporate mergers. The press and political leaders discredited labor actions as evidence of foreign (and hence "un-American") political radicalism and social disorder. Middle-class reformers concerned about the increasingly chaotic and diverse urban society saw worker action increasing class, ethnic, and gender conflict. With much of public opinion and official force arrayed against radical union and political activity, many workers (especially the native-born) backed away from radical groups. In 1900, the Massachusetts Bureau of Labor Statistics reported that while most workers believed in unions "in the abstract," many considered them "simply vehicles for the fomentation of incipient riots and disorderly conduct."

Fourth, the existing political system provided some channels for the redress of labor grievances. Universal manhood suffrage preceded industrialization in the United States, unlike in most European countries. The major parties vied for workingmen's votes in the large industrial cities and sometimes championed a few of their causes in state legislatures and Congress. The Republican and Democratic parties were large and diffuse enough to appeal to the diverse working force. Big-city political machines, with thousands of patronage jobs at their disposal, lured potential third-party supporters back into major-party ranks. After labor candidates won several offices in Chicago in 1886, Chicago Democrats hired more than four hundred Knights of Labor members for various city positions. Social critic Friedrich Engels, observing American labor from England, concluded in 1892 that "there is no place yet in America for a *third* party. . . . The divergence of interests even in the *same* class is so great . . . that wholly different groups and interests are represented in each of the two big parties."

Some states with large industrial work forces passed prolabor legislation as early as the 1880s. Massachusetts provided for arbitration of labor disputes, limits on the working hours of children and women, compensation for certain work-related accidents, and factory safety standards. New York passed similar measures during the 1880s. Southern states, with much fewer industrial workers, did not pass protective legislation until after 1900.

The federal government lagged behind the industrial states in significant prolabor legislation. Federal labor policy between 1877 and 1894 consisted primarily of mobilizing troops to put down worker uprisings. Congress appeased the fears of native-born workers about competition from Chinese immigrants with the **Chinese Exclusion Act** in 1882. Congress also established a bureau of labor in 1884,

Thomas Nast's "The Chinese Question" depicted Columbia, a common nineteenth-century symbol for American ideals, protecting a Chinese immigrant from an irate mob. Note the slogans posted behind Columbia. Nast particularly took issue with attacks on Chinese immigrants by labor unions and evangelical Protestants.

but at the outset the bureau viewed its role strictly as a compiler of statistics. After 1900, in response to the acceleration of corporate mergers and the continuation of labor unrest, states and the federal government increased surveillance over big business. Most states joined Massachusetts and New York in providing minimum protection for workers. Over the next fifteen years, additional state and federal legislation removed many important issues from labor's legislative agenda.

Fifth, the success of the AFL after 1890 kept more radical labor voices from emerging. Samuel Gompers urged his followers to reject radical programs to restructure industrial capitalism: "Whatever ideas we may have as to the future state of society . . . they must remain in the background, and we must subordinate our convictions . . . to the general good that the trades-union movement brings to the laborer." Gompers continued to stress short-term advances for workers rather than long-term solutions for the problems of urban industrial society. The AFL leadership had little interest in unifying workers across class or craft boundaries. Nor did they seek to appeal to African Americans, whom they saw as potential strikebreakers, or women, whom they saw as depressing wages and competing unfairly with men.

Perhaps another reason most American workers rejected socialism was the dramatic change in the industrial work force around 1900. As the large factories installed labor- and time-saving machinery, unskilled foreign-born labor flooded onto the shop floor. For many reasons, not least of which were the adjustments required for life in a new country, labor radicalism was not a high priority for many of the newcomers. Immigrants not only transformed the workplace, but also transformed the cities where they settled and the nation many eventually adopted. In the process, they changed themselves.

New Immigrants

The late nineteenth century was a period of unprecedented worldwide population movements. The United States was not the only New World destination for the migrants of this period. Many also found their way to Brazil, Argentina, and Canada.

Map 20-1 Patterns of Immigration, 1820–1914
The migration to the United States was part of a worldwide transfer of population that accelerated with the industrial revolution and the accompanying improvements in transportation.

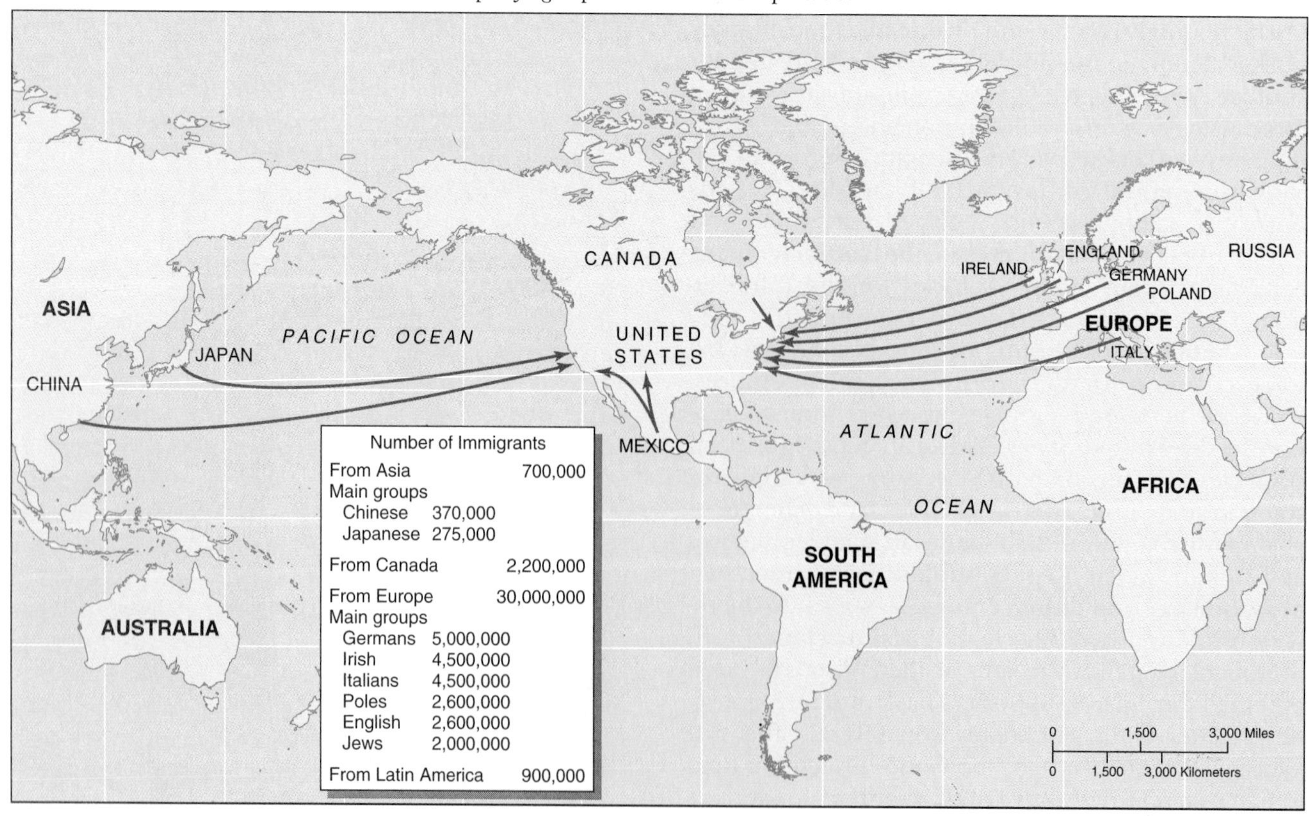

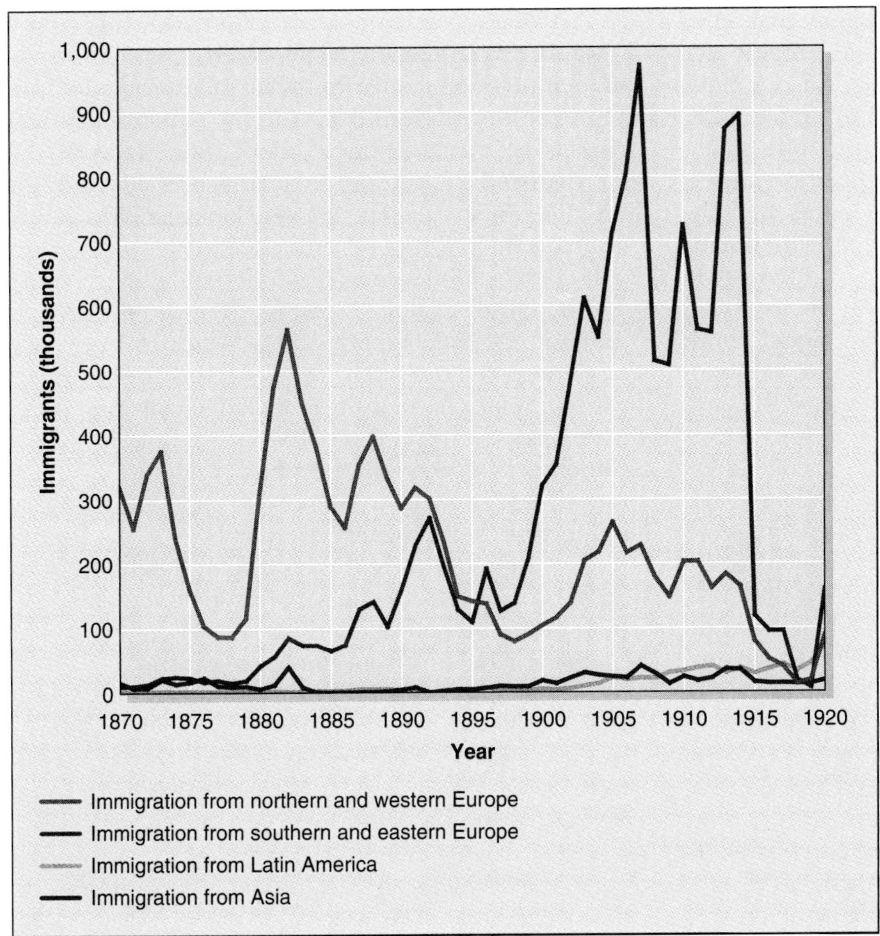

***Figure 20-2* Immigration to the United States, 1870–1915**
The graph illustrates the dramatic change in immigration to the United States during the late nineteenth and early twentieth centuries. As immigration from northern and western Europe slackened, the numbers of newcomers from southern and eastern Europe swelled. Latin American and Asian immigration also increased during this period.

The scale of overseas migration to the United States after 1870, however, dwarfed all that preceded it. Between 1870 and 1910, the country received more than 20 million immigrants. Before the Civil War, most immigrants came from northern Europe. Most of the new immigrants, in contrast, came from southern and eastern Europe. Swelling their ranks were migrants from Mexico and Asia, as well as internal migrants moving from the countryside to American cities (see Map 20-1 and Figure 20-2).

Old-World Backgrounds

The people of southern and eastern Europe had long been accustomed to migrating within Europe on a seasonal basis to find work to support their families. In the final quarter of the nineteenth century, however, several factors drove migrants beyond the borders of Europe and into the Western Hemisphere.

A growing rural population combined with unequal land distribution to create economic distress in late-nineteenth-century Europe. With land ownership concentrated in increasingly fewer hands, more and more people found themselves working ever-smaller plots as laborers rather than owners. In Poland, laborers accounted for 80 percent of the agricultural population in the 1860s. Similar conditions prevailed in the Mezzogiorno region of southern Italy, home of three out of four Italian emigrants to America. Declining farm commodity prices and the deterioration of the road system in southern Italy contributed to a general agricultural depression. Absentee landlords abused workers and neglected the land.

For Russian Jews, religious persecution compounded economic hardship. In tsarist Russia, Jews could not own real estate and were barred from work in farming, teaching, the civil service, and the law. Confined to designated cities, they struggled to support themselves. After the assassination of Tsar Alexander II in 1881, which some leaders falsely blamed on Jews, the government sanctioned a series of violent attacks on Jewish settlements known as **pogroms**. At the same time, the government forced Jews into fewer towns, deepening their poverty and making them easier targets for violence.

Economic hardship and religious persecution were not, of course, new to Europe. What made the late nineteenth century different was that new transportation technologies permitted people to leave. Railroad construction boomed in Europe during the 1870s and 1880s as Germany and Great Britain sought markets for their iron and steel. Steamship companies in several European countries built giant vessels to transport passengers quickly and safely across the Atlantic. The companies sent agents into Russia, Poland, Italy, and the Austro-Hungarian empire to solicit business.

Sometime during the 1880s, an agent from the Hamburg-American Line (HAPAG), a German steamship company, visited a village in the Russian Ukraine where the great grandparents of one of this book's authors lived. Shortly after his visit, they boarded a train to Austrian-occupied Poland and Hamburg. There they boarded a HAPAG steamer emblazoned with a large banner proclaiming "*Willkommen*" ("Welcome"). Just boarding that ship they felt they were entering the United States. Millions of others like them sailed on ocean liners from Germany, Italy, and Great Britain over the next thirty years.

Chinese and Japanese immigrants also came to the United States in appreciable numbers for the first time during the late nineteenth century. Most Chinese immigrants came from Canton in South China, a region of great rural poverty. They worked on railroads and in mines throughout the West and as farm laborers in California. Many eventually settled in cities such as San Francisco where they established residential enclaves referred to as Chinatowns. The Chinese population in the United States peaked at about 125,000 in 1882.

Japanese began immigrating to the United States beginning in the late 1880s, driven by a land shortage even more acute than that in Europe. The first wave came by way of Hawaii to work on farms in California, taking the place of Chinese workers who had moved to the cities. By 1900, there were some fifty thousand Japanese immigrants in the United States, nearly all on the West Coast.

Wherever they came from, most migrants saw the ocean as a two-way highway. They intended to stay only a year or two, long enough to earn money to buy land or, more likely, to enter a business back home and improve life for themselves and their families. Roughly half of all immigrants to the United States between 1880 and World War I returned to their country of origin. Some made several round trips. Jews, unwelcome in the lands they left, were the exception. No more than 10 percent of Jewish immigrants returned to Europe, and very few Jews from Russia, who accounted for almost 80 percent of Jewish immigrants after 1880, went back home.

Most newcomers were young men. (Jews again were the exception: Reflecting their intention to stay in their new home, they tended to migrate in families.) Immigrants easily found work in the nation's booming cities. The quickest way to make money was in the large urban factories with their voracious demands for unskilled labor. Except for the Japanese, few immigrants came to work on farms after 1880.

By 1900, women began to equal men among all immigrant groups as young men who decided to stay sent for their families. In a few cases, entire villages migrated, drawn by the good fortune of one or two compatriots, a process called **chain migration**. The success of Francesco Barone, a Buffalo tavern owner, convinced eight thousand residents of his former village in Sicily to migrate to that city, many arriving on tickets Barone purchased.

Immigrants tended to live in neighborhoods among people from the same homeland. Their native culture helped shape their response to their new home. For Italians from the Mezzogiorno, for example, the family was the basic institution for obtaining work and securing assistance in times of stress, death, or sickness. Family ties were so strong that voluntary associations in the towns of the Mezzogiorno were rare. In the United States, immigrants from southern Italy, almost alone among European and Asian migrants, rarely formed neighborhood or ethnic associations.

The desire of the new immigrants to retain their cultural traditions led contemporary observers to doubt their ability to assimilate into American society. Even sympathetic observers, such as social workers, marveled at the utterly foreign character of immigrant districts. In 1900, Philadelphia social worker Emily Dinwiddie visited an Italian neighborhood and described "black-eyed children, rolling and tumbling together, the gaily colored dresses of the women and the crowds of street vendors, that give the neighborhood a wholly foreign appearance."

The Neighborhood

Immigrants did not live in homogeneous communities isloated from the rest of society. Rarely did a particular ethnic group comprise more than 50 percent of a neighborhood. Chinese were the exception, but even the borders of Chinatowns usually overlapped with other neighborhoods. A particular apartment building might house families from Abruzzi in Italy, and Jews from Kiev might dominate a block of tenements in New York City's Lower East Side, but greater concentrations were rare. Even to call such districts "Jewish" or "Italian" distorts the reality. Most Italian immigrants identified not so much with

Mulberry Street, New York, 1905. The vibrant, predominantly Russian Jewish Lower East Side of New York at first reflected more the culture of the homeland than of America. Language, dress, ways of doing business, keeping house, and worshipping all followed Old-World patterns. Gradually, thanks especially to the influence of school-age children, a blend of Russian Jewish and American traditions emerged.

Italy—which had only recently been unified—as with the village of their birth. Only with time did they come to see themselves as "Italian" in the way the rest of American society saw them.

German Jews, long established in American cities, wanted little to do with their Russian coreligionists at first. Yet as the larger society conflated both groups, they began to help the newcomers assimilate into American society.

In smaller cities and in the urban South, where foreign-born populations were smaller, ethnic groups were more geographically dispersed, though occasionally they might inhabit the same neighborhood. In turn-of-the-century Memphis, for example, Irish, Italian, and Jewish immigrants lived cheek by jowl in a single immigrant district (called the "Pinch"), sharing schools and recreational space even as they led their singular institutional, religious, and family lives.

Immigrants maintained their cultural traditions through the establishment of religious and communal institutions. Charitable organizations were frequently connected to religious institutions. The church or synagogue became the focal point for immigrant neighborhood life. Much more than a place of worship, it was a school for transmitting Old World values and language to American-born children. The church or synagogue also functioned as a recreational facility and a gathering place for community leaders. In Jewish communities, associations called *landsmanshaften* arranged for burials, jobs, housing, and support for the sick, poor, and elderly.

Because religious institutions were so central to their lives, immigrant communities insisted on maintaining control over them. Polish parishioners wanted Polish priests, and Russian Jewish communities wanted Russian rabbis. The nationality of parish priests became such a heated topic for some Catholic national groups that they threatened to secede from the church, a movement the hierarchy squelched.

Religious institutions played a less formal role among Chinese and Japanese neighborhoods. For them, the family functioned as the source of religious activity and communal organization. Chinatowns were organized in clans of people with the same surname. An umbrella organization called the Chinese Consolidated Benevolent Association emerged; it functioned like the Jewish *landsmanshaften*. Perhaps most important, the association shipped the bones of deceased members back to China for burial in ancestral cemeteries. A similar association, the Japanese Association of America, governed the Japanese community in the United States. This organization was sponsored by the Japanese government, which was sensitive to mistreatment of its citizens abroad and anxious that immigrants set a good example. The Japanese Association, unlike other ethnic organizations, actively encouraged assimilation and stressed the importance of Western dress and learning English.

Ethnic newspapers, theaters, and schools supplemented associational life for immigrants. These institutions reinforced Old-World culture while informing immigrants about American ways. Thus the Jewish *Daily Forward,* first published in New York in 1897, reminded readers of the importance of keeping the Sabbath while admonishing them to adopt American customs.

The Job

If the neighborhood provided a familiar and supportive environment for the immigrant, work offered the ultimate reward for coming to America. All immigrants perceived the job as the way to independence and as a way out, either back to the Old World or into the larger American society.

Immigrants typically received their first job with the help of a countryman. Italian, Chinese, Japanese, and Mexican newcomers worked with contractors who placed them in jobs. These middlemen often provided housing, loans, and other services for recent arrivals. They exacted a fee, sometimes extortionate, for their services. In an era before employment agencies, however, they efficiently matched immigrants with jobs. Other immigrant groups, such as Poles and Russian Jews, often secured work through their ethnic associations or village or family connections. Poles in the meatpacking industries in Chicago, for example, recommended relatives to their bosses. Family members sometimes exchanged jobs with one another (see "American Views: Immigrants and Work").

The type of work available to immigrants depended on their skills, the local economy, and local discrimination. Mexican migrants to southern California, for example, concentrated in railroad construction. Mostly unskilled, they replaced Chinese laborers when the federal government excluded Chinese immigration after 1882. Mexicans built the interurban rail lines of Los Angeles in 1900 and established communities at their construction camps. Los Angeles businessmen barred Mexicans from other occupations. Similarly, Chinese immigrants were confined to work in laundries and restaurants within the boundaries of Los Angeles's Chinatown. There were no commercial laundries in China.

The Japanese who came to Los Angeles around 1900 were forced into sectors of the economy native-born white people had either shunned or failed to exploit. The Japanese turned this discrimination to their benefit when they transformed the cultivation of market garden crops into a major agricultural enterprise. By 1904, Japanese farmers owned more than fifty thousand acres in California. George Shima, who came to California from Japan in 1889 with a little capital, made himself the "Potato King" of the Sacramento Delta. By 1913, Shima owned 28,000 acres of farmland.

Other ethnic groups in other parts of the country had to conform to similar constraints. Greeks in Chicago, for example, restricted to food services, established restaurants, fruit distributorships, and ice-cream factories throughout the city.

Stereotypes also channeled immigrants' work options, sometimes benefiting one group at the expense of another. Jewish textile entrepreneurs, for example, sometimes hired only Italians because they thought them less prone to unionization than Jewish workers. Other Jewish bosses hired only Jewish workers, hoping that ethnic loyalty would overcome the lure of the unions. Pittsburgh steelmakers preferred Polish workers to the black workers who began arriving in northern cities in appreciable numbers after 1900. This began the decades-long tradition of handing down steel mill jobs through the generations in Polish families.

Jews, alone among European ethnic groups, found work almost exclusively with one another. Among the factors contributing to this pattern may have been the discrimination Jews faced in eastern Europe, the existence of an established Jewish community when they arrived, and their dominance of the needle trades. Jews comprised three-quarters of the more than half-million workers in New York City's garment industry in 1910. Jews were also heavily concentrated in the retail trade.

Like their native-born counterparts, few married immigrant women worked outside the home, but unlike the native-born, many Italian and Jewish women did piecework for the garment industry in their apartments. Unmarried Polish women often worked in factories or as domestic servants. Japanese women, married and single, worked with their families on farms. Until revolution in China in 1911 began to erode traditional gender roles, married Chinese immigrant women typically remained home.

The paramount goal for many immigrants was to work for themselves rather than someone else. Some immigrants, like George Shima, parlayed their skills and a small stake into successful businesses. Most new arrivals, however, had few skills and no resources beyond their wits with which to realize their dreams. Major banks at the time were unlikely to extend even a small business loan to a budding ethnic entrepreneur. Family members and small ethnic-based community banks provided the initial stake for most immigrant businesses. Many of these banks failed, but a few survived and prospered. For example, the Bank of Italy, established by Amadeo Pietro Giannini in San Francisco in 1904, eventually grew into the Bank of America, one of the nation's largest financial institutions today.

Immigrants could not fully control their own destinies in the United States any more than native-born Americans could. The vagaries of daily life, including death, disease, and bad luck, thwarted many immigrants' dreams. Hard work did not always ensure success. Add to these the difficulty of cultural adjustment to an unfamiliar environment, and the newcomer's confident hopes could fade quickly. Almost all immigrants, however, faced an obstacle that by its nature white native-born Americans did not. They faced it on the job, in the city at large, and even in their neighborhoods: the antiforeign prejudice of American **nativism**.

Nativism

Despite the openness of American borders in the nineteenth century and contrary to the nation's reputation as a refuge from foreign persecution and poverty, immigrants have not always received a warm reception. Ben Franklin groused about the "foreignness" of German immigrants during the colonial era. From the 1830s to 1860, nativist sentiment, directed mainly at Irish Catholic immigrants, expressed itself in occasional violence and job discrimination. Anti-immigrant sentiment gave rise to an important political party, the Know-Nothings, in the 1850s.

When immigration revived after the Civil War, so did antiforeign sentiment. But late-nineteenth-century nativism differed in two ways from its antebellum predecessor. First, the target was no longer Irish Catholics but the even more numerous Catholics and Jews of southern and eastern Europe, people whose language and usually darker complexions set them apart from the native-born majority. Second, late-nineteenth-century nativism had a pseudo-scientific underpinning. As we saw in Chapter 18, the so-called "scientific" racism of the period maintained that some people are inherently inferior to others. There was, in this view, a natural hierarchy of race. At the top, with the exception of the Irish, were northern Europeans, especially those of Anglo-Saxon descent. Following below them were French, Slavs, Poles, Italians, Jews, Asians, and Africans. Social Darwinism, which justified the class hierarchy, reinforced scientific racism.

When the "inferior" races arrived in the United States in significant numbers after 1880, nativists sounded the alarm. A prominent Columbia University professor wrote in 1887 that Hungarians and Italians were "of such a character as to endanger our civilization." Nine years later, the director of the U.S. census warned that eastern and southern Europeans were "beaten men from beaten races. They have none of the ideas and aptitudes which fit men to take up readily and easily the problem of self-care and self-government." The result of unfettered migration would be "race suicide."

The popular press translated these scientific pronouncements into blunter language. In the mid-1870s, a Chicago newspaper described recently arrived Bohemian immigrants (from the present-day Czech Republic) as "depraved beasts, harpies, decayed physically and spiritually, mentally and morally, thievish and licentious." A decade later, with eastern Europeans still pouring into Chicago, another newspaper suggested: "Let us whip these slavic wolves back to the European dens from which they issue, or in some way exterminate them." The *New York Times,* demurring from such an extreme, suggested instead some form of restriction. Referring to Russian Jewish and Italian immigrants, the *Times* concluded that Americans "pretty well agreed" that these foreigners were "of a kind which we are better without." The rhetoric of the scientific press was scarcely less extreme. *Scientific American* warned immigrants to "assimilate" quickly or "share the fate of the native Indians" and face "a quiet but sure extermination."

Such sentiments generated proposals to restrict foreign immigration. The treatment of the Chinese provided a precedent. Chinese immigrants had long worked for low wages under harsh conditions in mining and railroad construction in the West. Their different culture and their willingness to accept low wages provoked resentment among native- and European-born workers. Violence against Chinese laborers increased during the 1860s and 1870s. In 1870, the Republican-dominated Congress passed the **Naturalization Act**, which limited citizenship to "white persons and persons of African descent." The act was specifically intended to prevent Chinese from becoming citizens—a ban not lifted until 1943—but it affected other Asian groups also. The Chinese Exclusion Act of 1882, passed following another decade of anti-Chinese pressure, made the Chinese the only ethnic group in the world that could not emigrate freely to the United States. Even this drastic measure did not satisfy one Knights of Labor official, who in 1885 viewed the conflict between Chinese and native-born labor in the perspective of the 1850s sectional crisis (with a modern Darwinian twist): "This is the old irrepressible conflict between slave and white labor. God grant there may be survival of the fittest." Anti-Asian violence raced through mining communities in the West for the next two years.

Labor competition also contributed to the rise of another anti-immigrant organization. A group

American Views

Immigrants and Work

In 1906, a magazine called *The Independent* published a series of stories documenting immigrant work experiences, two of which are excerpted here. The first story is told by Rocco Corresca, an Italian immigrant whose first job in the United States was as a ragpicker. The second story is told in the halting English of a young Japanese immigrant who migrated to Portland, Oregon, and worked as a domestic servant. Their jobs typified what most immigrants could expect: not glamorous, not well-paying, and probably involving hard physical labor. Although the stories are generally upbeat, they reflect some of the hardships new immigrants faced.

As Corrersca's story indicates, immigrants often received their first jobs through an agent. The agents often extracted a fee, sometimes quite high, for this service. But the system enabled employers to find staff more efficiently than they could on their own.

- **Did the costs of the agent system outweigh its benefits?**
- **Do you think it is likely that Corrersca's English was as idiomatic as it appears here? Or do you think the editors of *The Independent* corrected it for him? If so, why do you think they didn't correct it for the Japanese immigrant? Is it significant that Corrersca is named and the Japanese immigrant isn't?**
- **Immigrants experienced considerable job and geographical mobility. Was this good or bad?**
- **Were these immigrants ever exploited? What recourse did they have to counter exploitation?**

Rocco Corrersca Becomes an Entrepreneur

We came to Brooklyn, New York, to a wooden house in Adams street that was full of Italians from Naples. Bartolo had a room on the third floor and there were fifteen men in the room, all boarding with Bartolo. . . . The next morning, early, Bartolo told us to go out and pick rags and get bottles. . . . Most of the men in our room worked at digging the sewer. Bartolo got them the work and they paid him about one-quarter of their wages. Then he charged them for board and he bought the clothes for them, too. So they got little money after all. . . .

of skilled workers and small businessmen formed the **American Protective Association (APA)** in 1887 and claimed half a million members a year later. The APA sought to limit Catholic civil rights in the United States to protect the jobs of Protestant workingmen.

The **Immigration Restriction League (IRL)**, formed in 1894 in the midst of a depression, took a more modest and indirect approach. The IRL proposed to require prospective immigrants to pass a literacy test that they presumed most southern and eastern Europeans would fail. Cynically reaching out to native-born workers, the IRL vowed that its legislation would protect "the wages of our workingmen against the fatal competition of low-price labor."

The IRL ultimately failed to have its literacy requirement enacted. The return of prosperity and the growing preference of industrialists for immigrant labor put an end to calls for formal restrictions on immigration for the time being. Less than thirty years later, however, Congress would enact major restrictive legislation aimed at southern and eastern European immigrants. In the meantime, IRL propaganda encouraged northern universities to establish quotas limiting the admission of new immigrants, especially Jews.

Immigrants and their communal associations fought attempts to restrict immigration. The Japanese government even hinted at violent retaliation if Congress ever enacted restrictive legislation

We went away one day to Newark [New Jersey] and got work on the street. . . . We paid a man five dollars each for getting us the work and we were with that boss for six months. He was Irish, but a good man and he gave us our money every Saturday night. We lived much better than with Bartolo, and when the work was done we each had nearly $200 saved. Plenty of the men spoke English and they taught us, and we taught them to read and write. . . .

We went back to Brooklyn to a saloon . . . where we got a job cleaning it out and slept in a little room upstairs. There was a bootblack named Michael on the corner and when I had time I helped him and learned the business. . . . Then [Francesco and I] thought we would go into business and we got a basement and put four chairs in it. . . . Outside we had a big sign that read:

THE BEST SHINE FOR TEN CENTS

We had said that when we saved $1,000 each we would go back to Italy and buy a farm, but now that the time is coming we are so busy and making so much money that we think we will stay.

A Japanese Immigrant Becomes a Servant

The desire to see America was burning at my boyish heart. . . . My destination was Portland, Ore., where my cousin is studying. . . . I can be any use here, but become a domestic servant, as the field for Japanese very narrow and limited. . . . The place where I got work in the first time was a boarding house. My duties were to peel potatoes, wash the dishes, a few laundry work, and also I was expected to do whatever mistress, waitress and cook has told me. . . .

My real objection was that the work was indeed too hard and unpleasant for me to bear and also there were no times even to read a book. But I thought it rather impolite to say so and partly my strange pride hated to confess my weakness. . . . At the end of the second week I asked my wages, but she refused on the ground that if she does I might leave her. . . . Believing the impossibility to obtain her sanction, early in the next morning while everybody still in the bed, I hide my satchel under the bush in the back yard. . . . Leaving the note and wages behind me, I hurried back to Japanese Christian Home.

Since then I have tried a few other places with a better success at each trial and in course of time I have quite accustomed to it and gradually become indifferent as the humiliation melted down. Though I never felt proud of this vocation, in several cases I have commenced to manifest the interest of my avocation as a professor of Dust and Ashes.

Sources: The Independent, *March and May 1906.*

similar to that imposed on the Chinese. But most immigrants believed that the more "American" they became, the less prejudice they would encounter. Accordingly, leaders of immigrant groups stressed the importance of assimilation.

In 1895, a group of American-born Chinese in California formed a communal association called the Native Sons of the Golden State (a deliberate response to a nativist organization that called itself the Native Sons of the Golden West). Stressing the need to assimilate, the association's constitution declared, "It is imperative that no members shall have sectional, clannish, Tong [a secret fraternal organization] or party prejudices against each other. . . . Whoever violates this provision shall be expelled." A guidebook written at the same time for immigrant Jews recommended that they "hold fast," calling that attitude "most necessary in America. Forget your past, your customs, and your ideals. . . . A bit of advice to you: do not take a moment's rest. Run, do, work, and keep your own good in mind." Although it is doubtful whether most Jewish immigrants followed this advice whole, it nonetheless reflects the way the pressure to conform modified the cultures of all immigrant groups.

Assimilation connotes the loss of one culture in favor of another. The immigrant experience of the late nineteenth and early twentieth centuries might better be described as a process of adjustment between old ways and new. It was a dynamic process that resulted in entirely new cultural forms. It rarely followed a straight line toward or from the culture of origin. The Japanese, for example, had not gone to Los Angeles to become truck farmers, but circumstances led them to that occupation, and they used their cultural heritage of hard work, strong family ties, and sober living to make a restricted livelihood successful. Sometimes economics and the availability of alternatives resulted in modifications of traditions that nonetheless maintained their spirit. In the old country, Portuguese held *festas* every Sunday honoring a patron saint. In New England towns, they confined the tradition to their churches instead of parading through the streets. And instead of baking bread themselves, Portuguese immigrant women were happy to buy all the bread they needed from local bakers.

In a few cases, the New World offered greater opportunities to follow cultural traditions than the Old. Young women who migrated from Italy's Abruzzi region to Rochester, New York, found that it was easier to retain their Old-World moral code in late-nineteenth-century Rochester, where young men outnumbered them significantly. At the same time, the enhanced economic prospects in Rochester enabled them to marry earlier than they would have in their hometown. It also allowed these young women to work outside the home, something women rarely did in Abruzzi. Financial security allowed them to construct the nuclear household that was the cultural ideal in the old country. In a similar way, Sicilians who migrated to lower Manhattan discovered that ready access to work and relatively high geographical mobility permitted them to live near and among their extended families much more easily than in Sicily.

Despite the antagonism of native-born white people toward recent immigrants, the greatest racial divide in America remained that between black and white. Newcomers quickly caught on to this distinction and sought to assert their "whiteness" as a common bond with other European immigrant groups and a badge of acceptance into the larger society. Nativists, however, often lumped immigrants into the "black" category. The word "guinea," for example, which originally referred to African slaves, emerged as a derogatory epithet for Italians and occasionally Greeks, Jews, and Puerto Ricans. When the Louisiana legislature debated disfranchisement in 1898, a lawmaker explained that "according to the spirit of our meaning when we speak of 'white man's government,' Italians are as black as the blackest negro in existence." For immigrants, therefore, becoming "white"—distancing themselves from African-American culture and people—was often part of the process of adjusting to American life, especially as increasing numbers of black Southerners began moving to northern cities.

Roots of the Great Migration

Nearly 90 percent of African Americans still lived in the South in 1900, most in rural areas. Between 1880 and 1900, however, black families began to move into the great industrial cities of the Northeast and Midwest. They were drawn by the same economic promise that attracted overseas migrants and were pushed by growing persecution in the South. They were also responding to the appeals of black Northerners. As a leading black newspaper, the ***Chicago Defender*** argued in the early 1900s, "To die from the bite of frost is far more glorious than at the hands of a mob. I beg you, my brother, to leave the benighted land." Job opportunities probably outweighed all other factors in motivating what became known as the **Great Migration**. Letters to the *Defender* spoke much less of the troubled life in the South than of the promise of a new, more productive life in the North.

In most northern cities in 1900, black people typically worked as common laborers or domestic servants. They competed with immigrants for jobs, and in most cases they lost. Immigrants even claimed jobs that black workers once dominated, like barbering and service work in hotels, restaurants, and transportation. Fannie Barrier Williams, a turn-of-the-century black activist in Chicago, complained that between 1895 and 1905, "the colored people of Chicago have lost . . . nearly every occupation of which they once had almost a monopoly."

Black women had particularly few options in the northern urban labor force outside of domestic service, although they earned higher wages than they had for similar work in southern cities. The retail and clerical jobs that attracted young working-class white women remained closed to black women. Employers rejected them for any job involving direct contact with the public. As one historian concluded, advertisers and corporate executives demanded "a pleasing physical appearance (or voice)—one that conformed to a native-born white American standard of female beauty [and served] as an important consideration in hiring office receptionists, secretaries, department store clerks, and telephone operators." Addie W. Hunter, who qualified for a civil service clerical position in Boston, could not find work to match her training. She concluded in 1916, "For the way things stand at present, it is useless to have the requirements. Color . . . will always be in the way."

The lack of options black migrants confronted in the search for employment matched similar frustrations in their quest for a place to live. Even more than foreign immigrants, they were restricted to segregated urban **ghettos**. Small black ghettos existed in antebellum northern cities. In 1860, four out of every five black residents of Detroit lived in a clearly defined district, for example. After the Civil War, black ghettos emerged in southern and border cities. In Washington, D.C., black residents comprised nearly 80 percent of the population in a twenty-block area in the southwest quadrant of the city. In the 1890s, black people dominated an area east of downtown Atlanta known as "Sweet Auburn" after the avenue that cut through the neighborhood. As black migration to northern cities accelerated after 1900, the pattern of residential isolation became more pronounced. The black districts in northern cities were more diverse than those of southern cities. Migration brought rural Southerners, urban Southerners, and West Indians (especially in New York) together with the black Northerners already living there. People of all social classes lived in these districts.

The difficulties that black families faced to make ends meet paralleled in some ways those of immigrant working-class families. Restricted job options, however, limited the income of black families, even with black married women five times more likely to work than married white women. In black families, moreover, working teenage children were less likely to stay home and contribute their paychecks to the family income.

Popular culture reinforced the marginalization of African Americans. Vaudeville and minstrel shows, popular urban entertainment around 1900, featured songs belittling black people and black characters with names like "Useless Peabody" and "Moses Abraham Highbrow." Immigrants frequented these shows and absorbed the culture of racism from them. The new medium of film perpetuated the negative stereotypes.

In the North as in the South, African Americans sought to counter the hostility of the larger society by building their own community institutions. An emerging middle-class leadership—including Robert Abbott, publisher of the *Chicago Defender*—sought to develop black businesses. Despite these efforts, chronic lack of capital kept black businesses mostly small and confined to the ghetto. Immigrant groups often pooled extended family capital resources or tapped ethnic banks. With few such resources at their disposal, black businesses failed at a high rate. Most black people worked outside the ghetto for white employers. Economic marginalization often attracted unsavory businesses—dance halls, brothels, and bars—to black neighborhoods. One recently arrived migrant from the South complained that in his Cleveland neighborhood, his family was surrounded by loafers, "gamblers [and] pocket pickers; I can not raise my children here like they should be. This is one of the worst places in principle you ever looked on in your life."

An African-American religious meeting, New York City, early 1900s. Black migrants from the South found vibrant communities in northern cities typically centered around black churches and their activities. Like immigrants from Asia and Europe who sought to transplant the cultures of their homelands within urban America, black migrants reestablished southern religious and communal traditions in their new homes.

Other black institutions proved more lasting than black businesses. In Chicago in 1891, black physician Daniel Hale Williams established Provident Hospital, the nation's first interracially staffed hospital, with the financial help of wealthy white Chicagoans. Although it failed as an interracial experiment, the hospital thrived, providing an important training ground for black physicians and nurses.

The organization of black branches of the Young Men's and Young Women's Christian Association provided living accommodations, social facilities, and employment information for black young people. Many black migrants to northern cities—perhaps a majority—were single, and the Y provided them guidance and a "home." White people funded many black Y projects but did not accept black members in their chapters. By 1910, black settlement houses modeled after white versions appeared in several cities.

New Cities

Despite the hardships associated with urban life, the American city continued to act, in the words of contemporary novelist Theodore Dreiser, as a "giant magnet." Immigration from abroad and migration from American farms to the cities resulted in an urban explosion during the late nineteenth century (see Map 20-2). In 1850, six cities had a population exceeding 100,000; by 1900, thirty-eight did. In 1850, only 5 percent of the nation's population lived in cities of more than 100,000 inhabitants; by 1900, the figure was 19 percent. The nation's population tripled between 1860 and 1920, but the urban population increased ninefold. Of the 1,700 cities listed in the 1900 census, less than 2 percent even existed in 1800.

In Europe, a few principal cities like Paris and Berlin absorbed most of the urban growth dur-

Map 20-2 The Growth of America's Cities, 1880–1900
Several significant trends stand out on this map. First is the development of an urban-industrial core stretching from New England to the Midwest where the largest cities were located. And second is the emergence of relatively new cities in the South and West, reflecting the national dimensions of innovations in industry and transportation.

ing this period. In the United States, in contrast, growth was more evenly distributed among many cities. In 1820, about 18 percent of the urban population of the United States lived in New York, the nation's largest city; by 1890, its share had fallen to 7 percent. Put another way, many U.S. cities experienced the pains of rapid growth and industrialization in the late nineteenth century.

Despite the relative evenness of growth, a distinctive urban system had emerged by 1900, with New York and Chicago anchoring an urban-industrial core extending in a crescent from New England to the cities bordering the Great Lakes. This region included nine of the nation's ten largest cities in 1920. Western cities such as Denver, San Francisco, and Los Angeles emerged as dominant urban places in their respective regions but did not challenge the urban core for supremacy. Southern cities, limited in growth by low consumer demand, low wages, and weak capital formation, were drawn into the orbit of the urban core. Atlanta, an offspring of the railroad, prospered as the region's major way station for funneling wealth into the urban North. Dallas emerged as Atlanta's counterpart in the western South (see Chapter 19).

Urban growth highlighted the growing divisions in American society. The crush of people and the emergence of new technologies expanded the city outward and upward as urban dwellers sorted themselves by social class and ethnic group. While the new infrastructure of water and sewer systems, bridges, and trolley tracks kept steel mills busy, it also fragmented the urban population by allowing settlements well beyond existing urban boundaries. The way people satisfied their needs for food, clothing, and shelter stimulated the industrial economy while distinguishing one class from another. Although urban institutions emerged to counter these divisive trends, they could not overcome them completely.

Centers and Suburbs

The centers of the country's great cities changed in scale and function in this era, achieving a prominence they would eventually lose in the twentieth century. Downtowns expanded up and out as tall buildings arose—monuments to business and finance—creating towering urban skylines. Residential neighborhoods were pushed out, leaving the center dominated by corporate headquarters and retail and entertainment districts.

Corporate heads administered their empires from downtown, even if their factories were located on the urban periphery or in other towns and cities. Banks and insurance companies clustered in financial centers like Atlanta's Five Points district to service the corporations. Department stores and shops clustered in retail districts in strategic locations along electric trolley lines. It was to these areas that urban residents usually referred when they talked about going "downtown." In the entertainment district, electric lights lit up theaters, dance halls, and restaurants into the night.

As retail and office uses crowded out dwellings from the city center, a new phenomenon emerged: the residential neighborhood. Advances in transportation technology, first the horse-drawn railway and, by the 1890s, the electric trolley, eased commuting for office workers. Some in the growing and increasingly affluent middle class left the crowded, polluted city altogether to live in new residential suburbs. These people did not abandon the city—they still looked to it for its jobs, schools, libraries, and entertainment—but they rejected it as a place to live, leaving it to the growing ranks of working-class immigrants and African Americans. This pattern contrasted with that of Europe, where the middle class remained in the city.

The suburb emerged as the preferred place of residence for the urban middle class after 1870. As early as 1873, Chicago boasted nearly one hundred suburbs with a combined population of more than fifty thousand. Smaller cities like Cleveland, Richmond, Memphis, Omaha, and San Francisco also sprouted large suburban communities. The ideals that had promoted modest suburban growth earlier in the nineteenth century—privacy, aesthetics, and home ownership—became increasingly important for the growing numbers of middle-class families after 1880.

Consider the Russells of Short Hills, New Jersey. Short Hills lay eighteen miles by railroad from New York City. William Russell; his wife, Ella Gibson Russell; and their six children moved there from Brooklyn in the late 1880s, seeking a "pleasant, cultured people whose society we could enjoy" and a cure for Russell's rheumatism. Russell owned and managed a small metal brokerage in New York and enjoyed gardening, reading, and socializing with his new neighbors. Ella Russell cared for their six children with the help of a servant and also found time for several clubs and charities.

The design of the Russells's home reflected the principles Catharine Beecher and Harriet Beecher Stowe outlined in their suburban home Bible, *American Woman's Home* (1869). The

As immigrants crowded into cities and as advances in transportation technology made commuting to work feasible, more and more middle-class families abandoned the noise, bustle, and diversity of the city for dream homes in the pastoral setting of the suburbs.

kitchen, according to Beecher and Stowe, should be organized for expedience and hygiene. The home's utilities should be confined to a central core, freeing wall areas for other functions. The new technology of central heating made it unnecessary to divide a house into many small rooms, each with its own fireplace or stove. Taking advantage of this change, Beecher and Stowe recommended that a home's ground floor have fewer but larger rooms to encourage the family to pursue their individual activities in a common space. Parlors and reception rooms disappeared, along with the rigid spatial segregation of the sexes. Such former standards as the children's wing, the male "smoking room," and the female parlor were not part of the new suburban home.

The once prevailing view that women were too frail for vigorous exercise was changing. Thus the entire Russell family was to be found enjoying the tennis, swimming, and skating facilities on the grounds of the Short Hills Athletic Club. Because the community bordered on undeveloped woodland traversed by trails, "wheel clubs" appeared in the 1880s to organize families for bicycle outings.

The emphasis on family togetherness also reflected the changing role of men in late-nineteenth-century society. Beecher and Stowe praised fathers who took active roles in child rearing and participated fully in the family's leisure activities. Women's roles also broadened, as Ella Russell's club work attested.

Suburbs differed not only from the city but also from one another. With the growth after 1890 of the electric trolley, elevated rail lines, and other relatively inexpensive forms of commuter travel, suburbs became accessible to a broader spectrum of the middle class. The social structure, architecture, and amenities of suburbs varied, depending on the rail service and distance from the city. The commuter railroad remained popular among people like the Russells who could afford the time and expense of commuting to and from the city center—a distance of fifteen miles or more. The trolley and elevated railroads generated modest middle-class urban neighborhoods and suburbs, with densities decreasing and income increasing toward the ends of the lines. But for the working class—even skilled artisans—suburban living remained out of reach.

The suburb underscored the growing fragmentation of life in and around American cities in the late nineteenth century. Residence, consumer habits, and leisure activities reflected growing social and class divisions. Yet, at the same time, the growing materialism of American society promised a common ground for its disparate ethnic, racial, and social groups.

The New Middle Class

From the colonial era, America's urban middle class had included professionals—physicians, lawyers, ministers, educators, editors—as well as merchants, shopkeepers, and skilled artisans (until they dropped from the middle class in the late nineteenth century). In the late nineteenth century, industrial technology and urban growth expanded the urban middle class to include salespeople, factory supervisors, managers, civil servants, technicians, and a broad range of "white-collar" office workers like insurance agents, bank tellers, and legal assistants. This newer middle class set national trends in residential patterns, consumption, and leisure.

The more affluent members of the new middle class, like the Russells, repaired to new subdivisions within and outside the city limits. Simple row houses sheltered the growing numbers of clerks and civil servants who remained in the city. These dwellings contrasted sharply with the crowded one- or two-room apartments that confined the working class. Rents for these apartments ran as much as $3 a week at a time when few workers made more than $9 or $10.

The new middle class transformed America into a consumer society. In earlier times, land had been a symbol of prestige. Now it was things. And the new industries obliged with a dazzling array of goods and technologies to make life easier and allow more time for family and leisure.

By 1910, the new middle class lived in all-electric homes, with indoor plumbing and appliances unavailable twenty years earlier. A typical kitchen might include a coffeepot, a hot plate, a chafing dish, and a toaster. These items eased food preparation. The modern city-dweller worked by the clock, not by the sun. Eating patterns changed: cold, packaged cereals replaced hot meats at breakfast; fast lunches of Campbell's soup—"a meal in itself"—or canned stews weaned Americans from the heavy lunch. Jell-O appeared in the 1890s, touted as America's "most quick and easy" dessert. In Nashville at the same time, Joel Cheek ground and blended coffee beans in his store for customers' convenience. He convinced the city's Maxwell House Hotel to serve his new concoction, and in 1907, when President Theodore Roosevelt visited the hotel and drained his cup, he turned to Cheek and declared that the coffee was "good to the very last drop." A slogan and Maxwell House coffee were born.

Advertising played an important role in the consumer society. Advertisers told Americans what they wanted; they created demand and developed loyalty for brand-name products. In early-twentieth-century New York, a six-story-high Heinz electric sign was a sensation, especially the forty-foot-long pickle at its top.

The middle class liked anything that saved time: trolleys, trains, electric razors, vacuum cleaners. The telephone replaced the letter for everyday communication; it was quicker and less formal. By 1900, some 1.4 million phones were in service, and many middle-class homes had one. The new technology introduced new terms that reflected the pace of urban life: "I'll give you a buzz" or "Give me a ring."

The middle class liked its news in an easy-to-read form. Urban tabloids multiplied after 1880, led by Joseph Pulitzer's *New York World* and William Randolph Hearst's *New York Journal.* The newspapers organized the news into topical sections, used bold headlines and graphics to catch the eye, ran human interest stories to capture the imagination, inaugurated sports pages to attract male readers, and offered advice columns for women. And they opened their pages to a wide range of attractive advertising, much of it directed at women, who did about 90 percent of the shopping in American cities by 1900.

As the visual crowded out the printed in advertising, newspapers, and magazines, these materials became more accessible to a wider urban audience. Although mainly middle-class in orientation, the tabloid press drew urban society together with new features such as the comic strip, which first appeared in the 1890s, and heart-rending personal sagas drawn from real life. Immigrants who might have had difficulty reading small-type newspapers received their initiation into the mainstream of American society through the tabloids.

In a similar manner, the department store, essentially a middle-class retail establishment, became one of the city's most democratic forums and the focus of the urban downtown after 1890. Originating in the 1850s and 1860s with the construction of retail palaces such as Boston's Jordan Marsh, Philadelphia's Wanamaker & Brown, New York's Lord & Taylor, and Chicago's Marshall Field, the department store came to epitomize the bounty of the new industrial capitalism. At the time of the Philadelphia Exposition in 1876, only thirty or so department stores existed; by 1920, there were thousands. They exuded limitless abundance with their extensive inventories, items for every budget, sumptuous surroundings, and efficient, trained personnel.

At first, most department store customers were middle-class married women. Not expected to work and with disposable income and flexible schedules, these women had the means and time to wander department store aisles. The stores catered to their tastes—and the current emphasis on home and domesticity—with such items as prefabricated household furnishings, ready-made clothing, toys, and stationery.

Industry churned out uniform, high-quality products in abundance, and middle-class salaries absorbed them. Department stores maintained consumers' interest with advertising campaigns arranged around holidays such as Easter and Christmas, the seasons, and the school calendar. Each event required new clothing and accessories, and the ready-made clothing industry changed fashions accordingly.

Soon the spectacle and merchandise of the department store attracted shoppers from all social strata, not just the middle class. "The principal cause of the stores' success," one shopper explained in 1892, "is the fact that their founders have understood the necessity of offering a new democracy whose needs and habits" are satisfied "in the cheapest possible way," providing "a taste for elegance and comfort unknown to previous generations." Though many less affluent women came merely to "window-shop" (a new expression inspired by the large plate glass display windows retailers installed in their stores to attract customers), some came to buy. After 1890, department stores increasingly hired young immigrant women to cater to their growing foreign-born clientele.

The department store was the turn-of-the-century shopping mall and provided inexpensive amusement for young working-class people, especially immigrants. Mary Antin recalled how she and her teenage friends and sister would spend their Saturday nights in 1898 patrolling "a dazzlingly beautiful palace called a 'department store.'" It was there that Mary and her sister "exchanged our hateful homemade European costumes . . . for real American machine-made garments, and issued forth glorified in each other's eyes."

By 1900, department stores had added sporting goods and hardware sections and were attracting male as well as female customers from a wide social spectrum. When Wanamaker's introduced a "bargain room" in 1888, other retail stores—including Filene's famous "Automatic Bargain Basement" in Boston—followed suit.

The expanding floor space devoted to sporting goods reflected the growth of leisure in urban society. And like other aspects of that society, leisure and recreation both separated and cut across social classes. The leisure activities of the wealthy increasingly removed them from the rest of urban society. For them, the good life required such prerequisites as a mansion on Fifth Avenue, carriages and horses for transportation, a pony for the younger children, a saddle horse for the older ones, and a yacht. As sports like football became important extracurricular activites at Harvard, Yale, and other elite universities, intercollegiate games became popular occasions for the upper class to congregate and, not incidentally, discuss business. For exercise and recreation, the elite gathered at the athletic clubs and country clubs that emerged as open spaces disappeared in the city. High fees and strict membership criteria kept these clubs exclusive. The first country club in the United States was founded in Brookline, Massachusetts, a Boston suburb, in 1882. Country clubs built golf courses for men and tennis courts primarily for women. The clubs offered a suburban retreat, away from the diverse middle- and working-class populations, where the elite could play in privacy.

Middle-class urban residents could not afford country clubs, but they rode electric trolleys to the end of the line to enjoy suburban parks and bicycle and skating clubs. Reflecting the emphasis on family togetherness in late-nineteenth-century America, both men and women participated in these sports. Bicycling in particular became immensely popular. New bikes cost at least $50, putting them beyond the reach of the working class.

If college football was the rage among the elite, baseball was the leading middle-class spectator sport. Organized baseball originated among the urban elite before the Civil War. The middle class took over the sport after the war. Baseball epitomized the nation's transition from a rural to an urban industrial society. Reflecting rural tradition, it was played on an expanse of green usually on the outskirts of the city. It was leisurely; unlike other games, it had no time limit. Reflecting industrial society, however, it had clearly defined rules and was organized into leagues. Professional leagues were profit-making enterprises, and, like other enterprises, they frequently merged. Initially, most professional baseball games were played on weekday afternoons, making it hard for working-class spectators to attend. After merging with the American Association (AA) in 1883, the National League adopted some of the AA's innovations to attract more fans, including beer sales, cheap admission, and, despite the objections of Protestant churches, Sunday games.

The tavern, or saloon, was the workingman's club. Typically an all-male preserve, the saloon provided drink, cheap food, and a place for workingmen to read a newspaper, socialize, and learn about job opportunities. Advances in refrigeration in the 1870s allowed large breweries such as Anheuser-Busch and Pabst to distribute their product nationwide. Alcoholism was a severe problem in

Thomas Eakins created this painting of baseball players practicing in 1875. Originating as a sport of urban gentlemen, baseball eventually broadened its appeal, drawing fans from all spectrums of city life.

cities, especially, though not exclusively, among working-class men, fueling the prohibition movement of the late nineteenth century.

Amusement parks, with their mechanical wonders, were another hallmark of the industrial city. Declining trolley fares made them accessible to the working class around 1900. Unlike taverns, they provided a place for working-class men and women to meet and date.

The most renowned of these parks was Brooklyn's Coney Island. In 1897, George C. Tilyou opened Steeplechase Park on Coney Island. He brought an invention by George Washington Ferris—a giant rotating vertical wheel equipped with swinging carriages—to the park from Chicago, and the Ferris Wheel quickly became a Coney Island signature. Together with such attractions as mechanical horses and 250,000 of Thomas Edison's light bulbs, Steeplechase dazzled patrons with its technological wonders. It was quickly followed by Luna Park and Dreamland, and the Coney Island attractions became collectively known as "the poor man's paradise." Immigrant entrepreneurs, seeing a good thing, flocked to Coney Island to set up sideshows, pool halls, taverns, and restaurants. One German immigrant opened a small café serving sausages that he named "frankfurters" after his native Frankfurt. Locals called them "Coney Island hots" or "hot dogs" because they resembled the dachshund, a German-bred dog.

After 1900, the wonders of Coney Island began to lure people from all segments of an increasingly diverse city. Sightseers came from around the world. Notables such as Herman Melville, Mark Twain, and even Sigmund Freud (what did he think of Dreamland?) rubbed shoulders with factory workers, domestics, and department store clerks. In much the same manner, baseball was becoming a national pastime as games attracted a disparate crowd of people with little in common but their devotion to the home team.

Increasing materialism had revealed great fissures in American urban society by 1900. Yet places like deparment stores, baseball parks, and amusement parks provided democratic spaces for some interaction. Newspapers and schools also indirectly offered diverse groups the opportunity to share similar experiences.

Conclusion

The new industrial order, the changing nature of work, the massive migrations of populations from the countryside and abroad, and the rise of great cities changed the American landscape in the late nineteenth century. By 1900, the factory worker and the department store clerk were more representative of the new America than the farmer and small shopkeeper. Industry and technology had created thousands of new jobs, but they also eliminated the autonomy many workers had enjoyed and limited their opportunities to advance.

Immigrants thronged to the United States to realize their dreams of economic and religious freedom. They found both to varying degrees but also discovered a darker side to the promise of American life. The great cities thrilled newcomers with their possibilities and their abundance of goods and activities. But the cities also bore witness to the growing divisions in American society. As the new century dawned, the prospects for urban industrial America seemed limitless, yet the stark contrasts that had appeared so vividly inside and outside the Centennial Exposition persisted and deepened.

Still, it would be wrong to depict the nation in 1900 as merely a larger and more divided version of itself in 1876. Although sharp ethnic, racial, and class differences persisted, the nation seemed better poised to address them in 1900 than it had a quarter-century earlier. Labor unions, ethnic organizations, government legislation, and new urban institutions promised ways to remedy the worst abuses of the new urban, industrial economy.

Review Questions

1. Were there ways to achieve the benefits of industrialization without its social costs, or did the nation's political and economic systems make that impossible?
2. Given the widespread grievances among unskilled workers in the late nineteenth and early twentieth centuries, why did so few turn to socialism?
3. When historians speak of immigrant groups adjusting rather than assimilating to American society, what do they mean?
4. The growing fragmentation of urban life reflected deep divisions in modern urban industrial society. At the same time, there were forces that tended to overcome these divisions. What were these forces, and were they sufficient to bridge the divisions?

Recommended Reading

Stuart M. Blumin, *The Emergence of the Middle Class: Social Experience in the American City, 1760–1900* (1989). Analyzes the key factors in the emergence of the urban middle class, especially in the late nineteenth century, and the impact of that class on urban society and culture.

John Bodnar, *The Transplanted: A History of Immigrants in Urban America* (1985). An excellent starting point for learning about the diverse immigrant experience in the United States that is also sensitive to conditions in the countries of origin.

Roger Daniels, *Coming to America: A History of Immigration and Ethnicity in American Life* (1990). Preferred by some to Bodnar's survey. The book's great virtue is its coverage of all immigrant groups; the discussion of Asian immigrants is especially good.

Theodore Dreiser, *Sister Carrie* (1900). One of the best novels to capture life in late-nineteenth-century Chicago and New York. Few detail so clearly the moral and economic dilemmas newcomers faced in the fast-evolving American urban environment.

David Goldfield and Blaine A. Brownell, *Urban America: A History* (1990). A comprehensive overview of the development of American cities that places particular emphasis on the interaction of social, economic, and geographical forces on urban growth.

John Higham, *Strangers in the Land: Patterns of American Nativism, 1860–1925* (1965). Despite its age, serves as an excellent overview of and introduction to the subject of nativism; especially good in setting the context of nativism in American society and politics.

Raymond A. Mohl, *A New City: Urban America in the Industrial Age, 1860–1920* (1985). A fine introduction to the relationship between urbanization and industrialization.

Additional Sources

New Industry

Mark Aldrich, *Safety First: Technology, Labor, and Business in the Building of American Work Safety, 1870–1939* (1997).

Edward Bellamy, *Looking Backward* (1888).

Susan Porter Benson, *Counter Cultures: Saleswomen, Managers, and Customers in American Department Stores, 1890–1940* (1986).

Eileen Boris, *Home to Work: Motherhood and the Politics of Industrial Homework in the United States* (1994).

Stanley Buder, *Pullman: An Experiment in Industrial Order and Community Planning, 1880–1930* (1967).

W. Bernard Carlson, *Innovation as a Social Process: Elihu Thomson and the Rise of General Electric, 1870–1900* (1991).

John Cumbler, *Working-Class Community in Industrial America: Work, Leisure, and Struggle in Two Industrial Cities* (1979).

Marjorie Davies, *Woman's Place Is at the Typewriter, 1870–1930* (1982).

Allan F. Davis, *Spearheads for Reform: The Social Settlements and the Progressive Movement, 1890–1914* (1967).

Nancy Schrom Dye, *As Equals and as Sisters: Feminism, the Labor Movement, and the Women's Trade Union League of New York* (1981).

Leon Fink, *Workingmen's Democracy: The Knights of Labor and American Politics* (1982).

Timothy J. Gilfoyle, *City of Eros: New York City, Prostitution, and the Commercialization of Sex, 1790–1920* (1992).

Herbert Gutman, *Work, Culture, and Society in Industrializing America* (1976).

Tamara Hareven, *Family Time and Industrial Time: The Relationship between Family and Work in a New England Industrial Community* (1982).

William H. Harris, *The Harder We Run: Black Workers since the Civil War* (1982).

Samuel P. Hays, *The Response to Industrialism: 1885–1914* (1957).

David A. Hounshell, *From the American System to Mass Production, 1800–1932* (1984).

Nathan I. Huggins, *Protestants against Poverty: Boston's Charities, 1870–1900* (1970).

Thomas J. Jablonsky, *Pride in the Jungle: Community and Everyday Life in Back of the Yards Chicago* (1993).

David M. Katzman, *Seven Days a Week: Women and Domestic Service in Industrializing America* (1978).

Stuart Kaufman, *Samuel Gompers and the Origins of the American Federation of Labor, 1848–1896* (1973).

Alice Kessler-Harris, *Out to Work: A History of Wage-Earning Women in the United States* (1982).

James B. Lane, *Jacob A. Riis and the American City* (1974).

Bruce Laurie, *Artisans into Workers: Labor in Nineteenth Century America* (1989).

W. David Lewis, *Sloss Furnaces and the Rise of the Birmingham District: An Industrial Epic* (1994).

Walter Licht, *Getting Work: Philadelphia, 1840–1950* (1992).

David Montgomery, *The Fall of the House of Labor: The Workplace, the State, and American Labor Activism, 1865–1925* (1987).

Allan Nevins, *A Study in Power: John D. Rockefeller* (2 vols., 1953).

Dominic A. Pacyga, *Polish Immigrants and Industrial Chicago: Workers on the South Side, 1880–1922* (1991).

Harold C. Passer, *The Electrical Manufacturers, 1875–1900* (1953).

Nick Salvatore, *Eugene V. Debs, Citizen and Socialist* (1982).

Upton Sinclair, *The Jungle* (1906).

John F. Stover, *American Railroads* (1970).

Shelton Stromquist, *A Generation of Boomers: The Pattern of Railroad Labor Conflict in Nineteenth-Century America* (1987).

Leslie Woodcock Tentler, *Wage-Earning Women: Industrial Work and Family Life, 1900–1930* (1979).

Jules Tygiel, *Workingmen in San Francisco, 1880–1901* (1992).

Kim Voss, *The Making of American Exceptionalism: The Knights of Labor and Class Formation in the Nineteenth Century* (1994).

Joseph F. Wall, *Andrew Carnegie* (1970).

New Immigrants

Josef Barton, *Peasants and Strangers: Italians, Rumanians, and Slovaks in an American City, 1890–1950* (1975).

Dag Blanck, *Becoming Swedish-American: The Construction of an Ethnic Identity in the Augustana Synod, 1860–1917* (1997).

Abraham Cahan, *The Rise of David Levinsky* (1917).

Albert Camarillo, *Chicanos in a Changing Society: From Mexican Pueblos to American Barrios in Santa Barbara and Southern California, 1848–1930* (1979).

Dino Cinel, *From Italy to San Francisco: The Immigrant Experience* (1982).

Dennis Clark, *The Irish in Philadelphia: Ten Generations of Urban Experience* (1973).

Roger Daniels, *Not Like Us: Immigrants and Minorities in America, 1890–1924* (1997).

Hasia Diner, *Erin's Daughters in America* (1983).

Donna Gabaccia, *From Sicily to Elizabeth Street: Housing and Social Change among Italian Immigrants, 1880–1930* (1984).

Donna Gabaccia, *From the Other Side: Women, Gender, and Immigrant Life in the U.S., 1820–1990* (1994).

Evelyn Nakano Glenn, *Issei, Nisei, War Bride: Three Generations of Japanese American Women in Domestic Service* (1986).

Christiane Harzig, ed., *Peasant Maids – City Women: From the European Countryside to Urban America* (1997).

Irving Howe, *World of Our Fathers* (1976).

Noel Ignatiev, *How the Irish Became White* (1995).

Thomas Kessner, *The Golden Door: Italian and Jewish Immigrant Mobility in New York City, 1880–1915* (1977).

Alan M. Kraut, *The Huddled Masses: The Immigrant in American Society, 1880–1921* (1982).

Kenneth Kusmer, *A Ghetto Takes Shape: Black Cleveland, 1870–1930* (1976).

Valeria Gennaro Lerda, ed., *From "Melting Pot" to Multiculturalism: The Evolution of Ethnic Relations in the United States and Canada* (1990).

Mario Maffi, *Gateways to the Promised Land: Ethnic Cultures on New York's Lower East Side* (1995).

David C. Mauk, *The Colony that Rose from the Sea: Norwegian Maritime Migration and Community in Brooklyn, 1850–1910* (1997).

Charles J. McClain, *In Search of Equality: The Chinese Struggle against Discrimination in Nineteenth-Century America* (1994).

John Modell, *The Economics and Politics of Racial Accommodation: The Japanese of Los Angeles, 1900–1942* (1977).

Walter Nugent, *Crossings: The Great Transatlantic Migration, 1870–1914* (1992).

Janet E. Rasmussen, *New Land, New Lives: Scandinavian Immigrants to the Pacific Northwest* (1993).

David R. Roediger, *The Wages of Whiteness: Race and the Making of the American Working Class* (rev. ed. 1999).

Betty Smith, *A Tree Grows in Brooklyn* (1943).

Gerald Sorin, *A Time for Building: The Third Migration, 1880–1920;* Vol. 3 of *The Jewish People in America*, ed. Henry L. Feingold (1992).

Daniel Soyer, *Jewish Immigrant Associations and American Identity in New York, 1880–1939* (1997).

Kenneth L. Stewart and Arnoldo De Leon, *Not Room Enough: Mexicans, Anglos, and Socio-Economic Change in Texas, 1850–1900* (1993).

Rudolph J. Vecoli and Suzanne M. Sinke, eds., *A Century of European Migrations, 1830–1930* (1991).

K. Scott Wong and Sucheng Chan, eds., *Claiming America: Constructing Chinese American Identities during the Exclusion Era* (1998).

Olivier Zunz, *The Changing Face of Inequality: Urbanization, Industrialization, and Immigrants in Detroit, 1880–1920* (1982).

New Cities

Gunther Barth, *Instant Cities: Urbanization and the Rise of San Francisco and Denver* (1975).

Gunther Barth, *City People: The Rise of Modern City Culture in Nineteenth-Century America* (1982).

Catherine W. Bishir and Lawrence S. Early, eds., *Early Twentieth-Century Suburbs in North Carolina* (1986).

Daniel Bluestone, *Constructing Chicago* (1991).

Edwin G. Burrows and Mike Wallace, *Gotham: A History of New York City to 1898* (1998).

David R. Contosta, *Suburb in the City: Chestnut Hill, Philadelphia, 1850–1990* (1992).

Francis G. Couvares, *The Remaking of Pittsburgh: Class and Culture in an Industrializing City, 1877–1919* (1984).

Michael H. Ebner, *Creating Chicago's North Shore: A Suburban History* (1988).

Robert Fishman, *Bourgeois Utopias: The Rise and Fall of Suburbia* (1987).

Jessica Foy and Thomas J. Schlereth, eds., *American Home Life, 1880–1930: A Social History of Spaces and Services* (1991).

Clifton Hood, 722 Miles: *The Building of the Subways and How They Transformed New York* (1993).

Kenneth T. Jackson, *Crabgrass Frontier: The Suburbanization of the United States* (1985).

Frederic C. Jaher, *The Urban Establishment: Upper Strata in Boston, New York, Charleston, Chicago, and Los Angeles* (1982).

John F. Kasson, *Amusing the Millions: Coney Island at the Turn of the Century* (1978).

Margaret Marsh, *Suburban Lives* (1990).

Donald L. Miller, *City of the Century: The Epic of Chicago and the Making of America* (1996).

David Nasaw, *Going Out: The Rise and Fall of Public Amusements* (1993).

Kathy Peiss, *Cheap Amusements: Working Women and Leisure in Turn-of-the-Century New York* (1986).

Harold L. Platt, *The Electric City: Energy and the Growth of the Chicago Area, 1880–1930* (1991).

Roy Rosenzweig, *Eight Hours for What We Will: Workers and Leisure in an Industrial City, 1870–1920* (1983).

David Schuyler, *The New Urban Landscape: The Redefinition of City Form in Nineteenth-Century America* (1986).

Richard Sennett, *Families against the City: Middle-Class Homes of Industrial Chicago, 1872–1890* (1970).

Kathryn Kish Sklar, *Catherine Beecher: A Study of Domesticity* (1973).

William R. Taylor, *In Pursuit of Gotham: Culture and Commerce in New York* (1992).

Alexander von Hoffman, *Local Attachments: The Making of an American Urban Neighborhood, 1850–1920* (1994).

David Ward, *Cities and Immigrants: A Geography of Change in Nineteenth-Century America* (1971).

Sam Bass Warner Jr., *Streetcar Suburbs: The Process of Growth in Boston, 1870–1900* (1962).

Gwendolyn Wright, *Moralism and the Model Home: Domestic Architecture and Cultural Conflict in Chicago, 1873–1913* (1980).

Where to Learn More

❖ **Edison National Historic Site, West Orange, New Jersey.** The site contains the Edison archives, including photographs, sound recordings, and industrial and scientific machinery. Its twenty historic structures dating from the 1880–1887 period include Edison's home and laboratory.

❖ **Japanese American National Museum, Los Angeles, California.** Housed in a converted Buddhist temple, this museum includes artifacts and photographs of early Japanese immigration and settlement. The core exhibit is "Issei Pioneers: Japanese Immigration to Hawaii and the Mainland from 1885 to 1924."

❖ **Missouri Historical Society, St. Louis, Missouri.** The Society displays a long-term exhibition accompanied by public programs called, "St. Louis in the Gilded Age," which focuses on the changes generated by industrialization and urban development in St. Louis from 1865 to 1900.

❖ **Senator John Heinz Pittsburgh Regional History Center, Pittsburgh, Pennsylvania.** Through its long-term exhibition, "Points in Time: Building a Life in Western Pennsylvania, 1750-Today," the Center explores the growth of the Pittsburgh metropolitan area, especially its expansion during the great industrial boom at the turn of the twentieth century.

❖ **Angel Island State Park, San Francisco Bay.** Angel Island served as a detention center from 1910 to 1940 for Asian immigrants who were kept there for days, months, and, in some cases, years, while immigration officials attempted to ferret out illegal entries. Exhibits depict the era through pictures and artifacts.

❖ **Strawbery Banke, Portsmouth, New Hampshire.** This museum includes an exhibit and audiovisual presentations on the adjustment of one immigrant family to American life: "Becoming Americans: The Shapiro Story, 1898-1929," presents the story of an immigrant Jewish family in the context of immigration to the small, coastal city of Portsmouth at the turn of the twentieth century.

❖ **Statue of Liberty National Monument and Ellis Island, New York, New York.** More than 12 million immigrants were processed at Ellis Island between 1892 and 1954. The exhibits provide a fine overview of American immigration history during this period. There is an ongoing oral history program as well.

TRANSFORMING THE WEST, 1865–1890

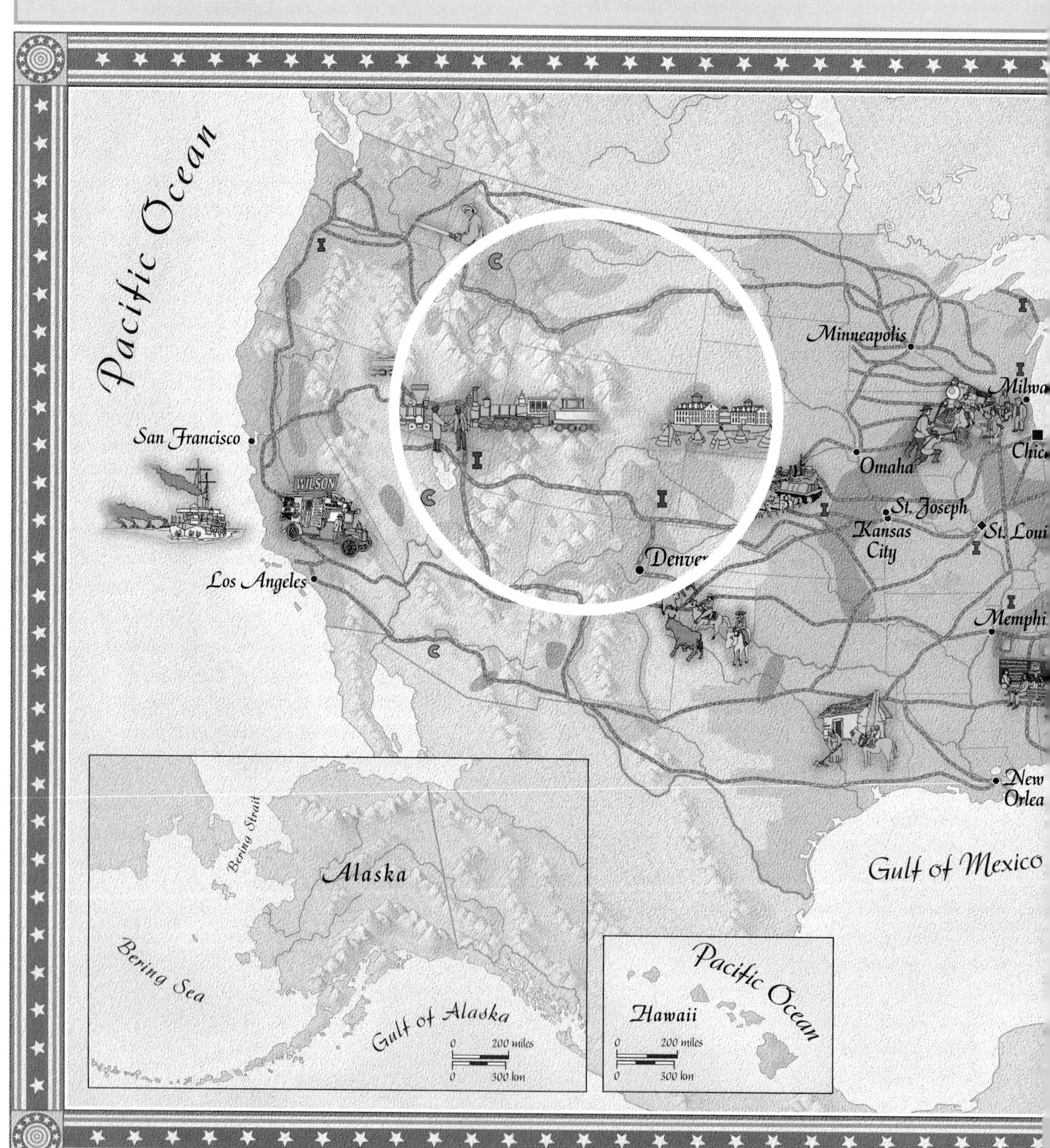

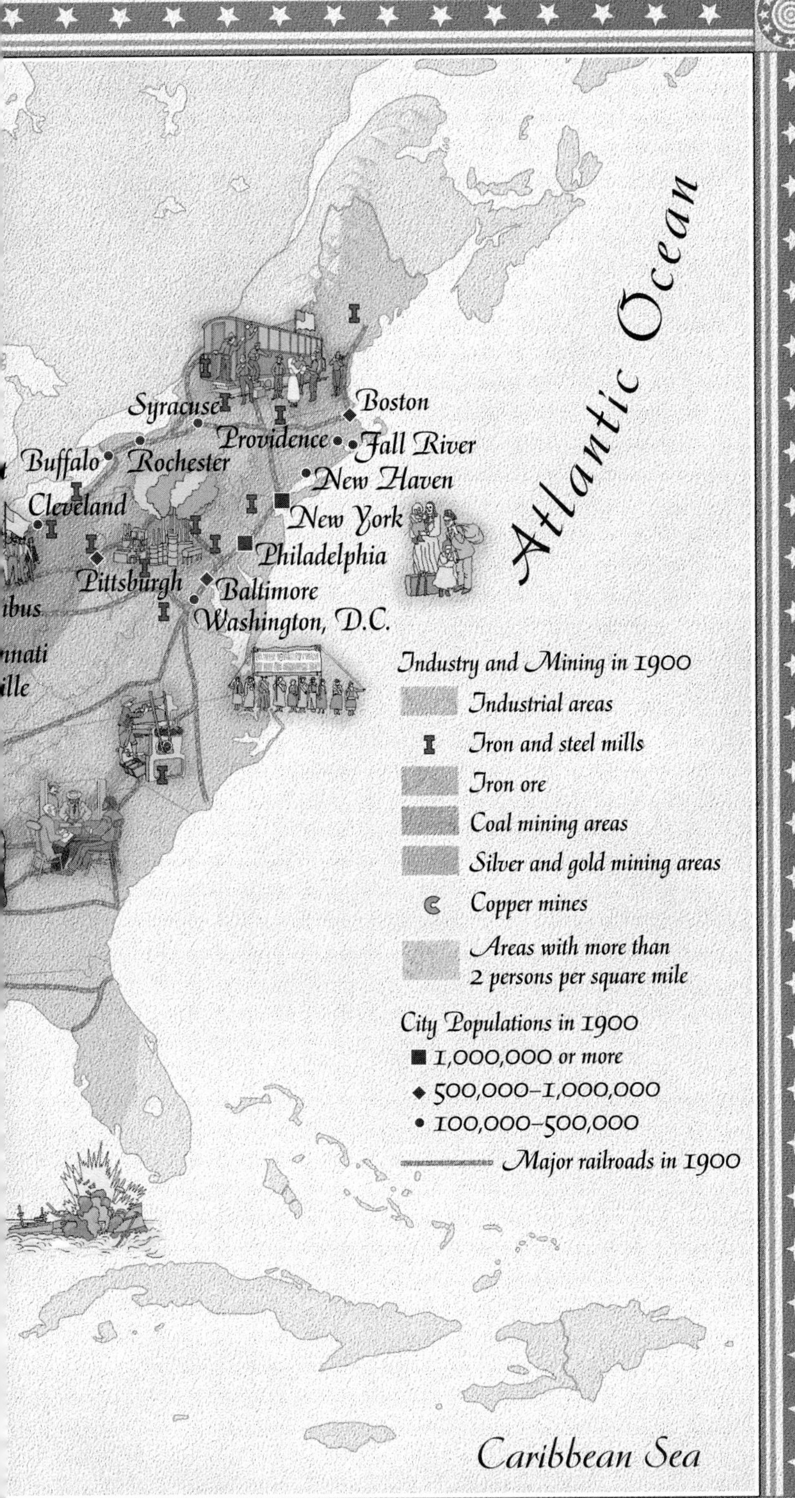

21

Chapter Outline

Key Topics

- ❖ The subjugation of Native Americans in the West, their confinement to reservations, and the attempted destruction of their culture
- ❖ The integration of the West into the national economy through the construction of transcontinental railroads
- ❖ The flood of migrants to the West in the late nineteenth century seeking work as railroad workers, miners, cowboys, and farmers
- ❖ The transformation of mining, ranching, and farming in the West from individual pursuits to corporate enterprises

The celebration began with a group of workers, soldiers, and railroad company officials at Promontory Point, a desolate sagebrush basin in western Utah. Chicago staged a seven-mile-long parade, Philadelphia rang the Liberty Bell, and New York held services in its greatest churches. The triumphal occasion was the completion of the nation's first transcontinental railroad, marked by the driving of a golden spike uniting the tracks of the Union Pacific and Central Pacific Railroads on May 10, 1869. The celebrations symbolized the nation's hopes, but the transcontinental railroad itself symbolized much more. It was, as the author Robert Louis Stevenson declared, "the one typical achievement of the age." It made the West as much a part of the nation as the East or the South and set a precedent for western development.

The two railroads were huge corporate enterprises, not individual efforts, and corporations would dominate western growth as much as they did eastern industrialization. But this corporate undertaking was scarcely private enterprise, for the federal government played a crucial role in railroad construction, as it did in virtually all aspects of western development. Congress had authorized the Union Pacific and Central Pacific to build the railroad link, given them the right-of-way for their tracks, and provided financial subsidies: For each mile of track laid, the companies received twenty square miles of land along the route and a loan of up to $48,000. With such backing, construction became a race between the companies to collect the largest subsidy. The Union Pacific worked westward from Omaha, Nebraska; the Central Pacific, eastward from Sacramento, California.

The separate companies that both railroads created to organize this construction siphoned money to a few major stockholders, foreshadowing the often corrupt methods by which the West would be developed. To shield these dishonest operations from government investigations, railroad officials bribed members of Congress and the Grant administration in Washington, D.C., forging yet another link between the exploitation of the West and events in the East.

The railroads' dependence on capital investment, engineering knowledge, technological innovations, and labor skills also typified western development. Their labor forces both reflected and reinforced the region's racial and ethnic diversity. Too few native-born Americans, white or black, were willing to build the roads, so the railroads looked elsewhere for workers. The Union Pacific recruited European immigrants, especially Irish; the Central Pacific hired Mexicans, Irish, and Paiute Indians, both male and female, but eventually relied on Chinese recruited in California and Asia. At the peak of construction, twelve thousand Chinese pushed the rails eastward, advancing as little as eight inches a day through the granite Sierras and as much as ten miles a day across the flat deserts of Nevada.

The railroads adopted callous and reckless construction tactics, resulting in waste, deaths, and environmental destruction. Laying track as quickly as possible to collect the subsidies awarded by the mile, each corporation built substandard railroads marked by improper grades, defective materials, dangerous curves, and flimsy bridges that might collapse under a locomotive's weight. Much of the work had to be redone almost immediately at the cost of millions of dollars. Such construction damaged the environment. Wood consumption alone was tremendous. Union Pacific tie cutters stripped the Platte Valley in Nebraska of its timber, and the Central Pacific used 64 million feet of timber just to build snowsheds. Finally, as the two corporations relentlessly drove their crews, even at night and in winter, perhaps as many as a thousand Chinese on the Central Pacific, and even more workers on the Union Pacific, died from accidents or exposure.

The construction of the transcontinental railroad was thus both a technological achievement that integrated the West into the rest of the nation and evidence that the development of the West, however fabled in folklore, was an integral part of the larger economic revolution that transformed America after the Civil War.

This contemporary engraving depicts the joining of the Central Pacific and Union Pacific railroads on May 10, 1869, at Promontory Point, Utah. Railroads transformed the American West, linking the region to outside markets, spurring rapid settlement, and threatening Indian survival.

Native Americans

The initial obstacle to exploiting the West was the people already living there, who used its resources in their own way and held different concepts of progress and civilization. For despite Easterners' image of the West as an unsettled wilderness, Native Americans had long inhabited it and had developed a variety of economies and cultures. As whites pressed westward, they attempted to subjugate the Indians, displace them from their lands, and strip them of their culture. Conquest gradually forced Indians onto desolate reservations, but efforts to destroy their beliefs and transform their way of life were less successful.

Tribes and Cultures

Throughout the West, Indians had adapted to their environment, developing subsistence economies ranging from simple gathering to complex systems of irrigated agriculture. Each activity encouraged their sensitivity to the natural world, and each had social and political implications.

In the Northwest, abundant food from rich waters and dense forests gave rise to complex and stable Indian societies. During summer fishing runs, the Tillamooks, Chinooks, and other tribes caught salmon that, after being dried in smokehouses, sustained them throughout the year. During the mild winters, they developed artistic handicrafts, elaborate social institutions, and a satisfying religious life.

At the opposite environmental extreme, the Cahuillas of the southern California desert survived only through their ability to extract food and medicines from desert plants. In the dry and barren Great Basin of Utah and Nevada, Shoshones and Paiutes ate grasshoppers and other insects to supplement their diet of rabbits, mice, and other small animals. Such harsh environments restricted the size, strength, and organizational complexity of societies. Needing to spend most of their time searching for food, these Indians lacked tribal unity. They lived in small family groups in flimsy huts rather than established villages.

In the Southwest, the Pueblos dwelled in permanent towns of adobe buildings and practiced intensive agriculture. Because tribal welfare depended on maintaining complex irrigation systems, the Zunis, Hopis, and other Pueblos emphasized community solidarity rather than individual ambition. Town living encouraged social stability and the development of complex effective governments, elaborate religious ceremonies, and creative arts. Navajos, Apaches, and other nomadic tribes in the region relied on sheepherding and hunting. They lacked the cohesion and structure of Pueblo society.

The most numerous Indian groups lived on the Great Plains. The largest of these tribes included the Lakotas or Sioux, who roamed from western Minnesota through the Dakotas; the Cheyennes and Arapahos, who controlled much of the central plains between the Platte and Arkansas

Chronology

1858 Gold is discovered in Colorado and Nevada.

1860 Gold is discovered in Idaho.

1862 Homestead Act is passed.
Gold is discovered in Montana.

1864 Militia slaughters Cheyennes at Sand Creek, Colorado.

1867 Cattle drives make Abilene the first cow town.

1868 Fort Laramie Treaty is signed.

1869 First transcontinental railroad is completed.

1874 Gold is discovered in the Black Hills.
Turkey Red wheat is introduced to Kansas.
Barbed wire is patented.

1876 Indians devastate U.S. troops in the Battle of the Little Bighorn.

1879 "Exodusters" migrate to Kansas.

1885 Chinese massacred at Rock Springs, Wyoming.

1887 Dawes Act is passed.

1890 Government troops kill two hundred Sioux at Wounded Knee, South Dakota.

1892 Mining violence breaks out at Coeur d'Alene, Idaho.

1893 Western Federation of Miners is organized.

Rivers; and the Comanches, predominant on the southern plains. Two animals dominated the lives of these peoples: the horse, which enabled them to move freely over the plains, and the buffalo, which provided meat, hides, bones and horns for tools, and a focus for spiritual life.

Despite their diversity, all tribes emphasized community welfare over individual interest. Their economies were based on subsistence rather than profit. They tried to live in harmony with nature to ward off sickness, injury, death, or misfortune. And they were intensely religious, absorbed with the need to establish proper relations with supernatural forces that linked human beings with all other living things. The connections among these basic values appeared in the frequent religious rituals regulating hunting. The Sioux, for example, performed ceremonies in which they accorded respect to the buffalo's soul, sought its forgiveness for having to kill it, and promised not to be wasteful, so that the animals would not depart and bring starvation on the tribe. These connections also shaped Indians' attitude toward land, which they regarded—like air and water—as part of nature to be held and used communally, not as an individual's personal property from which others could be excluded.

White and Indian cultural values were incompatible. Disdaining Native Americans and their religion, white people condemned them as "savages" to be converted or exterminated. Rejecting the concept of communal property, most settlers demanded land for the exclusive use of ambitious individuals. Ignoring the need for natural harmony, they followed their own culture's goal of extracting wealth from the land for a market economy.

No one expressed these cultural differences better than the great Sioux leader Sitting Bull. Referring to the forces of the spirit world, he declared:

> It is through this mysterious power that we too have our being and we therefore yield to our neighbors, even our animal neighbors, the same right as ourselves, to inhabit this land. Yet, hear me, people. We have now to deal with another race. . . . Possession is a disease with them. These people have made many rules that the rich may break but the poor may not. . . . They claim this mother of ours, the earth, for their own and fence their neighbors away; they deface her with their buildings. . . . That nation is like a spring freshet that overruns its banks and destroys all who are in its path. We cannot dwell side by side.

Federal Indian Policy

The government had in the 1830s adopted the policy of separating whites and Indians. Eastern tribes were moved west of Missouri and resettled on land then scorned as "the Great American Desert," unsuitable for white habitation and development. This division presumed a permanent frontier with perpetual Indian ownership of western America. It collapsed in the 1840s when the United States acquired Texas, California, and Oregon, and migrants crossed Indian lands to reach the West Coast. Mormons developed a trail through Indian country in 1847 and settled on Indian lands; gold and silver discoveries beginning in 1848 prompted miners to invade Indian lands. Rather than curbing white entry into Indian country, the government built forts along the overland trails and ordered the army to punish Indians who threatened travelers.

White migration devastated the Plains Indians. Livestock destroyed timber and pastures along streams in the semiarid region; trails disrupted buffalo grazing patterns and eliminated buffalo from tribal hunting ranges. The Pawnees in particular suffered from the violation of their hunting grounds. One observer reported that "their trail could be followed by the dead bodies of those who starved to death." The Plains Indians also suffered from diseases the white migrants introduced. Smallpox, cholera, measles, whooping cough, and scarlet fever, for which Indians had no natural immunity, swept through the tribes. Smallpox killed all but thirteen Mandans out of a population of sixteen hundred. Cholera killed more than half of the Comanches and Kiowas, and most other tribes lost up to 40 percent of their population from the new diseases. Emigrants along the Platte River routes came across "villages of the dead."

By the early 1850s, white settlers sought to occupy Indian territory. Recognizing that the Great American Desert could support agriculture, they pressed on the eastern edge of the plains and demanded the removal of the Indians. Simultaneously, railroad companies developed plans to lay tracks across the plains. To promote white settlement, the federal government decided to relocate the tribes to separate and specific reserves. In exchange for accepting such restrictions, the government would provide the tribes with annual payments of livestock, clothing, and other materials. To implement this policy, the government negotiated treaties, extinguishing Indian rights to millions of acres (see Map 21-1), and ordered the army to keep Indians on their assigned reservations.

These actions alarmed Native Americans. One Cherokee complained of a government official "with a pocket full of money and his mouth full of lies. Some chiefs he will bribe, some he will flatter and some he will make drunk; and the result . . . will be called a treaty." And the treaties the army enforced were not always what the Indians, however reluctantly, had accepted. Congress, for example, reduced by 70 percent the payments promised in the 1851 Fort Laramie Treaty. Similarly, the Comanches and Kiowas agreed in 1865 to exchange their traditional lands for new territory south of the Arkansas River, but Congress nullified the treaty provision for the new area. The commissioner of Indian affairs aptly described the Indians' lot: "By alternate persuasion and force these tribes have been removed, step by step, from mountain to valley, and from river to plain, until they have been pushed halfway across the continent. They can go no further; on the ground they now occupy the crisis must be met, and their future determined."

Warfare and Dispossession

Most smaller tribes accepted the government's conditions, but larger tribes resisted. From the 1850s to the 1880s, warfare engulfed the advancing frontier. The immediate initiative for conflict sometimes lay with Indians, especially in the form of small raids, but invading Americans bore ultimate responsibility for these wars. Even the men who led the white military assault conceded as much. General Philip Sheridan, for example, declared of the Indians: "We took away their country and their means of support, broke up their mode of living, their habits of life, introduced disease and decay among them, and it was for this and against this that they made war. Could anyone expect less?"

One notorious example of white aggression occurred in 1864 at Sand Creek, Colorado. Gold discoveries had attracted a flood of white miners and settlers onto land only recently guaranteed to the Cheyennes and Arapahos. Rather than enforcing the Indians' treaty rights, however, the government compelled the tribes to relinquish their lands, except for a small tract designated as the Sand Creek reservation. But white settlers wanted to eliminate the Indian presence altogether. John Chivington, a Methodist minister, led a militia force to the Sand Creek camp of a band of Cheyennes under Black Kettle, an advocate of peace and accommodation. An American flag flew over the Indian camp. Under Chivington's orders to "kill and scalp all, big and little," the militia attacked Black Kettle's sleeping camp without warning. With howitzers and rifles, the soldiers fired into the camp and then assaulted any survivors with swords and knives. One white trader later described the helpless Indians: "They were scalped, their brains knocked out; the [white] men used their knives, ripped open women, clubbed little children, knocked them in the head with their

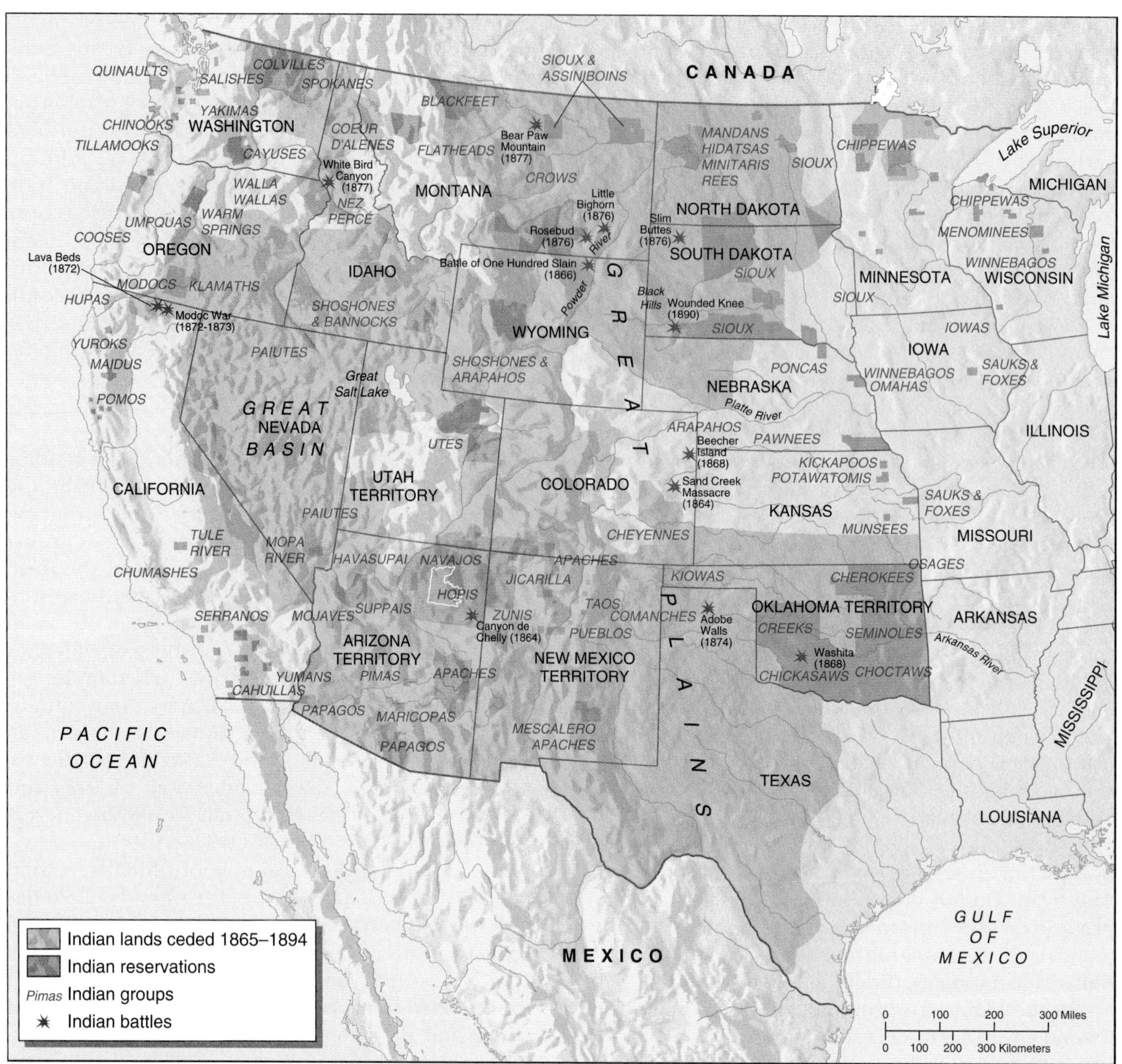

Map 21-1 Indian Land Cessions, 1860–1894
As white people pushed into the West to exploit its resources, Indians were steadily forced to cede their lands. By 1900 they held only scattered parcels, often in areas considered worthless by white people. Restricted to these reservations, tribes endured official efforts to suppress Indian customs and values.

guns, beat their brains out, mutilated their bodies in every sense of the word."

The **Sand Creek Massacre** appalled many Easterners. The Cheyennes, protested the commissioner of Indian affairs, were "butchered in cold blood by troops in the service of the United States." A congressional investigating committee denounced Chivington for "a foul and dastardly massacre which would have disgraced the veriest savage among those who were the victims of his cruelty." Westerners, however, justified the brutality as a means to secure their own opportunities. One western newspaper demanded, "Kill all the Indians that can be killed. Complete extermination is our motto."

While assaults on smaller tribes usually "succeeded," other tribes were more formidable.

None was more powerful than the Sioux, whose military skills had been honed in conflicts with other tribes. An army offensive against the Sioux in 1866 failed completely. Entire units deserted in fear and frustration; others were crushed by the Sioux. On the Bozeman Trail, in what the Lakotas called the **Battle of One Hundred Slain**, the Sioux wiped out an army detachment led by a captain who had boasted that he would destroy the Sioux nation. General William T. Sherman, who had marched through Georgia against Confederates, knew that the odds were different in the West. Fifty Plains Indians, he declared, could "checkmate" three thousand soldiers. General Philip Sheridan calculated that the army suffered proportionately greater losses fighting Indians than either the Union or the Confederacy had suffered in the Civil War.

With the army unable to defeat the Sioux and their allies, and with many Easterners shocked by both the military's indiscriminate aggression and the expense of the fighting, the government sued for peace. Describing white actions as "uniformly unjust," a federal peace commission in 1868 negotiated the **second Treaty of Fort Laramie**, in which the United States abandoned the Bozeman Trail and other routes and military posts on Sioux territory—one of the few times Indians forced the whites to retreat. The United States also guaranteed the Sioux permanent ownership of the western half of South Dakota and the right to inhabit and hunt in the Powder River country in Wyoming and Montana, an area to be henceforth closed to all white people.

For several years, peace prevailed on the northern plains, but in 1872, the Northern Pacific Railroad began to build westward on a route that would violate Sioux territory. Rather than stopping the railroad, the government sent an army to protect the surveyors. Sherman drew up plans for the war that he expected the construction to provoke. He regarded railroad expansion as the most important factor in defeating the Indians, for it would allow troops to travel as far in a day as they could march in weeks. Other technological developments, from the telegraph to rapid-fire weapons, also undercut the skills of the Indian warrior.

The destruction of the buffalo also threatened Native Americans. From 1872 to 1874, white hunters killed 4 million buffalo. Railroad survey and construction parties disrupted grazing areas, and hunters working for the railroads killed hordes of buffalo, both to feed construction crews and to prevent the animals from obstructing rail traffic. Hide hunters slaughtered even more of the beasts for their skins, leaving the bodies to rot. Reporters found vast areas covered with "decaying, putrid, stinking remains." Federal officials encouraged the buffalo's extermination because it would destroy the Indians' basis for survival.

The climactic provocation of the Sioux began in 1874 when Colonel George A. Custer led an invasion to survey the Black Hills for a military post and confirm the presence of gold. Thousands of white miners then illegally poured onto Sioux land. Ignoring Sioux demands that the government enforce the Fort Laramie treaty, the army insisted that the Indians leave their Powder River hunting grounds. When the Sioux refused, the army attacked. The Oglala Sioux under Crazy Horse repulsed one prong of this offensive at the Battle of the Rosebud in June 1876 and then joined a larger body of Sioux under Sitting Bull and their Cheyenne and Arapaho allies to overwhelm a second American column, under Custer, at the **Battle of the Little Bighorn**.

But the Indians could not follow up their dramatic victory. They had to divide their forces to find fresh grass for their horses and to hunt for their own food. Without such limitations, the U.S. Army relentlessly pursued the separate bands to exhaustion. "We have been running up and down in this country, but they follow us from one place to another," lamented Sitting Bull. He led his followers to Canada, but the other bands capitulated in

The scale of the destruction of the buffalo and its commercial organization are suggested by this photograph of a pile of buffalo skulls.

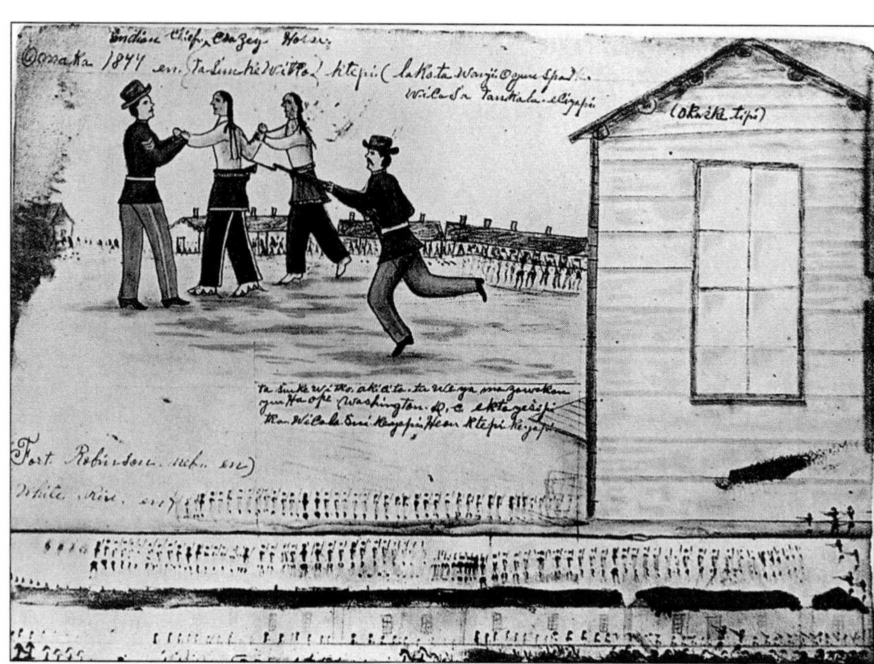

There is no photograph of Crazy Horse, but Amos Bad Heart Bull drew this pictograph of his murder at Fort Robinson, Nebraska, September 7, 1877. Bayoneted in the back, the great Sioux warrior told his followers: "It is no use to depend on me. I am going to die."

the winter of 1876–1877. In the end, the conquest of the northern plains came not through any decisive victory but through attrition and the inability of the traditional Indian economy to support resistance to the technologically and numerically superior white forces.

The defeat of the Sioux nearly completed the Indian Wars. Smaller tribes, among them the Kiowas, Modocs, and Utes, had been overrun earlier. In the Northwest, the Nez Percé resisted in 1877 when the government reneged on its agreement to protect their land. Outwitting and outfighting the larger forces of the U.S. Army over a 1,500-mile retreat toward Canada, the exhausted Nez Percé surrendered after being promised a return to their own land. But the government refused to honor that pledge, too, and imprisoned the tribe in Oklahoma, where more than a third perished within a few years.

In the Southwest, the Navajos and the Comanches were subdued, as the Sioux had been, by persistent pursuit that prevented them from obtaining food. The last to abandon resistance were the Apaches, under Geronimo. In 1886, he and thirty-six followers, facing five thousand U.S. troops, finally surrendered. Geronimo and other Apaches were sent to a military prison in Florida; the tribes were herded onto reservations. The Oglala chief Red Cloud concluded of the white invasion: "They made us many promises, more than I can remember, but they never kept but one. They promised to take our land, and they took it."

Life on the Reservation

Conquering the tribes and taking their land were only the initial objectives of government policy. The next goal was to require Indians to adopt white ways, instilled by education and religion and enforced when necessary by the military. This goal did not involve assimilation but merely "Americanization," an expression of cultural conquest.

The government received aid from many Christian denominations, which had long proposed nonviolent methods of controlling Indians. Beginning in the 1860s, they gained influence in reaction to the military's brutality. Religious groups helped staff the reservations as agents, missionaries, or civilian employees. Protestant philanthropists supervised Indian affairs and controlled several private organizations that worked to shape Indian policy, including the Indian Rights Association and the Women's National Indian Association. Reformers wanted to change Indian religious and family life, train Indian children in Protestant beliefs, and force Indians to accept private ownership and market capitalism.

Confined to reservations, Indians were a captive audience for white reformers. Furthermore, their survival depended on government rations and annual payments stipulated by treaties. Such dependence enabled government agents of the **Bureau of Indian Affairs** to control tribal life by withholding rations. The agents' power undermined tribal authority. White administrators sought to destroy traditional Indian government by prohibiting tribal councils from meeting and imprisoning tribal leaders.

White activists sought to destroy Indian religion because it was "pagan" and because it helped Indians resist assimilation. Protestant religious groups persuaded the Bureau of Indian Affairs to frame a criminal code prohibiting and penalizing tribal religious practices. Established in 1884, the code remained in effect until 1933. It was first invoked to ban the Sun Dance, the chief expression of Plains Indian religion. To enforce the ban, the government withheld rations and disrupted the religious ceremonies that transmitted traditional values. In 1890, the army even used machine guns to suppress the Ghost Dance religion, killing at least two hundred Sioux men, women, and children at **Wounded Knee**, South Dakota.

Missionaries attempted to convert Indians to Christianity but often found them reluctant to accept the creed of their conquerors. As one Crow Indian explained, "We found there were too many kinds of religion among white men for us to understand, and that scarcely any two white men agreed which was the right one to learn. This bothered us a good deal until we saw that the white man did not take his religion any more seriously than he did his laws, and that he kept both of them just . . . to use when they might do him good in his dealings with strangers. These were not our ways. We kept the laws we made and lived our religion."

The government and religious groups also used education to eliminate Indian values and traditions. They isolated Indian children from tribal influences at off-reservation boarding schools. Troops often seized Indian children for these schools, where they were confined until after adolescence. The schoolchildren were forced to speak English, attend Christian services, and profess white American values (see "American Views: Zitkala-Sa's View of Americanization").

Finally, the government and the religious reformers imposed the economic practices and values of white society on Indians. Government agents taught Indian men how to farm and distributed agricultural implements; Indian women were taught household tasks. These tactics reduced the status of Indian women, whose traditional responsibility for agriculture had guaranteed them respect and authority. Nor could men farm successfully on reservation lands, which whites had already rejected as unproductive. Kiowa chief Little Mountain suggested that if the president wanted Indians to raise corn, he should send them land fit for corn production. Whites, however, believed that the real obstacle to economic prosperity for the Indians was their rejection of private property. The Indians' communal values, the reformers argued, inhibited the pursuit of personal success that lay at the heart of capitalism. As one Bureau of Indian Affairs official declared, Indians must be taught to be more "mercenary and ambitious to obtain riches." To force such values on Indians, Congress in 1887 passed the **Dawes Act**, which divided tribal lands among individual Indians. Western settlers who had no interest in the Indians supported the law because it provided that reservation lands not allocated to individual Indians should be sold to white settlers. Under this "reform," the amount of land held by Indians declined by more than half by 1900.

White acquisition and exploitation of Indian land seemed to be the only constant in the nation's treatment of Native Americans. Assimilation itself failed because most Indians clung to their own values and rejected as selfish, dishonorable, and obsessively materialistic those favored by whites. But if it was not yet clear what place Native Americans would have in America, it was at least clear by 1900 that they would no longer stand in the way of western development.

Exploiting the Mountains: The Mining Bonanza

Migrants to the American West exploited the region's natural resources in pursuit of wealth and success. Some were rewarded; others met tragedy and failure. In either case, the challenges they confronted and the ventures they initiated gave rise to romantic images: the West as a land of adventure, opportunity, and freedom; pioneers as self-reliant individuals. Promoters, artists, and novelists developed these images into a heroic legend that movies, television, and politicians perpetuated. All too often, however, reality differed from legend. Opportunites were frequently short-lived and rarely available to all; individualism often gave way to group, corporate, or government action; nature and technology mocked self-reliance. The appeal of the cherished images made the reality harder to bear.

In the later nineteenth century, the West experienced several stages of economic development, but all of them transformed the environment, produced economic and social conflict, and integrated

FROM THEN TO NOW

The Legacy of Indian Americanization

The assumptions, objectives, and failures of the Americanization policies of the nineteenth century continue to affect American Indians more than a century later. Although periodically modified (see Chapter 27), these policies long persisted, as did their consequences. In the 1970s official investigations reported that the continuing attempts of the Bureau of Indian Affairs to use education to force Indians into an Anglo-American mold "have been marked by near total failure, haunted by prejudice and ignorance."

Similarly, the economic problems on reservations in the nineteenth century foreshadowed conditions a century later. Today Indians rank at the bottom of almost all measures of economic well-being. Lack of economic opportunity leaves isolated reservations with unemployment rates averaging 40 percent. Off the reservation, discrimination, limited skills, and inadequate capital further restrict Indians' job prospects.

Indians also continue to suffer from poor health standards. They have the highest rates of infant mortality, pneumonia, hepatitis, tuberculosis, and suicide in the nation and a life expectancy twenty-five years less than the national average.

Indian culture, however, did not succumb to the pressure to Americanize. In the words of a Shoshone writer, "Indian history didn't end in the 1800s. Indian cultures . . . evolve, grow, and continually try to renew themselves."

In recent decades, Indian peoples have begun to reclaim their past and assert control over their future. Dramatic protests—most notably a confrontation in 1973 between Indian activists and the FBI at Wounded Knee, the site of the notorious 1890 massacre—have called attention to Indian grievances. But Indians have also moved effectively to regain control of the institutions that define their cultural identity. They have established community schools and tribal community colleges that provide a bilingual, bicultural education, seeking to preserve traditions while opening new opportunities. They have built tribal museums and visitor centers in order to shape the presentation of their histories and cultures. By the late 1990s there were more than 200 such institutions, from the Seneca-Iroquois museum in upstate New York to the Makah Tribal Museum on the Olympic peninsula.

Indians have also secured legal recognition of their right to their cultural patrimony. The Native American Graves Protection and Repatriation Act of 1990 gives Indian communities the right to reclaim, or "repatriate," material artifacts and skeletal remains from museums and historical societies. The Native American Religious Freedom Act of 1978 affirmed their right to practice their traditional religions and have access to sacred sites. Indian dance—once suppressed by white authorities—has revived, and the powwow has become a national Indian institution and symbol of Indian identity.

With the help of historians and lawyers, Indians are also winning enforcement of long-ignored treaty provisions guaranteeing them land ownership and water, hunting, and fishing rights. Court decisions have recognized the right of tribes to permit gambling on their reservations, and some tribes have built profitable casinos, attracting economic development that creates new job opportunities for their people and permits them to stay on their land.

Indians still confront hostility and condescension reminiscent of attitudes a century ago. A white museum official, for example—seeking to prevent the repatriation of Pawnee artifacts—claimed recently that Indians do not have a real religion. But Indians have proved resilient in preserving their cultural heritage and keeping it vibrant for future generations.

On the Pine Ridge Reservation in South Dakota, the new government boarding school, designed to isolate Indian youth from their elders and their culture, looms over the old tribal lodgings in 1891.

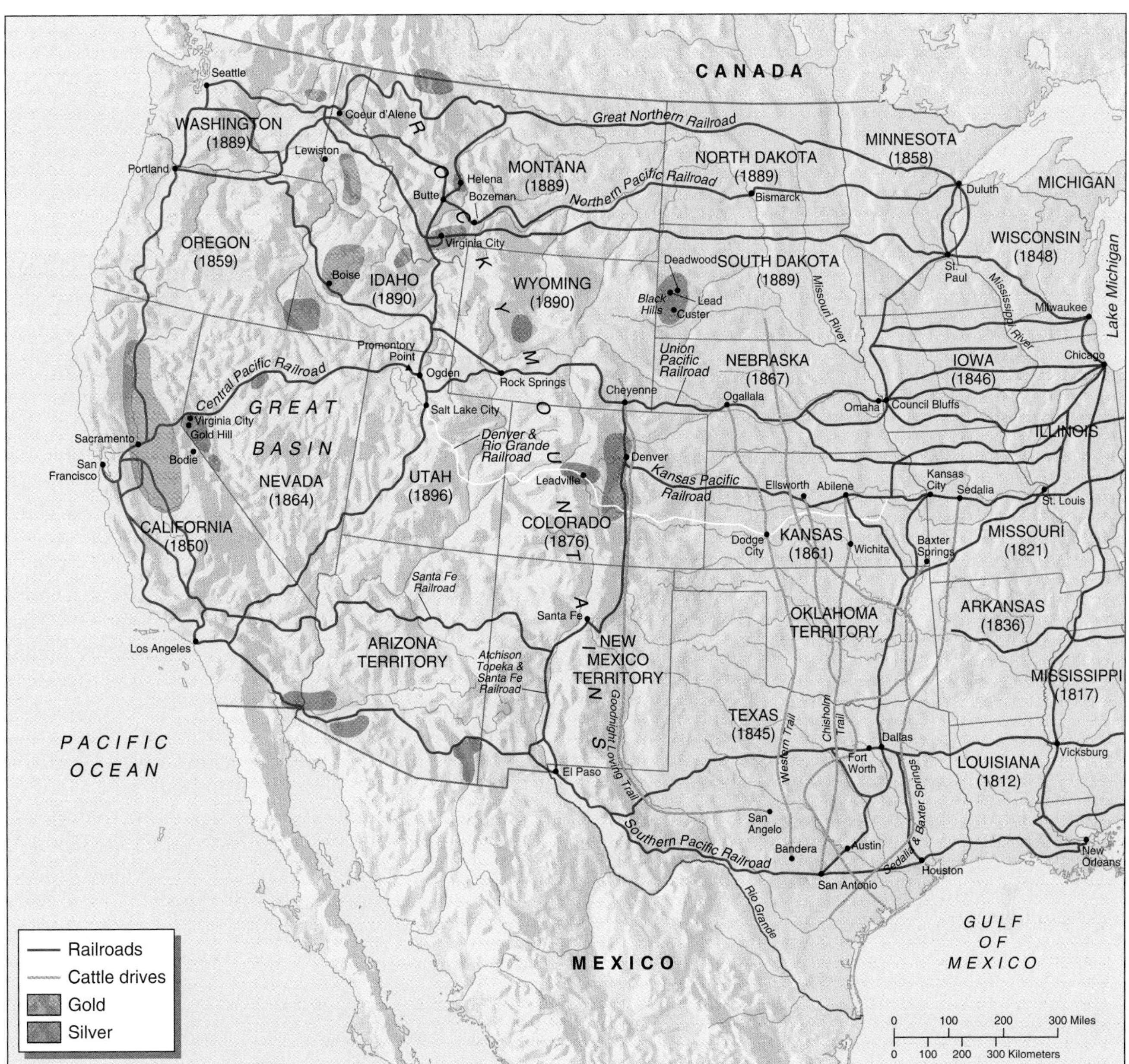

Map 21-2 Economic Development of the West: Railroads, Mining, and Cattle, 1860–1900
The spread of the railroad network across the West promoted economic development by providing access to outside markets for its resources. The discovery of precious metals often attracted the railroads, but stockraisers had to open cattle trails to reach the railheads.

the region into the modern national economy. The first stage of development centered on mining, which attracted swarms of eager prospectors into the mountains and deserts in search of gold and silver. They founded vital communities, stimulated the railroad construction that brought further development, and contributed to the disorderly heritage of the frontier (see Map 21-2). But few gained the wealth they had expected.

Rushes and Mining Camps

The first important gold rush in the Rocky Mountains came in Colorado in 1859. More than 100,000 prospectors crowded into Denver and the nearby mining camps. Simultaneously, the discovery of the famous Comstock Lode in Nevada produced an eastward rush of miners from California. Some seventeen thousand claims were made around Virginia City, Nevada, the main mining camp. Strikes in the

American Views

Zitkala-Sa's View of Americanization

Zitkala-Sa, or Red Bird, was an eight-year-old Sioux girl when she was taken from her South Dakota reservation in 1884 and placed in a midwestern missionary school, where she encountered what she called the "iron routine" of the "civilizing machine." Here she recalls her first day at the school.

❖ **What lessons were the missionaries trying to teach Zitkala-Sa by their actions?**

❖ **What lessons did Zitkala-Sa learn?**

Soon we were being drawn rapidly away by the white man's horses. When I saw the lonely figure of my mother vanish in the distance, a sense of regret settled heavily upon me. . . . I no longer felt free to be myself, or to voice my own feelings. The tears trickled down my cheeks, and I buried my face in the folds of my blanket. Now the first step, parting me from my mother, was taken, and all my belated tears availed nothing. . . . Trembling with fear and distrust of the palefaces . . . I was as frightened and bewildered as the captured young of a wild creature. . . .

[At the missionary school,] the constant clash of harsh noises, with an undercurrent of many voices murmuring an unknown tongue, made a bedlam within which I was securely tied. And though my spirit tore itself in struggling for its lost freedom, all was useless. . . .

We were placed in a line of girls who were marching into the dining room. . . . A small bell was tapped, and each of the pupils drew a chair from under the table. Supposing this act meant they were to be seated, I pulled out mine and at once slipped into it from one side. But when I turned my head, I saw that I was the only one seated, and all the rest at our table remained standing. Just as I began to rise, looking shyly around to see how chairs were to be used, a second bell was sounded. All were seated at last, and I had to crawl back into my chair again. I heard a man's voice at one end of the hall, and I looked around to see him. But all others hung their heads over their plates. As I glanced at the long chain of tables, I caught the eyes of a paleface woman upon me. Immediately I dropped my eyes, wondering why I was so keenly watched by the strange

northern Rockies followed in the 1860s. Boise City and Lewiston in Idaho and Helena in Montana became major mining centers, and other camps prospered briefly before fading into ghost towns. The last of the frontier gold rushes came in 1874 on the Sioux reservation in the Black Hills of South Dakota, where the roaring mining camp of Deadwood flourished. Later, other minerals shaped frontier development: silver in Nevada, silver and lead in Colorado and Idaho, silver and copper in Arizona and Montana.

Mining camps were often isolated by both distance and terrain. They frequently consisted of only flimsy shanties, saloons, crude stores, dance halls, and brothels, all hastily built by entrepreneurs. Such towns reflected the speculative, exploitive, and transitory character of mining itself. And yet they did contribute to permanent settlement by encouraging agriculture, industry, and transportation in the surrounding areas.

The camps had an unusual social and economic structure. Their population was overwhelmingly male. In 1860, for example, about 2,300 men and only 30 women lived in the Nevada mining camps of Virginia City and Gold Hill. Women found far fewer economic opportunities than men did on the mining frontier. Several opened hotels. Those with less capital worked as seamstresses and woman. The man ceased his mutterings, and then a third bell was tapped. Every one picked up his knife and fork and began eating. I began crying instead, for by this time I was afraid to venture anything more.

But this eating by formula was not the hardest trial in that first day. Late in the morning, my friend Judewin gave me a terrible warning. Judewin knew a few words of English; and she had overheard the paleface woman talk about cutting our long, heavy hair. Our mothers had taught us that only unskilled warriors who were captured had their hair shingled by the enemy. Among our people, short hair was worn by mourners, and shingled hair by cowards!

. . . I remember being dragged out, though I resisted by kicking and scratching wildly. In spite of myself, I was carried downstairs and tied fast in a chair. I cried aloud, shaking my head all the while until I felt the cold blades of the scissors against my neck, and heard them gnaw off one of my thick braids. Then I lost my spirit. . . . My long hair was shingled like a coward's. In my anguish I moaned for my mother, but no one came to comfort me. Not a soul reasoned quietly with me, as my own mother used to do; for now I was only one of many little animals driven by a herder. . . .

I blamed the hard-working, well-meaning, ignorant [missionary] woman who was inculcating in our hearts her superstitious ideas. Though I was sullen in all my little troubles, as soon as I felt better I was . . . again actively testing the chains which tightly bound my individuality like a mummy for burial. . . .

Many specimens of civilized peoples visited the Indian school. The city folks with canes and eyeglasses, the countrymen with sunburnt cheeks and clumsy feet, forgot their relative social ranks in an ignorant curiosity. Both sorts of these Christian palefaces were alike astounded at seeing the children of savage warriors so docile and industrious. . . .

In this fashion many [whites] have passed idly through the Indian schools during the last decade, afterward to boast of their charity to the North American Indian. But few there are who have paused to question whether real life or long-lasting death lies beneath this semblance of civilization.

Source: Zitkala-Sa, "The School Days of an Indian Girl" (1900). Reprinted in American Indian Stories *(Glorieta, NM: Rio Grande Press, 1976).*

cooks and took in washing. The few married women often earned more than their husbands by boarding other miners willing to pay for the trappings of family life.

But the largest source of paid employment for women was prostitution, a flourishing consequence of the gender imbalance. A few women prospered. Mary Josephine Welch, an entrepreneurial Irish immigrant, settled in Helena in 1867 and soon established the Red Light Saloon, the first of many saloons, dance halls, and brothels that she owned and operated. Most women who engaged in such activities, however, were far less successful. Many women became prostitutes because their other economic options were limited. A prostitute in Helena could earn five times more money than a saleswoman. And most prostitutes who entered brothels already suffered from economic hardship or a broken family. But prostitution usually only worsened their distress. By the 1890s, as men gained control of the vice trade from the madams, violence, suicide, alcoholism, disease, drug addiction, and poverty overcame most prostitutes. Public authorities showed little concern for the abuse and even murder of prostitutes, although they used "sporting women" to raise revenue by fining or taxing them. Condemning such moral indifference, middle-class Protestant women in Denver and other cities established "rescue homes" to protect or rehabilitate

Mary Josephine Welch adopted several names but prospered as "Chicago Joe," reigning over a red-light district that catered to miners in Helena, Montana.

prostitutes and dance-hall girls from male vice and violence. But their attempts to impose piety and purity had little success; male community leaders valued social order less than economic opportunity.

The gender imbalance in mining camps also made saloons prevalent among local businesses. An 1879 business census of Leadville, Colorado, reported 10 dry-goods stores, 4 banks, and 4 churches but 120 saloons, 19 beer halls, and 118 gambling houses. Saloons were social centers in towns where most miners lived in crowded and dirty tents and rooming houses. As Mark Twain wrote in *Roughing It* (1872), his account of Virginia City, "The cheapest and easiest way to become an influential man and be looked up to by the community at large, was to stand behind a bar, wear a cluster-diamond pin, and sell whiskey."

The male-dominated saloon society of mining camps generated social conflict. One observer of the Montana camps reported that men, "unburdened by families, drink whenever they feel like it, whenever they have money to pay for it, and whenever there is nothing else to do. . . . Bad manners follow, profanity becomes a matter of course. . . . Excitability and nervousness brought on by rum help these tendencies along, and then to correct this state of things the pistol comes into play." A Denver editor complained of "drunken men frequently firing pistols right and left, totally indifferent as to whom or what they hit." Disputes over mining claims could become violent, adding to the disorder. The California mining town of Bodie experienced twenty-nine killings between 1877 and 1883, a homicide rate higher than that of any U.S. city a century later. But such killings occurred only within a small group of males—young, single, surly, and armed—who were known as the Badmen of Bodie. Daily life for most people was safe.

Indeed, personal and criminal violence, which remains popularly associated with the West, was less pervasive than collective violence. This, too, affected mining camps and was aggravated by their ethnic and racial diversity. Irish, Germans, English, Chinese, Australians, Italians, Slavs, and Mexicans, among others, rushed into the mining regions. In many camps, half the population was foreign-born, and another fourth consisted of first-generation Americans. Virginia City was such a mixed community that Germans, Mexicans, Chinese, French, Cornish, and Welsh each had their own churches, bands, and other social organizations and celebrated their own national holidays.

The European immigrants who sometimes encountered nativist hostility in the East experienced less animosity in the West, but nonwhite minorities often suffered. In particular, white people frequently drove Mexicans and Chinese from their claims or refused to let them work in higher-paid occupations in the mining camps. The Chinese had originally migrated to the California gold fields and thereafter spread to the new mining areas of the Rockies and the Great Basin, where they worked in mining when possible, operated laundries and restaurants, and held menial jobs like hauling water and chopping wood. In 1870, more than a quarter of Idaho's population and nearly 10 percent of Montana's was Chinese. Where they were numerous, the Chinese built their own communities and maintained their customs.

But racism and fear of economic competition sparked hostility and violence against the Chinese almost everywhere. In Colorado, town leaders boasted of having driven all Chinese out of Leadville by 1879, and white citizens destroyed Denver's Chinatown in 1880. One Chinese leader observed that if such a riot had engulfed Americans in China, 100,000 "missionaries" would have been sent to "civilize the heathen." The worst anti-Chinese violence occurred in Rock

Springs, Wyoming, in 1885 when white miners killed twenty-eight unresisting Chinese miners and drove away all seven hundred residents from the local Chinatown. Although the members of the mob were well known, the grand jury, speaking for the white majority, found no cause for legal action: "Though we have examined a large number of witnesses, no one has been able to testify to a single criminal act committed by any known white person." Such community sanction for violence against racial minorities made mob attacks one of the worst features of the mining camps.

Labor and Capital

New technology had dramatic consequences for both miners and the mining industry. Initially, mining was an individual enterprise in which miners used simple tools, such as picks and shovels, wash pans, and rockers to work shallow surface deposits known as placers. Placer mining attracted prospectors with relatively little capital or expertise, but surface deposits were quickly exhausted. More complex and expensive operations were needed to reach the precious metal buried in the earth.

Hydraulic mining, for example, required massive capital investment to build reservoirs, ditches, and troughs to power high-pressure water cannons that would pulverize hillsides and uncover the mineral deposits. California's North Bloomfield Gravel Mining Company owned hundreds of miles of ditches and used more than a million gallons of water a day to feed its huge water nozzles. Still more formidable was quartz, or lode, mining, sometimes called hard rock mining. Time, money, and technology were required to sink a shaft into the earth, timber underground chambers and tunnels, install pumps to remove underground water and hoists to lower men and lift out rock, and build stamp mills and smelters to treat the ore.

Such complex, expensive, and permanent operations necessarily came under corporate control. Often financed with eastern or British capital, the new corporations integrated the mining industry into the larger economy. Hard rock mining produced more complex ores than could be treated in remote mining towns, but, with the new railroad network, they were shipped to smelting plants as far away as Kansas City and St. Louis and then to refineries in eastern cities. Western ores thus became part of national and international business. The mining industry's increasing development of lower-grade deposits led to greater capital investment and larger operations employing more workers and machinery.

Quartz mining thus helped usher the mining frontier into a more stable period. But the new corporate mining had disturbing effects. Its impact on the environment was horrendous. Hydraulic mining washed away hillsides, depositing debris in canyons and valleys to a depth of 100 feet or more, clogging rivers and causing floods, and burying thousands of

Chinese miners in Idaho operate the destructive water cannons used in hydraulic mining. Technological changes made most miners wage workers for companies.

acres of farmland. Such damage provoked an outcry and eventually led to government regulation. Fewer Westerners worried about sterile slag heaps or toxic fumes that belched from smelters and killed the vegetation for miles. They were the signs of progress. One Montana corporate leader even praised the arsenic fumes that permeated Butte for giving women "beautiful complexions."

Corporate mining also hurt miners, transforming them into wage workers with restricted opportunities. "It is useless to say that here all have an equal chance," conceded a Colorado newspaper in 1891. Miners' status declined as new machinery like power drills reduced the need for skilled laborers and prompted employers to hire cheaper workers from eastern and southern Europe. Mining corporations, moreover, did little to protect miners' health or safety. Miners died in cave-ins, explosions, and fires or from the great heat and poisonous gases in underground mines. Others contracted silicosis, lead poisoning, or other diseases or were crippled or killed by machines. Miners called power hoists "man killers" because they frequently crushed and dismembered workers. Investigating the new machinery in 1889, the Montana inspector of mines concluded that "death lurks even in the things which are designed as benefits."

To protect themselves, miners organized unions. These functioned as benevolent societies, using members' dues to pay benefits to injured miners or their survivors. Several unions established hospitals. Union halls offered an alternative to the saloons by serving as social and educational centers. The Miners' Union Library in Virginia City was the largest library in Nevada. Unions also promoted miners' interests on the job with strikes to protest wage cuts and with mine safety campaigns. They convinced states to pass mine safety laws and, beginning in the 1880s, to appoint mine inspectors. The chief role of these state officials was, in the words of a Colorado inspector, to decide "How far should an industry be permitted to advance its material welfare at the expense of human life?"

It was the industry itself, however, that often provided the answer to that question, for mining companies frequently controlled state power and used it to crush unions. Thus in 1892, in the Coeur d' Alene district of Idaho, mining companies locked out strikers and imported a private army, which battled miners in a bloody gunfight. Management next persuaded the governor and the president to send in the state militia and the U.S. Army. State officials then suppressed the strike and the union by confining all union members and their sympathizers in stockades.

Strikes, union busting, and violence continued for years. When mining companies in Utah, Colorado, and Montana pursued the same aggressive tactics of lockouts and wage cuts, the local miners' unions in the West united for strength and self-protection. In 1893, they formed one of the nation's largest and most militant unions, the Western Federation of Miners.

Violence and conflict were attributable not to frontier lawlessness but to the industrialization of the mines. Earlier, when the legal system was undeveloped, disputes rarely became violent. But as the law grew stronger and the owners adopted "legalized violence" as a repressive tool, miners turned to extralegal violence. In the western mines, then, both management's tactics—blacklisting union members, locking out strikers, obtaining court injunctions against unions, and using soldiers against workers—and labor's response mirrored conditions in the industrial East. In sum, western mining, reflecting the industrialization of the national economy, had been transformed from a small-scale prospecting enterprise characterized by individual initiative and simple tools into a large-scale corporate business characterized by impersonal management, outside capital, advanced technology, and wage labor.

Exploiting the Grass: The Cattle Kingdom

The development of the range cattle industry represented a second stage of exploitation of the late-nineteenth-century West. It reflected the needs of an emerging eastern urban society, the economic possibilities of the grasslands of the Great Plains, the technology of the expanding railroad network, and the requirements of corporations and capital. It also brought "cow towns" and urban development to the West. The fabled cowboy, though essential to the story, was only a bit player.

Cattle Drives and Cow Towns

The cattle industry originated in southern Texas, where the Spanish had introduced cattle in the eighteenth century. Developed by Mexican ranchers, "Texas longhorns" proved well adapted to the plains grasslands. By the 1860s, they numbered about 5 million head. Texans attempted to market these cattle as early as the 1850s, driving some herds on dusty journeys through New Mexico and Arizona to California and others to Missouri and Illinois. These latter drives disturbed local residents, angered farmers who feared that Texas cattle diseases might infect their own livestock, and prompted quarantine laws against the herds.

Following the Civil War, however, industrial expansion in the East and Midwest enlarged the urban market for food and increased the potential value of Texas steers. The extension of the railroad network into the West, moreover, opened the possibility of tapping that market without antagonizing farmers en route. The key was to establish a shipping point on the railroads west of the settled farming regions, a step first taken in 1867 by Joseph McCoy, an Illinois cattle shipper. McCoy selected Abilene, Kansas, in his words "a very small, dead place, consisting of about one dozen log huts." But Abilene was also the western railhead of the Kansas Pacific Railroad and was ringed by lush grasslands for cattle. McCoy bought 250 acres for a stockyard and imported lumber for stock pens, loading facilities, stables, and a hotel for cowhands. Texans opened the **Chisholm Trail** through Indian Territory to drive their cattle northward to Abilene. Within three years, a million and a half cattle arrived in Abilene, divided into herds of several thousand, each directed by a dozen cowhands on a "long drive" taking two to three months.

The cattle trade attracted other entrepreneurs who created a bustling town. Bankers prospered enough to convince one reporter in 1873 that "banks are as fat a thing as gold mines." Grocers, tailors, bootmakers, laundresses, barbers, druggists, blacksmiths, lawyers, and hotelkeepers provided consumer goods and services. Entertainments mushroomed: saloons, gambling rooms, dance halls, billiard parlors, and brothels. As both railroads and settlement advanced westward, a series of other cow towns—Ellsworth, Wichita, Dodge City, Cheyenne—attracted the long drives, cattle herds, and urban development.

As with the mining camps, the cow towns' reputation for violence was exaggerated. They adopted gun control laws, prohibiting the carrying of handguns within city limits, and established police forces to maintain order. The primary duties of law officers were arresting drunks, fixing sidewalks, and collecting fines. The cow towns regulated rather than prohibited prostitution and gambling, for merchants viewed these vices as necessary to attract the cattle trade. Thus the towns taxed prostitutes and gamblers and charged high fees for liquor licenses. By collecting such "sin taxes," Wichita was able to forgo general business taxes, thereby increasing its appeal to prospective settlers.

Not all cow towns became cities like Wichita, which by 1888 boasted of "Fine Educational Institutions, Magnificent Business Blocks, Elegant Residences, and Extensive Manufacturers"; most, like Abilene, dwindled into small towns serving farm populations. But cow towns, again like mining camps, contributed to the growth of an urban frontier. Railroads often determined the location and growth of western cities, providing access to markets for local products, transporting supplies and machinery for residents, and attracting capital for commercial and industrial development. When railroads reached El Paso, Texas, for example, it became a shipping point for cattle but then built its own packing houses and opened smelters to process Arizona ores. Its Mexican workers clustered in *barrios* and developed their own religious and social organizations—just as San Francisco's Chinese did in Chinatown or European immigrants did in eastern cities. This urbanization demonstrated how western developments paralleled those in older regions. The West, in fact, had become the most urban region in the nation by 1890, with two-thirds of its population living in communities of at least 2,500 people.

Rise and Fall of Open-Range Ranching

The significance of the long drive to the cow towns faded as cattle raising expanded beyond Texas. Indian removal and extension of the railroads opened land for ranching in Kansas, Nebraska, Wyoming, Colorado, Montana, and the Dakotas. Cattle reaching Kansas were increasingly sold to stock these northern ranges rather than for shipment to the packing houses. Ranches soon spread across the Great Plains and into the Great Basin, the Southwest, and even eastern Oregon and Washington. This expansion was helped by the initially low investment that ranching required. Calves were cheap, and grass was mostly free. Ranchers did not buy, but merely used, the grazing lands of the open range, which was public land. It sufficed to acquire title to the site for a ranch house and a water source because controlling access to water in semiarid lands gave effective control of the surrounding public domain "the same as though I owned it," as one rancher explained. Ranchers thus needed to invest only in horses, primitive corrals, and bunkhouses. Their labor costs were minimal: They paid cowboys in the spring to round up new calves for branding and in the fall to herd steers to market.

By the early 1880s, the high profits from this enterprise and an expanding market for beef attracted speculative capital and reshaped the industry. Eastern and European capital flooded the West, with British investors particularly prominent. Some investors went into partnership with existing ranchers, providing capital in exchange for expertise and management. On a larger scale, British and American corporations acquired, expanded, and managed huge ranches. In 1883, the Swan Land and Cattle Company controlled a tract in Wyoming 130 miles long and 40 to 100 miles wide with more than 100,000 cattle.

Large companies soon dominated the industry, just as they had gained control of mining. They also worked together to enhance their power, especially by restricting access to the range and by intimidating small competitors. Some large companies illegally began to enclose the open range, building fences to exclude newcomers and minimize labor costs by reducing the number of cowboys needed to control the cattle. One Wyoming newspaper complained that "some morning we will wake up to find that a corporation has run a wire fence about the boundary lines of Wyoming, and all within the same have been notified to move." And a Coloradan wondered, "Will the government protect us if we poor unite and cut down their fences and let our stock have some of Uncle Sam's feed as well as them?"

The corporate cattle boom overstocked the range, and the industry collapsed in an economic and ecological disaster. Overgrazing replaced nutritious grasses with sagebrush, Russian thistle, and other plants that livestock found unpalatable. Whereas five acres of land could support a steer in 1870, ten times as much was required by the 1880s. Droughts in the mid-1880s further withered vegetation and enfeebled the animals. Millions of cattle starved or froze to death in terrible blizzards in 1886 and 1887.

These ecological and financial disasters destroyed the open-range cattle industry. The surviving ranchers reduced their operations, restricted the size of their herds, and tried to ensure adequate winter feed by growing hay. To further reduce their dependence on natural vegetation, they introduced drought-resistant sorghum and new grasses; to reduce their dependence on rainfall, they drilled wells and installed windmills to pump water.

Cowhands

One constant in the cattle industry was the cowboy, but his conditions and opportunities changed sharply over time and corresponded little to the romantic image of a dashing individual free of social constraints. Cowboys' work was hard, dirty, seasonal, tedious, sometimes dangerous, and poorly paid. Many early cowboys were white Southerners unwilling or unable to return home after the Civil War. Black cowhands made up perhaps 25 percent of the trail-herd outfits. Many others, especially in Texas and the Southwest, were Mexicans. Indeed, Mexicans developed most of the tools, techniques, and trappings that characterized the cattle industry: from boots, chaps, and the "western" saddle to roundups and roping. Black and Mexican cowboys were often relegated to the more lowly jobs, such as wrangler, a "dust-eater" who herded horses for others to use, but most served as ordinary hands on ranch or trail. Except in the few all-black outfits, they were rarely ranch or trail bosses. Texas cowboys dominated the early years of ranching and trailing, but as the industry expanded northward, more cowboys came from rural Kansas, Nebraska, and neighboring states.

Initially, in the frontier-ranching phase dominated by the long drive, cowboys were seasonal employees who worked closely with owners. They were often the sons or neighbors of ranchers and frequently expected to become independent stock raisers themselves. They typically enjoyed the right to "maverick" cattle, or put their own brand on unmarked animals they encountered, and to "run a brand," or to own their own cattle while working for a ranch. These informal rights provided opportunities to acquire property and move up the social ladder.

As ranching changed with the appearance of large, corporate enterprises, so did the work and work relationships of cowhands. The power and status of employer and employees diverged, and the traditional rights of cowboys disappeared. Employers redefined mavericking as rustling and prohib-

Employees of the Prairie Cattle Company at the ranch headquarters in Dry Cimarron, New Mexico, in 1888. This company, a British corporation, held eight thousand square miles of land.

ited cowhands from running a brand of their own. One cowboy complained that these restrictions deprived a cowhand of his one way "to get on in the world." But that was their purpose: Cowboys were to be workers, not potential ranchers and competitors. To increase labor efficiency, some companies prohibited their cowboys from drinking, gambling, and carrying guns.

Cowboys sometimes responded to these structural transformations the same way skilled workers in the industrial East did—by forming unions and striking. Cowboy strikes broke out where corporate ranching was most advanced. The first strike occurred in Texas in 1883 when the Panhandle Stock Association, representing large operators, prohibited ranch hands from owning their own cattle and imposed a standard wage. More than three hundred cowboys struck seven large ranches for higher wages—$50 rather than $30 per month—and the right to brand mavericks for themselves and to run small herds on the public domain. Ranchers evicted the cowboys, hired scabs, and brought in the Texas Rangers for assistance. The strikers were forced to leave the region.

Other strikes also failed because corporate ranches and their stock associations had the power, and cowhands faced long odds in their efforts to organize. They were isolated across vast spaces and had little leverage in the industry. Members of the Northern New Mexico Cowboys Union, formed in 1886, recognized their weakness. After asking employers for "what we are worth after many years' experience," they conceded, "We are dependent on you."

The transformation of the western cattle industry and its integration into a national economy dominated by corporations thus made the cherished image of cowboy independence and rugged individualism more myth than reality. One visitor to America in the late 1880s commented: "Out in the fabled West, the life of the 'free' cowboy is as much that of a slave as is the life of his Eastern brother, the Massachusetts mill-hand. And the slave-owner is in both cases the same—the capitalist."

OVERVIEW

GOVERNMENT LAND POLICY

Legislation	Result
Railroad land grants (1850–1871)	Granted 181 million acres to railroads to encourage construction and development
Homestead Act (1862)	Gave 80 million acres to settlers to encourage settlement
Morrill Act (1862)	Granted 11 million acres to states to sell to fund public agricultural colleges
Other grants	Granted 129 million acres to states to sell for other educational and related purposes
Dawes Act (1887)	Allotted some reservation lands to individual Indians to promote private property and weaken tribal values among Indians and offered remaining reservation lands for sale to whites (by 1906, some 75 million acres had been acquired by whites)
Various laws	Permitted direct sales of 100 million acres by the Land Office

Exploiting the Earth: The Expansion of Agriculture

Even more than ranching and mining, agricultural growth boosted the western economy and bound it tightly to national and world markets. In this process, the government played a significant role, as did the railroads, science and technology, eastern and foreign capital, and the dreams and hard work of millions of rural settlers. The development of farming produced remarkable economic growth, but it left the dreams of many unfulfilled.

Settling the Land

Federal land grants to railroads had helped open the West to outside influences, and mining and cattle interests had also exploited public lands. To stimulate agricultural settlement, Congress passed the most famous land law, the Homestead Act of 1862 (see the overview table, "Government Land Policy"). The measure offered 160 acres of free land to anyone who

People from many countries migrated to the American West, bringing different beliefs and customs and contributing to the diversity of the region's population. Here Alsatian immigrants arrive at St. Paul, Minnesota, on their way further west.

The Homestead Act also reflected traditional eastern conceptions of the family farm, which were inappropriate in the West. A farm of 160 acres would have suited conditions in eastern Kansas or Nebraska, but farther west, larger-scale farming was necessary. And the law ignored the need for capital—for machinery, buildings, livestock, and fencing—successful farming on the Great Plains required.

Thus other forces assumed responsibility for promoting settlement. Newspaper editors trumpeted the prospects of their region. Land companies, eager to sell their speculative holdings, sent agents through the Midwest and Europe to encourage migration. Steamship companies, hoping to sell transatlantic tickets, advertised the opportunities in the American West across Europe. Religious and ethnic groups encouraged immigration. The Scandinavian Immigration Society generated both publicity and settlers for Minnesota;

would live on the plot and farm it for five years. The act promised opportunity and independence to ambitious farmers. The governor of Nebraska exclaimed, "What a blessing this wise and humane legislation will bring to many a poor but honest and industrious family."

Despite the apparently liberal land policy, however, prospective settlers found less land open to public entry than they expected. Federal land laws did not apply in much of California and the Southwest, where Spain and Mexico had previously transferred land to private owners, or in all of Texas. Elsewhere, the government had given away 181 million acres to railroads, transferred millions more to the states to sell for educational and other purposes (the Morrill Act provided the foundation for state agricultural colleges), and set aside millions of acres of former Indian land for sale rather than for homesteading. Moreover, other laws provided for easy transfer of public lands to cattle companies, to other corporations exploiting natural resources, and to land speculators.

Thus when settlers arrived in Kansas, Nebraska, Minnesota, and the Dakotas in the late 1860s and early 1870s, they often found most of the best land unavailable and much of the rest remote from transportation facilities and markets. Forty percent of the land in Kansas, for example, was closed to homesteading, which prompted the editor of the *Kansas Farmer* to complain that "the settlement of the state is retarded by land monopolists, corporate and individual." Although 375,000 farms were claimed by 1890 through the Homestead Act—a success by any measure—most settlers had to purchase their land.

Figure 21-1 The Growth of Western Farming, 1860–1900

Indian removal, railroad expansion, and liberal land policies drew farm families into the West from much of Europe as well as the East. Technological innovations like barbed wire and farm machinery soon enabled them to build farms, but economic, social, and environmental challenges remained.

Data Source: Historical Statistics of the United States (1975).

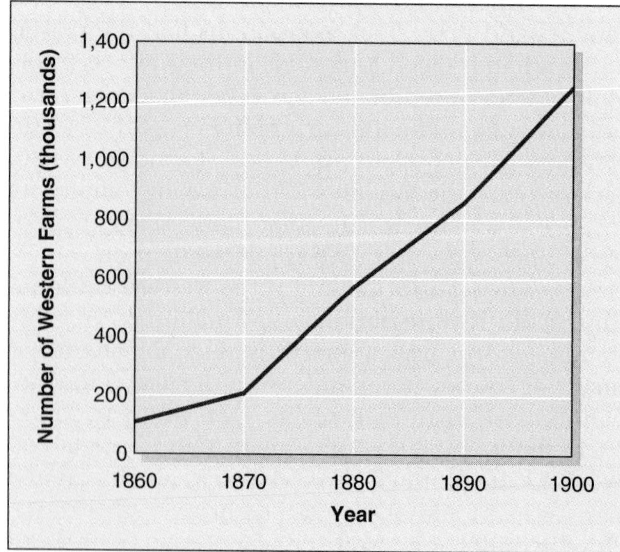

the Hebrew Emigrant Aid Society established Jewish agricultural colonies in Kansas and North Dakota. On a larger scale, the Mormons organized the Perpetual Emigrating Fund Company, which helped more than 100,000 European immigrants settle in Utah and Idaho. Their agricultural communities, relying on communal cooperation under church supervision, succeeded where individual efforts often failed in developing this region.

Most important, railroad advertising and promotional campaigns attracted people to the West. In 1882 alone, the Northern Pacific distributed more than 630,000 pieces of promotional literature in English, Swedish, Dutch, Danish, and Norwegian. "The glowing accounts of the golden west sent out by the R.R. companies," one pioneer later recalled, had convinced her that "they were doing a noble work to let poor people know there was such a grand haven they could reach." Only later did she realize the railroads' selfish motive. Not only would they profit from selling their huge land reserves to settlers, but a successful agricultural economy would produce crops to be shipped east and a demand for manufactured goods to be shipped west on their lines. The railroads therefore advanced credit to prospective farmers, provided transportation assistance, and extended technical and agricultural advice.

Thus encouraged, migrants poured into the West, occupying and farming more acres between 1870 and 1900 than Americans had in the previous 250 years (see Figure 21-1). Farmers settled in every region (see Map 21-3). Many went to California, Oregon, and Washington, where American development had begun much earlier. Some journeyed into the arid Great Basin and Rocky Mountains or the Southwest, where they often acquired land at the expense of the long-established Mexican population. Most, however, streamed into the Great Plains states, from

Map 21-3 Population Density and Agricultural Land Use in the Late Nineteenth Century

Economic integration of the West promoted regional agricultural specialization. Stockraising and grain production dominated the more sparsely settled West, while the South grew the labor-intensive crops of cotton, tobacco, and sugar cane, and other areas concentrated on dairy products, fruit, and other crops for nearby urban markets.

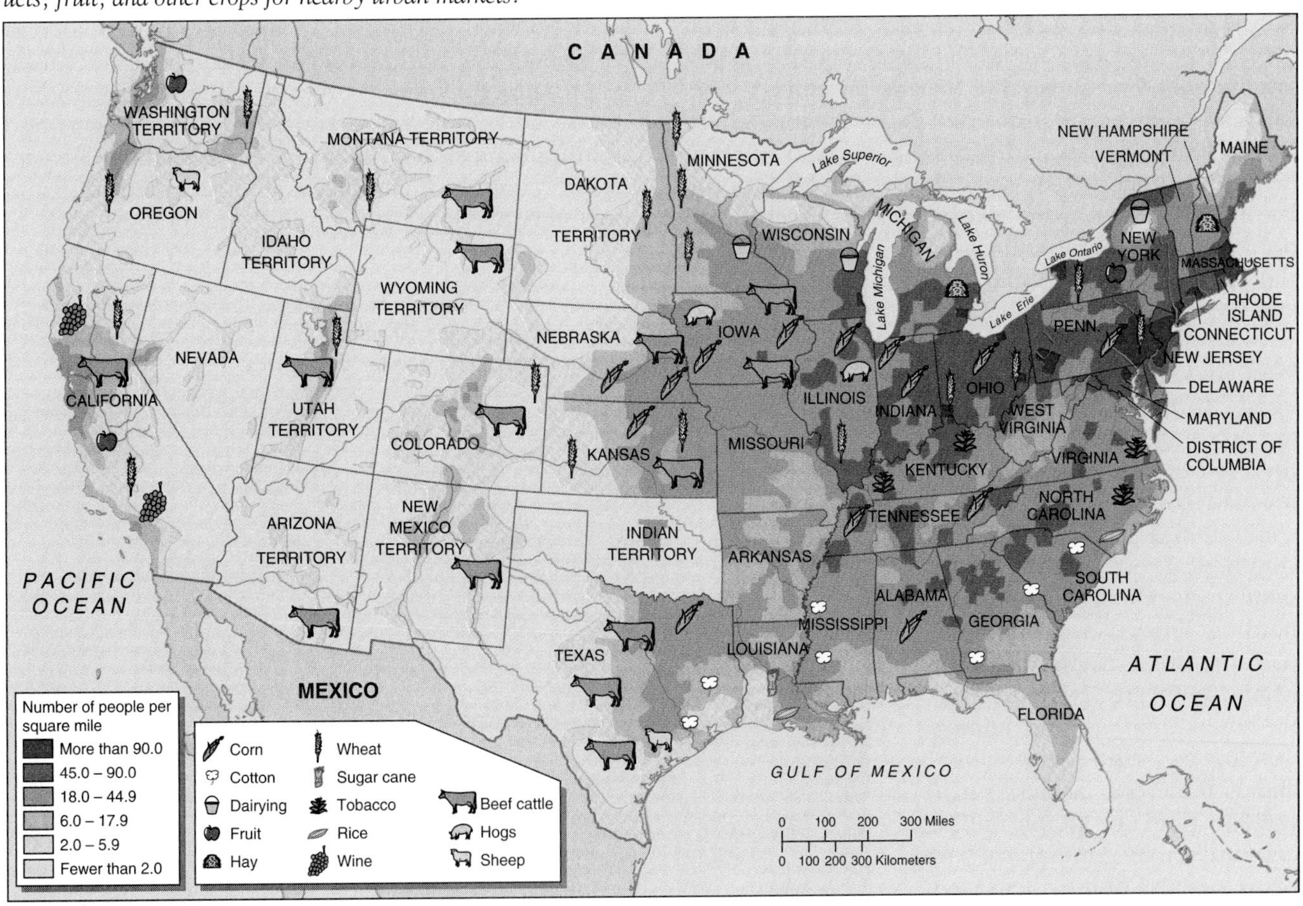

the Dakotas to Texas. Much of Oklahoma was settled in virtually a single day in 1889 when the government opened up lands previously reserved for Indians. A reporter described the wild land rush that created Oklahoma City in hours and claimed two million acres of land by nightfall: "With a shout and a yell the swift riders shot out, then followed the light buggies or wagons and last the lumbering prairie schooners and freighters' wagons, with here and there even a man on a bicycle and many too on foot—above all a great cloud of dust hovering."

So many Americans migrated west that many states east of the plains actually lost population during the 1870s. White migrants predominated in the mass migration, but African Americans initiated one of its most dramatic episodes, a millenarian folk movement they called the Exodus. Seeking to escape the misery and repression of the post-Reconstruction South, these poor "Exodusters" established several black communities in 1879 in Kansas and Nebraska on the agricultural frontier. But many of the new settlers came from Europe, sometimes in a chain migration of entire villages, bringing with them not only their own attitudes toward the land but also special crops, skills, settlement patterns, and agricultural practices. Peasants from Norway, Sweden, and Denmark flocked to Minnesota. Germans, Russians, and Irish put down roots across Texas, Kansas, Nebraska, and the Dakotas. French, Germans, and Italians developed vineyards, orchards, and nurseries in California, where laborers from Japan and Mexico arrived to work in fields and canneries. By 1890, the foreign-born population of North Dakota exceeded 40 percent, and nonnatives made up much of the population in California and other western states.

Migrants moved into the West in search of opportunity, which they sometimes seized at the expense of others already there. In the Southwest, Hispanics had long lived in village communities largely outside a commercial economy, farming small tracts of irrigated land and herding sheep on communal pastures. But as more Anglos, or white Americans, arrived as cattle raisers, railroad and mining developers, land speculators, and commercial farmers, their political and economic influence undermined traditional Hispanic society. Congress restricted the original Hispanic land grants to only the villagers' home lots and irrigated fields, throwing open most of their common lands to newcomers. Hispanic title was confirmed to only 2 million of the 37.5 million acres at stake. Anglo ranchers and settlers manipulated the federal land system to control these lands. The notorious Santa Fe Ring, a group of lawyers and land speculators, seized millions of acres through fraud and legal chicanery.

Spanish Americans resisted these losses, in court or through violence. *Las Gorras Blancas* (the White Caps) staged night raids to cut fences erected by Anglo ranchers and farmers and to attack the property of railroads, the symbol of the encroaching new order. "Our purpose," they announced, "is to protect the rights of the people in general and especially those of the helpless classes." Such resistance, however, had little success.

As their landholdings shrank, Hispanic villagers could not maintain their pastoral economy. Few turned to homesteading, for that would require dispersed settlement and abandoning the village and its church, school, and other cultural institutions. Thus many Hispanics became seasonal wage laborers in the Anglo-dominated economy, sometimes working as stoop labor in the commercial sugar beet fields that emerged in the 1890s, sometimes working on the railroads or in the mines. Women also participated in this new labor market. Previously crucial to the subsistence village economy, they now sought wage labor as cooks and domestic servants in railroad towns and mining camps. Such seasonal labor enabled Hispanics to maintain their villages and provided sufficient income to adopt some Anglo technology, such as

Mexican Americans had to adapt to changing conditions as the Southwest was developed, but they tried to preserve much of their traditional culture. This painting by Thomas Allen depicts Mexicanos *holding their market bazaar in the town plaza.*

Thomas Allen, Market Plaza, 1878–1879, oil on canvas, 26 × 39½," "Witte Museum, San Antonio, Texas.

cookstoves or sewing machines. But if Hispanics retained some cultural autonomy, they had little influence over the larger processes of settlement and development that restricted their opportunities and bound them to the western and national economy.

Home on the Range

In settling the West, farmers and their families encountered many difficulties, especially on the Great Plains, where they had to adapt to a radically new environment. The scarcity of trees on the plains meant that there was little wood for housing, fuel, and fencing. Until they had reaped several harvests and could afford to import lumber, pioneer families lived in houses made of sod. Though inexpensive and sturdy, sod houses were also dark and dirty. Snakes, mice, and insects often crawled out of the walls and roofs. One Nebraska homesteader recalled that her first sight of a sod house "sickened me."

For fuel, settlers often had to rely on buffalo or cattle "chips"—dried dung—which repelled some newcomers. One farmer reported in 1879 that "it was comical to see how gingerly our wives handled these chips at first. They commenced by picking them up between two sticks, or with a poker. Soon they used a rag, and then a corner of their apron. Finally, growing hardened, a wash after handling them was sufficient. And now? Now it is out of the bread, into the chips and back again—and not even a dust of the hands!"

The scarcity of water also complicated women's domestic labor. They often transported water over long distances, pulling barrels on "water sleds" or carrying pails on neck yokes. They melted snow on the stove for wash water and used the same water over again for different chores. Where possible, they also helped dig wells by hand.

Some women farmed the land themselves. Single women could claim land under the Homestead Act, and, in some areas, women claimants made up 18 percent of the total and succeeded more frequently than men in gaining final title. At times, married women operated the family farm by themselves while their husbands worked elsewhere to earn the money needed for seeds, equipment, and building supplies. In the 1870s, one Dakota woman recounted the demands women faced: "I had lived on a homestead long enough to learn some fundamental things: that while a woman had more independence here than in any other part of the world, she was expected to contribute as much as a man—not in the same way, it is true, but to the same degree; that people who fought the frontier had to be prepared to meet any emergency; that the person who wasn't willing to try anything once wasn't equipped to be a settler."

Isolation and loneliness troubled many early settlers on the plains. Women especially suffered because they frequently had less contact with other people than the farm men, who conducted their families' business in town and participated in such public activities as political meetings. One farm woman complained that "being cut off from everybody is almost too much for me." Luna Kellie recalled that from her Nebraska farm "there were no houses in sight and it seemed like the end of the world." The worst agony for many was the silence, unbroken by the sound of neighbors, the rush of water over rocks, or even—in the absence of trees—songbirds or rustling leaves. To break the silence, to provide some music and color, many homesteading families kept canaries among their few belongings.

Over time, conditions improved. Western settlers established churches and schools, both of which involved women in numerous social activities. They created rural social and economic organizations that

Each of the four Chrisman sisters claimed a homestead and built a sod house near Goheen, Nebraska. Farming on the Great Plains was typically a family operation, with all members of the family having important tasks.

encouraged community cooperation. Public institutions also developed to serve the rural population. Few were more important than **Rural Free Delivery**, started in 1896, which eventually brought letters, newspapers, magazines, and advertisements to farm families' doorsteps. Such changes helped incorporate Westerners into the larger society.

Farming the Land

Pioneer settlers had to make daunting adjustments to develop the agricultural potential of their new land. Advances in science, technology, and industry made such adjustments possible. The changes would not only reshape the agricultural economy but also bring their own great challenges to traditional rural values and expectations.

Fencing was an immediate problem, for crops needed to be shielded from livestock. But without timber, farmers could not build wooden fences. Barbed wire, developed in the mid-1870s, solved the problem. By 1900, farmers were importing nearly 300 million pounds of barbed wire each year from eastern and midwestern factories.

The aridity of most of the West also posed difficulties. In California, Colorado, and a few other areas, settlers used streams fed by mountain snowpacks to irrigate land. Elsewhere, enterprising farmers developed variants of the "dry farming" practices that the Mormons had introduced in Utah, attempting to maximize the limited rainfall. Some farmers built windmills to pump underground water.

Scarce rainfall also discouraged the cultivation of many of the crops that supported traditional general agriculture and encouraged farmers to specialize in a single cash crop for market. Gradually, many plains farmers turned from corn to wheat, especially the drought-resistant Turkey Red variety of hard winter wheat that German Mennonites had introduced into Kansas from Russia. Government agencies and agricultural colleges contributed to the success of such adaptations, and private engineers and inventors also fostered agricultural development. Technological advancements included grain elevators that would store grain for shipment and load it into rail cars mechanically and mills that used corrugated, chilled-iron rollers rather than millstones to process the new varieties of wheat.

Mechanization and technological innovations also made possible the large-scale farming practiced in semiarid regions. Farmers required special plows to break the tough sod, new harrows to prepare the soil for cultivation, grain drills to plant the crop, and harvesting and threshing machines to bring it in. Thanks to more and better machines, agricultural efficiency and productivity shot up. By the 1890s, machinery permitted the farmer to produce eighteen times more wheat than hand methods had. Nearly a thousand corporations were manufacturing agricultural machinery to meet the demands of farmers, who purchased implements in steadily mounting quantities.

These developments reflected both the expansion of agriculture and its increasing dependence on the larger society. Western commercial farmers needed the high demand of eastern and midwestern cities and the expanding world market. The rail network provided essential transportation for their crops; the nation's industrial sector produced necessary agricultural machinery. Banks and loan companies extended the credit and capital that allowed farmers to take advantage of mechanization and other new advances; and many other businesses graded, stored, processed, and sold their crops. In short, because of its market orientation, mechanization, and specialization, western agriculture relied on other people or impersonal forces as it was incorporated into the national and international economy.

When conditions were favorable—good weather, good crops, and good prices—western farmers prospered. Too often, however, they faced adversity. The early years of settlement were unusually wet, but, even then, periodic droughts brought crop failures. Other natural hazards also disrupted production. Especially alarming were plagues of grasshoppers, forming what one woman called a "cloud so dense that the sun was obscured and the earth was in darkness." Grasshoppers ate crops, clothing, and bedding; they attacked sod houses and chewed woodwork and furniture. "In a few hours," one newspaper reported, "many fields that had hung thick with long ears of golden maize were stripped of their value and left only a forest of bare yellow stalks that in their nakedness mocked the tiller of the soil." Private relief organizations distributed food, clothing, and seed to farm families suffering from droughts and grasshoppers in the 1870s, and state governments and Congress appropriated public funds to combat destitution on the agricultural frontier.

In the late 1880s, drought coincided with a slump in crop prices. The large European market that had encouraged agricultural expansion in the 1870s and early 1880s contracted after 1885 when several nations erected trade barriers to U.S. commodities. More important, America's production competed with that from Argentina, Canada, Australia, and Russia, and a world surplus of grain drove prices steadily downward. The average price of wheat dropped from $1.19 a bushel in 1881 to only $0.49 in 1894; prices for other farm commodities also declined.

Squeezed between high costs for credit, transportation, and manufactured goods and falling agricultural prices, western farmers faced disaster. They responded by lashing back at their points of contact with the new system. They especially condemned the railroads, believing that the companies exploited farmers' dependence by charging excessive and discriminatory freight rates. Luna Kellie complained of the railroads, "The minute you crossed the Missouri River your fate both soul and body was in their hands. What you should eat and drink, what you should wear, everything was in their hands and they robbed us of all we produced except enough to keep body and soul together and many many times not that."

Farmers censured the grain elevators in the local buying centers. Often owned by eastern corporations, including the railroads themselves, elevators allegedly exploited their local monopoly to cheat farmers by fixing low prices or misrepresenting the quality of wheat. A Minnesota state investigation found systematic fraud by elevators, which collectively cost farmers a massive sum.

Farmers also denounced the bankers and mortgage lenders who had provided the credit for them to acquire land, equipment, and machinery. Much of the money had come from eastern investors, seeking the higher interest rates in the West. With failing crops and falling prices, however, the debt burden proved calamitous for many farmers. Beginning in 1889, many western farms were foreclosed.

Stunned and bitter, western farmers concluded that their problems arose because they had been incorporated into the new system, an integrated economy directed by forces beyond their control. And it was a system that did not work well. "There is," one of them charged, "something radically wrong in our industrial system. There is a screw loose."

Conclusion

In a few decades, millions of people had migrated westward in search of new opportunities. With determination, ingenuity, and hard work they had settled vast areas, made farms and ranches, built villages and cities, brought forth mineral wealth, and imposed their values on the land. These were remarkable achievements, though tempered by a shameful treatment of Indians and an often destructive exploitation of natural resources. But if most Westerners took pride in their accomplishments, and a few enjoyed wealth and power, many also grew discontented with the new conditions they encountered as the "Wild" West receded.

The farmers' complaints indicted the major processes by which the West was developed and exploited in the late nineteenth century. Railroad expansion, population movements, eastern investment, corporate control, technological innovations, and government policies had incorporated the region fully into the larger society. Indians experienced this incorporation most thoroughly and most tragically, losing their lands, their traditions, and often their lives; the survivors were dependent on the decisions and actions of interlopers determined to impose "Americanization," the name itself implying the imposition of national patterns. Cowboys and miners also learned that the frontier merely marked the cutting edge of eastern industrial society. Both were wage workers, often for corporations controlled by eastern capital, and if industrial technology directly affected miners more than cowhands, neither could escape integration into the national economy by managerial decisions, transportation links, and market forces. Most settlers in the West were farmers, but they too learned that their distinctive environment did not insulate them from assimilation into larger productive, financial, and marketing structures.

Western developments, in short, reflected and interacted with those of eastern industrial society. The processes of incorporation drained away Westerners' hopes along with their products, and many of the discontented would demand a serious reorganization of relationships and power. Led by angry farmers, they turned their attention to politics and government, where they encountered new obstacles and opportunities.

Review Questions

1. What factors were most influential in the subjugation of American Indians?
2. What were the major goals of federal Indian policy, and how did they change?
3. How did railroads shape the settlement and development of the West?
4. How did technological developments affect Indians, miners, and farmers in the West?
5. How did the federal government help transform the West?

Recommended Reading

Robert R. Dykstra, *The Cattle Towns* (1968). A classic analysis of town building and social conflict in

Kansas cattle towns, both fascinating and fun to read.

Gilbert C. Fite, *The Farmers' Frontier, 1865–1900* (1966). A comprehensive account of agricultural settlement in all areas of the West.

Richard E. Lingenfelter, *The Hardrock Miners: A History of the Mining Labor Movement in the American West, 1863–1893* (1974). An important analysis of the relationship between the labor movement and the industrialization of the western mines.

Rodman W. Paul, *The Far West and the Great Plains in Transition* (1988). A valuable survey of regional development that devotes particular attention to mining.

Glenda Riley, *The Female Frontier: A Comparative View of Women on the Prairie and the Plains* (1988). A useful guide to women's experiences in the West.

Robert M. Utley, *The Indian Frontier of the American West, 1846–1890* (1984). A balanced survey of United States–Indian relations in the late nineteenth century.

Philip Weeks, *Farewell, My Nation: The American Indian and the United States, 1820–1890* (1990). Modern discussions of Indian policy that provide insights into the perspectives of the Indians.

Richard White, *"It's Your Misfortune and None of My Own": A New History of the American West* (1991). An important and original analysis of the development of the West that highlights environmental, ethnic, labor, and social history.

Mark Wyman, *Hard Rock Epic: Western Miners and the Industrial Revolution, 1860–1910* (1979). Miners experiencing the dual frontiers of the West and the industrial revolution.

Additional Sources

General Studies

Leonard J. Arrington, *Great Basin Kingdom: An Economic History of the Latter-day Saints* (1958).

Anne M. Butler, *Daughters of Joy, Sisters of Misery: Prostitutes in the American West* (1985).

William Cronon, *Nature's Metropolis: Chicago and the Great West* (1991).

Robert V. Hine, *Community on the American Frontier: Separate but Not Alone* (1980).

Julie Roy Jeffrey, *Frontier Women* (1998).

Patricia Nelson Limerick, *The Legacy of Conquest* (1987).

Clyde A. Milner, Carol A. O'Connor, and Martha A. Sandweiss, eds., *The Oxford History of the American West* (1994).

Sandra L. Myres, *Westering Women and the Frontier Experience* (1982).

Peggy Pascoe, *Relations of Rescue: The Search for Female Moral Authority in the American West* (1990).

William G. Robbins, *Colony and Empire: The Capitalist Transformation of the American West* (1994).

Elliott West, *The Way to the West* (1995).

Donald Worster, *Rivers of Empire: Water, Aridity, and the Growth of the American West* (1985).

Native Americans

David W. Adams, *Education for Extinction: American Indians and the Boarding School Experience* (1995).

Henry Fritz, *The Movement for Indian Assimilation, 1860–1890* (1963).

Arrell Morgan Gibson, *The American Indian, Prehistory to the Present* (1980).

Frederick E. Hoxie, *A Final Promise: The Campaign to Assimilate the Indians, 1880–1920* (1984).

Paul Hutton, *Phil Sheridan and His Army* (1985).

Peter Iverson, *The Navajos* (1990).

Alvin M. Josephy, Jr., *The Nez Percé Indians and the Opening of the Northwest* (1965).

Robert Mardock, *The Reformers and the Indian* (1971).

Janet McDonnell, *The Dispossession of the American Indian* (1991).

Robert M. Utley, *The Lance and the Shield: The Life and Times of Sitting Bull* (1993).

Robert M. Utley, *The Last Days of the Sioux Nation* (1963).

Wilcomb E. Washburn, *The Indian in America* (1975).

David Wishart, *An Unspeakable Sadness: The Dispossession of the Nebraska Indians* (1994).

Robert Wooster, *The Military and United States Indian Policy, 1865–1903* (1988).

The Mining Bonanza

David Emmons, *The Butte Irish: Class and Ethnicity in an American Mining Town* (1989).

Rodman W. Paul, *Mining Frontiers of the Far West, 1848–1880* (1963).

Richard H. Peterson, *The Bonanza Kings: The Social Origins and Business Behavior of Western Mining Entrepreneurs* (1977).

Paula Petrik, *No Step Backward: Women and Family on the Rocky Mountain Mining Frontier, Helena, Montana* (1987).

Malcolm Rohrbough, *Aspen: The History of a Silver-Mining Town* (1986).

Duane A. Smith, *Mining America: The Industry and the Environment* (1987).

Duane A. Smith, *Rocky Mountain Mining Camps: The Urban Frontier* (1967).

Clark Spence, *British Investments and the American Mining Frontier* (1958).

Elliott West, *The Saloon on the Rocky Mountain Mining Frontier* (1979).

The Cattle Kingdom

Lewis Atherton, *The Cattle Kings* (1961).

Edward Dale, *The Range Cattle Industry* (1969).

David Dary, *Cowboy Culture* (1981).

Philip Durham and Everett L. Jones, *The Negro Cowboys* (1965).

Gene M. Gressley, *Bankers and Cattlemen* (1966).

C. Robert Haywood, *Victorian West: Class and Culture in Kansas Cattle Towns* (1991).

David E. Lopez, "Cowboy Strikes and Unions," *Labor History* (1977).

H. Craig Miner, *Wichita: The Early Years, 1865–1880* (1982).

Jimmy M. Skaggs, *The Cattle Trailing Industry* (1973).

Don D. Walker, *Clio's Cowboys* (1981).

The Expansion of Agriculture

Allan G. Bogue, *Money at Interest: The Farm Mortgage on the Middle Border* (1955).

Cletus Daniel, *Bitter Harvest: A History of California Farmworkers* (1981).

Thomas Isern, *Bull Threshers and Bindlestiffs: Harvesting and Threshing on the North American Plains* (1990).

H. Craig Miner, *West of Wichita: Settling the High Plains of Kansas, 1865–1890* (1986).

Jane Taylor Nelsen, ed., *Prairie Populist: The Memoirs of Luna Kellie* (1992).

Nell Painter, *Exodusters: Black Migration to Kansas after Reconstruction* (1976).

Donald J. Pisani, *From the Family Farm to Agribusiness: The Irrigation Crusade in California and the West* (1984).

Donald J. Pisani, *To Reclaim a Divided West: Water, Law, and Public Policy* (1992).

Fred A. Shannon, *The Farmer's Last Frontier: Agriculture, 1860–1897* (1945).

Ethnic and Cultural Frontiers

Albert Camarillo, *Chicanos in a Changing Society* (1979).

Sucheng Chan, *This Bittersweet Soil: The Chinese in California Agriculture* (1986).

Sarah Deutsch, *No Separate Refuge: Culture, Class, and Gender on an Anglo-Hispanic Frontier in the American Southwest* (1987).

Mario T. Garcia, *Desert Immigrants: The Mexicans of El Paso, 1880–1920* (1981).

Jon Gjerde, *From Peasants to Farmers: The Migration from Balestrand, Norway, to the Upper Midwest* (1985).

Frederick C. Luebke, *Ethnicity on the Great Plains* (1980).

D. Aidan McQuillan, *Prevailing over Time: Ethnic Adjustment on the Kansas Prairies, 1875–1925* (1990).

Ronald Takaki, *Strangers from a Different Shore: A History of Asian Americans* (1989).

Where to Learn More

- **Bodie State Historic Park, Bodie, California.** The largest authentic ghost town in the West, Bodie was an important mining center from the 1860s to the 1880s. About 170 buildings remain, including a museum with mining equipment and artifacts of everyday life.
- **Little Bighorn Battlefield National Monument, Crow Agency, Montana.** The site of Custer's crushing defeat includes a monument to the Seventh Cavalry atop Last Stand Hill. A new authorized Indian Memorial will include sacred texts, artifacts, and pictographs of the Plains Indians.
- **American Historical Society of Germans from Russia Museum, Lincoln, Nebraska.** This unique museum, consisting of a complex of restored homes, exhibitions, and archives, preserves the history and culture of Germans who emigrated to Russia and then to the American Great Plains, where they contributed importantly to the development of a multicultural society and an agricultural economy.
- **National Museum of the American Indian, New York, New York.** Part of the Smithsonian Institution, this museum has a collection of artifacts illustrative of more than ten thousand years of the Native American culture.
- **National Cowboy Hall of Fame, Oklahoma City, Oklahoma.** This large institution contains an outstanding collection of Western art, displays of cowboy and Indian artifacts, and both kitschy exhibitions of the mythic, Hollywood West and serious galleries depicting the often hard realities of the cattle industry. Its many public programs also successfully combine fun with learning.
- **Fort Laramie, National Historic Site, near Guernsey, Wyoming.** A fur-trading post, stop on the Oregon Trail, site of treaty negotiations with the Plains Indians, and staging area for military campaigns, Fort Laramie is now a living history museum with many original buildings.

Politics and Government, 1877–1900

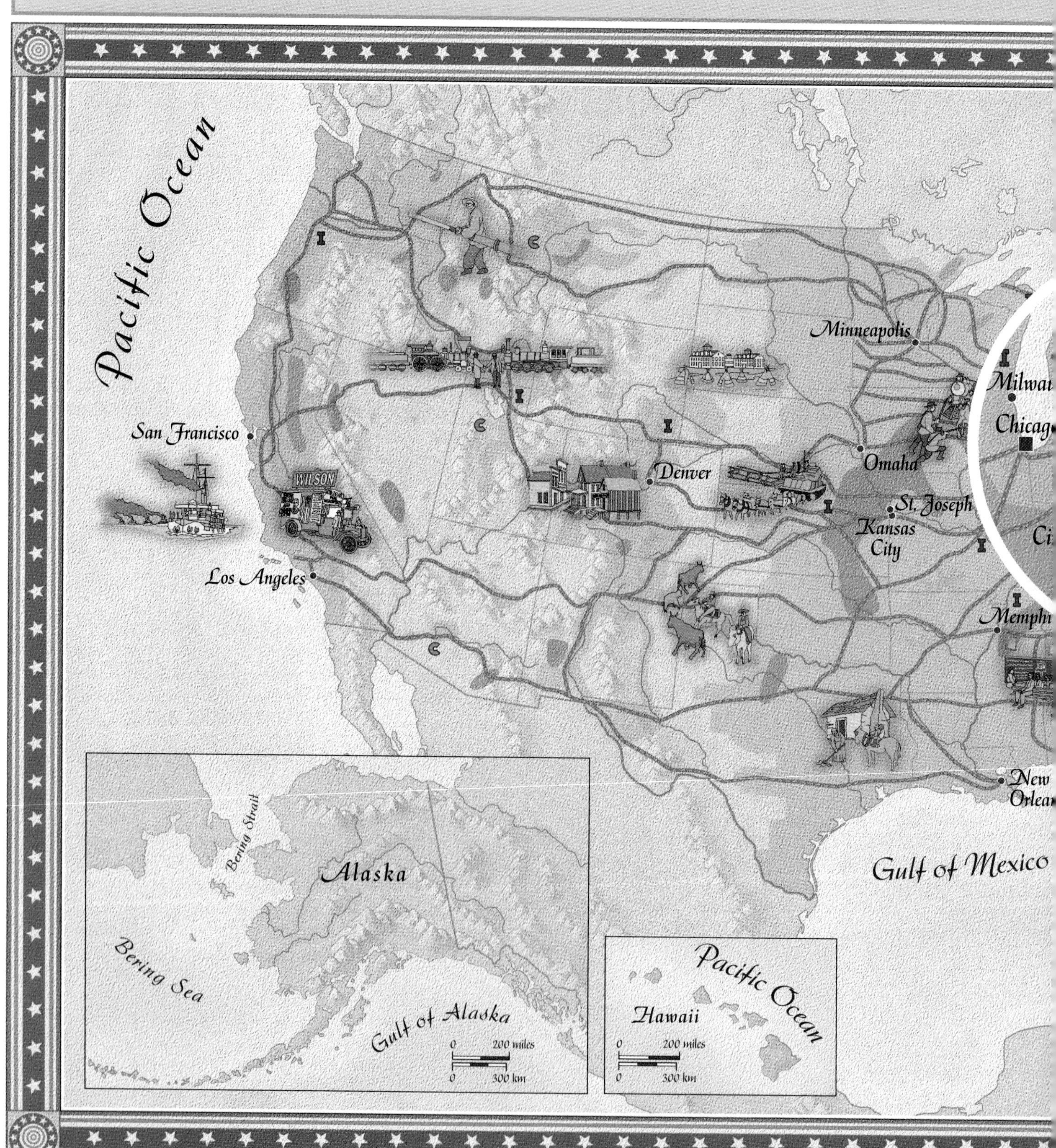

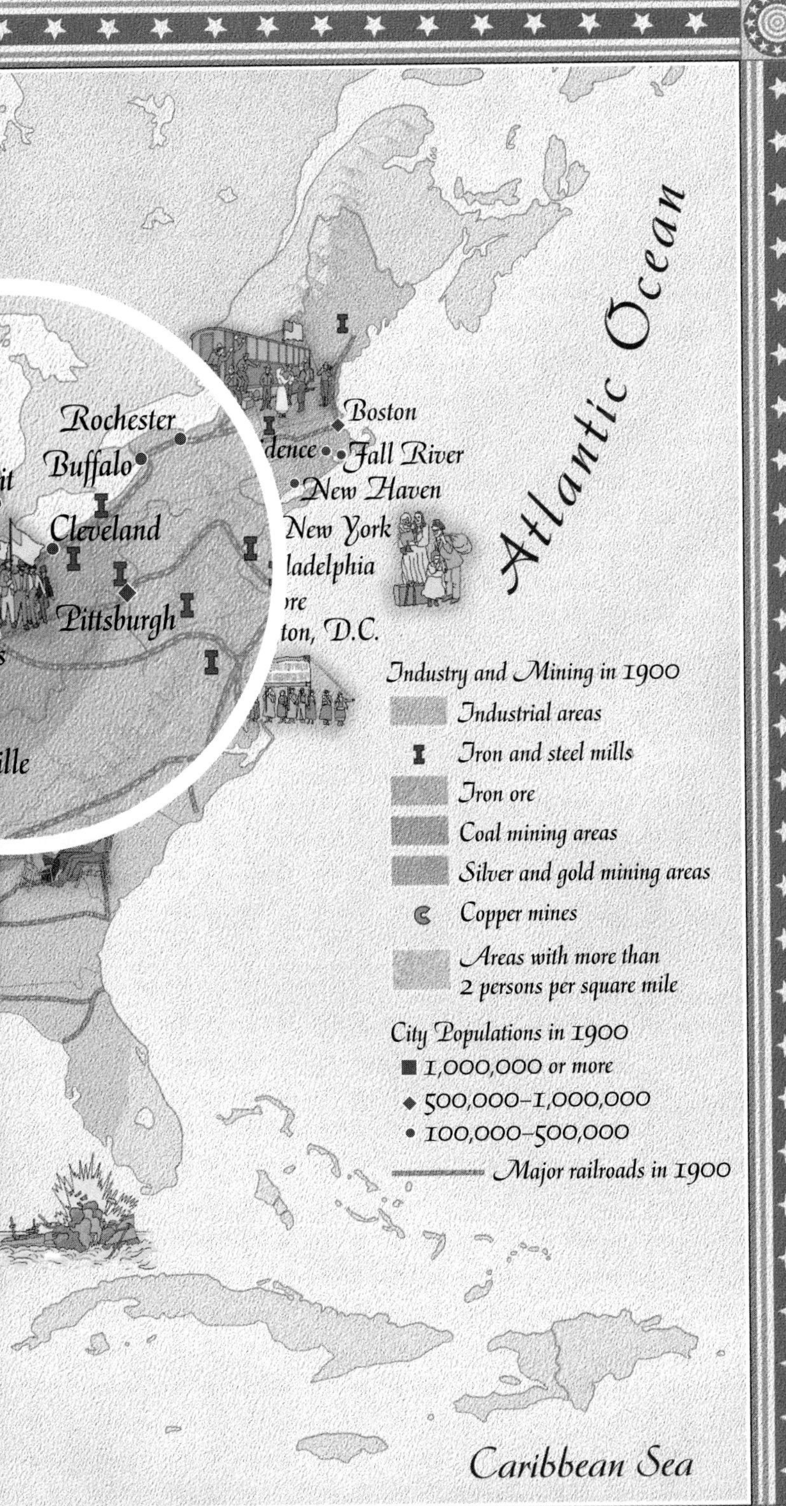

22

Chapter Outline

Key Topics

- The exuberant partisan politics and the close balance between parties in the late nineteenth century
- The inability of a weak federal government to address problems of America's industrializing economy
- The pressure for civil service reform
- The tariff issue
- Monetary policy and the call for free silver
- Agricultural protest and the emergence of the Populist party
- The end of political stalemate after the election of 1896

Cincinnati throbbed with excitement as the October 1884 congressional election approached. Republicans and Democrats staged mammoth campaign parades, each with more than twenty thousand torch-bearing marchers organized into uniformed companies, brigades, and divisions and accompanied by resplendent brass bands. Orators stirred the huge crowds with patriotic, religious, and cultural bombast. Partisans of the Anti-Monopoly party explained the dangers of corporate and money monopolies, but most voters ignored such complex issues amid the stirring spectacles presented by the major parties.

On October 14, in the dead of night, just hours before the polls opened, Cincinnati's police quietly entered the city's black neighborhoods. The police were a partisan force representing the Democratic-controlled city government. They arrested hundreds of African-American men and hurried them to jail. Those who promised to vote the Democratic ticket in exchange for 60 cents were escorted to the polls; those who remained steadfastly Republican were jailed until the polls closed and then released without charges. A thousand newly appointed Democratic deputies joined the police in attacking black Cincinnatians who tried to vote elsewhere in the city and arresting several hundred more Republicans at the polls.

Simultaneously, the U.S. marshal, a Republican, appointed nearly two thousand deputies, most of them paid and armed by the Lincoln Club, a Republican campaign organization. These deputies, "'roustabouts' and 'roughs,' men of no character or bad character," sought to incite violence in the city's Irish wards to keep Democratic voters from the polls. They too made mass arrests, often of Kentucky Democrats who had crossed the Ohio River to "colonize" Cincinnati's election. Several times deputies fired point-blank into Democratic crowds around the polls. Local Republican leader William Howard Taft, later a U.S. president, wrote his mother about witnessing a Democrat "shot & killed about fifteen feet from me at our polling place. . . . He drew a pistol on a Deputy Marshal but the Deputy was too quick for him." Although he considered the marshal's violence justified, Taft thought it risky for Republicans "to furnish revolvers to men who are close to or belong to the criminal class."

At the end of the day, according to the *Cincinnati Enquirer*, the "reign of terror" had left eight dead (including one federal deputy and one deputy sheriff), another two dozen with knife or bullet wounds, and "hundreds of cases of clubbing, sand-bagging, and brass-knuckle exercise." All in all, the newspaper concluded, it was a quiet election reflecting a "reasonably happy state of affairs."

As the *Enquirer* suggested, this Cincinnati election, though more riotous than some, was in many ways typical of late-nineteenth-century American politics. From the military-style campaign to the act of voting, elections were a masculine business. Marked by pageantry and hoopla, campaigns attracted mass participation but often avoided substantive policy issues. Third parties regularly challenged but rarely threatened the Democratic and Republican parties. These two major political parties shaped campaigns and controlled elections, which were usually tumultuous if not always violent. Partisan divisions overlapped with ethnic and racial divisions. The lack of a common national election day, which allowed Kentuckians to vote in Cincinnati's October election without missing their own in November, reflected localism—the belief that local concerns took precedence over national concerns. One newspaper even denied the legitimacy of federal involvement in the city's elections, declaring that federal deputies "can all be kicked and cuffed about like ordinary citizens, and will be compelled to take their chances with common people on election day."

These features of late-nineteenth-century politics would eventually be transformed in significant ways. But while they endured, they shaped not only campaigns and elections but the form and role of government as well.

The Structure and Style of Politics

Politics in the late nineteenth century was an absorbing activity. Campaigns and elections expressed social values as they determined who held the reins of government. Political parties dominated political life. They organized campaigns, controlled balloting, and held the unswerving loyalty of most of the electorate. While the major parties worked to maintain a sense of unity and tradition among their followers, third parties sought to activate those the major parties left unserved. Other Americans looked outside the electoral arena to fulfill their political goals.

Campaigns and Elections

Political campaigns and elections generated remarkable public participation and enthusiasm. They constituted a major form of entertainment at a time when recreational opportunities were limited. Campaign pageantry absorbed communities large and small. In cities and towns across the nation, thousands of men in elaborate uniforms marched in massive torch-lit parades to demonstrate partisan enthusiasm. The small town of Emporia, Kansas, once witnessed a campaign rally of twenty thousand people, several times its population. A parade of wagons stretched five miles, reported the proud local newspaper. "When the head of the procession was under the equator the tail was coming around the north pole." Political picnics and camp meetings served a comparable function in rural areas. Attending party meetings and conventions, listening to lengthy speeches appealing to group loyalties and local pride, gathering at the polls to watch the voting and the counting, celebrating victory and drowning the disappointment of defeat—all provided social enjoyment and defined popular politics.

The excitement of political contests prompted the wife of Chief Justice Morrison Waite to write longingly on election day, 1876, "I should want to vote all day." But women—though they often identified with and endorsed a political party—could not vote at all. Justice Waite himself had just a year earlier written the unanimous opinion of the Supreme Court (in *Minor* v. *Happersett*) that the Constitution did not confer suffrage on women. Men generally believed that weakness and sentimentality disqualified women from the fierce conflicts of the public realm.

Virtually all men participated in politics. In many states, even immigrants not yet citizens were eligible to vote and flocked to the polls. African Americans voted regularly in the North and irregularly in the South before being disfranchised at the end of the century. Overall, turnout was remarkably high, averaging nearly 80 percent of eligible voters in presidential elections between 1876 and 1900, a figure far greater than ever achieved thereafter (see Figure 22-1).

Political parties mobilized this huge electorate. They kept detailed records of voters, transported them to the polls, saw that they were registered where necessary, and sometimes even paid their poll

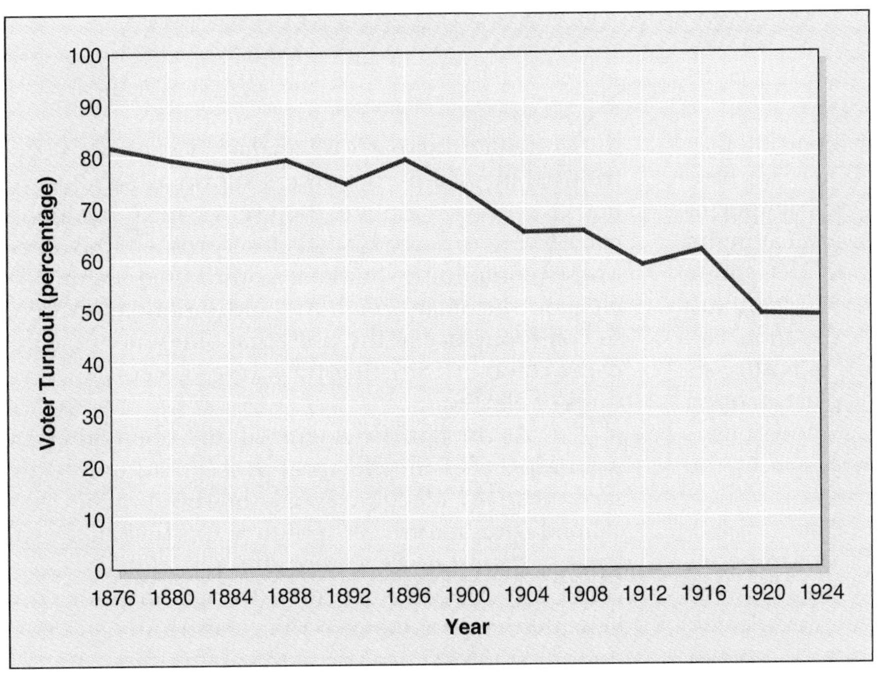

Figure 22-1 Voter Turnout in Presidential Elections, 1876–1924
The exciting partisan politics of the late nineteenth century produced very high voter turnouts, but as party competition declined and states enacted more restrictive voting regulations, popular participation in elections fell in the twentieth century.

Chronology

1867 Patrons of Husbandry (the Grange) is founded.

1869 Massachusetts establishes the first state regulatory commission.

1873 Silver is demonetized in the "Crime of '73."

1874 Woman's Christian Temperance Union is organized.

1875 U.S. Supreme Court, in *Minor* v. *Happersett,* upholds denial of suffrage to women.

1876 Greenback party runs presidential candidate.

1877 Rutherford B. Hayes becomes president after disputed election.
Farmers' Alliance is founded.
Supreme Court, in *Munn* v. *Illinois,* upholds state regulatory authority over private property.

1878 Bland-Allison Act obliges the government to buy silver.

1880 James A. Garfield is elected president.

1881 Garfield is assassinated; Chester A. Arthur becomes president.

1883 Pendleton Civil Service Act is passed.

1884 Grover Cleveland is elected president.

1886 Supreme Court, in *Wabash* v. *Illinois,* rules that only the federal government, not the states, can regulate interstate commerce.

1887 Interstate Commerce Act is passed.

1888 Benjamin Harrison is elected president.

1890 Sherman Antitrust Act is passed.
McKinley Tariff Act is passed.
Sherman Silver Purchase Act is passed.
National American Woman Suffrage Association is organized.
Wyoming enters the Union as the first state with woman suffrage.

1892 People's party is organized.
Cleveland is elected to his second term as president.

1893 Depression begins.
Sherman Silver Purchase Act is repealed.

1894 Coxey's Army marches to Washington.
Pullman strike ends in violence.

1895 Supreme Court, in *Pollock* v. *Farmers' Loan and Trust Company,* invalidates the federal income tax.
Supreme Court, in *United States* v. *E. C. Knight Company,* limits the Sherman Antitrust law to commerce, excluding industrial monopolies.

1896 William Jennings Bryan is nominated for president by Democrats and Populists.
William McKinley is elected president.

1900 Currency Act puts U.S. currency on the gold standard.

taxes or naturalization fees to make them eligible. With legal regulations and public machinery for elections negligible, parties dominated the campaigns and elections. Many states did not have meaningful registration laws, making it difficult to determine voter eligibility. Kentuckians swarmed to Cincinnati's polls in 1884 because Ohio had no registration law. Until the 1890s, most states had no laws to ensure secrecy in voting, and balloting often took place in open rooms or on sidewalks. Election clerks and judges were not public officials but partisans chosen by the political parties.

Nor did public authorities issue official ballots. Instead voters used party tickets, strips of paper printed by the parties. These had only the names of the candidates of the party issuing them and often varied in size and color. The voter's use of a ballot thus revealed his party allegiance. Tickets were distributed by paid party workers known as peddlers or hawkers, who stationed themselves near the polls, each trying to force his ticket on prospective voters. These contending hawkers contributed greatly to election day chaos. Fighting and intimidation were so commonplace at the polls that one state supreme court ruled in 1887 that they were "acceptable" features of elections.

As the court recognized, the open and partisan aspects of the electoral process did not necessarily lead to election fraud, however much they shaped the nature of political participation. In these circumstances, campaigns and elections provided opportunities for men to demonstrate publicly their commitment to their party and its values, thereby reinforcing their partisan loyalties.

Partisan Politics

A remarkably close balance prevailed between the two major parties in the elections of this era. Democrats and Republicans had virtually the same level of electoral support, one reason they worked so hard to get out the vote (see Map 22-1). Control of the presidency and Congress shifted back and forth between them. Rarely did either party control both branches of government at once (see the overview table, "Party Control of the Presidency and Congress, 1877–1900"). The party balance also gave great influence to New York, New Jersey, Ohio, and Indiana, whose evenly divided voters controlled electoral votes that could swing an election either way. Both parties tended to nominate presidential and vice presidential candidates from those states to woo their voters. The parties also concentrated campaign funds and strategy on the swing states. Thus Republican presidential candidate James Garfield of Ohio commented during the election campaign in 1880: "Nothing is wanting except an immediate and liberal supply of money for campaign expenses to make Indiana certain. With a victory there, the rest is easy." Garfield narrowly carried Indiana by six thousand votes and the nation by nine thousand out of 9.2 million cast. His victory was not the outcome of a contest over great issues but of carefully organized, tightly balanced parties mobilizing their supporters.

Map 22-1 ***The Two-Party Stalemate of the Late Nineteenth Century***
Strong parties, staunch loyalties, and an evenly divided electorate made for exciting politics but often stalemated government in the late nineteenth century. Most states voted consistently for one of the major parties, leaving the few swing states like New York and Indiana the scenes of fierce partisan battles.

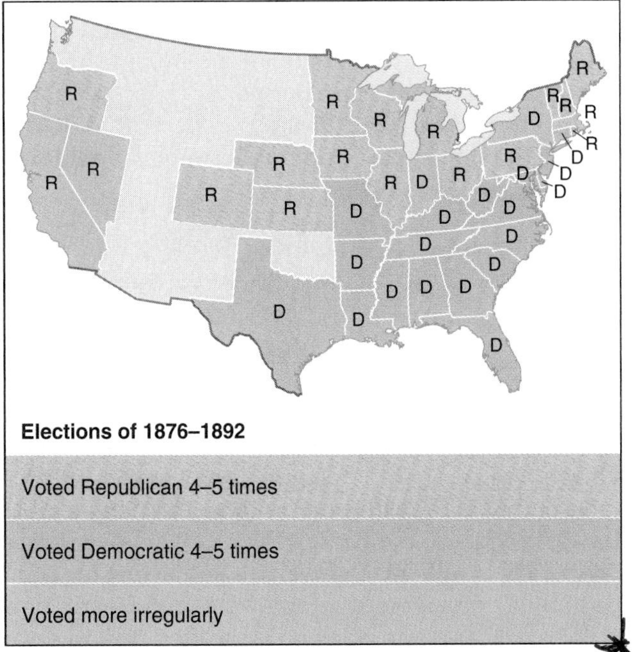

Interrelated regional, ethnic, religious, and local factors determined the party affiliations of most Americans. Economic issues, although important to the politics of the era, generally did not decide party ties. Farmers, for example, despite often shared economic concerns, affiliated with both major parties. Like religious belief and ethnic identity, partisan loyalty was largely a cultural trait passed from father to son, which helps explain the electoral stability of most communities.

Republicans were strongest in the North and Midwest, where they benefited from their party's role as the defender of the Union in the Civil War. But not all Northerners voted for the Grand Old Party, or GOP. The Republican party appealed primarily to old-stock Americans and other Protestants, including those of German and Scandinavian descent. African Americans, loyal to the party that had emancipated and enfranchised the slaves of the South, also supported the GOP where they could vote. Democrats were strongest in the South, where they stood as the defender of the traditions of the region's white population. But Democrats also drew support in the urban Northeast, especially from Catholics and recent immigrants.

Each major party thus consisted of a complex coalition of groups with differing traditions and interests. One observer of the Democratic party in California described it as "a sort of Democratic happy family, like we see in the prairie-dog villages, where owls, rattlesnakes, prairie dogs, and lizards all live in the same hole." This internal diversity often provoked conflict and threatened party stability. To hold its coalition together, each party identified itself with a theme that appealed broadly to all its constituents while suggesting that it was menaced by the members and objectives of the opposing party.

Republicans identified their party with nationalism and national unity and attacked the Democrats as an "alliance between the embittered South and the slums of the Northern cities." They combined a "bloody shirt" appeal to the memories of the Civil War with campaigns for immigration restriction and cultural uniformity. Seeing a threat to American society in efforts by Catholic immigrants to preserve their ethnic and cultural traditions, for example, Republican legislatures in several states in the 1880s and 1890s enacted laws regulating parochial schools, the use of foreign languages, and alcohol consumption.

OVERVIEW

PARTY CONTROL OF THE PRESIDENCY AND CONGRESS, 1877–1900

Period	Congress	House Majority Party		Senate Majority Party		Party of President	
1877–79	45th	D	153	R	39	R	Hayes
1879–81	46th	D	149	D	42	R	Hayes
1881–83	47th	D	147	R	37	R R	Garfield Arthur
1883–85	48th	D	197	R	38	R	Arthur
1885–87	49th	D	183	R	43	D	Cleveland
1887–89	50th	D	169	R	39	D	Cleveland
1889–91	51st	R	166	R	39	R	B. Harrison
1891–93	52nd	D	235	R	47	R	B. Harrison
1893–95	53rd	D	218	D	44	D	Cleveland
1895–97	54th	R	244	R	43	D	Cleveland
1897–99	55th	R	204	R	47	R	McKinley
1899–1901	56th	R	185	R	53	R	McKinley

Democrats portrayed themselves as the party of limited government and "personal liberties," a theme that appealed both to the racism of white Southerners and the resentment immigrants felt about the nativist meddling the Republicans favored. The Democrats' commitment to personal liberties had limits. They supported the disfranchisement of African Americans, the exclusion of Chinese immigrants, and the dispossession of American Indians. Nevertheless, their emphasis on traditional individualism and localism proved popular.

The partisan politics of both major parties culminated in party machines, especially at the local level. Led by powerful bosses like Democrat Richard Croker of New York or Republican George Cox of Cincinnati, these machines controlled not only city politics but municipal government. Party activists used well-organized ward clubs to mobilize working-class voters, who were rewarded by municipal jobs and baskets of food or coal doled out by the machine. Such assistance was often necessary given the lack of public welfare systems, but to buy votes the machine also sold favors. Public contracts and franchises were peddled to businesses whose high bids covered kickbacks to the machine.

The partisan politics of the era left room for several third parties organized around specific issues or groups. The **Prohibition party** persistently championed the abolition of alcohol but also introduced many important reform ideas. Some farmers and workers, fed up with the major parties, formed larger but shorter-lived third parties. These parties charged that Republicans and Democrats had failed to respond to economic problems caused by industrialization or, worse still, had deliberately promoted powerful business interests at the expense of ordinary Americans. The **Greenback party** of the 1870s denounced "the infamous financial legislation which takes all from the many to enrich the few." Its policies of labor reform and currency inflation (to stimulate and democratize the economy) attracted supporters from Maine to Texas. Other significant third parties included the Anti-Monopoly party, the Union Labor party, and, most important, the **People's** or **Populist** party of the 1890s. Although third parties often won temporary success at the local or regional level, they never permanently displaced the major parties or undermined traditional voter allegiances.

Associational Politics

Associations of like-minded citizens, operating outside the electoral arena, played an increasingly important role in late-nineteenth-century politics. These organizations worked to achieve public policies beneficial to their members. Farmers organized many such groups, most notably the Patrons of Husbandry, known familiarly as the Grange (see Chapter 19). Established in 1867, with both women and men eligible for membership, the Grange had 22,000 local lodges and nearly a million members by 1875. Its campaign for public regulation of the rates charged by railroads and grain elevators helped convince midwestern

FROM THEN TO NOW

Political Parties

Few things in contemporary American politics present a sharper contrast to the nineteenth century than the role of political parties. In the late nineteenth century, parties dominated politics. They commanded the allegiance of Americans, controlled the selection of candidates, mobilized voters, shaped voting behavior, provided ballots, and ran elections. They also shaped public policies and, through patronage, staffed government positions. At the beginning of the twenty-first century, parties do virtually none of these things.

This transformation began at the end of the nineteenth century. Extreme partisanship prompted states to assert control over elections. The corruption attributed to party machines led gradually to such changes as nonpartisan municipal elections and increased public control over parties. Restrictions on campaign expenditures reduced the party hoopla that had made politics so exciting and voter turnout so high. The connection between parties and voters declined further as new voters unfamiliar with the passions and loyalties of the past joined the electorate.

The inability of the major parties to deal effectively with important national problems, so evident in the depression of the 1890s, prompted Americans to find other ways to influence public policy. Associational groups that had acted outside the partisan arena evolved into effective special-interest lobbying groups. Civil service reform, beginning with the Pendleton Act, steadily reduced party influence in government. So did the growing reliance in the twentieth century on independent regulatory commissions, rather than partisan legislative committees, to make and implement policies.

In recent decades, party decline has accelerated. The introduction and spread of primary elections have stripped parties of their control over nominations. Individual candidates have come increasingly to rely more on personal organizations than party apparatus to manage campaigns. Candidates often appeal for votes as individuals rather than as party members and communicate directly to voters through the mass media, relying less on the old door-to-door personal campaign requiring party workers. Television, in particular, with its focus on dramatic and personal sound bites, is better at promoting individual candidates than abstract entities like parties.

Campaign finance reform laws have reduced party control over the funding of campaigns. So too has the rise of political action committees (PACs) as an important source of support for candidates. PACs represent particular interests, not a collection of interests the way parties do. Candidates dependent on specific interests find it harder to make broader partisan appeals.

Polls show fewer and fewer Americans identifying with a particular party and indicate that partisanship has greatly declined as a factor in voting decisions. Americans increasingly regard parties as neither meaningful nor even useful, let alone essential to democratic government. Nearly half of the electorate favors making all elections nonpartisan or even abolishing parties. More and more people believe that interest groups better represent their political needs than parties. At the same time, fewer and fewer Americans bother to vote. Those who do are much more likely than before to split their ticket, voting for candidates of different parties for different offices. This often results in divided government—with the presidency controlled by one party and Congress by the other. The resulting stalemate increases public cynicism about parties.

Of course, parties endure and retain some importance. Election laws favor the two established parties and obstruct independent candidacies. Public funds subsidize party activities, and party coffers harvest unregulated "soft money" campaign contributions. Congress and state legislatures continue to rely on party divisions to organize their leadership and committee structures, and party discipline still influences the way legislators vote. But while such institutional factors guarantee the continued presence of a two-party system, the parties themselves no longer enjoy the influence they had in the nineteenth century.

The campaign pageantry of a Republican parade in Canton, Ohio, in 1896 illustrates the central role played by political parties in entertaining, organizing, and mobilizing voters. A century later parties have lost many of their functions and much of their popular support.

states to pass the so-called **Granger laws**. The Grange also sought reforms in the nation's financial system. Although it inspired the formation of small independent farmers' parties in the Midwest and on the Pacific coast, the Grange itself remained nonpartisan.

To the Grangers' dismay, industrialists also formed pressure groups. Organizations such as the American Iron and Steel Association and the American Protective Tariff League lobbied Congress for high tariff laws and made campaign contributions to friendly politicians of both parties. A small group of conservative reformers known derisively as **Mugwumps** (the term derives from the Algonquian word for "chief") objected to both tariffs and the government regulations farmers favored. They saw both as interfering with "natural" economic laws. They devoted most of their efforts, however, to campaigning for honest and efficient government through civil service reform. They organized the National Civil Service Reform League to publicize their plans, lobby Congress and state legislatures, and endorse sympathetic candidates. Other pressure groups focused on cultural politics. The rabidly anti-Catholic American Protective Association, for example, agitated for laws restricting immigration, taxing church property, and inspecting Catholic religious institutions.

The Grange rejected partisanship but not politics. This sympathetic cartoon shows a Granger trying to warn Americans blindly absorbed in partisan politics of the dangers of onrushing industrialization.

Women were also active in associational politics. Susan B. Anthony and others formed groups to lobby Congress and state legislatures for constitutional amendments extending the right to vote to women. The leading organizations merged in 1890 as the **National American Woman Suffrage Association**. Despite the opposition of male politicians of both major parties, suffragists had succeeded by the mid-1890s in gaining full woman suffrage in four western states—Wyoming, Colorado, Idaho, and Utah—and partial suffrage (the right to vote in school elections) in several other states, east and west.

Other women influenced public issues through social service organizations. Although the belief that women belonged in the domestic sphere kept them out of electoral politics, it furnished a basis for political action focused on welfare and moral reform. With petition campaigns, demonstrations, and lobbying, women's social service organizations sought to remedy poverty and disease, improve education and recreation, and provide day nurseries for the children of workingwomen. The Illinois Woman's Alliance, organized in 1888 by suffragists, women assemblies of the Knights of Labor, and middle-class women's clubs, investigated the conditions of women and children in workshops and factories and campaigned for protective labor legislation and compulsory school attendance laws.

Women also combined domesticity and politics in the temperance movement. Alcoholism, widespread in American society, was thought to be a major cause of crime, wife abuse, and broken homes. The temperance movement thus invoked women's presumed moral superiority to address a real problem that fell within their accepted sphere. The Woman's Christian Temperance Union (WCTU) gained a massive membership campaigning for restrictive liquor laws. Under the leadership of Frances Willard, however, it built on traditional women's concerns to develop an important critique of American society. Reversing the conventional view, Willard argued that alcohol abuse was a result, not a cause, of poverty and social disorder. Under the slogan of "Home Protection," the WCTU inserted domestic issues into the political sphere with a campaign for social and economic reforms far beyond temperance. It particularly sought to strengthen and enforce laws against rape. Willard bitterly noted that twenty states fixed the age of consent at ten and that "in Massachusetts and Vermont it is a greater crime to steal a cow" than to rape a woman. The WCTU also pushed for improved health conditions and workplace and housing reforms. It eventually

A meeting in 1880 of the National Woman Suffrage Association protested the exclusion of women from electoral politics. Susan B. Anthony noted with regret that "to all men woman suffrage is only a side issue."

supported woman suffrage as well, on the grounds that women needed the vote to fulfill their duty to protect home, family, and morality.

The Limits of Government

Despite the popular enthusiasm for partisan politics and the persistent pressure of associational politics, government in the late nineteenth century was neither active nor productive by present standards. The receding government activism of the Civil War and Reconstruction years coincided with a resurgent belief in localism and laissez-faire policies. In addition, a Congress and presidency divided between the two major parties, a small and inefficient bureaucracy, and judicial restraints joined powerful private interests to limit the size and objectives of the federal government.

The Weak Presidency

The presidency was a weak and restricted institution. The impeachment of President Johnson at the outset of Reconstruction had undermined the office. Then President Grant clearly subordinated it to the legislative branch by deferring to Congress on appointments and legislation. Other factors contributed as well. The men who filled the office between 1877 and 1897—Republicans Rutherford B. Hayes (1877–1881), James A. Garfield (1881), and Chester A. Arthur (1881–1885); Democrat Grover Cleveland (1885–1889 and 1893–1897); and Republican Benjamin Harrison (1889–1893)—were all honest and generally capable. Each had built a solid political record at the state or federal level. But they were all conservatives with a narrow view of the presidency and proposed few initiatives. The most aggressive of them, Cleveland, used his energy in a singularly negative fashion, vetoing two-thirds of all the bills Congress passed, more than all his predecessors combined. Cleveland once vetoed a relief measure for drought-stricken Texas farmers with the statement that "though the people support the Government, the Government should not support the people." This attitude limited government action.

The presidents of this era viewed their duties as chiefly administrative. They made little effort to reach out to the public or to exert legislative leadership. In 1885, Woodrow Wilson, at the time a professor of history and government, described "the business of the president" as "not much above routine" and concluded that the office might "not inconveniently" be made purely administrative, its occupant a sort of tenured civil servant. (Wilson, who helped transform the presidency into a powerful office in the twentieth century, took a very different view when he became president himself in 1913.) Benjamin Harrison devoted as many as six hours a day to dealing with office seekers, and Garfield lamented, "My day is frittered away by the personal seeking of people, when it ought to be given to the great problems which concern the whole country."

The presidency was also hampered by its limited control over bureaus and departments, which responded more directly to Congress, and by its small staff. Indeed, the president's staff consisted of no more than half a dozen secretaries, clerks, and telegraphers. As Cleveland complained, "If the President has any great policy in mind or on hand he has no one to help him work it out."

The Inefficient Congress

Congress was the foremost branch of the national government. It exercised authority over the federal budget, oversaw the cabinet, debated public issues, and controlled legislation. Its members were often state and national party leaders who were strong-willed and, as one senator conceded, "tolerated no intrusion from the President or from anybody else."

But Congress was scarcely efficient. Its chambers were noisy and chaotic, and members rarely devoted their attention to the business at hand. Instead they played cards, read newspapers, or sent a page to get fruit or tobacco from the vendors who lined the hallways of the capitol. One senator from Nevada complained in 1881 that the "confusion, noise, and interruption" in the Senate chamber disrupted his efforts to write letters. The repeated shifts in party control of Congress also impeded effective action. So too did the loss of experienced legislators to rapid turnover. In some Congresses, a majority of members were first-termers.

Procedural rules, based on precedents from a simpler time and manipulated by determined partisans, impeded congressional action. Some rules restricted the introduction of legislation; others prevented its passage. The most notorious rule required that a quorum be not only present but voting. When the House was narrowly divided along party lines, the minority could block all business simply by refusing to answer when the roll was called.

But as a nationalizing economy required more national legislation, business before Congress grew relentlessly (see Figure 22-2). The expanding scale of congressional work prompted a gradual reform of procedures and the centralization of power in the speaker of the House and the leading committees. These changes did not, however, create a coherent program for government action.

The Federal Bureaucracy and the Spoils System

Reflecting presidential weakness and congressional inefficiency, the federal bureaucracy remained small and limited in the late nineteenth century. There were little more than fifty thousand government employees in 1871, and three-fourths of them were local postmasters scattered across the nation. Only six thousand, from President Grant to janitors, worked in Washington. The number of federal employees doubled to 100,000 in 1881 and grew again to 157,000 in 1891 and 239,000 in 1901. It was still the postal service, however, that absorbed most of this increase.

The system for selecting and supervising federal officials had developed gradually in the first half of the century. Known as the spoils system, its basic principle was that victorious politicians awarded government jobs to party workers, with little regard for qualifications, and ousted the previous employees. Appointees then typically promised part of their salary and time to the political interests of their patron or party. The spoils system played a crucial role in all aspects of politics. It enabled party leaders to strengthen their organizations, reward loyal party service, and attract the political workers that parties needed to mobilize the electorate. Supporters described it as a democratic system that offered opportunities to many citizens and prevented the emergence of an entrenched bureaucracy.

Critics, however, charged that the system was riddled with corruption, abuse, and inefficiency. Rapid turnover bred instability; political favoritism bred incompetence. One secretary of the navy, appointed at the behest of Indiana's Republican machine, was said to have exclaimed during his first official inspection of a ship: "Why, the thing's hollow!" Certainly the spoils system was ineffective for filling positions that required special clerical skills, like typing, or scientific expertise like that required by the Weather Bureau (established in 1870) or the U.S. Geological Survey (established in 1879). More serious, the spoils system also absorbed the president and Congress in unproductive conflicts over patronage.

Figure 22-2 Increase in Congressional Business, 1871–1901

Industrialization, urbanization, and western expansion brought increased demands for government action, but the party stalemate, laissez-faire attitudes, and inefficient public institutions often blocked effective responses.

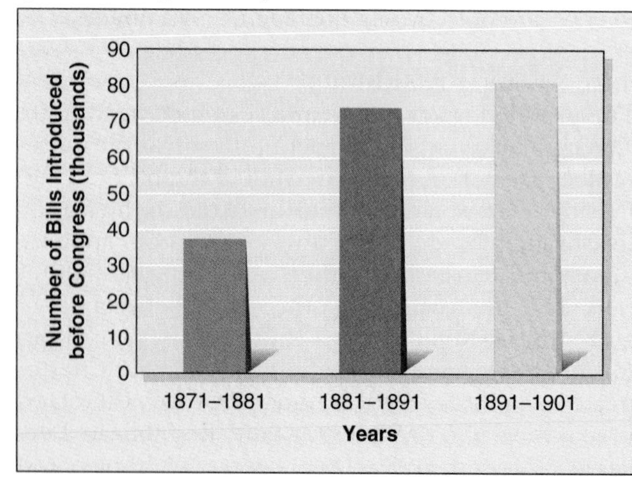

Inconsistent State Government

The public allowed state governments freer rein than the federal government. Considered closer and more responsible to the people, state governments had long exercised police power and regulatory authority. They collected taxes for education and public works, and they promoted private enterprise and public health. Still, they did little by today's standards. Few people thought it appropriate for government at any level to offer direct help to particular social groups. Some state governments contracted in the 1870s and 1880s following the wartime activism of the 1860s. Newly elected Democratic governors hewed to their party's narrow view of government, and new state constitutions restricted the scope of public authority. California's constitution of 1879, for example, limited the state government's authority so sharply that one wit even proposed abolishing the legislature, "and any person who shall be guilty of suggesting that a Legislature be held, shall be punished as a felon without the benefit of clergy."

But state governments gradually expanded their role in response to the stresses produced by industrialization. Following the lead of Massachusetts in 1869, a majority of states had by the turn of the century created commissions to investigate and regulate industry. Public intervention in other areas of the industrial economy soon followed. One observer noted in 1887 that state governments enacted many laws and established numerous state agencies in "utter disregard of the laissez-faire principle." In Minnesota, for example, the state helped farmers by establishing a dairy commission, prohibiting the manufacture or sale of margarine, creating a bureau of animal industry, and employing state veterinarians. In the lumber industry, state officials oversaw every log "floated downstream from the woods to the saw-mill." State inspectors examined Minnesota's steam boilers, oil production, and sanitary conditions. Other laws regulated railroads, telegraphs, and dangerous occupations, prohibited racial discrimination in inns, and otherwise protected the public welfare.

Not all such agencies and laws were effective, nor were all state governments as diligent as Minnesota's. Southern states especially lagged, and one Midwesterner complained that his legislature merely "meets in ignorance, sits in corruption, and dissolves in disgrace every two years." Still, the widening scope of state action represented a growing acceptance of public responsibility for social welfare and economic life and laid the foundation for more effective steps in the early twentieth century.

Public Policies and National Elections

Several great issues dominated the national political arena in the late nineteenth century, including civil service reform, tariffs, and business and financial regulation. Civil service reform attracted relatively little popular interest, but Americans argued passionately about even the smallest details of tariff, regulatory, and financial legislation. Rarely, however, did these issues clearly and consistently separate the major political parties. Instead they divided each party into factions along regional, interest, and economic lines. As a consequence, these leading issues often played only a small role in determining elections and were seldom resolved by government action.

Civil Service Reform

Reform of the spoils system emerged as a prominent issue during the Hayes administration. Reformers like the Mugwumps wanted a professional civil service based on merit and divorced from politics. They wanted officeholders to be selected on the basis of competitive written examinations and protected from removal on political grounds. They expected such a system to promote efficiency, economy, and honesty in government. But they also expected it to increase their own influence and minimize that of "mere politicians." As one Baltimore Mugwump said, civil service reform would replace ignorant and corrupt officeholders with "gentlemen . . . who need nothing and want nothing from government except the satisfaction of using their talents," or at least with "sober, industrious . . . middle-class persons who have taken over . . . the proper standards of conduct."

Not all Americans agreed with such haughty views. The *New York Sun* denounced "the proposition that men shall be appointed to office as the result of examinations in book learning and that they shall remain in office during life. . . . We don't want an aristocracy of office-holders in this country."

President Hayes favored civil service reform but did not fully renounce the spoils system. He rewarded those who had helped elect him, permitted party leaders to name or veto candidates for the cabinet, and insisted that his own appointees contribute funds to Republican election campaigns. But he rejected the claims of some machine leaders and office seekers and proposed reforms, which Congress promptly blocked. He struck a blow for change, however, when he fired Chester A. Arthur from his post as New York customs house collector after an investigation pronounced Arthur's patronage system to be

In this 1881 cartoon, the evil spirit of partisanship threatens a government clerk hesitating to kick back an assessed portion of his salary to the party in power. Civil service reformers wanted to eliminate political factors in staffing the federal bureaucracy.

"unsound in principle, dangerous in practice, . . . and calculated to encourage and perpetuate the official ignorance, inefficiency, and corruption. . . ."

The weakness of the civil service reformers was dramatically underscored in 1880 when the Republicans, to improve their chances of carrying the crucial state of New York, nominated Arthur for vice president on a ticket headed by James A. Garfield of Ohio. They won, and Garfield immediately found himself enmeshed in the demands of the unreformed spoils system. He once complained to his wife, "I had hardly arrived before the door-bell began to ring and the old stream of office-seekers began to pour in. They had scented my coming and were lying in wait for me like vultures for a wounded bison. All day long it has been a steeple chase, I fleeing and they pursuing." Within a few months of his inauguration in 1881, Garfield was assassinated by a disappointed and crazed office seeker, and Arthur became president.

Public dismay over this tragedy finally spurred changes in the spoils system. Arthur himself urged Congress to act, and in 1883, it passed the **Pendleton Civil Service Act**. This measure prohibited federal employees from soliciting or receiving political contributions from government workers and created the Civil Service Commission to administer competitive examinations to applicants for government jobs. The act gave the commission jurisdiction over only about 10 percent of federal positions but allowed presidents to extend its authority. And subsequent presidents did so, if sometimes only to prevent their own appointees from being turned out by a succeeding administration. A professional civil service free from partisan politics gradually emerged, strengthening the executive branch's ability to handle its increasing administrative responsibilities.

The new emphasis on merit and skill rather than party ties opened new opportunities to women. Federal clerks were nearly exclusively male as late as 1862, but by the early 1890s, women held a third of the clerical positions in the executive departments in Washington. These workers constituted the nation's first substantial female clerical labor force. Their work in public life challenged the conventional belief that a woman's ability and personality limited her to the domestic sphere. To succeed, clerks had to be assertive and competent, to acquire managerial skills, and to think of their careers as permanent, not temporary. Julia Henderson described her work as an examiner of accounts in the Interior Department in 1893 as "brain work of a character that requires a knowledge not only of the rulings of this Department, but also those of the Treasury, Second Auditor, Second Comptroller, and Revised Statutes; demanding the closest and most critical attention, together with a great deal of legal and business knowledge."

The Political Life of the Tariff

Americans debated heatedly over tariff legislation throughout the late nineteenth century. This complex issue linked basic economic questions to partisan, ideological, and regional concerns. Tariffs on imported goods provided revenue for the federal government and protected American industry from European competition. They thus promoted industrial growth but often allowed favored industries to garner high profits. By the 1880s, tariffs covered four thousand items and generated more revenue than the government needed to carry on its limited operations.

Reflecting its commitment to industry, the Republican party vigorously championed protective tariffs. Party leaders also claimed that American labor benefited from tariff protection. "Reduce the tariff, and labor is the first to suffer," declared William McKinley of Ohio. Most Democrats, by contrast, favored tariff reduction, a position that reflected their

OVERVIEW

ARGUMENTS IN THE TARIFF DEBATES

Area Affected	High-Tariff Advocates	Low-Tariff Advocates
Industry	Tariffs promote industrial growth.	Tariffs inflate corporate profits.
Employment	Tariffs stimulate job growth.	Tariffs restrict competition.
Wages and prices	Tariffs permit higher wages.	Tariffs increase consumer prices.
Government	Tariffs provide government revenue.	Tariffs violate the principle of laissez-faire and produce revenues that tempt the government to activism.
Trade	Tariffs protect the domestic market.	Tariffs restrict foreign trade.

party's relatively laissez-faire outlook. They argued that lower tariffs would encourage foreign trade and, by reducing the treasury surplus, minimize the temptation for the government to pursue activist policies. They pointed out the discriminatory effects of high tariffs, which benefited some interests, like certain manufacturers, but hurt others, like some farmers, while raising the cost of living for all (see the overview table, "Arguments in the Tariff Debates").

The differences between the parties, however, were often more rhetorical than substantial. They disagreed only about how great tariffs should be and what interests they should protect. Regardless of party position, congressmen of both parties voted for tariffs that would benefit their districts. California Democrats called for protective duties on wool and raisins, products produced in California; Massachusetts Republicans, to aid their state's shoe manufacturers, supported tariffs on shoes but opposed tariffs on leather. A Democratic senator from Indiana, elected on a campaign pledge to reduce tariffs, summed up the prevailing rule succinctly: "I am a protectionist for every interest which I am sent here by my constituents to protect."

In the 1884 campaign, Republican presidential candidate James G. Blaine maintained that prosperity and high employment depended on high duties. The Democrats' platform endorsed a lowered tariff, but their candidate, New York governor Grover Cleveland, generally ignored the issue. Unable to address this and other important issues, both parties resorted to scandalmongering. The Democrats exploited Blaine's image as a beneficiary of the spoils system, which convinced the Mugwumps to bolt to Cleveland. Republicans responded by exposing Cleveland as the father of an illegitimate child.

Cleveland continued to avoid the tariff issue for three years after his election, until the growing treasury surplus and rising popular pressure for tariff reduction prompted him to act. He devoted his entire 1887 annual message to attacking the "vicious, inequitable, and illogical" tariff, apparently making it the dominant issue of his 1888 reelection campaign. Once again, however, the distinctive political attribute of the period—intense and organized campaigning between closely balanced parties—forced both Democrats and Republicans to blur their positions. Cleveland proposed a Democratic platform that ignored his recent message and did not even use the word *tariff.* When the party convention adopted a tariff reduction plank, Cleveland complained bitterly and named high-tariff advocates to manage his campaign. "What a predicament the party is placed in," lamented one Texas Democrat, with tariff reform "for its battle cry and with a known protectionist . . . as our chairman." Cleveland won slightly more popular votes than his Republican opponent, Benjamin Harrison of Indiana, but Harrison carried the electoral college, indicating the decisive importance of strategic campaigning, local issues, and large campaign funds rather than great national issues.

The triumphant Republicans raised tariffs to unprecedented levels with the **McKinley Tariff Act** of 1890. McKinley praised the law as "protective in every paragraph and American on every page," but it provoked a popular backlash that helped return the Democrats to power. Still, the Democrats made little effort to push tariff reform. The *Atlanta Constitution* mused about such tariff politics in a bit of doggerel:

It's funny 'bout this tariff—how they've lost it or forgot;
They were rushing it to Congress once; their collars were so hot
They could hardly wait to fix it 'till we harvested a crop;
Was it such a burnin' question that they had to let it drop?

The Beginnings of Federal Regulation

While business leaders pressed for protective tariffs and other public policies that promoted their interests, they otherwise used their great political influence to ensure governmental laissez-faire. Popular pressure nonetheless compelled Congress to take the first steps toward the regulation of business with the passage of the **Interstate Commerce Act** in 1887 and the **Sherman Antitrust Act** in 1890.

The rapid growth of great industrial corporations and their disruptive effects on traditional practices and values profoundly alarmed the public (see Chapter 20). Farmers condemned the power of corporations over transportation facilities and their monopolization of industries affecting agriculture, from those that manufactured farm machinery to those that ran flour mills. Small business owners suffered from the destructive competition of corporations, workers were exploited by their control of the labor market, and consumers felt victimized by high prices. The result was a growing clamor to rein the corporations in.

The first target of this concern was the nation's railroads, the preeminent symbol of big business. Both farm groups and business shippers complained of discriminatory rates levied by railroads. Consumers condemned the railroads' use of pooling arrangements to suppress competition and raise rates. The resulting pressure was responsible for the Granger laws enacted in several midwestern states in the 1870s to regulate railroad freight and storage rates.

At first, the Supreme Court upheld this legislation, ruling in *Munn* v. *Illinois* (1877) that state governments had the right to regulate private property when it was "devoted to a public use." But in 1886, the Court ruled in *Wabash, St. Louis, and Pacific Railway Company* v. *Illinois* that only the federal government could regulate interstate commerce. This decision effectively ended state regulation of railroads but simultaneously increased pressure for congressional action. "Upon no public question are the people so nearly unanimous as upon the proposition that Congress should undertake in some way the regulation of interstate business," concluded a Senate committee. With the support of both major parties, Congress in 1887 passed the Interstate Commerce Act.

The act prohibited rebates, discriminatory rates, and pooling and established the **Interstate Commerce Commission (ICC)** to investigate and prosecute violations. The ICC was the first federal regulatory agency. But its powers were too limited to be effective. Senator Nelson Aldrich of Rhode Island, a leading spokesman for business interests, described the law as an "empty menace to great interests, made to answer the clamor of the ignorant." Presidents did little to enforce it, and railroads continued their objectionable practices. They frustrated the commission by refusing to provide required information and endlessly appealing its orders to a conservative judiciary. In its first fifteen years, only one court case was decided in favor of the ICC. Not surprisingly, then, popular dissatisfaction with the railroads continued into the twentieth century. Californian Frank Norris, in his novel *The Octopus* (1901), likened them to "a gigantic parasite fattening upon the lifeblood of an entire commonwealth."

Many people saw railroad abuses as indicative of the dangers of corporate power in general and demanded a broader federal response. As with railroad regulation, the first antitrust laws—laws intended to break up or regulate corporate monopolies—were passed by states. Exposés of the monopolistic practices of such corporations as Standard Oil forced both major parties to endorse national antitrust legislation during the campaign of 1888. In 1890, Congress enacted the Sherman Antitrust Act with only a single vote in opposition. But this near unanimity concealed real differences over the desirability and purpose of the law. Although it emphatically prohibited any combination in restraint of trade (any attempt to restrict competition), it was otherwise vaguely written and hence weak in its ability to prevent abuses. The courts further weakened it, and presidents of both parties made little effort to enforce it. Essentially still unfettered, large corporations remained an ominous threat in the eyes of many Americans.

The Money Question

Persistent wrangling over questions of currency and coinage made monetary policy the most divisive political issue in the late nineteenth century. President Garfield suggested the complexities of this subject when he wryly declared that a member of Congress had been committed to an asylum after "he devoted himself almost exclusively to the study of the currency, became fully entangled with the theories of the subject, and became insane." Despite the sometimes arcane and difficult nature of the money question, millions of Americans adopted positions on it and defended them with religious ferocity.

Creditors, especially bankers, as well as conservative economists and many business leaders favored limiting the money supply. They called this a **sound money** policy and insisted that it would ensure economic stability, maintain property values, and retain investor confidence. Farmers and other debtors complained that this deflationary monetary policy would exacerbate the trend toward depressed prices in the American economy. They feared it would depress already low crop prices, drive debtors further into debt, and restrict economic opportunities. They favored expanding the money supply to match the country's growing population and economy. They expected this inflationary policy to raise prices, stimulate the economy, reduce debt burdens, and increase opportunities.

The conservative leadership of both major parties supported the sound money policy, but their rank-and-file membership, especially in the West and the South, included many inflationists. As a result, the parties avoided confronting each other on the money issue.

The conflict between advocates of sound money and inflation centered on the use of paper money—"greenbacks"—and silver coinage. The greenback controversy had its roots in the Civil War. To meet its expenses during the war, the federal government issued $450 million in greenbacks—paper money backed only by the credit of the United States, not by gold or silver, the traditional basis of currency. After the war, creditors demanded that these greenbacks be withdrawn from circulation. Debtors and other Americans caught up in a postwar depression favored retaining the greenbacks and even expanding their use.

In 1875, sound money advocates in Congress enacted a deflationary law that withdrew some greenbacks from circulation and required that the remainder be convertible into gold after 1878. This action forced the money issue into electoral politics. Outraged inflationists organized the Greenback party. They charged that the major parties had "failed to take the side of the people" and instead supported the "great moneyed institutions." The Greenbackers polled more than a million votes in 1878 and elected fourteen members of Congress, nearly gaining the balance of power in the House. As the depression faded, however, so did interest in the greenback issue, and the party soon withered.

Inflationists then turned their attention to the silver issue, which would prove more enduring and disruptive. Historically, the United States had been on a bimetallic standard; that is, it used both gold and silver as the basis of its currency. But after the 1840s, the market price of silver rose above the currency value assigned to it by the government. Silver miners and owners began to sell the metal for commercial use rather than to the government for coinage, and little silver money circulated. In 1873, Congress passed a law "demonetizing" silver, making gold the only standard for American currency. Gold

"The Bosses of the Senate," a political cartoon of 1889, depicted the popular belief that huge corporate trusts controlled the government and corrupted public policy. This conviction helped fuel the demand for antitrust legislation but may not have been allayed by the weaknesses of the Sherman Act.

standard supporters hoped the law would promote international trade by aligning U.S. financial policy with that of Great Britain, which insisted on gold-based currency. But they also wanted to prevent new silver discoveries in the American West from expanding the money supply.

Indeed, silver production soon boomed, flooding the commercial market and dropping the value of the metal. Dismayed miners wanted the Treasury Department to purchase their surplus silver on the old terms and demanded a return to the bimetallic system. More important, the rural debtor groups seeking currency inflation joined in this demand, seeing the return to silver coinage as a means to reverse the long deflationary trend in the economy. Many passionately denounced the "Crime of '73" as a conspiracy of eastern bankers and foreign interests to control the money system to the detriment of ordinary Americans.

Again, both major parties equivocated. Eastern conservatives of both parties denounced silver; Southerners and Westerners demanded **free silver**, which meant unlimited silver coinage. One New York Democrat complained that western and southern members of his party were "mad as wild Texas steers on this silver dollar business. As we pass each other in the streets they seem to sneer, and hiss through their teeth the words 'gold bug,' and look as if they would like to spit upon [us]."

By 1878, a bipartisan coalition succeeded in passing the **Bland-Allison Act**. This compromise measure required the government to buy at least $2 million of silver a month. However, the government never exceeded the minimum, and the law had little inflationary effect. Republican President Arthur and Democratic President Cleveland recommended repealing the Bland-Allison Act, but the parties avoided the silver issue in their national platforms, fearing its divisive effect.

As hard times hit rural regions in the late 1880s, inflationists secured passage of the **Sherman Silver Purchase Act** of 1890. The Treasury now had to buy a larger volume of silver and pay for it with Treasury notes redeemable in either gold or silver. But this too produced little inflation because the government did not coin the silver it purchased, redeemed the notes only with gold, and, as western silver production increased further, had to spend less and less to buy the stipulated amount of silver. Debtors of both parties remained convinced that the government favored the "classes rather than the masses." Gold standard advocates (again of both parties) were even less happy with the law and planned to repeal it at their first opportunity. The division between them was deep and bitter.

The Crisis of the 1890s

In the 1890s, social, economic, and political pressures created a crisis for both the political system and the government. A third-party political challenge generated by agricultural discontent disrupted traditional party politics. A devastating depression spawned social misery and labor violence. Changing public attitudes led to new demands on the government and a realignment of parties and voters. These developments, in turn, set the stage for important political, economic, and social changes in the new century.

Agricultural Protest

The agricultural depression that engulfed the Great Plains and the South in the late 1880s brought misery and despair to millions of rural Americans. Falling crop prices and rising debt overwhelmed many people already exhausted from overwork and alarmed by the new corporate order. "At the age of 52 years, after a long life of toil, economy, and self-denial, I find myself and family virtual paupers," lamented one Kansan. Their farm, rather than being "a house of refuge for our declining years, by a few turns of the monopolistic crank has been rendered valueless." To a large extent, the farmers' plight stemmed from conditions beyond control, including bad weather and an international overproduction of farm products. Seeking relief, however, the farmers naturally focused on the inequities of railroad discrimination, tariff favoritism, a restrictive financial system, and apparently indifferent political parties.

Angry farmers particularly singled out the systems of money and credit that worked so completely against agricultural interests. Government rules for national banks directed credit into the urbanized North and East at the expense of the rural South and West and prohibited banks from making loans on farm property and real estate. As a result, farmers had to turn to other sources of credit and pay higher interest rates. In the West, farmers borrowed money from mortgage companies to buy land and machinery. Declining crop prices made it difficult to pay their debts and often required them to borrow more and at higher rates. In hard times, mortgage foreclosures crushed the hopes of many farmers. In the South, the credit shortage interacted with the practices of cotton marketing and retail trade to create the sharecropping system, which trapped more and more farmers, black and white, in a vicious pattern of exploitation. The government's policies of monetary deflation worsened the debt burden for all farmers.

Farmers protested other features of the nation's economic system as well. They shouldered railroad freight rates two or three times higher in the West and South than in the North and East. The near-monopolistic control of grain elevators and cotton brokerages in rural areas left farmers feeling exploited. Protective tariff rates on agricultural machinery and other manufactured goods further raised their costs. The failure of political parties and the government to devise effective regulatory and antitrust measures or to correct the inequities in the currency, credit, and tariff laws capped the farmers' anger. By the 1890s, many were convinced that the nation's great economic and political institutions were aligned against them.

In response, farmers turned to the **Farmers' Alliance**, the era's greatest popular movement of protest and reform. Originating in Texas, the Southern Farmers' Alliance spread throughout the South and across the Great Plains to the Pacific coast. By 1890, it had 1.2 million members. African-American farmers organized the Colored Farmers' Alliance. The Northwestern Farmers' Alliance spread westward and northward from Illinois to Nebraska and Minnesota. In combination, these groups constituted a massive grassroots movement committed to economic and ultimately political reform.

The Farmers' Alliance restricted its membership to men and women of the "producing class" and urged them to stand "against the encroachments of monopolies and in opposition to the growing corruption of wealth and power." At first, the Alliance attempted to establish farmers' cooperatives to market crops and purchase supplies. Although some co-ops worked well, most soon failed because of the opposition of established merchants and other business interests. Railroads suppressed Alliance grain elevators by refusing to handle their wheat. In Leflore County, Mississippi, when members of the Colored Farmers' Alliance shifted their trade to an Alliance store, local merchants provoked a conflict in which state troops killed twenty-five black farmers, including the local leaders of the Colored Alliance.

The Alliance also developed ingenious proposals to remedy rural credit and currency problems. In the South, the Alliance pushed the subtreasury system, which called on the government to warehouse farmers' cotton and advance them credit based on its value (see Chapter 19). In the West, the Alliance proposed a system of federal loans to farmers using land as security. This land-loan scheme, like the subtreasury system, was a political expression of greenbackism; it would have expanded the money supply while providing immediate relief for distressed farmers. These proposals were immensely popular among farmers, but the major parties and Congress rejected them. The Alliance also took up earlier calls for free silver, government control of railroads, and banking reform, again to no avail. Denouncing the indifference of the major political parties and the institutions of government, William A. Peffer, the influential editor of the Alliance newspaper the *Kansas Farmer,* declared that the "time has come for action. The people will not consent to wait longer. . . . The future is full of retribution for delinquents."

The People's Party

In the West, discontented agrarians organized independent third parties to achieve reforms the major parties had ignored. State-level third parties appeared in the elections of 1890 under many names. All eventually adopted the labels "People's" or "Populist," which were first used by a Kansas party that formed in June 1890. The founders of the Kansas People's Party included members of the Farmers' Alliance, the Knights of Labor, the Grange, and the old Greenback party. The new party's campaign, marked by grim determination and fierce rhetoric, set the model for Populist politics and introduced many of the movement's leaders. These people, women as well as men, were earnest organizers and powerful orators. One was *Kansas Farmer* editor Peffer. Others included "Sockless Jerry" Simpson, Annie Diggs, and Mary E. Lease. When hostile business and political leaders attacked the Populist

Established interests ridiculed the Populists unmercifully. This hostile cartoon depicts the People's Party as an odd assortment of radical dissidents committed to a "Platform of Lunacy."

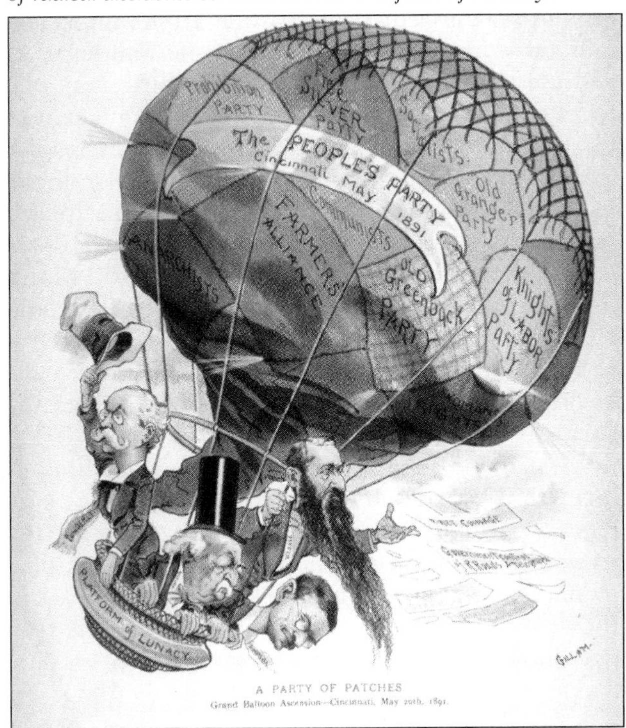

plans as socialistic, Lease retorted, "You may call me an anarchist, a socialist, or a communist. I care not, but I hold to the theory that if one man has not enough to eat three times a day and another has $25,000,000, that last man has something that belongs to the first." Lease spoke as clearly against the colonial status experienced by the South and West: "The great common people of this country are slaves, and monopoly is the master. The West and South are bound and prostrate before the manufacturing East."

The Populist parties proved remarkably successful. They gained control of the legislatures of Kansas and Nebraska and won congressional elections in Kansas, Nebraska, and Minnesota. Their victories came at the expense of the Republicans, who had traditionally controlled politics in these states, and contributed to a massive defeat of the GOP in the 1890 midterm elections after the passage of the McKinley Tariff and the Sherman Silver Purchase Act. Thereafter, Populists gained further victories throughout the West. In the mountain states, where their support came more from miners than farmers, they won governorships in Colorado and Montana. On the Pacific coast, angry farmers found allies among urban workers in Seattle, Tacoma, Portland, and San Francisco, where organized labor had campaigned for reform since the 1880s. The Populists elected a governor in Washington, congressmen in California, and legislators in all three states.

Even in the Southwest, where territorial status limited political activity, Populist parties emerged. In Oklahoma, the party drew support from homesteaders and tenant farmers; in Arizona, from miners and railroad workers. In New Mexico, the Southern Alliance established itself among small stockraisers who felt threatened by corporate ranches and land companies that were exploiting the confusion of old Spanish and Mexican land grants to expand their landholdings. The fear of corporate expansion even impelled Anglo New Mexicans to cooperate with poor Hispanics for whom they had previously shown little sympathy. One Alliance paper wrote of the need to defend Hispanics from the "mighty land monopoly which is surely grinding their bones into flour that it may make its bread." In the 1890 election, Populists gained the balance of power in the New Mexico legislature.

In the South, the Alliance did not initially form third parties but instead attempted to seize control of the dominant Democratic party by forcing its candidates to pledge support to the Alliance platform. The rural southern electorate then swept these "Alliance Democrats" into office, electing four governors, several dozen members of Congress, and a majority of legislators in eight states.

With their new political power, farmers enacted reform legislation in many western states. New laws regulated banks and railroads and protected poor debtors by capping interest rates and restricting mortgage foreclosures. Others protected unions and mandated improved workplace conditions. Still others made the political system more democratic. Populists were instrumental, for example, in winning woman suffrage in Colorado and Idaho, although the united opposition of Democrats and Republicans blocked their efforts to win it in other states. In the South, the Democratic party frustrated reform, and most Alliance Democrats repudiated their Alliance pledges and remained loyal to their party and its traditional opposition to governmental activism.

Populists soon realized that successful reform would require national action. They met in Omaha, Nebraska, on July 4, 1892, to organize a national party and nominated former Greenbacker James B. Weaver for president. The party platform, known as the **Omaha Platform**, is a remarkable statement of principles. Rejecting the laissez-faire policies of the old parties, it declared: "We believe that the powers of government—in other words, of the people, should be expanded . . . to the end that oppression, injustice, and poverty shall eventually cease in the land." The platform demanded government ownership of the railroads and the telegraph and telephone systems, a national currency issued by the government rather than private banks, the subtreasury system, free and unlimited silver coinage, a graduated income tax, and the redistribution to settlers of land held by railroads and speculative corporations. Accompanying resolutions endorsed the direct popular election of senators, the secret ballot, and other electoral reforms to make government more democratic and responsive to popular wishes. When the platform was adopted, "cheers and yells," one reporter wrote, "rose like a tornado from four thousand throats and raged without cessation for 34 minutes, during which women shrieked and wept, men embraced and kissed their neighbors . . . in the ecstasy of their delirium."

The Populists left Omaha to begin an energetic campaign. Weaver toured the western states and with Mary Lease invaded the Democratic stronghold of the South where some Populists like Tom Watson of Georgia tried to mobilize black voters. Southern Democrats, however, used violence and fraud to intimidate Populist voters and cheat Populist candidates out of office. Some local Populist leaders were murdered, and Weaver was driven from the South. One Democrat confessed that Alabama's Populist gubernatorial candidate "carried the state, but was swindled out of his victory . . . with unblushing trickery and corruption." Southern Democrats also appealed effectively to white supremacy, which undermined the Populist effort to build a biracial reform coalition.

Elsewhere, too, Populists met disappointment. Midwestern farmers unfamiliar with Alliance ideas and organization ignored Populist appeals and stood by their traditional political allegiances. So did most eastern working-class voters, who learned little of the Populist program beyond its demand for inflation, which they feared would worsen their own conditions.

The Populists lost the election but showed impressive support for a new organization. They got more than a million votes (one out of every twelve cast), carried several western states, and won hundreds of state offices throughout the West and in pockets of the South like Texas and North Carolina. Populist leaders began immediately working to expand their support, to the alarm of both southern Democrats and northern Republicans.

The Challenge of the Depression

The emergence of a significant third-party movement was but one of many developments that combined by the mid-1890s to produce a national political crisis. A harsh and lengthy depression began in 1893, cruelly worsening conditions not only for farmers but for most other Americans as well. Labor unrest and violence engulfed the nation, reflecting workers' distress but frightening more comfortable Americans. The persistent failure of the major parties to respond to serious problems contributed mightily to growing popular discontent. Together these developments constituted an important challenge to America's new industrial society and its government.

Although the Populists had not triumphed in 1892, the election nonetheless reflected the nation's spreading dissatisfaction. Voters decisively rejected President Harrison and the incumbent Republicans in Congress; turning again to the other major party, they placed the Democrats in control of Congress and Grover Cleveland back in the White House. But the conservative Cleveland was almost oblivious to the mounting demand for reform. He delivered an inaugural address championing the doctrine of laissez-faire and rejecting government action to solve social or economic problems.

Cleveland's resolve was immediately tested when the economy collapsed in the spring of 1893. Railroad overexpansion, a weak banking system, tight credit, and plunging agricultural prices all contributed to the disaster. So too did a depression in Europe, which reduced American export markets and prompted British investors to sell their American investments for gold. Within a few months, hundreds of banks closed, and thousands of businesses, including the nation's major railroads, went bankrupt. By winter, 20 percent of the labor force was unemployed, and the jobless scavenged for food in a country that had no public unemployment or welfare programs. "Never within memory," said one New York minister, "have so many people literally starved to death as in the past few months."

Churches, local charity societies, and labor unions tried to provide relief but were overwhelmed. Most state governments offered little relief beyond encouraging private charity to the homeless. In Kansas, however, the Populist governor insisted that traditional laissez-faire policies were inadequate: "It is the duty of government to protect the weak, because the strong are able to protect themselves." Cleveland disagreed and showed little sympathy for the struggling. The functions of the government, he said in 1893, "do not include the support of the people."

If Cleveland and Congress had no idea how the federal government might respond to the depression, some thoughtful Americans did. Jacob Coxey, a Populist businessman from Ohio, proposed a government public works program for the unemployed to be financed with paper money. This plan would improve the nation's infrastructure, create jobs for the unemployed, and provide an inflationary stimulus to counteract the depression's deflationary effects. In short, Coxey was advocating positive government action to combat the depression. Elements of his plan would be adopted for mitigating economic downturns in the twentieth century; in 1894, it was too untraditional for Congress to consider.

Coxey organized a march of the unemployed to Washington as "a petition with boots on" to support his ideas. **Coxey's Army** of the unemployed, as the excited press dubbed it, marched through the industrial towns of Ohio and Pennsylvania and into Maryland, attracting attention and support. Other armies formed in eastern cities from Boston to Baltimore and set out for the capital. Some of the largest armies organized in the western cities of Denver, San Francisco, and Seattle. Three hundred men in an army from Oakland elected as their commander Anna Smith, who promised to "land my men on the steps of the Capitol at Washington." "I am a San Francisco woman, a woman who has been brought up on this coast, and I'm not afraid of anything," Smith explained. "I have a woman's heart and a woman's sympathy, and these lead me to do what I have done for these men, even though it may not be just what a woman is expected to do."

Lewis Fry, the organizer of the Los Angeles army, declared: "If the government has a right to make us die in time of war, we have the right to demand of

Jacob Coxey's "Army" of the unemployed marches to Washington, D.C., in 1894. Many such "industrial armies" were organized during the depressed 1890s, revealing dissatisfaction with traditional politics and limited government.

her the right to live in time of peace." Fry's five hundred marchers captured a train to cross the desert regions of the Southwest and were feted and fed by townspeople from Tucson to El Paso. When the Southern Pacific uncoupled the train's locomotive and left the marchers stranded without food or water in West Texas for five days, the governor of Texas threatened to hold the railroad responsible for murder "by torture and starvation." Texas citizens quickly raised funds to speed the army on to St. Louis. From there it marched to Washington on foot.

The sympathy and assistance with which Americans greeted these industrial armies reflected more than anxiety over the depression and unemployment. As one economist noted, what distinguished the Populists and Coxeyites from earlier reformers was their appeal for federal action. Their substantial public support suggested a deep dissatisfaction with the failure of the government to respond to the country's social and economic needs.

Nonetheless, the government acted to suppress Coxey. When he reached Washington with six hundred marchers, police and soldiers arrested him and his aides, beat sympathetic bystanders in a crowd of twenty thousand, and herded the marchers into detention camps. Unlike lobbyists for business and finance, Coxey was not permitted to reach Congress to deliver his statement urging the government to assist "the poor and oppressed."

The depression also provoked labor turmoil. There were some 1,400 industrial strikes involving nearly 700,000 workers in 1894, the largest number of strikers in any year in the nineteenth century. Cleveland had no response except to call for law and order. One result was the government's violent suppression of the Pullman strike (see Chapter 20).

In a series of decisions in 1895, the Supreme Court strengthened the bonds between business and government. First, it upheld the use of a court-ordered injunction to break the Pullman strike. As a result, injunctions became a major weapon for courts and corporations against labor unions until Congress finally limited their use in 1932. Next, in *United States* v. *E. C. Knight Company,* the Court gutted the Sherman Antitrust Act by ruling that manufacturing, as opposed to commerce, was beyond the reach of federal regulation. The Court thus allowed the American Sugar Refining Company, a trust controlling 90 percent of the nation's sugar, to retain its great power. Finally, the Court invalidated an income tax that agrarian Democrats and Populists had maneuvered through Congress. The conservative Court rejected the reform as an "assault upon capital." A dissenting judge noted that the decision gave vested interests "a power and influence" dangerous to the majority of Americans. Not until 1913, and then only with an amendment to the Constitution, would it be possible to adopt an equitable system of taxation. Surveying these developments, farmers and workers increasingly concluded that the government protected powerful interests while ignoring the plight of ordinary Americans.

Certainly the callous treatment shown workers contrasted sharply with Cleveland's concern for bankers as he managed the government's monetary policy in the depression. Cleveland blamed the economic collapse on the Sherman Silver Purchase Act, which he regarded as detrimental to business confidence and a threat to the nation's gold reserve. He persuaded Congress in 1893 to repeal the law, enraging southern and western members of his own party. These Silver Democrats condemned Cleveland for betraying the public good to "the corporate interests." (See "American Views: A Westerner Views Sound Money and American Government.")

Cleveland's policy was ineffective at ending the depression. By 1894, the Treasury had begun borrowing money from Wall Street to bolster the gold reserve. These transactions benefited a syndicate of bankers headed by J. P. Morgan. It seemed to critics that an indifferent Cleveland was helping rich bankers profit from the nation's economic agony. "A set of vampires headed by a financial trust has control of our destiny," cried one rural newspaper.

The Battle of the Standards and the Election of 1896

The government's unpopular actions, coupled with the unrelenting depression, alienated workers and farmers from the Cleveland administration and the Democratic party. In the off-year elections of 1894, the Democrats suffered the greatest loss of congressional seats in American history. Populists increased their vote by 42 percent, making especially significant gains in the South, but the real beneficiaries of the popular hatred of Cleveland and his policies were the Republicans. Denouncing Cleveland's "utter imbecility," they gained solid control of Congress as well as state governments across the North and West. All three parties began to plan for the presidential election of 1896.

As hard times persisted, the silver issue came to overshadow all others. Some Populist leaders, hoping to broaden the party's appeal, had already begun to emphasize silver rather than the more radical but divisive planks of the Omaha Platform. Weaver declared the silver issue "the line upon which the battle should be fought. It is the line of least resistance and we should hurl our forces against it at every point." Many southern and western Democrats, who had traditionally favored silver inflation, also decided to stress the issue, both to undercut the Populists and to distance themselves and their party from the despised Cleveland. In 1895, leading Democrats began using the silver issue to reorganize their party and displace Cleveland and his conservative supporters. They held rallies and conventions across the South and West, distributed silver literature, and argued that free silver would finally end the depression.

The dissension among Democrats pleased Republicans. William McKinley, governor of Ohio and author of the McKinley Tariff Act of 1890, emerged as the leader of a crowd of hopeful Republican presidential candidates. His candidacy benefited particularly from the financial backing and political management of Marcus A. Hanna, a wealthy Ohio industrialist. Hanna thought McKinley's passion for high tariffs as the key to revived prosperity would appeal to workers as well as industry and business. As governor, McKinley had reached out to workers by supporting prolabor legislation and by avoiding the anti-Catholic positions that alienated immigrants from the Republicans. Nonetheless, he shared Hanna's conviction that government should actively promote business interests; he was not Hanna's puppet, as opponents sometimes claimed.

Republicans nominated McKinley on the first ballot at their 1896 convention. Their platform called for high tariffs but also endorsed the gold standard, placating eastern delegates but prompting several western Silver Republicans to withdraw from the party.

The Democratic convention met shortly thereafter. Embattled supporters of the gold standard soon learned that the silver crusade had made them a minority in the party. With a fervor that conservatives likened to "scenes of the French Revolution," the Silver Democrats revolutionized their party. They adopted a platform that repudiated the Cleveland administration and its policies and endorsed free silver, the income tax, and tighter regulation of trusts and

William Jennings Bryan in 1896. A powerful orator of great human sympathies, Bryan was adored by his followers as "the majestic man who was hurling defiance in the teeth of the money power." Nominated three times for the presidency by the Democrats, he was never elected.

American Views

A Westerner Views Sound Money and American Government

As a terrible depression engulfed America in 1893, Congress debated whether to repeal the Sherman Silver Purchase Act, as demanded by President Grover Cleveland. William Jennings Bryan, a young Democratic congressman from Nebraska, was a prominent opponent of repeal. In the following passages, excerpted from his congressional speeches, he eloquently outlines his views.

- **How does Bryan's rhetoric reflect the deep divisions over the money issue?**
- **What is Bryan's view of the role of government?**
- **In what ways might Populists find Bryan attractive?**
- **Can you explain why Bryan thought repeal would hurt Southerners and Westerners?**

The vote of this House on the subject under consideration may bring to the people of the West and South, to the people of the United States, and to all mankind, weal or woe beyond the power of language to describe or imagination to conceive. . . . [A vote to repeal means obeying] the dictation of the moneyed institutions of this country and those who want to appreciate the value of a dollar. . . . It means to increase by billions of dollars the debts of our people. It means a reduction in the price of our wheat and our cotton. . . .

If we who represent them consent to rob our people, the cotton-growers of the South and the wheat-growers of the West, we will be criminals whose guilt cannot be measured by words, for we will bring distress and disaster to our people. In many cases such a vote would simply be a summons to the sheriff to take possession of their property. . . .

The poor man is called a socialist if he believes that the wealth of the rich should be divided among the poor, but the rich man is called a financier if he devises a plan by which the pittance of the poor can be converted to his use. The poor man who takes property by force is called a thief, but the creditor who can by legisla-

railroads. A magnificent speech supporting this platform by William Jennings Bryan helped convince the delegates to nominate him for president. Bryan was only thirty-six years old but had already served in Congress, edited an important newspaper, and gained renown for his oratorical skills and popular sympathies.

Holding their convention last, the Populists now faced a terrible dilemma. The Democratic nomination of Bryan on a silver platform undercut their hopes of attracting into their own ranks disappointed reformers from the major parties. Bryan, moreover, had already worked closely with Nebraska Populists, who now urged the party to endorse him rather than split the silver vote and ensure the victory of McKinley and the gold standard. Other Populists argued that fusing—joining with the Democrats—would cost the Populists their separate identity and subordinate their larger political principles to the issue of free silver. After anguished discussion, the Populists nominated Bryan for president but named a separate vice presidential candidate, Tom Watson of Georgia, in an effort to maintain their identity. They hoped the Democrats would reciprocate by replacing their nominee with Watson, but the Democrats ignored the overture. The Populists' strength was in the South and West, regions that Bryan would control anyway. They could offer him tion make a debtor pay a dollar twice as large as he borrowed is lauded as the friend of a sound currency. The man who wants the people to destroy the Government is an anarchist, but the man who wants the Government to destroy the people is a patriot. . . .

Free government cannot long survive when the thousands enjoy the wealth of the country and the millions share its poverty in common. Even now you hear among the rich an occasionally expressed contempt for popular government, and among the poor a protest against legislation which makes them 'toil that others may reap.' I appeal to you to restore justice. . . .

Whence comes this irresistible demand for unconditional repeal? . . . Not from the workshop and the farm, not from the workingmen of this country, who create its wealth in time of peace and protect its flag in time of war, but from the middle-men, from what are termed the "business interests." . . . Go among the agricultural classes; go among the poor, whose little is as precious to them as the rich man's fortune is to him, and whose families are as dear, and you will not find the haste to destroy the issue of money or the unfriendliness to silver which is manifested in money centers.

We have come to the parting of the ways. . . . On the one side stand the corporate interests of the nation, its moneyed institutions, its aggregations of wealth and capital, imperious, arrogant, compassionless. They demand special legislation, favors, privileges, and immunities. They can subscribe magnificently to campaign funds; they can strike down opposition with their all-pervading influence, and, to those who fawn and flatter, bring ease and plenty. They demand that [Congress] . . . execute their merciless decrees.

On the other side stands the unnumbered throng. . . . Work-worn and dust-begrimed, they make their sad appeal. They hear of average wealth increased on every side and feel the inequality of its distribution. They see an overproduction of everything desired because of the underproduction of the ability to buy. They can not pay for loyalty except with their suffrages, and can only punish betrayal with their condemnation. Although the ones who most deserve the fostering care of Government, their cries for help too often beat in vain against the outer wall, while others less deserving find ready access to legislative halls. . . .

"Choose you this day whom ye will serve." What will the answer be?

Source: William Jennings Bryan, The First Battle *(Chicago: W. B. Conkey Company, 1896), 77, 81, 83, 103–104, 110–114.*

little help in the battle for the Midwest and East, what Bryan called "the enemy's country."

The campaign was intense and dramatic, with each side demonizing the other. Terrified by the thought of Bryan's election, eastern financial and business interests contributed millions of dollars to Hanna's campaign for McKinley. Standard Oil alone provided $250,000, about the same amount as the Democrats' total national expenses. Hanna used these funds to organize an unprecedented educational campaign, warning of economic disaster should Bryan be elected and the bimetallic standard be restored but promising that McKinley's election would finally end the depression. Republicans issued 250 million campaign documents, printed in a dozen languages. They were aided by a national press so completely sympathetic that many newspapers not only shaped their editorials but distorted their news stories to Bryan's disadvantage.

To counteract the Republicans' superior resources, the Democrats relied on Bryan's superb voice, oratorical virtuosity, and youthful energy. Bryan was the first presidential candidate to campaign systematically for election, speaking hundreds of times to millions of voters. By contrast, McKinley stayed home in Canton, Ohio, where he conducted a "front porch" campaign. Explaining his refusal to campaign outside Canton, McKinley

This Republican campaign poster of 1896 depicts William McKinley standing on sound money and promising a revival of prosperity. The depression of the 1890s shifted the electorate into the Republican column.

said, "I might just as well put up a trapeze . . . and compete with some professional athlete as go out speaking against Bryan." But Hanna brought groups of Republicans from all over the country to visit McKinley every day, and McKinley reiterated his simple promise of prosperity.

In the depression, that appeal proved enough. As the Democratic candidate, Bryan was ironically burdened with the legacy of the hated Cleveland administration. The intense campaign brought a record voter turnout. McKinley won decisively by capturing the East and Midwest as well as Oregon and California (see Map 22-2). Bryan carried the traditionally Democratic South and the mountain and plains states where Populists and silverites dominated. He failed to gain support in either the Granger states of the Midwest or the cities of the East. His silver campaign had little appeal to industrial workers. Hanna realized that Bryan was making a mistake in subordinating other popular grievances to silver: "He's talking silver all the time, and that's where we've got him."

Bryan immediately wrote a personal account of the campaign, which he optimistically titled *The First Battle.* But Bryan and the Democrats would not win subsequent battles, at least not on the issues of the 1890s. The elections of 1894 and 1896 ended the close balance between the major parties. Cleveland's failures, coupled with an economic recovery in the wake of the election of 1896, gained the Republicans a reputation as the party of prosperity and industrial progress, firmly establishing them in power for years to come. By contrast, the Democratic party receded into an ineffectual sectional minority dominated by southern conservatives, despite Bryan's liberal views.

The People's party simply dissolved. Demoralized by fusion with the Democrats, who had earlier violently repressed them, many southern Populists dropped out of politics. The Democrats' disfranchisement laws, directed at discontented poor white Southerners as well as poor black Southerners, further undermined the Populists in the South. In the West, the silver tide of 1896 carried many Populists

Map 22-2 The Election of 1896
William Jennings Bryan carried most of the rural South and West, but his free silver campaign had little appeal to more urban and industrial regions, which swung strongly to Republican candidate William McKinley.

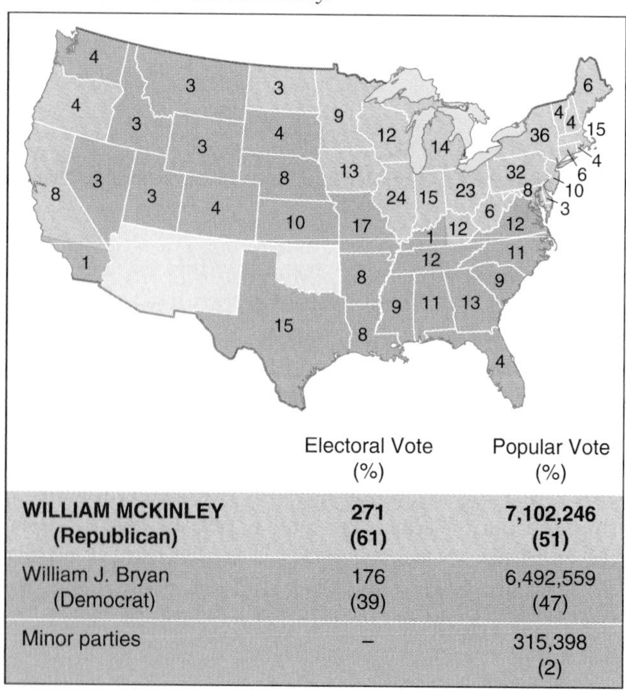

	Electoral Vote (%)	Popular Vote (%)
WILLIAM MCKINLEY (Republican)	**271 (61)**	**7,102,246 (51)**
William J. Bryan (Democrat)	176 (39)	6,492,559 (47)
Minor parties	–	315,398 (2)

into office, but with their party collapsing, they had no hope of retaining office. By 1898, the Populist party had virtually disappeared. Its reform legacy, however, proved more enduring. The issues it raised would continue to shape state and national politics.

McKinley plunged into his presidency. Unlike his predecessors, he had a definite, if limited, program, consisting of tariff protection, sound money, and overseas expansion. He worked actively to see it through Congress and to shape public opinion, thereby helping establish the model of the modern presidency. He had promised prosperity, and it returned, although not because of the record high tariff his party enacted in 1897 or the Currency Act of 1900, which firmly established the gold standard. Prosperity returned instead because of reviving markets and a monetary inflation that resulted from the discovery of vast new deposits of gold in Alaska, Australia, and South Africa. The silverites had recognized that an expanding industrial economy required an expanding money supply. Ironically, the new inflation was greater than would have resulted from free silver. With the return of prosperity and the decline of social tensions, McKinley easily won reelection in 1900, defeating Bryan a second time.

Conclusion

In late-nineteenth-century America, politics and government often seemed at cross-purposes. Political contests were exciting events, absorbing public attention, attracting high voter turnout, and often raising issues of symbolic or substantive importance. Closely balanced political parties commanded the zealous support of their constituents and wielded power and influence. The institutions of government, by contrast, were limited in size, scope, and responsibility. A weakened presidency and an inefficient Congress, hampered by a restrictive judiciary, were often unable to resolve the very issues that were so dramatically raised in the political arena. The persistent disputes over tariff and monetary policy illustrate this impasse. But the issue that most reflected it was civil service reform. The patronage system provided the lifeblood of politics but also disrupted government business.

The localism, laissez-faire, and other traditional principles that shaped both politics and government were becoming increasingly inappropriate for America's industrializing society. New challenges were emerging that state and local governments could not effectively solve on their own. The national nature of the railroad network, for example, finally brought the federal government into the regulatory arena, however imperfectly, with the Interstate Commerce Act of 1887. Both the depression of the 1890s and the popular discontent articulated most clearly by the Populist rejection of laissez-faire underscored the need for change and discredited the limited government of the Cleveland administration.

By the end of the decade, the political system had changed. The Republicans had emerged as the dominant party, ending the two-party stalemate of previous decades. Campaign hoopla in local communities had given way to information-based campaigns directed by and through national organizations. A new, activist presidency was emerging. And the disruptive currency issue faded with the hard times that had brought it forth. Still greater changes were on the horizon. The depression and its terrible social and economic consequences undermined traditional ideas about the responsibilities of government and increased public support for activist policies. The stage was set for the Progressive Era.

Review Questions

1. What were the social and institutional factors that shaped the disorderly nature of elections in the late nineteenth century?
2. What social and institutional factors determined the role of government? How and why did the role of government change during this period?
3. What factors determined the party affiliation of American voters? Why did so many third parties develop during this era?
4. How might the planks of the Omaha Platform have helped solve farmers' troubles?
5. What factors shaped the conduct and outcome of the election of 1896? How did that contest differ from earlier elections?

Recommended Reading

Paul Glad, *McKinley, Bryan, and the People* (1964). An excellent brief analysis of the issues and personalities in the 1896 election.

Morton Keller, *Affairs of State: Public Life in Late Nineteenth Century America* (1977). A detailed and fascinating account of the changing dimensions of government and politics.

Robert C. McMath, Jr., *American Populism: A Social History, 1877–1898* (1993). The best modern history of Populism; balanced and readable.

Mark Summers, *The Gilded Age* (1997). A useful survey that effectively captures the complexities of the era.

R. Hal Williams, *Years of Decision: American Politics in the 1890s* (1978). A valuable synthesis of the scholarship on the political currents of the 1890s.

Additional Sources

The Structure and Style of Politics

Peter H. Argersinger, *Structure, Process, and Party* (1992).

Paula Baker, "The Domestication of Politics: Women and American Political Society, 1780–1920," *American Historical Review 89* (1984): 620–647.

Ruth Bordin, *Frances Willard: A Biography* (1986).

Rebecca Edwards, *Angels in the Machinery: Gender in American Party Politics* (1997).

Michael Goldberg, *An Army of Women: Gender and Politics in Gilded Age Kansas* (1997).

Paul Kleppner, *The Third Electoral System, 1853–1892* (1979).

Richard L. McCormick, *The Party Period and Public Policy* (1986).

Michael McGerr, *The Decline of Popular Politics: The American North, 1865–1928* (1988).

Joel H. Silbey, *The American Political Nation, 1838–1893* (1991).

The Limits of Government

Cindy Aron, *Ladies and Gentlemen of the Civil Service: Middle-Class Workers in Victorian America* (1987).

William R. Brock, *Investigation and Responsibility: Public Responsibility in the United States, 1865–1900* (1984).

Ballard C. Campbell, *Representative Democracy: Public Policy and Midwestern Legislatures in the Late Nineteenth Century* (1980).

Sidney Fine, *Laissez-Faire and the General Welfare State* (1956).

John A. Garraty, *The New Commonwealth, 1877–1890* (1968).

Ari Hoogenboom, *Rutherford B. Hayes: Warrior and President* (1996).

David Rothman, *Politics and Power: The United States Senate* (1966).

Stephen Skowronek, *Building a New American State: The Expansion of National Administrative Capacities* (1982).

Margaret S. Thompson, *The "Spider Web": Congress and Lobbying* (1985).

Leonard D. White, *The Republican Era* (1958).

Public Policies and National Elections

Ari Hoogenboom, *Outlawing the Spoils: A History of the Civil Service Movement, 1865–1883* (1961).

Robert D. Marcus, *Grand Old Party: Political Structure in the Gilded Age, 1880–1896* (1971).

H. Wayne Morgan, *From Hayes to McKinley* (1969).

Walter Nugent, *Money and American Society, 1865–1880* (1968).

Joanne Reitano, *The Tariff Question in the Gilded Age: The Great Debate of 1888* (1995).

Gretchen Ritter, *Goldbugs and Greenbacks: The Antimonopoly Tradition and the Politics of Finance* (1997).

Homer E. Socolofsky and Allan B. Spetter, *The Presidency of Benjamin Harrison* (1987).

John Sproat, *"The Best Men": Liberal Reformers in the Gilded Age* (1968).

The Crisis of the 1890s

Peter H. Argersinger, *Populism and Politics: W. A. Peffer and the People's Party* (1974).

Gene Clanton, *Populism: The Humane Preference* (1991).

Lawrence Goodwyn, *The Populist Moment* (1978).

Richard Jensen, *The Winning of the Midwest: Social and Political Conflict, 1888–1896* (1971).

J. Morgan Kousser, *The Shaping of Southern Politics* (1974).

Robert W. Larson, *Populism in the Mountain West* (1986).

Samuel McSeveney, *The Politics of Depression* (1972).

Worth Robert Miller, *Oklahoma Populism* (1987).

Jeffrey Ostler, *Prairie Populism* (1993).

Carlos A. Schwantes, *Coxey's Army: An American Odyssey* (1985).

Barton Shaw, *The Wool-Hat Boys: Georgia's Populist Party* (1984).

Richard Welch, *The Presidencies of Grover Cleveland* (1988).

C. Vann Woodward, *Tom Watson, Agrarian Rebel* (1938).

James E. Wright, *The Politics of Populism: Dissent in Colorado* (1974).

Where to Learn More

❖ **Rest Cottage, Evanston, Illinois.** Frances Willard's home, from which she directed the Woman's Christian Temperance Union, is carefully preserved as a museum. The Willard Memorial Library contains more memorabilia and papers of Willard and the WCTU.

❖ **President Benjamin Harrison Home, Indianapolis, Indiana.** President Harrison's brick Italianate mansion, completed in 1875, has been completely restored with the family's furniture and keepsakes. The former third-floor ballroom serves as a museum with exhibits of many artifacts of the Harrisons' public and private lives.

❖ **Fairview, Lincoln, Nebraska.** A National Historic Landmark, Fairview was the home of William Jennings Bryan, who described it as "the Monticello of the West." Faithfully restored to depict the Bryan family's life in the early 1900s, it includes a museum and interpretive center.

❖ **Susan B. Anthony House National Historic Landmark, Rochester, New York.** This modest house was the home of the prominent suffragist and contains Anthony's original furnishings and personal photographs.

❖ **Rutherford B. Hayes Presidential Center, Fremont, Ohio.** This complex contains President Hayes's home, office, and extensive grounds together with an excellent library and museum holding valuable collections of manuscripts, artifacts, and photographs illustrating his personal interests and political career.

❖ **James A. Garfield Home, Mentor, Ohio.** Operated by the Western Reserve Historical Society as a museum, Garfield's home is the site of his successful 1880 front-porch campaign for president.

THE PROGRESSIVE ERA, 1900–1917

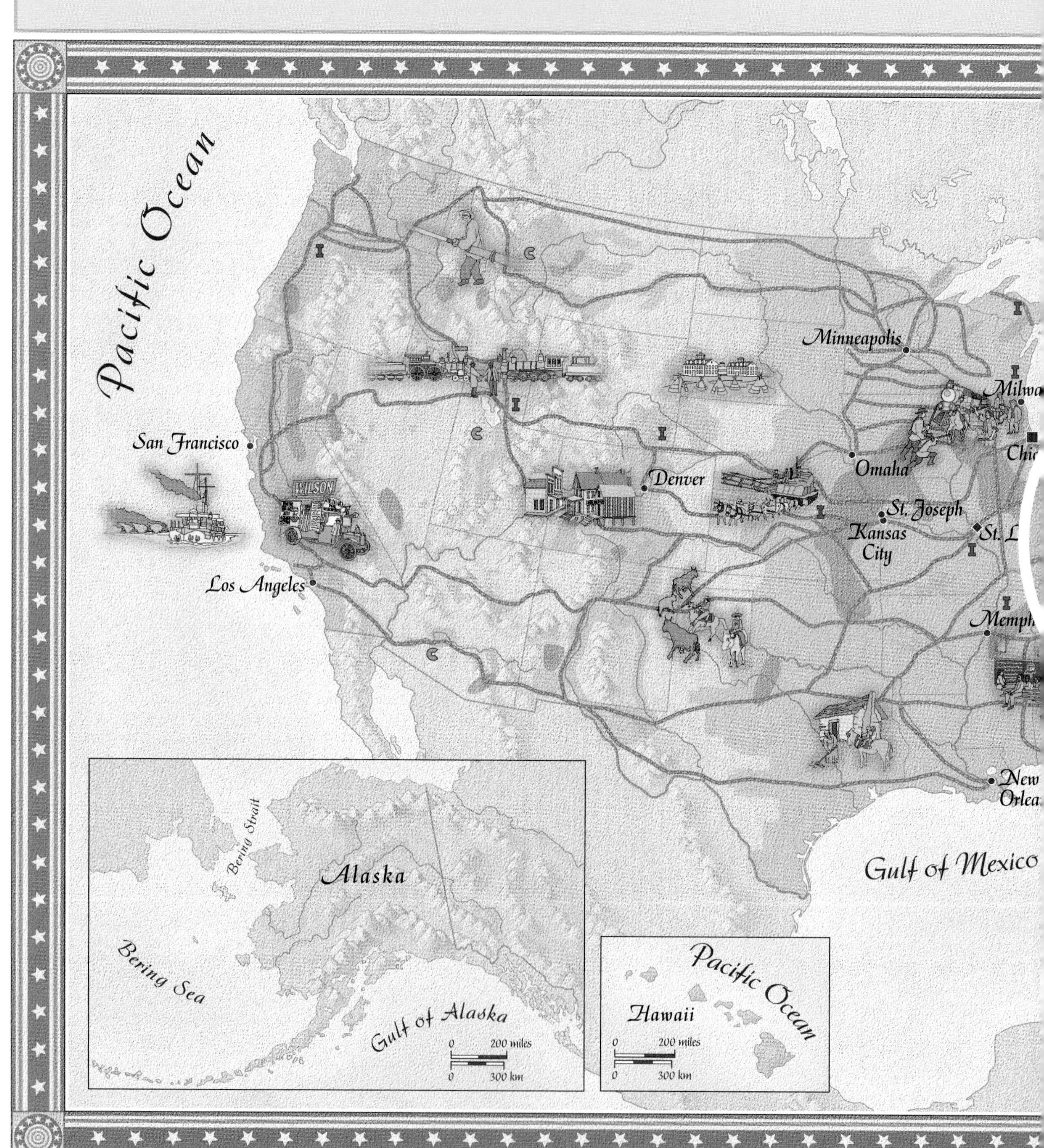

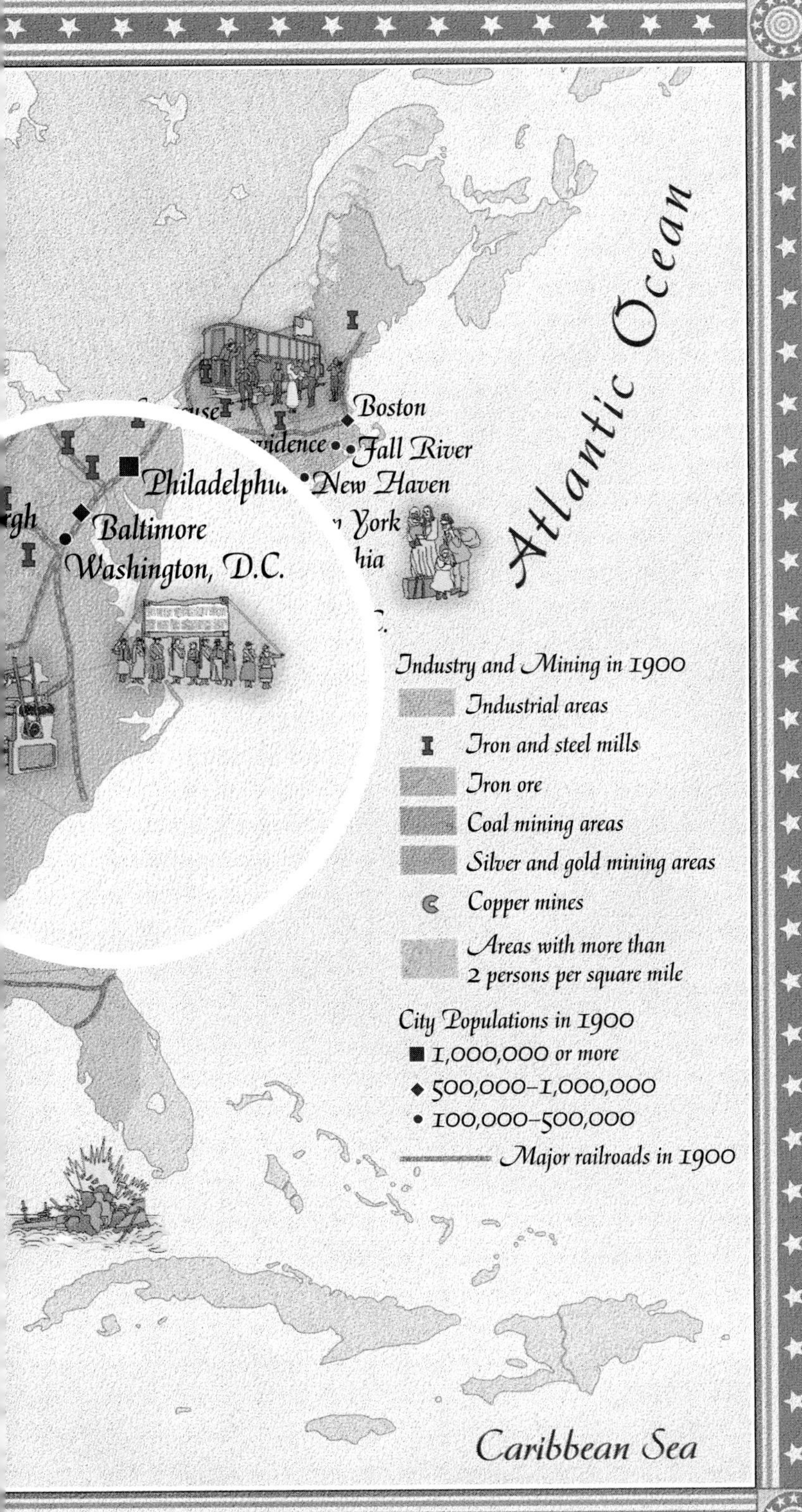

23

Chapter Outline

The Ferment of Reform
The Context of Reform
Church and Campus
Muckrakers
The Gospel of Efficiency
Labor's Demand for Rights
Extending the Woman's Sphere
Socialism/Opponents of Reform

Reforming Society
Settlement Houses and Urban Reform
Protective Legislation for Women and Children
Reshaping Public Education
Challenging Gender Restrictions
Reforming Country Life
Social Control and Moral Crusades
For Whites Only?

Reforming Politics and Government
Woman Suffrage/Electoral Reform
Municipal Reform
Progressive State Government

Roosevelt and the Progressive Presidency
TR and the Modern Presidency
Roosevelt and Labor
Managing Natural Resources
Corporate Regulation
Taft and the Insurgents

Woodrow Wilson and Progressive Reform
The Election of 1912
Implementing the New Freedom
The Expansion of Reform

Key Topics

- ❖ The nature of progressivism
- ❖ Women and progressivism
- ❖ Antidemocratic aspects of progressivism
- ❖ Strengthening of the executive under Roosevelt
- ❖ Climax of progressivism under Woodrow Wilson

Tomorrow Woodrow Wilson would be inaugurated as the nation's president. But today, March 3, 1913, Washington, D.C., belonged to America's women. Women had poured into the capital from across the country. The Army of the Hudson, a group of New York women, had marched for three weeks to reach Washington. Trains carried women of all social backgrounds from every state. Illinois women captured the public's attention with their "Manless Special," a train carrying—and run by—only women.

They came to participate in a great protest parade demanding **woman suffrage**—the right of women to vote—a reform that Woodrow Wilson declined to endorse. Before half a million spectators, the women set out down Pennsylvania Avenue. Behind a banner reading "Women of the World, Unite!" rolled elaborate floats representing countries where women already had the vote. Another column of floats portrayed working women: farmers, wage earners, homemakers, government employees, and professionals, including nurses, teachers, and social workers. Large groups of women paraded with each float. Two hundred striking garment workers fresh from their picket lines in Baltimore marched with a float depicting a sweatshop. In the education division, black women in caps and gowns from Howard University walked with students from Bryn Mawr, Goucher, and other colleges. Nine-month-old Mei Ching Wu, her mother a student at George Washington University, was the parade's youngest member. Bringing up the rear were members of the National Men's League for Woman Suffrage.

Many spectators cheered, but thousands of others insulted the suffragists, broke into their ranks, attacked their floats, and blocked their passage. The embattled women fought their way "foot by foot up Pennsylvania Avenue through two walls of antagonistic humanity," reported an astonished observer. They finally gained some help when male supporters counterattacked their assailants. Even so, the parade could not be completed until troops restored order. Hundreds were hospitalized. "No inauguration has ever produced such scenes," noted one reporter, "which in many instances amounted to nothing less than riots."

This remarkable incident dramatically illustrated critical features of life in the **Progressive Era**. Important movements challenged traditional relationships and attitudes—here involving women's role in American life—and often met strong resistance. "Progressives" seeking reforms organized their supporters across lines of class, education, occupation, geography, gender, and, at times, race and ethnicity—as the variety of groups in the suffrage parade demonstrated. Rather than rely on traditional partisan politics, reformers adopted new political techniques, including lobbying and demonstrating, as nonpartisan pressure groups. Reform work begun at the local and state levels—where the suffrage movement had already met some success—inexorably moved to the national level as the federal government expanded its authority and became the focus of political interest. Finally, this suffrage demonstration revealed the exceptional diversity of the progressive movement, for the women marched, in part, against Woodrow Wilson, who had campaigned for the presidency as a progressive.

However, woman suffrage did not define progressivism. Indeed, in a sense, there was no "progressive movement," for progressivism had no unifying organization, central leadership, or consensus on objectives. Instead, it represented the coalescing of different and sometimes even contradictory movements that sought changes in the nation's social, economic, and political life. But reformers did share certain convictions. They believed that industrialization and urbanization had produced serious social disorders, from city slums to corporate abuses. They believed that new ideas and methods were required to correct these problems. In particular, they rejected the ideology of individualism in favor of broader concepts of social responsibility, and they sought to achieve social order through organization and efficiency. Finally, most progressives believed that government itself, as the organized agent of public responsibility, should address social and economic problems.

Other Americans resisted the progressives' plans. The interaction among the reformers and the conflict with their opponents made the two decades before World War I a period of remarkable ferment and excitement. The progressives' achievements, and their failures, profoundly shaped America.

The great woman suffrage parade leaves Capitol Hill and heads for the White House, March 3, 1913. Dramatic tactics and careful organizing like those that marked this parade helped secure reform in the Progressive Era.

The Ferment of Reform

The diversity of progressivism reflected the diverse impulses of reform. Reformers responded to the tensions of industrialization and urbanization by formulating programs according to their own interests and priorities. Clergy and professors provided new ideas to guide remedial action. Journalists exposed corporate excesses and government corruption and stirred public demand for reform. Business leaders sought to curtail disorder through efficiency and regulation, while industrial workers struggled to improve the horrible conditions in which they worked and lived. Women organized to protect their families and homes from new threats and even to push beyond such domestic issues. Nearly every movement for change encountered fierce opposition. But in raising new issues and proposing new ideas, progressives helped America grapple with the problems of industrial society. (See the overview table, "Major Progressive Organizations and Groups.")

The Context of Reform: Industrial and Urban Tensions

The origins of progressivism lay in the crises of the new urban-industrial order that emerged in the late nineteenth century. The severe depression and consequent mass suffering of the 1890s, the labor violence and industrial armies, the political challenges of Populism and an obviously ineffective government shattered the complacency many middle-class Americans had felt about their nation and made them aware of social and economic inequities that rural and working-class families had long recognized. Many Americans began to question the validity of social Darwinism and the laissez-faire policies that had justified unregulated industrial growth. They began to reconsider the responsibilities of government and, indeed, of themselves for social order and betterment.

By 1900, a returning prosperity had eased the threat of major social violence, but the underlying problems intensified. Big business, which had disrupted traditional economic relationships in the late nineteenth century, suddenly became bigger in a series of mergers between 1897 and 1903, resulting in huge new business combinations. The formation in 1901 of the United States Steel Corporation, the world's largest firm, symbolized this development. Such giant corporations threatened to squeeze opportunities for small firms and workers, dominate markets, and raise social tensions. They also inspired calls for public control.

Industrial growth affected factory workers most directly. Working conditions were difficult and often dangerous. Most workers still toiled nine to ten hours a day; steelworkers and textile employees usually worked twelve-hour shifts. Wages were minimal; an economist in 1905 calculated that 60 percent of all adult male breadwinners made less than a living wage. Family survival, then, often required women and children to work, often in the lowest-paid, most exploited positions. Southern cotton mills employed children as young as seven; coal mines paid twelve-year-old slate pickers thirty-nine cents for a ten-hour day. Poor ventilation, dangerous fumes, open machinery, and an absence of safety programs threatened not only workers' health but their lives as well. Such conditions were gruesomely illustrated in 1911 when a fire killed 146 workers, most of them young women, trapped inside the factory of the **Triangle Shirtwaist Company** in New York because management had locked the exits. The fire chief found "skeletons bending over sewing machines." The United States had the highest rate of industrial accidents in the world. Half a million workers were injured and thirty thousand killed at work each year. These terrible conditions cried out for reform.

Other Americans saw additional social problems in the continuing flood of immigrants who were transforming America's cities. From 1900 to 1917,

OVERVIEW

MAJOR PROGRESSIVE ORGANIZATIONS AND GROUPS

Group	Activity
Social Gospel movement	Urged churches and individuals to apply Christian ethics to social and economic problems
Muckrakers	Exposed business abuses, public corruption, and social evils through investigative journalism
Settlement House movement	Attempted through social work and public advocacy to improve living and working conditions in urban immigrant communities
National Consumers League (1898)	Monitored businesses to ensure decent working conditions and safe consumer products
Women's Trade Union League (1903)	United workingwomen and their middle-class "allies" to promote unionization and social reform
National Child Labor Committee (1904)	Campaigned against child labor
Country Life movement	Attempted to modernize rural social and economic conditions according to urban-industrial standards
National American Woman Suffrage Association	Led the movement to give women the right to vote
Municipal reformers	Sought to change the activities and structure of urban government to promote efficiency and control
Conservationists	Favored efficient management and regulation of natural resources rather than uncontrolled development or preservation

more than 14 million immigrants entered the United States, and most became urban dwellers. By 1910, immigrants and their children comprised more than 70 percent of the population of New York, Chicago, Buffalo, Milwaukee, and other cities. Most of the arrivals were so-called new immigrants from southern and eastern Europe, rather than the British, Irish, Germans, and Scandinavians who had arrived earlier. More than 3 million Italians disembarked; another 2.5 million came from the diverse nationalities of the Russian empire. Several hundred thousand Japanese also arrived, primarily in California, as did increasing numbers of Mexicans. Crowding into urban slums, immigrants overwhelmed municipal sanitation, education, and fire protection services. One Russian described his new life as "all filth and sadness."

Many native-born Americans associated the immigrants with rampant urban crime and disease and with city bosses and government corruption. Ethnic prejudices abounded. Woodrow Wilson, then president of Princeton University, declared in 1902: "The immigrant newcomers of recent years are men of the lowest class from the South of Italy, and men of the meaner sort out of Hungary and Poland, men out of the ranks where there was neither skill nor energy, nor any initiative or quick intelligence." Americans of the Old Stock often considered the predominantly Catholic and Jewish newcomers a threat to social stability and cultural identity and so demanded programs to reform either the urban environment or the immigrants themselves.

Church and Campus

Many groups, drawing from different traditions and inspirations, responded to such economic and social issues. Reform-minded Protestant ministers were es-

CHRONOLOGY

1893–1898 Depression grips the nation.

1898 South Dakota adopts initiative and referendum.

National Consumers' League is organized.

1900 Robert La Follette is elected governor of Wisconsin.

1901 United States Steel Corporation is formed, the world's largest business at the time.

President William McKinley is assassinated; Theodore Roosevelt becomes president.

Socialist Party of America is organized.

Galveston, Texas, initiates the city commission plan.

1902 Antitrust suit is filed against Northern Securities Company.

Mississippi enacts the first direct primary law.

National Reclamation Act is passed.

Roosevelt intervenes in coal strike.

1903 Women's Trade Union League is organized.

1904 National Child Labor Committee is formed.

Roosevelt is elected president.

1905 Industrial Workers of the World is organized.

1906 Hepburn Act strengthens the Interstate Commerce Commission.

Meat Inspection Act extends government regulation.

Pure Food and Drug Act is passed.

1908 *Muller* v. *Oregon* upholds maximum workday for women.

William Howard Taft is elected president.

1910 National Association for the Advancement of Colored People is organized.

Ballinger-Pinchot controversy erupts.

1912 Children's Bureau is established.

Progressive Party organizes and nominates Roosevelt.

Woodrow Wilson is elected president.

1913 Sixteenth and Seventeenth Amendments are ratified.

Underwood-Simmons Tariff Act establishes an income tax.

Federal Reserve Act creates the Federal Reserve System.

1914 Federal Trade Commission is established.

Harrison Act criminalizes narcotics.

1915 National Birth Control League is formed.

1916 Keating-Owen Act prohibits child labor.

1917 Congress enacts literacy test for immigrants.

1920 Nineteenth Amendment is ratified.

pecially influential, creating the **Social Gospel movement**, which sought to introduce religious ethics into industrial relations and appealed to churches to meet their social responsibilities. Washington Gladden, a Congregational minister in Columbus, Ohio, was one of the earliest Social Gospelers. Shocked in 1884 by a bloody strike crushed by wealthy members of his own congregation, Gladden began a ministry to working-class neighborhoods that most churches ignored. He endorsed unions and workers' rights and proposed replacing a cruelly competitive wage system with profit sharing.

A more profound exponent of the Social Gospel was Walter Rauschenbusch, a Baptist minister who had served impoverished immigrants in New York's slums. In his book *Christianity and the Social Crisis* (1907), he argued that Christians should support social reform to alleviate poverty, slums, and labor exploitation. He attacked low wages for transforming workers "into lean, sallow, hopeless, stupid, and vicious young people, simply to enable some group of stockholders to earn 10 percent." Such ideas were popularized by Charles Sheldon, a Kansas minister whose book *In His Steps* sold 23 million copies and called on Americans to act in their daily lives as they believed Jesus Christ would in the same circumstances.

The Social Gospel was part of an emerging liberal movement in American religion. Scholars associated with this movement discredited the literal accuracy of the Bible and emphasized instead its general moral and ethical lessons. These modernists also abandoned theological dogmatism for a greater tolerance of other faiths and became more interested in social problems. To some extent, liberal Protestantism had its Jewish and Catholic counterparts. Reform Judaism renounced certain ancient religious practices and favored adapting to American life; liberal Catholics urged their church to modernize its theological and social positions, especially by showing sympathy for labor unions. But most Jewish immigrants followed Old World habits, and liberal Catholicism was checked in 1907 when Pope Pius X condemned modernism for questioning the church's authority.

Thus the Social Gospel movement flowered among certain Protestant denominations, especially Episcopalians, Congregationalists, and Methodists. It climaxed in 1908 in the formation of the Federal Council of Churches of Christ in America. The council, representing thirty-three religious groups, adopted a program that endorsed welfare and regulatory legislation to achieve social justice. By linking reform with religion (as "applied Christianity," in the words of Washington Gladden), the Social Gospel movement gave progressivism a powerful moral drive that affected much of American life.

The Social Gospel movement provided an ethical justification for government intervention to improve the social order. Scholars in the social sciences also gradually helped turn public attitudes in favor of reform by challenging the laissez-faire views of social Darwinists and traditional academics. In *Applied Sociology* (1906), Lester Ward called for social progress through rational planning and government intervention rather than through unrestrained and unpredictable competition. Economists rejected laissez-faire principles in favor of state action to accomplish social evolution. Industrialization, declared economist Richard T. Ely, "has brought to the front a vast number of social problems whose solution is impossible without the united efforts of church, state, and science."

Muckrakers

Journalists also spread reform ideas by developing a new form of investigative reporting known as **muckraking**. Technological innovations that sharply reduced production costs had recently made possible the mass circulation of magazines, and editors competed to attract an expanding urban readership. Samuel S. McClure was the first to introduce promotional gimmicks and serialized popular fiction in *McClure's Magazine;* he then sent his reporters to uncover political and corporate corruption. Sensational exposés sold magazines, and soon *Cosmopolitan, Everybody's,* and other journals began publishing investigations of business abuses, dangerous working conditions, and the miseries of slum life.

Muckraking articles aroused indignant public demands for reform. Lincoln Steffens detailed the corrupt links between "respectable" businessmen and crooked urban politicians in a series of articles called "The Shame of the Cities." Ida Tarbell revealed John D. Rockefeller's sordid construction of Standard Oil. Muckraking novels also appeared. *The Octopus* (1901), by Frank Norris, dramatized the Southern Pacific Railroad's stranglehold on California's farmers, and *The Jungle* (1906), by Upton Sinclair, exposed nauseating conditions in Chicago's meatpacking industry.

The Gospel of Efficiency

Many progressive leaders believed that efficiency and expertise could control or resolve the disorder of industrial society. President Theodore Roosevelt (1901–1909)—who called muckrakers irresponsible radicals—spoke for more moderate reformers by praising the "gospel of efficiency." Like many other progressives, he admired corporations' success in applying management techniques to guide economic growth. Drawing from science and technology as well as from the model of the corporation, many progressives attempted to manage or direct change efficiently. They used scientific methods to collect extensive data and relied on experts for analysis and recommendations. "Scientific management," a concept often used interchangeably with "sound business management," seemed the key to eliminating waste and inefficiency in government, society, and industry. Rural reformers thought that "scientific agriculture" could bring prosperity to the impoverished southern countryside; urban reformers believed that improvements in medical science and the professionalization of physicians through uniform state licensing standards could eradicate the cities' wretched health problems.

Business leaders especially advocated efficiency, order, and organization. Industrialists were drawn to the ideas of Frederick Taylor, a proponent of scientific management, for cutting factory labor costs. Taylor proposed to increase worker efficiency through imposed work routines, speedups, and mechanization. Workers, Taylor insisted, should "do what they are told promptly and without asking questions. . . . It is absolutely necessary for every man in our organization to become one of a train of gear wheels." By assigning workers simple and repetitive tasks on machines, Taylorization made their skills expendable and enabled managers to control the production, pace of work, and hiring and firing of personnel. Stripped of their influence and poorly paid, factory workers shared little of the wealth generated by industrial expansion and scientific management. When labor complained, one business leader declared that unions failed "to appreciate the progressivism of the age."

Sophisticated managers of big business combinations saw some forms of government intervention as another way to promote order and efficiency. In particular, they favored regulations that could bring about safer and more stable conditions in society and the economy. Government regulations, they reasoned, could reassure potential consumers, open markets, mandate working conditions that smaller competitors could not provide, or impose systematic procedures that competitive pressures would otherwise undercut.

Labor's Demand for Rights

Industrial workers with different objectives also hastened the ferment of reform. Workers resisted the new rules of efficiency experts and called for improved wages and working conditions and reduced work hours. They and their middle-class sympathizers sought to achieve some of these goals through state intervention, demanding laws to compensate workers injured on the job, curb child labor, and regulate the employment of women. Sometimes they succeeded. After the Triangle Shirtwaist fire, for example, urban politicians with working-class constituencies created the New York State Factory Commission and enacted dozens of laws dealing with fire hazards, machine safety, and wages and hours for women.

Workers also organized unions to improve their lot. The American Federation of Labor (AFL) claimed 4 million members by 1920. But it recruited mainly skilled workers, particularly native-born white males. New unions organized the factories and sweatshops where most immigrants and women worked. Despite strong employer resistance, the International Ladies Garment Workers Union (1900) and the Amalgamated Clothing Workers (1914) organized the garment trades, developed programs for social and economic reforms, and led their members—mostly young Jewish and Italian women—in spectacular strikes. The "Uprising of the 20,000," a 1909 strike in New York City, included months of massive rallies, determined picketing, and police repression. One observer marveled at the women strikers' "emotional endurance, fearlessness, and entire willingness to face danger and suffering."

A still more radical union tried to organize miners, lumberjacks, and Mexican and Japanese farm workers in the West, black dockworkers in the South, and immigrant factory hands in New England. Founded in 1905, the Industrial Workers of the World (IWW), whose members were known as "**Wobblies**," used sit-down strikes, sit-ins, and mass rallies, tactics adopted by other industrial unions in the 1930s and the civil rights movement in the 1960s. "Respectable people" considered the Wobblies violent revolutionaries, but most of the violence was committed against them. Private employers and public officials used every method, legal and illegal, to destroy the Wobblies, but broader labor unrest nonetheless stimulated the reform impulse.

Extending the Woman's Sphere

Women reformers and their organizations played a key role in progressivism. Women responded not merely to the human suffering caused by industrialization and urbanization but also to related changes in their own status and role. By the early twentieth century, more women than before were working outside the home—in the factories, mills, and sweatshops of the industrial economy and as clerks in stores and offices. In 1910, more than a fourth of all workers were women, increasing numbers of them married. Their importance in the

Striking garment workers and their supporters in the 1909 "Uprising" in New York City. Working women and their allies contributed to the growing pressure for improved working conditions.

workforce and participation in unions and strikes challenged assumptions that woman's "natural" role was to be a submissive housewife. Shrinking family size, laborsaving household equipment, and changing social expectations enabled middle-class women to find more time and opportunities to pursue activities outside the home. Better educated than previous generations, they also acquired interests, information, skills, and confidence relevant to a larger public setting.

The women's clubs that had begun multiplying in the late nineteenth century became seedbeds of progressive ideas in the early twentieth century. Often founded for cultural purposes, women's clubs soon adopted programs for social reform and gave their members a route to public influence. In 1914, an officer of the General Federation of Women's Clubs proudly declared that every cause for social reform had "received a helpful hand from the clubwomen." Generally, however, the clubs focused on public issues affecting women, home, and family.

Women also joined or created other organizations that pushed beyond the limits of traditional domesticity. "Woman's place is in the home," observed one progressive, but "no longer is the home encompassed by four walls." By threatening healthy and happy homes, urban problems required that women become "social housekeepers" in the community. The National Congress of Mothers, organized in 1897, worried about crime and disease and championed kindergartens, foster-home programs, juvenile courts, and compulsory school attendance.

Still more aggressive were the National Consumers' League, formed in 1898, and the Women's Trade Union League (WTUL; 1903), both of which organized women across class lines to promote social change. Led by the crusading Florence Kelley, the National Consumers' League tried to protect both women wage earners and middle-class housewives by monitoring stores and factories to ensure decent working conditions and safe products. The WTUL united working women and their self-styled middle-class "allies" to unionize women workers and eliminate sweatshop conditions. Its greatest success came in the 1909 garment workers' strike when the allies—dubbed by one worker the "mink brigade"—assisted strikers with relief funds, bail money, food supplies, and public relations campaign. This cooperation, declared one WTUL official, demonstrated the "sisterhood of women."

Although most progressive women stressed women's special duties and responsibilities as social housekeepers, others began to demand women's equal rights. In 1914, for example, critics of New York's policy of dismissing women teachers who married formed a group called the Feminist Alliance and demanded "the removal of all social, political, economic and other discriminations which are based upon sex, and the award of all rights and duties in all fields on the basis of individual capacity alone." With these new organizations and ideas, women gave important impetus and direction to the reform sentiments of the early twentieth century.

Socialism

The growing influence of socialist ideas also promoted the spirit of progressivism. Socialists never attracted a large following, even among workers (see Chapter 20), but their criticism of the industrial economy gained increasing attention in the early twentieth century. American socialists condemned social and economic inequities, criticized limited government, and demanded public ownership of railroads, utilities, and communications. They also campaigned for tax reforms, better housing, factory inspections, and recreational facilities for all. Muckrakers like Lincoln Steffens and Upton Sinclair were committed socialists, as were some Social Gospel ministers and labor leaders, but the most prominent socialist was Eugene Debs. In 1901, Debs helped organize the Socialist Party of America. In the next decade, the party won many local elections, especially in Wisconsin and New York, where it drew support from German and Russian immigrants, and in Oklahoma, among poor tenant farmers. Socialism was also promoted by newspapers and magazines, including the *Appeal to Reason* in Girard, Kansas, which had a circulation of 500,000 by 1906. "Socialism is coming," the *Appeal* proclaimed. "It's coming like a prairie fire and nothing can stop it."

Most progressives considered socialist ideas too drastic. Nevertheless, socialists contributed importantly to the reform ferment, not only by providing support for reform initiatives but often also by prompting progressives to push for some changes to undercut increasingly attractive radical alternatives.

Opponents of Reform

Not all Americans supported progressive reforms, and many people regarded as progressives on some issues opposed change in other areas. Social Gospeler Rauschenbusch, for instance, opposed expanding women's rights. More typically, opponents of reform held consistently traditional attitudes, like the conservatives who saw in feminism the orthodox bogies of "non-motherhood, free love, easy divorce, economic independence for all women, and other demoralizing and destructive theories."

Social Gospelers themselves faced opposition. Reacting to the rise of religious liberalism, Protestant traditionalists emphasized what they termed fundamental beliefs. Particularly strong among evangelical denominations with rural roots, these **fundamentalists** stressed personal salvation rather than social reform. "To attempt reform in the black depths of the great city," said one, "would be as useless as trying to purify the ocean by pouring into it a few gallons of spring water." Indeed, the urban and industrial crises that inspired Social Gospelers to preach reform drove many evangelical leaders to endorse social and political conservatism. The most famous evangelist, the crude but spellbinding Billy Sunday, scorned all reforms but prohibition and denounced labor unions, women's rights, and business regulation as violating traditional values. Declaring that the Christian mission was only to save individual souls, he condemned the Social Gospel as "godless social service nonsense" and attacked its advocates as "infidels and atheists."

The charismatic Eugene Debs, here speaking at Canton, Ohio, led American socialists in demanding radical economic and political changes. Debs twice received more than 900,000 votes for president.

Business interests angered by exposés of corporate abuse and corruption attacked muckrakers. To capture public opinion, business groups like the American Bankers' Association accused muckrakers of promoting socialism. Major corporations like Standard Oil created public relations bureaus to improve their image and to identify business, not its critics, with the public interest. "The voice of the public," one press agent proclaimed, was "spoken through the Chamber of Commerce." Advertising boycotts discouraged magazines from running critical stories, and credit restrictions forced some muckraking journals to suspend publication. By 1910, the heyday of muckraking was over.

Labor unions likewise encountered resistance. Led by the National Association of Manufacturers, business groups denounced unions as corrupt and radical, hired thugs to disrupt them, organized strikebreaking agencies, and used blacklists to eliminate union activists. The antiunion campaign peaked in Ludlow, Colorado, in 1914. John D. Rockefeller's Colorado Fuel and Iron Company used armed guards and the state militia to shoot and burn striking workers and their families. The courts aided employers by issuing injunctions against strikes and prohibited unions from using boycotts, one of their most effective weapons.

Progressives campaigning for government intervention and regulation also met stiff resistance. Many Americans objected to what they considered unwarranted interference in private economic matters. Their political representatives were called the "Old Guard," implying their opposition to political and economic change. The courts often supported these attitudes. In *Lochner* v. *New York* (1905), the Supreme Court overturned a maximum-hours law on the grounds that it deprived employers and employees of their "freedom of contract." Progressives constantly had to struggle with such opponents, and progressive achievements were limited by the persistence and influence of their adversaries.

Reforming Society

With their varied motives and objectives, progressives worked to transform society by improving living conditions, educational opportunities, family life, and social and industrial relations. (See the overview table, "Major Laws and Constitutional Amendments of the Progressive Era.") They sought what they called "social justice," but their plans for social reform sometimes also smacked of social control—coercive efforts to impose uniform standards on a diverse population. Organized women dominated the movement to reform society, but they

Overview

Major Laws and Constitutional Amendments of the Progressive Era

Legislation	Effect
New York Tenement House Law (1901)	Established a model housing code for safety and sanitation
Newlands Act (1902)	Provided for federal irrigation projects
Hepburn Act (1906)	Strengthened authority of the Interstate Commerce Commission
Pure Food and Drug Act (1906)	Regulated the production and sale of food and drug products
Meat Inspection Act (1906)	Authorized federal inspection of meat products
Sixteenth Amendment (1913)	Authorized a federal income tax
Seventeenth Amendment (1913)	Mandated the direct popular election of senators
Underwood-Simmons Tariff Act (1913)	Lowered tariff rates and levied the first regular federal income tax
Federal Reserve Act (1913)	Established the Federal Reserve System to supervise banking and provide a national currency
Federal Trade Commission Act (1914)	Established the FTC to oversee business activities
Harrison Act (1914)	Regulated the distribution and use of narcotics
Smith-Lever Act (1914)	Institutionalized the county agent system
Keating-Owen Act (1916)	Indirectly prohibited child labor
Eighteenth Amendment (1919)	Instituted prohibition
Nineteenth Amendment (1920)	Established woman suffrage

were supported, depending on the goal, by Social Gospel ministers, social scientists, urban immigrants, labor unions, and even some conservatives eager to regulate personal behavior.

Settlement Houses and Urban Reform

The spearheads for social reform were settlement houses, community centers in urban immigrant neighborhoods. Reformers created four hundred settlement houses, largely modeled after Hull House in Chicago, founded in 1889 by Jane Addams. Settlement houses often reflected the ideals of the Social Gospel. "A simple acceptance of Christ's message and methods," wrote Addams, "is what a settlement should stand for." Yet most were secular institutions, avoiding religion to gain the trust of Catholic and Jewish immigrants.

Most settlements were led and staffed primarily by middle-class young women, seeking to alleviate poverty and do useful, professional work when most careers were closed to them. Settlement work did not immediately violate prescribed gender roles because it initially focused on the "woman's sphere": family, education, domestic skills, and cultural "uplift." Thus settlement workers organized kindergartens and nurseries; taught classes in English, cooking, and personal hygiene; held musical performances and poetry readings; and sponsored recreation.

However, settlement workers soon saw that the root problem for immigrants was widespread poverty that required more than changes in individual behavior. Unlike earlier reformers, they regarded many of the evils of poverty as products of the social environment rather than of moral weakness. Slum-dwellers, Addams sadly noted, suffered from "poisonous sewage, contaminated water, infant mortality, adulterated food, smoke-laden air, juvenile crime, and unwholesome crowding." Thus settlement workers campaigned for stricter building codes to improve slums, better urban sanitation systems to enhance public health, public parks to revive the urban environment, and laws to protect women and children.

Their crusade for housing reform demonstrated the impact that social reformers often had on urban life. His work at the University Settlement in New York City convinced Lawrence Veiller that "the improvement of the homes of the people was the starting point for everything." Organizing pressure groups to promote tenement house reform, Veiller relied on settlement workers to help investigate housing conditions, prepare public exhibits depicting rampant disease in congested slums, and agitate for improvements. Based on their findings, Veiller drafted a new housing code limiting the size of tenements and requiring toilet facilities, ventilation, and fire protection. In 1901, the New York Tenement House Law became a model for other cities. To promote uniform building codes throughout the nation, the tireless Veiller founded the National Housing Association in 1910.

Protective Legislation for Women and Children

While settlement workers initially undertook private efforts to improve society, many reformers eventually concluded that only government power could achieve social justice. They demanded that state and federal governments protect the weak or disadvantaged. As Veiller insisted, it was "unquestionably the duty of the state" to enforce justice in the face of "greed on the part of those who desire to secure for themselves an undue profit."

The maiming and killing of children in industrial accidents made it "inevitable," Addams said, "that efforts to secure a child labor law should be our first venture into the field of state legislation." The National Child Labor Committee, organized in 1904, led the campaign to curtail child labor (see Figure 23-1). Reformers documented the problem with extensive investigations and also benefited from the public outrage stirred by socialist John Spargo's muckraking book *The Bitter Cry of the Children* (1906). In 1900, most states had no minimum working age; by 1914, every state but one had such a law. Effective regulation, however, required national action, for many state laws were weak or poorly enforced (see "American Views: Mother Jones and the Meaning of Child Labor in America").

Stiff resistance came from manufacturers who used child labor, conservatives who opposed government action as an intrusion into family life, and some poor parents who needed their children's income. But finally Congress in 1912 established the **Children's Bureau** to investigate the welfare of children. Julia Lathrop, from Hull House, directed the Bureau, the first government agency headed and staffed almost entirely by women. In 1916, the Keating-Owen Act prohibited the interstate shipment of goods manufactured by children. But the law was weaker than that of many states and did not cover most child workers. Even so, the Supreme Court declared the measure unconstitutional.

***Figure 23-1* Child labor, 1870–1930.**
Nearly 2 million children worked in factories and fields in 1900, twice the number as in 1870. Progressives' efforts to curtail child labor through laws for compulsory education and a minimum working age encountered resistance, and change came slowly.
Data Source: U.S. Bureau of the Census.

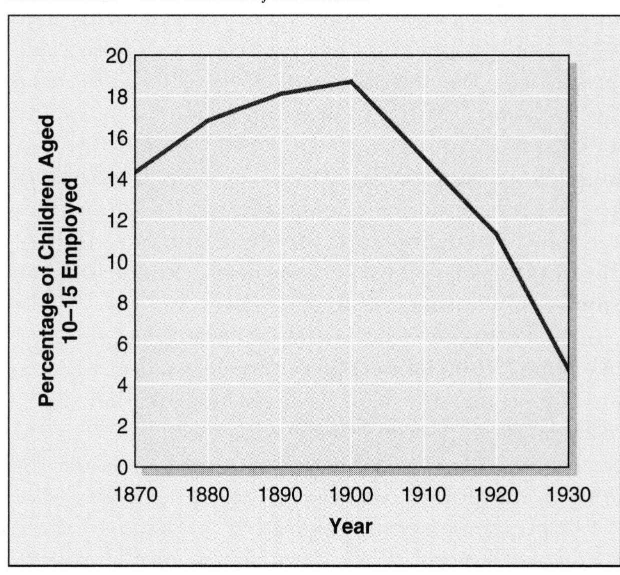

The famous photographer Lewis Hine used his camera to document child labor. The eight-year-old girl on the right in this 1911 photograph of women and children working in an Alabama canning factory had been shucking oysters for three years.

Social reformers also lobbied for laws regulating the wages, hours, and working conditions of women and succeeded in having states from New York to Oregon pass maximum-hours legislation. After the Supreme Court upheld such laws in *Muller* v. *Oregon* (1908), thirty-nine states enacted new or stronger laws on women's maximum hours between 1909 and 1917. Fewer states established minimum wages for women. In 1912, Massachusetts created a commission with the power to recommend such wages, and within a year, eight midwestern and western states authorized wage commissions to set binding rates. But few other states followed these examples.

Protective legislation for women posed a troubling issue for reformers. In California, for example, middle-class clubwomen favored protective legislation on grounds of women's presumed weakness. They wanted to preserve "California's potential motherhood." More radical progressives, as in the socialist-led Women's Trade Union League of Los Angeles, supported legislation to help secure economic independence and equality in the labor market for women, increase the economic strength of the working class, and serve as a precedent for laws improving conditions for all workers.

Progressive Era lawmakers adopted the first viewpoint. They limited protective legislation to measures reflecting the belief that women needed paternalist protection, even by excluding them from certain occupations. Laws establishing a minimum wage for women, moreover, usually set a wage level below what the wage commissions reported as subsistence rates. Protective legislation thus assured women not economic independence but continued dependence on husbands or fathers. In practice, then, the laws reinforced women's subordinate place in the labor force.

Social justice reformers forged the beginnings of the welfare state in further legislation. Prompted by both humanitarian and paternalistic urgings, many states began in 1910 to provide "mothers' pensions" to indigent widows with dependent children. Twenty-one states, led by Wisconsin in 1911, enacted workers' compensation programs, ending the custom of holding workers themselves liable for injuries on the job.

Compared to social insurance programs in western Europe, however, these were feeble responses to the social consequences of industrialization. Attempts by various reform groups to follow up workers' compensation laws with health insurance and old-age pension programs went nowhere. Business groups and other conservative interests curbed the movement toward state responsibility for social welfare. Few more advances would come until the New Deal (1930s) and the Great Society (1960s), both heirs of progressivism in their commitment to governmental activism.

Reshaping Public Education

Concerns about child labor overlapped with increasing attention to public schools. The rapid influx of immigrants, as well as the demands of the new corporate workplace, generated interest in education not only as a means of advancement but also as a tool for assimilation and the training of future workers. Middle-class women supported public school reforms. In 1900, for example, women's clubs in North Carolina launched a program to improve school buildings, increase teachers' salaries, and broaden the curriculum. Claiming efficiency and expertise, school administrators also pushed for changes, both to upgrade their own profession and to expand their public influence. And some intellectuals predicted that schools themselves could promote social progress and reform. Philosopher John Dewey sketched his plans for such progressive education in *The School and Society* (1899).

The modern urban public school system emerged between 1880 and 1920. Compulsory school attendance laws, kindergartens, age-graded elementary schools, professional training for teachers, vocational education, parent-teacher associations, and school nurses became standard elements in American education. School reformers believed in both the educational soundness of these measures and their importance for countering slum environments. As Jacob Riis contended, the kindergartner would "rediscover . . . the natural feelings that the tenement had smothered." Others supported the kindergarten as "the earliest opportunity to catch the little Russian, the little Italian, the little German, Pole, Syrian, and the rest and begin to make good American citizens of them." Further socialization came through vocational courses intended to instill discipline in poor students and prepare them to become productive adults.

Public education in the South lagged behind the North. An educational awakening, supported by northern philanthropy and southern reformers, brought improvements after 1900. Per capita expenditures for education doubled, school terms were extended, and high schools spread across the region. But the South frittered away its limited resources on a segregated educational system that shortchanged both races. Black Southerners particularly suffered, for the new programs increased the disparity in funding for white and black schools. South Carolina spent twelve times as much per white pupil as per black pupil. Booker T. Washington complained in 1906 that the educational reforms meant "almost nothing so far as the Negro schools are concerned." As a northern critic observed, "To devise a school system which shall save the whites and not the blacks is a task of such delicacy that a few surviving reactionaries are willing to let both perish together."

Challenging Gender Restrictions

Most progressives held fairly conservative, moralistic views about sexuality and gender roles. Margaret Sanger, however, radically challenged conventional ideas of the social role of women. Despite great opposition, she initiated the modern birth control movement. A public health nurse and an IWW organizer, she soon made the struggle for reproductive rights her personal crusade. Her mother had died at forty-nine after eighteen pregnancies, and Sanger saw in New York's immigrant neighborhoods the plight of poor women worn out from repeated pregnancies or injured or dead from self-induced knitting-needle abortions. Despite federal and state laws against contraceptives, Sanger began promoting birth control as a way to avert such tragedies. In 1914, Sanger published a magazine, *Woman Rebel*, in which she argued that "a woman's body belongs to herself alone. It does not belong to the United States of America or any other government on the face of the earth." Prohibiting contraceptives meant "enforced motherhood," Sanger declared. "Women cannot be on an equal footing with men until they have full and complete control over their reproductive function."

Sanger's crusade attracted support from many women's and labor groups, but it also infuriated those who regarded birth control as a threat to the family and morality. Indicted for distributing information about contraception, Sanger fled to Europe. Other women took up the cause, forming the National Birth Control League in 1915 to campaign for the repeal of laws restricting access to contraceptive information and devices. They had little immediate success, but their cause would triumph in later generations.

Reforming Country Life

Although most progressives focused on the city, others sought to reform rural life, both to modernize its social and economic conditions and to integrate it more fully into the larger society. They worked to improve rural health and sanitation, to replace inefficient one-room schools with modern consolidated ones under professional control, and to extend new roads and communication services into the countryside. To further these goals, President Theodore Roosevelt created the Country Life Commission in 1908. The country lifers had a broad program for social and economic change, involving expanded government functions, activist government agencies staffed by experts, and the professionalization of rural social services.

Agricultural scientists, government officials, and many business interests also sought to promote efficient, scientific, and commercial agriculture. A key innovation was the county agent system: the U.S. Department of Agriculture and business groups placed an agent in each county to teach farmers new techniques and encourage changes in the rural social

American Views

Mother Jones and the Meaning of Child Labor in America

Born in Ireland in 1830, the legendary Mother Jones (Mary Harris Jones) became one of America's greatest social activists, organizing workers, participating in strikes, and protesting social and industrial conditions from the 1870s through the 1920s. Here she recounts one of her efforts to end child labor, one of the most persistent reform goals of the Progressive Era. Using the techniques of exposure and publicity characteristic of the period and adroitly employing patriotic symbols and references, Jones skillfully raised troubling questions about the concepts of social and economic opportunity that many Americans associated with national development and identity.

❖ **How did Mother Jones direct public attention to child labor?**

❖ **How did she invoke the treasured American concept of opportunity to gain support for her goal?**

❖ **What did she argue was the relationship between child labor and the privileged status of other Americans?**

❖ **How successful was her crusade against child labor?**

In the spring of 1903 I went to Kensington, Pennsylvania, where 75,000 textile workers were on strike. Of this number at least 10,000 were little children. The workers were striking for more pay and shorter hours. Every day little children came into Union Headquarters, some with their hands off, some with the thumb missing, some with their fingers off at the knuckle. They were stooped little things, round shouldered and skinny. Many of them were not over ten years of age. . . .

We assembled a number of boys and girls one morning in Independence Park and from there we arranged to parade with banners to the court house where we would hold a meeting.

A great crowd gathered in the public square in front of the city hall. I put the little boys with their fingers off and hands crushed and maimed on a platform. I held up their mutilated hands and showed them to the crowd and made the statement that Philadelphia's mansions were built on the broken bones, the quivering hearts, and drooping heads of these children. . . .

I called upon the millionaire manufacturers to cease their moral murders, and I cried to

values that had spawned the Populist radicalism that most progressives decried. Farmers, it was hoped, would acquire materialistic values and learn "economy, order, . . . patriotism, and a score of other wholesome lessons," as one progressive put it in 1910. The Smith-Lever Act (1914) provided federal subsidies for county agents throughout the country. Its purpose, claimed Woodrow Wilson, was to produce "an efficient and contented population" in rural America.

Few farmers, however, welcomed these efforts. As one Illinois county agent said in 1915, "Farmers, as a whole, resent exceedingly those forces which are at work with missionary intent trying to uplift them." School consolidation meant the loss of community control of education; good roads would raise taxes and chiefly benefit urban business interests. Besides, most farmers believed that their problems stemmed not from rural life but from industrial society and its nefarious trusts, banks, and middlemen. Rural Americans did not want their lives revolutionized.

Even so, rural people were drawn into the larger urban-industrial society during the Progres-

the officials in the open windows opposite, "Some day the workers will take possession of your city hall, and when we do, no child will be sacrificed on the altar of profit."

The reporters quoted my statement that Philadelphia mansions were built on the broken bones and quivering hearts of children. The Philadelphia papers and the New York papers got into a squabble with each other over the question. The universities discussed it. Preachers began talking. That was what I wanted. Public attention on the subject of child labor.

The matter quieted down for a while and I concluded the people needed stirring up again. . . . I decided to go with the children to see President Roosevelt to ask him to have Congress pass a law prohibiting the exploitation of childhood. I thought that President Roosevelt might see these mill children and compare them with his own little ones who were spending the summer at the seashore at Oyster Bay. . . .

Everywhere we had meetings, showing up with living children, the horrors of child labor. . . . [In New Jersey] I called on the mayor of Princeton and asked for permission to speak opposite the campus of the University. I said I wanted to speak on higher education. The mayor gave me permission. A great crowd gathered, professors and students and the people; and I told them that the rich robbed these little children of any education of the lowest order that they might send their sons and daughters to places of higher education. . . . And I showed those professors children in our army who could scarcely read or write because they were working ten hours a day in the silk mills of Pennsylvania. . . .

[In New York] I told an immense crowd of the horrors of child labor in the mills around the anthracite region and . . . I showed them Gussie Rangnew, a little girl from whom all the childhood had gone. Her face was like an old woman's. Gussie packed stockings in a factory, eleven hours a day for a few cents a day. . . . "Fifty years ago there was a cry against slavery and men gave up their lives to stop the selling of black children on the block. Today the white child is sold for two dollars a week to the manufacturers."

. . . We marched down to Oyster Bay but the president refused to see us and he would not answer my letters. But our march had done its work. We had drawn the attention of the nation to the crime of child labor. And while the strike of the textile workers in Kensington was lost and the children driven back to work, not long afterward the Pennsylvania legislature passed a child labor law that sent thousands of children home from the mills, and kept thousands of others from entering the factory until they were fourteen years of age.

Source: The Autobiography of Mother Jones, *3rd ed. (Chicago: Kerr Publishing Company, 1977).*

sive Era. Government agencies, agricultural colleges, and railroads and banks steadily tied farmers to urban markets. Telephones and rural free delivery of mail lessened countryside isolation but quickened the spread of city values. Improved roads and the coming of the automobile eliminated many rural villages and linked farm families directly with towns and cities. Consolidated schools wiped out the social center of rural neighborhoods and carried children out of their communities, many never to return.

Social Control and Moral Crusades

The tendency toward social control evident in the movements to pass protective legislation and transform country life also marked other less attractive progressive efforts. These efforts, moreover, often meshed with the restrictive attitudes that conservative Americans held about race, religion, immigration, and morality. The result was widespread attempts to restrict certain groups and control behavior.

Many Americans wanted to limit immigration for racist reasons. Nativist agitation in California prompted the federal government to secure restrictions on Japanese immigration in 1907. Californians, including local progressives, also hoped to curtail the migration of Mexicans. A Stanford University researcher condemned Mexicans as an "undesirable class" compared to "the more progressive races," and in 1916 the Los Angeles County supervisors urged the federal government to deport Mexican immigrants.

Nationally, public debate focused on restricting the flow of new immigrants from southern and eastern Europe. Some labor leaders believed that immigration held down wages and impeded unionization; many sociologists thought it created serious social problems; other Americans disliked the newcomers on religious, cultural, or ethnic grounds. Many backed their prejudice with a distorted interpretation of Darwinism, labeling the Slavic and Mediterranean peoples "inferior races." As early as 1894, nativists had organized the Immigration Restriction League, which lobbied for a literacy test for admission, sure that it would "bear most heavily upon the Italians, Russians, Poles, Hungarians, Greeks, and Asiatics, and very lightly or not at all upon English-speaking immigrants or Germans, Scandinavians, and French." Congress enacted a literacy law in 1917.

Other nativists demanded the "Americanization" of immigrants already in the country. The Daughters of the American Revolution sought to inculcate loyalty, patriotism, and conservative values. Settlement workers and Social Gospelers promoted a gentler kind of Americanization by helping immigrants adapt to their new life with classes in English and home mission campaigns, but they too attempted to transfer their own values to the newcomers. The most prominent advocate of Americanization was a stereotypical progressive, Frances Kellor. She studied social work at the University of Chicago, worked in New York settlement houses, wrote a muckraking exposé of employment agencies that exploited women, and became director of the New York Bureau of Immigration. In 1915, she helped organize the National Americanization Committee and increasingly emphasized destroying immigrants' old-country ties and imposing an American culture.

Closely linked to progressives' worries about immigrants was their campaign for **prohibition**. This movement engaged many of the progressives' basic impulses. Social workers saw liquor as a cause of crime, poverty, and family violence; employers blamed it for causing industrial accidents and inefficiency; Social Gospel ministers condemned the "spirit born of hell" because it impaired moral judgment and behavior. But also important was native-born Americans' fear of new immigrants—"the dangerous classes, who are readily dominated by the saloon." Many immigrants, in fact, viewed liquor and the neighborhood saloon as vital parts of daily life, and so prohibition became a focus of nativist hostilities, cultural conflict, and Americanization pressures. In the South, racism also figured prominently. Alexander McKelway, the southern secretary for the National Child Labor Committee, endorsed prohibition as a way to maintain social order and white supremacy. McKelway himself drank, but he helped organize the North Carolina Anti-Saloon League to deny alcohol to African Americans, whom he considered naturally "criminal and degenerate."

Protestant fundamentalists also stoutly supported prohibition, working through the Anti-Saloon League, founded in 1893. Their nativism and antiurban bias surfaced in demands for prohibition to prevent the nation's cities from lapsing into "raging mania, disorder, and anarchy." With most urban Catholics and Jews opposing prohibition—the Central Conference of American Rabbis denounced it as "born of fanaticism"—the Anti-Saloon League justified imposing its reform on city populations against their will: "Our nation can only be saved by turning the pure stream of country sentiment . . . to flush out the cesspools of cities and so save civilization from pollution."

With these varied motivations, prohibitionists campaigned for local and state laws against the manufacture and sale of alcohol. Beginning in 1907, they proved increasingly successful, especially in the South, Midwest, and Far West. By 1917, twenty-six states had prohibition laws. Congress then approved the Eighteenth Amendment, which made prohibition the law of the land by 1920.

Less controversial was the drive to control narcotics, then readily available. Patent medicines commonly contained opium, heroin, and cocaine (popularly used for hay fever), and physicians known as "dope doctors" openly dispensed drugs to paying customers. Inaccurate assumptions that addiction was spreading in "the fallen and lower classes"—and particularly among black people and immigrants—prompted calls for restrictive legislation. In 1914, Congress passed the **Harrison Act**, prohibiting the distribution and use of narcotics for other than medicinal purposes.

California provided other examples of progressives' interest in social control and moral reform. The state assembly, described by the *San Francisco Chronicle* as "a legislature of progressive cranks," prohibited gambling, cardplaying, and prizefighting. Los Angeles—influenced by the aptly named Morals Efficiency League—banned premarital sex and introduced artistic censorship. One critic in 1913 complained that the reformers' "frenzy of virtue" made "Puritanism . . . the inflexible doctrine of Los Angeles."

For Whites Only?

Racism permeated the Progressive Era. In the South, progressivism was built on black disfranchisement and segregation. Like most white Southerners, progressives believed that racial control was necessary for social order and that it enabled reformers to address other social problems. Such reformers also invoked racism to gain popular support for their objectives. In Georgia, for instance, child labor reformers warned that while white children worked in the Piedmont textile mills, black children were going to school: Child labor laws and compulsory school attendance laws were necessary to maintain white supremacy.

Governors Hoke Smith of Georgia and James Vardaman, "the White Chief," of Mississippi typified the link between racism and reform in the South. They supported progressive reforms, but they also viciously attacked black rights. Their racist demagogy incited antiblack violence throughout the South. Antiblack race riots, like that produced in Atlanta by Smith's election in 1906, and lynching—defended on the floor of the U.S. Senate by a southern progressive—were part of the system of racial control that made the era a terrible time for African Americans.

Even in the North, where relatively few black people lived, race relations deteriorated. Civil rights laws went unenforced, black customers were excluded from restaurants and hotels, and schools were segregated. A reporter in Pennsylvania found "this disposition to discriminate against Negroes has greatly increased within the past decade." Antiblack race riots exploded in New York in 1900 and in Springfield, Illinois—Lincoln's hometown—in 1908.

But although most white progressives promoted or accepted racial discrimination and most black Southerners had to adapt to it, black progressive activism was growing. Even in the South, some African Americans struggled to improve conditions. In Atlanta, for example, black women created progressive organizations and established settlement houses, kindergartens, and day care centers. With public parks reserved for white people, the Gate City Day Nursery Association built and supervised a playground on the campus of Atlanta Baptist College. The women of the Neighborhood Union, organized in 1908, even challenged the discriminatory policies of Atlanta's board of education, demanding equal facilities and appropriations for the city's black schools. They had only limited success, but their efforts demonstrated a persisting commitment to reforming society.

In the North, African Americans more openly criticized discrimination and rejected Booker T. Washington's philosophy of accommodation. Ida Wells-Barnett, the crusading journalist who had fled the South for Chicago, became nationally prominent for her militant protests. She fought fiercely against racial injustices, especially school segregation, agitated for woman suffrage, and organized kindergartens and settlement houses for Chicago's black migrants.

Still more important was W. E. B. Du Bois, who campaigned tirelessly against all forms of racial discrimination. In 1905, Du Bois and other black activists met in Niagara Falls, Canada, to make plans to promote political and economic equality. In 1910, this **Niagara Movement** joined with a small group of white

A meeting of the Niagara Movement in Boston in 1907. W. E. B. Du Bois is seated on the left. Half of the delegates were women, indicating the important role that black women played in the struggle for racial justice.

reformers, including Jane Addams, to organize the National Association for the Advancement of Colored People. The NAACP sought to overthrow segregation and establish equal justice and educational opportunities. As its director of publicity and research, Du Bois launched the influential magazine *The Crisis* to shape public opinion. "Agitate," he counseled, "protest, reveal the truth, and refuse to be silenced." By 1918, the NAACP had 44,000 members in 165 branches. Two generations later, it would successfully challenge the racial discrimination that most early-twentieth-century white progressives either supported or tolerated.

Reforming Politics and Government

Progressives of all kinds clamored for the reform of politics and government. But their political activism was motivated by different concerns, and they sometimes pursued competing objectives. Many wanted to change procedures and institutions to promote greater democracy and responsibility. Others hoped to improve the efficiency of government, to eliminate corruption, or to increase their own influence. All justified their objectives as necessary to adapt the political system to the nation's new needs.

Woman Suffrage

One of the most important achievements of the era was woman suffrage. The movement had begun in the mid-nineteenth century, but suffragists had been frustrated by the prevailing belief that women's "proper sphere" was the home and the family. Males dominated the public sphere, including voting. Woman suffrage, particularly when championed as a step toward women's equality, seemed to challenge the natural order of society, and it generated much opposition, not only among men but among traditionalist-minded women as well. "Housewives," announced the Women's Anti-Suffrage Association of Massachusetts, "you do not need a ballot to clean out your sink spout. A handful of potash and some boiling water is quicker."

In the early twentieth century, suffragists began to outflank this opposition. Under a new generation of leaders like Carrie Chapman Catt, they adopted activist tactics, including parades, mass meetings, and "suffrage tours" by automobile. They also organized by political districts and attracted workingwomen and labor unions. By 1917, the National American Woman Suffrage Association had over 2 million members.

But some suffrage leaders shifted arguments to gain more support. They argued for woman suffrage within—not against—traditional ideas about women's role. Rather than insisting on the "justice" of woman suffrage or emphasizing equal rights, they spoke of the special moral and maternal instincts women could bring to politics if allowed to vote. The suffrage movement now appeared less a radical, disruptive force than a vehicle for extending traditional female benevolence and service to society. Many suffragists, particularly among working-class groups, remained committed to the larger possibilities they saw in suffrage, but the new image of the movement increased public support by appealing to conventional views of women. Noted one Nebraska undergraduate, women students no longer feared "antagonizing the men or losing invitations to parties by being suffragists."

Gradually, the suffrage movement began to prevail (see Map 23-1). In 1910, Washington became the first state to approve woman suffrage since the mid-1890s, followed by California in 1911 and Arizona, Kansas, and Oregon in 1912. Suffragists also mounted national action, such as the dramatic inaugural parade in March 1913 described at the beginning of this chapter. The violence surrounding that event outraged public opinion, revived interest in a federal constitutional amendment to grant women the vote, and prompted women to send petitions and organize pilgrimages to Washington from across the country. By 1919, thirty-nine states had established full or partial woman suffrage, and Congress finally approved an amendment. Ratified by the states in 1920, the **Nineteenth Amendment** marked a critical advance in political democracy.

Electoral Reform

Other electoral reforms changed the election process and the meaning of political participation. The so-called **Australian ballot** adopted by most states during the 1890s provided for secret voting, freeing voters from intimidation and making vote buying and other corruption more difficult. It also replaced the individual party tickets with an official ballot listing all candidates and distributed by public officials. The Australian ballot led to quiet, orderly elections. One Cincinnati editor, recalling the "howling mobs" and chaos at the polls in previous elections, declared: "The political bummer and thug has been relegated to the background . . . while good citizenship . . . has come to the front."

Government responsibility for the ballot soon led to public regulation of other parts of the electoral process previously controlled by parties. Be-

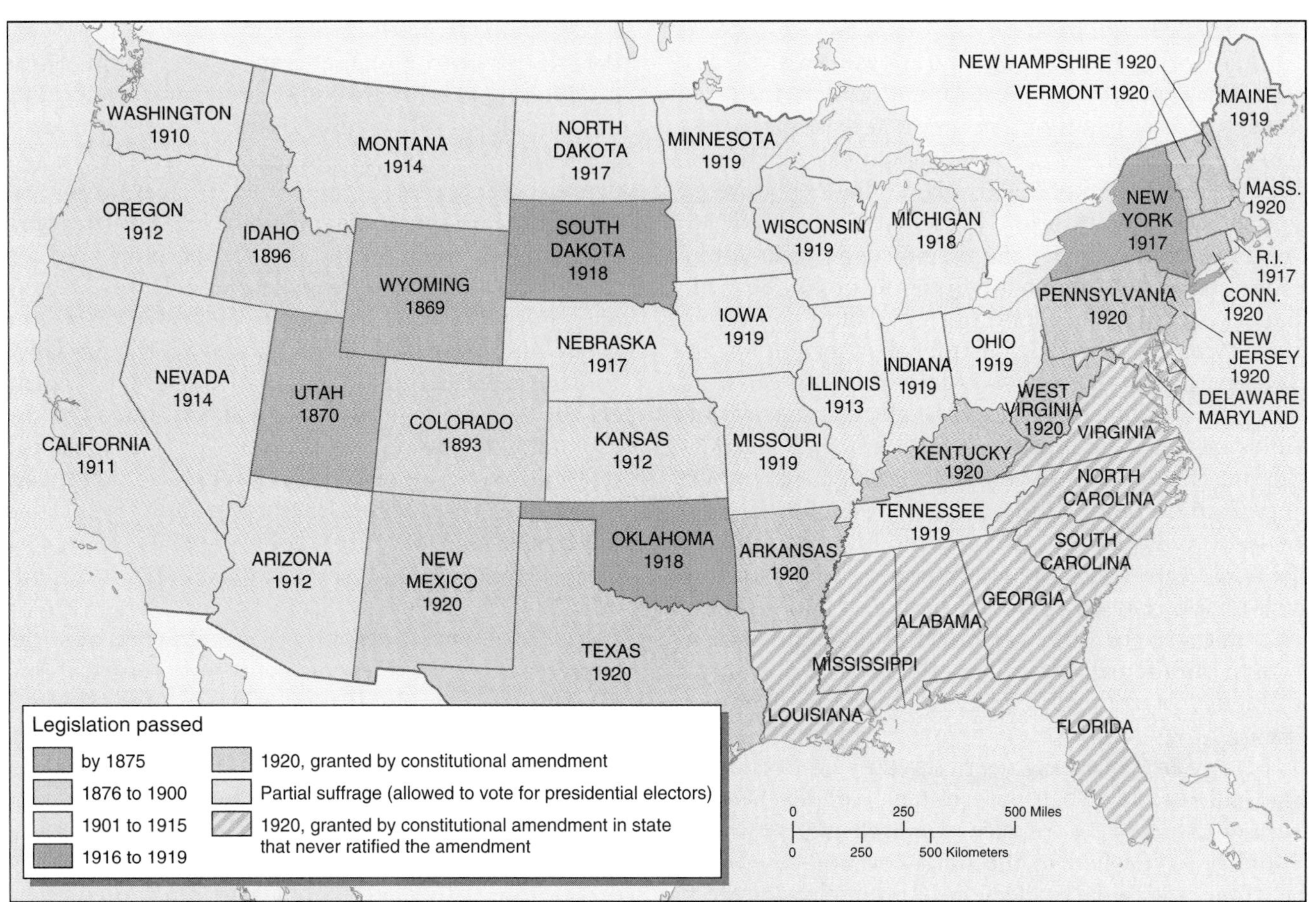

Map 23-1 Woman suffrage in the United States before the ratification of the Nineteenth Amendment.
Beginning with Wyoming in 1869, woman suffrage slowly gained acceptance in the West, but women in the South and much of the East got the ballot only when the Nineteenth Amendment was ratified in 1920.

ginning with Mississippi in 1902, nearly every state provided for direct primaries to remove nominations from the boss-ridden caucus and convention system. Many states also reformed campaign practices.

These reforms weakened the influence of political parties. Their decreasing ability to mobilize voters was reflected in a steady decline in voter participation, from 79 percent in 1896 to 49 percent in 1920. These developments had ominous implications, for parties and voting had traditionally linked ordinary Americans to their government. As parties contracted, nonpartisan organizations and pressure groups, promoting narrower objectives, gained influence. Thus the National Association of Manufacturers (1895) and the United States Chamber of Commerce (1912) lobbied for business interests; the National Farmers Union (1902) for commercial agriculture; the American Federation of Teachers (1916) for professional educators. Many of these special-interest groups represented the same middle- or upper-class interests that had led the attack on parties. Their organized lobbying would give them greater influence over government in the future and contribute to the declining popular belief in the value of voting or participation in politics.

Disfranchisement more obviously undermined American democracy. In the South, Democrats—progressive and conservative alike—eliminated not only black voters but many poor white voters from the electorate through poll taxes, literacy tests, and other restrictions. Republicans in the North adopted educational or literacy tests in ten states, enacted strict registration laws, and gradually abolished the right of aliens to vote. These restrictions reflected both the progressives' anti-immigrant prejudices and their obsessions with social control and with purifying politics and "improving" the electorate. Such electoral reforms reduced the political power of ethnic and working-class Americans, often stripping them of their political rights and means of influence.

Municipal Reform

Antiparty attitudes also affected progressives' efforts to reform municipal government, which they regarded as inefficient and corrupt, at least partly because of the power of urban political machines. Muckrakers had exposed crooked alliances between city bosses and business leaders that resulted in wasteful or inadequate municipal services. In some cities, urban reformers attempted to break these alliances and improve conditions for those suffering most from municipal misrule. For example, in Toledo, Ohio, Samuel "Golden Rule" Jones won enough working-class votes to be elected mayor four times despite the hostility of both major parties. Serving from 1897 to 1904, Jones opened public playgrounds and kindergartens, established the eight-hour day for city workers, and improved public services. Influenced by the Social Gospel, he also provided free lodging for the homeless and gave his own salary to the poor. Other reforming mayors also fought municipal corruption, limited the political influence of corporations, and championed public ownership of utilities.

More elitist progressives attempted to change the structure of urban government. Middle-class reformers worked to replace ward elections, which could be controlled by the neighborhood-based city machine, with at-large elections. To win citywide elections required greater resources and therefore helped swell middle-class influence at the expense of working-class wards. So did nonpartisan elections, which reformers introduced to weaken party loyalties.

Urban reformers developed two other structural innovations: the city commission and the city manager. Both attempted to institutionalize efficient, business-like government staffed by professional administrators. Galveston, Texas, initiated the city commission form in 1901 in response to a crisis in public services following a devastating tidal wave. Staunton, Virginia, appointed a professional city manager to run its government on a nonpartisan basis in 1908. By 1920, hundreds of cities had adopted one of the new plans.

Business groups often promoted these reforms. In Des Moines, for example, the Commercial Club dominated the movement for the city commission in 1906, and its president declared that "the professional politician must be ousted and in his place capable businessmen chosen to conduct the affairs of the city." Again, then, reform in municipal government often shifted political power from ethnic and working-class voters, represented however imperfectly by partisan elections, to smaller groups with greater resources.

Progressive State Government

Progressives also reshaped state government. Some tried to democratize the legislative process, regarding the legislature—the most important branch of state government in the nineteenth century—as ineffective and even corrupt, dominated by party bosses and corporate influences. The Missouri legislature reportedly "enacted such laws as the corporations paid for, and such others as were necessary to fool the people." Populists had first raised such charges in the 1890s and proposed novel solutions: the **initiative** and the **referendum**. The initiative enabled reformers themselves to propose legislation directly to the electorate, bypassing an unresponsive legislature; the referendum permitted voters to approve or reject legislative measures. South Dakota Populists established the first system of "direct legislation" in 1898, and progressives adopted these innovations in twenty other states between 1902 and 1915.

Conservative opponents and procedural difficulties, however, often blocked these reforms. And the reforms could be turned against progressives themselves. In the state of Washington in 1914, an initiative to establish an eight-hour workday was defeated by an electorate alarmed by conservative propaganda, and organized labor had to fight seven referendum measures, such as an antipicketing law, that conservative legislators had promoted. The head of the state federation of labor concluded that the people could be "fooled and confused" when they voted directly on legislation.

Other innovations also expanded the popular role in state government. The **Seventeenth Amendment**, ratified in 1913, provided for the election of U.S. senators directly by popular vote instead of by state legislatures. Beginning with Oregon in 1908, ten states adopted the **recall**, enabling voters to remove unsatisfactory public officials from office.

As state legislatures and party machines were curbed, dynamic governors like Robert La Follette in Wisconsin, Charles Evans Hughes in New York, and Hiram Johnson in California pushed progressive programs into law. Elected governor in 1900, "Fighting Bob" La Follette turned Wisconsin into "the laboratory of democracy." "His words bite like coals of fire," wrote one observer. "He never wearies and he will not allow his audience to weary." Overcoming fierce opposition from "stalwart" Republicans, La Follette established direct primaries, railroad regulation, the first state income tax, workers' compensation, and other important measures before being elected to the U.S. Senate in 1906.

Robert M. LaFollette was a relentless campaigner for progressive reform. Under his leadership, noted Theodore Roosevelt, Wisconsin surpassed all other states "in securing both genuine popular rule and the wise use of the collective power of the people."

La Follette also stressed efficiency and expertise. The Legislative Reference Bureau that he created was staffed by university professors to advise on public policy. He used regulatory commissions to oversee railroads, banks, and other interests. Most states followed suit, and expert commissions became an important feature of state government, gradually gaining authority at the expense of local officials. An observer in Virginia noted in 1912 that the emphasis on efficiency and expertise caused the government to "delegate all new functions, and some old ones, to state departments or commissions instead of to county officers."

"Experts" were presumed to be disinterested and therefore committed to the general welfare. In practice, however, regulators were subject to pressures from competing interest groups, and some commissions became captives of the very industries they were supposed to control. This irony was matched by the contradiction between the expansion of democracy through the initiative and referendum and the increasing reliance on nonelected professional experts to set and implement public policy. Such inconsistencies emphasize the complex mixture of ideas, objectives, and groups that were reshaping politics and government.

Theodore Roosevelt and the Progressive Presidency

When a crazed anarchist assassinated William McKinley in 1901, Theodore Roosevelt entered the White House, and the progressive movement gained its most prominent leader. Though only forty-two years old, Roosevelt had already had a remarkable career. The son of a wealthy New York family, he had been a New York legislator, U.S. civil service commissioner, and assistant secretary of the navy. After his exploits in the Spanish–American War, he was elected governor of New York in 1898 and vice president in 1900. His public life was matched by an active private life in which he both wrote works of history and obsessively pursued what he called the "strenuous life": boxing, wrestling, hunting, rowing, even ranching and chasing rustlers in Dakota Territory. His own son observed that Roosevelt "always wanted to be the bride at every wedding and the corpse at every funeral."

Roosevelt's frenetic activity, aggressive personality, and penchant for self-promotion worried some Americans. Mark Twain fretted that "Mr. Roosevelt is the Tom Sawyer of the political world of the twentieth century; always showing off; always hunting for a chance to show off; in his frenzied imagination the Great Republic is a vast Barnum circus with him for a clown and the whole world for audience." But Roosevelt's flamboyance and ambitions made him the most popular politician of the time and enabled him to dramatize the issues of progressivism and to become the first modern president.

TR and the Modern Presidency

Roosevelt rejected the limited role of Gilded Age presidents. He believed that the president could do anything to meet national needs that the Constitution did not specifically prohibit. "Under this interpretation of executive power," he later recalled, "I did and caused to be done many things not previously done. . . . I did not usurp power, but I did greatly broaden the use of executive power." Indeed, the expansion of government power and its consolidation in the executive branch were among his most significant accomplishments.

Rather than deferring to Congress, Roosevelt exerted legislative leadership. He spelled out his policy goals in more than four hundred messages to Congress, sent drafts of bills to Capitol Hill, and intervened to win passage of "his" measures. Some members of Congress resented such "executive arrogance" and "dictatorship." Roosevelt generally avoided direct challenges to the conservative Old Guard Republicans who controlled Congress, but his activities helped shift the balance of power within the national government.

Roosevelt also reorganized the executive branch. He believed in efficiency and expertise, which he attempted to institutionalize in special commissions and administrative procedures. To promote rational policymaking and public management, he staffed the expanding federal bureaucracy with able professionals. Here, too, he provoked opposition. The president, complained one Republican, was "trying to concentrate all power in Washington . . . and to govern the people by commissions and bureaus."

Finally, Roosevelt encouraged the development of a personal presidency by exploiting the public's interest in their exuberant young president. He established the first White House press room and skillfully handled the mass media. His endless and well-reported activities, from playing with his children in the White House to wrestling, hiking, and horseback-riding with various notables, made him a celebrity, "TR" or "Teddy." The publicity not only kept TR in the spotlight but also enabled him to mold public opinion.

Roosevelt and Labor

One sign of TR's vigorous new approach to the presidency was his handling of a coal strike in 1902. Members of the United Mine Workers Union walked off their jobs, demanding higher wages, an eight-hour day, and recognition of their union. The mine owners closed the mines and waited for the union to collapse. But led by John Mitchell, the strikers held their ranks. The prospect of a freezing winter frightened consumers. Management's stubborn arrogance contrasted with the workers' orderly conduct and willingness to negotiate and hardened public opinion against the owners. TR's legal advisers told him that the government had no constitutional authority to intervene.

As public pressure mounted, however, Roosevelt decided to act. He invited both the owners and the union leaders to the White House and declared that the national interest made government action necessary. Mitchell agreed to negotiate with the owners or to accept an arbitration commission appointed by the president. The owners, however, refused even to speak to the miners and demanded that Roosevelt use the army to break the union, as Cleveland had done in the Pullman strike in 1894.

Roosevelt was not a champion of labor, and he had favored shooting the Pullman strikers. But as president, he believed his role was to mediate social conflict for the public good. Furious with the owners' "arrogant stupidity" and "insulting" attitude toward the presidency, Roosevelt announced that he would use the army to seize and operate the mines, not to crush the union. Questioned about the constitutionality of such an action, Roosevelt bellowed: "To hell with the Constitution when the people want coal." Reluctantly, the owners accepted the arbitration commission they had previously rejected. The commission gave the miners a 10 percent wage increase and a nine-hour day, but not union recognition, and permitted the owners to raise coal prices by 10 percent. Roosevelt described his intervention as simply giving both labor and management a "square deal." It also set important precedents for an active government role in labor disputes and a strong president acting as a steward of the public.

Managing Natural Resources

Federal land policy had helped create farms and develop transportation, but it had also ceded to speculators and business interests much of the nation's forests, mineral deposits, waterpower sites, and grazing lands. Reckless exploitation of these resources alarmed a new generation that believed the public welfare required the **conservation** of natural resources through efficient and scientific management. Conservationists achieved early victories in the Forest Reserve Act (1891) and the Forest Management Act (1897), which authorized the federal government to withdraw timberlands from development and to regulate grazing, lumbering, and hydroelectric sites in the forests (see Map 23-2).

Roosevelt built on these beginnings and his friendship with Gifford Pinchot to make conservation a major focus of his presidency. Pinchot had been trained in French and German scientific forestry practices. Appointed in 1898 to head the new Division of Forestry (renamed the Forest Service in 1905), he brought rational management and regulation to resource development. With his advice, TR used presidential authority to triple the size of the forest reserves to 150 million acres, set aside another 80 million acres valuable for minerals and petroleum, and establish dozens of wildlife refuges. In 1908, Roosevelt held a White House conference of state and federal officials that led to the creation of

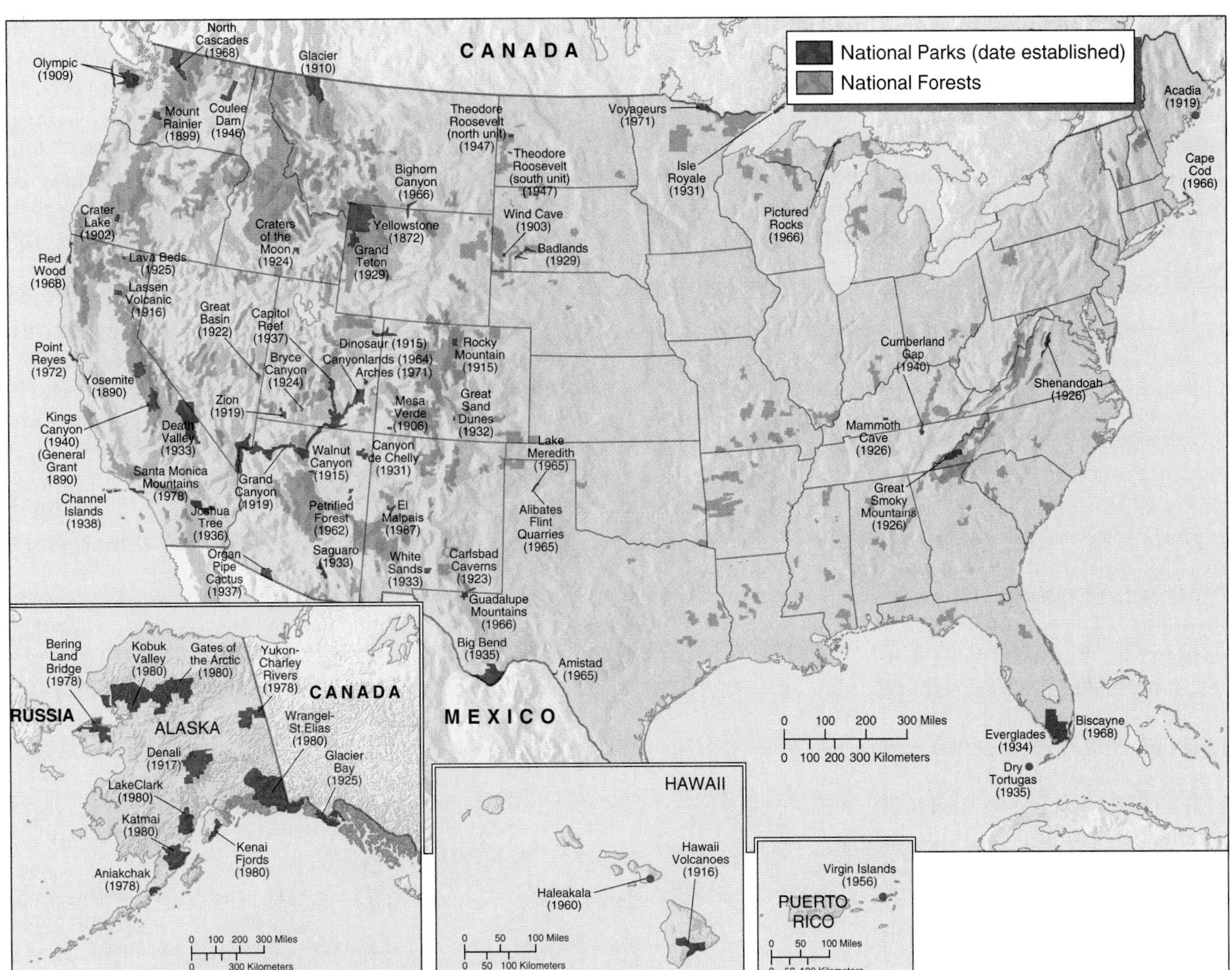

Map 23-2 The growth of National Forests and National Parks.
Rapid exploitation of the West prompted demands to preserve its spectacular scenery and protect its remaining forests. In 1872 Yellowstone became the first National Park, and the National Forest system began in the 1890s. Conservation became increasingly important during the Progressive Era but often provoked western hostility.

the National Conservation Commission, forty-one state conservation commissions, and widespread public support for the conservation movement.

Not everyone, of course, agreed with TR's conservationist policies. Some favored **preservation**, hoping to set aside land as permanent wilderness, whereas Roosevelt favored a scientific and efficient rather than uncontrolled use of resources. Pinchot declared, "Wilderness is waste." Preservationists won some victories, saving a stand of California's giant redwoods and helping create the National Park Service in 1916, but more Americans favored the utilitarian emphasis of early conservationists.

Other interests opposed conservation completely. While some of the larger timber and mineral companies supported conservation as a way to guarantee long-run profits, smaller western entrepreneurs cared only about quick returns. Many Westerners, moreover, resented having Easterners make key decisions about western growth and saw conservation as a perpetuation of this colonial subservience. Many ranchers refused to pay federal grazing fees. Colorado arsonists set forest fires to protest the creation of forest reserves.

But Westerners were happy to take federal money for expensive irrigation projects that private capital would not undertake. They favored the 1902 National Reclamation Act, which established what became the **Bureau of Reclamation**. Its engineers were to construct dams, reservoirs, and irrigation canals, and the government was to sell the irrigated lands in tracts no larger than 160 acres. The act helped shape the modern West. With massive dams and networks of irrigation canals, it reclaimed fertile valleys from the desert. Unfortunately, the bureau did not enforce the 160-acre limitation and thus helped create powerful corporate farms in the West.

Corporate Regulation

Nothing symbolized Roosevelt's active presidency better than his popular reputation as a "trust buster." TR took office at a time of public anxiety about corporate power, but he did not share that anxiety. On the contrary, he regarded the formation of large business combinations to be the result of a natural and beneficial process. But he understood the political implications of the public's concern. Although business leaders and Old Guard conservatives opposed any government intervention in the large trusts, Roosevelt knew better. "You have no conception of the revolt that would be caused if I did nothing," he said privately. To satisfy popular clamor, ensure social stability, and still retain the economic advantages of big modern corporations, TR proposed to "develop an orderly system, and such a system can only come through the gradually exercised right of efficient government control." Rather than invoking "the foolish antitrust law," he favored government regulation to prevent corporate abuses and defend the public interest. "Misconduct," not size, was the issue. Roosevelt preferred to use government agencies to work with corporations to avoid lawsuits. But he did sue some "bad trusts."

In 1902, the Roosevelt administration filed its most famous antitrust suit, against the Northern Securities Company, a holding company organized by J. P. Morgan to control the railroad network of the Northwest. For TR, this suit was an assertion of government power that reassured a worried public and made corporate responsibility more likely. In 1904, the Supreme Court ordered the dissolution of the Northern Securities Company. Ultimately, Roosevelt brought forty-four antitrust suits against business combinations, but, except for a few like Standard Oil, he avoided the giant firms. Many of the cases had inconclusive outcomes, but Roosevelt was more interested in establishing a regulatory role for government than in breaking up big businesses.

Elected president in his own right in 1904 over the colorless and conservative Democratic candidate, Judge Alton B. Parker, Roosevelt responded to the growing popular demand for reform by pushing further toward a regulatory government. He proposed legislation "to work out methods of controlling

Roosevelt enjoyed this cartoon illustrating his distinction between good trusts, restrained by government regulation for the public welfare, and bad trusts. On those he put his foot down.

FROM THEN TO NOW

The Environmental Movement

Many of the issues that concern environmentalists today were first raised by the conservationists and preservationists of the Progressive Era. Conservationists favored the planned and regulated management of America's natural resources for the public benefit. Led by Theodore Roosevelt, they dominated the new agencies like the Forest Service that were responsible for federal lands. In contrast, preservationists—like John Muir, who founded the Sierra Club in 1892—sought to protect wilderness from any development whatsoever. Opposing both were those who championed the uncontrolled development of public lands.

Preservationists' reasons for protecting wilderness were primarily aesthetic—to preserve natural splendors intact for future generations. By the second half of the twentieth century, however, the disturbing consequences of technological change, rapid economic development, and spiraling population growth began to raise the stakes. Air pollution from smokestack industries and automobile exhaust damaged natural vegetation and caused respiratory diseases; water pollution from sewage and chemical waste spread disease; and oil spills fouled beaches and devastated marine habitats.

Public concern over these problems gave birth to the environmental movement, which drew on the legacy of both the conservation and preservation movements but had wider interests and broader support than either. Responding to the environmental movement's quickly growing strength, Congress in the 1970s passed laws to protect endangered species, reduce pollution, limit the use of pesticides, and control hazardous waste. The Environmental Protection Agency, created in 1970, subsequently became the largest federal regulatory agency.

Again, however, as during the Progressive Era, efforts to protect the environment encountered opposition from proponents of unrestricted development, especially in the West. In the Sagebrush Rebellion in the late 1970s and 1980s, some Westerners condemned "outside" federal regulation and tried to seize control of public lands for private exploitation. One oil company dismissed catastrophic oil spills as merely "Mother Earth letting some oil come out."

Three Republican presidents from the West—Californians Richard Nixon and Ronald Reagan and Texan George Bush, all closely tied to oil and real estate interests—sought in varying degrees to curtail environmental policies, agencies, and budgets and to promote development. This repudiation of Theodore Roosevelt's conservationism reflected the shift of the party's base to the sunbelt. As one Nixon adviser said, when a pipeline across the Alaskan wilderness was approved, "Conservation is not in the Republican ethic."

Ronald Reagan in particular was convinced that environmental protection fundamentally conflicted with economic growth. The business executives and corporate lawyers he appointed to key federal positions rescinded or weakened environmental regulations.

Congress, the courts, and the public, however, resisted efforts to weaken environmental policy. "Green" groups proliferated, demanding greater attention to environmental issues; some, like Greenpeace, undertook direct action to protect the environment, and even Western communities organized to oppose strip-mining, nuclear power plants, and toxic waste dumping.

Despite fluctuations, public opinion and mainstream politics now appear to favor greater environmental protection. Debate is sure to continue over the cost and effectiveness of specific policies. But as ever more challenging ecological problems arise—like ozone depletion and global warming—Americans are increasingly inclined to stand with Theodore Roosevelt and John Muir in looking to the federal government for effective action to meet them.

Theodore Roosevelt and John Muir on a 1903 camping trip in Yosemite, which became a national park largely through Muir's activism.

the big corporations without paralyzing the energies of the business community." In 1906, Congress passed the Hepburn Act, the Pure Food and Drug Act, and the Meat Inspection Act. All three were compromises between reformers seeking serious government control of the industries and political defenders and lobbyists of the industries themselves.

The Hepburn Act authorized the Interstate Commerce Commission to set maximum railroad rates and extended its jurisdiction. It was a weaker law than many progressives had wanted, but it marked the first time the federal government gained the power to set rules in a private enterprise. The two other laws aimed at consumer protection in food and drugs. In part, this legislation reflected public demand, but many business leaders also supported government regulation, convinced that it would expand their markets by certifying the quality of their products and drive their smaller competitors out of business. The laws thus did extend government supervision and regulation over business to protect the public health and safety, but they also served some corporate purposes.

Despite the compromises and weaknesses in the three laws, TR contended that they marked "a noteworthy advance in the policy of securing federal supervision and control over corporations." In 1907 and 1908, he pushed for an eight-hour workday, stock market regulation, and inheritance and income taxes. Republican conservatives in Congress blocked such reforms, and tensions increased between the progressive and conservative wings of the party. Old Guard Republicans thought Roosevelt had extended government powers dangerously, but in fact his accomplishments had been relatively modest because of his need to compromise in Congress. As La Follette noted, Roosevelt's "cannonading filled the air with noise and smoke, which confused and obscured the line of action, but, when the battle cloud drifted by and the quiet was restored, it was always a matter of surprise that so little had really been accomplished."

Taft and the Insurgents

TR handpicked his successor as president: a loyal lieutenant, William Howard Taft. Member of a prominent Ohio political family, Taft had been a federal judge, governor-general of the Philippines, and secretary of war. Later he would serve as chief justice of the United States. But if Roosevelt thought that Taft would be a successful president, continuing his policies and holding the Republican party together, he was wrong. Taft's election in 1908, over Democrat William Jennings Bryan in his third presidential campaign, led to a Republican political disaster.

Taft did preside over important progressive achievements. His administration pursued a more active and successful antitrust program than Roosevelt's. He supported the Mann-Elkins Act (1910), which extended the ICC's jurisdiction to telephone and telegraph companies. Taft set aside more public forest lands and oil reserves than Roosevelt had. He also supported a constitutional amendment authorizing an income tax, which went into effect in 1913 under the **Sixteenth Amendment**. One of the most important accomplishments of the Progressive Era, the income tax would provide the means for the government to expand its activities and responsibilities.

Nevertheless, Taft soon alienated progressives and floundered into a political morass. His problems were twofold. First, the Republicans were divided. Midwestern reform Republicans, led by La Follette, clashed with more conservative Republicans led by Senator Nelson Aldrich of Rhode Island. Second, Taft was politically inept. He was unable to mediate between these two groups, and the party split apart.

Reformers wanted to restrict the power of the speaker of the House, "Uncle Joe" Cannon, a reactionary who blocked reform. After seeming to promise support, Taft backed down when conservatives threatened to defeat important legislation. The insurgents in Congress eventually restricted the speaker's powers, but they never forgave what they saw as Taft's betrayal. The tariff also alienated progressives from Taft. He had campaigned in 1908 for a lower tariff to curb inflation, and midwestern Republicans favored tariff reduction to trim the power of big business. But when they introduced tariff reform legislation, the president failed to support them, and Aldrich's Senate committee added 847 amendments, many of which raised tariff rates. Taft justified his inaction as avoiding presidential interference with congressional business, but this excuse clashed with TR's example and the reformers' expectations. Progressives concluded that Taft had sided with the Old Guard against real change.

That perception solidified when Taft stumbled into a controversy over conservation. Gifford Pinchot had become embroiled in a complex struggle with Richard Ballinger, Taft's secretary of the interior. Ballinger, who was closely tied to western mining and lumbering interests, favored private development of public lands. When Pinchot challenged Ballinger's role in a questionable sale of public coal lands in Alaska to a J. P. Morgan syndicate, Taft upheld Ballinger and fired Pinchot. Progressives concluded that Taft had repudiated Roosevelt's conservation policies.

Progressives determined to replace Taft, whom they now saw as an obstacle to reform. In 1911, the National Progressive League organized to champion La Follette for the Republican nomination in 1912. Roosevelt rejected an appeal for support, convinced that a challenge to the incumbent president was both doomed and divisive. Besides, his own position was closer to Taft's than to what he called "the La Follette type of fool radicalism." But Taft's political blunders increasingly angered Roosevelt. Condemning Taft as "disloyal to our past friendship . . . [and] to every canon of ordinary decency," TR began to campaign for the Republican nomination himself. In thirteen state primaries, he won 278 delegates to only 46 for Taft. But most states did not then have primaries; that allowed Taft to dominate the Republican convention and win renomination. Roosevelt's forces formed a third party—the Progressive party—and nominated the former president. The Republican split almost guaranteed victory for the Democratic nominee, Woodrow Wilson.

Woodrow Wilson and Progressive Reform

The pressures for reform called forth many new leaders. The one who would preside over progressivism's culmination, and ultimately its collapse, was Woodrow Wilson. Elected president in 1912 and 1916, he mediated among differing progressive views to achieve a strong reform program, enlarge the power of the executive branch, and make the White House the center of national politics.

The Election of 1912

Despite the prominence of Roosevelt and La Follette, progressivism was not simply a Republican phenomenon. In Congress, southern Democrats more consistently supported reform measures than Republicans did, and Democratic leader William Jennings Bryan surpassed Roosevelt as a persistent advocate of significant reform. As the Republicans quarreled during Taft's administration, Democrats pushed progressive remedies and achieved major victories in the state and congressional elections of 1910. To improve the party's chances in 1912, Bryan announced he would step aside. The Democratic spotlight shifted to the governor of New Jersey, Woodrow Wilson.

A portrait of Woodrow Wilson by Edward Charles Tarbell. A strong president, Wilson led Congress to enact sweeping and significant legislation.

Born in Virginia as the son and grandson of Presbyterian ministers, Wilson combined public eloquence with a cold personality; he balanced a self-righteousness that led to stubborn inflexibility with an intense ambition that permitted the most expedient compromises. Wilson first entered public life as a conservative, steeped in the limited government traditions of the South. As president of Princeton University, beginning in 1902, he became a prominent representative of middle-class respectability and conservative causes. In 1910, New Jersey's Democratic bosses selected him for governor to head off the progressives, but, once in office, Wilson championed popular reforms and immediately began to campaign as a progressive for the party's 1912 presidential nomination.

Wilson's progressivism differed from that of Roosevelt in 1912. TR emphasized a strong government to promote economic and social order. He defended big business as inevitable and healthy provided that government control ensured that it would benefit the entire nation. Roosevelt called this program the **New Nationalism**, reflecting his belief in a powerful state and a national interest. He also supported demands for social welfare, including workers' compensation and the abolition of child labor.

Wilson was horrified by Roosevelt's vision. His **New Freedom** program rejected what he called TR's "regulated monopoly." Wilson wanted "regulated competition," with the goverment's role limited to breaking up monopolies through antitrust action and preventing artificial barriers like tariffs from blocking free enterprise. Wilson opposed social welfare legislation as "paternalistic," reaching beyond the proper scope of the federal government, which he hoped to minimize. (This position, shot back the alarmed Roosevelt, meant the repeal of "every law for the promotion of social and industrial justice.")

Unable to add progressive Democrats to the Republicans who followed him into the Progressive party, TR could not win despite his personal popularity. Other reform voters embraced the Socialist candidate, Eugene V. Debs, who captured 900,000 votes—6 percent of the total. Taft played little role in the campaign. "I might as well give up as far as being a candidate," he lamented. "There are so many people in the country who don't like me."

Wilson won an easy electoral college victory, though he received only 42 percent of the popular vote and fewer popular votes than Bryan had won in any of his three campaigns (see Map 23-3). Roosevelt came in second, Taft third. The Democrats also gained control of Congress, giving Wilson the opportunity to enact his New Freedom program.

Implementing the New Freedom

As president, Wilson built on Roosevelt's precedent to strengthen executive authority. He summoned Congress into special session in 1913 and delivered his message in person, the first president to do so since John Adams. Wilson proposed a full legislative program and worked forcefully to secure its approval. He held regular conferences with Democratic leaders and had a private telephone line installed between the Capitol and the White House to keep tabs on congressional actions. When necessary, he appealed to the public for support or doled out patronage and compromised with conservatives. With such methods and a solid Democratic majority, Wilson gained approval of important laws.

Wilson turned first to the traditional Democratic goal of reducing the high protective tariff, the symbol of special privileges for industry. "The object of the tariff duties," he announced, "must be effective competition." He forced through the **Un-**

Map 23-3 **The Election of 1912.**
The split within the Republican party enabled Woodrow Wilson to carry most states and become president even though he won only a minority of the popular vote.

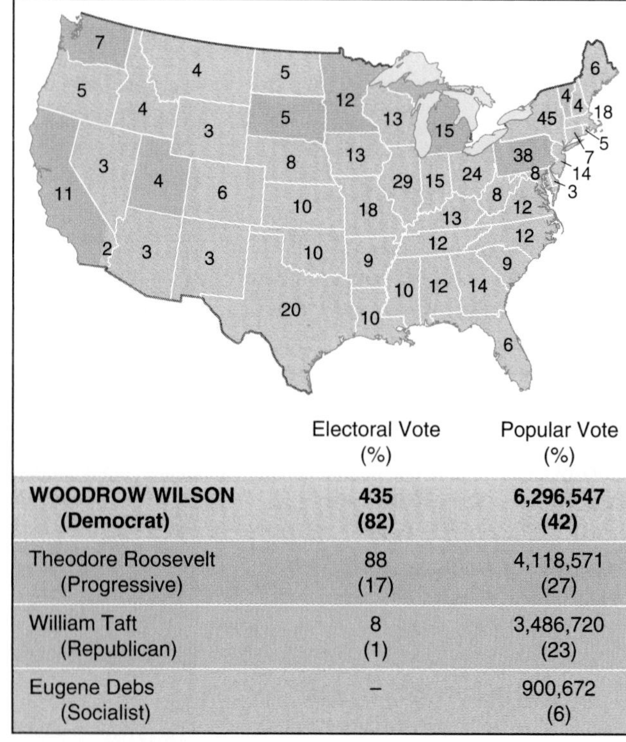

	Electoral Vote (%)	Popular Vote (%)
WOODROW WILSON (Democrat)	**435 (82)**	**6,296,547 (42)**
Theodore Roosevelt (Progressive)	88 (17)	4,118,571 (27)
William Taft (Republican)	8 (1)	3,486,720 (23)
Eugene Debs (Socialist)	–	900,672 (6)

derwood-Simmons Tariff Act of 1913, the first substantial reduction in duties since before the Civil War. The act also levied the first income tax under the recently ratified Sixteenth Amendment. Conservatives condemned the "revolutionary" tax, but it was designed simply to compensate for lower tariff rates. The top tax rate paid by the wealthiest was a mere 7 percent.

Wilson next reformed the nation's banking and currency system, which was inadequate for a modernizing economy. A panic in 1907 and a subsequent congressional investigation had dramatized the need for a more flexible and decentralized financial system. Wilson skillfully maneuvered a compromise measure through Congress, balancing the demands of agrarian progressives for government control with the bankers' desires for private control. The **Federal Reserve Act** of 1913 created twelve regional Federal Reserve banks that, although privately controlled, were to be supervised by the Federal Reserve Board, appointed by the president. The law also provided for a flexible national currency and improved access to credit. Serious problems remained, but the new system promoted the progressive goals of order and efficiency and fulfilled Wilson's New Freedom principle of introducing limited government regulation while preserving private business control.

Wilson's third objective was new legislation to break up monopolies. To this end, he initially supported the Clayton antitrust bill, which prohibited unfair trade practices and sharply restricted holding companies. But when business leaders and other progressives strenuously objected, Wilson reversed himself. Opting for continuous federal regulation rather than for the dissolution of trusts, Wilson endorsed the creation of the **Federal Trade Commission (FTC)** to oversee business activity and prevent illegal restrictions on competition.

The Federal Trade Commission Act of 1914 dismayed many of Wilson's early supporters because it embraced the New Nationalism's emphasis on positive regulation. Roosevelt's 1912 platform had proposed a federal trade commission; Wilson now accepted what he had earlier denounced as a partnership between trusts and the government that the trusts would dominate. Indeed, Wilson's conservative appointments to the FTC ensured that the agency would not seriously interfere with business, and by the 1920s, the FTC had become virtually a junior partner of the business community.

The fate of the Clayton antitrust bill after Wilson withdrew his support reflected his new attitude toward big business. Congressional conservatives gutted the bill with crippling amendments before permitting it to become law in 1914. As one senator complained, "When the Clayton bill was first written, it was a raging lion with a mouth full of teeth. It has degenerated to a tabby cat with soft gums, a plaintive mew, and an anemic appearance. It is a sort of legislative apology to the trusts, delivered hat in hand, and accompanied by assurances that no discourtesy is intended."

Wilson now announced that no further reforms were necessary—astonishing many progressives whose objectives had been completely ignored. Wilson refused to support woman suffrage and helped kill legislation abolishing child labor and expanding credits to farmers. Race relations provided a flagrant instance of Wilson's indifference to social justice issues. Raised in the South, he believed in segregation and backed the southern Democrats in his cabinet when they introduced formal segregation within the government itself. Government offices, shops, restrooms, and restaurants were all segregated; employees who complained were fired. Federal officials in the South discharged black employees wholesale. One Georgia official promised there would be no more government jobs for African Americans: "A Negro's place is in the cornfield."

The Expansion of Reform

Wilson had won in 1912 only because the Republicans had split. By 1916, Roosevelt had returned to the GOP, and Wilson realized that he had to attract some of TR's former followers. Wilson therefore abandoned his opposition to social and economic reforms aiding specific groups and promoted measures he had previously condemned as paternalistic and unconstitutional. But he had also grown in the White House and now recognized that some problems could be resolved only by positive federal action. "Old political formulas," he said, "do not fit the present."

To assist farmers, Wilson in 1916 convinced Congress to pass the Federal Farm Loan Act. This law, which Wilson himself had rejected twice earlier, provided farmers with federally financed, long-term agricultural credits. The Warehouse Act of 1916 improved short-term agricultural credit. The Highway Act of 1916 provided funds to construct and improve rural roads through the adoption of the "dollar-matching" principle by which the federal government would expand its power over state activities in the twentieth century.

Wilson and the Democratic Congress also reached out to labor. Wilson signed the Keating-Owen

Act prohibiting the interstate shipment of products made by child labor. In 1902, Wilson had denounced Roosevelt's intervention in the coal strike, but in 1916 he broke a labor-management impasse and averted a railroad strike by helping pass the Adamson Act establishing an eight-hour day for railway workers. Wilson also pushed the Kern-McGillicuddy Act, which achieved the progressive goal of a workers' compensation system for federal employees. Together, these laws marked an important advance toward government regulation of the labor market.

Wilson also promoted activist government when he nominated Louis Brandeis to the Supreme Court. Known as the "people's lawyer," Brandeis had successfully defended protective labor legislation before the conservative judiciary. The nomination outraged conservatives, including William Howard Taft and the American Bar Association. Brandeis was the first Jew nominated to the court, and anti-Semitism motivated some of his opponents. Wilson overcame a vicious campaign against Brandeis and secured his confirmation.

By these actions, Wilson brought progressivism to a culmination of sorts and consolidated reformers behind him for a second term. Less than a decade earlier, Wilson the private citizen had assailed government regulation and social legislation; by 1916, he had guided an unprecedented expansion of federal power. His own transformation symbolized the development of progressivism itself.

Conclusion

In the early twentieth century, progressive reformers responded to the tensions of industrial and urban development by moving to change society and government. Rejecting an earlier emphasis on individualism and laissez-faire, they organized to promote social change and an interventionist state. Programs and laws to protect women, children, and injured workers testified to their compassion; the creation of new agencies and political techniques indicated their interest in order and efficiency; campaigns to end corruption, whether perceived in urban political machines, corporate influence, drunkeness, or "inferior" immigrants, illustrated their self-assured vision of the public good.

Progressivism had its ironies and paradoxes. It called for democratic reforms—and did achieve woman suffrage, direct legislation, and popular election of senators—but helped disfranchise black Southerners and northern immigrants. It advocated social justice but often enforced social control. It demanded responsive government but helped create bureaucracies largely removed from popular control. It endorsed the regulation of business in the public interest but forged regulatory laws and commissions that tended to aid business. Some of these seeming contradictions reflected the persistence of traditional attitudes and the necessity to accommodate conservative opponents; others revealed the progressives' own limitations in vision, concern, or nerve.

But both the successes and the failures of progressivism revealed that the nature of politics and government had changed significantly. Americans had come to accept that government action could resolve social and economic problems, and the role and power of government expanded accordingly. The emergence of an activist presidency, capable of developing programs, mobilizing public opinion, directing Congress, and taking forceful action, epitomized this key development.

These important features would be crucial when the nation fought World War I, which brought new challenges and dangers to the United States. The Great War would expose many of the limitations of progressivism and the naiveté of the progressives' optimism.

Review Questions

1. How and why did the presidency change during the Progressive Era?
2. How did the progressive concern for efficiency affect social reform efforts, public education, government administration, and rural life?
3. How and why did the relationship between business and government change during this time?
4. Why did social reform and social control often intermingle in the Progressive Era? Can such objectives be separate?
5. What factors, old and new, stimulated the reform movements of progressivism?
6. How did the role of women change during the Progressive Era? How did that affect progressivism itself?

Recommended Reading

Jane Addams, *Twenty Years at Hull House* (1910). Jane Addams's own classic story of settlement work.

Kendrick A. Clements, *The Presidency of Woodrow Wilson* (1992). An excellent book that provides important new information on both Wilson and the presidency.

William Deverell and Tom Sitton, *California Progressivism Revisited* (1994). A valuable collection of essays that examines the complex motivations underlying progressivism in California.

Steven J. Diner, *A Very Different Age: Americans of the Progressive Era* (1998). An engaging survey of the era, stressing social history.

Lewis L. Gould, *The Presidency of Theodore Roosevelt* (1991). A balanced and comprehensive account of TR's presidency.

Arthur S. Link and Richard L. McCormick, *Progressivism* (1983). A superb brief analysis of the complexities and scholarly interpretations of progressivism.

Upton Sinclair, *The Jungle* (1906). The most famous muckraking novel.

Robert Wiebe, *The Search for Order, 1877–1920.* (1967). A masterful essay that emphasizes the organizational thrust of middle-class progressives.

Additional Sources

The Ferment of Reform

Karen Blair, *The Clubwoman as Feminist: True Womanhood Redefined, 1868–1914* (1980).

John W. Chambers, *The Tyranny of Change* (2nd ed., 1992).

Ellen Chesler, *Woman of Valor: The Life of Margaret Sanger* (1992).

Nancy Cott, *The Grounding of Modern Feminism* (1987).

Robert Crunden, *Ministers of Reform* (1982).

David B. Danbom, *"The World of Hope": Progressives and the Struggle for an Ethical Public Life* (1987).

Melvyn Dubofsky, *We Shall Be All: A History of the Industrial Workers of the World* (1969).

Susan A. Glenn, *Daughters of the Shtetl* (1990).

Eric Goldman, *Rendezvous with Destiny* (1952).

Alan Kraut, *The Huddled Masses: The Immigrant in American Society, 1880–1921* (1982).

George Marsden, *Fundamentalism and American Culture* (1980).

Henry May, *Protestant Churches and Industrial America* (1949).

Kathy Peiss, *Cheap Amusements: Working Women and Leisure in Turn-of-the-Century New York* (1986).

Nick Salvatore, *Eugene V. Debs: Citizen and Socialist* (1982).

Anne Firor Scott, *Natural Allies: Women's Associations in American History* (1991).

Elliott Shore, *Talkin' Socialism: J. A. Wayland and the Role of the Press in American Radicalism* (1988).

Margaret Spruill Wheeler, *New Women of the New South* (1993).

Reforming Society

Paul Boyer, *Urban Masses and Moral Order in America* (1978).

Mina Carson, *Settlement Folk: Social Thought and the American Settlement Movement* (1990).

Ruth H. Crocker, *Social Work and Social Order* (1992).

David Danbom, *The Resisted Revolution: Urban America and the Industrialization of Agriculture* (1979).

Allen F. Davis, *American Heroine: The Life and Legend of Jane Addams* (1973).

Allen F. Davis, *Spearheads of Reform: The Social Settlements and the Progressive Movement* (1968).

John Dittmer, *Black Georgia in the Progressive Era* (1977).

Lyle Dorsett, *Billy Sunday and the Redemption of Urban America* (1991).

Nancy S. Dye, *As Equals and as Sisters: Feminism, the Labor Movement, and the Women's Trade Union League of New York* (1980).

Noralee Frankel and Nancy S. Dye, *Gender, Class, Race, and Reform in the Progressive Era* (1991).

Louis Harlan, *Booker T. Washington: The Wizard of Tuskegee* (1983).

John Higham, *Strangers in the Land: Patterns of American Nativism* (1963).

Molly Ladd-Taylor, *Mother-Work: Women, Child Welfare, and the State, 1890-1930* (1994).

Kriste Lindenmeyer, *A Right to Childhood: The U.S. Children's Bureau and Child Welfare* (1997).

William A. Link, *The Paradox of Southern Progressivism* (1992).

Roy Lubove, *The Progressives and the Slums* (1962).

Robyn Muncy, *Creating a Female Dominion in American Reform, 1890–1935* (1991).

Daniel Nelson, *Frederick W. Taylor and the Rise of Scientific Management* (1980).

Elizabeth Anne Payne, *Reform, Labor, and Feminism: Margaret Dreier Robins and the Women's Trade Union League* (1988).

James Timberlake, *Prohibition and the Progressive Movement* (1963).

Nancy Woloch, *Women and the American Experience* (1984).

Reforming Politics and Government

John D. Buenker, *Urban Liberalism and Progressive Reform* (1973).

Ellen Carol DuBois, *Harriot Stanton Blatch and the Winning of Woman Suffrage* (1997).

Sara Hunter Graham, *Woman Suffrage and the New Democracy* (1996).

Dewey Grantham, *Southern Progressivism* (1983).

William F. Holmes, *The White Chief: James Kimble Vardaman* (1970).

Jack Temple Kirby, *Darkness at the Dawning: Race and Reform in the Progressive South* (1972).

J. Morgan Kousser, *The Shaping of Southern Politics* (1974).

Richard L. McCormick, *From Realignment to Reform: Political Change in New York State, 1893–1910* (1983).

Michael E. McGerr, *The Decline of Popular Politics* (1986).

John F. Reynolds, *Testing Democracy: Electoral Behavior and Progressive Reform in New Jersey* (1988).

Martin Schiesl, *The Politics of Efficiency: Municipal Administration and Reform in America* (1977).

David P. Thelen, *The New Citizenship: Origins of Progressivism in Wisconsin* (1972).

David P. Thelen, *Robert M. La Follette and the Insurgent Spirit* (1976).

Robert F. Wesser, *Charles Evans Hughes: Politics and Reform in New York State* (1967).

James E. Wright, *The Progressive Yankees: Republican Reformers in New Hampshire* (1987).

Theodore Roosevelt and the Progressive Presidency

John M. Blum, *The Republican Roosevelt* (1954).

David Burton, *The Learned Presidency: Theodore Roosevelt, William Howard Taft, Woodrow Wilson* (1988).

Paolo Coletta, *The Presidency of William Howard Taft* (1973).

William H. Harbaugh, *Power and Responsibility: The Life and Times of Theodore Roosevelt* (1961).

Samuel P. Hays, *Conservation and the Gospel of Efficiency: The Progressive Conservation Movement* (1962).

Morton Keller, *Regulating a New Economy* (1990).

Gabriel Kolko, *The Triumph of Conservatism* (1963).

Edmund Morris, *The Rise of Theodore Roosevelt* (1979).

George E. Mowry, *The Era of Theodore Roosevelt, 1900–1912* (1958).

Martin Sklar, *The Corporate Reconstruction of American Capitalism* (1988).

Donald Worster, *Rivers of Empire: Water, Aridity, and the Growth of the American West* (1985).

Woodrow Wilson and Progressive Reform

John M. Blum, *Woodrow Wilson and the Politics of Morality* (1956).

Kendrick A. Clements, *Woodrow Wilson* (1987).

John Milton Cooper, Jr., *The Warrior and the Priest: Woodrow Wilson and Theodore Roosevelt* (1983).

Lewis L. Gould, *Reform and Regulation: American Politics, 1900–1916* (1978).

August Heckshер, *Woodrow Wilson* (1991).

Arthur Link, *Woodrow Wilson and the Progressive Era* (1954).

James Livingston, *Origins of the Federal Reserve System* (1986).

David Sarasohn, *The Party of Reform: Democrats in the Progressive Era* (1989).

Melvin Urofsky, *Louis D. Brandeis and the Progressive Tradition* (1981).

Where to Learn More

❖ **John Muir National Historic Site, Martinez, California.** The architecture and furnishings of this seventeen-room house reflect the interests of John Muir, the writer and naturalist who founded the Sierra Club and led the preservationists in the Progressive Era.

❖ **National Museum of American History, Smithsonian Institution, Washington, D.C.** A permanent exhibition, "Parlor to Politics: Women and Reform, 1890–1925," uses design, artifacts, and recent scholarship to vividly illustrate the changing role of women in the Progressive Era. It effectively emphasizes their work in settlement houses and their growing politicization and demonstrates the importance of the work of black women's organizations.

❖ **Hull House, Chicago, Illinois.** This pioneering settlement house is now a museum on the campus of the University of Illinois, Chicago.

❖ **Lowell National Historic Park, Lowell, Massachusetts.** "The Working People," a permanent exhibition, uses artifacts and photographs to chart the activities of immigrant workers at different times in the past, particularly during the Progressive Era.

❖ **Lower East Side Tenement Museum, New York City, New York.** A six-story tenement building containing twenty-two apartments, this museum vividly illustrates the congested and unhealthy living conditions of urban immigrants from the 1870s to the early twentieth century.

❖ **Sagamore Hill, Oyster Bay, New York.** Theodore Roosevelt's home is now a National Historic Site and open to the public.

❖ **William Howard Taft National Historic Site, Cincinnati, Ohio.** Taft was born in this house, the only national Taft memorial. An informative tour focuses on Taft's public and private life.

❖ **Staunton, Virginia.** The birthplace and childhood home of Woodrow Wilson, restored with period furnishings, reveals many of the influences that shaped Wilson's career.

Creating an Empire, 1865–1917

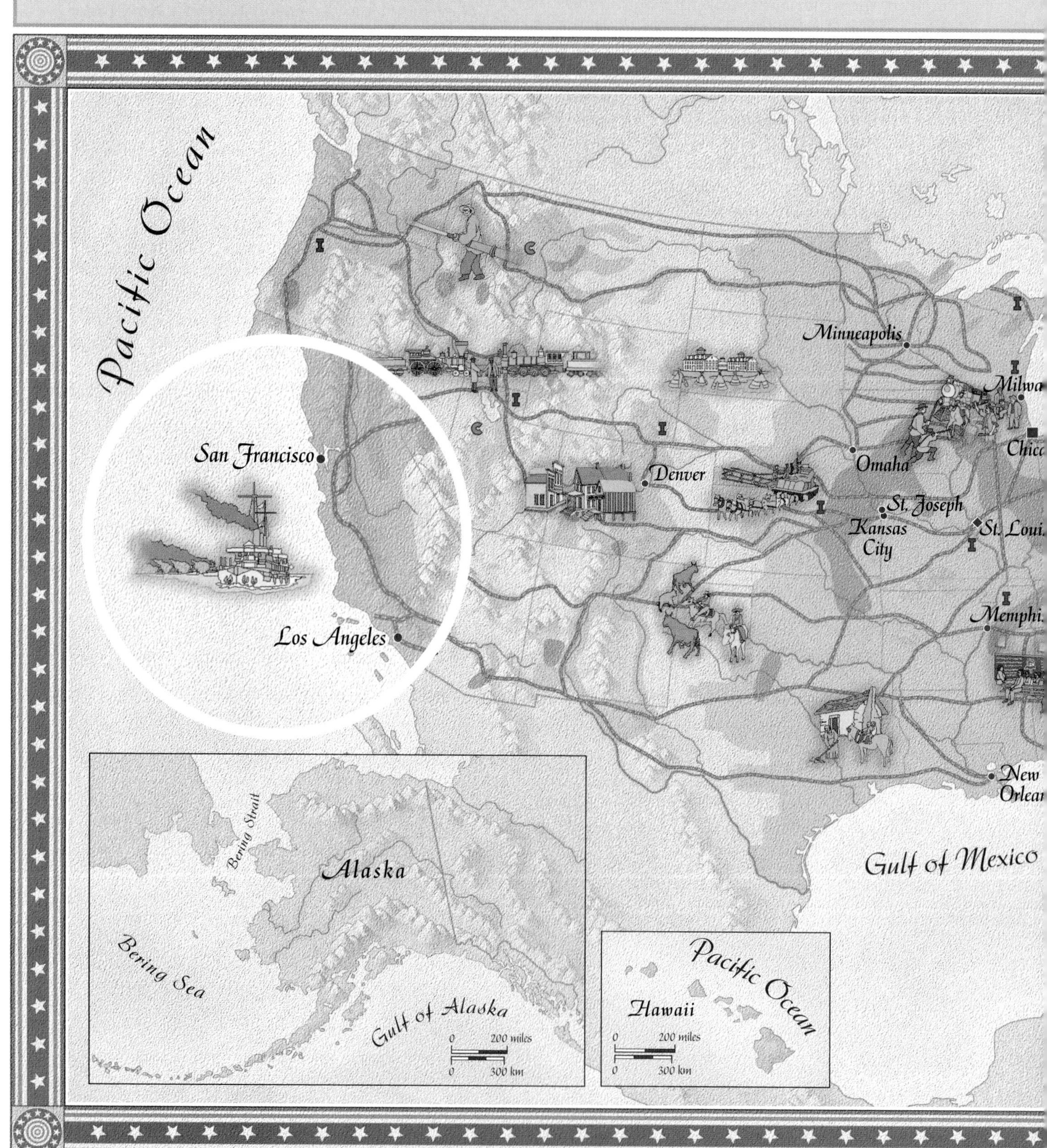

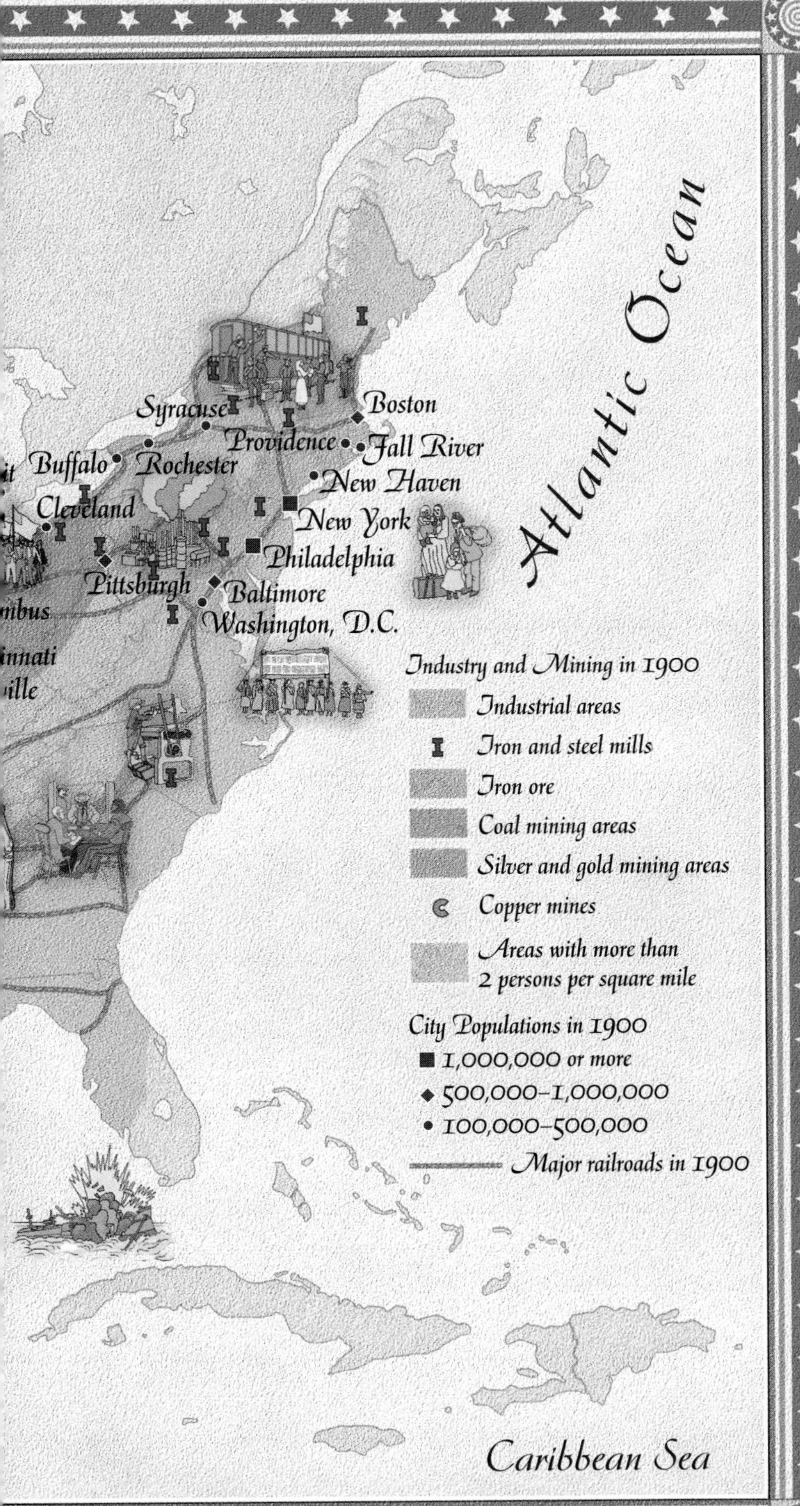

24

Chapter Outline

Key Topics

- Why the United States became an imperial power in the 1890s
- The Spanish-American War and the colonial empire the United States gained as a result
- U.S. involvement in Asia, and the tensions with Japan that resulted
- U.S. predominance in the Caribbean and Latin America

In 1898, the United States became embroiled in the **Spanish-American War** over Spanish policies in Cuba. The smashing U.S. victory in that conflict triggered a nationwide debate over the terms of the peace settlement in the **Treaty of Paris**. In the U.S. Senate, which had the constitutional duty to ratify or reject the treaty, in the nation's newspapers, and in the streets and pulpits, people argued vociferously over whether the country should acquire the Spanish colony of the Philippines. Many Americans opposed expanding beyond North America; some viewed the acquisition of a colony as repudiating America's historic political principles. Republican Albert Beveridge of Indiana responded to such arguments in speeches across the nation: America's acquisition of the Philippines, he declared, was "God's great purpose made manifest in the instincts of our race, whose present phase is our personal profit, but whose far-off end is the redemption of the world and the Christianization of mankind."

In a single sentence, Beveridge had linked the ideas that coalesced in the 1890s to propel the United States to broaden its role in world affairs. Demands for economic expansion, a belief in national mission, a sense of responsibility to help others, the missionary impulses of religion, and racist convictions combined in an uneasy mixture of self-interest and idealism. Such a variety of motives—to say nothing of the positive spin that orators like Beveridge could impart to them—helped garner support for the new policies that the nation's leaders adopted, including acquisition of the Philippines.

But even Beveridge presented too simple a picture. He did not anticipate the consequences, not just for Americans but for Filipinos, Cubans, Puerto Ricans, and others who rarely perceived American motives or American actions as positively as Beveridge and other proponents of imperial expansion. Military victory in the Spanish-American War provided the United States with an extensive empire, status as a world power, and opportunities and problems that would long shape American foreign policy.

The Roots of Imperialism

The United States had a long-established tradition of expansion across the continent. Through purchase, negotiation, or conquest, the vast Louisiana Territory, Florida, Texas, New Mexico, California, and Oregon had become U.S. territory. Indeed, by the 1890s, Republican Senator Henry Cabot Lodge of Massachusetts boasted that Americans had "a record of conquest, colonization, and territorial expansion unequalled by any people in the nineteenth century." Lodge now urged the country to build an overseas empire, emulating the European model of **imperialism** based on the acquisition and exploitation of colonial possessions. Other Americans favored a less formal empire, in which U.S. interests and influence would be assured through extensive trade and investments rather than through military occupation. Still others advocated a cultural expansionism in which the nation exported its ideals and institutions. All such expansionists could draw from many sources to support their plans. Some cited political, religious, and racial ideas; some were concerned with national security and power; others pointed to economic trends at home and abroad (see the overview table, "Rationales for Imperialism").

Ideological Arguments

Scholars, authors, politicians, and religious leaders provided interlocking ideological arguments for the new imperialism. Some intellectuals, for example, invoked social Darwinism, maintaining that the United States should engage in a competitive struggle for wealth and power with other nations. "The survival of the fittest," declared one writer, was "the law of nations as well as a law of nature." As European nations expanded into Asia and Africa in the 1880s and 1890s, seeking colonies, markets, and raw materials, these advocates argued that the United States had to adopt similar policies to ensure national success.

OVERVIEW

RATIONALES FOR IMPERIALISM

Category	Beliefs
Racism and social Darwinism	Convictions that "Anglo-Saxons" were racially superior and should dominate other peoples, either to ensure national success, establish international stability, or benefit the "inferior" races by imposing American ideas and institutions on them
Righteousness	The conviction that Christianity, and a supporting American culture, should be aggressively spread among the benighted peoples of other lands
Mahanism	The conviction, following the ideas advanced by Alfred Thayer Mahan, that U.S. security required a strong navy and economic and territorial expansion
Economics	A variety of arguments holding that American prosperity depended on acquiring access to foreign markets, raw materials, and investment opportunities

Related to social Darwinism was a pervasive belief in racial inequality and, particularly, in the superiority of people of English, or Anglo-Saxon, descent. To many Americans, the industrial progress, military strength, and political development of England and the United States were proof of an Anglo-Saxon superiority that carried with it a responsibility to extend the blessings of their rule to less-able people. John Fiske, a philosopher and historian, popularized these ideas in his oft-repeated lecture "Manifest Destiny." "The work which the English race began when it colonized North America," Fiske declaimed, "is destined to go on until every land on the earth's surface that is not already the seat of an old civilization shall become English in its language, in its religion, in its political habits and traditions, and to a predominant extent in the blood of its people." As a popular expression put it, colonialism was the "white man's burden," carrying with it a duty to aid and uplift other peoples. Such attitudes led some expansionists to favor imposing American ideas and practices on other cultures, regardless of those cultures' own values and customs. The political scientist John W. Burgess, for example, concluded that Anglo-Saxons "must have a colonial policy" and "righteously assume sovereignty" over "incompetent" or "barbaric races" in other lands.

American missionaries also promoted expansionist sentiment. Hoping to evangelize the world, American religious groups increased the number of Protestant foreign missions sixfold from 1870 to 1900. Women in particular organized foreign missionary societies and served in the missions. Missionaries publicized their activities throughout the United States, generating interest in foreign developments and support for what one writer called the "imperialism of righteousness." Abroad they pursued a religious transformation that often resembled a cultural conversion, for they promoted trade, developed business interests, and encouraged westernization through technology and education as well as religion. Sometimes, as in the Hawaiian Islands, American missionaries even promoted annexation by the United States.

Indeed, the American religious press endlessly repeated the themes of national destiny, racial superiority, and religious zeal. The Reverend J. H. Barrows in early 1898 lectured on the "Christian conquest of Asia," suggesting that American Christianity and commerce would cross the Pacific to fulfill "the manifest destiny of the Christian Republic." Missionaries also contributed to the imperial impulse by describing their work, as Barrows did, in terms of the "conquest" of "enemy" territory. Thus while missionaries were motivated by what they considered to be idealism and often brought real benefits to other lands, especially in education and health, religious sentiments reinforced the ideology of American expansion.

Strategic Concerns

Other expansionists were motivated by strategic concerns, shaped by what seemed to be the forces of history and geography. America's location in the Western Hemisphere, its coastlines on two oceans, and the ambitions and activities of other nations, particularly Germany and Britain, convinced some

An American missionary and her Chinese converts study the Bible in Manchuria in 1903 under a U.S. flag. American missionaries wanted to spread the Gospel abroad but inevitably spread American influence as well.

Americans that the United States had to develop new policies to protect and promote its national security and interests. Alfred Thayer Mahan, a naval officer and president of the Naval War College, emphasized the importance of a strong navy for national greatness in his book *The Influence of Sea Power upon History.* To complement that navy, Mahan proposed that the United States build a canal across the isthmus of Panama to link its coasts, acquire naval bases in the Caribbean and the Pacific to protect the canal, and annex Hawaii and other Pacific islands to promote trade and service the fleet. The United States must "cast aside the policy of isolation which befitted her infancy," Mahan declared, and "begin to look outward."

Mahanism found a receptive audience. President Benjamin Harrison declared in 1891 that "as to naval stations and points of influence, we must look forward to a departure from the too conservative opinions which have been held heretofore." Still more vocal advocates of Mahan's program were a group of nationalistic Republicans, predominantly from the Northeast. They included politicians like Henry Cabot Lodge and Theodore Roosevelt, journalists like Whitelaw Reid of the *New York Tribune* and Albert Shaw of the *Review of Reviews,* and diplomats and lawyers like John Hay and Elihu Root.

Conscious of European colonialism, such men favored imperial expansion, as Shaw wrote, "for the sake of our destiny, our dignity, our influence, and our usefulness." Roosevelt promoted Mahan's ideas when he became assistant secretary of the navy in 1897, but he was even more militaristic. Praising "the most valuable of all qualities, the soldierly virtues," Roosevelt declared in 1897: "No triumph of peace is quite so great as the supreme triumphs of war." One British observer concluded on the eve of the Spanish-American War that Mahan's influence had transformed the American spirit, serving "as oil to the flame of 'colonial expansion' everywhere leaping into life" (see "American Views: An Imperialist Views the World").

Even so, Mahan was not solely responsible for the large navy policy popular among imperialists. Its origins went back to 1881, when Congress established the Naval Advisory Board, which successfully lobbied for larger naval appropriations. An extensive program to replace the navy's obsolete wooden ships with modern cruisers and battleships was well under way by 1890 when the first volume of Mahan's book appeared. The United States soon possessed the formidable navy the expansionists wanted. This larger navy, in turn, demanded strategic bases and coaling stations. One writer indicated the circular nature of this development by noting in 1893 that Manifest Destiny now meant "the acquisition of such territory, far and near," that would secure "to our navy facilities desirable for the operations of a great naval power."

Economic Designs

One reason for the widespread support for a larger navy was its use to expand and protect America's international trade. Nearly all Americans favored economic expansion through foreign trade. Such a policy promised national prosperity: larger markets for manufacturers and farmers, greater profits for

Chronology

1861–1869	Seward serves as secretary of state.
1867	U.S. purchases Alaska from Russia.
1870	Annexation of the Dominican Republic is rejected.
1881	Naval Advisory Board is created.
1887	United States gains naval rights to Pearl Harbor.
1889	First Pan-American Conference is held.
1890	Alfred Thayer Mahan publishes *The Influence of Sea Power upon History.*
1893	Harrison signs but Cleveland rejects a treaty for the annexation of Hawaii.
1893–1897	Depression increases interest in economic expansion abroad.
1894–1895	Sino-Japanese War is fought.
1895	U.S. intervenes in Great Britain–Venezuelan boundary dispute. Cuban insurrection against Spain begins.
1896	William McKinley is elected president on an imperialist platform.
1898	Spanish-American War is fought. Hawaii is annexed. Anti-Imperialist League is organized. Treaty of Paris is signed.
1899–1902	Filipino-American War is fought.
1899	Open Door note is issued.
1901	Theodore Roosevelt becomes president.
1903	Platt Amendment restricts Cuban autonomy. Panama "revolution" is abetted by the United States.
1904	United States acquires the Panama Canal Zone. Roosevelt Corollary is announced.
1904–1905	Russo-Japanese War is fought.
1905	Treaty of Portsmouth ends the Russo-Japanese War through U.S. mediation.
1906–1909	United States occupies Cuba.
1907–1908	Gentlemen's Agreement restricts Japanese immigration.
1909	United States intervenes in Nicaragua.
1912–1933	United States occupies Nicaragua.
1914	Panama Canal opens.
1914–1917	United States intervenes in Mexico.
1915–1934	United States occupies Haiti.
1916–1924	United States occupies the Dominican Republic.
1917	Puerto Ricans are granted U.S. citizenship.
1917–1922	United States occupies Cuba.

merchants and bankers, more jobs for workers. Far fewer favored the acquisition of colonies that was characteristic of European imperialism. Commercial, as opposed to colonial, goals were the primary objective. As one diplomat declared in 1890, the nation was more interested in the "annexation of trade" than in the annexation of territory.

The United States had long aggressively fostered American trade, especially in Latin America and East Asia. As early as 1844, the United States had negotiated a trade treaty with China, and ten years later a squadron under Commodore Matthew Perry had forced the Japanese to open their ports to American products. In the late nineteenth century, the dramatic expansion of the economy caused many Americans to favor more government action to open foreign markets to American exports. Alabama Senator John Morgan had the cotton and textiles produced in the New South in mind when he warned in 1882: "Our home market is not equal to the demands of our producing and manufacturing classes and to the capital which is seeking employment. . . . We must either enlarge the field of our traffic, or stop the business of manufacturing just where it is." More ominous, a naval officer trying to open Korea to U.S. products declared in 1878, "At least one-third of our mechanical and agricultural products are now in excess of our wants, and we must *export* these products or *deport* the people who are creating them."

Exports, particularly of manufactured goods, which grew ninefold between 1865 and 1900, did increase greatly in the late nineteenth century. Still, periodic depressions fed these fears of overproduction. The massive unemployment and social unrest

American Views

An Imperialist Views the World

Theodore Roosevelt, Henry Cabot Lodge, Alfred Thayer Mahan, and other influential imperialists frequently corresponded with one another, expressing their views forcefully if not always in depth. The following excerpts are from Roosevelt's private correspondence in 1897, while he was assistant secretary of the Navy and before the Spanish-American War began.

❖ **In what ways does Roosevelt reflect the influence of Mahan?**

❖ **What is Roosevelt's view of war?**

❖ **How does Roosevelt view European nations?**

❖ **How does he view the independence of other nations in the Western Hemisphere?**

I suppose that I need not tell you that as regards Hawaii I take your views absolutely, as indeed I do on foreign policy generally. If I had my way we would annex those islands tomorrow. If that is impossible I would establish a protectorate over them. I believe we should build the Nicaraguan canal at once, and in the meantime that we should build a dozen new battleships, half of them on the Pacific Coast; and these battleships should have a large coal capacity and a consequent increased radius of action. . . . I think President Cleveland's action [in rejecting the annexation of Hawaii] was a colossal crime, and we should be guilty of aiding him after the fact if we do not reverse what he did. I earnestly hope we can make the President [McKinley] look at things our way. Last Saturday night Lodge pressed his views upon him with all his strength.

I agree with all you say as to what will be the result if we fail to take Hawaii. It will show that we either have lost, or else wholly lack, the masterful instinct which alone can make a race great. I feel so deeply about it I hardly dare express myself in full. The terrible part is to see that it is the men

that accompanied these economic crises also provided social and political arguments for economic relief through foreign trade.

In the depression of the 1890s, with the secretary of state seeing "symptoms of revolution" in the Pullman strike and Coxey's Army of unemployed workers (see Chapter 22), this interest in foreign trade became obsessive. More systematic government efforts to promote trade seemed necessary, a conclusion strengthened by new threats to existing American markets. In that tumultuous decade, European nations raised tariff barriers against American products, and Japan and the European imperial powers began to restrict commercial opportunities in the areas of China that they controlled. Many American leaders decided that the United States had to adopt decisive new policies or face economic catastrophe.

First Steps

Despite the growing ideological, strategic, and economic arguments for imperialism, the government only fitfully interested itself in foreign affairs before the mid-1890s. It did not pursue a policy of **isolationism** from international affairs, for the nation maintained normal diplomatic and trade ties and at times vigorously intervened in Latin America and East Asia. But in general the government deferred to the initiative of private interests, reacted haphazardly to outside events, and did little to create a professional foreign service.

Seward and Blaine

Despite this generally passive and ineffective approach, two secretaries of state, William H. Seward, secretary under Presidents Lincoln and Andrew of education who take the lead in trying to make us prove traitors to our race.

I fully realize the importance of the Pacific coast. . . . But there are big problems in the West Indies also. Until we definitely turn Spain out of those islands (and if I had my way that would be done tomorrow), we will always be menaced by trouble there. We should acquire the Danish Islands [in the West Indies], and by turning Spain out should serve notice that no strong European power, and especially not Germany, should be allowed to gain a foothold by supplanting some weak European power. I do not fear England; Canada is a hostage for her good behavior.

I wish we had a perfectly consistent foreign policy, and that this policy was that every European power should be driven out of America, and every foot of American soil, including the nearest islands in both the Pacific and the Atlantic, should be in the hands of independent American states, and so far as possible in the possession of the United States or under its protection.

To speak with a frankness which our timid friends would call brutal, I would regard a war with Spain from two standpoints: first, the advisability on the grounds both of humanity and self-interest of interfering on behalf of the Cubans, and of taking one more step toward the complete freeing of America from European dominion; second, the benefit done our people by giving them something to think of which isn't material gain, and especially the benefit done our military forces by trying both the Navy and the Army in actual practice. I should be very sorry not to see us make the experiment of trying to land, and therefore feed and clothe, an expeditionary force [on Cuba], if only for the sake of learning from our own blunders. I should hope that the force would have some fighting to do. It would be a great lesson, and we would profit much by it.

I wish there was a chance that the [U.S. battleship] *Maine* was going to be used against some foreign power; by preference Germany—but I am not particular, and I'd take even Spain if nothing better offered.

Source: The Letters of Theodore Roosevelt *selected and edited by Elting E. Morison, Cambridge: Harvard University Press.*

Johnson (1861–1869), and James G. Blaine, secretary under Presidents Garfield and Harrison (1881, 1889–1892), laid the foundation for a larger and more aggressive American role in world affairs. Seward possessed an elaborate imperial vision, based on his understanding of commercial opportunities, strategic necessities, and national destiny. In his concerns for opening East Asia to American commerce and establishing American hegemony over the Caribbean, he anticipated the subsequent course of American expansion. His hopes of annexing Canada and Greenland went unfulfilled, but he did purchase Alaska from Russia in 1867, approve the navy's occupation of the Midway Islands in the Pacific, push American trade on a reluctant Japan, and repeatedly try to acquire Caribbean naval bases (see Map 24-1). But his policy of expansion, as one observer noted, "went somewhat too far and too fast for the public," and many of his plans fizzled. Congressional opposition frustrated his efforts to obtain Haiti and the Dominican Republic and to purchase the Danish West Indies; Colombia blocked his attempt to gain construction rights for a canal across the isthmus of Panama.

The Grant administration (1869–1877) haphazardly pursued some of Seward's goals, but met resistance. When Grant attempted to take over the Dominican Republic in 1870, for example, the Senate defeated the annexation treaty. Opponents of overseas expansion complained of its cost, worried about the "alien races" it would incorporate into the nation, and above all condemned it as contrary to basic American principles. Such anticolonial sentiments would weaken, however, in the next generation.

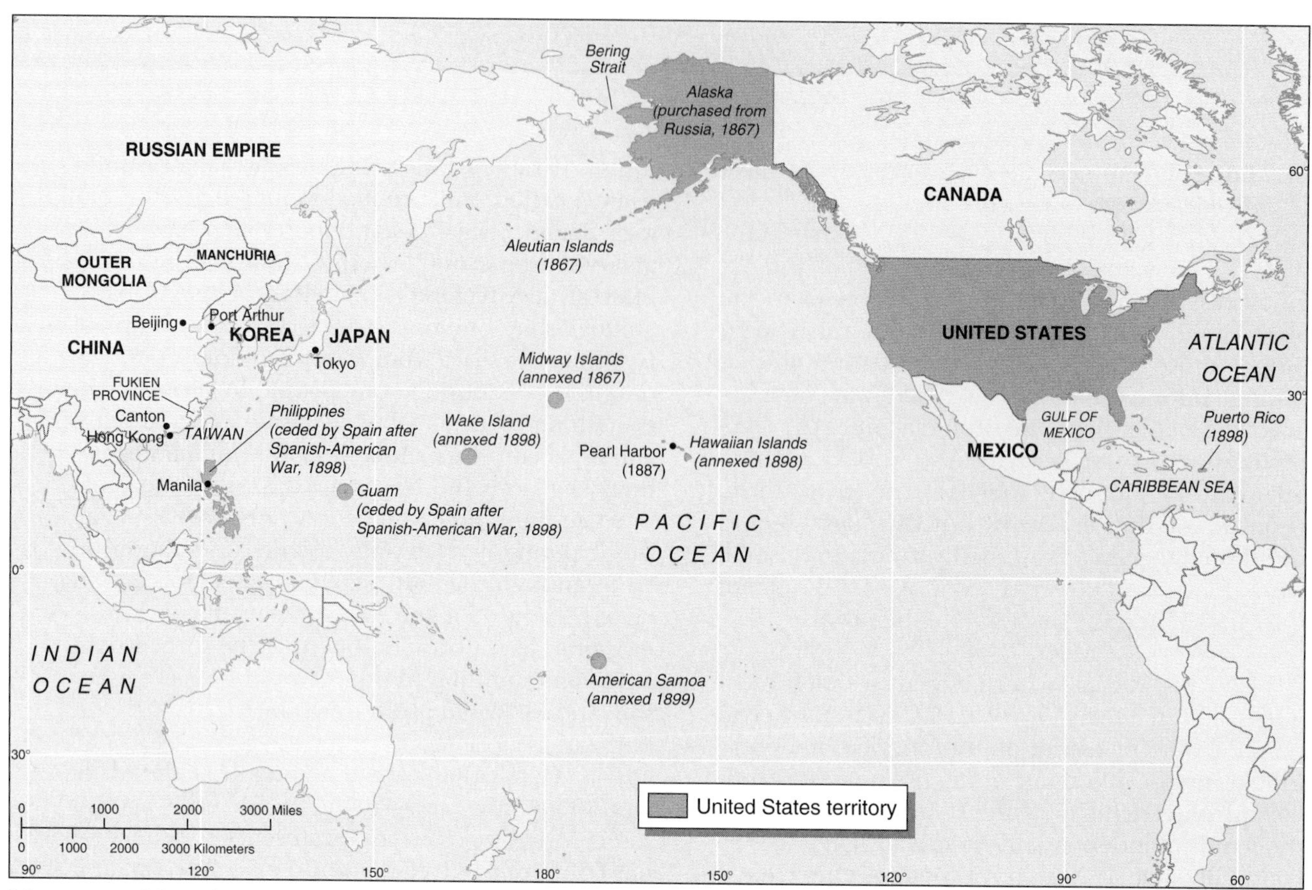

Map 24-1 United States Expansion in the Pacific, 1867-1899
Pursuing visions of a commercial empire in the Pacific, the United States steadily expanded its territorial possessions as well as its influence there in the late nineteenth century.

Blaine, though less thoughtful than Seward, was an equally vigorous, if inconsistent, advocate of expansion. He worked to extend what he called America's "commercial empire" in the Pacific. And he sought to ensure U.S. sovereignty over any canal in Panama, insisting that it be "a purely American waterway to be treated as part of our own coastline." In an effort to induce Latin American nations to import manufactured products from the United States rather than Europe, Blaine proposed a conference among the nations of the Western Hemisphere in 1881. The First International American Conference finally met in 1889. There Blaine called for the establishment of a customs union to reduce trade barriers. He expected this union to strengthen U.S. control of hemispheric markets. The Latin American nations, however, wary of economic subordination to the colossus of the north, rejected Blaine's plan. Instead, the conference established what eventually came to be known as the **Pan American Union**. Based in Washington, it helped promote hemispheric understanding and cooperation.

If U.S. officials were increasingly assertive toward Latin America and Asia, however, they remained little involved in Europe (one secretary of state declared in 1885 that he had no interest in European affairs, which he regarded "with impatience and contempt"). They were wholly indifferent to Africa, which the European powers were then carving up into colonies. In short, despite some important precedents for the future, much of American foreign policy remained undeveloped, sporadic, and impulsive.

Hawaii

Blaine regarded Hawaii as "indispensably" part of "the American system." As early as 1842, the United States had announced its opposition to European control of Hawaii, a key way station in the China trade where New England missionaries and whalers were active. Although the islands remained under native monarchs, American influence grew, particularly as other Americans arrived to establish sugar plantations and eventually dominate the economy.

Treaties in 1875 and 1887 integrated the islands into the American economy and gave the United States control over Pearl Harbor on the island of Oahu. In 1887, the United States rejected a proposal from Britain and France for a joint guarantee of Hawaii's independence and endorsed a new Hawaiian constitution that gave political power to wealthy white residents. The obvious next step was U.S. annexation, which Blaine endorsed in 1891.

A combination of factors soon impelled American planters to bid for annexation. The McKinley Tariff Act of 1890 effectively closed the U.S. market to Hawaiian sugar producers, facing them with economic ruin. At the same time, Queen Liliuokalani moved to restore native control of Hawaiian affairs. To ensure market access and protect their political authority, the American planters decided to seek annexation to the United States. In 1893, they overthrew the queen. John Stevens, the American minister, ordered U.S. Marines to help the rebels. He then declared an American protectorate over the new Hawaii government and wired Washington: "The Hawaiian pear is now fully ripe, and this is the golden hour for the United States to pluck it." A delegation from the new provisional government, containing no native Hawaiians, went to Washington to draft a treaty for annexation. President Harrison signed the pact but could not get Senate approval before the new Cleveland administration took office.

Cleveland immediately called for an investigation of the whole affair. Soon convinced that "the undoubted sentiment of the people is for the Queen, against the provisional Government, and against annexation," Cleveland apologized to the queen for the "flagrant wrong" done her by the "reprehensible conduct of the American minister and the unauthorized presence on land of a military force of the United States." But the American-dominated provisional government refused to step down, and Cleveland's rejection of annexation set off a noisy debate in the United States.

Many Republicans strongly supported annexation, which they regarded as merely part of a larger plan of expansion. One eastern Republican manufacturer called for the annexation of Hawaii as the first step toward making the Pacific "an American ocean, dominated by American commercial enterprise for all time." On the West Coast, where California business interests had close ties with the islands, the commercial and strategic value of Hawaii seemed obvious. The *San Francisco Examiner* declared, "Hoist the Stars and Stripes. It is a case of manifest destiny." Reflecting racial imperialism, others argued that annexation would both fittingly reward the enterprising white residents of Hawaii and provide an opportunity to civilize native Hawaiians.

Democrats generally opposed annexation. They doubted, as Missouri Senator George Vest declared, whether the United States should desert its traditional principles and "venture upon the great colonial system of the European powers." Most Democrats believed, as another argued, that "the mission of our nation is to build up and make a greater country out of what we have, instead of annexing islands."

The Hawaiian episode of 1893 thus foreshadowed the arguments over imperialism at the end of the century and emphasized the policy differences between Democrats and the increasingly expansionist Republicans.

Chile and Venezuela

American reactions to developments in other countries in the 1890s also reflected an increasingly assertive national policy and excitable public opinion. In 1891, American sailors on shore leave in Chile became involved in a drunken brawl that left two of them dead, seventeen injured, and dozens in jail. The incident heightened the already tense relations between the United States and Chile. After supporting the unpopular (and losing) side in a recent Chilean revolution, President Harrison had warned the new leaders that "sometime it may be necessary to instruct them." Now, encouraged by a combative navy, he threatened military retaliation against Chile, provoking an outburst of bellicose nationalism in the United States. Harrison relented only when Chile apologized and paid an indemnity.

A few years later, the United States again threatened war over a minor issue but against a more formidable opponent. Though opposed to annexing Hawaii, President Cleveland adopted an increasingly aggressive policy in Latin America. In 1895, he intervened in a boundary dispute between Great Britain and Venezuela over British Guiana. Cleveland was motivated not only by the long-standing U.S. goal of challenging Britain for Latin American markets but also by ever more expansive notions of the **Monroe Doctrine** and the authority of the United States. He also seized on this foreign policy issue to divert public attention from a severe economic depression. Secretary of State Richard Olney sent Britain a blunt note (a "twenty-inch gun," Cleveland called it) demanding arbitration of the disputed territory and stoutly asserting American supremacy in the Western Hemisphere. Cleveland urged Congress to establish

As other imperial powers look on, the United States abandons its traditional principles to rush headlong into world affairs. Uncle Sam would not always find it a smooth ride.

a commission to determine the boundary and enforce its decision by war if necessary. The astonished British ambassador reported an "extraordinary state of excitement into which the Congress of the United States and the whole country were thrown by the warlike Message . . . a condition of mind which can only be described as hysterical." As war fever swept the United States, Britain agreed to arbitration, recognizing the limited nature of the issue that so convulsed Anglo-American relations.

The United States' assertion of hemispheric dominance angered Latin Americans, and their fears deepened when it decided arbitration terms with Britain without consulting Venezuela, which protested before bowing to American pressure. The United States had intervened less to protect Venezuela from the British bully than to advance its own hegemony. The further significance of the Venezuelan crisis, as Captain Mahan noted, lay in its "awakening of our countrymen to the fact that we must come out of our isolation . . . and take our share in the turmoil of the world."

But if these bold steps in Hawaii, Chile, and Venezuela indicated an increasing role for the United States in world affairs, the nation had yet to adopt a consistent policy for expanding its influence. That would happen in the next few years.

The Spanish-American War

The forces pushing the United States toward imperialism and international power came to a head in the Spanish-American War. The war had its origins in Cuba's quest for independence from the oppressive colonial control of Spain. The struggle activated Americans' long-standing interest in the island. Many sympathized with the Cuban rebels' yearning for freedom, others worried that disorder in Cuba threatened their own economic and political interests, and some thought that United States intervention would increase its influence in the Caribbean and along key Pacific routes to Asian markets. But few foresaw that the war that finally erupted in 1898 would dramatically change America's relationships with the rest of the world and give it a colonial empire.

The Cuban Revolution

In the nineteenth century, Cubans rebelled repeatedly against Spanish rule. One rebellion, the Ten Years' War from 1868 to 1878, had been brutally suppressed, but not before drawing American interest and sympathy. Cuba was the last major European colony in Latin America, with an economic potential that attracted American business interests and a strategic significance for any Central American canal. In the 1880s, Spanish control became increasingly harsh even while American investors expanded their economic influence in Cuba. Cuban discontent erupted again in 1895 when the Cuban patriot José Martí launched another revolt.

The rebellion was a classic guerrilla war in which the rebels controlled the countryside and the Spanish army the towns and cities. American economic interests were seriously affected, for both Cubans and Spaniards destroyed American property and disrupted American trade. The Cleveland administration, motivated as much by a desire to protect American property and establish a safe environment for further investments as by a concern for Cuban rights, urged Spain to adopt reforms. But the brutality with which Spain attempted to suppress the revolt promoted American sympathy for the Cuban insurgents. Determined to cut the rebels off from their peasant supporters, the Spaniards herded most civilians into "reconcentration camps," where tens of thousands died of starvation and disease.

Americans' sympathy was further aroused by the sensationalist **yellow press**. To attract readers and boost advertising revenues, the popular press of the day adopted bold headlines, fevered editorials, and real or exaggerated stories of violence, sex, and corruption. A circulation war between William Randolph Hearst's *New York Journal* and Joseph Pulitzer's *New York World* helped stimulate interest in Cuban war. "Blood on the roadsides, blood on the fields, blood on the doorsteps, blood, blood, blood! The old, the young, the weak, the crippled—all are butchered without mercy," the *World* feverishly reported of Cuba. "Is there no nation wise enough, brave enough to aid this blood-smitten land?"

The nation's religious press, partly because it reflected the prejudice many Protestants held against Catholic Spain, also advocated American intervention. One religious newspaper endorsed an American war against Spain as God's instrument for attacking "that system of iniquity, the papacy." Another promised that if war came, "every Methodist preacher will be a recruiting officer" for the American military. The *Catholic Herald* of New York sarcastically referred to the "bloodthirsty preachers" of the Protestant churches, but such preachers undeniably influenced American opinion against Spain.

As the Cuban rebellion dragged on, more and more Americans advocated intervention to stop the carnage, protect U.S. investments, or uphold various principles. Expansionists like Roosevelt and Lodge clamored for intervention, but so did their opponents. Populists, for example, sympathized with a people seeking independence from colonial rule and petitioned Congress to support the crusade for Cuban freedom; conservative Democrats hoped that the excitement of intervention and war "might do much towards directing the minds of the people from imaginary ills, the relief of which is erroneously supposed to be reached by 'Free Silver.'" In the election of 1896, both major parties endorsed Cuban independence. The Democratic platform expressed "sympathy to the people of Cuba in their heroic struggle for liberty." The Republican platform not only wished Cubans success in "their determined contest for liberty" but urged intervention on the grounds that Spain was "unable to protect the property or lives of resident American citizens."

Growing Tensions

In his 1897 inaugural address, President William McKinley outlined an expansionist program ranging from further enlargement of the navy to the annexation of Hawaii and the construction of a Central American canal in Nicaragua, but his administration soon focused on Cuba. McKinley's principal complaint was that chronic disorder in Cuba disrupted America's investments and agitated public opinion. Personally opposed to military intervention, McKinley first used diplomacy to press Spain to adopt reforms that would settle the rebellion. Following his instructions, the U.S. minister to Spain warned the Spanish government that if it did not quickly establish peace, the United States would take whatever steps it "should deem necessary to procure this result." In late 1897, Spain modified its brutal military tactics and offered limited autonomy to Cuba. But Cubans insisted on complete independence, which Spain refused to grant.

Relations between the United States and Spain deteriorated. In early 1898, the *New York Journal* published a private letter from the Spanish minister to the United States that mocked McKinley as "weak and a bidder for the admiration of the crowd." (The *Journal* called the letter "the worst insult to the United States in its history.") McKinley found more troubling the letter's intimation that Spain was not negotiating in good faith. Only days later, on February 15, 1898, the U.S. battleship *Maine* blew up in Havana harbor, killing 260 men. The Spaniards were not responsible for the tragedy, which a modern naval inquiry has attributed to an internal accident. But many Americans agreed with Theodore Roosevelt, the assistant secretary of the navy, who called it "an act of dirty treachery on the part of the Spaniards" and told McKinley that only war was "compatible with our national honor."

Popular anger was inflamed, but the sinking of the *Maine* by itself did not bring war, though it did restrict McKinley's options. Other pressures soon began to build on the president. Increasingly, business interests favored war as less disruptive than volatile peace that threatened their investments. Senator Lodge reported a consensus "that this situation must end. We cannot go on indefinitely with this strain, this suspense, and this uncertainty, this tottering upon the verge of war. It is killing to business." McKinley also feared that a moderate policy would endanger congressional candidates. Again Senator Lodge, although hesitant to suggest "war for political reasons," nevertheless advised McKinley, "If the war in Cuba drags on through the summer with nothing done, we shall go down in the greatest [election] defeat ever known."

At the end of March 1898 (when the French ambassador in Washington reported that "a sort of bellicose fury has seized the American nation"), McKinley sent Spain an ultimatum. He demanded an armistice in Cuba, an end to the reconcentration policy, and the acceptance of American arbitration, which implied Cuban independence. Desperately, Spain made concessions, abolishing reconcentration and declaring a unilateral armistice. But McKinley had already begun war preparations, withdrawing American diplomats from Cuba and Spain, ordering the navy to prepare for war, and drafting a war message for

Congress. He submitted that message on April 11, asking for authority to use force against Spain "in the name of humanity, in the name of civilization, in behalf of endangered American interests." Congress declared war on Spain on April 25, 1898.

A few national leaders welcomed the war as a step toward imperialism, but there was little popular support for such a policy. Most interventionists were not imperialists, and Congress added the **Teller Amendment** to the war resolution, disclaiming any intention of annexing Cuba and promising that Cubans would govern themselves. Congress also refused to approve either a canal bill or the annexation of Hawaii. Nevertheless, the Spanish-American War did turn the nation toward imperialism.

War and Empire

The decisive engagement of the war took place not in Cuba but in another Spanish colony, the Philippines, and it involved the favored tool of the expansionists, the new navy (see Map 24-2). In 1897, McKinley had approved plans for an attack on the Philippines in the event of war with Spain. Once war was declared, Commodore George Dewey led the U.S. Asiatic squadron into Manila Bay and destroyed the much weaker Spanish fleet on May 1, 1898. This dramatic victory galvanized expansionist sentiment in the United States. The navy had long coveted Manila Bay as a strategic harbor, but other Americans, casting an eye on commercial opportunities in China, saw a greater significance in the victory. With Dewey's triumph, exulted one expansionist, "We are taking our proper rank among the nations of the world. We are after markets, the greatest markets now existing in the world." To expand this foothold in Asia, McKinley ordered troops to the Philippines, postponing the military expedition to Cuba itself.

Dewey's victory also precipitated the annexation of Hawaii, which had seemed hopeless only weeks before. Annexationists now pointed to the is-

Map 24-2 The Spanish-American War
The United States gained quick victories in both theaters of the Spanish-American War. Its naval power proved decisive, with Commodore Dewey destroying one enemy fleet in the Philippines and a second U.S. naval force cutting off the Spanish in Cuba.

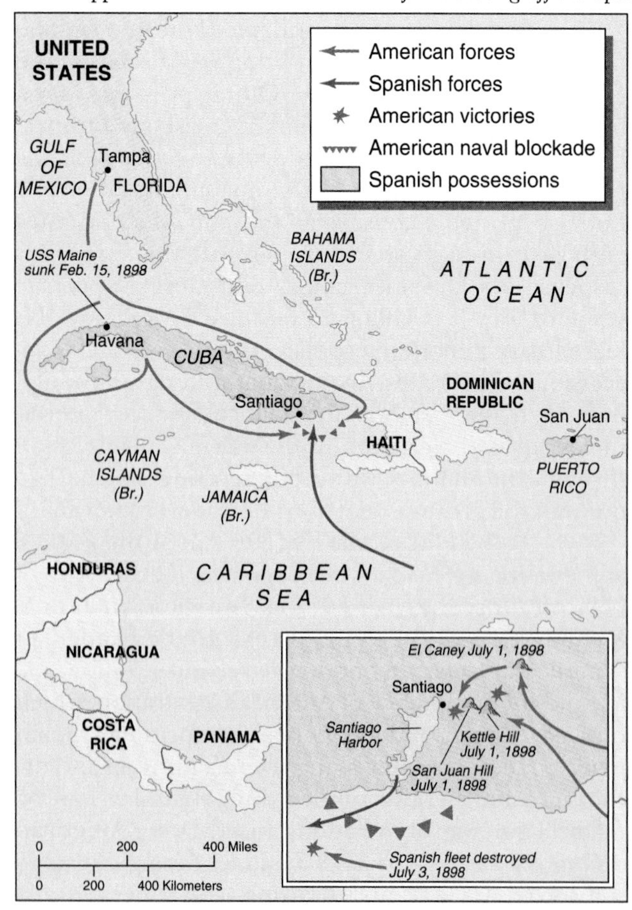

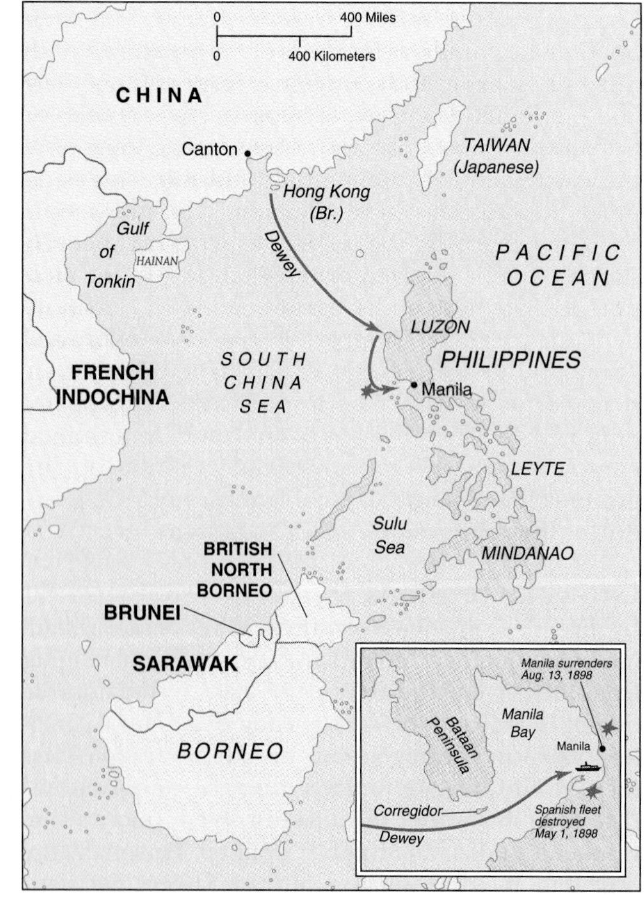

lands' strategic importance as stepping-stones to Manila. "To maintain our flag in the Philippines, we must raise our flag in Hawaii," the *New York Sun* contended. McKinley himself privately declared, "We need Hawaii just as much and a good deal more than we did California. It is Manifest Destiny." In July, Congress approved annexation, a decision welcomed by Hawaii's white minority. Natives solemnly protested this step taken "without reference to the consent of the people of the Hawaiian Islands." Filipinos would soon face the same American imperial impulse.

Military victory also came swiftly in Cuba, once the U.S. Army finally landed in late June. Victory depended largely on Spanish ineptitude, for the American army was poorly led, trained, and supplied. Troops had to fight with antiquated weapons and wear wool uniforms in the sweltering tropics. They were issued rotting and poisoned food by a corrupt and inefficient War Department. More than five thousand Americans died of diseases and accidents brought on by such mismanagement; only 379 were killed in battle. State militias supplemented the small regular army, as did volunteer units, such as the famous Rough Riders, a cavalry unit of cowboys and eastern dandies assembled by Theodore Roosevelt.

While the Rough Riders captured public attention, other units were more effective. The 10th Negro Cavalry, for example, played the crucial role in capturing San Juan Hill, a battle popularly associated with the Rough Riders. One war correspondent wrote of the black soldiers' charge: "They followed their leaders up the terrible hill from whose crest the

Fighting in Cuba in the Spanish-American War was brief but intense. This contemporary lithograph depicts the Ninth and Tenth Cavalry Regiments, African-American soldiers with white officers, charging the Spanish army at the Battle of Las Guasimos, June 24, 1898. Black soldiers composed nearly a fourth of the American army in Cuba.

desperate Spaniards poured down a deadly fire of shell and musketry. They never faltered. . . . Their aim was splendid, their coolness was superb. . . . The war had not shown greater heroism." Nevertheless, the Rough Riders gained the credit, thanks in part to Roosevelt's self-serving and well-promoted account of the conflict, which one humorist proposed retitling *Alone in Cuba.*

U.S. naval power again proved decisive. In a lopsided battle on July 3, the obsolete Spanish squadron in Cuba was destroyed, isolating the Spanish army and guaranteeing its defeat. U.S. forces then seized the nearby Spanish colony of Puerto Rico without serious opposition. Humbled, Spain signed an armistice ending the war on August 12.

Americans were delighted with their military achievements, but the *Philadelphia Inquirer* cautioned, "With peace will come new responsibilities, which must be met. We have colonies to look after and develop."

The Treaty of Paris

The armistice required Spain to accept Cuban independence, cede Puerto Rico and Guam (a Pacific island between Hawaii and the Philippines), and allow the Americans to occupy Manila pending the final disposition of the Philippines at a formal peace conference. The acquisition of Puerto Rico and Guam indicated the expansionist nature the conflict had assumed for the United States. So did the postponement of the Philippine issue. McKinley knew that delay would permit the advocates of expansion to build public support for annexation. Because the U.S. Army did not capture Manila until after the armistice had been signed, he could not claim the islands by conquest, as Spain pointed out.

McKinley defended his decision to acquire the Philippines in self-righteous imperialist rhetoric, promising to extend Christian influence and American values. But he was motivated primarily by a determination to use the islands to strengthen America's political and commercial position in East Asia. Moreover, he believed the Filipinos poorly suited to self-rule, and he feared that Germany or Japan might seize the Philippines if the United States did not. Meeting in Paris in December, American and Spanish negotiators settled the final terms for peace. Spain agreed—despite Filipino demands for independence—to cede the Philippines to the United States.

The decision to acquire the Philippines sparked a dramatic debate over the ratification of the Treaty of Paris. Imperialists invoked the familiar arguments of economic expansion, national destiny, and strategic necessity while asserting that Americans had religious and racial responsibilities to advance civilization by uplifting backward peoples. The *United States Investor* spoke for business leaders, for example, in demanding the Philippines as "a base of operations in the East" to protect American interests in China; other economic expansionists argued that the Philippines themselves had valuable resources and were a market for American goods or warned that "our commercial rivals in the Orient" would grab the islands if the United States did not. The *Presbyterian Banner* spoke for what it termed a nearly unanimous religious press in affirming "the desirability of America's retaining the Philippines as a duty in the interest of human freedom and Christian progress." The United States, it concluded, was "morally compelled to become an Asiatic power." Conveniently ignoring that most Filipinos were Catholic, the *Baptist Union* insisted: "The conquest by force of arms must be followed up by conquest for Christ."

Opponents of the treaty raised profound questions about national goals and ideals. They included such prominent figures as the civil service reformer Carl Schurz, steel baron Andrew Carnegie, social reformer Jane Addams, labor leader Samuel Gompers, and author Mark Twain. Their organizational base was the **Anti-Imperialist League**, which campaigned against the treaty, distributing pamphlets, petitioning Congress, and holding rallies. League members' criticisms reflected a conviction that imperialism was a repudiation of America's moral and political traditions embodied in the Declaration of Independence. The acquisition of overseas colonies, they argued, conflicted with the nation's commitment to liberty and its claim to moral superiority. They regarded as loathesome and hypocritical the transformation of a war to free Cuba into a campaign for imperial conquest and subjugation.

William Jennings Bryan ridiculed the imperialists' arguments of national destiny: "When the desire to steal becomes uncontrollable in an individual he is declared to be a kleptomaniac and is sent to an asylum; when the desire to grab land becomes uncontrollable in a nation we are told that the 'currents of destiny are flowing through the hearts of men.'" Some African Americans derided the rhetoric of Anglo-Saxon superiority that underlay imperialism and even organized the Black Man's Burden Association to promote Philippine independence.

But other arguments were less high-minded. Many anti-imperialists objected to expansion on the racist grounds that Filipinos were inferior and unassimilable. Gompers feared that cheap Asian labor would undercut the wages and living standards of

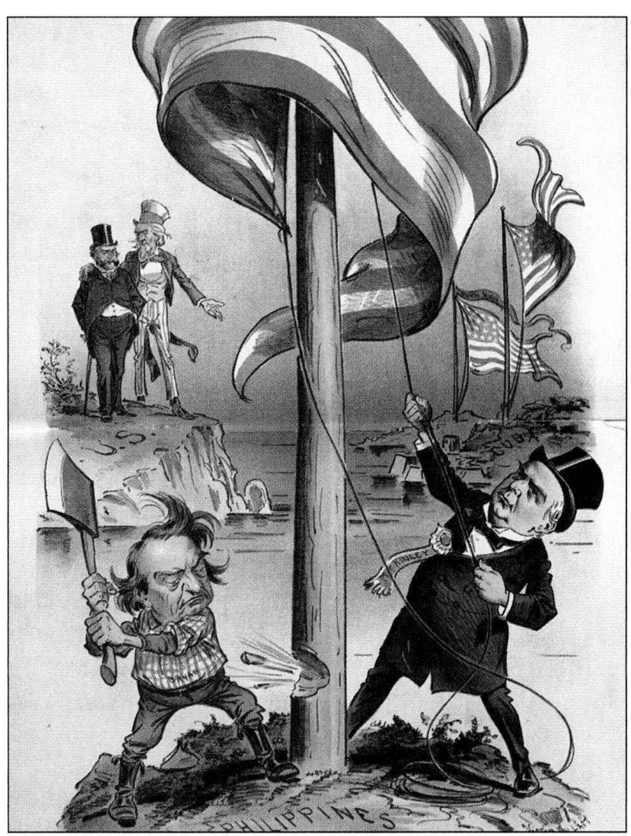

Republicans countered William Jennings Bryan's attempt to make imperialism an issue in 1900 by wrapping themselves in patriotism and the American flag. "Take Your Choice," a cartoon from Judge, *posed President McKinley raising Old Glory over the Philippines with a disheveled and frantic Bryan chopping down the symbol of American pride and power.*

American workers. The *San Francisco Call*, representing California-Hawaiian sugar interests, also wanted no competition from the Philippines.

The debate over the treaty became bitter. Furious at the opponents of empire, Roosevelt called them "little better than traitors." Carl Schurz responded that McKinley himself had earlier termed territorial annexation through conquest "a criminal act of aggression"; the president's seizure of the Philippines, Puerto Rico, and Hawaii, said Schurz, had perverted a legitimate concern for Cuba into "a war of selfish ambition and conquest."

Finally, on February 6, 1899, the Senate narrowly ratified the treaty. All but two Republicans supported the pact; most Democrats opposed it, although several voted for the treaty after Bryan suggested that approval was necessary to end the war and detach the Philippines from Spain. Thereafter, he hoped, a congressional resolution would give the Filipinos their independence. But by a single vote, the Republicans defeated a Democratic proposal for Philippine independence once a stable government had been established; the United States would keep the islands.

Bryan attempted to make the election of 1900 a referendum on "the paramount issue" of imperialism, promising to free the Philippines if the Democrats won. But many other issues determined the election. Some of the most ardent anti-imperialists were conservatives who remained loyal to McKinley because they could not tolerate Bryan's economic policies. Republicans also benefited from the prosperity the country experienced under McKinley after the hard 1890s, and they played on the nationalist emotions evoked by the war, especially by nominating the "hero of San Juan Hill," Theodore Roosevelt, for vice president. "If you choose to vote for America, if you choose to vote for the flag for which we fought," Roosevelt said, "then you will vote to sustain the administration of President

Roosevelt's well-advertised exploits in the Spanish-American War propelled his political career. After being elected governor of New York in 1898, he received the Republican nomination for vice president in 1900 and often seemed to overshadow President McKinley.

McKinley." Bryan lost again, as in 1896, and under Republican leadership, the United States became an imperial nation.

Imperial Ambitions: The United States and East Asia, 1899–1917

In 1899, as the United States occupied its new empire, Assistant Secretary of State John Bassett Moore observed that the nation had become "a world power. . . . Where formerly we had only commercial interests, we now have territorial and political interests as well." American policies to promote those expanded interests focused first on East Asia and Latin America, where the Spanish-American War had provided the United States with both opportunities and challenges. In Asia, the first issue concerned the fate of the Philippines, but looming beyond it were American ambitions in China, where other imperial nations had their own goals.

The Filipino-American War

Filipino nationalists, like Cuban insurgents, were already fighting Spain for their independence before the sudden American intervention. The Filipino leader, Emilio Aguinaldo, welcomed Dewey's naval victory as the sign of a de facto alliance with the United States; he then issued a declaration of independence and proclaimed the Philippine Republic. His own troops captured most of Luzon, the Philippines' major island, before the U.S. Army arrived. But the Filipinos' optimism declined as American officials acted in an increasingly imperious manner toward them, first refusing to meet with the "savages," then insisting that Filipino forces withdraw from Manila or face "forcible action," and finally dismissing the claims of Aguinaldo and "his so-called government." When the Treaty of Paris provided for U.S. ownership rather than independence, Filipinos felt betrayed. Mounting tensions erupted in a battle between American and Filipino troops outside Manila on February 4, 1899, sparking a long and brutal war.

Ultimately, the United States used nearly four times as many soldiers to suppress the Filipinos as to defeat Spain in Cuba and, in a tragic irony, employed many of the same brutal methods for which it had condemned Spain. Recognizing that "the Filipino masses are loyal to Aguinaldo and the government which he heads," U.S. military leaders adopted ever harsher measures, often directed at civilians, who were crowded into concentration camps in which perhaps 200,000 died. Americans often made little effort to distinguish between soldiers and noncombatants, viewing all Filipinos with racial antagonism. After reporting one massacre of a thousand men, women, and children, an American soldier declared, "I am in my glory when I can sight my gun on some dark skin and pull the trigger."

Before the military imposed censorship on war news, reporters confirmed U.S. atrocities; one wrote that "American troops have been relentless, have killed to exterminate men, women, and children, prisoners and captives, active insurgents and suspected people, from lads of 10 and up." A California newspaper defended such actions with remarkable candor: "There has been too much hypocrisy about this Philippine business. . . . Let us all be frank. WE DO NOT WANT THE FILIPINOS. WE DO WANT THE PHILIPPINES. All of our troubles in this annexation matter have been caused by the presence in the Philippine Islands of the Filipinos. . . . The more of them killed the better. It seems harsh. But they must yield before the superior race."

The overt racism of the war repelled African Americans. John Mitchell, a Virginia editor, condemned all the talk of "white man's burden" as deceptive rhetoric for brutal acts that could not be "defended either in moral or international law." Mitchell argued that white Southerners needed missionary work more than freedom-loving Filipinos. "With the government acquiescing in the oppression and butchery of a dark race in this country and the enslaving and slaughtering of a dark race in the Philippines," he concluded, "we think it time to call all missionaries home and have them work on our own people."

Other Americans also denounced the war. The Anti-Imperialist League revived, citing the war as proof of the corrosive influence of imperialism on the nation's morals and principles. Professors addressed antiwar rallies on college campuses. "Alas, what a fall," one University of Michigan professor told his audience. "Within the circuit of a single year to have declined from the moral leadership of mankind into the common brigandage of the robber nations of the world." By 1902, the realities of imperial policy—including American casualties—disillusioned most who had clamored to save Cuba.

By that time, however, the American military had largely suppressed the rebellion, and the United States had established a colonial government headed by an American governor general appointed by the president. Filipino involvement in the government was limited on educational and religious grounds.

The Filipino-American War was documented extensively by photographers. "First Position Near Manila" shows soldiers of the Twentieth Kansas Infantry Regiment deployed early in what would become a lengthy and brutal war.

Compared to the Americans' brutal war policies, U. S. colonial rule was relatively benign, though paternalistic. William Howard Taft, the first governor general, launched a program that brought the islands new schools and roads, a public health system, and an economy tied closely to both the United States and a small Filipino elite. Independence would take nearly half a century.

China and the Open Door

America's determined involvement in the Philippines reflected its preoccupation with China. By the mid-1890s, other powers threatened prospects for American commercial expansion in China. Japan, after defeating China in 1895, annexed Taiwan and secured economic privileges in the mainland province of Fukien (Fujian); the major European powers then competed aggressively to claim other areas of China as their own **spheres of influence**. In Manchuria, Russia won control of Port Arthur (Lüshun) and the right to construct a railway. Germany secured a ninety-nine year lease on another Chinese port and mining and railroad privileges on the Shandong Peninsula. The British wrung special concessions in Kowloon, opposite Hong Kong, and in other Chinese provinces, as well as a port facing the Russians in Manchuria. France gained a lease on ports and exclusive commercial privileges in southern China.

These developments alarmed the American business community. It was confident that given an equal opportunity, the United States would prevail in international trade because of its efficient production and marketing systems. But the creation of exclusive spheres of influence would limit the opportunity to compete. In early 1898, business leaders organized the Committee on American Interests in China to lobby Washington to promote American trade in the shrinking Chinese market. The committee persuaded the nation's chambers of commerce to petition the McKinley administration to act. This campaign influenced McKinley's interest in acquiring the Philippines, but the Philippines, in the words of Mark Hanna, were only a "foothold"; China was the real target. The State Department soon reported that, given overproduction for the home market, "the United States has important interests at stake in the partition of commercial facilities in regions which are likely to offer developing markets for its goods. Nowhere is this consideration of more interest than in its relation to the Chinese Empire."

In 1899, the government moved to advance those interests. Without consulting the Chinese, Secretary of State John Hay asked the imperial powers to maintain an **Open Door** for the commercial and financial activities of all nations within their Chinese spheres of influence. Privately, Hay had already approved a plan to seize a Chinese port for the United States if necessary to join in the partition of China, but equal opportunity for trade and investment would serve American interests far better. It would avoid the expense of military occupation, avert further domestic criticism of U.S. imperialism, and guarantee a wider sphere for American business.

The United States usually preferred the "annexation of trade" to the annexation of territory. The Open Door policy promised to advance American commercial expansion, but Uncle Sam had to restrain other imperialists with colonial objectives.

A FAIR FIELD AND NO FAVOR.
UNCLE SAM: "I'm out for commerce, not conquest."

The other nations replied evasively, except for Russia, which rejected the Open Door concept. In 1900, an antiforeign Chinese nationalist movement known as the Boxers laid seige to the diplomatic quarters in Beijing. The defeat of the Boxer Rebellion by a multinational military force, to which the United States contributed troops, again raised the prospect of a division of China among colonial powers. Hay sent a second Open Door note, reaffirming "the principle of equal and impartial trade" and respect for China's territorial integrity.

Despite Hay's notes, China remained a tempting arena for imperial schemes. But the Open Door became a cardinal doctrine of American foreign policy in the twentieth century, a means by which the United States sought to dominate foreign markets. The United States promoted an informal or economic empire, as opposed to the traditional territorial colonial empire that Americans preferred to identify with European powers. Henceforth, American economic interests expected the U.S. government to oppose any developments that threatened to close other nations' economies to American penetration and to advance "private enterprise" abroad.

Rivalry with Japan and Russia

At the turn of the twentieth century, both the Japanese and the Russians were more deeply involved in East Asia than the United States was. They expressed little support for the Open Door, which they correctly saw as favoring American interests over their own. But in pursuing their ambitions in China, the two came into conflict with each other. Alarmed at the threat of Russian expansion in Manchuria and Korea, Japan in 1904 attacked the Russian fleet at Port Arthur and defeated the Russians in Manchuria.

In this Russo-Japanese war, American sympathies lay with Japan, for the Russians were attempting to close Manchuria to foreign trade. President Theodore Roosevelt privately complained that a reluctant American public opinion meant that "we cannot fight to keep Manchuria open." He thus welcomed the Japanese attack in the belief that "Japan is playing our game." But he soon feared that an overwhelming Japanese victory could threaten American interests as much as Russian expansionism did, so he skillfully mediated an end to the war. In the Treaty of Portsmouth in 1905, Japan won control of Russia's sphere of influence in Manchuria, half the Russian island of Sakhalin, and recognition of its domination of Korea.

This treaty marked Japan's emergence as a great power, but ironically, it worsened relations with the United States. Anti-American riots broke out in Tokyo. The Japanese people blamed Roosevelt for obstructing further Japanese gains and blocking a Russian indemnity that would have helped Japan pay for the war. Tensions were further aggravated by San Francisco's decision in 1906 to segregate Asian schoolchildren to avoid affecting the "youthful impressions" of white children. Japan regarded this as a racist insult, and Roosevelt worried that "the infernal fools in California" would provoke war. Finally he got the school order rescinded in exchange for his limiting Japanese immigration, which lay at the heart of California's hostility. Under the **Gentlemen's Agreement**, worked out through a series of diplomatic notes in 1907 and 1908, Japan agreed not to issue passports to workers coming to the United States, and the United States promised not to prohibit Japanese immigration overtly or completely.

To calm their mutual suspicions in East Asia, the United States and Japan adopted other agreements but failed to halt the deteriorating relationship. The Taft-Katsura Agreement (1905), the Root-Takahira Agreement (1908), and the Lansing-Ishii Agreement (1917) seemed to trade grudging American acceptance of Japan's special interests in Manchuria and control of Korea for Japanese promises to respect American rule in the Philippines and maintain the Open Door in China. But these agreements were vague, if not contradictory, and produced discord rather than harmony between the two countries.

Increasingly, Japan began to exclude American trade from its territories in East Asia and to press for further control over China. Elihu Root, Roosevelt's secretary of state, insisted that the Open Door and American access be maintained but asserted also that the United States did not want to be "a protagonist in a controversy in China with Russia and Japan or with either of them." The problem was that the United States could not sustain the Open Door without becoming a protagonist in China. This paradox, and the unwillingness to commit military force, would plague American foreign policy in Asia for decades.

Imperial Power: The United States and Latin America, 1899–1917

In Latin America, where no major powers directly challenged American objectives as Japan and Russia did in Asia, the United States was more successful in exercising imperial power (see Map 24-3). In the two decades after the Spanish-American War, the United States intervened militarily in Latin America no fewer than twenty times to promote its own strategic and economic interests (see the overview table, "U.S. Interventions in Latin America, 1891–1933"). Policymakers believed that these goals required restricting the influence of European nations in the region, building an isthmian canal under American control, and establishing the order thought necessary for American trade and investments to expand. Intervention at times achieved these goals, but it often ignored the wishes and interests of Latin Americans, provoked resistance and disorder, and created lasting ill will.

U.S. Rule in Puerto Rico

Well before 1898, expansionists like James G. Blaine had advocated acquiring Puerto Rico because of its strategic location in the Caribbean. During the Spanish-American War, Roosevelt urged Washington, "Do not make peace until we get" Puerto Rico. Military invasion and the Treaty of Paris soon brought the island under American control, with mixed consequences. A military government improved transportation and sanitation and developed public health and education. But to the dismay of Puerto Ricans, who had been promised that American rule would bestow "the advantages and blessings of enlightened civilization," their political freedoms were curtailed. "We have suffered everything. No liberty, no rights," said José Henna. "We are Mr. Nobody from Nowhere."

In 1900, the United States established a civil government, but it was under U.S. control, and popular participation was even less than under Spain. In the so-called *Insular Cases* (1901), the Supreme Court upheld Congress's authority to establish an inferior status for Puerto Rico, as an "unincorporated territory" without promise of statehood. Disappointed Puerto Ricans pressed to end this colonial status, some advocating independence, others statehood or merely greater autonomy. This division would continue throughout the twentieth century. In 1917, the United States granted citizenship and greater political rights to Puerto Ricans, but their island remained an unincorporated territory under an American governor appointed by the president.

Economic development also disappointed most islanders, for American investors quickly gained control of the best land and pursued large-scale sugar production for the U.S. market. The landless peasants struggled to survive as workers on large plantations. By 1929, the new governor—ironically, Theodore Roosevelt, Jr.—found that under the domination of American capital, "poverty was widespread

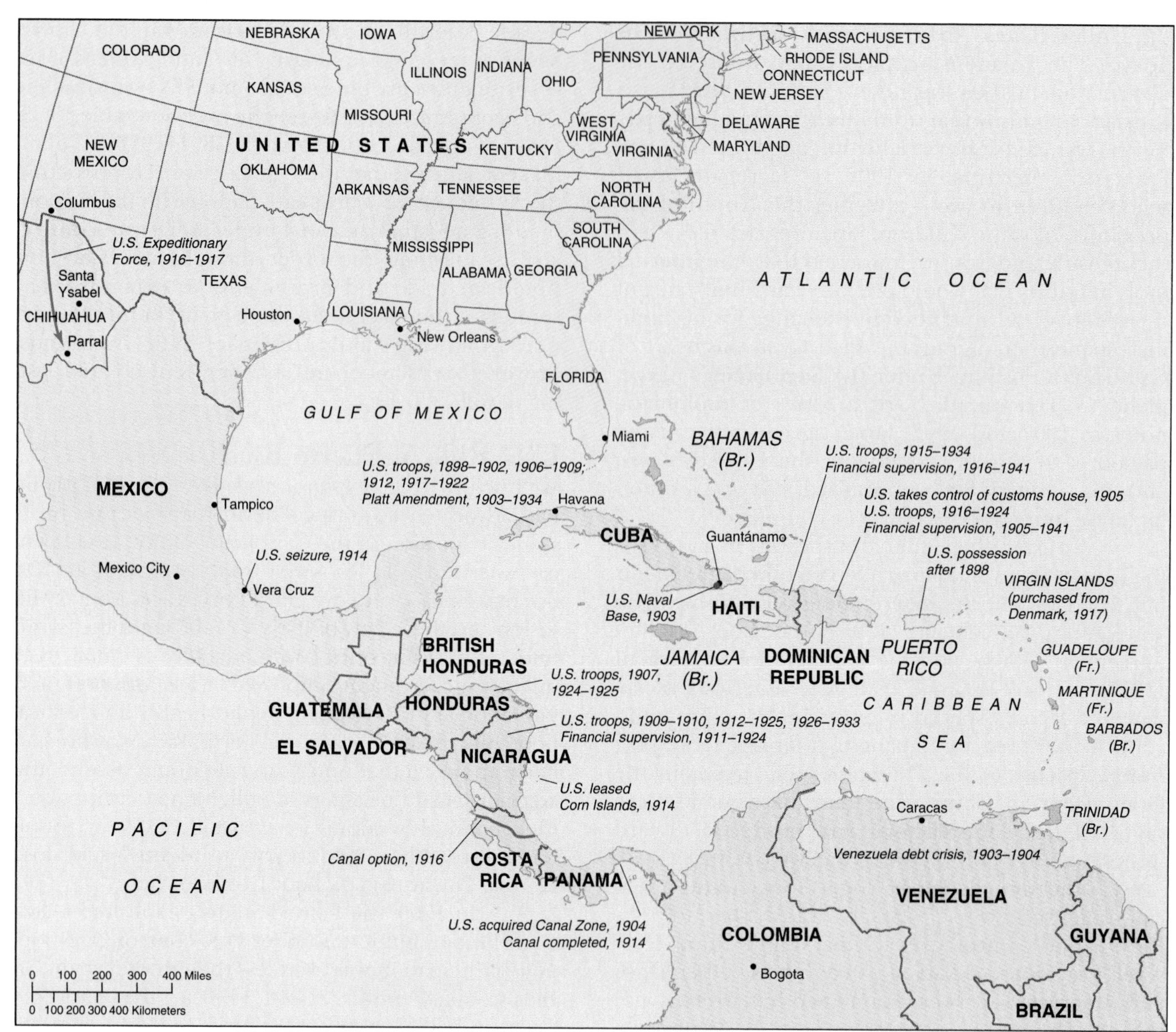

Map 24-3 The United States in the Caribbean

For strategic and economic reasons, the United States repeatedly intervened in the Caribbean in the first three decades of the twentieth century. Such interventions protected the U.S. claim to dominance but often provoked great hostility among Latin Americans.

and hunger, almost to the verge of starvation, common." A subsequent investigation concluded that while "the influx of capital has increased the efficiency of production and promoted general economic development," the benefits had gone largely to Americans, not to ordinary Puerto Ricans, whose conditions were "deplorable." Increasingly, they left their homes to seek work in the United States.

Cuba as a U.S. Protectorate

Despite the Teller Amendment, the Spanish-American War did not leave Cuba independent. McKinley opposed independence and distrusted the Cuban revolutionaries. Many Americans considered the Cubans racial inferiors, and one U.S. general in Cuba snorted, "Why those people are no more fit for self-government than gun-powder is for hell." Accordingly, a U.S. military government was established in the island. Only in 1900, when the Democrats made an issue of imperialism, did the McKinley administration move toward permitting a Cuban government and withdrawing American troops. McKinley summoned a Cuban convention to draft a constitution under the direction of the American military governor, General Leonard Wood. Reflecting the continuing U.S. fear of Cuban autonomy, this constitution

OVERVIEW

U.S. INTERVENTIONS IN LATIN AMERICA, 1891–1933

Country	Type of Intervention	Year
Chile	Ultimatum	1891–1892
Colombia	Military intervention	1903
Cuba	Occupation	1898–1902, 1906–1909, 1912, 1917–1922
Dominican Republic	Military and administrative intervention Occupation	1905–1907 1916–1924
Haiti	Occupation	1915–1934
Mexico	Military intervention	1914, 1916–1917
Nicaragua	Occupation	1912–1925, 1927–1933
Panama	Acquisition of Canal Zone	1904
Puerto Rico	Military invasion and territorial acquisition	1898

restricted suffrage on the basis of property and education, leaving few Cubans with the right to vote.

Even so, before removing its troops, the United States wanted to ensure its control over Cuba. It therefore made U.S. withdrawal contingent on Cuba's adding to its constitution the provisions of the **Platt Amendment**, drawn up in 1901 by the U.S. secretary of war. The Platt Amendment restricted Cuba's autonomy in diplomatic relations with other countries and in internal financial policies, required Cuba to lease naval bases to the United States, and most important, authorized U.S. intervention to maintain order and preserve Cuban independence. Cubans resented this restriction on their sovereignty. As General Wood correctly observed, "There is, of course, little or no independence left Cuba under the Platt Amendment."

Cubans quickly learned that when the United States prevented Cuba from extending the same trade privileges to the British that U.S. merchants enjoyed. The Open Door would not apply in the Caribbean, which was to be an American sphere of influence. To preserve that influence, the United States sent troops into Cuba three times between 1906 and 1917 (Roosevelt admitted his recurrent itch to "wipe its people off the face of the earth"). The last occupation lasted six years. Meanwhile, American property interests in Cuba increased more than fourfold, and American exports to the island increased eightfold from 1898 to 1917.

During their occupations of Cuba, the Americans modernized its financial system, built roads and public schools, and developed a public health and sanitation program that eradicated the deadly disease of yellow fever. But most Cubans thought these material benefits did not compensate for their loss of political and economic independence. The Platt Amendment remained the basis of American policy toward Cuba until 1934.

The Panama Canal

The Spanish-American War intensified the long American interest in a canal through Central America to eliminate the lengthy and dangerous ocean route around South America. Its commercial value seemed obvious, but the war emphasized its strategic importance. McKinley declared that a canal was now "demanded by the annexation of the Hawaiian Islands and the prospective expansion of our influence and commerce in the Pacific."

Theodore Roosevelt moved quickly to implement McKinley's commitment to a canal after becoming president in 1901. He was convinced that a strong presidential role was at least as important in foreign affairs as in domestic politics. Neither Congress nor "the average American," he believed, took "the trouble to think carefully or deeply" about international affairs. Roosevelt's canal diplomacy helped establish the assertive presidency that has characterized U.S. foreign policy in the twentieth century.

First, Roosevelt persuaded Britain to renounce its treaty right to a joint role with the United States in any canal venture. Britain's willingness reflected a growing friendship between the two nations, both wary of Germany's increasing aggressiveness. Where to build the canal was a problem. Some Americans favored Nicaragua, where a sea-level canal could be built. Another possibility was through Panama, which was part of Colombia. A canal through Panama would require an elaborate system of locks. But the French-owned Panama Canal Company had been unsuccessfully trying to build a canal in Panama and was now eager to sell its rights to the project before they expired in 1904.

In 1902, Congress directed Roosevelt to purchase the French company's claims for $40 million and build the canal in Panama if Colombia ceded a strip of land across the isthmus on reasonable terms. Otherwise, Roosevelt was to negotiate with Nicaragua for the alternate route. In 1903, Roosevelt pressed Colombia to sell a canal zone to the United States for $10 million and an annual payment of $250,000. Colombia, however, rejected the proposal, fearing the loss of its sovereignty in Panama and hoping for more money. After all, when the Panama Canal Company's rights expired, Colombia could then legitimately collect the $40 million so generously offered the company.

Roosevelt was furious. After warning "those contemptible little creatures" in Colombia that they were "imperiling their own future," he began writing a message to Congress proposing military action to seize the isthmus of Panama. Instead of using direct force, however, Roosevelt worked with Philippe Bunau-Varilla, a French official of the Panama Canal Company, to exploit long-smoldering Panamanian discontent with Colombia. Roosevelt's purpose was to get the canal zone, Bunau-Varilla's to get the American money. Roosevelt ordered U.S. naval forces to Panama; from New York, Bunau-Varilla coordinated a revolt against Colombian authority directed by officials of the Panama Railroad, owned by Bunau-Varilla's canal company. The bloodless "revolution" succeeded when U.S. forces prevented Colombian troops from landing in Panama, although the United States was bound by treaty to maintain Colombian sovereignty in the region. Bunau-Varilla promptly signed a treaty accepting Roosevelt's original terms for a canal zone and making Panama a U.S. protectorate, which it remained until 1939. Panamanians themselves denounced the treaty for surrendering sovereignty in the zone to the United States, but they had to acquiesce because their independence depended on American forces. The United States took formal control of the canal zone in 1904 and completed construction of the Panama Canal in 1914.

Many Americans were appalled by what the *Chicago American* called Roosevelt's "rough-riding assault upon another republic over the shattered wreckage of international law and diplomatic usage." But others, as *Public Opinion* reported, wanted a "canal above all things" and were willing to overlook moral questions and approve the acquisition of the canal zone as simply "a business question." Roosevelt himself boasted, "I took the Canal Zone and let Congress debate," but his unnecessary and arrogant actions generated resentment among Latin Americans that rankled for decades.

The Roosevelt Corollary

To protect the security of the canal, the United States increased its authority in the Caribbean. The objective was to establish conditions there that would both eliminate any pretext for European intervention and promote American control over trade and investment. The inability of Latin American nations to pay their debts to foreign lenders raised the possibility of European intervention, as evidenced by a German and British blockade of Venezuela in 1903 to secure repayment of debts to European bankers. "If we intend to say hands off to the powers of Europe," Roosevelt concluded, "then sooner or later we must keep order ourselves."

In his 1904 annual message to Congress, Roosevelt announced a new policy, the so-called **Roosevelt Corollary** to the Monroe Doctrine. "Chronic wrongdoing," he declared, would cause the United States to exercise "an international police power" in Latin America. The Monroe Doctrine had expressed American hostility to European intervention in Latin America; the Roosevelt Corollary attempted to justify U.S. intervention and authority in the region. Roosevelt invoked his corollary immediately, imposing American management of the debts and customs duties of the Dominican Republic in 1905. Commercial rivalries and political intrigue in that poor nation had created disorder, which Roosevelt suppressed for both economic and strategic reasons. Financial insolvency was averted, popular revolution prevented, and possible European intervention forestalled.

Latin Americans vigorously resented the United States' unilateral claims to authority. By 1907, the so-called Drago Doctrine (named after Argentina's foreign minister) was incorporated into international law, prohibiting armed intervention to collect debts. Still, the United States would continue to invoke the Roosevelt Corollary to advance its interests in the hemisphere. As Secretary of State Elihu Root asserted, "The inevitable effect of our building the Canal must be to require us to police the surrounding premises." He then added, "In the nature of things, trade and control, and the obligation to keep order which go with them, must come our way."

AMERICA'S JOURNEY

FROM THEN TO NOW

The Panama Canal

On December 31, 1999, almost a century after the United States took control of the Panama Canal Zone, Panama reclaimed it. "The canal is ours!" proclaimed Panamanian president Mireya Moscoso, just before her country's flag was raised over the canal area, resolving, for the moment at least, a contentious and complex issue.

From the beginning, Panamanians denounced the 1903 treaty—"the treaty that no Panamanian signed"—that had given the United States a perpetual lease over a strip of land that divided their country in two. American sovereignty prevailed in the zone, and the Americans who lived there and ran the canal enjoyed a life of privilege. Panamanians were mostly excluded from the zone; those who worked there were restricted to low-paying jobs and subject to American laws and courts.

Panamanians regularly demanded an end to this "Yankee colonialism," but, for a long time, few Americans spoke up for the return of the zone. As late as 1980, one Senator defended America's continued hold on the zone by declaring, "We stole it fair and square."

But in the 1960s, the United States began to negotiate the return of the Canal Zone to Panama. It had several reasons. The canal was gradually becoming obsolete. Its machinery was aging, and it was too small to accommodate ever-larger ships. From a military standpoint, it was increasingly vulnerable to terrorism and to missile attack. It could not accommodate aircraft carriers. And in any case, its strategic importance had declined since the United States had developed a two-ocean navy. American officials concluded that the canal was no longer of such vital strategic importance that the United States needed to maintain perpetual control and exclusive jurisdiction over it. At the same time, one official noted, the canal's "potential as a source of conflict with the Panamanians had increased."

Under President Jimmy Carter, the United States negotiated two treaties with Panama in 1978. The first returned jurisdiction over the Canal Zone to Panama but left the United States responsible for operating and defending the canal until December 31, 1999. The second gave the United States the permanent right to defend the "neutrality" of the canal. Conservative Republicans worried that the treaties were giving away "our canal" and nearly blocked Senate ratification. Approval came only after the administration agreed to a condition permitting the United States to send troops into Panama after 1999 if necessary to preserve open access to the canal. Panamanians objected that this condition violated their sovereignty and contradicted other treaty provisions that prohibited American intervention in Panama's internal affairs.

The treaties, then, did not end tensions between the United States and Panama. In 1989, President George Bush sent U.S. troops to overthrow Panamanian dictator Manuel Noriega, an erratic leader with close ties to both the CIA and the international drug trade. The United Nations and the Organization of American States condemned the intervention, but the United States justified it in part as protecting "the integrity of the Panama Canal Treaties."

In the 1990s, however, Panama gradually assumed territorial and legal jurisdiction over the canal. Panamanian administrators and workers were phased in to assume responsibilities previously held by Americans, and the Panamanian government collected an ever-larger proportion of the canal's revenues. But even as Panamanians celebrated the final transfer of authority, they worried about the continuing U.S. claim to the right to keep the canal open. After all, when asked how the United States would react if Panama closed down the canal "for repairs," a top U.S. official replied, "We will move in and close down the Panamanian government for repairs."

Theodore Roosevelt at the controls of a giant steam shovel during the construction of the Panama Canal in 1906. Roosevelt's aggressive acquisition of the Canal Zone and its subsequent control by the United States angered Panamanians for nearly a century.

The Roosevelt Corollary proclaimed the intention of the United States to police Latin America. Enforcement came, as this cartoon shows, with Roosevelt and subsequent presidents sending the U.S. Navy to one Caribbean nation after another.

Dollar Diplomacy

Roosevelt's successor as president, William Howard Taft, hoped to promote U.S. interests without such combative rhetoric and naked force. He described his plan as one of "substituting dollars for bullets"—using government action to encourage private American investments in Latin America to supplant European interests, promote development and stability, and gain profits for American bankers. Under this **dollar diplomacy**, American investments in the Caribbean increased dramatically during Taft's presidency from 1909 to 1913, and the State Department helped arrange for American bankers to establish financial control over Haiti and Honduras.

But Taft did not shrink from employing military force to protect American property or to establish the conditions he thought necessary for American investments. In fact, Taft intervened more frequently than Roosevelt had, with Nicaragua a major target. In 1909, Taft sent U.S. troops there to aid a revolution fomented by an American mining corporation and to seize the Nicaraguan customs houses. Under the new government, American bankers then gained control of Nicaragua's national bank, railroad, and customs service. To protect these arrangements, U.S. troops were again dispatched in 1912. To control popular opposition to the American client government, the marines remained in Nicaragua for two decades. Military power, not the social and economic improvement promised by dollar diplomacy, kept Nicaragua's minority government stable and subordinate to the United States.

Dollar diplomacy increased American power and influence in the Caribbean and tied underdeveloped countries to the United States economically and strategically. By 1913, American investments in the region reached $1.5 billion, and Americans had captured more than 50 percent of the foreign trade of Costa Rica, Cuba, the Dominican Republic, Guatemala, Haiti, Honduras, Nicaragua, and Panama. But this policy failed to improve conditions for most Latin Americans. U.S. officials remained primarily concerned with promoting American control and extracting American profits from the region, not with the well-being of its population. One American diplomat, for instance, casually described a Guatemalan president in whose government San Francisco bankers had invested heavily under the premises of dollar diplomacy as a cruel despot who had "the good sense to be civil to our country and its citizens and to keep his cruelties . . . for home consumption." Not surprisingly, dollar diplomacy proved unpopular in Latin America.

Wilsonian Interventions

Taking office in 1913, the Democrat Woodrow Wilson repudiated the interventionist policies of his Republican predecessors. He promised that the United States would "never again seek one additional foot of territory by conquest" but would instead work to promote "human rights, national integrity, and opportunity" in Latin America. Wilson also named as his secretary of state the Democratic symbol of anti-imperialism, William Jennings Bryan. Their generous intentions were apparent when Bryan signed a treaty with Colombia apologizing for Roosevelt's seizure of the Panama Canal Zone in 1903.

Nonetheless, Wilson soon became the most interventionist president in American history, for a number of reasons. He agreed that the United States had to expand its exports and investments abroad and that U.S. dominance of the Caribbean was strategically necessary. He also shared the racist belief that Latin Americans were inferior and needed paternalistic guidance from the United States. In providing that guidance, through military force if necessary, Wilson came close to assuming that American principles and objectives were absolutes, that different cultural traditions and national aspirations were simply wrong. His self-righteousness and determination to transform other peoples' behavior led his policies to be dubbed "missionary diplomacy," but they also contained elements of Roosevelt's commitment to military force and Taft's reliance on economic power.

In 1915, Wilson ordered U.S. Marines to Haiti. They went, explained Bryan, to restore order and preserve "American interests" that were "gravely menaced." The United States saved and even enhanced those interests by establishing a protectorate over Haiti and drawing up a constitution that increased U.S. property rights and commercial privileges. The U.S. Navy selected a new Haitian president, granting him nominal authority over a client government. Real authority, however, rested with the American military, which controlled Haiti until 1934, protecting the small elite who cooperated with foreign interests and exploited their own people. As usual, American military rule improved the country's transportation, sanitation, and educational systems, but the forced-labor program that the U.S. adopted to build such public works provoked widespread resentment. In 1919, marines suppressed a revolt against American domination, killing more than three thousand Haitians.

Wilson also intervened elsewhere in the Caribbean. In 1916, when the Dominican Republic refused to cede control of its finances to U.S. bankers, Wilson ordered the marines to occupy the country. The marines ousted Dominican officials, installed a military government to rule "on behalf of the Dominican government," and ran the nation until 1924. In 1917, the United States intervened in Cuba, which remained under American control until 1922.

Wilson also involved himself in the internal affairs of Mexico. The lengthy dictatorship of Porfirio Díaz had collapsed in 1911 in revolutionary disorder. The popular leader Francisco Madero took power and promised democratic and economic reforms that alarmed both wealthy Mexicans and foreign investors, particularly Americans. In 1913, General Victoriano Huerta seized control in a brutal counterrevolution backed by the landed aristocracy and foreign interests. Most nations recognized the Huerta government, but Wilson, despite strong pressure from American investors, refused to do so. He was appalled by the violence of Huerta's power grab and was aware that opponents had organized to reestablish constitutional government.

Wilson hoped to bring the Constitutionalists to power and "to secure Mexico a better government under which all contracts and business and concessions will be safer than they have been." He authorized arms sales to their forces, led by Venustiano Carranza; pressured Britain and other nations to deprive Huerta of foreign support; and blockaded the Mexican port of Vera Cruz. In April 1914 Wilson exploited a minor incident to have the marines attack and occupy Vera Cruz. This assault damaged his image as a promoter of peace and justice, and even Carranza and the Constitutionalists denounced the American occupation as unwarranted aggression. By August, Carranza had toppled Huerta, and Wilson shifted his support to Francisco ("Pancho") Villa, who seemed more susceptible to American guidance. But Carranza's growing popular support in Mexico and Wilson's preoccupation with World War I in Europe finally led the United States to grant de facto recognition to the Carranza government in October 1915.

Villa then began terrorizing New Mexico and Texas, hoping to provoke an American intervention that would undermine Carranza. In 1916, Wilson ordered troops under General John J. Pershing to pursue Villa into Mexico, leading Carranza to fear a permanent U.S. occupation of northern Mexico. Soon the American soldiers were fighting the Mexican army rather than Villa's bandits. On the brink of full-fledged war, Wilson finally ordered U.S. troops to withdraw in January 1917 and extended full recognition to the Carranza government. Wilson lamely defended these steps as showing that the United States had no intention of imposing on Mexico "an order and government of our own choosing." That had been Wilson's original objective, however. His aggressive tactics had not merely failed but also embittered relations with Mexico.

Conclusion

By the time of Woodrow Wilson's presidency, the United States had been expanding its involvement in world affairs for half a century. Several themes had emerged from this activity: increasing American domination of the Caribbean, continuing interest in East Asia, the creation of an overseas empire, and the evolution of the United States into a major world power. Underlying these developments were an uneasy mixture of ideas and objectives. The American involvement in the world reflected a traditional, if often misguided, sense of national rectitude and mission. Generous humanitarian impulses vied with ugly racist prejudices as Americans sought both to help other peoples and to direct them toward U.S. concepts of religion, sanitation, capitalist development, and public institutions. American motives ranged from ensuring national security and competing with European colonial powers to the conviction that the United States had to expand its economic interests abroad. But if imperialism, both informal and at times colonial, brought Americans greater wealth and power, it also increased tensions in Asia and contributed to anti-American hostility and revolutionary ferment in Latin America. It also entangled the United States in the Great Power rivalries that would ultimately result in two world wars.

Review Questions

1. What factors, old and new, shaped American foreign policy in the late nineteenth century? How were they interrelated?
2. How were individual politicians and diplomats able to affect America's foreign policy? How were they constrained by government institutions, private groups, and public opinion?
3. To what extent was the United States' emergence as an imperial power a break from, as opposed to a culmination of, its earlier policies and national development?
4. How effective were U.S. interventions in Latin America? What were the objectives and consequences?

Recommended Reading

Robert L. Beisner, *From the Old Diplomacy to the New, 1865–1900,* 2d ed. (1986). An excellent analysis of historiographical issues.

Charles S. Campbell, *The Transformation of American Foreign Relations, 1865–1900* (1976). A comprehensive and cautious survey that provides many insights in U.S. foreign policy.

David F. Healy, *Drive to Hegemony: The United States in the Caribbean, 1898–1917* (1988). A valuable account that highlights a key area of American foreign policy.

Walter LaFeber, *The American Search for Opportunity, 1865–1913* (1993). A fascinating study documenting the disruptive international consequences of America's rise to world power.

Walter LaFeber, *The New Empire: An Interpretation of American Expansion, 1860–1898* (1963). An influential study that emphasizes economic factors on American foreign policy.

John L. Offner, *An Unwanted War: The Diplomacy of the United States and Spain over Cuba, 1895–1898* (1992). A revisionist account maintaining that conflict over Cuba was inevitable.

Louis A. Perez, Jr., *The War of 1898: The United States and Cuba in History and Historiography* (1998). A brief book that emphasizes how relations between Cuba and the United States shaped the war and its meaning.

David Pletcher, *The Diplomacy of Trade and Investment: American Economic Expansion in the Hemisphere, 1865–1900* (1998). Stresses the complex but inconsistent and unsystematic nature of American economic expansion.

Additional Sources

Roots of Imperialism

David L. Anderson, *Imperialism and Idealism: American Diplomats in China, 1861–1898* (1985).

Stuart Anderson, *Race and Rapprochement: Anglo-Saxonism and Anglo-American Relations, 1895–1904* (1981).

Patrick J. Hearden, *Independence and Empire: The New South's Cotton Mill Campaign, 1865–1901* (1982).

Patricia R. Hill, *The World Their Household: The American Woman's Foreign Mission Movement and Cultural Transformation, 1870–1920* (1985).

Michael H. Hunt, *Ideology and U.S. Foreign Policy* (1987).

Edmund Morris, *The Rise of Theodore Roosevelt* (1979).

Ernest Paolino, *The Foundations of the American Empire: William Henry Seward and U.S. Foreign Policy* (1973).

Milton Plesur, *America's Outward Thrust: Approaches to Foreign Affairs, 1865–1890* (1971).

David M. Pletcher, *The Awkward Years: American Foreign Relations under Garfield and Arthur* (1962).

Ronald Spector, *Admiral of the New Empire* (1974).

William Widenor, *Henry Cabot Lodge and the Search for an American Foreign Policy* (1980).

William A. Williams, *The Roots of the Modern American Empire* (1969).

The Spanish-American War

Richard Challener, *Admirals, Generals, and American Foreign Policy, 1889–1914* (1973).

Graham A. Cosmas, *An Army for Empire: The United States Army and the Spanish-American War* (1971).

John Dobson, *Reticent Expansionism: The Foreign Policy of William McKinley* (1988).

Willard B. Gatewood, Jr., *Black Americans and the White Man's Burden, 1898–1903* (1975).

Lewis L. Gould, *The Spanish-American War and President McKinley* (1982).

David F. Healy, *U.S. Expansionism: The Imperialist Urge in the 1890s* (1970).

Gerald Linderman, *The Mirror of War: American Society and the Spanish-American War* (1974).

Joyce Milton, *The Yellow Journalists* (1989).

H. Wayne Morgan, *America's Road to Empire: The War with Spain and Overseas Expansion* (1965).

Julius W. Pratt, *Expansionists of 1898* (1936).

David R. Trask, *The War with Spain in 1898* (1981).

Anti-Imperialism

Robert L. Beisner, *Twelve against Empire: The Anti-Imperialists, 1898–1900* (1968).

Thomas J. Osborne, *"Empire Can Wait": American Opposition to Hawaiian Annexation, 1893–1898* (1981).

Daniel B. Schirmer, *Republic or Empire: American Resistance to the Philippine War* (1972).

E. Berkeley Tompkins, *Anti-Imperialism in the United States: The Great Debate, 1890–1920* (1970).

Imperial Ambitions: The United States and East Asia, 1899–1917

Charles S. Campbell, *Special Business Interests and the Open Door Policy* (1951).

Warren I. Cohen, *America's Response to China* (1989).

John M. Gates, *Schoolbooks and Krags: The United States Army in the Philippines* (1973).

Michael H. Hunt, *The Making of a Special Relationship: The U.S. and China to 1914* (1983).

Akira Iriye, *Pacific Estrangement: Japanese and American Expansion, 1897–1911* (1972).

Thomas McCormick, *China Market: America's Quest for Informal Empire* (1967).

Stuart Miller, *"Benevolent Assimilation": The American Conquest of the Philippines, 1899–1903* (1982).

Paul Varg, *The Making of a Myth: The United States and China, 1897–1912* (1968).

Richard E. Welch, *Response to Imperialism: The United States and the Philippine-American War* (1979).

Imperial Power: The United States and Latin America, 1899–1917

Howard K. Beale, *Theodore Roosevelt and the Rise of America to World Power* (1956).

Jules Benjamin, *Hegemony and Development: The United States and Cuba, 1890–1934* (1977).

Bruce Calder, *The Impact of Intervention: The Dominican Republic during the U.S. Occupation of 1916 to 1924* (1984).

Raymond Carr, *Puerto Rico: A Colonial Experiment* (1984).

Arturo Morales Carrion, *Puerto Rico* (1983).

John M. Cooper, Jr., *The Warrior and the Priest: Woodrow Wilson and Theodore Roosevelt* (1983).

John Eisenhower, *The United States and the Mexican Revolution, 1913–1917* (1993).

David F. Healy, *Gunboat Diplomacy in the Wilson Era: The U.S. Navy in Haiti* (1976).

James Hitchman, *Leonard Wood and Cuban Independence, 1898–1902* (1971).

Walter LaFeber, *Inevitable Revolutions: The United States in Central America* (1993).

Walter LaFeber, *The Panama Canal* (1990).

Lester Langley, *The Banana Wars: An Inner History of the American Empire, 1900–1934* (1983).

David McCullough, *The Path between the Seas: The Creation of the Panama Canal* (1977).

Allan R. Millett, *The Politics of Intervention: The Military Occupation of Cuba, 1906–1909* (1968).

Louis A. Perez, Jr., *Cuba under the Platt Amendment, 1902–1934* (1986).

Robert E. Quirk, *An Affair of Honor: Woodrow Wilson and the Occupation of Vera Cruz* (1962).

Where to Learn More

❖ **Mission Houses, Honolulu, Hawaii.** Built between 1821 and 1841, these buildings were homes and shops of missionaries sent to Hawaii by the American Board of Commissioners for Foreign Missions. Their exhibits include furnishings and memorabilia of a group important in developing American ties with Hawaii.

❖ **Funston Memorial Home, Iola, Kansas.** Operated as a museum by the Kansas State Historical Society, this is the boyhood home of General Frederick Funston, prominent in the Spanish-American War and the Filipino-American War.

❖ **James G. Blaine House, Augusta, Maine.** The Executive Mansion of Maine's governor since 1919, this house was formerly Blaine's home and still contains his study and furnishings from the time he served as secretary of state and U.S. senator.

❖ **Rough Riders Memorial and City Museum, Las Vegas, New Mexico.** Together with the nearby Castaneda Hotel, this site provides intriguing information on Roosevelt's volunteer cavalry, recruited primarily from the Southwest.

❖ **Seward House, Auburn, New York.** The home of William H. Seward contains furniture and momentos from his career as secretary of state.

AMERICA AND THE GREAT WAR, 1914–1920

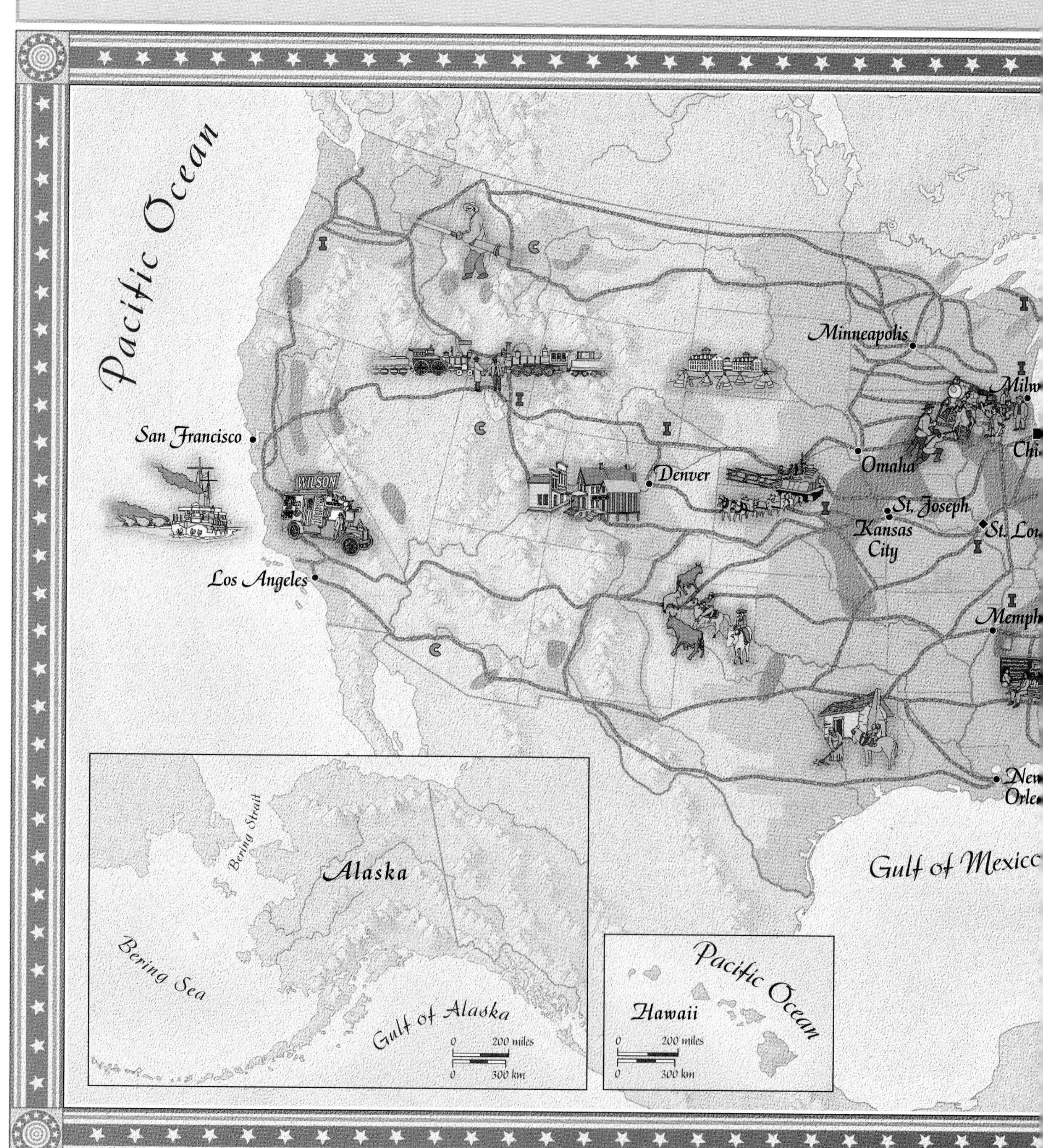

25

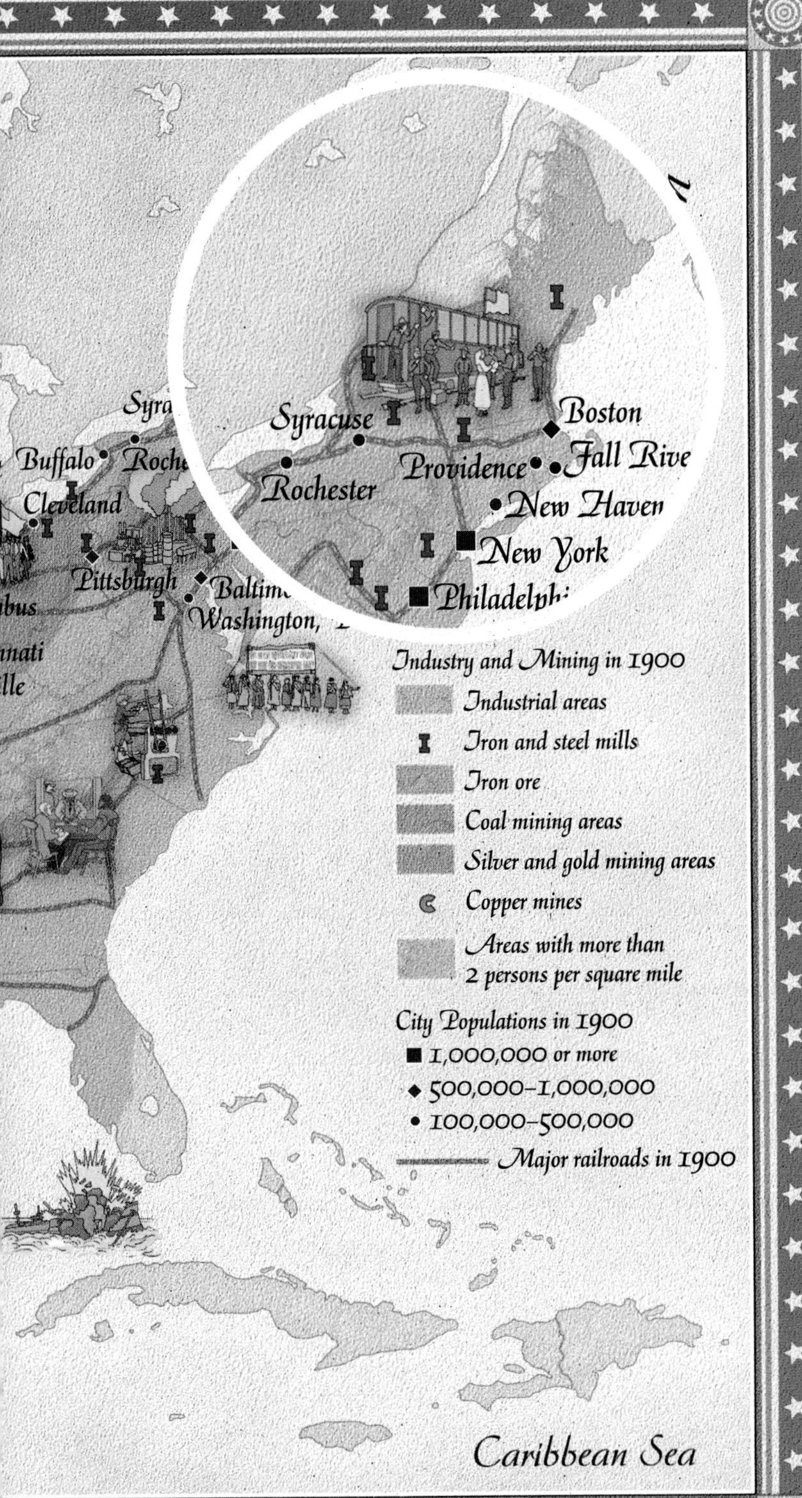

Chapter Outline

Key Topics

- How sympathy for the Allies and outrage over German submarine warfare undermined U.S. neutrality during World War I
- Wilson's decision to join the conflict on the side of the Allies
- The reorganization of the U.S. economy and the challenge to civil liberties that resulted from the war effort
- Wilson's influence on the Versailles Treaty and his failure to gain its ratification in the U.S. Senate
- The postwar backlash

On the evening of April 2, 1917, Woodrow Wilson, escorted by cavalry, drove through a misty rain down Pennsylvania Avenue to Capitol Hill, which was eerily illuminated by searchlights. All day, the antiwar Emergency Peace Federation had lobbied Congress; Senator Henry Cabot Lodge of Massachusetts had even punched one pacifist. Now mounted police with drawn sabers held back silent crowds as the president strode into the house chamber and asked Congress to declare war on Germany, a war that many Americans opposed and that Wilson conceded would sow death, misery, and reaction among them. He threatened "the firm hand of repression" against disloyalty—obviously foreseeing battles at home as well as abroad, clashes of opinion and will scarcely hinted at by Senator Lodge's fistfight. To justify such calamities, Wilson promised that the war would make the world "safe for democracy." Waving small American flags, many members of Congress broke into cheers, and Senator Lodge congratulated Wilson. The Senate passed a resolution for war on April 4, the House on April 6.

On July 10, 1919, Wilson made the same journey down Pennsylvania Avenue to Capitol Hill. This time he rode in brilliant sunshine through cheering crowds and flag-decorated streets. He asked the Senate to ratify a peace treaty that most Americans favored and that Wilson declared would prevent future wars. But many senators received Wilson's address in silence. Several refused even to stand when he entered the chamber. Senator Lodge concealed neither his hatred of the president nor his opposition to the treaty. Apparently affected by the hostility in the room, Wilson spoke without his usual eloquence. During the fierce political struggle over the treaty that followed, the president suffered a stroke that left him crippled. The Senate ultimately rejected the treaty and Wilson's peace.

Between these two presidential appearances, Americans experienced the horrors of the Great War, confronting and overcoming challenges but also sacrificing some of their national ideals and aspirations. Both the United States' intervention in the war and its failure to secure a lasting peace were consequences of serious disagreements over national interests, errors in judgment, and the pursuit of selfish as well as lofty goals. The war declaration came after a long period in which Americans tried to balance their desires for neutrality and peace with their ambitions for wealth, their sympathies for other countries, and their perceptions of America's security and world role. Not only was the war the United States' first major military conflict on foreign soil, but it also changed American life. With economic management and social control considered essential to the war effort, government authority increased sharply. Such changes, from efficiency to Americanization, often reflected prewar progressivism, and the war years did promote reforms. But the war also diverted reform energies into new channels, subordinated generous impulses to those that were more coercive, and strengthened the conservative opposition to reform. The results were often reactionary and contributed to a postwar mood that not only curtailed further reform but also helped defeat the peace treaty.

Waging Neutrality

Few Americans were prepared for the Great War that erupted in Europe in August 1914, but fewer still foresaw that their own nation might become involved in it. With near unanimity, they supported neutrality. But American attitudes, decisions, and actions, both public and private, undercut neutrality, and the policies of governments in Berlin, London, and Washington drew the United States into the war.

The Origins of Conflict

There had been plenty of warning. Since the 1870s, the competing imperial ambitions of the European powers had led to economic rivalries, military expansion, diplomatic maneuvering, and international tensions. A complex system of alliances divided the continent into two opposing blocs. In central Europe, the expansionist Germany of Kaiser Wilhelm II allied itself with the multinational Austro-Hungarian Empire. Confronting

President Woodrow Wilson reads his war message to Congress, April 2, 1917. He predicted "many months of fiery trial and sacrifice ahead of us."

stretching across France and Belgium from the English Channel to Switzerland. Little movement occurred despite great efforts and terrible casualties from artillery, machine guns, and poison gas. The British once suffered 300,000 casualties in an offensive that gained only a few square miles before being pushed back. Machine gunners went into shock at the carnage they inflicted. In the trenches, soldiers suffered in the cold and mud, surrounded by decaying bodies and human waste, enduring lice, rats, and nightmares and dying from disease and exhaustion. The belligerents subordinated their economies, politics, and cultures to military demands. The Great War, said one German soldier, had become "the grave of nations."

them, Great Britain and France formed alliances with Tsarist Russia. A succession of crises threatened this precarious balance of power, and in May 1914 an American diplomat reported anxiously, "There is too much hatred, too many jealousies." He predicted "an awful cataclysm."

The cataclysm began a month later. On June 28, a Serbian terrorist assassinated Archduke Franz Ferdinand, the heir to the Austro-Hungarian throne, in Sarajevo. With Germany's support, Austria declared war on Serbia on July 28. Russia then mobilized its army against Austria to aid Serbia, its Slavic client state. To assist Austria, Germany declared war on Russia and then on Russia's ally France. Hoping for a quick victory, Germany struck at France through neutral Belgium; in response, Britain declared war on Germany on August 4. Soon Turkey and Bulgaria joined Germany and Austria to form the **Central Powers**. The **Allies**—Britain, France, and Russia—were joined by Italy and Japan. Britain drew on its empire for resources, using troops from India, Canada, Australia, New Zealand, and South Africa. The war had become a global conflict, waged not only in Europe but also in Africa, the Middle East, and East Asia.

Mass slaughter enveloped Europe as huge armies battled to a stalemate. The British and French faced the Germans along a line of trenches

American Attitudes

Although the United States had also competed for markets, colonies, and influence, few Americans had expected this calamity. As one North Carolina congressman said, "This dreadful conflict of the nations came to most of us as lightning out of a clear sky." Most people believed that the United States had no vital interest in the war and would not become involved. "Our isolated position and freedom from entangling alliances," noted the *Literary Digest*, "inspire our press with the cheering assurance that we are in no peril of being drawn into the European quarrel." President Wilson issued a proclamation of neutrality and urged Americans to be "neutral in fact as well as in name . . . impartial in thought as well as in action."

However, neither the American people nor their president stayed strictly neutral. German Americans often sympathized with Germany, and many Irish Americans hoped for a British defeat that would free Ireland from British rule. But most Americans sympathized with the Allies. Ethnic, cultural, and economic ties bound most Americans to the British and French. Politically, too, most Americans felt a greater affinity for the democratic Western Allies—tsarist Russia repelled them—than for Germany's more authoritarian government and society. And whereas Britain and the United States had

FROM THEN TO NOW

The United States and the Balkans

The Great War was triggered by events in the Balkans, a corner of Europe long ravaged by violent conflict rooted in ethnic and religious hostility and political rivalry. The terrorists who assassinated Archduke Ferdinand in the Bosnian city of Sarajevo were hoping to create a greater Serbia at the expense of the Austro-Hungarian Empire. Because of a web of entangling alliances, their actions drew the nations of Europe, and eventually the United States, into a cataclysmic war. At the end of the twentieth century, deadly conflict again erupted in the Balkans, producing genocidal massacres and campaigns of "ethnic cleansing"—the forced removal of peoples from their homelands. Trying to decide how to respond to the humanitarian disaster and the threat of spreading conflict, U.S. and European leaders sought lessons from the past.

The United States ignored the troubles in the Balkans before 1914 and then long remained aloof from the war. Only during the peace conference did U.S. diplomats concern themselves with the peoples and issues of the region. The peace treaty created a new nation whose name—the Kingdom of Serbs, Croats, and Slovenes—reflected its factional tensions. (In 1929 it adopted the name Yugoslavia.) President Wilson assured Americans they would not be drawn into any new conflict in the region. "If you want to put out a fire in the Balkans," he promised, "you do not send to the United States for troops."

When violence broke out in the 1990s, the United States initially pursued the same course of noninvolvement. With the Cold War over, conflict in the Balkans seemed unlikely to draw in the major nations. "This is not 1914," insisted observers in 1991. Others suggested that the religious and ethnic factionalism of the region were so historically rooted that intervention was foolish.

The Bush administration accordingly kept a low profile as Yugoslavia disintegrated into separate republics. Even after Serbia invaded Slovenia and Croatia and Serbs began ruthless ethnic cleansing in Bosnia, the United States did little beyond endorsing U.N. proposals for economic sanctions against Serbia and an arms embargo in the region. Bill Clinton criticized Bush's inaction during the 1992 presidential campaign, but once in office he at first followed a similar policy. Like Wilson, Clinton saw nothing in the Balkans worth risking American troops.

But as the violence and atrocities worsened, calls for intervention increased. Fitfully, the Clinton administration and, even more reluctantly, European nations moved to confront Serbia, strengthening sanctions, enforcing no-fly zones, and finally in 1995 bombing Bosnian Serb military forces. American-sponsored peace talks in Dayton, Ohio, supported by Russians eager for Western economic assistance, brought an uneasy peace to Bosnia and temporarily ended the fighting throughout the region. But in 1998 the focus of the conflict shifted to Kosovo, still a province of what remained of Yugoslavia. Serbian forces began a murderous ethnic cleansing campaign against Kosovo's majority population of ethnic Albanians, who were seeking greater political autonomy. The United States, if again belatedly, led NATO in a bombing campaign that forced the Serbs out of Kosovo in 1999, then contributed troops to an international peacekeeping group in the region.

In contrast to its detached role eight decades before, then, the United States, however dilatory and indecisive, led in trying to contain the violence in the 1990s. "America—and America alone—can and should make the difference for peace," Clinton declared in Wilsonian rhetoric. "The need for American leadership is stark." The lesson of World War I, he had concluded, was that European stability, including stability in the Balkans, was a vital interest of the United States.

Gavrilo Princip is arrested after the Serbian terrorist assassinated Archduke Ferdinand in 1914. The subsequent Great War of 1914–1918 was only one of many violent conflicts that engulfed the Balkans in the twentieth century and often drew in other nations, including the United States.

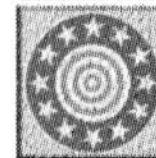

Chronology

1914 World War I begins in Europe.
President Woodrow Wilson declares U.S. neutrality.

1915 Germany begins submarine warfare.
Lusitania is sunk.
Woman's Peace Party is organized.

1916 Gore-McLemore resolutions are defeated.
Sussex Pledge is issued.
Preparedness legislation is enacted.
Woodrow Wilson is reelected president.

1917 Germany resumes unrestricted submarine warfare.
The United States declares war on Germany.
Selective Service Act establishes the military draft.
Espionage Act is passed.
Committee on Public Information, War Industries Board, Food Administration, and other mobilization agencies are established.
American Expeditionary Force arrives in France.
East St. Louis race riot erupts.
Bolshevik Revolution occurs in Russia.

1918 Wilson announces his Fourteen Points.
Sedition Act is passed.
Eugene Debs is imprisoned.
The United States intervenes militarily in Russia.
Armistice ends World War I.

1919 Paris Peace Conference is held.
Steel, coal, and other strikes occur.
Red Scare breaks out.
Prohibition amendment is adopted.
Wilson suffers a massive stroke.

1920 Palmer Raids round up radicals.
League of Nations is defeated in the U.S. Senate.
Woman suffrage amendment is ratified.
U.S. troops are withdrawn from Russia.
Warren Harding is elected president.

1921 United States signs a separate peace treaty with Germany.

enjoyed a rapprochement since 1895, Germany had repeatedly appeared as a potential rival. Many Americans considered it a militaristic nation, particularly after it violated Belgium's neutrality.

Wilson himself admired Britain's culture and government and distrusted Germany's imperial ambitions. Like other influential Americans, Wilson believed that a German victory would threaten America's economic, political, and perhaps even strategic interests. "England is fighting our fight," he said privately. Secretary of State William Jennings Bryan was genuinely neutral, but most officials favored the Allies. Robert Lansing, counselor of the State Department; Walter Hines Page, the ambassador to England; and Colonel Edward House, Wilson's closest adviser on foreign affairs, assisted British diplomats, undercut official U.S. protests against British violations of American neutrality, and encouraged Wilson's suspicions of Germany. Early in the war, House wrote Page, "I cannot see how there can be any serious trouble between England and America, with all of us feeling as we do." House and Lansing assured the Allies privately that "we considered their cause our cause."

British propaganda bolstered American sympathies. British writers, artists, and lecturers depicted the Allies as fighting for civilization against a brutal Germany that mutilated nuns and babies. Although German troops, like most other soldiers, did commit outrages, they were not guilty of the systematic barbarity claimed by Allied propagandists. Britain, however, shaped America's view of the conflict. It cut the only German cable to the United States and censored war news to suit itself. German propaganda directed at American opinion proved so ineffectual that the German ambassador concluded it might as well be abandoned.

Sympathy for the Allies, however, did not mean that Americans favored intervention. The British ambassador complained that it was "useless" to expect any "practical" advantage from the Americans' sympathy, for they had no intention of joining the conflict. Indeed, few Americans doubted that neutrality was the appropriate course and peace the proper goal. The carnage in France solidified their convictions. Wilson was determined to pursue peace as long as his view of national interests allowed.

The Economy of War

Economic issues soon threatened American neutrality. International law permitted neutral nations to sell or ship war material to all belligerents, and, with the economy mired in a recession when the war began, many Americans looked to war orders to spur economic recovery. But the British navy prevented trade with the Central Powers. Only the Allies could buy American goods. Their orders for steel, explosives, uniforms, wheat, and other products, however, pulled the country out of the recession. One journalist rejoiced that "war, for Europe, is meaning devastation and death; for America a bumper crop of new millionaires and a hectic hastening of prosperity revival."

Other Americans worried that this one-sided war trade undermined genuine neutrality. Congress even considered embargoing munitions. But few Americans supported that idea. One financial journal declared of the Allied war trade: "We need it for the profits which it yields." Whatever its justification, however, the war trade strengthened U.S. ties with the Allies and embittered Germans. As the German ambassador noted, American industry was "actually delivering goods only to the enemies of Germany."

A second economic issue complicated matters. To finance their war purchases, the Allies borrowed from American bankers. Initially, Secretary of State Bryan persuaded Wilson to prohibit loans to the belligerents as "inconsistent with the true spirit of neutrality." But as the importance of the war orders to both the Allies and the American economy became clear, Wilson ended the ban. Secretary of the Treasury William McAdoo argued that it would be "disastrous" *not* to finance the Allies' purchases, on which "our prosperity is dependent." By April 1917, American loans to the Allies exceeded $2 billion, nearly one hundred times the amount lent to Germany. These financial ties, like the war trade they underwrote, linked the United States to the Allies and convinced Germany that American neutrality was only a formality.

The Diplomacy of Neutrality

This same imbalance characterized American diplomacy. Wilson insisted on American neutral rights but acquiesced in British violations of those rights while sternly refusing to yield on German actions. Wilson argued that while British violations of international law cost Americans property, markets, and time, German violations cost lives. As the *Boston Globe* noted, the British were "a gang of thieves" and the Germans "a gang of murderers. On the whole, we prefer the thieves, but only as the lesser of two evils."

When the war began, the United States asked belligerents to respect the 1909 **Declaration of London** on neutral rights. Germany agreed to do so; the British refused. Instead, skirting or violating established procedures, Britain instituted a blockade of Germany, mined the North Sea, and forced neutral ships into British ports to search their cargoes and confiscate material deemed useful to the German war effort. These British actions infringed U.S. trading rights. Wilson branded Britain's blockade illegal and unwarranted, but by October he had conceded many of America's neutral rights to avoid conflict with Britain. This concession reflected both Wilson's English sympathies, for he thought it unfair and unrealistic to demand that Britain abandon its most effective weapon, and the profitable war trade with the Allies. He was also convinced that the Allied cause was vital to America's interests.

The British then prohibited food and other products that Germany had imported during peacetime, thereby interfering further with neutral shipping. Even the British admitted that these steps had no legal justification, and one American official complained privately: "England is playing a . . . high game, violating international law every day." But when the Wilson administration finally protested, it undermined its own position by noting that "imperative necessity" might justify a violation of international law. This statement virtually authorized the British to violate American rights. In January 1915, Wilson yielded further by observing that "no very important questions of principle" were involved in the Anglo-American quarrels over ship seizures and that they could be resolved after the war.

This policy tied the United States to the British war effort and provoked a German response. With its army stalemated on land and its navy no match for Britain's, Germany decided in February 1915 to use its submarines against Allied shipping in a war zone around the British Isles. Neutral ships risked being sunk by mistake, partly because British ships illegally flew neutral flags. Germany maintained that Britain's blockade and the acquiesence of neutral countries in British violations of international law made submarine warfare necessary.

Submarines could not readily follow traditional rules of naval warfare. These rules had been drawn up for surface ships and required them to identify enemy merchant ships and ensure the safety of passengers before attacking. But small and fragile submarines depended on surprise attacks. They could not surface without risking disaster from the deck guns of Britain's armed merchant ships, and they were too small to rescue victims of their sinkings. Yet Wilson refused to see the "imperative necessity" in German tactics that he found in British tactics, and he warned that he would hold Germany responsible for any loss of American lives or property.

In May 1915, a German submarine sank a British passenger liner, the *Lusitania*. It had been carrying arms, and the German embassy had warned Americans against traveling on the ship, but the loss of life—1,198 people, including 128 Americans—caused Americans to condemn Germany. "To speak of technicalities and the rules of war, in the face of such wholesale murder on the high seas, is a waste of time," trumpeted one magazine. Yet only six of a thousand editors surveyed called for war, and even the combative Theodore Roosevelt estimated that 98 percent of Americans still opposed war. Wilson saw he had to "carry out the double wish of our people, to maintain a firm front in respect of what we demand of Germany and yet do nothing that might by any possibility involve us in the war."

That was difficult. Wilson demanded that Germany abandon its submarine campaign. His language was so harsh that Bryan resigned, warning that by requiring more of Germany than of Britain, the president violated neutrality and threatened to draw the nation into war. Bryan argued that "Germany has a right to prevent contraband from going to the Allies," and he protested Britain's use of American passengers as shields to protect contraband cargo. "This country cannot be neutral and unneutral at the same time," he declared. "If it is to be neutral it cannot undertake to help one side against the other." Bryan proposed prohibiting Americans from traveling on belligerent ships. His proposal gained support in the South and West, and Senator Thomas Gore of Oklahoma and Representative Jeff McLemore of Texas introduced it in congressional resolutions in February 1916.

Wilson moved to defeat the Gore-McLemore resolutions, insisting that they impinged on presidential control of foreign policy and on America's neutral rights. In truth, the resolutions abandoned no vital national interest while offering to prevent another provocative incident. Moreover, neither law nor tradition gave Americans the right to travel safely on belligerent ships. Wilson's assertion of such a right committed him to a policy that could only lead to conflict. Of the nation's "double wish," then, Wilson placed more priority on confronting what he saw as the German threat than on meeting the popular desire for peace.

Arguments over submarine warfare climaxed in April 1916. A German submarine torpedoed the French ship *Sussex*, injuring four Americans. Wilson threatened to break diplomatic relations if Germany did not abandon unrestricted submarine warfare against all merchant vessels, enemy as well as neutral. This implied war. Germany promised not to sink merchant ships without warning but made its ***Sussex* Pledge** contingent on the United States' requiring Britain also to adhere to "the rules of international law universally recognized before the war." Wilson's diplomatic victory, then, was hollow. Peace for America would depend on the British adopting a course they rejected. As Wilson saw it, however, "any little German lieutenant can put us into the war at any time by some calculated outrage." Wilson's diplomacy had left the nation's future at the mercy of others.

The Battle over Preparedness

The threat of war sparked a debate over military policy. Theodore Roosevelt and a handful of other politicians, mostly northeastern Republicans convinced that Allied victory was in the national interest, advocated what they called **preparedness**, a program to expand the armed forces and establish universal military training. Conservative business groups also joined the agitation. The National Security League, consisting of eastern bankers and industrialists, combined demands for preparedness with attacks on progressive reforms.

But most Americans, certain that their nation would not join the bloody madness, opposed expensive military preparations. Many supported a large peace movement. Leading feminists like Jane Addams, Charlotte Perkins Gilman, and Carrie Chapman Catt formed the Woman's Peace Party in 1915, and other organizations like the American League to Limit Armaments also campaigned against preparedness. William Jennings Bryan denounced the militarism of Roosevelt as a "philosophy [that] can rot a soul" and condemned preparedness as a program for turning the nation into "a vast armory with skull and crossbones above the door." Most opponents agreed that military spending would undermine domestic reform and raise taxes while enriching arms merchants and financiers.

Wilson also opposed preparedness initially, but he reversed his position when the submarine crisis with Germany intensified. He also began to champion military expansion lest Republicans accuse him in the 1916 election of neglecting national defense. In early 1916, he made a speaking tour to generate public support for expanding the armed forces. Continuing opposition to preparedness, especially in the South and West, forced Wilson to drop his proposal

A preparedness parade winds its way through Mobile, Alabama, on July 4, 1916. By 1916, President Wilson, invoking the spirit of patriotism, had given his support to the preparedness program of military expansion.

for a national reserve force. Nevertheless, the National Defense Act and the Naval Construction Act increased the strength of the army and authorized a naval construction plan. Draped in the flag, Wilson marched at the head of a huge preparedness parade in Washington to celebrate the military program.

The Election of 1916

Wilson's preparedness plans stripped the Republicans of one issue in 1916, and his renewed support of progressive reforms (see Chapter 23) helped hold Bryan Democrats in line. Wilson continued his balancing act in the campaign itself, at first stressing "Americanism" and preparedness but then emphasizing peace. The slogan "He Kept Us Out of War" appealed to the popular desire for peace, and the Democratic campaign became one long peace rally. Wilson disliked the peace emphasis but exploited its political appeal. He warned, "The certain prospect of the success of the Republican party is that we shall be drawn, in one form or another, into the embroilments of the European war."

The Republicans were divided. They had hoped to regain their progressive members after Roosevelt urged the Progressive party to follow him back into the GOP. But many joined the Democratic camp instead, including several Progressive party leaders who endorsed Wilson for having enacted the party's demands of 1912. Roosevelt's frenzied interventionism had also alienated many midwestern Republicans opposed to preparedness and cost him any chance of gaining the nomination for himself. Instead, the GOP nominated Charles Evans Hughes, a Supreme Court justice and former New York governor. The platform denounced Wilson's "shifty expedients" in foreign policy and promised "strict and honest neutrality." Unfortunately for Hughes, Roosevelt's attacks on Wilson for not pursuing a war policy persuaded many voters that the GOP was a war party. The link with Roosevelt also kept Hughes from exploiting qualms about Wilson's own unneutrality. "If Hughes is defeated," wrote one observer, "he has Roosevelt to thank for it."

The election was the closest in decades (see Map 25-1). When California narrowly went for Wilson, it decided the contest. The results reflected sectional differences, with the South and West voting for Wilson and most of the Northeast and Midwest for Hughes. The desire for peace, all observers concluded, had determined the election.

Descent into War

Still, Wilson knew that war loomed, and he made a last effort to avert it. In 1915 and 1916, he had tried to mediate the European conflict, using Colonel House as a secret intermediary. Now he again appealed for an end to hostilities. In January 1917, he sketched out the terms of what he called a

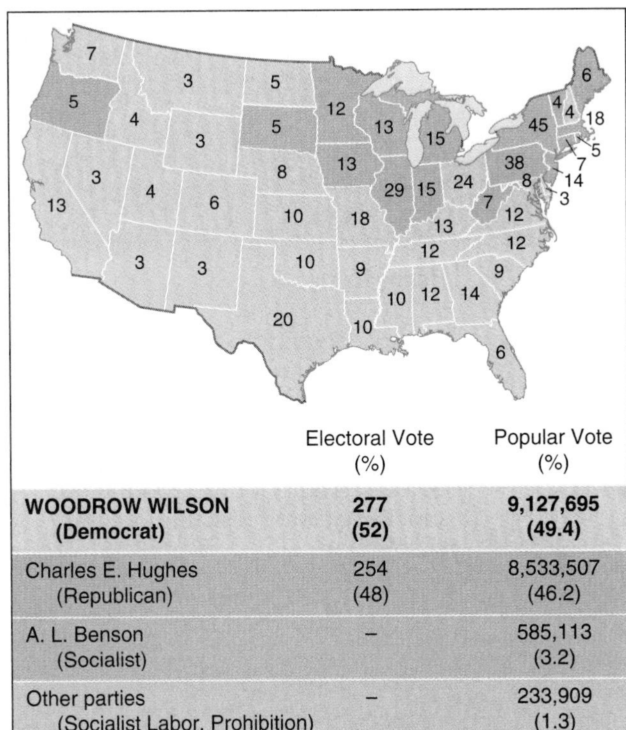

	Electoral Vote (%)	Popular Vote (%)
WOODROW WILSON (Democrat)	**277 (52)**	**9,127,695 (49.4)**
Charles E. Hughes (Republican)	254 (48)	8,533,507 (46.2)
A. L. Benson (Socialist)	–	585,113 (3.2)
Other parties (Socialist Labor, Prohibition)	–	233,909 (1.3)

Map 25-1 **The Election of 1916**
Woodrow Wilson won reelection in 1916 despite a reunified Republican party by sweeping the South and West on campaign appeals to peace and progressive reform.

"peace without victory." Anything else, he warned, would only lead to another war. The new world order should be based on national equality and **self-determination**, arms reductions, freedom of the seas, and an international organization to ensure peace. It was a distinctly American vision.

Neither the Allies nor the Central Powers were interested. Each side had sacrificed too much to settle for anything short of outright victory. Germany wanted to annex territory in eastern Europe, Belgium, and France and to take over Belgian and French colonies in Africa; Austria sought Balkan territory. The Allies wanted to destroy German military and commercial power, weaken the Austro-Hungarian empire, take Germany's colonies in Africa, and supplant Turkish influence in the Middle East. One British leader denounced Wilson as "the quintessence of a prig" for suggesting that after three years of "this terrible effort," the two sides should accept American principles rather than their own national objectives. Wilson's initiative failed.

Germany decided to resume unrestricted submarine warfare. German generals believed that even if the United States declared war, it could do little more in the short run to injure Germany than it was already doing. German submarines, they hoped, would end the war by cutting the Allies off from U.S. supplies before the United States could send an army to Europe. On January 31, Germany announced its decision to unleash its submarines in a broad war zone.

Wilson was now virtually committed to a war many Americans opposed. He broke diplomatic relations with Germany and asked Congress to arm American merchant vessels. When the Senate refused, Wilson invoked an antipiracy law of 1819 and armed the ships anyway. Although no American ships had yet been sunk, he also ordered the naval gun crews to shoot submarines on sight. Wilson's own secretary of the navy warned that these actions violated international law and were a step toward war; Wilson called his policy "armed neutrality." Huge rallies across America demanded peace.

Yet several developments soon shifted public opinion. On March 1, Wilson released an intercepted message from the German foreign minister, Arthur Zimmermann, to the German minister in Mexico. It proposed that in the event of war between the United States and Germany, Mexico should ally itself with Germany; in exchange, Mexico would recover its "lost territory in Texas, New Mexico, and Arizona." The Zimmermann note produced a wave of hostility toward Germany and increased support for intervention in the war, especially in the Southwest, which had opposed involvement. A revolution in Russia overthrew the tsarist regime and established a provisional government. Russia was now "a fit partner" for the United States, said Wilson. When submarines sank four American freighters in mid-March, anti-German feeling broadened.

On April 2, 1917, Wilson delivered his war message, declaring that neutrality was no longer possible, given Germany's submarine "warfare against mankind." To build support for joining a war that most people had long regarded with revulsion and as alien to American interests, Wilson set forth the nation's war goals as simple and noble. The United States would not fight for conquest or domination but for "the ultimate peace of the world and for the liberation of its peoples. . . . The world must be made safe for democracy." Interventionists like Senator Lodge were delighted with the decision for war but distanced themselves from any goal other than promoting national interests. Some progressives who had opposed involvement were won over by Wilson's appeal to idealism.

But others in Congress attacked war. Senator Robert La Follette assailed Wilson's policies as unneutral. Senator George Norris of Nebraska condemned the economic motives for American belligerency, crying out, "We are going to war upon the command of gold." Ridiculing Wilson's advocacy of war as a means to promote democracy, House Democratic leader Claude Kitchin of North Carolina insisted that the American people opposed war and requested a popular referendum on the question. After vigorous debate, the Senate passed the war resolution 82 to 6 and the House 373 to 50. On April 6, 1917, the United States officially entered the Great War, what Kitchin predicted would be "one vast drama of horrors and blood, one boundless stage upon which will play all the evil spirits of earth and hell."

OVERVIEW

MAJOR GOVERNMENT WARTIME AGENCIES

Agency	Purpose
War Industries Board	Reorganized industry to maximize wartime production
Railway Administration	Modernized and operated the nation's railroads
Food Administration	Increased agricultural production, supervised food distribution and farm labor
National War Labor Board	Resolved labor-management disputes, improved labor conditions, and recognized union rights as means to promote production and efficiency
Committee on Public Information	Managed propaganda to build public support for the war effort

Waging War in America

Mobilizing for military intervention was a massive undertaking. "It is not an army that we must shape and train for war," announced President Wilson; "it is a Nation." The government reorganized the economy to emphasize centralized management, developed policies to control public opinion and suppress dissent, and transformed the role of government itself. Mobilization often built on progressives' moralism and sense of mission and their work to resolve social and economic problems by government intervention. In other respects, however, the war experience undercut progressive achievements and withered the spirits of reformers. In many different ways, people on the home front—like soldiers in Europe—would participate in the Great War; all would find their lives changed.

Managing the War Economy

Surveying the nation's economy in May 1917, Secretary of War Newton Baker echoed Wilson. War no longer involved merely soldiers and weapons, he said. "It is the conflict of smokestacks now, the combat of the driving wheel and the engine." To harness those factories and machines for the war, federal and state governments developed a complex structure of agencies and controls for every sector of the economy, from industry and agriculture to transportation and labor (see the overview table, "Major Government Wartime Agencies"). Supervised by the Council of National Defense, these agencies shifted resources to war-related enterprise, increased production of goods and services, and improved transportation and distribution.

The most important agency was the **War Industries Board (WIB)**, established in July 1917 to set industrial priorities, coordinate military purchasing, and supervise business. Led by financier Bernard Baruch, the WIB exercised unprecedented powers over industry by setting prices, allocating scarce materials, and standardizing products and procedures to boost efficiency. The number of sizes and styles of plows was reduced by 80 percent; the number of colors of typewriter ribbon dropped from 150 to 5. The WIB even specified how many trunks traveling salesmen could carry and how many stops elevators could make. Yet Baruch was not an industrial dictator; he aimed at business–government integration. The WIB promoted major business interests, helped suspend antitrust laws, and guaranteed huge corporate profits. So many business leaders became involved in the WIB that there was a popular outcry against business infiltration of the government, and one corporate executive admitted, "We are all making more money out of this war than the average human being ought to." Some progressives began to see the dangers, and business leaders the advantages, of government economic intervention.

The **Railroad Administration** also linked business ambitions to the war economy. Under William McAdoo, it operated the nation's railroads as a unified system to move supplies and troops efficiently. Centralized management eliminated competition, permitted improvements in equipment, and brought great profits to the owners but higher prices to the general public. Progressive Republican Senator Hiram Johnson of California protested that the Railroad Administration was "outrageously generous to the railroads and shamefully unjust to the people."

Equally effective and far more popular was the **Food Administration**, headed by Herbert Hoover. Hoover had organized relief supplies for war-torn Belgium and now controlled the production and distribution of food for the United States and its allies. He persuaded millions of Americans to accept meatless and wheatless days so that the Food Administration could feed military and foreign consumers. Half a million women went door to door to secure food conservation pledges from housewives. City residents planted victory gardens in parks and vacant lots, and President Wilson even pastured sheep on the White House lawn.

Hoover also worked closely with agricultural processors and distributors, assuring profits in exchange for cooperation. Farmers profited from the war, too. To encourage production, Hoover established high prices for commodities, and agricultural income rose 30 percent. State and federal governments also provided commercial farmers with sufficient farm labor despite the military draft and competition from high-wage war industries. The Food Administration organized the Woman's Land Army to work in the fields. Most states formed units of the Boys' Working Reserve for agricultural labor. Many southern and western states required "loafers" or "slackers" to work in agriculture. Agribusinesses in the Southwest persuaded the federal government to permit them to import Mexicans to work under government supervision and be housed in special camps.

The **National War Labor Board** supervised labor relations. In exchange for labor's cooperation, this agency guaranteed the rights of unions to organize and bargain collectively. With such support, unions sharply increased their membership. The labor board also encouraged improved working conditions, higher wages, and shorter hours. War contracts stipulated an eight-hour day, and by the end of the war, nearly half

"Eat the potatoes, save the wheat; drive the Kaiser to defeat." Children in Wahoo, Nebraska, tend their victory garden. Government agencies tried to enlist everyone in the war effort.

the nation's workers had achieved the forty-eight-hour week. Wages rose, too, but often only as fast as inflation. These improvements limited labor disputes during the war, and Secretary of War Baker praised labor as "more willing to keep in step than capital." But when unions like the Industrial Workers of the World did not keep in step, the government suppressed them.

Although these and other government regulatory agencies were dismantled when the war ended, their activities reinforced many long-standing trends in the American economy, from the consolidation of business to the commercialization of agriculture and the organization of labor. They also set a precedent for governmental activism that would prove valuable during the crises of the 1930s and 1940s.

New Opportunities, Old Issues

The reorganization of the economy also had significant social consequences, especially for women and African Americans. In response to labor shortages, women took jobs previously closed to them. Besides farm work, they built airplanes, produced guns and ammunition, and manufactured tents and cartridge belts. More than 100,000 women worked in munitions plants and 40,000 in the steel industry. Women constituted 20 percent or more of all workers making electrical machinery, leather and rubber goods, and food. They operated drills and lathes, controlled cranes in steel mills, and repaired equipment in machine shops. "One of the lessons from the war," said one manufacturer, "has been to show that women can do exacting work." Harriot Stanton Blatch, a suffragist active in the Food Administration, estimated that a million women had replaced men in industry, where "their drudgery is for the first time paid for."

Many working women simply shifted to other jobs where their existing skills earned better wages and benefits. The reshuffling of jobs among white women opened new vacancies for black women in domestic, clerical, and industrial employment. As black women replaced white women in the garment and textile industries, social reformers spoke of "a new day for the colored woman worker." But such optimism was unwarranted. Racial as well as gender segregation continued to mark employment, and wartime improvements were temporary.

The war helped middle-class women reformers achieve two long-sought objectives: woman suffrage and prohibition. Women's support for the war effort prompted more Americans to support woman suffrage. Emphasizing the national cooperation needed to wage the war, one magazine noted that "arbitrarily to draw the line at voting, at a time when every man and woman must share in this effort, becomes an absurd anomaly." Even Woodrow Wilson finally endorsed the reform, terming it "vital to the winning of the war." Congress approved the suffrage amendment, which was ratified in 1920. Convinced that abstaining from alcohol would save grain and make workers and soldiers more efficient, Congress also passed the **prohibition** amendment, which was ratified in 1919.

The war also changed the lives of African Americans. The demand for industrial labor caused a huge migration of black people from the rural South, where they had had little opportunity, few rights, and no hope. In northern cities, they worked in shipyards, steel mills, and packing houses. Half a million African Americans moved north during the war, doubling and tripling the black populations of Chicago, Detroit, and other industrial cities.

Unfortunately, black people often encountered the kind of racial discrimination and violence in the North they had hoped to leave behind in the South. Fearful and resentful white people started race riots in northern cities. In East St. Louis, Illinois, where thousands of black Southerners sought defense work, a white mob in July 1917 murdered at least thirty-nine black people, sparing, as an investigating committee reported, "neither age nor sex in their blind lust for blood." Others placed the tragedy in a larger context. The *Literary Digest* noted, "Race-riots in East St. Louis afford a lurid background to our efforts to carry justice and idealism to Europe." And Wilson was told privately that the riot was "worse than anything the Germans did in Belgium."

Financing the War

To finance the war, the government borrowed money and raised taxes. Business interests favored the first course, but southern and western progressives argued that taxation was more efficient and equitable and would minimize war profiteering. Conservative and business opposition to progressive taxation prompted California Senator Johnson to note, "Our endeavours to impose heavy war profit taxes . . . have brought into sharp relief the skin-deep dollar patriotism of some of those who have been loudest in declamations on war and in their demands for blood." Nevertheless, the tax laws of 1917 and 1918 established a graduated tax structure with increased taxes on large incomes, corporate profits, and wealthy estates. Conservative opposition, however, would frustrate progressives' hopes for permanent tax reforms.

The government raised two-thirds of the war costs by borrowing. Most of the loans came from banks and wealthy investors, but the government also campaigned to sell **Liberty Bonds** to the general public. Celebrities went to schools, churches, and rallies to persuade Americans to buy bonds as their patriotic duty. "Every person who refuses to sub-

"Beat Back the Hun," a poster to induce Americans to buy Liberty Bonds, demonizes the enemy in a raw, emotional appeal. Liberty bond drives raised the immense sum of $23 billion.

scribe," Secretary of the Treasury McAdoo told a California audience, "is a friend of Germany." Using techniques of persuasion and control from advertising and mass entertainment, the Wilson administration thus enlisted the emotions of loyalty, fear, patriotism, and obedience for the war effort.

Conquering Minds

The government also tried to promote a war spirit among the American people by establishing propaganda agencies and enacting legislation to control social attitudes and behavior. This program drew from the restrictive side of progressivism: its impulses toward social control, behavior regulation, and nativism. It also reflected the interests of more conservative forces. The Wilson administration adopted this program of social mobilization because many Americans opposed the war: German Americans with ethnic ties to the Central Powers, Irish Catholics and Russian Jews who condemned the Allies for persecution and repression, Scandinavian immigrants averse to military service, pacifists who recoiled from what Wilson himself called "the most terrible and disastrous of all wars," radicals who denounced the war as capitalist and imperialist, and many others, especially among the rural classes of the South and Midwest, who saw no reason to participate in the distant war.

To rally Americans behind the war effort, Wilson established the **Committee on Public Information (CPI)** under George Creel. Despite its title, the CPI sought to manipulate, not inform, public opinion. Creel described his goal as winning "the fight for the *minds* of men, for the 'conquest of their convictions.'" The CPI flooded the country with press releases, advertisements, cartoons, and canned editorials. An average of six pounds of government publicity went each day to every newspaper in California, for example. The CPI made newsreels and war movies to capture public attention. It scheduled 75,000 speakers, who delivered a million speeches to 400 million listeners. Its women's division targeted American women in stereotyped emotional terms. It hired artists to draw posters, professors to write pamphlets in twenty-three languages, and poets to compose war poems for children.

Other government agencies launched similar campaigns. The Woman's Committee of the Council of National Defense established the Department of Educational Propaganda and Patriotic Education. Carrie Chapman Catt dropped her peace activism to head this bureau, in the hope that the war effort would increase support for woman suffrage. The agency worked to win over women who opposed the war, particularly in the rural Midwest, West, and South. It formed women's speakers' bureaus, developed programs for community meetings at country schools, and distributed millions of pamphlets.

Government propaganda had three themes: national unity, the loathsome character of the enemy, and the war as a grand crusade for liberty and democracy. Obsessed with national unity and conformity, Creel promoted fear, hatred, and prejudice in the name of a triumphant Americanism. Germans were depicted as brutal, even subhuman, rapists and murderers. The campaign suggested that any dissent was unpatriotic, if not treasonous, and dangerous to national survival. This emphasis on unreasoning conformity helped prompt hysterical attacks on German Americans, radicals, and pacifists.

Suppressing Dissent

The Wilson administration also suppressed dissent, now officially branded disloyalty. For reasons of their own, private interests helped shape a reactionary repression that tarnished the nation's professed idealistic war goals. The campaign also established unfortunate precedents for the future.

Congress rushed to stifle antiwar sentiment. The **Espionage Act** provided heavy fines and up to twenty years in prison for obstructing the war effort, a vague phrase but one "omnipotently comprehensive," warned one Idaho senator who opposed the law. "No man can foresee what it might be in its consequences." In fact, the Espionage Act became a weapon to crush dissent and criticism. In 1918, Congress passed the still more sweeping **Sedition Act**. Based on state laws in the West designed to suppress labor radicals, the Sedition Act provided severe penalties for speaking or writing against the draft, bond sales, or war production or for criticizing government personnel or policies. Congress emphasized the law's inclusive nature by *rejecting* a proposed amendment stipulating that "nothing in this act shall be construed as limiting the liberty or impairing the right of any individual to publish or speak what is true, with good motives, and for justifiable ends." Senator Hiram Johnson lamented: "It is war. But, good God, . . . when did it become war upon the American people?"

Postmaster General Albert Burleson banned antiwar or radical newspapers and magazines from the mail, suppressing literature so indiscriminately that one observer said he "didn't know socialism from rheumatism." Even more zealous in attacking radicals and presumed subversives was the reactionary attorney general, Thomas Gregory, who made little distinction between traitors and pacifists, war critics, and radicals. Eugene Debs was sentenced to ten years in prison for a "treasonous" speech in which he declared it "extremely dangerous to exercise the right of free speech in a country fighting to make democracy safe in the world." By war's end, a third of the Socialist party's national leadership was in prison, leaving the party in shambles. Other notable radicals imprisoned included Ricardo Flores Magon, a Mexican-American labor organizer who was sentenced to twenty years for publishing antiwar material in his Los Angeles Spanish-language newspaper, *Regeneracion.*

Gregory also enlisted the help of private vigilantes, including several hundred thousand members of the reactionary **American Protective League**, which sought to purge radicals and reformers from the nation's economic and political life. They wiretapped telephones, intercepted private mail, burglarized union offices, broke up German-language newspapers, harassed immigrants, and staged mass raids, seizing thousands of people they claimed were not doing enough for the war effort. Even George Creel conceded that "at all times their patriotism was a thing of screams, violence, and extremes, and their savage intolerances had the burn of acid."

State and local authorities also sought to suppress what they saw as antiwar, radical, or pro-German activities. They established 184,000 investigating and enforcement agencies known as councils of defense or public safety committees. They encouraged Americans to spy on one another, required people to buy Liberty Bonds, and prohibited teaching German in schools or using the language in religious services and telephone conversations (see "American Views: Mobilizing America for Liberty"). Indeed, suppression of all things German reached extremes. Germanic names of towns, streets, and people were changed; sauerkraut became liberty cabbage, and the hamburger the liberty sandwich. In Tulsa, a member of the council of defense killed someone for making allegedly pro-German remarks. The council declared its approval, and community leaders applauded the killer's patriotism. A midwestern official of the Council of National Defense noted, "All over this part of the country men are being tarred and feathered and some are being lynched. . . . These cases do not get into the newspapers nor is an effort ever made to punish the individuals concerned."

Members of the business community exploited the hysteria to promote their own interests at the expense of farmers, workers, and reformers. As one Wisconsin farmer complained, businessmen "now under the guise of patriotism are trying to ram down the farmers' throats things they hardly dared before." On the Great Plains from Texas to North Dakota, the business target was the Nonpartisan League, a radical farm group demanding state control or ownership of banks, grain elevators, and flour mills. Although the League supported the war, oversubscribed bond drives, and had George Creel affirm its loyalty, conservatives depicted it as seditious to block its advocacy of political and economic reforms, including the confiscation of large fortunes to pay for the war. Minnesota's public safety commission condemned members of the Nonpartisan League as traitors and proposed a "firing squad working overtime" to deal with them. Nebraska's council of defense barred League meetings. Public officials and self-styled patriots broke up the League's meetings and whipped and jailed its leaders.

In the West, business interests targeted labor organizations, especially the Industrial Workers of the World. In Arizona, for example, the Phelps-Dodge Company broke a miners' strike in 1917 by depicting the Wobblies as bent on war-related sabotage. A vigilante mob, armed and paid by the mining company, seized twelve hundred strikers, many of them Wobblies and one-third of them Mexican Americans, and herded them into the desert without food or water. Federal investigators found no evidence of sedition among the miners and reported that the company and its thugs had been inspired not by "patriotism" but by "ordinary strike-breaking motives." Corporate management was merely "raising the false cry of 'disloyalty'" to suppress workers' complaints.

Nonetheless, the government itself assisted the business campaign. It used the army to break loggers' support for the IWW in the Pacific Northwest, and it raided IWW halls across the country in September 1917. The conviction of nearly two hundred Wobblies on charges of sedition in three mass trials in Illinois, California, and Kansas crippled the nation's largest industrial union.

In the end, the government was primarily responsible for the war hysteria, regardless of how such fears were used. It encouraged suspicion and conflict by its own inflammatory propaganda, repressive laws, and violation of basic civil rights, by supporting extremists who used the war for their own purposes, and by not opposing mob violence against German Americans. This ugly mood would infect the postwar world.

Waging War and Peace Abroad

While mobilizing the home front, the Wilson administration undertook an impressive military effort to help the Allies defeat the Central Powers. Wilson also struggled to secure international acceptance for his plans for a just and permanent peace.

The War to End All Wars

When the United States entered the war, the Allied military position was dire. The losses from three years of trench warfare had sapped military strength and civilian morale. French soldiers mutinied and refused to continue an assault that had cost 120,000 casualties in five days; the German submarine campaign was devastating the British. On the eastern front, the Russian army collapsed, and the Russian government gradually disintegrated after the overthrow of the tsarist regime.

What the Allies needed, said French Marshal Joseph Joffre in April 1917, was simple: "We want men, men, men." In May, Congress passed the **Selective Service Act**, establishing conscription. More than 24 million men eventually registered for the draft, and nearly 3 million entered the army when their numbers were drawn in a national lottery. Almost 2 million more men volunteered, as did more than ten thousand women who served in the navy. Nearly one-fifth of America's soldiers were foreign-born (Europeans spoke of the "American Foreign Legion"); 367,000 were black.

Civilians were transformed into soldiers in hastily organized training camps operated according to progressive principles. Prohibition prevailed

The United States quickly raised, trained, and transported a large military force that helped to defeat Germany in the Great War. Within it were the black troops of the Fifteenth Infantry, shown here with their white officers on board ship.

American Views

Mobilizing America for Liberty

The war years witnessed official and popular efforts to repress dissent and diversity. Much of this repression was aimed at America's immigrant groups and sought to create national unity through coercive Americanization that trampled on the rights and values that the nation claimed to be defending. The following is an official proclamation of Governor W. L. Harding of Iowa, issued May 23, 1918.

- **What is the rationale for the governor's proclamation? What do you think of his interpretation of the constitutional guarantees of individual rights?**
- **What other "inconvenience or sacrifice" might the proclamation impose on minorities?**
- **How might the proclamation incite vigilantism?**

The official language of the United States and the State of Iowa is the English language. Freedom of speech is guaranteed by federal and State Constitutions, but this is not a guaranty of the right to use a language other than the language of this country—the English language. Both federal and State Constitutions also provide that "no laws shall be made respecting an establishment of religion or prohibiting the free exercise thereof." Each person is guaranteed freedom to worship God according to the dictates of his own conscience, but this guaranty does not protect him in the use of a foreign language when he can as well express his thought in English, nor entitle the person who cannot speak or understand the English language to employ a foreign language, when to do so tends in time of national peril, to create discord among neighbors and citizens, or to disturb the peace and quiet of the community.

in the camps; the poorly educated and largely working-class recruits were taught personal hygiene; worries about sin and inefficiency produced massive campaigns against venereal disease; and immigrants were taught English and American history. Some units were ethnically segregated: At Camp Gordon, Georgia, Italians and Slavs had separate units with their own officers. Racial segregation was more rigid, not only in training camps and military units but in assignments as well. The navy assigned black sailors to menial positions, and the army similarly used black soldiers primarily as gravediggers and laborers. But one black combat division was created, and four black regiments fought under French command. France decorated three of these units with its highest citations for valor. (White American officers urged the French not to praise black troops, treat black officers as equals, or permit fraternization.)

The first American troops landed in France in June 1917. This **American Expeditionary Force (AEF)** was commanded by General John J. Pershing, a career officer who had chased Pancho Villa across northern Mexico (see Chapter 24). Full-scale American intervention began in the late spring of 1918 (see Map 25-2). In June, the fresh American troops helped the French repulse a German thrust toward Paris at Château-Thierry. In July, the AEF helped defeat another German advance, at Rheims. The influx of American troops tipped the balance toward Allied victory. By July 18, the German chancellor later acknowledged, "even the most optimistic among us knew that all was lost. The history of the world was played out in three days."

Every person should appreciate and observe his duty to refrain from all acts or conversation which may excite suspicion or produce strife among the people, but in his relation to the public should so demean himself that every word and act will manifest his loyalty to his country and his solemn purpose to aid in achieving victory for our army and navy and the permanent peace of the world. . . .

The great aim and object of all should be unity of purpose and a solidarity of all the people under the flag for victory. This much we owe to ourselves, to posterity, to our country, and to the world.

Therefore, the following rules should obtain in Iowa during the war:

First. English should and must be the only medium of instruction in public, private, denominational, or other similar schools.

Second. Conversation in public places, on trains, and over the telephone should be in the English language.

Third. All public addresses should be in the English language.

Fourth. Let those who cannot speak or understand the English language conduct their religious worship in their homes.

This course carried out in the spirit of patriotism, though inconvenient to some, will not interfere with their guaranteed constitutional rights and will result in peace and tranquility at home and greatly strengthen the country in battle. The blessings of the United States are so great that any inconvenience or sacrifice should willingly be made for their perpetuity.

Therefore, by virtue of authority in me vested, I, W. L. Harding, Governor of the State of Iowa, commend the spirit of tolerance and urge that henceforth the within outlined rules be adhered to by all, that petty differences be avoided and forgotten, and that, united as one people with one purpose and one language, we fight shoulder to shoulder for the good of mankind.

Source: B. F. Shambaugh, ed., Iowa and War *(Iowa City: State Historical Society of Iowa, 1919).*

In July, Wilson also agreed to commit fifteen thousand American troops to intervene in Russia. Russia's provisional government had collapsed when the **Bolsheviks**, or communists, had seized power in November 1917. Under V. I. Lenin, the Bolsheviks had then signed an armistice with Germany in early 1918, which freed German troops for the summer offensive in France. The Allies' interventions were designed to reopen the eastern front and help overthrow the Bolshevik government. Lenin's call for the destruction of capitalism and imperialism alarmed the Allied leaders. One Wilson adviser urged the "eradication" of the Russian government. Soon American and British troops were fighting Russians in an effort to influence Russia's internal affairs. U.S. forces remained in Russia until 1920, even after Germany had surrendered in 1918. These military interventions failed, but they did promote lasting Russian distrust of the West.

The Allies were more successful on the western front. Having stopped the German offensive in July, they launched their own advance. The decisive battle began in late September when an American army over 1 million strong attacked German trenches in the Argonne Forest. The Americans were inexperienced; some had been drafted only in July and had spent more time traveling than training. One officer worried, "With their unfamiliarity with weapons, a gun was about as much use as a broom in their hands." Nevertheless, the Americans advanced steadily, despite attacks with poison gas and heavy artillery. Lieutenant Maury Maverick (later a Texas congressman) described

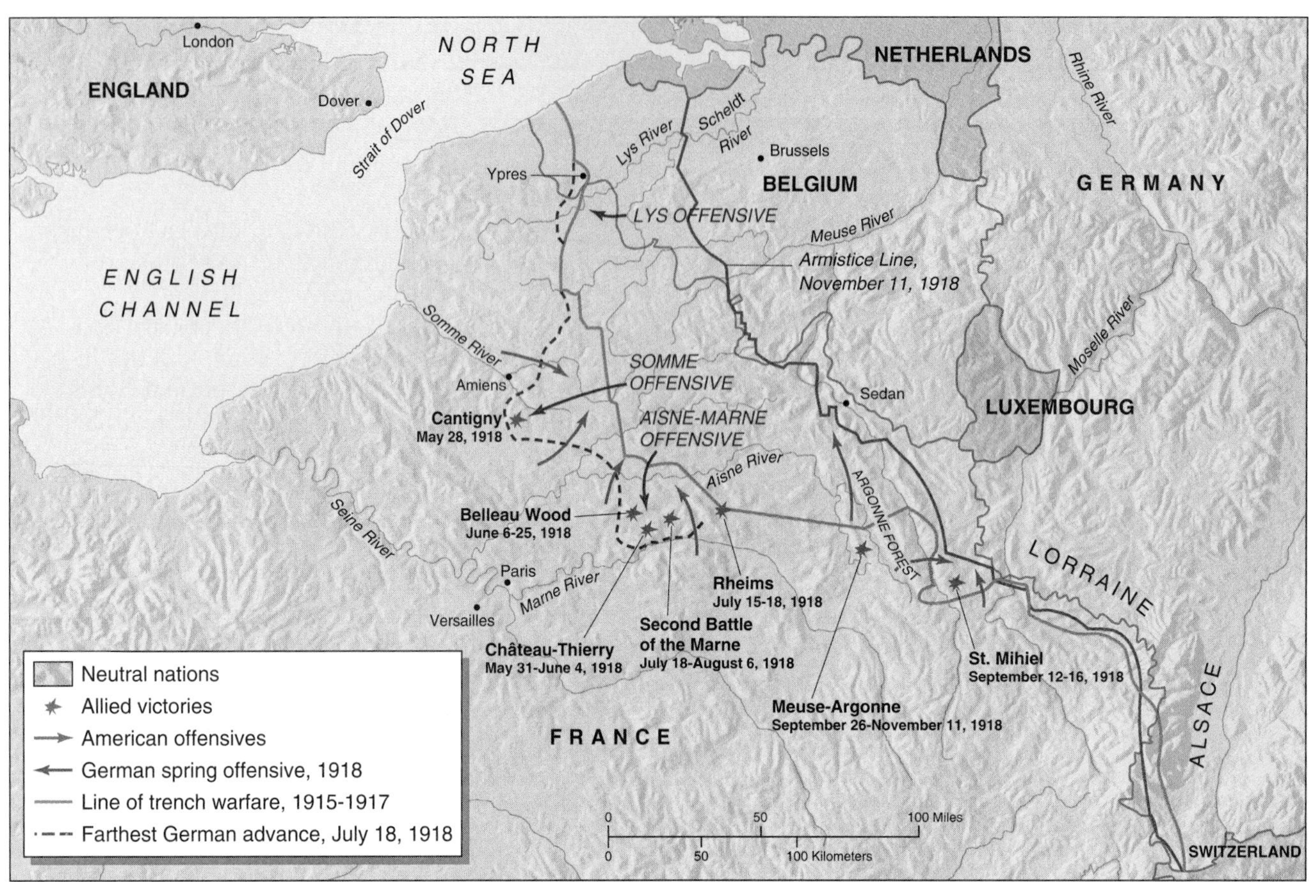

Map 25-2 The Western Front, 1918
After three years of trench warfare, the arrival of large numbers of American troops in 1918 enabled the Allies to launch an offensive that drove back the Germans and forced an armistice.

the shelling: "We were simply in a big black spot with streaks of screaming red and yellow, with roaring giants in the sky tearing and whirling and roaring." An exploding shell terrified him: "There is a great swishing scream, a smash-bang, and it seems to tear everything loose from you. The intensity of it simply enters your heart and brain, and tears every nerve to pieces."

The battle for the Argonne raged for weeks. One German general reported that his exhausted soldiers faced Americans who "were fresh, eager for fighting, and brave." But he found their sheer numbers most impressive. Eventually, this massive assault overwhelmed the Germans. Despite severe casualties, the AEF had helped the British and French defeat the enemy. With its allies surrendering, its own army in retreat, and revolution breaking out among war-weary residents in its major cities, Germany asked for peace. On November 11, 1918, an armistice ended the Great War. More than 115,000 Americans were among the 8 million soldiers and 7 million civilians dead.

The Fourteen Points

The armistice was only a step toward final peace. President Wilson had already enunciated American war objectives on January 8, 1918, in a speech outlining what became known as the Fourteen Points. In his 1917 war message, Wilson had advocated a more democratic world system, and this new speech spelled out how to achieve it. But Wilson also had a political purpose. The Bolsheviks had published the secret treaties the Allies had signed dividing up the economic and territorial spoils of war. Lenin called for an immediate peace based on the liberation of all colonies, self-determination for all peoples, and the rejection of annexations and punitive indemnities. Wilson's Fourteen Points reassured the American and Allied peoples that they were fighting for more than imperialist gains and offered an alternative to what he called Lenin's "crude formula" for peace.

Eight of Wilson's points proposed creating new nations, shifting old borders, or assuring self-determination for peoples previously subject to the Austrian, German, or Russian empires. The point about Russia would haunt Wilson after the Allied interventions there began, for it called on all nations to evacuate Russian territory and permit Russia "an unhampered and unembarrassed opportunity for the independent determination of her own political development" under "institutions of her own choosing." Another five points invoked principles to guide international relations: freedom of the seas, open diplomacy instead of secret treaties, reduction of armaments, free trade, and the fair settlement of colonial claims. Wilson's fourteenth and most important point proposed a league of nations to carry out these ideals and ensure international stability.

Wilson and the German government had these principles in mind when negotiating the armistice. The Allies, however, had never explicitly accepted the Fourteen Points, and framing a final peace treaty would be difficult. While Wilson favored a settlement that would promote international stability and economic expansion, he recognized that the Allies sought "to get everything out of Germany that they can." Indeed, after their human and economic sacrifices, Britain and France wanted tangible compensation, not pious principles.

Convinced of the righteousness of his cause, Wilson decided to attend the peace conference in Paris himself, though no president had ever gone to Europe while in office. But Wilson weakened his position before he even set sail. First, he urged voters to support Democratic candidates in the November 1918 elections to indicate approval of his peace plans. But the electorate, responding primarily to domestic problems like inflation, gave the Republicans control of both houses of Congress. This meant that any treaty would have to be approved by Senate Republicans angry that Wilson had tried to use war and peace for partisan purposes. Second, Wilson refused to consult with Senate Republicans on plans for the peace conference and failed to name important Republicans to the Paris delegation. It would be Wilson's treaty, but Republicans would feel no responsibility to approve it.

The Paris Peace Conference

The peace conference opened on January 18, 1919. Meeting at the Palace of Versailles, the delegations were dominated by the principal Allied leaders themselves: Wilson of the United States, David Lloyd George of Britain, Georges Clemenceau of France, and Vittorio Orlando of Italy. The Central Powers and Bolshevik Russia were excluded. The treaty would be one-sided except to the extent that Wilson could insist on the liberal terms of the Fourteen Points against French and British intransigence. As Clemenceau remarked, "God gave us the Ten Commandments and we broke them. Mr. Wilson has given us the Fourteen Points. We shall see."

Wilson himself had broken two of the Fourteen Points before the conference began. He had acquiesced in Britain's rejection of freedom of the seas. And he had sent U.S. troops to intervene in Russia in violation of its right to self-determination.

For months, the conference debated Wilson's other goals and the Allies' demands for compensation and security. Lloyd George later commented, with reference to the self-righteous Wilson and the assertive

The Big Four gather at the Paris Peace Conference. Vittorio Orlando of Italy, David Lloyd George of Great Britain, and Georges Clemenceau of France join Woodrow Wilson to discuss the terms of the treaty. The three Europeans had little interest in Wilson's Fourteen Points.

Clemenceau, "I think I did as well as might be expected, seated as I was between Jesus Christ and Napoleon Bonaparte." Under protest, Germany signed the **Treaty of Versailles** on June 28, 1919. Its terms were far more severe than Wilson had proposed or Germany had anticipated. Germany had to accept sole responsibility for starting the war, which all Germans bitterly resented. It was required to pay huge reparations to the Allies; to give up land to France, Poland, Belgium, and Denmark; to cede its colonies; to limit its army and navy to small self-defense forces; to destroy military bases; and to promise not to manufacture or purchase armaments.

Wilson gained some acceptance of self-determination. As the German, Austro-Hungarian, Turkish, and Russian empires had collapsed at the end of the war, nationalist groups had proclaimed their independence. On one hand, the peace settlement formally recognized these new nation-states: Poland, Finland, Estonia, Latvia, and Lithuania in eastern Europe and Austria, Hungary, Czechoslovakia, and Yugoslavia in central Europe (see Map 25-3). On the other hand, France, Italy, Romania, and Japan all annexed territory regardless of the wishes of the inhabitants. Germans were placed under Polish control in Silesia and Czech control in Bohemia. Austrians were not allowed to merge with Germany. And the conference sanctioned colonialism by establishing a trusteeship system that enabled France, Britain, and Japan to take over German colonies and Turkish territory.

Moreover, the Allied leaders endorsed the changes in eastern Europe in part because the new states there were anticommunist. Western leaders soon called these countries the **cordon sanitaire**, a barrier against Bolshevism. Indeed, the Allies at Versailles were preoccupied with Bolshevik Russia, which one of Wilson's aides called the "black cloud of the east, threatening to overwhelm and swallow up the world." Communist movements in early 1919 in Germany, Austria, and Hungary caused the Allies to fear that "the Russian idea was still rising in power," and they hoped to isolate and weaken Bolshevik Russia. Allied armies were in Russia during the peace conference, and Wilson and the other leaders agreed to provide further aid to fight the Bolsheviks. This hostility to Russia, like the punitive terms for Germany and the concessions to imperial interests, boded ill for a stable and just postwar order.

But Wilson hoped that the final section of the Versailles treaty would resolve the flaws of the agreement by establishing his great international organization to preserve peace: the **League of Nations**. The Covenant, or constitution, of the League was built into the treaty. Its crucial feature, Article Ten, bound the member nations to guarantee each other's independence, which was Wilson's concept of collective security. "At least," he told an aide, "we are saving the Covenant, and that instrument will work wonders, bring the blessing of peace, and then when the war psychosis has abated, it will not be difficult to settle all disputes that baffle us now." Sailing home, he mused: "Well, it is finished, and, as no one is satisfied, it makes me hope we have made a just peace; but it is all on the lap of the gods."

Waging Peace at Home

Wilson was determined to defeat opposition to the peace treaty. But many Americans were engaged in their own struggles with the new conditions of a nation suddenly at peace but riven by economic, social, and political conflict shaped by the war experience. Wilson's battle for the League of Nations would fail tragically. The other conflicts would rage until the election of 1920 restored a normalcy of sorts.

Battle over the League

Most Americans favored the Versailles treaty. A survey of fourteen hundred newspapers found fewer than two hundred opposed. Thirty-three governors and thirty-two state legislatures approved of the League of Nations. But when Wilson called for the Senate to accept "the moral leadership . . . and confidence of the world" by ratifying the treaty, he met resistance. Some Republicans wanted to prevent the Democrats from campaigning in 1920 as the party responsible for a victorious war and a glorious peace. But most Republican opponents of the treaty raised serious questions, often reflecting national traditions in foreign relations. Nearly all Democrats favored the treaty, but they were a minority; some Republicans had to be converted for the treaty to be approved.

Progressive Republican senators, such as Robert La Follette and Hiram Johnson, led one group of opponents. Called the **Irreconcilables**, they opposed participation in the League of Nations, which they saw as designed to perpetuate the power of imperialist countries. Article Ten, they feared, would require the United States to help suppress rebellions in Ireland against British rule or to enforce disputed European borders. Johnson declared, "I am opposed to American boys policing Europe and quelling riots in every new nation's backyard." Most of the Irreconcilables gave priority to restoring civil liberties and progressive reform at home.

A larger group of opponents had reservations about the treaty's provisions. These **Reservationists** were led by Henry Cabot Lodge, the chair of the Sen-

Map 25-3 Europe and the Middle East after the Treaty of Versailles
World War I and the Treaty of Versailles rearranged the borders of Europe and the Middle East. Germany, Russia, and the Austrian and Turkish empires all lost land, and new nations were recognized, but the principle of self-determination was only imperfectly observed.

ate Foreign Relations Committee. They regarded Article Ten as eroding congressional authority to declare war. They also fretted that the League might interfere with domestic questions, such as immigration laws. Lodge held public hearings on the treaty to rouse and focus opposition. German Americans resented the war guilt clause; Italian and Polish Americans complained that the treaty did not satisfy the territorial ambitions of Italy and Poland; Irish Americans condemned the treaty's failure to give self-determination to Ireland. Many progressives also criticized the treaty's compromises on self-determination, reparations, and colonies. Linking these failures with Wilson's domestic policies, one former supporter concluded; "The administration has become reactionary, and deserves no support from any of us."

Lodge's own opposition was shaped by both partisanship and deep personal hostility. "I never expected to hate anyone in politics with the hatred I feel toward Wilson," Lodge confessed. Wilson reciprocated, and when Lodge proposed reservations or amendments to the treaty, Wilson refused to compromise. He proposed "a direct frontal attack" on his opponents. If they wanted war, he said, he would "give them a belly full." In early September 1919, Wilson set out across the country to win popular support for the League. In three weeks, he traveled eight thousand miles and delivered thirty-seven speeches.

In poor health following a bout with influenza, he collapsed in Pueblo, Colorado. Confused and in tears, Wilson mumbled to his secretary, "I seem to have gone to pieces." Taken back to Washington, Wilson on October 2 suffered a massive stroke that paralyzed his left side and left him psychologically unstable and temporarily blind. Wilson's physician and his wife, Edith Galt Wilson, kept the nature of his illness secret from the public, Congress, and even the vice president and cabinet. Rumors circulated that Edith Wilson was running the administration, but she was not. Instead, it was immobilized.

By February 1920, Wilson had partially recovered, but he remained suspicious and quarrelsome. Bryan and other Democratic leaders urged him to accept Lodge's reservations to gain ratification of the treaty. Wilson refused. Isolated and inflexible, he ordered Democratic senators to vote with the Irreconcilables against the treaty as amended by Lodge. On March 19, 1920, the Senate killed the treaty.

Economic Readjustment and Social Conflict

The League was not the only casualty of the struggle to conclude the war. Grave problems shook the United States in 1919 and early 1920. An influenza epidemic had erupted in Europe in 1918 among the massed armies. It now hit the United States, killing perhaps 700,000 Americans, far more than had died in combat. Frightened authorities closed public facilities and banned public meetings in futile attempts to stop the contagion.

Meanwhile, the Wilson administration had no plans for an orderly reconversion of the wartime economy, and chaos ensued. The secretary of the Council of National Defense later reported with but slight exaggeration, "The magnificent war formation of American industry was dissipated in a day; the mobilization that had taken many months was succeeded by an instantaneous demobilization." The government canceled war contracts and dissolved the regulatory agencies. Noting that "the war spirit of cooperation and sacrifice" had disappeared with the Armistice, Bernard Baruch decided to "turn industry absolutely free" and abolished the War Industries Board as of January 1, 1919. Other agencies followed in such haste that turmoil engulfed the economy.

The government also demobilized the armed forces. The army discharged 600,000 soldiers still in training camps; the navy brought AEF soldiers home from France so fast that it had to expand the troop fleet to four times its peak size during the war. With no planning or assistance, troops were hustled back into civilian life. There they competed for scarce jobs with workers recently discharged from the war industries.

As unemployment mounted, the removal of wartime price controls brought runaway inflation. The cost of food, clothing, and other necessities more than doubled over prewar rates. The return of the soldiers caused a serious housing shortage, and rents skyrocketed. Democratic leaders urged Wilson to devote less time to the League of Nations and more to the cost of living and the tensions it unleashed. Farmers also suffered from economic readjustments. Net farm income declined by 65 percent between 1919 and 1921. Farmers who had borrowed money for machinery and land to expand production for the war effort were left impoverished and embittered.

Women also lost their wartime economic advances. Returning soldiers took away their jobs. Male trade unionists insisted that women go back to being housewives. One New York union maintained that "the same patriotism which induced women to enter industry during the war should induce them to vacate their positions after the war." At times, male workers struck to force employers to fire women and barred women from unions in jobs where union membership was required for employment. Most women were willing to relinquish their jobs to veterans who had previously held them but objected to being displaced by men without experience. "During the war they called us heroines," one woman complained, "but they throw us on the scrapheap now." By 1919, half of the women newly employed in heavy industry during the war were gone; by 1920, women constituted a smaller proportion of the work force than they had in 1910.

The postwar readjustments also left African Americans disappointed. During the war, they had agreed with W. E. B. Du Bois to "forget our special grievances and close our ranks shoulder to shoulder with our own white fellow citizens." Participation in the war effort, they hoped, might be rewarded by better treatment thereafter. African Americans had contributed to the fighting and home fronts. Now, the meagerness of their reward became clear.

Housing shortages and job competition interacted with racism in 1919 to produce race riots in twenty-six towns and cities, resulting in at least 120 deaths. In Chicago, thirty-eight people were killed and more than five hundred injured in a five-day riot that began when white thugs stoned to death a black youth swimming too near "their" beach. White rioters then fired a machine gun from a truck hurtling through black neighborhoods. But black residents fought back, no longer willing, the *Chicago Defender* reported, "to move along the line of least resistance as did their sires." The new militancy reflected both their experiences in the military and in industry and their exposure to propaganda about freedom and democracy. Racial conflict was part of a postwar battle between Americans hoping to preserve the new social relations fostered by the war effort and those wanting to restore prewar patterns of power and control.

Even more pervasive discontents roiled as America adjusted to the postwar world. More than 4 million angry workers launched a wave of 3,600 strikes in 1919. They were reacting not only to the soaring cost of living, which undermined the value of their wages, but also to employers' efforts to reassert their authority and destroy the legitimacy labor had won by its participation in the war effort. The abolition of government controls on industry enabled employers not only to raise prices but also to rescind their recognition of unions and reimpose objectionable working conditions. Employers also protected their rising profits by insisting that workers' wages remain fixed. In response, strikers demanded higher wages, better conditions, and recognition of unions and the right of collective bargaining.

The greatest strike involved the American Federation of Labor's attempt to organize steelworkers, who endured dangerous conditions and twelve-hour shifts. When the steel companies refused to recognize the union or even discuss issues, 365,000 workers went out on strike in September 1919. Strikers in Pennsylvania pointed out that they had worked "cheerfully, without strikes or trouble of any kind" during the war to "make the world safe for democracy" and that they now sought "industrial democracy." Employers hired thugs to beat the strikers, used strikebreakers to take their jobs, and exploited ethnic and racial divisions among them. To undercut support for the workers, management portrayed the strikers as disruptive radicals influenced by Bolshevism. After four months, the strike failed.

Employers used the same tactic to defeat striking coal miners, whose wages had fallen behind the cost of living. Refusing to negotiate with the United Mine Workers, coal operators claimed that Russian Bolsheviks financed the strike to destroy the American economy. Attorney General Mitchell Palmer secured an injunction against the strike under the authority of wartime legislation. Because the government no longer controlled coal prices or enforced protective labor rules, miners complained bitterly that the war had ended for corporations but not for workers.

Two municipal strikes in 1919 also alarmed the public when their opponents depicted them as revolutionary attacks on the social order. In Seattle in February, the Central Labor Council called a general strike to support 35,000 shipyard workers striking for higher wages and shorter hours. When 60,000 more workers from 110 local unions also walked out, the city ground to a halt. Workers behaved peacefully and protected public health and safety by operating garbage and fire trucks and providing food, water, and electricity. Nevertheless, Seattle's mayor, business leaders, and newspapers attacked the strikers as Bolsheviks and anarchists. Threatened with military intervention, the labor council called off the strike, but not before it had caused a public backlash against unions across the nation.

In Boston, the police commissioner fired police officers for trying to organize a union to improve their inadequate pay. In response, the police went on strike. As in Seattle, Boston newspapers, politicians,

Using eight different languages, a steel company poster combines patriotic and ethnic appeals with denunciations of "alien radicals" to urge workers to abandon their 1919 strike. The strikers were seeking union recognition and an end to twelve-hour days but were forcibly suppressed.

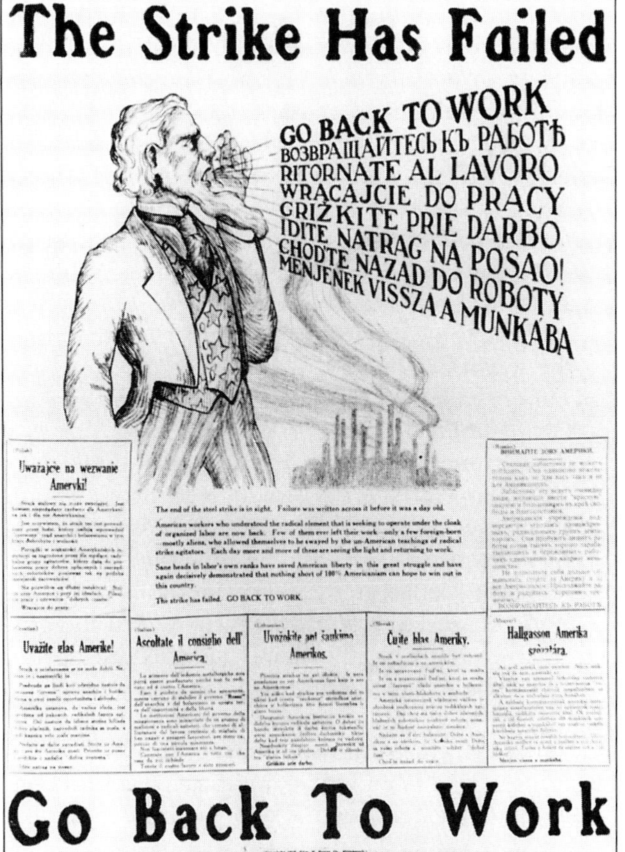

and business leaders attributed the strike to Bolshevism, although nothing indicated that the police wanted anything more than improved wages, conditions, and respect. Wilson denounced the Boston police strike as "a crime against civilization." Governor Calvin Coolidge mobilized the National Guard and gained nationwide acclaim when he stated, "There is no right to strike against the public safety by anybody, anywhere, anytime." The police were all fired; many of their replacements were war veterans.

Red Scare

The strikes contributed to an anti-Bolshevik hysteria that swept the country in 1919. This **Red Scare** reflected fears that the Bolshevik revolution in Russia might spread to the United States. Steeped in the antiradical propaganda of the war years, many Americans were appalled by Russian Bolshevism, described by the *Saturday Evening Post* as a "compound of slaughter, confiscation, anarchy, and universal disorder." Their alarm grew in 1919 when Russia established the **Third International** to foster revolution abroad, and a few American socialists formed the American Communist Party. But the Red Scare also reflected the willingness of antiunion employers, ambitious politicians, sensational journalists, zealous veterans, and racists to exploit the panic to advance their own purposes.

Fed by misleading reports about Russian Bolshevism and its influence in the United States, the Red Scare reached panic levels by mid-1919. Bombs mailed anonymously to several prominent people on May Day seemed proof enough that a Bolshevik conspiracy threatened America. The Justice Department, Congress, and patriotic organizations like the American Legion joined with business groups to suppress radicalism, real and imagined. The government continued to enforce the repressive laws against Wobblies, socialists, and other dissenters; a Minnesota senator warned that the nation was more imperiled than during the war itself. Indeed, Wilson and Attorney General Palmer called for more stringent laws and refused to release political prisoners jailed during the war. State governments harassed and arrested hundreds.

Palmer created a new agency, headed by J. Edgar Hoover, to suppress radicals and impose conformity. Its war on radicalism became the chief focus of the Justice Department. As an ambitious and ruthless bureaucrat, Hoover had participated in the government's assault on aliens and radicals during the war. Now he collected files on labor leaders and other "radical agitators" from Senator La Follette to Jane Addams, issued misleading reports on communist influence in labor strikes and race riots, and contacted all major newspapers "to acquaint people like you with the real menace of evil-thinking, which is the foundation of the Red Movement." Indeed, the Justice Department itself promoted the Red Scare hysteria, which Palmer hoped would lead to his presidential nomination and Hoover hoped would enhance his own power and that of his bureau.

In November 1919, Palmer and Hoover began raiding groups suspected of subversion. A month later, they deported 249 alien radicals, including the anarchist Emma Goldman, to Russia. Rabid patriots endorsed such actions. One minister favored deporting radicals "in ships of stone with sails of lead, with the wrath of God for a breeze and with hell for their first port." In January 1920, Palmer and Hoover rounded up more than four thousand suspected radicals in thirty-three cities. Without warrants, they broke into union halls, club rooms, and private homes, assaulting and arresting everyone in sight. People were jailed without access to lawyers; some were beaten into signing false confessions. In Lynn, Massachusetts, thirty-nine people meeting to organize a bakery were arrested for holding a revolutionary caucus. Other arrests were just as outrageous, but the *Washington Post* clamored, "There is no time to waste on hairsplitting over infringement of liberty."

Other Americans began to recoil from the excesses and illegal acts. Assistant Secretary of Labor Louis Post stopped further deportations by demonstrating that most of the arrested were "working men of good character, who are not anarchists or revolutionists, nor politically or otherwise dangerous in any sense." They had been arrested, he said, "for nothing more dangerous than affiliating with friends of their own race, country, and language." Support for the Red Scare withered. Palmer's attempt to inflame public emotions to advance his own candidacy for the presidency backfired. When his predictions of a violent attempt to overthrow the government on May 1, 1920, came to naught, most Americans could see that no menace had ever existed. They agreed with the *Rocky Mountain News*: "We can never get to work if we keep jumping sideways in fear of the bewhiskered Bolshevik." Even one conservative Republican concluded that "too much has been said about Bolshevism in America." But if the Red Scare faded in mid-1920, the hostility to immigrants, organized labor, and dissent it reflected would endure for a decade. During the 1920s, the most acceptable forms of social change would be derived from technological and commercial innovations.

The Election of 1920

Palmer failed to win the Democratic nomination, but it would have been an empty prize anyway. The Democratic coalition that Wilson had cobbled together on the issues of progressivism and peace came apart after the war. Workers resented the administration's hostility to the postwar strikes. Ethnic groups brutalized by the Americanization of the war years blamed Wilson for the war or condemned his peace settlement. Farmers grumbled about wartime price controls and postwar falling prices. Wartime taxes and the social and economic turmoil of 1919–1920 alienated the middle class. Americans were weary of great crusades and social sacrifices; in the words of Kansas journalist William Allen White, they were "tired of issues, sick at heart of ideals, and weary of being noble." They yearned for what Republican presidential candidate Warren Harding of Ohio called "normalcy."

The Republican ticket in 1920 symbolized the reassurance of simpler times. Harding was a genial politician who in a lengthy career had devoted more time to golf and poker than to public policy. An Old Guard conservative, he had stayed with the GOP when Theodore Roosevelt led the progressives out in 1912. His running mate, Calvin Coolidge, governor of Massachusetts, owed his nomination to his handling of the Boston police strike.

In a 1920 cartoon, "A. Mitchell Palmer Out for a Stroll," the Chicago Tribune *lampooned the Attorney General for his repeated but unfounded warnings about Bolshevik threats in America. The postwar Red Scare weakened civil liberties, promoted nativist hostilities, and undermined reform.*

Wilson called the election of 1920 "a great and solemn referendum" on the League of Nations, but such lofty appeals fell flat. Harding was ambiguous about the League, and the Democratic national platform endorsed it but expressed a willingness to accept amendments or reservations. The Democratic nominees, James Cox, former governor of Ohio, and the young Franklin D. Roosevelt, Wilson's assistant secretary of the navy, favored the League, but it was not a decisive issue in the campaign.

Harding won in a landslide reflecting the nation's dissatisfaction with Wilson and the Democratic party. "The Democrats are inconceivably unpopular," wrote Walter Lippmann, a prominent journalist. Harding received 16 million popular votes to Cox's 9 million. Running for president from his prison cell, Socialist Eugene Debs polled nearly a million votes. Not even his closest backers considered Harding qualified for the White House, but, as Lippmann said, the nation's "public spirit was exhausted" after the war years. The election of 1920 was "the final twitch" of America's "war mind."

Conclusion

The Great War disrupted the United States and much of the rest of the world. The initial American policy of neutrality yielded to sentimental and substantive links with the Allies and the pressure of German submarine warfare. Despite popular opposition, America joined the conflict when its leaders concluded that national interests demanded it. Using both military and diplomatic power, Woodrow Wilson sought to secure a more stable and prosperous world order, with an expanded role for the United States. But the Treaty of Versailles only partly fulfilled his hopes, and the Senate refused to ratify the treaty and its League of Nations. The postwar world order would be unstable and dangerous.

Participation in the war, moreover, had changed the American government, economy, and society. Some of these changes, including the centralization of the economy and an expansion of the regulatory role of the federal government, were already under way; some offered opportunities to implement progressive principles or reforms. Woman suffrage and prohibition gained decisive support because of the war spirit. But other consequences of the war betrayed both progressive impulses and the democratic principles the war was allegedly fought to promote. The suppression of civil liberties, manipulation of human emotions, repression of radicals and minorities, and exploitation of national crises by narrow interests helped disillusion the public. The repercussions of the Great War would linger for years, at home and abroad.

Review Questions

1. What were the major arguments for and against U.S. entry into the Great War? What position do you find most persuasive? Why?
2. How and why did the United States shape public opinion in World War I? What were the consequences, positive and negative, of the propaganda of the Committee on Public Information, Food Administration, and other government agencies?
3. How did other groups exploit the war crisis and the government's propaganda and repression?
4. Evaluate the role of Woodrow Wilson at the Paris Peace Conference. What obstacles did he face? How successful was he in shaping the settlement?
5. Discuss the arguments for and against American ratification of the Treaty of Versailles.

Recommended Reading

Kendrick A. Clements, *The Presidency of Woodrow Wilson* (1992). The best single volume on the Wilson presidency.

Edward M. Coffman, *The War to End All Wars* (1968). A valuable study of the U.S. military role in World War I.

Robert H. Ferrell, *Woodrow Wilson and World War I, 1917–1921* (1985). A useful synthesis that emphasizes diplomatic issues.

D. Clayton James and Anne Sharp Wells, *America and the Great War, 1914–1920* (1998). A fine, succinct synthesis of recent scholarship.

David M. Kennedy, *Over Here: The First World War and American Society* (1980). Thorough and illuminating discussion of the impact of World War I on American society.

Robert K. Murray, *The Red Scare: A Study in National Hysteria, 1919–1920* (1955). An important early study that retains much value.

Ronald Schaffer, *America in the Great War: The Rise of the War Welfare State* (1991). An effective and provocative summary that illuminates the expanding role of government.

Additional Sources

General Studies

John Whiteclay Chambers II, *The Tyranny of Change* (1992).

John M. Cooper, Jr., *Pivotal Decades: The United States, 1900–1920* (1990).

Otis L. Graham, Jr., *The Great Campaigns: Reform and War in America* (1971).

Ellis W. Hawley, *The Great War and the Search for a Modern Order* (1992).

Walter LaFeber, *The American Age* (1989).

Michael J. Lyons, *World War I: A Short History* (1994).

Neil Wynn, *From Progressivism to Prosperity: World War I and American Society* (1986).

Diplomacy of Neutrality, War, and Peace

Lloyd Ambrosius, *Woodrow Wilson and the American Diplomatic Tradition* (1987).

Thomas A. Bailey and Paul B. Ryan, *The Lusitania Disaster* (1975).

Kathleen Burk, *Britain, America, and the Sinews of War* (1985).

John Coogan, *The End of Neutrality* (1981).

John M. Cooper, Jr., *The Vanity of Power: American Isolationism and the First World War* (1969).

David S. Foglesong, *America's Secret War against Bolshevism: United States Intervention in the Russian Civil War, 1917–1920* (1995).

John A. Garraty, *Henry Cabot Lodge: A Biography* (1965).

Ross Gregory, *The Origins of American Intervention in the First World War* (1971).

Thomas J. Knock, *To End All Wars: Woodrow Wilson and the Creation of the League of Nations* (1992).

N. Gordon Levin, Jr., *Woodrow Wilson and World Politics: America's Response to War and Revolution* (1968).

Lawrence W. Levine, *Defender of the Faith: William Jennings Bryan, the Last Decade* (1965).

Arthur S. Link, *Woodrow Wilson and the Progressive Era, 1910–1917* (1954).

Ernest R. May, *The World War and American Isolation, 1914–1917* (1966).

David W. McFadden, *Alternative Paths: Soviets and Americans, 1917–1920* (1993).

Daniel M. Smith, *The Great Departure: The United States and World War I* (1965).

Ralph A. Stone, *The Irreconcilables* (1970).

Arthur Walworth, *Wilson and the Peacemakers* (1986).

The Military

Nancy Bristow, *Making Men Moral: Social Engineering During the Great War* (1996).

A. E. Barbeau and Florette Henri, *The Unknown Soldiers: Black American Troops in World War I* (1974).

John Whiteclay Chambers II, *To Raise an Army* (1987).

John Garry Clifford, *Citizen Soldiers: The Plattsburgh Training Camp Movement* (1972).

Edward M. Coffman, *The Hilt of the Sword: The Career of Peyton C. March* (1966).

Frank Freidel, *Over There: The Story of America's First Great Overseas Crusade* (1964).

Gerald W. Patton, *War and Race: The Black Officer in the American Military* (1981).

Laurence Stallings, *The Doughboys: The Story of the AEF, 1917–1918* (1963).

David Trask, *The AEF and Coalition Warmaking, 1917–1918* (1993).

Frank E. Vandiver, *Black Jack: The Life and Times of John J. Pershing* (1977).

Wartime Economy and Society

William J. Breen, *Uncle Sam at Home: Civilian Mobilization, Wartime Federalism, and the Council of National Defense, 1917–1919* (1984).

Valerie Connor *The National War Labor* (1983).

Robert D. Cuff, *The War Industries Board: Business-Government Relations during World War I* (1973).

David Danbom, *The Resisted Revolution: Urban America and the Industrialization of Agriculture* (1979).

Maurine Weiner Greenwald, *Women, War, and Work: The Impact of World War I on Women Workers in the United States* (1980).

Florette Henri, *Black Migration: The Movement North, 1900–1920* (1975).

Paul Koistinen, *Mobilizing for Modern War: The Political Economy of American Warfare, 1865–1919* (1997).

Frederick C. Luebke, *Bonds of Loyalty: German-Americans and World War I* (1974).

Elliot M. Rudwick, *Race Riot at East St. Louis, July 2, 1917* (1964).

John A. Thompson, *Reformers and War: American Progressive Publicists and the First World War* (1987).

Stephen L. Vaughn, *Holding Fast the Inner Lines: Democracy, Nationalism, and the Committee on Public Information* (1980).

Wartime Dissent and Repression

Christopher Gibbs, *The Great Silent Majority: Missouri's Resistance to World War I* (1989).

Robert Morlan, *Political Prairie Fire: The Nonpartisan League, 1915–1922* (1955).

H. C. Peterson and Gilbert Fite, *Opponents of War, 1917–1918* (1957).

William Preston, Jr., *Aliens and Dissenters: Federal Suppression of Radicals, 1903–1933* (1963).

Harry N. Scheiber, *The Wilson Administration and Civil Liberties* (1960).

James Weinstein, *The Decline of Socialism in America* (1967).

Postwar Conflict

David Brody, *Labor in Crisis: The Steel Strike of 1919* (1965).

Stanley A. Coben, *A. Mitchell Palmer, Politician* (1963).

Burl Noggle, *Into the Twenties: The United States from Armistice to Normalcy* (1974).

Athan Theoharis and John Stuart Cox, *The Boss: J. Edgar Hoover and the Great American Inquisition* (1988).

William M. Tuttle, Jr., *Race Riot: Chicago in the Red Summer of 1919* (1970).

Where to Learn More

❖ **National Infantry Museum, Fort Benning, Georgia.** This sprawling collection of weapons, uniforms, and equipment includes exhibits on World War I.

❖ **Fort George G. Meade Museum, Fort Meade, Maryland.** This museum contains unparalleled exhibits depicting U.S. military life during World War I, including artifacts, photographs, and French and American tanks designed for trench warfare.

❖ **General John J. Pershing Boyhood Home, Laclede, Missouri.** Maintained by the Missouri State Park Board, Pershing's restored nineteenth-century home exhibits some of his personal belongings and papers.

❖ **Wisconsin Veterans Museum, Madison, Wisconsin.** The most stunning museum of its size in the United States, this large building combines impressive collections of artifacts ranging from uniforms to tanks, with substantive exhibits and video programs based on remarkable historical research. It both documents and explains the participation of Wisconsin soldiers in the nation's wars, including the Spanish-American War and World War I.

Toward a Modern America: The 1920s

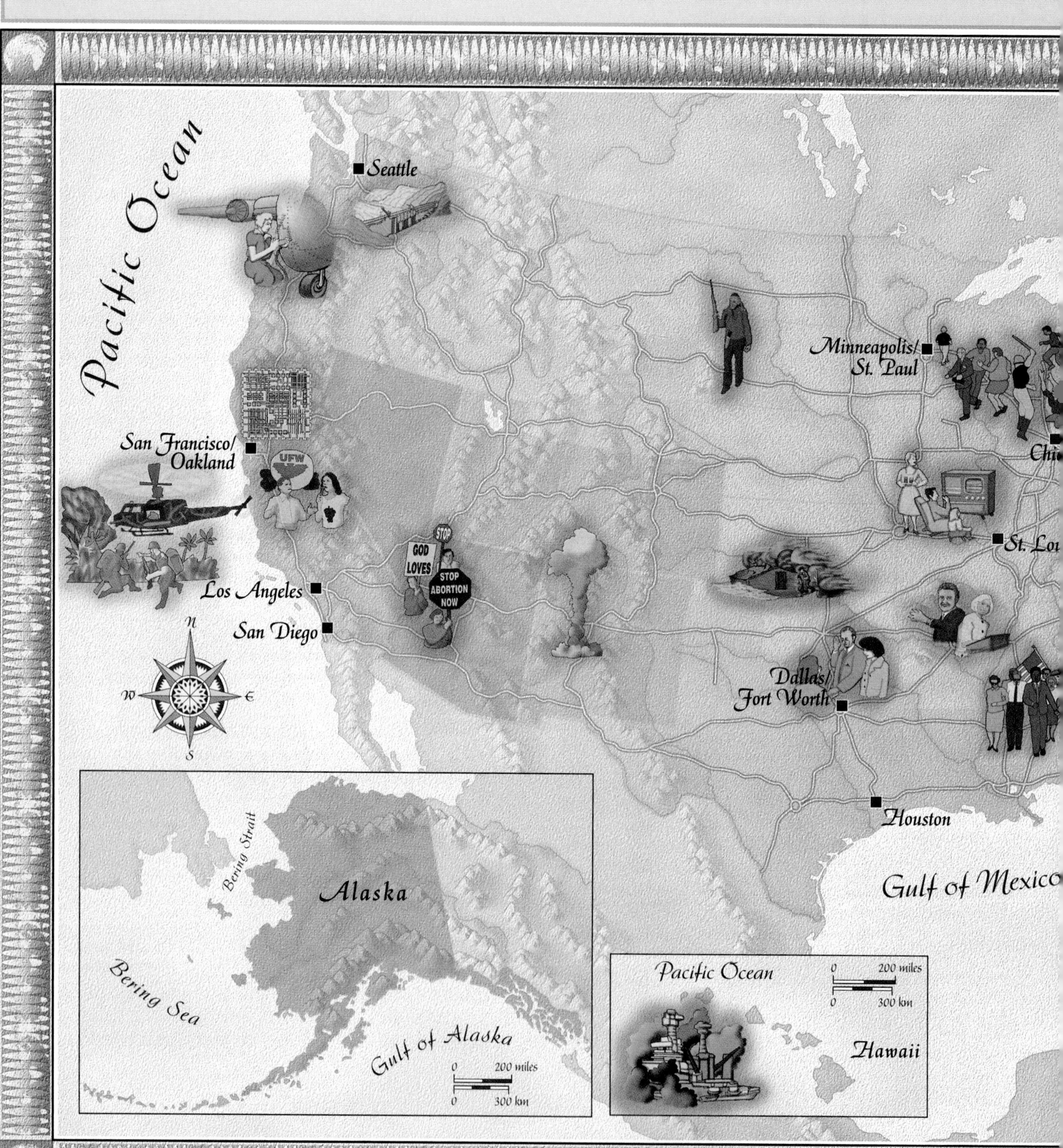

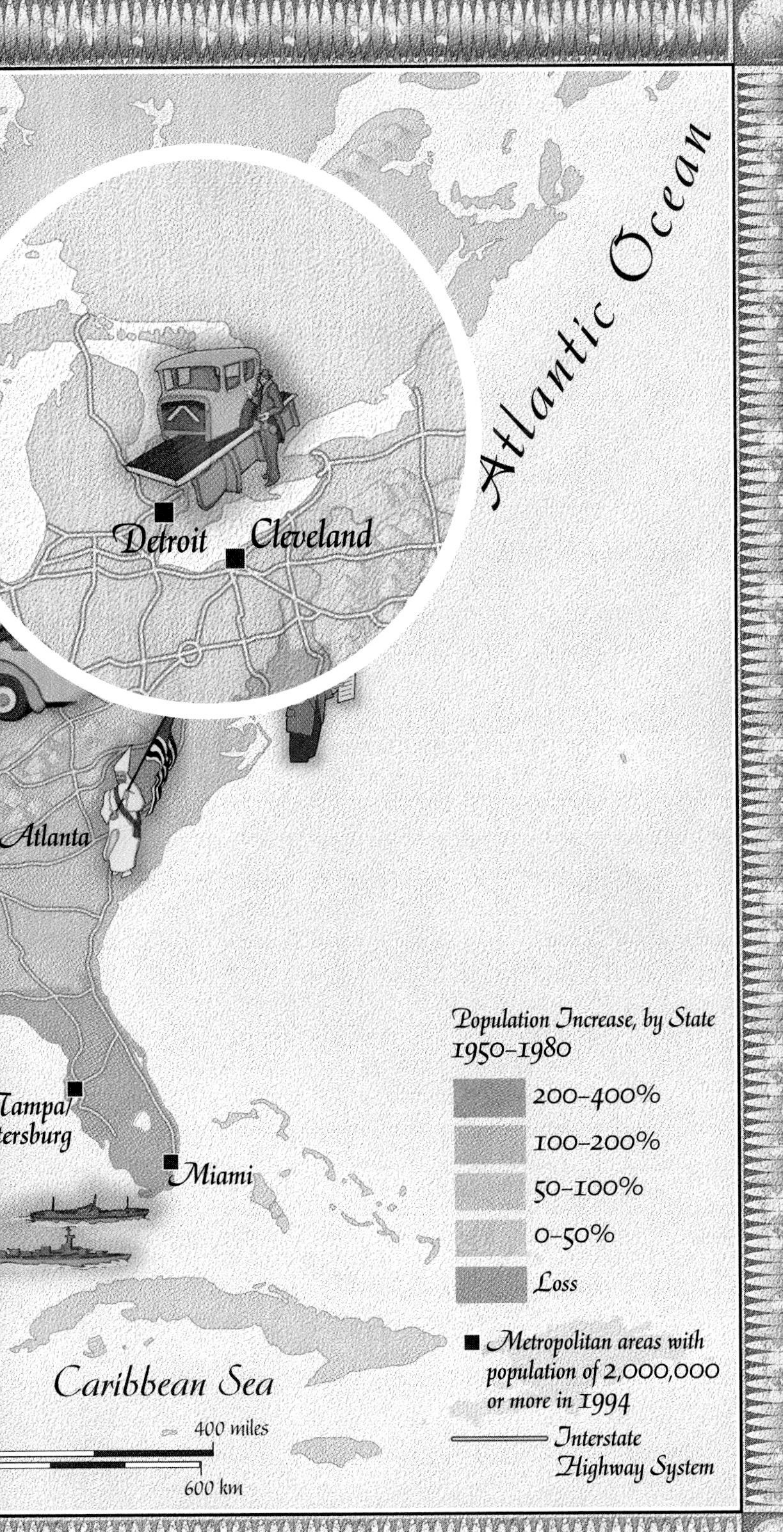

26

Chapter Outline

Key Topics

- ❖ The American economy in the 1920s
- ❖ The cult of business
- ❖ Change and social dislocation
- ❖ Materialism and mass culture
- ❖ The groups excluded from the prosperity of the 1920s

"Machinery," proclaimed Henry Ford, "is the new Messiah." Others in the 1920s thought Ford too deserved homage. "Just as in Rome one goes to the Vatican and endeavours to get audience of the Pope," noted one British observer, "so in Detroit one goes to the Ford Works and endeavours to see Henry Ford." Ford had introduced the moving assembly line at his automobile factory on the eve of World War I, and, by 1925, it was turning out a Model T every ten seconds. Mass production was becoming a reality; in fact, the term originated in Henry Ford's 1926 description of the system of flow production techniques popularly called "Fordism." The system symbolized the nation's booming economy: In the 1920s, Europeans used the word *Fordize* as a synonym for *Americanize.* Ford coupled machines and technology with managerial innovations. He established the "five-dollar day," twice the prevailing wage in Detroit's auto industry, and slashed the workweek from forty-eight to forty hours. These changes, Ford argued, would reduce the costs of labor turnover and boost consumer purchasing power, leading to further profits from mass production.

The assembly line, however, alienated workers. Fordism meant that skills, experience, and creativity were no longer necessary, that "upward mobility" was a meaningless phrase; all Ford wanted, said one observer, were machine tenders who "will simply do what they are told to do, over and over again from bell-time to bell-time." Even Ford conceded that the repetitive operations of the assembly line were "so monotonous that it scarcely seems possible that any man would care to continue long at the same job." Ford first tried to adapt his mostly immigrant workers to these conditions through an Americanization program. His "Education Department" taught classes in English, sobriety, obedience, and industrial efficiency to the unskilled laborers entering the factory. After the course, they participated in a symbolic pageant: They climbed into a huge "melting pot," fifteen feet across and seven feet deep. After Ford managers stirred the pot with ten-foot ladles, the workers emerged wearing new clothes and waving American flags—new Americans made for the factory. As one Ford leader said, "As we adapt the machinery in the shop to turning out the kind of automobile we have in mind, so we have constructed our educational system with a view to producing the human product in mind."

When the labor market became more favorable to management in the early 1920s, Ford abolished the Education Department and relied on discipline to control workers. To ensure efficiency, he prohibited talking, whistling, sitting, or smoking on the job. Wearing fixed expressions—"Fordization of the face"—workers could communicate only without moving their lips in the "Ford whisper." ("Ford employees are not really alive," noted one labor leader; "they are half dead.") Work under such conditions was for money, not fulfillment; workers would have to achieve personal satisfaction through consumption, not production.

Fordism, like the 1920s, had an even darker side. Henry Ford was an anti-Semite. His diatribes against Jews were reprinted by the Nazis in the 1930s. Ford also joined in the assault on labor unions that marked the 1920s. He declared that Jews organized unions to control industry. He banned unions and used spies and informants to prevent union activity, hiring an underworld thug to enforce a discipline that even involved searches of workers' homes. One observer said in 1924, "No one who works for Ford is safe from spies."

Fordism thus reflected the complexity of the 1920s. Economic growth and technological innovation were paired with social conflict as traditions were destroyed, values were displaced, and new people were incorporated into a society increasingly industrialized, urbanized, and dominated by big business. Industrial production and national wealth soared, buoyed by new techniques and markets for consumer goods. Business values pervaded society and dominated government, which promoted business interests. But not all Americans prospered. Many workers were unemployed, and the wages of still more were stagnant or falling. Farmers endured grim conditions and worse prospects. Social change brought pleasure to some and deep concern to others. City factories like the Ford Works attracted workers from the countryside, increasing urbanization; rapid suburbanization opened other horizons. Leisure activities flourished, and new mass media promoted modern ideas and stylish products. But such experiences often proved unsettling, and some Americans sought reassurance by imposing their cultural or religious values on everyone around them. The tumultuous decade thus had many unresolved issues, much like the complex personality of Henry Ford himself. And Ford so dominated the age that when college students were asked to rank the greatest people of all time, Ford came in third—behind Christ and Napoleon.

The Economy That Roared

Following a severe postwar depression in 1920 and 1921, the American economy boomed through the remainder of the decade. Gross domestic product soared nearly 40 percent; output per worker-hour, or productivity, rose 72 percent in manufacturing; average per capita income increased by a third. Although the prosperity was not evenly distributed and some sectors of the economy were deeply troubled, most Americans welcomed the industrial expansion and business principles of the "New Era."

Boom Industries

Many factors spurred the economic expansion of the 1920s. The huge wartime and postwar profits provided investment capital that enabled business to mechanize. Mass production spread quickly in American industry; machine-made standardized parts and the moving assembly line increased efficiency and production. Businesses steadily adopted the scientific management principles of Frederick W. Taylor (see Chapter 23). These highly touted systems, though often involving little more than an assembly-line "speed-up," also boosted efficiency. The nation more than doubled its capacity to generate electricity during the decade, further bolstering the economy. In factories, electric motors cut costs and improved manufacturing; in homes, electricity spurred demand for new products. Henry Ford was right: Mass production and consumption went hand in hand. Although not one in ten farm families had access to electric power, most other families did by 1929, and many bought electric sewing machines, vacuum cleaners, washing machines, and other labor-saving appliances.

Ford Motor Company's first moving assembly line in Highland Park, Michigan, in 1913. The increasing mechanization of work, linked to managerial and marketing innovations, boosted productivity in the 1920s and brought consumer goods within the reach of far more Americans than before.

Chronology

1915 Ku Klux Klan is founded anew.

1919 Volstead Act is passed.

1920 Urban population exceeds rural population for the first time.
Warren Harding is elected president.
Prohibition takes effect.
First commercial radio show is broadcast.
Sinclair Lewis publishes *Main Street.*

1921 Sheppard-Towner Maternity and Infancy Act is passed.
Washington Naval Conference limits naval armaments.

1922 Fordney-McCumber Act raises tariff rates.
Sinclair Lewis publishes *Babbitt.*
Country Club Plaza in Kansas City opens.

1923 Harding dies; Calvin Coolidge becomes president.

1924 National Origins Act sharply curtails immigration.
Coolidge is elected president.

1925 Scopes trial is held in Dayton, Tennessee.
F. Scott Fitzgerald publishes *The Great Gatsby.*

1927 Charles A. Lindbergh flies solo across the Atlantic.

1928 Kellogg-Briand Pact is signed.
Herbert Hoover is elected president.

1929 Ernest Hemingway publishes *A Farewell to Arms.*

The automobile industry drove the economy. Its productivity increased constantly, and sales rose from about 1.9 million vehicles in 1920 to nearly 5 million by 1929, when 26 million vehicles were on the road (see Figure 26-1). The automobile industry also employed one of every fourteen manufacturing workers and stimulated other industries from steel to rubber and glass. It created a huge new market for the petroleum industry and fostered oil drilling in Oklahoma, Texas, and Louisiana. It launched new businesses, from service stations (over 120,000 by 1929) to garages. It also encouraged the construction industry, a mainstay of the 1920s economy. Large increases in road building and residential housing, prompted by growing automobile ownership and migration to cities and suburbs, provided construction jobs, markets for lumber and other building materials, and profits.

New industries also sprang up. The aviation industry grew rapidly during the 1920s, with government support. The U.S. Post Office subsidized commercial air service by providing air mail contracts to private carriers. Congress then authorized commercial passenger service over the mail routes, with regular traffic opening in 1927 between Boston

Figure 26-1 Registered Motor Vehicles, 1913–1929
The rapid adoption of automobiles shaped the 1920s, stimulating demand for steel and gasoline, encouraging the use of credit, facilitating suburbanization, promoting tourism, and suggesting new cultural horizons.
Data Source: U.S. Bureau of Public Roads.

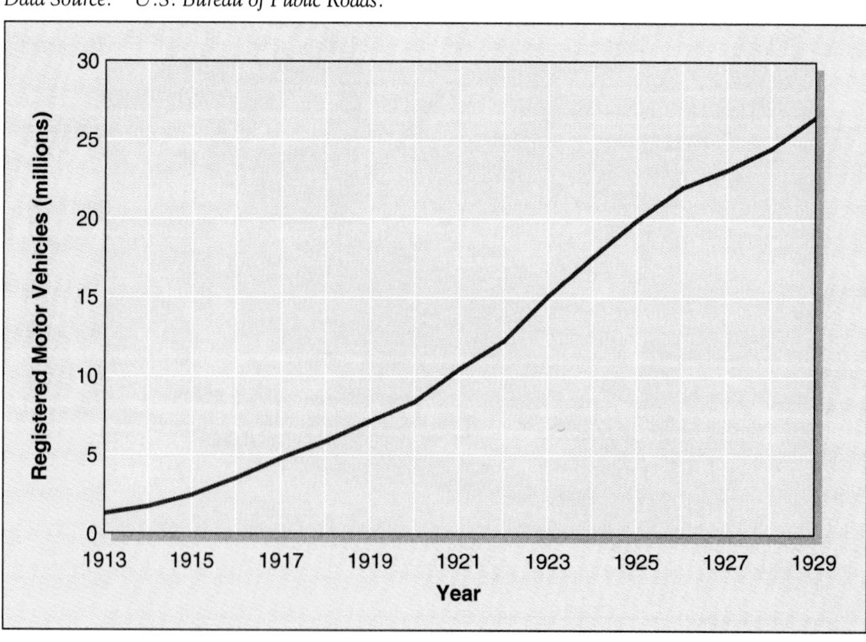

and New York. By 1930, more than one hundred airlines crisscrossed America.

The Great War also stimulated the chemicals industry. The government confiscated chemical patents from German firms that had dominated the field and transferred them to U.S. companies like Du Pont. With this advantage, Du Pont in the 1920s became one of the nation's largest industrial firms, a chemical empire producing plastics, finishes, dyes, and organic chemicals. It developed products for the commercial market: enamel for household appliances and automobile finishes, gasoline additives to eliminate engine knocks (many workers died from producing what the *New York World* called "loony gas"), rayon for women's clothing, cellophane to package consumer goods. Led by such successes, the chemicals industry became a $4 billion giant employing 300,000 workers by 1929.

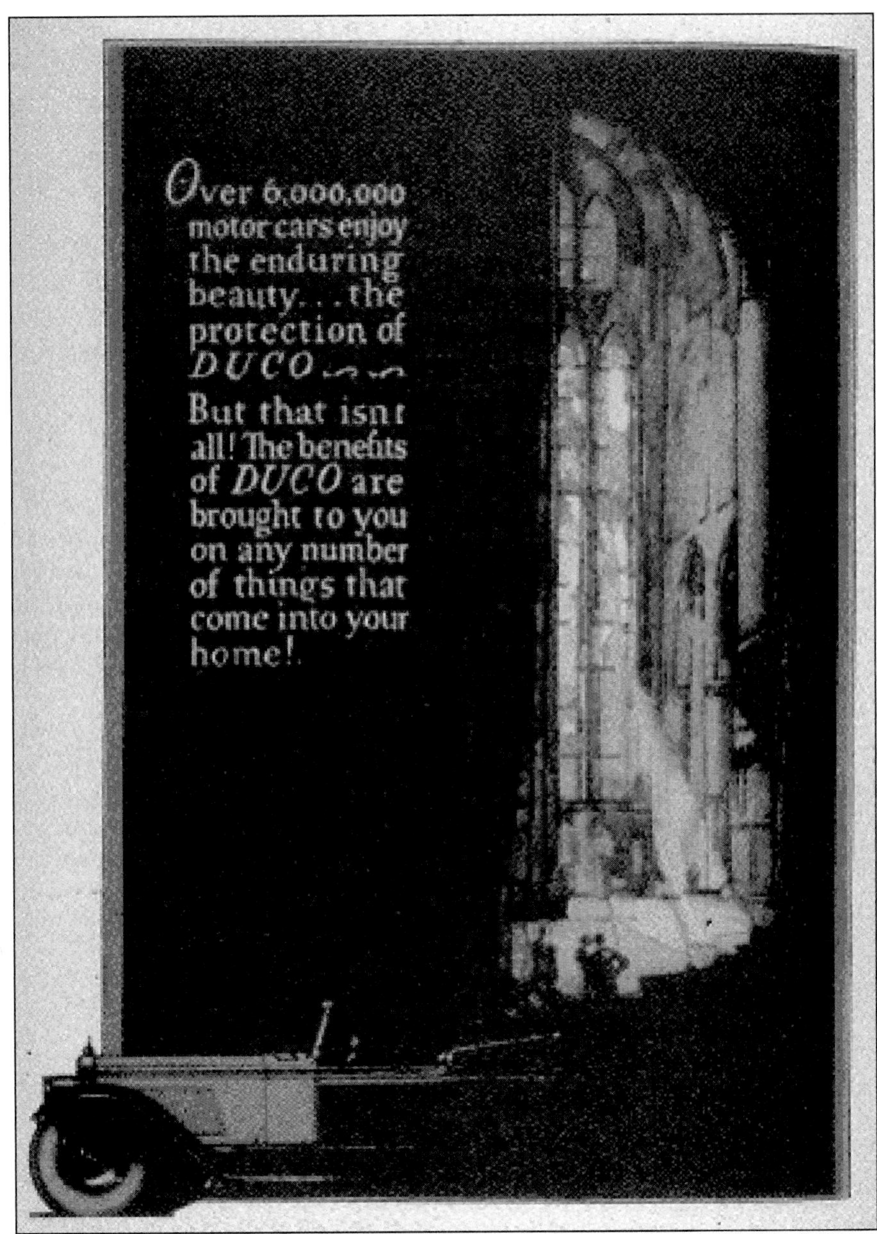

Du Pont became one of the nation's largest industrial corporations in the 1920s by developing new consumer products and marketing them aggressively. This advertisement for Duco automobile finishes blends images of a cathedral and an auto showroom, placing consumerism in a favorable light.

The new radio and motion picture industries also flourished. Commercial broadcasting began with a single station in 1920. By 1927, there were 732 stations, and Congress created the Federal Radio Commission to prevent wave band interference. The rationale for this agency, which was reorganized as the **Federal Communications Commission (FCC)** in 1934, was that the airwaves belong to the American people and not private interests. Nevertheless, corporations quickly dominated the new industry. Westinghouse, RCA, and General Electric began opening strings of stations in the early 1920s. Large corporations also came to control radio manufacturing. Factory-made crystal radio sets became available in 1920, and some 5 million sets were sold by middecade, but corporate pressure and patent control eliminated more than 90 percent of the 750 manufacturers by 1927.

The motion picture industry became one of the nation's five largest businesses, with twenty thousand movie theaters selling 100 million tickets a week. Hollywood studios were huge factories, hiring directors, writers, camera crews, and actors to produce films on an assembly-line basis. While Americans watched Charlie Chaplin showcase his comedic genius in films like *The Gold Rush* (1925), corporations like Paramount were integrating production with distribution and exhibition to maximize control and profit and eliminate independent producers and theaters. The advent of talking movies later in the decade brought still greater profits and power to the major studios, which alone could afford the increased engineering and production costs.

Corporate Consolidation

A wave of corporate mergers, rivaling that at the turn of the century, swept over the 1920s economy. Great corporations swallowed up thousands of small firms. Particularly significant was the spread of oligopoly—the control of an entire industry by a few giant firms. The number of automobile manufacturers dropped from 108 to 44, but three companies—Ford, General Motors, and Chrysler—produced 83 percent of the nation's cars. Their large-scale, integrated operations eliminated competition from small firms. In the electric light and power industry, nearly four thousand local utility companies were merged into a dozen holding companies. Mergers also expanded oligopoly control over other industries. By 1929, the nation's two hundred largest corporations controlled nearly half of all nonbanking corporate wealth.

Oligopolies also dominated finance and marketing. Big banks extended their control through mergers and by opening branches. By 1929, a mere 1 percent of the nation's banks controlled half of its banking resources. In marketing, national chain stores like A&P and Woolworth's displaced local retailers. With fifteen thousand grocery stores and an elaborate distribution system, A&P could buy and sell goods for less than many corner grocers.

The corporate consolidation of the 1920s provoked little public fear or opposition. Independent retailers campaigned for local zoning regulations and laws to restrict chain stores, but Americans mostly accepted that size brought efficiency and productivity.

Open Shops and Welfare Capitalism

Business also launched a vigorous assault on labor. In 1921, the National Association of Manufacturers organized an **open shop** campaign to break union shop contracts, which required all employees to be union members. Denouncing collective bargaining as un-American, businesses described the open shop, in which union membership was not required and usually prohibited, as the "American plan." They forced workers to sign so-called **yellow-dog contracts** that bound them to reject unions to keep their jobs. Business also used boycotts to force employers into a uniform antiunion front. Bethlehem Steel, for example, refused to sell steel to companies employing union labor. Where unions existed, corporations tried to crush them, using spies or hiring strikebreakers.

Some companies advocated a paternalistic system called **welfare capitalism** as an alternative to unions. Eastman Kodak, General Motors, U.S. Steel, and other firms provided medical services, insurance programs, pension plans, and vacations for their workers and established employee social clubs and sports teams. These policies were designed to undercut labor unions and persuade workers to rely on the corporation. Home-financing plans, for instance, increased workers' dependence on the company, and stock ownership plans inculcated business values among employees. Welfare capitalism, however, covered scarcely 5 percent of the workforce and often benefited only skilled workers already tied to the company through seniority. Moreover, it was directed primarily at men. General Electric, for example, dismissed women workers when they married. Women rarely built up enough seniority to obtain vacations and pensions.

Corporations in the 1920s also promoted company unions, management-sponsored substitutes for labor unions. But company unions were usually forbidden to handle wage and hour issues. Their function was to implement company policies and undermine real unionism. General Electric's management reported that through its company union, "we have been able to educate and secure sympathy and support from a large body of employees who, under the old arrangement of bargaining with [AFL] craft unions, could not have been reached."

Partly because of these pressures, membership in labor unions fell from 5.1 million in 1920 to 3.6 million in 1929. But unions also contributed to their own decline. Conservative union leaders neglected ethnic and black workers in mass-production industries. Nor did they try to organize women, by 1930 nearly one-fourth of all workers. And they failed to respond effectively to other changes in the labor market. The growing numbers of white-collar workers regarded themselves as middle class and beyond the scope of union action.

With increasing mechanization and weak labor unions, workers suffered from job insecurity and stagnant wages. Mechanization, *Fortune* concluded, meant that "from the purely productive point of view, a part of the human race is already obsolete." Unemployment reached 12 percent in 1921 and remained a persistent concern of many working-class Americans during the decade. And despite claims to the contrary, hours were long: The average workweek in manufacturing remained over fifty hours.

The promise of business to pay high wages proved hollow. Real wages (purchasing power) did improve, but most of the improvement came before

1923 and reflected falling prices more than rising wages. After 1923, American wages stabilized. Henry Ford made no general wage hike after 1919, although his workers would have needed an increase of 65 percent to recover the buying power they had enjoyed in 1914. Indeed, in 1928, Ford lowered wage rates. U.S. Steel also reduced weekly wages, even while its profits almost doubled between 1923 and 1929. The failure to raise wages when productivity was increasing threatened the nation's long-term prosperity. In short, rising national income largely reflected salaries and dividends, not wages.

Some workers fared particularly badly. Unskilled workers—especially southern and eastern Europeans, black migrants from the rural South, and Mexican immigrants—saw their already low wages decline relative to those of skilled workers. Southern workers earned much less than Northerners, even in the same industry, and women were paid much less than men, even for the same jobs. Male furniture assemblers, for example, earned 56 cents an hour; females, only 32 cents. Overall, the gap between rich and poor widened during the decade (see Figure 26-2). By 1929, fully 71 percent of American families earned less than what the U.S. Bureau of Labor Statistics regarded as necessary for a decent living standard. The maldistribution of income meant that eventually Americans would be unable to purchase the products they made.

The expansion of consumer credit, rare before the 1920s, offered temporary relief by permitting consumers to buy goods over time. General Motors introduced consumer credit on a national basis to create a mass market for expensive automobiles. By 1927, two-thirds of automobiles were purchased on the installment plan. By 1929, providing consumer credit had become the nation's tenth-largest business. Nevertheless, installment loans did not in the long run raise the purchasing power of an income; they simply added interest charges to the price of products.

Sick Industries

Despite the general appearance of prosperity, several "sick" industries dragged on the economy. Coal mining, textile and garment manufacturing, and railroads suffered from excess capacity (too many mines and factories), shrinking demand, low returns, and management–labor conflicts. For example, U.S. coal mines had a capacity of a billion tons, but scarcely half of that was needed because of increasing use of oil, natural gas, and hydroelectricity. Using company police, strikebreakers, and injunctions, mine operators broke the United Mine Workers and slashed wages by up to a third. Unemployment in the industry approached 30 percent; by 1928, a reporter found "thousands of women and children literally starving to death" in Appalachia and the remaining miners held in "industrial slavery."

Similarly, the textile industry coped with overcapacity and declining demand by shifting operations

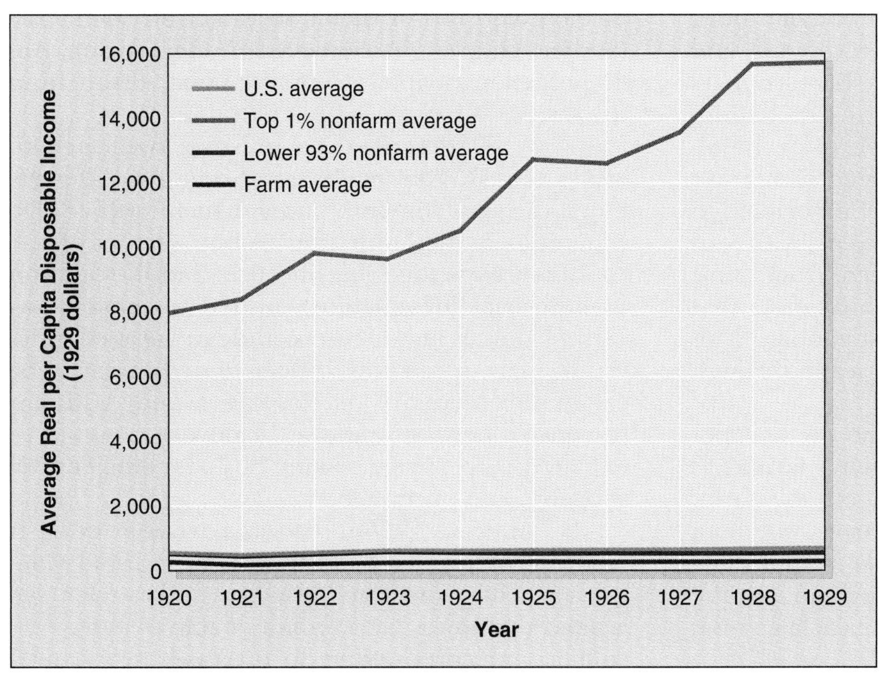

***Figure 26-2* Growing Income Inequality in the 1920s**
Despite the aura of prosperity in the 1920s, the vast majority of Americans received little or no increase in their real income. Farm families dragged the average down further while the wealthiest Americans doubled their own incomes.

Data Source: Charles Holt, "Who Benefited from the Prosperity of the Twenties?" *Explorations in Economic History*, 14 (1977).

from New England to the cheap-labor South, employing girls and young women for fifty-six-hour weeks at eighteen cents an hour. Textile companies, aided by local authorities, suppressed strikes in Tennessee and North Carolina. Ella May Wiggins sang of the worries in the mills:

> How it grieves the heart of a mother,
> You every one must know.
> For we can't buy for our children,
> Our wages are too low.

Wiggins was murdered by company thugs, leaving behind five small children. The textile industry, despite substandard wages and repressive policies, remained barely profitable.

American agriculture never recovered from the 1921 depression. In 1919, gross farm income amounted to 16 percent of the national income; by 1929, it had dropped to half that. Agricultural problems did not derive from inefficiency or low productivity. Mechanization (especially more tractors) and improved fertilizers and pesticides helped produce crop surpluses. But surpluses and shrinking demand forced down prices. After the war, foreign markets dried up, and domestic demand for cotton slackened. Moreover, farmers' wartime expansion left them heavily mortgaged in the 1920s. Small farmers, unable to compete with larger, better-capitalized farmers, suffered most. Many lost their land and became tenants or farm hands. By 1930, only 57 percent of American farmers owned the land they worked, the lowest percentage ever.

Racial discrimination worsened conditions for black and Hispanic tenants, sharecroppers, and farm workers. In the South, black sharecroppers trapped in grinding poverty endured segregation, disfranchisement, and violence. Mexican immigrants and Hispanic Americans labored as migrant farm workers in the Southwest and California. Exploited by a contract labor system pervasive in large-scale agriculture, they suffered from poor wages, miserable living conditions, and racism that created, in the words of one investigation, "a vicious circle" from which "few can escape through their own efforts."

By the end of the 1920s, the average per capita income for people on the nation's farms was only one-fourth that of Americans off the farm. "Widespread agricultural disaster," warned one Iowa newspaper, was producing "a highly dangerous situation." Like textile workers in New England and the Piedmont and coal miners in Appalachia, rural Americans suffered in the 1920s.

The Business of Government

The Republican surge in national politics also shaped the economy. In the 1920 election, the Republican slogan was "Less government in business, more business in government." By 1924, Calvin Coolidge, the decade's second Republican president, proclaimed, "This is a business country . . . and it wants a business government." Under such direction, the federal government advanced business interests at the expense of other objectives (see "American Views: The Cult of Business").

Republican Ascendancy

Republicans in 1920 had retained control of Congress and put Warren Harding in the White House. Harding was neither capable nor bright. One critic described a Harding speech as "an army of pompous phrases moving over the landscape in search of an idea." But he had a genial touch that contrasted favorably with Wilson. He pardoned Eugene Debs, whom Wilson had refused to release from prison, and he spoke out against racial violence. He also helped shape the modern presidency by supporting the Budget and Accounting Act of 1921, which gave the president authority over the budget and created the Budget Bureau and the General Accounting Office. Moreover, Harding recognized his own limitations and promised to appoint "the best minds" to his cabinet. Some of his appointees were highly accomplished, and two of them, Secretary of Commerce Herbert Hoover and Secretary of the Treasury Andrew Mellon, shaped economic policy throughout the 1920s.

A self-described progressive, dedicated to efficiency, Hoover made the Commerce Department the government's most dynamic office. He cemented its ties with the leading sectors of the economy, expanded its collection and distribution of industrial information, pushed to exploit foreign resources and markets, and encouraged innovation. His spreading influence led him to be called the secretary of commerce and "assistant secretary of everything else." Hoover's goal was to expand prosperity by making business efficient, responsive, and profitable.

Andrew Mellon had a narrower goal. A wealthy banker and industrialist, he pressed Congress to reduce taxes on businesses and the rich. He argued that lower taxes would enable wealthy individuals and corporations to increase their capital

One 1920s cartoon depicting a "View of Washington" showed Herbert Hoover everywhere at once. In fact, the talented and ambitious Secretary of Commerce was not a politician but a successful engineer, businessman, and administrator who symbolized to many Americans the best of the New Era.

investments, thereby creating new jobs and general prosperity. But Mellon's hope that favoring the rich would cause prosperity to trickle down to the working and middle classes proved ill-founded. Nevertheless, despite the opposition of progressives in Congress, Mellon succeeded in lowering maximum tax rates and eliminating wartime excess-profits taxes in 1921.

The Harding administration promoted business interests in other ways, too. The tariff of 1922 raised import rates to protect industry from foreign competition. High new duties on foreign aluminum, for instance, permitted manufacturers—including Mellon's own Alcoa Aluminum—to raise prices by 40 percent. But by excluding imports, high tariffs made it difficult for European nations to earn the dollars to repay their war debts to the United States. High rates also impeded American farm exports and raised consumer prices.

The Harding administration aided the business campaign against unions. Attorney General Harry Daugherty secured an injunction against a railroad strike in 1922 and promised to "use the power of the government to prevent the labor unions of the country from destroying the open shop."

The Republicans also curtailed government regulation. By appointing advocates of big business to the Federal Trade Commission, the Federal Reserve Board, and other regulatory agencies established earlier by the progressives, Harding made government the collaborator rather than the regulator of business. Progressive Republican Senator George Norris of Nebraska angrily asked, "If trusts, combinations, and big business are to run the government, why not permit them to do it directly rather than through this expensive machinery which was originally honestly established for the protection of the people of the country against monopoly?" Norris condemned the new appointments as nullifying "federal law by a process of boring from within" and as setting "the country back more than twenty-five years."

Finally, Harding reshaped the Supreme Court into a still more aggressive champion of business. He named the conservative William Howard Taft as chief justice and matched him with three other justices. All were, as one of them proclaimed, sympathetic to business leaders "beset and bedeviled with vexatious statutes, prying commissions, and government intermeddling of all sorts." The Court struck down much of the government economic regulation adopted during the Progressive Era, invalidated restraints on child labor and a minimum wage law for women, and approved restrictions on labor unions.

Government Corruption

The green light that Harding Republicans extended to private interests led to corruption and scandals. Harding appointed many friends and cronies who saw public service as an opportunity for graft. Attorney General Daugherty's associates in the Justice Department took bribes in exchange for pardons and government jobs. The head of the Veterans Bureau went to prison for cheating disabled veterans of $200 million. Albert Fall, the secretary of the interior, leased petroleum reserves set aside by progressive conservationists to oil companies in exchange for cash, bonds, and cattle for his New Mexico ranch. Exposed for his role in the **Teapot Dome scandal**, named after a Wyoming oil reserve, Fall became the first cabinet officer in history to go to jail. Daugherty escaped a similar fate by destroying records and invoking the Fifth Amendment.

Harding was appalled by the scandals. "My God, this is a hell of a job!" he told William Allen White. "I have no trouble with my enemies. . . . But my damned friends, . . . they're the ones that keep me walking the floor nights!" Harding died shortly thereafter, probably of a heart attack.

American Views

The Cult of Business

During the 1920s, publicists and politicians joined manufacturers and merchants in proclaiming that business promoted not only material but also social and even spiritual well-being. In his best-seller, *The Man Nobody Knows* (1924), advertising executive Bruce Barton portrayed Jesus Christ as the founder of modern business. The following excerpt from an article by Edward E. Purinton, a popular lecturer on business values and efficiency, makes even more extensive claims for business.

❖ **How accurate are Purinton's claims of great opportunity in the corporate world of the 1920s? Of occupational mobility in the factory economy?**

❖ **What does this view of business imply about the role of government in American life?**

❖ **How do you think Protestant fundamentalists might have viewed the cult of business?**

Among the nations of the earth today America stands for one idea: *Business.* National opprobrium? National opportunity. For in this fact lies, potentially, the salvation of the world.

Through business, properly conceived, managed, and conducted, the human race is finally to be redeemed. How and why a man works foretells what he will do, think, have, give, and be. And real salvation is in doing, thinking, having, giving, and being—not in sermonizing and theorizing. . . .

What is the finest game? Business. The soundest science? Business. The truest art? Business. The fullest education? Business. The fairest opportunity? Business. The cleanest philanthropy? Business. The sanest religion? Business.

You may not agree. That is because you judge business by the crude, mean, stupid, false imitation of business that happens to be located near you.

The finest game is business. The rewards are for everybody, and all can win. There are no favorites—Providence always crowns the career of the man who is worthy. And in this game there is no "luck"—you have the fun of taking chances but

Coolidge Prosperity

On August 3, 1923, Vice President Calvin Coolidge was sworn in as president by his father while visiting his birthplace in rural Vermont, thereby reaffirming his association with traditional values. This image reassured Americans troubled by the Harding scandals. Coolidge's calm appearance hid a furious temper and a mean spirit.

Coolidge supported business with ideological conviction. He opposed the activist presidency of the Progressive Era, cultivating instead a deliberate inactivity calculated to lower expectations of government. He endorsed Secretary of the Treasury Mellon's ongoing efforts to reverse the progressive tax policies of the Wilson years and backed Secretary of Commerce Hoover's persistent efforts on behalf of the business community (although he privately sneered at Hoover as the "Wonder Boy").

Like Harding, Coolidge installed business supporters in the regulatory agencies. To chair the Federal Trade Commission he appointed an attorney who had condemned the agency as "an instrument of oppression and disturbance and injury instead of help to business." Under this leadership, the FTC described its new goal as "helping business to help itself"—which meant approving trade associations and agreements to suppress competition. This attitude, endorsed by the Supreme Court, aided the mergers that occurred after 1925. The *Wall Street Journal* crowed, "Never before, here or anywhere else, has a government been so completely fused with business."

the sobriety of guaranteeing certainties. The speed and size of your winnings are for you alone to determine. . . .

The soundest science is business. All investigation is reduced to action, and by action proved or disproved. The idealistic motive animates the materialistic method. . . . Capital is furnished for the researches of "pure science"; yet pure science is not regarded pure until practical. Competent scientists are suitably rewarded—as they are not in the scientific schools. . . .

The fullest education is business. A proper blend of study, work and life is essential to advancement. The whole man is educated. Human nature itself is the open book that all business men study; and the mastery of a page of this educates you more than the memorizing of a dusty tome from a library shelf. In the school of business, moreover, you teach yourself and learn most from your own mistakes. What you learn here you live out, the only real test.

The fairest opportunity is business. You can find more, better, quicker chances to get ahead in a large business house than anywhere else on earth. . . . Recognition of better work, of keener and quicker thought, of deeper and finer feeling, is gladly offered by the men higher up, with early promotion the rule for the man who justifies it. There is, and can be, no such thing as buried talent in a modern business organization. . . .

The sanest religion is business. Any relationship that forces a man to follow the Golden Rule rightfully belongs amid the ceremonials of the church. A great business enterprise includes and presupposes this relationship. I have seen more Christianity to the square inch as a regular part of the office equipment of famous corporation presidents than may ordinarily be found on Sunday in a verbalized but not vitalized church congregation. . . . You can fool your preacher with a sickly sprout or a wormy semblance of character, but you can't fool your employer. I would make every business house a consultation bureau for the guidance of the church whose members were employees of the house. . . .

The future work of the businessman is to teach the teacher, preach to the preacher, admonish the parent, advise the doctor, justify the lawyer, superintend the statesman, fructify the farmer, stabilize the banker, harness the dreamer, and reform the reformer.

Source: Edward E. Purinton, "Big Ideas from Big Business," Independent, *April 16, 1921. National Weekly Corp., New York.*

And Coolidge confined the government's role to helping business. When Congress tried to raise farm prices through government intervention, Coolidge vetoed the measure as "preposterous" special-interest legislation. One economist said Coolidge's vetoes revealed "a stubborn determination to do nothing," but they revealed more. For on the same day that Coolidge vetoed assistance to farmers, he raised by 50 percent the tariff on pig iron, thereby increasing manufacturers' profits and farmers' costs for tools. Government action was acceptable for business but not for nonbusiness interests.

"Coolidge prosperity" determined the 1924 election. The Democrats, hopelessly divided, took 103 ballots to nominate the colorless, conservative Wall Street lawyer John W. Davis. His election prospects, Davis conceded, were less "than a snowball in hell." A more interesting opponent for Coolidge was Robert La Follette, nominated by discontented farm and labor organizations that formed a new Progressive party. La Follette campaigned against "the power of private monopoly over the political and economic life of the American people." The Progressive platform demanded government ownership of railroads and utilities, farm assistance, and collective bargaining. The Republicans, backed by immense contributions from business, denounced La Follette as an agent of Bolshevism. The choice, Republicans insisted, was "Coolidge or Chaos." Thus instructed, Americans chose Coolidge, though barely half the electorate bothered to vote.

The Fate of Reform

But progressive reform was not completely dead. Even Harding proposed social welfare measures, and, in the 1921 depression, he convened a conference on unemployment and helped spark voluntary relief. A small group in Congress led by La Follette and George Norris attacked Mellon's regressive tax policies and supported measures regulating agricultural processors, protecting workers' rights, and maintaining public ownership of a hydroelectric dam at Muscle Shoals, Alabama, that conservative Republicans wanted to privatize. Yet reformers' successes were few and often temporary.

The fate of women's groups illustrated the difficulties reformers faced in the 1920s. At first, the adoption of woman suffrage prompted politicians to champion women's reform issues. In 1920, both major parties endorsed many of the goals of the new **League of Women Voters**. Within a year, many states had granted women the right to serve on juries, several enacted equal pay laws, and Wisconsin adopted an equal rights law. Congress passed the **Sheppard-Towner Maternity and Infancy Act**, the first federal social welfare law, in 1921. It provided federal funds for infant and maternity care, precisely the type of protective legislation that the suffragists had described as women's special interest.

But thereafter women reformers gained little. As it became clear that women did not vote as a bloc but according to their varying social and economic backgrounds, Congress lost interest in "women's issues." In 1929, Congress killed the Sheppard-Towner Act. Nor could reformers gain ratification of a child labor amendment after the Supreme Court invalidated laws regulating child labor. Conservatives attacked women reformers as "Bolsheviks."

Disagreements among women reformers and shifting interests also limited their success. Led by the **National Woman's Party**, some feminists campaigned for an **Equal Rights Amendment**. But other reformers feared that such an amendment would nullify the progressive laws that protected working women. Reform organizations like the Consumers' League lost their energy and focus. The General Federation of Women's Clubs, always relatively conservative, promoted home economics and the use of electric appliances. Indeed, many younger women rejected the public reform focus of progressive feminists. The *Magazine of Business* even maintained that women valued the vacuum cleaner more than the vote. By 1927, the president of the Women's Trade Union League called the decade "hideous in the public life of our people and in the noisy flaunting of cheap hopes and cheaper materialism."

Cities and Suburbs

The 1920 census reported that, for the first time, more Americans lived in urban than in rural areas. The trend toward urbanization accelerated in the 1920s as millions of Americans fled the depressed countryside for the booming cities. This massive population movement interacted with technological innovations to reshape cities, build suburbs, and transform urban life (see Map 26-1).

Expanding Cities

Urbanization affected all regions of the country. In absolute terms, the older industrial cities of the Northeast and upper Midwest grew the most, attracting migrants from the rural South and distressed Appalachia. New York remained the nation's foremost metropolis. All other major cities expanded—none more spectacularly than Detroit, which grew to 1.6 million people. The "Motor City" thrived on the booming automobile industry and related industries like glass manufacturing. Old trees and wide lawns gave way to multilane highways as apartment houses and parking lots obliterated old Detroit.

Rural Southerners also headed for southern cities. In fact, the South was the nation's most rapidly urbanizing region. Migrants from the countryside poured into Atlanta, Birmingham, Memphis, and Houston. Little more than jungle before 1914, Miami became the fastest-growing city in the United States during the 1920s—"the Magic City." Not all Southerners welcomed urban growth and the values it represented. The novelist Thomas Wolfe cautioned against boosters in Asheville, North Carolina, "who shout 'Progress Progress Progress'—when what they mean is more Ford automobiles, more Rotary Clubs, more Baptist Ladies Social unions. . . . We are not necessarily four times as civilized as our grandfathers because we go four times as fast in automobiles, because our buildings are four times as tall."

In the West, Denver, Portland, and Seattle (each a regional economic hub) and several California cities grew rapidly. Los Angeles grew by 115 percent and by 1930 was the nation's fifth-largest city, with over 1.2 million people. Although it was the center of California's agricultural wealth and the motion picture industry and one of the world's busiest ports, Los Angeles was also linked to the automobile industry. The southern California oil fields and the demand for gasoline made it the nation's leading refining center.

The population surge transformed the urban landscape. As land values soared, developers built skyscrapers, giving Cleveland, Kansas City, San

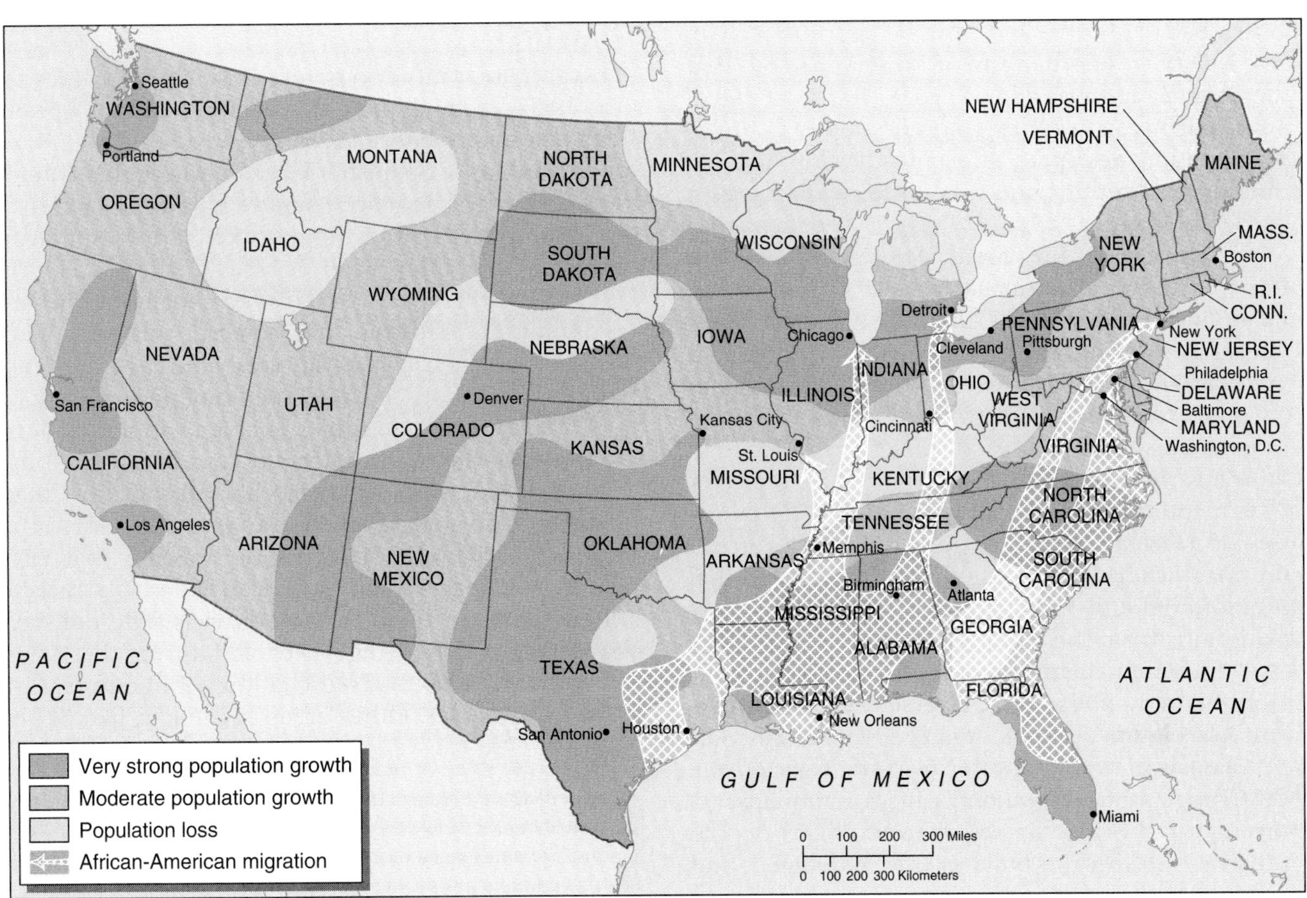

Map 26-1 Population Shifts, 1920–1930
Rural Americans fled to the cities during the 1920s, escaping a declining agricultural economy to search for new opportunities. African Americans in particular left the rural South for eastern and midwestern cities, but the urban population also jumped in the West and in the South itself.

Francisco, and many other cities modern skylines. By the end of the decade, American cities had nearly four hundred skyscrapers taller than twenty stories. The tallest, New York's 102-story Empire State Building, symbolized the urban boom.

The Great Black Migration

A significant feature of the rural-to-urban movement was the **Great Migration** of African Americans from the South. Like other migrants, they responded chiefly to economic factors. Southern segregation and violence made migration attractive, but job opportunities made it possible. Prosperity created jobs, and with the decline in European immigration, black workers filled the positions previously given to new immigrants. Though generally the lowest-paid and least secure jobs, they were better than sharecropping in the rural South. Black men worked as unskilled or semiskilled laborers; black women became domestics in white homes. The migrants often found adjustment to their new environment difficult. Southern rural black culture clashed with industrial work rhythms and discipline and with urban living. Still, more than a million and a half African Americans moved to northern cities in the 1920s.

There black ghettos usually developed, more because of prejudice than the wishes of the migrants. Although African Americans, like European immigrants, often wanted to live together to sustain their culture, racist restrictions meant that segregation, not congregation, most shaped their urban community. With thousands of newcomers limited to certain neighborhoods, housing shortages developed. Rapacious landlords charged ever-increasing rents for ever-declining housing. Rents doubled in New York's Harlem during the decade. In an example of the way racism exacerbated urban poverty, black workers earned less than working-class white workers but had to spend 50 percent more for housing. High rents and low wages forced black families to share inferior and unsanitary housing that threatened their health and safety. In Pittsburgh, only 20 percent of black houses had bathtubs, and only 50 percent had indoor toilets; in another city, an observer wrote that "the State would not allow cows to live in some of these apartments used by colored people." Continual migration disrupted efforts to develop a stable community; Harlem, said one social worker, was a "perpetual frontier."

However, the Great Migration also increased African Americans' racial consciousness, autonomy, and power. In 1928, for instance, black Chicagoans, using the ballot denied to African Americans in the South, elected the first black man to Congress since the turn of the century. Mutual aid societies and fraternal orders proliferated. Churches were particularly influential. A reporter in 1926 counted 140 black churches in a 150-block area of Harlem. Most of these were "storefront churches" where "cotton-field preachers" provided an emotional and fundamentalist religion familiar to migrants from the rural South.

Another organization also appealed to poor black ghetto dwellers. The **Universal Negro Improvement Association (UNIA)**, organized by Marcus Garvey, a Jamaican immigrant to New York, rejected the NAACP's goal of integration. A black nationalist espousing racial pride, Garvey exhorted black people to migrate to Africa to build a "free, redeemed, and mighty nation." In the meantime, he urged them to support black businesses. UNIA organized many enterprises, including groceries, restaurants, laundries, a printing plant, and the Black Star Steamship Line, intended as a commercial link between the United States, the West Indies, and Africa. UNIA attracted half a million members, the first black mass movement in American history. When Garvey was convicted of mail fraud and deported, however, the movement collapsed.

Racial pride also found expression in the **Harlem Renaissance**, an outpouring of literature, painting, sculpture, and music. Inspired by African-American culture and black urban life, writers and artists created works of power and poignancy. The poetry of Langston Hughes reflected the rhythm and mood of jazz and the blues. When a white patron complained that his writing was not "primitive" enough, Hughes responded, "I did not feel the rhythms of the primitive surging through me, and so I could not live and write as though I did. I was Chicago and Kansas City and Broadway and Harlem. And I was not what she wanted me to be." Other leading authors of the Harlem Renaissance who asserted their independence included Claude McKay, who wrote of the black working class in *Home to Harlem* (1928), Zora Neale Hurston, and James Weldon Johnson.

Barrios

Hispanic migrants also entered the nation's cities in the 1920s, creating their own communities, or *barrios*. Fifty thousand Puerto Ricans settled in New York, mostly in East ("Spanish") Harlem, where they found low-paying jobs. Far more migrants arrived from Mexico. Although many of them worked as migrant farm laborers, they often lived in cities in the off-season. Others permanently joined the expanding urban economy in industrial and construction jobs. The *barrios*, with their own businesses, churches, and cultural organizations, created a sense of permanency.

These communities enabled the newcomers to preserve their cultural values and build social institutions like *mutualistas* (mutual aid societies) that helped them get credit, housing, and health care. But the *barrios* also reflected the hostility that Hispanics encountered in American cities, for racism often restricted them to such districts. The number of Mexicans in Los Angeles tripled during the 1920s to nearly 100,000, but segregation confined them to East Los Angeles. Other areas of the city, like El Se-

Jessie Fauset, Langston Hughes, and Zora Neale Hurston stand at a memorial to Booker T. Washington. All authors prominent in the Harlem Renaissance, they represented a new generation of African Americans seizing what another black intellectual called their "first chances for group expression and self-determination."

gundo or Lynwood, boasted of being "restricted to the white race" and having "no Negroes or Mexicans." Los Angeles maintained separate schools for Mexicans, and a social worker reported that "America has repulsed the Mexican immigrant in every step he has taken" toward integration. As new migrants streamed in, conditions in the *barrios* deteriorated, for few cities provided adequate public services for them. Denver's *barrio* was described in 1924 as an area "both God and Denver had forgotten" with "no paving, no sidewalks, no sewers."

Some Hispanics fought discrimination. *La Orden de Hijos de America* (The Order of the Sons of America), organized in San Antonio in 1921, campaigned against inequities in schools and the jury system. In 1929, it helped launch the larger **League of United Latin American Citizens (LULAC)**, which would help advance civil rights for all Americans.

The Road to Suburbia

As fast as the cities mushroomed in the 1920s, the suburbs grew twice as fast. Park Ridge outside Chicago, Inglewood outside Los Angeles, Shaker Heights outside Cleveland, and many others expanded by 400 percent. New suburbs arose across the country. Fourteen hundred new subdivisions appeared in Los Angeles County during the 1920s; two-thirds of the new municipal incorporations in Illinois and Michigan were suburbs of Chicago, St. Louis, or Detroit. Some suburbs, such as Highland Park, where Henry Ford built his factory near Detroit, and Fairfield, Alabama, were industrial, but most were havens for the middle and upper classes.

Automobiles created the modern suburb. Nineteenth-century suburbs were small and linear, stretching along the street railway system. The new

Mexican Americans, like these farmworkers pitting apricots in Los Angeles County in 1924, often found jobs in the agribusiness enterprises of the Southwest but lived in barrios *in the expanding cities of the region. More Mexicans entered the United States in the 1920s than any other group of immigrants.*

developments were sprawling and dispersed, for the automobile enabled people to live in formerly remote areas. A single-family house surrounded by a lawn became the social ideal, a pastoral escape from the overcrowded and dangerous city. Many suburbs excluded African Americans, Hispanics, Jews, and working-class people. Shaker Heights, for instance, limited land sales to white buyers and required expensive building materials and professional architects. Suburbanites of more modest means found homes in places like Westwood, outside Chicago, the "World's Largest Bungalow Development."

Suburbanization and the automobile brought other changes. In 1922, J. C. Nichols opened the Country Club Plaza, the first suburban shopping center, in Kansas City; it provided free, off-street parking. Department stores and other large retailers began leaving the urban cores for the suburbs, where both parking and more affluent customers were waiting. Drive-in restaurants began with Royce Hailey's Pig Stand in Dallas in 1921. Later in the decade, the first fast-food franchise chain, White Tower, appeared, with its standardized menu and building. To serve the automobile, governments spent more on road construction and maintenance. By 1930, road construction was the largest single item in the national budget.

Mass Culture in the Jazz Age

The White Tower chain symbolized a new society and culture. Urbanization and the automobile joined with new systems of distributing, marketing, and communications to mold a mass culture of standardized experiences and interests. Not all Americans participated equally in the new culture, however, and some attacked it.

Advertising the Consumer Society

Advertising and its focus on increasing consumption shaped the new society. President Coolidge considered advertising "the most potent influence in adopting and changing the habits and modes of life, affecting what we eat, what we wear, and the work and play of the whole nation." A less complacent observer calculated that in 1925, nearly 50 percent more was spent "to educate consumers in what they may or may not want to buy" than on education from grade school through university.

Advertisers exhorted consumers via newspapers, billboards, streetcar signs, junk mail, radio, movies, and even skywriting. They sought to create a single market where everyone, regardless of region and ethnicity, consumed brand-name products. Advertisers attempted to stimulate new wants by ridiculing previous models or tastes as obsolete, acclaiming the convenience of a new brand, or linking the latest fashion with status or sex appeal. "If I wear a certain brand of underwear," observed one critic, "I have the satisfaction of knowing that my fellow-men not so fortunately clad are undoubtedly fouled swine."

The home became a focus of consumerism. Middle- and upper-class women purchased mass-produced household appliances, such as electric irons, toasters, vacuum cleaners, washing machines, and refrigerators. Working-class women bought packaged food, ready-made clothing, and other consumer goods to lighten their workload. Advertisers attempted to redefine the housewife's role as primarily that of a consumer, purchasing goods for her family. To promote sales of clothing and cosmetics, advertising depicted women as concerned with fashion, beauty, and sex appeal. It thus contributed to the declining interest in the larger social issues that the earlier women's movement had raised.

A shifting labor market also promoted mass consumption. The increasing number of white-collar workers had more time and money for leisure and consumption. Factory workers, whose jobs often provided little challenge, less satisfaction, and no prospect for advancement, found in consumption not only material rewards but, thanks to advertisers' claims, some self-respect and fulfillment as stylish and attractive people worthy of attention. Women clerical workers, the fastest-growing occupational group, found in the purchase of clothes and cosmetics a sign of social status and an antidote to workplace monotony. "People are seeking to escape from themselves," insisted a writer in *Advertising and Selling* in 1926. "They want to live in a more exciting world." Advertisers tried to portray popular fantasies rather than social realities.

Under the stimulus of advertising, consumption increasingly displaced the traditional virtues of thrift, prudence, and avoidance of debt. Installment buying became common. By 1928, fully 85 percent of furniture, 80 percent of radios, and 75 percent of washing machines were bought on credit. But with personal debt rising more than twice as fast as incomes, even aggressive advertising and the extension of credit could not indefinitely prolong the illusion of a healthy economy.

Leisure and Entertainment

During the 1920s, Americans also spent more on recreation and leisure, important features of the new mass society. Millions of people packed into movie theaters whose ornate style symbolized their social importance. In Chicago, the Uptown boasted a four thousand–seat theater, an infirmary, a nursery, and a restaurant; its turreted façade soared eight stories. Inside was a four-story lobby with twin marble staircases, crystal chandeliers, and an orchestra to entertain people waiting to enter. "It is beyond human dreams of loveliness," exclaimed one ad, "achieving that overpowering sense of tremendous size and exquisite beauty."

Movies helped spread common values and set national trends in dress, language, and behavior. Studios made films to attract the largest audiences and fit prevailing stereotypes. Cecil B. De Mille titilated audiences while reinforcing conventional standards with religious epics, like *The Ten Commandments* (1923) or *The King of Kings* (1927). Set in ancient times, such movies depicted both sinful pleasures and the eventual triumph of moral order. One Hollywood executive called for "passionate but pure" films that would give "the public all the sex it wants with compensating values for all those church and women groups."

The soup for men
who eat to win!
Campbell's
Condensed
Tomato Soup
MEN with the success-habit eat wisely and well, both. They enjoy Campbell's Tomato Soup regularly and they get from it a sparkle and zest, which tell in the day's work. All of the rich, tonic goodness. All of the famous tomato healthfulness. 12 cents a can.

Advertisements for brand-name products, like this 1929 ad for Campbell's tomato soup, often tried to link simple consumption with larger issues of personal success and achievement.

Radio also helped mold national popular culture. The first radio network, the National Broadcasting Company (NBC), was formed in 1926. Soon it was charging $10,000 to broadcast commercials to a national market. Networks provided standardized entertainment, personalities, and news to Americans across the nation. Radio incorporated listeners into a national society. Rural residents, in particular, welcomed the "talking furniture" for giving them access to the speeches, sermons, and business information available to city-dwellers.

The phonograph, another popular source of entertainment, allowed families to listen to music of their choice in their own homes. The phonograph business boomed. Manufacturers turned out more than 2 million phonographs and 100 million records annually. Record companies promoted dance crazes, such as the Charleston, and developed regional markets for country, or "hillbilly," music in the South and West as well as a "race market" for blues and jazz among the growing urban population, black and white. The popularity of the trumpet player Louis Armstrong and other jazz greats gave the decade its nickname, the **Jazz Age**.

Jazz derived from African-American musical traditions. The Great Migration spread it from New Orleans and Kansas City to cities throughout the nation. Its improvisational and rhythmic characteristics differed sharply from older and more formal music and were often condemned by people who feared that jazz would undermine conventional restraints on behavior. One group in Cincinnati, arguing that the music would implant "jazz emotions" in babies, won an injunction against its performance near hospitals. Middle-class black Chicagoans frowned on jazz and favored "the better class of music." But conductor Leopold Stokowski defended jazz as the music of modern America: "Jazz has come to stay because it is an expression of the times, of the breathless, energetic, superactive times in which we are living; it is useless to fight against it."

Professional sports also flourished and became more commercialized. Millions of Americans, attracted by the popularity of such celebrities as Babe Ruth of the New York Yankees, crowded into baseball parks to follow major league teams. Ruth treated himself as a commercial commodity, hiring an agent, endorsing Cadillacs and alligator shoes, and defending a salary in 1932 that dwarfed that of President Hoover by declaring, "I had a better year than he did."

Large crowds turned out to watch boxers like Jack Dempsey and Gene Tunney pummel each other; those who could not get tickets listened to radio announcers describe each blow. College football attracted frenzied followers among people with no interest in higher education. Universities built huge stadiums—Ohio State's had 64,000 seats. By 1929, the Carnegie Commission noted that the commercialization of college sports "overshadowed the intellectual life for which the university is assumed to exist."

Other crazes, from flagpole sitting to miniature golf, also indicated the spread of popular culture and its emphasis on leisure. Another celebrity who captured popular fascination was the aviator Charles Lindbergh, who flew alone across the Atlantic in 1927. In the *Spirit of St. Louis,* a tiny airplane built on a shoestring budget and nearly outweighed by the massive amount of fuel it had to carry, Lindbergh fought bad weather and fatigue for thirty-four hours before landing to a hero's welcome in Paris. Named its first "Man of the Year" by *Time,* one of the new mass-circulation magazines, Lindbergh won adulation and awards from Americans who still valued the image of individualism.

The New Morality

The promotion of consumption and immediate gratification weakened traditional self-restraint and fed a desire for personal fulfillment. The failure of wartime sacrifices to achieve promised glories deepened Americans' growing disenchantment with traditional values. The social dislocations of the war years and growing urbanization accelerated moral and social change. Sexual pleasure became an increasingly open objective. Popularization of Sigmund Freud's ideas weakened prescriptions for sexual restraint; the growing availability of birth control information enabled women to enjoy sex with less fear of pregnancy; and movie stars like Clara Bow, known as "the It Girl," and Rudolph Valentino flaunted sexuality to mass audiences. Traditionalists worried as divorce rates, cigarette consumption, and hemlines went up while respect for parents, elders, and clergy went down. A sociological study of Muncie, Indiana—the nation's "Middletown"—found that "religious life as represented by the churches is less pervasive than a generation ago."

Young people seemed to embody the new morality. Rejecting conventional standards, they embraced the era's frenzied dances, bootleg liquor, smoking, more revealing clothing, and sexual experimentation. They welcomed the freedom from parental control that the automobile afforded—although the car was hardly the "house of prostitution on wheels" that one critic called it. The "flapper"—a frivolous young woman with short hair and a skimpy skirt who danced, smoked, and drank in oblivious self-absorption—was a major obsession in countless articles, bearing such titles as "These Wild Young People" and "The Uprising of the Young." Few people were more alarmed than the president of the University of Florida. "The low-cut gowns, the rolled hose and short skirts are born of the Devil," he cried, "and are carrying the present and future generations to chaos and destruction." But feminists also condemned this symbol of changing standards. "It is sickening," Charlotte Perkins Gilman wrote in 1923, "to see so many of the newly freed abusing that freedom in mere imitation of masculine vice and weakness."

But the new morality was neither as new nor as widespread as its advocates and critics believed. Signs of change had appeared before the war in the popularity of new clothing fashions, social values, and public amusements among working-class and ethnic groups. And if it now became fashionable for the middle class to adopt such attitudes and practices, most Americans still adhered to traditional beliefs and values. Legislators in Utah and Virginia, for example, proposed laws requiring hemlines within three inches of the ankle and necklines within three inches of the throat. Moreover, as Gilman's comment suggests, the new morality offered only a limited freedom. It certainly did not promote social equality for women, who remained subject to traditional double standards, with marriage and divorce laws, property rights, and employment opportunities biased against them.

The Searching Twenties

Many writers rejected what they considered the materialism, conformity, and provincialism of the emerging mass culture. Their criticism made the postwar decade one of the most creative periods in American literature. The brutality and hypocrisy of the war stimulated their disillusionment and alienation. What Gertrude Stein called the **Lost Generation** considered, in the words of F. Scott Fitzgerald, "all Gods dead, all wars fought, all faiths in man shaken." Ernest Hemingway, wounded as a Red Cross volunteer during the war, rejected idealism in his novel *A Farewell to Arms* (1929), declaring that he no longer saw any meaning in "the words *sacred, glorious,* and *sacrifice.*"

Novelists also turned their attention to American society. In *The Great Gatsby* (1925), Fitzgerald traced the self-deceptions of the wealthy. Sinclair Lewis ridiculed middle-class society and its narrow business culture in *Babbitt* (1922), whose title character provided a new word applied to the smug and shallow. In 1930, Lewis became the first American to win the Nobel Prize in literature.

Other writers condemned the mediocrity and intolerance of mass society. The critic Harold Stearns edited *Civilization in the United States* (1922), a book of essays. Its depiction of a repressive society sunk in hypocrisy, conformity, and materialism prompted his departure for Paris, where he lived, like Hemingway and Fitzgerald, as an expatriate, alienated from America. H. L. Mencken made his *American Mercury* the leading magazine of cultural dissenters. Conventional and conservative himself, Mencken heaped vitriol on the "puritans," "peasants," and "prehensile morons" he saw everywhere in American life.

When President Coolidge declined a request to exhibit American paintings in Paris by declaring that there were none, he seemed to confirm for the critics the boorishness of American society. But many of the critics were as self-absorbed as their targets. When the old progressive muckraker Upton Sinclair complained that he found nothing "constructive" in Mencken's voluminous writings, Mencken was delighted. "Uplift," he retorted, "has damn nigh ruined the country." Fitzgerald claimed to have "no interest in politics at all." Such attitudes dovetailed with the society they condemned.

Culture Wars

Despite the blossoming of mass culture and society in the 1920s, conflicts divided social groups. Some of these struggles involved reactions against the new currents in American life, including technological and scientific innovations, urban growth, and materialism. But movements to restrict immigration, enforce prohibition, prohibit the teaching of evolution, and even sustain the Ku Klux Klan did not have simple origins, motives, or consequences. The forces underlying the culture wars of the 1920s would surface repeatedly in the future (see the overview table, "Issues in the Culture Wars of the 1920s").

Nativism and Immigration Restriction

For years, many Americans, from racists to reformers, had campaigned to restrict immigration. In 1917, Congress required immigrants to pass a literacy test. But renewed immigration after the war revived the anti-immigration movement, and the propaganda of the war and Red Scare years generated public support for more restriction. Depicting immigrants as radicals, racial inferiors, religious subversives, or criminals, nativists clamored for congressional action. The Emergency Quota Act of 1921 reduced immigration by about two-thirds and established quotas for nationalities on the basis of their numbers in the United States in 1910. Restrictionists, however, demanded more stringent action, especially against the largely Catholic and Jewish immigrants from southern and eastern Europe. Coolidge himself urged that America "be kept American," by which he meant white, Anglo-Saxon, and Protestant.

Congress adopted this racist rationale in the **National Origins Act of 1924**, which proclaimed its objective to be the maintenance of the "racial preponderance" of "the basic strain of our population." This law restricted immigration quotas to 2 percent of the foreign-born population of each nationality as recorded in the 1890 census, which was taken before the mass immigration from southern and eastern Europe. Another provision, effective in 1929, restricted total annual immigration to 150,000 with quotas that nearly eliminated southern and eastern Europeans. The law also completely excluded Japanese immigrants.

Other actions targeted Japanese residents in America. California, Oregon, Washington, Arizona, and other western states prohibited them from owning or leasing land, and in 1922, the Supreme Court ruled that, as nonwhites, they could never become naturalized citizens. A Japanese newspaper in Los Angeles criticized such actions as betraying America's own ideals. Dispirited by the prejudice of the decade, Japanese residents hoped for fulfillment through their children, the ***Nisei***, who were American citizens by birth.

Ironically, as a U.S. territory, the Philippines was not subject to the National Origins Act, and Filipino immigration increased ninefold during the 1920s. Most Filipino newcomers became farm laborers, especially in California, or worked in Alaskan fisheries. Similarly, because the law did not apply to immigrants from the Western Hemisphere, Mexican immigration also grew. Nativists lobbied to exclude Mexicans, but agribusiness interests in the Southwest blocked any restrictions on low-cost migrant labor.

The Ku Klux Klan

Nativism was also reflected in the popularity of the revived Ku Klux Klan, the goal of which, according to its leader, was to protect "the interest of those whose forefathers established the nation." Although founded in Georgia in 1915 and modeled on its Reconstruction predecessor, the new Klan was a national, not a southern, movement and claimed several million members by the mid-1920s. Admitting only native-born white Protestants, the Klan embodied the fears of a traditional culture threatened by social change. Ironically, its rapid spread owed

Overview

Issues in the Culture Wars of the 1920s

Issue	Proponent view	Opponent view
The new morality	Promotes greater personal freedom and opportunities for fulfillment	Promotes moral collapse
Evolutionism	A scientific advance linked to notions of progress	A threat to religious belief
Jazz	Modern and vital	Unsettling, irregular, vulgar, and primitive
Immigration	A source of national strength from ethnic and racial diversity	A threat to the status and authority of old-stock white Protestants
Great Migration	A chance for African Americans to find new economic opportunities and gain autonomy and pride	A threat to traditional white privilege, control, and status
Prohibition	Promotes social and family stability and reduces crime	Restricts personal liberty and increases crime
Fundamentalism	An admirable adherence to traditional religious faith and biblical injunctions	A superstitious creed given to intolerant interference in social and political affairs
Ku Klux Klan	An organization promoting community responsibility, patriotism, and traditional social, moral, and religious values	A group of religious and racial bigots given to violent vigilantism and fostering moral and public corruption
Mass culture	Increases popular participation in national culture; provides entertainment and relaxation	Promotes conformity, materialism, mediocrity, and spectacle
Consumerism	Promotes material progress and higher living standards	Promotes waste, sterility, and self-indulgence

much to modern business and promotional techniques as hundreds of professional recruiters raked in hefty commissions selling Klan memberships to those hoping to defend their way of life.

In part the Klan was a fraternal order, providing entertainment, assistance, and community for its members. Its picnics, parades, charity drives, and other social and family-oriented activities—perhaps a half million women joined the Women of the Ku Klux Klan—sharply distinguished the organization from both the small, secretive Klan of the nineteenth century and the still smaller, extremist Klan of the later twentieth century. Regarding themselves as reformers, Klan members supported immigration restriction and prohibition.

But the Klan also exploited racial, ethnic, and religious prejudices and campaigned against many social groups and what it called "alien creeds." It attacked African Americans in the South, Mexicans in Texas, Japanese in California, and Catholics and Jews everywhere. A twisted religious impulse ran through much of the Klan's organization and activities. It hired itinerant Protestant ministers to spread its message, erected altars and flaming crosses at its meetings, and sang Klan lyrics to the tunes of well-known hymns. One Klan leader maintained that "the Klan stood for the same things as the Church, but we did the things the Church wouldn't do." This included publishing anti-Catholic newspapers, boycotting Catholic and Jewish businesses, and lobbying

Indiana Klanswomen pose in their regalia in 1924. The Klan combined appeals to traditional family and religious values with violent attacks upon those who were not white, native-born Protestants.

for laws against parochial schools and for compulsory Bible reading in the public schools. The Klan also resorted to violence. In 1921, for example, a Methodist minister who belonged to the Klan murdered a Catholic priest on his own doorstep, and other Klansmen burned down Catholic churches. The leader of the Oregon Klan insisted that "the only way to cure a Catholic is to kill him."

To the Klan, Catholics and Jews symbolized not merely subversive religions but the ethnic diversity and swelling urban population that challenged traditional Protestant culture. To protect that culture, the Klan attempted to censor or disrupt "indecent" entertainment, assaulted those whom it accused of adultery, and terrorized doctors who performed abortions.

While the Klan's appeal seemed rooted in the declining countryside, it also attracted urban residents. Chicago had the largest Klan organization in the nation with fifty thousand members, and Houston, Dallas, Portland, Indianapolis, Denver, and the satellite communities ringing Los Angeles were also Klan strongholds. Urban Klansmen were largely lower or lower middle class, many recently arrived from the country and retaining its attitudes; others were long-term urban residents who feared being marginalized by social changes, especially by competition from immigrants and new ideas.

The Klan also ventured into politics, with some success. But eventually it encountered resistance. In the North, Catholic workers disrupted Klan parades. In the South, too, Klan excesses provoked a backlash. After the Klan in Dallas flogged sixty-eight people in a "whipping meadow" along the Trinity River in 1922, respect turned to outrage. Newspapers demanded that the Klan disband, district attorneys began to prosecute Klan thugs, and in 1924 Klan candidates were defeated by the ticket headed by Miriam "Ma" Ferguson, whose gubernatorial campaign called for anti-Klan laws and the loss of tax exemptions for churches used for Klan meetings. Elsewhere the Klan was stung by revelations of criminal behavior and corruption by Klan leaders who had been making fortunes pocketing membership fees and selling regalia to followers. The Klan crusade to purify society had bred corruption and conflict everywhere. By 1930, the Klan had nearly collapsed.

Prohibition and Crime

Like the Klan, prohibition both reflected and provoked social tensions in the 1920s. Reformers had long believed that prohibition would improve social conditions, reduce crime and family instability, increase economic efficiency, and purify politics. They rejoiced in 1920 when the Eighteenth Amendment, prohibiting the manufacture, sale, or transportation of alcoholic beverages, took effect. Congress then passed the **Volstead Act**, which defined the forbidden liquors and established the Prohibition Bureau to enforce the law. But many social groups, especially among urban ethnic communities, opposed prohibition, and the government could not enforce the law where public opinion did not endorse it.

Evasion was easy. By permitting alcohol for medicinal, sacramental, and industrial purposes, the Volstead Act gave doctors, priests, and druggists a huge loophole through which to satisfy their friends' needs. Hearing that the use of sacramental wines increased by 800,000 gallons under prohibition, one Protestant leader complained that "not more than one-quarter of this is sacramental—the rest is sacrilegious." City-dwellers made "bathtub gin," and rural people distilled "moonshine." Scofflaws frequented the "speakeasies" that replaced saloons or bought liquor from bootleggers and rumrunners, who imported it from Canada, Cuba, or Mexico. The limited resources of the Prohibition Bureau often allowed bootleggers to operate openly. Dozens met publicly in a Seattle hotel in 1922 and adopted "fair prices" for liquor and a code of ethics "to keep liquor runners within the limits of approved business methods."

The ethics and business methods of bootleggers soon shocked Americans, however. The huge profits encouraged organized crime—which had previously concentrated on gambling and prostitution—to develop elaborate liquor distribution networks. Operating outside the law, crime "families" used violence to enforce contracts, suppress competition, and attack rivals. In Chicago, Al Capone's army of nearly a thousand gangsters killed hundreds. Using the profits from bootlegging and such new tools as the automobile and the submachine gun, organized crime corrupted city governments and police forces.

Gradually, even many "drys"—people who had initially favored prohibition—dropped their support, horrified by the boost it gave organized crime and worried about a general disrespect for law that it promoted. A 1926 poll found that four-fifths of Americans wanted to repeal or modify prohibition. Yet it remained in force because it was entangled in party politics and social conflict. Many rural, Protestant Americans saw prohibition as a symbolic cultural issue. As the comedian Will Rogers said, "Mississippi will vote dry and drink wet as long as it can stagger to the polls." Prohibition represented their ability to control the newcomers in the expanding cities. Democrats called for repeal in their 1928 and 1932 platforms, and in 1933, thirty-six states ratified an amendment repealing what Herbert Hoover had called a "noble experiment."

Old-Time Religion and the Scopes Trial

Religion provided another fulcrum for traditionalists attempting to stem cultural change. Protestant fundamentalism, which emphasized the infallibility of the Bible, including the Genesis story of Adam and Eve, emerged at the turn of the century as a conservative reaction to religious modernism and the social changes brought by the mass immigration of Catholics and Jews, the growing influence of science and technology, and the secularization of public education. But the fundamentalist crusade to reshape America became formidable only in the 1920s.

Fundamentalist groups, colleges, and publications sprang up throughout the nation, especially in the South. The anti-Catholic sentiment exploited by the Klan was but one consequence of fundamentalism's insistence on strict biblical Christianity. A second was the assault on Darwin's theory of evolution, which contradicted literal interpretations of biblical Creation. The Southern Baptist Convention condemned "every theory, evolutionary or other, which teaches that man originated or came by way of lower animal ancestry." Fundamentalist legislators tried to prevent teaching evolution in public schools in at least twenty states. In 1923, Oklahoma banned Darwinian textbooks, and Florida's legislature denounced teaching evolution as "subversive." In 1925, Tennessee forbade teaching any idea contrary to the biblical account of human origins. The governor signed it, saying that "there is a widespread belief that something is shaking the fundamentals of the country,

Prohibition was a divisive issue, involving cultural values as much as alcoholic spirits. This 1920 cartoon depicts Prohibitionists as attempting to impose their own repressive values on all Americans.

"NOW THEN, ALL TOGETHER, 'MY COUNTRY 'TIS OF THEE'"

AMERICA'S JOURNEY

FROM THEN TO NOW

The Culture Wars

Cultural conflict raged through American society in the 1920s as people reacted to great social changes, including new roles for women, increasing ethnic and racial diversity, rapid urbanization, and the "new morality." Nativists demanded immigration restriction; the Ku Klux Klan played on fears of racial, ethnic, and religious minorities; prohibitionists grappled with the minions of Demon Rum; and Protestant fundamentalists campaigned to prohibit the teaching of evolution in public schools.

Such conflicts are rooted in the moral systems that give people identity and purpose. As a result, the challenges of the Great Depression and World War II dampened but did not extinguish them. Beginning in the 1960s, fueled as before by challenges to traditional values and beliefs—African-American demands for civil rights, opposition to the Vietnam War, the women's rights movement and women's growing presence in the workplace, a new wave of immigration (dominated this time by Asians and Latin Americans), the gay rights movement—cultural conflict flared again and continues to burn.

In the 1920s nativists succeeded in curtailing immigration with the passage of the National Origins Act of 1924. In 1994, the people of California approved Proposition 187, which barred undocumented aliens from public schools and social services. Again, as in the 1920s, fundamentalists are mounting an attack against the teaching of evolution in public schools, sometimes seeking to persuade local school boards to give equal time to the pseudoscience of creationism. And today rap and rock 'n' roll provoke the same kind of worried condemnation that jazz provoked in the 1920s.

The central battleground of today's culture wars, however, is women's rights, and especially abortion rights. Ever since the Supreme Court ruled in *Roe* v. *Wade* in 1973 that women had a right to an abortion, opponents, primarily religious conservatives, have sought to curtail or abolish that right in the name of "family values." Antiabortion protests became increasingly violent in the 1980s and 1990s. Demonstrators have harassed women trying to enter abortion clinics, clinics have been bombed, and several abortion providers have been murdered. Although the Supreme Court has upheld *Roe* v. *Wade* and laws restraining demonstrations at abortion clinics, it has also upheld state laws imposing limits on abortion rights. Abortions have become harder to obtain in many parts of the country.

Gay rights is another new battleground in the culture wars. Religious conservatives, again in the name of "family values," have sought to counter efforts to extend civil rights protections to gays and lesbians. In 1992, for example, Colorado approved a measure (overturned by the Supreme Court in 1996) that prohibited local governments from passing ordinances protecting gays and lesbians from discrimination.

The hostility to the Catholic Church and Catholic immigrants that had long been characteristic of American nativism has been largely absent from the current culture wars. On the contrary, conservative Catholics have joined forces with evangelical Protestants on many fronts, particularly on abortion and gay rights.

According to one popular analysis, the antagonists in today's culture wars are, on one side, those who find authority in transcendent universal sources like those that religious traditions lay claim to, and, on the other, those who find authority in society and human reason. From this perspective, perhaps the most prominent recent engagement in the culture wars was the impeachment of President Clinton. Republican leader Tom DeLay of Texas, for example, declared in 1999 that the impeachment debate was "about relativism versus absolute truth." Polls, however, showed that most Americans were more tolerant and flexible, willing to separate the president's public performance from his personal morality. With the failure to convict Clinton, one Republican lamented: "We probably have lost the culture war." But given the deeply rooted convictions that motivate it, cultural conflict is likely to remain a persistent undercurrent in American life.

The packed courtroom for the Scopes Trial in 1925 illustrates the intense interest that Americans have persistently taken in conflicts stemming from differing cultural values and ethical visions.

both in religion and in morals. It is the opinion of many that an abandonment of the old-fashioned faith and belief in the Bible is our trouble."

Social or political conservatism, however, was not an inherent part of old-time religion. The most prominent antievolution politician, William Jennings Bryan, continued to campaign for political, social, and economic reforms. Never endorsing the Klan, he served on the American Committee on the Rights of Religious Minorities and condemned anti-Semitism and anti-Catholicism. Bryan feared that Darwinism promoted political and economic conservatism. The survival of the fittest, he complained, elevated force and brutality, ignored spiritual values and democracy, and discouraged altruism and reform. How could a person fight for social justice "unless he believes in the triumph of right?"

The controversy over evolution came to a head when the **American Civil Liberties Union (ACLU)** responded to Tennessee's violation of the constitutional separation of church and state by offering to defend any teacher who tested the antievolution law. John Scopes, a high school biology teacher in Dayton, Tennessee, did so and was arrested. Scopes's trial riveted national attention after Bryan agreed to assist the prosecution and Clarence Darrow, a famous Chicago lawyer and prominent atheist, volunteered to defend Scopes.

Millions of Americans tuned their radios to hear the first trial ever broadcast. The judge, a fundamentalist, sat under a sign urging "Read Your Bible Daily." He ruled that scientists could not testify in support of evolution: Because they were not present at the Creation, their testimony would be "hearsay." But he did allow Darrow to put Bryan on the stand as an expert on the Bible. Bryan insisted on the literal truth of every story in the Bible, allowing Darrow to ridicule his ideas and force him to concede that some biblical passages had to be construed symbolically. Though the local jury took only eight minutes to convict Scopes, fundamentalists suffered public ridicule from reporters like H. L. Mencken, who sneered at the "hillbillies" and "yokels" of Dayton.

But fundamentalism was hardly destroyed, and antievolutionists continued their campaign. New organizations, such as the Bryan Bible League, lobbied for state laws and an antievolution amendment to the constitution. Three more states forbade teaching evolution, but by 1929 the movement had faltered. Even so, fundamentalism retained religious influence and would again challenge science and modernism in American life.

A New Era in the World?

Abroad, as at home, Americans in the 1920s sought peace and economic order. Rejection of the Treaty of Versailles and the League of Nations did not foreshadow isolationism. Indeed, in the 1920s, the United States became more deeply involved in international matters than ever before in peacetime. That involvement both produced important successes and sowed the seeds for serious future problems.

War Debts and Economic Expansion

The United States was the world's dominant economic power in the 1920s, changed by the Great War from a debtor to a creditor nation. The loans that the United States had made to its allies during the war troubled the nation's relations with Europe throughout the decade. American insistence on repayment angered Europeans, who saw the money as a U.S. contribution to the joint war effort against Germany. Moreover, high American tariffs blocked Europeans from exporting goods to the United States and earning dollars to repay their debts. Eventually, the United States readjusted the terms for repayment, and American bankers extended large loans to Germany, which used the money to pay reparations to Britain and France, whose governments then used the same money to repay the United States. This unstable system depended on a constant flow of money from the United States.

America's global economic role expanded in other ways as well. Exports, especially of manufactured goods, soared; by 1929, the United States was the world's largest exporter, responsible for one-sixth of all exports. American investment abroad more than doubled between 1919 and 1930. To expand their markets and avoid foreign tariffs, many U.S. companies became **multinational corporations**, establishing branches or subsidiaries abroad. Ford built assembly plants in England, Japan, Turkey, and Canada. International Telephone and Telegraph owned two dozen factories in Europe and employed more overseas workers than any other U.S. corporation.

Other companies gained control of foreign supply sources. American oil companies invested in foreign oil fields, especially in Latin America, where they controlled more than half of Venezuelan production. The United Fruit Company developed such huge operations in Central America that it often dominated national economies. In Costa Rica, the company had a larger budget than the national government.

Europeans and Latin Americans alike worried about this economic invasion; even Secretary of Commerce Hoover expressed concerns. Multinationals, he warned, might eventually take markets from American manufacturers and jobs from American workers. Business leaders, however, dismissed such reservations.

Hoover's concerns, moreover, did not prevent him from promoting economic expansion abroad. The government worked to open doors for American businesses in foreign countries, helping them secure access to trade, investment opportunities, and raw materials. Hoover's Bureau of Foreign Commerce opened fifty offices around the world to boost American business. Hoover also pressed the British to give U.S. corporations access to rubber production in the British colony of Malaya. Secretary of State Charles Evans Hughes negotiated access to Iraqi oil fields for U.S. oil companies. The government also authorized bankers and manufacturers to form combinations, exempt from antitrust laws, to exploit foreign markets.

Rejecting War

Although government officials cooperated with business leaders to promote American strategic and economic interests, they had little desire to use force in the process. Popular reaction against the Great War, strengthened by a strong peace movement, constrained policymakers. Having repudiated collective security as embodied in the League of Nations, the United States nonetheless sought to minimize international conflict and promote its national security. In particular, the State Department sought to restrict the buildup of armaments among nations.

At the invitation of President Harding, delegations from nine nations met in Washington at the Washington Naval Conference in 1921 to discuss disarmament. The conference drafted a treaty to reduce battleship tonnage and suspend the building of new ships for a decade. The terms virtually froze the existing balance of naval power, with the first rank assigned to Britain and the United States, followed by Japan and then France and Italy. Japan and the United States also agreed not to fortify their possessions in the Pacific any further and to respect the Open Door in East Asia. Public opinion welcomed the treaty; the U.S. Senate ratified it with only one dissenting vote, and the 1924 Republican platform hailed it as "the greatest peace document ever drawn."

The United States made a more dramatic gesture in 1928 when it helped draft the **Kellogg-Briand Pact**. Signed by sixty-four nations, the treaty renounced aggression and outlawed war. Without provisions for enforcement, however, it was little more than symbolic. The Senate reserved the right of self-defense, repudiated any responsibility for enforcing the treaty, and maintained U.S. claims under the Monroe Doctrine. These limitations on the treaty, Senator Hiram Johnson noted, "have made its nothingness complete."

Managing the Hemisphere

Senate insistence on the authority of the Monroe Doctrine reflected the U.S. claim to a predominant role in Latin America. The United States continued to dominate the hemisphere to promote its own interests. It exerted its influence through investments, control of the Panama Canal, invocation of the Monroe Doctrine, and, when necessary, military intervention.

In response to American public opinion, the peace movement, and Latin American nationalism, the United States did retreat from the extreme gunboat diplomacy of the Progressive Era, withdrawing troops from the Dominican Republic and Nicaragua. Secretary of State Hughes assured Latin Americans that "we covet no territory; we seek no conquest; the liberty we cherish for ourselves we desire for others; and we accept no rights for ourselves that we do not accord to others." But Haiti remained under U.S. occupation throughout the decade, American troops stayed in Cuba and Panama, and the United States directed the financial policies of other Latin American countries. Moreover, it sent the marines into Honduras in 1924 and back to Nicaragua in 1926. Such interventions could establish only temporary stability while provoking further Latin American hostility. "We are hated and despised," said one American businessman in Nicaragua. "This feeling has been created by employing American marines to hunt down and kill Nicaraguans in their own country."

Latin American resentment led to a resolution at the 1928 Inter-America Conference denying the right of any nation "to intervene in the internal affairs of another." The U.S. delegation rejected the measure, but the anger of Latin Americans prompted the State Department to draft the Clark Memorandum. This document, not published until 1930, receded from the Roosevelt Corollary and helped prepare the way for the so-called Good Neighbor Policy toward Latin America. Still, the United States retained the means, both military and economic, to dominate the hemisphere.

Herbert Hoover and the Final Triumph of the New Era

As the national economy steamed ahead in 1928, the Republicans chose as their presidential candidate Herbert Hoover, a man who symbolized the policies of prosperity and the New Era. Hoover was not a politician—he had never been elected to office—but a successful administrator who championed rational and efficient economic development. A cooperative government, he believed, should promote business interests and encourage corporations to form trade associations to assure stability and profitability. It should not regulate economic activities. Hoover's stiff managerial image was softened by his humanitarian record and his roots in rural Iowa.

The Democrats, in contrast, chose a candidate who evoked the cultural conflicts of the 1920s. Alfred E. Smith, four-term governor of New York, was a Catholic, an opponent of prohibition, and a Tammany politician tied to the immigrant constituency of New York City. He had failed to gain the presidential nomination in 1924 when the party split over prohibition and the Klan, but in 1928 he won the dubious honor of running against Hoover. His nomination plunged the nation into the cultural strife that had divided the Democrats in 1924. Rural fundamentalism, anti-Catholicism, prohibition, and nativism were crucial factors in the campaign. The fundamentalist assault was unrelenting. Billy Sunday attacked Smith and the Democrats as "the forces of hell," and a Baptist minister in Oklahoma City warned his congregation: "If you vote for Al Smith, you're voting against Christ and you'll all be damned."

But Hoover was in fact the more progressive candidate. Sympathetic to labor, sensitive to women's issues, hostile to racial segregation, and favorable to the League of Nations, Hoover had always distanced himself from what he called "the reactionary group in the Republican party." By contrast, despite supporting state welfare legislation to benefit his urban working-class constituents, Smith was essentially conservative and opposed an active government. Moreover, he was as parochial as his most rural adversaries and never attempted to reach out to them. H. L. Mencken, who voted for Smith, nevertheless said of him, "Not only is he uninterested in the great problems facing the nation, but he has never heard of them." Smith himself responded to a question about the needs of the states west of the Mississippi by asking, "What states *are* west of the Mississippi?"

Although many Americans voted against Smith because of his social background, those same characteristics attracted others. Millions of urban and ethnic voters, previously Republican or politically uninvolved, voted for Smith and laid the basis for a new Democratic coalition that would emerge in the 1930s. In 1928, however, with the nation still enjoying the economic prosperity so closely associated

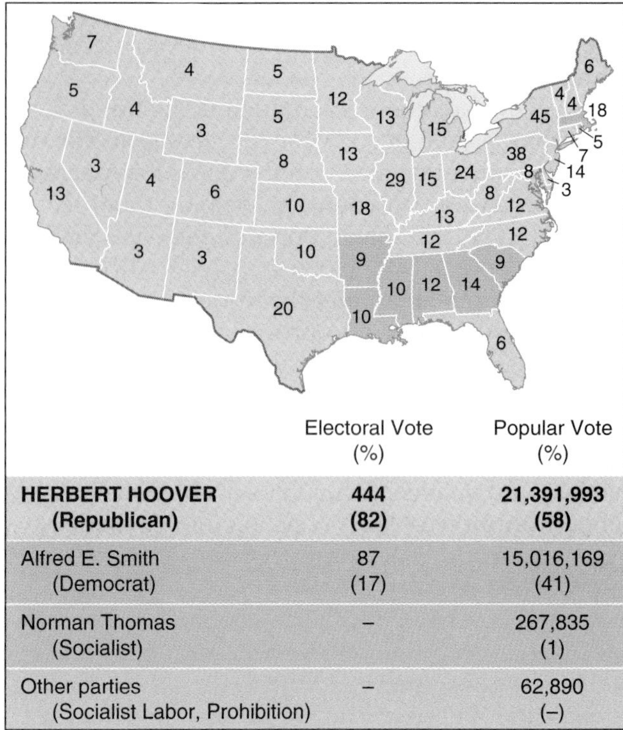

	Electoral Vote (%)	Popular Vote (%)
HERBERT HOOVER (Republican)	**444 (82)**	**21,391,993 (58)**
Alfred E. Smith (Democrat)	87 (17)	15,016,169 (41)
Norman Thomas (Socialist)	–	267,835 (1)
Other parties (Socialist Labor, Prohibition)	–	62,890 (–)

Map 26-2 The Election of 1928
The cultural conflicts of the 1920s shaped the 1928 election. Al Smith carried the largest cities, but Herbert Hoover swept most of the rest of the nation, even attracting much of the usually Democratic South.

with Hoover and the Republicans, the Democrats were routed (see Map 26-2).

In his campaign, Hoover boasted that Republican policies could bring America to "the final triumph over poverty." But 1928 would be the Republicans' final triumph for a long time. The vaunted prosperity of the 1920s was ending, and the country faced a future dark with poverty.

Conclusion

The New Era of the 1920s changed America. Technological and managerial innovations produced giant leaps in productivity, new patterns of labor, a growing concentration of corporate power, and high corporate profits. Government policies from protective tariffs and regressive taxation to a relaxation of regulatory laws reflected and reinforced the triumphs of a business elite over traditional cautions and concerns.

The decade's economic developments in turn stimulated social change, drawing millions of Americans from the countryside to the cities, creating an urban nation, and fostering a new ethic of materialism, consumerism, and leisure and a new mass culture based on the automobile, radio, the movies, and advertising. This social transformation swept up many Americans but left others unsettled by the erosion of traditional practices and values. The concerns of traditionalists found expression in campaigns for prohibition and against immigration, the revival of the Ku Klux Klan, and the rise of religious fundamentalism. Intellectuals denounced the materialism and conformity they saw in the new social order and fashioned new artistic and literary trends.

But the impact of the decade's trends was uneven. Mechanization increased the productivity of some workers but cost others their jobs; people poured into the cities while others left for the suburbs; prohibition, intended to stabilize society, instead produced conflict, crime, and corruption; government policies advanced some economic interests but injured others. Even the notion of a "mass" culture obscured the degree to which millions of Americans were left out of the New Era. With no disposable income and little access to electricity, rural Americans scarcely participated in the joys of consumerism; racial and ethnic minorities often were isolated in ghettos and *barrios*; and many workers faced declining opportunities. Most ominous was the uneven prosperity undergirding the New Era. Although living standards rose for many Americans and the rich expanded their share of national wealth, more than 40 percent of the population earned less than $1,500 a year and fell below the established poverty level. The unequal distribution of wealth and income made the economy unstable and vulnerable to a disastrous collapse.

Review Questions

1. How did the automobile industry affect the nation's economy and society in the 1920s?
2. What factors characterized the "boom industries" of the 1920s? The "sick industries"? How accurate is it to label the 1920s the "decade of prosperity"?
3. What were the underlying issues in the election of 1924? Of 1928? What role did politics play in the public life of the 1920s?
4. What were the chief points of conflict in the "culture wars" of the 1920s? What were the underlying issues in these clashes? Why were they so hard to compromise?
5. In what ways did the World War I experience shape developments in the 1920s?
6. What were the chief features of American involvement in world affairs in the 1920s? To what extent did that involvement constitute a new role for the United States?

Recommended Reading

John Braeman, Robert Bremner, and David Brody, eds., *Change and Continuity in Twentieth Century America: The 1920s* (1968). Stimulating essays that cover important features of economic, social, and political history.

Warren I. Cohen, *Empire without Tears: America's Foreign Relations, 1921–1933* (1987). A splendid brief analysis of diplomatic and economic policy.

James J. Flink, *The Car Culture* (1975). The fascinating history of the automobile and its social impact.

Ellis W. Hawley, *The Great War and the Search for a Modern Order* (1979). A valuable survey emphasizing economic and organizational changes.

Sinclair Lewis, *Babbitt* (1922). An important novel of the 1920s that ridicules the empty business values of the booster society.

Additional Sources

General Studies

John D. Hicks, *Republican Ascendancy, 1921–1933* (1960).

William Leuchtenberg, *The Perils of Prosperity* (1958).

Michael E. Parrish, *Anxious Decades: America in Prosperity and Depression, 1920–1941* (1992).

Geoffrey Perrett, *America in the Twenties* (1982).

Economic Developments

Jo Ann E. Argersinger, *Making the Amalgamated: Gender, Ethnicity, and Class in the Baltimore Clothing Industry* (1999).

Irving L. Bernstein, *The Lean Years: A History of the American Worker, 1920–1933* (1960).

James J. Flink, *The Automobile Age* (1988).

Alice Kessler-Harris, *Out to Work: A History of Wage-Earning Women* (1982).

Roland Marchand, *Advertising the American Dream* (1985).

Stephen Meyer III, *The Five Dollar Day: Labor Management and Social Control in the Ford Motor Company* (1981).

Ronald W. Schatz, *The Electrical Workers* (1983).

Susan Smulyan, *Selling Radio: The Commercialization of American Broadcasting, 1920–1934* (1994).

Susan Strasser, *Satisfaction Guaranteed: The Making of the American Mass Market* (1989).

Leslie Woodcock Tentler, *Wage-Earning Women: Industrial Work and Family Life in the United States, 1900–1930* (1979).

Robert H. Zieger, *American Workers, American Unions* (1994).

Politics and Government

David Burner, *Herbert Hoover: A Public Life* (1979).

David Burner, *The Politics of Provincialism* (1967).

Douglas B. Craig, *After Wilson: The Struggle for the Democratic Party* (1992).

Ellis W. Hawley (ed.), *Herbert Hoover as Secretary of Commerce* (1981).

Walter LaFeber, *Inevitable Revolutions: The United States in Central America* (1984).

Allan J. Lichtman, *Prejudice and the Old Politics: The Presidential Election of 1928* (1979).

Richard Lowitt, *George W. Norris: The Persistence of a Progressive* (1971).

Donald R. McCoy, *Calvin Coolidge* (1967).

Robert Murray, *The Politics of Normalcy* (1973).

Robert D. Schulzinger, *The Making of the Diplomatic Mind* (1975).

Eugene P. Trani and David L. Wilson, *The Presidency of Warren G. Harding* (1977).

Joan Hoff Wilson, *American Business and Foreign Policy, 1920–1933* (1968).

Joan Hoff Wilson, *Herbert Hoover: Forgotten Progressive* (1975).

Cities and Suburbs

Sarah Deutsch, *No Separate Refuge: Culture, Class, and Gender on an Anglo-Hispanic Frontier in the American Southwest* (1987).

Juan Garcia, *Mexicans in the Midwest, 1900-1932* (1996).

David Goldfield, *Cotton Fields and Skyscrapers* (1982).

Peter Gottlieb, *Making Their Own Way: Southern Blacks' Migration to Pittsburgh, 1916–30* (1987).

Kenneth T. Jackson, *Crabgrass Frontier: The Suburbanization of the United States* (1985).

Earl Lewis, *In Their Own Interests: Race, Class, and Power in Twentieth-Century Norfolk, Virginia* (1991).

Gilbert Osofsky, *Harlem: The Making of a Ghetto* (1968).

Ricardo Romo, *East Los Angeles: History of a Barrio* (1983).

John C. Teaford, *Cities of the Heartland* (1993).

William Worley, *J. C. Nichols and the Shaping of Kansas City* (1990).

Society and Culture

Charles C. Alexander, *The Ku Klux Klan in the Southwest* (1965).

Kathleen M. Blee, *Women and the Klan: Racism and Gender in the 1920s* (1991).

Paul Carter, *Another Part of the Twenties* (1977).

William H. Chafe, *The American Woman: Her Changing Social, Economic, and Political Roles* (1972).

Norman Clark, *Deliver Us from Evil: An Interpretation of American Prohibition* (1976).

Stanley Coben, *Rebellion against Victorianism* (1991).

Nancy F. Cott, *The Grounding of American Feminism* (1987).

Sara M. Evans, *Born for Liberty: A History of Women in America* (1989).

Stuart Ewen, *Captains of Consciousness: Advertising and the Social Roots of the Consumer Culture* (1976).

Paula Fass, *The Damned and the Beautiful: American Youth in the 1920s* (1977).

Fred Hobson, *Mencken: A Life* (1994).

Nathan Huggins, *Harlem Renaissance* (1971).

Kenneth T. Jackson, *The Ku Klux Klan in the City* (1967).

Bruce B. Lawrence, *Defenders of God: The Fundamentalist Revolt against the Modern Age* (1989).

Lawrence W. Levine, *Defender of the Faith: William Jennings Bryan, the Last Decade, 1915–1925* (1965).

David L. Lewis, *When Harlem Was in Vogue* (1981).

Nancy Maclean, *Behind the Mask of Chivalry: The Making of the Second Ku Klux Klan* (1994).

Lary May, Screening *Out the Past: The Birth of Mass Culture and the Motion Picture Industry* (1980).

Leonard Moore, *Citizen Klansmen: The Ku Klux Klan in Indiana* (1991).

Robyn Muncy, *Creating a Female Dominion in American Reform* (1991).

Kathy H. Ogren, *The Jazz Revolution* (1989).

Elizabeth A. Payne, *Reform, Labor, and Feminism: Margaret Dreier Robins and the Women's Trade Union League* (1988).

Benjamin G. Rader, *American Sports: From the Age of Folk Games to the Age of Spectators* (1983).

Robert Sklar, *Movie-Made America: A Cultural History of American Movies* (1994).

Judith Stein, *The World of Marcus Garvey* (1986).

David Wiggins, *Sport in America* (1995).

Where to Learn More

❖ **F. Scott and Zelda Fitzgerald Museum, Montgomery, Alabama.** The novelist and his wife lived a short while in this house in her hometown.

❖ **Smithsonian Institution, Washington, D.C.** "From Farm to Factory," a permanent exhibition at the National Museum of American History, splendidly portrays the human side of the Great Migration.

❖ **Herbert Hoover National Historic Site, West Branch, Iowa.** Visitors may tour Hoover's birthplace cottage, presidential library, and museum.

❖ **Henry Ford Museum and Greenfield Village, Dearborn, Michigan.** Among many fascinating exhibits, "The Automobile in American Life" particularly and superbly demonstrates the importance of the automobile in American social history.

❖ **George Norris Home, McCook, Nebraska.** This museum, operated by the Nebraska State Historical Society, is dedicated to a leading progressive Republican of the 1920s.

❖ **Warren G. Harding House, Marion, Ohio.** Harding's home from 1891 to 1921 is now a museum with period furnishings.

❖ **Rhea County Courthouse and Museum, Dayton, Tennessee.** The site of the Scopes Trial, the courtroom appears as it did in 1925; the museum contains memorabilia related to the trial.

❖ **Calvin Coolidge Homestead, Plymouth, Vermont.** Operated by the Vermont Division of Historic Sites, the homestead preserves the exact interiors and furnishings from when Coolidge took the presidential oath of office there in 1923.

THE GREAT DEPRESSION AND THE NEW DEAL, 1929–1939

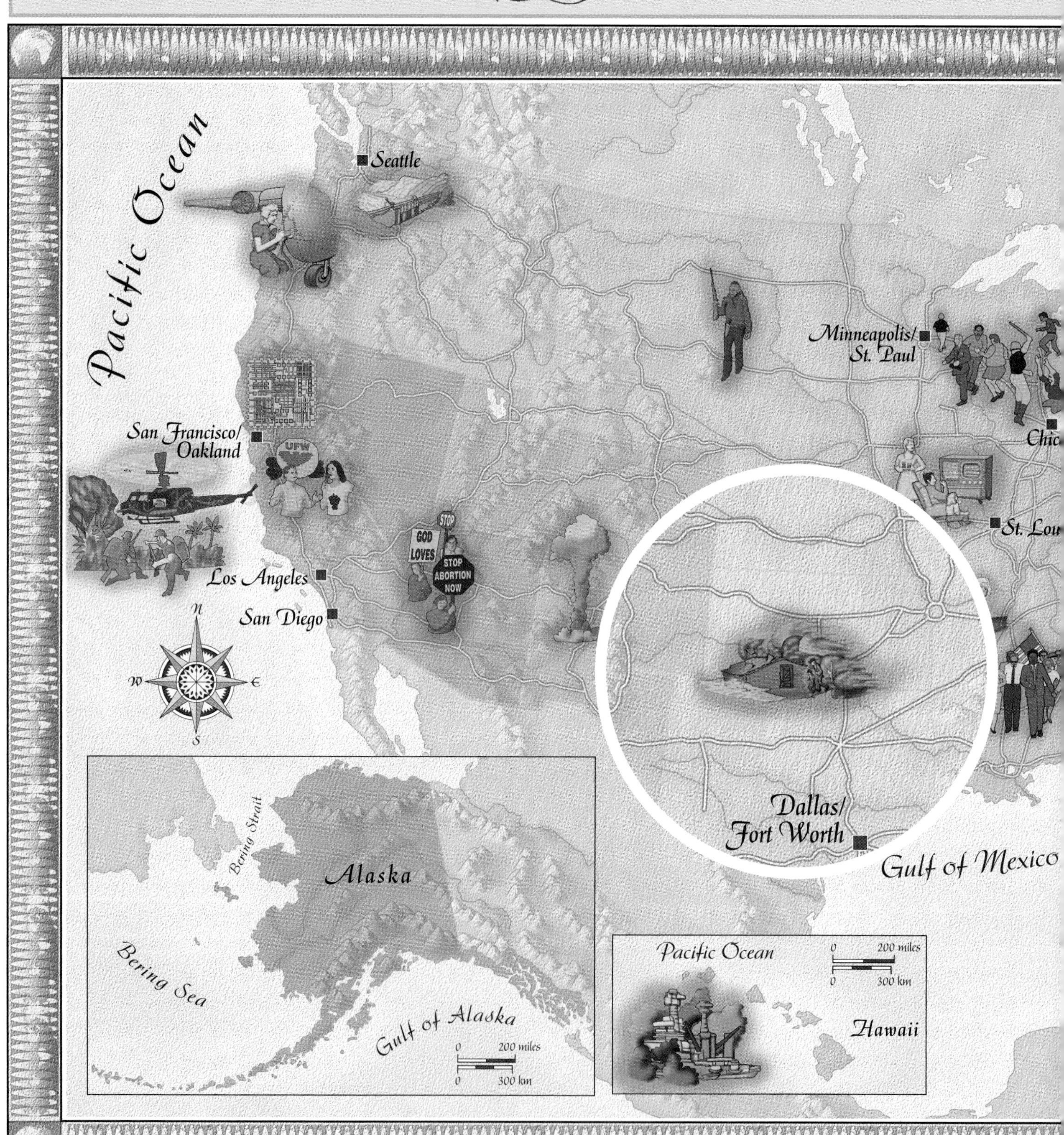

27

Chapter Outline

Hard Times in Hooverville
Crash!
The Depression Spreads
"Women's Jobs" and "Men's Jobs"
Families in the Depression
"Last Hired, First Fired"/Protest

Herbert Hoover and the Depression
The Limits of Voluntarism
Repudiating Hoover: The Election of 1932

Launching the New Deal
Action Now!/Relief
Helping Some Farmers
The Flight of the Blue Eagle
Critics Right and Left

Consolidating the New Deal
Lifting and Weeding/Expanding Relief
Election of 1936

The New Deal and American Life
Labor on the March
Women and the New Deal
Minorities and the New Deal
The New Deal for the South and West
The New Deal and Public Activism

Ebbing of the New Deal
Challenging the Court
More Hard Times
Political Stalemate

Key Topics

- The Great Depression
- Hoover's voluntary remedies
- FDR's New Deal
- The New Deal and organized labor, minorities, women, and farmers
- FDR's Democratic coalition of reformers, labor, urban ethnic groups, white Southerners, Westerners, and African Americans
- The faltering of the New Deal

In the summer of 1933, the signs were everywhere in the coal regions—on posters and billboards, in store windows: "The President wants you to join the union." In the 1920s, coal had been a sick industry, and its health had deteriorated with the onset of the **Great Depression** in 1929. Mounting unemployment and plummeting wages joined the industry's dangerous working conditions, arbitrary rules, and company domination. Membership in the United Mine Workers (UMW) had dropped from 400,000 in 1926 to barely 100,000 by 1933. Misery and hopelessness traveled in tandem. Yet now UMW officials spread the word that President Franklin Roosevelt favored the right to organize unions and bargain collectively.

The effect was electric. A UMW organizer in Pennsylvania found "a different feeling among the miners everywhere—they seem to feel that they are once more free men." In Kentucky, one organizer formed nine locals in a day, marveling that "the people have been so starved out that they are flocking into the Union by the thousands." Indeed, coal miners organized themselves spontaneously; union officials merely tried to keep up with the paperwork. The astonished governor of Pennsylvania told Roosevelt, "These people believe in you. . . . They trust you and all believe that you are working to get them recognition of the United Mine Workers of America."

The coal operators, accustomed to baronial control of the industry, vainly told their workers, "President Roosevelt is not an organizer for the United Mine Workers." But attitudes were changing. One organizer reported that whereas police had once chased union representatives out of Raton, New Mexico, "now the Mayor of the town gives us the city park for our meeting." Within two months, UMW membership numbered half a million.

Once organized, locals struck for union contracts and improved conditions. Some operators resisted, firing union leaders, recruiting strikebreakers, and employing police repression. When miners were shot, riots broke out. As one newspaper reported, "Miners' wives fought alongside their husbands, and sons joined with their fathers in battles with deputies." By September, the operators gave up, signing a contract that recognized the union, established the eight-hour day, and improved wages and working conditions. As the *New Yorker* noted, "The defeated mine-owners agreed to all the things that deputy sheriffs usually shoot people for demanding."

The union victory was not final, but these developments illustrated the forces that changed America in the 1930s. Responding to a crippling depression, the federal government—personalized by President Roosevelt—adopted an activist role in the economy and society. Its new reach seemed to extend everywhere—to the relief of those like the miners in Appalachia and the consternation of those like the coal operators. Federal activism restored hope and confidence for many Americans, often encouraging them to act for themselves.

The legislation that had spurred the miners' union drive was part of a massive and not always consistent program to promote economic recovery that in the process often promoted reform as well. The **New Deal**, as Roosevelt called his plan, achieved neither full recovery nor systematic reform, and its benefits were distributed unevenly. But it transformed American politics. The grateful union movement, for example, became an important part of Roosevelt's Democratic party. The Great Depression, Roosevelt's New Deal, and the behavior of the American people shaped the institutions and policies that would mark the nation for decades.

Hard Times in Hooverville

The prosperity of the 1920s ended in a stock market crash that revealed the flaws honeycombing the economy. As the nation slid into a catastrophic depression, factories closed, employment and incomes tumbled, and millions lost their homes, hopes, and dignity. Some protested and took direct action; others looked to the government for relief.

Crash!

The buoyant prosperity of the New Era, more apparent than real by the summer of 1929, collapsed in October when the stock market crashed. During the previous two years, the market had hit record highs, stimulated by optimism, easy credit, and speculators' manipulations. After peaking in September, it suffered several sharp checks, and on October 29, "Black Tuesday," panicked investors dumped their stocks at any price, wiping out the previous year's gains in one day. Confidence in the economy disappeared, and the slide continued for months, and then years. It hit bottom in July 1932. By then, the stock of U.S. Steel had plunged from 262 to 22, Montgomery Ward from 138 to 4. Much of the paper wealth of America had evaporated, and the nation sank into the Great Depression.

The Wall Street crash marked the beginning of the depression, but it did not cause it. The depression stemmed from weaknesses in the New Era economy. Most damaging was the unequal distribution of wealth and income. Workers' wages and farmers' incomes had fallen far behind industrial productivity and corporate profits; by 1929, the richest 0.1 percent of American families had as much total income as the bottom 42 percent (see Figure 27-1). With more than half the nation's people living at or below the subsistence level, there was not enough purchasing power to maintain the economy.

A second factor was that oligopolies dominated American industries. By 1929, the two hundred largest corporations (out of 400,000) controlled half the corporate wealth. Their power led to "administered prices," prices kept artificially high and rigid rather than determined by supply and demand. By not responding to purchasing power, this system not only helped bring on economic collapse but also dimmed prospects for recovery.

Weaknesses in specific industries had further unbalanced the economy. Agriculture suffered from overproduction, declining prices, and heavy debt; so did the coal and textile industries. These difficulties left the economy dependent on a few industries for expansion and employment; they could not carry the burden. Banking presented other problems. Poorly managed and regulated, banks had contributed to the instability of prosperity; they now threatened to spread the panic and depression.

International economic difficulties spurred the depression as well. Shut out from U.S. markets by high tariffs, Europeans had depended on American investments to manage their debts and reparation payments from the Great War. The stock market crash dried up the flow of American dollars to Europe, causing financial panics and industrial collapse and making the Great Depression global. In turn, European nations curtailed their imports of American goods and defaulted on their debts, further debilitating the U.S. economy. American exports fell by 70 percent from 1929 to

A coal miner greeting Franklin D. Roosevelt in West Virginia in 1932. Roosevelt's promise of a New Deal revived hope among millions of Americans trapped in hard times.

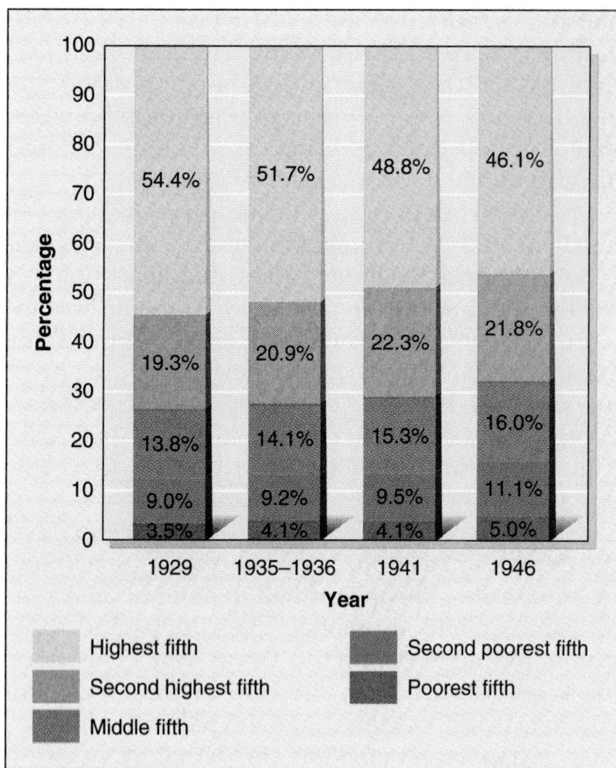

***Figure 27-1* Distribution of Income in the United States, 1929–1946**

An unequal distribution of income contributed to the Great Depression by limiting purchasing power. Only slight changes occurred until after World War II, but other factors gradually stabilized the national economy.

Data Source: U.S. Bureau of the Census.

1932. As foreign markets shrank, so did hopes for economic recovery.

Government policies also bore some responsibility for the crash and depression. Failure to enforce antitrust laws had encouraged oligopolies and high prices; failure to regulate banking or the stock market had permitted financial recklessness and irresponsible speculation. Reducing tax rates on the wealthy had also encouraged speculation and contributed to the maldistribution of income. Opposition to labor unions and collective bargaining helped keep workers' wages and purchasing power low. The absence of an effective agricultural policy and the high tariffs that inhibited foreign trade and reduced markets for agricultural products hurt farmers in the same way. In short, the same government policies that shaped the booming 1920s economy also pointed to economic disaster.

But the crash did more than expose the weaknesses of the economy. Business lost confidence and refused to make investments that might have brought recovery. Instead, banks called in loans and restricted credit, and depositors tried to withdraw their savings, which were uninsured. The demand for cash caused banks to fail, dragging the economy down further. And the Federal Reserve Board prolonged the depression by restricting the money supply.

The Depression Spreads

By early 1930, the effects of financial contraction were painfully evident. Factories shut down or cut back, and industrial production plummeted; by 1932, it was scarcely 50 percent of its 1929 level. Steel mills operated at 12 percent of capacity, auto factories at 20 percent. Unemployment skyrocketed, as an average of 100,000 workers a week were fired in the first three years after the crash. By 1932, one-fourth of the labor force was out of work (see Figure 27-2). In St. Louis, 75 percent of the workers in the building trades, a key sector of the 1920s economy, were jobless. Overall unemployment in Toledo reached 80 percent. The wages of those Americans lucky enough to work fell sharply. Personal income dropped by more than half between 1929 and 1932; by 1933, industrial workers had average weekly wages of only $16.73. Moreover, the depression began to feed on itself in a vicious circle: Shrinking wages and employment cut into purchasing power, causing business to slash production again and lay off workers, thereby further reducing purchasing power.

The depression particularly battered farmers. Commodity prices fell by 55 percent between 1929 and 1932, stifling farm income. Cotton farmers earned only 31 percent of the pittance they had received in 1929. Unable to pay their mortgages, many farm families lost their homes and fields. "We have no security left," cried one South Dakota farm woman. "Foreclosures and evictions at the point of sheriff's guns are increasing daily." The dispossessed roamed the byways, highways, and railways of a troubled country.

Urban families were also evicted when they could not pay their rent. Some moved in with relatives; others lived in **Hoovervilles**—the name reflects the bitterness directed at the president—shacks where people shivered, suffered, and starved. Oklahoma City's vast Hooverville covered a hundred square miles; one witness described its hapless residents as squatting in "old, rusted-out car bodies," orange crates, and holes in the ground.

Soup kitchens became standard features of the urban landscape, with lines of the hungry stretching for blocks. But charities and local communities could not meet the massive needs, and neither state nor federal governments had welfare or unemployment compensation programs. To survive, peo-

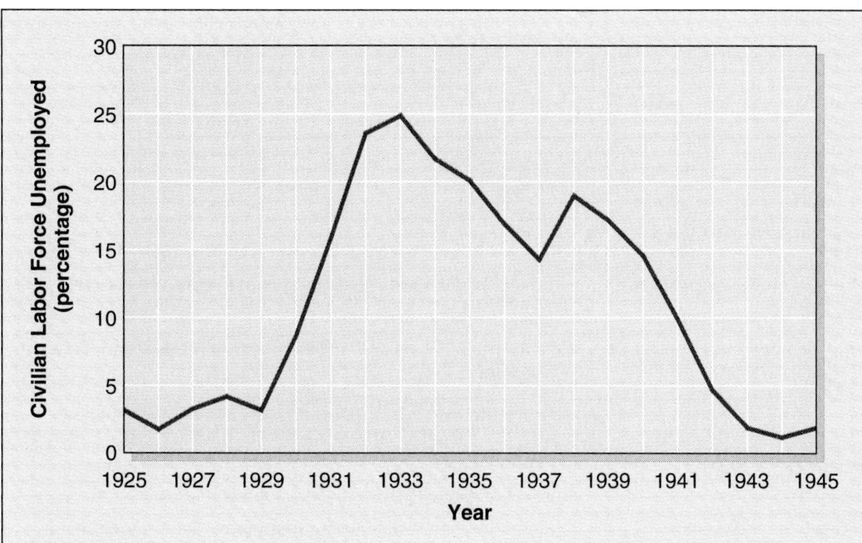

Figure 27-2 Unemployment, 1925–1945
Unemployment soared in the early 1930s, spreading distress and overwhelming charities and local relief agencies. Federal programs improved conditions, but only American entry into World War II really ended the problem.
Data Source: U.S. Bureau of the Census.

ple planted gardens in vacant lots and back alleys and tore apart empty houses or tapped gas lines for fuel. In immigrant neighborhoods, social workers found a "primitive communism" in which people shared food, clothing, and fuel in the belief that "what goes around comes around." Few Americans escaped hard times, but their experiences varied with their circumstances and expectations.

Homeless Americans gathered in squalid "Hoovervilles," like this one in Seattle, and struggled to survive.

"Women's Jobs" and "Men's Jobs"

The depression affected wage-earning women in complex ways. Although suffering 20 percent unemployment by 1932, women were less likely than men to be fired. Gender segregation had concentrated women in low-paid service, sales, and clerical jobs that shrank less than the heavy industries where men predominated. But while traditional attitudes somewhat insulated working women, they also reinforced opposition to female employment itself, especially that of married women. As one Chicago civic organization complained, "They are holding jobs that rightfully belong to the God-intended providers of the household." Nearly every state considered restricting the employment of married women, and the city council of Akron, Ohio, resolved that public agencies and private employers should stop employing wives. Three-fourths of the nation's school systems refused to hire married women as teachers, and two-thirds dismissed female teachers who married. Many private employers, especially banks and insurance companies, also fired married women.

Firing women, however, rarely produced jobs for men because few men sought positions in the fields associated

Chronology

1929 Stock market crashes.

1932 Farmers' Holiday Association organizes rural protests in the Midwest.

Reconstruction Finance Corporation is created to assist financial institutions.

Bonus Army is routed in Washington, D.C.

Franklin D. Roosevelt is elected president.

1933 Emergency Banking Act is passed.

Agricultural Adjustment Administration (AAA) is created to regulate farm production.

National Recovery Administration (NRA) is created to promote industrial cooperation and recovery.

Federal Emergency Relief Act provides federal assistance to the unemployed.

Civilian Conservation Corps (CCC) is established to provide work relief in conservation projects.

Public Works Administration (PWA) is created to provide work relief on large public construction projects.

Civil Works Administration (CWA) provides emergency winter relief jobs.

Tennessee Valley Authority (TVA) is created to coordinate regional development.

1934 Securities and Exchange Commission (SEC) is established.

Indian Reorganization Act reforms Indian policy.

Huey Long organizes the Share-Our-Wealth Society.

Democrats win midterm elections.

1935 Supreme Court declares NRA unconstitutional.

National Labor Relations Act (Wagner Act) guarantees workers' rights to organize and bargain collectively.

Social Security Act establishes a federal social insurance system.

Banking Act strengthens the Federal Reserve.

Revenue Act establishes a more progressive tax system.

Resettlement Administration is created to aid dispossessed farmers.

Rural Electrification Administration (REA) is created to help provide electric power to rural areas.

Soil Conservation Service is established.

Emergency Relief Appropriation Act authorizes public relief projects for the unemployed.

Works Progress Administration (WPA) is created.

Huey Long is assassinated.

1936 Supreme Court declares AAA unconstitutional.

Roosevelt is reelected president.

Sit-down strikes begin.

1937 Chicago police kill workers in Memorial Day Massacre.

FDR tries but fails to expand the Supreme Court.

Farm Security Administration (FSA) is created to lend money to small farmers to buy and rehabilitate farms.

National Housing Act is passed to promote public housing projects.

"Roosevelt Recession" begins.

1938 Congress of Industrial Organizations (CIO) is founded.

Fair Labor Standards Act establishes minimum wage and maximum hours rules for labor.

Roosevelt fails to "purge" the Democratic party.

Republicans make gains in midterm elections.

with women. Men did displace women as teachers, social workers, and librarians, but firing women simply aggravated the suffering of families already reeling from the depression. Disapproval of female employment implied that women did not deserve equal opportunities and probably stiffened the opposition to opening "men's jobs" to women when women were desperate for work. Despite such hostility, the proportion of married women in the work force increased in the 1930s as women took jobs to help their families survive.

Families in the Depression

"I have watched fear grip the people in our neighborhood around Hull House," wrote Jane Addams as the depression deepened in 1931 and family survival itself seemed threatened. Divorce declined because it was expensive, but desertion increased, and marriages were postponed. Birthrates fell. Husbands and fathers, the traditional breadwinners, were often humiliated and despondent when laid off from work. One social worker observed in 1931: "Like searing irons, the degradation, the sheer terror and panic which loss of job brings, the deprivation and the bitterness have eaten into men's souls." Unemployed men, sociologists reported, "lost much of their sense of time and dawdled helplessly and dully about the streets," dreading to return home.

Women's responsibilities, by contrast, often grew. The number of female-headed households increased sharply. Not only did some women become wage earners, but their traditional role as homemakers also gained new significance. To make ends meet, many women sewed their own clothing and raised and canned vegetables, reversing the trend toward consumerism. Some also took on extra work at home. In San Antonio, one in every ten families had boarders, and in Alabama, housewives took in laundry at 10 cents for a week's washload.

The depression also affected children. Some parents sacrificed their own well-being to protect their children. One witness described "the uncontrolled trembling of parents who have starved themselves for weeks so that their children might not go hungry." But children felt the tension and fear, and many went without food. In New York City, 139 people, most of them children, died of starvation and malnutrition in 1933. Boys and girls stayed home from school and church because they lacked shoes or clothing; others gave up their plans for college. As hope faded, family conflicts increased. Some parents nagged their children, even considering them burdens. Many teenagers left home, either to escape parental authority or so that younger children would have more to eat. These "juvenile transients" suffered from starvation, exposure, illness, and accidents. The California Unemployment Commission concluded that the depression had left the American family "morally shattered. There is no security, no foothold, no future."

"Last Hired, First Fired"

The depression particularly harmed racial minorities. With fewer resources and opportunities, they were less able than other groups to absorb the economic pain. African Americans were caught in a double bind, reported a sociologist at Howard University in 1932: They were "the last to be hired and the first to be fired." Black unemployment rates were more than twice the white rate, reflecting increased job competition and persistent racism. Jobless white workers now sought the menial jobs traditionally reserved for black workers, such as street cleaning and domestic service. In Atlanta, white citizens paraded with banners denouncing the hiring of black workers "Until Every White Man Has a Job."

Racism also limited the assistance African Americans received. Religious and charitable organizations often refused to care for black people. Local and state governments set higher requirements for black people than for white people to receive relief and provided them with less aid. One Memphis resident saw the result of such policies: "Colored men and women with rakes, hoes, and other digging tools, with buckets and baskets, digging around in the garbage and refuse for food." By 1932, most African Americans were suffering acute privation. "At no time in the history of the Negro since slavery," reported the Urban League, "has his economic and social outlook seemed so discouraging." African Americans were "hanging on by the barest thread."

Hispanic Americans also suffered. As mostly unskilled workers, they faced increasing competition for decreasing jobs paying declining wages. They were displaced even in the California agricultural labor force, which they had dominated. By the mid-1930s, they made up only a tenth of the state's migratory labor force, which increasingly consisted of white people who had fled the South and the Great Plains. Other jobs were lost when Arizona, California, and Texas barred Mexicans from public works and highway construction jobs. Vigilantes threatened employers who hired Mexicans rather than white Americans.

Economic woes and racism drove nearly half a million Mexican immigrants and their American-born children from the United States in the 1930s. Local authorities in the Southwest urged the federal government to deport Mexicans, offered free transportation to Mexico, and adopted discriminatory policies in providing relief. By 1931, a Los Angeles official announced that tens of thousands of Mexicans "have been literally scared out of southern California." Fear of deportation kept many Mexican-American families from seeking relief or even health care in Texas.

Protest

Bewildered and discouraged, most Americans reacted to the crisis without protest. Influenced by traditional individualism, many blamed themselves for their plight. But others did act, especially to protect their families. Protests ranged from small desperate gestures like stealing food and coal to more dramatic deeds. In Louisiana, women seized a train to call attention to the needs of their families; in New Jersey, in the "bloodless battle of Pleasantville," one hundred women held the city council hostage to demand assistance.

Communists, socialists, and other radicals organized more formal protests. Communists led the jobless into "unemployment councils" that staged hunger marches, demonstrated for relief, and blocked evictions. Mothers facing eviction in Chicago told their children: "Run quick and find the Reds." Socialists built similar organizations, including Baltimore's People's Unemployment League, which had twelve thousand members. Such groups provided protection and assistance. However, local authorities often suppressed their protests. In 1932, police fired on the Detroit Unemployment Council as it marched to demand food and jobs, killing four marchers and wounding many more.

Rural protests also broke out. Again, communists organized some of them, as in Alabama, where the Croppers' and Farm Workers' Union mobilized black agricultural laborers in 1931 to demand better treatment. In the Midwest, the Farmers' Holiday Association, formed among family farmers in 1932, stopped the shipment of produce to urban markets, hoping to drive up prices. A guerrilla war broke out as farmers blocked roads and halted freight trains, dumped milk in ditches, and fought bloody battles with deputy sheriffs. Midwestern farmers also tried to prevent foreclosure of their farms. In Iowa, farmers beat sheriffs and mortgage agents and nearly lynched a lawyer conducting foreclosure proceedings; in Nebraska, a Farmers' Holiday leader warned that if the state did not halt foreclosures, "200,000 of us are coming to Lincoln and we'll tear that new State Capitol Building to pieces."

Herbert Hoover and the Depression

The Great Depression challenged the optimism, policies, and philosophy that Herbert Hoover carried into the White House in 1929. The president took unprecedented steps to resolve the crisis but shrank back from the interventionist policies activists urged. His failures, personal as well as political and economic, led to his repudiation and opened the way to a new deal.

The Limits of Voluntarism

Hoover fought economic depression more vigorously than any previous president, but he believed that voluntary, private relief was preferable to federal intervention. The role of the national government, he thought, was to advise and encourage the voluntary efforts of private organizations, individual industries, or local communities. As secretary of commerce, Hoover had championed trade associations to achieve economic order and social progress. As president he persuaded Congress in 1929 to create the Federal Farm Board to promote voluntary agricultural cooperatives to raise farm income without government regulations. After the crash, he tried to apply this voluntarism to the depression.

Hoover first secured business leaders' pledges to maintain employment and wage levels. But most corporations soon repudiated these pledges, slashed wages, and laid off workers. An official of the Bureau of Labor Statistics complained that business leaders "are hell-bent to get wages back to the 1913 level." Hoover himself said, "You know, the only trouble with capitalism is capitalists; they're too damn greedy." Still, he rejected government action.

Hoover also depended on voluntary efforts to relieve the misery caused by massive unemployment. He created the President's Organization for Unemployment Relief to help raise private funds for voluntary relief agencies. Charities and local authorities, he believed, should help the unemployed; direct federal relief would expand government power and undermine the recipients' character. He vetoed congressional attempts to aid the unemployed. "The American way of relieving distress," said Hoover, was through "the voluntary agencies of self help in the community."

The depression rendered Hoover's beliefs meaningless. Private programs to aid the unemployed scarcely existed. Only a few unions like the Amalgamated Clothing Workers had unemployment funds, and these were soon spent. Company plans for unemployment compensation covered less than 1 percent of workers, revealing the charade of the welfare capitalism of the 1920s. Some business leaders rejected any responsibility: "Even God Almighty never promised anybody that he should not suffer from hunger," snorted the president of the Southern States Industrial Council. Private charitable groups like the Salvation Army, church associations, and ethnic societies quickly exhausted their resources. By 1931, the director of Philadelphia's Federation of Jewish Charities conceded, "Private philanthropy is no longer capable of coping with the situation." Tens of thousands of Philadelphians, he noted, had been reduced to "the status of a stray cat prowling for food. . . . What this does to the innate dignity of the human soul is not hard to guess."

Nor could local governments cope, and their efforts declined as the depression deepened. New York City provided relief payments of $2.39 a week for an entire family, and other cities much less. By

1932, more than one hundred cities made no relief appropriations at all, and the commissioner of charity in Salt Lake City reported that people were sliding toward starvation. Only eight state governments provided even token assistance. Constitutional restrictions on taxes and indebtedness stopped some from responding to the relief crisis. Others lacked the will. Texas refused to issue bonds to fund relief. (See "American Views: An Ohio Mayor on Unemployment and Relief.")

Hoover blundered not in first relying on charities and local governments for relief but in refusing to admit that they were inadequate. Even his advisers warned that voluntarism and "individual initiative" had become obsolete. Both his vision and his efforts fell short.

As the depression worsened, Hoover adopted more activist policies. He persuaded Congress to cut taxes to boost consumers' buying power, and he increased the public works budget. The Federal Farm Board lent money to cooperatives and spent millions trying to stabilize crop prices. Unable to control production, however, the board conceded failure by late 1931. More successful was the **Reconstruction Finance Corporation (RFC)**. Established in January 1932, the RFC lent federal funds to banks, insurance companies, and railroads so that their recovery could "trickle down" to ordinary Americans. Hoover still opposed direct aid to the general public, although he finally allowed the RFC to lend small amounts to state and local governments for unemployment relief.

But these programs satisfied few Americans. "While children starve," cried Pennsylvania's governor, Hoover "intends to let us have just as little relief as possible after the longest delay possible." Far more action was necessary, but Hoover remained committed to voluntarism and a balanced budget. The *New Republic* remarked in wonder: "Strangely enough, though he praises our government as representative and democratic, Mr. Hoover seems to regard most of the positive activities it might undertake as the intrusion of an alien sovereignty rather than the cooperative action of a people." Hoover's ideological limitations infuriated Americans who saw him as indifferent to their suffering and a reactionary protector of privileged business interests—an image his political opponents encouraged.

Repudiating Hoover: The 1932 Election

Hoover's treatment of the **Bonus Army** symbolized his unpopularity and set the stage for the 1932 election. In 1932, unemployed veterans of World War I gathered in Washington, demanding payment of service bonuses not due until 1945. Hoover refused to meet with them, and Congress rejected their plan. But ten thousand veterans erected a shantytown at the edge of Washington and camped in vacant public buildings. Hoover determined to evict the veterans, but General Douglas MacArthur disobeyed his cautious orders and on July 28 led cavalry, infantry, and tanks against the ragged Bonus Marchers. The troops cleared the buildings and assaulted the shantytown, dispersing the veterans and their families and setting their camp on fire.

This assault provoked widespread outrage. "What a pitiful spectacle is that of the great American Government, mightiest in the world, chasing unarmed men, women, and children with army tanks," commented the *Washington News*. The administration tried to brand the Bonus Marchers as communists and criminals, but official investigations refuted such claims. The marchers were anxious and discouraged Americans, not revolutionaries, and if any criminals were among them, noted one critic, they were proportionately fewer than in President Harding's cabinet. The incident confirmed Hoover's public image as harsh and insensitive.

In the summer of 1932, with no prospects for victory, Republicans renominated Hoover. Confident Democrats selected Governor Franklin D. Roosevelt of New York, who pledged "a new deal for the American people." A distant cousin of Theodore Roosevelt, FDR had prepared for the presidency. Born into a wealthy family in 1882, he had been educated at Harvard, trained in the law, and schooled in politics, as a state legislator, assistant secretary of the navy under Wilson, and the Democratic vice presidential nominee in 1920. In 1921, Roosevelt contracted polio, which paralyzed him from the waist down, leaving him dependent on braces or crutches. His struggle with this ordeal gave him greater maturity, compassion, and determination. His continued involvement in politics, meanwhile, owed much to his wife, Eleanor. A social reformer, she became a Democratic activist, organizing women's groups and campaigning across New York. In a remarkable political comeback, FDR was elected governor in 1928 and reelected in 1930.

The 1932 campaign gave scant indication of what Roosevelt's New Deal might involve. The Democratic platform differed little from that of the Republicans, and Roosevelt spoke in vague or general terms. He knew that the election would be a repudiation of Hoover more than an endorsement of himself. Still, observers gained clues from

American Views

An Ohio Mayor on Unemployment and Relief

Joesph Heffernan was the mayor of Youngstown, Ohio, when the nation sank into the Great Depression. Like other industrial cities, Youngstown soon confronted widespread unemployment and distress. In this document, written in 1932, Heffernan describes the obstacles he faced in responding to the suffering in Youngstown.

❖ **What would Heffernan think of President Hoover's belief that private charities and local authorities would provide unemployment relief?**

❖ **What did Heffernan see as obstacles to a public response to the depression?**

❖ **What did he fear would be the consequences of the failure to devise a rational and humane system of relief?**

[In 1930] I asked for a bond issue of $1,000,000 for unemployment relief. Many leading business men went out of their way to show their disapproval. One of them . . . said to me: "You make a bad mistake in talking about the unemployed. Don't emphasize hard times and everything will be all right." An influential newspaper chastised me for "borrowing trouble"; the depression would be over, the editor maintained, before relief would be needed. . . . The gravity of the situation was so deliberately misrepresented by the entire business community that when the bond issue finally came to a ballot, in November 1930, it was voted down.

Thus we passed into the early days of 1931—fourteen months after the first collapse—with no relief in sight except that which was provided by the orthodox charities. Not a single move had been made looking toward action by a united community.

Strange as it may seem, there was no way in which the city government could embark upon a program of its own. We had no funds available for emergency relief, and without specific authorization from the people we could not issue bonds. . . .

As time went on, business conditions showed no improvement. Every night hundreds of homeless men crowded into the municipal incinerator, where they found warmth even though they had to sleep on heaps of garbage. In January 1931, I obtained the cooperation of the City Council to con-

Roosevelt's record in New York, where he had created the first state system of unemployment relief and supported social welfare and conservation. More important was his outgoing personality, which radiated warmth and hope in contrast to Hoover's gloom. "If you put a rose in Hoover's hand," said one observer, "it would wilt."

FDR carried every state south and west of Pennsylvania (see Map 27-1). It was the worst rout of a Republican candidate ever (except in 1912 when the party had split). Yet Hoover would remain president for four more months, as the Constitution then required. And in those four months, the depression worsened, with rising unemployment, collapsing farm prices, and spreading misery. When teachers in Chicago, unpaid for months, fainted in their classrooms from hunger, it symbolized the imminent collapse of the nation itself. The final blow came in February 1933 when panic struck the banking system. Nearly six thousand banks had already failed, robbing 9 million depositors of their savings. Desperate Americans rushed to withdraw their funds from the remaining banks, pushing them to the brink as well. With the federal government under Hoover immobilized, state governments shut the banks to prevent vert an abandoned police station into a "flop house." The first night it was filled, and it has remained filled ever since. I made a point of paying frequent visits to this establishment so that I could see for myself what kind of men these down-and-outers were, and I heartily wish that those folk who have made themselves comfortable by ignoring and denying the suffering of their less fortunate neighbors could see some of the sights I saw. There were old men gnarled by heavy labor, young mechanics tasting the first bitterness of defeat, clerks and white-collar workers learning the equality of misery, derelicts who fared no worse in bad times than in good, Negroes who only a short time before had come from Southern cotton fields, now glad to find any shelter from the cold, immigrants who had been lured to Van Dyke's "land of youth and freedom"—each one a personal tragedy, and all together an overwhelming catastrophe for the nation. . . .

This descent from respectability, frequent enough in the best of times, has been hastened immeasurably by two years of business paralysis, and the people who have been affected in this manner must be numbered in millions. This is what we have accomplished with our bread lines and soup kitchens. I know, because I have seen thousands of these defeated, discouraged, hopeless men and women, cringing and fawning as they come to ask for public aid. It is a spectacle of national degeneration. That is the fundamental tragedy for America. If every mill and factory in the land should begin to hum with prosperity tomorrow morning, the destructive effect of our haphazard relief measures would not work itself out of the nation's blood until the sons of our sons had expiated the sins of our neglect.

Even now there are signs of rebellion against a system so out of joint that it can only offer charity to honest men who want to work. Sometimes it takes the form of social agitation, but again it may show itself in a revolt that is absolute and final. Such an instance was reported in a Youngstown newspaper on the day I wrote these lines:—

"FATHER OF TEN DROWNS SELF

. . . Out of work two years, Charles Wayne, aged 57, father of ten children, stood on the Spring Common bridge this morning. . . . He took off his coat, folded it carefully, and jumped into the swirling Mahoning River. Wayne was born in Youngstown and was employed by the Republic Iron and Steel Company for twenty-seven years as a hot mill worker. 'We were about to lose our home,' sobbed Mrs. Wayne. 'And the gas and electric companies had threatened to shut off the service.'"

Source: Joseph L. Heffernan, "The Hungry City: A Mayor's Experience with Unemployment," Atlantic Monthly, *May 1932, pp. 538–540, 546.*

their failure. By March, an eerie silence had descended on the nation. Hoover concluded, "We are at the end of our string."

Launching the New Deal

In the midst of national anxiety, Franklin D. Roosevelt pushed forward an unprecedented program to resolve the crises of a collapsing financial system, crippling unemployment, and agricultural and industrial breakdown and to promote reform. The early New Deal achieved successes and attracted support, but it also had limitations and generated criticism that suggested the need for still greater innovations.

Action Now!

On March 4, 1933, Franklin Delano Roosevelt became president and immediately reassured the American people. He insisted that "the only thing we have to fear is fear itself—nameless, unreasoning, unjustified terror, which paralyzes needed efforts to convert retreat into advance." And he promised "action, and action now!" Summoning Congress, Roosevelt pressed forward on a broad front. In the first

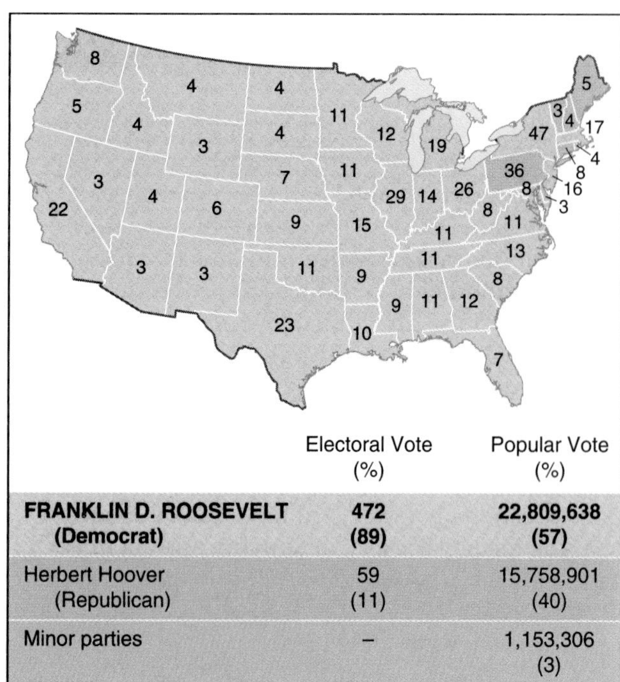

	Electoral Vote (%)	Popular Vote (%)
FRANKLIN D. ROOSEVELT (Democrat)	**472 (89)**	**22,809,638 (57)**
Herbert Hoover (Republican)	59 (11)	15,758,901 (40)
Minor parties	–	1,153,306 (3)

Map 27-1 The Election of 1932
In the midst of the Great Depression, only the most rock-ribbed Republican states failed to turn to Franklin D. Roosevelt and the Democrats for relief. The election of 1932 was a landslide.

three months of his administration, the famous Hundred Days of the New Deal, the Democratic Congress passed many important laws (see the overview table, "Major Laws of the Hundred Days").

Roosevelt's program reflected a mix of ideas, some from FDR himself, some from a diverse group of advisers, including academic experts dubbed the "brain trust," politicians, and social workers. It also incorporated principles from the progressive movement, precedents from the Great War mobilization, and even plans from the Hoover administration. Above all, the New Deal was a practical response to the depression. FDR had set its tone in his campaign when he declared, "The country needs, and, unless I mistake its temper, the country demands bold, persistent experimentation. . . . Above all, try something."

FDR first addressed the banking crisis. On March 5, he proclaimed a national bank holiday, closing all remaining banks. Congress then passed his **Emergency Banking Act**, a conservative measure that extended government assistance to sound banks and reorganized the weak ones. Prompt government action, coupled with a reassuring **fireside chat** over the radio by the president, restored popular confidence in the banks. When they reopened on March 13, deposits exceeded withdrawals. "Capitalism," said Raymond Moley of the brain trust, "was saved in eight days." In June, Congress created the **Federal Deposit Insurance Corporation (FDIC)** to guarantee bank deposits up to $2,500.

The financial industry was also reformed. The **Glass-Steagall Act** separated investment and commercial banking to curtail risky speculation. The Securities Act reformed the sale of stocks to prevent the insider abuses that had characterized Wall Street, and in 1934 the **Securities and Exchange Commission (SEC)** was created to regulate the stock market. Two other financial measures in 1933 created the Home Owners Loan Corporation and the Farm Credit Administration, which enabled millions to refinance their mortgages.

Relief

Roosevelt also provided relief for the unemployed. The Federal Emergency Relief Administration (FERA) furnished funds to state and local agencies. Harry Hopkins, who had headed Roosevelt's relief program in New York, became its director and one of the New Deal's most important members. FERA spent over $3 billion before it ended in 1935, and by then Hopkins and FDR had developed new programs that

The first "Hundred Days" of the New Deal brought a rush of important new laws to combat the depression. This 1933 cartoon captures the popular excitement generated by Roosevelt's commitment to action and leadership of Congress.

OVERVIEW

MAJOR LAWS OF THE HUNDRED DAYS

Law	Objective
Emergency Banking Act	Stabilized the private banking system
Agricultural Adjustment Act	Established a farm recovery program based on production controls and price supports
Emergency Farm Mortgage Act	Provided for the refinancing of farm mortgages
National Industrial Recovery Act	Established a national recovery program and authorized a public works program
Federal Emergency Relief Act	Established a national system of relief
Home Owners Loan Act	Protected homeowners from mortgage foreclosure by refinancing home loans
Glass-Steagall Act	Separated commercial and investment banking and guaranteed bank deposits
Tennessee Valley Authority Act	Established the TVA and provided for the planned development of the Tennessee River Valley
Civilian Conservation Corps Act	Established the CCC to provide work relief on reforestation and conservation projects
Farm Credit Act	Expanded agricultural credits and established the Farm Credit Administration
Securities Act	Required full disclosure from stock exchanges
Wagner-Peyser Act	Created a U.S. Employment Service and encouraged states to create local public employment offices

provided work rather than just cash. Work relief, they believed, preserved both the skills and the morale of recipients. In the winter of 1933–1934, Hopkins spent nearly $1 billion to create jobs for 4 million men and women through the Civil Works Administration (CWA). The CWA hired laborers to build roads and airports, teachers to staff rural schools, and singers and artists to give public performances. The Public Works Administration (PWA) provided work relief on useful projects to stimulate the economy through public expenditures. Directed by Harold Ickes, the PWA spent billions from 1933 to 1939 to build schools, hospitals, courthouses, dams, and bridges.

One of FDR's personal ideas, the **Civilian Conservation Corps (CCC)**, combined work relief with conservation. Launched in 1933, the CCC employed 2.5 million young men to work on reforestation and flood control projects, build roads and bridges in national forests and parks, restore Civil War battlefields, and fight forest fires. The men lived in isolated CCC camps and earned $30 a month, $25 of which had to be sent home. "I'd go anywhere," said one Baltimore applicant. "I'd go to hell if I could get work there." One of the most popular New Deal agencies, the CCC lasted till 1942.

Helping Some Farmers

Besides providing relief, the New Deal promoted economic recovery. In May 1933, Congress established the **Agricultural Adjustment Administration (AAA)** to combat the depression in agriculture caused by crop surpluses and low prices. The AAA subsidized farmers who agreed to restrict production. The objective was to boost farm prices to parity, a level that would restore farmers' purchasing power to what it had been in 1914. In the summer of 1933,

A Civilian Conservation Corps (CCC) poster offering relief work as a "young man's opportunity." Although the CCC was a popular and effective New Deal agency, some excluded women asked where was the "she-she-she." Most New Deal programs had a gender bias against women.

the AAA paid southern farmers to plow up 10 million acres of cotton and midwestern farmers to bury 9 million pounds of pork. Restricting production in hard times caused public outrage. "Farmers are not producing too much," said one critic. "What we have overproduction of is empty stomachs and bare backs." Secretary of Agriculture Henry Wallace defended production controls as analogous to corporations maximizing profits: "Agriculture cannot survive in a capitalistic society as a philanthropic enterprise."

Agricultural conditions improved. Farm prices rose from 52 percent of parity in 1932 to 88 percent in 1935, and gross farm income rose by 50 percent. Not until 1941, however, would income exceed the level of 1929, a poor year for farmers. Moreover, some of the decreased production and increased prices stemmed from devastating droughts and dust storms on the Great Plains. The AAA itself harmed poor farmers while aiding larger commercial growers. As southern planters restricted their acreage, they dismissed tenants and sharecroppers, and with AAA payments, they bought new farm machinery, reducing their need for farm labor. A reporter in 1935 found thousands of sharecroppers "along the highways and byways of Dixie, . . . lonely figures without money, without homes, and without hope." Thus while big producers moved toward prosperity, many small farmers were forced into a pool of rural labor for which there was decreasing need or into the cities, where there were no jobs.

The Supreme Court declared the AAA unconstitutional in 1936, but new laws established the farm subsidy program for decades to come. Increasing mechanization and scientific agriculture kept production high and farmers dependent on government intervention.

The Flight of the Blue Eagle

The New Deal attempted to revive American industry with the **National Industrial Recovery Act (NIRA)**, which created the **National Recovery Administration (NRA)**. The NRA sought to halt the slide in prices, wages, and employment by suspending antitrust laws and authorizing industrial and trade associations to draft codes setting production quotas, price policies, wages and working conditions, and other business practices. The codes promoted the interests of business generally and big business in particular, but Section 7a of the NIRA guaranteed workers the rights to organize unions and bargain collectively, which John L. Lewis of the United Mine Workers called an Emancipation Proclamation for labor.

Hugh Johnson became director of the NRA. He persuaded business leaders to cooperate in drafting codes and the public to patronize participating companies. The NRA Blue Eagle insignia and its slogan "We Do Our Part" covered workplaces, storefronts, and billboards. Blue Eagle parades marched down the nation's main streets and climaxed in a massive demonstration in New York City.

Support for the NRA waned, however. Corporate leaders used it to advance their own goals and discriminate against small producers, consumers, and labor. Minnesota's Governor Floyd Olson condemned the dominance within the NRA of the same selfish business interests he saw as responsible for the depression: "I am not satisfied with hanging a laurel wreath on burglars, thieves, and pirates and calling them code authorities."

Businesses also violated the labor rights specified in Section 7a. Defiant employers viewed collec-

New Deal agricultural programs stabilized the farm economy, but not all farmers benefited. Landowners receiving AAA payments evicted these black sharecroppers huddled in a makeshift roadside camp in Missouri in 1935.

tive bargaining as infringing their authority. Employers even used violence to smother unions. The NRA did little to enforce Section 7a, and Johnson—strongly probusiness—denounced all strikes. Workers felt betrayed.

Roosevelt tried to reorganize the NRA, but it remained controversial until the Supreme Court declared it unconstitutional in 1935.

Critics Right and Left

The early New Deal had not ended the depression. Recovery was fitful and uneven; millions of Americans remained unemployed. Nevertheless, the New Deal's efforts to grapple with problems, its successes in reducing suffering and fear, and Roosevelt's own skills carried the Democratic party to victory in the 1934 elections. But New Deal policies also provoked criticism, from both those convinced that too little had been achieved and those alarmed that too much had been attempted.

Despite the early New Deal's probusiness character, conservatives complained that the expansion of government activity and its regulatory role weakened the autonomy of American business. They also condemned the efforts to aid nonbusiness groups as socialistic, particularly the "excessive" spending on unemployment relief and the "instigation" of labor organizing. By 1934, as *Time* magazine reported, "Private fulminations and public carpings against the New Deal have become almost a routine of the business day." Industrialists and bankers organized the **American Liberty League** to direct attacks on the New Deal. The league distributed over 5 million copies of two hundred different pamphlets; it also furnished editorials and news stories to newspapers. These critics attracted little popular support, however, and their selfishness antagonized Roosevelt.

More realistic criticism came from the left. In 1932, FDR had campaigned for "the forgotten man at the bottom of the economic pyramid," and some radicals argued that the early New Deal had forgotten the forgotten man. Communists and socialists focused public attention on the poor, especially in the countryside. In California, Communists organized Mexican, Filipino, and Japanese farm workers into their Cannery and Agricultural Workers Union; in Arkansas and Tennessee, socialists in 1934 helped organize sharecroppers into the Southern Tenant Farmers Union, protesting the "Raw Deal" they had received from the AAA. Both unions encountered violent reprisals. Growers killed three picketers in California's San Joaquin Valley; in Arkansas, landlords shot union organizers and led vigilante raids on sharecroppers' shacks. This terrorism, however, created sympathy for farmworkers.

Even without the involvement of socialists or communists, however, labor militancy in 1934 pressed Roosevelt. Workers acted as much against the failure of the NRA to enforce Section 7a as against recalcitrant corporations. The number of workers participating in strikes leaped from 325,000 in 1932 (about the annual average since 1925) to 1.5 million in 1934. From dockworkers in Seattle and copper miners in Butte to streetcar drivers in Milwaukee and shoemakers in Boston, workers demanded their rights. Textile workers launched the largest single strike in the nation's history, shutting down the industry in twenty states.

Rebuffing FDR's pleas for fair treatment, employers moved to crush the strikes, often using complaisant police and private strikebreakers. In Minneapolis, police shot sixty-seven teamsters, almost all in the back as they fled an ambush arranged by employers; in Toledo, company police and National Guardsmen attacked autoworkers with tear gas, bayonets, and rifle fire; in the textile strike, police killed six picketers in South Carolina, and soldiers wounded another fifty in Rhode Island. At times, the workers held their ground, and they often attracted popular support, even in general strikes that paralyzed major cities like San Francisco. But against such powerful opponents, workers needed help to achieve their rights. Harry Hopkins and other New Dealers realized that labor's demands could not be ignored.

Popular discontent was also mobilized by four prominent individuals demanding government action to assist groups neglected by the New Deal. Representative William Lemke of North Dakota, an agrarian radical leader of the Nonpartisan League, called attention to rural distress. Lemke objected to the New Deal's limited response to farmers crushed by the depression. In his own state, nearly two-thirds of the farmers had lost their land through foreclosures. The AAA's strategy of simply restricting production, he thundered, was an "insane policy in the midst of hunger, misery, want, and rags."

Labor activism and its often violent suppression influenced New Deal policy. Here striking textile workers in Georgia in 1934 have been seized by National Guard troops to be taken to internment camps.

Francis Townsend, a California physician, proposed to aid the nation's elderly, many of whom were destitute. The Townsend Plan called for a government pension to all Americans over the age of 60, provided they retire from work and spend their entire pension. This promised to extend relief to the elderly, open jobs for the unemployed, and stimulate economic recovery. Townsend attracted people who in his words "believe in the Bible, believe in God, cheer when the flag passes by, the Bible Belt solid Americans." Over five thousand Townsend Clubs lobbied for government action to help the elderly poor.

Father Charles Coughlin, a Catholic priest in the Detroit suburb of Royal Oak, threatened to mobilize another large constituency against the limitations of the early New Deal. Thirty million Americans listened eagerly to his weekly radio broadcasts mixing religion with anti-Semitism and demands for social justice and financial reform. Coughlin had condemned Hoover for assisting banks but ignoring the unemployed and initially welcomed the New Deal as "Christ's Deal." But after concluding that FDR's policies favored "the virile viciousness of business and finance," Coughlin organized the National Union for Social Justice to lobby for his goals. With support among lower-middle-class, heavily Catholic, urban ethnic groups, Coughlin posed a real challenge to Roosevelt's Democratic party.

Roosevelt found Senator Huey P. Long of Louisiana still more worrisome. Alternately charming and autocratic, Long had modernized his state with taxation and educational reforms and an extensive public works program after his election as governor in 1928. Moving to the Senate and eyeing the White House, Long proposed more comprehensive social welfare policies than the New Deal had envisaged. In 1934, he organized the Share-Our-Wealth Society. His plan to end poverty and unemployment called for confiscatory taxes on the rich to provide every family with a decent income, health coverage, education, and old-age pensions. Long's appeal was enormous. Within months, his organization claimed more than 27,000 clubs and 7 million members.

These dissident movements raised complex issues and simple fears. They built on concerns about the New Deal, both demanding government assistance and fretting about government intrusion; their programs were often ill-defined or impractical—Townsend's plan would cost more than half the national income; and some of the leaders, like Coughlin and Long, approached demagoguery. Nevertheless, their popularity warned Roosevelt that government action was needed to satisfy reform demands and assure his reelection in 1936.

Consolidating the New Deal

Responding to the persistence of the depression and political pressures, Roosevelt in 1935 undertook economic and social reforms that some observers have called the **Second New Deal**. The new measures shifted the relative weights accorded to the constant objectives of recovery, relief, and reform. Nor did FDR's interest in reform simply reflect cynical politics. He had frequently championed progressive measures in the past, and many of his advisers had deep roots in reform movements. After the 1934 elections gave the president an even more Democratic Congress, Harry Hopkins exulted: "Boys—this is our hour. We've got to get everything we want—a works program, social security, wages and hours, everything—now or never."

Lifting and Weeding

"In spite of our efforts and in spite of our talk," Roosevelt told the new Congress in 1935, "we have not weeded out the overprivileged and we have not effectively lifted up the underprivileged." To do so, he developed "must" legislation, to which his allies in Congress added. One of the new laws protected labor's rights to organize and bargain collectively. Drafted by Senator Robert Wagner of New York to replace Section 7a, it received Roosevelt's endorsement only after it was clear that both Congress and the public favored it. The **Wagner National Labor Relations Act**, dubbed "Labor's Magna Carta," guaranteed workers' rights to organize unions and forbade employers to adopt unfair labor practices, such as firing union activists or forming company unions. The law also set up the **National Labor Relations Board (NLRB)** to enforce these provisions, protect workers from coercion, and supervise union elections.

Of greater long-range importance was the **Social Security Act**. Other industrial nations had established national social insurance systems much earlier, but only the Great Depression moved the United States to accept that the federal government should protect the poor and unemployed. Even so, the law was a compromise, framed by a nonpartisan committee of business, labor, and public representatives and then weakened by congressional conservatives. It provided unemployment compensation, old-age pensions, and aid for dependent mothers and children and the blind.

The conservative nature of the law appeared in its stingy benefit payments, its lack of health insurance, and its exclusion of more than a fourth of all workers, including many in desperate need of protection, such as farm laborers and domestic servants. Moreover, unlike in other nations, the old-age pensions were financed through a regressive payroll tax on both employees and employers rather than through general tax revenues. Thus the new system was more like a compulsory insurance program. Roosevelt conceded as much but defended the taxes on workers as a tactic to protect the reform itself: "We put those payroll contributions there so as to give the contributors a legal, moral, and political right to collect their pensions and their unemployment benefits. With those taxes in there, no damn politician can ever scrap my social security program."

Roosevelt was justifiably proud. Despite its weaknesses, the Social Security Act was one of the most important laws in American history. It provided, he pointed out, "at least some measure of protection to the average citizen and to his family against the loss of a job and against poverty-ridden old age." Moreover, by establishing federal responsibility for social welfare, it inaugurated a welfare system that subsequent generations would expand.

Another reform measure, the Banking Act of 1935, increased the authority of the Federal Reserve Board over the nation's currency and credit system and decreased the power of the private bankers whose irresponsible behavior had contributed to the depression and the appeal of Father Coughlin. The Revenue Act of 1935, passed after Roosevelt assailed the "unjust concentration of wealth and economic power," provided for graduated income taxes and increased estate and corporate taxes. Opponents called it the Soak the Rich Tax, but with its many loopholes, it was scarcely that and was certainly not a redistributive measure such as Huey Long had proposed. Nevertheless, it set a precedent for progressive taxation and attracted popular support.

The Second New Deal also responded belatedly to the environmental catastrophe that had turned much of the Great Plains from Texas to the Dakotas into a "Dust Bowl" (see Map 27-2). Since World War I, farmers had stripped marginal land of its native grasses to plant wheat. When drought and high winds hit the plains in 1932, crops failed, and nothing held the soil. Dust storms blew away millions of tons of topsoil, despoiling the land and darkening the sky a thousand miles away. Families abandoned their farms in droves. Many of these poor "Okies" headed for California, their plight captured in John Steinbeck's novel, *The Grapes of Wrath* (1939).

AMERICA'S JOURNEY

FROM THEN TO NOW

Social Security

No politician will "ever scrap my social security program." So predicted FDR when he signed the Social Security Act in 1935. He based his confidence on the provisions in the act that linked benefits to payroll deductions. Because workers contributed to the program, they would feel a "right to collect their pensions and unemployment benefits." But Roosevelt could not have imagined just how successful the Social Security program would become. Expanded over the years since the 1930s, it now assists 44 million Americans, including the elderly, the disabled, and the survivors of contributors to the program. Certain poverty would confront half the nation's elderly without their monthly checks.

But the successful expansion of the program has also called its future into question. By 2030, the number of eligible recipients will double, but the number of employees paying Social Security taxes will increase by only 17 percent. Annual funding deficits of more than $100 billion loom ahead.

Still, as FDR predicted, no political leader dares to propose "scrapping" Social Security. Rather, proposals to solve this problem reflect conflicting views about the expansion of the federal government—and especially its efforts to promote social welfare—that began with the New Deal. No longer does the public overwhelmingly endorse federal responsibility for solving social problems as it did during the economic crisis of the 1930s. On the contrary, an increasingly intense backlash against "big government" emerged in the 1960s, ultimately finding its champion in the 1980s in Republican President Ronald Reagan, who declared, "Government is not the solution to our problems; government is the problem." Reagan's administration sought to reduce the size of government and curtail its regulatory oversight of American business. This "Reagan Revolution" appealed to those who never supported government responsibility for social welfare and to those who had lost trust in the government's ability to fulfill that role. By the 1990s, even Democratic President Bill Clinton declared an end to the era of "big government."

Support has grown for private initiatives to replace government programs, and now critics are pressing to "privatize" the Social Security system itself. They have proposed such sweeping changes as limiting benefits to contributors only and requiring contributors to invest their Social Security accounts themselves, including in the stock market. The predicted payoff would be larger earnings.

Opponents of these critics argue for reforming, not overturning, the current Social Security system. Privatization, they argue, would undermine Social Security's fundamental principle: to guarantee retirees a dependable income base. Investing retirement savings in the stock market subjects them to market volatility, which might benefit some people but could leave others with serious losses just when they were ready to retire. Privatization would also eliminate the special assistance that Social Security provides to large families, couples with one partner who has had no or limited earnings, and low-income earners.

Rather than scrap the current system, reformers propose other changes. They suggest taxing all workers for Social Security; many, especially in state and local governments, are now outside the system. Extending the age of eligibility to receive benefits, justified by the increasing life expectancy of Americans, would also bolster the Social Security funds. Another proposal would abandon the current investment strategy but have a quasi-private government entity manage the system's portfolio. Such changes would enable Social Security to continue meeting the needs of all citizens.

The current argument over Social Security echoes the disputes of the 1930s about the role and function of our government and reflects continuing differences over the degree to which the government should attempt to make American society more equitable. Finding a solution to funding Social Security in the new century will require addressing the issue of America's core values.

FDR signs the Social Security Act in 1935, establishing a program that would grow in size and importance in subsequent decades. To the left in a dark suit is Senator Robert F. Wagner; behind FDR is Secretary of Labor Frances Perkins. All three were influential in shaping an activist federal government that some Americans would later decry as unnecessary.

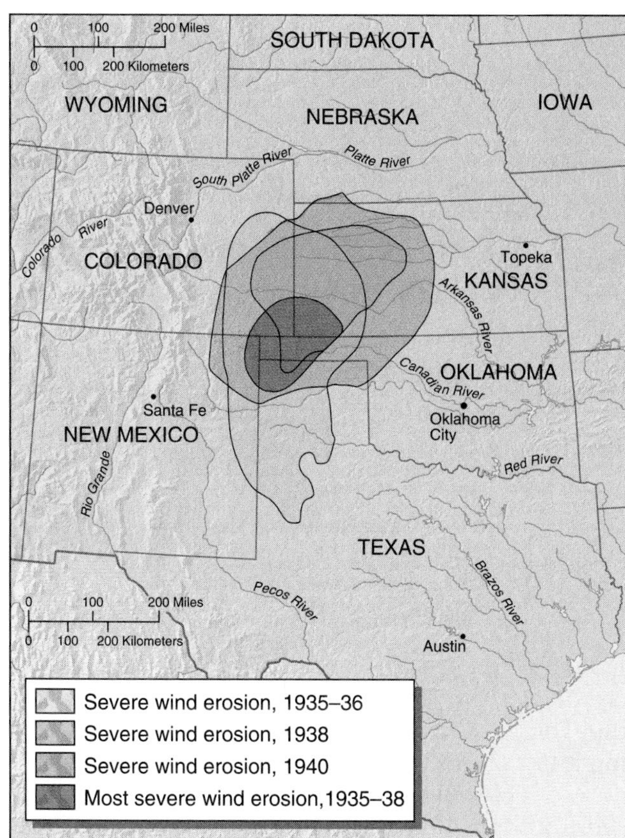

Map 27-2 The Dust Bowl
Years of overcultivation, drought, and high winds created the Dust Bowl, which most severely affected the southern Great Plains. Federal relief and conservation programs provided assistance, but many residents fled the area, often migrating to California.

In 1935, Roosevelt established the **Resettlement Administration** to focus on land reform and help poor farmers. Under Rexford Tugwell, this agency initiated soil erosion projects and attempted to resettle impoverished farmers on better land, but the problem exceeded its resources. Congress moved to save the land, if not its people, by creating the Soil Conservation Service in 1935.

Expanding Relief

If reform gained priority in the Second New Deal, relief remained critical. With millions still unemployed, Roosevelt pushed through Congress in 1935 the Emergency Relief Appropriation Act, authorizing $5 billion—at the time the largest single appropriation in history—for emergency public employment. Roosevelt created the **Works Progress Administration (WPA)** under Hopkins, who set up work relief programs to assist the unemployed and boost the economy. Before its end in 1943, the WPA gave jobs to 9 million people (more than a fifth of the labor force) and spent nearly $12 billion. Three-fourths of its expenditures went on construction projects that could employ manual labor: the WPA built 125,000 schools, post offices, and hospitals; 8,000 parks; nearly 100,000 bridges; and enough roads and sewer systems to circle the earth thirty times. From New York City's La Guardia Airport to Atlanta's sewer system to irrigation ditches in the Far West, the WPA laid much of the nation's basic infrastructure on which it still relies.

The WPA also developed work projects for unemployed writers, artists, musicians, and actors. "Why not?" said FDR. "They are human beings. They have to live." The Federal Writers' Project put authors to work preparing state guidebooks, writing historical pamphlets, and recording the memories of ex-slaves. The Federal Art Project hired artists to teach art in night schools, prepare exhibits at museums, and paint murals on post office walls. The Federal Theatre Project organized theatrical productions and drama companies that in four years played to 30 million Americans. The Federal Music Project hired musicians to collect and perform folk songs. These WPA programs allowed people to use their talents while surviving the depression, increased popular access to cultural performances, and established a precedent for federal support of the arts. "What has happened and in such a short time is almost incredible," said one reviewer. "From a government completely apathetic to art, we suddenly have a government very art conscious."

The National Youth Administration (NYA), another WPA agency, gave part-time jobs to students, enabling 2 million high school and college students to stay in school, learn skills, and do productive work. At the University of Nebraska, NYA students built an observatory; at Duke University, law student Richard M. Nixon earned 35 cents an hour doing research in the library. Lyndon Johnson, a Texas NYA official, believed that "if the Roosevelt administration had never done another thing, it would have been justified by the work of this great institution for salvaging youth."

The Roosevelt Coalition and the Election of 1936

The 1936 election gave Americans an opportunity to judge FDR and the New Deal. Conservatives alarmed at the expansion of government, businesspeople angered by regulation and labor legislation, and well-to-do Americans furious with tax reform decried the New Deal. But they were a minority. Even the presidential candidate they supported, Republican Governor Alf Landon of Kansas, endorsed much of the New Deal, criticizing merely the inefficiency and cost of some of its programs. (Roosevelt remarked whimsically that he

On work relief with the Federal Art Project, artist Eugene Trentham painted "Baling Hay in Holt County in Early Days" on a Nebraska post office wall in 1938. Roosevelt himself appraised the work of such muralists: "Some of it good, some of it not so good, but all of it native, human, eager, and alive."

thought he could defeat himself with such a campaign.) The New Deal's earlier critics on the left had also lost most of their following. The reforms of 1935 had undercut their arguments, and the assassination of Huey Long in the same year had removed their ablest politician. They formed the Union party and nominated William Lemke for the presidency, but they were no longer a threat.

The programs and politicians of the New Deal had created an invincible coalition behind Roosevelt. Despite ambivalence about large-scale government intervention, the New Deal's agricultural programs reinforced the traditional Democratic allegiance of white Southerners while attracting many western farmers. Labor legislation clinched the active support of the nation's workers; Sidney Hillman of the Amalgamated Clothing Workers promised his union would campaign for FDR "to see to it that we hold onto the gains labor has won." Middle-class voters, whose homes had been saved and whose hopes had been raised, also joined the Roosevelt coalition.

So did urban ethnic groups, who had benefited from welfare programs and appreciated the unprecedented recognition Roosevelt's administration gave them. FDR named the first Italian American to the federal judiciary, for example, and appointed five times as many Catholics and Jews to government positions as the three Republican presidents had during the 1920s (prompting anti-Semitic critics to speak of the "Jew Deal"). African Americans voted overwhelmingly Democratic for the first time. Women, too, were an important part of the Roosevelt coalition, and Eleanor often attracted their support as much as Franklin did. As one campaigner said to a roaring crowd in 1936, "Many women in this country when they vote for Franklin D. Roosevelt will also be thinking with a choke in the throat of Eleanor Roosevelt!"

This political realignment produced a landslide. Roosevelt polled 61 percent of the popular vote and the largest electoral vote margin ever recorded, 523 to 8. Landon even lost Kansas, his own state, and Lemke received fewer than 900,000 votes. Democrats also won huge majorities in Congress. Roosevelt's political coalition reflected a mandate for himself and the New Deal; it would enable the Democrats to dominate national elections for three decades.

The New Deal and American Life

The landslide of 1936 reflected the impact the New Deal had on Americans. Industrial workers mobilized to secure their rights, women and minorities gained increased, if still limited, opportunities to participate in American society, and Southerners and Westerners benefited from government programs they turned to their own advantage. Government programs changed daily life, and ordinary people often helped shape the new policies.

Labor on the March

The labor revival in the 1930s reflected both workers' determination and government support. Workers wanted not merely to improve their wages and benefits but also to gain union recognition and union contracts to limit arbitrary managerial authority and achieve some control over the workplace. This larger goal provoked opposition from employers and their allies and required workers to organize, strike, and become politically active. Their achievement was remarkable.

The Second New Deal helped. By guaranteeing labor's rights to organize and bargain collectively, the Wagner Act sparked a wave of labor activism. But if the government ultimately protected union rights, the unions themselves had to form locals, recruit members, and demonstrate influence in the workplace.

At first, those tasks overwhelmed the American Federation of Labor (AFL). Its reliance on craft-based unions and reluctance to organize immigrant, black, and women workers left it unprepared for the rush of industrial workers seeking unionization. More progressive labor leaders saw that industrywide unions were more appropriate for unskilled workers in mass-production industries. Forming the Committee for Industrial Organization (CIO) within the AFL, they campaigned to unionize workers in the steel, auto, and rubber industries, all notoriously hostile to unions. AFL leaders insisted that the CIO disband and then in 1937 expelled its unions. The militants reorganized as the separate **Congress of Industrial Organizations**. (In 1955, the two groups merged as the AFL-CIO.)

The split roused the AFL to increase its own organizing activities, but it was primarily the new CIO that put labor on the march. It inspired workers previously neglected. The CIO's interracial union campaign in the Birmingham steel mills, said one organizer, was "like a second coming of Christ" for black workers, who welcomed the union as a chance for social recognition as well as economic opportunity. The CIO also employed new and aggressive tactics, particularly the sit-down strike, in which workers, rather than picketing outside the factory, simply sat inside the plant, thereby blocking both production and the use of strikebreakers. Conservatives were outraged, but Upton Sinclair said, "For seventy-five years big business has been sitting down on the American people, and now I am delighted to see the process reversed."

Black and white laundry workers on strike in 1937. The new labor militancy helped organize workers previously neglected by unions and sometimes led to a sense of solidarity as well as better wages and working conditions.

The CIO won major victories, despite bitter opposition from industry and its allies. The issue was not wages but labor's right to organize and bargain with management. Sit-down strikes paralyzed General Motors in 1937 after it refused to recognize the United Auto Workers. GM tried to force the strikers out of its Flint, Michigan, plants by turning off the heat, using police and tear gas, threatening strikers' families, and securing court orders to clear the plant by military force. But the governor refused to order National Guardsmen to attack, and the strikers held out, aided by the Women's Emergency Brigade, working-class women who picketed the building, heckled the police, and smuggled food to the strikers. After six weeks, GM signed a contract with the UAW. Chrysler soon followed suit. Ford refused to recognize the union until 1941, often violently disrupting organizing efforts.

Steel companies also used violence against unionization. In the **Memorial Day Massacre** in Chicago in 1937, police guarding a plant of the Republic Steel Company fired on strikers and their families, killing ten people as they tried to flee. Scores more were wounded and beaten in a police frenzy so violent that theaters refused to show a newsreel of the event. A Senate investigation found that Republic and other companies had hired private police to attack workers seeking to unionize, stockpiled weapons and tear gas, and corrupted authorities. The investigators concluded that "private corporations dominate their employees, deny them their constitutional rights, promote disorder and disharmony, and even set at naught the powers of the government itself." Federal court orders finally forced the companies to bargain collectively.

New Deal labor legislation, government investigations and court orders, and the federal refusal to use force against strikes helped the labor movement secure basic rights for American workers. Union membership leaped from under 3 million in 1932 to 9 million by 1939, and workers won higher wages, better working conditions, and more economic democracy.

Women and the New Deal

As federal programs proliferated in 1933, a Baltimore women's group urged the administration to "come out for a square and new deal for women." Although women did gain increased attention and influence, government and society remained largely bound by traditional values.

New Deal relief programs had a mixed impact on workingwomen. Formal government policy required "equal consideration" for women and men, but local officials so flouted this requirement that Eleanor Roosevelt urged Harry Hopkins to "impress on state administrators that the women's programs are as important as the men's. They are so apt to forget us!" Women on relief were restricted to "women's work"—more than half worked on sewing projects, regardless of their skills—and were paid scarcely half what men received. WPA training programs also reinforced traditional ideas about women's work; black women, for example, were trained to be maids, dishwashers, and cooks. Although women constituted nearly a fourth of the labor force, they obtained only 19 percent of the jobs created by the WPA, 12 percent by the FERA, and 7 percent by the CWA. The CCC excluded women altogether. Still, relief agencies provided crucial assistance to women in the depression.

Other New Deal programs also had mixed benefits for women. Despite demands by the League of Women Voters and the Women's Trade Union League for "equal pay for equal work and equal opportunity for equal ability regardless of sex," many NRA codes mandated lower wage scales for women than for men, which officials justified as reflecting "long-established customs." But by raising minimum wages, the NRA brought relatively greater improvements to women, who were concentrated in the lowest-paid occupations, than to male workers. The Social Security Act did not cover domestic servants, waitresses, and women who worked in the home but did help mothers with dependent children.

Women also gained political influence under the New Deal, although Molly Dewson, the director of the Women's Division of the Democratic party, exaggerated when she exclaimed, "The change from women's status in government before Roosevelt is unbelievable." Dewson herself exercised considerable political power and helped shape the party's campaigns. Around Dewson revolved a network of women, linked by friendships and experiences in the National Consumers' League, Women's Trade Union League, and other progressive reform organizations. Appointed to many positions in the Roosevelt administration, they helped develop and implement New Deal social legislation. Secretary of Labor Frances Perkins was the first woman cabinet member and a key member of the network; other women were in the Treasury Department, the Children's Bureau, and relief and cultural programs.

Eleanor Roosevelt was their leader. Described by a Washington reporter as "a cabinet member without portfolio," she roared across the social and political landscape of the 1930s, pushing for women's rights, demanding reforms, traveling across the country, writing newspaper columns and speaking over the radio, developing plans to help unemployed miners in West Virginia and abolish slums in Washington, and lobbying both Congress and her husband. FDR used her as his eyes and ears and sometimes his conscience. He rebuffed her critics with a jaunty, "Well, that is my wife; I can't do anything about her." Indeed, Eleanor Roosevelt had become not merely the most prominent first lady in history but a force in her own right and a symbol of the growing importance of women in public life.

Eleanor Roosevelt campaigns with FDR in Fremont, Nebraska, in 1935. A visible activist for social and economic reform, she was also politically important in building the powerful Roosevelt coalition. "Previously," said journalist Ruby Black, "a President's wife acted as if she didn't know that a political party existed."

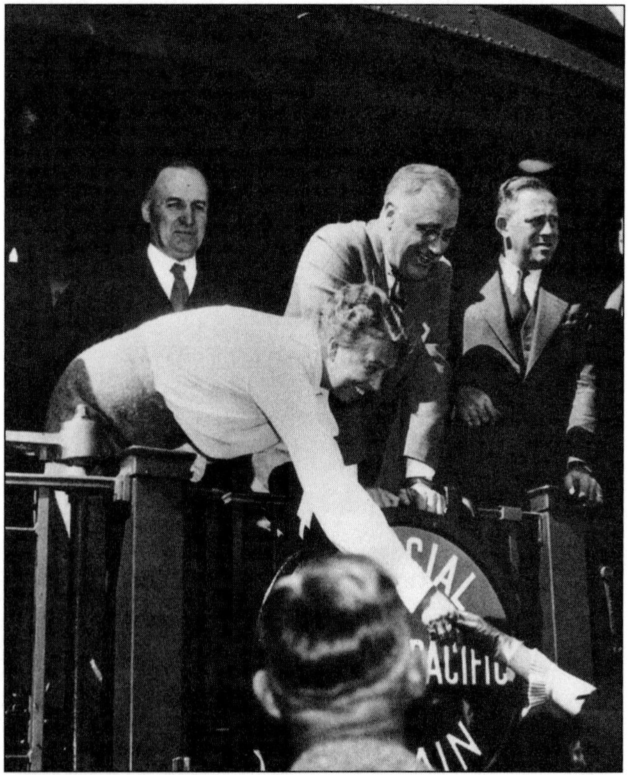

Minorities and the New Deal

Despite the move of African Americans into the Democratic party, the New Deal's record on racial issues was limited. Although Roosevelt deplored racial abuses, he never pushed for civil rights legislation, fearing to antagonize the influential Southern Democrats in Congress whose support he needed. For similar reasons, many New Deal programs discriminated against African Americans. The CCC segregated black workers; NRA codes so often specified lower wages and benefits for black workers relative to white workers or even excluded black workers from jobs that the black press claimed NRA stood for "Negro Run Around" or "Negroes Ruined Again." And racist officials discriminated in allocating federal relief. Atlanta, for instance, provided average monthly relief checks of $32.66 to white people but only $19.29 to black people.

However, disproportionately poor and unemployed, African Americans did benefit from the New Deal's welfare and economic programs. W. E. B. Du Bois asserted that "large numbers of colored people in the United States would have starved to death if it had not been for the Roosevelt policies." And key New Dealers campaigned against racial discrimination. Eleanor Roosevelt prodded FDR to appoint black officials, wrote articles supporting racial equality, and flouted segregationist laws. Attacked by white racists, she was popular in the black community. Harry Hopkins and Harold Ickes also promoted equal rights. Ickes, a former president of Chicago's NAACP chapter, insisted that African Americans receive PWA relief jobs in proportion to their share of the population and ended segregation in the Department of the Interior, prompting other cabinet secretaries to follow suit. As black votes in northern cities became important, more pragmatic New Dealers also began to pay more attention to black needs.

African Americans themselves pressed for reforms. Civil rights groups protested discriminatory policies, including the unequal wage scales in the NRA codes and the CCC's limited enrollment of black youth. African Americans demonstrated against racial discrimination in hiring and their exclusion from federally financed construction projects.

In response, FDR took more interest in black economic and social problems. He prohibited discrimination in the WPA in 1935, and the NYA adopted enlightened racial policies. Roosevelt also appointed black people to important positions, including the first black federal judge. Many of these officials began meeting regularly at the home of Mary McLeod Bethune of the National Council of Negro Women. Dubbed the Black Cabinet, they worked with civil rights organizations, fought discrimination in government, influenced patronage, and stimulated black interest in politics.

The New Deal improved economic and social conditions for many African Americans. Black illiteracy dropped because of federal education projects, and the number of black college students and graduates more than doubled, in part because the NYA provided student aid to black colleges. New Deal relief and public health programs reduced black infant mortality rates and raised life expectancy rates. Conditions for black people continued to lag behind those for white people, and discrimination persisted, but the black switch to the Roosevelt coalition reflected the New Deal's benefits.

Native Americans also benefited from the New Deal. The depression had imposed further misery on a group already suffering from poverty, wretched health conditions, and the nation's lowest educational level. Many New Deal programs had limited applicability to Indians, but the CCC appealed to their interests and skills. More than eighty thousand Indians received training in agriculture, forestry, and animal husbandry, along with basic academic subjects. CCC projects, together with those undertaken by the PWA and the WPA, built schools, hospitals, roads, and irrigation systems on reservations.

New Deal officials also refocused government Indian policy, which had undermined tribal authority and promoted assimilation by reducing Indian landholding and attacking Indian culture. Protests had been ignored. Appointed commissioner of Indian affairs in 1933, John Collier prohibited interference with Indian religious or cultural life, directed the Bureau of Indian Affairs to employ more Indians, and prevented Indian schools from suppressing native languages and traditions.

Collier also persuaded Congress to pass the **Indian Reorganization Act** of 1934, often called the Indians' New Deal. The act guaranteed religious freedom, reestablished tribal self-government, and halted the sale of tribal lands. It also provided funds to expand Indian landholdings, support Indian students, and establish tribal businesses. But social and economic problems persisted on the isolated reservations, and white missionaries and business interests attacked Collier's reforms as atheistic and communistic.

Hispanic Americans received less assistance from the New Deal. Its relief programs aided many Hispanics in California and the Southwest but ignored those who were not citizens. Moreover, local administrators often discriminated against Hispanics, especially by providing higher relief payments to Anglos. Finally, by excluding agricultural workers, neither the Social Security Act nor the Wagner Act gave Mexican Americans much protection or hope. Farm workers remained largely unorganized, exploited, and at the mercy of agribusinesses.

The New Deal for the South and West

The New Deal ironically offered special benefits to the South, traditionally averse to government activism, and to the West, which considered itself the land of rugged individualism.

The New Deal's agricultural program boosted farm prices and income more in the South than any other region. By controlling cotton production, it also promoted diversification; its subsidies financed mechanization. The resulting modernization helped replace an archaic sharecropping system with an emergent agribusiness. The rural poor were displaced, but the South's agricultural economy advanced.

The New Deal also improved southern cities. FERA and WPA built urban sewer systems, airports, bridges, roads, and harbor facilities. Whereas northern cities had already constructed such facilities themselves—and were still paying off their debts—the federal government largely paid for such modernization in the South, giving its cities an economic advantage.

Federal grants were supposed to be awarded to states in proportion to their own expenditures, but while southern politicians welcomed New Deal funds—"I'm gonna grab all I can for the state of Texas," said Governor Lee O'Daniel—they refused to contribute their share of the costs. Nationally, the federal proportion of FERA expenditures was 62 percent; in the South, it was usually 90 percent and never lower than 73 percent. Virginia officials refused to provide even 10 percent, declaring, "It takes people a long time to starve." Some southern cities and counties refused to contribute anything to relief, and Memphis spent less on relief—only 0.1 percent of its budget—than on maintaining public golf courses.

Federal money enabled southern communities to balance their own budgets, preach fiscal orthodoxy, and maintain traditional claims of limited government. Federal officials complained of the South's "parasitic" behavior in accepting aid but not responsibility, and even Southerners acknowledged the hypocrisy of the region's invocation of state's rights. "We recognize state boundaries when called on to give," noted the *Houston Press*, "but forget them when Uncle Sam is doing the giving."

The federal government had a particularly powerful impact on the South with the **Tennessee Valley Authority (TVA)**, launched in 1933 (see Map 27-3). Coordinating activities across seven states, the TVA built dams to control floods and generate hydroelectric power, produced fertilizer, fostered agricultural

Map 27-3 The Tennessee Valley Authority
By building dams and hydroelectric power plants, the TVA controlled flooding and soil erosion and generated electricity that did much to modernize a large region of the Upper South.

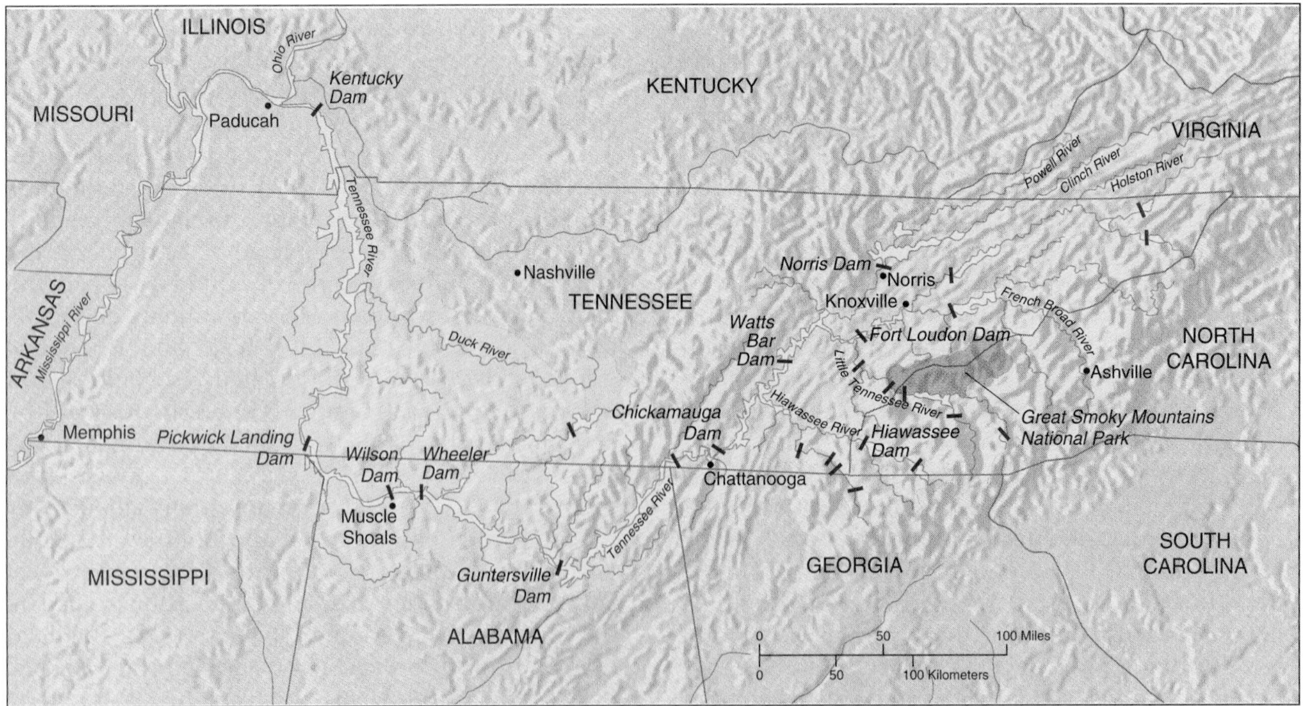

and forestry development, encouraged conservation, improved navigation, and modernized school and health systems. Private utility companies denounced the TVA as socialistic, but most Southerners supported it. Its major drawback was environmental damage that only became apparent later. Over a vast area of the South, it provided electricity for the first time.

The New Deal further expanded access to electricity by establishing the **Rural Electrification Administration (REA)** in 1935. Private companies had refused to extend power lines into the countryside because it was not profitable, consigning 90 percent of the nation's farms to drudgery and darkness. The REA revolutionized farm life by sponsoring rural nonprofit electric cooperatives. By 1941, 35 percent of American farms had electricity; by 1950, 78 percent. By providing electric power to light and heat homes and barns, pump water, and run refrigerators, washing machines, and radios, one Arkansas newspaper concluded, the REA had made "a reality" of what had been only a "utopian dream."

The New Deal also changed the West. Westerners received the most federal money per capita in welfare, relief projects, and loans. Like Southerners, they accepted federal aid and clamored for more. Utah, which received the most federal relief funds per capita, was the nation's "prize 'gimme state,'" said one FERA official. Western farmers and cattle raisers were saved by federal payments, and even refugees from the Dust Bowl depended on relief assistance and medical care in federal camps.

The Bureau of Reclamation, established in 1902, emerged as one of the most important government agencies in the West. It built huge dams to control the western river systems and promote large-scale development. The Hoover Dam on the Colorado River between Nevada and Arizona, completed in 1935; the Grand Coulee Dam on the Columbia River in Washington, finished in 1941; and other giant projects prevented flooding, produced cheap hydroelectric power, and created reservoirs and canal systems to bring water to farms and cities. By furnishing capital and expertise, the government subsidized and stimulated western economic development, particularly the growth of agribusiness.

Westerners welcomed such assistance but rarely shared the federal goals of rational resource management. Instead they often wanted to continue to exploit the land and resented federal supervision as colonial control. In practice, however, the government worked in partnership with the West's agribusinesses and timber and petroleum industries.

The New Deal and Public Activism

Despite Hoover's fear that government responsibility would discourage local initiative, the 1930s witnessed an upsurge in such activism. New Deal programs, in fact, often encouraged or empowered groups to shape public policy and social and economic behavior. Moreover, because the administration worried about centralization, some federal agencies fostered what New Dealers called "grassroots democracy." The AAA set up committees totaling more than 100,000 people to implement agricultural policy and held referendums on crop controls; local advisory committees guided the various federal arts projects; federal management of the West's public grasslands mandated cooperation with associations of livestock raisers.

At times, local administration of national programs enabled groups to exploit federal policy for their own advantage. Wealthy planters shaped AAA practices at the expense of poor tenant farmers; local control of TVA projects excluded black people. But federal programs often allowed previously unrepresented groups to contest traditionally dominant interests. By requiring that public housing projects be initiated locally, for example, New Deal programs prompted labor unions, religious and civic groups, neighborhood associations, and civil rights groups to form associations to overcome the hostility of realty agents and bankers to public housing. Often seeing greater opportunities for participation and influence in federal programs than in city and state governments, such community groups campaigned to expand federal authority. In short, depression conditions and New Deal programs actually increased citizen involvement in public affairs.

Ebbing of the New Deal

After his victory in 1936, Roosevelt committed himself to further reforms. "I see one-third of a nation ill-housed, ill-clad, ill-nourished," he declared in his second inaugural address. "The test of our progress is not whether we add more to the abundance of those who have much; it is whether we provide enough for those who have too little." But determined opponents, continuing economic problems, and the president's own misjudgments blocked his reforms and deadlocked the New Deal.

Challenging the Court

Roosevelt regarded the Supreme Court as his most dangerous opponent. During his first term, it had declared unconstitutional several important measures. FDR complained that the justices held "horse-and-buggy" ideas about government that prevented the president and Congress from responding to changes. Indeed, most of the justices were elderly conservatives appointed by Republicans and unsympathetic to an activist federal government. It seemed that the court would also strike down the Second New Deal.

Emboldened by the 1936 landslide, Roosevelt decided to restructure the federal judiciary. In early 1937, he proposed legislation authorizing the president to name a new judge for each one serving past the age of 70. Additional judges, he said, would increase judicial efficiency. But his real goal was to appoint new judges more sympathetic to the New Deal.

His court plan led to a divisive struggle. The proposal was perfectly legal: Congress had the authority, which it had used repeatedly, to change the number of judges on the Court. But Republicans and conservative Democrats attacked the plan as a scheme to "pack" the Court and subvert the separation of powers among the three branches of government. Some conservatives called the president a "dictator," but even many liberals expressed reservations about the plan or FDR's lack of candor in proposing it.

The Court itself undercut support for FDR's proposal by upholding the Social Security and Wagner Acts and minimum wage legislation. Moreover, the retirement of a conservative justice allowed Roosevelt to name a sympathetic successor. Congress rejected Roosevelt's plan.

Roosevelt's challenge to the Court hurt the New Deal. It worried the public, split the Democratic party, and revived conservatives. Opponents promptly attacked other New Deal policies, from support for unions to progressive taxation. Henceforth, a conservative coalition of Republicans and Southern Democrats in Congress blocked FDR's reforms.

More Hard Times

A sharp recession beginning in August 1937 added to Roosevelt's problems. The New Deal's deficit spending had reflected his desire to alleviate suffering, not a conviction that it would stimulate economic recovery. As the economy improved in 1936, Roosevelt decided to cut federal expenditures and balance the budget. But private investment and employment remained stagnant, and the economy plunged. A record decline in industrial production canceled the gains of the previous two years, and unemployment leaped from 7 million to 11 million within a few months. Republicans delighted in attacking the "Roosevelt recession," although it stemmed from retrenchment policies they themselves advocated.

In 1938, Roosevelt reluctantly increased spending. His decision was based on the principles of British economist John Maynard Keynes. As Marriner Eccles of the Federal Reserve Board explained, the federal government had to serve as the "compensatory agent" in the economy: It should use deficit spending to increase demand and production when private investment declined and raise taxes to pay its debt and cool the economy when business activity became excessive. New appropriations for the PWA and other government programs revived the faltering economy, but neither FDR nor Congress would spend what was necessary to end the depression. Only the vast expenditures for World War II would bring full recovery.

Political Stalemate

The recession interrupted the momentum of the New Deal and strengthened its opponents. In late 1937, their leaders in Congress issued a "conservative manifesto" decrying New Deal fiscal, labor, and regulatory policies. Holding seniority in a Congress malapportioned in their favor, they blocked most of Roosevelt's reforms. None of his "must" legislation passed a special session of Congress in December. In 1938, Congress rejected tax reforms and reduced corporate taxes.

The few measures that passed were heavily amended. The Fair Labor Standards Act established maximum hours and minimum wages for workers but authorized so many exemptions that one New Dealer asked "whether anyone is subject to this bill." The Farm Tenancy Act established the Farm Security Administration to lend money to tenant farmers and agricultural laborers to acquire their own land, but appropriations were so limited that centuries would have been required to meet the need. The National Housing Act created the United States Housing Authority to finance slum clearance and public housing projects, but its total funds were less than what was needed to demolish tenements in New York City alone.

To protect the New Deal, Roosevelt turned again to the public, with whom he remained immensely popular. In the 1938 Democratic primaries, he campaigned against the New Deal's conservative opponents. But FDR could not transfer his personal popularity to the political newcomers he supported. What his foes attacked as a "purge" failed. Roosevelt lost further political leverage when the Republicans gained seventy-five seats in the House and seven in the Senate and thirteen governorships.

The 1938 elections did not repudiate the New Deal, for the Democrats retained majorities in both houses of Congress. But the Republican revival and the survival of the conservative Southern Democrats guaranteed that the New Deal had gone as far as it ever would. With Roosevelt in the White House and his opponents controlling Congress, the New Deal ended in political stalemate.

Conclusion

The Great Depression and the New Deal mark a major divide in American history. The depression cast doubt on the traditional practices, policies, and attitudes that underlay not only the nation's economy but its social and political institutions and relationships as well. The New Deal failed to restore prosperity, but it did bring partial economic recovery. Moreover, its economic policies, from banking and securities regulation to unemployment compensation, farm price supports, and minimum wages, created barriers against another depression. The gradual adoption of compensatory spending policies also expanded the government's role in the economy. Responding to the failures of both private organizations and state and local governments, the federal government also assumed the obligation to provide social welfare. The New Deal established pensions for the elderly, aid for dependent mothers and children and the blind, public housing for the poor, and public health services. Although such programs were limited in scope and access, they helped establish a responsible government. "Better the occasional faults of a Government that lives in a spirit of charity," Roosevelt warned, "than the constant omission of a Government frozen in the ice of its own indifference."

Roosevelt also expanded the role of the presidency. As his White House took the initiative for defining public policy, drafting legislation, lobbying Congress, and communicating with the nation, it became the model for all subsequent presidents. Not only was the president's power increased, but Roosevelt made the federal government, rather than state or local governments, the focus of public interest and expectations. Under Hoover, one secretary had handled all the White House mail; under FDR, a staff of fifty was overwhelmed.

Roosevelt and the New Deal also revitalized the Democratic party, drawing minorities, industrial workers, and previously uninvolved citizens into a coalition with white Southerners. The tensions in such a coalition sometimes prevented effective public policies, but the coalition made the Democrats the dominant national party.

Political constraints explained some of the New Deal's failures. Conservative southern Democrats and northern Republicans limited its efforts to curtail racial discrimination or protect the rural and urban poor. But Roosevelt and other New Dealers were often constrained by their own vision, refusing to consider the massive deficit spending necessary to end the depression or not recognizing the need to end gender discrimination. But if the New Deal did not bring the revolution its conservative critics claimed—it did not redistribute wealth or income—it did change American life. By 1939, as international relations deteriorated, FDR was already considering a shift, as he later said, from Dr. New Deal to Dr. Win-the-War.

Review Questions

1. Why did President Hoover's emphasis on voluntarism fail to resolve the problems of the Great Depression?
2. Describe the relief programs of the New Deal. What were they designed to accomplish? What were their achievements and their limitations?
3. What were the major criticisms of the early New Deal? How accurate were those charges?
4. How did the policies of the New Deal shape the constituency and the prospects of the Democratic party in the 1930s?
5. Describe the conflict between management and labor in the 1930s. What were the major issues and motivations involved? How did the two sides differ in resources and tactics, and how and why did these factors change over time?
6. How did the role of the federal government change in the 1930s? What factors were responsible for those changes?

Recommended Reading

Paul Conkin, *The New Deal,* 3rd ed. (1992). A brief and insightful critique of FDR's programs.

Steve Fraser and Gary Gerstle, eds., *The Rise and Fall of the New Deal Order, 1930–1980* (1989). A valuable collection of essays that surveys the New Deal and explores its legacy.

Frank Freidel, *Franklin D. Roosevelt: A Rendezvous with Destiny* (1990). The best one-volume biography of FDR.

David Kennedy, *Freedom from Fear: The American People in Depression and War* (1999). The most recent and comprehensive survey of the period.

William Leuchtenburg, *Franklin D. Roosevelt and the New Deal, 1932–1940* (1963). The best single-volume study of FDR's policies during his first two terms as president.

Harvard Sitkoff, ed., *Fifty Years Later: The New Deal Evaluated* (1985). The New Deal analyzed in an excellent selection of essays.

John Steinbeck, *The Grapes of Wrath* (1939). The classic novel of Dust Bowl migrants; still makes gripping reading.

Additional Sources

Hard Times in Hooverville

Michael Bernstein, *The Great Depression* (1987).

Julia Kirk Blackwelder, *Women of the Depression: Caste and Culture in San Antonio* (1984).

William H. Chafe, *The American Woman, 1920–1970* (1972).

John Kenneth Galbraith, *The Great Crash: 1929* (1989).

John Garraty, *The Great Depression* (1986).

Robin D. G. Kelley, *Hammer and Hoe: Alabama Communists during the Great Depression* (1990).

Robert McElvaine, *The Great Depression: America, 1929–1941* (1984).

William Mullins, *The Depression and the Urban West Coast, 1929–1933* (1991).

Mark Reisler, *By the Sweat of Their Brow: Mexican Immigrant Labor in the United States* (1976).

Lois Scharf, *To Work and to Wed: Female Employment, Feminism, and the Great Depression* (1980).

John Shover, *Cornbelt Rebellion: The Farmers' Holiday Association* (1965).

Herbert Hoover and the Depression

David Burner, *Herbert Hoover: A Public Life* (1979).

Roger Daniels, *The Bonus March* (1971).

Martin L. Fausold, *The Presidency of Herbert C. Hoover* (1985).

David E. Hamilton, *From New Day to New Deal: American Farm Policy from Hoover to Roosevelt* (1991).

Donald Lisio, *The President and Protest* (1974).

Albert Romasco, *The Poverty of Abundance: Hoover, the Nation, the Depression* (1965).

Jordan A. Schwartz, *Interregnum of Despair* (1970).

Joan Hoff Wilson, *Herbert Hoover: Forgotten Progressive* (1975).

Launching the New Deal

Anthony J. Badger, *The New Deal: The Depression Years, 1933–1940* (1989).

Irving Bernstein, *Turbulent Years: A History of the American Worker, 1933–1941* (1970).

Edward C. Blackorby, *Prairie Rebel: William Lemke* (1963).

Alan Brinkley, *Voices of Protest: Huey Long, Father Coughlin, and the Great Depression* (1982).

David Conrad, *The Forgotten Farmers: The Story of the Sharecroppers in the New Deal* (1965).

Donald H. Grubbs, *Cry from the Cotton: The Southern Tenant Farmers Union and the New Deal* (1971).

Ellis Hawley, *The New Deal and the Problem of Monopoly* (1966).

William Leuchtenburg, *The FDR Years* (1995).

Leo P. Ribuffo, *The Old Christian Right: The Protestant Far Right from the Great Depression to the Cold War* (1983).

Albert Romasco, *The Politics of Recovery: Roosevelt's New Deal* (1983).

Theodore Saloutos, *The American Farmer and the New Deal* (1982).

Arthur M. Schlesinger, Jr., *The Coming of the New Deal* (1958).

T. Harry Williams, *Huey Long* (1969).

Consolidating the New Deal

John Allswang, *The New Deal and American Politics* (1978).

Kristi Andersen, *The Creation of a Democratic Majority* (1979).

Edward D. Berkowitz, *America's Welfare State* (1991).

Roger Biles, *A New Deal for the American People* (1991).

Gerald Gamm, *The Making of New Deal Democrats* (1989).

Colin Gordon, *New Deals: Business, Labor, and Politics in America* (1994).

Donald R. McCoy, *Landon of Kansas* (1966).

George McJimsey, *Harry Hopkins* (1987).

The New Deal and American Life

Jo Ann E. Argersinger, *Toward a New Deal in Baltimore: People and Government in the Great Depression* (1988).

Joseph L. Arnold, *The New Deal in the Suburbs* (1971).

John Barnard, *Walter Reuther and the Rise of the Auto Workers* (1983).

Roger Biles, *The South and the New Deal* (1994).

Lisabeth Cohen, *Making a New Deal: Industrial Workers in Chicago* (1990).

Elizabeth Faue, *Community of Suffering and Struggle: Women, Men, and the Labor Movement in Minneapolis* (1991).

Sidney Fine, *Sitdown: The General Motors Strike of 1936–1937* (1969).

Steven Fraser, *Labor Will Rule: Sidney Hillman and the Rise of American Labor* (1991).

James Gregory, *American Exodus: The Dust Bowl Migration and Okie Culture in California* (1989).

Laurence C. Kelly, *The Assault on Assimilation: John Collier and the Origins of Indian Policy Reform* (1983).

Nelson Lichtenstein, *The Most Dangerous Man in Detroit: Walter Reuther and the Fate of American Labor* (1995).

Richard Lowitt, *The New Deal and the West* (1984).

Bruce Nelson, *Workers on the Waterfront* (1988).

Harvard Sitkoff, *A New Deal for Blacks* (1978).

Douglas L. Smith, *The New Deal in the Urban South* (1988).

Catherine Stock, *Main Street in Crisis: The Great Depression and the Old Middle Class on the Northern Plains* (1992).

Graham Taylor, *The New Deal and American Indian Tribalism* (1980).

Susan Ware, *Beyond Suffrage: Women in the New Deal* (1981).

Susan Ware, *Holding Their Own: American Women in the 1930s* (1982).

Donald Worster, *Dust Bowl* (1979).

Donald Worster, *Rivers of Empire* (1985).

Robert Zieger, *The CIO, 1935–1955* (1995).

Robert Zieger, *John L. Lewis* (1988).

Ebbing of the New Deal

Alan Brinkley, *The End of Reform: New Deal Liberalism in Recession and War* (1995).

Melvyn Dubofsky, *The State and Labor in Modern America* (1994).

Mark Leff, *The Limits of Symbolic Reform: The New Deal and Taxation* (1984).

James T. Patterson, *Congressional Conservatism and the New Deal* (1967).

James T. Patterson, *The New Deal and the States* (1969).

Charles H. Trout, *Boston, the Great Depression, and the New Deal* (1977).

Where to Learn More

❖ **Center for New Deal Studies, Roosevelt University, Chicago, Illinois.** The center contains political memorabilia, photographs, papers, and taped interviews dealing with Franklin D. Roosevelt and the New Deal; it also sponsors an annual lecture series about the Roosevelt legacy.

❖ **Herbert Hoover National Historic Site, West Branch, Iowa.** This 186-acre site contains the birthplace cottage and grave of Herbert Hoover as well as his presidential library and museum, which contains a reconstruction of Hoover's White House office.

❖ **Labor Museum and Learning Center of Michigan, Flint, Michigan.** Exhibits trace the history of the labor movement, including the dramatic "Sit-Down Strike" of 1936–1937.

❖ **Franklin D. Roosevelt Home and Presidential Library, Hyde Park, New York.** The Roosevelt home, furnished with family heirlooms, and the spacious grounds, where FDR is buried, personalize the president and provide insights into his career. The nearby library has displays and exhibitions about Roosevelt's presidency, and the Eleanor Roosevelt Wing is dedicated to the career of ER.

❖ **Eleanor Roosevelt National Historic Site, Hyde Park, New York.** These two cottages, where Eleanor Roosevelt worked and, after 1945, lived, contain her furniture and memorabilia. Visitors can also watch a film biography of ER and tour the grounds of this retreat where she entertained personal friends and world leaders.

❖ **Civilian Conservation Corps Interpretive Center, Whidbey Island, Washington.** This stone and wood structure, built as a CCC project, now houses exhibits and artifacts illustrating the history of the CCC.

❖ **Bethune Museum and Archives National Historic Site, Washington, D.C.** This four-story townhouse was the home of Mary McLeod Bethune, a friend of Eleanor Roosevelt and the director of the New Deal's Division of Negro Affairs, and the headquarters of the National Council of Negro Women, which Bethune founded in 1935. Exhibits feature the contributions of black activist women and activities of the civil rights movement.

World War II, 1939–1945

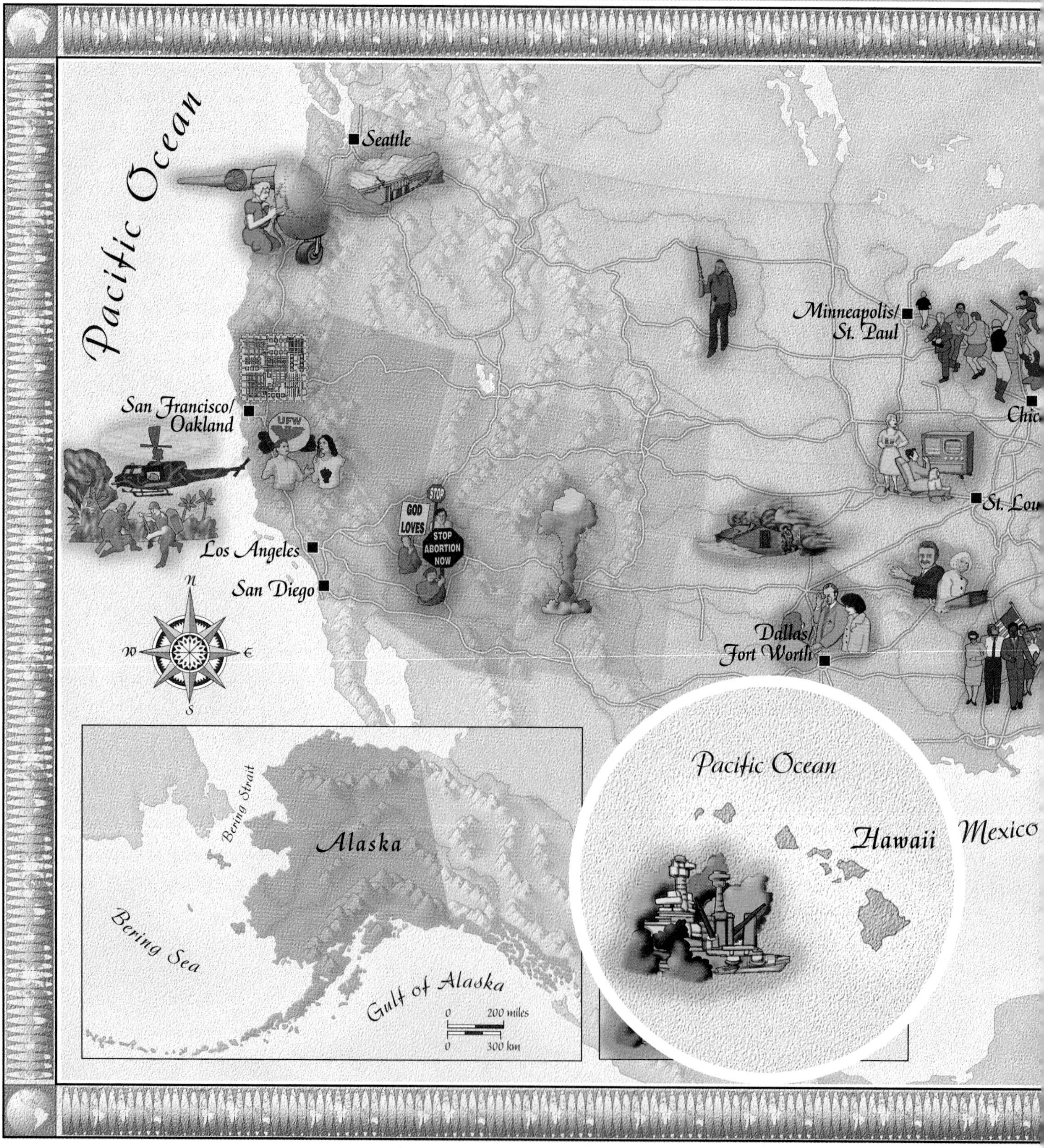

Pacific Ocean

Seattle

Minneapolis/ St. Paul

San Francisco/ Oakland

UFW

GOD LOVES

STOP

STOP ABORTION NOW

Los Angeles

San Diego

St. Lou

Chic

Dallas/ Fort Worth

N

W

E

S

Bering Strait

Alaska

Bering Sea

Gulf of Alaska

0 200 miles

0 300 km

Pacific Ocean

Hawaii

Mexico

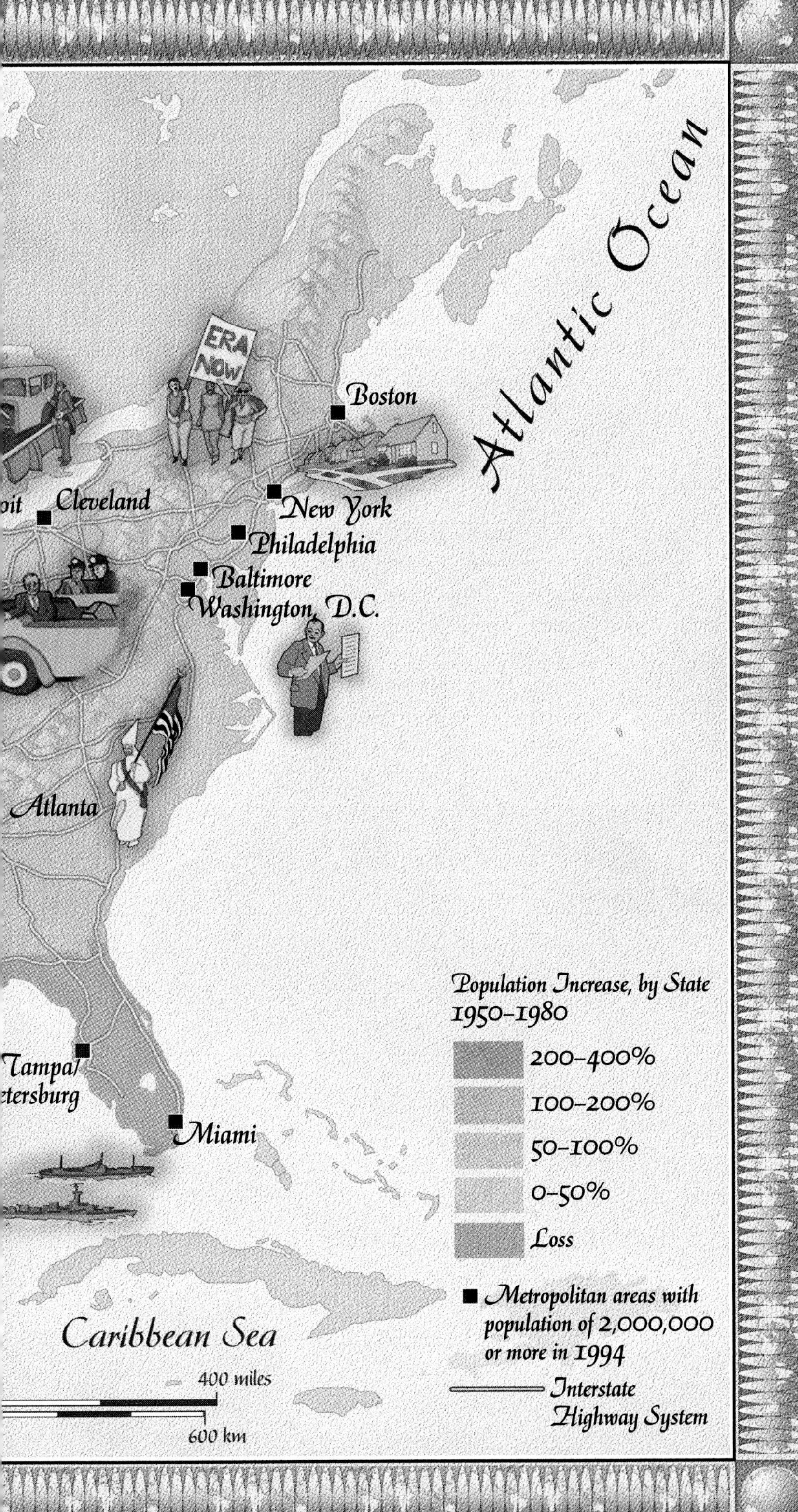

28

Chapter Outline

Key Topics

- The reluctance of most Americans to get involved in World War II
- FDR's effort to support Britain and pressure Japan despite isolationism
- The nation's strategy for a two-front war against Germany and Japan
- The social and economic transformation of the United States by the war
- The beginning of the Cold War and the emergence of the United States as the richest and most powerful nation in the world

Laura and Enrico Fermi arrived in the United States in 1939 as refugees from repression in **Fascist** Italy. In 1938, Enrico had earned a Nobel Prize in physics. By 1942, he was leading the efforts to develop an atomic bomb as the United States joined the ongoing global conflict of World War II. The next year found the Fermis, together with other atomic scientists and engineers and their families, at Los Alamos, a science city built hurriedly on a high plateau in northern New Mexico, where isolation was supposed to ensure secrecy.

The instant city was a cross between an army camp and a cheap subdivision. Big shots lived on "bathtub row," the few houses with full plumbing that were left over from a former boarding school. Most families lived in apartments awash in summer dust or winter mud. Scientists spent their days designing a bomb that would change world politics and returned to dinners cooked on wood-burning stoves. Despite the hardships, Laura Fermi and other residents remembered the sense of community. "I was in Los Alamos only a year and a half," she later wrote, "and still it seems such a big portion of my life . . . it was such intense living."

The Fermis were not the only family to give Los Alamos a multinational flavor. Britons and Canadians worked alongside U.S. scientists. So did Danes and Hungarians who had fled Nazi-dominated Europe. Workers from nearby Hispanic villages and Indian pueblos stoked the furnaces and swept the floors. Absent were scientists from the Soviet Union, which was bearing the worst of the fighting against Germany but was carefully excluded from the secret of the A-bomb.

The internationalism of Los Alamos mirrored the larger war effort. Japan's attack on Hawaii in December 1941 thrust the United States into a war that spanned the globe. U.S. allies against Japan in the Pacific and East Asia included Great Britain, Australia, and China. In Europe, its allies against Nazi Germany and Fascist Italy included Great Britain, the Soviet Union, and more than twenty other nations.

The men and women racing to perfect the atomic bomb knew that victory was far from certain. The **Axis Powers**—Germany, Italy, and Japan—had piled one conquest on another since the late 1930s, and they continued to seize new territories in 1942. Allied defeat in a few key battles could have resulted in standoff or Axis victory. Not until 1944 did American economic power allow the United States and its allies to feel confident of victory. A new weapon might end the war more quickly or make the difference between victory and defeat.

The war's domestic impacts were as profound as its international consequences. It highlighted racial inequalities, gave women new opportunities, and fostered growth in the South and West. By devastating the nation's commercial rivals, compelling workers to retrain and factories to modernize, World War II left the United States dominant in the world economy. It also increased the scope of the federal government and built an alliance among the armed forces, big business, and science that helped shape postwar America.

The Dilemmas of Neutrality

Americans in the 1930s wanted no part of another overseas war. According to a Gallup poll in 1937, 70 percent thought that the United States had made a mistake to fight in 1917. Despite two years of German victories and a decade of Japanese aggression against China, opinion polls in the fall of 1941 showed that most voters still hoped to avoid war. President Roosevelt's challenge was to lead the United States toward rearmament and support for Great Britain and China without alarming a reluctant public.

The Roots of War

The countdown to World War II started in 1931 when Japan invaded and soon conquered the northern Chinese province of Manchuria. Adding Manchuria to an empire that included Korea and Taiwan emboldened Japan's military. A full-scale invasion of China followed in 1937. Japan took many of the key cities and killed tens of thousands of civilians in the "rape of Nanking," but failed to dislodge the government of Jiang Jieshi (Chiang Kai-shek) and settled into a war of attrition.

Japan was determined to dominate Asia. Internal propaganda in the 1930s stressed the need to rebuild Japan's greatness. Japanese nationalists believed that the United States, Britain, and France after World War I had treated Japan unfairly, despite its participation against Germany. They believed that Japan should expel the French, British, Dutch, and Americans from Asia and create a **Greater East Asia Co-Prosperity Sphere** commanded by Japan.

In Germany, Adolf Hitler mixed the desire to reassert national pride and power after the defeat of World War I with an ideology of racial hatred. Coming to power by constitutional means in 1933 as the head of the **Nazi** party, Hitler quickly consolidated his grip as the German Führer, or absolute leader. Proclaiming the start of a thousand-year Reich (empire), he combined the historic German interest in eastward expansion with a long tradition of racialist thought about German superiority. In the Nazi scheme, Germany and other northern European nations ranked above the Slavs of eastern Europe. Special targets of Nazi hatred were Jews, who were prominent in German business and professional life but who soon faced persecution aimed at driving them from the country.

Germany's direct challenge to Europe began in 1936, when Hitler sent troops into the Rhineland, Germany's border region with France that had been demilitarized since 1918. The Reich absorbed German-speaking Austria in 1938. Hitler's next target was a German-speaking border district of Czechoslovakia known as the Sudetenland. As this crisis simmered in September 1938, French premier Edouard Daladier and British prime minister Neville Chamberlain flew to Munich to meet with Hitler. Chamberlain, claiming to have secured "peace in our time," agreed to German annexation of the Sudetenland in return for Hitler's pledge to make no more territorial claims. Hitler tossed aside this promise when Germany occupied the rest of Czechoslovakia six months later.

Italian aggression embroiled Africa and the Mediterranean. Benito Mussolini, Italy's leader since 1922, invaded and conquered Ethiopia in 1935–1936. To extend Italian influence in the Mediterranean, he sent arms and troops to General Francisco Franco's right-wing rebels when a civil war erupted in Spain in 1936. In the three years until Franco's victory, Spain became a bloody testing ground for new German military tactics and German and Italian ambitions against democratic Europe.

Germany and Italy formed the Rome–Berlin Axis in 1936 and the **Tripartite Pact** with Japan in 1940. Political dissidents in all three nations had already been suppressed. Mussolini boasted of burying the "putrid corpse of liberty." Politicians in Japan feared assassination if they spoke against the army, and the Thought Police intimidated the public. Hitler's Germany, however, was the most repressive. The Nazi **concentration camp** was a device for political terrorism where dissidents and "antisocials" could be separated from "pure" Germans. Hitler decreed that opponents should disappear into "night and fog." By 1939, concentration camps held 25,000 people—mostly socialists, homosexuals, and beggars—who were overworked, starved, and abused.

The raspy-voiced Adolf Hitler had a remarkable ability to stir the German people. He and his inner circle made skillful use of propaganda, exploiting German resentment over the country's defeat in World War I and, with carefully staged mass rallies such as this event in 1938, inspiring an emotional conviction of national greatness.

Chronology

1931	Japan invades Manchuria.
1933	Hitler takes power in Germany.
1934	Nye Committee opens hearings on international arms trade.
1935	Congress passes first of three Neutrality acts.
	Italy invades Ethiopia.
1936	Germany and Italy form the Rome–Berlin Axis.
	Civil war erupts in Spain.
1937	Japan invades China.
1938	Germany absorbs Austria.
	Munich agreement promises "peace in our time."
1939	Germany and the Soviet Union sign a nonaggression pact.
	Germany absorbs Czechoslovakia.
	Germany invades Poland; Great Britain and France declare war on Germany.
1940	Germany conquers Denmark, Norway, Belgium, the Netherlands, and France.
	Japan, Germany, and Italy sign the Tripartite Pact.
	The United States begins to draft men into the armed forces.
	Franklin Roosevelt wins an unprecedented third term.
1941	The United States begins a lend-lease program to make military equipment available to Great Britain and later the USSR.
	The Fair Employment Practices Committee is established.
	Germany invades the Soviet Union.
	Roosevelt and Churchill issue the Atlantic Charter.
	Japan attacks U.S. military bases in Hawaii.
1942	American forces in the Philippines surrender to Japan.
	President Roosevelt authorizes the removal and internment of Japanese Americans living in four western states.
	Naval battles in the Coral Sea and off the island of Midway blunt Japanese expansion.
	U.S. forces land in North Africa.
	Soviet forces encircle a German army at Stalingrad.
	The first sustained and controlled nuclear chain reaction takes place at the University of Chicago.
1943	U.S. and British forces invade Italy, which makes terms with the Allies.
	Race conflict erupts in riots in Detroit, New York, and Los Angeles.
	The landing of Marines on Tarawa initiates the island-hopping strategy.
	U.S. war production peaks.
	Roosevelt, Churchill, and Stalin confer at Tehran.
1944	Allied forces land in Normandy.
	The U.S. Navy destroys Japanese sea power in the battles of the Philippine Sea and Leyte Gulf.
	The Battle of the Bulge is the last tactical setback for the Allies.
1945	Roosevelt, Stalin, and Churchill meet at Yalta to plan the postwar world.
	The United States takes the Pacific islands of Iwo Jima and Okinawa.
	Franklin Roosevelt dies; Harry S Truman becomes president.
	Germany surrenders to the United States, Great Britain, and the USSR.
	The United Nations is organized at an international meeting in San Francisco.
	Japan surrenders after the detonation of atomic bombs over Hiroshima and Nagasaki.

Hitler's War in Europe

After annexing Austria and Czechoslovakia through diplomatic bullying and uncontested coups, Germany invaded Poland on September 1, 1939. Britain and France, Poland's allies, declared war on Germany but did nothing to stop the German war machine. Western journalists covering the three-week conquest of Poland coined the term ***Blitzkrieg***, or "lightning war," to describe the German tactics. Armored divisions with tanks and motorized infantry punched quick holes in defensive positions and raced forward thirty or forty miles per day. Dive bombers blasted defenses. Portable radios coordinated the tanks, trucks, and motorcycles. Ground forces with horse-drawn artillery and supply wagons encircled the stunned defenders.

Hitler's greatest advantage was the ability to attack when and where he chose. From September 1939 to October 1941, Germany marched from victory to victory (see Map 28-1). Striking from a central position against scattered enemies, Hitler chose the targets and timing of each new front: east to smash Poland in September 1939; north to capture Denmark and Norway in April and May 1940; west to defeat the Netherlands, Belgium, and France in May and June 1940, an attack that Italy also joined; south into the Balkans, enlisting Hungary, Romania, and Bulgaria as allies and conquering Yugoslavia and Greece in April and May 1941. He also launched the **Battle of Britain** in the second half of 1940, sending bombers in an unsuccessful effort to pound Britain into submission.

Hitler gambled once too often in June 1941. Having failed to knock Britain out of the war, he invaded the Soviet Union (officially the Union of Soviet Socialist Republics, or USSR). The attack caught the Red Army off guard. The Nazis and Soviets had signed a nonagression pact in 1939, and the USSR had helped dismember Poland. Soviet dictator

Map 28-1 Axis Europe, 1941, on the Eve of Hitler's Invasion of the Soviet Union
After almost two years of war, the Axis powers controlled most of Europe from the Atlantic Ocean to the Soviet border through annexation, military conquest, and alliances. Failure to force Britain to make peace caused Hitler to look eastward in 1941 to attempt the conquest of the Soviet Union.

Joseph Stalin thought his border was safe. But Hitler hoped that smashing the USSR and seizing its vast resources would make Germany invincible. From June until December 1941, more than 3 million Germans, Italians, and Romanians pushed through Belorus, Ukraine, and western Russia. They encircled and captured entire Soviet armies. Before desperate Soviet counterattacks and a bitter winter stopped the German tanks, they had reached the outskirts of Moscow and expected to finish the job in the spring.

Trying to Keep Out

"We Must Keep Out!" shouted the September 7, 1939, *Chicago Daily News*. As war erupted in Europe, most Americans wanted to avoid foreign quarrels. People who opposed intervention in the European conflict were sometimes called isolationists, but they considered themselves realists. Drawing their lessons from 1914–1918, they assumed that the same situation applied in 1939.

Much of the emotional appeal of neutrality came from disillusionment with the American crusade in World War I, which had failed to make the world safe for democracy. Many opponents of intervention wanted the United States to protect its traditional spheres of interest in Latin America and the Pacific. Charles A. Lindbergh and many others argued that the best way to assure the safety of the United States was to conserve resources to defend the Western Hemisphere. Like George Washington, whose Farewell Address they quoted, they wanted to avoid becoming entangled in the perpetual quarrels of the European nations.

Congressional hearings on munitions manufacturers and financiers had strengthened antiwar leanings in 1934–1936. Senator Gerald Nye's committee investigated whether New York bankers had dragged Americans into World War I to protect their loans to Britain and France. *Fortune* magazine and *Reader's Digest* published an exposé that blamed wars on arms manufacturers. *Merchants of Death* was a best-seller on the same theme. Neutrality acts in 1935, 1936, and 1937 forbade arms sales to nations at war. Other legislation prohibited loans to nations that had not paid their debts from World War I (including France and Great Britain).

The country's ethnic variety complicated U.S. responses to European conflict. Nazi aggression ravaged the homelands of Americans of Polish, Czech, Greek, and Norwegian ancestry. In contrast, 2.7 million Irish Americans, resentful of centuries of English rule over Ireland, applauded defeats that undermined Britain's empire. More than 5 million German Americans remembered the rabid anti-German sentiment of World War I and dreaded a second fight with Germany. Many of the 4.6 million Italian Americans admired Mussolini.

Edging toward Intervention

Despite the Nazi triumphs, nonintervention had direct emotional appeal. The case for supporting beleaguered Britain and China, in contrast, rested on abstract values like the worth of free societies and free markets. Still, Roosevelt's appeals to democratic values gained support in 1939 and 1940. Nazi persecution of minorities and Japanese atrocities in China struck most Americans as worse than British or French imperialism. Radio broadcasts from England describing London under German bombing heightened the sense of imperiled freedom. The importance of open markets also bolstered interventionism. As Roosevelt pointed out, "Freedom to trade is essential to our economic life. We do not eat all the food we produce; we do not burn all the oil we can pump; we do not use all the goods we can manufacture." U.S. business leaders had little doubt that Axis victories would bring economic instability and require crushing defense budgets to protect a Fortress America.

Because 85 percent of the American people agreed that the nation should fight only if directly attacked, Roosevelt had to chip away at neutrality. The first step came in October 1939. A month-long congressional debate inspired millions of letters and telegrams in favor of keeping the arms embargo against warring nations. Nevertheless, the lawmakers reluctantly allowed arms sales to belligerent nations on a "cash-and-carry" basis. In control of the Atlantic, France and Britain were the only expected customers.

Isolationism helps explain why the United States accepted only a few thousand Jewish refugees. American law strictly limited the numbers of Europeans who could enter the United States. Unthinking anti-Semitism at the State Department also contributed to tight enforcement of immigration quotas. Bureaucrats blocked entry to "undesirables," such as left-wing opponents of Hitler, and were unsympathetic to Jewish refugees. In 1939, officials turned the passenger ship *St. Louis* away from Miami and forced its 950 German Jewish refugees back to Europe. FDR made small gestures, such as allowing fifteen thousand German and Austrian refugees, including many scientists and artists, to remain in the United States on visitor permits, but polls showed that the public supported restricted immigration.

The collapse of France in June 1940 scared Americans into rearming. A year earlier, the United States army had ranked eighteenth in the world in size—on a par with Portugal's. However, the sudden defeat of France, which had survived four years of German attacks in World War I, made the new war seem far more serious. In the summer of 1940, Congress voted to expand the army to 2 million men, build 19,000 new war planes, and add 150 ships to the navy. September brought the nation's first peacetime draft, requiring 16.5 million men between the ages of twenty-one and thirty-five to register for military service.

In the same month, the United States concluded a "destroyer deal" with Britain. The British were desperate for small, maneuverable warships to guard imports of food and war materials against German submarines. The Americans had long wanted additional air and naval bases. Roosevelt met both needs by trading fifty old destroyers for the use of bases on British territories in the Caribbean, Bermuda, and Newfoundland.

In the presidential election of 1940, however, foreign policy was secondary. Wendell Willkie, the Republican nominee, was a successful lawyer and utility executive who had fought the New Deal. He shared Roosevelt's belief in the importance of aid to Britain. The big campaign issue was therefore whether FDR's unprecedented try for a third term represented arrogance or legitimate concern for continuity in a time of peril. The voters gave Roosevelt 55 percent of their votes. The president pledged that no Americans would fight in a foreign war. But if the United States were attacked, he said privately, the war would no longer be "foreign."

The Brink of War

After the election, FDR and his advisers edged the United States toward stronger support of Britain and put pressure on Japan. In January 1941, Roosevelt proposed the "lend-lease" program, which allowed Britain to "borrow" military equipment for the duration of the war. Roosevelt compared the program to lending a garden hose to a neighbor whose house had caught fire. Senator Robert Taft of Ohio countered that it was more like lending chewing gum—you wouldn't want it back after it was used. Behind the scheme was Britain's inability to pay for American goods. "Well boys," their ambassador explained to a group of reporters, "Britain's broke."

The lend-lease proposal triggered intense political debate. The Committee to Defend America by Aiding the Allies argued the administration's position. In opposition, the **America First Committee** claimed that lend-lease would allow the president to declare anything a "defense article." Charles Lindbergh protested that the United States should not surrender weapons that it might need to defend itself. Congress finally passed the measure in March 1941, giving Great Britain an unlimited line of credit.

FDR soon began an undeclared war in the North Atlantic, instructing the navy to report sightings of German submarines to the British. In September, the U.S. destroyer *Greer* clashed with a German submarine. The encounter allowed Roosevelt to proclaim a "shoot on sight" policy for German subs and to escort British convoys to within 400 miles of Britain. In reply, German submarines torpedoed and damaged the destroyer *Kearny* on October 17 and sank the destroyer *Reuben James* with the loss of more than one hundred lives on October 30. The United States was approaching outright naval war with Germany.

The **Atlantic Charter** of August 1941 provided a political umbrella for American involvement. Meeting off Newfoundland, Roosevelt and British prime minister Winston Churchill agreed that the first priority was to defeat Germany; Japan was secondary. Echoing Woodrow Wilson, Roosevelt also insisted on a commitment to oppose territorial change by conquest, to support self-government, to promote freedom of the seas, and to create a system of economic collaboration. Churchill signed to keep Roosevelt happy, but the document papered over sharp differences in U.S. and British expectations.

Roosevelt's intent in the North Atlantic remains uncertain. Some historians think that he hoped the United States could support Britain short of war. Others believe that he accepted the inevitability of war but hesitated to outpace public opinion (the House of Representatives renewed the draft in August 1941 by just one vote). In this second interpretation, FDR wanted to eliminate Hitler without going to war if possible, with war if necessary. "I am waiting to be pushed into the situation," he told his secretary of the treasury.

That final shove came in the Pacific rather than the Atlantic. In 1940, as part of its rearmament program, the United States decided to build a "two-ocean navy." This decision antagonized Japan, prodding it into a war that most U.S. leaders hoped to postpone or avoid. Through massive investment and national sacrifice, Japan had achieved roughly 70 percent of U.S. naval strength by late 1941. However, America's buildup promised to reduce that ratio to only 30 percent by 1944. Furthermore, the United States was restricting Japan's vital imports of steel, iron ore, and aluminum. In July 1941, after Japan occupied French Indochina, Roosevelt froze Japanese assets in the United States, blocked petroleum shipments, and began to build up U.S. forces in the Philippines. The actions caused Japan's rulers to consider war against the United States while Japan still had a petroleum reserve. Both militarily and economically, it looked in Tokyo as if 1942 was their last chance for victory.

The Japanese military made its choice in September. Unless the United States and Britain ended aid to China and acquiesced in Japanese dominance of southeast Asia—impossible conditions—war preparations would be complete in October. The Japanese General Staff defined its aims as "expelling American, Dutch, and British influences from East Asia, consolidating Japan's sphere of autonomy and security, and constructing a new order in greater East Asia." War planners never seriously considered an invasion of the United States or expected a decisive victory. They hoped that attacks on American Pacific bases would shock the United States into letting Japan have its way in Asia or at least win time to create impenetrable defenses in the central Pacific.

December 7, 1941

Since 1941, Americans have questioned Roosevelt's foreign policy. If he wanted an excuse for war, was the torpedoing of the *Reuben James* not enough? If

The Japanese attack on Pearl Harbor shocked the American people. Images of burning battleships confirmed the popular image of Japan as sneaky and treacherous and stirred a desire for revenge. The attack rendered the United States incapable of resisting Japanese aggression in southeast Asia in early 1942, but it failed to achieve its goal of destroying U.S. naval power in the Pacific.

he wanted to preserve armed neutrality, why threaten Japan by moving the Pacific fleet from California to Hawaii in 1940 and sending B-17 bombers to the Philippines in 1941? It now seems that Roosevelt wanted to restrain the Japanese with bluff and intimidation so that the United States could focus on Germany. FDR also recognized the possibility of a two-front war—at least a 20 percent chance, he told military advisers in January 1941. American moves were intended to be aggressive but measured in the Atlantic, firm but defensive in the Pacific. After July, however, Washington expected a confrontation with Japan over the oil and rubber of Southeast Asia. Because the United States cracked Japanese codes, it knew by November that Japanese military action was imminent but expected the blow to come in southeast Asia.

Instead, the Japanese navy launched a surprise attack on American bases in Hawaii. The Japanese fleet sailed a four-thousand-mile loop through the empty North Pacific, avoiding merchant shipping and American patrols. Before dawn on December 7, six Japanese aircraft carriers launched 351 planes in two unopposed bombing strikes on **Pearl Harbor**.

When the smoke cleared, Americans counted their losses: eight battleships, eleven other warships, and nearly all military aircraft damaged or destroyed; and 2403 people killed. They could also count their good fortune. Dockyards, drydocks, and oil storage tanks remained intact because the Japanese admiral had refused to order a third attack. And the American carriers, at sea on patrol, were unharmed. They proved far more important than battleships.

Speaking to Congress the following day, Roosevelt proclaimed December 7, 1941, "a date which will live in infamy." He asked for—and got—a declaration of war against the Japanese. Hitler and Mussolini declared war on the United States on December 11. On January 1, 1942, the United States, Britain, the USSR, and twenty-three other nations subscribed to the principles of the Atlantic Charter and pledged not to negotiate a separate peace.

Holding the Line

When Japan was considering war with the United States and Great Britain in 1940, Admiral Isoroku Yamamoto, the chief of Japan's Combined Fleet, weighed the chances of victory: "If I am told to fight regardless of the consequences, I shall run wild for the first six months or a year, but I have utterly no confidence for the second or third year." The admiral was right. Japan's armies quickly conquered most of southeast Asia; its navy forced the United States on the defensive in the central Pacific. As it turned out, Japan's conquests reached their limit after six months, but, in early 1942, it was far from clear that that would be so. In Europe, Allied fortunes went from bad to worse in the first half of 1942. Again, no one knew that German and Italian gains would peak at midyear. Decisive turning points did not come until November 1942, a year after the United States had entered the war.

Stopping Germany

In December 1941, the United States plunged into a truly global war that was being fought on six distinct fronts (see Map 28-2). In North Africa, the British battled Italian and German armies that were trying to seize the Suez Canal. On the **Eastern Front**, Soviet armies held defensive positions. In the North Atlantic, merchant ships dodged German submarines. In China, Japan controlled the most productive provinces but could not crush Chinese resistance, which was supported by supplies airlifted from British India. In Southeast Asia, Japanese troops attacked the Philippines, the Dutch East Indies, New Guinea, Malaya, and Burma. In the central Pacific, the Japanese fleet faced the U.S. Navy.

Despite the popular desire for revenge against Japan, the United States decided to defeat Germany first. The reasoning was simple: Germany was far stronger than Japan. Defeat of Japan would not assure the defeat of Germany, especially if it crushed the Soviet Union or starved Britain into submission. In contrast, a strategy that helped the Soviets and British survive and then destroyed German military power would doom Japan.

The strategy recognized that the Eastern Front held the key to Allied hopes. In 1941, Germany had seized control of 45 percent of the Soviet population, 47 percent of its grain production, and more than 60 percent of its coal, steel, and aluminum industries. Hitler next sought to destroy Soviet capacity to wage war. "Our aim," said Führer Directive No. 41, "is to wipe out the entire defense potential remaining to the Soviets, and to cut them off . . . from their most important centers of war industry." Hitler targeted southern Russia, an area rich in grain and oil. The German thrust was also designed to eliminate the British from the Middle East.

The scheme was easier to plot on a map than to carry out in the fields of Russia. The German offensive opened with stunning success. Every day's advance, however, stretched supply lines. Tanks ran out of fuel and spare parts. The horses that pulled German supply wagons died for lack of food.

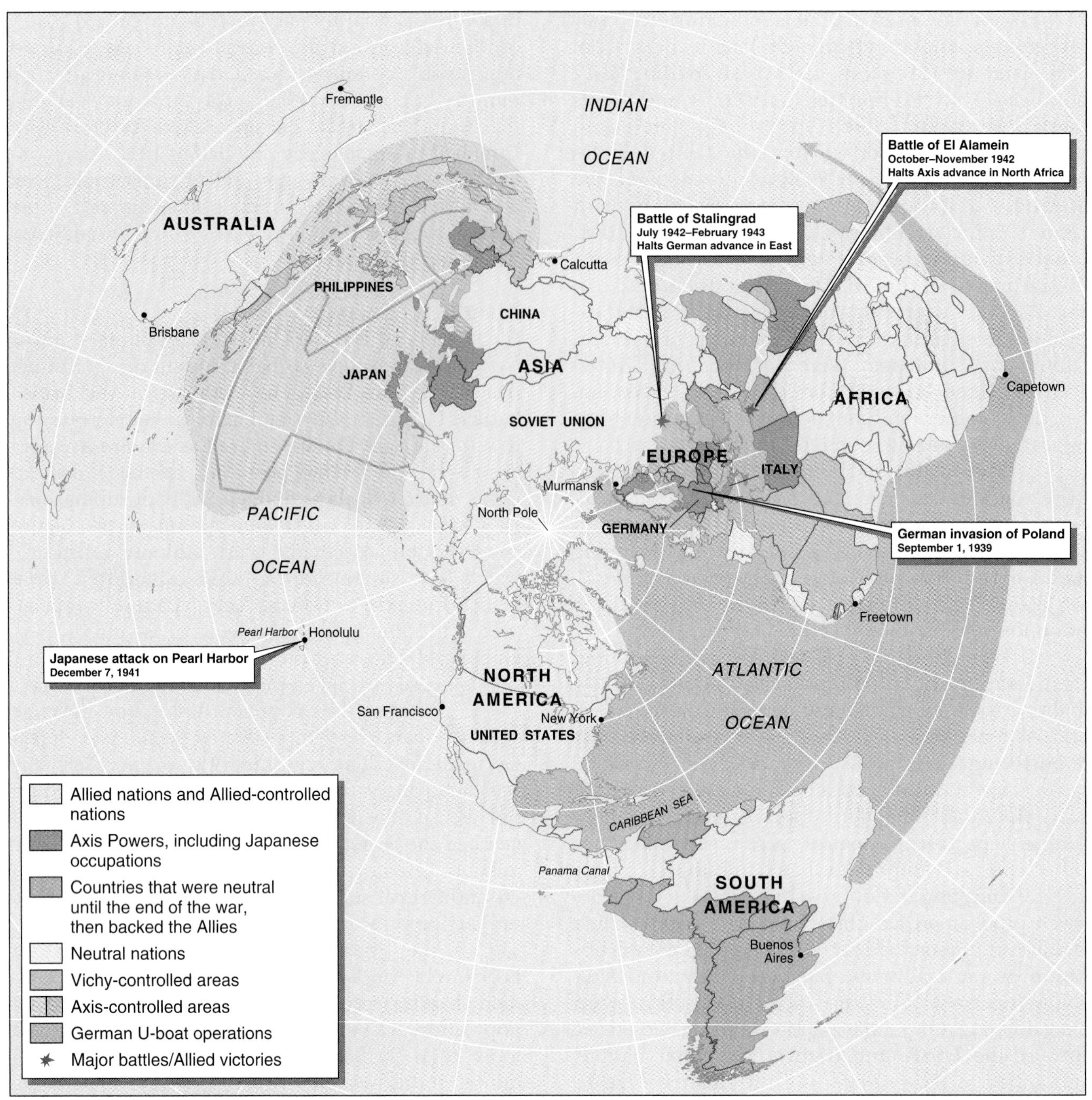

Map 28-2 A Global War
World War II was truly a global war. As this map indicates, fighting engulfed both sides of the Eurasian continent and spread deep into the Atlantic, Pacific, and Indian oceans. The United States was the only major belligerent nation that was insulated from the battle fronts by two oceans.

Disaster came at **Stalingrad** (present-day Volgograd), an industrial center on the western bank of the Volga River. The German armies had bypassed it, leaving a dangerous strongpoint on their flank that the German command decided to capture. In September and October, 1942, German, Italian, and Romanian soldiers fought their way house by house into the city. At night, the Soviets ferried their wounded across the Volga and brought in new ammunition. For both Hitler and Stalin, the city became a test of wills that outweighed even its substantial military importance.

The Red Army delivered a counterstroke on November 18 that cut off 330,000 Axis soldiers. Airlifts kept the Germans fighting for two more months, but they surrendered in February 1943. It was the first German mass capitulation, and it came at an immense human cost to both sides. Russians call the hills around Stalingrad "white fields" because human bones still turn up after spring thaws.

The Survival of Britain

After the failure of German air attacks in 1940, the British struggled to save their empire and supply themselves with food and raw materials. In World War I, German submarines (known as U-boats, from *Unterseeboot*) had nearly isolated Great Britain. In 1940 and 1941, they tried again. From bases in France, greatly improved U-boats intercepted shipments of oil from Nigeria, beef from Argentina, minerals from Brazil, and weapons from the United States. Through the end of 1941, German "tonnage warfare" sank British, Allied, and neutral merchant vessels faster than they could be replaced.

The British fought back in what became known as the **Battle of the Atlantic**. First, they reduced their reliance on the Atlantic supply lines. Between 1939 and 1944, planning and rationing cut Britain's need for imports in half. Second, the British organized protected convoys. Merchant ships sailing alone were defenseless against submarines. Grouping the merchant ships into convoys with armed escorts "hardened" the targets and made them more difficult to find in the wide ocean. Roosevelt's destroyer deal of 1940 and U.S. naval escorts in the western Atlantic in 1941 thus contributed directly to Britain's survival.

Nevertheless, German submarines dominated the Atlantic in 1942. U-boats operated as far as the Caribbean and the Carolinas, where the dangerous Cape Hatteras forced coastal shipping out to sea. In June, U-boats sank 144 ships; drowned sailors washed up on Carolina beaches. Only the extension of the convoy system to American waters forced the subs back toward Britain. Meanwhile, allied aircraft began to track submarines with radar, spot them with searchlights as they maneuvered on the surface, and attack them with depth charges. New sonar systems allowed escort ships to measure submarines' direction, speed, and depth. By the spring of 1943, American shipyards were also launching ships faster than the Germans could sink them.

British ground fighting in 1942 centered in North Africa, where the British operated out of Egypt and the Italians and Germans from the Italian colony of Libya. By October 1942, Field Marshal Erwin Rommel's German and Italian forces were within striking distance of the Suez Canal. At **El Alamein** between October 23 and November 5, 1942, however, General Bernard Montgomery, with twice Rommel's manpower and tanks, forced the enemy to retreat and lifted the danger to the Middle East.

Retreat and Stabilization in the Pacific

Reports from east Asia in the winter of 1942 were appalling. Striking the Philippines a few hours after Hawaii, the Japanese gained another tactical surprise (see Map 28-3). They destroyed most American air power on the ground and isolated U.S. forces. Between February 27 and March 1, Japan brushed aside a combined American, British, Dutch, and Australian fleet in the Battle of the Java Sea. Earlier in February, a numerically inferior Japanese force had seized Singapore, until then considered an anchor of Allied strength.

Spring brought no better news. Japan pushed the British out of Burma. In a three-month siege, they overwhelmed Filipino and U.S. defensive positions on the Bataan peninsula outside Manila. On May 6, the last American bastion, the island fortress of Corregidor in Manila Bay, surrendered.

The first check to Japanese expansion came on May 7–8, 1942, in the **Battle of the Coral Sea**, where U.S. aircraft carriers halted a Japanese advance toward Australia. In June, the Japanese struck at the island of Midway, fifteen hundred miles northwest of Honolulu. Their goal was to destroy American carrier forces. The plan included a diversionary invasion of the Aleutian Islands (the westernmost parts of Alaska) and a main assault on Midway to draw the Americans into battle on Japanese terms. Having cracked Japanese radio codes, U.S. forces were aware of the plan and refused the bait. On the morning of June 4, the Japanese and American carrier fleets faced off across 175 miles of ocean, each sending planes to search the other out. U.S. Navy dive bombers found the Japanese fleet and sank or crippled three aircraft carriers in five minutes; another Japanese carrier sank later in the day. The Battle of Midway ended Japanese efforts to expand in the Pacific.

Mobilizing the Home Front

News of the Japanese attack on Pearl Harbor shattered a bright Sunday afternoon. Twelve-year-old Jean Bartlett's family was headed to the movies when news of the attack came over the car radio. Elliott Johnson was eating in a Chinese restaurant in Portland, Oregon, when the proprietor burst from the kitchen with a portable radio; the line was two blocks long by the time he got to the marine recruiting office. In Cincinnati, the enormously popular Andrews Sisters found that no one had shown up for their Sunday matinee concert. "Where is Pearl Harbor?" Maxine Andrews asked the theater's doorman.

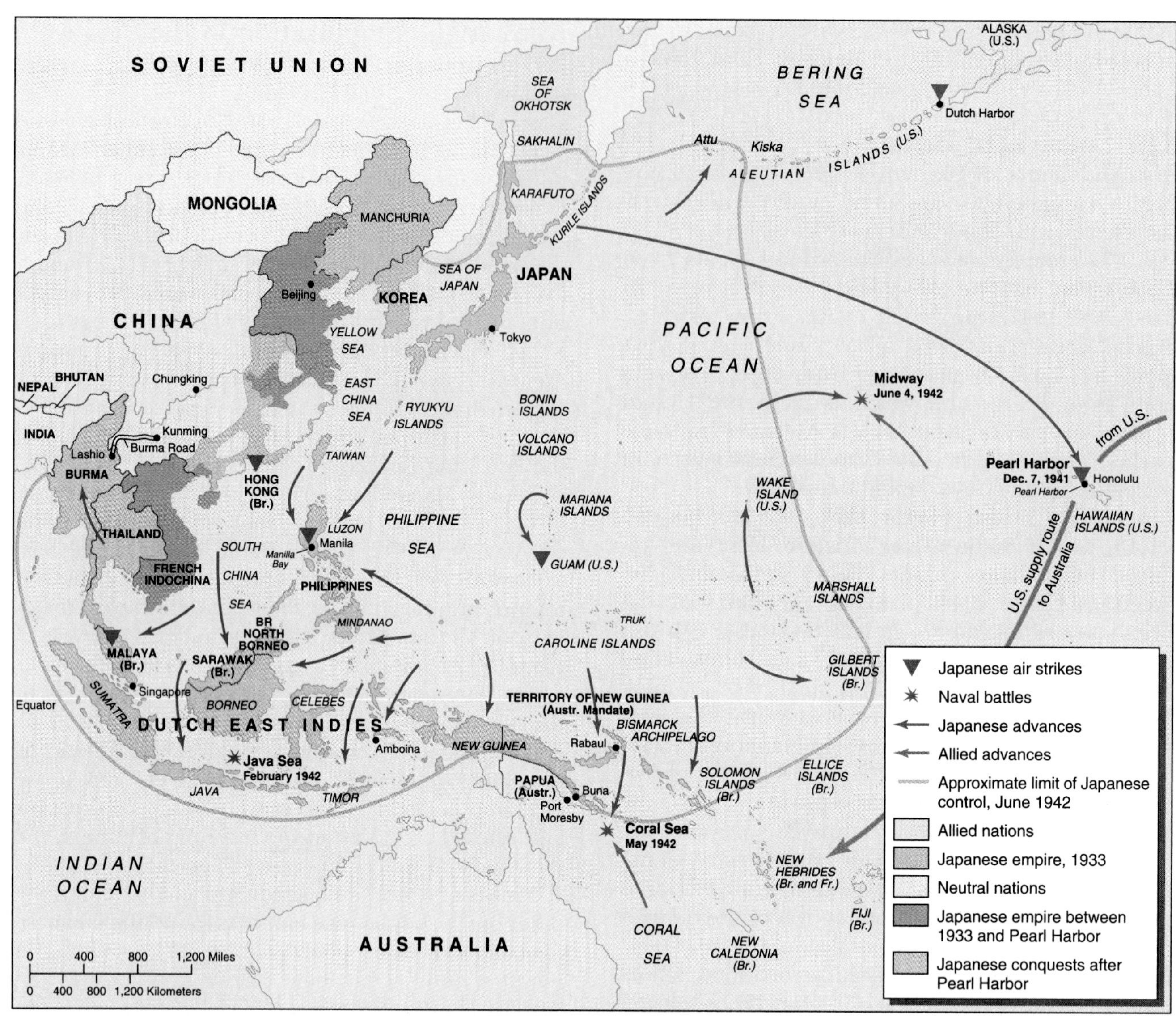

Map 28-3 World War II in the Pacific, from Pearl Harbor to Midway
The first six months after the Japanese attack on Pearl Harbor brought a string of Japanese victories and conquests in the Pacific, the islands southeast of Asia, and the British colonies of Malaya and Burma. Japan's advance was halted by a standoff battle in the Coral Sea, a decisive U.S. naval victory at Midway, and the length and vulnerability of Japanese supply lines to its most distant conquests.

War changed the lives of most Americans for the next four years—and for some forever. Some 350,000 woman and more than 16 million men served in the armed forces; 292,000 died in battle, 100,000 survived prisoner-of-war camps, and 671,000 returned wounded. More worked in defense industries. Youngsters saved tin foil, collected scrap metal, and followed the freedom-fighting stories of Wonder Woman in the comics. College science students might be recruited to work at scientific espionage against the Nazis. The breadth of involvement in the war effort gave Americans a common purpose that softened the divisions of region, class, and national origin while calling attention to continuing inequalities of race.

Warriors and Families

World War II required a thirtyfold expansion of the U.S. armed forces. By 1945, 8.3 million men and women were on active duty in the army and army air forces and 3.4 million in the navy and Marine Corps, totals exceeded only by the Soviet Union. The military establishment was four times larger than in World War I. Once in the military, sailors and GIs served an average of thirty-three months.

Many Americans put their lives on fast forward, as Judy Garland and Robert Walker did in the movie *The Clock* (1944). They played young people who meet in New York, fall in love, and are separated by the war in a matter of days. In real life, men and women often decided to beat the clock with instant matrimony. Couples who had postponed marriage because of the depression could afford to marry as the economy picked up. War intensified casual romances and heightened the appeal of marriage as an anchor in troubled times. Jewelers worried about running out of wedding rings. Altogether the war years brought 1.2 million "extra" marriages compared to the rate in 1920–1939.

The war's impact on families was gradual. The draft started with single men, then called up married men without children, and finally tapped fathers in 1943. Left at home were millions of "service wives," whose compensation from the government was $50 per month. Women who followed their husbands to stateside military posts and war factories often met cold welcomes from local residents. Harriet Arnow crafted a sensitive exploration of isolation from friends and family in her novel *The Dollmaker*, about a Kentucky farm woman who accompanied her husband to a Detroit war plant.

The war had mixed effects on children. Middle-class kids whose parents stayed home could treat it as an interminable scout project with salvage drives and campaigns to sell war bonds. Children in the rural Midwest picked milkweed pods to stuff life jackets; in coastal communities, they participated in blackout drills. Seattle high schools set aside one class period a day for the High School Victory Corps, training boys as messengers for air raid wardens while girls knitted sweaters and learned first aid. Between the end of school and suppertime, children listened as Captain Midnight, Jack Armstrong, and Hop Harrigan ("America's ace of the airways") fought the Nazis and Japanese on the radio.

The federal government tried to keep civilians of all ages committed to the war. It encouraged scrap drives and backyard victory gardens. The government also managed news about the fighting. Censors screened soldiers' letters. Early in the war, they blocked publication of most photographs of war casualties, although magazines such as *Life* were full of strong and haunting images. Worried about flagging commitment, censors later authorized photographs of enemy atrocities to incite the public.

Government officials had a harder time controlling Hollywood. The Office of War Information wanted propaganda in feature films, but not so heavy-handed that it drove viewers from theaters. Officials told movie directors to tone down car chases because screeching tires implied wasted rubber. War films revealed the nation's racial attitudes, often drawing distinctions between "good" and "bad" Germans but uniformly portraying Japanese as subhuman and repulsive. The most successful films dramatized the courage of the Allies. *Mrs. Miniver* (1942) showed the British transcending class differences in their battle with the Nazis. *So Proudly We Hail* (1943) celebrated the heroism of navy nurses in the Pacific theater.

Industry Gears Up

Industry had reluctantly begun to convert from consumer goods to defense production in 1940 and 1941. Although corporations hated to give up the market for toasters and automobiles just as Americans had more money, the last passenger car for the duration of the war rolled off the assembly line in February 1942. Existing factories retooled to make war equipment, and huge new facilities turned out thousands of planes and ships. Baltimore, Atlanta, Fort Worth, Los Angeles, and Seattle became centers for aircraft production. New Orleans, Portland, and the San Francisco Bay area were shipbuilding centers. Henry J. Kaiser, who had helped build vast projects like the Grand Coulee Dam, turned out cargo ships by the thousands. One of the Kaiser shipyards built a Liberty ship (a standard-model cargo carrier) in ten and a half days.

The results of war production were staggering (see Figure 28-1). One historian estimates that 40 percent of the world's military production was coming from the United States by 1944. Equally impressive is the 30 percent increase in the productivity of U.S. workers between 1939 and 1945. Surging farm income pulled agriculture out of its long slump. The rich certainly got richer, but overall per capita income doubled, and the poorest quarter of Americans made up some of the ground lost during the Great Depression.

Behind the scenes were new federal agencies. The War Manpower Commission allocated workers among vital industries and the military. The War Production Board invested $17 billion for new factories and managed $181 billion in war supply contracts. The Office of Price Administration (OPA) fought inflation with price controls and rationing that began with tires, sugar, and coffee and eventually included meat, butter, gasoline, and shoes. "Use it up, wear it out, make it do or do without" was the OPA's slogan. Consumers used ration cards and ration stamps to obtain scarce products. By slowing price increases, the OPA helped convince Americans to buy the war bonds that financed half the war spending. Americans also felt the bite of the first payroll deductions for income taxes as the government secured a steady of flow of revenues and soaked up some of the high wages that would have pushed inflation.

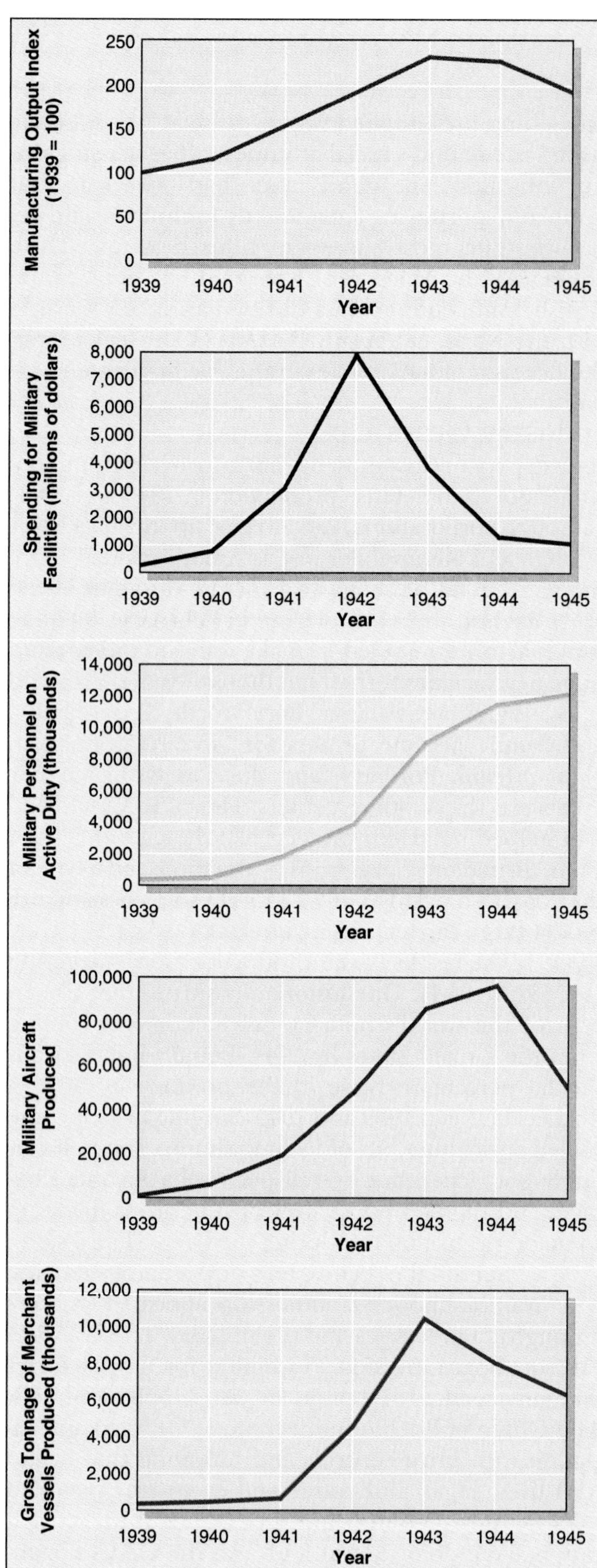

Figure 28-1 Making War: The United States Mobilizes, 1939–45
The U.S. economic mobilization for World War II reached its peak in 1943, the year in which the Allies prepared for the offensives against Germany and Japan that they hoped would end the war. The number of men and women in uniform continued to grow until 1945.

The Enlistment of Science

The war reached into scientific laboratories as well as shops and factories. "There wasn't a physicist able to breathe who wasn't doing war work," remembered Professor Philip Morrison. At the center of the scientific enterprise was Vannevar Bush, former dean at the Massachusetts Institute of Technology. As head of the newly established Office of Scientific Research and Development, Bush guided spending to develop new drugs, blood transfusion procedures, weapons systems, radar, sonar, and dozens of other military technologies. The scale of research and development dwarfed previous scientific work and set the pattern of massive federal support for science that continued after the war.

The biggest scientific effort was the drive to produce an atomic bomb. As early as 1939, Albert Einstein had written FDR about the possibility of such a weapon and the danger of falling behind the Germans. In late 1941, Roosevelt established what became known as the **Manhattan Project**. The work remained theoretical, however, until December 2, 1942, when scientists manipulated graphite rods inserted in a stack of uranium ingots until they were certain they could trigger and control a self-sustaining nuclear reaction. Because Enrico Fermi was in charge of the experiment, the coded message of scientific discovery recalled the voyages of Columbus—"The Italian navigator has landed in the new world."

The Manhattan Project moved from theory to practice in 1943. Physicist J. Robert Oppenheimer directed the young scientists at Los Alamos in designing a nuclear fission bomb. Engineers in other new science cities tried two approaches to producing the fissionable material. Richland, Washington, burgeoned into a sprawling metropolis that supported the creation of plutonium at the Hanford Engineer Works. Oak Ridge, Tennessee, near Knoxville, was built around gaseous diffusion plants that separated rare and vital uranium-235 from the more common uranium-238.

The Manhattan Project ushered in the age of atomic energy. Plutonium from Hanford fueled the first bomb tested at the Trinity site, 100 miles from Alamogordo, New Mexico, on July 16, 1945. The explosion astonished even the physicists; Oppenheimer quoted from Hindu scriptures as he tried to comprehend the results: "Now I am become death, destroyer of worlds."

Boom Times

The Manhattan Project was part of a regional tilt in the national economy; in effect, the war marked the takeoff of what Americans would later call the **Sunbelt** (see Map 28-4). Although most defense contracts went to established industrial states such as Michigan, New York, and Ohio, the relative impact was greatest in the South and West. Albuquerque, New Mexico, more than doubled in population during the 1940s. Wartime booms accelerated the growth of larger metropolitan areas like San Diego (up 92 percent in the decade), Phoenix (up 78 percent), Mobile (up 68 percent), and Dallas (up 54 percent).

War boom cities bustled with activity and hummed with tension. Factories operated three shifts, movies ran around the clock, and workers filled the streets after midnight. Most of the new industrial workers in 1941 and 1942 were unattached males—young men waiting for their draft call and older men separated from their families. They elbowed long-term residents in stores, snatched seats on the streetcars, and filled restaurants and theaters. Military and defense officials worried about sexually transmitted diseases and pressured cities to shut down their vice districts.

The hordes of war workers found housing scarce. Workers in Seattle's shipyards and Boeing plants scrounged for living space in offices, tents, chicken coops, and rooming houses where "hot beds" rented in shifts. When the Ford Motor Company began to build B-24 bombers at its new Willow Run plant in Michigan, the first of 42,000 workers made do with barns, garages, rented rooms, and trailers parked in thick mud. The situation was similar in small towns such as Seneca, Illinois, home to a company that normally made river barges. Between June 1942 and June 1945, it also built 157 LSTs—specialized ships to land tanks in amphibious assaults. Thousands of new workers flocked to Seneca. They lined up three deep at the bars with their Friday paychecks. Main Street clogged with cars and trucks. Residents would sometimes find a stranger rolled up in a blanket on their front porch.

Women in the War Effort

As draft calls took men off the assembly line, women changed the composition of the industrial work force. The war gave them new job opportunities that were embodied in the image of Rosie the Riveter. Women made up one-quarter of West Coast shipyard workers at the peak of employment and nearly half of Dallas

Map 28-4 States with Population Growth of 10 Percent or More, 1940–1943
The conversion of U.S. industry to defense production and the headlong expansion of the armed forces pulled Americans to coastal states and cities and to the South, where mild climate allowed year-round military training.

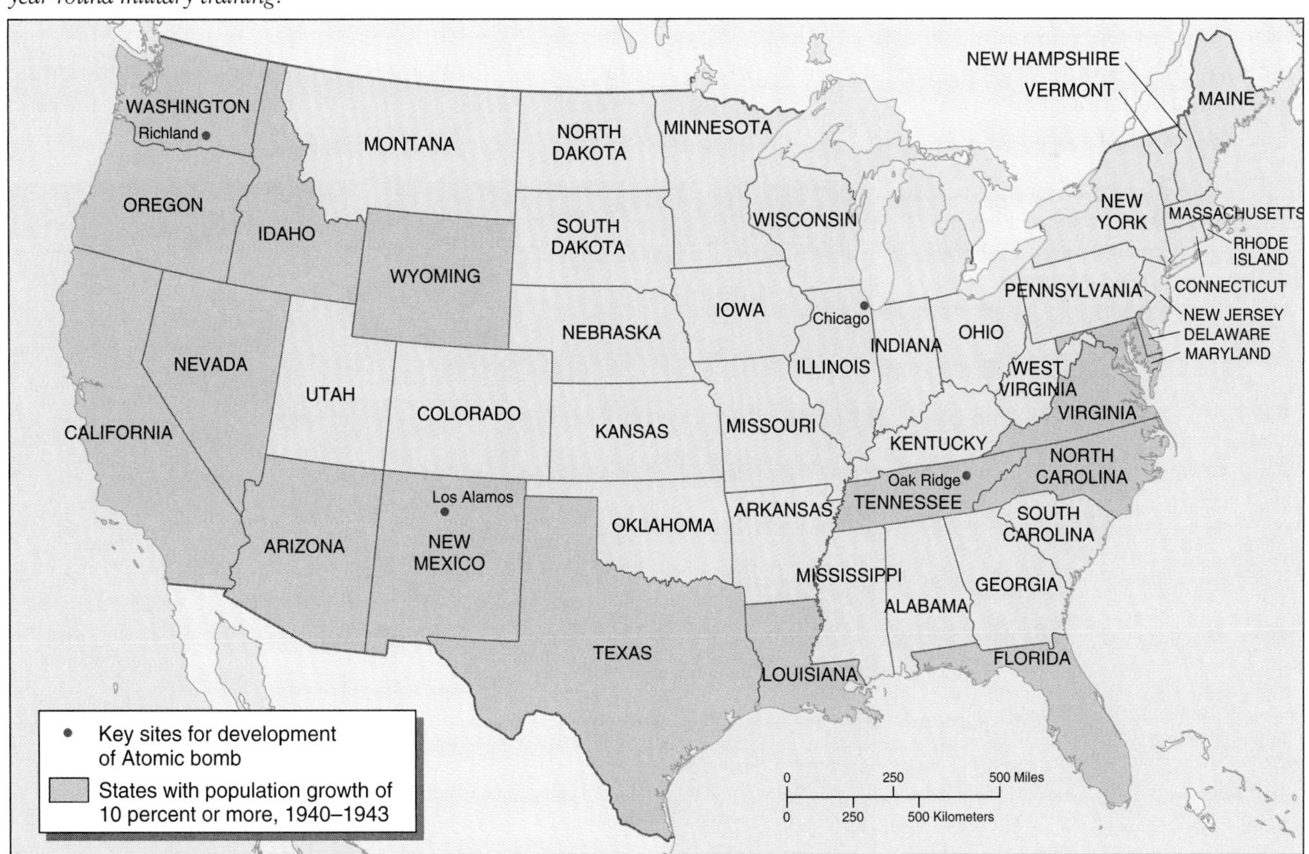

Members of Women Fliers of America examine an aircraft engine. The organization had been asked by the U.S. Army to identify women with more than 200 flying hours who might ferry planes, freeing military aviators for other duties.

and Seattle aircraft workers. Most women in the shipyards were clerks and general helpers. The acute shortage of welders and other skilled workers, however, opened thousands of journeyman positions to them as well—work that was far more lucrative than waiting tables or sewing in a clothing factory. Aircraft companies, which compounded labor shortages by stubborn "whites only" hiring, developed new power tools and production techniques to accommodate the smaller average size of women workers, increasing efficiency for everyone along the production line.

By July 1944, fully 19 million women held paid jobs, up 6 million in four years. Women's share of government jobs increased from 19 to 38 percent and their share of manufacturing jobs from 22 to 33 percent. Mirroring the sequence in which the military draft took men, employers recruited single women before turning to married women in 1943

In 1942, the federal government removed Japanese Americans from parts of four western states and interned them in isolated camps scattered through the West.

and 1944. Some women worked out of patriotism. Many others, however, needed to support their families. As one of the workers recalled of herself and a friend, "We both had to work, we both had children, so we became welders, and if I might say so, damn good ones" (see "American Views: A Woman Shipyard Worker Recalls Her Experience").

Americans did not know how to respond to the growing numbers of working women. The country needed their labor, but many worried that their employment would undermine families. The federal government assisted female entry into the labor force by funding day care programs that served 600,000 children. Employment recruitment posters showed strong, handsome women with rolled-up sleeves and wrenches in hand, but *Life* magazine reassured readers that women in factories could retain their sex appeal. Men and women commonly assumed that women would want to return to the home after victory; they were to work when the nation needed them and quit when the need was past.

The nation had the same mixed reaction to the women who joined the armed forces as army and navy nurses and as members of the WACS (Women's Army Corps), WAVES (Navy), and SPARS (Coast Guard). The armed services tried not to change established gender roles. Military officials told Congress that women in uniform could free men for combat. Most of the women hammered at typewriters, worked switchboards, inventoried supplies, and tended the ill and injured. WAC officers battled the tendency of the popular press to call females in the service "girls" rather than "women" or "soldiers" yet emphasized that military service promoted "poise and charm."

Unequal Opportunity

Not all Americans had the same chance to benefit from the economic boom. On February 19, 1942, President Roosevelt issued **Executive Order 9066**, which authorized the secretary of war to define restricted areas and remove civilian residents who were threats to national security. The targets were 110,000 Japanese Americans whom the army expelled from parts of Washington, Oregon, California, and Arizona in the spring of 1942. Those who had not moved voluntarily were sent to relocation camps in the West and Southwest. The removal satisfied anti-Japanese sentiment kindled into hatred by the war. Most evacuees left businesses and property that they were powerless to protect. Many in the camps would demonstrate their loyalty by joining the 442nd Regimental Combat Team, the most decorated American unit in the European war.

Although the U.S. Supreme Court sanctioned the removals in *Korematsu* v. *United States* (1944), the nation officially recognized its liability with the Japanese Claims Act of 1948 and its broader moral responsibility in 1988, when Congress approved redress payments to each of the sixty thousand surviving evacuees.

The internment of West Coast Japanese contrasted with the treatment of Japanese Americans by the military government of Hawaii. Despite the greater threat that Japan posed to Hawaii than to California, local residents and officials avoided panic. Hawaii's long history as a multiethnic society made residents disinclined to look for a racial scapegoat. Less than 1 percent of Hawaii's Japanese American population of 160,000 was interned.

The experience of African Americans was also mixed, particularly in the armed forces. As it had since the Civil War, the army organized black soldiers in segregated units. Towns adjacent to army posts were sometimes open to white soldiers but off limits to blacks. At some southern bases, German prisoners of war watched movies from the first rows along with white GIs while African American soldiers watched

Dorrie Miller, a mess attendant on the battleship Arizona, *received the Navy Cross for "extraordinary courage" during the Japanese attack on Pearl Harbor. Miller helped pull the* Arizona's *captain to safety and then manned a machine gun and shot down several Japanese planes. The War Department used Miller on recruiting posters such as this, but neglected to point out that it continued to restrict black recruits mostly to kitchen and other service jobs.*

"above and beyond the call of duty"
DORIE MILLER
Received the Navy Cross
at Pearl Harbor, May 27, 1942

American Views

A Woman Shipyard Worker Recalls Her Experience

World War II industry gave new opportunities to millions of women. Patricia Cain Koehler later recalled her work as a teenaged electrician who helped build escort aircraft carriers in Vancouver, Washington, from 1943 to 1945.

❖ **How did Koehler's experience challenge expectations about "women's work"?**

❖ **What impression does she give about the spirit with which Americans organized to win the war?**

❖ **How did the war change the patterns of everyday life?**

We girls wore leather jackets, plaid flannel shirts, and jeans we bought in the boys department of Meier & Frank. In was 1943, we were eighteen years old, our first year of college was over. My girlfriend and her mother had moved in with my mother and me for the duration of the war. Housing was tight because of the influx of war industry workers. Our fathers were overseas.

Three local shipyards were recruiting workers from the East Coast and the South. They advertised in Portland, too: HELP WANTED: WOMEN SHIPBUILDERS. Cartoons asked, "What are you doing to help the war?" They showed women sipping tea, playing cards, and relaxing. "THIS?" And then a smiling woman worker with lunch box, her hair tied up in a scarf, a large ship in the background, "Or THIS? . . .

Together my girlfriend and I applied to be electrician helpers at the Kaiser Vancouver Shipyards. . . . Twenty thousand workers labored

from the back. Private Charles Wilson wrote President Roosevelt that Davis-Monthan Army Air Force Base in Tucson was color-coded: Barracks for African Americans were coated with black tar paper, and those for white soldiers sported white paint. Military courts were quick to judge and harsh to punish when black GIs were the accused. Despite the obstacles, all-black units such as the 761st Tank Battalion and the 99th Pursuit Squadron earned distinguished records.

African Americans also found economic advancement through war jobs. Early in the mobilization, labor leader A. Philip Randolph of the Brotherhood of Sleeping Car Porters worked with Walter White of the NAACP to plan a "Negro March on Washington" to protest racial discrimination by the federal government. To head off a major embarrassment, Roosevelt issued **Executive Order 8802** in June 1941, barring racial discrimination in defense contracts and creating the **Fair Employment Practices Committee (FEPC)**; the order coined a phrase that reverberated powerfully through the coming decades: "no discrimination on grounds of race, color, creed, or national origin."

The FEPC's small staff resolved fewer than half of the employment discrimination complaints. White resistance to black coworkers remained strong. In Mobile, New Orleans, and Jacksonville, agreements between shipyards and segregated unions blocked skilled black workers from high-wage jobs. Attempts to overturn discrimination could lead to violence. When the Alabama Dry Dock Company integrated its work force in May 1943, white workers rioted. Transportation workers in Philadelphia struck the next year to protest upgrading of jobs held by black workers. Nevertheless, African American membership in labor unions doubled, and wartime prosperity raised the average black income from 41 percent of the white average in 1939 to 61 percent by 1950.

The war was also a powerful force for the assimilation of Native Americans. Twenty-five thousand Indians served in the armed forces. Some were around the clock to build ships—fast. At nights the yards were lit up as bright as day. . . . It was a world of strangers. . . . Coming from outside the Northwest, as most of them did, they spoke in accents we had never heard before. It became a game with us to listen and ask point of origin. Soon we could distinguish between a Brooklyn accent and one from New Jersey. . . .

The day came . . . when we graduated to journeyman-electrician at $1.20 per hour. We celebrated by applying for jobs on the hookup crews, which worked aboard ships at the outfitting dock. I was assigned to fire control. That meant guns! My leadman had never had a female working for him, and he was skeptical. Like a shadow, I followed his every move, anticipating what tool he needed next and handing it to him before he could ask. After a few days of this he relaxed and began teaching me the ropes—or, rather, the wires. . . .

We had watched some of the carriers launched, with wartime ceremony, gold braid, and ribbons. There was no glamour for us, though, as we slipped on the cluttered decks, dodged cables over our heads, and risked death crossing the tracks of the giant cranes. . . .

My first solo assignment was hooking up the forty-millimeter gun directors on the starboard side. . . . Occasionally I looked down into the swift current of the Columbia River and noticed small boats dragging for a worker who had fallen in. . . . Once when climbing down a ladder clogged with welding leads (large rubber hoses), I slammed a steel-toed boot against one of them and broke a toe. The doctor taped it to its neighbor and I went on working. On another occasion I broke my elbow in a fall, lost a day getting it set, and learned to work left-handed. . . .

Since every night we fell into bed exhausted, our hands chapped and our hair smelling of paint, there was really no time to spend our money. So we invested most of our earnings in war bonds to be cashed in for college.

Source: Patricia Cain Koehler, "Reminiscence: Pat Koehler on the Women Shipbuilders of World War II." Oregon Historical Quarterly, Fall 1990, pp. 285–291. Copyright © 1990 Oregon Historical Quarterly. Reprinted by permission.

members of radio combat-communication teams, known as "code-talkers," who transmitted vital information in Navajo and other Indian languages. Forty thousand other Native Americans moved to off-reservation jobs. The average cash income of Indian households tripled during the war. Many stayed in cities at its end. The stress of balancing tribal life and urban America is depicted in M. Scott Momaday's 1969 novel *House Made of Dawn*, which follows a World War II veteran as he moves between his home village in New Mexico and Los Angeles.

Clashing Cultures

As men and women migrated in search of work, they also crossed or collided with traditional boundaries of race and region. African-American migration out of the South accelerated in the early 1940s. Many of the migrants headed for well-established black neighborhoods in northern cities. Others created new African-American neighborhoods in western cities. White Southerners and black Northerners with different ideas of racial etiquette found themselves side by side in West Coast shipyards. In the Midwest, black migrants from the South and white migrants from Appalachia crowded into cities such as Cincinnati and Chicago, competing for the same high-wage jobs and scarce apartments.

Tensions between black and white residents exploded in at least fifty cities in 1943 alone. New York's Harlem erupted in a riot after rumors of attacks on black servicemen. In Detroit, the issue was the boundary between white and black territories. In June 1943, an argument over use of Detroit's Belle Isle Park set off three days of violence: Twenty-five black people and nine white people died in the most serious racial riot of the war.

Tensions were simultaneously rising between Mexican Americans and Anglos. In periods of labor shortage, the United States has repeatedly turned to Latin America for low-cost workers. World War II followed the pattern. In July 1942, the United States admitted hundreds of thousands of Mexican *braceros*, or temporary workers, to fill labor needs in the Southwest.

The Latino newcomers created ethnic tensions similar to those associated with the urbanization of African Americans. As the Mexican community in Los Angeles swelled to an estimated 400,000, newspapers published anti-Mexican articles. On June 6, 1943, off-duty sailors and soldiers attacked Latinos on downtown streets and invaded Mexican-American neighborhoods. The main targets were so-called *pachucos*—young Chicanos who wore flamboyant "zoot suits" with long, wide-shouldered jackets and pleated, narrow-cuffed trousers—whom the rioters considered delinquents. The "zoot suit" riots dragged on for a week of sporadic violence against black people and Filipinos as well as Latinos.

The End of the New Deal

Roosevelt's New Deal had run out of steam in 1938. The war had reinvigorated his political fortunes by focusing national energies on foreign policy, over which presidents have the greatest power. He declared that "Dr. Win the War" had replaced "Dr. New Deal." Especially after the 1942 election left Congress in the hands of Republicans and conservative southern Democrats, lawmakers followed the new tack. Conservative lawmakers ignored proposals that war emergency housing be used to improve the nation's permanent housing stock, abolished the National Resources Planning Board, curtailed rural electrification, and crippled the Farm Security Administration.

The presidential election of 1944 raised few new issues of substance. The Republicans nominated Governor Thomas Dewey of New York, who had made his reputation as a crime-fighting district attorney. The Democrats renominated Roosevelt for a fourth term. Missouri Senator Harry S Truman, a tough investigator of American military preparedness, replaced liberal New Dealer Henry Wallace as Roosevelt's running mate. The move appeased southern Democrats and moved the ticket toward the political center.

The most important issue was a fourth term for Roosevelt. Supporters argued that the nation could not afford to switch leaders in the middle of a war, but Dewey's vigor and relative youth (he was twenty years younger than FDR) pointed up the president's failing health and energy. Voters gave Roosevelt 432 electoral votes to 99, but the narrowing gap in the popular vote—54 percent for Roosevelt and 46 percent for Dewey—made the Republicans eager for 1948.

War and Peace

In January 1943, the U.S. War Department completed the world's largest office building, the Pentagon. The building housed 23,000 workers along 17.5

In the early 1940s, young Mexican-American men frequently dressed in "zoot suits" of baggy trousers, hip-length jackets with padded shoulders and wide lapels, and broad-brimmed hats. A badge of youthful defiance and ethnic identity, the style contrasted sharply with the tailored uniforms of the armed services. Zoot-suiters found themselves the targets of off-duty soldiers during the "zoot suit riots" in Los Angeles in 1943. This photo shows police arresting Mexican-American men, zoot suiters among them, in the wake of the riots.

Reproduced from Collection of the Library of Congress.

miles of corridors. While Congress was chipping away at federal programs, the war effort was massively expanding the government presence in American life. The gray walls of the Pentagon symbolized an American government that was outgrowing its prewar roots.

Gathering Allied Strength

The unanswered military question of 1942 and 1943 was when the United States and Britain would open a second front against Germany by attacking across the English Channel. Landings in north Africa in 1942 and Italy in 1943 satisfied the British desire to secure western influence in the Mediterranean and Middle East, and they gave U.S. forces invaluable battlefield experience. But they pleased neither American policymakers nor the Soviet Union. U.S. leaders wanted to justify massive mobilization with a war-winning campaign and to strike across Europe to occupy the heart of Germany. Stalin needed a full-scale invasion of western Europe to divert German forces from the Eastern Front.

In fact, 1943 was the year in which the Allies gained the edge in quality of equipment, capacity for war production, and military sophistication. The United States poured men and equipment into Britain. The Soviets recruited, rearmed, and upgraded new armies, despite enormous losses in 1941 and 1942. They learned to outfight the Germans in tank warfare and rebuilt munitions factories beyond German reach. They also made good use of 17.5 million tons of U.S. lend-lease assistance. As Soviet soldiers reconquered western Russia and the Ukraine, they marched in 13 million pairs of American-made boots and traveled in 51,000 jeeps and 375,000 Dodge trucks. "Just imagine how we could have advanced from Stalingrad to Berlin without [lend-lease vehicles]," future Soviet Premier Nikita Khrushchev later commented.

The Allies spent 1943 hammering out war aims and strategies. Meeting in Casablanca in January 1943, Roosevelt and Churchill demanded the "unconditional surrender" of Italy, Germany, and Japan; the phrase meant no deals that kept the enemy governments or leaders in power. Ten months later, the Allied leaders huddled again. Roosevelt and Churchill met with China's Jiang in Cairo and then flew on to meet Stalin in Tehran. Jiang and Stalin could not meet directly because the USSR was neutral in the east Asian war. At Tehran, the United States and Britain promised to invade France within six months. "We leave here," said the three leaders, "friends in fact, in spirit, in purpose."

The superficial harmony barely survived the end of the war. The Soviets had shouldered the brunt of the war for nearly two and a half years, suffering millions of casualties and seeing their nation devastated. Stalin and his generals scoffed at the small scale of early U.S. efforts. Roosevelt's ideal of self-determination for all peoples seemed naive to Churchill, who wanted the major powers to carve out realistic spheres of influence in Europe. It was irrelevant to Stalin, who wanted control of eastern Europe.

Turning the Tide in Europe

The United States had entered the ground war in Europe with **Operation TORCH**. Against little opposition, British and American troops under General Dwight Eisenhower landed in French Morocco and Algeria on November 8, 1942 (see Map 28-5). These were territories that the Germans had left under a puppet French government after the French military collapsed in 1940. This Vichy government, so named after its capital city, collaborated with the Nazis. With the TORCH landings, however, Vichy officials in Africa switched sides, giving the Allies footholds in north Africa.

Despite the easy landings, German troops taught U.S. forces hard lessons in tactics and leadership. German tanks in February 1943 counterattacked U.S. divisions at **Kasserine Pass** in the Atlas Mountains of Tunisia. The battle was a tactical defeat for the untested American army, but Axis forces lacked the strength to follow it up. Allied troops forced the Axis in Africa to surrender in May. Eisenhower had already demonstrated his ability to handle the politics of military leadership, skills he perfected commanding a multinational army for the next two and a half years. He also chose the right subordinates, giving operational command to Omar Bradley and George Patton. Bradley was low-keyed and rock solid; to relax he worked algebra and calculus problems. Patton was a much flashier figure with a mighty ego and a fierce commitment to victory.

The central Mediterranean remained the focus of U.S. and British action for the next year. The British feared military disaster from a premature landing in western Europe and proposed strikes in southern Europe, which Churchill inaccurately called the "soft underbelly" of Hitler's empire. U.S. Army Chief of Staff George Marshall and President Roosevelt agreed first to the action in north Africa and then to invade Italy in 1943, in part so that U.S. troops could participate in the ground fighting in Europe. In July and August, Allied forces led by Montgomery and Patton overran Sicily. The Italian mainland proved more difficult. As Sicily fell, the Italian king and army forced Mussolini from power and began to negotiate peace with Britain

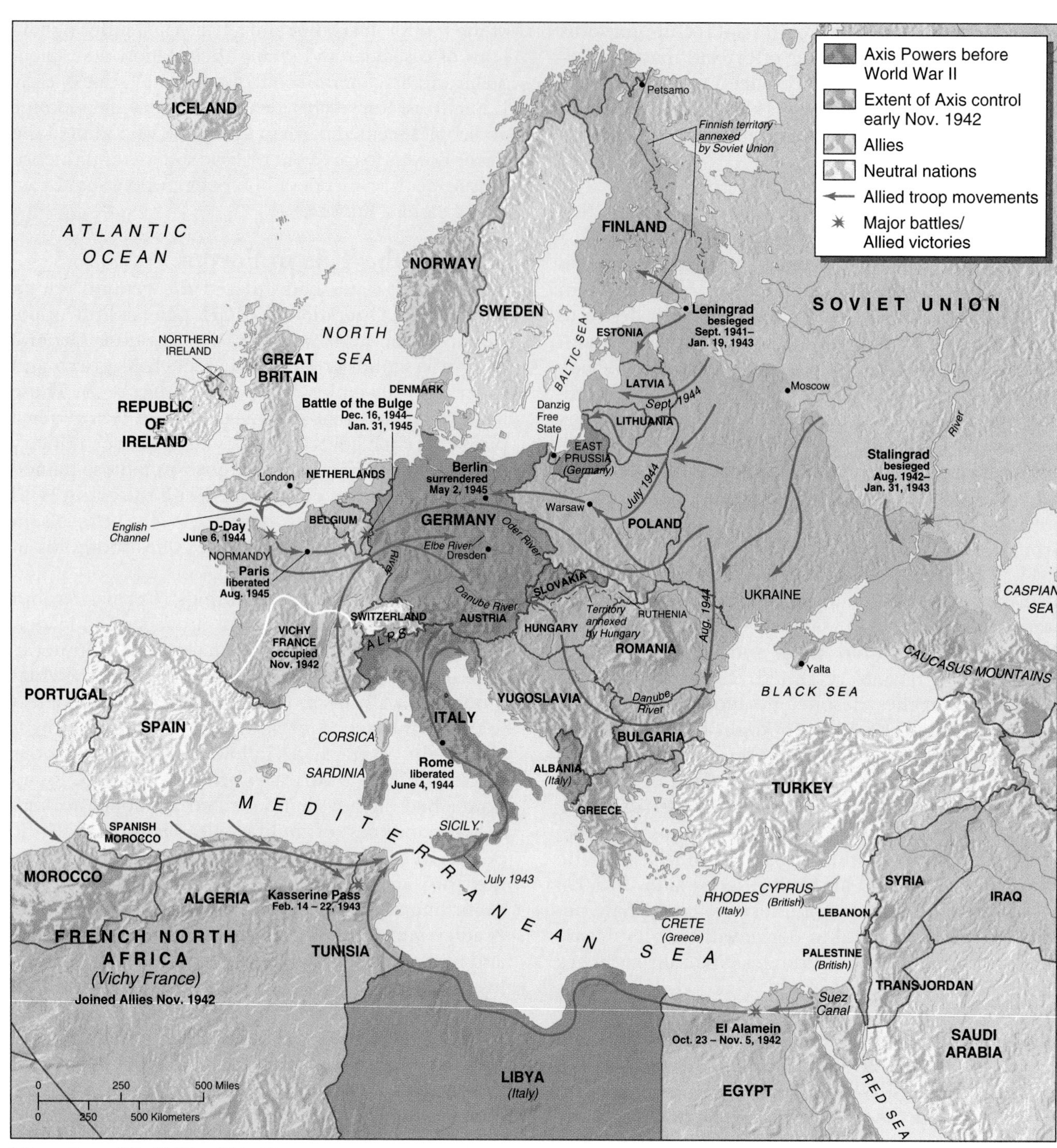

Map 28-5 World War II in Europe, 1942–1945
Nazi Germany had to defend its conquests on three fronts. Around the Mediterranean, American and British forces pushed the Germans out of Africa and Southern Italy, while guerrillas in Yugoslavia pinned down many German troops. On the Eastern Front, Soviet armies advanced hundreds of miles to drive the German army out of the Soviet Union and eastern Europe. In June 1944, U.S. and British landings opened the Western Front in northern France for a decisive strike at the heart of Germany.

and America (but not the Soviet Union). In September, the Allies announced an armistice with Italy, and Eisenhower's troops landed south of Naples. Germany responded by occupying the rest of Italy.

As American military planners had feared, the Italian campaign soaked up Allied resources. The mountainous Italian peninsula was one long series of defensive positions, and the Allies repeatedly bogged down. Week after week, the experience of GIs on the line was the same: "You wake up in the mud and your cigarettes are all wet and you have an ache in your joints and a rattle in your chest." Despite months of bitter fighting, the Allies controlled only two-thirds of Italy when the war there ended on May 1, 1945.

On the Eastern Front, the climactic battle of the German-Soviet war had erupted on July 5, 1943. The Germans sent three thousand tanks against the **Kursk Salient**, a huge wedge that the Red Army had pushed into their lines. In 1941 and 1942, such a massive attack would have forced the Soviets to retreat, but now Soviet generals had prepared a defense in depth with three thousand tanks of their own. When the attack finally stalled, it marked the last great German offensive until December 1944.

Operation OVERLORD

On **D-Day**—June 6, 1944—the western Allies landed on the coast of Normandy in northwestern France. Six divisions went ashore from hundreds of attack transports carrying four thousand landing craft. Dozens of warships and twelve thousand aircraft provided support. One British and two American airborne divisions dropped behind German positions. When the sun set on the "longest day," the Allies had a tenuous toehold in France.

The next few weeks brought limited success. The Allies secured their beachheads and landed 500,000 men and 100,000 vehicles within two weeks. However, the German defenders kept them pinned along a narrow coastal strip. **Operation OVERLORD**, the code name for the entire campaign across northern France, met renewed success in late July and August. U.S. troops improved their fighting skills through "experience, sheer bloody experience." They finally broke through German lines around the town of St.-Lô and then drew a ring around the Germans that slowly closed on the town of Falaise. The Germans lost a quarter of a million troops.

The German command chose to regroup closer to Germany rather than fight in France. The Allies liberated Paris on August 25; Free French forces (units that had never accepted Nazi or Vichy rule) led the entry. The drive toward Germany was the largest U.S. operation of the war. The only impediments appeared to be winter weather and getting enough supplies to the rapidly advancing armies.

The story was similar on the Eastern Front, where the Soviets relentlessly battered one section of the German lines after another. By the end of 1944, the Red Army had entered the Balkans and reached central Poland. With the end in sight, the Soviets

American, British, and Canadian forces opened the long-awaited "second front" against Germany on June 6, 1944—D-Day—when tens of thousands of troops landed on the coast of Normandy in France. The landings were the largest amphibious operation ever staged. Although the Germans had expected the landings further north, their defenses pinned the Allies to a narrow beachhead for several weeks.

Table 28.1 Military and Civilian Deaths in World War II

Nation	Victims (millions)
USSR	18–20
China	10–20
Germany and Austria	6
Poland	5
Japan	2.7
Yugoslavia	1.7
Romania	0.7
France	0.6
Great Britain	0.5
Hungary	0.5
Italy	0.4
Czechoslovakia	0.4
United States	0.3

had suffered nearly 20 million casualties and sustained the heaviest burden in turning back Nazi tyranny (see Table 28-1).

Victory and Tragedy in Europe

In the last months of 1944, massive air strikes finally reduced German war production. Early in the air war, flying at night, British bombers had aimed at entire cities—the smallest target they could be sure to hit. The American Eighth Air Force preferred to fly daylight raids from its bases in Britain with heavily armed B-17s ("Flying Fortresses") and B-24s ("Liberators") to destroy factories with precision bombing. On August 17, 1943, however, Germans shot down or damaged 10 percent of the bombers that attacked the aircraft factories of Regensburg and the ball-bearing factories of Schweinfurt. Air crews who were expected to fly mission after mission could count the odds, and the Americans had to seek easier targets. German war production actually increased during 1943 and much of 1944.

Gradually, however, the balance shifted. The new American P-51 escort fighter helped B-17s overfly Germany in relative safety after mid-1944. Thousand-bomber raids on railroads and oil facilities began to cripple the German economy. The raids also forced Germany to devote 2.5 million workers to air defense and damage repair and to divert fighter planes from the front lines. Politics rather than military need governed the final great action of the European air war. British and U.S. bombers in February 1945 staged a terror raid on the nonindustrial city of Dresden, packed with refugees, filled with great art, and undefended by the Germans; a firestorm fueled by incendiary bombs and rubble from blasted buildings killed tens of thousands of civilians without military justification.

Out of the bombing raids that pitted pilots and crews against unseen enemies would come some of the most vivid efforts to relive and comprehend the experience of war. The movie *Twelve O'Clock High* (1949) focused on successive commanders of a U.S. bomber unit in Britain who became too involved with their men to function effectively. The literature of the bomber campaigns included antiwar novels like Joseph Heller's *Catch-22* (1961) and poems like Randall Jarrell's "Death of the Ball Turret Gunner":

> From my mother's sleep I fell into the State,
> And I hunched in its belly until my wet fur froze.
> Six miles from earth, loosed from its dream of life,
> I woke to black flak and the nightmare fighters.
> When I died they washed me out of the turret with
> a hose.*

Even as the air bombardment intensified, Hitler struck a last blow. Stripping the Eastern Front of armored units, he launched twenty-five divisions against thinly held U.S. positions in the Ardennes Forest of Belgium on December 16, 1944. He hoped to split U.S. and British forces by capturing the Belgian port of Antwerp. The attack surprised the Americans, who had treated the Ardennes as a "ghost front" where nothing was going on. Taking advantage of snow and fog that grounded Allied aircraft, the Germans drove a fifty-mile bulge into U.S. lines. Although Americans took substantial casualties, the German thrust literally ran out of gas beyond the town of Bastogne. The **Battle of the Bulge** never seriously threatened the outcome of the war, but pushing the Germans back through the snow-filled forest gave GIs a taste of the conditions that had marked the war in the Soviet Union.

The Nazi empire collapsed in the spring of 1945. American and British divisions crossed the Rhine in March and enveloped Germany's industrial

*"The Death of a Ball Turret Gunner" from *The Complete Poems,* by Randall Jarrell, Copyright © 1969, renewed 1997 by Mary von S. Jarrell. Reprinted by permission of Farrar, Straus, Giroux, LLC.

core. The Soviets drove through eastern Germany toward Berlin. On April 25, American and Red Army troops met on the Elbe River. Hitler committed suicide on April 30 in his concrete bunker deep under devastated Berlin, which surrendered to the Soviets on May 2. The Nazi state formally capitulated on May 8.

The defeat of Germany revealed appalling evidence of the evil at the heart of the Nazi ideology of racial superiority. After occupying Poland in 1939, Nazi officials had begun to force Jews to wear yellow six-pointed stars. Homosexuals had to wear a pink triangle. Nazis also expanded concentration camps into forced labor camps where overwork, starvation, and disease killed hundreds of thousands of Jews, Gypsies, Poles, Russians, and others the Nazis classed as subhuman. Labor conscripts from both eastern and western Europe provided forced labor in fields, factories, mines, and repair crews.

The "final solution" to what Hitler thought of as the "Jewish problem" went far beyond slave labor. The elite SS, Hitler's personal army within the Nazi party, in 1942 set out to eliminate all of Europe's Jews. The evidence of genocide—systematic racial murder—is irrefutable. At Auschwitz and Treblinka, the SS organized the efficient extermination of up to 6 million Jews and 1 million Poles, Gypsies, and others who failed to fit the Nazi vision of the German master race. Prisoners arrived by forced marches and cattle trains. Those who were not worked or starved to death were herded into gas chambers and then incinerated in huge crematoriums. Soviet troops could scarcely believe what they saw as they overran the death camps and freed the few survivors of what we now call the **Holocaust**.

The Pacific War

In the Pacific, as in Europe, the United States used 1943 to probe enemy conquests and to build better submarines, bigger aircraft carriers, and superior planes. Washington divided responsibilities in the Pacific theater. General Douglas MacArthur operated in the islands that stretched between Australia and the Philippines. Admiral Chester Nimitz commanded in the central Pacific. The Allies planned to isolate Japan from its southern conquests. The British moved from India to retake Burma. The Americans advanced along the islands of the southern Pacific to retake the Philippines. With Japan's army still tied down in China, the Americans then planned to bomb Japan into submission.

The Pacific campaigns of 1944 are often called **island hopping**. This was the American naval version of the Blitzkrieg. Planes from American carriers controlled the air, allowing the navy and land forces to isolate and capture the most strategically located Japanese-held islands while bypassing the rest. The process started in November 1943, when Marines took Tarawa (see Map 28-6). It worked to perfection with the assault on Saipan in June 1944. When the Japanese fleet challenged the attack, U.S. Navy flyers destroyed three aircraft carriers and hundreds of planes.

When Soviet troops liberated Poland and the western allies entered Germany in 1945, they found appalling evidence of the Nazi political and racial terror that had killed millions of people, including six million Jews. A handful of victims survived the death factories and concentration camps—among them these inmates of the Buchenwald concentration camp in central Germany—to bear witness to the horror.

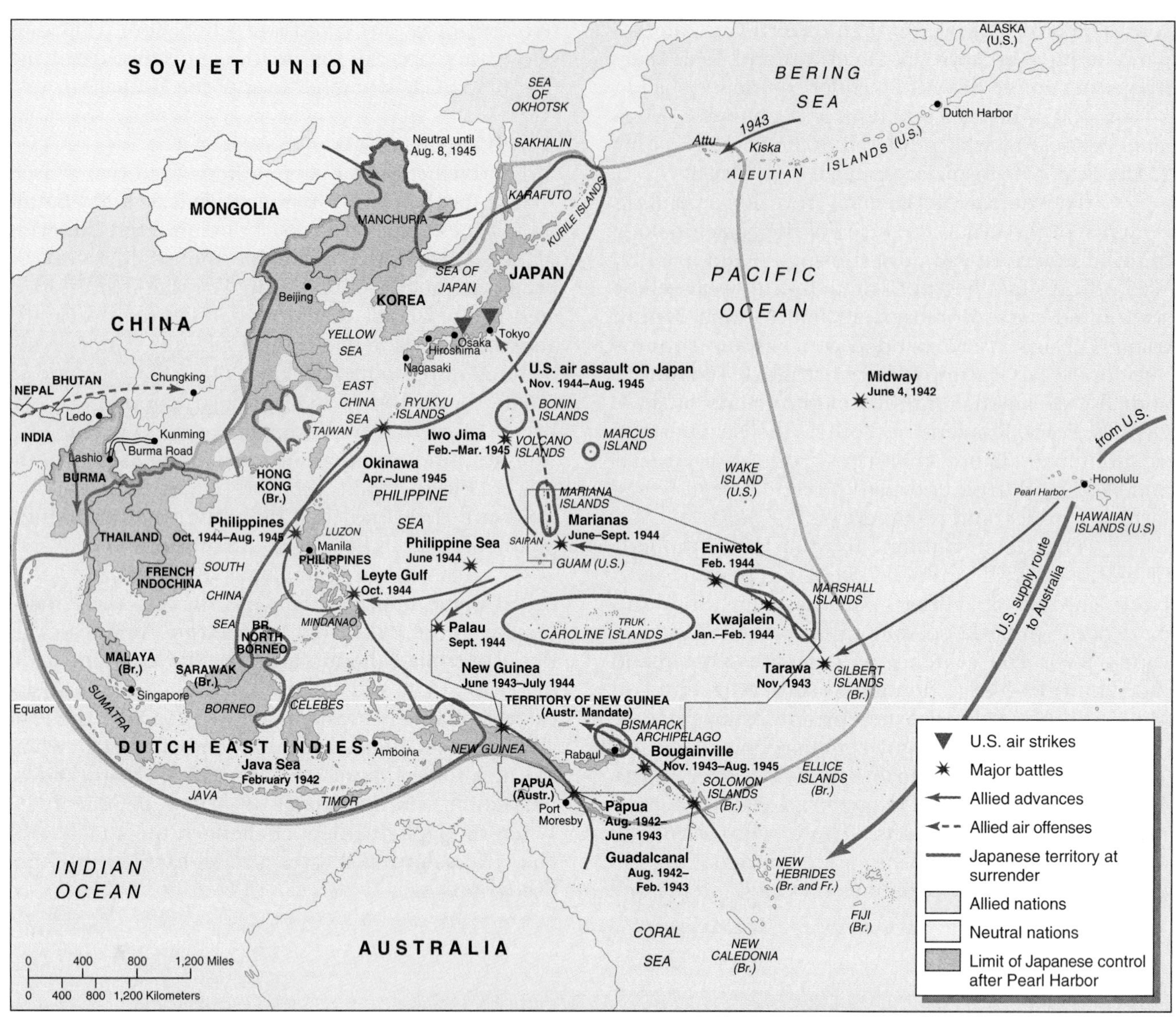

Map 28-6 World War II in the Pacific, 1942–1945
The Allied strategy against Japan was to cut off Japan's southern conquests by retaking the central Pacific islands, the Philippines, and Burma and then to strike at the Japanese home islands. Submarine warfare and massive air attacks from November 1944 to August 1945 crippled Japan's capacity to wage war. The detonation of atomic bombs over Hiroshima and Nagasaki then forced surrender on August 15, 1945.

Racial hatred animated both sides in the Pacific war and fueled a "war without mercy." Americans often characterized Japanese soldiers as vermin. Political cartoons showed Japanese as monkeys or rats, and some Marines had "Rodent Exterminator" stenciled on their helmets. In turn, the Japanese depicted themselves as the "leading race" with the duty to direct the rest of Asia. Chinese, Filipinos, and other conquered peoples were treated with contempt and brutality. Japanese viewed Americans as racial mongrels and called them demons. Each side expected the worst of the other and frequently lived up to expectations.

MacArthur used a version of the bypass strategy in the Solomon Islands and New Guinea, leapfrogging over Japanese strong points. The invasion of the Philippines repeated the approach by landing on Leyte, in the middle of the island chain. The Philippine campaign also destroyed the offensive capacity of the Japanese fleet. In the **Battle of Leyte Gulf**, the U.S. military sank four Japanese battleships, four carriers, and ten cruisers. The Japanese home islands were left with no defensive screen against an expected invasion.

During 1943 and 1944, the U.S. also savaged the Japanese economy. Submarines choked off food, oil, and raw materials bound for Japan and island bases. By 1945, imports to Japan were one-eighth of the 1940 level. Heavy bombing of Japan began in early 1944. Japan's dense wooden cities were more vulnerable than their German counterparts, and Japanese air defenses were much weaker. A fire-bomb raid on Tokyo on the night of March 9, 1945, killed 124,000 people and left 1 million homeless; it was perhaps the single biggest mass killing of all time. Overall, conventional bombing destroyed 42 percent of Japan's industrial capacity. By the time the United States captured the islands of Iwo Jima and Okinawa in fierce fighting (April–June 1945) and neared the Japanese home islands, Japan's position was hopeless.

Searching for Peace

At the beginning of 1945, the Allies sensed victory. Conferring from February 4 to 11 in the Ukrainian town of Yalta, Roosevelt, Stalin, and Churchill planned for the postwar world. The most important American goal was to enlist the USSR in finishing off the Pacific war. Americans hoped that a Soviet attack on Manchuria would tie down enough Japanese troops to reduce U.S. casualties in invading Japan. Stalin repeated his intent to declare war on Japan within three months of victory in Europe, in return for a free hand in Manchuria.

In Europe, the Allies had decided in 1944 to divide Germany and Austria into French, British, American, and Soviet occupation zones. The Red Army already controlled Bulgaria, Romania, and Hungary, countries that had helped the Germans; Soviet officials were installing sympathetic regimes there. Soviet armies also controlled Poland. The most that Roosevelt could coax from Stalin were vague pledges to allow participation of noncommunists in coalition governments in eastern Europe. Stalin also agreed to join a new international organization, the **United Nations**, whose foundations were laid at a conference in San Francisco in the spring of 1945.

Conservative critics later charged that the western powers "gave away" eastern Europe at the **Yalta Conference**. In fact, the Soviet Union gained little that it did not already control. In east Asia as well, the Soviets could seize the territories that the agreements granted them. Roosevelt overestimated his ability to charm Stalin, but the Yalta talks could not undo the results of four years of fighting by the Soviet Army.

On April 12, two months after Yalta, Roosevelt died of a cerebral hemorrhage. Harry Truman, the new president, was a shrewd politician, but his experience was limited; Roosevelt had not even told him about the Manhattan Project. Deeply distrustful of the Soviets, Truman first ventured into personal international diplomacy in July 1945 at a British-Soviet-American conference at Potsdam, near Berlin. Most of the sessions debated the future of Germany. The leaders endorsed the expulsion of ethnic Germans from eastern Europe and moved the borders of Poland one hundred miles west into historically German territory. Truman also made it clear that the United States expected to dominate the occupation of Japan. Its goal was to democratize the Japanese political system and reintroduce Japan into the international community—a policy that succeeded. The **Potsdam Declaration** on July 26 summarized U.S. policy and gave Japan an opening for surrender. However, the declaration failed to guarantee that Emperor Hirohito would not be tried as a war criminal. The Japanese response was so cautious that Americans read it as rejection.

Secretary of State James Byrnes now urged Truman to use the new atomic bomb, tested just weeks earlier. Japan's ferocious defense of Okinawa had confirmed American fears that the Japanese would fight to the death. Thousands of suicide missions by *kamikaze* pilots who tried to crash their planes into U.S. warships seemed additional proof of Japanese fanaticism. Prominent Americans were wondering if unconditional surrender was worth another six or nine months of bitter fighting. In contrast, using the bomb to end the conflict quickly would ensure that the United States could occupy Japan without Soviet participation, and the bomb might intimidate Stalin (see the overview table, "The Decision to Use the Atomic Bomb"). In short, a decision not to use atomic weapons was never a serious alternative in the summer of 1945.

In early August, the United States dropped two of three available nuclear bombs on Japan. On August 6 at Hiroshima the first bomb killed at least eighty thousand people and poisoned thousands more with radiation. A second bomb three days later at Nagasaki took another forty thousand lives. Japan ceased hostilities on August 14 and surrendered formally on September 2. The world has wondered ever since if the United States might have defeated Japan without resorting to atomic bombs, but recent research shows that the bombs were the shock that allowed the Emperor and peace advocates to overcome military leaders who wanted to fight to the death.

FROM THEN TO NOW

Nuclear Weapons

On May 11 and 12, 1998, India tested five nuclear weapons in its western desert. Two weeks later, Pakistan tested its own nuclear weapons. Neighbors and bitter rivals, the two became the sixth and seventh nations to publicly acknowledge the possession of a nuclear arsenal. Now the tensions between them, which had long fueled border clashes and twice erupted in open warfare, had become another factor in the delicate calculus of nuclear terror that has confronted the world since Hiroshima.

It has been a central goal of U.S. policy since 1945 to limit the number of nations with atomic weapons and place ceilings on the size of nuclear arsenals. The goal became more urgent when the Soviet Union deployed its own nuclear weapons after 1949, establishing the "balance of terror" that haunted the decades-long Cold War between the United States and the Soviet Union.

Two key steps toward reducing the nuclear threat were the Limited Test Ban Treaty of 1963—in which the United States, Britain, and the USSR outlawed atmospheric nuclear testing (see Chapter 30)—and the Nuclear Non-Proliferation Treaty, which was signed in 1968 and extended indefinitely in 1995. One hundred eighty nations have agreed not to acquire nuclear weapons, and five acknowledged nuclear powers—the United States, Russia, Britain, France, China—have agreed to eventual elimination of their own weapons.

The power of international opinion was clearly not enough to convince India and Pakistan to abandon their nuclear weapons programs, but it has been effective elsewhere in the 1990's. One justification of the Gulf War in 1991 (see Chapter 33) was to prevent Iraq from developing nuclear arms, and Iraqi interference with United Nations inspection teams triggered bombing raids on Iraq in 1998–99. The United States also orchestrated pressure on North Korea to cancel a suspected nuclear weapons program and admit international inspectors.

The 1990s saw advances in efforts to reduce the huge nuclear stockpiles of the United States and Russia. The first Strategic Arms Limitation Treaty (START I) went into effect in 1994. The United States and Russia agreed to retain a maximum of eight thousand warheads each. START II, if implemented, would cut the total to three thousand each. The breakup of the Soviet Union and the economic challenges that have confronted its constituent republics have created fears about the diversion of warheads into the hands of terrorists. The United States, however, has helped to pay for dismantling of Russian warheads and their removal from Ukraine and Kazakhstan, both formerly parts of the Soviet Union.

The frightening proliferation and growth of nuclear arsenals that began with the Manhattan Project and continued into the 1980s may be ending. The 1990s, on the contrary, may have marked the beginning of a new era of shrinking nuclear capacity, despite reversals like those in India and Pakistan. South Africa, for example, announced in 1993 that it had destroyed six warheads that it had manufactured secretly. And planned reductions in the largest nuclear arsenals offer hope that the trend will continue in the new century.

Hiroshima in the aftermath of the atomic bomb. Atomic bombs, dropped first on Hiroshima and a few days later on Nagasaki in August 1945, instantly destroyed much of both cities. Now one airplane with one bomb could wreak the kind of devastation massive fire bombing raids had inflicted on cities such as Hamburg, Dresden, and Tokyo, adding new terror to the idea of total war.

OVERVIEW

THE DECISION TO USE THE ATOMIC BOMB

Americans have long argued whether the use of atomic bombs on the Japanese cities of Hiroshima and Nagasaki was necessary to end the war. Several factors probably influenced President Truman's decision to use the new weapon.

Military necessity	Truman later argued that the use of atomic bombs was necessary to avoid an invasion of Japan that would have cost hundreds of thousand of lives. Military planners expected Japanese soldiers to put up the same kind of suicidal resistance in defense of the home islands as they had to American landings at the Philippines, Iwo Jima, and Okinawa. More recently, historians have argued that the Japanese military was near collapse and that an invasion would have met far less resistance than feared.
Atomic diplomacy	Some historians believe that Truman used atomic weapons to overawe the Soviet Union and induce it to move cautiously in expanding its influence in Europe and east Asia. Truman and his advisers were certainly aware of how the bomb might influence the Soviet leadership.
Domestic politics	President Roosevelt and his chief military advisers had spent billions on the secret atomic bomb project without the knowledge of Congress or the American public. The managers of the Manhattan Project may have believed that only proof of its military value would quiet critics and justify the huge cost.
Momentum of war	The United States and Britain had already adopted wholesale destruction of German and Japanese cities as a military tactic. Use of the atomic bomb looked like a variation on fire bombing, not the start of a new era of potential mass destruction. In this context, some historians argue, President Truman's choice was natural and expected.

Conclusion

World War II changed the lives of tens of millions of Americans. It made and unmade families. It gave millions of women new responsibilities and then sent them back to the kitchen. It put money in pockets that had been emptied by the Great Depression and turned struggling business owners into tycoons.

Most of the 16 million men and women in uniform served in support jobs that keep the war machine going. They repaired airplanes and built runways, tracked supplies, and counted coffins. Poet John Ciardi wrote out commendations for valor. Bill Mauldin drew cartoons for the Army newspaper *Stars and Stripes.*

For many readers, Mauldin's cartoon GIs, Willie and Joe, came to represent the experience of the front lines. It was loyalty to the men in their own unit that kept fighting men steady. "The only thing that kept you going was your faith in your buddies," recalled a Marine from the Pacific theater. "You couldn't let 'em down. It was stronger than flag and country."

Whether on the home front or the fighting front, Americans knew that victory was uncertain. World War II adventure movies in which Americans always win leave the impression that triumph was necessary and inevitable. In fact, victory was the hard-fought result of public leadership and military effort. Under other leaderships, the United States might have stood aside until it was too late to reverse the Axis conquest of Europe and east Asia. The collapse of the Soviet Union or failure of the North Atlantic convoy system might have made Germany unbeatable. In 1941 and 1942 in particular, Americans faced each day with fear and uncertainty.

The war unified the nation in new ways while confirming old divisions. People of all backgrounds shared a common cause. Farm boys mixed with city slickers, Northerners with Southerners. "When I woke up the first morning on the troop train in Fulton, Kentucky," recalled one Midwesterner, "I thought I was in Timbuktu." The war narrowed the distance between native-born, small-town Americans and recent European immigrants from the big cities. The chasms between Protestant, Catholic, and Jewish Americans were far narrower in 1945 than they had been in 1940.

But nothing broke the barriers that separated white and black Americans. Unequal treatment in a war for democracy outraged black soldiers, who returned to fight for civil rights. The uprooting of Japanese Americans was another reminder of racial prejudice. After the war, however, memories of the contrast between the nation's fight against Axis tyranny and the unequal treatment of American citizens fueled a gradual shift of public attitudes that climaxed in the civil rights movements of the 1950s and 1960s.

The insecurities of the war years influenced the United States for decades. A nation's current leaders are often shaped by its last war. Hitler, Mussolini, Churchill, and Truman all served in World War I and carried its memories in World War II. The lessons of World War II would similarly influence the thinking of presidents from Eisenhower in the 1950s to Bush in the 1990s. Even though the United States ended 1945 with the world's mightiest navy, biggest air force, and only atomic bomb, the instability that had followed World War I made Western leaders nervous about the shape of world politics.

One result in the postwar era was conflict between the United States and the Soviet Union, whose only common ground had been a shared enemy. After Germany's defeat, their wartime alliance gave way to hostility and confrontation in the Cold War. At home, international tensions fed pressure for social and political conformity. The desire to enjoy the fruits of victory after fifteen years of economic depression and sacrifice made the postwar generation sensitive to perceived threats to steady jobs and stable families. For the next generation, the unresolved business of World War II would haunt American life.

Review Questions

1. What motivated German, Italian, and Japanese aggression in the 1930s? How did Great Britain, the USSR, and other nations respond to the growing conflict?
2. What arguments did Americans make against involvement in the war in Europe? Why did President Roosevelt and many others believe it necessary to block German and Japanese expansion? What steps did Roosevelt take to increase U.S. involvement short of war?
3. What was the military balance in early 1942? What were the chief threats to the United States and its allies? Why did the fortunes of war turn in late 1942?
4. Assess how mobilization for World War II altered life in the United States. How did the war affect families? How did it shift the regional balance of the economy? What opportunities did it open for women?
5. Did World War II help or hinder progress toward racial equality in the United States? How did the experiences of Japanese Americans, African Americans, and Mexican Americans challenge American ideals?
6. What factors were decisive in the defeat of Germany? How important were Soviet efforts on the Eastern Front, the bomber war, and the British-American landings in France?
7. What was the U.S. strategy against Japan, and how well did it work? What lay behind President Truman's decision to use atomic bombs against Japanese cities?

Recommended Reading

Beth Bailey and David Farber, *The First Strange Place: The Alchemy of Race and Sex in World War II Hawaii* (1992). Explores the effects of the war on American ideas about the proper roles of men and women, black people, white people, and Asian Americans.

Doris Kearns Goodwin, *No Ordinary Time: Franklin and Eleanor Roosevelt, the Home Front in World War II* (1994). A prize-winning study that presents the tensions and crises of World War II through the daily lives of President Roosevelt, his wife Eleanor, and others in the White House.

John Hersey, *Hiroshima* (1946). Recounts the atomic bombing through the eyes of victims and survivors.

John Keegan, *The Second World War* (1990). A comprehensive and readable account giving a strong sense of the relative importance of the various fronts.

William L. O'Neill, *A Democracy at War: America's Fight at Home and Abroad in World War II* (1993). An insightful summary that explores the choices that the United States made in mobilizing and conducting the war.

Martin J. Sherwin, *A World Destroyed: The Atomic Bomb and the Grand Alliance* (1975). Explains why American leaders never seriously considered alternatives to the atomic bomb.

Studs Terkel, *The Good War: An Oral History of World War II* (1984). Eloquent testimony about the effects of the war on both ordinary and extraordinary Americans.

Additional Sources

The Politics of War

Wayne S. Cole, *Roosevelt and the Isolationists* (1983).

Robert Dallek, *Franklin D. Roosevelt and American Foreign Policy, 1932–1945* (1979).

Waldo Heinrichs, *Threshold of War: Franklin D. Roosevelt and American Entry into World War II* (1988).

Akira Iriye, *Power and Culture: The Japanese-American War, 1941–1945* (1981).

Warren Kimball, *The Juggler: Franklin Roosevelt as Wartime Statesman* (1991).

James Schneider, *Should America Go to War? The Debate over Foreign Policy in Chicago, 1939–1941* (1989).

Military Operations

Stephen E. Ambrose, *D-Day, June 6, 1944: The Climactic Battle of World War II* (1994).

Anthony Beevor, *Stalingrad* (1998).

John D. Chappell, *Before the Bomb: How Americans Approached the Pacific War* (1997).

John Keegan, *Six Armies in Normandy; From D-Day to the Liberation of Paris* (1982).

Samuel Eliot Morrison, *The Two-Ocean War: A Short History of the United States Navy in the Second World War* (1963).

Gordon Prange, *At Dawn We Slept: The Untold Story of Pearl Harbor* (1981).

John Ray Skates, *The Invasion of Japan: Alternative to the Bomb* (1994).

Ronald H. Spector, *Eagle against the Sun: The American War with Japan* (1985).

David Syrett, *The Defeat of the German U-Boats: The Battle of the Atlantic* (1994).

Barbara W. Tuchman, *Stillwell and the American Experience in China, 1911–1945* (1970).

Russell Weigley, *Eisenhower's Lieutenants* (1981).

H.P. Willmott, *The Great Crusade: A New Complete History of the Second World War* (1989).

The Experience of War

Craig M. Cameron, *American Samurai: Myth, Imagination, and the Conduct of Battle in the First Marine Division, 1941–1951* (1994).

Michael Doubler, *Closing with the Enemy: How GIs Fought the War in Europe, 1944–1945* (1994).

Paul Fussell, *Wartime: Understanding and Behavior in the Second World War* (1989).

Harold P. Leinbaugh and John D. Campbell, *The Men of Company K: The Autobiography of a World War II Rifle Company* (1985).

William Manchester, *Goodbye Darkness: A Memoir of the Pacific War* (1980).

Harrison Salisbury, *The 900 Days: The Siege of Leningrad* (1969).

Mobilizing the Home Front

John M. Blum, *V Was for Victory: Politics and American Culture during World War II* (1976).

Thomas Doherty, *Projections of War: Hollywood, American Culture, and World War II* (1994).

Mark Foster, *Henry J. Kaiser: Builder in the Modern American West* (1989).

Clayton Koppes and Gregory Black, *Hollywood Goes to War* (1987).

Nelson Lichtenstein, *Labor's War at Home: The CIO in World War II* (1983).

Gerald Nash, *The American West Transformed: The Impact of the Second World War* (1985).

Richard Polenberg, *War and Society: The United States, 1941–1945* (1972).

Richard Rhodes, *The Making of the Atomic Bomb* (1986).

William M. Tuttle, *Daddy's Gone to War: The Second World War in the Lives of America's Children* (1993).

Harold Vatter, *The U.S. Economy in World War II* (1985).

Women and the War Effort

Karen Anderson, *Wartime Women: Sex Roles, Family Relations, and the Status of Women during World War II* (1981).

D'Ann Campbell, *Women at War with America: Private Lives in a Patriotic Era* (1984).

Susan Hartmann, *The Home Front and Beyond: American Women in the 1940s* (1982).

Amy Kesselman, *Fleeting Opportunities: Women in Portland and Vancouver Shipyards during World War II and Reconversion* (1990).

Judy Barrett Litoff, *We're in This War Too: World War II Letters of American Women in Uniform* (1994).

Racial Attitudes and U.S. Policy

Roger Daniels, *Concentration Camps U.S.A.: Japanese Americans and World War II* (1971).

John Dower, *War without Mercy: Race and Power in the Pacific War* (1986).

Dominic J. Capeci, Jr., *Race Relations in Wartime Detroit: The Sojourner Truth Controversy of 1942* (1984).

David S. Wyman, *The Abandonment of the Jews: America and the Holocaust, 1941–1945* (1984).

Where to Learn More

❖ **USS *Arizona* Memorial and Submarine Memorial Park, Pearl Harbor, Hawaii.** The memorial commemorates the men who died in the Japanese attack of December 7, 1941, and recounts the events of the day.

❖ **Air Force Museum, Dayton, Ohio.** Visitors can walk among World War II fighter planes and bombers, including the B-29 that dropped the atomic bomb on Nagasaki, and learn about the role of aviation in the war.

❖ **Japanese-American Historical Plaza, Portland, Oregon.** The plaza uses landscaping and haiku (Japanese-style poems) to convey the meaning of internment for Japanese Americans.

❖ **Los Alamos County Historical Museum and Bradbury Science Museum, Los Alamos, New Mexico.** The museum traces the origins of atomic energy for military and civilian uses. Nearby is the Los Alamos County Historical Museum, which gives the feel of everyday life in the atomic town.

❖ **United States Holocaust Memorial Museum, Washington, D.C.** The Holocaust Museum gives visitors a deeply moving depiction of the deadly impacts of Nazi ideas in the 1930s and 1940s.

THE COLD WAR AT HOME AND ABROAD, 1946–1952

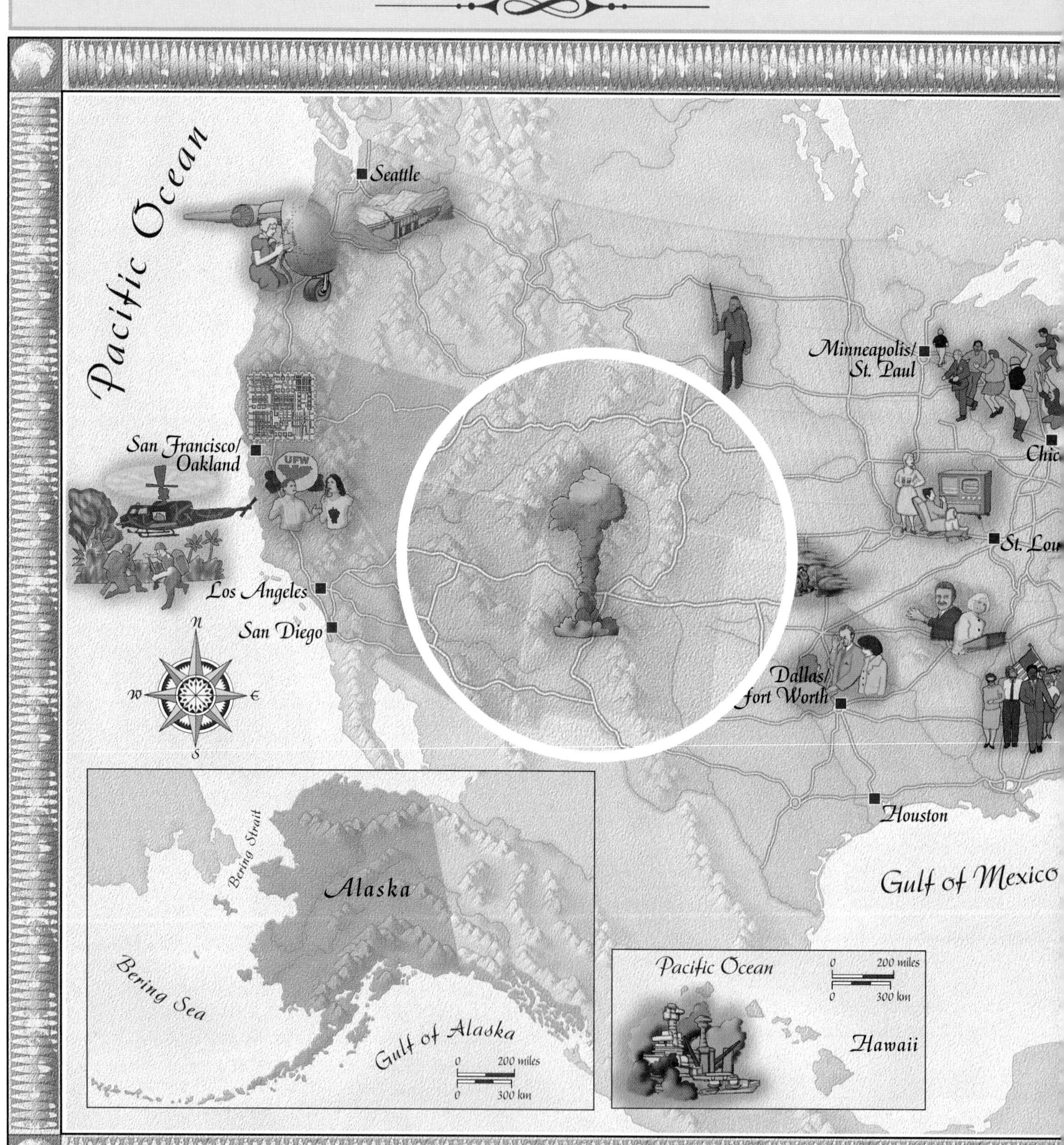

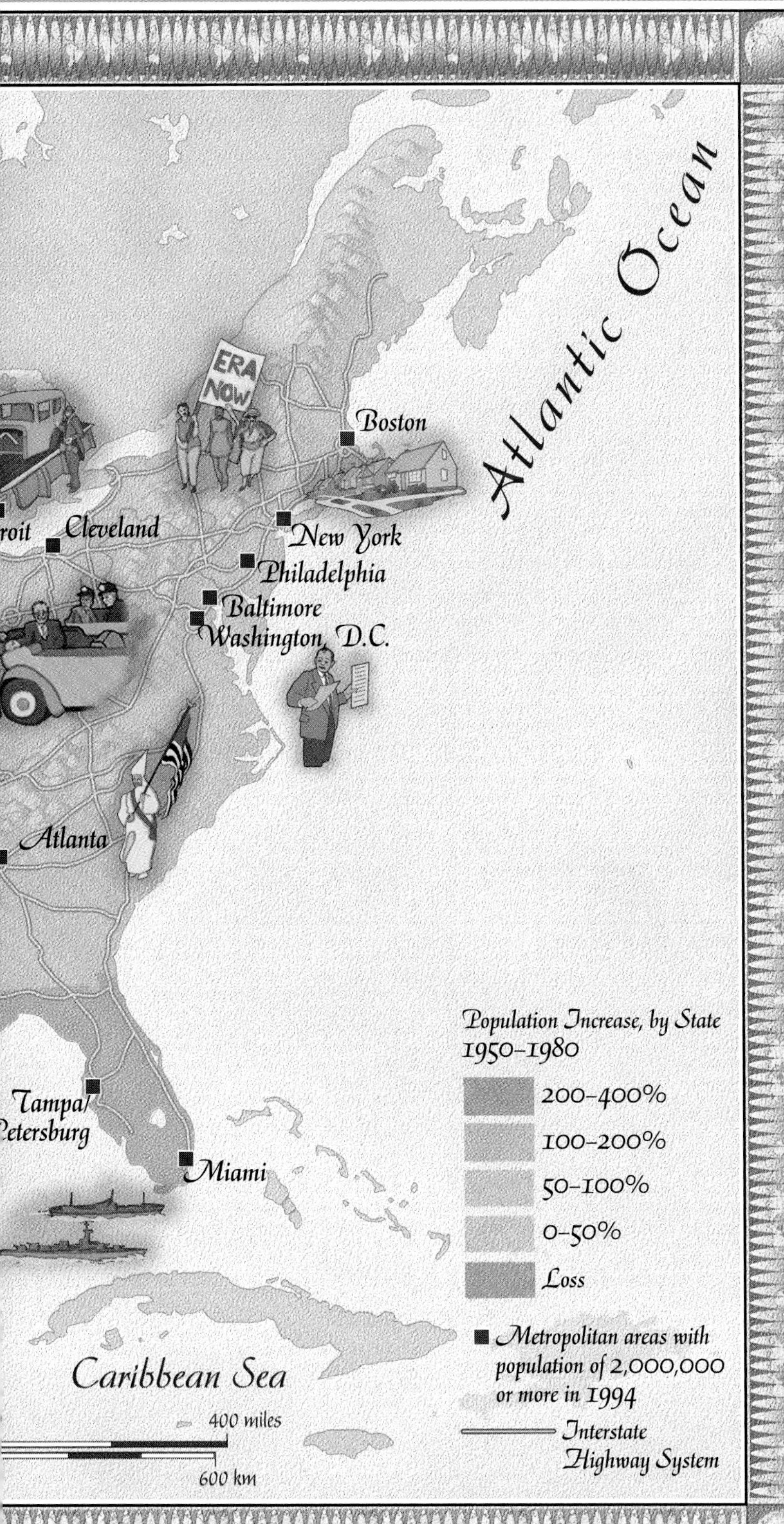

29

Chapter Outline

Key Topics

- Post-war shortages and the massive exit of women from the workforce
- The beginning of a twenty-five-year economic boom
- The beginning of the postwar civil rights movement
- The origins of the Cold War
- The reelection of Harry Truman
- The Korean War and the nuclear arms race
- McCarthy and the Second Red Scare

In 1947, *The Best Years of Our Lives* swept the Academy Awards. The film won seven Oscars, including best picture, best director, and best actor. The immensely popular movie dealt with the problems of returning veterans as squarely as Hollywood could. It follows three veterans as they try to readjust to civilian life. The plot cuts between the personal problems of reconnecting with wives and sweethearts and the social challenge of finding meaningful work.

Behind the story line was nagging concern about the future. "Hard times are coming," one character predicts. The film reminded audiences of their own difficulties with postwar inflation, shortages, and strikes and their fears of another economic depression. The end, however, is upbeat. Wandering through a junkyard for discarded bombers, one of the veterans relives the nightmare of bombing runs over Germany but ends up with a job recycling the planes into building materials for new houses. After months spent in a bar trying to figure out the postwar world, he will now be able to marry his girlfriend and grab a share of the American dream.

Most Americans in 1946 wanted to follow the same script and put together the best years of their lives. After years of hardship, they defined American ideals in terms of economic opportunity and the chance to enjoy national prosperity. Even President Truman replaced the model gun on his White House desk with a model plow.

This compelling desire to enjoy the promise of American life after years of sacrifice helps explain why Americans reacted so fiercely to new challenges and threats. They watched as congressional conservatives and President Truman fought over the fate of New Deal programs. More worrisome was the confrontation with the Soviet Union that was soon being called the **Cold War**. Triggered by the Soviet Union's imposition of communist regimes throughout eastern Europe, the Cold War grew into a global contest in which the United States tried to counter Soviet influence around the world. By the time real war broke out in Korea in 1950, many Americans were venting their frustration by blaming international setbacks on internal subversion and by trying to root out suspected "reds."

The Cold War began in the late 1940s, but it would shape the United States and the world for another generation. Massive rearmament allowed U.S. presidents to act as international policemen in the name of democratic values—a vast change from earlier American foreign relations. Defense spending also reshaped American industry and helped stimulate twenty-five years of economic growth. The Cold War narrowed the range of political discussion, making many of the left-wing ideas of the 1930s taboo by the 1950s. It also made racial segregation and limits on immigration into international embarrassments and thus nudged the nation to live up to its ideals.

Launching the Great Boom

When World War II ended, Americans feared that demobilization would bring a rerun of the inflation and unemployment that had followed World War I. In the first eighteen months of peace, rising prices, labor–management strife, and shortages of everything from meat to automobiles confirmed their anxiety. In 1947 and 1948, however, an economic expansion began that lasted for a quarter century. The resulting prosperity would finance a military buildup and an activist foreign policy. It also supported continuity in domestic politics from the late 1940s to the mid-1960s.

Reconversion Chaos

Japan's sudden surrender took U.S. officials by surprise. They had planned on taking two years to phase out military spending and reintroduce veterans to the domestic economy. Now their plans were obsolete. The Pentagon, already scaling back defense spending, canceled $15 billion in war contracts in the first two days after Japanese surrender. Public pressure demanded that the military release the nation's

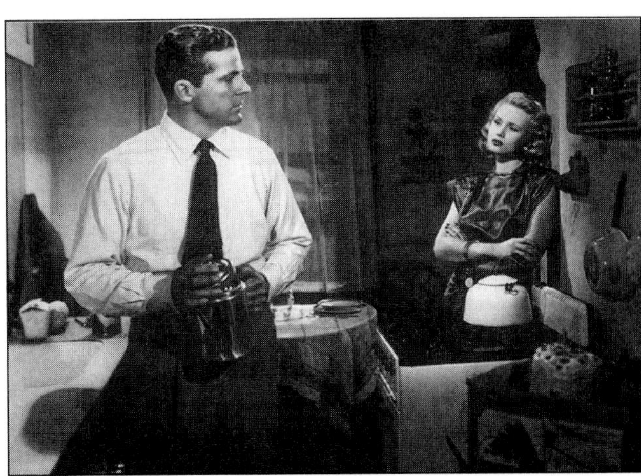

The Best Years of Our Lives *dealt realistically with the problems facing veterans trying to readjust to civilian life. Director William Wyler strove for a feeling of accuracy, shooting on location in Cincinnati and costuming the actors in clothing bought in local stores.*

12 million servicemen and servicewomen as rapidly as possible. GIs in Europe and the South Pacific waited impatiently for their turn on slow, crowded troop ships and calculated their order of discharge according to length of time in uniform, service overseas, combat decorations, and number of children. Even at the rate of 25,000 discharges a day, it took a year to get veterans back to the States and civilian life.

Veterans came home to shortages of food in the grocery stores and consumer goods in the department stores. High demand and short supply meant inflationary pressure, checked temporarily by continuing the Office of Price Administration until October 1946. Meanwhile, producers, consumers, and retailers scrambled to evade price restrictions and scarcities. Farmers sold meat on the black market, bypassing the big packing companies for one-on-one deals at higher prices. Automobiles were especially scarce; the number of vehicles registered in the United States had declined by 4 million during the war. For the privilege of spending a few hundred dollars on a junker, consumers sometimes had to pay used-car dealers for so-called accessories like $150 batteries and $100 lap robes.

A wave of strikes made it hard to retool factories for civilian products. Inflation squeezed factory workers, who had accepted wage controls during the war effort. Since 1941, prices had risen twice as fast as base wages. In the fall of 1945, more and more workers went on strike to redress the balance; the strikes interrupted the output of products from canned soup to copper wire. By January 1946, some 1.3 million auto, steel, electrical, and packinghouse workers were off the job. Strikes in these basic industries shut other factories down for lack of supplies. Presidential committees finally crafted settlements that allowed steel and auto workers to make up ground lost during the war, but they also allowed corporations to pass on higher costs to consumers. One Republican senator complained of "unionists who fatten themselves at the expense of the rest of us." Bill Nation, who inspected window moldings at a GM plant in Detroit, wondered who the senator was talking about. The strike gave him an hourly raise of 18 cents, pushing his weekly income to $59. After paying for food, housing, and utilities, that left $13.44 for Bill, his wife, and five children to spend on clothes, comic books, and doctor bills.

Economic Policy

The economic turmoil of 1946 set the stage for two major—and contradictory—efforts to deal more systematically with peacetime economic readjustment. The **Employment Act of 1946** and the **Taft-Hartley Act** of 1947 represented liberal and conservative approaches to the peacetime economy.

The Employment Act was an effort by congressional liberals to ward off economic crisis by fine-tuning government taxation and spending. It started as a proposal for a full-employment bill that would have committed the federal government to ensure everyone's "right to a useful and remunerative job." Watered down in the face of business opposition, it still defined economic growth and high employment as national goals. It also established the **Council of Economic Advisers** to assist the president. Even this weak legislation, putting the federal government at the center of economic planning, would have been unthinkable a generation earlier.

In the short term, the Employment Act aimed at a problem that didn't materialize. Economists had predicted that the combination of returning veterans and workers idled by cancelled defense work would bring depression-level unemployment of 8 to 10 million. In fact, more than 2 million women provided some slack by leaving the labor force outright. Federal agencies hastened their departure by publishing pamphlets asking men the pointed question, "Do you want your wife to work after the war?" In addition, consumer spending from a savings pool of $140 billion in bank accounts and war bonds created a huge demand for workers to fill. Total employment rose rather than fell with the end of the war, and unemployment in 1946–1948 stayed below 4 percent.

From the other end of the political spectrum, the Taft-Hartley Act climaxed a ten-year effort by conservatives to reverse the gains made by organized labor in the 1930s. The act passed in 1947 because of anger about continuing strikes. For many Americans,

Chronology

1944 Servicemen's Readjustment Act (GI Bill) is passed.

1945 United Nations is established.

1946 Employment Act creates Council of Economic Advisers.

George Kennan sends his "long telegram."

Winston Churchill delivers his "iron curtain" speech.

1947 Truman Doctrine is announced.

Truman establishes a federal employee loyalty program.

Kennan explains containment policy in an anonymous article in *Foreign Affairs.*

Marshall Plan begins providing economic aid to Europe.

HUAC holds hearings on Hollywood.

Taft-Hartley Act rolls back gains of organized labor.

National Security Act creates the National Security Council and the Central Intelligence Agency.

1948 Communists stage coup in Czechoslovakia.

Berlin airlift overcomes Soviet blockade.

Truman orders desegregation of the armed forces.

Selective Service is reestablished.

Truman wins reelection.

1949 North Atlantic Treaty Organization is formed.

Communist Chinese defeat Nationalists.

Soviet Union tests an atomic bomb.

Department of Defense is established.

1950 Senator McCarthy begins his Red hunt.

Alger Hiss is convicted of perjury.

NSC-68 is drafted and accepted as U.S. policy.

Korean War begins.

1951 Senate Internal Security Subcommittee begins hearings.

Truman relieves MacArthur of his command.

Julius and Ethel Rosenberg are convicted of conspiring to commit espionage.

Truce talks begin in Korea.

1952 United States tests the hydrogen bomb.

Eisenhower is elected president.

the chief culprit was John L. Lewis, head of the United Mine Workers, who had won good wages for coal miners with a militant policy that included wartime walkouts. In a country that still burned coal for most of its energy, the burly, bushy-browed, and combative Lewis was instantly recognizable—loved by his workers and hated by nearly everyone else. In April 1946, a forty-day coal strike hampered industrial production. The coal settlement was only days old when the nation faced an even more crippling walkout by railroad workers. Truman asked for the unprecedented power to draft strikers into the army; the threat led to a quick and dramatic settlement. Many middle-class Americans were convinced that organized labor needed to be curbed.

In November 1946, Republicans capitalized on the problems of reconversion chaos, labor unrest, and dissatisfaction with Truman. Their election slogan was simple: "Had enough?" The GOP won control of Congress for the first time since the election of 1928, continuing the political trend toward the right that had been apparent since 1938.

Adopted by the now firmly conservative Congress, the Taft-Hartley Act was a serious counterattack by big business against large unions. It outlawed several union tools as "unfair labor practices." It barred the closed shop (the requirement that all workers hired in a particular company or plant be union members) and blocked secondary boycotts (strikes against suppliers or customers of a targeted business). The federal government could postpone a strike by imposing a "cooling-off period," which gave companies time to stockpile their output. Officers of national unions had to swear they were not communists or communist sympathizers, even though corporate executives had no similar obligation. The bill passed over Truman's veto.

The GI Bill

Another landmark law for the postwar era passed Congress without controversy. The Servicemen's Readjustment Act of 1944 was designed to ease veterans back into the civilian mainstream. Popularly known as the **GI Bill of Rights**, it was one of the federal government's most successful public assistance programs. Rather than pay cash bonuses to veterans, as after previous wars, Congress tied benefits to specific public goals. The GI Bill guaranteed loans of up to $2,000 for buying a house or farm or starting a business, a substantial sum at a time when a new house cost $6,000. The program encouraged veterans to attend college with money for tuition and books plus monthly stipends.

The GI Bill democratized American higher education by making college degrees accessible to men with working-class backgrounds. It brought far more students into higher education than could otherwise have enrolled. In the peak year of 1947, veterans made up half of all college students. "We're all trying to get where we would have been if there hadn't been a war," one vet attending Indiana University told *Time* magazine. Veterans helped convert the college degree—once available primarily to the socially privileged—into a basic business and professional credential.

College life in 1946 and 1947 meant close quarters. Universities were unequipped to deal with older or married students. Prefabricated apartments from the wartime atomic energy project at Richland, Washington, were trucked to college campuses around the West to house newly enrolled veterans. Recycled Quonset huts became as much a part of campus architecture as gothic towers and ivy-covered halls. States rented surplus defense facilities for big-city extension campuses that would be easier for veterans to attend than traditional small-town universities. Many of these campuses evolved into major public universities, such as the University of Illinois at Chicago and Portland State University in Oregon.

An unfortunate side effect of the GI tide was to crowd women out of classrooms, although sixty thousand servicewomen did take advantage of educational benefits. In 1946, Cornell University made room for veterans by limiting women to 20 percent of its entering class. The University of Wisconsin closed its doors to women from out of state. Women's share of bachelor's degrees dropped from 40 percent in 1940 to 25 percent in 1950. The most common female presence on many campuses was working wives trying to make up the gap between Veterans Administration (VA) checks and the expenses of new families.

Assembly-Line Neighborhoods

Americans faced a housing shortage after the war. In 1947, fully 3 million married couples were unable to set up their own households. Most doubled up with relatives while they waited for the construction industry to respond.

Hunger for housing was fierce. Eager buyers lined up for hours and paid admission fees to tour model homes or to put their names in drawings for the opportunity to buy. When in 1946 the *Des Moines Register and Tribune* ran a fake apartment ad to check real estate industry claims that the housing crisis was over, 351 people answered it. Fifty-six of them said they lived in a hotel or rented room; sixty-eight lived with parents.

The solution started with the federal government and its VA mortgage program. By guaranteeing repayment, the VA allowed veterans to get home purchase loans from private lenders without a down payment. Neither the VA program nor the New Deal–era Federal Housing Administration (FHA) mortgage insurance program, however, could do any good unless there were houses to buy. Eyeing the mass market created by the federal programs, innovative private builders devised their own solution. In 1947, William Levitt, a New York builder who had developed defense housing projects, built two thousand rental houses for veterans on suburban Long Island. His basic house had eight hundred square feet of living space in two bedrooms, living room, kitchen, and bath, a sixty-by-one-hundred-foot lot, and an unfinished attic waiting for the weekend handyman. It gave new families a place to start. There were six thousand **Levittown** houses by the end of 1948 and more than seventeen thousand by 1951.

Other successful builders worked on the same scale. They bought hundreds of acres of land, put in utilities for the entire tract, purchased materials by the carload, and kept specialized workers busy on scores of identical houses. Floor plans were square, simple, and easy for semiskilled workers to construct. For the first time, kitchens across America were designed for preassembled cabinets and appliances in standard sizes. "On-site fabrication" was mass production without an assembly line. Work crews at the Los Angeles suburb of Lakewood started a hundred houses a day as they moved down one side of the street and back up the other, digging foundation trenches, pouring concrete, and working through the dozens of other stages of home building.

From 1946 through 1950, the federal government backed $20 billion in VA and FHA loans, approximately 40 percent of all home mortgage debt. Housing starts neared 2 million in the peak year of 1950. New subdivisions were starting places for couples in their late twenties or early thirties making up for lost time on a tight budget. By the end of the 1940s, 55 percent of American households owned their homes. The figure continued to climb until the 1980s, broadening access to the dream of financial security for many families. All during this time, the suburban population grew much faster

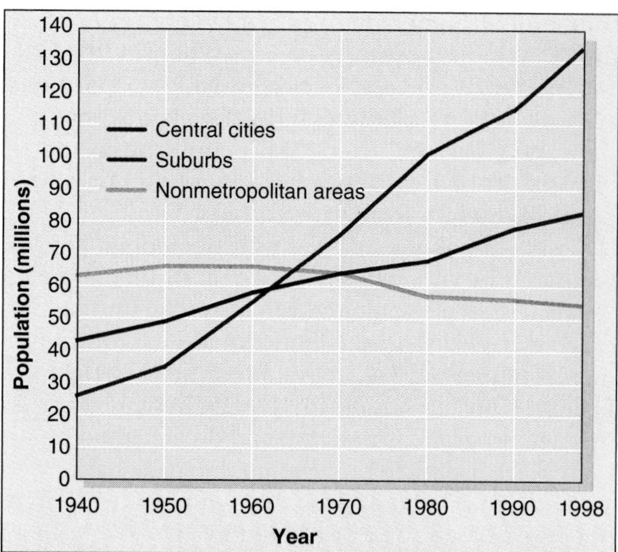

Figure 29-1 The Suburbanizing Nation
In the decades after World War II, Americans moved in unprecedented numbers to new communities surrounding established cities. In the early 1960s, the combined population of suburban areas passed the populations of large central cities and of smaller towns and rural areas.

than the population of central cities, and the population outside the growing reach of metropolitan areas actually declined (see Figure 29-1).

Unfortunately, the suburban solution to housing shortages also had costs. Vast new housing tracts tended to isolate women and children from traditional community life. They also did little to help African Americans. As the migration of black workers and their families to northern and western cities continued after the war, discrimination excluded them from new housing. As late as 1960, the 82,000 residents of Levittown had no African American neighbors; not until 1957 did a black family move into a second Levittown near Philadelphia. Federal housing agencies and private industry worsened the problem by **redlining** older neighborhoods, which involved withholding home purchase loans and insurance coverage from inner-city areas.

Public and private actions kept African Americans in deteriorating inner-city ghettos. When severe flooding in 1948 drove thousands of African Americans from leftover wartime housing in Portland, Oregon, for example, their only choice was to crowd into the city's small black neighborhood. Chicago landlords squeezed an estimated 27,000 black migrants per year into run-down buildings, subdividing larger apartments into one-room "kitchenette" units with sinks and hot plates but no private bathrooms. One tenant commented that rats came "in teams." Families who tried to find new homes in white neighborhoods on the edge of black ghettos often met violence—rocks through windows, firebombs, angry white mobs.

Steps toward Civil Rights

The problem of securing decent housing fueled a demand for civil rights for African Americans. The wartime experience of fighting for freedom abroad while suffering discrimination at home steeled a new generation of black leaders to reduce the gap between America's ideal of equality and its performance. As had also been true after World War I, some white Americans had the opposite view, hoping to reaffirm racial segregation. A wave of racist violence surged across the South after the war; special targets were black veterans who tried to register to vote. However, many white Americans felt uneasy about the contradiction between a crusade for freedom abroad and racial discrimination at home.

In this era of rapid change and racial tension, the Truman administration recognized the importance of securing civil rights for all Americans. Caught between pressure from black leaders and the fear of alienating southern Democrats, the president in 1946 appointed the Committee on Civil Rights, whose report developed an agenda for racial justice that would take two decades to put into effect. The Justice Department began to support antisegregation lawsuits filed by the NAACP. The administration ordered federal housing agencies to modify their racially restrictive policies and prohibited racial discrimination in federal employment.

The president also ordered "equality of treatment and opportunity" in the armed services in July 1948. The army in particular dragged its feet, hoping to limit black enlistees to 10 percent of the total. Manpower needs and the record of integrated units in Korea from 1950 to 1953 persuaded the reluctant generals. Over the next generation, African Americans would find the military an important avenue for career opportunities.

Changes in national policy were important for ending racial discrimination, but far more Americans were interested in the lowering of racial barriers in professional team sports. Americans had applauded individual black champions, such as heavyweight boxer Joe Louis and sprinter Jesse Owens, but team sports required their members to travel, practice, and play together. The center of attention was Jack Roosevelt (Jackie) Robinson, a gifted African American athlete who opened the 1947 baseball season as a member of the Brooklyn Dodgers. Black baseball players had previously displayed their talents

Jackie Robinson with white teammates in the Dodger dugout at Ebbets Field, Brooklyn.

in the Negro leagues, but Robinson broke the color line that had reserved the modern major leagues for white players. His ability to endure taunting and hostility and still excel on the ball field opened the door for other African Americans and Latinos. In the segregated society of the 1940s, Robinson also found himself a powerful symbol of racial change.

Consumer Boom and Baby Boom

The housing boom was a product of both pent-up demand and a postwar "family boom." Americans celebrated the end of the war with weddings; the marriage rate in 1946 surpassed even its wartime high. Many women who left the labor force opted for marriage, and at increasingly younger ages. By 1950, the median age at which women married would be just over 20 years—lower than at any previous time in the twentieth century. Movies in the 1930s had abounded with independent career women. By the late 1940s, Hollywood reflected new attitudes and social patterns by portraying women as helpless victims or supportive wives and publicizing hard-edged stars, such as Joan Crawford, as homebodies at heart. The United States ended the 1940s with 7 million more married couples than at the decade's start.

New marriages jump-started the "baby boom," as did already married couples who decided to catch up after postponing childbearing during the war. In the early 1940s, an average of 2.9 million children per year were born in the United States; in 1946–1950, the average was 3.6 million. Those 3.5 million "extra" babies needed diapers, swing sets, lunch boxes, bicycles, and schoolrooms (see Figure 29-2).

Fast-growing families also needed to stock up on household goods. Out of an average household income of roughly $4,000 in 1946 and 1947, a family of four had $300 to $400 a year for furnishings and appliances. A couple who studied *Consumer Reports* might equip their new Levittown kitchen with a Dripolator coffee maker for $2.45 and Mirro-Matic pressure cooker for $12.95. The thrifty family could get along with a Motorola table radio in brown plastic for under $30; for $100, they could have a massive radio-phonograph combination in a four-foot console—the centerpiece of a well-equipped living room before the arrival of television.

Truman, Republicans, and the Fair Deal

From new radios to new homes to new jobs, the economic gains of the postwar years propelled Americans toward the political center. After fifteen years of economic crisis and world war, they wanted to enjoy prosperity. They wanted to keep the gains of the New Deal—but without risking new experiments. William Levitt tried to humorously capture the American satisfaction with the fruits of free en-

Figure 29-2 The Post-War Baby Boom: The U.S. Birthrate, 1930–1995
The baby boom after World War II was a product of high marriage rates and closely spaced children. The generation of Americans born between 1945 and 1960 has strongly affected American society and politics as its members have gone to school and college, entered the workforce, started their own families, and begun to plan for retirement in the twenty-first century.

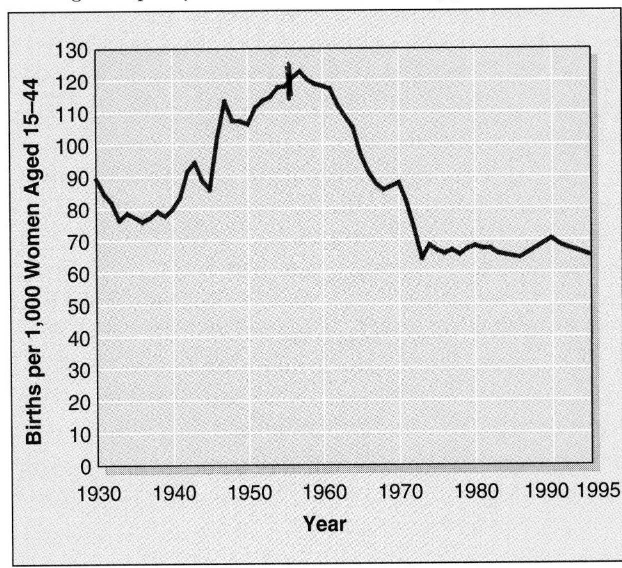

Americans were eager to enjoy the most modern appliances and houses. Manufacturers promoted streamlined kitchens to make life easier for housewives and their families.

terprise when he said in 1948 that "no man who owns his house and lot can be a Communist; he has too much to do."

Recognizing this attitude, Harry Truman and his political advisers tried to define policies acceptable to moderate Republicans as well as Democrats. This meant creating a bipartisan coalition to block Soviet influence in western Europe and defending the core of the New Deal's social and economic agenda at home.

This political package is known as the strategy of the "vital center," after the title of a 1949 book by Arthur Schlesinger, Jr. The book linked anticommunism in foreign policy with efforts to enact inclusive social and economic policies—to extend freedom abroad and at home at the same time. The vital center reflected the political reality of the Cold War years, when Democrats had to prove that they were tough on communism before they could enact domestic reforms. The approach defined the heart of the Democratic party for twenty years and found full expression in the administrations of John Kennedy (1961–1963) and Lyndon Johnson (1963–1969).

Truman's Opposition

Truman had unexpected luck in his campaign for a full term as president in 1948. Besides the Republicans, he faced new fringe parties on the far right and far left that allowed him to position himself in the moderate center. The blunt, no-nonsense Missourian entered the campaign an underdog, but, compared to his rivals, he soon looked like the country's best option for steering a steady course.

Truman's opponents represented the left-leaning American Progressive party, the **Dixiecrats** (officially the States' Rights Democrats), and the Republicans. The president also ran against the Republican-controlled "do-nothing 80th Congress," which he used as a punching bag at every opportunity. The Progressive candidate was Henry Wallace, who had been FDR's vice president from 1941 to 1945 before being dumped in favor of Truman himself; more recently, he had been Truman's secretary of commerce. The Dixiecrat, Governor Strom Thurmond of South Carolina, had bolted the Democratic party over civil rights. The most serious challenger was Republican Thomas Dewey, who had run against Roosevelt in 1944.

Wallace cast himself as the prophet for "the century of the common man." His background as a plant geneticist and farm journalist prepared him to deal with domestic policy but not world affairs. After Truman fired him from the cabinet in 1946 for advocating a conciliatory stance toward the Soviet Union, Wallace went to Europe to praise the USSR and denounced U.S. foreign policy. On his return, enthusiastic college crowds raised his sights—from "scaring the Democratic Party leftward" to running for president. Most liberal Democrats ran the other way when Wallace organized the Progressive party, leaving the Communist party to supply many of his campaign workers.

Wallace argued that the United States was forcing the Cold War on the Soviet Union and undermining American ideals by diverting attention from poverty and racism at home. He wanted to repeal the draft and destroy atomic weapons. His arguments had merit, for the United States was becoming a militarized society, but Wallace was the wrong person to change American minds. With his shy personality, disheveled appearance, and fanaticism about health food, he struck most voters as a kook rather than a statesman. Although a small core of supporters clung to his message of international reconciliation, Wallace made skepticism about the Cold War increasingly vulnerable to right-wing attack.

At the other political extreme were the Southerners who walked out when the 1948 Democratic National Convention called for full civil rights for African Americans. The raucous convention debate previewed the politics of the 1960s. Mayor Hubert Humphrey of Minneapolis challenged the Democratic party "to get out of the shadow of states' rights and walk forthrightly into the bright sunshine of human rights." His speech foreshadowed Humphrey's twenty years of liberal influence in the Democratic party, culminating in his presidential nomination in 1968.

When the angry Southerners met to nominate their own candidate, however, the South's important politicians stayed away. They had worked too long to throw away seniority and influence in Congress and the Democratic party. Major southern newspapers called the revolt futile and narrow-minded. Strom Thurmond claimed that the Dixiecrats were really trying to defend Americans against government bureaucracy, not fighting to preserve racial segregation, but few listened outside the deep South.

Tom Dewey, Truman's real opponent, had a high opinion of himself. He had been an effective governor of New York and represented the moderate eastern establishment within the Republican party. Fortunately for Truman, Dewey lacked the common touch. Smooth on the outside, he alienated people who should have been his closest supporters; as one political acquaintance put it, "You have to know Dewey really well to dislike him." He was an arrogant campaigner, refusing to interrupt his morning schedule to talk to voters. He acted like a snob and dressed like the groom on a wedding cake.

Dewey was also saddled with the results of the 80th Congress (1947–1948). Truman used confrontation with Congress to rally voters who had supported the New Deal. He introduced legislation that he knew would be ignored, and he used his veto even when he knew Congress would override it. All the while he was building a list of campaign issues by demonstrating that the Republicans were obstructionists. Vote for me, Truman argued, to protect the New Deal, or vote Republican to bring back the days of Herbert Hoover. After his nomination in July 1948, Truman called Congress back into session and dared Republicans to enact all the measures for which their party claimed to stand. Congress did nothing, and Truman had more proof that the Republicans were all talk and no show.

Whistle-Stopping across America

The 1948 presidential campaign mixed old and new. For the last time, a major candidate crisscrossed the nation by rail and made hundreds of speeches from the rear platforms of trains. For the first time, national television broadcast the two party conventions, although the primitive cameras showed the handful of viewers little more than talking heads. The Republican campaign issued a printed T-shirt that read "Dew-It With Dewey"—the earliest advertising T-shirt in the collections of the Smithsonian Institution.

Truman ran on both character and issues. He was a widely read and intelligent man who cultivated the image of a backslapper. "I'll mow 'em down . . . and I'll give 'em hell," he told his vice presidential running mate. Crowds across the country greeted him with "Give 'em hell, Harry!" He covered 31,700 miles in his campaign train and gave ten speeches a day. Republicans belittled the small towns and cities he visited, calling them "whistle-stops." Democrats made the term a badge of pride for places like Laramie, Wyoming, and Pocatello, Idaho.

Truman brought the campaign home to average Americans. On the advice of political strategist Clark Clifford, he tied Dewey to inflation, housing shortages, and fears about the future of Social Security. In industrial cities, he hammered at the Taft-Hartley Act. In the West, he pointed out that Democratic administrations had built dams and helped turn natural resources into jobs. He called the Republicans the party of privilege and arrogance.

Harry Truman greets supporters and railroad workers in Pittsburgh at the start of an eighteen-state campaign tour in June 1948. Truman's grassroots campaign and down-home style helped him pull out an unexpected victory in November 1948.

The Democrats, he said, offered opportunity for farmers, factory workers, and small business owners.

Truman got a huge boost from Dewey's unwillingness to fight. Going into the fall with a huge lead in the public opinion polls, Dewey sought to avoid mistakes. He failed to counter Truman's attacks and packed his speeches with platitudes: "Our streams abound with fish." "You know that your future is still ahead of you." "Peace is a blessing that we all share." The results astounded the poll takers, who had stopped sampling opinion in mid-October—just as a swing to Truman gathered strength. Wallace and Thurmond each took just under 1.2 million votes. Dewey received nearly 22 million popular votes and 189 electoral votes, but Truman won more than 24 million popular votes and 303 electoral votes (see Map 29-1).

Truman's Fair Deal

Truman hoped to build on the gains of the New Deal. In his State of the Union address in January 1949, he called for a **Fair Deal** for all Americans. He

Map 29-1 The Election of 1948
Harry Truman won a narrow victory in the presidential election of 1948 by holding many of the traditionally Democratic states of the South and West and winning key industrial states in the Middle West. His success depended on the coalition of rural and urban interests that Franklin Roosevelt had pulled together in the 1930s.

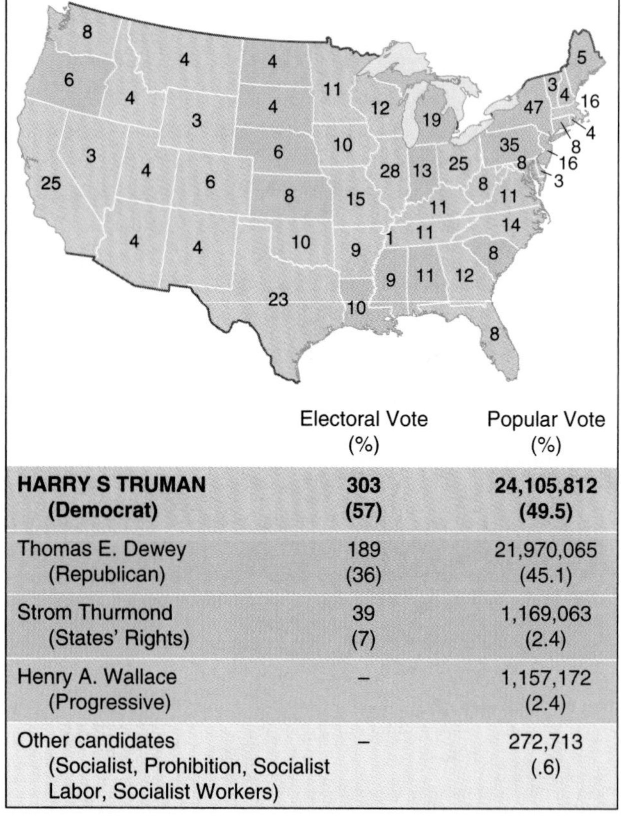

	Electoral Vote (%)	Popular Vote (%)
HARRY S TRUMAN (Democrat)	**303 (57)**	**24,105,812 (49.5)**
Thomas E. Dewey (Republican)	189 (36)	21,970,065 (45.1)
Strom Thurmond (States' Rights)	39 (7)	1,169,063 (2.4)
Henry A. Wallace (Progressive)	–	1,157,172 (2.4)
Other candidates (Socialist, Prohibition, Socialist Labor, Socialist Workers)	–	272,713 (.6)

promised to extend the New Deal and ensure "greater economic opportunity for the mass of the people." Over the next four years, however, conservative Republicans and southern Democrats forced Congress to chose carefully among Truman's proposals, accepting those that expanded existing programs but rejecting new departures.

In the Housing Act of 1949, the federal government reaffirmed its concern about families who had been priced out of the private market. Passed with the backing of conservative Senator Robert Taft—"Mr. Republican" to his admirers—the act provided money for local housing agencies to buy, clear, and resell land for housing. The intent was to clear "substandard and blighted areas" and replace them with affordable modern apartments. The program never worked as intended because of scanty appropriations and poor design of the replacement housing, but it established the goal of decent housing for all Americans.

In 1950, Congress revitalized the weak Social Security program. Benefits went up by an average of 80 percent, and 10.5 million additional people received old-age and survivors' insurance. Most of the new coverage went to rural and small-town people, thus consolidating the broad support that has made it politically difficult to change Social Security ever since, even in the face of projected shortages in the twenty-first century.

Congress rejected other Fair Deal proposals that would remain on the national agenda for decades. A plan to alter the farm subsidy system to favor small farmers rather than agribusiness went nowhere. A Senate filibuster killed a permanent Fair Employment Practices Commission to fight racial discrimination in hiring, halting progress toward civil rights. The medical establishment blocked a proposal for national health insurance as "socialistic," leaving the issue to be revisited in the 1960s (with the passage of Medicare and Medicaid) and 1990s (with Bill Clinton's proposals for health care reform). The overall message from Truman's second term was clear: Americans liked what the New Deal had given them but were hesitant about new initiatives.

Confronting the Soviet Union

In 1945, the United States and the Soviet Union were allies, victorious against Germany and planning the defeat of Japan. By 1947, they were engaged in a diplomatic and economic confrontation and soon came close to war over the city of Berlin. Business tycoon and presidential adviser Bernard Baruch characterized the conflict in April 1947 as a "cold war," and newspaper columnist Walter Lippmann quickly popularized the term.

Over the next forty years, the United States and the USSR contested for economic, political, and military influence around the globe. The heart of Soviet policy was control of eastern Europe as a buffer zone against Germany. The centerpiece of American policy was to link the United States, western Europe, and Japan into an alliance of overwhelming economic power. Both sides spent vast sums on conventional military forces and atomic weapons that held the world in a balance of terror. They also competed for political advantage in Asia and Africa as newly independent nations replaced European colonial empires. For the United States, the Cold War was simultaneously an effort to promote democracy in Europe, maintain a strategically favorable military position in relation to the USSR, and preserve its leadership of the world economy.

Each party in the Cold War thought the worst of the other. Behind the conflicts were Soviet insecurity about an aggressive West and American fear of communist expansionism. Americans and Soviets frequently interpreted each other's actions in the most threatening terms, turning miscalculations and misunderstandings into crises. A U.S. public that had suffered through nearly two decades of economic depression and war reacted to international problems with frustration and anger. The emotional burdens of the Cold War warped and narrowed a generation of American political life around the requirements of anticommunism.

The End of the Grand Alliance

The Yalta Conference of February 1945 had recognized military realities by marking out rough spheres of influence. The Soviet defeat of Germany on the Eastern Front had made the USSR the only military power in eastern Europe. The American and British attacks through Italy and France had made the Western allies dominant in western Europe and the Mediterranean. The Soviets, Americans, British, and French shared control of defeated Germany, each with its own occupation zone and its own sector of Berlin. The Western allies had the better of the bargain. Defeated Italy and Japan, whose reconstruction was firmly in Western hands, had far greater economic potential than Soviet-controlled Bulgaria, Romania, or Hungary. In addition, the British, French, and American occupation zones in western Germany had more people and industrial potential than the Russian zone in eastern Germany.

As the victorious powers tried to put their broad agreements into operation, they argued bitterly about Germany and eastern Europe. Was the Soviet Union to dominate eastern Europe, or was the region to be open to Western economic and political influence? For Poland, Truman and his advisers claimed that Yalta had assumed open elections on the American model. The Soviet Union saw Poland as the historic invasion route from the west; it claimed that Yalta had ensured that any Polish government would be friendly to Soviet interests and acted to guarantee that this would be so.

Facing Soviet intransigence over eastern Europe, Truman decided that the United States should "take the lead in running the world in the way the world ought to be run." One technique was economic pressure. The State Department "mislaid" a Soviet request for redevelopment loans. The United States and Britain objected to Soviet plans to take industrial equipment and raw materials from the western occupation zones in Germany, compensation that the Soviets thought they had been promised.

The United States also tried to involve the USSR and eastern Europe in new international organizations. The Senate approved American membership in the newly organized United Nations (UN) with only two opposing votes, a sharp contrast to its rejection of the League of Nations in 1920. The Washington-based **International Monetary Fund (IMF)** and the **World Bank** were designed to revive international trade. The IMF stabilized national currencies against the short-term pressures of international trade. The World Bank drew on the resources of member nations to make economic development loans to governments for such projects as new dams or agricultural modernization. These organizations ensured that a reviving world economy would revolve around the industrial and technological power of the United States.

In 1946, the United States also presented a plan in the United Nations to control atomic energy. Bernard Baruch suggested that an international agency should oversee all uranium production and research on atomic explosives. The Baruch plan emphasized enforcement and inspections that would have opened the Soviet nuclear effort to American interference, an unacceptable prospect for a nation trying to catch up with the United States by building its own atomic bombs. On-site inspection would remain a problem in arms control negotiations for the next half-century.

While UN delegates debated the future of atomic energy, American leaders were becoming convinced of Soviet aggressiveness. In February

1946, George Kennan, a senior American diplomat in Moscow, sent a "long telegram" to the State Department. He depicted a USSR driven by expansionist communist ideology. The Soviets, he argued, would constantly probe for weaknesses in the capitalist world. The best response was firm resistance to protect the western heartlands.

The British encouraged the same tough stand. Lacking the strength to shape Europe on its own, Great Britain repeatedly nudged the United States to block Soviet influence. Speaking at Westminster College in Missouri in March 1946, Winston Churchill warned that the USSR had dropped an "iron curtain" across the middle of Europe and urged a firm Western response.

Churchill's speech matched the mood in official Washington. Truman's foreign policy advisers shared the belief in an aggressive Soviet Union, and the president himself saw the world as a series of either-or choices. Administration leaders did not fear an immediate Soviet military threat to the United States itself, for they knew that World War II had exhausted the USSR. But they also knew that the Soviets were strong enough to brush aside the U.S. occupation forces in Germany. Added to military apprehension were worries about political and economic competition. Communist parties in war-ravaged Europe and Japan were exploiting discontent. In Asia and Africa, the allegiance of nationalists who were fighting for independence from France, Great Britain, and the Netherlands remained in doubt. America's leaders worried that much of the Eastern Hemisphere might fall under Soviet control and turn its back on North America.

Were Truman and his advisers right about Soviet intentions? The evidence is mixed. In their determination to avoid another Munich, Truman and the "wise men" who made up his foreign policy circle ignored examples of Soviet caution and conciliation. The Soviets withdrew troops from Manchuria in northern China and acquiesced in America's control of defeated Japan. They allowed a neutral but democratic government in Finland and technically free elections in Hungary and Czechoslovakia (although it was clear that communists would do well there). They demobilized much of their huge army and reduced their forces in eastern Europe while expecting a falling out between capitalist Britain and the United States.

However, the Soviet regime also did more than enough to justify American fears. The USSR could not resist interfering in the Middle East. It pressured Turkey to give it partial control of the exit from the Black Sea. It retained troops in northern Iran until warned out by the United States. The Soviets were ruthless in support of communist control in Bulgaria, Romania, and Poland. U.S. policymakers read these Soviet actions as a rerun of Nazi aggression and determined not to let a new totalitarian threat undermine Western power.

The Truman Doctrine and the Marshall Plan

Whatever restraint the USSR showed was too late or too little. Early in 1947, Truman and his advisers decided on decisive action. The British could no longer afford to back the Greek government that was fighting communist rebels, and U.S. officials feared that a communist takeover in Greece would threaten the stability of Italy, France, and the Middle East. Truman coupled his case for intervention in Greece with an appeal for aid to Turkey, which lived under the shadow of the USSR. On March 12, he told Congress that the United States faced a "fateful hour." Taking the advice of Senator Arthur Vandenberg to "scare the hell out of the country," he said that only the appropriation of $400 million to fight communism in Greece and Turkey could secure the free world. Congress agreed, and the United States became the dominant power in the eastern Mediterranean.

Framing the specific request was a sweeping declaration that became known as the **Truman Doctrine**. The president pledged to use U.S. economic power to help free nations everywhere resist internal subversion or aggression. "It must be the policy of the United States," he said, "to support free peoples who are resisting attempted subjugation by armed minorities or by outside pressures. . . . I believe that our help should be primarily through economic and financial aid, which is essential to economic stability and orderly political processes."

Meanwhile, Europe was sliding toward chaos. Germany was close to famine after the bitter winter of 1946–1947. Western European nations were bankrupt and unable to import raw materials for their factories. Overstressed medical systems could no longer control diseases such as tuberculosis. Communist parties had gained in Italy, France, and Germany. Winston Churchill, again sounding the alarm, described Europe as "a rubble-heap, a charnel house, a breeding ground of pestilence and hate."

The U.S. government responded with unprecedented economic aid. Secretary of State George C. Marshall announced the European Recovery Plan on June 5, 1947. What the press quickly dubbed the **Marshall Plan** committed the United States to help rebuild Europe. The United States invited Soviet and eastern European participation, but under terms that would have reduced Moscow's control over its satellite economies. The Soviets refused, fearing that the United States wanted to undermine its influence, instead organizing their eastern European satellites in their own association for Mutual Economic Assistance, or **Comecon**, in 1949. In western Europe, the Marshall Plan was a success. Aid totaled $13.5 billion over four years. It met many of Europe's economic needs and quieted class conflict. Unlike the heavy-handed Soviet role in eastern Europe, the Marshall Plan expanded American influence through cooperative efforts. Because Europeans spent much of the aid on U.S. goods and machinery and because economic recovery promised markets for U.S. products, business and labor both supported it. In effect, the Marshall Plan created an "empire by invitation" in which Americans and Europeans jointly planned European recovery.

U.S. policy in Japan followed the pattern set in Europe. As supreme commander of the Allied Powers, General Douglas MacArthur acted as Japan's postwar dictator. He tried to change the values of the old war-prone Japan through social reform, democratization, and demilitarization. At the end of 1947, however, the United States decided that democracy and pacifism could go too far. Policymakers were fearful of economic collapse and political chaos, just as in Europe. The "reverse course" in occupation policy aimed to make Japan an economic magnet for other nations in East Asia, pulling them toward the American orbit and away from the Soviet Union. MacArthur reluctantly accepted the new policy of "economic crank-up" by preserving Japan's corporate giants and encouraging American investment. At American insistence, the new Japan accepted American bases and created its own "self-defense force" (with no capacity for overseas aggression).

George Kennan summed up the new American policies in the magazine *Foreign Affairs* in July 1947. Writing anonymously as "X," Kennan argued that the Soviet leaders were committed to a long-term strategy of expanding communism. The proper posture of the United States, he said, should be an equally patient commitment to "firm and vigilant containment of Russian expansive tendencies." Kennan warned that the emerging Cold War would be a long conflict with no quick fixes.

Soviet Reactions

The bold American moves in the first half of 1947 put the USSR on the defensive. In response, Soviet leaders orchestrated strenuous opposition to the Marshall Plan by French and Italian communists. East of the iron curtain, Hungarian communists expelled noncommunists from a coalition government. Bulgarian communists shot opposition leaders. Romania, Bulgaria, and Hungary signed defense pacts with the Soviet Union.

In early 1948, the Soviets targeted Czechoslovakia. For three years, a neutral coalition government there on the model of Finland had balanced trade with the West with a foreign policy friendly to the USSR. In February 1948, while Russian forces assembled on the Czech borders, local communists pushed aside Czechoslovakia's democratic leadership and turned the nation into a dictatorship and Soviet satellite within a week.

The climax of the Soviet reaction came in divided Berlin, located 110 miles inside the Soviet Union's East German occupation zone. On June 24, 1948, Soviet troops blockaded surface traffic into Berlin, cutting off the U.S., British, and French sectors. The immediate Soviet aim was to block Western plans to merge their three occupation zones into an independent federal republic (West Germany). Rather than abandon 2.5 million Berliners or shoot their way through, the Western nations responded to the **Berlin blockade** by airlifting supplies to the city. Planes landed every two minutes at Berlin's Tempelhof Airport. Stalin decided not to intercept the flights. After eleven months, the Soviets abandoned the blockade, making the Berlin airlift a triumph of American resolve.

Berlin in 1948 was still a devastated city of gutted buildings and heaps of rubble. When the Soviet Union shut off ground access to Berlin's British, French, and American occupation zones, the city also became a symbol of the West's Cold War resolve. Allied aircraft lifted in food, fuel, and other essentials for West Berliners for nearly a year until the Soviets ended the blockade.

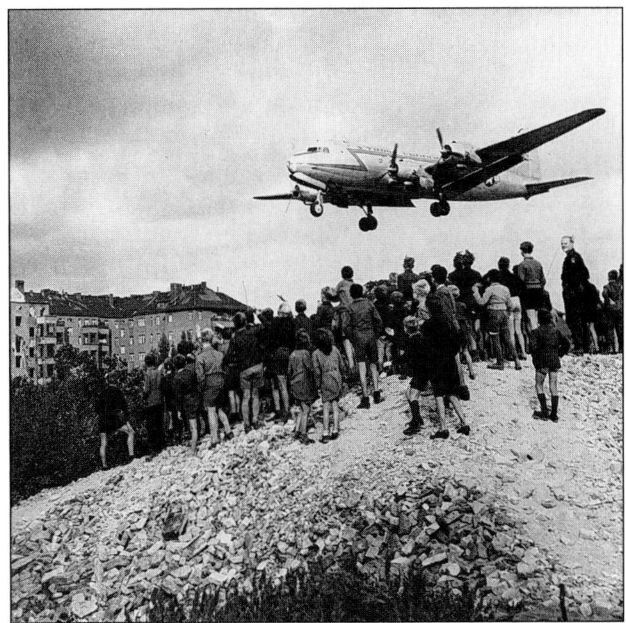

American Rearmament

The coup in Czechoslovakia and the Berlin blockade shocked American leaders and backfired on the Soviets. The economic assistance strategy of 1947 now looked inadequate. Congress responded in 1948 by reinstating the military draft and increasing defense spending. Much of the money bought new war planes, as thrifty congressmen decided that air power was the easiest way for the United States to project its military power abroad.

The United States had already begun to modernize and centralize its national security apparatus, creating the institutions that would run foreign policy in the second half of the century. The National Security Act of July 1947 created the **Central Intelligence Agency (CIA)** and the **National Security Council (NSC)**. The CIA handled intelligence gathering and covert operations. The NSC assembled top diplomatic and military advisers in one committee. In 1949, legislation also created the Department of Defense to oversee the army, navy, and air force (independent from the army since 1947). The new post of chairman of the Joint Chiefs of Staff was supposed to coordinate the rival branches of the military.

In April 1949, ten European nations, the United States, and Canada signed the North Atlantic Treaty as a mutual defense pact. American commitments to the **North Atlantic Treaty Organization (NATO)** included military aid and the deployment of U.S. troops in western Europe. As Republican Senator Robert Taft warned in the ratification debate, NATO was the sort of "entangling alliance" that the United States had avoided for 160 years. It was also the insurance policy that western Europeans required if they were to accept the dangers as well as the benefits of a revived Germany, which was economically and militarily necessary for a strong Europe. In short, NATO was a sort of marriage contract between Europe and the previously standoffish United States. After 1955, its counterpart would be the **Warsaw Pact** for mutual defense among the USSR and its European satellites (see Map 29-2).

Two years later, the United States signed similar but less comprehensive agreements in the western Pacific: the ANZUS Pact with Australia and New Zealand and a new treaty with the Philippines. The alliances reassured Pacific allies who were nervously watching the United States negotiate a unilateral peace treaty with Japan (ignoring the Soviet Union). The United States overcame opposition from nations that Japan had attacked in World War II by promising to assist their defense and maintaining military bases in Japan. Taken together, peacetime rearmament and mutual defense pacts amounted to a revolution in American foreign policy.

Cold War and Hot War

The first phase of the Cold War reached a crisis in the autumn of 1949. The two previous years had seen an uneasy equilibrium in which American success in southern and western Europe and the standoff over Berlin (the blockade ended in May 1949) balanced the consolidation of Soviet power in eastern Europe. Now, suddenly, two key events seemed to tilt the world balance against the United States and its allies. In September, Truman announced that the Soviet Union had tested its own atomic bomb. A month later, the Chinese communists under Mao Zedong (Mao Tse-tung) took power in China. The following summer, civil war in Korea sucked the United States into a fierce war with communist North Korea and China. While Americans studied maps that showed communism spreading across Europe and Asia, their government accelerated a forty-year arms race with the Soviet Union.

The Nuclear Shadow

Experts in Washington had known that the Soviets were working on an A-bomb, but the news dismayed the average citizen. As newspapers and magazines scared their readers with artists' renditions of the effects of an atomic bomb on New York or Chicago, the shock tilted U.S. nuclear policy toward military uses. In 1946, advocates of civilian control had won a small victory when Congress gave control of atomic energy to the new **Atomic Energy Commission (AEC)**. The AEC tried to balance research on atomic power with continued testing of new weapons. Now Truman told the AEC to double the output of fissionable uranium and plutonium for "conventional" nuclear weapons.

A more momentous decision soon followed. Truman decided in January 1950 to authorize work on the "super" bomb—the thermonuclear fusion weapon that would become the hydrogen bomb (H-bomb). The debate over the "super" pitted a cautious scientific advisory committee and J. Robert Oppenheimer against powerful political figures and a handful of scientists who believed correctly that the Soviets were already at work on a similar weapon. As would be true in future nuclear defense debates, the underlying question was how much capacity for nuclear destruction was enough.

Nuclear weapons proliferated in the early 1950s. The United States exploded the first hydro-

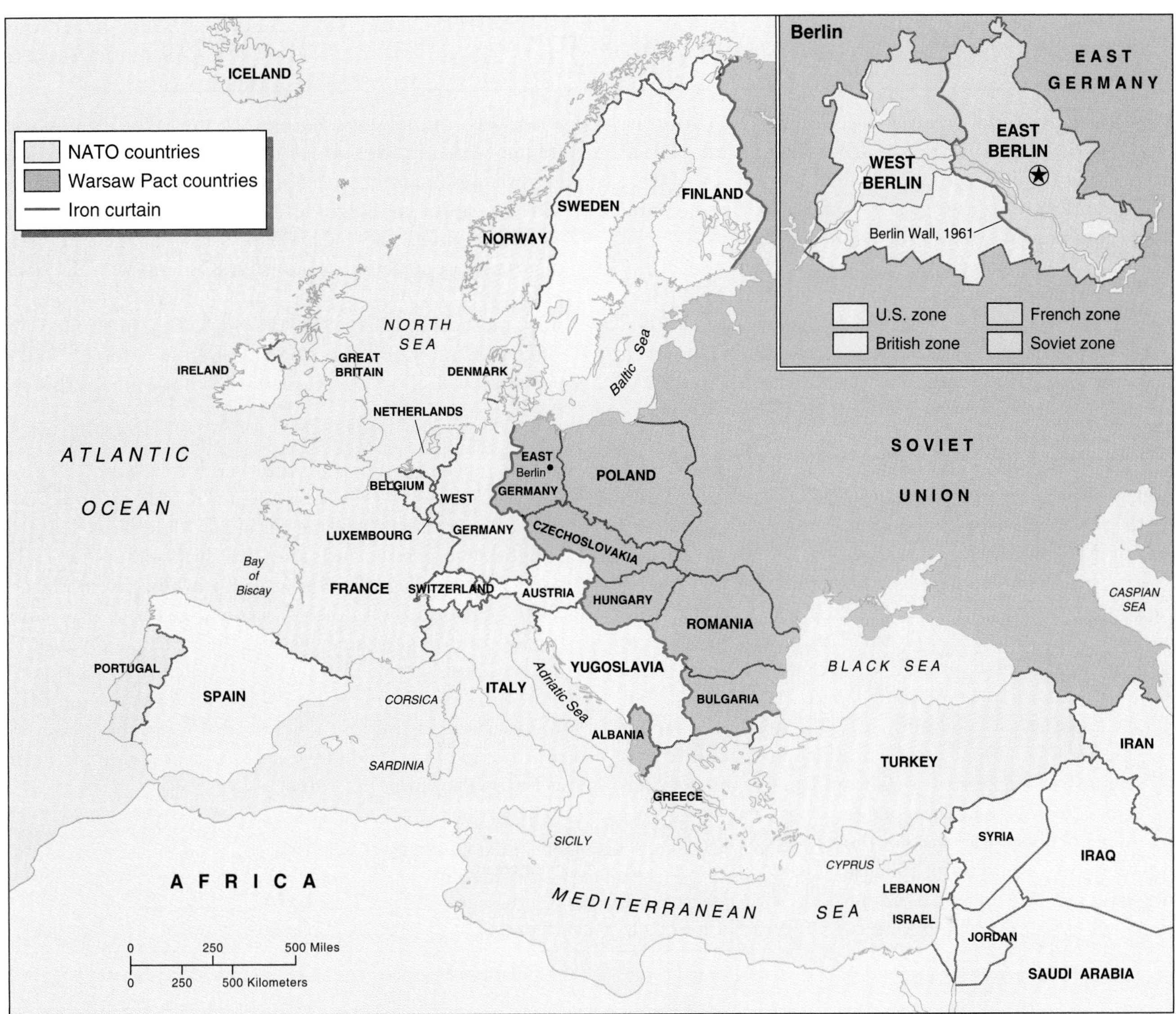

Map 29-2 Cold War in Europe
In the late 1940s and 1950s, the Cold War split Europe into rigidly divided western and eastern blocs. Members of NATO allied with the United States to oppose Soviet expansion. The Soviet Union directed the military and foreign policies of members of the Warsaw Pact.

gen bomb in the South Pacific in November 1952. Releasing one hundred times the energy of the Hiroshima bomb, the detonation tore a mile-long chasm in the ocean floor. Great Britain became the third nuclear power in the same year. The Soviet Union tested its own hydrogen bomb only nine months after the U.S. test. Americans who remembered the attack on Pearl Harbor now worried that the Soviets might send fleets of bombers over the Arctic to surprise U.S. military forces and smash its cities into radioactive powder.

The nuclear arms race and the gnawing fear of nuclear war multiplied the apprehensions of the Cold War. Under the guidance of the Federal Civil Defense Administration, Americans learned that they should always keep a battery-powered radio and tune to 640 or 1240 on the AM dial for emergency information when they heard air raid sirens. Schoolchildren learned to hide under their desks when they saw the blinding flash of a nuclear detonation. Popular literature in the 1950s was filled with stories in which nuclear war destroyed civilization and left a handful of survivors to pick through the rubble.

More insidiously, nuclear weapons development generated new environmental and health problems. Soldiers were exposed to post-test radiation with minimal protection. Nuclear tests in the South Pacific dusted fishing boats with radioactivity

FROM THEN TO NOW

NATO

The North Atlantic Treaty Organization (NATO) celebrated its fiftieth anniversary at a meeting of heads of state in Washington in April 1999. Four thousand miles away, British and American warplanes under NATO command were bombing Yugoslav army units in the province of Kosovo, trying to prevent the wholesale expulsion of the province's 2 million ethnic Albanians (out of a total population of 2.2 million). A few weeks later, in June 1999, NATO ground forces entered Kosovo to maintain order in place of withdrawing Yugoslav troops. The NATO peacekeeping contingents came from Britain, France, Germany, Italy, the Netherlands, and the United States.

The seventy-eight-day air war and the occupation of Kosovo by fifty thousand NATO troops were dramatic evidence of the transformation of NATO after the end of the Cold War.

In 1949, the new North Atlantic Treaty Organization had three purposes. The first was to unite noncommunist nations of western Europe in an alliance against the Soviet Union. The second was to formally commit the United States and Canada to the defense of western Europe, a commitment that involved placing substantial U.S. military forces in Europe. The third was to establish a framework that would make the rearmament of West Germany acceptable to other European nations. For the next forty years—until the collapse of eastern European communism—NATO coordinated western European defense planning and remained a foundation stone of U.S. foreign policy.

The new NATO is a product of the new Europe of the 1990s. A key step was expansion into the former Soviet sphere in eastern Europe. At the anniversary summit in 1999, NATO formally admitted Poland, Hungary, and the Czech Republic. Over the objections of Russia, the action erased the last vestige of the buffer of satellite nations that the USSR had created after World War II.

The other fundamental change was a redefinition of NATO's purpose from defense against outside invasion to peacekeeping within Europe. The focus in the later 1990s was southeastern Europe. In the 1990s, Yugoslavia fragmented into five independent nations (the name Yugoslavia was retained by the predominantly Serbian nation with its capital at Belgrade). Bitter civil war erupted in Bosnia in middecade. Christian Serbs engaged in massacres and deportations of Muslim Bosnians with the goal of creating "ethnically clean" Serbian districts. Too late to stop most bloodshed, NATO eventually intervened in 1995. U.S. and European troops arrived to enforce a shaky peace accord and division of the territory into Serb and Bosnian sectors.

After this tentative first step, NATO in 1999 found it easier to agree on intervention in Kosovo. Here too, the issue was ethnic cleansing. A militant independence movement among ethnic Albanians led to Yougoslav reprisals and another civil war. NATO air strikes against Yugoslav forces in Kosovo began in March 1999 and eventually totaled more that thirty thousand sorties. In order to satisfy Russia, the peacekeeping force that entered Kosovo in June was technically a U.S. operation. But it was a reinvented NATO that negotiated with Yugoslavia. Insisting on "essential NATO participation in peacekeeping," the alliance defined a new role for itself as Europe's own police force.

The United States has maintained a naval presence in the Mediterranean Sea since World War II and the era of the Cold War. Shown here in June 1998, the assault carrier USS Wasp and its warplanes are engaged in a show of force by NATO along the borders of Yugoslavia with the goal of changing its government's policies toward non-Serb minorities.

and forced islanders to abandon contaminated homes. Las Vegas promoted tests in southern Nevada as tourist attractions, but radioactive fallout contaminated large sections of the West and increased cancer rates among "downwinders" in Utah. Weapons production and atomic experiments contaminated vast tracts in Nevada, Washington, and Colorado and left huge environmental costs for later generations (see Map 29-3).

The Cold War in Asia

Communist victory in China's civil war was as predictable as the Soviet nuclear bomb but no less controversial. American military and diplomatic missions in the late 1940s pointed out that the collapse of Jiang Jieshi's Nationalist regime was nearly inevitable, given its corruption and narrow support. Nevertheless, Americans looked for a scapegoat when Jiang's anticommunist government and fragments of the Nationalist army fled to the island of Taiwan off China's southern coast.

Advocates for Jiang, mostly conservative Republicans from the Midwest and West, were certain that Truman's administration had done too little. "China asked for a sword," complained one senator, "and we gave her a dull paring knife." Critics looked for scapegoats. Foreign service officers who had honestly analyzed the weakness of the Nationalists were accused of communist sympathies and hounded from their jobs. The results were tragedy for those unfairly branded as traitors and damage to the State Department—a weakness that would haunt the United States as it became entangled in southeast Asia in the 1950s and 1960s.

Mao's victory expanded a deep fissure between "Europe first" and "Asia first" approaches to American foreign policy. Both during and after World War II, the United States had made Europe its first priority. Strong voices, however, had persistently argued that America's future lay with China, Japan, and the Pacific nations. Influential senators claimed that the "loss of China" was the disastrous result of putting the needs of England and France above the long-term interests of the United States.

NSC-68 and Aggressive Containment

The turmoil of 1949 led to a comprehensive statement of American strategic goals. In April 1950, the State Department prepared a sweeping report known as **National Security Council Paper 68 (NSC-68)**. The document described a world divided between the forces of "slavery" and "freedom" and assumed that the Soviet Union was actively aggressive, motivated by greed for territory and a "fanatic faith" in communism. To defend civilization itself, said the experts, the United States should use as much force as needed to resist communist expansion anywhere and everywhere.

The authors of NSC-68 thought in terms of military solutions. Truman and his advisers in 1947 and 1948 had hoped to contain the Soviets by diplomacy and by integrating the economies of Europe and Japan with that of the United States. Now that the Soviets had the atomic bomb, however, the American atomic shield might be neutralized. Instead, NSC-68 argued that the United States needed to press friendly nations to rearm and to make its former enemies into military allies. It also argued that

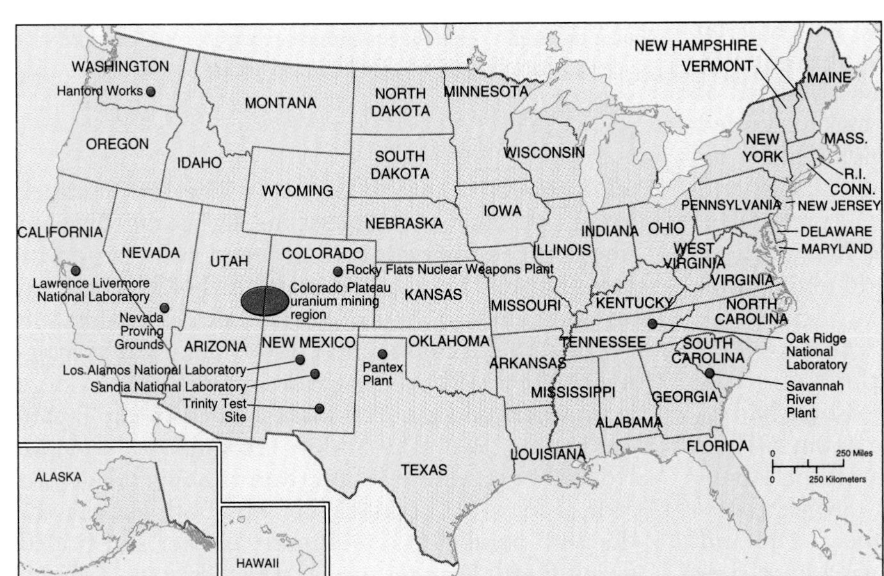

Map 29-3 The Landscape of Nuclear Weapons
The development and production of nuclear weapons concentrated in the West and South. The World War II sites of Hanford, Los Alamos, and Oak Ridge remained active after the war. Workers at Savannah River, Rocky Flats, and Pantex produced nuclear materials. Scientists and engineers at Lawrence-Livermore and Sandia laboratories designed and assembled weapons that were tested at the Nevada Proving Grounds. Prospectors with Geiger counters swarmed over the canyons of southwestern Colorado and southeastern Utah in a uranium mining rush in the early 1950s.

the nation needed expensive conventional forces to defend Europe on the ground and to react to crises as a "world policeman." NSC-68 thus advocated nearly open-ended increases in the defense budget (which in fact tripled between 1950 and 1954).

NSC-68 summed up what many people already believed. Although it was not a public document, its portrait of implacable communist expansion would have made sense to most Americans; it certainly did to Harry Truman. The outbreak of war in Korea at the end of June 1950 seemed to confirm that communism was a military threat. The thinking behind the report led the United States to approach the Cold War as a military competition and to view political changes in Africa and Asia as parts of a Soviet plan. The need for a flexible military response became the centerpiece of an American policy of active intervention that led eventually to the jungles of Vietnam in the 1960s. And the report's implied strategy of bankrupting the communists through competitive defense spending helped destroy the Soviet Union at the end of the 1980s.

War in Korea, 1950–1953

The success of Mao and the Chinese communists forced the Truman administration to define national interests in east Asia and the western Pacific. The most important U.S. interest was Japan, still an industrial power despite its devastating defeat. The United States had denied the Soviet Union any part in the occupation of Japan in 1945 and had shaped a more democratic nation that would be a strong and friendly trading partner. Protected by American armed forces, Japan would be part of a crescent of offshore strong points that included Alaska, the Philippines, Australia, and New Zealand.

Two questions remained at the start of 1950 (and were still troublesome at the turn of the century). One was the future of Taiwan and the remnants of Jiang's regime. Some American policymakers wanted to defend Jiang against the communists. Others assumed that his tattered forces would collapse and allow Mao to complete the communist takeover of Chinese territory. The other question was Korea, whose own civil war would soon bring the world to the brink of World War III.

The Korean peninsula is the closest point on the Asian mainland to Japan. With three powerful neighbors—China, Russia, and Japan—Korea had always had to fight for its independence. From 1910 to 1945, it had been an oppressed colony of the Japanese empire. As World War II ended, Soviet troops moved down the peninsula from the north and American forces landed in the south, creating a situ-

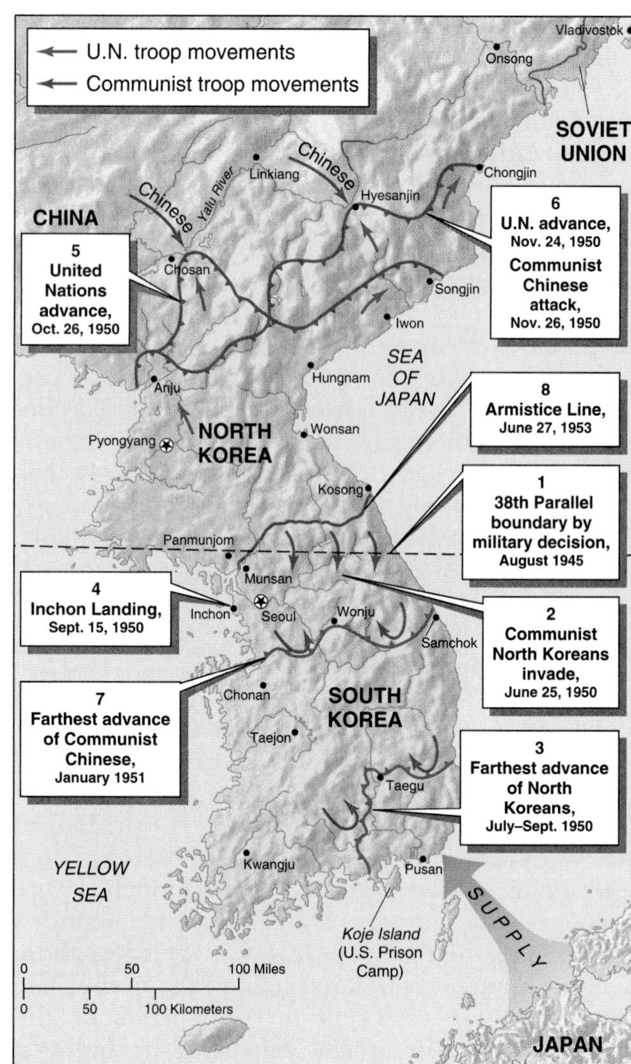

Map 29-4 The Korean War
After rapid reversals of fortune in 1950 and early 1951, the war in Korea settled into stalemate. Most Americans agreed with the need to contain communist expansion but found it deeply frustrating to fight for limited objectives rather than total victory.

ation similar to that in Germany. The 38th parallel, which Russians and Americans set as the dividing line between their zones of occupation, became a de facto border. The United States in 1948 recognized an independent South Korea, with its capital at Seoul, under a conservative government led by Syngman Rhee. Rhee's support came from large landowners and a police force trained by the Japanese before 1945. The Soviets recognized a separate North Korea, whose leader, Kim Il Sung, advocated radical social and political change. Both leaders saw the 38th parallel as a temporary barrier and hoped to unify all Koreans under their own rule. Each crushed political dissent and tried to undermine the other with economic pressure and commando raids.

As early as 1947, the United States had decided that Korea itself was not essential to American military strategy. Planners assumed that U.S. air power in Japan could neutralize unfriendly forces on the Korean peninsula. But Korea remained politically important as the only point of direct confrontation with the Soviet Union in Asia. In January 1950, Secretary of State Dean Acheson carefully excluded Korea from the primary "defensive perimeter" of the United States but kept open the possibility of international guarantees for Korean security.

On June 25, 1950, North Korea, helped by Soviet equipment and Chinese training, attacked South Korea, starting the **Korean War**, which lasted until 1953 (see Map 29-4). Truman and Acheson believed that Moscow lay behind the invasion. They worried that the attack was a ploy to suck America's limited military resources into Asia before a bigger war came in Europe or the Middle East. Republicans blamed Acheson's speech for inviting an invasion, but the war was really an intensification of an ongoing civil war that Stalin was willing to exploit. In fact, Kim originated the invasion plan and spent a year persuading Stalin to agree to it. Stalin hoped that the conquest of South Korea would force Japan to sign a favorable treaty with the USSR.

The explosion of a hot war after five years of world tension seemed to American leaders to demand a military response. As the South Korean army collapsed, Truman committed American ground troops from Japan on June 30. The United States also had the good fortune of securing an endorsement from the United Nations. Because the USSR was boycotting the UN (hoping to force the seating of Mao's People's Republic of China in place of Jiang's government), it could not use its veto when the Security Council asked UN members to help South Korea. The Korean conflict remained officially a United Nations action, although U.S. Generals Douglas MacArthur, Matthew Ridgway, and Mark Clark ran the show as the successive heads of the UN command.

The Politics of War

Fortunes in the first year of the Korean conflict seesawed three times. The first U.S. combat troops were outnumbered, outgunned, and poorly trained. They could not stop the North Koreans. By early August, the Americans clung to a narrow toehold around the port of Pusan on the tip of the Korean peninsula. As reinforcements arrived from the United States, however, MacArthur transformed the war with a daring amphibious counterattack at Inchon, 150 miles behind North Korean lines. The North Korean army was already overextended and exhausted. It collapsed and fled north.

United Nations forces in Korea fought the weather as well as communist North Koreans and Chinese. Baking summer heat alternated with fierce winters. Snow and cold were a major help to the Chinese when they surprised United States troops in November 1950 and drove the American forces southward.

The temptation to push across the 38th parallel and unify the peninsula under Syngman Rhee was irresistible. MacArthur and Washington officials disregarded warnings by China that it would enter the war if the United States tried to reunite Korea by force. U.S. and South Korean troops rolled north, drawing closer and closer to the boundary between North Korea and China.

Chinese forces attacked MacArthur's command in late October but then disappeared. MacArthur dismissed the attacks as a token gesture. In fact they were a final warning. On November 26, the Chinese struck the overextended American columns. They had massed 300,000 troops without detection by American aviation. Their assault drove the UN forces into a two-month retreat that again abandoned Seoul.

Despite his glaring mistake, MacArthur remained in command until he publicly contradicted national policy. In March 1951, with the UN forces again pushing north, Truman prepared to offer a cease-fire that would have preserved the separate nations of South and North Korea. MacArthur tried to preempt the president by demanding that China admit defeat or suffer the consequences. He then published a direct attack on the administration's policy of limiting the Asian war to ensure the security of Europe.

President Truman had no choice. To protect civilian control of the armed forces, he relieved MacArthur of his commands on April 11, 1951. The general returned to parades and a hero's welcome when he addressed a joint session of Congress. He quoted a line from an old barracks song: "Old soldiers never die; they just fade away." The song was soon heard on the radio, but Truman remained in charge of the war.

In Korea itself, U.S. and South Korean forces stabilized a strong defensive line that cut diagonally across the 38th parallel. Here the conflict settled into trench warfare. UN and communist armies faced each other across steep bare hills that choked in clouds of summer dust and froze in winter. For two years, boredom alternated with fierce inch-by-inch battles for territory with names like Heartbreak Ridge and Pork Chop Hill. The war's only glamour was in the air, where the arrival of new F-86 Saberjets in 1952 allowed American pilots to clear the skies of Chinese aviators in Russian-made MIG 15s.

Stabilization of the Korean front ushered in two years of truce negotiations beginning in July 1951, for none of the key actors wanted a wider war. The Chinese were careful to keep their war planes north of the ground combat zone. The Russians had stayed out of the war. The United States learned a painful lesson in 1950 and was willing to accept a divided Korea.

Negotiations stalled over thousands of Chinese prisoners of war who might not want to return to China. The political decision to turn free choice for POWs into a symbol of resistance to communism left Truman's administration bogged down in a grinding war. Nearly half of the 140,000 U.S. casualties came after the truce talks started. The war was a decisive factor behind the Republican victory in the November 1952 elections and dragged on until June 1953, when an armistice returned the peninsula roughly to its prewar political division.

The blindly ambitious attack into North Korea was one of the great failures of intelligence and strategic leadership in American military history. Nearly everyone in Washington shared the blame for letting the excitement of battlefield victories obscure limited war aims. Civilian leaders couldn't resist the desire to roll back communism. Truman hoped for a striking victory before the 1950 congressional elections. The Joint Chiefs of Staff failed to question a general with MacArthur's heroic reputation. MacArthur himself allowed ambition and wishful thinking to jeopardize his army.

The war in Korea was a preview of Vietnam fifteen years later. American leaders propped up an undemocratic regime to defend democracy. Both North Koreans and South Koreans engaged in savage political reprisals as the battlefront shifted back and forth. American soldiers found it hard distinguish between allied and enemy Koreans. American emphasis on the massive application of firepower led U.S. forces to demolish entire villages to kill single snipers. The air force tried to break North Korean resistance by pouring bombs on cities, power stations, factories, and dams; General Curtis Le May estimated that the bombings killed a million Koreans.

The Korean War had global consequences. It helped to legitimize the United Nations. In Washington, it confirmed the ideas behind NSC-68, with its call for the United States to expand its military and to lead an anticommunist alliance. Two days after the North Korean invasion, President Truman ordered the Seventh Fleet to protect the Nationalist Chinese on Taiwan, a decision that guaranteed twenty years of hostility between the United States and the People's Republic of China. In the same month, the United States began to aid France's struggle to retain control over its southeast Asian colony of Indochina, which included Laos, Cambodia, and Vietnam.

In Europe, the United States pushed to rearm West Germany as part of a militarized NATO and sent

American Views

Integrating the Army in Korea

Racial integration of the armed forces became official policy in 1948, but President Truman's directive was not fully implemented until during and after the war in Korea. Two veterans of that war—white G.I. Harry Summers and black officer Beverly Scott—recall some of the steps toward integration.

❖ **What do these recollections say about the pervasiveness of racism in midcentury American life?**

❖ **How has the experience of minority soldiers changed from the 1950s to the 1990s?**

Harry Summers: When they first started talking about integration, white soldiers were aghast. They would say, How can you integrate the army? How do you know when you go to the mess hall that you won't get a plate or a knife or a spoon that was used by a Negro? Or when you go to the supply room and draw sheets, you might get a sheet that a Negro had slept on. . . .

I remember a night when our rifle company was scheduled to get some replacements. I was in a three-man foxhole with one other guy, and they dropped this new replacement off at our foxhole. The other guy I was in the foxhole with was under a poncho, making coffee. It was bitterly cold. And pitch dark. He got the coffee made, and he gave me a drink, and he took a drink, and then he offered some to this new replacement, who we literally couldn't see, it was that dark. And the guy said, "No, I don't want any."

"What the hell are you talking about, you don't want any? You got to be freezing to death. Here, take a drink of coffee."

"Well," he said, "you can't tell it now, but I'm black. And tomorrow morning when you find out I was drinking out of the same cup you were using, you ain't gonna be too happy."

Me and this other guy kind of looked at each other. "You silly son of a bitch," we told him, "here, take the goddam coffee."

Beverly Scott: The 24th Regiment was the only all-black regiment in the division, and as a black officer in an all-black regiment commanded by whites I was always super sensitive about standing my ground. Being a man. Being honest with my soldiers. . . .

Most of the white officers were good. Taken in the context of the times, they were probably better than the average white guy in civilian life. But there was still that patronizing expectation of failure. White officers came to the 24th Regiment knowing or suspecting or having been told that this was an inferior regiment.

[In September 1951, members of the regiment were integrated into other units.] I was transferred to the 14th [Regiment] and right away I experienced some problems. People in the 14th didn't want anybody from the 24th. I was a technically qualified communications officer, which the 14th said they needed very badly, but when I got there, suddenly they didn't need any commo officers.

Then their executive officer said, "We got a rifle platoon for you. Think you can handle a rifle platoon?"

What the hell do you mean, can I handle a rifle platoon? I was also trained as an infantry officer. He knew that. I was a first lieutenant, been in the army six years . . . If I had been coming in as a white first lieutenant the question never would have been asked.

Source: Rudy Tomedi, No Bugles, No Drums: An Oral History of the Korean War *(NY: John Wiley & Sons 1993).*

troops to Europe as a permanent defense force. It increased military aid to European governments and secured a unified command for the national forces allocated for NATO. The unified command made West German rearmament acceptable to France and the smaller nations of western Europe. Rearmament also stimulated German economic recovery and bound West Germany to the political and economic institutions of the North Atlantic nations. In 1952, the European Coal and Steel Community marked an important step toward economic cooperation that would evolve into the European Union by the end of the century. Dwight Eisenhower, who had led the Western allies in the invasion of France and Germany, became the new NATO commander in April 1951; his appointment symbolized the American commitment to western Europe.

The Second Red Scare

The Korean War reinforced the second Red Scare, an assault on civil liberties that stretched from the mid-1940s to the mid-1950s and dwarfed the Red Scare of 1919–1920. The Cold War fanned fears of communist subversion on American soil. Legitimate concerns about espionage mixed with suspicions that communist sympathizers in high places were helping Stalin and Mao. The scare was also a weapon that the conservative wing of the Republican party used against men and women who had built Roosevelt's New Deal (see the overview table, "The Second Red Scare").

Efforts to root out suspected subversives operated on three tracks. National and state governments established loyalty programs to identify and fire suspect employees. The courts punished members of suspect organizations. Congressional and state legislative investigations followed the whims of committee chairs. Anticommunist crusaders often relied on dubious evidence and eagerly believed the worst. They also threatened basic civil liberties.

The Communist Party and the Loyalty Program

The Communist party in the United States was in rapid decline after World War II. Many intellectuals had left the party over the Nazi–Soviet Pact in 1939. The wartime glow of military alliance with the Soviet Union helped the party recover to perhaps eighty thousand members—still fewer than one in every fifteen hundred Americans—but the postwar years brought a series of failures. In 1946, Walter Reuther defeated a Communist for the presidency of the huge United Auto Workers union, and other CIO unions froze Communists out of leadership positions. Communist support for Henry Wallace reduced the party's influence and separated it from the increasingly conservative mainstream of American politics.

Nevertheless, Republicans used **Red-baiting** as a campaign technique in 1944 and 1946, setting the stage for a national loyalty program. In 1944 they tried to frighten voters about "commydemocrats" by linking FDR, CIO labor unions, and communism. Democrats slung their own mud by trying to convince voters that Hitler preferred the Republicans. Two years later, Republican campaigners told the public that the basic choice was "between Communism and Republicanism." Starting a thirty-year political career, a young Navy veteran named Richard Nixon won a southern California congressional seat by hammering on his opponent's connections to supposedly "Communist-dominated" organizations.

President Truman responded to the Republican landslide with the **Executive Order 9835** in March 1947, initiating a loyalty program for federal employees. Truman may have been trying to head off more drastic action by Congress. Nevertheless, Order 9835 was a blunt instrument. It authorized the attorney general to prepare a list of "totalitarian, Fascist, Communist, or subversive" organizations and made membership or even "sympathetic association" with such groups grounds for dismissal. The loyalty program applied to approximately 8 million Americans working for the federal government or defense contractors; similar state laws affected another 5 million.

Loyalty was a moving target. The attorney general's list grew in fits and starts with often arbitrary additions. Many accusations were just malicious gossip, but allegations stayed in a worker's file even if refuted. Appointment to a new job in the federal government triggered a new investigation in which officials might paw through the same old material. Many New Dealers and people associated with presumably liberal East Coast institutions were targets. An Interior Department official boasted that he had been especially effective in squeezing out graduates of Harvard and Columbia.

Federal employees worked under a cloud of fear. Would the cooperative store they had once patronized or the protest group they'd joined in college suddenly appear on the attorney general's list? Would someone complain that they had disloyal books on their shelves? Loyalty boards asked about religion, racial equality, and a taste for foreign films; they also tried to identify homosexuals, who were thought to be targets for blackmail by foreign agents. The loyalty program resulted in 1,210 firings and

OVERVIEW

THE SECOND RED SCARE

Type of Anticommunist Effort	Key Tools	Results
Employee loyalty programs	U.S. attorney general's list of subversive organizations	Thousands of federal and state workers fired, careers damaged
Congressional investigations	HUAC McCarren Committee Army-McCarthy hearings	Employee blacklists, harassment of writers and intellectuals
Criminal prosecutions	Trials for espionage and conspiracy to advocate violent overthrow of the U.S. government	Convictions of Communist party leaders (1949), Rosenbergs (1951)

6,000 resignations under Truman and comparable numbers during Dwight Eisenhower's first term from 1953 to 1956.

Naming Names to Congress

Congress was even busier than the executive branch. The congressional hunt for subversives had its roots in 1938, when Congressman Martin Dies, a Texas Democrat, created the Special Committee on Un-American Activities. Originally intended to ferret out pro-Fascists, the Dies Committee evolved into the permanent **House Committee on Un-American Activities (HUAC)** in 1945. It investigated "un-American propaganda" that attacked constitutional government.

One of HUAC's juiciest targets was Hollywood. In the last years before television, the movie industry stood at the height of its capacity to influence public opinion. In 1946, Americans bought an average of 90 million tickets every week. But Hollywood's reputation for loose morals, foreign-born directors, Jewish producers, and left-leaning writers aroused the suspicions of many congressmen. HUAC sought to make sure that no un-American messages were being peddled through America's most popular entertainment.

When the hearings opened in October 1947, studio executives, such as Jack Warner of Warner Brothers and Louis B. Mayer of MGM, assured HUAC of their anticommunism. So did popular actors Gary Cooper and Ronald Reagan. In contrast, eight screenwriters and two directors—the Hollywood Ten—refused to discuss their past political associations, citing the free speech protections of the First Amendment to the Constitution. HUAC countered with citations for contempt of Congress. The First Amendment defense failed when it reached the Supreme Court, and the Ten went to jail in 1950.

HUAC changed the politics of Hollywood. Before 1947, it had been fashionable to lean toward the left; even *The Best Years of Our Lives* contained criticism of American society. After the hearings, it was imperative to tilt the other way. Humphrey Bogart apologized for being a "dope" about politics. The government refused to let British-born Charlie Chaplin reenter the United States in 1952 because of his left-wing views. Other actors, writers, and directors found themselves on the Hollywood blacklist, banned from jobs where they might insert communist propaganda into American movies.

At the start of 1951, the new Senate Internal Security Subcommittee joined the sometimes bumbling HUAC. The **McCarran Committee**, named for the Nevada senator who chaired it, targeted diplomats, labor union leaders, professors, and schoolteachers. Both committees turned their investigations into rituals. The real point was not to force personal confessions from witnesses but to badger them into identifying friends and associates who might have been involved in suspect activities.

The only sure way to avoid "naming names" was to respond to every question by citing the Fifth Amendment to the Constitution, which protects Americans from testifying against themselves. When the states adopted the Fifth Amendment in 1791, they wanted to protect citizens against false confessions coerced by intimidation and torture. The ordeal triggered by a congressional subpoena was certainly intimidating. Many Americans assumed that citing the amendment was a sure sign of guilt, not a matter of principle, and talked about Fifth Amendment communists. "Taking the Fifth" couldn't protect jobs and reputations.

State legislatures imitated Congress by searching for "Reducators" among college faculty in such states as Oklahoma, Washington, and California. College presidents frequently fired faculty who took the Fifth Amendment. Harvard apparently used its influence to stay out of the newspapers, cutting a deal in which the FBI fed it information about suspect faculty, whom the university quietly fired. More common was the experience of the economics professor fired from the University of Kansas City after testimony before the McCarran Committee. He found it hard to keep any job once his name had been in the papers. A local dairy fired him because it thought its customers might be uneasy having a radical handle their milk bottles.

The moral dilemma posed by the investigations was revisited in 1954's Oscar-winning movie *On the Waterfront.* The director, Elia Kazan, and the scriptwriter, Budd Schulberg, had both named names. They used the movie as a parable to justify their actions. The film's hero, played by Marlon Brando, agonizes about informing against corrupt officials in a dockworkers union. He finally speaks out at the urging of an activist priest. Most Americans called before HUAC and the McCarran Committee thought that Kazan and Schulberg had missed the point, for witnesses were usually being asked about previous political affiliations and beliefs, not current criminal activity.

Subversion Trials

In 1948, the Justice Department indicted the leaders of the American Communist party under the Alien Registration Act of 1940. Eleven men and women were convicted in 1949 of conspiring to advocate the violent overthrow of the United States government through their speech and publications. Some of the testimony came from Herbert Philbrick, an advertising manager and FBI informer who had posed as a party member. Philbrick parlayed his appearance into a bestseller titled *I Led Three Lives* and then into a popular television series on which the FBI foiled communist spies every Friday night.

The case of Alger Hiss soon followed. In 1948, former Communist Whittaker Chambers named Hiss as a Communist with whom he had associated in the 1930s. Hiss, who had held important posts in the State Department, first denied knowing Chambers but then admitted to having known him under another name. He continued to deny any involvement with Communists and sued Chambers for slander. As proof, Chambers gave Congressman Richard Nixon microfilms that he had hidden inside a pumpkin on his Maryland farm. Tests seemed to show that the "pumpkin papers" were State Department documents that had been copied on a typewriter that Hiss had once owned. With the new evidence, the Justice Department indicted Hiss for perjury—lying under oath. A first perjury trial ended in deadlock, but a second jury convicted Hiss in January 1950.

Hiss was more important as a symbol than as a possible spy. For more than forty years, the essence of his case was a matter of faith, not facts. Even his enemies agreed that any documents he might have stolen were of limited importance. What was important, they said, was the sort of disloyalty and "weak thinking" that Hiss represented. Moreover, his smugness as a member of the East Coast establishment enraged them. To his opponents, Hiss stood for every wrong turn that the nation had taken since 1932. In contrast, his supporters found a virtue in every trait that his enemies hated, from his refined taste to his education at Johns Hopkins University and Harvard Law School. Many supporters believed that he had been framed. Both sides claimed support from Soviet records that became public in the 1990s.

The case of Julius and Ethel Rosenberg represented a similar test of belief. In 1950, the British arrested nuclear physicist Klaus Fuchs, who confessed to passing atomic secrets to the Soviets when he worked at Los Alamos in 1944 and 1945. The "Fuchs spy ring" soon implicated the Rosenbergs, New York radicals of strong beliefs but limited sophistication. Convicted in 1951 of the vague charge of conspiring to commit espionage, they were sent to the electric chair in 1953 after refusing to buy a reprieve by naming other spies.

As with Alger Hiss, the government had a plausible but not airtight case. After their trial, the Rosenbergs became a cause for international protest. Their small children became pawns and trophies in political demonstrations, an experience recaptured in E. L. Doctorow's novel *The Book of Daniel* (1971). There is no doubt that Julius Rosenberg was a convinced Communist, and he was likely a minor figure in an atomic spy net, but Ethel Rosenberg was charged to pressure her husband into confessing.

Richard Nixon (right) and the chief investigator for the House Committee on Un-American Activities inspect microfilm of the "pumpkin papers." Hidden inside a pumpkin on the Maryland farm of committee informant Whittaker Chambers, the papers helped convict Alger Hiss of perjury. Nixon's role in pursuing Hiss launched a political career that took him to the White House.

Senator McCarthy on Stage

The best-remembered participant in the second Red Scare was Senator Joseph McCarthy of Wisconsin. Crude, sly, and ambitious, McCarthy had ridden to victory in the Republican landslide of 1946. His campaign slogan—"Congress needs a tail gunner"—claimed a far braver war record than he had earned. He burst into national prominence on February 9, 1950. In a rambling speech in Wheeling, West Virginia, he latched on to the issue of communist subversion. Although no transcript of the speech survives, he supposedly stated: "I have here in my hand a list of 205 that were known to the Secretary of State as being members of the Communist Party and who, nevertheless, are still working and shaping the policy of the State Department." In the following days, the 205 Communists changed quickly to 57, to 81, to 10, to 116. McCarthy's rise to fame climaxed with an incoherent six-hour speech to the Senate. He tried to document the charges by mixing previously exposed spies with people who no longer worked for the government or who had never worked for it. Over the next several years, his speeches were moving targets full of multiple untruths. He threw out so many accusations, true or false, that the facts could never catch up.

The Senate disregarded McCarthy, but the public heard only the accusations, not the lack of evidence. Senators treated McCarthy as a crude outsider in their exclusive club, but voters in 1950 turned against his most prominent opponents. Liberal politicians ran for cover; conservatives were happy for McCarthy to attract media attention away from HUAC and the McCarran Committee. In 1951, McCarthy even called George Marshall, now serving as secretary of defense, an agent of communism. The idea was ludicrous. Marshall was one of the most upright Americans of his generation, the architect of victory in World War II and a key contributor to the stabilization of Europe. Nevertheless, McCarthy was so popular that the Republicans featured him at their 1952 convention. That fall, the Republicans' presidential candidate, Dwight Eisenhower, appeared on the same campaign platform with McCarthy and conspicuously failed to defend George Marshall—who was chiefly responsible for Eisenhower's fast-track career.

McCarthy's personal crudeness made him a media star but eventually undermined him. Given control of the Senate Committee on Government Operations in 1953, he investigated dozens of agencies from the Government Printing Office to the Army Signal Corps. Early in 1954, he began to harass the U.S. Army about the promotion of an army dentist with a supposedly subversive background. The confrontation turned into two months of televised hearings that revealed the emptiness of the charges.

Hank Walker, *Life Time Magazine.*

Senator Joe McCarthy shown here with his aide Roy Cohn, used press releases and congressional committee hearings to attack suspected communists. By 1954 he was reaching to more and more extreme accusations to keep his name before the public.

The cameras also put McCarthy's style on trial. "Have you no decency?" asked the army's lawyer Joseph Welch at one point.

The end came quickly. McCarthy's "favorable" rating in the polls plummeted. The comic strip *Pogo* began to feature a foolishly menacing figure with McCarthy's face named Simple J. Malarkey. The U.S. Senate finally voted 67 to 22 in December 1954 to condemn McCarthy for conduct "unbecoming a Member of the Senate." Until his death from alcoholism in 1957, he was an increasingly isolated figure, repudiated by the Senate and ignored by the media who had built him up.

Understanding McCarthyism

The antisubversive campaign that everyone now called **McCarthyism**, however, died a slower death. Legislation, such as the Internal Security Act (1950) and the Immigration and Nationality Act (1952), remained as tools of political repression. HUAC continued to mount investigations as late as the 1960s.

Fear of communist subversion reached deep into American society. In the early 1950s, Cincinnati's National League baseball team was phasing in a new double-play duo of second baseman Johnny Temple and shortstop Roy McMillan. The team was also trying out a new name, for it was important not to let the national game be tainted by communism. Harking back to its origins as the Red Stockings, the team was now the "Redlegs," not the "Reds." The brief revision of baseball history was one example of how the fear of communists spread from Washington through the grassroots. Cities and states required loyalty oaths from their employees; Ohio even required oaths from recipients of unemployment compensation.

In retrospect, at least four factors made Americans afraid of communist subversion. One was a legitimate but exaggerated concern about atomic spies. A second was an undercurrent of anti-Semitism and nativism, for many labor organizers and Communist party members (like the Rosenbergs) had Jewish and eastern European backgrounds. Third was southern and western resentment of the nation's Ivy League elite. Most general, finally, was a widespread fear that the world was spinning out of control. Many people sought easy explanations for global tensions. It was basically reassuring if Soviet and Chinese communist successes were the result of American traitors rather than communist strengths.

Partisan politics mobilized the fears and resentments into a political force. From 1946 through 1952, the conservative wing of the Republican party used the Red Scare to attack New Dealers and liberal Democrats. HUAC, the McCarran Committee, and McCarthy were all tools for bringing down the men and women who had been moving the United States toward a more active government at home and abroad. The Republican elite used McCarthy until they won control of the presidency and Congress in 1952 and then abandoned him.

The broader goal of the second Red Scare was conformity of thought. Many of the professors and bureaucrats targeted for investigation had indeed been Communists or interested in communism, usually in the 1930s and early 1940s. Most saw it as a way to increase social justice, and they sometimes excused the failures of communism in the Soviet Union. Unlike the handful of real spies, however, they were targeted not for actions but for ideas. The investigations and loyalty programs were efforts to ensure that Americans kept any left-wing ideas to themselves.

Conclusion

In the face of confrontation over Berlin, fighting in Korea, and growing numbers of nuclear weapons, the Cold War stayed cool because each side achieved its essential goals. The Soviet Union controlled eastern Europe, while the United States built increasingly strong ties with the NATO nations and Japan. Though the result was a stalemate that would last through the 1980s, it nevertheless absorbed huge shares of Soviet and American resources and conditioned the thinking of an entire generation.

The shift from prewar isolationism to postwar internationalism was one of the most important changes in the nation's history. To many of its advocates, internationalism represented a commitment to spread political democracy to other nations. As the 1950s and 1960s would show, the results often contradicted the ideal when the United States forcibly imposed its will on other peoples. Even as the results overseas fell short of the ideal, however, the new internationalism highlighted and helped change domestic racial attitudes.

The Truman years brought increasing stability. The economic chaos of 1946 faded quickly. By identifying liberalism at home with anticommunism abroad, Truman's efforts to define a vital center helped protect the New Deal. Americans in the early 1950s could be confident that New Deal and Fair Deal programs to expand economic opportunity and increase economic security were permanent, if incomplete, setting the stage for new social activism in the 1960s. If the Republicans had won in 1948, they might have dismantled the New Deal. By 1952, both presidential candidates affirmed the consensus that placed economic opportunity at the center of the national agenda. The suburban housing boom seemed to turn the dream of prosperity into reality for millions of families.

Despite the turmoil and injustice of the second Red Scare and deep worries about nuclear war, the United States emerged from the Truman years remarkably prosperous. It was also more secure from international threats than many nervous Americans appreciated. The years from 1946 to 1952 set the themes for a generation that believed that the United States could do whatever it set its mind to: end poverty, land an astronaut on the moon, thwart communist revolutions in other countries. There was a direct line from Harry Truman's 1947 declaration that the United States would defend freedom around the world to John Kennedy's 1961 promise that the nation would bear any burden necessary to protect free nations from communism. As the world moved slowly toward greater stability in the 1950s, Americans were ready for a decade of confidence.

Review Questions

1. What were the key differences between Harry Truman and congressional Republicans about the legacy of the New Deal? Why did regulating labor unions become a central domestic issue in the late 1940s? Why did Truman manage to win the presidential election of 1948 despite starting as an underdog?
2. How did the postwar years expand opportunity for veterans and members of the working class? How did they limit opportunities for women? How did they begin to challenge racial inequities in American society? How did the postwar readjustment create a suburban society?
3. What foreign policy priorities did the United States set after 1945? To what extent did the United States achieve its most basic objectives? How did mutual mistrust fuel the origins and deepen the Cold War?
4. How did the Cold War change character in 1949 and 1950? What were key actions by the Soviet Union and China, and how did the United States respond? What was the effect of the chaotic fighting in Korea on U.S. domestic politics and diplomacy?
5. What factors motivated an increasingly frantic fear of domestic subversion in the late 1940s and early 1950s? Who were the key actors in the second Red Scare? What was its long-term impact on American society?

Recommended Reading

Paul Boyer, *By the Bomb's Early Light: American Thought and Culture at the Dawn of the Atomic Age* (1985). Examines the mixture of hopes and fears with which Americans greeted the arrival of the atomic age, giving detailed attention to popular culture as well as national policy.

Joseph C. Goulden, *The Best Years, 1945–1950* (1976). A very readable portrayal of the ways in which Americans adjusted to the postwar years, drawing heavily on contemporary magazine accounts.

Melvyn Leffler, *A Preponderance of Power: National Security, the Truman Administration, and the Cold War* (1992). Provides a balanced interpretation of responsibility for the Cold War in a detailed but readable account of American policy.

Samuel Lubell, *The Future of American Politics* (1952). An incisive analysis of the social forces that shaped the American political scene in the 1940s, giving insights that are still telling after more than four decades.

David McCullough, *Truman* (1992). A readable and sympathetic biography of the thirty-third president.

Victor Navasky, *Naming Names* (1980). The impact of HUAC on Hollywood and the entertainment industry, told by a strong opponent of the Committee.

Arnold Rampersad, *Jackie Robinson* (1997). Presents Jackie Robinson as a pioneer of racial integration on and off the ball field.

Additional Sources

Foreign and Military Policy

John L. Gaddis, *The United States and the Cold War* (1992).

Greg Herken, *The Winning Weapon: The Atomic Bomb in the Cold War, 1945–1950* (1980).

Michael Hogan, *Cross of Iron: Harry S. Truman and the Origins of the National Security State, 1945-54* (1998).

Michael Hogan, *The Marshall Plan* (1987).

Walter Le Feber, *America, Russia, and the Cold War* (1985).

Ernest R. May, ed., *American Cold War Strategy: Interpreting NSC-68* (1993).

Thomas G. Paterson, *On Every Front: The Making of the Cold War* (1979).

Richard Rhodes, *Dark Sun: The Making of the Hydrogen Bomb* (1995).

Michael Schaller, *The American Occupation of Japan* (1985).

Herbert F. York, *The Advisors: Oppenheimer, Teller and the Super* (1976).

Vladislav Zubok and Constantine Pleshkanov, *Inside the Kremlin's Cold War: From Stalin to Khrushchev* (1996).

Korean War

Bruce Cumings, *The Origins of the Korean War* (1981, 1990).

Rosemary Foot, *The Wrong War: American Policy and the Dimensions of the Korean Conflict, 1950–1953* (1985).

D. Clayton James, *Refighting the Last War: Command and Crisis in Korea, 1950–1953* (1992).

Burton I. Kaufman, *The Korean War: Challenges in Crisis, Credibility, and Command* (1986).

William Stueck, *The Korean War: An International History* (1995).

Society and Politics at Home

Steven Gillon, *Politics and Vision: The ADA and American Liberalism* (1987).

Eric F. Goldman, *The Crucial Decade and After: America, 1945–1960* (1960.

Alonzo Hamby, *A Man of the People: A Life of Harry Truman* (1995).

Barbara M. Kelly, *Expanding the American Dream: Building and Rebuilding Levittown* (1993).

Donald R. McCoy and Richard Ruetten, *Quest and Response: Minority Rights and the Truman Administration* (1973).

James Patterson, *Mr. Republican: A Biography of Robert A. Taft* (1972).

Graham White and John Maze, *Henry A. Wallace: His Search for a New World Order* (1995).

Gwendolyn Wright, *Building the Dream: A Social History of Housing in America* (1981).

Red Scare

David Caute, *The Great Fear* (1978).

Richard Fried, *Nightmare in Red: The McCarthy Era in Perspective* (1990).

Robert Griffith, *The Politics of Fear: Joseph R. McCarthy and the Senate* (1970).

Stanley Kutler, *The American Inquisition* (1982).

Michael Paul Rogin, *The Intellectuals and McCarthy: The Radical Spectre* (1967).

Ellen Schrecker, *No Ivory Tower: McCarthyism and the Universities* (1986).

Athan Theoharis and John Stuart Cox, *The Boss: J. Edgar Hoover and the Great American Inquisition* (1988).

Where to Learn More

- ❖ **Harry S Truman National Historic Site, Library and Museum, Independence, Missouri.** The museum has exhibits and materials on Truman's political career and American history during his administration. Also in Independence is the Harry S Truman Courtroom and Office, with exhibits focusing on his early career.
- ❖ **General Douglas MacArthur Memorial, Norfolk, Virginia.** The MacArthur Memorial in downtown Norfolk commemorates the career of a key figure in the shaping of the postwar world.
- ❖ **United Nations Headquarters, New York, New York.** A tour of the United Nations complex in New York is a reminder of the new organizations for international cooperation and coordination that emerged from World War II.

THE CONFIDENT YEARS, 1953–1964

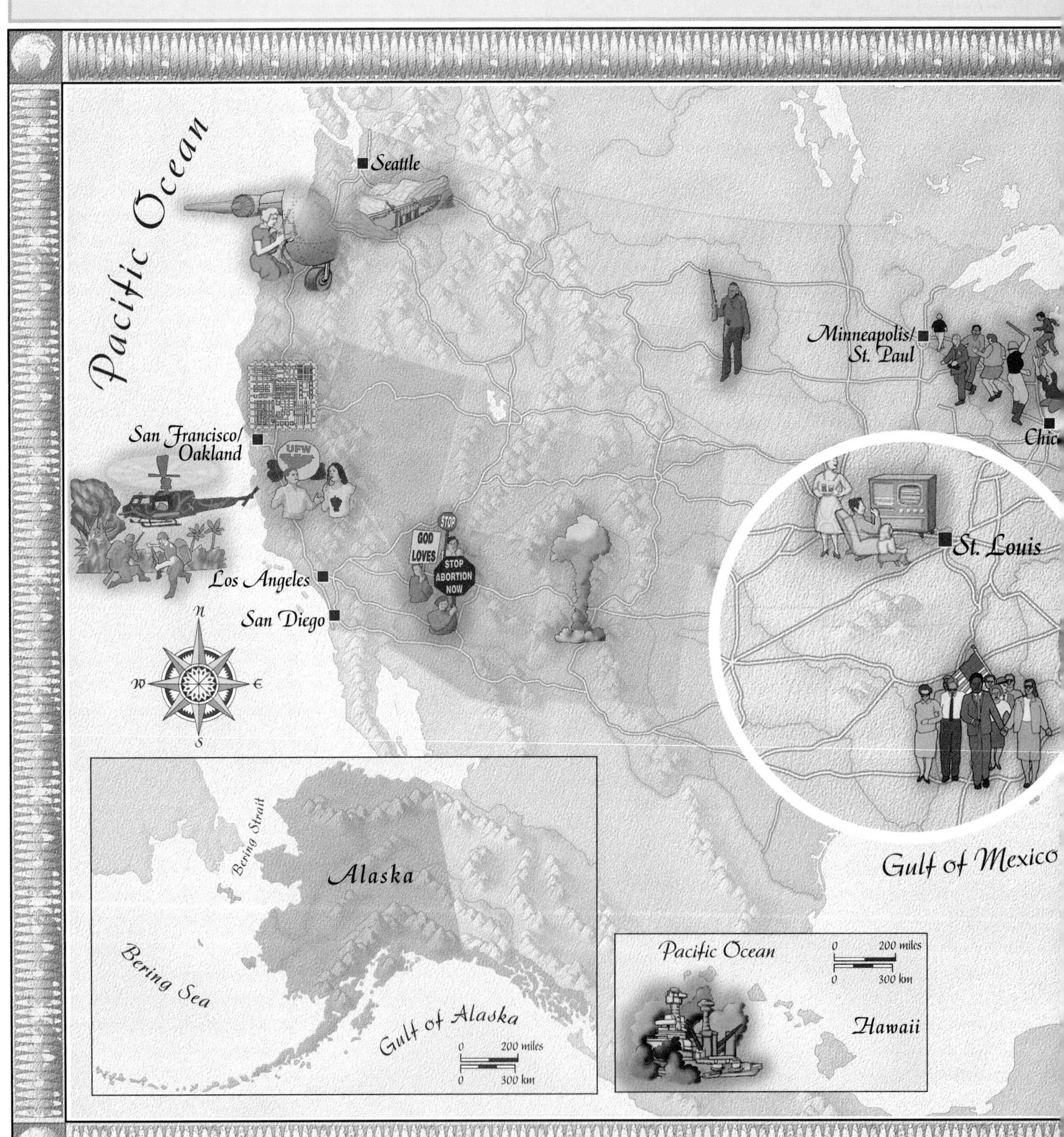

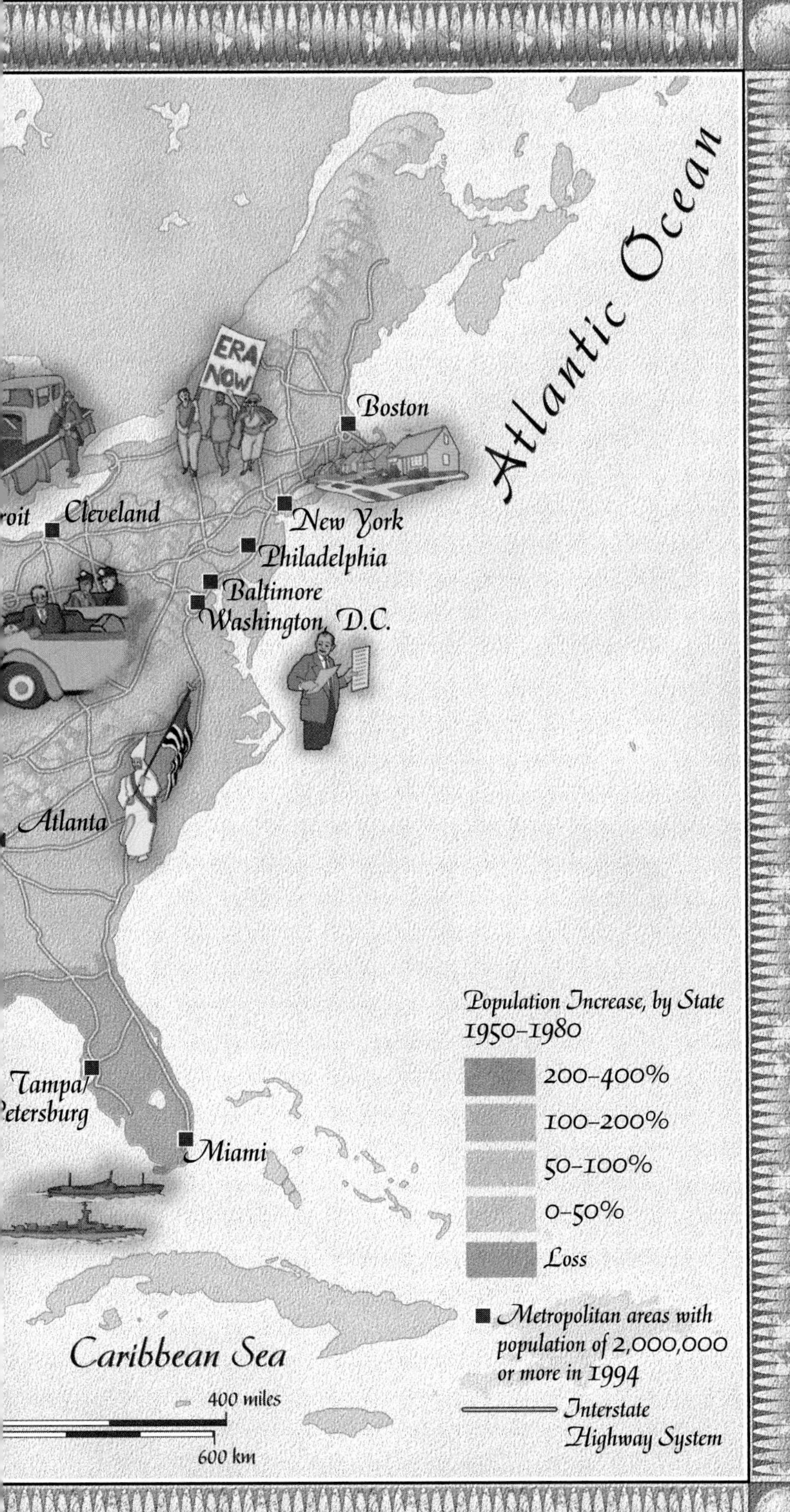

30

Chapter Outline

Key Topics

- ❖ Affluence and conformity in the middle class during the 1950s
- ❖ The Cold War confrontation with the USSR during the Eisenhower and Kennedy administrations
- ❖ The struggle for African-American civil rights
- ❖ Lyndon Johnson and the Great Society

The United States gained a new hero on April 12, 1955, when Dr. Jonas Salk announced an effective vaccine for polio. In the confident mid-1950s, the polio vaccine seemed another proof of American ability to improve the world.

Poliomyelitis, or infantile paralysis, can paralyze the legs or kill by short-circuiting muscles in the throat and chest. Before 1900, infants had often encountered the polio virus in their first months and developed lifelong immunity. In the twentieth century, cleaner houses and streets delayed contact with polio until preschool years or later, when the disease could be devastating. The virus sometimes struck adults—it cost Franklin Roosevelt the use of his legs when he was in his thirties—but most victims were children.

Fear of polio haunted American families. The disease killed fewer people than heart disease or cancer, but it seemed grossly unfair. Most Americans knew at least one child who hobbled through life on crutches and metal leg braces. Hospitals filled with new cases every summer—58,000 in 1952 alone. Many children clung to life inside iron lungs, metal cylinders that pumped air in and out of a hole in the throat.

Polio season peaked in July and August. Worried parents kept their children out of movie theaters and swimming pools, but the disease struck even the most careful families. "Polio?" one girl remembered from the 1950s. "That was the big fear when I was young. . . . I remember going to Dallas and seeing television for the first time. . . . Every day they would report 'another so many polio cases today.'"

Salk's announcement was welcome news. Hundreds of thousands of children had participated in vaccine field trials, and millions of Americans had funded the research with contributions to the March of Dimes. A generation later, President Ronald Reagan would list the polio vaccine with the steam engine and silicon chip as one of the great modern discoveries.

Salk's triumph affirmed American faith in the future. The prosperous years from 1953 to 1964 spread the economic promise of the 1940s across American society. Young couples could afford large families and new houses. Labor unions grew conservative because cooperation with big business offered immediate gains for their members. Corporations used scientific research to craft new products for eager customers.

The Cold War consensus that paired strength at home with strength abroad guided U.S. foreign policy. Few leaders questioned the rightness or necessity of fighting the Cold War—or America's ultimate triumph. The consensus gave U.S. policy an overarching goal of containment but also narrowed its options by casting every issue in terms of U.S.–Soviet rivalry. When events challenged U.S. preeminence, as when the USSR launched the first artificial space satellite in 1957, the response was shock followed by redoubled efforts to regain what Americans considered their rightful world leadership.

But agreement at the top did not always bring harmony. Social dissenters argued that the United States was misusing its wealth. They criticized fifties society for ignoring the talents of women and leaving millions of Americans in poverty. Critics also spoke for a civil rights movement that sprang from deep roots in southern black communities and demanded equal access to opportunity for all Americans.

A Decade of Affluence

Americans in the 1950s believed in the basic strength of the United States. Television's *General Electric Theater* was third in the ratings in 1956–1957. Every week, its host, Ronald Reagan, a popular Hollywood lead from the late 1930s, stated, "At General Electric, progress is our most important product." It made sense to his viewers. Large, technologically sophisticated corporations were introducing new marvels: Orlon sweaters and Saran Wrap, long-playing records and Polaroid cameras. As long as the United States defended free enterprise, Reagan told audiences on national speaking tours, the sky was the limit.

Many Americans valued economic policy and family life for their contributions to the anti-communist crusade. Social and intellectual confor-

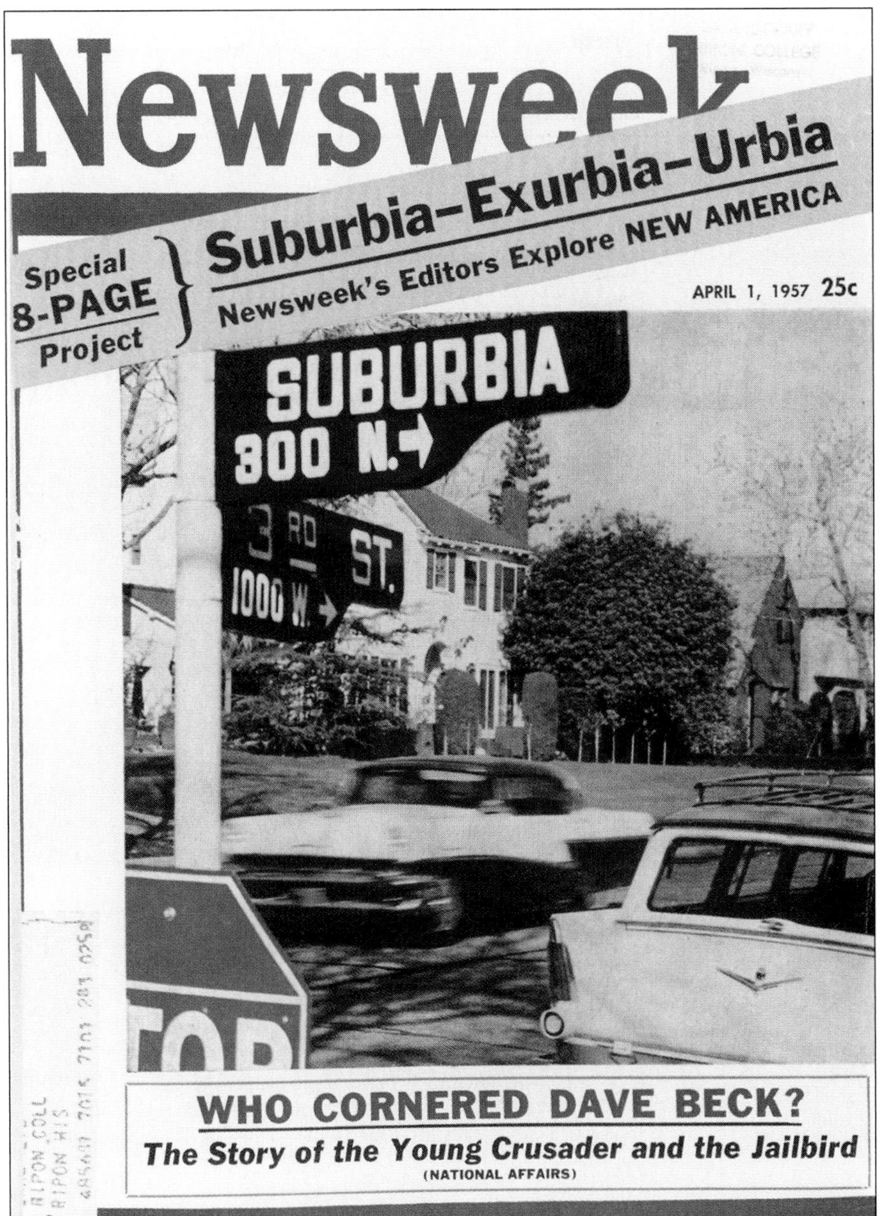

In 1957 Newsweek *ran a special story on the American move to the suburbs, the dominant population movement of the decade. The cover showed new cars (with tail fins and two-tone paint jobs) and older houses that mark this neighborhood as upper middle class. Most new suburbs offered far more modest housing.*

mity assured a united front. Congress established Loyalty Day in 1955. National leaders argued that strong families were bulwarks against communism and that churchgoing inoculated people against subversive ideas. Under the lingering cloud of McCarthyism, the range of political ideas that influenced government policy was narrower than in the 1930s and 1940s. Nevertheless, disaffected critics began to voice the discontents that exploded in the 1960s and 1970s.

What's Good for General Motors

Dwight Eisenhower presided over the prosperity of the 1950s. Both Democrats and Republicans had courted him as a presidential candidate in 1948. Four years later, he picked the Republicans and easily defeated Democrat Adlai Stevenson, the moderately liberal governor of Illinois. Stevenson was a thoughtful politician, a witty campaigner, and a favorite in academic circles. He also carried Truman's negative legacy of domestic policy confrontation, the hated war in Korea, and the "loss" of China, and he had no chance of winning.

Over the next eight years, Eisenhower claimed the political middle for Republicans. Publicists tried a variety of labels for his domestic views: "progressive moderation," "**New Republicanism**," "dynamic conservatism." Satisfied with postwar America, Eisenhower accepted much of the New Deal but saw little need for further reform. In a 1959 poll, liberals considered him a fellow liberal and conservatives thought him a conservative.

Eisenhower's first secretary of defense, "Engine Charlie" Wilson, had headed General Motors. At his Senate confirmation hearing, he proclaimed, "For years, I thought what was good for the country was good for General Motors and vice versa." Wilson's statement captured a central theme of the 1950s. Not since the 1920s had Americans been so excited about the benefits of big business. When *Fortune* magazine began in 1957 to publish an annual list of the 500 largest American corporations, it tapped a national fascination with America's productive capacity.

The economy in the 1950s gave Americans much to like. Between 1950 and 1964, output grew by a solid 3.2 percent per year. Automobile production, on which dozens of other industries depended,

Chronology

1953 CIA-backed coup returns the Shah to power in Iran.
USSR detonates hydrogen bomb.

1954 Vietnamese defeat the French.
Geneva conference divides Vietnam.
United States and allies form SEATO.
Supreme Court decides *Brown* v. *Board of Education of Topeka.*
CIA overthrows the government of Guatemala.
China provokes a crisis over Quemoy and Matsu.

1955 Salk polio vaccine is announced.
Black citizens boycott Montgomery, Alabama, bus system.
USSR forms the Warsaw Pact.
AFL and CIO merge.

1956 Interstate Highway Act is passed.
Soviets repress Hungarian revolt.
Israel, France, and Britain invade Egypt.

1957 U.S. Army maintains law and order in Little Rock.
Soviet Union launches Sputnik.

1958 U.S. and USSR voluntarily suspend nuclear tests.

1959 Fidel Castro takes power in Cuba.
Nikita Khrushchev visits the United States.

1960 U-2 shot down over Russia.
Sit-in movement begins in Greensboro, North Carolina.

1961 Bay of Pigs invasion fails.
Kennedy establishes the Peace Corps.
Vienna summit fails.
Freedom rides are held in the Deep South.
Berlin crisis leads to construction of the Berlin Wall.

1962 John Glenn orbits the earth.
Cuban missile crisis brings the world to the brink.
Michael Harrington publishes *The Other America.*

1963 Civil rights demonstrations rend Birmingham.
Civil rights activists march in Washington.
Betty Friedan publishes *The Feminine Mystique.*
Limited Test Ban Treaty is signed.
Ngo Dinh Diem is assassinated in South Vietnam.
President Kennedy is assassinated.

1964 Civil Rights Act is passed.
Freedom Summer is organized in Mississippi.
Office of Economic Opportunity is created.
Gulf of Tonkin Resolution is passed.
Wilderness Act launches the modern environmental movement.

1965 Medical Care Act establishes Medicare and Medicaid.
Elementary and Secondary Education Act extends direct federal aid to local schools.
Selma-Montgomery march climaxes era of nonviolent civil rights demonstrations.
Voting Rights Act suspends literacy tests.

neared 8 million vehicles per year in the mid-1950s; less than 1 percent of new car sales were imports.

American workers in the 1950s had more disposable income than ever before. Their productivity, or output per worker, increased steadily. Average wages rose faster than consumer prices in nine of eleven years between 1953 and 1964. Rising productivity made it easy for corporations to share gains with large labor unions. The steel and auto industries gave their workers a middle-class way of life. In turn, labor leaders lost interest in radical changes in American society. In 1955, the older and politically more conservative American Federation of Labor absorbed the younger Congress of Industrial Organizations. The new AFL-CIO positioned itself as a partner in prosperity and foe of communism at home and abroad.

For members of minority groups with regular industrial and government jobs, the fifties were also economically rewarding. Industrial cities offered them factory jobs at wages that could support a family. Black people worked through the Urban League, the National Association of Colored Women, and other race-oriented groups to secure fair employment laws and jobs with large corporations. Many Puerto Rican migrants to New York found steady work in the Brooklyn Navy Yard. Mexican-American families in San Antonio benefited from maintenance jobs at the city's military bases. Steady employment allowed black people and Latinos to build strong community institutions and vibrant neighborhood business districts.

However, there were never enough family-wage jobs for all of the African-American and Latino workers who continued to move to northern and western cities. Many Mexican Americans were still migrant farm laborers and workers in nonunionized sweatshops. Minority workers were usually the first to suffer from the erosion of industrial jobs that began in the 1960s.

Native Americans faced equally daunting prospects. To cut costs and accelerate assimilation, Congress pushed the policy of termination between 1954 and 1962. The government sold tribal land and assets, distributed the proceeds among tribal members, and terminated its treaty relationship with the tribe. Termination gave thousands of Indians one-time cash payments but cut them adrift from the security of tribal organizations. The Bureau of Indian Affairs also encouraged Indians to move to large cities, but jobs were often unavailable. The new urban populations would nourish growing militancy among Native Americans in the 1960s and 1970s.

Reshaping Urban America

If Eisenhower's administration opted for the status quo on many issues, it nevertheless reshaped American cities around an agenda of economic development. In 1954, Congress transformed the public housing program into urban renewal. Cities used federal funds to replace low-rent businesses and run-down housing on the fringes of their downtowns with new hospitals, civic centers, sports arenas, office towers, and luxury apartments. Urban renewal temporarily revitalized older cities in the Northeast and Midwest that were already feeling the competition of the fast-growing South and West. *Fortune* in 1956 concluded that some of the largest cities were the best run—Cincinnati, New York, Philadelphia, Detroit, Milwaukee.

Only a decade later, the same cities would top the list of urban crisis spots, in part because of accumulating social costs from urban renewal. The bulldozers often leveled minority neighborhoods in the name of downtown expansion. Los Angeles demolished the seedy Victorian mansions of Bunker Hill, just northwest of downtown, for a music center and bank towers. A mile to the north was Chavez Ravine, whose Mexican-American population lived in substandard housing but maintained a lively community. When conservative opposition blocked plans for public housing, the residents were evicted, and Dodger Stadium was built. Here as elsewhere, urban showplaces rose at the expense of minority groups.

The Eisenhower administration also revolutionized American transportation. By the early 1950s, Americans were fed up with roads designed for Model A Fords: They wanted to enjoy their new V-8 engines. The solution was the **Federal Highway Act of 1956**, creating a national system of Interstate and Defense Highways. The legislation wrapped a program to build 41,000 miles of freeways in the language of the Cold War. The roads would be wide and strong enough for trucks hauling military hardware; they were also supposed to make it easy to evacuate cities in case of a Soviet attack.

Although the first interstate opened in Kansas in 1956, most of the mileage came in use in the 1960s and 1970s. Interstates halved the time of city-to-city travel. They were good for General Motors, the steel industry, and the concrete industry, requiring the construction equivalent of sixty Panama Canals. The highways promoted long-distance trucking at the expense of railroads. They also wiped out hundreds of homes per mile when they plunged through large cities. As with urban renewal, the bulldozers most often plowed through African-American or Latino neighborhoods, where land was cheap and white politicians could ignore protests. Some cities, such as Miami, used the highways as barricades between white and black neighborhoods.

Interstates accelerated suburbanization. The beltways or perimeter highways that began to ring most large cities made it easier and more profitable to develop new subdivisions and factory sites than to reinvest in city centers. Federal grants for sewers and other basic facilities further cut suburban costs. Continuing the pattern of the late 1940s, suburban growth added a million new single-family houses per year.

Comfort on Credit

Prosperity transformed spending habits. The 1930s had taught Americans to avoid debt. The 1950s taught them to buy on credit. Families financed their new houses with 90 percent FHA mortgages and 100 percent VA mortgages. They filled the rooms by signing installment contracts at furniture and appliance stores and charging the drapes and carpeting on department store credit cards. The value of consumer debt, excluding home mortgages, tripled from 1952 to 1964.

New forms of marketing facilitated credit-based consumerism. The first large-scale suburban shopping center was Northgate in Seattle, which assembled all the pieces of the full-grown mall—small stores facing an interior corridor between anchor department stores and surrounded by parking. By the end of the decade, developers were building malls with 1 million square feet of shopping floor. At the start of the 1970s, the universal credit card (Visa, MasterCard) made shopping even easier.

Surrounding the new malls were the servants and symbols of America's car culture. Where cities of the early twentieth century had been built around the public transportation of streetcars and subways, the 1950s depended on private automobiles. Interstate highways sucked retail business from small-town main streets to interchanges on the edge of town. Nationally franchised motels and fast-food restaurants sprang up along suburban shopping strips, pioneered by Holiday Inn (1952) and McDonald's (nationally franchised in 1955). Many Americans identified consumption with the process of driving rather than the place of the old downtown.

More extreme than the mall were entirely new environments for high-intensity consumption and entertainment that appeared in the Southwest. Mobster Bugsy Siegel transformed Las Vegas with the Flamingo Hotel in 1947. Other hotel-casinos soon turned Vegas into a middle-class adult fantasyland. Disneyland was Las Vegas for the whole family, a walk-through fantasy designed to outperform wide-screen movies as a "real" experience. Opening in Orange County, California, in 1955, Disneyland was safe and artificial—a never-ending state fair without the smells and dust.

The New Fifties Family

Family life in the Eisenhower years departed from historic patterns. Prosperity allowed children to finish school and young adults to marry right after high school. Young women faced strong social pressure to pursue husbands rather than careers; women went to college, people said, to get the "Mrs." degree rather than the B.A. In a decade when the popular press worried about "latent homosexuality," single men were also suspect. The proportion of single adults reached its twentieth-century low in 1960. At all social levels, young people married quickly and had an average of three children spaced closely together, adding to the number of baby boomers whose needs would influence American society for the rest of the century. Family activities replaced the street corner for kids and the neighborhood tavern for men. Strong families, said experts, defended against communism by teaching American values.

Television was made to order for the family-centered fifties. By 1960, fully 87 percent of households had sets (see Figure 30-1). Popular entertainment earlier had been a community activity; people saw movies as part of a group, cheered baseball teams as part of a crowd. TV was watched in the privacy of the home.

Situation comedies were the most successful programs. Viewers liked continuing characters who resolved everyday problems in half an hour. A few shows dealt with characters outside the middle-class mainstream, but most successful shows depicted the ideal of family togetherness. Lucille Ball and Desi Arnaz in *I Love Lucy* (1951–1955) started a family and left New York for suburbia. The families on *The Adventures of Ozzie and Harriet* (1952–1966), *Father Knows Best* (1954–1962), and *Leave It to Beaver* (1957–1962) were white, polite, and happy. The Nelsons, Andersons, and Cleavers bore northern Euro-

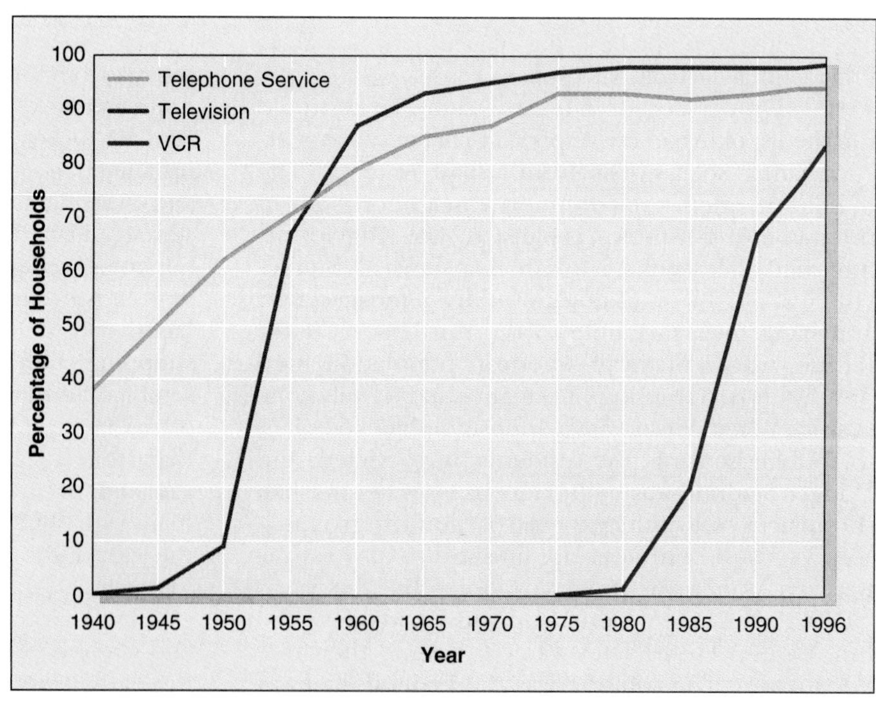

Figure 30-1 Households with Telephones, Televisions, and VCRs *American life in the twentieth century was transformed by a sequence of electronic consumer goods, from telephones to laptop computers. Entertainment items (televisions and videocassette recorders) spread even more rapidly among consumers than did the home telephone.*

Data Source: Statistical Abstract of the United States.

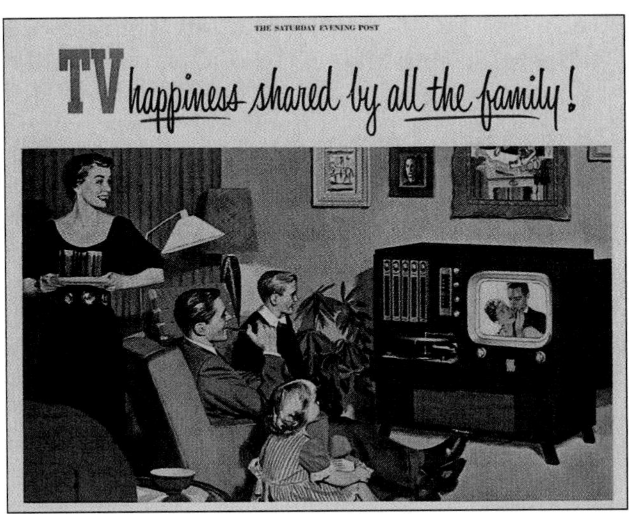

Television sets were major pieces of living room furniture in the 1950s. This 1951 Motorola ad from Woman's Home Companion *emphasizes television as a source of family togetherness, a popular theme in the 1950s.*

pean names and lived in single-family houses with friendly neighbors. Thousands of school-aged baby boomers wondered why their families didn't have similar good times.

Television programming helped limit women's roles by power of example. Women in the fifties gave up some of their earlier educational gains. Their share of new college degrees and professional jobs fell. Despite millions of new electric appliances, the time spent on housework increased. Magazines proclaimed that proper families maintained distinct roles for dad and mom, who was urged to find fulfillment in a well-scrubbed house and children. Television actresses assured readers that they were housewives first and career women second.

In fact, far from allowing women to stay home as housewives, family prosperity in the 1950s often depended on their earnings. The number of employed women reached new highs. By 1960, nearly 35 percent of all women held jobs, including 7.5 million mothers with children under 17 (see Figure 30-2).

Teenagers in the 1950s joined adults as consumers of movies, clothes, and automobiles. Advertisers tapped and expanded the growing youth market by promoting a distinct "youth culture," an idea that became omnipresent in the 1960s and 1970s. While psychologists pontificated on the special problems of adolescence, many cities matched their high schools to the social status of their students: college-prep curricula for middle-class neighborhoods, vocational and technical schools for future factory workers, and separate schools or tracks for African Americans and Latinos. "Maturity" in middle-class high schools meant self-confidence and leadership; at vocational schools, it meant neatness and respect for authority. In effect, the schools trained some children to be doctors and officers and others to be mechanics and enlisted men.

All teenagers shared rock-and-roll, a new music of the mid-1950s that adapted black urban rhythm-and-blues for a white mass market. Rock music drew vitality from poor white Southerners (Buddy Holly, Elvis Presley), Hispanics (Richie

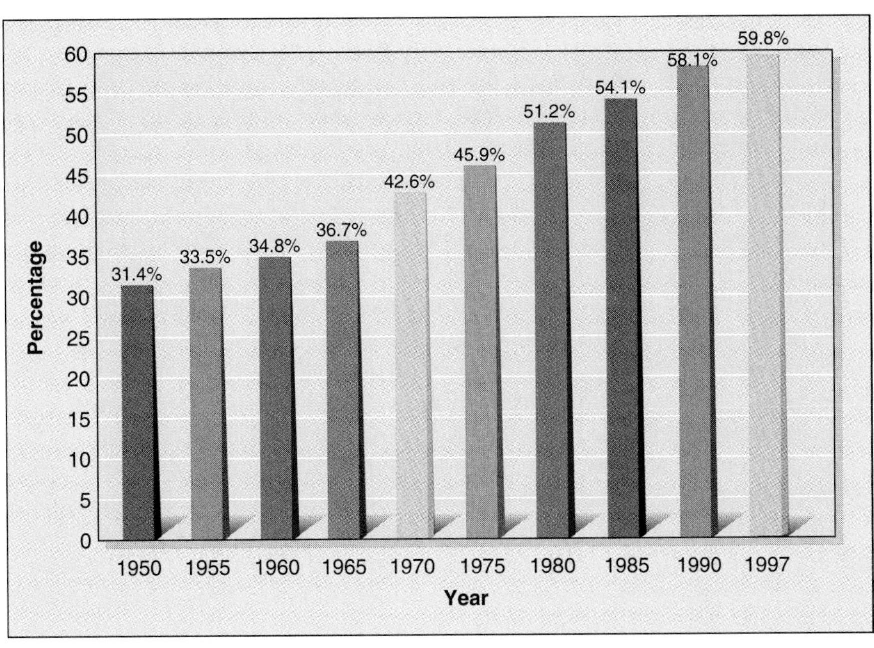

Figure 30-2** **Working Women as a Percentage of All Women, 1950–1997
The proportion of American women who are part of the labor force (working or looking for work) has increased steadily since 1950, with the fastest increase between 1965 and 1985.

Valens), and, in the 1960s, the British working class (the Beatles). Record producers played up the association between rock music and youthful rebellion. The 1955 movie *Blackboard Jungle* depicted juvenile delinquency to the music of Bill Haley's "Rock Around the Clock." Elvis Presley's meteoric career, launched in 1956 with "Heartbreak Hotel," depended both on his skill at blending country music with rhythm-and-blues and the sexual suggestiveness of his stage act.

Portable phonographs and 45-rpm records made rock-and-roll portable, letting kids listen in their own rooms. Car radios and transistor radios (first marketed around 1956) let disc jockeys reach teenagers outside the home. The result was separate music for young listeners and separate advertising for teenage consumers, the roots of the teenage mall culture of the next generation.

Turning to Religion

Leaders from Dwight Eisenhower to FBI Director J. Edgar Hoover advocated churchgoing as an antidote for communism. Regular church attendance grew from 48 percent of the population in 1940 to 63 percent in 1960. Moviegoers flocked to biblical epics: *The Robe* (1953), *The Ten Commandments* (1956), *Ben-Hur* (1959). *Newsweek* talked about the "vast resurgence of Protestantism," and *Time* claimed that "everybody knows that church life is booming in the U.S."

The situation was more complex. Growing church membership looked impressive at first, but the total barely kept pace with population. In some ways, the so-called return to religion was new. Congress created new connections between religion and government when it added "under God" to the Pledge of Allegiance in 1954 and required currency to bear the phrase "In God We Trust" in 1955.

Radio and television preachers added a new dimension to religious life. Bishop Fulton J. Sheen brought vigorous anticommunism and Catholic doctrine to millions of TV viewers who would never have entered a Catholic church. Norman Vincent Peale blended popular psychology with Protestantism, presenting Jesus Christ as "the greatest expert on human nature who ever lived." His book *The Power of Positive Thinking* (1952) told readers to "stop worrying and start living" and sold millions of copies.

Another strand in the religious revival was revitalized evangelical and fundamentalist churches. During the 1950s, the theologically and socially conservative Southern Baptists became the largest Protestant denomination. Evangelist Billy Graham continued the grand American tradition of the mass revival meeting. In auditoriums and stadiums, he preached personal salvation in words that everyone could understand. Graham was a pioneer in the resurgence of evangelical Christianity that stressed an individual approach to belief and social issues. "Before we can solve the economic, philosophical, and political problems in the world," he said, "pride, greed, lust, and sin are going to have to be erased."

African-American churches were community institutions as well as religious organizations. With limited options for enjoying their success, the black middle class joined prestigious churches. Black congregations in northern cities swelled in the postwar years and often supported extensive social service programs. In southern cities, churches were centers for community pride and training grounds for the emerging civil rights movement.

Boundaries between many Protestant denominations blurred as church leaders emphasized national unity, paving the way for the ecumenical movement and denominational mergers. Supreme Court decisions sowed the seeds for later political activism among evangelical Christians. In *Engel* v. *Vitale* (1962), the Court said that public schools could not require children to start the school day with group prayer. *Abington Township* v. *Schempp* (1963) prohibited devotional Bible reading in the schools. Such decisions alarmed many evangelicals; within two decades, school prayer would be a central issue in national politics.

The Gospel of Prosperity

Writers and intellectuals often marveled at the prosperity of Eisenhower's America. For scholars and journalists who had grown up during the Great Depression, the lack of economic hardship was the big story. William H. Whyte, Jr., searched American corporations for the changing character of the United States in *The Organization Man* (1956). Historian David Potter brilliantly analyzed Americans in *People of Plenty* (1954), contending that their national character had been shaped by the abundance of natural resources. In *The Affluent Society* (1958), economist John Kenneth Galbraith predicted that the challenge of the future would be to ensure the fair distribution of national wealth.

At times in these years, production and consumption even outweighed democracy in the American message to the world. Officially, the argument was that abundance was a natural by-product of a free society. In fact, it was easy to present prosperity as a goal in itself, as Vice President Richard Nixon did when he represented the United States at a technology exposition in Moscow in 1959. The American exhibit included twenty-one models of automobiles

The United States exhibit at a technology exposition in Moscow in 1959 displayed a wide range of American consumer goods, from soft drink dispensers to sewing machines. It included a complete six-room ranch house with an up-to-date kitchen where, in a famous encounter dubbed the "kitchen debate," Richard Nixon and Soviet Communist party chairman Nikita Khrushchev disputed the merits of capitalism and communism.

and a complete six-room ranch house. In its "miracle kitchen," Nixon engaged Soviet Communist party chairman Nikita Khrushchev in a carefully planned "kitchen debate." The vice president claimed that the "most important thing" for Americans was "the right to choose": "We have so many different manufacturers and many different kinds of washing machines so that the housewives have a choice."

Khrushchev heard a similar message when he visited the United States in September 1959. He went to a farm in Coon Rapids, Iowa, a machine shop in Pittsburgh, and Hollywood movie studios. Although Khrushchev never believed that ordinary workers had miracle kitchens, he returned to Moscow knowing that America meant "business."

The Underside of Affluence

The most basic criticism of the ideology of prosperity was the simplest—that affluence concealed vast inequalities. Michael Harrington had worked among the poor before writing *The Other America* (1962). He reminded Americans about the "underdeveloped nation" of 40 to 50 million poor people who had missed the last two decades of prosperity. The poor were walled off in urban and rural backwaters. They were old people living on stale bread in bug-infested hotels. They were white families in the valleys of Appalachia, African Americans in city ghettos who could not find decent jobs, and Hispanic migrant workers whose children went for months without a glass of milk.

If Harrington found problems at the bottom of U.S. society, C. Wright Mills found dangers in the way that the Cold War distorted American society at the top. *The Power Elite* (1956) described an interlocking alliance of big government, big business, and the military. The losers in a permanent war economy, said Mills, were economic and political democracy. His ideas would reverberate in the 1960s during the Vietnam War.

Other critics targeted the alienating effects of consumerism and the conformity of homogeneous suburbs. Sociologist David Riesman saw suburbia as the home of "other-directed" individuals who lacked inner convictions. Although the antisuburban rhetoric was based on intellectual snobbery rather than research, it represented significant dissent from the praise of affluence.

There was far greater substance to increasing dissatisfaction among women, who faced conflicting images of the perfect woman in the media. On one side was the comforting icon of Betty Crocker, the fictional spokeswoman for General Mills who made housework and cooking look easy. On the other side were sultry sexpots, such as Marilyn Monroe and the centerfold women of *Playboy* magazine, which first appeared in 1953. Women wondered how to be both Betty and Marilyn.

In 1963, Betty Friedan's book *The Feminine Mystique* recognized that thousands of middle-class housewives were seething behind their picture windows. It followed numerous articles in *McCall's*, *Redbook*, and the *Ladies' Home Journal* about the unhappiness of college-educated women who were expected to find total satisfaction in kids and cooking.

Friedan repackaged the message of the women's magazines along with results of a survey of her Smith College classmates who were then entering their forties. What Friedan called "the problem that has no name" was a sense of personal emptiness. "I got up one morning," remembered Geraldine Bean, "and I got my kids off to school. I went in to comb my hair and wash my face, and I stood in front of the bathroom mirror crying . . . because at eight-thirty in the morning I had my children off to school. I had my housework done. There was absolutely nothing for me to do the rest of the day." She went on to earn a Ph.D. and win election to the board of regents of the University of Colorado.

Eventually, the critical analysis of Harrington, Mills, and Friedan would fuel radical politics; in the short run, it inspired radical art. New York and San Francisco had long sheltered cultural rebels who liked to confront the assumptions of mainstream Americans. The artsy bohemians of New York's Greenwich Village used Pop Art to satirize consumer culture. The **Beats** came together in San Francisco, where poets, artists, and musicians drifted in and out of the City Lights bookstore. They attracted national attention in 1955 when Allen Ginsberg first chanted his poem "Howl," with its blistering attack on stifling materialism.

Facing Off with the Soviet Union

Americans got a reassuring new face in the White House in 1953, but not new policies toward the world. As had been true since 1946, the nation's leaders weighed every foreign policy decision for its effect on the Cold War. The United States pushed ahead in an arms race with the Soviet Union, stood guard on the borders of China and the Soviet empire, and judged political changes in Latin America, Africa, and Asia for their effect on the global balance of power.

U.S. and Soviet actions created a bipolar world that mimicked the effects of a magnet on a scattering of iron filings. The two poles of a magnet draw some filings into tightly packed clusters, pull others into looser alignments pointing toward one pole or the other, and leave a few in the middle unaffected. In the later 1950s and early 1960s, the United States and the USSR were the magnetic poles. Members of NATO, the Warsaw Pact, and other formal alliances made up the tight clusters. The **third world** of officially uncommitted nations felt the influence of both blocs, sometimes aligning with one or the other and sometimes struggling to remain neutral.

Why We Liked Ike

In the late twentieth century, few leaders were able to master both domestic policy and foreign affairs. Some presidents, such as Lyndon Johnson, have been more adept at social problems than diplomacy. In contrast, Richard Nixon and George Bush were more interested in the world outside the United States.

Dwight Eisenhower was one of these "foreign policy presidents." As a general, he had understood that military power should serve political ends. He had helped hold together the alliance that defeated Nazi Germany and built NATO into an effective force in 1951–1952. He then sought the Republican nomination, he said, to ensure that the United States kept its international commitments. He sealed his victory in 1952 by emphasizing foreign policy expertise, telling a campaign audience that "to bring the Korean war to an early and honorable end . . . requires a personal trip to Korea. I shall make that trip . . . I shall go to Korea."

What makes Eisenhower's administration hard to appreciate is that many of its accomplishments were things that didn't happen. Eisenhower refused to dismantle the social programs of the New Deal. He exerted American political and military power around the globe but avoided war. Preferring to work behind the scenes, he knew how to delegate authority and keep disagreements private.

In his "hidden-hand" presidency, Eisenhower sometimes masked his intelligence. It helped his political agenda if Americans thought of him as a smiling grandfather. The "Ike" who gave rambling, incoherent answers at White House press conferences knew exactly what he was doing—controlling information and keeping the opposition guessing. When his press secretary advised him to duck questions at one press conference, Ike replied, "Don't worry, I'll just confuse them." He was easily reelected in 1956, when Americans saw no reason to abandon competent leadership.

A Balance of Terror

The backdrop for U.S. foreign policy was the growing capacity for mutual nuclear annihilation. The rivalry between the United States and the USSR was therefore carried out within a framework of deterrence, the knowledge that each side could launch a devastating nuclear attack. The old balance of power had become a balance of terror.

The Eisenhower administration's doctrine of massive retaliation took advantage of America's superior technology while economizing on military spending. Eisenhower and his advisers worried that matching the land armies of China and the Soviet Union would inflate the role of the federal government in American society (see Figure 30-3). Eisen-

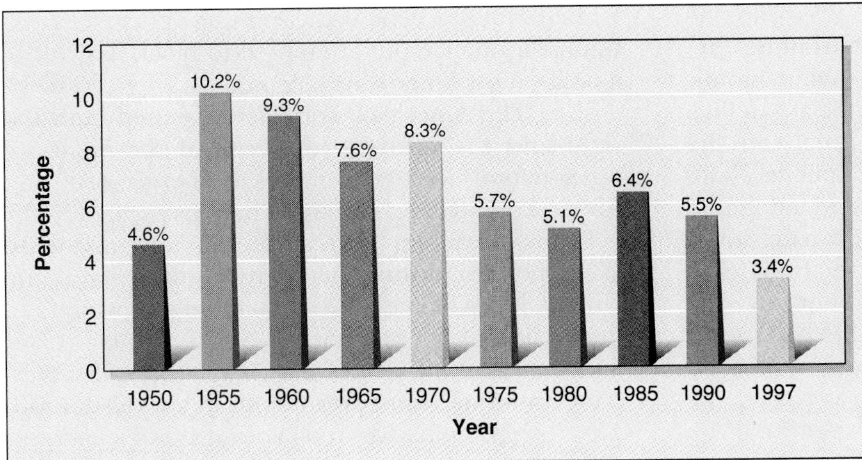

Figure 30-3 ***Defense Spending as a Percentage of Gross Domestic Product, 1950–1997***
Defense spending has been an important force for economic development and innovation. The impact of the defense budget in the domestic economy was greatest in the mid-1950s at the height of the Cold War. Lesser peaks came during the Vietnam War in the late 1960s and the Reagan administration defense buildup in the early 1980s.

Data Source: Statistical Abstract of the United States.

hower compared uncontrolled military spending to crucifying humankind on a "cross of iron." "Every gun that is fired," he warned, "every warship launched, every rocket fired signifies . . . a theft from those who hunger and are not fed, those who are cold and not clothed." The administration concentrated military spending where the nation already had the greatest advantage—on atomic weapons. In response to any serious attack, the United States would direct maximum force against the homeland of the aggressor.

The massive retaliation doctrine treated nuclear weapons as ordinary or even respectable. It put European and American cities on the frontline in the defense of Germany, for it meant that the United States would react to a Soviet conventional attack on NATO by dropping nuclear bombs on the Soviet Union, which would presumably retaliate in kind. The National Security Council in 1953 made reliance on "massive retaliatory damage" by nuclear weapons official policy.

The doctrine grew even more fearful as the Soviet Union developed its own hydrogen bombs. The chairman of the Atomic Energy Commission terrified the American people by mentioning casually that the Soviets could now obliterate New York City. Dozens of nuclear weapons tests in the late 1950s made the atomic threat immediate. So did signs for air raid shelters posted on downtown buildings and air raid drills

Schoolchildren in the 1950s regularly practiced taking cover in case of atomic attack. If there was warning, they were to file into interior hallways, crouch against the walls, and cover their heads with their jackets as protection from flying glass. If they saw the blinding flash of an atomic explosion without warning, they were to "duck and cover" under their school desks.

in schools. Radioactivity carried by fallout appeared in milk supplies in the form of the isotope strontium 90.

The USSR added to worries about atomic war by launching the world's first artificial satellite. On the first Sunday of October 1957, Americans discovered that Sputnik—Russian for "satellite"—was orbiting the earth. The Soviets soon lifted a dog into orbit while U.S. rockets fizzled on the pad. Soviet propagandists claimed that their technological "first" showed the superiority of communism, and Americans wondered if the United States had lost its edge. Schools beefed up science courses and began to introduce the "new math," Congress passed the National Defense Education Act to expand college and postgraduate education, and the new **National Aeronautics and Space Administration (NASA)** took over the satellite program in 1958.

The crisis was more apparent than real. Eisenhower had rejected using available military rockets for the U.S. space program in favor of developing new launch vehicles, and he overlooked the symbolic impact of Sputnik. He thus built himself into a political box, for the combination of Soviet rocketry and nuclear capacity created alarm about a missile gap. The USSR was said to be building hundreds of intercontinental ballistic missiles (ICBMs) to overwhelm American air defenses designed to intercept piloted bombers. By the early 1960s, critics charged, a do-nothing administration would have put the United States in peril. Although there was no such gap, Eisenhower was unwilling to reveal secret information that might have allayed public anxiety.

Containment in Action

Someone who heard only the campaign speeches in 1952 might have expected sharp foreign policy changes under Eisenhower, but there was more continuity than change. John Foster Dulles, Eisenhower's secretary of state, had attacked the Democrats as defeatists and appeasers. He demanded that the United States liberate eastern Europe from Soviet control and encourage Jiang Jieshi to attack communist China. Warlike language continued after the election. In 1956, Dulles proudly claimed that tough-minded diplomacy had repeatedly brought the United States to the verge of war: "We walked to the brink and looked it in the face. We took strong action." Critics protested that such "brinkmanship" endangered the entire world.

In fact, Eisenhower viewed the Cold War in the same terms as Truman. Caution replaced campaign rhetoric about "rolling back" communism. Around the periphery of the communist nations, from eastern Asia to the Middle East to Europe, the United States accepted the existing sphere of communist influence but attempted to block its growth, a policy most Americans accepted.

The American worldview assumed both the right and the need to intervene in the affairs of other nations, especially in Latin America, Asia, and Africa. Policymakers saw these nations as markets for U.S. products and sources of vital raw materials. When political disturbances arose in these states, the United States blamed Soviet meddling to justify U.S. intervention. If communism could not be rolled back in eastern Europe, the CIA could still undermine anti-American governments in the third world. The Soviets themselves took advantage of local revolutions even when they did not instigate them; they thus confirmed Washington's belief that the developing world was a gameboard on which the superpowers carried on their rivalry by proxy.

Twice during Eisenhower's first term, the CIA subverted democratically elected governments that seemed to threaten U.S. interests. In Iran, which had nationalized British and U.S. oil companies in an effort to break the hold of western corporations, the CIA in 1953 backed a coup that toppled the government and helped the young Shah, or monarch, gain control. The Shah then cooperated with the United States until his overthrow in 1979. In Guatemala, the leftist government was upsetting the United Fruit Company. When the Guatemalans accepted weapons from the communist bloc in 1954, the CIA imposed a regime friendly to U.S. business (see Map 30-1).

For most Americans in 1953, democracy in Iran was far less important than ending the war in Korea and stabilizing relations with China. Eisenhower declined to escalate the Korean War by blockading China and sending more U.S. ground forces. Instead he shifted atomic bombs to Okinawa, only four hundred miles from China. The nuclear threat, along with the continued cost of the war on both sides, brought the Chinese to a truce that left Korea divided into two nations.

The next year, China began to shell the small islands of Quemoy and Matsu, from which the Nationalist Chinese on Taiwan were launching commando raids on the mainland. Again Secretary Dulles rattled the atomic saber, and China stopped the attacks. Evidence now suggests that Washington misread the situation. Mao's "theatrical" shelling was a political statement, not a prelude to military assault. Stepping to the "brink of war" did not deter Chinese aggression, because China never planned to attack.

In Vietnam, on China's southern border, France was fighting to maintain its colonial rule

FROM THEN TO NOW

Space Exploration and Science

In December 1998, astronauts joined the first two segments of the International Space Station. Scheduled for completion in 2003, the station is projected to cost $10 billion dollars. Japan, Brazil, Canada, and European nations, as well as the United States, are contributing to its construction. With an operating crew of seven, the orbiting laboratory will allow long-running scientific experiments in six pressurized modules and dozens of external payload sites.

The International Space Station represents a basic transformation of the American space effort from adventure to science. In 1961, President Kennedy committed the United States to be the first nation to send a human being to the moon and to do it by 1970. Cold War rivalry with the Soviet Union motivated this ambitious decision. The USSR had alarmed the United States by its early successes in space. It was the first nation to launch an artificial satellite, and it sent cosmonaut Yuri Gagarin into orbit around the earth ten months before the United States matched the feat and sent astronaut John Glenn into orbit.

Most Americans and most politicians who promoted the space program understood it as a new phase in the history of human exploration and saw the astronauts as modern-day pioneers. Thus when Neil Armstrong set foot on the lunar surface in 1969, he was seen to be following the tradition of Francis Drake, Meriwether Lewis, Charles Lindbergh, and the polar explorers of the twentieth century.

In the decades since Armstrong's famous "giant leap for mankind," the national attitude toward space has changed. From Velcro to satellite communication, many by-products of the space race have become parts of everyday life. Our lives would be far different without government and commercial satellites. Remote sensing helps geologists locate potential petroleum deposits, geographers map the destruction of rain forest, and military specialists pinpoint bombing targets in Iraq and Kosovo. Without the satellite technology developed under the pressure of the Cold War, there would be no global positioning systems for ships, no overhead pictures of storm fronts and hurricanes on The Weather Channel.

But as the world has grown increasingly accustomed to the benefits of space-centered technology, space exploration has shifted away from a focus on manned to unmanned voyages. Despite the expectations of science fiction, the landings on the moon were not followed by efforts to send humans to other planets. Instead, we have sent payloads of instruments to bring back scientific data and often stunning pictures of the surface of Venus, the moons of Jupiter, and the rings of Saturn. We have visited the surface of Mars through the lenses and sensors of special landing craft. The International Space Station is a long way from both the race to the moon and the Starship *Enterprise*, but its model of scientific cooperation may be at least a small step toward the United Federation of Planets.

Astronaut Buzz Aldrin, one of three crewmwn for Apollo 11, was the second human to walk on the moon in July 1969. In the 1980s and 1990s, space exploration shifted from manned flights to remotely controlled landers and remotely monitored instruments.

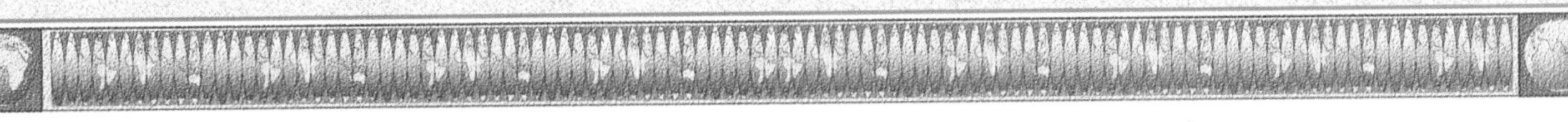

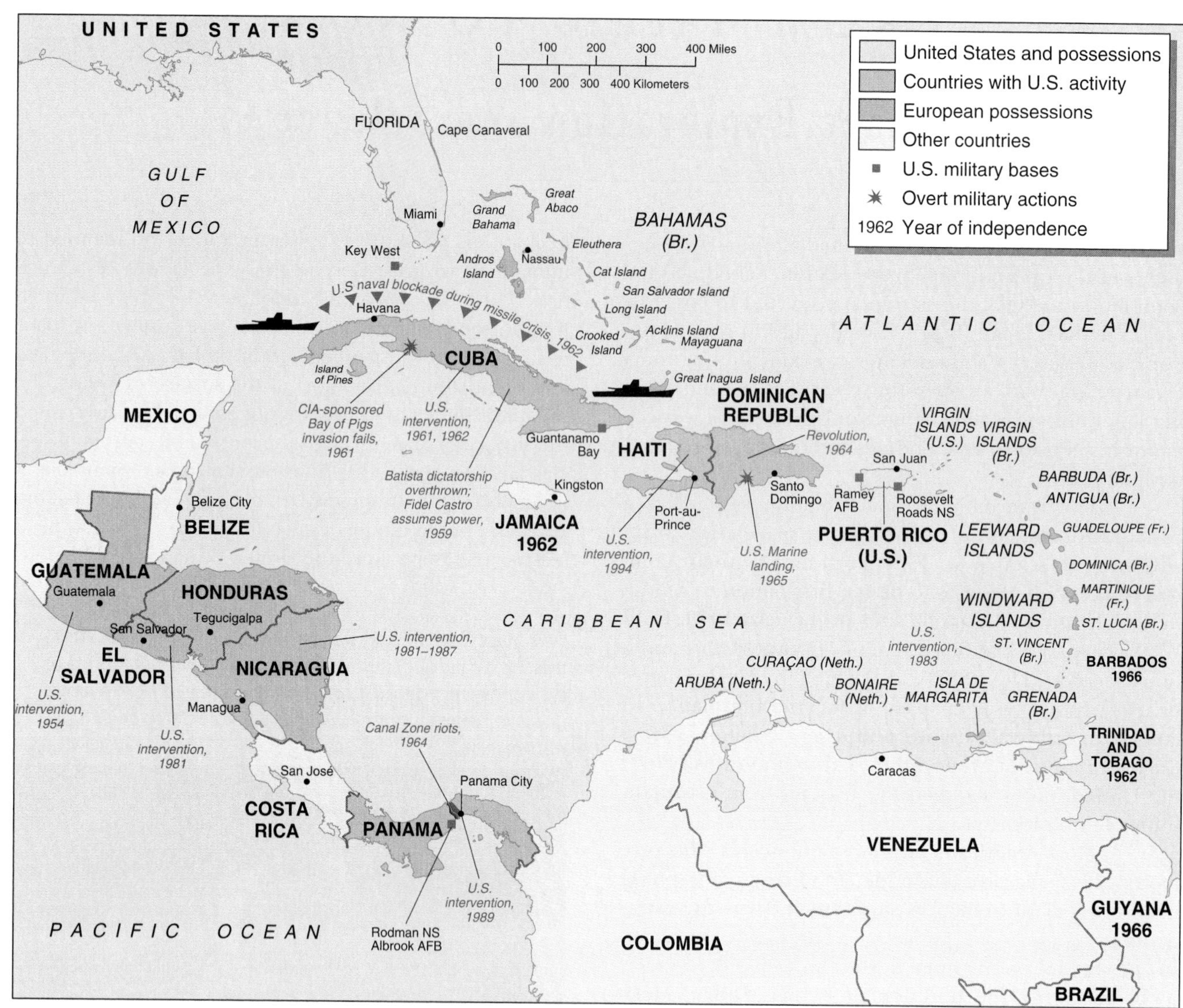

Map 30-1 U.S. Intervention around the Caribbean since 1954
The United States has long kept a careful eye on the politics of neighboring nations to its south. In the second half of the twentieth century, the United States frequently used military assistance or force to influence or intervene in Caribbean and Central American nations. The most common purpose has been to counter or undermine left-leaning governments; some interventions, as in Haiti, have been intended to stabilize democratic regimes.

against rebels who combined communist ideology with fervor for national independence under the leadership of Ho Chi Minh. The United States picked up three-quarters of the costs, but the French military position collapsed in 1954 after Vietnamese forces overran the French stronghold at Dien Bien Phu. The French had had enough, and Eisenhower was unwilling to join another Asian war. A Geneva peace conference in 1954 "temporarily" divided Vietnam into a communist north and a noncommunist south and scheduled elections for a single Vietnamese government.

The United States then replaced France as the supporter of pro-Western Vietnamese in the south. Washington's client was Ngo Dinh Diem, an anticommunist from South Vietnam's Roman Catholic elite. U.S. officials encouraged Diem to put off the elections and backed his efforts to construct an authoritarian South Vietnam. Ho meanwhile consolidated the northern half as a communist state that claimed to be the legitimate government for all Vietnam. The United States further reinforced containment in Asia by bringing Thailand, the Philippines, Pakistan, Australia, New Zealand, Britain, and

France together in the **Southeast Asia Treaty Organization (SEATO)** in 1954 (see Map 30-2).

Halfway around the world, there was a new crisis when three American friends—France, Britain, and Israel—ganged up on Egypt. France was angry at Egyptian support for revolutionaries in French Algeria. Britain was even angrier at Egypt's nationalization of the British-dominated Suez Canal. And Israel wanted to weaken its most powerful Arab enemy. On October 29, 1956, Israel attacked Egypt. A week later, British and French forces attempted to seize the canal. The United States forced a quick cease-fire, partly to maintain its standing with oil-producing Arab nations. The war left Britain and France dependent on American oil that Eisenhower would not provide until they left Egypt.

In Europe, Eisenhower accepted the status quo because conflicts there could result in nuclear war. In 1956, challenges to communist rule arose in East Germany, Poland, and Hungary and threatened to break up the Soviet empire. The Soviets replaced liberal communists in East Germany and Poland with hard-liners. In Hungary, however, open warfare broke out. Hungarian freedom fighters in Budapest used rocks and firebombs against Soviet tanks for several days, while pleading in vain for Western aid. NATO would not risk war with the USSR. Tens of thousands of Hungarians died, and 200,000 fled when the Soviets crushed the resistance.

Global Standoff

The Soviet Union, China, and the United States and its allies were all groping in the dark as they maneuvered for influence in the 1950s and 1960s. In one international crisis after another, each player misinterpreted the other's motivations and diplomatic signals. As documents from both sides of the Cold War become available, historians have realized what

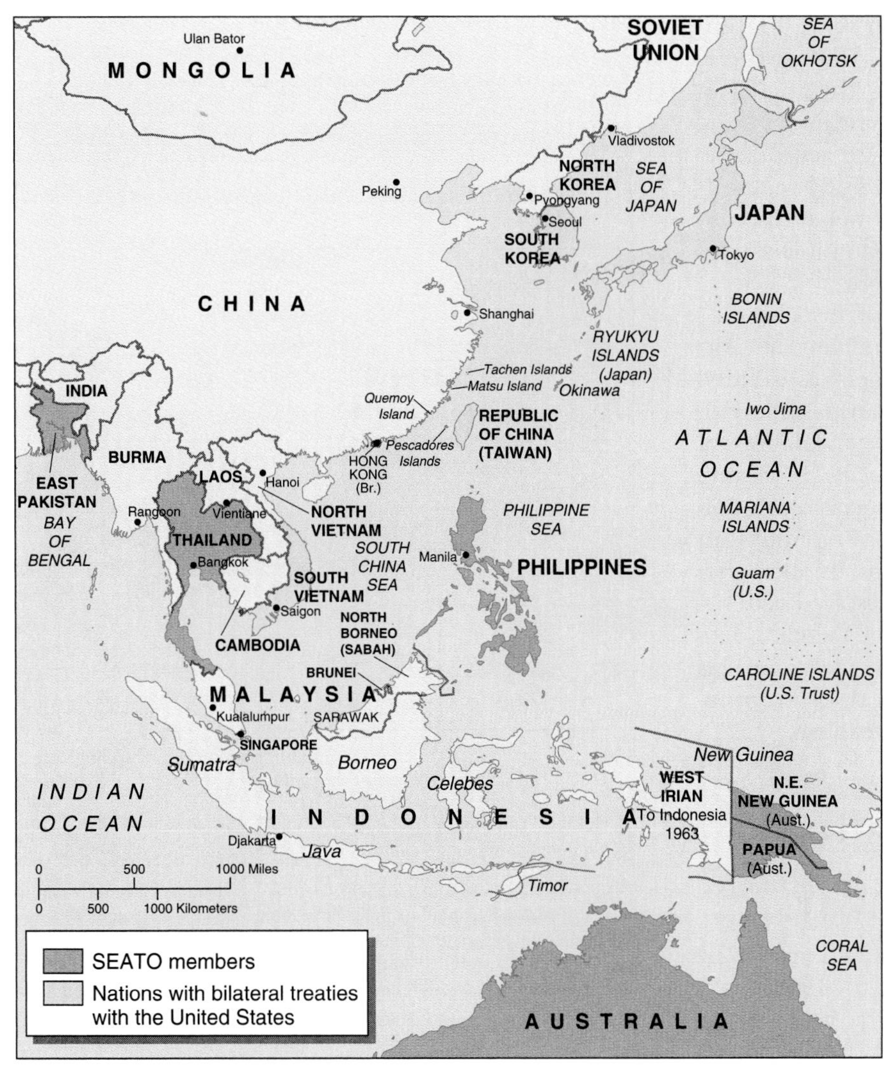

Map 30-2 SEATO and Other East Asian Countries with Ties to the United States
In East Asia and the western Pacific, the United States in the 1950s constructed a series of alliances to resist Soviet and Chinese communist influence.

dangerously different meanings the two sides gave to confrontations between 1953 and 1964.

A good example was the U-2 affair of 1960, which derailed progress toward nuclear disarmament. The Kremlin was deeply worried that West Germany and China might acquire nuclear bombs. Washington wanted to reduce military budgets and nuclear fallout. Both countries voluntarily suspended nuclear tests in 1958 and prepared for a June 1960 summit meeting in Paris, where Eisenhower intended to negotiate a test ban treaty.

But on May 1, 1960, Soviet air defenses shot down an American U-2 spy plane over the heart of Russia and captured the pilot, Francis Gary Powers. Designed to soar above the range of Soviet antiaircraft missiles, U-2s had assured American officials that there was no missile gap.

When Moscow trumpeted the news of the downing, Eisenhower took personal responsibility in hopes that Khrushchev would accept the U-2 as an unpleasant reality of international espionage. Unfortunately, the planes meant something very different to the Soviets, touching their festering sense of inferiority. They had stopped protesting the flights in 1957 because complaints were demeaning. The Americans thought that silence signaled acceptance. Khrushchev had staked his future on good relations with the United States; when Eisenhower refused to apologize in Paris, Khrushchev stalked out. Disarmament was set back for years.

The most important aspect of Eisenhower's foreign policy was continuity. Despite militant rhetoric, the administration pursued containment as defined under Truman. The Cold War consensus, however, prevented the United States from seeing the nations of the developing world on their own terms. By viewing every independence movement and social revolution as part of the competition with communism, American leaders created unnecessary problems. In the end, Eisenhower left troublesome and unresolved issues—upheaval in Latin America, civil war in Vietnam, tension in Germany, a nuclear arms race—for his successor, John Kennedy, who wanted to confront international communism even more vigorously.

John F. Kennedy and the Cold War

John Kennedy was a man of contradictions. Many Americans recall his presidency (1961–1963) as a golden age, but we are more taken by his memory than we were by Kennedy himself. A Democrat, he presided over policies whose direction was set under Eisenhower. Despite stirring rhetoric about leading the nation toward a **New Frontier** of scientific and social progress, he recorded his greatest failures and successes in the continuing Cold War.

The Kennedy Mystique

Kennedy won the presidency over Richard Nixon in a cliffhanging election that was more about personality and style than substance (see Map 30-3). Both candidates were determined not to yield another inch to communism. The charming and eloquent Kennedy narrowly skirted scandal in his personal life. Well publicized as a hero from World War II, he tempered ruthless ambition with respect for public service. His forthright campaigning allayed voter concern about his Roman Catholicism. Nixon had wider experience and was a shrewd tactician, but he was also self-righteous and awkward. Eisenhower had

Map 30-3 The Election of 1960
The presidential election of 1960 was one of the closest in American history. John Kennedy's victory depended on his appeal in northern industrial states with large Roman Catholic populations and his ability to hold much of the traditionally Democratic South. Texas, the home state of his vice-presidential running mate Lyndon Johnson, was vital to the success of the ticket.

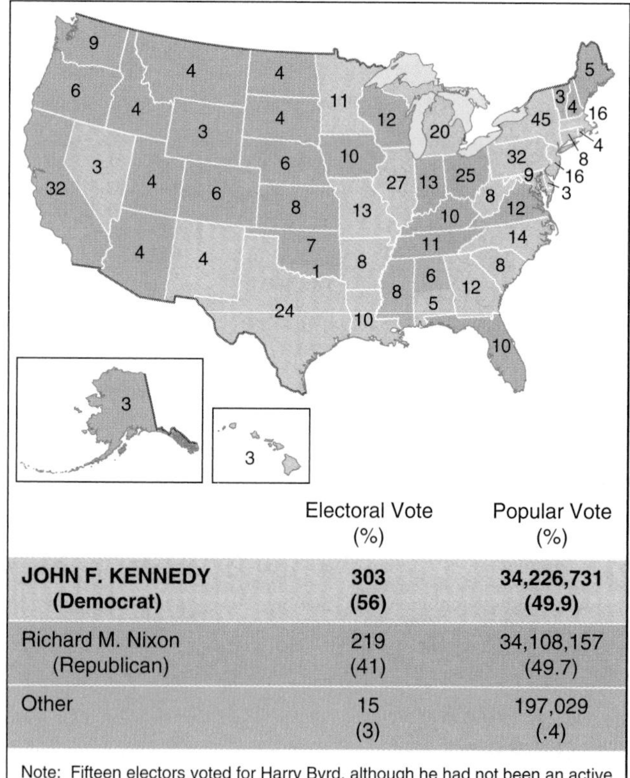

	Electoral Vote (%)	Popular Vote (%)
JOHN F. KENNEDY (Democrat)	**303 (56)**	**34,226,731 (49.9)**
Richard M. Nixon (Republican)	219 (41)	34,108,157 (49.7)
Other	15 (3)	197,029 (.4)

Note: Fifteen electors voted for Harry Byrd, although he had not been an active candidate. Minor party candidates took a tiny percentage of the popular vote.

wanted to drop Nixon as vice president in 1956 and gave him only lukewarm support in 1960—when a reporter asked Eisenhower to cite important decisions to which Nixon had contributed, Ike replied, "Give me a week and I might think of one."

Television was crucial to the outcome. The campaign featured the first televised presidential debates. In the first session, Nixon actually gave better replies, but his nervousness and a bad makeup job turned off millions of viewers who admired Kennedy's energy. Nixon never overcame the setback. Kennedy's televised inauguration was the perfect setting for his impassioned plea for national unity: "My fellow Americans," he challenged, "ask not what your country can do for you—ask what you can do for your country."

Kennedy brought dash to the White House. His beautiful and refined wife, Jackie, made sure to seat artists and writers next to diplomats and businessmen at White House dinners. Kennedy's staff and large family played touch football, not golf. No president had shown such verve since Teddy Roosevelt. People began to talk about Kennedy's "charisma," his ability to lead by sheer force of personality.

Behind the glamorous façade, Kennedy remained a puzzle. One day he could propose the Peace Corps, which gave thousands of idealistic young Americans a chance to help developing nations; another day he could approve plots to assassinate Fidel Castro. Visitors who expected a shallow glad-hander were astonished to meet a sharp, hardworking man who was eager to learn about the world. One savvy diplomat commented, "I have never heard of a president who wanted to know so much."

Kennedy's Mistakes

Kennedy and Khrushchev perpetuated similar problems. Talking tough to satisfy more militant countrymen, they pushed each other into corners, continuing the problems of mutual misunderstanding that had marked the 1950s. When Khrushchev promised in January 1961 to support "wars of national liberation," he was really fending off Chinese criticism. But Kennedy overreacted in his first State of the Union address by asking for more military spending.

Three months later, Kennedy fed Soviet fears of American aggressiveness by sponsoring an invasion of Cuba. At the start of 1959, Fidel Castro had toppled corrupt dictator Fulgencio Batista, who had made Havana infamous for Mafia-run gambling and prostitution. Castro then nationalized American investments, and thousands of Cubans fled to the United States.

When fourteen hundred anti-Castro Cubans landed at Cuba's **Bay of Pigs** on April 17, 1961, they were following a plan from the Eisenhower administration. The CIA had trained and armed the invaders and convinced Kennedy that the landing would trigger spontaneous uprisings. But when Kennedy refused to commit American armed forces to support them, Cuban forces captured the attackers.

Kennedy followed the Bay of Pigs debacle with a hasty and ill-prepared summit meeting with Khrushchev in Vienna in June, where Khrushchev saw no need to bargain and subjected him to intimidating tirades. The meeting left the Soviets with the impression that the president was weak and dangerously erratic.

To exploit Kennedy's perceived vulnerability, the USSR renewed tension over Berlin, deep within East Germany. The divided city served as an escape route from communism for hundreds of thousands of East Germans. Khrushchev now threatened to transfer the Soviet sector in Berlin to East Germany, which had no treaty obligations to France, Britain, or the United States. If the West had to deal directly with East Germany for access to Berlin, it would have to recognize a permanently divided Germany. Kennedy sounded the alarm; he doubled draft calls, called up reservists, and warned families to build fallout shelters. Boise, Idaho, families paid $100 for a share in a community shelter with its own power plant and hospital. Outside New York, Art Carlson and his son Claude put up a prefabricated steel shelter in four hours; Sears planned to sell the same model for $700.

Rather than confront the United States directly, however, the Soviets and East Germans on August 13, 1961, built a wall around the western sectors of Berlin while leaving the access route to West Germany open. The **Berlin Wall** thus isolated East Germany without challenging the Western allies in West Berlin itself. In private, Kennedy accepted the wall as a clever way to stabilize a dangerous situation: "A wall," he said, "is a hell of a lot better than a war." Tensions remained high for months as the two sides tested each other's resolve. Berlin remained a point of East-West tension until East German communism collapsed in 1989 and Berliners tore down the hated wall.

Another indirect consequence of the Vienna summit was growing American involvement in South Vietnam. Kennedy saw South Vietnam as a promising arena for containment. The anticommunist Diem controlled the cities with the help of a large army and a Vietnamese elite that had worked with the French. In the countryside, communist insurgents known as the **Viet Cong** were gaining strength. The United States stepped up its supply of weapons and sent advisers, including members of one of

Kennedy's military innovations, the Army Special Forces Group (Green Berets).

U.S. aid did not work. Despite overoptimistic reports and the help of sixteen thousand American troops, Diem's government by 1963 was losing the loyalty—"hearts and minds"—of many South Vietnamese. North Vietnamese support for the Viet Cong canceled the effect of U.S. assistance. Diem courted a second civil war by violently crushing opposition from Vietnamese Buddhists. Kennedy's administration tacitly approved a coup on November 1 that killed Diem and his brother and installed an ineffective military junta.

Missile Crisis: A Line Drawn in the Waves

The escalating tensions of 1961 in Southeast Asia, the Caribbean, and Germany were a prelude to the crisis that came closest to triggering a nuclear war. In the summer of 1962, congressional Republicans had hounded Kennedy about the Soviet military presence in Cuba. On October 15, reconnaissance photos revealed Soviets at work on launching sites from which nuclear missiles could hit the United States. Top officials spent five exhausting and increasingly desperate days sorting through the options. Doing nothing was never considered: The missiles would be political disaster and a threat to national security. Full-scale invasion of Cuba was infeasible on short notice, and "surgical" air strikes were technically impossible. Either sort of military operation would kill hundreds of Soviet personal and force Moscow to react. Secretary of Defense Robert McNamara suggested demanding removal of the missiles and declaring a naval "quarantine" against the arrival of further offensive weapons. A blockade would buy time for diplomacy.

Kennedy imposed the blockade in a terrifying speech on Monday, October 22. He emphasized the "deceptive" deployment of the Russian missiles and raised the specter of nuclear war. Americans would have been even more afraid had they known that some of the missiles were operational and that Soviets in Cuba were authorized to use them in self-defense. While Khrushchev hesitated, Soviet ships circled outside the quarantine line. On Friday, Khrushchev offered to withdraw the missiles in return for an American pledge not to invade Cuba. On Saturday, a second communication raised a new complaint about American missiles on the territory of NATO allies. The letter was the result of pressure by Kremlin hard-liners and Khrushchev's own wavering. Kennedy decided to accept the first letter and ignore the second. The United States pledged not to invade Cuba and secretly promised to remove obsolete Jupiter missiles from Turkey. Khrushchev accepted these terms on Sunday, October 28.

Why did Khrushchev risk the Cuban gamble? One reason was to protect Castro as a symbol of Soviet commitment to anti-Western regimes in the developing world. Americans hated the Castro government out of proportion to its geopolitical importance, but they rightly feared that Cuba would try to export revolution throughout Latin America. Kennedy had tried to preempt Castroism in 1961 by launching the **Alliance for Progress**, an economic development program for Latin America that tied aid to social reform. However, the United States had also orchestrated the Bay of Pigs invasion and funded a CIA campaign to sabotage Cuba and assassinate its leaders. High American officials were not contemplating a full-scale invasion, but Castro and Khrushchev had reason to fear the worst.

Khrushchev also hoped to redress the strategic balance. As Kennedy discovered on taking office, the United States actually led the world in the deployment of strategic missiles. Intermediate-range rockets gave the USSR a nuclear club over western Europe, but in October 1962, the USSR had fewer than fifty ICBMs to aim at the United States and China. The United States was creating a defensive triad of a thousand land-based Minuteman missiles, five hundred long-range bombers, and six hundred Polaris missiles on nuclear submarines targeted on the USSR. The strategic imbalance had sustained NATO during the Berlin confrontation, but forty launchers in Cuba with two warheads each would have doubled the Soviet capacity to strike at the United States.

Soviet missiles in Cuba thus flouted the Monroe Doctrine and posed a real military threat. Kennedy and Khrushchev had also backed each other into untenable positions. In September, Kennedy had warned that the United States could not tolerate Soviet offensive weapons in Cuba, never dreaming that they were already there. Had Khrushchev acted openly (as the United States had done in siting missiles in Turkey), the United States would have been hard pressed to object under international law. By acting in secret and breaking previous promises, the Soviets outsmarted themselves. When the missiles were discovered, Kennedy had to act.

In the end, both sides were cautious. Khrushchev backed down rather than fight. Kennedy fended off hawkish advisers who wanted to destroy Castro. The world had trembled, but neither nation wanted war over "the missiles of October."

After the missile crisis showed his toughness, Kennedy had enough political maneuvering room to respond to pressure from liberal Democrats and groups like Women Strike for Peace and the Committee for a Sane Nuclear Policy by giving priority to disarmament. In July 1963, the United States, Britain, and the USSR signed the **Limited Test Ban Treaty**, which outlawed nuclear testing in the atmosphere, in outer space, and under water, and invited other nations to join in. A more comprehensive treaty was impossible because the Soviet Union refused the on-site inspections the United States deemed necessary to distinguish underground tests from earthquakes. France and China, the other nuclear powers, refused to sign, and the treaty did not halt weapons development, but it was the most positive achievement of Kennedy's foreign policy.

Righteousness Like a Mighty Stream: The Struggle for Civil Rights

Supreme Court decisions are based on abstract principles, but they involve real people. One was Linda Brown of Topeka, Kansas, a third-grader whose parents were fed up with sending her past an all-white public school to attend an all-black school a mile away. The Browns volunteered to help the NAACP challenge Topeka's school segregation by trying to enroll Linda in their neighborhood school, beginning a legal case that reached the Supreme Court. Three years later, on May 17, 1954, the Court decided ***Brown* v. *Board of Education of Topeka***, opening a new civil rights era. The justices reversed the 1896 case of *Plessy* v. *Ferguson* by ruling that sending black children to "separate but equal" schools denied them equal treatment under the Constitution. Linda's mother heard about the decision on the radio while she was ironing and told her daughter when she got home from school; when Linda's father heard the news, his eyes filled with tears, and he said, "Thanks be to God."

The Brown decision made the growing effort to secure equal legal treatment for African Americans an inescapable challenge to American society. The first phase of the civil rights struggle built from the Supreme Court's decision in 1954 to a vast gathering at the Lincoln Memorial in 1963. In between, African Americans chipped away at the racial segregation of schools, universities, and public facilities with marches, boycotts, sit-ins, and lawsuits, forcing segregated communities to choose between integration and violent defiance. In the two years following the 1963 March on Washington, the federal government passed landmark legislation.

Getting to the Supreme Court

The Brown decision climaxed a twenty-five-year campaign to reenlist the federal courts on the side of equal rights (see the Overview table, "Civil Rights in the South: The Struggle for Racial Equality"). The work began in the 1930s when Charles Hamilton Houston, dean of Howard University's law school, trained a corps of civil rights lawyers. Working on behalf of the NAACP, he hoped to erode *Plessy* by suits focused on interstate travel and professional graduate schools (the least defensible segregated institutions, because states seldom provided alternatives). In 1938, Houston's student Thurgood Marshall, a future Supreme Court justice, took over the NAACP job. He and other NAACP lawyers such as Constance Baker Motley risked personal danger crisscrossing the South to file civil rights lawsuits wherever a local case emerged. In 1949, Motley was the first black lawyer to argue a case in a Mississippi courtroom since Reconstruction.

The Brown case combined lawsuits from Delaware, Virginia, South Carolina, the District of Columbia, and Kansas. In each instance, students and families braved community pressure to demand equal access to a basic public service. Chief Justice Earl Warren brought a divided Court to unanimous agreement. Viewing public education as central for the equal opportunity that lay at the heart of American values, the Court weighed the consequences of segregated school systems and concluded that separate meant unequal. The reasoning fit the temper of a nation that was proud of making prosperity accessible to all.

Brown also built on efforts by Mexican Americans in the Southwest to assert their rights of citizenship. After World War II, Latino organizations such as the League of United Latin American Citizens battled job discrimination and ethnic segregation. In 1946, the federal courts had prohibited segregation of Mexican-American children in California schools. Eight years later, the Supreme Court forbade Texas from excluding Mexican Americans from juries. These cases provided precedents for civil rights arguments.

Deliberate Speed

Racial segregation by law was largely a southern problem, the legacy of Jim Crow laws from early in the century. The civil rights movement therefore first focused on the South and allowed Americans elsewhere to think of racial injustice as a regional issue.

Overview

Civil Rights in the South: The Struggle for Racial Equality

Area of Concern	Key Actions	Results
Public school integration	Federal court cases	*Brown* v. *Board of Education of Topeka* (1954) Enforcement by presidential action, Little Rock (1957) Follow-up court decisions, including mandatory busing programs
Equal access to public facilities	Montgomery bus boycott (1955) Lunch counter sit-ins (1960) Freedom rides (1961) Birmingham demonstrations (1963) March on Washington (1963)	Civil Rights Act of 1964
Equitable voter registration	Voter registration drives, including Mississippi Summer Project (1964) Demonstrations and marches, including Selma to Montgomery march (1965)	Voting Rights Act of 1965

Southern responses to Brown emphasized regional differences. Few southern communities desegregated schools voluntarily, for to do so undermined the entrenched principle of a dual society. Their reluctance was bolstered in 1955 when the Supreme Court allowed segregated states to carry out the 1954 decision "with all deliberate speed" rather than immediately. The following year, 101 southern congressmen and senators issued the **Southern Manifesto**, which asserted that the Court decision was unconstitutional. President Eisenhower privately deplored the desegregation decision, which violated his sense of states' rights and upset Republican attempts to gain southern votes; he called both those who resisted the decision and those who wanted to enforce it "extremists."

Eisenhower's distaste for racial integration left the Justice Department on the sidelines. Courageous parents and students had to knock on schoolhouse doors, often carrying court orders. Responses varied: School districts in border states, such as Maryland, Kentucky, and Oklahoma, desegregated relatively peacefully; farther south, African-American children often met taunts and violence.

The first crisis came in Little Rock, Arkansas, in September 1957. The city school board admitted nine African Americans to Central High, only to be upstaged by Governor Orval Faubus. Claiming to fear violence, he surrounded Central with the National Guard and turned the new students away. Meanwhile, segregrationists stirred up white fears. Under intense national pressure, Faubus withdrew the Guard, and a howling crowd surrounded the school. When the black students entered anyway, the mob threatened to storm the building. The police had to sneak the students out after two hours. Fuming at the governor's defiance of federal authority, which bordered on insurrection, Eisenhower reluctantly nationalized the National Guard and sent in the 101st Airborne Division to keep order. Eight of the students endured a year of harassment in the hallways of Central.

Change came slowly to state universities. Border states desegregated colleges and professional schools with few incidents. Again, the story was differ-

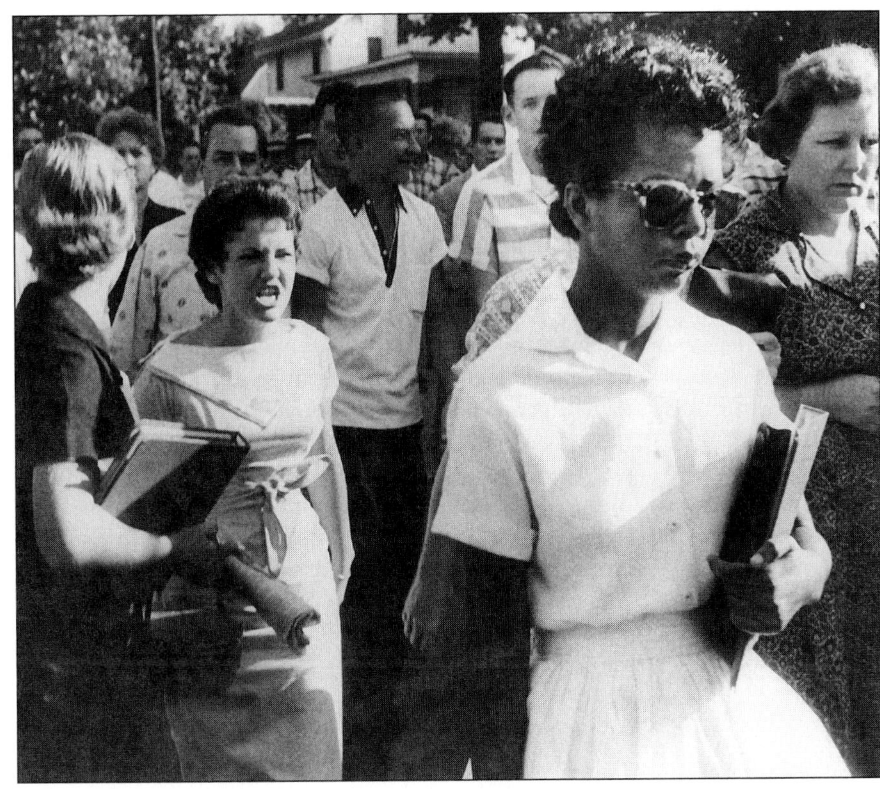

Elizabeth Eckford, one of the first black students to attend Central High in Little Rock, Arkansas, in 1957, enters the school amid taunts from white students and bystanders.

ent in the lower South. In 1956, the University of Alabama admitted Autherine Lucy under court order but then expelled her before she could attend class. In September 1962, James Meredith tried to enter the University of Mississippi, igniting a riot that the state refused to control. President Kennedy sent in the army. A year later, Governor George Wallace of Alabama grabbed headlines by "standing in the schoolhouse door" to prevent integration of the University of Alabama, gaining a national prominence that culminated in a third-party candidacy for president in 1968.

The breakthrough in school integration did not come until the end of the 1960s, when the courts rejected further delays, and federal authorities threatened to cut off education funds. As late as 1968, only 6 percent of African-American children in the South attended integrated schools. By 1973, the figure was 90 percent. Attention thereafter shifted to northern communities, whose schools were segregated not by law but by the divisions between white and black neighborhoods and between white suburbs and multiracial central cities, a situation known as de facto segregation.

Public Accommodations

The civil rights movement also sought to integrate public accommodations. Most southern states separated the races in bus terminals and movie theaters. They required black riders to take rear seats on buses. They labeled separate restrooms and drinking fountains for "colored" users. Hotels denied rooms to black people, and restaurants refused them service.

The struggle to end segregated facilities started in Montgomery, Alabama. On December 1, 1955, Rosa Parks, a seamstress who worked at a downtown department store, refused to give up her bus seat to a white passenger and was arrested. Parks acted spontaneously, but she was part of a network of civil rights activists who wanted to challenge segregated buses and was the secretary of the Montgomery NAACP. As news of her action spread, the community institutions that enriched southern black life went into action. The Women's Political Council, a group of college-trained black women, initiated a mass boycott of the privately owned bus company. Martin Luther King, Jr., a twenty-six-year-old pastor, led the boycott. He galvanized a mass meeting with a speech that quoted the biblical prophet Amos: "We are determined here in Montgomery to work and fight until justice runs down like water, and righteousness like a mighty stream."

Montgomery's African Americans organized their boycott in the face of white outrage. A car pool substituted for the buses despite police harassment. As the boycott survived months of pressure, the national media began to pay attention. After nearly a year, the Supreme Court agreed that the bus segregation law was unconstitutional.

Victory in Montgomery depended on the steadfastness of African-American involvement. Leaders included Ralph Abernathy, other black preachers, and faculty from Alabama State College. Participants cut across the class lines that had divided black Southerners. Success also revealed the discrepancy between white attitudes in the Deep South and national opinion. For white Southerners, segregation was a local concern best defined as a legal or constitutional matter. For other Americans, it was increasingly an issue of the South's deviation from national moral norms.

The Montgomery boycott won a local victory and made King famous, but it did not propel a wave of immediate change. King formed the **Southern Christian Leadership Conference (SCLC)** and sparred with the NAACP about community-based versus court-based civil rights tactics, but four African-American college students in Greensboro, North Carolina, started the next phase of the struggle. On February 1, 1960, they sat down at the segregated lunch counter in Woolworth's, waiting through the day without being served. Their patient courage brought more demonstrators; within two days, eighty-five students packed the store. Nonviolent sit-ins spread throughout the South.

The sit-ins had both immediate and long-range effects. In comparatively sophisticated border cities like Nashville, Tennessee, sit-ins integrated lunch counters. Elsewhere they precipitated white violence and mass arrests. Like soldiers on a battlefield, nervous participants in sit-ins and demonstrations drew strength from one another. "If you don't have courage," said one young woman in Albany, Georgia, "you can borrow it." King welcomed nonviolent confrontation. SCLC leader Ella Baker helped the students form a new organization, the **Student Nonviolent Coordinating Committee (SNCC)**. (See "American Views: Nonviolent Action for Civil Rights: Mississippi 1961.")

The year 1961 brought "freedom rides" to test the segregation of interstate bus terminals. The

Students from North Carolina A&T, an all-black college, began the lunch counter sit-in movement in February 1960. Here four of the students sit patiently in the Greensboro Woolworth's without being served. Participants wore their best clothes and suffered politely through days of verbal and sometimes physical abuse.

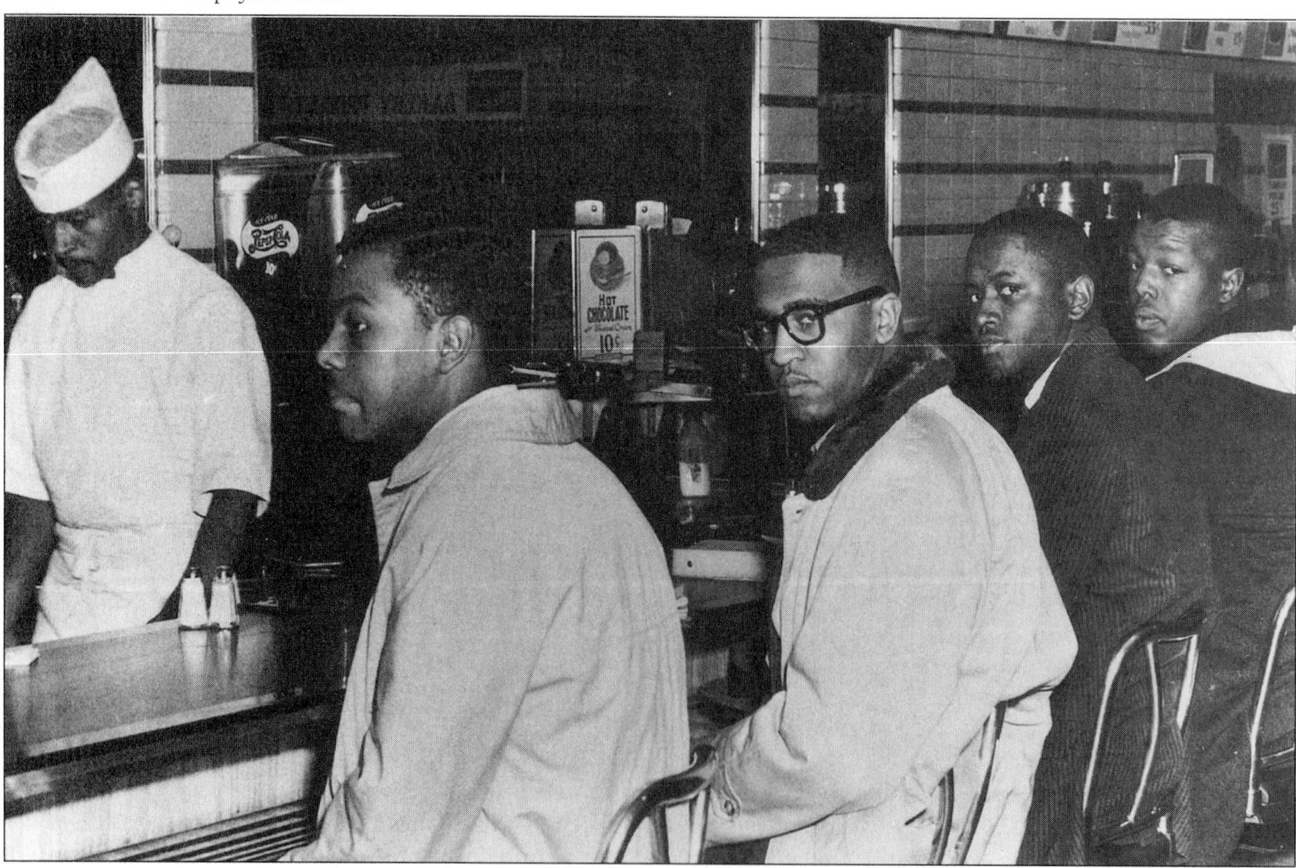

American Views

Nonviolent Action for Civil Rights: Mississippi 1961

As sit-ins and other nonviolent civil rights protests spread across the South, Burgland High School, in McComb, Mississippi, expelled two students after they tried to integrate the local Greyhound bus station. Many fellow students boycotted the school in sympathy, attending "Nonviolent High," classes taught by workers from the Student Nonviolent Coordinating Committee. One of these students was Suzette Miller, who explained her motivations in a class assignment.

❖ **What does the episode suggest about the local roots of the civil rights movement?**

❖ **What does the statement show about the role of religion in American reform efforts?**

Suzette Miller
Subject: English
Instructor: C. McDew

Why I walked out of Burgland High School:

I am Suzette Miller, a student of the present Freshman class. I don't have much to lose, but I do have a lot to gain. That is my equal rights.

Brenda Travis is a female that made a protest in McComb Bus Station. She was also a student at Burgland Hi, but is now an ex-student.

I was in the walk out because I am A student at Burgland just like Brenda. Because she wasn't allowed back in school I don't feel that I should allow myself to go back.

I walked out and to be readmitted I have to sign a paper saying that if I walk out any more I will be expelled, and if I didn't sign the paper asking for readmittance back in school.

Now I am expelled for the remainder of the school year. But I will keep protesting until the battle is won.

I am now a student of The Nonviolent High School. In my heart I believe where there is a will there is a way.

Now is the time to put God first and to let him lead us.

Our white brothers and sisters think that we want war. War is not needed now in Mississippi. If we ever needed any thing we need God. He is the way and the light.

If we would stop and think we could see what we need and what we are doing to try to get it.

We as a race come face to face with our enemies kind and willing to have them as brothers and sisters. We would have better families, homes, churches, towns, and states.

May God forever bless us all over land and country. "Oh God show us the right way."

Source: Staughton Lynd, Nonviolence in America: A Documentary History *(Bobbs-Merrill, 1966).*

idea came from James Farmer of the **Congress of Racial Equality (CORE)**, who copied a little-remembered 1947 Journey of Reconciliation that had tested the integration of interstate trains. Two buses carrying black and white passengers met only minor problems in Virginia, the Carolinas, and Georgia, but Alabamians burned one of the buses and attacked the riders in Birmingham, where they beat demonstrators senseless and clubbed a Justice Department observer. The governor and police refused to protect the freedom riders. The riders traveled into Mississippi under National Guard protection but were arrested at the Jackson bus terminal. Despite Attorney General Robert Kennedy's call for a cooling-off period, freedom rides continued through the summer. The rides proved that African Americans were in charge of their own civil rights revolution.

March on Washington, 1963

John Kennedy was a tepid supporter of the civil rights movement and entered office with no civil rights agenda. He appointed segregationist judges to mollify southern congressmen and would have preferred that African Americans stop disturbing the fragile Democratic party coalition. As Eisenhower did at Little Rock, Kennedy intervened at the University of Mississippi in 1962 because of a state challenge to federal authority, not to further racial justice.

In the face of slow federal response, the SCLC concentrated for 1963 on rigidly segregated Birmingham. April began with sit-ins and marches that aimed to integrate lunch counters, restrooms, and stores and secure open hiring for some clerical jobs. Birmingham's commissioner of public safety, Bull Connor, used fire hoses to blast demonstrators against buildings and roll children down the streets. When demonstrators fought back, his men chased them with dogs. Continued marches brought the arrest of hundreds of children. King's own "Letter from Birmingham City Jail" stated the case for protest: "We have not made a single gain in civil rights without determined legal and nonviolent pressure. . . . Freedom is never voluntarily given by the oppressor; it must be demanded by the oppressed."

The Birmingham demonstrations were inconclusive. White leaders accepted minimal demands on May 10 but delayed enforcing them. Antiblack violence continued, including a bomb that killed four children in a Birmingham church. Meanwhile, the events in Alabama had forced President Kennedy to board the freedom train with an eloquent June 11 speech and to send a civil rights bill to Congress. "Are we to say . . . that this is the land of the free, except for Negroes, that we have no second-class citizens, except Negroes . . . ? Now the time has come for the nation to fulfill its promise."

On August 28, 1963, a rally in Washington transformed African-American civil rights into a national cause. A quarter of a million people, black and white, marched to the Lincoln Memorial. The day gave Martin Luther King, Jr., a national pulpit. His call for progress toward Christian and American goals had immense appeal. Television cut away from afternoon programs for his "I Have a Dream" speech.

The March on Washington demonstrated the mass appeal of civil rights and its identification with national values. It also papered over growing tensions within the civil rights movement. John Lewis of SNCC wanted to challenge Kennedy for doing "too little, too late" but dropped the criticism under intense pressure. He was the only speaker at the march to talk about "black people" rather than "Negroes," an indication of growing militancy that split the civil rights effort in the mid-sixties and moved younger African Americans, as well as Latinos and Native Americans, to emphasize their own distinct identities within American society.

"Let Us Continue"

The two years that followed King's speech mingled despair and accomplishment. The optimism of the March on Washington shattered with the assassination of John Kennedy in November 1963. In 1964 and 1965, however, President Lyndon Johnson pushed through Kennedy's legislative agenda and much more. Federal legislation brought victory to the first phase of the civil rights revolution, launched the **War on Poverty**, expanded health insurance and aid to education, and opened an era of environmental protection, government activism unmatched since the 1930s.

Dallas, 1963

In November 1963, President Kennedy visited Texas to patch up feuds among Texas Democrats. On November 22, the president's motorcade took him near the Texas School Book Depository building in Dallas, where Lee Harvey Oswald had stationed himself at a window on the sixth floor. When Kennedy's open car swung into the sights of his rifle, Oswald fired three shots that wounded Texas Governor John Connally and killed the president. As doctors vainly treated the president in a hospital emergency room, Dallas police arrested Oswald. Vice President Lyndon Johnson took the oath of office as president on Air Force One while the blood-spattered Jacqueline

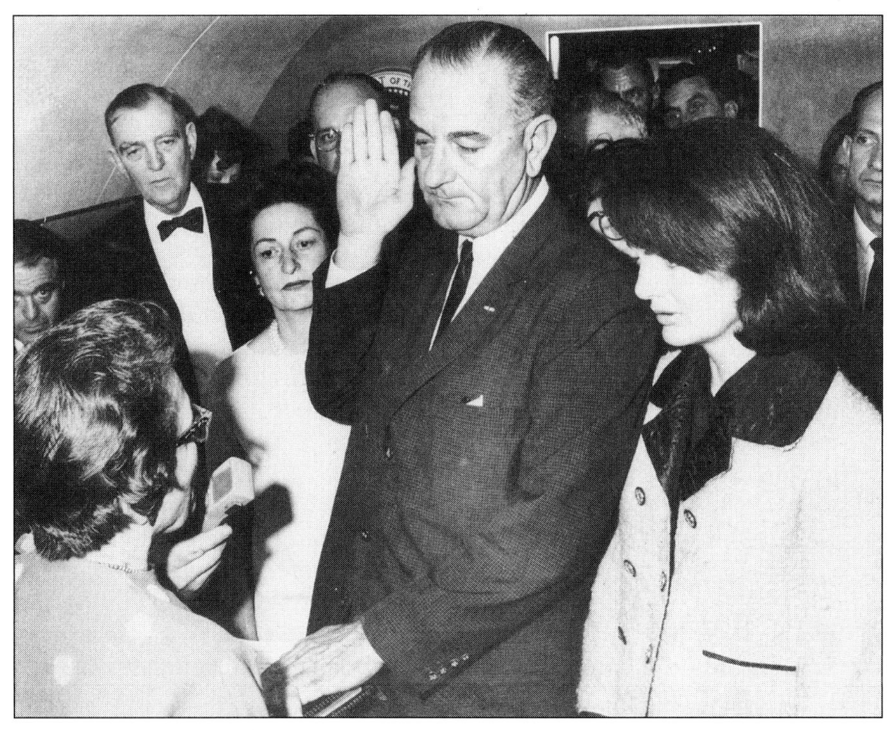

After the assassination of John Kennedy in Dallas, Lyndon Johnson, with Jackie Kennedy looking on, took the oath of office as president aboard Air Force One at Love Field in Dallas.

Kennedy looked on. Two days later, as Oswald was being led to a courtroom, Texas nightclub owner Jack Ruby killed Oswald with a handgun, in full view of TV cameras.

Lee Oswald was a twenty-four-year old misfit. He had served in the Marines and worked maintaining U-2 spy planes before defecting to the Soviet Union, which he found to be less than a workers' paradise. He returned to the United States after three years with a Russian wife and a fervent commitment to Fidel Castro's Cuban revolution. It was later learned that he had tried to shoot a right-wing general in 1963. He visited the Soviet and Cuban embassies in Mexico City in September trying to drum up a job, but neither country thought him worth hiring.

Some Americans believe there is more to the story. Why? One possibility is the expectation that important events should have great causes. Oswald seems too insignificant to be responsible on his own for the murder of a charismatic president. The sketchy job done by the Warren Commission, appointed to investigate the assassination, also bred doubts in some minds. The commission hurried to complete its work before the 1964 election. It also sought to assure Americans that Kennedy had not been killed as part of a communist plot. The Warren Commission calmed fears in the short run but left loose ends that have fueled conspiracy theories.

All of the theories remain unproved. Until they are, logic holds that the simplest explanation for cutting through a mass of information is usually the best. Oswald was a social misfit with a grievance against American society. Ruby was an impulsive man who told his brother on his deathbed that he thought he was doing the country a favor. Like presidents Garfield and McKinley before him, Kennedy died at the hands of one unbalanced man acting alone.

War on Poverty

Five days after the assassination, Lyndon Johnson claimed Kennedy's progressive aura for his new administration. "Let us continue," he told the nation, promising to implement Kennedy's policies. In fact, Johnson was vastly different from Kennedy. He was a professional politician who had reached the top through Texas politics and congressional infighting. As Senate majority leader during the 1950s, he had built a web of political obligations and friendships. Johnson's presence on the ticket in 1960 had helped elect Kennedy by attracting southern voters, but the Kennedy entourage loathed him. He lacked Kennedy's polish and easy relations with the eastern elite. He knew little about foreign affairs but was deeply committed to social equity. He had entered public life with the New Deal in the 1930s and believed in its principles. Johnson, not Kennedy, was the true heir of Franklin Roosevelt.

Johnson inherited a domestic agenda that the Kennedy administration had defined but not enacted. Kennedy's New Frontier had met the same fate as Truman's Fair Deal. Initiatives in education, medical insurance, tax reform, and urban affairs had stalled or been gutted by conservatives in Congress.

Kennedy's farthest-reaching initiative was rooted in the acknowledgment that poverty was a persistent American problem. Michael Harrington's study *The Other America* became an unexpected best-seller. As poverty captured public attention, Kennedy's economic advisers devised a community action program that emphasized education and job training, a national service corps, and a youth conservation corps. They prepared a package of proposals to submit to Congress in 1964 that downplayed the option of large-scale income transfers as politically unpopular. Instead, they focused on social programs to alter behaviors that were thought to be passed from generation to generation, thus following the American tendency to attribute poverty to the failings of the poor themselves.

Johnson made Kennedy's antipoverty package his own. Adopting Cold War rhetoric, he declared "unconditional war on poverty." The core of Johnson's program was the **Office of Economic Opportunity (OEO)**. Established under the direction of Kennedy's brother-in-law R. Sargent Shriver in 1964, the OEO operated the **Job Corps** for school dropouts, the Neighborhood Youth Corps for unemployed teenagers, the **Head Start** program to prepare poor children for school, and **VISTA** (Volunteers in Service to America), a domestic Peace Corps. OEO's biggest effort went to Community Action Agencies. By 1968, more than five hundred such agencies provided health and educational services. Despite flaws, the War on Poverty improved life for millions of Americans.

Civil Rights, 1964–1965

Johnson's passionate commitment to economic betterment accompanied a commitment to civil rights. In Johnson's view, segregation not only deprived African Americans of access to opportunity but also distracted white Southerners from their own poverty and underdevelopment. As he complained in a speech in New Orleans, southern leaders ignored the region's economic needs in favor of racial rabble-rousing.

One solution was the **Civil Rights Act of 1964**, which Kennedy had introduced but Johnson got enacted. The law prohibited segregation in public accommodations, such as hotels, restaurants, gas stations, theaters, and parks, and outlawed employment discrimination on federally assisted projects. It also created the **Equal Employment Opportunity Commission (EEOC)** and included gender in list of categories protected against discrimination, a provision whose consequences were scarcely suspected in 1964.

Even as Congress was debating the 1964 law, **Freedom Summer** moved political power to the top of the civil rights agenda. Organized by SNCC, the Mississippi Summer Freedom Project was a voter registration drive that sent white and black volunteers to the small towns and back roads of Mississippi. The target was a political system that used rigged literacy tests and intimidation to keep black Southerners from voting. In Mississippi in 1964, only 7 percent of eligible black citizens were registered voters. Local black activists had laid the groundwork for a registration effort with years of courageous effort through the NAACP and voter leagues. Now an increasingly militant SNCC took the lead. The explicit goal was to increase the number of African-American voters. The tacit intention was to attract national attention by putting middle-class white college students in the line of fire. Freedom Summer gained sixteen hundred new voters and taught two thousand children in SNCC-run Freedom Schools at the cost of beatings, bombings, church arson, and the murder of three project workers.

Another outgrowth of the SNCC effort was the Mississippi Freedom Democratic Party (MFDP), a biracial coalition that bypassed Mississippi's all-white Democratic party, followed state party rules, and sent its own delegates to the 1964 Democratic convention. To preserve party harmony, President Johnson refused to expel the "regular" Mississippi Democrats and offered instead to seat two MFDP delegates and enforce party rules for 1968. The MFDP walked out, seething with anger. Fannie Lou Hamer, a MFDP delegate who had already suffered in the struggle for voting rights, remembered, "We learned the hard way that even though we had all the law and all the righteousness on our side—that white man is not going to give up his power to us. We have to build our own power."

Freedom Summer and political realities both focused national attention on voter registration. Lyndon Johnson and Martin Luther King, Jr., agreed on the need for federal voting legislation when King visited the president in December 1964 after winning the Nobel Peace Prize. For King, power at the ballot box would help black Southerners take control of their own communities. For Johnson, voting reform would fulfill the promise of American democracy. It would also benefit the Democratic party by replacing with black voters the white Southerners who were drifting toward anti-integration Republicans.

The target for King and the SCLC was Dallas County, Alabama, where only 2 percent of eligible black residents were registered, compared with 70 percent of white residents. Peaceful demonstrations started in January 1965. By early February, jails in the county seat of Selma held 2,600 black people whose offense was marching to the courthouse to demand the vote. The campaign climaxed with a march from Selma to the state capital of Montgomery. SNCC leader John Lewis remembered, "I don't know what we expected. I think maybe we thought we'd be arrested and jailed, or maybe they wouldn't do anything to us. I had a little knapsack on my shoulder with an apple, a toothbrush, toothpaste, and two books in it: a history of America and a book by [Christian theologian] Thomas Merton."

On Sunday, March 7, five hundred marchers crossed the bridge over the Alabama River to meet a sea of state troopers. The troopers gave them two minutes to disperse and then attacked on foot and horseback "as if they were mowing a big field." The attack drove the demonstrators back in bloody confusion while television cameras rolled.

After being attacked and dispersed by Alabama state police as they attempted a fifty-three mile march from Selma to Montgomery, Alabama, civil rights demonstrators regrouped. Under the glare of national press coverage, Alabama authorities let the march proceed. Here the leaders—including Martin Luther King, Jr., Coretta Scott King, Hosea Williams, Bayard Rustin, and Ralph Bunche—enter Montgomery.

As violence continued, Johnson addressed a joint session of Congress to demand a voting rights law: "Our mission is at once the oldest and the most basic of this country: to right wrong, to do justice, to serve man." He ended with the refrain of the civil rights movement: "We shall overcome."

Johnson signed the **Voting Rights Act** on August 6, 1965. The law outlawed literacy tests and provided for federal voting registrars in states where registration or turnout in 1964 was less than 50 percent of eligible population. It applied initially in seven southern states. Black registration in these states jumped from 27 percent to 55 percent within the first year. In 1975, Congress extended coverage to Hispanic voters in the Southwest. By the end of 1992, Virginia had elected a black governor and nearly every southern state had elected black Representatives to Congress. Less obvious but just as revolutionary were the thousands of black and Latino candidates who won local offices and the new moderation of white leaders who had to satisfy black voters.

War, Peace, and the Landslide of 1964

Lyndon Johnson was the peace candidate in 1964. Johnson had maintained Kennedy's commitment to South Vietnam. On the advice of Kennedy holdovers like Defense Secretary Robert McNamara, he stepped up commando raids and naval shelling of North Vietnam on the assumption that North Vietnam controlled the Viet Cong. On August 2, North Vietnamese torpedo boats attacked the U.S. destroyer *Maddox* in the Gulf of Tonkin while it was eavesdropping on North Vietnamese military signals. Two days later, the *Maddox* and the *C. Turner Joy* reported another torpedo attack (probably false sonar readings). Johnson ordered a bombing raid in reprisal and asked Congress to authorize "all necessary measures" to protect American forces and stop further aggression. Congress passed the **Gulf of Tonkin Resolution** with only two nay votes, effectively authorizing the president to wage undeclared war.

Johnson's militancy paled beside that of his Republican opponent. Senator Barry Goldwater of Arizona represented the new right wing of the Republican party, which was drawing strength from the South and West. A department store heir, Goldwater wanted minimal government interference in free enterprise. As a former Air Force pilot, he also wanted aggressive confrontation with communism. Campaign literature accurately described him as "a choice, not an echo." He declared that "extremism in the defense of liberty is no vice," raising visions of vigilantes and mobs. Goldwater's campaign made Johnson look moderate. Johnson pledged not "to send American boys nine or ten thousand miles from home to do what Asian boys ought to be doing for themselves" while Goldwater proposed an all-out war.

The election was a landslide. Johnson's 61 percent of the popular vote was the greatest margin ever recorded in a presidential election. Democrats racked up two-to-one majorities in Congress. For the first time in decades, liberal Democrats could enact their domestic program without begging votes from conservative Southerners or Republicans, and Johnson could achieve his goal of a **Great Society** based on freedom and opportunity for all.

The result in 1965 was a series of measures that Johnson rushed through Congress before his political standing began to erode and Vietnam distracted national attention. The **National Endowment for the Humanities**, **National Endowment for the Arts**, and highway beautification were part of the Great Society for the middle class. The Wilderness Act (1964), an early success of the modern environmental movement, preserved 9.1 million acres from all development.

More central to Johnson's vision of the Great Society were efforts to increase opportunity for all Americans, a goal that stirred the president deeply. As he told a July 1965 news conference, "When I was young, poverty was so common that we didn't know it had a name. An education was something that you had to fight for. . . . It is now my opportunity to help every child get an education, to help every Negro and every American citizen have an equal opportunity, to have every family get a decent home, and to help bring healing to the sick and dignity to the old." The Elementary and Secondary Education Act was the first general federal aid program for public schools, allocating $1.3 billion for textbooks and special education. The Higher Education Act funded low-interest student loans and university research facilities. The Medical Care Act created federally funded health insurance for the elderly **(Medicare)** and helped states offer medical care to the poor **(Medicaid)**. The Appalachian Regional Development Act funded economic development in the depressed mountain counties of twelve states from Georgia to New York and proved a long-run success.

It is sometimes said that the United States declared war on poverty and lost. In fact, the nation came closer in to winning the war on poverty than the war in Vietnam. New or expanded social insurance and income support programs, such as Medicare, Medicaid, Social Security, and food stamps, cut the

Figure 30-4 Poverty Rate, 1960–1997
With the improvement of federal health insurance, assistance for the elderly, and antipoverty programs, the proportion of Americans living in poverty dropped dramatically in the later 1960s. It began to inch upward again in the 1980s when the priorities of the federal government shifted.
Data Source: Statistical Abstract of the United States.

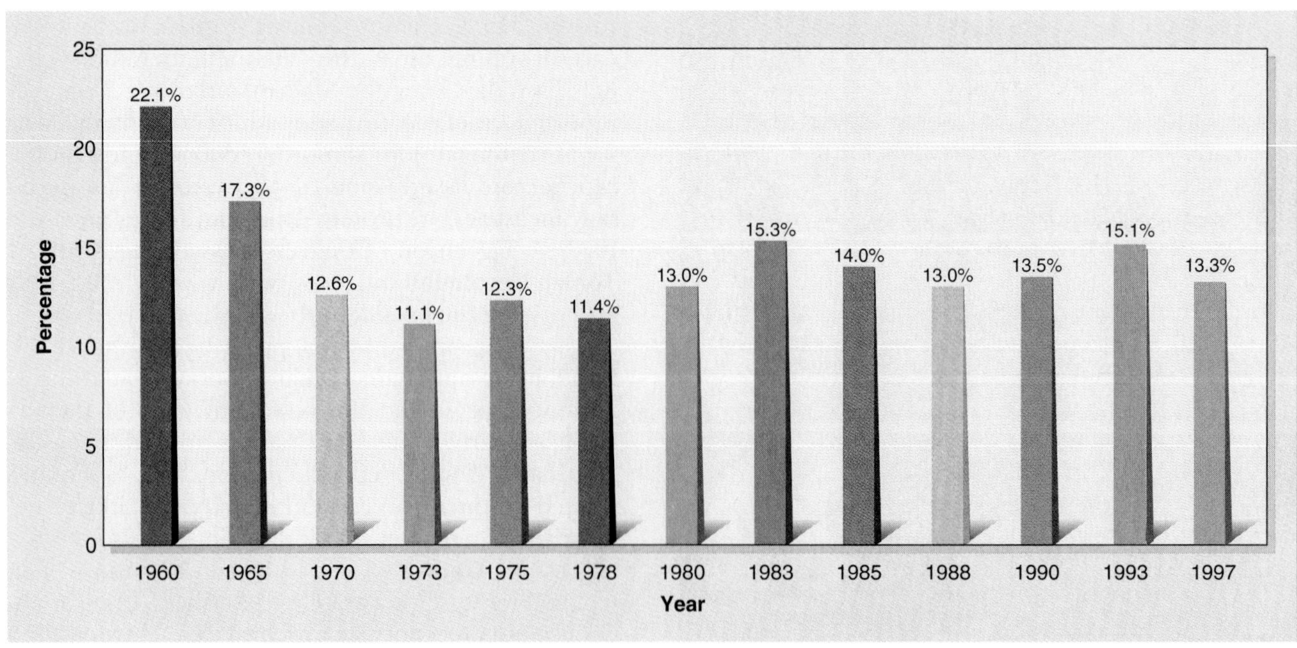

proportion of poor people from 22 percent of the American population in 1960 to 13 percent in 1970 (see Figure 30-4). Infant mortality dropped by a third because of improved nutrition and better access to health care for mothers and children. Taken together, the political results of the 1964 landslide moved the United States far toward Lyndon Johnson's vision of an end to poverty and racial injustice.

Conclusion

The era commonly remembered as "the fifties" stretched from 1953 to 1964. Consistent goals guided American foreign policy through the entire period, including vigilant anticommunism and the confidence to intervene in trouble spots around the globe. At home, the Supreme Court's *Brown* decision introduced a decadelong civil rights revolution. However, many patterns of personal behavior and social relations remained unchanged. Women faced similar expectations from the early fifties to the early sixties. Churches showed more continuity than change.

In retrospect, it is remarkable how widely and deeply the Cold War shaped U.S. society. Fundamental social institutions, such as marriage and religion, got extra credit for their contributions to anticommunism. The nation's long tradition of home-grown radicalism was virtually silent in the face of the Cold War consensus. Even economically meritorious programs like more money for science and better roads went down more easily if linked to national defense.

But the consistency and stability of the fifties were fragile. The larger world was too complex to fit forever within the narrow framework of bipolar conflict. American society was too disparate and dynamic for Cold War conformity. In the later 1960s and the 1970s, contradictions burst through the surface of the American consensus. Foreign competitors, resource scarcities, and environmental damage diminished economic abundance and sapped national confidence. Nations from Vietnam to Iran refused to cooperate with American plans for the world. Corrupt politicians threatened the constitutional order.

Under these pressures, the national consensus splintered after 1964. Some members of minority groups turned their back on integration. Some younger Americans dropped out of mainstream society to join the aptly named counterculture. Others sought the security of religious commitment and community. Perhaps most divisively, "hawks" battled "doves" over Vietnam. If civil rights and Cold War had been the defining issues for "the fifties," Vietnam would define "the sixties," which stretched from 1965 to 1974.

Review Questions

1. What were the sources of prosperity in the 1950s and 1960s? How did prosperity shape cities, family life, and religion? What opportunities did it create for women and for young people? How did it affect the American role in the world? Why did an affluent nation still need a war on poverty in the 1960s?
2. What assumptions about the Soviet Union shaped U.S. foreign policy? What assumptions about the United States shaped Soviet policy? What did American leaders think was at stake in Vietnam, Berlin, and Cuba?
3. Who initiated and led the African-American struggle for civil rights? What role did the federal government play? What were the goals of the civil rights movement? Where did it succeed, and in what ways did it fall short?
4. How did the growth of nuclear arsenals affect international relations? How did the nuclear shadow affect American politics and society?
5. In what new directions did Lyndon Johnson take the United States? Were there differences in the goals of the New Frontier and the Great Society?

Recommended Reading

Michael Beschloss, *May-Day: Eisenhower, Khrushchev, and the U-2 Affair* (1986). The drama and confusion of the U-2 affair used to interpret the meaning of the Cold War for the United States and the Soviet Union.

William Graebner, *Coming of Age in Buffalo* (1990). In words and pictures, places the complexity of teenage life in the 1950s within the American patterns of class and race.

David Halberstam, *The Fifties* (1993). Provides a readable and detailed account of political and social change.

Michael Harrington, *The Other America* (1962). Published early in the Kennedy years, an impassioned study that reminded Americans of continuing economic inequality and helped launch the War on Poverty.

Gerald Posner, *Case Closed* (1993). As close as we are likely to get to a definitive analysis of John

Kennedy's death; convincingly refutes the most popular conspiracy theories.

Theodore White, *The Making of the President, 1960* (1961). A vivid account of the issues and personalities of the 1960 campaign.

Juan Williams, *Eyes on the Prize: America's Civil Rights Years, 1954–1965* (1988). A graphic and fast-moving account of the civil rights movement, written in conjunction with a PBS television series.

Tom Wolfe, *The Right Stuff* (1979). An irreverent account of the early years of the U.S. space program that captures the atmosphere of the 1950s and early 1960s.

Additional Sources

The Eisenhower Presidency

Stephen E. Ambrose, *Ike's Spies: Eisenhower and the Espionage Establishment* (1981).

H. W. Brands, *Cold Warriors: Eisenhower's Generation and American Foreign Policy* (1988).

Robert Divine, *Eisenhower and the Cold War* (1981).

Fred Greenstein, *The Hidden-Hand Presidency: Eisenhower as Leader* (1982).

Walter Hixson, *Parting the Curtain: Propaganda, Culture and the Cold War* (1997).

Richard Immerman, *The CIA in Guatemala: The Foreign Policy of Intervention* (1982).

Chester Pach, *The Presidency of Dwight David Eisenhower* (1991).

Science, Politics, and Society

Barbara Clowse, *Brainpower for the Cold War: The Sputnik Crisis and the National Defense Education Act* (1981).

Robert Divine, *The Sputnik Challenge* (1993).

Robert Kleidman, *Organizing for Peace: Neutrality, the Test Ban, and the Freeze* (1993).

Walter McDougall, *The Heavens and the Earth: A Political History of the Space Age* (1985).

Jane Smith, *Patenting the Sun* (1990).

M. Costandina Titus, *Bombs in the Backyard: Atomic Testing and American Politics* (1986).

Allan Winkler, *Life under a Cloud: American Anxiety about the Atom* (1993).

The Politics of Growth

Carl Abbott, *The New Urban America: Growth and Politics in Sunbelt Cities* (1986).

Elizabeth Fones-Wolf, *Selling Free Enterprise: The Business Assault in Labor and Liberalism,* 1945–1960 (1994).

Kenneth Jackson, *The Crabgrass Frontier* (1985).

Kim McQuaid, *Uneasy Partners: Big Business in American Politics, 1945–1990* (1993).

William L. O'Neill, *American High: The Years of Confidence, 1945–1960* (1986).

Mark Rose, *Interstate: Express Highway Politics* (1990).

Jon Teaford, *The Rough Road to Renaissance: Urban Revitalization in America* (1990).

Family Life and Culture

Glenn Altschuler and David Grossvogel, *Changing Channels: America in TV Guide* (1992).

Wini Breines, *Young, White and Miserable: Growing Up Female in the 1950s* (1992).

Daniel Horowitz, *Vance Packard and American Social Criticism* (1994).

Eugenia Kaledin, *Mothers and More: American Women in the 1950s* (1984).

Elaine Tyler May, *Homeward Bound: American Families in the Cold War Era* (1988).

Leila Rupp and Verta Taylor, *Survival in the Doldrums: The American Women's Rights Movement, 1945 to the 1960s* (1987).

William Whyte, *The Organization Man* (1956).

The Early 1960s

Michael Beschloss, *The Crisis Years: Kennedy and Khrushchev, 1960–1963* (1991).

David Burner, *John F. Kennedy and a New Generation* (1988).

James Giglio, *The Presidency of John F. Kennedy* (1991).

Robert Alan Goldberg, *Barry Goldwater* (1995).

Elizabeth Cobbs Hoffman, *All You Need Is Love: The Peace Corps and the Spirit of the 1960s* (1998).

Doris Kearns, *Lyndon Johnson and the American Dream* (1976).

Edward Moise, *Tonkin Gulf and the Escalation of the Vietnam War* (1996).

James T. Patterson, *America's Struggle against Poverty, 1900–1985* (1986).

Mark Stern, *Calculating Visions: Kennedy, Johnson, and Civil Rights* (1992).

Peter Wyden, *Bay of Pigs: The Untold Story* (1979).

Struggles for Equal Rights

Rudolfo Acuña, *Occupied America: A History of Chicanos* (1988).

Taylor Branch, *Parting the Waters: America in the King Years, 1954–1963* (1988).

Eric Burner, *And Gently He Shall Lead Them: Robert Parris Moses and Civil Rights in Mississippii*(1994).

Claybourne Carson, *In Struggle: SNCC and the Black Awakening of the 1960s* (1981).

William Chafe, *Civilities and Civil Rights: Greensboro, North Carolina, and the Black Struggle* (1980).

John Dittmer, *Local People: A History of the Mississippi Movement* (1994).

John Egerton, *Speak Now against the Day: The Generation before the Civil Rights Movement in the South* (1994).

David Garrow, *Bearing the Cross: Martin Luther King Jr. and the Southern Christian Leadership Conference* (1986).

Roger Goldman and David Gallen, *Thurgood Marshall: Justice for All* (1993).

David Halberstam, *The Children* (1998).

Elizabeth Huckaby, *Crisis at Central High: Little Rock, 1957–1958* (1980).

Richard Kluger, *Simple Justice: The History of* Brown *v.* Board of Education (1976).

Charles Marsh, *God's Long Summer: Stories of Faith and Civil Rights* (1998).

Kay Mills, *This Little Light of Mine: The Life of Fannie Lou Hamer* (1993).

Charles Payne, *I've Got the Light of Freedom: The Organizing Tradition and the Mississippi Freedom Struggle* (1995).

Harvard Sitkoff, *The Struggle for Black Equality; 1954–1992* (1992).

Where to Learn More

❖ **National Air and Space Museum, Washington, D.C.** Part of the Smithsonian Institution's complex of museums in Washington, the Air and Space Museum is the richest source for artifacts and discussion of the American space program.

❖ **Kansas Cosmosphere, Hutchinson, Kansas.** This is a rich collection of artifacts and equipment from the American space program.

❖ **Sixth Floor Museum, Dallas, Texas.** Occupying the sixth floor of the former Texas School Book Depository building, exhibits examine the life, death, and legacy of John F. Kennedy.

❖ **Birmingham Civil Rights Institute, Birmingham, Alabama.** This museum and archive deal with the background of southern racial segregation, civil rights activism, and the 1963 demonstrations in Birmingham.

❖ **Martin Luther King, Jr., National Historic Site, Atlanta, Georgia.** The birthplace and grave of Reverend King are the nucleus of a park set in the historic black neighborhood of Auburn.

❖ **National Civil Rights Museum, Memphis, Tennessee.** Located in the Lorraine Motel, where Martin Luther King, Jr., was killed, the museum traces the participants, background, and effects of key events in the civil rights movement.

❖ **National Afro-American Museum and Cultural Center, Wilberforce, Ohio.** The exhibit, "From Victory to Freedom: Afro-American Life in the Fifties," looks at home, family, music, and religion as well as politics and civil rights.

❖ **New Museum at the John F. Kennedy Library, Boston, Massachusetts.** Exhibits offer a sympathetic view of Kennedy's life and achievements.

SHAKEN TO THE ROOTS, 1965–1980

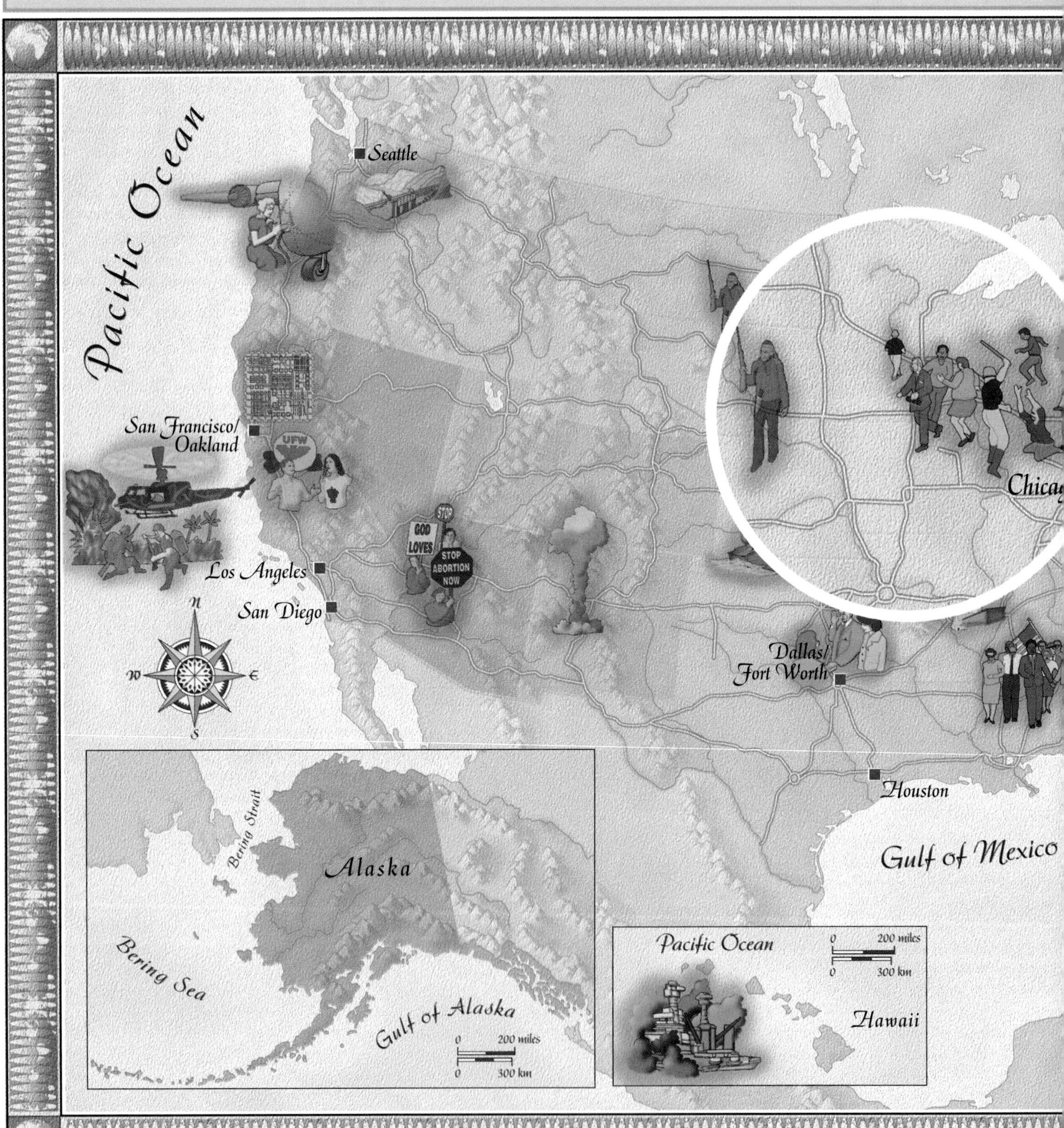

31

Chapter Outline

Key Topics

- ❖ Vietnam, civil rights, and the unraveling of the national consensus
- ❖ The escalating war in Vietnam and the growing opposition it provoked
- ❖ The unraveling of the New Deal coalition
- ❖ Nixon and the Watergate scandal
- ❖ The growing militance of the struggle for civil rights among African Americans, Hispanic Americans, and Native Americans

PLEIKU IS A TOWN 240 MILES NORTH OF SAIGON (NOW HO CHI MINH CITY). IN 1965, PLEIKU WAS THE SITE OF A SOUTH VIETNAMESE ARMY HEADQUARTERS AND AMERICAN MILITARY BASE. AT 2 A.M. ON FEBRUARY 7, THE VIET CONG ATTACKED THE U.S. base with mortars and grenades, killing eight Americans, wounding a hundred, and destroying ten planes and helicopters. National security advisor McGeorge Bundy, in Saigon on a fact-finding visit; Ambassador Maxwell Taylor; and military commander General William Westmoreland quickly recommended a retaliatory air strike against North Vietnam. President Johnson concurred, and navy bombers roared off aircraft carriers in Operation FLAMING DART. A month later, Johnson ordered a full-scale air offensive code-named ROLLING THUNDER.

The attack at Pleiku triggered plans that were waiting to be put into effect. The official reason for the bombing was to pressure North Vietnam to negotiate an end to the war. As the South Vietnamese government lost control of the countryside, air strikes on North Vietnam looked like an easy way to shore up South Vietnamese morale. In the back of President Johnson's mind were the need to prove his toughness and the mistaken assumption that China was aggressively backing North Vietnam.

The air strikes pushed the United States over the line from propping up the South Vietnamese government to leading the war effort. A president who desperately wanted a way out of southeast Asia kept adding American forces. Eventually, the war in Vietnam would distract the United States from the goals of the Great Society and drive Johnson from office. It hovered like a shadow over the next two presidents, set back progress toward global stability, and divided the American people.

The war eroded the nation's confidence. Most Americans had agreed about the goals of the Cold War, the benefits of economic growth, and the value of equal opportunity. Stalemate in Vietnam, an oil supply crisis, and political changes in other nations outside the framework of the Cold War challenged U.S. influence in the world. Frustrated with slow progress toward racial equality, many minority Americans advocated separation rather than integration. Political scandals, summarized in three syllables as "Watergate," undercut faith in government. Fifteen years of turmoil forced a grudging recognition of limits to American military power, economic capacity, governmental prerogatives, and even the ideal of a single American dream.

The End of Consensus

Nineteen sixty-five was a confusing year. In Washington, it brought triumphal progress for the goals of the Great Society with such measures as the Voting Rights Act and Medicare. Elsewhere, however, things began to go wrong. The Viet Cong gained strength in the villages of Vietnam. African Americans rioted in Los Angeles. Well-educated and articulate young people left their button-down shirts or high heels in the closet and pursued goals outside the mainstream. The cumulative effect was to unravel the national consensus of the 1950s and early 1960s.

Deeper into Vietnam

Lyndon Johnson faced limited options in Vietnam (see Map 31-1). The pervasive American determination to contain communism and Kennedy's commitments there hemmed Johnson in. Advisers persuaded him that controlled military escalation—a middle course between withdrawal and all-out war—could secure Vietnam. They failed to understand the extent of popular opposition to the official government in Saigon and the willingness of North Vietnam to sacrifice to achieve national unity.

ROLLING THUNDER put the United States on the up escalator to war. Because an air campaign required ground troops to protect bases in South Viet-

Map 31-1 The War in Vietnam *The United States attacked North Vietnam with air strikes but confined large-scale ground operations to South Vietnam and Cambodia. In South Vietnam, U.S. forces faced both North Vietnamese army units and Viet Cong rebels, all of whom received supplies by way of the so-called "Ho Chi Minh Trail," named for the leader of North Vietnam. The coordinated attacks on cities and towns throughout South Vietnam during the Tet Offensive in 1968 surprised the United States.*

nam, Marines landed on March 8. Over the next four months, General Westmoreland wore away Johnson's desire to contain American involvement. More bombs, a pause, an offer of massive U.S. aid—nothing brought North Vietnam to the negotiating table. Meanwhile, defeat loomed. Johnson dribbled in new forces and expanded their mission from base security to combat. On July 28, he finally gave Westmoreland doubled draft calls and an increase in U.S. combat troops from 75,000 to 275,000 by 1966 (see Figure 31-1).

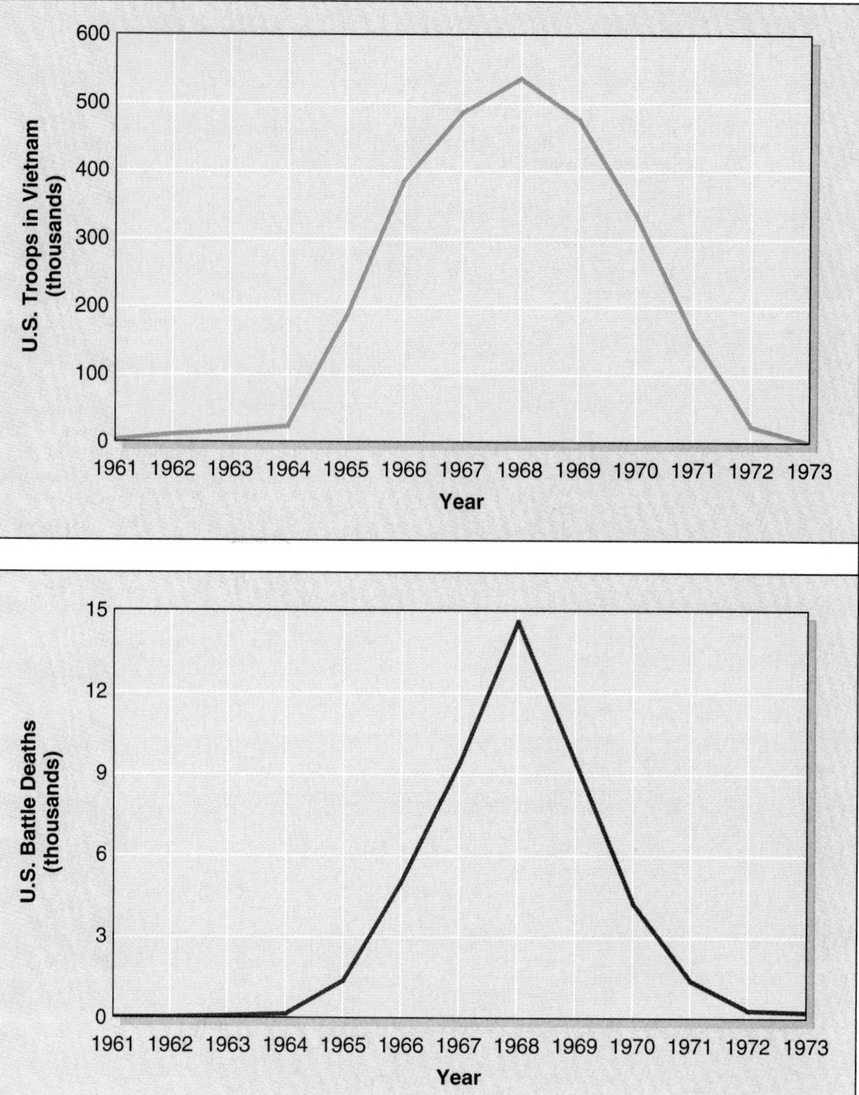

Figure 31-1 The United States in Vietnam
American involvement in Vietnam grew slowly in the Kennedy administration from 1961 to 1963, expanded rapidly under Lyndon Johnson from 1964 to 1968, and fell just as rapidly under Richard Nixon from 1969 to 1973. The "Nixon Doctrine" tried to substitute American weapons and equipment for American military personnel but failed to prevent North Vietnamese victory in 1975 after United States withdrawal.
Data Source: Statistical Abstract of the United States.

Johnson's decision turned a South Vietnamese war into an American war. Secretary of Defense McNamara was clear about the change: "We have relied on South Vietnam to carry the brunt. Now we would be responsible for a satisfactory military outcome." At the end of 1967, American forces in South Vietnam totaled 485,000; they reached their maximum of 543,000 in August 1969. In all, more than 2 million Americans served in Vietnam.

The U.S. strategy on the ground was **search and destroy**. As conceived by Westmoreland, it used sophisticated surveillance and heavily armed patrols to locate enemy detachments, which could then be destroyed by air strikes, artillery, and reinforcements carried in by helicopter. The approach made sense when the opposition consisted of North Vietnamese troops and large Viet Cong units. It worked well in the sparsely populated Ia Drang Valley where the First Air Cavalry chewed up North Vietnamese regulars in November 1965.

However, most opponents were not North Vietnamese divisions but South Vietnamese guerrillas. The Viet Cong avoided "set-piece" battles. Instead, they forced the United States to make repeated sweeps through farms and villages. The enemy were difficult for Americans to recognize among farmers and workers, making South Vietnamese society itself the target. The American penchant for massive firepower killed thousands of Vietnamese and made millions refugees. Because the South Vietnamese government was unable to secure areas after American sweeps, the Viet Cong often reappeared after the Americans had crashed through a district.

Chronology

1962 Rachel Carson publishes *Silent Spring*.
Port Huron Statement launches Students for a Democratic Society.

1965 Congress approves Wilderness Act.
Malcolm X is assassinated.
Residents of Watts neighborhood in Los Angeles riot.

1967 African Americans riot in Detroit and Newark.

1968 Viet Cong launches Tet Offensive.
James Earl Ray kills Martin Luther King, Jr.
Lyndon Johnson declines to run for reelection.
SDS disrupts Columbia University.
Sirhan Sirhan kills Robert Kennedy.
Peace talks start between the United States and North Vietnam.
Police riot against antiwar protesters during the Democratic National Convention in Chicago.
Richard Nixon is elected president.

1969 Neil Armstrong walks on the moon.

1970 United States invades Cambodia.
Earth Day is celebrated.
National Guard units kill students at Kent State and Jackson State Universities.
Environmental Protection Agency is created.

1971 *New York Times* publishes the secret "Pentagon Papers."
President Nixon freezes wages and prices.
"Plumbers" unit is established in the White House.

1972 Nixon visits China.
United States and Soviet Union adopt SALT I.
Operatives for Nixon's reelection campaign break into Democratic headquarters in the Watergate complex in Washington, D.C.

1973 Paris accords end direct U.S. involvement in South Vietnamese war.
United States moves to all-volunteer armed forces.
Watergate burglars are convicted.
Senate Watergate hearings reveal the existence of taped White House conversations.
Spiro Agnew resigns as vice president, is replaced by Gerald Ford.
Arab states impose an oil embargo after the third Arab-Israeli War.

1974 Nixon resigns as president, is succeeded by Gerald Ford.

1975 Communists triumph in South Vietnam.
United States, USSR, and European nations sign the Helsinki Accords.

1976 Jimmy Carter defeats Gerald Ford for the presidency.

1978 Carter brings the leaders of Egypt and Israel to Camp David for peace talks.

1979 SALT II agreement is signed but not ratified.
OPEC raises oil prices.
Three Mile Island nuclear plant comes close to disaster.
Iranian militants take U.S. embassy hostages.

1980 Iranian hostage rescue fails.
Soviet troops enter Afghanistan.
Ronald Reagan defeats Jimmy Carter for the presidency.

The American air war also had limited results. Pilots dropped tons of bombs on the "Ho Chi Minh Trail," a network of supply routes from North Vietnam to South Vietnam through the mountains of neighboring Laos. Despite the bombing, thousands of workers converted rough paths into roads that were repaired as soon as they were damaged. Air assault on North Vietnam itself remained "diplomatic," intended to force North Vietnam to stop intervening in the South Vietnamese civil war. Because Ho Chi Minh considered North and South to be one country, the American goal was unacceptable. Attacking North Vietnam's poorly developed economy, the United States soon ran out of targets. The CIA estimated that it cost nearly $10 to inflict every $1 of damage.

At home, protest against the war mounted (see "American Views: An Antiwar Protester Describes the Generation Gap"). A March 24, 1965, "teach-in" at the University of Michigan—a nightlong sequence of speeches and seminars—signaled the disaffection. In the 1950s, dissenters on the left had been too intimidated by McCarthyism to protest overcommitment to the Cold War. Now a coalition of experienced antiwar workers and new college activists openly challenged the Cold Warriors. The first national antiwar march took place in Washington on

Antiwar protests were simultaneously symbolic and disruptive. Some activists dumped jars of animal blood over draft board records. Others tried to block munitions trains. In October 1967, 100,000 people marched on the Pentagon and surrounded it with the light of burning draft cards. Some in front stuck flowers in the rifle barrels of the soldiers ringing the building; others kicked and spat. The troops and police cleared the grounds with tear gas and clubs.

April 17. Twenty-five thousand people picketed the White House, assembled at the Washington Monument for speeches by Senator Ernest Gruening of Alaska (one of the two dissenting votes on the Gulf of Tonkin Resolution) and African-American leaders, and walked up the Mall to the Capitol.

Over the next two years, antiwar activity changed to direct confrontations. Much of the anger was directed at the military draft administered by the **Selective Service System**. In theory, the Selective Service picked the young men who could best serve the nation as soldiers and deferred induction of those with vital skills. In fact, deferral criteria helped make Vietnam a working-class war. Full-time college enrollment was good for a deferment; so was graduate school until 1967. Draftees and enlistees tended to be small-town and working-class youth who had few opportunities outside the military. They were also young. The average GI in World War II had been in his midtwenties; the typical soldier in Vietnam was 19 or 20. Women who served as military nurses tended to come from the same backgrounds, where patriotism was unquestioned.

The black community supplied more than its share of combat soldiers. In 1965, when African Americans made up 11 percent of the nation's population, 24 percent of the soldiers who died in Vietnam were black. This disparity forced the Defense Department to revise its combat assignments. Martin Luther King, Jr., joined the protest in 1967. King called the war a moral disaster whose costs weighed most heavily on the poor and a new form of colonialism that was destroying Vietnamese society.

New Left and Community Activism

The antiwar movement was part of a growing grassroots activism that took much of its tone from the university-based **Students for a Democratic Society (SDS)**. The group was important for its ideas, not its size. Its **Port Huron Statement**, largely written by Tom Hayden and adopted in 1962, called for grassroots action and "participatory democracy." Building on ideas of 1950s dissenters such as C. Wright Mills, SDS tried to harness youthful disillusionment about consumerism, racism, and imperialism. It wanted to counter the trends that seemed to be turning Americans into tiny cogs in the machinery of big government, corporations, and universities. An example was its Economic Research and Action Project in which students moved to poor neighborhoods in cities such as Newark and tried to help residents protest inequitable living conditions. SDS thought of itself as a "New Left" that was free from doctrinal squabbles that hampered the old left of the 1930s and 1940s.

Many of the original SDS leaders were also participants in the civil rights movement. The same was true of Mario Savio, founder of the **Free Speech Movement (FSM)** at the University of California at Berkeley. Savio hoped to build a multi-issue "community of protest" around the idea of "a free university in a free society." FSM protests climaxed with a December sit-in that led to 773 arrests and stirred protest on other campuses.

What SDS wanted to do with its grassroots organizing resembled the federal community action programs associated with the war on poverty. The

Model Cities Program (1966) invited residents of poor neighborhoods to write their own plans for improving local housing, education, health services, and job opportunities. Model Cities assemblies challenged the racial bias in programs like urban renewal and helped train community leaders.

In the 1970s and 1980s, when SDS was long gone and Model Cities was fading, the lessons of grassroots reform would still be visible in alternative organizations and political movements that strengthened democracy from the bottom up. Activists staffed food cooperatives, free clinics, women's health groups, and drug counseling centers across the country. Community-based organization was a key element in self-help efforts by African Americans, Asian Americans, and Latinos. Neighborhood associations and community development corporations that provided affordable housing and jobs extended the "backyard revolution" into the 1980s and beyond. Social conservatives, such as antiabortionists, used the same techniques on behalf of their own agendas.

Youth Culture and Counterculture

The popular context for the serious work of the New Left was the growing youth culture and **counterculture**. Millions of young people in the second half of the 1960s expressed their alienation from American society by sampling drugs or chasing the rainbow of a youth culture. Some just smoked marijuana, grew long hair, and listened to psychedelic rock. Others plunged into ways of life that scorned their middle-class backgrounds. The middle-aged and middle-class ignored the differences and dubbed the rebellious young **hippies**.

The youth culture took advantage of the affluence of the 1950s. It was consumerism in a tie-dyed T-shirt. A high point was the 1969 Woodstock rock festival in New York State, a weekend of "sex, drugs, and rock-and-roll" for 400,000 young people. But Woodstock was an excursion, not a life-altering commitment. Members of the **Woodstock Generation** were consumers in a distinct market niche, dressing but not living like social reformers or revolutionaries. The musical *Hair* (1968) and the film *Easy Rider* (1969) harnessed their social ferment for the box office as mass culture absorbed the youth culture.

Within the youth culture was a smaller and more intense counterculture that added Eastern religion, social radicalism, and evangelistic belief in the drug LSD. Harvard professor Timothy Leary and writer Aldous Huxley claimed that hallucinogenic or psychedelic drugs, such as mescaline and LSD, would swing open the "doors of perception." Rock lyrics began to reflect the drug culture in 1966 and 1967, and young people talked about Leary's advice to "tune in, turn on, and drop out."

The mecca of the dropouts was San Francisco's Haight-Ashbury district. In the early 1960s, its cheap apartments had housed African Americans, beatniks, and homosexuals. Its radical atmosphere attracted a sudden influx of students and college dropouts in 1966. In 1967's "Summer of Love," the Haight was home to perhaps seven thousand permanent hippies and seventy thousand short-time visitors.

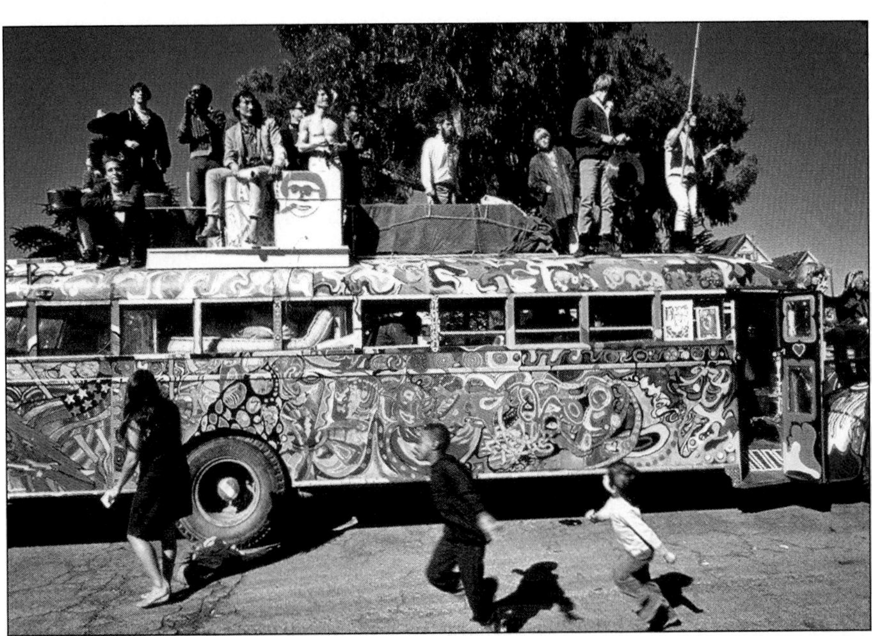

Writer Ken Kesey and the self-defined Merry Pranksters toured the country in a brightly painted bus, parked here in San Francisco's Golden Gate Park. They sometimes threw open parties where they served punch laced with psychedelic drugs in the hope of inciting radical social change.

American Views

An Antiwar Protester Describes the Generation Gap

Robert S. McNamara was one of the architects of the war in Vietnam as secretary of defense for John Kennedy and Lyndon Johnson from 1961 to 1968. Like thousands of other parents, including many Washington officials, McNamara found opposition to the war within his own family. Here his son, Craig McNamara, describes his actions as an antiwar demonstrator and his decision to drop out of mainstream society (he eventually became a farmer in northern California). In 1995, Robert McNamara revealed that he had serious but silent doubts about the wisdom of the war long before he left the Defense Department.

❖ **What do Craig McNamara's recollections tell us about the "generation gap" of the 1960s?**

❖ **What do they suggest about the connection between political dissent and decisions to drop out of mainstream culture?**

You know, things were so split in the Sixties. You were either for the war or against it, and I was definitely against it. My father knew where I stood, but we didn't discuss it. . . . It just wasn't possible during those years for us to talk about the issues of the war. . . .

Not long after I got to Stanford, I began taking part in antiwar demonstrations. . . . I participated in a major event at the San Francisco airport. A group of students had got together to read a list of the California men who had been killed in Vietnam. We just stood in one of the main terminal

"If you're going to San Francisco," said one song, "be sure to wear some flowers in your hair." Drugs and violence soon took over the streets, psychedelic businesses closed, and a respectable middle class bought the cheap real estate. Meanwhile, hippie districts sprang up around university campuses across the country.

The cultural rebels of the late 1950s and early 1960s had been trying to combine personal freedom with new social arrangements. Many hippies were more interested in altering their minds with drugs than with politics or poetry. Serious exploration of societal alternatives was left for a minority who devoted themselves to the political work of the New Left, communal living, women's liberation, gay liberation, and other movements.

Racial Rioting

In contrast to the youth culture, African Americans and Hispanics who rioted in city streets weren't dabbling; they were in deadly earnest. Prominent black writers, such as James Baldwin in *The Fire Next Time* (1963), had warned of mounting anger. Suddenly the fires were real. Riots in Rochester, Harlem, and Brooklyn in July 1964 opened four years of racial violence. Before they subsided, the riots scarred most big cities and killed two hundred people, most of them African Americans.

The explosion of the Watts neighborhood in Los Angeles fixed the danger of racial unrest in the public mind. Trouble started on August 11, 1965, when a white highway patrol officer arrested a young African American for drunken driving. Loud complaints drew a crowd, and the arrival of Los Angeles police turned the bystanders into an angry mob that attacked passing cars. Rioting, looting, and arson spread through Watts for two days until the National Guard cordoned off the trouble spots and occupied the neighborhood on August 14 and 15.

The outburst frightened white Americans. In most previous race riots, white people had used violence to keep black people "in their place." In Watts, black people were the instigators. The primary tar-

buildings on a marble floor, with thirty-foot ceilings above and all the traffic of people going back and forth. It became very clear to us immediately that we were antagonizing a lot of people. . . . It was amazing to realize how threatening one person reading a list of the war dead in Vietnam could be to other people. And it was a tremendous list. . . . Each of us would read for two or three hours at a time, and then the next person would take over.

I remember a variety of men coming up to me at various times during those hours, men in their mid-fifties saying, "You son of a bitch!" or "We're going to kick your knees in!" or "You haven't been there. What do you know?" I just remember taking a deep breath and keeping on reading and feeling sad, tremendously sad. . . . I think that is the feeling that we probably all share now about Vietnam: what sadness, what tremendous sadness.

[After being physically disqualified from military service], I left for South America. Two friends and I went on motorcycles down to Texas with our shoulder-length hair and ponytails and leather pants. Nobody stopped us. We just kept going until we got into Mexico, and started the long journey to the south. When we got to Bogotá [Colombia], my two friends decided they'd gone far enough. They were going to stay, and I was on my own. I decided to send my motorcycle home. To me it represented imperialism. I set out myself, into the unknown, and traveled for the next few months on trucks, buses, trains, hitchhiking. . . .

While I was in Santiago [Chile], my father came down to a big United Nations conference on trade. He was head of the World Bank at that time. I was staying probably a mile away from where he was, but we didn't see each other. I think it was probably a decision on both our parts, that we were in different worlds and those worlds couldn't seem to come together.

Source: Joan Morrison and Robert K. Morrison, From Camelot to Kent State: The Sixties Experience in the Words of Those Who Lived It.

gets were the police and ghetto businesses that had reputations for exploiting their customers. The National Advisory Commission on Civil Disorders concluded in 1968 that most property damage was the "result of deliberate attacks on white-owned businesses characterized in the Negro community as unfair or disrespectful." In short, the riots were protests about the problems of ghetto life.

After Watts, Americans expected "long hot summers" and got them. Scores of cities suffered riots in 1966, including a riot by Puerto Ricans in Chicago that protested the same problems black people faced. The following year, the worst violence was in Newark, New Jersey, and in Detroit, where forty-three deaths and blocks of blazing buildings stunned television viewers.

Rioting in the midsixties followed a consistent scenario. A routine police action would spark rumors or draw a crowd. It might be a raid on an illegal bar, intervention in a fight, or the shooting of a crime suspect. Angry onlookers would turn into rioters when they saw that the police could not disperse crowds, enforce curfews, or even protect themselves. After the police withdrew, looting might turn into a serious assault on property. Disorder would continue until the National Guard or the army scared the crowds off the streets. Many deaths came in the last days when heavily armed and fearful soldiers fired on nonexistent snipers and killed bystanders.

Few politicians wanted to admit that African Americans and Hispanics had serious grievances. Their impulse was to blame riffraff and outside agitators—"lawbreakers and mad dogs," to quote California Governor Ronald Reagan. This theory was wrong. Almost all participants were neighborhood residents. Except that they were younger, they were representative of the African-American population, and their violence came from the frustration of rising expectations. Despite the political gains of the civil rights movement, unemployment remained high, and the police still treated all African Americans as potential criminals. The urban riots were political actions to force the problems of African-Americans onto the national agenda. "What are these people rioting about?" asked one resident. "They want recognition, and the only way they're going to get it is to riot."

Minority Separatism

Minority separatism tapped the same anger that fueled the urban riots. Separatists challenged the central goal of the civil rights movement, which sought full participation in American life. The phrase "**Black Power**" summed up the new alternative. The term came from frustrated SNCC leader Stokely Carmichael in 1966: "We've been saying freedom for six years—and we ain't got nothing. What we're going to start saying now is 'Black Power'!"

Black power translated many ways—control of one's own community through the voting machine, celebration of African-American heritage, creation of a parallel society that shunned white institutions. At the personal level, it was a synonym for black pride. It propelled the successful political campaigns of Richard Hatcher in Gary, Indiana, and Carl Stokes in Cleveland, the first African Americans elected mayors of large northern cities.

Black Power also meant increased interest in the **Nation of Islam**, or Black Muslims. Organized in 1931 by Elijah Muhammad, the Black Muslims combined a version of Islam with radical separatism. They called for self-discipline, support of black institutions and businesses, and total rejection of white America. The Nation of Islam appealed to black people who saw no future in integration. It was strongest in northern cities, such as Chicago, where it offered an alternative to the life of the ghetto streets.

In the early 1960s, Malcolm X emerged as a leading Black Muslim. Growing up as Malcolm Little, he was a streetwise criminal until he converted to the Nation of Islam in prison. After his release, Malcolm preached that black people should stop letting white people set the terms by which they judged their appearance, communities, and accomplishments. He emphasized the African cultural heritage and economic self-help and proclaimed himself an extremist for black rights. In the last year of his life, however, he returned from a pilgrimage to Mecca willing to temper his rejection of white society. Rivals within the movement assassinated him in February 1965, but his ideas lived on in *The Autobiography of Malcolm X.*

The **Black Panthers** pursued similar goals. Bobby Seale and Huey Newton grew up in the Oakland, California, area and met as college students. They saw African-American ghettos as internal colonies in need of self-determination. They created the Panthers in 1966, began to carry firearms, and recruited Eldridge Cleaver as chief publicist.

The Panthers asserted their equality. They shadowed police patrols to prevent mistreatment of African Americans and carried weapons into the California State Legislature in May 1967 to protest gun control. As Seale recalled, the goal was "to read a message to the world" and use the press to "blast it across the country." The Panthers also promoted community-based self-help efforts, such as a free breakfast program and medical clinics, and ran political candidates. In contrast to the rioters in Watts, the Panthers had a political program, if not the ability to carry it through. The movement was shaken when Newton was convicted of manslaughter for killing a police officer, Cleaver fled to Algeria, and an unjustified police raid killed Chicago Panther leader Fred Hampton. Panther chapters imploded when they attracted thugs and shakedown artists as well as visionaries. Nevertheless, the Panthers survived as a political party into the 1970s. Former Panther Bobby Rush entered Congress in 1992.

Latinos in the Southwest developed a similar "brown power" movement in the late 1960s. Led by Reies López Tijerina, Hispanics in rural New Mexico demanded the return of lands that had been lost to Anglo Americans despite the guarantees of the Treaty of Guadalupe Hidalgo in 1848. Tijerina's "Letter from the Santa Fe Jail" denounced the "rich people from outside the state with their summer homes and ranches" and "all those who have robbed the people of their land and culture for 120 years." Mexican Americans in the 1970s organized for political power in southern Texas communities where they were a majority. In Denver, Rodolfo Gonzales established the Crusade for Justice. His "Plan for the *Barrio*" emphasized Hispanic cultural traditions, community control of schools, and economic development. Best known among the Latino activists was César Chávez, who organized the multiracial United Farm Workers in California (see Chapter 32).

Latino political activism had strong appeal for young people. Ten thousand young Chicanos stormed out of Los Angeles high schools in March 1968 to protest poor education and racist teachers. Some students organized as Brown Berets to demand more relevant education and fairer police treatment. Many rejected assimilation in favor of community self-determination and began to talk about *la Raza* ("the people"), whose language and heritage descended from centuries of Mexican history. *Chicano* itself was a slang term with insulting overtones that was now adopted as a badge of pride and cultural identity.

The Black Panthers hoped to gain political power and to provide social services in black ghettos. Police repression and arrests of Panther leaders diverted much of their energy to raising money to pay legal costs.

Native Americans fought both for equal access to American society and to preserve cultural traditions through tribal institutions. Congress in 1968 restored the authority of tribal laws on reservations. A few years later, it granted native Alaskans 40 million acres to settle claims for their ancestral lands. Legally sophisticated tribes sued for compensation and enforcement of treaty provisions, such as fishing rights in the Pacific Northwest. Larger tribes established their own colleges, such as Navajo Community College (1969) and Oglala Lakota College (1971). Navajo Community College, said its catalog, "exists to fulfill many needs of the Navajo people. . . . It provides a place where Navajo history and culture can be studied and learned; it provides training in the skills necessary for many jobs on the reservation which today are held by non-Navajos."

A second development was new media-oriented protest. Chippewas in Minneapolis created the **American Indian Movement (AIM)** in 1968 to increase economic opportunity and stop police mistreatment. AIM dramatized the needs of Native Americans by seizing the abandoned Alcatraz Island as a cultural and educational center (1969–1971) and leading the cross-country Broken Treaties Caravan, which occupied the Bureau of Indian Affairs in Washington (1972).

In the early 1970s, AIM allied with Sioux traditionalists on the Pine Ridge Reservation in South Dakota against the tribe's elected government. In 1973, they took over the village of Wounded Knee, where the U.S. Army in 1890 had massacred three hundred Indians. They held out for seventy days before leaving peacefully. Although AIM itself soon collapsed, Native Americans continued to assert their distinctiveness within American society.

The slogans of Black Power, Brown Power, and Red Power spanned goals that ran from civil rights to cultural pride to revolutionary separatism. They were all efforts by minorities to define themselves through their own heritage and backgrounds, not simply by looking in the mirror of white society. They thus questioned the American assumption that everyone wanted to be part of the same homogeneous society.

The American Indian Movement (AIM) drew its strength from young Indians in the cities. In 1972 AIM led a march of Indians along the "Trail of Broken Treaties" to Washington, D.C., where members occupied the offices of the Bureau of Indian Affairs. The occupation ended after a week but succeeded in publicizing Native American grievances.

The Year of the Gun, 1968

Some years are turning points that force society to reconsider its basic assumptions. In 1914, the violence of World War I undermined Europe's belief in progress. In 1933, Americans had to rethink the role of government. In 1968, mainstream Americans turned against the war in Vietnam, student protest and youth counterculture turned ugly, and political consensus shattered.

The Tet Offensive

The longer the Vietnam War continued and the less interest that China or the Soviet Union showed in it, the less valid the conflict seemed to the American people. It looked more and more like a war for pride, not national security.

The Viet Cong's Tet Offensive on January 30, 1968, undermined that pride. At the end of 1967, U.S. officials were over-confidently predicting victory. They also fell for a North Vietnamese feint by committing U.S. forces to the defense of Khe Sanh, a strongpoint near the North–South border. The defense was a tactical success for the United States but thinned its forces elsewhere in South Vietnam. Then, at the beginning of Tet, the Vietnamese New Year, the Viet Cong attacked thirty-six of forty-four provincial capitals, the historic city of Hue, and the capital, Saigon. They hit the U.S. embassy and reached the runways of Tan Son Nhut air base. If the United States was winning, the Tet offensive should not have been possible.

As a military effort, the attacks failed. U.S. and South Vietnamese troops repulsed the attacks and cleared the cities. But the offensive was a psychological blow that convinced the American public that the war was quicksand.

Television coverage of the Tet battles made the bad publicity worse. During World War II, officials had censored pictures from the front. Images from Vietnam went direct to the evening news; it was a "living room war." At least until Tet, the commentary from network news anchors had supported the American effort, but the pictures undermined civilian morale. Viewers could hear cigarette lighters clicking open to set villages in flames. A handful of images stayed in people's memories—a Buddhist monk burning himself to death in protest; a child with flesh peeled off by napalm; a South Vietnamese official executing a captive on the streets of Saigon.

In the wake of the Tet crisis, General Westmoreland's request for 200,000 more troops forced a political and military reevaluation. Clark Clifford, a dedicated Cold Warrior, was the new secretary of defense. Now he had second thoughts. Twenty "wise men"—the big names of the Cold War—told the president that the war was unwinnable on terms acceptable to America's allies and to many Americans. By devouring resources and souring relations with other nations, it endangered rather than enhanced American security. Most scholars have agreed with this assessment. The best option, the wise men told LBJ, was disengagement. "He could hardly believe his ears," Clifford remembered.

LBJ's Exit

The president was already in political trouble. After other prominent Democrats held back, Minnesota's liberal Senator Eugene McCarthy had decided to challenge Johnson in the presidential primaries. Because he controlled the party organizations in two-

GIs evacuate a wounded comrade from fighting near the border between Vietnam and Cambodia.

thirds of the states, Johnson didn't need the primary states for renomination and ignored the first primary in New Hampshire. Enthusiastic college students staffed McCarthy's campaign. McCarthy won a startling 42 percent of the popular vote and twenty of twenty-four delegates in the March 16 election. The vote was a protest against Johnson's Vietnam policy rather than a clear mandate for peace. As an unknown, McCarthy attracted voters who wanted the United States out of Vietnam and those who wanted all-out victory. Nevertheless, the vote proved that the political middle ground would no longer hold.

By showing Johnson's vulnerability, New Hampshire also drew Robert Kennedy into the race. Younger brother of the former president, Kennedy inspired both fervent loyalty and strong distaste. In the 1950s, he had worked for Senator Joe McCarthy and had been a reluctant supporter of civil rights during his brother's administration. He was arrogant and abrasive but also bright and flexible. More than other mainstream politicians of the 1960s, he touched the hearts of Hispanic and African-American voters as well as the white working class. He had left his position as attorney general to win election to the Senate from New York in 1964. Now he put the Kennedy mystique on the line against a man whom he despised.

Facing political challenges and an unraveling war, on March 31, 1968, Johnson announced a halt to most bombing of North Vietnam, opening the door for negotiations. He then astounded the country by withdrawing from the presidential race. It was a statesmanlike act by a man who had been consumed by a war he didn't want, had never understood, and couldn't end. As he told an aide, the war made him feel like a hitchhiker in a hailstorm: "I can't run, I can't hide, and I can't make it stop." Hoping to save his domestic program, he served out his term with few friends and little credit for his accomplishments.

Red Spring

In the months that followed the Tet crisis, much of the industrial world was in ferment. Grassroots rebellion shook the Soviet grip on eastern Europe. University students in Poland protested the stifling of political discussion. Alexander Dubček, the new leader of the Czech Communist party, brought together students and the middle class around reforms that caused people to talk about "Prague Spring"—a blossoming of democracy inside the iron curtain. In August, the Soviets sent in their tanks to crush the reforms and bring Czechoslovakia back into line.

Western Europe was also in turmoil. Students rioted in Italy and Berlin. Workers and students protested against the Franco regime in Spain. In Paris, student demonstrations against the Vietnam War turned into attacks on the university system and the French government. One slogan proclaimed: "Professors, you are past it, and so is your culture." Students fought police in the Paris streets in the first days of May. Radical industrial workers called a general strike. The government nearly toppled.

Students at Columbia University in New York echoed Europe with their own rebellion. Columbia's African-American students and its SDS chapter had several grievances. One was the university's cooperation with the Pentagon-funded Institute for Defense Analysis. Another was its plan to build a gymnasium on park land that might better serve the residents of Harlem. Some students wanted changes in university policy, others a confrontation that would recruit new radicals. They occupied five university buildings, including the library and the president's office, for a week in April until police evicted them. A student strike and additional violence lasted until June. The "battle of Morningside Heights" (the location of Columbia) was tame when compared to the events in Warsaw or Paris, but it gave Americans a glimpse of the gap that divided radicalized students from national institutions.

Violence and Politics

Red Spring in France, Prague Spring in Czechoslovakia, and turmoil in New York were background for the violent disruption of American politics through assassination and riot. On April 4, 1968, ex-convict James Earl Ray shot and killed Martin Luther King, Jr., as he stood on the balcony of a Memphis motel. King's death was the product of pure racial hatred, and it triggered a climactic round of violence in black ghettos. Fires devastated the West Side of Chicago and downtown Washington, D.C. The army guarded the steps of the Capitol, ready to protect Congress from its fellow citizens.

The shock of King's death was still fresh when another political assassination stunned the nation. On June 5, Robert Kennedy won California's primary election. He was still behind Vice President Hubert Humphrey in the delegate count but coming on strong. As Kennedy walked out of the ballroom at his headquarters in the Ambassador Hotel in Los Angeles, a Jordanian immigrant named Sirhan Sirhan put a bullet in his brain. Sirhan may have wanted revenge for America's tilt toward Israel in that country's victorious Six-Day War with Egypt and Jordan in 1967.

Kennedy's death ensured the Democratic nomination for Humphrey, a liberal who had loyally supported Johnson's war policy. After his nomination, Humphrey faced Republican Richard Nixon and Independent George Wallace. Nixon positioned himself as the candidate of the political middle. Wallace appealed to white Southerners and working-class Northerners who feared black militancy and hated "the ivory-tower folks with pointed heads."

Both got great help from the Democratic Convention, held in Chicago on August 26–29. While Democrats feuded among themselves, Chicago Mayor Richard Daley and his police department monitored antiwar protesters. The National Mobilization Committee to End the War in Vietnam drew on the New Left and on older peace activists—sober and committed people who had fought against nuclear weapons in the 1950s and the Vietnam War throughout the 1960s. They wanted to embarrass the Johnson-Humphrey administration by marching to the convention hall on nomination night. Mixed in were the **Yippies**. The term supposedly stood for Youth International Party, but the idea of "hippies making yippie!" came first and the word later. The Yippies planned to attract young people to Chicago with a promise of street theater, media events, and confrontation that would puncture the pretensions of the power structure. To the extent they had a program, it was to use youth culture to attract converts to radical politics.

The volatile mix was ready for a spark. On August 28, the same night that Democratic delegates were nominating Humphrey, tensions exploded in a police riot. Protesters and Yippies had congregated in Grant Park, across Michigan Avenue from downtown hotels. Undisciplined police waded into the crowds with clubs and tear gas. Young people fought back with rocks and bottles. Television caught the hours of violence that ended when the National Guard separated police from demonstrators. On the convention floor, Senator Abraham Ribicoff of Connecticut decried "Gestapo tactics" on the streets of Chicago. Mayor Daley shouted back obscenities. For Humphrey, the convention was a catastrophe, alienating liberal Democrats and associating Democrats with disorder in the public mind.

The election was closer than Humphrey had any right to hope (see Map 31-2). Many Americans who liked Wallace's message were unwilling to vote for a radical third party. Nixon appealed to the white middle class and claimed he had a secret plan to end the war. Humphrey picked up strength in October after he separated himself from Johnson's war policy. Election day gave Wallace 13.5 percent of the popular vote, Humphrey 42.7 percent of the popular vote and 191 electoral votes, and Nixon 43.4 percent of the popular vote and 301 electoral votes.

The Wallace candidacy was a glimpse of the future. The national media saw Wallace in terms of bigotry and backlash against civil rights, getting only part of the story. Many of Wallace's northern backers were unhappy with both parties. Liberal on economic issues but conservative on family and social issues, many of these working-class voters evolved into "Reagan Democrats" by the 1980s. In the South, Wallace was a way station for conservative voters who would eventually transfer their allegiance from the Democratic to the Republican party.

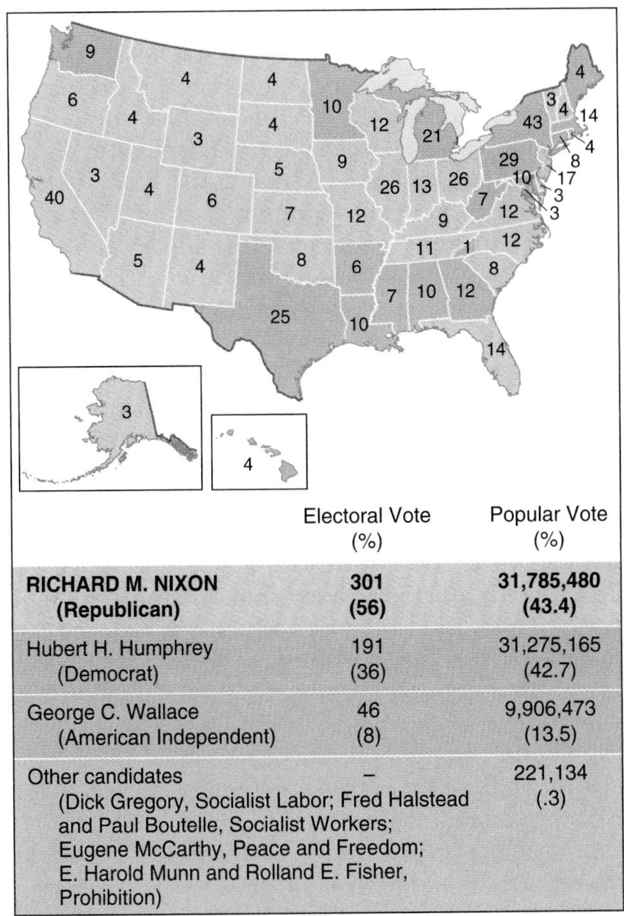

	Electoral Vote (%)	Popular Vote (%)
RICHARD M. NIXON (Republican)	**301 (56)**	**31,785,480 (43.4)**
Hubert H. Humphrey (Democrat)	191 (36)	31,275,165 (42.7)
George C. Wallace (American Independent)	46 (8)	9,906,473 (13.5)
Other candidates (Dick Gregory, Socialist Labor; Fred Halstead and Paul Boutelle, Socialist Workers; Eugene McCarthy, Peace and Freedom; E. Harold Munn and Rolland E. Fisher, Prohibition)	–	221,134 (.3)

Map 31-2 The Election of 1968
Richard Nixon won the presidency with the help of American Independent party candidate George Wallace. Wallace won several southern states, offering an alternative to white Southerners unhappy with the Democratic party but not yet prepared to vote Republican. He also drew northern working class votes away from Hubert Humphrey and helped Nixon take several midwestern states.

Nixon and Watergate

The new president was an unlikely politician, ill-at-ease in public and consumed by a sense of inferiority. A product of small-town California, he felt rejected by the eastern elite. After losing a 1962 race for governor of California, he announced that he was quitting politics and that the press would no longer have Dick Nixon "to kick around." In 1968, he skillfully sold a "new Nixon" to the media. Seven years later, the press was his undoing as it uncovered the Watergate scandal.

Nixon's painful public presence and dishonesty have tended to obscure his administration's accomplishments. He reduced tensions in the Cold War. He reluctantly upgraded civil rights enforcement, set goals for minority hiring by federal contractors, and presided over impressive environmental legislation.

Getting Out of Vietnam, 1969–1973

After 1968, things got worse in southeast Asia before they got better. Nixon had no secret plan to end the war. Protests culminated in 1969 with the Vietnam Moratorium on October 15, when 2 million protesters joined rallies across the country. Disaffection also mounted in Vietnam. Nurses found their idealism strained as they treated young men maimed in thousands of nasty skirmishes in the jungles and mountains. Racial tensions sapped morale on the front lines. Troops lost discipline, took drugs, and hunkered down waiting for their tours of duty to end. Soldiers "fragged" (killed) their own gung-ho or racist officers, and the high command had to adapt its code of justice to keep an army on the job.

Nixon and Vice President Spiro Agnew responded by trying to isolate the antiwar opposition, but Nixon also reduced the role of U.S. ground forces. He claimed that his policies represented "the great silent majority of my fellow Americans." Agnew blamed bad morale on journalists and intellectuals—on "nattering nabobs of negativism" and "an effete corps of impudent snobs." The administration arranged for a "spontaneous" attack by construction workers on antiwar protesters in New York. The hard-hat counterattack was a cynically manipulated symbol, but Nixon and Agnew tapped genuine anger about failure in Asia and rapid change in American society.

The New Left had already split into factions. Many activists continued to focus on peace work, draft resistance, and other efforts to link radical and liberal agendas. About a hundred angry SDS members, however, declared themselves the **Weather Underground** in 1969, taking their name from a Bob Dylan lyric ("You don't need a weatherman to know which way the blows"). They tried to disrupt Chicago and Washington with window-smashing "days of rage." Three Weatherpeople blew themselves up with a homemade bomb in New York in 1970. Others robbed a Boston bank to get money for the revolution. Still others bombed a University of Wisconsin building and killed a student.

Nixon's secretary of defense, Melvin Laird, responded to the antiwar sentiment with "Vietnamization," withdrawing U.S. troops as fast as possible without undermining the South Vietnamese government. In July 1969, the president announced the "Nixon Doctrine." The United States would help other countries fight their wars with weapons and money but not soldiers. The policy substituted machines for men. Americans rearmed and expanded the South Vietnamese army and surreptiously bombed communist bases in neutral Cambodia.

The secret war against Cambodia culminated on April 30, 1970, with an invasion. Americans who had hoped that the war was fading away were outraged. Students shut down hundreds of colleges. At Kent State University in Ohio, the National Guard was called in to maintain order. Taunts, tossed bottles, and the recent record of violence put them on edge. On May 4, one unit unexpectedly fired on a group of nonthreatening students and killed four of them. At Jackson State University in Mississippi, two unsuspecting students were killed when troops fired on their dormitory.

The Cambodian "incursion" extended the military stalemate in Vietnam to United States policy. Beginning in December 1969, a new lottery system for determining the order of draft calls by birth date let two-thirds of young men know they would not be drafted. In December 1970, Congress repealed the Gulf of Tonkin Resolution and prohibited use of U.S. ground troops outside South Vietnam. Cambodia, however, was already devastated. The U.S. invasion had destabilized its government and opened the way for the bloodthirsty Khmer Rouge, who killed millions of Cambodians in the name of working-class revolution. Vietnamization continued; only ninety thousand U.S. ground troops were still in Vietman by early 1972. A final air offensive in December smashed Hanoi into rubble and helped force four and a half years of peace talks to a conclusion.

The cease-fire began on January 27, 1973. It confirmed American withdrawal from Vietnam. North Vietnamese and Viet Cong forces would remain in control of the territory they occupied in South Vietnam, but they were not to be reinforced or substantially reequipped. The United States promised not to increase its military aid to South Vietnam. There were no solid guarantees for the South Vietnamese government. Immediately after coming to terms with North Vietnam, Nixon suspended the draft in favor of an all-volunteer military.

Nixon and the Wider World

To his credit, Richard Nixon took American foreign policy in new directions even while he was struggling to escape from Vietnam and Cambodia. Like Dwight Eisenhower before him, Nixon's reputation as an anticommunist allowed him to improve relations with China and the USSR. Indeed, he hoped to distract the American people from frustration in southeast Asia with accomplishments elsewhere.

Nixon's first foreign policy success was a gift from Kennedy and Johnson. NASA had been working

The shootings at Kent State University in May 1970 reflected the deep divisions in American society created by the Vietnam War, including those between antiwar college students and young people serving in the armed forces.

since 1961 to meet Kennedy's goal of an American on the moon before the end of the decade. The trial runs were Apollo 8, which sent American astronauts in orbit around the moon on Christmas Eve of 1968, and Apollo 10 in May 1969. The following summer, a Saturn V booster lifted the Apollo 11 crew of Edwin Aldrin, Neil Armstrong, and Michael Collins toward the untouched world. On July 20, the lunar lander Eagle detached from the command module circling the moon and landed on the level plain known as the Sea of Tranquillity. Six hours later, Armstrong was the first human to walk on the moon. Astronauts made five more trips to the moon between 1969 and 1972 and restored American prestige as the world's technological leader.

Back on earth, Nixon and Henry Kissinger, his national security adviser (and later secretary of state), shared what they considered a realistic view of foreign affairs. For both men, foreign policy was not about crusades or moral stands. It was about the balance of world economic and military power and securing the most advantageous agreements, alliances, and military positions. In particular, they hoped to trade improved relations with China and the USSR for help in settling the Vietnam War.

Since 1950, the United States had acted as if China didn't exist, refusing economic relations and insisting that the Nationalist regime on Taiwan was the legitimate Chinese government. But China was increasingly isolated within the communist world. In 1969, it almost went to war with the USSR. Nixon was eager to take advantage of Chinese–Soviet tension. Secret talks led to an easing of the American trade embargo in April 1971 and a tour of China by a U.S. table tennis team. Kissinger then arranged for Nixon's startling visit to Mao Zedong in Beijing in February 1972.

Playing the "China card" helped improve relations with the Soviet Union. The Soviets needed increased trade with the United States and a counterweight to China, the United States was looking for help in getting out of Vietnam, and both countries wanted to limit nuclear armaments. In 1969, the Senate came within one vote of stopping the development of defensive antiballistic missiles (ABMs). Opponents feared that strong antimissile defenses would encourage the idea that a nation could launch a first strike and survive the retaliation. Nixon treated the ABM program as a bargaining chip. Protracted negotiations led to arms agreements known as **SALT**—the Strategic Arms Limitation Treaty—that Nixon signed in Moscow in May 1972. The agreements blocked creation of extensive ABM systems but failed to limit bombers, cruise missiles, or multiple independently targeted warheads on single missiles.

Diplomats used the French word ***détente*** to describe the new U.S. relations with China and the Soviet Union. *Détente* means an easing of tensions, not friendship or alliance. It facilitated travel between the United States and China. It allowed U.S. farmers to sell wheat to the Soviets. More broadly, *détente* implied that the United States and China recognized mutual interests in Asia and that the United States acknowledged the Soviet Union as an equal in world affairs. *Détente* made the world safer.

Courting Middle America

Nixon designed domestic policy to help him win reelection. His goal was to solidify his "Middle American" support; the strategy targeted the suburbs and the South. Political writers Richard Scammon and Ben Wattenberg warned the Democrats that blue-collar voters were ready to defect to law-and-order Republicans.

The Nixon White House preferred to ignore troubled big cities. Spokesmen announced that the "urban crisis" was over and then dismantled the urban initiatives of Johnson's Great Society, even though programs like Model Cities had never been given enough money to work. Instead, Nixon tilted federal assistance to the suburbs. The centerpiece of his **New Federalism** was General Revenue Sharing (1972). By 1980, it had transferred more than $18 billion from the federal treasury to the states and more than $36 billion to local governments. Revenue sharing was a suburban aid program. Its "no-strings" grants supplemented the general funds of every full-service government, whether a city of 2 million or a suburban town of five hundred.

Nixon pursued the southern strategy through the symbolism of Supreme Court nominations. His first nominees were Clement Haynsworth of Florida and G. Harrold Carswell of Alabama. Although the Senate rejected both as unqualified, the nominations nonetheless gave Nixon a reputation as a champion of the white South. He hoped to move cautiously in enforcing school desegregation, but a task force led by Secretary of Labor George Shultz crafted an approach that allowed substantial desegregation. In this instance, as elsewhere with his domestic policies, Nixon was inflammatory in speeches but moderate in action, increasing the funding of federal civil rights agencies.

More troublesome was inflation, one of Lyndon Johnson's unpleasant legacies (see Figure 31-2). The cost of living began to outpace wages in the late 1960s. Economists saw the situation as a classic

FROM THEN TO NOW

Affirmative Action

In 1996, California voters approved a ballot measure to eliminate state-sponsored affirmative action. One effect was to prohibit state-funded colleges and universities from using race or ethnicity as a factor in deciding which applicants to admit. In the same year, the Supreme Court let stand a lower court ruling that had forbidden the University of Texas to consider race in admission decisions. The number of black freshmen in the University Texas at Austin dropped by half in 1997, and the number of black and Hispanic students entering its law school dropped by two-thirds. At the law school of the University of California at Berkeley, where the number of entering black students dropped from twenty to one.

These events were part of a widespread reaction in the 1990s against policies that emerged in the 1960s as part of an effort to redress inequalities that handicapped minorities in American society. An executive order by Johnson required businesses that received federal contracts to "take affirmative action to ensure that applicants are employed, and that employees are treated during employment without regard for their race, creed, color, or national origin." By the 1970s, many states and cities had adopted similar policies and had extended affirmative action to women as well as minorities. Colleges and universities adopted affirmative action policies for faculty recruitment and admissions.

As affirmative action spread, it evolved from an effort to prevent discrimination to an active ("affirmative") effort to increase diversity in schools and the workplace. Government agencies began to set aside a certain small percentage of contracts for woman-owned or minority-owned firms. Cities actively worked to hire more minority police officers and firefighters. Colleges made special efforts to attract minority students.

In the late 1970s, however, affirmative action began to face court challenges. In a landmark case, Allan Bakke, an unsuccessful applicant to the medical school of the University of California at Davis, claimed the university had improperly set aside places in its entering class for minority students, thereby engaging in reverse discrimination against white applicants. In a narrow decision, the U.S. Supreme Court in 1978 ordered Bakke admitted because the only basis for his rejection had been race. At the same time, the Court stated that college and universities could legally base admissions decisions on race and ethnicity among other factors.

Since *Bakke*, affirmative action has come under increasing scrutiny and attack. The Supreme Court has narrowed the scope of affirmative action, and states like California and Texas have acted to curtail their affirmative action programs. The problem is that the goal of diversity seems to conflict with the fundamental American value of individual opportunity. Americans reject the idea that past injustice and unequal opportunity can justify special consideration for all members of a group. Instead they believe that individual merit should be the sole basis for getting into school or getting a job. Many minority group members worry that affirmative action undermines their own success by suggesting that it resulted from preferential treatment rather than merit.

Yet the concerns that affirmative action has addressed since its inception are still valid. The nation surely benefits when members of minority groups are able to build successful businesses. A city with large minority populations benefits when members of those groups are serving on its police force and working in its classrooms. Students benefit when they interact with people of diverse backgrounds and opinions in the course of their studies. As a result, affirmative action programs are likely to endure, if in a substantially limited form, into the twenty-first century.

Students demonstrate while University of California Regents consider affirmative action programs in 1995.

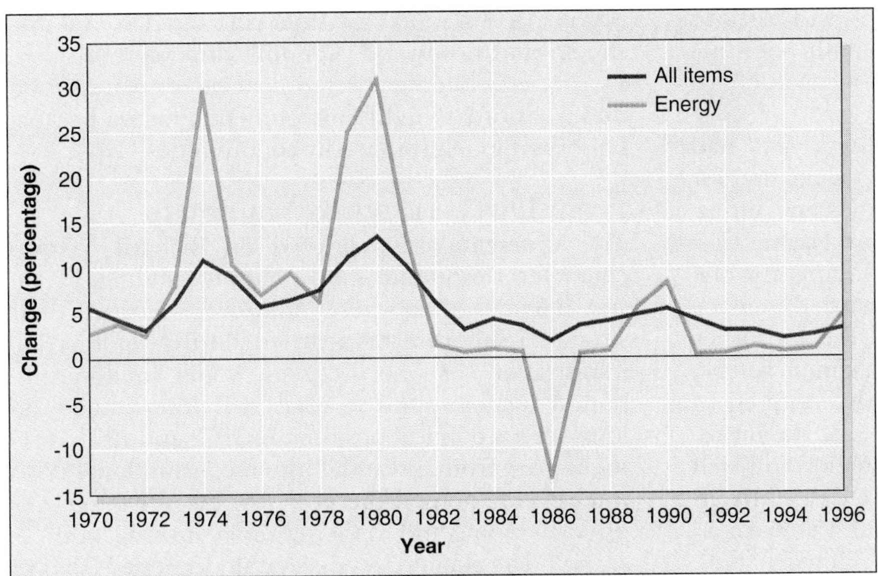

***Figure 31-2* Changes in the Consumer Price Index and Energy Prices**

From 1974 to 1982, price inflation was one of the nation's most serious problems. Spikes in energy prices in 1974 and 1979 were one cause. Another was the effort to fight a war in southeast Asia without raising taxes to offset federal defense spending. Inflation eroded the value of savings and hurt people on fixed incomes, such as the elderly.

Data Source: U.S. Bureau of Labor Statistics.

example of "demand-pull" inflation in which too many dollars from government and consumers were chasing too few goods and services. One of the causes was LBJ's decision to fight in Vietnam without tax increases until 1968. An income tax cut in 1969, supported by both parties, made the situation worse. Inflation eroded the value of savings and pensions. It also made U.S. goods too expensive for foreign buyers and generated a trade deficit.

In August 1971, Nixon detached the dollar from the gold standard. The Treasury would no longer sell gold at $35 an ounce, a practice that had made the dollar the anchor around which other currencies fluctuated. The dollar could now float in value relative to other currencies, making U.S. exports more competitive. Nixon took the action without consulting America's allies, even though it triggered drastic readjustments of international markets. It was an example of the political expediency behind his economic policy.

After the 1972 election, inflation came roaring back in the form of "cost-push" inflation in which a price increase for one key product raises the cost of producing other items. The main cause was sharp increases in the cost of energy, an input to every product and service. Angry at American support for Israel in the Arab-Israeli War of October 1973, Arab nations imposed an embargo on oil exports that lasted from October 1973 to March 1974. Gasoline and heating oil became scarce and expensive. Long lines at gas pumps and hurried rationing systems panicked auto-dependent Americans. The shortages eased when the embargo ended, but the **Organization of Petroleum Exporting Countries (OPEC)** had challenged the ability of the industrial nations to dictate world economic policy.

Rising energy prices forced Americans to switch off unused lights, turn down thermostats, and put on sweaters. Consumers compared the efficiency ratings of appliances and the gas mileage of cars. Congress required states to enforce a highway speed limit of 55 miles per hour to get federal highway funds. Congress also enacted the first fuel economy standards for automobiles. The fuel efficiency of the average new car doubled from 14 miles per gallon in 1973 to 28 miles per gallon by the late 1980s, and more efficient imports captured a third of the U.S. car market by 1980.

While Nixon searched for short-term political advantage, the underlying problems of the American economy went untreated. After thirty years at the top, the United States could no longer dominate the world economy by itself. Germany and Japan now had economies as modern as that of the United States. Declining rates of saving and investment in industrial capacity seemed to put the United States in danger of following the British road to economic obsolescence and second-level status. Indeed, a new term entered the popular vocabulary in 1971. **Stagflation** was the painful combination of inflation, high unemployment, and flat economic growth that matched no one's economic theory but everyone's daily experience.

Americans as Environmentalists

In the turbulent 1970s, Americans found one issue they could agree on. In the 1970s, resource conservation grew into a multifaceted environmental movement. Environmentalism dealt with serious problems. It was broad enough for both scientific experts and activists, for both Republican Richard Nixon and Democrat Jimmy Carter.

After the booming 1950s, Americans had started to pay attention to "pollution," a catchall for the damage that advanced technologies and industrial production did to natural systems. Rachel Carson's *Silent Spring* in 1962 pushed pollution onto the national agenda. Carson, a well-regarded science writer, described the side effects of DDT and other pesticides on animal life. In her imagined future, spring was silent because all the birds had died of pesticide poisoning. Other side effects of the industrial economy made headlines. An offshore oil well polluted the beaches of Santa Barbara, California, in 1969. Fire danced across the Cuyahoga River in Cleveland when industrial discharges ignited.

Environmentalism gained strength among Americans in 1970. On April 22, students and teachers from ten thousand schools as well as 20 million other people took part in Earth Day, an occasion first conceived by Wisconsin Senator Gaylord Nelson. Earth Day gained a grassroots following in towns and cities across the country. New York closed Fifth Avenue to automobiles for the day. Companies touted their environmental credentials.

The American establishment had been looking for a safe and respectable crusade to divert the idealism and discontent of the 1960s. Now the mainstream media discovered the ravaged planet. So did a politically savvy president. An expedient proenvironmental stance might attract some of the antiwar constituency. Nixon had already signed the National Environmental Policy Act on January 1, 1970, and later in the year created the **Environmental Protection Agency (EPA)** to enforce environmental laws. The rest of the Nixon years brought legislation on clean air, clear water, pesticides, hazardous chemicals, and endangered species (see the overview table, "The Environmental Decades") that made environmental management and protection part of governmental routine.

As Americans became more aware of human-caused environmental hazards, they realized that low-income and minority communities had more than their share of problems. Residents near the Love Canal in Buffalo discovered in 1978 that an entire neighborhood was built on land contaminated by decades of chemical dumping. Activists sought to understand the health effects and force compensation, paving the way for the **Superfund** cleanup legislation.

In other areas of industrial contamination, such as the Louisiana petrochemical belt along the Mississippi River, African Americans often lived downstream and downwind. Landfills and waste disposal sites were frequently located near minority neighborhoods. Efforts to fight environmental racism became important in many minority communities.

From Dirty Tricks to Watergate

The **Watergate** crisis pivoted on Richard Nixon's character. Despite his solid political standing, Nixon saw enemies everywhere and overestimated their strength. Subordinates learned during his first administration that the president would condone dishonest actions—"dirty tricks"—if they stood to improve his political position. In 1972 and 1973, dirty tricks grew from a scandal into a constitutional crisis when Nixon abused the power of his office to cover up wrongdoing and hinder criminal investigations.

The chain of events that undermined Nixon's presidency started with the **Pentagon Papers**. In his last

The first Earth Day in 1970 tapped growing concern about the environment. It helped turn the technical field of pollution control into the broad-based environmental movement.

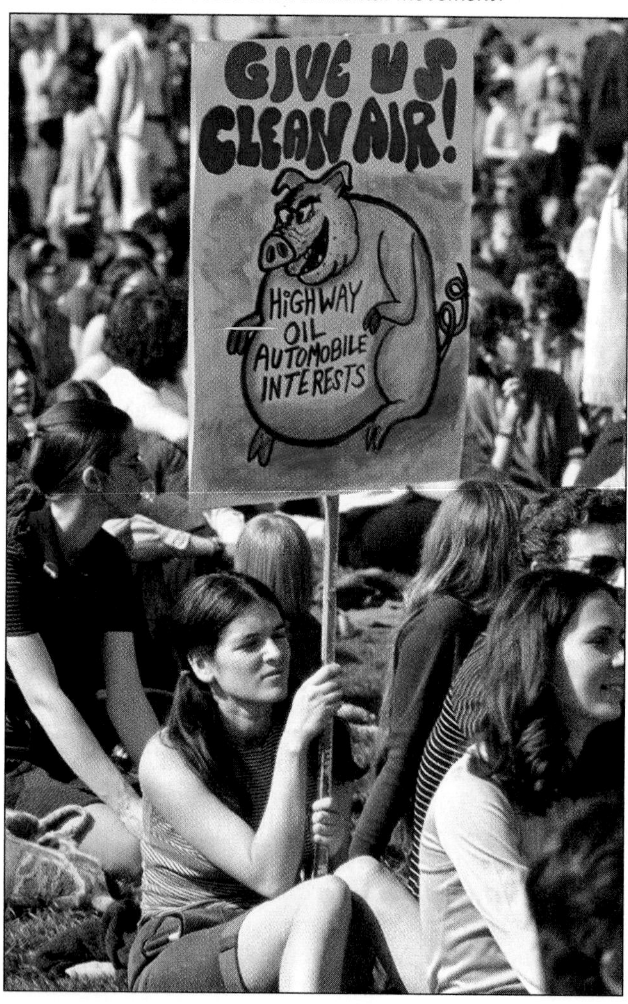

OVERVIEW

THE ENVIRONMENTAL DECADES

Administration	Focus of Concern	Legislation
Johnson	Wilderness and wildlife	Wilderness Act (1964) National Wildlife Refuge System (1966) Wild and Scenic Rivers Act (1968)
Nixon	Pollution control and endangered environments	National Environmental Policy Act (1969) Environmental Protection Agency (1970) Clean Air Act (1970) Occupational Safety and Health Act (1970) Water Pollution Control Act (1972) Pesticide Control Act (1972) Coastal Zone Management Act (1972) Endangered Species Act (1973)
Ford	Energy and hazardous materials	Toxic Substances Control Act (1976) Resource Conservation and Recovery Act (1976)
Carter	Energy and hazardous materials	Energy Policy and Conservation Act (1978) Comprehensive Emergency Response, Compensation, and Liability Act (Superfund) (1980)

year as secretary of defense, Robert McNamara had commissioned a report on America's road to Vietnam. The documents showed that the country's leaders had planned to expand the war even while they claimed to be looking for a way out. In June 1971, one of the contributors to the report, Daniel Ellsberg, leaked it to the *New York Times.* Its publication infuriated Nixon.

In response, the White House compiled a list of journalists and politicians who opposed Nixon. As White House staffer John Dean put it, the president's men could then "use the available federal machinery [Internal Revenue Service, FBI] to screw our political enemies." Nixon set up a special investigations unit in the White House. Former CIA employees E. Howard Hunt and G. Gordon Liddy became the chief "plumbers," as the group was known because its job was to prevent leaks of information. The plumbers contributed to an atmosphere of lawlessness in the White House. They cooked up schemes to embarrass political opponents and ransacked the office of Ellsberg's psychiatrist.

Early in 1972, Hunt went to work for CREEP—the Committee to Re-Elect the President—while Liddy took another position on the presidential staff. CREEP had already raised millions from corporations and was hatching plans to undermine Democrats with rumors and pranks. Then, on June 17, 1972, five inept burglars hired with CREEP funds were caught breaking into the Democratic National Committee office in Washington's Watergate apartment building. The people involved knew that an investigation would lead directly to CREEP and then to the White House. Nixon felt too insecure to ride out what would probably have been a small scandal. Instead, he initiated a coverup. On June 23, he ordered his assistant H. R. Haldeman to warn the FBI off the case with the excuse that national security was involved. Nixon compounded this obstruction of justice by arranging a $400,000 bribe to keep the burglars quiet.

The coverup worked in the short run. As midlevel officials from the Justice Department pursued their investigation, the public lost interest in what looked more like slapstick than a serious crime. Nixon's opponent in the 1972 election was South Dakota Senator George McGovern, an impassioned opponent of the Vietnam War. McGovern was honest, intelligent, and well to the left on issues like the defense budget and legalization of marijuana. He did not appeal to the white Southerners and blue-collar Northerners whom Nixon and Agnew were luring from the Democrats. An assassination attempt that took George Wallace out of national politics also helped Nixon win in a landslide.

The coverup began to come apart with the trial of the Watergate burglars in January 1973. Federal Judge John Sirica used the threat of heavy sentences to pressure one burglar into a statement that implied that higher-ups had been involved. Meanwhile, the *Washington Post* was linking Nixon's people to dirty tricks and illegal campaign contributions. The White House scrambled to find a defensible story. John Dean, who coordinated much of the effort, reported to Nixon in March that the scandal and coverup had become a "cancer on the presidency." Nixon was aware of many of the actions that his subordinates had undertaken. He now began to coach people on what they should tell investigators, claimed his staff had lied to him, and tried to set up Dean to take the fall.

In the late spring and early summer, attention shifted to the televised hearings of the Senate's Select Committee on Presidential Campaign Activities. Its chair was Sam Ervin of North Carolina, whose down-home style masked a clever mind. A parade of White House and party officials described their own pieces in the affair, often accusing each other and revealing the plumbers and the enemies list. The real questions, it became obvious, were what the president knew and when he knew it. It seemed to be John Dean's word against Richard Nixon's.

A bombshell turned the scandal into a constitutional crisis. A midlevel staffer told the committee that Nixon made tape recordings of his White House conversations. Both the Senate and the Watergate special prosecutor, Archibald Cox, subpoenaed the tapes. Nixon refused to give them up, citing executive privilege and the separation of powers. In late October, after he failed to cut a satisfactory deal, he fired his attorney general and the special prosecutor. This "Saturday night massacre" caused a storm of protest, and many Americans thought that it proved that Nixon had something to hide. In April 1974, he finally issued edited transcripts of the tapes, with foul language deleted and key passages missing; he claimed that his secretary had accidentally erased crucial material. Finally, on July 24, 1974, the U.S. Supreme Court ruled unanimously that Nixon had to deliver sixty-four tapes to the new special prosecutor.

Congress was now moving to impeach the president. On July 27, the House Judiciary Committee took up the specific charges. Republicans joined Democrats in voting three articles of impeachment: for hindering the criminal investigation of the Watergate break-in, for abusing the power of the presidency by using federal agencies to deprive citizens of their rights, and for ignoring the committee's subpoena for the tapes. Before the full House could vote on the articles of impeachment and send them to the Senate for trial, Nixon delivered the tapes. One of

The Watergate story captured national attention in 1973 and 1974. Here, Senator Sam Ervin (with his back to the camera) swears in White House aide John Dean III. Dean's decision to testify about his role in the Watergate coverup helped break the story open.

them contained the "smoking gun," direct evidence that Nixon had participated in the coverup on June 23, 1972, and had been lying ever since. On August 8 he announced his resignation, effective the next day.

Watergate was two separate but related stories. On one level, it was about individuals who deceived or manipulated the American people. Nixon and his cronies wanted to win too badly to play by the rules and repeatedly broke the law. Nixon paid for his overreaching ambition with the end of his political career; more than twenty others paid with jail terms.

On another level, the crisis was a lesson about the Constitution. The separation of powers allowed Congress and the courts to rein in a president who had spun out of control. The Ervin Committee hearings in 1973 and the House Judiciary Committee proceedings in 1974 were rituals to assure Americans that the system still worked. Nevertheless, the sequence of political events from 1968 to 1974 disillusioned many citizens.

The Ford Footnote

Gerald Ford was the first president who had been elected neither president nor vice president. Ford was Nixon's appointee to replace Spiro Agnew, who resigned and pleaded no contest to charges of bribery and income tax evasion in 1973 as Watergate was gathering steam. Ford was competent but unimaginative. His first major act was his most controversial. On September 8, he pardoned Richard Nixon for "any and all crimes" committed while president. Because Nixon had not yet been indicted, the pardon saved him from future prosecution. To many Americans, it looked like a payoff. Ford insisted that the purpose was to clear the decks so that the nation could think about the future rather than the past. He also offered clemency to thousands of draft resisters.

In 1975, South Vietnam collapsed. Only the American presence had kept its political, ethnic, and religious factions together. For the first two years after the Paris agreement, North Vietnam quietly rebuilt its military capacity. In the spring of 1975, it opened an offensive, and South Vietnamese morale evaporated. Resistance crumbled so rapidly that the United States had to evacuate its embassy in Saigon by helicopter while frantic Vietnamese tried to join the flight.

Elsewhere in the world, *détente* continued. American diplomats joined the Soviet Union and thirty other European nations in the capital of Finland to sign the **Helsinki Accords**. The agreements called for increased commerce between the Eastern and Western blocs and human rights guarantees. They also legitimized the national boundaries that had been set in eastern Europe in 1945.

At home, the federal government did little new during Ford's two and a half years in office. The economy slid into recession; unemployment climbed above 10 percent; inflation diminished the value of savings and wages. Ford beat back Ronald Reagan for the Republican presidential nomination, but he was clearly vulnerable.

His Democratic opponent was a political enigma. James Earl Carter, Jr., had been a navy officer, a farmer, and governor of Georgia. He was one of several new-style politicians who transformed southern politics in the 1970s. Carter and the others left race-baiting behind to talk like modern New Dealers, emphasizing that white and black Americans all needed better schools and economic growth. He appealed to Democrats as someone who could reassemble LBJ's political coalition and return the South to the Democratic party. In his successful campaign, Carter presented himself as an alternative to party hacks and Washington insiders (see Map 31-3).

Map 31-3 The Election of 1976
Georgian Jimmy Carter ran in 1976 as an outsider to Washington politics. He capitalized on a reputation as a progressive governor and on the Watergate scandal, which had damaged the Republican party.

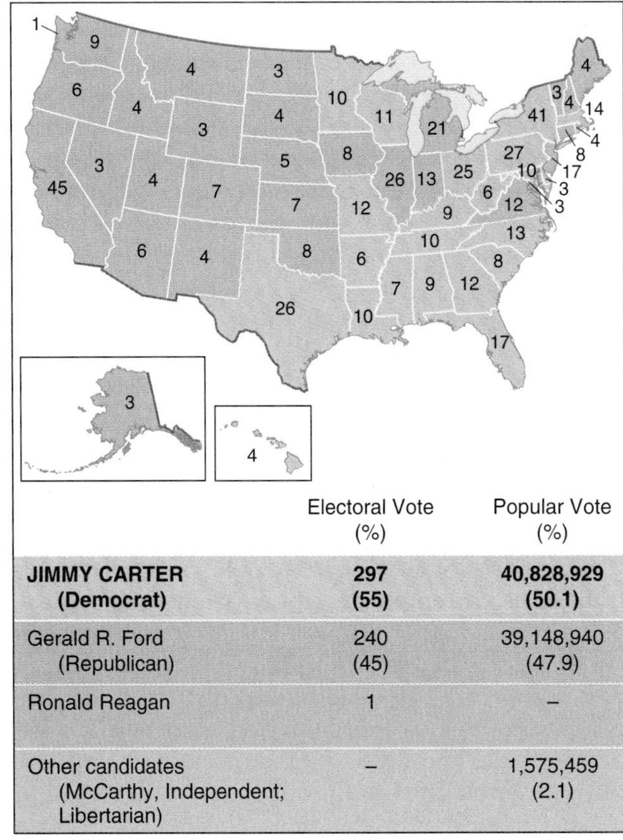

	Electoral Vote (%)	Popular Vote (%)
JIMMY CARTER (Democrat)	**297 (55)**	**40,828,929 (50.1)**
Gerald R. Ford (Republican)	240 (45)	39,148,940 (47.9)
Ronald Reagan	1	–
Other candidates (McCarthy, Independent; Libertarian)	–	1,575,459 (2.1)

Jimmy Carter: Idealism and Frustration in the White House

Johnson and Nixon had both thought of themselves as outsiders even after nearly thirty years in national politics. Carter was the real thing, a stranger to the national policy establishment that revolves around Washington think tanks and New York law firms. As an outsider, Carter had one great advantage: freedom from the narrow mind-set of experts who talk only to each other. However, he lacked both the knowledge of key political players and the experience to resolve legislative gridlock.

The new president's personal background compounded his problems. Intellectuals found this devout Baptist hard to fathom. Labor leaders and political bosses didn't know what to make of a deep Southerner. The national press was baffled. It was only after his presidency, when Americans took a clear look at Carter's moral character, that they decided they liked what they saw.

Even had he been the most skilled of politicians, however, Carter took office with little room to maneuver. Watergate bequeathed him a powerful and self-satisfied Congress and a combative press. OPEC oil producers, Islamic fundamentalists, and Soviet generals followed their own agendas. The American people themselves were fractionalized and quarrelsome, uneasy with the new advocacy of equality for women, uncertain as a nation whether they shared the same values and goals. Carter's attempt to govern like a preacher, with appeals to moral principles, did more to reveal divisions than establish common ground.

Carter, Energy, and the Economy

Carter was refreshingly low-key. After his inauguration, he walked from the Capitol to the White House as Jefferson had. He preferred sweaters to tuxedos and signed official documents "Jimmy." He tended to tell the public what he thought rather than what pollsters said the people wanted to hear.

Carter's approach to politics reflected his training as an engineer. He was analytical, logical, and given to breaking a problem into its component parts. He was better at working with details than at defining broad goals. He filled his cabinet with experts rather than political operators. He failed to understand the importance of personalities and was uncomfortable with compromise. Carter even found it hard to deal with the Democrats who ran Congress. He didn't seem to understand the basic rules of Washington politics. For example, he and his cabinet officers developed policies and made appointments without consulting key congressional committee chairs.

Carter got into political trouble in his first month in office. Federal water and land policy in the West had long subsidized big agricultural businesses. Carter's team decided to kill a long list of wasteful water projects. Westerners in Congress were astonished when the proposal arrived without warning, for it attacked powerful interests. Carter eventually managed to get half of what he wanted, but the battle soured relations between the White House and Capitol Hill.

The biggest domestic problem remained the economy, which slid into another recession in 1978. Another jump in petroleum prices helped make 1979 and 1980 the worst years for inflation in the postwar era. Interest rates surged past 20 percent as the Federal Reserve tried to reduce inflation by squeezing business and consumer credit. Carter himself was a fiscal conservative whose impulse was to cut federal spending. This worsened unemployment and alienated liberal Democrats, who wanted to revive the Great Society.

Carter simultaneously proposed a comprehensive energy policy. He asked Americans to make energy conservation the moral equivalent of war—to accept individual sacrifices for the common good. Congress created the Department of Energy but refused to raise taxes on oil and natural gas to reduce consumption. However, the Energy Policy and Conservation Act (1978) did encourage alternative energy sources to replace foreign petroleum. Big oil companies poured billions of dollars into western Colorado to squeeze a petroleum substitute from shale. Solar energy research prospered. Breezy western hillsides sprouted "wind farms" to wring electricity out of the air.

However, antinuclear activism blocked one obvious alternative to fossil fuels. The antinuclear movement had started with concern about the ability of the Atomic Energy Commission to monitor the safety of nuclear power plants and about the disposal of spent fuel rods. In the late 1970s, activists staged sit-ins at the construction sites of nuclear plants. A near-meltdown at the Three Mile Island nuclear plant in Pennsylvania in March 1979 stalemated efforts to expand nuclear power capacity. Utilities were soon worrying about the costs of shutting down and dismantling their old nuclear plants rather than trying to build new ones.

When the OPEC price hikes undermined the inflation-fighting effort in the summer of 1979,

Carter told the nation that a "moral and spiritual crisis" demanded a rebirth of the American spirit. He also proposed new steps to solve the energy crisis. The public did not know whether he had preached a sermon or given them marching orders. A cabinet reshuffle a few days later was supposed to show that he was firmly in charge. Instead, the media painted the president as inconsistent and incompetent.

Carter's problems were both personal and structural. In effect, opinion leaders by 1979 had decided that he was not capable of leading the nation and then interpreted every action as confirming that belief. There was also the practical problem of trying to hold the loyalty of Democratic liberals while attracting middle-of-the-road voters.

Building a Cooperative World

Despite troubles on the home front, Carter's first two years brought foreign policy success that reflected a new vision of a multilateral world. As a relative newcomer to international politics, Carter was willing to try to work with African, Asian, and Latin American nations on a basis of mutual respect. He appointed Andrew Young—a fellow Georgian with long experience in the civil rights movement—as ambassador to the United Nations, where he worked effectively to build bridges to third-world nations.

Carter's moral convictions were responsible for a new concern with human rights around the globe. He criticized the Soviet Union for preventing free speech and denying its citizens the right to emigrate, angering Soviet leaders, who didn't expect the human rights clauses of the Helsinki Accords to be taken seriously. Carter was also willing to criticize some (but not all) American allies. He withheld economic aid from South Africa, Guatemala, Chile, and Nicaragua, which had long records of human rights abuses. In Nicaragua, the change in policy helped left-wing Sandinista rebels topple the Somoza dictatorship.

The triumph of the new foreign policy was the **Camp David Agreement** between Egypt and Israel. Carter risked his reputation and credibility in September 1978 to bring Egyptian President Anwar el-Sadat and Israeli Prime Minister Menachem Begin together at Camp David, the presidential retreat. He refused to admit failure and dissuaded the two leaders from walking out. A formal treaty was signed in Washington on March 26, 1979. The pact normalized relations between Israel and its most powerful neighbor and led to Israeli withdrawal from the Sinai Peninsula. It was a vital prelude to further progress toward Arab-Israeli peace in the mid 1990s.

Return of the Cold War

The Cold War was a noxious weed that détente trimmed but did not uproot. In the last two years of Carter's administration, it sprang back to life around the globe and smothered the promise of a new foreign policy. The Soviets ignored the human rights provisions of the Helsinki Accords. Soviet advisers or Cuban troops intervened in African civil wars. At home, Cold Warriors who had never accepted *détente* found it easier to attack Carter than Nixon.

Carter inherited negotiations for SALT II—a strategic arms limitation treaty that would have reduced both the American and Soviet nuclear arsenals—from the Ford administration. SALT II met stiff resistance in the Senate. Opponents claimed it would create a "window of vulnerability" in the 1980s that would invite the Soviets to launch a nuclear first strike. Carter tried to counter criticism by stepping up defense spending, starting a buildup that would accelerate under Ronald Reagan.

Hopes for SALT II vanished on January 3, 1980, when Soviet troops entered Afghanistan, a neutral Muslim nation on the southern border of the USSR. Muslim tribespeople unhappy with modernization had attacked Afghanistan's procommunist government, which invited Soviet intervention. The situation resembled the American involvement in South Vietnam. Similar too was the inability of Soviet forces to suppress the Afghan guerrillas, with their American weapons and control of the mountains. In the end, it took the Soviets a decade to find a way out.

The final blow to Carter's foreign policy came in Iran. Since 1953, the United States had strongly backed Iran's monarch, the Shah. The Shah modernized Iran's economy but jailed political opponents. U.S. aid and oil revenues helped him build a vast army, but the Iranian middle class despised his authoritarianism, and Muslim fundamentalists opposed modernization. Revolution toppled the Shah at the start of 1979.

The upheaval installed a nominally democratic government, but the Ayatollah Ruhollah Khomeini, a Muslim cleric who hated the United States, exercised real power. Throughout 1979, Iran grew increasingly anti-American. After the United States allowed the exiled Shah to seek medical treatment in New York, a mob stormed the U.S. embassy in Tehran on November 4, 1979, and took more than sixty Americans hostage. They demanded that Carter surrender the Shah.

Television brought pictures of blindfolded hostages and anti-American mobs burning effigies of Uncle Sam and wrapping American flags around garbage. Americans returned the hate. The administration tried economic pressure and diplomacy, but Khomeini had no desire for accommodation. When Iran announced in April 1980 that the hostages would remain in the hands of the militants rather than be transferred to the government, Carter ordered an airborne rescue. Even a perfectly managed effort would have been difficult. The hostages were held in the heart of a city of 4 million hostile Iranians, hundreds of miles from the nearest aircraft carrier and thousands of miles from U.S. bases. The attempt misfired when three of eight helicopters malfunctioned and one crashed in the Iranian desert. The fiasco added to the national embarrassment. The United States and Iran finally reached agreement on the eve of the 1980 election. The hostages gained their freedom after 444 days at the moment Ronald Reagan took office as the new president.

The hostage crisis consumed Jimmy Carter the way that Vietnam had consumed Lyndon Johnson. It gripped the public and stalemated other issues. For weeks, Carter limited public appearances to statements in the White House Rose Garden. The public blamed him for problems literally beyond his control, for failing to use military force, and then for using it and failing. Carter's tragedy was that "his" Iranian crisis was the fruit of policies hatched by the Eisenhower administration and pursued by every president since then, all of whom overlooked the Shah's despotic government because of his firm anticommunism.

After thirty years in which the United States had viewed the entire world as a Cold War battlefield, Carter was willing to accept the developing world on its own terms. His human rights efforts showed that evangelical religious convictions could be tied to progressive aims. He wanted to prevent overreliance on oppressive regimes, but the past was too burdensome. Iranian rage at past policies of the sort Carter hoped to change destroyed his ability to direct a new course.

The Iran hostage crisis reflected intense anti-American feelings in Iran and provoked an equally bitter anti-Iranian reaction in the United States. Fifty-two of the more than sixty U.S. embassy employees first seized were held for 444 days, giving the United States a painful lesson about the limits on its ability to influence events around the world.

Conclusion

In the mid-1970s, Americans encountered real limits to national capacity. From 1945 to 1973, they had enjoyed remarkable prosperity. That ended in 1974. Long lines at gas stations suggested that prosperity was fragile. Cities and regions began to feel the costs of obsolete industries. Environmental damage caused many Americans to reconsider the goal of economic expansion.

The nation also had to recognize that it could not run the world. American withdrawal from Vietnam in 1973 and the collapse of the South Vietnamese government in 1975 were defeats; the United States ended up with little to show for a long and painful war. SALT I stabilized the arms race, but it also recognized that the Soviet Union was an equal. The American nuclear arsenal might help deter a third world war, but it could not prevent the seizure of hostages in Iran.

These challenges came amid profound social and economic revolutions in the United States. Renewed immigration was changing the mix of the American population. The ways that Americans made their livings, built their families, ran their personal lives, and sought spiritual reassurance were in flux. The nation finished the 1970s more egalitarian than it had been in the early 1960s but also more divided. More citizens had the opportunity to advance economically and to seek political power, but there were deepening fissures between social liberals and cultural conservatives, old and new views about roles for women, rich and poor, white and black. In 1961, John Kennedy had called on his fellow citizens to "bear any burden, pay any price" to defend freedom. By 1980, the nation had neither the economic capacity to pay any price nor the unity to agree on what burdens it should bear.

Review Questions

1. Why did the United States fail to achieve its objectives in Vietnam? What factors limited President Johnson's freedom of action there? How did the Tet Offensive affect U.S. policy? How did antiwar protests in the United States influence national policy?
2. How did racial relations change between 1965 and 1970? What were the relationships between the civil rights movement and minority separatism? What were the similarities and differences among African-American, Latino, and Native American activism?
3. In what ways was 1968 a pivotal year for American politics and society?
4. What were the implications of *détente*? Why did the Cold War reappear in the late 1970s? How and why did U.S. influence over the rest of the world change during the 1970s?
5. How did Richard Nixon's political strategy respond to the growth of the South and West? How did it respond to the shift of population from central cities to suburbs?
6. How did the backgrounds of Presidents Johnson, Nixon, and Carter shape their successes and failures as national leaders?
7. What political and constitutional issues were at stake in the Watergate scandal? How did it change American politics?

Recommended Reading

Tom Bates, *Rads: The 1970 Bombing of the Army Math Research Center at the University of Wisconsin and Its Aftermath* (1992). Uses a specific episode to understand the collapse of the New Left.

John Morton Blum, *Years of Discord: American Politics and Society, 1961–1974* (1991). Shares with McQuaid (below) a disillusionment with America's development since the hope of the 1960s.

David Caute, *Year of the Barricades* (1988). Tours the events of 1968 on both sides of the Atlantic.

Gloria Emerson, *Winners and Losers* (1976). The impact of the war in Vietnam on American society, told through the stories of individuals changed by the war.

David Farber, *The Age of Great Dreams: America in the 1960s* (1994). A positive assessment of the legacy of the 1960s.

David Farber, *Chicago '68* (1988). Contrasts the perspectives and language of city officials and protesters.

David Halberstam, *October 1964* (1994). Uses the baseball season of 1964 and the World Series between the St. Louis Cardinals and New York Yankees to encapsulate the impacts of changing racial relations on American society.

Stanley Karnow, *Vietnam: A History* (1983). A comprehensive history of American involvement in Vietnam that details the collapse of French rule and early U.S. relations with Vietnam.

Kim McQuaid, *The Anxious Years: America in the Vietnam-Watergate Era* (1989). Tries to understand how the United States turned aside from the promise of the early 1960s.

Haskell Wexler, director, *Medium Cool* (1969). A film that captures the tension of Chicago in the hot summer of 1968 through the eyes of a reporter.

Additional Sources

War in Vietnam

Christian Appy, *Working-Class War: American Combat Soldiers and Vietnam* (1993).

Albert Auster and Leonard Quart, *How the War Was Remembered: Hollywood and Vietnam* (1988).

Robert Buzzanco, *Masters of War* (1996).

Francis Fitzgerald, *Fire on the Lake* (1972).

George Herring, *America's Longest War* (1986).

David W. Levy, *The Debate over Vietnam* (1991).

Robert Schulzinger, *A Time for War. The United States and Vietnam, 1941–1975* (1997).

William Shawcross, *Sideshow: Kissinger, Nixon, and the Destruction of Cambodia* (1979).

Neil Sheehan, *A Bright Shining Lie: John Paul Vann and America in Vietnam* (1988).

Brian Van De Mark, *Into the Quagmire: Johnson and the Escalation of the Vietnam War* (1991).

Lynda Van Devanter, *Home before Morning* (1984).

Tom Wells, *The War Within: America's Battle over Vietnam* (1994).

Marilyn Young, *The Vietnam Wars, 1945–1990* (1991).

The Revolt of the Young

Terry Anderson, *The Movement and the Sixties* (1995).

Wini Breines, *Community and Organization in the New Left, 1962–1968* (1982).

Sara Evans, *Personal Politics: The Roots of Women's Liberation in the Civil Rights Movement and the New Left* (1979).

Todd Gitlin, *The Sixties: Years of Hope, Days of Rage* (1987).

Kenneth Heineman, *Campus Wars: The Peace Movement at American State Universities in the Vietnam Era* (1993).

Marty Jezer, *Abbie Hoffman: American Rebel* (1992).

James Miller, *"Democracy Is in the Streets": From Port Huron to the Siege of Chicago* (1987).

Charles Perry, *The Haight-Ashbury* (1985).

William Rorabaugh, *Berkeley at War* (1989).

Kirkpatrick Sale, *SDS* (1973).

Minority Rights and Minority Separatism

Paula Giddings and Cornel West, *Regarding Malcolm X* (1994).

Peter Mathiesson, *In the Spirit of Crazy Horse* (1983).

Russell Means, *Where White Men Fear to Tread* (1995).

Felix Padilla, *Puerto Rican Chicago* (1987).

Donald Parman, *Indians and the American West in the Twentieth Century* (1994).

Piri Thomas, *Down These Mean Streets* (1967).

William L. Van Deburg, *New Day in Babylon: The Black Power Movement and American Culture, 1965–1975* (1993).

Foreign Policy in the 1970s

James A. Bill, *The Eagle and the Lion: The Tragedy of American-Iranian Relations* (1988).

Raymond Garthoff, *Détente and Confrontation* (1985).

Walter Isaacson, *Kissinger: A Biography* (1992).

Walter Le Feber, *The Panama Canal: The Crisis in Historical Perspective* (1978).

Robert Litwak, *Détente and the Nixon Doctrine* (1984).

Keith Nelson, *The Making of Détente* (1995).

William B. Quando, *Camp David: Peacemaking and Politics* (1986).

Robert Schulzinger, *Henry Kissinger: Doctor of Diplomacy* (1989).

Gaddis Smith, *Morality, Reason, and Power* (1986).

Strobe Talbot, *Endgame: The Inside Story of SALT II* (1979).

Watergate and Politics in the Nixon Years

Stephen E. Ambrose, *Nixon: Ruin and Recovery, 1973–1990* (1991).

Dan T. Carter, *The Politics of Rage: George Wallace, the Origins of the New Conservatism, and the Transformation of American Politics* (1996).

John Robert Greene, *The Limits of Power: The Nixon and Ford Administrations* (1992).

Stanley Kutler, *The Wars of Watergate* (1990).

Michael Schudson, *Watergate in American Memory: How We Remember, Forget, and Reconstruct the Past* (1992).

Jimmy Carter and His Presidency

Jimmy Carter, *Keeping Faith: Memoirs of a President* (1982).

Betty Glad, *Jimmy Carter, In Search of the Great White House* (1980).

Erwin C. Hargrove, *Jimmy Carter as President: Leadership and the Politics of the Public Good* (1988).

Charles O. Jones, *The Trusteeship Presidency: Jimmy Carter and the United States Congress* (1988).

Burton I. Kaufman, *The Presidency of James Earl Carter, Jr.* (1993).

William Lee Miller, *Yankee from Georgia: The Emergence of Jimmy Carter* (1978).

Environmental Politics

Robert Gottlieb, *Forcing the Spring: The Transformation of the American Environmental Movement* (1993).

Samuel Hays, *Beauty, Health, and Permanence: Environmental Politics in the United States, 1955–1985* (1987).

Kirkpatrick Sale, *The Green Revolution: The American Environmental Movement, 1962–1992* (1993).

Where to Learn More

❖ **Lyndon B. Johnson National Historical Park, Johnson City, Texas.** Johnson's ranch, southwest of Austin, gives visitors a feeling for the open landscape in which Johnson spent his early years.

❖ **Vietnam Veterans Memorial, Washington, D.C.** A simple wall engraved with the names of the nation's Vietnam War dead is testimony to one of the nation's most divisive wars.

❖ **Richard Nixon Library and Birthplace, Yorba Linda, California.** Exhibits trace Nixon's political career and related world events with a sympathetic interpretation.

❖ **Titan Missile Museum, Green Valley, Arizona.** The Green Valley complex near Tucson held eighteen Titan missiles. They were deactivated after SALT I, and the complex is now open to visitors.

SHAPING A NEW AMERICA, SINCE 1965

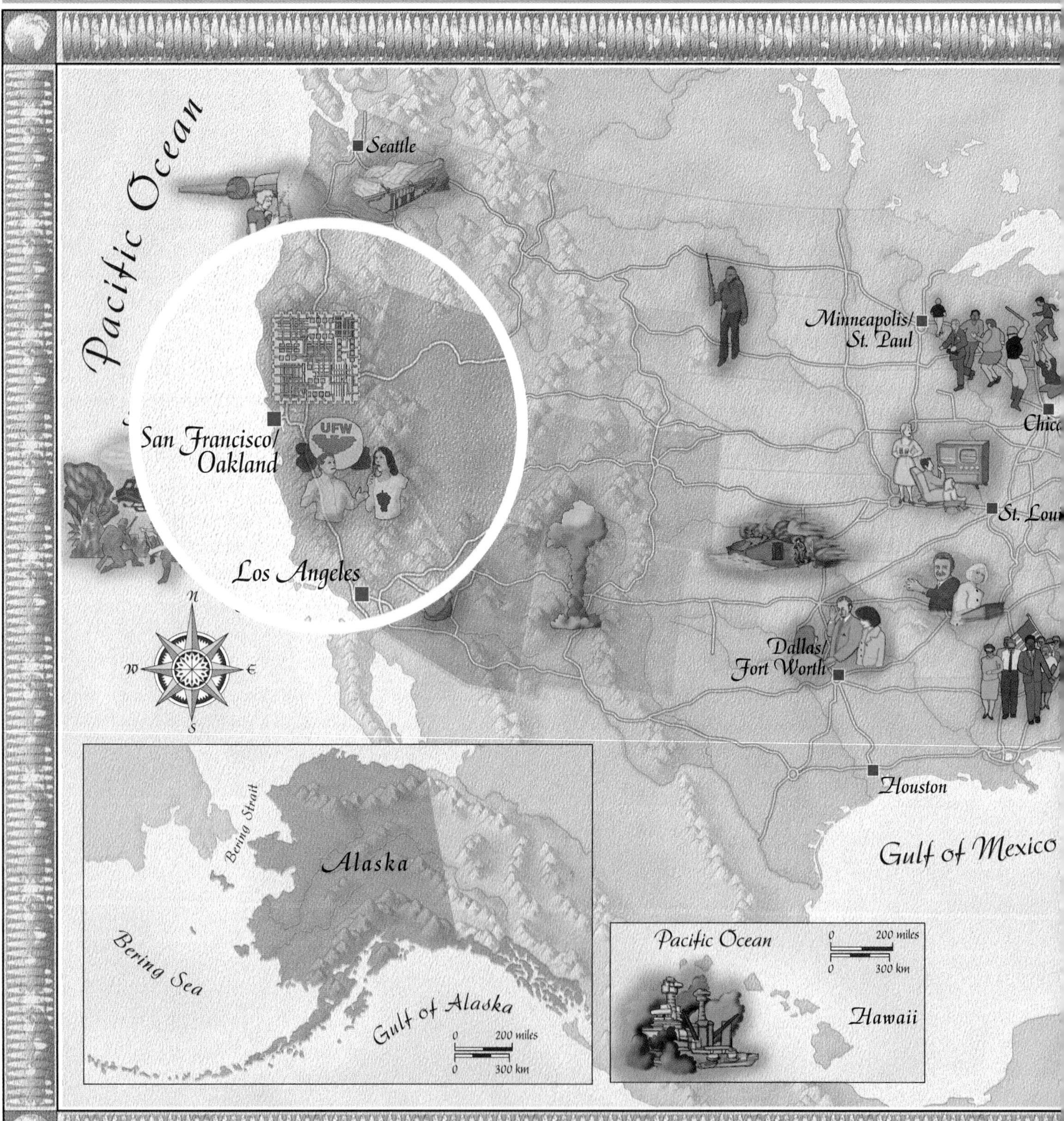

32

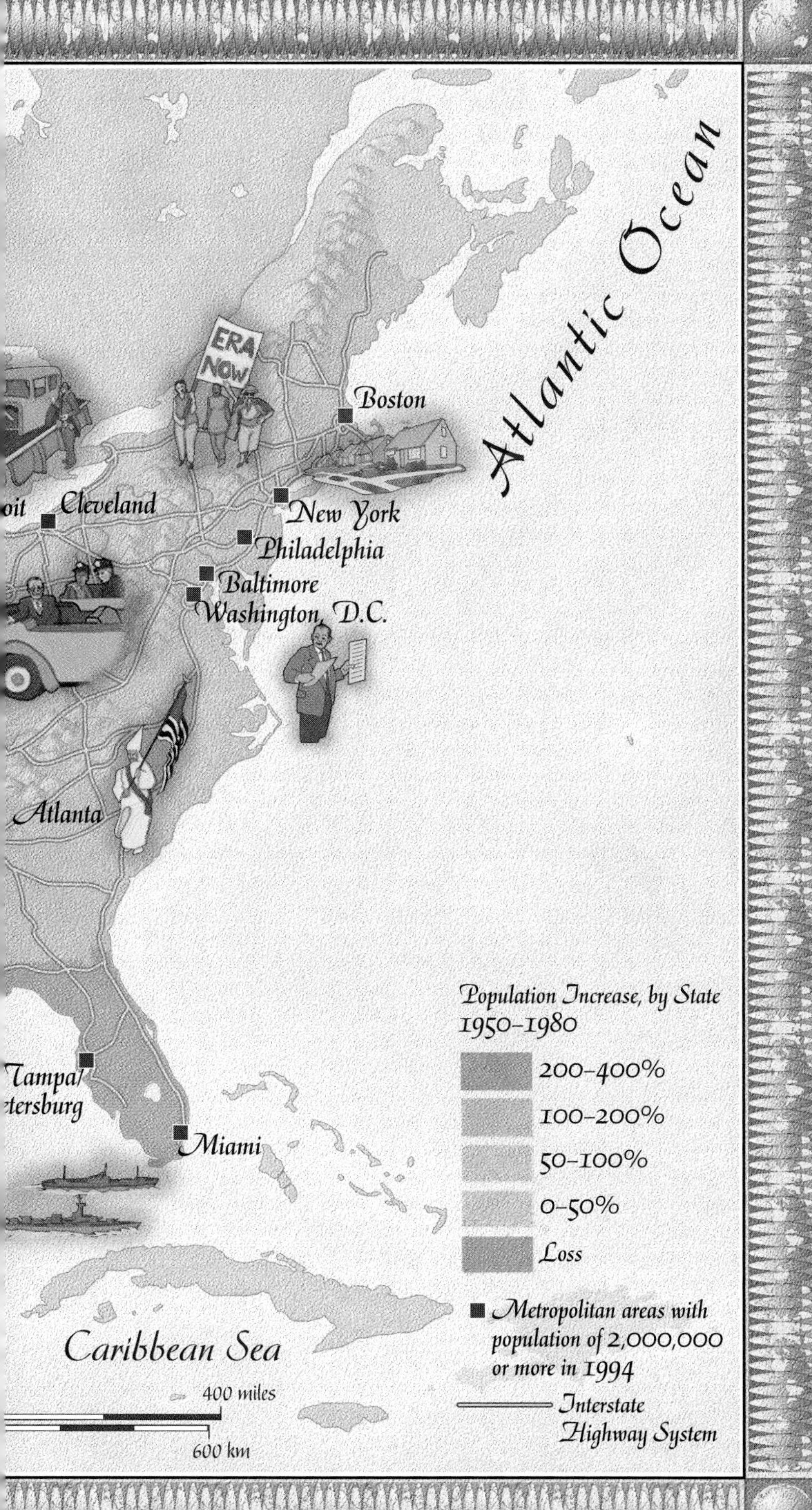

Chapter Outline

Key Topics

- ❖ Changes in immigration policy and the resulting new wave of immigration from Latin America, the Caribbean, and Asia after 1965
- ❖ The effect of global competition on the U.S. economy
- ❖ The shift from the Rustbelt to the Sunbelt
- ❖ The changing role of women
- ❖ The culture wars

In June 1992, Hiroshi Yamauchi paid $100 million for a controlling interest in the Seattle Mariners baseball team, using a fortune acquired as head of American-based but Japanese-owned Nintendo America. The purchase of the M's demonstrated the growing international dimension of American society. So did other aspects of professional baseball, such as the prominence of players from Latin America, the 1993 World Series victory of Canada's Toronto Blue Jays, and a Baltimore Orioles exhibition game in Havana in 1999, and major league games played in Japan in 2000.

Globalization is not the only way that baseball has responded to changes in the United States. Starting in 1958, when the New York Giants moved to San Francisco and the Brooklyn Dodgers to Los Angeles, the big leagues followed population and business southward and westward, adding teams in cities such as San Diego, Atlanta, and Miami to balance old factory towns like Milwaukee and Detroit. In 1994–1995, a long players' strike mirrored renewed labor–management battles in other industries. Baltimore, Cleveland, San Francisco, and Denver joined the national shift from manufacturing to service employment by leveling old warehouses and factories to build downtown stadiums that could boost tourism and convention business.

Baseball's new look was part of a broad transformation of American society after 1965. After twenty years of relative social and economic stability, seeds of change that were sown in the Eisenhower and Kennedy years began to blossom. Just as the nation entered a decade of political turmoil, Americans reopened basic questions about their personal lives and communities. Who constituted the American people? What were the best ways to earn a living and the preferred places to live? Where could individuals find a sense of reassurance in troubled times? The answers were different by the 1980s and 1990s than they had been in the 1950s; the new voices and ideas were unsettling, but they were also proof of the strength of American democracy.

A globalizing economy was one powerful engine of change. As leader of the Western nations, the United States opened itself to a world developing beyond American control. Immigration reshaped and revitalized cities. Foreign competition accelerated the transition from old industries to new. One effect was to decentralize the United States: Central cities declined relative to their suburbs; the Northeast declined relative to the South and West; mass-production manufacturing declined relative to competitors in Asia and Latin America.

Americans also explored new ways to find their identity as individuals and members of groups. The outcome of such profound questioning was decentering—an erosion of the unspoken assumption that tight, white, middle-class families were the national norm. Growing immigration made the benefits and perils of a multicultural society a topic of concern. As the new economy made it difficult for a single wage earner to support a family, individuals increasingly defined themselves not only as fathers, mothers, and children but also by age group, gender, and sexual orientation. Millions of Americans followed old or new avenues to spiritual assurance and a sense of community, generating conflicts over cultural values that entered the political arena as battles over affirmative action, abortion, or religion in the schools.

A Globalized America

In the years after 1965, the United States reacquainted itself with the world. Nineteenth-century America depended on Europe for immigrants, investment capital, and markets for raw materials, only to turn a cold shoulder to much of the world through high tariffs and immigration restrictions after World War I. Since 1965, however, the United States has built new international connections at every level from the corporate to the personal.

A few examples show the extent of the change. Foreign tourism became big business, exploding from a few hundred thousand annual visitors from outside North America in the 1950s to 20 million a year in the mid-1990s. Thousands of cities

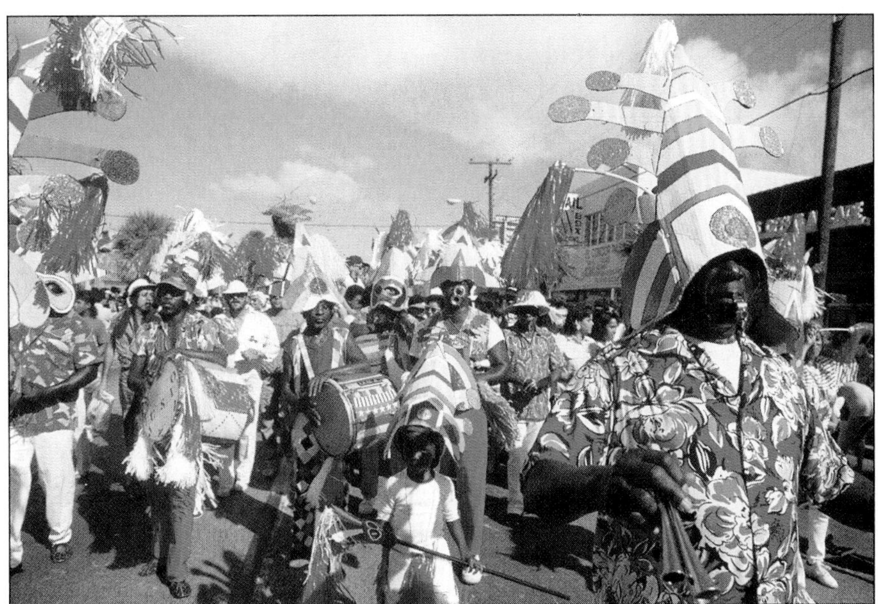

Costumed dancers celebrate during Carnaval Miami along Calle Ocho, or Eighth Street. The two-week celebration of Hispanic culture includes parades and open air performances. The event is typical of the revival of ethnic community culture with the new immigration of the late twentieth century.

and towns now maintain "sister city" exchanges with communities around the globe. Governors and mayors jet off to Seoul and Shanghai on development junkets. Foreign involvement in the U.S. economy benefits New York and San Francisco but also such unexpected places as Greenville and Spartanburg, South Carolina, deeply American communities where the chamber of commerce rolls out the red carpet for German executives and forty thousand residents work for European corporations.

New Americans

Few Americans anticipated the effects of the **Immigration and Nationality Act of 1965**. The new law initiated a change in the composition of the American people by abolishing the national quota system in effect since 1924. Quotas had favored immigrants from western Europe and limited those from other parts of the world. The old law's racial bias contradicted the self-proclaimed role of the United States as a defender of freedom, making immigration reform an episode in the propaganda battles of the Cold War. The new law gave preference to family reunification and welcomed immigrants from all nations equally. The United States also accepted refugees from communism outside the annual limits.

Immigration reform opened the doors to Mediterranean Europe, Latin America, and Asia. Legal migration to the United States surged from 1.1 million in 1960–1964 to nearly 4 million in 1990–1994. Nonlegal immigrants may have doubled the total number of newcomers in the 1970s and early 1980s. Not since World War I had the United States absorbed so many new residents from other countries. By the early 1990s, legal immigration accounted for 37 percent of all American population growth, compared with 10 percent before 1965. Meanwhile, over 2 million nonlegal immigrants had taken advantage of the **Immigration Reform and Control Act of 1986** to legalize their presence in the United States.

Immigration changed the nation's ethnic mix. Members of officially defined ethnic and racial minorities accounted for one out of every four Americans in 1990. Roughly 20 million Americans had been born in other countries. Asians and Hispanics were the fastest-growing groups. Hispanics are likely to pass African Americans as the largest minority in a decade or two (see Table 32-1).

New immigrant groups did not distribute themselves evenly across American states and regions (see Map 32-1). Most Mexican immigrants moved to the states adjacent to Mexico. The East Coast has meanwhile welcomed migrants from the West Indies and Central America. Many Puerto Ricans, who hold U.S. citizenship, came to Philadelphia and New York in the 1950s and 1960s. The 110th Street subway station in East Harlem marked the center of *El Barrio de Nueva York* for that city's 600,000 Puerto Ricans. Other countries sending large numbers of immigrants include Haiti, the Dominican Republic, Guatemala, Honduras, Nicaragua, El Salvador, and Jamaica. Many immigrants have come as tourists and stayed to live and work in the anonymity of large cities.

In contrast to Puerto Ricans and Mexicans, who can easily travel back and forth between their old and new homes, Cubans have been one-way migrants. Fidel Castro's Cuban revolution pushed 250,000 Cuban businessmen, white-collar workers, and their families to the United States. As many as six planeloads a day touched down in Miami from 1959 to 1962. Another round of "freedom flights" carried 150,000 Cubans to the United States from 1966 to 1973, and a third round added 125,000 in

TABLE 32.1

MAJOR RACIAL AND ETHNIC MINORITIES IN THE UNITED STATES

	1960 Population (in millions)	Percentage of total	1990 Population (in millions)	Percentage of total
American Indians	.5	0.3	2.0	0.8
Asians and Pacific Islanders	1.1	0.6	7.3	2.9
African Americans	18.9	10.5	30.0	12.1
Hispanics	not available		22.4	9.0

1980. Virtually all Cubans settled in Florida or in major cities, such as New York and Chicago.

Another great immigration has occurred eastward across the Pacific. Chinese, Filipinos, Koreans, Samoans, and other Asians and Pacific Islanders constituted only 6 percent of newcomers to the United States in 1965 but nearly half of all arrivals in 1990.

The numbers of ethnic Chinese in the United States jumped from a quarter of a million in 1965 to 1,645,000 in 1990. Immigrants from Taiwan, Hong Kong, and the People's Republic created new Chinatowns in Houston and San Diego and crowded into the historic Chinatowns of New York and San Francisco. Social and economic divisions appeared between upwardly mobile and assimilating students and professionals, Chinatown businessmen, and isolated immigrant workers in sweatshops and service jobs.

The most publicized Asian immigrants were refugees from Indochina after communist victories in 1975. The first arrivals tended to be highly educated professionals who had worked with the Americans. Another 750,000 Vietnamese, Laotians, and Cambodians arrived after 1976 by way of refugee camps in Thailand. Most settled on the West Coast. The San Francisco Bay area, for example, had more than a dozen Vietnamese-language newspapers, magazines, and cable television programs.

The United States has provided economic opportunity for millions of newcomers. More than half the Cuban households in Miami are homeowners. The 130,000 Vietnamese immigrants of 1975 now have an average adjusted income above the national average. Asians in the early 1980s constituted 20 percent of the students in California's public universities and were moving into the professions. Many black West Indians, Asians, and second-generation Mexicans are now comfortable members of the middle class (see "American Views: Growing Up Mexican American").

The new immigration spread entrepreneurial talent and ambition throughout the country. Like earlier European immigrants, many newcomers have opened groceries, restaurants, and other businesses that serve their own group before expanding into larger markets. Juan Fernandez found it easier to set up a successful car repair shop in Gary, Indiana, than in Guadalajara, Mexico, because his fellow immigrants prefer a Spanish-speaking mechanic. Asian-born business owners have filled retail vacuums in central city neighborhoods abandoned by chain stores. One Korean told a typical story: "A friend of mine came over with his family. He invested a few dollars in a vegetable stand in downtown Manhattan. He and his sons got up early, went to the market early. . . . He took some of his earnings and invested in a candy store. Then he bought two more vegetable and fruit stands. . . . Their kids work hard too and they make a lot of money."

In the World Market

Expanding foreign commerce became a deliberate goal of national policy with the **General Agreement on Tariffs and Trade (GATT)** in 1947. GATT regularized international commerce after World War II and helped ensure that world markets remained open to American industry. The Trade Expansion Act in 1962 authorized President Kennedy to make reciprocal trade agreements to cut tariffs by up to 50 percent to keep American companies competitive in the new European Common Market. Although both measures were aimed at trade with Europe, they also helped expand American commerce across the Pacific.

The value of American imports and exports more than doubled from 7 percent of the gross domestic product in 1965 to 16 percent in 1990—the largest percentage since World War I. Americans in the 1970s began to worry about a "colonial" status in which the United States exported food, lumber, and

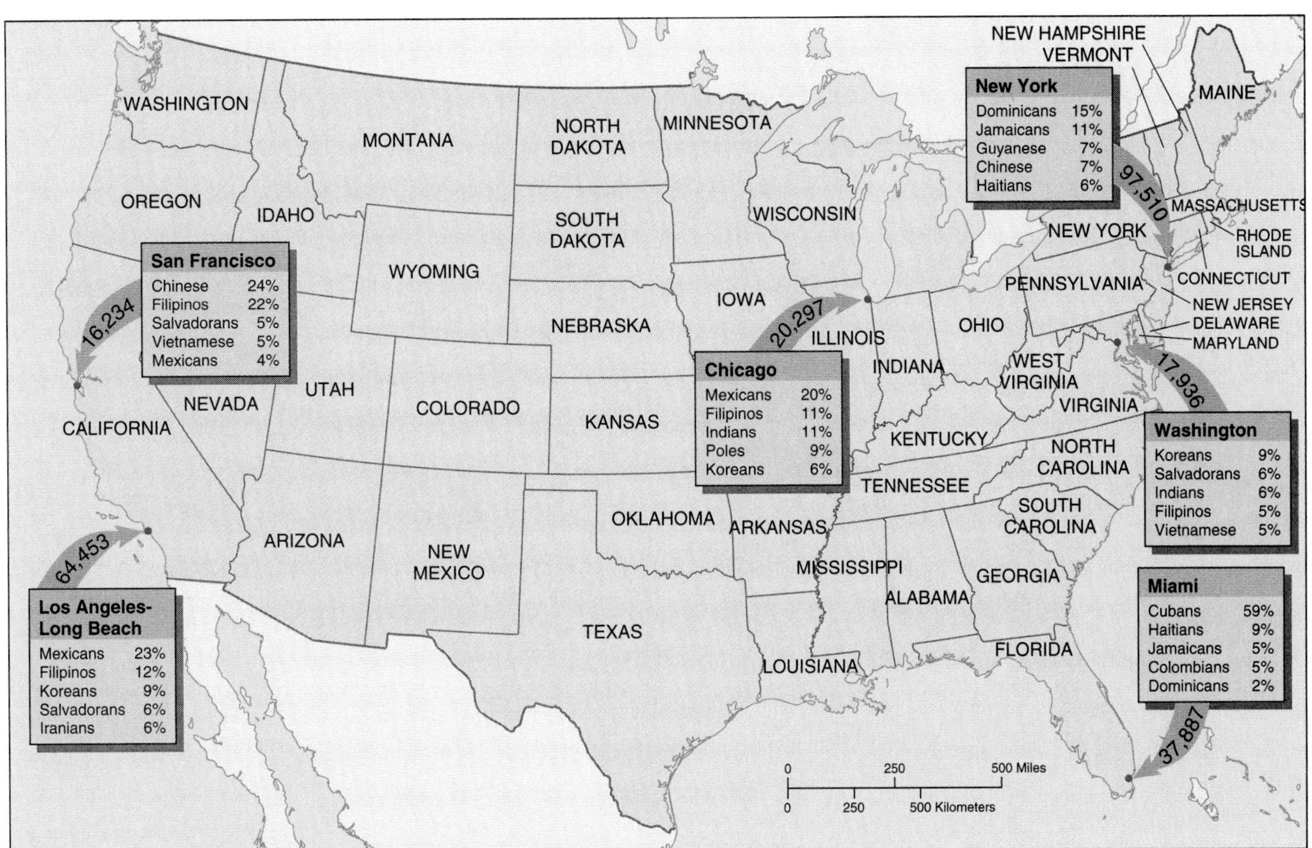

Map 32-1 Sources of Immigrants to Six Major Metropolitan Areas in 1987
Immigrants to the United States in the 1980s and 1990s largely settled in large cities. This map shows the sources of immigrants to six major metropolitan areas for a typical year. Immigrants tend to settle in cities that are convenient to their homelands and already have large communities from the same country. Note the contrast between San Francisco's attractiveness for Asian immigrants and Miami's popularity with immigrants from the Caribbean nations.
Data Source: Ruben Rumbaut and Alejandro Portes, Immigrant America, *1990.*

minerals and imported automobiles and television sets. By the 1980s, foreign economic competitiveness and trade deficits, especially with Japan, became issues of national concern.

The effects of international competition were more complex than "Japan-bashers" acknowledged. Mass-production industries, such as textiles and aluminum, suffered from cheaper and sometimes higher-quality imports, but many specialized industries and services—such as Houston's oil equipment and exploration firms—thrived. Globalization also created new regional winners and losers. In 1982, the United States began to do more business with Pacific nations than with Europe.

More recent steps to expand the global reach of the American economy were the **North American Free Trade Agreement (NAFTA)** in 1993 and a new worldwide GATT approved in 1994. Negotiated by Republican George Bush and pushed through Congress in 1993 by Democratic Bill Clinton, NAFTA combined 25 million Canadians, 90 million Mexicans, and 250 million U.S. consumers in a single "common market" similar to that of western Europe. GATT cut tariffs among one hundred nations.

NAFTA revived the old debate between free traders and protectionists. Support was strongest from professional businesses and industries that sought foreign customers, including agriculture and electronics. Opponents included organized labor, communities already hit by industrial shutdowns, and environmentalists worried about lax regulations in Mexico. In contrast to the nineteenth-century arguments for protecting infant industries, new industries now looked to foreign markets, while older and uncompetitive firms hoped for protected domestic markets. Evidence from the early years favored NAFTA supporters, indicating that few manufacturing jobs relocated to Mexico.

Chronology

1960 Birth control pill is marketed.

1962 *Baker* v. *Carr* establishes the principle of "one person, one vote" for creating state legislative districts.

1963 Betty Friedan publishes *The Feminine Mystique.*

1964 Beatles make first visit to the United States.

1965 Immigration reform eases immigration for Asians and Latin Americans.

1966 National Organization for Women is founded.

1969 Stonewall Inn riot opens era of gay militancy.

1971 Twenty-Sixth Amendment lowers the voting age to eighteen.

U.S. Supreme Court, in *Swann* v. *Charlotte-Mecklenburg Board of Education,* approves busing for racial integration of public schools.

Walt Disney World opens near Orlando, Florida.

1972 Equal Rights Amendment is sent to the states for ratification.

1973 *Roe* v. *Wade* decision expands abortion rights.

1975 Busing plan is implemented to integrate Boston public schools.

1978 People's Temple adherents commit mass suicide at Jonestown, Guyana.

1981 AIDS is recognized as new disease.

1982 Equal Rights Amendment fails to achieve ratification.

1986 Immigration Reform and Control Act regularizes illegal immigration.

1993 Branch Davidian followers die in flames at Waco, Texas.

North American Free Trade Agreement is ratified.

1996 *Romer* v. *Evans* overturns a Colorado constitutional amendment limiting the legal recourse of homosexuals against discrimination.

Old Gateways and New

The globalization of the United States had its most striking effects in coastal and border cities. New York again became the great mixing bowl of the American population. Between 1965 and 1980, it received a million legally recorded immigrants and between 500,000 and 750,000 illegal newcomers. By 1990, some 28 percent of the population of New York City was foreign-born, compared to 42 percent at the height of European immigration in 1910. Journalist Andy Logan described the new immigrants' impact by the early 1970s: "A third of the children now in the city's public schools are said to be the children of parents who were born in other countries. . . . Whole areas of the city, such as Washington Heights, in Manhattan, and Elmhurst, in Queens, would be half empty without the new arrivals." ZIP code 11373 in North Queens was reportedly the most diverse neighborhood in the world.

Just as important was the transformation of southern and western cities into gateways for immigrants from Latin America and Asia. Los Angeles emerged as "the new Ellis Island." As *Time* magazine put it in 1983, the arrival of more than 2 million immigrants in greater Los Angeles altered "the collective beat and bop of L.A." In 1960, a mere 1 percent of the Los Angeles County population was Asian and 11 percent was Hispanic. By 1990, the figures for a population of 8.8 million were 11 percent Asian and 37 percent Hispanic. The sprawling neighborhoods of East Los Angeles make up the second-largest Mexican city in the world. New ethnic communities appeared in Los Angeles suburbs—Iranians in Beverly Hills, Chinese in Monterey Park, Japanese in Gardena, Thais in Hollywood, Samoans in Carson, Cambodians in Lakewood. A hundred languages are spoken among students entering Los Angeles schools.

New York and Los Angeles are world cities as well as immigrant destinations. Like London and Tokyo, they are capitals of world trade and finance, with international banks and headquarters of multinational corporations. They have the country's greatest concentrations of international lawyers, accounting firms, and business consultants. The deregulation of international finance and the explosive spread of instant electronic communication in the 1980s confirmed their importance as global decision centers.

Smaller international cities dot the southern border of the United States. Latin American connections have altered the character of Miami, where Hispanics now constitute nearly half of the metropolitan-area population. Cubans by the late 1970s owned about one-third of the area's retail stores and many of its other businesses. Access to the Caribbean and South America make Miami an international banking and commercial center with hundreds of offices for corporations engaged in U.S.–Latin American trade. Two million Latin American tourists and shoppers a year patronized its stores and hotels during the 1980s. Miami is the economic capital of the Caribbean.

Cross-border communities in the Southwest, such as El Paso, Texas, and Juarez, Mexico, or San Diego, California, and Tijuana, Mexico, are "Siamese twins joined at the cash register." Employees with work permits commute from Mexico to the United States. American popular culture flows southward. Bargain hunters and tourists pass in both directions. A shopping center near San Diego makes 60 percent of its sales to Mexicans. In the other direction, most of the signs for roadside attractions for two hours south from Tijuana read in English rather than Spanish.

Both nations have promoted the cross-border economy. The Mexican government in the mid-1960s began to encourage a "platform economy" by allowing companies on the Mexican side of the border to import components and inputs duty-free as long as 80 percent of the items were reexported and 90 percent of the workers were Mexicans. The intent is to encourage American corporations to locate assembly plants south of the border. Such factories can employ lower-wage workers and avoid strict antipollution laws (leading to serious threats to public health on both sides of the border). For Mexico, the so-called *maquila* industries were the second-largest earner of foreign exchange by 1990. From the Gulf of Mexico to the Pacific Ocean, eighteen hundred *maquiladora* plants employed half a million workers. North of the border, U.S. factories supplied components under laws that meshed with the Mexican regulations.

Ethnic Identity and Conflict

Despite its positive economic contributions, the new immigration revived old American racisms and created new racial tensions. It also continued the longstanding process by which immigrants coalesced and identified themselves as members of American ethnic groups.

Some of the deepest conflicts arose between old and new minorities. African Americans have resented special services for political refugees and ambitious immigrants who seem to be shoving their way to the head of the line for economic and political influence. In Miami, Cubans asserted political leverage at the perceived expense of African Americans, who consider Cubans part of the exploitative majority. Black people in every major city have resented Asian immigrant storekeepers who run convenience stores and markets in ghettos, often replacing Jewish retailers as the "middleman minority" between mainstream businesses and African-American and Latino customers. In the Los Angeles riots of 1992, angry black people targeted Korean and Vietnamese shops as symbols of economic discrimination.

White people in the 1980s expressed their own discomfort with the new immigration by moving. In the 1950s, they had fled the growing African-American populations of large cities for segregated suburbs. A generation later, they seemed to be fleeing concentrations of Asians and Hispanics by moving across state borders. Between 1985 and 1990, a net of 1 million white people left the high-immigrant states of New York, Illinois, and Texas. Hundreds of thousands of others left California for "whiter" states, such as Utah, Oregon, and Nevada. These moves may create a new regional pattern in which the ethnically diverse northeast, southeast, and southwest corners of the United States are out of sync with a racially homogeneous heartland.

A second reaction against the new immigration has been discrimination against Latinos. The Immigration Reform and Control Act requires employers to verify the citizenship or immigration status of their workers. Some employers stopped hiring anyone who looked or sounded Hispanic as a way to avoid illegal immigrants. The Immigration and Naturalization Service (INS) under the Reagan and Bush administrations (1981–1993) treated refugees from civil war in El Salvador and murderous dictatorships in Guatemala and Haiti as economic rather than political immigrants; they were denied political asylum and deported. Officials were more likely to grant legal entry to similarly motivated white immigrants from the Soviet Union.

The INS acted while Americans were arguing over the economic impact of illegal immigration. Advocates of tight borders assert that illegal immigrants take jobs away from legal residents and eat up public assistance. Many studies, however, find that illegal immigrants fill jobs that nobody else wants. Over the long run, high employment levels among immigrants mean that their tax contributions through sales taxes and Social Security taxes

American Views

Growing Up Mexican American

Three Americans of Mexican heritage—Richard Rodriguez, Dolores Huerta, and Ana Caballero—recall experiences during their school years that have shaped their identification with American culture and their sense of ethnic identity. Rodriguez grew up in Sacramento, the son of immigrants from Mexico who had found steady jobs. He entered school with limited English; his family spoke Spanish at home. He would become a professional writer and scholar. Huerta's family has lived in the United States for many generations. She grew up in Stockton, California, in the 1950s, became a Chicano activist in college, and served as vice president of the United Farm Workers. Here she recalls two formative experiences from her teens. Caballero's grandparents moved to El Paso in 1958; her father, César, became a successful professional as a library director at the University of Texas–El Paso. She was sixteen when the family was interviewed in the late 1980s.

❖ **How do the psychological pressures on new immigrants differ from those that affect Mexican-American families long established in the United States?**

❖ **Do differences between the stories of Dolores Huerta in the 1950s and Ana Caballero in the 1980s result from their different economic positions or from changes in American society?**

❖ **How does the ability to speak a second language, either English or Spanish, affect each person's sense of identity?**

❖ **What does "being Mexican" mean to each individual?**

Richard Rodriguez

When I first entered a classroom, [I was] able to understand some fifty stray English words. . . . Half a year passed. Unsmiling, ever watchful, my teachers noted my silence. They began to connect my behavior with the difficult progress my older brother and sister were having. Until one Saturday morning three nuns arrived at the house to talk to our parents. Stiffly, they sat on the blue living room sofa. . . . I overheard one voice gently wondering, "Do your children speak only Spanish at home, Mrs. Rodriguez? . . . Is it possible for you and your husband to encourage your children to practice their English when they are home?" Of course my parents complied. What would they not do for their children's well-being?

Again and again in the days following, increasingly angry, I was obliged to hear my mother and father: "Speak to us en ingles" . . . Only then did I determine to learn classroom English. Weeks after, it happened: One day in school I raised my

and payroll deductions more than pay for their use of welfare, food stamps, and unemployment benefits (which illegal immigrants are often afraid to claim for fear of calling attention to themselves). Nevertheless, high immigration can strain local government budgets even if it benefits the nation as a whole. Partly for this reason, 60 percent of California voters approved Proposition 187 in 1994, cutting off access to state-funded public education and health care for illegal immigrants. The mostly white supporters of the measure said it was about following the rules; Hispanic opponents saw it as racism.

In struggling for their place in American society, immigrants have added new panethnic identities to their national identities. In the nineteenth century, English-speaking Americans looked at European immigrants from widely separated regions and backgrounds and saw "Italians" or "Jews." In turn, newcomers found economic and political strength by making common cause across their differences, molding identities as hand to volunteer an answer. I spoke out in a loud voice. And I did not think it remarkable when the entire class understood. . . . At last, seven years old, I came to believe what had been technically true since my birth: I was an American citizen.

Dolores Huerta

When I got to high school, then it was really segregated. There was the real rich and the real poor. We were poor too, and I got hit with a lot of racial discrimination. . . . I got straight A's in all of my compositions. . . . But the teacher told me at the end of the year she couldn't give me an A because she knew that somebody else was writing my papers for me. That really discouraged me, because I used to stay up all night and think, and try to make every paper different, and try to put words in there that I thought were nice. Well, it just kind of crushed me. . . .

I was the only Chicano at Stockton Junior College. . . . I was frustrated . . . because I seemed to be out of step with everybody and everything. You're trying to go to school and yet you see all of these injustices. . . .

Then my mother took me to Mexico City when I was about seventeen. She had never been there either. It was our first trip. But that opened my eyes to the fact that there was nothing wrong with Chicanos.

Ana Caballero and her father, César

Ana: Most of the kids in my high school are Anglo. I'm the only Mexican-American girl on my cheerleading team. I'm the only cheerleader with black hair. . . . There's a lot of competition within the school, but other kids accept me for who I am rather than for my background or nationality.

César: Busing had a lot to do with that. Ana was involved in one of the last phases of court-ordered integration of the schools. . . . There was some tension. But as time moved on, busing has worked really well. . . .

Ana: When I moved to this neighborhood, I felt strange getting started. My first day in fifth grade in the new school, it seemed so different. Not only because they were new kids, but the way they talked. There were so many blondes! Then, when I began to get used to everyone, I was bused to a new school. There were a lot of blondes there, too. But they were the children of doctors and the rich. The way they looked down on certain styles was very upsetting for me. After seventh grade, I started to fit in with them. I became more relaxed. There are a few kids who come from Mexico, so I get to speak some Spanish. . . . I don't speak Spanish as fluently as I should. I'm studying Spanish in school now, because I don't write it well. I was born here, but I'll always feel part Mexican. . . . I think I'll always have a little of both cultures.

Sources: Richard Rodriguez, Hunger of Memory. *Reprinted by permission of David R. Godine, Publisher, Inc. Copyright © 1982 by Richard Rodriguez; Joan M. Jensen, ed.,* With These Hands: Women Working on the Land *(Feminist Press, 1981). Reprinted by permission of the Feminist Press at The City University of New York. Translation copyright © 1981. The Spanish original was first published in La Voz del Pueblo (Nov./Dec. 1972); Al Santoli,* New Americans, An Oral History. *© 1988 by Al Santoli. Used by permission of Viking Penguin, a division of Penguin Putnam, Inc.*

ethnic groups within the U.S. context. Along with Native Americans, newer immigrants have gone through a parallel process. Hispanic activists revived the term *Chicano* to bridge the gap between recent Mexican immigrants and Latinos whose families had settled in the Southwest before American conquest in 1848. Great gaps of experience and culture separate Chinese, Koreans, Filipinos, and Vietnamese, but they gain political recognition and influence if they deal with other Americans as "Asians."

Making a Living

The American economy after 1965 told two stories. Fast-growing "sunrise industries" shouldered aside declining industries making obsolete products. Booming southern and western states stood next to shell-shocked industrial states full of padlocked factories and double-digit unemployment (see Figure 32-1). Yuppies with MBAs steered their BMWs along the fast lane to success while displaced mill

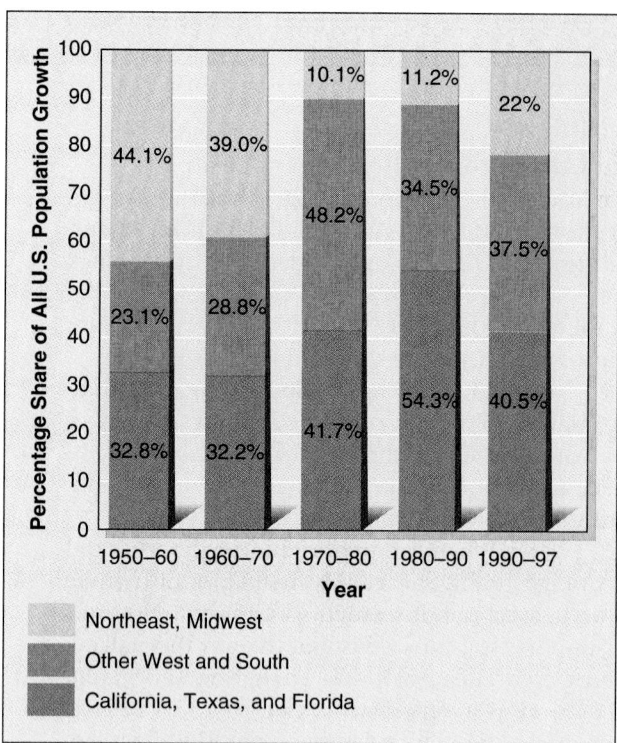

Figure 32-1 ***Regional Patterns in American Growth*** *The regional balance of American growth shifted substantially from the 1950s to the 1980s. The figures reflect the national "tilt" toward the South and West as a result of immigration, defense spending, and new industries such as electronics.*

hands drove battered pickups along potholed roads to nowhere.

Communities divided between white-collar and working-class worlds. Teenagers in Hamilton, Ohio, recognized the social chasm. On one side were kids with new cars and cashmere sweaters, on the other the girls who planned to be beauticians and the boys who expected to work in the plant. One young woman described the country club set: "The girls act like they don't know you if you're not one of them. You don't have their clothes, you're not in their college prep classes, and you better not go out with their brothers. . . . Not one of my ten best friends is going to college."

The winners and losers among industries and the class division between workers and managers were tied to the U.S. role in the world. The need to project an American military presence around the world fueled a prosperous defense economy. Foreign competitors undercut established industries, but markets abroad helped high-end service industries, such as engineering and professional consulting.

The Defense Economy

The Vietnam buildup and reinvestment in the military during the Carter (1977–1981) and Reagan (1981–1989) administrations made the defense budget one of the most direct paths to prosperity. Over the forty years from the Korean conflict to the **Persian Gulf War**, the United States made itself the mightiest military power ever known. Military bases and defense contractors remolded the economic landscape, as mild winters and clear skies for training and operations helped the South and West attract more than 75 percent of military payrolls (see Map 32-2).

Defense dependents included big cities and small. Southern California thrived on 500,000 jobs in the aircraft industry (the 1967 figure). Lockheed's huge Burbank plant drew thousands of families to the San Fernando Valley; McDonnell-Douglas shaped the area around Los Angeles International Airport. Twelve thousand smaller firms and a third of the area's jobs depended on defense spending. Visitors to Colorado Springs could drive past sprawling Fort Carson and visit the new Air Force Academy, opened in 1958. Sunk deep from view was the North American Air Defense command post beneath Cheyenne Mountain. Malmstrom Air Force Base transformed Great Falls, Montana, into a coordinating center for Minuteman missiles targeted at Moscow and Beijing. Dark blue Air Force vans carried crews from Great Falls to missile sites dotted over a swath of rolling plains as vast as Maryland.

Besides the men and women in uniform, defense employed 4 million civilians through federal agencies and military contractors by the late 1960s. The aggregate impact on metropolitan areas can be calculated by subtracting the taxes that go for defense from the amount spent in each area for military payrolls and supplies. Approximately two-thirds of American metropolitan areas came up losers and one-third winners in the late 1970s. The ten biggest gainers included only two in the old industrial belt, compared to eight in the South and West.

Defense spending underwrote the expansion of American science and technology. Nearly one-third of all engineers worked on military projects. Large universities, such as MIT, Michigan, Cal Tech, and Stanford, were leading defense contractors. The modern electronics business started in Boston and the San Francisco Bay Area with research and development for military uses, such as guided-missile controls. The space component of the aerospace industry was equally reliant on the defense economy, with NASA spending justified by competition with the USSR. NASA's centers of gravity were scattered across

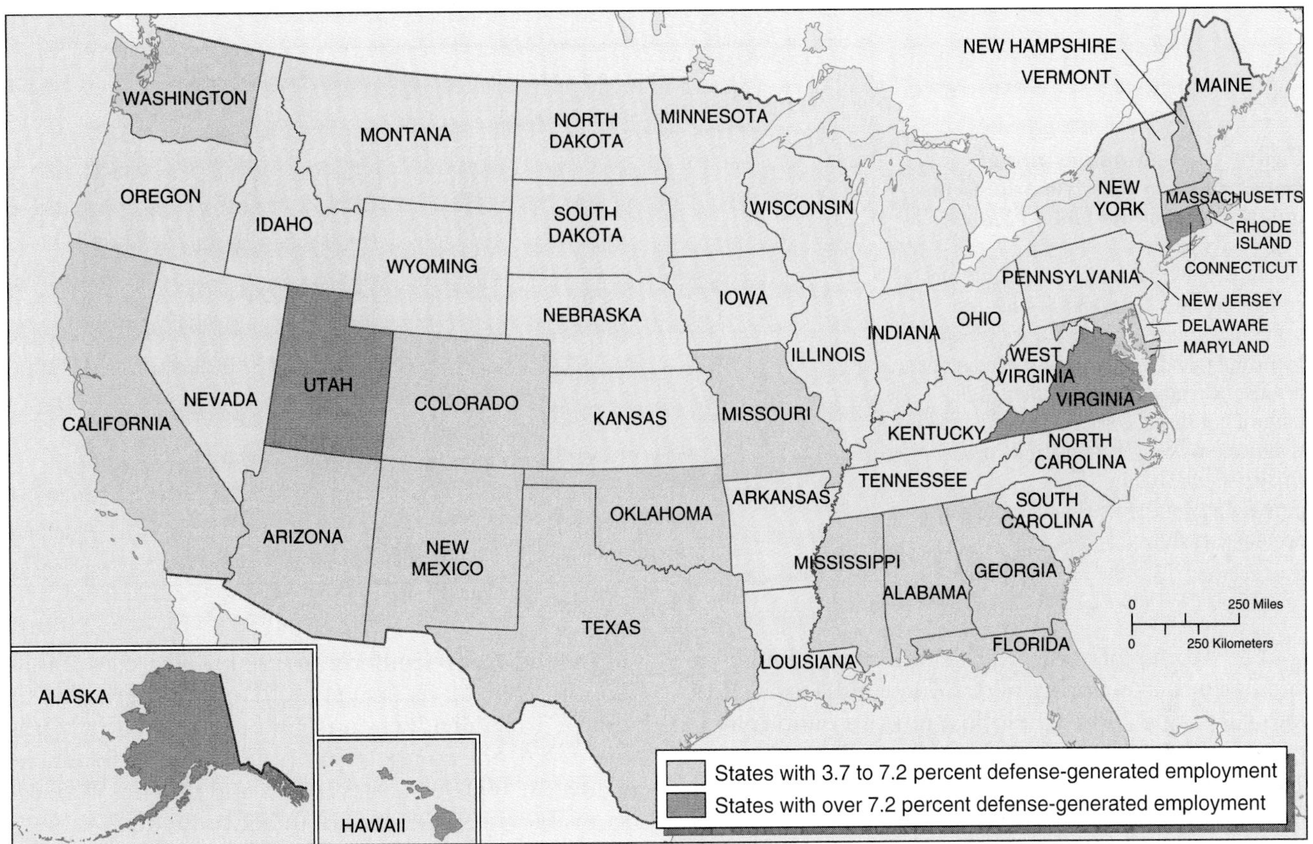

Map 32-2 Defense Dependent States, 1968
The federal defense budget benefited primarily the states of the South and West, helping to fuel the sunbelt boom. This map shows the twenty-one states (and Washington, D.C.) where defense-generated employment exceeded the national average of 3.6 percent of the civilian work force.
Data Source: Statistical Abstract of the United States, 1970.

the South—launch facilities at Cape Canaveral, Florida, research labs at Huntsville, Alabama; and Houston's Manned Spacecraft Center, itself the product of an alliance among Texas politicians, Rice University, and Houston corporations.

Deindustrialization

Here's how novelist John Updike described the fictional city of Brewer, Pennsylvania, at the start of the 1970s:

> Railroads and coal made Brewer. Everywhere in this city, once the fourth largest in Pennsylvania but now slipped to seventh, structures speak of expended energy. Great shapely stacks that have not issued smoke for half a century. . . . The old textile plants given over to discount clothing outlets teeming with a gimcrack cheer of banners FACTORY FAIR and slogans Where a Dollar Is Still a Dollar. . . . All this had been cast up in the last century by what now seem giants, in an explosion of iron and brick still preserved intact in this city where the sole new buildings are funeral parlors and government offices.

Updike's Brewer is like dozens of specialized industrial cities that fell behind a changing economic world in the 1960s and 1970s. Industrial decay stalked "gritty cities" like Allentown, Pennsylvania; Trenton, New Jersey; and Gary, Indiana. Communities whose businesses and workers had made products in high volume for mass markets found that technological revolutions made them obsolete. When radial tires replaced bias-ply tires, Akron rubber workers paid the price. Merchants who replaced mechanical cash registers with electronic models left Dayton with block after block of outmoded factories. Asian steelmakers undercut the aging mills of Pittsburgh and Birmingham. Two dozen metropolitan areas lost population during the 1970s. Critics renamed the old manufacturing region of the Northeast and Middle West the **Rustbelt** in honor of its abandoned factories (see Figure 32-2).

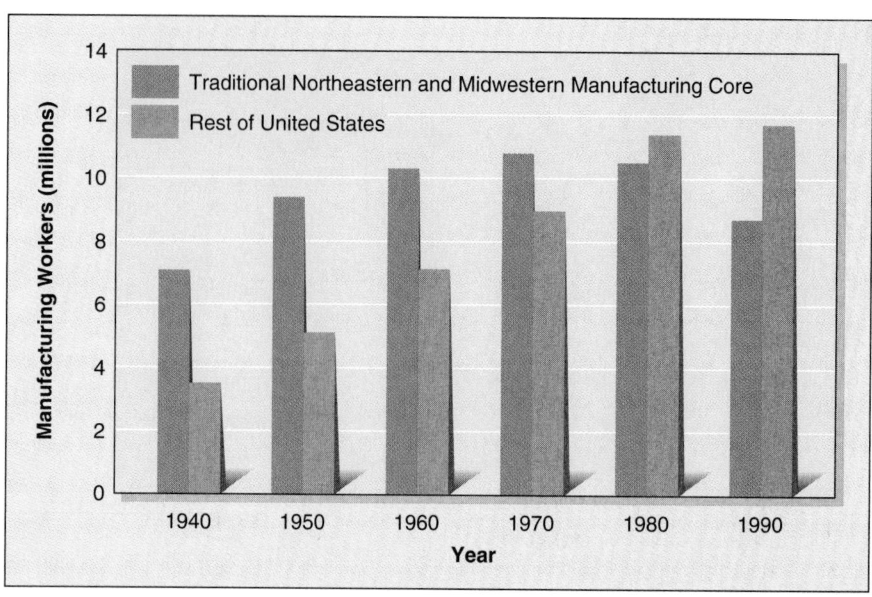

Figure 32-2 Manufacturing Employment in the Industrial Core and the Rest of the United States, 1940–1990
In 1940, the traditional manufacturing core of Northeastern and Midwestern states accounted for two-thirds of manufacturing workers; by 1990 it accounted for just over 40 percent. Although the majority of major corporate headquarters remained in New York and Chicago, cities such as Atlanta, Dallas, and Los Angeles had emerged as new centers of economic power.
Data Source: U.S. Bureau of the Census.

Stories of industrial decline were similar in small cities like Springfield, Ohio, and large cities like Cleveland. Springfield lost ten thousand manufacturing jobs and four thousand people during the 1970s, suffered unemployment of 17 percent, and needed $30 million in public subsidies to keep its largest factory going in 1982. Cleveland had built a century of prosperity on oil refining, steel, and metalworking; the metropolitan area had grown from 1.3 million in 1940 to 2.1 million in 1970. In the 1970s, however, it lost 165,000 people. As high-paying jobs in unionized industries disappeared, sagging income undermined small businesses and neighborhoods. Falling tax revenue brought the city to the verge of bankruptcy in 1978; bankers forced public service cuts and tax increases, which meant further job losses.

Plant closures were only one facet of nationwide efforts to increase productivity by substituting machinery for employees. Between 1947 and 1977, American steelmakers doubled output while cutting their work force from 600,000 to 400,000. Lumber companies used economic recession in the early 1980s to automate mills and rehired only a fraction of their workers when the economy picked up. White-collar industries like insurance computerized operations and farmed out routine work to part-time employees. In the late 1980s and early 1990s, corporations continued to downsize by firing managers who now had fewer workers to supervise.

Parallel to the decline of heavy industry was the continuing transformation of American agriculture from small, family enterprises to corporate "agribusinesses" (see Figure 32-3). The number of farms slid from 4 million in 1960 to just over 2 million in 1998. Many farmers sold out willingly, glad to escape from drudgery and financial insecurity. Others could not compete in an agricultural system in which the 600,000 largest farms and ranches were responsible for 94 percent of total production.

Fewer than 2 percent of all American workers now make their living from farming, down from 8 percent in 1960. Farmers in the Midwest suffered from a roller-coaster economy. Many overinvested in land and equipment when commodity prices climbed in the 1970s, only to be haunted with unpayable debts when prices slumped in the 1980s. Farm bankruptcies in Iowa reached levels unseen since the 1930s. Some family farmers found that they had to farm more acreage to stay competitive; individually owned wheat farms in the western states might total thousands of acres. Other farmers kept their land by working full time in factories and raising crops and livestock on the side.

Corporate farming substituted capital investment for labor in the time-tested manner of industrial maturity. Big farms were also the greatest beneficiaries of federal farm subsidy programs. The downside of corporate investment was excessive irrigation and massive use of pesticides and fertilizers. Wildlife was destroyed, groundwater was contaminated, underground water supplies were exhausted, and flowing streams, such as the lower Colorado River, were polluted with chemical-laden agricultural runoff.

Despite the despairing headlines, some older industries and their workers did find new roles in the sink-or-swim environment of technological and international competition. Buffalo, New York, lost much of its steel industry but retained smaller and more flexible factories making diverse products. The auto industry went through a similar cycle of crisis and response. Prosperity in the 1950s had led automobile executives to believe that they knew how to manipulate U.S. consumers. Booming imports of well-made Toyotas and Hondas and customer demand for smaller cars destroyed that complacency in the fuel-short 1970s. In response, Ford, Chrysler, and finally General Motors remade themselves on the Japanese model as lean and flexible manufacturers. They cast off old plants, workers, and executives, started over, often in new locations, and forced Japanese companies to shift production to U.S. localities and workers.

Sunrise Industries and Service Jobs

Concealed within the story of economic decline was a more complex narrative of changes in the demand for goods and services and adaptation to new markets and technologies. With its fierce competition, the capitalist economy involves what is sometimes called "creative destruction," in which new enterprises push aside inefficient and outmoded industries. After 1965, the pressures for change included both foreign competition and technological breakthroughs that opened new opportunities even while they undermined old industries.

The epitome of the "sunrise" economy was electronics. Employment in computer manufacturing rose in the mid-1960s. California's **Silicon Valley**, north of San Jose, took off with corporate spinoffs and civilian applications of military

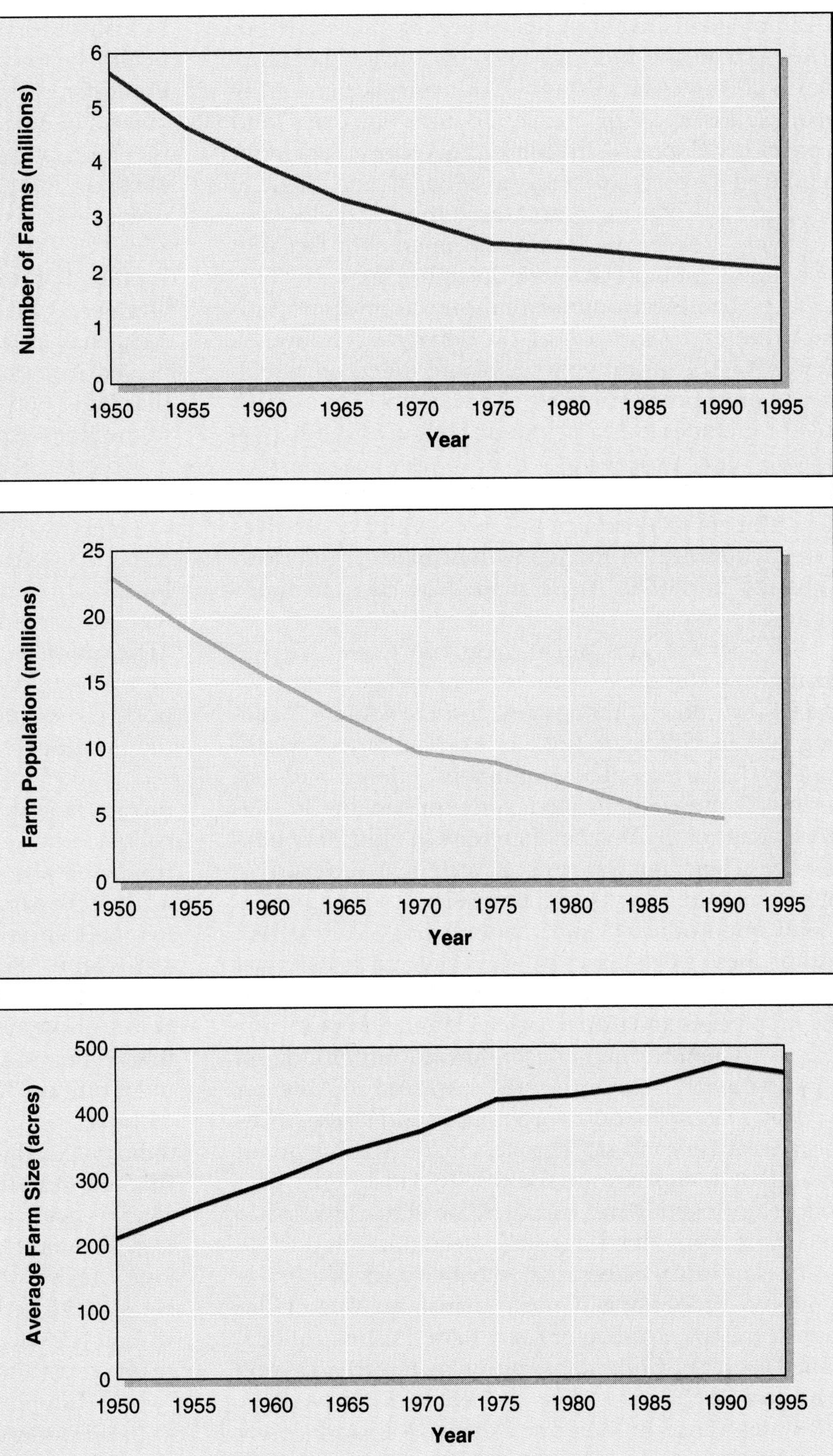

Figure 32-3 **The Transformation of American Farming**
Since 1950, American agriculture has been producing more and more food with fewer and fewer workers. As farm population and the number of farms have dropped, the average farm size has more than doubled. Large-scale agriculture has vastly increased the efficiency of farming at the expense of small family farms.

Data Source: Statistical Abstract of the United States, 1995.

technologies. Invention of the microprocessor in 1971 kicked the industry into high gear. The farmlands of Santa Clara County, California, became a "silicon landscape" of neat one-story factories and research campuses. In 1950, the county had eight hundred factory workers. In 1980, it had 264,000 manufacturing workers and three thousand electronics firms. Related hardware and microchip factories spread the industry through the entire West.

The electronic revolution was an important contributor to the rise of the service economy. As fewer Americans drove tractors and toiled on assembly lines, more became service workers. The service sector includes everyone not directly involved in producing and processing physical products. Service workers range from lawyers to hairstylists, from police officers to theater employees. In 1965, services already accounted for more than half of American jobs. By the 1990s, their share had risen to more than 70 percent.

Service jobs varied greatly in quality. At the bottom of the scale were minimum-wage jobs held mostly by women, immigrants, and the young—cleaning people, child care workers, hospital orderlies, and fast-food workers. These positions offered little in terms of advancement, job security, or benefits. In contrast, many of the best new jobs were in information industries. Teaching, research, government, advertising, mass communications, and professional consulting depend on producing and manipulating information. All of these fields have grown. They add to national wealth by creating and applying new ideas rather than by supplying standardized products and services.

The information economy flourishes in large cities with libraries, universities, research hospitals, advertising agencies, and corporate headquarters. New York's bankers and stockbrokers made Manhattan an island of prosperity in the 1980s. Pittsburgh, with major universities and corporate headquarters, made the transition to the information economy even while its steel industry failed. A good benchmark of a brain-powered economy is if more than a quarter of the adults (people aged 25 or over) have finished college. The District of Columbia, with its high-priced lawyers and lobbyists, ranked first in 1990 with 35 percent. Next was Massachusetts (28 percent), followed closely by California, Colorado, Connecticut, Maryland, New Jersey, Vermont, and Virginia.

The rise of the service economy had political consequences. Rapid expansion of jobs in state and local government triggered popular revolts against state taxes that started in 1978 with passage of California's Proposition 13, which limited property taxes, and continued into the 1990s. Another growth industry was health care. Spending on medical and health services amounted to 12 percent of the gross domestic product in 1990, up from 5 percent in 1960. The need to share this huge expense fairly was the motivation for Medicare and Medicaid in the 1960s and the search for a national health insurance program in the 1990s.

Crisis for Organized Labor

Organized labor counted a million fewer members in 1989 than in 1964, even though the number of employed Americans had nearly doubled. Many unions that had been the mainstays of the labor movement in the Roosevelt and Truman years found themselves in trouble, saddled with leaders who were unable to cope with change. The rank and file in unions like the Steel Workers and Mine Workers had to fight entrenched and unimaginative leadership. Ed Sadlowski, who lost a bid for the presidency of the United Steelworkers in 1976, thought he knew the problem: "The unions missed the boat by not taking unionism beyond the gates and into the community. . . . The pork choppers wanted to become 'part of' rather than 'change' the whole political and social system."

Meanwhile, corporations seized the opportunity for "union busting." They often demanded wage rollbacks and concessions on working conditions as trade-offs for continued employment, squeezing workers in one plant and then using the settlement to pressure another. Hanging over workers in the 1970s and 1980s was the threat that employers might move a factory to a new site elsewhere in the United States or overseas. Or a company might sell out to a new owner, who could close a plant and reopen without a union contract. The wave of corporate consolidations and mergers in the 1980s had especially damaging effects on the workplace. One sixteen-year-old described the changes in the grocery chain where her father worked for twenty-six years: "They're letting people go with no feelings for how long they've worked there, just lay 'em off. It's sad. He should be getting benefits after all these years and all the sacrifices he's made. Now they're almost ready to lay him off without a word."

Immigration, both legal and illegal, added to the numbers of nonunion workers. In the Southwest, for example, low-paid immigrants filled the workforces of the electronics and garment industries. People in Silicon Valley knew the electronics company Hewlett-Packard as "Little Vietnam" in the mid-1980s and Advanced Micro Devices as "Little Manila." By one estimate, two-thirds of the workers in the Los Angeles garment trade were undocumented immigrants. Most worked for small, nonunion firms in basements and storefronts, without health insurance or pensions.

Another cause for shrinking union membership was the overall decline of blue-collar jobs—from 36 percent of the American work force in 1960 to 25 percent in 1997. Unionization of white-collar workers made up only part of the loss from manufacturing. Unions were most successful recruiting government workers, such as police officers, teachers, and bus drivers. By the late 1980s, the American Federation of State, County, and Municipal Employees had twice the membership of the United Steel Workers. In the private sector, however, many white-collar jobs were in small firms and offices that were difficult to organize. In the 1990s, microcomputers and electronic communication allowed companies to create even greater barriers to unionization by turning many of their employees into part-timers or home-based workers paid by output rather than hours.

The union effort that best recaptured the crusading spirit of earlier generations and partly renewed the labor movement was the United Farm Workers, led by César Chávez. Committed to nonviolent action for social justice and to the labor movement, Chávez organized the UFW among Mexican-American farm workers in California in 1965. Their demands included better wages and safer working conditions, such as less exposure to pesticides. UFW Vice President Dolores Huerta spoke for the special needs of women who labored in the fields. Because farm workers were not covered by the National Labor Relations Act of 1935, the issue was whether farm owners would recognize the union as a bargaining agent and sign a contract. Chávez supplemented work stoppages with national boycotts against table grapes, lettuce, and certain brands of wine, making *la huelga* ("the strike") into *la causa* for urban liberals. Rival organizing by the Teamsters Union and the short attention span of the national public gradually undermined the UFW's initial success. Nevertheless, Chávez's dogged toughness and self-sacrifice gave both Chicanos and the country a new hero.

The Rise of the Sunbelt

The rise of the American Sunbelt in the 1970s and 1980s reflected the new economy. In contrast to troubled industrial cities in the Northeast and Midwest, journalists and scholars found headlong prosperity in cities like Orlando, Charlotte, Atlanta, Dallas, and Phoenix (see Map 32-3). Another example was Houston. Its sprawling and unplanned growth, business spinoffs from NASA, and purring air conditioners epitomized the booming metropolitan areas of the South and West. It was, said one reporter in 1976, "the place that scholars flock to for the purpose of seeing what modern civilization has wrought."

The westward and southward tilt dated to the mobilization for World War II, but it caught popular attention with the publication of Kevin Phillips's analysis *The Emerging Republican Majority* in 1969. Phillips described a region of conservative voting habits where Republicans might solidify their status as a majority party (a process that continued in the 1990s). National publications deluged the public with discussions of the Sunbelt's economic and demographic patterns, environmental problems, and impact on the national balance of power.

The Sunbelt benefited from each of the leading economic trends of the years since 1965: Asian and Latin American immigration, defense

Dolores Huerta and César Chávez confer at the 1973 convention of the United Farm Workers. Chávez and Huerta tried to build a union that welcomed workers of all ethnic backgrounds, but the UFW leaders were largely Hispanic, and the union took much of its symbolism from the Mexican heritage shared by most of its membership.

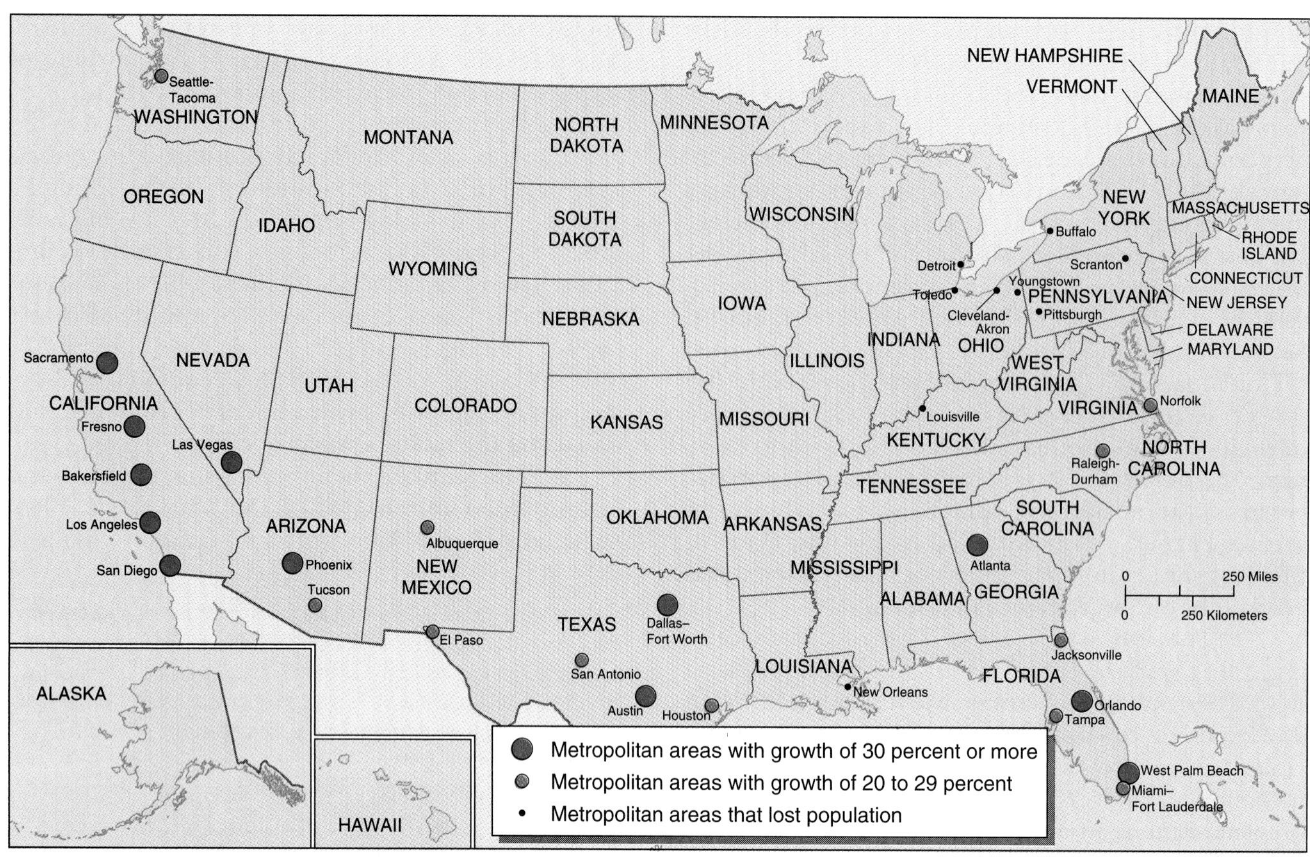

Map 32-3 Fast-Growing and Shrinking Metropolitan Areas, 1980–1990
In the 1980s, boom cities were found in the Southeast, Southwest, and on the West Coast. In contrast, seven of the nine large metropolitan areas that lost population were located on or near the Great Lakes, the region hit hardest by the decline of employment in established manufacturing industries.

spending, high-tech industries, and recreation and retirement spending that supported service employment. The South and Southwest also gained from industrial flight from the Northeast. Corporations that wanted to escape union contracts liked the business climate of the Sunbelt, which promised weak unions and low taxes. New factories dotted the southern landscape, often in smaller towns rather than cities. General Motors closed factories in Flint, Michigan, but invested in a new Saturn plant in Spring Hill, Tennessee.

California, Texas, and Florida anchored the Sunbelt. The common definition sets the regional boundary at the line of state borders that runs along the northern edges of North Carolina, Tennessee, Arkansas, Oklahoma, New Mexico, and Arizona with an extension to include greater Los Angeles. However, at least three other areas have shared the underlying patterns of economic change and metropolitan growth: the Pacific coast from Monterey, California, north to Seattle; the central Rocky Mountains of Colorado and Utah; and the Chesapeake Bay region. These areas enjoy at least two of the three big S's—sun, sea, and skiing.

However, economic shadows cooled parts of the Sunbelt in the 1980s and 1990s. Oil-producing Texas, Oklahoma, and the Rocky Mountain states felt severe recession from declining oil prices in the 1980s. California suffered from defense cutbacks before recovering in the 1990s. Despite the prosperity and global connections of cities like Atlanta, poverty in the rural South remained as bad as in northern slums. Despite the massive shifts of regional activity, in short, the United States remained a society of economic haves and have-nots, of fast-track cities and industries and places left by the wayside.

It was also increasingly decentered and decentralized. Driven in part by new industries, Pacific trade, and non-Atlantic migrations, the rise of the Sunbelt helped open an insular nation to a wider world and to broaden the cultural range subsumed by the word American. Sections of the South and West, historically controlled from the northeastern industrial core, developed as independent centers of

Seattle in the 1980s and 1990s prospered from the globalizing economy and the rise of the information industries. Only oldtimers noticed the disappearance of fish canneries and lumber mills. Taking their place were Boeing, which fueled an international travel revolution; Microsoft, which made Seattle a high-tech capital; and the many foreign companies that used Seattle's port for access to the U.S. market.

economic change. Income per capita in the South neared the national average in the mid-1990s, ending several generations when it was the poor cousin among American regions. In the 1990s, the region's economic power would be reflected in a conservative tone in both the Republican and Democratic parties and in the prominence of southern political leaders.

Cities and Suburbs

Between 1965 and 1990, the proportion of Americans living in metropolitan areas (large cities and their suburbs) rose from 66 percent to just under 80 percent. Despite social problems and racial riots, urban areas remained the centers of commerce and job creation in the fast-changing economy. New businesses benefit from cities' specialized manufacturers and wholesalers. Corporate executives, bankers, and attorneys depend on easy access to each other's expertise. The diverse urban labor force, including millions of immigrants, meet the employment needs of new and old businesses.

Urban growth itself stimulated the economy. As city officials rebuilt urban centers and new suburbs sprawled over surrounding farmland, the United States had to provide freeways, schools, shopping centers, and housing for 66 million new metropolitan residents. It was the equivalent of building an entire new Paris every three and a half years, a new Singapore every thirteen months.

This immense growth also meant decentralization of metropolitan areas that paralleled the regional decentralization of the Sunbelt. Most of the new development pushed the suburban frontier further into open countryside, spreading people and their daily environments more and more thinly over the landscape. Like the Rustbelt in competition with the South and West, the old central cities had to fight to remain viable against the suburban tide.

Urban Crisis

In the confident years after World War II, big cities had an upbeat image. The typical movie with a New York setting opened with a shot of the towering Manhattan skyline and plunged into the bustling business or theater districts. By the 1970s, slums and squalid back streets dominated popular imagery. *The French Connection* (1971) followed a drug dealer from Fifth Avenue to empty and menacing warehouses. *Klute* (1971) and *Taxi Driver* (1976) took moviegoers through the twilight world of prostitution. *Blade Runner* (1982) showed a Los Angeles driven mad by corporate violence and social isolation. Television cop shows like *Hill Street Blues* (1981–1987) and *Miami Vice* (1984–1990) repeated the message that cities were places of random and frequent violence.

Popular entertainment reflected Americans' growing discomfort with their cities. The nation entered the 1960s with the assumption that urban problems were growing pains. Exploding metropolitan areas needed money for streets, schools, and sewers. Politicians viewed the difficulties of central cities as byproducts of exuberant suburban growth, which left outmoded downtowns in need of physical redevelopment. In middecade, however, TV networks and newsmagazines began to run stories of the "Battlefield,

The movie Taxi Driver *(1976), in which Jodie Foster played a young prostitute, showed a New York in which isolated individuals lived out desperate lives within failing communities. It reflected the pessimism with which many Americans regarded not only their cities but their larger society in the 1970s.*

USA" and "Crisis in the Cities" type. The public heard that American cities were sinking under racial violence, crime, and unemployment.

Central cities had the double responsibility of helping immigrants adjust to a new country and caring for the domestic poor. Baltimore had 27 percent of the Maryland population in 1970 but 66 percent of the state's welfare recipients. Boston had 14 percent of the Massachusetts population but 32 percent of the welfare clients. Impoverished and often fragmented families needed schools that would serve as social work agencies as well as educational institutions. Poor people with no other access to health care treated city hospital emergency rooms as the family doctor.

Many urban problems were associated with the "second ghettos" created by the migration of 2.5 million African Americans from southern farms to northern and western cities in the 1950s and 1960s. At the start of World War II, black Americans had been much more rural than white Americans. By 1970, they were more urban. Fully one-third of all African Americans lived in the twelve largest cities, crowding into ghetto neighborhoods dating from World War I.

Postwar black migrants found systems of race relations that limited their access to decent housing, to the best schools, and to many unionized jobs. Many families also arrived just in time to face the consequences of industrial layoffs and plant closures in the 1970s and 1980s. Already unneeded in the South because of the mechanization of agriculture, the migrants found themselves equally unwanted in the industrial North, caught in decaying neighborhoods and victimized by crime.

The residential ghetto trapped African-American families who tried to follow the expectations of mainstream society. Because ghettos grew block by block, middle-class families had to pioneer as intruders into white neighborhoods and then see ghetto problems crowd in behind them. Their children faced the seductions of the street, which became increasingly violent with the spread of handguns and trade in illegal drugs. Successful African-American families began to flee to suburbs when fair housing laws slowly opened the real estate market, leaving ghettos with fewer middle-class leaders.

Central cities faced additional financial problems unrelated to poverty and race. Many of their roads, bridges, fire stations, and water mains were fifty to one hundred years old. By the 1960s and 1970s, they were wearing out. Closure of the elevated West Side Highway along the Hudson River in Manhattan after huge chunks fell out of the roadway symbolized a spreading urban problem. Decay of the urban infrastructure of utility and transportation systems was a byproduct of market forces and public policy. Private developers often borrowed money saved through northeastern bank accounts, insurance policies, and pension funds to finance new construction in the Sunbelt. The defense budget pumped tax dollars from the old industrial cities into the South and West.

High local taxes in older cities were one result, for the American system of local government demands that cities—and the poor—help themselves. By the early 1970s, the average resident of a central city paid roughly twice the state and local taxes per $1,000 of income as the average suburbanite. As Mayor Moon Landrieu of New Orleans commented, "We've taxed everything that moves and everything that stands still; and if anything moves again, we tax that, too."

In part because of their need to increase the value of the real estate on which they collected property taxes, big-city leaders fought back by emphasizing the renewal of downtowns. Office construction booms in the late 1970s and again in the mid-1980s filled skylines with the tracery of steel skeletons and twenty-story cranes. An example of the strategy was Boston. From 1930 to 1960, the city's historic core had attracted virtually no private investment. One banker stated in 1957 that "no one can buy land within the city of Boston, put up an office building, and make money." In the 1960s, the city used urban renewal to level run-down blocks for a new city hall and office buildings. In the 1970s, redevelopment extended to the waterfront, where investors converted nineteenth-century wharves and huge granite warehouses into condominiums and restaurants. The historic Faneuil Hall market reopened in 1976 as an upscale "festival market" for tourists and suburbanites. A private building boom doubled downtown office space. Downtown Boston by 1980 was cramped, crowded, and confusing; it was also a diverse and lively mixture of old and new buildings, districts, and people.

Revitalized cities had clear winners and losers. Obvious beneficiaries were downtown property owners, retailers, metropolitan newspapers, and utilities with huge investments in facilities serving older parts of city. Revitalization also favored managers and professionals who could enjoy the attractions and convenience of strong downtowns. The same benefits largely bypassed men and women who lacked the education the information economy demanded. With fewer unskilled and semiskilled jobs available in manufacturing and construction, undereducated city people either tended the wants of the elite or did nothing. At its worst, the redeveloped city was a community of dangerous extremes, where enormous wealth contrasted with hopeless poverty. In New York, the real incomes of people on the lower third of the economic ladder declined during the 1980s, while those of the top 10 percent rose by 40 percent. Novelist Tom Wolfe fictionalized the cold statistics in his bestselling novel *The Bonfire of the Vanities* (1987), depicting a New York where the art dealers and stockbrokers of glitzy Manhattan meet the poor of the devastated South Bronx only through an automobile accident—to their mutual incomprehension and ruin.

Suburban America

Downtown revitalization ran against the tide of metropolitan sprawl. In the mid-1960s, the United States became a suburban nation. The 1970 census found more people living in the suburban counties of metropolitan areas (37 percent) than in central cities (31 percent) or in small towns and rural areas (31 percent). Just after World War II, most new suburbs had been bedroom communities that depended on the jobs, services, and shopping of central cities. By the late 1960s, suburbs were evolving into "outer cities" whose inhabitants had little need for the old central city. The *New York Times* in 1978 found that 40 percent of the residents of New York's Long Island and New Jersey suburbs visited the city fewer than three times a year, and most denied that they were part of the New York area.

One key to the changing character of the suburbs was a shift in their sources of population. In the first decades after the war, "white flight" described the hundreds of thousands of young families who left old walk-up apartments and row houses for bright new tract houses, distancing themselves from minority and racially changing neighborhoods. After the mid-1960s, however, new residents in a suburban ring typically moved from other suburbs and felt no personal connection to or responsibility for old city neighborhoods. For them, suburban malls and shopping strips were the new American Main Street and suburban communities the new Middle America.

Suburbs captured most new jobs. In the fifteen largest metropolitan areas, the number of central city jobs fell by 800,000 in the 1960s, while the number of suburban jobs rose by 3.2 million. The shift from rail to air for business travel accentuated suburban job growth. Sales representatives and executives could arrive at airports on the edge of town rather than railroad stations at the center and transact business without ever going downtown. The trend was first obvious at Chicago's O'Hare Airport in the 1960s; by the 1970s, every major airport had a fringe of hotels, office parks, and corporate offices.

Suburban rings gained a growing share of public facilities intended to serve the entire metropolitan area. As pioneered in California, community colleges served the suburban children of the baby boom. Many of the new four-year schools that state university systems added in the 1960s and early 1970s were also built for suburbanites, from George Mason University and the University of Maryland–Baltimore County in the Washington-Baltimore area to California State University campuses at Northridge and Fullerton. New sports complexes in the 1980s were as likely to be suburban as urban. The California Angels in baseball and New York Islanders in hockey gave suburban regions exclusive claims to their own major league sports franchises.

In the 1980s and 1990s, suburban retailing, employment, and services fused into so-called **edge cities**. Examples are the Galleria–Post Oak district in Houston and the Tysons Corner area in northern Virginia. Huge complexes of shopping malls, high-rise hotels, and glass-sided office buildings have far more space than old business districts in cities like Fort Wayne or Wichita. Even in edge cities, however, population remained more scattered than in older city neighborhoods. "I live in Garden Grove," one southern Californian reported, "work in Irvine, shop in Santa Ana, go to the dentist in Anaheim, . . . and used to be president of the League of Women Voters in Fullerton."

Suburbs and Politics

Suburban political power grew along with economic clout. In 1962, the Supreme Court handed down a landmark decision in the case of ***Baker* v. *Carr***. Overturning laws that treated counties or other political subdivisions as the units to be represented in state legislatures, Baker required that legislative seats be apportioned on the basis of population. This principle of "one person, one vote" broke the stranglehold of rural counties on state governments, but the big beneficiaries were not older cities but fast-growing suburbs.

School integration controversies in the 1970s reinforced a tendency for suburbanites to separate themselves from city problems. In ***Swann* v. *Charlotte-Mecklenburg Board of Education*** (1971), the U.S. Supreme Court held that crosstown busing was an acceptable solution to de facto segregation that resulted from residential patterns within a single school district. When school officials around the country failed to achieve racial balance, federal judges ordered their own busing plans. Although integration through busing occurred peacefully in dozens of cities, many white people resented it. Working-class students who depended on public schools found themselves on the front lines of integration, while many middle-class families switched to private education. For many Americans, the image of busing for racial integration was fixed in 1975 when white citizens in Boston reacted with violence against black students who were bused to largely white high schools in the South Boston and Charlestown neighborhoods. The goal of equal opportunity clashed with equally strong values of neighborhood, community, and ethnic solidarity.

Because the Supreme Court also ruled that busing programs normally stopped at school district boundaries, suburbs with independent districts escaped school integration. One result was to make busing self-defeating, for it caused white families to move out of the integrating school district or to place their children in private academies, as happened frequently in the South. Busing also caused suburbanites to defend their political independence fiercely. In Denver, for example, a bitter debate lasted from 1969 until court-ordered busing in 1974. By-products included incorporation or expansion of several large suburbs and a state constitutional amendment that blocked further expansion of the city boundaries (and thus of the Denver school district).

Zoning was another powerful tool of suburban self-defense. Restrictive building codes, requirements for large lots, and expensive subdivision fees could price all but the rich out of the local housing market. Many suburbs refused to allow apartments. The various limitations added up to snob zoning. As one Connecticut suburbanite put it, for a moderate-income family to hope to move into one of the state's most exclusive suburbs was "like going into Tiffany and demanding a ring for $12.50. Tiffany doesn't have any rings for $12.50. Well, Greenwich is like Tiffany."

Few suburbs, however, were so privileged. As continued decentralization pushed the suburban share of the U.S. population toward 50 percent in the 1990s, suburban areas displayed the full range of American society. Older suburbs struggled with the same economic problems as central cities, and their minority populations grew. Sprawling new suburbs imposed "urban" costs of traffic congestion and pollution on their residents. As these problems grew, it increasingly appeared that national politics was becoming suburban politics.

New Meanings for American Families

The political and social changes of the 1960s altered the patterns and meaning of family life. Americans began to rethink ideas about families and to emphasize personal identities in addition to traditional family roles. Women redefined themselves as individuals and workers as well as wives and mothers. Gays and lesbians asserted that their sexual orientations were not aberrations from "normal" family patterns but were valid in their own right. As average life spans lengthened, older Americans found personal satisfaction and political influence as members of their own communities and interest groups.

If one result of changing family patterns was new political groupings and new policies, another was deep confusion. In 1992, Vice President Dan Quayle earned headlines, and some derision, by criticizing the television comedy *Murphy Brown* for a positive and unrealistic portrayal of its lead character as a single mother. In the same year, however, opinion pollsters found strong disagreement about what counts as a family. A married couple living with their children was easy; 98 percent of Americans agreed that the label "family" was appropriate in that case. Less reassuring to Quayle was the 81 percent who also applied "family" to the *Murphy Brown* scenario of an unwed mother living with her child. More than a quarter were comfortable using "family" for two lesbian women or two gay men living together and raising children.

The Feminist Critique

The growing dissatisfaction of many women with the domestic role expected of them in the 1950s helped set the stage for a revived feminism. Important steps in this revival included the Presidential Commission on the status of women in 1961; the addition of gender was one of the categories protected by the Civil Rights Act of 1964 (see Chapter 30); and creation of the **National Organization for Women (NOW)** in 1966.

Mainstream feminism targeted unequal opportunity in the job market. Newspapers in the early 1960s segregated help-wanted ads by sex, listing "Girl Friday" jobs in one column and professional work in another. College-educated baby boomers encountered "glass ceilings" and job discrimination in which companies hired less qualified men who "needed the job" rather than more qualified women who supposedly did not. Throughout the 1970s, activists battled to open one job category after another to women who proved that they could indeed use tools, run computers, or pick stocks on Wall Street. They also battled for equal pay for everyone with equal qualifications and responsibilities.

Changes in sexual behavior paralleled efforts to equalize treatment in the workplace. More reliable methods of contraception, especially birth control pills introduced in the early 1960s, gave women greater control over childbearing. In some ways a replay of ideas from the 1920s, a new sexual revolution eroded the double standard that expected chastity of women but tolerated promiscuity among men. Starting in the 1960s, women began to catch up to men by acting as if marriage was not necessary to sanction sexual relations. One consequence was a singles culture that accepted sexual activity between unmarried men and women.

More radical versions of the feminist message came from women who had joined the civil rights and antiwar movements only to find themselves working the copy machine and coffee maker while men plotted strategy. Radicals caught the attention of the national media with a demonstration against the 1968 Miss America pageant. Protesters crowned a sheep as Miss America and encouraged women to make a statement by tossing their bras and makeup in the trash.

Women's liberation took off as a social and political movement in 1970 and 1971. Theoretical works that probed the roots of gender inequality commanded the attention of national reviewers. Women shared their stories and ideas in small "consciousness-raising sessions." *Ms.* magazine gave the movement a national voice in 1972. Within a few years, millions of women had recognized events and patterns in their lives as discrimination based on gender.

Women's Rights and Public Policy

Congress wrote key goals of the feminist movement into law in the early 1970s. Title IX of the Educational Amendments (1972) to the Civil Rights Act prohibited discrimination by sex in any educational program receiving federal aid. The most visible result was the expansion of athletic opportunities for women; another was a slow equalization in the balance of women and men in faculty positions. In the same year, Congress sent the **Equal Rights Amendment (ERA)** to the states for ratification. The amendment read, "Equal rights under the law shall not be denied or abridged by the United States or by any state on account of sex." More than twenty states ratified quickly in the first few months and another dozen after increasingly tough battles in state legislatures. The ERA then stalled, three states short, until the time limit for ratification expired in 1982.

In January 1973, the U.S. Supreme Court expanded the debate about women's rights with the case of ***Roe* v. *Wade*.** Voting 7 to 2, the Court struck down state laws forbidding abortion in the first three months of pregnancy and set guidelines for abortion during the remaining months. Drawing on the earlier decision of *Griswold* v. *Connecticut*, which dealt with access to information about birth control, the justices held that the Fourteenth Amendment includes a right to privacy that blocks states from interfering with a woman's right to terminate a pregnancy. In later decisions, the court upheld congressional limitations on the use of federal funds for abortion in *Webster* v. *Reproductive Health Services* (1989) and allowed some state restrictions in *Planned Parenthood* v. *Casey* (1992). Nevertheless, the Roe decision remained in place.

The feminist movement and specific policy measures related to it put equal rights and the fight against sexism (a word no one knew before 1965) on the national agenda and gradually changed how Americans thought about the relationships between men and women. Feminists focused attention on rape as a crime of violence, calling attention to the burdens the legal system placed on rape victims. In the 1980s and 1990s, they also challenged sexual harassment in the workplace, gradually refining the boundaries between acceptable and unacceptable behavior.

These changes came in the context of increasingly sharp conflict over the feminist agenda. Both the ERA and *Roe* stirred impassioned support and equally

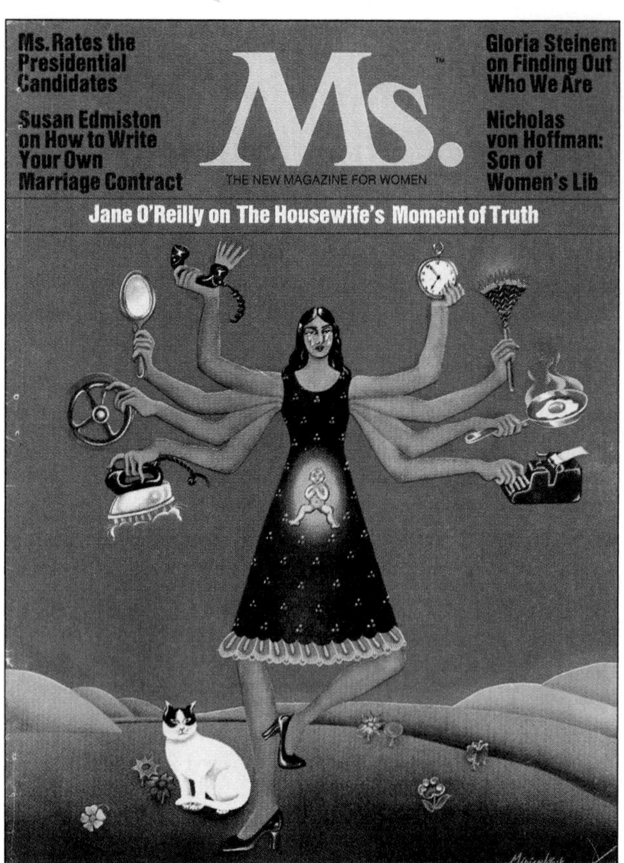

Ms. magazine published its first issue in 1972. Edited by Gloria Steinem, the magazine attempted to bring a radical feminist message to a wide audience. Ms. emphasized the need for women to have equal access with men to education, health care, and employment and tried to help Americans rethink traditional gender roles.

passionate opposition. Opponents of the ERA worried about unisex restrooms (not a problem on commercial airliners) and women in the military (not a problem in the Persian Gulf War). Behind the rhetoric were male fears of increased job competition during a time of economic contraction and concern about changing families. Also fueling the debate was a deep split between the mainstream feminist view of women as fully equal individuals and the contrary belief that women had a special role as anchors of families, an updating of the nineteenth-century idea of separate spheres. The debate about abortion drew on the same issue of women's relationship to families but also tapped such deep emotion that the two sides could not even agree on a common language, juxtaposing a right to life against rights to privacy and freedom of choice.

Women in the Labor Force, Women in Poverty

The most sweeping change in the lives of American women did not come from federal legislation or court cases but from the growing likelihood that a woman would work outside the home. In 1960, some 32 percent of married women were in the labor force; thirty-five years later, 62 percent were working or looking for work (along with 67 percent of single women) Federal and state governments slowly responded to the changing demands of work and family with new policies such as a federal child care tax credit.

One reason for more working women was inflation in the 1970s and declining wages in the 1980s, both of which eroded the ability of families to live comfortable lives on one income. Between 1979 and 1986, fully 80 percent of married households saw the husband's income fall in constant dollars. The result, headlined the *Wall Street Journal* in 1994: "More Women Take Low-Wage Jobs Just So Their Families Can Get By." One young woman juggled community college courses and full-time work as an insurance company clerk, earning more than her husband brought home as a heavy equipment operator. Another worked at the drive-up window of a shopping center bank and cleaned offices on Saturdays to help pay the mortgage on a house purchased before her husband's employer imposed pay cuts.

A second reason for the increase in working women from 29 million in 1970 to 64 million in 1998 was the broad shift from manufacturing to service jobs, reducing demand for factory workers and manual laborers and increasing the need for "women's jobs" like data entry clerks, reservation agents, and nurses. Indeed, the American economy still divides job categories by sex. There was some movement toward gender-neutral hiring in the 1970s because of legal changes and the pressures of the women's movement. Women's share of lawyers more than quadrupled, of economists more than tripled, and of police detectives more than doubled. Nevertheless, job types were more segregated by sex than by race in the early 1990s.

Nor could most women, even those working full time, expect to earn as much as men. In the 1960s and 1970s, the average workingwoman earned just 60 percent of the earnings of the average man (see Figure 32-4). Only part of the wage gap could be explained by measurable factors, such as education or experience. The gap narrowed in the 1980s, with women's earnings rising to 73 percent of men's by 1998. About half of the change was the result of bad news, namely, a decline of earnings among men as high-wage factory jobs disappeared. The other half was the positive result of better-educated younger women finding better jobs. Indeed, women took 57 percent of the four-year college degrees awarded in 1995 (up from 38 percent in 1960) and 41 percent of first professional degrees (up from 3 percent).

Despite gains at the top, the low earning capacity of women with limited educations meant that

FROM THEN TO NOW

Women and Work in American Offices

At the end of the twentieth century, women filled the majority of America's office-based jobs. More women than men worked as office managers, receptionists, library administrators, bank tellers, travel agents, administrative assistants, insurance agents, bookkeepers, and other desk-and-computer occupations.

In 1997, women made up 46 percent of the American labor force. Seven out of ten of these women worked in professional, managerial, technical, administrative support, and sales positions. They ranged from corporate CEOs and college professors to clerks in state motor vehicle offices and the voices that take your orders and reservations when you dial 800.

This employment pattern, which most Americans now take for granted, is the product of 140 years of gradual change that began with, and was triggered by, the Civil War. Before the Civil War, American women found employment as domestic servants, sometimes as mill operatives, and increasingly as schoolteachers, but not as office workers. Clerks were men—sometimes settled into lower-status white-collar careers and sometimes learning a business from the inside before rising into management. Their jobs consisted of copying letters and documents by hand, tracing orders and correspondence, and keeping financial records.

The Civil War, however, sharply increased the flow of government paperwork while diverting young men into military service. The U.S. Treasury Department in Washington responded in 1862 by hiring women to sort and package federal bonds and currency. Treasury officials fretted about the moral implications of mixing men and women in offices but overcame these concerns when they found that women were both cheap and reliable workers. By 1870, several hundred women worked in Washington's federal offices, enough for a character in a novel about the Hayes administration (1877–1881) to comment that he could learn from a glance to "single out the young woman who supported her family upon her salary, and the young woman who bought her ribbons with it; the widow who fed half-a-dozen children."

As the national economy grew in the late nineteenth century, it generated ever-increasing flows of information. New technologies such as telephones and typewriters routinized clerical work. These trends increased the need for desk workers, a need largely filled by middle-class women, whose literacy was often guaranteed by the high school diplomas that went disproportionately to women in the later nineteenth century. As women workers filled new downtown skyscrapers, the central districts of large cities lost some of their rough edges and grew more respectable as centers of shopping and entertainment.

Women clerks at the U.S. Treasury Department sort through used greenbacks and check for counterfeit bills. When this picture was taken around 1890, four thousand women worked in federal offices in Washington, leading the way for the shift of most office work from men to women.

By 1900, the division of labor that would characterize the first half of the twentieth century was in place. Women comprised 76 percent of the nation's stenographers and typists and 29 percent of its cashiers, bookkeepers, and accountants. For the most part, however, they occupied the lower echelons of the office hierarchy. It was men who determined what was to be said; women who transcribed, transmitted, recorded, and filed their messages. Only in recent decades have women begun successfully to challenge that established order.

women were far more likely than men to be poor. Women constituted nearly two-thirds of poor adults at the end of the 1980s. Only 6 percent of married-couple households were below poverty level, but 32 percent of households headed by a woman without a husband present were poor. The feminization of poverty and American reliance on private support for child rearing also meant that children had a higher chance of living in poverty than adults and that poor American children were worse off than their peers in other advanced nations.

Coming Out

New militancy among gay men and lesbians drew on several of the social changes of the late 1960s. Willingness to talk about nonstandard sexual behavior was part of a change in public values. Tactics of political pressure came from the antiwar and civil rights movements. The timing, with a series of key events from 1969 to 1974, coincided with that of women's liberation.

Gay activism spread from the biggest cities to smaller communities, from the coasts to Middle America. New York police had long harassed gay bars and their customers. When police raided Manhattan's Stonewall Inn in June 1969, however, patrons fought back in a weekend of disorder. The "Stonewall rebellion" was a catalyst for homosexuals to assert themselves as a political force. San Francisco also became a center of gay life. Its large homosexual community dated to World War II, when gays discharged from the armed forces in the Pacific theater were processed out through San Francisco. Openly gay poets and artists were prominent in the city's avant-garde circles. By the late 1970s, the city had more than three hundred business and social gathering places identified as gay and lesbian.

Figure 32-4 Median Salary of Women and Men, 1960–1998

Since the 1960s, the gap between the earnings of women and men working full time and year round has narrowed. One reason is better pay for jobs traditionally considered "women's work," but another has been the declining earning power of men without college educations. Nevertheless, the gender gap in earning power remains an important economic problem.

Data Source: Institute for Women's Policy Research.

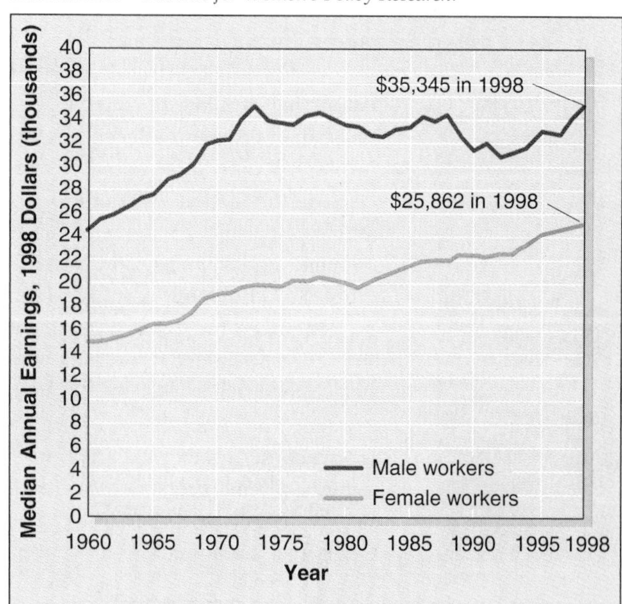

With New Yorkers and San Franciscans as examples, more and more gay men and lesbians "came out," or went public about their sexual orientation. They published newspapers, organized churches, and lobbied politicians. They staged "gay pride" days and marches. In 1974, the American Psychiatric Association eliminated homosexuality from its official list of mental disorders.

The character of life in gay communities took an abrupt turn in the 1980s when the worldwide **AIDS** epidemic began to have an impact on the United States. Scientists first identified a new disease pattern, acquired immune deficiency syndrome, in 1981. The name described the symptoms resulting from the human immunodeficiency virus (HIV), which destroys the body's ability to resist disease. HIV is transferred through blood and semen. In the 1980s, the most frequent American victims were gay men or intravenous drug users. By the end of 1998, AIDS had been responsible for 411,000 deaths in the United States, and transmission to heterosexual women was increasing. The U.S. Centers for Disease Control and Prevention estimated forty thousand new cases of HIV infection in 1995, bringing the total close to 1 million. HIV infection had spread to every American community.

AIDS triggered many of the same intense emotions as polio. It struck people in their prime and gradually wasted their strength; by the early 1990s, it had become the leading cause of death for men aged 25 to 44. Because many gay men were estranged from their families, death from AIDS was often preceded by social isolation. The spread of the epidemic gave new ammunition to people opposed to homosexuality, who called the plague God's punishment. It inspired intense anger among gays who believed that straight society and government agencies were indifferent to their plight and had failed to fund sufficient research on vaccines and treatment, although spending rose substantially in the late 1980s and 1990s. The public health establishment stressed that the most effective preventive measures were changes in personal behavior.

The Graying of America

Between 1965 and 1990, the number of Americans aged sixty-five and over jumped from 18.2 million to 31.3 million. For the first time, most Americans could

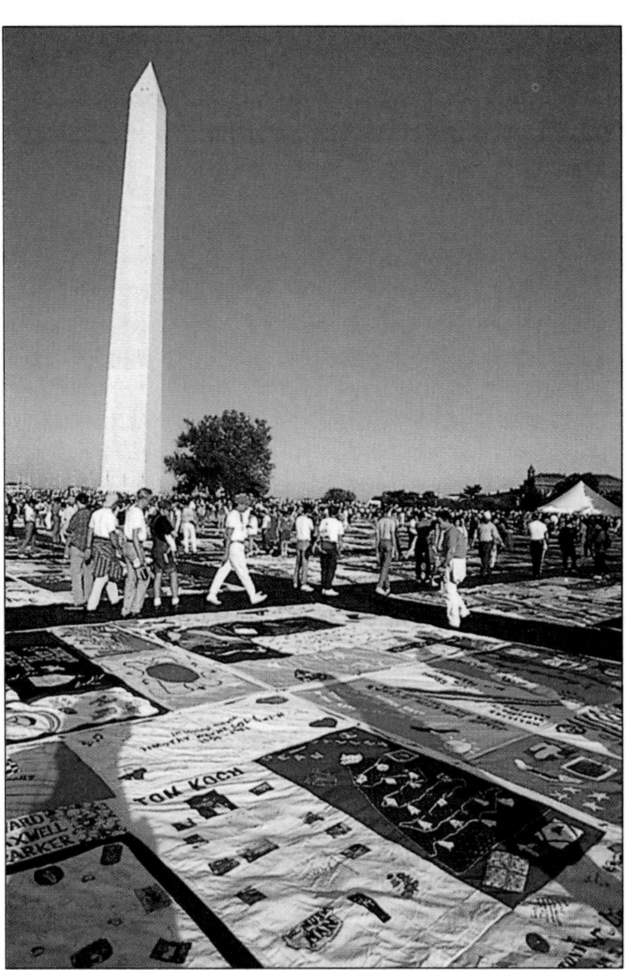

The AIDS Quilt, displayed in Washington in October 1992, combined individual memorials to AIDS victims into a powerful community statement. The quilt project reminded Americans that AIDS had penetrated every American community.

expect to survive into old age. The "young old" are people in their sixties and early seventies who remain sharp, vigorous, and financially secure because of better private pensions, Social Security, and Medicare. The "old old" are people in their eighties and nineties who often require daily assistance. Their increasing numbers—9 million in 1998—have made older and retired Americans both a problem for American society and a force to reckon with.

Older Americans have become a powerful voice in public affairs. They tend to vote against local taxes but fight efforts to slow the growth of Social Security, even though growing numbers of the elderly are being supported by a relatively smaller proportion of working men and women. By the 1990s, observers noted increasing resentment among younger Americans, who fear that public policy is biased against the needs of men and women in their productive years. In turn, the elderly fiercely defend the programs of the 1960s and 1970s that have kept many of them from poverty. Protecting Medicare and Social Security was one of the Democrats' best campaign issues in 1996 after Republicans suggested cuts in spending growth.

Retired Americans changed the social geography of the United States, moving steadily to attractive Sunbelt communities. Much growth in the South and Southwest has been financed by money earned in the Northeast and Midwest and transferred by retirees. Florida in the 1980s absorbed nearly 1 million new residents aged sixty or older. California, Arizona, Texas, the Carolinas, and the Ozark Mountains of Missouri and Arkansas have all attracted retirees.

Sunbelt developers invented age-segregated new towns in the 1960s as full-service environments for people aged fifty or older. The first Sun City opened south of Tampa and another near Phoenix in 1960. Close behind were several Leisure World communities in California. Sun City's physical characteristics and national advertising helped define retirement as a distinct stage of life offering "an unending treasure of perfect days, filled with interesting activities." Attractions included golf, clean air, low-maintenance housing, and an escape from urban minorities. On a smaller scale, thousands of small retirement developments, many church sponsored, offer apartments, assisted living, and health care.

Large or small, these unprecedented developments substitute organized services and voluntary association with other older people for traditional reliance on care within families. The result changed the balance of responsibility for elder care between families and the broader public. In 1968, more than two-middle aged children (aged forty to fifty-five) were available to care for every elderly person; twenty years later, there was fewer than one middle-aged child for each elderly person. With too many elders and not enough adult family members, the elderly increasingly rely on specially designed institutions and communities.

The Search for Spiritual Grounding

Americans picture mining frontiers as rip-roaring places where a handful of women hold the fort while the men work hard, drink deep, and carry on. Modern Grand Junction, Colorado, however, is far less exciting. Between 1980 and 1984, efforts to develop the oil shale resources of western Colorado pushed the population of Grand Junction from sixty thousand to eighty thousand. Hopes were high and money was easy, but there was also a boom in religion. Newcomers to

Grand Junction, a fast-changing city within a rapidly evolving society, searched for family stability and a sense of community by joining established congregations and organizing new churches. The telephone book in 1985 listed twenty-eight mainstream Protestant and Catholic churches, twenty-four Baptist churches (reflecting the Oklahoma and Texas roots of many oil workers), five more liberal churches (such as Unitarians and Bahais), and more than fifty Pentecostal, Bible, and Evangelical churches. Nearly a dozen Christian schools supplemented the public schools.

Grand Junction's religious bent is typical of the contemporary United States, where religion is prominent in daily lives, institutions, and public policy debates. Americans take their search for spiritual grounding much more seriously than citizens of other industrial nations. Roughly half of privately organized social activity (such as charity work) is church related. In the mid-1970s, 56 percent of Americans said that religion was "very important" to them, compared to only 27 percent of Europeans.

Spiritual searches have followed both the well-marked routes of established denominations and new paths through avant-garde philosophies and feel-good therapies. One pathway has led individuals to isolate themselves from the larger society in communities of fellow believers. Another route, strong among many evangelical Protestants, emphasizes the personal search for salvation and individual relationships with God. A third path leads believers to seek to remold American society in accord with their understanding of divine intention.

Communes and Cults

Self-isolating communes and cults represent a long heritage of American utopian communities. Out of the half-secular, half-spiritual vision of the counterculture came people who not only dropped out of mainstream institutions but also tried to drop into miniature societies built on new principles. Thousands of Americans in the late 1960s and 1970s formed "intentional communities" or "communes." Their members usually tried to combine individual freedom and spontaneity with cooperative living. Upper New England and the Southwest were commune country. The northern California coast and the Pacific Northwest were attractive because of their fine climate for growing marijuana. Rural communes usually located on marginal land too poor to support commercial farming; members pored over *The Whole Earth Catalog* (1968) to figure out how to live on the land.

A few communes followed coherent social theories, but most were free form. It is easy to make fun of them in retrospect, with their tepees, log cabins, and eccentric architecture. Children ended up with off-the-tent names like Catnip, Psyche Joy, and Hummingbird. Adults practiced odd combinations of vegetarianism, Asian religion, and campfire sing-alongs. Journalist Sara Davidson described one California commune in 1970:

> Women in long skirts and shawls, men in lace-up boots, coveralls, and patched jeans tied with pieces of rope, sitting on the grass playing banjos, guitars, lyres, wood flutes, dulcimers, and an accordion. . . . Nine-year-old Michelle is prancing around in a pink shawl and a floppy hat warbling "It's time for the feast." Nancy says, "The pickin's are sort of spare, because tomorrow is welfare day and everybody's broke." She carries from the outdoor wood stove pots of brown rice.

As the description implies, communes were artificial families, financed by inheritances, food stamps, and handicraft sales and suffered from the same inequality between men and women that was fueling the feminist revolt. Like natural families, they were emotional hothouses; most collapsed because their members had incompatible goals.

Similar to communes but far more organized were exotic religious communities. Following an American tradition, they have offered tightly knit group membership and absolute answers to basic questions of human life. One of the most successful has been the Holy Spirit Association for the Unification of World Christianity (Unification Church), which Sun Myung Moon brought from Korea to the United States in 1973. Converts ("Moonies") have never numbered more than a few tens of thousands, but Moon amassed a huge fortune and dabbled in conservative politics.

Americans usually hear about cults only if they clash with authorities or end in disaster. Most tragic was the case of Jim Jones, who founded the People's Temple in California on a program of social justice but became increasingly dictatorial and abusive. He moved nearly a thousand followers to Guyana in South America and violently resisted authorities' efforts to penetrate his walls of secrecy. A congressional investigation of abuses within the colony led to the murder of Congressman Leo Ryan and mass suicide by nine hundred of Jones's followers, who drank cyanide-laced punch on November 18, 1978. On a smaller scale was the 1993 siege and shootout at the Branch Davidian compound near Waco, Texas, when a raid and a seige by federal agents triggered a fire that killed dozens of cult members.

Personal Religion

"The sixties" opened Americans to new spiritual experiences. Many young people in their twenties and thirties had left conventional Christian churches but had not

OVERVIEW

RELIGION AND POLITICS

Americans in the 1980s and 1990s battled over abortion, the teaching of evolution, limits to artistic expression, and other social values. Much of the conflict in social expectations and political goals stems from opposing tendencies in religious belief: the traditional impulse versus the progressive impulse.

	The Traditional Impulse	**The Progressive Impulse**
Religious basis	Orthodox theology that relies on unchanging truths and moral traditions	Theology that reconciles belief with findings of science and respects multiple ways to know the divine
Subscribers	Evangelical and fundamentalist Protestants, Orthodox Jews, conservative Roman Catholics	Mainline and liberal Protestants, Conservative and Reform Jews, Roman Catholics influenced by changes introduced by the Second Vatican Council
Social assumption	Traditional family as the basic social unit	Acceptance of diverse groups and treatment of individuals as equal before God as basis for a just society
Moral imperative	Responsibility to order one's personal life in accord with religious teaching	Responsibility to heed scriptural calls to end inequality and social injustice
Political goals	Protection of opportunities for religious expression (such as prayer in schools), protection of rights of individual economic initiative, support for nuclear families	Strict separation of church and state, protection of individual freedom of expression and belief, assistance for the poor at home and abroad
Political technique	Grassroots organizing and campaigning	Legislative lobbying

lost their spiritual hunger. Some turned to Sufis, Zen Buddhists, Hare Khrishnas, and others who adapted Asian religious traditions for modern Americans. The counterculture softened and blended into human potential movements of the 1970s and **New Age** movements of the 1980s. The secular-minded could pursue a quest for fuller lives through vigorously marketed spiritual therapies like est and encounter groups. For understanding American culture, the particular answers are less important than the strength of the search for greater self-realization and spiritual meaning.

One important change in national religious life has been the continuing "Americanization" of the Roman Catholic church following the **Second Vatican Council** in 1965, in which church leaders sought to respond to postwar industrial society. In the United States, Roman Catholicism moved toward the center of American life, helped by the popularity of John Kennedy and by worldly success that made Catholics the economic peers of Protestants. The tight connection between Catholicism and membership in particular immigrant communities gradually faded. Church practice lost some of its distinctiveness; celebrating Mass in English rather than Latin was symbolic of numerous changes that split the church between reformers and traditionalists.

The mainline Protestant denominations that traditionally defined the center of American belief struggled after 1960. The United Methodist Church, the Presbyterian Church U.S.A., the United Church of Christ, and the Episcopal Church battled internally over the morality of U.S. foreign policy, the role of women in the ministry, and the reception of gay and lesbian members. They were strengthened by the ecumenical impulse, which united denominational branches that had been divided by ethnicity or regionalism. However, they gradually lost their position among American churches, perhaps because ecumenism diluted the certainty of their message. Liberal Protestantism has also historically been strongest in the slow-growing Northeast and Midwest.

In contrast, evangelical churches have benefited from the direct appeal of their message and from strong roots in the booming Sunbelt. Members of evangelical churches (25 percent of white Americans) now outnumber the members of mainline Protestant churches (20 percent). Major evangelical denominations include Baptists, the Church of the Nazarene, and the Assemblies of God. Fundamentalists, defined by a belief in the literal truth of the Bible, are a subset of evangelicals. So are 8 to 10 million Pentecostals and charismatics, who accept "gifts of the spirit," such as healing by faith and speaking in tongues.

Outsiders know evangelical Christianity through "televangelists." Spending on religious television programming rose from $50 to $600 million in the 1970s. The "electronic church" built on the radio preaching and professional revivalism of the 1950s. By the 1970s, it reached 20 percent of American households. Americans everywhere recognized the Big Four. Oral Roberts had a television show and Oral Roberts University in Oklahoma. Pat Robertson had the 700 Club and the Christian Broadcasting Network in Virginia. Jerry Falwell claimed leadership of the Moral Majority. Jim and Tammy Faye Bakker had grand plans for real estate development before their schemes collapsed in fraud.

Behind the glitz and hype of the television pulpit, evangelical churches emphasized religion as an individual experience focused on personal salvation. Unlike many of the secular and psychological avenues to fulfillment, however, they also offered communities of faith that might stabilize fragmented lives. The conservative nature of their theology and social teaching in a changing society offered certainty that was especially attractive to many younger families.

Values in Conflict

In the 1950s and 1960s, Americans argued most often over foreign policy, racial justice, and the economy. Since the mid-1970s, they have also quarreled over beliefs and values. Religious belief has reentered politics as individuals and groups try to shape America around their particular, and often conflicting, ideas of the godly society. One expert talks about a division between cultural liberals and conservatives, another about "culture wars" between progressivism and orthodoxy. Americans who are undogmatic in religion are often liberal in politics as well, hoping to lessen economic inequities and

Evangelist and politician Pat Robertson works delegates at the 1988 Republican convention. In the late 1980s and 1990s, evangelical Christians became a major constitutency of the Republican party.

strengthen individual social freedom. Religious and political conservatism also tend to go together. To some degree, this cultural division runs all the way through American society, dividing liberal North from conservative South, cities from small towns, and college professors from Kiwanis Club members (see the overview table, "Religion and Politics").

The division on social issues is related to theological differences within Protestantism. The "conservative" emphasis on personal salvation and the literal truth of the Bible also expresses itself in a desire to restore "traditional" social patterns. Conservatives worry that social disorder occurs when people follow personal impulses and pleasures. In contrast, the "liberal" or "modern" emphasis on the universality of the Christian message restates the Social Gospel with its call to build the Kingdom of God through social justice and may recognize divergent pathways toward truth. Liberals worry that rampaging greed in the unregulated marketplace creates disorder and injustice.

The cultural conflict transcends the historic three-way division of Americans among Protestants, Catholics, and Jews. Instead, the conservative–liberal division now cuts through each group. For example, conservative Catholics, fundamentalist Protestants, and Orthodox Jews may find themselves in agreement on issues of cultural values despite theologies that are worlds apart. The same may be true of Catholic reformers, liberal Protestants, and Reform Jews.

The Reverend Jesse Jackson used his religious training and convictions to good effect in trying to build a "Rainbow Coalition" of politically progressive voters from all ethnic backgrounds.

Conservatives have initiated the culture wars, trying to stabilize what they fear is an American society spinning out of control because of personal sexual indulgence. In fact, the evidence on the sexual revolution is mixed. Growing numbers of teenagers reported being sexually active in the 1970s, but the rate of increase tapered off in the 1980s. The divorce rate began to drop after 1980; births to teenagers dropped after 1990, and the number of two-parent families increased. Most adults remained staid and monogamous, according to a survey published in 1994, but sexual self-help and advice books proliferated. Perhaps the logical extension of reading about sex in the 1970s was an astonishing eagerness to talk about sex in the 1990s, a decade whose soap opera story lines and talk shows covered everything from family violence to exotic sexual tastes.

The explosion of explicit attention to sexual behavior set the stage for religiously rooted battles over two sets of issues. One cluster revolves around so-called "family values," questioning the morality of access to abortion, the acceptability of homosexuality, and the roles and rights of women. The debates are a response to changing personal behaviors and family patterns, such as the large increase in the number of children living with a never-married parent, from 2 million in 1980 to 6.3 million in 1993, although the rate of births outside marriage leveled off in the 1990s. A second set of concerns has focused on the supposed role of public schools in undermining morality through sex education, unrestricted reading matter, nonbiblical science, and the absence of prayer. Opinion polls show clear differences among religious denominations on issues such as censorship of library books, acceptability of racially segregated neighborhoods, freedom of choice in terminating pregnancy, and homosexuality.

Not all issues of the culture wars carry the same weight. Censorship of art exhibits and library collections has mostly been an issue for political grandstanding. U.S. senators grabbed headlines beginning in 1989 by attacking the National Endowment for the Arts for funding "obscene" art, but a local jury in Cincinnati proved tolerant of sexually explicit images in a photographic exhibition. Efforts to restrict legal access to abortion mobilized thousands of "right to life" advocates in the late 1980s and early 1990s, but illegal acts remained the work of a radical fringe. A culturally conservative issue with great popular appeal in the early 1990s was an effort to prevent states and localities from protecting homosexuals against discrimination. Using the slogan "No special rights," antigay measures passed in Cincinnati, Colorado, and communities in Oregon in 1993 and 1994, only to have the Supreme Court overturn the Colorado law in ***Romer* v. *Evans*** (1996).

On the national level, President Ronald Reagan gave respectability to what critics called a "politics of nostalgia," but the movement's strength came from outside the political establishment. For example, Jerry Falwell was an outsider to politics before he founded the Moral Majority in 1979 and influenced the 1980 election. Television appeals and direct-mail fund-raising became powerful tools for both sides in the 1980s—for the liberal People for the American Way and the American Civil Liberties Union as well as for the Moral Majority.

A good occasion for observing the full spectrum of religiously based politics came in 1988, when two different preachers sought a presidential nomination. Pat Robertson's campaign for the Republican nomination tapped deep discontent with social change. He used the mailing list from his 700 Club program to mobilize evangelical and charismatic Christians and pushed the Republican party further to the right on family and social issues. Jesse Jackson's grassroots campaign had the opposite goal of moving the Democratic party to the left on social and economic policy. With roots in the black civil rights movement, he assembled a "Rainbow Coalition" that included militant labor unionists, feminists, gay activists, and others whom Robertson's followers feared. Both Jackson and Robertson used their powerful personalities and religious convictions to inspire support from local churches and churchgoers, but the sharp divergence of their goals is a reminder about the continuing variety of American religious beliefs.

Conclusion

After twenty years of consensus, Americans since the mid-1960s have revisited basic questions about our character as a nation and people: Who is an American? How can we earn our livelihoods? Where do we want to live? What values and principles should guide our lives?

Both Pat Robertson and Jesse Jackson are reminders that the countertrend to decentralization and decentering was a search for community and connection. In the face of economic and cultural dislocation, some Americans moved to self-contained suburbs or constructed entirely new communities. Others turned to a wide range of religious organizations. Groups as different as feminists, gays, and evangelicals forged grassroots political movements to place their own concerns on the national agenda.

Even as Americans rallied around conflicting visions of the good society, the clamor of new voices and new concerns demonstrated the strength of American democracy. What remained to be tested was the continuing viability of the political process—the nation's capacity to recognize the values of diverse groups while enlisting them around a common vision of the public good.

Review Questions

1. Describe how the United States has become more international since 1965. What policy changes have promoted globalization? How have increased foreign trade and immigration affected American cities and states? What political conflicts stem from the nation's growing international connections?
2. How did the changing economy affect the various regions of the United State? How does an economy based on information and services differ from the earlier manufacturing economy? Have recent economic changes helped or hurt organized labor?
3. Why did Americans in the 1960s come to believe that larger cities were in crisis? What have been the major trends in suburban growth since the 1960s? How has this growth affected prominent political issues and the balance of political power?
4. Describe key changes in American family patterns since the 1960s. To what extent are these changes the result of economic forces? Of changing social values? How is an aging population likely to affect national politics in the twenty-first century?
5. Describe the variety of ways in which recent Americans have searched for spiritual connection and community. How does the social and political role of religion in the United States differ from that in other industrialized nations? What key issues have brought religious groups into the political arena? What positions do different groups take on these issues?

Recommended Reading

Elijah Anderson, *Streetwise: Race, Class, and Change in an Urban Community* (1990). A deeply troubling portrait of the culture of the streets in the Philadelphia ghetto.

Stephanie Coontz, *The Way We Never Were* (1992) and *The Way We Really Are* (1997). Two books that place modern family patterns in accurate historical context, puncturing a series of myths and preconceptions about family decline.

Peter Davis, *Hometown: A Contemporary American Chronicle* (1982). Profiles the small city of Hamilton, Ohio, in the late 1970s.

Francis Fitzgerald, *Cities on a Hill* (1986). Incisive portraits of new American communities in the 1980s, including retirees' Sun City, Florida; gay San Francisco; and the religious commune of Rajneeshpuram.

Joel Garreau, *Edge City: Life on the New Frontier* (1991). Argues that suburban rings are developing their own "downtowns."

Milton Rogovin and Michael Frisch, *Portraits in Steel* (1993). The transformation of an American industrial city (Buffalo), told through photographs and interviews.

Wade Clark Roof, *A Generation of Seekers: The Spiritual Journeys of the Baby Boom Generation* (1993). Examines the range of religious and spiritual experiences of contemporary Americans.

Additional Sources

Globalization and Economic Change

Barry Bluestone and Bennett Harrison, *The Deindustrialization of America* (1982).

David Calleo, *The Imperious Economy* (1982).

Barbara Ehrenreich, *Fear of Falling: The Inner Life of the Middle Class* (1989).

Thomas Kessner and Betty Boyd Caroli, *Today's Immigrants: Their Stories* (1981).

Tracy Kidder, *The Soul of a New Machine* (1981).

Frank Levy, *Dollars and Dreams: The Changing American Income Distribution* (1987).

Ann Markusen, Scott Campbell, Peter Hall, and Sabina Dietrich, *The Rise of the Gunbelt: The Military Remapping of Industrial America* (1991).

Everett Rogers, *Silicon Valley Fever* (1984).

Hobart Rowen, *Self-Inflicted Wounds: From LBJ's Guns and Butter to Reagan's Voodoo Economics* (1994).

Ruben Rumbaut and Alejandro Portes, *Immigrant America* (1990).

Saskia Sassen, *The Global City* (1991).

William Serrin, *Homestead: The Glory and Tragedy of an American Steel Town* (1992).

Studs Terkel, *Working* (1972).

Urban Growth

Carl Abbott, *The Metropolitan Frontier: Cities in the Modern American West* (1993).

Mike Davis, *City of Quartz: Excavating the Future in Los Angeles* (1992).

John Findlay, *Magic Lands: Western Cityscapes and American Culture since 1940* (1992).

Bernard Frieden and Lynn Sagalyn, *Downtown, Inc.: How America Rebuilds Its Cities* (1989).

Myron Orfield, *Metropolitics: A Regional Agenda for Community and Stability* (1997).

Neal Peirce and Robert Guskind, *Breakthrough: Re-Creating the American City* (1993).

Jon Teaford, *The Rough Road to Renaissance: Urban Revitalization in America, 1940–1985* (1990).

Cities as Places of Ethnic Contact and Conflict

Ronald Formisano, *Boston against Busing: Race, Class, and Political Action* (1991).

Paul Jargowsky, *Poverty and Place: Ghettos, Barrios, and the American City* (1997).

Peter Kwong, *The New Chinatown* (1987).

Nicholas Lemann, *The Promised Land: The Great Black Migration and How It Changed America* (1991).

J. Anthony Lukas, *Common Ground: A Turbulent Decade in the Lives of Three American Families* (1985).

Douglas Massey and Nancy Denton, *American Apartheid: Segregation and the Making of the Underclass* (1993).

Alejandro Portes and Alec Stepick, *City on the Edge* (1992).

Brett Williams, *Upscaling Downtown* (1988).

William Julius Wilson, *The Truly Disadvantaged* (1987).

Women's Rights and Family Change

Sara Evans, *Personal Politics: The Women's Liberation in the Civil Rights Movement and the New Left* (1980).

Jo Freeman, *The Politics of Women's Liberation* (1979).

Blanche Linden-Ward and Carol Hurd Green, *American Women in the 1960s* (1993).

Arlene Skolnick, *Embattled Paradise: The American Family in an Age of Uncertainty* (1991).

The Experience of Sexual Minorities

Margaret Cruikshank, *The Gay and Lesbian Liberation Movement* (1992).

Eric Marcus, *Making History: The Struggle for Gay and Lesbian Equal Rights, 1945–1990, An Oral History* (1992).

Randy Shilts, *And the Band Played On: Politics, People, and the AIDS Epidemic* (1987).

Religion and Public Life

Robert Bellah, Richard Madsen, William Sullivan, and Steven Tipton, *Habits of the Heart: Individualism and Commitment in American Life* (1985).

Paul Boyer, *When Time Shall Be No More: Prophecy Belief and Modern American Culture* (1992).

Allen D. Hertzke, *Echoes of Discontent: Jesse Jackson, Pat Robertson, and the Resurgence of Populism* (1993).

James Davison Hunter, *Culture Wars: The Struggle to Define America* (1991).

Wade Clark Roof and William McKinney, *American Mainline Religion: Its Changing Shape and Future* (1987).

John Woodridge, *The Evangelicals* (1975).

Robert Wuthnow, *The Restructuring of American Religion: Society and Faith since World War II* (1988).

Where to Learn More

- ❖ **Museum of Broadcast Communication, Chicago, Illinois.** Exhibits on the rise of broadcasting plus a library of television and radio programs and commercials offer a window into American popular culture.
- ❖ **Downtown Baltimore, Maryland.** A visit to the Harborplace festival market, the revitalized waterfront, the old Lexington Market food market, and the new Camden Yards baseball stadium is a quick way to see the sort of "new downtown" that cities tried to build after 1975.
- ❖ **Youngstown Historical Center of Industry and Labor, Youngstown, Ohio.** A permanent exhibit, "Forging the Steel Valley," focuses on the daily lives of steelworkers and the decline of the industry.

SEARCHING FOR STABILITY IN A CHANGING WORLD, SINCE 1980

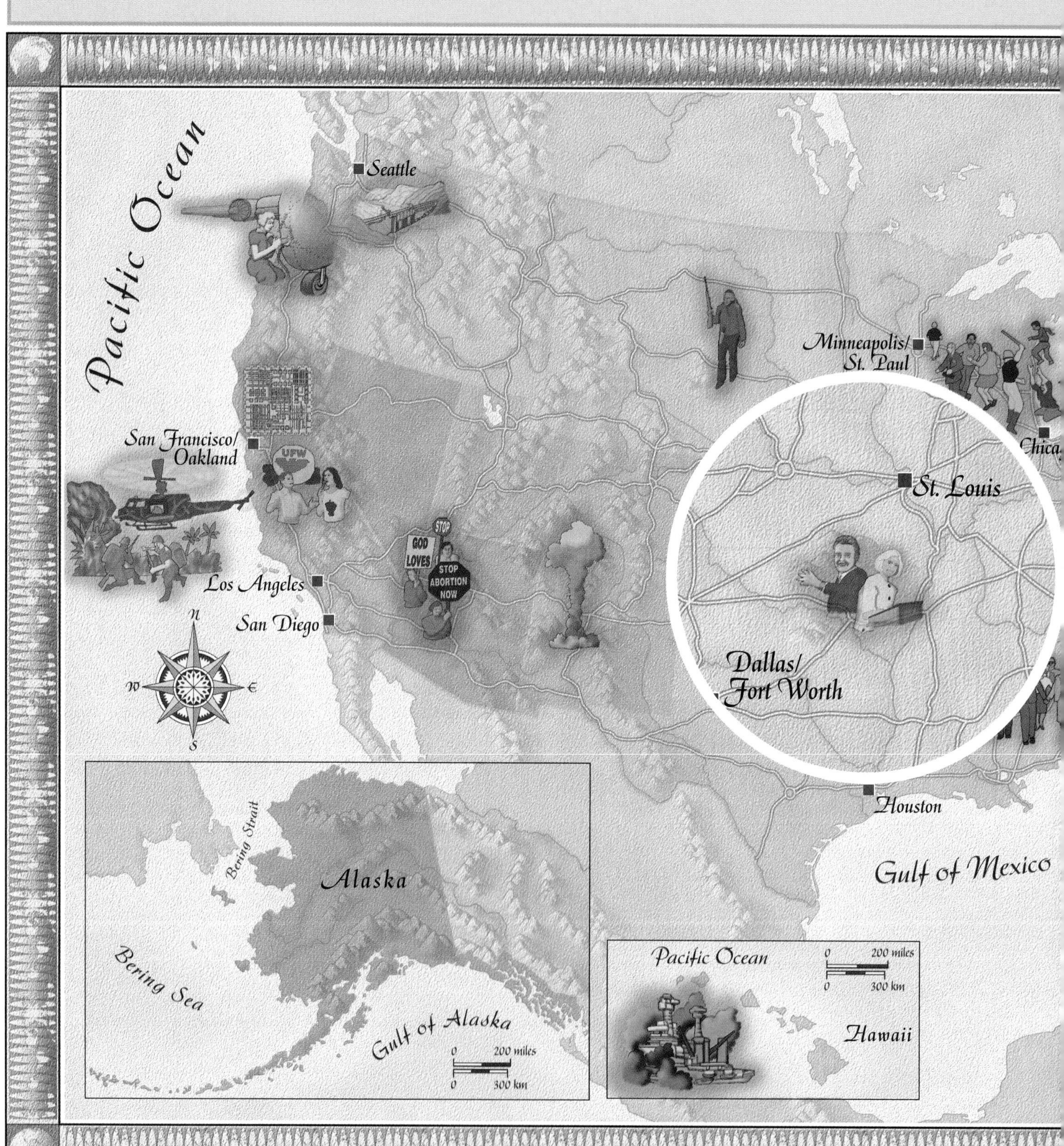

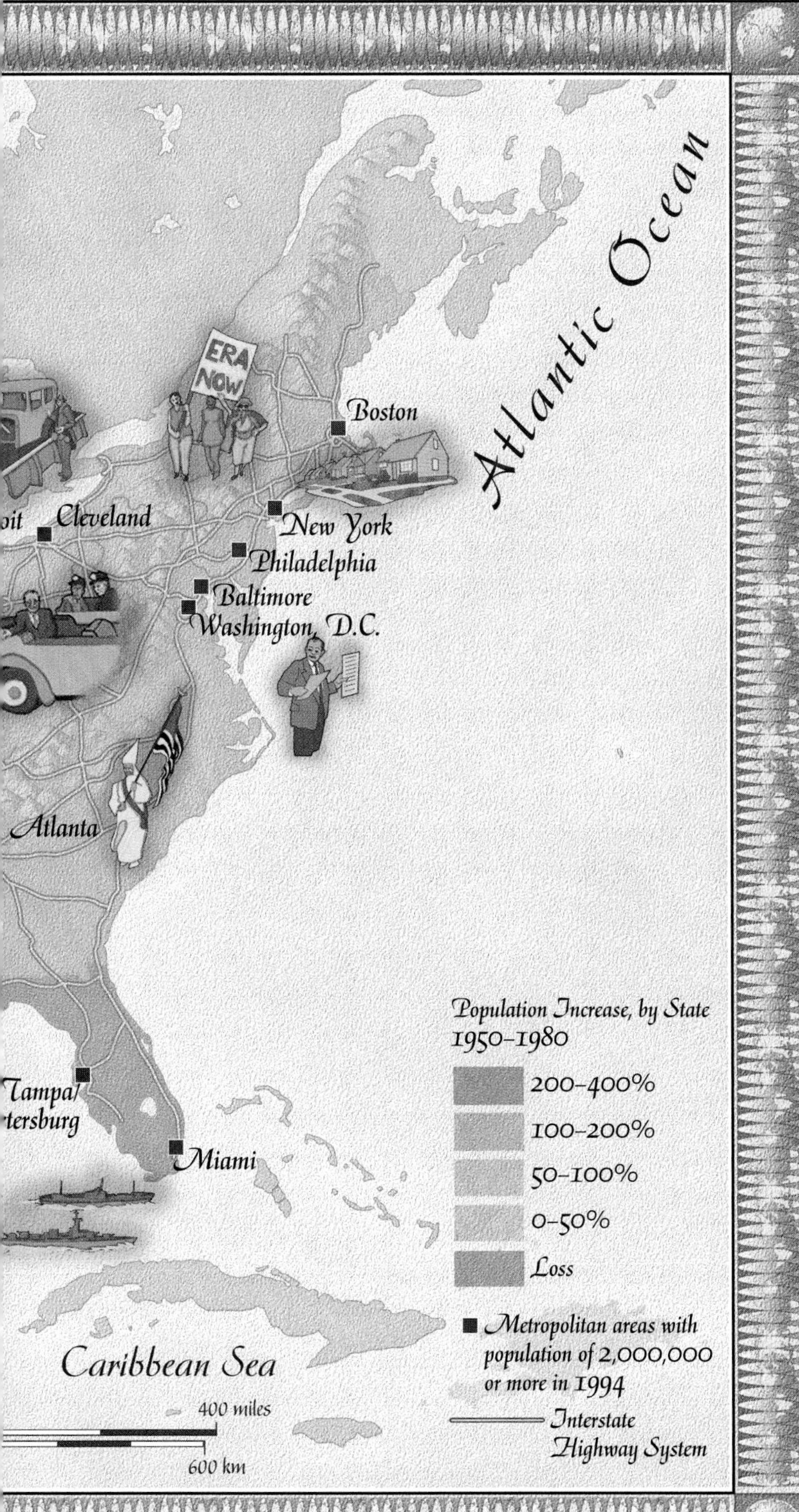

33

Chapter Outline

Key Topics

- ❖ Economic and social change during the Reagan Revolution
- ❖ The collapse of the USSR and the end of the Cold War
- ❖ Concern for the economy, the desire for stability, and the election and re-election of Bill Clinton

On June 1, 1980, CNN—Cable News Network—gave television viewers their first chance to watch news coverage twenty-four hours a day. Newscasters Bernard Shaw and Mary Alice Williams brought instant information to an initial audience of 1.7 million subscribers; a decade later, CNN had hundreds of millions of viewers in more than seventy-five countries. Business executives in Zurich, college students in Nairobi, and farmers in Omaha all tuned in to the version of world events pulled together in CNN's Atlanta headquarters.

Fourteen months after CNN came another new cable channel with immediate impact—MTV: Music Television. By the time it reached the key New York and Los Angeles markets in January 1983, MTV's round-the-clock programming of music videos had created a new form of popular art and advertising. With its own programming aimed at viewers aged eighteen to thirty-four, MTV inspired Nickelodeon for kids and VH-1 for baby boomers.

CNN, MTV, and the rest of cable television reflected both the pace of change and the fragmentation of American society in the 1980s and 1990s. As late as 1980, ordinary Americans had few choices for learning about their nation and world—virtually identical newscasts on NBC, CBS, and ABC and similar stories in *Time* and *Newsweek.* Fifteen years later, they had learned to surf through dozens of cable channels in search of specialized programs and were beginning to explore the Internet. Hundreds of magazines for niche markets had replaced the general-circulation periodicals of the postwar generation. Vast quantities of information were more easily available, but much of it was packaged for a subdivided marketplace of specialized consumers.

The new cable channels are also reminders of the powerful connections between the United States and the rest of the world. MTV by 1990 had spawned MTV Europe, MTV Australia, MTV Japan, and MTV Latin America. CNN made a global reputation with live reporting on the student revolt in Beijing in 1989. People in many developing nations prefer CNN news to their local government-controlled stations. When American bombs began to fall on Baghdad in January 1991, White House officials watched CNN to find out how their war was going.

Broadcasting was not the only field where the rules changed. From the mid-1940s to the mid-1970s, politics had followed a well-thumbed script. Lessons about full employment or the communist menace that were learned in 1948 were still applicable in 1968 or 1972. By the end of Ronald Reagan's presidency, however, new rules governed foreign affairs and the national economy. Even as the world grew safer with the breakup of the Soviet Union, it also grew more complicated. Americans had to learn new principles for understanding diplomatic relations when nations no longer had to choose sides in the Cold War. At home, Americans decided to reverse the growth of federal government responsibilities that had marked both Republican and Democratic administrations since the 1930s. By the later 1990s, the center of U.S. politics had shifted substantially to the right, with conservative Republicans recycling arguments from generations earlier and "liberal" Democrat Bill Clinton sounding like an Eisenhower Republican.

The Reagan Revolution

Political change began in 1980, when Ronald Reagan rode the tide of American discontent to a narrow but decisively important victory in the presidential election (see Map 33-1). Building on a conservative critique of American policies and on issues that Jimmy Carter had placed on the national agenda, he presided over revolutionary changes in American government and policies. Reagan was a "Teflon president" who managed to take credit for successes but avoid blame for problems and rolled to a landslide reelection in 1984. The consequences of his two terms were startling. They included an altered role for government, powerful but selective economic growth, and a shift of domestic politics away from bread-and-butter issues toward moral or lifestyle concerns.

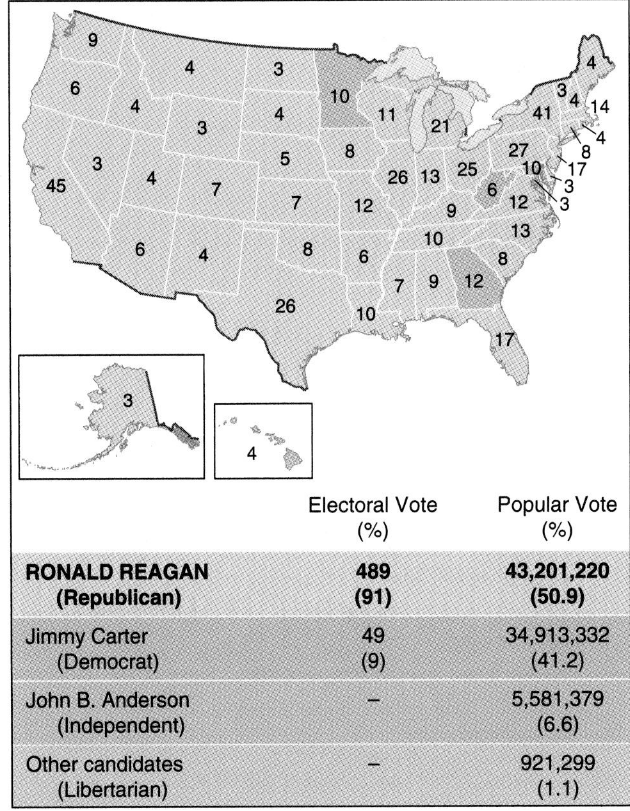

	Electoral Vote (%)	Popular Vote (%)
RONALD REAGAN (Republican)	**489 (91)**	**43,201,220 (50.9)**
Jimmy Carter (Democrat)	49 (9)	34,913,332 (41.2)
John B. Anderson (Independent)	–	5,581,379 (6.6)
Other candidates (Libertarian)	–	921,299 (1.1)

Map 33-1 Election of 1980
Ronald Reagan won in a landslide in 1980. Independent candidate John Anderson took more votes from Jimmy Carter than from Reagan, but Reagan's personal magnetism was a powerful political force. His victory confirmed the shift of the South to the Republican party.

Reagan's Majority

Reagan won in 1980 because many Americans felt buffeted by forces beyond their control. They worried about inflation at home and declining power abroad. A CBS News–*New York Times* poll found that only 11 percent of Reagan's supporters voted for him because of his conservative platform. Fully 38 percent pulled the Reagan lever simply because he was not Jimmy Carter. Reagan's majority was a tenuous alliance of groups with little in common except dissatisfaction with the status quo.

Some of Reagan's most articulate support came from anticommunist conservatives of both parties who feared that the United States was losing influence in the world. Despite Carter's tough actions in 1979 and 1980 and increases in defense spending, such conservatives didn't trust him to do enough. The inability to free the hostages in Iran grated. The Panama Canal and SALT II treaties seemed to give away American power. The Soviet military buildup, charged the critics, was creating a "window of vulnerability"—a dangerous period when the Soviet Union might threaten the United States with a first strike by nuclear weapons.

Other Reagan voters directed their anger at government bureaucracies. Christian conservatives worried that social activists were using the federal courts to alter traditional values to the detriment of American society. One young woman from Houston perceived "a parallel [between] the amount of government taking religion out and also America's debt getting worse, crime getting greater." Wealthy entrepreneurs from the Sunbelt states believed that Nixon-era federal offices like the Environmental Protection Agency and the Occupational Safety and Health Administration were choking their businesses in red tape. Many of these critics had amassed fortunes in oil, real estate, retailing, and electronics and hated the taxes that funded social programs. In many ways, the two groups were mismatched. Christian moralists as individuals had little in common with the high-rolling hedonists and Hollywood tycoons with whom Reagan rubbed shoulders. But they shared a deep distrust of the federal establishment.

Foreign policy activists and antiestablishment crusaders would have been unable to elect Reagan without disaffected blue collar and middle-class voters who deserted the Democrats. Reagan's campaign hammered on the question: "Are you better off than you were four years ago?" Many white working-class voters believed that minorities were getting an unfair edge in hiring and social services. The same voters worried about inflation, which had halted growth in the average family's spending

Ronald Reagan and his wife Nancy celebrate Reagan's inauguration as President.

Chronology

1980 Ronald Reagan is elected president.
CNN begins cable broadcasting.

1981 Reagan breaks strike by air traffic controllers.

1982 Nuclear freeze movement peaks.
United States begins to finance Contra rebels against the Sandinista government in Nicaragua.

1983 241 Marines are killed by a terrorist bomb in Beirut, Lebanon.

1984 Reagan wins reelection.

1985 Mikhail Gorbachev initiates reforms in the USSR.

1986 Economic Recovery Tax Act is adopted.

1987 Congress holds hearings on the Iran-Contra scandal.
Reagan and Gorbachev sign the Intermediate Nuclear Force treaty.

1988 George Bush is elected president.

1989 Communist regimes in eastern Europe collapse; Germans tear down Berlin Wall.
Financial crisis forces federal bailout of many savings and loans.
United States invades Panama to capture General Manuel Noriega.

1990 Iraq invades Kuwait; and United States sends forces to the Persian Gulf.
West Germany and East Germany reunite.

1991 Operation Desert Storm drives the Iraqis from Kuwait.
Soviet Union dissolves into independent nations.
Strategic Arms Reduction Treaty (START) is signed.
Clarence Thomas is seated on the Supreme Court.

1992 Acquital of officers accused of beating Rodney King triggers Los Angeles riots.
Bill Clinton defeats George Bush for the presidency.

1993 Congress approves the North American Free Trade Agreement.

1994 Independent Counsel Kenneth Starr begins investigation of Bill and Hilary Clinton.
Paula Jones files sexual harassment lawsuit against Bill Clinton.
Republicans sweep to control of Congress.
Federal government temporarily shuts down for lack of money.

1995 United States sends troops to Bosnia.

1996 Clinton wins a second term as president.

1998 Paula Jones lawsuit dismissed.
House of Representatives impeaches Clinton.

1999 Senate acquits Clinton of impeachment charges.
United States leads NATO intervention in Kosovo.

power since 1973, and blamed their difficulties on runaway government spending.

These political responses gained in influence as conservative intellectuals offered a coherent critique of the New Deal–New Frontier approach to American government. Edward Banfield's radical ideas about the failures of the Great Society set the tone of the **neoconservative** analysis. In *The Unheavenly City* (1968), he questioned the basic idea of public solutions for social problems. He argued that liberal programs failed because inequality is based on human character and rooted in the basic structure of society; government action can solve only the problems that require better engineering, such as pollution control, better highways, or the delivery of explosives to military targets.

By the late 1970s and early 1980s, other conservatives were elaborating the Banfield thesis. Some were academics, such as Irving Kristol, editor of the magazine *The Public Interest.* Others were journalists, such as Charles Murray, who attacked the welfare system in the book *Losing Ground.* Still others were political activists, such as Reagan's secretary of education, William Bennett. They found support in new conservative think tanks and political lobbying organizations. The *Wall Street Journal* evolved from a narrow business newspaper into a national conservative forum by devoting its editorial page to strident versions of neoconservatism.

The common themes were simple: Free markets work better than government programs; government intervention does more harm than good; government assistance may be acceptable for property owners, but it saps the initiative of the poor. In 1964, three-quarters of Americans had trusted Washington "to do what is right." By 1980, three-quarters were convinced that the federal government wasted tax money. The neoconservatives agreed and offered the details to support Reagan's own summary: "Government is not the solution to our problems; government is the problem."

The president's Hollywood background made it easy for him to use films to make his points. He once threatened to veto unwanted legislation by challenging Congress with Clint Eastwood's "Make my day." Many blockbuster movies reinforced two of Reagan's messages. One was the importance of direct confrontation with the bad guys: communists (*Rambo*), global terrorists (*Die Hard*), drug dealers (*Lethal Weapon*). The second was the incompetence or dishonesty of government bureaucracies from the CIA to local police, whose elitist mistakes could only be set right by average but tough individuals like "Dirty Harry Callahan" and "John Rambo."

Taxes, Deficits, and Deregulation

The heart of the 1980s revolution was the **Economic Recovery and Tax Act of 1981 (ERTA)**, which reduced personal income tax rates by 25 percent over three years. The explicit goal was to stimulate business activity by lowering taxes overall and slashing rates for the rich. Cutting the government's total income by $747 billion over five years, ERTA meant less money for federal programs and more money in the hands of consumers and investors to stimulate economic growth. Most Americans recognized the strategy's unequal impacts on the poor and still thought the benefits were worth the price.

Reagan's first budget director, David Stockman, later revealed a second goal. ERTA would lock in deficits by "pulling the revenue plug." Because defense spending and Social Security were politically untouchable, Congress would find it impossible to create and fund new programs without cutting old ones. The first year's tax reductions were accompanied by cuts of $40 billion in federal aid to mass transit, school lunches, and similar programs. If Americans still wanted social programs, they could enact them at the local or state level, but Washington would no longer pay the tab.

The second part of the economic agenda was to free capitalists from government regulations to increase business initiative, innovation, and efficiency. The **deregulation** revolution built on a head start from the 1970s. A federal antitrust case had split the unified Bell System of AT&T and its subsidiaries into seven regional telephone companies and opened long-distance service to competition. Congress also deregulated air travel in 1978. During the first forty years of commercial air service, the Federal Aviation Administration (FAA) had matched airlines and routes (treating air service like a public utility). Deregulation now allowed air carriers to start and stop service at will. The result has been cheaper and more frequent air service for major hubs and poorer and more expensive service for small cities. Economists tend to be satisfied that the net gains have outweighed the costs. The transformation of telecommunications similarly meant more choices for sophisticated consumers but higher prices for basic phone service.

As the movie character John Rambo, actor Sylvester Stallone in the early 1980s gave voice to American frustrations with the country's place in the world. The "Rambo" movies clearly distinguished the good guys from the bad guys and suggested that stronger determination could have brought victory in Vietnam.

Corporate America used the Reagan administration to attack environmental legislation as "strangulation by regulation." Reagan's new budgets sliced funding for the Council on Environmental Quality and the Environmental Protection Agency. Vice President George Bush headed the White House Task Force on Regulatory Relief, which delayed or blocked regulations on hazardous wastes, automobile emissions, and exposure of workers to chemicals on the job.

Most attention, however, went to the instantly controversial appointment of Colorado lawyer James Watt as Secretary of the Interior. Watt had long worked to open up federal lands in the West to more intensive development. He was sympathetic to a western movement known as the **Sagebrush Rebellion**, which wanted the vast federal land holdings in the West transferred to the states for more rapid economic use. The sagebrush rebels faded in the early 1980s, in part because western resource industries found Watt so sympathetic. He blamed air pollution on natural emissions from trees and compared environmentalists to both Nazis and Bolsheviks. Federal resource agencies sold trees to timber companies at a loss to the Treasury, expanded offshore oil drilling, and expedited exploration for minerals.

The early 1980s also transformed American financial markets. **Individual Retirement Accounts (IRAs)**, a creation of the 1981 tax act, made millions of households into new investors. A new generation of Americans learned to play the stock market through mutual funds and direct stock purchases. Dollars poured from savings accounts into higher-paying money market funds. Savings and loans had traditionally been conservative financial institutions that funneled individual savings into safe home mortgages. Under new rules, they began to compete for deposits by offering high interest rates and reinvested the money in much riskier commercial real estate. By 1990, the result would be a financial crisis in which bad loans destroyed hundreds of S&Ls, especially in the Southwest. American taxpayers were left to bail out depositors to the tune of hundreds of billions of dollars to prevent a collapse of the nation's financial and credit system.

Wide-open financial markets were made to order for corporate consolidations and mergers. Corporate raiders snapped up "cash cows," profitable and cash-rich companies that could be milked of profits and assets. Dealmakers, such as Ivan Boesky and Michael Milken, brought together often mismatched companies into huge conglomerates. They raised money with "junk bonds," high-interest, high-risk securities that could be paid off only in favorable conditions. The merger mania channeled capital into paper transactions rather than investments in new equipment and products. Another effect was to damage the economies of small and middle-sized communities by transferring control of local companies to outside managers.

The flip side of corporate consolidation was another round in the Republican offensive against labor unions. President Reagan set the tone when he fired more than eleven thousand members of PATCO—the Professional Air Traffic Controllers Organization—for violating a no-strike clause in their hiring agreements with the FAA. Reagan claimed to be enforcing the letter of the law, but the message to organized labor was clear. Over the next eight years, the National Labor Relations Board and other federal agencies weakened the power of collective bargaining. The administration's policies reinforced the vigorous effort by American corporations to cut costs by relocating operations to nonunion plants and shifting to part-time workers.

The Election of 1984

An unresolved question is whether Ronald Reagan planned these economic changes as parts of a single strategy. Did he direct an economic revolution, or did he simply preside over changes initiated by others? Most memoirs by White House insiders suggest the latter; so do journalists who titled books about the Reagan administration *Sleepwalking through History*, *The Acting President*, and *The Role of a Lifetime*. Even if Reagan was acting out a role that was scripted by others, however, he was a hit at the polling place. If Americans had voted against Carter in 1980, they voted for Reagan in 1984.

A sharp recession in 1981–1982 had helped the Democrats slow the progress of Reagan's initiatives in Congress, but the national Democratic party continued to have a problem. National political parties in the United States are coalitions. They bring together people from different regions and ethnic backgrounds, with different social values and ways of making a living. The Democrats' problem was to hold key voting groups, such as labor unions and African Americans, without being labeled the party of "special interests." Indeed, conservatives in the 1980s had trashed the word *liberal* and convinced Americans that oil tycoons, defense contractors, and other members of Reagan's coalition were not special interests.

Democrats faced a special dilemma with the deepening tension between working-class white voters and black voters. Democrats needed both groups to win but found white blue-collar voters deeply alienated by affirmative action and busing for school integration. In one set of focused interviews, pollsters read white Detroiters a statement from Robert Kennedy that called on Americans to recognize special obligations to black citizens who had endured racial discrimination. The responses were vehement: "I can't go along with that." "That's bull!" "No wonder they killed him."

A further Democratic challenge was Ronald Reagan's personal popularity. The president won over many Americans by surviving a 1981 assassination attempt in fine spirits. Reagan's popularity compounded the Democrats' inability to excite younger voters. Polls in the mid-1980s consistently showed that roughly two-thirds of people in their twenties and early thirties were choosing the Republicans as the party of energy and new ideas, leaving the Democrats to the middle-aged and elderly.

Democrats sealed their fate in 1984 by nominating Walter Mondale, who had been vice president under Carter. Mondale was earnest, honest, and dull. He assumed that Americans cared enough about the exploding federal deficit to accept an across-the-board tax increase. With the economy growing and inflation in check, most voters didn't want Mondale to remind them of long-range financial realities. Reagan took 59 percent of the popular vote and 98 percent of the electoral votes.

Progress and Poverty

The national economy boomed in the mid-1980s. Deregulated credit and massive deficit spending fueled exuberant growth. The decade as a whole brought nearly 20 million new jobs. Inflation dipped to 3 percent per year. The stock market mirrored the overall prosperity; the Dow Jones average of blue-chip industrial stock prices more than tripled from August 1982 to August 1987.

However, federal tax and budget changes had different effects on rich and poor (see Figure 33-1). The 1981 tax cuts came with sharp increases in the Social Security tax, which hit lower-income workers the hardest. The tax changes meant that the average annual income of households in the bottom 40 percent declined and that many actually paid higher taxes. In contrast, Americans at the upper end of the economic scale increased their share of after-tax income at the expense of everyone else. The 2.5 million Americans at the very top of the heap (the richest 1 percent) saw their share of all privately held wealth grow from 31 percent to 37 percent.

The new income fueled lavish living by the upper crust and a fascination with the "lifestyles of the rich and famous." With a few exceptions, the "middle class" in television sitcoms enjoyed lives available only to the top 20 percent of Americans. The national media discovered "yuppies"—the "young urban professionals" who supposedly defined themselves by elitist consumerism. Consumers wanted imported beer and ice cream with made-up foreign names. Middle-line retailers like Sears had clothed Americans for decades and furnished their homes. Now consumers who could flocked to upscale retailers like Nieman-Marcus, Bloomingdale's, and Nordstrom. *GQ* and *Metropolitan Home* advised readers on stylish consumption. Dispatches from the consump-

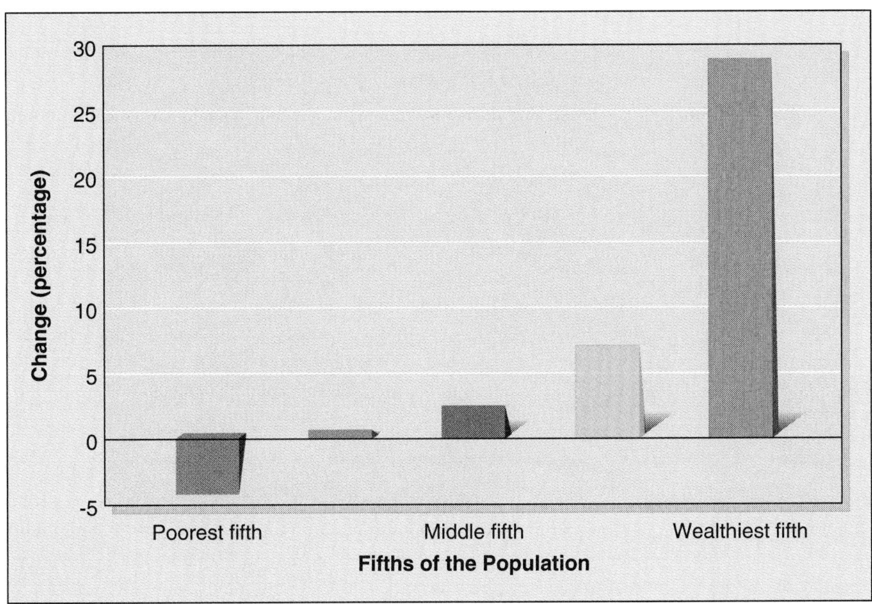

***Figure 33-1* Changes in Real Family Income, 1980–1990**
In the 1980s, the poor got poorer, the middle class made slight gains, and the most affluent 20 percent of the American people did very well. Tax changes that helped well-off households were one factor. Another factor was the erosion of "family-wage jobs" in manufacturing.

tion capitals of Manhattan and Beverly Hills reported that cocaine was now the intoxicant of choice.

The budget changes that fueled conspicuous consumption put pressure on American cities. Cities and their residents absorbed approximately two-thirds of the cuts in the 1981–1982 federal budget. Provisions for accelerated depreciation (tax write-offs) of factories and equipment in the 1981 tax act encouraged the abandonment of center-city factories in favor of new facilities in the suburbs. Meanwhile, federal aid recognized both the economic independence and political power of America's suburbs. By 1975, suburbanites held the largest block of seats in the House of Representatives—131 suburban districts, 130 rural, 102 central-city, and 72 mixed. Reapportionment in 1982, based on the 1980 census, produced a House that was even more heavily suburban. For a trip to the U.S. Senate, most politicians in earlier generations had needed rural roots or a big-city power base. By the 1980s, however, the Senate included residents of suburbs like Mill Valley, California; Aurora, Colorado; and Island Park, New York.

Federal tax and spending policies made life even harder for middle-class families who were caught by industrial restructuring. The squeeze put pressure on traditional family patterns and pushed into the workforce women who might otherwise have stayed home. By 1992, more than half of younger married women, aged 18 to 33, contributed between 30 and 70 percent of total household income. Even with two incomes, many families found it hard to buy a house because of skyrocketing prices in urban markets and sky-high interest rates. The national home ownership rate actually fell for the first time in almost fifty years, from 66 to 64 percent of American households. Many Americans no longer expected to surpass their parents' standard of living.

An affluent family pedals by a group of homeless people in Santa Barbara, California. In the 1980s a combination of rising housing prices and the closure of most mental hospitals pushed increasing numbers of Americans onto the streets. Estimates of the number of homeless Americans in the late 1980s ranged from 300,000 to 3 million, depending on the definition of homelessness and the political goals of the estimator.

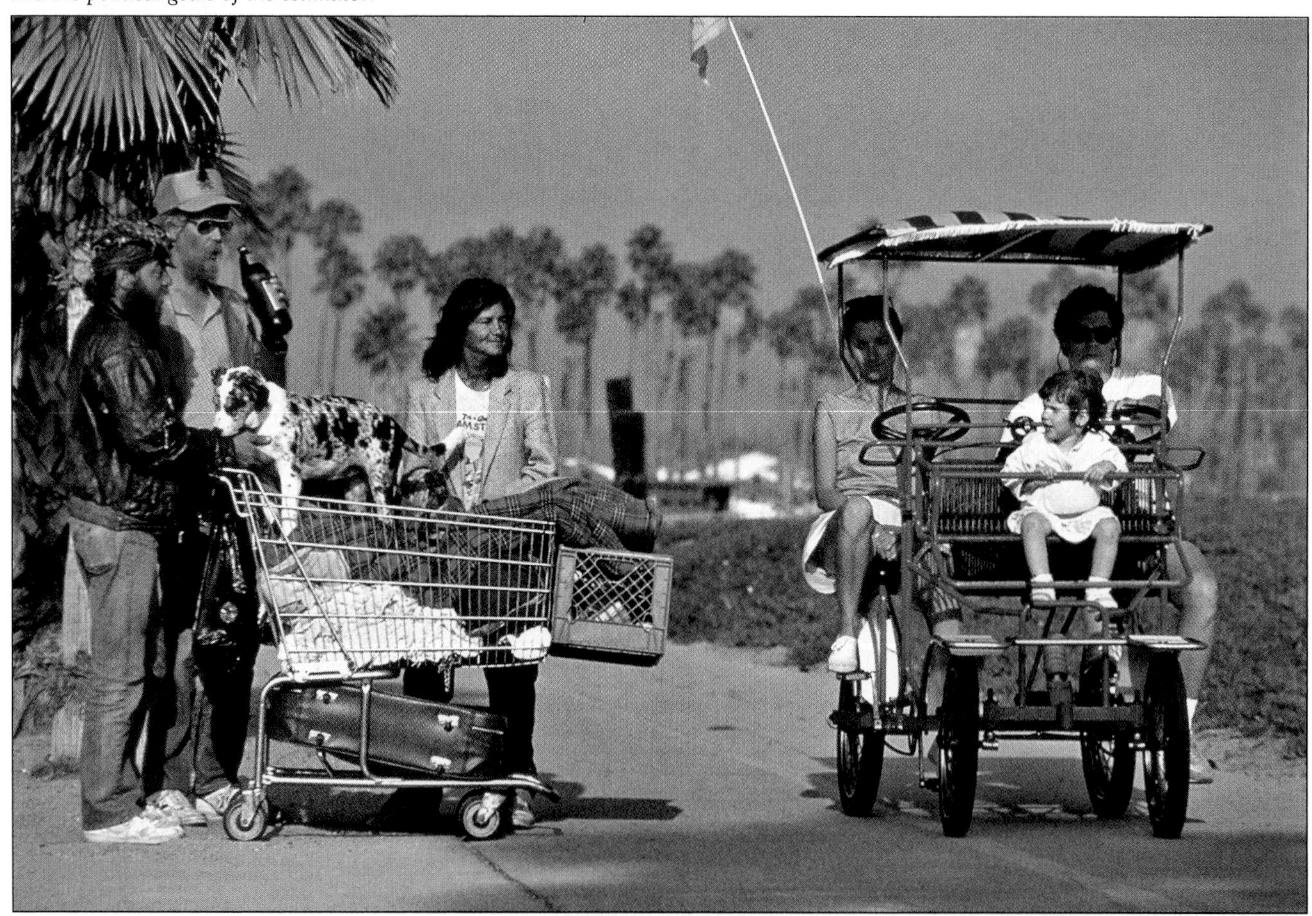

OVERVIEW

WHY ARE 35 MILLION AMERICANS POOR?

	Culture of Poverty Theory	**Malfunctioning Economy Theory**
Explanation of poverty	Poverty is the result of learned behaviors that are transmitted through families and communities. Individuals learn to scorn education and saving, expect instant gratification, and fall into laziness.	The economy is not structured to generate decent-paying jobs for all Americans who want to work. Economic and social changes have repeatedly yanked opportunity away from African-American families.
Focus of Attention	Individual behavior, poor neighborhoods	Location and availability of family wage jobs, effects of discrimination on employment chances
Political Bias	Conservative	Progressive
Policy Suggestions	Reduce welfare, food stamps, and other public assistance to encourage individuals to behave responsibly.	Ensure equal access to the job market; make the tax system more family-friendly; adequately fund public education and job training.
Buzzwords	"welfare queen," "underclass"	"blaming the victim," "housing-jobs mismatch"

At the lower end of the economic ladder, the proportion of Americans living in poverty increased. After declining steadily from 1960 to a low of 11.1 percent in 1973, the poverty rate climbed back to the 13 to 15 percent range. Conservative critics began to talk about an "underclass" of Americans permanently outside the mainstream economy because of poor education, drug abuse, or sheer laziness. In fact, most of the nation's millions of poor people lived in households with employed adults. In 1992, fully 18 percent of all full-time jobs did not pay enough ($13,091 in 1992 dollars) to lift a family of four out of poverty, a jump of 50 percent over the proportion of underpaid jobs in 1981 (see the overview table, "Why Are 35 Million Americans Poor?").

Falling below even the working poor were growing numbers of homeless Americans. Large cities have always had derelict alcoholics and the voluntarily homeless—tramps, hobos, and transient laborers. In the 1980s, several factors made homelessness more visible and pressing. A new approach to the treatment of the mentally ill reduced the population of mental hospitals from 540,000 in 1960 to only 140,000 in 1980. Deinstitutionalized patients were supposed to receive community-based treatment, but many ended up on the streets and in overnight shelters. New forms of self-destructive drug abuse, such as crack addiction, joined alcoholism. A boom in downtown real estate destroyed old skid row districts with their bars, employment offices, missions, and dollar-a-night hotels.

These factors tripled the number of permanently homeless people during the early and middle 1980s, from 200,000 to somewhere between 500,000 to 700,000. Twice or three times that many may have been homeless for part of a given year. For every person in a shelter on a given night, two people were sleeping on sidewalks, in parks, in cars, and in abandoned buildings. Because homeless people made middle-class Americans uncomfortable, it was reassuring to assume they were outsiders attracted by local conditions, such as tolerant attitudes (as some claimed in Seattle) or mild climate (as some claimed in Phoenix). In fact, few among the down-and-out have the resources to move from town to town. Bag ladies, panhandlers, working people, and yuppies were all parts of the same communities, neighbors in the broadest sense.

The Second (Short) Cold War

Ronald Reagan entered office determined not to lose the Cold War. He considered the Soviet Union not a coequal nation with legitimate world interests but an "evil empire," like something from the *Star Wars* movies. After the era of détente, global tensions had started to mount in the late 1970s. They were soon higher than they had been since the 1960s.

Confronting the USSR

Who renewed the Cold War after Nixon's diplomacy of détente and Carter's early efforts at negotiation? The Soviets had pursued military expansion in the 1970s, triggering the fear that they might stage a nuclear Pearl Harbor. The USSR in 1980 was supporting Marxist regimes in civil wars in Angola, Ethiopia, Nicaragua, and especially Afghanistan. Were these actions parts of a careful plan? Or did they result from the Cold War inertia of a rudderless nation that reacted to situations one at a time? Given the aging Soviet leadership and the economic weaknesses revealed in the late 1980s, it makes more sense to see the Soviets as muddling along rather than executing a well-planned global strategy.

On the American side, Reagan's readiness to confront "the focus of evil in the modern world" reflected the views of many conservative supporters that the USSR was a monolithic and ideologically motivated foe bent on world conquest. In hindsight, some Reaganites claim that the administration's policies were part of a deliberate and coordinated scheme to check a Soviet offensive and bankrupt the USSR by pushing it into a new arms race. Compared with spending patterns in effect in 1980, the Reagan administration shifted $70 billion per year from domestic to military programs (see Map 33-2). It is just as likely, however, that the administration's defense and foreign policy initiatives were a set of discrete but effective decisions.

The new administration reemphasized central Europe as the focus of superpower rivalry. To counter improved Soviet armaments, the United States began to place cruise missiles and midrange Pershing II missiles in Europe in 1983. NATO governments approved the action, but it frightened millions of their citizens. By the mid-1980s, many Europeans saw the United States as the dangerous and aggressive force in world affairs and the Soviet Union as the voice of moderation.

The controversy over the new missile systems was part of new thinking about nuclear weaponry. Multiple warheads on U.S. missiles already allowed Washington to target 25,000 separate places in the Soviet Union. National Security Directive D-13 (1981) stated that a nuclear war might be winnable, despite its enormous costs. A reactivated civil defense program also suggested that the United States was serious about nuclear war. All Americans needed for survival, said one administration official, were "enough shovels" to dig fallout shelters.

Escalation of the nuclear arms race reinvigorated the antiwar and antinuclear movement in the United States as well as Europe. Drawing on the experience of the antiwar movement, the **nuclear freeze** campaign caught the imagination of many

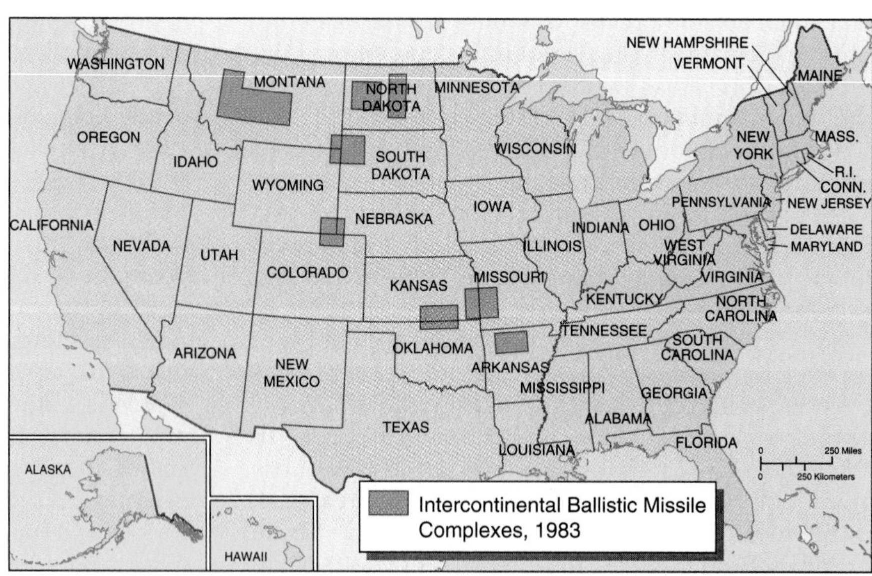

Map 33-2 Intercontinental Ballistic Missile Sites, 1983
In the early 1980s, the United States aimed hundreds of ballistic missiles with nuclear warheads at the Soviet Union. The hardened underground silos that housed the missiles were distributed across sparsely populated sections of the middle states between the Rocky Mountains and the Mississippi River.

Americans in 1981 and 1982. It sought to halt the manufacture and deployment of new atomic weapons by the great powers. The movement gained urgency when distinguished scientists argued that the smoke and dust thrown up by an atomic war would devastate the ecology of the entire globe by triggering "nuclear winter." Nearly a million people turned out for a nuclear freeze rally in New York in 1982. Voters in several states approved the idea. Hundreds of local communities endorsed the freeze or took the symbolic step of declaring themselves "nuclear-free zones."

In response, Reagan announced the **Strategic Defense Initiative (SDI)** or "Star Wars" program in 1983. SDI was to deploy new defenses that could intercept and destroy ballistic missiles as they rose from the ground and arced through space. Ideas included superlasers, killer satellites, and clouds of projectiles to rip missiles to shreds before they neared their targets. All of the technologies were untested; some existed only in the imagination. Few scientists thought that SDI could work. Many arms control experts thought that defensive systems were dangerous and destabilizing, because strong defenses suggested that a nation might be willing to risk a nuclear exchange. Nevertheless, President Reagan found SDI appealing, for it offered a way around the balance of terror that he hated.

Risky Business: Foreign Policy Adventures

The same administration that sometimes seemed reckless in its grand strategy also took risks to assert U.S. influence in global trouble spots. Nevertheless, Reagan kept the United States out of a major war and backed off in the face of serious trouble. Foreign interventions were designed to achieve symbolic victories rather than change the global balance of power. The exception was the Caribbean and Central America, the "backyard" where the United States had always claimed an overriding interest and where left-wing action infuriated Reagan's conservative supporters.

Lebanon was the model for Reagan's small-scale military interventions. Israel invaded Lebanon in 1982 to clear Palestinian guerrillas from its borders and set up a friendly Lebanese government. In fact, Lebanon was divided between Christian Arabs and Muslims and influenced by Israel's enemies Syria and the Palestine Liberation Organization (PLO). The Israeli army bogged down in a civil war. Reagan sent U.S. Marines to preserve the semblance of a Lebanese state and provide a face-saving exit for Israel. Although the Marines arrived in Beirut to interpose themselves between Israeli tanks and the Lebanese, they remained on an ill-defined "presence mission" that angered Arabs. In October 1983, a car bomb killed 241 Marines. The remainder were soon gone, confirming the Syrian observation that Americans were "short of breath" when it came to Middle East politics.

The administration had already found an easier target. On October 25, 1983, only days after the disaster in Beirut, U.S. troops invaded the small independent Caribbean island of Grenada. A left-leaning government had invited Cuban help in building an airfield, which the United States feared would turn into a Cuban military base. Two thousand American troops overcame Cuban soldiers who were thinly disguised as construction workers, "rescued" American medical students, and put a more sympathetic and locally popular government in power.

The Caribbean was also the focus of a secret foreign policy operated by the CIA and then by National Security Council staff. They engaged not just in espionage but in attempts to implement policy. The target was Nicaragua, the Central American country where leftist Sandinista rebels had overthrown the Somoza dictatorship in 1979. Reagan and his people were determined to prevent Nicaragua from becoming "another Cuba," especially when Sandinistas helped left-wing insurgents in neighboring El Salvador. The CIA organized perhaps ten thousand "Contras" from remnants of Somoza's national guard. From bases in Honduras, they harassed the Sandinistas with sabotage and raids. Reagan called the Contras "freedom fighters," listened to stories of their exploits, and hunched over maps to follow their operations in detail. Meanwhile, other Americans aided refugees from the war zones of Central America through the church-based sanctuary movement ("sanctuary" could imply both legal economic assistance and direct defiance of efforts to deport refugees).

Constitutional trouble started when an unsympathetic Congress blocked U.S. funding for the Contras. Under the direction of CIA director William Casey, Lieutenant Colonel Oliver North flouted the law by organizing aid from private donors while serving on the staff of the National Security Council. The arms pipeline operated until a supply plane was shot down in 1986.

Even shadier were the administration's arms-for-hostages negotiations with Iran. Using questionable Middle Eastern arms dealers as go-betweens, the United States in 1985 joined Israel in selling five hundred antitank missiles to Iran. The deal followed stern public pronouncements that the United States would never negotiate with terrorists, and it violated this nation's official trade embargo against Iran. In

May 1986, National Security adviser Robert McFarlane flew to Iran to negotiate a second deal, carrying a chocolate cake and a Bible autographed by Reagan to present to the Ayatollah Khomeini. The tit-for-tat was Iran's help in securing the release of several Americans held hostage in Lebanon by pro-Iranian radicals; they were released, but other hostages were soon taken. Just as startling was the revelation that Colonel North funneled proceeds from the arms sales to the Contras, in a double evasion of the law.

As had been true with Watergate, the Iran-Contra affair was a two-sided scandal. First was the blatant misjudgment of operating a secret and bumbling foreign policy that depended on international arms dealers and ousted Nicaraguan military officers. Second was a concerted effort to cover up the actions. North shredded relevant documents and lied to Congress. In his final report in 1994, Special Prosecutor Lawrence Walsh found that President Reagan and Vice President Bush were aware of much that went on and participated in efforts to withhold information and mislead Congress.

American policy in Asia was a refreshing contrast with Central America and the Middle East. In the Philippines, American diplomats helped push corrupt President Ferdinand Marcos out and opened the way for a popular uprising to put Corazon Aquino in office. Secretary of State George Shultz made sure that the United States supported popular democracy while reassuring the Philippine military. In South Korea, the United States similarly helped ease out an unpopular dictator by firmly supporting democratic elections that brought in a more popular but still pro-U.S. government.

Embracing *Perestroika*

Thaw in the Cold War started in Moscow. Mikhail Gorbachev became general secretary of the Communist party in 1985. Gorbachev was the picture of vigor compared to his three sick or elderly predecessors, Leonid Brezhnev, Yuri Andropov, and Constantin Chernenko. He was a master of public relations who charmed western Europe's leaders and public. He was also a modernizer in a long Russian tradition that stretched back to Tsar Peter the Great in the eighteenth century. Gorbachev startled Soviet citizens by urging ***glasnost***, or political openness and free discussion of issues. He followed by setting the goal of ***perestroika***, or restructuring of the painfully bureaucratic Soviet economy.

Gorbachev decided that he needed to reduce the crushing burden of Soviet defense spending if the USSR was to have any chance of modernizing. In turn, such reductions required basic changes in superpower relations. During Reagan's second term, the Soviets offered one concession after another in a relentless drive for arms control. They agreed to cut the number of land-based strategic weapons in half. They gave up their demand for a stop to SDI research. In negotiations on conventional forces in Europe, they accepted bigger cuts for the Warsaw Pact nations than for NATO. They even agreed to on-site inspections to control chemical weapons.

Reagan had the vision (or audacity) to embrace the new Soviet position. He cast off decades of belief in the dangers of Soviet communism and took Gorbachev seriously. One of his reasons for SDI had been his personal belief that the abolition of nuclear weapons was better than fine-tuning the balance of terror. Now he was willing to forget his own rhetoric and abandon many of his most fervent supporters. He frightened his own staff when he met Gorbachev in Iceland in the summer of 1986 and accepted the principle of deep cuts in strategic forces. A new attitude was clear. Reagan explained that when he railed against the "evil empire," he had been talking about Brezhnev and the bad old days; Gorbachev and *glasnost* were different.

In the end, Reagan negotiated the Intermediate Nuclear Force (INF) agreement over the strong objections of the CIA and the Defense Department but with the support of Secretary of State Shultz. INF was the first true nuclear disarmament treaty (see the overview table, "Controlling Nuclear Weapons: Four Decades of Progress"). Previous treaties had only slowed the growth of nuclear weapons; they were "speed limits" for the arms race. The new pact matched Soviet SS-20s with American cruise missiles as an entire class of weapons that would be destroyed, with on-site inspections for verification.

Mikhail Gorbachev and Ronald Reagan sign the Intermediate Nuclear Forces treaty at the White House in 1987. The treaty marked a radical transformation in Reagan's approach to relations with the Soviet Union and lessened the military tension between NATO and the Soviet bloc in Europe.

OVERVIEW

CONTROLLING NUCLEAR WEAPONS: FOUR DECADES OF PROGRESS

Limiting the Testing of Nuclear Weapons	Limited Test Ban Treaty (1963)	Banned nuclear testing in the atmosphere, ocean, and outer space.
	Comprehensive Test Ban Treaty (1996)	Bans all nuclear tests, including underground tests. Rejected by U.S. Senate in 1999.
Halting the Spread of Nuclear Weapons	Nuclear Non-Proliferation Treaty (1968)	Pledged five recognized nuclear nations (United States, USSR, Britain, France, China) to pursue disarmament in good faith, and 140 other nations not to acquire nuclear weapons.
	Strategic Arms Limitation Treaty (SALT I, 1972)	Limited the number of nuclear-armed missiles and bombers maintained by the United States and USSR. Closely associated with United States–USSR agreement to limit deployment of antiballistic missile systems to one site each.
	Strategic Arms Limitation Treaty (SALT II, 1979)	Further limited the number of nuclear-armed missiles and bombers. Not ratified but followed by Carter and Reagan administrations.
Reducing the Number of Nuclear Weapons	Intermediate Nuclear Force Agreement (1987)	Required the United States to eliminate 846 nuclear armed cruise missiles, and the Soviet Union to eliminate 1846 SS-20 missiles.
	Strategic Arms Reduction Treaty (START I, 1991)	By July 1999, led to reductions of approximately 2750 nuclear warheads by the United States and 3725 warheads by the nations of the former USSR.
	Strategic Arms Reduction Treaty (START II, 1993)	Set further cuts in nuclear arsenals. Ratified by Russia in April 2000.

Data Source: Warhead data from Arms Control Association.

Government by Gestures

George Bush, Reagan's vice president and successor as president, loved to run the world by Rolodex. When someone's name came up at a formal dinner, he was likely to grab a phone and ring the person up. He upgraded the hot line to Moscow from a teletype machine to a modern communications system. When Congress was heading in the wrong direction, he started dialing senators and representatives. When a crisis threatened world peace, he had the same reaction—pick up the phone and start chatting with presidents and prime ministers. He viewed diplomacy as a series of conversations and friendships among leaders, not the reconciliation of differing national interests.

This view of national and world politics reflected a background in which personal connections counted. He was raised as part of the New England elite, built his own oil business in Texas, and then held a series of high-level federal appointments that produced a résumé with little impact on American politics. As someone who had survived twenty years of bureaucratic infighting, his watchword was prudence. Using a comparison from baseball, he described himself as the sort of guy who'd play the averages and "bunt 'em over" rather than go for the big inning. The result was a caretaker administration at home and abroad until forced to act by the pressure of events in the Soviet Union and the Middle East.

George Bush, Willie Horton, and Manuel Noriega

Michael Dukakis, the Democratic nominee in 1988, was a dry by-the-numbers manager who offered the American people "competence." The Bush campaign painted him as a liberal ideologue. Campaign Director Lee Atwater looked for "hot button" issues that could fit onto a three-by-five card. He found that Dukakis as governor of Massachusetts had delayed cleanup of Massachusetts Bay, favored gun control, and had vetoed a bill requiring schoolchildren to recite the Pledge of Allegiance (arguing correctly that it would be overturned in the courts). Even more damaging was that Massachusetts officials had allowed a murderer named Willie Horton a weekend furlough from prison, during which he had committed a brutal rape.

The Republican campaign exploited all of these issues. The goal was to hold the blue-collar and independent suburban voters who had gone with Reagan. Pro-Bush advertisements tapped real worries among the voters—fear of crime, racial tension (Willie Horton was black), worry about eroding social values. George Bush, despite his background in prep schools and country clubs, came out looking tough as nails while the Democrats looked like effete snobs.

The ads also locked Bush into a rhetorical war on crime and drugs that was his major domestic policy. Americans had good cause to be worried about public safety, but most were generally unaware that the victimization rate—the likelihood of becoming the target of a violent crime—had leveled off and would continue to fall in the 1990s and that crime was far worse in minority communities than elsewhere, in part due to gang- and drug-related activities.

The Bush administration stepped up the fight against illegal drugs. In his first televised speech from the White House, the president showed a bag of crack purchased just across the street from the White House. He failed to mention that the Drug Enforcement Agency had decoyed a dealer so that the president would have a prop. The federal drug control budget tripled. In the early 1980s, a quarter of federal prison inmates were in jail for drug offenses. Longer sentences, mandatory jail time, and tougher parole terms for drug crimes pushed the proportion over 50 percent by 1990. The United States tried to stop the flow of cocaine by blockading its borders with airplanes, sea patrols, and sniffer dogs at airport customs lines. Casual and middle-class use of cocaine and marijuana began to decline in the mid-1980s. Drug use and drug sales were increasingly a problem of poor and minority neighborhoods.

The drug war strained relations with Latin America. The United States pressured South American nations like Colombia and Peru to uproot coca plants grown by poor farmers. Bush also parlayed the war on drugs into war on Panama. General Manuel Noriega, the Panamanian strongman, had once been on the CIA payroll. He had since turned to international drug sales in defiance of United States antismuggling efforts. On December 20, 1989, American troops invaded Panama, hunted down Noriega, and brought him back to stand trial in the United States on drug-trafficking charges. A handful of Americans and thousands of Panamanians died, many of them civilians caught in cross fire.

Otherwise, George Bush had little domestic policy, believing that Americans wanted government to leave them alone. He ignored a flood of new ideas from entrepreneurial conservatives, such as HUD Secretary Jack Kemp and "drug tsar" William Bennett. He surrounded himself with advisers who valued short-term political advantage over long-term strategies. He used dozens of vetoes to court favor with special interests, such as antiabortionists and big business.

Major legislation from the Bush years featured two environmental laws and one civil rights measure. Congress reauthorized and strengthened the **Clean Air Act**, passed a transportation bill that shifted federal priorities from highway building toward mass transit, and wrote the **Americans with Disabilities Act** (1990) to prevent discrimination against people with physical handicaps. In the areas of crime and health care, however, Bush's lack of leadership left festering problems.

The administration expected private individuals to take up the slack. Bush's often ridiculed but sincere vision was of a "kinder and gentler America" in which personal acts of social responsibility would shine like a "thousand points of light." If individuals failed to respond, however, Bush did not think that government should step in. He vetoed an extension of unemployment benefits in October 1991 and expressed his concern for "families in America that are having difficulty making ends meet" just before he teed off for Sunday afternoon golf at a suburban country club. George Bush saw little that was wrong with an America that had been so good to him and his friends.

The same attitude produced weak economic policies. The national debt had amounted to 50 percent of personal savings in 1980 but swelled to 125 percent by 1990. The massive budget deficits of the 1980s combined with growing trade deficits to turn the United States from an international creditor to a debtor nation. When Reagan took office, foreigners owed the United States and its citizens the equivalent of $2,500 for every American family. When Bush took office, the United States had used up its foreign assets and become the world's biggest debtor, with liabilities that averaged $7,000 per family. Yet the Bush administration was uninterested in dealing with either the national debt or inequitable taxes. After pledging "no new taxes" in his campaign, Bush backed into a tax increase in 1990. Voters found it hard to forget not the taxes themselves, which a strong leader might have justified to the nation, but the president's waffling and trying to downplay the importance of his decision. Thereafter, Bush ducked the political dangers of a balanced budget and tried not to rock the boat.

Crisis and Democracy in Eastern Europe

As a believer in personal diplomacy, George Bush based much of his foreign policy on his changing attitudes toward Mikhail Gorbachev. He started lukewarm, talking tough to please the Republican right wing. Bush feared that Gorbachev was being imprudent. Before 1989 was over, however, the president had decided that Gorbachev was OK. For the next two years, the United States pushed reform in Europe while being careful not to gloat in public or damage Gorbachev's position at home.

The people of eastern Europe overcame both American and Soviet caution. Gorbachev had urged his eastern European allies to emulate *perestroika* and proclaimed what his foreign ministry called the "Sinatra doctrine," alluding to the ballad "My Way," popularized by Frank Sinatra. Each communist nation could "do it their way" without fearing the Soviet tanks that had crushed change in Hungary in 1956 and Czechoslovakia in 1968. Instead of controlled reform, the Warsaw Pact system collapsed. Poland and Hungary were the first satellite nations to eject their communist leadership in favor of democracy in mid-1989. When East Germans began to flee westward through Hungary, the East German regime bowed to mounting pressure and opened the Berlin Wall on November 9. By the end of 1989, there were new governments in Czechoslovakia, Romania, Bulgaria, and East Germany.

The wall that divided East from West Berlin from 1962 to 1989 was a hated symbol of the Cold War. When the communist government of East Germany collapsed in November 1989, jubilant Berliners celebrated the opening of the wall and the reuniting of the divided city.

These largely peaceful revolutions destroyed the military and economic agreements that had harnessed the satellites to the Soviet economy. The USSR swallowed hard, accepted the loss of its satellites, and slowly withdrew its army from eastern Europe.

Events in Europe left German reunification as a point of possible conflict. Soviet policy since 1945 had sought to prevent the reemergence of a strong united Germany. West German Chancellor Helmut Kohl removed one obstacle when he reassured Poland and Russia that Germany would seek no changes in the boundaries drawn after World War II. By July 1990, the United States and USSR had agreed that a reunited Germany would belong to NATO. The decision satisfied France and Britain that a stronger Germany would still be under the influence of the Western allies. In October, the two Germanies completed their political unification, although it would be years before their mismatched economies functioned as one. Reunification was the final step in the diplomatic legacy of World War II.

Throughout these events, the Bush administration proceeded cautiously. The president wondered if a moderate communist might not be better for Poland than radical reformer Lech Walesa of the Solidarity labor movement; an abrupt change to Walesa might be "more than the market will bear." Asked whether the United States had a new foe after the end of the Cold War, Bush answered without hesitation: "The enemy is unpredictability. The enemy is instability." He tried not to push the Soviet Union too hard and infuriate Russian hard-liners. "I don't want to do something that would inadvertently set back the progress," Bush said.

The same desire not to create "big problems" affected U.S. policy as the Soviet Union itself began to break up. The USSR had absorbed the small Baltic republics of Estonia, Lithuania, and Latvia during World War II. In 1990, they reasserted their independence. When Gorbachev refused to recognize the action, Bush said little. In August 1991, Bush visited the USSR and disappointed an independence-minded crowd in the Ukrainian capital of Kiev by warning against "suicidal nationalism based on ethnic hatred." Critics quickly labeled it the "Chicken Kiev" speech. The administration's desire to work with a known leader also caused the United States to favor Gorbachev over his challenger Boris Yeltsin, who spoke for the Russian Republic rather than the larger USSR.

The Persian Gulf War

On August 2, 1990, President Saddam Hussein of Iraq seized the small neighboring country of Kuwait. The conquest gave Iraq control of 20 percent of the world's oil production and reserves. Bush demanded unconditional withdrawal, enlisted European and Arab allies in an anti-Iraq coalition, and persuaded Saudi Arabia to accept substantial U.S. forces for its protection against Iraqi invasion. Within weeks, the Saudis were host to tens of thousands of U.S. soldiers and hundreds of aircraft.

The background for Iraq's invasion was a simmering dispute over border oil fields and islands in the Persian Gulf. Iraq was a dictatorship that had just emerged from an immensely costly eight-year war with Iran. Saddam Hussein had depended on help from the United States and Arab nations in this war, but Iraq was now economically exhausted. Kuwait itself was a small, rich nation whose ruling dynasty enjoyed few friends but plenty of oil royalties. The U.S. State Department had signaled earlier in 1990 that it might support some concessions by Kuwait in the disputes. Saddam Hussein read the signal as an open invitation to do what he wanted; having been favored in the past by the United States, he probably expected denunciations but no military response.

The Iraqis gave George Bush a golden opportunity to assert America's world influence. The importance of Middle Eastern oil helped enlist France and Britain as military allies and secure billions of dollars from Germany and Japan. A short-term oil glut also meant that the industrial nations could boycott Iraqi production. Iraq itself had antagonized nearly all its neighbors. The collapse of Soviet power and Gorbachev's interest in cooperating with the United States meant that the Soviets would not interfere with U.S. plans.

Bush and his advisers offered a series of justifications for American actions. First and most basic were the desire to punish armed aggression and the presumed need to protect Iraq's other neighbors. In fact, there was scant evidence of Iraqi preparations against Saudi Arabia. The buildup of American air power plus the effective economic sanctions would have accomplished both protection and punishment. Sanctions and diplomatic pressure might also have brought withdrawal from most or all of Kuwait. However, additional American objectives—to destroy Iraq's capacity to create atomic weapons and to topple Saddam's regime—would require direct military action.

The Persian Gulf itself offered an equally golden opportunity to the American and allied armed forces. Here were no tangled jungles, invisible guerrillas, or civilians caught in a civil war. The terrain was open and nearly uninhabited. The enemy had committed regular forces to traditional battle, where the superiority of American equipment and training would be telling. Indeed, the United States

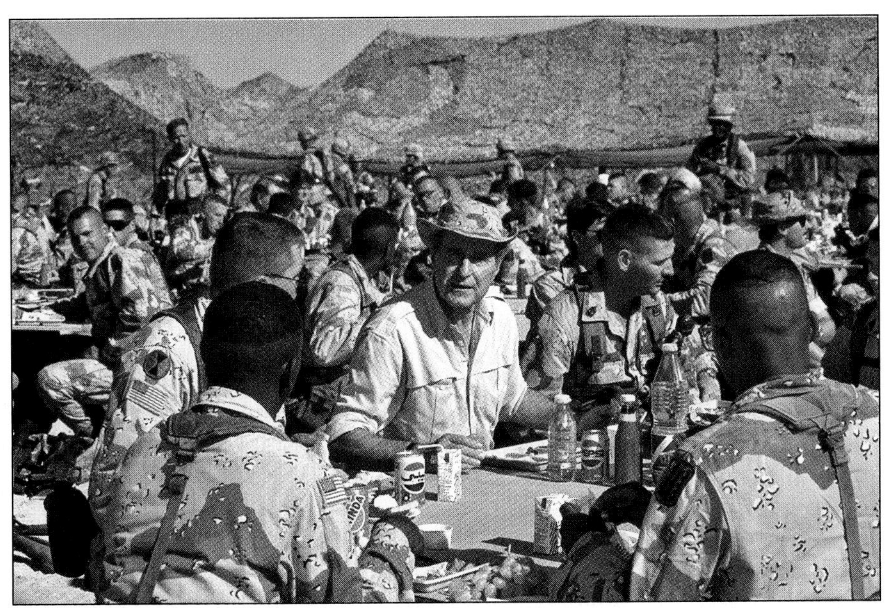

George Bush visits American troops in Saudi Arabia on Thanksgiving Day, 1990. The United States had countered Iraq's seizure of Kuwait in August by rushing forces to protect Saudi Arabia's vital oil fields. The buildup lasted until January, when U.S. planes began a systematic air assault on Iraq.

could try out the tactics of armored maneuver and close land–air cooperation that the Pentagon had devised to protect Germany against Soviet invasion.

Bush probably decided on war in October, eventually increasing the number of American troops in Saudi Arabia to 580,000. The United States stepped up diplomatic pressure by securing a series of increasingly tough United Nations resolutions that culminated in November 1990 with Security Council Resolution 678, authorizing "all necessary means" to liberate Kuwait. The president convinced Congress to agree to military action under the umbrella of the UN. The United States also ignored compromise plans floated by France and last-minute concessions from Iraq.

War began one day after the UN's January 15 deadline for Iraqi withdrawal from Kuwait. **Desert Storm** opened with massive air attacks on command centers, transportation facilities, and Iraqi forward positions. The air war destroyed 40 to 50 percent of Iraqi tanks and artillery by late February. The attacks also seriously hurt Iraqi civilians by disrupting utilities and food supplies.

Americans found the new war fascinating. They bought millions of Middle East maps to follow the conflict. They watched CNN's live transmission of Baghdad under bombardment and stared in fascination at pictures of Patriot missiles presumably intercepting Iraqi Scud missiles. They read about Stealth fighter bombers that were invisible to radar and precision-guided missiles that could home in on specified targets (although most of the damage came from traditional bombing and low-tech A-10 antitank aircraft).

The forty-day rain of bombs was the prelude to a ground attack (see Map 33-3). Despite Saddam Hussein's threats that the coalition faced the "mother of all battles," the Iraqi military made the land war easy. They concentrated their forces near

Map 33-3 Persian Gulf War

Ground operations against Iraq in the Persian Gulf War followed six weeks of aerial bombardment. The ground attack, which met quick success, was a multinational effort by the United States, Britain, France, Saudi Arabia, and other Arab nations threatened by an aggressive Iraq. The war freed Kuwait from Iraqi occupation but stopped before forcing a change in Iraq's government.

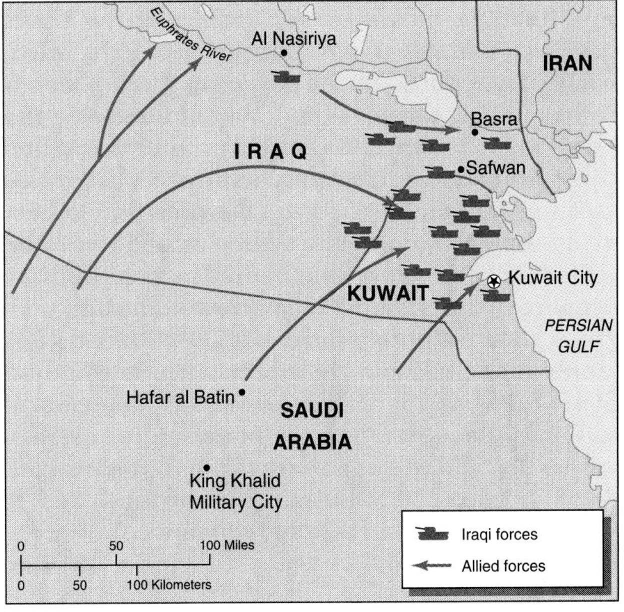

the Persian Gulf in Kuwait itself because they expected an amphibious landing near Kuwait City and a direct strike north along the coast. Instead, the allies moved 235,000 U.S., French, and British soldiers far into the interior. On February 24, 1991, these forces swept into Iraq in a great arc. Americans, Saudis, Syrians, and Egyptians advanced directly to liberate Kuwait. A cease-fire came one hundred hours after the start of the ground war. The Iraqis had been driven out of Kuwait, but the relatively slow advance of the left wing failed to prevent many of the Iraqi troops from escaping. Allied forces suffered only 240 deaths in action, compared to perhaps 100,000 for the Iraqis.

Bush directed Desert Storm with the "Vietnam syndrome" in mind, believing that Americans were willing to accept war only if it involved overwhelming U.S. force and ended quickly. The desire for a quick war, however, posed a problem. The United States hoped to replace Saddam Hussein without disrupting Iraqi society. Instead, the hundred-hour war incited armed rebellions against Saddam by Shi'ite Muslims in southern Iraq and by ethnically distinct Kurds in the north. Because Bush and his advisers were unwilling to get embroiled in a civil war, they stood by while Saddam crushed the uprisings. In one sense, the United States won the war but not the peace. Saddam Hussein became a hero to many in the Islamic world simply by remaining in power. In another sense, Bush had accomplished exactly what he wanted—the restoration of the status quo.

A New World Order?

There was no such status quo in the Soviet Union. The final act in the transformation of the USSR began with an attempted coup against Mikhail Gorbachev in August, 1991. The trigger was a planned vote on a new constitution that would decrease the power of the central Soviet government. Old-line communist bureaucrats arrested Gorbachev in his vacation house and tried to take over the government apparatus in Moscow. They turned out to be bumblers and drunks who hadn't secured military support and even failed to take over radio and television stations. Boris Yeltsin, president of the Russian Republic, organized the resistance. The United States cautiously deplored the coup as "extraconstitutional," then gradually hardened its line as Muscovites flocked to support Yeltsin and defied tank crews in front of the Russian parliament building. Within three days, the plotters themselves were under arrest.

The coup hastened the fragmentation of the Soviet Union. Before the month was out, the Soviet parliament banned the Communist party. By December, Gorbachev had resigned, and all of the fifteen component republics of the Soviet Union had declared their independence. The superpower Union of Soviet Socialist Republics ceased to exist. Russia remained the largest and strongest of the new states, followed by Ukraine and Kazakhstan.

The end of the Cold War leaves the historical assessment of the last half-century of U.S. foreign policy open to debate. Analysts agree that the relentless pressure of American defense spending helped bankrupt and undermine the USSR. It is an open question whether this same American defense spending also weakened the United States' economy and its ability to compete in the world marketplace. Some scholars see the demise of the Soviet empire as ultimate justification for forty years of Cold War. Dissenters argue the opposite—that the collapse of European communism shows that American leaders had magnified its threat. Before we can choose among differing views, we will need to wait for scholars to explore Russian archives and Soviet Cold War policy to place alongside our understanding of U.S. policy.

The end of the Cold War created a multisided world system. Since the 1940s, diplomats and politicians had judged every choice in terms of the great standoff between the United States and the USSR. Now they had to understand the complex interactions of new centers of power—not only the United States and Russia but also Japan, the European Union, and rising economies like China, Brazil, and Mexico.

What role would the United States find? President Bush saw a new world order in which the United States would be a global police force. The problem was no longer the global balance of power but rather disciplining renegade nations like Iraq. In his 1991 State of the Union speech, Bush talked about the necessity for the United States to "bear a major share of leadership" in keeping the world orderly, for only the United States had "both the moral standing and the means" to do so. He seemed to be calling for something like the Pax Britannica of the nineteenth century, when the British navy enforced a British-dominated peace on small nations around the globe.

The debate about foreign policy influenced another debate about the future of American armed forces. In the 1990s, the Pentagon closed dozens of military bases and facilities, disrupting local economies and reducing the military establishment. Military and civilian employment directly related to defense dropped from 7.2 million in 1987 to 4.5 million in 1997. In this context, it is important to remember that the Persian Gulf War cured the "Vietnam syndrome" but not the "Vietnam problem." Public excitement about the successful campaign made future military action more feasible. But Desert Storm did not solve the problem of how to intervene and retain the initiative in civil wars. The "doctrine of invincible force" is not so easy to apply in peacekeeping situations or civil war quagmires. In the mid-1990s, conflict in Somalia, Bosnia, Rwanda, Haiti, and Kosovo presented the United States with far harder choices than Saddam Hussein had offered George Bush. Bill Clinton faced a legacy of expectations about an activist foreign policy but little guidance about how to meet those expectations.

Searching for the Center

In Bill Clinton's race for president in 1992, the "war room" was the decision center where Clinton and his staff planned tactics and countered Republican attacks. On the wall was a sign with a simple message: "It's the economy, stupid." The short sentence was a reminder that victory lay in emphasizing everyday problems that George Bush neglected.

The message also revealed an insight into the character of the United States in the 1990s. What mattered most were down-to-earth issues, not the distant problems of foreign policy. As voters worried about the changing economy and its social consequences, they were eager for leaders who promised practical responses to problems that spanned the left and right. The mid-1990s brought erratic swings between the two major parties, but the most reliable position was the center. As had happened time and again, the nation's two-party system punished extremes and rewarded leaders who claimed the middle of the road with issues such as economic growth.

Political Generations

Every fifteen to twenty years, a new group of voters and leaders comes to power, driven by the desire to fix the mess that the previous generation left behind. The agenda for the Reagan and Bush years arose from the disillusion and crises of the late 1960s and 1970s. The leaders who dominated the 1980s believed that the answer was to turn the nation's social and economic problems over to the market while asserting America's influence and power around the world.

The mid-1990s brought another generation into the political arena. The members of "Generation X" came of voting age with deep worries about the foreclosing of opportunities. They worried that previous administrations had neglected social problems and let the competitive position of the United States deteriorate. The range of suggested solutions differed widely—individual moral reform, a stronger labor movement, leaner competition in world markets—but the generational concern was clear.

This turmoil of generational change made 1992 one of the most volatile national elections in decades. Young and successful but not widely known as governor of Arkansas, Democrat Bill Clinton decided that George Bush was vulnerable. His campaign for the nomination overcame minimal name recognition, accusations of womanizing, and his use of a student deferment to avoid military service in Vietnam. Clinton made sure that the Democrats fielded a full baby boomer (and southern) ticket by choosing the equally youthful Tennessean Albert Gore, Jr., as his running mate.

Bush won renomination by beating back archconservative Patrick Buchanan, who claimed that the last twelve years had been a long betrayal of true conservatism. The Republican National Convention in Houston showed how important cultural issues had become to the Republican party. The party platform conformed to the beliefs of the Christian right. Pat Buchanan called for right-thinking Americans to crusade against unbelievers. Buchanan's startling speech was a reminder of the multiple ways that religious belief was reshaping American politics (see "American Views: The Religious Imperative in Politics").

The wild card was Texas billionaire Ross Perot, whose independent campaign started with an appearance on a television talk show. Perot loved flip charts, distanced himself from professional politicians, and claimed to talk sense to the American people. He also tried to occupy the political center, appealing to the middle of the middle-class—to small business owners, middle managers, and professionals who had approved of Reagan's antigovernment rhetoric but distrusted his corporate cronies. In May, Perot outscored both Bush and Clinton in opinion polls, but his behavior became increasingly erratic. He withdrew from the race and then reentered after floating stories that he was the target of dark conspiracies.

American Views

The Religious Imperative in Politics

The strong religious faith of many Americans frequently drives them to different stands on political issues. The first of these two documents, a letter by Jerry Falwell to potential supporters of the Moral Majority, reflects the politically conservative outlook of many evangelical Christians. Falwell is pastor of the Thomas Road Baptist Church in Lynchburg, Virginia. He founded the Moral Majority, a conservative religious lobbying and educational organization, in 1979 and served as its president until 1987, the year he wrote the letter reprinted here. The second document, from an open letter issued by the Southside United Presbyterian Church in Tucson in 1982, expresses the conviction of other believers that God may sometimes require civil disobedience to oppose oppressive government actions. The letter explains the church's reasons for violating immigration law to offer sanctuary to refugees from repressive Central American regimes supported by the United States.

- **How do Falwell and the Southside Presbyterian Church define the problems that demand a religious response?**
- **Are there any points of agreement?**
- **How does each statement balance the claims of God and government?**

From the Reverend Jerry Falwell

I believe that the overwhelming majority of Americans are sick and tired of the way that amoral liberals are trying to corrupt our nation from its commitment to freedom, democracy, traditional morality, and the free enterprise system.

And I believe that the majority of Americans agree on the basic moral values which this nation was founded upon over 200 years ago.

Today we face four burning crises as we continue in this Decade of Destiny—the 1980s—loss of our freedom by giving in to the Communists; the destruction of the family unit; the deterioration of the free enterprise system; and the crumbling of basic moral principles which has resulted in the legalizing of abortion, wide-spread pornography, and a drug problem of epidemic proportions.

That is why I went to Washington, D.C., in June of 1979, and started a new organization—The Moral Majority

Right now you may be wondering: "But I thought Jerry Falwell was the preacher on the Old-Time Gospel Hour television program?"

Bush campaigned as a foreign policy expert. He expected voters to reward him for the end of the Cold War, but he ignored anxieties about the nation's direction at home. In fact, voters in November ranked the economy first as an issue, the deficit second, health care third, and foreign policy eighth. Clinton hammered away at economic concerns and the need for change from the Reagan-Bush years, appealing to swing voters, such as suburban independents and blue-collar Reagan Democrats. He presented himself as the leader of new, pragmatic, and livelier Democrats. He put on sunglasses and played the saxophone on a late-night talk show. He answered questions from viewers on MTV. His campaign theme song came from Fleetwood Mac, one of the favorite rock groups of thirty-something Americans: "Don't stop thinking about tomorrow. . . . Yesterday's gone. Yesterday's gone."

Election day gave the Clinton-Gore ticket 43 percent of the popular vote, Bush 38 percent, and Perot 19 percent (see Map 33-4). Clinton held the Democratic core of northern and midwestern industrial states

You are right. For over twenty-four years I have been calling the nation back to God from the pulpit on radio and television.

But in recent months I have been led to do more than just preach—I have been compelled to take action.

I have made the commitment to go right into the halls of Congress and fight for laws that will save America. . . .

I will still be preaching every Sunday on the Old-Time Gospel Hour—and I still must be a husband and father to my precious family in Lynchburg, Virginia.

But as God gives me the strength, I must do more. I must go into the halls of Congress and fight for laws that will protect the grand old flag . . . for the sake of our children and grandchildren.

From Southside United Presbyterian Church

We are writing to inform you that Southside Presbyterian Church will publicly violate the Immigration and Nationality Act, Section 274 (A). . . .

We take this action because we believe the current policy and practice of the United States Government with regard to Central American refugees is illegal and immoral. We believe our government is in violation of the 1980 Refugee Act and international law by continuing to arrest, detain, and forcibly return refugees to the terror, persecution, and murder in El Salvador and Guatemala.

We believe that justice and mercy require the people of conscience actively assert our God-given right to aid anyone fleeing from persecution and murder. . . .

We beg of you, in the name of God, to do justice and love mercy in the administration of your office. We ask that "extended voluntary departure" be granted to refugees from Central America and that current deportation proceedings against these victims be stopped.

Until such time, we will not cease to extend the sanctuary of the church. . . . Obedience to God requires this of us all.

Sources: Gary E. McCuen, ed., The Religious Right *(G. E. McCuen Publishers, 1989); Ann Crittenden,* Sanctuary *(Weidenfeld and Nicolson, 1988).*

and loosened the Republican hold on the South and West. Millions who voted for Perot were casting a protest vote for "none of the above" and against "politics as usual" rather than hoping for an actual Perot victory. Clinton ran best among voters over 65, who remembered FDR and Harry Truman, and voters under 30.

Minorities at the Ballot Box

Beyond the highly publicized realm of presidential elections, the 1990s saw the continued emergence of new participants in American government. Clinton's first cabinet, in which three women and four minority men balanced seven white men, marked the maturing of minorities and women as distinct political constituencies. In both cases, their new prominence in the national government followed years of growing success in cities and states.

After the racial violence of the 1960s, many black people had turned to local politics to gain control of their own communities. The first black mayor of a major twentieth-century city was Carl Stokes in Cleveland in 1967, followed closely by

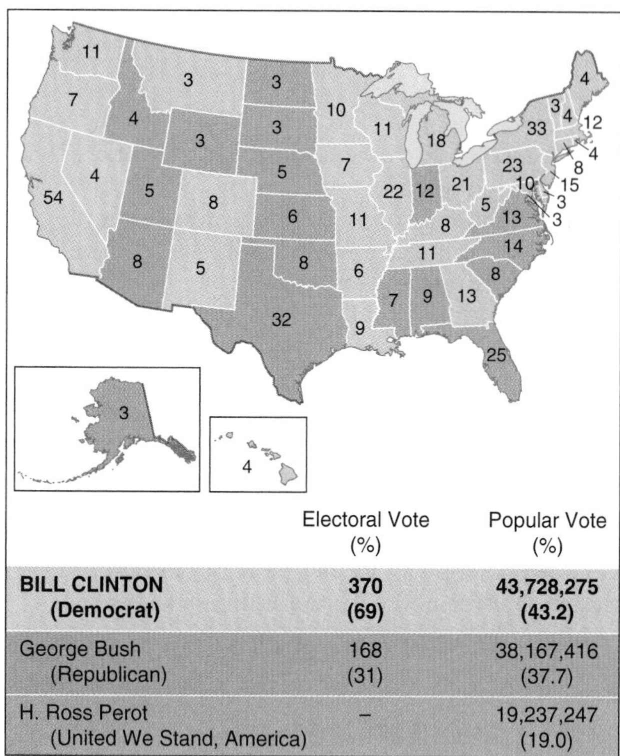

	Electoral Vote (%)	Popular Vote (%)
BILL CLINTON (Democrat)	**370 (69)**	**43,728,275 (43.2)**
George Bush (Republican)	168 (31)	38,167,416 (37.7)
H. Ross Perot (United We Stand, America)	–	19,237,247 (19.0)

Map 33-4 Election of 1992
Bill Clinton defeated George Bush in 1992 by reviving the Democratic party in the industrial Northeast and enlisting new Democratic voters in the western states, where he appealed both to Hispanic immigrants and to people associated with fast-growing high tech industries. He won reelection in 1996 with the same pattern of support. However, the coalition is an unstable combination of "Old Democrats" associated with older industries and labor unions and "New Democrats" favoring economic change, free trade, and globalization.

Richard Hatcher in Gary, Indiana. The 1973 election brought victories for Tom Bradley in Los Angeles, Maynard Jackson in Atlanta, and Coleman Young in Detroit. By 1983, three of the nation's four largest cities had black mayors (Harold Washington in Chicago, Wilson Goode in Philadelphia, and Bradley in Los Angeles). In 1989, Virginia made Douglas Wilder the first black governor in any of the United States since Reconstruction.

The election of a minority mayor was sometimes more important for its symbolism than for the transfer of real power. Efforts to restructure the basis of city council elections, however, struck directly at the balance of power. Most midsized cities had stopped electing city councils by wards or districts during the first half of the twentieth century. Voting at large shifted power away from geographically concentrated ethnic groups. It favored business interests who claimed to speak for the city as a whole but who could assign most of the costs of economic growth to older and poorer neighborhoods.

In the 1970s, minority leaders and community activists realized that a return to district voting could convert neighborhood segregation from a liability to a political resource. As amended in 1975, the federal Voting Rights Act allowed minorities to use the federal courts to challenge at-large voting systems that diluted the impact of their votes. Blacks and Mexican Americans used the act to reestablish city council districts in the late 1970s and early 1980s in city after city across the South and Southwest. By the 1980s and 1990s, younger Latino and African-American mayors, such as Henry Cisneros in San Antonio, Andrew Young in Atlanta, and Dennis Archer in Detroit, won election on positive platforms of growth and equity; they mended fences with local business leaders and promised newly empowered minorities a fair share of an expanding economic pie.

At the national level, minorities gradually increased their representation in Congress. Ben Nighthorse Campbell of Colorado, a Cheyenne, brought a Native American voice to the U.S. Senate in 1992. The number of African Americans in the House of Representatives topped forty after 1992 with the help of districts drawn to concentrate black voters. Even after a series of Supreme Court cases invalidated districts drawn with race as the "predominant factor," however, African Americans and Latinos held their gains in 1996 and 1998 (see Figure 33-2).

Women from the Grassroots to Congress

A second quiet political change was the increasing prominence of women and family issues in national politics. The period opened with two actions that were both symbolic and substantive. In 1981, President Reagan appointed Arizona judge Sandra Day O'Connor to be the first woman on the United States Supreme Court. In 1984, Walter Mondale chose New York Congresswoman Geraldine Ferraro as his vice presidential candidate.

As with Latinos and African Americans, political gains for women at the national level reflected their growing importance in grassroots politics. The spreading suburbs of postwar America were "frontiers" that required concerted action to solve immediate needs like adequate schools and decent parks. Because pursuit of such community services has often been viewed as "woman's work" (in contrast to the "man's work" of economic development), postwar metropolitan areas offered numerous opportunities for women to engage in volunteer civic work, learn political skills, and run

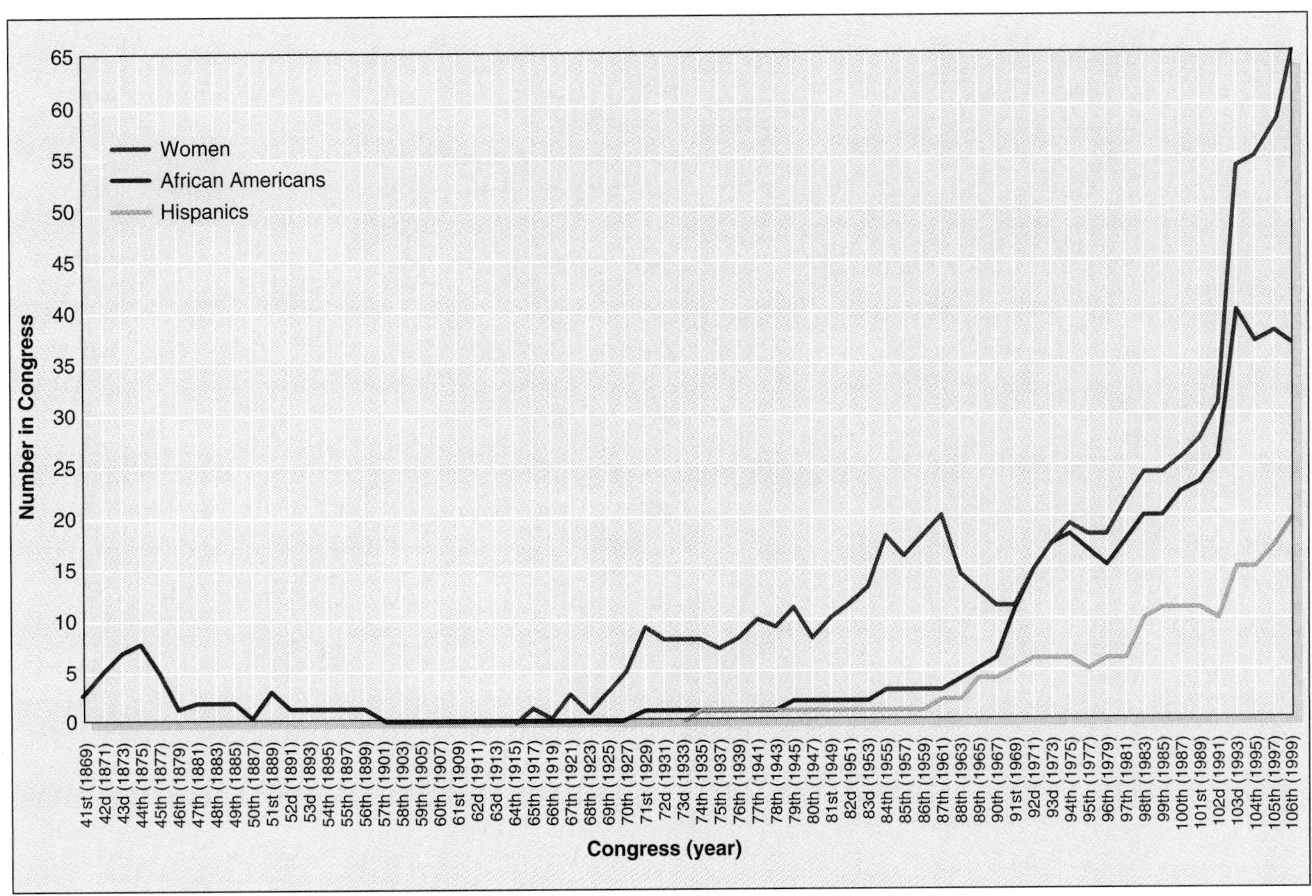

***Figure 33-2* Minorities and Women in Congress, 1869–1999**
The number of African Americans, Hispanics, and women serving in the House of Representatives and Senate increased rapidly in the 1980s and early 1990s and more slowly in the middle 1990s. The increases reflected changing attitudes, the impact of the Voting Rights Act, and decades of political activism at the grassroots.

for local office. Moreover, new cities and suburbs had fewer established political institutions, such as political machines and strong parties; their politics were open to energetic women.

The entry of more women into politics was a bipartisan affair. Important support and training grounds were the League of Women Voters, which did nonpartisan studies of basic issues, and the **National Women's Political Caucus**, designed to support women candidates of both parties. Most women in contemporary politics have been more liberal than men, a difference that political scientists attribute to women's interest in the practical problems of schools, neighborhoods, and two-earner families. But women's grassroots mobilization, especially through evangelical churches, has also strengthened groups committed to conservative social values.

Regional differences have affected women's political gains. The West has long been the part of the country most open to women in state and local government and in business (see Map 33-5). Several western states granted voting rights to women before the adoption of the Nineteenth Amendment. Westerners have been more willing than voters in the East or South to choose women as mayors of major cities and as members of state legislatures.

In 1991, the nomination of Judge Clarence Thomas to the U.S. Supreme Court ensured that everyone knew that the terms of American politics were changing. Thomas, an African American, was controversial because of his conservative positions on social and civil rights issues. Controversy deepened when law professor Anita Hill accused Thomas of harassing her sexually while she had served on his staff at the U.S. Civil Rights Commission. The accusations led to riveting hearings before a U.S. Senate committee. Critics tried to discredit Hill with vicious attacks on her character but failed to shake her story. Thomas presented himself as the victim of false accusations and a media lynching. The public was left with Hill's

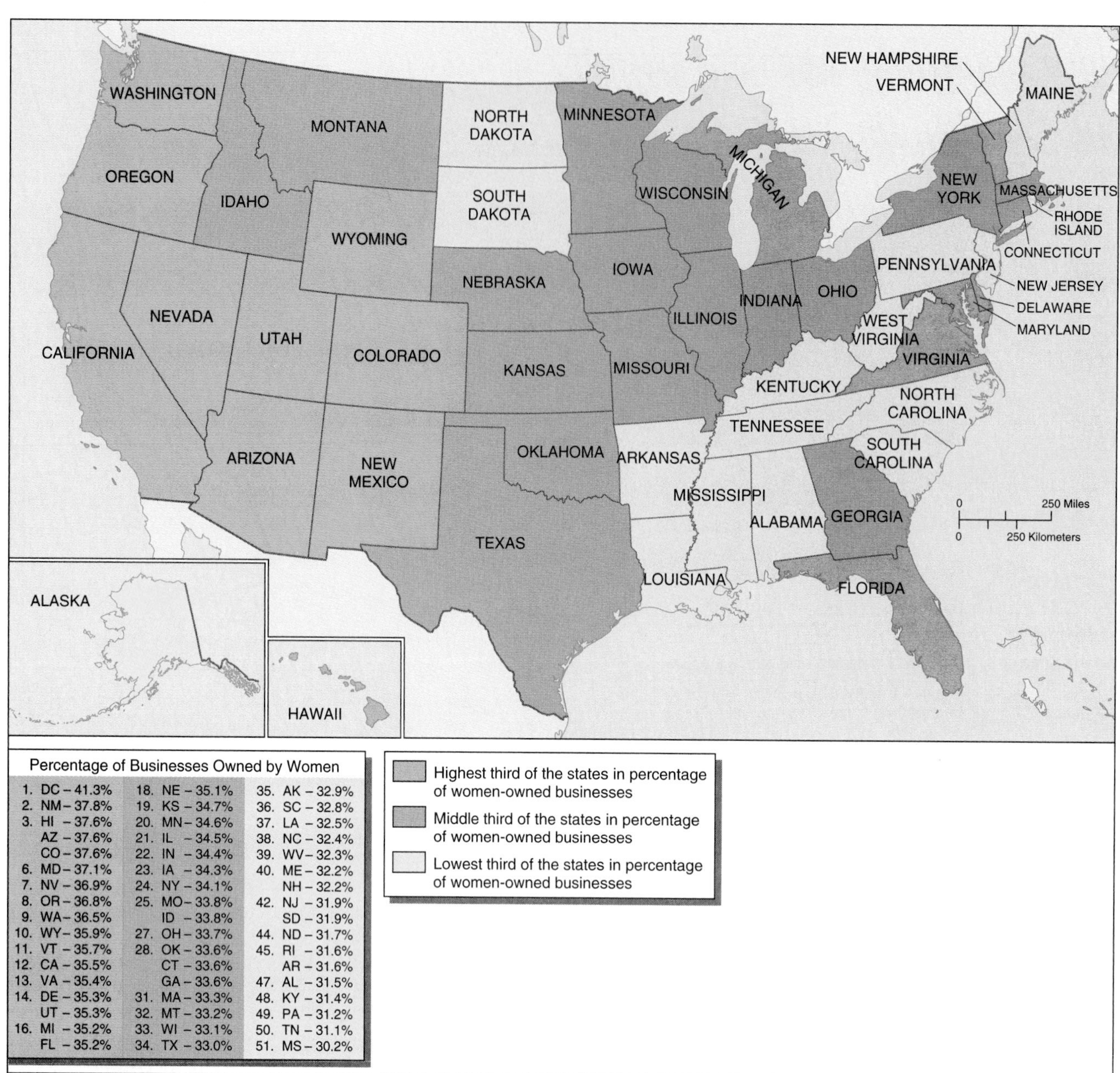

Percentage of Businesses Owned by Women

1. DC – 41.3%	18. NE – 35.1%	35. AK – 32.9%
2. NM – 37.8%	19. KS – 34.7%	36. SC – 32.8%
3. HI – 37.6%	20. MN – 34.6%	37. LA – 32.5%
AZ – 37.6%	21. IL – 34.5%	38. NC – 32.4%
CO – 37.6%	22. IN – 34.4%	39. WV – 32.3%
6. MD – 37.1%	23. IA – 34.3%	40. ME – 32.2%
7. NV – 36.9%	24. NY – 34.1%	NH – 32.2%
8. OR – 36.8%	25. MO – 33.8%	42. NJ – 31.9%
9. WA – 36.5%	ID – 33.8%	SD – 31.9%
10. WY – 35.9%	27. OH – 33.7%	44. ND – 31.7%
11. VT – 35.7%	28. OK – 33.6%	45. RI – 31.6%
12. CA – 35.5%	CT – 33.6%	AR – 31.6%
13. VA – 35.4%	GA – 33.6%	47. AL – 31.5%
14. DE – 35.3%	31. MA – 33.3%	48. KY – 31.4%
UT – 35.3%	32. MT – 33.2%	49. PA – 31.2%
16. MI – 35.2%	33. WI – 33.1%	50. TN – 31.1%
FL – 35.2%	34. TX – 33.0%	51. MS – 30.2%

Map 33-5 *Women as Business Owners, 1992*
Some parts of the nation are more inviting to woman-owned businesses than are others. The western and Great Lakes states, with reputations for innovative politics and flexible social environments, stand out as supportive of business opportunities for women.
Data Source: Institute for Women's Policy Research.

plausible but unproved allegations and Thomas's equally vigorous but unproved denials. The Senate confirmed Thomas to the Supreme Court. Partisans on each side continued to believe the version that best suited their preconceptions and agendas.

Whatever the merits of her charges, Hill's badgering by skeptical senators angered millions of women. In the shadow of the hearings, women made impressive gains in the 1992 election, when the number of women in the U.S. Senate jumped from two to six (and grew further to six Democrats and three Republicans after November 1996). Successful candidates ranged from savvy and experienced politicians like California's Barbara Boxer and Dianne Feinstein to Washington's Patty Murray, who ran as a "mom in tennis shoes." The 1992 election pushed women's share of seats in the fifty state legislatures above 20 percent (it was 22 percent in

Law professor Anita Hill became a national symbol when she accused Clarence Thomas, a nominee to the Supreme Court, of sexual harassment. Her testimony at Thomas's Senate confirmation hearing failed to prevent the Senate from approving him. After confirmation, Thomas became one of the Court's most conservative members.

1999). Bill Clinton appointed women to 37 percent of the five hundred or so high-level jobs in the White House and federal departments (see Figure 33-3). That is far higher than Jimmy Carter's 15 percent or Lyndon Johnson's 4 percent.

Women have influenced national politics as voters as well as candidates and cabinet members. Since the 1980s, voting patterns have shown a widening gender gap. Women in the 1990s identified with the Democratic party and voted for its candidates at a markedly higher rate than men. The reasons include concerns about the effects of government spending cuts and interest in measures to support families rather than conservative rhetoric. This gender gap has helped keep Democrats competitive and dampened the nation's conservative swing.

Clinton as President

Bill Clinton's first term and his reelection in 1996 show the attraction of the political center. The middle and later 1990s also suggest that national politics may be stabilizing around a relatively even balance between political parties and partisan agendas, somewhat like the years from 1876 to 1896. In his first inaugural address in January 1993, Clinton pledged "an end to the era of deadlock and drift—and a new season of American renewal." What he found in his first four years in office was an equilibrium that resulted in narrow, bipartisan victories and defeats. In 1996, voters showed that they liked the nation's break from an activist government by keeping the balance of a Democratic White House and Republican Congress, although they whittled away Republican strength in 1998.

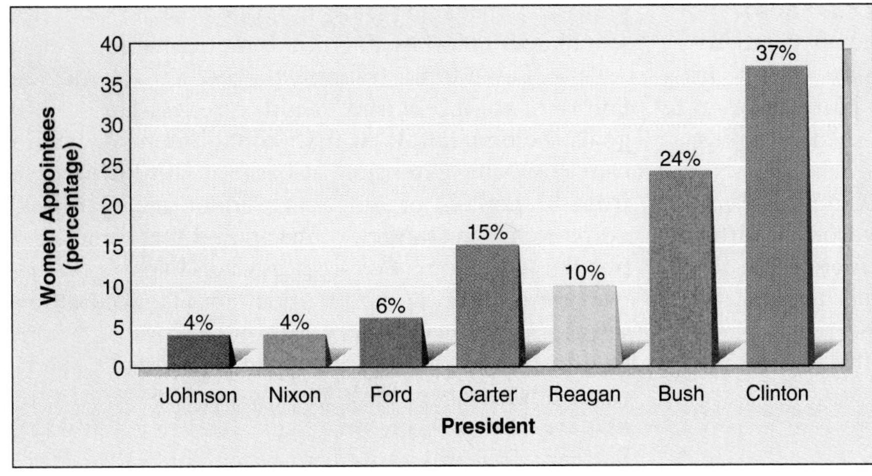

Figure 33-3 Women as a Percentage of Initial High-Level Presidential Appointments: Johnson to Clinton

By the 1990s, Americans were willing to accept women in positions that would have been reserved for "men only" in earlier decades, such as Attorney General and Secretary of State.

Data Source: Portland Oregonian, 28 September 1993.

In foreign affairs, Clinton inherited Bush's New World Order and the expectation that the United States could keep the world on an even keel and counter ethnic hatred. During the administration's first years, U.S. diplomats helped broker an Israel–PLO accord that gave Palestinians self-government in Gaza and the West Bank, only to watch extremists on both sides undermine the accords, which remained fragile but alive in 2000. The United States in 1994 used firm diplomatic pressure to persuade North Korea to stop building nuclear weapons, calming a potentially explosive trouble spot. The world also benefited from a gradual reduction of nuclear arsenals and from a 1996 treaty to ban the testing of nuclear weapons.

Elsewhere in the world, Clinton used American military power with caution. Given the national distaste for overseas entanglements, he responded far more effectively than critics expected. He inherited a U.S. military presence in Somalia (in northeastern Africa) because of a postelection decision by Bush; he withdrew American forces when their humanitarian mission of guarding food relief to starving Somalis was overshadowed by the need to take sides in civil war. Clinton intervened decisively in Haiti to restore an elected president. He reluctantly committed the United States to a multinational effort to end bloody civil war in ethnically and religiously divided Bosnia (in southeastern Europe), where U.S. troops monitored a brittle peace agreement.

The American military revisited the same part of Europe in 1999, when the United States and Britain led NATO's intervention in Kosovo. The majority of people in this Yugoslav province are ethnic Albanians who have chafed under the control of the Serb-controlled Yugoslav government since the breakup of the rest of Yugoslavia. When a Kosovar independence movement began a rebellion, the Yugoslav government responded with brutal repression that threatened to drive over one million ethnic Albanians out of the province. To protect the Kosovars, NATO began a bombing campaign that targeted Yugoslav military bases and Serb forces in Kosovo. In June, Yugoslavia agreed to withdraw its troops and make way for a multinational NATO peacekeeping force, marking a measured success for U.S. policy.

In Washington, Clinton's first four years divided into two parts. In 1993–1994, he worked with a Democratic majority in Congress to modernize the American economy. In 1995 and 1996, however, he faced solid Republican majorities, the result of an unanticipated Republican tide in the November 1994 elections.

The heart of Clinton's agenda was efforts to make the United States economy more equitable domestically and more competitive internationally; these goals marked Clinton as a **neoliberal** who envisioned a partnership between a leaner government and a dynamic private sector. Efforts to "reinvent" government cut federal employment below Reagan administration levels. A new tax bill reversed some of the inequities of the 1980s by increasing taxes on the well-off who had benefited from Reagan's policies (the top 1.2 percent of households). At the other end of the income scale was expansion of the Earned Income Tax Credit, a Nixon-era program that helps lift working Americans out of poverty. An improved college student aid program spread benefits to more students by allowing direct federal loans. The National and Community Service Trust Act created a pilot program for a domestic Peace Corps, although it was hampered by its small size (twenty thousand participants in 1994–1995) and limits on types of work.

The administration's most important victory was the approval of the treaty creating a North American Free Trade Agreement (NAFTA) (see Chapter 32). To overcome Democratic reluctance, Clinton lobbied reluctant Representatives. Al Gore took a political risk and convincingly defended NAFTA against treaty opponent Ross Perot in a debate on CNN. In November 1993, NAFTA finally passed as a measure of the political center with roughly equal numbers from each party outvoting Republican isolationists and Democratic protectionists.

The administration's record in pursuing a broad set of liberal civil rights goals was mixed in its first two years. The Department of Energy began to make public the record of Cold War tests and experiments that had subjected unknowing citizens to nuclear radiation, opening the possibility of medical treatment or compensation. The administration lifted a ban on abortion counseling in federally assisted family planning clinics. It backpedaled on the issue of gays in the military, but Congress and the Pentagon accepted a policy that made engaging in homosexual acts, but not sexual orientation itself, grounds for discharge.

The administration's biggest setback was the failure of comprehensive health care legislation. The goals seemed simple at first: containment of health care costs and extension of basic medical insurance from 83 percent of Americans under age 65 to 100 percent. In the abstract, voters agreed that something needed to be done. So did individuals like the twenty-five-year-old photographer's assistant who found herself facing cancer surgery without savings or health insurance: "I work full-time, and because it's a very small business, we don't get any benefits. . . . It just devastated everybody financially. And that shouldn't happen. That's the American dream that's lost."

Unfortunately, the plan that emerged from the White House ran to 1,342 pages of complex regulations with something for everyone to dislike. Senior citizens worried about limits on Medicare spending. Insurance companies didn't want more regulations. Businesses didn't want the costs of insuring their workers. Taxpayers liked the idea of wider medical insurance coverage but not the idea of paying for it through higher taxes or rationing of medical services.

If Reagan avoided blame for mistakes, Clinton in his first two years in office seemed to avoid credit for successes. Despite his legislative accomplishments, the press emphasized his difficulty in reaching decisions. Perhaps because he sometimes started with absolute statements and positions, what might look in another leader like a willingness to compromise looked like waffling in Clinton. Both the president and his wife attracted extreme and bitter hatred from the far right, of a sort previously reserved for Franklin and Eleanor Roosevelt and the Kennedy family. Indeed, Hillary Rodham Clinton became a symbol of discomfiting changes in American families.

Personal animosity was part of the setting for an extraordinary off-year election in 1994, in which voters defeated dozens of incumbents and gave Republicans control of both House and Senate. For most of 1995, the new speaker of the House, Newt Gingrich of Georgia, dominated political headlines as he pushed the **Contract with America**, the official Republican campaign platform for the 1994 elections, which called for a revolutionary reduction of federal responsibilities.

Clinton took a page from *B'rer Rabbit.* He laid low and let the new Congress attack environmental protections, propose cuts in federal benefits for the elderly, and push a cut in the capital gains tax to help the rich. As Congress and president battled over the budget, congressional Republicans refused to authorize interim spending and forced the federal government to shut down for more than three weeks between November 1995 and January 1996. Gingrich was the clear loser in public opinion, both for the shutdowns and his ideas. Democrats painted Gingrich and his congressional allies as a radical fringe who wanted to gut Medicare and Medicaid, undermine education, punish legal immigrants, and sell off the national parks—core values and programs that most Americans wanted to protect. Democrats, of course, proclaimed themselves the defenders of national values.

After the budget confrontations, 1996 brought a series of measures to reward work—a centrist position acceptable to most Americans. The minimum wage increased. Congress made pension programs easier for employers to create and made health insurance portable when workers changed jobs. After tough negotiations and two Clinton vetos, a welfare reform bill that emphasized work as a condition for public assistance shifted responsibilities to the states. The number of welfare recipients has fallen dramatically, but there are doubts that many of the former recipients have found jobs adequate to support their families.

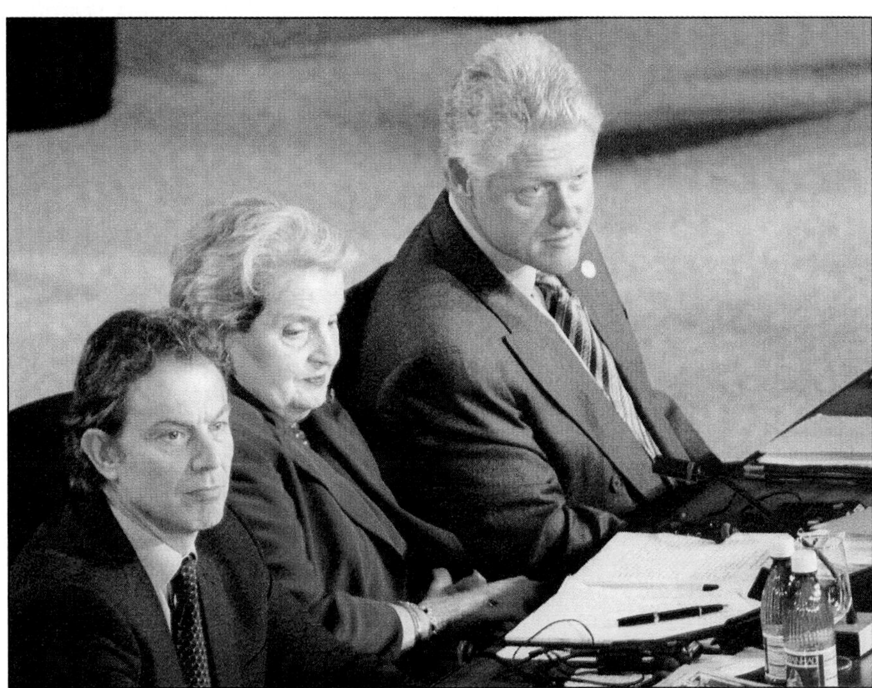

Bill Clinton significantly expanded the number of women appointed to cabinet offices and other high positions in the federal government. Madeleine K. Albright took office in 1997 as the nation's first woman Secretary of State and the nation's highest-ranking woman official. She appears here with the president and British Prime Minister Tony Blair during NATO's fiftieth anniversary summit.

Underlying politics were continued efforts to cope with a globalizing economy and technological change in a world shaped by CNN and MTV, the unification of Europe, and the rise of East Asian nations. Both the Clinton-Gore team and Gingrich were eager to take on the task. Clinton pushed for free trade and deregulation of the telecommunications industry, Gore promoted wide access to the Internet, and Gingrich preached a new frontier of entrepreneurial energy.

Clinton's reelection in 1996 was a virtual replay of 1992. His opponent, Robert Dole, represented an earlier political generation. Dole's Republican party was uncertain whether to stress free markets or morality. The party tried to paper over its uneasy mix of traditional country club Republicans (probusiness and socially moderate), radical proponents of unregulated markets, and religious conservatives affiliated with the Christian Coalition. Evangelicals dominated state parties from Minnesota to Texas, but they made many traditional party regulars uncomfortable and carried few statewide elections. The Republicans thus displayed many of the internal fractures that characterized American society as a whole.

Because the nation was prosperous and at peace, and because Clinton had claimed the political center (allowing him to sound like Dwight Eisenhower), the results were never in doubt. The Clinton-Gore ticket took 70 percent of the electoral votes and 49 percent of the popular vote (versus 41 percent for Dole and 9 percent for a recycled Ross Perot). Clinton easily won the Northeast, the industrial Midwest, and the Far West; Hispanic voters alienated by anti-immigrant rhetoric from the Republicans helped Clinton also take usually Republican states, such as Florida and Arizona.

A New Prosperity?

In 2000, Americans entered a tenth year of continuous economic expansion. Unemployment dropped from 7.2 percent in 1992 to 4.0 percent at the start of 2000 as American businesses created more than 12 million new jobs. Key states like California rebounded from economic recession with new growth driven by high-tech industries, entertainment, and foreign trade. The stock market soared during the nineties; rising demand for shares in established blue-chip companies and new Internet firms swelled the value of individual portfolios, IRA accounts, and pension funds. The rate of homeownership rose after declining for fifteen years. The proportion of Americans in poverty dropped to 13 percent, and the gap between rich and poor began to narrow (slightly) for the first time in two decades.

The economic boom was good news for the federal budget. Tight spending and rising personal income turned perennial deficits into surpluses for 1998 and 1999. Reduced borrowing by the U.S. Treasury resulted in low interest rates, which further fueled corporate expansion and consumer spending. Both political parties anticipated a growing surplus for the next decade and debated whether to offer massive tax cuts, to buy down the national debt, or to shore up Social Security and Medicare.

Behind the statistics were substantial gains in the efficiency of the American economy. International rivals—especially Japan—experienced severe economic slumps in the mid-1990s. In the United States, in contrast, by the end of the decade the productivity of manufacturing workers was increasing more than 4 percent per year. Part of the gain was the payoff from the painful business restructuring and downsizing of the 1970s and 1980s. Another cause was improvements in efficiency from the full incorporation of personal computers and electronic communication into everyday life and business practice.

It remains to be seen whether the growth of the 1990s marked the beginning of a new wave of sustained economic expansion like earlier waves triggered by technological innovation. In the past, such waves have followed fifty-year cycles that begin with a thirty-year period of rapid expansion followed by two decades of consolidation and slow growth. From 1945 to 1974, for example, the automobile and aerospace industries helped Europe, Japan, and the United States enjoy an era of sustained growth that was followed by two decades of painful economic readjustment and problems. In the later 1990s, fast-growing information-based industries such as electronic communications, software, biotechnology, and medicine may have jump-started another era of prosperity.

Morality and Partisanship

If the economy was the fundamental news of the later 1990s, Bill Clinton's personal life was the hot news. In 1998 and 1999, the United States was riveted by revelations about the president's busy sex life, doubts about his integrity, and debates about his fitness for high office. Years of rumors, innuendoes, and law suits culminated in 1999 in the nation's second presidential impeachment trial.

Clinton's problems began in 1994 with the appointment of a special prosecutor to investigate possible fraud in the Whitewater development, an Arkansas land promotion in which Bill and Hillary Clinton had invested in the 1980s. The probe by Kenneth Starr, the Independent Counsel, however, expanded beyond Whitewater into a wide-ranging

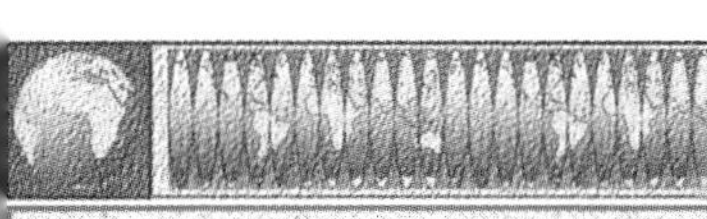

FROM THEN TO NOW

Impeachment

Bill Clinton was the third president to be enmeshed in a serious impeachment process. He was the second to have been formally impeached by the House of Representatives, tried by the Senate, and acquitted of the impeachment charges.

The framers of the Constitution designed impeachment as one of its many checks and balances. Impeachment was to be a method for holding the judicial and executive branches accountable and particularly to assure that the presidency could not turn into a kingship. The Constitution thus included a procedure for charging the president with treason or bribery and removing him from office if the charges held. The makers of the Constitution added "high crimes and misdemeanors" to the list of impeachable offenses based on five hundred years of experience in Britain; the phrase meant actions that undermined the integrity or stability of the government.

As legal historian Stanley Kutler has pointed out, a successful and legitimate impeachment process needs to be bipartisan rather than blatantly political. It also must be a response to a genuine threat to the integrity of the political and governmental process.

The impeachment and trial of Andrew Johnson in 1868 clearly failed the first of these tests, for the affair was driven by a faction of the Republican Party and was defeated by the defection of moderate Republicans. The case did revolve around a basic constitutional issue—Johnson's refusal to accept the Tenure of Office Act—but it also nonetheless failed the second test because the law in question actually altered the political balance in favor of Congress rather than the president.

The impeachment of Bill Clinton also failed both tests. Partisanship in the House Judiciary Committee drove the passage of two articles of impeachment, and the votes of moderate Republicans, as in 1868, provided the margin for acquittal. The Clinton impeachment was flawed as well by the nature of the charges, which had only the faintest relationship to the conduct of government. Clinton was certainly dishonest in shading and withholding the truth before a grand jury, but his actions undermined only his personal reputation, not the stability of the nation.

In comparison, the near impeachment of Richard Nixon more closely meets the two standards. First, the House Judiciary Committee hearings in 1974 were careful and bipartisan, as were its recommendations of impeachment to the full House. Members worked quietly for eight months before they were satisfied that impeachment was the only option. It was conservative Republicans such as Barry Goldwater who told Nixon that resignation was the only alternative to conviction and removal from office. Second, Nixon's active efforts to conceal political cheating did carry a serious threat to the political system. His lies did not just reflect on his character, they also undermined the integrity of national elections.

William Rehnquist, Chief Justice of the Supreme Court, is sworn in as the presiding judge for the impeachment trial of Bill Clinton.

investigation that encompassed the firing of the White House travel office staff, the suicide of White House aide Vincent Foster, and the sexual behavior of the president. Meanwhile, Paula Jones had brought a lawsuit claiming sexual harassment by then-governor Clinton while she was a state worker in Arkansas. The investigation of Whitewater brought convictions of several friends and former associates of the Clintons, but no evidence pointing directly at either Bill or Hilary Clinton themselves.

The legal landscape changed in January 1998 when allegations surfaced about an affair between the president and Monica Lewinsky, a former White House intern. Lewinsky admitted to the relationship privately and then to Starr's staff after the president had denied it in a sworn deposition for the Paula Jones case. This opened him to charges of perjury and obstruction of justice. Although a federal judge dismissed Jones's suit in April, the continued unfolding of the Lewinsky affair treated the nation to a barrage of personal details about Bill Clinton and to semantic debates over what exactly constituted a "sexual relationship." The affair certainly revealed deep flaws in Clinton's character and showed his willingness to shade the truth. Newspaper editorials, radio talk shows, and politicians debated whether such flaws were relevant to his ability to perform his Constitutional duties.

In the fall of 1998, the Republican leaders who controlled Congress decided that Clinton's statements and misstatements justified the Constitutional process of impeachment. In December, the Republican majority on the House Judiciary Committee recommended four articles of impeachment, or specific charges against the president, to the House of Representatives. By a partisan vote, the full House approved two of the charges and forwarded them to the Senate. The formal trial of the charges by the Senate began in January 1999 and ended on February 12. Moderate Republicans joined Democrats to assure that the Senate would fall far short of the two-thirds majority required for conviction and removal from office. Article 1, charging that the president had perjured himself, failed by a vote of 45 to 55. Article 2, charging that he had obstructed justice, failed by a vote of 50 to 50.

Why did Congressional Republicans pursue impeachment to the bitter end? It was clear by the end of 1998 that a majority of Americans strongly disapproved of Clinton's conduct but did not think that his personal behavior merited removal from office. The 1998 election, which reduced the Republican majority in the House and resulted in the resignation of Newt Gingrich, confirmed the opinion polls. At the same time, 25 to 30 percent of Americans remained convinced that Clinton was a disgrace whose presence in the White House demeaned the nation. It was not so much that they disliked his policies, which were often quite conservative, but that they felt that his personal flaws and sins made him unfit to lead and represent the nation. In other words, although impeachment was certainly motivated by politics (anti-Clinton people are a powerful force within the Republican Party), it was also another battle in America's continuing culture wars.

Conclusion

Americans entered the 1980s searching for stability. The 1970s had brought unexpected and uncomfortable change. Soviet actions in Asia and Africa seemed to be destabilizing the world. The memory of defeat in Vietnam left a bitter taste, and hostages in Tehran seemed to signal the end to America's global postwar dominance. Energy crises, inflation, and boarded-up factories eroded purchasing power and undermined confidence in the future. Traditional values seemed under siege. Ronald Reagan's presidential campaign played to these insecurities by promising to revitalize the older ways of life and restore the United States to its former influence.

Instead of time out from change, the 1980s brought new uncertainties and new efforts to articulate the nation's core values. The political liberalization and then the astonishing collapse of the Soviet Union ended forty years of Cold War. New political leadership in Washington reversed the fifty-year expansion of federal government programs to deal with economic and social inequities. Prosperity alternated with recessions that shifted the balance between regions. The stock market rode a roller coaster, familiar corporate names vanished, and the national media made temporary heroes of business tycoons. Middle-class Latinos and African Americans made substantial gains while many other minority Americans sank deeper into poverty. The outbreak of violence in Los Angeles in 1992, after the acquittal of police officers accused of beating Rodney King, showed that race relations were as tense as they had been in the 1960s.

In the 1990s, the United States found itself with uncontested political and military influence in the world. Despite its growing dependence on foreign goods, it remained a nation of rich resources. It had one of the world's most broadly educated populations and the greatest concentration of scientific and technical capacity. After struggling in the 1980s, its highly flexible economy was outperforming most rivals.

Politics rewarded the pragmatic center rather than extreme positions. Voters were cautious about the radical free-market advocates on the extreme right, showing little interest in having Republicans actually put the Contract with America into practice. They were equally unimpressed by liberal advocates of extensive entitlements on the European model. What voters wanted was to continue the reduction of the federal role in domestic affairs that began in the 1980s without damaging social insurance programs. Successful new initiatives included such middle-of-the-road measures as NAFTA and welfare reform.

Left unsolved were two challenges to basic American values. One was the challenge of equality. The American system distributed the benefits of prosperity less equally than other major industrial nations. Americans also struggled to reconcile their belief in equal opportunity with the realities of long-term poverty and racial discrimination. Insecurity among working families prompted calls in the mid-1990s to restrict immigration and end affirmative action as "reverse discrimination." While most Americans believed in giving everyone a fair chance, they disagreed about how to define and assure that chance.

The second task was to strengthen the nation's civic life. Here, too, Americans disagreed. Was the solution to social problems for individuals to be more upright or for communities to take more responsibility for common needs? Many Americans in the mid-1990s distrusted government but were still willing to attack problems through grassroots organizations. The job for citizens and leaders was to revive faith in public institutions and in the belief that Americans of all backgrounds could work together to achieve common national goals.

Review Questions

1. Is it accurate to talk about a Reagan Revolution in American politics? Did Reagan's presidency change the economic environment for workers and business corporations? How did economic changes in the 1980s affect the prospects of the richest and poorest Americans?
2. What caused the breakup of the Soviet Union and the end of the Cold War? Did U.S. foreign policy under Reagan and Bush contribute significantly to the withdrawal of Soviet power from eastern Europe? Did the collapse of the USSR show the strength of the United States and its allies or the weakness of Soviet communism?
3. Was the American political system more polarized and divided in 1996 than in 1980? How did religiously conservative Americans understand issues of foreign relations and economic policy? How did religiously liberal Americans understand these same issues? What was the gender gap in national politics in the 1990s? Why were Republicans unable to appeal to most black and Hispanic voters in 1992 and 1996?
4. What were Bill Clinton's major policy accomplishments? Do these represent "liberal," "moderate," or "conservative" positions? What was the Contract with America? What are other examples of a conservative political trend in the 1990s?

Recommended Reading

Michael Beschloss and Strobe Talbott, *At the Highest Levels* (1993). A dramatic narrative of the last years of the Cold War, based on detailed interviews with American and Soviet participants.

Susan Bibler Coutin, *The Culture of Protest: Religious Activism and the U.S. Sanctuary Movement* (1993). Examining foreign policy from the grassroots, sympathetically portrays the meanings that participants in the sanctuary movement gave their actions.

Thomas Byrne Edsall and Mary D. Edsall, *Chain Reaction: The Impact of Race, Rights, and Taxes on American Politics* (1991). Argues that the Democratic party has systematically alienated its working-class supporters.

Sara Lawrence-Lightfoot, *I've Known Rivers: Lives of Loss and Liberation* (1994). Conveys the experiences of black women in the changing postwar world.

Elliot Liebow, *Tell Them Who I Am: The Lives of Homeless Women* (1993). A sensitive depiction of "street people" and "bag ladies" as complex individuals coping with personal problems and economic crisis.

Kevin Phillips, *Boiling Point: Democrats, Republicans, and the Decline of Middle-Class Prosperity* (1992). Expresses the belief that the economic policies of the Reagan and Bush administrations systematically damaged working- and middle-class families.

Lillian Rubin, *Families on the Fault Line: American's Working Class Speaks about the Family, the Economy, Race, and Ethnicity* (1994). Interviews with American families about their efforts to cope with economic and social change.

Garry Wills, *Reagan's America: Innocents at Home* (1987). A biography critical of Reagan's ideas but insightful about his personality.

Additional Sources

Economic Change: Opportunity and Inequality

William Bowen and Derek Bok, *The Shape of the River: The Long-Term Consequences of Considering Race in College and University Admissions* (1998).

Michael Lee Cohen, *The Twenty-Something American Dream* (1993).

Andrew Hacker, *Two Nations: Black and White, Separate, Hostile, Unequal* (1992).

William Robbins, *Hard Times in Paradise* (1988).

Daphne Spain and Suzanne Bianchi, *Balancing Act: Motherhood, Marriage and Employment among American Women* (1996).

Ida Susser, *Norman Street: Poverty and Politics in an Urban Neighborhood* (1982).

Sharon Zukin, *Loft Living: Culture and Capital in Urban Change* (1982).

African-American Experiences

Pierre Clavel and Wim Wiewel, eds., *Harold Washington and the Neighborhoods* (1991).

Daniel Coyle, *Hardball: A Season in the Projects* (1993).

Mitchell Duneier, *Slim's Table: Race, Respectability and Masculinity* (1992).

Steven F. Lawson, *In Pursuit of Power: Southern Blacks and Electoral Politics* (1985).

William Julius Wilson, *The Truly Disadvantaged* (1987).

The New Conservatism

William Bennett, *The De-Valuing of America: The Fight for Our Culture and Our Children* (1992).

Lee Edwards, *The Conservative Revolution* (1999).

John Ehrman, *The Rise of Neo-Conservative Intellectuals and Foreign Affairs, 1945-1994* (1995).

J. David Hoeveler, Jr., *Watch on the Right: Conservative Intellectuals in the Reagan Era* (1991).

Linda Kintz, *Between Jesus and the Market: The Emotions That Matter in Right-Wing America* (1997).

Irving Kristol, *Neoconservatism: The Autobiography of an Idea* (1995).

Theodore J. Lowi, *The End of the Republican Era* (1995).

Charles Murray, *Losing Ground: American Social Policy, 1950–1980* (1984).

Politics, Society, and the Mass Media

R. Serge Denisoff, *Inside MTV* (1988).

Don Flournoy, *CNN World Report: Ted Turner's International News Coup* (1992).

Todd Gitlin, *Watching Television* (1987).

Andrew Goodwin, *Dancing in the Distraction Factory: Music Television and Popular Culture* (1992).

Military and Foreign Policy

Dana H. Allin, *Cold War Illusions: America, Europe, and Soviet Power, 1969–1989* (1998).

David Cortright, *Peace Works: The Citizen's Role in Ending the Cold War* (1993).

Theodore Draper, *A Very Thin Line* (1991).

Lawrence Freedman and Efraim Karsh, *The Gulf Conflict, 1990–1991: Diplomacy and the New World Order* (1993).

John L. Gaddis, *Now We Know; Rethinking Cold War History* (1997).

Stephen Graubard, *Mr. Bush's War* (1992).

Michael J. Hogan, ed., *The End of the Cold War: Its Meaning and Implications* (1992).

Christian Smith, *Resisting Reagan: The U.S. Central American Peace Movement* (1997).

Robert W. Tucker and David C. Hendrickson, *The Imperial Temptation: The New World Order and America's Purposes*(1992).

Daniel Wirls, *Buildup: The Politics of Defense in the Reagan Era*(1992).

Politics and Politicians in the 1980s

Martin Anderson, *Revolution* (1989).

William Berman, *America's Right Turn: From Nixon to Bush* (1994).

Michael Duffy and Dan Goodgame, *Marching in Place: The Status Quo Presidency of George Bush* (1992).

Steven M. Gillon, *The Democrats' Dilemma: Walter F. Mondale and the Liberal Legacy* (1992).

Haynes Johnson, *Sleepwalking through History: America in the Reagan Years* (1991).

William Pemberton, *Exit with Honor: The Life and Presidency of Ronald Reagan* (1997).

Peggy Noonan, *What I Saw at the Revolution: A Political Life in the Reagan Era* (1990).

Michael Schaller, *Reckoning with Reagan: American and Its President in the 1980s* (1992).

John W. Sloan, *The Reagan Effect: Economics and Presidential Leadership* (1999).

David Stockman, *The Triumph of Politics: How the Reagan Revolution Failed* (1986).

Politics in the 1990s

Dan Balz and Ronald Brownstein, *Storming the Gates: Protest Politics and the Republican Revival* (1996).

E. J. Dionne, Jr., *Why Americans Hate Politics* (1991).

Mark Rozell and Clyde Wilcox, *Second Coming: The New Christian Right in Virginia Politics* (1996).

Where to Learn More

❖ **Ronald Reagan Boyhood Home, Dixon, Illinois.** The home where Reagan lived from 1920 to 1923 tells relatively little about Reagan himself but a great deal about the small-town context that shaped his ideas.

❖ **State Humanities Councils.** Every state has a council or committee for the humanities that is affiliated with the National Endowment for the Humanities. They sponsor a wide variety of events and publications that often link historical perspectives to current social issues of importance in each state.

❖ **C-SPAN.** The Cable Satellite Public Affairs Network allows cable television viewers to observe the public workings of the national government in ways previously available only to Washington insiders.

APPENDIX

The Declaration of Independence

When in the course of human events it becomes necessary for one people to dissolve the political bands which have connected them with another and to assume, among the powers of the earth, the separate and equal station to which the laws of nature and of nature's God entitle them, a decent respect to the opinions of mankind requires that they should declare the causes which impel them to the separation.

We hold these truths to be self-evident, that all men are created equal; that they are endowed by their Creator with certain unalienable rights; that among these are life, liberty, and the pursuit of happiness. That, to secure these rights, governments are instituted among men, deriving their just powers from the consent of the governed; that, whenever any form of government becomes destructive of these ends, it is the right of the people to alter or to abolish it, and to institute a new government, laying its foundation on such principles, and organizing its powers in such form, as to them shall seem most likely to effect their safety and happiness. Prudence, indeed, will dictate that governments long established should not be changed for light and transient causes; and, accordingly, all experience hath shown that mankind are more disposed to suffer, while evils are sufferable, than to right themselves by abolishing the forms to which they are accustomed. But when a long train of abuses and usurpations, pursuing invariably the same object, evinces a design to reduce them under absolute despotism, it is their right, it is their duty, to throw off such government and to provide new guards for their future security. Such has been the patient sufferance of these colonies, and such is now the necessity which constrains them to alter their former systems of government. The history of the present King of Great Britain is a history of repeated injuries and usurpations, all having, in direct object, the establishment of an absolute tyranny over these States. To prove this, let facts be submitted to a candid world:

He has refused his assent to laws the most wholesome and necessary for the public good.

He has forbidden his governors to pass laws of immediate and pressing importance, unless suspended in their operation till his assent should be obtained; and, when so suspended, he has utterly neglected to attend to them.

He has refused to pass other laws for the accommodation of large districts of people, unless those people would relinquish the right of representation in the legislature, a right inestimable to them and formidable to tyrants only.

He has called together legislative bodies at places unusual, uncomfortable, and distant from the depository of their public records, for the sole purpose of fatiguing them into compliance with his measures.

He has dissolved representative houses, repeatedly for opposing, with manly firmness, his invasions on the rights of the people.

He has refused, for a long time after such dissolutions, to cause others to be elected; whereby the legislative powers, incapable of annihilation, have returned to the people at large for their exercise; the state remaining, in the meantime, exposed to all the danger of invasion from without and convulsions within.

He has endeavored to prevent the population of these States; for that purpose, obstructing the laws for naturalization of foreigners, refusing to pass others to encourage their migration hither, and raising the conditions of new appropriations of lands.

He has obstructed the administration of justice by refusing his assent to laws for establishing judiciary powers.

He has made judges dependent on his will alone for the tenure of their offices and the amount and payment of their salaries.

He has erected a multitude of new offices and sent hither swarms of officers to harass our people and eat out their substance.

He has kept among us, in time of peace, standing armies, without the consent of our legislatures.

He has affected to render the military independent of, and superior to, the civil power.

He has combined with others to subject us to a jurisdiction foreign to our Constitution and unacknowledged by our laws, giving his assent to their acts of pretended legislation—

For quartering large bodies of armed troops among us;

For protecting them by a mock trail from punishment for any murders which they should commit on the inhabitants of these States;

For cutting off our trade with all parts of the world;

For imposing taxes on us without our consent;

For depriving us, in many cases, of the benefit of trial by jury;

For transporting us beyond seas to be tried for pretended offences;

For abolishing the free system of English laws in a neighboring province, establishing therein an arbitrary government, and enlarging its boundaries, so as to render it at once an example and fit instrument for introducing the same absolute rule into these colonies;

For taking away our charters, abolishing our most valuable laws, and altering, fundamentally, the powers of our governments.

For suspending our own legislatures and declaring themselves invested with power to legislate for us in all cases whatsoever.

He has abdicated government here by declaring us out of his protection and waging war against us.

He has plundered our seas, ravaged our coasts, burnt our towns, and destroyed the lives of our people.

He is, at this time, transporting large armies of foreign mercenaries to complete the works of death, desolation, and tyranny already begun with circumstances of cruelty and perfidy scarcely paralleled in the most barbarous ages, and totally unworthy the head of a civilized nation.

He has constrained our fellow citizens, taken captive on the high seas, to bear arms against their country, to become the executioners of their friends and brethren, or to fall themselves by their hands.

He has excited domestic insurrections amongst us and has endeavored to bring on the inhabitants of our frontiers, the merciless Indian savages, whose known rule of warfare is an undistinguished destruction of all ages, sexes, and conditions.

In every stage of these oppressions, we have petitioned for redress in the most humble terms; our repeated petitions have been answered only by repeated injury. A prince whose character is thus marked by every act which may define a tyrant is unfit to be the ruler of a free people.

Nor have we been wanting in attention to our British brethren. We have warned them, from time to time, of attempts made by their legislature to extend an unwarrantable jurisdiction over us. We have reminded them of the circumstances of our emigration and settlement here. We have appealed to their native justice and magnanimity, and we have conjured them, by the ties of our common kindred, to disavow these usurpations, which would inevitably interrupt our connections and correspondence. They, too, have been deaf to the voice of justice and consanguinity. We must, therefore, acquiesce in the necessity which denounces our separation, and hold them, as we hold the rest of mankind, enemies in war, in peace, friends.

We, therefore, the representatives of the United States of America, in general Congress assembled, appealing to the Supreme Judge of the world for the rectitude of our intentions, do, in the name and by the authority of the good people of these colonies, solemnly publish and declare, that these united colonies are, and of right ought to be, free and independent states: that they are absolved from all allegiance to the British Crown, and that all political connection between them and the state of Great Britain is, and ought to be, totally dissolved; and that, as free and independent states, they have full power to levy war, conclude peace, contract alliances, establish commerce, and to do all other acts and things which independent states may of right do. And, for the support of this declaration, with a firm reliance on the protection of Divine Providence, we mutually pledge to each other our lives, our fortunes, and our sacred honor.

The Articles of Confederation and Perpetual Union*

Between the states of New Hampshire, Massachusetts-bay Rhode Island and Providence Plantations, Connecticut, New York, New Jersey, Pennsylvania, Delaware, Maryland, Virginia, North Carolina, South Carolina, and Georgia.

Article I

The Stile of this Confederacy shall be "The United States of America."

Article 2

Each state retains its sovereignty, freedom, and independence, and every power, jurisdiction, and right, which is not by this Confederation expressly delegated to the United States, in Congress assembled.

Article 3

The said States hereby severally enter into a firm league of friendship with each other, for their common defense, the security of their liberties, and their mutual and general welfare, binding themselves to assist each other, against all force offered to, or attacks made upon them, or any of them, on account of religion, sovereignty, trade, or any other pretense whatever.

Article 4

The better to secure and perpetuate mutual friendship and intercourse among the people of the different States in this Union, the free inhabitants of each of these States, paupers, vagabonds, and fugitives from justice excepted, shall be entitled to all privileges and immunities of free citizens in the several States; and the people of each State shall have free ingress and regress to and from any other State, and shall enjoy therein all the privileges of trade and commerce, subject to the same duties, impositions, and restrictions as the inhabitants thereof respectively, provided that such restrictions shall not extend so far as to prevent the removal of property imported into any State, to any other State of which the owner is an inhabitant; provided also that no imposition, du-

*Agreed to in Congress November 15, 1777; ratified March 1781.

ties or restriction shall be laid by any State, on the property of the United States, or either of them.

If any person guilty of, or charged with, treason, felony, or other high misdemeanor in any State, shall flee from justice, and be found in any of the United States, he shall, upon demand of the Governor or executive power of the State from which he fled, be delivered up and removed to the State having jurisdiction of his offense.

Full faith and credit shall be given in each of these States to the records, acts, and judicial proceedings of the courts and magistrates of every other State.

Article 5

For the more convenient management of the general interests of the United States, delegates shall be annually appointed in such manner as the legislatures of each State shall direct, to meet in Congress on the first Monday in November, in every year, with a power reserved to each State to recall its delegates, or any of them, at any time within the year, and to send others in their stead for the remainder of the year.

No State shall be represented in Congress by less than two, nor by more than seven members; and no person shall be capable of being a delegate for more than three years in any term of six years; nor shall any person, being a delegate, be capable of holding any office under the United States, for which he, or another for his benefit, receives any salary, fees or emolument of any kind.

Each State shall maintain its own delegates in a meeting of the States, and while they act as members of the committee of the States.

In determining questions in the United States in Congress assembled, each State shall have one vote.

Freedom of speech and debate in Congress shall not be impeached or questioned in any court or place out of Congress, and the members of Congress shall be protected in their persons from arrests or imprisonments, during the time of their going to and from, and attendence on Congress, except for treason, felony, or breach of the peace.

Article 6

No State, without the consent of the United States in Congress assembled, shall send any embassy to, or receive any embassy from, or enter into any conference, agreement, alliance or treaty with any King, Prince or State; nor shall any person holding any office of profit or trust under the United States, or any of them, accept any present, emolument, office or title of any kind whatever from any King, Prince or foreign State; nor shall the United States in Congress assembled, or any of them, grant any title of nobility.

No two or more States shall enter into any treaty, confederation or alliance whatever between them, without the consent of the United States in Congress assembled, specifying accurately the purposes for which the same is to be entered into, and how long it shall continue.

No State shall lay any imposts or duties, which may interfere with any stipulations in treaties, entered into by the United States in Congress assembled, with any King, Prince or State, in pursuance of any treaties already proposed by Congress, to the courts of France and Spain.

No vessel of war shall be kept up in time of peace by any State, except such number only, as shall be deemed necessary by the United States in Congress assembled, for the defense of such State, or its trade; nor shall any body of forces be kept up by any State in time of peace, except such number only, as in the judgement of the United States in Congress assembled, shall be deemed requisite to garrison the forts necessary for the defense of such State; but every State shall always keep up a well-regulated and disciplined militia, sufficiently armed and accoutered, and shall provide and constantly have ready for use, in public stores, a due number of filed pieces and tents, and a proper quantity of arms, ammunition and camp equipage.

No State shall engage in any war without the consent of the United States in Congress assembled, unless such State be actually invaded by enemies, or shall have received certain advice of a resolution being formed by some nation of Indians to invade such State, and the danger is so imminent as not to admit of a delay, till the United States in Congress assembled can be consulted; nor shall any State grant commissions to any ships or vessels of war, nor letters of marque or reprisal, except it be after a declaration of war by the United States in Congress assembled, and then only against the Kingdom or State and the subjects thereof, against which war has been so declared, and under such regulations as shall be established by the United States in Congress assembled, unless such State be infested by pirates, in which case vessels of war may be fitted out for that occasion, and kept so long as the danger shall continue, or until the United States in Congress assembled shall determine otherwise.

Article 7

When land forces are raised by any State for the common defense, all officers of or under the rank of colonel, shall be appointed by the legislature of each State respectively, by whom such forces shall be raised, or in such manner as such State shall direct, and all vacancies shall be filled up by the State which first made the appointment.

Article 8

All charges of war, and all other expenses that shall be incurred for the common defense or general welfare, and allowed by the United States in Congress assembled, shall be defrayed out of a common treasury, which shall be supplied by the several States in proportion to the value of all land within each State, granted to or surveyed for any person, as such land and the buildings and improvements thereon shall be estimated according to such mode as the United States in Congress assembled, shall from time to time direct and appoint.

The taxes for paying that proportion shall be laid and levied by the authority and direction of the legislatures of the several States within the time agreed upon by the United States in Congress assembled.

Article 9

The United States in Congress assembled, shall have the sole and exclusive right and power of determining on peace and war, except in the cases mentioned in the sixth article; of sending and receiving ambassadors; entering into treaties and alliances, provided that no treaty of commerce shall be made whereby the legislative power of the respective States shall be restrained from imposing such imposts and duties on foreigners, as their own people are subjected to, or from prohibiting the exportation or importation of any species of goods or commodities whatsoever; of establishing rules for deciding in all cases, what captures on land or water shall be legal, and in what manner prizes taken by land or naval forces in the service of the United States shall be divided or appropriated; of granting letters of marque and reprisal in times of peace; appointing courts for the trial of piracies and felonies committed on the high seas and establishing courts for receiving and determining finally appeals in all cases of captures, provided that no member of Congress shall be appointed a judge of any of the said courts.

The United States in Congress assembled shall also be the last resort on appeal in all disputes and differences now subsisting or that hereafter may arise between two or more States concerning boundary, jurisdiction or any other causes whatever; which authority shall always be exercised in the manner following. Whenever the legislative or executive authority or lawful agent of any State in controversy with another shall present a petition to Congress stating the matter in question and praying for a hearing, notice thereof shall be given by order of Congress to the legislative or executive authority of the other State in controversy, and a day assigned for the appearance of the parties by their lawful agents, who shall then be directed to appoint by joint consent, commissioners or judges to constitute a court for hearing and determining the matter in question: but if they cannot agree, Congress shall name three persons out of each of the United States, and from the list of such persons each party shall alternately strike out one, the petitioners beginning, until the number shall be reduced to thirteen; and from that number not less than seven, nor more than nine names as Congress shall direct, shall in the presence of Congress be drawn out by lot, and the persons whose names shall be so drawn or any five of them, shall be commissioners or judges, to hear and finally determine the controversy, so always as a major part of the judges who shall hear the cause shall agree in the determination: and if either party shall neglect to attend at the day appointed, without showing reasons, which Congress shall judge sufficient, or being present shall refuse to strike, the Congress shall proceed to nominate three persons out of each State, and the secretary of Congress shall strike in behalf of such party absent or refusing; and the judgement and sentence of the court to be appointed, in the manner before prescribed, shall be final and conclusive; and if any of the parties shall refuse to submit to the authority of such court, or to appear or defend their claim or cause, the court shall nevertheless proceed to pronounce sentence, or judgement, which shall in like manner be final and decisive, the judgement or sentence and other proceedings being in either case transmitted to Congress, and lodged among the acts of Congress for the security of the parties concerned: provided that every commissioner, before he sits in judgment, shall take an oath to be administered by one of the judges of the supreme or superior court of the State, where the cause shall be tried, "well and truly to hear and determine the matter in question, according to the best of his judgement, without favor, affection or hope of reward:" provided also, that no State shall be deprived of territory for the benefit of the United States.

All controversies concerning the private right of soil claimed under different grants of two or more States, whose jurisdictions as they may respect such lands, and the States which passed such grants are adjusted, the said grants or either of them being at the same time claimed to have originated antecedent to such settlement of jurisdiction, shall on the petition of either party to the Congress of the United States, be finally determined as near as may be in the same manner as is before prescribed for deciding disputes respecting territorial jurisdiction between different States.

The United States in Congress assembled shall also have the sole and exclusive right and power of regulating the alloy and value of coin struck by their own authority, or by that of the respective States; fixing the standards of weights and measures throughout the United States; regulating the trade and managing all affairs with the Indians not members of any of the States; provided that the legislative right of any State within its own limits be not infringed or violated; establishing or regulating post offices from one State to another, throughout all the United States, and exacting such postage on the papers passing through the same as may be requisite to defray the expenses of the said office; appointing all officers of the land forces in the service of the United States, excepting regimental officers; appointing all the officers of the naval forces, and commissioning all officers whatever in the service of the United States; making rules for the government and regulation of the said land and naval forces, and directing their operations.

The United States in Congress assembled shall have authority to appoint a committee, to sit in the recess of Congress, to be denominated "A Committee of the States," and to consist of one delegate from each State; and to appoint such other committees and civil officers as may be necessary for managing the general affairs of the United States under their direction; to appoint one of their members to preside, provided that no person be allowed to serve in the office of president more than one year in any term of three years; to ascertain the necessary sums of money to be raised for the service of the United States, and to appropriate and apply the same for defraying the public expenses; to borrow money, or emit bills on the credit of the United States, transmitting every half year to the respective States an account of the sums of money so borrowed or emitted; to build and equip a navy; to agree upon the number of land forces, and to make requisitions from each State for its quota, in proportion to the number of white inhabitants in such State; which requisition shall be binding, and thereupon the legislature of each State shall appoint the regimental officers, raise the men and cloath, arm and equip them in a soldier-like manner, at the expense of the United States; and the officers and men so cloathed, armed and equipped shall march to the place appointed, and within the time agreed on by the United States in Congress assembled; but if the United States in Congress assembled shall, on consideration of circumstances judge proper that any State should not raise men, or should raise a smaller number of men than the quota thereof, such extra number shall be raised, officered, cloathed, armed and equipped in the same manner as the quota of such State, unless the legislature of such State shall judge that such extra number cannot be safely spared out in the same, in which case they shall raise, officer, cloath, arm and equip as many of such extra number as they judge can be safely spared. And the officers and men so cloathed, armed, and equipped, shall march to the place appointed, and within the time agreed on by the United States in Congress assembled.

The United States in Congress assembled shall never engage in a war, nor grant letters of marque or reprisal in time of peace, nor enter into any treaties or alliances, nor coin money, nor regulate the value thereof, nor ascertain the sums and expenses necessary for the defense and welfare of the United States, or any of them, nor emit bills, nor borrow money on the credit of the United States, nor appropriate money, nor agree upon the number of vessels of war, to be built or purchased, or the number of land or sea forces to be raised, nor appoint a commander in chief of the army or navy, unless nine States assent to the same: nor shall a question on any other point, except for adjourning from day to day be determined, unless by the votes of the majority of the United States in Congress assembled.

The Congress of the United States shall have power to adjourn to any time within the year, and to any place within the United States, so that no period of adjournment be for a longer duration than the space of six months, and shall publish the journal of their proceedings monthly, except such parts thereof relating to treaties, alliances or military operations, as in their judgment require secrecy; and the yeas and nays of the delegates of each State on any question shall be entered on the journal, when it is desired by any delegates of a State, or any of them, at his or their request shall be furnished with a transcript of the said journal, except such parts as are above excepted, to lay before the legislatures of the several States.

Article 10

The Committee of the States, or any nine of them, shall be authorized to execute, in the recess of Congress, such of the powers of Congress as the United States in Congress assembled, by the consent of the nine States, shall from time to time think expedient to vest them with; provided that no power be delegated to the said Committee, for the exercise of which, by the Articles of Confederation, the voice of nine States in the Congress of the United States assembled is requisite.

Article 11

Canada acceding to this confederation, and adjoining in the measures of the United States, shall be admitted into, and entitled to all the advantages of this Union; but no other colony shall be admitted into the same, unless such admission be agreed to by nine States.

Article 12

All bills of credit emitted, monies borrowed, and debts contracted by, or under the authority of Congress, before the assembling of the United States, in pursuance of the present confederation, shall be deemed and considered as a charge against the United States, for payment and satisfaction whereof the said United States, and the public faith are hereby solemnly pledged.

Article 13

Every State shall abide by the determination of the United States in Congress assembled, on all questions which by this confederation are submitted to them. And the Articles of this Confederation shall be inviolably observed by every State, and the Union shall be perpetual; nor shall any alteration at any time hereafter be made in any of them; unless such alteration be agreed to in a Congress of the United States, and be afterwards confirmed by the legislatures of every State.

These articles shall be proposed to the legislatures of all the United States, to be considered, and if approved of by them, they are advised to authorize their delegates to ratify the same in the Congress of the United States; which being done, the same shall become conclusive

The Constitution of the United States of America

We the people of the United States, in order to form a more perfect union, establish justice, insure domestic tranquillity, provide for the common defense, promote the general welfare, and secure the blessings of liberty to ourselves and our posterity, do ordain and establish this Constitution for the United States of America.

Article I

SECTION 1. All legislative powers herein granted shall be vested in a Congress of the United States, which shall consist of a Senate and House of Representatives.

SECTION 2. 1. The House of Representatives shall be composed of members chosen every second year by the people of the several States, and the electors in each State shall have the qualifications requisite for electors of the most numerous branch of the State legislature.

2. No person shall be a representative who shall not have attained to the age of twenty-five years, and been seven years a citizen of the United States, and who shall not, when elected, be an inhabitant of that State in which he shall be chosen.

3. Representatives and direct taxes[1] shall be apportioned

[1]See the Sixteenth Amendment.

among the several States which may be included within this Union, according to their respective numbers, which shall be determined by adding to the whole number of free persons, including those bound to service for a term of years, and excluding Indians not taxed, three fifths of all other persons.[2] The actual enumeration shall be made within three years after the first meeting of the Congress of the United States, and within every subsequent term of ten years, in such manner as they shall by law direct. The number of representatives shall not exceed one for every thirty thousand, but each State shall have at least one representative; and until such enumeration shall be made, the State of New Hampshire shall be entitled to choose three, Massachusetts eight, Rhode Island and Providence Plantations one, Connecticut five, New York six, New Jersey four, Pennsylvania eight, Delaware one, Maryland six, Virginia ten, North Carolina five, South Carolina five, and Georgia three.

4. When vacancies happen in the representation from any State, the executive authority thereof shall issue writs of election to fill such vacancies.

5. The House of Representatives shall choose their speaker and other officers; and shall have the sole power of impeachment.

SECTION 3. 1. The Senate of the United States shall be composed of two senators from each State, chosen by the legislature thereof,[3] for six years; and each senator shall have one vote.

2. Immediately after they shall be assembled in consequence of the first election, they shall be divided as equally as may be into three classes. The seats of the senators of the first class shall be vacated at the expiration of the second year, of the second class at the expiration of the fourth year, and of the third class at the expiration of the sixth year, so that one third may be chosen every second year; and if vacancies happen by resignation, or otherwise, during the recess of the legislature of any State, the executive thereof may make temporary appointments until the next meeting of the legislature, which shall then fill such vacancies.[4]

3. No person shall be a senator who shall not have attained to the age of thirty years, and been nine years a citizen of the United States, and who shall not, when elected, be an inhabitant of that State for which he shall be chosen.

4. The Vice President of the United States shall be President of the Senate, but shall have no vote, unless they be equally divided.

5. The Senate shall choose their other officers, and also a president pro tempore, in the absence of the Vice President, or when he shall exercise the office of the President of the United States.

6. The Senate shall have the sole power to try all impeachments. When sitting for that purpose, they shall be on oath or affirmation. When the President of the United States is tried, the chief justice shall preside: and no person shall be convicted without the concurrence of two thirds of the members present.

[2]See the Fourteenth Amendment.
[3]See the Seventeenth Amendment.
[4]See the Seventeenth Amendment.

7. Judgment in cases of impeachment shall not extend further than to removal from office, and disqualification to hold and enjoy any office of honor, trust or profit under the United States: but the party convicted shall nevertheless be liable and subject to indictment, trial, judgment and punishment, according to law.

SECTION 4. 1. The times, places, and manner of holding elections for senators and representatives, shall be prescribed in each State by the legislature thereof; but the Congress may at any time by law make or alter such regulations, except as to the places of choosing senators.

2. The Congress shall assemble at least once in every year, and such meeting shall be on the first Monday in December, unless they shall by law appoint a different day.

SECTION 5. 1. Each House shall be the judge of the elections, returns and qualifications of its own members, and a majority of each shall constitute a quorum to do business; but a smaller number may adjourn from day to day, and may be authorized to compel the attendance of absent members, in such manner, and under such penalties as each House may provide.

2. Each House may determine the rules of its proceedings, punish its members for disorderly behavior, and, with the concurrence of two thirds, expel a member.

3. Each House shall keep a journal of its proceedings, and from time to time publish the same, excepting such parts as may in their judgment require secrecy; and the yeas and nays of the members of either House on any question shall, at the desire of one fifth of those present, be entered on the journal.

4. Neither House, during the session of Congress, shall, without the consent of the other, adjourn for more than three days, nor to any other place than that in which the two Houses shall be sitting.

SECTION 6. 1. The senators and representatives shall receive a compensation for their services, to be ascertained by law, and paid out of the Treasury of the United States. They shall in all cases, except treason, felony, and breach of the peace, be privileged from arrest during their attendance at the session of their respective Houses, and in going to and returning from the same; and for any speech or debate in either House, they shall not be questioned in any other place.

2. No senator or representative shall, during the time for which he was elected, be appointed to any civil office under the authority of the United States, which shall have been created, or the emoluments whereof shall have been increased, during such time; and no person holding any office under the United States shall be a member of either House during his continuance in office.

SECTION 7. 1. All bills for raising revenue shall originate in the House of Representatives; but the Senate may propose or concur with amendments as on other bills.

2. Every bill which shall have passed the House of Representatives and the Senate, shall, before it become a law, be presented to the President of the United States; If he approves he shall sign it, but if not he shall return it, with his objections, to that House in which it shall have originated, who shall enter the objections at large on their journal, and proceed to reconsider it. If after such reconsideration two thirds

of that House shall agree to pass the bill, it shall be sent, together with the objections, to the other House, by which it shall likewise be reconsidered, and if approved by two thirds of that House, it shall become a law. But in all such cases the votes of both Houses shall be determined by yeas and nays, and the names of the persons voting for and against the bill shall be entered on the journal of each House respectively. If any bill shall not be returned by the President within ten days (Sundays excepted) after it shall have been presented to him, the same shall be a law, in like manner as if he had signed it, unless the Congress by their adjournment prevent its return, in which case it shall not be a law.

3. Every order, resolution, or vote to which the concurrence of the Senate and the House of Representatives may be necessary (except on a question of adjournment) shall be presented to the President of the United States; and before the same shall take effect, shall be approved by him, or being disapproved by him, shall be repassed by two thirds of the Senate and House of Representatives, according to the rules and limitations prescribed in the case of a bill.

SECTION 8. 1. The Congress shall have the power

1. To lay and collect taxes, duties, imposts, and excises, to pay the debts and provide for the common defense and general welfare of the United States; but all duties, imposts, and excises shall be uniform throughout the United States.

2. To borrow money on the credit of the United States;

3. To regulate commerce with foreign nations, and among the several States, and with the Indian tribes;

4. To establish a uniform rule of naturalization, and uniform laws on the subject of bankruptcies throughout the United States;

5. To coin money, regulate the value thereof, and of foreign coin, and fix the standard of weights and measures;

6. To provide for the punishment of counterfeiting the securities and current coin of the United States;

7. To establish post offices and post roads;

8. To promote the progress of science and useful arts, by securing for limited times to authors and inventors the exclusive right to their respective writings and discoveries;

9. To constitute tribunals inferior to the Supreme Court;

10. To define and punish piracies and felonies committed on the high seas, and offenses against the law of nations;

11. To declare war, grant letters of marque and reprisal, and make rules concerning captures on land and water;

12. To raise and support armies, but no appropriation of money to that use shall be for a longer term than two years;

13. To provide and maintain a navy;

14. To make rules for the government and regulation of the land and naval forces;

15. To provide for calling forth the militia to execute the laws of the Union, suppress insurrections and repel invasions;

16. To provide for organizing, arming, and disciplining the militia, and for governing such part of them as may be employed in the service of the United States, reserving to the States respectively, the appointment of the officers, and the authority of training the militia according to the discipline prescribed by Congress;

17. To exercise exclusive legislation in all cases whatsoever, over such district (not exceeding ten miles square) as may, by cession of particular States, and the acceptance of Congress, become the seat of the government of the United States, and to exercise like authority over all places purchased by the consent of the legislature of the State in which the same shall be, for the erection of forts, magazines, arsenals, dockyards, and other needful buildings; and

18. To make all laws which shall be necessary and proper for carrying into execution the foregoing powers, and all other powers vested by this Constitution in the government of the United States, or any department or officer thereof.

SECTION 9. 1. The migration or importation of such persons as any of the States now existing shall think proper to admit, shall not be prohibited by the Congress prior to the year one thousand eight hundred and eight, but a tax or duty may be imposed on such importation, not exceeding ten dollars for each person.

2. The privilege of the writ of habeas corpus shall not be suspended, unless when in cases of rebellion or invasion the public safety may require it.

3. No bill of attainder or ex post facto law shall be passed.

4. No capitation, or other direct, tax shall be laid, unless in proportion to the census or enumeration herein-before directed to be taken.[5]

5. No tax or duty shall be laid on articles exported from any State.

6. No preference shall be given by any regulation of commerce or revenue to the ports of one State over those of another: nor shall vessels bound to, or from, one State be obliged to enter, clear, or pay duties in another.

7. No money shall be drawn from the treasury, but in consequence of appropriations made by law; and a regular statement and account of the receipts and expenditures of all public money shall be published from time to time.

8. No title of nobility shall be granted by the United States: and no person holding any office of profit or trust under them, shall, without the consent of the Congress, accept of any present, emolument, office, or title, of any kind whatever, from any king, price, or foreign State.

SECTION 10. 1. No State shall enter into any treaty, alliance, or confederation; grant letters of marque and reprisal; coin money; emit bills of credit; make any thing but gold and silver coin a tender in payment of debts; pass any bill of attainder, ex post facto law, or law impairing the obligation of contracts, or grant, any title of nobility.

2. No State shall, without the consent of the Congress, lay any imposts or duties on imports or exports, except what may be absolutely necessary for executing its inspection laws: and the net produce of all duties and imposts laid by any State on imports or exports, shall be for the use of the treasury of the United States; and all such laws shall be subject to the revision and control of the Congress.

3. No State shall, without the consent of the Congress, lay any duty of tonnage, keep troops, or ships of war in time of peace, enter into any agreement or compact with another State, or with a foreign power, or engage in war, unless actually invaded, or in such imminent danger as will not admit of delay.

[5]See the Sixteenth Amendment.

Article II

Section 1. 1. The executive power shall be vested in a President of the United States of America. He shall hold his office during the term of four years, and, together with the Vice President, chosen for the same term, be elected, as follows:

2. Each State shall appoint, in such manner as the legislature thereof may direct, a number of electors, equal to the whole number of senators and representatives to which the State may be entitled in the Congress: but no senator or representative, or person holding any office of trust or profit under the United States, shall be appointed an elector.

The electors shall meet in their respective States, and vote by ballot for two persons, of whom one at least shall not be an inhabitant of the same State with themselves. And they shall make a list of all the persons voted for, and of the number of votes for each; which list they shall sign and certify, and transmit sealed to the seat of the government of the United States, directed to the president of the Senate. The president of the Senate shall, in the presence of the Senate and House of Representatives, open all the certificates, and the votes shall then be counted. The person having the greatest number of votes shall be the President, if such number be a majority of the whole number of electors appointed; and if there be more than one who have such majority, and have an equal number of votes, then the House of Representatives shall immediately choose by ballot one of them for President; and if no person have a majority, then from the five highest on the list the said House shall in like manner choose the President. But in choosing the President, the votes shall be taken by States, the representation from each State having one vote; a quorum for this purpose shall consist of a member or members from two thirds of the States, and a majority of all the States shall be necessary to a choice. In every case after the choice of the President, the person having the greatest number of votes of the electors shall be the Vice President. But if there should remain two or more who have equal votes, the Senate shall chose from them by ballot the Vice President.[6]

3. The Congress may determine the time of choosing the electors, and the day on which they shall give their votes; which day shall be the same throughout the United States.

4. No person except a natural born citizen, or a citizen of the United States, at the time of the adoption of this Constitution, shall be eligible to the office of President; neither shall any person be eligible to the office who shall not have attained to the age of thirty-five years, and been fourteen years a resident within the United States.

5. In case of the removal of the President from office, or of his death, resignation, or inability to discharge the powers and duties of the said office, the same shall devolve on the Vice President, and the congress may by law provide for the case of removal, death, resignation or inability, both of the President and Vice President, declaring what officer shall then act as President, and such officer shall act accordingly until the disability be removed, or a President shall be elected.

6. The President shall, at stated times, receive for his services a compensation which shall neither be increased nor diminished during the period for which he shall have been elected, and he shall not receive within that period any other emolument from the United States, or any of them.

7. Before he enter on the execution of his office, he shall take the following oath or affirmation:—"I do solemnly swear (or affirm) that I will faithfully execute the office of President of the United States, and will to the best of my ability, preserve, protect and defend the Constitution of the United States."

Section 2. 1. The President shall be commander in chief of the army and navy of the United States, and of the militia of the several States, when called into the actual service of the United States; he may require the opinion in writing, of the principal officer in each of the executive departments, upon any subject relating to the duties of their respective offices, and he shall have power to grant reprieves and pardons for offenses against the United States, except in cases of impeachment.

2. He shall have power, by and with the advice and consent of the Senate, to make treaties, provided two thirds of the senators present concur; and he shall nominate, and by and with the advice and consent of the Senate, shall appoint ambassadors, other public ministers and consuls, judges of the Supreme Court, and all other officers of the United States, whose appointments are not herein otherwise provided for, and which shall be established by law; but the Congress may by law vest the appointment of such inferior officers, as they think proper, in the President alone, in the courts of laws, or in the heads of departments.

3. The President shall have power to fill up all vacancies that may happen during the recess of the Senate, by granting commissions which shall expire at the end of their next session.

Section 3. He shall from time to time give to the Congress information of the state of the Union, and recommend to their consideration such measures as he shall judge necessary and expedient; he may, on extraordinary occasions, convene both Houses, or either of them, and in case of disagreement between them with respect to the time of adjournment, he may adjourn them to such time as he shall think proper; he shall receive ambassadors and other public ministers; he shall take care that the laws be faithfully executed, and shall commission all the officers of the United States.

Section 4. The President, Vice President, and all civil officers of the United States, shall be removed from office on impeachment for, and conviction of, treason, bribery, or other high crimes and misdemeanors.

Article III

Section 1. The judicial power of the United States shall be vested in one Supreme Court, and in such inferior courts as the Congress may from time to time ordain and establish. The judges, both of the Supreme and inferior courts, shall hold their offices during good behavior, and shall, at stated times, receive for their services, a compensation, which shall not be diminished during their continuance in office.

Section 2. 2. The judicial power shall extend to all cases, in law and equity, arising under this Constitution, the laws of the United States, and treaties made, or which shall be made,

[6]Superseded by the Twelfth Amendment.

under their authority;—to all cases of admiralty and maritime jurisdiction;—to controversies to which the United States shall be a party;[7]—to controversies between two or more States;—between a State and citizens of another State;—between citizens of different States;—between citizens of the same State claiming lands under grants of different States, and between a State, or the citizens thereof, and foreign States, citizens or subjects.

2. In all cases affecting ambassadors, other public ministers and consuls, and those in which a State shall be party, the Supreme Court shall have original jurisdiction. In all the other cases before mentioned, the Supreme Court shall have appellate jurisdiction, both as to law and fact, with such exceptions, and under such regulations as the Congress shall make.

3. The trial of all crimes, except in cases of impeachment, shall be by jury; and such trial shall be held in the State where the said crimes shall have been committed; but when not committed within any State, the trial shall be such place or places as the congress may by law have directed.

SECTION 3. 1. Treason against the United States shall consist only in levying war against them, or in adhering to their enemies, giving them aid and comfort. No person shall be convicted of treason unless on the testimony of two witnesses to the same overt act, or on confession in open court.

2. The Congress shall have power to declare the punishment of treason, but no attainder of treason shall work corruption of blood, or forfeiture except during the life of the person attained.

Article IV

SECTION 1. Full faith and credit shall be given in each State to the public acts, records, and judicial proceedings of every other State. And the Congress may by general laws prescribe the manner in which such acts, records and proceedings shall be proved, and the effect thereof.

SECTION 2. 1. The citizens of each State shall be entitled to all privileges and immunities of citizens in the several States.[8]

2. A person charged in any State with treason, felony, or other crime, who shall flee from justice, and be found in another State, shall on demand of the executive authority of the State from which he fled, be delivered up to be removed to the State having jurisdiction of the crime.

3. No person held to service or labor in one State under the laws thereof, escaping into another, shall, in consequence of any law or regulation therein, be discharged from such service or labor, but shall be delivered up on claim of the party to whom such service or labor may be due.[9]

SECTION 3. 1. New States may be admitted by the Congress into this Union; but no new State shall be formed or erected within the jurisdiction of any other State, nor any State be formed by the junction of two or more States, or parts of States, without the consent of the legislatures of the States concerned as well as of the Congress.

2. The Congress shall have power to dispose of and make all needful rules and regulations respecting the territory or other property belonging to the United States; and nothing in this Constitution shall be so construed as to prejudice any claims of the United States, or of any particular State.

SECTION 4. The United States shall guarantee to every State in this Union a republican form of government, and shall protect each of them against invasion; and on application of the legislature, or of the executive (when the legislature cannot be convened) against domestic violence.

Article V

The Congress, whenever two thirds of both Houses shall deem it necessary, shall propose amendments to this Constitution, or, on the application of the legislatures of two thirds of the several States, shall call a convention for proposing amendments, which in either case shall be valid to all intents and purposes, as part of this Constitution, when ratified by the legislatures of three fourths of the several States, or by conventions in three fourths thereof, as the one or the other mode of ratification may be proposed by the Congress; Provided that no amendment which may be made prior to the year one thousand eight hundred and eight shall in any manner affect the first and fourth clauses in the ninth section of the first article; and that no State, without its consent, shall be deprived of its equal suffrage in the Senate.

Article VI

1. All debts contracted and engagements entered into, before the adoption of this Constitution, shall be as valid against the United States under this Constitution, as under the Confederation.[10]

2. This Constitution, and the laws of the United States which shall be made in pursuance thereof; and all treaties made, or which shall be made, under the authority of the United States, shall be the supreme law of the land; and the judges in every State shall be bound thereby, any thing in the Constitution or laws of any State to the contrary notwithstanding.

3. The senators and representatives before mentioned, and the members of the several State legislatures, and all executive and judicial officers, both of the United States and of the several States, shall be bound by oath or affirmation to support this Constitution; but no religious test shall ever be required as a qualification to any office or public trust under the United States.

Article VII

The ratification of the conventions of nine States shall be sufficient for the establishment of this Constitution between the States so ratifying the same.

Done in Convention by the unanimous consent of the States present the seventeenth day of September in the year of our Lord one thousand seven hundred and eighty-seven, and of the independence of the United States of America the twelfth. In witness whereof we have hereunto subscribed our names.

[Signatories names omitted]

* * *

[7]See the Eleventh Amendment.
[8]See the Fourteenth Amendment, Sec. 1.
[9]See the Thirteenth Amendment.

[10]See the Fourteenth Amendment, Sec. 4.

Articles in addition to, and amendment of, the Constitution of the United States of America, proposed by Congress, and ratified by the legislatures of the several States, pursuant to the fifth article of the original Constitution.

Amendment I

[First ten amendments ratified December 15, 1791]

Congress shall make no law respecting an establishment of religion, or prohibiting the free exercise thereof; or abridging the freedom of speech, or of the press; or the right of the people peaceably to assemble, and to petition the government for a redress of grievances.

Amendment II

A well regulated militia, being necessary to the security of a free State, the right of the people to keep and bear arms, shall not be infringed.

Amendment III

No soldier shall, in time of peace be quartered in any house, without the consent of the owner, nor in time of war, but in a manner to be prescribed by law.

Amendment IV

The right of the people to be secure in their persons, houses, papers, and effects, against unreasonable searches and seizures, shall not be violated, and no warrants shall issue, but upon probable cause, supported by oath or affirmation, and particularly describing the place to be searched, and the persons or things to be seized.

Amendment V

No person shall be held to answer for a capital or otherwise infamous crime, unless on a presentment or indictment of a grand jury, except in cases arising in the land or naval forces, or in the militia, when in actual service in time of war or public danger; nor shall any person be subject for the same offense to be twice put in jeopardy of life or limb; nor shall be compelled in any criminal case to be a witness against himself, nor be deprived of life, liberty, or property, without due process of law; nor shall private property be taken for public use, without just compensation.

Amendment VI

In all criminal prosecutions, the accused shall enjoy the right to a speedy and public trial, by an impartial jury of the State and district wherein the crime shall have been committed, which district shall have been previously ascertained by law, and to be informed of the nature and cause of the accusation; to be confronted with the witnesses against him; to have compulsory process for obtaining witnesses in his favor, and to have the assistance of counsel for his defense.

Amendment VII

In suits at common law, where the value in controversy shall exceed twenty dollars, the right of trial by jury shall be preserved, and no fact tried by a jury shall be otherwise reexamined in any court of the United States, than according to the rules of the common law.

Amendment VIII

Excessive bail shall not be required, nor excessive fines imposed, nor cruel and unusual punishments inflicted.

Amendment IX

The enumeration in the Constitution of certain rights shall not be construed to deny or disparage others retained by the people.

Amendment X

The powers not delegated to the United States by the Constitution, nor prohibited by it to the States, are reserved to the States respectively, or to the people.

Amendment XI [January 8, 1798]

The judicial power of the United States shall not be construed to extend to any suit in law or equity, commended or prosecuted against one of the United States by citizens of another State, or by citizens or subjects of any foreign State.

Amendment XII [September 25, 1804]

The electors shall meet in their respective States, and vote by ballot for President and Vice President, one of whom, at least, shall not be an inhabitant of the same State with themselves; they shall name in their ballots the person voted for as President, and in distinct ballots, the person voted for as Vice President, and they shall make distinct lists of all persons voted for as President and of all persons voted for as Vice President, and of the number of votes for each, which lists they shall sign and certify, and transmit sealed to the seat of the government of the United States, directed to the President of the Senate;—The President of the Senate shall, in the presence of the Senate and House of Representatives, open all the certificates and the votes shall then be counted;—The person having the greatest number of votes for President, shall be the President, if such number be a majority of the whole number of electors appointed; and if no person have such majority, then from the persons having the highest numbers not exceeding three on the list of those voted for as President, the House of Representatives shall choose immediately, by ballot, the President. But in choosing the President, the votes shall be taken by States, the representation from each State having one vote; a quorum for this purpose shall consist of a member or members from two thirds of the States, and a majority of all the States shall be necessary to a choice. And if the House of Representatives shall not choose a President whenever the right of choice shall devolve upon them, before the fourth day of March next following, then the Vice President shall act as President, as in the case of the death or other constitutional disability of the President. The person having the greatest number of votes as Vice President shall be the Vice President, if such number be a majority of the whole number of electors appointed, and if no person have a majority, then from the two highest numbers on the list, the Senate shall choose the Vice President; a quorum for the purpose shall consist of two thirds of the whole number of Senators, and a majority of the whole number shall be necessary to a choice. But no person constitutionally ineligible to the office of President shall be eligible to that of Vice President of the United States.

Amendment XIII [December 18, 1865]

SECTION 1. Neither slavery nor involuntary servitude, except as a punishment for crime whereof the party shall have been duly convicted, shall exist within the United States, or any place subject to their jurisdiction.

SECTION 2. Congress shall have power to enforce this article by appropriate legislation.

Amendment XIV [July 28, 1868]

SECTION 1. All persons born or naturalized in the United States, and subject to the jurisdiction thereof, are citizens of the United States and of the State wherein they reside. No State shall make or enforce any law which shall abridge the privileges or immunities of citizens of the United States; nor shall any State deprive any person of life, liberty, or property, without due process of law; nor deny to any person within its jurisdiction the equal protection of the laws.

SECTION 2. Representatives shall be apportioned among the several States according to their respective numbers, counting the whole number of persons in each State, excluding Indians not taxed. But when the right to vote at any election for the choice of electors for President and Vice President of the United States, representatives in Congress, the executive and judicial officers of a State, or the members of the legislature thereof, is denied to any of the male inhabitants of such State, being twenty-one years of age, and citizens of the United States, or in any way abridged, except for participating in rebellion, or other crime, the basis of representation there shall be reduced in the proportion which the number of such male citizens shall bear to the whole number of male citizens twenty-one years of age in such State.

SECTION 3. No person shall be a senator or representative in Congress, or elector of President and Vice President, or hold any office, civil or military, under the United States, or under any State, who having previously taken an oath, as a member of Congress, or as an officer of the United States, or as a member of any State legislature, or as an executive or judicial officer of any State, to support the Constitution of the United States, shall have engaged in insurrection or rebellion against the same, or given aid or comfort to the enemies thereof. But Congress may by a vote of two thirds of each House, remove such disability.

SECTION 4. The validity of the public debt of the United States, authorized by law, including debts incurred for payment of pensions and bounties for services in suppressing insurrection or rebellion; shall not be questioned. But neither the United States nor any State shall assume or pay any debt or obligation incurred in aid of insurrection or rebellion against the United States, or any claim for the loss or emancipation of any slave; but all such debts, obligations, and claims shall be held illegal and void.

SECTION 5. The Congress shall have the power to enforce, by appropriate legislation, the provisions of this article.

Amendment XV [March 30, 1870]

SECTION 1. The right of citizens of the United States to vote shall not be denied or abridged by the United States or by any State on account of race, color, or previous condition of servitude.

SECTION 2. The Congress shall have power to enforce this article by appropriate legislation.

Amendment XVI [February 25, 1913]

The Congress shall have power to lay and collect taxes on incomes, from whatever source derived, without apportionment among the several States, and without regard to any census or enumeration.

Amendment XVII [May 31, 1913]

The Senate of the United States shall be composed of two senators from each State, elected by the people thereof, for six years; and each senator shall have one vote. The electors in each State shall have the qualifications requisite for electors of the most numerous branch of the State legislature.

When vacancies happen in the representation of any State in the Senate, the executive authority of such State shall issue writs of election to fill such vacancies: Provided, That the legislature of any State may empower the executive thereof to make temporary appointments until the people fill the vacancies by election as the legislature may direct.

This amendment shall not be so construed as to affect the election or term of any senator chosen before it becomes valid as part of the Constitution.

Amendment XVIII[11] [January 29, 1919]

After one year from the ratification of this article, the manufacture, sale, or transportation of intoxicating liquors within, the importation thereof into, or the exportation thereof from the United States and all territory subject to the jurisdiction thereof for beverage purposes is thereby prohibited.

The Congress and the several States shall have concurrent power to enforce this article by appropriate legislation.

This article shall be inoperative unless it shall have been ratified as an amendment to the Constitution by the legislatures of the several States, as provided in the constitution, within seven years from the date of the submission hereof to the States by Congress.

Amendment XIX [August 26, 1920]

The right of citizens of the United States to vote shall not be denied or abridged by the United States or by any State on account of sex.

Congress shall have the power to enforce this article by appropriate legislation.

Amendment XX [January 23, 1933]

SECTION 1. The terms of the President and Vice President shall end at noon on the 20th day of January and the terms of Senators and Representatives at noon on the 3d day of January, of the years in which such terms would have ended if this article had not been ratified; and the terms of their successors shall then begin.

SECTION 2. The Congress shall assemble at least once in every year, and such meeting shall begin at noon on the 3d day of January, unless they shall by law appoint a different day.

SECTION 3. If, at the time fixed for the beginning of the term of President, the President-elect shall have died, the

[11] Repealed by the Twenty-first Amendment.

Vice President-elect shall become President. If a President shall not have been chosen before the time fixed for the beginning of his term, or if the President-elect shall have failed to qualify, then the Vice President-elect shall act as President until a President shall have qualified; and the Congress may by law provide for the case wherein neither a President-elect nor a Vice President-elect shall have qualified, declaring who shall then act as President, or the manner in which one who is to act shall be selected, and such person shall act accordingly until a President or Vice President shall have qualified.

SECTION 4. The Congress may by law provide for the case of the death of any of the persons from whom, the House of Representatives may choose a President whenever the right of choice shall have devolved upon them, and for the case of the death of any of the persons from whom the Senate may choose a Vice President whenever the right of choice shall have devolved upon them.

SECTION 5. Sections 1 and 2 shall take effect on the 15th day of October following the ratification of this article.

SECTION 6. This article shall be inoperative unless it shall have been ratified as an amendment to the Constitution by the legislatures of three-fourths of the several States within seven years from the date of its submission.

Amendment XXI [December 5, 1933]

SECTION 1. The Eighteenth Article of amendment to the Constitution of the United States is hereby repealed.

SECTION 2. The transportation or importation into any State, Territory, or possession of the United States for delivery or use therein of intoxicating liquors in violation of the laws thereof, is hereby prohibited.

SECTION 3. This article shall be inoperative unless it shall have been ratified as an amendment to the Constitution by conventions in the several States, as provided in the Constitution, within seven years from the date of the submission thereof to the States by the Congress.

Amendment XXII [March 1, 1951]

No person shall be elected to the office of the President more than twice, and no person who has held the office of President, or acted as President, for more than two years of a term to which some other person was elected President shall be elected to the office of the President more than once.

But this article shall not apply to any person holding the office of President when this article was proposed by the Congress, and shall not prevent any person who may be holding the office of President, or acting as President, during the term within which this article becomes operative from holding the office of President or acting as President during the remainder of such term.

This article shall be inoperative unless it shall have been ratified as an amendment to the Constitution by the legislatures of three-fourths of the several States within seven years from the date of its submission to the States by the Congress.

Amendment XXIII [March 29, 1961]

SECTION 1. The District constituting the seat of Government of the United States shall appoint in such manner as the Congress may direct.

A number of electors of President and Vice President equal to the whole number of Senators and Representatives in Congress to which the District would be entitled if it were a State, but in no event more than the least populous State; they shall be in addition to those appointed by the States, but they shall be considered, for the purposes of the election of President and Vice President, to be electors appointed by a State; and they shall meet in the District and perform such duties as provided by the twelfth article of amendment.

SECTION 2. The Congress shall have power to enforce this article by appropriate legislation.

Amendment XXIV [January 23, 1964]

SECTION 1. The right of citizens of the United States to vote in any primary or other election for President or Vice President, for electors for President or Vice President, or for Senator or Representative in Congress, shall not be denied or abridged by the United States or any State by reason of failure to pay any poll tax or other tax.

SECTION 2. The Congress shall have power to enforce this article by appropriate legislation.

Amendment XXV [February 10, 1967]

SECTION 1. In case of the removal of the President from office or of his death or resignation, the Vice President shall become President.

SECTION 2. Whenever there is a vacancy in the office of the Vice president, the President shall nominate a Vice President who shall take office upon confirmation by a majority of both Houses of Congress.

SECTION 3. Whenever the President transmits to the President pro tempore of the Senate and the Speaker of the House of Representatives his written declaration that he is unable to discharge the powers and duties of his office, and until he transmits to them a written declaration to the contrary, such powers and duties shall be discharged by the Vice President as Acting President.

SECTION 4. Whenever the Vice president and a majority of either the principal officers of the executive departments or of such other body as Congress may by law provide, transmit to the President pro tempore of the Senate and the Speaker of the House of Representatives their written declaration that the President is unable to discharge the powers and duties of his office, the Vice President shall immediately assume the powers and duties of the office as Acting President.

Thereafter, when the President transmits to the President pro tempore of the Senate and the Speaker of the House of Representatives his written declaration that no inability exists, he shall resume the powers and duties of his office unless the Vice President and a majority of either the principal officers of the executive departments or of such other body as

Congress may by law provide, transmit within four days to the President pro tempore of the Senate and the Speaker of the House of Representatives their written declaration that the President is unable to discharge the powers and duties of his office. Thereupon Congress shall decide the issue, assembling within forty-eight hours for that purpose if not in session. If the Congress, within twenty-one days after receipt of the latter written declaration, or, if Congress is not in session, within twenty-one days after Congress is required to assemble, determines by two-thirds vote of both Houses that the President is unable to discharge the powers and duties of his office, the Vice President shall continue to discharge the same as Acting President; otherwise, the President shall resume the powers and duties of his office.

Amendment XXVI [June 30, 1971]

SECTION 1. The right of citizens of the United States who are eighteen years of age or older to vote shall not be denied or abridged by the United States or by any State on account of age.

SECTION 2. The Congress shall have power to enforce this article by appropriate legislation.

Amendment XXVII[12] [May 7, 1992]

No law, varying the compensation for services of the Senators and Representatives, shall take effect until an election of Representatives shall have intervened.

[12]James Madison proposed this amendment in 1789 together with the ten amendments that were adopted as the Bill of Rights, but it failed to win ratification at the time. Congress, however, had set no deadline for its ratification, and over the years—particularly in the 1980s and 1990s—many states voted to add it to the Constitution. With the ratification of Michigan in 1992 it passed the threshold of 3/4ths of the states required for adoption, but because the process took more than 200 years, its validity remains in doubt.

Presidential Elections

Year	Number of States	Candidates	Party	Popular Vote*	Electoral Vote†	Percent-age of Popular Vote
1789	11	GEORGE WASHINGTON	No party designations		69	
		John Adams			34	
		Other Candidates			35	
1792	15	GEORGE WASHINGTON	No party designations		132	
		John Adams			77	
		George Clinton			50	
		Other Candidates			5	
1796	16	JOHN ADAMS	Federalist		71	
		Thomas Jefferson	Democratic-Republican		68	
		Thomas Pinckney	Federalist		59	
		Aaron Burr	Democratic-Republican		30	
		Other Candidates			48	
1800	16	THOMAS JEFFERSON	Democratic-Republican		73	
		Aaron Burr	Democratic-Republican		73	
		John Adams	Federalist		65	
		Charles C. Pinckney	Federalist		64	
		John Jay	Federalist		1	
1804	17	THOMAS JEFFERSON	Democratic-Republican		162	
		Charles C. Pinckney	Federalist		14	
1808	17	JAMES MADISON	Democratic-Republican		122	
		Charles C. Pinckney	Federalist		47	
		George Clinton	Democratic-Republican		6	
1812	18	JAMES MADISON	Democratic-Republican		128	
		DeWitt Clinton	Federalist		89	
1816	19	JAMES MONROE	Democratic-Republican		183	
		Rufus King	Federalist		34	
1820	24	JAMES MONROE	Democratic-Republican		231	
		John Quincy Adams	Independent Republican		1	
1824	24	JOHN QUINCY ADAMS	Democratic-Republican	108,740	84	30.5
		Andrew Jackson	Democratic-Republican	153,544	99	43.1
		William H. Crawford	Democratic-Republican	46,618	41	13.1
		Henry Clay	Democratic-Republican	47,136	37	13.2
1828	24	ANDREW JACKSON	Democrat	647,286	178	56.0
		John Quincy Adams	National Republican	508,064	83	44.0
1832	24	ANDREW JACKSON	Democrat	687,502	219	55.0
		Henry Clay	National Republican	530,189	49	42.4
		William Wirt	Anti-Masonic	33,108	7	2.6
		John Floyd	National Republican		11	

**Percentage of popular vote given for any election year may not total 100 percent because candidates receiving less than 1 percent of the popular vote have been omitted.*

†Prior to the passage of the Twelfth Amendment in 1904, the electoral college voted for two presidential candidates; the runner-up became Vice-President. Data from Historical Statistics of the United States, Colonial Times to 1957 (1961), pp. 682–683, and The World Almanac.

Presidential Elections
(continued)

Year	Number of States	Candidates	Party	Popular Vote	Electoral Vote	Percentage of Popular Vote
1836	26	MARTIN VAN BUREN	Democrat	765,483	170	50.9
		William H. Harrison	Whig	739,795	73	49.1
		Hugh L. White	Whig		26	
		Daniel Webster	Whig		14	
		W. P. Mangum	Whig		11	
1840	26	WILLIAM H. HARRISON	Whig	1,274,624	234	53.1
		Martin Van Buren	Democrat	1,127,781	60	46.9
1844	26	JAMES K. POLK	Democrat	1,338,464	170	49.6
		Henry Clay	Whig	1,300,097	105	48.1
		James G. Birney	Liberty	62,300		2.3
1848	30	ZACHARY TAYLOR	Whig	1,360,967	163	47.4
		Lewis Cass	Democrat	1,222,342	127	42.5
		Martin Van Buren	Free Soil	291,263		10.1
1852	31	FRANKLIN PIERCE	Democrat	1,601,117	254	50.9
		Winfield Scott	Whig	1,385,453	42	44.1
		John P. Hale	Free Soil	155,825		5.0
1856	31	JAMES BUCHANAN	Democrat	1,832,955	174	45.3
		John C. Frémont	Republican	1,339,932	114	33.1
		Millard Fillmore	American ("Know Nothing")	871,731	8	21.6
1860	33	ABRAHAM LINCOLN	Republican	1,865,593	180	39.8
		Stephen A. Douglas	Democrat	1,382,713	12	29.5
		John C. Breckinridge	Democrat	848,356	72	18.1
		John Bell	Constitutional Union	592,906	39	12.6
1864	36	ABRAHAM LINCOLN	Republican	2,206,938	212	55.0
		George B. McClellan	Democrat	1,803,787	21	45.0
1868	37	ULYSSES S. GRANT	Republican	3,013,421	214	52.7
		Horatio Seymour	Democrat	2,706,829	80	47.3
1872	37	ULYSSES S. GRANT	Republican	3,596,745	286	55.6
		Horace Greeley	Democrat	2,843,446	*	43.9
1876	38	RUTHERFORD B. HAYES	Republican	4,036,572	185	48.0
		Samuel J. Tilden	Democrat	4,284,020	184	51.0
1880	38	JAMES A. GARFIELD	Republican	4,453,295	214	48.5
		Winfield S. Hancock	Democrat	4,414,082	155	48.1
		James B. Weaver	Greenback-Labor	308,578		3.4
1884	38	GROVER CLEVELAND	Democrat	4,879,507	219	48.5
		James G. Blaine	Republican	4,850,293	182	48.2
		Benjamin F. Butler	Greenback-Labor	175,370		1.8
		John P. St. John	Prohibition	150,369		1.5
1888	38	BENJAMIN HARRISON	Republican	5,447,129	233	47.9
		Grover Cleveland	Democrat	5,537,857	168	48.6
		Clinton B. Fisk	Prohibition	249,506		2.2
		Anson J. Streeter	Union Labor	146,935		1.3

**Because of the death of Greeley, Democratic electors scattered their votes.*

Presidential Elections (continued)

Year	Number of States	Candidates	Party	Popular Vote	Electoral Vote	Percentage of Popular Vote
1892	44	GROVER CLEVELAND	Democrat	5,555,426	277	46.1
		Benjamin Harrison	Republican	5,182,690	145	43.0
		James B. Weaver	People's	1,029,846	22	8.5
		John Bidwell	Prohibition	264,133		2.2
1896	45	WILLIAM MCKINLEY	Republican	7,102,246	271	51.1
		William J. Bryan	Democrat	6,492,559	176	47.7
1900	45	WILLIAM MCKINLEY	Republican	7,218,491	292	51.7
		William J. Bryan	Democrat; Populist	6,356,734	155	45.5
		John C. Woolley	Prohibition	208,914		1.5
1904	45	THEODORE ROOSEVELT	Republican	7,628,461	336	57.4
		Alton B. Parker	Democrat	5,084,223	140	37.6
		Eugene V. Debs	Socialist	402,283		3.0
		Silas C. Swallow	Prohibition	258,536		1.9
1908	46	WILLIAM H. TAFT	Republican	7,675,320	321	51.6
		William J. Bryan	Democrat	6,412,294	162	43.1
		Eugene V. Debs	Socialist	420,793		2.8
		Eugene W. Chafin	Prohibition	253,840		1.7
1912	48	WOODROW WILSON	Democrat	6,296,547	435	41.9
		Theodore Roosevelt	Progressive	4,118,571	88	27.4
		William H. Taft	Republican	3,486,720	8	23.2
		Eugene V. Debs	Socialist	900,672		6.0
		Eugene W. Chafin	Prohibition	206,275		1.4
1916	48	WOODROW WILSON	Democrat	9,127,695	277	49.4
		Charles E. Hughes	Republican	8,533,507	254	46.2
		A. L. Benson	Socialist	585,113		3.2
		J. Frank Hanly	Prohibition	220,506		1.2
1920	48	WARREN G. HARDING	Republican	16,143,407	404	60.4
		James M. Cox	Democrat	9,130,328	127	34.2
		Eugene V. Debs	Socialist	919,799		3.4
		P. P. Christensen	Farmer-Labor	265,411		1.0
1924	48	CALVIN COOLIDGE	Republican	15,718,211	382	54.0
		John W. Davis	Democrat	8,385,283	136	28.8
		Robert M. La Follette	Progressive	4,831,289	13	16.6
1928	48	HERBERT C. HOOVER	Republican	21,391,993	444	58.2
		Alfred E. Smith	Democrat	15,016,169	87	40.9
1932	48	FRANKLIN D. ROOSEVELT	Democrat	22,809,638	472	57.4
		Herbert C. Hoover	Republican	15,758,901	59	39.7
		Norman Thomas	Socialist	881,951		2.2
1936	48	FRANKLIN D. ROOSEVELT	Democrat	27,752,869	523	60.8
		Alfred M. Landon	Republican	16,674,665	8	36.5
		William Lemke	Union	882,479		1.9
1940	48	FRANKLIN D. ROOSEVELT	Democrat	27,307,819	449	54.8
		Wendell L. Willkie	Republican	22,321,018	82	44.8
1944	48	FRANKLIN D. ROOSEVELT	Democrat	25,606,585	432	53.5
		Thomas E. Dewey	Republican	22,014,745	99	46.0

PRESIDENTIAL ELECTIONS
(continued)

Year	Number of States	Candidates	Party	Popular Vote	Electoral Vote	Percentage of Popular Vote
1948	48	HARRY S. TRUMAN	Democrat	24,105,812	303	49.5
		Thomas E. Dewey	Republican	21,970,065	189	45.1
		J. Strom Thurmond	States' Rights	1,169,063	39	2.4
		Henry A. Wallace	Progressive	1,157,172		2.4
1952	48	DWIGHT D. EISENHOWER	Republican	33,936,234	442	55.1
		Adlai E. Stevenson	Democrat	27,314,992	89	44.4
1956	48	DWIGHT D. EISENHOWER	Republican	35,590,472	457*	57.6
		Adlai E. Stevenson	Democrat	26,022,752	73	42.1
1960	50	JOHN F. KENNEDY	Democrat	34,227,096	303†	49.9
		Richard M. Nixon	Republican	34,108,546	219	49.6
1964	50	LYNDON B. JOHNSON	Democrat	42,676,220	486	61.3
		Barry M. Goldwater	Republican	26,860,314	52	38.5
1968	50	RICHARD M. NIXON	Republican	31,785,480	301	43.4
		Hubert H. Humphrey	Democrat	31,275,165	191	42.7
		George C. Wallace	American Independent	9,906,473	46	13.5
1972	50	RICHARD M. NIXON‡	Republican	47,165,234	520	60.6
		George S. McGovern	Democrat	29,168,110	17	37.5
1976	50	JIMMY CARTER	Democrat	40,828,929	297	50.1
		Gerald R. Ford	Republican	39,148,940	240	47.9
		Eugene McCarthy	Independent	739,256		
1980	50	RONALD REAGAN	Republican	43,201,220	489	50.9
		Jimmy Carter	Democrat	34,913,332	49	41.2
		John B. Anderson	Independent	5,581,379		
1984	50	RONALD REAGAN	Republican	53,428,357	525	59.0
		Walter F. Mondale	Democrat	36,930,923	13	41.0
1988	50	GEORGE BUSH	Republican	48,901,046	426	53.4
		Michael Dukakis	Democrat	41,809,030	111	45.6
1992	50	BILL CLINTON	Democrat	43,728,275	370	43.2
		George Bush	Republican	38,167,416	168	37.7
		H. Ross Perot	United We Stand, America	19,237,247		19.0
1996	50	BILL CLINTON	Democrat	45,590,703	379	49.0
		Bob Dole	Republican	37,816,307	159	41.0
		H. Ross Perot	Reform	7,866,284		8.0

**Walter B. Jones received 1 electoral vote.*

†Harry F. Byrd received 15 electoral votes.

‡Resigned August 9, 1974: Vice President Gerald R. Ford became President.

Presidential Administrations

The Washington Administration (1789–1797)

Vice President	John Adams	1789–1797
Secretary of State	Thomas Jefferson	1789–1793
	Edmund Randolph	1794–1795
	Timothy Pickering	1795–1797
Secretary of Treasury	Alexander Hamilton	1789–1795
	Oliver Wolcott	1795–1797
Secretary of War	Henry Knox	1789–1794
	Timothy Pickering	1795–1796
	James McHenry	1796–1797
Attorney General	Edmund Randolph	1789–1793
	William Bradford	1794–1795
	Charles Lee	1795–1797
Postmaster General	Samuel Osgood	1789–1791
	Timothy Pickering	1791–1794
	Joseph Habersham	1795–1797

The John Adams Administration (1797–1801)

Vice President	Thomas Jefferson	1797–1801
Secretary of State	Timothy Pickering	1797–1800
	John Marshall	1800–1801
Secretary of Treasury	Oliver Wolcott	1797–1800
	Samuel Dexter	1800–1801
Secretary of War	James McHenry	1797–1800
	Samuel Dexter	1800–1801
Attorney General	Charles Lee	1797–1801
Postmaster General	Joseph Habersham	1797–1801
Secretary of Navy	Benjamin Stoddert	1798–1801

The Jefferson Administration (1801–1809)

Vice President	Aaron Burr	1801–1805
	George Clinton	1805–1809
Secretary of State	James Madison	1801–1809
Secretary of Treasury	Samuel Dexter	1801
	Albert Gallatin	1801–1809
Secretary of War	Henry Dearborn	1801–1809
Attorney General	Levi Lincoln	1801–1805
	Robert Smith	1805
	John Breckinridge	1805–1806
	Caesar Rodney	1807–1809
Postmaster General	Joseph Habersham	1801
	Gideon Granger	1801–1809
Secretary of Navy	Robert Smith	1801–1809

The Madison Administration (1809–1817)

Vice President	George Clinton	1809–1813
	Elbridge Gerry	1813–1817
Secretary of State	Robert Smith	1809–1811
	James Monroe	1811–1817
Secretary of Treasury	Albert Gallatin	1809–1813
	George Campbell	1814
	Alexander Dallas	1814–1816
	William Crawford	1816–1817
Secretary of War	William Eustis	1809–1812
	John Armstrong	1813–1814
	James Monroe	1814–1815
	William Crawford	1815–1817
Attorney General	Caesar Rodney	1809–1811
	William Pinkney	1811–1814
	Richard Rush	1814–1817
Postmaster General	Gideon Granger	1809–1814
	Return Meigs	1814–1817
Secretary of Navy	Paul Hamilton	1809–1813
	William Jones	1813–1814
	Benjamin Crowninshield	1814–1817

The Monroe Administration (1817–1825)

Vice President	Daniel Tompkins	1817–1825
Secretary of State	John Quincy Adams	1817–1825
Secretary of Treasury	William Crawford	1817–1825
Secretary of War	George Graham	1817
	John C. Calhoun	1817–1825
Attorney General	Richard Rush	1817
	William Wirt	1817–1825
Postmaster General	Return Meigs	1817–1823
	John McLean	1823–1825
Secretary of Navy	Benjamin Crowninshield	1817–1818
	Smith Thompson	1818–1823
	Samuel Southard	1823–1825

The John Quincy Adams Administration (1825–1829)

Vice President	John C. Calhoun	1825–1829
Secretary of State	Henry Clay	1825–1829
Secretary of Treasury	Richard Rush	1825–1829
Secretary of War	James Barbour	1825–1828
	Peter Porter	1828–1829
Attorney General	William Wirt	1825–1829
Postmaster General	John McLean	1825–1829
Secretary of Navy	Samuel Southard	1825–1829

The Jackson Administration (1829–1837)

Vice President	John C. Calhoun	1829–1833
	Martin Van Buren	1833–1837
Secretary of State	Martin Van Buren	1829–1831
	Edward Livingston	1831–1833
	Louis McLane	1833–1834
	John Forsyth	1834–1837
Secretary of Treasury	Samuel Ingham	1829–1831
	Louis McLane	1831–1833
	William Duane	1833
	Roger B. Taney	1833–1834
	Levi Woodbury	1834–1837
Secretary of War	John H. Eaton	1829–1831
	Lewis Cass	1831–1837
	Benjamin Butler	1837
Attorney General	John M. Berrien	1829–1831
	Roger B. Taney	1831–1833
	Benjamin Butler	1833–1837
Postmaster General	William Barry	1829–1835
	Amos Kendall	1835–1837

Presidential Administrations
(continued)

Secretary of Navy	John Branch	1829–1831
	Levi Woodbury	1831–1834
	Mahlon Dickerson	1834–1837

The Van Buren Administration (1837–1841)

Vice President	Richard M. Johnson	1837–1841
Secretary of State	John Forsyth	1837–1841
Secretary of Treasury	Levi Woodbury	1837–1841
Secretary of War	Joel Poinsett	1837–1841
Attorney General	Benjamin Butler	1837–1838
	Felix Grundy	1838–1840
	Henry D. Gilpin	1840–1841
Postmaster General	Amos Kendall	1837–1840
	John M. Niles	1840–1841
Secretary of Navy	Mahlon Dickerson	1837–1838
	James Paulding	1838–1841

The William Harrison Administration (1841)

Vice President	John Tyler	1841
Secretary of State	Daniel Webster	1841
Secretary of Treasury	Thomas Ewing	1841
Secretary of War	John Bell	1841
Attorney General	John J. Crittenden	1841
Postmaster General	Francis Granger	1841
Secretary of Navy	George Badger	1841

The Tyler Administration (1841–1845)

Vice President	None	
Secretary of State	Daniel Webster	1841–1843
	Hugh S. Legaré	1843
	Abel P. Upshur	1843–1844
	John C. Calhoun	1844–1845
Secretary of Treasury	Thomas Ewing	1841
	Walter Forward	1841–1843
	John C. Spencer	1843–1844
	George Bibb	1844–1845
Secretary of War	John Bell	1841
	John C. Spencer	184t–1843
	James M. Porter	184–1844
	William Wilkins	1844–1845
Attorney General	John J. Crittenden	1841
	Hugh S. Legaré	1841–1843
	John Nelson	1843–1845
Postmaster General	Francis Granger	1841
	Charles Wickliffe	1841
Secretary of Navy	George Badger	1841
	Abel P. Upshur	1841
	David Henshaw	1843–1844
	Thomas Gilmer	1844
	John Y. Mason	1844–1845

The Polk Administration (1845–1849)

Vice President	George M. Dallas	1845–1849
Secretary of State	James Buchanan	1845–1849
Secretary of Treasury	Robert J. Walker	1845–1849
Secretary of War	William L. Marcy	1845–1849
Attorney General	John Y. Mason	1845–1846
	Nathan Clifford	1846–1848
	Isaac Toucey	1848–1849
Postmaster General	Cave Johnson	1845–1849
Secretary of Navy	George Bancrocft	1845–1846
	John Y. Mason	1846–1849

The Taylor Administration (1849–1850)

Vice President	Millard Fillmore	1849–1850
Secretary of State	John M. Clayton	1849–1850
Secretary of Treasury	William Meredith	1849–1850
Secretary of War	George Crawford	1849–1850
Attorney General	Reverdy Johnson	1849–1850
Postmaster General	Jacob Collamer	1849–1850
Secretary of Navy	William Preston	1849–1850
Secretary of Interior	Thomas Ewing	1849–1850

The Fillmore Administration (1850–1853)

Vice President	None	
Secretary of State	Daniel Webster	1850–1852
	Edward Everett	1852–1853
Secretary of Treasury	Thomas Corwin	1850–1853
Secretary of War	Charles Conrad	1850–1853
Attorney General	John J. Crittenden	1850–1853
Postmaster General	Nathan Hall	1850–1852
	Sam D. Hubbard	1852–1853
Secretary of Navy	William A. Graham	1850–1852
	John P. Kennedy	1852–1853
Secretary of Interior	Thomas McKennan	1850
	Alexander Stuart	1850–1853

The Pierce Administration (1853–1857)

Vice President	William R. King	1853–1857
Secretary of State	William L. Marcy	1853–1857
Secretary of Treasury	James Guthrie	1853–1857
Secretary of War	Jefferson Davis	1853–1857
Attorney General	Caleb Cushing	1853–1857
Postmaster General	James Campbell	1853–1857
Secretary of Navy	James C. Dobbin	1853–1857
Secretary of Interior	Robert McClelland	1853–1857

The Buchanan Administration (1857–1861)

Vice President	John C. Breckinridge	1857–1861
Secretary of State	Lewis Cass	1857–1860
	Jeremiah S. Black	1860–1861
Secretary of Treasury	Howell Cobb	1857–1860
	Philip Thomas	1860–1861
	John A. Dix	1861
Secretary of War	John B. Floyd	1857–1861
	Joseph Holt	1861
Attorney General	Jeremiah S. Black	1857–1860
	Edwin M. Stanton	1860–1861
Postmaster General	Aaron V. Brown	1857–1859
	Joseph Holt	1859–1861
	Horatio King	1861

Presidential Administrations
(continued)

Secretary of Navy	Isaac Toucey	1857–1861
Secretary of Interior	Jacob Thompson	1857–1861

The Lincoln Administration (1861–1865)

Vice President	Hannibal Hamlin	1861–1865
	Andrew Jackson	1865
Secretary of State	William H. Seward	1861–1865
Secretary of Treasury	Salmon P. Chase	1861–1864
	William P. Fessenden	1864–1865
	Hugh McCulloch	1865
Secretary of War	Simon Cameron	1861–1862
	Edwin M. Stanton	1862–1865
Attorney General	Edward Bates	1861–1864
	James Speed	1864–1865
Postmaster General	Horatio King	1861
	Montgomery Blair	1861–1864
	William Dennison	1864–1865
Secretary of Navy	Gideon Welles	1861–1865
Secretary of Interior	Caleb B. Smith	1861–1863
	John P. Usher	1863–1865

The Andrew Johnson Administration (1865–1869)

Vice President	None	
Secretary of State	William H. Seward	1865–1869
Secretary of Treasury	Hugh McCulloch	1865–1869
Secretary of War	Edwin M. Stanton	1865–1867
	Ulysses S. Grant	1867–1868
	Lorenzo Thomas	1868
	John M. Schofield	1868–1869
Attorney General	James Speed	1865–1866
	Henry Stanbery	1866–1868
	William M. Evarts	1868–1869
Postmaster General	William Dennison	1865–1866
	Alexander Randall	1866–1869
Secretary of Navy	Gideon Welles	1865–1869
Secretary of Interior	John P. Usher	1865
	James Harlan	1865–1866
	Orville H. Browning	1866–1869

The Grant Administration (1869–1877)

Vice President	Schuyler Colfax	1869–1873
	Henry Wilson	1873–1877
Secretary of State	Elihu B. Washburne	1869
	Hamilton Fish	1869–1877
Secretary of Treasury	George S. Boutwell	1869–1873
	William Richardson	1873–1874
	Benjamin Bristow	1874–1876
	Lot M. Morrill	1876–1877
Secretary of War	John A. Rawlins	1869
	William T. Sherman	1869
	William W. Belknap	1869–1876
	Alphonso Taft	1876
	James D. Cameron	1876–1877
Attorney General	Ebenezer Hoar	1869–1870
	Amos T. Ackerman	1870–1871
	G. H. Williams	1871–1875
	Edwards Pierrepont	1875–1876
	Alphonso Taft	1876–1877
Postmaster General	John A. J. Creswell	1869–1874
	James W. Marshall	1874
	Marshall Jewell	1874–1876
	James N. Tyner	1876–1877
Secretary of Navy	Adolph E. Borie	1869
	George M. Robeson	1869–1877
Secretary of Interior	Jacob D. Cox	1869–1870
	Columbus Delano	1870–1875
	Zachariah Candler	1875–1877

The Hayes Administration (1877–1881)

Vice President	William A. Wheeler	1877–1881
Secretary of State	William M. Evarts	1877–1881
Secretary of Treasury	John Sherman	1877–1881
Secretary of War	George W. McCrary	1877–1879
	Alex Ramsey	1879–1881
Attorney General	Charles Devens	1877–1881
Postmaster General	David M. Key	1877–1880
	Horace Maynard	1880–1881
Secretary of Navy	Richard W. Thompson	1877–1880
	Nathan Goff, Jr.	1881
Secretary of Interior	Carl Schurz	1877–1881

The Garfield Administration (1881)

Vice President	Chester A. Arthur	1881
Secretary of State	James G. Blaine	1881
Secretary of Treasury	William Windom	1881
Secretary of War	Robert T. Lincoln	1881
Attorney General	Wayne MacVeagh	1881
Postmaster General	Thomas L. James	1881
Secretary of Navy	William H. Hunt	1881
Secretary of Interior	Samuel J. Kirkwood	1881

The Arthur Administration (1881–1885)

Vice President	None	
Secretary of State	F. T. Frelinghuysen	1881–1885
Secretary of Treasury	Charles J. Folger	1881–1884
	Walter Q. Gresham	1884
	Hugh McCulloch	1884–1885
Secretary of War	Robert T. Lincoln	1881–1885
Attorney General	Benjamin H. Brewster	1881–1885
Postmaster General	Timothy O. Howe	1881–1883
	Walter Q. Gresham	1883–1884
	Frank Hatton	1884–1885
Secretary of Navy	William H. Hunt	1881–1882
	William E. Chandler	1882–1885
Secretary of Interior	Samuel J. Kirkwood	1881–1882
	Henry M. Teller	1882–1885

The Cleveland Administration (1885–1889)

Vice President	Thomas A. Hendricks	1885–1889
Secretary of State	Thomas F. Bayard	1885–1889

PRESIDENTIAL ADMINISTRATIONS (continued)

Secretary of Treasury	Daniel Manning	1885–1887
	Charles S. Fairchild	1887–1889
Secretary of War	William C. Endicott	1885–1889
Attorney General	Augustus H. Garland	1885–1889
Postmaster General	William F. Vilas	1885–1888
	Don M. Dickinson	1888–1889
Secretary of Navy	William C. Whitney	1885–1889
Secretary of Interior	Lucius Q. C. Lamar	1885–1888
	William F. Vilas	1888–1889
Secretary of Agriculture	Norman J. Colman	1889

THE BENJAMIN HARRISON ADMINISTRATION (1889–1893)

Vice President	Levi P. Morton	1889–1893
Secretary of State	James G. Blaine	1889–1892
	John W. Foster	1892–1893
Secretary of Treasury	William Windom	1889–1891
	Charles Foster	1891–1893
Secretary of War	Redfield Proctor	1889–1891
	Stephen B. Elkins	1891–1893
Attorney General	William H. H. Miller	1889–1891
Postmaster General	John Wanamaker	1889–1893
Secretary of Navy	Benjamin F. Tracy	1889–1893
Secretary of Interior	John W. Noble	1889–1893
Secretary of Agriculture	Jeremiah M. Rusk	1889–1893

THE CLEVELAND ADMINISTRATION (1893–1897)

Vice President	Adlai E. Stevenson	1893–1897
Secretary of State	Walter Q. Gresham	1893–1895
	Richard Olney	1895–1897
Secretary of Treasury	John G. Carlisle	1893–1897
Secretary of War	Daniel S. Lamont	1893–1897
Attorney General	Richard Olney	1893–1895
	James Harmon	1895–1897
Postmaster General	Wilson S. Bissell	1893–1895
	William L. Wilson	1895–1897
Secretary of Navy	Hilary A. Herbert	1893–1897
Secretary of Interior	Hoke Smith	1893–1896
	David R. Francis	1896–1897
Secretary of Agriculture	Julius S. Morton	1893–1897

THE MCKINLEY ADMINISTRATION (1897–1901)

Vice President	Garret A. Hobart	1897–1901
	Theodore Roosevelt	1901
Secretary of State	John Serman	1897–1898
	William R. Day	1898
	John Hay	1898–1901
Secretary of Treasury	Lyman J. Gage	1897–1901
Secretary of War	Russell A. Alger	1897–1899
	Elihu Root	1899–1901
Attorney General	Joseph McKenna	1897–1898
	John W. Griggs	1898–1901
	Philander C. Knox	1901
Postmaster General	James A. Gary	1897–1898
	Charles E. Smith	1898–1901
Secretary of Navy	John D. Long	1897–1901
Secretary of Interior	Cornelius N. Bliss	1897–1899
	Ethan A. Hitchcock	1899–1901
Secretary of Agriculture	James Wilson	1897–1901

THE THEODORE ROOSEVELT ADMINISTRATION (1901–1909)

Vice President	Charles Fairbanks	1905–1909
Secretary of State	John Hay	1901–1905
	Elihu Root	1905–1909
	Robert Bacon	1909
Secretary of Treasury	Lyman J. Gage	1901–1902
	Leslie M. Shaw	1902–1907
	George B. Cortelyou	1907–1909
Secretary of War	Elihu Root	1901–1904
	William H. Taft	1904–1908
	Luke E. Wright	1908–1909
Attorney General	Philander C. Knox	1901–1904
	William H. Moody	1904–1906
	Charles J. Bonaparte	1906–1909
Postmaster General	Charles E. Smith	1901–1902
	Henry C. Payne	1902–1904
	Robert J. Wynne	1904–1905
	George B. Cortelyou	1905–1907
	George von L. Meyer	1907–1909
Secretary of Navy	John D. Long	1901–1902
	William H. Moody	1902–1904
	Paul Morton	1904–1905
	Charles J. Bonaparte	1905–1906
	Victor H. Metcalf	1906–1908
	Truman H. Newberry	1908–1909
Secretary of Interior	Ethan A. Hitchcock	1901–1907
	James R. Garfield	1907–1909
Secretary of Agriculture	James Wilson	1901–1909
Secretary of Labor and Commerce	George B. Cortelyou	1903–1904
	Victor H. Metcalf	1904–1906
	Oscar S. Straus	1906–1909
	Charles Nagel	1909

THE TAFT ADMINISTRATION (1909–1913)

Vice President	James S. Sherman	1909–1913
Secretary of State	Philander C. Knox	1909–1913
Secretary of Treasury	Franklin MacVeagh	1909–1913
Secretary of War	Jacob M. Dickinson	1909–1911
	Henry L. Stimson	1911–1913
Attorney General	George W. Wickersham	1909–1913
Postmaster General	Frank H. Hitchcock	1909–1913
Secretary of Navy	George von L. Meyer	1909–1913
Secretary of Interior	Richard A. Ballinger	1909–1911
	Walter L. Fisher	1991–1913
Secretary of Agriculture	James Wilson	1909–1913

Presidential Administrations (continued)

Secretary of Labor and Commerce	Charles Nagel	1909–1913

The Wilson Administration (1913–1921)

Vice President	Thomas R. Marshall	1913–1921
Secretary of State	William J. Bryan	1913–1915
	Robert Lansing	1915–1920
	Bainbridge Colby	1920–1921
Secretary of Treasury	William G. McAdoo	1913–1918
	Carter Glass	1918–1920
	David F. Houston	1920–1921
Secretary of War	Lindley M. Garrison	1913–1916
	Newton D. Baker	1916–1921
Attorney General	James C. McReyolds	1913–1914
	Thomas W. Gregory	1914–1919
	A. Mitchell Palmer	1919–1921
Postmaster General	Albert S. Burleson	1913–1921
Secretary of Navy	Josephus Daniels	1913–1921
Secretary of Interior	Franklin K. Lane	1913–1920
	John B. Payne	1920–1921
Secretary of Agriculture	David F. Houston	1913–1920
	Edwin T. Meredith	1920–1921
Secretary of Commerce	William C. Redfield	1913–1919
	Joshua W. Alexander	1919–1921
Secretary of Labor	William B. Wilson	1913–1921

The Harding Administration (1921–1923)

Vice President	Calvin Coolidge	1921–1923
Secretary of State	Charles E. Hughes	1921–1923
Secretary of Treasury	Andrew Mellon	1921–1923
Secretary of War	John W. Weeks	1921–1923
Attorney General	Harry M. Daugherty	1921–1923
Postmaster General	Will H. Hays	1921–1922
	Hubert Work	1922–1923
	Harry S. New	1923
Secretary of Navy	Edwin Denby	1921–1923
Secretary of Interior	Albert B. Fall	1921–1923
	Hubert Work	1923
Secretary of Agriculture	Henry C. Wallace	1921–1923
Secretary of Commerce	Herbert C. Hoover	1921–1923
Secretary of Labor	James J. Davis	1921–1923

The Coolidge Administration (1923–1929)

Vice President	Charles G. Dawes	1925–1929
Secretary of State	Charles E. Hughes	1923–1925
	Frank B. Kellogg	1925–1929
Secretary of Treasury	Andrew Mellon	1923–1929
Secretary of War	John W. Weeks	1923–1925
	Dwight F. Davis	1925–1929
Attorney General	Harry M. Daugherty	1923–1924
	Harlan F. Stone	1924–1925
	John G. Sargent	1925–1929
Postmaster General	Harry S. New	1923–1929
Secretary of Navy	Edwin Derby	1923–1924
	Curtis D. Wilbur	1924–1929
Secretary of Interior	Hubert Work	1923–1928
	Roy O. West	1928–1929
Secretary of Agriculture	Henry C. Wallace	1923–1924
	Howard M. Gore	1924–1925
	William M. Jardine	1925–1929
Secretary of Commerce	Herbert C. Hoover	1923–1928
	William F. Whiting	1928–1929
Secretary of Labor	James J. Davis	1923–1929

The Hoover Administration (1929–1933)

Vice President	Charles Curtis	1929–1933
Secretary of State	Henry L. Stimson	1929–1933
Secretary of Treasury	Andrew Mellon	1929–1932
	Ogden L. Mills	1932–1933
Secretary of War	James W. Good	1929
	Patrick J. Hurley	1929–1933
Attorney General	William D. Mitchell	1929–1933
Postmaster General	Walter F. Brown	1929–1933
Secretary of Navy	Charles F. Adams	1929–1933
Secretary of Interior	Ray L. Wilbur	1929–1933
Secretary of Agriculture	Arthur M. Hyde	1929–1933
Secretary of Commerce	Robert P. Lamont	1929–1932
	Roy D. Chapin	1932–1933
Secretary of Labor	James J. Davis	1929–1930
	William N. Doak	1930–1933

The Franklin D. Roosevelt Administration (1933–1945)

Vice President	John Nance Garner	1933–1941
	Henry A. Wallace	1941–1945
	Harry S. Truman	1945
Secretary of State	Cordell Hull	1933–1944
	Edward R. Stettinius, Jr.	1944–1945
Secretary of Treasury	William H. Woodin	1933–1934
	Henry Morgenthau, Jr.	1934–1945
Secretary of War	George H. Dern	1933–1936
	Henry A. Woodring	1936–1940
	Henry L. Stimson	1940–1945
Attorney General	Homer S. Cummings	1933–1939
	Frank Murphy	1939–1940
	Robert H. Jackson	1940–1941
	Francis Biddle	1941–1945
Postmaster General	James A. Farley	1933–1940
	Frank C. Walker	1940–1945
Secretary of Navy	Claude A. Swanson	1933–1940
	Charles Edison	1940
	Frank Knox	1940–1944
	James V. Forrestal	1944–1945
Secretary of Interior	Harold L. Ickes	1933–1945
Secretary of Agriculture	Henry A. Wallace	1933–1940
	Claude R. Wickard	1940–1945

Presidential Administrations
(continued)

Secretary of Commerce	Daniel C. Roper	1933–1939
	Harry L. Hopkins	1939–1940
	Jesse Jones	1940–1945
	Henry A. Wallace	1945
Secretary of Labor	Frances Perkins	1933–1945

The Truman Administration (1945–1953)

Vice President	Alben W. Barkley	1949–1953
Secretary of State	Edward R. Stettinius, Jr.	1945
	James F. Byrnes	1945–1947
	George C. Marshall	1947–1949
	Dean G. Acheson	1949–1953
Secretary of Treasury	Fred M. Vinson	1945–1946
	John W. Snyder	1946–1953
Secretary of War	Robert P. Patterson	1945–1947
	Kenneth C. Royall	1947
Attorney General	Tom C. Clark	1945–1949
	J. Howard McGrath	1949–1952
	James P. McGranery	1952–1953
Postmaster General	Frank C. Walker	1945
	Robert E. Hannegan	1945–1947
	Jesse M. Donaldson	1947–1953
Secretary of Navy	James V. Forrestal	1945–1947
Secretary of Interior	Harold L. Ickes	1945–1946
	Julius A. Krug	1946–1949
	Oscar L. Chapman	1949–1953
Secretary of Agriculture	Clinton P. Anderson	1945–1948
	Charles F. Brannan	1948–1953
Secretary of Commerce	Henry A. Wallace	1945–1946
	W. Averell Harriman	1946–1948
	Charles W. Sawyer	1948–1953
Secretary of Labor	Lewis B. Schwellenback	1945–1948
	Maurice J. Tobin	1948–1953
Secretary of Defense	James V. Forrestal	1947–1949
	Louis A. Johnson	1949–1950
	George C. Marshall	1950–1951
	Robert A. Lovett	1951–1953

The Eisenhower Administration (1953–1961)

Vice President	Richard M. Nixon	1953–1961
Secretary of State	John Foster Dulles	1953–1959
	Christian A. Herter	1959–1961
Secretary of Treasury	George M. Humphrey	1953–1957
	Robert B. Anderson	1957–1961
Attorney General	Herbert Brownell, Jr.	1953–1958
	William P. Rogers	1958–1961
Postmaster General	Arthur E. Summerfield	1953–1961
Secretary of Interior	Douglas McKay	1953–1956
	Freed A. Seaton	1956–1961
Secretary of Agriculture	Ezra T. Benson	1953–1961
Secretary of Commerce	Sinclair Weeks	1953–1958
	Lewis L. Strauss	1958–1959
	Frederick H. Mueller	1959–1961
Secretary of Labor	Martin P. Durkin	1953
	James P. Mitchell	1953–1961
Secretary of Defense	Charles E. Wilson	1953–1957
	Neil H. McElroy	1957–1959
	Thomas S. Gates Jr.	1959–1961
Secretary of Health, Education, and Welfare	Oveta Culp Hobby	1953–1955
	Marion B. Folsom	1955–1958
	Arthur S. Flemming	1958–1961

The Kennedy Administration (1961–1963)

Vice President	Lyndon B. Johnson	1961–1963
Secretary of State	Dean Rusk	1961–1963
Secretary of Treasury	C. Douglas Dillon	1961–1963
Attorney General	Robert F. Kennedy	1961–1963
Postmaster General	J. Edward Day	1961–1963
	John A. Gronouski	1963
Secretary of Interior	Stewart I. Udall	1961–1963
Secretary of Agriculture	Orville L. Freeman	1961–1963
Secretary of Commerce	Luther H. Hodges	1961–1963
Secretary of Labor	Arthur J. Goldberg	1961–1962
	W. Willard Wirtz	1962–1963
Secretary of Defense	Robert S. McNamara	1961–1963
Secretary of Health, Education, and Welfare	Abraham A. Ribicoff	1961–1962
	Anthony J. Celebrezze	1962–1963

The Lyndon Johnson Administration (1963–1969)

Vice President	Hubert H. Humphrey	1965–1969
Secretary of State	Dean Rusk	1963–1969
Secretary of Treasury	C. Douglas Dillon	1963–1965
	Henry H. Fowler	1965–1969
Attorney General	Robert F. Kennedy	1963–1964
	Nicholas Katzenbach	1965–1966
	Ramsey Clark	1967–1969
Postmaster General	John A. Gronouski	1963–1965
	Lawrence F. O'Brien	1965–1968
	Marvin Watson	1968–1969
Secretary of Interior	Stewart L. Udall	1963–1969
Secretary of Agriculture	Orville L. Freeman	1963–1969
Secretary of Commerce	Luther H. Hodges	1963–1964
	John T. Connor	1964–1967
	Alexander B. Trowbridge	1967–1968
	Cyrus R. Smith	1968–1969
Secretary of Labor	W. Willard Wirtz	1963–1969
Secretary of Defense	Robert F. McNamara	1963–1968
	Clark Clifford	1968–1969
Secretary of Health, Education, and Welfare	Anthony J. Celebrezze	1963–1965
	John W. Gardner	1965–1968
	Wilbur J. Cohen	1968–1969
Secretary of Housing and Urban Development	Robert C. Weaver	1966–1969
	Robert C. Wood	1969
Secretary of Transportation	Alan S. Boyd	1967–1969

PRESIDENTIAL ADMINISTRATIONS
(continued)

THE NIXON ADMINISTRATION (1969–1974)

Vice President	Spiro T. Agnew	1969–1973
	Gerald R. Ford	1973–1974
Secretary of State	William P. Rogers	1969–1973
	Henry Kissinger	1973–1974
Secretary of Treasury	David M. Kennedy	1969–1970
	John B. Connally	1972–1974
	George P. Schultz	1972–1974
	William E. Simon	1974
Attorney General	John N. Mitchell	1969–1972
	Richard G. Kleindienst	1972–1973
	Elliot L. Richardson	1973
	William B. Saxbe	1973–1974
Postmaster General	Winton M. Blount	1969–1971
Secretary of Interior	Walter J. Hickel	1969–1970
	Rogers Morton	1971–1974
Secretary of Agriculture	Clifford M. Hardin	1969–1971
	Earl L. Butz	1971–1974
Secretary of Commerce	Maurice H. Stans	1969–1972
	Peter G. Peterson	1972–1973
	Frederick B. Dent	1973–1974
Secretary of Labor	George P. Shultz	1969–1970
	James D. Hodgson	1970–1973
	Peter J. Brennan	1973–1974
Secretary of Defense	Melvin R. Laird	1969–1973
	Eliot L. Richardson	1973
	James R. Schelsinger	1973–1974
Secretary of Health, Education, and Welfare	Robert H. Finch	1969–1970
	Elliot L. Richardson	1970–1973
	Caspar W. Weinberger	1973–1974
Secretary of Housing and Urban Development	George Romney	1969–1973
	James T. Lynn	1973–1974
Secretary of Transportation	John A. Volpe	1969–1973
	Claude S. Brinegar	1973–1974

THE FORD ADMINISTRATION (1974–1977)

Vice President	Nelson A. Rockefeller	1974–1977
Secretary of State	Henry A. Kissinger	1974–1977
Secretary of Treasury	William E. Simon	1974–1977
Attorney General	William Saxbe	1974–1975
	Edward Levi	1975–1977
Secretary of Interior	Rogers Morton	1974–1975
	Stanley K. Hathaway	1975
	Thomas Kleppe	1975–1977
Secretary of Agriculture	Earl I. Butz	1974–1976
	John A. Knebel	1976–1977
Secretary of Commerce	Frederick B. Dent	1974–1975
	Rogers Morton	1975–1976
	Elliot L. Richardson	1976–1977
Secretary of Labor	Peter J. Brennan	1974–1975
	John T. Dunlop	1975–1976
	W. J. Usery	1976–1977
Secretary of Defense	James R. Schlesinger	1974–1975
	Donald Rumsfeld	1975–1977
Secretary of Health, Education, and Welfare	Caspar Weinberger	1974–1975
	Forrest D. Mathews	1975–1977
Secretary of Housing Urban Development	James T. Lynn	1974–1975
	Carla A. Hills	1975–1977
Secretary of Transportation	Claude Brinegar	1974–1975
	William T. Colemn	1975–1977

THE CARTER ADMINISTRATION (1977–1981)

Vice President	Walter F. Mondale	1977–1981
Secretary of State	Cyrus R. Vance	1977–1980
	Edmund Muskie	1980–1981
Secretary of Treasury	W. Michael Blumenthal	1977–1979
	G. William Miller	1979–1981
Attorney General	Griffin Bell	1977–1979
	Benjamin R. Civiletti	1979–1981
Secretary of Interior	Cecil D. Andrus	1977–1981
Secretary of Agriculture	Robert Bergland	1977–1981
Secretary of Commerce	Juanita M. Kreps	1977–1979
	Philip M. Klutznick	1979–1981
Secretary of Labor	F. Ray Marshall	1977–1981
Secretary of Defense	Harold Brown	1977–1981
Secretary of Health, Education, and Welfare	Joseph A. Califano	1977–1979
	Patricia R. Harris	1979
Secretary of Health and Human Services	Patricia R. Harris	1979–1981
Secretary of Education	Shirley M. Hufstedler	1979–1981
Secretary of Housing and Urban Development	Patricia R. Harris	1977–1979
	Moon Landrieu	1979–1981
Secretary of Transportation	Brock Adams	1977–1979
	Neil E. Goldschmidt	1979–1981
Secretary of Energy	James R. Schlesinger	1977–1979
	Charles W. Duncan	1979–1981

THE REAGAN ADMINISTRATION (1981–1989)

Vice President	George Bush	1981–1989
Secretary of State	Alexander M. Haig	1981–1982
	George P. Schultz	1982–1989
Secretary of Treasury	Donald Regan	1981–1985
	James A. Baker III	1985–1988
	Nicholas F. Brady	1988–1989
Attorney General	William F. Smith	1981–1985
	Edwin A. Meese III	1985–1988
	Richard Thornburgh	1988–1989
Secretary of Interior	James Watt	1981–1983
	William P. Clark, Jr.	1983–1985
	Donald P. Hodel	1985–1989
Secretary of Agriculture	John Block	1981–1986
	Richard E. Lyng	1986–1989
Secretary of Commerce	Malcolm Baldridge	1981–1987
	C. William Verity, Jr.	1987–1989
Secretary of Labor	Raymond Donovan	1981–1985
	William Brock	1985–1987
	Ann D. McLaughlin	1987–1989

PRESIDENTIAL ADMINISTRATIONS
(continued)

Secretary of Defense	Caspar Weinberger	1981–1987
	Frank C. Carlucci	1987–1989
Secretary of Health and Human Services	Richard Schweiker	1981–1983
	Margaret Heckler	1983–1985
	Otis R. Bowen	1985–1989
Secretary of Education	Terrel H. Bell	1981–1985
	William J. Bennett	1985–1988
	Laura F. Cavazos	1988–1989
Secretary of Housing and Urban Development	Samuel Pierce	1981–1989
Secretary of Transportation	Drew Lewis	1981–1983
	Elizabeth Dole	1983–1987
	James H. Burnley	1987–1989
Secretary of Energy	James Edwards	1981–1982
	Donald P. Hodel	1982–1985
	John S. Herrington	1984–1989

THE BUSH ADMINISTRATION (1989–1993)

Vice President	J. Danforth Quayle	1989–1993
Secretary of State	James A. Baker III	1989–1992
	Lawrence S. Eagleburger	1992–1993
Secretary of Treasury	Nicholas F. Brady	1989–1993
Attorney General	Richard Thornburgh	1989–1991
	William P. Barr	1991–1993
Secretary of Interior	Manuel Lujan	1989–1993
Secretary of Agriculture	Clayton K. Yeutter	1989–1991
	Edward Madigan	1991–1993
Secretary of Commerce	Robert A. Mosbacher	1989–1992
	Barbara H. Franklin	1992–1993
Secretary of Labor	Elizabeth Dole	1989–1991
	Lynn M. Martin	1991–1993
Secretary of Defense	Richard B. Cheney	1989–1993
Secretary of Health and Human Services	Louis W. Sullivan	1989–1993
Secretary of Education	Laura F. Cavazos	1989–1991
	Lamar Alexander	1991–1993
Secretary of Housing and Urban Development	Jack F. Kemp	1989–1993
Secretary of Transportation	Samuel K. Skinner	1989–1992
	Andrew H. Card	1992–1993
Secretary of Energy	James D. Watkins	1989–1993
Secretary of Veterans Affairs	Edward J. Derwinski	1989–1993

THE CLINTON ADMINISTRATION (1993–)

Vice President	Albert Gore, Jr.	1993–
Secretary of State	Warren M. Christopher	1993–1997
	Madeleine Albright	1997–
Secretary of Treasury	Lloyd M. Bentsen, Jr.	1993–1995
	Robert E. Rubin	1995–1999
	Lawrence H. Summer	1999–
Attorney General	Janet Reno	1993–
Secretary of Interior	Bruce Babbitt	1993–
Secretary of Agriculture	Mike Espy	1993–1995
	Daniel R. Glickman	1995–
Secretary of Commerce	Ronald H. Brown	1993–1996
	William M. Daley	1997–
Secretary of Labor	Robert B. Reich	1993–1997
	Alexis M. Herman	1997–
Secretary of Defense	Les Aspin	1993–1994
	William Perry	1994–1996
	William S. Cohen	1996–
Secretary of Health and Human Services	Donna E. Shalala	1993–
Secretary of Education	Richard W. Riley	1993–
Secretary of Housing and Urban Development	Henry G. Cisneros	1993–1997
	Andrew Cuomo	1997–
Secretary of Energy	Hazel R. O'Leary	1993–1997
	Federico Pena	1997–1998
	Bill Richardson	1998–
Secretary of Transportation	Federico Pena	1993–1997
	Rodney Slater	1997–
Secretary of Veterans Affairs	Jesse Brown	1993–1997
	Togo D. West, Jr.	1998–

Supreme Court Justices

Name*	Years on Court	Appointing President
JOHN JAY	1789–1795	Washington
James Wilson	1789–1798	Washington
John Rutledge	1790–1791	Washington
William Cushing	1790–1810	Washington
John Blair	1790–1796	Washington
James Iredell	1790–1799	Washington
Thomas Jefferson	1792–1793	Washington
William Paterson	1793–1806	Washington
JOHN RUTLEDGE†	1795	Washington
Samuel Chase	1796–1811	Washington
OLIVER ELLSWORTH	1796–1800	Washington
Bushrod Washington	1799–1829	J. Adams
Alfred Moore	1800–1804	J. Adams
JOHN MARSHALL	1801–1835	J. Adams
William Johnson	1804–1834	Jefferson
Brockholst Livingston	1807–1823	Jefferson
Thomas Todd	1807–1826	Jefferson
Gabriel Duvall	1811–1835	Madison
Joseph Story	1812–1845	Madison
Smith Thompson	1823–1843	Monroe
Robert Trimble	1826–1828	J. Q. Adams
John McLean	1830–1861	Jackson
Henry Baldwin	1830–1844	Jackson
James M. Wayne	1835–1867	Jackson
ROGER B. TANEY	1836–1864	Jackson
Philip P. Barbour	1836–1841	Jackson
John Cartron	1837–1865	Van Buren
John McKinley	1838–1852	Van Buren
Peter V. Daniel	1842–1860	Van Buren
Samuel Nelson	1845–1872	Tyler
Levi Woodbury	1845–1851	Polk
Robert C. Grier	1846–1870	Polk
Benjamin R. Curtis	1851–1857	Fillmore
John A. Campbell	1853–1861	Pierce
Nathan Clifford	1858–1881	Buchanan
Noah H. Swayne	1862–1881	Lincoln
Samuel F. Miller	1862–1890	Lincoln
David Davis	1862–1877	Lincoln
Stephen J. Field	1863–1897	Lincoln
SALMON P. CHASE	1864–1873	Lincoln
William Strong	1870–1880	Grant
Joseph P. Bradley	1870–1892	Grant
Ward Hunt	1873–1882	Grant
MORRISON R. WAITE	1874–1888	Grant
John M. Harlan	1877–1911	Hayes
William B. Woods	1881–1887	Hayes
Stanley Matthews	1881–1889	Garfield
Horace Gray	1882–1902	Arthur
Samuel Blatchford	1882–1893	Arthur
Lucious Q. C. Lamar	1888–1893	Cleveland
MELVILLE W. FULLER	1888–1910	Cleveland
David J. Brewer	1890–1910	B. Harrison
Henry B. Brown	1891–1906	B. Harrison
George Shiras, Jr.	1892–1903	B. Harrison
Howel E. Jackson	1893–1895	B. Harrison
Edward D. White	1894–1910	Cleveland
Rufus W. Peckman	1896–1909	Cleveland
Joseph McKenna	1898–1925	McKinley

Supreme Court Justices
(continued)

Name*	Years on Court	Appointing President
Oliver W. Holmes	1902–1932	T. Roosevelt
William R. Day	1903–1922	T. Roosevelt
William H. Moody	1906–1910	T. Roosevelt
Horace H. Lurton	1910–1914	Taft
Charles E. Hughes	1910–1916	Taft
EDWARD D. WHITE	1910–1921	Taft
Willis Van Devanter	1911–1937	Taft
Joseph R. Lamar	1911–1916	Taft
Mahlon Pitney	1912–1922	Taft
James C. McReynolds	1914–1941	Wilson
Louis D. Brandeis	1916–1939	Wilson
John H. Clarke	1916–1922	Wilson
WILLIAM H. TAFT	1921–1930	Harding
George Sutherland	1922–1938	Harding
Pierce Butler	1923–1939	Harding
Edward T. Sanford	1923–1930	Harding
Harlan F. Stone	1925–1941	Coolidge
CHARLES E. HUGHES	1930–1941	Hoover
Owen J. Roberts	1930–1945	Hoover
Benjamin N. Cardozo	1932–1938	Hoover
Hugo L. Black	1937–1971	F. Roosevelt
Stanley F. Reed	1938–1957	F. Roosevelt
Felix Frankfurter	1939–1962	F. Roosevelt
William O. Douglas	1939–1975	F. Roosevelt
Frank Murphy	1940–1949	F. Roosevelt
HARLAN F. STONE	1941–1946	F. Roosevelt
James F. Brynes	1941–1942	F. Roosevelt
Robert H. Jackson	1941–1954	F. Roosevelt
Wiley B. Rutledge	1943–1949	F. Roosevelt
Harold H. Burton	1945–1958	Truman
FREDERICK M. VINSON	1946–1953	Truman
Tom C. Clark	1949–1967	Truman
Sherman Minton	1949–1956	Truman
EARL WARREN	1953–1969	Eisenhower
John Marshall Harlan	1955–1971	Eisenhower
William J. Brennan, Jr.	1956–1990	Eisenhower
Charles E. Whittaker	1957–1962	Eisenhower
Potter Stewart	1958–1981	Eisenhower
Byron R. White	1962–1993	Kennedy
Arthur J. Goldberg	1962–1965	Kennedy
Abe Fortas	1965–1970	L. Johnson
Thurgood Marshall	1967–1991	L. Johnson
WARREN E. BURGER	1969–1986	Nixon
Harry A. Blackmun	1970–1994	Nixon
Lewis F. Powell, Jr.	1971–1987	Nixon
William H. Rehnquist	1971–1986	Nixon
John Paul Stevens	1975–	Ford
Sandra Day O'Connor	1981–	Reagan
WILLIAM H. REHNQUIST	1986–	Reagan
Antonin Scalia	1986–	Reagan
Anthony Kennedy	1988–	Reagan
David Souter	1990–	Bush
Clarence Thomas	1991–	Bush
Ruth Bader Ginsburg	1993–	Clinton
Stephen Breyer	1994–	Clinton

**Capital letters designate Chief Justices*

†Never confirmed by the Senate as Chief Justice

Admission of States into the Union

State	Date of Admission	State	Date of Admission
1. Delaware	December 7, 1787	26. Michigan	January 26, 1837
2. Pennsylvania	December 12, 1787	27. Florida	March 3, 1845
3. New Jersey	December 18, 1787	28. Texas	December 29, 1845
4. Georgia	January 2, 1788	29. Iowa	December 28, 1846
5. Connecticut	January 9, 1788	30. Wisconsin	May 29, 1848
6. Massachusetts	February 6, 1788	31. California	September 9, 1850
7. Maryland	April 28, 1788	32. Minnesota	May 11, 1858
8. South Carolina	May 23, 1788	33. Oregon	February 14, 1859
9. New Hampshire	June 21, 1788	34. Kansas	January 29, 1861
10. Virginia	June 25, 1788	35. West Virginia	June 20, 1863
11. New York	July 26, 1788	36. Nevada	October 31, 1864
12. North Carolina	November 21, 1789	37. Nebraska	March 1, 1867
13. Rhode Island	May 29, 1790	38. Colorado	August 1, 1876
14. Vermont	March 4, 1791	39. North Dakota	November 2, 1889
15. Kentucky	June 1, 1792	40. South Dakota	November 2, 1889
16. Tennessee	June 1, 1796	41. Montana	November 8, 1889
17. Ohio	March 1, 1803	42. Washington	November 11, 1889
18. Louisiana	April 30, 1812	43. Idaho	July 3, 1890
19. Indiana	December 11, 1816	44. Wyoming	July 10, 1890
20. Mississippi	December 10, 1817	45. Utah	January 4, 1896
21. Illinois	December 3, 1818	46. Oklahoma	November 16, 1907
22. Alabama	December 14, 1819	47. New Mexico	January 6, 1912
23. Maine	March 15, 1820	48. Arizona	February 14, 1912
24. Missouri	August 10, 1821	49. Alaska	January 3, 1959
25. Arkansas	June 15, 1836	50. Hawaii	August 21, 1959

Demographics of the United States

Population Growth

Year	Population	Percent Increase
1630	4,600	
1640	26,600	478.3
1650	50,400	90.8
1660	75,100	49.0
1670	111,900	49.0
1680	151,500	35.4
1690	210,400	38.9
1700	250,900	19.2
1710	331,700	32.2
1720	466,200	40.5
1730	629,400	35.0
1740	905,600	43.9
1750	1,170,800	29.3
1760	1,593,600	36.1
1770	2,148,100	34.8
1780	2,780,400	29.4
1790	3,929,214	41.3
1800	5,308,483	35.1
1810	7,239,881	36.4
1820	9,638,453	33.1
1830	12,866,020	33.5
1840	17,069,453	32.7
1850	23,191,876	35.9
1860	31,443,321	35.6
1870	39,818,449	26.6
1880	50,155,783	26.0
1890	62,947,714	25.5
1900	75,994,575	20.7
1910	91,972,266	21.0
1920	105,710,620	14.9
1930	122,775,046	16.1
1940	131,669,275	7.2
1950	151,325,798	14.5
1960	179,323,175	18.5
1970	203,302,031	13.4
1980	226,542,199	11.4
1990	248,718,301	9.8
1998	270,561,000	8.8

Source: *Historical Statistics of the United States* (1975); *Statistical Abstract by the United States* (1999).
Note: Figures for 1630–1780 include British colonies within limits of present United States only; Native American population included only in 1930 and thereafter.

Work Force

Year	Total Number Workers (1000s)	Farmers as % of Total	Women as % of Total	% Workers in Unions
1810	2,330	84	(NA)	(NA)
1840	5,660	75	(NA)	(NA)
1860	11,110	53	(NA)	(NA)
1870	12,506	53	15	(NA)
1880	17,392	52	15	(NA)
1890	23,318	43	17	(NA)
1900	29,073	40	18	3
1910	38,167	31	21	6
1920	41,614	26	21	12
1930	48,830	22	22	7
1940	53,011	17	24	27
1950	59,643	12	28	25
1960	69,877	8	32	26
1970	82,049	4	37	25
1980	106,940	3	43	23
1990	125,840	3	45	16
1998	137,673	2	46	14

Source: *Historical Statistics of the United States* (1975); *Statistical Abstract of the United States* (1999).

Vital Statistics
(in thousands)

Year	Births	Deaths	Marriages	Divorces
1800	55	(NA)	(NA)	(NA)
1810	54.3	(NA)	(NA)	(NA)
1820	55.2	(NA)	(NA)	(NA)
1830	51.4	(NA)	(NA)	(NA)
1840	51.8	(NA)	(NA)	(NA)
1850	43.3	(NA)	(NA)	(NA)
1860	44.3	(NA)	(NA)	(NA)
1870	38.3	(NA)	9.6 (1867)	0.3 (1867)
1880	39.8	(NA)	9.1 (1875)	0.3 (1875)
1890	31.5	(NA)	9.0	0.5
1900	32.3	17.2	9.3	0.7
1910	30.1	14.7	10.3	0.9
1920	27.7	13.0	12.0	1.6
1930	21.3	11.3	9.2	1.6
1940	19.4	10.8	12.1	2.0
1950	24.1	9.6	11.1	2.6
1960	23.7	9.5	8.5	2.2
1970	18.4	9.5	10.6	3.5
1980	15.9	8.8	10.6	5.2
1990	16.7	8.6	9.8	4.7
1997	14.6	8.6	8.9	4.3

Source: *Historical Statistics of the United States* (1975); *Statistical Abstract of the United States* (1999).

Racial Composition of the Population

(in thousands)

Year	White	Black	Indian	Hispanic	Asian
1790	3,172	757	(NA)	(NA)	(NA)
1800	4,306	1,002	(NA)	(NA)	(NA)
1820	7,867	1,772	(NA)	(NA)	(NA)
1840	14,196	2,874	(NA)	(NA)	(NA)
1860	26,923	4,442	(NA)	(NA)	(NA)
1880	43,403	6,581	(NA)	(NA)	(NA)
1900	66,809	8,834	(NA)	(NA)	(NA)
1910	81,732	9,828	(NA)	(NA)	(NA)
1920	94,821	10,463	(NA)	(NA)	(NA)
1930	110,287	11,891	(NA)	(NA)	(NA)
1940	118,215	12,866	(NA)	(NA)	(NA)
1950	134,942	15,042	(NA)	(NA)	(NA)
1960	158,832	18,872	(NA)	(NA)	(NA)
1970	178,098	22,581	(NA)	(NA)	(NA)
1980	194,713	26,683	1,420	14,609	3,729
1990	208,727	30,511	2,065	22,372	2,462
1998	223,001	34,431	2,360	30,250	10,507

Source: U.S. Bureau of the Census, U.S. *Census of Population: 1940*, vol. II, part 1, and vol. IV, part 1; *1950*, vol. II, part 1; *1960*, vol. I, part 1; *1970*, vol. I, part B; and *Current Population Reports*, P25-1095 and P25-1104; *Statistical Abstract of the United States* (1999) and unpublished data.

The Economy and Federal Spending

Year	Gross National Product (GNP) (in billions)	Foreign Trade (in millions): Exports	Imports	Balance of Trade	Federal Budget (in billions)	Federal Surplus/Deficit (in billions)	Federal Debt (in billions)
1790	(NA)	$ 20	$ 23	$ −3	$ 0.004	$+0.00015	$ 0.076
1800	(NA)	71	91	−20	0.011	+0.0006	0.083
1810	(NA)	67	85	−18	0.008	+0.0012	0.053
1820	(NA)	70	74	−4	0.018	−0.0004	0.091
1830	(NA)	74	71	+3	0.015	+0.100	0.049
1840	(NA)	132	107	+25	0.024	−0.005	0.004
1850	(NA)	152	178	−26	0.040	+0.004	0.064
1860	(NA)	400	362	−38	0.063	−0.01	0.065
1870	$ 7.4	451	462	−11	0.310	+0.10	2.4
1880	11.2	853	761	+92	0.268	+0.07	2.1
1890	13.1	910	823	+87	0.318	+0.09	1.2
1900	18.7	1,499	930	+569	0.521	+0.05	1.2
1910	35.3	1,919	1,646	+273	0.694	−0.02	1.1
1920	91.5	8,664	5,784	+2,880	6.357	+0.3	24.3
1930	90.7	4,013	3,500	+513	3.320	+0.7	16.3
1940	100.0	4,030	7,433	−3,403	9.6	−2.7	43.0
1950	286.5	10,816	9,125	+1,691	43.1	−2.2	257.4
1960	506.5	19,600	15,046	+4,556	92.2	+0.3	286.3
1970	992.7	42,700	40,189	+2,511	195.6	−2.8	371.0
1980	2,631.7	220,783	244,871	+24,088	590.9	−73.8	907.7
1990	5,524.5	394,030	494,042	−101,012	1,251.8	−220.5	3,233.3
1998	8,490.5	933,907	1,098,189	−164,282	1,652.5	+69.2	5,478.7

Source: U.S. *Office of Management and Budget, Budget of the United States Government, annual; Statistical Abstract of the United States*, 1996; *census bureau web site www.gov/foreign-trade/Press-Release/2000pr/01/exh7.txt*

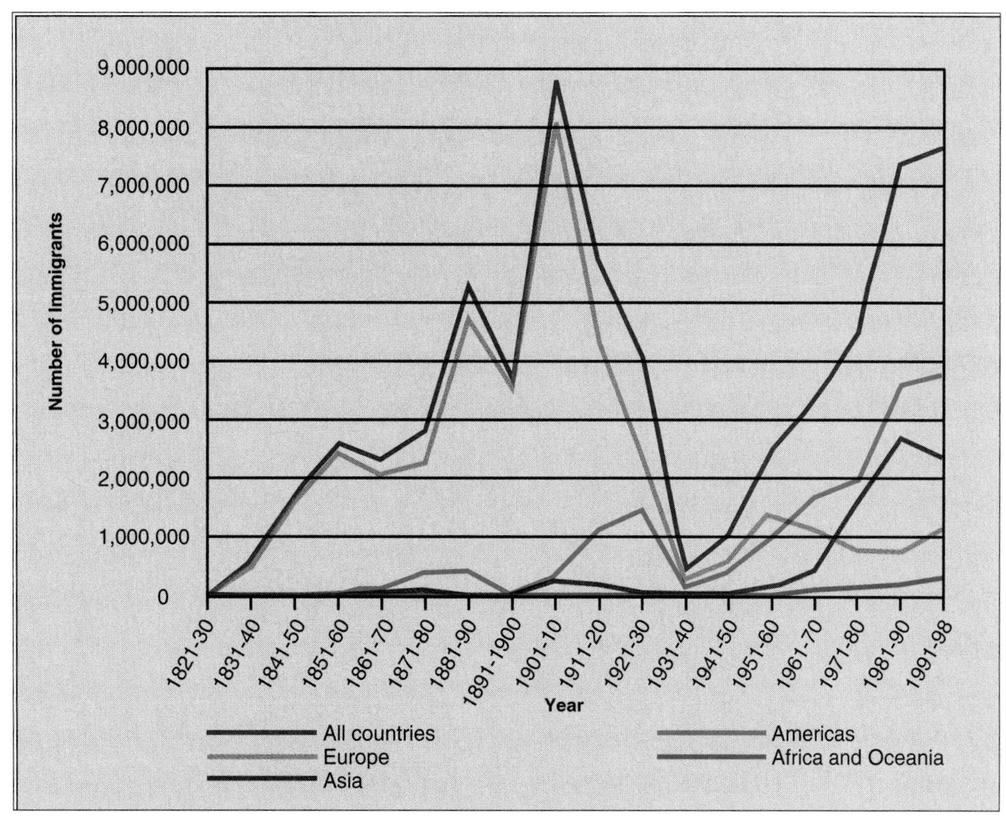

Immigration to the United States since 1820, by decade
Source: *Statistical Yearbook of the Immigration and Naturalization Service, 1997; Annual Report of the Immigration and Naturalization Service: Legal Immigration, Fiscal year 1998.*

GLOSSARY

Abolitionist movement A radical antislavery crusade committed to the immediate end of slavery that emerged in the three decades before the Civil War.

Acquired immune deficiency syndrome (AIDS) A complex of deadly pathologies resulting from infection with the human immunodeficiency virus (HIV).

Act for Religious Toleration The first law in America to call for freedom of worship for all Christians. It was enacted in Maryland in 1649 to quell disputes between Catholics and Protestants, but it failed to bring peace.

Actual representation The practice whereby elected representatives normally reside in their districts and are directly responsive to local interests.

Administration of Justice Act One of the **Coercive** or **Intolerable Acts** passed by Parliament in 1774 in response to the **Boston Tea Party**. It provided that British officials accused of capital crimes could be tried in England.

African Methodist Episcopal (AME) Church Religious body founded by black people for black people in the North during the early nineteenth century that gained adherents among former slaves in the South after the Civil War.

Age of Enlightenment Major intellectual movement occurring in western Europe in the late seventeenth and early eighteenth centuries. Inspired by recent scientific advances, thinkers emphasized the role of human reason in understanding the world and directing its events. Their ideas placed less emphasis on God's role in ordering worldly affairs.

Agricultural Adjustment Administration (AAA) **New Deal** agency that attempted to regulate agricultural production through farm subsidies.

Agricultural Wheel One of several farmer organizations that emerged in the South during the 1880s. It sought federal legislation to deal with credit and currency issues.

Alamo Franciscan mission at San Antonio, Texas, that was the site in 1836 of a siege and massacre of Texans by Mexican troops.

Albany Congress Intercolonial congress called in 1754 in Albany, New York, to deal with Iroquois grievances against the English. At the congress, prominent colonists proposed the **Albany Plan of Union**.

Albany Plan of Union Plan put forward in 1754 by Massachusetts Governor William Shirley, Benjamin Franklin, and other colonial leaders, calling for an intercolonial union to manage defense and Indian affairs. The plan was rejected by participants at the **Albany Congress**.

Albany Regency Popular name after 1820 for the state political machine in New York headed by Martin Van Buren.

Alien and Sedition Acts Collective name given to four acts passed by Congress in 1798 that curtailed freedom of speech and the liberty of foreigners resident in the United States.

Alien Enemies Act Law passed by Congress in 1798 authorizing the president in the event of war to deport aliens suspected of endangering the public peace; one of the **Alien and Sedition Acts**.

Alien Friends Act Law passed by Congress in 1798 authorizing the president during peacetime to expel aliens suspected of subversive activities; one of the **Alien and Sedition Acts**.

Alliance for Progress Program of economic aid to Latin America during the Kennedy administration.

Allies Britain, France, Russia, Italy, and other belligerent nations fighting against the **Central Powers** in World War I but not including the United States.

America First Committee Officially the Committee to Defend America First, organized in 1940 to promote the policy of building and defending "Fortress America."

American and Foreign Anti-Slavery Society Antislavery organization formed in 1840 when a group of moderate abolitionists split off from the **American Anti-Slavery Society** in protest of the radicalism of William Lloyd Garrison and his support of women's rights.

American Anti-Slavery Society The first national organization of abolitionists, founded in 1833. *See also* **American and Foreign Anti-Slavery Society**.

American Civil Liberties Union (ACLU) Organization formed in 1920 to guard the constitutional rights of Americans against government infringement.

American Colonization Society Organization, founded in 1817 by antislavery reformers, that called for gradual emancipation and the removal of freed blacks to Africa.

American Equal Rights Association Association formed by women's rights activists in 1866 to advocate universal **suffrage** at the state level after the **Fourteenth Amendment** failed to provide federal guarantees for women's voting rights.

American Expeditionary Force (AEF) The American army that fought with but was independent of the Allied armies in World War I.

American Federation of Labor (AFL) Union formed in 1886 that organized skilled workers along craft lines and emphasized a few workplace issues rather than a broad social program.

American Female Moral Reform Society Organization founded in 1839 by female reformers that established homes of refuge for prostitutes and petitioned for state laws that would criminalize adultery and the seduction of women.

American Indian Movement (AIM) Group of Native American political activists who used confrontations with the federal government to publicize their case for Indian rights.

American Liberty League Business group organized to sway popular opinion against the **New Deal**.

American Protective Association (APA) Association formed in 1893 by skilled workers and small businessmen in response to increasing immigration from eastern and southern Europe; sought to limit Catholic civil rights and save jobs for Protestant workers.

American Protective League One of the leading vigilante organizations that suppressed dissent while promoting reactionary causes during World War I.

American Railway Union (ARU) Union led by Eugene V. Debs; supported the **Pullman strike**.

American Revenue Act Commonly known as the **Sugar Act**, law passed in 1764 to raise revenue in the American colonies. It lowered the duty from 6 pence to 3 pence per gallon on foreign molasses imported into the colonies and increased the restrictions on colonial commerce.

Americans with Disabilities Act Legislation in 1992 that banned discrimination against physically handicapped persons in employment, transportation, and public accommodations.

American System The program of government subsidies favored by Henry Clay and his followers to promote American economic growth and protect domestic manufacturers from foreign competition.

American system of manufacturing A technique of production pioneered in the United States in the first half of the nineteenth century that relied on precision manufacturing with the use of interchangeable parts.

American Temperance Society National organization established in 1826 by evangelical Protestants that campaigned for total abstinence from alcohol and was successful in sharply lowering per capita consumption of alcohol.

Anarchist A person who believes that all government interferes with individual liberty and should be abolished by whatever means.

Anglican Of or belonging to the Church of England, a Protestant denomination.

Anglo–American Accords Series of agreements reached in the British–American Convention of 1818 that fixed the western boundary between the United States and Canada at the 49th parallel, allowed for the joint occupation of the Oregon Country, and restored to Americans fishing rights off Newfoundland.

Anglo-Saxon Broadly, a person of English descent.

Annapolis Convention Conference of state delegates at Annapolis, Maryland, that issued a call in September 1786 for a convention to meet at Philadelphia in May 1787 to consider fundamental changes to the **Articles of Confederation**.

Antietam, Battle of Narrow strategic Union victory in the Civil War in September 1862 that turned back the first Confederate invasion of the North and enabled President Lincoln to issue the **Emancipation Proclamation**.

Antifederalist An opponent of the **Constitution** in the debate over its ratification.

Anti-Imperialist League Organization, established in 1898, that opposed the annexation of the Philippines and the ratification of the **Treaty of Paris**.

Anti-Masons Third party formed in 1827 in opposition to the presumed power and influence of the Masonic order.

Antinomian A person who believes that salvation comes through faith alone and that individuals who are saved obey the spirit within them rather than the moral law.

Appeal to the Colored Citizens of the World Pamphlet published in 1829 by David Walker, a Boston free black, calling for slaves to rise up in rebellion.

Appomattox Court House Town in south-central Virginia where Confederate general Robert E. Lee surrendered to Union general Ulysses S. Grant on April 9, 1865, ending the Civil War.

Apprentice A person, usually a young male, bound by a legal agreement to serve an employer for a specified amount of time in return for training in a craft, trade, or business.

Archaic The period roughly between 8000 and 1500 B.C., during which time Native Americans adapted to a changed continental climate, developed larger communities, and, in several regions, adopted agriculture.

Articles of Confederation Written document setting up the loose confederation of states that comprised the first national government of the United States from 1781 to 1788.

Atlanta Campaign Decisive Civil War campaign in 1864 in which Union general William T. Sherman maneuvered past Confederate general Joseph E. Johnson from northwestern Georgia toward Atlanta until President Davis replaced Johnson with General John B. Hood, who promptly engaged Sherman and lost this vital rail junction to the Union.

Atlanta Compromise Booker T. Washington's policy accepting segregation and **disfranchisement** for African Americans in exchange for white assistance in education and job training.

Atlantic, Battle of the A struggle for control of the North Atlantic (1940–1943) between German submarines and British and American naval and air forces.

Atlantic Charter Statement of common principles and war aims developed by President Franklin Roosevelt and British Prime Minister Winston Churchill at a meeting in August 1941.

Atomic Energy Commission (AEC) Civilian agency created in 1946 to develop and control military and civilian uses of atomic energy; its functions were transferred to the Nuclear Regulatory Commission in 1975.

Australian ballot Secret voting and the use of official ballots rather than party tickets.

Axis Powers The opponents of the United States and its allies in World War II. The Rome–Berlin Axis was formed between Germany and Italy in 1936 and included Japan after 1940.

Backcountry The western edges of settlement in colonies from Pennsylvania south to the Carolinas. Colonists first began moving to this region in the eighteenth century, developing a society that was at first somewhat cruder than longer-settled eastern communities.

Bacon's Rebellion Violent conflict in Virginia (1675–1676), beginning with settler attacks on Indians but culminating in a rebellion led by Nathaniel Bacon against Virginia's government.

Baker* v. *Carr U.S. Supreme Court decision in 1962 that allowed federal courts to review the apportionment of state legislative districts and established the principle that such districts should have roughly equal populations ("one person, one vote").

Banking Act of 1935 Law that strengthened the authority of the Federal Reserve Board over the nation's currency and credit system.

Bank War The political struggle between President Andrew Jackson and the supporters of the **Second Bank of the United States**.

Bay of Pigs Site in Cuba of an unsuccessful landing by fourteen hundred anti-Castro Cuban refugees in April 1961.

Beats Nonconformists in the late 1950s who came together in large cities to reject conventional dress and sexual standards and cultivate poetry, jazz, and folk music; also known as *beatniks*.

Beaver Wars Series of bloody conflicts, occurring between 1640s and 1680s, during which the Iroquois fought the French and their Indian allies for control of the fur trade in eastern North America and the Great Lakes region.

Benevolent empire Network of reform associations affiliated with Protestant churches in the early nineteenth century dedicated to the restoration of moral order.

Berlin blockade Three-hundred-day Soviet blockade of land access to United States, British, and French occupation zones in Berlin, 1948–1949.

Berlin Wall Wall erected by East Germany in 1961 and torn down in 1989 that isolated West Berlin from the surrounding areas in Communist-controlled East Berlin and East Germany.

Bicameral legislature A legislative body composed of two houses.

Bill of rights A written summary of inalienable rights and liberties.

Black codes Laws passed by states and municipalities denying many rights of citizenship to free blacks. Also, during **Reconstruction**, laws passed by newly elected southern state legislatures to control black labor, mobility, and employment.

Black Death Outbreak of the pneumonic form of bubonic plague in Europe between 1347 and 1351 that killed perhaps a third of Europe's population.

Black Hawk's War Short 1832 war in which federal troops and Illinois militia units defeated the Sauk and Fox Indians led by Black Hawk.

Black Panthers Political and social movement among black Americans, founded in Oakland, California, in 1966 and emphasizing black economic and political power.

Black Power Philosophy emerging after 1965 that real economic and political gains for African-Americans could come only through self-help, **self-determination**, and organizing for direct political influence. Latinos and Native Americans developed their own versions as Brown Power and Red Power, respectively.

Bland-Allison Act An 1878 compromise currency law that provided for limited silver coinage.

"Bleeding Kansas" Violence between pro- and antislavery forces in Kansas Territory after the passage of the **Kansas-Nebraska Act** in 1854.

Blitzkrieg German war tactic in World War II ("lightning war") involving the concentration of air and armored firepower to punch and exploit holes in opposing defensive lines.

Board of Indian Commissioners A nonpartisan board established in 1869 as an advisory agency to eliminate politics and corruption from the government bureaucracy dealing with Indian affairs.

Board of Trade Committee set up by King William in 1696 that replaced the Lords of Trade as overseers of colonial affairs. The board gathered information about the colonies and recommended policy changes but had no executive authority.

Bolshevik Member of the communist movement in Russia that established the Soviet government after the 1917 Russian Revolution; hence, by extension, any radical or disruptive person or movement seeking to transform economic and political relationships.

Bonus Army A group of unemployed veterans who demonstrated in Washington for the payment of service bonuses, only to be violently dispersed by the U.S. Army in 1932.

Boston Massacre Incident that occurred in Boston on March 5, 1770, in which British soldiers fired on a crowd that had been harassing them. Five civilians were killed.

Boston Port Act One of the **Coercive Acts** passed by Parliament in 1774 in response to the **Boston Tea Party**. It closed the port of Boston until townspeople paid for the tea and the duties on it.

Boston Seamen's Aid Society Female reform organization founded in 1833 to assist widows and orphans of sailors.

Boston Tea Party Incident that occurred on December 16, 1773, in which Bostonians, disguised as Indians, destroyed £9,000 worth of tea belonging to the British East India Company in order to prevent payment of the duty on it.

Brandywine Creek, Battle of Revolutionary War engagement on September 11, 1777, in southeastern Pennsylvania in which British forces under Sir William Howe defeated Americans under General George Washington, thereby clearing the way for the British occupation of Philadelphia.

Britain, Battle of Series of air engagements in 1940 during World War II that pitted British interceptor fighter planes against German bombers attacking British cities and industry.

British Constitution The principles, procedures, and precedents that governed the operation of the British government. These could be found in no single written document; Parliament and the king made the Constitution by their actions.

Broad constructionist Person who favors reading implied powers into the **Constitution**.

Brook Farm A utopian community and experimental farm established in 1841 near Boston.

Brooklyn Heights, Battle of Revolutionary War battle fought on August 27, 1776, when Sir William Howe landed a large British force on Long Island, New York, outflanked the American defenders, and attacked their rear. Although the Americans suffered heavy casualties, General George Washington was later able under cover of darkness to withdraw his forces to Manhattan Island.

Brown* v. *Board of Education of Topeka Supreme Court decision in 1954 that declared that "separate but equal" schools for children of different races violated the **Constitution**.

Bulge, Battle of the German counteroffensive in December 1944 during World War II that slowed the Allied advance on Germany.

Bull Run, First Battle of The first major battle of the Civil War in July 1861; a disaster for Federal forces.

Bull Run, Second Battle of Federal Civil War defeat in August 1862 one year after a similar loss at the same place.

Bunker Hill, Battle of Revolutionary War battle actually fought on nearby Breed's Hill, overlooking Boston Harbor, on June 17, 1775. It was a costly engagement for the British, who suffered more than a thousand casualties.

Bureau of Indian Affairs Government agency, within the U.S. Department of the Interior, responsible for carrying out official Indian policy.

Bureau of Reclamation Federal agency established in 1902 providing public funds for irrigation projects in arid regions; played a major role in the development of the West by constructing dams, reservoirs, and irrigation systems, especially beginning in the 1930s.

Business unionism The **American Federation of Labor** stance that members should avoid political activism and concentrate on basic workplace issues.

Cabinet The body of secretaries appointed by the president to head executive departments and serve as advisers.

Californio A person of Spanish descent in California.

Camden, Battle of Decisive British victory at Camden, South Carolina, on August 16, 1780, with more than one thousand Americans killed or wounded and many captured. A second battle near Camden on April 25, 1781, was more nearly a draw.

Camp David Agreement Agreement to reduce points of conflict between Israel and Egypt, hammered out in 1977 with the help of U.S. President Jimmy Carter.

Carpetbaggers Northerners who came to the post–Civil War South, initially for economic reasons, and then became involved in Republican politics; a disparaging term.

Cattle Kingdom The open-range cattle industry that stretched from Texas into Montana in the 1870s and 1880s.

Centennial Exposition Fair held in Philadelphia in 1876 to celebrate the hundredth anniversary of the United States and to showcase American industry and technology.

Central Intelligence Agency (CIA) Agency that coordinates the gathering and evaluation of military and economic information on other nations, established in 1947.

Central Powers Germany and its World War I allies Austria, Turkey, and Bulgaria.

Chain migration Process common to many immigrant groups whereby one family member brings over other family members, who in turn bring other relatives and friends and occasionally entire villages.

Chancellorsville Battle ending in a Confederate victory in Virginia in May 1863 during which General Thomas "Stonewall" Jackson was mortally wounded.

Charles River Bridge* v. *Warren Bridge Supreme Court decision of 1837 that promoted economic competition by ruling that the broader rights of the community took precedence over any presumed right of monopoly granted in a corporate charter.

Charleston, Battle of Revolutionary War engagement that began on February 11, 1780, when Sir Henry Clinton, leading eight thousand British troops from New York, encircled and laid siege to Charleston, South Carolina. On May 12, of that year, 5,400 American defenders under Benjamin Lincoln surrendered in the costliest American defeat of the Revolutionary War.

Chattanooga Site of a series of Civil War campaigns culminating in a smashing Union victory in November 1863 as federal troops broke a Confederate siege of the city and opened the road to Georgia.

Cherokee War Conflict (1759–1761) on the southern frontier between the Cherokee Indians and colonists from Virginia southward. It caused South Carolina to request the aid of British troops and resulted in the surrender of more Indian land to white colonists.

Cherry Valley Site of a Revolutionary War incident that occurred on November 11, 1778, when Joseph Brant of the Mohawks and Captain Walter Butler led seven hundred Indians and **Tories** on a raid of a New York valley that left as many as fifty **Whig** settlers dead.

***Chesapeake* Incident** Attack in 1807 by the British ship *Leopard* on the American ship *Chesapeake* in American territorial waters that nearly provoked an Anglo-American war.

Chicago Defender A major black newspaper that encouraged black migration from the South to the urban North.

Children's Bureau Federal agency established in 1912 to investigate and report on matters pertaining to the welfare of children.

Chinese Consolidated Benevolent Association Umbrella social service organization for Chinese immigrants that pooled their resources to assist in such activities as job hunting, housing, support for the sick or poor, and burial.

Chinese Exclusion Act Law passed by Congress in 1882 prohibiting Chinese immigration to the United States; overturned in 1943.

Chisholm Trail The route followed by Texas cattle raisers driving their herds north to markets at Kansas railheads.

Church of God A religious movement that emerged from the mountains of Tennessee and North Carolina in 1886 as part of the **Holiness movement**. It accepted women, and sometimes black people, on an equal basis with white men.

Church of Jesus Christ of Latter-day Saints *See* **Mormon Church.**

Civilian Conservation Corps (CCC) Popular **New Deal** program that provided young men with relief jobs working on reforestation, flood control, and other **conservation** projects.

Civil Rights Act of 1866 Law that defined national citizenship and specified the civil rights to which all national citizens were entitled.

Civil Rights Act of 1875 Law that prohibited racial discrimination in jury selection, public transportation, and public accommodations; declared unconstitutional by the U.S. Supreme Court in 1883.

Civil Rights Act of 1964 Federal legislation that outlawed discrimination in public accommodations and employment on the basis of race, skin color, sex, religion, or national origin.

Civil Works Administration (CWA) Government agency under Harry Hopkins that created 4 million relief jobs for the unemployed during the winter of 1933–1934.

Claims club A group of local settlers on the nineteenth-century frontier who banded together to prevent the price of their land claims from being bid up by outsiders at public land auctions.

Clean Air Act Legislation in 1970 that set federal standards for air quality.

Coercive Acts Legislation passed by Parliament in 1774; included the **Boston Port Act**, the **Massachusetts Government Act**, the **Administration of Justice Act**, and the **Quartering Act** of 1774.

Cold Harbor Crossroads ten miles northeast of Richmond where, in June 1864, General Ulysses S. Grant launched a disastrous assault on Confederate positions during the Civil War.

Cold War The political and economic confrontation between the Soviet Union and the United States that dominated world affairs from 1946 to 1989.

Collective bargaining Representatives of a union negotiating with management on behalf of all members.

Colored Farmers' Alliance An organization of southern black farmers formed in Texas in 1886 in response to the **Southern Farmers' Alliance**, which did not accept black people as members.

Columbian exchange The transatlantic exchange of plants, animals, and diseases that occurred after the first European contact with the Americas.

Comecon The Council for Mutual Economic Assistance, established in 1949 by the Soviet Union and its eastern European satellites.

Committee of Safety Any of the extralegal committees that directed the Revolutionary movement and carried on the functions of government at the local level in the period between the breakdown of royal authority and the establishment of regular governments under the new state constitutions. Some Committees of Safety continued to function throughout the Revolutionary War.

Committee on Public Information (CPI) Government agency during World War I that sought to shape public opinion in support of the war effort through newspapers, pamphlets, speeches, films, and other media.

Committees of correspondence Committees formed in Massachusetts and other colonies in the pre-Revolutionary period to keep Americans informed about British measures that would affect the colonies.

Committee to Defend America by Aiding the Allies Group organized to support Franklin Roosevelt's policy of resisting **Nazi** Germany by actively aiding the British war effort.

Common Sense Influential pamphlet by Thomas Paine. Published in Philadelphia in January 1776, it convinced many Americans that common sense dictated that the colonies should be independent of Great Britain.

Commonwealth* v. *Hunt Case in which the Massachusetts Supreme Court in 1842 ruled that labor unions were not inherently criminal conspiracies guilty of restraining trade.

Communism A social structure based on the common ownership of property.

Community Action Agencies Locally based antipoverty organizations created under federal legislation in 1964 and intended to allow poor people to help plan programs and services.

Competency In colonial New England, the possession of enough property to maintain a family's independent economic existence. Later, a secure income from an independent trade.

Compromise of 1850 Congressional solution to the controversy over California's admission to the Union as a free state; it granted the populations of other territories the right to decide on slavery **(popular sovereignty)** and established the **Fugitive Slave Act**.

Compromise of 1877 A deal that settled the contested presidential election of 1876 by installing Republican Rutherford B. Hayes in the White House and returning home rule to the South. It formally ended **Reconstruction** and left the fate of the freedmen in the hands of southern white people.

Concentration camp A prison camp for political dissenters and social undesirables, used extensively in **Nazi** Germany.

Conciliatory Proposition Plan proposed by Lord North and adopted by the House of Commons in February 1775 whereby Parliament would "forbear" taxation of Americans in colonies whose assemblies imposed taxes considered satisfactory by the British government. The Continental Congress rejected this plan on July 31, 1775.

Confederate States of America Nation proclaimed in Montgomery, Alabama, in February 1861 after the seven states of the Lower South seceded from the United States.

Confiscation Act of 1862 Second confiscation law passed by Congress, ordering the seizure of land from disloyal Southerners and the emancipation of their slaves.

Congressional Reconstruction Name given to the period 1867–1870 when the Republican-dominated Congress controlled **Reconstruction** policy. It is sometimes known as Radical Reconstruction, after the radical faction in the **Republican party**.

Congress of Industrial Organizations An alliance of industrial unions that spurred the 1930s organizational drive among the mass-production industries.

Congress of Racial Equality (CORE) Civil rights group formed in 1942 and committed to nonviolent civil disobedience, such as the 1961 "freedom rides."

Conquistador Spanish for "conqueror," applied to a Spanish soldier who participated in the conquest and colonization of America.

Conscience Whigs Primarily northern members of the **Whig party** who opposed the extension of slavery in the territories. When the party disintegrated after 1852, many of these Whigs eventually joined the **Republican party**.

Conservation The efficient management and use of natural resources, such as forests, grasslands, and rivers, as opposed to **preservation** or uncontrolled exploitation.

Constitutional Convention Convention that met in Philadelphia in 1787 and drafted the **Constitution of the United States**.

Constitutional Union party National party formed in 1860, mainly by former **Whigs**, that emphasized allegiance to the Union and strict enforcement of all national legislation.

Constitution of the United States The written document providing for a new central government of the United States, drawn up at the **Constitutional Convention** in 1787 and ratified by the states in 1788.

Continental Army The regular or professional army authorized by the Second Continental Congress and commanded by General George Washington during the Revolutionary War. Better training and longer service distinguished its soldiers from the state militiamen.

Continental Association Agreement, adopted by the **First Continental Congress** in 1774 in response to the **Coercive Acts**, to cut off trade with Britain until the objectionable measures were repealed. Local committees were established to enforce the provisions of the association.

Continental dollars Paper money issued by the Continental Congress to finance the Revolution. Lacking tax revenues to back it up, this money depreciated rapidly. By mid-1781, it was literally worthless, but it had served its purpose by helping Congress conduct the war for six years.

Contrabands Slaves who escaped from their masters to Union lines during the Civil War.

Contract theory of government The belief that government is established by human beings to protect certain rights—such as life, liberty, and property—that are theirs by natural, divinely sanctioned law and that when government protects these rights, people are obligated to obey it. But when government violates its part of the bargain (or contract) between the rulers and the ruled, the people are no longer required to obey it and may establish a new government that will do a better job of protecting them. Elements of this theory date back to the ancient Greeks; John Locke used it in his *Second Treatise on Government* (1682), and Thomas Jefferson gave it memorable expression in the Declaration of Independence, where it provides the rationale for renouncing allegiance to King George III.

Contract with America Platform on which many Republican candidates ran for Congress in 1994. Associated with House Speaker Newt Gingrich, it proposed a sweeping reduction in the role and activities of the federal government.

Cooperative An organization that allowed a group of farmers to buy tools, seed, livestock, and other farm-related products at discounted prices in bulk.

Copperhead A term Republicans applied to Northern war dissenters and those suspected of aiding the Confederate cause during the Civil War.

Coral Sea, Battle of the Battle between U.S. and Japanese aircraft carriers that halted the Japanese advance toward Australia in May 1942 during World War II.

Cordon sanitaire The belt of anticommunist eastern European nations that separated western Europe from the Soviet Union after World War I.

Council of Economic Advisers Board of three professional economists established in 1946 to advise the president on economic policy.

Council of National Defense The government body, consisting of **cabinet** officials and economic leaders, that oversaw the wartime agencies controlling the nation's economy during World War I.

Counterculture Various alternatives to mainstream values and behaviors that became popular in the 1960s, including experimentation with psychedelic drugs, communal living, a return to the land, Asian religions, and experimental art.

Country (Real Whig) ideology Strain of thought first appearing in England in the late seventeenth century in response to the growth of governmental power and a national debt. Main ideas stressed the threat to personal liberty posed by a standing army and high taxes and emphasized the need for property holders to retain the right to consent to taxation.

Coureur de bois French for "woods runner," an independent fur trader in New France.

Covenant A formal agreement or contract. The idea of a covenant became an important organizing principle in early New England. Settlers believed that they made a covenant with the Lord to create a godly society, and, in their towns and churches, settlers made covenants whereby they agreed to live and worship in harmony.

Cowpens, Battle of January 17, 1781, engagement in upstate South Carolina during the Revolutionary War involving approximately one thousand men on each side, in which Americans won a resounding victory over the British under Banastre Tarleton, thereby compromising his reputation for invincibility and boosting American morale.

Coxey's Army A protest march of unemployed workers, led by Populist businessman Jacob Coxey, demanding inflation and a public works program during the depression of the 1890s.

Creole A slave of African descent born in the colonies.

Criollo A person of Spanish descent born in the Americas or the West Indies.

Crittenden Plan Series of measures submitted to Congress in January 1861 by John Crittenden of Kentucky to permit slavery below the **Missouri Compromise** line.

Crop lien A claim against all or a portion of a farmer's crop as security against a debt.

Crop lien laws In the Reconstruction and post-Reconstruction South, laws that gave merchants the right to sharecroppers' future cotton crop in exchange for credit.

Cult of domesticity The belief that women, by virtue of their sex, should stay home as the moral guardians of family life.

Culture area A geographical region inhabited by peoples who share similar basic patterns of subsistence and social organization.

Currency Act Law passed by Parliament in 1764 to prevent the colonies from issuing **legal tender** paper money, which often depreciated.

Dartmouth College* v. *Woodward Supreme Court decision of 1819 that prohibited states from interfering with the privileges granted to a private corporation.

Dawes Act An 1887 law terminating tribal ownership of land and allotting some parcels of land to individual Indians with the remainder opened for white settlement.

D-Day June 6, 1944, the day of the first paratroop drops and amphibious landings on the coast of Normandy, France, in the first stage of **Operation OVERLORD** during World War II.

Declaration of Independence The document by which the Second Continental Congress announced and justified its decision (reached July 2, 1776) to renounce the colonies' allegiance to the British government. Drafted mainly by Thomas Jefferson and adopted by Congress on July 4, the declaration's indictment of the king provides a remarkably full catalog of the colonists' grievances, and Jefferson's eloquent and inspiring statement of the **contract theory of government** makes the document one of the world's great state papers.

Declaration of London Statement drafted by an international conference in 1909 to clarify international law and specify the rights of neutral nations.

Declaration of Rights and Grievances Resolves, adopted by the **Stamp Act Congress** at New York in 1765, asserting that the **Stamp Act** and other taxes imposed on the colonists without their consent, given through their colonial legislatures, were unconstitutional.

Declaration of Sentiments The resolutions passed at the **Seneca Falls Convention** in 1848 calling for full female equality, including the right to vote.

Declaration of the Causes and Necessity of Taking Up Arms Document, written mainly by John Dickinson of Pennsylvania and adopted on July 6, 1775, by which the Second Continental Congress justified its armed resistance against British measures.

Declaratory Act Law passed in 1766 to accompany repeal of the **Stamp Act** that stated that Parliament had the authority to legislate for the colonies "in all cases whatsoever." Whether "legislate" meant tax was not clear to Americans.

Deism Religious orientation that rejects divine revelation and holds that the workings of nature alone reveal God's design for the universe.

Democratic party Political party formed in the 1820s under the leadership of Andrew Jackson; favored states' rights and a limited role for the federal government, especially in economic affairs.

Denmark Vesey's Conspiracy The most carefully devised slave revolt, named after its leader, a free black in Charleston. The rebels planned to seize control of Charleston in 1822 and escape to freedom in Haiti, a free black republic, but they were betrayed by other slaves, and seventy-five conspirators were executed.

Deregulation Reduction or removal of government regulations and encouragement of direct competition in many important industries and economic sectors.

Desert Storm Code name for the successful offensive against Iraq by the United States and its allies in the Persian Gulf War (1991).

Deskilling A decline in workforce skills due to discrimination, as for southern black people in the late nineteenth century, or to mechanization, as for white industrial workers in the same period.

Détente A lessening of tension, applied to improved American relations with the Soviet Union and China in the mid-1970s.

Direct Tax of 1798 A national tax levied on land, slaves, and dwellings.

Disfranchisement The use of legal means to bar individuals or groups from voting.

Dixiecrats Southern Democrats who broke from the party in 1948 over the issue of civil rights and ran a presidential ticket as the States' Rights Democrats.

Dollar diplomacy The U.S. policy of using private investment in other nations to promote American diplomatic goals and business interests.

Dominion of New England James II's failed plan of 1686 to combine eight northern colonies into a single large province, to be governed by a royal appointee (Sir Edmund Andros) with an appointed council but no elective assembly. The plan ended with James's ouster from the English throne and rebellion in Massachusetts against Andros's rule.

***Dred Scott* decision** Supreme Court ruling, in a lawsuit brought by Dred Scott, a slave demanding his freedom based on his residence in a free state and a free territory with his master, that slaves could not be U.S. citizens and that Congress had no jurisdiction over slavery in the territories.

Dutch West India Company Trading enterprise that established and governed the Dutch colony of New Netherlands from its first permanent settlement at Fort Orange in 1624 until it was seized by the English in 1664.

Eastern Front The area of military operations in World War II located east of Germany in eastern Europe and the Soviet Union.

Economic Recovery and Tax Act of 1981 (ERTA) A major revision of the federal income tax system.

Edge city A suburban district that has developed as a center for employment, retailing, and services comparable to a traditional downtown.

El Alamein, Battle of British victory during World War II that checked the advance of the German army into Egypt in June 1942.

Elementary and Secondary Education Act Federal legislation in 1965 that provided the first large-scale federal aid for needy public school districts.

Emancipation Proclamation Decree announced by President Abraham Lincoln in September 1862 and formally issued on January 1, 1863, freeing slaves in all Confederate states still in rebellion.

Embargo Act of 1807 Act passed by Congress in 1807 prohibiting American ships from leaving for any foreign port.

Emergency Banking Act of 1933 A law that stabilized the banking system through government aid and supervision.

Emergency Relief Appropriation Act of 1935 Law authorizing a massive program of public work relief projects for the unemployed.

Employment Act of 1946 Federal legislation that committed the United States to the goal of "maximum employment, production and purchasing power."

Empresario An agent who received a land grant from the Spanish or Mexican government in return for organizing settlements.

Encomienda In the Spanish colonies, the grant to a Spanish settler of a certain number of Indian subjects, who would pay him tribute in goods and labor.

Enforcement Act of 1870 Largely ineffectual law passed in response to growing political violence in the South, enabling the federal government to appoint supervisors where states failed to protect citizens' voting rights.

Engel* v. *Vitale Supreme Court decision in 1962 that found that reading a nondenominational prayer in public schools violated the First Amendment to the Constitution.

Enrollment Act A law passed by the U.S. Congress in 1863 during the Civil War subjecting all able-bodied men between the ages of twenty and forty-five to the draft. Its unpopularity contributed to the **New York Draft Riot** later that year.

Enumerated products Items produced in the colonies and enumerated in acts of Parliament that could be legally shipped from the colony of origin only to specified locations, usually England and other destinations within the British empire.

Environmental Protection Agency (EPA) Federal agency created in 1970 to oversee environmental monitoring and cleanup programs.

Equal Employment Opportunity Commission (EEOC) Federal commission established by the **Civil Rights Act of 1964** to monitor and enforce nondiscrimination in employment.

Equal Rights Amendment (ERA) A proposed but never adopted amendment to the **Constitution** to prevent abridgment of rights on account of a person's sex.

Era of Good Feelings The period from 1817 to 1823 in which the disappearance of the **Federalists** enabled the **Republicans** to govern in a spirit of seemingly nonpartisan harmony.

Espionage Act of 1917 Law whose vague prohibition against obstructing the nation's war effort was used to crush dissent and criticism during World War I.

Established church A church supported in part by public taxes.

Executive Order 8802 Presidential order in 1943 that required racial nondiscrimination clauses in war contracts and subcontracts.

Executive Order 9066 Presidential order in February 1942 that authorized the forcible relocation of Japanese Americans from portions of four western states.

Executive Order 9835 Presidential order by President Truman in 1947 implementing a loyalty program for federal employees.

Fair Deal Program for expanded economic opportunity and civil rights proposed by President Truman in 1949.

Fair Employment Practice Committee (FEPC) Federal agency established in 1941 to curb racial discrimination in war production jobs and government employment.

Fallen Timbers, Battle of Battle fought in northern Ohio in August 1794, in which an American army led by General Anthony Wayne decisively defeated an Indian confederation.

Farm Credit Administration Government agency established in 1933 to refinance farm mortgages, thereby saving farms and protecting banks.

Farmers' Alliance A broad mass movement in the rural South and West during the late nineteenth century, encompassing several organizations and demanding economic and political reforms; helped create the **Populist party**.

Fascist Subscribing to a philosophy of governmental dictatorship that merges the interests of the state, armed forces, and big business; associated with the dictatorship of Italian leader Benito Mussolini between 1922 and 1943 and also often applied to **Nazi** Germany.

Federal Communications Commission (FCC) Government agency established in 1934 with authority to regulate radio and television.

Federal Deposit Insurance Corporation (FDIC) Government agency that guarantees bank deposits, thereby protecting both depositors and banks.

Federal Emergency Relief Administration (FERA) Agency set up to provide direct federal grants to the states for assisting the unemployed in the **Great Depression**.

Federal Highway Act of 1956 Measure that provided federal funding to build a nationwide system of interstate and defense highways.

Federalism The sharing of powers between the national government and the states.

Federalist A supporter of the **Constitution** who favored its ratification.

The Federalist A series of eighty-five essays, written anonymously and individually by Alexander Hamilton, James Madison, and John Jay, published in New York in 1787 and 1788 to rally support for the ratification of the **Constitution**.

Federalist party Political party organized within the Washington administration by supporters of Alexander Hamilton who favored a strong national government, commercial development, and a pro-British stance in foreign policy.

Federal Reserve Act The 1913 law that revised banking and currency by extending limited government regulation through the creation of the Federal Reserve System.

Federal Trade Commission (FTC) Government agency established in 1914 to provide regulatory oversight of business activity.

Fence laws Legislation that required the penning of animals so that they would not disturb crops.

Field Order No. 15 Order by General William T. Sherman in January 1865 to set aside abandoned land along the southern Atlantic coast for forty-acre grants to freedmen; rescinded by President Andrew Johnson later that year.

Fifteenth Amendment **Reconstruction** amendment passed by Congress in February 1869 guaranteeing the right of all American male citizens to vote regardless of race.

Fireside chats Speeches broadcast nationally over the radio in which President Franklin Roosevelt explained complex issues and programs in plain language, as though his listeners were gathered around the fireside with him.

First Continental Congress Meeting of delegates from most of the colonies held in 1774 in response to the **Coercive Acts**. The Congress endorsed the **Suffolk Resolves**, adopted the **Declaration of Rights and Grievances**, and agreed to establish the **Continental Association** to put economic pressure on Britain to repeal its objectionable measures. The Congress also wrote addresses to the king, the people of Britain, and the American people.

Fletcher* v. *Peck Supreme Court decision of 1810 that overturned a state law by ruling that it violated a legal contract.

Food Administration The agency that sought to increase agricultural production and food conservation to supply the U.S. military and the **Allies** during World War I.

Fort Donelson With **Fort Henry**, one of two strategic forts on the Tennessee and Cumberland Rivers; site of a January 1862 Union victory during the Civil War.

Fort Henry With **Fort Donelson**, one of two strategic forts on the Tennessee and Cumberland Rivers; site of a January 1862 Union victory during the Civil War.

Fort Laramie Treaty Treaty of 1851 in which the United States attempted to establish definite boundaries for each of the major Indian tribes on the Central Plains.

Fort Sumter Begun in the late 1820s to protect Charleston, South Carolina, it became the center of national attention in April 1861 when President Lincoln attempted to provision federal troops at the fort, triggering a hostile response from on-shore Confederate forces, opening the Civil War.

Fort Ticonderoga Strategically important fort between Lake George and Lake Champlain in New York State. Benedict Arnold and Ethan Allen, leading forces from Massachusetts and Vermont, respectively, captured the fort, its fifty defenders, and its military stores on May 10, 1775, at the outset of the Revolutionary War.

Fort Wagner Confederate installation guarding the entrance to Charleston harbor during the Civil War and site of a failed Federal assault in July 1863 during which a black Union regiment, the 54th Massachusetts, distinguished itself.

Forty-Niners Miners who rushed to California after the discovery of gold in the northern part of the territory in 1848.

Fourierist communities Short-live utopian communities in the 1840s based on the ideas of economic cooperation and self-sufficiency popularized by the Frenchman Charles Fourier.

Fourteenth Amendment Constitutional amendment passed by Congress in April 1866 incorporating some of the features of the **Civil Rights Act of 1866**. It prohibited states from violating the civil rights of its citizens and offered states the choice of allowing black people to vote or losing representation in Congress.

Frame of Government William Penn's 1682 plan for the government of Pennsylvania, which created a relatively weak legislature and a strong executive. It also contained a provision for religious freedom.

Franco-American Accord of 1800 Settlement reached with France that brought an end to the **Quasi-War** and released the United States from its 1778 alliance with France.

Franklin, Battle of Confederate general John B. Hood's disastrous frontal assault on well-entrenched Union positions south of Nashville in November 1864 during the Civil War.

Fredericksburg Site of a Union setback in late 1862 that ended another Federal attempt to march on Richmond during the Civil War.

Freedmen's Bureau Agency established by Congress in March 1865 to provide social, educational, and economic services, advice, and protection to former slaves and destitute whites; lasted seven years.

Freedom Summer Voter registration effort in rural Mississippi organized by black and white civil rights workers in 1964.

Freedom's Journal The first African-American newspaper, founded in 1827 by John Russwurm and Samuel Cornish.

Freeport Doctrine Illinois Senator Stephen A. Douglas's statement during the 1858 **Lincoln–Douglas debates** that slavery could exist in a territory only if residents passed a law to protect it and that, if residents did not pass such a law, there would be no slavery.

Free silver Philosophy that the government should expand the money supply by purchasing and coining all the silver offered to it.

Free-Soil party Anti-Southern party centered on keeping slavery out of the territories.

Free Speech Movement (FSM) Student movement at the University of California, Berkeley, formed in 1964 to protest limitations on political activities on campus.

French and Indian War The last of the Anglo-French colonial wars (1754–1763) and the first in which fighting began in North America. The war (which merged with the European conflict known as the **Seven Years' War**) ended with France's defeat and loss of its North American empire.

Fries's Rebellion An armed attempt to block enforcement of the **Direct Tax of 1798** in the eastern counties of Pennsylvania, named for an auctioneer who played a prominent role.

Fugitive Slave Act Law, part of the **Compromise of 1850**, that required that authorities in the North to assist southern slave catchers and return runaway slaves to their owners.

Fundamental Constitutions of Carolina A complex plan for organizing the colony of Carolina, drafted in 1669 by Anthony Ashley Cooper and John Locke. Its provisions included a scheme for creating a hierarchy of nobles who would own vast amounts of land and wield political power; below them would be a class of freedmen and slaves. The provisions were never implemented by the Carolina colonists.

Fundamentalists Religious conservatives who believe in the literal accuracy and divine inspiration of the Bible; the name derives from an influential series of pamphlets, *The Fundamentals* (1909–1914).

Fundamental Orders Design for Connecticut government, adopted in 1639, that was modeled on that of Massachusetts Bay, except that voters did not have to be church members.

Funded debt Means by which governments allocate a portion of tax revenues to guarantee payment of interest on loans from private investors. England used this process to begin paying debts incurred during the first two Anglo-French wars, thereby harnessing private capital to serve the nation's military needs.

Fusion Political strategy adopted by Populists and Republicans in North Carolina during their successful 1894 election campaign.

Gabriel Prosser's Rebellion Slave revolt that failed when Gabriel Prosser, a slave preacher and blacksmith, organized a thousand slaves for an attack on Richmond, Virginia, in 1800. A thunderstorm upset the timing of the attack, and a slave informer alerted the whites. Prosser and twenty-five of his followers were executed.

Gag rule Procedural rule passed in the House of Representatives that prevented discussion of antislavery proposals from 1836 to 1844.

Gang system The organization and supervision of slave field hands into working teams on southern plantations.

Gaspee British revenue schooner burned in Narragansett Bay by Rhode Islanders in 1772. The incident led to the appointment of a British commission of inquiry whose powers prompted Americans to establish **committees of correspondence**.

General Agreement on Tariffs and Trade (GATT) International agreement aimed at lowering barriers to international trade, first signed in 1947 and updated periodically.

General Court The legislature of the colony of Massachusetts.

General Union for Promoting the Observance of the Christian Sabbath Reform organization founded in 1828 by Congregationalist and Presbyterian ministers that lobbied for an end to the delivery of mail on Sundays and other Sabbath violations.

Gentlemen's Agreement A diplomatic agreement in 1907 between Japan and the United States curtailing but not abolishing Japanese immigration.

Gettysburg Town in Pennsylvania; site of a pivotal Union victory in July 1863 during the Civil War.

Ghent, Treaty of Treaty signed in December 1814 between the United States and Britain that ended the **War of 1812**.

Ghetto A neighborhood or district in which members of a particular racial or ethnic group are forced to live by law or as a result of economics or social discrimination.

GI World War II slang for a U.S. soldier, derived from the words *government issue* stamped on equipment and supplies.

GI Bill of Rights Legislation in June 1944 that eased the return of veterans into American society by providing educational and employment benefits.

Gibbons* v. *Ogden Supreme Court decision of 1824 involving coastal commerce that overturned a steamboat monopoly granted by the state of New York on the grounds that only Congress had the authority to regulate interstate commerce.

Gilded Age Term applied to late-nineteenth-century America that refers to the shallow display and worship of wealth characteristic of the period.

Glasnost Russian for "openness," applied to Mikhail Gorbachev's encouragement of new ideas and easing of political repression in the Soviet Union.

Glass-Steagall Act of 1933 Law that separated investment from commercial banking to limit speculation by bankers and created the **Federal Deposit Insurance Corporation**.

Glorieta Pass Mountain pass in New Mexico; site of an important Civil War battle in April 1862 that maintained the Southwest under Union control.

Glorious Revolution Bloodless revolt that occurred in England in 1688 when parliamentary leaders invited William of Orange, a Protestant, to assume the English throne and James II fled to France. James's ouster was prompted by fears that the birth of his son would establish a Catholic dynasty in England.

Goliad Town in Texas where Mexican troops put to death over three hundred American prisoners on March 27, 1836, during the Texas War for Independence.

Gospel of Wealth Thesis that hard work and perseverance lead to wealth, implying that poverty is a character flaw.

Grand Settlement of 1701 Separate peace treaties negotiated by Iroquois diplomats at Montreal and Albany that marked the beginning of Iroquois neutrality in conflicts between the French and the British in North America.

Grandfather clause Rule that required potential voters to demonstrate that their grandfathers had been eligible to vote; used in some southern states after 1890 to limit the black electorate, as most black men's grandfathers had been slaves.

Grange The National Grange of the Patrons of Husbandry, a national organization of farm owners formed after the Civil War.

Granger laws State laws enacted in the Midwest in the 1870s that regulated rates charged by railroads, grain elevator operators, and other middlemen.

Great Awakening Tremendous religious revival in colonial America. Sparked by the tour of the English evangelical minister George Whitefield, the Awakening struck first in the Middle Colonies and New England in the 1740s and eventually spread to the southern colonies by the 1760s.

Great Bridge Causeway near Norfolk, Virginia, that on December 9, 1775, was the site of a Revolutionary War battle between Americans and a British force composed mostly of African-Americans and other **Loyalists** who had joined the governor of Virginia, Lord Dunmore. Victory by the Americans enabled them to occupy Norfolk shortly thereafter.

Great Compromise Plan proposed by Roger Sherman of Connecticut at the 1787 **Constitutional Convention** for creating a national **bicameral legislature** in which all states would be equally represented in the Senate and proportionally represented in the House.

Great Depression The nation's worst economic crisis, extending throughout the 1930s, producing unprecedented bank failures, unemployment, and industrial and agricultural collapse and prompting an expanded role for the federal government.

Greater East Asia Co-Prosperity Sphere Japanese goal of an East Asian economy controlled by Japan and serving the needs of Japanese industry.

Great Migration The mass movement of African Americans from the rural South to the urban North, spurred especially by new job opportunities during World War I and the 1920s.

Great Society Theme of Lyndon Johnson's administration, focusing on poverty, education, and civil rights.

Great Uprising Unsuccessful railroad strike of 1877 to protest wage cuts and the use of federal troops against strikers; the first nationwide work stoppage in American history.

Greenback party A third party of the 1870s and 1880s that garnered temporary support by advocating currency inflation to expand the economy and assist debtors.

Greenville, Treaty of Treaty of 1795 in which Indians in the Old Northwest were forced to cede most of the present state of Ohio to the United States.

Guadalupe Hidalgo, Treaty of Treaty signed in 1848 that ended the **Mexican War**; Mexico surrendered its claim to Texas above the Rio Grande and, in the **Mexican Cession of 1848**, ceded New Mexico and Alta California to the United States in return for a payment of $15 million.

Guilford Court House, Battle of A fiercely fought Revolutionary War engagement that occurred on March 15, 1781, near modern Greensboro, North Carolina, in which British forces under Lord Cornwallis and Americans commanded by General Nathanael Greene both sustained heavy losses. The British technically won but were forced to withdraw to Wilmington, North Carolina.

Gulf of Tonkin Resolution Congressional resolution in August 1964 that authorized the president to take all necessary steps to protect South Vietnam, adopted after reports of North Vietnamese attacks on U.S. ships in the Gulf of Tonkin off North Vietnam.

Habeas corpus Writ that requires arresting authorities to explain the grounds for a person's imprisonment or detention before a court of law.

Halfway Covenant Plan adopted in 1662 by New England clergy to deal with the problem of declining church membership. It allowed adults who had been baptized because their parents were church members but who had not yet experienced conversion to have their own children baptized. Without the Halfway Covenant, these third-generation children would remain unbaptized until their parents experienced conversion.

Harlem Renaissance A new African-American cultural awareness that flourished in literature, art, and music in the 1920s.

Harrison Act The 1914 law that prohibited the dispensing and use of narcotics for other than medicinal purposes.

Hartford Convention A meeting of New England **Federalists** in late 1814 in which they protested the **War of 1812** and demanded constitutional changes to protect the commercial interests of New England.

Haymarket Square Location in Chicago where workers gathered in May 1886 to protest the slayings of colleagues who had struck for an eight-hour workday; a bomb exploded, throwing the gathering into chaos and resulting in the arrest and execution of strike leaders and the decline of the **Knights of Labor**.

Headright system Adopted first in Virginia and later in Maryland, a system of land distribution during the early colonial era that granted settlers 50 acres for themselves and another 50 for each "head" (or person) they brought with them to the colony.

Head Start Federal program that since 1965 has helped prepare children from disadvantaged backgrounds for success in school.

Helsinki Accords Agreement in 1975 among **NATO** and **Warsaw Pact** members that recognized European national boundaries as set after World War II and included guarantees of human rights.

Higher Education Act Federal legislation in 1965 that provided federal financial aid for college students.

High Federalists Followers of Alexander Hamilton who wanted President John Adams to declare war against France in 1798 and stamp out political dissent within the United States.

Hippie A person who dropped out of mainstream society or adopted some of the styles associated with the **counterculture** of the 1960s and early 1970s.

Holiness movement Religious movement originating in the antebellum North and revived among Texas farmers in the 1880s that stressed simplicity in lifestyle and appealed especially to the poor.

Holocaust The systematic murder of millions of European Jews and others deemed undesirable by **Nazi** Germany.

Holy Roman Empire The loose confederation of German and Italian territories under the authority of an emperor that existed from the ninth or tenth century until 1806.

Home mission societies Organizations founded by white Methodist Church women in the South during the 1870s to promote industrial education among the southern poor and help working-class women become self-sufficient.

Home Owners Loan Corporation Federal agency that rescued individual homeowners from foreclosure by refinancing mortgage loans.

Homestead Act Law passed by Congress in May 1862 providing homesteaders (mainly in the West) with 160 acres of free land in exchange for improving the land (as by cultivating it and erecting a house) within five years of the grant.

Homestead strike A bloody, lengthy, and ultimately unsuccessful strike against Andrew Carnegie's Homestead, Pennsylvania, steelworks in 1892.

Hooverville Shantytown, sarcastically named after President Hoover, in which unemployed and homeless people lived in makeshift shacks, tents, and boxes. Hoovervilles cropped up in many cities in 1930 and 1931.

Horizontal integration The merger of competitors in the same industry.

House Committee on Un-American Activities (HUAC) Congressional committee (1938–1975) that investigated suspected **Nazi** and communist sympathizers.

House of Burgesses The legislature of colonial Virginia. First organized in 1619, it was the first institution of representative government in the English colonies.

House of Commons The lower house of the British Parliament, which included representatives elected by England's propertied class.

House of Lords The upper house of the British Parliament, where members of the aristocracy were represented.

Hull House Chicago **settlement house** that became part of a broader neighborhood revitalization project led by Jane Addams.

Immigrant Restriction League (IRL) New England–based organization formed in 1894 to restrict immigration from southern and eastern Europe by mandating a literacy test for every immigrant.

Immigration and Nationality Act of 1965 Federal legislation that replaced the national quota system for immigration with overall limits of 170,000 immigrants per year from the Eastern Hemisphere and 120,000 per year from the Western Hemisphere.

Immigration Reform and Control Act of 1986 Legislation that granted legal status to 2,650,000 undocumented immigrants and established penalties for employers who knowingly hire illegal immigrants.

Impeachment The formal charging of a public official with improper conduct.

Imperialism The policy and practice of exploiting nations and peoples for the benefit of an imperial power either directly through military occupation and colonial rule or indirectly through economic domination of resources and markets.

Indenture A contract binding a person to the legal service of another for a specified period.

Indentured servant An individual—usually male but occasionally female—who contracted to serve a master for a period of four to seven years in return for payment of the servant's passage to America. Indentured servitude was the primary labor system in the Chesapeake colonies for most of the seventeenth century.

Independent Treasury System Fiscal arrangement first instituted by President Martin Van Buren in which the federal government kept its money in regional vaults ("pet banks") and transacted its business entirely in hard money.

Indian Removal Act Legislation passed by Congress in 1830 that provided funds for removing and resettling eastern Indians in the West. It granted the president the authority to use force if necessary.

Indian Reorganization Act of 1934 Law that reversed previous Indian policy by guaranteeing religious freedom and tribal self-government and providing economic assistance.

Individual Retirement Accounts (IRAs) Personal saving and investment accounts that allow workers and their spouses to accumulate retirement savings on a tax-deferred basis.

Industrial Workers of the World (IWW) Militant labor organization founded in 1905 that attracted mostly recent immigrants and espoused a class-conscious program and ideology. Its members were known as **Wobblies**.

Initiative Procedure by which citizens can introduce a subject for legislation, usually through a petition signed by a specific number of voters.

Intendant A royally appointed government official in New France.

Intermediate Nuclear Force Agreement (INF) Disarmament agreement between the United States and the Soviet Union under which an entire class of missiles would be removed and destroyed and on-site inspections would be permitted for verification.

International Monetary Fund (IMF) International organization established in 1945 to assist nations in maintaining stable currencies.

Interstate Commerce Act The 1887 law that expanded federal power over business by prohibiting pooling and discriminatory rates by railroads and establishing the first federal regulatory agency, the **Interstate Commerce Commission**.

Interstate Commerce Commission (ICC) The first federal regulatory agency, established in 1887 to oversee railroad practices.

Intolerable Acts American term for the **Coercive Acts** and the **Quebec Act**.

Iroquois League The union of five Indian nations (Mohawks, Oneidas, Onondagas, Cayugas, and Senecas) formed around 1450, also known as the League of Five Nations. Essentially a religious organization, its purpose was to maintain peace among the five nations and unite them to fight against other enemies. After the Tuscarora War (1713–1715), the Tuscaroras joined the league, thereafter known as the League of Six Nations.

Irreconcilables Group of U.S. senators adamantly opposed to ratification of the **Treaty of Versailles** after World War I.

Island hopping In the Pacific theater during World War II, the strategy in which U.S. land and amphibious forces seized selected Japanese-held islands while bypassing and isolating other islands held by Japan.

Isolationism The belief that the United States should not involve itself in international (especially European) political and military developments.

Jacksonian Democrats *See* **Democratic party**.

Japanese Association of America Social service organization for Japanese immigrants that stressed assimilation.

Jay's Treaty Treaty with Britain negotiated in 1794 in which the United States made major concessions to avert a war over the British seizure of American ships.

Jazz Age The 1920s, so called for the popular music of the day as a symbol of the many changes taking place in the mass culture.

Jeffersonian Republicans See **Republican party (Jeffersonian)**.

Jim Crow laws **Segregation** laws that became widespread in the South during the 1890s, named for a minstrel show character portrayed satirically by white actors in blackface.

Job Corps Antipoverty program created in 1964 that has provided job training and public service work for young people aged 16 to 21 in residential centers.

John Brown's Raid New England abolitionist John Brown's ill-fated attempt to free Virginia's slaves with a raid on the federal arsenal at Harpers Ferry, Virginia, in 1859.

Joint Committee on the Conduct of the War Committee created by the Republican-dominated Congress in December 1861 to examine and monitor Civil War military policy, although it ultimately devoted itself more to harassing Democratic officers and promoting the political agenda of **Radical Republican** congressmen.

Joint-stock company Business enterprise in which a group of stockholders pooled their money to engage in trade or to fund colonizing expeditions. Joint-stock companies participated in the founding of the Virginia, Plymouth, and Massachusetts Bay colonies.

Journeyman A person who has completed an apprenticeship in a trade or craft and is now a qualified worker in another person's employ.

Judicial review A power implied in the **Constitution** that gives federal courts the right to review and determine the constitutionality of acts passed by Congress and state legislatures.

Judiciary Act of 1789 Act of Congress that implemented the judiciary clause of the **Constitution** by establishing the Supreme Court and a system of lower federal courts.

Judiciary Act of 1801 Law passed by a **Federalist**-dominated Congress that created new judgships and judicial offices that outgoing President John Adams filled with prominent **Federalists**.

Kansas-Nebraska Act Law passed in 1854 creating the Kansas and Nebraska Territories but leaving the question of slavery open to residents, thereby repealing the **Missouri Compromise**.

Kaskaskia Illinois town on the Mississippi River occupied on July 4, 1778, during the Revolutionary War, by George Rogers Clark, commanding troops from Virginia; Cahokia, Illinois, and Vincennes, Indiana, soon capitulated, though the British later reoccupied Vincennes before Clark recaptured it on February 23, 1779. Clark's operations strengthened American claims to the areas at the end of the war.

Kasserine Pass Site of the first large-scale World War II encounter between U.S. and German ground forces, in February 1942 in North Africa.

Kellogg-Briand Pact International treaty negotiated in 1928 to outlaw war but containing no enforcement provisions.

Kettle Creek, Battle of Revolutionary War engagement in upstate Georgia on February 14, 1779, in which Americans under General Andrew Pickens defeated a band of about seven hundred **Tories** from North and South Carolina. This victory boosted American morale and intimidated **Tories** in the area.

King George's War The third Anglo-French war in North America (1744–1748), part of the European conflict known as the **War of the Austrian Succession**. During the North American fighting, New Englanders captured the French fortress of Louisbourg, only to have it returned to France after the peace negotiations.

King Philip's War Conflict in New England (1675–1676) between Wampanoags, Narragansetts, and other Indian peoples against English settlers; sparked by English encroachments on native lands.

Kings Mountain, Battle of Decisive American Revolutionary War victory in northwestern South Carolina on October 7, 1780, when nine hundred American militia from Virginia, the western Carolinas, and eastern Tennessee annihilated or captured over one thousand **Loyalists**, an important turning point in the southern campaign.

King William's War The first Anglo-French conflict in North America (1689–1697), the American phase of Europe's **War of the League of Augsburg**. Ended in negotiated peace that reestablished the balance of power.

Kiva A Pueblo Indian ceremonial structure, usually circular and underground.

Knights of Labor Labor union that included skilled and unskilled workers irrespective of race or gender; founded in 1869, peaked in the 1880s, and declined when its advocacy of the eight-hour workday led to violent strikes in 1886.

Know-Nothing party Anti-immigrant party formed from the wreckage of the **Whig party** and some disaffected northern Democrats in 1854.

Korean War War between North Korea and South Korea (1950–1953) in which the People's Republic of China fought on the side of North Korea and the United States and other nations fought on the side of South Korea under the auspices of the **United Nations**.

Ku Klux Klan Perhaps the most prominent of the vigilante groups that terrorized black people in the South during **Reconstruction**, founded by Confederate veterans in 1866.

Ku Klux Klan Act of 1871 Law that held the perpetrators responsible for denying a citizen's civil rights and allowed the federal government to prosecute and send military assistance if states failed to act.

Kursk Salient Site of the largest tank battle in World War II (July 1943), when Germans failed to throw back Soviet forces that had pushed a huge bulge or salient into German lines.

Ladies' Memorial Associations Women's organizations formed in the South after the Civil War to commemorate Confederate soldiers.

Lancaster, Treaty of Negotiation in 1744 whereby Iroquois chiefs sold Virginia land speculators the right to trade at the Forks of the Ohio. Although the Iroquois had not intended this to include the right to settle in the Ohio Country, the Virginians assumed that it did. Ohio Valley Indians considered this treaty a great grievance against both the English and the Iroquois.

Land Grant College Act Law passed by Congress in July 1862 awarding proceeds from the sale of public lands to the states for the establishment of agricultural and mechanical (later engineering) colleges. Also known as the Morrill Act, after its sponsor, Congressman Justin Morrill of Vermont.

Land Ordinance of 1785 Act passed by Congress under the **Articles of Confederation** that created the grid system of surveys by which all subsequent public land was made available for sale.

Landsmanshaften Jewish associations that provided social and economic services for their members.

Las Gorras Blancas Hispanic villagers ("the White Caps") in New Mexico who disguised themselves and employed violent tactics to resist Anglo capitalist disruptions of their traditional life.

Lawes Divine, Morall and Martiall A harsh code of laws in force in Virginia between 1609 and 1621, intended to use military discipline to bring order to the struggling colony.

League of Armed Neutrality Association of European powers (Russia, Denmark, Sweden, Austria, Netherlands, Portugal, Prussia, and Sicily), formed between 1780 and 1782 to protect their rights as neutral traders against British attempts to impose a blockade on its enemies. Britain declared war on the Dutch on December 20, 1780, in an effort to cut off their trade with the United States.

League of Freedom African-American organization formed in Boston in 1851 to protect blacks against the **Fugitive Slave Act**.

League of Nations International organization created by the **Versailles Treaty** after World War I to ensure world stability.

League of United Latin American Citizens (LULAC) Organization for Hispanic Americans formed in 1928 to fight segregation and promote equal rights and opportunities.

League of Women Voters Group formed in 1920 from the **National American Woman Suffrage Association** to encourage informed voting and social reforms.

Lecompton Constitution Proslavery draft written in 1857 by Kansas territorial delegates elected under questionable circumstances; it was rejected by two governors, supported by President Buchanan, and decisively defeated by Congress.

Legal tender An attribute of money that results from legislation declaring it to be, as in the case of modern United States currency, "legal tender for all debts public and private." Creditors must therefore accept it at face value.

Levittown Large post–World War II housing developments built by William Levitt and Sons outside New York and Philadelphia.

Lexington and Concord, Battles of First skirmishes of the Revolutionary War, April 19, 1775. British forces, determined to destroy American supplies, fired on American militia at Lexington, then pushed on to Concord, where they themselves came under attack. On the long retreat back to Boston, the British suffered 273 dead, wounded, or missing, inflicted by some four thousand American militiamen.

Leyte Gulf, Battle of World War II naval engagement in October 1944 in which the Japanese navy tried to disrupt U.S. landings in the Philippines and suffered a decisive defeat.

Liberal Republicans Members of a reform movement within the **Republican party** in 1872 that promoted measures to reduce government influence in the economy and restore control of southern governments to local white elites.

The Liberator The best-known and most influential abolitionist newspaper; founded in 1831 by William Lloyd Garrison.

Liberty Association African-American organization formed in Chicago in 1851 that patrolled the city to spot slavecatchers.

Liberty Bonds Interest-bearing certificates sold by the U.S. government to finance the American World War I effort.

Liberty party The first antislavery political party, formed in 1840.

Limited Test Ban Treaty Agreement in 1963 between the United States, Britain, and the Soviet Union to halt atmospheric and underwater tests of nuclear weapons.

Lincoln-Douglas debates Series of debates in the 1858 Illinois senatorial campaign during which Democrat Stephen A. Douglas and Republican Abraham Lincoln staked out their differing opinions on the issue of slavery in the territories.

Little Bighorn, Battle of the Battle in which Colonel George A. Custer and the Seventh Cavalry were defeated by the Sioux and Cheyennes under Sitting Bull and Crazy Horse in Montana in 1876.

Localism The belief prevalent during much of the nineteenth century that local concerns took precedence over national concerns and that people and institutions should generally resolve issues without the involvement of the national government.

Lords of Trade A standing committee of the Privy Council, appointed to oversee colonial affairs; created by Charles II in 1675.

Lost Cause The phrase many white Southerners applied to their Civil War defeat. They viewed the war as a noble cause but only a temporary setback in the South's ultimate vindication.

Lost Generation The intellectuals of the 1920s, disillusioned by the brutality of World War I and alienated by the materialism and conformity of the new mass culture.

Louisiana Purchase The U.S. purchase from France in 1803 of a huge tract of land between the Mississippi River and the Rocky Mountains.

Loyalist An American supporter of the British crown during the Revolution. *See also* **Tories**.

Lynching Execution, usually by a mob, without trial.

Macon's Bill No. 2 Act passed by Congress in 1810 that reopened American trade with Britain and France but stipulated that if either nation lifted its restrictions on American shipping, trading sanctions would be reimposed on the other.

Mahanism The ideas advanced by Alfred Thayer Mahan, stressing U.S. naval, economic, and territorial expansion.

Manhattan Project The effort, using the code name Manhattan Engineer District, to develop an atomic bomb under the management of the U.S. Army Corps of Engineers during World War II.

Manifest Destiny Doctrine, first expressed in 1845, that the expansion of white Americans across the continent was inevitable and ordained by God.

Marbury* v. *Madison Supreme Court decision of 1803 that created the precedent of judicial review by ruling as unconstitutional part of the **Judiciary Act of 1789**.

Marshall Plan The European Recovery Program (1949), which provided U.S. economic assistance to European nations; named for Secretary of State George Marshall.

Massachusetts Government Act Law passed in 1774 in response to the **Boston Tea Party** and directed at Massachusetts; one of the **Coercive** or **Intolerable Acts**. It provided for an appointed rather than an elected upper house of the legislature and restricted the number and kind of town meetings that a community might hold.

Matrilineal Descriptive of societies in which family descent is traced through the mother's line.

Mayflower Compact Document creating a civil government for Plymouth Colony. The compact was signed by all adult males before their ship, the *Mayflower*, landed in 1620.

McCarran Committee The Senate Internal Security Subcommittee, chaired by Senator Pat McCarran and charged to investigate potentially subversive activities.

McCarthyism Anticommunist attitudes and actions associated with Senator Joe McCarthy in the early 1950s, including smear tactics and innuendo.

McCulloch* v. *Maryland Supreme Court decision of 1819 that established the supremacy of federal over state authority by declaring that states could not tax federal institutions.

McKinley Tariff Act A Republican enactment of 1890 that sharply raised tariff rates to protect American manufacturers but thereby provoked a political backlash against the GOP.

Medicaid Supplementary medical insurance for the poor, financed through the federal government; program created in 1965.

Medicare Basic medical insurance for the elderly, financed through the federal government; program created in 1965.

Memorial Day Massacre A murderous attack on striking steelworkers and their families by Chicago police in 1937.

Mercantilism Economic system whereby the government intervenes in the economy for the purpose of increasing national wealth. Mercantilists advocated possession of colonies as places where the mother country could acquire raw materials not available at home.

Mestizo A person of mixed Spanish and Indian ancestry.

Mexican Cession of 1848 The ceding of New Mexico and Alta California to the United States by Mexico as a result of the U.S. victory in the **Mexican War**. *See also* **Guadalupe Hidalgo, Treaty of**.

Mexican War War fought between the United States and Mexico from May 1846 to February 1848. *See also* **Guadalupe Hidalgo, Treaty of; Mexican Cession of 1848**.

Middle Passage The voyage between West Africa and the New World slave colonies.

Midway, Battle of World War II naval and air battle in which the United States turned back a Japanese effort to seize Midway Island in June 1942 and inflicted severe damage on the Japanese navy.

Military Reconstruction Acts The first major legislation in the period known as **Congressional Reconstruction**. Passed in March 1867 over President Johnson's veto, these laws divided the ten remaining ex-Confederate states into five military districts each headed by a general who was charged to conduct voter registration drives among black people and bar white people who had held office before the Civil War and who had supported the Confederacy. The remaining voters would elect a constitutional convention to write a new state constitution that guaranteed **universal manhood suffrage**. If a majority of voters ratified both the new constitution and the **Fourteenth Amendment**, their state would be readmitted into the Union.

Minute Men Special companies of militia formed in Massachusetts and elsewhere beginning in late 1744. These units were composed of men who were to be ready to assemble with their arms at a minute's notice.

Mission system Chain of missions established by Franciscan monks in the Spanish Southwest and California that forced Indians to convert to Catholicism and work as agricultural laborers.

Missouri Compromise Sectional compromise in Congress in 1820 that admitted Missouri to the Union as a slave state and Maine as a free state and prohibited slavery in the **Louisiana Purchase** territory above 36°30′ north latitude.

Model Cities Program Effort to target federal funds to upgrade public services and economic opportunity in specifically defined urban neighborhoods between 1966 and 1974.

Molasses Act Law passed by Parliament in 1733 that taxed sugar products from foreign sources in order to encourage British colonists to buy sugar and molasses only from the British West Indies.

Monmouth Court House, Battle of Last major Revolutionary War engagement between the main British and American forces in the North; occurred on June 28, 1778, in central New Jersey as the British withdrew from Philadelphia toward their headquarters at New York City. The Americans under General George Washington and the British under Sir Henry Clinton each suffered about 350 casualties.

Monroe Doctrine Declaration by President James Monroe in 1823 that the Western Hemisphere was to be closed off to further European colonization and that the United States would not interfere in the internal affairs of European nations.

Moore's Creek Bridge, Battle of Revolutionary War engagement that occurred on February 27, 1776, near Wilmington, North Carolina, when an American force of approximately one thousand militia clashed with about eighteen hundred **Loyalists**, most of them Highland Scots. The smashing American victory disrupted British plans for the **Loyalists** to link up with a large British expedition that sailed from Ireland to North Carolina during the winter of 1775–1776.

Mormon Church (Church of Jesus Christ of Latter-day Saints) Church founded in 1830 by Joseph Smith and based on the revelations in a sacred book he called the Book of Mormon.

Muckraking Journalism exposing economic, social, and political evils, so named by Theodore Roosevelt for its "raking the muck" of American society.

Mugwumps Elitist and conservative reformers who favored **sound money** and limited government and opposed tariffs and the **spoils system**.

Muller* v. *Oregon Supreme Court decision (1908) upholding a maximum-hour law for women workers; opened the way to an expansion of state regulation.

Multinational corporation Firm with direct investments, branches, factories, and offices in a number of countries.

Nashville, Battle of Union general George H. Thomas's destruction of the Confederacy's Army of Tennessee in December 1864 during the Civil War.

National Aeronautics and Space Administration (NASA) Federal agency created in 1958 to manage American space flights and exploration.

National American Woman Suffrage Association The organization, formed in 1890, that coordinated the ultimately successful campaign to achieve women's right to vote.

National and Community Service Trust Act Legislation in 1994 creating a pilot program for a domestic Peace Corps for young Americans.

National Association for the Advancement of Colored People (NAACP) National interracial organization founded in 1910 and dedicated to restoring African-American political and social rights.

National Association of Colored Women Group founded in 1896 as an umbrella organization for black women's clubs that worked to improve the lives of black women, especially in the rural South.

National Banking Act Law passed in 1863 authorizing certain banks to issue bank notes backed by U.S. bonds and guaranteed by Washington. It brought order to a chaotic monetary system and raised the creditworthiness of the federal government.

National Black Convention A prominent gathering of northern black leaders in 1853, called to protest the **Fugitive Slave Act**.

National Endowment for the Arts Federal agency created in 1965 to fund research, public programs, and museum exhibits dealing with the performing arts, visual arts, and design arts.

National Endowment for the Humanities Federal agency created in 1965 to fund research, publications, and museum exhibits dealing with history, literature, and related fields.

National Industrial Recovery Act (NIRA) A 1933 law that created the National Recovery Administration and, in Section 7a, guaranteed workers the rights to organize unions and bargain collectively.

Nationalists Group of leaders in the 1780s who spearheaded the drive to replace the **Articles of Confederation** with a stronger central government.

National Labor Relations Board (NLRB) Federal board established in 1935 to enforce workers' rights to organize, supervise union elections, and oversee **collective bargaining**.

National Organization for Women (NOW) Group organized in 1966 to expand civil rights for women.

National Origins Act A 1924 law sharply restricting immigration on the basis of immigrants' national origins and discriminating against southern and eastern Europeans and Asians.

National Recovery Administration (NRA) Federal agency established in 1933 to promote economic recovery by promulgating codes to control production, prices, and wages.

National Republican party Short-lived political party opposed to Andrew Jackson that unsuccessfully ran John Quincy Adams for the presidency in 1828 and Henry Clay in 1832.

National Security Council (NSC) The formal policymaking body for national defense and foreign relations, created in 1947 and consisting of the president, the secretary of defense, the secretary of state, and others appointed by the president.

National Security Council Paper 68 (NSC-68) Policy statement that committed the United States to a military approach to the **Cold War**.

National War Labor Board Government agency that supervised labor relations during World War I, guaranteeing union rights in exchange for industrial stability.

National Women's Party Political organization formed in 1916 that campaigned aggressively first for **woman suffrage** and thereafter for the **Equal Rights Amendment**.

National Women's Political Caucus Political organization formed in 1971 to help elect women to local, state, and federal offices.

Nation of Islam Religious movement among black Americans that emphasizes self-sufficiency, self-help, and separation from white society.

Nativist Favoring the interests and culture of native-born inhabitants over those of immigrants.

Nat Turner's Rebellion Uprising of slaves in Southampton County, Virginia, in the summer of 1831 led by Nat Turner that resulted in the death of fifty-five whites.

Naturalization Act of 1798 Law passed by Congress in 1798 that extended the residency requirement of alien residents for U.S. citizenship from five to fourteen years. One of the **Alien and Sedition Acts**.

Naturalization Act of 1870 Law passed by Congress in 1870 that limited citizenship to "white persons and persons of African descent."

Natural rights Political philosophy that maintains that individuals have an inherent right, found in nature and preceding any government or written law, to life and liberty.

Navigation Act of 1651 First piece of mercantilist legislation passed to regulate colonial commerce; called for imperial trade to be conducted using English or colonial ships with mainly English crews.

Navigation Act of 1696 Law that closed loopholes in earlier mercantilist legislation and also created **vice-admiralty courts** in the colonies.

Nazi Truncated form of the name of the National Socialist German Workers' party, led by Adolf Hitler, which ruled Germany from 1933 to 1945.

Neighborhood Union Organization founded by Lugenia Burns Hope, a middle-class black woman, in Atlanta in 1908 and modeled on similar efforts in the urban North, that provided playgrounds, a health center, and education for young urban black people.

Neighborhood Youth Corps Antipoverty program that recruited young people from low-income areas for community projects.

Neoconservative Advocate of or participant in the revitalized conservative politics of the 1980s and 1990s, calling for a strong government role in defense and foreign policy and a limited role in social and economic policy.

Neoliberal Advocate of or participant in the effort to reshape the **Democratic party** for the 1990s around a policy emphasizing economic growth and competitiveness in the world economy.

New Age Term applied to a wide range of ideas and practices that seek to enhance individual potential and spiritual well-being outside the boundaries of traditional religion.

New Deal The economic and political policies of the Roosevelt administration in the 1930s.

New England Non-Resistant Society Pacifist organization founded by Garrisonian abolitionists in 1838 that was opposed to all authority resting on force.

New Federalism President Richard Nixon's policy to shift responsibilities for government programs from the federal level to the states.

New Freedom Woodrow Wilson's 1912 program for limited government intervention in the economy to restore competition by curtailing the restrictive influences of trusts and protective tariffs, thereby providing opportunities for individual achievement.

New Frontier John F. Kennedy's domestic and foreign policy initiatives, designed to reinvigorate a sense of national purpose and energy.

New Harmony Short-lived utopian community established in Indiana in 1825, based on the socialist ideas of Robert Owen, a wealthy Scottish manufacturer.

New immigrants Immigrants from southern and eastern Europe, predominantly Catholic and Jewish and often unskilled and poorly educated, who entered the United States in increasing numbers after the 1880s.

New Jersey Plan Proposal of the New Jersey delegation at the 1787 **Constitutional Convention** for a strengthened national government in which all states would have equal representation in a **unicameral legislature**.

New Lights People who experienced conversion during the revivals of the **Great Awakening**.

New Nationalism Theodore Roosevelt's 1912 program calling for a strong national government to foster, regulate, and protect business, industry, workers, and consumers.

New Orleans, Battle of Decisive American **War of 1812** victory over British troops in January 1815 that ended any British hopes of gaining control of the lower Mississippi River Valley.

New Republicanism Dwight Eisenhower's vision of the Republicans as a relatively moderate party of the political center.

New York Draft Riot A mostly Irish-immigrant protest against conscription in New York City in July 1863 that escalated into class and racial warfare that had to be quelled by federal troops.

Niagara Movement African-American group organized in 1905 to promote racial integration, civil and political rights, and equal access to economic opportunity.

Nineteenth Amendment Constitutional revision that in 1920 established women citizens' right to vote.

Nisei U.S. citizens born of immigrant Japanese parents.

Nonimportation A tactical means of putting economic pressure on Britain by refusing to buy its exports to the colonies. Initiated in response to the taxes imposed by the **Sugar** and **Stamp Acts**, it was used again against the **Townshend duties** and the **Coercive Acts**. The nonimportation movement popularized resistance to British measures and deepened the commitment of many ordinary people to a larger American community.

Nonintercourse Act Law passed by Congress in 1809 that prohibited American trade with Britain and France.

Nonpartisan League A radical farmers' movement in the Great Plains states after 1915 that sought to restrain railroads, banks, elevators, and other major corporations.

North American Free Trade Agreement (NAFTA) Agreement reached in 1993 by Canada, Mexico, and the United States to substantially reduce barriers to trade.

North Atlantic Treaty Organization (NATO) Military alliance of the United States, Canada, and western European nations created in 1949 to protect Europe against possible Soviet aggression.

North Carolina Mutual Life Insurance Company Insurance company founded in Durham, North Carolina, in 1898 that eventually became the largest black-owned business in the nation.

The North Star Antislavery newspaper established by Frederick Douglass in Rochester, New York, in 1847.

Northwest Ordinance of 1787 Legislation passed by Congress under the **Articles of Confederation** that prohibited slavery in the Northwest Territories and provided the model for the incorporation of future territories into the Union as coequal states.

Nuclear freeze Proposal that the United States and the Soviet Union should stop further production and deployment of nuclear weapons.

Nullification A constitutional doctrine holding that a state has a legal right to declare a national law null and void within its borders.

Nullification crisis Sectional crisis in the early 1830s in which a **states' rights** party in South Carolina attempted to nullify federal law.

Office of Economic Opportunity (OEO) Federal agency that coordinated many programs of the **War on Poverty** between 1964 and 1975.

Office of Price Administration (OPA) Federal agency during World War II that fixed price ceilings on all commodities, controlled rents in defense areas, and rationed scare goods such as sugar, fuel, and automobile tires.

Office of Scientific Research and Development Federal agency established in 1941 to mobilize American science on behalf of national defense.

Old Stock European ethnic groups prominent in the eighteenth-century United States, especially English, Dutch, German, and Scots-Irish.

Olive Branch Petition Petition, written largely by John Dickinson and adopted by the Second Continental Congress on July 5, 1775, as a last effort of peace that avowed America's loyalty to George III and requested that he protect them from further aggressions. Congress continued military preparations, and the king never responded to the petition.

Omaha Platform The 1892 platform of the **Populist party** repudiating laissez-faire and demanding economic and political reforms to aid distressed farmers and workers.

One Hundred Slain, Battle of An 1866 Sioux defeat of the U.S. Army on the Bozeman Trail that whites call the Fetterman Massacre.

Oneida Community Utopian community established in upstate New York in 1848 by John Humphrey Noyes and his followers.

Open Door American policy of seeking equal trade and investment opportunities in foreign nations or regions.

Open shop Factory or business employing workers whether or not they are union members; in practice, such a business usually refuses to hire union members and follows antiunion policies.

Operation OVERLORD U.S. and British invasion of France in June 1944 during World War II.

Operation TORCH U.S. and British landings in French North Africa in November 1942 during World War II.

Order of the Heroes of America Loosely knit group of pro-Unionists in the Piedmont and mountain sections of North Carolina who demonstrated for peace and sometimes violently opposed Confederate authorities during the Civil War.

Orders in Council Decrees of the British ministry setting up a naval blockade of Europe and controls over neutral shipping during the Napoleonic Wars.

Ordinance of 1784 Act passed but never put into effect by the Congress under the **Articles of Confederation** that embodied the proposals of Thomas Jefferson for dividing the public domain into states and immediately granting settlers the right of self-government.

Oregon Trail Overland trail of more than two thousand miles that carried American settlers from the Midwest to new settlements in Oregon, California, and Utah.

Organization of Petroleum Exporting Countries (OPEC) Cartel of oil-producing nations in Asia, Africa, and Latin America that gained substantial power over the world economy in the mid- to late 1970s by controlling the production and price of oil.

Ostend Manifesto Message sent by U.S. envoys to President Franklin Pierce from Ostend, Belgium, in 1854, stating that the United States had a "divine right" to wrest Cuba from Spain.

Paleo-Indians The first human inhabitants of the Americas, who crossed the land bridge from Asia perhaps as long as fifty thousand years ago and survived by hunting large mammals.

Pan American Union International organization originally established as the Commercial Bureau of American Republics by Secretary of State James Blaine's first Pan-American Conference in 1889 to promote cooperation among nations of the Western Hemisphere through commercial and diplomatic negotiations.

Panic of 1819 A severe tightening of credit set off by a fall in cotton prices and more restrictive financial policies by the **Second Bank of the United States**.

Panic of 1837 A sharp contraction in credit and currency triggered by a fall in cotton prices.

Panic of 1857 Banking crisis that caused a credit crunch in the North; it was less severe in the South, where high cotton prices spurred a quick recovery.

Pan-Indian resistance movement Movement calling for the political and cultural unification of Indian tribes in the late eighteenth and early nineteenth centuries.

Paris, Treaty of The 1898 treaty that ended the **Spanish-American War** and transferred the Spanish colonies of Puerto Rico, Guam, and the Philippines to the United States while recognizing the independence of Cuba.

Paris, Treaty of Treaty concluded in 1763 to end the **French and Indian War (Seven Years' War)**. Its principal feature was France's loss of nearly all of its North American empire, retaining only its West Indian possessions.

Parson's Cause Series of developments (1758–1763) that began when the Virginia legislature modified the salaries of Anglican clergymen, who complained to the crown and sued to recover damages. British authorities responded by imposing additional restrictions on the legislature. Virginians, who saw this as a threat, reacted by strongly reasserting local autonomy.

Party caucus A meeting of party leaders to decide questions of policy or to select candidates running for office.

Patent medicines Trademarked concoctions, often of little medical value, available for purchase without a physician's prescription.

Patriarchal Descriptive of societies in which fathers are the heads of clans or families, women and children are legally dependent on husbands and fathers, and family descent and inheritance follow the male line.

Patrilineal Descriptive of societies in which family descent is traced through the father's line.

Patriot Term usually used to refer to Americans during the Revolutionary period whose resistance to British measures included a willingness to resort to arms and, ultimately, a commitment to American independence. However, many **Loyalists** were also patriotic in their allegiance to Great Britain.

Patronage The power to appoint individuals to governmental positions.

Patroonship The grant of a vast estate of land in New Netherlands, offered by Dutch authorities as a way to attract settlers. Very few patroonships were actually created.

Paxton Boys Frontiersmen from Paxton township (near modern Harrisburg, Pennsylvania) who responded in 1763 to **Pontiac's Rebellion** by massacring nearby Indians; later they marched toward Philadelphia to demand greater military protection for the frontiers.

Peace of Paris Treaties signed in 1783 by Great Britain, the United States, France, Spain, and the Netherlands that ended the Revolutionary War. First in a preliminary agreement and then in the final treaty with the United States, Britain recognized the independence of the United States, agreed that the Mississippi River would be its western boundary, and permitted it to fish in some Canadian waters. Prewar debts owed by the inhabitants of one country to those of the other were to remain collectible, and Congress was to urge the states to return property confiscated from **Loyalists**. British troops were to evacuate United States territory without removing slaves or other property. In a separate agreement, Britain relinquished its claim to East and West Florida to Spain.

Pearl Harbor Site of a United States naval base in Hawaii attacked from Japanese aircraft carriers on December 7, 1941, during World War II.

Pendleton Civil Service Act A law of 1883 that reformed the **spoils system** by prohibiting government workers from making political contributions and creating the Civil Service Commission to oversee their appointment on the basis of merit rather than politics.

Peninsula Campaign Civil War campaign launched by Union general George B. McClellan in the spring of 1862 with Richmond as its objective; it failed despite superior numbers of Federal troops.

Pentagon Papers Classified Defense Department documents on the history of the United States' involvement in Vietnam, prepared in 1968 and leaked to the press in 1971.

People's party *See* **Populist party**.

Pequot War Conflict between English settlers (who had Narragansett and Mohegan allies) and Pequot Indians over control of land and trade in eastern Connecticut. The Pequots were nearly destroyed in a set of bloody confrontations, including a deadly English attack on a Mystic River village in May 1637.

Perestroika Russian for "restructuring," applied to Mikhail Gorbachev's efforts to make the Soviet economic and political systems more modern, flexible, and innovative.

Persian Gulf War War (1991) between Iraq and a U. S. led coalition that followed Iraq's invasion of Kuwait and resulted in the expulsion of Iraqi forces from that country.

Petersburg During the Civil War, a key Confederate rail and supply center that guarded the Confederate capital of Richmond thirty miles to the north; besieged by Union forces from June 1864 to March 1865.

Pietists Protestants who stress a religion of the heart and the spirit of Christian living.

Pilgrims Settlers of Plymouth Colony, who viewed themselves as spiritual wanderers.

Pinckney's Treaty Treaty with Spain in 1795 in which Spain recognized the 31st parallel as the boundary between the United States and Spanish Florida and opened the Mississippi River through the port of New Orleans to American shipping.

Platt Amendment A stipulation the United States had inserted into the Cuban constitution in 1901 restricting Cuban autonomy and authorizing U.S. intervention and naval bases.

Plattsburg, Battle of American naval victory on Lake Champlain in September 1814 in the **War of 1812** that thwarted a British invasion from Canada.

Plessy* v. *Ferguson The 1896 case in which the U.S. Supreme Court ruled that providing "separate but equal" facilities for white and black people did not violate the **Constitution**.

Plymouth Company One of two **joint-stock companies** chartered in 1606 to establish English colonies in America. Composed of merchants from England's western ports, the company organized the founding of Plymouth Colony in 1620.

Pogroms Government-directed attacks against Jewish citizens, property, and villages in tsarist Russia beginning in the 1880s; a primary reason for Russian Jewish migration to the United States.

Poll tax A tax imposed on voters as a requirement for voting. Most southern states imposed poll taxes after 1900 as a way to disfranchise black people; the measures also restricted the white vote.

Pontiac's Rebellion Indian uprising (1763–1766) led by Pontiac of the Ottawas and Neolin of the Delawares. Fearful of their fate at the hands of the British after the French had been driven out of North America, the Indian nations of the Ohio River Valley and the Great Lakes area united to oust the British from the Ohio-Mississippi Valley. They failed and were forced to make peace in 1766.

Popular sovereignty The notion that territorial residents should have the right to decide whether they wanted slavery.

Populist party A major third party of the 1890s, also known as the **People's party**. Formed on the basis of the **Southern Farmers' Alliance** and other reform organizations, it mounted electoral challenges against the Democrats in the South and the Republicans in the West.

Port Huron Statement Founding document of **Students for a Democratic Society**, proclaiming an idealistic vision of grassroots democracy.

Potsdam Declaration Statement issued by the United States during a meeting of U.S. President Harry Truman, British Prime Minister Winston Churchill, and Soviet Premier Joseph Stalin held at Potsdam, near Berlin, in July 1945 to plan the defeat of Japan and the future of eastern Europe and Germany. In it, the United States declared its intention to democratize the Japanese political system and reintroduce Japan into the international community and gave Japan an opening for surrender.

Praying towns Villages established in Massachusetts for Indian converts to Christianity. The inhabitants were expected to follow an English way of life as well as the **Puritan** religion.

Predestination The belief that God decided at the moment of Creation which humans would achieve salvation.

Preparedness Military buildup in preparation for possible U.S. participation in World War I.

Preservation Protecting forests, land, and other features of the natural environment from development or destruction, often for aesthetic appreciation.

Presidio A military post established by the Spanish in the Southwest.

Princeton, Battle of Revolutionary War battle fought on January 3, 1777. Eluding the main British forces under Cornwallis, General Washington attacked a British column near Princeton, New Jersey, inflicting heavy losses before withdrawing into winter quarters not far away at Morristown. The battles of **Trenton** and Princeton greatly improved **patriot** morale.

Proclamation Line Boundary, decreed as part of the **Proclamation of 1763**, that limited British settlements to the eastern side of the Appalachian Mountains, thereby threatening colonial expansionists and causing resentment. It proved unenforceable.

Proclamation of 1763 Royal proclamation setting the boundary known as the **Proclamation Line**.

Progressive Era The period of the twentieth century before World War I when many groups sought to reshape the nation's government and society in response to the pressures of industrialization and urbanization.

Prohibition A ban on the production, sale, and consumption of liquor, achieved temporarily through state laws and the Eighteenth Amendment.

Prohibition party A venerable third party still in existence that has persistently campaigned for the abolition of alcohol but has also introduced many important reform ideas into American politics.

Proprietary colony A colony created when the English monarch granted a huge tract of land to an individual or group of individuals, who became "lords proprietor." Many lords proprietor had distinct social visions for their colonies, but these plans were hardly ever implemented. Examples of proprietary colonies are Maryland, Carolina, New York (after it was seized from the Dutch), and Pennsylvania.

Protective legislation Measures designed to protect women from labor exploitation that also served to narrow their employment opportunities.

Protective tariff A tax on imported goods specifically intended to raise their price high enough to protect domestic producers of those goods from foreign competition.

Provincial congress An extralegal, Revolutionary representative body that conducted government and waged the Revolution at the state level in the period between the breakdown of royal authority and the establishment of regular legislatures under new state constitutions. Many members of these congresses had been members of the old colonial assemblies; the Massachusetts **General Court** and the Virginia **House of Burgesses**, in fact, transformed themselves into provincial congresses or conventions. (The terms were used interchangeably at first.)

Public Utility Holding Company Act of 1935 Law giving the **Securities and Exchange Commission** extensive regulatory powers over public utility companies.

Public Works Administration (PWA) Federal agency under Harold Ickes that provided work relief by building schools, hospitals, roads, and other valuable projects during the 1930s.

Pueblo Revolt Rebellion in 1680 of Pueblo Indians in New Mexico against their Spanish overlords, sparked by religious conflict and excessive Spanish demands for tribute.

Pullman strike Violent 1894 worker protest against wage cuts at the Pullman Palace Sleeping Car Company outside Chicago.

Puritan An individual who believed that Queen Elizabeth's reforms of the Church of England had not gone far enough in improving the church, particularly in ensuring that church members were among the saved. Puritans led the settlement of Massachusetts Bay Colony.

Put-in-Bay, Battle of American naval victory on Lake Erie in September 1813 in the **War of 1812** that denied the British strategic control over the Great Lakes.

Putting-out system System of manufacturing in which merchants furnished households with raw materials for processing by family members.

Quakers Members of the Society of Friends, a radical religious group that arose in the mid-seventeenth century. Quakers rejected formal theology and an educated ministry, focusing instead on the importance of the "Inner Light," or Holy Spirit that dwelt within them. Quakers were important in the founding of Pennsylvania.

Quartering Acts Acts of Parliament requiring colonial legislatures to provide supplies and quarters for the troops stationed in America. Americans considered this taxation in disguise and objected. None of these acts passed during the pre-Revolutionary controversy required that soldiers be quartered in an occupied house without the owner's consent.

Quasi-War Undeclared naval war of 1797 to 1800 between the United States and France.

Quebec Act Law passed by Parliament in 1774 that provided an appointed government for Canada, enlarged the boundaries of Quebec southward to the Ohio River, and confirmed the privileges of the Catholic Church. Alarmed Americans termed this act and the **Coercive Acts** the **Intolerable Acts**.

Quebec, Siege of An attempt during the Revolutionary War by American forces under Richard Montgomery and Benedict Arnold to capture Quebec City during the winter of 1775–1776. In an abortive attack on the city on December 31, 1775, Arnold was wounded and Montgomery killed. The siege failed, and Canada remained in British hands, serving as a base for later British expeditions down the Hudson River Valley.

Queen Anne's War American phase (1702–1713) of Europe's **War of the Spanish Succession**. At its conclusion, England gained Nova Scotia.

Queenston Heights, Battle of Major defeat in October 1812 for an American army attempting to invade Canada along the Niagara frontier during the **War of 1812**.

Quiet Period The apparently calm years (1770–1773) between Britain's repeal of most of the **Townshend duties** and the **Boston Tea Party.** No general grievances against Britain united Americans during this period, though many localized disputes continued.

Radical Republicans A shifting group of Republican congressmen, usually a substantial minority, who favored the abolition of slavery from the beginning of the Civil War and later advocated harsh treatment of the defeated South.

Railroad Administration Federal agency that operated and modernized the nation's railways to improve transportation related to the World War I war effort.

Real Whig ideology *See* **Country (Real Whig) ideology**.

Recall The process of removing an official from office by popular vote, usually after using petitions to call for such a vote.

Reconquista The long struggle (ending in 1492) during which Spanish Christians reconquered the Iberian peninsula from Muslim occupiers, who first invaded in the eighth century.

Reconstruction The era (1865–1877) when the resolution of two major issues—the status of the former slaves and the terms of the Confederate states' readmission into the Union—dominated political debate.

Reconstruction Finance Corporation (RFC) Federal agency established in 1932 to provide funds to financial institutions to save them from bankruptcy.

Red-baiting Accusing a political opponent of sympathizing with or being "soft on" Communism.

Redeemers Southern Democrats who wrested control of governments in the former Confederacy, often through electoral fraud and violence, from Republicans beginning in 1870.

Redemptioners Similar to **indentured servants**, except that redemptioners signed labor contracts in America rather than in Europe, as indentured servants did. Shipmasters sold redemptioners into servitude to recoup the cost of their passage if they could not pay the fare upon their arrival.

Redlining Refusing mortgage loans and insurance to properties in designated inner-city neighborhoods.

Red Scare Post–World War I public hysteria over **Bolshevik** influence in the United States directed against labor activism, radical dissenters, and some ethnic groups.

Referendum Submission of a law, proposed or already in effect, to a direct popular vote for approval or rejection.

Reformation Sixteenth-century movement to reform the Catholic Church that began with Martin Luther's critique of church practices in 1517. The Reformation ultimately led to the founding of a number of new Protestant Christian religious groups.

Regulators Vigilante groups active in the 1760s and 1770s in the western parts of North and South Carolina. The South Carolina Regulators attempted to rid the area of outlaws; the North Carolina Regulators sought to protect themselves against excessively high taxes and court costs. In both cases, westerners lacked sufficient representation in the legislature to obtain immediate redress of their grievances. The South Carolina government eventually made concessions; the North Carolina government suppressed its Regulator movement by force.

Renaissance Major cultural movement in Europe during the fifteenth and sixteenth centuries that began in the city-states of Italy and spread to other parts of the continent. Sharing a "rebirth" of interest in the classical civilizations of ancient Greece and Rome, many artists of the period produced notable works in painting, sculpture, architecture, writing, and music.

Repartimiento In the Spanish colonies, the assignment of Indian workers to labor on public works projects.

Republicanism A complex, changing body of ideas, values, and assumptions, closely related to **country ideology**, that influenced American political behavior during the eighteenth and nineteenth centuries. Derived from the political ideas of classical antiquity, **Renaissance** Europe, and early modern England, republicanism held that self-government by the citizens of a country, or their representatives, provided a more reliable foundation for the good society and individual freedom than rule by kings. The benefits of monarchy depended on the variable abilities of monarchs; the character of republican government depended on the virtue of the people. Republicanism therefore helped give the American Revolution a moral dimension. But the nature of republican virtue and the conditions favorable to it became sources of debate that influenced the writing of the state and federal constitutions as well as the development of political parties.

Republican party Party that emerged in the 1850s in the aftermath of the bitter controversy over the **Kansas-Nebraska Act**, consisting of former **Whigs**, some northern Democrats, and many **Know-Nothings**.

Republican party (Jeffersonian) Party headed by Thomas Jefferson that formed in opposition to the financial and diplomatic policies of the **Federalist party**; favored limiting the powers of the national government and placing the interests of farmers and planters over those of financial and commercial groups; supported the cause of the French Revolution.

Rescate Procedure by which Spanish colonists would pay ransom to free Indians captured by rival natives. The rescued Indians then became workers in Spanish households.

Reservationists Group of U.S. senators favoring approval of the **Treaty of Versailles**, the peace agreement after World War I, after amending it to incorporate their reservations.

Resettlement Administration Federal agency established in 1935 to provide financial assistance and social services to displaced tenants and farm workers.

Revenue Act of 1935 Law establishing a more progressive tax system by setting graduated taxes on corporate income and increasing the top tax rates on personal income.

Rhode Island system During the industrialization of the early nineteenth century, the recruitment of entire families for employment in a factory.

Roe* v. *Wade U.S. Supreme Court decision in 1973 that disallowed state laws prohibiting abortion during the first three months (trimester) of pregnancy and established guidelines for abortion in the second and third trimesters.

Romer* v. *Evans U.S. Supreme Court decision in 1996 that overturned an antigay measure adopted in Colorado.

Roosevelt Corollary President Theodore Roosevelt's policy asserting U.S. authority to intervene in the affairs of Latin American nations; an expansion of the **Monroe Doctrine**.

Rural Electrification Administration (REA) Federal agency that transformed American rural life by making electricity available in areas that private companies had refused to service.

Rural Free Delivery (RFD) Government delivery of mail directly to farmsteads rather than merely to village post offices to which rural residents would then have to travel to retrieve their mail.

Rush–Bagot Agreement Treaty of 1817 between the United States and Britain that effectively demilitarized the Great Lakes by sharply limiting the number of ships each power could station on them.

Rustbelt The states of the Midwest and Northeast affected adversely by the decline of manufacturing in the 1970s and 1980s, named for the image of machinery rusting in abandoned factories.

Sabbatarian movement *See* **General Union for Promoting the Observance of the Christian Sabbath**.

"Sack of Lawrence" Vandalism and arson committed by a group of proslavery men in Lawrence, the free-state capital of Kansas Territory.

Sagebrush Rebellion Political movement in the western states in the early 1980s that called for easing of regulations on the economic use of federal lands and the transfer of some or all of those lands to state ownership.

Saint A **Puritan** who had experienced religious conversion and had been admitted to membership in a **Puritan** church.

SALT Strategic Arms Limitation Treaty signed in 1972 by the United States and the Soviet Union to slow the nuclear arms race.

Sand Creek Massacre The near annihilation in 1864 of Black Kettle's Cheyenne band by Colorado troops under Colonel John Chivington's orders to "kill and scalp all, big and little."

San Jacinto, Battle of Battle fought in eastern Texas on April 21, 1836, in which Texas troops under General Sam Houston overwhelmed a Mexican army and forced its commander, General Antonio López de Santa Anna, to recognize the independence of Texas.

San Lorenzo, Treaty of *See* **Pinckney's Treaty**.

Santa Fe Ring A group of lawyers and land speculators who dominated New Mexico Territory in the late nineteenth century and amassed great wealth through political corruption and financial chicanery.

Santa Fe Trail Overland trail across the southern Plains from St. Louis to New Mexico that funneled American traders and goods to Spanish-speaking settlements in the Southwest.

Saratoga, Battle of Two engagements (September 19 and October 7, 1777) during the Revolutionary War in the vicinity of Saratoga, New York, that resulted in the surrender on October 17 of 5,700 troops commanded by General John Burgoyne to American forces under General Horatio Gates. This stunning American victory contributed to the French decision to sign an alliance with the United States on February 6, 1778.

Savannah, Battles of Series of Revolutionary War encounters that began when British forces routed American militia and occupied Savannah on December 29, 1778. A French fleet under the Comte d'Estaing and American forces under General Benjamin Lincoln then tried to recapture the city by siege, beginning on September 3, 1779, but an assault on October 9 failed, with heavy casualties. D'Estaing, wounded, departed with this fleet on October 28, leaving the way open for the British attack on **Charleston**, South Carolina.

Scalawags Southern whites, mainly small landowning farmers and well-off merchants and planters, who supported the southern **Republican party** during **Reconstruction** for diverse reasons; a disparaging term.

Search and destroy U.S. military tactic in South Vietnam, using small detachments to locate enemy units and then massive air, artillery, and ground forces to destroy them.

Second Bank of the United States A national bank chartered by Congress in 1816 with extensive regulatory powers over currency and credit.

Second Great Awakening Series of religious revivals in the first half of the nineteenth century characterized by great emotionalism in large public meetings.

Second New Deal The policies adopted by the Roosevelt administration from 1935 to 1937 that emphasized social and economic reform.

Second party system The national two-party competition between **Democrats** and **Whigs** from the 1830s through the early 1850s.

Second Treaty of Fort Laramie The treaty acknowledging U.S. defeat in the Great Sioux War in 1868 and supposedly guaranteeing the Sioux perpetual land and hunting rights in South Dakota, Wyoming, and Montana.

Second Vatican Council A 1965 meeting of the leadership of the Roman Catholic Church that liberalized many church practices.

Secret Six Group of prominent New England abolitionists who financially supported John Brown's scheme to attack the federal arsenal at Harpers Ferry, Virginia, and foment a slave rebellion in the South.

Securities and Exchange Commission (SEC) Federal agency with authority to regulate trading practices in stocks and bonds.

Sedition Act Law passed by Congress in 1798 that provided fines and imprisonment for anyone found guilty of saying or writing anything false or malicious about the government or one of its officers. One of the **Alien and Sedition Acts**.

Sedition Act of 1918 Broad law restricting criticism of America's involvement in World War I or its government, flag, military, taxes, or officials.

Segregation A system of racial control that separated the races, initially by custom but increasingly by law during and after **Reconstruction**.

Selective Service Act of 1917 The law establishing the military draft for World War I.

Selective Service System Federal agency that coordinated military conscription before and during the Vietnam War.

Selectmen Group of men (usually seven) selected annually to run local affairs in a New England town.

Self-determination The right of a people or nation to decide on its own political allegiance or form of government without external influence.

Seneca Falls Convention The first convention for women's equality in legal rights, held in upstate New York in 1848. *See also* **Declaration of Sentiments**.

Separatist Member of an offshoot branch of Puritanism. Separatists believed that the Church of England was too corrupt to be reformed and hence were convinced that they must "separate" from it to save their souls. Separatists helped found Plymouth Colony.

Settlement house A multipurpose structure in a poor neighborhood that offered social welfare, educational, and homemaking services to the poor or immigrants; usually under private auspices and directed by middle-class women.

Seven Days' Battles Weeklong series of fierce engagements in June and July 1862 along Virginia's peninsula that resulted in a Federal retreat during the Civil War.

Seven Years' War Conflict (1756–1763) that pitted France, Austria, and Russia against England and Prussia; in 1762, Spain entered the war on France's side. Often called the first "world war" because fighting occurred in Europe, India, the Philippines, and North America. The American phase was known as the **French and Indian War**.

Seventeenth Amendment Constitutional change that in 1913 established the direct popular election of U.S. senators.

Shakers The followers of Mother Ann Lee, who preached a religion of strict celibacy and communal living.

Sharecropping Labor system that evolved during and after **Reconstruction** whereby landowners furnished laborers with a house, farm animals, and tools and advanced credit in exchange for a share of the laborers' crop.

Shays's Rebellion An armed movement of debt-ridden farmers in western Massachusetts in the winter of 1786–1787. The rebellion shut down courts and created a crisis atmosphere, strengthening the case of **nationalists** that a stronger central government was needed to maintain civil order in the states.

Sheppard-Towner Maternity and Infancy Act of 1921 The first federal social welfare law; funded infant and maternity health care programs in local hospitals.

Sherman Antitrust Act The first federal antitrust measure, passed in 1890; sought to promote economic competition by prohibiting business combinations in restraint of trade or commerce.

Sherman Silver Purchase Act An 1890 law that required the government to increase silver purchases sharply, but other provisions restricted its inflationary effect; its repeal in 1894 caused a political uproar.

Sherman's March Three-month army march during the Civil War in late 1864 led by Union general William T. Sherman from Atlanta to Savannah and the sea, destroying property as well as the morale of Georgians.

Shiloh Church Site of a Union victory along the Tennessee–Mississippi border in April 1862 that enabled Federal forces to capture Corinth, Mississippi, an important rail junction, during the Civil War.

Silicon Valley The region of California between San Jose and San Francisco that holds the nation's greatest concentration of electronics firms.

Sixteenth Amendment Constitutional revision that in 1913 authorized a federal income tax.

***Slaughterhouse* cases** Group of cases resulting in one sweeping decision by the U.S. Supreme Court in 1873 that contradicted the intent of the **Fourteenth Amendment** by decreeing that most citizenship rights remained under state, not federal, control.

Slave codes Sometimes known as "black codes." A series of laws passed mainly in the southern colonies in the late seventeenth and early eighteenth centuries to define the status of slaves and codify the denial of basic civil rights to them. Also, after American independence and before the Civil War, state laws in the South defining slaves as property and specifying the legal powers of masters over slaves.

Slave Power A key concept in abolitionist and northern antislavery propaganda that depicted southern slaveholders as the driving force in a political conspiracy to promote slavery at the expense of white liberties.

Slum A poor neighborhood with many dwellings in bad repair.

Social Darwinism The application of Charles Darwin's theory of biological evolution to society, holding that the fittest and the wealthiest survive, the weak and the poor perish, and government action is unable to alter this "natural" and beneficial process.

Social Gospel movement An effort by leading Protestants to apply religious ethics to industrial conditions and thereby alleviate poverty, **slums**, and labor exploitation.

Socialism A social order based on government ownership of industry and worker control over corporations as a way to prevent worker exploitation.

Socialist Party of America Political party formed in 1901 with a strong representation from immigrants; provided a political outlet for worker grievances but fared poorly beyond a few local elections in industrial areas.

Social Security Act A 1935 law that initiated a federal social insurance system with unemployment compensation, old-age pensions, and aid for dependent mothers and children and the blind.

Society for the Relief of Poor Widows with Small Children Female benevolent organization founded in New York City in 1797 to assist widows and orphans.

Soil Conservation Service A branch of the Department of Agriculture created in 1935 to undertake **conservation** projects on individual farms as well as on a broader national basis.

Solid South The one-party (Democratic) political system that dominated the South from the 1890s to the 1950s.

Sons of Liberty Secret organizations in the colonies formed to oppose the **Stamp Act**. From 1765 until independence, they spoke, wrote, and demonstrated against British measures. Their actions often intimidated stamp distributors and British supporters in the colonies.

Sound money Misleading slogan that referred to a conservative policy of restricting the money supply and adhering to the gold standard.

Southeast Asia Treaty Organization (SEATO) Mutual defense alliance signed in 1954 by the United States, Britain, France, Thailand, Pakistan, the Philippines, Australia, and New Zealand.

Southern Christian Leadership Conference (SCLC) Black civil rights organization founded in 1957 by Martin Luther King, Jr., and other clergy.

Southern Farmers' Alliance The largest of several organizations that formed in the post-Reconstruction South to advance the interests of beleaguered small farmers.

Southern Homestead Act Largely unsuccessful law passed in 1866 that gave black people preferential access to public lands in five southern states.

Southern Manifesto A document signed by 101 members of Congress from southern states in 1956 that argued that the Supreme Court's decision in ***Brown* v. *Board of Education of Topeka*** itself contradicted the **Constitution**.

Southwest Ordinance of 1790 Legislation passed by Congress that set up a government with no prohibition on slavery in U.S. territory south of the Ohio River.

Spanish-American War Brief 1898 conflict in which the United States defeated Spanish forces in Cuba and the Philippines and forced Spain to relinquish control over Cuba and cede the Philippines, Puerto Rico, and other territories to the United States.

Specie Circular Proclamation issued by President Andrew Jackson in 1836 stipulating that only gold or silver could be used as payment for public land.

Sphere of influence A region dominated and controlled by an outside power.

Spoils system The awarding of government jobs to party loyalists.

Spotsylvania, Battle of Another in a series of dogged attacks in Virginia by Union general Ulysses S. Grant and entrenched Confederate positions during May 1864. Despite high casualties and mounting public criticism, Grant continued to push on until the disaster at **Cold Harbor** later in the month caused him to reconsider his tactics.

Squatters Settlers who moved onto public land before it had been surveyed for sale.

Stagflation Economic condition of the 1970s in which price inflation accompanied slow economic growth.

Stalingrad, Battle of World War II battle of attrition between German and Soviet armies in Stalingrad, on the Volga River, August 1942–February 1943, ending with the surrender of the encircled German army.

Stamp Act Law passed by Parliament in 1765 to raise revenue in America by requiring taxed, stamped paper for legal documents, publications, and playing cards. Americans opposed it as "taxation without representation" and prevented its enforcement. Parliament repealed it a year after its enactment.

Stamp Act Congress October 1765 meeting of delegates sent by nine colonies, held in New York City, that adopted the **Declaration of Rights and Grievances** and petitioned against the **Stamp Act**.

States' rights Favoring the rights of individual states over rights claimed by the national government.

Stono Rebellion Uprising in 1739 of South Carolina slaves against whites; inspired in part by Spanish officials' promise of freedom for American slaves who escaped to Florida.

Strategic Arms Reduction Treaty (START) Agreement between the United States and the Soviet Union in 1991 to substantially reduce the number of long-range nuclear weapons held by each side.

Strategic Defense Initiative (SDI) President Reagan's program, announced in 1983, to defend the United States against nuclear missile attack with untested weapons systems and sophisticated technologies; also known as "Star Wars."

Strict constructionist Person who holds that the national government has only those powers specifically delegated to it in the **Constitution**.

Student Nonviolent Coordinating Committee (SNCC) Black civil rights organization founded in 1960 and drawing heavily on younger activists and college students.

Students for a Democratic Society (SDS) The leading student organization of the New Left of the early and mid-1960s.

Subtreasury plan A program promoted by the **Southern Farmers' Alliance** in response to low cotton prices and tight credit. Farmers would store their crop in a warehouse (or "subtreasury") until prices rose, in the meantime borrowing up to 80 percent of the value of the stored crops from the government at a low interest rate.

Suffolk Resolves Militant resolves adopted in September 1774 in response to the **Coercive Acts** by representatives from the towns in Suffolk County, Massachusetts, including Boston. They termed the **Coercive Acts** unconstitutional, advised the people to arm, and called for economic sanctions against Britain. The **First Continental Congress** endorsed these resolves.

Suffrage The right to vote in a political election.

Sugar Act *See* **American Revenue Act**.

Sunbelt The states of the American South and Southwest.

Superfund Federal fund devoted to the cleanup of the nation's most severely contaminated industrial and toxic waste sites.

***Sussex* Pledge** Germany's pledge during World War I not to sink merchant ships without warning, on the condition that Britain also observe recognized rules of international law.

Swann* v. *Charlotte-Mecklenburg Board of Education U.S. Supreme Court decision in 1971 that upheld cross-city busing to achieve the racial integration of public schools.

Sweatshops Small, poorly ventilated shops or apartments crammed with workers, often family members, who pieced together garments.

Taft-Hartley Act Federal legislation of 1947 that substantially limited the tools available to labor unions in labor–management disputes.

Tallmadge Amendment Proposed amendment to the Missouri statehood bill in 1819 that mandated the gradual end of slavery in Missouri.

Tammany Hall New York City's **Democratic party** organization, dating from well before the Civil War, that evolved into a powerful political machine after 1860, using **patronage** and bribes to maintain control of the city administration.

Taos Revolt Uprising of Pueblo Indians in New Mexico that broke out in January 1847 over the imposition of American rule during the **Mexican War**; the revolt was crushed within a few weeks.

Tariff Act of 1798 Law placing a duty of 5 percent on most imported goods, designed primarily to generate revenue and not to protect American goods from foreign competition.

Tariff of 1816 The first openly protective tariff passed by Congress.

Tea Act of 1773 Act of Parliament that permitted the East India Company to sell tea through agents in America without paying the duty customarily collected in Britain, thus reducing the retail price. Americans, who saw the act as an attempt to induce them to pay the Townshend duty still imposed in the colonies, resisted this act through the **Boston Tea Party** and other measures.

Teapot Dome scandal A scandal of the 1920s that sent the secretary of the interior to prison for taking bribes to lease naval oil reserves to private companies.

Tejano A person of Spanish or Mexican descent born in Texas.

Teller Amendment A congressional resolution adopted in 1898 renouncing any American intention to annex Cuba.

Temperance Reform movement originating in the 1820s that sought to eliminate the consumption of alcohol.

Tenement Four- to six-story residential dwelling, once common in New York and certain other cities, built on a tiny lot without regard to providing ventilation or light.

Tennessee Valley Authority (TVA) Federal regional planning agency established to promote **conservation**, produce electric power, and encourage economic development in seven southern states.

Ten Percent Plan Plan devised by President Lincoln in 1863 as a method for readmitting the seceding states to the Union; required 10 percent of a state's prewar voters to swear allegiance to the Union and a new state constitution that banned slavery. Many congressional Republicans considered this standard too thin to support a general reconstruction of the Union and responded with the **Wade-Davis Bill**.

Tenure of Office Act Law Congress passed in 1867 prohibiting the president from removing certain officeholders without the Senate's consent; President Andrew Johnson's defiance of the act led to an **impeachment** trial in the Senate that narrowly failed to remove him from office.

Termination Federal policy of withdrawing official recognition from American Indian tribes and dividing tribal assets among the tribe's members.

Thames, Battle of the American victory in October 1813 over combined British and Indian forces in southern Ontario during the **War of 1812**.

Third International International organization of Communist parties created in 1919 under **Bolshevik** control.

Third world Nations that were aligned with neither the communist bloc (the "second world") nor the West (the "first world").

Thirteenth Amendment Constitutional amendment ratified in 1865 that freed all slaves throughout the United States.

Tippecanoe, Battle of American victory in November 1811 over Shawnee Indians at Prophetstown in the Indiana Territory that provoked Indians into warfare along the western frontier.

Tonnage Act of 1789 Duty levied on the tonnage of incoming ships to U.S. ports; tax was higher on foreign-owned ships to favor American shippers.

Tordesillas, Treaty of Treaty negotiated by the pope in 1494 to resolve the territorial claims of Spain and Portugal. It drew a north–south line approximately 1,100 miles west of the Cape Verde Islands, granting all lands west of the line to Spain and all lands east of the line to Portugal. This limited Portugal's New World empire to Brazil but confirmed its claims in Africa and Asia.

Tories A derisive term applied to **Loyalists** in America who supported the king and Parliament just before and during the American Revolution. The term derived from late-seventeenth-century English politics when the Tory party supported the Duke of York's succession to the throne as James II. Later the Tory party favored the Church of England and the crown over dissenting denominations and Parliament.

Townshend Duty Act Act of Parliament, passed in 1767, imposing duties on colonial tea, lead, paint, paper, and glass. Designed to take advantage of the supposed American distinction between internal and external taxes, the Townshend duties were to help support government in America. The act prompted a successful colonial **nonimportation** movement.

Trail of Tears The forced march in 1838 of the Cherokee Indians from their homelands in Georgia to the Indian Territory in the West; thousands of Cherokees died along the way.

Transcendentalism A philosophical and literary movement centered on an idealistic belief in the divinity of individuals and nature.

Trans-Continental Treaty of 1819 Treaty between the United States and Spain in which Spain ceded Florida to the United States, surrendered all claims to the Pacific Northwest, and agreed to a boundary between the **Louisiana Purchase** territory and the Spanish Southwest.

Transportation revolution Dramatic improvements in transportation that stimulated economic growth after 1815 by expanding the range of travel and reducing the time and cost of moving goods and people.

Trenton, Battle of Revolutionary War clash that occurred on December 26, 1776, when General George Washington, who had withdrawn his forces into Pennsylvania, recrossed the Delaware River and surprised approximately fourteen hundred Hessians at Trenton, New Jersey, capturing or killing nearly one thousand.

Triangle Shirtwaist Company Clothing manufacturer whose New York factory burned in 1911, prompting outrage over unsafe working conditions and the passage of remedial legislation.

Tripartite Pact An alliance of Germany, Italy, and Japan signed in September 1941 in which each nation agreed to help the others in the event of an attack by the United States.

Truman Doctrine President Harry Truman's statement in 1947 that the United States should assist other nations that were facing external pressure or internal revolution; an important step in the escalation of the **Cold War**.

Tuskegee Institute Educational institution founded by Booker T. Washington in 1881 in rural Alabama to train black people in agricultural and industrial skills.

Uncle Tom's Cabin Novel about slave life in the South by Harriet Beecher Stowe.

Underground Railroad Support system set up by antislavery groups in the Upper South and the North to assist fugitive slaves in escaping the South.

Underwood-Simmons Tariff Act The 1913 reform law that lowered tariff rates and levied the first regular federal income tax.

Unicameral legislature A legislative body composed of a single house.

Union League A **Republican party** organization in northern cities that became an important organizing device among freedmen in southern cities after 1865.

United Daughters of the Confederacy (UDC) Organization founded in 1892 to preserve southern history and honor its heroes; it reflected the growing role of middle-class white women in public affairs.

United Nations During World War II, the name adopted by the United States, Britain, and their allies against Germany and Italy; after 1945, an international organization joined by nearly all nations.

United States* v. *Cruikshank The 1876 case in which the U.S. Supreme Court nullified the **Enforcement Act of 1870**, overturning the convictions of white people accused of violence against black people in Louisiana and declaring that the **Fifteenth Amendment** did not sanction federal interference in matters that were clearly reserved for the states.

Universal manhood suffrage The right of all male U.S. citizens to vote; a key element of **Radical Republican** policy in the South after 1867.

Universal Negro Improvement Association (UNIA) A black nationalist movement organized by Marcus Garvey to promote black pride, unity, and economic **self-determination**.

U.S. Sanitary Commission Private, voluntary medical organization founded in May 1861 and dedicated to tending Union wounded and improving soldier comfort and morale during the Civil War.

Valley Forge Area of Pennsylvania approximately 20 miles northwest of Philadelphia where General George Washington's continental troops were quartered from December 1777 to June 1778 while British forces occupied Philadelphia during the Revolutionary War. Approximately 2,500 men, about a quarter of those encamped there, died of hardship and disease.

Versailles, Treaty of The treaty ending World War I and creating the **League of Nations**.

Vertical integration The consolidation of numerous production functions, from the extraction of the raw materials to the distribution and marketing of the finished products, under the direction of one firm.

Vice-admiralty courts Royal courts established in the colonies to handle maritime cases and enforce the Acts of Trade. The enlarged role of these bodies, which operated without juries, was considered a grievance.

Vicksburg Key Mississippi River port and rail junction that fell in July 1863 to a brilliant Union campaign by Ulysses S. Grant, commander of the Army of Tennessee, during the Civil War.

Viet Cong Communist rebels in South Vietnam who fought the pro-American government established in South Vietnam in 1954.

Vincennes, Treaty of Treaty of 1804 in which Americans claimed that Indian leaders ceded most of southern Indiana to the United States.

Virginia Company One of two **joint-stock companies** chartered in 1606 to establish English colonies in America. Also known as the London Company, it organized the founding of the Virginia Colony. The company went bankrupt in 1624, and a year later Virginia became a royal colony.

Virginia Plan Proposal of the Virginia delegation at the 1787 **Constitution Convention** calling for a national legislature in which the states would be represented according to population. The national legislature would have the explicit power to veto or overrule laws passed by state legislatures.

Virtual representation The notion, current in eighteenth-century England, that parliamentary members represented the interests of the nation as a whole, not those of the particular district that elected them.

VISTA Volunteers in Service to America, the "domestic Peace Corps" of the 1960s that gave individuals an opportunity to work on behalf of low-income communities in the United States.

Volstead Act The 1920 law defining the liquor forbidden under the Eighteenth Amendment and giving enforcement responsibilities to the Prohibition Bureau of the Department of the Treasury.

Voting Rights Act Legislation in 1965 that overturned a variety of practices by which states systematically denied voter registration to minorities.

Wade-Davis Bill Congressional alternative to Lincoln's **Ten Percent Plan**, passed in 1864; required 50 percent of prewar voters to pledge their loyalty and demanded guarantees for black equality. The president exercised a pocket veto, and it never became law.

Wagner National Labor Relations Act The 1935 law guaranteeing workers' rights to organize unions and establishing the **National Labor Relations Board**.

Waltham system During the industrialization of the early nineteenth century, the recruitment of unmarried young women for employment in factories.

War Hawks Members of Congress, predominantly from the South and West, who aggressively pushed for a war against Britain after their election in 1810.

War Industries Board (WIB) The federal agency that reorganized industry for maximum efficiency and productivity during World War I.

War Manpower Commission Federal agency established in 1942 to allocate workers among the armed services, defense industries, and essential civilian industries.

War of 1812 War fought between the United States and Britain from June 1812 to January 1815 largely over British restrictions on American shipping.

War of the Austrian Succession A small conflict between Britain and Spain that began in 1739 and widened into a larger European war in 1740 (lasting until 1748) when the king of Prussia attacked lands claimed by Austria's ruling family. Known in America as **King George's War**.

War of the League of Augsburg Conflict in Europe (1688–1697) that pitted France against Spain, Sweden, the Holy Roman Empire, the Dutch republic, various German principalities, and, in 1689, England. The principal aim was to halt the growing power of France's Louis XIV. In America, this was known as **King William's War**.

War of the Spanish Succession European conflict (1702–1713) that began in a struggle between the king of France and the Holy Roman emperor over claims to the Spanish throne. England, Holland, and the Holy Roman Empire fought France and Spain in a war known in America as **Queen Anne's War**.

War on Poverty Set of programs introduced by Lyndon Johnson between 1963 and 1966 designed to break the cycle of poverty by providing funds for job training, community development, nutrition, and supplementary education.

War Production Board Federal agency established in 1942 to coordinate defense production and allocate scarce resources to serve the war effort.

Warsaw Pact Military alliance of the Soviet Union and communist nations in eastern Europe from 1955 to 1989.

Washington Temperance Societies **Temperance** associations dominated by mechanics and laborers that first formed in Baltimore in 1840.

Watergate A complex scandal involving attempts to cover up illegal actions taken by administration officials and leading to the resignation of President Richard Nixon in 1974.

Weather Underground Fringe group of former members of **Students for a Democratic Society**, 1969–1970, who emphasized confrontation and violence.

Webster–Ashburton Treaty Treaty signed by the United States and Britain in 1842 that settled a boundary dispute between Maine and Canada and provided for closer cooperation in suppressing the African slave trade.

Welfare capitalism A paternalistic system of labor relations emphasizing management responsibility for employee well-being. While providing some limited benefits, its function was primarily to forestall the formation of unions or public intervention.

Wesley Houses Organizations modeled after the **settlement houses** of the North that began appearing in southern cities under the auspices of the Methodist Church in the 1890s to serve working-class neighborhoods.

Western Federation of Miners A large and radical union of western miners formed in Butte, Montana, in 1893 to coordinate local unions' resistance to corporate threats to workers' wages, working conditions, and health.

Whig party Political party, formed in the mid-1830s in opposition to the **Jacksonian Democrats,** that favored a strong role for the national government in promoting economic growth.

Whigs The name used by advocates of colonial resistance to British measures during the 1760s and 1770s. The Whig party in England unsuccessfully attempted to exclude the Catholic Duke of York from succession to the throne as James II; victorious in the **Glorious Revolution**, the Whigs later stood for religious toleration and the supremacy of Parliament over the crown.

Whiskey Rebellion Armed uprising in 1794 by farmers in western Pennsylvania who attempted to prevent the collection of the excise tax on whiskey.

White League One of several military organizations operating openly and in concert with the **Democratic party** in the South to thwart black voting rights during **Reconstruction**.

White Plains, Battle of Revolutionary War engagement that took place on October 28, 1776, between General George Washington's troops, evacuating New York City, and British forces under Sir William Howe. Washington sustained more than three hundred casualties before withdrawing his troops.

Wide Awakes Group of red-shirted, black-caped young men who paraded through city streets in the North extolling the virtues of the **Republican party** during the 1860 presidential election campaign.

Wilderness Act Law, the Wilderness Areas Act, that in 1964 designated certain federal lands as parts of the National Wilderness Preservation System, consisting originally of 9.1 million acres.

Wilderness, Battle of the Civil War clash between Confederate and Union forces near Chancellorsville in May 1864 marked by fierce hand-to-hand combat in dense woods.

Wilmot Proviso Never-approved amendment to a **Mexican War** appropriations bill that would ban slavery from any territory acquired from Mexico, submitted to Congress by Pennsylvania Democrat David Wilmot.

Wobblies Popular name for the members of the **Industrial Workers of the World (IWW)**.

Woman suffrage The right of women to vote, achieved in the **Nineteenth Amendment**.

Women's Christian Temperance Union (WCTU) National organization formed after the Civil War dedicated to prohibiting the sale and distribution of alcohol.

Woodstock Generation Members of the late 1960s **counterculture**, named for a rock festival held in New York State in August 1969.

Workingmen's movement Associations of urban workers who began campaigning in the 1820s for free public education and a ten-hour workday.

Works Progress Administration (WPA) Key **New Deal** agency that provided work relief for the unemployed.

World Bank Officially the International Bank for Reconstruction and Development, an international organization established in 1945 that assists governments around the world in economic development efforts.

Wounded Knee Massacre The U.S. Army's brutal winter massacre in 1890 of at least two hundred Sioux men, women, and children as part of the government's assault on the tribe's Ghost Dance religion.

Writs of assistance Documents issued by a court of law that gave British officials in America the power to search for smuggled goods wherever they wished. The legality of these writs became an important cause of controversy in Massachusetts in 1761 and 1762.

Wyoming Valley Pennsylvania site where, in June and July 1778, a force comprised of Iroquois Indians and **Tories** under colonel John Butler routed **Patriot** defenders and laid waste to settlements during the Revolutionary War.

XYZ Affair Diplomatic incident in 1798 in which Americans were outraged by the demand of the French for a bribe as a condition for negotiating with American diplomats.

Yalta Conference Meeting of U.S. President Franklin Roosevelt, British Prime Minister Winston Churchill, and Soviet Premier Joseph Stalin held in February 1945 to plan the final stages of World War II and postwar arrangements.

Yellow-dog contracts Employment agreements binding workers not to join a union.

Yellow press A deliberately sensational journalism of scandal and exposure designed to attract an urban mass audience and increase advertising revenues.

Yippies Fringe group of radical activists, 1968–1972, who emphasized media events.

Yorktown, Siege of Final major decisive engagement of the Revolutionary War in which American and French forces under Generals Washington and Rochambeau laid siege to British forces under Lord Cornwallis at Yorktown, Virginia, from August 30 to October 19, 1781. The surrender of approximately eight thousand British troops on October 19 led to the British government's decision to end the war.

Young America Mid-nineteenth-century movement that espoused strong nationalistic views and the desire to expand American influence overseas.

PHOTO CREDITS

COVER AND TITLE PAGE: Everett Longley Warner (1877–1963) "Along the River Front, New York," 1912. Oil on canvas, 32 x 10 inches. The Toledo Museum of Art, Toledo, Ohio, Museum Purchase.

CHAPTER 1: The Granger Collection, 3; Danny Lehman Photography, 8; Cahokia Mounds State Historic Site, 9; National Geographic Society, 13; The Granger Collection, 15; University of Toronto-Thomas Fisher Rare Book Library, 17; University of Minnesota, James Ford Bell Library, 19; Courtesy of the Library of Congress, 20; Courtesy of the Library of Congress, 22; The Granger Collection, 29.

CHAPTER 2: British Library, 35; Picture Collection, The Branch Libraries, The New York Public Library, 38; Courtesy of the Library of Congress, 40; Jonathan Carver, A TREATISE ON THE CULTURE OF THE TOBACCO PLANT (London, 1779), Swem Library, College of William and Mary, 41; Courtesy, American Antiquarian Society, 46; The Fine Arts Museums of San Francisco, 49; Courtesy of the National Library of Jamaica; 53, Courtesy of the National Library of Jamaica, 53; Carolina Art Association/Gibbes Museum of Art, 56; AP/Wide World Photos, 57.

CHAPTER 3: The South Carolina Historical Society, 65; Courtesy of the Library of Congress, 66; Courtesy of the Library of Congress, 70; Fruitlands Museums, 72; Photo by Thomas L. McKnight, 73; The Baltimore Museum of Art, 75; (c)The British Museum, 78; The New York Public Library, Research Libraries, 79; The British Museum, 83; Colonial Williamsburg Foundation, 84.

CHAPTER 4: Washington and Lee University, 95; Museum of Fine Arts, Boston, 100; Museum of Fine Arts, Boston, 101; National Gallery of Art, Washington D.C., 103; Harvard University Museums, 105; Collection of The New-York Historical Society, 107; National Portrait Gallery, London, 108; Henry Glasse, Pattern in the Material Folk Culture of the Eastern United States, 116; Art Resource, N.Y., 117; Courtesy of the Library of Congress, 120; North Wind Picture Archives, 121; National Gallery of Canada, 124.

CHAPTER 5: Courtesy of the Library of Congress, 131; The Library Company of Philadelphia, 134; North Wind Picture Archives, 135; New York Public Library, 137; Museum of Fine Arts, Boston, 140; The Granger Collection, 141; Philadelphia Museum of Art, 143; Courtesy of the Library of Congress, 145; Christie's Images Inc., 145.

CHAPTER 6: The Henry Francis DuPont Winterthur Museum, 159; The Granger Collection, 161; Courtesy of the Library of Congress, 163; The Granger Collection, 163; The Henry Francis DuPont Winterthur Museum, 168; Courtesy of the Library of Congress, 169; The New-York Historical Society, 175; Yale University Art Gallery, 179; The Henry Francis DuPont Winterthur Museum, 180; Anne S. K. Brown Military Collection, Brown University, 183.

CHAPTER 7: The Granger Collection, 191; Corbis, 192; Courtesy of the Library of Congress, 193; The Library Company of Phladelphia, 194; The Granger Collection, 199; Courtesy of the Historical Society of Pennsylvania, 201; Charles Allen Munn Collection, Fordham University Library, Bronx, N.Y., 208; The Granger Collection, 214; Print and Picture Collection, The Free Library of Philadelphia, 215.

CHAPTER 8: Colonial Williamsburg Foundation, 221; National Gallery of Art, Washington, D.C., 223; The New York Public Library, 226; The New-York Historical Society, 229; U. S. Bureau of Engraving and Printing, 230; Chicago Historical Society, 237; The Granger Collection, 240; Collection of The New-York Historical Society, 241; The White House Collection, (c) White Historical Historical Association, 242, The New-York Historical Society, 244.

CHAPTER 9: Courtesy of the Library of Congress, 251; The Granger Collection, 252; Missouri Historical Society, 255; North Wind Picture Archives, 258; Courtesy of the Library of Congress, 259; McCord Museum of Canadian History, 264; National Graphic Society, 265; Courtesy of the Library of Congress, 267; The Boston Athenaeum, 269.

CHAPTER 10: The Henry Francis DuPont Winterthur Museum, 279; The New-York Historical Society, 282; Detroit Institute of Arts, 284; The Corcoran Gallery of Art, 285; Courtesy of the Library of Congress, 286; The Granger Collection, 287; Courtesy of the Library of Congress, 292; The New-York Historical Society, 294; Smithsonian Institution, 299.

CHAPTER 11: The New York Public Library Prints Division, 312; The Granger Collection, 318; American Textile History Museum, 319; Museum of Fine Arts, Boston, 322; Corbis, 324; Museum of Fine Arts, Boston, 329; Museum of Fine Arts, Boston, 331; Museum of the City of New York, 333.

CHAPTER 12: The Granger Collection, 342; The Old Print Shop, 343; Denver Art Museum, 346; The Denver Public Library, 348; Colorado Historical Society, 351; The Walter Art Gallery, Baltimore, 352; Art Resource, 353; Christie's Images, Inc., 360; Amon Carter Museum, 361.

CHAPTER 13: "Courtesy of The New-York Historical Society, New York City," 372; The New-York Historical Society, 373; Louisiana State Museum, 378; Courtesy of the Library of Congress, 381; Sophia Smith Collection, Smith College, 381; Hunter Museum of Art, 385; Daughters of the Republic of Texas Library, Yanaguana Society Collection, 386; Jay P. Altmayer, 389; Courtesy of the Library of Congress, 390.

CHAPTER 14: Courtesy of American Bible Society Library/Archives, 397; Courtesy of the Library of Congress, 400; Museum of Fine Arts, Boston, 405; Paul Rocheleau, Photographer, 407; Courtesy of the Library of Congress, 410; The Library Company of Philadelphia, 411; The Granger Collection, 416; Corbis, 418; The Granger Collection, 419.

CHAPTER 15: Courtesy of the California History Room, California State Library, Sacramento, California, 425; Courtesy of the Library of Congress, 430; The Metropolitan Museum of Art, 431; The Newberry Library, 436; The New York Public Library, 436; Stock Montage, Inc./ Historical Pictures Collection, 438; Courtesy of the Library of Congress, 440; The Granger Collection, 447.

CHAPTER 16: Museum of Fine Arts, Boston, 461; By Courtesy of The Trustees of The Boston Public Library, 463; The Metropolitan Museum of Art, 470; Corbis, 472; The Metropolitan Museum of Art, 478; Chicago Historical Society, 479; Courtesy of the Library of Congress, 482; Corbis, 487.

CHAPTER 17: Culver Pictures, Inc., 495; Culver Pictures, Inc, 496; Center of Military History, U.S. Army, 497; Corbis, 499; National Archives, 501; Courtesy of the Library of Congress, 505; Harper's Weekly, March 18, 1865, Courtesy of William Hine, 508; Courtesy of the Library of Congress, 509.

CHAPTER 18: The Granger Collection, 515; The Granger Collection, 517; Courtesy of Hampton University Archives, 519; The Granger Collection, 521; The Granger Collection, 524; Courtesy of the Library of Congress, 531; Courtesy of the Library of Congress, 533; Harper's Weekly, 1874, 535; The Granger Collection, 540.

CHAPTER 19: T. E. Armistead Collection, University of South Alabama Archives, 547; Courtesy of the North Carolina Division of Archives and History, 555; Library of Congress, 560; Courtesy of the Library of Congress, 562; The Granger Collection, 563; The New-York Historical Society, 568; North Carolina Mutual Life Insurance Company, 569; The Granger Collection, 571 (left); The Granger Collection, 571 (right).

CHAPTER 20: Library of Congress, 580; U.S. Department of the Interior, National Park Service, Edison National Historic Site, 580; Culver Pictures, Inc., 585; The Granger Collection, 588; Stock Montage, Inc./Historical Pictures Collection, 591; Library of Congress, 595; Brown Brothers, 601; Library of Congress, 604; Museum of Art, Rhode Island School of Design, 607.

CHAPTER 21: The Granger Collection, 615; Courtesy of the Burton Historical Collection, Detroit Public Library, 619; A Pictographic History of the Oglala Sioux, The University of Nebraska Press, 620; Library of Congress, 622; Montana Historical Society, Helena, 626; Idaho State Historical Society, 627; The Denver Public Library, Western History Department, 630; Corbis, 632; Witte Museum, 634; Solomon D. Butcher Collection, Nebraska State Historical Society, 635.

CHAPTER 22: Reproduced from the collections of the Ohio Historical Society Archives/Library, 647; The Granger Collection, 648; The Granger Collection, 649; Stock Montage, Inc./Historical Pictures Collection, 652; Library of Congress, 655; Kansas State Historical Society, 657; Library of Congress, 660; Culver Pictures, Inc., 661; The Granger Collection, 664.

CHAPTER 23: Brown Brothers, 671; Cornell University School of Industrial and Labor Relations, 675; Corbis, 677; Courtesy National Archives, photo no. 102-LH-1986, 680; Special Collections and Archives, W.E.B. Du Bois Library, University of Massachusetts Amherst, 685; State Historical Society of Wisconsin, 689; The Granger Collection, New York, 692; Portrait #65, The Bancroft Library, University of California at Berkeley, 693; The Granger Collection, 695.

CHAPTER 24: By permission of the Houghton Library, Harvard University, 706; Corbis, 712; The Granger Collection, 715; Library of Congress,

717; Theodore Roosevelt Collection, Harvard College Library, 717; Kansas State Historical Society, Topeka, Kansas, 719; Stock Montage, Inc./Historical Pictures Collection, 720; Theodore Roosevelt Collection, Harvard College Library, 725; The Granger Collection, 726.

CHAPTER 25: Library of Congress, 733; Corbis, 734; University of South Alabama Archives, 738; Nebraska State Historical Society, 741; The Granger Collection, 743; Culver Pictures, Inc., 745; The Granger Collection, 749; Carnegie Library of Pittsburgh, 753; The Chicago Tribune, 755.

CHAPTER 26: Culver Pictures, Inc., 761; By permission of DuPont Automotive, 763; The Granger Collection, 767; Yale Collection of American Literature, Beinecke Rare Book and Manuscript Library, 772; Library of Congress, 773; By permission of Campbell Soup Company, 775; Courtesy W. A. Swift Photograph Collection; Archives and Special Collections, Ball State University, 779; The Granger Collection, 780; AP/Wide World Photos, 781.

CHAPTER 27: Corbis, 791; Special Collections Division, University of Washington Libraries, Neg # Lee 20102, 793; The Granger Collection, 800; The Granger Collection, 802; Corbis, 803; Corbis, 804; AP/Wide World Photos, 806; Nebraska State Historical Society, 808; Walter P. Reuther Library, Wayne State University, 809; Corbis, 810.

CHAPTER 28: Bildarchiv Preussischer Kulturbesitz, 821; National Archives, 826; Hulton Getty/Liaison Agency, Inc. 834; AP/Wide World Photos, 834; Courtesy of the Library of Congress, 835; Library of Congress, 838; Corbis, 841; Margaret Bourke-White, Life Magazine (c) Time Warner, Inc., 843; Liaison Agency, Inc., 846.

CHAPTER 29: RKO Radio Pictures/Archive Photos, 853; AP/Wide World Photos, 857; The Granger Collection, 858; AP/Wide World Photos, 859; Bildarchiv Preussischer Kulturbesitz, 863; AP/Wide World Photos, 866; National Archives, 869; Corbis, 875; Time Life Syndication, 876.

CHAPTER 30: (c) 1957, Newsweek, Inc. All rights reserved. Reprinted by permission, 883; Motorola, Inc., 887; Magnum Photos, Inc. 889; FPG International, LLC, 891; NASA/SCIENCE Photo Library /Photo Researchers, Inc., 893; AP/Wide World Photos, 901; Greensboro News & Record, 902; AP/Wide World Photos, 905; (c) 1976, Matt Herron/Take Stock–Images of Change, 907.

CHAPTER 31: Corbis, 918; Black Star, 919; Leonard Freed, Magnum Photos, Inc., 923; Corbis, 924; Corbis, 925; (c) John Paul Filo/Archive Photos, 928; AP/Wide World Photos, 930; Black Star, 932; Corbis, 934; SIPA Press, 938.

CHAPTER 32: Corbis, 945; Archives of Labor and Urban Affairs, Wayne State University, 957; Corbis Digital Stock, 959; Photofest, 960; Reprinted by permission of Ms. Magazine (c) 1972, 964; Culver Pictures, Inc., 965; Black Star, 967; Pearson Education/PH College, 970; Magnum Photos, Inc., 971.

CHAPTER 33: Corbis, 977; Photofest, 979; P. F. Bentley, Time Magazine (c) Time, Inc., 982; Corbis, 986; Corbis Sygma Photo News, 989; Liaison Agency, Inc., 991; Liaison Agency, Inc., 999; Liaison Agency, Inc., 1001; Corbis, 1003.

Index

C

D

O

T

160°
140°
120°
100°
80°
60°
40°
20°
80°
GREENLAND (DENMARK)
Arctic Circle
U.S.
CANADA
60°
ALEUTIAN ISLANDS
UNITED KINGDOM
IRELAND
ANDORRA
UNITED STATES
ATLANTIC OCEAN
PACIFIC OCEAN
40°
PORTUGAL
MOROCCO
MEXICO
BAHAMAS
WESTERN SAHARA (MOROCCO)
Tropic of Cancer
CUBA
U.S.
20°
HAITI
PUERTO RICO (U.S.)
JAMAICA
BELIZE
HONDURAS
DOMINICAN REPUBLIC
ST. KITTS AND NEVIS
ANTIGUA AND BARBUDA
DOMINICA
ST. VINCENT AND THE GRENADINES
BARBADOS
MAURITANIA
CAPE VERDE
SENEGAL
GAMBIA
GUINEA-BISSAU
GUINEA
SIERRA LEONE
LIBERIA
IVORY COAST
GHANA
GUATEMALA
EL SALVADOR
NICARAGUA
GRENADA
TRINIDAD AND TOBAGO
COSTA RICA
GUYANA
PANAMA
VENEZUELA
SURINAME
FRENCH GUIANA (FR)
COLOMBIA
0°
Equator
GALAPAGOS ISLANDS (ECUADOR)
ECUADOR
CENTRAL AFRICAN REP
SÃO TOMÉ AND PR
EQUATORIAL G
PERU
BRAZIL
WESTERN SAMOA
TONGA
BOLIVIA
20°
Tropic of Capricorn
PARAGUAY
CHILE
ARGENTINA
URUGUAY
PACIFIC OCEAN
ATLANTIC OCEAN
40°
60°
Antarctic Circle
80°